Major Companies of the USA 1988/89

Major Companies of the USA 1988/89

Managing Editor
R M Whiteside

Editors
A Wilson
S Blackburn

Assistant
J Dunmall

Graham & Trotman
Sterling House, 66 Wilton Road, London SW1V 1DE
A member of the Kluwer Academic Publishers Group

Second edition published in 1988 by Graham & Trotman Limited
Sterling House, 66 Wilton Road, London SW1V 1DE.

abdp

Graham & Trotman Ltd is a member of the
Association of British Directory Publishers

British Library Cataloguing in Publication Data

Major companies of the USA — 1988/89
1. Corporations — United States —
Directories
338.7'4'02573 HF3010

ISBN 978-94-010-7077-5 ISBN 978-94-009-1297-7 (eBook)
DOI 10.1007/978-94-009-1297-7

ISSN 0268-2338

CONTENTS

INTRODUCTION

Major Companies of the USA provides useful information in a succinct, standardised form on over 5,200 of the largest manufacturing and service companies in the United States. The companies have been selected for inclusion on the size of their sales revenues or their balance sheet.

The information published about each company is intended to provide a convenient descriptive reference to those companies in the top slice of American industry and commerce.

The data published in Major Companies of the USA is the result of an extensive and careful research operation which it would not have been possible to pursue without the assistance and cooperation of many of the companies in this directory which provided the publishers with information about themselves.

Major Companies of the USA will be updated and published annually. Any US company not included in this edition and which considers itself eligible for inclusion in the next edition, should write to the publishers at the address below. No charge is made to any company submitting data for inclusion in this directory.

GUIDE TO THE ARRANGEMENT OF THE BOOK

Company entries are listed alphabetically. There then follows the Index section on blue pages, consisting of:

1. Index to major companies throughout the USA
2. Index to companies within each state of the USA
3. Index to companies classified by business activity within each state of the USA.

ABOUT THE PUBLISHER

Graham & Trotman, one of Europe's leading business information publishers, is headquartered in London and has US offices in Boston. Other company reference annuals published by Graham & Trotman include:

- Major Companies of Europe
- Major Companies of the Arab World
- Major Companies of the Far East

A full catalogue describing the more than 300 titles published by Graham & Trotman, is available on request from the publisher's UK or USA addresses given below.

Graham & Trotman Ltd
Sterling House
66 Wilton Road
London SW1V 1DE
England

Graham & Trotman Inc
Kluwer Academic Publishers Group
101 Philip Drive
Assinippi Park
Norwell, MA 02061
USA

Major Companies of the UNITED STATES OF AMERICA

1ST SOURCE CORPORATION

PO Box 1602, 100 North Michigan, South Bend, IN 46601
Tel: (219) 236 8275

Chairman: Ernestine M Raclin (and Subsidiary Officer)
President: Christopher J Murphy III (and Subsidiary Officer)
Senior Executive Officers: Vincent A Tamburo (Secretary and General Counsel), Larry E Lentych (Treasurer and Subsidiary Officer)

PRINCIPAL ACTIVITIES: Banking
Principal Subsidiaries: 1st Source Bank; 1st Source Bank of Starke County
Principal Bank: 1st Source Bank
Financial Information:

	Dec 31 1986	Dec 31 1987
	$'000	$'000
Income before taxes	7,174	9,770
Net income	7,125	8,068
Common dividends	1,256	1,447
Dividends per common share	$0.44	$0.44
Earnings per share	$1.97	$2.12
Common stock	3,318	3,418
Retained income	25,744	30,773
Shareholders equity	64,220	69,159
Deposits	867,891	908,944
Total assets	1,033,509	1,072,372

Principal Shareholders: Ernestine M Raclin; Christopher J Murphy III
No of Employees: 672

20TH CENTURY INDUSTRIES

6301 Owensmouth Avenue, Suite, 700, Woodland Hills, CA 91367
Tel: (818) 704 3700

Chairman: Louis W Foster (and Chief Executive Officer)
President: G Robert Thompson (and Chief Operating Officer)
Senior Executive Officers: A Kobayashi (Senior VP and Secretary), John W Wallen (Senior VP), Neil H Ashley (Group VP and Legal Counsel), Kay Bell (VP), Paul S Castellani (VP), William G Crain (VP), Gregory A Foster (VP), Willian L Mellick (VP), Margaret Chang (Treasurer), Joseph J Urist (Controller)

PRINCIPAL ACTIVITIES: Insurance including homeowner and private passenger automobile insurance
Principal Subsidiaries: 20th Century Insurance Co
Financial Information:

	$'000
Sales revenues	281,860

3COM CORPORATION

1365 Shorebird Way, Mountain View, CA 94043
Tel: (415) 961 9602

Chairman: Robert M Metcalfe (and Senior VP and General Manager)
President: L William Krause (and Chief Executive Officer)
Senior Executive Officers: Howard S Charney (Senior VP, General Manager, Legal Counsel and Secretary), Lazar Birenbaum (VP), Bob Bressler (VP), Debra Engel (VP), John Marman (VP Sales and Marketing), Chris Paisley (VP Finance and Chief Financial Officer), J Daniel Robertson (VP)

PRINCIPAL ACTIVITIES: Data processing systems
Principal Bank: Bank of America
Financial Information:

	$'000
Sales revenues	64,000

No of Employees: 400

3M

Minnesota Mining & Manufacturing Co

3M Center, St Paul, MN 55144-1000
Tel: (612) 733-1110
Cable: TRIMINCO
Telex: 29-7023

Chairman: Allan F Jacobson (and Chief Executive Officer)
Senior Executive Officers: L D DeSimone (Executive VP Industrial and Consumer), Allan J Huber (Executive VP Electronics and Information Technologies), Jerry E Robertson (Executive VP Life Sciences), Manuel J Monteiro (Executive VP International Operations), Kenneth A Schoen (Executive VP Graphic Technology), Stanley W Thiele (Senior VP Administration), Donn R Osmon (VP Marketing and Public Affairs)

PRINCIPAL ACTIVITIES: Manufacture of a wide range of products including chemicals, healthcare products, medical equipment, plastic films, sheeting and insulation products, photographic materials, adhesives, abrasives, household cleaning, personal care and electrical products
Trademarks/Trade Names: Buf (personal cleaning sponges), Cantata (music units), Centerlite (reflective paint compounds), Coban (elastic bandage), Color-Key (imaging films), Controltac (film markings), Dynatel (telecommunications devices), Fabricut (coated abrasives), Fluorad (fluorochemical surfactants), Fluorinert (electronic liquids), Jet-melt (hot melt adhesives), Littmann (stethoscopes, anesthescopes, ECG accessories), Magic (transparent tape), Microfragrance (encapsulated fragrances), Micropore (surgical tape), Photogard (protective coatings), Post-it (note pads), Production (coated abrasives), Rescue (soap-filled cleaning pads), Safety-Walk (antislip surfacing materials), Scotch (brand psa tapes, magnetic tapes, laminating films and other products), Scotch-Brite (cleaning materials), Scotchcal (films), Scotchcast (cable splicing materials), Scotchgard (fabric treatments), Scotchlite (reflective sheetings), Scotchlok (splice connectors), Scotchtint (sun control films), Scotch-Weld (structural adhesives), Steri-Drape (surgical drapes), Textool (electronic sockets/carriers), Thinsulate (insulation material), 3M (abrasives, adhesives, chemical additives, respirators, industrial filter materials, visual communication systems, static shielding systems and other products), Underseal (auto underbody protective coatings) are but a few of the hundreds of trade names used to identify 3M products in many countries
Principal Subsidiaries: United States: D L Auld Inc/3M; Dorran Photonics Inc; Unitek/3M; C.M.T.L. Corporation; Media Networks Inc; Cable Networks Inc; AVI Inc; National Advertising Company; Riker Laboratories Inc; 3M Diagnostic Systems; Sarns Inc/3M; 3M Media Services Inc; Trim-Line Inc. Outside United States: 3M Belgium NV/SA; 3M Canada Inc; 3M France; 3M Deutschland GMBH; 3M Italia SPA; Sumitomo 3M Limited (Japan); 3M South Africa (Pty) Ltd; 3M United Kingdom PLC and more than 40 companies marketing 3M products through manufacturing and sales subsidiaries in OUS locations
Principal Banks: First Trust Company Inc, St Paul, MN; Morgan Guaranty Trust Company of New York, NY
Financial Information:

	Dec 31 1985	Dec 31 1986
	$'000	$'000
Sales revenues	7,846,000	8,602,000
Income before taxes	1,097,000	1,348,000
Net income	664,000	779,000
Dividends	403,000	412,000
Dividends per share	$3.50	$3.60
Earnings per share	9.7%	8.3%
Common stock*	112,100	106,000
Retained income	4,389,000	4,900,000
Shareholders equity	4,008,000	4,463,000

*number of stockholders

No of Employees: 81,847

UNITED STATES OF AMERICA

A A BRUNELL ELECTROPLATING CORPORATION
See BRUNELL, A A, ELECTROPLATING CORPORATION

A B DICK COMPANY
See DICK, A B, COMPANY

A C NIELSEN CO
See NIELSEN, A C, CO

A E STALEY MFG CO
See STALEY, A E, MFG CO

A G EDWARDS INC
See EDWARDS, A G, INC

A H BELO CORPORATION
See BELO, A H, CORPORATION

A H ROBINS COMPANY, INC
See ROBINS, A H, COMPANY, INC

A JOHNSON & COMPANY, INC
See JOHNSON, A, & COMPANY, INC

A L WILLIAMS CORPORATION (THE)
See WILLIAMS, A L, CORPORATION (THE)

A M CASTLE & CO
See CASTLE, A M, & CO

A O SMITH CORPORATION
See SMITH, A O, CORPORATION

A P GREEN REFRACTORIES CO
See GREEN, A P, REFRACTORIES CO

A SCHULMAN INC
See SCHULMAN, A, INC

A T CROSS CO
See CROSS, A T, CO

A Y MCDONALD INDUSTRIES, INC
See MCDONALD, A Y, INDUSTRIES, INC

A&E PRODUCTS GROUP, INC
1460 Route 9 N., Woodbridge, NJ 07095
Tel: (201) 738-4900
Telex: TWX 7109980881 Warbern Keas

President: Nicholas H Carlozzi
Senior Executive Officers: Bernard Schwarz (Executive VP), Stephen Melnik (VP and Controller), Howard Samuels (VP Sales), Richard Peck (VP), Stephen Biroczky (VP Manufacturing)

PRINCIPAL ACTIVITIES: Manufacture of plastic clothes hangers
Principal Bank: Citicorp Industrial Credit, Inc
Financial Information:

	$'000
Sales revenues	60,000

No of Employees: 1,200

A&M FOOD SERVICES INC
1924 South Utica Ave, Suite 1018, Tulsa, OK 74104
Tel: (918) 749-4423

Chairman: W S Atherton (and Chief Executive Officer); Vice Chairman: Pat M Murphy
President: William C Ferril
Senior Executive Officers: Robert C Taft (Executive VP and Chief Operating Officer), Mike E Staten (Chief Financial Officer and Controller), C E Meyer (VP), P R Hughes Jr (VP), R A Boer (VP), G K Meinheit (VP), David J Davenport (Secretary)

PRINCIPAL ACTIVITIES: Fast food restaurants; franchise operations
Trade Names: Pepsico Inc
Principal Bank: Utica National Bank & Trust Co
Financial Information:

	$'000
Sales revenues	54,000

No of Employees: 1,650 (full-time)

AAI CORPORATION
Box 6767, Baltimore, MD 21204
Tel: (301) 666-1400
Cable: AAICKYVL, Baltimore, Md, USA
Telex: WUT 87849 aai coye

President: Irwin R Barr
Senior Executive Officers: Stuart M Macht (VP and Controller), Thomas J Holden (VP,Secretary and Treasurer)

PRINCIPAL ACTIVITIES: Manufacture of simulation and testing equipment for defense systems, ammunition and armaments; mechanical handling equipment
Parent Company: United Industrial Corporation
Principal Bank: Maryland National Bank
Financial Information:

	Dec 31 1985	Dec 31 1986
	$'000	$'000
Sales revenues	224,164	228,770

No of Employees: 3,300

AAR/BROOKS & PERKINS CORPORATION
17515 W Nine Mile Road, Southfield, MI 48075
Tel: (313) 559-3500

Chairman: Edward H Perkins Jr
President: Arthur C Richards
Senior Executive Officers: Raymond Kurtz (VP Finance), Ronald C Karzmar (VP Operations), Ralph G Gillespie (VP Planning and Development), Ben Brostoff (Secretary), L F Dinsmoore (Director Advertising)

PRINCIPAL ACTIVITIES: Manufacture of containers for air transportation and handling machinery
Parent Company: AAR Corporation, Elk Grove Village, IL
Principal Bank: Comerica Bank - Detroit
Financial Information:

	$'000
Sales revenues	70,000

No of Employees: 700

AAR CORPORATION
1111 Nicholas Boulevard, Elk Grove Village, IL 60007
Tel: (312) 439-3939

Chairman: Ira A Eichner
President: Barton J Levin (also Chief Operating Officer)
Senior Executive Officers: A L Hall (Group VP), Arthur C Richards (Group VP), Robert A Cameron (VP Finance and Treasurer), Ben C Brostoff (VP and Secretary), Jan Van den Berg (VP International Operations), Joseph J Dzurinko (VP and Controller), John Debenedictis (VP Marketing)

PRINCIPAL ACTIVITIES: Manufacturing and services for the aviation industry
Principal Bank: The First National Bank of Chicago
Financial Information:

	$'000
Sales revenues	219,000

No of Employees: 1,400

AARON RENTS, INC

1100 Aaron Building, 3001 North Fulton Drive NE, Atlanta, GA 30363
Tel: (404) 231-0011

Chairman: R Charles Loudermilk Sr (and President and Chief Executive Officer)
Senior Executive Officers: J Ray Minchew (Financial VP and Secretary), Lee Danbig (VP, Real Estate Development), Roderick McDonald (VP, Manufacturing), D Bruce Cox (VP, Residential Furniture Sales), Doug S McKenzie (VP, Office Furniture), Keith C Groen (VP, Legal), H Lee Burgin (Treasurer), E Randall Lee (Comptroller)

PRINCIPAL ACTIVITIES: Aaron Rents, Inc, the nation's largest furniture rental and sales company, is a vertically integrated furniture company engaged in the rental and sale of both residential and office furniture from 129 stores in 38 major metropolitan areas, primarily located in the Southeast and Southwest. The Company also manufactures residential and office furniture at four company-owned manufacturing facilities in Georgia and Florida
Trade Names: Aaron Rents Furniture, Aaron Sells Furniture, Aaron Rents & Sells Office Furniture, MacTavish Furniture Industries, Aaron Rents Electronices
Principal Bank: Trust Company Bank; First National Bank of Atlanta
Financial Information:

	$'000
Sales revenues	110,300

No of Employees: 1,205

AARQUE COMPANIES

111 W Second Street, Jamestown, NY 14701
Tel: (716) 664 6014
Telex: TWX 5102466260 aarque jame

Chairman: R Q Anderson (also President Aarque Steel Group); Vice Chairman: John T Thompson
Senior Executive Officers: Wilbur J Berner (President Aarque Management Corp), Jack E Smith (President Kordex Systems Inc), Thomas E Thayer (President Western Capital Group)

PRINCIPAL ACTIVITIES: Manufacture of steel tubes and strips, filing cabinets and metal products
Financial Information:

	$'000
Sales revenues	400,000

No of Employees: 3,100

ABBOTT LABORATORIES

Abbott Park, North Chicago, IL 60064
Tel: (312) 937-6100
Telex: (312)-1511
Telefax: (312) 937-3863

Chairman: Robert A Schoellhorn (and Chief Executive Officer); Vice Chairman: Duane L Burnham (and Chief Financial Officer)
President: Jack W Schuler (and Chief Operating Officer)
Corporate Officers: Charles J Aschauer Jr (Executive VP), Thomas R Hodgson (Executive VP and President Abbott International Ltd), Laurence R Lee (Senior VP Administration and Secretary), Paul N Clark (VP, Pharmaceutical Operations), John E Condon (VP, Corporate Quality Assurance), O Ralph Edwards Jr (VP, Personnel), James L Farlander (VP, Corporate Materials Management), Kenneth W Farmer (VP, Management Information Services), Richard W Gast (VP, Ross Products), Richard B Hamilton (VP, Public Affairs), Lester E Hammar (VP and Controller), James A Hanley (VP and Treasurer), Robert S Janicki (VP, Pharmaceutical Products Research and Development), Joseph S Jenckes (VP, Washington, DC), Lael F Johnson (VP and General Counsel), John C Kane (VP, Chemical and Agricultural Products), John G Kringel (VP, Hospital Products), John F Lussen (VP, Taxes), J Duncan McIntyre (VP), David V Milligan (VP, Diagnostic Products Research and Development), Richard H Morehead (VP, Corporate Planning and Development), Daniel O Struble (VP, Corporate Engineering), David A Thompson (VP, Diagnostic Operations), Joseph M Bernik (Assistant Secretary), Peter E Jansen (Assistant Treasurer), Louis Korom Jr (Assistant Treasurer)

PRINCIPAL ACTIVITIES: Pharmaceutical and nutritional products including a broad line of adult and pediatric pharmaceuticals, nutritionals, vitamins and hematinics, which are sold primarily on prescription or recommendation of physicians or other health care professionals; and personal care products, agricultural and chemical products and bulk pharmaceuticals
Trade Names: Abbokinase(R), Abbott Spectrum(R), ADD-Vantage(R), Amidate(R), Bremax, Cartrol(R), Commander(R), Depakote(R), DiBeta(R), Dipel(R), Enduron(R), Enduronyl(R), Envacor, Erythrocin(R), Ethrane(R), Faultless(R), Flexiflo(R) II, Forane(R), Forta(R), Hytrin(R), K-Lor, K-Tab(R), LifeCare(R), Loftyl(R), Lupron(R), Murine(R), Nutrimix(R), Ogen(R), Osmolite(R), Oximetrix(R), PCE, Pedialyte(R), Pediazole(R), Pentothal(R), Pro-Gibb(R), Promalin(R), ProMod(R), Pulmocare, Quantum(R), Quantumatic, Rondec(R), Selsun Blue(R), Similac(R), Similator, TDx(R), TestPack, Thymone(R), Transpac(R) II, Tranxene(R), Tronolane(R), Vectobac(R), Vi-Daylin(R), Vision
Principal Subsidiaries: Abbott Caribbean Inc; Abbott Chemicals Inc; Abbott Energy Inc; Abbott Export Co; Abbott International Ltd; Abbott Laboratories International Co; Abbott Laboratories Pacific Ltd; Abbott Laboratories Services Corp; Abbott Laboratories Utility Corp; Abbott Pharmaceutical Inc; AHI Holding Co; Abbott Hospitals Inc; CMM Transportation Inc; Haven Leasing Corp; Havtex Leasing Corp; M & R Dietetic Laboratories; Murine Co Inc; Ross Laboratories Inc; Sorenson Research Co Inc; Swan-Myers Inc; Takeda-Abbott Products; TB Prevention Pdts (Hong Kong); Tobal Products Inc; Wichita Chemicals Inc
Financial Information:

	Dec 31 1986 $'000	Dec 31 1987 $'000
Sales revenues	3,807,634	4,387,876
Income before taxes	818,698	937,125
Net income	540,460	632,559
Dividends	194,099	228,078
Dividends per share	$0.84	$1.00
Earnings per share	$2.32	$2.78
Common stock	181,317	187,979
Retained income	1,702,502	1,926,800
Shareholders equity	1,778,921	2,093,453

No of Employees: 37,828

ABBOTTS DAIRIES

33rd and Arch Street, Philadelphia, PA 19104
Tel: (215) 386-0200

President: William G Shafer
Senior Executive Officers: Dale Beckman (VP Operations), Randall P Nielson (VP Administration), Don Holt (Comptroller), John Kovarovic (Marketing Manager)

PRINCIPAL ACTIVITIES: Manufacture and sale of dairy products
Principal Bank: Philadelphia National Bank
Financial Information:

	$'000
Sales revenues	100,000

No of Employees: 400

ABERDEEN MANUFACTURING CORPORATION

16 E 34th St, New York, NY 10016
Tel: (212) 889-8380

President: Jud R Lober

Senior Executive Officers: Norman La Peters (Assistant to President and Treasurer)

PRINCIPAL ACTIVITIES: Manufacture of soft furnishings and garden furniture
Parent Company: Henry Crown & Co
Principal Bank: Manufacturers Hanover Trust Co
Financial Information:

	$'000
Sales revenues	90,000

No of Employees: 1,800

ABEX CORPORATION

Six Landmark Sq, Box 10268, Stamford, CT 06904
Tel: (203) 328-3200
Telex: WUT 643010

President: Stephen S Conway Jr
Senior Executive Officers: Donald W Grinter (Executive VP), A A Borin (Group VP), K R Mayne (Group VP), G E Stinson (Group VP), C J Moisen (VP and Treasurer), Charles W Grinnell (VP, General Counsel and Secretary), E E Berry (VP Defense Systems), John Berkenkamp (VP Planning), D C Christensen (VP Human Resources), Arvind G Paranjpe (VP International)

PRINCIPAL ACTIVITIES: Manufacture of a range of brake equipment, pumps and valves; metal castings, aircraft and railroad equipment
Parent Company: IC Industries Inc, Chicago, IL
Financial Information:

	$'000
Sales revenues	700,000

No of Employees: 10,500

ABRAMS INDUSTRIES INC

P O Box 76600, Atlanta, GA 30328
Tel: (404) 256-9785

Chairman: Bernard W Abrams (and Chief Executive Officer)
President: Edward M Abrams
Senior Executive Officers: Joseph H S Rubin (Treasurer)

PRINCIPAL ACTIVITIES: Building and construction; electrical contracting; fire prevention equipment
Principal Subsidiaries: Abrams Construction Inc; Abrams Fixture Corp; Abrams Investments Inc; Columbia Engineering & Services; Financial Prpts. Developers; Jones Piping Inc; South Elmec Inc
Financial Information:

	$'000
Sales revenues	46,000

No of Employees: 500

ACADEMY INSURANCE GROUP INC

1 Valley Forge Plaza, Valley Forge, PA 19487
Tel: (215) 337-1400

Chairman: Richard D Barger
President: Fred M Dolin (and Chief Executive Officer and Chief Operating Officer)
Senior Executive Officers: John I Barringer (VP), Stephen A Cohen (VP Legal Counsel), Anthony A Geyelin (VP Assistant General Counsel), Samuel J Walsh (Senior VP), Thomas P Casalnova (Treasurer), Michael F Beausang Jr (Secretary)

PRINCIPAL ACTIVITIES: Life, health and accident insurance
Financial Information:

	Dec 31 1985
	$'000
Revenues	123,335

No of Employees: 600

ACCEL INTERNATIONAL CORPORATION

475 Metro Place North, Dublin, OH 43017
Tel: (614) 764-7000
Telefax: (614) 764-7196

Chairman: Brian L Howell (and Chief Financial Officer)
President: R Max Williamson (and Chief Executive Officer)
Senior Executive Officers: Nicholas Z Alexander (VP, Secretary and General Counsel), William L Gesler (VP and Actuary), James M Bernard (VP and Treasurer), Larry L Main (VP-Accounting), Barry E Hunlock (VP-Taxes and Reinsurance), H W (Tripp) Marshall (VP-Marketing)

PRINCIPAL ACTIVITIES: Insurance services
Trade Names: COSTGUARD, ACCELERATION (Logo)
Principal Subsidiaries: Acceleration Life Insurance Company; Acceleration National Insurance Company; Acceleration National Service Corporation; Acceleration Insurance Company Limited (UK)
Principal Bank: Fifth Third Bank, Columbus, Ohio
Financial Information:

	Dec 31 1985	Dec 31 1986
	$'000	$'000
Premium income	78,555	95,444
Investment income	9,186	9,346
Income before taxes	3,297	2,125
Net income	3,110	4,304
Earnings per share	$0.60	$0.83
Common stock	485	517
Retained income	18,080	20,187
Stockholders equity	39,389	43,786

No of Employees: 130

ACCO INTERNATIONAL INC

770 S Acco Plaza, Wheeling, IL 60090
Tel: (312) 541-9500
Telex: TWX 9106512085 acco 2 whlg

Chairman: Douglas K Chapman
President: William L Walter (and Chief Operating Officer)
Senior Executive Officers: Raymond Stamm (Senior VP), James E Cullen (VP International), Fred Schomer (VP Finance and Secretary)

PRINCIPAL ACTIVITIES: Manufacture of data processing equipment and office equipment
Parent Company: Acco World Corporation, Northbrook, IL
Principal Bank: Continental Illinois National Bank and Trust Company of Chicago
Financial Information:

	$'000
Sales revenues	90,000

No of Employees: 950

ACCO WORLD CORPORATION

2215 Sanders Rd, Northbrook, IL 60062
Tel: (312) 480-9700

Chairman: D K Chapman (and Chief Executive Officer)
President: D R LaPlace (and Chief Operating Officer)
Senior Executive Officers: William Walter (VP and President US Division), Robert L Hanson (VP), Gershen M Abraham (VP Manufacturing and Engineering), Norman H Wesley (VP Corporate Planning), Fred K Schomer (VP, Secretary and Treasurer), Donald W Rogers (Controller)

PRINCIPAL ACTIVITIES: Manufacture of office products including paper clips and binders
Principal Subsidiaries: Acco International Inc; Polyblend Corp; Systems Furniture Co
Principal Bank: Continental Illinois Bank
Financial Information:

	$'000
Sales revenues	160,000

No of Employees: 2,800

ACE HARDWARE CORPORATION

2200 Kensington, Oakbrook, IL 60521
Tel: (312) 887 6600
Telex: TWX 910 651 01 86 ace hdwe oakr

Chairman: Theodore Costoff; Vice Chairman: Gregg Ziegler
President: Lawrence R Gavin
Senior Executive Officers: Roger E Peterson (Executive VP), David F Hodnik (VP Finance and Treasurer), William A Loftus (VP Sales), Frank A Szymanek (VP Merchandising)

PRINCIPAL ACTIVITIES: Cooperative association with interests in the supply of hardware
Principal Bank: Northern Trust Company
Financial Information:

	Dec 31 1985	Dec 31 1986
	$'000	$'000
Sales revenues	1,008,970	1,060,632
Shareholders equity	102,780	109,881

No of Employees: 2,253

ACETO CHEMICAL CO INC

126-02 Northern Blvd, Flushing, NY 11368
Tel: (718) 898-2300
Telex: ITT 423159 acet ui; RCA 234965 aceto ur; TWX 7105824900 aceto nyk

Chairman: Arnold J Frankel (and Secretary/Treasurer)
President: Seymour Mann
Senior Executive Officers: Robert E Parsont (Executive VP), Richard Amitrano (VP), Anthony Baldi (President, Agricultural Chemicals Division), William Blank (VP), Thomas Brunner (Senior VP), Steven Chepow (VP, Pfaltz & Bauer Division), Gary Conte (Products Manager), Frank Debenedittis (Products Manager), James Dillon (VP, Arsynco Division), Michael Feinman (VP, Agricultural Chemicals Division), Roy Goodman (Assistant VP), Donald Horowitz (VP and Controller), Curtis Koeppe (Products Manager), John Larocca (Assistant Controller), Leonard Lawton (Assistant VP), Henry Mellett (Products Manager), Vincent Miata (Products Manager), Harry Olenberg (VP, Roehr Chemicals Division), Rita Pasternack (VP and Traffic Manager), Leonard Schwartz (VP), Terry Steinberg (Assistant VP)

PRINCIPAL ACTIVITIES: Manufacture of chemicals; The Company's product line includes chemicals for a wide variety of uses. They are used to synthesize colors for use in photography, textiles, plastics, paints and printing inks. In the pharmaceutical industry the company supplies bulk pharmaceuticals for both human and veterinary use, as well as specialty chemicals to be used as raw materials to synthesize pharmaceuticals and antibiotics. Other specialty chemicals are supplied to a wide variety of customers for use in hundreds of applications for myriads of end products
Principal Subsidiaries: Arsynco, Inc; Roehr Chemicals, Inc; Pfaltz & Bauer, Inc
Financial Information:

	Jun 30 1985	Jun 30 1986
	$'000	$'000
Sales revenues	93,068	105,926
Income before taxes	9,215	9,574
Net income	4,796	4,937
Dividends(1)	181	412
Dividends per share(1)	8%	8%
Earnings per share net(2)	$1.46	$1.49
Common stock	30	32
Retained income	22,573	22,918
Shareholders equity	36,121	41,210

(1) common stock
(2) fully diluted

No of Employees: 175

ACF INDUSTRIES INC

3301 Rider Trail S, Hazelwood, MO 63045
Tel: (314) 344-4500
Telex: WUT 447612; WUT 447691

Chairman: Carl C Icahn (and Chief Executive Officer); Vice Chairman: Alfred D Kingsley
President: D Joseph Corr
Senior Executive Officers: John F McCarthy (Senior VP, Sales and Marketing), Henry N Parrish (Senior VP), Donald E Reese (Senior VP), James J Unger (Senior VP Finance and Chief Financial Officer), Robert F Allen (VP Labor Relations), William L Finn (VP Fleet Operations), David R Sutliff (VP Engineering), Roger D Wynkoop (VP Sls Leasing), Robert J Mitchell (Treasurer

PRINCIPAL ACTIVITIES: Manufacture of railroad freight cars, sale and leasing
Principal Subsidiaries: ACF America Corp; ACF Canada Ltd; ACF International Sales Corp; ACF Leasing Co; Carter Automotive Products Corp; Carter Precision Parts Inc; Corning Distribution Co; SHPX Fifth Corp
Financial Information:

	$'000
Sales revenues	400,000

No of Employees: 1,900

ACME ELECTRIC CORPORATION

20 Water Street, Cuba, NY 14727
Tel: (716) 968-2400
Telex: WUT 916451 acme el cuba

Chairman: James W McLaughlin
President: G Wayne Hawk (and Chief Executive Officer)
Senior Executive Officers: R Hartley Bond (VP of Marketing and Corporate Planning), J Thomas Odell (VP), Daniel K Corwin (VP and Corporate Controller), David G Anderson (Secretary, Treasurer and General Counsel), Thomas G Long (VP and General Manager Acme Transformer Group), Joseph Pinker (Vice President and General Manager, Commercial Products Group), Thomas P Sullivan (VP and General Manager Power Products Group), Dale G Guilford (Group Sales Manager, Power Products Group), William A Boyd (President, ACME URDC, Inc), Robert W McGinnis (President, SAFE Power Systems Inc)

PRINCIPAL ACTIVITIES: Acme Electric Corporate designs, manufactures and markets power conversion equipment for electronic and electrical systems. This is considered to be one line of business. Principal markets encompass computers, test equipment, information systems and telecommunications, as well as a variety of industrial, commercial and residential applications requiring conversion of electrical energy from one useable state to another
Principal Subsidiaries: Safe Power Systems Inc; Acme-URDC Inc
Principal Bank: First Wachovia
Financial Information:

	Jun 30 1986	Jun 30 1987
	$'000	$'000
Sales revenues	69,578	67,471
Income before taxes	3,369	1,365
Net income	1,883	663
Dividends	1,244	1,305
Dividends per share	$0.30	$0.32
Earnings per share	$0.45	$0.16
Common stock	4,016	4,254
Retained income	5,589	3,516
Shareholders equity	22,680	22,297

No of Employees: 1,000

ACME PRECISION PRODUCTS INC

3750 East Outer Drive, Detroit, MI 48234
Tel: (313) 891-3400

Chairman: Thomas M Wheeler (and Executive VP)
President: Raymond A McCarroll
Senior Executive Officers: Raymond A Burger (Group President), Vincent J Spedale (Group President), Richard M Tanghe (Secretary and Treasurer)

PRINCIPAL ACTIVITIES: Manufacture of machine tools
Principal Bank: Bank of New York
Financial Information:

	$'000
Sales revenues	41,235

No of Employees: 50

ACME UNITED CORPORATION
425 Post Road, Fairfield, CT 06430
Tel: (203) 255-2744

President: Henry C Wheeler (and Treasurer and Chief Executive Officer)
Senior Executive Officers: Joseph H Edgeworth (VP, Controller and Assistant Treasurer), John D Hoeveler (Senior VP and Secretary), Dwight C Wheeler II (Executive VP and Chief Operating Officer), James F Farrington (Senior VP Marketing), Edward J Sharkany (Senior VP Manufacturing), Andrew T Harrison (Senior VP Group Relations), William O'B. Warren (VP), Charles F Murphy (VP Sales), John V Moran (VP), Donald E Wenderoth (VP Sales), Kenneth S Green (VP Sales), William F O'Dell (VP Marketing)

PRINCIPAL ACTIVITIES: Manufacture of scissors, shears and medical equipment
Principal Bank: The Connecticut National Bank
Financial Information:

	$'000
Sales revenues	36,410

No of Employees: 850

ACME VISIBLE RECORDS INC
Crozet, VA 22932
Tel: (804) 823-4351
Telex: WUT 822455 acme vis crzt

Chairman: John P Clark (and Chief Executive Officer)
President: V S Schroeder (and Real Estate Executive)
Senior Executive Officers: V S Schroeder (Executive VP)

PRINCIPAL ACTIVITIES: Manufacture of office equipment and printing of business forms
Parent Company: Wilson Jones Co
Principal Bank: Sovran Bank
Financial Information:

	$'000
Sales revenues	50,000

No of Employees: 900

ACME-CLEVELAND CORPORATION
30195 Chagrin Blvd, Cleveland, OH 44124
Tel: (216) 292-2100

Chairman: B C Ames (and Chief Executive Officer)
President: James T Bartlett (and Chief Operating Officer)
Senior Executive Officers: Francis R Appeldorn (VP), David L Swift (VP), Richard B Ainsworth Jr (VP)

PRINCIPAL ACTIVITIES: Manufacture of machine tools and electrical and electronic equipment
Principal Bank: Ameritrust Company
Financial Information:

	$'000
Sales revenues	220,000

No of Employees: 3,100

ACORN BUILDING COMPONENTS INC
12620 Westwood Avenue, Detroit, MI
Tel: (313) 272-5700

Chairwoman: Ruth E Rich (and President)
Senior Executive Officers: Keith Pietila (Chief Operating Officer), Robert A Rich (Senior VP and Chief Executive Officer), Wilmer Frazier (VP Sales), Kent Bathurst (VP Manufacturing), Joseph DiFazio (VP), Arthur Zapico (VP)

PRINCIPAL ACTIVITIES: Manufacture of aluminum and glass products for the building industry
Principal Subsidiaries: Acorn Distributing Co Inc
Financial Information:

	$'000
Sales revenues	70,000

No of Employees: 1,200

ACTION INDUSTRIES INC
460 Nixon Road, Cheswick, PA 15024
Tel: (412) 782-4800
Telex: WUT 866144 actionind chsw

Chairman: Amos Comay (and Treasurer); Vice Chairman: S B Buchwach
President: Ernest S Berez (and Chief Executive Officer)
Senior Executive Officers: Raymond A Hutchinson (Executive VP, Finance and Administration), Sholom D Comay (Senior VP), Ronald A Gagnon (Senior VP Proprietary Products), Gerhard J Mueller (VP Plastics Manufacturing), Robert Robinson (VP Information Systems), Kenneth L Campbell (VP and Controller), Jack Gershowitz (VP Proprietary Products Sales), Carl P Maurantonio (VP Proprietary Products Sales), Michael L Merlo (VP Proprietary Products Sales), Thomas L Ranieri (VP Proprietary Products Sales), James G Meehan (VP Proprietary Products Sales Service), Jack Winemiller (VP Marketing Services), Linda S Wilson (VP Legal and Assistant Secretary)

PRINCIPAL ACTIVITIES: Manufacture, wholesale and retail trade in household goods
Principal Subsidiaries: Action International Ltd
Principal Bank: Union National Bank of Pittsburgh
Financial Information:

	$'000
Sales revenues	167,000

No of Employees: 960

ACTIVISION INC
2350 Bayshore Frontage Road, Mountain View, CA 94043
Tel: (415) 960-0410
Telex: WUT 17 2758 actvision mntv

Chairman: J H Levy (and President and Chief Executive Officer)
Senior Executive Officers: Gregory Fishback (Senior VP), Joseph Avery (VP Operations and Administration), Kenneth Coleman (VP Product Development), R L Smith McKeithen (VP, General Counsel and Secretary), Edward Roffman (VP Finance and Controller)

PRINCIPAL ACTIVITIES: Manufacture and sale of software for home computers
Financial Information:

	$'000
Sales revenues	70,000

No of Employees: 240

ACTMEDIA INC
30 Old Kings Highway S, Darien, CT 06820
Tel: (203) 655-2211

Chairman: Bruce F Failing Sr
President: Bruce F Failing Jr
Senior Executive Officers: Elizabeth F Failing (Executive VP), Marxianna M Moe (VP), Leighton H York Jr (VP), Ross W McKeon (VP Finance), J H Stevenson (VP), J C Sturgess (VP)

PRINCIPAL ACTIVITIES: Advertising
Principal Bank: Long Island Trust Co

Financial Information:

	$'000
Sales revenues	45,000

No of Employees: 600

ACUSHNET CO

700 Belleville Avenue, New Bedford, MA 02745
Tel: (617) 997-2811

President: John T Ludes (and Chief Executive Officer)
Senior Executive Officers: J W Jepson (Executive VP), W R Uihlein (Senior VP), R B Forbush (VP), J G DeMello (VP Sales-Rubber Division), D M Shenk (VP and Controller)

PRINCIPAL ACTIVITIES: Manufacture of precision-molded natural and synthetic rubber goods and golf equipment
Trade Names: Titleist, Pinnacle, Bulls Eye, Dead Center, Foot-Joy
Parent Company: American Brands, Inc
Principal Bank: Shawmut Bank of Boston
Financial Information:

	1986
	$'000
Sales revenues	261,985

No of Employees: 2,240

ADAC LABORATORIES

540 Alder Dr, Milpitas, CA 95035-7443

Chairman: Q T Wiles
President: Charles W Cantoni
Senior Executive Officers: Stephen J Weiss (Executive VP), William Ross (VP Engineering), Bob Dienhammer (VP Operations), Ralph Andreas (VP Sales and Marketing), Victor Hersone (VP Field Resources)

PRINCIPAL ACTIVITIES: Manufacture of medical equipment for radiation treatment and radiography
Principal Bank: Union Bank
Financial Information:

	$'000
Sales revenues	60,000

No of Employees: 500

ADAGE INC

1 Fortune Drive, Billerica, MA 01821
Tel: (617) 667-7070

President: Richard N Spann
Senior Executive Officers: Henry H Rich (VP), John P Cunningham (Executive VP and Treasurer), James H Hardie (VP Marketing), Fredrick E Shirk (Senior VP Sales), Peter H Emery (VP Manufacturing), Brijeshwari Prasad (Executive VP Marketing), J N England III (VP Product Area), Richard D Fiorentino (VP Product Area), Seymour Yalen (VP)

PRINCIPAL ACTIVITIES: Manufcture of electronic data processing equipment
Principal Bank: Bank of New England
Financial Information:

	$'000
Sales revenues	37,000

No of Employees: 430

ADAMS PACKING ASSOCATION INC

625 Bridgers Avenue, Auburndale, FL 33823
Tel: (813) 967-4431

President: John F Wise
Senior Executive Officers: Charles W Adams (VP and Secretary), Fred A Harman (Treasurer)

PRINCIPAL ACTIVITIES: Manufacture of frozen and canned fruit juice
Parent Company: Royal Crown Companies Inc, Atlanta, GA
Principal Bank: Barnett Bank of East Polk County
Financial Information:

	$'000
Sales revenues	70,000

No of Employees: 750

ADAMS RESOURCES AND ENERGY INC

6910 Fannin, Houston, TX 77030
Tel: (713) 797-9966

Chairman: K S Adams Jr (and President and Chief Executive Officer)
Executive Vice President: E H Laws (and Chief Operating Officer)
Senior Executive Officers: Richard B Abshire (VP Finance), David B S Hurst (Legal), Claude L Lewis (VP Land Transportation), William R Sharp (VP Oil and Gas)

PRINCIPAL ACTIVITIES: Production of oil and gas; distribution of petroleum products; truck transportation industry
Trade Names: Ada Resources
Financial Information:

	Dec 31 1985	Dec 31 1986
	$'000	$'000
Revenues	127,916	67,031
Income before taxes	3,175	1,964
Net income	1,944	1,964
Earnings per share	$0.22	$0.23
Common stock	691	696
Retained (deficit)	(28,705)	(27,136)
Shareholders (deficit)	(7,916)	(6,223)

No of Employees: 207

ADAMS RUSSELL CO, INC

1380 Main Street, Waltham, MA 02154
Tel: (617) 894-8450
Fax: (617) 893-0069
Telex: TWX 7103246450 adamsrussb whe

Chairman: Gerald J Adams
President: John J Lynch (and Chief Executive Officer)
Senior Executive Officers: Joseph S Batal (VP), James J Connolly (VP), William C Henchy (VP), Trevor Lambert (VP), Harold H Leach (VP), David McLachlan (VP and Secretary)

PRINCIPAL ACTIVITIES: Manufacture of electronic and commmunications equipment
Trade Names: Anzac
Principal Subsidiaries: Adams Russell Cable Services
Principal Bank: First National Bank of Boston
Financial Information:

	$'000
Sales revenues	129,000

Principal Shareholders: Telecable (11.5%); Continental Cablevision (8%); T Rowe-Price (7.4%)
No of Employees: 1,440

ADAMS-MILLIS CORPORATION

225 N Elm Street, High Point, NC 27260
Tel: (919) 889-7071
Telex: 510-9261923 Adm Millis HIP

Chairman: James H Millis Sr
President: Robert M Bundy Jr
Senior Executive Officers: M Neel Harrison (Senior VP-Finance), Michael L Ryan (Senior VP-Administration and Human Resources), Lawrence Smith (Senior VP-Sales), Jon Wallner (Senior VP-Manufacturing), James H Millis Jr (Senior VP-Marketing and Product Development), N G Harris Jr (VP and Financial Controller), E D Denny (VP and Operations), C D Oakes (VP Administrative Services)

PRINCIPAL ACTIVITIES: Major marketer and manufacturer of hosiery products for the entire family
Trade Names: Private Label. Licensee for hosiery under the following names: Hanes, Field & Stream, Playmate, Jockey,

Yves St Laurent, Colours by Alexander Julian. Brand names owned by Adams-Millis: Weekender, Sweatout
Principal Subsidiaries: Silver Knit Industries Inc; Drexel Knitting Mills Inc
Principal Bank: Wachovia Bank & Trust
Financial Information:

	$'000
Sales revenues	116,300

No of Employees: 2,100

ADC TELECOMMUNICATIONS INC
5501 Green Valley Drive, Bloomington, MN 55437
Tel: (612) 835-6800
Telex: TWX 9105762832 adc mc

Chairman: C M Denny Jr
President: F R Boswell (and Chief Executive Officer)
Senior Executive Officers: R C Wagner (Senior VP), D A Leese (VP Sales), L J Morgan (VP Finance), D H Moersch (VP Human Resources), L J Davis (VP Manufacturing), W C Hamer (VP Technology), C R Bigham (VP Information Services), R G Martin (VP Quality), C M Johnson (VP Product Management)

PRINCIPAL ACTIVITIES: Manufacture of electronic equipment for the telecommunications industry
Principal Bank: Norwest Bank
Financial Information:

	$'000
Sales revenues	125,000

No of Employees: 1,800

ADDISON-WESLEY PUBLISHING CO
South Street, Reading, MA 01867
Tel: (617) 944-3700
Cable: JACOB WAY, READING, MA 01867
Telex: 94916 ADIWES

Chairman: Donald R Hammonds
President: R Wayne Oler (and Chief Executive Officer)
Senior Executive Officers: J L Jones (Executive VP), R W Oler (Executive VP), Warren R Stone (Executive VP), Ronald N Woodward (Executive VP, Finance), Ann E Dilworth (Executive VP), Robert E Podsen (Senior VP)

PRINCIPAL ACTIVITIES: Publishing of educational books
Principal Bank: Bank of Boston
Financial Information:

	Nov 30 1985	Dec 31 1986
	$'000	$'000
Sales revenues	139,402	150,118
Income before taxes	11,735	13,852
Net income	6,666	7,998
Dividends	1,901	2,185
Dividends per share	$0.75	$0.85
Earnings per share	$2.63	$3.12
Common stock	4,241	7,326
Retained income	51,197	55,534
Shareholders equity	57,438	62,860

No of Employees: 1,300

ADDRESSOGRAPH FARRINGTON INC
Randolph Industrial Park, Randolph, MA 02368
Tel: (617) 963-8500
Telex: RCA 294007 Afir ur

President: Charles W Doulton
Senior Executive Officers: Robert P Axline (VP), Peter D Lock (VP Marketing), Ed Langley (VP), Robert E McManus (VP Finance and Administration, Secretary and Treasurer)

PRINCIPAL ACTIVITIES: Manufacture of printing machinery and imprinting equipment for the production of credit cards
Parent Company: DBS Inc, Randolph, MA
Principal Bank: Bank of New England
Financial Information:

	$'000
Sales revenues	100,000

No of Employees: 1,650

ADIA SERVICES INC
64 Willow Place, Menlo Park, CA 94025
Tel: (415) 324-0696
Telex: 34872

Chairman: Yves J Paternot
President: Walter W Macauley (and Chief Executive Officer)
Senior Executive Officers: John W Hamachek (Senior VP and Chief Financial Officer), Doreen Penfield (VP Administration), Carl Mianecke (VP)

PRINCIPAL ACTIVITIES: Provision of temporary help services
Parent Company: Adia SA, Switzerland
Principal Bank: Bank of America
Financial Information:

	$'000
Sales revenues	220,000

No of Employees: 500

ADOBE OIL & GAS CORPORATION
1100 Western United Life Building, Midland, TX 79701
Tel: (915) 683-4701

President: B J Pevehouse
Senior Executive Officers: Loyd G Whitley (Senior VP Finance), M D Rogers (Senior VP Operations)

PRINCIPAL ACTIVITIES: Holding company with interests in the exploration for, and production of oil, gas, coal and uranium
Principal Bank: Chase Manhattan Bank
Financial Information:

	$'000
Sales revenues	167,000

No of Employees: 260

ADOLPH COORS CO
See COORS, ADOLPH, CO

ADRIA LABORATORIES INC
5000 Post Road, Dublin, OH 43017
Tel: (614) 764-8100
Telex: WUT 246620 adrialabl dbo

President: David E Robinson
Senior Executive Officers: James M McCormick (VP Marketing), Robert L Fleming (VP Operations), James A Page (VP Medical), Robert J Little (VP Finance)

PRINCIPAL ACTIVITIES: Manufacture and sale of pharmaceuticals
Principal Bank: BancOhio National Bank
Financial Information:

	$'000
Sales revenues	125,000

No of Employees: 700

ADT INC
One World Trade Center, New York, NY 10048
Tel: (212) 558-1100

Chairman: Raymond B Carey Jr
President: Ulysses J Brualdi (and Chief Operating Officer)
Senior Executive Officers: Edward M Liddy (Executive VP and Chief Financial Officer), Daniel C Colin (VP Marketing and New Construction Systems), Glenn T Dallas (VP Operations), Robert O Donnelly (VP and General Counsel), Anthony J Grosso (VP, National Accounts), William F Halpin (VP Administration, Treasurer and Secretary), John P Mercer (VP Operations), Selma Rossen (VP Engineering), Ronald F Thornley (VP Operations), Norman H Whitman (VP Service)

PRINCIPAL ACTIVITIES: Production of electronic surveillance and security equipment
Trade Names: FOCUS, SAFEWATCH, UNIMODE
Financial Information:

	$'000
Sales revenues	470,600

No of Employees: 9,800

ADVANCE CIRCUITS INC

560 16th Ave South, Hopkins, MN 55343
Tel: (612) 935 5695

President: Thomas F Leahy
Senior Executive Officers: Robert W Heller (Executive VP), George E Kline (VP, Secretary and Treasurer), Clarence E Wordehoff (VP Operations), John P Kerrick (VP Engineering)

PRINCIPAL ACTIVITIES: Manufacture of electronic components including printed circuits
Principal Bank: National City Bank of Minneapolis
Financial Information:

	$'000
Sales revenues	57,600

No of Employees: 725

ADVANCED MICRO DEVICES, INC

901 Thompson Pl, Sunnyvale, CA 94086
Tel: (408) 732-2400
Telex: RCA 278261 amdsv ur

Chairman: W J Sanders III (and President and Chief Executive Officer)
Senior Executive Officers: Anthony Holbrook (Executive VP and Chief Operating Officer), James B Downey (Senior VP), Richard Previte (Senior VP Finance), George Scalise (Senior VP Administration), Steve Zelenick (Senior VP Sales and Marketing)

PRINCIPAL ACTIVITIES: Manufacture of data processing equipment peripherals
Principal Bank: Bank of America
Financial Information:

	Mar 31 1986 $'000
Sales revenues	576,124
Net (loss)	(36,624)
Earnings per share	$1.23
Shareholders equity	389,178

No of Employees: 15,000

ADVANCED SYSTEMS INC

155 East Algonquin Road, Arlington Heights, IL 60005
Tel: (312) 981-1500

Chairman: Arthur H Stromberg
President: William R Roach (and Chief Executive Officer)
Senior Executive Officers: Horst J Gallus (VP Europe), John A Kirkham (Senior VP), Gareth G Morris (VP General Counsel and Secretary), Geoffrey C Murphy (VP Finance and Chief Financial Officer and Treasurer), Elizabeth E Tomaszewicz (VP Sales), Robert M Dussault (VP), Daniel P Brosman (VP Training Management)

PRINCIPAL ACTIVITIES: Production of multimedia training courses
Principal Subsidiaries: ASI Domestic International Sales Corp; VAI Study Centers Inc
Principal Bank: Harris Trust & Savings
Financial Information:

	$'000
Sales revenues	51,515

No of Employees: 550

ADVANCED TELECOMMUNICATIONS CORPORATION

148 International Blvd, Suite 500, Atlanta, GA 30303
Tel: (404) 688-2475

Chairman: Stephen E Raville
President: John D Phillips
Senior Executive Officers: H Hobart Corwin (VP-Finance and Treasurer), Dennis E Bay (VP-Marketing), Robert P Chastain (VP-Network Engineering), Joan C Merrill (VP-Administraton and Secretary), Stephen M Rawls (VP-Transmission)

PRINCIPAL ACTIVITIES: Long distance telephone service
Trade Names: ATC/TRANSCALL, ATC/DIRECTLINE, ATC/SATELCO
Principal Subsidiaries: Transcall America Inc; Directline Austin Inc; Satelco Inc
Principal Bank: First Union Bank of Georgia
Financial Information:

	Mar 31 1986 $'000	Mar 31 1987 $'000
Sales revenues	45,616	67,206
Income before taxes	6,481	9,685
Net income	3,485	5,129
Earnings per share	$0.58	$0.75
Common stock	5,996	22,703
Retained income	8,396	13,525
Shareholders equity	14,392	36,228

No of Employees: 360

ADVEST GROUP INC

6 Central Row, Hartford, CT 06103
Tel: (203) 525-1421

Chairman: Anthony A Lacroix (and President and Chief Executive Officer)
Senior Executive Officers: A Clinton Allen III (Executive VP), George A Boujoukos (Executive VP), John Everets Jr (Executive VP), Barton Ferris (Managing Director), Martin M Lilienthal (VP and Treasurer), Melvin I Schiloni (Senior VP Marketing and Advertising), Allen G Botwinick (Senior VP Administration and Special Investment Service), John D Reynolds (Group VP), Robert L Thomas (Executive VP), Allen Weintraub (Senior Executive VP and Chief Operating Officer), Lee G Kuckroe (Secretary and VP), Arnold E Amstutz (Executive VP Investments)

PRINCIPAL ACTIVITIES: A wide range of financial and investment services
Principal Subsidiaries: Advest Bank; Advest Credit Corp; Advest Inc; Billings & Co Inc; Burgess & Leith/Advest Co Inc; Central Row Corp; T E Desmond Co
Principal Bank: The Connecticut Bank & Trust Co
Financial Information:

	$'000
Revenues	146,585

No of Employees: 1,450

AEC, INC

850 Pratt Blvd, Elk Grove Village, IL 60007
Tel: (312) 593-5000
Telex: 28-7426

Chairman: Michael A Waters (and Chief Executive Officer)
President: Donald C Williams (and Chief Operating Officer)
Senior Executive Officers: Richard R Aevermann (VP), D W Swanson (Treasurer)

PRINCIPAL ACTIVITIES: Manufacture of water treatment equipment; manufacture of mechanical handling equipment
Principal Subsidiaries: Application Engineering Corporation; Whitlock, Inc; Nelmor Co, Inc
Principal Bank: Continental Illinois National Bank

Financial Information:

	Oct 31 1985	Oct 31 1986
	$'000	$'000
Sales revenues	59,458	64,505
Income before taxes	320	1,989
Net income	405	987
Dividends	529	529
Dividends per share	$0.32	$0.32
Earnings per share	$0.25	$0.25
Common stock	1,655	1,654
Retained income	9,828	10,296
Shareholders equity	11,876	12,328

No of Employees: 606

AEL AMERICAN ELECTRONIC LABORATORIES, INC

305 Richardson, Lansdale, PA 19446
Tel: (215) 822-2929
Cable: AMERLAB
Telex: 476-1188 AELABS

Chairman: Conrad J Fowler
President: Mark Ronald (and Chief Operating Officer)
Senior Executive Officers: C B Cronin (VP Marketing), George King (VP Finance), Harold Musnitsky (VP Manufacturing), Stephen Lipsky (VP Engineering), Jesse H Riebman (VP Treasurer and Secretary)

PRINCIPAL ACTIVITIES: Manufacture of defense electronic equipment and systems
Parent Company: AEL Industries, Inc
Principal Subsidiaries: Elisra Electronic Systems Ltd (Israel)
Principal Bank: Meridian Bank of Pennsylvania
Financial Information:

	$'000
Sales revenues	60,000

No of Employees: 1,475

AEL INDUSTRIES INC

305 Richardson Road, Lansdale, PA 19446
Tel: (215) 822-2929

Chairman: Conrad J Fowler
President: Dr Leon Riebman (and Chief Executive Officer)
Senior Executive Officers: George King (VP Finance and Administration), Jesse H Riebman (VP), Raymond Gutowski (VP), John F Sharkey (VP)

PRINCIPAL ACTIVITIES: AEL is a leading supplier of electronic defense systems and subsystems. The Company designs and manufactures sophisticated countermeasure, simulation and receiving systems, engages in the installation and integration of electronic and avionics equipment into military aircraft and provides state of the art antenna, microwave and integrated circuit components equipment
Principal Subsidiaries: AEL American Electronic Laboratories, Inc
Principal Bank: Meridian Bank of Pennsylvania
Financial Information:

	Feb 28 1986
	$'000
Sales revenues	104,909
Net income	4,739
Earnings per share	$1.01
Common stock*	4,671

*average shares outstanding in thousands

No of Employees: 1,475

AEP INDUSTRIES INC

20 Knickerbocker Road, Moonachie, NJ 07074
Tel: (201) 935-6500

Chairman: J Brendon Barba (and President)
Senior Executive Officers: Robert W Cron (VP), Jack Emmanuele (VP), David J McFarland (Executive VP and Secretary), Ralph Young (VP Manufacturing)

PRINCIPAL ACTIVITIES: Manufacture of polythene products including shrink film, bags and sheeting
Principal Bank: Banks Trust Company
Financial Information:

	$'000
Sales revenues	54,215

No of Employees: 230

AERO SERVICES INTERNATIONAL INC

111 Charles A Lindberg Drive, Teterboro Airport, Teterboro, NJ 07608
Tel: (201) 641-1770

Chairman: Orlando E Panfile (and President and Chief Executive Officer)
Senior Executive Officers: John Kennedy (VP Operations), A Brown Moore (Secretary), Howard F Zick (Treasurer and Comptroller), John L Carlen (Director Administration)

PRINCIPAL ACTIVITIES: Hangars, fueling and servicing of aircraft
Principal Bank: Hibernia National Bank
Financial Information:

	$'000
Sales revenues	45,465

No of Employees: 835

AEROFLEX LABORATORIES INC

35 South Service Road, Plainview, NY 11803
Tel: (516) 694-7400

Chairman: Julius D Winer
President: Milton Brenner
Senior Executive Officers: Arthur J Hendler (Executive VP), Jack Tusinski (VP Finance), Frank Dimaio (Secretary and Treasurer), Richard Casper (VP Engineering), Thomas Guerriere (VP Technical), Chester Gilbert (VP Product Area)

PRINCIPAL ACTIVITIES: Manufacture of springs
Principal Subsidiaries: Aeroflex Systems Corp; Filtron Co Inc; Huxley Envelope Corp; Vibration Mountings & Controls Inc
Principal Bank: Barclays Bank
Financial Information:

	$'000
Sales revenues	48,000

No of Employees: 600

AEROJET ORDNANCE CO

2521 Michelle Dr, Tustin, CA 92680
Tel: (714) 730-6004

President: E R Elko
Senior Executive Officers: R E Ochs (VP and General Manager), E L Smith (VP Communications), E L Johnson (VP Engineering), R L Bivens (VP and Comptroller), G F Kriska (VP Industrial Relations), J Somberg (VP Contracts), R B Lyons (VP Business Development)

PRINCIPAL ACTIVITIES: Manufacture of military ordnance
Parent Company: Aerojet General Corporation-Ultimate Holding Company-Gencorp
Financial Information:

	$'000
Sales revenues	120,000

No of Employees: 800

AEROJET-GENERAL CORPORATION

10300 N Torrey Pines Road, La Jolla, CA 92037
Tel: (619) 455-8500
Telex: WUT 181774 aerojet ljla

President: George W Leisz

Senior Executive Officers: Rex Warden (Executive VP)

PRINCIPAL ACTIVITIES: Manufacture of aerospace and defense equipment
Trade Names: Aerojet
Parent Company: GenCorp, Akron, OH
Financial Information:

	1985	1986
	$'000	$'000
Sales revenues	760,000	861,000
Income before taxes	70,000	69,000

Principal Shareholders: GenCorp (100%)
No of Employees: 8,000

AERONAUTICAL ELECTRIC CO
5656 Northwest Hwy, Chicago, IL 60646
Tel: (312) 774-5200

President: Wm R Nordlof

PRINCIPAL ACTIVITIES: Electrical equipment
Principal Bank: Continental Illinois National Bank and Trust Company of Chicago
Financial Information:

	$'000
Sales revenues	700,000

No of Employees: 30

AERONCA INC
7415 Pineville-Matthews Road, Charlotte, NC 28226
Tel: (704) 541-1700

Chairman: Joe L Miller (and President and Chief Executive Officer)
Senior Executive Officers: J Lamont Crosby (VP and Chief Financial Officer), Clifton W Phillips (VP and Division President), Michael Rahman (VP Operations), Billy C Layton (Controller), John R Stewart (Treasurer), John E Hackett (VP Human Resources)

PRINCIPAL ACTIVITIES: Manufacture of aircraft components and related equipment
Parent Company: Fleet Aerospace Corporation
Principal Subsidiaries: Aeronca Electronics Inc
Principal Bank: Trust Co Bank of Middle Georgia
Financial Information:

	$'000
Sales revenues	65,200

No of Employees: 830

AEROQUIP CORPORATION
300 S East Avenue, Jackson, MI 49203
Tel: (517) 787-8121
Telex: WUT 223412 aeroquip jkn

President: G W Moody
Senior Executive Officers: J R Morgan (Group VP Administration), D E Rainey (Group VP International Operations), E Loll (Group VP European Operations), J L Price (Group VP U.S. Industrial), R E Ritchie (Group VP, Aerospace)

PRINCIPAL ACTIVITIES: Manufacture of clamps, seals, couplings, ball and swivel joints, flexible hose and molded rubber goods
Parent Company: Trinova Corporation

No of Employees: 7,000

AEROSPACE CORPORATION
2350 E El Segundo Blvd, El Segundo, CA 90245
Tel: (213) 648-5000
Telex: WUT 664460 aerospace elsd

Chairman: James W Plummer; Vice Chairman: Russell E Dougherty
President: Eberhardt Rechtin
Senior Executive Officers: David J Griep (Group VP Administration) George A Paulikas (Group VP Development), Samuel M Tennant (Group VP Programs), Ernest L Laporte (Group VP Engineering), Arthur J Schiewe (VP), Richard A Hartunian (VP Space Launch Vehicle Operations), Allan J Boardman (VP Advanced Orbital Systems Operations), Edward M Lassiter (VP Space Flight Operations)

PRINCIPAL ACTIVITIES: Military space research
Financial Information:

	$'000
Sales revenues	300,000

No of Employees: 4,200

AETNA LIFE & CASUALTY COMPANY
151 Farmington Avenue, Hartford, CT 06156
Tel: (203) 273-0123
Telex: 99-241 Aetna LC HFD

Chairman: James T Lynn
President: William O Bailey
Senior Executive Officers: Donald G Conrad (Executive VP and Chief Financial Officer), Burton E Burton (Senior VP, Employee Benefits Division), Robert J Clark (Senior VP, Commercial Insurance Division), Dean E Wolcott (Senior VP, Personal Financial Security Division)

PRINCIPAL ACTIVITIES: Group life; health and pensions; health and annuities; person casualty-property; casualty-property reinsurance
Principal Subsidiaries: Aetna Life Insurance Company; Aetna Casualty & Surety Company; Aetna Casualty & Surety Company of Illinois; Aetna Casualty & Surety Company of America; Automobile Insurance Company; American Reinsurance Company; Standard Fire; Aetna Life Insurance Company of Illinois; Aetna Life & Casualty of Canada Limited; Excelsior Life Insurance Company; Aetna Casualty Company of Canada; Aetna Life Insurance and Annuity Company; Aetna Life & Casualty (Bermuda) Limited
Financial Information:

	Dec 31 1986
	$'000
Revenues	20,482,900
Earnings per share	$9.12
Shareholders equity	5,697,200
Total assets	66,829,900

No of Employees: 45,100

AETNA LIFE INSURANCE & ANNUITY CO
151 Farmington Avenue, Hartford, CT 06156
Tel: (203) 272-0123
Telex: RCA 221055 aetna ur

President: Dean E Wolcott
Senior Executive Officers: Donald G Conrad (Executive VP), Dean E Wolcott (Senior VP), J H Fitzsimmons (VP and Controller), Joseph F Crowe (VP Life and Health Operations), John O Alden (VP Life and Health Operations), J Douglas Azar (VP Annuity and Pension Marketing), Charles N Dawkins (VP Investment), Edward B Eliason (VP and Actuary), James C Hamilton (VP, Actuary and Treasurer), Otmar A Klee (VP Systems), John J Martin (VP Field Management), Michael E Mateja (VP and Actuary), Robert G Maxon (VP and Actuary), Richard C Murphy (VP, Field Management and Marketing), M Stanley Niehaus Jr (VP Health Products), John J Michael (VP Western Region), Robert F Phillips (VP Northeast Region), Hylan T Habbard III (VP South/Central Region), William B Stephenson (VP Marketing, Field Management Department), Stanley I Strouch (VP Health Products, Life and Health Operations), Thomas L West Jr (VP Annuity and Pension Operations)

PRINCIPAL ACTIVITIES: Life insurance
Parent Company: Aetna Life & Casualty Co

Financial Information:

	Dec 31 1985	Dec 31 1986
	$'000	$'000
Premium income	674,690	986,995
Investment income	260,870	312,460

No of Employees: 12,480

AETNA LIFE INSURANCE CO

151 Farmington Avenue, Hartford, CT 06156

Tel: (203) 273-0123

Telex: RCA 221055 aetna ur

Chairman: James T Lynn (and President)

Senior Executive Officers: Donald G Conrad (Executive VP), Burton E Burton (Senior VP Employee Benefits Division), Robert J Clark (Senior VP Commercial Insurance Division), Dean E Wolcott (Senior VP Personal Financial Security Division), Louis Capozzi (VP Corporate Communications), Ronald E Compton (Senior VP), Robert B Nicholas (Senior VP, Corporate Planning and Development), Philip R Roberts (Senior VP, Investments), Gary G Bananav (VP Finance and Treasurer), J Heath Fitzsimmons (VP and Corporate Actuary), Stephen B Middlebrook (VP and General Counsel), Louise L McCormick (Corporate Secretary)

PRINCIPAL ACTIVITIES: Individual life, health and annuities and group accident and health insurance

Parent Company: Aetna Life and Casualty Company

Financial Information:

	Dec 31 1985	Dec 31 1986
	$'000	$'000
Premium income	3,594,100	10,506,900
Investment income	3,021,500	3,130,200

No of Employees: 16,000

AFFILIATED BANK CORPORATION OF WYOMING

P O Box 2799, Casper, WY 82602

Tel: (307) 235-7797

Chairman: William H Brown; Vice Chairman: Axel R Ostlund

President: Robert W Miracle (and Chief Executive Officer)

Senior Executive Officers: Donald R Drummer (Senior VP, Chief Financial Officer and Secretary), Deborah S Sneve (Controller), Lund Galbraith (Senior VP and Senior Credit Administrator), Theodore A Ernst (VP and Manager, Special Assets), James S Saunders (VP-Special Assets), Roger M Trupp (VP-Special Assets), Ted L Hall (Assistant VP, Special Assets), Michael L Franck (Special Assets Officer), Robert T Noel (Senior VP-Operations and Data Processing), Vance M Zuerlein (VP-Operations and Data Processing), Charles L Tangney (Treasurer and Assistant Secretary), Don R Brookshire (VP-Human Resources), Jerome C Overmier (Assistant VP-Human Resources), Donald E Hole (VP-Marketing), Jeffrey A Walker (VP-Audit/Loan Review), Jim Glover (Corporate Auditor), Scott H Moore (Assistant VP-Loan Review), Hans Nelson (VP-Investments)

PRINCIPAL ACTIVITIES: Affiliated Bank Corporation of Wyoming is a Casper-based registered bank holding company formed in August, 1970. Its eight Norwest banks are located in Casper, Cheyenne, Gillette, Kemmerer and Wheatland, Wyoming

Principal Subsidiaries: Norwest Banks - Casper, Cheyenne, Gillette, Kemmere and Wheatland, Wyoming

Financial Information:

	30.9.87 (9mths)
	$'000
(Loss) before taxes	(1,163)
Net (loss)	(1,148)
(Loss) per share	($0.97)
Common stock	1,190
Retained income	6,919
Stockholders equity	19,869
Deposits	364,356
Total assets	421,937

No of Employees: 404

AFFILIATED BANKSHARES OF COLORADO

1125 17th Street, Denver, CO 80202

Tel: (303) 296-7788

Chairman: Leo Hill (and Chief Executive Officer)

President: Kent O Olin (and Chief Operating Officer)

Senior Executive Officers: Gordon M Pedersen (Senior VP Finance and Treasurer), Charles L Ferguson (Executive VP), Steven D Barnett (VP and Secretary),

PRINCIPAL ACTIVITIES: Banking

Principal Subsidiaries: Affiliated Banks Service Co; Affiliated Banks Building Co; Alameda National Bank; Bank of Manitou; Cache National Bank; Farmers National Bank of Avlt; First Colorado Bank & Trust; First Colorado Bank; First Colorado Bank of Greeley; First Colorado Bankshares Insurance Co; First National Bank; First National Bank of Lafayette; First National Bank of Louisville; Fort Carson National Bank; Greeley National Bank; Intermountain Bankshares Colorado; Chaffee County Bank; Colorado Bank & Trust Co; Fruita State Bank; Montrose State Bank; Lakeside National Bank; Littleton National Bank; Moffatt County State Bank; University National Bank; Westlake First National Bank

Financial Information:

	Dec 31 1985
	$'000
Revenues	278,000
Net income	10,000
Total assets	2,552,000

No of Employees: 2,300

AFFILIATED FOOD STORES, INC

100 Nat Gibbs Drive, Keller, TX 76248

Tel: (817) 281-4417

Chairman: Nat Gibbs (and Chief Executive Officer)

Senior Executive Officers: Don Smith (VP Marketing), Jackie W Brewer (Comptroller), John Myrick (General Manager)

PRINCIPAL ACTIVITIES: Wholesale trade in food products, tobacco and cigarettes, dairy products, meat, frozen food products

Principal Bank: First City Bank of Dallas

Financial Information:

	$'000
Sales revenues	700,000

No of Employees: 1,000

AFFILIATED HOSPITAL PRODUCTS, INC

1920 St Jefferson Avenue, St Louis, MO 63104

Tel: (312) 772-7000

Telex: WUT 434256 affilhospa stl

Chairman: Bernard Fein (and President)

Senior Executive Officers: Leon Fern (Executive VP), Frank R Rauch (VP), Michael A Chalverus (VP), Gustav A Scheuble (VP), Howard M Bloch (Treasurer)

PRINCIPAL ACTIVITIES: Manufacture of surgical equipment and medical supplies

Parent Company: Industrial Corporation, New York, NY

Principal Bank: The Boatmens National Bank
Financial Information:

	$'000
Sales revenues	64,000

No of Employees: 1,350

AFFILIATED PUBLICATIONS, INC

135 Morrissey Blvd, Boston, MA 02107
Tel: (617) 929-3035

Chairman: William O Taylor (and Chief Executive Officer and Director)
President: John P Giuggio (and Chief Operating Officer and Director)
Senior Executive Officers: Arthur F Kingsbury (Senior VP, Treasurer and Chief Financial Officer), Catherine E C Henn (Corporate Counsel and Clerk), Timothy Leland (VP), Daniel Orr (VP), William B Huff (VP and Controller), James I Cash Jr (Professor, Harvard Business School and Director), Robert T H Davidson (Attorney and Director), Roland D Grimm (President, Faneuil Management Corp and Director), Robert Haydock Jr (Of Counsel, Bingham, Dana & Gould and Director), Robert A Lawrence (Executive VP State Street Research and Management Company and Director), Adele Simmons (President, Hampshire College and Director), Ralph Z Sorenson (Chairman, President and Chief Executive Officer, Barry Wright Corporation and Director), Charles H Taylor (Vice Chairman of the Board, Psychotherapist and Director)

PRINCIPAL ACTIVITIES: Affiliated Publications, Inc is the parent company of Globe Newspaper Company, publisher of New England's largest newspapers, The Boston Globe and The Boston Sunday Globe. Through its association with McCaw Communications Companies, Inc of Kirkland, Washington, Affiliated also has major interests in the personal communications fields of paging and cellular radio telephones. In addition, Affiliated owns The Globe Pequot Press Inc, a publisher and retailer of fine books.
Principal Subsidiaries: Globe Newspaper Co; McCaw Communications Companies (joint venture); The Globe Pequot Press Inc
Principal Bank: The First National Bank of Boston
Financial Information:

	Dec 28 1985	Dec 28 1986
	$'000	$'000
Sales revenues	350,699	401,109
Income before taxes	67,530	84,439
Net income	30,958	66,092
Dividends	7,514	8,653
Dividends per share	$0.20	0.22
Earnings per share	$0.84	$1.85
Common stock	182	354
Retained income	142,349	169,740
Shareholders equity	161,355	190,253

No of Employees: 2,200

AFG INDUSTRIES, INC

18200 Von Karman Avenue, Suite 700, Irvine, CA 92715
Tel: (714) 553-9026
Telex: WUT 553436 afg int kst

Chairman: Randall D Hubbard (and Chief Executive Officer)
President: Wayne G Basler (and Chief Operating Officer)
Senior Executive Officers: R C Cunningham (Executive VP), J W Bradford Jr (VP, Secretary and General Counsel), L C Kaufman (VP-Sales), D R Kennedy (VP-Marketing), R G McMasters (Executive VP), G G Miller (VP-Finance), J F Nee (Assistant Treasurer), F C Paulsen (VP-Engineering), P A Ruth (Assistant Secretary)

PRINCIPAL ACTIVITIES: AFG is an integrated manufacturer and fabricator of flat glass products, primarily for the residential, remodeling and non-residential construction markets, as well as the retail market. The company's product line emphasizes a broad range of value-added, specialty glass products including tempered, laminated safety, appliance, low-emissivity, solar and energy-absorbing colored glass for the United States and overseas markets
Principal Subsidiaries: Gemtron Corp; New Jersey Float Glass; Southern Wholesale Glass; American Flat Glass Distributors
Principal Banks: Bank of America; Chase; Wells Fargo
Financial Information:

	Dec 31 1985	Dec 31 1986
	$'000	$'000
Sales revenues	320,034	405,885
Income before taxes	35,292	92,790
Net income	21,102	53,322
Dividends	-	2,025
Dividends per share	-	$0.12
Earnings per share(1)	$1.41	$3.35
Earnings per share(2)	$1.33	$3.04
Common stock	26,830	65,828
Retained income	86,727	138,024
Shareholders equity	113,557	203,852

(1) primary
(2) fully diluted

Principal Shareholders: R D Hubbard; W G Basler; Leo Zuckerberg
No of Employees: 4,000

AG PROCESSING INC

11235 Davenport Street, Omaha, NE 68154-2627
Tel: (402) 334-8010

Chairman: Urban Knobbe (and President); Vice Chairmen: James Rainey (1st Vice Chairman and VP), Ronald Ostby (2nd Vice Chairman and VP); Secretary: James E Higgs (and Treasurer)
Senior Executive Officers: James W Lindsay (Chief Executive Officer and General Manager), Kenneth S Grubbe (Chief Financial Officer, Assistant Treasurer, VP), Kenneth J McQueen (Assistant Secretary, VP Administration), James Yeates (VP Operations), Anthony "Tony" Porter (VP Marketing and Transportation), Joseph Meyer (VP Vegetable Oils and Meal Exports), William C Lester (VP Member and Public Relations), Gordon Dorff (VP Human Resources)

PRINCIPAL ACTIVITIES: The Company is a soybean processing agricultural cooperative operating for the mutual benefit of its members.
Principal Subsidiaries: AGPEX Inc; AGPI Ltd; AGP Grain Company
Financial Information:

	Aug 31 1985	Aug 31 1986
	$'000	$'000
Sales revenues	643,469	625,404
Income before taxes (1)	8,141	2,048
Net income	7,816	2,016
Dividends (2)	793	-
Common stock	1,530	2,420
Retained earnings	3,852	2,016
Total members' equity	67,286	69,713

(1) and extraordinary item
(2) Cash distributions to members

No of Employees: 630

AGENCY-RENT-A-CAR INC

30000 Aurora Road, Solon, OH 44139
Tel: (216) 349-1000

Chairman: Samuel J Frankino (and President and Chief Executive Officer)
Senior Executive Officers: Vincent T Garrenton Jr (Executive VP), Bruce W Hockman (VP), Philip D Rash (VP), Louis H Rice (VP and Secretary), G Beard (VP), Edward D Hammer (Treasurer)

PRINCIPAL ACTIVITIES: Operation of car rental services

Principal Subsidiaries: Agency Chrysler Plymouth; Agency Ford; Agency Rent-a-Car Systems Ltd; Altra Chevrolet; Trans Automative Insurance Co
Principal Bank: National City Bank
Financial Information:

	$'000
Sales revenues	118,265

No of Employees: 1,470

AGRI INDUSTRIES

2829 Westown Pkway, West Des Moines, IA 50265
Tel: (515) 223-3700
Telex: TWX 910 520 2627 agri wdms

Chairman: Dennis Lundsgaard
President: Harrold Richard
Senior Executive Officers: Ovel Johnsrud (VP), Gene Peters (Controller)

PRINCIPAL ACTIVITIES: Cereal products, edible oils; leasing of vehicles
Principal Bank: Bank for Cooperatives
Financial Information:

	$'000
Sales revenues	2,000,000

No of Employees: 480

AGRIPAC INC

PO Box 5346, Salem, OR 97304
Tel: (503) 363-9255
ESL: 62933671
Fax: (503) 371-5666

President: Paul E Solari
Senior Executive Officers: Donald P Heffernan (Secretary, Treasurer and VP Finance), Dennis Delaye (VP Sales and Marketing), Robert Isaac (VP Operations)

PRINCIPAL ACTIVITIES: Processing and marketing of canned and frozen fruits and vegetables
Trade Names: Diamond A(R), Jack 'N' The Beanstalk(R), Oregon's Finest(R)
Principal Subsidiaries: Woodburn Foods Corp
Principal Banks: Spokane Bank for Cooperatives; US National Bank of Oregon
Financial Information:

	1986 $'000
Sales revenues	77,429
(Loss) before taxes	(28)
Net (loss)	(28)
Shareholders equity	19,671

No of Employees: 700

AGS COMPUTERS INC

1139 Spruce Drive, Mountainside, NJ 07092
Tel: (201) 654-4321

Chairman: Lawrence J Schoenberg (also Treasurer)
President: Joseph P Abrams (also Chief Operating Officer)
Senior Executive Officers: Anthony F Stepanski (Executive VP), David B Levine (VP), Robert V Trocchio (VP), Richard D W Thatcher Jr (VP), Frances Mann (VP), Mario Incalicchio (Controller), Leonard Ostfield (Chief Financial Officer), Allen Pearl (Legal Counsel)

PRINCIPAL ACTIVITIES: Development of computer equipment; programming; software; training services
Principal Bank: First Fidelity Bank
Financial Information:

	$'000
Sales revenues	278,870

No of Employees: 2,000

AGWAY INC

Box 4933, Syracuse, NY 13221
Tel: (315) 477-7061
Telex: WUT 937379 agy feed

Chairman: Richard Croner; Vice Chairman: Richard Call
President: William A Hiller (and Chief Executive Officer)
Senior Executive Officers: Richard G Radey (Senior VP Finance), Arnon C Greif (Senior VP), Arthur J Fogerty (Senior VP), Edward J Hartnett (Group VP), Gilbert H Porter (VP Research and Development), Charles F Saul (VP Food Group), Robert J Kutil (VP Energy), Robert J Ryan (VP and Treasurer)

PRINCIPAL ACTIVITIES: Manufacture and trade in agricultural feeds and fertilizers; fuel distribution
Principal Subsidiaries: Agway Life Insurance Co; Agway Insurance Co Inc; Agway Petroleum Corp; Texas City Refining Inc; HP Hood Inc; Empire Cheese Inc; Telmark Inc
Financial Information:

	Jun 30 1986 $'000
Sales revenues	3,510,506
Shareholders equity	322,163

No of Employees: 9,000

AHMANSON, H F, & CO

3731 Wilshire Blvd, Los Angeles, CA 90010
Tel: (213) 736-8705

Chairman: William H Ahmanson
President: Richard H Deihl (and Chief Executive Officer)
Senior Executive Officers: Robert M DeKruif (Vice Chairman), Warren L Androus (Senior VP), Michael Brent (Senior VP), George G Gregory (Senior VP and General Counsel), F Anthony Kurtz (Senior VP and Treasurer), Norman L Parker (Senior VP), Gayle D Morris (VP-Investor Relations)

PRINCIPAL ACTIVITIES: H F Ahmanson & Company is a holding company owning subsidiaries engaged principally in savings and loan operations and insurance operations consisting of property and liability insurance operations and life insurance operations. In addition, Ahmanson has other minor subsidiaries which are engaged primarily in related financial activities, including mortgage origination and mortgage banking activities and trust services
Principal Subsidiaries: Savings and Loan:- Home Savings of America, FA; Savings of America, a division of Home Savings of America, FA; Ahmanson Commercial Development Company; Ahmanson Developments; Discount Investments of America, Inc; HS of A Insurance Services; Oxford Investment Corporation. Ahmanson Services, Inc:- Ahmanson Commercial Brokerage Company; Ahmanson Equities; Ahmanson Marketing, Inc; Ahmanson Mortgage Company; Oxford Travel Service, Inc; The Griffin Agency. Property and Liability Insurance:-National American Insurance Company; National American Insurance Company of California; National American Insurance Company of New York. Life Insurance:- Bankers National Life Insurance Company; National American Life Insurance Company of California; National American Life Insurance Company of Pennsylvania; Trans-Oceanic Life Insurance Company. Trust Services:-Ahmanson Trust Company
Principal Bank: Union Bank
Financial Information:

	Dec 31 1986 $'000
Net income	303,604
Earnings per share	$3.22
Shareholders equity	1,677,418
Deposits	21,687,190
Total assets	27,592,294

No of Employees: 10,162

AID CORPORATION

0701 5th Avenue, Des Moines, IA 50309
Tel: (515) 280-4211

Chairman: John E Evans (and President and Subsidiary Officer)
Senior Executive Officers: Bob O Myers (VP), Jamie H Schaffer (Treasurer and Subsidiary Officer), B Rees Jones (Secretary)

PRINCIPAL ACTIVITIES: Insurance
Parent Company: Allied Mutual Insurance Co
Principal Bank: Bankers Trust Co
Financial Information:

	$'000
Revenues	101,120

No of Employees: 1,035

AIFS

American Institute for Foreign Study

102 Greenwich Ave, Greenwich, CT 06830
Tel: (203) 869 9090
Telex: WUT 965932 worldstudy grch

President: R O Walther
Senior Executive Officers: R Dayan (Treasurer), K F Morgan (Secretary)

PRINCIPAL ACTIVITIES: Educational and sightseeing tours of foreign countries for students
Financial Information:

	$'000
Sales revenues	38,000

No of Employees: 280

AILEEN, INC

331 E 38th Street, New York, NY 10016
Tel: (212) 679-7010

Chairman: Abe Oberlin (and President and Chief Executive Officer)
Senior Executive Officers: Harold Lash (VP and Treasurer), Alvin Stein (Secretary)

PRINCIPAL ACTIVITIES: Manufacture of clothing
Principal Subsidiaries: Aileen Factory Outlet Stores
Principal Bank: Manufacturers Hanover Trust Company
Financial Information:

	$'000
Sales revenues	54,000

No of Employees: 1,750

AIR CONDITIONING COMPANY, INC

6265 San Fernando Road, Glendale, CA 91201
Tel: (818) 244-6571

Chairman Emeritus: Kenneth D Simon
Chairman: Theodore M Seidman (and President and Chief Executive Officer)
Senior Executive Officers: Carl H Johnson (Senior VP), Robert P Vlick (Senior VP), William B McNamara (VP and Treasurer), Lester L Miller (VP and Senior Project Manager), John P Aversano (VP, Senior Project Management Southern California), Jon M Bernard (VP, Senior Project Management), Richard F Loman (VP Senior Project Management), Vahe Markarian (VP Senior Project Management), Robert T Hammond (VP Senior Project Management), S Ronald Krassensky (VP Project Management), Roy E Packard (VP Project Management), Geoffrey Beecroft (VP Purchasing), Merrill R Hess (VP ACCO Energy Saving Division), Charles K Richter (VP), Robert E Kokenda (VP and Manager Customer Division)

PRINCIPAL ACTIVITIES: Air conditioning and ventilation services
Principal Bank: Union Bank; First Interstate Bank
Financial Information:

	$'000
Sales revenues	60,000

No of Employees: 440

AIR EXPRESS INTERNATIONAL CORPORATION

120 Tokeneke Rd, Darien, CT 06820
Tel: (203) 655-7900

Chairman: Hendrik J Hartsong Jr (and Chief Executive Officer)
President: Guenter Rohrmann (and Chief Operating Officer)
Senior Executive Officers: Frank Cassi (Senior VP), Fred Schwartzstein (VP Finance and Treasurer), Martin Hoffenberg (VP Administration), Richard Friedl (VP Southern Divison), Michael Patermaster (VP Belgium, France, Spain and Africa), Bryan Bullman (VP Germany, Holland, Scandinavia and Middle East), Michael Claydon (VP United Kingdom), Robert Lim (VP Asia), Philip Rosso (VP Domestic Operations), Frank De Matlachowski (VP North American Gateway Operations), S Alan Kettle (VP Midwest Division), John Russo (VP Eastern Division), Louis Mobilia (VP Latin America), Reginald Tuthill (VP Executive Sales), John D Kennedy (VP International Executive Sales), Arthur M Stephenson (VP Ocean Services), Colin Cook (VP Data Processing), Siegfried Kratzer (VP Executive Sales), Charles Seymour (VP Western Division), Jeremy Zeitlyn (VP South Pacific), Herbert Bremer (VP Financial Services), Richard Sun (VP)

PRINCIPAL ACTIVITIES: Freight forwarding by air
Principal Subsidiaries: Air Charter Express International Ltd; Air Express International USA; Air Express International Airlines; Air Express Warehousing Corp; Couriaire Express International; Service Freight Corp Miami
Principal Bank: Chemical Bank
Financial Information:

	$'000
Sales revenues	309,000

No of Employees: 2,300

AIR MIDWEST INC

20 West, 2203 Air Cargo Rd, PO Box 7724, Wichita, KS 67209
Tel: (316) 942-8137

Chairman: Calvin C Hermann
President: Gary M Adamson (and Chief Executive Officer)
Senior Executive Officers: Charles E Bowman (VP Operations), David L Ewing (VP Operations), Michael G Freeman (VP Operations), Benjamin F Oxley (VP Operations), Jo Lynn C Foster (Controller), John S Myers (VP Finance and Chief Financial Officer and Treasurer)

PRINCIPAL ACTIVITIES: Air transportation services
Principal Bank: Boatmen's Bank & Trust Co
Financial Information:

	$'000
Sales revenues	60,635

No of Employees: 1,100

AIR PRODUCTS AND CHEMICALS, INC

Box 538, Allentown, PA 18105
Tel: (215) 481-4911
Telex: 847-416

Chairman: Edward Donley (and Chief Executive Officer); Vice Chairman: Leon C Holt Jr (and Chief Administrative Officer)
President: Dexter F Baker (and Chief Operating Officer)
Senior Executive Officers: A P Dyer (Group VP Gas Group), J R Lovett (President Air Products Europe Inc), Arthur W Mellen (President Stearns Catalytic World Corporation), Frank J Ryan (Group VP Chemicals Group), W J Scharle (Group VP Process Systems Group), J H Agger (VP and General Counsel), R D Barclay (VP and Treasurer), P L Thibaut Brian (VP-Engineeering), R A Gray Jr (VP and Corporate Secretary), A H Kaplan (VP and Corporate Controller), W J Kendrick (VP-

Public Affairs), P W C Mather (VP-Management Information Services), C P Powell (VP-Taxes), B M Rushton (VP-Research and Development), D T Shire (VP-Energy and Materials), H A Wagner (VP-Planning), G A White (VP-Finance)

PRINCIPAL ACTIVITIES: Air Products and Chemicals, Inc is a major international supplier of industrial gases and related equipment, chemicals and engineering services

Principal Subsidiaries: Stearns Catalytic World Corporation; Stearns Catalytic Corporation; Catalytic Inc; Stearns-Roger Inc; Project Construction Corporation; Stearns Catalytic Architects Ltd; Stearns Catalytic Equipment Co; Stearns Catalytic International Ltd; Stearns Catalytic Ltd; Kinhill Stearns

Financial Information:

	Sep 30 1986
	$'000
Sales revenues	1,982,134
Net income	4,735
Earnings per share	$0.08
Shareholders equity	1,100,141

No of Employees: 19,000

AIR WIS SERVICES INC

Outagamie Airport, Appleton, WI 54915
Tel: (414) 739-5123

President: Preston H Wilbourne (and Chief Executive Officer and Subsidiary Officer)

Senior Executive Officers: Peter A Doering (Subsidiary Officer), James G Jansen (Subsidiary Officer), Patrick J Thopson (Subsidiary Officer), Watson Whiteside (Subsidiary Officer), William H Geenen (VP and Treasurer and Subsidiary Officer), Kathy Comins (Secretary and Subsidiary Officer)

PRINCIPAL ACTIVITIES: Air transportation services

Principal Subsidiaries: Air Wisconsin Inc operating as United Express

Principal Bank: Continental Illinois National Bank, Chicago, IL

Financial Information:

	Dec 31 1985	Dec 31 1986
	$'000	$'000
Sales revenues	120,165	119,191
Income (loss) before taxes	(124)	4,256
Net income	1,336	4,869
Earnings per share	$0.18	$0.66
Common stock*	39,544	39,544
Retained income	21,051	25,920
Shareholders equity	60,595	65,464

*and paid in capital

No of Employees: 1,150

AIRBORNE FREIGHT CORPORATION

3101 Western Avenue, PO Box 662, Seattle, WA 98111
Tel: (206) 285-4600
Telex: 329543

Chairman: Robert S Cline (and Chief Executive Officer)

President: Robert G Brazier (and Chief Operating Officer)

Senior Executive Officers: Kent W Freudenberger (Executive VP, Marketing Division), Roy C Liljebeck (Executive VP, Chief Financial Officer-Treasurer), Raymond T Van Bruwaene (Executive VP, Operations Division), John J Cella (Executive VP, International Division), Frank C Steele (Senior VP, Sales), David A Billings (VP, Corporate Systems), James J Guiod (VP, Eastern Sales Division), Dick Goodwin (VP, Human Resources), Lanny H Michael (Controller), Earl L Richardson (VP, Mid-Continent Region), Ken McCumber (VP, Corporate Marketing), David H Scheevel (VP, Revenue and Property Control), Don A Smith (VP, Operations Division II), Harry K Sprague (Assistant VP, Traffic), Bill Simpson (VP, Operations Division I), Jack Wilbourne (Secretary), J Vernon Williams (Assistant Secretary), William E York (VP, Southeast Region). Subsidiary: Graham E Dorland (Chairman, Airborne Express, Inc), Albert Wiseman (President, Airborne Express, Inc)

PRINCIPAL ACTIVITIES: Airborne Express is an integrated air and ground transportation company, principally providing door-to-door express, next morning delivery of small packages and documents throughout the United States. The Company operates its own airline, and a fleet of ground transportation vehicles. Each weekday night the Airline flies approximately 54,000 air miles serving 115 major cities in the United States, providing next day service to over 20,300 cities, of which most receive service before noon. The Company also provides air freight services for shipments of any size on a worldwide basis using a combination of commercial air carriers, its Airline and its own or independent ground transporation services. In all instances the Company's commitment begins with pickup at point of origin and extends through final delivery

Trade Names: Airborne Express

Principal Subsidiaries: Company Subsidiaries:- Airborne Express Inc; Awawago Delivery Inc; Australia Airborne Pty Ltd (Australia); Airborne Forwarding Corp; Airborne Freight Ltd (New Zealand); Airborne Freight Corporation (UK) Ltd (UK). Airline Subsidiaries:- Wilmington Air Park Inc; Airborne FTZ Inc; Aviation Fuel Inc; Sound Suppression Inc

Principal Bank: Seattle First National Bank - Main Branch

Financial Information:

	Dec 31 1985	Dec 31 1986
	$'000	$'000
Total revenues	465,991	541,627
Earnings before taxes	15,089	23,687
Net earnings	8,169	13,215
Dividends	3,494	3,512
Dividends per share	$0.60	$0.60
Earnings per share*	$1.39	$2.11
Common stock	6,001	6,023
Retained earnings	46,757	56,460
Shareholders equity	81,581	91,751

*fully diluted

Principal Shareholders: TNT Ltd (14%)

No of Employees: 6,500

AIRCAL INC

3636 Birch Street, Newport Beach, CA 92660
Tel: (714) 752-7000

Chairman: William Lyon (and Chief Executive Officer)

President: David A Banmiller (and Chief Operating Officer)

Senior Executive Officers: George L Argyros (Chairman of Executive Board and Secretary), Peter M Deiser (Senior VP Administration), Fred K von Husen (Senior VP Operations), Brett M Clark (Controller), Denis P Kalscheur (Senior VP Finance, Treasurer and Chief Financial Officer), William D Slattery (Senior VP Marketing), Michael P Coffman (VP Technical Services), Bruce B Wetsel (VP), William R Bell (VP Corporate Affairs and Public Affairs), Frantz B Lipsey (VP Corporate Services)

PRINCIPAL ACTIVITIES: Air transportation services

Parent Company: ACI Holdings Inc

Financial Information:

	$'000
Sales revenues	344,505

No of Employees: 3,575

AJ INDUSTRIES, INC

11454 San Vicente Blvd, Los Angeles, CA 90049
Tel: (213) 879-0370

Chairman: Raymond M O'Keefe (and President and Chief Executive Officer); Vice Chairman: Walter B Chaffee

Senior Executive Officers: Harland E Holman (VP and Secretary), Joseph H Breuer (VP Finance)

PRINCIPAL ACTIVITIES: Manufacture of heavy vehicle and aircraft components; aviation refueling equipment; heating systems; steel; cast brass products

Principal Bank: First National Bank of Chicago

Financial Information:

	$'000
Sales revenues	99,000

No of Employees: 1,400

AJAX MAGNETHERMIC CORPORATION

1745 Overland Avenue, NE Warren, OH 44482
Tel: (216) 372-8511
Telex: WUT 982482 ajax mag war

President: Norman C Harbert (and Chief Operating Officer)
Senior Executive Officers: J V Ackerman (VP Finance), R E Jennings (VP Heating), John W Cook (VP Melting)

PRINCIPAL ACTIVITIES: Manufacture of industrial heaters and furnaces
Parent Company: Guthrie North America Inc
Principal Bank: Pittsburg National Bank
Financial Information:

	$'000
Sales revenues	60,000

No of Employees: 550

AKZO COATINGS AMERICA INC

650 Stephenson Hwy, Troy, MI 48083
Tel: (313) 589-3660
Telex: 211847 WPMI UR

Chairman: C Zaal
President: Charles A Brethren III (and Chief Executive Officer)
Senior Executive Officers: John Gardon (VP, Research and Development), Taki Anagnostou (VP, Quality Assurance), John Wood (VP, Manufacturing), Robert Jurczyszyn (VP, Engineering, Safety and Environmental), George Findling (VP Finance, Planning and Control), Mary Durham (Corporate Director, Human Resources), John Walker (President, Akzo Coating Canada, Ltd)

PRINCIPAL ACTIVITIES: Manufacture of paints and coatings
Parent Company: Akzo America Inc
Principal Bank: National Bank Wyandotte-Taylor
Financial Information:

	$'000
Sales revenues	100,000

No of Employees: 600

AKZONA INC

Sand Hill Road, Enka, NC 28728
Tel: (704) 667 6400

President: G J Coli
Senior Executive Officers: Jan-Michiel Hessels (Executive VP), Vinson A Parsons (VP and Chief Financial Officer)

PRINCIPAL ACTIVITIES: Manufacture of man-made fibers, leather, chemicals, pharmaceuticals
Parent Company: Akzo NV, Arnhem, Netherlands
Principal Subsidiaries: Akzo Chemie America; Noury Chemical Corp; Armira Corp; Ghia Corp; International Salt Co; Organon Inc. Divisions: American Enka Co
Principal Bank: Wachovia Bank & Trust Company NA
Financial Information:

	$'000
Sales revenues	1,200,000

No of Employees: 9,500

AL LABORATORIES, INC

One Executive Drive, Box 1399, Fort Lee, NJ 07024
Tel: (201) 947 7774

Chairman: Einar W Sissener
President: I R Cohen
Senior Executive Officers: Bernard B Brown (VP Research and Development), Jeffrey E Smith (VP Finance and Chief Financial Officer), Karl L Winter (VP Sales), Kenneth D Walter (VP Production and Engineering), David E Cohen (VP Marketing)

PRINCIPAL ACTIVITIES: Manufacture of pharmaceuticals and veterinary products
Principal Bank: United Jersey Bank
Financial Information:

	$'000
Sales revenues	97,000

No of Employees: 800

ALAMITO COMPANY

3567 E Sunrise Drive, Tucson, AZ 85718
Tel: (602) 577-3747

Chairman: Theodore M Welp (and Chief Executive Officer)
President: J Robert Johnston
Senior Executive Officers: Carol Breckner (VP and Treasurer), Roland F Hoch (Senior VP, Legal Counsel and Secretary), John Van Egmond (VP and Controller), Albert Warner (VP Operations)

PRINCIPAL ACTIVITIES: Supply of electricity
Parent Company: Catalyst Energy Development Corp
Financial Information:

	$'000
Sales revenues	269,825

No of Employees: 150

ALAMO IRON WORKS

PO Box 231, San Antonio, TX 78291
Tel: (512) 223-6161
Telex: TWX 910 871 1184 alamo iron snt

Chairman: John C Holmgreen (and Chief Executive Officer); Vice Chairman: Baxter Grier
President: Carl Shenken Jr
Senior Executive Officers: Patrick M Cowles (VP Finance), Edward R Lenz (Senior VP), Steven R Smith (VP), Warren S Wilkinson (VP Operations), Roger W Malek (VP Human Resources), James E Baxter (VP Marketing), Larry D Castleberry (VP Sales)

PRINCIPAL ACTIVITIES: Processing of iron and steel; fabricated steel and supplies for the steel industry; steel service center
Principal Bank: National Bank of Commerce
Financial Information:

	$'000
Sales revenues	50,000

No of Employees: 540

ALAMO SAVINGS ASSOCIATION OF TEXAS

901 Northeast, Loop 410, San Antonio, TX 78209
Tel: (512) 828-7171

Chairman: Richard L Fite; Vice Chairman: William W Ochse
President: Michael J Minihan (and Chief Executive Officer)
Senior Executive Officers: Charles L Rackley (Executive VP and Chief Operating Officer), Barry L Brock (Senior VP), Marie C Collier (Senior VP), John S Crossman (Senior VP), Joe B Eanes (Senior VP), Wayne Wesley (Senior VP Purchasing), Margaret Courtney (VP Personnel)

PRINCIPAL ACTIVITIES: Financial services
Principal Bank: Frost National Bank
Financial Information:

	Dec 31 1985
	$'000
Revenues	91,930

No of Employees: 300

ALASKA AIR GROUP INC
PO Box 68947, Seattle, WA 98168
Tel: (206) 433-3200
Telefax: (206) 433-3350

Chairman: Bruce R Kennedy (and Chief Executive Officer and President)
Senior Executive Officers: J Ray Vingo (VP Finance, Chief Financial Officer and Treasurer), Marjorie E Laws (Corporate Secretary), Jan David Blais (General Counsel and Assistant Secretary), Paul T Nishimura (Controller)

PRINCIPAL ACTIVITIES: Holding company with interests in air transportation
Principal Subsidiaries: Alaska Airlines Inc; Horizon Air Industries Inc
Principal Bank: Seattle First National Bank
Financial Information:

	Dec 31 1985	Dec 31 1986
	$'000	$'000
Sales revenues	433,187	468,264
Income before taxes	33,786	27,918
Net income	25,935	17,713
Dividends	1,911	1,979
Dividends per share	$0.155	$0.16
Earnings per share(1)	$1.85	$1.30
Common stock(2)	15,141	15,977
Retained income	81,892	97,626
Shareholders equity	161,011	177,179

(1) fully diluted
(2) average shares outstanding

Principal Shareholders: Various institutional investors
No of Employees: 9 (5,813 including subsidiaries)

ALASKA AIRLINES, INC
19300 Pacific Highway South, Seattle, WA 98188
Tel: (206) 433-3200

Chairman: Bruce R Kennedy (and President and Chief Executive Officer)
Senior Executive Officers: Raymond J Vecci (Executive VP and Chief Operating Officer), Robert E Gray (Senior VP/Industrial Relations), James A Johnson (Senior VP/Public Affairs), Patrick L Glenn (VP/Flight Operations), John F Kelly (VP/Marketing), Majorie E Laws (Corporate Secretary), Harry G Lehr (VP/Planning), Frederick P Schubel (VP/Maintenance and Engineering), Douglas L Versteeg (VP/Administration), J Ray Vingo (VP Finance and Chief Financial Officer), Clifford T Argue (Staff VP/Properties and Facilities), Jan David Blais (Staff VP/Legal, General Counsel and Assistant Secretary), William MacKay (Regional VP), Robert H Putman (Staff VP/Personnel)

PRINCIPAL ACTIVITIES: Air transportation services
Parent Company: Alaska Air Group Inc
Principal Subsidiaries: Alaska Coastal Airlines, Inc; Northstar Hotel; Alyeska Ski Corp; Cordova Airlines, Inc; Alaska General Properties, Inc; Golden Nugget Motel, Inc
Financial Information: Figures for Alaska Air Group

No of Employees: 3,280

ALASKA MUTUAL BANCORPORATION
Pouch 4-9003, Anchorage, AK 99509
Tel: (907) 274-3561

Chairman: Richard L Silberer (and Subsidiary Officer)
President: Joseph C Miller (and Chief Executive Officer and Subsidiary Officer)
Senior Executive Officers: H Lee Carter (Executive VP), Lynn Hammond (Chief Financial Officer and Subsidiary Officer), Richard E Anglemyer (Secretary and Subsidiary Officer), Craig Floerchinger (Comptroller)

PRINCIPAL ACTIVITIES: Banking
Principal Subsidiaries: Alaska Mutual Bank
Financial Information:

	Dec 31 1985
	$'000
Revenues	92,815
Net income	8,600

No of Employees: 300

ALASKAN COPPER COMPANIES
3223 6th Avenue S, Seattle, WA 98124
Tel: (206) 623-98124

Chairmen: William Rosen, Kermit Rosen
President: William M Rosen (and Chief Executive Officer)
Senior Executive Officers: Kermit Rosen Jr (Executive VP), Douglas C Rosen (VP Corporate Development)

PRINCIPAL ACTIVITIES: Manufacture and distribution of stainless steel and copper pipes
Principal Subsidiaries: Stainless Piping Systems Inc. Divisions: Alaskan Copper Works; Alaskan Copper & Brass Co
Principal Bank: Seattle First National Bank
Financial Information:

	$'000
Sales revenues	54,000

No of Employees: 450

ALATENN RESOURCES INC
PO Box 918, Florence, AL 35631
Tel: (205) 383-3631

Chairman: M D Prouty Jr
President: Jerry A Howard (and Chief Executive Officer)
Senior Executive Officers: Lewis C Bartmess (VP), R M Lawson (VP, Secretary and Treasurer)

PRINCIPAL ACTIVITIES: Exploration and distribution of natural gas
Principal Bank: First National Bank of Florence
Financial Information:

	$'000
Sales revenues	125,425

No of Employees: 40

ALBA WALDENSIAN INC
201 Saint Germain Ave Southwest, PO Box 100, Valdese, NC 28690
Tel: (704) 874-2191

Chairman: William D Schubert (and President)
Senior Executive Officers: J Michael Bridges (Division President), Ronald W Scott (VP and Division President), J Edward Garrou (VP Finance and Secretary), Van C Irwin (Treasurer and Assistant Secretary)

PRINCIPAL ACTIVITIES: Manufacture of underwear and hosiery
Principal Bank: Wachovia Bank & Trust Co
Financial Information:

	$'000
Sales revenues	41,525

No of Employees: 1,490

ALBERT PIPE SUPPLY CO
101 Varick Avenue, Brooklyn, NY 11237
Tel: (718) 497-4900
Telex: RCA 233573 alb ur

Chairman: Colin Halpern
Senior Executive Officers: Sean McKeown (VP Sales), Charles J Joseph (VP)

PRINCIPAL ACTIVITIES: Manufacture of industrial pipes, valves and fittings for a variety of industries
Principal Bank: Chemical Bank

Financial Information:

	$'000
Sales revenues	50,000

No of Employees: 180

ALBERT TROSTEL & SONS CO

See TROSTEL, ALBERT, & SONS CO

ALBERTO-CULVER COMPANY

2525 Armitage Avenue, Melrose Park, IL 60160
Tel: (312) 450-3000
Telex: WUT 721478 ac intl mlpk

Chairman: Leonard H Lavin (and President and Chief Executive Officer)
Senior Executive Officers: George Polk (Senior VP), Howard Bernick (Executive VP), David D Lewis (Group VP Professional Products), Malcolm R Lloyd (Group VP Consumer Products), Bernice E Lavin (Secretary and Treasurer), Andrew W Donnelly (VP International), Robert Winton (VP Law), Carol M Bernick (VP New Business Development), Henry Wittemann (VP Advertising Services), Arthur E DeShon (VP Merchandising), Albert M Swayne (VP Personnel), William J Cerrugel (VP Finance and Controller), Nicholas Z Malhem (VP Imformation Systems), Thomas J Pallone (VP Research and Development)

PRINCIPAL ACTIVITIES: Manufacture of beauty products for the hair and other toiletries; household and grocery products, food service, maintenance chemicals
Trade Names: Alberto VO5, Alberto Mousse, FDS, SUGARTwin, Mrs Dash, STATIC GUARD, BAKER'S JOY, KLEEN GUARD, ALBERTO NATURAL SILK
Principal Subsidiaries: Sally Beauty Company, Inc; Masury-Columbia Co; Phillippe of California, Inc; Draper Daniels Media Services, Inc
Principal Bank: First National Bank of Boston
Financial Information:

	Sep 30 1985	Sep 30 1986
	$'000	$'000
Sales revenues	368,576	439,049
Net income	7,879	8,631
Earnings per share	$1.35	$0.68
Shareholders equity	69,404	116,066

Principal Shareholders: L H Lavin; B E Lavin
No of Employees: 3,600

ALBERTSON'S INC

250 Parkcenter Blvd, PO Box 20, Boise, ID 83726
Tel: (208) 344-7441

Chairman: Warren E McCain (and Chief Executive Officer); Chairman of Executive Committee: Joseph A Albertson; Vice Chairman: Gary G Michael (and Chief Financial Officer)
President: John B Carley
Senior Executive Officers: Kenneth R Huff (Executive VP), Alec R Gloth (Senior VP Store Planning), Wendell E Hornecker (Senior VP Design and Construction), W L Jordan (Senior VP Oregon, Rocky Mountain-Omaha), C Clint Joyce (Senior VP Management Information Systems), Robert G Miller (Senior VP Texas/Florida), Michael F Reuling (Senior VP Real Estate), Marvin W Robertson (Senior VP South/North California/Western Wash/New Mexico), Gerald R Rudd (Senior VP Human Resources), Thomas R Saldin (Senior VP, General Counsel and Assistant Secretary), Ronald D Walk (Senior VP Idaho, Utah and Inland Empire)

PRINCIPAL ACTIVITIES: Supermarkets, specialty supermarkets, superstores and drug stores
Principal Bank: Idaho First National Bank
Financial Information:

	Dec 31 1985	Dec 31 1986
	$'000	$'000
Sales revenues	5,060,265	5,379,643
Net income	85,110	100,152
Earnings per share	$2.57	$3.00
Shareholders equity	-	594,379

No of Employees: 40,000

ALC COMMUNICATIONS CORPORATION

30300 Telegraph Road, Birmingham, MI 48010
Tel: (313) 647-6920

Chairman: Melvyn J Goodman
President: George J Vasilakos (and Chief Executive Officer)
Senior Executive Officers: William A Maloney (VP), Andrew J Margeson (VP), James P Dorn (VP Human Resources), Donald W Sessamen (Senior VP), Robert A Peiser (VP, Chief Financial Officer), James M Tobin (VP, Legal Counsel and Secretary), Gerry Finefrock (VP Network Planning), Marshall Hanno (VP Sales), Bradley Heap (VP), John Henson Jr (VP Operations), Janice Loichle (VP and Comptroller), Derrald Pick (VP Engineering)

PRINCIPAL ACTIVITIES: Telecommunications
Principal Bank: Continental Illinois National Bank and Trust Co
Financial Information:

	$'000
Sales revenues	72,000

No of Employees: 2,345

ALCAN ALUMINUM CORPORATION

100 Erieview Plaza, Cleveland, OH 44114
Tel: (216) 523-6800
Telex: WUT 985324 alcan clv b

President: Timothy C Tuff
Senior Executive Officers: D G Schurman (VP Finance), Stephen R Brown (Executive VP), S Bruce Heister (Executive VP), Ian Rugeroni (Executive VP), Francois Senecal-Trembley (Executive VP), Dennis D Foley (VP Technology), James P Monaghan (VP Government Affairs), R Terry Olbrysh (VP Public Relations), Herbert Taber (VP Rail Transportation), Sandford Yosouritz (VP, Secretary and Legal Counsel)

PRINCIPAL ACTIVITIES: Manufacture of aluminum and aluminum products
Parent Company: Aluminum Company of Canada
Principal Subsidiaries: Alcan Rolled Products Company
Financial Information:

	$'000
Sales revenues	2,000,000

No of Employees: 7,500

ALCO CONTROLS DIVISION

Box 12700, St Louis, MO 63141
Tel: (314) 569-4500
Telex: WUT 447162 alco contl stl

Chairman: Charles Knight
President: Robert Ogrodnick
Senior Executive Officers: D H Hannasch (VP Sales and Marketing), C E O'Rourke (VP Manufacturing), J L Behr (VP Engineering), Jack Marchiano (VP Finance)

PRINCIPAL ACTIVITIES: Manufacture of controls and regulators for air conditioning and refrigeration; valves
Parent Company: Emerson Electric Co, St Louis, MO
Principal Bank: Centerre Bank
Financial Information:

	$'000
Sales revenues	73,000

No of Employees: 1,000

ALCO HEALTH SERVICES CORPORATION

PO Box 959, Valley Forge, PA 19482
Tel: (215) 296-4480

Chairman: John H Kennedy
President: Joseph B Churchman
Senior Executive Officers: Robert L Aitchison (VP), John F McNamara (Executive VP)

PRINCIPAL ACTIVITIES: Wholesale supply of pharmaceutical products, beauty products and medical supplies
Financial Information:

	Dec 31 1986
	$'000
Sales revenues	1,285,811
Net income	15,640
Earnings per share	$1.20
Shareholders equity	129,475

No of Employees: 2,282

ALCO POWER INC

100 Orchard Street, Auburn, NY 13021
Tel: (315) 253-3241
Telex: WUT 937300 alco abur

President: Roland Gagnon
Senior Executive Officers: Jacques Savard (VP, Finance), Robert Dunton (VP, Engineering), A A Meo (VP, Sales), P K Hunt (VP, Manufacturing)

PRINCIPAL ACTIVITIES: Manufacture of diesel engines and parts
Parent Company: Bombadier Inc
Principal Bank: Mellon Bank NA
Financial Information:

	$'000
Sales revenues	90,000

No of Employees: 500

ALCO STANDARD CORPORATION

PO Box 834, Valley Forge, PA 19482
Tel: (215) 296-8000

Chairman: Ray B Mundt (and President and Chief Executive Officer); Vice Chairman: William F Drake Jr
Senior Executive Officers: O Gordon Brewer Jr (VP and Treasurer), J Kenneth Croney (VP-Law and Secretary), Anthony DiGiovanni (VP), William F Drake Jr (Vice Chairman), Richard C Gozon (VP), John H Kennedy (Senior VP and Chief Financial Officer), William P Kirby (VP-Human Resources), Larry L Leedy (VP-Investor Relations), Thomas J McCann Jr (VP-Acquisitions), Robert K McClain (VP and Controller), Hugh G Moulton (Senior VP-Administration and General Counsel), B Patrick O'Rourke (VP-Business Planning), Edward N Patrone (Executive VP-Corporate Planning), Edward J Phillips (VP), George R Shelley (VP), Tinkham Veale III (VP-Investments)

PRINCIPAL ACTIVITIES: Wholesale trade in paper, distilled spirits and wines, steel, consumer goods including giftware, glassware and containers, medical supplies, toiletries and cosmetics, restaurant equipment; coal mining
Principal Bank: Philadelphia National Bank
Financial Information:

	Sep 30 1986
	$'000
Sales revenues	4,334,020
Net income	56,963
Earnings per share	$3.24
Shareholders equity	425,590

No of Employees: 18,700

ALCON LABORATORIES, INC

PO Box 6600, Fort Worth, TX 76115
Tel: (817) 293-0450
Telex: WUT 758549 alcon actg ftw

Chairman: Edgar H Schollmaier (and President and Chief Executive Officer)
Senior Executive Officers: George F Leone (Senior VP, Science and Technology), T R Sear (Senior VP, International Operations), Richard H Sisson (Senior VP, Ophthalmology and Dermatology), Robert R Montgomery (VP and Chief Financial Officer)

PRINCIPAL ACTIVITIES: Manufacture of pharmaceuticals, opthalmic care products and contact lens solutions, medical equipment and surgical instruments
Parent Company: Nestlé SA, Vevey, Switzerland
Principal Bank: Texas American Bank
Financial Information:

	$'000
Sales revenues	380,000

No of Employees: 4,000

ALEX BROWN INC

See BROWN, ALEX, INC

ALEXANDER & ALEXANDER SERVICES INC

1211 Avenue of the Americas, New York, NY 10036
Tel: (212) 840-8500

Chairman: John A Bogardus Jr
President: Tinsley H Irvin (and Chief Executive Officer)
Senior Executive Officers: John C Sienkiewicz (Senior VP), Kenneth W S Soubry (Former Chairman of the Board), Michael K White (Executive VP), Paul E Rohner (Senior VP-Chief Financial Officer), Peter M Densen (Senior VP and Chief of Staff), Joseph E Morahan Jr (Senior VP), Bobby J Cline (Senior VP), John B Devine (Senior VP), David C French (Senior VP), Cedric G E Gyles (Senior VP), Ronald A Iles (Senior VP), James A McCormick (Senior VP), William M Wilson (Executive VP), Maurice F Greaver III (VP and Chief Internal Auditor), James Y Paulding (Senior VP), Ernest J Maddox (Assistant Treasurer, Risk Management), James B Lockhart III (VP and Treasurer), Jayne D Maas (VP and Director of Taxes), Dr Robert H Moore (Senior VP Corporate Relations), Mark E Oleksik (VP and Controller, Chief Accounting Officer), Ronald J Roessler (VP and General Counsel), Frank R Wieczynski (Secretary)

PRINCIPAL ACTIVITIES: Alexander & Alexander Services Inc is the second largest international insurance brokerage company. Through its 18,000 employees, it provides a broad range of risk management and financial services to companies of all kinds and sizes. A&A plans, places and services all types of insurance programs-principally casualty, property, marine, life and group. The corporation and its subsidiaries provide reinsurance placement, underwriting management, risk analysis and management and self-insurance services. In addition, A&A offers a variety of human resource management consulting services, including actuarial and administrative services for pension, compensation and benefit plans, employee communications consulting and management consulting. A&A also provides property tax consulting and premium finance services. A&A serves clients through offices in more than 158 cities in the United States, Canada and the United Kingdom, and operates in over 70 countries and territories worldwide through subsidiaries, joint ventures and correspondent relationships
Principal Subsidiaries: Alexander & Alexander Services Inc Major Operating Units;- Alexander & Alexander Inc; Alexander & Alexander International Inc; Alexander Howden Group Ltd; Alexander Howden North America Inc; The Alexander Consulting Group Inc; Risk Management Services Group; Shand, Morahan & Company Inc; Thomas A Greene & Company Inc; TIFCO Inc. Alexander & Alexander Inc Major Subsidiary and Operating Units:- Albert G Ruben & Co Inc; Alexander & Associates Inc; Alexsis Inc; Barros & Carrion Inc; Corporate Service Inc; Mel McReynolds Company Inc; PBA Inc; Property Tax Service Company; S Hammond Story Agency Inc; Summit Consulting Inc; Turner and Shepard Inc.

Alexander & Alexander International Inc Major Subsidiary and Operation Units:- Alexander Stenhouse Europe Ltd (Continental Europe); Alexander Stenhouse Ltd (Asia Pacific); Alexander Stenhouse Ltd (UK); Reed Stenhouse Ltd (Canada). Alexander Howden Group Ltd Major Subsidiary and Operating Units:- Alexander Howden Ltd; Alexander Howden Reinsurance Brokers Ltd; Alexander Howden & Beck Ltd; Halford, Shead & Co Ltd; Holmes Johnson Lessiter Ltd. The Alexander Consulting Group Inc Major Subsidiary and Operating Units:- Alexander & Alexander Benefits Services Inc; Alexander & Alexander Consulting Group Inc; Alexander & Alexander Securities Corp; The Alexander Consulting Group Ltd (Australia and New Zealand); The Alexander Consulting Group Ltd (Canada); The Alexander Consulting Group Ltd (UK and Europe); Benefacts Inc. Risk Management Services Group Major subsidiary and Operating Units:- Anistics Inc; Anistics Ltd (UK); Anistics Pty Ltd (Australia); Alexander Insurance Managers Ltd; Alexander International Insurance Services Ltd; Alexander Trade Services; Hemisphere Marine & General Assurance Company Ltd. Alexander & Alexander operates in: Argentina, Australia, Austria, Bahamas, Barbados, Belgium, Bermuda, Bolivia, Brazil, Brunei, Cameroon, Canada, Cayman Islands, Channel Islands, Chile, Colombia, Costa Rica, Curacao, Denmark, Dominican Republic, Ecuador, Finland, Fiji, France, Greece, Guadeloupe, Guatemala, Hong Kong, India, Indonesia, Ireland, Isle of Man, Italy, Jamaica, Japan, Malaysia, Mexico, Netherlands, New Zealand, Nigeria, Norway, Panama, Papua New Guinea, Peru, Philippines, Portugal, Puerto Rico, Saudi Arabia, Singapore, South Korea, Spain, Swaziland, Sweden, Switzerland, Taiwan, Thailand, Trinidad & Tobago, Turkey, United Arab Emirates, United Kingdom, United States, Venezuela, West Germany, Zaire

Financial Information:

	Dec 31 1985	Dec 31 1986
	$'000	$'000
Operating revenues	913,600	1,068,000
Income before tax*	96,900	146,700
Net income (loss)	(7,300)	43,200
Dividends	36,800	41,000
Dividends per share	$1.00	$1.00
Net income (loss) per share	($0.19)	$1.05
Common stock	32,500	35,400
Retained income	13,000	14,700
Shareholders equity	284,000	324,400

* from continuing operations

No of Employees: 18,000

ALEXANDER & BALDWIN, INC

82 Bishop Street, PO Box 3440, Honolulu, HI 96813
Tel: (808) 525-6611

Chairman: R J Pfeiffer (and Chief Executive Officer)
President: J C Couch (and Chief Operating Officer)
Senior Executive Officers: Robert F Clarke (Senior VP), Edwin S Wong (Senior VP), F L Fleischmann (Senior VP Industrial Relations), N J Marks (Senior VP, Legal Counsel and Secretary), G S Holaday (VP, Treasurer and Controller), J B Kelley (VP Public and Investor Relations), R K Sasaki (VP Property)

PRINCIPAL ACTIVITIES: Shipping; road transportation; warehousing; sugar cane growing, and refining of molasses and sugar; property development
Financial Information:

	Dec 31 1986
	$'000
Sales revenues	536,668
Net income	92,380
Earnings per share	$3.30
Shareholders equity	559,659

No of Employees: 3,250

ALEXANDER'S INC

500 7th Avenue, New York, NY 10018
Tel: (212) 560-2121

Chairman: Robin L Farkas (and Chief Executive Officer); Vice Chairman: Bruce R Farkas
Presidents: Roger A Barrer (and Executive VP and General Manager), Louis Powell
Senior Executive Officers: Robert E Geber (Senior VP Operations), Francis S Leichtman (Senior VP, Divisional Manager), Leon Peck (Senior VP and Controller), Albert A Seedman (VP Security), Murray Cohen (VP Divisional Merchandise), Robert G Spevak (VP Divisional Merchandise), Joan R Carstens (VP Divisional Merchandise), Joseph Kramer (VP Divisional Merchandise), David C Rubin (VP Divisional Merchandise), Stephen E Markowitz (VP Human Resources), Raphael Present (VP, Director Stores), Donald Sharon (VP, Director Wholesale), John A Donovan (VP Planning and Research), Donald W Madsen (VP Construction), Brian M Kurtz (VP and Group Controller), Harvey B Weston (VP Store Planning), Thomas M Coleman (VP Finance Administration), Patrick C Raccioppi (VP Advertising)

PRINCIPAL ACTIVITIES: Department stores
Principal Bank: Manufacturers Hanover Trust
Financial Information:

	$'000
Sales revenues	520,050

No of Employees: 10,000

ALFA-LAVAL, INC

2115 Linwood Avenue, Ft Lee, NJ 07024
Tel: (201) 592-7800
Telex: WUT 135526 alfalaval fort

Chairman: Harry Faulkner
President: Bjorn Fagerstrom (and Chief Executive Officer)
Senior Executive Officers: Terry Blanks (Senior VP), Robert E Wiltz (Senior VP), Hans Bernunger (VP Finance), Michael Rosenberg (VP and Legal Counsel)

PRINCIPAL ACTIVITIES: Manufacture of dairy equipment and food processing machinery
Parent Company: Alfa Laval AB, Sweden
Principal Bank: Chemical Bank
Financial Information:

	$'000
Sales revenues	150,000

No of Employees: 1,200

ALL AMERICAN GOURMET COMPANY

1 City Boulevard West, Suite 308, Orange, CA 92668
Tel: (714) 978-0772

Chairman: Harris J Ashton (and Chief Executive Officer)
President: Ernest W Townsend (and Chief Operating Officer)
Senior Executive Officers: A Stephen Diamond (VP), John F Donnelly (VP), E Darton Greist Jr (VP), Henry L Nichols (VP), David E Lewis (Controller), Robert G Kuhbach (Secretary)

PRINCIPAL ACTIVITIES: Frozen fruit, vegetables and other food products
Financial Information:

	$'000
Sales revenues	91,250

No of Employees: 730

ALL SEASONS RESORTS INC

3050 152nd Ave NE, Suite 600, Redmond, WA 98053
Tel: (206) 885-6233

Chairman: Leonard H Gross (and President and Chief Executive Officer)
Senior Executive Officers: Ralph F Sites (Executive VP, Chief Operating Officer and Treasurer), Woodrow J O'Rourke (VP Sales), Robert C Pappas (Senior VP Marketing and

Secretary), Donald G Mitchell (VP Product Area), J Michael Moyer (VP Public Affairs)

PRINCIPAL ACTIVITIES: Hotels and motels; trailer parks and camp sites

Financial Information:

	$'000
Sales revenues	35,520

No of Employees: 530

ALLEGHANY CORPORATION

Park Avenue Plaza, New York, NY 10055
Tel: (212) 752-1356

Chairman: F M Kirby (and Chief Executive Officer)
President: John J Burns Jr
Senior Executive Officers: David B Cuming (VP), Jared C Horton (VP, Secretary and Treasurer), Theodore E Somerville (VP and General Counsel), John E Conway (Controller and Assistant Secretary)

PRINCIPAL ACTIVITIES: Interests in financial services and insurance
Principal Subsidiaries: Chicago Title & Trust Company; Shelby Insurance Company; MSL Industries
Principal Bank: Manufacturers Hanover
Financial Information:

	Dec 31 1985*	Dec 31 1986
	$'000	$'000
Sales revenues	349,615	623,414
Income before taxes	14,117	117,712
Net income	7,052	79,465
Earnings per share	$0.95	$12.36
Common stock	7,419	6,430
Retained income	6,802	69,465
Shareholders equity	404,355	497,241

*restated

Principal Shareholders: F M Kirby; Allan P Kirby; Grace Kirby Culbertson; Ann Kirby Kirby
No of Employees: 4,786

ALLEGHENY & WESTERN ENERGY CORPORATION

1600 Kanawha Valley Building, Charleston, WV 25301
Tel: (304) 343-4567

Chairman: Reeves Lewenthal
President: Anthony F Altmann (and Chief Executive Officer)
Senior Executive Officers: Roland Baer Jr (Executive VP, Treasurer and Subsidiary Officer), George D Bailey Jr (VP and Controller), James W S Deer (Legal), Dennis Mann (VP), Richard L Mann (VP and Group President)

PRINCIPAL ACTIVITIES: Exploration and production of crude oil and natural gas
Principal Bank: First National Bank of Boston
Financial Information:

	$'000
Sales revenues	240,000

No of Employees: 520

ALLEGHENY BEVERAGE CORPORATION

Mackey Circle, Cheverly, MD 20781
Tel: (301) 341-6000

Chairman: Edward A Weisman
President: Morton M Lapides (and Chief Executive Officer)
Senior Executive Officers: David Barr (Executive VP), John E Baker (Senior VP and Chief Financial Officer), Milton H Neidlinger (Senior VP), A J Hering (Senior VP and Treasurer), Jeffrey R Lapides (Senior VP), Mark A Garfinkel (VP and Legal Counsel), J Tighe Merkert (VP), Frank E Silvestro (VP and Controller)

PRINCIPAL ACTIVITIES: Manufacture and sale of soft drinks; food and drink service equipment; commercial cleaning; laundries; retail trade in office furniture
Principal Bank: The Riggs National Bank
Financial Information:

	Mar 31 1986
	$'000
Sales revenues	1,138,832
Net income	59,842
Earnings per share	$8.57
Shareholders equity	151,126

No of Employees: 32,000

ALLEGHENY INTERNATIONAL INC

PO Box 456, Pittsburgh, PA 15230
Tel: (412) 562-4000

Chairman: Olver S Travers (and Chief Executive Officer and Chief Operating Officer)
Senior Executive Officers: Thomas J Albani (Executive VP), Timothy L Guzzle (Executive VP), Anthony D Shanagher (Executive VP and Chief Executive Officer), F George Scott (Senior VP), George C Oehmler (VP)

PRINCIPAL ACTIVITIES: Manufacture of a wide range of consumer goods and sports equipment; electronics; industrial equipment; safety equipment; manufacture of metals and metallurgical products
Financial Information:

	Dec 31 1985	Dec 31 1986
	$'000	$'000
Sales revenues	2,180,060	1,924,194
Net (loss)	(109,143)	(164,000)
Shareholders equity	176,109	66,142

No of Employees: 30,800

ALLEGHENY LUDLUM CORPORATION

1000 Six PPG Place, Pittsburgh, PA 15222
Tel: (412) 394-2800

Chairman: Richard P Simmons (and Chief Executive Officer)
President: Robert P Bozzone (and Chief Operating Officer)
Senior Executive Officers: R C O'Sullivan (Senior VP, Finance)

PRINCIPAL ACTIVITIES: Manufacture of specialty steel products including stainless steel, silicon electrical steel and specialty alloys
Principal Subsidiaries: Alstrip
Principal Bank: Pittsburg National Bank
Financial Information:

	Dec 31 1985	Dec 31 1986*
	$'000	$'000
Sales revenues	716,360	732,453

*on May 8 1987 Allegheny Ludlum made an Initial Public Offering (IPO) of common stock and as a result became a "public" company. Its stock trades on the NYSE (symbol ALS). Further, as of December 28 1986 the company effected a recapitalization which, in effect, resulted in it becoming a "new" company with "no prior financial history".

Principal Shareholders: R P Simmons; R P Bozzone; R C O'Sullivan
No of Employees: 5,600

ALLEGHENY POWER SYSTEM, INC

320 Park Avenue, New York, NY 10022
Tel: (212) 752-2121

Chairman: Charles B Finch
President: Klaus Bergman (and Chief Executive Officer)
Senior Executive Officers: John Adams (Senior VP Finance), Frank J Eppich (Senior VP)

PRINCIPAL ACTIVITIES: Electricity supply
Principal Subsidiaries: Allegheny Power Service Corp; Monongahela Power Co; Potomac Edison Co; West Penn Power Co
Financial Information:

	Dec 31 1985	Dec 31 1986
	$'000	$'000
Sales revenues	1,830,650	1,704,093
Net income	178,420	203,746
Earnings per share	$3.59	$4.03
Shareholders equity	-	1,605,549

No of Employees: 5,837

ALLEGRETTI & CO

9200 Mason Avenue, Chatsworth, CA 91311
Tel: (818) 341-4800
Telex: WUT 696417 allegreti chca

Chairman: Joseph B Allegretti
President: James M Warren
Senior Executive Officers: George Welford (Executive VP), Steve Farley (VP Finance), George V Jiran (VP and Plant Manager), Charles Mattson (VP Operations), A E Eggly (VP Marketing), Art Weiss (VP Distribution)

PRINCIPAL ACTIVITIES: Manufacture of electrical appliances for the home and electrical garden equipment including lawn trimmers
Principal Bank: Security Pacific National Bank
Financial Information:

	$'000
Sales revenues	80,000

No of Employees: 1,400

ALLEN GROUP INC

534 Broadhollow Road, Melville, NY 11746
Tel: (516) 293-5500
Telex: WUT 961 357 allen melv

Chairman: Walter B Kissinger (and President and Chief Executive Officer); Vice Chairman: J Chisholm Lyons
Senior Executive Officers: R Michael Briggs (Senior VP), Donald E Bindler (Senior VP), Richard P Motta (VP and Treasurer), Stephen E Gilhuley (VP, Secretary and Legal Counsel), Andris Grants (VP Corporate Development), Sheldon Gross (VP), Frederick D Heiman (VP Administration), Robert G Paul (VP), G Watton Cottrell (VP Finance), Robert A Youdelman (VP Taxation), Stuart M Wilens (VP and Controller), Carlos I Diaz (VP), John McCusker (VP)

PRINCIPAL ACTIVITIES: Manufacture of equipment and components for the automotive industry
Principal Bank: Manufacturers Hanover Trust
Financial Information:

	Dec 31 1986
	$'000
Sales revenues	423,220
Net (loss)	(8,553)
(Loss) per share	($1.23)
Shareholders equity	147,823

No of Employees: 5,000

ALLIANCE MANUFACTURING COMPANY, INC

22790 Lake Park Blvd, Alliance, OH 44601
Tel: (216) 821-44601
Telex: TWX 810 4339157 alncmfg alce

Chairman: F L Randall Jr
President: John Gray
Senior Executive Officers: Stanley I Cundey (Treasurer), W E Collins (Secretary)

PRINCIPAL ACTIVITIES: Manufacture of domestic electrical equipment and telecommunications equipment
Parent Company: North American Philips Corporation, New York, NY
Principal Bank: Irving Trust Company
Financial Information:

	$'000
Sales revenues	50,000

No of Employees: 500

ALLIED BANCSHARES, INC

1000 Louisiana, Houston, TX 77002
Tel: (713) 224-6611

Chairman: Walter M Mischer
President: D K Anderson
Senior Executive Officers: Gerald H Smith (Chief Executive Officer), Jay C Crager Jr (Executive VP and Chief Financial Officer), Paul W Carlisle Jr (Senior VP), Robert B Goldstein (Senior VP), Michael C Baker (Senior VP), Frank C McDowell (Senior VP), Thomas Y Hamilton (Senior VP)

PRINCIPAL ACTIVITIES: Banking
Principal Bank: Allied Bank of Texas
Financial Information:

	Dec 31 1985	Dec 31 1986
	$'000	$'000
Net income (loss)	122,030	(17,593)
Earnings (loss) per share	$2.95	($0.42)
Retained income	-	613,158
Deposits	8,171,030	8,103,275
Total assets	10,245,507	9,863,646

No of Employees: 3,350

ALLIED BANK OF TEXAS

Travis & Rusk Avenue, Houston, TX 77001
Tel: (713) 224-6611
Telex: WUT 792193 albank int hou

Chairman: Jack T Trotter; Chairman of Executive Committee: Gerald H Smith; Vice Chairman: Bob D Ward
President: Walter E Johnson
Senior Executive Officers: Jay C Crager Jr (Executive VP), D K Andersen (Executive VP), Edwin E Smith (Executive VP), Yale Smith (Executive VP), Robert B Goldstein (Executive VP), James W Little (Senior VP International), Paul W Carlisle (Executive VP Operations), Michael C Baker (Executive VP)

PRINCIPAL ACTIVITIES: Bank
Parent Company: Allied Bancshares Inc, Houston, TX

No of Employees: 760

ALLIED/EGRY BUSINESS SYSTEMS, INC

PO Box 125, W C Br, Dayton, OH 45449
Tel: (513) 866-7421

President: W H Ames
Senior Executive Officers: E J Klimczak (VP), R Dean (VP), J Feeley (VP, Secretary and Treasurer), R Lytle (VP Sales)

PRINCIPAL ACTIVITIES: Manufacture of business forms
Parent Company: SCM Corporation through Allied Paper Inc

Financial Information:

	$'000
Sales revenues	85,000

No of Employees: 700

ALLIED MATERIALS CORPORATION

PO Box 18760, Oklahoma City, OK 73154-0760
Tel: (405) 842 4403

President: Jerry Plant
Senior Executive Officers: Ralph Wilkie (Executive VP)

PRINCIPAL ACTIVITIES: Manufacture of roofing materials
Parent Company: Entex Inc, Houston, Texas
Principal Bank: Liberty National Bank and Trust Company of Oklahoma City
Financial Information:

	$'000
Sales revenues	40,000

No of Employees: 150

ALLIED PAPER INC

2030 Portage Street, Kalamazoo, MI 49003
Tel: (616) 345-7131
Telex: TWX 8102772629 allied ppr kzo

President: Ernest J Klimczak
Senior Executive Officers: George E Hall (VP), W Ames (VP Allied Energy), P F Kraushaar (VP Industrial Relations), Paul Harvey (VP), Eugen C Kowall (VP and Controller), Thomas Riley (VP and Legal Counsel)

PRINCIPAL ACTIVITIES: Manufacture of a wide range of paper and paper products
Parent Company: SCM Corporation, New York, NY
Financial Information:

	$'000
Sales revenues	350,000

No of Employees: 2,000

ALLIED PRODUCTS COMPANY

PO Box 36130, Birmingham, AL 35211
Tel: (205) 988-8200

President: Mack A Rikard
Senior Executive Officers: William R Stephenson (VP, Treasurer and Comptroller), Jerry Wheeler (VP)

PRINCIPAL ACTIVITIES: Manufacture of cement and concrete products
Principal Bank: Birmingham Trust National Bank
Financial Information:

	$'000
Sales revenues	55,000

No of Employees: 550

ALLIED PRODUCTS CORPORATION

10 S Riverside Plaza, Chicago, IL 60606
Tel: (312) 454-1020

Chairman: S S Sherman; Chairman of Exeuctive Committee: Lloyd Drexler
President: Richard A Drexler (and Chief Executive Officer)
Senior Executive Officers: Charles W Lunger (Senior Executive VP and Chief Operating Officer), Kenneth B Light (Executive VP Administration), James Hayden (Executive VP and Chief Financial Officer), Bob Middlebrooks (Senior VP), Harold C Jenseth (Senior VP), Edward E Carlson (Senior VP)

PRINCIPAL ACTIVITIES: Manufacture of agricultural implements and equipment; manufacture of industrial presses; heavy stamping and die work
Trade Names: Bush Hog, New Idea, White Farm Equipment, Continental Cotton, Verson, South Bend Stamping, Littell
Principal Bank: Continental Illinois National Bank and Trust Co
Financial Information:

	Dec 31 1985	Dec 31 1986
	$'000	$'000
Sales revenues	276,112	420,846
Net income*	10,603	16,173
Earnings per share	$3.33	$3.36
Shareholders equity	87,129	156,132

*after extraordinary credits

No of Employees: 3,900

ALLIED SECURITY INC

2840 Library Road, Pittsburgh, PA 15234
Tel: (412) 884-2636

Chairman: Neal H Holmes (and Chief Executive Officer)
President: Steven B Stein (and Chief Operating Officer)
Senior Executive Officers: Kenneth B Slutzky (VP Operations), Glenn A Pifer (Treasurer), Vincent J Papi (VP Marketing)

PRINCIPAL ACTIVITIES: Security services
Financial Information:

	$'000
Sales revenues	47,660

No of Employees: 3,900

ALLIED STORES CORPORATION

1114 Avenue of the Americas, New York, NY 10036
Tel: (212) 764-2000
Telex: 12-7630

Chairman: Thomas M Macioce (and Chief Executive Officer); Vice Chairman: John T Cullen (and Chief Merchandising Officer)
President: James A Walsh (and Chief Operating Officer)
Senior Executive Officers: Howard E Hassler (Executive VP Finance), Frank R D'Elia (Senior VP Secretary and Corporate Attorney), Donald F Dunn (Senior VP, Executive Group Manager), Benjamin Frank (Senior VP, Legal and Governmental Affairs), Frank W Harvey (Senior VP, Executive Group Manager and President of Maas Brothers), Joseph M Lesser (Senior VP, Executive Group Manager), Frank T Reilly (Senior VP, President of Brooks Brothers), Alfred J Schwarz (Senior VP, Personnel and Executive Development), Joseph J Calandro Jr (VP Taxes), Wilbur J Fix (VP, President of The Bon), Frank S Fuino Jr (VP and Treasurer), Charles B James II (VP, Executive Group Manager), Orren F Knauer (VP, Investor Relations), Robert L Mettler (VP, President of Joske's), John P Murphy (VP, Financial and Security Audit), Ralph Nofi (VP, President of Allied Stores Marketing Corporation), William S Ruben (VP, Executive Group Manager and President of Bonwit Teller), Ruben L Slape (VP, Credit), Leonard M Snyder (VP, Executive Group Manager and President of Donaldson's), William J Stapleton (VP, EDP and Management Information Services), Elliot J Stone (VP, President of Jordan Marsh, Boston), Lawrence Stone (VP, President of Stern's), Robert Tanner (VP, Construction and Store Planning), Frank J Zamboni (VP, Real Estate), Robert J Strechay (Controller), JoAnn Abma (Assistant VP), Phillip Silverman (Assistant VP), Lawrence Saunders (Assistant Treasurer)

PRINCIPAL ACTIVITIES: Department stores
Principal Subsidiaries: Allied Central Stores, Inc (Missouri), d/b/a/Donaldson's and Heer's Donaldson's Distributing Corporation (Minnesota); Allied International Management Services, Inc (New York); Allied Stores Credit Corporation (Delaware), Allied Stores Credit Corporation of New York (New York); Allied Stores-East, Inc (New York), d/b/a Bonwit Teller, Joske's, Plymouth Shops, Read's and Stern's; Allied Stores International, Inc (New York); Allied Stores International Sales Company, Inc (New York); Allied Stores Marketing Corp (New York); Allied Stores of Penn-Ohio, Inc (Ohio), d/b/a Block's, Herpolsheimer's and Pomeroy's; Retail Service, Inc (Michigan); ASC Stores III, Inc (Delaware), d/b/a Brooks Brothers, Miller & Rhoads, Miller's Garfinckel's,

Catherine's Stout Shoppe, Clothes for Eve, Ann Taylor and Plus-Size; Brooks Brothers (Japan) Ltd (Japan); The Garland Shirt Company, Inc (Delaware); The Cain-Sloan Company (Tennessee); Delivery Services, Inc (Florida); Jerry Leonard, Inc (Nebraska); Jordan Marsh Company (Massachusetts); Jordan Marsh Insurance Agency, Inc (Massachusetts); Maas Brothers, Inc (Florida); Jor-Mar, Inc (Delaware); The Muller Company, Limited (Louisiana); Tukwila Warehousing Services Corporation (Washington); Alstores Realty Corporation (Delaware); Aliana Realty Corp (Indiana); Al-Jordan Realty Corp (Massachusetts), Bay Colony Shopping Center, Inc (Massachusetts); Baygertz Realty Corp (New York); Boncom Corporation (Washington); Broadway & Charnelton, Inc (Oregon); Clearmaas Realty Corp (Florida); Columbia Shopping Center, Inc (Washington); Jo-Line Relaty Corp (Texas); Jordan Servicenter, Inc (Massachusetts); Laudermarsh Realty Corp (Florida); The Northgate Company (Washington); Northgate Centers, Inc (Washington); Northgate Apartments, Inc (Washington), Saramaas Realty Corp (Florida); Shoppers' World, Inc (Massachusetts); Realbon Corporation (Washington); Southcenter Shopping Center Corporation (Washington); Tacoma Mall Corporation (Washington)

Principal Bank: Manufacturers Hanover Trust Co

Financial Information:

	Feb 1 1986
	$'000
Sales revenues	4,135,027
Income before taxes	289,875
Net income	159,275
Common dividends	46,297
Dividends per share*	$1.07
Earnings per share primary*	$3.70
Common stock	46,102
Retained income	960,382
Shareholders equity	1,258,470

* all per share data reflects the 2 for 1 stock split on March 20 1986

No of Employees: 65,000

ALLIED VAN LINES, INC

25th Avenue & Roosevelt Road, Broadview, IL 60153
Tel: (312) 681-8000
Telex: WUT 728483 avlic brdva

Chairman: Dennis I Mudd; Vice Chairman: Richard Ryan
President: Sidney Epstein (and Chief Operating Officer)
Senior Executive Officers: Peter P Mazzetti (Senior VP), Williams Weity (VP Finance), Terry G Fewell (VP and Legal Counsel), Perry Anthony (VP Household Goods), Larry L Stein (VP Marketing and Sales), Frank W Borta (VP and Managing Director Allied Van Lines International Corp), Dave Southard (VP Specialty Products), Marshall Felbein (VP, Vanguard Insurance Agency), Robert McClure (VP and General Manager Vanguard Insurance Agency)

PRINCIPAL ACTIVITIES: Trucking and freight forwarding
Principal Bank: Harris Bank and Trust Co
Financial Information:

	Dec 31 1985	Dec 31 1986
	$'000	$'000
Sales revenues	546,780	562,208
Net income	4,750	3,656
Earnings per share	$4.56	$3.51
Shareholders equity	33,615	36,722

No of Employees: 1,050

ALLIED-LYONS NORTH AMERICA CORPORATION

PO Box 2736, Huntington, CT 06484
Tel: (203) 929-9200

President: James Johnson Jr
Senior Executive Officers: J W Granucci (VP Finance)

PRINCIPAL ACTIVITIES: Holding company with interests in tea, coffee, cookies and food mixes
Parent Company: Allied-Lyons PLC, UK
Principal Bank: Manufacturers Hanover Trust Co
Financial Information:

	$'000
Sales revenues	1,500,000

ALLIED-SIGNAL AEROSPACE COMPANY

1000 Wilson Boulevard, Arlington, VA 22209
Tel: (703) 276-2000

President: Robert L Kirk (and Chief Executive)

PRINCIPAL ACTIVITIES: Allied-Signal Aerospace is one of the world's ten largest aerospace companies. About 80 percent of the company's business is in aircraft equipment. About 60 percent of its sales are from the military and 40 percent from commercial customers. US Customers account for 75 percent of sales, with the balance from the international market. The company is a market leader in small turbine engines, auxiliary power units and aircraft brake equipment. It manufactures turbofan and turboprop engines, advanced avionics and engine controls, electrical and mechanical power systems, environmental heat transfer equipment, fluid propulsion systems, secure communications and anti-submarine warfare systems, It also provides a wide range of other products and services for aircraft, missiles and space applications.
Trade Names: Bendix, Garrett, Bendix/King, AiResearch
Parent Company: Allied-Signal Inc, Morristown, NJ
Principal Subsidiaries: Garrett Turbo Inc (Japan); Garrett GmbH (Germany)
Financial Information:

	$'000
Sales revenues	4,500,000

No of Employees: 60,000

ALLIED-SIGNAL, INC

PO Box 4000R, Morristown, NJ 07960
Tel: (201) 455-2000

Chairman: Edward L Hennessy Jr (and Chief Executive Officer); Vice Chairman: Forrest N Shumway
Senior Executive Officers: Alan Belzer (Executive VP, Operations), Daniel W Derbes (Executive VP, Operations), William C Purple (Executive VP, Operations), J Mason Reynolds (Executive VP, Operations), Gerald L Seelig (Executive VP, Operations), John A Teske (Executive VP, Operations), Nicholas A Cameron (Senior VP, Planning and Development), L James Colby Jr (Senior VP, Technology), Brian D Forrow (Senior VP, General Counsel and Secretary), Edwin M Halkyard (Senior VP, Human Resources), Donald R Kayser (Senior VP and Chief Financial Officer), David G Powell (Senior VP, Public Affairs)

PRINCIPAL ACTIVITIES: Allied-Signal, Inc is a holding company formed by the merger of Allied Corporation and The Signal Companies, Inc on September 19th 1985. A high technology company, Allied-Signal serves a broad spectrum of industries through its strategic businesses, which are engaged in the aerospace, automotive, chemical, electronics and oil and gas industries
Principal Subsidiaries: Allied Corporation; The Signal Companies, Inc; Union Texas Petroleum; Industrial Products Company; Allied Health & Scientific Products Company; The Garrett Corporation
Financial Information:

	Dec 31 1985	Dec 31 1986
	$'000	$'000
Sales revenues	9,115,000	11,794,000
Net income (loss)	(279,000)	605,000
Earnings (loss) per share	($3.28)	$3.26
Shareholders equity	6,130,000	3,686,000

No of Employees: 143,800

ALLIS-CHALMERS CORPORATION

PO Box 512, Milwaukee, WI 53201-0512
Tel: (414) 475-2000

Chairman: Wendell F Bueche (and President and Chief Executive Officer)
Senior Executive Officers: Richard A Buese (VP), Charles W Parker Jr (VP Communications and Public Affairs), Ronald J Burns (VP, Chief Financial Officer and Treasurer), John J Platner (VP), Donald E Machenberg (VP), Jacques F Trevillyan (VP), Dale L Matschullat (VP and General Counsel, Secretary)

PRINCIPAL ACTIVITIES: Allis-Chalmers provides specialized technologies that help the world meet basic needs in the areas of air quality control, fluids handling, solid materials processing and material handling. Its operating companies serve four general markets: the processing industries-such as mining, chemicals and pulp and paper-energy production, construction and general industry. Allis has strong positions in a number of major market areas and can source equipment in every important market location. Its operating philosophy today emphasizes technological and marketing strengths backed by worldwide sourcing flexiblility
Principal Subsidiaries/ Divisions: American Air Filter; Allis-Chalmers Fluid Products Company; Allis-Chalmers Energy and Minerals Systems Company; Allis Chalmers Solids Process Equipment Company; Industrial Truck Division
Financial Information:

	Dec 31 1985	Dec 31 1986
	$'000	$'000
Sales revenues	886,064	771,188
Net (loss)	(168,383)	(8,581)
Net (loss) per share	($12.27)	($1.09)

No of Employees: 12,000

ALLSTATE INSURANCE GROUP

Allstate Plaza, Northbrook, IL 60062
Tel: (312) 291-5000

Chairman: Donald J Craib Jr (and Chief Executive Officer)

PRINCIPAL ACTIVITIES: Allstate Insurance Group, provides personal and business property and casualty insurance, and individual and group life and health products
Parent Company: Sears, Roebuck & Co, Chicago, IL
Principal Subsidiaries: Group Companies: Allstate Insurance Co; Allstate Development Corp Inc; Allstate Indemnity Co; Allstate Life Insurance Co; General Underwriting Agency Inc; Harbridge House Inc; Lincoln Benefit Life Co; Northbrook Indemnity Co; Northbrook Life Insurance Co; Northbrook National Insurance Co; Northbrook Property Casualty Insurance; Surety Life Insurance Co
Financial Information:

	Dec 31 1985
	$'000
Total revenues	10,378,900
Premium income(1)	7,465,400
Premium income(2)	1,840,600
Investment income(3)	1,026,400
Income before taxes(4)	292,000
Group income	604,800

(1) Property-liability
(2) Life-health
(3) less investment expense
(4) and net realized capital gains, equity in net income of unconsolidated companies and minority interests

ALLTEL CORPORATION

100 Executive Parkway, Hudson, OH 44236
Tel: (216) 650-7000

Chairman: Weldon W Case (and Chief Executive Officer)
President: Joe T Ford (and Chief Operating Officer)
Senior Executive Officers: Max E Bobbitt (Executive VP and Chief Financial Officer), Robert D Bonnar (Senior VP and Controller), Charles W Miller (Executive VP), Tom Orsigny (VP), Nick F Arena (Treasurer), George C McConnaughey (Secretary), Nelson H Case (Executive VP Communications)

PRINCIPAL ACTIVITIES: Operation of telephone systems
Financial Information:

	$'000
Sales revenues	672,045

No of Employees: 5,600

ALMA PLASTICS COMPANIES

303 Valley Avenue, Alma, MI 48801
Tel: (517) 463-1191

President: Roger L Plew
Senior Executive Officers: Frederick D Hay (Executive VP), Darrel Hampton (VP Sales), Dennis Howell (VP Sales), Robert Davie (VP Manufacturing), Pat Fleming (VP Manufacturing), Thomas J Fellrath (Comptroller), Douglas P Hamilton (VP and Treasurer), Roger M Bougie (VP and General Counsel), Ronald F Thompson (Secretary)

PRINCIPAL ACTIVITIES: Manufacture of plastic products
Principal Bank: Commercial National Bank of Alma
Financial Information:

	$'000
Sales revenues	108,000

No of Employees: 1,150

ALOHA INC

PO Box 30028, Honolulu International Airport, Honolulu, HI 96820
Tel: (808) 836-4200

Chairman: Hung Wo Ching; Vice Chairman: Sheridan C F Ing
President: J R O'Gorman (and Chief Executive Officer)
Senior Executive Officers: P N Economou (Executive VP), John L Garibaldi (VP Finance and Chief Financial Officer), Eleanor S Urakawa (Secretary), William T Henderson (VP Marketing), James I Williamson (VP)

PRINCIPAL ACTIVITIES: Air transportation of passengers, freight and mail
Principal Subsidiaries: Aloha Airlines Inc
Financial Information:

	$'000
Sales revenues	95,075

No of Employees: 990

ALPHA CORPORATION OF TENNESSEE

Hwy 57 E, Collierville, TN 38017
Tel: (901) 853-2450

Chairman: William D Watkins (and Chief Executive Officer)
President: J D Burriss (and Chief Operating Officer)
Senior Executive Officers: Joe B Simpson Jr (VP Finance and Chief Financial Officer), Bernard J Froelich (VP Sales), George W Carey Jr (VP Operations), Gerald P Griffith (VP, Research and Development and Technology), Jerry Stauffer (VP and General Counsel)

PRINCIPAL ACTIVITIES: Manufacture of electrical insulators, laminates and resins
Principal Bank: Security Pacific Business Credit Inc
Financial Information:

	$'000
Sales revenues	96,000

No of Employees: 400

ALPHA INDUSTRIES INC

20 Sylvan Road, Woburn, MA 01801
Tel: (617) 935-5150
Telex: RCA 200206 alpha ur

Chairman: George S Kariotis (and Chief Executive Officer)

President: Martin J Reid (and Chief Operating Officer)

Senior Executive Officers: Allan L Coon (Senior VP, Treasurer and Chief Financial Officer), Constantine Kamnitsis (Senior VP), Robert E Goldwasser (VP), Howard J Hall (VP), Frank A Leith (VP), Donald Paulson (Secretary), John A Hanna Jr (Assistant Treasurer), Paul E Vincent (Controller)

PRINCIPAL ACTIVITIES: Alpha Industries Inc designs, manufactures and markets microwave semiconductor devices, components, subsystems and microwave ferrite and other microwave ceramic materials primarily for the defense electronics, commercial telecommunications and other commercial markets

Principal Bank: First National Bank of Boston

Financial Information:

	Mar 31 1986
	$'000
Sales revenues	70,996
(Loss) before taxes	(3,391)
Net (loss)	(876)
Dividends	178
Dividends per share	$0.025
(Loss) per share	($0.12)
Common stock	1,857
Retained income	26,893
Shareholders equity	54,667

No of Employees: 1,370

ALPHA METALS, INC

600 Rte 440, Jersey City, NJ 07304

Tel: (201) 434-6778

President: Raymond P Sharpe

Senior Executive Officers: Karl Mount (VP, Finance and Administration), Victor Coppola (Executive VP International), Tom Marks (VP Sales), James Bralla (VP Operations), Richard Hilsinger (VP Corporate Development and Planning)

PRINCIPAL ACTIVITIES: Manufacture of solder and solder related products

Parent Company: Cookson America Inc

Principal Subsidiaries: Alpha Metals, UK, France, Italy, Hong Kong

Principal Bank: Chemical Bank

Financial Information:

	$'000
Sales revenues	75,000

Principal Shareholders: Cookson PLC, UK

No of Employees: 500

ALPHA MICROSYSTEMS

PO Box 25059, Santa Ana, CA 92799-5059

Chairman: Richard A Cortese (and President and Chief Executive Officer)

Senior Executive Officers: John F Glade (VP and Secretary), Nyoka L Criner (Comptroller)

PRINCIPAL ACTIVITIES: Manufacture of microcomputer systems

Principal Subsidiaries: Alpha Microsystems Europe

Financial Information:

	$'000
Sales revenues	48,100

No of Employees: 455

ALPINE GROUP INC

1290 Avenue of the Americas, New York, NY 10104

Tel: (212) 489-0110

Chairman: Steven S Elbaum (and Chief Executive Officer)

President: Terence P Swain (and Chief Operating Officer and Subsidiary Officer)

Senior Executive Officers: Alan J Nickerson (VP Secretary and Treasurer)

PRINCIPAL ACTIVITIES: Manufacture of industrial machinery

Principal Subsidiaries: Alpine Petroleum Corp; Marine Petroleum Corp; Precision Products Inc; Rochester Button Co Inc

Principal Bank: Colonial Bank

Financial Information:

	$'000
Sales revenues	30,000

No of Employees: 450

ALTOS COMPUTER SYSTEMS

2641 Orchard Park Way, San Jose, CA 95134

Tel: (408) 946-6700

Telex: WTX 176782 altos snj

Chairman: David Jackson (and President and Chief Executive Officer)

Senior Executive Officers: David Liggett (Executive VP Operations), Phillip E White (Senior VP Marketing and Sales), David Zacarius (Senior VP, Chief Operating Officer and Secretary), Kapil Nanda (VP Engineering), Colin Goble (VP Software Engineering), Thomas Anthony (VP Sales), Rene Aenishaenslin (VP European Operations), Sandy Holt (VP)

PRINCIPAL ACTIVITIES: Manufacture and sale of data processing equipment

Principal Subsidiaries: Australian Altos Computer Systems Pty Ltd

Principal Bank: Bank of America NT and SA

Financial Information:

	$'000
Sales revenues	124,500

No of Employees: 430

ALTUS BANK, A FEDERAL SAVINGS BANK (FORMERLY FIRST SOUTHERN FEDERAL

851 S Beltline Hwy, Mobile, AL 36606

Tel: (205) 473-0500

Fax: (205) 473-0554

Chairman: Arthur Tonsmeire Jr

President: Gerald M Czarnecki (and Chief Executive Officer)

Senior Executive Officers: Robert F Polk (Managing Director of Capital Markets Division), Kenneth L Gould (Executive VP, Chief Executive Officer of the Consumer Services Group), Robert S Moore Jr (Executive VP, Managing Director and Chief Executive Officer Mortgage Bank), Harry M Barnes Jr (Senior VP), Alfred K Seibt (Senior VP), Roland V Lee Jr (Senior VP), John L Sullivan (Senior VP and Treasurer), W Phillip Givens (Senior VP), Robert J Ziner (Senior VP), Douglas W Graham (Senior VP)

PRINCIPAL ACTIVITIES: Financial services including savings and loans

Principal Subsidiaries: The Mitchell Company

Financial Information:

	Dec 31 1985	Dec 31 1986
	$'000	$'000
Income before taxes	10,144	18,636
Net income	10,144	18,636
Earnings per share	$3.31(1)	$3.84(2)
Common stock(3)	43,377	43,478
Retained income	40,117	58,753
Shareholders equity	83,494	102,231
Deposits	1,487,942	1,607,013
Total assets	2,074,246	2,535,435

(1) total after extraordinary item-before extraordinary item $1.55, extraordinary item $1.76

(2) total after extraordinary item-before extraordinary item $3.35, extraordinary item $0.49

(3) and additional paid in capital

No of Employees: 1,063

ALUMAX, INC

400 S El Camino Real, San Mateo, CA 94402
Tel: (415) 348-3400
Telex: WTX 34791 alumax smt

Chairman: Allen Born; Vice Chairman: Mamoru Tabuchi
President: Paul E Drack (and Chief Executive Officer)
Senior Executive Officers: Craig A Davis (Executive VP), Shiro Nakagaura (Senior VP), Herbert C Clough (Group VP), V B Evans (Executive VP), John A Brader (VP and Controller)

PRINCIPAL ACTIVITIES: Holding company with interests in the production of aluminum
Parent Company: AMAX Inc
Principal Subsidiaries: Alumax Extrusions Inc; Alumax Fabricated Products Inc; Alumax Mill Products Inc; Alumax of SC Inc; Alumax Pacific Corp; Alumax Recycling Group Inc; Alumet Holding Corp; Alumet Corp; Alumax Aluminium Corp; Eastalco Aluminium Co; Intalco Aluminium Corp; Kawneer Co Inc
Principal Bank: Bank of America NT and SA
Financial Information:

	Dec 31 1985	Dec 31 1986
	$'000	$'000
Sales revenues	1,887,072	1,974,333
Net income	62,876	70,120
Shareholders equity	786,301	782,945

No of Employees: 13,300

ALUMAX MILL PRODUCTS, INC

5555 East Hwy 6, Morris, IL 60450
Tel: (815) 942 3420

President: Roy J Steward
Senior Executive Officers: John A Brader (VP), Craig A Davis (VP and Secretary), V B Evans (VP), Francis G Foster (VP and Treasurer)

PRINCIPAL ACTIVITIES: Manufacture of aluminum products
Parent Company: Alumax Inc
Financial Information:

	$'000
Sales revenues	300,000

No of Employees: 830

ALUMINUM CO OF AMERICA
ALCOA

1501 Alcoa Bldg, Pittsburgh, PA 15219
Tel: (412) 553-4545

Chairman: Charles W Parry (and Chief Executive Officer); Vice Chairman: James S Pasman Jr
President: C F Fetterolf
Senior Executive Officers: Robert D Hornbeck (Executive VP), Richard L Fischer (Senior VP), Donald R Whitlow (Senior VP), James W Wirth (Senior VP), Harold S Evans (Group VP International), Clyde R Gillespie (Group VP), Ronald R Hoffman (Group VP), Vincent R Scorsone (Group VP), Bruce R Barstow (VP and Director General Grupo Alumino), John L Diederich (Group VP Metals and Chemicals), Charles K Lignon (Group VP Material Science)

PRINCIPAL ACTIVITIES: Bauxite mining, refining and smelting; processing of aluminum and manufacture of aluminum products
Financial Information:

	Dec 31 1985	Dec 31 1986
	$'000	$'000
Sales revenues	5,162,700	4,667,200
Net income (loss)	(16,600)	254,100
Earnings per share	$2.03	$2.96
Shareholders equity	3,307,900	3,721,600

No of Employees: 40,100

ALUMINUM SMELTING & REFINING CO

5463 Dunham Road, Maple Heights, OH 44137
Tel: (216) 662-3100

President: Richard B Barnett
Senior Executive Officers: Terrence P Szarka

PRINCIPAL ACTIVITIES: Smelting and refining of aluminum; aluminum and zinc alloys
Parent Company: Delaware North Companies Inc, Buffalo, NY
Financial Information:

	$'000
Sales revenues	100,000

No of Employees: 400

AM GENERAL CORPORATION

31744 Enterprise Drive, Livonia, MI 48151
Tel: (313) 523-0400

President: Robert L Kirk (and Chief Executive Officer)
Senior Executive Officers: Eugene Zembrzuski (VP Finance), George Scharbach (VP), Werner H Jean (VP), Frank S Besson (VP), Jeffrey C Wright (VP)

PRINCIPAL ACTIVITIES: Manufacture of commercial vehicles
Parent Company: LTV Corporation
Principal Bank: Bank of America
Financial Information:

	$'000
Sales revenues	400,000

No of Employees: 1,800

AM INTERNATIONAL, INC

333 W Wacker Drive, Chicago, IL 60606 - 1265
Tel: (312) 558-1966
Telex: 3734857 AMINT

Chairman: Merle H Banta (and President and Chief Executive Officer)
Senior Executive Officers: Gerald G McConnell (Senior VP and President Multigraphics Division), Donald A Biesack (VP Human Resources), Marion G Durk (VP Corporate Relations), John H Shuey (VP Finance and Chief Financial Officer), Jim Corcoran (Treasurer), Anthony Spier (VP and President International Division), Joseph A Verderber (VP and President Varityper Division), Jerry O Williams (VP and President Bruning Division)

PRINCIPAL ACTIVITIES: AM International, Inc is a worldwide sales/service/distribution organization serving the image systems and reprographics markets. AM International is engaged in the sale and service of over 11,000 products for the image systems and reprographics markets. AM International's products and supplies reach a worldwide customer base totaling more than 150,000. The reprographics segment is composed of products and services sold under the "Bruning" and "Multigraphics" names. Activities are conducted by the Domestic Bruning Division, which produces and markets equipment and supplies for the preparation, storage and reproduction of architectural and engineering designs; the Multigraphics Division, which manufactures and distributes offset duplicating machines and related supply products. The image systems segment is comprised of products and services sold under the "BruningCAD" and "Varityper" names. Activities are conducted by the domestic Bruning Division, which also markets equipment and software for computer aided drafting and design (CAD); the Varityper Division, which produces computer-based composing and phototypesetting systems that produce finished typeset copy for printing. In the latter part of fiscal 1985 the Company refocused the direction of its CAD business to take advantage of increased product availability. The CAD business has been marked by slowing market growth and the proliferation of low cost CAD software packages. Thus, this redirection will result in the Company selling to its customer base CAD software and related products supplied in large part of other companies. Accordingly, the Company discontinued its internal CAD software development operations. This will reduce in the near term future revenues in the Image Systems Segment but will not have a significant effect on this Segment's or the Company's operating profits. The Company's International Division sells and services products from both market segments through its 15 subsidiaries in 16 foreign countries. The division also maintains an ongoing relationship with over 100 independent dealers who distribute AM International products and supplies

Trade Names: "AM International", "Bruning", "Comp/Edit", "Comp/Set", "Multigraphics", "Multigraph", "Multilith", "Varityper", "EasyDraf", "PD"

Principal Subsidiaries: (100% owned unless stated): AM International Inc (Canada); AM International Ltd (New Zealand); Addressograph Multigraph (1979) Ltd (New Zealand); AM International Pty Ltd (Australia); Tetota Pty Ltd (Australia); AM Disco Inc; AM Foreign Sales Corp; AM International Export Corp; AM Export Corp; AM Distribution Services Corp; AM International AG (Switzerland); AM International (Pty) Ltd (South Africa); AM International SA Spain (Spain); AM International (Holdings) Ltd (UK); Admel International Ltd (UK); AM Admel Ltd (from AM Bruning Ltd) (UK); AM Jacquard Systems Ltd (UK); AM Varityper Ltd (UK); Addressograph-Multigraph Ltd (UK); AM International Leasing Ltd (UK); AM International GmbH (Germany); AM Bruning GmbH (Germany); AM International Corporation NV (Netherlands Antilles); Grafcon Corp; Multigraphics Advertising Corp; Addressograph-Multigraph Corp; AM International Leasing Corp; AM Finance Canada Ltd (Canada); AM Puerto Rico Inc; AM International (Denmark) AS (Denmark); AM International OY (Finland); AM Japan Company Ltd (67%) (Japan); AM International SA de CV (Mexico); AM International BV (Netherlands); AM Varityper BV (Netherlands); AM International AB (Sweden); AM International SA (France); AM Varityper and Co; AM International SA/NV (Belgium); Addressograph-Multigraph Ltd (Zambia); AM Holdings Inc; Harris-Marinoni SA (France); Harris Graphics SARL (France) Harris Graphics International Corp; Harris Graphics De Mexico SA De CV

Principal Banks: Security Pacific National Bank of Los Angeles; Continental Illinois National Bank of Chicago

Financial Information:

	May 3 1986 (9 mths) $'000	May 2 1987 (9 mths) $'000
Sales revenues	460,459	843,498
Income before taxes*	19,405	6,051
Net income	17,692	2,638
Earnings (loss) per share	$0.40	($0.05)
Common stock	505	508
Accumulated (deficit)	(72,718)	(72,255)
Shareholders equity	249,670	256,356

*and extraordinary item

No of Employees: 9,492

AMALGAMATED SUGAR CO

PO Box 1520, Ogden, UT 84402
Tel: (801) 399-3431
Telex: TWX 910-971-5914 tasco ogd

Chairman: Harold C Simmons (and Chief Executive Officer)
President: Allan M Lipman Jr
Senior Executive Officers: Quentin Smelzer Jr (VP), K P Chertudi (VP), Larry L Corry (VP), Robert C Lane (Treasurer), John R Lemke (Secretary)

PRINCIPAL ACTIVITIES: Manufacturer of sugar and molasses; animal feedstuffs
Parent Company: Amalgamated Group Inc
Financial Information:

	Jun 30 1986 $'000
Sales revenues	492,843
Net income	12,290
Earnings per share	$1.88
Shareholders equity	125,682

No of Employees: 1,300

AMANA REFRIGERATION, INC

Amana, IA 52204
Tel: (319) 622-5511
Telex: WUT 464450 amana ref amna

Chairman: Charles W Schmidt
President: Henry J Meyer (and Chief Executive Officer)
Senior Executive Officers: Wayne A Giddings (Senior VP), John Kammerer (Senior VP), Alex A Meyer (Senior VP Special Projects), C A Thompson (Senior VP), Allan J Glasford (Senior VP), Charles R Heyn (Treasurer)

PRINCIPAL ACTIVITIES: Manufacture of refrigerators, freezers and ovens; air conditioning equipment
Parent Company: Raytheon Co, Lexington, MA
Principal Bank: Merchants National Bank
Financial Information:

	$'000
Sales revenues	400,000

No of Employees: 2,900

AMAX INC

Amax Center, Greenwich, CT 06836-1700
Tel: (203) 629-6000
Telex: 996-480-Domestic; ITT Telex 4750114 Intnt'l

President: Allen Born
Senior Executive Officers: Malcolm Bayliss (Executive VP and General Counsel), Thomas McKeever (Executive VP), David Ball (Senior VP)

PRINCIPAL ACTIVITIES: AMAX is a worldwide supplier of minerals and energy, with its primary production located in the United States. The Company explores for, mines, refines and sells a wide variety of minerals and metals. Alumax Inc, its wholly owned subsidiary, is one of the major integrated aluminum companies in North America, while Amax Coal Company is the third largest coal producer in the United

States. AMAX's principal products are aluminum, coal, gold and molybdenum. The Company is also involved in the production of oil and natural gas. Other businesses in which the Company participates include silver, tungsten, magnesium, specialty metals and zinc. As part of its long-range strategy, AMAX is concentrating its operations in three core businesses-aluminum, coal and gold-but will continue to invest in other businesses as it deems appropriate

Current Trademarks: AMAX, AMAX EHC (& Design), AMAX LOGO, AMAX MSHC (& Design), AMAX TAXTICS, AMAX-LP, AMAX-MZC, AMAX-XLP, AMCO (& Diamond Device), AMCROM, AMIXALOGY, AMNIC, AMPHOS, AMSIL, AMSULF, AMTEL, AMTITE, AMZIRC, BRIX, C (& Design), CDP (Stylized), CLIMAX, CLIMAX MOLYBDENUM (& Design), CLIMELT, CLIMELT-MOLY-MESH, DIKAL, DRW, HIGH-K (& Design), KMAX-50, MOLYHIBIT, MOLYSULFIDE (Stylized), OFHC (In Rectangle), UNI-SCREEN

Principal Subsidiaries and Divisions: Alumax Inc (aluminum); AMAX Coal Company (Coal); AMAX Petroleum Corporation (oil and gas); AMAX Metal Products (Sales, conversion and development); AMAX Mineral Resources (molybdenum, tungsten, gold, magnesium; AMAX Pacific Inc/AMETALCO; Metal Refining Operations

Principal Banks: Chase Manhattan; National Westminster; Swiss Bank Corp

Financial Information:

	Dec 31 1985	Dec 31 1986
	$'000	$'000
Sales revenues	1,178,000	1,307,000
Profit (loss) before taxes	(106,000)	89,000
Net income (loss)	(621,000)	14,000
Dividends	5,100	-
Dividends per share*	$0.10	-
Earnings (loss) per share*	($9.35)	$0.05
Common stock	71,800	77,400
Retained (deficit)	(411,400)	(397,100)
Shareholders equity	888,400	884,600

*common shares

No of Employees: 12,571

AMBRIT INC

5400 118th Ave N, Clearwater, FL 33520
Tel: (813) 576-8424

Chairman: Henry Clarke Jr
President: L James Santerre (and Chief Executive Officer)
Senior Executive Officers: Thomas G Dixcy (Executive VP and Division President), H William Isaly (VP), George N Derhofer (VP Finance and Treasurer), David L Downes (Secretary)

PRINCIPAL ACTIVITIES: Production of ice cream and frozen foods

Financial Information:

	$'000
Sales revenues	51,000
Net income	50

No of Employees: 120

AMC ENTERTAINMENT INC

106 West 14th Street, Kansas City, MO 64105
Tel: (816) 474-6150

Chairman: S H Durwood (and Chief Executive Officer)
President: R D Leslie (and Chief Operating Officer)
Senior Executive Officers: William B Doeren (VP Operations), Edward D Derwood (VP), Ron D Lesilie (Executive VP), Joel H Resnick (Executive VP), Frank Rutkowski (Senior VP), Steven P Zell (VP Finance and Treasurer), Alan K Benjamin (Secretary)

PRINCIPAL ACTIVITIES: Operation of motion picture theaters

Financial Information:

	$'000
Sales revenues	200,000

No of Employees: 4,050

AMCA INTERNATIONAL LTD

Dartmouth National Bank Bldg, Hanover, NH 03755
Tel: (603) 643-5454

Chairman: Kenneth S Barclay
President: William R Holland (and Chief Executive Officer)
Senior Executive Officers: F J Stevenson (Executive VP), R E Chamberlain (Senior Group VP), R H Elman (Senior Group VP), John A Davis (Senior VP and Secretary)

PRINCIPAL ACTIVITIES: Design and manufacture of machinery for wide range of industrial outlets; manufacture of steel and machine tools

Principal Bank: Royal Bank of Canada

Financial Information:

	$'000
Sales revenues	1,600,000

No of Employees: 16,200

AMCAST INDUSTRIAL CORPORATION

3931 S Dixie Avenue, Dayton, OH 45439
Tel: (513) 298-5251
Telex: 383082

Chairman: Leo W Ladehoff (and Chief Executive Officer)
President: Raymond J Birkholz (and Chief Operating Officer)
Senior Executive Officers: T G Amato (VP Finance, Secretary), W J Durbin (VP Human Resources), Y P Telang (VP Technology), W R Hennig (Controller), M R Higgins (Treasurer)

PRINCIPAL ACTIVITIES: Manufacture of metal products; pipe fittings and hardware for utilities

Principal Subsidiaries: Stanley G Flagg & Co Inc; Amcast of Canada Ltd; Elkhart Products Corporation; Wheeltek Inc; Helmet Steel Casting Corp

Principal Bank: Bank One, NA, Dayton

Financial Information:

	Aug 30 1986	Aug 30 1987
	$'000	$'000
Sales revenues	229,728	264,310
Income (loss) before taxes	(15,183)	3,563
Net income (loss)	(7,927)	1,815
Dividends	2,920	3,110
Dividends per share	$0.44	$0.44
Earnings (loss) per share	($1.20)	$0.26
Common stock	6,995	7,442
Retained income	40,805	39,512
Shareholders equity	78,965	82,957

Principal Shareholders: FMR Corp; The Jeffrey Company; Alex Brown Investment Management; Batterymarch Financial Management Corp; Entregrowth International Limited

No of Employees: 3,300

AMCHEM PRODUCTS INC

Brookside Avenue, Ambler, PA 19002
Tel: (215) 628-1000
Telex: WUI 6851092 amchem ambler

Chairman: D Ambros
President: F M Procopio
Senior Executive Officers: G L Gibson (Senior VP), C J Roberts (VP Finance), J W Harrison (VP International), N E McDonald (VP Manufacturing)

PRINCIPAL ACTIVITIES: Manufacture of a wide range of specialty chemicals

Parent Company: Henkel KGaA, Germany

Financial Information:

	$'000
Sales revenues	60,000

No of Employees: 450

AMDAHL CORPORATION

1250 E Arques Avenue, PO Box 3470, Sunnyvale, CA 94088-3470
Tel: (408) 746-6000

Chairman: John C Lewis (and Chief Executive Officer)
President: E Joseph Zemke (and Chief Operating Officer)
Senior Executive Officers: E Joseph Zemke (Chief Operating Officer), Bruce O Beebe (Senior VP Product Operations), Joseph J Francesconi (Senior VP Marketing, Services and Communications Systems), William F O'Connell Jr (Senior VP Corporate Strategy), Anthony M Pozos (Senior VP Industrial Relations and Corporate Services), Edward F Thompson (VP, Chief Financial Officer and Secretary), David L Beamer (VP US Sales Operations), David M Brewer (VP Processor Products), Michael R Clements (VP, Advanced Development Chief Technical Officer), William Flanagan (VP Manufacturing), Paul M Hachigian (VP Communications), David J Horton (VP and General Manager Communications Systems Division), O J Nutt (VP Corporate Marketing), Thomas F O'Rourke (VP and General Manager Peripheral Products Division), Ernest B Thompson (VP and Controller), Daniel W Tierney (VP Corporate Operations and Administration Systems), Frederick M Trapnell Jr (VP Systems Products), Dean Witter III (VP and Treasurer)

PRINCIPAL ACTIVITIES: Amdahl Corporation, based in Sunnyvale, California, develops, manufactures, markets and supports large-scale computer systems, storage products, communications systems, software programs and educational services
Principal Bank: Bank of America
Financial Information:

	Dec 27 1985 $'000	Dec 27 1986 $'000
Sales revenues	862,032	966,349
Income before taxes	35,806	68,829
Net income	28,706	41,829
Dividends per share	$0.20	$0.20
Earnings per share net	$0.60	$0.86
Common stock*	277,032	287,721
Retained income	180,728	212,983
Shareholders equity	457,760	500,704

*and paid-in capital

No of Employees: 7,500

AMECOM

5115 Calvert Road, College Park, MD 20740
Tel: (301) 864-5600
Telex: TWX 710 8260457 liton purcork

President: Charles B Hofmann
Senior Executive Officers: Michael R Brown (VP), Irwin Nepo (VP), R E Hess (VP), J O Harmon (VP), J W Beakes (VP), John A Becka (VP Finance), Anthony M Corrado (VP Operations), J L Walker (VP EA-6B Program)

PRINCIPAL ACTIVITIES: Manufacture of electronic communications and navigation equipment for the defense industry
Parent Company: Litton Industries Inc, Beverly Hills, CA
Principal Bank: Maryland National Bank
Financial Information:

	$'000
Sales revenues	85,000

No of Employees: 1,600

AMEDCO INC

143235 South Outer Forty Drive, Chesterfield, MO 63017
Tel: (314) 576 7404

Chairman: B D Hunter (and President)
Senior Executive Officers: C E Luedde (Executive VP), Robert J Marischen (Executive VP Finance and Treasurer), James F Moore (Executive VP), Wayne A Scheer (Executive VP), David F Beck (VP and Controller), William J Kortz (VP Insurance)

PRINCIPAL ACTIVITIES: Manufacture of goods for health care and funeral services
Parent Company: Service Corporation International
Principal Subsidiaries: Abco Wire and Metal Products Inc; Amedco Casket Stamping Co; Amedco Contract Inc; Amedco Controls Inc; Amedco Healthcare Inc; Amedco Steel Inc; American Funeral Computer Inc; Amjet Inc; Belmont Casket Co; Brenner Casket Co; Control Chemical Corp; Edwards Equipment Co Inc; Halmark Casket Co; Imperial Casket; L H Kellogg Chemical Co; Kelco Supply Co; Lewis Industries; Lockwoven Co; Jaeger Funeral Supplies; Marshfield Casket Co; Mastercraft Casket; Merit Co; Midwest Products Inc; Olsen & Co; Oxycon Inc; Practical Burial Footwear; Professional Securities Corp; Royal Bond Inc; Naturo Manufacturing Corp; S & D Medical Products; Sessions Co; Smith & Davis Manufacturing Co; Spartan Casket Shell Inc; Spartan East; Stainless Medical Products; Universal Flowers Inc; York Casket Co
Principal Bank: Mercantile Trust Company
Financial Information:

	$'000
Sales revenues	240,000

No of Employees: 2,430

AMELCO CORPORATION

19208 S Vermont Ave, Gardena, CA 90248
Tel: (213) 327-3070

Chairman: George Murphy (and President)
Senior Executive Officers: H E Steinseifer (VP), S M Angelich (VP), V O Bortz (Secretary)

PRINCIPAL ACTIVITIES: Construction industry; electrical and mechanical engineering; manufacture of prefabricated concrete products
Principal Bank: Bank of Hawaii
Financial Information:

	$'000
Sales revenues	74,000

No of Employees: 700

AMERACE CORPORATION

Newburgh Road, Hackettstown, NJ 07840
Tel: (201) 852 1122
Telex: 6853377

President: Shirley D Brinsfield (and Chief Executive Officer)
Senior Executive Officers: William H Ward (Executive Vice President and Chief Operating Officer), Matthew M Craig (Senior VP and Chief Financial Officer)

PRINCIPAL ACTIVITIES: Manufacture of electrical equipment; safety products
Principal Subsidiaries: Amerace Export Corp
Financial Information:

	$'000
Sales revenues	270,000

No of Employees: 4,100

AMERADA HESS CORPORATION

1185 Avenue of the Americas, New York, NY 10036
Tel: (212) 997-8500

Chairman: Leon Hess (and Chief Executive Officer)
President: Robert F Wright (and Chief Operating Officer)

Senior Executive Officers: A T Jacobson (Group VP), Bernard T Deverin (Senior VP), R K Stafford (Senior VP Finance), John B Hess (Senior Executive VP), Norman Goldberg (Executive VP), J Barclay Collins II (Senior VP and General Counsel)

PRINCIPAL ACTIVITIES: Exploration for and production of oil and natural gas; distribution of oil and gas
Principal Subsidiaries: Amerada Petrocorp of UK Ltd; Atlantis Agency Corp; Ira S Bushey & Sons Inc; College Point Dry Dock Supply Co; Diesel Vessel Operators Inc; Red Star Marine Service Inc; Red Star Towing & Transport Co; Hess Oil Virgin Islands Corp; Hess Pipeline Co; New Jersey Barging Corp; Spentonbush Transport Services
Principal Bank: Chase Manhattan Bank
Financial Information:

	Dec 31 1985	Dec 31 1986
	$'000	$'000
Sales revenues	7,653,440	4,014,671
Net (loss)	(260,409)	(219,443)
(Loss) per share	-	($2.60)
Shareholders equity	2,260,590	2,050,482

No of Employees: 8,900

AMERFORD INTERNATIONAL CORPORATION
218-01 Merrick Boulevard, Jamaica, NY 11413
Tel: (718) 528-0800

Chairman: Hector Garcia (and Chief Executive Officer); Vice Chairman: Milton Gratt (and Secretary)
President: Walter Marx (and Chief Operating Officer)
Senior Executive Officers: Jacob Avnir (VP Division), Richard Garcia (VP), Gordon Keats (VP), Albert J Murphy (VP), Don Smith (VP), Richard Chassman (VP Finance, Treasurer and Chief Financial Officer), Harold Belser (VP Sales), David Marx (VP Sales), John Kearns (VP), Roy W Hecterman (VP Group Relations)

PRINCIPAL ACTIVITIES: Freight forwarding services; air cargo and shipping
Principal Subsidiaries: Amerford Airways Inc
Principal Bank: Chase Manhattan Bank
Financial Information:

	$'000
Sales revenues	81,800

No of Employees: 550

AMERIBANC INC
5th and Francis Streets, St Joseph, MO 64502
Tel: (816) 233-2000

Chairman: William F Enright Jr; Vice Chairman: Darwin H Deaver (and Chairman of Executive Committee)
President: Clark G McCorkle (and Chief Executive Officer)
Senior Executive Officers: Glenn Bellamy (Senior VP), James R Bocell (Executive VP), Milton Tootle Jr (VP, Secretary and Legal Counsel), Urban G Wise (Executive VP), Sue A Gallatin (Treasurer), Harry J Johnson (Controller)

PRINCIPAL ACTIVITIES: Banking
Principal Subsidiaries: Ameribank Data Service Corp; Ameribank Life Assurance Co; American Bancorp Inc; American Bank & Trust Co; Price Bank Building Corp; American Bank; Manufacturers Redevelopment Corp; American Leasing of St Joseph; Belt American Bank; Laurel American Bank
Financial Information:

	Dec 31 1985
	$'000
Revenues	126,930

No of Employees: 800

AMERICA WEST AIRLINES INC
222 South Mill Avenue, Tempe, AZ 85281
Tel: (602) 894-0800

Chairman: Edward R Beauvais (and Chief Executive Officer)
President: Michael J Conway (and Chief Operating Officer)
Senior Executive Officers: Don Montieth (Senior VP Operations), T Raymond Nakano (VP and Controller), E Patrick Thurston (VP Operations), Patricia A Burr (Treasurer), Alphonse E Frei (Senior VP Finance and Chief Financial Officer), Richard Delafield (VP and Legal), Michael W Margrave (Secretary), Thomas P Burns (VP Marketing), Russell A Bleil (VP Purchasing), Leroy A Paulson (VP Technical Services), Trevor Van Horn (VP), Mark J Coleman (Senior VP Planning and Advertising), Donald R Neilson (Senior VP Planning)

PRINCIPAL ACTIVITIES: Operation of airline services
Principal Bank: First Interstate Bank of Arizona
Financial Information:

	Dec 31 1986
	$'000
Sales revenues	328,926
Net income	3,027
Earnings per share	$0.11
Shareholders equity	57,933

No of Employees: 3,978

AMERICAL CORPORATION
PO Box 1419, Henderson, NC 27536
Tel: (919) 492-2166

Chairman: Robert J Froeber; Vice Chairman: Manuel J Oliveira
President: Robert L Hubbard
Senior Executive Officers: Glen E Wilcox (VP Sales), Felix C McDaniel (VP and Treasurer)

PRINCIPAL ACTIVITIES: Manufacture of hosiery
Principal Bank: Wachovia Bank
Financial Information:

	$'000
Sales revenues	65,000

No of Employees: 2,000

AMERICAN & EFIRD MILLS, INC
PO Box 507, Mount Holly, NC 28120
Tel: (704) 827-4311
Telex: WUI 6843014 amerfird mthy

Chairman: Alan J Dickson; Vice Chairman: J F Love Jr
President: John W Copeland
Senior Executive Officers: W H Moore (Senior VP Finance), James A Scott (Senior VP), Joe E Dawn (Senior VP)

PRINCIPAL ACTIVITIES: Manufacture of cotton and synthetic threads and yarns
Parent Company: Ruddick Corporation, Charlotte, NC
Principal Bank: North Carolina National Bank
Financial Information:

	$'000
Sales revenues	100,000

No of Employees: 2,000

AMERICAN ADVENTURE INC
12910 Kingsgate Way NE, Kirkland, WA 98083
Tel: (206) 821-7766

Chairman: Jerald C Hall (and Chief Executive Officer)
President: John M Nye
Senior Executive Officers: M P Dyer (VP, Legal Counsel and Secretary), Kent W Mordy (Executive VP, Chief Financial Officer and Treasurer), Richard O Nichols (VP Sales), Joseph McAree (Director Accounting), Gary Whitney (Director Management Information Services), John C Martin (Director Public Affairs), David M Hall (Director Budget and Planning), Meredith Doran (Director Recreation)

PRINCIPAL ACTIVITIES: Trailer parks and camp sites
Principal Bank: Seattle First National Bank

Financial Information:

	$'000
Sales revenues	59,000

No of Employees: 800

AMERICAN AGGREGATES CORPORATION

300 Garst Avenue, Greenville, OH 45331

Tel: (513) 548-2111

Chairman: Walter I Thieme

President: William E Hole

Senior Executive Officers: John W Spidel (VP Advertising), Dudley D Steinhilber (VP), Robert L Schooley (Treasurer), David T Feltman (Secretary), William D Brewster (VP Operations)

PRINCIPAL ACTIVITIES: Quarrying and processing aggregates, sand and gravel

Principal Subsidiaries: American Materials Corp; Brown-Huffstetter Materials Co; Grant Contracting Co; Permacrete Products Corp

Principal Bank: Greenville National Bank

Financial Information:

	$'000
Sales revenues	78,000

No of Employees: 760

AMERICAN AGRONOMICS CORPORATION

4600 W Cypress Street, Tampa, FL 33607

Tel: (813) 872-9909

Telex: TWX 810-876-9142 amer agron tpa

President: Michael Brenner (and Chief Executive Officer and Corporate Counsel)

Senior Executive Officers: Cecil Miles (Controller and Chief Financial Officer)

PRINCIPAL ACTIVITIES: Citrus fruit growers; manufacturers of citrus products

Principal Subsidiaries: American Orange Corp; California Fresh-Pak Inc; Florida Fresh-Pak; Juice Tree Inc; Myakka Processors Inc; National Papaya Corp; Syndyne Corp; Carroll Oil Co; Star Timber Products Co

Principal Bank: Chase Manhattan Bank NA

Financial Information:

	$'000
Sales revenues	88,000

No of Employees: 400

AMERICAN BAKERIES COMPANY

633 Third Avenue, New York, NY 10017

Tel: (212) 687-7225

Chairman: E G Bewkes Jr (and President and Chief Executive Officer)

Senior Executive Officers: Castle N Day (Executive VP), Joseph V McGinley (Executive VP), William K Hood (Senior VP), Phillip S Lyddon (Senior VP), Richard L Metrick (Senior VP, Treasurer and Chief Financial Officer), Charles A Sullivan (Senior VP), Don K Vance (Senior VP)

PRINCIPAL ACTIVITIES: Manufacture of bakery products, sauces, relishes and pickles

Principal Subsidiaries: Camp Coast to Coast Inc; Cotton Bros Inc; Bakery Equipment Services Inc; Cotton Brothers Baking Co Inc; Cottons Hosum Bakery New Orleans; Hearts Farms Inc

Principal Bank: Manufacturers Hanover Trust Co

Financial Information:

	Dec 31 1985
	$'000
Sales revenues	461,568
Net income	7,600
Earnings per share	$2.56
Shareholders equity	62,074

No of Employees: 7,600

AMERICAN BANK NOTE CO

70 Broad Street, New York, NY 10004

Tel: (212) 425-5100

Telex: ITT 421795 inbnkno

Chairman: Edward H Weitzen (and Chief Executive Officer)

President: Salvatore F D'Amato

Senior Executive Officers: Edwin J Deadrick (Executive VP), Annabelle W Model (Senior VP), L O McGehee (Senior VP), Richard C Sennett (Senior VP), Robert F Ivey (VP and Secretary)

PRINCIPAL ACTIVITIES: Security printing; checks, stamps and banknotes

Parent Company: International Banknote Company, New York, NY

Financial Information:

	$'000
Sales revenues	165,000

No of Employees: 3,100

AMERICAN BANK STATIONERY CO

Executive Plaza III, Hunt Valley, MD 21031

Tel: (301) 667-6700

Telex: WUT 87854 abs coye

Chairman: William A Marquard; Vice Chairman: Keith D Brunnel

President: William B Boyd (and Chief Operating Officer)

Senior Executive Officers: Alan C Root (Senior VP), Hugh Ronalds (VP Finance), Richard H Francis (VP and Chief Financial Officer)

PRINCIPAL ACTIVITIES: Printing of checks for banking

Parent Company: American Standard Inc

Principal Bank: Union Trust of Maryland

Financial Information:

	$'000
Sales revenues	115,000

No of Employees: 2,200

AMERICAN BANKERS INSURANCE GROUP INC

11222 Quail Roost Drive, Miami, FL 33157

Tel: (305) 253-2244

Chairman: R Kirk Landon (and Chief Executive Officer)

President: Gerald N Gaston (and Vice Chairman and Chief Operating Officer)

Senior Executive Officers: Arthur W Heggen (VP and Treasurer), J B Shumate (Executive VP and Treasurer), Faye S Albert (Senior VP Finance), Eugene E Becker (Executive VP Finance), George R Van Wyck (Secretary), Frank C Baiamonte (Executive VP Marketing and Subsidiary Officer)

PRINCIPAL ACTIVITIES: Insurance holding company; subsidiaries are engaged in all classes of insurance

Principal Subsidiaries: American Bankers Insurance Co of Florida; American Bankers Life Assurance Co of Florida

Principal Bank: Continental Illinois National Bank & Trust Co

Financial Information:

	$'000
Revenues	382,200

No of Employees: 900

AMERICAN BILTRITE INC

57 River Street, Wellesley Hils, MA 02181

Tel: (617) 237-6655

Telex: WUT 951311 ambilt well

Chairman: Robert G Marcus; Vice Chairman: Roger S Marcus (and Chief Executive Officer)

President: Richard G Marcus

Senior Executive Officers: William M Marcus (Executive VP and Treasurer)

PRINCIPAL ACTIVITIES: Manufacture of rubber and plastic products for the footwear industry and flooring

Trade Names: Armtico, Bulldog, TransferRite, ProtecRite

Principal Subsidiaries: American Biltrite (Canada) Ltd

Principal Bank: Bank of Boston

Financial Information:

	Dec 31 1985	Dec 31 1986
	$'000	$'000
Sales revenues	99,269	110,081
Income before taxes	4,769	6,046
Net income	4,024	5,017
Dividends	358	327
Dividends per share	$0.15	$0.15
Earnings per share	$1.68	$2.28
Common stock*	2,392	2,134
Retained income	12,335	17,025
Shareholders equity	55,687	69,675

*Shares outstanding

No of Employees: 850

AMERICAN BRANDS, INC

1700E Putnam Avenue, PO Box 811, Old Greenwich, CT 06870-0811

Tel: (203) 698-5000

Chairman: Edward W Whittemore (and Chief Executive Officer)

President: Virginius B Lougee III (and Chief Operating Officer)

Senior Executive Officers: William J Alley (Vice Chairman), Robert L Plancher (Senior VP and Chief Accounting Officer), Paul A Randour (Senior VP and General Counsel), Robert L Austin (Senior VP and Chief Administrative Officer), Thomas C Hays (VP-Tobacco), John T Ludes (VP-Operations), Robert J Rukeyser (VP-Office Products), Russell P Truitt (VP-Operations), Peter Reed Jr (VP and Treasurer), Louis F Fernous Jr (Secretary), Theresa B Fealey (Assistant Secretary), Dudley L Bauerlein Jr (Assistant Treasurer), Everett W Partin Jr (Assistant Treasurer), Sebastian M Cicitta (Assistant Controller)

PRINCIPAL ACTIVITIES: American Brands core businesses are consumer packaged goods and financial services

Trade Names: Jim Beam Bourbon, Master Locks, Sunshine crackers and cookies, Titleist, Pinnacle and Foot-Joy golf products, Jergens Aloe & Lanolin Skin Conditioning Lotion, Jergens Lotion, Case cutlery, Pall Mall Cigarettes, Carlton Cigarettes, Lucky Strike Cigarettes, Tareyton Cigarettes, Antonio y Cleopatra Cigars, Swingline Staplers, Prestige Housewares, Pinkerton, Franklin Life, Southland Life

Principal Subsidiaries and Divisions: Acushnet Company; The American Tobacco Company; James B Beam Distilling Co; The Franklin Life Insurance Company; Gallaher Ltd (UK); Golden Belt Manufacturing Company; The Andrew Jergens Company; Master Lock Company; MCM Products Inc; Pinkerton's Inc; Southland Life Insurance Company; Sunshine Biscuits Inc; Swingline Inc; Wilson Jones Company

Financial Information:

	Dec 31 1985	Dec 31 1986
	$'000	$'000
Sales revenues net	7,308,311	8,469,641
Income before taxes	750,733	670,368
Net income	420,870	365,304
Dividends-common stock	214,920	224,054
Dividends per common share	$1.95	$2.03875
Earnings per common share*	$3.59	$3.12
Common stock	179,352	358,703
Retained income	2,509,537	2,455,314
Common shareholders equity	2,378,063	2,540,879

*fully diluted

No of Employees: 74,800

AMERICAN BROADCASTING COMPANIES, INC

1330 Avenue of the Americas, New York, NY 10019

Tel: (212) 887-7777

President: John B Sias (and Chief Operating Officer)

Senior Executive Officers: Michael P Mallardi (Executive VP and Chief Financial Officer), Mark H Cohen (Senior VP), Ronald J Doerfler (VP), Robert T Goldman (VP Administration and Real Estate), John E Frisoli (VP Human Resources), Alfred R Schneider (VP Policy and Standards), Richard L Freund (VP Labor Relations), Warren D Schaub (VP Finance), Arnold H Agree (VP Taxes), Ann M Gray (VP Corporate Planning), Edward D Williams (VP Management Information Systems), Patricia J Matson (VP Corporate Communications), Stephen J Soloman (VP), David J Vondrak (VP and Treasurer), William E Pierson (VP and Comptroller)

PRINCIPAL ACTIVITIES: Television and radio broadcasting; leisure services

Parent Company: Capital Cities Communications

Principal Subsidiaries: ABC Leisure Magazine Inc; ABC News Inc; ABC Sports Inc; ABC Schwann Publications Inc; ABC Wide World of Learning Inc; Ambroad Inc; Hitchcock Publishing Co; Kaum Inc; Los Angeles Magazine Inc; Miller Publishing Co; National Price Service Co; Nils Codes and Regulations Inc; Park City Communications; Prairie Farmer Publishing Co; Wisconsin Farmers Co Inc; Silver Springs Inc; WLS Inc; R L White Co Inc; WMAL Inc; WXYZ Inc

Principal Bank: Chase Manhattan Bank

Financial Information:

	$'000
Sales revenues	3,710,000

No of Employees: 13,000

AMERICAN BUILDING MAINTENANCE INDUSTRIES INC

333 Fell Street, San Francisco, CA 94102

Tel: (415) 864-5150

Chairman: Sydney J Rosenberg

President: R David Anacker (and Chief Executive Officer)

Senior Executive Officers: William C Banner (VP), J E Benton III (VP), John F Egan (VP), Eleanor A Elrod (VP, General Counsel and Secretary), David H Hebble (VP and Chief Financial Officer), Harry H Kahn (VP and Legal Counsel), William W Steel (VP), Tony Vernava (VP)

PRINCIPAL ACTIVITIES: Provision of security and general maintenance services for business and industrial premises

Principal Subsidiaries: American Building Maintenance Company; American Security & Investigative Services Inc; Ampco Auto Parks Inc; Amtech Lighting Services Co; Amtech Mechanical Services Co; Amtech Reliable Elevator Co; Easterday Supply Co of California; Rose Exterminator Co

Principal Bank: Security Pacific National Bank

Financial Information:

	$'000
Sales revenues	424,000

No of Employees: 26,000

AMERICAN BUILDINGS CO

State Docks Road, Eufaula, AL 36026
Tel: (205) 687-2032

President: James D Murphy Jr
Senior Executive Officers: Alvan E Richey Jr (VP), Richard W Mullin (VP), Lyle L Wilson (VP), Christian W Page (VP), Roger L Pritts (VP), William P Cole (Treasurer)

PRINCIPAL ACTIVITIES: Manufacture of sectional buildings
Parent Company: Cronus Industries Inc, Dallas, TX
Principal Bank: Eufaula Bank & Trust Co
Financial Information:

	$'000
Sales revenues	180,000

No of Employees: 900

AMERICAN BUSINESS PRODUCTS, INC

100 Riveredge Pkwy, Atlanta, GA 30328
Tel: (404) 953-8300

Chairman: W J Biggers (and Chief Executive Officer)
President: Thomas R Carmody
Senior Executive Officers: Richard A LeFeber (VP and Secretary), W C Downer (VP Finance and Chief Financial Officer)

PRINCIPAL ACTIVITIES: Printing of business forms, books and office stationery
Financial Information:

	$'000
Sales revenues	300,000

No of Employees: 3,800

AMERICAN CAN COMPANY

American Lane, Greenwich, CT 06836
Tel: (203) 552-2000

Chairman: Gerald Tsai Jr (and Chief Executive Officer)
President: Frank J Connor
Senior Executive Officers: Kenneth A Yarnell Jr (Senior Executive VP and Chief Financial Officer), Alfred G Goldstein (Executive VP), John G Polk (Executive VP), Robert Abramson (Senior VP), James A Long (Senior VP), Michael I Roth (Senior VP), C Richard Pedersen (Senior VP, General Counsel and Secretary), David A Frank (VP and Treasurer), David I Chemerow (VP and Corporate Controller)

PRINCIPAL ACTIVITIES: Manufacture of containers and packaging; insurance and financial services; specialty retailing
Principal Subsidiaries: American Capital Corp; Associated Madison Companies; Fingerhut Companies Inc; Goody Sam Inc; Michigan Bulb Co; Penncorp Financial Inc; Pickwick International Inc; Sumter & Choctaw Railway Co
Principal Bank: Bankers Trust Company
Financial Information:

	Dec 31 1985	Dec 31 1986
	$'000	$'000
Sales revenues	2,854,800	4,292,800
Net income	149,100	196,300
Earnings per share	$2.53	$3.21
Shareholders equity	1,266,600	1,354,100

No of Employees: 24,300

AMERICAN CAPITAL CORPORATION

5555 Biscayne Blvd, Miami, FL 33137
Tel: (305) 754-5555

Chairman: Robert M Marlin
President: Jack D Burstein (and Chief Executive Officer)
Senior Executive Officers: Steven R Cook (Executive VP Finance), Samuel I Adler (Secretary and Treasurer), Anthony Triola (Executive VP Real Estate)

PRINCIPAL ACTIVITIES: Financial services, savings; interests in real estate development
Principal Subsidiaries: AAC Development Corp; First Global Investors Inc; TransOhio Financial Corp; TransOhio Savings Bank
Principal Bank: Sun Bank of Miami
Financial Information:

	Dec 31 1986
	$'000
Net income	8,683
Earnings per share	$0.55
Shareholders equity	103,623
Deposits	3,390,684
Total assets	5,099,789

No of Employees: 2,200

AMERICAN CARRIERS, INC

9393 W 110th Street, Overland Park, KS 66210
Tel: (913) 451-2811

Chairman: L H Robertson (and President and Chief Executive Officer)
Senior Executive Officers: B G Cott (Senior VP Finance), J P Bigger (Senior VP), D R Glancy (VP and Treasurer)

PRINCIPAL ACTIVITIES: Trucking services
Principal Subsidiaries: American Freight System, Inc; Midwest Coast Transport, Inc; USA Eastern, Inc; USA Western, Inc; Sioux Falls Service Center, Inc
Principal Banks: Irving Trust Company; Norwest National Bank
Financial Information:

	Dec 31 1985	Dec 31 1986
	$'000	$'000
Sales revenues	380,808	401,917
Income before taxes	2,401	8,753
Net income	2,231	5,553
Earnings per share	$0.53	$1.04
Common stock	6,559	30,536*
Retained income	34,659	40,212
Shareholders equity	54,028	83,558

*number of shares outstanding = 6,068,078

No of Employees: 5,000

AMERICAN CAST IRON PIPE CO

Box 2727, Birmingham, AL 35202
Tel: (205) 325-7701
Telex: WUT 59736 acipco bhm

President: P W Green
Senior Executive Officers: E E Langner (VP Works), V L Richey (VP Sales and Secretary), R M Bragdon (VP Engineering)

PRINCIPAL ACTIVITIES: Manufacture of iron and steel pipes, tubes and castings
Principal Subsidiaries: American Valve & Hydrant Manufacturing Co; Kristin Shipping Co; Specification Rubber Products
Principal Bank: First National Bank of Birmingham
Financial Information:

	$'000
Sales revenues	250,000

No of Employees: 2,500

AMERICAN CENTURY CORPORATION

1300 Commerce Plaza, 111 Soledad, San Antonio, TX 78205
Tel: (512) 226-2222

Chairman: John C Kerr (and Chief Executive Officer)
President: Roger D Harrison (and Chief Operating Oficer)

Senior Executive Officers: Gerald H Stool (Executive Officer), John H Bethel (Executive VP), Steven L Prichard (Executive VP)

PRINCIPAL ACTIVITIES: Financial services including savings and loans and real estate investment
Principal Subsidiaries: Commerce Savings Association; Commerce Service Corp
Principal Bank: Barnett Bank of Jacksonville
Financial Information:

	$'000
Revenues	101,700

No of Employees: 130

AMERICAN CITY BUSINESS JOURNALS INC

3535 Broadway, Kansas City, MO 64111
Tel: (816) 753-4300

Chairman: Michael K Russell; Vice Chairman: William H Worley
President: William H Worley
Senior Executive Officers: Carolyn Ashford (Executive VP and Chief Operating Officer), James R Bergfalk (VP), Clifford W Donnelly (VP and Treasurer), Glenn A Etherington (VP and Controller), Richard J Koch (VP, Secretary and Legal Counsel)

PRINCIPAL ACTIVITIES: Publication of business newspapers
Financial Information:

	Dec 31 1985	Dec 31 1986
	$'000	$'000
Sales revenues	18,564	27,481
(Loss) before taxes	(3,653)	(7,166)
Net (loss)	(4,366)	(7,389)
(Loss) per share	($1.70)	($2.36)
Common stock*	2,564	3,132
Retained (deficit)	(6,270)	(8,540)
Shareholders equity (deficit)	(1,010)	9,883

*weighted average shares outstanding in thousands

No of Employees: 1,660

AMERICAN COMMERCIAL LINES, INC

1701 E Market Street, Jeffersonville, IN 47130
Tel: (812) 288-0100

Chairman: H T Watkins
President: H J Bobzien Jr (and Chief Executive Officer)
Senior Executive Officers: Robert W Greene (Executive VP and President Jeffboat Inc), Kenneth W Peters (Senior VP and President Watercom), Frank J Haendiges (VP and Treasurer), Michael L Harris (Vice President and Secretary), Thomas Frazier III (Senior VP American Commercial Barge Line Company), W Norb Whitlock (Senior VP American Commercial Barge Line Company), Kent E Hoffmeister (Executive VP Jeffboat Inc), D Ray Miller (President American Commercial Terminals Inc), Richard A Baker (Executive VP Watercom), Michael C Hagan (VP-Sales American Commercial Barge Line Company), Charles F Lehman (VP-Public Affairs)

PRINCIPAL ACTIVITIES: Barge transportation
Parent Company: CSX Corporation, Richmond, VA
Principal Bank: Chase Manhattan Bank
Financial Information: American Commercial Lines and subsidiaries

	$'000
Revenue	270,000

No of Employees: 2,520

AMERICAN CONTINENTAL CORPORATION

2735 East Camelback Road, Phoenix, AZ 85016
Tel: (602) 957-7170

Chairman: Charles H Keating Jr (and Chief Executive Officer)
President: Judy J Wischer
Senior Executive Officers: Robert J Kielty (Senior VP, Secretary and General Counsel), Andrew F Ligget (VP and Chief Financial Officer), Charles H Keating III (Executive VP), Andre A Niebling (Senior VP and Treasurer), Robert M Wurzelbacher Jr (Senior VP)

PRINCIPAL ACTIVITIES: Financial services including mortgage broking, savings and loans
Principal Subsidiaries: First Lincoln Corp; American Continental Mortgage Co
Principal Bank: United Bank of Arizona
Financial Information:

	Dec 31 1985	Dec 31 1986
	$'000	$'000
Net income	42,540	24,330
Earnings per share	$2.71	$1.51
Shareholders equity	121,920	128,591
Deposits	-	2,821,375
Total assets	4,114,907	4,575,171

No of Employees: 1,355

AMERICAN CRYSTAL SUGAR CO

101 N Third Street, Moorhead, MN 56560
Tel: (218) 236-4400
Telex: WUT 292230 sugarbeet moor

Chairman: Clark Ewen; Vice Chairman: Rodney Webster
President: Ronald G Hayes
Senior Executive Officers: A C Bloomquist (VP Public Affairs), J G Lackman (VP), S E Bichsel, E H Christensen (VP), J J Horvath (VP), R W Levos (VP), M F Richardson (VP) (VP), R J Pearson (VP)

PRINCIPAL ACTIVITIES: Manufacture of beet sugar, pulp, molasses and dietary fiber
Trade Names: Crystal Sugar, DuoFiber
Principal Bank: St Paul Bank for Cooperatives
Financial Information:

	1986
	$'000
Sales revenues	354,000
Income before taxes	169,346
Net income	174,368
Common stock	18
Retained income	18,835
Shareholders equity	115,203

No of Employees: 1,200

AMERICAN CYANAMID CO

One Cyanamid Plaza, Wayne, NJ 07470
Tel: (201) 831-2000
Telex: 130400

Chairman: George J Sella Jr (and President and Chief Executive Officer); Vice Chairman: William A Liffers
Senior Executive Officers: Frank V Attlee (Executive VP), Jack L Bowman (Executive VP), Albert J Costello (Executive VP)

PRINCIPAL ACTIVITIES: Cyanamid is a research-based biotechnology and chemical company which develops medical, agricultural, chemical and consumer products and manufactures and markets them throughout the world
Financial Information:

	Dec 31 1985	Dec 31 1986
	$'000	$'000
Sales revenues	3,536,100	3,815,900
Income before taxes	134,000	275,300
Net income	129,100	202,500
Dividends	91,400	88,200
Dividends per share	$1.90	$1.90
Earnings per share	$2.68	$4.36
Common stock	245,500	245,500
Retained income	1,588,900	1,703,200
Shareholders equity	1,644,300	1,720,600

No of Employees: 36,462

AMERICAN DISTRICT TELEGRAPH CO INC

One World Trade Center, New York, NY 10048
Tel: (212) 558-1100
Telex: WUT 125056 adt nyk

Chairman: Raymond B Carey Jr (and President)
Senior Executive Officers: James A Synk (Senior VP), U J Brualdi (Senior VP), Dennis P Flynn (VP Finance)

PRINCIPAL ACTIVITIES: Manufacture of security systems
Principal Bank: Chemical Bank
Financial Information:

	$'000
Sales revenues	500,000

No of Employees: 9,600

AMERICAN ECOLOGY CORPORATION

30423 Canwood Street, Suite 201, Agoura Hills, CA 91301
Tel: (818) 9917361

Chairman: W E Prachar (and President)
Senior Executive Officers: R Lee Armbruster (VP and General Counsel), J J Scovill (Group VP), Charles A Simms (VP Finance and Administration), Karl J Eimer (Treasurer and Secretary)

PRINCIPAL ACTIVITIES: Disposal of radioactive waste
Principal Subsidiaries: National Ecology Inc
Principal Bank: First Interstate Bank of California
Financial Information:

	$'000
Sales revenues	57,840

No of Employees: 350

AMERICAN ELECTRIC POWER CO INC

One Riverside Plaza, Columbus, OH 43215
Tel: (614) 223-1000

Chairman: W S White Jr (and Chief Executive Officer)
President: Richard E Disbrow
Senior Executive Officers: G P Maloney (VP Finance), Peter H DeMaria (Treasurer), A J Dowd (Secretary)

PRINCIPAL ACTIVITIES: Electricity supply
Principal Subsidiaries: Wheeling Electric Co; Michigan Power Co; Ohio Power Co; Kingsport Power Co; Kentucky Power Co; Indiana and Michigan Electric Co; Columbus and Southern Ohio Electric Co; Appalachian Power Co
Financial Information:

	Dec 31 1985	Dec 31 1986
	$'000	$'000
Sales revenues	4,847,980	4,842,801
Net income	418,650	507,171
Earnings per share	$2.19	$2.62
Shareholders equity	-	4,007,922

No of Employees: 23,315

AMERICAN ENKA CO

Enka, NC 28728
Tel: (704) 667-7110
Telex: WUT 577410 amerenka enka

President: Harold C Encloe
Senior Executive Officers: Sidney M Smith (Senior VP Marketing), James H Miller (VP Finance)

PRINCIPAL ACTIVITIES: Manufacture of synthetic fibers
Parent Company: Akzo NV, Arnhem, Netherlands
Principal Bank: Wachovia Bank and Trust Co
Financial Information:

	$'000
Sales revenues	500,000

No of Employees: 5,000

AMERICAN EXCELSIOR CO

850 Avenue H E, Arlington, TX 76011
Tel: (817) 640-1555

Chairman: W E Johnson (and President)
Senior Executive Officers: R L Gregerson (VP Sales), M S Heil (Treasurer)

PRINCIPAL ACTIVITIES: Manufacture of synethetic foam for a variety of applications including bedding and upholstered furniture, packaging and the building industry
Principal Bank: First National Bank
Financial Information:

	1986
	$'000
Sales revenues	56,000
Income before taxes	1,200
Net income	790

Principal Shareholders: Employee Stock Ownership Plan
No of Employees: 750

AMERICAN EXPRESS COMPANY

American Express Tower, World Financial Center, New York, NY 10285
Tel: (212) 640-2000

Chairman: James D Robinson III (and Chief Executive Officer)
President: Louis V Gerstner Jr (and Chairman American Express Travel Related Services Company Inc)
Senior Executive Officers: Peter A Cohen (Chairman and Chief Executive Officer, Shearson Lehman Brothers Inc), Harvey Golub (President and Chief Executive Officer, IDS Financial Services Inc), Robert F Smith (Chairman and Chief Executive Officer, American Express Bank Ltd), Gary A Beller (Executive VP and General Counsel, American Express Company), Howard L Clark Jr (Executive VP and Chief Financial Officer, American Express Company), Harry L Freeman (Executive VP, Corporate Affairs and Communications, American Express Company)

PRINCIPAL ACTIVITIES: Founded in 1850, American Express Company is a diversified financial and travel-related services company. It is a leader in the charge card, Travelers Cheque, travel, international banking, brokerage, investment banking, personal financial planning, life insurance and asset management industries
Trade Names: Trademarks and Service Marks: "AMERICAN EXPRESS", "AMERICAN EXPRESS Box Logo", "AMERICAN EXPRESS Box Logo and CARDS WELCOME"*, "AMERICAN EXPRESS Card Design"*, "AMERICAN EXPRESS WORLD SERVICE and Design", CAUSE RELATED MARKETING", "FOOD & WINE", "Gladiator Head", "GOLD CARD", "HEALTH CARECARD", "IDS", "MMP", "MONEY MARKET PREFERRED", "PLATINUM CARD", "PREMIER SERVICES", PRESTIGE PLUS", "TRAVEL & LEISURE", *Mark is also a copyrighted property of American Express
Financial Information:

	Dec 31 1986
	$'000
Revenues	14,652,000
Income before taxes	1,110,000
Net income	1,250,000
Dividends per common share	$1.38
Earnings per share net	$5.55
Shareholders equity	5,726,000
Total assets	99,476,000

No of Employees: 78,747

AMERICAN EXPRESS CREDIT CORPORATION

One Rodney Square, Wilmington, DE 19801
Tel: (302) 594-3350

Chairman: F G Fitzgerald
President: Vincent P Lasanke (and Chief Executive Officer)

Senior Executive Officers: Ronald J Yoo (Senior VP Finance)

PRINCIPAL ACTIVITIES: Financial services including short term business finance

Parent Company: American Express Co

Financial Information:

	$'000
Revenues	705,000

No of Employees: 30

AMERICAN EXPRESS TRAVEL RELATED SERVICES COMPANY, INC

723 W 7th St, Los Angeles, CA 90017

Tel: (213) 488-1301

Chairman: Louis V Gerstner Jr (and Chief Executive Officer); Vice Chairmen: James F Calvano, Jonathan S Linen, Aldo Papone

Senior Executive Officers: Raymond J Larkin (Executive VP, Operations, Credit and Quality Assurance), G Richard Thoman (Executive VP, Finance and Planning), Jerry C Welsh (Executive VP, Worldwide Marketing and Communications), Lawrence R Ricciardi (General Counsel), Peter Ellis (Senior VP, Human Resources)

PRINCIPAL ACTIVITIES: American Express Travel Related Services Company, Inc, provides an unmatched selection of payment, travel and communications products designed to meet the lifestyle and business needs of its clients, whether individuals or companies. It offers two of the world's best-known consumer financial products: The American Express Card and the American Express Travelers Cheque. More than 1,200 owned and representative travel offices make it one of the world's largest travel companies

Parent Company: American Express Company

Principal Subsidiaries: Divisions: US Payment Systems Division; International Division; US Travel Services; First Data Resources, Inc (American Express Travel Related Services Co Inc Owns approx 75% of the capital stock)

Financial Information:

	$'000
Revenues	3,600,000

AMERICAN FAMILY CORPORATION

1932 Wynnton Road, Columbus, GA 31906

Tel: (404) 323-3431

Chairman: John B Amos (and Chief Executive Officer); Vice Chairman: Paul S Amos

President: Salvador Diaz-Verson Jr

Senior Executive Officers: Daniel P Amos (Executive VP and Chief Financial Officer), Herbert A Bowick (Executive VP), George W Jeter (Executive VP), R Lee Anderson (VP Advertising and Stockholder Relations)

PRINCIPAL ACTIVITIES: Holding company with interests in insurance, advertising, television broadcasting, printing

Principal Subsidiaries: American Blackhawk Broadcast; American Blackhawk Food Services; Display Inc; KTIV-TV Inc; American Family Laws; American Family Life Assurance; American Family Laws Life Assurance Co; American Family Reinsurance Co; American Hirsch Broadcasting Co; American SAV Broadcasting Co; Hotel Columbus Inc; American Self Care Corp; American Valley Broadcasting Co Inc; Communicorp Inc; Health Cost Management Inc; Medical Cost Management Systems

Principal Bank: Trust Company of Columbus

Financial Information:

	$'000
Revenues	954,800

No of Employees: 2,400

AMERICAN FILTRONA CORPORATION

8401 Jefferson Davis Highway, PO Box 34668, Richmond, VA 23234

Tel: (804) 275-2631

Telex: RCA 279928 AM FLTRNA RH

Chairman of the Board: R H Bunzl

President: John L Morgan

Senior Executive Officers: John D Barlow Jr (VP-Finance), L C Drozeski Jr (VP-Plastic Products), Randall L Hagan (VP-Bonded Fiber Products), Ken L Sandy (VP-Air and Fluid Filter Products)

PRINCIPAL ACTIVITIES: American Filtrona Corporation sells bonded fiber, air and fluid filter and plastic products to a variety of industries. Bonded fiber products (consisting of cigarette and cigar filters, ink reservoirs and tips for writing instruments and other specialties such as filters, reservoirs and applicators) are developed and manufactured in Richmond, Virginia. Air and fluid filter products consisting of a broad line of industrial filters and filtration systems are developed and manufactured in Rochester, New York, Chicago, Illinois, Santa Fe Springs, California, Stanley, North Carolina and Killarney, Ireland. Plastics products consisting of sheets, profiles, tubes and printed flexible packaging materials are manufactured in Columbia, South Carolina, Des Plaines, Illinois, and Montreal, Quebec

Trade Names: FILTRONA, DURAYL, TECHNOLAB, TRANSWICK, UNIPHASE, TRANSORB, TRANSTIP, TRANSTUBE, DOLLINGER, STAYNEW, UAC, UNITED, TRI-PHASE, MAXI-FLO, (All Registered trademarks)

Principal Subsidiaries and Divisions: American Filtrona Company; Dollinger Corporation; Filpac, Inc; Porth Plastic Company; Southern Plastics Company; Technolab; United Air Cleaner Company; United Engine Life Company

Principal Bank: Sovran Bank

Financial Information:

	Dec 31 1985 $'000	Dec 31 1986 $'000
Sales	104,347	114,358
Income before taxes	11,450	11,709
Net income	6,275	6,434
Dividends	2,558	2,687
Dividends per share	$0.68*	$0.71
Earnings per share	$1.67*	$1.70
Common stock	1,804	3,679
Retained income	48,165	47,976
Shareholders equity	48,922	50,645

*Reflects 1986 two-for-one stock split

No of Employees: 1,075

AMERICAN FINANCIAL CORPORATION

One E 4th Street, Cincinnati, OH 45202

Tel: (513) 579-2121

Chairman: Carl H Lindner (and Chief Executive Officer)

President: Ronald E Walker (and Chief Operating Officer)

Senior Executive Officers: Robert D Lindner (Senior VP), James E Evans (VP and Secretary), Robert A Johnston (VP and Treasurer)

PRINCIPAL ACTIVITIES: Insurance and financial services

Principal Subsidiaries: American Financial Enterprises; American Money Management Corp; Great American Holding Corp; Great American Insurance Co; Agricultural Insurance Co; American Alliance Insurance Co; Dempsey & Siders Agency Inc; Great American Life Insurance Co; Great American Management Services; Great American Surplus Lines Insurance Co; KCC Holding Inc; Moore Group Inc; American Deposit Insurance Co; Southeastern Fidelity Insurance Co; Georgia American Insurance Co; Republic Indemnity Co; Stonewall Insurance Co; Atlanta Casualty Co; MR Agency of Georgia Inc; Boca Grande Club Inc; Dixie Auto Insurance Co; Dixie Insurance Co; Stonewall Underwriters; Transport

Insurance Co; Transport Underwriters Association; Transport Indemnity Co; United Liberty Life Insurance Co; Hunter Savings Association; American Home Development Corp; Hunter Financial Inc; Utotem Inc; Monterre Properties Inc
Principal Bank: Continental Illinois National Bank and Trust Co
Financial Information:

	Dec 31 1986
	$'000
Revenues	3,190,212
Net income	178,650
Shareholders equity	291,259
Total assets	7,325,962

No of Employees: 44,300

AMERICAN FIRST CORPORATION OKLAHOMA

American First Tower Suite 1340, Oklahoma City, OK 73102
Tel: (405) 270-5300

Chairman: J David Markley (and President and Chief Executive Officer)
Senior Executive Officers: Cecile Carter (VP and Controller), John W Cox (VP and Treasurer), Danny S Baze (Senior VP Insurance)

PRINCIPAL ACTIVITIES: Holding company with interests in insurance, real estate and securities broking
Principal Subsidiaries: American First Title and Trust Co; First Affiliated Securities; First In First Travel; Park Avenue Securities Inc; First Life Assurance Co Inc; Florida Life Assurance Co; Leo Oppenheim & Co Inc
Principal Bank: First National Bank & Trust Co of Oklahoma City
Financial Information:

	$'000
Revenue	80,050

No of Employees: 240

AMERICAN FLETCHER CORPORATION

111 Monument Circle, Indianapolis, IN 46277
Tel: (317) 639 3000

Chairman: Frank E McKinney Jr (and Chief Executive Officer). Vice Chairman: Walter W Ogilvy Jr (and Chief Financial Officer and Subsidiary Officer)
President: Joseph D Barnett Jr
Senior Executive Officers: Richard I Horen (Senior VP and Controller), Wade A Roth (Senior VP and Treasurer), Eugene E Henn (VP and Secretary), J Albert Smith Jr (VP)

PRINCIPAL ACTIVITIES: Banking
Principal Subsidiaries: American Fletcher National Bank and Trust Co; American Fletcher Leasing Corporation; American Fletcher Financial Services; American Fletcher Mortgage Co; Circle Realty Corp
Financial Information:

	Dec 31 1985
	$'000
Revenues	376,500
Net income	36,790

No of Employees: 2,330

AMERICAN FOODSERVICE CORPORATION

400 Drew Ct, King of Prussia, PA 19406
Tel: (215) 277-5010
Telex: WUT 846476 amfoodsrv kopr

Chairman: John F Ireton
President: Donald F Blackburn
Senior Executive Officers: Richard S Downs (VP and Treasurer), Ronald Allen (VP and Secretary), Ed McGroarty (Comptroller)

PRINCIPAL ACTIVITIES: Production of meat and prepared products
Principal Bank: The First Pennsylvania Banking and Trust Co
Financial Information:

	$'000
Sales revenues	90,000

No of Employees: 170

AMERICAN FRUCTOSE CORPORATION

41 Harbor Plaza Dr, Stamford, CT 06904
Tel: (203) 356-9000

Chairman: William Ziegler III; Vice Chairmen: Leslie Liabo; John C McCormick
President: Patric J McLoughlin
Senior Executive Officers: Alan J Edly (VP Finance)

PRINCIPAL ACTIVITIES: Producers of corn syrup
Parent Company: American Maize Products Corp, Stamford, CT
Principal Bank: Citibank
Financial Information:

	$'000
Sales revenues	128,000

No of Employees: 200

AMERICAN FURNITURE CO INC

Hairston Street off Starling, Martinsville, VA 24112
Tel: (703) 632-2061
Telex: WUT 829347 american mavl

Chairman: R M Simmons Jr (and President)
Senior Executive Officers: Roy Mitchell (VP Sales), R W England (VP Purchasing), F L Schuermann Jr (VP and Chief Financial Officer), Mike Haley (VP Contracting), A R Brock (VP, Secretary and Treasurer)

PRINCIPAL ACTIVITIES: Manufacture of a wide range of furniture
Principal Bank: Wachovia Bank and Trust
Financial Information:

	$'000
Sales revenues	96,500

No of Employees: 2,700

AMERICAN GAGE & MACHINE CO

853 Dundee Avenue, Elgin, IL 60120
Tel: (312) 379-1121

Chairman: Wallace E Carroll (and President)
Senior Executive Officers: Harold Miller (Executive VP), Warren A Furst (VP and Secretary), William H Murphy (VP and Treasurer), William Barrett (VP)

PRINCIPAL ACTIVITIES: Manufacture of electrical and electronic components and equipment and scientific instruments; aircraft and automotive equipment; pumping equipment and valves
Parent Company: Katy Industries, Inc, Elgin, IL
Principal Bank: Continental Illinois National Bank and Trust Co
Financial Information:

	$'000
Sales revenues	30,000

No of Employees: 1,500

AMERICAN GENERAL CORPORATION

2929 Allen Pkwy, Houston, TX 77019
Tel: (713) 522-1111

Chairman: Harold S Hook (and Chief Executive Officer); Vice Chairmen: Henry S Romaine, Don W Hutson
President: Michael J Poulos
Senior Executive Officers: Charles M Kelso (Executive VP), Nicholas R Rasmussen (Executive VP), Kurt G Schreiber (Executive VP), Howard Arner (Executive VP), Edwin G Pickett (Executive VP and Chief Financial Officer), Stephen J Bickel (Executive VP and Chief Actuary)

PRINCIPAL ACTIVITIES: Insurance and financial services
Principal Bank: Texas Commerce Bank

Financial Information:

	Dec 31 1985	Dec 31 1986
	$'000	$'000
Premium income	4,001,000	4,388,000
Investment income	1,551,000	1,656,000
Income before taxes	463,000	571,000
Net income	506,000	669,000
Dividends(1)	177,000	165,000
Dividends per share(2)	$1.00	$1.12
Earnings per share(3)	$3.12	$3.60
Common stock	58,000	78,000
Retained income	2,191,000	2,694,000
Shareholders equity	3,866,000	4,477,000

(1) paid
(2) annualized
(3) operating earnings

No of Employees: 16,000

AMERICAN GENERAL LIFE & ACCIDENT INSURANCE CO (FORMERLY NATIONAL LIFE &

American General Center, Nashville, TN 37250
Tel: (615) 749-1000

Senior Chairmen: Harold S Hook; Michael J Paulos; Chairman: Carroll D Shanks (and Chief Executive Officer)
President: James R Tuerff (and Chief Operating Officer)
Senior Executive Officers: Leo Lebos Jr (Executive VP), William B Pardue (Executive VP), Robert M Devlin (Executive VP), Roland R Strickert (Senior VP Financial Services)

PRINCIPAL ACTIVITIES: Life, accident and health insurance services
Parent Company: American General Corporation
Financial Information:

	Dec 31 1985	Dec 31 1986
	$'000	$'000
Premium income	427,508	410,285
Investment income	288,228	287,759

No of Employees: 8,534

AMERICAN GREETINGS CORPORATION

10500 American Road, Cleveland, OH 44144
Tel: (216) 252-7300
Telex: WUT 980371 agc clv

Chairman: Irving I Stone (and Chief Executive Officer); Vice Chairman: Morris S Stone
President: Morry Weiss (and Chief Operating Officer)
Senior Executive Officers: Morton Wyman (Executive VP American Greetings Division), Rubin Feldman (Senior VP), Henry Lowenthal (Senior VP Chief Financial Officer), Packy Nespeca (Senior VP Corporate Trade Development), Al J Stenger (Senior VP), William L Powell (Senior VP Carlton and Subsidiary Operations), Ronald E Clouse (Senior VP International and Subsidiary Operations), Ralph L White (VP Chief Human Resource Officer), Allan J Goodfellow (General Counsel and Secretary), John M Klipfell (Controller), Eugene B Scherry (Treasurer)

PRINCIPAL ACTIVITIES: Manufacture of greetings cards, wrapping paper, paper party goods, stationery, giftware, candles, novelties, toys and ceramics
Trade Names: American Greetings, Forget-Me-Not, Designers Collection, Carlton Cards, Rust Craft, Plus Mark, AmToy
Principal International and Subsidiary Operations: United States:-A.G.Industries, Inc; AmToy, Inc; Carlton Cards, Inc; Plus Mark, Inc; The Summit Corporation; Those Characters From Cleveland, Inc; Tower Products Company, Inc; Acme Frame Products, Inc; P A Plymouth Inc. Canada:- Carlton Cards Ltd; Plus Mark Canada; Rust Craft Canada, Inc. Continental Europe:-Grako Oy (Finland); A/S Muva Grafiske Produkter (Norway); Muva Greetings B.V. (Netherlands); Muva Greetings SA (Belgium). Mexico:- Felicitaciones Nacionales SA de CV. Monaco:- Rust Craft International SA. United Kingdom:-Rust Craft Greeting Cards (UK) Ltd; Andrew Valentine Holdings Ltd; Celebration Arts Group Ltd; Denison Colour Ltd. Division: American Greetings Division
Principal Banks: National City Bank; AmeriTrust; Society National Bank; Manufacturers Hanover Trust; Chase Manhattan Bank; National Bank of Detroit; Citizens & Southern National Bank; Continental Illinois Bank; First Republic Bank
Financial Information:

	Feb 28 1986	Feb 28 1987
	$'000	$'000
Sales revenues	1,035,651	1,125,995
Income before taxes	136,060	102,195
Net income	74,425	63,361
Dividends	19,910	21,288
Dividends per share	$0.62	$0.66
Earnings per share	$2.32	$1.97
Common stock	125,240	119,449
Retained income	357,724	404,994
Shareholders equity	482,964	524,443

No of Employees: 22,000

AMERICAN HARDWARE SUPPLY CO

PO Box 1510, Butler, PA 16001
Telex: WUT 550428 am hdwe but

Chairman: Joseph Sweterlitsch; Vice Chairman: Clyde Wilber
President: Lawrence T Zehfuss
Senior Executive Officers: Donald Cotton (Senior VP Marketing), Albert Mielcuszny (Senior VP Finance, Data Processing and Treasurer), Alan Jeveret (Senior VP Operations), Paul Pentz (VP Merchandising and Advertising), Russell Thomas (VP Personnel), Bernard Smith (VP Investment Control), Donald Belt (VP Sales)

PRINCIPAL ACTIVITIES: Cooperative association with interests in the supply of home hardware
Financial Information:

	Jun 30 1986
	$'000
Sales revenues	669,653
Shareholders equity	56,669

No of Employees: 1,010

AMERICAN HEALTHCARE MANAGEMENT INC

14160 Dallas Parkway, Suite 900, Dallas, TX 75240
Tel: (214) 385 7000

Chairman: John A Bradley (and Chief Executive Officer)
President: David A Huff (and Chief Operating Officer)
Senior Executive Officers: Philip Flame (Executive VP), Edward J Spillane (Senior VP), Grace D Dilworth (Senior VP Auditing), Mark L Plaumman (Senior VP Finance Administration and Chief Financial Officer), Joseph W Atkinson (VP Corporate Counsel and Secretary)

PRINCIPAL ACTIVITIES: Provision of a wide range of medical services through hospitals and related care facilities
Principal Bank: Chase Manhattan Bank
Financial Information:

	$'000
Sales revenues	413,410

No of Employees: 6,000

AMERICAN HERITAGE LIFE INVESTMENT CORPORATION

American Heritage Life Bldg, 11 E Forsyth St, Jacksonville, FL 32202
Tel: (904) 354 1776

Chairman: J E Davis
President: W Ashley Verlander (and Chief Executive Officer)
Senior Executive Officers: John W Alexander (VP), Charles T Boswell (VP Actuarial), Doyle Russell Burch (Group Senior

Vice President), T O'Neal Douglas (Executive VP), Richard B Franz II (VP and Controller), William P Montgomery (Group Senior Vice President), Don C Smith (Group Senior Vice President), James R Tabor (Senior VP Administration), Judson S Wharton (Senior VP and Treasurer), William E Mayhew (Senior VP Finance), Norman J Harrison (Senior VP Employment Affairs), Embert G Sosnin (VP Insurance), Chris A Verlander (Senior VP Investments and Secretary)

PRINCIPAL ACTIVITIES: Life insurance

Principal Subsidiaries: American Heritage Life Insurance Co; Florida Associated Services

Principal Bank: Barnett Bank of Jacksonville

Financial Information:

	Dec 31 1985
	$'000
Revenue	189,900
Net income	8,440

No of Employees: 420

AMERICAN HOIST & DERRICK CO

Suite 1800, 345 St Peter St, St Paul, MN 55102
Tel: (612) 293-4904

President: Robert H Nassau (and Chief Executive Officer)

Senior Executive Officers: Charles G Truzinski (VP Finance), Jerry A Morgan (VP)

PRINCIPAL ACTIVITIES: Manufactures hydrants, valves, fire pumps; scrap balers and shears; fittings for wire rope and chain; vacuum chambers

Trade Names: Waterous, Harris Press & Shear, HRB, Crosby, McKissick, Laughlin, Lebus, Vac-Tec Systems

Principal Subsidiaries: Waterous Company; Harris Press & Shear; Crosby Group; Vac-Tec Systems

Financial Information:

	Nov 30 1987
	$'000
Sales revenues	279,000
Income before taxes	9,000
Net income	15,000
Earnings per share	$2.01
Shareholders equity	66,500

No of Employees: 2,365

AMERICAN HOME PRODUCTS CORPORATION

685 Third Avenue, New York, NY 10017
Tel: (212) 986-1000

Chairman: John W Culligan (and Chief Executive Officer); Chairman of Executive Committee: William F LaPorte

President: John R Stafford

Senior Executive Officers: Robert G Blount (Senior VP), Ernest T Harper (VP), Joseph R Bock (VP Development), Charles D Canevari (VP Tax), George DeMott (VP), John G Horsman Jr (VP), Charles F Hagan (VP and General Counsel), Albert R Pezzillo (VP), Herbert A Bly (VP Engineering), William F Emswyler (VP and Treasurer)

PRINCIPAL ACTIVITIES: Manufacture and sale of pharmaceuticals, food specialties, confectionery and household products

Principal Subsidiaries: American Home Foods Inc; API Leasing Inc; Ayerst International Inc; Ayerst Laboratories Inc; Ayerst Laboratories Research; Boyle-Midway Inc; Boyle-Midway International Inc; E J Brach & Sons Inc; Brucarla Building Corp; Corometrics Medical Systems; Fort Dodge Laboratories Inc; Franklin Laboratories Inc; Home Products (Japan) Inc; Home Products Inc; Home Products Overseas Inc; Household Research Institute; International Floor Machine; Ives Laboratories Inc; Laboratorios Wyeth Inc; Lucks Inc; John F Murray Advertising Agency; Sherwood Medical Co Inc; Whitehall International Inc; Whitehall Laboratories Inc; Wyeth International Ltd; Wyeth Laboratories Inc; Wyeth Nutritionals Inc

Principal Bank: Manufacturers Hanover Trust Co

Financial Information:

	Dec 31 1985	Dec 31 1986
	$'000	$'000
Sales revenues	4,684,740	4,926,512
Net income	717,140	778,824
Earnings per share	$10.21	$5.18
Shareholders equity	2,291,758	2,380,846

No of Employees: 47,240

AMERICAN INCOME LIFE INSURANCE COMPANY

1200 Wooded Acres Drive, PO Box 2608, Waco, TX 76797
Tel: (817) 772 3050

Chairman: Bernard Rapoport (and Chief Executive Officer); Vice Chairman: Pat Beard

President: Charles B Cooper (and Chief Operating Officer)

Senior Executive Officers: George R Dethlefsen (VP, Controller and Treasurer), Fred Hudson (Executive VP Agency), Joyce Lillard (VP Agency), Alvin Adelman (VP and Secretary), Bun Raley (VP Postal Division)

PRINCIPAL ACTIVITIES: Life insurance

Principal Bank: Mid-America Bank of Louisville and Trust Co

Financial Information:

	Dec 31 1985
	$'000
Revenue	120,440
Net income	18,540

No of Employees: 1,110

AMERICAN INDEMNITY FINANCIAL CORPORATION

1 American Indemnity Plaza, Galveston, TX 77550
Tel: (409) 766 4600

Chairman: J F Seinsheimer Jr (and Chief Executive Officer)

President: J Fellman Seinsheimer III (and Chief Operating Officer)

Senior Executive Officers: Synott L McNeel (Senior VP, Secretary and Treasurer)

PRINCIPAL ACTIVITIES: Provision of casualty and property insurance through subsidiary companies

Principal Subsidiaries: American Indemnity Co

Financial Information:

	Dec 31 1985
	$'000
Revenues	84,380

No of Employees: 415

AMERICAN INDUSTRIES, INC

4033 NW Yeon Avenue, Portland, OR 97210
Tel: (503) 226-1511

Chairman: Howard Hedinger

President: Neil Thornton

Senior Executive Officers: Gerald Hoover (VP), Bob Duffy (VP Finance)

PRINCIPAL ACTIVITIES: Metal processing

Principal Bank: United States National Bank of Oregon

Financial Information:

	$'000
Sales revenues	100,000

No of Employees: 400

AMERICAN INFORMATION TECHNOLOGIES CORPORATION
Ameritech
30 S Wacker Dr, Chicago, IL 60606
Tel: (312) 750-5000

Chairman: W L Weiss; Vice Chairman: W H Springer
Presidents: O J Wade (Bell Group); R L Barnett (Enterprise Group)
Directors: J F Beré, W R Christopherson, E M de Windt, M Gillett, H H Gray, J A Henderson, H C Kuehl, F P Lloyd, G J Morgan, J D Ong, R C Ernest, W L Weiss, W H Springer, O J Wade, R L Barnett. Senior Executive Officers: Bruce B Howat (Secretary)

PRINCIPAL ACTIVITIES: Operation of telephone systems
Trade Names: Ameritech
Principal Subsidiaries: Illinois Bell Telephone Co; Illinois Bell communications Inc; Indiana Bell Telephone Co Inc; Indiana Bell Communications Inc; Michigan Bell Telephone Co; Michigan Bell Communications Inc; The Ohio Bell Telephone Co; Ohio Bell Communications Inc; Wisconsin Bell Telephone Co; Wisconsin Bell Communications Inc; Ameritech Services Inc; Ameritech Communications Inc; Ameritech Credit Corpn; Ameritech Development Corpn; Ameritech Mobile Communications Inc; Ameritech Publishing Inc; Applied Data Research Inc
Financial Information:

	Dec 31 1985	Dec 31 1986
	$'000	$'000
Sales revenues	9,021,100	9,362,100
Net income	1,077,700	1,138,400
Dividends per share*	$4.40	$4.79
Earnings per share*	$7.35	$7.87
Shareholders equity	7,449,500	7,609,000

*per share data reflects 3-for-2 stock split effective December 31 1986

No of Employees: 77,538

AMERICAN INTERNATIONAL GROUP, INC
70 Pine Street, New York, NY 10270
Tel: (212) 770-7000
Telex: ITT 420627 aiu ui

President: Maurice R Greenberg (and Chief Executive Officer)
Senior Executive Officers: Edward E Matthews (Executive VP, Finance), John J Roberts (Executive VP), Robert B Sanborn (Executive VP), Gordon O'Brien (Senior VP Human Resources)

PRINCIPAL ACTIVITIES: Diversified insurance and financial interests
Principal Subsidiaries: A I Credit Corp; AICCO Inc; AIG Consultants Inc; AIG Data Center; AIG Equipment Lessors; AIG Realty Inc; AIG Risk Management Inc; AIG Oilrig Inc; AIU Insurance Co; Agency Management Corp; AIG Energy Inc; American Home Assurance Co; Transatlantic Reinsurance Co; American International Adjustment Co; American International Life Assurance Co; American International Underwriters Corp; American International Marine Agency; American Life Insurance Co Inc; Delaware American Life Insurance Co; American Life Insurance Co; Audubon Indemnity Co; Audubon Insurance Co; Birmingham Fire Insurance Co; Commerce & Industry Insurance Co; Insurance Company of the State; Landmark Insurance Co; Lexington Insurance Co; Marketpac International Inc; MT Mansfield Co Inc; Stowe Country Club Corp; National Union Fire Insurance Pittsburgh; New Hampshire Insurance Co; AI Network Corp; AIG Life Insurance Co; Alaska Insurance Co; American Fidelity Co; Granite State Insurance Co; Illinois National Insurance Co; International Computer Service; North American Manager Inc; Pacific Union Assurance Co Inc; Risk Specialists Co Inc; Midtown Risk Specialists Inc; Eastern Risk Specialists Inc; Louisiana Risk Specialists Inc; North East Risk Specialists Inc; Southeastern Risk Specialists Inc; Western Risk Specialists Inc; CV Starr & Co; United Guaranty Corp, United Guaranty Commercial Insurance; United Guaranty Residential Insurance NC Inc
Financial Information:

	Dec 31 1985	Dec 31 1986
	$'000	$'000
Revenues	5,782,254	9,704,119
Net income	420,470	795,827
Earnings per share	$2.75	$4.90
Shareholders equity	-	4,867,797
Total assets	15,570,720	21,022,868

No of Employees: 28,000

AMERICAN MAIZE-PRODUCTS CO
250 Harbour Plaza Drive, Stamford, CT 06904
Tel: (203) 356-9000

Chairman: William Ziegler III (and Chief Executive Officer)
President: John C McCormack (and Chief Operating Officer)
Senior Executive Officers: Alan J Edly (VP Finance), Charles A Koons (VP Corporate Development and Planning), Edward P Norris (VP and Controller), Donald E McNicol (Secretary)

PRINCIPAL ACTIVITIES: Manufacture of a wide range of corn products; cigars; distribution of building materials and home inprovement items
Principal Subsidiaries: J N O Swisher & Son, Inc; American Fructose Corporation; Lloyd Home & Building Centers; Helme Tobacco Company
Principal Bank: Irving Trust Company
Financial Information:

	Dec 31 1986
	$'000
Sales revenues	509,544
Income before taxes*	27,065
Net income	9,732
Dividends	2,777
Dividends per share	$0.52
Earnings per share	$1.82
Shareholders equity	126,343

*and minority interest

No of Employees: 2,800

AMERICAN MANAGEMENT SYSTEMS INC
1777 North Kent Street, Arlington, VA 22209
Tel: (703) 841-6000

Chairman: Ivan Selin
President: Charles O Rossotti (and Chief Executive Officer)
Senior Executive Officers: Patrick W Gross (Chief Executive and Secretary), Frank A Nicolai (Executive VP and Treasurer)

PRINCIPAL ACTIVITIES: Supply of computer software and services
Principal Subsidiaries: American Management Systems; AMS Technical
Principal Bank: Sovran Bank
Financial Information:

	$'000
Sales revenues	88,450

No of Employees: 1,400

AMERICAN MEDICAL INTERNATIONAL, INC
414 N Camden Drive, Beverly Hills, CA 90210
Tel: (213) 278-6200

Chairman: Royce Diener (and Chief Executive Officer)
President: Walter L Weisman (and Chief Operating Officer)
Senior Executive Officers: R B Andrews (Executive VP Finance), Thomas E Donahue Jr (Executive VP), Charles P Reilly (Executive VP), Andre Dimitriadis (Senior VP and Chief Financial Officer)

PRINCIPAL ACTIVITIES: Provision and management of hospitals
Financial Information:

	Aug 31 1986
	$'000
Sales revenues	2,569,893
Net (loss)	(97,279)
(Loss) per share	($1.12)
Shareholders equity	886,748

No of Employees: 47,000

AMERICAN MEDICAL SERVICES INC

1051 East Ogden Avenue, Milwaukee, WI 53202
Tel: (414) 271 1300

Chairman: Harry E Samson
President: Harold Nash
Senior Executive Officers: Allen L Samson (Executive VP, Chief Executive Officer and Secretary), R Max Samson (Executive VP and Chief Operating Officer), Stanley J Cohen (VP and Chief Financial Officer), Mary Jo Pencikowski (VP)

PRINCIPAL ACTIVITIES: Nursing homes
Principal Bank: First National Bank
Financial Information:

	$'000
Sales revenues	60,110

No of Employees: 3,400

AMERICAN MOTOR INNS INC

1917 Franklin Rd SW, Box 14100 Roanoke, VA 24022
Tel: (703) 342-4531

Chairman: A O Krisch
President: Joel P Krisch
Senior Executive Officers: Sydney Shaftman (Executive VP and Treasurer), William H Hancock Jr (Senior VP Finance), John Poff (Senior VP Operations), Ben M Richardson (Senior VP Law)

PRINCIPAL ACTIVITIES: Operation of motels and restaurants
Parent Company: Prime Motor Inns, Inc
Principal Subsidiaries: AMI Resorts Ltd; American Trayer Inc; Argus Motor Inns Inc; Atlas Motor Inns Inc; Baltimore Hotels Inc; Civic Motor Inns Inc; Coliseum Motor Inns Inc; Connecticut Motor Inns; Eden Motor Inns Inc; Federal Motor Inns; Flamboyant Investment Co; General Motor Inns Inc; Hartford Motor Inns Inc; Krisch Corp; Lion Motor Inns Inc; Metropolitan Motor Inns Inc; Motel Co of Gastonia Inc; Motels of MD Inc; Republic Motor Inns Inc; State Motor Inns Inc; Universal Communication Systems Inc; Digi-Stat Ltd
Financial Information:

	$'000
Sales revenues	200,000

No of Employees: 4,000

AMERICAN MOTORS CORPORATION

27777 Franklin Road, Southfield, MI 48034
Tel: (313) 827-1000

Chairman: Pierre Semerena
President: Jose J Dedeurwaerder (and Chief Executive Officer)
Senior Executive Officers: Richard A Calmes (VP-Personnel and Industrial Relations), Joseph E Cappy (Executive VP-Operations), François J Castaing (VP-Products Engineering and Development), Tod O Clare (VP-International Operations), A Keith Ebersole (VP-Supply), Gerard Gastaut (VP-Business Planning and Corporate Affairs), Peter G Guptill (VP-US Sales), Kenneth A Lawton (VP and Treasurer), John P Tierney (VP and Chief Financial Officer), Jesus Peon (VP-Manufacturing), John W Mowrey (VP-Product Planning and Design), Jerry L Sloan (VP-Public Relations), Marvin W Stuckey (VP-Civic and Government Affairs)

PRINCIPAL ACTIVITIES: Manufacture of automobiles, trucks and related parts
Trade Names: American Motors Eagle, Renault Alliance and Encore, Jeep Cherokee, Jeep Wagoneer, Jeep CJ-7, Jeep Grand Wagoneer, Jeep J-10 and J-20 pickup truck, Jeep Comanche
Principal Subsidiaries: Jeep Corporation; American Motors Sales Corporation; American Motors (Canada) Inc; American Motors Leasing Corporation; American Motors Pan American Corporation; American Motors Realty Corporation; Coleman Products Company; Evart Products Company; MacDonald Molding Inc; Mercury Plastics Company; Rantoul Products Inc
Principal Bank: The Chase Manhattan Bank of New York
Financial Information:

	Dec 31 1986
	$'000
Sales revenues	3,462,504
Net (loss)	(91,319)
(Loss) per share	($0.99)
Shareholders equity	378,538

No of Employees: 23,500

AMERICAN NATIONAL BANK

1325 19th Street, Bakersfield, CA 93301
Tel: (805) 861-5396

Chairman: Rayburn S Dezember
President: D L Wiley (and Chief Executive Officer)
Senior Executive Officers: John H Tait (Executive VP), Lucille T Finley (Executive VP), Edward J Biebrich Jr (Executive VP), Rollin Winslow (Senior VP), Kris E Holt (Public Relations Director)

PRINCIPAL ACTIVITIES: Banking services
Parent Company: Central Pacific Corporation

No of Employees: 630

AMERICAN NATIONAL CAN COMPANY

8101 Higgins Road, Chicago, IL 60631
Tel: (312) 399-3000
Telex: WUT 726425 NCC EXEC CGO

Chairman: Frank W Considine (and President and Chief Executive Officer); Vice Chairmen: Roland H Meyer, Louis F Umsted
Senior Executive Officers: Steven J Friesen (Executive VP, Performance Plastics Packaging-Barrier Plastics, Flexible, Tube), John F Hildner (Executive VP, Food Sales and Marketing Metal Container), Walter T Stelzel (Executive VP, Finance and Chief Financial Officer), Jack H Turner (Executive VP, International), J Richard Woods (Executive VP, Diversified Packaging-Glass, Plastics, Closure), William K Zoon (Executive VP, Operations Services), Neil N Chernikoff (Senior VP, Engineering), Leonard C Everson (Senior VP and General Counsel), Jerald L Pangborn (Senior VP, Human Resources), William J Baker (VP, Personnel), Donald G Brungard (VP, Management Information Systems), William A Francois (VP, Associate General Counsel and Secretary), Gilbert M Kapelman (VP and Associate General Counsel), Arnold A Kopetz (VP, Research and Development), John M Schemm Jr (VP, Industrial Relations), E James Schneiders (VP, Planning), Alan H Schumacher (VP and Controller), Stanley Shapiro (VP, Research and Development Operations), Patrick F Van Keuren (VP, Government Affairs), Donald G Wanfalt (VP, Corporate Finance), Larry R Williams (VP, Purchasing and Distribution), Richard A Kabaker (Assistant Secretary), Donald L Rice (Assistant Treasurer), Shirley L Rice (Assistant Controller), Colin R Silvester (Assistant Treasurer), Robert A Stenzel (Assistant Secretary), Robert F Thompson (Assistant Treasurer). International Division: Antonio Bove (Managing Director-National Can Italiana SpA), Martin J Clegg (VP and Managing Director, UK), Pantelis Constantinides (Managing Director, National Can Cyprus Ltd), Keith B Cooper (VP, Sales), Charles J Davis (General Manager, National Can

Puerto Rico, Inc), Manfred Graf (Managing Director, National Can Iberica SA), Arturo Grullon (President-Envases Antillanos C Por A), Michael J Herdman (VP, Latin America and Business Development), John J McLaine (VP, Finance and Control), Emilio Morganti (Managing Director, Nacanco Italiana SpA), Joseph K Prevloski (Managing Director, Nacanco Deutschland GmbH), Daniel J Spillane (Managing Director, Nacanco Ireland Division, Nacanco Netherlands BV), Richard G Sturdevant (VP, European Operations), Samuel T Telerico (VP, Licensing and Machinery Sales), Luke vanWidenfelt (VP, Far East Operations), Malcolm F White (VP, Business Development)

PRINCIPAL ACTIVITIES: Manufacture of containers made of glass, plastic and metal; metal and plastic closures; barrier, flexible, tube plastic packaging

Parent Company: Triangle Industries, Inc

Principal Subsidiaries: Bernadin of Canada Ltd (Canada); The Magic Can Co; Metal Containers Ltd of Cyprus (Cyprus); Nacanco Deutschland GmbH (Germany); Nacanco (Holdings) Ltd (UK); Nacanco Ltd (UK); Nacanco Ireland Ltd (Eire); National Can Italiana SpA (Italy); Nacanco SpA (Italy); Natadco Ltd; National Can Iberica SA, (Spain); National Can Overseas Corporation; National Can Puerto Rico Inc; National Trading Corp; NCC International Sales Corp; National Can Services Corp

No of Employees: 22,000 (American National Can only)

AMERICAN NATIONAL HOLDING COMPANY

136 East Michigan Avenue, Kalamazoo, MI 49007
Tel: (616) 383 6700

Chairman: Harold H Holland (and President and Chief Executive Officer)

Senior Executive Officers: James H Walters (Executive VP), Bonnie E Yates (Senior VP Loan Review), Richard W Cook (VP Marketing), Gerard J Molitor (VP and Controller), Larry E Blanchard (VP and Auditor)

PRINCIPAL ACTIVITIES: Banking services

Parent Company: Old Kent Financial Corporation

Principal Subsidiaries: American Bank; American National Bank; American National Bank and Trust Co; American National Bank West; America National Bank Western MI; American National Mortgage Co; Central National Bank; Great Lakes Computer Center; Ludington Bank & Trust Co; Superior Life Insurance Co

Principal Bank: American National Bank and Trust Co

Financial Information:

	Dec 31 1985
	$'000
Revenues	79,100
Net income	6,240

No of Employees: 660

AMERICAN NATIONAL INSURANCE CO

One Moody Plaza, Galveston, TX 77550-7999
Tel: (409) 763-4661
Telex: WUT 765430 anico c gal

Chairman: Robert L Moody

President: O C Clay (and Chief Executive Officer)

Senior Executive Officers: R A Banks (Executive VP), W K Nicol (Executive VP), C R Robertson (Senior Executive VP), V E Soler Jr (VP and Controller)

PRINCIPAL ACTIVITIES: Life insurance and health insurance

Principal Subsidiaries: American National Life Insurance Co of Texas; Commonwealth Life & Accident Insurance Co; Standard Life & Accident Insurance Co; American National Property & Casualty Co; American National General Insurance Co; ANREM Corp; Securities Management & Research

Principal Bank: First City National Bank, Houston

Financial Information:

	Dec 31 1985	Dec 31 1986
	$'000	$'000
Premium income	356,351	363,944
Investment income	221,297	226,245
Other income	4,026	15,909
Income before taxes	131,079	125,095
Net income	158,432	241,338
Dividends	32,162	35,533
Dividends per share	$1.11	$1.23
Earnings per share	$8.35	$5.47
Common stock	28,974	28,888
Retained income	1,110,291	1,316,097
Shareholders equity	1,116,340	1,319,330

Principal Shareholders: Moody Foundation (7,238,500 shares); The Libbie S Moody Trust (9,949,585 shares)

No of Employees: 7,599

AMERICAN NATURAL RESOURCES CO

One Woodward Avenue, Detroit, MI 48226
Tel: (313) 965-1200

Chairman: James R Paul; Vice Chairman: S K Smith Jr

President: James F Cordes

Senior Executive Officers: D A Arledge (Senior VP and Treasurer), Jules W Breslow (VP Taxes), P C Iribe (VP Corporate Planning), R E Moss (VP Federal Affairs), Thomas M Murray (VP Personnel)

PRINCIPAL ACTIVITIES: Exploration, production and sale of natural gas and coal; freight forwarding and trucking

Parent Company: The Coastal Corporation

Principal Subsidiaries: ANR Coal Co Inc; ANR Coal Sales Inc; Apache Mining Co Inc; Brooks Run Coal Co; Enterprise Coal Co Inc; VICC Land Co; Virginia Iron, Coal & Coke Co; ANR Storage Co; ANR Intrastate Storage Co; ANR MI Storage Co; ANR Western Storage Co; ANG Coal Gasification Co; ANR Freight System Inc; Associated Truck Lines Inc; Garrett Freightlines Inc; Graves Truck Line Inc; Neuendorf Transportation Co; Road Equipment Inc; United Truck Rental Inc; ANR Gasification Properties Co; ANR Gathering Co; ANR Pipeline Co; American Natural Offshore Co; ANR Technology Co; ANR Energy Conversion Co; ANR Western Coal Development Co

Principal Bank: Citibank NA

Financial Information:

	$'000
Sales revenues	3,500,000

No of Employees: 10,900

AMERICAN OIL AND GAS CORPORATION

2370 M Corp Plaza, 333 Clay Street, Houston, TX 77002
Tel: (713) 650 0510

Chairman: David M Carmichael (and President and Chief Executive Officer)

Senior Executive Officers: William P Conner (Senior VP, Chief Financial Officer, Secretary and Treasurer), Byron L Blackwell (VP), Gary A McElroy (VP and Subsidiary Officer), Albert F Richmond Jr (VP Secretary and Treasurer), Dean A Zimmerman (VP and Subsidiary Officer), David W Rucker (Controller and Chief Accounting Officer)

PRINCIPAL ACTIVITIES: Supply of natural gas

Principal Bank: Bankers Trust Co

Financial Information:

	$'000
Sales revenues	106,550

No of Employees: 290

AMERICAN OLEAN TILE CO

1000 Cannon Avenue, Lansdale, PA 19446
Tel: (215) 855-1111
Telex: WUT 846407 amnolean lans

President: W L Snyder
Senior Executive Officers: E M Adams (Executive VP Development), R S Siock (VP and Controller), W M Pye (VP Personnel and Administration), W H Hoaglund (VP Manufacturing), J F Monney (VP Research and Development), D W Sewell (VP Engineering), M J Cerruti (VP Sales), W S King (Secretary and Treasurer)

PRINCIPAL ACTIVITIES: Manufacture of tiles for walls and floors
Parent Company: National Gypsum Co, Dallas, TX
Principal Bank: Philadelphia National Bank
Financial Information:

	$'000
Sales revenues	150,000

No of Employees: 2,600

AMERICAN OPTICAL CORPORATION

14 Mechanic Street, Southbridge, MA 01550
Tel: (617) 765-9711
Telex: 920334 AMEROPT SOUT

Chairman: Maurice J Cunniffe
President: James J O'Connor
Senior Executive Officers: J W Van Dyke (Senior Vice President and Chief Financial Officer), J P Flanagan (President, Safety Products Business), J N Berinstein (President, Ophthalmic Business), R Levesque (President, International Business), J L Bala (President, Precision Products Business), S J Beckett (Treasurer)

PRINCIPAL ACTIVITIES: Manufacture of lenses and spectacles, eye protection products, respiratory and hearing protection and custom molded plastics and industrial abrasives and polishing materials
Trade Names: Aolite, Truvision, M3, Duraguard, Aerosite, Geosite, Radiac
Principal Subsidiaries: AoCo Ltd (Canada); IALO SA (Brazil); ALL OPTIC GmbH (Germany); AO International AG (Switzerland); American Optical Co (Singapore) Pty (Singapore); British American Optical Co Ltd (UK); UKO International Plc (UK); UKO Ltd (UK); Raphael Taylor Group (UK); Ouest Optique SA (France); M Wiseman & Co Pty (Australia); American Optical de Mexico SA de CV (Mexico); Radiac Abrasives (USA); National Grinding Wheel (USA); Universal Grinding Wheel (USA)
Principal Bank: Irving Trust Co
Financial Information:

	Mar 31 1986	Mar 31 1987
	$'000	$'000
Sales revenues	220,000	221,000

AMERICAN PACESETTER

4540 Campus Drive, Newport Beach, CA 92660
Tel: (714) 756-8168

Chairman: John W Klug (and President and Chief Executive Officer)
Senior Executive Officers: Landon M Exley (VP), Richard F Holland (VP), John R Polen (Secretary and Chief Financial Officer)

PRINCIPAL ACTIVITIES: Manufacture of electronic, mechanical and electro-mechanical components; real estate development
Principal Subsidiaries: American Electronics Inc; Pacesetter Homes Inc; San Clemente Savings and Loan Association
Principal Bank: First Interstate Bank
Financial Information:

	$'000
Sales revenues	120,000

No of Employees: 400

AMERICAN PACKAGING CORPORATION

Grant & Ashton, Philadelphia, PA 19114
Tel: (215) 698-4800

Chairman: S A Shottland (and Chief Executive Officer)
President: S B Schottland
Senior Executive Officers: R L Coleman (VP Manufacturing), C B Shottland (VP), D Howley (VP and General Manager Coated and Laminated Products Division)

PRINCIPAL ACTIVITIES: Manufacture of packaging
Principal Bank: Philadelphia National Bank
Financial Information:

	$'000
Sales revenues	110,000

No of Employees: 800

AMERICAN PETROFINA, INCORPORATED

PO Box 2159, Dallas, TX 75221
Tel: (214) 750-2400

Chairman: Paul D Meek
President: Kenneth W Perry (and Chief Executive Officer)
Senior Executive Officers: Ronald W Haddock (Executive VP and Chief Operating Officer), Joe A Moss (VP and General Counsel), Samuel R West (VP and Controller), Neil A Smoak (VP-Exploration and Production), Michael J Couch (VP-Supply and Transportation), Jerry G Jenkins (VP), Glenn E Selvidge (VP-Employee Relations), Willem Willemstyn (VP-Audit and Compliance), R J Comeaux (VP-Chemical Manufacturing), Stuart M Pearman (VP-Marketing), Christian Buggenhout (VP-Finance), Linda Middleton (Secretary), Cullen M Godfrey (Assistant Secretary), Brendan M O'Connor (Treasurer), Andrew Wang (Assistant Treasurer), Gerald Wise (Assistant Treasurer, Assistant Secretary), Ray Been (Assistant Treasurer). Directors: Paul D Meek, Ken W Perry, R I Galland, Pierre de Tillesse, François Cornelis, Jean-Pierre Amory, Georges Vander Straetan, David C Treen, Robert L Mitchell, Ronald W Haddock

PRINCIPAL ACTIVITIES: Through its operating company, Fina Oil and Chemical Company, exploration for and production of crude oil and natural gas, refining marketing and transportation of petroleum products and the manufacture and marketing of petrochemicals and plastics
Trade Names: Fina, Cosden
Principal Subsidiaries: Fina Oil and Chemical Company; FinaServe, Inc; American Protectorate, Inc; Fina Exploration, Inc
Principal Bank: First RepublicBank Dallas, NA
Financial Information:

	Dec 31 1985	Dec 31 1986
	$'000	$'000
Sales revenues	2,408,502	1,960,030
(Loss) before taxes	(48,803)	(40,863)
Net (loss)	(10,163)	(24,569)
Dividends	25,133	-
Dividends per share	$2.10	-
(Loss) per share	$(0.85)	($2.03)
Common stock	11,978	12,210
Retained income	384,046	359,477
Shareholders equity	624,513	654,220

No of Employees: 3,419

AMERICAN PIONEER SAVINGS BANK

135 West Central Boulevard Suite 700, Orlando, FL 32801
Tel: (305) 423 7300

Chairman: Richard R Swann (and Chief Executive Officer); Vice Chairman: Samuel P Bell III, William T Wallis
President: Richard L Paul (and Chief Operating Officer)
Senior Executive Officers: H E Davis (Executive VP), William P Valenti (Executive VP), David C Hall (VP and Controller), J A Huggins (Senior VP and Treasurer), Phillip J Wise Jr (VP and Secretary), John Waters (VP and Chief Accounting Officer), Richard T Grelecki (Senior VP Marketing and Corporate Planning), J Rudy Spears (VP Human Resources)

PRINCIPAL ACTIVITIES: Financial services; subsidiaries have interests in insurance

Principal Subsidiaries: American Pioneer Corporation; American Pioneer Life Insurance Co

Financial Information:

	Dec 31 1985
	$'000
Revenues	145,625
Net income	3,825

No of Employees: 1,000

AMERICAN PRECISION INDUSTRIES INC

2777 Walden Avenue, Buffalo, NY 14225

Tel: (716) 684-9700

President: Robert J Fierle

Senior Executive Officers: Richard P Becht (Senior VP-Operations and Treasurer), James W Bevevino (Corporate VP and President-Heat Transfer Equipment Group), William A Donovan (Secretary), Donald C McElheny (Corporate VP, President-Electronic Components Group), Richard S Warzala (Corporate VP, President-Motion Control Group), Robert E Weld (VP-Finance and Corporate Controller), Virginia C Pursell (Assistant Secretary)

PRINCIPAL ACTIVITIES: API American Precision Industries is people, and through their efforts, its divisions and subsidiaries develop, manufacture, and sell high quality products to industry and government. The Industrial Process Equipment segment of the business produces heat transfer products for manufacturers of gas compressors, steam and gas turbines, diesel engines, compressed air dryers, air conditioning equipment and hydraulic systems. The Elctronic Products segment manufactures and sells high reliability micro-miniature coils, capacitors, electromagnetic clutches, brakes and step motors to the industrial, telecommunications, computer, military, aerospace and business machine markets

Principal Subsidiaries: (100% owned unless stated): American Precision Industries (UK) Ltd (UK); API Development Corporation; API-FS Corporation (US Virgin Islands); API of Canada Inc (Canada); Nitta-Apitron Co Ltd (50%) (Japan)

Financial Information:

	Dec 27 1985	Jan 2 1987
	$'000	$'000
Sales revenues net	34,106	33,655
Income before taxes	2,747	1,181
Net income	1,595	813
Dividends	728	812
Dividends per share	$0.16	$0.18
Earnings per share net	$0.35	$0.18
Common stock	2,061	3,108
Retained income	5,839	5,840
Shareholders equity	18,936	18,719

No of Employees: 600

AMERICAN PRESIDENT COMPANIES LTD

1800 Harrison Street, Oakland, CA 94612

Tel: (415) 272-8000

Telex: ITT 470174 apl ui

Chairman: W B Seaton (and President and Chief Executive Officer)

Senior Executive Officers: Joji Hayashi (Executive VP), Richard L Tavrow (Senior VP), Michael T Maher (VP), Derek A Medcalf (VP), Timothy J Rhein (VP), Roger A Barnes (VP and Controller)

PRINCIPAL ACTIVITIES: Holding company with interests in cargo shipping and property

Principal Bank: Chase Manhattan Bank

Financial Information:

	Dec 31 1985	Dec 31 1986
	$'000	$'000
Sales revenues	1,170,720	1,466,714
Net income	38,486	17,956
Earnings per share	$1.86	$0.71
Shareholders equity		640,562

No of Employees: 3,970

AMERICAN SAFETY RAZOR COMPANY

PO Box 500, Staunton, VA 24401

Tel: (703) 248-8000

Telex: 82 2435 AMCORAZ VEVA

President: J G Ferguson (and Chief Executive Officer)

Senior Executive Officers: Earl C Howell (VP Finance), Joseph F Hackett (Director of Marketing and Sales, Branded Products), Richard E Bonin (VP Operations)

PRINCIPAL ACTIVITIES: Manufacturer and distributor of high quality shaving blades and razors and broad variety of industrial blades used in cutting, slitting, scraping, trimming applications

Trade Names: American Line, Personna, Flicker, Gem, Pal, Treet, Ever-Ready, Burma Shave, Face Guard

Principal Subsidiaries: Personna International Limited; Personna International of Puerto Rico; American Safety Razor of Canada Ltd

Principal Bank: Bankers Trust

Financial Information:

	$'000
Sales revenues	125,000

No of Employees: 700 (approx)

AMERICAN SAVINGS & LOAN ASSOCIATION OF FLORIDA

17801 NW 2nd Avenue, Miami, FL 33169

Tel: (305) 653-5353

Telex: TWX 810 8454015 money mia

Chairman: Morris N Broad (and Chief Executive Officer)

President: Edward P Mahoney (and Chief Operating Officer)

Senior Executive Officers: Robert A Luther (Executive VP and Chief Financial Officer), Thomas Cusick (Executive VP), Nicholas L S Cross (Senior VP), Thomas Duane (Senior VP Savings and Marketing), Barbara Mirabile (Senior VP Operations), M H Fernandez (Senior VP and Secretary)

PRINCIPAL ACTIVITIES: Savings and loans

Financial Information:

	Sep 30 1985	Sep 30 1986
	$'000	$'000
Net income (loss)	(33,240)	50,242
Earnings (loss) per share	($6.76)	$6.11
Shareholders equity	94,710	150,552
Deposits	-	2,094,066
Total assets	2,775,208	2,600,032

No of Employees: 832

AMERICAN SAVINGS BANK, FSB

380 Madison Avenue, New York, NY 10017

Tel: (212) 880-7600

Chairman: John T Morgan (and Chief Executive Officer)

President: William G Lillis (and Chief Operating Officer)

PRINCIPAL ACTIVITIES: Savings bank

Principal Bank: Chemical Bank

Financial Information:

	Dec 31 1986
	$'000
Revenues	339,021
Income before taxes	45,591
Net income	40,570
Earnings per share	$6.11
Common stock	5,980
Retained income	156,269
Shareholders equity	291,380
Deposits	2,981,894
Total assets	3,833,200

No of Employees: 1,070

AMERICAN SEATING CO

901 Broadway NW, Grand Rapids, MI 49504
Tel: (616) 456-0600
Telex: WUT 22632 6 amseco gdr

President: Edward J Clark (and Chief Executive Officer)
Senior Executive Officers: Glen A Harper (Executive VP), Robert S Perry (Senior VP)

PRINCIPAL ACTIVITIES: Manufacture of seats and furniture including motor vehicle seats, office and institutional furniture
Parent Company: Fuqua Industries Inc, Atlanta, GA
Principal Bank: First Union National Bank
Financial Information:

	$'000
Sales revenues	100,000

No of Employees: 1,400

AMERICAN SECURITY CORPORATION

730 15th Street NW, Washington, DC 20013
Tel: (202) 624-4000

Chairman: Daniel J Callahan III (and Chief Executive Officer)
Senior Executive Officers: Douglas T Ledwith (Executive VP and Chief Financial Officer), William C Yowell Jr (Executive VP), Frank B Holloway (Senior VP), John M Sanders (Senior VP), Clement Geitner (Senior VP), Junius S Morgan (Senior VP), Edward J Stark (VP and Secretary)

PRINCIPAL ACTIVITIES: All banking services; insurance; travel interests
Principal Bank: American Security Bank NA
Financial Information:

	Dec 31 1985
	$'000
Net income	25,410
Earnings per share	$2.17
Deposits	3,077,970
Total assets	4,154,600

No of Employees: 1,500

AMERICAN SHIP BUILDING CO

2502 Rocky Point Road, Tampa, FL 33607
Tel: (813) 885-5537

Chairman: George M Steinbrenner III; Vice Chairman: Leonard L Kleinman
President: H Allen Fernstrom (and Chief Executive Officer)
Senior Executive Officers: Philip A McNiff (VP Administration), Edward J Lasko (VP Finance)

PRINCIPAL ACTIVITIES: Ship building and ship repairing; building materials; metal fabrication
Principal Subsidiaries: Nashville Bridge Co; Tampa Shipyards Inc
Principal Bank: First National Bank of Florida
Financial Information:

	$'000
Sales revenues	194,400

No of Employees: 2,260

AMERICAN STANDARD INC

40 W 40th Street, New York, NY 10018
Tel: (212) 703-5100
Telex: 234144; 234116

Chairman: William B Boyd (and Chief Executive Officer); Vice Chairman: Keith D Bunnel
President: William G Roth (and Chief Operating Officer)
Senior Executive Officers: Alan C Root (Senior VP), James C Huntington Jr (Senior VP, Human Resources), Emmanuel A Kampouris (Senior VP, Building Products), Nicholas M Georgitsis (Senior VP, Railway, Auto and Fluid Power Products), Richard H Francis (Senior VP and Chief Financial Officer), James C Workman (Senior VP, Air Conditioning Products)

PRINCIPAL ACTIVITIES: Manufacture and distribution of air conditioning equipment; manufacture of building materials including plumbing equipment; manufacture of automotive and railroad equipment; printing
Trade Names: "TRANE", "TYLER", "AMERICAN-STANDARD", "IDEAL-STANDARD", "STANDARD", "STEELCRAFT", "PERMA-DOOR", "WABCO", "WABCO WESTINGHOUSE", "CLAYTON DEWANDRE"
Principal Subsidiaries: A-S Energy Inc; American Standard International Inc; American Standard Trane Ltd; Amstam Trucking Inc; Mosler Safe Co; Standard Wabco Export Ltd; Trane Co; Trane CAC Inc; Trane Export Inc; Trane Sentinel Inc; Tyler Refrigeration Corp; Tyler Refrigeration Capital; Tyler-Kalt Inc; AH Witt Inc; Wabco Trade Co Inc; Wabco Westinghouse International Co; Wabco Westinghouse International Trade Co; Wabco-Standard Export Ltd; Westinghouse Air Brake Co; Westinghouse Air Brake International Corp
Financial Information:

	Dec 31 1985	Dec 31 1986
	$'000	$'000
Sales revenues	2,912,438	3,324,592
Net income	22,051	188,467
Earnings per share	$0.56	$5.15
Shareholders equity	923,846	840,958

No of Employees: 40,000

AMERICAN STERILIZER CO

2222 W Grandview Blvd, Erie, PA 16514
Tel: (814) 452-3100
Telex: WUT 914495 amsco x eri

Chairman: Henry E Fish (and Chief Executive Officer)
President: B J Walker (and Chief Operating Officer)
Senior Executive Officers: Frank DeFazio (Senior VP Finance and Administration), E R Bindseil (Senior VP), Leo M Storey Jr (Group VP), James A Nally (Group VP), James R Thomas (VP Marketing), W R Miller (VP Research and Development), Richard B Yeager (VP Administration), Lawrence X Webb (VP Manufacturing)

PRINCIPAL ACTIVITIES: Medical and surgical equipment
Principal Subsidiaries: Amsco International Sales Corp
Principal Bank: Morgan Guaranty Trust Company
Financial Information:

	$'000
Sales revenues	257,000

No of Employees: 3,500

AMERICAN STORES CO

PO Box 27447, 709 East South Temple, Salt Lake City, UT 84127-0447
Tel: (801) 539-0112

Chairman: L S Skaggs; Vice Chairman: Richard G Dunlop (and Treasurer)
President: Thomas A King (and Chief Operating Officer)
Senior Executive Officers: Thomas H Sunday (Executive VP and General Counsel), Michael T Miller (Senior VP Public

Relations), Victor Lund (Senior VP), Mike Miller (VP), Robert Salmon (VP), Alan D Stewart (VP)

PRINCIPAL ACTIVITIES: Retailing of food and drugs through superdrug centers, drug/food stores, food stores and drugstores
Principal Subsidiaries: Alpha Beta Company; Skaggs Companies Inc; Rea & Derrick Inc; Acme Markets Inc, Buttery Food Stores; Jewel Food Stores; Osco Drug Inc; Sav-on-Drugs Inc; Skaggs Alpha Beta Inc; Star Market Company
Principal Bank: First Interstate Bank
Financial Information:

	Dec 31 1985 $'000	Dec 31 1986 $'000
Sales revenues	13,889,530	14,021,484
Net income	154,470	144,528
Earnings per share	$4.11	$3.79
Shareholders equity	761,810	1,094,520

No of Employees: 129,000

AMERICAN SYNTHETIC RUBBER CORPORATION

PO Box 32960, Louisville, KY 40232
Tel: (502) 448-2761
Telex: TWX 810 535 3329 asrc lou

Chairman: Dake W Dodrill (and President)
Senior Executive Officers: William R Tennill (VP Finance, Secretary and Treasurer), Gene Trott (VP Technical), Donald Schmidt (VP Manufacturing)

PRINCIPAL ACTIVITIES: Production of synthetic rubber
Principal Bank: Citizens Fidelity Bank and Trust Co (Louisville)
Financial Information:

	$'000
Sales revenues	80,000

Principal Shareholders: W R Grace Co; Michelin Corp
No of Employees: 300

AMERICAN TARA CORPORATION

5667 New Peachtree Road, Atlanta, GA 30341
Tel: (404) 452-7521
Telex: WUT 707 320 amer tara cham

Chairman: Albert M Bridell
President: Robert J Bridell
Senior Executive Officers: Robert A Slad (Executive VP), Jack Pfeiffer (VP), Mak Kawano (VP), Alex Sartini (VP)

PRINCIPAL ACTIVITIES: Production of carbon paper and carbon inks
Principal Banks: Continental Illinois National Bank; Trust Company of Chicago
Financial Information:

	$'000
Sales revenues	50,000

No of Employees: 300

AMERICAN TELEPHONE & TELEGRAPH CO AT&T

550 Madison Avenue, New York, NY 10022
Tel: (212) 605-5500

Chairman: James E Olson; Vice Chairmen: Charles Marshall, Morris Tanenbaum, Randall L Tobias (and Chairman and Chief Executive Officer, AT&T Communications and Information Systems)
President: Robert E Allen (and Chief Operating Officer)
Senior Executive Officers: John E Berndt (President and Chief Executive Officer, AT&T International, Inc), James R Billingsley (Senior VP Federal Regulation), W Frank Blount (President Network Operations Group), Michael A Brunner (Executive VP Federal Systems), Harold W Burlingame (Senior VP Personnel), Vittorio Cassoni (Senior VP Data Systems Division), Robert M Kavner (Senior VP and Chief Financial Officer), Marilyn Laurie (Senior VP Public Relations and Employee Information), Gerald M Lowrie (Senior VP Public Affairs), John M Nemecek (Executive VP Components and Electronic Systems), John T O'Neill (Executive VP Network Systems Products), Alfred C Partoll (Senior VP External Affairs), Victor A Pelson (President General Markets Group), Ian M Ross (President AT&T Bell Laboratories), John L Segall (Senior VP Corporate Strategy and Development), John R Smart (Senior VP Business Sales), Alexander C Stark Jr (Senior VP Communications Systems), Thomas R Thomsen (President AT&T Technology Systems Group), Paul M Villiere (Executive VP Network Systems Marketing and Customer Operations), E Wayne Weeks Jr (President AT&T Network Systems Group), Sam R Willcoxon (President Business Markets Group), John D Zeglis (Senior VP and General Counsel), Lydell L Christensen (Corporate VP and Secretary), C Perry Colwell (Corporate VP and Controller), S Lawrence Prendergast (Corporate VP and Treasurer)

PRINCIPAL ACTIVITIES: AT&T's business activities-from reserch and development, through manufacturing and network operations, to marketing, sales and service-are focused on providing solutions to meet customer needs for the movement and management of information . The company is building on its strength in network design and systems engineering to develop data networking solutions for customers that will help them to connect their equipment and information sources through fully integrated systems that they can direct and control themselves. To make AT&T a truly international business, the company is establishing itself in key global markets by working with-and through-strategic overseas partners. The company has been reorganized into business units that serve the needs of businesses, consumers, telephone companies and other communications suppliers. Services and products include voice, data and image telecommunication services; telephone products, ranging from voice instruments to complex switching and transmission systems; computers for integrated networks and for stand-alone uses; and components for high technology products and systems.
Principal Subsidiaries: AT&T Communications; AT&T Technology Inc; ATP&T Communications and Information Systems; American Transtech Inc; AT&T International Inc; AT&T Bell Laboratories Inc; AT&T Network Systems; AT&T Credit Corporation; Actuarial Sciences Associates; AT&T Foundaton
Financial Information:

	Dec 31 1985 $'000	Dec 31 1986* $'000
Sales revenues	34,417,000	34,087,000
Income before taxes	2,546,000	121,000
Net income	1,557,000	139,000
Preferred dividends	110,000	86,000
Dividends per common share	$1.20	$1.20
Earnings per common share	$1.37	$0.05
Common stock	1,069,000	1,072,000
Retained income	5,081,000	3,934,000
Shareholders equity	14,633,300	13,550,000

*Results for 1986 were significantly affected by major charges for business restructuring, an accounting change and other actions, which reduced net income by $1.7 billion. The actions are designed to strengthen the company and make it more competitive, building a base for greater returns to shareowners in the future.

No of Employees: 316,900

AMERICAN THREAD CO

High Ridge Park, Stamford, CT 06905
Tel: (203) 329-8111
Telex: TWX 7104741750

Chairman: A G Hilton
President: M L Morgan
Senior Executive Officers: J W Calby (VP Industrial Thread Sales), R L Cothran (VP Manufacturing), R V Budnick (VP Finance)

PRINCIPAL ACTIVITIES: Manufacture of yarns of cotton and synthetic fibers and threads; market leaders in spun polyester
Parent Company: Tootal Group plc, Manchester, UK
Principal Bank: The Connecticut Bank and Trust Company
Financial Information:

	$'000
Sales revenues	150,000

No of Employees: 3,500

AMERICAN TRADING AND PRODUCTION CORPORATION

Blaustein Building, Baltimore, MD 21203
Tel: (301) 685-4230

Chairman: Marton K Blaustein (and Chief Executive Officer); Vice Chairman: David Hirschhorn
President: Louis B Thalheimer
Senior Executive Officers: Robert Ihrie (Senior VP), J W Weiss (Senior VP and Chief Financial Officer), Charles Koblenz (Senior VP), Samuel R Wells Jr (Senior VP and General Manager, Real Estate Subsidiaries), Charles E Payton (VP and General Manager, Oil and Gas Division), William A Collinge (VP and Treasurer), William D Savitsky (VP and Controller), Paul W McGillicuddy (VP Employee Relations), Alan G Choate (VP Law and Secretary)

PRINCIPAL ACTIVITIES: Exploration and production of oil and natural gas; interests in shipping and real estate; manufacture of housewares and giftware
Principal Subsidiaries: American Trading Real Estate; American Trading Transportation Co; Lamination Specialties Inc
Principal Bank: Union Trust Co of Maryland
Financial Information:

	$'000
Sales revenues	150,000

No of Employees: 1,300

AMERICAN TRANSIT CORPORATION

120 S Central Avenue, St Louis, MO 63105
Tel: (314) 726-9200

President: D A Richter
Senior Executive Officers: H C Ashby (Executive VP, Administration and Secretary), Arnold Burkhart (Executive VP Operations), Gerald Hausman (VP Bus Sales), Eugene Tarkoff (VP and Assistant Secretary), Bill Weist (VP Part Sales), Don Boyles (VP Airport Services and Sightseeing) Alan Woolard (VP Treasurer and Controller)

PRINCIPAL ACTIVITIES: Holding company with interests in bus services and the manufacture and sale of bus parts
Parent Company: Chromalloy American Corporation, St Louis, MO
Financial Information:

	$'000
Sales revenues	106,000

No of Employees: 2,500

AMERICAN UNIFORM CO

Parker Street NE, Cleveland, TN 37311
Tel: (615) 476-6561
Telex: WUT 558341 amuniform cend

President: Gary K Smith
Senior Executive Officers: T Roy James (VP Sales), Elwood Sperry (VP Merchandising), John P Ward (VP Finance and Secretary)

PRINCIPAL ACTIVITIES: Manufacture of industrial clothing
Financial Information:

	$'000
Sales revenues	72,000

No of Employees: 1,680

AMERICAN UNITED LIFE INSURANCE CO

PO Box 368, Indianapolis, IN 46206-0368
Tel: (317) 263-1877

Chairman: Jack E Reich (and Chief Executive Officer)
President: Jerry D Semler (and Chief Operating Officer)
Senior Executive Officers: Alfred J Stokely (Chairman, Finance Committee), Edgar W Pattison (Executive VP), J W Murphy (Senior VP Corporate Finance), Rodney R Petterson (Senior VP Reinsurance), Leonard D Schutt (Senior VP Investments), Richard F Aller (Senior VP Group Operations), J P Shanahan (Senior VP Pension Operations), John H Barbre (Senior VP Marketing), James R Hetherington (VP Corporate Communications)

PRINCIPAL ACTIVITIES: Life insurance
Principal Bank: American Fletcher National Bank
Financial Information:

	31.12.85
	$'000
Premium income	441,912
Investment income	221,951

No of Employees: 800

AMERICAN V MUELLER DIVISION

6600 W Touhy Avenue, Chicago, IL 60648
Tel: (312) 647-9383

President: David Makarewicz
Senior Executive Officers: Jay Hawthorne (VP Manufacturing), R B Hayes (VP Marketing), Robert Moss (VP Operations), Carl Gatewood (VP Sales)

PRINCIPAL ACTIVITIES: Manufacture and distribution of medical supplies and equipment
Parent Company: American Hospital Supply Corporation, Evanston, IL
Principal Bank: Harris Trust and Savings Bank
Financial Information:

	$'000
Sales revenues	100,000

No of Employees: 500

AMERICAN WATER WORKS COMPANY INC

3908 Kennett Pike, PO Box 3539 Greenville Branch, Wilmington, DE 19807
Tel: (302) 656 1681

Chairman: Samuel H Ballam Jr
President: James V Lafrankie
Senior Executive Officers: Loren D Melendorf (Executive VP), J James Barr (Treasurer), Henry A Riddle Jr (Secretary)

PRINCIPAL ACTIVITIES: Supply of water
Principal Subsidiaries: Alton Water Co Inc; American Water Works Sv Co Inc; Kentucky-American Water Co; Maryland Water Works Co Inc; California-American Water Co; Clinton Water Works Co; Commonwealth Water Co Inc; Davenport Water Co; Greenwick Water System Inc; Bristol County Water Co; Connecticut American Water Co; Dedham Water Co; New York-American Water Co Inc; Wannacomet Water Co; Hershiey Water Co; Huntington Water Corp; Illinois-American Water Co; Indiana-American Water Co; Keystone Water Co; Missouri-American Water Co; Monmouth Consolidated Water Co; New Jersey Water Co; Ohio American Water Co; Paradise Valley Water Co; Riverton Consolidated Water Co;

Salisbury Water Supply Co Inc; St Joseph Water Co; Tennessee American Water Co Inc; Virginia American Water Co Inc; West Virginia Water Co; Western PA Water Co

Financial Information:

	$'000
Sales revenues	430,000

No of Employees: 3,660

AMERICAN WELDING & MFG CO

100 Dietz Road, Warren, OH 44481
Tel: (216) 393-2531
Telex: WUT 982455 amer wel war

Chairman: John P Lynn
President: D R Fountain (and Chief Executive Officer)
Senior Executive Officers: Forrest W Johnson (VP and General Manager, Industrial Products Division), Paul E Emmerling (VP Sales and Marketing, Industrial Products Division), Richard H Reddinger (Controller)

PRINCIPAL ACTIVITIES: Metal welding and fabrication of building products; aircraft parts and engines
Parent Company: Hoover Universal Inc, Arbor, MI
Principal Bank: Bank One of Eastern Ohio
Financial Information:

	$'000
Sales revenues	85,000

No of Employees: 650

AMERICAN WESTERN CORPORATION

1208 W Elkhorn, PO Box 5009, Sioux Falls, SD 57117
Tel: (605) 334 0334

Chairman: John L Mulligan (and Chief Executive Officer)
President: Rodney D Skillman
Senior Executive Officers: Lawrence J Isom (Executive VP), Jonathan E Summerton (Executive VP), Daniel K Afdahl (VP, Secretary and Treasurer)

PRINCIPAL ACTIVITIES: Manufacture of a range of plastic products
Principal Bank: First Bank of South Dakota
Financial Information:

	$'000
Sales revenues	48,370

No of Employees: 500

AMERICAN WOOLEN COMPANY

7290 NW 32nd Street, Box 521399, Miami, FL 33152
Tel: (305) 594-0001
Telex: 4940944 Merino

Chairman: Richard S Marcus (and Treasurer)
President: Richard S Marcus (and Treasurer)
Senior Executive Officers: Leonard S Marcus (Secretary)

PRINCIPAL ACTIVITIES: Textile manufacture; fabrics for household furnishing and high performance fabrics for specialized applications; wool, cotton and synthetic blankets, upholstery fabrics, drapery fabrics
Principal Bank: Florida National Bank
Financial Information:

	Dec 30 1987 $'000
Sales revenues	60,000

No of Employees: 450

AMERICARE HEALTH CORPORATION

2600 V Street, Sacramento, CA 95818
Tel: (916) 456 7000

Chairman: James J Schubert
President: George Deubel (and Chief Executive Officer)
Senior Executive Officers: L Arno Lejnieks (VP), R Steven Shean (VP and Chief Financial Officer), Steven R Tough (VP Operations), S R Robertson (VP)

PRINCIPAL ACTIVITIES: Healthcare services
Financial Information:

	$'000
Revenues	87,000

No of Employees: 430

AMERIFIRST FEDERAL SAVINGS & LOAN ASSOCIATION

One SE Third Ave, Miami, FL 33131
Tel: (305) 577-6100

Chairman: Thomas R Bomar (also Chief Executive Officer)
President: Carlos Garcia-Velez
Senior Executive Officers: William H Walker III (Vice Chairman and Secretary), Robert W Benner (Executive VP Finance), Sherry Barrat (Senior VP Retail Banking), Vivian A Decker (Senior VP Marketing), Joyce A Denny (Senior VP Consumer Lending), Richard M Hattler (Senior VP Commercial Banking), C Stephen Kinnear (Senior VP and Treasurer), Richard L Labbe (VP and Controller), W Hamilton Hayes (VP Personnel)

PRINCIPAL ACTIVITIES: Banking services, savings and loans
Principal Subsidiaries: AmeriFirst Development Corp; AmeriFirst F L Trust Co; AmeriFirst Mortgage Corp; AmeriFirst Securities Corp
Principal Bank: Southeast Bank
Financial Information:

	Sep 30 1986 $'000
Net (loss)	(47,847)
Stockholders equity	104,466
Deposits	2,827,009
Total assets	4,082,464

No of Employees: 2,373

AMERITRUST CORPORATION

900 Euclid Avenue, Cleveland, OH 44101
Tel: (216) 687-5000
Telex: WUT 980198 ameritrust clv

Chairman: Jerry V Jarrett (and Chief Executive Officer); Vice Chairman: Benjamin H Paddock
President: James D Rode
Senior Executive Officers: John F Miller (Senior Executive VP), Larry Glasscock (Group Executive VP), Peter R Osenar (Group Executive VP), Frederick W Ramsey II (Executive VP), Robert L Yoder (Executive VP and Chief Financial Officer), E William Haffke (Executive VP), Andrew P Strada (Senior VP and Comptroller), George T Sutherland (Senior VP), Peter G Kratt (Secretary)

PRINCIPAL ACTIVITIES: AmeriTrust Corporation is a bank holding company with total assets at year end 1985 of $7.8 billion. It is among the most strongly capitalized of the 100 largest US banking companies. Its principal subsidiary is AmeriTrust Company National Association, one of the nation's major regional banks, headquartered in Cuyahoga County, Ohio, with branch systems in major population centers throughout the state. Other subsidiaries maintain offices in Indiana, Illinois, Texas, Florida and New York. Through its 120 banking offices, AmeriTrust Company National Association offers a full range of banking services on a local, regional, national and international basis to individuals and business customers. In addition to the bank, the corporation also owns a non-voting limited partnership interest in Central Bankcorporation, Inc, a Colorado bank holding company
Principal Subsidiaries: AmeriTrust Company, N.A.

Financial Information:

	Dec 31 1986 (12 mths) $'000	Jun 30 1987 (6 mths) $'000
Income (loss) before taxes	110,013	(57,695)
Net income (loss)*	88,480	(37,140)
Dividends	34,878	19,786
Dividends per share	$1.72	$0.47
Earnings (loss) per share	$4.28	($0.88)
Common stock	69,499	70,200
Retained income	530,854	473,928
Shareholders equity	828,200	775,729
Deposits	7,972,168	8,457,462
Total assets	11,068,113	10,567,528

*In June, 1987, AmeriTrust added an extra $78,344,000 to its provision for loan losses, the greatest portion of which was allocated to the international loan portfolio. This action was taken in response to recent developments in regard to bank loans to troubled countries. In addition, Central Bancorporation, Inc, a Denver-based multi-bank holding company in which AmeriTrust has an economic interest, recorded a loss for the quarter resulting from a special provision for loan losses of $29,485,000 and write-downs of certain other assets of $8,350,000. As a result of the extra provision recorded by AmeriTrust and the actions taken by CBI, earnings for AmeriTrust were reduced by $81,190,000 or $1.93 per share

No of Employees: 5,180

AMERIWEST FINANCIAL CORPORATION

6501 Americas Parkway, Albuquerque, NM 87110
Tel: (505) 889-1000

Chairman: James T Graves (and Chief Executive Officer)
President: Douglas M Brown (and Chief Operating Officer)
Senior Executive Officers: Kenneth T Nagle (Senior VP and Chief Financial Officer)

PRINCIPAL ACTIVITIES: Savings, loans and other financial services
Principal Subsidiaries: Albuquerque Federal Savings and Loan; AmeriWest Corp; AmeriWest Homes; Amrock Enterprises; Energy Engineering Inc; AmeriWest Mortgage Securities Corp; Independent Southwest; Inter-Mountain Constructors Inc

No of Employees: 640

AMERON, INC

4700 Ramona Boulevard, PO Box 3000, Monterey Park, CA 91754
Tel: (213) 268-4111
Telex: 421274 AMERONMYPK

President: Lawrence R Tollenaere (and Chief Executive Officer)
Senior Executive Officers: Roger F Barrett (Senior VP, Finance and Administration), William R Dana (Senior VP, Technology), Kenneth J Pace (VP, Communications and Marketing Services), Richard H Jenner (VP and Treasurer), William W Craven (VP, Employee Relations), John S Volpe (VP, Manufacturing), D A Hausmann (Group VP), David W Thomas Jr (Group VP), Thomas J Keefe (Group VP), Javier Solis (VP and Secretary)

PRINCIPAL ACTIVITIES: Large diameter concrete pressure pipe; high performance protective coatings; product finishes; protective linings; fiberglass pipe and fittings; steel and concrete traffic and lighting poles; concrete construction products; steel and wire construction and manufacturing products; equipment fabrication; steel rod and billets
Trade Names: Bondstrand, T-Lock, Amercoat, Dimetcote, Nu-Klad, Tideguard, Amerlock, Amershield
Principal Subsidiaries: Ameron BV (Netherlands); Ameron Canada Inc; Ameron do Brasil; American Pipe and Construction International (Colombia); Ameron (Pte) Ltd (Singapore); Ameron (UK) Ltd; Amercoat Espana SA (Spain); Amercoat Mexicana (Mexico); Ameron Gulf Ltd (United Arab Emirates); Ameron Saudi Arabia Ltd; Bondstrand, Ltd (Saudi Arabia); CIM-Spunline (Brazil); Fuji Bonstrand Co Ltd (Japan); Gifford-Hill-American (Texas); Oasis-Ameron Ltd (Saudi Arabia); Tamco (California); Tubolining SA (France)
Principal Bank: Morgan Guaranty Trust Co
Financial Information:

	Nov 30 1985 $'000	Nov 30 1986 $'000
Sales revenues	305,315	314,705
Income before taxes	9,425	8,931
Net income	12,551	13,022
Common dividends	3,812	4,443
Dividends per common share	$0.80*	$0.92*
Earnings per share	$2.63*	$2.70*
Common stock	11,959	12,111
Retained income	115,565	124,144
Shareholders equity	133,433	143,457

*prior year amounts have been restated to reflect a two-for-one exchange of stock effective March 25, 1986

No of Employees: 3,000

AMERON PROTECTIVE COATINGS DIVISION

201 N Berry Street, Brea, CA 92621
Tel: (213) 625-7742
Telex: WUT 655342 ameron brea

President: James F Slatic
Senior Executive Officers: P S Nathan (VP and General Manager, Americas, Asia), Anton V Landen (VP and General Manager, Europe, Africa, Middle East), Raymond E Foscante (VP Technical)

PRINCIPAL ACTIVITIES: Manufacture of protective coatings and linings for industrial applications
Parent Company: Ameron Inc
Principal Bank: First Interstate Bank
Financial Information:

	$'000
Sales revenues	75,000

No of Employees: 650

AMES CO

PO Box 1774, Parkersburg, WV 26101
Tel: (304) 424-3000
Telex: WUT 869422 o ames pkb

Chairman: Douglas E Cochran
President: Richard G Mason
Senior Executive Officers: D R Langfitt (VP Finance, Secretary and Treasurer), I R Phillips (VP Manufacturing), J T Baxley (VP Sales

PRINCIPAL ACTIVITIES: Manufacture of garden tools

Parent Company: H M Acquisition Corp
Principal Bank: Mellon Bank
Financial Information:

	$'000
Sales revenues	80,000

No of Employees: 1,000

AMES DEPARTMENT STORES INC

2418 Main Street, Rocky Hill, CT 06067
Tel: (203) 563 8234

Chairman: Herbert Gilman (and Chief Executive Officer)
President: Gerald Kanter (and Chief Operating Officer)
Senior Executive Officers: Kenneth H Cooper (Executive VP), Charles H Lytle (Executive VP), Earl M Spector (Executive VP, Real Estate and Legal and Secretary), Lawrence H Gofberg (Senior VP and General Merchandise Manager), John Kearney (Senior VP and Director Store Operations), Eugene Senecal (Senior VP, Management Information Systems), Stewart J Shapiro (Senior VP Distribution), Ralph M Schulansky (Senior VP Finance and Administration and Chief Financial Officer)

PRINCIPAL ACTIVITIES: Retail department stores
Principal Subsidiaries: ADK Inc; Matthews and Boucher; G C Murphy Co; Eastern Retailers Service Corp; Joseph Leavitt Warehousing Co; Andrew Lewis Importing Corp; Northeast Carriers Inc
Principal Bank: Shawmut Worcester County Bank
Financial Information:

	Dec 31 1986 $'000
Sales revenues	1,888,471
Net income	27,129
Earnings per share	$0.73
Shareholders equity	394,205

No of Employees: 25,000

AMETEK, INC

Station Square Two, Paoli, PA 19301
Tel: (215) 647-2121
Telex: 834637 AME PAOLI

Chairman: Dr John H Lux (and Chief Executive Officer)
President: Robert L Noland
Senior Executive Officers: Corporate Officers: John P Dandalides (Executive VP, Eastern Operations), Gerald G Loehr (Executive VP, Western Operations), Wallace E Cowan (Secretary of the Company), Robert W Yannarell (Treasurer and Assistant Secretary), Allan Kornfeld (Senior VP and Chief Financial Officer), Otto W Richards (Comptroller), Murray A Luftglass (Senior VP, Corporate Development), Robert A Russel (VP, Marketing), Neal R Stark (VP, Compliance). Operating Officers: Senior Vice Presidents:- Walter E Blankley, Roger K Derr, Gary M Noland, Charles E Rausch, Henry Schladen Jr. Vice Presidents:- Lee J Barthold, H Dudley Barton, Harold E Cosson, Herman C Koch, Thomas Laidlaw, Morris P Molinero, Raymond J Moore, William H Spencer, Donald L Whitehead

PRINCIPAL ACTIVITIES: Industrial manufacturer. Operating groups: Precision Instruments; Electromechanical Devices; Process Equipment; Industrial Materials
Trade Names: Instruments: US Gauge, Panalarm. Motors: Lamb Electric. Robot Submarines: SCARAB, SCORPIO, GEMINI. Computerspacegraphic Plotters: Houston Instrument. Packaging Materials: MICROFOAM. Replacable-Cartridge Water-filters: Plymouth. Composite Materials: Haveg, Carsonite
Principal Subsidiaries and Divisions: Precision Instruments: Controls Division; Mansfield & Green Division; McCrometer Division; Panalarm Division; SIOC (Canada); SCAMA Ltd (UK); Panalarm GmbH (Austria); Rodan Division; Thermox Instruments Division; US Gauge Division. Electro-Mechanical: Eastport International; Houston Instrument Division; L.A. Die Casting Division; Lamb Electric Division; Offshore Research and Engineering Division; Straza Division; Ametek Offshore (Scotland) Co (Scotland, UK). Industrial Materials: Aluminum Extrusion Division; Carsonite Division; Composite Materials Division; Haveg Division; Microfoam Division; Plymouth Products Division; Special Filaments Division; Westchester Plastics Division. Process Equipment: Heat Transfer Equipment Division; Process Equipment/US Bellows Division; Schutte & Koerting Division; Valley Foundry Division. Research and Development: Computer Research; Electrical Systems; Electronic Systems; Microelectronics; Photovoltaics/Applied Materials
Principal Bank: Chase Manhattan NA; Chemical Bank
Financial Information:

	Dec 31 1985 $'000	31 Dec 1986 $'000
Sales revenues	502,789	568,493
Income before taxes	54,464	61,768
Net income	34,935	36,584
Dividends	18,684	21,975
Dividends per share	$0.85	$1.00
Earnings per share	$1.59	$1.66
Common stock*	22,016	21,905
Retained income	203,988	249,066
Shareholders equity	219,693	231,067

*shares outstanding in thousands, decrease as company bought in some

No of Employees: 6,700

AMFAC FOODS INC

6600 SW Hampton Street, Portland, OR 97223
Tel: (503) 620-3720

President: Ronald H Dykehouse
Senior Executive Officers: Frederick J Bolthouse (Senior VP), W W Phillips Jr (Senior VP and Controller), John Geist (Senior VP)

PRINCIPAL ACTIVITIES: Food processing including cheese and vegetable processing; frozen food products
Parent Company: Amfac Inc
Financial Information:

	$'000
Sales revenues	500,000

No of Employees: 6,400

AMFAC, INC

44 Montgomery Street, San Francisco, CA 94104
Tel: (415) 772-3300

Chairman: Henry A Walker Jr
President: Ronald R Sloan (and Chief Executive Officer)
Senior Executive Officers: John E Gomena (Executive VP), Thomas L Braje (Senior Chief VP Financial Officer), Daniel A Curry (Senior VP and General Counsel), Harry Matte (Senior VP), John R Stamps (Senior VP), Richard R Bacigalupi (VP, Controller), Coy F Baugh (VP and Treasurer), Ronald H Dykehouse (Chairman and CEO), Donald C Onasch (Chairman and CEO), Richard A Naille II (Chairman and CEO), Richard L Griffith (Chairman and CEO), Keith V Mabee (VP Public Corporate Communications)

PRINCIPAL ACTIVITIES: Wholesale trade in pharmaceutical products and electrical products; food production and processing; retail trade; hotels and resorts; agriculture; sugar production; real estate management
Principal Subsidiaries: Amfac Distribution Corporation; Amfac Foods Inc; Amfac Stores Inc; Amfac Hotels & Resorts Inc; Amfac Hawaii Inc

Financial Information:

	Dec 31 1985 $'000	Dec 31 1986 $'000
Sales revenues	1,921,975	1,962,204
Income (loss) before taxes	45,527	(15,687)
Net income (loss)	17,912	(66,599)
Earnings (loss) per share	$1.09	($4.27)
Common stock	16,636,622	16,679,635
Shareholders equity	423,581	404,038

Principal Shareholders: Fort Associates Limited Partnership (9.66%); Southeastern Asset Management Inc (9.17%); Robert E Torray & Co (7.8%); Batterymarch Financial Management (6.3%); Sasco Capital Inc (5.06%) (Proxy Statement-May 14 1987)
No of Employees: 21,000

AMFESCO INDUSTRIES INC
2 Amfesco Drive, Plainview, NY 11803
Tel: (516) 694-7272
Telex: WUT 144 603 amfesco plvw

Chairman: David Greenblatt (and Chief Executive Officer)
Senior Executive Officers: Joseph Kantrowitz (Senior VP and Chief Financial Officer), Eric S Weil (Senior VP), Michael Greenblatt (VP and Treasurer)

PRINCIPAL ACTIVITIES: Manufacture of footwear
Principal Subsidiaries: American Felt Slipper Co; Amfesco-Duramil Div Inc; Rest Right Slipper Co Inc
Principal Bank: Irving Trust Company
Financial Information:

	$'000
Sales revenues	69,500

No of Employees: 2,850

AMGEN INC
1900 Oak Terrace Lane, Thousand Oaks, CA 91320
Tel: (805) 499-5725
Telex: 4994440

Chairman: George B Rathmann (and President)
Senior Executive Officers: Gordon Binder (Senior VP and Chief Financial Officer), Robert Weist (Senior VP, Administration), Harry Hixson, Ph.D. (Senior VP, Business Operations), Daniel Vapnek, Ph.D. (VP Research), Marvin Caruthers, Ph.D, (VP Research, Boulder)

PRINCIPAL ACTIVITIES: Amgen Inc is a major biotechnology company which is poineering the development of novel and innovative products based on advances in recombinant DNA and molecular biology for the human health care, animal health care and specialty chemical markets. Since its inception, Amgen has focused on building an integrated health care business based on recombinant DNA technology. The Company's primary focus has been on pharmaceutical product development. During this past year, Amgen continued to establish itself as one of the premier companies within the biotechnology industry. The Company's demonstrated successes at bringing its products out of the laboratory and into clinical testing distinguishes it as one of the most productive of the emerging biotechnology based pharmaceutical companies. With six of its products undergoing human clinical testing, Amgen continues on its plan to build a new generation pharmaceutical company based on the advances of molecular biology
Trade Names: Projects/Products currently under development: Human Pharmaceuticals:- Erythropoietin, Granulocyte colony stimulating factor, Hepatitis B vaccine, Consensus interferon, Interleukin 2, Gamma interferon, Granulocyte-macrophage colony stimulating factor, Epidermal growth factor, Platelet-derived growth factor, Fibroblast growth factor, Insulin-like growth factor 1. Human Diagnostics:- DNA probes, Immunoassays. Animal Health Care:- Bovine somatotropin, Porcine somatotropin. Poultry: Specialty Chemicals, Indigo, Certain vitamins, Certain enzymes, Certain hydrocarbons
Principal Subsidiaries: Amgen Development Inc
Principal Bank: Investment Banks: PaineWebber; Kidder Peabody; Montgomery Securities
Financial Information:

	Mar 31 1986 $'000	Mar 31 1987 $'000
Sales turnover	23,359	34,722
Income before taxes	672	1,595
Net income	548	1,137
Earnings per share	$0.05	$0.08
Common stock*	11,644	14,933
Shareholders funds	80,580	83,959
*number of share in thousands		

No of Employees: 300

AMKOR ELECTRONICS INC
Box 801, Valley Forge, PA 19482
Tel: (215) 666-9040
Telex: ITT 476 1041 amkor b ntw

Chairman: James J Kim
President: Anthony P Perrotta
Senior Executive Officers: John Boruch (VP), Frank J Marcucci (VP Finance and Administration), John E Schaefer (VP)

PRINCIPAL ACTIVITIES: Electrical and electronic products
Principal Bank: Korea Exchange Bank
Financial Information:

	$'000
Sales revenues	100,000

No of Employees: 100

AMOCO CHEMICALS COMPANY
200 E Randolph Drive, Chicago, IL 60601
Tel: (312) 856-3200

President: R D Cadieux
Senior Executive Officers: R M Winters (VP Marketing, Chemical Intermediates), J V Peterson (VP Plastic Products and Specialty Chemicals), S J Wommack (VP Technical and Development), B M Otto (VP Planning and Administration), R C Jagel (VP Manufacturing and Engineering), F G Andrusko (VP Olefins and Polymers), G A Nersesian (VP President Amoco Chemicals, Far East), W A Miller (VP Business Development), G E Light (VP Managing Director, Europe), J A Maish (VP Central and South America Region), W R Hutchinson (Treasurer)

PRINCIPAL ACTIVITIES: Manufacturer of chemical intermediates, synthetic fabrics and fibers, styrenic products, petroleum additives, oil production chemicals
Trade Names: Torlon, Amofoam, Marquesa Lana, Amocor (all Registered Trademarks)
Parent Company: Amoco Corporation, Chicago, IL
Financial Information:

	$'000
Sales revenues	2,800,000

No of Employees: 13,000

AMOCO CORPORATION (FORMERLY STANDARD OIL COMPANY INDIANA)
200 E Randolph Drive, Chicago, IL 60601
Tel: (312) 856-6111
Telex: 25-3731
Fax: (312) 856-2450

Chairman: Richard M Morrow (Chairman of the Board)
President: H Laurance Fuller (Member of the Board)
Senior Executive Officers: *James W Cozad (Vice Chairman of the Board and Chief Financial Officer), *Arthur E Rasmussen, *Richard D Wood, *Walter R Peirson (Executive VP), *Robert H Malott, *Ruth S Block, *Karl D Bays, *Richard J Ferris, *Frederick G Jaicks, *John H Bryan Jr, *Walter E Massey, *Richard H Leet (Executive VP), *Patrick J Early (President-

Amoco Production Company), Robert D Cadieux (President-Amoco Chemical Company), Lawrason D Thomas (President-Amoco Oil Company), Rady A Johnson (VP Public and Government Affairs), Edward A Mason (VP-Research), L Bates Lea (VP and General Counsel), Frederick S Addy (VP-Finance), R Wayne Anderson (VP-Human Resources), Richard L Fisher (VP-Government Affairs), John R Lyman (VP-Planning, Economics, and Development), William K Hutchinson (VP and Controller), Ronald E Callahan (Secretary), James E Allard (VP and Treasurer), *Member of Board of Directors

PRINCIPAL ACTIVITIES: Exploration, development, and production of crude oil and natural gas. Refining, marketing, and transporting of petroleum and related products. Manufacture and sale of chemical products

Trade Names: Major Trademarks of Amoco Corporation and Subsidiaries:-AMOCO, AMOCO with design of torch & oval, OMEGA, RAINBO, AMERICAN, PREMIER, PERMALUBE, ULTIMATE, LDO, PANASOL, INDOPOL, TORLON, AMOLUBE, POLY-BAC, PROPEX, PATLON, MARQUESA LANA, SYNERA, SOLAREX, ACTIONBAC, AMOCOR, ARTCOR, CERTICARE, AMOPAVE, AMOFOAM, SOFT-CELL, SOFT-PAK, AMOCAMS, SNACKER, AMOWEVE, WELCHEM, DRILLAID, WELLAID, AMOCO SILVER, THORNEL, UDEL, RADEL, ZENDEL

Principal Subsidiaries: Amoco Company; Amoco Production Company; Amoco Oil Company; Amoco Chemical Company

Principal Banks: Transfer Agents and Registrars:- The Chase Manhattan Bank; The First National Bank of Chicago; The National Trust Company (Toronto)

Financial Information:

	Dec 31 1985	31 Dec 1986
	$'000	$'000
Sales revenues*	28,537,000	20,034,000
Income before taxes	3,811,000	1,588,000
Net income	1,953,000	747,000
Cash dividends	872,000	849,000
Dividends per share	$3.30	$3.30
Earnings per share	$7.42	$2.91
Common stock	2,234,000	1,875,000
Retained income	12,142,000	9,610,000
Shareholders equity	11,588,000	11,324,000

*includes consumer excise taxes

No of Employees: 46,775

AMOSKEAG BANK SHARES INC

875 Elm Street, Manchester, NH 03105
Tel: (603) 624 3200

Chairman: William S Bushnell (and President and Chief Executive Officer); Vice Chairman: Milton Machinist

Senior Executive Officers: Eugene H Tellier Jr (Senior VP and Chief Financial Officer), John H Giffin Jr (VP, Secretary and Subsidiary Officer), Howard W Keegan (Subsidiary Officer), John S Perley (Subsidiary Officer), Donald H Sargent (VP and Treasurer)

PRINCIPAL ACTIVITIES: Banking

Principal Subsidiaries: Amoskeag Bank

Principal Bank: Amoskeag National Bank & Trust Co

Financial Information:

	Dec 31 1985
	$'000
Revenues	121,300
Net income	13,830

No of Employees: 690

AMOSKEAG COMPANY

Prudential Center Suite 4500, Boston, MA 02199
Tel: (617) 262 4000

Chairman: Albert B Hunt

President: Joseph B Ely II (and Chief Executive Officer and Subsidiary Officer)

Senior Executive Officers: F C Dumaine (Chief Executive), James M Fitzgibbons (Executive VP), W R Mitchell Jr (VP Treasurer, Chief Financial Officer and Subsidiary Officer), Frederic P Melzer (Secretary), M W Stewart (VP Investments)

PRINCIPAL ACTIVITIES: Operation of railroad services

Principal Subsidiaries: Bangor & Aroostook Railroad Co; Moores Falls Corp; Westville Homes Corp

Financial Information:

	$'000
Sales revenues	39,900

No of Employees: 520

AMP INC

PO Box 3608, (Mail Stop 176-43), Harrisburg, PA 17105

Tel: (717) 564-0100

Telex: 842313 AMP INC HBG A

Chairman: Walter F Raab (and Chief Executive Officer); Vice Chairman: Harold A McInnes

President: James E Marley

Senior Executive Officers: W Bennett Conner (VP, Director of Marketing), Gerald F Englehart (Executive VP), Benjamin Savidge (VP and Chief Financial Officer), Joseph P Sweeney (VP, Technology), Mark L Miller (Treasurer), Hugo A Walfred (Secretary)

PRINCIPAL ACTIVITIES: AMP Incorporated is a producer of electrical/electronic terminations, interconnection and switching devices. Product lines include: terminals and splices, printed circuit board connectors, multiple position connectors, coaxial connector, fiber optic and EMI/RFI connectors and filters, electronic packaging and interconnection devices, switches and programming systems, touch entry devices and a complete line of customer application tools and machines. AMP products and technological capabilities serve customers worldwide in a wide range of industries-communications, aerospace and military, industrial and commercial electronics, computer and office equipment, semiconductor, consumer goods, transportation and electrical equipment. AMP serves over 30,000 manufacturers of electrical and electronic equipment, and tens of thousands of customers who install, maintain and upgrade that equipment.

Trade Names: AMP is a copyright for AMP Incorporated

Principal Subsidiaries: Pamcor Inc (Puerto Rico); AMP Keyboard Technologies Inc; AMP Products Corp; Carroll Touch Inc; AMP Packaging systems Inc; Mark Eyelet; AMP SA Argentina (Argentina); AMP do Brasil Ltda (Brazil); AMP of Canada Ltd (Canada); AMP de Mexico SA (Mexico); AMP Österreich Handelsges mbH (Austria); AMP Belgium (Belgium); AMP Danmark (Denmark); AMP Finland Oy (Finland); AMP de France SA (France); AMP of Great Britain Ltd (UK); AMP-Holland BV (Netherlands); AMP Ireland Ltd (Eire); AMP Italia Spa (Italy); AMP Norge A/S (Norway); AMP Española SA (Spain); AMP Svenska AB (Sweden); AMP (Schweiz) AG (Switzerland); AMP (Deutschland) GmbH (Germany); Australian AMP Pty Ltd (Australia); AMP Products Pacific Ltd (Hong Kong); AMP (Japan) Ltd (Japan); AMP Korea (Korea); New Zealand AMP Ltd (New Zealand); AMP Singapore Pte Ltd (Singapore); AMP Taiwan (Taiwan)

Principal Bank: Chase Bank

Financial Information:

	Dec 31 1985 $'000	Dec 31 1986 $'000
Sales revenues	1,636,100	1,933,100
Income before taxes	192,500	294,000
Net income	108,000	164,300
Dividends	77,700	80,000
Dividends per share	$0.72	$0.74
Earnings per share	$1.00	$1.52
Common stock	12,480	12,480
Retained income	1,016,600	1,101,000
Shareholders equity	996,900	1,134,900

No of Employees: 22,000

AMPACET CORPORATION

250 S Terrace Avenue, Mt Vernon, NY 10550
Tel: (212) 597-5700
Cable: CHEMPROD NYK
Telex: 62588 CHEMPROD NYK

President: David S Weil
Senior Executive Officers: Howard England (VP Manufacturing), Martin Fernandi (VP Marketing), Donald Fleischman (VP Finance)

PRINCIPAL ACTIVITIES: Manufacture of plastic products
Trade Names: MASTERCOLOR, POLYGRADE, KROMAPLAST
Principal Subsidiaries: Ampacet Europe, Messancy, Belgium
Principal Banks: Chase Manhattan Bank; Manufacturers Hanover
Financial Information:

	$'000
Sales revenues	150,000

No of Employees: 425

AMPAD CORPORATION

104 Lower Westfield Road, Holyoke, MA 01040
Tel: (413) 536-3511

Chairman: Francis J Guiliano (and President and Chief Executive Officer); Vice Chairman: Henry A Fifield
Senior Executive Officers: Robert Antrasian (Executive VP), David J Cairns (VP Sales and General Manager), William J Callahan (VP Marketing), Jerre Hoffman (VP National Accounts), George D Becher Jr (VP Engineering and Construction)

PRINCIPAL ACTIVITIES: Manufacture of paper products for domestic and office use
Principal Bank: Shawmut First Bank & Trust Co
Financial Information:

	$'000
Sales revenues	115,000

No of Employees: 710

AMPAL-AMERICAN ISRAEL CORPORATION

10 Rockefeller Plaza, New York, NY 10020
Tel: (212) 586 3232

Chairman: Ephraim Reiner
President: Michael Jaffe
Senior Executive Officers: Yair Youtzis (Assistant VP Operations), Hillel Peled (VP Finance and Treasurer), Shlomo Recht (VP Accounting), Alan L Shaffer (Controller), Lawrence Lefkowitz (VP Legal and Secretary), David Mersky (VP Marketing)

PRINCIPAL ACTIVITIES: Provision of credit and financial services to Israel
Parent Company: Bank Hapoalim B.M.
Financial Information:

	Dec 31 1985 $'000
Revenues	91,280
Net income	6,100

AMPCO METAL

PO Box 2004, Milwaukee, WI 53201
Tel: (414) 645-3750
Telex: WUT 26623

President: Kimbell J Norman
Senior Executive Officers: James J Seibert (VP Marketing), Patrick A Tully (VP Operations), Kenneth A Warren (VP Finance)

PRINCIPAL ACTIVITIES: Metal castings; wire
Parent Company: Ampco Pittsburgh Corporation
Financial Information:

	$'000
Sales revenues	60,000

No of Employees: 700

AMPCO-PITTSBURGH CORPORATION

700 Porter Bldg, Pittsburgh, PA 15219
Tel: (412) 456-4400

Chairman: Marshall L Berkman (and Chief Executive Officer); Vice Chairman Irving J Berkman
President: Robert A Paul (and Chief Operations Officer)
Senior Executive Officers: Ernest G Siddons (Senior VP Finance and Treasurer), James Huber (VP Purchasing), Edward H Moores (VP Legal and Secretary), Sidney Wasser (VP Controller), John R Young (VP Administration)

PRINCIPAL ACTIVITIES: Railroad cars, metal fabrication, steel products, machine tools and agricultural equipment
Principal Subsidiaries: Ampco-Pittsburgh Overseas Corp; Buffalo Forge Co; Aerofin Corp; Greenville Steel Car Co; Pittsburgh Forgings Co; Union Electric Steel Corp; New Castle Industries Inc; Union Rolls Corp; Vulcan Inc; Parnell Precision Products Inc; Shepard Niles Inc
Principal Bank: Mellon Bank
Financial Information:

	Dec 31 1985 $'000
Sales revenues	461,343
Net income	3,434
Earnings per share	$0.36
Shareholders equity	192,280

No of Employees: 5,270

AMPEX CORPORATION

401 Broadway, Redwood City, CA 94063
Tel: (415) 367-2011
Telex: WUT 348464 ampex pwc 3

Chairman: Arthur H Hausman
President: Roy H Ekrom (and Chief Executive Officer)
Senior Executive Officers: Charles A Steinberg (Executive VP and Chief Operations Officer), David A Bocchini (VP and Chief Financial Officer)

PRINCIPAL ACTIVITIES: Manufacture of Winchester disk drives, video display terminals and storage back-up systems for use with personal computers
Trade Names: Ampex, Alar, PC Megastore
Parent Company: The Signal Companies Inc, La Jolla, CA
Principal Bank: Wells Fargo Bank
Financial Information:

	$'000
Sales revenues	500,000

No of Employees: 6,650

AMR CORPORATION

PO Box 619616, Dallas/Fort Worth Airport, TX 75261-9616
Tel: (817) 355-1234

Chairman: Robert L Crandall (and President, Chief Executive Officer)
Senior Executive Officers: Richard A Lempert (Senior VP and General Counsel), John C Pope (Senior VP Finance), Donald

J Cary (Senior VP Airline Planning), Max D Hopper (Senior VP Information Systems), Michael W Gunn (Senior VP Marketing), Richard D Pearson (Senior VP Field Services), Gene E Overbeck (Senior VP Government Relations), Wesley G Kaldahl (Senior VP International)

PRINCIPAL ACTIVITIES: Holding company with interests in passenger airline services; ground handling services for the airlines; direct marketing; information services
Principal Subsidiaries: AMR Services Corporation; A A Direct Marketing Corporation; AMR Information Services
Financial Information:

	Dec 31 1985	Dec 31 1986
	$'000	$'000
Sales revenues	6,131,028	6,018,175
Income before taxes	519,046	418,662
Net income	345,840	279,132
Earnings per share	$5.94	$4.63
Retained income	1,092,110	1,367,669
Shareholders equity	2,180,914	2,484,896

No of Employees: 54,300

AMREP CORPORATION

10 Columbus Circle, New York, NY 10019
Tel: (212) 541 7300

Chairman: Howard W Friedman (and Chief Executive Officer)
President: Lawrence T Perlmutter (and Chief Operating Officer)
Senior Executive Officers: Daniel Friedman (Senior VP), Rudolph J Skalka (VP), Mitchell Roberts (Secretary)

PRINCIPAL ACTIVITIES: Real estate development; magazine and book distribution
Principal Subsidiaries: Albuquerque Utilities Corp; Kable News Co Inc
Financial Information:

	$'000
Sales revenues	89,000

No of Employees: 800

AMRON CORPORATION

525 Progress Avenue, Waukesha, WI 53186
Tel: (414) 547-1661

President: Arthur J Williams
Senior Executive Officers: Arthur W Nesbitt (VP), Phillip F Lange (VP Contract Administration), Richard R Peters (VP and General Manager), Charles Lubochinski (VP), Ronald G Strackbein (VP), Steven B Lapin (VP and Assistant Secretary), Carl G Dobratz (Secretary and Treasurer), Paul G Brett (VP Engineering)

PRINCIPAL ACTIVITIES: Armaments manufacture
Parent Company: Nasco International Inc
Principal Bank: Independence Bank of Waukesha
Financial Information:

	$'000
Sales revenues	59,000

No of Employees: 640

AMSOUTH BANCORPORATION

PO Box 11007, Birmingham, AL 35288
Tel: (205) 326-5771

Chairman: John W Woods (and Chief Executive Officer)
President: William A Powell Jr
Senior Executive Officers: Thomas J Tucker (Executive VP), Maria B Campbell (Executive VP), Douglas B Nunnelley (Executive VP)

PRINCIPAL ACTIVITIES: Banking
Principal Subsidiaries: AmSouth Bank; AmSouth Bank International; AmSouth Capital Inc; AmSouth Financial Corp; AmSouth Mortgage Co Inc; AmSouth of LA Inc; First National Bank
Principal Bank: AmSouth Bank NA

Financial Information:

	Dec 31 1985	Dec 31 1986
	$'000	$'000
Net income	46,510	61,012
Earnings per share	$2.77	$3.13
Shareholders equity	-	385,428
Deposits	3,740,350	4,449,827
Total assets	5,227,040	5,942,706

No of Employees: 4,325

AMSTAR CORPORATION

1251 Avenue of the Americas, New York, NY 10020
Tel: (212) 489-9000
Telex: 12-5863

Chairman: Howard B Wentz Jr (President and Chief Executive Officer)
Senior Executive Officers: F F Coons (Senior VP), Charles W Bradbury Jr (VP and Controller), John C Reynolds (VP and General Counsel), Raymond C Guth (VP and Secretary)

PRINCIPAL ACTIVITIES: Sugar refining; corn wet milling; prepared foods; packaging materials; portable electric hand tools; industrial equipment
Parent Company: Amstar Technical Products Co; Milwaukee Electric Tool Co; Duff-Norton Co Inc
Principal Subsidiaries: Amstar Technical Products Co Inc; Duff-Norton Co Inc; Milwaukee Electrical Tool Corp
Financial Information:

	Jun 30 1986
	$'000
Sales revenues	1,321,502
Net income	34,713
Shareholders equity	163,798

No of Employees: 7,700

AMSTED INDUSTRIES INC

3700 Prudential Plaza, Chicago, IL 60601
Tel: (312) 645-1700
Telex: WUT 254187 amsted ind cgo

President: Robert H Wellington (and Chief Executive Officer)
Senior Executive Officers: Frank Marold (VP), Warren W Rasmussen (VP), Gordon R Lohman (VP), O J Sopranos (VP) Gerald K Walter (VP)

PRINCIPAL ACTIVITIES: Cast steel products; railroad equipment; pipes
Financial Information:

	Sep 30 1986
	$'000
Sales revenues	700,664

No of Employees: 8,800

AMTROL INC

1400 Division Road, West Warwick, RI 02893
Tel: (401) 884-6300
Telex: WUT 927716 amtrol wrlok

Chairman: Chester H Kirk (and Chief Executive Officer); Vice Chairman: Kenneth L Kirk
Senior Executive Officers: Edward Cooney (VP Financial Planning and Treasurer), John J McCann (Chief Operating Officer), Albert N D'Amico (Chief Finance Officer and Treasurer)

PRINCIPAL ACTIVITIES: Heating, ventilation and refrigeration equipment
Principal Subsidiaries: Automatic Metal Blanking Co
Principal Bank: Fleet National Bank
Financial Information:

	$'000
Sales revenues	75,000

No of Employees: 1,000

AMWAY CORPORATION
7575 East Fulton Road, Ada, MI 49355
Tel: (616) 676-6000
Telex: 432-0146 Amway Corporation

Chairman: Jay Van Andel
President: Richard M DeVos
Senior Executive Officers: William W Nicholson (Chief Operating Officer), Otto Stolz (Executive VP), Roger E Beutner (Senior VP), Nan Van Andel (VP-Communications) Dick DeVos (VP-International), Casey Wondergem (Director-Public Relations)

PRINCIPAL ACTIVITIES: Amway Corporation manufactures and/or markets more than 300 products in such fields as home care, housewares, nutrition and diet, personal care, commercial lines and a Personal Shoppers Catalog. The products are sold through personal selling by independent contractors who own and operate their own independent Amway businesses. Amway is one of the largest direct selling firms in the world, with more than one million independent distributors.
Trade Names: Amway, Nutrilite, Artistry Cosmetics
Principal Subsidiaries: Amway itself operates in more than 44 countries and territories, with the world headquarters in Ada, Michigan. Subsidiaries are:- Nutrilite Products Inc; the Amway Grand Plaza Hotel (Grand Rapids, Michigan); The Peter Island Resort (British Virgin Islands); Mutual Satellite Service.
Principal Bank: Michigan National Bank
Financial Information:

	$'000
Retail sales*	1,200,000

*estimated figure

No of Employees: 7,000 worldwide

ANACOMP INC
11550 North Meridian Street, PO Box 40888, Indianapolis, IN 46240
Tel: (317) 844 9666

Chairman: Louis P Ferrero (and President and Chief Executive Officer)
Senior Executive Officers: Thomas R Simmons (Executive VP and Chief Operating Officer), William C Ater (VP Administration and Secretary), Neil M Bardach (VP, Chief Financial Officer and Treasurer), Dennis R Johnson (VP), Marion G Tomlin (VP and Group President), Donald L Viles (VP and Controller), J Mark Woods (Executive VP), Paul R Chapman (VP Finance), K Gordon Fife (VP Tax and Accounting), John B Gray Jr (VP)

PRINCIPAL ACTIVITIES: Provision of data processing services
Principal Subsidiaries: Info Optics Inc
Financial Information:

	$'000
Revenues	123,120

No of Employees: 2,000

ANADITE, INC
5301 Roosevelt Road, Chicago, IL 60650
Tel: (312) 656-8558

Chairman: Felix T Grossman (and President and Chief Executive Officer)
Senior Executive Officers: Ronald E Bailitz (Treasurer and Chief Financial Officer), Ralph B Perry III (Secretary)

PRINCIPAL ACTIVITIES: Cast metal products; metal processing
Principal Bank: Bank of America NT & SA
Financial Information:

	$'000
Sales revenues	57,700

No of Employees: 1,000

ANALOG DEVICES, INC
Rte One Industrial Park, Norwood, MA 02062
Tel: (617) 329-4700
Telex: WUI 6817042 anand uw

Chairman: Ray Stata (and President)
Senior Executive Officers: Joseph M Hinchey (Senior VP Finance), Lawrence T Sullivan (Senior VP Corporate Development), Jerald G Fishman (Group VP Components), Melvin J Sallen (Group VP Sales), Heinrich F Krabbe (VP New Business Development), Arnold Kanarick (VP Human Resources), A G Sterling (VP Strategic Planning)

PRINCIPAL ACTIVITIES: Production of components for electronic and data processing systems
Principal Bank: Bank of Boston
Financial Information:

	$'000
Sales revenues	322,400

No of Employees: 4,760

ANALOGIC CORPORATION
8 Centennial Drive, Peabody, MA 01961
Tel: (617) 246-0300
Telex: 681-7021; 94-9307 ANAPBDY

Chairman: Bernard M Gordon (and President and Chief Executive Officer); Vice Chairman: Bernard M Friedman
Senior Executive Officers: John A Tarello (Senior VP, Administration), Edmund Becker (VP), Ross Brown (VP Operations), Daniel Abenheim (VP), Leopold Neumann (VP), Richard Powell (VP), Julian Soshnick (VP and General Counsel), Thomas J Dempsey (VP)

PRINCIPAL ACTIVITIES: Manufacturer high-speed, high-precision measurement, signal translation, and data manipulation equipment
Trade Names: Monitroller, Measurometer, Digi-Cal, APL, AP400, NucMed
Principal Subsidiaries: 3H Industries, Inc; Computer Design & Applications, Inc; Analogic GmbH (Germany); Analogic Limited (UK)
Principal Bank: Bank of New England
Financial Information:

	Jul 31 1985	Jul 31 1986
	$'000	$'000
Sales revenues	132,019	148,211
Income before taxes*	14,334	18,769
Net income	9,940	10,075
Earnings per share net	$0.53	$0.53
Common stock	990	1,008
Retained income	78,255	88,330
Shareholders equity	142,185	157,335

*and extraordinary credit

No of Employees: 1,800

ANALYSTS INTERNATIONAL CORPORATION
7615 Metro Boulevard, Minneapolis, MN 55435
Tel: (612) 835 2330

President: Frederick W Lang (and Chief Executive Officer)
Senior Executive Officers: Victor C Benda (Executive VP), John T Paprocki (VP and Treasurer), Thomas R Mahler (Secretary and General Counsel)

PRINCIPAL ACTIVITIES: Provision of computer services including software
Principal Bank: National Bank of Detroit
Financial Information:

	$'000
Sales revenues	44,000

No of Employees: 800

ANCHOR BRUSH CO

209 DeSoto Ave, Morristown, TN 37814
Tel: (615) 586-9711

President: B F Bouldin
Senior Executive Officers: Fred Fassler (VP Manufacturing), Bob Slaughter (VP Sales), C J Kyker (VP and Controller)

PRINCIPAL ACTIVITIES: Manufacture of toothbrushes and nailbrushes; scrub brushes for surgeons; medical products; molded plastic bottles and cosmetic packaging
Parent Company: North American Philips Corporation
Principal Bank: Continental Illinois National Bank and Trust Company of Chicago
Financial Information:

	$'000
Sales revenues	60,000

No of Employees: 1,150

ANCHOR CONTINENTAL, INC

2000 South Beltline Blvd, Columbia, SC 29205
Tel: (803) 799-8800
Telex: TWX 810 666 2105 anchorcont db

President: Curtis H Easter Jr
Senior Executive Officers: Calvin H Shuford (Senior VP), William Roberts (Executive VP), E H Milner (VP Sales), Richard Butcher (VP Finance), Grover Pilot (VP Engineering), William Norwood (VP Human Resources), Lacy Hayes (VP Manufacturing)

PRINCIPAL ACTIVITIES: Manufacture of pressure sensitive tapes
Parent Company: Camber Holdings Inc
Principal Bank: South Carolina National Bank
Financial Information:

	1986
	$'000
Sales revenues	80,000
Income before taxes	4,500
Net income	3,000
Shareholders equity	10,100

Principal Shareholders: Curtis H Easter Jr; William L Roberts
No of Employees: 800

ANCHOR FASTENERS

PO Box 2548, Waterbury, CT 06720
Tel: (203) 574-1800
Telex: WUT 962410 anchorfast wby

President: Vincent Largay
Senior Executive Officers: P D Becker (VP Engineering), Alfred Kachergis (VP Sales), Edward Wilson (VP Operations), James M Barkley (Secretary and Treasurer)

PRINCIPAL ACTIVITIES: Manufacture of fasteners for industrial applications
Parent Company: Buell Industries Inc
Principal Bank: The Colonial Bank and Trust Company
Financial Information:

	$'000
Sales revenues	50,000

No of Employees: 600

ANCHOR GLASS CONTAINER CORPORATION

One Anchor Place, 1100 Anchor Street, Tampa, FL 33607-1765
Tel: (813) 870-6120

Chairman: Vincent J Naimoli (and President and Chief Executive Officer)
Senior Executive Officers: D Richard Barry (VP), Richard J Brown (VP), James W Carpenter (VP), Raymond H Cox (VP), Richard D Everett (VP, General Counsel and Secretary), James S Luci (VP), James H Smith (VP and Chief Financial Officer), Franklin E Whitmore (VP), Edward M Jonas (Comptroller), Gary L Matter (Treasurer)

PRINCIPAL ACTIVITIES: Manufacture of glass products, principally containers
Principal Bank: Wells Fargo
Financial Information:

	Dec 31 1985	Dec 31 1986
	$'000	$'000
Sales revenues	564,673	587,492
Income before taxes	13,760	40,722
Net income	7,744	22,137
Dividends	1,500	-
Dividends per share	$0.15	-
Earnings per share net	$0.73	$1.84
Common stock	50	133
Retained income	7,945	29,934
Shareholders equity	8,963	58,366

Principal Shareholders: As of September 30, 1987: Fidelity Management & Research Company 992,400 shares and Vincent J Naimoli 841,864 shares
No of Employees: 9,900

ANCHOR HOCKING CORPORATION

109 N Broad Street, Lancaster, OH 43132-0001
Tel: (614) 687-2111

President: J R Topper (and Chief Executive Officer)
Senior Executive Officers: Corporate Officers: J R Topper (President and Chief Executive Officer), F T Carlin (Senior VP Finance and Administration), R P Ellwood (Senior VP Household Products Group), J E Biafore (VP and General Manager-Consumer and Industrial Division), L E Gloyd (VP and General Manager, Hardware Products Group and President, Amerock Corporation), R L Hollaway (VP Hardware Products Group and Packaging Products Group), S C Hurley III (VP and Treasurer), D J Libert (VP and General Counsel), E L Rowe (VP and President, Carr-Lowrey Division), D B Sutton (VP and General Manager-Packaging Products Group), D R Timberlake (VP and President Anchor Hocking Foodservice & Trading Co), J D Voss (VP and General Manager-International Division), R H Seeley (VP, Secretary and Associate General Counsel), D S Snyder (VP and Controller). Divisional Officers: R W Armen (VP and General Manager, Metal Closure Division), C J Arnsbarger (VP, Director of Public Affairs), W K Berry (VP Sales and Marketing-Industrial Markets-Consumer and Industrial Division), H S Bobroff (VP Marketing-Consumer and Industrial Markets), K G Burchmore (VP Carr-Lowrey Division), R C Darling (VP Marketing-Household Products), R T Dawson (VP Human Resources), J S Eaton (VP Hardware Products and Packaging Products), J S Eaton (VP Sales-Consumer and Industrial Division), J E Goodman (VP Sales-Consumer and Industrial Division), R H Horn (President and General Manager Plastic Products Division), D N Ingram (VP Engineering and Development-Consumer and Industrial Division), V B Martin Jr (VP International Division), D D Powell (VP and Comptroller- Household Products Group), W J Rolo (VP Operations-Consumer and Industrial Division), W M Schaar (VP Factories Manager-Consumer and Industrial Division), D E Shane (VP Sales-Packaging Products Group), W C Swift (VP Marketing-Packaging Products Group), M L Weil (VP Administrative Services). Subsidiary and Division Officers: R F Lehner (VP Finance-Anchor Hocking Foodservice & Trading Co), W J Marks (President Anchor Cap & Closure Corp of Canada, Ltd), E C Schams (VP and General Manager-Moldcraft Division), R I Shrode (VP and General Manager-Gibson Division), E B Stevens (President and Chief Executive Officer-Embassy Industrial Corporation), L H Storck (VP and General Manager-Anchor Hocking Foodservice & Trading Co), A F Tomburo (VP Technical-Gibson Division), D A Sell (President and General Manager-Amerock, Inc), J S Waddell (VP and General Manager-Shenango China), A E Lewis (Manager Corporate Public Relations), S M Bussmann (Manager Investor Relations)

PRINCIPAL ACTIVITIES: Manufacture of china, glass and plastic products for domestic and industrial use; container and packaging products; importers of ceramics and domestic hardware.
Principal Subsidiaries: Amerock Corporation; Anchor Hocking Plastic Packaging Inc; Anchor Hocking Puerto Rico Ltd; Brand Manufacturing Company; Capstan Transportation Company; Embassy Industrial Corporation; Gas Transport Inc; Hocking Industries Inc; Hocking Valley Leasing Co; Imperial Arts Corporation; Plastics Inc International; Amerock Inc; Anchor Cap & Closure Corpn of Canada Ltd; Anchor Hocking International Corpn Ltd; Kenneth M Smith Inc; Plasticap Ltd; Premier Plastics Ltd
Financial Information:

	Dec 31 1985	Dec 31 1986
	$'000	$'000
Sales revenues	720,347	757,820
Net income	2,388	6,562
Earnings per share	$0.23	$0.63
Shareholders equity	254,754	247,250

No of Employees: 10,800

ANCHOR SAVINGS BANK
5323 Fifth Avenue, Brooklyn, NY 11220
Tel: (718) 439-7300

Chairman: Donald L Thomas (and Chief Executive Officer); Vice Chairman: Eugene G Schulz Jr (and General Counsel)
President: William G Schneider Jr (and Chief Operating Officer)
Senior Executive Officers: Patricia K Dawley (Executive VP and Secretary)

PRINCIPAL ACTIVITIES: Savings bank
Principal Subsidiaries: Mortgage Resources Inc; Standard of GA Insurance Agency; Suburban Coastal Corp

No of Employees: 2,000

ANDAL CORPORATION
60 Madison Avenue, New York, NY 10010
Tel: (212) 683-9191

Chairman: Andrew J Frankel (and Chief Executive Officer)
President: Alan N Cohen
Senior Executive Officers: Charles R Dickie (VP, General Counsel and Secretary), Stuart B Freeman (VP, Treasurer and Chief Financial Officer, Walter N Kreil Jr (Assistant VP and Controller)

PRINCIPAL ACTIVITIES: Metals trading; manufacture of tin plate and steel tube
Principal Subsidiaries: Olsher Metals Corp; Olsher Metals Processing Corp
Principal Bank: Manufacturers Hanover Trust Co
Financial Information:

	$'000
Sales revenues	41,580

No of Employees: 1,800

ANDERSEN CORPORATION
Foot N 5th Avenue, Bayport, MN 55003
Tel: (612) 439-5150

Chairman: W A Wellman
President: Harold C Meissner
Senior Executive Officers: A D Hulings (Chairman, Executive Committee), Gerry A Hoel (Executive VP Operations), George Hoel (VP Sales), L W Kedrowski (Treasurer and Controller)

PRINCIPAL ACTIVITIES: Manufacture of windows and doors
Principal Bank: First National Bank
Financial Information:

	$'000
Sales revenues	330,000

No of Employees: 2,800

ANDERSEN GROUP INC
1280 Blue Hills Avenue, Bloomfield, CT 06002
Tel: (203) 242 0761

Chairman: Oliver R Grace
President: Francis E Baker
Senior Executive Officers: Ernest P Hodur (Subsidiary Officer), Kenneth T Kelley (VP and General Counsel), Spencer M Vawter (Subsidiary Officer), Timothy E Griffin (Treasurer and Chief Financial Officer), Elmer J Dahl (Secretary)

PRINCIPAL ACTIVITIES: Manufacture of specialty electronic components for commercial, medical and defense applications
Principal Subsidiaries: Andersen Laboratories Inc; Bio Sound Inc; Cardiac Datacorp Inc; Microtime Inc; Seratronics Inc
Financial Information:

	$'000
Sales revenues	43,400

No of Employees: 560

ANDERSON CLAYTON & CO
121 W Florence Blvd, Casa Grande, AZ 85222
Tel: (602) 836-2189
Telex: Wut 762917 anderclay holl

Chairman: T J Barlow (and Chairman of Executive Committee)
President: W F Giunee Jr (and Chief Executicе Officer)
Senior Executive Officers: John L Fichter (Executive VP), J A Atar (VP Commodity Trading), R R Bachman (VP Consumer Products), Roy T Bogan (VP Systems and Computer Services), W M Glasgow (VP Corporate Development)

PRINCIPAL ACTIVITIES: Food products including edible oils and fats; animal feedstuffs; insurance; warehousing services
Trade Names: Quaker Oats Co
Principal Bank: Morgan Guaranty Trust Company
Financial Information:

	Jun 30 1986
	$'000
Sales Revenues	1,056,497
Net income	16,766
Shareholders equity	581,081

ANDERSON CO OF INDIANA (THE)
402 Royal Road, Michigan City, IN 46360
Tel: (219) 872-5150
Telex: WUT 725 419 anderson gary

Chairman: R A Stranahan Jr
General Manager: G M Stace
Other Directors: R C Fox (Director of Manufacturing Services), W H Harbison (Director of Technical Services), C H Murphy (Director of Purchasing), R W Ostrega (Controller), W F Rister (Director of Personnel), J A Mann (Director of Operating Services), W P Fekete (Director of Manufacturing)

PRINCIPAL ACTIVITIES: Motor vehicle components and accessories
Trade Names: ANCO
Parent Company: Champion Spark Plug Company, Toledo, OH
Principal Subsidiaries: Jordan Products, Inc
Principal Bank: United Bank of Grand Junction, Denver, CO

No of Employees: 980

ANDERSON GREENWOOD & CO
5425 S Rice Avenue, Houston, TX 77036
Tel: (713) 668-0631
Telex: WUT 775 219 agco valve hou

Chairman: James H Elder Jr (and President and Chief Executive Officer)
Senior Executive Officers: Gerald A Sears (VP Finance and Chief Financial Officer), Walter W Powell (VP Engineering), G F Bright (VP Sales, Special Projects), Thomas C Dolson (VP Planning and Operations), M E Jones (VP), A W Luedtke (VP

Corporate Development), Christopher B Reale (VP Marketing and Sales)

PRINCIPAL ACTIVITIES: Manufacture of valves
Parent Company: Keystone International Inc
Principal Subsidiaries: Anderson Greenwood International Inc; Anderson Greenwood Europe Inc; Anderson Greenwood USA Inc; Instrumentation Products Inc; Prince Valve Inc; Lumac Inc; Rutherford Co Inc; West Holdings Inc; AG General Agency
Principal Bank: Bank of the Southwest
Financial Information:

	$'000
Sales revenues	76,000

No of Employees: 670

ANDERSON JACOBSON, INC

521 Charcot Avenue, San Jose, CA 95131
Tel: (408) 263-8520
Telex: TWX 910 3380 136 andn jcb snj

Chairman: Raymond E Jacobson (and President)
Senior Executive Officers: Thomas B Zmach (VP), Wayne C Seppeler (VP Operations), Kent M Wilkins (VP and Controller), James W A Jacobson (VP Quality and Product Assurance)

PRINCIPAL ACTIVITIES: Data processing equipment
Principal Bank: Bank of California
Financial Information:

	$'000
Sales revenues	47,000

No of Employees: 460

ANDREW CORPORATION

10500 W 153rd Street, Orland Park, IL 60462
Tel: (312) 349-3300
Cable: WERDNA CHICAGO
Telex: 25-3897; TWX 910 651 33 40 andrew chi

Chairman: E J Andrew
President: Floyd L English (and Chief Executive and Chief Operating Officer)
Senior Executive Officers: George R Forbes (Senior VP, Corporate Staff), Eric Brooker (VP Research and Development), E T Weber (VP Government Group), C R Nicholas (VP Finance and Chief Financial Officer), F R Roddy (VP Commercial Group), H Johnson (VP Corporate Development)

PRINCIPAL ACTIVITIES: Andrew Corporation's principal products include microwave antennas for point-to-point communications systems; antennas and complete earth stations for satellite communication systems, electronic radar and communication reconnaissance systems, special purpose antennas for commercial, government and military end use, coaxial cables, and related ancillary items and services
Trade Names: Heliax
Principal Banks: Continental Illinois National Bank; Trust Company of Chicago
Financial Information:

	Sep 30 1985 $'000	Sep 30 1986 $'000
Sales revenues	215,528	197,659
Income before taxes	24,623	16,353
Net income	14,117	9,518
Earnings per share	$1.41	$0.95
Common stock	10,051	10,078
Retained income	113,878	123,396
Shareholders equity	134,840	144,049

No of Employees: 2,331

ANGELES CORPORATION

10301 West Pico Boulevard, Los Angeles, CA 90064
Tel: (213) 277 4900

Chairman: William H Elliott (and President and Chief Executive Officer); Vice Chairmen: Joseph Cattivera, Richard E Landau, William E Tuthill, Lawrence J Winston
Senior Executive Officers: Robert S Sedor (VP Finance), John C Burrow (Executive VP), Villiga V Butkys (VP Manager Tax), Derek D'Sa (VP and Treausrer), Claudine L Kalin (VP and Secretary), Anna Merguerian (VP), Steven L Tanner (Senior VP and Chief Accounting Officer), Richard A Wollin (Senior VP), Vivian P Wong (VP), Guadaloupe Cabral (VP Finance), Michael H Rothman (VP Finance and Corporate Planning), Walter S Losk (VP Communications)

PRINCIPAL ACTIVITIES: Securities investment managers; broker dealer services; investment product services including management of property and real estate
Principal Subsidiaries: Angeles/Quinoco Securities Inc
Principal Bank: Bank of America
Financial Information:

	$'000
Revenues	192,000

No of Employees: 1,100

ANGELICA CORPORATION

10176 Corporate Square Drive, St Louis, MO 63132
Tel: (314) 991-4150

Chairman: Leslie F Loewe (and Chief Executive Officer); Vice Chairman: John D Levy
President: Earl F Neely (and Chief Operating Officer)
Senior Executive Officers: Lawrence J Young (Executive VP), James E Stetoff (Executive VP), Theodore M Armstrong (Senior VP and Chief Financial Officer)

PRINCIPAL ACTIVITIES: Linen rental services; manufacture of uniforms
Principal Subsidiaries: Angelica Healthcare Services; Life Uniform Co; Southern Service Co
Principal Bank: Centerre Bank
Financial Information:

	$'000
Sales revenues	270,000

No of Employees: 6,700

ANGLO ENERGY LIMITED

71 Murray Street, New York, NY 10007
Tel: (212) 619 4242

Chairman: Peter O Lawson-Johnston; Vice Chairman: Louis Putze
President: Allen F Rhodes (and Chief Executive Officer)
Senior Executive Officers: Kenneth G Reed (Senior VP and Treasurer), Thomas A McKay (VP), Francis J Nestor (VP, General Counsel and Secretary), Richard A Stratton (VP and Controller)

PRINCIPAL ACTIVITIES: Oilfield services
Principal Subsidiaries: Anglo Alaska Construction Inc; Anglo Hearne Co Inc
Financial Information:

	$'000
Sales revenues	91,570

No of Employees: 800

ANHEUSER-BUSCH COMPANIES, INC

One Busch Pl, St Louis, MO 63118
Tel: (314) 577-2000

Chairman: August A Busch III (and President)
Senior Executive Officers: Luke L Meatte (Senior VP), Michael J LaMonica (Senior VP Industry Affairs), Dennis P Long (VP), Jerry E Ritter (VP), Barry H Beracha (VP), Patrick T Stokes (VP), John H Purnell (VP), W R Baker (VP)

PRINCIPAL ACTIVITIES: Brewing; baking; sports and recreational services; railroad operations and repairs

Trade Names: Anheuser-Busch, A & Eagle design, Budweiser, Bud, Bud Light, King of Beers, Michelob, Michelob Light, Michelob Classic Dark, Mich, Busch, Natural Light, LA, King Cobra, Busch Gardens, Dark Continent, Old Country, Adventure Island, Kingsmill, Busch Corporate Centre, Cardinals, Eagle, Honey Roast, Rainbo, Colonial, Earth Grains, El Charrito
Principal Subsidiaries: Anheuser-Busch Inc; Metal Container Corpn; Container Recovery Corpn; Busch Entertainment Corpn; Busch Properties Inc; St Louis Refrigerator Car Co; St Louis National Baseball Club Inc; Anheuser-Busch International Inc; Busch Agricultural Resources Inc; Busch Creative Services Corpn; Civic Center Corpn; Manufacturers Railway Co; Campbell Taggart Inc; Eagle Snacks Inc; Busch Industrial Products Corpn
Financial Information:

	Dec 31 1985	Dec 31 1986
	$'000	$'000
Sales revenues	7,000,300	7,677,200
Net income	443,700	518,000
Earnings per share	$2.84	$1.69
Shareholders equity	2,173,000	2,313,700

No of Employees: 39,770

ANITEC IMAGE TECHNOLOGY CORPORATION
40 Charles Street, PO Box 4444, Binghampton, NY 13902
Tel: (607) 774 3333

Chairman: Gerhard R Andlinger (and President)
Senior Executive Officers: Anthony P Crupi (Senior VP), Carl R Ernst (Senior VP), James H Kruegel (Senior VP and Assistant Secretary), Kenneth L Gottlieb (Senior VP), William A Bellnier (VP), Robert C Kleinbauer (VP), Harry J Boswell (Treasurer), Frank Fotia Jr (Controller), Stephen A Magida (Secretary)

PRINCIPAL ACTIVITIES: Supply of photographic equipment and related products
Financial Information:

	Dec 31 1985
	$'000
Sales revenues	107,370
Net income	9,420

No of Employees: 1,000

ANIXTER BROS, INC
4711 Golf Road, Skokie, IL 60076
Tel: (312) 677-2600
Telex: WUT 289464 anixter sko

Chairman: Alan B Anixter (and Chief Executive Officer); Vice Chairmen: William R Anixter, Bruce Van Wagner, James R Anixter
President: John A Pigott
Senior Executive Officers: John Egan (President Anixter Communications and Product Sales), Raymond J Geraci (VP Advertising), Roland Watkins (VP Engineering), John J Mariana (VP Information Services), Kenneth E Morton (VP Manufacturing), Herbert L Pruzan (VP), William S Race (VP Finance), Albert Smith (VP and Controller)

PRINCIPAL ACTIVITIES: Telephone, telecommunications and television equipment
Principal Subsidiaries: Anixter Financial Corp; Anixter of Texas Inc; Anixter-New Orleans Inc; Anixter-OHM International; Anixter-Pruzan Inc; Anixter-San Francisco Inc; Illinois Cable Corp; OHM International Inc
Principal Bank: The First National Bank of Chicago
Financial Information:

	$'000
Sales revenues	650,950

No of Employees: 2,500

ANR PIPELINE COMPANY
500 Renaissance Center, Detroit, MI 48243
Tel: (313) 496 0200

Chairman: James F Cordes (and President and Chief Executive Officer); Vice Chairman: Kinnie S Smith Jr
Senior Executive Officers: William J Haener (Executive VP), David A Arledge (Senior VP), Daniel F Collins (Senior VP), Michael G Morris (Senior VP), Austin M O'Toole (Senior VP)

PRINCIPAL ACTIVITIES: Supply of natural gas
Parent Company: American Natural Resources Co
Financial Information:

	$'000
Sales revenues	1,980,000

No of Employees: 2,720

ANSUL FIRE PROTECTION
Ansul Fire Protection, Division of Wormald US, Inc
One Stanton Street, Marinette, WI 54143
Tel: (715) 735-7411
Telex: 4941581 ANSULINTL
Fax: (715) 732-3477

Chairman: Geoffrey Davis (and Chief Executive Officer)
President: Marc V Gross (and Chief Operating Officer)
Senior Executive Officers: Philip Alman (VP, Marketing) Larry Christensen (VP, Sales) Robert L Oberle (VP, Operations), Gerald Poquette (Controller), Sara M Lambrecht (Public Relations Manager)

PRINCIPAL ACTIVITIES: Manufacture of fire safety apparatus and related chemicals; fire fighting training services
Trade Names: Ansul, Met-L-X, Ansulite, Ansulex, Plus-Fifty, Checkfire, Autopulse, Automan, Spill-X, Spill-Gun, Sentry
Parent Company: Wormald International, Ltd
Principal Bank: Continental Illinois National Bank & Trust Company of Chicago

Principal Shareholders: Wormald International, Ltd
No of Employees: 650

ANTA CORPORATION
101 N Robinson, One Galleria Tower St 1400, Oklahoma City, OK 73102
Tel: (405) 272-9321
Telex: TWX 910 831 4004 anta corp okc

Chairman: J R Tolbert III (and President, Chief Financial Officer and Treasurer)
Senior Executive Officers: Robert S Savage (Executive VP Operations)

PRINCIPAL ACTIVITIES: Aluminum fabrication; oil and gas exploration; building materials
Financial Information:

	$'000
Sales revenues	185,000

No of Employees: 1,000

ANTHEM ELECTRONICS INC
174 Component Drive, San Jose, CA 95131
Tel: (408) 946 8000

Chairman: Robert S Throop (and Chief Executive Officer)
President: Peyton L Gannaway (and Chief Operating Officer)
Senior Executive Officers: Bobby G Pipkin (Senior VP), Paul Eder (VP, Chief Financial Officer and Secretary)

PRINCIPAL ACTIVITIES: Sale of semiconductors
Principal Bank: Bank of America
Financial Information:

	$'000
Sales revenues	104,500

No of Employees: 250

ANTHONY INDUSTRIES, INC

4900 Triggs Street, City of Commerce, CA 90022

Tel: (213) 268-4877

Telex: WUT 67239 an inds

Chairman: Bernard I Forester (and President and Chief Executive Officer)

Senior Executive Officers: Myron P Anthony (Chairman Executive Committee), John G Templeton (Senior VP), Hilton R Leibow (Senior VP), Richard Rodstein (VP Finance), Marilyn E Lane (VP and Treasurer)

PRINCIPAL ACTIVITIES: Manufacture of sports equipment and clothing

Principal Subsidiaries: Shakespeare Co; Columbia Products Co

Principal Bank: Security Pacific National Bank

Financial Information:

	$'000
Sales revenues	218,000

No of Employees: 2,600

AOI COAL COMPANY

1100 Western United Life Building, Midland, TX 79701

Tel: (915) 683 4701

President: B J Pevehouse (and Chief Executive Officer)

Senior Executive Officers: Robert L Herndon (Senior VP), Loyd Whitley (Senior VP and Treasurer), James Sartori (VP)

PRINCIPAL ACTIVITIES: Mining and marketing of coal

Principal Bank: Mellon Bank

Financial Information:

	$'000
Sales revenues	55,960

No of Employees: 260

AON CORPORATION (FORMERLY COMBINED INTERNATIONAL CORPORATION)

123 North Wacker Drive, Chicago, IL 60606

Tel: (312) 701-3000

Chairman: W C Stone

President: Patrick G Ryan (and Chief Executive Officer)

Senior Executive Officers: Ronald K Holmberg (Executive VP, Chief Administrative Officer), Raymond I Skilling (Executive VP and Chief Counsel), Wallace J Buya (VP and Secretary), H R Powell (Executive VP and Chief Investment Officer), Harvey N Medvin (Executive VP and Chief Financial Officer and Treasurer), George W Lawler (VP and Corporate Internal Auditor), Donald D McDonald (VP and Assistant Treasurer), Bruce L Miller (VP-Information Service), John R Stone (VP-Personnel), James D White (VP and Controller)

PRINCIPAL ACTIVITIES: Aon Corporation is a leading insurance marketing organization with strong market positions in life insurance, accident and health and specialty property/casualty lines. In addition Aon Corporation's insurance brokerage business, the 7th largest in the country, has built a reputation as the premier broker in many of the markets it serves.

Principal Subsidiaries: Combined Insurance Company of America; Union Fidelity Life Insurance Company; Rollins Burdick Hunter Company; Ryan Insurance Group Inc; The Life Insurance Company of Virginia

Principal Bank: First National Bank of Chicago

Financial Information:

	Dec 31 1985 $'000	Dec 31 1986 $'000
Revenues	1,359,824	1,805,626
Premium income	1,027,494	1,303,019
Investment income	172,961	310,614
Income before taxes	230,036	262,710
Net income	181,995	247,249
Common dividends	69,293	72,497
Dividends per common share	$2.14	$2.22
Earnings per share	$5.48	$7.40
Common stock	32,488	32,910
Retained income	847,766	1,021,791
Shareholders equity	972,914	1,142,005
Total assets	3,195,687	5,904,802

No of Employees: 15,000

APACHE CORPORATION

Foshay Tower, Minneapolis, MN 55402

Tel: (612) 332-7222

Telex: TWX 910 5763 129 apachecorp mps

Chairman: Raymond Plank (and Chief Executive Officer)

President: John A Kocur (and Chief Operating Officer)

Senior Executive Officers: J W Cunningham (Executive VP Production), Darrell J Egertson (Executive VP Corporate Development), Albert B Perlin (Senior VP Legal), Henry W See (Senior VP Marketing), G C Hann (VP Product and Program Development), Dean G Newman (VP Employee Relations), Beatrice L Huston (VP and Secretary), James E Kneser (VP Acquisitions), Stanley F Schindler (VP Exploration), Edwin E Cain (VP Government Relations), Donald F Wivchar (VP Producing and Drilling Operations), James R Bauman (VP Wyoming Operations), Roger K Tromanhauser (VP APC Program Management), William Anderson (VP MIS), Roland E Monk (VP Internal Audit), Reggie L Medley (VP), Vincent H Buckley (VP Venture Development), William N Lundberg (VP and Assistant Secretary), William E Sheridan (VP Controller)

PRINCIPAL ACTIVITIES: Oil and gas exploration; financial services; lumber; engineering products

Principal Subsidiaries: Apache Programs Inc; Midwest Walnut Co of IA; S & J Ranch Inc; Ucross Land Co

Financial Information:

	$'000
Sales revenues	130,000

No of Employees: 1,430

APEX INTERNATIONAL ALLOYS, INC

2340 Des Plaines Avenue, Des Plaines, IL 60018

Tel: (312) 297-1360

Telex: WUT 726318 apex alumx dsp

President: Milton Richmond

Senior Executive Officers: Robert R Goble (VP); Craig A Davis (Secretary)

PRINCIPAL ACTIVITIES: Aluminum and aluminum products

Parent Company: Alumax Inc

Principal Bank: Bank of America

Financial Information:

	$'000
Sales revenues	100,000

No of Employees: 400

APL CORPORATION

6917 Collins Avenue, Miami Beach, FL 33141

Tel: (305) 866-7771

Chairman: Victor Posner (and President and Chief Executive Officer); Vice Chairman: Steven Posner

Senior Executive Officers: Leonard Leifert (Executive VP and Chief Operations Officer), A H Fishman (Executive VP), Donald J Glazer (Executive VP), Jack Coppersmith (Senior VP and Chief Financial Officer), Renee Mottram (Senior VP),

Melvin R Colvin (VP), John Luby (VP), Orville Sims (VP), Michael Fishman (VP), Phillip A Smalley (VP Human Resources), Harry T Clew (VP), Tracy Posner (VP and Assistant Secretary-Treasurer), Charles L Nielsen Jr (VP and Treasurer), Edward A Christensen (VP and Secretary), Stephen A Hurwitz (VP Controller and Assistant Secretary)

PRINCIPAL ACTIVITIES: Manufacture of tissue paper, packaging and giftware
Parent Company: NVF Company
Principal Bank: Continental Bank
Financial Information:

	$'000
Sales revenues	263,500

No of Employees: 3,140

APOGEE ENTERPRISES, INC

7900 Xerxes Avenue S, Minneapolis, MN 55431
Tel: (612) 835-1874

Chairman: Russell H Baumgardner; Vice Chairman: Laurence J Niederhofer
President: Donald W Goldfus (and Chief Executive Officer)
Senior Executive Officers: Gerald K Anderson (Executive VP), James L Martineau (VP), William G Gardner (Treasurer)

PRINCIPAL ACTIVITIES: Building materials and fittings; glass products
Trade Names: Harmon Glass, Wausau Metals Corporation; Viracon, Inc; Nanik
Principal Subsidiaries: Viracon, Inc; Wausau Metals Corporation; Harmon Glass; Harmon Contract (WSA Inc)
Principal Bank: First National Bank of Minneapolis
Financial Information:

	Jan 3 1985	Feb 28 1987
	$'000	$'000
Sales revenues	249,570	279,097
Income before taxes	15,682	16,142
Net income	8,233	8,523
Dividends	1,342	1,516
Dividends per share	$1.01	$0.112
Earnings per share	$0.62	$0.64
Common stock*	12,362	13,698
Shareholders equity	55,381	62,561

*and Paid in Capital

Principal Shareholders: Russell H Baumgardner, Chairman
No of Employees: 2,902

APOLLO COMPUTER INC

15 Elizabeth Drive, Chelmsford, MA 01824
Tel: (617) 256-6600
Telex: TWX 710 343 6803 apollo chfd

President: J W Poduska Sr (and Chief Executive Officer)
Senior Executive Officers: C P Spector (Executive VP and Chief Operating Officer), Richard P Bond (Senior VP and Chief Financial Officer), R M Antonuccio (VP), B J Fidelman (VP), J M Greata (VP), D L Nelson (VP)

PRINCIPAL ACTIVITIES: Data processing equipment
Financial Information:

	$'000
Sales revenues	295,600

No of Employees: 450

APPLE BANK FOR SAVINGS

205 East 42nd St, New York, NY 10017
Tel: (212) 573-8000

Chairman: Jerome McDougal (also President and Chief Executive Officer)
Senior Executive Officers: Spiros Voutsinas (Executive VP), Mrs Joyce Wynn (VP Personnel)

PRINCIPAL ACTIVITIES: Savings bank
Financial Information:

	Dec 31 1986
	$'000
Net income	22,487
Earnings per share	$4.90
Stockholders equity	176,584
Deposits	2,451,764
Total assets	2,699,331

No of Employees: 930

APPLE COMPUTER, INC

20525 Mariana Avenue, Cupertino, CA 95014
Tel: (408) 996-1010

Chairman: John Sculley (and President and Chief Executive Officer)
Senior Executive Officers: William V Campbell (Executive VP Sales), Delbert W Yocam (Executive VP and General Manager, Apple II Division), Albert A Eisenstat (VP, Secretary and General Counsel), David J Barram (VP and Chief Financial Officer), J J Marano (VP), Michael Muller (VP and General Manager, Accessory Products), Michael Spindler (VP and General Manager, Europe), Roy Weaver Jr (VP Field Operations), Kenneth R Zerbe (VP Americas, Far East and Africa)

PRINCIPAL ACTIVITIES: Manufacture of personal computers and associated services and products
Principal Bank: Bank of America
Financial Information:

	Sep 30 1985	Sep 30 1986
	$'000	$'000
Sales revenues	1,918,280	1,901,898
Net income	61,223	153,963
Earnings per share	$0.99	$2.39
Shareholders equity	550,487	694,087

No of Employees: 4,300

APPLETON PAPERS INC

825 E Wisconsin Avenue. Appleton, WI 54912
Tel: (414) 734-9841
Telex: WUT 2627 52 ap co b aple

Chairman: John W Turner (and Chief Executive Officer)
President: Dale H Schumaker
Senior Executive Officers: James E Grabow (VP Finance), Paul G Meier (VP Human Resources), Ronald C Jezerc (VP Research and Development Engineering), E F McKinney (VP, Secretary and General Counsel), Lawrence J Casey (VP Manufacturing), Daniel W McIntosh (VP Marketing and Sales), John L Tucker (VP Inforamtion Services)

PRINCIPAL ACTIVITIES: Manufacture of paper
Parent Company: Batus Inc
Principal Bank: Valley Bank
Financial Information:

	$'000
Sales revenues	693,000

No of Employees: 3,600

APPLIED BIOSYSTEMS INC

850 Lincoln Center Drive, Foster City, CA 94404
Tel: (415) 570 6667

Chairman: Sam H Eletr (and Chief Executive Officer)
President: Andre Marion (and Chief Operating Officer)
Senior Executive Officers: Nancy T Montgomery (VP Finance), Kathy A San Roman (Secretary), James M Schlater (VP Marketing)

PRINCIPAL ACTIVITIES: Manufacture of biochemicals, reagents and scientific instruments for diagnostic applications

Financial Information:

	$'000
Sales revenues	36,000

No of Employees: 270

APPLIED DIGITAL DATA SYSTEMS, INC

100 Marcus Blvd, Hauppauge, NY 117887
Tel: (516) 231-5400
Telex: TWX 510227 9886 appldigit haup

President: David G Laws (and Chief Executive Officer)
Senior Executive Officers: A W Saunders (VP Operations and General Manager), R T White (VP and General Manager, Systems), E Schenk (VP and General Manager, Displays), W F Miller (VP Finance)

PRINCIPAL ACTIVITIES: Products include a broad line of computer video-display terminals and small business computer systems
Parent Company: NCR Corporation
Principal Bank: Marine Midland Bank
Financial Information:

	$'000
Sales revenues	80,000

No of Employees: 600

APPLIED MAGNETICS CORPORATION

75 Robin Hill Road, Goleta, CA 93117
Tel: (805) 683-5353
Telex: 910 334-1195
Answerback: AMC Goleta CAL

Chairman: Harold R Frank; Vice Chairman: Ben J Newitt (and Chief Executive Officer)
President: William R Anderson
Senior Executive Officers: G P Sprague Jr (Executive VP and Chief Financial Officer), Robert Tetherow (Executive VP), Thomas W Russell (VP), Raymond P Le Blanc (VP, Secretary and General Counsel), O M Fundingsland (VP, Sales and Marketing), Louis W Rayer (VP-General Manager, Materials)

PRINCIPAL ACTIVITIES: The Company designs, manufactures and markets magnetic heads used in tape, rigid disk and floppy-disk drives and sells primarily to OEM's in the peripheral memory segment of the computer industry
Principal Subsidiaries: Applied Magnetics Belgium; Applied Magnetics Ireland; Applied Magnetics Japan; Applied Magnetics Korea; Applied Magnetics Singapore
Principal Bank: First Interstate Bank of California
Financial Information:

	Sep 30 1985	Sep 30 1986
	$'000	$'000
Sales revenues	120,751	128,119
Income before taxes	2,048	4,863
Net income	3,087	5,487
Earnings per share	$0.48	$0.81
Common stock	630	633
Retained income	33,021	39,573
Shareholders equity	92,714	99,874

No of Employees: 3,462

APPLIED MATERIALS INC

3050 Bowers Avenue, Santa Clara, CA 95051
Tel: (408) 727-5555

President: James C Morgan (and Chief Executive Officer)
Senior Executive Officers: James W Bagley (Senior VP), James M Ellick (VP, Sales and Marketing), Dan Mayden (VP, Etch and CVD Engineering and Technology), Glen Toney (VP)

PRINCIPAL ACTIVITIES: Production of semiconductors and related devices
Principal Subsidiaries: Applied Materials International Inc
Principal Bank: Bank of America NT & SA

Financial Information:

	$'000
Sales revenues	174,600

No of Employees: 1,470

APPLIED POWER INC

1300 W Silver Spring Drive, Butler, WI 53007
Tel: (414) 781-6600
Telex: WUT 26765 apowr mil bkfd

Chairman: Philip G Brumder
President: Richard G Sim
Senior Executive Officers: Kenneth D Miller (VP), Robert T Foote Jr (VP), Dale A Knutson (VP), H Gary Martin (VP)

PRINCIPAL ACTIVITIES: Manufacture of hydraulic equipment, pumps and valves; labor and cost saving products and systems
Trade Names: Enerpac, Power-Packer
Principal Bank: Manufacturers Hanover; Continental Illinois
Financial Information:

	Aug 30 1985	Aug 31 1986
	$'000	$'000
Sales revenues	99,908	113,039
Income before taxes	5,731	9,397
Net income	3,946	5,782
Common dividends	855	915
Dividends per share	$0.183	$0.20
Earnings per share*	$0.76	$1.18
Common stock	1,804	1,804
Additional capital	6,334	6,336
Retained income	32,698	35,414
Shareholders equity	40,514	43,193

*primary

No of Employees: 1,200

APPLIED TECHNOLOGY

645 Almanor Avenue, Sunnyvale, CA 94088
Tel: (408) 773-0777
Telex: TWX 910 379 69 35 applied techsv

President: Vincent Battaglia
Senior Executive Officers: H W Wilson (VP Administration), J R Peletta (VP Finance), K E Verble (VP Business Development), Lawrence E Langley (VP Engineering), L Max Bowery (VP Operations), Stan Denton (VP Product Assurance)

PRINCIPAL ACTIVITIES: Electronic defense and armaments systems
Parent Company: Litton Industries Inc
Financial Information:

	$'000
Sales revenues	120,000

No of Employees: 1,600

AQUA-CHEM INC

PO Box 421, Milwaukee, WI 53201
Tel: (414) 962-0100
Cable: Aqua Mil
Telex: 26679 aqua mil

Chairman: George A Chandler (and President and Chief Executive Officer)
Senior Executive Officers: Thomas J Nissen (VP and Treasurer), Robert W Agnew (VP and President, Water Technology Division), John M Plant (VP and President, Cleaver Brooks Division), Terry B Hanna (VP and President, Industrial Combustion Division), James F Tucker (VP and President Turbo Refrigerating Co)

PRINCIPAL ACTIVITIES: Manufacture of water purification plant; boilers and ancillary equipment; ice makers, packaged ice machines, ice storage, ice distribution and thermal storage systems
Parent Company: Lyonnaise des Eaux, Paris, France

Principal Bank: Marine Bank
Financial Information:

	$'000
Sales revenues	160,000

No of Employees: 1,800

ARA HOLDING

Independence Square West, Philadelphia, PA 19106
Tel: (215) 574-5000
Telex: ITT 4761043 ara svc pha

Chairman: Joseph Neubauer (and President and Chief Executive Officer); Vice Chairman: Alan K Campbell
Senior Executive Officers: William S Fishman (Chairman, Executive Committee), Francis J Palamara (Executive VP, Finance and Chief Financial Officer), Martin W Spector (Senior VP and General Counsel), Howard A Cohen (VP), John R Farquarson (VP), Claude Feninger (VP International), Edward J Fitzsimmons (VP Tax), Robert J Franco (VP) Glendon E French (VP), Francis X McCoy (VP), William J O'Kane (VP and Secretary), Gene P Remoff (VP), Charles D Scudder (VP), Anthony J Tanzola (VP, Controller and Chief Accounting Officer), Richard H Vent (VP Marketing), Gerald Willis (VP)

PRINCIPAL ACTIVITIES: Provision of management services in catering, distribution and health care
Principal Bank: Chemical Bank
Financial Information:

	Sep 30 1986 $'000
Sales revenues	3,748,750
Net income	15,502
Shareholders equity	114,384

No of Employees: 115,000

ARA MANUFACTURING COMPANY OF DELAWARE, INC

PO Box 534002, 606 Fountain Parkway, Grand Prairie, TX 75050
Tel: (214) 647-4111
Telex: 730372 ARAMCO

Chairman: Robert L Baccus
President: Donald E Green
Senior Executive Officers: William R Marcom (Senior VP), Raymond W Hergott (Senior VP), Jo Gesme (VP of Finance), Adel Jeske (Treasurer)

PRINCIPAL ACTIVITIES: Manufacturer of automotive aftermarket products and accessories including air conditioning systems, sound systems, speed controls, cellular telephones, power door locks and power windows
Trade Names: ARA
Parent Company: Schick Inc
Principal Subsidiaries: ARA Automotive Accessories
Principal Bank: InterFirst Bank Dallas
Financial Information:

	$'000
Sales revenues	140,000

No of Employees: 1,500

ARBOGAST & BASTIAN, INC

1 Hamilton Street, Allentown, PA 18105
Tel: (215) 435-4771
Telex: WUT 847 442 axb inc atv

Chairman: Robert G Tallman (and General Counsel)
President: Richard A Strouce (and Chief Operating Officer)
Senior Executive Officers: Lorin A Hoffman (Executive Vice President and Chief Operating Officer), Ray W Biondi (VP, Purchasing and Secretary)

PRINCIPAL ACTIVITIES: Meat products and meat processing
Principal Bank: Bank of Pennsylvania
Financial Information:

	$'000
Sales revenues	110,000

No of Employees: 650

ARBOR DRUGS INC

1818 Maplelawn, Troy, MI 48084
Tel: (313) 643 9420

Chairman: Eugene Applebaum (and President)
Senior Executive Officers: Markus M Ernst (Executive VP), Robert R Beale (VP), Gilbert C Gerhard (VP, Secretary and Treasurer), Donald M Stutrud (VP)

PRINCIPAL ACTIVITIES: Operation of drug store
Financial Information:

	$'000
Sales revenues	120,490

No of Employees: 1,620

ARCATA CORPORATION

Suite 1800, 601 California Street, San Francisco, CA 94108
Tel: (415) 781-4200

Chairman: Edward L Scarff (and Chief Executive Officer)
Presidents: Robert L Swam (President, Arcata Graphics Company), Burnette Henry (President, Arcata Forest Products Company)

PRINCIPAL ACTIVITIES: Magazine, book and commercial printing; redwood lumber and forest products
Financial Information:

	Dec 31 1985 $'000	Dec 31 1986 $'000
Sales revenues	540,000	550,000

No of Employees: 6,800

ARCHER-DANIELS-MIDLAND CO

4666 Faries Pkwy, Decatur, IL 62525
Tel: (217) 424-5200
Telex: TWX 910 243 0452 artco dtr

Chairman: Dwayne O Andreas (and Chairman of the Executive Committee and Chief Executive Officer)
President: James R Randall
Senior Executive Officers: Michael D Andreas (Group VP and Assistant to the President), D F Benson (VP Employee Relations), Richard E Burket (VP and Assistant to Chairman), Thomas A Duffield (VP), James R Feddick (VP), Burnell D Kraft (VP), Roy L Erickson (VP, Secretary and General Counsel), D P Poboisk (VP and Treasurer), O K Nelson (VP) Jack Reed (VP), James W Stowell (VP)

PRINCIPAL ACTIVITIES: Flour milling; edible oils; fruit syrups
Principal Subsidiaries: ADM Milling Co; River Canyon Ranch Co; American River Transportation Co; Archer-Daniels-Midland (Canada) Ltd; Ardanco Inc; Coeval Inc; Fleischman Malting Co; Bauer-Schweitzer Malting Co; Rickel Malting Co; Gooch Feed Mill Co; Gooch Foods Inc; Miller Hauling Co Inc; Supreme Sugar Co Inc; Tabor Grain Co; Farmer City Grain Co Inc; Smoot Grain Co Inc; Albin Elevator Co; Asherville Grain Co Inc; Brownell Grain Co Inc; Canton Elevator Co; Central KS Elevator Co Inc; Central KS Terminal Inc; Farmers Elevator Co Inc; Feuquay Elevator Co; Genesco Grain Co Inc; Goodland Grain Inc; Grainfield Elevator Inc; Longford Lumber & Grain Co Inc; Oakley Elevator Co Inc; Palco Grain Inc; Park Grain Co Inc; Reid Grain of Kanorado Inc; Rush County Elevator Co Inc; Sherman County Grain Co Inc; Snell Grain and Feed Inc; Snell Grain Co; Snell Grain of Arriba Inc; Tri-County Elevator

Financial Information:

	Jun 30 1986 $'000
Sales revenues	5,335,975
Net income	230,386
Earnings per share	$1.43
Shareholders equity	2,075,887

No of Employees: 9,446

ARCHIVE CORPORATION

1650 Sunflower Avenue, Costa Mesa, CA 92626
Tel: (714) 641 0279

Chairman: D Howard Lewis (and Chief Executiv Officer)
President: J Peter Wilson (and Chief Operating Officer)
Senior Executive Officers: William R Miller (VP), William J Kreidler (VP Operations), Joseph I Martin (VP Finance, Secretary and Treasurer), M Thomas Makmann (VP Marketing), Kenneth C Campbell (VP Engineering), J V Howell (VP Research and Development)

PRINCIPAL ACTIVITIES: Manufacture of 1/4 inch streaming cartridge tape drives for computers
Financial Information:

	$'000
Sales revenues	57,840

No of Employees: 600

ARCO CHEMICAL CO

1500 Market Street, Philadelphia, PA 19101
Tel: (215) 557-2000
Telex: WUT 834297 homarco pha

President: Harold A Sorgenti
Senior Executive Officers: J G Johnson Jr (Senior VP Oxygenates), D W Wood Sr (Senior VP International), M Gelb (VP Research), J L Cobb (VP Polystyrenics), E Y Zenzola (VP Planning and Control), F W Welsh (VP Employee Relations)

PRINCIPAL ACTIVITIES: Manufacture of functional/specialty chemicals, oxygenates and polystyrenics; biotechnology; agricultural research and chemicals; building materials including prefabricated wall systems and window frames
Trade Names: ARCOSOLV, Poly bd, OXINOL, DYLITE, ARCEL, CHEMLINK, FLO, SUNXAN, CERALOX, WALLFRAME, DYLARK
Parent Company: Atlantic Richfield Company
Principal Subsidiaries: Sartomer; ARCO Seed Company; Plant Cell Research Institute; Arrahona SA (Spain)
Principal Bank: Barnett Bank
Financial Information:

	$'000
Sales revenues	2,000,000

No of Employees: 6,400

ARCO PIPE LINE CO

Arco Building, Independence, KS 67301
Tel: (316) 331-1300
Telex: WUT 910 740 1602 arcopl ind ks

President: Daniel O Gallas
Senior Executive Officers: R B Hastie (Senior VP), G M Stout (Senior VP), D R Dozier (VP), K A Baden (Secretary, Treasurer and Controller)

PRINCIPAL ACTIVITIES: Transporter of crude oil and refined products by pipeline; also operates a carbon dioxide pipeline
Parent Company: Atlantic Richfield Company
Financial Information:

	$'000
Sales revenues	873,000

No of Employees: 860

ARDEN GROUP, INC

220 South Central Avenue, Compton, CA 90220
Tel: (213) 638-2842
Facsimile: (213) 631-0950

Chairman: Curtis H Palmer
President: Bernard Briskin (and Chief Executive Officer)
Senior Executive Officers: M H Barker (VP), Ernest T Klinger (VP, Chief Financial Officer and Treasurer)

PRINCIPAL ACTIVITIES: Operation of supermarkets; production of specialty chemicals; telecommunications equipment
Trade Names: Omnifax
Principal Subsidiaries: Arden Mayfair Inc; Gelson's Markets; Telautograph Corporation
Financial Information:

	Jan 31 1987 $'000
Sales revenues	398,834
Income before taxes	9,838
Net income	4,609
Earnings per share	$1.89
Common stock	1,075
Retained income	23,779
Shareholders equity	40,925

No of Employees: 2,600

ARGOSYSTEMS, INC

884 Hermosa Ct, Sunnyvale, CA 94086
Tel: (408) 737-2000
Telex: WUT 352 077 argosystm suvl

President: Kenneth P Miles
Senior Executive Officers: Bill B May (Chief Executive Officer), Gary D Kimmel (Chief Financial Officer), Joyce E Maas-Schmietow (Secretary)

PRINCIPAL ACTIVITIES: Electronic engineering
Principal Bank: Bank of America NT & SA
Financial Information:

	$'000
Sales revenues	65,000

No of Employees: 700

ARISTAR, INC

3655 N W 87th Avenue, Miami, FL 33178
Tel: (305) 594-3000

Chairman: James F Montgomery
President: Robert B Holmes (and Chief Executive Officer)
Senior Executive Officers: Carl F Geuther (Executive VP and Chief Financial Officer), Bruce F Antenberg (Senior VP, Finance and Treasurer), Stephen F Adams (VP, Secretary and General Counsel), Joel D Baumgarten (VP), Roger G Metcalf (VP and Controller), Charles M Havican (VP)

PRINCIPAL ACTIVITIES: Interests in financial services and insurance
Parent Company: Great Western Financial Corporation
Principal Bank: First National Bank of Chicago
Financial Information:

	$'000
Revenues	550,000

No of Employees: 2,500

ARIZONA BANCWEST CORPORATION

101 North First Avenue, Phoenix, AZ 85003
Tel: (602) 262 2000

Chairman: Don B Tostenrud (and Chief Executive Officer); Vice Chairmen: F Lee Jacquette (and Treasurer), Todd H Langley, E Danson Perin, Eugene L Thomas
President: Robert L Matthews (and Chief Operating Officer)
PRINCIPAL ACTIVITIES: Banking services

Financial Information:

	Dec 31 1985
	$'000
Revenues	371,020
Net income	28,500

ARIZONA CHEMICAL CO

200 S Sudduth Pl, Panama City, FL 32404
Tel: (904) 785-6700
Telex: WUT 130321 acintol faln

Chairman: D I Wang
President: M L Snapp Jr
Senior Executive Officers: Ernie Spinner (VP Sales), G A Midwood (Treasurer)

PRINCIPAL ACTIVITIES: Chemical manufacture
Parent Company: International Paper Co
Principal Bank: Manufacturers Hanover Trust Company
Financial Information:

	$'000
Sales revenues	50,000

No of Employees: 350

ARIZONA PUBLIC SERVICE CO

PO Box 21666, Phoenix, AZ 85036
Tel: (602) 271-7900
Telex: WUT 165 094 az pubsvc phx

Chairman: Keith L Turley (and Chief Executive Officer)
President: O M De Michele (and Chief Operating Officer)
Senior Executive Officers: Karl Eller (Chairman, Executive Committee), Jaron B Norberg (Executive VP and Chief Financial Officer), Edwin Van Brunt Jr (Executive VP Arizona Nuclear Power Projects), Walter F Ekstrom (VP Fossil Fuel Supply), David W Ellis (VP Research, Development and Alternate Energy Applications), Joseph A Gelinas (VP Employee Relations), B H Hart (VP Rates), Russell D Hulse (VP Resources Planning), Jerry P Human (VP Customer Services, State Region), Charles D Jarman (VP Engineering and Construction), Guy W Lunt (VP Customer Service, Metro Region), John C Ogden (VP Customer Administration Services), Shirley A Richard (VP Corporate Relations) Paul A Williams (VP and Treasurer)

PRINCIPAL ACTIVITIES: Generation and distribution of electricity; gas supply
Parent Company: AZP Group Inc
Financial Information:

	Dec 31 1985
	$'000
Sales revenues	1,174,500
Net income	279,550

No of Employees: 8,320

ARKANSAS BEST CORPORATION

1000 S 21st Street, Fort Smith, AR 72901
Tel: (501) 785-6000
Telex: TWX 910 723 7686 abc ft sm

Chairman: Hugh L Hembree (and Chief Executive Officer); Vice Chairman: Herman J Udouj
President: Robert A Young III (and Chief Operating Officer)
Senior Executive Officers: Roger E Curtis (Senior VP Administration), Donald L Neal (Senior VP and Comptroller), Robert M Powell (Senior VP Specialized Trucking), David E Stubblefield (Senior VP Marketing), J A Yarbrough (Senior VP Operations), Richard J Udouj (Senior VP Manufacturing), Robert P Dougherty (VP Insurance and Assistant Secretary), John R Meyers (VP and Treasurer)

PRINCIPAL ACTIVITIES: Road transportation; furniture manufacture; computer services; real estate interests
Principal Bank: Citibank NA
Financial Information:

	Dec 31 1985	Dec 31 1986
	$'000	$'000
Sales revenues	581,620	689,815
Net income	16,570	18,205
Earnings per share	$1.65	$1.79
Shareholders equity	-	110,328

No of Employees: 10,492

ARKANSAS RICE GROWERS COOPERATIVE ASSOCIATION

2120 Park Avenue, Stuttgart, AR 72160
Tel: (501) 673-5481
Telex: WUT 536464 arkango st gt

Chairman: R E Short Jr; Vice Chairman: Stewart E Jessup
President: Richard E Bell (and Chief Executive Officer)
Senior Executive Officers: Charles A Gunnell (VP Finance, Secretary and Treasurer), W L Knoll (VP Marketing), Carl Brothers (VP Export & Industrial Markets)

PRINCIPAL ACTIVITIES: Rice milling
Principal Bank: St Louis Bank for Coop
Financial Information:

	$'000
Sales revenues	300,000

No of Employees: 1,070

ARKLA INC

Arkla Building, 525 Milam, Shreveport, LA 71101
Tel: (318) 429 2700
Telex: (318) 429-2793

Chairman: Thomas F McLarty III (and President and Chief Executive Officer)
Senior Executive Officers: Michael B Bracy (Executive VP Finance and Administration), Alan M Warren (President-Arkla Exploration Co), Michael T Hunter (President-Arkla Energy Resources), T Milton Honea Jr (President-Arkansas Louisiana Gas Co), Thomas A Agee (VP Auditing), Bradford G Keithley (VP and General Counsel), Joe D Kruse (VP and Controller), Jim O Wilhite (President-Mississippi River Transmission Corp), B D Kline (VP Finance, Secretary and Treasurer)

PRINCIPAL ACTIVITIES: Supply, transmission and distribution of natural gas
Principal Subsidiaries: Arkla Exploration Co; Arkla Chemical Corp; Mississippi River Transmission Corp
Principal Bank: Morgan Guaranty Trust Co of America
Financial Information:

	Dec 31 1985	Dec 31 1986
	$'000	$'000
Sales revenues	993,420	999,560
Income before taxes	116,145	113,346
Net income	69,490	64,179
Dividends	54,345	58,393
Dividends per share	$1.08	$1.08
Earnings per share	$1.38	$1.20
Common stock*	50,267	53,472
Retained income	435,994	441,779
Shareholders equity	480,597	616,368
*weighted average common shares outstanding in thousands		

No of Employees: 3,650

ARLEY MERCHANDISE CORPORATION

42 Adams Street, Taunton, MA 02780
Tel: (617) 822 7133

Chairman: David M Susswein (and Chief Executive Officer)
President: Arnold N Nathanson (and Chief Operating Officer)
Senior Executive Officers: Clifford Seresky (Executive VP and Treasurer), Arthur R Booth (Senior VP), Paul D O'Reilly

(Senior VP Finance and Chief Financial Officer), David I Reimer (Finance), James Park (Senior VP Sales)

PRINCIPAL ACTIVITIES: Manufacture of household textiles and soft furnishings
Financial Information:

	$'000
Sales revenues	75,000

No of Employees: 1,450

ARMADA CORPORATION
600 Buhl Building, Detroit, MI 48226
Tel: (313) 963-3100

President: Jerry D Luptak
Senior Executive Officers: Raymond N Anderson (VP Alloys Group), Lowell V Robinson Jr (VP Finance), Robert A Wasik (VP Exhaust Group), Eugene Sokoloff (VP and Treasurer), Arthur J Giese Jr (Secretary)

PRINCIPAL ACTIVITIES: Alloy production; automobile exhaust systems
Principal Bank: Manufacturers National Bank of Detroit
Financial Information:

	$'000
Sales revenues	69,394

No of Employees: 764

ARMATRON INTERNATIONAL INC
2 Main Street, Melrose, MA 02176
Tel: (617) 321-2300
Telex: 949425

Chairman: Edward L Houseman
President: Anthony A Goodchild (and Chief Executive Officer)
Senior Executive Officers: Herbert E Houseman (Executive VP), Stephen J McCabe (VP), Robert W Snow (VP), James J Hickey (VP Finance), Charles Houseman (Treasurer)

PRINCIPAL ACTIVITIES: Manufacture of auto radios and telecommunications equipment
Principal Bank: Shawmut Bank of Boston, NA
Financial Information:

	$'000
Sales revenues	59,587

No of Employees: 800

ARMCO INC
300 Interpace Parkway, Parsippany, NJ 07054-0324
Tel: (201) 316-5200
Telex: 810-451-2040 (Middletown)

Chairman: Robert E Boni (and Chief Executive Officer)
President: Robert L Purdum (and Chief Operating Officer)
Senior Executive Officers: Wallace B Askins (Executive VP and Chief Financial Officer), John M Bilich (VP Corporate Human Resources), Kempton B Jenkins (VP International and Government Affairs), Robert W Kent (VP Law, General Counsel and Secretary), J W Albright (VP and President, Armco Assets Management), Carl R Fiora (VP and President, Eastern Steel Division), L W Hicks (VP and President, Midwestern Steel Division), J R Bartol (VP and President Latin American Division), D E Todd (VP and President Specialty Steels Division), W L Trubeck (VP and Corporate Treasurer), W H Schaar (VP and Corporate Controller), D L Chalk (VP Research and Technology)

PRINCIPAL ACTIVITIES: Armco is a producer of carbon, electrical and stainless steels, steel products, and oilfield machinery and equipment. Armco reports results in four broad lines of business: Carbon Steel, Specialty Steels, Oilfield Equipment, and Other Operations (primarily the Latin American Division).
Principal Bank: Chase Manhattan Bank
Financial Information:

	Dec 31 1985 $'000	Dec 31 1986 $'000
Sales revenues	2,936,100	2,640,500
(Loss) before taxes	(52,200)	(350,500)
Net income (loss)	44,800	(472,000)
Dividends	8,100	8,000
Dividends per share(1)	$2.10	$2.10
Dividends per share(2)	$4.50	$4.50
Earnings (loss) per share	$0.54	$(7.04)
Common stock	340,200	342,600
Retained income (deficit)	229,800	(250,200)
Shareholders equity	901,400	479,300

(1) Preferred stock-Class A
(2) Preferred stock-Class B

No of Employees: 22,000

ARMIN CORPORATION
301 West Side Ave, Jersey City, NJ 07305
Tel: (201) 432-8032
Telex: 238402

Chairman: John F Fort
President: Armin Kaufman
Senior Executive Officers: Irving Gutin (Senior VP), Bernard Elefant (VP), Ari Perlow (VP Finance)

PRINCIPAL ACTIVITIES: Plastic packaging and products including plastic pallets and shrinkable plastic pallet covers; printed bags; film for agricultural and construction applications; disposable plastic gloves
Parent Company: Tyco Laboratories Inc, Exeter, NH
Financial Information:

	$'000
Sales revenues	105,000

No of Employees: 500

ARMOR ELEVATOR CO INC
5534 National Turnpike, Louisville, KY 40214
Tel: (502) 361-7181
Telex: WUT 204126 armoreler ivl

President: Robert M Page
Senior Executive Officers: Alan A Floyd (Executive VP), Werner Walter (Senior VP), Dennis McCabe (VP Manufacturing), William Lippman (VP Marketing), R L Bodart (VP, Secretary and Treasurer)

PRINCIPAL ACTIVITIES: Manufacture of elevators and equipment; elevator maintenance services
Parent Company: Kone Corporation, Helsinki, Finland through Kone Holding Inc
Principal Bank: First National Bank
Financial Information:

	$'000
Sales revenues	70,000

No of Employees: 800

ARMSTRONG CONTAINERS, INC
10330 Roosevelt Road, Westchester, IL 60153
Tel: (312) 344-5580

Chairman: Roland V McPherson (and Chief Executive Officer)
President: Ted Rohde (and Chief Operating Officer)
Senior Executive Officers: Duncan J McCallum (VP Engineering), Don Brown (VP Marketing and Sales), Edward J Flemming (Treasurer)

PRINCIPAL ACTIVITIES: Metal products including packaging; flat sheet coating
Financial Information:

	$'000
Sales revenues	70,000

No of Employees: 400

ARMSTRONG RUBBER CO

500 Sargent Drive, New Haven, CT 06536
Tel: (203) 562-1161
Telex: TWX 710 465 2389 armstrong nun

Chairman: Frank R O'Keefe (and President and Chief Executive Officer)
Senior Executive Officers: Robert M Kuhn (Senior VP, Finance and Administration), G R Millar (VP Personnel and Corporate Relations)

PRINCIPAL ACTIVITIES: Manufacture of rubber products including tires; manufacture of automobile wheels
Principal Subsidiaries: Arco Wheel Inc; Armstrong Acceptance Co Inc; Armstrong Rubber Export Ltd; Copolymer Rubber Chemical Corp; Jackson Distribution Center; Richmond Converters Inc
Principal Bank: Chemical Bank
Financial Information:

	Sep 30 1985	Sep 30 1986
	$'000	$'000
Sales revenues	767,844	800,136
Net income (loss)	16,026	(37,608)
Earnings (loss) per share	$1.52	($3.64)
Shareholders equity	239,063	182,647

No of Employees: 8,000

ARMSTRONG WORLD INDUSTRIES INC

PO Box 3001, West Liberty Street, Lancaster, PA 17604
Tel: (717) 397-0611
Telex: 84 8411

Chairman: Joseph L Jones (and President and Chief Executive Officer)
Senior Executive Officers: William W Adams (Executive VP), Lawrence E Bish (Executive VP), R H Caldwell (Executive VP), E A Deaver (Group VP Corporate Technology and Venture Management), John B Helmer (Group VP Industrial Products and Corporate Markets), William W Locke (Group VP International Operations), George A Lorch (Group VP Carpet Operations), Alfred B Strickler Jr (Group VP Floor Products Operations), Phillip W Unger (Group VP Building Products Operations), F H Burgess (VP Information)

PRINCIPAL ACTIVITIES: Production of heavy-duty floor coverings; specialty products for the construction industry and textiles for the automobile industries
Principal Subsidiaries: Armstrong-Cape Girardeau Inc; Applied Color International Sales Corpn; Armstrong Finance Corpn; Armstrong Cork Co (Del); Armstrong Cork Finance Corpn; Armstrong Export Sales Corpn; I W Investments Inc; Thomasville Furniture Industries Inc; Applied Color Systems Inc; Fayette Enterprises Inc; Armstrong Ventures Inc; ArmStar; Armstrong World Industries Pty Ltd (Australia); Armstrong World Industries Canada Ltd (Canada); Armstrong World Industries Ltd (UK); Armstrong Cork (Ireland) Ltd (Eire); Armstrong Europe Services (UK); Inarco Ltd (India); Armstrong World Industries GmbH (Germany); Armstrong Nylex Pty Ltd (Australia); Armstrong World Industries SA (Spain); Trefinos SA (Spain); Armstrong do Brasil Industria e Comercio Ltda (Brazil); Armstrong (Japan) KK (Japan); Armstrong AWI Ltd (Hong Kong); Armstrong (Singapore) Pte Ltd (Singapore); Armstrong FSC Inc (Virgin Islands); Tubarit Isolierungstechnik AG (Switzerland)
Financial Information:

	Dec 31 1985	Dec 31 1986
	$'000	$'000
Sales revenues	1,679,213	1,920,345
Net income	100,892	122,423
Earnings per share	$4.20	$2.54
Shareholders equity	733,372	812,964

No of Employees: 20,780

ARNOLD CORPORATION (THE)

PO Box 577, Akron, OH 44309-0577
Tel: (216) 896-2365

President: Wayne Jira (and Chief Executive Officer)
Senior Executive Officers: John Lautzenheiser (VP-Finance and Chief Financial Officer), George Martin (Executive VP-Procurement), William M J Moser (VP-Marketing), Thomas Shatzer (VP-M.I.S.), Robert Gellatly (VP-Human Resources)

PRINCIPAL ACTIVITIES: Printing and manufacture of: business forms; computer forms; direct mail; lottery, gaming and entertainment tickets; large volume job printing
Parent Company: Reynolds & Reynolds Company
Financial Information:

	$'000
Sales revenues	175,000

No of Employees: 1,400

ARNOLD INDUSTRIES, INC

625 S 5th Ave, Lebanon, PA 17042
Tel: (717) 274-2521

President: E H Arnold
Senior Executive Officers: Kenneth F Leedy (VP), Alvin D Hershey (VP), Ronald E Walborn (Treasurer)

PRINCIPAL ACTIVITIES: Trucking
Financial Information:

	$'000
Sales revenues	84,500

No of Employees: 1,095

ARO CORPORATION

One Aro Center, Bryan, OH 43506
Tel: (419) 636-4242
Telex: TRT 196 120 aro o ut

Chairman: Frederick W Schwier (and President and Chief Executive Officer)
Senior Executive Officers: M J Anderson (Chairman of Executive Committee), L D Black (Executive VP Engineering), D E Moore (Group VP Manufacturing), W C House (VP Finance and Treasurer)

PRINCIPAL ACTIVITIES: Manufacture of power-driven hand tools; power equipment; pneumatic equipment
Parent Company: Todds Shipyards Corp
Financial Information:

	$'000
Sales revenues	100,000

No of Employees: 1,775

ARROW AUTOMOTIVE INDUSTRIES, INC

5 Speen Street, Framingham, MA 01701
Tel: (617) 872-3711

President: Harry A Holzwasser
Senior Executive Officers: David L Koontz (Executive VP Finance, Treasurer and Chief Financial Officer), James Ragan (Executive VP), Marshall L Gralnick (VP), Robert A Holzwasser (VP), Joel D Holzwasser (VP), Jimmy L Osment (VP), Lawrence G Szuhy (VP), L M Levinson (Secretary)

PRINCIPAL ACTIVITIES: Electrical equipment including renovated generators; automobile components; pumps and compressors
Principal Bank: The First National Bank of Boston
Financial Information:

	$'000
Sales revenues	100,150

No of Employees: 1,300

ARROW ELECTRONICS, INC

25 Huls Drive, Melville, NY 11747
Tel: (516) 391-1300

Chairman: John C Waddell
President: Stephen P Kaufman (and Chief Executive Officer)
Senior Executive Officers: Thomas M Davidson (Executive VP Finance and Administration), T W Anthony (VP), Robert E Klatell (VP and General Counsel), Dominic A Polmeni (VP and Chief Financial Officer)

PRINCIPAL ACTIVITIES: Electronic components and computer products; refining of non-ferrous metals
Financial Information:

	Dec 31 1986
	$'000
Sales revenues	529,621
(Loss) before taxes	(28,267)
Net (loss)	(31,899)*
(Loss) per share	($5.38)
Common stock	6,563,081
Shareholders equity	102,406

*includes an extraordinary charge of $3,632

No of Employees: 2,100

ARROW INDUSTRIES, INC
2625 Belt Line Road, Carrollton, TX 75006
Tel: (214) 242-0525
Telex: WUT 730618 arrowind carn

President: Marcus Rosenberg
Senior Executive Officers: David Rosenberg (Executive VP and Secretary), Andrew Sigal (VP Charcoal Division), Fred Roy (VP Sales), Michael Petrak (VP Purchasing)

PRINCIPAL ACTIVITIES: Manufacture and sale of dried vegetables, cereal products, coffee and packaging materials
Principal Bank: RepublicBank Dallas
Financial Information:

	$'000
Sales revenues	150,000

No of Employees: 600

ARROWHEAD DRINKING WATER COMPANY
2 Cupania Circle, Monterey Park, CA 91754
Tel: (213) 728-6636

President: A J Peever
Senior Executive Officers: W R Dahlman (Executive VP), F H Schiller (VP Production), M E Frandsen (VP Marketing), A N Alderson (VP and Controller), R M Sturdy (VP Personnel)

PRINCIPAL ACTIVITIES: Still and sparkling bottled water; water purification equipment; electric water cooler rentals
Parent Company: Beatrice Companies Inc
Principal Bank: Bank of America
Financial Information:

	$'000
Sales revenues	120,000

No of Employees: 1,600

ART METAL USA, INC
300 Passaic Street, Newark, NJ 07104
Tel: (201) 485-5310
Telex: WUT 138 363 art metal nwk

President: Philip J Kurens (and Chief Operating Officer)
Senior Executive Officers: Irving Cooperstein (Chief Financial Officer, Executive VP, Secretary and Treasurer), Joseph Markowitz (VP Finance and Comptroller)

PRINCIPAL ACTIVITIES: Steel industry; manufacture of steel office furniture and shelving for libraries
Principal Bank: First National State Bank of New Jersey
Financial Information:

	$'000
Sales revenues	50,000

No of Employees: 1,000

ARTHUR D LITTLE INC
See LITTLE, ARTHUR D, INC

ARTHUR J GALLAGHER AND COMPANY
See GALLAGHER, ARTHUR J, AND COMPANY

ARTRA GROUP INC
500 Central Avenue, Northfield, IL 60093
Tel: (312) 441-6650
Telex: TWX 910 99 20 686 artra noth

Chairman: John J Harvey
President: Peter R Harvey
Senior Executive Officers: K Earl Abel (VP and Treasurer), John G Hamm (VP Finance), Robert S Gruber (VP Corporate Relations), James D Doerling (VP and Controller)

PRINCIPAL ACTIVITIES: Medical equipment for ultrasound scanning; manufacture of costume jewelry
Financial Information:

	$'000
Sales revenues	60,351

No of Employees: 1,550

ARUNDEL CORPORATION (THE)
110 West Road, Baltimore, MD 21204
Tel: (301) 296-6400
Telefax: (301) 337-7406

Chairman: Henry J Knott
President: Francis X Knott
Senior Executive Officers: Walter K Duncan (Executive VP Construction Materials Division), David P Scheffenacker (Senior VP Real Estate Division), T Edgie Russell III (Executive VP Finance and Treasurer), Richard H Bowden (VP), Thomas F X Grover (VP and Controller), Harry W Schlegelmilch (VP), William H Quigley (Assistant VP), Charlotte A Waters (Corporate Secretary and Legal Administrator)

PRINCIPAL ACTIVITIES: The Arundel Corporation is engaged in the production and marketing of construction materials and the acquisition, development and sale of real estate
Trade Names: Arundel, Tidewater, S & G, Sadler
Principal Subsidiaries: ARL Development Corp; Arundel Materials Corp; Arundel Products Inc; Arundel Risk Managers Inc; Arundel Sand and Gravel Company; BWIP Inc; Blades Materials Inc; Landel/Arundel Inc; The Maryland Slag Company; Mid-Atlantic Ash Company; Patapsco Properties Inc; S & G Concrete Co; S & G Prestress Company; Sadler Materials Corporation; Scenic Hill Inc; TBS Enterprises Inc; Tidewater Holding Company; Tidewater Materials Corporation; Tidewater Quarries Inc
Principal Bank: Maryland National Bank
Financial Information:

	Dec 31 1985	Dec 31 1986
	$'000	$'000
Sales revenues	81,907	94,293
Income before taxes	5,747	8,137
Net income	5,340	7,815
Earnings per share	$2.34	$3.47
Common stock	6,937	6,954
Retained income	19,213	27,028
Shareholders equity	39,497	41,081

No of Employees: 1,000

ARVEY CORPORATION
3450 N Kimball Avenue, Chicago, IL 60641
Tel: (312) 463-0030

Chairman: Joseph Regenstein Jr (and Chief Executive Officer); Vice Chairman: Robert S Hartman
President: James S Minnis (and Chief Operating Officer)

Senior Executive Officers: James L Krebaum (VP Finance), James K Arthur (VP Law and Secretary), T J Eischeid (VP and Controller)

PRINCIPAL ACTIVITIES: Manufacture of paper and paper products; operation of retail outlets
Principal Bank: First National Bank
Financial Information:

	$'000
Sales revenues	150,000

No of Employees: 1,600

ARVIN INDUSTRIES, INC

1531 13th Street, Columbus, IN 47201
Tel: (812) 379-3000
Telex: TWX 810 352 1270 arvinautocol

Chairman: James K Baker (and Chief Executive Officer)
President: Loren K Evans (and Chief Operating Officer)
Operating Officers: Joe T Atkins (President of North American Automotive and Arvin VP), Dr H Robert Leland (President of Calspan Corp and Arvin VP), David N Lewis (President of Aftermarket Products Div and Arvin VP), Francis J Myers (President of Arvin Electronics and Arvin VP), J Kevin Nameth (President of Schrader Automotive and Arvin VP), Byron O Pond (President of Maremont Corp and Arvin VP), Ronald J Rosin (President of ArvinAir and Arvin VP), James S Smith (President of Roll Coater, Inc and Arvin VP), Charles H Watson (President of Arvinyl and Arvin VP). Corporate Officers: John P Sohn (Executive VP), W F Meyer (VP Public Affairs), Haren B Thakor (VP Finance), V W Hunt (VP Administration and Secretary)

PRINCIPAL ACTIVITIES: Manufacture of automobile components; domestic electrical equipment and electronic equipment; metal fabricating, government and private research
Trade Names: Arvin, Maremont (R), Gabriel (R), Visualizer (R), Arvin (R), Bendafit (R) AK Tubing, Exostar (R), Orange Peeler (R), Super "C" (R)/AK Mufflers, Supreme, Turbo.e., ARVEX (R), Arvinyl (R), AVDEC (R), Roll Coater, Alpine (R), Arctic Circle (R), Arvin (TM), CariHeat (R), Heat Stream (R), MasterCool (R), MasterCool 2-Stage (TM), ThermOil (TM), Thermoquest (R), TravelAire (R), Universal (R), Wispercool (R), Wright (R)
Principal Subsidiaries: Calspan Corporation; Maremont Corporation; Schrader Automotive Inc; Roll Coater Inc
Principal Bank: The First National Bank of Chicago
Financial Information:

	Dec 29 1985 $'000	Dec 28 1986 $'000
Sales revenues	820,995	995,620
Income before taxes	63,715	76,027
Net earnings	35,872	41,207
Dividends	9,747	10,583
Dividends per share	$0.61	$0.65
Earnings per share(1)	$2.21	$2.46
Common stock(2)	16,632	16,160
Common stock(3)	16,084	16,669
Retained income	171,589	202,037
Shareholders equity	249,938	260,942

(1) primary
(2) end of period
(3) average shares outstanding

No of Employees: 17,823

ASARCO INC

180 Maiden Lane, New York, NY 10038
Tel: (212) 510-2000
Cable: SMELTER MINEDEPART (Mining Dept); FARWINN (Traffic Dept); BRUSHAMER (Sales Dept)
Telex: ITT 420585; RCA 232378

Chairman: Richard de J Osborne (and President and Chief Executive Officer); Vice Chairman: Alexander J Gillespie Jr
Senior Executive Officers: George W Anderson (Executive VP), Thomas C Osborne (Executive VP), William A Bennis (VP Administration), Richard L Brown (VP Exploration), John R Corbett (VP Industrial Relations), Augustus B Kinsolving (VP and General Counsel), Robert J Kupsch (VP Mining), W Scott Latimer (VP Ore Department), Francis R McAllister (VP Finance and Administration and Chief Financial Officer), Stephen P McCandless (VP and Treasurer), Robert J Muth (VP Government and Public Affairs), Robert J Bothwell Jr

PRINCIPAL ACTIVITIES: Mining of non-ferrous metals, coal and minerals; metal smelting and recycling; production of specialty chemicals
Trade Names: ASARCO
Principal Subsidiaries: (100% owned unless stated): American Limestone Co; Capco Pipe Co Inc; Enthone Inc; Federated Metals Corpn; Lac d'Amiante du Quebec Ltee; Mexico Desarrollo Industrial Minero SA (34%) (Mexico); Midland Coal Co Inc; MIM Holdings Ltd (19%) (Australia); Southern Peru Copper Corpn (52.3%) (Peru); Corparación Minera Nor Peru SA; Lone Star Lead Construction Corpn; Federated Genco Ltd (60%) (Canada)
Financial Information:

	Dec 31 1985 $'000	Dec 31 1986 $'000
Sales revenues	1,166,921	1,056,538
Profit (loss) before taxes	(59,923)	13,406
Net income (loss)	(62,184)	9,140
(Loss) per share(1)	($2.87)	($0.46)
Common stock(2)	502,355	502,355
Retained income	438,473	426,123
Shareholders equity(1)	641,479	655,274

(1) common
(2) number of shares in thousands

Principal Shareholders: MIM Holdings Limited (24.4%)
No of Employees: 7,000

ASEA INC

4 New King Street, White Plains, NY 10604
Tel: (914) 428-6000
Telex: WUT 137401 asea elec whp

Chairman: William Lockwood
President: Paul A Brunner
Senior Executive Officers: Anthony C Recchia (VP Finance and Administration, Secretary and Treasurer), John J O'Hara (VP Sales and Sales Manager, Power Systems)

PRINCIPAL ACTIVITIES: Electrical engineering; mining machinery; railroad vehicles
Principal Bank: Citibank
Financial Information:

	$'000
Sales revenues	100,000

No of Employees: 230

ASH GROVE CEMENT CO

PO Box 25900, Overland Park, KS 66225
Tel: (913) 381-8900

Chairman: Robert Sunderland
President: James P Sunderland
Senior Executive Officers: Richard E Willis (Senior Vice President, Operations), B R Raines (VP Finance), Graham D Jones (VP Production), Richard F Ladd (VP Materials), Ronald V Deleenheer (VP Marketing), John H Ross III (VP and Secretary)

PRINCIPAL ACTIVITIES: Production of lime and cement
Principal Subsidiaries: Ash Grove Cement West Inc; Cedar Creek Investment Co Inc; Cedar Creek Properties Co Inc; Century Concrete Inc; Chemseco; Fordyce Concrete Co Inc;

Lime Transport Co; Subsurface Development Co; Union Quarries Inc; Material Transport Co
Principal Bank: First National Bank
Financial Information:

	$'000
Sales revenues	175,000

No of Employees: 1,400

ASHLAND OIL, INC
PO Box 391, Ashland, KY 41114
Tel: (606) 329-3333

Chairman: John R Hall (and Chief Executive Officer); Vice Chairmen: Robert T McCowan (External Affairs), William R Seaton (and Chief Financial Officer)
President: Charles J Luellen (and Chief Operating Officer)
Senior Executive Officers: Paul W Chellgren (Senior VP, Group Operating Officer: Ashland Chemical Company, Ashland Coal Inc and Ashland Development Inc), William C Voss (Senior VP, Group Operating Officer: APAC Inc, Arch Mineral Corporation, Ashland Exploration Inc and Ashland Technology Corp, President, Ashland Exploration Inc), Richard W Spears (Senior VP, Human Resources and Law), John A Brothers (Senior VP, and President, Ashland Chemical Company), Robert E Yancey Jr (Senior VP and President, Ashland Petroleum Company), John F Boehm (VP, and President, Valvoline Oil Company), Charles D Hoertz (VP, and President, Ashland Development Inc), Richard A Jensen (VP, and President, Super America), John B Kebblish (VP, and President, Ashland Coal Inc), William R Sawran (VP and President, Ashland Services Company). Administrative Officers: Kenneth B Denton (Administrative VP and Controller), William E Perrine (Administrative VP), Charles M Russell Jr (Administrative VP), Harry M Zachem (Administrative VP), John W Dansby (VP), Thomas L Feazell (VP and General Counsel), William Harkins (VP), Frank P Justice Jr (VP), J Dan Lacy (VP), J Marvin Quin (Treasurer), John P Ward (Secretary), John H Wallace Jr (Auditor)

PRINCIPAL ACTIVITIES: Ashland Oil Inc is a diversified energy company with operations in petroleum refining, transportation and marketing; chemicals; coal; highway construction; engineering services; and oil and gas exploration and production. Based in Ashland, Ky, the company employs more than 34,000 people worldwide and ranks in sales among the 50 largest industrial corporations in America
Trade Names: (100% owned unless stated): Ashland Petroleum Co; Ashland Chemical Co; Ashland Coal Inc (65%); Ashland Exploration Inc; Ashland Development Inc; APAC/Ashland Technology Inc; Arch Mineral Corpn (50%); Valvoline Oil Co; Ashland Services Co; Ashland (Bermuda) Ltd
Financial Information:

	Sep 30 1985	Sep 30 1986
	$'000	$'000
Sales revenues (1)	8,183,733	7,282,659
Income before taxes	218,708	372,351
Net income	146,722	208,571
Dividends(2)	45,052	52,478
Dividends per share(2)	$1.60	$1.70
Earnings per share	$4.12	$6.15
Common stock	28,672	32,941
Retained income	690,621	831,271
Shareholders equity	929,411	971,044

(1) including excise taxes
(2) common stock

No of Employees: 34,400

ASHLAND TECHNOLOGY, INC
3340 Peachtree Rd NE, Atlanta, GA 30326
Tel: (404) 261-2610

Chairman: John R Hall (and Chief Executive Officer); Vice Chairmen: William R Seaton (and Chief Financial Officer), Robert T McCowan
President: William C Voss (and Chief Operating Officer)
Senior Executive Officers: James P Kressler (Senior VP Finance and Planning), William E Adams (Group VP Metal Fabrication and Casting Group), Albert A Doorman (Group VP Engineering and Power Group), Paul J Miller (Group VP Process Instruments Group), Karel A Weits (Group VP Environmental Systems Group), Ronald E Gustafson (VP Human Resources), Allan E Johnson (VP and Treasurer), Todd R Wilkins (VP Columbia Cement Corporation), J H Murphy (VP and General Counsel), William V Rice (VP International Operations), Frank J Schmidt (VP Financial Services), Joseph F Tartaglia (VP Operations Services)

PRINCIPAL ACTIVITIES: Services to the energy industries; manufacture of generators
Parent Company: Ashland Oil Inc, Ashland, KY
Principal Bank: Morgan Guaranty Trust Company
Financial Information:

	$'000
Sales revenues	500,000

No of Employees: 4,000

ASK COMPUTER SYSTEMS INC
730 Distel Drive, Los Altos, CA 94022
Tel: (415) 969 4442

Chairman: Sandra L Kurtzig
President: Ronald W Braniff (and Chief Executive Officer)
Senior Executive Officers: Robert J Riopel (Executive VP, Chief Financial Officer and Assistant Secretary), Kenneth A Fox (Executive VP Research and Development), James T Manion (VP), Larry W Sonsini (Secretary), David Sohm (VP Marketing), Martin R Browne (VP Software Systems)

PRINCIPAL ACTIVITIES: Provision of computer software and related services
Financial Information:

	$'000
Sales revenues	79,000

No of Employees: 470

ASLESEN CO
2700 E 28th Street, Minneapolis, MN 55406
Tel: (612) 721-2981

Chairman: Emory Williams
President: F R Murphy
Senior Executive Officers: R W Lannan (Executive VP and Treasurer), Gerald Cooper (VP Marketing and Distribution)

PRINCIPAL ACTIVITIES: Production of food catering packs; food processing equipment and associated services
Parent Company: Chicago Milwaukee Corporation
Principal Bank: Midland National Bank
Financial Information:

	$'000
Sales revenues	50,000

No of Employees: 200

ASSOCIATED BANC-CORP
222 Cherry Street, Green Bay, WI 54301
Tel: (414) 433 3166

Chairman: John M Rose
President: Harry B Conlon (and Chief Executive Officer)
Senior Executive Officers: Clifford J Crockford Jr (Senior VP), Robert C Gallagher (Senior VP), Gerald L Schaper (Senior VP), Edward C Fordney (VP), James H Lewis (VP), Frank W Norris (Subisidiary Officer), Richard D Julian (VP Auditing), Joseph B Selner (VP Finance), Howard F Kiley (Secretary and Treasurer)

PRINCIPAL ACTIVITIES: Banking
Principal Subsidiaries: Associated Citizens Bank NA

Financial Information:

	Dec 31 1985
	$'000
Revenues	122,910
Net income	10,530

ASSOCIATED COCA-COLA BOTTLING CO, INC

320 Orange Avenue, Daytona Beach, FL 32015
Tel: (904) 258-3355

President: Thomas Dannemiller
Senior Executive Officers: Robert L Voges (VP), Fredric F Gruber (VP and Treasurer)

PRINCIPAL ACTIVITIES: Coca-Cola bottling
Parent Company: The Coca-Cola Company, Atlanta, GA
Principal Bank: The Philadelphia National Bank
Financial Information:

	$'000
Sales revenues	353,000

No of Employees: 2,400

ASSOCIATED HOSTS INC

8447 Wilshire Boulevard, Suite 200, Beverly Hills, CA 90211
Tel: (213) 653 6010

Chairman: Joseph Bulaski (and Chief Executive Officer)
President: Paul Rothman
Senior Executive Officers: Nathan Winters (Executive VP, Chief Financial Officer and Treasurer), Howard W Dicker (VP Secretary and General Counsel), Irving Jacobson (VP and Controller), Paul A Sandbloom (VP)

PRINCIPAL ACTIVITIES: Operation of restaurants, hotels and a motel
Financial Information:

	$'000
Sales revenues	89,510

No of Employees: 3,300

ASSOCIATED MILK PRODUCERS, INC

PO Box 32287, San Antonio, TX 78284
Tel: (512) 340-9100

President: Irvin Elkin
Senior Executive Officers: Lee Wolf (VP), Gregory Blaska (VP), Clifford Schumacher (VP), William Lenschow (Treasurer)

PRINCIPAL ACTIVITIES: Cooperative association for milk producers
Financial Information:

	Dec 31 1986
	$'000
Sales revenues	2,535,873
Shareholders equity	135,672

No of Employees: 3,731

ASSOCIATED MILLS, INC

111 N Canal Street, Chicago, IL 60606
Tel: (312) 454-5400
Cable: POLLENEX CHICAGO USA
Telex: TWX 910 2212197 pollenex sgo

President: Richard J Stern
Senior Executive Officers: Jefferson Gentry (Senior VP), John G McDowall (VP Finance)

PRINCIPAL ACTIVITIES: Manufacture of water and air filter units; electrical equipment for personal care and health care
Trade Names: POLLENEX
Principal Bank: Harris Trust and Savings Bank
Financial Information:

	$'000
Sales revenues	70,000

No of Employees: 600

ASSOCIATED PRODUCTS INC

445 Park Avenue, New York, NY 10022
Tel: (212) 751 1690

President: Noel Levine
Senior Executive Officers: H C Van Lanen (Executive VP), Richard A Guggenheimer (Senior VP), Donald Stevens (VP and Treasurer), Richard Silberman (VP and Secretary)

PRINCIPAL ACTIVITIES: Manufacture of household plastic products including bathroom accessories
Parent Company: Dawson International
Principal Bank: Manufacturers Hanover Trust Company
Financial Information:

	$'000
Sales revenues	69,000

No of Employees: 1,000

ASSOCIATED SAND & GRAVEL CO, INC

6300 Glenwood Avenue, Everett, WA 98201
Tel: (206) 355-2111

President: John Hutsell
Senior Executive Officers: Alfred Schlicker (Executive VP), E D Dowden (Executive VP)

PRINCIPAL ACTIVITIES: Quarrying; manufacture of construction materials including cement and concrete products
Parent Company: ARC America
Principal Bank: Seattle-First National Bank
Financial Information:

	$'000
Sales revenues	50,000

No of Employees: 330

ASSOCIATES CORPORATION OF NORTH AMERICA

One Gulf & Western Plaza, New York, NY 10023
Tel: (212) 233-4744
Telex: TWX 710 581 2087 aic treas ny

Chairman: Reece A Overcash Jr
President: Ronald J Krause
Senior Executive Officers: Keith W Hughes (Senior Executive VP, Consumer Finance), Alan B Lerner (Senior Executive VP, Corporate Staff), Harold D Marshall (Senior Executive VP, Commercial Finance), James E Jack (Executive VP and Chief Financial Officer), Joseph M McQuillan (Executive VP and Comptroller)

PRINCIPAL ACTIVITIES: Financial services
Parent Company: Associates First Capital Corporation-Ultimate Holding Company-Gulf & Western Inc
Principal Bank: Chase Manhattan Bank
Financial Information:

	Jul 31 1986	Jul 31 1987
	$'000	$'000
Revenues	1,687,300	1,777,500
Operating income	289,500	324,100

Principal Shareholders: Gulf & Western Inc (wholly owned)
No of Employees: 7,700

AST RESEARCH INC

2121 Alton Avenue. Irvine, CA 92714
Tel: (714) 863-1333
Telex: WUT 858252 astr ud

President: S U Quereshey
Senior Executive Officers: A C Wong (Executive VP and Secretary), B C Edwards (VP Finance), T K Yuen (Executive VP)

PRINCIPAL ACTIVITIES: Manufacture of data processing equipment
Trade Names: SixPakPlus, Rampage!, Advantage!

Principal Subsidiaries: AST Europe Limited; AST Research (Far East) Limited
Principal Bank: Bank of America
Financial Information:

	$'000
Sales revenues	138,576

No of Employees: 850

ASTEN GROUP, INC

999 W Valley Road, Roswell, GA 30077
Tel: (404) 993 5100

Chairman: E A Walther
Senior Executive Officers: W A Finn (VP and General Manager, Asten Hill Company), E Walther (VP Marketing), J A Flynn (VP Finance), G T Chapman (VP and Secretary)

PRINCIPAL ACTIVITIES: Production of textiles
Principal Subsidiaries: Ascoe Felts; Wisconsin Wires Inc
Principal Bank: Philadelphia National Bank
Financial Information:

	$'000
Sales revenues	70,000

No of Employees: 1,300

ASTRA PHARMACEUTICAL PRODUCTS, INC

50 Otis Street, Westborough, MA 01581
Tel: (617) 366-1100

Chairman: Mats G Nilsson
President: Lars Bildman (and Chief Executive Officer)
Senior Executive Officers: Stefan Solvell (Treasurer)

PRINCIPAL ACTIVITIES: Pharmaceutical products
Trade Names: XYLOCAINE
Parent Company: Astra AB, Sweden
Principal Bank: State Street Bank and Trust Company
Financial Information:

	$'000
Sales revenues	75,000

No of Employees: 600

ASTRONAUTICS CORPORATION OF AMERICA

4115 N Teutonia, Milwaukee, WI 53201
Tel: (414) 447-8200
Telex: WUT 910 262 3153 aca mil

Chairman: Nathaniel K Zelazo
President: Dr R E Zelazo
Senior Executive Officers: Norma Paige (VP), R E Zelazo (Treasurer and General Manager)

PRINCIPAL ACTIVITIES: Manufacture of electronic instruments, data processing equipment and telecommunications equipment for the aircraft industry
Trade Names: Pathfinder Auto Pilot
Principal Subsidiaries: Astro GmbH; Astro Ltd
Principal Bank: First Wisconsin National Bank of Milwaukee
Financial Information:

	1987
	$'000
Sales revenues	122,000

No of Employees: 1,400

ASTROTECH INTERNATIONAL CORPORATION

Two Chatham Center, Pittsburgh, PA 15219
Tel: (412) 391-1896

Chairman: Willard F Rockwell Jr (and Chief Executive Officer)
President: E D Ward
Senior Executive Officers: Robert F Kastelic (Executive VP, Treasurer and Chief Financial Officer), S W Brown (VP Operations), Willard F Rockwell III (VP Operations Space), P A Wick (VP and Treasurer), E M Randolph (VP and Controller)

PRINCIPAL ACTIVITIES: Aerospace equipment and components
Principal Subsidiaries: Astrotech Space Operations Inc; Quasitronics Inc; Special Metals Corporation
Principal Bank: Mellon Bank
Financial Information:

	$'000
Sales revenues	122,000

No of Employees: 850

AT&T NASSAU METALS CORPORATION

PO Box 218, Gaston, SC 29053
Tel: (803) 796-4720
Telex: 272595

President: Robert E Cornelia
Senior Executive Officers: Robert P Dawson (Chief Financial Officer), Edward E Heslin (Marketing Director)

PRINCIPAL ACTIVITIES: Precious metal products, precious metals plating products, copper products; non-ferrous metal recycling
Parent Company: AT&T Technologies Inc, New York, NY
Financial Information:

	$'000
Sales revenues	300,000

No of Employees: 1,000

AT&T TECHNOLOGIES INC

One Oak Way, Berkeley Heights, NJ 07922
Tel: (201) 771-2000

Chairman: James E Olson (and Chief Executive Officer); Vice Chairman: Donald E Procknow (and Chief Operating Officer)
Presidents: Thomas R Thompsen (Technical Systems), Victor A Pelson (Consumer Products), E W Weeks Jr (Network Systems)
Senior Executive Officers: Michael A Brunner (Executive VP Federal Systems), John M Nemecek (Executive VP Components and Electronic Systems), Robert S Kern (Executive VP Planning and Administration), John T O'Neill (Executive VP Network Systems Products), Paul M Villiere (Executive VP Network Systems Marketing and Customer Operations), John D Zeglis (Executive VP and General Counsel)

PRINCIPAL ACTIVITIES: Manufacture of telecommunications equipment and cables
Parent Company: American Telephone & Telegraph Company
Financial Information:

	$'000
Sales revenues	12,000,000

No of Employees: 139,000

ATC PETROLEUM, INC

One Parade Mall, Portsmouth, NH 03801
Tel: (603) 431-5131

President: James M Cox (and Chief Executive Officer)

PRINCIPAL ACTIVITIES: Refining and marketing of oil
Principal Bank: Bank of New England
Financial Information:

	$'000
Sales revenues	120,000

No of Employees: 150

ATCOR INC

16100 South Lathrop Avenue, Harvey, IL 60426
Tel: (312) 955 6000

Chairman: Theodore H Krengel (and President and Chief Executive Officer)

Senior Executive Officers: Sherman J Rosen (Senior VP), Gerald J Stein (Senior VP), Robert F Erazmus (VP and Treasurer), John M Lison (VP, General Counsel and Secretary), Michael L Lowenthal (Subsidiary Officer), John R Ranelli (VP and Treasurer)

PRINCIPAL ACTIVITIES: Manufacture of wires and cables
Financial Information:

	Sep 30 1986
	$'000
Sales revenues	458,377
Net (loss)	(3,688)
(Loss) per share	($0.65)
Shareholders equity	90,645

No of Employees: 2,200

ATHLONE INDUSTRIES, INC

200 Webro Road, Parsippany, NJ 07054
Tel: (201) 887-9100
Telex: TWX 710 9868 257 athlone papy

Chairman: Harold J Miller (and President)
Senior Executive Officers: Daniel J Lyons (Executive VP), Fred Engelhardt (VP Finance and Treasurer), Alan Shaw (VP, Secretary and General Counsel), Stanley Harris (VP Henschel Shoe Division), Raymond P Fisher (VP), Charles E Quinby (VP and Controller), Robert L Wood (VP)

PRINCIPAL ACTIVITIES: Steel industry; manufacture of steel products including industrial fasteners; manufacture of sports and leisure apparel and footwear and sports goods
Principal Subsidiaries: CSI Corp; Lee-Mar of CA; Valley Sportswear Manufacturing Co; Gelfo Manufacturing Co; Green River Steel Corp; Jessop Steel Co; Jessop Steel of CA; Reynolds Fastener Inc; Sea Fashions Inc
Principal Bank: Manufacturers Hanover Trust Company
Financial Information:

	$'000
Sales revenues	217,265

No of Employees: 3,300

ATKINSON, GUY F, CO OF CALIFORNIA

10 W Orange Avenue, South San Francisco, CA 94080
Tel: (415) 876-1000
Telex: WUT 34297 atkinson ssf

Chairman: T W Halligan (and President and Chief Executive Officer); Vice Chairman: Ray N Atkinson
Senior Executive Officers: Richard F Byers (Senior VP), Jonathan Goodier Jr (Senior VP), T J Henderson (Senior VP), J J Agresti (Senior VP), Michael H Heys (Senior VP and Chief Financial Officer), Bryant K Zimmerman (Senior VP, Secretary and Chief Legal Counsel), J D Stevens (VP and Chief Administrative Officer), W P Hart Jr (Senior VP and General Controller)

PRINCIPAL ACTIVITIES: Construction; steel manufacture; mechanical engineering and manufacture of pumps
Principal Subsidiaries: Guy F Atkinson Co; Atkinson Construction Co; Atkinson Development Co; Guy F Atkinson Construction Ltd; Guy F Atkinson Export Co; Atkinson International Dominican Republic Inc; Atkinson International Venezuela Inc; Columbia Service Co; Commercial Welding Co; Atkinson Land Co; Mine Industries Inc; Tyger Construction Co; Wismer & Becker Constructing Engineers
Principal Bank: Bank of America
Financial Information:

	Dec 31 1986
	$'000
Sales revenues	857,618
Net income	8,526
Earnings per share	$0.97
Shareholders equity	187,953

No of Employees: 8,726

ATLANTA DAIRIES CO-OPERATIVE INC

777 Memorial Drive SE, Atlanta, GA 30316
Tel: (404) 688-2671

President: William A Neel
Senior Executive Officers: Forrest N Davenport (Executive VP and General Manager), H D Thames (First VP), R M Paxon (Second VP)

PRINCIPAL ACTIVITIES: Cooperative organisation for the production and distribution of dairy products
Principal Bank: Trust Company Bank
Financial Information:

	$'000
Sales revenues	75,000

No of Employees: 650

ATLANTA GAS LIGHT COMPANY

235 Peachtree Street Northeast, Atlanta, GA 30302
Tel: (404) 584 4000

Chairman: Joe T Laboon (and Chief Executive Officer)
President: David R Jones (and Chief Operating Officer)
Senior Executive Officers: W James Goldin (Senior VP Operations), William F Norman (Senior VP Operations and Engineering), B L Fackler (Senior VP Finance), Charles W Bass (VP Division), Thomas H Benson (VP Division), L J Hill Jr (VP Division), John C Mayson (VP Division), Charles B Seymour (VP Division), Harold C Weathers (VP Division), J M Johnson (Treasurer), Kimsey McKinley (Controller), R H Person (Secretary)

PRINCIPAL ACTIVITIES: Supply of natural gas
Financial Information:

	$'000
Sales revenues	1,164,710

No of Employees: 3,260

ATLANTA NEWSPAPERS

72 Marietta Street NW, Atlanta, GA 30303
Tel: (404) 526-5151
Telex: TWX 810751 3325 journalcon atl

Chairman: Anne C Chambers
President: Minor J Ward
Senior Executive Officers: Tom Giuffrida (VP and General Manager), James G Minter Jr (VP and Editor), Ferguson Rood (VP Advertising and Marketing), Ellen L Gilbert (VP Community Affairs), David Steward (VP Business Manager)

PRINCIPAL ACTIVITIES: Publishing of newpapers
Parent Company: Cox Enterprises Inc
Principal Bank: Fulton National Bank
Financial Information:

	$'000
Sales revenues	100,000

No of Employees: 2,500

ATLANTIC AMERICAN CORPORATION

4370 Peachtree Road Northeast, Atlanta, GA 30319
Tel: (404) 266 5500

Chairman: J Mack Robinson (and President)
Senior Executive Officers: A H Dyess (Division President), H Y Hutcheson Jr (VP), K R Stricklin (Senior VP), J R Copeland (Secretary and Treasurer)

PRINCIPAL ACTIVITIES: Provision of insurance services
Principal Subsidiaries: Atlantic American Life Insurance Co; Bankers Fidelity Life Insurance Co; Georgia Casualty & Surety Co
Principal Bank: Trust Co Bank of Middle Georgia
Financial Information:

	$'000
Revenues	130,400

No of Employees: 2,200

ATLANTIC AVIATION CORPORATION

PO Box 15000, Wilmington, DE 19850
Tel: (302) 322-7000
Telex: WUT 835 370 atlantiavi wil

Chairman: Edward B duPont
President: William L Patrick (and Chief Executive Officer)
Senior Executive Officers: Malcolm S Graham (Executive VP), Donald R Romano (Senior VP and Treasurer), Franklin S Eyster II (Senior VP Secretary and General Counsel)

PRINCIPAL ACTIVITIES: Aerospace equipment and components; aircraft maintenance; sale and charter of aircraft; related services
Principal Bank: Bankers Trust Company
Financial Information:

	$'000
Sales revenues	225,000

No of Employees: 1,000

ATLANTIC BUILDING SYSTEMS, INC

2001 Orchard, PO Box 1108, Hannibal, MO 63401
Tel: (314) 221 2715
Telex: TWX 810 731 8320

Chairman: H F McCarley
Senior Executive Officers: John Cullens (VP Marketing), B E Ellison (VP Engineering), R T Gross (VP Operations), Jerry Kirkland (Treasurer)

PRINCIPAL ACTIVITIES: Manufacture of steel products including welded tubing and steel structures
Principal Bank: Trust Company of Georgia
Financial Information:

	$'000
Sales revenues	50,000

No of Employees: 500

ATLANTIC CITY ELECTRIC COMPANY

PO Box 1264, 1199 Black Horse Pike, Pleasantville, NJ 08232
Tel: (609) 645-4100

Chairman: John D Feehan (and Chief Executive Officer)
President: E Douglas Huggard (and Chief Operating Officer)
Senior Executive Officers: J G Salomone (Senior VP Finance and Treasurer), Jerrold L Jacobs (Senior VP), Michael A Jarrett (Senior VP)

PRINCIPAL ACTIVITIES: Electricity supply
Principal Bank: Irving Trust Co
Financial Information:

	$'000
Sales revenues	580,000

No of Employees: 2,100

ATLANTIC FEDERAL SAVINGS & LOAN ASSOCIATION

1750 East Sunrise Blvd, Fort Lauderdale, FL 33304
Tel: (305) 764-2111

Chairman: Charlie C Winningham II; Vice Chairman: Philip Morgaman
Senior Executive Officers: Robert D Knight (Senior VP), Suzanne S Coleman (VP Advertising and Marketing), Robert L Elifritz (VP Purchasing), Patricia Page (VP Personnel), C Nick Preble (VP Data Processing), Robert F DeLong Jr (VP and Treasurer), Jean M Teson (VP and Secretary), Michael V Matrone (VP and Comptroller)

PRINCIPAL ACTIVITIES: Savings and loan association
Principal Bank: Sun Bank

No of Employees: 586

ATLANTIC FINANCIAL FEDERAL

50 Monument Road, Bala Cynwyd, PA 19004
Tel: (215) 668-6600
Telecopy: (215) 668-9529

Chairman: Calvin D Baker
President: Donald R Caldwell (and Chief Executive Officer)
Senior Executive Officers: Richard A Guttendorf Jr (Executive VP Finance and Chief Financial Officer), Ronald S Murray (Executive VP Operations), James J Rizzo (Executive VP Lending), Joshua D Thompson (Executive VP Retail Banking)

PRINCIPAL ACTIVITIES: Savings and loan association
Trade Names: Atlantic Financial
Principal Subsidiaries: Atlantic Financial Savings Bank, FSB, California; Atlantic Financial Savings, Nevada; Atlantic Financial Mortgage Corporation, Texas
Financial Information:

	Sep 30 1986 (12 mths) $'000	Jun 30 1987 (9 mths) $'000
Income before taxes	16,775	19,336
Net income	16,453	17,774
Dividends	535	819
Dividends per share	$0.15	$0.19
Earnings per share	$3.39	$3.60
Common stock	4,313	4,315
Retained income	114,549	129,297
Shareholders equity	186,595	199,118
Deposits	3,842,627	3,987,251
Total assets	5,208,146	7,416,257

Principal Shareholders: FMR Corporation, Boston, MA; MacKay-Shields Financial, New York, NY
No of Employees: 2,200

ATLANTIC RESEARCH CORPORATION

5390 Cherokee Avenue, Alexandria, VA 22312-2302
Tel: (703) 642-4000
Cable: AFTRECO
Telex: RCA 248893 arc ur
Telefax: (703) 642-4021

President: William H Borten (and Chief Executive Officer)
Senior Executive Officers: W Gerald Hamm (Executive VP and Chief Operating Officer), Christopher W Robertson (Senior VP and Chief Financial Officer), Carlyle C Ring (VP and General Counsel), Robert S Hinton (VP, Human Resources/Administration), Alfred P Principe (VP and Corporate Controller), James R Sides (Senior VP and ARC Group President), Harvey D Kushner (Senior VP and ORI Group President), Richard C Barron (VP and General Manager, ARC/Teleproducts), Donald R Burklew (VP and ORI, Inc President), Dr Howard Eisner (VP and ORI/INTERCON President), Art R Milkes (VP and Chief Financial Officer, ORI Group), Paul F Lumbye (VP and General Manager, ARC/Tempest), E Eugene Sharer (ORI/CALCULON President), Stephen J Hostettler (VP and General Manager, ARC/Virginia Propulsion), Keith B Mullin (VP and General Manager, ARC/Arkansas Propulsion), Jon H Cowell (VP and General Manager, SASC)

PRINCIPAL ACTIVITIES: ARC Group: Atlantic Research's product-oriented operating Group includes four Divisions: Virginia Propulsion and Arkansas Propulsion:- research, design, and manufacture of solid rocket propellants, gas generators, composite materials, advanced aerospace programs; Teleproducts:- research, development, and manufacture of data communications test equipment; TEMPEST:- design, manufacture, and testing of secure electronics and communications products/systems. ORI Group: Atlantic Research's professional and technical services operating Group includes ORI, Inc, ORI/CALCULON, ORI/INTERCON, Systems and Applied Sciences (SASC) and Atlantic Research Services Corporation (ARSCO). The Group's services to government and industry apply advanced science and technology to support C3I systems; software development, implementation and maintenance; operational and administrative support; training systems development; knowledge engineering (AI); and telecommunications engineering and support

Parent Company: Sequa Corporation, New York, NY

Principal Subsidiaries: Systematics General Corporation, Sterling, VA; ORI Group Inc, Rockville, MD

Principal Bank: National Bank of Washington, D.C.

Financial Information:

	Dec 31 1986
	$'000
Sales revenues	375,400
Income before taxes	29,744
Net income	17,382
Earnings per share	$1.84
Retained earnings	74,480
Shareholders equity	99,518

No of Employees: 5,500

ATLANTIC RICHFIELD CO

515 South Flower Street, Los Angeles, CA 900071
Tel: (213) 486-3511

Chairman: Robert O Anderson (and Chairman Executive Committee); Vice Chairmen: Edward M Benson Jr, Joseph P Downer

President: W F Kieschnik (and Chief Executive Officer)

Senior Executive Officers: Lodwrick M Cook (Chief Operating Officer Products), Ralph F Cox (Chief Operating Officer Resources), Robert E Wycoff (Chief Corporate Officer), Ronald J Arnault (Senior VP and Chief Financial Officer), Hiram E Bond (Senior VP President, ARCO Transportation Co), Willard T Chamberlain (Senior VP President, ARCO Metals Co), Claude O Goldsmith (Senior VP, Acquisitions and Divestments), Bob G Gower (Senior VP, Planning and Advanced Technology), Harry C Jamison (Senior VP President, ARCO Exploration Co), James L Marvin (Senior VP President, Anaconda Minerals Co), Francis X McCormack (Senior VP and General Counsel), James A Middleton (Senior VP President, ARCO Oil and Gas Co), James S Morrison (Senior VP President, ARCO Petroleum Products Co), Stuart C Mut (Senior VP, Senior VP, ARCO Resources Technology), Paul Ravesies (Senior VP President, ARCO International Oil and Gas Co), Howard A Slack (Senior VP, Technology), Dwaine H Smith (Senior VP, Employee Relations), Harold A Sorgenti (Senior VP President, ARCO Chemical Co), Richard P Van Horne (Senior VP Public Affairs), Michael R Bowlin (VP Senior VP, ARCO Resources Administration), Camron Cooper (VP and Treasurer), Brack W Duker, (VP, Special Asset Transactions), William M Fischbach (VP and General Tax Officer), Donald A Henriksen (VP, Constituency Relations), Harold C Heinze (VP President, ARCO Alaska, Inc), William D Leake (VP, Information Technolgoy and Corporate Services), William H Magee (VP and Controller), William M Marcussen (VP and Assistant to the President), Douglas G McNair (VP International Coordination), Paul B Norgaard (VP Public Affairs Operations), Howard H Ockelmann (VP and Investment Officer), Rodney W Rood (VP and Assistant to the Chairman of the Board), Howard L Edwards (Secretary)

PRINCIPAL ACTIVITIES: In 1984, Atlantic Richfield's operations were reorganized into two major groups, each with a chief operating officer. The Resources Group, which includes domestic and international oil and gas exploration and production, and minerals, is responsible for finding, developing and profitably producing resources. Working together, these operations benefit from common technological and management structures. In the Products Group, the second of Atlantic Richfield's two major operating units, refining and marketing, transportation, chemicals and solar operations share a market-driven orientation

Principal Subsidiaries: ARCO Transportation Co; ARCO Metals; ARCO Exploration Co; Anaconda Minerals Co; ARCO Oil & Gas Co; ARCO Petroleum Products Co; ARCO International Oil & Gas Co; ARCO Chemical Co; ARCO Alaska Inc

Financial Information:

	Dec 31 1986
	$'000
Revenues	14,585,802
Net income	615,116
Earnings per share	$3.38
Shareholders equity	5,258,730

No of Employees: 39,400

ATLANTIC SERVICE CO INC

711 Caton Avenue, Brooklyn, NY 11218
Tel: (718) 633-0100

Chairman: Walter K McManus

President: Robert J Edmondson

Senior Executive Officers: Joseph J Fetzner (VP and Chief Financial Officer), George T Bowers (VP Marketing)

PRINCIPAL ACTIVITIES: Manufacture of equipment for the meat preparation industry; equipment for supermarkets

Trade Names: Hook-Eye

Parent Company: ASC Investors

Principal Subsidiaries: Atlantic Service Co Ltd (Canada); Atlantic Service Co Ltd (UK); Sniders Atlantic Service Co Inc (USA); Euro-Atlantic SA (France); ASCO Cutting Equipment BV (Netherlands)

Principal Bank: Manufacturers Hanover

Financial Information:

	Dec 31 1985
	$'000
Sales revenues	50,000
Income before taxes	1,761
Net income	1,301
Dividends	144
Retained income	2,976
Shareholders equity	3,982

No of Employees: 250

ATLANTIC SOFT DRINK CO

PO Box 261, Columbia, SC 29202
Tel: (803) 786-7710

President: James Moore

Senior Executive Officers: Robert M Buys (VP Operations), Dave Bush (VP Finance, Secretary and Treasurer), Leonard Rosinski (VP Marketing), Ronald K Runkle (VP Sales), R Simmons (VP Personnel)

PRINCIPAL ACTIVITIES: Bottling of soft drinks; Pepsi-Cola and Canada Dry franchise operations

Parent Company: Grandmet USA Inc

Financial Information:

	$'000
Sales revenues	125,000

Principal Shareholders: Grand Metropolitan PLC, London, UK

No of Employees: 900

ATLANTIC SOUTHEAST AIRLINES INC

1688 Phoenix Parkway, College Park, GA 30349
Tel: (404) 996 4562

Chairman: Alan M Voorhees

President: George F Pickett (and Chief Executive Officer)

Senior Executive Officers: Robert L Priddy (Senior VP Administration), Ronald V Sapp (VP Finance, Treasurer and Chief Financial Officer), John W Beiser (Senior VP Sales and Secretary)

PRINCIPAL ACTIVITIES: Operation of air transportation services

Financial Information:

	$'000
Sales revenues	75,320

No of Employees: 300

ATLANTIC STEEL CO

PO Box 1714, Atlanta, GA 30301
Tel: (404) 897-4500
Telex: WUT 542504 asco atl

President: J J Webb (and Chief Executive Officer)
Senior Executive Officers: R B Webb (VP Sales), R J Dervales (VP Industrial Relations), Charles W Mynard (VP Finance and Treasurer), E M Vannerson (VP Operations)

PRINCIPAL ACTIVITIES: Steel industry
Parent Company: Ivaco Inc, Canada
Principal Bank: Trust Company of Georgia

No of Employees: 1,150

ATLAS CORPORATION

353 Nassau Street, Princeton, NJ 08540
Tel: (609) 921 2000

Chairman: Edward R Farley Jr (and President)
Senior Executive Officers: Richard R Weaver (Executive VP and Division President), John M Devaney (VP Finance, Treasurer and Assistant Secretary), Edgar M Mascinter (Secretary)

PRINCIPAL ACTIVITIES: Exploration and production of uranium and other natural resources
Principal Subsidiaries: Tri Valley Silica Sand Co Inc
Principal Bank: Manufacturers Hanover Trust co
Financial Information:

	$'000
Sales revenues	39,000

No of Employees: 4,400

ATLAS POWDER CO

15301 Dallas Pkwy, Dallas, TX 75248
Tel: (214) 387-2400
Telex: TWX 910 860 5237 atlas pwdr dal

President: H Joseph Burchell (and Chief Executive Officer)
Senior Executive Officers: W W Caldwell (Senior VP Sales), P J Martikes (Senior VP Finance), David G Fiore (VP Manufacturing), Joseph V Urenovitch (VP Research and Development), Jack E Downen (VP), Charles W Miller (VP)

PRINCIPAL ACTIVITIES: Manufacture of explosives for commercial applications
Parent Company: Tyler Corporation
Principal Bank: Interfirst Bank
Financial Information:

	$'000
Sales revenues	150,000

No of Employees: 1,200

ATV SYSTEMS, INC

2921 S Daimler, Santa Ana, CA 92705
Tel: (714) 261-2390

Chairman: Philip J Gomez (and President)
President: Douglas O'Connor
Senior Executive Officers: Frank Gleason (Executive VP Finance and Chief Financial Officer), Robert F Brown (VP Marketing and Sales), James File (VP Engineering), John Nicholas (VP Legal Counsel and Secretary), Steve Williams (VP Personnel)

PRINCIPAL ACTIVITIES: Manufacture of microprocessors including point-of-sale systems and office information systems

Financial Information:

	$'000
Sales revenues	30,000

No of Employees: 250

ATWOOD OCEANICS INC

15835 Park Ten Place Drive, PO Box 218350, Houston, TX 77084
Tel: (713) 492 2929

President: Robert E Turrentine (and Chief Operating Officer)
Senior Executive Officers: James W Ferguson (VP, Secretary and General Counsel), John R Irwin (VP Operations), Pete L Gonzalez (Treasurer), James M Holland (VP Finance), Larry P Till (VP)

PRINCIPAL ACTIVITIES: Oil and gas exploration and production
Principal Subsidiaries: Atwood Oceanics Drilling Co; Eagle Oceanics Inc
Principal Bank: First National Bank of Chicago
Financial Information:

	$'000
Sales revenues	42,000

No of Employees: 900

ATWOOD VACUUM MACHINE CO

1400 Eddy Avenue, Rockford, IL 61101
Tel: (815) 877-5771
Telex: TWX 910 631 3405 atwood rkfd

Chairman: Seth G Atwood
President: Robert B Rosecrance
Senior Executive Officers: Michael J Delany (Executive VP Mobile Products), Roy McCleary (Executive VP Auto and Contract Division), J R Henriksen (VP, Secretary and Treasurer)

PRINCIPAL ACTIVITIES: Automobile parts and accessories
Principal Subsidiaries: United Realty Corp
Principal Bank: United Bank of Illinois
Financial Information:

	$'000
Sales revenues	53,000

No of Employees: 2,000

AUBURN STEEL CO, INC

PO Box 2008, Auburn, NY 13021
Tel: (315) 253-4561
Telex: WUT 937484 austeel abur

Chairman: T Ogawa; Vice Chairman: K Takashima
President: K Numaguchi
Senior Executive Officers: W Humes Jr (Senior VP), J Rossi (VP Operations), M Fanning (VP Industrial Relations), K Mifhiguchi (VP Planning), Y Yasuda (VP, Secretary and Treasurer)

PRINCIPAL ACTIVITIES: Steel industry
Principal Bank: Bank of Auburn
Financial Information:

	$'000
Sales revenues	80,000

No of Employees: 300

AUDIO/VIDEO AFFILIATES INC

2875 Needmore Road, Dayton, OH 45414
Tel: (513) 276 3931

Chairman: Stuart Rose (and Chief Executive Officer)
President: Alvin P Sotoloff (and Treasurer)
Senior Executive Officers: Lawrence Tomchin (Executive VP and Chief Operating Officer), Ronald Durbin (VP Finance and Chief Financial Officer), William Jung (Controller), Edward Kress (Secretary)

PRINCIPAL ACTIVITIES: Retail trade in television, video and other home entertainment equipment

Principal Bank: National Bank of Detroit
Financial Information:

	£'000
Sales revenues	250,000

No of Employees: 3,000

AUDIOVOX CORPORATION

150 Marcus Blvd, Hauppauge, NY 11788
Tel: (516) 231-7750
Telex: WUT 967794 audio voxhaup

President: John J Shalam (and Chief Executive Officer)
Senior Executive Officers: Philip Christopher (Senior VP), Michael Stoehr (VP Finance), Martin Novick (VP Sales), Ann Boutcher (VP Marketing)

PRINCIPAL ACTIVITIES: Manufacture of stereo equipment and telephones for automobiles
Trade Names: Hi Comp, Audiovox
Principal Subsidiaries: Audiovox West Corp
Principal Bank: Manufacturers Hanover Trust Co
Financial Information:

	Nov 30 1986 $'000
Sales revenues	203,000
Income before taxes	7,019
Net income	3,453
Earnings per share	$0.51
Common stock	68
Retained income	16,976
Shareholders equity	27,032

No of Employees: 900

AUGAT INC

89 Forbes Blvd, PO Box 448, Mansfield, MA 02048
Tel: (617) 543-4300
Telex: 710-346-0596 AUGAT INC MNSF

Chairman: Roger D Wellington
President: William P Miller
Senior Executive Officers: Gerald F Barrett (Executive VP and Chief Financial Officer), Frank Angelis (Group VP), John A Braun (Group VP), Richard J Eaton (Corporate VP), Richard M Grubb (Corporate Senior VP), John E Lynch Jr (Treasurer), Daniel J Maher Jr (Corporate Controller), Richard P Prybyl (Group VP)

PRINCIPAL ACTIVITIES: Designers and manufacturers of a broad range of electromechanical components for the electronics industry and a major supplier of related services. The Company's principal products and services are integrated circuit sockets and accessories, coaxial cable network and fiberoptic interconnection products, subminiature switches, high reliability packages for microcircuits, packaging panels, computer aided design and wiring services, interconnection test probes and systems, and custom connector assemblies for the automotive and telecommunications industry.
Trade Names: Augat, Alcoswitch, Altair, Telzon
Principal Subsidiaries: Alco Electronic Products Inc; Altair International Inc; Broadband Engineering Inc; Datatex Corporation; Electronic Systems & Programming Inc; Isotronics Inc; LRC Electronics; Microtec; Pylon Company; Reed Devices Inc; Richfield Isotronics Tooled Products; Telzon Inc; Augat AB (Sweden); Augat AG (Switzerland); Augat Electronics (Canada); Augat GMBH (West Germany); Augat Israel (Israel); Augat KK (Japan); Augat Ltd (UK); Augat SA (France); Augat SRL (Italy); Electroform SA (Switzerland)
Principal Bank: Bank of New England
Financial Information:

	$'000
Sales revenues	255,000

No of Employees: 3,800

AURORA PUMP

800 Airport Road, North Aurora, IL 60542
Tel: (312) 859-7000
Telex: 720411 AUR PUMP AUR

President: D N Patterson
Senior Executive Officers: F P McGorty (VP Finance), P J Beyer (VP Manufacturing), W Scott (VP and Manager)

PRINCIPAL ACTIVITIES: Manufacture of pumps
Parent Company: General Signal Corporation, Stamford, CT
Financial Information:

	$'000
Sales revenues	55,000

No of Employees: 800

AUSTIN CO

Hall & Cutler, Greeneville, TN 37743
Tel: (615) 638-4124
Telex: WUT 553433 austin co gvle

Chairman: Tom N Austin; Vice Chairman: Robert C Austin
President: Fred A Serral
Senior Executive Officers: E B Smith (Chairman, Executive Committee), Sam J Calvert Jr (VP), Hans Andersen (VP), William D Payne (VP), C B Austin III (VP and Treasurer), Carroll Sasscer (VP Production), Jan Van Galen (VP), James H Felts (VP), Larry R Corbett (VP)

PRINCIPAL ACTIVITIES: Tobacco and tobacco products
Principal Subsidiaries: Austin Carolina Co; Cigar Supply Co Inc; Mullins Leaf Tobacco Co Inc
Principal Bank: Commerce Union Bank
Financial Information:

	$'000
Sales revenues	200,000

No of Employees: 250

AUSTIN, NICHOLS & CO, INC

1290 Avenue of the Americas, New York, NY 10019
Tel: (212) 903-9400
Telex: TWX 710 581 5578 nichaust nyk

President: Marshall L Berkowitz (and Chief Executive Officer)
Senior Executive Officers: Sylvester T Ribaudo (Executive VP Administration and Manufacturing), Edward L Golden (VP Sales), Robert W Beck (VP and Comptroller), James E Brewer (VP Marketing), Pierre de Champfleury (Executive VP Sales and Marketing)

PRINCIPAL ACTIVITIES: Production and distribution of wines and spirits
Parent Company: Pernod Ricard SA, Paris, France
Principal Bank: Manufacturers Hanover Trust Company
Financial Information:

	$'000
Sales revenues	70,000

No of Employees: 300

AUTOCLAVE ENGINEERS INC

2930 West 22nd Street, PO Box 4007, Erie, PA 16506
Tel: (814) 838 2071

Chairman: James C Levinson (and President and Chief Executive Officer)
Senior Executive Officers: Joseph F Allison (Executive VP, General Manager and Group President), Robert F Ruyak (Senior VP), Charles W Smith Jr (Senior VP), John G Sontag (Treasurer and Chief Financial Officer), Paul T Bowser (Senior VP Sales), David M Sample (VP)

PRINCIPAL ACTIVITIES: Manufacture of temperature and high pressure equipment, autoclaves and scientific instruments for engineering, laboratory and industrial use
Principal Bank: Marine Bank

Financial Information:

	$'000
Sales revenues	36,700

No of Employees: 490

AUTODIE CORPORATION

44 Coldbrook Northwest, Grand Rapids, MI 49503
Tel: (616) 454 9361

President: Joseph N Spruit (and Chief Executive Officer)
Senior Executive Officers: John C Kennedy (VP, Secretary and Treasurer), Florence L Spruit (VP), John C Zoodsma (Manager Finance), Leland J Sprute (Chief Engineer)

PRINCIPAL ACTIVITIES: Manufacture of special dies and molds
Principal Bank: National Bank of Detroit
Financial Information:

	$'000
Sales revenues	39,220

No of Employees: 460

AUTOMATIC DATA PROCESSING, INC

One ADP Blvd, Roseland, NJ 07068
Tel: (201) 994-5000
Telex: 710-989-7069

Chairman: Josh Weston (and Chief Executive Officer)
President: William Turner (and Chief Operating Officer)
Senior Executive Officers: Ric Duques (Group President), Robert J Levenson (Group President), Fred S Lafer (Senior VP, Secretary and General Counsel), Arthur F Weinbach (Senior VP Administration and Finance), Arthur S Kranseler (VP), David L Perlman (VP), Garen K Staglin (VP), David J Torrance (Group VP), George J Eklund (VP)

PRINCIPAL ACTIVITIES: ADP's mission is to serve an ever-increasing number of clients with computing and management information services that help them advance their business goals. Today, some 150,000 commercial companies, financial institutions and government agencies of all sizes are ADP clients.
Trade Names: ADP
Financial Information:

	Jun 30 1985	Jun 30 1986
	$'000	$'000
Sales revenues	1,031,491	1,204,246
Income before taxes	154,583	183,500
Net income	87,600	105,960
Dividends	22,603	25,490
Dividends per share	$0.3175	$0.3500
Earnings per share*	$1.22	$1.45
Common stock	7,275	7,394
Retained income	398,949	479,419
Shareholders equity	557,370	664,848

*primary

No of Employees: 21,000

AUTOMATIC SWITCH CO

50-56 Hanover Road, Florham Park, NJ 07932
Tel: (201) 966-2000
Telex: WUI 6853068 a sc of uw

Chairman: Edward R Ehrhard (and Chief Executive Officer)
President: Hans R Naumann (and Chief Executive Officer)
Senior Executive Officers: Herbert H Kaemmer (VP Valve Department), George A Franklin (VP Industrial Relations and Secretary), Raymond L Walter (VP Advertising and Public Information), Edmund Z Berdela (VP Planning and Statistical Control), Frank J Manna (VP and Treasurer), Robert G Campbell (VP Accounting), Victor C Squitieri Jr (VP International Operations)

PRINCIPAL ACTIVITIES: Manufacture of valves and industrial controls
Parent Company: Emerson Electric Co Inc, St Louis, MO
Principal Bank: Horizon Bank
Financial Information:

	$'000
Sales revenues	160,000

No of Employees: 1,800

AUTOMATION INDUSTRIES, INC

500 W Putnam Avenue, Greenwich, CT 06830
Tel: (203) 629-3780
Telex: WUT 643417 autom inds grc

President: Eugene G Swartz (and Chief Executive Officer)
Senior Executive Officers: Gerald Bomstad Jr (Executive VP Manufactured Products), Larry G Morris (Senior VP), Thomas L Flattery (Senior VP, Secretary and General Counsel), Thomas W Powers (Senior VP Technical Services), Doyle M Canaday (VP and Chief Financial Officer), Ronald H Rothman (VP)

PRINCIPAL ACTIVITIES: Precision engineering; heating and ventilation equipment; weapons systems; aircraft components
Parent Company: The Penn Central Corporation through GK Technologies Inc
Principal Bank: Bank of America
Financial Information:

	$'000
Sales revenues	500,000

No of Employees: 9,000

AUTOMOTIVE & CONSUMER GROUP

4450 Cranwood Ct, Cleveland, OH 44128
Tel: (216) 475-3600
Telex: 98259

President: Larry Kauchek (and Chief Executive Officer)
Senior Executive Officers: Ron Stibich (VP Marketing), Doug Kanter (VP/General Manager Auto Aftermarket Sales Division), Pat Reddington (VP Finance), Nat Cooke (VP Manufacturing), Dave Dunn (VP Research and Development), Larry Gisondi (VP/General Manager Consumer Division), Dave Schaar (VP/General Manager Specialized Dist. Sales Division)

PRINCIPAL ACTIVITIES: Manufacture of adhesives and home DIY products and products for car and boat maintenance
Trade Names: DURO (TM), PERMATEX (TM), LOCTITE (TM)
Parent Company: Loctite Corporation
Financial Information:

	$'000
Sales revenues	100,000

No of Employees: 500

AUTO-TROL TECHNOLOGY CORPORATION

12500 N Washington Street, PO Box 33815, Denver, CO 80223
Tel: (303) 452-4919

Chairman: Howard B Hillman (and President)
Senior Executive Officers: James T Hammock (Senior VP Marketing), Carnig Izmirian Sr (Senior VP Operations), Paul J Jerde (VP Finance), Jerry Sisson (VP International)

PRINCIPAL ACTIVITIES: Manufacture of data processing equipment
Principal Bank: Colorado National Bank of Denver
Financial Information:

	$'000
Sales revenues	65,400

No of Employees: 666

AVANTEK, INC

4401 Great America Parkway, Santa Clara, CA 95054-1211
Tel: (408) 727-0700
Telex: 3103718717 AVANTEK SNT

Chairman: Dr E Oran Brigham (and President)

Senior Executive Officers: Robert W Busch, Robert E Goff, Gary G Harmon, Lionel A Kirton

PRINCIPAL ACTIVITIES: Avantek, Inc was incorporated in California in 1965. It is engaged in the design, manufacture and marketing of solid-state microwave and lower frequency components, subsystems, equipment and systems sold to approximately 3,000 customers in the defense and space, commercial communications and test and instrumentation markets. The company produces over 600 separate proprietary products, the majority of which utilize microwave semiconductors manufactured by it which operate throughout the microwave frequency range (1-60 Gigahertz). While it currently sells some of its microwave semiconductors to outside customers, Avantek is a vertically integrated manufacturer and uses the bulk of these components in its own subassemblies such as amplifiers, oscillators, modules, mixers and multifunction assemblies which are then sold to other microwave equipment and system manufacturers. These subassemblies are also used in the production of Avantek's telecommunication subsystems, satellite earth station products and in its digital microwave radio network systems

Trade Names: Registered Trade Names:- Avantek, MICamp, UNIT. Trade Marks:-PlanarPak, IMFET, Avanpak, MODAMP

Financial Information:

	Dec 31 1985	Dec 31 1986
	$'000	$'000
Sales revenues	168,277	208,184
Income before taxes	31,373	29,410
Net income	18,338	16,116
Earnings per share	$0.95	$0.84

No of Employees: 3,200

AVATAR HOLDINGS INC

201 Alhambra Circle, Coral Gables, FL 33134
Tel: (305) 442 7000

Chairman: Leon Levy
President: Lawrence Wilkov

Senior Executive Officers: Peter Sharp (Chief Executive Officer and Chairman Executive Committee), Dennis J Gedman (Executive VP), Peter R Kleinerman (Executive VP, Treasurer and Chief Financial Officer), Juanita I Kerrigan (VP and Secretary), Barbara J McGlynn (VP Finance), Charles R McNairy (VP Finance), John Sladkus (Executive VP)

PRINCIPAL ACTIVITIES: Management of property and real estate

Principal Subsidiaries: Avatar Properties Inc; Country Club Inn Inc; Fort Myers Construction Co Inc; Gulf Communications Inc; Phoenix Advertising Associates; River Ranch Acres Club Inc; Sun Country Resorts Inc; Avatar Realty Inc; Mailman Development Corp; Avatar Utilities Inc; Consolidated Water Co Inc; Indiana Cities Water Corp; Missouri Cities Water Co; Northern MI Water Co; Ohio Suburban Water Co; Cape Coral Realty Inc; GAC Finance Inc of NY; GAC Utilities Inc of FL; Florida Cities Water Co; Parkway Mortgage Co Inc; T&T Co Holding Co; Title & Trust Co of FL; Abstract & Title Corp FL; Home Owners Title Co; Lauderdale Title Insurance

Principal Bank: Manufacturers Hanover Trust Co

Financial Information:

	$'000
Sales revenues	68,230

No of Employees: 930

AVCO FINANCIAL SERVICES, INC

3349 Michelson Center Drive, PO Box 19701, Irvine, CA 92713-9701
Tel: (714) 553-1200

Chairman: H Wallace Merryman
President: Charles R Rhinehart (and General Manager)

Senior Executive Officers: Robert P Bauman (Director, Vice Chairman of Textron Inc), Robert D Brazeau (Senior VP and Director), George H Breslin Jr (Director, President of Avco Financial Insurance Group), Ronald Bukow (Senior VP, Treasurer and Director), Donald K Farrar (Director, Senior Executive VP of Textron Inc and President of AVCO Operation), Gary L Fite (Senior VP, Controller and Director), Dennis G Little (Director, Executive VP and Chief Financial Officer of Textron Inc), Warren R Lyons (Senior VP and Director), Herbert F Smith (Senior VP, General Counsel, Secretary and Director), R Murray Smith (Senior VP and Director), Thomas D Soutter (Director, Executive VP and General Counsel of Textron Inc)

PRINCIPAL ACTIVITIES: Financial services including consumer credit operations, leasing and insurance

Parent Company: Paul Revere Corporation

Principal Subsidiaries: Avco Financial Services Group; Avco Financial Insurance Group; Paul Revere Life Insurance Group

Financial Information:

	Dec 31 1985
	$'000
Total revenues	1,545,884
Income before taxes	125,778
Net income	76,847
Dividends	49,400
Common stock	500
Retained income	783,973
Shareholders equity	807,362

No of Employees: 8,000

AVCO SYSTEMS

201 Lowell Street, Wilmington, MA 01887
Tel: (617) 657-5111
Telex: WUT 951531 avcosdl wili

Senior Executive Officers: H K McCard (VP and General Manager), R E Bibaud (VP Computer Services), J E Stevens (VP Operations), P B Kenyon (VP Tactical Systems), J J Siegel (VP), R L Townsend (VP Finance), H S Flickinger (VP Advanced Technology and Support Systems), R G Kitson (VP Operations, Washington DC), W A Fitzgerald Jr (VP Engineering), R A Robertson (VP Manufacturing and Procurement), S Zorfas, (VP Contract Management), R Feinberg (VP Strategic Laser Systems)

PRINCIPAL ACTIVITIES: Manufacture of missiles and aerospace equipment

Parent Company: Textron Inc

Financial Information:

	$'000
Sales revenues	240,000

No of Employees: 3,600

AVEMCO CORPORATION

411 Aviation Way, Frederick, MD 21701
Tel: (301) 694 5700

Chairman: William P Condon (and President and Chief Executive Officer)

Senior Executive Officers: John R Yuska (VP Finance and Treasurer), Thomas J Schwab (Secretary), John M St Peter (VP Marketing), Thomas H Chero (VP Legal), Dan L Jonson (VP Systems and Administration)

PRINCIPAL ACTIVITIES: Provision of a wide range of insurance services

Principal Subsidiaries: Avemco Insurance Co; Avemco Aircraft Investment Corp; Avemco Brokerage Inc; Avemco Sales Corp; Brooks-Shettle Co; Eastern AVI MAR Underwriters; Linden Corp; Loss Management Services Inc; National Insurance Underwriters

Principal Bank: Maryland National Bank

Financial Information:

	Dec 31 1985
	$'000
Revenues	59,410
Net income	7,590

No of Employees: 320

AVERY INTERNATIONAL CORPORATION

150 N Orange Grove Blvd, Box 7090, Pasadena, CA 91109
Tel: (818) 304-2000
Telex: WUT 675444 averycorp psd

Chairman: R S Avery (Founder); Chairman: Charles D Miller (and Chief Executive Officer)
President: Richard J Pearson (and Chief Operating Officer)
Senior Executive Officers: H R Smith (Chairman Executive Committee), Ralph F Baxter (Senior VP Manufacturing and Engineering), Philip M Neal (Senior VP Finance and Chief Financial Officer), Gerard Van Den Akker (Group VP Fasson Europe), Donald D Belcher (Group VP Consumer and Office Products), Robert D Fletcher (Group VP Avery Label), Richard J Hartl (Group VP Specialty Tapes and Adhesives), R Gregory Jenkins (Group VP Materials Division), John M Sergey (Group VP Sobar Division)

PRINCIPAL ACTIVITIES: Manufacture of adhesive labels for home, office and industrial use; printing and ancillaries
Principal Bank: Security Pacific National Bank
Financial Information:

	Nov 30 1985	Nov 30 1986
	$'000	$'000
Sales revenues	932,670	1,131,204
Net income	48,260	48,634
Earnings per share	$2.44	$2.45
Shareholders equity	314,455	350,010

No of Employees: 9,350

AVESTA INC

S.R. 38 W, PO Box 370, New Castle, Indianapolis, IN 47362
Tel: (317) 257-0584
Telex: WUT 501578 avesta ud

President: E Wayne Pokorney (and Chief Executive Officer)
Senior Executive Officers: John M Whitcomb (VP Administration)

PRINCIPAL ACTIVITIES: Steel industry
Parent Company: Avesta AB, Stockholm, Sweden
Financial Information:

	$'000
Sales revenues	100,000

No of Employees: 350

AVIALL, INC

4000 McEwen N, Dallas, TX 75244
Tel: (214) 357-1811

Chairman: Andrew G Galef; Vice Chairman: Frank D Hintze
President: Robert F Lambert
Senior Executive Officers: Peter D Blakely (Executive VP Engine and Aircraft Servicing), Donald T Koch (Executive VP International and Distribution Group), John L Wallace (Executive VP and Chief Operating Officer), Edward A Harris (VP Finance and Administration, Chief Financial Officer and Controller), Gerald F Price (VP Light and Medium Turbine Engine Division), Robert F Hanrahan (VP Aircraft Servicing Division), R F Leftwich (VP Heavy Turbine Engine Division), Ronald O Gall (VP Turbine Servicing Division), Larry J Schultz (VP General Aviation Distribution), Ronald L Patrick (VP Airline Distribution), William R Dexter (VP Human Resources), Roger A Hanna (VP Information Services), Steven J Maybury (VP Strategic Planning)

PRINCIPAL ACTIVITIES: Aircraft engineering and maintenance services

Financial Information:

	$'000
Sales revenues	400,000

No of Employees: 2,300

AVIS INDUSTRIAL CORPORATION

123 N Main Street, Upland, IN 46989
Tel: (317) 988-2706

Chairman: Leland E Boren
President: Gene L Hainen
Senior Executive Officers: Jacquelyn S Duggan (VP Finance), Dana H Dillard (Treasurer), Judith E Owen (Secretary)

PRINCIPAL ACTIVITIES: Interests in the manufacture of automobile products and accessories; production of electrical generators
Principal Bank: Indiana Bank and Trust Company of Fort Wayne
Financial Information:

	$'000
Sales revenues	72,000

No of Employees: 1,000

AVNET, INC

767 Fifth Avenue, New York, NY 10153
Tel: (212) 644-1050

Chairman: Anthony R Hamilton (and Chief Executive Officer)
President: Leon Machiz (and Vice Chairman and Chief Operating Officer)
Senior Executive Officers: Albert Snider (Executive VP), Jordan S Berman (Senior VP), Sylvester Herlihy (Senior VP and Secretary), Richard Deutsch (VP), Milt Graham (VP), Walter Hyjek (VP), Irwin Lubalin Sr (VP), Alvin A Odintz (VP), William Rose (VP and General Counsel), David S Shaw Sr (VP), Stanley Benerofe (VP), John Regazzi Sr (VP, Chief Financial Officer and Treasurer), Edward Kaniger Sr (VP), Daniel M Robbin (VP), Donald Sweet (VP), Anthony DeLuca (VP), Richard Berger (VP), San Farhg (VP), William Page (VP), Burton Katz (VP), George Kokkinakis (VP), John Lane (Senior VP), Steven Menefee (VP), Raymond Sadowski (VP and Controller), Morton Vogel (VP)

PRINCIPAL ACTIVITIES: Distribution of electronic components and computer products for industrial and military customers
Principal Bank: The Bank of New York
Financial Information:

	Jun 30 1986	Jun 30 1987
	$'000	$'000
Sales revenues	1,415,600	1,539,300
Income before taxes	42,300	46,600
Net income	23,900	22,800
Dividends per share	$0.50	$0.50
Earnings per share	$0.67	$0.64
Shareholders equity	646,900	657,900

No of Employees: 9,500

AVON PRODUCTS, INC

9 W 57th Street, New York, NY 10019
Tel: (212) 546-6015
Telex: 233568 AVONUR

Chairman: Hicks B Waldron (and Chief Executive Officer)
President: John S Chamberlin (and Chief Operating Officer)
Senior Executive Officers: James E Preston (Executive VP and President Avon Div), W Thomas Knight (Senior VP, Secretary and General Counsel), Jules Zimmerman (Senior VP and Chief Financial Officer), Robert W Pratt Jr (Senior VP, Planning and Administration Avon Div), Paul B Markovits (Executive VP, Avon Div, US), Stuart A Ochiltree (Executive VP, Avon Div, International), William R Henn (Senior VP, Planning and Development), John F Cox (Senior VP, Communications), Cam Starrett (Senior VP, Human Resources)

PRINCIPAL ACTIVITIES: A leading marketer and manufacturer of beauty products and supplier of health care services.
Trade Names: Avon Products Inc
Principal Subsidiaries: Foster Medical Corporation; The Mediplex Group Inc; Retirement Inns of America
Financial Information:

	Dec 31 1985	Dec 31 1986
	$'000	$'000
Sales revenues	2,470,100	2,883,100
Income before taxes	224,300	273,600
Net income (loss)	(59,900)	158,700
Dividends	925,500	706,300
Dividends per share	$2.00	$2.00
Earnings (loss) per share	($0.76)	$2.23
Retained income	706,300	606,800
Shareholders equity	926,400	681,300

No of Employees: 35,200

AVONDALE MILLS

Avondale Avenue, Sylacauga, AL 35150
Tel: (205) 245-5221
Telex: WUT 59861 avondale slga

Chairman: G Stephen Felker (and President and Chief Executive Officer)
Senior Executive Officers: Donald Comer Jr (Chairman Executive Committee), D R Bess (Senior VP Finance and Administration), R L Edmunds (VP, Secretary and Treasurer), Lorton S Livingston (VP Credit), T W Spraggins (VP Manufacturing Service), C S Crockard (VP Corporate Planning and Development)

PRINCIPAL ACTIVITIES: Manufacture of knitting yarns
Principal Bank: The First National Bank of Birmingham
Financial Information:

	$'000
Sales revenues	238,263

No of Employees: 4,690

AVONDALE SHIPYARDS, INC

PO Box 50280, New Orleans, LA 70150
Tel: (504) 436-2121
Telex: RCA 266070 avon ur

President: Albert L Bossier Jr (and Chief Executive Officer)
Senior Executive Officers: Richard F Brunner (Senior VP and Senior Operating Officer), Edward A Blanchard (Group VP Production Operations), James R Wilkins Jr (Group VP Engineering), W A Harmeyer (Group VP Production), Robert S Miller (Group VP Administration), V J Baricev (VP Purchasing), M McCain Jr (VP Repairs and Conversions), Clarence Geier (VP Harvey Plant), Ernest F Griffin (VP Personnel), J W Oberfell (VP and Chief Financial Officer), Kenneth Dupont (VP Bayon Black Division), R Dean Church (VP and Assistant Secretary), F J Roth (VP Security), E E Blanchard (VP Production Engineering), M Colen (VP Corporate Marketing Management), Alan Nierenberg (VP and Chief Engineer), P D Mitchell (VP Estimating), E L Landry (VP Steel Sales Division), C J Starkenburg (VP Production Planning), R P Meric Jr (VP Contract Administration), William W Lewis (VP Industrial Marketing)

PRINCIPAL ACTIVITIES: Avondale Shipyards, Inc, designs, engineers, builds, modernizes and repairs Naval and commercial oceangoing vessels, non-oceangoing craft, offshore structures, and drilling vessels; and modular units for oil exploration and production, chemical and petroleum processing plants, and hydraulic facilities
Parent Company: Ogden Corporation, New York, NY
Principal Bank: Whitney National Bank
Financial Information:

	$'000
Sales revenues	420,000

No of Employees: 5,000

AVX CORPORATION

60 Cutter Mill Road, Great Neck, NY 11021
Tel: (516) 829-8500
Telex: TWX 510 2230 856 avx grnk

Chairman: Marshall D Butler (and Chief Executive Officer)
President: Donald Thostenson (and Chief Operating Officer)
Senior Executive Officers: Benedict P Rosen (Executive VP), John S Gilbertson (VP), Joe Norwood (VP), John Mann (VP), Kim Ritchie (VP), John Winn (VP)

PRINCIPAL ACTIVITIES: Manufacture of electronic ceramic capacitors
Principal Subsidiaries: Central Machine Products Inc
Principal Bank: Bankers Trust Company
Financial Information:

	$'000
Sales revenues	178,700

No of Employees: 5,100

AXIA INC

122 W 22nd Street, Oak Brook, IL 60523
Tel: (312) 654-3350

Chairman: D W Sheehan (and President and Chief Executive Officer)
Senior Executive Officers: D B Moritz (Executive VP), H J Vogt (VP Finance, Treasurer and Controller), Uma N Aggarwal (VP and President and General Manager Jensen Tools Inc), R J Robinson (VP and President and General Manager Ames Taping Tool Systems Company), R J Kulla (VP and General Counsel), Terry E Williams (President and General Manager Goldblatt Tool co), H O Hayes (President and General Manager Nestaway Division), E Curtis Johnson (President and General Manager Dave Fischbein Co)

PRINCIPAL ACTIVITIES: Manufacture of steel products; furniture components; tools
Parent Company: New Axia Holding Corp
Principal Subsidiaries: Ames Taping Tools Systems Co; Goldblatt Tool Co; Jensen Tools Inc
Principal Bank: Marine Midland Bank NA
Financial Information:

	$'000
Sales revenues	120,000

No of Employees: 1,100

AYDIN CORPORATION

700 Dresher Road, Box 349, Horsham, PA 19044
Tel: (215) 657-7510
Telex: 685 1211 AYDIN UW

Chairman: Ayhan Hakimoglu (and President)
Senior Executive Officers: P Christensen, W L Creech, L Goetz, J Lohr, B J Miller, J Vanderslice, J Landis, J Clements, D Wennerstrom, R Clancy, G Hakimoglu, H Welber

PRINCIPAL ACTIVITIES: Telecommunications-including satellite earth stations, digital telecommunications, line-of-sight microwave radios, T-I Multiplexers, troposcatter terminals, anti-jam communications, data acquisition and receive systems, transceivers, computer networking equipment, avionics, and complete telecommunications systems. Color Terminals and Computer Systems-color display terminals, high resolution color monitors, computer systems for military communications, including Full-Mil systems, anti-submarine warfare display systems, air traffic control and air space management systems, and supervisory control systems for telecom networks. Radars, EW and Support Components-2-Dimensional and 3-Dimensional radars for tactical applications, air defense systems, and electronic warfare equipment, self protection electronic decoys, threat simulation systems; printed circuit boards and sheet metal cabinetry
Trade Names: Patriot (Line of High Resolution Color Monitors)
Principal Subsidiaries: Aydin Controls (UK) Ltd; Aydin International UK

Principal Banks: Citibank; Mellon Bank (East) NA; American Express; Security Pacific
Financial Information:

	Dec 31 1985	Dec 31 1986
	$'000	$'000
Sales revenues	133,019	136,791
Income before taxes	4,877	12,164
Net income	3,799	6,952
Earnings per share	$0.86	$1.81
Common stock*	4,119,481	3,723,021
Retained income	57,228	56,342
Shareholders equity	61,348	60,065

*number of shares

Principal Shareholders: A Hakimoglu (21.45%); Prudential Insurance Co of America (8.53%)
No of Employees: 2,000

AZP GROUP INC

411 North Central Avenue, Phoenix, AZ 85004
Tel: (602) 250-1000

Chairman: Keith L Turley (and President)
Senior Executive Officers: Henry B Sargent (Executive VP, Treasurer and Chief Financial Officer), Edward E Van Brunt Jr (Executive VP Nuclear Operations), Jaron B Norberg (Senior VP and Corporate Counsel), O Mark De Michele (VP), Walter F Ekstrom (VP Electric Operations), David W Ellis (VP Research and Development and Alternative Energy Applications), Joseph A Gelinas (VP Employee Relations), B Paul Hart (VP Rates and Regulations), Russell D Hulse (VP Resources Planning), Jerry Human (VP Customer Services State Region), Charles D Jarman (VP Construction), Donald B Karner (VP Engineering), Guy W Lunt (VP Customer Services Metro Region), John C Ogden (VP Cusomter and Administrative Services), William J Post (VP and Controller), Shirley Richard (VP Corporate Relations), Henry B Sargent Jr (VP and Treasurer), Paul A Williams II (VP and Treasurer, Finance and Tax Services)

PRINCIPAL ACTIVITIES: Supply of gas and electricity
Principal Subsidiaries: Arizona Public Service Co; El Dorado Investment Co; Malapai Resources Co; SunCor Development Co; APS Finance Co NV; APS Fuels Co; Bixco Inc; Energy Development Co
Principal Bank: Valley National Bank
Financial Information:

	Dec 31 1986
	$'000
Sales revenues	1,249,912
Net income	234,184
Earnings per share	$3.04
Shareholders equity	2,069,347

No of Employees: 11,300

AZS CORPORATION

762 Marietta Blvd NW, Atlanta, GA 30318
Tel: (404) 873-1850

Chairman: Tozo Morishima
President: Robert G Short (and Chief Executive Officer)
Senior Executive Officers: Joel L Padgett (Secretary and Treasurer)

PRINCIPAL ACTIVITIES: Manufacture of specialty chemicals and plastics
Parent Company: Toyo Soda Manufacturing Co Ltd
Principal Bank: Bank of the South
Financial Information:

	$'000
Sales revenues	50,000

No of Employees: 200

B B WALKER COMPANY

See WALKER, B B, COMPANY

B F GOODRICH COMPANY (THE)

See GOODRICH, B F, COMPANY (THE)

BABBITT BROTHERS TRADING CO

Box 1328, Flagstaff, AZ 86001
Tel: (602) 774-8711

Chairman: John G Babbitt
President: Paul Babbitt Jr
Senior Executive Officers: J L Roubal (VP Credit), Michael D'Mura (VP), Raymond Lopp (VP Wholesale Division), James E Babbitt (VP Personnel), Robert E Nimmons (Treasurer and Controller)

PRINCIPAL ACTIVITIES: General trading; operation of department stores; hardware wholesale; timber sales
Principal Subsidiaries: Cedar Ridge Trading Post Co; Oraibi Trading Post Co; Redlake Trading Post Co Inc; Tuber Trading Post Co Inc; Warren Trading Post Co
Principal Bank: The Valley National Bank
Financial Information:

	$'000
Sales revenues	60,000

No of Employees: 500

BACARDI CORPORATION

2100 Biscayne Blvd, Miami, FL 33131
Tel: (305) 573 8511
Telex: WUT 519292 Bacardi Mia

PRINCIPAL ACTIVITIES: Manufacture of alcoholic beverages
Parent Company: Bacardi Corporation, San Juan, Puerto Rico
Financial Information:

	$'000
Sales revenues	270,000

No of Employees: 740

BADCOCK, W S, CORPORATION

200 Phosphate Blvd, Mulberry, FL 33860
Tel: (813) 425-4921

Chairman: Wogan S Badcock Sr
President: Wogan S Badcock Jr
Senior Executive Officers: William K Pou (Executive VP), Evelyn C Badcock (Executive VP), William T Daughtrey (VP, Secretary and Assistant to President), Richard P Barnes (VP Live Oak Operations), Robert E Elliot (VP Operations and Systems), Luther N Pipkin (VP Appliance and Electronics), William Seigler (VP Dealer Operations), Frank Lunsford (VP Wholesale Operations), William L Girtman (VP Finance and Treasurer), William E Sparkman (VP Customer Relations)

PRINCIPAL ACTIVITIES: Manufacture and sale of furniture and furniture components
Principal Bank: Atlantic National Bank of Jacksonville
Financial Information:

	$'000
Sales revenues	140,000

No of Employees: 500

BADGER METER, INC

4545 W Brown Deer Road, Milwaukee, WI 53223
Tel: (414) 355-0400
Telex: WUT 26757 badgmet bandr

Chairman: J O Wright (and Chief Executive Officer)
President: James L Forbes
Senior Executive Officers: R Robert Howard (VP Finance and Treasurer), W E Bidgood (VP), W H Vander Heyden (VP), W C Howland (VP International), Rebecca L Rush (Secretary), John J Janik (VP Operations), Ron H Dix (VP Personnel)

PRINCIPAL ACTIVITIES: Manufacture of measurement and control systems
Principal Subsidiaries: Badger Meter International Sales
Principal Bank: Marshall & Ilsley

Financial Information:

	Dec 31 1985
	$'000
Sales revenues	55,586
Income before taxes	1,695
Net income	1,339
Dividends	584
Dividends per share	$0.40
Earnings per share	$0.92
Common stock	1,460
Retained income	17,622
Shareholders equity	20,054

No of Employees: 1,050

BADGER PAPER MILLS INC
200 West Front Street, PO Box 149, Peshtigo, WI 54157
Tel: (715) 582 4551

Chairman: Edwin A Meyer Jr (and Chief Executive Officer)
President: Bennie C Burish (and Chief Operating Officer)
Senior Executive Officers: Duane U Stehle (VP, Director Sales and Advertising), Miles L Kresl Jr (Secretary and Treasurer), Raymond C Andersen (VP Manufacturing)

PRINCIPAL ACTIVITIES: Paper production
Principal Bank: Harris Bank & Trust Co
Financial Information:

	$'000
Sales revenues	49,070

No of Employees: 430

BADISCHE CORPORATION
600 Palisade Avenue, Englewood, NJ 07631
Tel: (201) 568-6354
Telex: TWX 710 8821255 baco wmbg

Chairman: Detlef Dibbern
President: H H Kopper (and Chief Executive Officer)
Senior Executive Officers: R R Zoccolillo (Group VP Fibers and Yarns), J R Pinotti (Group VP Chemicals), K H Messinger (VP Finance), W K Martin (VP Technical), A R Trevarthen (VP Human Resources)

PRINCIPAL ACTIVITIES: Manufacture of chemicals and synthetic fibers
Parent Company: BASF AG, Ludwigshafen, Germany
Financial Information:

	$'000
Sales revenues	700,000

No of Employees: 4,283

BAIRD CORPORATION
125 Middlesex Turnpike, Bedford, MA 01730
Tel: (617) 276 6000

President: John M Dempsey Jr
Senior Executive Officers: George J Lilley (VP Operations), Jack M Medzorian (VP and Treasurer), Robert A Trevisani (Secretary), I D'Arcy Brent II (VP Production), Arthur S Turner (VP Nuclear), John A Fitzmaurice (VP Corporate Development), Donald R Walker (VP)

PRINCIPAL ACTIVITIES: Manufacture of scientific instruments for technical and engineering research purposes
Principal Subsidiaries: Labtest Equipment Co; Miller-Holzwarth Inc
Principal Bank: Bank of New England
Financial Information:

	$'000
Sales revenues	49,225

No of Employees: 700

BAIRD-WARD PRINTING CO, INC
PO Box 539, Nashville, TN 37202
Tel: (615) 385-0460

Senior Executive Officers: William J Hepler (VP Manufacturing)

PRINCIPAL ACTIVITIES: Commercial printing; telephone directories, magazines and periodicals
Parent Company: Arcata Corporation, Arcata, CA
Financial Information:

	$'000
Sales revenues	50,000

No of Employees: 900

BAIRNCO CORPORATION
200 Park Avenue, New York, NY 10166
Tel: (212) 490-8722

Chairman: Glenn W Bailey (and President)
Senior Executive Officers: Frank Metzger (VP Administration), Robert J Prata (VP Secretary and Treasurer)

PRINCIPAL ACTIVITIES: Holding company with interests in electronic equipment and domestic lighting fixtures, industrial products
Principal Subsidiaries: Genlyte Group Inc; KCS Lighting Inc; Lightolier Inc; Basic Concept Ltd; Wide-Lite International Corp; Keene Corp
Principal Bank: Chemical Bank
Financial Information:

	Dec 31 1985	Dec 31 1986
	$'000	$'000
Sales revenues	537,240	585,055
Net income	21,900	22,530
Earnings per share	$2.33	$2.20
Shareholders equity	167,528	185,656

No of Employees: 5,000

BAKER COMMODITIES INC
4020 Bandini Blvd, Los Angeles, CA 90023
Tel: (213) 268-2801
Telex: TWX 9103213987 bakercom blsa

President: James M Andreoli (and Chief Executive Officer)
Senior Executive Officers: Raymond F Kelly (Executive VP Operations and Secretary), George L Congleton (VP Marketing), Edward S Murakami (VP Research and Quality Assurance), James K Reynolds (VP Finance and Chief Financial Officer), William Sikes (VP Production), Joseph Keeler (VP)

PRINCIPAL ACTIVITIES: Processing of oils and fats; production of animal feedstuffs
Principal Bank: Bank of America
Financial Information:

	$'000
Sales revenues	200,000

No of Employees: 600

BAKER INDUSTRIES, INC
1633 Littleton Road, Parsippany, NJ 07054
Tel: (201) 267-5300

Chairman: James J Gavin Jr (and President and Chief Executive Officer)
Senior Executive Officers: Charles R Schneider (Group VP Physical Security), James C Hensler (Group VP Electronic Security), Kenneth W Oringer (VP Finance), Paul L Rathblott (VP Secretary and General Counsel)

PRINCIPAL ACTIVITIES: Fire alarm and detection systems; transportation and courier service
Parent Company: Borg Warner Corporation, Chicago, IL
Principal Bank: Chemical Bank
Financial Information:

	$'000
Sales revenues	1,000,000

No of Employees: 60,000

BAKER INTERNATIONAL CORPORATION

500 City Parkway West, Orange, CA 92668
Tel: (714) 634-2333
Telex: WUT 181616 baker int orge

Chairman: Ernest H Clark Jr (and Chief Executive Officer)
President: James D Woods (and Chief Operating Officer)
Senior Executive Officers: John F Schaefer (Executive VP), Joel V Staff (Senior VP), Ronald G Turner (VP), R Robert Harris (VP, Secretary and General Counsel), Max L Lukens (VP and Chief Financial Officer)

PRINCIPAL ACTIVITIES: Manufacture of tools and equipment for gas and oil industry; mining equipment
Principal Subsidiaries: Totco; Tri-State Oil Tool Industries Inc; Reed Tool Company; Baker Oil Tools Inc; Baker CAC Inc; Baker Production Technology; Magna Corporation; Baker Mining Equipment Company; Chas S Lewis & Co Inc; Ramsey Engineering Company; Reed Mining Tools Inc; GLI Inc; Baker Drilling Equipment Company; Baker Tubular Services; Exploration Logging Inc; Milchem Inc
Financial Information:

	Sep 30 1985	Sep 30 1986
	$'000	$'000
Sales revenues	1,904,320	1,557,211
Net income (loss)	87,740	(272,987)
Earnings (loss) per share	$1.25	($3.89)
Shareholders equity	1,010,166	683,201

No of Employees: 20,580

BAKER, MICHAEL, CORPORATION

4301 Dutch Ridge Road, Box 280, Beaver, PA 15009
Tel: (412) 495 7711

Chairman: William J Copeland; Vice Chairman: Phillip A Koonce
President: Richard L Shaw (and Chief Executive Officer)
Senior Executive Officers: Charles I Homan (President Northern Division), Donald J Nelson (Treasurer and Secretary)

PRINCIPAL ACTIVITIES: Civil engineering and related consultancy services
Principal Subsidiaries: Michael Baker Jr Inc; Baker Engineering Inc; Michael Baker Jr of NY Inc
Principal Bank: Mellon Bank
Financial Information:

	$'000
Sales revenues	40,000

No of Employees: 740

BALDOR ELECTRIC CO

5711 South 7th Street, Fort Smith, AR 72902
Tel: (501) 646-4711
Telex: TWX 910 7237650 baldor fts

Chairman: Roland S Boreham Jr (and Chief Executive Officer)
President: William T Kirkpatrick (and Chief Operating Officer)
Senior Executive Officers: Quentin Ponder (Executive VP Operations), Robert L Qualls (Executive VP Finance and Planning), William O Parris (Senior VP Operations), Robert E Bender (VP Sales), Robert G DeVinney (VP Marketing), Orville W Dodson (VP Quality and Production Engineering), Henry W Endres Jr (VP St Louis Operations), Gregory C Kowert (VP and Controller)

PRINCIPAL ACTIVITIES: Production of electric motors, grinders and dental equipment
Principal Subsidiaries: ASR Inc; ASR Servotron Inc; Baldor International Inc; Baldor-Osseo Inc; RA Boehm Co; Carolina Capacitors Inc; Southwestern Die Castings Co
Principal Bank: The Boatmen's National Bank of St Louis
Financial Information:

	$'000
Sales revenues	174,700

No of Employees: 2,470

BALDWIN & LYONS INC

3100 North Meridian Street, Indianapolis, IN 46208
Tel: (317) 925 3501

Chairman: John C Aldin (and Chief Executive Officer)
President: Gary W Miller
Senior Executive Officers: Patrick G Corydon (VP and Treasurer), James E Kirschner (VP and Secretary), James W Good (VP Marketing), Gregory A Bonnell (VP Insurance), Daniel P Colombo (VP Sales)

PRINCIPAL ACTIVITIES: Insurance
Principal Subsidiaries: AMLI Realty Co Inc; Protective Insurance Co; Sagamore Insurance Co
Principal Bank: Merchants National Bank & Trust Co
Financial Information:

	Dec 31 1985
	$'000
Revenues	100,665

No of Employees: 225

BALFOUR, L G, COMPANY, INC

25 County Street, Attleboro, MA 02703
Tel: (617) 222-3600
Telex: WUT 927799 balfour abor

Chairman: Thomas G Wyman
President: James S Cook (and Chief Executive Officer)
Senior Executive Officers: Richard L Yale (VP Finance and Administration), Timothy B Sullivan (VP Educational Products Group), Kenneth H Klein (VP Recognition Products Group)

PRINCIPAL ACTIVITIES: Manufacture of educational products
Principal Bank: Fleet National Bank
Financial Information:

	$'000
Sales revenues	100,000

No of Employees: 2,000

BALL CORPORATION

345 S High Street, Muncie, IN 47302
Tel: (317) 747-6100
Telex: TWX 8103441680 ball corp

Chairman: Richard M Ringson (and President and Chief Executive Officer)
Senior Executive Officers: Edmund F Ball (Chairman Executive Committee), D E Emerson (Senior VP Administration), William L Peterson (Senior VP and Chief Financial Officer), Frank A Bracken (Group VP Glass Containers), D A Davis (Group VP Metal Containers), John H Snyder (Group VP Industrial Products), D B Hicks (Group VP Technical Products)

PRINCIPAL ACTIVITIES: Manufacture of glass, metal and plastic containers; data processing equipment components; ophthalmic products; aerospace equipment
Principal Subsidiaries: Ball International Sales Corp; Ball Packaging Products Inc; Muncie & Western Railroad Co
Principal Bank: Continental Illinois National Bank & Trust co
Financial Information:

	Dec 31 1985	Dec 31 1986
	$'000	$'000
Sales revenues	1,106,230	1,070,300
Net income	51,200	58,900
Earnings per share	$14.29	$2.56
Shareholders equity	-	365,300

No of Employees: 9,000

BALLY MANUFACTURING CORPORATION

8700 W Bryn Mawr, Chicago, IL 60631
Tel: (312) 399-1300
Telex: WUT 253076 balfan cgl

Chairman: Robert E Mullane (and President and Chief Executive Officer)

Senior Executive Officers: Roger N Keesee (Executive VP), Paul Johnson (VP, Chief Financial Officer and Treasurer), William H Peltier (VP, Communications), Charles T Powell (VP Administration), James M Rochford (VP), Neil Jenkins (VP, Secretary and General Counsel)

PRINCIPAL ACTIVITIES: Manufacture of coin operated amusement and gaming machines; operation of amusement arcades, casinos and hotels and health clubs
Principal Bank: Continental Illinois National Bank
Financial Information:

	Dec 31 1985	Dec 31 1986
	$'000	$'000
Sales revenues	1,294,830	1,638,969
Net income	25,640	24,009
Earnings per share	$0.95	$0.81

No of Employees: 47,000

BALLY'S PARK PLACE INC

Park Place and the Boardwalk, Atlantic City, NJ 08401
Tel: (609) 340 2000

Chairman: Richard Gillman (and Chief Executive Officer)
President: William S Weinberger
Senior Executive Officers: Dorothy Attanasio (Senior VP), Wallace R Barr (Senior VP), James D Carr (Senior VP), C Patrick McKoy (VP and Treasurer), Charles Tannenbaum (Senior VP), Dennis P Venuti (VP, Secretary and Legal Counsel)

PRINCIPAL ACTIVITIES: Casino and hotel operators
Parent Company: Bally Manufacturing Corporation
Principal Bank: First Fidelity Bank of South Jersey
Financial Information:

	$'000
Revenues	260,320

No of Employees: 3,800

BALTIMORE BANKCORP

Baltimore and Charles Streets, Baltimore, MD 21202
Tel: (301) 244 3360

President: Harry L Robinson (and Chief Executive Officer)
Senior Executive Officers: Jerome P Baroch (VP), John Haigh (VP)

PRINCIPAL ACTIVITIES: Banking
Financial Information:

	Dec 31 1985
	$'000
Revenues	183,130
Net income	17,315

No of Employees: 765

BALTIMORE GAS & ELECTRIC CO

Gas and Electric Bldg, Charles Center, PO Box 1475, Baltimore, MD 21203
Tel: (301) 234-5000

Chairman: Bernard C Trueschler
President: George V McGowan
Senior Executive Officers: Herbert D Coss Jr (VP, General Services), Michael J Chesser (VP, Consumer Services), Edward A Crooke (VP, Finance and Accounting and Secretary), John M Files (VP, Management and Staff Services), John W Gore, Jr (VP, Electric Interconnection and Operations), Arthur E Lundvall Jr (VP, Fossil Energy), George D England (VP, Distribution), Joseph A Tiernan (VP, Nuclear Energy), Charles W Shivery (Treasurer and Assistant Secretary), Thomas F Brady (Assistant Secretary and Assistant Treasurer)

PRINCIPAL ACTIVITIES: Primarily in the business of producing and selling electricity and purchasing and selling natural gas
Principal Subsidiaries: Safe Harbor Water Power Corporation; Constellation Holdings, Inc; BNG Inc
Principal Bank: Maryland National Bank-Baltimore
Financial Information:

	Dec 31 1985	Dec 31 1986
	$'000	$'000
Sales revenues	1,754,772	1,834,020
Net Income before taxes	403,872	428,581
Net income	247,300	274,619
Dividends common stock	131,692	139,567
Dividends per share declared	$1.675	$1.775
Earnings per common share	$2.80	$3.15
Common stock	78,622	78,640
Retained earnings	712,280	820,156
Shareholders equity	1,521,960	1,629,867

No of Employees: 8,833

BALTZ BROS PACKING CO

1612 Elm Hill Pike, Nashville, TN 37210
Tel: 615 244-9480

President: Robert J Baltz Jr
Senior Executive Officers: Frank J Baltz (VP), Dennis L Baltz (VP Plant, Secretary and Treasurer), Douglas M Baltz (VP Engineering), John P Baltz (VP Distribution)

PRINCIPAL ACTIVITIES: Meat and meat processing; meat packing
Principal Bank: Third National Bank
Financial Information:

	$'000
Sales revenues	65,000

No of Employees: 450

BANC ONE CORPORATION

100 E Broad Street, Columbus, OH 43215
Tel: (614) 463-5944

Chairman: John F Havens
President: John B McCoy (and Chief Executive and Operations Officer)
Senior Executive Officers: Roman J Gerber (Executive VP and Secretary), John F Fisher (Senior VP), P P Handley (VP)

PRINCIPAL ACTIVITIES: Holding company with interests in banking
Principal Subsidiaries: Banc One Capital Corp; Banc One Financial Corp; Banc One Life Insurance Co; Banc One Mortgage Co; Banc One Realty Corp; Bank One; Miami Bank
Financial Information:

	Dec 31 1985	Dec 31 1986
	$'000	$'000
Net income	130,362	164,738
Earnings per share	$2.01	$2.29
Shareholders equity	772,380	960,359
Deposits	8,140,636	10,195,497
Total assets	10,823,485	12,661,761

No of Employees: 9,945

BANCAL TRI-STATE CORPORATION

400 California Street, San Francisco, CA 94104
Tel: (415) 765-0400

President: Ross P Williams (and Chief Operating Officer)
Senior Executive Officers: Eugene F McKelligan (VP Treasurer and Controller), Bonnie H Hemmerling (VP and Secretary)

PRINCIPAL ACTIVITIES: Bank holding company
Parent Company: Mitsubishi Bank Limited
Principal Bank: The Bank of California NA

No of Employees: 2,230

BANCOHIO NATIONAL BANK

155 E Broad St, Columbus, OH 43251
Tel: (614) 463-8100

Chairman: Arthur D Herrmann (and Chief Executive Officer)

President: David A Daberko
Senior Executive Officers: Alan J Davidson (Executive VP), Willis I Else (Executive VP)

PRINCIPAL ACTIVITIES: Banking
Parent Company: National City Corporation

No of Employees: 5,750

BANCOKLAHOMA CORPORATION

BancOklahoma Tower, Box 2300, Tulsa, OK 74192
Tel: (918) 588-6000
Telex: WUT 492388 boktu

Chairman: Leonard J Eaton Jr (and Chief Executive Officer)
President: Samuel B Hayes III (and Chief Operating Officer)
Senior Executive Officers: William B Fader (Executive VP Finance and Chief Financial Officer)

PRINCIPAL ACTIVITIES: Banking
Principal Subsidiaries: Bank of Oklahoma, Tulsa, NA
Financial Information:

	Dec 31 1985
	$'000
Revenues	319,682
Net income	6,150

No of Employees: 1,600

BANCORP HAWAII, INC

111 S King St, PO Box 2900, Honolulu, HI 96846
Tel: (808) 537-8111

Chairman: Frank J Manaut (and Chief Executive Officer)
President: Howard H Stephenson
Senior Executive Officers: Lawrence M Johnson (Vice Chairman), Thomas W Mahoney (Senior VP), Thomas J Kappock III (Executive VP and Treasurer), John K Tsui (Executive VP), Richard J Dahl (Executive VP and Chief Financial Officer)

PRINCIPAL ACTIVITIES: Banking, leasing and insurance interests
Principal Subsidiaries: Bank of Hawaii; Bank of Hawaii International, Inc; Bank of Hawaii International Corporation, New York; Bankoh Advisory Corp; Bankoh Corporation; Bankoh Equipment Leasing Corporation; S I L Inc; Hawaiian Hong Kong Holdings Ltd; Arbella Leasing Corporation; Bancorp Business Systems of Hawaii Inc; Bancorp Leasing of Hawaii Inc; Bancorp Finance of Hawaii Inc; Bancorp Finance of Hawaii-(Guam) Inc; Bancorp Life Insurance Company of Hawaii Inc; Bancorp Insurance Agency of Hawaii Inc; Bancorp Hawaii Small Business Investment Company Inc; Bancorp Investment Advisory Services Inc; Bancorp Hawaii Service Corp; Investors Pacific Ltd; Hawaiian Trust Company Ltd
Principal Bank: Bank of Hawaii
Financial Information:

	Dec 31 1985	Dec 31 1986
	$'000	$'000
Income(1)	485,856	485,475
Investment income	68,753	60,058
Income before taxes	50,061	64,598
Net income	38,561	46,185
Dividends	11,627	13,504
Dividends per share	$1.30	$1.48
Earnings per share(2)	$4.31	$5.07
Earnings per share(3)	$4.25	$4.97
Common stock	18,061	18,461
Retained income	180,045	212,726
Shareholders equity	262,032	303,908
Deposits	3,857,284	4,342,847
Total assets	4,438,585	5,060,018

(1) Total interest income and non interest income
(2) Primary
(3) Fully diluted

No of Employees: 3,258

BANCORP OF MISSISSIPPI INC

1 Mississippi Plaza, Tupelo, MS 38802
Tel: (601) 842 6661

Chairman: J C Whitehead (and Chief Executive Officer); Vice Chairman: Aubrey B Patterson Jr (and President)
Senior Executive Officers: L Nash Allen (Treasurer and Chief Financial Officer), Cornelia B Emmons (Secretary)

PRINCIPAL ACTIVITIES: Banking services
Principal Bank: Bank of Mississippi
Financial Information:

	Dec 31 1985
	$'000
Revenues	68,050
Net income	7,550

No of Employees: 590

BANCTEC INC

4435 Spring Valley Road, Dallas, TX 75244
Tel: (214) 450 7700

Chairman: Grahame N Clark (and Chief Executive Officer)
President: Norton A Stuart (and Chief Operating Officer)
Senior Executive Officers: G Wesley Mayland (Senior VP and Chief Financial Officer), Wm E Bassett (Senior VP and General Manager)

PRINCIPAL ACTIVITIES: Manufacture, sale and service of a broad line of document processing systems
Trade Names: BancTec
Principal Subsidiaries: BTI Systems Inc; BancTec Supplies & Manufacturing PR Inc; Scan-Data GmbH (Germany); OCR Scan-Data Ltd (UK)
Principal Bank: First Republic Bank Dallas
Financial Information:

	Mar 31 1986	Mar 31 1987
	$'000	$'000
Sales revenues	76,441	85,571
Income before taxes	3,365	5,247
Net income	2,617	3,815
Earnings per share*	$0.45	$0.71
Common stock	44	45
Retained income	2,036	5,851
Shareholders equity	27,989	26,754

*fully diluted

No of Employees: 960

BANCTEXAS GROUP INC

PO Box 50972, 1601 Elm Street, Dallas, TX 75250
Tel: (214) 969-6109

Chairman: Vance C Miller
President: Richard L Ripley (and Chief Executive Officer)
Senior Executive Officers: Alfred W Bowman Jr (Executive VP), Richard H Braucher (Senior VP), Daniel S Piggott (Senior VP and Controller), Charles W Kay (Senior VP Operations and Administration), Gerald Pavlas (Senior VP Supervised Loans and Corporate Administration)

PRINCIPAL ACTIVITIES: Banking
Principal Subsidiaries: BancTexas, Dallas, NA
Financial Information:

	Dec 31 1985
	$'000
Revenues	197,250

No of Employees: 1,240

BANDAG, INC

Bandag Center, Muscatine, IA 52761
Tel: (319) 262-1400
Telex: WUT 468459 bandag musc

Chairman: Martin G Carver (and Chief Executive Officer)
Senior Executive Officers: Donald Chester (Senior VP International), Thomas Dvorchak (Senior VP and Chief

Financial Officer), William Herd (Senior VP North American Sales), Hendrik A Glazener (Senior VP, General Manager, Eastern Hemisphere Retread Group), Madis Sulg (Senior VP Planning and Development)

PRINCIPAL ACTIVITIES: Manufacture of precured tread rubber, equipment and supplies for the retreading of tires, primarily truck and bus, by exclusive franchised dealers using the patented Bandag method of retreading

Trade Names: Bandag (R)

Principal Subsidiaries: Bandag AG (Switzerland); Bandag Europe NV (Belgium); Bandag Canada Ltd; Bandag Licensing Corporation (doing business as Master Processing Corp)

Principal Bank: Northern Trust Co, Chicago, IL

Financial Information:

	Dec 31 1985	Dec 31 1986
	$'000	$'000
Sales revenues	329,591	370,396
Income before taxes (1)	81,402	92,016
Net income (2)	43,254	48,464
Dividends	10,355	11,236
Dividends per share	$0.60(3)	$0.6625
Earnings per share	$2.51(3)	$2.85
Common stock	8,631	8,432
Retained income	150,263	178,853
Shareholders equity	163,879	191,948

(1) and extraordinary credit
(2) before extraordinary credit and reversal of deferred DISC income taxes
(3) adjusted for 2:1 stock split Jan 16 1987

Principal Shareholders: The Carver Family

No of Employees: 2,113

BANGOR HYDROELECTRIC COMPANY

33 State Street, Bangor, ME 04401
Tel: (207) 945 5621

Chairman: Thomas A Greenquist (and President and Chief Executive Officer)

Senior Executive Officers: Robert S Briggs (VP and Legal Counsel), John P O'Sullivan (VP and Treasurer), Carroll R Lee (VP Engineering and Operations)

PRINCIPAL ACTIVITIES: Production and supply of electricity

Principal Bank: Manufacturers Hanover Trust Co

Financial Information:

	$'000
Sales revenues	95,750

No of Employees: 420

BANGOR PUNTA CORPORATION

One Greenwich Plaza, Greenwich, CT 06830
Tel: (203) 622-8100
Telex: WUT 965909 bnkgrc

Chairman: Robert T Campion (and President)

Senior Executive Officers: Dudley C Phillips (Senior VP and General Counsel), Max E Black (Senior VP), Gerald B Brewer (Senior VP), L J Deters (Senior VP), Jonathan Lushing (Senior VP), Morgan C Brown III (VP and Secretary)

PRINCIPAL ACTIVITIES: Holding company with interests in aviation and aerospace equipment and sporting equipment including guns

Parent Company: Lear Siegler Inc, Santa Monica, CA

Financial Information:

	$'000
Sales revenues	620,000

No of Employees: 14,000

BANK BUILDING & EQUIPMENT CORPORATION OF AMERICA

3630 S Geyer Road, St Louis, MO 63127
Tel: (314) 821-2265

President: Carl J Weis (and Chief Executive Officer)

Senior Executive Officers: Myron A Carpenter (Senior VP, Chief Financial Officer and Secretary), Rex H Dunlap (Executive VP and Chief Operating Officer), Charles M Biscan (VP and Corporate Counsel), Richard P Miller (VP Construction and Estimating), Charles P Guariglia (VP Architecture)

PRINCIPAL ACTIVITIES: Building and construction of business and commercial property

Principal Subsidiaries: Loughman Cabinet Company; BBC Manufactured Buildings Inc; Accesseron Products Inc

Principal Bank: Centerre Bank, St Louis, MO

Financial Information:

	Oct 31 1986	Oct 31 1987
	$'000	$'000
Sales revenues	94,942	76,157
Income before taxes (1)	2,360	5,517
Net income (1)	1,329	3,177
Net (loss) (2)	(1,222)	(371)
Net Income	107	2,806
Dividends	653	646
Dividends per share	$0.40	$0.40
Earnings per share	0.07	$1.86
Common stock	3,021	3,039
Retained income	9,229	11,389
Shareholders equity	10,279	5,672

(1) Continuing operations
(2) Discontinued operations

No of Employees: 600

BANK OF AMERICA NATIONAL TRUST & SAVINGS ASSOCIATION

555 California Street, San Francisco, CA 94104
Tel: (415) 622-3456
Telex: WUT 34346 bancamer sfo a

Chairman: Samuel H Armacost (and Chief Executive Officer); Chairman of the Executive Committee: Leland S Prussia

President: Thomas A Cooper (and Chief Operating Officer)

Senior Executive Officers: John S Poelker (Executive VP, Chief Financial Officer, Cashier and Treasurer), Robert W Frick (Vice Chairman, World Banking Division), Glenhall E Taylor Jr (Vice Chairman, Credit Policy), James B Wiesler (Vice Chairman, Global Consumer Markets)

PRINCIPAL ACTIVITIES: Banking

Parent Company: BankAmerica Corporation, San Francisco, CA

Principal Subsidiaries: (100% owned unless stated): Direct holdings of Bank of America NT & SA; B.A. Leasing Corporation; BA Pacific Properties, Inc; BA Properties I, Inc; BA Properties III, Inc; BameriLease Capital Corporation; BameriLease, Inc; Banca d'America e d'Italia (98.13%); BankAmerica Options, Inc (80%); BankAmerica International (BI); BankAmerica International Financial Corporation (BIFC); BankAmerica Nominees (Hong Kong) Ltd; BankAmerica Nominees Limited (London); BankAmerica Nominees (Singapore) PTE Ltd; BankAmerica Ventures, Inc; Bankhaus Centrale Credit AG; Bank of America Canada; Bank of America International SA; Bank of America (Jersey) Limited; Bank of America S.A.E. (BofA 50%; BI 50%); Continental Auxiliary Company; Davenport Data Processors, Inc; The Electronic Payments Exchange, Inc; Lease Holding VIII, Inc; Managistics Incorporated; NADRE II, Inc; Republic Drilling Company

Principal Bank: Bank of America National Trust & Savings Association

Financial Information:

	Dec 31 1985 $'000
(Loss) before taxes	(426,726)
Net (loss)	(337,215)
Dividends	246,737
Dividends per share	$1.16
(Loss) per share	($2.68)
Common stock	240,610
Retained income	2,802,654
Shareholders equity	4,547,057
Deposits	94,210,950
Total assets	118,541,125

No of Employees: 83,299

BANK OF BOSTON CORPORATION

100 Federal Street, Boston, MA 02110
Tel: (617) 434-2200

Chairman: William L Brown; Vice Chairman: Charles K Gifford
President: Ira Stepanian (and Chief Executive Officer)
Senior Executive Officers: Alan L McKinnon (Executive VP and Chief Financial Officer), Lawrence K Fish (Executive VP), Clark W Miller (Executive VP), Edwin B Morris III (Executive VP), Peter C Read (Executive VP)

PRINCIPAL ACTIVITIES: Bank holding company
Principal Subsidiaries: First National Bank of Boston; Casco Northern Bank N.A. (Maine); Bank of Boston Connecticut; Rhode Island Hospital Trust National Bank
Financial Information:

	Dec 31 1985 $'000	Dec 31 1986 $'000
Income before taxes	289,500	368,395
Net income	173,800	232,764
Dividends	48,000	55,076
Dividends per share*	$0.82	$0.91
Earnings per share*	$2.82	$3.69
Common stock	208,628	208,436
Retained income	971,450	1,135,665
Shareholders equity	1,474,590	1,769,000
Deposits	19,214,060	21,725,000
Total assets	28,296,340	34,045,000

*adjusted to reflect two-for-one stock split in March 1986; three-for-two stock split declared in November 1986 in the form of a dividend payable in January 1987

No of Employees: 20,000

BANK OF DELAWARE CORPORATION

300 Delaware Avenue, PO Box 788, Wilmington, DE 19899
Tel: (302) 429 2200

Chairman: Jeremiah P Shea (and Chief Executive Officer)
President: David McMillan (and Chief Operating Officer)
Senior Executive Officers: John J Corrigan (Executive VP and Chief Financial Officer), Hugh A George (Executive VP), Calvert A Morgan Jr (Senior VP), Joseph N Sgroi Jr (Secretary)

PRINCIPAL ACTIVITIES: Banking services
Principal Subsidiaries: Bank of Delaware
Financial Information:

	Dec 31 1985 $'000
Revenues	144,600
Net income	12.560

No of Employees: 1,065

BANK OF NEW ENGLAND CORPORATION

28 State Street, Boston, MA 02109
Tel: (617) 742-4000

Chairman: Walter J Connolly Jr; Vice Chairman: Gordon I Ulmer
President: Peter H McCormick
Senior Executive Officers: Joseph J Whiteside (Executive VP and Treasurer)

PRINCIPAL ACTIVITIES: Banking
Principal Subsidiaries: Bank of New England County; Bank of New England Interntional; Bank of New England; New England Capital Corp; New England Merchants Leasing; New England Merchants Funding; Beacon Asset Inc; BNE Mortgage Corp; Cape Ann Bank & Trust Co; New England Commercial Finance Corp
Principal Bank: Bank of New England
Financial Information:

	Dec 31 1985 $'000	Dec 31 1986 $'000
Net income	131,190	171,800
Earnings per share	$3.11	$3.52
Shareholders equity	-	1,152,000
Deposits	14,055,000	17,677,000
Total assets	17,804,000	22,473,000

No of Employees: 14,827

BANK OF NEW ENGLAND, NA

28 State Street, Boston, MA 02109
Tel: (617) 742-4000
Cable: BKNE INT BSN (International)
Telex: WUT 940610 BKNE BANK BSN
FAX: (617) 973 6273

Chairman: Peter H McCormick (and Chief Executive Officer)
President: Richard D Driscoll
Senior Executive Officers: Robert T McAlear (Executive VP Commercial Banking), Ralph D Gordon (Executive VP Staff Services), Arthur H Meehan Jr (Executive VP), John N Rees (Executive VP), Richard G Scheide (Executive VP), Joseph J Whiteside (Executive VP and Chief Financial Officer), Millard T Wilson Jr (Executive VP), Hugh M Taylor (Executive VP Commercial Banking)

PRINCIPAL ACTIVITIES: Banking
Parent Company: Bank of New England Corporation (100%)
Financial Information:

	Dec 31 1985 $'000
Net income	26,787
Deposits	3,739,216
Total assets	5,044,607

No of Employees: 2,777

BANK OF NEW HAMPSHIRE CORPORATION

300 Franklin Street, Manchester, NH 03105
Tel: (603) 624 6600

Chairman: Davis P Thurber (and President)
Senior Executive Officers: Edward Baines (Senior VP Operations), Gerald G Gaucher (Senior VP and Treasurer), Alice L DeSouza (Senior VP Marketing), Paul R Shea (Senior VP Corporate Development), Frederic R Pilch (Senior VP Investment), Arnold E Green II (VP), Gregory D Landroche (VP and Controller), Robert B Field Jr (Secretary)

PRINCIPAL ACTIVITIES: Banking services
Principal Subsidiaries: Bank of New Hampshire N.A.
Financial Information:

	Dec 31 1985 $'000
Revenues	53,425
Net income	5,500

No of Employees: 470

BANK OF NEW YORK CO, INC

48 Wall Street, New York, NY 10015
Tel: (212) 530-1784

Chairman: J Carter Bacot (and Chief Executive Officer)
President: Peter Herrick
Senior Executive Officers: Newton P Merrill (Executive VP), Deno D Papageorge (Executive VP Finance), Robert E Keilman (Senior VP, Comptroller)

PRINCIPAL ACTIVITIES: Holding company whose activities include banking and general financial services
Principal Subsidiaries: The Bank of New York; The Bank of New York (Delaware); The Bank of New York Trust Company; The Bank of New York Trust Company of Florida, NA; Beacon Capital Management Co Inc; ARCS Mortgage Co Inc; BNY Leasing Inc; The Bank of New York Life Insurance Company Inc
Financial Information:

	Dec 31 1985 $'000	Dec 31 1986 $'000
Income before taxes	173,918	182,865
Net income	130,256	155,218
Dividends(1)	40,047	46,859
Dividends per share	$1.40	$1.56
Earnings per share(2)	$4.02	$4.54
Common stock	343,755	372,347
Retained income	516,958	619,189
Shareholders equity	960,713	1,091,536
Deposits	12,369,021	15,112,849
Total assets	18,486,000	20,708,850

(1) Common
(2) Fully diluted

No of Employees: 9,304

BANK OF NEW YORK (THE)

48 Wall Street, New York, NY 10286
Tel: (212) 495-1784
Cable: BANKONE NEW YORK
Telex: TWX 7105814506 bank of nynyk

Chairman: J C Bacot (and Chief Executive Officer)
President: Peter Herrick (and Chief Operating Officer)
Senior Executive Officers: Gregory W Spurr Jr (Senior Executive VP and Chief Credit and Commercial Banking Officer), Deno D Papageorge (Senior Executive VP and Chief Financial Officer), Sheldon Harrison (Senior Executive VP and Chief Operations Officer), Richard D Field (Executive VP, Retail Banking), Alan R Griffith (Executive VP, Special Industries and International Banking), Newton P S Merrill (Executive VP, US Commercial Banking), Douglas F Adams (Executive VP and Chief Trust Officer), Charles L Booth (Executive VP and Chief Investment Officer)

PRINCIPAL ACTIVITIES: Banking
Parent Company: The Bank of New York Company Inc
Principal Subsidiaries: The Bank of New York (Delaware)
Financial Information:

	Dec 31 1985 $'000	Dec 31 1986 $'000
Income before taxes	173,918	182,865
Net income	130,256	155,218
Dividends	47,897	53,059
Dividends per share	$1.40	$1.56
Earnings per share	$4.02	$4.54
Common stock	151,268	231,867
Retained income	516,958	619,189
Shareholders equity	921,241	1,052,519
Deposits	12,369,021	15,112,849
Total assets	18,486,200	20,708,850

No of Employees: 8,000

BANK OF TOKYO TRUST CO

100 Broadway, New York, NY 10005
Tel: (212) 766-3400
Telex: WUD 126365; RCA 222967 TOHBANK

Chairman: Tomatsu Yamaguchi
President: Tomonori Naruse
Senior Executive Officers: Hiroshi Hayashi (Vice Chairman), Eiji Seiki (Executive VP), T Fujino (Executive VP), J Rene Prat (Senior VP), H Clifton Whiteman (Executive VP), Takashi Tatsuno (Chief Credit Officer), John Clark (Senior VP), Gerald Jagendorf (Senior VP), Robert E Hand (Senior VP and Counsel), Katsu Yamaguchi (Senior VP),

PRINCIPAL ACTIVITIES: Banking and trust business
Principal Subsidiaries: The Bank of Tokyo Trust; Cayman Limited; TOHLEASE Corporation, NY
Financial Information:

	Dec 31 1985 $'000	Dec 31 1986 $'000
Income before taxes	42,769	38,962
Net income	25,529	30,356
Dividends	11,113	14,904
Dividends per share	$14.14	$18.22
Earnings per share	$31.21	$35.38
Common stock	81,788	85,805
Retained income	68,274	83,686
Shareholders equity	297,447	327,800
Deposits	4,560,762	5,168,657
Total assets	5,379,498	5,874,302

Principal Shareholders: Bank of Tokyo, Ltd
No of Employees: 495

BANK SOUTH CORPORATION

55 Marietta Street, Atlanta, GA 30303
Tel: (404) 529 4521

President: Robert P Guyton (and Chief Executive Officer)
Senior Executive Officers: Franklin L Burke (Executive VP), Rod W Cook (Senior VP), Robert A Carper (Senior VP Marketing), Ralph E Hutchins Jr (Executive VP and Chief Financial Officer), John W Aldridge (Senior VP General Sales), Edward B Grimball (Senior VP and Comptroller), Huw S Williams (Senior VP Secretary and Controller)

PRINCIPAL ACTIVITIES: Holding company with interests in banking
Principal Subsidiaries: Bank South N.A.
Financial Information:

	Dec 31 1985 $'000
Revenues	270,915
Net income	23,480

No of Employees: 2,025

BANKAMERICA CORPORATION

Bank of America Center, 55 California St, San Francisco, CA 94104
Tel: (415) 622-3456

Chairman: Leland S Prussia; Vice Chairman: Arthur V Toupin
President: Samuel H Armacost (and Chief Executive Officer)
Senior Executive Officers: George W Coombe Jr (Executive VP and General Counsel), John S Poelker (Executive VP and Treasurer)

PRINCIPAL ACTIVITIES: Bank holding company
Principal Subsidiaries: Direct subsidiaries of BankAmerica Corporation: BA Agency, Inc (dba BA Insurance Agency,Inc); BA Appraisals, Inc; BA Cheque Corporation; BA Commercial Credit Corporation; BA Futures, Incorporated; BA Insurance (Cayman) Ltd; BA Investment Management Corporation; BA Mortgage and International Realty Corporation; BancAmerica Commercial Corporation; BancAmerica Lease Holding, Incorporated; BankAmerica Capital Corporation; BankAmerica Capital Investments, Inc; BankAmerica Overseas Finance

Corporation NV; BankAmerica Realty Services, Inc; BankAmerica Trust Company of New York; BankAmerica World Trade Corporation; Bank of America NT & SA; The Charles Schwab Corporation; Overseas Asset Holdings Inc; Seafirst Corporation

Principal Bank: Bank of America National Trust & Savings Association

Financial Information:

	Dec 31 1985	Dec 31 1986
	$'000	$'000
Net (loss)	(337,215)	(518,000)
(Loss) per share	($2.68)	($3.74)
Shareholders equity	4,547,057	4,038,000
Deposits	94,210,950	82,205,000
Total assets	118,541,125	104,189,000

No of Employees: 73,465

BANKEAST CORPORATION

1 Wall Street, Manchester, NH 03105

Tel: (603) 624 6000

Chairman: Walter N De Witt

President: John I Snow (and Chief Executive Officer)

Senior Executive Officers: David Blake (VP Marketing), Victor J Tremblay (VP Corporate Development), Daniel Glasner (VP Human Resources), Lawrence Hookeyl (VP Data Processing), Charles Palm (VP and Controller)

PRINCIPAL ACTIVITIES: Banking and financial services

Principal Subsidiaries: BankEast

Financial Information:

	Dec 31 1985
	$'000
Revenues	90,700
Net income	8,215

No of Employees: 770

BANKERS FIRST CORPORATION

945 Broad Street, PO Box 1332, Augusta, GA 30913

Tel: (404) 823-3200

Telefax: (404) 823-3377

Chairman: H M Osteen Jr (and President and Chief Executive Officer)

Senior Executive Officers: James L LaBoon Jr (Chairman, President and Chief Executive Officer of Athens Federal Savings Bank), A Byrnes Bryant Jr (Chairman, President and Chief Executive Officer of Southeast Federal Savings Bank), Larry De Meyers (President and Chief Operating Officer of Bankers First Federal Savings and Loan Association, South Eastern Mortgage Corporation, Lafayette Marketing Inc, Bankers First Data Services Inc and Bankers First Life Insurance Co) Robert L Smalley (VP and Chief Financial Officer), Ronald E Minor (Treasurer), Charles O Parker (VP)

PRINCIPAL ACTIVITIES: Multiple savings and loan holding company

Principal Subsidiaries: Bankers First Federal Savings and Loan Association; Athens Federal Savings Bank; Southeast Federal Savings Bank

Financial Information:

	Dec 31 1985	Dec 31 1986
	$'000	$'000
Income before taxes	6,503	13,054
Net income	4,240	8,024
Earnings per share net	$1.30	$1.66
Common stock	44	57
Retained earnings(1)	22,650	30,674
Stockholders equity	63,286	95,221
Deposits(2)	476,710	955,984
Total assets	655,413	1,201,223

(1) substantially restricted

(2) and repurchase agreements

No of Employees: 700

BANKERS TRUST COMPANY

280 Park Avenue, New York, NY 10017

Tel: (212) 775-2500

Chairman: Charles S Sanford Jr

Senior Executive Officers: James J Baechle (Executive VP), Philip M Hampton (Vice Chairman), Edward A Lesser (Executive VP), Ralph L MacDonald Sr (Managing Director), Joseph A Manganello Jr (Executive VP), Eugene B Shanks (Managing Director), George J Vojta (Executive VP)

PRINCIPAL ACTIVITIES: Banking

Parent Company: Bankers Trust New York Corporation

Principal Bank: Bankers Trust Company

No of Employees: 11,069

BANKERS TRUST NEW YORK CORPORATION

280 Park Avenue, New York, NY 10017

Tel: (212) 250-2500

Chairman: Charles S Sanford Jr

Senior Executive Officers: Philip M Hampton (Vice Chairman), Edward A Lesser (Executive VP), James J Baechle (Executive VP and General Counsel), David O Beim (Executive VP), Jan R Brumm (Executive VP), William S Epstein (Executive VP), Peter E Lengyel (Executive VP), Ralph L MacDonald Sr (Managing Director), Joseph A Manganello Jr (Executive VP), Eugene B Shanks (Managing Director), George J Vojta (Executive VP)

PRINCIPAL ACTIVITIES: Bank holding company which co-ordinates policies and activities of subsidiary and affiliated banks and bank related subsidiaries

Principal Subsidiaries: Domestic: Bankers Trust Company; Bankers Trust Company of Florida; BT Commercial Corporation; BT Equipment Leasing, Inc; BT Futures Corp N.A.; BT International Trading Corp; BT Southwest, Inc; BT Investment Managers, Inc; BT Brokerage Corporation; BT Capital Corporation; Bankers Trust (Delaware); BT Private Clients Corp. International: Bankers Trust International Ltd (UK); BT Investment Management Ltd (UK); Bankers Trust (France) SA; Bankers Trust Finanziaria SpA (Italy); Bankers Trust AG (Switzerland); Bankers Trust GmbH (Germany); Bancho Iochpe de Investimento SA (Brazil); BT Bank of Canada; Bankers Trust (Cayman) International Ltd (Cayman Islands); BT Australia Limited; BT Asia Limited (Hong Kong); Bankers Trust International (Asia) Ltd (Singapore); BT Futures (Singapore); Thai Investment and Securities Company Ltd (Thailand); United Bank for Africa Ltd (Nigeria); Japan Bankers Trust Co Ltd

Principal Bank: Bankers Trust Company

Financial Information:

	Dec 31 1985	Dec 31 1986
	$'000	$'000
Income before taxes	487,800	520,100
Net income	371,200	427,900
Common dividends	106,200	91,600
Dividends per common share	$1.38	$1.53
Earnings per share	$5.39	$6.01
Common stock	683,300	701,900
Retained income	1,600,000	1,900,000
Shareholders equity	2,500,000	2,700,000
Deposits	28,700,000	29,500,000
Total assets	50,600,000	56,400,000

No of Employees: 11,069

BANNER INDUSTRIES, INC

24500 Chagrin Blvd, Cleveland, OH 44122
Tel: (216) 464-3650

Chairman: Jeffrey Steiner (and Chief Executive Officer); Vice Chairman: Samuel J Krasney (and Chief Operating Officer)
President: William C Hunt (and Chief Operating Officer)
Senior Executive Officers: Michael T Alcox (VP Finance), Sam Spector (VP Corporate Development), Melvin K Allen (VP), Robert Todd (VP)

PRINCIPAL ACTIVITIES: Manufacture of mining machinery and equipment, aviation equipment; water and sewage pumps
Principal Subsidiaries: Banner Aircraft International; Banner Aviation Inc; Adams Industries Inc; Adams Industries International Inc; Bannerair Inc; Banner Aircraft Inc; Banner Aircraft International Inc; Burbank Aircraft International Inc; Burbank Aircraft Supply Inc; Thompson Aircraft Tire Corp; Benner Industrial Products Inc; Banner Energy Corp; Banner Energy Corp of KY Inc; Jenkins Coal Dock Co; Banner Energy of IN Inc; Banner International Inc; Commercial Casting Inc; Dubie-Clark International Inc; Patterson Pump Co; Plymouth Locomotive Works Inc; Reymond Machinery Inc; Skinner Engine Co Inc
Principal Bank: Huntington National Bank of N E Ohio
Financial Information:

	$'000
Sales revenues	128,000

No of Employees: 1,100

BANQUET FOODS CORPORATION

13515 Beritt Pkwy, Ballwin, MO 63011
Tel: (314) 957-4000
Telex: TWX 9107601903 banquet stl a

President: John Philips (and Chief Operating Officer)
Senior Executive Officers: Donald P Rasche (Executive VP), Donald V Granneman (VP Sales), James F Carl (VP Industrial Relations), C M Stamper (VP Manufacturing), Gordon Stevenes (VP Engineering), Gerald E Keathley (VP Purchasing), Jim Kennedy (VP Marketing), John Graft (Public Relations Director)

PRINCIPAL ACTIVITIES: Manufacture of frozen food products and poultry
Parent Company: ConAgra Inc, Omaha, NE
Principal Subsidiaries: Banta Co; Banta Co Inc-Harrisonburg; Clark Printing Co Inc; Color Response Inc; Daniels Packaging Co Inc; Hartpress Inc; KCS Industries Inc; Ling Products inc; Northwestern Colorgraphics Inc
Financial Information:

	$'000
Sales revenues	280,000

No of Employees: 4,000

BANTA, GEORGE, COMPANY, INC

Curtis Reed Plaza, Menasha, WI 54952
Tel: (414) 722-7771
Telex: TWX 910 27 31 236 geo banta mnsh

Chairman: Harry W Earle (and President and Chief Executive Officer)
Senior Executive Officers: William B Dresser (VP), Anton G Stepanek (VP), Dean E Bergstrom (VP and Secretary), Gerald A Henseler (VP and Treasurer)

PRINCIPAL ACTIVITIES: Printing and binding services
Principal Subsidiaries: Banta Co; Banta Co Inc-Harrisonburg; Clark Printing Co Inc; Color Response Inc; Daniels Packaging Co Inc; Hartpress Inc; KCS Industries Inc; Ling Products Inc; Northwestern Colorgraphics Inc
Principal Bank: First Wisconsin National Bank of Milwaukee
Financial Information:

	$'000
Sales revenues	276,000

No of Employees: 2,260

BANTAM DOUBLEDAY DELL PUBLISHING GROUP, INC

666 Fifth Avenue, New York, NY 10019
Tel: (212) 765-6500
Telex: WUT 12402 bantambks nyk

Chairman: Olaf Paeschke
President: Alberto Vitale (and Chief Exeuctive Officer)
Senior Executive Officers: Linda Grey (President and Publisher of Bantam Books), Nancy Evans (President and Publisher of Doubleday & Co), Carole Baron (President and Publisher of Dell Publishing), Jack Hoeft (President, Sales & Marketing Division), Alun Davies (President and Publisher, International Division), John Choi (VP, Chief Financial Officer), William Wright (Senior VP, Chief Administrative Officer), Harriette K Dorsen (VP, Secretary and General Counsel)

PRINCIPAL ACTIVITIES: Book publishers
Parent Company: Bertelsmann Publishing Group Inc
Principal Bank: Chase Manhattan Bank

Principal Shareholders: Bertelsmann AG, Gütersloh, Germany
No of Employees: 1,200

BARBER-COLMAN CO

555 Colman Center Drive, Rockford, IL 61125
Tel: (815) 397-7400
Telex: 257417

President: R M Sampson (and Chief Executive Officer)
Senior Executive Officers: C W Carroll (Executive VP Operations), G R McMillin (Group VP Energy Management), J W Mink (VP Corporate Manufacturing), R T Leighton (VP Finance), R T Hardy (VP Industrial Relations), L C Jon Moll (VP Marketing), F J Norton (VP International Marketing)

PRINCIPAL ACTIVITIES: Manufacture of textile machinery; machine tools; control systems including aircraft controls; environmental equipment; industrial equipment
Principal Subsidiaries: Colman AC Motors Inc; Colman Motor Products; Colman OEM Inc; E A Gould Co Inc; Robicom Corp
Principal Bank: First National Bank of Rockford
Financial Information:

	$'000
Sales revenues	250,000

No of Employees: 5,000

BARBER-GREENE CO

400 N Highland Avenue, Aurora, IL 60507
Tel: (312) 859-2200
Telex: RCA 210055 barg ur

Chairman: R C Johnson (and President and Chief Executive Officer)
Senior Executive Officers: P A Barber (VP Sales), W E Putz (VP Product Support), R L DeVore (Treasurer and Controller), R A Landl (VP Engineering)

PRINCIPAL ACTIVITIES: Manufacture of construction machinery and equipment

Parent Company: Astec Industries
Principal Bank: First National Bank
Financial Information:

	Aug 31 1985 $'000	Aug 31 1986 $'000
Sales revenues	102,183	97,662
(Loss) before taxes	(3,031)	(5,907)
Net (loss)	(3,062)	(5,571)
(Loss) per share	($1.34)	$(2.44)
Common stock	11,598	11,598
Retained (deficit)	(6,244)	(11,815)
Shareholders equity (deficit)	1,428	(3,823)

No of Employees: 479

BARCLAYS BANK OF NEW YORK

75 Wall Street, New York, NY 10265
Tel: (212) 412-4000

Chairman: Albert Bush-Brown
President: John S Spencer (and Chief Executive Officer)
Senior Executive Officers: Christopher J Lendrum (Executive VP), Peter V Nash (Executive VP), Richard M Webb (Executive VP), E C Flanagan (VP and Secretary)

PRINCIPAL ACTIVITIES: Banking
Parent Company: Barclays Bank International Limited
Principal Bank: Manufacturers Hanover Trust Company

No of Employees: 1,700

BARCLAYSAMERICAN CORPORATION

201 S Tryon St, Box 31488, Charlotte, NC 28231
Tel: &04) 372-0060

Chairman: Graeme M Keith (also President and Chief Executive Officer)
Senior Executive Officers: Roger B Hendrix (Exeuctive VP Legal and Management Services and Secretary), Bruce C McMillen (Executive VP), Jack A Reeder (Executive VP Retail Group), C David Biswell (Senior VP and Controller), Edward L Boyd (Senior VP Factoring), H B Hirsch (Senior BP Business Finance), Robert V Knight Jr (Senior VP Administration), Dale Peters (Senior VP Leasing), Irwin Teich (Senior VP Business Finance), James T Verfurth (Senior VP Commercial Finance), J D Wedhams (Senor VP Real Estate), E Douglas M Schacher (Chief Financial Officer)

PRINCIPAL ACTIVITIES: Financial services; factoring; commercial finance; consumer lending and sale finance
Parent Company: Barclays Bank PLC
Financial Information:

	Dec 31 1986 $'000
Revenues	479,608
Net income	22,692
Shareholders equity	537,420
Total assets	4,147,990

No of Employees: 3,314

BARD, C R, INC

731 Central Avenue, Murray Hill, NJ 07974
Tel: (201) 277-8000
Telex: TRT 178157 crbard

Chairman: Robert H McCaffrey (and Chief Exeuctive Officer)
President: George T Maloney (and Chief Operating Officer)
Senior Executive Officers: William G Little (Group Executive), Edward A Leskanic (Group VP), David W Prigmore (Group VP), George A Davis (VP Finance)

PRINCIPAL ACTIVITIES: Manufacture of medical and surgical equipment and supplies
Principal Subsidiaries: C R Bard International Inc; Davol Inc; Electro Medical Systems Inc; USCI International Inc
Principal Bank: Morgan Guaranty Trust Company
Financial Information:

	Dec 31 1985 $'000	Dec 31 1986 $'000
Sales revenues	465,480	547,994
Net income	41,948	51,194
Earnings per share	$2.78	$1.72
Shareholders equity	256,776	265,919

No of Employees: 6,350

BARDEN CORPORATION

200 Park Avenue, Danbury, CT 06810
Tel: (203) 744-2211
Telex: TWX 710 456 0098 barden corp

President: Stanley Noss (and Chief Executive Officer)
Senior Executive Officers: Donald K Brush (VP and General Manager-Manufacturing), Robert H Buch (VP and General Manager-Marketing), Robert P More (VP and General Manager Lacey Manufacturing Co), Thomas R Hensal (VP Administration and Finance)

PRINCIPAL ACTIVITIES: The Barden Corporation is a world leader in the engineering, design and manufacture of precision ball bearings and bearing components. In addition, Barden produces linear bearings, precision balls, stampings and surgical and other mechanical assemblies
Principal Subsidiaries: Divisions:- Barden Precision Bearings; Lacey Manufacturing Company; Winsted Precision Ball Company. Subsidiary:- The Barden Corporation (UK) Limited (UK)
Principal Bank: First National Bank of Boston
Financial Information:

	Oct 31 1985 $'000	Oct 31 1986 $'000
Sales revenues	72,686	74,027
Income before taxes	9,186	5,804
Net income	5,534	3,205
Dividends	1,755	1,609
Dividends per share	$1.00	$1.00
Earnings per share	$3.16	$2.00
Common stock	5,613	5,613
Retained income	53,287	54,883
Shareholders equity	48,859	49,183

No of Employees: 1,520

BARNES GROUP INC

123 Main Street, Bristol, CT 06010
Tel: (203) 583-7070
Telex: 643121

Chairman: Wallace Barnes (and Chief Executive Officer); Chairman Executive Committee: Carlyle F Barnes
President: William R Fenoglio (and Chief Operating Officer)
Senior Executive Officers: Mary Louise Beardsley (Assistant General Counsel and Assistant Secretary), John E Besser (VP Administration, General Counsel and Secretary), Francis C Boyle Jr (Assistant Controller), William R Coombes (Senior VP), George J Crowley (VP-Treasurer), John J Locher (VP-Controller), Robert F O'Connor (VP Corporate Development and Planning), A Stanton Wells (Executive VP-Finance), Jack C Williams (VP-Human Resources). Operations: Richard D Hines (Group VP-Associated Spring), John M Knapp (Group VP-Bowman Distribution), Alexander Jackson, III (Group VP-Aerospace Components), Charles G Rowley (VP-Associated Spring Operations), Werner H Schuele (VP-Associated Spring Operations)

PRINCIPAL ACTIVITIES: Barnes Group Inc, is a diversified manufacturer and distributor of critical parts and supplies for a wide range of applications in virtually every industry. Our manufactured products are precision metal components-springs and complex machined parts-that perform vital operations within larger assemblies. The products and services provided by our distribution businesses are used by thousands of customers to repair and maintain all types of equipment. The company consists of three operating groups, each a leader in its particular market. Bowman Distribution-is a direct-to-user distributor of expendable parts and supplies for industrial, transportation and heavy equipment maintenance markets. Associated Spring-manufactures close-tolerance springs and other custom metal parts for durable goods markets, including automotive, appliances, farm and construction equipment and machinery. Aerospace Components-highly specialized manufacturing and repair operations serving the gas turbine market

Principal Subsidiaries: Autoliaisons France SA; Bowman Products (Canada) Ltd; Motalink Ltd (UK); Resortes Mecanicos SA (Mexico); Stumpp & Schuele do Brasil Industria e Comercio Ltda (Brazil); Associated Spring-Asia Pte Ltd (Singapore); Resortes Industriales del Norte SA (Mexico)

Financial Information:

	Dec 31 1985	Dec 31 1986
	$'000	$'000
Sales revenues	431,762	439,727
Income* before taxes	33,574	35,336
Net income	12,093	16,603
Dividends	6,202	6,469
Dividends per share	$0.85	$1.00
Earnings per share	$1.67	$2.57
Common stock	15,730	15,737
Retained income	105,858	115,992
Shareholders equity	113,978	123,025

*from continuing operations

No of Employees: 4,697

BARNETT BANKS OF FLORIDA, INC

100 Laura Street, Jacksonville, FL 32202
Tel: (904) 791-7720

Chairman: Charles E Rice (and President and Chief Executive Officer); Vice Chairmen: Albert D Ernest Jr, Earl B Hadlow (and General Counsel), Thomas H Jacobsen, Allen L Lastinger Jr

Senior Executive Officers: Stephen A Hansel (Executive VP and Chief Financial Officer), Paul T Kerins (Executive VP Human Resources), William M Fackler (Executive VP Marketing), R David Barnett (Executive VP Consumer Credit), Hinton F Nobles Jr (Executive VP Special Services), C Royce Hough (Executive VP Corporate and International Banking), Timothy Lane (Executive VP Investment and Funds Management), Arthur L Shealy Jr (Executive VP and Controller), Conrad W Acosta (Senior VP Bond Portfolio), John M Godfrey (Senior VP and Chief Economist), Paul J McConnell (Senior VP Compensation and Benefits), Thomas H Yochum (Senior VP Productivity Management), Robert A Hawkins (Senior VP Commercial Real Estate), Andrew L Higgins (Senior VP Corporate Services), Benjamin H Turnbull (Senior VP International Banking), James W Covington Jr (Senior VP Retail Marketing), Charles W Newman (Senior VP and Deputy Controller)

PRINCIPAL ACTIVITIES: Banking and financial services

Principal Subsidiaries: Banking: Barnett Bank of Alachua County NA; Barnett Bank of Central Florida NA; Barnett Bank of Citrus County NA; Barnett Bank of Columbia County; Barnett Bank of Highlands County; Barnett Bank of Indian River County: Barnett Bank of Jacksonville NA; Barnett Bank of the Keys; Barnett Bank of Lake County NA; Barnett Bank of Lake Okeechobee; Barnett Bank of Lee County NA; Barnett Bank of Manatee County NA; Barnett Bank of Marion County NA; Barnett Bank of Martin County NA; Barnett Bank of Naples; Barnett Bank of Nassau County; Barnett Bank of Palm Beach County; Barnett Bank of Pasco County; Barnett Bank of Pinnellas County NA; Barnett Bank of Polk County; Barnett Bank of Putnam County; Barnett Bank of South Florida NA; Barnett Bank of Southwest Florida; Barnett Bank of St Johns County; Barnett Bank of Tallahassee; Barnett Bank of Tampa NA; Barnett Bank of Volusia County; Barnett Bank of West Florida; Florida Coast Bank. Non-Banking: Barnett Banks Trust Co NA; Barnett Brokerage Service Inc; Barnett Computing Company; Barnett Credit Services Inc; Barnett Mortgage Co; Barnett Operations Company; Barnett Overseas Finance NV; StateWide Collection Corporation; Verifications Inc; Barnett Banks Insurance Inc

Financial Information:

	Dec 31 1985	Dec 31 1986
	$'000	$'000
Net income	128,267	157,495
Earnings per share	$2.65	$2.91
Shareholders equity	-	1,035,763
Deposits	13,082,310	17,736,767
Total assets	14,829,080	20,228,950

No of Employees: 16,902

BARR, W M, CO INC

PO Box 1879, Memphis, TN 38101
Tel: (901) 775-0100
Telex: TWX 810 591 1499 wmbarr mfs

President: George E Conaway

Senior Executive Officers: A V Richmond (Executive VP, Secretary and Treasurer), Raymond J Berckes (VP Merchandise), Michael D Wells (VP Sales), Ron Riley (VP Corporate Development)

PRINCIPAL ACTIVITIES: Specialty chemicals for paint manufacture; packaging

Principal Bank: First Tennessee Bank NA

Financial Information:

	$'000
Sales revenues	60,000

No of Employees: 200

BARRY, R G, CORPORATION

13405 Yarmouth Road NW, Pickerington, OH 43147
Tel: (614) 864-6400

Chairman: Gordon Zacks (and Chief Executive Officer)

President: Wade M Harn (and Chief Operting Officer)

Senior Executive Officers: Robert Woodruff (VP Human Resources), Richard L Burrell (VP Finance, Secretary and Treasurer), Matthew Chamlin (VP Marketing), Larry Knudsen (VP Sales)

PRINCIPAL ACTIVITIES: Manufacture of footwear

Principal Bank: The Huntington National Bank of Columbus

Financial Information:

	$'000
Sales revenues	95,700

No of Employees: 2,000

BARRY WRIGHT CORPORATION

One Newton Executive Park, Newton Lower Falls, MA 02162
Tel: (617) 965-5800
Telex: 710-335-7700 BARRYCORP NEW

Chairman: Ralph Z Sorenson (and President and Chief Executive Officer)

Senior Executive Officers: P Norman Roy (Executive VP), John F Quinn (VP, President Industrial and Aero Products Group), Philip M Croel (VP, President Wright Line Inc), Milton E Gilbert (VP, General Counsel and Secretary), Jack L Manes Jr (VP, Human Resources), Charles H Sellman (VP, Controller and Treasurer), Eustis Walcott Jr (VP, Corporate Relations), Patricia A Irwin (Assistant Treasurer and Assistant Secretary), William H Gorham (Clerk)

PRINCIPAL ACTIVITIES: Barry Wright Corporation is a diversified industrial company with two operating groups. Wright Line Inc is a worldwide marketer of high quality specialized filing systems and devices which facilitate the management, filing, handling and protection of information media. The Industrial and Aero Products Group provides engineered components and systems to control vibration and specialized products which improve the efficiency, productivity and safety of industrial equipment. Manufacturing Divisions: Barry Controls, Dolan-Jenner, Vlier Engineering, Zero-Max

Trade Names: Duo-Plexx(R), SafeScan(R), Dojen (TM), Sensoflex(R), Documate(R), Roh'Lix(R), Quasi-Vision (TM), Tape-Seal(R), Optimedia(R), PC Work Center (TM), PC WorkCenter (TM)

Principal Subsidiaries: Wright Line Inc; Barry Controls Ltd; Schmidt Couplings Inc; Visu-Flex Company; Dolan-Jenner Industries; Zero-Max Industries Inc; Datafile Inc and other subsidiary companies in Canada, Germany and UK and joint ventures in Germany and Japan

Financial Information:

	Dec 31 1985 $'000	Dec 31 1986 $'000
Sales revenues	196,872	195,142
Earnings before taxes	19,546	13,831
Net earnings	10,519	7,036
Dividends	5,475	5,087
Dividends per share	$0.60	$0.60
Earnings per share net	$1.16	$0.81
Common stock	9,185	9,188
Retained earnings	77,278	79,227
Shareholders equity	107,907	90,238

No of Employees: 2,220

BARRY'S JEWELERS INC

1430 Huntington Drive, Duarte, CA 91010
Tel: (818) 303 4741

Chairman: David Blum
President: Terry L Burman
Senior Executive Officers: Jay A Johnson (VP), Jack Reid (VP), Hugh C Rose (VP), Jack Woolf (VP), Charlotte K Burch (Controller), Gerson I Fox (Secretary and Treasurer)

PRINCIPAL ACTIVITIES: Retail jewelry stores
Principal Bank: Citibank
Financial Information:

	$'000
Sales revenues	65,000

No of Employees: 915

BARTLETT AGRI ENTERPRISES INC

4800 Main Street, Kansas City, MO 64112
Tel: (816) 531-6235
Telex: TWX 9107712021 bartlett kcmo

President: Paul D Bartlett
Senior Executive Officers: W R Berg (VP, Secretary and Treasurer)

PRINCIPAL ACTIVITIES: Grain processing and milling; production of animal feedstuffs; commodity trading; warehousing of farm products
Principal Bank: United Missouri Bank of Kansas City
Financial Information:

	$'000
Sales revenues	450,000

No of Employees: 500

BARTON BRANDS LTD

55 E Monroe Street, Chicago, IL 60603
Tel: (312) 346-9200
Telex: 910/221-5158 BARTONDSTG

Chairman: Ellis M Goodman (and President and Chief Executive Officer)
Senior Executive Officers: Edward L Golden (Executive VP), Michael J Mazzoni (Executive VP), Paul L Kraus (Executive VP), John C Negri (Executive VP), Ralph D Silver (Executive VP), Fred R Mardell (Executive VP and Secretary)

PRINCIPAL ACTIVITIES: Spirits and beers
Parent Company: Barton Incorporated
Principal Subsidiaries: Barton Beers Ltd; Barton Brands of California, Inc; Barton Brands of Georgia, Inc
Principal Bank: American National Bank and Trust Company of Chicago
Financial Information:

	$'000
Sales revenues	300,000

Principal Shareholders: Barton Incorporated
No of Employees: 500

BASF CORPORATION

8 Campus Drive, Parsippany, NJ 07054
Tel: (201) 397-2700
Telex: 988-036
Telecopier: (201) 397-2737

Chairman: Dr Juergen F Strubbe (and President) (Dr Dieter Stein will become President and CEO on May 1 1988 and Chairman on Sept 1 1988)
President: Edwin L Stenzel (and Chief Executive Officer)
Senior Executive Officers: Frederick W Bernthal (Vice Chairman and Chief Administrative Officer), Peter R Heinze (President, Chemicals Division), J Larry Jameson (President, Inmont Division), R Wayne Godwin (President, Fibers Division), Nicola W Palmieri-Egger (Group VP Human Resources, General Counsel), Werner Praetorius (Group VP, Strategic Business Development), Dietrich von Hanstein (SR VP-Controller), Christoph von Krafft (SR VP-Treasurer), Helmuth von Moltke (VP, Corporate Communications), Frank Mueller (VP, Corporate Engineering), Gerhard W Paul (VP, Corporate Research and Development), Manfred Buller (Group VP Finance)

PRINCIPAL ACTIVITIES: Production of chemicals for automobile, agriculture, food processing and textile industries; petrochemicals, specialty chemicals; dyes and pigments, magnetic storage media; pharmaceuticals; coatings and inks
Parent Company: BASFIN Corporation, Parsipanny, NJ, a subsidiary of BASF AG, Ludwigshafen, West Germany
Principal Subsidiaries: BASF K&F Corporation; BASG Canada Inc; BASF Structural Materials Inc
Financial Information:

	Dec 31 1985 $'000	Dec 31 1986 $'000
Sales revenues	2,600,600	3,645,400
Income before taxes	68,500	188,500
Net income	38,200	104,500
Shareholders equity	944,900	923,000

Principal Shareholders: BASFIN Corporation, which is owned by BASF AG, Ludwigshafen, West Germany
No of Employees: 4,200

BASF CORPORATION INFORMATION SYSTEMS

Crosby Drive, Bedford, MA 01730
Tel: (617) 271-4000
Telex: WUT 951856 basf uw bfrd

President: Dieter O Heuer
Senior Executive Officers: Juergen Blank (VP Audio and Video Marketing and Sales), Manfred Rinke (VP Finance and Administration and Treasurer), Eckhard Reuther (VP Operations), Dieter Mayer (VP Manufacturing), John Healion (VP Computer Media, Marketing and Sales)

PRINCIPAL ACTIVITIES: Magnetic tapes for audio and video use; data processing accessories and equipment
Principal Bank: European American Bank
Financial Information:

	$'000
Sales revenues	130,000

Principal Shareholders: BASF AG, Ludwigshafen, Germany
No of Employees: 1,300

BASIC AMERICAN MEDICAL INC

4000 East Southport Road, PO Box 27249, Indianpolis, IN 46227
Tel: (317) 783 5461

Chairman: Ethan Jackson; Vice Chairman: Franklin L Jackson
President: Brady R Justice Jr
Senior Executive Officers: Joe L Scott (Senior VP), Robert D West (Senior VP), Jay Jarrell (VP), Ronald Hicks (Treasurer), John C Stark (Secretary and Legal Counsel)

PRINCIPAL ACTIVITIES: Operation and management of hospitals
Principal Bank: American Fletcher National Bank
Financial Information:

	$'000
Sales revenues	250,350

No of Employees: 5,200

BASIX CORPORATION

110 E 59th Street, New York, NY 10022
Tel: (212) 758-1990

Chairman: Donald T Beldock (and Chief Executive Officer)
Senior Executive Officers: A S Isenberg (Executive VP), Jeffrey Henderickson (Senior VP), Lee J Royle (VP Finance)

PRINCIPAL ACTIVITIES: Holding company with interests in oil and gas exploration and development; highway traffic control systems and toll collecting systems; access control systems; legal, financial and commercial printing and publishing
Principal Subsidiaries: Automatic Toll Systems Inc; The Winko-Matic Signal Company; Multisonics Corporation; BASIX Controls Systems Corporation; CRA Inc; Packard Press Corporation; The R J Brown Companies; White Shield Greece Oil Corporation; Ocean Thermal Corporation; Basix Communications Inc; Basco Energy Inc; Basix Arizona Energy Corporation
Principal Bank: Marine Midland
Financial Information:

	$'000
Sales revenues	140,000
*5% stock	

No of Employees: 1,198

BASLER ELECTRIC CO

Box 269, Rte 143, Highland, IL 62249
Tel: (618) 654-2341
Telex: TWX 910 9962522 baselecthigh

Chairman: William L Basler (and Chief Executive Officer and Treasurer)
President: Floyd J Basler (and Chief Operating Officer)
Senior Executive Officers: Arthur E Johnson (Executive VP), Robert P Roepke (VP Marketing and Corporate Planning), Raymond M Vollet (VP Finance and Corporate Secretary), Edward Leird (VP Engineering), Herbert R Roach (VP Industrial Relations)

PRINCIPAL ACTIVITIES: Electrical and electronic machinery, equipment and supplies including transformers and switchgear
Principal Subsidiaries: Basler Electric Circuits Inc; Summit Electronics Inc
Principal Bank: City Bank
Financial Information:

	$'000
Sales revenues	55,000

No of Employees: 900

BASS, G H, & CO

Weld Street, 218 Main Street, Wilton, ME 04294
Tel: (207) 645-3131

Chairman: Ralph E Ward
President: Richard H Bourtet
Senior Executive Officers: William Keaton (VP Manufacturing), Donald E Poole (Controller)

PRINCIPAL ACTIVITIES: Manufacture and retail of footwear
Parent Company: Chesebrough-Pond's Inc, Greenwich, CT
Financial Information:

	$'000
Sales revenues	125,000

No of Employees: 2,000

BASSETT FURNITURE INDUSTRIES, INC

Hwy 257, Bassett, VA 24055
Tel: (703) 629-7511
Telex: 829 445 BASSETT BSET

Chairman: R H Spilman (and President and Chief Executive Officer)
Senior Executive Officers: B M Brammer (Senior VP and Treasurer), G A Hunsucker (Senior VP), J R Meadows (Senior VP), J C Philpott (Senior VP), J E Bassett Jr (Group VP), J L Franklin Jr (Group VP), H H White (Group VP)

PRINCIPAL ACTIVITIES: Manufacture of domestic furniture and components
Trade Names: Bassett Table, Bassett Upholstery, National/Mt airy, Weiman, Montclair, Commonwealth Contract Furnishings, Impact Furniture, Bassett Bedding, Bassett Juvenile, Bassett Contract Industries
Principal Subsidiaries: Bassett Furniture Industries of N.C. Inc; E B Malone Corp; Impact Furniture, Inc
Principal Bank: Dominion Bank, Roanoke, VA
Financial Information:

	Nov 30 1985	Nov 30 1986
	$'000	$'000
Sales revenues	408,499	421,612
Net income	25,070	19,478
Earnings per share	$3.01	$2.32
Shareholders equity	237,974	248,974

No of Employees: 8,300

BASSETT-WALKER, INC

Rives Road Extension, Martinsville, VA 24112
Tel: (703) 632-5601
Telex: TWX 7108733651 bas walk mavl

President: L D Walker
Senior Executive Officers: James B Montgomery (Executive VP Sales), Walter W Flythe (Senior VP Administration), George H Box (VP Sales), Thomas L Butler (VP, Robert S Gauldin (VP Personnel), George S Wade (VP Manufacturing), G B Piland (Treasurer and Controller)

PRINCIPAL ACTIVITIES: Manufacture of knitted clothing and knitted fabrics
Parent Company: V F Corporation
Financial Information:

	$'000
Sales revenues	222,000

No of Employees: 6,000

BASTIAN INDUSTRIES INC

150 E 58th Street, New York, NY 10155
Tel: (212) 889-8424
Telex: WUT 126220 bbco nyk

Chairman: Benson A Selzer
President: Samuel Ofrichter (and Secretary)
Senior Executive Officers: Robert Komenda (VP and Treasurer), John Gioioso (VP and Controller), John Selzer (VP)

PRINCIPAL ACTIVITIES: Manufacture of oil exploration equipment; rubber hoses; metal and electronic components
Principal Subsidiaries: Bastion Energy Corp; Bradford Pipe and Supply Co; Branchland Pipe and Supply Co; Northern Energy Supply Co Inc; Nytronics Inc; Hi-G Co Inc; Electronica Allu SA; Nytronics Components Group Inc

Principal Bank: Citibank
Financial Information:

	$'000
Sales revenues	143,600

No of Employees: 1,500

BATA SHOE CO

U.S. Route 40, Pulaski Hwy, Belcamp, MD 21017
Tel: (301) 272-2000
Telex: RCA 240 195 bata ur

Chairman: J G Janssen (Canada)
Senior Executive Officers: Dennis Sanderson (VP), Peter J Nicholls (VP), E W Hielke (VP Administration, Secretary and Comptroller)

PRINCIPAL ACTIVITIES: Manufacture of footwear
Principal Bank: Citibank NA
Financial Information:

	$'000
Sales revenues	85,000

No of Employees: 1,500

BATH IRON WORKS CORPORATION

700 Washington Street, Bath, ME 04530
Tel: (207) 443-3311
Telex: WUT 944455 bath iron bthm

Chairman: Eddy G Nicholson
President: William E Haggett (and Chief Executive Officer)
Senior Executive Officers: James M Blenkhorn (Senior VP Business and Technical Development), Royce A Young (Senior VP Operations), Ronald M Bancroft (Senior VP Administration and Finance), James A McGregor (Public Relations Director), William E Graham (VP Contracts), Clifford F Bolster (VP Human Resources and Community Relations), Steven G Buttner (VP Program Management), Carl G Buzawa (VP and Legal Counsel), Howard J Yates (VP Finance), William E Potter (VP Engineering), Dennis K Dugan (VP Management Information Services)

PRINCIPAL ACTIVITIES: Ship building; ship repairing; marine engineering
Parent Company: Congoleum Corporation
Principal Bank: Manufacturers Hanover Trust Company
Financial Information:

	$'000
Sales revenues	400,000

No of Employees: 7,000

BATSON-COOK CO

116 Fourth Avenue, West Point, GA 31833
Tel: (404) 643-2101

Chairman: Cliff C Glover (and Chief Executive Officer)
President: Edmund C Glover
Senior Executive Officers: W H Huguley III (Executive VP and Treasurer), William H Huguley IV (Senior VP), Donald E Hand (VP Jacksonville Office), Paul L Yantis Jr (VP Atlanta Office), A D Cotney (VP West Point Foundry and Machine Company Division), John C McCraney (VP Tampa Office), J L Glover Sr (VP), J L Glover Jr (VP)

PRINCIPAL ACTIVITIES: General building contractors; manufacture of textile machinery; wholesale construction materials
Principal Subsidiaries: Able Construction Co Inc
Principal Bank: Trust Company of Georgia
Financial Information:

	$'000
Sales revenues	105,000

No of Employees: 500

BATTERY STREET ENTERPRISES, INC

617 Mission Street, San Francisco, CA 94105
Tel: (415) 730-1005

Chairman: Peter E Haas
President: Leo Isotalo
Senior Executive Officers: David K Lelewer (Senior VP Human Resources), David D Smith (Treasurer), Katherine B Durgin (Secretary), Karl F Slacik (Chief Financial Officer)

PRINCIPAL ACTIVITIES: Clothing manufacture
Parent Company: Levi Strauss & Company, San Francisco, CA
Financial Information:

	$'000
Sales revenues	275,000

No of Employees: 5,000

BATTLE MOUNTAIN GOLD COMPANY

700 Milam Street, Suite 1300, Houston, TX 77002
Tel: (713) 227 6330

Chairman: Douglas J Bourne (and Chief Executive Officer)
President: Theodore H Pate Jr (and Chief Operating Officer)
Senior Executive Officers: Joseph L Mazur (VP), Frank W Schweizer Jr (VP), John I Sharpe (VP), Richard A Sumin (VP), George W Mitchell (VP Finance, Chief Financial Officer and Treasurer), Robert J Quinn (Secretary and Legal Counsel)

PRINCIPAL ACTIVITIES: Mining of precious metals
Financial Information:

	$'000
Sales revenues	77,640

No of Employees: 460

BATUS INC

2000 Citizens Plaza, Louisville, KY 40202
Tel: (502) 581-8000
Telex: WUT 204177 batus inc lvl

Chairman: P Sheehy
President: H F Frigon (and Chief Executive Officer)
Senior Executive Officers: J A McDonough (VP and Treasurer), L W Arentsen (VP and Controller), T G Hall (VP Human Resources), D A Schlechter (VP and General Counsel), D H Roe (VP Planning), J D Tyson (VP Public Affairs), B D Cummins (VP and Controller), J R Clifford (VP Planning), J H Bullis (VP Management and Organisation Development), L E Lyles (VP Minority Affairs)

PRINCIPAL ACTIVITIES: Holding company with interests in retailing
Parent Company: BAT Industries PLC, London, UK (100%)
Principal Bank: Morgan Guaranty Trust Co
Financial Information:

	Dec 31 1985 $'000
Sales revenues excluding tax	5,881,408
Net income	163,532
Shareholders equity	1,400,420

No of Employees: 62,754

BAUSCH & LOMB INC

One Lincoln First Square, Rochester, NY 14601
Tel: (716) 338-6000
Telex: WUT 978 231 bauschlomb roc

Chairman: Daniel E Gill (and President and Chief Executive Officer)
Senior Executive Officers: Thomas C McDermott (Executive VP, President US Operations), Jay T Holmes (Senior VP Corporate Affairs, Secretary and General Counsel), Harold O Johnson (Senior VP, President Interntional Operations), James E Kanaley (Senior VP, President Professional Eye Care Products Group), Stephen P Kelbley (Senior VP Finance), Stanley W Merrell (Senior VP Administration), W Richard Clark (VP, President Sunglass Division), George L

Foster (VP, President Optical Systems Division), Henry L Foster (VP, President Charles River Laboratories Inc), Diane C Harris (VP Corporate Development), Stephen A Hellrung (VP and Legal Counsel), Randy D Hoffman (VP, President Bushnell Division), Franklin T Jepson (VP Community and Investor Relations), Jon M Larson (VP Technical Services International Division), Robert J Palmisano (VP Human Resources), Alan H Resnick (VP President, Personal Products Division), Frank E Rumpeltin (VP, President Personal Products Division), James J Ward (VP and Controller), Ronald L Zarrella (VP Subsidiary Operations)

PRINCIPAL ACTIVITIES: Optical instruments and soft contact lenses; ophthalmic goods; scientific instruments
Principal Subsidiaries: Bausch & Lamb Opticare Inc; Charles River Laboratories Inc; Charles River Biotechnical Services Inc; Charles River Res Primate; Key Lois Inc; Polymer Technology Corp
Principal Bank: Lincoln First Bank NA
Financial Information:

	Dec 31 1985 $'000	Dec 31 1986 $'000
Sales revenues	596,150	698,867
Net income	66,765	74,695
Earnings per share	$10.76	$2.47
Shareholders equity	-	490,761

No of Employees: 7,600

BAXTER TRAVENOL LABORATORIES INC

One Baxter Parkway, Deerfield, IL 60015
Tel: (312) 948-2000
Telex: 724497 Baxter LB DFLD

Chairman: Vernon R Loucks Jr (President and Chief Executive Officer)
President: Wilbur H Gantz
Senior Executive Officers: G Marshall Abbey (Senior VP and General Counsel), Richard B Egen (Senior VP), Robert J Lambrix (Senior VP and Chief Financial Officer), Lawrence H N Kinet (Group VP), C A (Lance) Piccolo (Executive VP), Will R Pierie (Group VP), Thomas H Quinn (Group VP), Robert J Simmons (Executive VP), Dale A Smith (Group VP), James R Tobin (Group VP), Charles H Blanchard (VP), Wayne G Custead (VP), Michael S Estes (VP), Michael S Heschel (VP), Thomas W Hodson (VP), Warren D Johnson (VP), Melvyn R Kalas (VP and Controller), Brien Laing (VP), Roger F Lewis (VP), Terence J Mulligan (VP), Robert L Rain (VP), Anthony J Rucci (Senior VP), Ellen A Rudnick (VP), Arthur F Staubitz (VP and Deputy General Counsel), Tony L White (VP), Donna C E Williamson (VP), James G Connelly (VP), Patrick J Fortune (VP), Darnell Martin (VP), Gerard Moufflet (VP), David A Nelson (VP), William A Schmidt (VP), Barbara Young Morris (Treasurer), John F Gaither Jr (Secretary and Deputy General Counsel)

PRINCIPAL ACTIVITIES: The Company is engaged in the worldwide development, manufacture and distribution of a diversified line of products, systems and services used and consumed primarily in the health-care field. Products are manufactured by the company in 22 countries and sold in more than 100 countries. Health care is concerned with the preservation of health and with the diagnosis, cure, mitigation, treatment and prevention of disease and body defects and deficiencies. The Company's more than 120,000 products are used principally by hospitals, clinical and medical research laboratories, blood and dialysis centers, rehabilitation centers, nursing homes, doctors' offices and at home under physician supervision. Some of the Company's products have uses other than for health care and, accordingly, the Company sells products for industrial use.
Principal Subsidiaries: (100% owned unless stated): Baxter Travenol Finance Corporation; Baxter World Trade Corporation; American Hospital Supply Deutschland GmbH (West Germany); Baxter Travenol Ltd (Japan); Baxter Travenol World Trade Corporation; Travenol Export Corporation; Baxter Laboratories (1960) Ltd (50%) (UK); Baxter Travenol SA (Belgium); International Reagents Corporation (50%) (Japan); Laboratoires AHS/France SA (France); Travenol Canada Inc (Canada); Travenol Laboratories SA (Panama); Travenol Laboratories (Ireland) (Eire); Travenol Sales Corporation; Travenol Laboratories Inc (Alaska); Travenol Laboratories Inc (Utah); Baxter Healthcare Corporation; American Bentley Inc; SKBL Inc (27.5%)
Principal Bank: The First National Bank of Chicago; Morgan Guaranty Trust Company of New York
Financial Information:

	Dec 31 1985 $'000	Dec 31 1986 $'000
Sales revenues	2,348,000	5,543,000
Income before taxes(1)	136,000	260,000
Net income(1)	137,000	444,000
Dividends	60,000	86,000
Dividends per share	$0.37	$0.40
Earnings per share(2)	$0.85	$1.70
Common stock	211,000	217,000
Retained income	955,000	1,253,000
Shareholders equity	2,963,000	3,370,000

(1) and extraordinary item
(2) primary

Number of Shareholders: 79,000
No of Employees: 61,600

BAY PACIFIC HEALTH CORPORATION

1111 Bayhill Drive, Suite 300, San Bruno, CA 94066
Tel: (415) 952 5000

Chairman: Ernest A Dernberg
President: Stephen C Schwarz (and Chief Executive Officer)
Senior Executive Officers: Allan J Chernov (VP), Michael F Fedor (VP), Denise C Hanson (VP), Maria Orth (VP), Bruce Carp (Treasurer and Senior VP), Richard J Levy (Secretary)

PRINCIPAL ACTIVITIES: Health insurance services
Financial Information:

Net income	1,035

No of Employees: 120

BAY STATE GAS COMPANY

120 Royall Street, Canton, MA 02021
Tel: (617) 828 8650

Chairman: Charles H Tenney II (and Chief Executive Officer)
President: Roger A Young (and Chief Operating Officer)
Senior Executive Officers: Eugene H Owen (Chairman of Executive Committee), Thomas W Sherman (Executive VP and Controller), Charles T Eliss (Senior VP), Charles G Setian (Senior VP), James A Burke (VP), R I Peairs II (VP), Paul G Ford (VP), Walter C Ivancevic (VP), S Robert Jeffrey (VP), Joseph S Raffaele (VP), John D Sampson (VP), John R Snow (VP), Joseph A Teves (VP), Angela P Carlson (Finance), James J Flanagan III (Treasurer)

PRINCIPAL ACTIVITIES: Supply of natural gas
Principal Subsidiaries: Bay State Exploration Inc; Northern Utilities Inc; Granite State Gas Transmission
Principal Bank: First National Bank of Boston
Financial Information:

	$'000
Sales revenues	314,000

No of Employees: 1,110

BAY STATE MILLING CO

541 Main Street, S Weymouth, MA 02190-1857

Chairman: Bernard J Rothwell II
President: William Sheskey
Senior Executive Officers: Robert F Alcarez (Treasurer), John Hillman (Secretary)

PRINCIPAL ACTIVITIES: Milling; flour products

Financial Information:

	$'000
Sales revenues	130,000

No of Employees: 400

BAYBANKS INC

175 Federal Street, Boston, MA 02110
Tel: (617) 482-1040
Telex: WUT 921840 baybank bsn

Chairman: William M Crozier Jr (and President and Chief Executive Officer); Vice Chairmen: Richard F Pollard, William T Sandalls Jr
Senior Executive Officers: Ilene Beal (Senior VP), Donald L Isaacs (Senior VP Public Relations), Galena U Jeffrey (Senior VP), Michael W Vasily (Senior VP), Thomas M Whitney (Senior VP), Joan E Tonra (Senior VP)

PRINCIPAL ACTIVITIES: Bank holding company
Principal Subsidiaries: BayBank Boston; BayBank First Easthampton; BayBank Harvard Trust Co; BayBank Merrimac Valley; BayBank Middlesex; BayBanks Finance and Leasing Co Inc; BayBank Norfolk County Trust Co; BayBanks Credit Corp; BayBanks Mortgage Corp; BayBank Southeast; BayBank Valley Trust Co; BayBanks Systems Inc
Financial Information:

	Dec 31 1985	Dec 31 1986
	$'000	$'000
Net income	48,580	58,852
Earnings per share	$3.81	$4.10
Shareholders equity	315,540	420,370
Deposits	5,081,852	6,348,201
Total assets	6,269,012	7,627,668

No of Employees: 5,565

BAYER USA INC

Mobay Rd, Pittsburgh, PA 15205
Tel: (412) 777-2000

President: K M Weis

PRINCIPAL ACTIVITIES: Holding company whose subsidiaries are engaged in the manufacture and marketing of chemical products, pharmaceuticals, diagnostic systems, biotechnology products, consumer products and hospital products
Parent Company: Bayer AG, Leverkisen, West Germany
Principal Subsidiaries: Miles Laboratories Inc; Miles Laboratories Ltd (Canada); Cutter Japan Ltd (Japan); Mobay Corporation; Helena Chemical Company
Financial Information:

	Oct 31 1986
	$'000
Sales revenues	3,409,997
Net income	93,790
Shareholders equity	805,422

Principal Shareholders: Bayer AG (100%)

BAYLY CORPORATION

5500 S Valentia Way, Denver, CO 80111
Tel: (303) 773-3850
Telex: TWX 910 9350 794 bayly denver

Chairman: David T Marantette III (and Chief Executive Officer)
President: Richard P Thrush
Senior Executive Officers: W L Bullard (VP Operations), Kenneth R Delk (VP), William Harrington (VP Retail Operations), Joseph L Holgerson (VP Ocean Pacific Division)

PRINCIPAL ACTIVITIES: Clothing manufacture inclduing ladies' ready-to-wear; sportswear and sporting equipment
Principal Subsidiaries: Aspen Leaf Inc; Baywood Transport Inc; Waco Apparel Inc
Principal Bank: First Interstate Bank of Denver

Financial Information:

	$'000
Sales revenues	158,000

No of Employees: 3,100

BBC BROWN BOVERI INC

1460 Livingston Avenue, North Brunswick, NJ 08902
Tel: (201) 932-6000
Telex: TRT 178026 brown bov nbru

President: George Gyssler (and Chief Executive Officer)
Senior Executive Officers: Kanwal K Mathur (VP), H E Weinrich (VP), Z S Stys (VP), Ben L Swanson (VP), Hans Heine (VP), Peter Giller (VP), Rudolph J Thurnes (VP and Treasurer), Edward H Stauffer (VP and Secretary)

PRINCIPAL ACTIVITIES: Manufacture of a range of industrial power equipment
Parent Company: BBC Brown, Boveri & Co Ltd, Baden, Switzerland
Principal Bank: Fidelity Union Bancorp
Financial Information:

	$'000
Sales revenues	150,000

No of Employees: 370

BDM INTERNATIONAL INC

7915 Jones Branch Drive, McLean, VA 22102
Tel: (703) 821 5000

President: Earle C Williams
Senior Executive Officers: Stanley E Harrison (Executive VP Advertising and Marketing), Florian N Hofer (Senior VP Administration), David T Bailey (VP), Joseph V Braddock (VP), Robert B Buchanan (VP), James C Hughes (VP General Counsel), Laurence B Jacobs (VP), William R MacDonald (VP), John F McCabe (VP and General Counsel), Daniel F McDonald (VP), George S Newman (VP), Samuel R Strickland (VP and Controller), Charles R Wasaf (VP), John P Riceman (Treasurer)

PRINCIPAL ACTIVITIES: Provision of consultancy and technical services to the defense, communications, space, energy and transportation industries
Principal Subsidiaries: BDM Corp; BDM Engineering Support Services Co; BDM Management Services Co; BDM Services Co Inc; Zapex Corp
Principal Bank: Manufacturers Hanover Trust
Financial Information:

	$'000
Sales revenues	250,300

No of Employees: 3,770

BEACON MANUFACTURING CO

PO Box 395, Swannanoa, NC 28778
Tel: (704) 686-3861
Telex: WUT 577458 beacon swoa

Senior Executive Officers: Forrest Wilkerson (Executive VP), Drew Ansley (VP Merchandising), W Berner (VP and Controller)

PRINCIPAL ACTIVITIES: Textile manufacture
Financial Information:

	$'000
Sales revenues	65,000

No of Employees: 1,000

BEACON MILLING CO, INC

River Road, Cayuga, NY 13034
Tel: (315) 253-7331

President: Wilbur L Townsend

Senior Executive Officers: Alem B Smith (Executive VP), Olin A Rowoth (VP), Theodore G Wright Jr (VP), Edson K Murdock (VP)

PRINCIPAL ACTIVITIES: Production of livestock and animal feeds

Principal Bank: Marine Midland Bank NA

Financial Information:

	$'000
Sales revenues	60,000

No of Employees: 300

BEAMAN CORPORATION

800 West Smith Street, Greensboro, NC 27420

Tel: (919) 271 4400

Chairman: Hugh B Maness (and Chief Administration Officer, Secretary and Treasurer)

President: Donald S Jay (and Chief Operating Officer)

Senior Executive Officers: Robert R Campbell (Senior VP Operations), C Grayson Willard (Senior VP), James J Ebert (VP Manufacturing)

PRINCIPAL ACTIVITIES: Building and construction of non-residential properties

Principal Bank: North Carolina National Bank

Financial Information:

	$'000
Sales revenues	63,050

No of Employees: 750

BEAR AUTOMOTIVE SERVICE EQUIPMENT COMPANY

12121 West Feerick Place, Milwaukee, WI 53222

Tel: (414) 527 3200

President: John F Stolle

Senior Executive Officers: Russell W H Bailey (Senior VP Marketing), Joseph A Marino (Senior VP Engineering), John J Gaskell (VP, Legal Counsel and Secretary), James D Henkhaus (VP and Treasurer)

PRINCIPAL ACTIVITIES: Manufacture of service and diagnostic equipment for the motor vehicle industry

Principal Bank: Continental Illinois National Bank & Trust Co

Financial Information:

	$'000
Sales revenues	73,745

No of Employees: 1,265

BEAR STEARNS & CO

55 Water St, New York, NY 10041

Tel: (212) 952-5000

Chairman: Alan C Greenberg (and Chief Executive Officer)

Senior Executive Officers: Alvin H Einbender (Executive VP and Chief Operating Officer), Thomas R Anderson (Executive VP), Livio M Borghese (Executive VP), Denis P Coleman Jr (Executive VP), Michael L Tarnopol (Executive VP), Carleton A Holstrom (Senior VP Finance)

PRINCIPAL ACTIVITIES: Financial services including security broking and dealing; commodity broking

Parent Company: The Bear Stearns Companies Inc

Principal Subsidiaries: Singer & Mackie Inc; Battery Park Settlement Corp

Principal Bank: Morgan Guaranty Trust Co

Financial Information:

	Apr 30 1986 $'000
Revenues	1,188,950
Net income	89,474
Earnings per share	$1.11
Shareholders equity	651,435
Total assets	26,939,440

No of Employees: 5,650

BEARINGS, INC

3600 Euclid Ave, Cleveland, OH 44115

Tel: (216) 881-2828

Chairman: John R Cunin (and Chief Executive Officer)

President: George L LaMore (and Chief Operating Officer)

Senior Executive Officers: Raymond E Smiley (VP Finance and Treasurer), Thomas L Bradley (VP Corporate Administration), Fred L Mohr (VP Sales and Marketing), E Park Spence (VP Branch Administration), Bryan Sanders (VP Information Services)

PRINCIPAL ACTIVITIES: Wholesale trade in roller and ball bearings, machine tools, hardware and other industrial supplies

Principal Subsidiaries: Bruening Bearings Inc; Dixie Bearings Inc

Principal Bank: AmeriTrust Co

Financial Information:

	$'000
Sales revenues	500,000

No of Employees: 3,300

BEATRICE COMPANIES INC

2 N LaSalle Street, Chicago, IL 60602

Tel: (312) 782-3820

Chairman: Donald P Kelly (and Chief Executive Officer)

Senior Executive Officers: William G Karnes (Chairman Executive Committee), Frank E Grzelecki (Executive VP), David E Lipson (Executive VP and Chief Financial Officer), Anthony Luiso (Executive VP), William S Mowry Jr (Executive VP), Richard J Pigott (Executive VP and Chief Administration Officer), Fred M Adamany (Senior VP), Nolan D Archibald (Senior VP), John R Attwood (Senior VP), Reuben W Berry (Senior VP Human Resources), Thomas P Kemp (Senior VP), William E Reidy (Senior VP), Hercules P Sotos (Senior VP), Richard F Vitkus (Senior VP and General Counsel), Richard S Williamson (Senior VP Corporate Relations)

PRINCIPAL ACTIVITIES: Holding company with interests in dairy products, ice cream, meat products, agricultural products, wines, soft drinks, cold storage warehouses

Parent Company: BCI Holdings Corp

Principal Subsidiaries: Allison Manufacturing Co; Arrowhead Drinking Water Co; Artistic Texturing Corp; Aunt Nellies Foods Inc; Brookside Enterprises Inc; Certified Transportation Co; Coca Cola Bottling Co Mid-America; Coca Cola Bottling Co Omaha; Culligan International Co Inc; CWC Inc; Culligan Dayton Inc; Culligan Des Plaines Valley Water Conditioning; Culligan Water Conditioning Houston Inc; Culligan Water Conditioning Beaver Inc; Culligan Water Conditioning Glendale Inc; Culligan Water Conditioning Inc WI; Culligan Water Conditioning Jacksonville Inc; Culligan Water Consitioning South Bend Inc; Culligan Water Conditioning Greater Pittsburgh Inc; Culligan Water Conditioners Orange City Inc; Culligan Water Conditioning Greater Detroit Inc; Culligan Water Conditioning Inland Empire Inc; Culligan Water Conditioning Robinsdale Inc; Culligan-Nassau Water Conditioning Co; Everpure Inc; Greater Chicago Culligan Water Conditioning Inc; Greater Kansas City Culligan Water Conditioning Inc; Indiana Soft Water Service Inc; Softwater Service Inc; St Louis Soft Water Service Inc; Day-Timers Inc; Dri-Print Foils Inc; Peter Eckrich & Sons Inc; Esmark Inc; Beatrice Meats Inc; Personnel & Labor Consultants;

Strongheart Products Inc; Swift & Co; DRE Interstate Aviation Inc; Eschem Inc; Eschem International Sales Corp; National Wax Co; St Johns Oil Co; Esmark International Inc; Esmark Investments Inc; Estech Inc; Estech Investments Inc; Esgen Phosphate Corp; Estech of Japan Inc; Montan Transport (USA) Inc; Trans-Pacific Resources Inc; Weskem Inc; Estronics Inc; Custom Technologies Corp; Comark Inc; Dycutec Inc; Escast Inc; Federal Stampings Inc; Oklahoma Comex Building Corp; Washington Manufacturing Co; Wellman Dynamics Corp; Eesco Inc; International Jensen Inc; International Audio Sales Corp; Jensen Sound Laboratories International; Southern Electrical Distributors; Pemcor International Inc; Georgetown Interstate Aviation; International Playtex Inc; Almay Inc; BG Marketing Corp; Danskin FL Inc; Danskin Inc; Danskin TX Inc; Fiberite Corp; Fiberite West Coast Corp; Playtex Export Corp; Playtex Holdings Inc; Jhirmack Enterprises Inc; Playtex TX Inc; Tailby-Nason Co Inc; KBH Holdings Inc; Norton Simon Inc; Avis Inc; Avis Leasing Corp; Avis Rent-a-Car System Inc; We Try Harder Inc; Max Factor & Co; Stephen Burrows Frangrance Inc; Parfums Corday Inc; Halston Enterprises Inc; Hunt Foods & Industries Inc; McCall Pattern Co; Norton Simon Communications; Norton Simon International Southern Cotton Oil Co Inc; United Can Co; NSI Transitory Inc; Everain Industries Inc; Hunt-Wesson Foods Inc; Hunt-Wesson Foods Export Corp; J Smith Hungerford Corp; KSS Transportation Corp; Kelley Manufacturing Co; E W Kneip Inc; Liquid Nitrogen Processing; Louvredrape Inc; Martha White Foods Inc; Metallic Lubricants Ltd; Mid-America Container Corp; Nehi-Royal Crown Bottling Co; Pepcol Manufacturing Co; Quincy Market Cold Store Warehouse Co; James J Gallery Inc; North East Cold Storage Corp; Samsonite Corp; Southwestern Investment Co; Premium Funding Co; St Johns Inc; Termicold Corp; Terminal Refrigeration Co; Tropicana Products Inc; Tropicana Transportation Corp; Waterloo Industries Inc

Principal Bank: Continental Illinois National Bank & Trust Co
Financial Information:

	$'000
Sales revenues	12,600,000

No of Employees: 100,000

BECKETT PAPER CO

400 Dayton Street, Hamilton, OH 45012
Tel: (513) 863-5641

President: David L Belew
Senior Executive Officers: James E Reid (VP Marketing), William J Copeland (VP Sales), William R Birri (Controller)

PRINCIPAL ACTIVITIES: Paper manufacture including printing papers and fine papers
Parent Company: Hammermill Paper Company, Erie, PA
Financial Information:

	$'000
Sales revenues	50,000

No of Employees: 400

BECOR WESTERN INC

1100 Milwaukee Avenue, South Milwaukee, WI 53172
Tel: (414) 768-4000

Chairman: Norris K Ekstrom (and Chief Executive Officer)
President: William B Winter (and Chief Operating Officer)
Senior Executive Officers: Thomas G Folliard (VP Finance and Controller), Ray G Olander (VP and Secretary)

PRINCIPAL ACTIVITIES: Manufacture of machinery for mining and construction industries; aerospace components
Principal Subsidiaries: Brad Foote Gear Works Inc; Pittsburgh Gear Co Inc; Bucyrus Disc Inc; Bucyrus International Inc; Western Gear Corp; Western Gear Machinery Co; Sky Climber Inc
Financial Information:

	$'000
Sales revenues	381,070

No of Employees: 3,500

BECTON, DICKINSON & CO

Mack Centre Drive, Paramus, NJ 07652
Tel: (201) 967-3700
Telex: TWX 710 990 6627 bd para

Chairman: Wesley J Howe (and President and Chief Executive Officer); Vice Chairman: Henry P Becton
Senior Executive Officers: Photios T Paulson (Executive VP and Chief Operating Officer), Raymond V Gilmartin (Senior VP), James S Burns (Group President), Herbert B Morote (Group President), Richard F Carey (Group President), Clateo Castollini (Group VP), Robert P Denise (VP and Treasurer)

PRINCIPAL ACTIVITIES: Manufacture of medical and surgical equipment and medical supplies
Principal Subsidiaries: Becton, Dickinson Latin America
Principal Bank: Citibank
Financial Information:

	Sep 30 1985 $'000	Sep 30 1986 $'000
Sales revenues	1,143,790	1,311,570
Net income	88,000	121,930
Earnings per share	$4.20	$2.85
Shareholders equity	681,050	803,925

No of Employees: 16,900

BEE CHEMICAL COMPANY

2700 E 170th Street, Lansing, IL 60438
Tel: (312) 474-7000
Telex: TWX 910 6510591 beechemical

President: George D Lutz
Senior Executive Officers: Joseph Klein (VP Marketing), John Harigan (VP Automotive Operations), G Craig Vincent (VP Administration), Rodney K Sohrbeck (VP Operations and Engineering), Richard Jarzombek (VP Research and Development)

PRINCIPAL ACTIVITIES: Manufacture of paint and office products
Parent Company: Morton Thiokol Inc
Principal Bank: La Salle National Bank
Financial Information:

	$'000
Sales revenues	65,000

No of Employees: 400

BEEBA'S CREATIONS INC

9220 Activity Road, San Diego, CA 92126
Tel: (619) 549 2922

Chairman: Arjun C Waney (and President and Chief Executive Officer)
Senior Executive Officers: Thomas P Baumann (VP and Chief Financial Officer), Murli Hathiramani (VP), Ronald Herron (VP), Eugene B Price II (VP), Rebekah Roth (VP), Ervin Tullman (VP)

PRINCIPAL ACTIVITIES: Manufacture of women's and children's clothing
Financial Information:

	$'000
Sales revenues	46,565

BEECH AIRCRAFT CORPORATION

PO Box 85, Wichita, KS 67201
Tel: (316) 681-7111
Telex: WUT 417 422 beechcraft wic

Chairman: Thomas L Philips
President: Max E Bleck

Senior Executive Officers: C W Dieker (Executive VP-Marketing), Joseph T Giardina (VP-Comptroller), Glenn Ehling (Executive VP-President's Staff), Jack Braly (VP-Operations), Dick Griffiths (VP-Industrial Relations), James P Woolnough (VP-Aerospace Division)

PRINCIPAL ACTIVITIES: Aircraft manufacture; aerospace equipment and components
Parent Company: Raytheon Company, Lexington, MA
Principal Subsidiaries: Beech Acceptance Corporation Inc; Beech Aerospace Services Inc; Beech Holdings Inc; Travel Air Insurance; Scaled Composites Inc
Principal Bank: The Fourth National Bank and Trust Company
Financial Information:

	1986
	$'000
Sales revenues	868,000

No of Employees: 8,500

BEECHAM INC

3 Garret Mountain Plaza, West Patterson, NJ 07424
Tel: (201) 881-3000
Telex: TRT 178044 beecham inc

Chairman: J W Robb (and President)
Senior Executive Officers: Robert E McEntee (President), R P Tatman (President), C A Pergola (President), Charles A Kapp (President), R A Fallon (President), J K Morris (President), Paul Hawran (Treasurer)

PRINCIPAL ACTIVITIES: Manufacture of pharmaceutical preparations; domestic cleaning products
Parent Company: Beecham Group plc, Brentford, Middlesex, UK
Principal Bank: Citibank NA
Financial Information:

	$'000
Sales revenues	765,000

No of Employees: 6,000

BEGLEY COMPANY

PO Box 1000, Richmond, KY 40475
Tel: (606) 623 2550

Chairman: Robert J Begley (and President)
Senior Executive Officers: Donald R Snyder (Executive VP and Treasurer), W W Lake (Senior VP Division), Orlando F Segneri (Senior VP Operations), Conley C Congleton (VP and Secretary), Ronald C Clasgens (Controller and Assistant Treasurer), C E Fain (VP Distribution), Bill R Masters (VP Management Information Systems), Mitch Jacobs (VP Marketing)

PRINCIPAL ACTIVITIES: Drug store chain
Principal Subsidiaries: B & B Equipment & Supply Co; Convenience Manufacturing Co
Principal Bank: The Central Trust Co
Financial Information:

	$'000
Sales revenues	66,000

No of Employees: 1,450

BEKER INDUSTRIES CORPORATION

PO Box 5700, Greenwich, CT 06836
Tel: (203) 622-5700
Telex: WUT 643414 beker a grc

Presidents: Erol Y Beker (and Vice Chairman), Perry B Duryea Jr (and Chief Executive Officer)
Senior Executive Officers: Mack A Barber (Senior VP Engineering), Larry C Dearing (Senior VP Domestic Sales), John J Fitteron (Senior VP Finance and Treasurer), Gary D Greer (Senior VP Manufacturing), Lawrence B Kessler (Senior VP General Counsel and Secretary), M S Pansini (Senior VP), Louis M Whitlock (Senior VP Corporate Affairs)

PRINCIPAL ACTIVITIES: Production of agricultural chemicals particularly concentrated phosphate fertilizers
Principal Subsidiaries: Beker Export Corp; Beker International Corp; Beker Maritime Co; Beker Phosphate Corp; Beker Shipping Co; Beker Transportation Co
Principal Bank: Citibank NA
Financial Information:

	$'000
Sales revenues	264,000

No of Employees: 1,000

BELDING HEMINWAY CO, INC

1430 Broadway, New York, NY 10018
Tel: (212) 944-6040
Telex: TWX 710 5816166 beld heminway

Chairman: Richard D Hausman (and Chief Executive Officer); Senior Vice Chairman: Bruce Hausman (VP and Corporate Counsel)
President: Robert H Brown Jr
Senior Executive Officers: Jack Hausman (Vice Chairman), Leo Hausman (Vice Chairman) Samuel Hausman (Vice Chairman), Bernard A Hellman (Vice President), Ronald V Kaplan (Vice President and Treasurer), Charles L Randazzo (Vice President and Secretary), Charles J Palermo (VP and Controller)

PRINCIPAL ACTIVITIES: Manufacture of sewing threads, fabrics, buttons, zippers and sewing notions
Principal Subsidiaries: Belding Chemical Industries; Belgin Hausman Inc; B Blumenthal & Co Inc; Elmore Corp; Pentapco Inc
Principal Bank: Morgan Guaranty Trust Company of New York
Financial Information:

	$'000
Sales revenues	113,202

No of Employees: 1,600

BELL & HOWELL CO

5215 Old Orchard Road, Skokie, IL 60077-1076
Tel: (312) 470-7100

Chairman: Donald N Frey (and Chief Executive Officer)
President: Gerald E Schultz (and Chief Operating Officer)
Senior Executive Officers: Gary W Ampulski (VP), W James Donaldson (VP), Gary D Eisenberger (VP), Jerome B Herb (VP Finance), William C Jackson Jr (VP), John B Kambanis (VP), Eugene F Sikorovsky (VP, General Counsel and Secretary), Nils A Johansson (Treasurer), Joseph S Secker (Controller), Richard O Becker (Assistant Secretary), Patrick J Graver (Assistant Treasurer), Philip P Haag (Assistant Controller), Lynn E Straley (Assistant Secretary)

PRINCIPAL ACTIVITIES: Bell Howell is a publishing and information services company with four lines of business: Publishing; Document/Mail Processing; Information Storage and Retrieval; and International Marketing Services
Trade Names: Bell & Howell, DeVRY, Merrill Publishing Co, UMI, ID2000, Mailstar, Data Search, Merrill and many others
Principal Subsidiaries: Major Domestic Divisions and Subsidiaries: Business Data Products Division; Business Records Management Companies; DeVRY INC; Document Management Products Division; Merrill Publishing Company; Phillipsburg Division; Publication Systems Division; Quintar Division; University Microfilms Inc. Major International Offices: Chatswood, Australia; São Paulo, Brazil; Friedberg, West Germany; Milan, Italy; Ashford and Wembley, Middlesex, England; Paris, France; Tokyo, Japan; Weston, Ontario, Canada

Financial Information:

	Dec 31 1985	Jan 3 1986
	$'000	$'000
Sales revenues	759,832	853,409
Income before taxes	47,811	50,835
Net income	32,186	32,895
Dividends	6,252	6,736
Dividends per share	$0.62	$0.575
Earnings per share	$3.06	$3.10
Common stock	33,941	36,742
Retained income	217,912	244,071
Shareholders equity	236,921	272,951

No of Employees: 9,000

BELL ATLANTIC CORPORATION

1600 Market St, Philadelphia, PA 19103
Tel: (215) 963-6000

Chairman: Thomas E Bolger (and Chief Executive Officer); Vice Chairman: Raymond W Smith (and Chief Financial Officer)
President: Philip A Campbell (President Network Services)
Senior Executive Officers: Robert A Levetown (Executive VP and General Counsel), Raymond W Smith (VP and Chief Financial Officer)

PRINCIPAL ACTIVITIES: Operation of telephone communications services, computer maintenance and financial services
Principal Subsidiaries: New Jersey Bell; Bell of Pennsylvania; C&P Telephone Companies; Bell Atlantic Systems Leasing International; Bell Atlantic International; Bell Atlantic Tricon Leasing; Sorbus; MAI Canada
Financial Information:

	Dec 31 1985	Dec 31 1986
	$'000	$'000
Sales revenues	9,084,200	9,920,800
Income before taxes	1,903,300	2,071,600
Net income	1,092,900	1,167,100
Dividends per share	$3.40	$3.60
Earnings per share	$5.47	$5.85
Common stock*	199,800	199,600
Shareholders equity	7,921,300	8,320,700

*shares outstanding in thousands

No of Employees: 80,105

BELL FIBRE PRODUCTS CORPORATION

3102 S Boots Street, Marion, IN 46953
Tel: (317) 664-1261

Chairman: John L Bell (and Chief Executive Officer)
President: F H East
Senior Executive Officers: M J Day (VP Manufacturing), R W McMullen (VP Industrial Relations), Vern Tinkle (Manager)

PRINCIPAL ACTIVITIES: Manufacture of paper and board packaging products
Financial Information:

	$'000
Sales revenues	100,000

No of Employees: 900

BELL INDUSTRIES, INC

11812 San Vincente Blvd, Los Angeles, CA 90049
Tel: (213) 826-6778

Chairman: Theodore E Williams (and President)
Senior Executive Officers: Howard Franklin (Senior VP), Nathan Landgarten (Senior VP and Treasurer), Bruce M Jaffe (Senior VP Finance and Secretary), Sam Essick (VP), Paul F Doucette (VP), Vern Severy (VP), D J Hough (VP), Gordon Graham (VP), Dennis Hoertt (VP), Marcus Labe (VP)

PRINCIPAL ACTIVITIES: Electronic equipment including computer disks; heating and ventilation products; motor vehicle parts and accessories; film, chemicals and printing supplies
Principal Subsidiaries: Graham Electronics Supply Inc; Fort Wayne Electronics Supply Inc
Principal Bank: Union Bank
Financial Information:

	$'000
Sales revenues	304,000

No of Employees: 2,000

BELL NATIONAL CORPORATION

155 Sansome Street, San Francisco, CA 94104
Tel: (415) 989-8750

Chairman: Miles A Cobb
President: Nicholas E Toussaint (and Chief Executive Officer)
Senior Executive Officers: John Y Chiang (Treasurer and Chief Financial Officer)

PRINCIPAL ACTIVITIES: Holding company; financial services including savings and loans; interests in real estate
Principal Subsidiaries: Bell Savings & Loan Association
Principal Bank: Bank of America
Financial Information:

	$'000
Revenues	127,000

No of Employees: 400

BELL, W, & CO INC

12401 Twinbrook Parkway, Rockville, MD 20852
Tel: (301) 468 5662

Chairman: Walter Bell (and President)
Senior Executive Officers: Bernard M Blum (Executive VP), Frederic J Bell (Senior VP), Desmond J Karmolinski (VP Merchandising), Warren L Lawhon (VP Advertising), Larry McPherson (VP Corporate Services), Martin S Phiefer (VP Finance and Treasurer), Thomas E Tatum (VP Operations)

PRINCIPAL ACTIVITIES: Retail trade in jewelry
Financial Information:

	$'000
Sales revenues	148,000

No of Employees: 1,300

BELLSOUTH CORPORATION

115 Peachtree Street NE, Atlanta, GA 30367-6000
Tel: (404) 420-8600

Chairman: John L Clendenin (and President and Chief Executive Officer); Vice Chairman: William O McCoy
Senior Executive Officers: Norman C Frost (Executive VP and General Counsel), John B White Jr (Executive VP-Finance and Administration), Raymond L McGuire (Senior VP-Governmental Affairs), C Sidney Boren (VP-Corporate Planning and Budget), Malcolm L Campbell (VP-Corporate Affairs and Secretary), Roy B Howard (VP-Industrial Relations and Benefits), David J Markey (VP-Federal Regulatory Affairs), Raymond K Nolin (VP-Federal Relations), Vincent L Sgrosso (VP and Associate General Counsel), Richard J Sharp (VP-Corporate Human Resources), Owen K Williamson (VP-Senior Financial Officer), C Richard Yarbrough (VP-Public Relations), Winford H Guin (Comptroller), Arlen G Yokley (Treasurer)

PRINCIPAL ACTIVITIES: Telephone services
Principal Subsidiaries: Telephone Subsidiaries: South Central Bell Telephone Company; Southern Bell Telephone and Telegraph Company; BellSouth Services Incorporated. Other Subsidiaries: BellSouth Enterprises Inc. BellSouth Enterprises Companies:- Advertising and Publishing Group: BellSouth Advertising & Publishing Corporation; L M Berry and Company; BellSouth Information Systems Inc; Stevens Graphics Inc (Not wholly owned); TechSouth Inc (Not wholly owned). Communications Systems Group: BellSouth

Advanced Systems Inc; BellSouth Government Systems Inc; BellSouth Systems Technology Inc; FiberLAN Inc (Joint Venture). Corporate Enterprises Group: BellSouth Mobility Inc; BellSouth International Inc; Sunlink Corporation; American Cellular Communications (Joint Venture). Other Bell South Corporation Subsidiary: BellSouth Financial Services Corporation

Financial Information:

	Dec 31 1985 $'000	Dec 31 1986 $'000
Sales revenues	10,663,900	11,441,100
Income before taxes	2,481,500	2,891,600
Net income	1,417,800	1,588,700
Dividends	847,100	954,600
Dividends per share	$1.88	$2.04
Earnings per share	$3.13	$3.38
Common stock	309,800	481,500
Retained income	3,167,700	3,902,200
Shareholders equity	10,198,100	11,261,900

No of Employees: 96,900

BELO, A H, CORPORATION

Communications Center, Dallas, TX 75265
Tel: (214) 745-8730

Chairman: James M Moroney Jr (and Chief Executive Officer)
President: Robert W Decherd (and Chief Operating Officer)
Senior Executive Officers: James P Sheehan (Executive VP and Chief Financial Officer), Michael J McCarthy (VP, Secretary and General Counsel), Robert G Norvell (VP and Treasurer), Michael D Perry (VP and Controller), Walter G Mullins (VP Administration)

PRINCIPAL ACTIVITIES: Publishing of newspapers; broadcasting services including radio, television and cable television
Principal Subsidiaries: Belo Broadcasting Corp; Great Western Broadcasting Corp; Gulf Television Corp; KOTV Inc; WVEC Television Inc; News Texan Inc
Principal Bank: Interfirst
Financial Information:

	$'000
Sales revenues	385,000

No of Employees: 2,050

BELTRAN CORPORATION

One Acton Place, Acton, MA 01720
Tel: (612) 264-4900

President: George A Ethier
Senior Executive Officers: Peter W Clegg (VP and Treasurer), E W Kelley (Chief Executive Officer)

PRINCIPAL ACTIVITIES: Manufacture of snack products; meat and meat products
Principal Bank: Citibank
Financial Information:

	$'000
Sales revenues	35,000

No of Employees: 845

BEMIS COMPANY, INC

800 Northstar Center, Minneapolis, MN 55402
Tel: (612) 340-6000
Telex: WUT 290141 bemis go mps

Chairman: Edward W Asplin (and Chief Administrative Officer)
President: Howard J Curler (and Chief Executive Officer)
Senior Executive Officers: John H Roe (Executive VP), John N Dempsey (VP Science and Technology), Edwin S McBride (VP Operations), George W Andrews (VP, Secretary and General Counsel), Benjamin R Field (VP and Treasurer), LeRoy F Bazany (VP and Controller)

PRINCIPAL ACTIVITIES: Packaging; paper; related products
Principal Subsidiaries: Accraply Inc; Curwood Inc; Custom Resins Inc; Haysson Manufacturing Co; Louissiana Plastics Inc; Lustour Corp; Mankato Corp; Morgan Adhesives Co; Mactac US; Perry Industries Inc; Pervel Industries Inc; Ross and Roberts Inc; Sackner Products Inc; Western Litho Plate & Supply Co
Financial Information:

	Dec 31 1985 $'000	Dec 31 1986 $'000
Sales revenues	787,028	846,670
Net income	23,005	25,631
Shareholders equity	183,785	194,010

No of Employees: 7,720

BENCH CRAFT, INC

State Hwy 15, Box 86, Blue Mountain, MS 38610
Tel: (601) 685-4711

Chairman: H W McLarty (and President)
Senior Executive Officers: Keith Franklin (Executive VP, Sales and Marketing), S L Owen (Senior VP), J L Cochran (VP, Finance)

PRINCIPAL ACTIVITIES: Furniture manufacture
Principal Bank: Peoples Bank
Financial Information:

	$'000
Sales revenues	106,000

No of Employees: 1,050

BENDER, MATTHEW, & CO

1275 Broadway, Albany, NY 12201
Tel: (518) 462-3331
Telex: WUI 6711090 matbdr uw

President: Larry W Peterson (and Chief Executive Officer)
Senior Executive Officers: William A Musso (VP), Ernest D Fiore (VP), T K Holland (VP), Lloyd C Spear (VP Finance and Planning)

PRINCIPAL ACTIVITIES: Publication of books on law and tax; wholesale trading
Parent Company: The Times Mirror Company, Los Angeles, CA
Principal Bank: State Bank
Financial Information:

	$'000
Sales revenues	100,000

No of Employees: 1,300

BENEFICIAL CORPORATION

400 Bellevue Parkway, Wilmington, DE 19809
Tel: (302) 798-0800
Telex: 466286
Telecopy: 792-4071

Chairman: Finn M W Caspersen (and Chief Executive Officer)
Senior Executive Officers: Andrew C Halvorsen (Member of the Office of the President and Chief Financial Officer), David J Farris (Member of the Office of the President and Chief Operating Officer), William H H Ely Jr (Senior VP and Treasurer), James H Gilliam Jr (Senior VP and General Counsel, Corporate Secretary Legal), Thomas P McGough (Senior VP and Corporate Controller), Bruce A Olster (Senior VP-Tax and Audit), Maryann Schneider (Senior VP-Planning and Administration)

PRINCIPAL ACTIVITIES: Beneficial Corporation is one of the world's leading consumer financial services companies. Consumer finance, with over $5.5 billion in receivables, is the cornerstone of Beneficial's business and the basis of the Company's market franchise. Financial services are provided to consumers through more than 1,000 loan offices in the United States, Canada, the United Kingdom and West Germany. Within consumer finance, real estate secured loans, including first and second mortgages and equity lines of credit, represent Beneficial's key growth markets. The Company also markets unsecured personal loans and sales finance contracts, and owns a full service commercial bank and several consumer banking operations

Principal Subsidiaries: Beneficial Management Corporation of America; Beneficial Insurance Group; Beneficial National Bank; Beneficial Mortgage Corporation

Financial Information:

	Dec 31 1986
	$'000
Revenue	1,134,100
Net (loss)	(171,600)
Dividends per share	$2.00
(Loss) per share	($8.30)
Common stock	22,900
Retained income	510,000
Shareholders equity*	808,100
Total assets	7,274,200

*includes redeemable preferred stock of $125 million

No of Employees: 7,000

BENIHANA NATIONAL CORPORATION

8685 Northwest 53rd Terrace, Miami, FL 33166
Tel: (305) 593 0770

Chairman: Rochy H Aoki
President: Joel A Schwarz
Senior Executive Officers: Anthony J Carvalho (VP, Treasurer and Assistant Secretary), Hideaki Kobayashi (VP), Glen Simoes (VP), Darwin C Dornbush (Secretary)

PRINCIPAL ACTIVITIES: Operation of Japanese restaurants; distribution of frozen foods
Parent Company: Benihana of Tokyo Inc
Principal Bank: Southeast Bank
Financial Information:

	$'000
Sales revenues	76,000

No of Employees: 750

BENTLY NEVADA CORPORATION

1617 Water Street, Minden, NV 89423
Tel: (702) 782-3611
Telex: TRT 160415 benv corp mdn

President: Donald E Bently
Senior Executive Officers: Roger Harker (General VP), Raymond J Case (VP Finance), George E Palmatier (VP Marketing), Earl R Nino (VP Sales and Servicing), David H Biggs (VP Manufacturing and Product Development)

PRINCIPAL ACTIVITIES: Electrical measuring and control systems
Principal Bank: Wells Fargo Bank
Financial Information:

	$'000
Sales revenues	57,000

No of Employees: 900

BERCOR INC

14450 Industry Circle, La Mirada, CA 90638
Tel: (714) 670 7644

Chairman: Richard I Berger (and President and Chief Executive Officer); Vice Chairman: William D Rollnick
Senior Executive Officers: Paul A Schur (Executive VP and Secretary), Stuart R Schaefer (Senior VP, Treasurer and Chief Financial Officer), Lucas S Fafara (VP)

PRINCIPAL ACTIVITIES: Manufacture of sports equipment and toys
Principal Bank: Union Bank
Financial Information:

	$'000
Sales revenues	136,000

No of Employees: 350

BERGEN BRUNSWIG CORPORATION

400 Metropolitan Drive, Orange, CA 92668
Tel: (714) 385-4000

Chairman: Emil P Martini Jr (and Chief Executive Officer)
President: Robert E Martini
Senior Executive Officers: George E Reinhardt Jr (VP, Finance and Chief Financial Officer), Dwight A Steffensen (Executive VP), John Calasibetta (Senior VP), Douglas A Chadwick Jr (VP, Secretary and Corporate Counsel), John T Fay Jr (VP, Corporate Affairs), Michael W Fipps (Treasurer), Richard G Gerlach (Controller), Jerome O Gutman (VP, Human Resources), Bernard J Hale (VP, Distribution Services), Gary Rockhold (President, Commtron), Lloyd D Thompson (VP, Corporate Planning and Development), Anthony A Vallario (VP, Corporate Information Resources)

PRINCIPAL ACTIVITIES: Bergen Brunswig Corporation is a diversified and rapidly growing national distributor of health care and consumer electronics products. The Company's business is carried out through three wholly owned subsidiaries. Bergen Brunswig Drug Company is one of the nation's largest distributors of pharmaceuticals and other products sold by pharmacies. The Drug Company serves 10,000 independent, chain and hospital pharmacies. Bergen Brunswig Medical Supply distributes medical and surgical supplies to some 2,000 hospitals, HMOs, emergency centers and other health care facilities. Commtron Corp, a national distributor of consumer electronics products and the nation's largest distributor of video software, serves more than 15,000 customers ranging from small family-owned stores to mass merchandisers
Trade Names: Trade Marks and Registered Trade Names: ULTRAPHASE, MICROPHASE, COMPUPHASE 2, The SPACE MANAGER, The GOOD NEIGHBOR PHARMACY
Principal Subsidiaries: Bergen Brunswig Drug Company; Bergen Brunswig Medical Supply; Commtron Corp
Principal Bank: Security Pacific National Bank
Financial Information:

	Aug 8 1985	Aug 31 1986
	$'000	$'000
Sales revenues	2,434,861	3,065,536
Net income	23,270	20,661
Earnings per share net	$1.83	$1.54
Shareholders equity	159,555	176,839

No of Employees: 4,552

BERGER INDUSTRIES

74-16 Grand Avenue, Maspeth, NY 11378
Tel: (718) 335-8000
Telex: WUT 126004 bergerind nyk

Chairman: Robert I Steiner (and President)
Corporate Officers: Robert I Steiner (Chairman and President), Robert W Berger (VP and Secretary), Morton Lazarus (VP Finance and Treasurer). Staff Officers: Sami Shemtov (VP Manufacturing), Lawrence Steiner (VP Marketing)

PRINCIPAL ACTIVITIES: Manufacture of welded pipes and tubes and electrical fittings
Trade Names: E.T.P.
Principal Bank: Manufacturers Hanover

Financial Information:

	Dec 31 1985	Dec 31 1986
	$'000	$'000
Sales revenues	64,561	58,313
Income (loss) before taxes	888	(431)
Net income (loss)	504	(246)
Earnings (loss) per share	$0.66	($0.33)
Common stock	824	824
Retained income	7,804	7,557
Shareholders equity	10,617	10,312

No of Employees: 550

BERKEY INC

One Water Street, White Plains, NY 10601
Tel: (914) 997-9700

Chairman: A M Victory
President: Jerry J Burgdoerfer (and Chief Executive Officer)
Senior Executive Officers: Richard Darrow (Senior VP), Ronald L Walsworth (Senior VP), Steven P Foerder (VP and Chief Financial Officer), Robert E Goldblatt (VP), Elizabeth R Clancy (VP and Secretary)

PRINCIPAL ACTIVITIES: General photographic services
Principal Subsidiaries: B & E Sales Co Inc; Circu Print Inc; Berkey Film Processing San Francisco; Berkey Film Processing of PA; Berkey Photo Services Washington DC; Direct Photo Inc; Kelly Film Express Inc; Yuletide Concepts Inc
Principal Bank: Manufacturers Hanover Trust Company
Financial Information:

	$'000
Sales revenues	216,000

No of Employees: 2,900

BERKLEY INC

One Berkley Drive, Spirit Lake, IA 51360
Tel: (712) 336-1520
Telex: WUT 480 135
Answerback: Berkleyco stle

President: Tom Bedell (and Chief Executive Officer)
Senior Executive Officers: Paul Johnson (VP Special Services), Charles R Haning (VP Finance and Treasurer), Chuck Skogerboe (VP Human Resources), Bob McMickle (VP Research and Development), Dennis Stule (VP Marketing), Michael Brenny (VP Sales)

PRINCIPAL ACTIVITIES: Manufacture of ropes and fishing tackle
Principal Subsidiaries: Berkley International Co Ltd (Taiwan); Berkley Ltd (Canada)
Principal Bank: First National Bank of Minneapolis
Financial Information:

	$'000
Sales revenues	60,000

No of Employees: 900

BERKLEY, W R, CORPORATION

165 Mason Street, PO Box 2518, Greenwich, CT 06836
Tel: (203) 629 2880

Chairman: William R Berkley (and President)
Senior Executive Officers: Frederick H Brown (Senior VP), Robert V Mendelsohn (Executive VP and Secretary), John D Vollaro (Senior VP), Robert G Walter (Senior VP), Charles E Collins (VP), Stephen G Franks (VP and Controller), E Leroy Heer (VP and Actuary), Brian C Kelly (VP and Legal Counsel), Ira S Lederman (VP and Insurance Counsel)

PRINCIPAL ACTIVITIES: Insurance
Principal Subsidiaries: Jersey/International Group Inc; Admiral Insurance Co; Reinsurance Underwriters Corporation; Tri-State Insurance Co MN; Union Insurance Co; Union Standard Insurance Co
Principal Bank: Chemical Bank
Financial Information:

	$'000
Revenues	214,600

No of Employees: 860

BERKLINE CORPORATION (THE)

One Berkline Drive, Morristown, TN 37814
Tel: (615) 586-1461

Chairman: Alan E Budnick
President: Charles S Shaughnessy Jr (and Chief Executive Officer)
Senior Executive Officers: Timothy Bobo (VP, Support Operations), John V Labarowski (VP, Sales and Merchandising), Richard W Laws (VP, Finance), Larry R Musick (VP, Administration)

PRINCIPAL ACTIVITIES: Holding company whose interests include manufacture of domestic furniture and household hardware
Trade Names: Autoglide, Automotion, LIV-IN-Room, Rock-A-Lounger, Wall-A-Way
Principal Bank: The Chase Manhattan Bank NA
Financial Information:

	Jun 28 1986
	$'000
Sales revenues	86,052
Income before taxes	3,044
Net income	1,748
Dividends	760
Dividends per share	$0.50
Earnings per share	$1.15
Common stock	1,520
Retained income	19,316
Shareholders equity	22,477

No of Employees: 1,650

BERKSHIRE HATHAWAY INC

1440 Kiewit Plaza, Omaha, NE 68131
Tel: (402) 342-4110

Chairman: W E Buffet; Vice Chairman: Charles T Munger
Senior Executive Officers: Michael A Goldberg (VP), J V McKenzie (VP Secretary and Treasurer), Robert H Bird (VP), J William Scott (VP)

PRINCIPAL ACTIVITIES: Holding company with interests in textile manufacture, retail chain stores, the manufacture of candy, publishing, financial services and insurance
Principal Subsidiaries: Associated Retail Stores Inc; Blue Chip Stamps Inc; Buffalo Evening News Inc; Wesco Financial Corp; Mutual Savings & Loan Association; Precision Steel Warehouse Inc; Columbia Insurance Co; Southern Casualty Insurance Co; Cypress Insurance Co; Gateway Underwriters Agency Inc; Home and Automobile Insurance Co; National Fire and Marine Insurance Co; Redwood Fire and Casualty Co; National Indemnity Co; American Condor Insurance Services Inc; Continental Divide Insurance Co; Cornhusker Casualty Co; Kansas Fire and Casualty Co; Lakeland Fire and Casualty Co; Sun Newspapers Inc; Waunbec Mills Inc; WSC Insurance Agency of Pasadena CA; Nebraska Furniture Mart Inc; Scott Fetzer Co; SFZ Transportation Inc; Scott Fetzer Europe Inc; United Computer Services Ltd; World Book Finance Inc; World Book Inc; World Book Life Insurance Co Inc; See's Candy Shops Inc
Principal Bank: First National Bank of Boston

Financial Information:

	Dec 31 1985	Dec 31 1986
	$'000	$'000
Sales revenues	832,200	2,058,236
Net income	435,820	282,361
Earnings per share	$379.99	$246.19
Shareholders equity	1,885,330	2,377,800

No of Employees: 23,200

BERRIE, RUSS, & CO, INC

111 Bauer Drive, Oakland, NJ 07436
Tel: (201) 891-7500

Chairman: Russell Berrie (and President)
Senior Executive Officers: A C Cooke (Executive VP, Chief Financial Officer and Secretary)

PRINCIPAL ACTIVITIES: Manufacture of soft toys, other giftware and greetings cards
Financial Information:

	Dec 31 1985	Dec 31 1986
	$'000	$'000
Sales revenues	204,666	229,278
Income before taxes	45,745	54,201
Net income	25,573	30,434
Dividends	-	5,950
Dividends per share	-	$0.40
Earnings per share	$1.74	$2.05
Common stock	14,736	14,888
Retained income	81,867	106,351
Shareholders equity	97,494	125,040

No of Employees: 1,600

BERRY CONTRACTING, INC

PO Box 4858, Corpus Christi, TX 78408
Tel: (512) 289-2100
Telex: WUT 778446 beconbefab coc

President: Marvin L Berry
Senior Executive Officers: Walter H Kluge (Executive VP), Bruce Daniels (VP), Don Spangler (VP Finance), Paul Lemmons (VP), B F McDonald Jr (VP & General Counsel)

PRINCIPAL ACTIVITIES: Civil engineering and construction; metal fabrication; mechanical engineering and construction
Principal Subsidiaries: Bay Inc; Berry Engineering Inc
Principal Banks: Citizen State Bank; MBank
Financial Information:

	$'000
Sales revenues	50,000

No of Employees: 1,000

BERWIND CORPORATION

1500 Market Street, Philadelphia, PA 19102
Tel: (215) 563-2800

Chairman: C G Berwind Jr (and President and Chief Executive Officer)
Senior Executive Officers: J C Krallinger (VP), W J Eckenrode (VP Finance and Controller), R D Rivers (VP and General Counsel), W W Heilig (VP and Treasurer)

PRINCIPAL ACTIVITIES: Interests in property leasing; industrial equipment; coal and coal products; process equipment; motor vehicle components
Principal Subsidiaries: Bepex Corp; Berwind Instrument Group; Berwind Land Co; Berwind Railway Service Co; Berwind Realty Services Inc; Colorcon Inc; Kentland Co; Layland Coal Co; Perfect Equipment Corp; Reclasource Corp; Agglomeration of Dayton; Redaform Inc; Reitz Coal Co Inc; Rockingham Light, Heat & Power Co
Principal Bank: First Pennsylvania Bank NA
Financial Information:

	$'000
Sales revenues	300,000

No of Employees: 2,000

BEST PRODUCTS CO, INC

PO Box 26303, Richmond, VA 23260
Tel: (804) 261-2000

Chairman: Andrew M Lewis (and Chief Executive Officer)
President: Robert E Huntley (and Chief Operating Officer)
Senior Executive Officers: Sydney L Lewis (Chairman Executive Committee), Francis A Lewis (Executive VP), J L Hawks (Senior VP Operations), Fred A Wollenberg (Senior VP Planning and Management Services), Dudley L Parker Jr (Senior VP Administration), Robert A Rubinoff (Senior VP Merchandising), William F Costello (Senior VP and Chief Financial Officer), James D Staudohar (VP and Controller), Stuart R Golde (VP Ashby's), John Penn (VP Real Estate), E Woodrow Fleming (VP Jewelry Group), Thomas H Schunk (VP Hardlines Group), H Marvin Beasley (VP Jewelry), Dennis Huyck (VP Self Service Merchandise), Lawrence Maxwell (VP Hardlines), George G Seitzinger (VP Publicity), Sanat K Dutta (VP Distribution), Robert A Kendig (VP Field Merchandising), Daniel J Rubin (VP Management Information Systems), Wayne T Tennent (VP Human Resources), Mark M Murphy (VP Corporate Communications), Norman M Laskin (VP Business Systems Planning), Myron H Ginsberg (VP Diamonds), Bruce A Milbrett (VP Loss Prevention and Shortage Control), Richard T Riley (VP and General Manager East Coast Region), W David Hiner (VP and General Manager South/Southwest Region), Richard D Robertson (VP and Geneal Manager West Coast Region), Robert N Thompson (VP and General Manager Mid-West Region)

PRINCIPAL ACTIVITIES: Retailing of a wide range of consumer goods including household appliances, household furnishings, clothing, jewelry and leather goods
Principal Subsidiaries: Ashby's Ltd; Land Builders Inc; Modern Merchandising Inc
Principal Bank: Bank of Virginia Central
Financial Information:

	Dec 31 1985	Dec 31 1986
	$'000	$'000
Sales revenues	2,234,770	2,200,517
Net income (loss)	2,220	(25,593)
Earnings (loss) per share	$0.08	($0.95)
Shareholders equity	415,400	387,158

No of Employees: 20,500

BETHLEHEM STEEL CORPORATION

Martin Tower, Eighth & Eaton Avenues, Bethlehem, PA 18016
Tel: (215) 694-2424
Telex: 215-694-5780

Chairman: Walter F Williams (and Chief Executine Officer)
Senior Executive Officers: D Sheldon Arnot (Executive VP, Steel Commercial), Curtis H Barnette (Senior VP, General Counsel and Secretary, Law and Public Affairs), John A Jordan Jr (Senior VP, Steel Services), Gary L Millenbruch (Senior VP, Chief Financial Officer), Roger P Penny (Senior VP, Steel Operations), Larry L Adams (VP, Union Relations), Lonnie A Arnett (VP and Controller, Accounting), Benjamin C Boylston (VP, Human Resources), Robert W Cooney (VP, Steel Planning), George T Fugere (VP, Information Services), James F Kegg (VP, Materials Management), C Adams Moore (VP, Steel Sales), James C Van Vliet (VP, Steel Marketing), Andrew M Waller (Treasurer, Finance)

PRINCIPAL ACTIVITIES: Bethlehem is a large integrated steel producer which makes and sells a wide variety of steel mill and manufactured steel products. Bethlehem is also engaged in the production and sale of coal and other raw materials; in the construction and servicing of mobile offshore drilling rigs and ships; in the manufacture of railroad cars and parts; in

the sale of equipment and supplies to the oil and gas industries
Principal Subsidiaries: BethEnergy Mines Inc
Financial Information:

	Dec 31 1985	Dec 31 1986
	$'000	$'000
Sales revenues net	5,117,700	4,332,900
(Loss) from operations	(69,800)	(36,300)
Net (loss)	(196,000)	(152,700)
Dividends	14,500	-
Dividends per share	$14.5	-
(Loss) per share	($4.37)	($3.37)
Common stock*	51,981	52,080
Shareholders equity	1,011,300	849,000

*outstanding at year end in thousands

No of Employees: 37,500

BETTER-BILT ALUMINUM PRODUCTS

Smyrna Industrial Park, Smyrna, TN 37167
Tel: (615) 459-4161

President: L M Moffatt (and Chief Executive Officer)
Senior Executive Officers: Gale Swett (Senior VP and General Manager), Hosea Magee (VP Marketing), Roy Anderson (VP Finance), Floyd Boren (VP Engineering), Robert Waycaster (VP Management Information Systems), James Sanders (VP Personnel), Gaylon Austin (VP Manufacturing), Fran Lyons (VP Sales), Randy Cook (VP Sales), Larry Rockovich (VP Purchasing), Dave Jordan (VP Distribution)

PRINCIPAL ACTIVITIES: Manufacture of building products including aluminum windows and doors
Parent Company: Indal Ltd
Principal Bank: Mellon Bank
Financial Information:

	$'000
Sales revenues	82,000

No of Employees: 1,000

BETZ LABORATORIES, INC

4636 Somerton Road, Trevose, PA 19047
Tel: (215) 355-3300
Telex: RCA 244904 betz ur

Chairman: John R McCaughan (and President and Chief Executive Officer)
Senior Executive Officers: Edward W Ross (VP Administration), Hillel Lieberman (VP Research), Robert D Voncanon (VP Finance), James R Marquiss (VP Production), William C Brafford (VP Secretary and General Counsel), Clarence Williams (VP Information Services), Hillel Lieberman (VP Research), Bobby C Moore (VP Marketing), Richard E Fruit (VP Engineering Services)

PRINCIPAL ACTIVITIES: The business of Betz Laboratories, Inc is the engineered chemical treatment of water, wastewater, and process systems operating in a wide variety of industrial and commercial applications, with particular emphasis on the chemical, pertoleum refining, paper, automotive, electrical utility, and steel industries. Betz produces and markets a wide range of specialty chemical products, including the technical and laboratory services necessary to utilize Betz products effectively. Chemical treatment programs are applied for use in boilers, cooling towers, heat exchangers, paper and petroleum process streams and both influent and effluent systems.
Principal Subsidiaries: Betz Energy Chemicals, Inc; Betz Entec, Inc; Betz PaperChem, Inc; Betz Process Chemicals, Inc; Betz International, Inc; Betz Europe, Inc; Betz Inc (Canada); Betz Limited (UK); Betz GmbH (West Germany); Betz NV (Belgium); Betz Sud SpA (Italy); Betz Pte, Ltd (Singapore); Betz Laboratores Pty, Ltd (Australia); Betz GesmbH (Austria); Betz Industries sa (France)
Principal Bank: Provident National Bank
Financial Information:

	Dec 31 1985	Dec 31 1986
	$'000	$'000
Sales revenues	319,381	344,377
Income before taxes	64,864	66,788
Net income	36,792	35,544
Dividends	19,831	21,647
Dividends per share	$1.26	$1.36
Earnings per share	$2.33	$2.23
Common stock	1,689	1,688
Retained income	188,427	202,044
Shareholders equity	19,793	204,040

No of Employees: 2,540

BEVERAGE MANAGEMENT, INC

1001 Kingsmill Pkwy, Columbus, OH 43229
Tel: (614) 846-9800

Chairman: Henry M O'Neill Jr (and Chief Executive Officer)
President: Albert L Coughlin (and Chief Operating Officer)
Senior Executive Officers: Frederick H DiRenzo (VP Manufacturing), Peter P Sullivan (VP Finance), Charles R Gibson (VP Industrial Relations), Paul J Quinn (VP Group)

PRINCIPAL ACTIVITIES: Production of non-alcoholic beverages
Principal Bank: Banc Ohio National Bank
Financial Information:

	$'000
Sales revenues	185,000

No of Employees: 2,000

BEVERLY ENTERPRISES

99 So Oakland Avenue, Pasadena, CA 91101
Tel: (818) 577-6111

Chairman: Robert Van Tuyle (and Chief Exeuctive Officer)
President: David R Banks (and Chief Operating Officer)
Senior Executive Officers: Charles Jordan (Senior VP), William M Wright (Executive VP Finance), George Wagner (Executive VP Operations), Larry B Cornish (Senior VP General Counsel and Secretary), Sherri E Lee (VP and Controller), Jack MacDonald (VP)

PRINCIPAL ACTIVITIES: Provision of health-care services including in-home nursing
Principal Bank: First Interstate Bank of California
Financial Information:

	Dec 31 1985	Dec 31 1986
	$'000	$'000
Sales revenues	1,690,740	2,019,262
Net income	59,820	44,943

No of Employees: 116,000

BGA INTERNATIONAL

440 W 8th South Street, Salt Lake City, UT 84110
Tel: (801) 359-8731

President: Stephen T Harcrow
Senior Executive Officers: A R Nelson (Executive VP and Chief Financial Officer), Edward deBoer (executive VP Marketing), Donald Blohm (VP Manufacturing), Charles Horne (VP Engineering), Gary Draper (VP)

PRINCIPAL ACTIVITIES: Manufacture of pumps and other equipment for the oil industry
Parent Company: Baker International Corp
Principal Bank: First Security Bank of Utah
Financial Information:

	$'000
Sales revenues	100,000

No of Employees: 1,000

BIBB CO

237 Coliseum Drive, Macon, GA 31201
Tel: (912) 743-3731
Telex: TWX 810 7835533 bibb macon

Chairman: Thomas C Foley
President: Roland K Knight (and Chief Operating Officer)
Senior Executive Officers: Alan V Davis (Senior VP and Chief Financial Officer), Steve Boyter (VP Manufacturing), Lowell W Belk (VP Administration and Secretary), Donald G Vereen (VP Data Processing and Controller)

PRINCIPAL ACTIVITIES: Manufacture of cotton and synthetic fibers and fabrics for the home
Parent Company: National Textile Corp
Principal Bank: The Citizens and Southern National Bank
Financial Information:

	$'000
Sales revenues	250,000

No of Employees: 5,200

BIC CORPORATION

Wiley Street, Milford, CT 06460
Tel: (203) 783-2000
Telex: TWX 7104620135 bic mfrd

Chairman: Marcel L Bich
President: Bruno Bich (and Chief Executive Officer and Chief Operating Officer)
Senior Executive Officers: Alex Alexiades (VP and Treasurer)

PRINCIPAL ACTIVITIES: Manufacture of writing equipment, lighters, razors and leisure goods
Principal Bank: Irving Trust Company
Financial Information:

	$'000
Sales revenues	262,700

No of Employees: 2,500

BIDDLE SAWYER CORPORATION

2 Pennsylvania Plaza, New York, NY 10001
Tel: (212) 736-1580
Telex: ITT 420080 bsc edc

President: Wallace Chavkin
Senior Executive Officers: Jack D Haim (Executive VP), Robert Chavkin (VP Sales), Benjamin Benveniste (VP Sales), Arthur L Friedman (Treasurer), George Bovit (VP Sales-Chemicals), Robert Unrath (VP Sales-Essential Oils), Philip Nelson (VP Sales-Enzymes)

PRINCIPAL ACTIVITIES: Manufacture of chemicals
Principal Bank: The Bank of New York
Financial Information:

	$'000
Sales revenues	73,000

No of Employees: 130

BIG B INC

PO Box 10166, Birmingham, AL 35202
Tel: (205) 424-3421

Chairman: Joseph S Bruno
President: Anthony J Bruno
Senior Executive Officers: Arthur M Jones Sr (Executive VP Finance, Secretary and Treasurer), Vincent J Bruno (VP Merchandising and Advertising), John F Hight Jr (VP Pharmacy), Bobby W Little (VP)

PRINCIPAL ACTIVITIES: Operation and management of drug stores
Financial Information:

	$'000
Sales revenues	175,430

No of Employees: 2,000

BIG BEAR INC

770 West Goodale Boulevard, Columbus, OH 43212
Tel: (614) 464 6500

President: Michael J Knilans (and Chief Executive Officer)
Senior Executive Officers: David W Godfrey (VP Discount Department Stores), Richard L Vogel (VP Supermarket Store Operations), W T Flyg (VP Finance, Treasurer and Assistant Secretary), Samuel J Soponto Sr (VP)

PRINCIPAL ACTIVITIES: Supermarkets and discount stores
Principal Subsidiaries: Big Bear Stores Inc; Big Bear Bakeries Inc; Hart Stores Inc
Principal Bank: BancOhio National Bank
Financial Information:

	$'000
Sales revenues	828,100

No of Employees: 8,630

BIG DRUM, INC

PO Box 1819, Columbus, OH 43216
Tel: (614) 294-4931
Telex: TWX 8104821656 big drum cols

Chairman: Thomas L Parker
President: R E Janis (and Chief Executive Officer)
Senior Executive Officers: Richard E Estell (VP), Ralph Drenisco (VP Sales), J R Orrell (VP), David May (VP)

PRINCIPAL ACTIVITIES: Manufacture of food packaging
Parent Company: Alco Standard Corporation, Valley Forge, PA
Principal Bank: BancOhio National Bank
Financial Information:

	$'000
Sales revenues	50,000

No of Employees: 600

BIG THREE INDUSTRIES INC

3535 W Twelfth Street, Houston, TX 77008
Tel: (713) 868-0333
Telex: WUT 775805 gib 3 co hou

Chairman: Harry K Smith (and Chief Executive Officer); Co Chairman: Albert K Smith; Vice Chairman: William M Boren
President: Thomas E Sands (and Chief Financial Officer)
Senior Executive Officers: Harold E Purdom (Executive VP Sales), Kenneth Miller (Executive VP), Paul H Galton (VP and General Manager), Roy Mellor (VP Engineering), James W Clinton (VP), Milton Kuhn (VP Production and Distribution Industrial Gas Division), James Fry (VP Administration and Real Estate Officer), Calvin Hodges (VP Louisiana Operation), John Porter (VP), Russell K Smith (VP)

PRINCIPAL ACTIVITIES: Manufacture of industrial gases, welding machinery and oilfield equipment and services
Principal Subsidiaries: Bayou Cogeneration Plant; Big Three Cogeneration; Big Three International Inc; Big Three Lincoln AK Inc; Bowen Tools Inc; Dia-Log Co; Industrial Water Treatment Co; Lincoln Big Three Inc; Noursco Services Inc
Principal Bank: Texas Commerce Bank National Association
Financial Information:

	Dec 31 1985	Dec 31 1986
	$'000	$'000
Sales revenues	834,170	645,962
Net income (loss)	14,537	(4,505)
Shareholders equity	511,546	464,675

No of Employees: 5,210

BIG V SUPERMARKETS INC

176 North Main Street, Florida, NY 10921
Tel: (914) 651 4411

Chairman: William Rosenberg
President: A Richard Rosenberg (and Chief Executive Officer)
Senior Executive Officers: David G Bronstein (Executive VP and Chief Operating Officer), John W Beisel Jr (VP Operations),

Gary S Koppele (VP Administration, Treasurer and Chief Financial Officer), Richard A Rantala (VP Merchandising), Cornelius J J Madera Jr (VP Corporate Development, Legal Counsel and Secretary), Erwin J Fox (VP Industrial Relations)

PRINCIPAL ACTIVITIES: Supermarkets

Principal Bank: Bank of New York

Financial Information:

	$'000
Sales revenues	560,630

No of Employees: 4,000

BIGELOW-SANFORD, INC

PO Box 3089, Greenville, SC 29602

Tel: (803) 299-2000

Telex: TWX 8102812179 big low grv

Chairman: C R Goulet (and Chief Executive Officer)

President: Anthony O Kelly (and Chief Operating Officer)

Senior Executive Officers: Steven K Bordeaux (Senior VP Marketing), Roy Guess (Senior VP Products and Technical Services), J P Kitchens (Senior VP Manufacturing), Robert W Liptak (Senior VP Finance and Administration), Don B Noell (VP Contract Sales), Richard A Moore (VP Customer Service and Production Planning), Theodore Betsch (VP Technical Services), Philip Haney (VP Residential Sales), J E Meredith (VP Plant Operations), P B Norman (VP Marketing Services), R P Strawhorn (VP and Controller)

PRINCIPAL ACTIVITIES: Manufacture of materials handling equipment

Principal Bank: Chemical Bank

Financial Information:

	$'000
Sales revenues	200,000

No of Employees: 2,400

BILTRITE CORPORATION

PO Box 9045, Waltham, MA 02254-1524

Tel: (617) 884-1700

Chairman: S J Bernstein (and Chief Executive Officer)

President: S A Fine (and Chief Operating Officer)

Senior Executive Officers: H F McKeon Jr (VP and Treasurer), G H Weinstein (VP and Secretary), E A Beawieu (VP), F W Foshage Jr (VP), W Matfess (VP), J T Mooney (VP), F W Trezise (VP)

PRINCIPAL ACTIVITIES: Manufacture of products for shoe repairs

Financial Information:

	$'000
Sales revenues	62,700

No of Employees: 750

BINDLEY WESTERN INDUSTRIES, INC

4212 West 71st St, Indianapolis, IN 46268

Tel: (317) 298-9900

Chairman: William E Bindley (and President)

Senior Executive Officers: David D Swaim (Senior VP and Treasurer), Richard Zartman (VP), James P Keller (VP), James E Miller (Controller)

PRINCIPAL ACTIVITIES: Wholesale trade in drugs principally for warehousing drug chains

Trade Names: Bindley Western Drug Company, Inc

Principal Subsidiaries: Bindley Western Drug Company, Inc

Principal Bank: Indiana National Bank

Financial Information:

	Dec 31 1985	Dec 31 1986
	$'000	$'000
Sales revenues	626,900	711,020
Net income	5,150	4,340
Earnings per share	$0.76	$0.67
Shareholders equity	40,991	44,684

Principal Shareholders: William E Bindley

No of Employees: 355

BINGHAM-WILLAMETTE CO

2800 NW Front Avenue, Portland, OR 97210

Tel: (503) 226-5200

Telex: TWX 9104648031 bing will db

Chairman: T J Henderson

President: J W Reece (and General Manager)

Senior Executive Officers: W L Hallmark (VP Nuclear Sales and Engineering), W J Muller (VP Pump Sales and Marketing), A R Sadewic (VP Maufacturing), H T Williams (VP Finance and Administration), R G Hamreus (VP Pump Engineering)

PRINCIPAL ACTIVITIES: Manufacture of pumps; products for the nuclear industry

Parent Company: Guy F Atkinson Co

Principal Bank: The Bank of California National Association

Financial Information:

	$'000
Sales revenues	140,000

No of Employees: 1,600

BINKS MANUFACTURING CO

9201 W Belmont Avenue, Franklin Park, IL 60131

Tel: (312) 671-3000

Telex: 728367

Chairman: Burke B Roche (and President)

Senior Executive Officers: Doran J Unschuld (VP and Secretary), W W Roche (Assistant Secretary and Director), G W Zoellick (Treasurer), S R Kennedy (Assistant Secretary and Assistant Treasurer), Ernest J Magnus (Assistant VP), Ernest Watts (VP)

PRINCIPAL ACTIVITIES: Manufacture and sale of coating application equipment

Trade Names and Registered Trademarks: Wren, Pogo, Rotojet, Dynaprecipitor, Lo-Boy, Re-Trak, Moe-Air, Superbee, Predator, Spray-Tainer and the Corporate Mark, Binks

Principal Subsidiaries: Foreign Subsidiaries with warehouse facilities:-Binks Manufacturing Company of Canada Ltd (Canada); Binks de Mexico SA (Mexico); Binks-Bullows Ltd (UK); Binks-Bullows Sweden AB (Sweden); Binks-Bullows (Aust) Pty Ltd (Australia); Binks International SA (Belgium); Binks Deutschland GmbH (Germany); Binks International (Italia) Srl (Italy); Binks Japan Ltd (Japan); *Binks International (France), *Branch sales office of Binks International SA. Domestic Subsidiary:- Binks Research and Development Corporation. Division:- Poly-Craft Systems

Principal Bank: Continental Illinois National Bank and Trust Company

Financial Information:

	$'000
Sales revenues	142,000

No of Employees: 1,400

BINNEY & SMITH INC

1100 Church Lane, Easton, PA 18042

Tel: (215) 253-6271

Telex: ITT 4761084 b+s inc eat

Chairman: Jack F Kofoed (and Chief Executive Officer)

President: Richard Gurin (and Chief Operating Officer)

Senior Executive Officers: Terrence Schmoyer (VP Operations), Steve Yanklowitz (VP Crayola Products Division and General Manager), Paul E Keane (VP International), Drew W Landis

(VP Human Resources), Neil E Glickstein (VP Finance), Lindley Scarlett (VP Strategic Planning), Stan Strauss (VP Educational Products Division and General Manager), Roger Cooley (VP Art Products Division and General Manager)

PRINCIPAL ACTIVITIES: Manufacture of artists' materials, games and toys
Parent Company: Hallmark Cards Inc, Kansas City, MO
Principal Bank: Morgan Guaranty Trust of New York
Financial Information:

	$'000
Sales revenues	125,000

No of Employees: 1,500

BIO-LAB, INC

627 E College Avenue, Decatur, GA 300310
Tel: (404) 378-1753
Telex: TWX 810 751-3318 bio lab decr

Chairman: Marshall Bloom
President: Larry Bloom
Senior Executive Officers: Joel Grayson (VP Pool and Spa), Rod Sterling (VP Diversified Products)

PRINCIPAL ACTIVITIES: Manufacture of specialty chemicals and pool and spa chemicals
Parent Company: Lonza, Inc
Principal Bank: Bank of the South
Financial Information:

	1986 $'000
Gross sales revenues	80,000

No of Employees: 350

BIO-RAD LABORATORIES, INC

1000 Alfred Nobel Drive, Hercules, CA 94547
Tel: (415) 724-7000
Telex: ITT 470179 biordclem rcmd

President: David Schwartz
Senior Executive Officers: James J Bennett (VP Diagnostics Products Group), Guy Gerard (VP European Operations), Gregory K Hinckley (VP Finance), Warren R Howell (VP Analytical Instrumentation Group), Burton A Zabin (VP Research Products Group), Norman Schwartz (Treasurer), Peter V Leigh (Controller)

PRINCIPAL ACTIVITIES: Since its inception in 1957, Bio-Rad has become a recognized world leader in chemical separations and identifications, in clinical diagnosis and in analytical instrumentation. With facilities and offices in 13 countries, Bio-Rad serves the scientific research and healthcare communities, and industry worldwide. Bio-Rad serves four major market places, universities, biotechnology, healthcare and semiconductors. The company develops, makes, sells, and services a range of more than 3,500 products and systems delivered to over 10,000 customers in over 50 countries: specialty chemicals and related equipment used to separate complex mixtures into individual components and identify those components; test kits, instruments and controls used to diagnose human disorders; and analytical instrumentation and materials to detect, examine, measure and identify minute amounts of individual chemicals.
Principal Divisions and Subsidiaries: Divisions: Research Products Division; Clinical Division; Digilab Division; ECS Division; Ophthalmic Division; Polaron Division (UK); Sadtler Research Laboratories Division. Subsidiaries and Branches: Bio-Rad Laboratories Pty, Limited (Australia); Bio-Rad Laboratories GesmbH (Austria); Bio-Rad Laboratories (Belgium); Bio-Rad Laboratories (Canada) Ltd (Canada); Bio-Rad Lasersharp Ltd (UK); Bio-Rad Laboratories Ltd (UK); Polaron Equipment Limited (UK); Orimbio SA (France); Bio-Rad Pacific (Hong Kong); Bio-Rad Laboratories SRL (Italy); Elfiplast SRL (Italy); Nippon Bio-Rad Laboratories KK (Japan); Bio-Rad Laboratories BV (Netherlands); Bio-Rad Laboratories AG (Switzerland); Bio-Rad Laboratories GmbH (West Germany)
Principal Bank: First National Bank of Chicago
Financial Information:

	Dec 31 1985 $'000	Dec 31 1986 $'000
Sales revenues	102,000	127,000
Income before taxes	6,000	9,500
Net income	4,300	5,800
Earnings per share	$0.65	$0.80
Common stock	7,131	7,540
Retained income	15,999	21,773
Shareholders equity	29,856	43,305

No of Employees: 1,500

BIRD INC

Washington Street, East Walpole, MA 02032
Tel: (617) 668-2500
Telex: WUT 924429 birdson wpol

Chairman: George J Haufler (and President and Chief Executive Officer)
Senior Executive Officers: Peter H Buttler (VP Business Development), William C Kinsey (VP and General Manager Housing Group), Richard C Maloof (VP and General Manager North East Roofing Division), Paul A Lacy (VP, Treasure and Controller), Frank S Anthony (VP Real Estate, Secretary and Legal Counsel), James J Palermo (VP, President Industrial Group), Joseph G LaCroix (VP, President Plastic Products Group)

PRINCIPAL ACTIVITIES: Manufacture of building and roofing materials, equipment for the pulp and paper industry and filtration machinery
Principal Subsidiaries: Bird Machine Co Inc; Southwest Express Inc
Principal Bank: Bank of New England
Financial Information:

	$'000
Sales revenues	191,700

No of Employees: 2,000

BIRD MACHINE CO

Neponset Street, South Walpole, MA 02071
Tel: (617) 668-0400
Telex: WUT 924428

Chairman: George G Haufler
President: James J Palermo
Senior Executive Officers: T O San Giacomo (VP Marketing), Edward V Garner (VP Engineering), W F White (New Business Development), Jerry M Moyer (VP Administration and Secretary)

PRINCIPAL ACTIVITIES: Manufacture of machines for the paper, mining and chemical industries
Parent Company: Bird Inc
Principal Bank: Bank of New England
Financial Information:

	$'000
Sales revenues	50,000

No of Employees: 600

BIRD-JOHNSON COMPANY

110 Norfolk Street, Walpole, MA 02081
Tel: (617) 668-9610
Telex: WUT 6817294 birdjohn wpol

Chairman: Richard E McGinnis
President: Charles A Orem (and Chief Executive Officer)
Senior Executive Officers: Donald E Ridley (Senior VP Marine Division), Joseph J Riley (VP Finance)

PRINCIPAL ACTIVITIES: Manufacture of marine propellers and subcontract precision machinery
Parent Company: A Johnson & Co Inc, New York, NY
Principal Bank: Bay Bank/Norfolk County Trust Co
Financial Information:

	$'000
Sales revenues	50,000

No of Employees: 280

BIRDSBORO CORPORATION

Furnace Street, Birdsboro, PA 19508
Tel: (215) 582-2011
Telex: WUT 836412 birdsboro bdso

Chairman: Victor Posner (and President and Chief Executive Officer); Vice Chairman: Steven Posner; Deputy Vice Chairman: Austin J Paddock
Senior Executive Officers: Walter Seickman (Executive VP and Chief Operations Officer), A F McLean (Executive VP), Peter J Gibson (Executive VP and General Manager, Machines Division), Bernard Posner (Senior VP), Bernard M Krakower (Senior VP), Jack Coppersmith (Senior VP and Chief Financial Officer), Mitchell V Gregory (VP), Melvin R Colvin (VP), Hans A Schmidt (VP and General Manager Founding Division), Anthony L Lombardo (VP and Controller), Tracy Posner (VP and Assistant Secretary)

PRINCIPAL ACTIVITIES: Manufacture of machinery for the steel industry and manufacture of castings
Parent Company: Pennsylvania Engineering Corporation, Pittsburgh, PA
Principal Bank: Mellon Bank NA
Financial Information:

	$'000
Sales revenues	50,000

No of Employees: 750

BIRDVIEW SATELLITE COMMUNICATIONS INC

315 North Lindenwood, Olathe, KS 66062
Tel: (913) 829 0400

Chairman: Charles A Ross (and President)
Senior Executive Officers: Roger L Mason (Senior VP Division)

PRINCIPAL ACTIVITIES: Manufacture of satellite TV systems and security equipment
Principal Bank: Security Pacific National Bank
Financial Information:

	$'000
Sales revenues	60,000

No of Employees: 740

BIRMINGHAM STEEL CORPORATION

PO Box 1208, Birmingham, AL 35201
Tel: (205) 871-9290
Telex: TWX 810 733 5548 boltsusco bhm

President: James A Todd Jr (and Chief Executive Officer)
Senior Executive Officers: J C Nuckels (Executive VP), T E Kerlin (Executive VP)

PRINCIPAL ACTIVITIES: Operates steel mini mills producing steel and steel products and steel roof support systems for underground coal mining
Principal Bank: Manufacturers Hanover Trust
Financial Information:

	$'000
Sales revenues	50,000

No of Employees: 1,000

BISSELL INC

2345 Walker Road NW, Grand Rapids, MI 49504
Tel: (616) 453-4451
Telex: WUT 226413 bissell gdr

President: J M Bissell (and Chief Executive Officer)
Senior Executive Officers: H J Bloem (Executive VP US Division), J W Conway (VP Finance), R W Ball (VP European Division), K J Klaver (VP Marketing), J S Hughes Jr (VP Sales), W J Systema (VP Graphics Division), T L Aldrich (VP Healthcare Group), D E McDowell (VP Product Development)

PRINCIPAL ACTIVITIES: Manufacture of a wide range of carpet cleaning equipment, toys, cleaning chemicals
Principal Subsidiaries: Atlantic Precision Works Inc; Atlas Tag & Label Inc; Bissell International Corp; Bissell Printed Products Inc; Imperial Business Forms Inc; Marion Manufacturing Inc; Maxi-Vac Manufacturing Co; Penn Champ Inc; Fred Sammons Inc; Slip-X Safety Treads Inc; Venturi Inc
Principal Bank: Old Kent Bank and Trust Company
Financial Information:

	$'000
Sales revenues	85,000

No of Employees: 1,400

BIW CABLE SYSTEMS, INC

22 Joseph E Warner Blvd, North Dighton, MA 02764
Tel: (617) 822 6600
Telex: 94-0604 BOSBIW

Chairman: H B Burley Jr
President: E Manchester Jr
Senior Executive Officers: F C Schwelm Jr (VP Operations), R Kruger (VP Marketing and Sales), R Weintraub (Treasurer and Controller)

PRINCIPAL ACTIVITIES: Manufacture of electrical wire and cables, connectors, and cable assemblies
Principal Subsidiaries: Boston Insulated Wire & Cable Company Ltd (Canada); Boston Insulated Wire (UK) Ltd (UK)
Principal Bank: The First National Bank of Boston
Financial Information:

	Dec 31 1985	Dec 31 1986
	$'000	$'000
Sales revenues	48,749	45,974
(Loss) before taxes	(351)	(6,831)
Net income (loss)	49	(6,613)
Dividends	226	113
Dividends per share	$0.100	$0.050
Earnings (loss) per share	$0.02	($2.93)
Common stock	904	904
Retained income	10,460	3,374
Shareholders equity	16,488	9,420

No of Employees: 629

BLACK & DECKER CORPORATION

701 E Joppa Road, Towson, MD 21204
Tel: (301) 583-3900

Chairman: Laurence J Farley
President: N D Archibald
Senior Executive Officers: William E Stevens (Executive VP), James F Barcus Jr (Senior VP Worldwide Information Services), George M Sherman (Senior VP Power Tools Group), Dennis G Heiner (Senior VP Household Products Group), Arnold L Breidenbaugh (Group VP Pan American Region), Roger H Thomas (Group VP Eastern Hemisphere), Stephen F Page (VP Finance and Treasurer), Francis J Rosenthal (VP Global Manufacturing and Technical Development), Barbara B Lucas (VP and Secretary), David R Stone (VP European Marketing), Leonard A Strom (VP Human Resources)

PRINCIPAL ACTIVITIES: Manufacture of power tools for the home, garden and workshop
Principal Bank: Morgan Guaranty Trust Co

Financial Information:

	Sep 30 1985	Sep 30 1986
	$'000	$'000
Sales revenues	1,732,280	1,791,633
Net income (loss)	(158,425)	6,304
Shareholders equity	504,848	616,660

No of Employees: 22,400

BLACK CLAWSON CO
666 Third Avenue, New York, NY 10017
Tel: (212) 972-4440

Chairman: Carl C Landegger
President: E T Zimmerman
Senior Executive Officers: D E Parker (VP and Controller)

PRINCIPAL ACTIVITIES: Manufacture of machines for the paper and pulp industry and other industrial equipment
Parent Company: Landegger Industries Inc
Principal Bank: Citibank NA
Financial Information:

	$'000
Sales revenues	135,000

No of Employees: 2,000

BLACK HILLS CORPORATION
625 Ninth Street, Rapid City, SD 57709
Tel: (605) 348 1700

Chairman: Larry M Owen (and President and Chief Executive Officer)
Senior Executive Officers: Daniel P Landguth (Senior VP and Chief Operating Officer), E F Pompy (VP Human Resources), Richard J Tupper (Senior VP Corporate Development), Jeffrey E Wood (Controller), Louise S Kelley (Secretary and Treasurer), Mack J West (VP Engineering and Operations), R E Furois (VP Customer Services), Joseph E Rovere (VP Public Affairs)

PRINCIPAL ACTIVITIES: Holding company with interests in electricity, oil and gas, coal mining and trucking services
Principal Bank: Norwest Bank South Dakota
Financial Information:

	$'000
Sales revenues	113,915

No of Employees: 550

BLAIR, JOHN, COMPANY
1290 Avenue of the Americas, New York, NY 10104
Tel: (212) 603-5000

President: Jack W Fritz (and Chief Executive Officer)
Senior Executive Officers: Hugh R Beath (Executive VP), James C Hilliard (Senior VP), John A Valentine (Senior VP), Harry Smart (VP Television), Richard Leberman (VP and Chief Financial Officer), Gary I Klein (VP), Thomas J McKee (VP and Legal Counsel), R Peter Zimmermann (VP and Controller)

PRINCIPAL ACTIVITIES: The company has interests in radio and television broadcasting
Principal Subsidiaries: Advo-System Inc; Alden Press Inc; American Printers & Lithogrphers Inc; Blair Broadcasting Corp; John Blair Marketing Inc; Blair Spanish Television FL Inc; Blair/RAR Inc; Blairspan Inc; JBMT Printing Corp; RPR Productions; WHDH Corp
Principal Bank: Manufacturers Hanover Trust Co
Financial Information:

	$'000
Sales revenues	630,630

No of Employees: 8,090

BLANDIN PAPER CO
115 First Street SW, Grand Rapids, MN 55744
Tel: (218) 328-6200
Telex: TWX 910 5612550 blandin 02 gra

Chairman: K P Benson
President: A C Wallace
Senior Executive Officers: T S McKeon (VP Sales), A E Radecki (VP Finance and Administration), Clarence Blaine (VP Operations)

PRINCIPAL ACTIVITIES: Manufacture of paper
Parent Company: British Columbia Forest Products Ltd
Principal Bank: Norwest Bank of Minneapolis
Financial Information:

	$'000
Sales revenues	200,000

No of Employees: 1,300

BLASIUS INDUSTRIES INC
1600 Peninsula Drive, Erie, PA 16505
Tel: (814) 838 2044

Chairman: Harold H George (and Chief Executive Office)
President: Chester M Kempinski (and Chief Operating Officer)
Senior Executive Officers: Julian Gravino (Executive VP and Chief Operating Officer), Frank N Hiza (VP Finance, Treasurer and Chief Financial Officer), Kenneth I Greenstein (Secretary), Arnold W MacAlonan (VP), George R Bessette (VP Finance)

PRINCIPAL ACTIVITIES: Manufacture of a wide range of rubber and metal products for the automobile, plumbing, electrical and appliance industries
Principal Bank: Horizon Bank
Financial Information:

	$'000
Sales revenues	41,000

No of Employees: 675

BLAW-KNOX CORPORATION
One Oliver Plaza, Pittsburgh, PA 15222
Tel: (412) 263-2200
Telex: TWX 710 664 4228 bk exec pg

Chairman: Robert J Tomsich
President: Jon J O'Connor
Senior Executive Officers: Eugene F Finkin (Executive VP), Richard A McIntyre (VP Finance),

PRINCIPAL ACTIVITIES: Manufacture of machines and equipment for iron and steel rolling mills; steel castings
Financial Information:

	$'000
Sales revenues	250,000

BLESSINGS CORPORATION
5527-33 N Maplewood Ave, Chicago, IL 60625
Tel: (312) 728-4700

Chairman: Otto E Scherer; Chairman of Executive Committee: C D Williamson
President: David E Lewis (also Chief Executive Officer)
Senior Executive Officers: Mary E Hart (VP Publicity), Ivan E Becker (VP Plastics), Richard Jannoni (VP Geri-Care), James P Luke (VP Finance, Secretary and Treasurer)

PRINCIPAL ACTIVITIES: Manufacture of plastic products including baby diapers; publishing of a baby magazine
Parent Company: Williamson-Dickie Manufacturing Co, Fort Worth, TX
Principal Bank: Chase Manhattan Bank
Financial Information:

	$'000
Sales revenues	64,000

No of Employees: 300

BLOCK DRUG CO
257 Cornelison Avenue, Jersey City, NJ 07302
Tel: (201) 434-3000
Telex: TRT 1780 11 block drug jcty

Chairman: Leonard Block (and Chief Executive Officer)
President: James A Block
Senior Executive Officers: Thomas R Block (Executive VP and Treasurer), Donald Le Sieur (Executive VP Marketing), Peter C Mann (Senior VP Marketing and New Products), G A McMullen (VP Sales), John Perry (VP Marketing), John Goodman (VP Dental Operations and Planning), Melvin Kopp (VP and Comptroller), Gilbert Seymann (VP Operations), Colin Abbott (VP International), John E Peters (VP and Corporate Counsel), Edward G Brady (VP Corporate Development), Richard C Brogle (VP Research and Development), John S Smith (VP Quality Assurance), Arthur A Looney (VP New Products), James B Purcell (VP Professional Relations), John B Bennett (VP International), Hermann Reyes (VP International)

PRINCIPAL ACTIVITIES: Manufacture of pharmaceuticals and household cleaning products
Trade Names: Polident, Caffree
Principal Subsidiaries: Block Drug Corp; Block Household Products Inc; Dentco Inc; Reedco Inc; Stafford Miller International Inc
Financial Information:

	$'000
Sales revenues	238,000

No of Employees: 2,330

BLOCK, H & R, INC
4410 Main Street, Kansas City, MO 64111
Tel: (816) 753-6900

President: Henry W Bloch (and Chief Executive Officer)
Senior Executive Officers: Jerome B Grossman (Executive VP and Chief Operating Officer), Donald W Ayers (VP Finance and Treasurer), Thomas M Bloch (VP), Harry W Buckley (VP and Director Field Operations), James J Moran (VP Corporate Development), William T Ross (VP Supply and Secretary), Ozzie Wenich (Corporate Controller and Assistant Treasurer)

PRINCIPAL ACTIVITIES: Provision of financial and personnel services and general management activities; preparation of income tax returns
Principal Subsidiaries: Block Management Co; CompuServe Inc; Path Management Industries; Personnel Pool of America Inc; Richfield Agency Inc
Principal Bank: Commerce Bank
Financial Information:

	$'000
Sales revenues	493,000

No of Employees: 2,000

BLOCKER ENERGY CORPORATION
16225 Park Ten Place, Houston, TX 77084
Tel: (713) 578 3677

Chairman: John R Blocker (and Chief Executive Officer)
President: James H Morris
Senior Executive Officers: John R Blocker Jr (Chief Operating Officer), James W Allen (VP), Jack M Lane (VP), Richard M Pilgrim (VP), Paul A Bragg (Chief Financial Officer)

PRINCIPAL ACTIVITIES: Exploration and production of oil and gas
Principal Bank: InterFirst Bank
Financial Information:

	$'000
Sales revenues	46,540

No of Employees: 480

BLOUNT, INC
4520 Executive Park Drive, Montgomery, AL 36116
Tel: (205) 272-8020
Cable: 513
Telex: TWX 810 7283 252 blount mgy

Chairman: Winton M Blount (and Chief Executive Officer)
President: Oscar J Reak (and Chief Operating Officer)
Senior Executive Officers: J Lee Ledbetter (Executive VP and Chief Financial Officer), Frank H McFadden (Senior VP), D J McInnes (VP Human Resources), Peter C Robinson (VP Planning and Marketing)

PRINCIPAL ACTIVITIES: Manufacture and sale of industrial and agricultural equipment; consultants for the construction and engineering industries
Principal Subsidiaries: Blount International Ltd
Principal Bank: Continental Illinois National Bank and Trust Co of Chicago
Financial Information:

	Feb 28,1986 $'000
Sales revenues	1,165,693
Net income	12,213
Earnings per share	$1.01
Shareholders equity	137,170

No of Employees: 10,700

BLUE BELL, INC
301 N Elm Street, Greensboro, NC 27401
Tel: (919) 373-3400
Telex: WUI 6827061 bblsl uw

Chairman: Edward J Bauman (and President and Chief Executive Officer)
Senior Executive Officers: P B Thompson (VP), B T Toben Jr (VP Diversified Brand), K E Tutterow (VP and Chief Financial Officer), H R Watkins (VP Human Resources), H Varnell Moore (VP Wrangler Group), Gary Patterson (VP), Jerome Pool (VP), Gary D Carter (VP Manufacturing)

PRINCIPAL ACTIVITIES: Manufacture of jeans, work clothing, sportswear and uniforms
Trade Names: Wrangler
Parent Company: Blue Bell Holding Co Inc
Principal Subsidiaries: Jantzen Inc; Brenton Textiles Inc
Financial Information:

	$'000
Sales revenues	1,070,000

No of Employees: 20,000

BLUE CIRCLE INC (FORMERLY ATLANTIC CEMENT CO INC)
One Parkway Center-Suite 1000, 1850 Parkway Place, Marietta, GA 30067
Tel: (404) 427-8701

Chairman: P Malozemoff (New York)
President: Jack L Gordon (and Chief Executive Officer)
Senior Executive Officers: Louis U Spellman (Executive VP), Daniel P McGeehan (VP Marketing), George R French Jr (VP Distribution), Arthur C Thompson Jr (VP Sales), E Glen Irwin (VP Production), L C Leonard (VP and Treasurer)

PRINCIPAL ACTIVITIES: Blue Circle Inc operates a 1,500,000-ton-per-year portland cement plant on the Hudson River at Ravena, New York, and an 800,000-ton-per-year slag cement plant at Sparrows Point, Maryland. It serves a 16-state market along the Eastern Seaboard by means of a fleet of barges delivering its products to coastal distribution terminals
Principal Bank: The Chase Manhattan Bank
Financial Information:

	$'000
Sales revenues	120,000

No of Employees: 500

BLUE DIAMOND GROWERS
1802 C Street, PO Box 1768, Sacramento, CA 95812
Tel: (916) 442-0771

Chairman: William McFarlane

President: Roger I Baccigaluppi (and Chief Executive Officer)
Senior Executive Officers: Alfred D DeGregory (VP Finance and Treasurer), Steven W Easter (VP Member and Government Relations and Secretary), Walter F Payne (VP Sales and Marketing)

PRINCIPAL ACTIVITIES: Production and marketing of almond products
Trade Names: Registered trademarks: Blud Diamond, The Almond People, Smokehouse, Almond Plaza, One Niblle is Never Enough, Celebration, Invitation, Almond Facts
Financial Information:

	June 30 1986	June 30 1987
	$'000	$'000
Sales Revenues	425,178	418,347
Income before taxes	5,369	1,799
Income*	4,309	1,228
Members' equity	18,535	19,763

No of Employees: 2,160

BLUEFIELD SUPPLY COMPANY

100 Bluefield Avenue, Bluefield, WV 24701
Tel: (304) 325 6131

Chairman: C I Johnston Jr
President: B W Harvey (and Chief Executive Officer)
Senior Executive Officers: James E Gillenwater (Executive VP and Chief Administration Officer), Thomas E Rhodes (VP), Roy L Scales (VP Secretary and Treasurer)

PRINCIPAL ACTIVITIES: Manufacture of equipment for the construction and mining industries
Principal Subsidiaries: Crawford Equipment Co; Dixie Appliance Co; Rish Equipment Co
Principal Bank: Flat Top National Bank of Bluefield
Financial Information:

	$'000
Sales revenues	65,565

No of Employees: 520

BMC INDUSTRIES, INC

1100 American National Bank Building, St Paul, MN 55101
Tel: (612) 228-6310
Telex: 297022

Chairman: Robert J Carlson (and President)
Senior Executive Officers: Robert J Bateman (VP and President of Interconics), Carl A Bergmann (VP and President of Optical Products), Gerald M Bestler (VP and President of Special Products), Paul B Burke (VP and General Counsel), Michael P Hawks (Corporate Controller), Merle D Kerr (VP, Finance and Chief Financial Officer), Kenneth W Lewis (VP, Human Resources and Administration)

PRINCIPAL ACTIVITIES: BMC Industries designs, manufacturers and markets precision electronic components and systems and related manufacturing equipment and optical products such as eyewear frames and lenses
Principal Subsidiaries: Interconics:- Buckbee Mears Operation; Bussing Systems Operation; Cirpack Design & Prototype Operation; Cirtel Circuits Operation; IMC Microcircuits Operation; IMC Tampa Operation; Nashua Flexible Circuits Operation; Precision Stamping Operation; Industries Singapore Pte Ltd. Special Products:- Advanced Controls; Buckbee-Mears; Buckbee-Mears Europe GmbH (Germany). Optical Products:- Buckbee-Mears Europe Optics (Germany); Kelley & Hueber; Pennsylvania Optical; Univis Eyewear; Vision-Ease Lens
Principal Bank: First National Bank of St Paul
Financial Information:

	$'000
Sales revenues	100,000

No of Employees: 4,500

BMJ FINANCIAL CORPORATION

243 Route 130, Bordentown, NJ 08505
Tel: (609) 298 5500

Chairman: William H Wells
President: Robert H Deacon
Senior Executive Officers: John C Hall (Senior VP), Albert P Mainka III (Senior VP), John H O'Neill (Senior VP), R Joseph Foster Jr (VP and Treasurer), Rosemarie Hobson (Secretary)

PRINCIPAL ACTIVITIES: Banking services
Financial Information:

	Dec 31 1985
	$'000
Revenues	36,405
Net income	3,870

No of Employees: 390

BMY DIVISION

PO Box 1512, York, PA 17405
Tel: (717) 225-4781
Telex: TWX 510 657 4212 bmy inc yrk

President: R P Cordes
Senior Executive Officers: Victor J Gongola (VP Business and Product Planning), W R Jairett (VP Engineering), B A Forinash (VP), P E Byrne (VP International Sales), J R Spearing (VP Business Development), Roger E Snodgrass (VP Employee Relations), T B Van Wyk (Divisional VP and General Manager Tracked Vehicle Operations)

PRINCIPAL ACTIVITIES: Manufacture of military vehicles
Parent Company: Harsco Corporation, Camp Hill, PA
Financial Information:

	$'000
Sales revenues	300,000

No of Employees: 2,100

BOATMEN'S BANCSHARES, INC

100 N Broadway, St Louis, MO 63102
Tel: (314) 425-7527
Telex: 209891 (RCA NO) BOATM UR; 434277 (WESTERN UNION NO) BOATMENS STL

Chairman: Donald N Brandin (and Chief Executive Officer)
President: Andrew B Craig III
Senior Executive Officers: Ethan A H Shepley Jr (Vice Chairman of the Board), Gordon E Wells (Vice Chairman of the Board), Robert J Bennett (Executive VP), John M Brennan (Executive VP), William J Huhmann (Executive VP), Larry D Bayliss (Senior VP), James W Kienker (Senior VP and Controller), Philip N McCarty (Senior VP, Secretary and Treasurer), Gregory L Curl (Senior VP), Earl R Fell (Senior VP), Norville R Gish (Senior VP), Marvin W Smith (Senior VP), Leland M Walker (Senior VP)

PRINCIPAL ACTIVITIES: Registered bank holding company which owns substantially all of the outstanding capital stock of 39 commercial banks, a trust company, a mortgage banking company and a credit life insurance company
Trade Names: Boatmen's, Boatmen's HOMEQUITY, Boatmen's Super 60's, Boatmen's SUPERCHECK, Boatmen's OPTION twenty-four, SUPERCHECK, Super 60's, OPTION twenty-four, HOMEQUITY, Boatmen's NOW Account, Boatmen's Funds Management Account
Principal Subsidiaries: Banking Subsidiaries: St Louis Region:- The Boatmen's National Bank of St Louis; Boatmen's Bank of Concord Village; Boatmen's Bank of Crestwood; Boatmen's Bank of DeSoto; Boatmen's Hampton Bank; Boatmen's Bank of Jefferson County; Boatmen's Bank of Jennings; Boatmen's National Bank of North St Louis County; Boatmen's Bank of O'Fallon; Boatmen's Bank of St Louis County; Boatmen's Bank of Troy; Boatmen's Bank of Webster Groves; Boatmen's Bank of West County. Southeast Region:- Boatmen's Bank of Cape Girardeau. Kansas City Region:- Boatmen's First National Bank of Kansas City; Boatmen's

Bank of Belton; Boatmen's National Bank of Boonville; Boatmen's Bank of Butler; Boatmen's Bank of Clinton; Boatmen's Bank of Excelsior Springs; Boatmen's Bank of Independence; Boatmen's Bank of Lee's Summit; Boatmen's Bank of Lexington; Boatmen's Livestock National Bank; Boatmen's Bank of Nevada; Boatmen's North Hills Bank; Boatmen's Raytown Bank; Boatmen's National Bank of Richmond; Boatmen's Bank of South Raytown. Southwest Region:- The Boatmen's National Bank of Springfield; Boatmen's Bank of Aurora; Boatmen's Bank of Carthage; Boatmen's National Bank of Cassville; Boatmen's National Bank of Lebanon; Boatmen's Bank of Lockwood; Boatmen's Mountain Grove National Bank; Boatmen's Bank of Pulaski County; Boatmen's Bank of Taney County. Non-Banking Subsidiaries:- Missouri Mortgage & Investment Co; Boatmen's Life Insurance Company; Boatmen's Trust Company

Principal Bank: The Boatmen's National Bank of St Louis

Financial Information:

	Dec 31 1986
	$'000
Income before taxes	78,052
Earnings per share	$4.00
Shareholders equity	621,108
Deposits	7,472,492
Total assets	9,919,003

No of Employees: 5,600

BOB EVANS FARMS, INC

See EVANS, BOB, FARMS, INC

BOBBIE BROOKS, INC

3830 Kelley Avenue, Cleveland, OH 44114
Tel: (216) 881-5300
Telex: ITT 433 20 52 brooks ch a

Chairman: Maurice Saltzman (and Chief Executive Officer)
President: Robert H Kanner (and Chief Operating Officer)
Senior Executive Officers: Stephen Kalette (Secretary), Joseph A Woolf (Treasurer and Chief Financial Officer)

PRINCIPAL ACTIVITIES: Manufacture of women's clothes including sportswear
Principal Subsidiaries: Bryn Mawr Sportswear Inc
Principal Bank: Ameritrust Company N.A.
Financial Information:

	$'000
Sales revenues	67,000

No of Employees: 100

BOC GROUP, INC

85 Chestnut Ridge Road, Montvale, NJ 07645
Tel: (201) 573-0800
Telex: WUT 134307 boc montvale

Chairman: Richard V Giordano (and Chief Executive Officer); Vice Chairman: Paul Bosonnet
Senior Executive Officers: David J Craig (MD Engineering and Technology), James G Baldwin (MD Carbon Diversified Business), Desmond H O'Connell Jr (MD Health Care), David W Troast (Group VP), Charles A Bonnes (VP Legal Counsel and Secretary), Joseph Carter (VP Human Resources), Angelo N Tarallo (Senior VP Administration)

PRINCIPAL ACTIVITIES: Manufacture of industrial gases, welding machinery and gases and equipment for hospitals
Parent Company: BOC Group PLC, London, UK
Financial Information:

	$'000
Sales revenues	1,130,000

No of Employees: 11,400

BOEHRINGER INGELHEIM LTD

90 E Ridge, Ridgefield, CT 06877
Tel: (203) 438-0311
Telex: RCA 221091 brgi ur

Chairman: Hansjerg Gauger
Senior Executive Officers: Digby Barrios (Executive VP), P B Stewart (Senior VP, Research and Development), Werner Gerstenberg (Senior VP, Finance and Administration)

PRINCIPAL ACTIVITIES: Manufacture of pharmaceuticals
Principal Bank: Citibank
Financial Information:

	$'000
Sales revenues	230,000

No of Employees: 1,500

BOEHRINGER MANNHEIM CORPORATION

9115 Hague Road, Indianapolis, IN 46250
Tel: (317) 845-2000

Chairman: Curt Engelhorn
President: J Van Kampen (Chief Executive Officer)
Senior Executive Officers: R F Schwindt (VP Administration and Chief Financial Officer), L McCarthy (VP), J A Lent (VP), Gerald Moeller (VP)

PRINCIPAL ACTIVITIES: Manufacture of medical equipment
Parent Company: Corange Ltd
Principal Bank: Indiana National Bank
Financial Information:

	$'000
Sales revenues	280,000

No of Employees: 1,900

BOEING CO

7755 E Marginal Way S, Seattle, WA 98108
Tel: (206) 655-2121

Chairman: T A Wilson (and Chief Executive Officer); Vice Chairman: Malcolm T Stamper
President: Frank A Shrontz
Senior Executive Officers: H W Haynes (Executive VP and Chief Financial Officer), Lionel D Alford (Senior VP), K F Holtby (Senior VP), R W Tharrington (Senior VP), D D Thornton (Senior VP), D P Beighle (Senior VP, Secretary and Legal Counsel), A H Lowell (VP and Controller)

PRINCIPAL ACTIVITIES: Manufacture of aircraft and aerospace equipment
Principal Subsidiaries: Boeing Aerospace Co; Boeing Vertol Co; Boeing Commercial Airplane Co; Boeing Computer Services Co; Boeing Military Airplane Co; Boeing Marine Systems; Boeing Electronics Co
Financial Information:

	Dec 31 1985	Dec 31 1986
	$'000	$'000
Sales revenues	13,636,000	16,341,000
Net income	366,000	665,000
Shareholders equity	4,364,000	4,826,000

No of Employees: 104,000

BOHEMIA INC

2280 Oakmont Way, Eugene, OR 97401
Tel: (503) 342-6262
Telex: WUT 36442 bohemia eug

President: Strayer E Pittman (and Chief Executive Officer)
Senior Executive Officers: Frederick G Gent (Senior VP Finance), Thomas W Coiner (Senior VP), C D Fisher (VP Timber), Vernon L Williams (VP Manufacturing), Keith M Wright (VP Marketing)

PRINCIPAL ACTIVITIES: Manufacture of forest products, lumber and building materials
Principal Subsidiaries: Century Park Inc

Principal Bank: First National Bank of Oregon
Financial Information:

	$'000
Sales revenues	163,900

No of Employees: 2,080

BOISE CASCADE CORPORATION

One Jefferson Square. Boise, ID 83728
Tel: (208) 384-6161
Telex: WUT 368437 boiseadmin bse

Chairman: John B Fery (and Chief Executive Officer)
President: Jon H Miller (and Chief Operating Officer)
Senior Executive Officers: George J Harad (Senior VP and Chief Financial Officer), John E Clute (Senior VP), William Bridenbaugh (Senior VP), Peter G Danis Jr (Senior VP), K P Norrie (Senior VP), J R Forrest (Senior VP), Alice E Hennessey (Senior VP and Secretary)

PRINCIPAL ACTIVITIES: Manufacture of paper and packaging products
Principal Subsidiaries: Beaver Falls Power Co; International Bridge and Terminal Co; Boise Cascade Home and Land Corp; Boise Cascade Trucking Inc; Boise Cascade World Headquarters Co Inc; Boise National Leasing Inc; Boise Southern Co; Boville Inc; Clearfield Insurance Ltd; Ebasint International Inc; International Falls Power Co; Lowville and Beaver River Railroad Co; MD & W Railway Co; Oxford Paper Co; Rumford Falls Power Co; Sheldon Springs Power Co; Valley & Siletz Railroad Co
Financial Information:

	Dec 31 1985	Dec 31 1986
	$'000	$'000
Sales revenues	3,737,220	3,739,970
Net income	104,290	101,540
Earnings per share	$3.45	$3.32
Shareholders equity	1,450,026	1,575,063

No of Employees: 22,960

BOLAR PHARMACEUTICAL COMPANY INC

130 Lincoln Street, Copiague, NY 11726
Tel: (516) 842 8383

President: Bob Schulman
Senior Executive Officers: Carlos Rodriguez (Finance), Dorothy Roubal (Chief Accounting Officer), Sid Stuchin (Controller), Charles Dicola (Manager Production), Gena Finelli (Director), Seymour Inkles (Director), Arnold Mendell (Director Quality Control)

PRINCIPAL ACTIVITIES: Manufacture of pharmaceuticals
Financial Information:

	$'000
Sales revenues	38,355

No of Employees: 180

BOLT BERANEK AND NEWMAN INC

10 Fawcett Street, Cambridge, MA 02238
Tel: (617) 491 1850

Chairman: Stephen R Levy (and Chief Executive Officer)
President: Michael P Lavigna (and Chief Operating Officer)
Senior Executive Officers: W B Barker (Senior VP), Bruce D Glabe (Senior VP, Chief Financial Officer and Treasurer), David C Walden (Senior VP), Terry Fagin (VP), Michael Nacey (VP Administration), Ean M Ranking (VP), E R Santoro (VP), R A Goldwasser (Controller), John Montjoy (General Counsel)

PRINCIPAL ACTIVITIES: Manufacture of defense electronics and other electronic equipment including electronic training simulators, artificial intelligence systems
Principal Subsidiaries: BBN Communications Corp
Principal Bank: First National Bank of Boston
Financial Information:

	1986
	$'000
Sales revenues	178,000
Net income	11,000

No of Employees: 1,830

BOND, JUDY, INC

330 W 34th St, New York, NY 10001
Tel: (212) 921-4800
Telex: ITT 422819 judy b

President: Robert Postal
Senior Executive Officers: Elaine Postal (Executive VP), Louis Eaccarino (VP Regional Sales), Andrew Postal (VP), Neil J Ronga (Chief Financial Officer)

PRINCIPAL ACTIVITIES: Manufacture of ladies' clothing
Financial Information:

	$'000
Sales revenues	50,000

No of Employees: 1,200

BONGARDS CREAMERIES

N Main Street, Bongards, MN 55368
Tel: (612) 466-5521
Telex: WUT 291065 ww 1483 telex

President: Donald Herrmann
Senior Executive Officers: Edwin W Brudggemeier (VP), Duane Heuer (Secretary and Treasurer)

PRINCIPAL ACTIVITIES: Manufacture of dairy products
Principal Bank: First National Bank of Minneapolis
Financial Information:

	$'000
Sales revenues	100,000

No of Employees: 200

BONNELL, WILLIAM L, CO

PO Box 428, Newnan, GA 30264
Tel: (404) 253-2020

President: E M Harvey
Senior Executive Officers: J C Dunn (VP and General Sales Manager), D R Monk (VP Operations and Finance)

PRINCIPAL ACTIVITIES: Manufacture of aluminum products
Parent Company: Ethyl Corporation, Richmond, VA
Principal Bank: First National Bank
Financial Information:

	$'000
Sales revenues	150,000

No of Employees: 1,450

BOOTH NEWSPAPERS, INC

PO Box 2168, Grand Rapids, MI 49501
Tel: (616) 459-3826

President: Werner Veit (and Chief Executive Officer)

PRINCIPAL ACTIVITIES: Publication of newspapers
Principal Bank: Old Kent Bank
Financial Information:

	$'000
Sales revenues	158,700

No of Employees: 2,400

BOOTHE FINANCIAL CORPORATION

100 Bush Street, Suite 1700, San Francisco, CA 94104
Tel: (415) 989 6580

Chairman: Brian P Burns (and Chief Executive Officer)
President: Harold M Messmer Jr (and Chief Operating Officer)
Senior Executive Officers: Stuart B Aronoff (Senior VP), John M Price (Senior VP, Legal Counsel and Secretary), Robert G

Sharpe (Senor VP, Treasurer and Chief Financial Officer), Stanley E Zimmerman Jr (Senior VP)

PRINCIPAL ACTIVITIES: Provision of a wide range of financial services including leasing, loans and mortgages
Principal Subsidiaries: Boothe Credit Corporation; Boothe Financial Services Inc; Lease Marketing Inc
Financial Information:

	Dec 31 1985
	$'000
Revenues	32,810
Net income	6,860

No of Employees: 20

BORDEN CHEMICAL DIVISION
180 E Broad Street, Columbus, OH 43215
Tel: (614) 225-4000

President: R J Ventres
Senior Executive Officers: J S Bellecci (Group VP Basic Chemicals), H A Reed (Group VP Adhesives, Canadian and Graphics), T C Walker (Group VP Vinyl Resins and Petrochemical Marketing), F J Proto (Controller)

PRINCIPAL ACTIVITIES: Manufacture of chemicals, resins and vinyl products
Parent Company: Borden Inc, New York, NY
Financial Information:

	$'000
Sales revenues	1,000,000

BORDEN INC
277 Park Avenue, New York, NY 10172
Tel: (212) 573-4000

Chairman: R J Ventres (and President and Chief Executive Officer)
President: R J Ventres
Senior Executive Officers: A S D'Amato (Executive VP and President Chemical Division), Jon G Hettinger (Executive VP and President Grocery Division), H Wayne Mosley (Executive VP and President Dairy Division), George J Waydo (Executive VP and President Snacks Division), Lawrence O Doza (Senior VP and Chief Financial Officer), David A Kelly (VP and Treasurer)

PRINCIPAL ACTIVITIES: Manufacture of food, dairy and chemical products
Trade Names: Over 100 brands
Financial Information:

	Dec 31 1985	Dec 31 1986
	$'000	$'000
Sales revenues	4,716,172	5,002,097
Income before taxes	324,504	390,212
Net income	193,804	223,312
Dividends	76,501	81,347
Dividends per share	$0.987	$1.093
Earnings per share	$2.50	$3.00
Shareholders equity	1,407,795	1,438,743

No of Employees: 33,800

BORG-WARNER CORPORATION
200 South Michigan Avenue, Chicago, IL 60604
Tel: (312) 322-8500
Telex: 25-3450

Chairman: James F Bere
President: Clarence E Johnson
Senior Executive Officers: Malcolm F Baker (VP Protective Services), James R Deters (VP Finance), Richard J Doyle (Executive VP Air Conditioning), Neal F Farrell (VP Taxes), Robert J M Fisher (VP International and President, Chief Executive Officer Air Conditioning), James J Gavin Jr (Vice Chairman), Leonard A Harvey (Executive VP Chemicals, Air Conditioning, Automotive, Industrial Products), Robert E LaRoche (Executive VP Financial Services and Borg-Warner Australia, Ltd), Robert A Morris (VP Communications), Keith D Schulz (VP and General Counsel), Donald C Trauscht (VP Corporate Planning), William M Valiant (VP Treasurer), Peter C Valli (Corporate VP and President Industrial Products), William H Weltyk (VP Technology), Timothy M Wood (Controller)

PRINCIPAL ACTIVITIES: Air Conditioning:- light commercial and residential air conditioning and heating systems; engineered machinery. Automotive:-automotive components supplied to original equipment manufacturers. Chemicals and Plastics:- engineering thermoplastics and chemicals which are primarily polymer additives. Financial Services:- wholesale, retail and receivables financing; credit life, disability and property insurance; real estate development; and leasing of vehicles and equipment for commercial, industrial and institutional use. Industrial Products:- primarily pumps, valves, mechanical seals, hydraulic and pneumatic actuators to the power and petroleum markets and other markets including aerospace, agriculture, general industry and municipal water systems. Protective Services:- armored car, alarm and guard services (Wells Fargo); small-package delivery service (Pony Express Courier); smoke and fire detection equipment systems (Pyrotronics); security and loss-prevention services (Burns International Security Services); and ground courier business (Gelco Corporation)
Trade Names: Air Conditioning:- York, Fraser-Johnston, Luxaire, Moncrief. Automotive:- Hy-Vo, Borg & Beck, Morse. Chemicals and Plastics:- Cycolac, Blendex, Prevex, FyRid, Weston. Financial Services:- BWAC. Industrial Products:- Byron Jackson. Protective Services:- Wells Fargo, Pony Express (all names are Registered trademarks)
Principal Subsidiaries: Borg-Warner Air Conditioning, Inc; Borg-Warner Automotive, Inc; Borg-Warner Chemicals, Inc; Borg-Warner Financial Services, Inc; Borg-Warner Industrial Products, Inc; Borg-Warner Protective Services, Inc
Principal Banks: Morgan Guaranty; Citibank; First National Bank of Chicago; Continental; Chemical; Barclays
Financial Information:

	Dec 31 1986
	$'000
Sales revenues	3,623,400
Net income	206,300
Earnings per share	$2.35
Shareholders equity	1,524,800

No of Employees: 80,700

BORMAN'S INC
PO Box 33446, Detroit, MI 48232
Tel: (313) 270-1000

President: Paul Borman
Senior Executive Officers: Daniel Church (VP Finance), Ted Simon (VP Real Estate)

PRINCIPAL ACTIVITIES: Supermarkets
Trade Names: Farmer Jack Supermarkets
Principal Bank: National Bank of Detroit
Financial Information:

	$'000
Sales revenues	987,190

No of Employees: 6,600

BOSE CORPORATION
The Mountain, Framingham, MA 01701
Tel: (617) 879-7330
Telex: ITT 4430058 boseco

Chairman: Amar G Bose
President: Sherwin Greenblatt
Senior Executive Officers: Dan Grady (VP Finance), Joseph Veranth (VP Engineering), John Geheran (VP Marketing and Sales)

PRINCIPAL ACTIVITIES: Manufacture of electronic equipment including Hi-Fi systems
Principal Subsidiaries: Stereo Advertising Corp
Principal Bank: First National Bank of Chicago
Financial Information:

	$'000
Sales revenues	108,000

No of Employees: 1,000

BOSS MANUFACTURING COMPANY

221 West First Street, Kewanee, IL 61443
Tel: (309) 852-2131
Telex: (Easylink) 5101001689 BOSSCO KEW UD

Chairman: Milton Falkoff
President: Barry F Kane
Senior Executive Officers: Norman Kronenberg (VP Sales and Marketing), Kenneth A Fristad (VP Operations), Beverly J Williams (VP Administration), Douglas H Lay (VP Manufacturing), James C Kelley (VP and Controller)

PRINCIPAL ACTIVITIES: Boss Manufacturing Company is a 93 year old manufacturing and distributing company serving consumer and industrial markets with premium quality personal apparel and protective products. The consumer unit manufactures and markets the industry's most comprehensive line of gloves and a variety of related personal use products for sale through retailers. The major products include an extensive line of work, utility and garden gloves, jackets, umbrellas, stretch rubbers, ponchos and children's backpacks, as well as sports gloves, down-filled clothing, backpacks and sleeping bags for outdoor enthusiasts. The industrial unit manufactures and distributes job-related safety products including an extensive line of industrial gloves, boots and rainwear as well as protective clothing, eye, ear, head and respiratory protective products. Corporate headquarters are in Kewanee, Illinois. Manufacturing plants are in Alabama, Florida, Texas, Mexico and Canada. The Corporation has seven additional distribution centers strategically located throughout the United States
Trade Names: BOSS, LADYFINGER, TURFMAN, ROUND TOWNERS, JOBMASTER, MONKEFACE, BIG APE, TRAILWISE, PLASTIC DOT, MORRIS FEEL, GREEN APE, GREEN MUNK, SNYDER
Principal Subsidiaries: Boss de Mexico, SA (Mexico); M L Dnyder Inc (Canada)
Principal Bank: Standard Chartered Bank PLC
Financial Information:

	$'000
Sales revenues	34,800

No of Employees: 850

BOSTON EDISON CO

800 Boylston St, Boston, MA 02199
Tel: (617) 424-2000

Chairman: Thomas J Galligan Jr
President: Stephen P Sweeney (and Chief Executive Officer)
Senior Executive Officers: James M Lydon (Executive VP), Joseph P Tyrell (Executive VP), William D Harrington (Senior VP), Thomas J May (VP and Treasurer), Robert T Parry (VP Employee Relations), Benjamin H Weiner (VP Power Supply Administration), Eleanor T Daly (VP and Assistant to Chairman), J Edward Howard (VP Nuclear), David J O'Connor Jr (VP Corporate Information Services), L Carlisle Gustin (VP Corporate Relations), John R Stevens (VP Corporate Relations), Victor H Kazanjian (VP and Legal Counsel), C Bruce Damrell (VP Engineering and Distribution), Craig D Peffer (VP Commercial)

PRINCIPAL ACTIVITIES: Electricity supply
Principal Subsidiaries: Reco Fuel Co Inc

Financial Information:

	1986
	$'000
Sales revenues	1,100,000
Net income	91,000

No of Employees: 4,250

BOSTON FIVE CENTS SAVINGS BANK, FSB

10 School Street, Boston, MA 02108
Tel: (617) 742-6000

Chairman: Robert J Spiller (and Chief Executive Officer)
President: Peter J Blampied (and Chief Operating Officer)
Senior Executive Officers: William P Morrissey (Executive VP, Corporate Affairs), Kathryn M Hinderhofer (Senior VP Retail Banking), Vernon L Blodgett Jr (Senior VP Finance and Development), Deborah E Byron (VP Human Resources), Ruth E Kadlec (VP and Corporate Secretary), Joseph Guido (VP Information Services), Karen Q Hammond (VP Investment)

PRINCIPAL ACTIVITIES: Financial services including savings and loans
Principal Bank: First National Bank of Boston

No of Employees: 800

BOURNS INC

1200 Columbia Avenue, Riverside, CA 92507
Tel: (714) 781-5690
Telex: TWX 910 3321252 bourns riv

Chairman: Marlan E Bourns
President: Albert R Snider
Senior Executive Officers: Marshall Bartlett (Executive VP Corporate Operations), Guy S Forney (Senior VP Trimpot Division), Larry L White (Senior VP Finance and Administration), Robert Salrin (Senior VP Technical Products Group), R A Beck (Senior VP), Gary T Barbera (Senior VP Resistive Components Group), Raymond T Lloyd (VP and Treasurer), Robert J Bluell (VP and Controller), George Harding (VP Networks Division)

PRINCIPAL ACTIVITIES: Manufacture of precision instruments and components for the electronics industry
Principal Subsidiaries: Bourns Instruments Inc; Precision Monolithics Inc; Analog Integrated Micro-Systems Inc; Recon-Optical Inc
Principal Bank: Security Pacific National Bank
Financial Information:

	$'000
Sales revenues	350,000

No of Employees: 7,000

BOWATER INCORPORATED

One Parklands Drive, Box 4012, Darien, CT 06820-4012
Tel: (203) 656-7200
Cable: NUSEPRINT
Telex: 96-4297 BOWATER-DRN

Chairman: Anthony P Gammie (and President and Chief Executive Officer)
Senior Executive Officers: Richard D McDonough (Senior VP-Finance and Chief Financial Officer), David G McMaster (VP, President-Pulp and Paper Group), Ronald W Toelle (VP Corporate-Development), Donald J D'Antuono (VP-Investor Relations), John P Fucigna (VP-Treasurer), Ronald E Gustafson (VP-Human Resources and Administration), Thomas G Hart (VP-General Counsel), Arthur H King (VP-Corporate Relations), Robert C Lancaster (VP-Controller), Robert J Pascal (VP, General Manager-Business Forms Group), Leonard M Saari (Secretary and Assistant General Counsel)

PRINCIPAL ACTIVITIES: Bowater Incorporated is a major integrated producer of newsprint, coated publication paper and market pulp. It is the largest producer of newsprint in the

United States and third largest producer in North America. Other operations include production of continuous computer business forms and the production of construction grade lumber

Trade Names: Bowater

Principal Subsidiaries: US Divisions:- Bowater Carolina Company; Bowater Lumber Company; Bowater Sales Company; Catawba Timber Company; Hiwassee Land Company; Bowater Southern Paper Company. US Subsidiaries:- Bowater Computer Forms Inc; Calhoun Energy Inc; Carolina Export Corporation; Catawba Newsprint Company; Terrain Incorporated; Bowater Foreign Sales Corporation. Bowater Canadian Ltd:- Bowater Mersey Paper Co Ltd

Principal Bank: Morgan Guaranty Trust Co of New York

Financial Information:

	Dec 31 1985	Dec 31 1986
	$'000	$'000
Sales revenues	904,004	919,690
Income before taxes	114,843	90,949
Net income	67,520	49,444
Dividends	21,068	21,149
Dividends per share	$0.72	$0.72
Earnings per share(1)	$2.21	$1.49
Common stock(2)	29,271	29,470
Retained income	291,365	314,566
Shareholders equity	131,592	137,357

(1) fully diluted
(2) number of shares in thousands

Principal Shareholders: State of Wisconsin Investment Board

No of Employees: 4,800

BOWATER SOUTHERN PAPER COMPANY

US Hwy 11, Calhoun, TN 37309
Tel: (615) 336-2211
Telex: WUT 558406 bowaters calh

President: W C Grater (and General Manager)

Senior Executive Officers: L A Eldredge (Treasurer), C L Gobble (Purchasing and Stores Manager), E N Scott (Paper Production Manager), William M Share (Pulp Manager), Robert Wright (Legal Counsel), R J Hall (Mill Manager), Clarence Streetman (Public Relations Manager), R M Gibson Jr (Major Project Manager), R G Anderson (Woods Manager), J B Bates (Industrial Relations Manager), L H Camisa (Land Management Forester), J Dan Crook Jr (Forest Engineer), R J Burns (Chief Engineer)

PRINCIPAL ACTIVITIES: Manufacture of pulp and paper

Parent Company: Bowater Inc, Darien, CT

Financial Information:

	$'000
Sales revenues	144,000

No of Employees: 1,450

BOWMAR INSTRUMENT CORPORATION

531 Main Street, Acton, MA 01720
Tel: (617) 263 8365

Chairman: Edward A White (and Chief Executive Officer)

President: Charles S Krakauer (and Chief Operating Officer)

Senior Executive Officers: John C Maag (Secretary, Treasurer and Controller)

PRINCIPAL ACTIVITIES: Manufacture of electronic equipment for the computing and telecommunications industries

Principal Subsidiaries: Bowmar Ali Inc; Haroe Servo Controls Inc

Principal Bank: Fort Wayne National Bank

Financial Information:

	$'000
Sales revenues	42,620

No of Employees: 890

BOWNE & CO, INC

345 Hudson Street, New York, NY 10014
Tel: (212) 924-5500

Chairman: Franz von Ziegesar (and Chief Executive Officer)

President: Richard H Koontz (and Chief Operating Officer)

Senior Executive Officers: James P O'Neil (VP Finance), Allen D Marold (VP Human Resources), Thomas J Vos (VP Marketing), Douglas F Bauer (Corporate Secretary and Counsel)

PRINCIPAL ACTIVITIES: Financial and commercial printing services

Principal Bank: The Bank of New York

Financial Information:

	Oct 31 1985	Oct 31 1986
	$'000	$'000
Sales revenues	142,498	177,413
Income before taxes	20,946	38,873
Net income	11,889	19,671
Dividends	4,031	4,025
Dividends per share	$0.22	$0.22
Earnings per share	$1.07	$1.15
Common stock	9,139	9,158
Retained income	79,026	94,672
Shareholders equity	92,551	108,223

No of Employees: 1,600

BOZZUTO'S INC

275 Schoolhouse Road, Cheshire, CT 06410
Tel: (203) 272 3511

Chairman: Adam J Bozzuto (and President)

Senior Executive Officers: Michael Bozzuto (Executive VP and Treasurer), Nicholas Halzack (Controller, Assistant Secretary and Assistant Treasurer), Robert H Wood (VP Finance), Patricia S Houlse (Assistant Secretary and Assistant Treasurer), Jayne A Bozzuto (VP Marketing), William E Hoskins (VP Merchandising)

PRINCIPAL ACTIVITIES: Wholesale trade in grocery products

Principal Bank: Colonial Bank

Financial Information:

	$'000
Sales revenues	221,000

No of Employees: 340

BRAD RAGAN INC

4404-G Stuart Andrew Blvd, Charlotte, NC 28210
Tel: (704) 529 6666

Chairman: James W Barnett

Senior Executive Officers: R Melvin Morrison (Chief Executive Officer), Roy E Everett (Executie VP Sales and Marketing), Clyde W Granberry (VP Division), W Sam Smoak (VP Finance and Chief Financial Officer), Donald R Dodson (Secretary and Treasurer), Homer L Huskings (VP)

PRINCIPAL ACTIVITIES: Manufacture of tires and inner tubes

Principal Bank: North Carolina National Bank

Financial Information:

	$'000
Sales revenues	191,500

No of Employees: 1,700

BRADBURY & STAMM CONSTRUCTION CO

1217 First Street, NW, Albuquerque, NM 87125
Tel: (505) 765-1200

Chairman: Robert J Stamm (also President)

Senior Executive Officers: James N King (Executive VP), Robert H McAfee (VP), Alvin C Scrivner (VP), Richard Vittow (VP), Allen Stecker (VP Finance)

PRINCIPAL ACTIVITIES: Building and construction

Principal Bank: The First National Bank

Financial Information:

	$'000
Sales revenues	50,000

No of Employees: 400

BRADFORD-WHITE CORPORATION

24th & Ellsworth, Philadelphia, PA 19146
Tel: (215) 546-3800
Telex: TWX 710 670 1632 brad white pha

President: M R DeLuca
Senior Executive Officers: A R Carnevale (Senior VP), J T Borzoni (VP Marketing), R L Milock (VP and General Manager), F G Saunders (VP)

PRINCIPAL ACTIVITIES: Manufacture of household and commercial water heaters
Principal Bank: Central Penn National Bank
Financial Information:

	$'000
Sales revenues	94,000

No of Employees: 800

BRADNER CENTRAL CO

333 S Desplaines Street, Chicago, IL 60606
Tel: (312) 454-1852

Chairman: Richard S Bull Jr (President and Treasurer)
Senior Executive Officers: Terence J Shea (VP, President Bradner Smith & Co)

PRINCIPAL ACTIVITIES: Manufacture of paper
Principal Subsidiaries: Bradner Smith & Co
Principal Bank: The First National Bank of Chicago
Financial Information:

	$'000
Sales revenues	134,000

No of Employees: 150

BRADY, W H, CO

727 W Glendale Avenue, Milwaukee, WI 53201
Tel: (414) 332-8100
Telex: WUT 26677 brady milglen

Chairman: William H Brady Jr
President: James E Larson (and Chief Executive Officer)
Senior Executive Officers: Paul G Gengler (Executive VP, Chief Operating Officer and Director), Joseph C Barbieri (Group VP-International), H Joseph Wise (Group VP), Donald P McConnell (VP-Personnel), Philip L Pearson (Treasurer and VP-Finance), Sterling F Strause (VP-Research), Thomas L Turner (VP-Information Services)

PRINCIPAL ACTIVITIES: The Company develops, manufactures and sells a broad range of stock and customized products employing its knowledge of surface chemistry, principally in adhesives, coatings and graphics technologies. Brady's products include over 20,000 stock items and a wide variety of custom items, which are used primarily to identify, inform or instruct, including pressure-sensitive identification, labeling and marking systems for electrical wires and pipes; membrance switches and keyboards; self-bonding nameplates, faceplates, and control panels; safety and instructional signs; specialized tapes used in audio, video and computer applications; dispensers, packaging tapes and supplies; building and grounds maintenance supplies; and a line of miniature coils, transformers and electronic assemblies
Principal Subsidiaries: Domestic Locations: Glendale (WI); Milwaukee (WI); Hillsborough (NC); Branford (CT); Ft Lauderdale (FL); Solon (OH); Arizona City (AZ). International Locations: W H Brady Pty Ltd (Australia); W H Brady nv (Belgium); W H Brady inc (Canada); Revere-Seton Inc (Canada); W H Brady Co Ltd (UK); Seton Ltd (UK); W H Brady sarl (France); Nippon Brady KK (Japan); Brady AB (Sweden); W H Brady GmbH (West Germany)

Financial Information:

	Jul 31 1986	Jul 31 1987
	$'000	$'000
Sales revenues	108,364	126,420
Income before taxes	17,320	16,379
Net income	9,447	8,844
Dividends(1)	569	1,142
Dividends(2)	-	177
Dividends per share(1)	$0.10	$0.20
Dividends per share(2)	-	$0.10
Earnings per share(1)	$1.26	$1.17
Earnings per share(2)	$1.16	$1.07
Common stock	56	57
Retained income	60,878	68,131
Shareholders equity	66,791	76,044

(1) Class A Nonvoting
(2) Class B Voting

No of Employees: 1,000

BRAE CORPORATION

Four Embarcadero Center, Suite 3100, San Francisco, CA 94111
Tel: (415) 951 1500

Chairman: Ian M Cumming
President: Joseph S Steinberg
Senior Executive Officers: Feroze A Waheed (VP Finance), Thomas E Mara (VP)

PRINCIPAL ACTIVITIES: Communications systems; leasing of railcars and trailers
Principal Subsidiaries: American Sign and Indicator Corp; Brae Trailers; Cargo Inc; Integrated Systems Engineering Inc; Intermodal Brokerage Services; Transportation Resources Inc
Financial Information:

	$'000
Sales revenues	146,000

No of Employees: 1,200

BRANCH CORPORATION

223 West Nash Street, Wilson, NC 27893
Tel: (919) 399 4291

President: L Vincent Lowe Jr (and Chief Executive Officer and Subsidiary Officer)
Senior Executive Officers: John A Allison (Senior VP), Jerome C Herring (VP and Secretary), Henry G Williamson Jr (Senior VP), Scott E Reed (Treasurer)

PRINCIPAL ACTIVITIES: Banking services
Principal Subsidiaries: Branch Banking and Trust Company
Financial Information:

	Dec 31 1985
	$'000
Revenues	288,675
Net income	23,130

No of Employees: 2,460

BRAND INSULATIONS INC

1420 Renaissance Drive, Park Ridge, IL 60068
Tel: (312) 298 1200

Chairman: Eugene L Barnett (and Chief Executive Officer and Subsidiary Officer)
President: Alvin K Eaton (and Chief Operating Officer)
Senior Executive Officers: Melvin J Corbeil (VP and Division President), Richard C Keeley (VP and Treasurer), Sandra S Seelman (VP and Secretary)

PRINCIPAL ACTIVITIES: Installation of insulation products; services for the construction industry
Principal Bank: Harris Trust and Savings Bank

Financial Information:

	$'000
Sales revenues	119,150

No of Employees: 1,000

BRAND-REX COMPANY

90 Progress Drive, Manchester, CT 06040
Tel: (203) 643 2435

President: Peter Petruchik
Senior Executive Officers: Richard G Boyle (Executive VP), George C Graeber (President Electronic Industrial Wire and Cable Group), Bruce W Gardner (President Telecommunications Wire, Cable and Electronic Group), John J Finnerty (President Interconnection Group), Reginald W Barrett (President Connector Group), Philip R Nack (President Harness Group)

PRINCIPAL ACTIVITIES: Manufacture of electronic equipment, electric wire and cable and insulating materials
Financial Information:

	$'000
Sales revenues	250,000

No of Employees: 4,000

BRANIFF, INC

7701 Lemmon Avenue, PO Box 7035, Dallas, TX 75209
Tel: (214) 358-6011
Telex: 73376 BRANWAYS DAL

Chairman: Jay A Pritzker; Vice Chairman: J Patrick Foley (and Chief Executive Officer)
Senior Executive Officers: R Lawrence Hughes (Senior VP-Marketing and Sales), Scott A Keeshin (VP, General Cousel and Secretary), H Kirk Mueller (VP-Personnel), William C Oliver (VP-Customer Service), John R Olson (VP-Operations), Mark W Osterberg (VP-Finance and Controller), Peter D Connolly (VP), Harold S Handelsman (VP), Shelley M Starr (Treasurer)

PRINCIPAL ACTIVITIES: Airline transportation-national carrier-U.S. and Mexico
Trade Names: Braniff Inc
Principal Bank: First RepublicBank, Dallas, Texas
Financial Information:

	Jan 31 1986	Jan 31 1987
	$'000	$'000
Total revenues	244,311	239,490
Income (loss) before taxes	23,048	(9,022)
Net income (loss)	23,048	(9,022)
Earnings (loss) per share	$1.87	($0.74)
Common stock	122	123
Retained (deficit)	(63,345)	(72,367)
Shareholders equity	54,241	45,560

No of Employees: 1,931

BRASS-CRAFT MANUFACTURING CO

27700 N W Hwy, Southfields, MI 48034
Tel: (313) 827-1100
Telex: WUT 810 2219447 brascraft sofd

Chairman: Stanley Q Rosen (and Chief Executive Officer)
President: Murray W Snyder (and Treasurer)
Senior Executive Officers: James Greiner (VP Sales), Leonard C Andrus (VP Marketing), Alan H Barry (VP Administration), Fred Hyman (VP), Reginald Maxwell (VP), Charles Wellnitz (VP Sales)

PRINCIPAL ACTIVITIES: Manufacture of plumbing supplies
Parent Company: Masco Corporation, Taylor, MI
Principal Bank: National Bank of Detroit
Financial Information:

	$'000
Sales revenues	90,000

No of Employees: 1,100

BRAUN ENGINEERING CO

19001 Glendale, Detroit, MI 48223
Tel: (313) 270-1700
Telex: ITT 4320118 braun eng det

Chairman: Russell L Bearss (and Chief Executive Officer)
President: William J Storen (and Chief Operating Officer)
Senior Executive Officers: Michael J Taormino (VP Manufacturing Services), James J Pike (VP Sales), William A Bietler (VP Manufacturing Services), Albert L Hoffmanner (VP Engineering and Development), Paul R Biondi (VP Purchasing)

PRINCIPAL ACTIVITIES: Manufacture of components for the automotive industry
Parent Company: Masco Industries Inc
Principal Bank: National Bank of Detroit
Financial Information:

	$'000
Sales revenues	78,000

No of Employees: 550

BRENNAND-PAIGE INDUSTRIES, INC

745 Fifth Avenue, New York, NY 10022
Tel: (212) 688-2774

President: J L Stern (and Treasurer)
Senior Executive Officers: Herbert Levine (VP), L W Grotta (VP)

PRINCIPAL ACTIVITIES: Distribution of cable and wire and hardware for the building industry; distribution of florists' supplies
Principal Subsidiaries: Atlantic Hardware and Supply Corp; BPI International Corp; Thackeray Corp; Paige Electric Corp
Principal Bank: Fidelity Union Trust Company
Financial Information:

	$'000
Sales revenues	63,000

No of Employees: 300

BRENTON BANKS INC

Capital Square, 400 Locust, Suite 300, Des Moines, IA 50309
Tel: (513) 283 2394

Chairman: William H Brenton
President: C Robert Brenton
Senior Executive Officers: Junius C Brenton (Executive VP, Treasurer and Subsidiary Officer), Robert L De Meulenaere (Senior VP Division), R Dean Duben (Senior VP and Subsidiary Officer), Robert D McKee (Senior VP Administration), Thomas R Smith (VP and Subsidiary Officer), Roger D Winterhof (Senior VP Division), Steven T Schuler (VP and Secretary), Craig V McGarry (VP Trusts), Richard N Strang (VP Investment), W Michael Heilbronn (VP Marketing), Philip L Risley (VP Data Processing)

PRINCIPAL ACTIVITIES: Holding company with interests in banking and data processing services
Principal Subsidiaries: Brenco Automation Center Inc; Brenton Agri-Credit Corporation; Brenton Bank and Trust Company; Brenton First National Bank; Brenton Funds Transfer System; Brenton Insurance Services Inc; Brenton Mortgages Inc; Brenton National Bank; Brenton Properties Inc; Brenton State Bank; Community National Bank and Trust Company; Fidelity Brenton Bank and Trust Company; Palo Alto Community State Bank; Warren Community Brenton Bank and Trust
Principal Bank: Brenton National Bank
Financial Information:

	Dec 31 1985
	$'000
Revenues	105,810

No of Employees: 880

BREWER, C, & CO LTD

827 Fort Street, Honolulu, HI 96813
Tel: (808) 536-4461

Chairman: John W Buyers (and President)

Senior Executive Officers: James S Andrasick (VP Finance and Administration), J A Kugle (Executive VP), M J Tilker (Executive VP), William B Case (Senior VP Agricultural Products), R L Herberg (Senior VP Land Resources), Harold S Y Hee (VP Industrial Relations), James G Higgins (VP Administration and Secretary), Mark W Melidosian (VP Central America Operations)

PRINCIPAL ACTIVITIES: Holding company with interests in sugar, coffee and spices; transport; insurance; chemicals

Parent Company: IU International Corporation, Philadelphia, PA

Principal Bank: Bank of Hawaii

Financial Information:

	$'000
Sales revenues	195,000

No of Employees: 6,000

BRIDGFORD FOODS CORPORATION

1308 N Patt Street, Anaheim, CA 92801

Tel: (714) 526-5533

Chairman: H W Bridgford; Chairman of Executive Committee: H H Bridgford

President: Allan L Bridgford

Senior Executive Officers: Homer Morris (VP Sales), Salvatore DeGeorge (VP Sales), Larry English (VP Processed Meat Sales), Robert E Schulze (VP and Treasurer)

PRINCIPAL ACTIVITIES: Manufacture of pre-packed meat and cheese; frozen and snack food products

Principal Bank: Bank of America

Financial Information:

	$'000
Sales revenues	50,580

No of Employees: 420

BRIGADIER INDUSTRIES CORP

1800 W Loop S, Houston, TX 77027

Tel: (713) 877-2311

Chairman: Chris B Redigen

Senior Executive Officers: R Strudlen (Senior VP), Isaac Heinbenden (Senior VP Finance), Jon L Andersen (VP and Treasurer)

PRINCIPAL ACTIVITIES: Manufacture of mobile homes

Parent Company: US Home Corporation, Houston, TX

Principal Bank: Bank of Thomson

Financial Information:

	$'000
Sales revenues	100,000

No of Employees: 1,600

BRIGGS & STRATTON CORPORATION

3300 N 124 Street, Wauwatosa, WI 53222

Tel: (414) 259-5333

Telex: WUT 26776 basco mil wosa

Chairman: Frederick P Stratton Jr (and Chief Executive Officer)

President: George A Senn (and Chief Operating Officer)

Senior Executive Officers: L W Dewey Jr (Executive VP), William Rollo (VP and General Manager Lock Division), Michael D Hamilton (VP International), Charles L Fricke (VP Service), Bernard O Davis (VP and Controller)

PRINCIPAL ACTIVITIES: Manufacture of petrol engines

Financial Information:

	Jun 30 1986 $'000	Jun 30 1987 $'000
Sales revenues	745,831	784,665
Income before taxes	61,930	45,564
Net income	34,080	26,614
Dividends	23,142	23,142
Dividends per share	$1.60	$1.60
Earnings per share	$2.36	$1.84
Common stock	43,391	43,391
Retained income	251,218	254,690
Shareholders equity	293,517	296,260

Principal Shareholders: Publicly traded-NYSE

No of Employees: 8,611

BRILLION IRON WORKS, INC

200 Park Avenue, Brillion, WI 54110

Tel: (414) 756-2121

Telex: TWX 510 3889781 brilliron brll

President: Karl F Gabler

Senior Executive Officers: Kenneth Wagner (VP Sales and Marketing Foundry), Richard Larson (VP Administration), Dennis Graven (VP Finance)

PRINCIPAL ACTIVITIES: Manufacture of iron castings and agricultural implements

Financial Information:

	$'000
Sales revenues	100,000

No of Employees: 1,000

BRINTEC CORPORATION

1600 West Main Street, Willimantic, CT 06226

Tel: (203) 456 8000

President: Peter Petruchik (and Chief Executive Officer)

Senior Executive Officers: R Guy Boyle (Executive VP and Chief Financial Officer), Reginald W Barrett (VP), Bruce W Gardner (VP), George C Graeber (VP), Frank H Barnes (VP Communications)

PRINCIPAL ACTIVITIES: Manufacture of cables and wires

Financial Information:

	$'000
Sales revenues	299,600

No of Employees: 4,100

BRISTOL STEEL & IRON WORKS, INC

300-328 King Street, Bristol, VA 24201

Tel: (703) 466-2241

Chairman: W J Tilley Sr

President: Otis Hurt (and Chief Executive Officer)

Senior Executive Officers: Kenneth H Cullum (Executive VP), John A Hawkins (VP Sales), Richard D McCullum (VP Bridge Construction), J G Tilley III (VP Operations), Ned Shaw (Treasurer)

PRINCIPAL ACTIVITIES: Manufacture of structural steel for the construction industry

Principal Subsidiaries: Bristol Concrete Products Corp; Tri-State Concrete Products Co Inc; Bristol Steel Corp; Chattanooga Boiler and Tank Co; Holston Steel Structures Inc

Principal Bank: Dominion National Bank

Financial Information:

	$'000
Sales revenues	130,000

No of Employees: 1,000

BRISTOL-MYERS CO

345 Park Avenue, New York, NY 10154

Tel: (212) 546-4000

Telex: ITT 420 160 brmy ui

Chairman: Richard L Gelb (and Chief Executive Officer)
Senior Executive Officers: Bruce S Gelb (Vice Chairman), William R Miller (Vice Chairman), Michael E Autera (Senior VP Administration), J R Edmondson (Senior VP and General Counsel), Wayne A Davidson (Senior VP), Garth F Dimon (Senior VP), N M Evans (Senior VP), Chas A Heimbold (Senior VP), Marvin H Koslow (Senior VP), Joseph E Maroun (Senior VP), A Virgilio (Senior VP)

PRINCIPAL ACTIVITIES: Manufacture of pharmaceuticals, nutritional products, consumer products and other medical products
Principal Subsidiaries: Clairol Inc; Drackett Co; Mead Johnson Co; Zimmer USA.
Financial Information:

	Dec 31 1985	Dec 31 1986
	$'000	$'000
Sales revenues	4,444,000	4,836,000
Net income	531,400	589,500
Earnings per share	$3.86	$4.13
Shareholders equity	2,451,000	2,703,000

No of Employees: 35,700

BROADVIEW FINANCIAL CORPORATION

6000 Rockside Woods Blvd, Cleveland, OH 44131
Tel: (216) 447-1900

Chairman: William F Ford (and Chief Executive Officer)
President: William R Heideloff (Chief Operating Officer)
Senior Executive Officers: William Abbott (Treasurer and Chief Financial Officer), F R O'Keefe (Secretary and Legal Counsel)

PRINCIPAL ACTIVITIES: Financial services
Principal Subsidiaries: Broadview Savings & Loan Co; Broadview Service Corp; Brighton Litho Inc; Broadview Management Co; Broadview Mortgage Corp
Principal Bank: Central National Bank
Financial Information:

	Dec 31 1985
	$'000
Revenues	212,000

No of Employees: 660

BROAN MFG CO, INC

926 W State Street, Hartford, WI 53027
Tel: (414) 673-4340
Telex: 919 260-3845

President: Donald E Schlegel (and Chief Executive Officer)
Senior Executive Officers: L T Lopina (Senior VP, Finance), J G Santowski (Senior VP, Sales and Marketing), R E Dunlap (Senior VP, Manufacturing)

PRINCIPAL ACTIVITIES: Manufacture of extractor fans and ventilation equipment for residential and commercial applications
Trade Names: Broan, Nautilus, Monarch
Parent Company: Nortek Inc, Providence, RI
Principal Bank: First Wisconsin National Bank
Financial Information:

	$'000
Sales revenues	100,000

No of Employees: 700

BROCK HOTEL CORPORATION

4441 West Airport Freeway, Irving, TX 75062
Tel: (214) 258-8500

Chairman: Anthony J Gumbiner
President: Thomas J Corcoran Jr (and Chief Executive Officer)
Senior Executive Officers: Richard M Frank (Executive VP, Chairman and Chief Executive Officer of ShowBiz), Lewis B Kilbourne (Senior VP and Chief Financial Officer), Ronald F Saupe (Senior VP, General Counsel and Secretary), Bruce G Wiles (Senior VP-Corporate Development), Vincent Sikora (Executive VP, President-Hotel Division), Richard T Huston (Executive VP-Director of Marketing), J Terry Spaight (Executive VP and Director of Operations for ShowBiz)

PRINCIPAL ACTIVITIES: Brock Hotel Corporation, a Delaware corporation, and its consolidated subsidiaries are engaged in the restaurant and lodging business. The lodging operations consist of Holiday Inn, Days Inn, Park Suite, Park Inn International, Embassy Suite, Ramada Inn and Residence Inn hotels. The restaurant operations consist of ShowBiz Pizza Place, Chuck E Cheese's Pizza Time Theatre, and Monterey House Mexican Restaurants. The various locations consist of Company owned properties, franchise operations, and managed properties
Trade Names: Hotels: Holiday Inn, Days Inn, Park Suite, Park Inn International, Embassy Suite, Ramada Inn franchise, Residence Inn franchise. Restaurants: ShowBiz Pizza Place, Chuck E Cheese's Pizza Time Theatre, Monterey House Mexican Restaurants
Principal Subsidiaries: Showbiz Pizza Time Inc; Brock Suite Hotels Inc; BHC Acquisition Corporation
Principal Bank: National Westminster
Financial Information:

	Dec 27 1985	Jan 2 1987
	$'000	$'000
Sales revenues	228,591	178,670
(Loss) before taxes	(85,144)	(6,389)
Net income (loss)	(73,994)	29,028(1)
Earnings (loss) per share	($268.48)	$7.41
Common stock(2)	28	681
Retained (deficit)	(91,512)	(62,988)
Shareholders equity (deficit)	(62,688)	55,103

(1) Income taxes were $370,000 with extraordinary items totaling $35,787,000
(2) Issued 6,811,209 and 282,736 shares at year end 1986 and 1985 respectively. On June 25, 1986 the Company consummated a plan of financial restructuring. The Company also effected a 1-for-50 reverse stock split at the consummation of the Restructuring Plan. The number of shares of common stock issued were adjusted for the reverse split

No of Employees: 9,600 (varies seasonally)

BROCKWAY, INC (NY)

225 Water St, PO Box 44058, Jacksonville, FL 32231-4058
Tel: (904) 797-400
Telex: TWX 5106934041 broc glas broc

Chairman: John J McMackin (and President and Chief Executive Officer)
Senior Executive Officers: DeVere L Sheesley Jr (Senior VP Finance, and Corporate Marketing, Development and Planning), P R Burnaman (Senior VP, General Counsel and Secretary), Lawrence J Beighey (VP, President Brockway Standard Division), B Hancel Bonds (VP, President Plastics Division), Robert S Coakley (Group VP, President Glass Container Division), John T Stirrup (Group VP, Plastics and Metal), Harry D Jackson (VP, President International Division), John A Sullivan (VP, President Airline Division), James W Hysong (VP, Human Resources), James A Kline (VP, Controller), Peter R Osterman (Treasurer) Planning)

PRINCIPAL ACTIVITIES: Brockway is a leading producer of plastic, metal and glass containers, lids and closures manufactured through a network of plants and support facilities nationwide. Brockway's airline operations, in association with USAir and Piemont Airlines, provide passenger air service linking more than two dozen regional airports with major air centers throughout the northeast corridor. Brockway also sells technology and production expertise to foreign manufacturers of packaging and related products

Principal Subsidiaries/Divisions: Brockway Glass; Brockway Plastics; Brockway Standard; Brockway International; Brockway Captainer; Brockway Airlines; Brockway Air; Crown Airways, Inc

Principal Bank: Manufacturers Hanover Trust Co

Financial Information:

	Dec 31 1985	Dec 31 1986
	$'000	$'000
Sales revenues	1,032,773	1,065,618
Income before taxes	32,019	59,088
Net income	17,926	30,284
Dividends	10,791	10,912
Dividends per share	$0.88(1)	$0.88
Earnings per share	$1.46(1)	$2.44
Common stock(2)	12,255	12,390
Retained income	170,022	189,394
Shareholders equity	223,919	245,533

(1) restated to reflect three-for-two stock split in December 1986

(2) shares outstanding in thousands

No of Employees: 12,000

BRODART CO

500 Arch St, Williamsport, PA 17705
Tel: (717) 326-2461
Telex: 510-655-523

Chairman: Arthur Brody (and Chief Executive Officer)

President: Joseph Largen

Senior Executive Officers: Christopher Daly (Treasurer and Chief Financial Officer), Joseph Pugliese (VP Furniture), John Schaub (VP Automated Services), John Weir (VP Book Division), Jack O'Neill (VP Manufacturing), Richard Belzer (VP Retail Division)

PRINCIPAL ACTIVITIES: Brodart Co is engaged in the distribution of books, supplies, equipment and furniture to libraries and the operation of retail stores which sell books, greeting cards and gifts, office, art and engineering supplies

Principal Bank: Commonwealth Bank & Trust Co

Financial Information:

	1985	1986
	$'000	$'000
Sales revenues	124,000	126,000

No of Employees: 1,700

BROOKLYN UNION GAS COMPANY

195 Montague Street, Brooklyn, NY 11201
Tel: (718) 403-2000

Chairman: Eugene H Lunty (and Chief Executive Officer)

President: Elwin S Larson (and Chief Operating Officer)

Senior Executive Officers: Robert B Catell (Executive VP), Malcolm M Chesney Jr (Senior VP), Robert V Delaney (Senior VP), Fred J Gentile (Senior VP and Chief Accounting Officer), Fred W McPhilliamy (Senior VP), Helmut W Peter (Senior VP and Chief Engineer), Joseph A Pinnola (Senior VP), Maurice K Shaw (Senior VP), Richard M Coddington (VP), James W Dunlop (VP), Edward J Sondey (VP), Craig G Matthews (VP and Chief Financial Officer)

PRINCIPAL ACTIVITIES: Supply of natural gas

Principal Subsidiaries: Fuel Resource Inc; Gas Energy Inc; Methane Development Corp; Star Enterprises Inc; Delaware Valley Propane Company

Financial Information:

	Sep 30 1986
	$'000
Sales revenues	1,000,000
Net income	37,000

No of Employees: 3,780

BROWN & BIGELOW

345 Plato Blvd. E, St Paul, MN 55104
Tel: (612) 293-7000
Telex: WUT 297030

President: Paul Charron

Senior Executive Officers: Milan G Gersting (Senior VP), Roger Greenwald (VP Sales), William O'Reilly (VP Marketing), Robert Head (VP and Treasurer), Richard Knight (VP Administrative Services)

PRINCIPAL ACTIVITIES: Manufacture of stationery, calendars and greeting cards; smokers' requisites; giftware

Parent Company: Atwater Group Inc

Principal Bank: Chase Manhattan Bank

Financial Information:

	$'000
Sales revenues	100,000

No of Employees: 2,000

BROWN & SHARPE MFG CO

Precision Park, North Kingstown, RI 02852
Tel: (401) 886-2000
Telex: WUT 92 7771 sharpe nktn a

Chairman: Henry D Sharpe Jr

President: Donald A Roach (and Chief Executive Officer)

Senior Executive Officers: John H Hubbard (Executive VP), Richard J Duncan (VP Finance), Hans Baertschi (VP, Managing Director Rhode Island Tesa SA), John G Gordon (VP Human Resources)

PRINCIPAL ACTIVITIES: Manufacture of pumps, valves and machine tools

Principal Subsidiaries: Brown & Sharpe Disc Inc; Brown & Sharpe Financial Co; Brown & Sharpe International Capital Inc; Tools Capital Corp

Principal Bank: RIHT Financial Corp

Financial Information:

	$'000
Sales revenues	120,920

No of Employees: 2,000

BROWN & WILLIAMSON TOBACCO CORPORATION

1500 Brown & Williamson Tower, Louisville, KY 40202
Tel: (502) 568-7011
Telex: TWX 810 5353278 bw tobco lvl

Chairman: R J Pritchard (and Chief Executive Officer)

President: T E Sandefur Jr (and Chief Operating Officer)

Senior Executive Officers: C J Heger (Senior VP Finance), W L DeWitt (Senior VP Planning and Administration), B M Lowdenback (Senior VP Human Resources), Ernest Pepples (Senior VP Law), J S Hedewicz (VP Corporate Communications), H A Roeder (VP Manufacturing), R H Sachs (VP Law), E E Kohnhorst (VP Research and Development), T E Whitehair Jr (VP Corporate Marketing), J R Anders (VP International), W B Knable (VP License Operations), C D White (VP Leaf Buying), C H Teague (VP Quality Systems and Customer Services)

PRINCIPAL ACTIVITIES: Manufacture of cigarettes and tobacco

Parent Company: BAT Industries plc, London, UK (100%)

Financial Information:

	$'000
Sales revenues	2,300,000

No of Employees: 5,000

BROWN, ALEX, INC
135 East Baltimore Street, Baltimore, MD 21202
Tel: (301) 727-1700

Chairman: F Barton Harvey Jr; Vice Chairmen: Benjamin H Griswold, Jack S Griswold
President: Donald B Hebb Jr (and Chief Executive Officer)
Senior Executive Officers: Joseph R Hardiman (Secretary and Treasurer)

PRINCIPAL ACTIVITIES: Financial and investment services
Principal Subsidiaries: Alex Brown & Sons Inc

No of Employees: 1,220

BROWN GROUP, INC
8400 Maryland Avenue, St Louis, MO 63105
Tel: (314) 854-4000
Telex: TWX 9107611191 brown grp stl

Chairman: B A Bridgewater Jr (and Chief Executive Officer)
Senior Executive Officers: Harry E Rich (Senior VP and Chief Financial Officer), Erik R Risman (Senior VP), J J Cramer (VP), David L Bowman (VP), William S Frederick (VP and Controller), Robert D Pickle (VP), Douglas W Walrod (VP), Donald G Lenoard (VP), Robert D Gibbs (VP), Andrew M Rosen (Treasurer)

PRINCIPAL ACTIVITIES: Retailing and manufacturing/wholesaling of footwear and specialty retailing
Trade Names: Women's Footwear: Naturalizer, Connie, Fanfare, Jones New York, Life Stride. Men's & Children's Footwear: Regal, Buster Brown
Principal Bank: Centerre Bank, NA St Louis, MO
Financial Information:

	Feb 1 1986	Jan 31 1987
	$'000	$'000
Sales revenues	1,406,215	1,406,527
Income before taxes	93,054	69,515
Net income	51,573	39,503
Dividends	27,033	26,646
Dividends per share	$1.38	$1.455
Earnings per share	$2.65	$2.16
Common stock	89,176	85,597
Retained income	285,553	267,492
Shareholders equity	374,729	353,089

No of Employees: 25,500

BROWN, H H, SHOE CO
8400-T Maryland Ave, PO Box 29, St Louis, MO 63166
Tel: (314) 854-4000

Chairman: Richard W Shomaker
President: Raymond B Shlora
Senior Executive Officers: F Mark Lemp (Executive VP), Curtis R Johnson (Executive VP Production and Purchasing), David L Bowman (Senior VP Advertising), James A Flynn (Senior VP Marketing and Planning), James P Marrs (Senior VP Retail Operations), Robert T Bahn (Senior VP Merchandising), Edward Miser (Senior VP Purchasing), Phillip F Fried (Senior VP Marketing Group Coordinator), Morton P Tucker (Senior VP Women's Marketing), Richard N Stone (Senior VP Men's Marketing), John Grose (VP Children's Marketing), David Dean (VP Administration)

PRINCIPAL ACTIVITIES: Manufacture of footwear for men and boys
Parent Company: Brown Group Inc
Principal Subsidiaries: ITS Inc; Lauriel Press Inc; Reunion Inc
Principal Bank: Bank of New England
Financial Information:

	$'000
Sales revenues	100,000

No of Employees: 1,300

BROWN, JOHN, INC
333 Strawberry Field Road, Warwick, RI 02887
Tel: (401) 739-7100

President: Dr Alastair C Gowan (and Chief Executive Officer)
Senior Executive Officers: Charles E Buckley (VP Finance and Chief Financial Officer), Gerald T Dwyer (Division President Brown Machine), James H Sharpe (Division President Cumberland Engineering), Robert V Lucke (Division President Egan Machinery), Ronald A Schroeder (Division President EPCO), Ross A Slater (Division President Leesona Textile Machinery), Arrigo Manara (Division President Negri Bossi), W B Zehner III (Division President Worldwide Plastics Sales)

PRINCIPAL ACTIVITIES: Manufacture of textile machinery and plastics processing machinery
Parent Company: John Brown PLC, London, UK
Principal Bank: Shawmut Bank
Financial Information:

	$'000
Sales revenues	200,000

No of Employees: 2,800

BROWN-FORMAN CORPORATION
850 Dixie Hwy, PO Box 1080, Louisville, KY 40201
Tel: (502) 585-1100
Telex: TWX 8105353430 brn form lvl

Chairman: W L Lyons Brown Jr (and Chief Executive Officer); Vice Chairmen: Owsley Brown Frazier, William M Street
President: Owsley Brown II
Senior Executive Officers: Russell C Buzby (Senior VP Human Resources and Information Systems), John S Moremen (Senior VP and Secretary), John P Bridendall (Senior VP, Corporate Development), Lois Musselman (Senior VP, Corporate Communications), Clifford G Rompf Jr (Senior VP Financial Operations), Vernon L Boylan (VP, Corporate Services), Robert S Lyons (VP, Information Systems), Charles E Muntan (VP and Controller), Larry W Perry (VP, Tax), Michael G Smith (VP, Human Resources), Christopher A Sailer (Treasurer), Robinson S Brown III (Assistant VP, Computer Operations), Jay R Colvin (Assistant VP, Executive Search), John J Davis III (Assistant VP, Senior Attorney), Stephen T Fox (Assistant VP, Information Systems), Milton B Gillis (Assistant VP, Benefits), Gregory P Givan (Assistant VP, Investment Analysis), John S Harston (Assistant VP, Employee Relations), John W Hagan (Assistant VP, Corporate Accounting), James F Lancaster (Assistant VP, Management Development and Training), Harold G McManaway (Assistant VP, Information Systems), Lawrence K Probus (Assistant VP, Planning and Analyses), John G Spanyer (Assistant VP, Corporate Services), Leon R Timmons (Assistant Secretary, Senior Attorney)

PRINCIPAL ACTIVITIES: Manufacture and import of wines and spirits; manufacture and trade in consumer goods including jewelry, crystalware, fine china and luggage
Trade Names: Jack Daniels
Principal Subsidiaries: Brown-Forman Beverage Company; Brown-Forman International Ltd; Lenox, Incorporated

No of Employees: 6,550

BROWN-FORMAN INC
850 Dixie Hwy, PO Box 1080, Louisville, KY 40201
Tel: (502) 585-1100

Chairman: W L Lyons Brown Jr (and Chief Executive Officer); Vice Chairman: Owsley B Frazier
Senior Executive Officers: Owsley Brown II (VP and Treasurer), John S Moreman (Secretary)

PRINCIPAL ACTIVITIES: Brown-Forman, founded in 1870, is a diversified producer and marketer of fine quality consumer products. Its Brown-Forman Beverage Company division markets Jack Daniel's Tennessee Whiskey, Early Times Old Style Kentucky Whisky, Old Forester Kentucky Straight

Bourbon Whiskies, Canadian Mist Canadian Whisky, Martell Cognacs, Usher's Green Stripe Scotch Whisky, Old Bushmills Irish Whiskey, Pepe Lopez Tequilas, Southern Comfort, Korbel California Champagnes, California Cooler, Bolla, Cella, and Fontana Candida Italian Wines, Parducci Premium California Wines, Korbel California Brandy, Bols Liqueurs, Noilly Prat Vermouths, and Black Bush, a specialty malt whiskey from Ireland, Through Lenox, Incorporated, Brown-Forman also manufactures and markets Lenox fine china, crystal, and giftware, Hartmann luggage, and ArtCarved jewelry. White oak barrels, essential in the maturation of fine whiskies, and bottle closures are also produced by divisions of the Company.

Principal Subsidiaries: Brown-Forman Corporation; Brown-Forman Brands, Ltd (1); Jack Daniel Distillery, Lem Motlow, Prop, Inc (1); Blue Grass Cooperage Company, Inc (2); Lenox, Incorporated (3); Mt Eagle Corporation (1); Canadian Mist Distillers, Limited (1); The Jos Garneau Co, SA (1)(4); Thoroughbred Plastics Corporation (1); Longnorth, Limited (1)(4); Clintock, Limited (4)(5); Early Times Distillers Company (1); Brown-Forman International FSC, Ltd (1); (1) A wholly-owned subsidiary of Brown-Forman Corporation; (2) A wholly-owned subsidiary of Jack Daniel Distillery, Lem Motlow, Prop, Inc;(3) A wholly-owned subsidiary of Brown-Forman Brands, Ltd; (4) Includes directors' qualifying shares assigned to Brown-Forman Corporation; (5) A wholly-owned subsidiary of Longnorth Limited

Financial Information:

	Apr 30 1986	Apr 30 1987
	$'000	$'000
Sales revenues	1,288,808	1,404,465
Net sales*	994,864	1,098,110
Income before taxes	163,244	161,815
Net income	86,376	89,584
Total cash dividends	21,848	29,347
Dividends per common share	$0.67	$0.90
Earnings per share	$2.68	$2.78
Common stock Class A	1,809	1,809
Common stock Class B	4,000	4,000
Retained income	542,468	602,705
Shareholders equity	528,144	589,717

*less excise taxes

No of Employees: 6,600

BROWNING

Rte 1, Morgan, UT 84050
Tel: (801) 543-3200
Telex: WUT 388409 browning mgan

Chairman: Jacques Germay
President: Don W Gobel (and Chief Executive Officer)
Senior Executive Officers: Donald E Jones (VP and Chief Financial Officer), Ron Mosier (VP Sales)

PRINCIPAL ACTIVITIES: Distribution of guns, archery and fishing equipment, sports equipment and leisure goods; manufacture of archery bows, golf carts and raquet ball raquets
Trade Names: Browning, Ektelon, Bag Boy
Parent Company: FN America
Principal Subsidiaries: Browning Manufacturing Co; Jarman Company; Ektelon; Browning Canada Sports Ltd/Ltee
Principal Bank: Generale Bank, New York Branch
Financial Information:

	Dec 31 1985	Dec 31 1986
	$'000	$'000
Sales revenues	133,622	128,361
Income before taxes	1,859	1,180
Net income	761	544
Common stock	9,132	9,132
Retained income	22,283	21,494
Shareholders equity	31,415	30,626

Principal Shareholders: FN America
No of Employees: 440

BROWNING-FERRIS INDUSTRIES INC

14701 St Mary's Lane, Houston, TX 77079
Tel: (713) 870-8100

Chairman: Harry J Phillips Sr (and Chief Executive Officer); Vice Chairman: Norman A Myers (and Chief Marketing Officer)
President: John E Drury (and Chief Operating Officer)
Senior Executive Officers: George R Farris (Executive VP and Chief Financial Officer), Howard S Hoover Jr (Senior VP), Oscar M Holland (Senior VP), Harry J Phillips Jr (Senior VP, Solid Waste Operations North America), Edward J Crane (VP General Sales), Bruce Hendrickson (VP Engineering Services), Robert A Johnson (VP), Robert W Lary (VP), Michael P Lawlor (VP Landfill Operations), C P J Mooney III (VP Employee Relations), Stephen L Thomas (VP Operations Administration)

PRINCIPAL ACTIVITIES: Waste disposal for industry, commerce and households
Principal Subsidiaries: American Waste Removal Inc; BFI Waste Systems of IN Inc; Joe Ball Sanitation Service Inc; Browning-Ferris Industrial Chemical Services Inc; Cardinal Land Corp; Cecos Environmental Inc; Cecos International Inc; Comet Enterprises Inc; Dallas Refuse Service Inc; Disposal Specialist Inc; Dooley Equipment Corp; ESI Inc; Ecco Contractors Inc; Environmental Equipment Corp; Heavy Equipment Leasing Services Co; Highway 36 Land Development Co; HL-NIW Inc; Indoco Inc; International Disposable Corp; International Disposal Corp; Jeffco Land Reclamation Inc; Louis Kmito & Son Inc; Landfill Inc; Lanham Waste Control Inc; Lyon Development Inc; Modern Waste Removal Inc; National Disposal Service of NE Inc; Newco Waste Systems Inc; Niagara Landfill Inc; Niagara Recycling Inc; Niagara Sanitation Co Inc; Orchard Mesa Landfill Inc; Phoenix Inc; Resource Recovery Corp; Resource Recovery Inc; Ricks Repair and Manufacturing Co; Robins Refuse Service Inc; Transworld Hospital Consultants; Waste Disposal Inc; West Roxbury Crushed Stone Co; Woodlake Sanitary Service Inc
Principal Bank: Republic Bank Dallas
Financial Information:

	Sep 30 1985	Sep 30 1986
	$'000	$'000
Sales revenues	1,144,510	1,328,390
Net income	111,830	136,853
Earnings per share	$1.60	$1.90
Shareholders equity	-	746,867

No of Employees: 14,000

BROYHILL FURNITURE INDUSTRIES, INC

Broyhill Park, Lenoir, NC 28633
Tel: (704) 758-3111
Telex: WUT 375167 broyhill lenr

Chairman: Paul H Broyhill
President: Gene Gunter (and Chief Executive Officer)
Senior Executive Officers: Brent B Kincaid (VP Purchasing), E D Beach (VP Finance), Jack Ludwig (VP Dining Room and Bedroom), Guy Walters (VP Occasional/Casual), Tom Cunningham (VP Upholstery), Bruce Hardy (VP Operations)

PRINCIPAL ACTIVITIES: Manufacture of furniture
Principal Bank: First Union National Bank of North Carolina
Financial Information:

	$'000
Sales revenues	280,000

No of Employees: 7,700

BRUCE, ROBERT, INC

C & Westmoreland, Philadelphia, PA 19134
Tel: (215) 426-0300
Telex: TWX 7106701230 robt bruce pha

Chairman: I L Feinberg
President: Thomas T Brumm

Senior Executive Officers: Gary Thorpe (Executive VP Marketing), Dick Selman (Senior VP Manufacturing), Jay Ehrensaal (VP Sales), Aaron Gelstine (VP), John Sabin (VP and Chief Financial Officer)

PRINCIPAL ACTIVITIES: Manufacture of clothing including sportswear and knitted goods

Parent Company: Savoy Industries Inc, New York, NY

Principal Bank: The Fidelity Bank

Financial Information:

	$'000
Sales revenues	69,000

No of Employees: 1,000

BRUNELL, A A, ELECTROPLATING CORPORATION

41 Sutton Lane, Worcester, MA 01603

Tel: (617) 752-7595

Chairman: Arthur B Brunell (and President and Sales and Advertising Manager)

Senior Executive Officers: Paul Brunell (VP), Jonathan Brunell (Treasurer)

PRINCIPAL ACTIVITIES: Electroplating in a range of finishes

Principal Bank: First Safety Fund National Bank

Financial Information:

	$'000
Sales revenues	800,000

No of Employees: 30

BRUNO'S INC

300 Research Pkwy, PO Box 2486, Birmingham, AL 35201-2486

Tel: (025) 940-9400

Chairman: Angelo J Bruno (and Chief Executive Officer); Vice Chairman: Lee J Bruno (Senior VP)

President: Ronald G Bruno (and Chief Operating Officer)

Senior Executive Officers: Paul F Garrison (Executive VP), Paschal P Vacca (VP and Counsel), Glenn J Griffin (Senior VP and Chief Financial Officer, Secretary)

PRINCIPAL ACTIVITIES: Supermarkets

Financial Information:

	Jun 28 1986	Jun 27 1987
	$'000	$'000
Sales revenues	1,018,431	1,143,235
Income before taxes	48,761	57,717
Net income	30,251	31,010
Dividends	6,304	7,102
Dividends per share	$0.16	$0.18
Earnings per share	$0.77	$0.79
Common stock	394	395
Retained income	106,694	130,602
Shareholders equity	177,184	201,320

No of Employees: 12,000

BRUNSWICK CORPORATION

One Brunswick Plaza, Skokie, IL 60077

Tel: (312) 470-4700

Telex: 190 127

Chairman: Jack F Reichert (and President and Chief Executive Officer)

Senior Executive Officers: Richard J Jordan (Executive VP), Frederick J Florjancic Jr (VP Finance), Robert T McNaney (General Counsel), Henry H Marvin (VP Technology), William R McManaman (Controller), Dianne M Yaconetti (Corporate Secretary)

PRINCIPAL ACTIVITIES: Brunswick Corporation is a recreation/leisure company with interests in defense/aerospace and industrial products. It serves worldwide markets in the marine power, pleasure boat, fishing tackle, bowling equipment and supplies, retail bowling center, defense/aerospace, filtration, specialty materials, energy and transportation areas

Trade Names: Mercury Outboards, Mariner Outboards, MerCruiser Stern Drives/Inboards, Quicksilver Marine Parts and Accessories, Bayliner, Force Outboards, US Marine Power, Blue Fin, Sea Ray, Zebco, Quantum, MotorGuide, Brunswick Making Bowling Better, BRC Brunswick Recreation Centers, Brunswick Defense, Filtration Technology, Filterite, Fluid Dynamics, Brunswick Technetics Engineered Materials, Circle Seal Controls, Brunswick Golf, Texsteam TXT, Cooper Valve Company, Vapor, GPE, RCS Raymond Control Systems, HSI Hydro Steam Industries

Principal Bank: First National Bank of Chicago

Financial Information:

	Dec 31 1985	Dec 31 1986
	$'000	$'000
Sales revenues	1,538,538	1,717,361
Income before taxes	163,114	185,416
Net income	100,310	110,316
Dividends per share*	$0.2275	$0.275
Earnings per share*	$1.17	$1.32
Common stock*	86,000	83,800
Retained income	482,460	568,604
Shareholders equity	523,186	690,779

*stock split 2:1 on 9 June 1987

No of Employees: 26,800

BRUNSWICK PULP & PAPER CO

PO Box 1438, Brunswick, GA 31520

Tel: (912) 265-5780

Telex: TWX 8107825069 bpp b brwk

Chairman: W A Enouen

President: P F Marsden (and Chief Executive Officer)

Senior Executive Officers: J D Wethern (VP Planning and Development), A D Correll (VP), C H Martin Jr (VP Woods Division), W H Nelson III (VP), A N Bakhru (Treasurer), J F McLeod (VP), R W Neal (VP)

PRINCIPAL ACTIVITIES: Manufacture of pulp and paper products

Principal Subsidiaries: Brunswick Chemical Co Inc

Principal Bank: Pacific National Bank

Financial Information:

	$'000
Sales revenues	300,000

No of Employees: 1,000

BRUSH WELLMAN INC

1200 Hanna Building, Cleveland, OH 44115

Tel: (216) 443-1000

Telex: TWX 810 4218284 bw hanna clv

Chairman: H G Piper (and Chief Executive Officer)

President: Raymond A Foos

Senior Executive Officers: James Dudziak (VP), James E Gulick (VP), C G Waite (VP Finance)

PRINCIPAL ACTIVITIES: Manufacture of alloys and special metals

Principal Bank: AmeriTrust

Financial Information:

	Dec 31 1986
	$'000
Sales revenues	241,428
Income before taxes	40,253
Net income	22,675
Dividends	10,337
Dividends per share	$0.55
Earnings per share	$1.20
Common stock	51,501
Retained income	183,224
Shareholders equity	234,725

No of Employees: 2,630

BSD BANCORP INC

225 Broadway, Suite 1320, San Diego, CA 92101
Tel: (619) 237 5365

Chairman: James S Brown (and Chief Executive Officer)
Senior Executive Officers: E Lynn Caswell (Senior Executive VP), Alan B Lord (Executive VP and Secretary), Bradford J Hanson (Chief Financial Officer), Vito J Guarino Jr (Chief Operating Officer)

PRINCIPAL ACTIVITIES: Banking services
Principal Bank: Security Pacific National Bank
Financial Information:

	Dec 31 1985
	$'000
Revenues	43,000
Net income	780

No of Employees: 300

BTK INDUSTRIES, INC

9033 Billy The Kid Road, El Paso, TX 79907
Tel: (915) 545-4000

Chairman: Daniel J Manella (and Chief Executive Officer)
Senior Executive Officers: Ken Leccesse (VP Finance)

PRINCIPAL ACTIVITIES: Manufacture of clothing
Principal Bank: Manufacturers Hanover Trust
Financial Information:

	$'000
Sales revenues	75,000

No of Employees: 1,400

BTR INC

2200 Hospital Trust Tower, Providence, RI 02903
Tel: (401) 272-7000

Chairman: Owen Green
President: John C Cahill (and Chief Executive Officer)
Senior Executive Officers: Edgar E Sharp (Group VP), Max H Buzzell (VP Taxation), Joseph T Gentile (VP)

PRINCIPAL ACTIVITIES: Manufacture of supplies and equipment for the paper and textile industries; machine tools
Parent Company: BTR PLC
Principal Bank: First National Bank of Boston
Financial Information:

	$'000
Sales revenues	500,000

Principal Shareholders: BTR PLC, UK
No of Employees: 5,500

BTU ENGINEERING CORPORATION

Esquire Road, Billerica, MA 01862
Tel: (617) 667-4111
Telex: WUT 947489 btuengcor nbil

President: Paul J van der Wansem
Senior Executive Officers: Peter H Goebel (VP), David H Barry (VP), John H Fabricius (VP), A D Velardocchia (VP), J Neal Armstrong (VP)

PRINCIPAL ACTIVITIES: Manufacture of furnace equipment for a range of applications and process equipment for semiconductor manufacture
Trade Names: BTU Systems, Bruce Systems
Principal Subsidiaries: BTU International, Inc
Principal Bank: First National Bank of Boston
Financial Information:

	$'000
Sales revenues	50,000

No of Employees: 600

BUCKEYE FINANCIAL CORPORATION

36 E Gay Street, Columbus, OH 43215
Tel: (614) 225-2100

Chairman: D S Cook
President: B G Glass
Senior Executive Officers: Raymond F Van De Weghe (VP and Treasurer), R H McNaughten (VP)

PRINCIPAL ACTIVITIES: Financial services and property interests
Principal Subsidiaries: Buckeye Federal Savings & Loan Association; B F Mortgage Co; Buckeye Consumer Plan Inc; Buckeye Service Corp
Principal Bank: Huntington National Bank
Financial Information:

	Dec 31 1985
	$'000
Revenues	138,240
Net income	2,080

No of Employees: 440

BUCKHORN INC

PO Box 689, 3592 Corporate Drive, Columbus, OH 43216
Tel: (614) 895 1895

Chairman: Richard P Johnston (and President)
Senior Executive Officers: Richard R Halsor (Group Vice President), Larry R Martin (Senior VP and Treasurer), Michael F Simon (Senior VP Division), Thomas A Bruser (VP Human Resources), James A Fellows (Group VP Materials Handling International), Michael H Blackburn (Group VP Materials Handling Domestic), Charles F Metzger (VP Communications), David R Best (VP and Controller)

PRINCIPAL ACTIVITIES: Manufacture of plastic products including storage products; shipping containers; industrial rubber prodcuts
Principal Subsidiaries: Buckhorn Rubber Products Group (Division); Buckhorn Materials Handling Group Inc; Buckhorn Metal Products Inc
Principal Bank: First National Bank of Chicago
Financial Information:

	$'000
Sales revenues	45,540

No of Employees: 560

BUCYRUS-ERIE CO

W Quinn Road, Pocatello, ID 83201
Tel: (208) 238 2000

Chairman: N K Ekstom (and Chief Executive Officer)
President: W B Winter (and Chief Operating Officer)
Senior Executive Officers: T G Folliard (VP Finance and Controller)

PRINCIPAL ACTIVITIES: Manufacture of construction and mining machinery, oil and gas exploration equipment and aerospace systems
Financial Information:

	$'000
Sales revenues	407,000

No of Employees: 4,050

BUDD COMPANY

3155 W Big Beaver Road, Box 2601, Troy, MI 48084
Tel: (313) 643-3500
Telex: TRT 164107 buddcohq trmi

Chairman: James H McNeal Jr (and Chief Executive Officer); Vice Chairman: Siegfried Buschmann (and Chief Financial Officer)
President: David P Williams (and Chief Operating Officer)
Senior Executive Officers: James S Roth (VP and President, Stamping and Frame Division), George J Schuster (VP and President, Wheel and Brake Division), Jerry E Purcell (VP and President, Plastics Division)

PRINCIPAL ACTIVITIES: Manufacture of components for the automotive industry
Parent Company: Thyssen AG, Duisburg, Germany
Principal Bank: National Bank of Detroit

No of Employees: 14,000

BUEHLER INTERNATIONAL INC

41 Waukegan Road, Lake Bluff, IL 60044
Tel: (312) 295 6500

Chairman: Philip E Beck
President: Daniel E Albrecht (and Director and Chief Executive Officer)
Senior Executive Officers: Dereck B Gange (Chief Operating Officer), Michael L Bryant (Secretary)

PRINCIPAL ACTIVITIES: Manufacture of scientific instruments and equipment for laboratories and industrial applications for materials analysis
Principal Subsidiaries: Buehler Inc
Financial Information:

	$'000
Revenues	57,440

No of Employees: 500

BUELL INDUSTRIES, INC

130 Huntingdon Avenue, Waterbury, CT 06708
Tel: (203) 574-1800
Telex: WUT 962410 anchorfast wby

Chairman: Vincent B Largay (and Chief Executive Officer)
President: George H Largay II
Senior Executive Officers: George H Largay II (VP), Edward S Wilson (VP), James M Barkley (Secretary and Treasurer)

PRINCIPAL ACTIVITIES: Manufacture of a range of industrial fasteners including nuts and screws
Principal Bank: The Colonial Bank and Trust Company
Financial Information:

	$'000
Sales revenues	75,000

No of Employees: 730

BUFFALO FORGE CO

490 Broadway, Buffalo, NY 14204
Tel: (716) 847-5121
Telex: WUT 91234 bufloforge buf

President: J R Adare
Senior Executive Officers: G H Johnson (VP), R Jorgensen (VP Engineering), Dennis M O'Connor (VP and Treasurer), S A Young (VP Manufacturing), G C Morris (VP Sales)

PRINCIPAL ACTIVITIES: Manufacture of pumps, heating and ventilation equipment and machine tools
Parent Company: Ampco-Pittsburgh Corporation, Pittsburgh, PA
Principal Bank: Mellon Bank NA
Financial Information:

	$'000
Sales revenues	119,000

No of Employees: 1,600

BUILDERS TRANSPORT INC

PO Box 500, US Highway 1, Camden, SC 29020
Tel: (803) 432 1400

Chairman: Charles C Gay (and Chief Executive Officer); Vice Chairman: Lee A Gay (and Chief Administrative Officer and Assistant Secretary)
President: B M Shirley (and Chief Operating Officer)
Senior Executive Officers: Charles C Gay Jr (Executive VP Operations), George L Corbin Jr (Senior VP, Chief Financial Officer and Assistant Secretary), John R Morris (Senior VP Operations), Donald A Michael (Treasurer and Assistant Secretary), Robert E Lee Garner (Secretary), P Michael Davis (Senior VP Sales and Marketing)

PRINCIPAL ACTIVITIES: Long-distance road haulage services
Principal Bank: Citizens & Southern
Financial Information:

	$'000
Sales revenues	130,720

No of Employees: 1,960

BULOVA WATCH COMPANY, INC

Bulova Park, Flushing, NY 11370
Tel: (718) 565-4200

Chairman: Harry B Henshel
President: Andrew H Tisch
Senior Executive Officers: Herbert C Hofmann (Chief Operating Officer), James S Waterwash (VP), Lawrence F Cordraro (VP and Secretary), Paul S Sayegh (VP Finance), Thomas P Hickerson (VP and Controller)

PRINCIPAL ACTIVITIES: Manufacture of watches and clocks
Parent Company: Loews Corporation, New York, NY
Financial Information:

	$'000
Sales revenues	145,000

No of Employees: 1,600

BUNDY CORPORATION

12345 E Nine Mile Road, Warren, MI 48090
Tel: (313) 758-6500
Telex: WUT 230661 bundy warn a

Chairman: Wendell W Anderson Jr (and Chief Executive Officer); Vice Chairman: John W Anderson II
President: William E Eckhardt (and Chief Operating Officer)
Senior Executive Officers: Michael N Counen (VP, International), Raymond H Steben Jr (VP, Finance), James F Mueller (Group VP, Tubing Operations), Donald J Mesdor (Group VP, Performance Plastics)

PRINCIPAL ACTIVITIES: Manufacture of steel, plastic and metal tubes, hoses, plastic components and pressure sensitive tape
Financial Information:

	Jul 31 1985	Jul 31 1986
	$'000	$'000
Sales revenues	208,440	216,336
Net income	970	8,896

No of Employees: 3,026

BUNGE CORPORATION

1 Chase Manhattan Plaza, New York, NY 10005
Tel: (212) 943-6600
Telex: TRT 177655 bunge ut

Chairman: Walter C Klein
President: John E Klein
Senior Executive Officers: John Hofmann (Senior VP), Richard G Kerwin (Senior VP), John Phillips (Senior VP), David C Thompson (Senior VP)

PRINCIPAL ACTIVITIES: Manufacture of grain products and edible oils

Principal Subsidiaries: Bunge Edible Oil Corp; International Grain Stevedores Inc; International Produce Inc; Lauhoff Grain Co; Produce Grain Inc
Principal Bank: Chase Manhattan Bank
Financial Information:

	$'000
Sales revenues	4,000,000

No of Employees: 3,000

BUREAU OF NATIONAL AFFAIRS, INC

1231 25th Street NW, Washington, DC 20037
Tel: (202) 452-4200
Telex: WUT 892692 bnai wsh

Chairman: John D Stewart
President: William A Beltz (and Chief Executive Officer)
Senior Executive Officers: George F Knight (VP Sales), Ralph J Wall (VP and Chief Financial Officer), Hugh J Yarrington (VP and General Counsel), Stanley E Degler (VP and Executive Editor), John P Boylan Jr (VP Administration), John V Schappi (VP Human Resources)

PRINCIPAL ACTIVITIES: Publishing
Trade Names: BNA
Principal Subsidiaries: Tax Management Inc; The McArdle Printing Co Inc
Principal Bank: First American Bank of Washington
Financial Information:

	Dec 31 1986 $'000
Sales revenues	122,567
Income before taxes	15,999
Net income	5,122
Dividends	3,835
Shareholders equity	39,527

No of Employees: 1,600

BURLINGTON COAT FACTORY WAREHOUSE CORPORATION

Rte 130 N, Burlington, NJ 08016
Tel: (609) 386-3314

Chairman: Monroe G Milstein (and President)
Senior Executive Officers: Henrietta Milstein (VP, Secretary), Steven Milstein (VP), Mark A Nesci (VP), Robert L LaPenta Jr (VP, Chief Accounting Officer and Controller), Elisabeth Stout (Treasurer)

PRINCIPAL ACTIVITIES: Retail trade in clothing
Trade Names: Modecraft Fashions
Principal Subsidiaries: 111 Operating subsidiaries in 32 States
Principal Banks: Chemical Bank; Mellon Bank; Bank Ohio
Financial Information:

	Nov 2 1985 $'000	Nov 1 1986 $'000
Sales revenues	352,060	391,608
Income before taxes	29,171	32,940
Net income	16,088	17,326
Earnings per share	$1.38	$1.48
Common stock	11,700,000	11,731,000
Retained income	57,636	74,962
Shareholders equity	112,120	130,060

No of Employees: 10,000

BURLINGTON INDUSTRIES, INC

3330 W Friendly Avenue, Greensboro, NC 27410
Tel: (919) 379-2000

Chairman: Frank S Greenberg (and Chief Executive Officer); Vice Chairman: Donald R Hughes (and Chief Financial Officer)
President: Lanty L Smith
Senior Executive Officers: George C Waldrep Jr (Executive VP for Manufacturing). Group Vice Presidents: Roger F Anthony, Robert L Barnes, Clarence C Finley, George W Henderson III, William deR Holt Jr, Bernard A Leventhal, Marvin J Pinson Jr, Abraham B Stenberg, Arthur C Wiener. Management Committee: Richard M Altman, Roger F Anthony, Agustin J Diodati, John D Englar, Frank S Greenberg, George W Henderson III, William deR Holt, Donald R Hughes, Peyton R Latimer, J Kenneth Lesley, Bernard A Leventhal, Lanty L Smith, Abraham B Stenberg, George C Waldrep Jr, Arthur C Wiener. Staff Officers: Agustin J Diodati (Controller), John D Englar (VP, General Counsel and Secretary), E Barry James (VP, Fibers Purchasing), Peyton R Latimer (VP and Treasurer), J Kenneth Lesley (VP, Personnel and Public Relations), Robert T Abbott (Assistant Treasurer), Park R Davidson (Assistant VP, Finance), Barbara K Eisenberg (Assistant General Counsel), Emil F Garda (Assistant Treasurer, Credit), William D Lusk (Assistant Controller), Roy M Phipps, Jr (Assistant Treasurer), Roger M Rheaume (Assistant Controller), Robert H Stevens Jr (Assistant General Counsel). Ben F Tennille (Associate General Counsel), Robert B Underhill (Associate General Counsel)

PRINCIPAL ACTIVITIES: Burlington is the nation's largest and most diversified manufacturer of textiles and related products for apparel, the home and industry. The company manufactures and merchandises apparel fabrics, yarns, carpets, rugs, mattress tickings, draperies, upholstery fabrics, bedspreads, comforters, automotive fabrics and carpets and fabrics for industrial uses.
Principal Subsidiaries: Domestic: Burlington Automotive Fabrics; Burlington Blended Fabrics; Burlington Denim; Burlington Formed Fabrics; Burlington Glass Fabrics; Burlington Greige Sales; Burlington Home Sewing Fabrics; Burlington House Area Rugs; Burlington House Carpets; Burlington House Converter Fabrics; Burlington House Draperies; Burlington House Tickings; Burlington House Upholstery Fabrics; Burlington Impression Fabrics; Burlington Industrial Fabrics; Burlington Knitted Fabrics; Burlington Madison Yarn; Burlington Menswear; Burlington Performance Fabrics; Burlington Prints; Klopman Fabrics; Lees Carpets; Lees Commercial Carpets; C H Masland & Sons; Military Fabrics; Monticello Carpet Mills. International: Burlington Canada Inc (Canada); Burlington Carpet Mills Canada (Canada); Burlington Industries (Ireland) Limited (Eire); Burlington Sportswear Fabrics Limited (Eire); Klopman International SpA (Italy); Leedye, Inc (Canada); Masland of Canada, Ltd (Canada); Mitsubishi-Burlington Co Ltd (Japan); Nobilis-Lees SA de CV (Mexico); Textiles Morelos SA de CV (Mexico). Other: BI Transportation, Inc; Burlington Trading Company; Insuratex, Ltd (Bermuda); Valley Forge Information Service
Financial Information:

	Sep 28 1985 $'000	Sep 27 1986 $'000
Sales revenues	2,802,134	2,778,132
Income before taxes	7,505	106,435
Net income	12,574	56,531
Dividends	46,907	46,332
Dividends per share	$1.64	$1.64
Earnings per share*	$0.44	$1.98
Common stock	28,898	28,898
Retained income	992,371	1,002,570
Shareholders equity	1,158,811	1,188,423

*fully diluted

No of Employees: 43,000

BURLINGTON NORTHERN INC

999 Third Avenue, Seattle, WA 98104-4097
Tel: (206) 467-3838

Chairman: Richard M Bressler (and President and Chief Executive Officer); Vice Chairmen: Thomas H O'Leary, Gerald Grinstein, Travis H Petty
Senior Executive Officers: Christopher T Bayley (Senior VP Corporate Affairs), Allan R Boyce (Senior VP Human Resources), Luino Dell'Osso (Senior VP Finance and Planning)

PRINCIPAL ACTIVITIES: Burlington Northern Inc, through operating subsidiaries, is primarily engaged in transportation and natural resource businesses. The Company's principal business activities are a rail carrier system, a natural gas pipeline, the exploration, development, and production of oil, gas, coal, and other minerals, the sale of timber and logs primarily from land owned by the Company, the manufacture and sale of forest products, and motor carrier operations
Principal Subsidiaries: Meridian Oil Inc; Burlington Northern Railroad Co; El Paso Natural Gas Co; Glacier Park Co; Plum Creek Timber Co; Burlington Northern Motor Carriers Inc; Meridian Minerals Co
Financial Information:

	Dec 31 1985	Dec 31 1986
	$'000	$'000
Sales revenues	8,650,927	6,941,413
Income (loss) before taxes	1,040,196	(454,544)
Net income (loss)	596,488	(860,485)(1)
Dividends(2)	162,045	152,146
Dividends per common share	$1.40	$1.70(3)
Earnings (loss) per share	$7.19(4)	($12.07)(1)
Common stock(5)	797,523	808,636
Retained income	3,714,484	2,725,678
Shareholders equity	4,512,007	3,534,314

(1) after asset writedowns and accounting change. Pro forma net income excluding these items was $289.1 million or $3.46 per share
(2) total paid including preferred
(3) current dividend rate is $2.20 per share
(4) Pro forma net income and earnings per share assuming retroactive effect of change in railroad depreciation method of accounting would be $556,701 and $6.65 per share respectively
(5) less Treasury stock

No of Employees: 44,200

BURNDY CORPORATION

Richards Avenue, Norwalk, CT 06856
Tel: (203) 838-4444

Chairman: David Dibner
President: Theodore York
Senior Executive Officers: Frederick H McLenaghan (VP), Donald F Keating (VP Human Resources), Ramon V Nicholl (VP Management Systems Services), Ernest Fanwick (VP Legal Counsel and Secretary), Stanley J Aris (VP and Chief Financial Officer), Thomas H Pluff (VP, General Manager Electrical Group), William M Nuckols (VP, General Manager Electronics Group)

PRINCIPAL ACTIVITIES: Manufacture of electrical and electronic equipment
Principal Subsidiaries: Burndy International Inc
Principal Bank: Bankers Trust Company
Financial Information:

	$'000
Sales revenues	219,000

No of Employees: 4,350

BURNHAM CORPORATION

2 Main Street, Box 255, Irvington, NY 10533
Tel: (914) 591-8800

Chairman: John W Murray Jr
President: Richard E Olson
Senior Executive Officers: C Robert Jenkins (VP), John A McDonald (VP), Albert Morrison III (VP), Peter F Sherwood (VP and Treasurer)

PRINCIPAL ACTIVITIES: Manufacture of glazed buildings and glazing supplies; manufacture of cast iron products and heating and air conditioning equipment
Principal Subsidiaries: Lutton Co Inc
Principal Bank: Citibank NA
Financial Information:

	$'000
Sales revenues	119,000

No of Employees: 1,300

BURNHAM SERVICE CORPORATION

5000 Burnham Blvd, PO Box 7966, Columbus, GA 31908
Tel: (404) 563-1120

Chairman: Ray E Crowley (and Chief Executive Officer)
President: Chris J Martin
Senior Executive Officers: Calvin J Martin Jr (Executive VP), Mokhtar S Bazaraa (VP), William M Cole (VP), Gary R Manning (VP), Charles E Sasser (Senior VP), Joyce L Curry (Secretary), John H Karr (Treasurer), Samuel H Grubbs (Controller). Additional Subsidiary Officers: James B Herndon Jr (VP), Joseph C Hortman (VP), Paul F Keating (VP), Marvin J Schneider (VP), Len J Beaudoin (Assistant VP), Phil E Harris (Assistant VP), Laura G Rainer (Assistant VP)

PRINCIPAL ACTIVITIES: Burnham Service Corporation provides distribution, transportation, and related systems services for major corporations throughout the United States and for the relocation of personal effects for their employees. The company operates approximately 50 branch facilities in major US markets. This branch service network is supplemented by agents operating under Burnham's ICC authority
Principal Subsidiaries: Burnham Van Services Inc
Financial Information:

	Dec 31 1985	Dec 31 1986
	$'000	$'000
Revenues	103,268	110,201
Income before taxes	6,558	8,563
Net income	3,660	4,777
Dividends	976	1,065
Dividends per share	$0.22	$0.24
Earnings per share*	$0.82	$1.07
Common stock	22	22
Retained income	14,097	17,809
Shareholders equity	27,822	31,534

*primary

No of Employees: 1,000

BURNUP & SIMS INC

PO Box 15070, Plantation, FL 33318
Tel: (305) 587-4512

Chairman: Riley V Sims
President: Nick A Caporella (and Chief Executive Officer)
Senior Executive Officers: Leo J Hussey (Senior VP Operations), George B Bracken (VP Financial Planning), Edward L Grant (VP Business Development), Jack Brown (VP and Controller), John J Ekstrom (VP Financial Administration)

PRINCIPAL ACTIVITIES: Operation of television and telecommunications services
Principal Subsidiaries: Burnup & Sims Cablecom Inc; Burnup & Sims Comtec Inc; Burnup & Sims Engineering Inc; GDSI Inc; Burnup & Sims of CA Inc; Burnup & Sims of TX Inc; Burnup & Sims Telcom Inc; Capscan Cableco Inc; Deviney Construction Co; Fitton & Pittman Inc; Floyd Theatres Inc; Lectro Products Inc; Southeastern Printing Co Inc; Southwest Bottlers of FL Inc; Telink Inc
Principal Bank: Chemical Bank

Financial Information:

	$'000
Sales revenues	190,000

No of Employees: 3,900

BURR-BROWN CORPORATION

6730 S Tucson Blvd, PO Box 11400, Tucson, AZ 85706
Tel: (602) 746-1111
Cable: 666491
Telex: 759027

Chairman: Thomas R Brown Jr; Vice Chairman: Thomas J Troup (and Chief Financial Officer)
President: James J Burns (also Chief Executive Officer)
Senior Executive Officers: Frank M Myers (VP-Component Operations), Thomas W Fern (Senior VP-Strategic Sales Development), D Atkinson (VP-Finance), John Wyman (VP-Systems Products Operations), William Craft (Controller)

PRINCIPAL ACTIVITIES: Burr-Brown Corporation designs, manufactures and markets precision, highly reliable microelectronic components, subassemblies and microprocessor-based systems
Principal Subsidiaries and Divisions: Analog Products Division; Data Products Division; Microtechnology Division; Burr Brown Limited; Military Products Division; Data Acquisition and Control Systems Division
Principal Banks: Valley National Bank; First Interstate Bank
Financial Information:

	Dec 31 1985	Dec 31 1986
	$'000	$'000
Sales revenues	94,503	112,788
Income before taxes	7,484	6,820
Net income	4,768	3,736
Earnings per share	$0.50	$0.39
Common stock	24,878	25,200
Retained income	28,854	32,590
Shareholders equity	53,214	58,290

No of Employees: 1,445

BUSH HOG

PO Box 1039, Selma, AL 36701
Tel: (205) 872-6261

President: Bob Middlebrooks
Senior Executive Officers: Russell Buster (Executive VP)

PRINCIPAL ACTIVITIES: Manufacture of agricultural implements
Parent Company: Allied Products Corp
Principal Bank: Continental Illinois National Bank and Trust Co of Chicago
Financial Information:

	$'000
Sales revenues	50,000

No of Employees: 520

BUSH INDUSTRIES INC

312 Fair Oak Street, Little Valley, NY 14755
Tel: (716) 939 9101
Telex: WUT 919 177

Chairman: Paul S Bush (and President)
Senior Executive Officers: Harold R Andersen (Executive VP), William S Schaeffer (Executive VP), David G Messinger (VP), Donald F Hauck (VP Finance, Chief Financial Officer, Secretary and Treasurer)

PRINCIPAL ACTIVITIES: Manufacture of wooden furniture for household use
Financial Information:

	$'000
Sales revenues	41,670

No of Employees: 800

BUSINESS MENS ASSURANCE COMPANY OF AMERICA

BMA Tower, 700 Karnes Blvd, Kansas City, MO 64108
Tel: (816) 753-8000

Chairman: W D Grant (and Chief Executive Officer)
President: W T Grant II
Senior Executive Officers: Oscar R Klein (Executive VP and Chief Financial Officer), J K Bales (Executive VP and Secretary), R D Bates Sr (Senior VP Individual Insurance), R E Gunter (Senior VP Administration), P Anthony Jacobs (Senior VP Investment), R C Johnson (Senior VP Financial Management), G P Luger (Senior VP Corporate Research and Planning), R R Raynolds (Senior VP Administrative Services), J W Sayler Jr (Senior VP Group Insurance), J E Walker (Senior VP Reinsurance and Related Services), V W Voorhees II (Senior VP Finance)

PRINCIPAL ACTIVITIES: Life and health insurance; interests in property development and television broadcasting
Principal Subsidiaries: BMA Properties Inc; Assurance Life Co; Rebma CA Six Inc
Financial Information:

	Dec 31 1985
	$'000
Revenues	414,774
Net income	35,060
Earnings per share	$3.31
Shareholders equity	312,100

No of Employees: 2,110

BUTLER INTERNATIONAL, INC

110 Summit Ave, PO Box 460, Montvale, NJ 07645
Tel: (201) 573-8000

Chairman: N G Widmark; Vice Chairman: F R Einsidler (and President and Chief Executive Officer)
Senior Executive Officers: Reginald F Woods (Executive VP), Gary M Cademartori (Senior VP Finance), Dominick A Dattilo (Senior VP and Legal Counsel), Robert J Maguire (VP Taxes), Gerald R Cioci (VP and Treasurer), Marie Wolfson (VP Information Systems)

PRINCIPAL ACTIVITIES: Trucking services; aircraft services
Principal Subsidiaries: Butler Aviation International Inc; Butler Aviation Inc; Butler Aviation Commuter Services Inc; Butler Service Group Inc; Butler Telecommunications Group Inc; Butler Computer Graphics Inc; Scouthern Design Services Inc
Principal Bank: Chase Manhattan Bank
Financial Information:

	$'000
Sales revenues	365,000

No of Employees: 4,500

BUTLER, JOHN O, CO

4635 West Foster Avenue, Chicago, IL 60630
Tel: (312) 777 4000

Chairman: Emanuel B Tarrson (and Chief Executive Officer)
President: Ronald E Tarrson (and Chief Operating Officer and Treasurer)
Senior Executive Officers: Jordan H Krugel (Executive VP, Secretary and Chief Financial Officer), Gerry R Munroe (VP Division), Anita Sperry (VP Europe), David E Gordon (VP Marketing and Sales), James M Kowalczyk (VP Sales)

PRINCIPAL ACTIVITIES: Manufacture of dental supplies and equipment; brushes and brooms
Financial Information:

	$'000
Sales revenues	34,680

No of Employees: 400

BUTLER MANUFACTURING CO
BMA Tower, Kansas City, MO 64141
Tel: (816) 968-3000

Chairman: Robert H West
President: Donald H Pratt
Senior Executive Officers: Richard O Ballentyne (VP, Secretary and Legal Counsel), Robert J Kronschnabel (VP Manufacturing), Leslie V Rist (VP Finance and Treasurer), John R Moran (VP Systems), William D Chapman (VP International), John J Holland (VP and Controller)

PRINCIPAL ACTIVITIES: Manufacture of sectional buildings, agricultural equipment and electrical equipment
Principal Subsidiaries: Bucon Inc
Financial Information:

	Dec 31 1985	Dec 31 1985
	$'000	$'000
Sales revenues	497,892	576,850
Net income	10,630	3,625
Earnings per share	$2.01	$0.71
Shareholders equity	139,230	133,178

No of Employees: 3,800

C & J CLARK INC
See CLARK, C & J, INC

C 3 INC
11425 Isaac Newton Square S, Reston, VA 22090
Tel: (703) 471-6000
Telex: TWX 621 04470

Chairman: John G Ballenger (and President and Treasurer)
Senior Executive Officers: William E Gesell (VP Finance), Joseph Kenney (VP Manufacturing), Al Iwersen (VP Field Engineering)

PRINCIPAL ACTIVITIES: Computer systems, software and services
Principal Bank: United Virginia Bank
Financial Information:

	$'000
Sales revenues	72,000

No of Employees: 540

C A NORGREN CO
See NORGREN, C A, CO

C B FLEET CO, INC
See FLEET, C B, CO, INC

C BREWER & CO LTD
See BREWER, C, & CO LTD

C F HATHAWAY CO
See HATHAWAY, C F, CO

C H HEIST CORPORATION
See HEIST, C H, CORPORATION

C H MASLAND & SONS
See MASLAND, C H, & SONS

C R BARD INC
See BARD, C R, INC

C SCHMIDT & SONS, INC
See SCHMIDT, C, & SONS, INC

C&R CLOTHIERS INC
8660 Hayden Place, Culver City, CA 90232
Tel: (213) 559 8200

Chairman: Paul S Reisbord (and President)
Senior Executive Officers: Burton L Kieffer (Executive VP and Secretary), Joel S Adelman (VP Finance)

PRINCIPAL ACTIVITIES: Retail trade in men's clothing
Principal Bank: Union Bank
Financial Information:

	$'000
Sales revenues	57,240

No of Employees: 700

CABLE TV INDUSTRIES
5922 Bowcroft St, Los Angeles, CA 90016
Tel: (213) 202-2746

Chairman: George M Acker (and Chief Executive Officer)
President: Mark A Engler (and Chief Operating Officer and Chief Financial Officer)
Senior Executive Officers: Paul A Acker (Secretary and Director Marketing), H Frederick Bergamo (and VP Finance), William Krempasky (VP Sales)

PRINCIPAL ACTIVITIES: Manufacture of electrical and electronic equipment for cable TV
Principal Bank: Imperial Bank
Financial Information:

	$'000
Sales revenues	34,640

No of Employees: 125

CABLEVISION SYSTEMS CORPORATION
1 Media Crossways, Woodbury, NY 11797
Tel: (516) 364-8450

Chairman: Charles F Dolan (and Chief Executive Officer); Vice Chairmen: William J Bell, Francis F Randolph Jr
President: John Tatta (and Chief Operating Officer)
Senior Executive Officers: James A Kofalt (Executive VP), Marc A Lustgarten (Executive VP), Daniel T Sweeney (Senior VP), Robert S Lemie (VP, Legal Counsel and Secretary), Barry J O'Leary (VP and Treasurer), Jerry Shaw (Controller)

PRINCIPAL ACTIVITIES: Cable television
Financial Information:

	Dec 31 1986
	$'000
Sales revenues	151,000
Net (loss)	(7,000)

No of Employees: 1,000

CABOT CORPORATION
125 High Street, Boston, MA 02110
Tel: (617) 423-6000
Telex: WUT 940 975 cablak bsn A

Chairman: Louis W Cabot
President: Robert A Charpie
Senior Executive Officers: William D Manley (Executive VP), Norton Q Sloan (Executive VP), John G Cabot (Executive VP), Samuel B Coco Jr (Executive VP), Walter F Greeley (VP, Secretary and General Counsel)

PRINCIPAL ACTIVITIES: Production of carbon blacks, interests in oil and gas and pipelines, specialty metals, and engineered products
Principal Subsidiaries: Cabot Berylco Inc; Cabot International Capital Inc; Cabot Oil and Gas Corp; Cranberry Pipeline Corp; Distrigas Corp; Distrigas of MA Corp; Industrial Gas Corp; Big Sandy Gas Corp; Tuco Inc
Principal Bank: Chase Manhattan Bank

Financial Information:

	Sep 30 1986 $'000
Sales revenues	1,309,920
Net income	71,051
Earnings per share	$2.49
Shareholders equity	591,130

No of Employees: 7,700

CACI INTERNATIONAL INC

1700 N Moore St, 23rd Floor, Arlington, VA 22209
Tel: (703) 841 7800
Telex: 824416
Telefax: (703) 841-4645

Chairman: Herbert W Karr
President: J P London (and Chief Executive Officer)
Senior Executive Officers: John H Baker (Executive VP and Chief Financial Officer), Michael L Holshey (Executive VP), Jim Topping (Operating Division President), George Krikorian (Operating Division President), Ray Oleson (Operating Division President)

PRINCIPAL ACTIVITIES: CACI International is a high technology and professional services corporation. Founded in 1962, CACI is a leader in advanced information systems, systems engineering, logistics sciences, proprietary analytical software products, and market analysis consultancy services, information products, and systems. CACI markets include defense, aerospace, communications, energy, transportation and distribution, financial institutions, real estate, retailing, and many other sectors of public and private enterprise
Trade Names: CACI
Principal Subsidiaries: CACI Inc Federal
Principal Bank: Signet Bank
Financial Information:

	Jun 30 1986 $'000	Jun 30 1987 $'000
Sales revenues	98,699	118,830
Income before taxes	1,468	5,013
Net income	1,054	2,706
Earnings per share	$0.09	$0.22
Common stock	11,753	12,026
Retained income	15,953	18,658
Shareholders equity	16,653	19,385

Number of Shareholders: 2,100
No of Employees: 2,500

CADENCE INDUSTRIES CORPORATION

21 Hendersen Drive, West Caldwell, NJ 07006
Tel: (201) 227-5100

Chairman: Sheldon Feinberg (and President)
Senior Executive Officers: Paul Hindin (Executive VP Finance and Administration), James Foy (VP Financial Services), Joseph Calamari (VP and Associate Counsel)

PRINCIPAL ACTIVITIES: Publishing; pharmaceuticals; stationery supplies; theater management
Principal Subsidiaries: CC Studios Inc; CDE Inc; CDE Realty Co GSS Stamps Ltd; Saxon Theatre Corp of Boston; Gary Theatre Inc; Capri Theatre Inc; Sack Cheri II Inc; Sack Cheri III Inc; Sack Cheri Inc; Savoy II Inc; Curtis Books Inc; Curtis Circulation Co; Dash Inc; Hudson Pharmaceutical Corp; Hudson Pharmaceutical Corp NV; Vitamin Quota Inc; VPS Inc; Magazine Management Inc; Alexander Film Services Corp; Astro Profile Ltd; Perfect Subscription Co; Keystone Readers Service Inc; Moore-Cottrel Subscription Agency; US Pencil and Stationery Co; US Pen Co; US Pencil Co Inc
Principal Bank: The First National Bank of Boston
Financial Information:

	$'000
Sales revenues	97,000

No of Employees: 2,500

CADILLAC PLASTIC & CHEMICAL CO

530 Stephenson Hwy, Troy, MI 48007
Tel: (313) 583-1200
Telex: TWX 810 232 1886 cadco det

Chairman: William D Benkelman
President: Jack Nichols
Senior Executive Officers: Stephen M Augustyn (Executive VP and Treasurer)

PRINCIPAL ACTIVITIES: Plastics and plastic products
Trade Names: CADCO
Parent Company: Day International
Financial Information:

	$'000
Sales revenues	100,000

No of Employees: 1,000

CADILLAC RUBBER & PLASTICS, INC

05 W Seventh Street, Cadillac, MI 49601
Tel: (616) 775-1345
Telex: TWX 810 2913383 cad rub plas

President: Peter Barry (and Chief Operating Officer)
Senior Executive Officers: Steven Frisbie (VP Administration), William A Paul (VP Industrial Relations and Secretary), John Raffaele (VP and Treasurer), Michael Frederick (VP Marketing), Paul Taylor (VP and General Manager)

PRINCIPAL ACTIVITIES: Rubber and rubber products; plastic products
Principal Bank: National Bank of Detroit
Financial Information:

	$'000
Sales revenues	50,000

No of Employees: 800

CADMUS COMMUNICATIONS CORPORATION

2901 Byrdhill Road, Richmond, VA 23230
Tel: (804) 264 2885

Chairman: Wallace Stettinius (and Chief Executive Officer)
President: Don Davidson
Senior Executive Officers: Sherrill M Capps (VP and Secretary), C Stephenson Gillispie Jr (Group President), Arthur R Myers Jr (VP and Treasurer), John H Phillips (Group President), H Edward Stone (Division President)

PRINCIPAL ACTIVITIES: Printing services
Financial Information:

	$'000
Sales revenues	93,000

No of Employees: 1,300

CAESARS WORLD, INC

1801 Century Park East, Los Angeles, CA 90067
Tel: (213) 552-2711

Chairman: Henry Gluck (and Chief Executive Officer); Vice Chairman: M P Schweitzer
President: J T Lanni (and Chief Operating Officer)
Senior Executive Officers: Philip L Ball (Senior VP, Secretary and General Counsel), Roger Lee (Senior VP, Finance and Administration), Joseph LaGumina (VP Construction), Edwin L Getz (VP, Taxes), Jack Leone (VP Communications), Warren Salisbury (Senior VP, Corporate Security), Bruce Hinckley (VP, Controller)

PRINCIPAL ACTIVITIES: The operating entities of Caesars World, Inc and its subsidiaries provide domestic and international customers with a broad rnage of entertainment, gaming and resort experiences. Caesars World includes three renowned destination gaming resorts-Caesars Palace in Las Vegas, Nevada; and, through the Company's subsidiary, Caesars New Jersey Inc, Caesars Atlantic City. We also have four resorts in the Pocono mountains of Pennsylvania:

Caesars Cove Haven, Caesars Paradise Stream, Caesars Pocono Palace, and Caesars Brookdale
Principal Subsidiaries: Caesars New Jersey Inc (86.6%)
Principal Bank: Security Pacific National Bank
Financial Information:

	Jul 31 1986	Jul 31 1987
	$'000	$'000
Sales revenues	688,225	779,693
Income before taxes	80,349	83,497
Net income	41,017	33,695
Earnings per share	$1.36	$1.08
Common stock	161,247	275,577
Retained income	108,736	142,431
Shareholders equity	269,774	417,441

No of Employees: 9,981

CAGLE'S INC

1155 Hammond Drive N E, Atlanta, GA 30328
Tel: (404) 394-8223

Chairman: W E Strain
President: J D Cagle (and Chief Executive Officer)
Senior Executive Officers: James M Evans (VP), C W May (VP, Sales), Kenneth R Bardley (Secretary and Treasurer)

PRINCIPAL ACTIVITIES: Rearing of poultry; processing of poultry products
Principal Subsidiaries: Strain Poultry Farms Inc
Financial Information:

	$'000
Sales revenues	133,000

No of Employees: 2,150

CAI DIVISION

550 W Northwest Hwy, Barrington, IL 60010
Tel: (312) 381-2400
Telex: TWX 910 6511 904 cai recop bgtn

President: L G Larson
Senior Executive Officers: R J Kay (Senior VP Finance and Administration), K M Jackson (VP Contracts), R P Hansen (VP Manufacturing), F J Wilmers (VP Engineering), R Broda (VP Quality Assurance), E Kazubowski (VP Marketing), R Gillespie (VP Business Development), W L Owens (VP Program Management)

PRINCIPAL ACTIVITIES: Photographic equipment and supplies for aerial photography
Parent Company: Bourns Inc through Recon-Optical Inc
Principal Bank: Harris Trust Company
Financial Information:

	$'000
Sales revenues	96,000

No of Employees: 1,000

CAIN & BULTMAN

2145 Dennis Street, Jacksonville, FL 32202
Tel: (904) 356-4812
Telex: TWX 810 827 0343 c & b inc jax

Chairman: Norwood H Sandifer
President: Thomas N Sandifer
Senior Executive Officers: Edward C Spivey (Executive VP Personnel and Purchasing and Comptroller), W R Faircloth (VP Sales), P J Serino (VP Tampa Division), Don Gies (VP Miami Division), J H Swanson (VP Sales), J B Teeters (VP Sales), R Ashby (VP Sales), B W O'Steen (VP Sales), M W Griese (VP Orlando Division), L Bauer (VP Atlanta Division)

PRINCIPAL ACTIVITIES: Trade in domestic electrical appliances and data processing equipment
Principal Bank: Barnett Bank of Jacksonville
Financial Information:

	$'000
Sales revenues	183,000

No of Employees: 550

CAIN, JOHN E, CO

Cains Corner, Ayer, MA 01432
Tel: (617) 772-0300

Chairman: Robert H Cain
President: Eugene E Wejman
Senior Executive Officers: Sidney W Farnsworth (VP Manufacturing), George M Herrick (VP Finance and Treasurer)

PRINCIPAL ACTIVITIES: Sauces and other relishes
Principal Bank: Brown Brothers Harriman & Co
Financial Information:

	$'000
Sales revenues	50,000

No of Employees: 300

CALCASIEU-MARINE NATIONAL BANK

844 Ryan Street, Lake Charles, LA 70601
Tel: (318) 439-4541
Telex: TWX 510 9717 513 mj calbank lkc

Chairman: William B Lawton; Vice Chairman: Jack E Lawton
President: J L McGough
Senior Executive Officers: W W Thompson (Executive VP), J M Duhon (Senior VP and Chief Operating Officer), Wayne Gabbert (Senior VP and Chief Commercial Loan Officer), Arthur T Burch (Senior VP and Cashier), Andrew Reed (Senior VP and Branch Manager), Robert W Enos (Senior VP Personnel), Herbert L Ryder (Senior VP), Steve Broussard (Senior VP Loan), Gordon Steen (Senior VP Computer Services)

PRINCIPAL ACTIVITIES: Banking

No of Employees: 650

CALCOMP INC

2411 W La Palma Avenue, Anaheim, CA 92801
Tel: (714) 821-2000 or (800) CALCOMP
Telex: 188746 CALCOMP
Telefax: TWX: 910-591-1154

President: William P Conlin
Senior Executive Officers: Roger M Damphousse (VP/General Manager, Display Products Division), Gary R Long (VP/General Manager, Digitizer Products Division), Larry Sanders (VP, Sales and Marketing), James R Gowan (VP, Sales), Carolyn M Monfore (VP, Marketing Services), William O'Brien (VP, Customer Service), Joseph E Smith (VP, Marketing Operations), David L Schlotterbeck (VP/General Manager, Plotter Products Division), Kenneth D Van Kleeck (VP, Finance and Administration), Charles Furniss (VP, Human Resources), Roy A Young (VP, Information Services)

PRINCIPAL ACTIVITIES: Manufacture of computer graphics peripherals
Trade Names: CalComp, ColorMaster, Vistagraphic, Vistagraf, Enviroclean
Parent Company: Lockheed Corporation, Calabasas, CA
Principal Bank: Wells Fargo Bank
Financial Information:

	$'000
Sales revenues	355,000

No of Employees: 2,800

CALFED INC

5670 Wilshire Boulevard, Los Angeles, CA 90036
Tel: (213) 932-4200
Telex: (213) 932-2869

Chairman: Robert R Dockson

President: Gorge P Rutland
Senior Executive Officers: William L Callender (Executive VP, General Counsel and Corporate Secretary), Thomas H Dooley (Executive VP, Chief Financial Officer and Treasurer), James B Jacobson (Executive VP), David W Glenn (Senior VP Strategic Planning and Acquisitions), Jerry A St Dennis (Senior VP Chief Econimist, Asset-Liability Management), James R Wegge Jr (Senior VP Tax Planning and Research), James F Hurley (VP Corporate Communications), Omar F Johnson Jr (VP Internal Audit), Thomas E Smith (VP Special Projects)

PRINCIPAL ACTIVITIES: Consumer banking, commercial banking, home mortgage lending, life insurance and annuity products, trust and investment services, consumer finance
Principal Subsidiaries: Beneficial Standard Insurance Company; California Federal Savings and Loan Association; California Thrift and Loan; Trust Services of America Inc
Financial Information:

	Dec 31 1986
	$'000
Net income	164,400
Earnings per share	$7.03
Shareholders equity	1,168,900
Deposits	15,486,500
Total assets	20,552,900

No of Employees: 6,800

CALIFORNIA & HAWAIIAN SUGAR CO

One California Street, San Francisco, CA 94111
Tel: (415) 772-3800
Telex: TWX 910 372 6117 ch sugar sfo

Chairman: J W Buyers; Vice Chairman: R J Pfeiffer
President: John B Bunker (and Chief Executive Officer)
Senior Executive Officers: H R Somerset (Executive VP), J C Jaeger (Senior VP Finance and Treasurer), James M Burt (Senior VP Sales and Marketing), William H Stewart (Senior VP Operations), Richard A DeTata (VP Industrial Products), Daniel C Croker (VP Grocery Products), R L Knecht (VP Refinery Operations), D T Hanson (VP Personnel and Industrial Relations), G A Nelson (VP and Controller), T W Rowland (VP, Secretary and Legal Counsel)

PRINCIPAL ACTIVITIES: Sugar refining
Financial Information:

	Dec 31 1986
	$'000
Sales revenues	526,260
Shareholders equity	51,070

No of Employees: 1,400

CALIFORNIA CEDAR PRODUCTS CO

1345 W Washington Street, Stockton, CA 95201
Tel: (209) 944-5800
Telex: WUT 35 94 83 cedarprod st o

Chairman: Charles P Berolzheimer
President: Philip C Berolzheimer
Senior Executive Officers: James Baker (VP), R W Stewart (Treasurer), D R Wilson (Secretary)

PRINCIPAL ACTIVITIES: Timber products
Principal Bank: Bank of California
Financial Information:

	$'000
Sales revenues	55,000

No of Employees: 650

CALIFORNIA FIRST BANK

350 California Street, San Francisco, CA 94104
Tel: (415) 445-0200
Telex: RCA 278452 cf bk ur

Chairman: Toshio Nagamura
President: Seishichi Itoh (and Chief Executive Officer)
Senior Executive Officers: James R Gibson (Executive VP), Taisuke Shimizu (Executive VP and Chief Financial Officer), Yoshiaki Shibusawa (Executive VP), Donald A Burnell Jr (Senior VP and Treasurer)

PRINCIPAL ACTIVITIES: Banking
Parent Company: Bank of Tokyo Ltd (77%)
Principal Subsidiaries: Bankers Commercial Corporation; Cal First Properties Inc; CFB Venture Capital Corp
Financial Information:

	Dec 31 1985	Dec 31 1986
	$'000	$'000
Net income	25,580	30,733
Earnings per share	$2.26	$2.61
Shareholders equity	282,410	311,105
Deposits	4,698,330	5,268,106
Total assets	5,401,040	5,995,907

No of Employees: 3,942

CALIFORNIA MICROWAVE, INC

990 Almanor Avenue, Sunnyvale, CA 94086
Tel: (408) 732-4000
Telex: WUT 352016 calmic a suvl

Chairman: David B Leeson
President: Gilbert J Johnson (and Chief Operating Officer)
Senior Executive Officers: Dave E Hershberg (VP, President Satellite Transmission Systems Inc), Joseph Russell (VP, President Government Electronics Division), George L Spillane (VP Finance and Chief Financial Officer)

PRINCIPAL ACTIVITIES: Manufacture of communications and intelligence equipment; electronic equipment
Principal Subsidiaries: Satellite Transmission Systems Inc
Principal Bank: Bank of America
Financial Information:

	Jun 30 1986	Jun 30 1987
	$'000	$'000
Sales revenues	104,421	97,657
Income (loss) before taxes	7,881	(12,520)
Net income (loss)	4,418	(7,193)
Earnings (loss) per share	$0.55	($0.91)
Common stock	1,962	1,983
Number of shares*	8,086	7,910
Retained income	29,614	22,421
Shareholders equity	46,438	40,137

*average

No of Employees: 780

CALIFORNIA MILLING CORPORATION

1861 E 55th Street, Los Angeles, CA 90058
Tel: (213) 585-0131
Telex: WUT 698 264 calif mill lsa

Chairman: Frank Viault Jr
President: Clifton Capps (and Treasurer)
Senior Executive Officers: Edward F Stapelton (Senior VP and Secretary), Dennis R Tofte (VP Finance), Ron Miller (VP Marketing and Sales), John Ruland (VP Manufacturing)

PRINCIPAL ACTIVITIES: Milling; cereal products; snack products
Parent Company: Pillsbury Co
Principal Bank: Security Pacific National Bank
Financial Information:

	$'000
Sales revenues	60,000

No of Employees: 200

CALIFORNIA PORTLAND CEMENT CO

3200 San Fernando Road, Los Angeles, CA 90065
Tel: (213) 680-2316

Senior Executive Officers: Ronald E Evans (Executive VP and General Manager), W B Jager (VP California Sales), Anthony E Sarris (VP Operations and Engineering), M D Ross (VP Coal), Skit Corley (VP Arizona Sales), Robert Lamp (VP Manufacturing)

PRINCIPAL ACTIVITIES: Manufacture and sale of portland cement; coal mining; limestone products
Parent Company: CalMat Company, Los Angeles, CA
Financial Information:

	$'000
Sales revenues	160,000

No of Employees: 1,000

CALIFORNIA WATER SERVICE COMPANY

1720 North First Street, San Jose, CA 95112
Tel: (408) 298 1414

Chairman: Ralph D Lindberg (and Chief Executive Officer)
President: C H Stump (and Chief Operating Officer)
Senior Executive Officers: Donald L Houck (VP), Harold C Ulrich (VP, Chief Financial Officer and Treasurer), Jeptha A Wade Jr (VP), Gerald F Feeney (Controller, Assistant Secretary and Assistant Treasurer), Lester E Saxe (Secretary)

PRINCIPAL ACTIVITIES: Water supply
Principal Bank: Wells Fargo Bank
Financial Information:

	$'000
Sales revenues	104,650

No of Empioyees: 530

CALLON PETROLEUM COMPANY

200 North Canal Street, Natchez, MS 39120
Tel: (601) 442 1601

Chairman: John S Callon (and Chief Executive Officer)
President: Fred L Callon (and Chief Operating Officer)
Senior Executive Officers: I Meade Hufford (Senior VP), Wayne A Potter (Senior VP Finance), George Beylouni Jr (Senior VP Marketing), H Michael Tatum Jr (VP), John G Warren (VP and Controller), John S Weatherly (VP and Treasurer), William D Cheyney Jr (VP Production), Dennis W Christian (VP), Ed R Killian (Senior VP Exploration and Production)

PRINCIPAL ACTIVITIES: Exploration and production of petroleum and natural gas
Principal Subsidiaries: Callon Energy Services Inc
Principal Bank: Continental Illinois National Bank and Trust Company
Financial Information:

	$'000
Sales revenues	34,000

No of Employees: 380

CAL-MAINE FOODS, INC

3320 Woodrow Wilson, Jackson, MS 39207
Tel: (601) 948-6813
Telex: TWX 810 9662745 cal-maine jks

Chairman: Fred Adams Jr (and President and Chief Executive Officer)
Senior Executive Officers: R K Looper (Executive VP and Chief Operating Officer), Bobby J Rains (VP, Treasurer and Chief Financial Officer), Joe Wyatt (VP), Bob Johns (VP), Jack Self (VP)

PRINCIPAL ACTIVITIES: Poultry and egg processing; food products
Principal Subsidiaries: Dairy Fresh Products Co; Demler Farms Inc; EVPA Inc; Market Produce Co Albuquerque; Nationwide Distributors and Broking Co
Principal Bank: First National Bank of Jackson
Financial Information:

	$'000
Sales revenues	165,000

No of Employees: 1,000

CALMAR INC

40 Stirling Road, Watchung, NJ 07060
Tel: (201) 561-7700

Chairman: William J Koslo
President: Donald E Knox (and Chief Executive Officer)
Senior Executive Officers: Richard L Harris (Senior VP Marketing and Sales), C R Huebner (VP Finance), Douglas Corsette (VP Technical Services, Albert J Bailer (VP Manufacturing)

PRINCIPAL ACTIVITIES: Plastics and plastic products including bottle closures and pump sprayers
Principal Bank: Wachovia Bank and Trust Co
Financial Information:

	$'000
Sales revenues	99,000

No of Employees: 1,000

CALMAT CO

3200 San Fernando Road, Los Angeles, CA 90065
Tel: (213) 258-2777

Chairman: William Jenkins (and Chief Executive Officer); Vice Chairman: Michael A Morphy
President: A F Gerstell (and Chief Operating Officer)
Senior Executive Officers: R E Evans (Executive VP and General Manager California Portland Cement Division), M J Kerstetter (Executive VP and General Manager ConRock Division), Thomas M Linden (Executive VP and General Manager Properties Division), Ronald C Hadfield (Senior VP Finance and Chief Financial Officer), S J Wilcott (Senior VP and Secretary), G R Block (VP Property), D S Cahn (VP), Wilbur B Jager (VP Marketing), John G S Mills (VP and Chief Accounting Officer), Anthony E Sarris (VP Technical Services)

PRINCIPAL ACTIVITIES: Production of cement; mining and quarrying; real estate
Principal Subsidiaries: California Portland Cement Co; ConRock Co; CalMat Co of AZ; CalMat Properties Co; Palomar Transit Mix Co; Reliance Transport Co; Sloan Canyon Sand Co; Statex Petroleum Inc; Valley Reclamation Co
Principal Bank: Security Pacific National Bank
Financial Information:

	Dec 31 1986 $'000
Sales revenues	605,928
Net income	44,100
Earnings per share	$1.44
Shareholders equity	370,720

No of Employees: 2,500

CALNY INC

1650 Borel Place, Suite 101, San Mateo, CA 94402
Tel: (415) 574 2455

Chairman: Virgil D Dardi; Vice Chairman: Marvin C Bonine
President: R T Larive (and Chief Executive Officer)
Senior Executive Officers: William F Ahern (Executive VP and Chief Financial Officer), John C O'Donnell (Senior VP), James B Thompson (Secretary), K R Massara (VP Marketing and Public Relations), James W Walker (VP and Chief Operating Officer), John R Diehl (VP, Treasurer and Chief Financial Officer)

PRINCIPAL ACTIVITIES: Restaurant chain and franchising services
Principal Bank: Bank of America

Financial Information:

	$'000
Sales revenues	44,000

No of Employees: 2,000

CALSPAN CORPORATION

PO Box 400, Buffalo, NY 14225
Tel: (716) 632-7500

President: H R Leland
Senior Executive Officers: Robert J Walker (VP Marketing), Wallace R Vaughn (VP Finance), Paul V Marrone (VP Experimental Research), D B Dahm (VP Electronic Warfare and Space), Miles W Hall (VP Systems ATC), Charles E Treanor (VP Chief Scientist ATC), Paul J Brodnicki (VP Systems), King D Bird (VP AEDC Division ATC), Anthony L Russo (VP Franklin Research Centre), Charles K Akers (VP Chemical Defense Programs)

PRINCIPAL ACTIVITIES: Research and development services; automobile components; domestic electrical equipment; home entertainment equipment
Parent Company: Arvin Industries, Columbus, IN
Principal Bank: Manufacturers and Traders Trust Company
Financial Information:

	$'000
Sales revenues	100,000

No of Employees: 2,000

CALUMET INDUSTRIES, INC

303 E Wacker Drive, Chicago, IL 60601
Tel: (312) 726-6171

Chairman: S M Salvino (and President and Chief Executive Officer)
Senior Executive Officers: Roger W Garey (Senior VP and Secretary), Gerald L Lepinske (VP Research), Walter W Little (VP and Treasurer), Miller Williams (VP), John M Dillon (Controller), Henry L Vornkahl (VP)

PRINCIPAL ACTIVITIES: Oil refining; production of petrochemicals and oil related products
Principal Bank: Continental Illinois National Bank and Trust Company of Chicago
Financial Information:

	$'000
Sales revenues	60,000

No of Employees: 160

CAMCO, INC

7010 Ardmore Street, Houston, TX 77021
Tel: (713) 747-4000
Telex: WUT 790 528 camco hou

Chairman: David M Veit
President: Gilbert H Tausch (and Chief Executive Officer)
Senior Executive Officers: Dick Koons (Senior VP Operations), Merle Muckleroy (Senior VP Sales and Servicing), Herb Yates (VP Finance), Steve Fotiades (VP Sales Eastern Hemisphere), Steve Smith (VP Subsidiary Operations), Roy Caldwell (VP Engineering and Research), Bill Pursell (VP Manufacturing), Jack Hill (VP Marketing), Don Eastwood (VP Western Hemisphere)

PRINCIPAL ACTIVITIES: Manufacture of valves; control equipment; data processing equipment; oilfield services
Principal Subsidiaries: Camco International Capital Corp; Camco International Sales Corp; Camco Services International Inc; Camco Trading Corp; Comco Wireline Line; Tejas Controls Inc
Principal Bank: First City National Bank
Financial Information:

	$'000
Sales revenues	175,000

No of Employees: 2,400

CAMDEN WIRE CO, INC

12 Masonic Avenue, Camden, NY 13316
Tel: (315) 245-2000

Chairman: Frank M Crawford (and Chief Executive Officer)
President: Samuel J Lanzafame
Senior Executive Officers: Terry M French (Executive VP and Chief Operating Officer), M E Fenton (VP Administration), Henry Hilliker (VP Manufacturing), Donald R Buck (VP Sales), Scott J McLallen (VP Finance and Treasurer), Karl E Anna (VP Procurement)

PRINCIPAL ACTIVITIES: Camden Wire Co, Inc, a supplier of copper conductor wire, produces bare or tinned copper wire in concentric bunched rope, stranded, braided and extra flexible stranded forms, as well as tin or alloy electroplated wire. Camden's customers include manufacturers of insulated wire and cable, carbon brushes and circuit-breaking resistors and capacitors for use in transformers, generators, motors and appliances. Camden also produces a variety of cables used in the aircraft industry and braided cables used extensively in the automotive field
Parent Company: Oneida Ltd, Oneida, NY
Principal Bank: Oneida National Bank and Trust
Financial Information:

	$'000
Sales revenues	87,000

No of Employees: 870

CAMERON IRON WORKS, INC

PO Box 1212, Houston, TX 77251
Tel: (713) 939-2211
Telex: WUT 775 422 camiron hou a

Chairman: P J Burguieres (and President and Chief Executive Officer)
Senior Executive Officers: John D Deakins (Senior VP Finance), K L Hardcastle (Senior VP and General Manager Forged Products), C B King (Senior VP and General Manager Oil Tool)

PRINCIPAL ACTIVITIES: Cameron Iron Works Inc is a vertically integrated company engaged in designing, manufacturing and marketing a broad range of oil tools, ball valves and forged products. These products are used by many industries, including oi and gas drilling and production, aviation and power generation
Principal Bank: Texas Commerce Bank
Financial Information:

	Jun 30 1986	Jun 30 1987
	$'000	$'000
Sales revenues	616,209	485,027
Income (loss) before taxes	12,131	(106,325)
Net income (loss)	4,639	(110,657)
Dividends	3,639	1,219
Dividends per share	$0.12	$0.04
Earnings (loss) per share	$0.15	($3.62)
Common stock	6,375	6,377
Retained income	426,010	314,626
Shareholders equity	361,481	335,672

Principal Shareholders: George Anderson Robinson 1967 Trust(1) (23.51%); Jamie Abercrombie Robinson 1967 Trust(1) (23.51%); Josephine E Abercrombie (8.33%); Directors and Officers (10.24%)
No of Employees: 4,578

CAMPBELL INDUSTRIES

501 Harbor Drive, San Diego, CA 92112
Tel: (714) 233-7115

Chairman: Peter G Schmidt (and President)
Senior Executive Officers: Robert Allen (VP and General Manager), Paul A Gilliland (VP), Howard Raymond (VP)

PRINCIPAL ACTIVITIES: Shipbuilding and marine engineering
Parent Company: Marine Construction and Design Co

Principal Bank: Bank of America
Financial Information:

	$'000
Sales revenues	50,000

No of Employees: 500

CAMPBELL SOUP COMPANY

Campbell Place, Camden, NJ 08101
Tel: (609) 964-4000
Telex: ITT 476 1154 camelsp cmdn

Chairman: William S Cashel Jr
President: R Gordon McGovern (and Chief Executive Officer)
Senior Executive Officers: A M Williams (Executive VP and President, Campbell International), Arnold E Denton (Senior VP and President, Campbell Institute for Research and Technology), Herbert M Baum (Senior VP and President, Campbell USA), Edwin L Harper (Senior VP and Chief Financial Officer), Carl V Stinnett (VP, Sales and Marketing)

PRINCIPAL ACTIVITIES: Manufacture of canned foods, fish, pet foods, food ingredients, canned vegetables, fruit juices, frozen foods, bakery products, dry foods, candy, pickles, sauces, cheese specialties; health and fitness products; mail order, retail snack shop and restaurants; distributor of fresh fruits and vegetables
Principal Subsidiaries: United States:- CSC Advertising Inc; Campbell Finance Corp; Campbell Hospitality Inc; Campbell Investment Company; Campbell Sales Company; Campbell Soup Company (Sumter Plant) Inc; Campbell Soup (Texas) Inc; Camsco Produce Company Inc; Casera Foods, Inc; Champion Valley Farms Inc; Dixon Canning Corp; Domsea Farms Inc; Fine Oven Products Inc; Godiva Chocalatier Inc; Herider Farms Inc; Joseph Campbell Company; Juice Bowl Products Inc; Martino's Bakery Inc; Mendelson-Zeller Co Inc; Mrs Paul's Kitchens Inc; Pepperidge Farm Incorporated; Pepperidge Farm Mail Order Company Inc; Pietro's Corp; Snow King Frozen Foods Inc; Southeastern Wisconsin Products Company Inc; Triangle Manufacturing Corp; Valley Tomato Products Inc; Vlasic Foods Inc; Win Schuler Foods Inc. Other Countries:-Swift-Armour Sociedad Anonima Argentina (Argentina); Campbell's Soups (Aust) Pty Limited (Australia); NV Biscuits Delacre SA (Belgium); Continental Foods Company SA (Belgium); Campbell Soup Company Ltd (Canada); Campbell's Soups Limited (UK); Unger Meats Limited (UK); Société Française des Biscuits Delacre SA (France); Conservanfabrik Eugen Lacroix GmbH (West Germany); D Lazzaroni & C.SpA (Italy); Campbell's Soups SpA (Italy); Campbell Japan Incorporated (Japan); Campbell's de Mexico SA de CV (Mexico); Sinalopasta SA de CV (Mexico); Campbell Nederland BV (Netherlands); Campbell Soup Overseas Finance NV (Netherlands Antilles)
Financial Information:

	Jul 28 1985	Jul 31 1986
	$'000	$'000
Sales revenues	3,988,705	4,378,714
Net income	197,824	223,223
Earnings per share	$3.06	$3.45
Shareholders equity	1,382,487	1,538,880

No of Employees: 44,716

CAMPBELL TAGART, INC

6211 Lemmon Avenue, Dallas, TX 75209
Tel: (214) 358-9211
Telex: WUT 730 728 camtag dal

President: C B Lane Jr (and Chief Executive Officer)
Senior Executive Officers: Jose M Rubi (Executive VP Bakery Division), David S Leavenworth (Executive VP Administration and Diversified), Henry J Himmelberg (VP and Controller), B L Bowden (VP Cost Control), Thomas E Burnett (VP Marketing and Operations), Howard Chambers (VP Education), R C Clack Jr (VP Labor Relations), Frank R Goley (VP Engineering), Richard L Green (VP Risk Management), Jaime Iglesias (VP International), Michael D Kafoure (VP National Accounts), Bill M Keith (VP Special Marketing Projects), James Lannom (VP Management Information Systems), R Gordon Manning (VP Western Bakery Operations), T E Mason (VP and Treasurer), Ellis W McCracken Jr (VP and Legal Counsel), William R Palmer (VP Eastern Bakery Operation), John Piotrowski (VP Planning and Development), Ken Schierling (VP Office Services), Harold D Slankard (VP Human Resources), Paul A Wright (VP Product Services), Eugene Wisakowsky (VP Quality Control)

PRINCIPAL ACTIVITIES: Bakery products
Parent Company: Anheuser-Busch Companies Inc
Principal Bank: Interfirst Bank Dallas
Financial Information:

	$'000
Sales revenues	1,260,000

No of Employees: 22,000

CANANDAIGUA WINE CO INC

116 Buffalo Street, Canandaigua, NY 14424
Tel: (716) 394-3630

President: Marvin Sands
Senior Executive Officers: Richard Sands (Executive VP), Bertram E Silk (VP Winery Operations), Joseph McDonald (VP Advertising and Marketing Services), Robert I Huntington (VP Marketing and Sales), Raymond C Bumpus (VP National Sales), Stafford H Krause (Secretary and Treasurer)

PRINCIPAL ACTIVITIES: Production of wine
Principal Subsidiaries: Batavia Wine Cellars Inc; Bisceglia Brothers Wine Co; Richard Wine Cellars Inc; Tenner Brothers Inc
Principal Bank: Lincoln First Bank of Rochester
Financial Information:

	$'000
Sales revenues	134,000

No of Employees: 460

CANNON GROUP INC

640 San Vicente Boulevard, Los Angeles, CA 90048
Tel: (213) 658 2100

Chairman: Menahem Golan
President: Yoram Globus (and Chief Executive Officer)
Senior Executive Officers: Barry Lublin (Executive VP and Chief Financial Officer), Christopher Pearce (Executive VP and Chief Operating Officer), Tom Berman (Executive VP National Sales, Cannon Releasing Corp), Henry Weinstein (Executive VP, Production Head Camon Films Inc), Lisbeth Aschenbrenner (VP, Legal Counsel and Secretary), David Burkhardt (VP), Elizabeth Mackiewicz (VP and Assistant Secretary), William Steinbach (VP and Treasurer), Richard Nissenbaum (Controller), Barry Jenkins (VP Managing Director Cannon Classic Cinemas Ltd), Priscilla McDonald (VP Advertising and Publicity Cannon Films Inc)

PRINCIPAL ACTIVITIES: Production and distribution of motion pictures
Principal Bank: Wells Fargo Bank
Financial Information:

	$'000
Sales revenues	150,830

No of Employees: 1,300

CANTOR, EDWARD A, AFFILIATED INTERESTS

1203 West St George Avenue, Linden, NJ 07036
Tel: (201) 925-6650

Chairman: Edward A Cantor (and President)
Senior Executive Officers: Leo Masin (Executive VP), Irving Fabricant (VP and Comptroller), Robert D Fair (Assistant VP Engineering and Construction)

PRINCIPAL ACTIVITIES: Edward A Cantor and its many affiliated corporations are involved in four general aspects of the real estate business as well as manufacturing. The four areas are: Constructing properties to realize an immediate profit or to maintain an interest in their future appreciation; Sale of properties from its portfolio after long holding periods; Managing properties acquired and those of others with a view toward enhancing their economic value and marketability; Acquiring real estate properties or real estate companies
Principal Subsidiaries: (100% owned unless stated): Edward Construction Corp and its subsidiaries: N J Industrial Properties (80%); Milweed Industrials Inc (80%); Edward A Cantor Affiliated Interests Inc (80%); Lupas Corporation (80%); Space Products Corp (85%); P B W Inc (80%); Industrial Previews Inc (80%); Edward Leasing Corporation
Principal Bank: National State Bank
Financial Information:

	$'000
Group revenues	108,000

No of Employees: 160

CAPITAL CITIES COMMUNICATIONS/ABC INC

24 E 51st Street, New York, NY 10022
Tel: (212) 421-9595
Telex: TWX 710 5815646 cap cities nyk

Chairman: Thomas S Murphy (and Chief Executive Officer)
President: Daniel B Burke (and Chief Operating Officer)
Senior Executive Officers: Joseph P Dougherty (Executive VP), John B Fairchild (Executive VP), William R James (Executive VP), John B Sias (Executive VP), Ronald J Doerfler (Senior VP and Chief Financial Officer), Andrew E Jackson (VP Community Relations)

PRINCIPAL ACTIVITIES: Radio and television broadcasting including cable television; publishing of newspapers
Principal Subsidiaries: Capital Cities Cable Inc; Tele Hi Fi Co Inc; Capital Cities Media Inc; Clear Cablevision Inc; Institutional Investor Inc; Kansas City Star Co; Marks Cablevision of Green Inc; Oakland Press Co; Omnicom of MI Inc; Sandoval County Cable TV Inc; Satellite Cablevision Inc; Securities Data Corp
Financial Information:

	Dec 31 1985	Dec 31 1986
	$'000	$'000
Sales revenues	1,020,880	4,124,374
Net income	142,222	447,689
Earnings per share	$10.87	$27.55
Shareholders equity	889,260	1,948,627

No of Employees: 19,960

CAPITAL HOLDING CORPORATION

Commonwealth Bldg, Louisville, KY 40202
Tel: (502) 560-2000

Chairman: Thomas C Simons (and Chief Executive Officer)
President: Robert T Rakich
Senior Executive Officers: John A Franco (President Agency Group), Irving W Bailey II (Executive VP and Chief Investment Officer), Theodore S Rosky (Executive VP and Chief Financial Officer), Stephen B Bonner (Executive VP and General Counsel), Robert W Crispin (Senior VP)

PRINCIPAL ACTIVITIES: Holding company with interests in financial services, life insurance and fire, accident, health and casualty insurance
Principal Subsidiaries: Capital Enterprise Insurance Group; Capital Ventures Corp; Commonwealth Building Inc; Commonwealth Life Insurance Co; Georgia International Life Insurance Co; Home Security Life Insurance Co Inc; Home Security Fire and Casualty Insurance Co; National Home and Life Assurance Co; National Liberty Corp; National Liberty Marketing Inc; Valley Forge Associates Inc; National Standard Life Insurance Co; Peoples Life Insurance Co

Financial Information:

	Dec 31 1986
	$'000
Revenues	2,300,000
Net income	148,000

No of Employees: 8,500

CAPITAL WIRE & CABLE CORPORATION

910 10th Street, Plano, TX 75074
Tel: (214) 423-6565

President: Vincent A Rego
Senior Executive Officers: Donald M Spurgin (Executive VP), Charles J Woodward (VP Sales), Billy E Lewis (VP Purchasing), Phil Pringle (VP Engineering), Joe Gibson (VP Manufacturing), J D Ward (VP Finance), James Grier (VP Plastics)

PRINCIPAL ACTIVITIES: Manufacture of cables and wires
Principal Bank: First National Bank of Dallas
Financial Information:

	$'000
Sales revenues	70,000

No of Employees: 300

CAPITOL BANCORPORATION

1 Bullfinch Place, Boston, MA 02114
Tel: (617) 723 5300

Chairman: Sherwood J Tarlow (and President)
Senior Executive Officers: James R Degiacomo (Financial), John E Parigian (Treasurer)

PRINCIPAL ACTIVITIES: Banking
Principal Subsidiaries: Capitol Bank and Trust Co; Globe Financial Services Inc
Principal Bank: Shawmut Bank
Financial Information:

	Dec 31 1985
	$'000
Revenues	58,685
Net income	10,915

No of Employees: 120

CAPITOL COMPANIES, INC

304 E Rand Road, Arlington Heights, IL 60004
Tel: (312) 259-9200

Chairman: Joseph J Freed
President: Marvin Goldblatt
Senior Executive Officers: Seymour Cohen (VP), Thomas Callaghan (VP), Donald Langkan (VP), Arthur Paullin (VP), Joseph Thornton (VP), Scott F Sternfield (Secretary)

PRINCIPAL ACTIVITIES: Store fittings and interiors; building contractors
Principal Bank: First National Bank of Chicago
Financial Information:

	$'000
Sales revenues	60,000

No of Employees: 500

CAPITOL FEDERAL SAVINGS & LOAN ASSOCIATION OF DENVER

3300 South Parker Road, Aurora, CO 80014
Tel: (303) 671 1000

Chairman: Richard D Heiserman (and President)
Senior Executive Officers: David M Bruining (Executive VP and Chief Financial Officer), Keith E Key (Executive VP), Richard L Smith (Executive VP, Manager Finance), David G Marberry (Senior VP), Frances J Steele (Senior VP), Joann L Carson (Secretary)

PRINCIPAL ACTIVITIES: Financial services including savings and loans

Principal Subsidiaries: Capitol Insurance Services Inc; First Capitol Corporation; Capitol Building Group; First Capitol Leasing Inc
Principal Bank: Chase Manhattan Bank

No of Employees: 460

CAPITOL LIFE INSURANCE CO
1600 Sherman Street, Denver, CO 80203
Tel: (303) 861-4065

Chairman: Paul R Dupee Jr
President: Edward J Baran
Senior Executive Officers: Jospeh L Blattner (Executive VP), Warren L Berg (Senior VP), Fred J Farris (Senior VP), James E Nuss (Senior VP and Treasurer), Joel S Feldman (Senior VP)

PRINCIPAL ACTIVITIES: Life insurance
Parent Company: Providence Capitol Corporation
Financial Information:

	$'000
Premium income	375,000

No of Employees: 3,000

CAPITOL PRODUCTS CORPORATION
PO Box 3070, Harrisburg, PA 17105
Tel: (717) 766-7661

Chairman: E M Harvey (and President)
Senior Executive Officers: George L Anton (Executive VP, General Manager), Wallace Fremont (VP Sales), Lawrence E Blanchard Jr (VP), Neil Barr (VP Operations), Frank X Matunis (Treasurer)

PRINCIPAL ACTIVITIES: Manufacture of aluminum products including windows and doors
Parent Company: Ethyl Corporation, Richmond, VA
Principal Bank: Dauphin Deposit Bank and Trust Co
Financial Information:

	$'000
Sales revenues	100,000

No of Employees: 1,200

CAPITOL STEEL CORPORATION
1726 Sth Agnew Avenue, PO Box 26487, Oklahoma City, OK 73126
Tel: (405) 634-6381

Chairman: Michael Tarr (and President and Chief Executive Officer)
Senior Executive Officers: James Rooney (Executive VP and Treasurer), David L Stegmann (VP and Product Manager), John H Nesom (VP Sales and General Sales Manager)

PRINCIPAL ACTIVITIES: Manufacture of fabricated steel structural products for the construction industry
Principal Bank: Liberty National Bank and Trust Co
Financial Information:

	$'000
Sales revenues	40,000

No of Employees: 235

CARDINAL DISTRIBUTION INC
655 Metro Place North, Suite 300, Dublin, OH 43017
Tel: (614) 766 6662

Chairman: Robert D Walter (and Chief Executive Officer)
President: Edward D Esping
Senior Executive Officers: Charles E Reisner (Senior VP and Chief Financial Officer), Alan B Satterwhite (VP Finance and Treasurer), Michael E Moritz (Secretary), Douglas E Linton (VP Purchasing)

PRINCIPAL ACTIVITIES: Wholesale trade in food, cosmetics, medical supplies and drugs
Principal Bank: Bank One
Financial Information:

	$'000
Sales revenues	430,000

No of Employees: 500

CARDIS CORPORATION
9401 Wilshire Boulevard, Suite 500, Beverly Hills, CA 90212
Tel: (213) 275 3866

Chairman: Jack I Salzberg (and Chief Executive Officer); Vice Chairman: A Michael Victory
President: Richard F Norman (and Chief Operating Officer)
Senior Executive Officers: James E Lane (Senior VP Operations, Assistant Secretary and Assistant Treasurer), Isaac S Salzberg (VP and Secretary), R Jack Sharkey (VP, General Manager Regional), Roger G Ruppert (VP Finance and Chief Financial Officer), Steven D Gilman (VP Marketing), Richard J Burrell (VP Human Resources), Ronald Ahlstrom (VP and Regional Manager)

PRINCIPAL ACTIVITIES: Distribution of motor vehicle components; machine tools
Principal Bank: Security Pacific
Financial Information:

	$'000
Sales revenues	130,430

No of Employees: 1,000

CARE CORPORATION
200 Trust Building, Grand Rapids, MI 49503
Tel: (616) 459 1071

Chairman: Robert W Browne (and Chief Executive Officer and President)
Senior Executive Officers: Fred E Vandenberg (Executive VP), John D Bouwer (Senior VP), John J Donnelly Jr (VP Corporate Development), Charles M Bloom (VP and Treasurer), David Coates (VP Administrative Services)

PRINCIPAL ACTIVITIES: Nursing homes; medical personnel agencies; property interests; bowling centers
Principal Bank: Michigan National Bank
Financial Information:

	$'000
Sales revenues	107,095

No of Employees: 6,100

CARE ENTERPRISES
23046 Avenida de la Carlotta, Laguna Hills, CA 92653
Tel: (714) 837 8800

Chairman: Lee R Bangarter (and President); Co-Chairmen: Dee R Bangarter; Ted D Nelson
Senior Executive Officers: Boyd W Hendrickson (Executive VP), Derwin L Williams (Senior VP and Chief Financial Officer), Gary W Sanders (VP, Secretary and General Counsel), David K Juberg (VP Operations), David S Rubardt (VP Human Resources and Administration)

PRINCIPAL ACTIVITIES: Operation of facilities for the provision of skilled nursing and rehabilitation services
Principal Bank: Crocker National Bank
Financial Information:

	$'000
Sales revenues	239,000

No of Employees: 11,730

CAREMARK INC
4340 Von Karman, Newport Beach, CA 92660
Tel: (714) 851 2311

Chairman: James M Sweeney (and Chief Executive Officer); Vice Chairman: Paul M Gertman
President: Gordon Clemons (and Chief Operating Officer)

Senior Executive Officers: Dick P Allen (VP and Secretary), David Rosenbloom (President, Health Data Institute), William F Walker (VP Finance and Chief Financial Officer), Richard B Fontain (President, Americas Pharmacy)

PRINCIPAL ACTIVITIES: Domestic health care services
Principal Bank: Bank of America
Financial Information:

	$'000
Sales revenues	74,000

No of Employees: 950

CARESSA, INC
3601 NW 54th Street, Miami, FL 33142
Tel: (305) 633-8605
Telex: RCA 2640 14 carsa ur

Chairman of the Board: Donald Taicher (and President and Chief Executive Officer)
Senior Executive Officers: R Brian Fifer (Executive VP), Miguel A Hernandez (Executive VP), Raymond S Matko (Executive VP Administration and Finance), Arthur Stamberg (Senior VP), Stuart Weitzmann (VP), Edward de la Paz (VP)

PRINCIPAL ACTIVITIES: Manufacture of ladies' shoes
Trade Names: Caressa, S.R.O., Allure
Parent Company: Footwear Holding Inc
Principal Banks: Chase Manhattan Bank; Morgan Guaranty
Financial Information:

	$'000
Sales revenues	73,000

No of Employees: 150

CARISBROOK INDUSTRIES INC
1114 Avenue of the Americas, New York, NY 10036
Tel: (212) 398-1180
Telex: 12-59-95

Senior Executive Officers: Joseph G McNicholas (President Yarn Group), David Krivitsky (President Fabric Group), George S Goffe (VP, Treasurer and Secretary)

PRINCIPAL ACTIVITIES: Manufacture of fibers and textiles
Parent Company: Hanson Trust PLC, London, UK
Principal Subsidiaries: Tubular Textile Machy Corp
Principal Bank: Chemical Bank
Financial Information:

	Sep 30 1985	Sep 30 1986
	$'000	$'000
Sales revenues	171,847	180,763
Income before taxes	6,955	11,831
Net income	4,438	6,470
Dividends	12,000	-
Common stock	1	1
Retained income	38,935	45,405
Shareholders equity	45,829	52,299

Principal Shareholders: Hanson Trust PLC
No of Employees: 3,000

CARL KARCHER ENTERPRISES INC
See KARCHER, CARL, ENTERPRISES INC

CARLIN FOODS CORPORATION
230 W Monroe, Chicago, IL 60606
Tel: (312) 853-6070

Chairman: John J Anton (and President)
Senior Executive Officers: Mark A Waldron Jr (VP, Secretary and Treasurer), Jerome Berge (Comptroller)

PRINCIPAL ACTIVITIES: Manufacture of special ingredients for the food industry
Principal Bank: American National Bank & Trust Company
Financial Information:

	$'000
Sales revenues	76,000

CARLISLE COMPANIES INCORPORATED
250 E Fifth Street, Cincinnati, OH 45202
Tel: (513) 241-2500

Chairman: George F Dixon Jr; Vice Chairman: Malcolm C Myers (and Chief Executive Officer)
President: Robert J Deffeyes (and Chief Operating Officer)
Senior Executive Officers: Jerome H Eichert (Executive VP, Treasurer and Chief Financial Officer), Gerald L Doerger (VP), Edwin M North (Secretary), Robert J Westerkamp (Controller)

PRINCIPAL ACTIVITIES: Manufacture of a wide variety of products serving construction materials, data communications/electronics, and automotive/industrial markets
Principal Subsidiaries and Divisions: Braemar Corporation; Carlisle SynTec Systems; Carlisle Tire & Rubber Company; Continental Carlisle Inc; Digital Controls Corporation; Geauga Company; Graham Magnetics Inc; International Wire Products Company; Motion Control Industries; Tensolite Company; Zetaco, Inc; Data Electronics Inc; DSI Inc
Financial Information:

	Dec 31 1985	Dec 31 1986
	$'000	$'000
Sales revenues	481,881	466,075
Income before taxes	46,787	34,647
Net income	24,137	19,672
Dividends	9,663	9,952
Dividends per share	$1.05	$1.09
Earnings per share	$2.61	$2.16
Common stock	9,833	9,833
Retained income	195,894	205,613
Shareholders equity	197,388	181,375

No of Employees: 4,949

CARLISLE SYNTEC SYSTEMS
PO Box 7000, Carlisle, PA 17013
Tel: (717) 245-7000
Telex: 84-2511 SynTec CLSL

Chairman: George F Dixon Jr
President: Robert A Brown
Senior Executive Officers: Hugh C Kenney (Senior VP), John H Ensign (Senior VP Finance and Administration)

PRINCIPAL ACTIVITIES: Manufacture and sale of rubber roofing products and accessories
Trade Names: Carlisle, Sureseal
Parent Company: Carlisle Corporation, Cincinnati, OH
Principal Bank: Harris Trust Compnany
Financial Information:

	$'000
Sales revenues	140,000

No of Employees: 800

CARLSON COMPANIES, INC
12755 State Hwy 55, Minneapolis, MN 55441
Tel: (612) 540-5000
Cable: CARLINTER
Telex: 29 0996 CARLSON PLOH

Chairman: Curtis L Carlson (and Chief Executive Officer)
President: E C Gage (and Chief Operating Officer)
Senior Executive Officers: Juergen Bartels (President Hospitality Group), Lee Bearmon (VP and General Counsel), Joel E Burke (President Consumer Promotions), Terry M Butorac (VP-Personnel), Kenneth Gudorf (VP and Chief Financial Officer), John A Norlander (President-Radisson Hotel Corp), James K Pfleider (President-Carlson Marketing), E F MacDonald, Kurt Retzler (VP-Acquisitions), Ann Richardson (VP-Administration and President CSA), John Ueberroth (President Carlson Travel Group), Rodney M Wilson (VP and President-Investment Group), Thomas D Jardine (VP-Public Relations/Public Affairs), John Dignan (VP and Controller), Darrel Hamann (VP-Corp Tax)

PRINCIPAL ACTIVITIES: Interests include hotels, restaurants, property, travel agencies, marketing, incentives, training
Principal Subsidiaries: Carlson Marketing Group Inc; Radisson Hotel Corporation; Carlson Travel Group; Carlson Real Estate Co
Principal Bank: First Bank of St Paul
Financial Information:

	1985	1986
	$'000	$'000
Sales revenues	2,600,000	3,500,000

No of Employees: 50,000

CARLSON, G O, INC

Marshalton Road, Thorndale, PA 19372
Tel: (215) 384-2800
Telex: WUT 835 341 gocarlson tndl

Chairman: A F Travaglini; Vice Chairman: B C Travaglini
President: H L Kephart
Senior Executive Officers: G F Stanko (VP Sales), G C Travaglini (VP Production), L B Turner (VP Finance)

PRINCIPAL ACTIVITIES: Manufacture of non-ferrous alloys, stainless steel and titanium products
Principal Bank: Girard Bank
Financial Information:

	$'000
Sales revenues	50,000

No of Employees: 200

CARNATION CO

5045 Wilshire Blvd, Los Angeles, CA 90036
Tel: (213) 932-6000
Telex: TWX 910 3212 830 carcust lsa

President: Timm F Crull (and Chief Executive Officer)
Senior Executive Officers: J M Weller (Executive VP), J N Kvamme (Executive VP, Chief Administration Officer), M W Malone (Senior VP and Chief Financial Officer), F T Hull (Senior VP Food Services and Processed Potatoes), P D Argentine (VP and Treasurer)

PRINCIPAL ACTIVITIES: Manufacture of dairy foods, groceries and animal feedstuffs
Parent Company: Carnation Company Holdings Inc
Principal Subsidiaries: Bon Bon Co of America Inc; Camera Art School Photographers; Carnaco Transport Inc; Contadina Foods Inc; Dayton Reliable Tool & Manufacturing Co; Favorite Foods Inc; Hawaiian Grain Corp; McGraw Colorgraph Co; Princeton Industries Corp; Tomorrow Products Inc; Yolo Transport Co Inc
Principal Bank: Morgan Guaranty Trust Co
Financial Information:

	$'000
Sales revenues	3,340,000

No of Employees: 10,000

CAROLINA FREIGHT CORPORATION

PO Box 545, Cherryville, NC 28021
Tel: (704) 435-6811

Chairman: J L Fraley
President: K G Younger (and Chief Executive Officer)
Senior Executive Officers: K E Mayhew Jr (Executive VP and Chief Operating Officer), P E Huffstetler (Senior VP), Carlisle Jackson (Treasurer), James D Carlton (Senior VP), James R Eaton (Senior VP)

PRINCIPAL ACTIVITIES: Holding company with interests in trucking
Principal Subsidiaries: Carolina Freight Carriers Corporation; G.I. Trucking Company; Red Arrow Freight Lines Inc; Cardinal Freight Carriers Inc
Principal Bank: Citicorp
Financial Information:

	Dec 31 1985	Dec 31 1986
	$'000	$'000
Sales revenues	523,369	591,324
Income before taxes	25,911	29,556
Net income	14,448	16,644
Common dividends	2,468	2,835
Dividends per common share	$0.40	$0.44
Earnings per share*	$2.25	$2.45
Common stock	3,208	3.234
Retained income	58,657	72,377
Shareholders equity	105,623	120,558

*fully diluted

No of Employees: 9,525

CAROLINA MILLS, INC

618 Carolina Avenue, Maiden, NC 28650
Tel: (704) 428-9911
Telex: WUT 572500 caromaid maid

President: Ed Schrum
Senior Executive Officers: Jerry Harbison (VP Administration), T P Pruitt Jr (VP Weaving Division), George A Moretz (VP Yarn Division), Kenneth Isaac (VP Circular Knit Finishing Division)

PRINCIPAL ACTIVITIES: Manufacture of fabrics, yarns and knitted goods
Principal Subsidiaries: Null Manufacturing Corp
Principal Bank: North Carolina National Bank
Financial Information:

	$'000
Sales revenues	150,000

No of Employees: 2,400

CAROLINA POWER & LIGHT CO

411 Fayetteville Street, Raleigh, NC 27602
Tel: (919) 836-6111
Telex: 910-380-3760 CPL RALNC

Chairman: Sherwood H Smith Jr (and President)
Senior Executive Officers: William E Graham Jr (Vice Chairman), E E Utley (Senior Executive VP), Edward G Lilly (Executive VP), Wilson W Morgan (Senior VP), M A McDuffie (Senior VP), Lynn W Eury (Senior VP), James M Davis Jr (Senior VP), Charles D Barham Jr (Senior VP)

PRINCIPAL ACTIVITIES: Generation, transmission, distribution and sale of electricity
Trade Names: CP & L
Principal Bank: Wachovia Bank & Trust Company
Financial Information:

	Dec 31 1985	Dec 31 1986
	$'000	$'000
Sales revenues	1,934,715	2,040,798
Income before taxes	567,186	591,247
Net income	331,446	357,774
Dividends(1)	236,448	257,853
Dividends per share(2)	$2.60	$2.68
Earnings per share(3)	$3.86	$3.96
Common stock(4)	72,866	78,939
Retained income	87,143	98,526
Common shareholders equity	2,094,586	2,305,845

(1) common and preferred
(2) common share
(3) per average common share outstanding
(4) average number of shares outstanding in thousands

No of Employees: 9,475

CAROLINA STEEL CORPORATION

1451 S Elm-Eugene Street, Greensboro, NC 27420
Tel: (919) 275-9711

Chairman: John B Poindexter
President: N G Ridenhour (and Chief Executive Officer)
Senior Executive Officers: John W Robinson (Executive VP and Chief Operating Officer), Ronald H Davis (VP Administration), William J Bolton (VP Finance and Chief Financial Officer)

PRINCIPAL ACTIVITIES: Manufacture and sale of structural steel; steel service centers
Principal Subsidiaries: CSC Erectors Inc
Principal Bank: Wachovia Bank and Trust
Financial Information:

	$'000
Sales revenues	200,000

No of Employees: 1,300

CARON INTERNATIONAL, INC

Avenue E & S 2nd Street, Rochelle, IL 61068
Tel: (815) 562-4121
Telex: TWX 910 6420 390 caron rchl

Chairman: John B Caron (and President)
Senior Executive Officers: Leo Gildea (VP Manufacturing), Alec Kaplanes (Chief Financial Officer)

PRINCIPAL ACTIVITIES: Manufacture of knitted goods and knitting and carpet wools
Trade Names: Caron, Aunt Mary's Yarns
Principal Bank: Harris Bank and Trust of Chicago
Financial Information:

	$'000
Sales revenues	100,000

No of Employees: 1,700

CARPENTER TECHNOLOGY CORPORATION

101 W Bern Street, Reading, PA 19601
Tel: (215) 371-2000
Telex: WUT 836432 cartech rdg

Chairman: Paul R Roedel (and Chief Executive Officer)
President: Dr Adolph J Lena (and Chief Operating Officer)

PRINCIPAL ACTIVITIES: Manufacture of a wide range of steel products
Principal Bank: Morgan Guaranty Trust Co
Financial Information:

	Jun 30 1987
	$'000
Sales revenues	480,501
Income before taxes	9,194
Net income	4,491
Dividends	19,019
Dividends per share	$2.10
Earnings per share	$0.50
Common stock	82,931*
Retained income	217,269
Shareholders equity	300,200

*9,096,111 shares issued

No of Employees: 3,782

CARRIAGE INDUSTRIES INC

S Industrial Blvd, Calhoun, GA 30701
Tel: (404) 629-9234

Chairman: C E Harris (and Chief Executive Officer)
Executive Vice President: Stephen R Dickinson
Senior Executive Officers: K D Bryson (VP), S G Jones (VP Finance)

PRINCIPAL ACTIVITIES: Manufacture of carpets
Trade Names: Carriage Carpets, Tower Carpets, Suncraft Mills
Principal Subsidiaries: Carriage Transport, Inc; Carriage Designs Inc
Principal Bank: Bank of Boston
Financial Information:

	Jul 29 1986	Jun 28 1987
	$'000	$'000
Sales revenues	75,324	76,582
Income before taxes	7,040	4,674
Net income	3,801	2,243
Dividends	-	493
Dividends per share	-	$0.10
Earnings per share	$0.85	$0.45
Common stock	101	101
Retained income	15,773	17,523
Shareholders equity	27,649	28,488

Principal Shareholders: C E Harris
No of Employees: 550

CARROLS CORPORATION

968 James Street, Syracuse, NY 13203
Tel: (315) 424 0513

Chairman: Herbert N Slotnick
President: David J Connor
Senior Executive Officers: Daniel T Accordino (Senior VP Operations), Richard V Cross (Senior VP and Treasurer), Paul P Drotar (VP and Controller), Jack B Talsky (VP, Legal Counsel and Secretary), Melvin M Slotnick (Assistant Secretary), Steven A F Cox (VP Purchasing), Kenneth M Fagnant (VP Distribution), Stuart L Needel (VP Real Estate), Richard W Wessels (VP Information Systems)

PRINCIPAL ACTIVITIES: Restaurants and catering services
Principal Subsidiaries: Quanta Advertising Corporation
Principal Bank: Merchants National Bank and Trust Co
Financial Information:

	$'000
Sales revenues	146,000

No of Employees: 5,400

CARSON PIRIE SCOTT AND COMPANY

1 South State Street, Chicago, IL 60603
Tel: (312) 245 8000

Chairman: Peter S Willmott (and President and Chief Executive) Officer); Vice Chairmen: Dennis S Bookshester; Robert P Bryant; Carroll E Ebert
Senior Executive Officers: Charles T Reice (VP and Treasurer), Bruce R Rismiller (VP Customer Satisfaction), Robert F Doak (VP and Controller)

PRINCIPAL ACTIVITIES: Department stores; provision of catering services
Principal Subsidiaries: CPS Credit Corporation; Carson International Inc; Dobbs Houses Inc; Dobbs-Paschal Midfield Corporation; Dobbs Houses Restaurants Inc
Principal Bank: Continental Illinois
Financial Information:

	$'000
Sales revenues	1,300,000

No of Employees: 25,000

CARTER DAY INDUSTRIES, INC

555 Madison Avenue, New York, NY 10022
Tel: (212) 980 3700

President: John R Thomas
Senior Executive Officers: Michael Trachtenberg (VP and Treasurer)

PRINCIPAL ACTIVITIES: Manufacture of pollution control equipment including filtering, conveying and combustion equipment
Principal Subsidiaries: Carter Day International Inc; CEA Combustion Inc; Combe Fill Corp; Hart-Carter Co; Carter Day Co Inc; CEA Carter Overseas Inc; Ind-O-Chem Construction Corp; International Boiler Works Co
Principal Bank: Marine Midland Bank

Financial Information:

	$'000
Sales revenues	91,400

No of Employees: 1,400

CARTER HAWLEY HALE STORES INC

550 S Flower Street, Los Angeles, CA 90071

Tel: (213) 620-0150

Telex: WUT 67264 chh stores lsa

Chairman: Philip M Hawley (and Chairman of Executive Committee and Chief Executive Officer)

President: Waldo H Burnside (Chief Operating Officer)

Senior Executive Officers: Arthur L Crowe (Executive VP), J H Lyon (Executive VP), John M Gailys (Executive VP and Chief Financial Officer), Edward S Waterburg (Senior VP)

PRINCIPAL ACTIVITIES: Retail trade through department stores, high fashion stores and bookshops

Principal Subsidiaries: Bergdorf Goodman Inc; CHH Holdings Inc; Carter Hawley Hale Credit Corp; Carter Hawley Hale Properties; CHH Realty Inc; Contempo Casuals Inc; Private Business Air Service; Thalhimer Brothers Inc; Thalhimers Azalea Inc; Thalhemers Danville Inc; Thalheimers NC; Thalheimers Riverside Inc; John Wanamaker Philadelphia; Cleland Simpson Co

Principal Bank: Bank of America

Financial Information:

	Dec 31 1985	Dec 31 1986
	$'000	$'000
Sales revenues	3,977,913	4,089,794
Net income	48,030	18,000
Earnings (loss) per share	$0.92	($1.27)
Shareholders equity	359,354	324,207

No of Employees: 46,000

CARTER, WILLIAM, COMPANY

963 Highland Avenue, Needham Heights, MA 02194

Tel: (617) 444-7500

Telex: WUT 922 430 wm carter nedm

Chairman: Manson H Carter (and Chief Executive Officer)

President: Richard G Holland Jr (and Chief Operating Officer)

Senior Executive Officers: Donald J Griffin (Executive VP-Marketing), William H Carter II (Senior VP-International), James B Haymes (Senior VP-Finance), James F Mulcahy Jr (Senior VP-Sales), Thomas W Roberts Jr (Senior VP-Manufacturing), John G Heald (VP-National Accounts), Richard P Kirchner (VP-Corporate Planning), John J Cash (VP-Sales Midwestern Region), L Terry Louis (VP-Sales, Eastern Region), John A MacEachern (VP-Sales, Western Region), Robert S Miller (VP-Sales, Special Research), Stephen W Carter (Clerk), David Y Gardner (Controller), Thomas A Moore (Treasurer), Fred L Morse (Assistant Treasurer, Assistant Secretary)

PRINCIPAL ACTIVITIES: The Company is a children's apparel manufacturer which sells its products nationally to retailers which include leading department and specialty stores. The Company also operates factory outlet stores that are used to market both irregulars and closeout merchandise and non-Company products. This product mix provides each outlet store with a broad range of merchandise

Trade Names: Carter's

Principal Bank: The First National Bank of Boston

Financial Information:

	Dec 28 1985	Jan 3 1987
	$'000	$'000
Sales revenues	211,453	184,989
Income before taxes*	5,055	275
Net income	3,063	206
Dividends	1,380	1,382
Dividends per share	$0.80	$0.80
Earnings per share net	$1.78	$0.12
Common stock	8,645	8,672
Retained income	65,223	64,047
Shareholders equity	73,900	72,844

*and extraordinary item

No of Employees: 5,800

CARTERET SAVINGS BANK

200 South Street, Morristown, NJ 07960

Tel: (201) 326-1000

Chairman: Robert B O'Brien Jr (and Chief Executive Officer); Vice Chairman: Robert D Pierson

President: Robert J Mueller

Senior Executive Officers: Dennis M Mahoney (Executive VP and Treasurer), Arthur E Gilgar (Executive VP Customer Service), James F Redfern (Executive VP Corporate Lending), Joseph B Tockarshewsky (Executive VP Real Estate Lending), Valentine F Emmich (Senior VP Information Service), Frank A Willis (Senior VP and Controller), Michael H Albano (Senior VP Florida Corporate Lending), Brian M Duffy (Senior VP Marketing and Planning), Joseph L Grabowski (Senior VP Consumer Lending), Herbert W Korfe Jr (Senior VP Corporate Services), Thomas T McMurrain (Senior VP Marketing and Administration Florida Division), Lawrence Sachs (Senior VP Service Corp), P Christian Yates (Senior VP NE/SE Income Property Lending)

PRINCIPAL ACTIVITIES: Financial services including savings and loans

Principal Bank: First National State Bank

Financial Information:

	Sep 30 1985	Sep 30 1986
	$'000	$'000
Net income	25,220	46,090
Earnings per share	$2.73	$4.21
Shareholders equity	185,765	260,762
Deposits	-	4,165,587
Total assets	5,121,800	5,537,547

No of Employees: 1,700

CARTER-WALLACE, INC

767 Fifth Avenue, New York, NY 10022

Tel: (212) 758-4500

Telex: TWX 710 5813916 carter ny

Chairman of the Executive Committee: Henry H Hoyt; Chairman: Henry H Hoyt Jr (and Chief Executive Officer); Vice Chairman: Charles O Hoyt

President: Daniel J Black (and Chief Operating Officer)

Senior Executive Officers: Michael J Kopec (VP Manufacturing), Joseph S Harun (VP Medical and Scientific Affairs), Miguel Fernandez (VP International), Herbert Sosman (VP Pharmaceuticals), John D Mack (VP Consumer Products US), Robert A Cuthbert (VP Pet Products US), John Bridgen (VP Diagnostics US), Peter J Griffin (VP and Controller), Donald R Daoust (VP Quality Control), C Richard Stafford (VP Corporate Development), Lyman C Conant (VP Organisation and Development), James L Wagar (VP and Treasurer), Ralph Levine (VP and Secretary), Paul A Veteri (VP Finance)

PRINCIPAL ACTIVITIES: Manufacture of pharmaceuticals and beauty products

Financial Information:

	1986 $'000
Sales revenues	451,000
Net income	32,000

No of Employees: 3,000

CASABLANCA INDUSTRIES INC

450 North Baldwin Park Boulevard, City of Industry, CA 91746
Tel: (818) 369 6441

Chairman: Burton A Burton (and President)
Senior Executive Officers: Richard Y Fisher (VP and Secretary), Jerry C Holland (VP and Chief Financial Officer), Donald D Barr (Assistant Secretary)

PRINCIPAL ACTIVITIES: Ceiling fans
Principal Bank: Manufacturers Hanover Trust Co
Financial Information:

	$'000
Sales revenues	62,700

No of Employees: 300

CASCADE CORPORATION

2020 SW Fourth Ave, Portland, OR 97201
Tel: (503) 297-2287

Chairman: Robert C Warren
President: Joseph J Barclay (and Chief Executive Officer)
Senior Executive Officers: Richard L Matson (VP Marketing), Jack E Kahle (VP Manufacturing), Stanley E Farmer (VP Engineering), Richard C Hire (VP Finance), Robert C Warren Jr (VP Corporate Projects)

PRINCIPAL ACTIVITIES: Manufacture of hydraulic equipment for materials handling
Principal Bank: Bank of America
Financial Information:

	$'000
Sales revenues	63,000

No of Employees: 1,100

CASCADE NATURAL GAS CORPORATION

222 Fairview Avenue North, Seattle, WA 98109
Tel: (206) 624 3900

Chairman: O Marshall Jones (and Chief Executive Officer)
President: Arthur R Mitchell
Senior Executive Officers: Melvin C Clapp (Executive VP), James S Dickinson (VP Administration), Jonathon Youk Jr (VP Operations), Donald E Bennett (VP Finance), James E Haug (Treasurer), Lucille R Walsh (Secretary), O Leroy Beaudry (VP Sales), Jon T Stoltz (VP Supply, Special Projects and Consumer Affairs)

PRINCIPAL ACTIVITIES: Supply of natural gas
Principal Bank: Canadian Imperial Bank of Commerce
Financial Information:

	$'000
Sales revenues	218,615

No of Employees: 430

CASCADE STEEL ROLLING MILLS INC

3200 N Hwy 99, McMinnville, OR 97128
Tel: (503) 472-2911

Senior Executive Officers: Richard Kuntz (VP and General Manager), Claudia Burnett (Controller), Glenn Peterson (Sales Manager)

PRINCIPAL ACTIVITIES: Manufacture of steel bars
Parent Company: Schnitzer Steel Products Co
Principal Bank: Oregon Bank
Financial Information:

	$'000
Sales revenues	82,000

No of Employees: 450

CASE, J I, COMPANY

700 State Street, Racine, WI 53404
Tel: (414) 636-6011
Telex: WUI 6878015 csr cn uw

Chairman: J P Diesel
President: J K Green (and Chief Executive Officer)
Senior Executive Officers: J F Boylan (Executive VP Construction Equipment), J J Gill (Executive VP Technology), J D Michaels (Executive VP Agricultural Equipment), J A Borden (Executive VP Finance and Corporate Planning), R W Ayres Jr (Senior VP Service Parts Supply), R R Riebau (Senior VP, General Manager, Components), Richard D Sibbernsen (Senior VP Corporate Relations), D B Falstad (Senior VP and Secretary), John S Gleason (Senior VP Sales and Marketing North America), Richard M Christman (Senior VP European Sales and Marketing), Richard A Seagrave (Senior VP Manufacturing Europe)

PRINCIPAL ACTIVITIES: Manufacture of tractors and contractors' vehicles
Parent Company: Tenneco Inc, Houston, TX
Financial Information:

	$'000
Sales revenues	2,200,000

No of Employees: 29,350

CASE, J I, WAUSAU PLANT

Box 1087, Wausau, WI 54401
Tel: (715) 359-6511

Senior Executive Officers: D George (Plant Manager), Jim Von Rueden (Controller)

PRINCIPAL ACTIVITIES: Manufacture of cranes and excavators
Parent Company: Tenneco Inc through J I Case Company
Principal Bank: First Wisconsin Bank
Financial Information:

	$'000
Sales revenues	95,000

No of Employees: 250

CASE-HOYT CORPORATION

800 St Paul Street, Rochester, NY 14601
Tel: (716) 232-6840

Chairman: David H Billing
Senior Executive Officers: Richard J Agostinelli (Executive VP), Laurence C Glazer (Executive VP), Bryan King (Executive VP), John E Lovenheim (Executive VP), Louis A Callegari (Executive VP), Robert G Galbreath (VP Finance and Administration)

PRINCIPAL ACTIVITIES: Commercial printing and packaging
Principal Bank: Marine Midland Bank-Rochester
Financial Information:

	$'000
Sales revenues	100,000

No of Employees: 1,000

CASEY'S GENERAL STORES INC

1299 Northeast Broadway Avenue, Des Moines, IA 50313
Tel: (515) 263 3700

President: Donald F Lamberti
Senior Executive Officers: Ronald M Lamb (VP), Walter J Carlson (Secretary and Treasurer)

PRINCIPAL ACTIVITIES: Operation of convenience stores; franchise services

Financial Information:

	$'000
Sales revenues	247,000

No of Employees: 1,990

CASS-CLAY CREAMERY, INC

PO Box 2947, Fargo, ND 58108
Tel: (701) 232-1566

Chairman: Chester Kolstad
President: Donald Ommodt
Senior Executive Officers: Art Beckman (Executive VP of Production), Bob Gregory (Executive VP of Sales and Marketing), Mel Verbout (Executive VP of Procurement)

PRINCIPAL ACTIVITIES: Dairy
Trade Names: Cass-Clay
Principal Bank: Farm Credit Services; First Bank Fargo
Financial Information:

	1985	1986
	$'000	$'000
Sales revenues	100,000	105,000
Income before taxes	510	797

No of Employees: 400

CASTLE & COOKE, INC

50 California Street, San Francisco, CA 94111
Tel: (415) 986-3000
Telex: RCA 278617 casc ur

Chairman: David H Murdock (and Chief Executive Officer)
President: Robert D Cook (and Chief Operating Officer)
Senior Executive Officers: Raymond F Henze III (Executive VP), Leonard Marks Jr (Executive VP), William H Frank (Senior VP Finance)

PRINCIPAL ACTIVITIES: Production of sugar, fruit, vegetables, processed and canned seafoods
Principal Subsidiaries: Antle Bud Inc; Barclay Hollander Corp; Castle & Cooke Development Inc; Hawaiian Plantations Inc; West Foods Inc; Castle & Cooke Fresh Vegetables; Castle & Cooke Terminals Ltd; Kohala Corp; Oceanic Properties Inc; Mililani Town Inc; Oceanic CA Inc; Pan-Alaska Fisheries Inc; Standard FT Steamship Inc; Standard Fruit Co; Waialua Sugar Co Inc
Principal Bank: Morgan Guaranty Trust Co
Financial Information:

	Dec 31 1986
	$'000
Sales revenues	1,809,175
Net income	43,925
Earnings per share	$0.56
Shareholders equity	507,437

No of Employees: 34,600

CASTLE, A M, & CO

3400 North Wolf Road, Franklin Park, IL 60131
Tel: (312) 455-7111

Chairman: Michael Simpson
President: Richard A Virzi (and Chief Executive Officer)
Senior Executive Officers: Richard P Briscoe (VP South Central Region), Edward F Culliton (VP Finance), Leonard G O'Connor (VP Marketing), Corky L Read (VP Western Region), William F Reichert (VP Operations and Administration), Richard G Mork (VP Eastern Region)

PRINCIPAL ACTIVITIES: Production of a wide range of specialty metals which include stainless steel, copper, titanium and nickel
Principal Subsidiaries: Hy-Alloy Steels Co
Principal Bank: First National Bank of Chicago
Financial Information:

	$'000
Sales revenues	307,200

No of Employees: 1,300

CATALYST ENERGY DEVELOPMENT CORPORATION

180 Maiden Lane, New York, NY 10038
Tel: (212) 968-1700

Chairman: J J Lowrey (and Chief Executive Officer)
President: J D Kuhns (and Chief Operating Officer)
Senior Executive Officers: M H Best (Executive VP), L S Coben (Senior VP and Secretary), R L Torrens (Senior VP)

PRINCIPAL ACTIVITIES: Power production including steam supply and liquefied gas production
Principal Subsidiaries: Alamito Company
Financial Information:

	$'000
Sales revenues	36,530

CATERPILLAR INC

100 NE Adams Street, Peoria, IL 61629
Tel: (309) 675-1000
Telex: TRT 190 177 caterpillar peo

Chairman: G A Schaefer (and Chief Executive Officer)
President: P Donis
Senior Executive Officers: P C Guarindon (Executive VP), D V Fites (Executive VP), D S Gould (Executive VP), J W Wogsland (Executive VP)

PRINCIPAL ACTIVITIES: Manufacture of earthmoving, materials handling and construction industry equipment and engines
Financial Information:

	Dec 31 1985	Dec 31 1986
	$'000	$'000
Sales revenues	6,725,000	7,321,000
Income before taxes	216,000	99,000
Net income	198,000	76,000
Dividends	49,000	62,000
Dividends per share	$0.50	$0.50
Earnings per share	$2.02	$0.77
Common stock	696,000	714,000
Retained income	2,349,000	2,363,000
Shareholders equity	3,068,000	3,149,000

No of Employees: 53,731

CAVENHAM (USA) INC

25 Old Kings HiWay North, Darien, CT 06820
Tel: (203) 655-6211

Chairman: Floyd Hall (and President and Chief Executive Officer)
Senior Executive Officers: Kenneth R Baum (VP and Controller), Robert Terence Galvin (VP Chief Financial Officer and Secretary), Roger W Kennedy (VP and Treasurer)

PRINCIPAL ACTIVITIES: Operation of retail food outlets
Parent Company: Générale Occidentale, France
Principal Subsidiaries: The Grand Union Co
Principal Bank: First National Bank of New Jersey
Financial Information:

	Mar 31 1986
	$'000
Sales revenues	2,614,226
Shareholders equity	127,760

No of Employees: 21,000

CB&T BANCSHARES INC

1148 Broadway, PO Box 120, Columbus, GA 31901
Tel: (404) 649 2387

Chairman: James H Blanchard
President: H Lynn Page

Senior Executive Officers: James D Yancey (President of Subsidiary), Kenneth E Evans (Executive VP and Secretary), Stephen L Burts Jr (Senior VP and Treasurer), Charles G Harbour (Senior VP and Auditor), Jack B Parker (Senior VP, Loan Administration)

PRINCIPAL ACTIVITIES: Banking services
Trade Names: CB&T Bcsh
Principal Subsidiaries: CB&T and Total System Services, Inc
Financial Information:

	Dec 31 1985	Dec 31 1986
	$'000	$'000
Income before taxes	19,372	25,004
Net income	16,721	19,302
Dividends	5,152	6,291
Dividends per share	$0.287	$0.34
Earnings per share	$0.91	$1.04
Common stock	18,568	18,629
Retained income	62,117	75,128
Stockholders equity	98,594	112,515
Deposits	1,150,480	1,269,075
Total assets	1,328,440	1,471,367

No of Employees: 600

CBI INDUSTRIES, INC
800 Jorie Blvd, Oak Brook, IL 60521
Tel: (312) 654-7000

Chairman: William A Pogue (and President and Chief Executive Officer); Vice Chairman: John E Jones
Senior Executive Officers: James P Gage (Executive VP), F G Butterfield (Executive VP), J R Mansell (Senior VP), C W Bauer (Senior VP), C O Ziemer (Senior VP), R L Bruno (Senior VP Finance)

PRINCIPAL ACTIVITIES: Holding company with interests in the oil and gas industry, forestry, metal plate fabrication and construction, waste water treatment equipment and real estate
Principal Subsidiaries: CBI Offshore Inc; Sea-Con Services Inc; Atlantic Sea-Con Ltd; CBI Terminal Co; Chicago Bridge & Iron Co; Atlantis Oceanic Sales Corp; CBI Caribe Ltd; CBI Co Ltd; CBI Nuclear Co; CBI Sales Corp; Fairmac Realty Corp; Fibre Making Processes Inc; Indelco Inc; Integrated Drilling & Exploration Inc; Quarles Drilling Inc; NA-Con Services Inc; Walker Process Corp
Principal Bank: Continental Illinois National Bank and Trust Co of Chicago
Financial Information:

	Dec 31 1985	Dec 31 1986
	$'000	$'000
Sales revenues	1,571,491	1,155,230
Net income (loss)	(46,964)	8,000
Shareholders equity	500,013	584,624

No of Employees: 12,160

CBS/FOX VIDEO INC
1211 Avenue of the Americas, New York, NY 10036
Tel: (212) 819 3200

President: Lawrence B Hilford (and Chief Executive Officer)
Senior Executive Officers: Leonard White (President Consumer Products Division), Ralston Coffin (President CBS/Fox Video International), W G Barker Jr (Senior VP Operations), Todd Leavitt (Senior VP Legal and Business Affairs), Fred Fehlauer (Senior VP Commercial Products Division)

PRINCIPAL ACTIVITIES: Producer and marketer of theatrical motion pictures on video-cassette
Parent Company: CBS (50%); Twentieth Century-Fox (50%)
Principal Subsidiaries: Operating units: Playhouse Video; CBS/Fox Video; Key Video
Principal Bank: Chemical Bank

No of Employees: 400

CBS INC
51 W 52 Street, New York, NY 10019
Tel: (212) 975-4321
Telex: RCA 232068 chs ur

Chairman: William S Paley
President: Laurence A Tisch (Chief Executive Officer)
Officers: Gene F Jankowski (VP and President, CBS/Broadcast Group), Walter R Yetnikoff (VP and President, CBS/Records Group), Haskell P MacCowatt (Senior VP, Administration), Fred J Meyer (Senior VP, Finance), James F Sirmons (Senior VP, Industrial Relations), Louis Dorfsman (VP, Creative Director, Advertising and Design), Laurence B Glasberg (VP and General Auditor), Peter W Keegan (VP and Controller), Louis J Rauchenberger Jr (VP and Treasurer), Peter J Schementi (VP, Management Information Systems), Joan Showalter (VP, Personnel), Nathan Snyder (VP, Acquisitions), George Vradenburg III (VP and General Counsel), Marilyn Walsh (VP and Director of Taxes), Charles T Bates (Secretary)

PRINCIPAL ACTIVITIES: Broadcasting; producer, manufacturer and marketer of recorded music; makes and distributes video games and personal computer software; publishes music; and markets video cassettes through a joint venture
Principal Subsidiaries: Aspenfair Music Inc; Beverlyfax Music Inc; Cadisco Inc; CBS/Australia Pty Ltd (Australia); CBS Productions Pty Ltd (Australia); CBS Records Australia Ltd (Australia); Entertainment Distributors Co Pty Ltd (50%) (Australia); Music Publishing Co of Australia Pty Ltd (50%) (Australia); CBS Broadcast International of Canada Ltd (Canada); CBS Columbia CA (Venezuela); CBS Columbia AG (Switzerland); CBS Disques/Grammofoonplaten SA/NV (Belgium); CBS Grammofoonplaten BV (Netherlands); CBS Records AB (Sweden); CBS Records ApS (Denmark); Grammofonselskabs Distributions Centralen A/S (25%) (Denmark); CBS Records A/S (Norway); CBS Records Inc (Baar) (Switzerland); CBS Records Ltd (Israel); CBS Schallplatten GmbH (Germany); Discos CBS SA (Spain); Funckler BV (Netherlands); Industria de Discos Centroamericana SA (Costa Rica); Distribuidora Salvadorena de Discos SA (El Salvador); Distribuidora Panamena de Discos SA (Panama); Distribuidora Guatemalteca de Discos SA (Guatemala); CBS/Columbia Internacional SA (Mexico); CBS Dischi SpA (Italy); CBS Discos del Peru SA (Peru); CBS Epic (Thailand) Ltd (60%) (Thailand); CBS FMX Stereo Inc; The CBS/FOX Company (General Partnership) (50%); CBS/FOX VIDEO (Holdings) Ltd (UK); CBS/FOX VIDEO Ltd (UK); CBS/FOX VIDEO (Germany) GmbH (Germany); CBS/FOX VIDEO (South Pacific) Pty Ltd (Australia); CBS/FOX VIDEO (Canada) Ltd (Canada); CBS/FOX VIDEO (Espanola) SA (90%) (Spain); CBS/FOX VIDEO French Film Licensing Corp; CBS/FOX VIDEO (France) SA (99%) (France); CBS/FOX VIDEO International SARL (99%) (France); CBS/FOX VIDEO (New Zealand) Ltd (99.99%) (New Zealand); CBS/FOX VIDEO (Far East) KK (Japan); CBS Gramophone Records and Tapes (India) Ltd (40%) (India); CBS International SA (France); CBS Disques SA (86.62%) (France); Gilda SARL (25%) (France); CBS Electronics Ltd (95%) (Greece); Music and Video Enterprises Ltd (95%) (Greece); CBS/MTM Company (General Partnership) (50%); CBS Music (Thailand) Ltd (60%) (Thailand); CBS Nigeria Ltd (60%) (Nigeria); CBS Overseas Inc; CBS (Portugal) Musica y Discos Ltda (Portugal); CBS Records Canada Ltd (Canada); CBS Music Products Inc (Canada); CBS Records Chile Ltda (98%) (Chile); CBS Records International Ltd (UK); CBS Records (Kenya) Ltd (70%) (Kenya); CBS Records (Malaysia) Sdn Bhd (Malaysia); CBS Records OY (Finland); PEC Musiikkitukku OY (33.3%) (Finland); CBS Schallplattengesellschaft mbH (Austria); Music Service Center Gesellschaft mbH (33.3%) (Austria); CBS Singapore (Pte) Ltd (Singapore); CBS/SONY Group Inc (50%) (Japan); April Music Inc (Japan); CBS/SONY Inc (Japan); CBS/SONY California Inc; CBS/SONY Family Club Inc (Japan); CBS/SONY Hong Kong Ltd (51%) (Hong Kong); CBS/Sony Publishing Inc (Japan); CBS/SONY Records Inc

(Japan); EPIC/SONY Inc (Japan); Japan Record Distribution System Inc (50%) (Japan); Music Plaza Inc (Japan); SD Hokkaido Inc (Japan); SD Kansai Inc (Japan); CBS United Kingdom Ltd (UK); Diski CBS AEBE (Greece); CBS Urban Renewal Corp; CJG Productions Inc; Columbia Television Inc; Discos CBS Industria e Comercio Ltda (Brazil); Discos CBS International de Puerto Rico Inc (Puerto Rico); Discos CBS SAICF (Argentina); Discos CBS SA (Colombia); Eleni Films Ltd (UK); Filmvision Inc; Houston Motion Picture Entertainment Inc; Mainstrean Communications Corp (50%); Maindata Inc (70%); Sportscene Chicago Inc; SportsChannel Chicago Associates (General Partnership) (33.3%); Sportscene New England Inc; Cablevision Programming New England Corporation (33.3%); Sportscene New York Inc; SportsChannel Associates (General Partnership) (33.3%); Sportscene Prism Inc; SportsChannel Prism Associates (General Partnership) (33.3%); Vista Marketing Inc; Winterland Concessions Co (50%); Winterland Productions Ltd
Principal Bank: Morgan Shareholder Services Trust Co
Financial Information:

	Dec 31 1985	Dec 31 1986
	$'000	$'000
Total revenues	4,452,000	4,753,700
Income before taxes	334,200	284,600
Net income	27,400	375,100
Common dividends	79,800	70,600
Dividends per common share	$3.00	$3.00
Earnings per share	$0.81	$15.42
Common stock	59,800	59,900
Retained income	251,400	543,200
Shareholders equity	481,300	806,500

Principal Shareholders: As of Dec 31 1986-Wm S Paley (7.72%); Loews Corporation (24.89%)
No of Employees: 18,300

CBT CORPORATION CONNECTICUT

One Constitution Plaza, Hartford, CT 06115
Tel: (203) 244-5000

Chairman: W J Connolly Jr
Senior Executive Officers: Seymore M Smith (Executive VP and Treasurer), E Lane-Reticker (Secretary)

PRINCIPAL ACTIVITIES: Banking and financial services
Principal Subsidiaries: CBT Data Services Corp; CBT Business Credit Corp; CBT Clearing Corp; CBT Realty Corp; Connecticut Bank & Trust Co; CBT Leasing Corp; Connecticut Bank International; General Discount Corp; Lazere Financial Corp; CBT Factors Corp
Financial Information:

	$'000
Revenues	720,400

No of Employees: 5,800

CCB FINANCIAL CORPORATION

111 Corcoran Street, PO Box 931, Durham, NC 27701
Tel: (919) 683 7777

Chairman: George Watts Hill
President: W L Burns Jr (and Chief Executive Officer)
Senior Executive Officers: Edward W Back Jr (Executive VP and Chief Administration Officer), Edward J Cunningham (Senior VP), J Scott Edwards (Senior VP), Richard L Furr (Senior VP), James L Nicholson Jr (Senior VP), Richard L Furr (Senior VP), James L Nicholson Jr (Senior VP), A B Taylor (Senior VP and Controller), Norwood A Thomas Jr (Senior VP and Senior Financial Officer), David P Shaw (First VP Funds), Michael H Chappell (First VP Leasing), John J Zenner (First VP Marketing), J Kent Fawcett (First VP Personnel), Lee R Williams (First VP Centra Line)

PRINCIPAL ACTIVITIES: Banking services
Principal Bank: Central Carolina Bank & Trust Co
Financial Information:

	Dec 31 1985
	$'000
Revenues	28,015
Net income	14,395

No of Employees: 1,090

CCNB CORPORATION

331 Bridge Street, New Cumberland, PA 17070
Tel: (717) 774 7000

Chairman: John L Witner; Vice Chairman: Wilhelm E Shissler
President: Ronald H Smith (and Chief Executive Officer)
Senior Executive Officers: John E Hakes (VP), Donald E Stoner (Treasurer), John D Stoner (Secretary)

PRINCIPAL ACTIVITIES: Holding company with interests in banking
Principal Subsidiaries: CCNB Bank
Financial Information:

	Dec 31 1985
	$'000
Revenues	55,320
Net income	4,825

No of Employees: 430

CCX INC

1 Old Country Road, Carle Place, NY 11514
Tel: (516) 294 3380

Chairman: Barry Silverstein (and Chief Executive Officer); Vice Chairman: William J O'Brien
President: James A Loveland
Senior Executive Officers: Charles F Mansfield (Chairman Executive Committee), James P Connelly (Executive VP), Miguel Flores (VP, Controller and Assistant Secretary), Francis J Kenney (Treasurer and Secretary)

PRINCIPAL ACTIVITIES: Manufacture of steel; castings, forgings, wire cloth and mesh screens
Principal Bank: Marine Midland Bank
Financial Information:

	$'000
Sales revenues	50,500

No of Employees: 1,000

CD MEDICAL, INC

14600 NW 60th Avenue, Miami Lakes, FL 33014
Tel: (305) 823-5240

President: R E Monica (and Chief Executive Officer)
Senior Executive Officers: A E Jarvis (VP Regional Affairs), L Miller (VP Manufacturing), G Mandlesman (VP Marketing), Roger Hornby (VP Research and Development)

PRINCIPAL ACTIVITIES: Manufacture of medical equipment for kidney dialysis, surgical equipment and medical disposables
Parent Company: Dow Chemical Co
Principal Bank: Northern Trust Bank of Florida
Financial Information:

	$'000
Sales revenues	65,000

Principal Shareholders: Dow Chemical Company, Midland, MI
No of Employees: 650

CDI CORPORATION

10 Penn Center, Philadelphia, PA 19103-1670
Tel: (215) 569-2200

Chairman: Walter R Garrison (and President)
Senior Executive Officers: Christian M Hoechst (Executive VP), Edgar D Landis (Senior VP Finance and Treasurer), Arlington A Nagel Jr (VP), Ilmars Ritins (VP), Joseph R Seiders (VP and Secretary)

PRINCIPAL ACTIVITIES: Holding company with interests in technical and management services for a wide range of industries
Principal Subsidiaries: CDI Marine Co; CDI Telecommunications Inc; CDI Temporary Services Inc; CompData Services Corp; Management Recruiters International Inc; Midwest Technical Inc; Modern Engineering Service Co; Modern Prototype Co; Stubbs Overbeck & Associates Inc
Principal Bank: First Pennsylvania Bank
Financial Information:

	$'000
Sales revenues	433,600

No of Employees: 8,000

CECO INDUSTRIES, INC
1400 Kensington Road, Oak Brook, IL 60521
Tel: (312) 789-1400

Chairman: Erwin E Schulze (and President and Chief Executive Officer)
Senior Executive Officers: Howard E Jessen (Senior VP, Planning and Development), Larry L Funk (Senior VP), George L Faulstrich Jr (Senior VP and Chief Financial Officer), Charles F Brown III (VP and Assistant to the Chief Executive Officer), Donald J Cisek (VP Labor Relations), J Arthur Gustafson (VP Long Range Planning), Randall S Hintz (VP Human Resources), Nicole S Williams (VP and Treasurer)

PRINCIPAL ACTIVITIES: Holding company with interests in steel building components and steel buildings and concrete products
Principal Subsidiaries: Ceco Corporation; Adams Products Co; Arrow Tru-Line Inc; Engineered Components Inc; NC Products Corp; Tyee Lumber & Manufacturing Co; Formwork Services Inc; Linden Post-Tensioning Corp; Research Systems Group Inc
Principal Bank: First National Bank of Chicago
Financial Information:

	Dec 31 1985 $'000
Sales revenues	613,310
Net income	13,133
Shareholders equity	152,805

No of Employees: 7,150

CEILCOTE CO
140 Sheldon Road, Berea, OH 44017
Tel: (216) 243-0700
Telex: WUI 6873036 celcote bera

President: G R Bent
Senior Executive Officers: Stanton V Sheppard (VP and General Manager, Air Pollution Control Division), T Priest (VP, Purchasing Agent, General Manager, Corrosion Control Division), R C Drabik (VP Finance), A E Feucht (VP and General Manager Construction Division)

PRINCIPAL ACTIVITIES: Manufacture of anti-corrosion products and equipment for the control of air pollution
Parent Company: General Signal Corporation
Principal Bank: National City Bank
Financial Information:

	$'000
Sales revenues	50,000

No of Employees: 400

CELERON CORPORATION
1250 Capital of Texas Highway South, Austin, TX 78746
Tel: (512) 328 2275

Chairman: Gale L Galloway (and President and Chief Executive Officer)
Senior Executive Officers: Carl S Quinn (Executive VP and Secretary), Ronald L Hinn (Group Senior VP), Carl E Jameson (Group Senior VP)

PRINCIPAL ACTIVITIES: Transmission of natural gas; oil and gas exploration, production and refining
Parent Company: Goodyear Tire & Rubber Company
Principal Bank: Citibank
Financial Information:

	$'000
Sales revenues	760,000

No of Employees: 600

CELINA FINANCIAL CORPORATION
1 Insurance Square, Celina, OH 45822
Tel: (419) 586 5181

Chairman: Don W Montgomery (and President)
Senior Executive Officers: Robert H Broski (VP), Eugene F Cloninger (VP), L P Hanni (VP and Secretary), Martin A Herf (VP), W H Williamson (VP Administration, Treasurer and Assistant Secretary), Theodore K Knott (VP Investments)

PRINCIPAL ACTIVITIES: Provision of a wide range of insurance services; computer services
Principal Subsidiaries: Celina National Life Insurance Company; Congregation Insurance Company; First Ohio Financial Corp; Midwest Data Systems Inc; National Technical Services Inc; Ohio Reinsurance Corp; West Virginia Fire Casualty Company; National City Bank
Principal Bank: National City Bank
Financial Information:

	Dec 31 1985 $'000
Revenues	50,745

No of Employees: 680

CEMENT DIVISION
PO Box 887, Southfield, MI 48037
Tel: (313) 354-9050

President: J M Piecuch
Senior Executive Officers: P E Herguth (VP Sales and Marketing), G M Stewart (VP Sales West), D C Jones (VP Marketing Services), R J Trahey (Controller)

PRINCIPAL ACTIVITIES: Production of cement including portland cement
Parent Company: National Gypsum Company, Dallas, TX
Principal Bank: National Bank of Detroit
Financial Information:

	$'000
Sales revenues	140,000

No of Employees: 1,200

CENCOR INC
12th and Baltimore, City Center Sq, PO Box 26610, Kansas City, MO 64196
Tel: (816) 474 4750

Chairman: Robert F Brozman (and President)
Senior Executive Officers: Molly M McCarthy (VP), William J Turner (VP), Nora K Gosney (Treasurer and Secretary), Paul J Vadovicky (Controller)

PRINCIPAL ACTIVITIES: Financial services including loans and credit services
Principal Subsidiaries: Century Acceptance Corporation; Century Finance Co Kansas
Principal Bank: Boatmens First National Bank
Financial Information:

	$'000
Revenues	55,755

No of Employees: 7,005

CENERGY CORPORATION
10210 North Central Expressway, Suite 500, Dallas, TX 75231
Tel: (214) 692 3800

President: H S Erskine (and Chief Operating Officer)

Senior Executive Officers: Robert I Smith (Senior VP Administration), Richard H Roda (Senior VP Exploration and Production), Stephen M Clark (VP Accounting and Treasurer), David L Smith (VP Communications), James M Wilson Jr (VP, Legal Counsel and Secretary), Robert C Boyd (VP Finance)

PRINCIPAL ACTIVITIES: Exploration and production of petroleum and natural gas

Financial Information:

	$'000
Sales revenues	68,400

No of Employees: 120

CENTEL CORPORATION

O'Hare Plaza, 8725 Higgins Rd, Chicago, IL 60631

Tel: (312) 399-2500

Chairman: Robert P Reuss

President: John P Frazee Jr (and Chief Executive Officer)

Senior Executive Officers: James A Lovell Jr (Executive VP and Director), Karl Berolzheimer (Senior VP, General Counsel and Secretary), Eugene H Irminger (Senior VP-Finance), A Allan Kurtze (Senior VP-Planning Staff), William J Laggett (Senior VP and President Centel Services), Samuel E Leftwich (President-Central Telephone Company), J Stephen Vanderwoude (Executive VP), George B Kemple (President-Centel Business Systems), David A Bohmer (President-Centel Cable Television Company)

PRINCIPAL ACTIVITIES: Telephone; electric; cable television; business systems and supply; cellular mobile telephone

Principal Subsidiaries and Divisions: Telephone: Central Telephone Company: Iowa Division, Minnesota Division, Nevada Division, North Carolina Division; Central Telephone Company of Florida; Central Telephone Company of Illinois; Central Telephone Company of Virginia; Centel-Texas Inc; Central Telephone Company of Ohio. Business Systems and Supply: Centel Communications Company; Communications Systems Division; Centel Information Systems Inc; Centel Financial Systems Inc; Centel Supply Company. Cable Television: Centel Cable Television Company of Florida; Centel Cable Television Company of Illinois; Centel Cable Television Company of Iowa; Centel Cable Television Company of Kentucky (1); Centel Cable Television Company of Michigan; Centel Cable Television Company of Ohio; Perry Cable Companies Inc; Centel Videopath Inc. Electric: Centel Electric-Colorado; Centel Electric-Kansas. Cellular (2) and Other: Cental Cellular Company; Centel Network Company: Investments in Microtel Inc and LCI Communications Inc; Centel Credit Company. (1) Central Cable Television Company of Kentucky includes cable operations in Indiana. (2) Centel Cellular Company operates and is the managing partner for cellular systems in Greensboro and Hickory, North Carolina, Lynchburg, Danville and Charlottesville, Virginia, Killeen/Temple and Waco, Texas, Tallahassee and Fort Walton Beach, Florida, Las Vegas, Nevada, Omaha, Nebraska and Peoria, Illinois. In addition, Centel Cellular Company has limited partnership investments in Chicago, Illinois, Houston and Austin, Texas, Richmond, Virginia and Cleveland, Ohio

Principal Bank: Harris Bank

Financial Information:

	Dec 31 1985	Dec 31 1986
	$'000	$'000
Sales revenues	1,331,649	1,369,912
Income before taxes	222,611	211,815
Net income	128,743	109,002
Dividends(1)	66,256	68,707
Dividends per share(1)(2)	$1.597	$1.637
Earnings per share(2)	$3.07	$2.59
Common stock	284,401	350,401
Retained income	561,465	601,174
Shareholders funds	845,620	951,575

(1) common stock dividends

(2) restated to reflect the October, 1987 three-for-two stock split

No of Employees: 12,825

CENTERIOR ENERGY CORPORATION

55 Public Square, Cleveland, OH 44101

Tel: (216) 622 9800

Chairman: Robert M Ginn (and Chief Executive Officer)

President: Richard A Miller (and Chief Operating Officer)

Senior Executive Officers: Robert J Farling (Executive VP), Paul M Smart (Executive VP), Edgar H Maugans (VP Finance), Alan D Wright (VP Public Information), Murray R Edelman (VP Nuclear), Richard P Crouse (VP Fossil Engineering and Operations), William D Masters (VP Systems Engineering), Stanley E Wertheim (VP Administration Services), Victor F Greenslade (VP and General Counsel)

PRINCIPAL ACTIVITIES: Supply of electricity

Principal Subsidiaries: The Cleveland Electric Illuminating Co; Toledo Edison Co

Financial Information:

	Nov 30 1987
	$'000
Sales revenues	1,990,000
Net income	409,000
Dividends per share(1)	$2.56
Earnings per share(2)	$3.10
Common stock	2,200,000
Retained income	893,000
Shareholders equity	3,093,000

(1) annual

(2) 12 months to Nov 30 1987

Number of shareholders: 187,000

No of Employees: 8,900

CENTERRE BANCORPORATION

One Centerre Plaza, St Louis, MO 63101

Tel: (314) 554-6000

Chairman: Clarence C Barksdale (and Chief Executive Officer)

President: John P MacCarthy

Senior Executive Officers: John H Biggs (Executive VP), Dan L Huffer (Executive VP and Chief Financial Officer), James L Kerley (Executive VP), Walter D Schmitz (Executive VP), John W Rowe (Executive VP), Wayne D Muskopf (VP), W L Rives (Executive VP), Lonnie L Kinchen (VP and Group Manager), R L Uptegrove (VP)

PRINCIPAL ACTIVITIES: Banking services

Principal Bank: Centerre Bank

Financial Information:

	Dec 31 1985	Dec 31 1986
	$'000	$'000
Income before taxes	32,354	29,391
Net income	27,180	30,125
Dividends	13,852	13,908
Dividends per share	$1.80	$1.80
Earnings per share	$3.53	$3.90
Common stock	90,030	91,003
Retained income	229,605	245,822
Shareholders equity	319,635	335,825
Deposits	3,682,753	3,983,641
Total assets	5,171,671	5,664,526

No of Employees: 3,581

CENTEX CORPORATION

Republicbank Tower, Dallas, TX 75201
Tel: (214) 748-7901

Chairman: Paul R Seegers (and Chief Executive Officer); Vice Chairman: Frank M Crossen
President: Laurence E Hirsh (and Chief Operating Officer)
Senior Executive Officers: James E Lewis (Executive VP), Harry J Leonhardt (Executive VP), Paul Woodberry (Executive VP), John A Wacker (Executive VP), John G Jones (VP, Secretary and General Counsel), Richard C Harvey (VP), Harold E Norris (VP), Jeffery W Seel (VP and Treasurer)

PRINCIPAL ACTIVITIES: Residential and general construction; production of cement; oil and gas products
Principal Subsidiaries: C & C Properties Inc; Cenergy Corp; Centex Aggregates Inc; Centex American Gypsum Co Inc; Centex Cement Corp; Centex Development Co; Centex Enterprises Inc; J W Bateson Co Inc; Cardinal Contracting Co; Centex Construction Co Inc; J W Bateson Enterprises Inc; Rooney Enterprises Inc; Great Southwest Corp; Frank J Rooney Inc; Centex Financial Corp; Centex Homes Corp; Centex Homes Northwest Inc; III E Chestnut Corp; Centex Materials Inc; Centex West Inc; Constructional Chemicals Inc; Fox & Jacobs Inc; Plavco Mortgage Co Inc; M H Golden Co; Great Southwest Construction; Hillis Homes Inc; Illinois Cement Co; Mathews Readymix Inc; Nevada Cement Co; Eugene Simpson & Brother Inc; Texas Cement Co
Principal Bank: Republic Bank
Financial Information:

	Mar 31 1986	Mar 31 1987
	$'000	$'000
Sales revenues	1,427,200	1,300,000
Net income	47,600	44,000

No of Employees: 4,600

CENTOCOR INC

244 Great Valley Parkway, Malvern, PA 19355
Tel: (215) 296-4488

Chairman: Michael A Wall
President: Hubert J P Shoemaker (and Chief Executive Officer)
Senior Executive Officers: Vincent R Zurawski Jr (Executive VP and Secretary), Bruce A Peacock (VP Finance, Assistant Secretary and Treasurer), David Hoverg (VP Marketing and Planning), Harvey Belzek (VP), Jacques Fonteyne (VP Entertainment), Bert Del Villaro (VP Sales)

PRINCIPAL ACTIVITIES: Laboratories; biotechnology
Principal Bank: Mercantile Bank & Trust
Financial Information:

	Dec 31 1986
	$'000
Sales revenues	27,000
Net (loss)	(39,000)

No of Employees: 180

CENTRAL & SOUTH WEST CORPORATION

Box 660164, 2121 San Jacinto Street, Dallas, TX 75266
Tel: (214) 754-1000

Chairman: Durwood Chalker (and Chief Executive Officer); Vice Chairman: Merle L Borchelt
President: Bill J Harris (and Chief Operating Officer)
Senior Executive Officers: John E Taulbee (Executive VP Finance), Stanley P Wilson (Senior VP and General Counsel), Philip I McConnell (VP and Secretary)

PRINCIPAL ACTIVITIES: Electricity generation and distribution
Principal Subsidiaries: Central & South West Services Corp; Central Power & Light Co; Public Service Co of OK; Ash Creek Mining Co; Southwestern Electric Power Co; Transok Inc; West Texas Utilities Co
Principal Bank: Bankers Trust Company
Financial Information:

	Dec 31 1986
	$'000
Sales revenues	2,555,102
Net income	389,280
Earnings per share	$3.75
Shareholders equity	2,359,742

No of Employees: 9,202

CENTRAL BANCORPORATION INC

Central Trust Center, 5th & Main Streets, Cincinnati, OH 45202
Tel: (513) 651-8915

President: Oliver W Birckhead (and Chief Executive Officer)
Senior Executive Officers: Gary N Kocher (Executive VP), Noble O Carpenter (Executive VP), J Clay Stinneth (Executive VP), Robert A Ries (Senior VP and Chief Financial Officer)

PRINCIPAL ACTIVITIES: Banking
Principal Subsidiaries: Central Trust Co; Centralbanc Realty Co
Principal Bank: Central Trust Co
Financial Information:

	Dec 31 1985
	$'000
Revenues	391,000
Net income	33,500
Total assets	3,856,000

No of Employees: 2,500

CENTRAL BANCSHARES OF THE SOUTH INC

701 South 20th St, Birmingham, AL 35296
Tel: (205) 933-3000

Chairman: Harry B Brock (and Chief Executive Officer and Treasurer); Vice Chairmen: Philip C Jackson Jr; Paul D Jones (and Secretary and General Counsel)
President: Terence C Brannon
Senior Executive Officers: W Dan Puckett (Executive VP)

PRINCIPAL ACTIVITIES: Banking services
Principal Subsidiaries: Central Bank of the South
Financial Information:

	Dec 31 1986
	$'000
Revenues	354,000
Net income	36,000

No of Employees: 2,400

CENTRAL BANKING SYSTEM INC

1450 Treat Boulevard, Box 8050, Walnut Creek, CA 94596

Chairman: Michael G Rafton (and President)
Senior Executive Officers: Grace H Foster (VP and Secretary), A Ray Freeman (VP and Chief Financial Officer), Fred C Sharna (VP and General Auditor)

PRINCIPAL ACTIVITIES: Banking

Principal Subsidiaries: CB Insurance Agency Inc; Central Bank; Central Hawaiian Leasing Co; Cenval Leasing Corp; Central Banking System Credit Corp

No of Employees: 1,535

CENTRAL CONTAINER DIVISION

PO Box 2008, Milwaukee, WI 53201
Tel: (414) 264-8100

Senior Executive Officers: J C Walker (VP Production), H K Broxey (VP Sales)

PRINCIPAL ACTIVITIES: Manufacture of shipping containers
Parent Company: Longview Fibre Company, Longview, WA
Financial Information:

	$'000
Sales revenues	60,000

No of Employees: 500

CENTRAL FIDELITY BANKS INC

PO Box 27602, Broad at Third Street, Richmond, VA 23261
Tel: (804) 782-4000

Chairman: Carroll L Saine (and Chief Executive Officer)
President: Lewis N Miller
Senior Executive Officers: Kenneth W Farmer (President Eastern Region), Rodger W Fauber (President Western Region), Philip G Hug (President Central Region), Charles H Rotert Jr (Executive VP), William F Shumadine (Executive VP), Howard B Sivils Jr (Executive VP), Donald F Delaney (Corporate Executive Officer Finance and Treasurer), Warren L Emerson (Corporate Executive Officer Marketing), John T Percy Jr (Corporate Executive Officer Investment)

PRINCIPAL ACTIVITIES: Banking services
Principal Subsidiaries: Cencor Insurance Agency Inc; Central Fidelity Bank; Central Fidelity Mortgage Co; Central Fidelity Services Inc; Fidelity American Leasing Corp
Principal Bank: Central Fidelity Bank
Financial Information:

	Dec 31 1986
	$'000
Revenues	380,000
Net income	42,000

No of Employees: 2,800

CENTRAL HUDSON GAS & ELECTRIC CORPORATION

284 South Ave, Poughkeepsie, NY 12601
Tel: (914) 452-2000

Chairman: Theodore J Carlson; Vice Chairman: Ernest Althouse
President: John E Mack III (and Chief Executive Officer), Paul J Ganci (Senior VP Operations)
Senior Executive Officers: L Wallace Cross (Senior VP Finance)

PRINCIPAL ACTIVITIES: Distribution of electricity and natural gas
Financial Information:

	Dec 31 1986
	$'000
Sales revenues	439,000
Net income	59,000

No of Employees: 1,300

CENTRAL ILLINOIS PUBLIC SERVICE CO

607 E Adams St, Springfield, IL 62701
Tel: (217) 523-3600

President: Donald G Raymer (and Chief Executive Officer)
Senior Executive Officers: Goff Smith (Chairman Executive Committee), R W Jackson (Senior VP Finance and Secretary), C L Greenwalt (Senior VP Operations), C F Logan (VP), Robert G Lane (VP Power Supply), William R Morgan (VP Corporate Services), Lowell A Dodd (VP Corporate Planning), Clyde S Heaton (VP Public Relations), J C Fiaush (Controller)

PRINCIPAL ACTIVITIES: Distribution of natural gas
Principal Bank: First National Bank of Chicago
Financial Information:

	Dec 31 1985	Dec 31 1986
	$'000	$'000
Sales revenues	701,000	626,000
Net income	74,300	67,000

No of Employees: 2,800

CENTRAL JERSEY BANCORP

Route 9, Freehold, NJ 07728
Tel: (201) 462 0011

Chairman: Elsie Sokol (and President)
Senior Executive Officers: John W Bisbee (Executive VP), Robert W Buck (Secretary and Treasurer)

PRINCIPAL ACTIVITIES: Banking
Principal Subsidiaries: Central Jersey Bank & Trust Company
Financial Information:

	Dec 31 1985
	$'000
Revenues	89,870
Net income	13,270

No of Employees: 810

CENTRAL LOUISIANA ELECTRIC COMPANY INC

Box 5000, 415 Main Street, Pineville, LA 71360
Tel: (318) 484-7400

Chairman: William F Terbot (and President and Chief Executive Officer)
Senior Executive Officers: Scott O Brame (Senior VP and Secretary), Robert L Duncan (Senior VP), Gregory L Nesbitt (Senior VP), E L Barron (VP), D M Eppler (VP), Charles S Goodgame (VP), William J Thevenote (VP), D K Warner (VP), Charles E LeBlanc (Treasurer), D E Williams (Controller)

PRINCIPAL ACTIVITIES: Supply of electricity
Principal Bank: Citibank
Financial Information:

	Dec 31 1986
	$'000
Sales revenues	297,000
Net income	36,000

No of Employees: 1,200

CENTRAL MAINE POWER COMPANY

Edison Drive, Augusta, ME 04336
Tel: (207) 623 3521

Chairman: John W Rowe (and President and Chief Executive Officer)
Senior Executive Officers: Charles E Monty (Executive VP and Chief Operating Officer), Charles D Frizzle Jr (VP Operations), Joseph R Moran (VP Operations), Gerald C Poulin (Assistant VP and Manager Engineering), Richard A Crabtree (VP Finance and Chief Financial Officer), Robert S Howe (Controller), John L Lacrosse (Assistant Treasurer and VP Insurance), David E Marsh (Treasurer), Carol W Oliva (Assistant Treasurer), Arthur W Adelberg (Legal Counsel), William M Finn (Secretary), David T Flanagan (VP Legal and Administration), Ralph L Bean (VP Engineering), R Edward Hanson (Assistant VP Production), Donald F Kelly (VP Energy), Patrick S Lydon (VP Nuclear Operations and Administration), John B Randazza (VP Nuclear), Douglas Stevenson (Assistant VP Resources and Budget)

PRINCIPAL ACTIVITIES: Supply of electricity
Principal Subsidiaries: Maine Electric Power Company; Maine Yankee Atomic Power Company; Union Water Power Company

Principal Bank: First National Bank of Boston
Financial Information:

	Dec 31 1986
	$'000
Sales revenues	509,000
Net income	35,000

No of Employees: 2,060

CENTRAL PACIFIC CORPORATION

5016 California Avenue, Bakersfield, CA 93309
Tel: (805) 861 5324

Chairman: Rayburn S Dezember (and President and Chief Executive Officer)
Senior Executive Officers: Edward J Biebrich Jr (Chief Financial Officer), Edward M Carpenter (Legal Counsel and Secretary)

PRINCIPAL ACTIVITIES: Banking
Principal Subsidiaries: American National Bank; Bankers Funding Corporation; Human Resources Dimension Inc; Sacramento Valley Bank
Principal Bank: Bank of America National Trust and Savings Association
Financial Information:

	Dec 31 1985
	$'000
Revenues	70,290

No of Employees: 540

CENTRAL RESERVE LIFE CORPORATION

343 West Bagley Road, Berea, OH 44017
Tel: (216) 826 4100

Chairman: Leo D Stone
President: Fred Lick Jr
Senior Executive Officers: Frank W Grimone (Executive VP, Treasurer and Chief Financial Officer), Charles W Johnson (Secretary)

PRINCIPAL ACTIVITIES: Life insurance services
Principal Bank: National City Bank
Financial Information:

	Dec 31 1985
	$'000
Revenues	70,340
Net income	4,850

No of Employees: 280

CENTRAL SOYA COMPANY, INC

1300 Ft Wayne National Bank Building, Ft. Wayne, IN 46802
Tel: (219) 425-5100
Telex: WUT 276170 censoya fwa a

Chairman: Douglas G Fleming: Vice Chairman: Joseph W Gillespie
President: Donald P Eckrich (and Chief Executive Officer)
Senior Executive Officers: William W Wilkinson (Executive VP), Robert E Gillis (Executive VP), Willis S Clark (Executive VP), C L Marine (Group VP), Richard J Sager (Senior VP Finance and Secretary), Harley J Donnell (VP Agribusiness Development), Milo C Fritzsche (VP Personnel), John F Moran Jr (VP International), Samuel C Arnold (VP), Thomas C Griffith (VP Refined Oil), Robert G Gallaway (VP Domestic Feed), William M Myrhang (VP Manufacturing), Leamon D Williams (VP Research), Jerry R James (VP Grain), Charles M Freeland (VP Food Development), Calvin R Shields (VP Engineering)

PRINCIPAL ACTIVITIES: Livestock and animal feeds; soybean products
Principal Bank: First National Bank of Chicago
Financial Information:

	Aug 31 1986
	$'000
Sales revenues	1,475,500
Net income	1,797

No of Employees: 8,000

CENTRAL STATES CAN CO

700 16th Street SE, Massillon, OH 44646
Tel: (216) 833-1011
Telex: WUT 983455 cs can co maln

President: George M Smart
Senior Executive Officers: David E Blizzard (VP Engineering and Research and Development), Gerald L Bowman (VP Administration), Paul H Weston (VP Sales), Arthur J Boske (VP Manufacturing), Patrick L Ferron (VP Materials)

PRINCIPAL ACTIVITIES: Production of metal cans; printing machinery
Parent Company: Van Dorn Co
Financial Information:

	$'000
Sales revenues	60,000

No of Employees: 500

CENTRAL STATES DIVERSIFIED INC

9322 Manchester Road, St Louis, MO 63119
Tel: (314) 261-8000

Chairman: J Russell Flowers; Vice Chairman: H Velkoff
President: R Prince
Senior Executive Officers: N Thomas (Senior VP and Secretary), Jerry Becker (VP Healthcare Display and Divisional Manager), Marshall Marcus (VP Sales), Charles F Aebel (VP Finance)

PRINCIPAL ACTIVITIES: Production of paper bags; paper and plastic packaging; medical disposables
Principal Bank: The Boatmen's National Bank of St Louis
Financial Information:

	$'000
Sales revenues	50,000

No of Employees: 500

CENTRAL STEEL TUBE CO

PO Box 551, Clinton, IA 52732
Tel: (319) 243-2102

President: Leonard Fruchtman
Senior Executive Officers: Robert Lardon (Executive VP), Len Eller (VP and General Manager), Gary Fruchtman (VP Sales), Morris Fruchtman (VP)

PRINCIPAL ACTIVITIES: Oil and gas services and equipment
Parent Company: Donovan Wire & Iron Company
Principal Bank: Camanche State Bank
Financial Information:

	$'000
Sales revenues	60,000

No of Employees: 350

CENTRAL VERMONT PUBLIC SERVICE CORPORATION

77 Grove Street, Rutland, VT 05701
Tel: (802) 773 2711

Chairman: F Ray Keyser Jr
President: Thomas C Webb (and Chief Executive Officer)
Senior Executive Officers: Donald L Rushford (VP and Legal Counsel), Jonathan W Boorame (Treasurer), Theodore W Millspaugh (Controller), Olga G Laird (Secretary), Darrow R McLeod (VP Engineering and Operations), Thomas J Hurcomb (VP External Affairs)

PRINCIPAL ACTIVITIES: Supply of electricity

Principal Subsidiaries: Connecticut Valley Electric Company Inc; Vermont Electric Power Company
Principal Bank: First National Bank of Boston
Financial Information:

	Dec 31 1985
	$'000
Sales revenues	169,100
Net income	23,600

No of Employees: 630

CENTRAL WISCONSIN BANKSHARES INC

500 Third Street, Wausau, WI 54401
Tel: (715) 845 3133

Chairman: William H Rodd (and Chief Executive Officer)
President: Edwin J Zagzebski (and Chief Operating Officer)
Senior Executive Officers: Andrew W Sigl (Secretary and Controller), Gary D Maples (VP)

PRINCIPAL ACTIVITIES: Banking
Principal Subsidiaries: Community First Bank; Community State Bank; Eagle River State Bank; First American National Bank; First National Bank; Mosinee Commercial Bank; Northern National Bank; Tri-County State Bank; Union National Bank; Wisconsin Valley Trust Company
Principal Bank: First American National Bank
Financial Information:

	Dec 31 1985
	$'000
Revenues	69,370
Net income	4,835

No of Employees: 520

CENTRILIFT-HUGHES, INC

200 W Stuart Roosa Drive, Claremore, OK 74017
Tel: (918) 341-9600
Telex: WUT 796269 centrilift tul

President: J L Cox (and Chief Executive Officer)
Senior Executive Officers: D R Forgerson (Senior VP Marketing), J L Hastings (Senior VP Pump Operations), C A Boyd (Senior VP Power Supply and Control Operations), H E Oelklaus (VP Human Resources), J E Vandevier (VP Engineering), G P Ferry (Secretary and Controller)

PRINCIPAL ACTIVITIES: Manufacture of pumps and pumping equipment
Parent Company: Hughes Tool Company
Financial Information:

	$'000
Sales revenues	90,000

No of Employees: 1,000

CENTRONICS DATA COMPUTER CORPORATION

One Wall Street, Hudson, NH 03051
Tel: (603) 883-0111
Telex: TWX 710 2227 525 centronichsun

Chairman: Stephen D Weinroth; Vice Chairman: Thomas G Kamp
President: Robert Stein (and Chief Executive Officer)
Senior Executive Officers: Robert Kilcullen (VP Business Management Organisation), Richard Williams (VP Engineering), Piero Falchero (VP), Jeffrey Weinstein (VP, Secretary and General Counsel), R J Holbrook (VP and General Manager), Donald L O'Bryant (VP Quality Assurance), Ronald Fox (VP Operations), Yoon Paek (VP Offshore Procurement)

PRINCIPAL ACTIVITIES: Manufacture of line printers and serial dot matrix printers for computers
Principal Subsidiaries: Centronics Export Sales Corp; Centronics Sales & Service Corp
Principal Bank: The First National Bank of Boston
Financial Information:

	$'000
Sales revenues	216,000

No of Employees: 1,850

CENTRUST SAVINGS BANK

101 E Flagler Street, Miami, FL 33131
Tel: (305) 376-33131

Chairman: David L Paul (and President and Chief Executive Officer); Vice Chairmen: Joel D Ware (and Executive VP); Edward L Abbott (and Secretary)
Senior Executive Officers: Alfred L Teti (Senior Executive VP and Chief Operating Officer), Walter D Shealy III (Senior Executive VP Capital Markets), Angel Cortina Jr (Senior Executive VP and Treasurer), Earl Baldwin (Executive VP Capital Markets), Robert R Bartolini (Executive VP Branch Administration), Richard A Bondie (Executive VP Residential Mortgage Lending), Robert Ciani (Executive VP), Winthrop F Davis (Executive VP Commercial Real Estate), Alan Merkur (Executive VP Real Estate Equities)

PRINCIPAL ACTIVITIES: Savings and loan association and diversified financial services
Principal Bank: Southeast First National Bank of Miami
Financial Information:

	Sep 30 1985	Sep 30 1986
	$'000	$'000
Net income	36,640	55,906
Earnings per share	$8.10	$7.84
Shareholders equity	156,536	296,807
Deposits	-	3,400,244
Total assets	4,711,000	6,142,788

No of Employees: 1,882

CENTURI, INC

300 Plaza Drive, Binghamton, NY 13903
Tel: (607) 729 5313

Chairman: Milton Koffman; Vice Chairman: Martin Altman (and Chief Operating Officer and Secretary)
Senior Executive Officers: Robert W Feyler (VP Finance), Ivan Rothstein (VP Sales), Martin Sasso (VP Operations)

PRINCIPAL ACTIVITIES: Manufacture of amusement machines and electronic equipment
Principal Subsidiaries: Allied Leisure Export Corp; Outdoor Sports Headquarters Inc; Virginia Capes Seafood Inc
Principal Bank: United National Bank of Miami
Financial Information:

	$'000
Sales revenues	187,600

No of Employees: 1,200

CENTURY COMMUNICATIONS CORPORATION

51 Locust Avenue, New Canaan, CT 06840
Tel: (203) 966-8746

Chairman: Larry C Ballard
President: Leonard Tow (and Chief Executive Officer, Chief Operating Officer and Chief Financial Officer)
Senior Executive Officers: Michael G Harris (VP), Robert E Morrison (VP), Eugene Weinrich (VP and Assistant Secretary), Scott N Schneider (Controller), David Z Rosenweig (Secretary)

PRINCIPAL ACTIVITIES: Provision of cable television services
Financial Information:

	$'000
Sales revenues	64,000

No of Employees: 640

CENTURY FURNITURE CO

408 12th Street Dr NW, Hickory, NC 28601
Tel: (704) 328-1851
Telex: WUT 800549 century hiko

Chairman: Harley F Shuford Sr
President: Harley F Shuford Jr
Senior Executive Officers: David L Leffler (VP and General Sales Manager), William S Lamparter (VP Export Sales), Samuel M Hemphill (VP Finance, Secretary and Treasurer), A A Shuford (VP and Manager), George K Snow Jr (VP Case Good Products), Robert E Bliss (VP Upholstery Products)

PRINCIPAL ACTIVITIES: Manufacture of domestic furniture
Principal Subsidiaries: Arthur Laskys Carriage House Inc
Principal Bank: First Union National Bank
Financial Information:

	$'000
Sales revenues	60,000

No of Employees: 1,350

CENTURY PAPERS INC

4211 Southwest Freeway, Houston, TX 77027
Tel: (712) 877 1100

Chairman: Jules Maltz
President: Herschel G Maltz (and Chief Executive Officer)
Senior Executive Officers: Charles Maltz (Senior VP), Maurice Maltz (VP and Assistant Secretary), Michael G Moncrief (Assistant VP Administration), Werner J Pratka (Treasurer and Assistant Secretary), Jack L Thomas (Chief Financial Officer and Secretary), Joseph A Giardina (VP Marketing), Harvey Glanzrock (VP Marketing and Manager Functional Area), Ronald L Lardinois (VP Marketing), Walter G Gafner (VP Functional Area)

PRINCIPAL ACTIVITIES: Manufacture of hygienic paper products and packaging supplies
Principal Subsidiaries: Arizona Paper Company Inc; Best Sanitary Supply; Century Papers of Colorado Inc
Principal Bank: First City National Bank
Financial Information:

	$'000
Sales revenues	103,000

No of Employees: 460

CENTURY TELEPHONE ENTERPRISES INC

520 Riverside Drive, Monroe, LA 71201
Tel: (318) 387 5541

Chairman: Clarke M Williams (and Chief Executive Officer); Vice Chairman: Clarke M Williams Jr (and President and Chief Operating Officer)
Senior Executive Officers: R L Hargrove Jr (Executive VP), Harvey P Perry (Senior VP, Legal Counsel and Secretary), Glen F Post III (Senior VP, Treasurer and Chief Financial Officer), Jim D Reppond (Senor VP Operations), W Bruce Hanks (Senior VP Finance and External Affairs), David E Hogan (Senior VP Marketing and Business Relations), C Kenneth Conrad Sr (Senior VP Research and Development), Tony R Davis (Senior VP Business Development), Stewart R Ewing Jr (VP and Controller)

PRINCIPAL ACTIVITIES: Provision of telecommunications services
Principal Subsidiaries: Adamsville Telephone Company Inc; Athens Telephone Company Inc; Au Gres Telephone Company; Butler Telephone Company Inc; Caddoan Telephone Company Inc; Central Indiana Telephone Company Inc; Central Louisiana Telephone Company; Central Telephone Company Inc; Century Area Long Lines Inc; Century Cablenet Inc; Century Printing & Publishing Company; Century Service Group Inc; Century Supply Group Inc; Century Telephone Company Inc; Century Telephone Midwest; Century Telephone of Idaho Inc; Century Telephone of Michigan Inc; Century Telephone of Wisconsin Inc; Century Teleview of Arkansas; Century Teleview of Louisiana; Century Teleview of Michigan; Century Teleview of Missouri; Century Teleview of Tennessee; Century Teleview of Wisconsin; Claiborne Telephone Company; Coastal Telephone Electronic Corporation; Evangeline Telephone Company; Falcon Communication Inc; Hadley Telephone Company Inc; Holway Telephone Company; Home Telephone Company Inc; Liberty Tele & Communications; Liberty Telephone Company; Louisiana Western Telephone Company; Midwest Computer Services Inc; Mississippi Tele Communications; Mountain Home Telephone Company; Mustang Telephone Company; Myrtle Telephone Company Inc; Northwest Louisiana Telephone Company Inc; Plain Dealing Telephone Compay Inc; Redfield Telephone Company Inc; Union Telephone Company Inc; Union Telephone Company Louisiana; War Telephone Company; Wyandotte Telephone Company
Principal Bank: Mercantile National Bank
Financial Information:

	$'000
Sales revenues	135,000

No of Employees: 1,650

CERBERONICS INC

5600 Columbia Pike, Bailey's Crossroads, VA 22041
Tel: (703) 379 4500

Chairman: Robert W Erikson (and President)
Senior Executive Officers: George W Erikson (Executive VP, Legal Counsel and Secretary), Charles M Mills (Executive VP and Chief Operating Officer), Walter T Laws (VP), John Ludes Jr (VP), David N Walker (Treasurer)

PRINCIPAL ACTIVITIES: Provision of consultancy services in the fields of architecture, engineering and surveying
Principal Bank: American Security Bank
Financial Information:

	$'000
Sales revenues	36,000

No of Employees: 210

CEROCK WIRE AND CABLE GROUP, INC

285 Nicoll Street, New Haven, CT 06511
Tel: (203) 7722-2250
Telex: WUT 95 6042 rckbstint wfod

President: R A Pritzker
Senior Executive Officers: G A Jones (Executive VP), W F Hogan (VP Finance and Assistant Secretary), E Barth (VP Manufacturing), R C Gluth (VP)

PRINCIPAL ACTIVITIES: Manufacture of cables and wires; copper tubing
Financial Information:

	$'000
Sales revenues	120,000

No of Employees: 1,000

CERRO METAL PRODUCTS

PO Box 388, Bellefonte, PA 16823
Tel: (814) 355-6217
Telex: TWX 510 670 3523 cerrp befo

President: D A Gardiner

PRINCIPAL ACTIVITIES: Metal fabrication
Parent Company: The Marmon Group Inc
Financial Information:

	$'000
Sales revenues	100,000

No of Employees: 1,400

CERRO SALES CORPORATION

540 Madison Avenue, New York, NY 10222
Tel: (212) 888-2100
Telex: WUI 620460
Telefax: cerro 620460

Chairman: R A Pritzker
President: Jaime Claro
Senior Executive Officers: Salvatore De Micoli (Senior VP), R C Gluth (VP), Rigo Cardenas (VP and Assistant Secretary), Michael Fannon (VP), Barry Feldman (VP), Dino Barone (Controller)

PRINCIPAL ACTIVITIES: Sale of non-ferrous and precious metals
Parent Company: Marmon Group Inc
Principal Bank: Chase Manhattan Bank
Financial Information:

	1987 (11mths) $'000
Sales revenues	271,000

Principal Shareholders: Fully owned by Marmon Group Inc
No of Employees: 24

CERTAINTEED CORPORATION

750 E Swedesford Road, PO Box 860, Valley Forge, PA 19482
Tel: (215) 341-7000
Telefax: (215) 341-7797

Chairman: John T Gurash (Chairman of the Board)
President: Michel L Besson (President and Chief Executive Officer)
Senior Executive Officers: Michel L Besson (President and Chief Executive Officer), Myron P Simmons (Senior VP, Chief Administrative Officer and President Pipe and Plastics Group), Michel J Lecomte (Senior VP, Chief Financial Officer), John W Belt Jr (VP, President, Vinyl Building Products Division), Peter R Dachowski (VP, President, Shelter Materials Group), Thomas A Decker (Corporate VP and General Counsel and Secretary), Dwight F Deinchik (VP and Controller), Thomas A Dougherty (VP Employee and Industrial Relations), Rene Goutte (VP, President Insulation Group), Donald S Huml (VP, President, Utility Supply Group and Building Materials Distribution Group), Lester F Kaas (VP Administration), John D Keohane (VP Internal Audit), Theodore F Merkel (VP Information Systems), Douglas E Potter (VP, President, Fiber Glass Reinforcements Division), Carl C Rue (VP, Planning and Development), Michael J Walsh (VP and Treasurer)

PRINCIPAL ACTIVITIES: Fiber Glass Products:- thermal and acoustical insulation materials, and fiber glass products for reinforcement applications. Building Materials:- residential roofing, vinyl building products, (solid vinyl siding and accessory items, and solid vinyl profiles for replacement windows), filtered ridge vents, and aluminum doors and windows. The Company also distributes a broad line of building materials in the state of Texas. Piping Products:- piping for water, sewer, irrigation and electrical applications; PVC residential water well products; and water meters. The Company also distributes pipe and pipe system components.
Trade Names: Registered Trade Names and Trade Marks:- Insul-Safe III fiber glass blown insulation, Hallmark Shangle roofing shingles, Horizon Shangle roofing shingles, Hearthstead roofing shingles, Glasstex roofing shingles, Glassguard roofing shingles, Snap*On fiber glass pipe insulation, Punchline fiber glass air duct with integral hanger, Ideal millwork, Vinyl-iron PVC pressure pipe
Principal Subsidiaries: Air Vent Inc; Certain-teed Agricultural Systems Inc; Certain-teed Corporation Foundation; CertainTeed Foreign Sales Corporation; Certain-teed Weaving Corporation; CRT Inc; Fluid Systems Hawaii Inc; Gustin Bacon Company; Precision Meters Inc; Wm Cameron Company; Bay Mills Ltd; CertainTeed Canada Inc; CertainTeed Limited
Primary Banks: Banque National de Paris; Banque Indosuez; Barclays Bank PLC; Chemical Bank; Crédit Industriel et Commercial; Crédit du Nord; Crédit Lyonnais; Commerzbank; Crédit Suisse; European American Bank; First Pennsylvania Bank; Manufacturers Hanover Trust Company; Morgan Guaranty; National Westminster Bank; Philadelphia National Bank; Security Pacific; Société Générale; Union Bank of Switzerland; Westdeutsche Landesbaank; Westpac Banking Corporation
Financial Information:

	Dec 31 1985 $'000	Dec 31 1986 $'000
Sales revenues	1,109,678	1,114,242
Income before taxes	90,010	105,379
Net income	53,380	57,274
Dividends(1)	14,880	17,079
Dividends per common share	$0.70	$0.90
Earnings per share	$2.73	$3.02
Common stock(2)	18,970	18,977
Retained income	251,135	291,330
Shareholders equity	458,857	499,277

(1) Preferred and Common Stock
(2) Average shares outstanding in thousands

No of Employees: 7,250

CESSNA AIRCRAFT COMPANY

PO Box 1521, Wichita, KS 67201
Tel: (316) 685-9111

Chairman: Russell W Meyer Jr (and Chief Executive Officer)
Senior Executive Officers: Brian E Barents (Senior VP Marketing), John E Moore (Senior VP Personnel), Carl G Miller (VP, Finance and Controller), Bruce Peterman (VP Operations)

PRINCIPAL ACTIVITIES: Manufacturing aircraft, aircraft equipment and components; hydraulic systems
Parent Company: General Dynamics Corporation
Principal Subsidiaries: Fluid Power Division; McCauley Accessory Division
Financial Information:

	Dec 31 1986 $'000
Sales revenues	539,000
(Loss) before taxes	(486)

No of Employees: 5,000

CETEC CORPORATION

9900 Baldwin Place, El Monte, CA 91731
Tel: (818) 442-8840
Telex: 910 587 3539 cetec corp elm

Chairman: Hugh P Moore
President: Robert A Nelson
Senior Executive Officers: Rodney K Madsen, Rodney C Minium, George M McCollister (Secretary and Treasurer)

PRINCIPAL ACTIVITIES: Cetec Corporation enters its Silver Anniversary year with nine operating divisions in diversified high technology industries-ranging from communications equipment to precision plastics to the automotive aftermarket and business software. Most occupy leadership positions in their respective fields, based on unique capabilities and a strong technological base. Many market worldwide with US-made products in successful competition with foreign producers
Trade Names: Cetec Vega, Cetec Raymer, Cetec Software Services, Cetec Ivie, Cetec Benmar, Cetec Gauss, Cetec Original Cylinder, Cetec Anco, Cetec Guardian
Principal Subsidiaries: Cetec International Ltd; Original Cylinder Corporation
Principal Bank: Security Pacific National Bank

Financial Information:

	Dec 31 1985 $'000	Dec 31 1986 $'000
Sales revenues	33,598	31,002
(Loss) before taxes	(2,994)	(248)
Net income (loss)	(1,258)	50
Dividends	441	394
Dividends per share	$0.20	$0.20
Earnings (loss) per share	($0.57)	$0.02
Common stock	636	22
Retained income	7,165	6,408
Shareholders equity	13,523	11,731

No of Employees: 446

CETUS CORPORATION

1400 Fifty-Third St, Emeryville, CA 94608
Tel: (415) 420-3300

Chairman: Ronald E Cape (and Chief Executive Officer)
President: Robert A Fildes (and Chief Operating Officer)
Senior Executive Officers: Robert E Havranek (VP Operations), Michael S Ostrach (VP and General Counsel), Hollings C Renton (Executive VP Finance and Chief Financial Officer), William F Amon Jr (VP Business Development and Industrial Products), Winston J Brill (VP Research and Development, Agracetus), Brian F Issell (VP Research Cetus Immune Corp), Behzad Khosrovi (VP Development), Jeffrey S Price (VP Research and Development), James E Rurka (VP Marketing and Commercial Development), Thomas J White (VP Research)

PRINCIPAL ACTIVITIES: Laboratories for clinical research and development; manufacture of drugs
Principal Subsidiaries: Cetus Healthcare Limited Partnership, Cetus Immune Corp; Cetus Madison Corp; Cetus Palo Alto
Principal Bank: Wells Fargo Bank
Financial Information:

	$'000
Sales revenues	40,000

No of Employees: 640

CF & I STEEL CORPORATION

PO Box 316, Pueblo, CO 81002
Tel: (303) 561-6000
Telex: TWX 910 9399586 cf & i pub

Chairman: Crocker Nevin
President: F J Yaklich Jr
Senior Executive Officers: Gene A Strasheim (VP Finance and Treasurer), Richard L Head (VP Commercial), J D Houghton (VP Operations), K Uttelman (VP Corporate Services)

PRINCIPAL ACTIVITIES: Steel producer (rails, pipe, wire, rod and Rebar)
Principal Bank: Security Pacific
Financial Information:

	Dec 31 1985 $'000	Dec 31 1986 $'000
Sales revenues	253,292	197,055
(Loss) before taxes	(8,631)	(25,119)
Net (loss)	(4,426)	(20,971)
(Loss) per share	($1.12)	($5.29)
Common stock	19,829	19,829
Retained (deficit)	(3,782)	(24,753)
Shareholders equity	82,597	61,626

Principal Shareholders: Employees through an E.S.O.P (40% of outstanding shares)
No of Employees: 2,000

CF INDUSTRIES, INC

Salem Lake Drive, Long Grove, IL 60047
Tel: (312) 438-9500
Telex: WUT 254180 cfindinc lngr

President: R C Liuzzi (and Chief Executive Officer)
Senior Executive Officers: L H Devereaux (Senior VP, Chief Financial Officer and Treasurer), P R Obert (VP, General Counsel and Secretary)

PRINCIPAL ACTIVITIES: Manufacture of fertilizers
Principal Bank: First National Bank of Chicago
Financial Information:

	Dec 31 1986 $'000
Sales revenues	766,140
Shareholders equity	466,033

No of Employees: 1,720

CFS CONTINENTAL, INC

100 S Wacker Drive, Chicago, IL 60606
Tel: (312) 368-7500

Chairman: Robert H Cohn; Vice Chairman: Stanley Owens (and Senior VP)
President: Alvin W Cohn
Senior Executive Officers: Donald W Hansen (Executive VP), R K Scott (VP and General Counsel), R J Hershenhorn (VP Administration), R A Agostinelli (VP Treasurer and Controller), R W Pirsein (VP Human Resources), R C Morgan (VP Tax)

PRINCIPAL ACTIVITIES: Manufacture and wholesale distribution of institutional food, coffee, frozen foods, bakery products and edible fats
Parent Company: A E Staley Mfg Company
Principal Bank: Continental Illinois National Bank and Trust Company of Chicago
Financial Information:

	$'000
Sales revenues	1,500,000

No of Employees: 5,500

CFS FINANCIAL CORPORATION

4020 University Drive, Fairfax, VA 22030
Tel: (703) 691 4400

Chairman: J A Riddle Jr; Vice Chairman: J L Patton
President: Allan R Plumley Jr (and Chief Executive Officer)
Senior Executive Officers: Craig W Anderson (Senior Executive VP, Treasurer and Chief Financial Officer), Jerry R Baugh Jr (Senior Executive VP and Chief Operating Officer), Robert E Johnson (Senior Executive VP), William E Borcherding (Executive VP), Eugene F Dunn (Executive VP and Chief Financial Officer), Ernest L Tressler (Executive VP), W N Ball (Senior VP)

PRINCIPAL ACTIVITIES: Financial services including savings and loans
Principal Subsidiaries: Rocky Mountain Brokerage Co
Financial Information:

	$'000
Revenues	84,000

No of Employees: 430

CHALLENGE-COOK BROS, INC

15421 E Gale Avenue, Industry, CA 91745
Tel: (213) 330-0666
Telex: WUT 670436 chal cook coid

Chairman: Charles E Cook
President: Daniel J McCluer
Senior Executive Officers: James Johnston (Senior VP Engineering), R B Slight (VP Administration and Secretary), L Tackington (VP Construction Machinery)

PRINCIPAL ACTIVITIES: Manufacture of construction equipment; commercial drying and cleaning equipment; concrete pumps
Parent Company: Cook Bros Equipment Co
Principal Bank: Community Bank

Financial Information:

	$'000
Sales revenues	100,000

No of Employees: 1,400

CHAMBERLAIN MANUFACTURING CORPORATION

845 Larch Avenue, Elmhurst, IL 60126

Tel: (312) 279-3600

Telex: WUT 721476 chambhqts elms

Chairman: Richard L Duchossois

President: J J Bergstrom (and Chief Executive Officer)

Senior Executive Officers: J M Palermo (VP, Secretary and General Counsel), F M Nipper (VP), Robert J Ladecky (VP and Controller), E Smith (VP), M J Balcerzak (VP), L S Minkel (VP Finance)

PRINCIPAL ACTIVITIES: Building components and fittings; radio control equipment

Parent Company: Duchossois Industries Inc

Principal Bank: Continental Illinois National Bank and Trust Company of Chicago

Financial Information:

	$'000
Sales revenues	200,000

No of Employees: 4,000

CHAMPION HOME BUILDERS CO

5573 North Street, Dryden, MI 48428

Tel: (313) 796-2211

Telex: 228539

Chairman: Stanley R Day

President: Joseph J Morris (and Chief Executive Officer)

Senior Executive Officers: Operations Officers: Donald B Fisher (Senior VP Manufacturing Operations), Stephen E Summers (VP Sales Operations-Manufactured Housing), William D Ballard (VP Community Sales), Marc A Glova (VP Champion Home Communities Inc, a subsidiary), Thomas L Jensen (VP Manufactured Home Sales-Eastern Region), Jerome B Light (VP Western Manufactured Housing Divisions), Donald J Pascoe (VP-Retail Sales and Chairman Global Homes, Inc a subsidiary), Dwane I Schmer (VP Eastern Manufactured Housing Divisions), David C Struck (VP Manufactured Home Sales-Western Region), Clare G Wentworth (VP Recreation and Commercial Vehicles and President Champion Motor Coach, Inc, a subsidiary). Staff Officers: Robert A Post (VP Finance and Treasurer), Louis M Balius (VP Counsel for Governmental Affairs), Rodger A Dotson (VP Purchasing), Rodney A Knight (VP Legal Affairs and Secretary), Thomas C Krueger (Assistant Treasurer), Charles E Muessig (VP Engineering and Quality Assurance), Gerald W Paga (VP Financial and Accounting Services), John G Sims (Assistant Secretary), J Craig Wiles (Controller)

PRINCIPAL ACTIVITIES: Champion Home Builders Co produces and markets manufactured homes, motor homes and medium-duty buses through a nation-wide network of more than 1,200 independent retailers

Trade Names: Manufactured Homes:- Atlantic, Champion, Concord, Huntington, Manatee, Meadow Creek, Metamora, Park River, Parkridge, Piedmont, Sequoia, Sun Belt, Sunview, Tamarack, Titan, Wolverine, Woodlake. Motor Homes:- Eurocoach, LaSalle, Sun-Seeker, TelStar, Titan, Trans-Van. Park Models:-Parkridge, Park River, Sunview II. Medium-Duty Buses:- Champion; Eurobus

Principal Subsidiaries: Champion Home Communities Inc; Global Homes Inc; North American Insurance Agency Corporation; Builders Credit Corporation; Champion Acceptance Corporation; Hawk Sales Co Inc; Champion Motor Coach Inc

Principal Bank: National Bank of Detroit

Financial Information:

	Feb 28 1986	Feb 27 1987
	$'000	$'000
Revenues	333,609	300,869
(Loss) before taxes	(6,021)	(3,340)
Net (loss)	(2,828)	(1,439)
(Loss) per share net	($0.08)	($0.04)
Common stock	35,841	36,179
Retained income	14,537	13,098
Shareholders equity	52,307	51,566

No of Employees: 3,200

CHAMPION INTERNATIONAL CORPORATION

One Champion Plaza, Stamford, CT 06921

Tel: (203) 358-7000

Cable: CHAMP INT STAMFORD

Telex: 965958

Teletype: 710-474-3197

Chairman: Andrew C Sigler (and Chief Executive Officer and Director)

President: Robert F Longbine (and Chief Operating Officer and Director)

Senior Executive Officers: Aubrey L Cole (Vice Chairman and Director), William R Haselton (Vice Chairman and Director), Gerald J Beiser (Senior VP-Finance), Marvin H Ginskey (Senior VP and General Counsel), Philip R O'Connell (Senior VP and Secretary), John A Ball (Senior VP), Kenwood C Nichols (Senior VP), Judson Hannigan (Senior VP), William H Burchfield (Executive VP), B Taggart Edwards (Executive VP), Mark A Fuller Jr (Executive VP), L C Heist (Executive VP), Austin A Moore Jr (VP-Corporate Controller), Frank Kneisel (VP-Treasurer)

PRINCIPAL ACTIVITIES: Champion has restructured its paper, packaging, and building products business since its acquisition of St Regis Corporation late in 1984. The following description of Champion's business activities reflects divestitures thru 1986. 1. Paper:- A. Manufacturing: Bleached kraft market pulp; coated and uncoated free-sheet printing and writing grades; lightweight coated publications papers; uncoated groundwood grades; newsprint; bleached paperboard. B. Converting: Milk and juice cartons; ovenable trays. C. Distribution: Printing and writing papers; packaging products; publishing and printing, industrial, retail and institutional users' supply items; food service products. 2. Packaging:- Champion sold most of its packaging operations effective in January 1986. Remaining operations will include the following products: Kraft bag paper; linerboard; shopping bags; gift wrap. 3. Building products:- Plywood; lumber and studs. Champion is a broad-spectrum white paper company with substantial lumber and plywood capacity and only a limited position in packaging. The number of employees was substantially reduced when previously announced divested operations and certain facilities closures were completed

Trade Names: Champion; Nationwide Papers, for distribution operations; DairyPak, for milk and juice cartons; Weldwood, for Canadian building products

Principal Subsidiaries: Champion Papel e Celulose, SA (99%) (Brazil); Weldwood of Canada Limited (73%) (Canada)

Principal Bank: Morgan Guaranty Trust Company; Chemical Bank

Financial Information:

	Dec 31 1985 $'000	Dec 31 1986 $'000
Sales revenues	5,769,759	4,387,623
Income before taxes	245,469	312,980
Net income	163,139	200,832
Common dividends-declared(1)	42,719	48,793
Common dividends per share(1)	$0.46	$0.52
Earnings per common share(2)	$1.59	$2.05
Common stock(3)	92,890	94,202
Retained income	1,331,648	1,463,795
Shareholders equity	2,599,088	2,592,395

(1) declared
(2) diluted
(3) shares outstanding at year-end

No of Employees: 32,200

CHAMPION PARTS REBUILDERS INC

2525 22nd Street, Oak Brook, IL 60521
Tel: (312) 986 6100

Chairman: Charles P Schwartz Jr (and President)
Senior Executive Officers: Donato A Savini (Executive VP), Leonard D O'Brien (VP Finance, Secretary and Treasurer), Robert C Mikolashek (VP Manufacturing)

PRINCIPAL ACTIVITIES: Manufacture of components for motor vehicles
Principal Subsidiaries: Champion/Party
Financial Information:

	$'000
Sales revenues	100,900

No of Employees: 2,360

CHAMPION PRODUCTS INC

3141 Monroe Avenue, Rochester, NY 14618
Tel: (716) 385-3200
Telex: WUT 978222 champion roc

Chairman: John J Tanis
President: Roger Holland (and Chief Executive Officer)
Senior Executive Officers: Harold Feinbloom (Senior VP), William Loftus (VP Research and Development), Thomas D Sheehy (VP Operations), Fred Lulof (VP International), A J Paridon (VP and General Manager), John F Hackett (Treasurer)

PRINCIPAL ACTIVITIES: Manufacture of leisurewear and sportswear; retail clothing
Principal Subsidiaries: CP International Sales Co; Champion Finishing Co Inc; Champion Knitwear Co Inc; Champion Products Export Co; Pensic Corp
Principal Bank: Chemical Bank
Financial Information:

	$'000
Sales revenues	119,000

No of Employees: 2,530

CHAMPION SPARK PLUG CO

900 Upton Avenue, Toledo, OH 43661
Tel: (419) 535-2567
Telex: RCA 212532 chsp ur

Chairman: R A Stranahan Jr (and Chief Executive Officer)
President: O L Henry
Senior Executive Officers: R J Brotje Jr (Chief Executive Officer), D A Ramsdell (VP US Automobile Products Operation), D M Stevens (VP Finance and Administration), R D Kudner (VP Advertising/Merchandising), R L Black (VP Research and Product Development), N P Atherton (VP Spark Plug Manufacturing Operations)

PRINCIPAL ACTIVITIES: Motor vehicle spark plugs and windshield wipers; fabricated and cold drawn steel products; medical equipment
Principal Subsidiaries: Anderson Co of IN; Anco Domestic International Sales Corp; Westchester Industrial Park; Baron Drawn Steel Corp; Champion Spark Plug (Far East) Ltd; Champion Spark Plug International Sales Corp; Champion World Air Inc; Devilbiss Electronics Corp; Devilbiss Leasing Co; Iowa Industries Inc; PB Marketing Inc
Financial Information:

	Dec 31 1985 $'000	Dec 31 1986 $'000
Sales revenues	829,400	883,840

No of Employees: 12,450

CHAMPLIN PETROLEUM CO

345 Park Avenue, New York, NY 10154
Tel: (212) 418-7800

Chairman: W L Adams (and Chief Executive Officer)
President: R F Cox (and Chief Operating Officer)
Senior Executive Officers: W S Cook (Chairman Executive Committee), L W Marshall (Senior VP Manufacturing and Marketing), W F Surette (VP Corporate Finance), J P Halan (VP Benefit Plan Administration), D W Bossert (VP and Regional Manager Denver), G J Casler (VP Supply and Transport), W G Christensen (VP Natural Gas Sales), M S Kraemer (VP and Regional Manager Gulf Coast Area, Houston), J R Mendenhall (VP Taxes), J M Pachman (VP Planning and Administration), L D Prescott (VP Government Relations and Public Affairs), R S Jackson (VP Finance), R K Russell (VP Industrial Relations), W M Westhoff (VP Petrochemicals), B J Zimmerman (VP and General Counsel)

PRINCIPAL ACTIVITIES: Oil and gas exploration and production; petrochemicals
Parent Company: Union Pacific Corporation, New York, NY
Principal Bank: InterFirst Bank Fort Worth
Financial Information:

	$'000
Sales revenues	3,800,000

No of Employees: 3,000

CHARLES, CHARLOTTE, INC

2501 North Elston Avenue, Chicago, IL 60647
Tel: (312) 772 8310

Chairman: Steve Reich (and President)
Senior Executive Officers: Margrit S Reich (Executive VP), Stewart H Reich (VP), David A Reich (Treasurer)

PRINCIPAL ACTIVITIES: Supply of grocery products including jellies, preserves, bakery products and gourmet food items
Principal Bank: Continental Illinois National Bank and Trust Company
Financial Information:

	$'000
Sales revenues	33,870

No of Employees: 250

CHARLES MACHINE WORKS, INC

PO Box 66, 1959 W Fir Avenue, Perry, OK 73077
Tel: (405) 336-4404
Telex: TWX 910 830 6580 dich wich peyr

Chairman: Ed Malzahn (and President); Vice Chairman: Mary Malzahn
Senior Executive Officers: Jim Roth (VP), J D Sadler (Secretary and Treasurer)

PRINCIPAL ACTIVITIES: Manufacture of earth moving machinery
Principal Bank: First National Bank of Perry

Financial Information:

	$'000
Sales revenues	80,000

No of Employees: 750

CHARLES OF THE RITZ GROUP LTD

40 West 57th Street, New York, NY 10019
Tel: (212) 621-7300
Telex: ITT 423516 squbui

Chairman: Martin H Schmidt
President: Robert H Miller (and Chief Executive Officer)
Senior Executive Officers: Kristina Wrba (Group VP SL and Cosmetic Collection), Philip D Brazier (Senior VP Finance), John V Grace (Senior VP Worldwide Marketing), Timothy A Hogan (Senior VP Operations), David S Mosteller (Senior VP, Secretary and Legal Counsel), Richard C Berke (Senior VP Personnel and Administration), John Siebert (Senior VP Research and Development)

PRINCIPAL ACTIVITIES: Manufacture of cosmetics, perfumes and toiletries
Parent Company: Squibb Corporation, Princeton, NJ
Principal Bank: Manufacturers Hanover Trust Company
Financial Information:

	$'000
Sales revenues	400,000

No of Employees: 4,000

CHARLOTTE CHARLES INC

See CHARLES, CHARLOTTE, INC

CHARLOTTE PIPE & FOUNDRY CO

PO Box 35430, Charlotte, NC 28235
Tel: (704) 372-5030

Chairman: Roddey Dowd
President: Edward H Hardison (and Treasurer)
Senior Executive Officers: Frank Dowd Jr (Chairman Executive Committee), William F Austin (Senior VP Foundry Operations), Barton Hodges (Senior VP Plastics), James R Latham (VP and Secretary), John A Biggers (VP), Thomas H Hobbs (VP)

PRINCIPAL ACTIVITIES: Manufacture of iron and plastic pipes
Financial Information:

	$'000
Sales revenues	58,000

No of Employees: 800

CHARMING SHOPPES INC

450 Winks Lane, Bensalem, PA 19020
Tel: (215) 245 9100

Chairman: David V Wachs (and Secretary)
President: Morris Sidewater (and Chief Executive Officer)
Senior Executive Officers: Arthur Sidewater (Senior Executive VP), Ellis Wachs (Senior Executive VP)

PRINCIPAL ACTIVITIES: Retail of women's clothing and specialty products
Principal Subsidiaries: Charming Shoppes; Fashion Bug
Principal Bank: American Bank & Trust Co
Financial Information:

	1986 $'000
Sales revenues	521,000
Net income	40,000

No of Employees: 4,800

CHARTER COMPANY

One Charter Plaza, Box 2017, Jacksonville, FL 32202
Tel: (904) 358-4111

Chairman: Raymond K Mason
President: Thomas Moody (and Chief Executive Officer)
Senior Executive Officers: Norman K Green (Senior VP International Affairs), Ray M Van Landingham (Senior VP), Larry Singleton (VP Corporate Taxes and Chief Accounting Officer), Wallace A Patzke Jr (VP and Comptroller), John Brent (VP and Treasurer)

PRINCIPAL ACTIVITIES: Oil refining; broadcasting; publishing
Principal Subsidiaries: Charter Crude Oil Co; Charter International Oil Co; Charter Land Co; Charter Marine Corp; Charter Oil (AK) Inc; Charter Oil Co; Acorn Pipeline Co; Charter Coal Co; Northeast Petroleum Industries Inc; Charter Marine Fuels Inc; Charter Marketing Co; Luqua Inc; Manchester Terminal Co; Riffe Petroleum Co; Investors Drilling Exploration Co; Riffe Marine Corp; Charter Security Life Insurance Co; Charter Security Life Insurance Co Inc; New England Petroleum Corp; Nepco Terminal Corp
Principal Bank: Jacksonville National Bank
Financial Information:

	Dec 31 1986 $'000
Sales revenues	1,329,260
Net income	153,180
Earnings per share	$3.23
Shareholders equity	47,490

No of Employees: 2,780

CHARTER FEDERAL SAVINGS & LOAN ASSOCIATION

110 Piedmont Avenue, Bristol, VA 24201
Tel: (703) 669 5101

Chairman: Frank Leonard
President: E L Byington (and Chief Executive Officer)
Senior Executive Officers: S Spencer Edmunds (Senior VP), Robert A Glover (Senior VP), Clifton E Noble (Senior VP), S C Sumner (Senior VP), Audrey H Ketron (VP and Treasurer), Julie E Powell (Secretary and Assistant VP)

PRINCIPAL ACTIVITIES: Financial services including savings and loans
Principal Bank: Dominion Bank

No of Employees: 265

CHARTER MARKETING CO

21 W Church, Jacksonville, FL 32202
Tel: (904) 358-4111

President: Joseph Leonardo
Senior Executive Officers: Arthur L Cahoon (VP), C A Cary (Senior VP Operations), Ronald R Johnson (VP Marketing), William O Schwind (VP Marketing Development), W R Booth (VP Supply and Transfers)

PRINCIPAL ACTIVITIES: Operation of gasoline service stations; fuel and petrochemical distribution
Parent Company: Charter Oil Company, Jacksonville, FL
Principal Bank: Community State Bank
Financial Information:

	$'000
Sales revenues	465,000

Principal Shareholders: Charter Company, Jacksonville, FL
No of Employees: 2,500

CHARTER MEDICAL CORPORATION

577 Mulberry Street, Post Office Box 209, Macon, GA 31298
Tel: (912) 742-1161

Chairman: William A Fickling Jr (and President)
Senior Executive Officers: James D Daher (Executive VP Hospital Operations), C Michael Ford (Executive VP Finance and Secretary), J Rodney Laughlin (Executive VP Planning and Development), Ben G Porter (Senior VP Public Affairs and International), Ronald L Doley (Senior VP Human Resources)

PRINCIPAL ACTIVITIES: Operation of hospitals and clinics; provision of a wide range of medical services
Principal Bank: Bank of America
Financial Information:

	Sep 30 1986	Sep 30 1987
	$'000	$'000
Sales revenues	803,188	1,009,471
Income before taxes	85,871	101,856
Net income	43,655	52,043
Dividends	5,934	7,403
Dividends per share	$0.19	$0.24
Earnings per share	$1.40	$1.69
Common stock	31,140	30,877
Retained income	172,201	213,328
Shareholders equity	225,928	263,043

No of Employees: 14,800

CHARTER OIL CO

21 W Church Street, Jacksonville, FL 32202
Tel: (904) 358-4395
Telex: WUI 6827065 charter jax b

Chairman: Alexander Zechella
President: James D Francis
Senior Executive Officers: Richard J Bastien (Executive VP Marketing), Alistair H McNaughton (Executive VP Supply and Manufacturing), K C Caldabaugh (VP), Fred G McGinnis (VP Administration), Wallace A Patzke Jr (VP and Controller), Howard C Serkin (VP), John W Brent (VP and Treasurer)

PRINCIPAL ACTIVITIES: Oil refining; gasoline stations
Parent Company: The Charter Company, Jacksonville, FL
Principal Bank: First National Bank of Boston
Financial Information:

	$'000
Sales revenues	4,000,000

No of Employees: 3,000

CHARVOZ-CARSEN CORPORATION

5 Daniel Road East, Fairfield, NJ 07006
Tel: (201) 227 6500

Chairman: Charles M Diker (and President and Chief Executive Officer)
President: James H Slater
Senior Executive Officers: Claude Bernard (Senior VP), Edward E Meltz (VP Finance and Treasurer), William W Greene (Secretary), Darwin C Dornbush (Assistant Secretary)

PRINCIPAL ACTIVITIES: Supply of optical and audio equipment, photographic, scientific and medical equipment
Principal Bank: Irving Trust Company
Financial Information:

	$'000
Sales revenues	45,820

No of Employees: 200

CHAS LEVY CIRCULATING CO

See LEVY, CHAS, CIRCULATING CO

CHASE MANHATTAN CORPORATION

One Chase Manhattan Plaza, New York, NY 10081
Tel: (212) 552-2222
Telex: WUI 62910 cmb uw

Chairman: Willard C Butcher (and Chief Executive Officer); Vice Chairmen: Robert R Douglass, Arthur F Ryan, Anthony P Terracciano
President: Thomas G Labrecque (and Chief Operating Officer)
Senior Executive Officers: A F Allinson (Executive VP), James W Bergford (Executive VP), Donald L Boudreau (Executive VP), Richard J Boyle (Executive VP), A W Elliott (Executive VP), M P Esposito Jr (Executive VP and Controller), Joseph J Harkins (Executive VP), Robert M Lichten (Executive VP), Wolfgang Schoellkopf (Executive VP and Treasurer), Francis X Stankard (Executive VP), Michael Urkowitz (Executive VP), P T Walker (Executive VP), L Edward Shaw (Executive VP and Legal Counsel)

PRINCIPAL ACTIVITIES: Banking
Principal Subsidiaries: CCC Holding Inc; Chase Commercial Corp; Chase Home Mortgage Corp; Chase Investors Management Corp; Chase Manhattan Bank; Chase Bank International; Chase Econometrics; Chase Manhattan Capital Corp; Chase Manhattan Overseas Bank Corp; Computer Power Inc; Interactive Data Corp; Chase Manhattan Realty Leasing; Chase Manhattan Service Corp; Chase T/C Service Corp; Chase US Consumer Services; CMRCC Inc; Duval County Properties Inc; Half Moon Towers of Miami Inc; PPW Inc; Villa Del Sol of Stuart
Principal Bank: Chase Manhattan Bank
Financial Information:

	Dec 31 1985	Dec 31 1986
	$'000	$'000
Net income	564,820	585,360
Earnings per share	$6.39	$6.63
Shareholders equity	4,397,136	4,280,310
Deposits	61,353,050	66,002,844
Total assets	87,685,442	94,765,815

No of Employees: 47,480

CHATHAM CORPORATION

1200 Shermer Road, Northbrook, IL 60062
Tel: (312) 498-4495

President: Garry Brainin
Senior Executive Officers: Robert J Bond Jr (VP and Secretary), John F Guy (VP), T Kelly (Controller)

PRINCIPAL ACTIVITIES: Holding company with interests in the manufacture of industrial equipment; food manufacturing plant; electrical and electronic equipment; telecommunications equipment; broadcasting
Principal Subsidiaries: Altair Corp; Harvest Industries Inc; W-P Milling Co; Hurletron Inc; Vacudyne Inc
Principal Bank: American National Bank and Trust Company of Chicago
Financial Information:

	$'000
Sales revenues	50,000

No of Employees: 400

CHATHAM MFG CO

E Main Street, Elkin, NC 28621
Tel: (919) 835-2211
Telex: TWX 5109227195 chatham elkn

Chairman: Calder W Womble
President: Alan L Payne
Senior Executive Officers: W F Altemueller (Executive VP), David H Cline III (VP Finance and Treasurer), C L Neaves (VP Blanket Division), W F Williams (VP Manufacturing), D N Lowe (VP Industrial Relations), R F Callaway (VP Purchasing), C J Moore (VP Engineering), Lucy C Everett (VP Administration and Secretary), A D Andrews (VP Furniture Upholstery), J L Loew (VP Automotive Upholstery)

PRINCIPAL ACTIVITIES: Manufacture of household textiles including blankets and upholstery fabrics
Principal Bank: Wachovia Bank & Trust Co

Financial Information:

	Dec 31 1985	Dec 31 1986
	$'000	$'000
Sales revenues	119,983	124,399
Income before taxes	5,666	9,121
Net income	3,199	5,189
Dividends	1,433	1,367
Dividends per share	$0.88	$0.80
Earnings per share	$1.79	$3.07
Common stock	1,800	1,800
Retained income	52,610	56,432
Shareholders equity	53,218	57,037

No of Employees: 2,345

CHATTEM, INC

1715 W 38th Street, Chattanooga, TN 37409
Tel: (615) 821-4571
Telex: WUT 558463 chattem cta

President: Alex Guerry
Senior Executive Officers: Zan Guerry (Executive VP and Chief Financial Officer), Charles Jolly (VP Legal Affairs), G H Behling (VP Personnel), D C Harvey (VP Accounting), H E Ottley (VP Consumer Products), Gary H Henderson (VP Consumer Products), James G Brown (VP Chemicals), Robert E Bosworth (VP and Chief Financial Officer)

PRINCIPAL ACTIVITIES: Manufacture of toiletries and cosmetics; specialty chemicals
Principal Bank: American National Bank and Trust Company
Financial Information:

	$'000
Sales revenues	64,000

No of Employees: 400

CHB FOODS, INC

7351 Crider Avenue, PO Box 218, Pico Rivera, CA 90660
Tel: (213) 949 6634
Telex: TWX 910-345-7466

Chairman: Robert J Pasarow (and President)
Senior Executive Officers: Michael Pasarow (VP), Earl W Deharak (Secretary and Treasurer)

PRINCIPAL ACTIVITIES: Canned meat and fish; canned pet foods; mayonnaise, relishes and sauces; canned fruit and vegetables
Principal Bank: Bank of America
Financial Information:

	$'000
Sales revenues	290,000

No of Employees: 3,500

CHECKER MOTORS CORPORATION

2016 N Pitcher Street, Kalamazoo, MI 49007
Tel: (616) 343-6121
Telex: TWX 810 2775779 checker kmz

President: David R Markin
Senior Executive Officers: L Temple (VP Engineering and Factory), J J Love (VP Sales), R A Yealin (VP and Treasurer), A E Samson (Assistant VP Personnel), S Wilson (Assistant VP Materials), B F Lewis (Assistant VP Sales)

PRINCIPAL ACTIVITIES: Metal fabrication; operation of taxicab and airport bus services
Principal Subsidiaries: Airlines Transportation Co; American Country Insurance Co; Cab Service & Parts Corp; Checker Motor Sales Corp; Parmelee Motor Fuel Co; Yellow Cab Co
Principal Bank: Continental Illinois National Bank and Trust Company of Chicago
Financial Information:

	$'000
Sales revenues	96,000

No of Employees: 1,500

CHEF FRANCISCO INC

Box 1187, Eugene, OR 97440
Tel: (503) 484-2182
Telex: TWX 510 5970377 cgefr ab eug

President: Frank Elsener
Senior Executive Officers: Charles Koenig (Executive VP Manufacturing), Nick Chilton (VP Grocery Products), Walter Dundon (VP Research and Development), Gary Knight (VP Finance), Donald Kerr (VP Operations), Theodore Scherer (VP Sales)

PRINCIPAL ACTIVITIES: Manufacture of frozen foods including ready-made-meals
Parent Company: John Labatt Ltd
Financial Information:

	$'000
Sales revenues	100,000

No of Employees: 1,000

CHELSEA INDUSTRIES, INC

1360 Soldiers Field Road, Boston, MA 02135
Tel: (617) 787-9010

Chairman: Ronald G Casty (and President and Chief Executive Officer)
Senior Executive Officers: Norman S Dunn (Executive VP and Treasurer), David L Phillips (VP Plastics), Milton Graff (VP Administration), Emil S Bernstein (VP Finance and Corporate Development)

PRINCIPAL ACTIVITIES: Plastic and plastic products; footwear; coated textiles; electronic components
Principal Subsidiaries: Bes-Pak & Co Inc; R S Electronics Inc
Principal Bank: First National Bank of Boston
Financial Information:

	$'000
Sales revenues	184,527

No of Employees: 1,900

CHEMED CORPORATION

1200 DuBois Tower, Cincinnati, OH 45202
Tel: (513) 762-6900

Chairman: J Peter Grace Jr
President: Edward L Hutton (and Chief Executive Officer)
Senior Executive Officers: Paul C Voet (Executive VP and Chief Operating Officer), John L Kenrich (Executive VP and Chief Administrative Officer), Ronald J Brickner (Senior VP and Controller), Kevin J McNamara (VP and Secretary), Anthony C Hutton (VP), Joseph Hutton (VP), Sandra E Laney (VP), Samuel K Wait (VP), Thomas E Westerfield (VP)

PRINCIPAL ACTIVITIES: Chemed Corporation is a specialty chemical company with leading positions in Industrial cleaning and maintenance; janitorial supply products and services; laundry detergents and related specialties; water treatment products; residential and industrial sewer, drain and pipe cleaning
Principal Subsidiaries: Fabrilife Chemicals Inc; National Sanitary Supply Co; Roto-Rooter Inc (62%)
Principal Bank: Fifth Third Bank
Financial Information:

	Dec 31 1985	Dec 31 1986
	$'000	$'000
Sales & service revenues	326,354	359,476
Income before taxes	35,013	17,400
Net income	21,858	37,633
Dividends	13,368	13,959
Dividends per share	$1.52	$1.56
Earnings per share	$2.49	$4.21
Common stock	9,292	9,440
Retained income	28,922	52,596
Shareholders equity	90,540	119,832

No of Employees: 4,783

CHEMICAL ENTERPRISES, INC

8582 Katy Freeway, Houston, TX 77024
Tel: (713() 461-0606
Telex: WUT 775687 cei hou

President: Dallas Cantwell
Senior Executive Officers: G C Mathiesen (Executive VP), Gary D McSwain (VP Finance), Jim L Hight (VP Industrial Chemicals), M G Warthan (VP Product Systems and Development)

PRINCIPAL ACTIVITIES: Manufacture of fertilizers
Principal Subsidiaries: Sun-Vue Fertilizer Inc
Principal Bank: RepublicBank Houston
Financial Information:

	$'000
Sales revenues	80,000

No of Employees: 135

CHEMICAL EXPRESS COMPANY

4645 N Central Expwy, Dallas, TX 75205
Tel: (214) 559-0580

Chairman: Stratton J Georgoulis (and Chief Executive Officer)
Senior Executive Officers: T O'Roark (VP Finance)

PRINCIPAL ACTIVITIES: Rental and leasing of motor carrier equipment
Parent Company: TIC United Corporation, Dallas, TX
Principal Bank: Interfirst Bank
Financial Information:

	$'000
Sales revenues	50,000

No of Employees: 1,000

CHEMICAL FABRICS CORPORATION

701 Daniel Webster Highway, Merrimac, NH 03054
Tel: (603) 424 9000

President: Duane C Montopali (and Chief Financial Officer)
Senior Executive Officers: Charles P O'Leary (Executive VP and Treasurer), Edwin J Emmet (VP), John D Masters (VP and Secretary), John A Effenberger (VP Technology)

PRINCIPAL ACTIVITIES: Manufacture of synthetic fabrics
Principal Subsidiaries: Birdair Structures Inc
Principal Bank: Morgan Guaranty Trust Company
Financial Information:

	$'000
Sales revenues	25,000

No of Employees: 280

CHEMICAL LEAMAN CORPORATION

102 Pickering Way, Lionville, PA 19353
Tel: (215) 363 4200

President: S F Miness Jr (and Chief Executive Officer)
Senior Executive Officers: Charles E Fernald Jr (Senior VP Finance), William O'Kane (Secretary and Legal Counsel)

PRINCIPAL ACTIVITIES: Operation of road transport and haulage services
Principal Subsidiaries: Chemical Leaman Tank Lines Inc; Chemical Properties Inc; Tank Service Company
Principal Bank: Philadelphia National Bank
Financial Information:

	$'000
Sales revenues	163,130

No of Employees: 2,300

CHEMICAL NEW YORK CORPORATION

277 Park Avenue, New York, NY 10172
Tel: (212) 310-6161

Chairman: Walter V Shipley (and Chief Executive Officer); Vice Chairman: Richard K LeBlond II
Presidents: Robert J Callander, Thomas S Johnson, Robert I Lipp
Senior Executive Officers: Alan H Fishman (Senior Executive VP), Kenneth N LaVine Jr (Executive VP), John J Higgins (Controller)

PRINCIPAL ACTIVITIES: Banking
Principal Subsidiaries: Bach Holding Corp; Brown & Co Securities Corp; Chemadvertising Inc; Chemco International Inc; Chemgraphics Systems Inc; Chemical Bank; Chem Credit Inc; Chem Lease Worldwide Inc; Chem Network Processing Services Inc; Chemco International Leasing; Chemical Bank International; Chemical International Finance Ltd; Chemical Mortgage Co; Chemical Business Credit Corp; Chemical Equity Inc; Chemical First State Corp; Chemexec Relocation Systems; Chemical Futures Inc; Chemical Real Holdings Inc; Chemical Realty Corp; Chemical Venture Capital Corp; Favia Hill & Associates Inc; Investment & Capital Management Inc; ICM of the South Inc; Portfolio Group Inc; Pronto Inc; Pronton Link Corp; Alexander Scriver & Associates Inc; Sunamerica Corp; Sunamerica Financial Corp; Sentry Acceptance Corp; Van Deventer & Hoch Inc
Financial Information:

	Dec 31 1985	Dec 31 1986
	$'000	$'000
Net income	390,187	402,430
Earnings per share	$7.33	$7.57
Shareholders equity	2,819,980	3,119,854
Deposits	34,503,315	39,054,910
Total assets	56,990,170	60,564,123

No of Employees: 20,993

CHEMLAWN CORPORATION

8275 North High Street, Columbus, OH 43085
Tel: (614) 888 3572

Chairman: L Jack Van Fossen (and President and Chief Executive Officer)
Senior Executive Officers: Don L Luke (Executive VP and Chief Operating Officer), Richard W Ballantyne (Senior VP and Chief Financial Officer), Mary Jane Goldthwaite (Secretary), John H Perdue (Treasurer and Assistant Secretary)

PRINCIPAL ACTIVITIES: Horticultural equipment and services
Principal Subsidiaries: Chemlawn Supply Corporation
Principal Bank: Bank One
Financial Information:

	$'000
Sales revenues	330,000

No of Employees: 4,500

CHEMTECH INDUSTRIES, INC

1655 Des Peres Road, St Louis, MO 63131
Tel: (314) 966-9900
Telex: TWX 910 7601488 chemtichhq stl

Chairman: William F Schierholz (and Chief Executive Officer)
President: Fletcher N Anderson
Senior Executive Officers: R S McCambridge (Executive VP and General Manager Manufacturing Products Group), J Dwight Bell (Executive VP and Chief Operating Officer), C F Luft (VP and General Manager Distribution), D A Kunz (VP Finance and Treasurer), D M Davis (VP and Secretary)

PRINCIPAL ACTIVITIES: Chemical manufacture
Principal Bank: Centerre Bank
Financial Information:

	$'000
Sales revenues	87,000

No of Employees: 300

CHEROKEE GROUP

12544 Saticoy Street, North Hollywood, CA 91605
Tel: (213) 875-1002

Chairman: James P Argyropoulos (and Chief Executive Officer)
President: Robert Margolis (and Chief Operating Officer)
Senior Executive Officers: Arthur P Argyris (VP of Manufacturing, Shoes), Terrance J Smith (Chief Financial Officer, Secretary), Jay L Kester (Executive VP), Charles R Campbell (VP of Production of Cherokee Apparel), Gloria G Goldberg Teague (VP Marketing/Merchandising), Richard L Ashbee (President, Licensing)

PRINCIPAL ACTIVITIES: Manufacturers of women's, children's and men's apparel, shoes and accessories
Trade Names: Cherokee
Principal Subsidiaries: Cherokee Apparel Corporation; Cherokee Trading Corporation
Principal Bank: Wells Fargo Bank
Financial Information:

	$'000
Sales revenues	83,000

No of Employees: 651

CHERRY ELECTRICAL PRODUCTS CORPORATION

3600 Sunset Avenue, Waukegan, IL 60087
Tel: (312) 662-9200
Telex: TWX 910 235 1572 cherry elect

Chairman: Walter L Cherry (and Chief Executive Officer)
President: Peter B Cherry (and Chief Operating Officer)
Senior Executive Officers: Charles Heyward (VP Materials and Services), Donald Straka (VP Manufacturing), Grant T Hollett (VP Production), Fred Ebert (VP Engineering), Edward Mass (VP Finance, Secretary and Treasurer)

PRINCIPAL ACTIVITIES: Manufacture of electrical equipment including switches and semiconductors
Principal Subsidiaries: Cherry Display Products Corp; Cherry Semiconductor Corp
Principal Bank: Harris Trust and Savings Bank
Financial Information:

	$'000
Sales revenues	126,000

No of Employees: 2,800

CHESAPEAKE CORPORATION

19th & Main Sts, Box 311, West Point, VA 23181
Tel: (804) 843-5000
Telex: 82-7308; 82-7452

Chairman: Sture G Olsson
President: J Carter Fox (and Chief Executive Officer)
Senior Executive Officers: Paul A Dresser Jr (Group VP-Finance & Administration and Chief Financial Officer), J Paul Harper (Group VP-Woodlands & Wood Products), Frederick V Ernst (Group VP-Kraft Products), Robert S Argabright II (Group VP-Containers), James D Nagy (VP, Production-Kraft Products), Peter R Chiericozzi (VP, Sales-Kraft Products), Alvah H Eubank Jr (Corporate Treasurer), J P Causey Jr (Corporate Secretary and General Counsel), John W Kirk (Controller), Thomas A Smith (VP-Human Resources) Louis K Matherne Jr (Assistant Treasurer)

PRINCIPAL ACTIVITIES: Chesapeake Corporation, an integrated paper and forest products company, is a major manufacturer of pulp and paper products, including unbleached kraft linerboard and paper, bleached hardwood market pulp and commercial and industrial tissue products. It converts paperboard and other materials into corrugated containers, displays and other packaging products. Chesapeake also converts timber into lumber. It also operates a real estate subsidiary. Chesapeake, its divisions and subsidiaries, operate from 22 company-owned locations in nine states. The company owns 362,000 acres of timberland in three states
Trade Names: OXY-BRITE, TRI-KRAFT, TRI-LITE, TRI-BRITE
Principal Subsidiaries: Wisconsin Tissue Mills Inc; Delmarva Properties Inc
Principal Bank: United Virginia Bank
Financial Information:

	Dec 31 1986 $'000
Sales revenues	599,800
Income before taxes	21,900
Net income	13,700
Dividends	8,600
Dividends per share	$0.86
Earnings per share	$1.36
Common stock*	10,137
Retained income	5,100
Shareholders equity	215,200

*number of shares in thousands

No of Employees: 4,556

CHESAPEAKE UTILITIES CORPORATION

350 South Queen Street, Dover, DE 19901
Tel: (302) 734 6700

President: John W Jardine Jr (and Chief Executive Officer)
Senior Executive Officers: Ralph J Adkins (VP and Treasurer), Frederick A Phillips (VP and Assistant Secretary), Wayne L Hart (Secretary and Assistant Treasurer), James R Lowe (Assistant Secretary)

PRINCIPAL ACTIVITIES: Supply of natural gas
Principal Subsidiaries: Eastern Shore Natural Gas Company; Sharpgas Inc
Principal Bank: Maryland National Bank
Financial Information:

	$'000
Sales revenues	45,900

No of Employees: 160

CHESEBROUGH-POND'S INC

Westport, CT 06881-0851
Tel: (203) 222-3000
Telex: (203) 222-4435

Chairman: Ralph E Ward
President: George F Goebeler (President, Consumer Products Group), Roy Sambrook (President, Chemical Products Group)
Senior Executive Officers: Donald G Wiesen (Vice Chairman and Chief Financial Officer), Richard P Schiefele (Vice Chairman), Robert M Phillips (Vice President), Robert H Mann (Senior VP, Secretary and General Counsel), Richard H Bourret (VP, President, Bass Division), Anthony J Butterworth (VP, President International Division, Consumer Products Group), Robert E Crow (VP, President, Basic Chemicals Division), Carl R Garr (VP, President, Polymer Division), Robert E Karlson (VP, President, Hospital Products Division), Conrad S Kent (VP, President, Specialty and Food Products Division), Gary N Malloch (VP, President Health and Beauty Products Division), Joseph P Monteleone (VP, President, International Division, Chemical Products Group), Edward I Rabin (VP, President Prince Matchabelli Division), Charles B Strauss (VP, President, Packaged Foods Division), John M Sullivan (VP, Prince Division), Milan Turk (VP, President, Agricultural Products Division), Ethan E Galloway (Executive VP), Rocco Balestriere (VP Controller), Melvin I Davis (VP), Edward C Hughes (VP), Kenneth R Lightcap (VP, Public Relations), George J Luby (VP), Richard I Mateles (VP), Theodore C Mullins (VP), Richard J Rolzhausen (VP and Treasurer), William M Schmitt (VP), Stephen R Walls (VP)

PRINCIPAL ACTIVITIES: Manufacturer and marketer of branded consumer products. Divisions include Packaged Foods, Health and Beauty, Bass, Prince, Prince Matchabelli, Hospital Products, International Health and Beauty, also manufacturer and marketer of agricultural, specialty and basic chemicals, hybrid seeds and food ingredients

Trade Names: Ragu, Adolph's, Cutex, Pond's, Q-tips, Rave, Intensive Care, Vaseline, Cachet, Wind Song, Bass, Aziza, Prince Matchebelli, Prince Tennis Racquets and Apparel, Erno Laszlo, Ballo & Faichney Thermometers, Kangaroo Entral Feeding Systems, Corvel Coating Powders, Nylaflow & Piranaho Hose Products. International:- Clyo Fragrances, Cotrino Cotton Swabs, Durban's Toothpaste, Lysoform Cleanser

Principal Subsidiaries: Prince; Bass; Prince Matchabelli; Stauffer Chemical; Polymer Corporation; Applied Solar Energy Corporation

Principal Banks: Morgan Guarantee; Chase Manhattan Bank

Financial Information:

	Dec 31 1986 $'000
Sales revenues	312,000

No of Employees: 21,500

CHEVRON CHEMICAL COMPANY

6001 Bollinger Canyon Rd, San Ramon, CA 94583
Tel: (415) 842-5500
Telex: 470074 CHEV UI

President: R W Davis (and Chief Executive Officer)

Senior Executive Officers: J E Peppercorn (Senior VP), J R Dixon (VP Finance, Secretary and Treasurer), D A Newell (VP Law), R F Dennison (VP and General Manager Ortho Agricultural Chemicals Division), J R Lieto (VP and General Manager Ortho Consumer Products Division), P McCrea (VP and General Manager Ortho Fertilizer Division), J R Sanders (VP and General Manager Oronite Additives Division), E M Kura (VP and General Manager Aromatics and Derivatives Division), G T Scott (VP and General Manager Olefins and Derivatives Division)

PRINCIPAL ACTIVITIES: Production of petrochemicals, agricultural chemicals and industrial chemicals

Parent Company: Chevron Corporation, San Francisco, CA

Principal Bank: Bank of America

Financial Information:

	1986 $'000
Sales revenues	2,152,000
Net income	108,000

No of Employees: 4,900

CHEVRON CORPORATION

225 Bush Street, San Francisco, CA 94104
Tel: (415) 894-7700

Chairman: George M Keller (and Chief Executive Officer); Vice Chairmen: K T Derr, James E Lee

Senior Executive Officers: J Dennis Bonney (VP Logistics and Trading), Lawrence W Funkhouser (VP Exploration and Production), W Jones McQuinn (VP Foreign), Willis J Price (VP), Rodney E Willoughby (VP and Treasurer), L Fernandez Jr (VP Human Resources), W E Grier (VP Canada), E R Lowry (VP Foreign, Corporate Planning and Development), A V Martini (VP), L C McGraw (VP Information Technology), W K Morris (VP Public Affairs), H A Navis (VP), C B Renfrew (VP Law), G A Schurman (VP Production), C M Short (VP and Treasurer), Sellers Stough (VP Finance), J N Sullivan (VP Engineering and Environmental Affairs), J R Sylla (VP, President Chevron USA Inc)

PRINCIPAL ACTIVITIES: Exploration and production of oil and gas; production of petrochemicals and agricultural chemicals

Trade Names: Chevron

Principal Subsidiaries: (100% owned unless stated): USA: Chevron USA Inc; Gulf Corporation; Chandeleur Pipe Line Company; Chevron Capital USA Inc; Chevron Chemical Company; Chevron Industries Inc; Chevron Land and Development Company; Chevron Oil Field Research Company; Chevron Pipe Line Company; Chevron Research Company; Chevron Resources Company; Chevron Shale Oil Company; Chevron Shipping Company; Chevron Stations Inc; Standard Pipe Line Company; Huntington Beach Company; American Gilsonite Company; Kenai Pipe Line Company (50%); Plantation Pipe Line Company (27.13%); UNC Resources Inc (36.6%); AMAX Inc (22.1%). Canada: Chevron Asphalt Ltd; Chevron Canada Ltd; Chevron Canada Resources Limited; Chevron Chemical (Canada) Ltd; Irving Oil Ltd (48.9%). Mexico, Central and South America, Caribbean Area: Chevron Chemical Pan American Company; Chevron Petroleum Company of Colombia; Chevron do Brasil Ltda. Other foreign areas: Arabian American Oil Company (28.33%); Bermaco Insurance Company Ltd; California Asiatic Oil Company; Chevron International Oil Company Inc; Chevron Oil Company of Spain; Chevron Oil Company of Sudan; Chevron Oil Trading Company; Chevron Overseas Finance Company; Chevron Overseas Petroleum Inc; Chevron Overseas Petroleum Ltd; Chevron Petroleum (UK) Limited; Chevron Tankers (Nederland) BV; Chevron Transport Corporation; International Bitumen Emulsions Corporation; PT Caltex Pacific Indonesia (50%)

Financial Information:

	Dec 31 1985 $'000	Dec 31 1986 $'000
Sales revenues	41,741,905	24,351,000
Net income	1,547,360	715,000
Earnings per share	$4.52	$2.09
Shareholders equity	15,554,525	15,493,000

No of Employees: 60,845

CHEVRON USA INC

575 Market Street, San Francisco, CA 94105
Tel: (415) 894-7700
Telex: ITT 470 074 soco ui

President: J R Sylla

Senior Executive Officers: W J Price (Senior VP Manufacturing, Supply and Marketing), F W Bradley (VP Washington DC Office), C H Mackdanz (VP Industrial Relations), P S Hobin (VP Legal and General Counsel), D G Henderson (VP Finance), Paul R Larson (VP Manufacturing), L E Elkins (VP Production), W E Crain (VP Exploration), R L Hartung (VP Public Affairs), R F Walsh (VP Supply and Distribution), L Taigen (VP Marketing)

PRINCIPAL ACTIVITIES: Oil and gas exploration and production; refining and distribution

Parent Company: Chevron Corporation, San Francisco, CA

Financial Information:

	$'000
Sales revenues	18,000,000

No of Employees: 35,000

CHICAGO MILWAUKEE CORPORATION

547 W Jackson Boulevard, Chicago, IL 60606
Tel: (312) 822-0400

Chairman: Clarence G Frame

President: Edwin Jacobson

Senior Executive Officers: Leon F Fiorentino (VP Finance, Secretary and Treasurer)

PRINCIPAL ACTIVITIES: Chicago-Milwaukee is a non-operating holding company whose subsidiaries are engaged in:- food service equipment manufacturing; concrete paving-operating as a subcontractor; metal fabrication

Trade Names: Wolf Range, Ultra-Serve, Moffat, Vulcan-Hart, Foster Refrigerator

Principal Subsidiaries: Vulcan-Hart Corporation; Hi-Way Paving; Southern Boiler & Tank Works; Aslesen Co; Hanson Porcelain Co Inc

Principal Bank: Continental Illinois National Bank and Trust Company of Chicago

Financial Information:

	$'000
Sales revenues net	159,000

No of Employees: 2,000

CHICAGO PACIFIC CORPORATION

200 South Michigan Avenue, Chicago, IL 60604
Tel: (312) 435 7300
Telefax: (312) 435-7646

Chairman: Harvey Kapnick (and President)
Senior Executive Officers: Edward J Harrison (Executive VP and Legal Counsel), John F Pastrone (Executive VP-Furniture), Frank E Vaughn (Executive VP-Appliances), William C Terpstra (Executive VP-Finance), Clarence B Lozaw (VP and Treasurer), Daniel R Murray (Secretary), Howard E Buker (VP Public Affairs), Thomas J Gavin (VP-Taxes), Steven Khaner (VP Controller)

PRINCIPAL ACTIVITIES: Manufacturer and marketer of home products
Trade Names: Hoover, Rowenta, Kittinger, Pennsylvania House, McGuire, Gunlocke, Brown Jordan
Principal Subsidiaries: Chicago Pacific Far East Co; Hoover Holdings Inc; Phase IV Products Inc; The Gunlocke Company; Brown Jordan Company; Rowenta (USA) Inc
Financial Information:

	1986 $'000
Sales revenues	954,936
Income before taxes	46,563
Net income	28,788
Earnings per share (1)	$3.34
Earnings per share (2)	$3.14
Common stock (3)	9,637
Retained income	163,721
Shareholders equity	330,313

(1) primary
(2) fully diluted
(3) shares outstanding in thousands

Principal Shareholders: As of March 13, 1987 Lester Crown 1,009,707 shares beneficially owned; as of February 10, 1987 Southeastern Asset Management 1,230,900 shares
No of Employees: 21,000

CHICAGO PNEUMATIC TOOL CO

6 E 44th Street, New York, NY 10017
Tel: (212) 850-6800

Chairman: Steven M Rales (and Chief Executive Officer)
President: Mitchell P Rales
Senior Executive Officers: Thomas Ammer (VP), James J Carey (VP Industrial Relations and Personnel), Robert Cecchini (VP and Controller), Joseph M Walsh Jr (VP and Legal Counsel), Ralph T Brandifino (VP Finance), Gerald Northern (VP)

PRINCIPAL ACTIVITIES: Manufacture of tools and industrial components for the transportation and construction industries
Principal Subsidiaries and Divisions: Chicago Pneumatic Tool Division; Consolidated Pneumatic Tool Company Ltd; Allied Steel Tractor Products Inc; Hennessy Industries Inc; The Jacobs Manufacturing Company; The Jacobs Manufacturing Company Ltd (UK); The Allen Manufacturing Company Dynapar Corporation; The Partlow Corporation; Qualitrol Corporation; Consolidated Pneumatic Tool Company SA (Pty) Ltd (South Africa); Chicago Pneumatic de Mexico SA; Chicago Pneumatic Systems Division; Matco Tools; Chicago Pneumatic Credit Corporation; Chicago Pneumatic Latinoamerica SA (Mexico); Consolidated Pneumatic Tool Company (India) Ltd; Bhagwati Foundries Ltd (India); Revathi-CP Equipment Company Limited; Toku-Hambai KK (Japan); Mechanics Acceptance Corporation; Chicago Pneumatic Equipment Division; CP/Coats Diagnostic Equipment Division; The Canadian Pneumatic Tool Company Ltd; Chicago Pneumatic Construction Equipment Division

Principal Bank: Chase Manhattan Bank
Financial Information:

	$'000
Sales revenues	408,000

No of Employees: 4,000

CHI-CHI'S INC

10002 Shelbyville Rd, PO Box 32338, Louisville, KY 40223
Tel: (502) 244 1800

Chairman: Shelly Frank (and Chief Executive Officer)
President: Joseph P Smaha (and Chief Operating Officer)
Senior Executive Officers: John R Bifone (Executive VP Administration), John R Weaver (Executive VP Operations), Wayne P Jones (Executive VP Marketing and Business Development), Ronald W Stebelton (Group VP), Richard A Sanks (Senior VP, Legal Counsel and Secretary), Saundra C Nelson (Senior VP Finance and Chief Financial Officer), Guy W Van Dyke (Senior VP Development), Charles E Fioretti (VP Division), Michael F Fiori (VP Division), James M Mulrooney (VP and Treasurer), Terrance A Smith (VP International), Glenn D Drasher (VP Marketing), Thomas A Grote (VP Construction), Stephen D Fenstermacher (VP Planning), Kerry A Kramp (VP Product Area and Research and Development), Gary L McCartin (VP Real Estate), George F Theisen (VP Human Resources)

PRINCIPAL ACTIVITIES: Restaurants specializing in Mexican food franchising services
Principal Bank: Citizens Fidelity Bank and Trust Company
Financial Information:

	$'000
Sales revenues	270,000

No of Employees: 16,500

CHICKASHA COTTON OIL CO

6100 Western Place, PO Box 511, Fort Worth, TX 76101
Tel: (817) 732-76101
Telex: WUT 794847 chickasha ftw

Chairman: Hiroshi Narita
President: C C Wisler Jr
Senior Executive Officers: Jim Wilkerson (Executive VP), Shoji Hasegawa (Executive VP, Treasurer and Secretary), M D Tucker (VP), W A Podsednik Jr (VP and Secretary), Riftin Curtis (VP), J D Smith (VP)

PRINCIPAL ACTIVITIES: Cottonseed products including edible oils, livestock and animal feed; cotton ginning, compressing and storage
Parent Company: Toyo Menka Kaisha Ltd
Principal Bank: InterFirst Bank
Financial Information:

	$'000
Sales revenues	120,000

No of Employees: 800

CHIEF
CHIEF INDUSTRIES, INC.

CHIEF INDUSTRIES, INC

Old West Hwy 30, PO Box 2078, Grand Island, NE 68802
Tel: (308) 382-8820
Telex: TWX 910 6293713 chief ind grid
Telefax: (308) 381-8475

Chairman: Virgil R Eihusen (and Chief Executive Officer)
Senior Executive Officers: Robert Eihusen (Executive VP, Operations), Mel R Auch (President and Chief Operating Officer Housing Division). Corporate Officer: Thomas D Potter (Executive VP, Finance and Planning)

PRINCIPAL ACTIVITIES: Fabricated metal buildings and grain storage bins; mobile homes; pollution control equipment
Trade Names: "Chief", "BonnaVilla" Homes, "King of the Road" (recreational vehicles)
Principal Subsidiaries: Chief Industries, UK, Ltd (UK)
Principal Bank: Centerre Bank, St. Louis, Missouri
Financial Information:

	Jun 27 1986	Jun 26 1987
	$'000	$'000
Sales revenues	73,500	85,900
Income before taxes	2,750	26,500
Net income	1,800	17,000
Earnings per share	$1.52	$14.03
Common stock	130	130
Retained income	27,270	44,070
Shareholders equity	27,400	44,200

No of Employees: 1,000

CHILD WORLD INC

25 Littlefield Street, Avon, MA 02322
Tel: (617) 588 7300

Chairman: Dennis H Barron
President: Gilbert Wachsman
Senior Executive Officers: Richard J Ryan (Executive VP and Chief Financial officer), Thomas T S Kaung (Senior VP), Robert W Antall (VP), Stanley R Walsh (VP), Steve Robinson (VP), Linda Goodman (VP), Cathy Wells (VP), Larry E Cook (VP), Herbert J Hodus (VP), David J Nace (VP and Controller), John Nugent (VP), Tracy L Burmeister (Treasurer), John F Downie (Financial)

PRINCIPAL ACTIVITIES: Retail trade in toys and games
Parent Company: Cole National Corporation
Principal Bank: Central National Bank of Cleveland
Financial Information:

	Feb 1 1986	Jan 31 1987
	$'000	$'000
Sales revenues	513,148	628,834
Income before taxes	20,802	26,012
Net income	9,368	10,949
Earnings per share	$0.91	$0.95
Common stock	11,500	11,500
Retained income	10,928	21,877
Shareholders equity	170,859	181,808

No of Employees: 4,821

CHILI'S INC

8350 Meadow Road, Dallas, TX 75321
Tel: (214) 369 0918

Chairman: Norman E Brinker (and Chief Executive Officer)
President: Hal W Smith (and Chief Operating Officer)
Senior Executive Officers: James R Parish (Executive VP, Chief Financial Officer and Treasurer), Ronald A McDougall (Executive VP Marketing and Strategic Planning), Creed L Ford III (Senior VP Operations), Richard Spellman (Secretary and Legal Counsel), John W Titus (VP Real Estate)

PRINCIPAL ACTIVITIES: Restaurant operators
Principal Bank: InterFirst Bank
Financial Information:

	$'000
Sales revenues	69,000

No of Employees: 3,600

CHITTENDEN CORPORATION

2 Burlington Square, Burlington, VT 05402
Tel: (802) 864-7968

Chairman: George E Little Jr
President: William H Burett Jr
Senior Executive Officers: John T Rider (Senior VP and Treasurer), Robert D Siff (Executive VP Loans), Dale W Good (Executive VP Trust and Investment Division), Richard Chapman (Executive VP and Chief Operations Officer), Doreen J Sheridan (Executive VP Consumer Banking and Municipal Division)

PRINCIPAL ACTIVITIES: Banking
Trade Names: Chittenden Bank
Principal Subsidiaries: Chittenden Trust Company; Chittenden Realty Credit Corporation; Chittenden Consulting Corporation; Chittenden Leasing Corp
Principal Bank: Chittenden Bank
Financial Information:

	Dec 31 1985	Dec 31 1986
	$'000	$'000
Income before taxes	6,104	11,096
Net income(1)	5,620	7,246
Dividends(2)	2,316	3,028
Dividends per share	$1.00	$1.08
Earnings per share	$3.02	$3.06
Common stock	16,434	23,422
Retained income and surplus	23,923	45,395
Shareholders equity(3)	46,357	74,817
Deposits	775,158	838,991
Total assets	851,486	980,495

(1) before preferred
(2) common and preferred
(3) including preferred

No of Employees: 889

CHLORIDE INC

3507 S 50th Street, Tampa, FL 33601
Tel: (813) 248-3161
Telex: WUT 52715 chloride tpa

Chairman: Alexander H Stitt (and President and Chief Executive Officer)
Senior Executive Officers: Daniel M Burns (VP Finance and Secretary)

PRINCIPAL ACTIVITIES: Manufacture of industrial and automotive batteries
Parent Company: Chloride Group plc, London, UK
Principal Bank: European-American Bank and Trust Company
Financial Information:

	$'000
Sales revenues	156,000

No of Employees: 2,400

CHOCK FULL O'NUTS CORPORATION

370 Lexington Avenue, New York, NY 10017
Tel: (212) 532-0300
Telex: TWX 710 5815301 chock full nyk

Chairman: Leon Pordy (and Chief Executive Officer); Vice Chairman: George Rudy
President: Howard Leitner (and Chief Financial Officer)
Senior Executive Officers: Max Apfelbaum (Senior VP), Martin Cullen (VP and Treasurer), Jeffrey Morris (VP Sales), Ismar Reich (VP Research and Development), Martin Slater (VP Real Estate Operations), Joseph A Breslin (VP Corporate Affairs), Raymond Hickey (VP Manufacturing), Peter Baer (VP Labor Relations)

PRINCIPAL ACTIVITIES: Processing and sale of coffee; fresh and frozen cakes and other bakery products
Principal Bank: Manufacturers Hanover Trust Company
Financial Information:

	$'000
Sales revenues	118,000

No of Employees: 300

CHRIS-CRAFT INDUSTRIES, INC

600 Madison Avenue, New York, NY 10022
Tel: (212) 421-0200

Chairman: Herbert J Siegel (and President and Chief Executive Officer)
Senior Executive Officers: James J Rochlis (Executive VP, President Industrial Division), Lawrence R Barnett (Executive VP), Barry S Greene (VP, Secretary and General Counsel), Laurence M Kashdin (VP Finance and Controller)

PRINCIPAL ACTIVITIES: Television broadcasting; plastic and plastic products
Principal Subsidiaries: BHC Inc; United Television Inc; Chris-Craft Industrial Products Inc; KCOP Television Inc; Oregon Television Inc; United Television Inc
Principal Bank: Philadelphia National Bank
Financial Information:

	Dec 31 1986 $'000
Sales revenues	224,000
Net income	14,000

No of Employees: 1,200

CHROMALLOY AMERICAN CORPORATION

120 S Central Avenue, St Louis, MO 63105
Tel: (314) 726-9200

Chairman: Norman E Alexander (and Chief Executive Officer)
President: William E Stevens (and Chief Operating Officer)
Senior Executive Officers: Geoffrey L Phillips (Executive VP Operations Administration), John P Denneen (Executive VP, Secretary and General Counsel), T G Barnett (Executive VP Finance), A W Clubb (VP), Ernest M Felago (VP Human Resources), Del G Maine (VP Texas), Thomas Phelps (VP Business Planning), John J Quickie (VP and Controller), James A Silkwood (VP Corporate Development)

PRINCIPAL ACTIVITIES: Gray iron castings; agricultural machinery; vehicle components; oilfield equipment
Principal Subsidiaries: Airport Service Inc; American Transit Corp; Chromalloy Finance Corp; National Seating Co; American Universal Insurance Co; Assurers Service Inc; Canadian Universal Insurance Co Inc; Canadian Universal Insurance Co; Maurice H Saval Inc; Cro-Marine Inc; Flowers Transportation Inc; ERK Manufacturing Inc; Hausman Bus Parts Co Inc; Missouri River Barge Lines Inc; Evco Marine Inc; Hou-Tex Barge Co; Sabine Towing & Transport Co Inc; Saval Group Inc; American Universal Insurance Co; Security Barge Line Inc; A & M Fleeting & Towing Inc; Swiss Albe Inc; Valley Line Co; Island Terminal Co; MVBL Terminal Co; Mead Johnson Terminal Corp; Valley Line Supply Equipment Co; Valley Terminal Co Inc
Principal Bank: Irving Trust Company
Financial Information:

	Dec 31 1985 $'000	Dec 31 1986 $'000
Sales revenues	917,123	813,000

No of Employees: 14,700

CHRYSLER CORPORATION

PO Box 1919, Detroit, MI 48288
Tel: (313) 956-5252
Telex: 810-243-4051/52

Chairman: Lee A Iacocca (and Chief Executive Officer)
President: Harold K Sperlich
Senior Executive Officers: Gerald Greenwald (Vice Chairman), Bennett E Bidwell (Executive VP), Richard E Dauch (Executive VP-Manufacturing), Richard Goodyear (VP, General Counsel and Secretary), Robert S Miller (Executive VP-Finance and Administration and Chairman of Chrysler Financial Corporation), Stephan Sharf (Executive VP-International Business Development), Frederick W Zuckerman (VP and Treasurer)

PRINCIPAL ACTIVITIES: Chrysler Corporation (Chrysler) and its subsidiaries manufacture, assemble and sell in the United States and Canada, Chrysler, Dodge and Plymouth passenger cars, Dodge trucks, and related qutomotive parts and accessories. Chrysler produces trucks only in light-duty and van/wagon models, which represent the largest segment of the truck market. The passenger cars are offered in various size classes and models. In addition, Chrysler imports and distributes under the Dodge and Plymouth trade names, certain small passenger cars and trucks manufactured in Japan by Mitsubishi Motors Corporation (MMC), a company in which Chrysler has a 15% interest. Chrysler currently participates in markets outside the United States and Canada principally through its subsidiary, Chrysler de Mexico SA (Chrysler de Mexico), and through minority investments in MMC, and Peugeot SA (PSA) a company in which Chrysler has a 14% interest. Chrysler and its subsidiaries also sell part of their production of automatic and manual transmission, transfer cases, electronic equipment, chemical and plastic products and powder metal components to unaffiliated companies, principally in the United States
Trade Names: Chrysler, Dodge, Plymouth
Principal Subsidiaries: Chrysler Canada Ltd; Chrysler de Mexico SA; Chrysler Financial Corporation; Chrysler Aerospace Corporation
Principal Bank: Manufacturers Hanover Trust Company
Financial Information:

	Dec 31 1986 $'000
Sales revenues	22,513,500
Net income	1,403,600
Earnings per share	$9.47
Shareholders equity	5,344,800

No of Employees: 100,435 (worldwide)

CHRYSLER FINANCIAL CORPORATION

901 Wilshire Drive, Troy, MI 48084
Tel: (313) 244-3000

Chairman: J P Tierney; Vice Chairman: R E Baker
President: J E Farrell (President of Chrysler Credit)
Senior Executive Officers: T P Capo (VP and Controller), J J Madden Jr (VP Marketing and Operational Services Chrysler Credit), D A Robison (VP and Treasurer), A L Ronquillo (VP and General Counsel), R J Pear (VP Personnel and Administration), D M Cantwell (VP Strategic Planning and Development), M R Cooper (VP Financial Sales)

PRINCIPAL ACTIVITIES: Chrysler Financial Corporation (CFC) is a wholly-owned unconsolidated subsidiary of Chrysler Corporation. CFC's primary functions are to provide wholesale, retail and lease financing to Chrysler-AMC franchised dealers; direct consumer lending, wholesale and retail financing of consumer goods, small business loans, commercial leasing and lending and insurance products
Principal Subsidiaries: Chrysler Credit Corporation; Chrysler First Inc; Chrysler Capital Corporation; Chrysler Insurance; Chrysler Realty
Financial Information:

	Dec 31 1985 $'000	Dec 31 1986 $'000
Total revenues	1,478,200	2,376,800
Income before taxes	256,200	315,100
Net income	154,300	200,000
Common stock	-	25,000
Retained income	-	837,900
Shareholders equity	-	1,971,100
Total assets	15,873,400	21,028,300

No of Employees: 5,530

CHUBB CORPORATION

15 Mountain View Road, Box 1615, Warren, NJ 07061
Tel: (201) 580-2000

Chairman: Henry U Harder (and President and Chief Executive Officer); Vice Chairman: Percy Chubb III
President: Dean R O'Hare

Senior Executive Officers: Thomas V Kelsey (Senior VP), Samuel V Gilman Jr (Senior VP), Newell G Alford Jr (Senior VP and General Counsel), Richard D Smith (Senior VP)

PRINCIPAL ACTIVITIES: Holding company with interests in insurance and property investment
Principal Subsidiaries: Associated Insurers Corp; Chubb & Son Inc; Associated Aviation Inc; Associated Aviation Underwriters Inc; Chubb Custom Market Inc; Chubb Institute for Computer Technology; Chubb Life Insurance Co of America Federal Insurance Co; Bellemead Development Corp; Bellemead Construction Corp; Oceans Racquet Club Inc; Reliance Realty Inc; Chubb Custom Insurance Co; Chubb Insurance Co of NJ; Chubb Life Insurance Co; Chubb America Service Corp; Chubb Securities Corp; Colonial Life Insurance Company of America; UPA Inc; Hampshire Funding Inc; United Life & Accident Insurance Co; Volunteer State Life Insurance Co; Chubb Lloyds Insurance Co of Texas; Chubb Syndicate Inc; Great Northern Insurance Co; KGMG Inc; J & H WF Syndicate; Pacific Indemnity Co; Texas Pacific Indemnity Co; Touchette Corp; Vigilant Insurance Co
Principal Bank: Citibank
Financial Information:

	Dec 31 1985 $'000	Dec 31 1986 $'000
Revenues	2,394,020	3,208,760
Net income	70,540	267,940
Earnings per share	$1.92	$7.05
Shareholders equity	-	1,575,530

No of Employees: 9,600

CHURCH & DWIGHT CO, INC

469 N Harrison St, Princeton, NJ 08540
Tel: (609) 683-5900

Chairman: Dwight C Minton (and Chief Executive Officer)
Senior Executive Officers: A Elliott Archer (VP and General Manager Chemcials Division), Zvi Eiref (VP Finance), Wendell J Harkleroad (VP Operations), James I Rogula (VP and General Manager ARM & HAMMER Division), Wayne R Sorenson (VP Research and Development), Robert H Bidwell (Secretary and General Counsel), David E Breithaupt (VP Marketing ARM & HAMMER Division), Gary P Halker (Controller), Dennis M Moore (VP Human Resources), Albert R Nicusanti Jr (VP Sales ARM & HAMMER Division), Martin A Pickus (Treasurer), Ralph E Wulff (VP Manufacturing), C Herbert Crews Jr (President DeWitt International Corporation), Donald J Bowman (President Church & Dwight Ltd/Ltée)

PRINCIPAL ACTIVITIES: Founded in 1846, Church & Dwight Co, Inc is the world's leading producer of sodium bicarbonate, popularly known as baking soda, a versatile chemical which performs a broad range of functions such as cleaning, deodorizing, leavening and buffering. The Company specializes in sodium bicarbonate and sodium bicarbonate-based products, along with other produts which use the same raw materials or technology, or are sold into the same markets
Trade Names: ARM & HAMMER (R)
Principal Bank: Morgan Guaranty Trust Company of New York
Financial Information:

	Dec 31 1985 $'000	Dec 31 1986 $'000
Sales revenues net	231,367	275,424
Income before taxes	7,106	19,686
Net income	4,662	12,777
Dividends	3,905	4,254
Dividends per share	$0.195	$0.205
Earnings per share	$0.23	$0.60
Common stock	10,060	10,849
Retained income	62,279	70,802
Shareholders equity	74,103	104,812

No of Employees: 645

CHURCH'S FRIED CHICKEN INC

PO Box BH 001, San Antonio, TX 78284
Tel: (512) 735 9392

Chairman: J David Bamberger (and Chief Executive Officer)
President: Richard F Sherman (and Chief Operating Officer)
Senior Executive Officers: James S Parker (Executive VP), Robert E Hilgenfeld (Senior VP), Lewis B Kilbourne (Senior VP Finance), John F Barteau (Senior VP Construction and Manufacturing), Thomas Wayne Baker (VP Operations), Dorian W Gibbs (VP), James R Hale (Secretary), Joseph A Cote (VP Production), Thomas H Turkett (VP Production), Neil D Frumkin (VP Development), Norman D Mecham (VP Personnel Affairs), George N Samaras (VP Franchising)

PRINCIPAL ACTIVITIES: Drive-in and take-out food stores specializing in chicken dishes
Principal Bank: Frost National Bank of San Antonio
Financial Information:

	Dec 31 1986 $'000
Sales revenues	468,000
Net income	17,000

No of Employees: 14,000

CIBA-GEIGY CORPORATION

444 Saw Mill River Road, Ardsley, NY 10502
Tel: (914) 478-3131
Telex: WUT 131 411 ciba geigy yks

Chairman: O Sturzenegger
President: R Barth (and Chief Executive Officer)
Senior Executive Officers: C O O'Brien (Executive VP and Chief Operating Officer), J Schneller (Senior VP, President Plastics and Additives Division), J T Sullivan (Senior VP)

PRINCIPAL ACTIVITIES: Manufacture of agricultural chemicals, dyestuffs, pharmaceuticals and specialty chemicals
Parent Company: CIBA-GEIGY AG, Basle, Switzerland
Principal Bank: Irving Trust
Financial Information:

	$'000
Sales revenues	2,400,000

No of Employees: 12,000

CIGNA CORPORATION

One Logan Square, Philadelphia, PA 19101
Tel: (215) 557-5000
Telex: 834442

Chairman: Robert D Kilpatrick (and Chief Executive Officer)
President: Hartzel Z Lebed
Senior Executive Officers: John K Armstrong (Executive VP, Chief Investment Officer and President CIGNA Investment Group), Thomas H Dooley (Executive VP and President Individual Financial Group), G Robert O'Brien (Executive VP and President Employee Benefits and Health Care Group), Andrew M Rouse (Executive VP), James G Stewart (Executive VP and Chief Financial Officer), Wilson H Taylor (Executive VP and President Property and Casualty Group), James W Walker Jr (Executive VP and General Counsel), Donald M Levinson (Senior VP), Allan Z Loren (Senior VP), Robert L Robinson (Senior VP and Corporate Secretary), Charles H Stamm III (Senior VP), Barry F Wiksten (Senior VP), Paul B Lukens (Controller), Paul H Rohrkemper (Treasurer)

PRINCIPAL ACTIVITIES: Insurance, health care, employee benefits and financial services
Principal Subsidiaries: Connecticut General Life Insurance Company; Insurance Company of North America and several hundred other subsidiaries
Principal Bank: Morgan Guaranty Trust Co

Financial Information:

	Dec 31 1986
	$'000
Premium income	17,100,000
Net income	483,000

No of Employees: 49,400

CILCORP INC

300 Liberty Street, Peoria, IL 61602
Tel: (309) 672 5271

President: William R Vogelsang (and Chief Executive Officer and Subsidiary Officer)
Senior Executive Officers: Charles W Cox (Senior VP), R O Viets (VP and Controller), W L Barton (Treasurer and Assistant Secretary), M J Murray (Secretary and Assistant Treasurer)

PRINCIPAL ACTIVITIES: Holding company with interests in the supply of electricity and natural gas
Principal Bank: Commercial National Bank
Financial Information:

	Dec 31 1986
	$'000
Sales revenues	490,000
Net income	42,000

No of Employees: 1,510

CIMARRON INVESTMENT CO, INC

101 N Main Street, Cimarron, KS 67835
Tel: (316) 855-7711

Chairman: Leigh Warner
President: Sidney Warner
Senior Executive Officers: William R Docking (VP), Gerald Vogel (Treasurer)

PRINCIPAL ACTIVITIES: Holding company with interests in insurance
Principal Subsidiaries: Cimarron Finance Co Inc; Cimarron Insurance Co Inc
Principal Bank: First National Bank
Financial Information:

	$'000
Revenues	51,000

No of Employees: 340

CINCINNATI BELL INC

201 E 4th Street, Cincinnati, OH 45202
Tel: (513) 397-9900
Telefax: (513) 421-5973

Chairman: Dwight H Hibbard (and Chief Executive Officer)
President: John T LaMacchia (and Chief Operating Officer)
Senior Executive Officers: Raymond R Clark (Executive VP and President-Cincinnati Bell Telephone), Dennis J Sullivan Jr (Executive VP and Chief Financial Officer), Richard L Dewey (Secretary and Treasurer), Robert L Layton (VP Corporate Development)

PRINCIPAL ACTIVITIES: Cincinnati Bell Telephone: The core business of Cincinnati Bell Inc. It is a fully integrated provider of telecommunication equipment and services, offering a wide range of information services including voice, data, text and video. Cincinnati Bell Telephone has more than one billion dollars invested in plant...nearly 600,000 business and residence customers and 662,000 main access lines. Cincinnati Bell Information Systems: Designs, markets and manages information systems for three separate areas of telecommunications: business operations for telecommunications companies, communications management for corporations and other large organizations, and billing and management systems for cellular mobile telephone companies. Anixter-Cincinnati: A joint venture with Anixter Brothers of Chicago. The partnership distributes telecommunications, electrical, construction, mining and cable TV supplies. It also reconditions used telephone equipment. Material Recycling: Buys, sells and brokers new, used and reconditioned telecommunications equipment. Salvages, reclaims and recycles scrap material from telecommunications equipment. RESTOR: Repairs and tests printed circuit boards. Service centers in Cincinnati, Ohio, Portland Oregon, and Jacksonville, Florida. ComQuest: Provides specialized market research, and technical assistance in the form of product evaluation, testing and training programs to US and foreign communications manufacturers. Cincinnati Bell Long Distance: A reseller of long distance service. Telephone Marketing Services: A telemarketing firm specializing in full-account handling of wholesale, retail and industrial markets. Cincinnati Bell Cellular Systems: Oversees Cincinnati Bell Inc.'s investment as a minority partner with Ameritech Mobile Communications. The partnership offers cellular mobile telephone service. Abacus Computer Stores: A dealership in microcomputers, accessory hardware and software including training, program development, service and support
Trade Names: CMS-1000,2000,3000 Call accounting for private networks, CMS-5000 Multi-tenant resale/billing system, CMS-900 Call traffic analysis for private networks, CMS System Telemanagement system for private networks, CHAT PC communications link, COCRIS Centralized online customer records system, COMMIS Cellular/paging equipment inventory system, CRIS Customer records billing system, Cellware, Macro/Cell CompuCellular Cellular management, engineering and billing systems, Inside Line Real-time call message processing system, LUCAS Facilities management system, MPS Message Processing System, OS/Connector Mainframe-to-minicomputer interface, FAS* PC force access system, OS/Force Plus Construction force management system, OS/Order Customer service order processing system, OS/Plant Outside plant facilities administration, OS/CableNet Small-telco outside plant facilities administration system, SOCRATES Service order entry and billing system, Staffstats Sickness, accident, and disability information system, Switch Manager Cellular switch interface, Taxmit Electronic income tax transmission system, *A joint development of CBIS and Phoenix Telecom, Inc.
Principal Subsidiaries: Cincinnati Bell Telephone; Cincinnati Bell Information Systems; Cincinnati Bell Enterprises Inc
Principal Bank: Central Trust Company
Financial Information:

	Dec 31 1985	Dec 31 1986
	$'000	$'000
Sales revenues	466,900	492,600
Income before taxes	85,100	97,600
Net income	51,600	58,200
Dividends	28,000	28,800
Dividends per share	$0.78	$0.88
Earnings per share	$1.55	$1.77
Common stock	173,200	176,800
Retained income	222,200	246,400
Shareholders equity	395,400	423,200

No of Employees: 5,100

CINCINNATI ELECTRONICS CORPORATION

2630 Glendale-Milford Road, Cincinnati, OH 45241
Tel: (513) 733-6100
Cable: CECCINO
Telex: TWX 810 464 8151 ce corp cin

President: Douglas G Dwyre Jr
Senior Executive Officers: Byron G Fehler Jr (VP and General Manager Aerospace Division), Robert D Smith (VP and General Manager C31 Division), Dr P J Kenny (VP Government Affairs), Laurence I Annear (Secretary/Treasurer and VP Human Resources and Support Services), Kenneth J Gilkey (VP Marketing)

PRINCIPAL ACTIVITIES: Tactical communications, aerospace electronics, infrared, radar, electronic warfare systems and

equipment, integrated logistics support, contract manufacturing
Parent Company: The General Electric Company plc, UK
Principal Bank: Central Trust Company

No of Employees: 1,000

CINCINNATI ENQUIRER

617 Vine Street, Cincinnati, OH 45201
Tel: (513) 721-2700

Chairman: William J Keating
President: John P Zanotti (and Publisher)
Senior Executive Officers: George R Blake (VP and Editor), Craig A Moon (VP Advertising), William R Johnston (VP Circulation), Francis M Price (VP Production), James A Schwartz (Treasurer)

PRINCIPAL ACTIVITIES: Publishing of newspapers
Parent Company: Gannett Satellite Information Network Inc
Principal Bank: Fifth Third Bank
Financial Information:

	$'000
Sales revenues	130,000

CINCINNATI FINANCIAL CORPORATION

11295 Princeton Pike, PO Box 14567, Cincinnati, OH 45214
Tel: (513) 771-2000

Chairman: John J Schiff (and Chief Executive Officer); Vice Chairman: William H Zimmer Jr
President: Robert B Morgan
Senior Executive Officers: Robert J Driehaus (VP Finance)

PRINCIPAL ACTIVITIES: Insurance services
Principal Subsidiaries: CFC Investment Co Inc; Cincinatti Insurance Co; Life Insurance Co of Cincinnatti; Queen City Indemnity Co; Inter-Ocean Insurance Co
Principal Bank: The Fifth Third Bank
Financial Information:

	Dec 31 1985	Dec 31 1986
	$'000	$'000
Revenues	607,890	775,804
Net income	54,990	93,470
Earnings per share	$3.64	$6.08
Shareholders equity	470,330	580,174

No of Employees: 1,600

CINCINNATI GAS & ELECTRIC CO

139 E Fourth St, Cincinnati, OH 45202
Tel: (513) 381-2000

President: Jackson H Randolph (and Chief Executive Officer)
Senior Executive Officers: Earl A Borgmann (Senior VP), Robert E Byrnes (VP Administration), C Robert Everman (VP Finance and Treasurer), R Gregory Graham (VP Customer Relations), C Larry Schmidt (VP Gas Operations), Milton L Van Schoik (VP Corporate Planning and Information Services), Robert P Wiwi (VP Electrical Operations)

PRINCIPAL ACTIVITIES: Distribution of electricity and natural gas
Principal Subsidiaries: Union Light, Heat & Power Co
Financial Information:

	Dec 31 1985	Dec 31 1986
	$'000	$'000
Sales revenues	1,397,000	1,400,000
Net income	168,500	150,000

No of Employees: 4,600

CINCINNATI MICROWAVE, INC

One Microwave Plaza, Cincinnati, OH 45242
Tel: (513) 489-5400
Telex: WUT 24-1486 cin microwave

Chairman: James L Jaeger (and Chief Executive Officer)
President: John A O'Steen (and Chief Operating Officer)
Senior Executive Officers: Paul M Allen (Senior VP Marketing and Secretary), Michael C Koetters (Senior VP Finance and Treasurer), R Gregory Blair (VP Operations), Dana D Glasgo (VP Sales), John W Grether (VP Marketing)

PRINCIPAL ACTIVITIES: Manufacture of radar equipment
Principal Bank: Central Trust Company
Financial Information:

	$'000
Sales revenues	113,000

No of Employees: 500

CINCINNATI MILACRON INC

4701 Marburg Avenue, Cincinnati, OH 45209
Tel: (513) 841-8100
Telex: TWX 810 4612463 cme hqcin

Chairman: James A Geier (and Chief Executive Officer)
Executive Vice President: Donald G Shively
Senior Executive Officers: George T Rehfeldt (Group VP), George S Carper (Group VP), Daniel J Meyer (VP Finance and Administration), Richard C Messinger (VP Research and Development), David E Noffsinger (Group VP), Michael Clabaugh (VP Machine Tools Europe)

PRINCIPAL ACTIVITIES: Manufacture of machine tools; process engineering
Principal Subsidiaries: Cincinnati Milacron Marketing Co; Amertool Services, Inc; Amertool Services Corp; Cincinnati Milacron Japan Ltd (Japan); Cincinnati Milacron UK Co; Cincinnati Milacron Ltd (UK); LK Tool USA Inc; LK Tool Co Limited (UK); LK Tool Metrology Systems Limited (UK); LK Measurement & Control Systems Limited (UK); Cincinnati Milacron International Marketing Company; Coge AG (Switzerland); Cincinnati Milacron Holding Gesellschaft mbH (Austria); Cincinnati Milacron Austria Aktiengesellschaft (Austria); Cincinnati Milacron Handelsgesellschaft mbH (Austria); Cincinnati Milacron Semiconductor Materials Inc; The Factory Power Company (91.9%); Cincinnati Milacron Assurance Ltd (Bermuda); Cincinnati Milacron-Heald Corp; Cincinnati Milacron Commercial Corp; Cincinnati Milacron-Canada Ltd (Canada); Cincinnati Milacron BV (Netherlands); NV Vlaardingse Hattschappijtot Verhuur van Fabrieksgebouwen (Netherlands); Cincinnati Milacron Srl (Italy); Cincinnati Milacron Foreign Sales Corp (Virgin Islands)
Principal Bank: Central Trust
Financial Information:

	Dec 28 1985	Dec 28 1986
	$'000	$'000
Sales revenues	732,152	849,994
Net income (loss)	(44,767)	23,328
Earnings (loss) per share	($1.92)	$0.98
Shareholders equity	268,427	289,143

No of Employees: 9,568

CINCINNATI MILACRON-HEALD CORPORATION

10 New Bond Street, Worcester, MA 01606
Tel: (617) 853-2121

Chairman: James E Kroencke
President: Alfred J Purcell Jr
Senior Executive Officers: James N Heald II (VP Grinding Division), Donald B Sampson (VP Manager Machining Center), James V Casella (VP Secretary and Treasurer)

PRINCIPAL ACTIVITIES: Machine tools
Parent Company: Cincinnati Milacron Inc, Cincinnati, OH
Principal Bank: Shawmut National Bank
Financial Information:

	$'000
Sales revenues	735,000

No of Employees: 1,000

CINTAS CORPORATION

11255 Reed Hartman Hwy, Cincinnati, OH 45241
Tel: (513) 489-4000

Chairman: Richard T Farmer (and Chief Executive Officer)
President: Robert J Kohlhepp (and Chief Operating Officer)
Senior Executive Officers: Joseph A Detzel (Senior VP Rental), Robert R Buck (Senior VP Finance), Scott D Farmer (Senior VP Sales), Fred A Aberlin (Senior VP Corporate Development), John S Kean III (Senior VP, Red Stick Services)

PRINCIPAL ACTIVITIES: Manufacture and sale of uniforms; uniform rental services
Principal Bank: Fifth Third Bank
Financial Information:

	May 31 1986 $'000	May 31 1987 $'000
Revenues	123,726	163,375
Income before taxes	20,014	25,087
Net income	11,256	13,936
Dividends	978	1,173
Dividends per share	$0.075	$0.09
Earnings per share	$0.86	$1.07
Common stock	16,267	16,387
Retained income	48,567	61,330
Shareholders equity	64,834	77,717

No of Employees: 1,800

CIPHER DATA PRODUCTS, INC

9715 Business Park Ave, San Diego, CA 92131
Tel: (619) 693-7200

Chairman: Don M Muller
President: Gary E Liebl (and Chief Executive Officer)
Senior Executive Officers: Thomas R Anderson (Corporate VP, Shareholder Relations), Henry G Kohlmann (Corporate VP, General Counsel), Larry D Hemmerich Sr (VP, Product/Market Development), Richard P Ottaviano (Corporate VP, Human Resources), Robert F Prether (Corporate VP, Operations), Don Lundell (Corporate VP, Engineering), Dan E Steimle (Corporate VP, Chief Financial Officer), Jack Andersen (Corporate VP, Sales and Service)

PRINCIPAL ACTIVITIES: Electronic data storage equipment
Principal Subsidiaries: OPTIMEM
Principal Bank: Citicorp
Financial Information:

	Jun 30 1986 $'000	Jun 30 1987 $'000
Sales revenues	163,005	178,192
Income before taxes	10,560	211
Net income	7,196	4,331
Earnings per share	$0.50	$0.30
Common stock	88,281	89,285
Retained income	44,226	49,208
Shareholders equity	132,507	138,493

No of Employees: 1,881

CIRCLE EXPRESS INC

9001 Wesleyan Road, Suite 104, Indianapolis, IN 46268
Tel: (317) 872 4011

Chairman: Arthur L Belford (and President and Chief Executive Officer)
Senior Executive Officers: Judith R Belford (VP and Assistant Secretary), Merle E Bright (Treasurer)

PRINCIPAL ACTIVITIES: Operation of motor freight transportation services
Principal Bank: Merchants National Bank
Financial Information:

	$'000
Sales revenues	100,980

No of Employees: 90

CIRCLE K CORPORATION

1601 North Seventh St, Phoenix, AZ 85006
Tel: (602) 253-9600

Chairman: Karl Eller (and Chief Executive Officer); Vice Chairman: Fred Hervey
President: Robert M Reade (and Chief Operating Officer)
Senior Executive Officers: Bill Farmer (Senior VP Finance and Treasurer), William H Remmers (Senior VP International Operations), Ray Cox (Senior VP Corporate Affairs), Gehl Babinic (Senior VP, General Counsel and Assistant Treasurer), Charles A Shoumaker (Senior VP Human Resources)

PRINCIPAL ACTIVITIES: Retail trade including convenience grocery stores and gasoline self service; canning and bottling of soft drinks
Principal Subsidiaries: Circle K Convenience Stores; UtoteM Inc; Circle K General Inc; Shop and Go Inc; Circle K International Inc
Financial Information:

	Apr 30 1986 $'000	Apr 30 1987 $'000
Sales revenues	2,111,267	2,289,444
Income before taxes	69,603	94,296
Net income	39,222	49,430
Dividends	9,876	12,959
Dividends per share	$0.25	$0.28
Earnings per share	$0.74	$0.85
Common stock	21,468	49,740
Retained income	83,984	94,967
Shareholders equity	200,102	310,013

No of Employees: 20,983

CIRCUIT CITY STORES INC

2040 Thalbro Street, Richmond, VA 23230
Tel: (804) 257-4292

Chairman: Alan L Wurtzel; Vice Chairman: Samuel S Wurtzel
President: Richard L Sharp (and Chief Executive Officer)
Senior Executive Officers: Daniel M Rexinger (Executive VP), William D Rivas (Executive VP), Walter Bruckart (Senior VP), Edward Villanueva (VP and Treasurer), Gertrude M Gibson (Secretary), William E Zierden (VP Human Resources)

PRINCIPAL ACTIVITIES: Retail trade in domestic electrical appliances and electronic equipment
Principal Subsidiaries: Acme Commercial Corporation
Principal Bank: Bank of Virginia
Financial Information:

	1986 $'000
Sales revenues	1,000,000
Net income	35,000

No of Employees: 3,800

CIRCUS CIRCUS ENTERPRISES INC

2880 Las Vegas Boulevard S, Las Vegas, NV 89109
Tel: (702) 734-0410

Chairman: William G Bennett (and Chief Executive Officer)
President: William N Pennington
Senior Executive Officers: Richard P Banis (Executive VP and Chief Financial Officer), Glenn Schaeffer (Senior VP)

PRINCIPAL ACTIVITIES: Operation of casinos; hotels
Principal Subsidiaries: Slots-a-Fun
Financial Information:

	1986 $'000
Sales revenues	374,000
Net income	36,000

No of Employees: 5,600

CIT GROUP HOLDINGS (THE)

135 W 50th St, New York, NY 10020
Tel: (212) 408-6000

Chairman: C L Wingfield (and Chief Executive Officer)
Senior Executive Officers: James J Egan Jr (Executive VP, Secretary and General Counsel), H Anthony Ittelson (Executive VP, Corporate Development), William M O'Grady (Executive VP Administration), Thomas J O'Rourke (Senior VP Marketing), Jay R Simons (VP Treasury Operations)

PRINCIPAL ACTIVITIES: Holding company with interests in financial services, leasing, factoring and insurance
Parent Company: Manufacturers Hanover Corporation, New York, NY
Principal Subsidiaries: The CIT Group Inc; The CIT Group Business Credit Inc; The CIT Group/Sales Financing Inc; The CIT Group/Factoring Inc; The CIT Group/Capital Financing Inc; The CIT Group/Equipment Financing Inc
Financial Information:

	$'000
Revenues	950,000

No of Employees: 3,500

CITADEL HOLDING CORPORATION

600 N Brand Blvd, Glendale, CA 91203
Tel: (818) 956-7100

Chairman: J A Taylor
President: G D Barrone (and Chief Executive Officer)
Senior Executive Officers: S C McCarver (Executive VP and Treasurer), David Hooker (Senior VP and Controller)

PRINCIPAL ACTIVITIES: Financial services; savings institution
Principal Bank: First Interstate Bank of California
Financial Information:

	Dec 31 1985	Dec 31 1986
	$'000	$'000
Net income	26,040	29,030
Earnings per share	$7.73	$8.43
Shareholders equity	119,088	148,243
Deposits	-	2,400,294
Total assets	3,139,990	3,273,980

No of Employees: 688

CITATION-WALTHER CORPORATION

648 Monroe Avenue N.W., Grand Rapids, MI 49503
Tel: (616) 451-2581

Chairman: Daniel Walther (and Chief Executive Officer)
President: Fred Walther (and Chief Operating Officer)
Senior Executive Officers: J Vance (VP and Treasurer)

PRINCIPAL ACTIVITIES: Plumbers' supplies
Parent Company: Dayton-Walther Corporation, Dayton, OH
Principal Bank: Old Kent Bank
Financial Information:

	$'000
Sales revenues	70,000

No of Employees: 1,000

CIT-CON OIL CORPORATION

PO Box 1578, Lake Charles, LA 70602
Tel: (318) 491-8581

Chairman: C A Mattei (and President)
Senior Executive Officers: R E Funk (VP), G W Edwards (VP), F J Gangi (Treasurer)

PRINCIPAL ACTIVITIES: Oils and petroleum products
Parent Company: Citgo Petroleum Corporation, Tulsa, OK
Financial Information:

	$'000
Sales revenues	400,000

Principal Shareholders: Southland Corporation, Dallas, TX

CITICORP

399 Park Avenue, New York, NY 10043
Tel: (212) 559-1000

Chairman: John S Reed; Vice Chairmen: H H Angermueller, J D Farley, T C Theobald

Senior Executive Officers: Lawrence R Glenn (Chairman Corporate Policy Committee), William R Rhodes (Chairman Restructuring Committee), Richard S Braddock (Sector Executive), Lawrence M Small (Sector Executive)

PRINCIPAL ACTIVITIES: Financial services and banking

Principal Subsidiaries: BHC Resources Inc; Capital Markets Sources Inc; Citibank; Aspirations Inc; Lebanon Properties Inc; Regency Associates Inc; Yorktowne Development Corp; Citibank International; Citibank NY State; CIRI Corp; Carte Blanche Corp; Prestige Gifts Corp; Citicorp Investment Management; Citicorp Leasing Inc; Citicorp Leasing International; Citicorp Real Estate Inc; FNCB Capital Corp; Flex Inc; Inter-Continental Computing Corp; Maria Real Estate Inc; Citibank SD; Citicorp Associates Inc; CU Resources Inc; Citicorp Business Credit Inc; Citicorp Commercial Inc; Citicorp Homeowners Inc; Citicorp Latino Inc; Citicorp Leasing Inc; Citicorp Person-to-Person Inc; Citicorp Real Estate Inc; Citicorp Remote Computing Services; Citicorp Retail Services Inc; Citicorp Financial Inc; Citicorp Services Inc; Citicorp USA Inc; Citicorp Venture Capital Ltd; Citicors Commercial Inc; Computer Professionals Unlimited; Correspondent Resources Inc; Lexar Business Communications Inc; Mission Park Corp; Nationwide Finance Co of Portland; Retail Consumer Services Inc; Services Management Group IL; Thrift Resources Inc; Bankers Data Processing Inc; Thrift Services Inc; Transaction Technology Inc

Principal Bank: Citibank NA; Citicorp Holdings Inc; Citicorp Banking Corporation; Citibank (New York State) NA; Citicorp Trust NA; Citicorp (Maine); Citicorp International Group Inc; Citilease Inc; Citicorp Retail Services Inc

Financial Information:

	Dec 31 1985	Dec 31 1986
	$'000	$'000
Net income	998,000	1,058,000
Earnings per share	$7.12	$7.14
Shareholders equity	7,765,000	9,060,000
Deposits	104,959,000	114,689,000
Total assets	173,597,000	196,124,000

No of Employees: 88,500

CITIZENS & SOUTHERN GEORGIA CORPORATION

35 Broad Street, Atlanta, GA 30303
Tel: (404) 581-2121

Chairman: Bennett A Brown (and Chief Executive Officer); Vice Chairman: John W McIntyre

President: John S Poelker (and Chief Financial Officer)

Senior Executive Officers: William J Van Landingham (Executive VP North Georgia Banking Group), Lee M Sessions Jr (Executive VP and Assistant to Chairman), Willard A Alexander (General VP, Credit Administration), Henry T Collinsworth (General VP Administration), Archie H Davis (General VP), A G Oliver (General VP Community Banking Group), William L Mathis (General VP South Georgia Banking Group)

PRINCIPAL ACTIVITIES: Bank holding company

Principal Subsidiaries: Citizens & Southern Agency Inc; Citizens & Southern Bank; Citizens & Southern National Bank; Citizens & Southern International Bank; Family Credit Services Inc; Citizens & Southern Financial Corp; Citizens Southern Equity Mortgaging; Citizens Southern Insurance Co; First Southeastern Co; Landmark Bank

Financial Information:

	Dec 31 1985	Dec 31 1986
	$'000	$'000
Dividends	124,590	155,850
Earnings per share	$2.38	$2.63
Shareholders equity	-	1,091,340
Deposits	9,651,880	14,026,050
Total assets	13,590,530	18,757,410

No of Employees: 13,320

CITIZENS BANKING CORPORATION

One Citizens Banking Center, Flint, MI 48502
Tel: (313) 766-7500

Chairman: Donald E Johnson Jr
President: Charles R Weeks (and Chief Executive Officer)
Senior Executive Officers: Alvin G Benson (Vice Chairman), John W Ennest (Executive VP), John E Birky (Executive VP), R T Carley (Executive VP and Secretary to Board), Gary O Clark (Executive VP), David A Thomas Jr (Executive VP), Robert J Vitito (Executive VP), Nicholas J Cilfone (VP), Gary P Drainville (Senior VP), Richard J Mitsdarfer (VP and General Auditor), Edward H Newman (VP), Wayne G Schaeffer (VP, Chief Financial Officer and Treasurer)

PRINCIPAL ACTIVITIES: Banking
Principal Subsidiaries: Citizens Commercial & Savings Bank; Second National Bank of Saginaw
Financial Information:

	1985	1986
	$'000	$'000
Income before taxes	18,715	18,423
Net income	17,368	17,961
Dividends	4,451	6,278
Dividends per share	$0.80	$0.95
Earnings per share	$2.62	$2.71
Common stock	44,209	66,311
Retained income	77,040	88,723
Shareholders equity	150,281	161,950
Deposits	1,646,414	1,695,275
Total assets	1,980,470	2,012,545

No of Employees: 1,790

CITIZENS FEDERAL SAVINGS & LOAN ASSOCIATION

3605 132nd Avenue, Bellevue, WA
Tel: (206) 644 1133

Chairman: David P Thompson (and President)
Senior Executive Officers: William A Taylor (Senior VP Asset Management, and Secretary), George Chambers (Senior VP Marketing), William V Read (Senior VP Retail Sales), Pamela J Barngrover (Senior VP), William G Filler II (VP and Controller), Joseph Rogers (VP), J William Wood (VP), Eugene H Brus (VP Commercial Insurance)

PRINCIPAL ACTIVITIES: Savings and loans and other financial services
Principal Subsidiaries: Citizens Service Corp
Principal Bank: Peoples National Bank

No of Employees: 200

CITIZENS FIDELITY CORPORATION

Citizens Plaza, 500 W Jefferson St, Louisville, KY 40202
Tel: (502) 581-2100

Chairman: David J Grissom (and President and Chief Executive Officer)
Senior Executive Officers: Charles J Thayer (Executive VP and Chief Financial Officer), Michael N Haneld (Executive VP), Frederick E Zopp (Secretary)

PRINCIPAL ACTIVITIES: Banking services
Principal Subsidiaries: C F Financial Services Inc; Citizens Fidelity (OH); Citizens Fidelity Bank & Trust Co; Citizens Fidelity Leasing Corp
Principal Bank: Citizens Fidelity Bank & Trust Co
Financial Information:

	Dec 31 1985
	$'000
Revenues	379,000
Net income	41,000
Total assets	3,980,000

No of Employees: 2,250

CITIZENS FINANCIAL GROUP, INC

870 Westminster Street, Providence, RI 02902
Tel: (401) 456-7000
Telex: WUT 952077 citizens pvd

President: George Graboys (and Chief Executive Officer)
Senior Executive Officers: Herbert W Cummings (Executive VP), Kenneth E Hogberg (Senior VP and Treasurer), Robert C Sanderson Jr (VP). Senior Officers of Citizens Savings Bank, FSB & Citizens Trust Company: George Graboys (Chairman and Chief Executive Officer), Herbert W Cummings (President), Kenneth E Hogberg (Vice Chairman and Chief Financial Officer Corporate Planning and Finance Group), Richard E Benson (Executive VP Corporate Banking Group), Bernard P Campbell (Executive VP Trust and Investment Management Group), George E Kilguss Jr (Executive VP Retail Banking Group), Edward J Parry Jr (Executive VP Banking Services Group), Vincent Balasco (Senior VP Data Processing Administration), Jeffrey R Carlson (Senior VP Asset-Based Loan Division), Robert A Crowley (Senior VP Commercial Real Estate Department), Salvatore C DiSanto (Senior VP Trust and Investment Management Group), Michael Edwards (Senior VP Funds Management Department), James C Fahey (Senior VP and Commercial Loan Supervisor), Denise S Hartman (Senior VP Marketing Department), Thomas W Hoagland (Senior VP Corporate Banking Group), Thomas J Kean (Senior VP Trust Operations), Edward J Muldowney (Senior VP Special Projects), Robert S Nelson (Senior VP Corporate Banking Group), Robert C Sanderson Jr (Senior VP Corporate Development Department), Richard J Wischnowsky (Senior VP Banking Services Group), John T Wiseman (Senior VP Municipal Finance)

PRINCIPAL ACTIVITIES: Bank holding company
Trade Names: Citizens Bank
Principal Subsidiaries: Citizens Savings Bank, FSB; Citizens Trust Company
Principal Bank: Citizens Savings Bank, FSB
Financial Information:

	Dec 31 1985	Dec 31 1986
	$'000	$'000
Income before taxes	32,213	45,986
Net income	21,987	30,471
Dividends paid	1,653	7,476
Dividends per share paid (1)	$0.115	$0.52
Earnings per share (1)	N/M(2)	$2.10
Common stock (1)(3)	14,375	14,383
Retained income	20,334	22,995
Shareholders equity	270,631	293,424
Deposits	1,345,528	1,546,770
Total assets	1,865,165	2,539,499

(1) All figures have been restated to reflect the 2-for-1 common stock split effective May 15, 1987
(2) Not meaningful as the company converted to stock on June 19, 1985
(3) number of shares in thousands

Principal Shareholders: 1. FMR Corp (6.62%); 2. Harris Associates L.P; TRI-Partners Corporation (7.43%)
No of Employees: 1,192

CITIZENS FIRST BANCORP INC

208 Harristown Road, Glen Rock, NJ 07452
Tel: (201) 445 3400

Chairman: Richard G Kelley (and Chief Executive Officer)
President: Rodney T Verblaauw (and Chief Administrative Officer)
Senior Executive Officers: Joseph W Fitzpatrick (Secretary and Treasurer)

PRINCIPAL ACTIVITIES: Holding company with interests in banking
Principal Subsidiaries: Citizens First National Bank of New Jersey
Principal Bank: Midlantic National Bank
Financial Information:

	Dec 31 1985
	$'000
Revenues	144,660
Net income	17,450

No of Employees: 800

CITIZENS SAVINGS FINANCIAL CORPORATION

999 Brickell Avenue, Miami, FL 33131
Tel: (305) 577-0400

Chairman: Charles B Stuzin (and President)
Senior Executive Officers: Morton Trilling (Executive VP and Treasurer and Assistant Secretary), Thomas A Christensen (Senior VP and Assistant Secretary), Richard Hawkshead (Assistant Secretary), Dennis B Holthaus (VP and Chief Accounting Officer and Assistant Secretary)

PRINCIPAL ACTIVITIES: Citizens Savings Financial Corporation is a savings and loan holding company
Principal Subsidiaries: Citizens Federal Savings and Loan Association
Principal Bank: Federal Home Loan Bank, Atlanta
Financial Information:

	Dec 31 1985	Dec 31 1986
	$'000	$'000
Revenues	218,975	234,383
Income before taxes	9,985	14,083
Net income	5,492	11,332
Earnings per share	$2.83	$5.62
Common stock	7,016	7,285
Retained income	30,860	42,161
Shareholders equity	36,980	106,759
Deposits	1,363,983	1,903,638
Total assets	2,009,408	2,577,079

No of Employees: 696

CITIZENS UTILITIES COMPANY

High Ridge Park, PO Box 3801, Stamford, CT 06905
Tel: (203) 329-8800

Chairman: Richard L Rosenthal
President: Ishier Jacobson (and Chief Executive Officer)
Senior Executive Officers: John H Engel (Assistant VP), Richard K Robinson (Assistant VP and Controller), Boyd T Townsley (VP Division), Hampton D Graham Jr (Treasurer and Chief Financial Officer), Robert L O'Brien (VP Finance), George H Rivard (Assistant Treasurer), Budd S Schwartz (Assistant Treasurer), Gary T Snyder (Assistant Treasurer), Brigid M Smith (Assistant Secretary), Theresa M Walsh (Assistant Secretary), David S Chardavoyne (Assistant VP Functional Area), Richard B Hieber (VP Functional Area)

PRINCIPAL ACTIVITIES: Public services including the supply of water, gas, electricity and telephone services
Principal Subsidiaries: Big Run Telephone Company; Blue Mountain Consolidated Water Company; Brimfield Water Company; Citizens Utilities Home Water Company; Citizens Utilities Company California; Citizens Utilities Company of Illinois; Citizens Utilities Company of Pennsylvania; Citizens Utilities Rural Company; Citizens Utilities Water Company Pennsylvania; Flowing Wells Inc; Francis Land & Water Company; Glen Alsace Water Company; Jacksons Waterworks Inc; Lake Heritage Utilities Inc; Larkfield Water Company; Ohio Utilities Company; Sun City Sewer Company; Sun City Water Company; Sun City West Utilities Company; Tubac Valley Water Company Inc; Valley Utility Company
Principal Bank: Marine Midland Bank
Financial Information:

	Dec 31 1986
	$'000
Sales revenues	268,900
Net income	58,000

No of Employees: 1,560

CITRUS CENTRAL INC

North Hwy 441, PO Box 17774, Orlando, FL 32860
Tel: (305) 889-4101
Telex: WUT 564348 citruscent orl

Chairman: Joseph D Marshburn (and President); Vice Chairman: John F Nelson Jr
Senior Executive Officers: Jack Z Randall (Executive VP and General Manager Supply Division), John St John (Senior VP), James R Terrill (Senior VP, Secretary and Treasurer), Paul H Waller Jr (Senior VP Corporate Services and Assistant Secretary)

PRINCIPAL ACTIVITIES: Manufacture of containers
Principal Bank: First Fidelity Savings and Loan
Financial Information:

	$'000
Sales revenues	100,000

No of Employees: 400

CITY GAS COMPANY OF FLORIDA

955 East 25th Street, Hialeah, FL 33013
Tel: (305) 691 8710

Chairman: S W Langer (and President)
Senior Executive Officers: Alice M Harris (Executive VP), Larry I Hixon (VP and Divisional Manager), David Langer (Senior VP), Jack Langer (VP), Jerry A Wutzler (Assistant VP and Controller), Harry Blumin (Treasurer), Salvatore Bertolo (VP Operations), Charles S Roberts (Secretary)

PRINCIPAL ACTIVITIES: Supply of natural gas
Principal Subsidiaries: Essel Corporation
Principal Bank: Panamerican Bank
Financial Information:

	$'000
Sales revenues	40,000

No of Employees: 200

CITY INVESTING COMPANY

59 Maiden Lane, New York, NY 10038
Tel: (212) 530-7300
Telex: WUT 125467 cic nyk

Chairman: George T Scharffenberger (and Chief Executive Officer)
President: Peter C Huang (and Chief Operating Officer)
Senior Executive Officers: Gerald S Armstrong (Senior VP), John C Herndon (Senior VP), Steven H Newman (Senior VP), Richard W Ohman (Senior VP), John J Quirk (Senior VP and Treasurer), John D Russell (Senior VP), Edward P Sheridan (Senior VP), William H Tucker III (Senior VP)

PRINCIPAL ACTIVITIES: Holding company with interests in housing construction, metal fabrication and financial services

Principal Bank: Citibank
Financial Information:

	$'000
Sales revenues	6,000,000

No of Employees: 63,000

CITY NATIONAL CORPORATION

400 N Roxbury Drive, Beverly Hills, CA 90210
Tel: (213) 550-5400
Telex: WUT 67-7653 cinabnkho bvhl

Chairman: Bram Goldsmith (and Chief Executive Officer City National Bank and City National Corporation)
President: Alexander L Kyman (and Chief Operating Officer City National Bank, VP City National Corporation)
Senior Executive Officers: James P Del Guercio (Executive VP and General Counsel, and Secretary City National Bank; VP, Secretary and General Counsel City National Corporation), Jerome F Schulte (Executive VP and Chief Financial Officer City National Bank; VP and Treasurer City National Corporation), Nell A Cox (Senior VP and General Manager City National Information Systems), Newton Gore (Executive VP Marketing and Sales, City National Information Systems), Jeffrey Cove (Senior VP and Manager Real Estate Loans), Marjorie Luttenbacher (Senior VP Human Resources), Edward B Linsley (Senior VP Head Office Loans), Roberta J Swan (Senior VP and Senior Operations Officer Operations Administration), Thomas G O'Mara (Senior VP Investments), Geoffrey B Williams (Senior VP and Senior Trust Officer), Jack Cummings (Regional Senior VP), Roger A Sharp (Regional Senior VP), Irene Romero (Senior VP Entertainment)

PRINCIPAL ACTIVITIES: Banking
Principal Subsidiaries: City National Bank
Financial Information:

	Dec 31 1985	Dec 31 1986
	$'000	$'000
Total revenue	258,653	275,735
Income before taxes	36,321	41,497
Net income	24,179	29,734
Dividends	7,691	9,180
Dividends per share	$0.420	$0.50
Earnings per share	$1.32	$1.62
Common stock	9,158	18,371
Surplus	-	68,145
Retained income	62,093	82,647
Shareholders equity	147,995	169,163
Deposits	1,990,791	2,668,796
Total assets	2,473,169	3,141,551

Principal Shareholders: Bram Goldsmith Group (17%); City National Bank, Trustee Profit Sharing Retirement Plan of City National Bank Employees (5%); Wellington Management Company/Thorndike, Doran, Paine & Lewis (6%)
No of Employees: 2,200

CITYFED FINANCIAL CORP

293 South County Road, PO Box 2872, Palm Beach, FL 33480
Tel: (305) 655-5919 (Corporate Offices); (201) 658-4100 (Administrative Offices)

Chairman: Gilbert G Roessner
President: Alfred J Hedden (and Chief Executive Officer)
Senior Executive Officers: John W Atherton Jr (Vice Chairman), John K Darr (Vice Chairman and Chief Financial Officer), Ronald J Tell (Secretary), Glenn J Ohl (Controller)

PRINCIPAL ACTIVITIES: CityFed Financial Corp is a financial services holding company. Through its operating units, it is a leading, nationwide mortgage banker with total first mortgage production in the first six months of 1987 of more than $3 billion and with an $18 billion loan servicing portfolio. It also has major interstate banking operations, with assets of $10.8 billion and with nearly 1,000,000 customer accounts through retail banking operations in New Jersey and Florida

Principal Subsidiaries: City Federal Savings and Loan Association
Principal Bank: City Federal Savings and Loan Association
Financial Information:

	Dec 31 1985	Dec 31 1986
	$'000	$'000
Income before taxes (1)	71,969	44,100
Net income	62,110	37,524
Dividends per share (2)	$0.40	$0.40
Earnings per share (3)	$2.63	$1.46
Common stock (4)	13,780	18,472
Retained income	192,238	213,601
Shareholders equity	360,543	356,956
Deposits	6,280,536	6,843,992
Total assets	8,234,216	10,728,053

(1) and extraordinary items
(2) common stock
(3) fully diluted
(4) shares outstanding at year end in thousands

No of Employees: 6,500

CITYTRUST BANKCORP INC

945 Main Street, Bridgeport, CT 06601
Tel: (203) 384 5400

Chairman: George F Taylor (and Chief Executive Officer)
President: Jonathan A Topham (and Chief Operating Officer)
Senior Executive Officers: Edward J McNabb (VP and Chief Financial Officer), Reid C Spencer (Executive VP Finance), Frank W Estes (Secretary), M James Geraghty (VP), Murray H Morse (VP), E Cortright Phillips (VP)

PRINCIPAL ACTIVITIES: Holding company with interests in banking
Principal Subsidiaries: Capital Impact Corporation; Citytrust; LWC Corporation
Financial Information:

	Dec 31 1985
	$'000
Revenues	192,340
Net income	17,110

No of Employees: 1,140

CLABIR CORPORATION

485 W Putnam Avenue, Old Greenwich, CT 06870
Tel: (203) 625-0300
Telex: WUT 99-6468 clabir oldg

Chairman: Henry D Clarke Jr (and President and Chief Executive Officer)
Senior Executive Officers: Jeffrey J Kaplan (Executive VP), David L Downs (VP and Secretary), James W Schell (VP and Chief Financial Officer)

PRINCIPAL ACTIVITIES: Holding company whose subsidiaries are engaged in the manufacture of precision machined products, military equipment and ice cream
Principal Subsidiaries: Clabir Corp CA; Isaly Co Inc; Hanover Klondike Co Inc; Isaly Co; Klondike Southeast Corp
Principal Bank: Citibank
Financial Information:

	$'000
Sales revenues	51,000

No of Employees: 2,800

CLAIBORNE,, LIZ, INC

1441 Broadway, New York, NY 10018
Tel: (212) 354-4900
Telex: 423-221

Co-Chairmen: Arthur Ortenberg (and Secretary), Jerome A Chazen
President: Elizabeth Claiborne Ortenberg

Senior Executive Officers: H L Falk (Executive VP of Finance), John Consolini (Executive VP of Operations)

PRINCIPAL ACTIVITIES: Production of women's clothing
Trade Names: Claiborne, Lizsport, Lizwear, Liz Claiborne, Dana Buchman, Liz
Principal Subsidiaries: Liz Claiborne Licensing Inc; Liz Claiborne Sales Inc; Liz Claiborne Export Inc; Liz Claiborne Foreign Holdings Inc; Liz Claiborne Accessories Inc; Liz Claiborne Accessories-Sales Inc
Principal Banks: Chase Manhattan; Citibank
Financial Information:

	Dec 28 1985	Dec 27 1986
	$'000	$'000
Sales revenues	556,553	813,497
Income before taxes	119,600	169,302
Net income	60,580	86,194
Dividends	6,942	9,980
Dividends per share	$0.16	$0.23
Earnings per share	$1.42	$2.00
Common stock	42,904	43,279
Retained income	106,960	183,104
Shareholders equity	162,729	247,787

No of Employees: 3,000

CLAIRE'S STORES INC

PO Box 9312, Miami, FL 33014
Tel: (305) 558-2577

Chairman: Rowland Schaefer (and President)
Senior Executive Officers: Ira D Kaplan (Treasurer), Harold E Berritt (Secretary), Sylvia Schaefer (VP), Charlotte G Fischer (President Claire's Boutiques, Inc), Theodore Adler (VP Real Estate Claire's Boutiques, Inc), Leslie D Dunavant (VP Store Operations Claire's Boutiques, Inc), Alexander M Winiecki (VP Administration Claire's Boutiques, Inc)

PRINCIPAL ACTIVITIES: Retailer specializing in women's fashion accessories
Principal Subsidiaries: Claire's Boutiques, Inc; Dara Michelle, Inc
Principal Bank: Southeast Bank
Financial Information:

	Jan 2 1986	Jan 31 1987
	$'000	$'000
Sales revenues	74,456	87,205
Income before taxes	13,770	10,415
Net income	7,479	5,323
Dividends	1,338	1,587
Dividends per share	$0.083	$0.10
Earnings per share	$0.45	$0.33
Common stock	805	809
Retained income	13,494	17,231
Shareholders equity	20,257	23,618

No of Employees: 4,000

CLARE DIVISION

3101 Pratt Blvd, Chicago, IL 60645
Tel: (312) 262-7700
Telex: WUT 253775 cpclare co cgo

Senior Executive Officers: David M Schwarz (VP and General Manager)

PRINCIPAL ACTIVITIES: Manufacture of electrical switchgear and apparatus
Parent Company: General Instrument Corporation, New York, NY
Financial Information:

	$'000
Sales revenues	50,000

No of Employees: 3,000

CLARK, C & J, INC

2201 W 11th Street, Wilmington, DE 19805
Tel: (302) 654-2106

President: Stephen Clark (and Secretary and Treasurer)

PRINCIPAL ACTIVITIES: Holding company with interests in the manufacture of footwear
Trade Names: Hanover, Bostonian
Parent Company: C & J Clark Ltd, Street, Somerset, UK
Principal Bank: Chase Manhattan Bank
Financial Information:

	$'000
Sales revenues	200,000

No of Employees: 3,400

CLARK CONSOLIDATED INDUSTRIES INC

20575 Center Ridge Road, Cleveland, OH 44116
Tel: (216) 333 8200

Chairman: W S Beckenbach (and Chief Executive Officer)
President: R W Haskins (and Treasurer)
Senior Executive Officers: W C Beckenbach (Executive VP), Joseph H Persky (Secretary)

PRINCIPAL ACTIVITIES: Wholesalers of electrical products for the construction industry including wires and cables
Principal Subsidiaries: JC Baxter Company; Clark Pulley Corporation; Duellman Electric Company; Elgee Electric Company
Principal Bank: Central National Bank
Financial Information:

	$'000
Sales revenues	48,230

No of Employees: 325

CLARK EQUIPMENT CO

100 N Michigan Street, 7008 South Bend, IN 46634
Tel: (219) 239 0100
Telex: WUT 234033 clark bcan a

President: Leo J McKernan
Senior Executive Officers: F M Sims (Executive VP Servicing and Chief Operating Officer), T C Clarke (Senior VP, Secretary and Chief Administration Officer), E A Dippo (Senior VP and Group Executive), W T Hjorth (Senior VP and Chief Financial Officer)

PRINCIPAL ACTIVITIES: Components for heavy vehicles and earth moving machines including transmissions and axles
Principal Subsidiaries: Clark Business Services Corp; Clark Automotive Products Corp; Clark Equipment Overseas Financial Corp; Clark Equipment Credit Corp; Clark Equipment Realty Corp; Clark Financial Marketing Corp; Clark Rental Corp; Clark Rental System Inc; Horizon Creditcorp; Clark Information Technologies; Clark International Marketing SA Inc; Clark MI Co Inc; Cortez Custom Brokerage Co
Financial Information:

	Dec 31 1985	Dec 31 1986
	$'000	$'000
Sales revenues	964,093	954,043
Net (loss)	(85,472)	(60,600)
Shareholders equity	428,800	393,168

No of Employees: 10,063

CLARK, J L, MFG CO

2300 6th Street, Box 7000, Rockford, IL 61125
Tel: (815) 962-8861
Telex: TWX 910 631 3446 jl clark rk

President: W O Nelson (and Chief Executive Officer)
Senior Executive Officers: R W Malmgren (Executive VP), T P Harnois (VP Corporate Development), J F Newman (VP Manufacturing), L Ax (VP Industrial Engineering), D M Carter (VP Sales), D R Galinat (VP Filter Manufacturing), D J Schmitz (VP Plant, Lancaster Division), S K Nolt (VP Sales, Lancaster

Division), R T Gibbs (VP Sales, Rockford Division), W K McKenzie (VP Sales, J A Baldin Subsidiary), V E Zumhagen (VP Finance)

PRINCIPAL ACTIVITIES: Manufacture of metal, plastic and paper tubes and containers and filters
Principal Subsidiaries: J A Baldwin Manufacturing Co
Financial Information:

	$'000
Sales revenues	155,000

No of Employees: 1,940

CLARK PRODUCTS, INC
1850 Arthur Avenue, Elk Grove Village, IL 60007
Tel: (312) 956-1730

Chairman: Don J Hindman (and President)
Senior Executive Officers: Andre D Andrews (Senior VP Finance and Administration), George W Sengstock (VP Purchasing), Douglas L Young (VP)

PRINCIPAL ACTIVITIES: Industrial paper and plastic products; manufacture of sauces, salad dressings and pickles
Principal Subsidiaries: Mrs Clark's Food Inc
Principal Bank: Continental Illinois National Bank of Chicago
Financial Information:

	$'000
Sales revenues	200,000

No of Employees: 600

CLARKE DIVISION
2800 Estes Street, Muskegon, MI 49441
Tel: (616) 759-8545

Senior Executive Officers: Robert Buroker (VP and General Manager), Randy Curran (VP Finance), Len Roessler (VP International Marketing), L S Bacon (VP Human Resources)

PRINCIPAL ACTIVITIES: Manufacture of industrial cleaning and maintenance equipment
Parent Company: Cooper Industries Inc
Financial Information:

	$'000
Sales revenues	70,000

No of Employees: 1,700

CLARKSON INDUSTRIES, INC
950 Third Avenue, New York, NY 10022
Tel: (212) 355-7722
Telex: WUT 645 377 clarkind nyk

Chairman: Hugh Laughland
President: Lester Lieberman
Senior Executive Officers: Frederick P Finck (VP, President Highfield Division), James L Rothkopf (VP Finance), Thomas J Mitchell (VP and General Counsel)

PRINCIPAL ACTIVITIES: Valves and pipe fittings; ventilation equipment; safety equipment, aviation ground support equipment; computer room air conditioning; baggage handling equipment
Parent Company: BTR plc, UK
Principal Bank: Morgan Bank
Financial Information:

	$'000
Sales revenues	100,000

No of Employees: 900

CLASSIC CORPORATION
8214 Wellmore Court, Jessup, MD 20794
Tel: (301) 953 1133

Chairman: Isaac Fogel (and President and Chief Executive Officer)
Senior Executive Officers: L Wride (VP Sales and Marketing), Dennis M Baker (VP, Treasurer and Controller), Jo Benson Fogel (Secretary), R Magill (VP Manufacturing)

PRINCIPAL ACTIVITIES: Manufacture of beds
Principal Bank: Maryland National Bank
Financial Information:

	$'000
Sales revenues	38,000

No of Employees: 500

CLAUSING CORPORATION
6401 Quail Run Drive, Oshtemo, MI 49077
Tel: (616) 372-1450
Telex: WUT 224415 clauscorp k mz

President: A C Shauer (and Chief Operating Officer)
Senior Executive Officers: Douglas P Bergmoser (Group VP), D D Paulson (Group VP), W J Nancarrow (Group VP), J A Mais (VP Personnel), H Swan (VP Productivity)

PRINCIPAL ACTIVITIES: Manufacture of molded plastic products; process engineering; distribution of machine tools
Parent Company: Rexnord
Principal Bank: First National Bank of Chicago
Financial Information:

	$'000
Sales revenues	95,000

No of Employees: 1,300

CLAYTON HOMES, INC
PO Box 15169, Knoxville, TN 37912
Tel: (615) 970-7200

Chairman: J L Clayton (and President and Chief Executive Officer); Vice Chairman: B J Clayton
Senior Executive Officers: E T Kelly (Executive VP), R B Ray Jr (Executive VP Finance)

PRINCIPAL ACTIVITIES: Manufacture of sectional buildings and mobile homes
Trade Names: Clayton Mobile Homes, LUV Homes, International Homes, Crossland Homes
Principal Subsidiaries: Vanderbilt-Mortgage & Finance Inc; Vanderbilt Life Insurance Co
Principal Bank: First American Bank in Knoxville
Financial Information:

	Jun 30 1986 $'000	Jun 30 1987 $'000
Sales revenues	161,444	178,585
Income before taxes	13,726	17,956
Net income	8,376	10,356
Earnings per share*	$0.64	$0.75
Common stock	19,526	19,913
Retained income	29,731	40,087
Shareholders equity	49,257	58,530

*fully diluted

Principal Shareholders: James L Clayton; J P Morgan & Co
No of Employees: 2,000

CLC OF AMERICA INC
1655 Des Peres Road, St Louis, MO 63131
Tel: (314) 966 3757

Chairman: Donald E Peiser
President: L Warren Golden (and Chief Executive Officer)
Senior Executive Officers: Michael T Hayo (Executive VP), Dennis R Eichholz (Controller and Secretary), David T Hawkins (Treasurer)

PRINCIPAL ACTIVITIES: Transport services on inland waterways
Principal Subsidiaries: Morgan Drive Away Inc; Wisconsin Barge Line Inc
Principal Bank: Continental Illinois National Bank and Trust Company

Financial Information:

	$'000
Sales revenues	82,280

No of Employees: 650

CLEVELAND PNEUMATIC CO

3781 E 77 Street, Cleveland, OH 44105
Tel: (216) 341-1700
Telex: TWX 810 4218267 pneumo cp cl

Chairman: G A Fulham
President: Philip A Greco
Senior Executive Officers: James A Wood (VP), William F Grun (VP Overhaul, Overhaul Division), John C Schrecongost (VP Engineering), Myron J Bieber (VP Advanced Technology), Dale A Kulbago (VP Finance), L W Lowd (VP Marketing), D L Schuyler (VP Procurement), Patrick T Osborne (VP Employee Relations), Richard A Lachance (VP Quality Assurance)

PRINCIPAL ACTIVITIES: Aerospace equipment and components; telecommunications equipment
Parent Company: Pneumo Corporation, Boston, MA
Financial Information:

	$'000
Sales revenues	200,000

No of Employees: 1,000

CLEVELAND-CLIFFS INC

1100 Superior Avenue, Cleveland, OH 44114-2589
Tel: (216) 694-5700

Chairman: Samuel K Scovil
President: M T Moore (and Chief Executive Officer)
Senior Executive Officers: Directors: Samuel K Scovil (Chairman), Harry J Bolwell, E M deWindt, James D Ireland III, E Bradley Jones, M Thomas Moore, Donald C Platten, David V Ragone, Richard S Sheetz, Jeptha A Wade, Alton W Whitehouse Jr. Officers: M T Moore (President and Chief Executive Officer), W R Calfee (Group Executive VP), R McInnes (Group Executive VP), F S Forsythe (Executive VP), J S Brinzo (Senior VP-Finance), R Emmet (VP and Treasurer), J L Kelley (VP-Public Affairs), T C Levan (VP-Corporate Development), R F Novak (VP-Human Resources), F L Hartman (Corporate Counsel), M E Jackson (Secretary), J A Trethewey (Controller), J E Lenhard (Assistant Corporate Counsel and Assistant Secretary), J F Gribben (Assistant Treasurer), M J Kirwan (Assistant Treasurer), N Kochan (Cash Manager)

PRINCIPAL ACTIVITIES: Cleveland-Cliffs Inc produces and sells iron ore, coal, and hardwood lumber and veneer, supplies turnkey contract services for oil and gas drilling, provides management services for natural resource development, sells purchased commodities
Principal Subsidiaries: Subsidiaries of which there exists a 50% or greater interest: The Ashtabula & Buffalo Dock Company; Carroll County Coal Company; Cleveland-Cliffs Company; The Cleveland-Cliffs Iron Company; The Cleveland-Cliffs Steamship Company; Cleveland-Cliffs Ore Corporation; Cliffs Biwabik Ore Corporation; Cliffs Copper Corp; Cliffs Drilling Company; Cliffs Electric Service Company; Cliffs Empire Inc; Cliffs Engineering Inc; Cliffs Exploration Company; Cliffs Forest Company; Cliffs Fuel Service Company; Cliffs IH Empire Inc; Cliffs Incorporated; Cliffs Marquette Inc; Cliffs McEmpire Inc; Cliffs Mining Company; Cliffs Oil Shale Corp; Cliffs Synfuel Corporation; Cliffs Tilden Inc; Cliffs TIOP Inc; Cliffs Western Development Inc; Crawford Coal Company; Escanaba Properties Company; FCDC Coal Inc; Ishpeming Mining Company; Lake State Land Company; Lake Superior & Ishpeming Railroad Co; Mesabi Radio Corporation; Peninsula Land Corporation; Pickands Erie Corporation; Pickands Hibbing Corporation; Pickands Mather & Co; Pickands Mather & Co International; Pickands Mather Services Inc; Pickands Radio Co Ltd; Robert Coal Company; Seignelay Resources Inc; Splint Coal Company; Study Butte Mining Company; Syracuse Mining Company; Taconite Contracting Corporation; Tetapaga Mining Company Limited; The Erie Dock Company; Toledo Coke Inc; Turner Elkhorn Mining Company; Tuscaloosa Management Corporation; Upper Peninsula Generation Company
Principal Bank: AmeriTrust Company, N.A.
Financial Information:

	Dec 31 1985 $'000	Dec 31 1986 $'000
Sales revenues	343,800	296,400
Income (loss) before taxes	16,800	(55,900)
Net income (loss)	17,200	(41,700)
Common dividends	12,400	4,400
Dividends per common share	$1.00	$0.35
Earnings (loss) per share	$1.23	($3.76)
Common stock	12,800	12,800
Retained income	313,300	262,200
Shareholders equity	363,900	325,500

No of Employees: 8,306 (Company-wide)

CLEVEPAK CORPORATION

2500 Westchester Avenue, Purchase, NY 10577
Tel: (914) 694-1230

Chairman: A E Ditri (and Chief Executive Officer)
Senior Executive Officers: Philip L Fondy (Executive VP), A H Songer (VP and Chief Financial Officer)

PRINCIPAL ACTIVITIES: Manufacture of packaging; industrial ceramics; process equipment
Parent Company: Madison Management Group Inc
Principal Bank: Manufacturers Hanover Trust Company
Financial Information:

	$'000
Sales revenues	290,000

No of Employees: 5,600

CLIMAX MOLYBDENUM CO

1 Greenwich Plaza, Greenwich, CT 06830
Tel: (303) 234-9020
Telex: WUT 450 000 clmxnolyd gldn

Chairman: Pierre Gousseland
President: Charles E Stott Jr

PRINCIPAL ACTIVITIES: Molybdenum products
Parent Company: Amax Inc
Principal Bank: Manufacturers Hanover Trust
Financial Information:

	$'000
Sales revenues	670,000

No of Employees: 2,600

CLINTON MILLS, INC

600 Academy Street, Clinton, SC 29325
Tel: (803) 833-5500
Telex: TWX 810 3992071 clin mills

Chairman: Robert M Vance
President: George H Cornelson
Senior Executive Officers: C B Dixon (VP Engineering), J R Swetenburg (VP Manufacturing), G T Williams (VP Finance, Secretary and Treasurer), Steve Warren (VP Marketing), Claude A Crocker (VP Industrial and Public Relations), W A Sigman Jr (VP and Controller)

PRINCIPAL ACTIVITIES: Textile manufacture
Principal Subsidiaries: Clinton Mills of Geneva Inc; Mid-America Yarn Mills Inc
Principal Bank: M S Bailey and Son
Financial Information:

	$'000
Sales revenues	125,000

No of Employees: 2,000

CLOPAY CORPORATION

101 E Fourth Street, Cincinnati, OH 45202
Tel: (513) 381-4800
Telex: WUT 214701 clopay rdc cin

Chairman: Robert B Goergen (and Chief Executive Officer)
President: George A Strutz Jr (and Chief Operating Officer)
Senior Executive Officers: Edward C Zepf (Senior VP Finance), Leo V Cancio (Senior VP), Edward R Gaw (Senior VP Household Products Division), David B Lopez (Senior VP, Secretary and General Counsel), Christopher C Metcalf (VP and Controller), Clifford H Lahner (VP Human Resources), Raymond T Hagedorn (VP Management Information Services)

PRINCIPAL ACTIVITIES: Building materials and fittings
Principal Bank: The First National Bank of Cincinnati
Financial Information:

	$'000
Sales revenues	139,000

No of Employees: 1,600

CLOROX COMPANY (THE)

1221 Broadway, PO Box 24305, Oakland, CA 94623
Tel: (415) 271-7000
Telex: 336-423 CLOROX OPD OAK

Chairman: C R Weaver (and Chief Executive Officer)
President: J W Collins (and Chief Operating Officer)
Senior Executive Officers: Sheldon N Lewis (Executive VP-Technology), William F Ausfahl (Group VP and Chief Financial Officer), Robert A Bolingbroke (Group VP), Anthony W Biebl (VP-Food Service Products), Bryant C Blewett (VP-Taxes), John J Calderini (VP-Human Resources), Edward A Cutter (VP-General Counsel and Secretary), Robert J Diaz (VP-Controller), Raymond H Johnson (VP-Information Services), David L Goodman (VP-Public Affairs and Marketing Services), Lee Griffey (VP-Purchasing and Distribution), Charles E Harder (VP-Technical Services), Lyle L Hoover (VP-Treasurer), Rodric A Lorimer (VP-Manufacturing and Engineering), W E Lynn (VP-Kingsford Products), Donald C Murray (VP-International), Glynn M Phillips (VP-Sales), Ralph C Richter (VP-Olympic HomeCare Products), R A Steiner (VP-Prince Castle), G Craig Sullivan (VP-Household Products), Eugene N Wheeler (VP-Product Research and Development)

PRINCIPAL ACTIVITIES: The Clorox Company is a growing, diversified firm whose principal business is the development, manufacture and marketing of premium quality household products sold through grocery stores and other retail outlets. Additionally, many of these products are marketed to food service customers, such as restaurants, hotels and schools. The Company also manufactures and markets a full line of high quality interior and exterior architectural coatings sold through paint and building supply centers and other retail operations. The Company markets in more than 60 countries and operates more than 35 manufacturing facilities in the United States and Puerto Rico, Canada, Mexico, Barbados, Saudi Arabia, Colombia, Egypt, Yemen Arab Republic and Panama
Trade Names: Principal Brand Names used in USA:- Clorox, Clorox 2, Clorox Pre-Wash, Formula 409, Fresh Step, Hidden Valley Ranch, K.C. Masterpiece, Kingsford, Kingsford with Mesquite, Kitchen Bouquet, Liquid-plumr, Litter Green, Lucite, Match Light, Moore's, Olympic, Olympic Overcoat, Salad Crispins, Soft Scrub, Tackle, Tilex, Twice As Fresh, Prince Castle
Principal Subsidiaries: (100% owned unless stated): The Clorox Company of Canada Ltd; The Clorox Company of Puerto Rico; The Clorox International Company; Clorox International Trading Ltd; Food Service Products Company; The Household Cleaning Products Company of Egypt Ltd (49%); The Household Products Company; The HVR Company; Industrias Lesedo SA de CV (49%) (Mexico); The Kingsford Products Company; National Cleaning Products Ltd (40%) (Saudi Arabia); The Olympic HomeCare Products Company; Prince Castle Inc; Taurel Industries Ltd (51%) (Barbados); Tecnoclor SA (49%) (Colombia); Progar SA (49%) (Argentina)
Financial Information:

	Jun 30 1986 $'000	Jun 30 1987 $'000
Sales revenues	1,089,070	1,126,044
Earnings before taxes	175,308	186,586
Net earnings	95,610	104,899
Dividends	37,201	42,224
Dividends per share	$0.70(1)	$0.79(1)
Earnings per share(2)	$1.75(1)	$1.90(1)
Common stock	55,034(1)	55,385(1)
Retained earnings	424,547	487,222
Shareholders equity	549,793	616,477

(1) assuming full dilution
(2) all per-share and share amounts are restated for the June 1987 2-for-1 stock split

No of Employees: 4,500

CLOTHESTIME INC

5325 East Hunter Avenue, Anaheim, CA 92807
Tel: (714) 779 5881

Chairman: Michael P DeAngelo (and Chief Executive Officer); Vice Chairmen: Raymond A DeAngelo, John Ortega II
President: Gordon Nielson
Senior Executive Officers: Joel T Doti (Senior VP Operations and Public Affairs), William W Mowbray (Senior VP Finance and Administration), Roger C Johnson (VP and Manager Exploration), August DeAngelo (Secretary), Jeffrey R Dake (VP Real Estate and Engineering)

PRINCIPAL ACTIVITIES: Retailing of women's clothing
Principal Bank: Union Bank
Financial Information:

	$'000
Sales revenues	126,530

No of Employees: 2,300

CLOVER CLUB FOODS CO

1st E 2nd N, Kaysville, UT 84037
Tel: (801) 546-1201

President: Peter Duggan
Senior Executive Officers: Carl Caughran (General Manager/VP), Otto Clements (VP Operations), Raymond E Barkley (Controller)

PRINCIPAL ACTIVITIES: Snack foods
Trade Names: Clover Club, Little Pancho, Wise, El Molino, Spud Chips
Parent Company: Borden's Inc
Principal Subsidiaries: El Molino Foods Co
Principal Bank: First Interstate
Financial Information:

	$'000
Sales revenues	56,000

No of Employees: 420

CLOW CORPORATION

5050 Stepp Avenue, Jacksonville, FL 32216
Tel: (904) 731-3220

Chairman: Gilbert L Feltel (President and Chief Executive Officer)
Senior Executive Officers: J L Kelly (Senior VP), R K Phelps (VP), M Chopro (VP Financial Planning and Treasurer), K R McManes (VP Development), W V Gebhart (Controller), D Williams (Director Management Information Services), E J Crowley (VP Valve), E J Powers (VP Special Projects), R W Smith (Senior VP and General Manager), D A Schwartz (VP Water), A Mickevicius (Senior VP and General Manager)

PRINCIPAL ACTIVITIES: Manufacture of pipes, fittings and valves; pollution control chemicals and equipment
Parent Company: McWane Inc
Principal Bank: Continental Bank
Financial Information:

	$'000
Sales revenues	165,000

No of Employees: 1,770

CLUETT, PEABODY & CO, INC

510 Fifth Avenue, New York, NY 10036
Tel: (212) 930-3000
Telex: WUI 620019

Chairman: Henry H Henley Jr (and Chief Executive Officer)
President: Richard Q Armstrong (and Chief Operating Officer)
Senior Executive Officers: Irwin W Winter (Senior VP Finance, Treasurer and Chief Financial Officer), Robert D Krumme (Senior VP and General Counsel), Cochran B Supplee (VP Corporate Relations), D M Roark (VP Personnel), Roy E Green (VP and Controller), Ronald G Heller (VP, Secretary and Legal Counsel)

PRINCIPAL ACTIVITIES: Manufacture of clothing and sportswear
Parent Company: West Point-Pepperell Inc
Principal Bank: Manufacturers Hanover Trust Company
Financial Information:

	$'000
Sales revenues	961,700

No of Employees: 19,000

CMI CORPORATION

1-40 & Morgan Road, PO Box 1985, Oklahoma City, OK 73101
Tel: (405) 787-6020
Telex: 747167 CMI OKC

Chairman: Bill Swisher
President: Jay T Edwards
Senior Executive Officers: Jim D Holland (VP and Treasurer), Thane Swisher (VP and Secretary), Robert S Morrison (President, CMI Load King Division and Transport Trailers Manufacturing Company), Murray Rowe (President, CMI Bid-Well Division), Jim Furey (Executive VP, CMI Corporation-OKC), Charles Mencel (President, RayGo Inc)

PRINCIPAL ACTIVITIES: Manufacture road construction and pavement equipment. Have divisions and subsidiaries which manufacture lowboy and bottom dump trailers, bridge finishing equipment and soil and compaction equipment. Sixty percent of manufactured goods are manufactured for Caterpillar Tractor Co and sold under Caterpillar tradename
Principal Subsidiaries: CMI Load King Division; CMI Bid-Well Division; CMI Corporation (OKC); RayGo Inc
Principal Bank: Liberty National Bank & Trust Company of Oklahoma City
Financial Information:

	Dec 31 1985	Dec 31 1986
	$'000	$'000
Sales revenues	135,159	168,780
Net income (loss)	9,068	(7,469)
Earnings (loss) per share	$0.67	($0.58)
Common stock	13,281	13,670
Retained income (deficit)	(938)	(7,018)
Shareholders equity	47,366	39,779

No of Employees: 1,000

CML GROUP INC

524 Main Street, Acton, MA 01720
Tel: (617) 264 4155

Chairman: Charles M Leighton (and Chief Executive Officer)
President: G Robert Tod (and Chief Operating Officer)
Senior Executive Officers: Glenn E Davis (Controller), George W Duncklee (Treasurer), William F Harris (VP Finance), Paul P Brountas (Secretary), Patricia K Peters (VP Investor Relations)

PRINCIPAL ACTIVITIES: Retail trade in clothing and accessories
Trade Names: Boston Whaler, Britches of Georgetowne, Carroll Reed, The Nature Company, NordicTrack, SuperVision
Principal Bank: Citibank, NA
Financial Information:

	Jul 31 1986	Jul 31 1987
	$'000	$'000
Sales revenues	232,282	282,972
Income before taxes	12,546	17,463
Net income	6,838	9,035
Earnings per share	$1.04	$1.35
Common stock*	6,585	6,711
Retained income	24,491	33,526
Shareholders equity	50,298	60,084
*number of shares in thousands		

No of Employees: 4,000

CNA FINANCIAL CORPORATION

CNA Plaza, Chicago, IL 60685
Tel: (312) 822 5000

Chairman: Lawrence A Tisch
President: Edward J Noha (Chairman, President and Chief Executive Officer, CNA Insurance Officer)
Senior Executive Officers: Dennis H Chookaszian (VP and Controller), Thomas R Igleski (VP and Corporate Secretary)

PRINCIPAL ACTIVITIES: Provision of a wide range of insurance services
Parent Company: Loews Corporation
Principal Subsidiaries: Continental Casualty Company
Financial Information:

	1986
	$'000
Investment income net	896,243
Net income	403,526
Earnings per share	$6.25
Shareholders equity	2,738,217

No of Employees: 14,000

CNB BANCSHARES INC

20 Northwest Third Street, Evansville, IN 47708
Tel: (812) 464 3400

Chairman: H Lee Cooper (and Chief Executive Officer)
President: William E Veith
Senior Executive Officers: Ralph L Alley (Treasurer), David L Knapp (Secretary)

PRINCIPAL ACTIVITIES: Banking services
Financial Information:

	Dec 31 1985
	$'000
Revenues	64,780
Net income	6,160

No of Employees: 400

CNW CORPORATION

165 N Canal Street, Chicago, IL 60606
Tel: (312) 559-7000
Telex: WUT 253557 cnwdivbura cgo

Chairman: James R Wolfe
Senior Executive Officers: John M Butler Senior VP Finance and Accounting), Jerome W Conlon (Senior VP Governmant Affairs, Acquisitions and Planning), James P Daley (Senior VP Law and Real Estate), Louis T Duerinck (Senior VP Traffic), Robert W Schmiege (Senior VP Administration), Robert D

Smith (Senior VP Investor Relations), James A Zito (Senior VP Operations)

PRINCIPAL ACTIVITIES: Railroad services and manufacturing
Trade Names: Western and Fisher Snowplows (Douglas Dynamics, Inc)
Parent Company: CNW
Principal Subsidiaries: Douglas Dynamics Inc; Western Railroad Properties Inc; 400 Freight Services Inc
Principal Bank: Continental Illinois National Bank and Trust Company of Chicago
Financial Information:

	Dec 31 1985	Dec 31 1986
	$'000	$'000
Sales revenues	897,710	959,500
Net income (loss)	(27,410)	43,000
Earnings (loss) per share	($1.70)	$2.31
Shareholders equity	287,690	397,275

No of Employees: 9,000

COACHMEN INDUSTRIES, INC

601 E Beardsley Ave, Box 3300, Elkhart, IN 46515
Tel: (219) 262 0123
Telex: 258495

Chairman: Thomas H Corson (and Chief Executive Officer)
President: Philip G Lux (and Chief Operating Officer)
Senior Executive Officers: Gary L Groom (Executive VP and Secretary), Gene E Stout (Executive VP), Robert M Wasieko (Executive VP), Robert A Gottschalk (Executive VP), Lewis G Rawles (Executive VP), James Frahm (VP Personnel), L Tinley (VP Coachmen of Georgia), L Pavel (VP Kenco Engineering Division), B Snook (VP Coachmen Van Conversions), N Roberts (VP Coachmen Housing of Oregon), J Nicholson (VP Shasta Industries), C Corson (VP Coachmen-Indiana), M Johnson (VP Coachmen California), W Weaver (VP Coachmen Oregon), J Long (VP Coachmen Housing of Indiana), J Laughlin (VP Shadow Interiors), R Towry (VP Coachmen Texas), N Sayers (VP Coachmen Housing of PA), F Cullifer (VP Auranco), John C Huft (VP Facilities)

PRINCIPAL ACTIVITIES: Manufacture of trailers, campers and motor homes
Principal Subsidiaries: All American Homes Inc; Coachmen Housing of IN Inc; Coachmen Industries; Fan Coach Co Inc; Lux Co Inc; Shasta Industries of PA Inc; Sportscoach Corp America; Viking Recreational Vehicles
Principal Bank: Citibank
Financial Information:

	$'000
Sales revenues	356,000

No of Employees: 3,300

COAST FEDERAL SAVINGS & LOAN ASSOCIATION

1777 Main Street, Sarasota, FL 33577
Tel: (813) 366-7000

Chairman: R E Arnold
President: R W Antrim (and Chief Executive Officer)
Senior Executive Officers: J F Hutchinson (Senior VP, Chief Investment Officer and Treasurer), Richard Franz (Executive VP), H F Baird (Executive VP), W D Branham (Senior VP), C E Bruin (Senior VP), W L Childs (Senior VP), B G Glazener (Senior VP), G W Houts (Senior VP), R F Reinert (Senior VP), J E Roberts (Senior VP)

PRINCIPAL ACTIVITIES: Financial services including savings and loans
Principal Subsidiaries: Golden Eagle Service Corp
Principal Bank: Federal Home Loan Bank

No of Employees: 400

COAST SAVINGS & LOAN ASSOCIATION

855 S Hill St, Los Angeles, CA 90014
Tel: (213) 624-2110

Chairman: Ross M Blakely
President: Ray Martin
Senior Executive Officers: Jerome Nussbaum (Executive VP and Chief Financial Officer), Gilbert L Farley (Executive VP), John M Yunker (VP Administration and Operations), William S Bradway III (VP Marketing and Planning), Sim C Hixon (VP Lending)

PRINCIPAL ACTIVITIES: Savings and loan association
Principal Subsidiaries: Coast Mortgage and Realty Investors Corp
Financial Information:

	Dec 31 1986
	$'000
Net income	50,380
Earnings per share	$3.84
Shareholders funds	399,250
Deposits	5,931,130
Total assets	9,725,360

No of Employees: 1,800

COASTAL CORPORATION

Nine Greenway Plaza E, Houston, TX 77046
Tel: (713) 877-1400
Telex: WUT 77-4254 coastal d hou

Chairman: Oscar S Wyatt Jr (and Chief Executive Officer)
President: James R Paul (and Chief Operating Officer)
Senior Executive Officers: David A Arledge (Senior VP and Chief Financial Officer), Austin M O'Toole (Senior VP, Secretary and General Counsel), Dan J Hill (Senior VP Marketing), Kenneth O Johnson (Senior VP Subsidiary President Belcher Oil Company), John B McElreath (Senior VP and Controller), W E Spencer (Senior VP), Sam F Willson Jr (Senior VP Eastern Hemisphere Supply), James L Van Lanen (Senior VP Coal Operations)

PRINCIPAL ACTIVITIES: Oil and gas exploration and production; refining; petrochemicals; coal mining
Principal Subsidiaries: Coastal Capital Corp; Coastal Oil & Gas Corp; Border Exploration Co; Coastal Indonesia Inc; Coastal Uranium Inc; Syrian American Oil Corp; Coastal Refining Co; CIC Industries Inc; Derby Refining Co; Pacific Refining Co; Wycon Chemical Co Inc; Coastal States Petroleum Co; Coastal State Crude Gathering Co; Coastal States Marketing Inc; Coastal States Energy Co; Utah Fuel Co; Coastal States Management Corp; Coastal States Trading Inc; Colorado Interstate Corp; Colorado Interstate Gas Co; CIG Exploration Inc; Cosbel Petroleum Corp; Belcher Co of NY Inc; Belcher New England Inc; Belcher NJ Inc; Belcher Oil Co; Belcher Co of TN Inc; Poly-Products Inc; Southern Petroleum Co; Belcher Terminals Inc; Belcher Towing Co; Manatee Towing Co Inc; Coscol Petroleum Corp; Coscol Marine Corp; Texas Tank Ship Agency Inc; McCoy Caney Coal Co; Texcol Gas Services Inc
Principal Bank: Continental Illinois National Bank and Trust Company of Chicago
Financial Information:

	Dec 31 1985	Dec 31 1986
	$'000	$'000
Sales revenues	7,254,300	6,668,200
Net income	142,400	71,600
Earnings per share	$3.61	$0.84
Shareholders equity	772,000	788,900

No of Employees: 6,660

COASTAL LUMBER CO

Elm Street, Weldon, NC 27890
Tel: (919) 536-4211
Telex: TWX 510-929 0701 costallbr weln

President: Paul B Barringer (and Chief Executive Officer)
Senior Executive Officers: S H Conger (Executive VP Marketing and International Operations), J G Williams (VP Operations), L C shipley (VP Sales), R Seay (VP and Treasurer)

PRINCIPAL ACTIVITIES: Timber products; furniture
Principal Bank: United Virginia Bank
Financial Information:

	$'000
Sales revenues	130,000

No of Employees: 1,300

COATS & CLARK INC

72 Cummings Point Road, Stamford, CT 06902
Tel: (203) 327-3005

President: R G Laidlaw
Senior Executive Officers: W J Bruce (VP Manufacturing), G A Burnett (VP Finance), W A Waller (VP Administration and Secretary), F E Bradley (VP Personnel)

PRINCIPAL ACTIVITIES: Leisure and craft products; home sewing products; precision engineering and diecasting; industrial sewing products
Parent Company: Coats Patons plc, Glasgow, UK
Principal Subsidiaries: Gries/Dynacast Division
Principal Bank: Manufacturers Hanover Trust Company
Financial Information:

	$'000
Sales revenues	225,000

No of Employees: 3,400

COBANCO INC

55 River Street, Santa Cruz, CA 95060
Tel: (408) 423 8200

Chairman: E Reese Davis (and President and Chief Executive Officer)
Senior Executive Officers: Melvyn Switzer Jr (Executive VP and Chief Administrative Officer), Bonnie G Dodd (Senior VP and Chief Operating Officer), George R Galluci (Senior VP and Chief Financial Officer)

PRINCIPAL ACTIVITIES: Banking services
Financial Information:

	Dec 31 1985 $'000
Revenues	57,570
Net income	2,860

No of Employees: 500

COBE LABORATORIES, INC

1185 Oak Street, Lakewood, CO 80215
Tel: (303) 232-6800
Telex: 4322040 COBE UI

Chairman: Robert M Collins (and President)
Senior Executive Officers: Randall F Bellows (Executive VP), Robert S Timmins (Senior VP)

PRINCIPAL ACTIVITIES: Design manufacture and market medical products and services used in the treatment of kidney disease (nephrology), in open heart surgery, and monitoring (cardiovascular), in auto-immune disease (theraputic plasma exchanges), and in blood cell processing (cell treatment)
Trade Names: Centry as in Centry 2, Centry 2RX, Centry 2000, Centry 2000RX, Centry RO etc, COBE CML, COBE VPCML, COBE CDX, COBE 2991 and COBE 2997, COBE Computerized Perfusion Controller System
Principal Subsidiaries: NV COBE Laboratories Europe SA (Belgium); COBE Laboratories Deutschland (Germany); COBE SA (France); COBE Canada (Canada); COBE Laboratories Ltd (UK); COBE Laboratories Pty Ltd (Australia); Gradatim Medical Management Inc; COBE ASDT

Financial Information:

	$'000
Sales revenues	152,000

No of Employees: 1,700

COCA-COLA BOTTLING CO CONSOLIDATED

PO Box 31487, Charlotte, NC 28231
Tel: (704) 334-6851

Chairman: J F Harrison (and Chairman Executive Committee); Vice Chairmen: James V Johnson, Reid M Henson, William H Dougherty Jr (and Chief Financial Officer)
President: Marvin W Griffin Jr (and Chief Executive Officer)
Senior Executive Officers: Mike Bascle (Senior VP Marketing), Ron Barrett (Senior VP Soft Drinks), Kim Sheelar (VP Soft Drink Greensboro and Raleigh Division), Charles H Beach (Senior VP Operations/Soft Drinks), James A Jernigan (Senior VP Business Development), Grant L Hamrick (VP and Corporate Controller), Robert D Pettus (VP Human Resources), David V Singer (VP and Treasurer)

PRINCIPAL ACTIVITIES: Manufacture and wholesale of soft drinks; vending machine sales
Principal Subsidiaries: Consolidated Coin Caterers Inc
Principal Bank: North Carolina National Bank
Financial Information:

	$'000
Sales revenues	428,000

No of Employees: 3,000

COCA-COLA BOTTLING CO OF CHICAGO

7400 N Oak Park Avenue, Chicago, IL 60648
Tel: (312) 775-0900

President: Marvin J Herb
Senior Executive Officers: William F O'Rourke (Executive VP), William A Fullerton (VP and Controller)

PRINCIPAL ACTIVITIES: Soft drink manufacture
Principal Bank: First National Bank of Chicago
Financial Information:

	$'000
Sales revenues	55,000

No of Employees: 1,000

COCA-COLA BOTTLING CO OF MEMPHIS, TENN.

499 S Hollywood, Memphis, TN 38111
Tel: (901) 324-3611

President: G R Pidgeon (and Treasurer)
Senior Executive Officers: William R Sledge (VP), Nat Baxter (VP and General Manager)

PRINCIPAL ACTIVITIES: Coca-Cola bottling
Principal Bank: First Tennesse Bank
Financial Information:

	$'000
Sales revenues	60,000

No of Employees: 600

COCA-COLA BOTTLING CO OF MIAMI, INC

3440 Hollywood Blvd, Hollywood, FL 33021
Tel: (305) 985 5080

Chairman: Robert Spindler (and Chief Executive Officer)
President: Larry Smith
Senior Executive Officers: Amiel Brown (VP), William T Williams (VP and Treasurer), Raymond S Mathews (VP), Winston F Scherer (VP), Amiram Basevitch (VP), Robert J Feeley (VP), David A Zachry (VP), Danny Moskovitz (VP), David J Waluer (VP), Howard D Houchins (VP), G R Beachley (VP), Stephen D Worth (VP)

PRINCIPAL ACTIVITIES: Soft drink bottling and wholesale

Financial Information:

	$'000
Sales revenues	162,000

No of Employees: 670

COCA-COLA BOTTLING CO OF MID-AMERICA INC

PO Box 500, Shawnee Mission, KS 66201
Tel: (913) 492-8100

President: James E Waller
Senior Executive Officers: George F Lake (VP), Robert W Johnson (VP), David R Burks (VP), Stephen O Hulcomb (VP), L J Pickert (VP and Controller)

PRINCIPAL ACTIVITIES: Manufacture and bottling of soft drinks
Parent Company: Beatrice Companies Inc, Chicago, IL
Principal Bank: Commerce Bank of Kansas City
Financial Information:

	$'000
Sales revenues	100,000

No of Employees: 1,000

COCA-COLA BOTTLING CO OF NEW YORK, INC

20 Horseneck Lane, Greenwich, CT 06830
Tel: (203) 625-4000

Chairman: Charles E Millard (and Chief Executive Officer)
President: Edward F O'Reilly (and Chief Operating Officer)
Senior Executive Officers: Walter W Hemming (Executive VP and Chief Financial Officer), W W Gibbons (Executive VP), George R Heinold (Senior VP), Bruce E Mommsen (Senior VP), Paul D Cunningham (Senior VP), Morris E Haney (Senior VP), William Pearce (Senior VP Customer Relations), William C Gouldsbury (Senior VP and Secretary), Peter D Heberling (VP and General Counsel), Andres J Scanlon (VP and Controller)

PRINCIPAL ACTIVITIES: Bottling and wholesale trade in soft drinks
Principal Bank: Morgan Guaranty Trust Company
Financial Information:

	$'000
Sales revenues	575,000

No of Employees: 4,000

COCA-COLA BOTTLING MIDWEST INC

2750 Eagandale Blvd, St Paul, MN 55121
Tel: (612) 454-5460
Telex: WUT 29-8450 cokemwinc stp

Chairman: Summerfield K Johnston Jr
President: Henry A Schimberg
Senior Executive Officers: John Alm (VP Finance), Marvin Richards (VP Manufacturing)

PRINCIPAL ACTIVITIES: Coca-Cola bottling
Parent Company: Johnston Midwest Inc
Principal Bank: The First National Bank of Minneapolis
Financial Information:

	$'000
Sales revenues	175,000

No of Employees: 1,000

COCA-COLA COMPANY

310 North Avenue NW, Atlanta, GA 30313
Tel: (404) 676-2121

Chairman: Roberto C Goizueta (and Chief Executive Officer)
President: Donald R Keough (and Chief Operating Officer)
Senior Executive Officers: Claus M Halle (Senior Executive VP), Eugene V Amoroso (Executive VP), A G Hamby (Executive VP), Ira C Herbert (Executive VP), M D Ivester (Senior VP Finance)

PRINCIPAL ACTIVITIES: Manufacture of soft drinks; interests in motion pictures and home entertainment
Trade Names: Coca Cola, Minute Maid, Five Alive, Bright and Early, Hi-C, Maryland Club, Butter-Nut
Principal Subsidiaries: (100% owned unless stated): Belmont Springs Water Company Inc; Presto Products Inc; Coca Cola USA; Coca Cola Ltd (Canada); Tri-Star Pictures (33.3%); Embassy Communications; Tandem Productions; Colombia Pictures Industries
Financial Information:

	Dec 31 1985	Dec 31 1986
	$'000	$'000
Sales revenues	8,138,904	8,668,556
Net income	722,300	734,350
Earnings per share	$5.51	$2.42
Shareholders equity	2,979,060	3,514,980

No of Employees: 39,600

COHERENT INC

3210 Porter Drive, Palo Alto, CA 94304
Tel: (415) 493-2111
Telex: WUT 348 304

Chairman: James L Hobart
President: Henry E Gauthier (and Chief Executive Officer)
Senior Executive Officers: Robert J Quillinan (VP and Chief Financial Officer), Larry W Sonsini (Secretary)

PRINCIPAL ACTIVITIES: Electro-optical products including lasers for theraputic and diagnostic uses
Principal Subsidiaries: Coherent General Sturbridge; Lambda Physik
Principal Bank: Bank of America
Financial Information:

	$'000
Sales revenues	132,000

No of Employees: 1,300

COLECO INDUSTRIES, INC

999 Quaker Lane S, West Hartford, CT 06110
Tel: (203) 725-6000

Chairman: Arnold C Greenberg; Vice Chairman: Melvin Y Gershman (and Chief Operating Officer)
President: J Brian Clarke (and Chief Operating Officer)
Senior Executive Officers: Mark L Yoseloff (Executive VP), Philip Cohen (Executive VP Sales), George V Goudreault (Executive VP Operations), Morton E Handel (Executive VP Administration and Finance), Alfred Kahn (Executive VP Marketing), David J Ruggles (Executive VP and Chief Financial Officer), Michael S Schwefel (Senior VP, Legal Counsel and Secretary), Eric D Bromby (Senior VP Advanced Research and Development), Martin Ehrlich (Senior VP Orient Operations), Jeffrey S Jacobson (Senior VP International Sales), Paul C Meyer (Senior VP Operations Planning and Controller), Martin Nadborny (Senior VP Operations), Marvin A Posner (Senior VP Sales)

PRINCIPAL ACTIVITIES: Manufacture of toys; leisure and entertainment goods
Financial Information:

	Dec 31 1985	Dec 31 1986
	$'000	$'000
Sales revenues	776,000	500,660
Net income (loss)	82,915	(111,250)
Shareholders equity (deficit)	102,352	(7,664)

No of Employees: 3,000

COLEMAN COMPANY, (THE)

250 N St Francis Avenue, Wichita, KS 67201
Tel: (316) 261-3211
Telex: TWX 910 7416921 coleman wich

Chairman: Sheldon Coleman (and President and Office of Chief Executive); Vice Chairman: Clarence Coleman

Senior Executive Officers: Lawrence M Jones (Chairman Executive Committee), Donald V Berchtold (Executive VP and General Manager) Frank Shaw (Executive VP and General Manager Outing Products), Richard A Curry (Senior VP Finance), Clair McCurdy (Senior VP Acquisitions and Group Manager), John M Reiff (Senior VP Law and Personnel), Robert Cooper (VP and General Manager Canadian Coleman), Mel Adams (VP and General Manager Recreational Vehicle Group), Doug Campbell (VP and General Manager Coast Catamaran), James C Minson (VP and Managing Director International), Roger Hetrick (VP Personnel), Charles B Mcllwaine (VP Corporate Communications), Jon C Dell'Antonia (VP-MIS)

PRINCIPAL ACTIVITIES: Manufacture of camping and picnic equipment; heating and air conditioning units
Financial Information:

	Dec 31 1985	Dec 31 1986
	$'000	$'000
Sales revenues	442,710	501,589
Income before taxes	19,407	33,228
Net income	10,119	17,300
Dividends	8,241	8,375
Dividends per share	$1.20	$1.20
Earnings per share	$1.46	$2.48
Common stock	6,877	7,015
Retained income	126,248	135,173
Shareholders equity	158,948	172,966

No of Employees: 5,678

COLGATE-PALMOLIVE COMPANY

300 Park Avenue, New York, NY 10022-7499
Tel: (212) 310-2000

Chairman: Reuben Mark (and President and Chief Executive Officer)
Senior Executive Officers: William S Shanahan (Senior Executive VP, Chief of Operations-Colgate), J Dale Sherratt (Senior Executive VP, Chief of Operations-Kendall), Roderick L Turner (Senior Executive VP, Chief of Operations-Specialty Marketing), John M Watkins (Senior Executive VP), Robert M Agate (Executive VP, Chief Financial Officer), William G Cooling (Executive VP, Chief Technological Officer), Silas M Ford (Executive VP, Office of the Chairman), Jules Blake (VP Corporate, Scientific Affairs) Benjamin C Davis Jr (VP Human Resources), Brian J Heidtke (VP, Financial and Corporate Treasurer), Peter D McLeod (VP, Corporate Manufacturing), Harold Obstler (VP, General Counsel and Secretary), A Courtenay Shepard (VP, President-Colgate-US), Frederick O Cowles (Associate General Counsel, Assistant Secretary), William R Peters (Associate General Counsel, Assistant Secretary)

PRINCIPAL ACTIVITIES: Manufacture of household, personal care and health care products; specialty marketing
Trade Names: Household Products:- Hand Dishwashing Liquids: Palmolive, Axion, Ajax, Paic Citron. Automatic Dishwasher: Palmolive Automatic, Galaxy. Heavy Duty Detergents: Ajax, Dinamo, Fab, Fresh Start, Cold Power, ABC, Genie. Fabric Softeners: Soflan, Soupline, Sta-Soft, Suavitel. Cleaners: Ajax, Fabuloso, Spray'n Wipe. Laundry Soap: Ola, Odex, Bingo, Ajax, Octagon. Personal Care Products:- Toothpaste: Colgate, Ultra Brite, Tonigencyl, Dentagard, Defend. Toothbrushes: Colgate. Bath Soap: Palmolive, Irish Spring, Protex, Colgate, Cashmere Bouquet, Cleopatra, Cadum. Hair Care: Palmolive, Gard, Halo, Caprice. Deodorants: Irish Spring, Palmolive, Soft'n Gentle. Shave Creams: Colgate, Palmolive. Health Care:- Wound Care: Curad, Kerlix, Telfa, Tendersorb, Excilon, Versalon, Wet Pruf. Hospital Care and Home Health Care: Kenguard, Boundary, Kendall-McGaw, TED, Futuro, Curity. Respiratory Care: Concha, Aquapak, Circapak. Tapes: Tough Stuff, Web-Lock, Polyken. Specialty Marketing:- Princess House: Princess House, Princess Heritage, Fantasia, Highlights in Lead Crystal. Hill's: Science Diet, Prescription Diet. CPL: Sterno, Handy Fuel.
Principal Subsidiaries: The Kendall Company; Pakman (Australia); Mediquip (Malaysia); Hill's Pet Products; Princess House; Fiesta International (UK); CPL Industries
Financial Information:

	Dec 31 1985	Dec 31 1986
	$'000	$'000
Net sales revenues	4,523,678	4,984,576
Income before taxes	275,455	297,010
Net income	109,442	177,465
Common dividends	100,756	95,123
Dividends per common share	$1.32	$1.36
Earnings per share	$1.39	$2.52
Common stock	83,211	83,485
Retained income	1,342,036	1,423,845
Shareholders equity	907,048	979,916

No of Employees: 37,900

COLLECTIVE FEDERAL SAVINGS AND LOAN ASSOCIATION

158 Philadelphia Avenue, Egg Harbor, NY 08215
Tel: (609) 965 1234

President: Thomas H Hamilton (and Chief Executive Officer)
Senior Executive Officers: James E Franz (Executive VP), Edward J McColgan (Executive VP and Chief Financial Officer), Arthur L Foster (Senior VP and Treasurer), Richard J Ims (Senior VP), Albert A Kuehner (Senior VP), Scott T Page (VP and Secretary)

PRINCIPAL ACTIVITIES: Financial services including savings and loans
Financial Information:

	$'000
Revenues	127,000

No of Employees: 360

COLLEGE-TOWN

Collegetown Drive, Braintree, MA 02184
Tel: (617) 848-1200
Telex: TRT 174114

Chairman: Arthur M Sibley
President: Peter Culberton
Senior Executive Officers: William Packer (VP Finance), Joseph Moccia (VP Administration)

PRINCIPAL ACTIVITIES: Manufacture of sportswear for women
Parent Company: Interco Inc, St Louis, MI
Principal Bank: State Street Bank & Trust Co
Financial Information:

	$'000
Sales revenues	150,000

No of Employees: 500

COLLINGWOOD GRAIN INC

Wiley Building, Hutchinson, KS 67501
Tel: (316) 663-7121
Telex: WUT 417 304

Chairman: Mrs Edna E Collingwood
President: William R Morand
Senior Executive Officers: Kirby Clawson (VP), Keith L Zody (VP Finance and Secretary)

PRINCIPAL ACTIVITIES: Suppliers of grain, animal feeds and general agricultural supplies
Financial Information:

	$'000
Sales revenues	185,000

No of Employees: 400

COLLINS & AIKMAN CORPORATION

210 Madison Avenue, New York, NY 10016
Tel: (212) 578-1200
Telex: TWX 710 5815176 c and a nyk

Chairman: Donald F McCullough (and Chief Executive Officer)
President: Alfred S Crimmins
Senior Executive Officers: William D Armstrong (VP-President, Wallcoverings Group), Warren B Irwin (VP-President, Automotive Division), Andrew Major (VP-President, Decorative Fabrics Division), Charles H Scherer (VP, Secretary and General Counsel), Charles E Doran (Treasurer), John J Hopkins (Controller)

PRINCIPAL ACTIVITIES: Collins & Aikman is a major producer of specialty products which fall into three reportable business segments: non-fabricated textile products (i.e. requiring further processing before use), fabricated textile products and wallcoverings. Products include Decorative Fabrics:-residential and contract upholstery fabrics, pile apparel fabrics, toy plush, industrial fabrics and transportation products. Floor Coverings:-commercial/institutional carpeting and carpet tiles. Wallcoverings:-residential and commercial wallcoverings. Yarn:- spun yarns, textured yarns, dyed yarns and sewing threads. Automotive and Specialty Products:-automotive upholstery and carpet, industrial fabrics and lining fabrics. Fashion Fabrics:- wrap knit fabrics. Bath Fashions:- bathroom carpeting, area rugs, shower curtains and accessories
Trade Names: Registered Trade Names and Trade Marks: Colonnade, Eligère, Powerbond, Pro-Gym, Tex-Tiles, Imperial, United, Carefree, Milbrook, Color House, Quality House
Principal Subsidiaries: Ack-Ti-Linings Inc; Ackerman Associates Inc; Collins & Aikman Export Corp; Imperial Manufacturing Co; Kinney Bros of CA Inc; Kinney Wallcoverings
Principal Bank: Branch Bank & Trust Co
Financial Information:

	Feb 28 1986
	$'000
Sales revenues	1,100,700
Net income	66,370
Earnings per share	$3.06
Shareholders equity	343,209

No of Employees: 11,300

COLLINS FOODS INTERNATIONAL, INC
PO Box 92092, Los Angeles, CA 90009
Tel: (213) 827-2300

Chairman: James A Collins (and Chief Executive Officer); Vice Chairman: Rushton O Backer
President: Richard P Bermingham (and Chief Operating Officer)
Senior Executive Officers: Melvyn J Schulman (VP and General Counsel)

PRINCIPAL ACTIVITIES: Kentucky Fried Chicken franchises and foodservice distribution services to restaurants; Sizzler Restaurants and Naugles Mexican food
Principal Subsidiaries: CFI Insurers Ltd; CFI Pty Ltd; Collins Food Services Inc; Collins Foods International Pty Ltd; Collins Management and Systems Inc; Kentucky Fried Chicken of CA Inc; Sizzler Restaurants International Inc
Principal Bank: Security Pacific National Bank
Financial Information:

	1986
	$'000
Sales revenues	522,000
Net income	21,000

No of Employees: 13,500

COLLINS INDUSTRIES INC
700 First National Centre, One North Main, Hutchinson, KS 67501
Tel: (316) 663 5551

Chairman: Don L Collins (and President and Chief Executive Officer)
Senior Executive Officers: Donald Lynn Collins (VP, Treasurer and Chief Financial Officer), Lewis W Ediger (VP), Charles F Crews (Secretary), Gary G Goetsch (VP Sales)

PRINCIPAL ACTIVITIES: Manufacture of specialised vehicles for passenger transport and commercial use; related components
Principal Subsidiaries: Capacity of Texas Inc
Principal Bank: Allied Bank of Dallas
Financial Information:

	$'000
Sales revenues	85,310

No of Employees: 1,200

COLLINS PINE CO
Terminal Sales Building, Portland, OR 97205
Tel: (503) 227-1219

President: Robert J Lastofka (and Chief Executive Officer)
Senior Executive Officers: Joe Connolly Jr (Executive VP), Eugene E Sharp (VP and Treasurer), Robert M Hathaway (VP), Michael M Collins (VP)

PRINCIPAL ACTIVITIES: Timber products, wholesale and retail
Principal Bank: The United States National Bank of Oregon
Financial Information:

	$'000
Sales revenues	50,000

No of Employees: 600

COLLOIDS, INC
394 Frelinghuysen Avenue, Newark, NJ 07114
Tel: (201) 926-6100
Telex: WUT 139248

President: William F Mann Jr
Senior Executive Officers: Charles K Schramm (VP Research and Development and Textiles), W F MacAdam Jr (VP Production), Warren F Jones (VP Production), William E Mann III (VP Marketing), Stanley D Schwartz (VP Sales, Industrial)

PRINCIPAL ACTIVITIES: General and specialty chemicals
Parent Company: Interchem Inc
Principal Bank: Midlantic National Bank
Financial Information:

	$'000
Sales revenues	54,000

No of Employees: 200

COLONIAL BEEF CO
Food Distribution Center, Philadelphia, PA 19148
Tel: (215) 467-0900
Telex: TWX 710 6700235 colbeco pha

Chairman: Louis E Waxman (and President)
Senior Executive Officers: Ron Davis (Executive VP), William Hardiman (Senior VP), Marvin Samson (VP), Joe Delfini (VP and Secretary)

PRINCIPAL ACTIVITIES: Meat and meat processing
Principal Subsidiaries: Colonial Frozen Foods Co
Principal Bank: The First Pennsylvania Banking and Trust Company
Financial Information:

	$'000
Sales revenues	50,000

No of Employees: 200

COLONIAL GAS COMPANY
40 Market Street, Lowell, MA 01853
Tel: (617) 458 3171

Chairman: Frederic L Putnam Jr
President: Eugene P Hart
Senior Executive Officers: Albert C Dudley (Senior VP Gas Supply), Frederic L Putnam III (VP and Divisional Manager), Charles O Swanson II (VP and Divisional Manager), Rinald A Asbjornson (Treasurer), Carol E Elden (Financial), Charles A Cook (VP Human Resources), Ralph H Jannini (VP Internal Audit)

PRINCIPAL ACTIVITIES: Supply of natural gas
Principal Subsidiaries: Transgas Inc
Principal Bank: Chase Manhattan Bank
Financial Information:

	$'000
Sales revenues	128,165

No of Employees: 520

COLONIAL GROUP INC (THE)

One Financial Center, Boston, MA 02111
Tel: (617) 225-2365

Chairman: John A McNeice Jr (and Chief Executive Officer)
President: C Herbert Emilson
Senior Executive Officers: Charles J Mohr (Executive VP), Davey S Scoon (VP Finance and Treasurer), Arthur O Stern (VP Legal and Clerk)

PRINCIPAL ACTIVITIES: Management and service of mutual funds and advisory accounts
Principal Subsidiaries: Colonial Management Associates Inc
Principal Bank: Bank of New England
Financial Information:

	Dec 31 1985	Dec 31 1986
	$'000	$'000
Revenues	51,260	76,250
Income before taxes	16,617	23,844
Net income	8,561	12,654
Earnings per share net	$1.07	$1.59
Common stock class A	769	769
Common stock class B	31	31
Retained income	9,983	22,637
Stockholders equity	12,918	24,613
Total assets	67,771	129,100

No of Employees: 620

COLONIAL LIFE AND ACCIDENT INSURANCE COMPANY

1200 Colonial Life Boulevard West, PO Box 1365, Columbia, SC 29210
Tel: (803) 798 7000

Chairman: Gayle O Averyt (and Chief Executive Officer)
President: Stephen G Hall (and Chief Operating Officer)
Senior Executive Officers: Paul H Clifton Jr (Executive VP), Robert O Best (VP Operations), Milton M Faulk (VP), Robert E Staton (VP and Legal Counsel), David B Arial (VP Marketing and Actuary), Donald E Ward (VP Sales), Terry P Miller (VP Management Information and Software Systems), Frank S Smith Jr (Senior VP Investment and Secretary), Ned L Threatt (VP Compliance and Government Relations), George E Reeder (VP Office Services)

PRINCIPAL ACTIVITIES: Insurance services
Principal Bank: Citizens and Southern National Bank
Financial Information:

	Dec 31 1985
	$'000
Revenues	175,470
Net income	18,690

No of Employees: 850

COLONIAL METALS CO

217 Linden, Box 311, Columbia, PA 17512
Tel: (717) 684-2311
Telex: WUT 848428

President: David Serls
Senior Executive Officers: Richard J Sanger (Executive VP), Kenneth E McClure (VP Sales), Michael R Mann (VP Purchasing), John R McMiller (VP Finance and Administration)

PRINCIPAL ACTIVITIES: Smelting and refining of brass, bronze and aluminum
Financial Information:

	$'000
Sales revenues	50,000

No of Employees: 240

COLONIAL PENN GROUP, INC

5 Penn Center Plaza, Philadelphia, PA 19181
Tel: (215) 988-8000

Chairman: John J MacWilliams (and Chief Executive Officer)
President: Daniel F Crough
Senior Executive Officers: Richard E Bird (Assistant Secretary and Senior Associate General Counsel), Harold W Booth (Senior VP, Colonial Penn Group Inc), J Richard Boylan (Vice Chairman, PNC Financial Corp), James E Brennan (Executive VP and Chief Financial Officer), Walter M Foody Jr (Senior VP), Alan Hahn (Senior VP, Marketing), Russell A Glicksman (Senior VP, Human Resources), Joseph J Gallagher (VP, Taxes), Michael T Chambers (VP, Investments), John G Heimann (Vice Chairman of Merrill Lynch Capital Markets), Anthony A Latini (Senior VP and Treasurer), John Laurino (President and Chief Executive Officer, Bay Loan and Investment Bank), James P Morrison (Senior VP, Secretary and General Counsel), Kenneth C Otis (Senior VP Life/Health Operations), Harry F Perlet (VP), Norman L Phelps (Senior VP, Property/Casualty and Data Processing Operations)

PRINCIPAL ACTIVITIES: Colonial Penn's primary business is the development and marketing of personal lines insurance-property and liability, life and health-sold on a group or individual basis. The Company markets to all age groups and uses a variety of sales and distribution methods
Parent Company: FPL Group Inc
Principal Subsidiaries: Member Companies of Colonial Penn Group Inc:-Colonial Penn Holdings Inc; Colonial Penn Franklin Insurance Company; Colonial Penn Insurance Company; Colonial Penn Life Insurance Company; Colonial Penn Group Data Corp; Colonial Penn Services Corp; Colonial Penn Underwriters Inc; Hawthorne Advertising Inc; Group Association Plans Inc; National Association Plans Inc; Grand Circle Travel Inc; REDI/Multi-List Inc; Real Estate Data Inc; Multi-List Inc; Colonial Exchange Inc; Colonial Penn Properties Inc; Colonial Penn Corporation; Colonial Penn Distributors Corp; Colonial Penn Investment Advisors Corp
Principal Bank: Provident National Bank
Financial Information:

	$'000
Revenues	1,260,000

No of Employees: 3,200

COLONIAL PROVISION CO, INC

1100 Massachusetts Avenue, Boston, MA 02125
Tel: (617) 442-6886

Chairman: Jack Satter
President: George Pile
Senior Executive Officers: Joel Satter (Senior VP), Samuel Levy (VP)

PRINCIPAL ACTIVITIES: Meat and meat processing
Principal Bank: BayBank Corporation
Financial Information:

	$'000
Sales revenues	93,000

No of Employees: 650

COLONIAL SUGARS, INC

PO Box 1646, Mobile, AL 36633
Tel: (205) 433-0454
Telex: TWX 810 741 4902 colsugars mbl

President: H T Morrissette Sr
Senior Executive Officers: G D Vega (Executive VP Raw Sugar), Arthur V Yarosh (Executive VP), W R Tucon (VP Operations),

Thomas A Tate (VP General Sales), Edmund M Mofyka (VP Sales and Marketing)

PRINCIPAL ACTIVITIES: Sugar refining
Principal Bank: Chase Manhattan Bank
Financial Information:

	$'000
Sales revenues	300,000

No of Employees: 600

COLOR TILE, INC

515 Houston St, Fort Worth, TX 76102
Tel: (817) 870-9630

Chairman: John A Wilson (and President and Chief Executive Officer)
Senior Executive Officers: Eddie M Lesok (Executive VP and Secretary), Barry W Witt (VP and Treasurer)

PRINCIPAL ACTIVITIES: Retail trade in floor coverings, wall tiles and paint
Principal Subsidiaries: C Tile Transportation Inc; Color Tile Manufacturing Inc; Color Tile Supermart Inc
Principal Bank: Interfirst Bank
Financial Information:

	$'000
Sales revenues	380,000

No of Employees: 4,500

COLORADO NATIONAL BANKSHARES, INC

950 Seventeenth Street, Denver, CO 80202
Tel: (303) 893-1862
Telex: 4322016
Fax: (303) 893 1862

Chairman: Will F Nicholson Jr (and President)
Senior Executive Officers: John R Shaddock (Senior VP Administration), James L Basey (Senior VP and Controller), Frank J Brainerd (Senior VP), William R Frogge III (Senior VP Subsidiaries and Administration), A A Jones (Senior VP Subsidiaries and Administration)

PRINCIPAL ACTIVITIES: Banking
Principal Subsidiaries: Colorado National Bank of Denver (100%)

No of Employees: 3,000

COLORITE PLASTICS CO

101 Railroad Avenue, Ridgefield, NJ 07657
Tel: (201) 941-2900
Telex: WUT 134442 colorite ride

Chairman: Milton Weiss
President: Jules R Besserman
Senior Executive Officers: Norman Perry (Executive VP), Donald Larris (VP Finance), Raymond Mistretta (VP Marketing), Edward Plank (VP Sales), George Kaufman (VP Production), Charles Fox (VP Production), Tony Santola (VP Sales), Nate Sofor (VP Operations)

PRINCIPAL ACTIVITIES: Manufacture of plastics and plastic products
Parent Company: Plastic Specialties and Technologies Inc
Financial Information:

	$'000
Sales revenues	75,000

No of Employees: 450

COLT INDUSTRIES INC

430 Park Avenue, New York, NY 10022
Tel: (212) 940-0400
Telex: 125897

Chairman: David I Margolis (and President and Chief Executive Officer)

Senior Executive Officers: Salvatore J Cozzolino (Executive VP), Andrew C Hilton (Executive VP), Guy C Shafer (Executive VP), George W Townsend (Group VP), C Edward Warner (Group VP), Phil Berkowitz (VP Personnel), John F Campbell (VP Public Relations), Anthony J diBuono (VP General Counsel), Julius Levinson (VP Taxes), Jospeh P Lisa (VP and Controller), James J McHugh (VP Labor Relations), Hershell B Murray (VP Government Relations)

PRINCIPAL ACTIVITIES: Manufacture of automotive equipment:- Fuel delivery and fuel management systems; special products; replacement parts; truck products; sealing systems; engine accessories. Aerospace equipment:-aircraft landing gear, flight control systems; jet engine fuel controls; gas turbine products; compaction metals. Machinery and equipment:- diesel engines; distribution transformers; air compressors; bearings, valves, plastics, cylinders; compressor components. Materials and components:- industrial seals, packings, gasketing; military, security commemorative, sporting arms

Trade Names: Holley, Stemco, Farnam, Fairbanks Morse, Menasco, Chandler Evans, Delavan, Crucible, Central Moloney, Fairbanks, Quincy, Pratt & Garlock, France, Colt

Principal Subsidiaries and Divisions: Automotive: Holley Carburetor Division; Holley Replacement Parts Division; Holley Special Products Division; Stemco Truck Products Division; Farnams Sealing Systems Division; Fairbanks Morse Engine Accessories Operation. Aerospace:- Chandler Evans Control Systems Division; Menasco Aerosystems Division; Menasco Overhaul Division; Delavan Gas Turbine Products Division. Machinery and Equipment:-Fairbanks Morse Engine Division; Central Moloney Transformer Division; Quincey Compressor Division; Fairbanks Morse Pump Division; Garlock Special Products Division; France Compressor Products Division. Materials and Components:- Garlock Mechanical Packing Division. Colt Firearms Division; International Operations:- Menasco Aerospace Ltd; Garlock of Canada Ltd, Canada; Delavan Ltd; Garlock (Great Britain) Ltd, UK; Garlock AG, Switzerland; Liard SA, France; Garlock GmbH, Germany; Garlock SA, Spain; Garlock de Mexico SA de CV, Mexico; Garlock Pty Ltd, Australia

Financial Information:

	Dec 31 1986	Dec 31 1987
	$'000	$'000
Sales revenues	1,616,267	1,641,596
Income before taxes	209,892	250,742
Net income	89,270	75,045
Earnings per share	$0.66	$2.15

No of Employees: 22,400

COLUMBIA GAS SYSTEM, INC

20 Montchanin Road, Wilmington, DE 19807
Tel: (302) 429-5000

Chairman: John H Croom (and President and Chief Executive Officer)

Senior Executive Officers: John P Cornell (Executive VP and Chief Financial Officer), J D Little (Executive VP)

PRINCIPAL ACTIVITIES: Purchase and distribution of natural gas and by-products

Principal Subsidiaries: Big Marsh Oil Co Inc; Columbia Ak Gas Transmission Corp; Columbia Coal Gasification Corp; Columbia Gas Brokerage Corp; Columbia Gas Development Corp; Columbia Gas Inc; Columbia Gas Systems Service Corp; Columbia Gulf Transmission Co; Columbia Hydrocarbon Corp; Commonwealth Gas Pipeline Corp; Commonwealth Gas Services Inc; Commonwealth Propane Inc; Inland Gas Co Inc

Financial Information:

	Dec 31 1986 $'000
Sales revenues	3,369,580
Net income	88,000
Earnings per share	$1.82
Shareholders equity	1,498,640

No of Employees: 10,600

COLUMBIA GENERAL CORPORATION
5750 Pineland Drive, Dallas, TX 75231
Tel: (214) 373-6991

Chairman: W R Cowan
President: Edward O Boshell Jr (and Chief Executive Officer)
Senior Executive Officers: John F Anderson (VP Finance, Secretary and Treasurer)

PRINCIPAL ACTIVITIES: Manufacture of industrial fasteners; wholesale trade in welding supplies, bearings, fasteners, hardware and industrial products
Principal Subsidiaries: Bering Sales Inc; C L Gransden Co; Lewis Screw Co; Rice Supply Co Inc; Servisio de Baleros SA
Principal Bank: American National Bank & Trust Co
Financial Information:

	$'000
Sales revenues	62,900

No of Employees: 300

COLUMBIA LNG CORPORATION
20 Montchanin Road, Wilmington, DE 19807
Tel: (302) 429-5000

President: J E Towle
Senior Executive Officers: R A Oswald

PRINCIPAL ACTIVITIES: Liquid gas production
Parent Company: The Columbia Gas System Inc, Wilmington, DE
Principal Subsidiaries: Commerce Bank of Kansas City, N.A. (99.96%)
Financial Information:

	$'000
Sales revenues	90,000

No of Employees: 100

COLUMBIA MANUFACTURING COMPANY
One Cycle Street, Westfield, MA 01085
Tel: (413) 562-3664
Telex: WUT 955407 columbia wefd

President: Kenneth Howard
Senior Executive Officers: Richard A Armstrong (VP Sales), Stanley M Dangert (VP Sales and Marketing), Richard B Huntoon (Treasurer)

PRINCIPAL ACTIVITIES: Manufacture of bicycles and mopeds; furniture for schools and colleges
Parent Company: MTD Products Inc, Valley City, OH
Financial Information:

	$'000
Sales revenues	50,000

No of Employees: 700

COLUMBIA NEWSPAPERS, INC
Stadium Road, Columbia, SC 29201
Tel: (803) 771-6161

President: Ben R Morris (and Publisher)
Senior Executive Officers: R S Crim (VP and General Manager), Paul B Barringer II (VP), Channing S Joye (Treasurer)

PRINCIPAL ACTIVITIES: Publishing of newspapers
Parent Company: State-Record Co
Principal Bank: The Citizens and Southern Bank of South Carolina
Financial Information:

	$'000
Sales revenues	50,000

No of Employees: 500

COLUMBIA NITROGEN CORPORATION
PO Box 1483-13, Augusta, GA 30913
Tel: (404) 832-4000
Telex: WUT 545448

Chairman: William P Copenhaver (and President)
Senior Executive Officers: W C Moye (VP Marketing), B B Mullins (VP Manufacturing), M J van Campen (VP Finance), William B Paschal (VP Industrial Relations), R A Sisk (VP Marketing Industrial Chemicals)

PRINCIPAL ACTIVITIES: Manufacture of fertilizers and industrial chemicals
Parent Company: Nipro Inc
Financial Information:

	$'000
Sales revenues	150,000

No of Employees: 800

COLUMBIA PICTURES INDUSTRIES, INC
711 Fifth Avenue, New York, NY 10022
Tel: (212) 751-4400
Telex: ITT 420975

Chairman: Francis T Vincent Jr (and Chief Executive Officer)
President: Richard C Gallop (and Chief Operating Officer)
Senior Executive Officers: Peter S Sealey (Executive VP), Patrick M Williamson (Executive VP), Peter C Kells (Executive VP and Chief Financial Officer), Kenneth L Lemberger (Senior VP and General Counsel), Paul M Cholak (VP Personnel and Administration), Raymond A Boyce (VP Corporate Communications), Hugh K Switzer (VP Management Information Systems), Kenneth S Williams (VP and Treasurer), Jay M Green (VP and Controller), Susan B Garelli (VP Human Resources), Patrick M Wilkinson (VP Compensation Benefits)

PRINCIPAL ACTIVITIES: Production and distribution of films and television programs; coin operated amusement machines
Parent Company: The Coca-Cola Company, Atlanta, GA
Principal Bank: Manufacturers Hanover Trust Company
Financial Information:

	$'000
Sales revenues	850,000

No of Employees: 3,300

COLUMBIA SAVINGS & LOANS ASSOCIATION
8800 Wilshire Blvd, Beverly Hills, CA 90211
Tel: (213) 657-6303

Chairman: Abraham Spiegel
President: Thomas Spiegel (and Chief Executive Officer)
Senior Executive Officers: Seymour Fagan (Executive VP Real Estate, Equities and Major Loan Division), Wendell Ruppe (Executive VP and Chief Administration Officer), David Rosenthal (Executive VP and Chief Financial Officer), Lee Eckel (Senior VP and Legal Counsel), Hillel Aronson (Senior VP Taxes and Financial Planning), Bernard J Lynch (Senior VP Major Loan Division), L W Reed (Senior VP Residential Loan Division)

PRINCIPAL ACTIVITIES: Savings and loan association
Principal Bank: California First Bank

Financial Information:

	Dec 31 1985 $'000	Dec 31 1986 $'000
Net income	122,280	193,530
Earnings per share	$7.91	$5.40
Shareholders equity	269,280	499,730
Deposits	-	5,192,585
Total assets	7,116,427	10,222,652

No of Employees: 830

COLUMBIAN ENTERPRISES INC

299 Park Ave, New York, NY 10171
Tel: (212) 303-9500

Chairman: Ladislaus von Hoffman (and President)
Senior Executive Officers: Kurt B Eckrich (Executive VP), Manuel Iraola (VP)

PRINCIPAL ACTIVITIES: Manufacture of carbon black; metal trading
Principal Subsidiaries: Columbian Chemicals Co
Principal Bank: Bank of Oklahoma
Financial Information:

	$'000
Sales revenues	400,000

No of Employees: 60

COLUMBUS COATED FABRICS

1230 N Grant Avenue, Columbus, OH 43216
Tel: (614) 225-4000
Telex: WUT 246 670 colfabs col a

Senior Executive Officers: R T Paul (VP Wallcovering), D S Gordon (VP Industrial), K J Licht (Comptroller)

PRINCIPAL ACTIVITIES: Vinyl coated wall paper and fabrics
Parent Company: Borden Chemical Division
Principal Bank: Chemical Bank
Financial Information:

	$'000
Sales revenues	70,000

No of Employees: 1,000

COLUMBUS MILLS, INC

PO Box 1560, Columbus, GA 31993
Tel: (404) 324-0111
Telex: TWX 810 758 4304 colsmills clo

Chairman: George P Swift Jr
President: W J Dixon
Senior Executive Officers: Charles Parham (Executive VP), W H Parham (VP Purchasing), Lawrence P Cooper (VP Carpet Sales), Marvin Youngerman (VP Marketing), James T Tapscott (Secretary and Treasurer)

PRINCIPAL ACTIVITIES: Carpet manufacture
Principal Bank: National Bank and Trust Company
Financial Information:

	$'000
Sales revenues	146,000

No of Employees: 1,000

COMAIR, INC

PO Box 75021, Greater Cincinnati Airport, Cincinnati, OH 45275
Tel: (606) 525 2550

Chairman: Raymond A Mueller
President: David R Mueller (and Chief Executive Officer)
Senior Executive Officers: David A Siebenburgen (Executive VP and Chief Operating Officer), Kermit M Stuart (Senior VP Operations), Randy D Rademacher (Controller), Richard D Siegel (Secretary), Charles E Curran III (Senior VP Marketing), Linda D Landers (VP Customer Service), Linda E Noble (VP Human Resources), Kenneth W Marshall (VP Flight Operations)

PRINCIPAL ACTIVITIES: Air transport services
Principal Subsidiaries: CVG Aviation Inc; Comair Investment Company
Principal Bank: First National Bank of Cincinnati
Financial Information:

	Mar 31 1986 $'000	Mar 31 1987 $'000
Operating revenues	61,546	62,391
Income (loss) before taxes	3,758	(993)
Net income (loss)	3,472	(942)
Earnings (loss) per share	$0.47	($0.10)
Common stock	26,491	43,187
Retained income	10,432	9,489
Shareholders equity	36,922	52,677

No of Employees: 1,300

COMARCO INC

160 South Old Springs Road, Anaheim, CA 92808
Tel: (714) 921 0672
Telefax: (714) 283-0604

Chairman: Walter V Sterling (and President and Chief Executive Officer)
Senior Executive Officers: Peter McKane (VP, Treasurer and Chief Financial Officer), Mark L Fagerlin (VP), Marion O Greene Jr (VP), Harlan D Parode (VP), Robert E Wattenberg (VP), Harrison Young II (VP), Don M Bailey (Secretary), Robert L O'Leary (Assistant Secretary)

PRINCIPAL ACTIVITIES: Computer services and related software
Trade Names: COMPUDOC
Principal Subsidiaries: International Business Services Inc
Principal Bank: Wells Fargo Bank
Financial Information:

	Jan 1 1986 $'000	Jan 1 1987 $'000
Sales revenues	41,701	78,284
Income (loss) before taxes	2,541	(2,495)
Net income (loss)	1,965	(1,145)
Earnings (loss) per share*	$0.65	($0.40)
Common stock	275	286
Retained income	6,631	5,486
Shareholders equity	7,735	7,177

*fully diluted

No of Employees: 1,400

COMB COMPANY

14605 28th Avenue North, Minneapolis, MN 55441
Tel: (612) 559 8000

Chairman: Theodore Deikel (and Chief Executive Officer)
President: J Clinton Shaver
Senior Executive Officers: Ralph P Klein (Senior VP and Division President), Grant E Oppegaard (Senior VP and VP Operations), George L Walters (Senior VP and Division President), Roger R Cloutier (VP and Chief Financial Officer), Stephen Winnick (Secretary), W Stephen Platt (VP), Gregory D Lerman (VP Purchasing)

PRINCIPAL ACTIVITIES: General retailing
Principal Bank: Norwest Bank
Financial Information:

	$'000
Sales revenues	114,475

No of Employees: 1,320

COMBUSTION ENGINEERING INC

PO Box 9308, Stamford, CT 06904
Tel: (203) 329-8771
Telex: WUT 965950 combeng std

Chairman: Arthur J Santry Jr
President: Charles E Hugel (and Chief Executive Officer)

Senior Executive Officers: George S Kimmel (Executive VP and Chief Financial Officer), Charles E Barnett (VP and General Counsel), Joseph F Condon (VP), William J Connolly (VP), James B Kelly (VP), Mitchell Kiamie (VP), John F Mangold (VP), Robert H Masson (VP and Treasurer), Dudley C Mecum (VP), John R Peterson (VP), Jeffrey S Rubin (VP and Controller), Jack T Sanderson (VP), Eugene T Yon (VP)

PRINCIPAL ACTIVITIES: Manufacture of generators; oil and gas production equipment; pollution control systems; industrial process engineering and industrial equipment and services

Principal Subsidiaries: American Pole Structures Corp; Beaumont Forged Products; C-E Air Preheater Inc; C-E Bauer; C-E Elgin Electronics; C-E Minerals; C-E Tyler; C-E/KSB Pump Co Inc; C-E/MHI Fan Co Inc; Combustion Engineering Simcon; Construction Equipment; Electro Mechanics Inc; Globe Refractories Inc; Gray Tool Co; Impell Corp; Invalco Measurement & Control; Jamesbury Corp; Lummus Crest Inc; Oil Field Construction; Process Analytics; Q Dot Corp; Randall Process Sytems; Taylor Instrument Co; Ken Thelen Co; Thermotect Co Inc; Vetco Offshore Inc; Vetco Inc; C-E Vetco Inc; C-E Vetco Services; Vetco Inspection Service Inc

Financial Information:

	Dec 31 1986
	$'000
Sales revenues	2,551,470
Net income	50,866
Earnings per share	$1.53
Shareholders equity	686,880

No of Employees: 36,390

COMCAST CORPORATION

One Belmont Ave, Suite 227, Bala Cynwd, PA 19004

Tel: (215) 667-4200

Chairman: Ralph J Roberts (and President); Vice Chairman: Daniel Aaron

Senior Executive Officers: Julian A Brodsky (Senior VP and Chief Financial Officer), Robert B Clasen (VP, President Comcast Cable Communications Inc); Bernard P Gallagher (VP and Treasurer), Stanley Wang (VP and Legal Counsel), Anthony A Clifton (VP), F Jerome Purcell (VP, President Comcast Sound Communications Inc)

PRINCIPAL ACTIVITIES: Cable television services and background music services

Principal Subsidiaries: Comcast Cablevision Corp; Comcast Sound Communications Inc

Principal Bank: Philadelphia National Bank

Financial Information:

	Dec 31 1986
	$'000
Sales revenues	131,000
Net income	1,000

No of Employees: 1,000

COMDATA NETWORK INC

2209 Crestmoor Road, Nashville, TN 37215

Tel: (615) 385 0400

Chairman: R Lewis Jones (and President and Chief Executive Officer)

Senior Executive Officers: Alan C Abrams (Senior VP Marketing), Patricia Fulton (VP Credit Collections and Secretary), Jimmy Pemberton (VP Data Processing), Jerry L Yoder (Chief Operating Officer), James G Gregoric (Senior VP), Douglas L Wise (VP)

PRINCIPAL ACTIVITIES: Financial services for the banking industry; computer services

Principal Subsidiaries: Comdata Financial Service; Comdata Telegraph and Telecommunications

Principal Bank: First American National Bank

Financial Information:

	$'000
Sales revenues	91,730

No of Employees: 1,000

COMDIAL CORPORATION

2340 Commonwealth Drive, Charlottesville, VA 22906

Tel: (804) 978 2506

Chairman: Ted B Westfall (and Chief Executive Officer)

President: Ronald C Whigham (and Chief Operating Officer)

Senior Executive Officers: L P Harnois (VP, Treasurer and Chief Financial Officer), David Boland (VP), Larry Tate (VP, President of Comdial Business Communications Corp), Wayne R Wilver (VP and Chief Financial Officer)

PRINCIPAL ACTIVITIES: Manufacture of electrical equipment and telephone equipment

Principal Subsidiaries: Comdial Telephone Systems Inc; R&G Communications Inc; American Phone Centers Inc

Financial Information:

	$'000
Sales revenues	85,000

No of Employees: 1,800

COMDISCO, INC

6400 Shafer Court, Rosemont, IL 60018

Tel: (312) 698-3000

Telex: ITT 433 0257 comd ui

Chairman: Kenneth N Pontikes (and President)

Senior Executive Officers: Michael J Brown (Executive VP Administration), Robert A Bardagy (Senior VP Marketing), Michael Joseph (Senior VP Europe), William N Pontikes (Senior VP Operations), Frank D Trznadel (Senior VP), John J Vosicky (Senior VP, Treasurer and Chief Financial Officer)

PRINCIPAL ACTIVITIES: Leasing of used computer equipment; placement of new and used data processing equipment

Principal Subsidiaries: Bay Area Computer Corp; Comdisco Disaster Recovery Services Inc; Comdisco Financial Services Inc; Comdisco Technical Services

Principal Bank: Continental Illinois National Bank

Financial Information:

	Sep 30 1986
	$'000
Sales revenues	869,000
Net income	78,808
Earnings per share	$1.91
Shareholders equity	350,590

No of Employees: 930

COMERICA INC

211 W Fort Street, Detroit, MI 48275

Tel: (313) 222-3300

Telex: 23-5393

Chairman: Donald R Mandich (and Chief Executive Officer); Vice Chairman: James R Waterston

President: Eugene A Miller (and Chief Administration Officer)

Senior Executive Officers: John A Simonson (Executive VP and Chief Financial Officer), Joseph G Horonzy (Executive VP and Chief Loan Officer), Cleveland Thurber Jr (Executive VP), Robert L London (Executive VP), Manown Kisom Jr (Executive VP)

PRINCIPAL ACTIVITIES: Banking services

Principal Subsidiaries: Comerica Bank, Detroit

Financial Information:

	Dec 31 1985 $'000	Dec 31 1986 $'000
Income before taxes	-	71,717
Net income	57,000	61,911
Dividends	28,000	27,853
Dividends per share	$2.13	$2.20
Earnings per share	$4.85	$5.45
Common stock*	199,970	205,930
Retained income*	231,486	293,528
Shareholders equity*	491,456	559,458
Deposits*	8,073,000	8,310,545
Total assets*	9,769,000	9,982,511

*year end

No of Employees: 6,070

COMET RICE, INC

PO Box 1681, Houston, TX 77001
Tel: (713) 447-7423

Chairman: A A Barnett
President: G E Prchal
Senior Executive Officers: D E Wiggins (VP Export Sales), J L Beeson (VP Domestic Sales), C H Peterson (VP Production), Gerald D Murphy (VP), Gerard P Thomas (VP), C B Schultz (VP Finance), J S Poole (VP Rough Rice Purchasing)

PRINCIPAL ACTIVITIES: Processing of rice and manufacture of rice products
Parent Company: Erly Industries
Principal Bank: The Chase Manhattan Bank NA
Financial Information:

	$'000
Sales revenues	145,000

No of Employees: 400

COMMERCE BANCSHARES, INC

720 Main Street, Kansas City, MO 64199
Tel: (816) 234-2000

Chairman: James M Kemper Jr (and Chief Executive Officer)
President: David W Kemper
Senior Executive Officers: James H Linn (Executive VP), Jonathan Ford (Senior VP), T Alan Peschka (VP, Secretary and Treasurer)

PRINCIPAL ACTIVITIES: Banking and financial services
Principal Subsidiaries: (100% owned unless stated): Commerce Bank of Kansas City, N.A. (99.96%); Capital for Business Inc; Commerce Mortgage Co Inc; Mid-America Financial Corp; Plaza Bank & Trust Co
Principal Bank: Commerce Bank of Kansas City NA
Financial Information:

	Dec 31 1985 $'000	Dec 31 1986 $'000
Net income	37,910	39,178
Earnings per share	$3.61	$3.75
Shareholders equity	321,080	343,856
Deposits	4,065,984	4,441,590
Total assets	4,923,886	5,293,463

No of Employees: 4,000

COMMERCE CLEARING HOUSE, INC

700 Lake Cook Road, Riverwoods, IL 60015
Tel: (312) 583-8500
Telex: TWX 910 2212587 cch chgo

Chairman: Oakleigh B Thorne
President: Richard T Merrill (and Chief Executive Officer)
Senior Executive Officers: Edward L Massie (Executive VP), James R McNelis (VP Washington Office), Raymond P Myrvold (VP Los Angeles Sales), Victor F Bittner Jr (VP General Sales), Vernon B Lussky (VP Marketing), Bernard Elafros (VP and Treasurer), Donald B Izban (VP Subscription Services), Thaddeus A Kowalski (VP Production), Daniel L Newquist (VP Federal Tax and Managing Editor), Justus H Schlichting (VP Research and Development), Wilbert J Schroeder (VP Printing), Allen E Schechter (VP Business Law and Senior Managing Editor), Theodore E Heimer (VP Quail Hill Office), Howard F Reblitz (VP Electronic Publishing), John L Randolph (VP and Secretary), Thomas C Conoscenti (VP and Controller), Mary Ann Hynes (VP and Legal Counsel), Thomas N Taylor (VP St Petersburg Office)

PRINCIPAL ACTIVITIES: Publication of legal reports; computer services
Principal Subsidiaries: CT Corp System Inc; Corporation Co; Household Finance Corp; CCH Computax Inc; CCH Computax Systems Inc; CT Law Technology Inc; Commerce Clearing House Inc NJ; Facts on File inc; National Quotation Bureau Inc; State Capitol Information Service; Washing Service Bureau Inc
Principal Bank: Continental Illinois National Bank and Trust Co of Chicago
Financial Information:

	Dec 31 1985 $'000	Dec 31 1986 $'000
Sales revenues	453,950	505,345
Net income	44,844	47,550
Earnings per share	$4.98	$2.64
Shareholders equity	134,230	159,987

No of Employees: 5,500

COMMERCE UNION CORPORATION

One Commerce Plaza, Nashville, TN 37219
Tel: (615) 749-3333

Chairman: Dennis C Bottorff (and President and Chief Executive Officer); Vice Chairmen: James A Rainey (and Chief Administration Officer), George E Bivins Jr
Senior Executive Officers: H Carey Brown (Executive VP and General Manager), John H Dillon (Executive VP, Executive Lending), Dale W Polley (Executive VP and Chief Financial Officer), LeRoy A Reeder (Executive VP Corporate Development), Doyle Rippee (Executive VP and General Manager), Robert H Smith (Executive VP and General Auditor), T Hal Bishop (Senior VP), William A Caldwell (Senior VP Personnel), Michael T Christian (Senior VP Community Banking), D Todd Christofferson (Senior VP and Secretary), William R DeBerry (Senior VP Metro Retail Banking), John D Kottmeyer (Senior VP Asset Liability Planning), John E Krueger (Senior VP Corporate and Investment Services), Cynthia Pyle (Senior VP Corporate Administration), James L Springer Jr (Senior VP and Controller)

PRINCIPAL ACTIVITIES: Banking
Principal Subsidiaries: Commerce Union Bank; Commerce Union Realty Services Corp; Tennessee Valley Life Insurance Co
Financial Information:

	Dec 31 1985 $'000
Revenues	313,000
Net income	23,300
Total assets	3,120,000

No of Employees: 2,100

COMMERCIAL ALLIANCE CORPORATION

770 Lexington Avenue, New York, NY 10021
Tel: (212) 421 3600

Chairman: Bernard G Palitz
President: Clarence Y Palitz Jr
Senior Executive Officers: Gerard Loewenstein (Senior VP and Treasurer), Jacob M Mehl (Senior VP and Secretary), Martin Rothman (VP Administration, Controller and Assistant Treasurer)

PRINCIPAL ACTIVITIES: Financial services including credit facilities

Parent Company: First Interstate Bancorp
Financial Information:

	$'000
Revenues	82,000

No of Employees: 300

COMMERCIAL BANCSHARES INC NEW JERSEY

15 Exchange Place, Jersey City, NJ 07302
Tel: (201) 434 5100

Chairman: John G Collins (and President and Chief Executive Officers); Vice Chairmen: Ronald C Brown (and Executive VP), Robert Ranzinger (and Executive VP)
Senior Executive Officers: Peter J O'Brien (Senior VP and Treasurer), Joseph E DesMarais (VP and Secretary), Dennis J Flanagan (VP and Controller), William V Peacok (VP)

PRINCIPAL ACTIVITIES: Banking services
Principal Subsidiaries: Commercial Trust Company of New Jersey; Fidelity Bank and Trust Company of New Jersey; Trico Mortgage Company; Wood Ridge National Bank
Principal Bank: Commercial Trust Company of New Jersey
Financial Information:

	Dec 31 1985 $'000
Revenues	145,630
Net income	15,170

No of Employees: 900

COMMERCIAL CREDIT COMPANY

300 St Paul Pl, Baltimore, MD 21202
Tel: (301) 332-3000
Telex: WUT 87428
Telefax: ccec bal

Chairman: Joseph D Minutilli (and President and Chief Executive Officer)
Senior Executive Officers: Peter G Bailey (Senior VP Realty and Corporate Services), Howard R Fricke (Senior VP Insurance Services), Fred W Meier (Senior VP Risk Administration), William J Miller (Senior VP Consumer Banking Services), George P Shaw (Senior VP International Financial Services), Roger D Shober (Senior VP Business Services), George K Bardos (VP Corporate Marketing), Charles W Brooks Jr (VP Investment), John R Eickhoff (VP Financial Planning and Controller), Hugh Henig (VP Operational Services), Stephen R Leskovsky (VP), Ronald C Mickelberg (VP Corporate Development), John P Moe (VP Personnel), Charles O Prince III (VP), W B Quackenbush (VP Finance and Treasurer), Patrick M Sheridan (VP and Chief Financial Officer), William B Turley (VP Consumer Banking Services), Robert S Volland (VP Debt Management)

PRINCIPAL ACTIVITIES: Provision of a wide range of financial services including credit and loans; leasing; insurance
Parent Company: Control Data Corp
Financial Information:

	$'000
Revenues	1,300,000

No of Employees: 8,900

COMMERCIAL FEDERAL CORPORATION

2120 South 72nd St, Omaha, NE 68124
Tel: (402) 554-9200

Chairman: William F Fitzgerald
President: William A Fitzgerald
Senior Executive Officers: Gene R Boba (Senior VP, Chief Financial Officer and Treasurer), Robert M Ames (Senior VP), George A Grieb (Senior VP)

PRINCIPAL ACTIVITIES: Financial services including savings and loans
Principal Subsidiaries: Commercial Federal Savings and Loan Association Inc
Principal Bank: Federal Home Loan Bank
Financial Information:

	Jun 30 1986
Net income	17,325
Earnings per share	$3.16
Shareholders equity	99,418
Deposits	1,666,218
Total assets	3,067,980

No of Employees: 978

COMMERCIAL INTERNATIONAL CORPORATION

1445 Nebraska Avenue, Selma, CA 93662
Tel: (209) 896 5961

Chairman: Sidney W Schuman Jr (and President and Assistant Secretary)
Senior Executive Officers: Bruce R Baker (Treasurer), Eugene L Walker (Secretary and Assistant Treasurer)

PRINCIPAL ACTIVITIES: Supply of processed fruit products, nuts, seeds and raisins
Principal Bank: Valley National Bank
Financial Information:

	$'000
Sales revenues	45,000

No of Employees: 215

COMMERCIAL METALS COMPANY

7800 Stemmons Freeway, Dallas, TX 75247
Tel: (214) 689-4300
Telex: 730813 COMCDAL

President: Stanley A Rabin (and Chief Executive Officer)
Senior Executive Officers: Marvin Selig (President, CMC Steel Group), Jacob Feldman (Director), A Leo Howell (VP, Chairman of Executive Committee and President of Howell Metal Co), Harry Bauer (VP and President of Cometals Inc), Bert Romberg (Senior VP and President of Dallas Trading Division), Walter F Kammann (VP International Operations and Managing Director CMC (Int'l) AG), Jack T Mulos (Controller), Milton L Davis (Assistant Controller), Louis A Federle (Assistant Treasurer), Robert H Maier (VP-Administration and Chief Personnel Officer), David M Sudbury (VP, Secretary and General Counsel), Lawrence A Engels (VP, Treasurer and Chief Financial Officer)

PRINCIPAL ACTIVITIES: Commercial Metals Company, headquartered in Dallas is a diversified leader in manufacturing, processing, fabrication, trading and distribution of steel, primary and secondary metals and numerous raw materials. Through its network of trading offices around the world, the Company markets and trades primary and secondary metals, steel, ores and concentrates, industrial minerals, ferroalloys, chemicals, and other materials used by a variety of industries. The manufacturing group includes a copper tube plant, two steel mini-mills, fabrication shops, service centers, fence post manufacturing plants and a railroad car rebuilding facility. Recycling operations include 18 metals processing plants across the Sunbelt and a railroad salvage company products
Principal Subsidiaries: American Steel Sales Company; CMC (Australia) Pty Ltd; CMC Comercio de Metais Ltda; CMC Fareast Ltd; CMC Finanz AG; CMC (International) AG; CMC International (SE Asia) Pte Ltd; CMC Steel Inc; CMC Steel Fabricators Inc; CSC Engineering Inc; Capitol City Steel Company; Cometals (Canada) Ltée; Cometals China Inc; Cometals Far East Inc; Cometals Inc; Commercial Metals-Austin Inc; Commercial Metals (Belgium) SA; Commercial Metals Company, Holding AG; Commercial Metals Overseas Export Company; Commercial Metals Overseas Export (FSC) Corp; Commercial Metals Railroad Salvage Company; Commonwealth Metal Corporation; Daltrading Limited; Electro

Extraction Inc; Enterprise Metal Corporation; Eurintrade SA; Howell Metal Company; Mini-Mill Consultants Inc; Ramasco AG; Regency Advertising Agency Inc; SMI Steel Inc; Structural Metals Inc; Texas Cold Finished Steel Inc; Zenith Finance and Construction Company

Principal Bank: Bank of America

Financial Information:

	Aug 31 1986	Aug 31 1987
	$'000	$'000
Sales revenues	885,411	872,830
Income before taxes	22,538	17,528
Net income	14,226	10,208
Dividends	2,495	2,863
Dividends per share	$0.28	$0.32
Earnings per share	$1.60	$1.14
Common stock	45,378	45,378
Retained income	101,191	109,474
Shareholders equity	146,569	154,852

No of Employees: 3,100

COMMERCIAL NATIONAL CORPORATION LOUISIANA

PO Box 21119 Shreveport, LA 71152

Tel: (318) 429 4614

Chairman: N H Wheless Jr

President: James E Burt III (and Chief Executive Officer)

Senior Executive Officers: C W Holtsclaw Jr (Executive VP and Secretary), P Michael Adkins (Senior VP and Chief Financial Officer), David H Nordyke (Senior VP), Hines S Vaughan (Senior VP), Steven C Walker (Senior VP)

PRINCIPAL ACTIVITIES: Banking and financial services

Principal Subsidiaries: Commercial National Bank in Shreveport

Financial Information:

	Dec 31 1985	Dec 31 1986
	$'000	$'000
Income (loss) before taxes	5,149	(13,813)
Net income	8,116	577
Dividends	4,200	4,200
Dividends per share	$1.00	$1.00
Earnings per share	$1.93	$0.14
Common stock	21,000	21,000
Retained income	53,790	50,167
Stockholders equity	88,790	85,167
Deposits	1,013,638	981,799
Total assets	1,197,875	1,193,061

Principal Shareholders: N W Wheless Jr (12.59%); Willis L Meadows (8.07%); William G Anderson (6.01%); Commercial National Bank in Shreveport, Trustee (4.5%)

No of Employees: 599

COMMERCIAL SHEARING INC

1775 Logan Avenue, Youngstown, OH 44501

Tel: (216) 746-8011

Telex: TWX 8104 352910 commercialyo

Chairman: John Nelson (and Chief Executive Officer)

President: Paul J Powers (and Chief Operating Officer)

Senior Executive Officers: Don E Tucker (Senior VP and Chief Administration Officer), Philip N Winkelstern (Senior VP and Chief Financial Officer), William G Welker (Group VP), Leon Blank (VP), William W Cushwa (VP), Leonard N Ganchar (VP), Patrick C Reardon (VP), Kenneth C Hou (VP Research and Development), Hans W Lange (VP, President Cuno Inc)

PRINCIPAL ACTIVITIES: Manufacture of pumps, valves, motors and other industrial equipment

Principal Subsidiaries: Commercial Stamping & Forging Inc; Orange County Machine Works Inc

Financial Information:

	$'000
Sales revenues	192,000

No of Employees: 2,700

COMMODORE CORPORATION (THE)

64654 U.S. 33 East, PO Box 577, Goshen, IN 46526

Tel: (219) 642-3646

Chairman: Barry S Shein

President: Thomas L Underwood (and Chief Executive Officer)

Senior Executive Officers: Bobby G Hatley (VP Treasurer/Secretary), J Charles Follett (Executive VP)

PRINCIPAL ACTIVITIES: Manufacture and sale of mobile homes

Parent Company: Great American Management & Investment Inc

Principal Subsidiaries: Commodore Home Systems Inc; Premier Plastic Products Inc

Principal Bank: Continental Illinois National Bank and Trust Co of Chicago

Financial Information:

	Jul 31 1986	Jul 31 1987
	$'000	$'000
Sales revenues	58,928	75,755
Income (loss) before taxes*	(2,540)	1,420
Net income	11,186	1,380
Earnings per share	-	$18.158
Retained income (deficit)	(10)	1,370
Shareholders equity	9,990	11,370

*and extraordinary items

Sole Shareholder: Great American Management & Investment Inc

No of Employees: 700

COMMODORE INTERNATIONAL LTD

1200 Wilson Drive, Westchester, PA 19380

Tel: (215) 431-9100

Telex: WUT 701206 cil wch ud

Chairman: I Gould (and Chief Executive Officer)

Senior Executive Officers: Joseph C Benedetti (VP, Secretary and General Counsel), Henri Rubin (Executive VP and Chief Operating Officer), Harald Speyer (VP), Mikiu Izumi (VP), David Spiers (VP), Thomas Matson (VP and Controller), Carden Welsh (Assistant Treasurer), Frances Moffitt (Assistant Secretary)

PRINCIPAL ACTIVITIES: Commodore International Limited is a fully integrated manufacturer of advanced microcomputer systems, semiconductor components and consumer electronic products. Manufacturing facilities are located in North America, Europe and the Far East. Marketing is worldwide. Reasearch is devoted primarily to the devlopment of new products using solid state integrated circuitry, computer technology and consumer electronics

Operating Subsidiaries: Commodore AB (Sweden); Commodore AG (Switzerland); Commodore BV (Netherlands); Commodore SA (Spain); Commodore-Amiga, Inc; Commodore Buromaschinen GmbH (West Germany); Commodore Buromaschinen (Austria) GmbH (Austria); Commodore Business Machines Inc; Commodore Business Machines Limited (Canada); Commodore Business Machines UK Limited (UK); Commodore Business Machines (Asia Pacific) Ltd (Hong Kong); Commodore Business Machines Pty Ltd (Australia); Commodore Computers Norge A/S (Norway); Commodore Computers NV/SA (Belgium); Commodore Data A/S (Denmark); Commodore Electronics Limited (Bahamas); Commodore Electronics (Taiwan) Limited (Taiwan); Commodore France SARL (France); Commodore Italiana SpA (Italy); Commodore Japan Ltd (Japan); Commodore Semiconductor Group

Principal Bank: Canadian Imperial Bank of Commerce Trust Co (Bahamas) Ltd

Financial Information:

	Jun 30 1986	Jun 30 1987
	$'000	$'000
Sales revenues	889,300	806,700
Income (loss) before taxes	32,400	(123,700)
Net income(loss)	28,600	(127,900)
Earnings (loss) per share	$0.89	($4.08)
Common stock	32,300	32,300
Retained income	117,500	88,900
Shareholders equity	145,000	105,000

No of Employees: 3,000

COMMONWEALTH BANCSHARES CORPORATION

101 West Third Street, Williamsport, PA 17701
Tel: (717) 327 5011

Chairman: W D Davis (and Chief Executive Officer)
President: J T Detwiler (and Chief Operating Officer)
Senior Executive Officers: Emerson W Kryrim (VP), Charles J Lydon (VP), David W Poch (VP), John H Turpish (VP)

PRINCIPAL ACTIVITIES: Banking services
Principal Subsidiaries: Commonwealth Bank and Trust Company; Susquehannah Life Insurance Company
Principal Bank: Federal Reserve Bank

No of Employees: 650

COMMONWEALTH EASTERN MORTGAGE CORPORATION

430 Westfield Avenue, Elizabeth, NJ 07207
Tel: (201) 354-8000

President: Sefton Stallard (and Chief Executive Officer)
Senior Executive Officers: Robert G Guempel (Executive VP), Edward J Goldberg (Senior VP Spot Residential Loans), Richard Utzinger (Senior VP Income Loans), Nicholas F Panza (1st VP Income Loan Originations), Guido Giannotti (VP and Controller)

PRINCIPAL ACTIVITIES: Financial services
Principal Bank: United Counties Trust Company

No of Employees: 300

COMMONWEALTH EDISON CO

PO Box 767, Chicago, IL 60690
Tel: (312) 294-4321

Chairman: James J O'Connor (and President and Chief Executive Officer); Vice Chairman: Wallace B Behnke Jr
Senior Executive Officers: Byron Lee Jr (Executive VP), Bide L Thomas (Executive VP), Robert J Schultz (VP), James W Johnson (VP), Preston B Kavanagh (VP)

PRINCIPAL ACTIVITIES: Electricity supply
Principal Subsidiaries: Chicago and IL Midland Railroad Co; Commonwealth Edison Co of IN; Commonwealth Research Corp; Cotter Corp; Edison Development Canada Inc; Edison Development Co Inc
Principal Bank: Continental Illinois National Bank
Financial Information:

	Dec 31 1985	Dec 31 1986
	$'000	$'000
Sales revenues	4,964,151	5,478,510
Net income	955,736	1,049,595
Earnings per share	$4.45	$4.69
Shareholders equity	-	6,855,742

No of Employees: 18,110

COMMONWEALTH ENERGY SYSTEMS

675 Massachusetts Avenue, Cambridge, MA 02139
Tel: (617) 864 3100

Chairman: Robert E Siegfried
President: Gerald E Anderson (and Chief Executive Officer and Subsidiary Officer)
Senior Executive Officers: Michael P Sullivan (VP, Secretary and General Attorney), Earl G Cheney (VP Finance and Treasurer), John A Whalen (Controller)

PRINCIPAL ACTIVITIES: Supply of electricity and natural gas
Principal Subsidiaries: Cambridge Electric Light Company; Canal Electric Company; Com/Energy Acushnet Realty; Com/Energy Cambridge Realty; Com/Energy Realty Company; Com/Energy Reasearch Park Realty; Com/Energy Services Company; Com/Energy Steam Company; Commonwealth Electric Company; Commonwealth Gas Company; Darvel Realty Trust
Principal Bank: First National Bank of Boston
Financial Information:

	$'000
Sales revenues	678,100

No of Employees: 2,510

COMMONWEALTH METAL CORPORATION

560 Sylvan Avenue, Englewood Cliffs, NJ 07632
Tel: (201) 569-2000
Telex: ITT 424 330 cmwl a ui

President: Robert L Prosnitz
Senior Executive Officers: Charles Shrem (Executive VP), Philip Marchant (VP), Henry Shrem (VP and Secretary), Elia Danon (VP), Steven Shur (VP), Richard Cork (VP and Controller)

PRINCIPAL ACTIVITIES: Manufacture of non-ferrous metals
Parent Company: Commercial Metals Co, Dallas, TX
Principal Bank: Algemene Bank
Financial Information:

	$'000
Sales revenues	121,000

No of Employees: 55

COMMUNICATIONS CORP OF AMERICA

500 Twin Towers South, 8585 North Stemmons Freeway, Dallas, TX 75247
Tel: (214) 638 5444

Chairman: Bill G Grubbs (and Chief Executive Officer)
President: J Robert Bozman (and Chief Operating Officer)
Senior Executive Officers: Sheri G Grubbs (Secretary and Director Stockholder Relations), E Wade Griffin (VP Customer Service), David M Hagen (VP Finance and Treasurer)

PRINCIPAL ACTIVITIES: Design, sale, installation and maintenance of business telecommunications systems
Principal Bank: BancTexas Dallas
Financial Information:

	Jun 30 1986	Jun 30 1987
	$'000	$'000
Sales revenues	40,008	27,062
(Loss)(1)	(12,308)	(6,347)
Net (loss)	(12,308)	(1,816)
Net (loss) per share	($2.36)	($0.27)
Common stock(2)	5,224	6,819
Retained (deficit)	(29,063)	(30,879)
Shareholders (deficit)	(7,207)	(8,286)

(1) before extraordinary item
(2) weighted average number of common shares outstanding in thousands

Principal Shareholders: Albalec SA (10.8%); Executive Life Insurance Co (9.3%); Lord Abbett & Co (15.9%); Merrill Lynch Asset Management Corporate Bond Fund-High Yield Portfolio (7.9%)
No of Employees: 300

COMMUNICATIONS INDUSTRIES, INC

3811 Turtle Creek Blvd, Dallas, TX 75219
Tel: (214) 651-4250

Chairman: Clayton E Niles (and Chief Executive Officer)
President: Roger D Linquist (and Chief Operating Officer)
Senior Executive Officers: Louis E Brown (VP Research and Development), Michael H Barnes (VP Finance and Treasurer)

PRINCIPAL ACTIVITIES: Manufacture of telephone equipment; telephone and communications services
Parent Company: Pacific Telesis Group
Principal Bank: InterFirst Bank Dallas
Financial Information:

	$'000
Sales revenues	98,000

No of Employees: 1,340

COMMUNICATIONS SATELLITE CORPORATION

950 L'Enfant Plaza SW, Washington, DC 20024
Tel: (202) 863-6000
Telex: TRT 197604 comsat wsh ut

Chairman: Irving Goldstein (and Chief Executive Officer)
President: Marcel P Joseph (and Chief Operating Officer); President (Comsat World Systems Division): Joel R Alper; President (Communications Services Division): Robert W Kinzie
Senior Executive Officers: Robert F Allnut (VP Government Affairs), Robert W Baumann (VP Human Resources and Organisational Development), Jerome W Breslow (VP and Assistant to Chairman and Chief Executive Officer), Ronald J Mario (VP Corporate Services), Susan Meyer (VP Corporate Development), Richard L McGraw (VP Corporate Affairs), William R Nichols (VP, Secretary and Legal Counsel), Robert J Perry (VP and Chief Financial Officer), Joseph M Quigley (VP Management Information Services)

PRINCIPAL ACTIVITIES: Satellite communications services
Principal Subsidiaries: Comsat General Corp; Comsat International Communications; Comsat Technology Products; Amplica Inc; Environmental Research and Technology Inc; Satellite Television Corp; Telesystems
Principal Bank: Citibank
Financial Information:

	$'000
Sales revenues	460,000

No of Employees: 2,670

COMMUNICATIONS SYSTEMS, INC

213 S Main Street, Hector, MN 55342
Tel: (612) 848-6231

President: Curtis A Sampson (and Chief Executive Officer)
Senior Executive Officers: Ronald W Wisenheart (Executive VP Apparatus Marketing and Engineering), Hubertus Sarrazin (Executive VP North American Cable Systems), Paul N Hanson (VP Finance, Treasurer and Chief Financial Officer), Charles J Kish (VP Apparatus Manufacturing), Steven H Sjogren (VP and General Manager), Wendell E Dietrich (VP Cable Spinning Equipment and Berry Electronics Inc), Glenn W Thompson (VP Sales, Suttle Apparatus), John C Ortman (VP Special Accounts, Suttle Apparatus), Robert W Davis (VP Telecommunications Products), Michael L Fannin (VP Finance, Suttle Apparatus)

PRINCIPAL ACTIVITIES: Manufacture of equipment for the telecommunications industry; cable television
Principal Subsidiaries: Berry Electronics Inc; North American Communications; Suttle Apparatus Corp
Principal Bank: First Bank St Paul
Financial Information:

	$'000
Sales revenues	33,600

No of Employees: 800

COMMUNITY BANK SYSTEM INC

5790 Widewaters Parkway, DeWitt, NY 13214
Tel: (315) 445 2282

Chairman: William D Stadler; Vice Chairman: Jack Scott
President: Edwin J Lyons (and Chief Executive Officer)
Senior Executive Officers: John A Lanahan (First VP), Leon K Jackson (Senior VP Finance and Treasurer), Avis L Exelby (VP and Secretary), Augustine J Guarino (VP), Barry S Kublin (VP Human Resources)

PRINCIPAL ACTIVITIES: Holding company with interests in banking
Principal Subsidiaries: Exchange National Bank; Horizon Bank; Northeastern Computer Services Inc
Principal Bank: Saint Lawrence National Bank
Financial Information:

	Dec 31 1985 $'000
Revenues	42,460
Net income	3,160

No of Employees: 425

COMMUNITY PSYCHIATRIC CENTERS

517 Washington St, San Francisco, CA 9411
Tel: (415) 397-6151

Chairman: Robert L Green (and Chief Financial Officer)
President: James W Conte (and Chief Executive Officer)
Senior Executive Officers: James P Smith (Senior VP and Treasurer)

PRINCIPAL ACTIVITIES: Operation of psychiatric hospitals, dialysis centers and home nursing services
Financial Information:

	Nov 30 1986 $'000
Sales revenues	246,771
Income before taxes	93,695
Net income	51,339
Dividends	310
Dividends per share	$0.31
Earnings per share	$1.71
Common stock	30,436
Retained income	180,987
Shareholders equity	271,469

No of Employees: 4,514

COMPACT VIDEO INC

2813 West Alameda Avenue, Burbank, CA 91505
Tel: (818) 840 7000

Chairman: Arthur N Ryan; Vice Chairmen: Raymond A Gaul, Wendell B Sell
President: John H Dollan (and Chief Operating Officer)
Senior Executive Officers: Jim Bullard (VP Finance, Chief Financial Officer and Treasurer), John H Oliphant (Secretary and Legal Counsel)

PRINCIPAL ACTIVITIES: Provision of a range of services for the film industry including rental of mobile video tape systems
Principal Bank: Continental Bank International
Financial Information:

	$'000
Sales revenues	37,000

No of Employees: 300

COMPAQ COMPUTER CORPORATION

20555 Fm 149, Houston, TX 77070
Tel: (713) 370-7040

Chairman: Benjamin M Rosen
President: Joseph R Canion (and Chief Executive Officer)
Senior Executive Officers: James M Eckhart (Senior VP Operations), Wayne F Collins (VP Materials and Resources), James D D'Arezzo (VP Corporate Communications), B Kevin

Ellington (VP Personal Computer Division, Wilson D Fargo (VP, Legal Counsel and Secretary), J Steven Flannigan (VP Systems Engineering), John F Gribi (VP Finance and Chief Financial Officer), William H Murto (VP Corporate Marketing), Cecil C Parker (VP Human Resources), Mike Swavely (VP Product Marketing), Robert E Vieau (VP Manufacturing), Eckhard Pfeiffer (VP International), Max E Toy (VP Sales), James M Harris (VP Engineering)

PRINCIPAL ACTIVITIES: Data processing equipment and services
Principal Bank: Bank of America
Financial Information:

	Dec 31 1985	Dec 31 1986
	$'000	$'000
Sales revenues	503,880	625,240
Net income	26,595	42,900
Earnings per share	$0.97	$1.52
Shareholders equity	136,608	183,302

No of Employees: 1,500

COMPCO CORPORATION
1800 N Spaulding Avenue, Chicago, IL 60647
Tel: (312) 384-1000

President: L G Zagel
Senior Executive Officers: E F Zurawski (Executive VP)

PRINCIPAL ACTIVITIES: Manufacture of a wide range of lighting equipment
Financial Information:

	$'000
Sales revenues	130,000

No of Employees: 70

COMPO INDUSTRIES, INC
125 Roberts Road, Waltham, MA 02154
Tel: (617) 899-3000
Telex: WUT 923469 compo ind wha

Chairman: Peter Weiss; Vice Chairman: Henry Hardy
President: Leonard Rosenblatt (and Chief Executive Officer)
Senior Executive Officers: Robert J Cobuzzi (Executive VP and Chief Financial Officer), Henry R Lasman (VP), Norman A Sessler (VP), Irwin Shapiro (VP), Joel Sugarman (VP)

PRINCIPAL ACTIVITIES: Manufacture of synthetic leather and machinery for the footwear and clothing industries; manufacture of chemicals, adhesives, sound proofing materials, plastics
Principal Subsidiaries: Compo Chemical Co Inc; Compo Leasing Corp; Compo Salpa Inc; International Vulcanizing Corp; Middlesex Import Inc; Pandel Chemical Inc
Principal Bank: The First National Bank of Boston
Financial Information:

	$'000
Sales revenues	132,000

No of Employees: 2,100

COMPREHENSIVE CARE CORPORATION
18551 Von Karman Ave, Irvine, CA 92715
Tel: (714) 851 2273

Chairman: B Lee Karns; Vice Chairman: W James Nicol (and Secretary and Chief Administrative Officer)
President: Richard A Santoni (and Chief Operating Officer)
Senior Executive Officers: Edward J Johnson (Executive VP Operations), Edward J Carels (Executive VP Communications), Stephen R Munroe (Senior VP and Chief Financial Officer), John J Acurso (Treasurer), Cheryl A Arnold (Assistant Secretary), Joseph A Pursch (Director Medical)

PRINCIPAL ACTIVITIES: Healthcare services
Principal Bank: Union Bank
Financial Information:

	$'000
Sales revenues	190,000

No of Employees: 3,500

COMP-U-CARD INTERNATIONAL INC
707 Summer Street, Stamford, CT 06901
Tel: (203) 324 9261

Chairman: Walter A Forbes (and President and Chief Executive Officer); Vice Chairman: Henry C McCall
Senior Executive Officers: Stuart L Bell (Executive VP, Treasurer and Chief Financial Officer), E Kirk Shelton (Executive VP), Christopher K McLeod (Senior VP Operations), John H Fullmer (Senior VP Marketing), Vincent R D'Agostino (Senior VP Information Systems)

PRINCIPAL ACTIVITIES: Computerized shopping, travel and insurance services
Financial Information:

	$'000
Sales revenues	87,460

No of Employees: 150

COMPUDYNE CORPORATION
391 Greendale Road, York, PA 17403
Tel: (717) 843-4020

Chairman: David W Clark Jr; Vice Chairman: Millard H Pryor Jr
President: David W Stevens
Senior Executive Officers: Bruce Chandler (VP)

PRINCIPAL ACTIVITIES: Manufacture of heating and ventilating equipment, air cleaning equipment, illuminated products for advertising and information; machine tools
Principal Bank: Maryland National Bank
Financial Information:

	$'000
Sales revenues	110,000

No of Employees: 1,650

COMPUGRAPHIC CORPORATION
200 Ballardvale Street, Wilmington, MA 01887
Tel: (617) 658-5600
Telex: RCA 200263 cmpg ur

Chairman: John Bisschops
President: Carl E Dantas (and Chief Executive Officer)
Senior Executive Officers: James McTeague (VP, Quality and Customer Satisfaction), Fred J Butler (Senior VP, Finance and Treasurer), David E Costa (VP, Corporate and Product Planning), John M Duker (Senior VP, Sales and Marketing), Vincent M Kaseta (Senior VP, Human Resources), David B Lundquist (Senior VP, Business Development Group), Frank J Perpiglia (Senior VP, Engineering Division), Richard Renwick (Senior VP, Operations), Donald C Wile (Senior VP, Graphic Products Group), Thomas E Kerr (General Counsel and Clerk), Raymond A Melillo (Assistant Treasurer)

PRINCIPAL ACTIVITIES: Manufacture of machinery and equipment for photocomposition and typesetting
Parent Company: Agfa-Gevaert NV; Bayer AG
Principal Subsidiaries: Compugraphic International Products Ltd (Eire); Compugraphic Canada Inc
Principal Bank: State Street Bank & Trust

Financial Information:

	Dec 28 1985	Jan 31 1987
	$'000	$'000
Sales revenues	400,807	341,082
Income before taxes	28,454	5,208
Net income	21,797	3,385
Dividends	4,888	4,998
Dividends per share	$0.60	$0.60
Earnings per share	$2.63	$0.41
Common stock	419	419
Retained income	123,356	121,195
Shareholders equity	194,693	193,520

Principal Shareholders: Agfa-Gevaert Graphics, Inc (82%)
No of Employees: 3,992

COMPUTER & COMMUNICATIONS TECHNOLOGY CORPORATION

9177 Sky Park Ct, San Diego, CA 92123-4341
Tel: (619) 279-8973

Chairman: Everett T Bahre (and President and Chief Executive Officer)
Senior Executive Officers: Robert L McKay (VP Finance), Jerry F Smith (VP Personal)

PRINCIPAL ACTIVITIES: Manufacture of components and equipment for computers
Principal Bank: Bank of America
Financial Information:

	$'000
Sales revenues	62,000

No of Employees: 2,400

COMPUTER ASSOCIATES INTERNATIONAL INC

711 Stewart Ave, Garden City, NY 11530
Tel: (516) 227 3300
Telex: 981 293
Telefax: (516) 227 3937

Chairman: Charles B Wang (and Chief Executive Officer)
President: Anthony W Wang (and Chief Operating Officer)
Senior Executive Officers: Beldon A Frease (Division President) Secretary), Abraham Poznansky (Division President), Russell M Artzt (Senior VP Development), David A Tory (Senior VP Planning), David J Wardle (Division President), Charles P McWade (Treasurer), Peter A Schwartz (VP Finance), William Labermaas (VP Research and Special Projects)

PRINCIPAL ACTIVITIES: Computer software
Principal Bank: J Henry Schroder Bank & Trust
Financial Information:

	Mar 31 1986	Mar 31 1987
	$'000	$'000
Sales revenues	321,985	452,289
Income before taxes	56,302	94,812
Net income	37,055	50,227
Earnings per share	$0.51	$0.64
Common stock	73,036	78,250
Retained income (deficit)	(15,165)	41,266
Shareholders equity	296,669	357,836

No of Employees: 4,000

COMPUTER AUTOMATION, INC

2181 Dupont Drive, Irvine, CA 92713
Tel: (714) 833 8830
Telex: TWX 910 9400 991

Chairman: George Pratt (and Chief Executive Officer)
President: Douglas L Cutsforth
Senior Executive Officers: Stuart F Dale (Senior VP), William L Osmundsen (VP Finance, Treasurer and Chief Financial Officer), Ira L Robinson (VP, Legal Counsel and Secretary)

PRINCIPAL ACTIVITIES: Manufacture of a range of computers and computer products
Principal Bank: First Interstate Bank of California
Financial Information:

	$'000
Sales revenues	40,000

No of Employees: 400

COMPUTER CONSOLES, INC

97 Humboldt Street, Rochester, NY 14609
Tel: (716) 482-5000
Telex: WUT 978 463 comp com roc

Chairman: John F Cunningham (and Chief Executive Officer); Vice Chairman: Herman A Affel Jr
Senior Executive Officers: Gary Haynes (Senior VP Sales and Marketing), Eileen Abare (VP Manufacturing), B Denison Olmsted (VP Marketing and Customer Services), John P Jacobson (VP World Wide Sales), Richard I Krieger (VP and Chief Financial Officer), Thomas I Nientimp (VP Administration), Harold S Koplow (VP Development Planning), David Moros (VP Corporate Development), Frank L Brandvold (VP Western Operations), Richard P Adam (VP International Distribution Operations)

PRINCIPAL ACTIVITIES: Development of computer systems for government departments, industry, commerce and the legal profession
Principal Bank: Chase Lincoln Bank of Rochester
Financial Information:

	$'000
Sales revenues	112,000

No of Employees: 1,200

COMPUTER DATA SYSTEMS INC

One Curie Court, Rockville, MD 20850
Tel: (301) 921 7000

Chairman: Clifford M Kendall (and President)
Senior Executive Officers: Gordon S Glenn (Executive VP Professional Services), Harold J Johnson Jr (Executive VP Operations), Wyatt D Tinsley (Executive VP Administration), Donald E Ziegler (Secretary and Treasurer), Barbara Perry (VP Human Resources)

PRINCIPAL ACTIVITIES: Data processing services and software
Principal Bank: Maryland National Bank
Financial Information:

	$'000
Sales revenues	55,000

No of Employees: 1,125

COMPUTER DEPOT INC

7450 West Flying Cloud Drive, Eden Prairie, MN 55344
Tel: (612) 944 8787

Chairman: Richard W McEwen (and Chief Executive Officer)
President: Frederick S Larson (and Chief Operating Officer)
Senior Executive Officers: Paul J Larson (VP, Chief Financial Officer and Treasurer), E T Rossing (VP Sales), George R A Johnson (Secretary)

PRINCIPAL ACTIVITIES: Retail of computer products and related equipment
Principal Bank: First National Bank of St Paul
Financial Information:

	$'000
Sales revenues	76,000

No of Employees: 550

COMPUTER ENTRY SYSTEMS CORPORATION

2141 Industrial Parkway, Silver Spring, MD 20904
Tel: (301) 622 3500

Chairman: Brian T Cunningham (and Chief Executive Officer)
President: Michael J King (and Chief Operating Officer)
Senior Executive Officers: Robert F Gibbs (VP Operations and Secretary), Craig E Nichols (Treasurer and Assistant Secretary), John G Guthrie (VP Engineering), George L Rusnak (VP Manufacturing)

PRINCIPAL ACTIVITIES: Supply of computer products
Principal Subsidiaries: Amer-o-Matic Corporation
Principal Bank: Maryland National Bank
Financial Information:

	$'000
Sales revenues	39,085

No of Employees: 1,000

COMPUTER FACTORY INC
399-A Executive Boulevard, Elmsford, NY 10523
Tel: (914) 347 5000

Chairman: Jay Gottlieb (and President)
Senior Executive Officers: Rochelle Cochin (Secretary and Treasurer), Edward R Anderson (VP Marketing), Russell L Madris (VP Sales)

PRINCIPAL ACTIVITIES: Retail trade in computer products
Principal Bank: Citibank
Financial Information:

	$'000
Sales revenues	104,000

No of Employees: 440

COMPUTER HORIZONS CORPORATION
747 Third Avenue, New York, NY 10017
Tel: (212) 371 9600

Chairman: John J Cassese (and President)
Senior Executive Officers: Martin E Pelcyger (Executive VP and Secretary), Bernhard Hubert (Senior VP), John J Murray (Senior VP), E D Fleury (Senior VP), Carl T Bergeman (VP), David W Bialick (VP, Treasurer and Assistant Secretary), Peter D Colgan (VP), Robert J Palmieri (VP), Richard Yagoda (VP)

PRINCIPAL ACTIVITIES: Computer services including programs and software
Principal Bank: Chase Manhattan Bank
Financial Information:

	$'000
Sales revenues	51,000

No of Employees: 680

COMPUTER LANGUAGE RESEACH INC
2395 Midway Road, Carrollton, TX 75006
Tel: (214) 250 7000

Chairman: Francis W Winn
President: Stephen T Winn (and Chief Executive Officer)
Senior Executive Officers: James J Charles (Group VP), R Michael Howard (Group VP), Michael D Radice (Group VP), J Eugene Stubbs (Group VP), Jan P Taylor (VP Operations), Nancy D Gardner (Controller), Terry D Bland (Secretary and General Counsel), Robert N McFarland (VP Sales), William E Nicholson (VP Sales), Richard J Weincek (VP Manufacturing), Robert M Flanagan (VP Business Development), Sarah A Helber (VP Corporate Planning), John L Eaton (VP Corporate Services)

PRINCIPAL ACTIVITIES: Provision of a range of a computer services
Principal Bank: InterFirst Dallas
Financial Information:

	$'000
Sales revenues	98,730

No of Employees: 1,370

COMPUTER MEMORIES INC
9216 Eton Avenue, Chatsworth, CA 91311
Tel: (818) 709 6445

Chairman: Rubin Irwin (and Chief Executive Officer and President)
Senior Executive Officers: Frederic A Heim (Senior VP), Frederic T Boyer (VP Finance and Administration and Chief Financial Officer)

PRINCIPAL ACTIVITIES: Manufacture of data processing equipment
Principal Bank: Security Pacific National Bank
Financial Information:

	$'000
Sales revenues	109,000

No of Employees: 450

COMPUTER PERIPHERALS, INC
8100 34th Avenue, Minneapolis, MN 55440
Tel: (612) 853-8100

Chairman: T G Kamp
Senior Executive Officers: F J Skilton (Treasurer), D P Hedberg (Secretary)

PRINCIPAL ACTIVITIES: Manufacture of tape drives for computers
Parent Company: Control Data Corporation, Minneapolis, MN
Principal Bank: Northwestern National Bank of Minneapolis
Financial Information:

	$'000
Sales revenues	100,000

No of Employees: 1,000

COMPUTER PRODUCTS, INC
2900 Gateway Drive, Pompano Beach, FL 33069
Tel: (305) 974-5500

Chairman: David C Yoder (and President and Chief Executive Officer)
Senior Executive Officers: Edward J Schneider (VP, President and General Manager Power Conversion Group), Keith F Vreeland (VP Finance, Secretary and Treasurer)

PRINCIPAL ACTIVITIES: Manufacture of a range of electronic equipment
Principal Bank: State Street Bank and Trust
Financial Information:

	$'000
Sales revenues	89,000

No of Employees: 2,100

COMPUTER SCIENCES CORPORATION
2100 E Grand Avenue, El Segundo, CA 90245
Tel: (213) 615-0311
Telex: (910) 348-6286 CSC ELSD UD

Chairman: William R Hoover (and President)
Senior Executive Officers: George Barratt (VP and Chief Financial Officer), Denis M Crane (VP Controller), Albert Gluckson (VP and General Counsel and Secretary), Alvin E Nashman (VP and President of Systems Group), Roy Nutt (VP), Lawrence Parkus (VP-Corporate Development), L Scott Sharpe (VP-Personnel), Arthur B Sims (VP and President of Industry Services Group)

PRINCIPAL ACTIVITIES: Federal Systems and Services:- Designs, engineers and integrates computer-based systems and communications systems, providing all of the hardware, software, communications, training and related elements necessary to develop, operate and maintain a system. Software development for aerospace and defense systems. Systems engineering and technical assistance in satellite communications, intelligence, aerospace, logistics and related high-technology fields. Multi-disciplinary technical services in engineering, software development, data processing and range operations. Health and Administrative Systems:- Large-scale claims processing for property casualty and health-care programs. Also turnkey (ie, software & hardware sold as a package) business information systems for managed-health care organizations. Credit Services:- Consumer credit reports and accounts receivable management services for credit grantors; data processing services for credit bureaus. Professional Services:- Consulting and technical services in the development, integration and operation of computer information systems and communications systems for clients other than the US government. Network Services:- Electronic messaging and data transport services via the company's worldwide communications network, called INFONET. Complementary Services:- Turnkey business information systems for manufacturers, and processing of income tax returns for chartered accountants

Trade Names: INFONET: International value-added communications network. INFO-SCAN: Data acquisition and control system for large-scale applications in energy management, process control and security. ComCare: Business management system for managed-health care organizations. MAN-FACT II: Material requirements planning and business information system for manufacturers. IV-D("Four-D"): Software package for automated development of interactive videodiscs and courseware for technical training, sales promotion and computer-aided instruction

Principal Subsidiaries: Associated Credit Services, Inc; Computer Partners, Inc; CSC Compufact, Inc; CSC Comtec, Inc; Computer Sciences Canada Ltd (Canada); Computer Sciences Company Limited (UK); CSID-Computer Sciences International Deutschland GmbH (West Germany); CSC Computer Sciences Europe SA (Belgium); CSC Computer Sciences Nederland BV (Netherlands); CSC Computer Sciences (Schweiz) AG (Switzerland)

Principal Bank: Citibank

Financial Information:

	Mar 31 1986 $'000	Mar 31 1987 $'000
Sales revenues	838,587	1,031,459
Income before taxes	42,764	58,096
Net income	23,948	32,243
Earnings per share(1)	$1.69	$2.08
Earnings per share(2)	$1.61	$2.06
Common stock	14,020	15,400
Retained income	192,150	224,393
Shareholders equity	213,853	284,813

(1) primary
(2) fully diluted

No of Employees: 14,100

COMPUTER TASK GROUP INC

800 Delaware Avenue, Buffalo, NY 14209
Tel: (716) 882 8000

Chairman: David N Campbell (and Chief Executive Officer)
President: John P Courtney (and Chief Operating Officer)
Senior Executive Officers: John A Lozan (VP Human Resources), Stephen P Keider (VP), William P Adamucci (VP Finance, Secretary and Treasurer)

PRINCIPAL ACTIVITIES: Provision of a wide range of computer services including programs and software
Principal Bank: Marine Midland Bank
Financial Information:

	$'000
Sales revenues	115,710

No of Employees: 2,275

COMPUTERCRAFT INC

1616 South Voss Road, Suite 900, Houston, TX 77057
Tel: (713) 977 8419

Chairman: William E Ladin Jr (and Executive VP Marketing)
President: Paul M Frison (and Chief Executive Officer)
Senior Executive Officers: H W Berkowitz (Senior VP), Phylis Cohen (VP and Secretary), Isaac Levanon (VP)

PRINCIPAL ACTIVITIES: Retailing of microcomputers
Financial Information:

	$'000
Sales revenues	137,000

No of Employees: 200

COMPUTERVISION CORPORATION

15 Crosby Drive, Bedford, MA 01730
Tel: (617) 275-1800
Telex: WUI 6817 236 cvops bfrd

Chairman: Martin Allen
President: Robert L Gable (and Chief Executive Officer)
Senior Executive Officers: Philip Read (Senior VP), Robert L Callaway (VP), David Friedman (VP), Lon F Bonczek Jr (VP Human Resources), Derick V Mauro (VP Finance and Chief Financial Officer), Victor Larkin (VP and Controller), Karl H Geng (VP and General Manager Worldwide Services), Robert P Gothie (VP and General Manager International Sales), Bardwell C Salmon (VP and General Manager Marketing), Patrick A Alias (VP North American Sales)

PRINCIPAL ACTIVITIES: Design and manufacture of automation equipment
Principal Subsidiaries: CIS Inc; OIR Inc; Organization for Industrial Resources
Financial Information:

	Dec 31 1986 $'000
Sales revenues	494,672
Net (loss)	(5,770)
(Loss) per share	($0.20)
Shareholders equity	182,870

No of Employees: 4,770

COMPUTONE SYSTEMS INC

1 Dunwoody Pk, Suite 200, 1-285 & Chamblee Dunwoody Rd, Atlanta, GA 30338
Tel: (404) 393 3010

President: Jay M Rosovsky (and Chief Operating Officer and Chief Executive Officer)
Senior Executive Officers: Edward J Ramos (Senior VP), Thomas J Petrigliano (VP), Frank B Thomason (VP and Treasurer), Walter M Keel (VP Finance), David J Harris (Secretary)

PRINCIPAL ACTIVITIES: Supply of specialty computer services and equipment
Principal Bank: National Bank of Georgia
Financial Information:

	$'000
Sales revenues	61,000

No of Employees: 355

COMSHARE INC

3001 South State Street, Ann Arbor, MI 48106
Tel: (313) 994 4800

President: Richard L Crandall (and Chief Executive Officer)
Senior Executive Officers: Ian G McNaught-Davis (Group VP), T Wallace Wrathall (Group VP and Secretary), Jesse W Caravello (VP Hardware Division), Peter Gray (VP Operations), Donald J Walker (VP Sales), James G Wyllie (VP and Controller), Robert A Feldman (VP and Counsel), Charles J Palmer (VP Eastern Sales), Norman R Neuman Jr (VP Product Development), William J Barkley (VP 4-1-1 Sales), Ronald E Jeffries (VP Information Systems), Stanley R Starkey (VP Western Sales), Mary Danforth (VP Research and Development)

PRINCIPAL ACTIVITIES: Provision of a range of data processing services
Principal Subsidiaries: Computer Research Co
Principal Bank: National Bank of Detroit
Financial Information:

	$'000
Sales revenues	69,000

No of Employees: 1,000

COMSTOCK GROUP INC

38 Old Ridgebury Road, Danbury, CT 06810
Tel: (203) 792 9800

Chairman: Charles L Scharfe (and Chief Executive Officer)
President: George Scharfe
Senior Executive Officers: John Halecki Jr (Executive VP and Chief Financial Officer), George E Wrage (Senior VP), Charles W McFarland (VP and Treasurer), Peter Alan Pasch (VP), Harvey Cohen (Secretary)

PRINCIPAL ACTIVITIES: Electrical installations for the construction industry
Financial Information:

	$'000
Sales revenues	469,240

No of Employees: 3,000

CONAGRA, INC

One Central Park Plaza, Omaha, NE 68102
Tel: (402) 978-4000
Telex: WUT 484556 conagra oma

Chairman: Charles M Harper (and Chief Executive Officer)
Presidents and Chief Operating Officers: George W Doering (Conagra Agri-Prod Companies), Philip B Fletcher (Conagra Frozen Prepared Food Companies), R F Morrison (Conagra Grain Processing Companies), John B Phillips (Conagra Refrigerated Prepared Food Companies)
Senior Executive Officers: Harold F Schuler (Senior VP Human Resources), M S Colladay (VP Public Affairs), Walter W Casey (VP Corporate Communications)

PRINCIPAL ACTIVITIES: Manufacture of food products, animal feedstuffs and fertilizers; processing of cereals and meat
Principal Bank: The First National Bank of Chicago
Financial Information:

	May 31 1987 $'000
Sales revenues	9,001,553
Income before taxes	271,526
Net income	148,726
Dividends	42,825
Dividends per share	$0.56
Earnings per share	$1.85
Common stock	394,379
Retained income	352,672
Shareholders equity	2,482,520

No of Employees: 30,410

CONAIR CORPORATION

11 Executive Avenue, Edison, NJ 08817
Tel: (201) 287-4800
Telex: RCA 253127 conair ur

Chairman: Leandro P Rizzuto (and President)
Senior Executive Officers: Maurice Lucas (Executive VP), Salvatore T Di Mascio (Senior VP Finance), John Raab (Senior VP Operations), R Diamond (VP Consumer Appliances), John Bernhart (VP Professionals), J J Mayorek (VP Administration), Francis Lindsey (VP Appliance Marketing), Ronald Diamond (VP Consumer Toiletries), Patrick Yannotta (VP and Treasurer)

PRINCIPAL ACTIVITIES: Manufacture of electrical equipment for hair care; cosmetics and toiletries
Principal Bank: Citibank NA
Financial Information:

	$'000
Sales revenues	260,000

No of Employees: 500

CONCEPT DEVELOPMENT INC

12811 Q Street, Omaha, NE 68137
Tel: (402) 896 0997

Chairman: Norman A Lies
President: R E Smith
Senior Executive Officers: Jack D Harris (Executive VP), William B Dukes (VP), John B Tatum (VP Division), D L Amundson (VP), Roy J Schumacher (Secretary and Treasurer)

PRINCIPAL ACTIVITIES: Restaurants
Financial Information:

	$'000
Sales revenues	40,000

No of Employees: 1,400

CONCORD FABRICS, INC

1411 Broadway, New York, NY 10018
Tel: (212) 840-2300
Telex: TWX 710 581 4391 concordtex nyk

Chairman: Alvin Weinstein; Vice Chairman: Frank Weinstein
President: Earl Kramer
Senior Executive Officers: David Silver (VP Personnel), Paul Cohen (VP), Martin Wolfson (VP and Treasurer)

PRINCIPAL ACTIVITIES: Manufacture of fabrics for clothing and furnishing
Financial Information:

	$'000
Sales revenues	110,300

No of Employees: 560

CONDEC CORPORATION

630 Fifth Avenue, Suite 2607, New York, NY 10020-0334
Tel: (212) 582-0800

Chairman: William F Farley (and Chief Executive Officer)
Senior Executive Officers: Richard M Cion (VP Finance and Legal), William H Vrba (Senior VP, Secretary and Treasurer)

PRINCIPAL ACTIVITIES: Manufacture of machinery for the rubber and plastic industries; manufacture of valves and controls; production of alternators; equipment and vehicles for the armed forces
Parent Company: Farley/Northwest Industries Inc
Principal Bank: The Chase Manhattan Bank NA
Financial Information:

	$'000
Sales revenues	343,000

No of Employees: 4,900

CONDUCTRON CORPORATION

9 Mohawk Drive, Leominster, MA 01453
Tel: (617) 534-0040

Chairman: Thomas H Lee
President: Joseph J Incandela (and Chief Executive Officer)
Senior Executive Officers: Frank W Miller (Executive VP), Joseph Banafato (VP and Treasurer and Chief Financial Officer)

PRINCIPAL ACTIVITIES: Manufacture of electrical and electronic equipment
Principal Subsidiaries: Oxford Precision Inc
Principal Bank: State Street Bank

Financial Information:

	$'000
Sales revenues	35,000

No of Employees: 440

CONERGICS CORPORATION

4350 Shawnee Mission Parkway, Fairway, KS 66205
Tel: (913) 362-7900

Chairman: Joseph P Forte (and President and Chief Executive Officer)
Senior Executive Officers: F A Norden (Executive VP Finance)

PRINCIPAL ACTIVITIES: Manufacture of industrial handling equipment, conveyors and conveying equipment
Parent Company: Foster Wheeler Corp
Financial Information:

	$'000
Sales revenues	150,000

No of Employees: 1,200

CONIFER GROUP INC

370 Main St, Worcester, MA 01608
Tel: (617) 752-5661

Chairman: William D Ireland Jr (and Chief Executive Officer)
President: Kenneth J McIlraith (and Chief Operating Officer)
Senior Executive Officers: Theodore W Potter (Senior VP Finance), Earl H Mason (Senior VP and Treasurer), James H Wright (Senior VP, General Counsel and Clerk), John C VanAken (Senior VP Human Resources), Thomas C Roberts (Senior VP Marketing)

PRINCIPAL ACTIVITIES: Banking services
Financial Information:

Total assets	2,540,000

No of Employees: 3,250

CONNECTICUT ENERGY CORPORATION

880 Broad Street, Bridgeport, CT 06604
Tel: (203) 382 8111

President: George B Uihlein
Senior Executive Officers: John H Larson (VP Finance), Robert J Smith (Secretary and Treasurer)

PRINCIPAL ACTIVITIES: SUpply of natural gas
Principal Subsidiaries: SCG Gas Quest Inc; Southern Connecticut Gas Company
Principal Bank: Connecticut National Bank
Financial Information:

	$'000
Sales revenues	163,850

No of Employees: 620

CONNECTICUT GENERAL LIFE INSURANCE CO

Hartford, CT 06152
Tel: (203) 726-6000
Telex: WUT 643206 c g invo blcn

President: Hartzel Z Lebed
Senior Executive Officers: Thomas H Dooley (Senior VP), Marvin A Levins (Senior VP), G R O'Brien (Senior VP), Richard J Shepler (Senior VP), James H Vineburgh (Senior VP), Allan Z Loren (Senior VP Cigna Systems Division)

PRINCIPAL ACTIVITIES: Life insurance
Parent Company: Cigna Corporation, Philadelphia, PA
Principal Bank: Morgan Guaranty Trust Co
Financial Information:

	Dec 31 1985	Dec 31 1986
	$'000	$'000
Premium income	3,922,070	2,869,640
Investment income	1,420,240	1,544,120

No of Employees: 12,537

CONNECTICUT MUTUAL LIFE INSURANCE CO

140 Garden Street, Hartford, CT 06115
Tel: (203) 727-6500
Telex: WUT 99214 conmuco hfd

Chairman: Denis F Mullane (and Chief Executive Officer): Vice Chairman: Albert E Reavill Jr
President: S Caesar Raboy
Senior Executive Officers: Executive Vice Presidents: Robert K Dickson Jr, Robert R Googins, Robert E Stevens, David D Whelehan: Senior Vice Presidents: Gregory A Boyko, Robert E Casey, Jerry J Coursey Jr, Walter J Gorski, Robert F Granquist, Robert N Hunter, Marnie W Mueller, Paul E Petry, Donald H Pond Jr, Gerald J Randall, John A Weber

PRINCIPAL ACTIVITIES: Life insurance
Trade Names: CM Alliance
Principal Subsidiaries: CM Life Insurance Co
Principal Bank: Connecticut Bank and Trust Co
Financial Information:

	Dec 31 1985	Dec 31 1986
	$'000	$'000
Income before taxes	1,507,900	1,654,200
Premium income	899,900	982,400
Investment income	650,200	732,000
Net income	274,900	297,000
Dividends	251,400	262,200
Retained income	23,500	34,800

No of Employees: 6,532

CONNECTICUT NATURAL GAS CORPORATION

100 Columbus Boulevard, PO Box 1500, Hartford, CT 06144
Tel: (203) 727 3459

Chairman: Robert H Willis (and Chief Executive Officer)
President: Victor H Frauenhofer (and Chief Operating Officer)
Senior Executive Officers: James P Boldac (Group VP), Alexander J Kennedy (Group VP, Treasurer and Chief Financial Officer), Donato P Lauria (Group VP), Frank H Livingston (Group VP), John P Brennan (VP Regional), John S Filbert (VP Operations), Anthony C Mirabella (VP)

PRINCIPAL ACTIVITIES: Supply of natural gas
Principal Subsidiaries: Affiliated Resources Corporation; ARC Energy Systems Inc; ARC Service Company; Energy Networks Inc; Fuels Inc; Hatford Steam Co; CNG Realty Corproation
Principal Bank: Connecticut Bank and Trust Company
Financial Information:

	$'000
Sales revenues	195,695

No of Employees: 600

CONNECTICUT SAVINGS BANK

55 Church Street, New Haven, CT 06501
Tel: (203) 773-4200

President: Paul H Johnson (and Chief Executive Officer)
Senior Executive Officers: Beverley H Lapham Jr (Senior VP Lending), Robert C Davis Jr (Senior VP and Treasurer), F P Wilson Jr (Senior VP), John R Matheny (VP Marketing), John E Wright (VP Branch Administration), Richard P Wood (VP Data Processing), Robert L Theve (VP Commercial Mortgage),

B Patrick Madden (VP Corporate Loans), Walter P Hrabstock (VP Resident Mortgage)

PRINCIPAL ACTIVITIES: Savings bank

No of Employees: 300

CONNELLY CONTAINERS, INC

Righters Ferry Road & Schuylkill River, Bala-Cynwyd, PA 19004
Tel: (215) 839-6400

Chairman: John F Connelly
President: Thomas S Connelly
Senior Executive Officers: Charles Boy (VP Engineering), Harry D Heaps Jr (VP Containers), Charles J Lagrossa (VP Production), Robert J Murphy (VP Containers), Leon A Wojnowski (Secretary and Treasurer)

PRINCIPAL ACTIVITIES: Manufacture of a wide range of containers
Trade Names: Mrs Schlorer's, Bulk Board
Principal Subsidiaries: Connelly Containers, Inc of Phila; Venice Maid Co, Inc
Principal Bank: Philadelphia National Bank
Financial Information:

	Dec 31 1985	Dec 31 1986
	$'000	$'000
Sales revenues	50,500	52,400
Income before taxes	3,913	1,304
Net income	2,071	620
Earnings per share	$1.75	$0.53
Common stock*	1,185,988	1,163,360
Retained income	11,911	12,318
Shareholders equity	12,702	13,098

*weighted average

No of Employees: 470

CONNER CORPORATION

PO Box 520, Newport, NC 28570
Tel: (919) 223-5121

Chairman: Wallace J Conner (and President)
Senior Executive Officers: Larry M Dinkins (Senior VP Finance), John Swecker (Senior VP), David M Booth (Senior VP Marketing), James A Ross (VP), Doug Goines (VP and Legal Counsel)

PRINCIPAL ACTIVITIES: Manufacture and sale of mobile homes
Principal Bank: First Union National Bank
Financial Information:

	$'000
Sales revenues	119,000

No of Employees: 1,800

CONOCO INC

1007 Market Street, Wilmington, DE 19898
Tel: (302) 594-3400
Telex: WUT 90 5602 conoco std b

Chairman: R E Bailey (and Chief Executive Officer)
Presidents: B R Brown (Coal Operations), C S Nicandros (Petroleum Operations)
Senior Executive Officers: A W Dunham (Executive VP), E J Grivetti (Executive VP), F E Ellis (Executive VP), C H Lee (Executive VP), S Schwartz (Executive VP), A L Cleveland (Senior VP and General Counsel), M L Sharrah (Senior VP)

PRINCIPAL ACTIVITIES: Manufacture of oil and petroleum products, coal, gas and chemicals
Trade Names: Conoco
Parent Company: E I du Pont de Nemours & Company, Wilmington, DE
Financial Information:

	$'000
Sales revenues	18,800,000

No of Employees: 43,140

CONRAC CORPORATION

Three Landmark Square, Stamford, CT 06901
Tel: (203) 348-2100
Telex: WUT 965978 conrac std

Chairman: Donald H Putnam (and Chief Executive Officer)
President: Paul E Graf (and Chief Operating Officer)
Senior Executive Officers: L M Ryan (VP), C W Kaericher (VP Finance and Treasurer), Joseph M O'Donnell (VP)

PRINCIPAL ACTIVITIES: Manufacture of telecommunications equipment and electrical display products
Principal Subsidiaries: Code-a-Phone Corp
Principal Bank: Security Pacific National Bank
Financial Information:

	$'000
Sales revenues	150,000

No of Employees: 1,400

CONSOLIDATED ALUMINUM CORPORATION CONALCO

63146 Westline Industrial Drive, St Louis, MO 63141
Tel: (314) 878-6950
Telex: WUT 447738 cons alum stl

President: Theodore M Tschopp
Senior Executive Officers: James E Hughes (Executive VP), R J Willis (VP Finance), R E Kopf (VP Sales and Marketing), G E Thym (VP Core Group)

PRINCIPAL ACTIVITIES: Primary aluminum, semi-finished products, foil, finished products
Parent Company: ALUSUISSE, Zurich, Switzerland (96%)
Financial Information:

	$'000
Sales revenues	600,000

No of Employees: 4,500

CONSOLIDATED CIGAR CORPORATION

400 Plaza Drive, Secaucus, NJ 07094
Tel: (201) 392 5000

President: Theodore W Fold
Senior Executive Officers: George F Gershel Jr (Senior VP), Gordon F Sutliff (VP), Robert S Wilkins (VP), Nick Amon (VP Finance)

PRINCIPAL ACTIVITIES: Manufacture of tobacco products and lighters
Principal Bank: Citibank NA
Financial Information:

	$'000
Sales revenues	150,000

No of Employees: 3,000

CONSOLIDATED CONTROLS CORPORATION

15 Durant Avenue, Bethel, CT 06801
Tel: (203) 743-6721
Telex: TWX 710 4560 446 cons control

President: Hans W Kretsch
Senior Executive Officers: John K Engelberger (VP East Coast Operations), Joseph A Fontana (VP West Coast Operations), Walter Dudnick (VP New Jersey), J E Hall (VP Production)

PRINCIPAL ACTIVITIES: Manufacture of controls for aviation and industrial equipment
Parent Company: Eaton Corporation
Principal Bank: Bank of Boston
Financial Information:

	$'000
Sales revenues	100,000

No of Employees: 1,200

CONSOLIDATED EDISON CO OF NEW YORK, INC

4 Irving Place, New York, NY 10003
Tel: (212) 460-4600

Chairman: Arthur Hauspurg (and President and Chief Executive Officer); Vice Chairman: John V Thornton
Senior Executive Officers: John T Conway (Executive VP Corporate Affairs), Raymond J McCann (Executive VP Divisional Operations), Eugene R McGrath (Executive VP Central Operations), Charles F Soutar (Executive VP Central Services), Joseph T Hydok (Senior VP Gas and Steam Operations), Joy Tannian (Senior VP and General Counsel)

PRINCIPAL ACTIVITIES: Distribution of natural gas and electricity
Financial Information:

	Dec 31 1985	Dec 31 1986
	$'000	$'000
Sales revenues	5,497,920	5,197,736
Net income	563,731	546,407
Earnings per share	$4.26	$4.26
Shareholders equity	4,551,195	4,633,455

No of Employees: 20,698

CONSOLIDATED FREIGHTWAYS, INC

3240 Hillview Avenue, Palo Alto, CA 94303
Tel: (415) 494-2900
Telex: TWX 910 3732 105 cf inc pla

Chairman: Raymond F O'Brien (and President and Chief Executive Officer); Vice Chairman: Donald E Moffitt
President: Larry Scott (and Chief Operating Officer)
Senior Executive Officers: Frank E Roberts (VP and Treasurer), John P Kelly (VP, Secretary and General Counsel), Norman Benke (Senior VP Finance)

PRINCIPAL ACTIVITIES: Transportation of freight by air; trucking services
Principal Subsidiaries: CF Air Freight Inc; Consolidated Freightways Corp; Road Systems Inc
Financial Information:

	Dec 31 1985	Dec 31 1986
	$'000	$'000
Sales revenues	1,882,142	2,124,470
Net income	79,291	89,109
Earnings per share	$3.10	$2.31
Shareholders equity	-	655,050

No of Employees: 24,600

CONSOLIDATED MARKETING, INC

253 N Common, Shreveport, LA 71102
Tel: (318) 424-7715

Chairman: Lionel W Eltis
President: Sam F Loeb (and Chief Executive Officer)
Senior Executive Officers: Jim Michael (VP Administration)

PRINCIPAL ACTIVITIES: Distribution of paper and paper products
Parent Company: Great Northern Nekoosa Corporation, Stamford, CT
Principal Bank: City Corp
Financial Information:

	$'000
Sales revenues	80,000

No of Employees: 400

CONSOLIDATED NATURAL GAS CO

Four Gateway Center, Pittsburgh, PA 15222
Tel: (412) 227-1000

Chairman: George A Davidson Jr (and Chief Executive Officer)
President: Ralbern H Murray (and Chief Operating Officer)
Senior Executive Officers: Paul H Dudley Jr (Senior VP), Henry P Sullivan (Senior VP and General Council), A M Abramovic (VP, Secretary and Assistant to Chairman), Lester D Johnson (VP and Chief Financial Officer), James L Douglass (VP Human Resources), Thomas H Stewart (VP Accounting and Internal Auditing)

PRINCIPAL ACTIVITIES: Exploration, production and sale of natural gas
Principal Subsidiaries: Consolidated Natural Gas Service Company Inc; The East Ohio Gas Company; The Peoples Natural Gas Company; The River Gas Company; West Ohio Gas Company; CNG Producing Company; Consolidated System LNG Company; CNG Development Company; CNG Research Company; CNG Coal Company; CNG Energy Company; Consolidated Gas Transmission Corporation; Hope Gas Inc
Principal Bank: The Chase Manhattan Bank
Financial Information:

	Dec 31 1986
	$'000
Sales revenues	2,600,000
Net income	175,000

No of Employees: 7,550

CONSOLIDATED PACKAGING CORPORATION

333 W Lake Street, Chicago, IL 60606
Tel: (312) 984-1024

President: Andre E Holtzman (and Chief Executive and Operating Officer)
Senior Executive Officers: Michael W Carrender (VP, Secretary/Treasurer)

PRINCIPAL ACTIVITIES: Manufacture of packaging materials and containers; electronic equipment
Principal Subsidiaries: Lestronics, Inc
Principal Bank: Maryland National Bank
Financial Information:

	Dec 31 1985
	$'000
Sales revenues	42,902

Principal Shareholders: Gidwitz Family (72%)
No of Employees: 451

CONSOLIDATED PAPERS, INC

231 First Ave N, PO Box 50, Wisconsin Rapids, WI 54494
Tel: (715) 422-3111
Telex: 026-3442

Chairman: G W Mead
President: L H Boling
Senior Executive Officers: L A Engelhardt (VP, Finance), G T Beckley (VP Marketing, Enamel Printing Papers), Groff Collett (VP), H M Hughson (VP, Manufacturing), W P Orcutt (VP, Manufacturing), P F Brennan (VP), P G Meyers (Secretary and Corporate Attorney), E E Smiley (Controller), L O Jaeger (Treasurer)

PRINCIPAL ACTIVITIES: Enamel printing papers manufacturing
Principal Subsidiaries: Consolidated Water Power Company
Principal Banks: Citibank; First Wisconsin National Bank; Harris Bank and Trust Company
Financial Information:

	Dec 31 1985	Dec 31 1986
	$'000	$'000
Sales revenues	715,744	653,040
Income before taxes	186,323	153,428
Net income	106,881	87,542
Dividends	31,315	34,199
Dividends per share	$1.43	$1.57
Earnings per share	$4.91	$4.02
Common stock	68,051	68,077
Retained income	420,320	473,633
Shareholders equity	492,898	546,722

No of Employees: 4,901

CONSOLIDATED STORES CORPORATION

2020 Corvair Avenue, PO Box 627, Columbus, OH 43207
Tel: (614) 224 1297

Chairman: Sol A Shenk (and Chief Executive Officer)
President: Charles H Shenk (and Treasurer)
Senior Executive Officers: Sol Norflus (Executive VP), William B Snow (Executive VP and Chief Financial Officer), Brady Churches (VP), Eli Goldach (VP), Irving Tromberg (VP), John A Gabelman (Controller and Secretary)

PRINCIPAL ACTIVITIES: Wholesale and retail trade in motor vehicle components
Principal Subsidiaries: Automotive Merchandisers Texas; CI Merchandising Corporation; Consolidated International Export Corporation; Corvairs Inc
Principal Bank: BancOhio National Bank
Financial Information:

	1986
	$'000
Sales revenues	397,100
Net income	19,000

No of Employees: 2,000

CONSTELLATION BANCORP

68 Broad Street, Elizabeth, NJ 07207
Tel: (201) 354 4080

President: John J Connolly (and Subsidiary Officer)
Senior Executive Officers: John L Joseph (Senior VP and Treasurer)

PRINCIPAL ACTIVITIES: Banking
Financial Information:

	Dec 31 1985
	$'000
Revenues	140,035
Net income	12,625

No of Employees: 1,445

CONSTRUCTION SPECIALTIES INC

55 Winans Avenue, Cranford, NJ 07016
Tel: (201) 272-5200

Chairman: Ellen H Geortner
President: Robert H Thomson
Senior Executive Officers: Frederick Smith (VP Finance), Jack Geortner (VP Sales), Ronald F Dadd (VP Group)

PRINCIPAL ACTIVITIES: Manufacture of a range of products for the construction industry
Principal Subsidiaries: Construction Specialties CA; Data Aire Inc; Datasphere Inc; Special Erection Services Inc
Principal Bank: Toronto Dominion Bank
Financial Information:

	$'000
Sales revenues	77,000

No of Employees: 600

CONSUL RESTAURANT CORPORATION

4815 West 77th Street, Minneapolis, MN 55435
Tel: (612) 893 0230

Chairman: James H Crivits (and Chief Executive Officer)
President: William D Etter (and Chief Operating Officer)
Senior Executive Officers: William C Kuhlmann (VP Administration, Legal Counsel and Secretary), Theodore J O'Shaughnessy (VP), David C Stevens (VP), John M Hamburger (VP Finance), Robert A Lamp (Treasurer), Joseph R Finnigan (Controller)

PRINCIPAL ACTIVITIES: Restaurant chain specializing in Mexican food
Principal Bank: Norwest Bank of Minneapolis
Financial Information:

	$'000
Sales revenues	87,000

No of Employees: 6,500

CONSUMERS POWER CO

212 W Michigan Avenue, Jackson, MI 49201
Tel: (517) 788-0550

Chairman: William T McCormick Jr (and President and Chief Executive Officer); Vice Chairmen: Joseph F Paquette Jr (and Chief Financial Officer), S Kinnie Smith Jr (and General Counsel)
Senior Executive Officers: Jack W Reynolds (Executive VP, Energy Supply), John W Clark (Senior VP, Communications), Rann C Lincoln (Senior VP, Energy Distribution)

PRINCIPAL ACTIVITIES: Supply of electricity and natural gas
Parent Company: CMS Energy Corporation
Principal Subsidiaries: Michigan Gas Storage Company
Financial Information:

	Dec 31 1985	Dec 31 1986
	$'000	$'000
Sales revenues	3,298,328	3,108,414
Net income (loss)	(269,772)	177,849
Earnings (loss) per share	($4.42)	$0.74
Shareholders equity	2,586,421	2,548,284

No of Employees: 9,920

CONSUMERS WATER COMPANY

4 Canal Plaza, Portland, ME 04112
Tel: (207) 773 6438

Chairman: David R Hastings II; Vice Chairman: John W L White
President: John Van C Parker (and Chief Executive Officer and Subsidiary Officer)
Senior Executive Officers: William D Holmes (Executive VP Functional Area), John F Isacke (Senior VP Real Estate), Robert W Phelps (VP and Treasurer), Judith W Hayes (Controller), Brian R Mullany (Secretary), Paul F Noran (VP Engineering), Paul F Noran (VP Engineering)

PRINCIPAL ACTIVITIES: Water supply
Principal Subsidiaries: Burlington Homes of New England; Camden & Rockland Water Co; Consumer Illinois Water Co; Dartmouth Co; Garden State Water Co Inc; Kankakee Water Co; Maine Water Co; Ohio Water Service Co; Pennsylvania Water Co; Schiaji Homes Corporation; Shenango Valley Water Co; Southern New Hampshire Water Co Inc; Wanakah Water Co
Principal Bank: Maine National Bank
Financial Information:

	$'000
Sales revenues	70,635

No of Employees: 600

CONTAINER CORPORATION OF AMERICA

One First National Plaza, Chicago, IL 60603
Tel: (312) 580-5500

President: Joe L Cooper (and Chief Executive Officer)
Senior Executive Officers: R W Graham (Group VP Administration), J D Tovin (Group VP Boxboard and Plastics), T V Brown (Group VP Containerboard, Timberlands/Wood Products), Raymond V Miezelis (Group VP International), M Eugene Perry (Senior VP Employee Relations), H A Johnson (Senior VP and Legal Counsel), D E Beeman (Senior VP Carton Division), D B Johnston (Senior VP Container Division), R S Silva (Senior VP Containerboard Mills)

PRINCIPAL ACTIVITIES: Manufacture and sale of corrugated and solid fiber shipping containers, folding cartons, fiber drums, paper bags, industrial plastic containers, and paperboard in the form of containerboard and boxboard
Parent Company: Mobil Corporation

Financial Information:

	$'000
Sales revenues	1,850,000

No of Employees: 22,600

CONTEL CORPORATION (FORMERLY CONTINENTAL TELECOM)

245 Perimeter Center Parkway, P O Box 105194, Atlanta, GA 30348
Tel: (404) 391-8000

Chairman: Charles Wohlstetter (New York, NY)
President: Donald W Weber (and Chief Executive Officer)
Senior Executive Officers: Malcolm Holmes (Executive VP and Chief Financial Officer), William P Kamachaitis (Executive VP, President Federal Systems Sector), Irvin W Maloney (Executive VP, President Information Systems Sector), William Y O'Connor (Executive VP, President Business Systems Sector), Robert C Abrams (VP Western Region Telephone), James L Carroll (VP Central Region Telephone), Michael B Esstman (VP Eastern Region Telephone), Norman Brust (VP Corporate Communications), William Friedman (VP Government Relations), Walter M Grant (VP, Secretary and Legal Counsel), John C McDonald (VP and Chief Scientist), Don D Pitts (VP and Treasurer), John P Dawley (VP Human Resources)

PRINCIPAL ACTIVITIES: Manufacture of electronic data processing, computer and communications equipment and services
Principal Subsidiaries: Contel Business Network; Contel Credit Corporation; Contel Data Services Corporation
Principal Bank: Bank of America
Financial Information:

	Dec 31 1985	Dec 31 1986
	$'000	£'000
Sales revenues	2,556,617	3,073,977
Net income	239,858	232,878
Earnings per share	$3.21	$3.04
Shareholders equity	1,412,070	1,496,379

No of Employees: 23,098

CONTICO INTERNATIONAL, INC

1101 Warson Road, St Louis, MO 63132
Tel: (314) 997-5900
Telex: WUT 442315 cont mfgco stl

Chairman: Lester Miller; Vice Chairman: M B Levy
President: L M Hill
Senior Executive Officers: Bill Miller (Executive VP), James P Flynn (VP Finance and Secretary)

PRINCIPAL ACTIVITIES: Manufacture of home hardware and sanitary equipment, chemicals and plastic products
Principal Bank: First City National Bank of Houston
Financial Information:

	$'000
Sales revenues	100,000

No of Employees: 1,800

CONTINENTAL AIRLINES CORPORATION

P O Box 60450, Houston, TX 77060
Tel: (713) 780 3344

Chairman: Francisco A Lorenzo (and Chief Executive Officer); Vice Chairman: Howard P Swanson
President: Philip J Bakes (and Chief Operating Officer)
Senior Executive Officers: James W Arpey (Senior VP Operations and Technical Services), Donald J Breeding (VP Operations), Richard A Schroeter (VP and Treasurer), Barry P Simon (VP, Legal Counsel and Secretary), Mickey P Foret (VP Finance and Chief Financial Officer), Dan J Thompson (VP Technical Services), James C Bacon (VP), Douglas C Birdsall (VP Marketing Planning), Larry S Dickenson (VP Aircraft Programs), Chester H Miller (VP), Richard E Murray (VP Automated Marketing Programs), William C Neary (VP Sales and Service, Central Region), James O'Donnell (VP Market Development)

PRINCIPAL ACTIVITIES: Air transportation services
Parent Company: Continental Airlines Inc
Financial Information:

	Dec 31 1985
	$'000
Sales revenues	1,704,775
Net income	60,885

No of Employees: 11,500

CONTINENTAL ASSURANCE CO

CNA Plaza, Chicago, IL 60685
Tel: (312) 822-5000

Chairman: Edward J Noha (and President)
Senior Executive Officers: William J Gilmartin (Senior VP), Dennis H Chookaszian (VP and Controller)

PRINCIPAL ACTIVITIES: Life insurance
Parent Company: Loews Corporation, New York, NY
Financial Information:

	Dec 31 1985	Dec 31 1986
	$'000	$'000
Premium income	1,374,859	1,488,613
Investment income	162,648	178,575

No of Employees: 11,000

CONTINENTAL BANCORPORATION

1500 Market Street, Philadelphia, PA 19102
Tel: (215) 564-7000

Chairman: Roy T Peraino (and Chief Executive Officer); Vice Chairmen: Glenn Y Forney, R F Laux, John C Schmidt, John T Wagner
President: Richard C Rishel (and Chief Administration Officer)
Senior Executive Officers: Russell E Fitzgerald (Executive VP), E V Caruso (Executive VP), James Kelly (Senior VP and Treasurer)

PRINCIPAL ACTIVITIES: Bank
Principal Subsidiaries: Continental Bank; Lincoln National Leasing Inc; Lenders Life Insurance Co; York Bank & Trust Co
Financial Information:

	Dec 31 1985	Dec 31 1986
	$'000	$'000
Net income	51,009	34,740
Earnings per share	$4.65	$3.15
Shareholders equity	-	326,900
Deposits	4,042,666	4,508,373
Total assets	4,717,962	5,311,046

No of Employees: 3,000

CONTINENTAL BOILER WORKS, INC

5620 W Park Avenue, St Louis, MO 63110
Tel: (314) 781-8500
Telex: TWX 910 7610 552 continental

President: Robert G Fournie
Senior Executive Officers: Joseph O'Brien (Secretary and Comptroller), Robert G Fournier Jr (Sales Manager), Manuel R Moon (Works Manager)

PRINCIPAL ACTIVITIES: Manufacture of metal products and pollution control equipment
Principal Subsidiaries: Brooks Erection & Construction Co; Gulf States Fabricators Inc
Principal Bank: Centerre Bank
Financial Information:

	$'000
Sales revenues	80,000

No of Employees: 800

CONTINENTAL CONVEYOR & EQUIPMENT COMPANY, INC

4th Avenue South, Winfield, AL 35594
Tel: (205) 487-6492
Telex: WUT 59769 conveco wifd

President: C E Bryant Jr
Senior Executive Officers: John B Jeans (Senior VP Marketing), Ray McGaha (VP Sales), J D Dickinson (VP Finance), Alex Saliba (VP Conveyor Systems), Bob Wheeler (VP Manufacturing), James A Key (VP Advertising)

PRINCIPAL ACTIVITIES: Manufacture of conveyors, chemicals and plastics
Financial Information:

	$'000
Sales revenues	60,000

No of Employees: 500

CONTINENTAL CORPORATION

80 Maiden Lane, New York, NY 10038
Tel: (212) 440-3980

Chairman: John Mascotte (and Chief Executive Officer)
President: John H Bretherick Jr
Senior Executive Officers: Walter H Hallowell (Executive VP), Richard A Liddy (Executive VP), William E Thiele (Executive VP), Charles A Parker (Executive VP), Steven J Smith (Executive VP and Secretary)

PRINCIPAL ACTIVITIES: Holding company with interests in insurance, consumer finance and data processing services
Principal Subsidiaries: American Title Insurance Co; Columbia RE Title Insurance Co; Boston Old Colony Insurance Co; Equitable Fire Insurance Co; Buffalo Reinsurance Co; CIC Financial Corp; Commercial Life Insurance Co; Continental Insurance Co; AFCO Credit Corp; Buckeye Union Insurance Co Inc; Casualty Insurance Co; Continental Insurance Co; Kansas City Fire & Marine Insurance Co; Fidelity & Casualty Co NY; Firemens Insurance Co Newark NJ; Commercial Insurance Co Newark NJ; Continental Reinsurance Corp; Glens Falls Insurance Co; Niagara Fire Insurance Co; First Insurance Co of HI; Foremark Corp; Harbor Insurance Co; Insurnet Inc; Kansas City Fire & Marine Insurance Co; Loyalty Life Insurance Co; Marine Office of America Corp; Hull & Cargo Surveyors Inc; United States P & I Agency Inc; National Reinsurance Corp; National-Ben Franklin Insurance IL; National-Ben Franklin Insurance MI; Title Insurance Corp of PA Inc; Underwriters Adjusting Co; Quality Adjustment & Service Co; William Penn Life Insurance Co NY
Financial Information:

	Dec 31 1985	Dec 31 1986
	$'000	$'000
Revenues	5,119,157	6,002,273
Net income	61,270	215,000
Earnings per share	$1.01	$7.42
Shareholders equity	2,001,066	2,550,890
Total assets	11,494,806	13,623,230

No of Employees: 17,000

CONTINENTAL ILLINOIS CORPORATION

231 S LaSalle Street, Chicago, IL 60697
Tel: (312) 828-2345

Chairman: Thomas C Theobold (and Chief Executive Officer); Vice Chairman: Edward S Bottum
Senior Executive Officers: Richard S Brennan (Executive VP, General Counsel and Secretary), Eugene R Croisant (Executive VP, Retail Banking), Leo C de Grijs (Executive VP, Country Exposure and Sovereign Risk Management), Alfred F Miossi (Executive VP International Finance), Hillis W Rademacher (Executive VP and Chief Credit Officer), Caren L Reed (Executive VP Corporate and Institutional Banking-East), Garry J Scheuring (Executive VP Corporate and Institutional Banking, Sector II), Leonard W Busse (Executive VP International Banking), Kenneth K Chalmers (Executive VP Special Industries), William E Gibson (Executive VP, Asset and Liability Management Committee), William L Gunlicks (Executive VP Investment/Merchant Banking), Paul M Homan (Executive VP Planning), Michael J Murray (Corporate and Institutional Banking, Midwest), David O Nordby (Executive VP, FDIC Asset Administration), Michael O Rigg (Executive VP and Treasurer)

PRINCIPAL ACTIVITIES: Banking services
Principal Subsidiaries: Continental Illinois National Bank and Trust Company of Chicago; Continental Bank Buffalo Grove; Continental Bank Oakbrook Terrace; Continental Illinois Commercial Corp; Continental IL Corp Financial Futures; Continental IL Energy Development Corp; Continental IL Equity Corp; Continental IL Leasing Corp; Continental Bank International; Continental International Finance Corp; Continental IL Trust Co; Continental IL Trust Co of FL; Continental IL Venture Corp
Principal Bank: Continental Illinois National Bank and Trust Company of Chicago
Financial Information:

	Dec 31 1985	Dec 31 1986
	$'000	$'000
Net income	151,000	165,200
Earnings per share	$0.53	$0.60
Shareholders equity	1,872,000	2,048,000
Deposits	17,759,000	18,030,000
Total assets	30,528,000	32,809,000

No of Employees: 9,480

CONTINENTAL MATERIALS CORPORATION

325 N Wells Street, Chicago, IL 60610
Tel: (312) 661-7200

Chairman: James G Gidwitz (and Chief Executive Officer); Vice Chairmen: Joseph L Gidwitz
President: William A Ryan
Senior Executive Officers: Melvin Pollack (VP and Treasurer)

PRINCIPAL ACTIVITIES: Mining and quarrying natural resources; manufacture of furnaces and coolers
Principal Subsidiaries: Arco Corp; Castle Concrete Co; Continental Catalina Inc; Continental Copper Inc; Continental Mining & Minerals Corp; Continental Mining & Minerals Ltd; Continental Quicksilver Inc; Continental Uranium Inc; Edens Industrial Park Inc; Florida Rental Tool & Equipment Corp; Leland Co; Phoenix Manufacturing Inc; Transit Mix Concrete Co; Kay Tee Inc; Williams Furnace; Williams Furnace International Corp; Woodmont Inc
Principal Bank: The Northern Trust Bank
Financial Information:

	$'000
Sales revenues	70,000

No of Employees: 780

CONTINENTAL STEEL CORPORATION

151 N Delaware St, 1770 Market Sq, Indianapolis, IN 46204-2526

Chairman: Jack R Wheeler (and President and Chief Executive Officer); Vice Chairman: David Polla
Senior Executive Officers: J R Fager (VP Marketing), H H Herin (VP Operations), M E Chinski (VP and Controller), D E Brooks (VP Employee Relations)

PRINCIPAL ACTIVITIES: Processing of steel and manufacture of steel products
Principal Bank: Trefoil Capital Corp
Financial Information:

	$'000
Sales revenues	125,000

No of Employees: 1,500

CONTINUUM COMPANY INC

3429 Executive Center Drive, Austin, TX 78731

Tel: (512) 345 5700

Chairman: Ronald C Carroll (and President and Chief Executive Officer)

Senior Executive Officers: W Michael Long (Executive VP Sales), A Gale Hasselmeier (Senior VP and Actuary), Alan J Garland (VP Division), Thomas F Gomolski (VP Management Information Systems), Robert W Willingham (VP Division), Lou Ann Gilmore (Controller and Assistant Secretary)

PRINCIPAL ACTIVITIES: Data processing services including programs and software for the insurance industry

Principal Bank: Texas Commerce Bank

Financial Information:

	$'000
Sales revenues	30,000

No of Employees: 400

CONTRAVES-GOERZ CORPORATION

620 Epsilon Drive, Pittsburgh, PA 15238

Tel: (412) 967-7700

Telex: 247628 ctrz corp pgh

President: James Colker

Senior Executive Officers: George Economou (VP), Charles L Malone (VP), R A Peterson (VP), Charles Gregory (VP), John Landis (VP), Harry J Noss Jr (Treasurer and VP Finance)

PRINCIPAL ACTIVITIES: Manufacture of optical equipment including fire control systems for anti-aircraft and field artillery; naval anti-aircraft defense systems; trajectory measuring systems; testing equipment; satellite assemblies; computer aided design; measuring and medical systems; electronic components; electronic drive systems and motors

Parent Company: Oerlikon-Bürhrle USA Inc

Principal Bank: Mellon Bank

Financial Information:

	$'000
Sales revenues	80,000

Principal Shareholders: Oerlikon Bührle Holding AG, Zürich, Switzerland

No of Employees: 950

CONTROL DATA CORPORATION

PO Box 0, Minneapolis, MN 55440-4700

Tel: (612) 853-8100

Chairman: Robert M Price (and President and Chief Executive Officer); Deputy Chairman: Norbert R Berg

Senior Executive Officers: John K Buckner (Executive VP and Chief Financial Officer), Franklin R Dawe (VP Human Resources), Larry E Jodsaas (Senior VP Quality and Operations Effectiveness), Boyd T Jones (President Government Systems Group), Daniel R Pennie (VP, General Counsel and Secretary), Lawrence Perlman (Executive VP and President, Data Storage Products Group), Thomas C Roberts (Executive VP and President, Computer Systems and Services Group), George F Troy (President Training and Education Group), David P White (Executive VP and President, Business Services Group)

PRINCIPAL ACTIVITIES: Computer systems and services; government systems; data storage products; business services; training and education

Principal Bank: Chase Manhattan Bank

Financial Information:

	Dec 31 1985 $'000	Dec 31 1986 $'000
Total revenues	3,679,700	3,346,700
(Loss) before taxes	(484,000)	(280,600)
Net (loss)	(567,500)	(264,500)
Dividends per share	$0.54	-
(Loss) per share	($14.56)	($6.48)
Common stock	20,680	20,700
Retained income	763,900	498,900
Shareholders equity	1,202,600	991,100

No of Employees: 34,409

CONVENIENT/CONNA CORPORATION

6060 Dutchmans Ln, Louisville, KY 40205-3221

Tel: (502) 584-1281

Chairman: Joe P Peden (and Chief Executive Officer)

President: Robert T Johnson (and Chief Operating Officer)

Senior Executive Officers: Douglas A Vetter (Senior VP and Chief Financial Officer), R J Stewart (Senior VP Real Estate), James E Shallcross (President Food Mart Division), Michael Merrifield (VP Franchise Relations), Bernard J Finneran (VP Marketing), C B Wunderlich III (VP Administrative Services)

PRINCIPAL ACTIVITIES: Gas stations; food retailing

Principal Subsidiaries: Conna Australia Pty Ltd; Convenient Food Marts of Indiana; Convenient Gasoline; Convenient Industries of America; CFM of Illinois Inc; CFM of New England Inc; CIA Food Mart Inc; Convenient Equipment Inc; Financial Opportunities Inc; Ewing Oscar Inc; Food Merchandisers Inc; Remote Services Inc; Remstar Corporation

Principal Bank: Citizens Fidelity Bank and Trust Co

Financial Information:

	$'000
Sales revenues	200,000

No of Employees: 500

CONVENT CHEMICAL CORPORATION

6100 Oak Tree Blvd, Cleveland, OH 44131

Tel: (216) 447-1650

Chairman: Patrick C Ross

President: Raymond E Pasquali

Senior Executive Officers: Louis J Weisz (VP)

PRINCIPAL ACTIVITIES: Manufacture of chemicals

Parent Company: B F Goodrich Co, Akron, OH

Principal Bank: First National Bank

Financial Information:

	$'000
Sales revenues	117,000

No of Employees: 220

CONVERGENT TECHNOLOGIES

2700 North First St, PO Box 6685, San Jose, CA 95150-6685

Tel: (408) 434-2848

Telex: TWX 910-338-2149

Chairman: Paul C Ely Jr (President and and Chief Executive Officer)

Senior Executive Officers: John M Russell (VP and Chief Financial Officer), Richard G Meise (VP Sales), Jiro Abe (VP Asia), Jack Kay (VP Eastern Division Sales), Jim Greenup (VP Western Division Sales), Roger Cooper (VP European Sales), Mike Lambert (VP Intercontinental Sales)

PRINCIPAL ACTIVITIES: Manufacture of computer systems and microprocessors

Principal Bank: Bank of America

Financial Information:

	Dec 31 1985	Dec 31 1986
	$'000	$'000
Sales revenues	395,000	306,000
Net income (loss)	11,500	(33,000)

No of Employees: 1,994

CONVERSE INC

55 Fordham Road, North Reading, MA 01864
Tel: (617) 664 0194

Chairman: Richard B Loynd
President: John P O'Neil
Senior Executive Officers: Gib Ford (Executive VP Marketing and Sales), John McQuaid (VP Manufacturing), Richard Wolfe (Senior VP Finance), Jack Green (Senior VP), Richard Conforti (VP Business Development and General Manager, Hamptons Division), Riney Lochmann (VP Sales), Joe Dean (VP), Kevin Loftus (VP International), Joseph Henry (VP Materials Management), Vincente Dordal (VP and General Manager, Converse de Puerto Rico)

PRINCIPAL ACTIVITIES: Manufacture of footwear
Principal Bank: The First National Bank of Boston
Financial Information:

	$'000
Sales revenues	220,000

No of Employees: 3,500

CONWOOD CORPORATION

813 Ridge Lake Blvd, Memphis, TN 38117
Tel: (901) 761-2050
Telex: WUT 53859 conwood mfs

President: William M Rosson (and Chief Executive Officer)
Senior Executive Officers: B C Parker (VP Sales), W G Dean (VP Leaf), A D Harris Jr (VP Administration), E C Powell (VP Marketing), W E Ingram (VP), J A Bracey (VP)

PRINCIPAL ACTIVITIES: Manufacture of tobacco products and insecticides
Principal Bank: Morgan Guaranty Trust Co
Financial Information:

	$'000
Sales revenues	198,000

No of Employees: 1,320

COOK UNITED INC

16501 Rockside Road, Cleveland, OH 44137
Tel: (216) 475 1000

Chairman: Russell A Hansen (and President and Chief Executive Officer)
Senior Executive Officers: Lawrence A Reznick (VP Distribution and Management Information Systems), Edward J Lewis (Controller), Adam Talarek (Executive VP Administration), Gary N Nebinger (Senior VP Operations), Donald J Rhine (Senior VP Merchandising), Walter Jones (VP Finance and Chief Financial Officer), Ralph R Luffler (VP and Treasurer), John W Edstrom (VP, Secretary and General Counsel)

PRINCIPAL ACTIVITIES: Retail department stores
Principal Subsidiaries: Cook-Car Inc; Nickman Myron Inc
Principal Bank: Ameritrust Company
Financial Information:

	$'000
Sales revenues	300,000

No of Employees: 4,500

COOPER BIOMEDICAL INC

197 Airport Boulevard, Burlingame, CA 94010
Tel: (415) 342 0123

Chairman: P G Montgomery
President: J L Edwards
Senior Executive Officers: James A Edlund (Executive VP), Richard K Leute (Senior VP), Michael K Ullman (Senior VP), Dennis L Winger (VP, Treasurer and Controller)

PRINCIPAL ACTIVITIES: Manufacture of drugs and products for laboratories
Financial Information:

	$'000
Sales revenues	88,000

No of Employees: 580

COOPER INDUSTRIES, INC

PO Box 4446, Houston, TX 77210
Tel: (713) 739-5400

Chairman: Robert Cizik (and President)
Senior Executive Officers: Joseph R Coppola (Senior VP, Manufacturing Services), Dewain K Cross (Senior VP, Finance), C Baker Cunningham (Executive VP Operations), Alan E Riedel (Senior VP, Administration), H John Riley Jr (Executive VP, Operations), Michael J Sebastian (Executive VP, Operations), Edgar A Bircher (VP and General Counsel), Thomas W Campbell (VP, Public Affairs), Alan J Hill (VP and Treasurer), D Bradley McWilliams (VP, Taxes), Carl J Plesnicher Jr (VP, Employee Relations and Environmental Affairs), Laurence H Polsky (VP, Personnel), Roger A Scott (VP, Secretary and Corporation Counsel), Donald R Sheley Jr (Controller)

PRINCIPAL ACTIVITIES: Cooper Industries manufactures equipment for primary and secondary distribution of electricity to industrial and commercial users; wire and cable for electronic transportation and consumer markets; equipment, hardware, and hand and power tools for consumer use, commercial and industrial construction, automotive assembly and aftermarket; and a broad line of machinery and aftermarket support services for oil and natural gas drilling and compression markets and for the mining and construction industries
Principal Subsidiaries and Divisions: Electrical & Electronic Products: Belden Wire and Cable; Bussmann; Cooper Lighting Products; Crouse-Hinds Electrical Construction Materials; Cooper Electrical Distribution Equipment; McGraw-Edison Power Systems. Commercial & Industrial Products: Apex; Cooper Air Tools; The Cooper Group (hand tools); Kirsch; Wagner. Compression & Drilling Products: Demco; Energy Services Group; Ajax; Cooper-Bessemer Reciprocating; Cooper-Bessemer Rotating; Superior; Funk; Gardner-Denver Mining & Construction; Industrial Machinery Division; Martin-Decker
Principal Bank: First City National Bank
Financial Information:

	Dec 31 1985	Dec 31 1986
	$'000	$'000
Sales revenues	3,067,169	3,433,296
Income before taxes	258,168	285,172
Net income	135,080	147,722
Dividends	64,253	77,033
Dividends per share	$1.52	$1.60
Earnings per share net	$2.79	$3.04
Common stock	225,513	242,044
Retained income	926,561	997,200
Shareholders equity	1,381,001	1,419,946

No of Employees: 40,200

COOPER LABORATORIES, INC

3145 Porter Drive, Palo Alto, CA 94304
Tel: (415) 856-5000
Telex: WUT 334424 cooper cli pla

Chairman: Parker G Montgomery (and President and Chief Executive Officer)
Senior Executive Officers: George J Fields (VP and Chief Financial Officer), Joseph A Dorrily Jr (VP Secretary and

Chief Administration Officer), D Hungerford (VP Personnel), Marshall W Bautz (VP), Charles Dore (VP), Robert J Dran (VP)

PRINCIPAL ACTIVITIES: Manufacture of medical and dental supplies

Principal Bank: Manufacturers Hanover Trust Co

Financial Information:

	$'000
Sales revenues	156,000

No of Employees: 1,900

COOPER LASERSONICS INC

3420 Central Expressway, Santa Clara, CA 95051

Tel: (408) 720 1100

Chairman: Parker G Montgomery; Vice Chairman: A K Nilsson

President: M M Koffel

Senior Executive Officers: Ira J Fertik (Executive VP), William D Hyatt (Executive VP), Joseph A Doring (VP and Secretary), Michael Mitzmacher (VP, Treasurer and Controller)

PRINCIPAL ACTIVITIES: Manufacture of medical and surgical instruments and equipment

Financial Information:

	$'000
Sales revenues	81,145

No of Employees: 800

COOPER, PETER, CORPORATIONS

7401 Carmel Executive Park, Charlotte, NC 28226

Tel: (704) 542-7474

Telex: WUT 572 313 petercoop cha

Chairman: Alexis Lavion

President: Georges Larroux

Senior Executive Officers: Eugene Thordahl (Executive VP), H J Laude (VP and General Manager Adhesives), Joseph Vocca (Secretary)

PRINCIPAL ACTIVITIES: Manufacture of adhesives and gelatine

Parent Company: Rousselot SA, Paris, France

Principal Bank: First Union National Bank

Financial Information:

	$'000
Sales revenues	70,000

No of Employees: 350

COOPER TIRE & RUBBER COMPANY

Lima & Western Avenues, Findlay, OH 45840

Tel: (419) 423-1321

Telex: 419/424-4108

Chairman: Edward E Brewer

President: Ivan W Gorr

Senior Executive Officers: William T Fitzgerald (Executive VP), J Alec Reinhardt (VP-Finance)

PRINCIPAL ACTIVITIES: Cooper produces a wide variety of carbon black and fabric reinforced parts for consumers and industry. It manufactures and markets automobile and truck tires, inner tubes, reinforced hose, high technology rubber-to-metal bonded parts, and complex molded and extruded rubber products

Trade Names: COOPER, FALLS/MASTERCRAFT, GIANT

Principal Subsidiaries: Cooper International Holding Corporation; Cooper International Rubber Ltd

Financial Information:

	Dec 31 1985 $'000	Dec 31 1986 $'000
Sales revenues	522,639	577,517
Income before taxes	31,151	43,138
Net income	18,471	23,018
Dividends	4,013	4,146
Dividends per share	$0.40	$0.41
Earnings per share	$1.84	$2.28
Common stock*	10,078	10,144
Retained income	175,711	195,151
Shareholders equity	175,711	195,151
*number of shares in thousands		

No of Employees: 5,400

COOPERATIVE FARM CHEMICALS ASSOCIATION

PO Box 308, Lawrence, KS 66044

Tel: (913) 843-7300

Telex: TWX 910 7496 570 c f c a

President: W J Harwell

Senior Executive Officers: Eric Thompson (VP), Allen Hoffman (VP and General Manager), R W Lind (Treasurer)

PRINCIPAL ACTIVITIES: Manufacture of chemicals

Principal Bank: United Missouri Bank of Kansas City

Financial Information:

	$'000
Sales revenues	70,000

No of Employees: 270

COOPERVISION, INC

3145 Porter Drive, Palo Alto, CA 94304

Tel: (415) 856 5000

Chairman: P G Montgomery (and Chief Executive Officer)

President: J H Williford

Senior Executive Officers: A R McMillen (Executive VP), Peter Riepenhausen (Executive VP), Jack R Blair (Executive VP), J A Dornig Jr (VP and Secretary), J T McKinley (VP and Treasurer)

PRINCIPAL ACTIVITIES: Manufacture of optical and ophthalmic products, pharmaceuticals, medical and surgical instruments and equipment

Parent Company: Cooper Laboratories Inc, Palo Alto, CA

Principal Bank: Manufacturers Hanover Trust Co

Financial Information:

	Oct 31 1986 $'000
Sales revenues	560,096
Net income	9,000
Earnings per share	$0.41
Shareholders equity	220,960

No of Employees: 4,800

COORS, ADOLPH, CO

Golden, CO 80401

Tel: (303) 279-6565

Telex: TWX 9109340118 coorsbrew gldn

Chairman: William K Coors

President: Jeffrey H Coors; Division President: Peter Coors (Brewing Division),

Senior Executive Officers: Bob L Mornin (Executive VP, Corporate Development), Max W Goodwin (Executive VP, Allied Operations), Robert A Rechholtz (Executive VP, Sales and Marketing), Harold R Smethills (Executive VP, Corporate Finance and Administraton), Alvin C Babb (Executive VP, Brewing Division, Plant Operations)

PRINCIPAL ACTIVITIES: Brewing of beer

Principal Subsidiaries: Golden Aluminium Co; Coors Packaging Co; Coors Transportation Co; Coors Food Products Co; Coors Energy Co; Coors Porcelain Company; Coors Distributing Co
Principal Bank: The First National Bank of Denver
Financial Information:

	Dec 29 1985	Dec 28 1986
	$'000	$'000
Sales revenues excl. tax	1,281,122	1,314,930
Income before taxes	1,424,533	1,464,881
Net income	53,416	59,393
Dividends	14,039	17,956
Dividends per share	$0.40	$0.50
Earnings per share	$1.52	$1.65
Shareholders equity	936,461	996,140

No of Employees: 9,800

COPCO PAPERS INC
525 N Nelson Road, Columbus, OH 43216
Tel: (614) 251-7000

President: J F Page Jr
Senior Executive Officers: R I Dennis (Executive VP Copco Columbus), G L Straus (Executive VP Chope Stevens), R H Noble (VP Administration), C M Wolfe (VP Systems), R E Hill (VP Industrial Marketing), D E Howell (VP Fine Marketing), R E Hill (VP Industrial Marketing), K Buckham (VP Information Products Marketing), D J McMullen (VP Copco Cleveland), M J Miller (VP Copco Dayton), R A Fieher (VP Copco Pittsburgh), R L Henderson (VP Copco Indianapolis), S White (VP Copco Charleston), J Boling (VP Dudley Division, Lansing), V A Roekle (VP Dudley Division, Saginaw), G L Strang (VP Chope Stevens Division, Detroit), R V Honka (VP Union Paper Division, Detroit), M S Kuhr (Controller)

PRINCIPAL ACTIVITIES: Manufacture of paper and paper products
Parent Company: Paper Corp of America
Financial Information:

	$'000
Sales revenues	175,000

No of Employees: 420

COPELAND CORPORATION
Campbell Road, Sidney, OH 045365
Tel: (513) 498-3011
Telex: WUT 288267 copelander sdyo

Chairman: Henry L Hillman
President: Matthew O Diggs Jr (and Chief Executive Officer)
Senior Executive Officers: R M Hartnett (VP Finance), Earl B Muir (VP Research), Bill F Dittman (VP Engineering and Research), Dean M Ruwe (VP Operations), Paul H Boorman (VP Human Resources), Hartmut Schmied (VP International), T G Ralph Jr (VP Sales)

PRINCIPAL ACTIVITIES: Manufacture of condensing equipment and compressors
Parent Company: Hillman Company
Financial Information:

	$'000
Sales revenues	368,000

No of Employees: 4,250

COPLAY CEMENT CO
PO Box 32, Nazareth, PA 18064
Tel: (215) 837-6725

Chairman: Roger W Mullin Jr; Chairman of Executive Committee: Philippe Ronsin
President: George Uding (and Chief Executive Officer)
Senior Executive Officers: Marcel G Mallet (VP Operations), Edwin C Colwell (VP Marketing), Jules R Cattie Jr (VP Finance and Treasurer)

PRINCIPAL ACTIVITIES: Manufacture of cement
Parent Company: Société des Ciments Français
Financial Information:

	$'000
Sales revenues	160,000

No of Employees: 825

COPOLYMER RUBBER & CHEMICAL CORPORATION
PO Box 2591, Baton Rouge, LA 70821
Tel: (504) 355-5655
Telex: TWX 510 9933 564 copo mkt btr

President: S D Lyon (and Chief Executive Officer)
Senior Executive Officers: D H Neufeld (Senior VP Finance), W A Bishop (VP Research and Development), T M Sarsfield (VP Marketing), B D Butler (VP Manufacturing)

PRINCIPAL ACTIVITIES: Manufacture and sale of synthetic rubber
Parent Company: Armstrong Rubber Company, New Haven, CT
Financial Information:

	$'000
Sales revenues	160,000

No of Employees: 700

COPPERWELD CORPORATION
Four Gateway Center, Pittsburgh, PA 15222
Tel: (412) 263-3200
Telex: TWX 710 6642 022 copperweld pgh

Chairman: Anthony J Bryan (and Chairman of Executive Committee and President and Chief Executive Officer)
Senior Executive Officers: John D Turner (VP Operations), William S Cook (VP Strategic Planning and Development), John G Roberts (VP Operations Copperweld Steel Co), William A Wolfe (VP Operations Regal Tube Division), Alan A Smith (VP Operations Bimetallics Division), Guillermo Gomez (VP International), Donald P DeLuca (VP and Treasurer), Paul C Borland (VP and General Manager Ohio Steel Tubes Co)

PRINCIPAL ACTIVITIES: Manufacture of a wide range of steel products
Parent Company: Imetal
Financial Information:

	$'000
Sales revenues	350,000

No of Employees: 3,000

CORAL PETROLEUM, INC
908 Town & Country Blvd, Box 19666, Houston, TX 77224
Tel: (713) 827-5700
Telex: TWX 910 8817 269 Coral pat hou c

Chairman: David B Chalmers Sr (and President and Chief Executive Officer)
Senior Executive Officers: William T Hamilton (Executive VP Exploration and Production), Young J Boozer III (Senior VP Finance and Corporate Development), Frank De Weese (VP and Controller), Dave T Davies (VP and Treasurer)

PRINCIPAL ACTIVITIES: Manufacture of crude oil, petroleum and related products
Principal Bank: Banque de Paris et des Pays Bas, New York
Financial Information:

	$'000
Sales revenues	6,000,000

No of Employees: 2,500

CORDIS CORPORATION
PO Box 025700, Miami, FL 33102
Tel: (305) 551-2000
Telex: WUT 519 592 cordiscpr milk

Chairman: Alexander T Daignault

President: Norman R Weldon (and Chief Executive Officer)
Senior Executive Officers: Harold Hershenson (Executive VP), Frank M Fischer (President Implantable Products Division), Richard T Spencer (President Marketing Division), Rudolph J Kranys (Executive VP and President Angiographic Products Division), George Von Klan (VP European Marketing), Robert R Strauss (VP Finance), David C MacGregor (VP Medical Research and President Cordis Research Corp), J L de Ruyter Van Steveninck (VP European Operations), C Stewart Finch (VP Marketing, Planning and Devleopment), Allan R Freelon (VP Community Relations), Bonnie R Leetmaa (VP Clinical Research), David M Link (VP Corporate Product Assurance), Charles R McDowell (VP Corporate Relations), Bruce L Nickerson (VP Implantable Division), John N Pagones (VP Product Assurance), Melvyn A Saslow (VP Corporate Development), Stanley H Saulson (VP Engineering)

PRINCIPAL ACTIVITIES: Manufacture of medical and surgical equipment
Principal Subsidiaries: Cordis International Corp; Cordis Laboratories Inc; Hyperion Inc; Medical Devices International (Barbados); Motion Control Inc; Neurometrics Inc; Norland Corp; Electro Tek Corp
Principal Bank: Southeast First National Bank of Miami
Financial Information:

	$'000
Sales revenues	202,400

No of Employees: 3,200

CORDURA CORPORATION

2029 Centry Park East, Los Angeles, CA 90067
Tel: (213) 553 4646

Chairman: Norman E Friedmann (and Chief Executive Officer)
President: Robert G Sims (and Chief Operating Officer)
Senior Executive Officers: George C Evanoff (Senior VP), Walter G Cleveland (VP), Robert R Parker (VP), Rodney F Sloss (VP Finance and Treasurer)

PRINCIPAL ACTIVITIES: Publishing services
Principal Subsidiaries: Cordura Publications Inc; Derivation and Tabulation Assoication; Harrington R E Inc; Mitchellmatix Inc
Principal Bank: First Interstate Bank
Financial Information:

	$'000
Sales revenues	53,440

No of Employees: 695

CORDUROY RUBBER CO

Fuller Avenue, Grand Rapids, MI 49501
Tel: (616) 459-4541
Telex: TWX 810 27 36 948 corduroy grr

President: Robert E Murphy (and Chief Executive Officer)
Senior Executive Officers: Richard D Murphy (Executive VP), W J Baldwin (VP Engineering), Charles McCallum (Secretary)

PRINCIPAL ACTIVITIES: Manufacture of rubber products
Principal Subsidiaries: Cadillac Molded Rubber Inc
Principal Bank: Union Bank and Trust Co
Financial Information:

	$'000
Sales revenues	50,000

No of Employees: 450

CORE INDUSTRIES INC

PO Box 2000, 500 N Woodward Avenue, Bloomfield, MI 48013
Tel: (313) 642-3400

Chairman: Harold M Marko
President: Richard T Walsh
Senior Executive Officers: Wendel Calderwood (VP), Lawrence J Murphy (VP Finance and Secretary), Thomas G Hooper (Treasurer and Controller)

PRINCIPAL ACTIVITIES: Manufacture of electrical and electronic equipment, agricultural machinery, fluid control and construction products, and industrial products
Principal Subsidiaries: Anilam Electronics; Robert Carter Corporation; Cherokee International; Feterl Manufacturing Co; GSE Inc; Hilton Industries Inc; Pasar Inc; Poly-Craft Inc; Sunflower Manufacturing Co; SOSS of Singapore Pte Ltd
Principal Bank: National Bank of Detroit
Financial Information:

	Aug 31 1986
	$'000
Sales revenues	163,513
Income before taxes(1)	16,120
Net income(1)	9,320
Dividends	5,758
Dividends per share	$0.59
Earnings per share(1)	$0.96
Common stock(2)	5,209
Retained income	89,052
Shareholders equity	94,261

(1) from continuing operations
(2) includes common stock and additional paid-in capital, less cost of treasury stock

No of Employees: 2,000

CORESTATES FINANCIAL CORP

Broad & Chestnut Streets, PO Box 7618, Philadelphia, PA 19101
Tel: (215) 629-3553
Telex: 244-477 bankphil ur

Chairman: G Morris Dorrance Jr (and Chief Executive Officer)
President: Terrence A Larsen (and Chief Operating Officer)
Senior Executive Officers: CoreStates Vice Chairmen, Managing Committee: Gregory C Dillett (Finance and Administration), Roland K Bullard (Commercial and Investment Banking), Bipin C Shah (Processing Services and Systems Group, National Electronic and Card Services Group), John H Walther (Consumer Banking and Chairman of New Jersey National Bank), Frederick Heldring (Chairman and Chief Executive Officer of Philadelphia National Bank), Wilson B McElhinny (Chairman, Hamilton Bank), Richard S Ravenscroft. CoreStates Financial Corp Executive Vice Presidents: Rolland K Bullard, Donald M Cooper, Gregory C Dillett (Chief Financial Officer), Paul G Finegan, Joseph K Gordon (Chief Counsel), A Gilbert Heebner (Economist), Rosemary O'Malley Laphen, Terrence A Larsen, George D Norton, Bipin C Shah, Robert D Siff (Chief Credit Policy Officer). Philadelphia National Bank President: Robert B Palmer. Philadelphia Natioanl Bank Executive Vice Presidents: Charles L Coltman (Executive Director of National and International Banking), Robert B Murray (Regional Banking Group), Robert P Spencer (Chief Credit Policy Officer). Philadelphia National Limited Executive Vice President: James Hildabrandt (Chief Executive Officer). Hamilton Bank President: William M Fenimore Jr. New Jersey National Bank Resident: John D Wallace. New Jersey National Bank Executive Vice President: Robert B Murray (Credit Policy)

PRINCIPAL ACTIVITIES: Banking: Philadelphia National Bank and Hamilton Bank, the principal banking subsidiaries of the corporation, provide businesses, banks, government entities and individuals a variety of financial services including credit, deposit, transactional, international, correspondent, trust and investment management services. In cooperation with each other the banks manage their own dealer and trading activities. The banks market their services extensively in the CoreStates region including Pennsylvania, New Jersey, Delaware, Maryland and Virginia, and selectively around the world with offices in key financial centers. They deliver comprehensive retail services through branch networks in southeastern and south central Pennsylvania. CoreStates Bank of Delaware NA, based in Wilmington, conducts the corporation's credit card and certain related consumer lending businesses. Commercial Finance: Congress Financial Corporation provides factoring secured lending services nationwide from offices in seven states and Puerto Rico. Consumer Finance: Signal Financial Corporation makes direct, personal installment loans and secured personal loans, issues consumer investment certificates, purchases consumer sales finance contracts and provides credit-related insurance in six states. Other Financial Services: CoreStates Capital Markets Group conducts investment dealer activities, underwriters and assists with state and local government bond issues. Philadelphia Capital Advisors performs corporate financial advisory services including valuations mergers and acquisitions, and private placements. International Finance: Philadelphia International Investment Corporation engages in foreign investment and financing activities, including holding equity interests in foreign financial institutions

Trade Names: CoreStates Financial Corp, Philadelphia National Bank, New Jersey National Bank; Hamilton Bank, CoreStates Bank of Delaware NA, Congress Financial, New Jersey National Bank Corporation, Signal Financial Corporation

Principal Subsidiaries: CoreStates Financial Corp; CoreStates Capital Corp; Philadelphia National Bank; New Jersey National Bank; Hamilton Bank; CoreStates Bank of Delaware NA; Congress Financial Corporation; Congress Factors Corporation; Signal Financial Corporation; CoreStates Capital Markets Group; Philadelphia Capital Advisors; Philadelphia International Bank; Phildelphia International Investment Corporation

Principal Bank: Philadelphia National Bank

Financial Information:

	Dec 31 1985(1)	Dec 31 1986
	$'000	$'000
Income before taxes(2)	122,196	177,425
Net income(3)	202,021	114,997
Dividends declared(3)	40,770	47,122
Dividends per share(4)	$1.14	$1.27
Earnings per share(5)	$5.22	$2.94
Earnings per share(6)	$2.74	$3.57
Common stock(4)	307,507	317,794
Retained income	536,590	605,302
Shareholders equity	900,396	978,877
Deposits	9,614,151	10,636,974
Total assets	13,122,321	14,595,402

(1) restated to reflect the October 30 1986 merger with New Jersey National Corporation under the pooling of interests method of accounting

(2) income from continuing operations before tax and extraordinary items

(3) applicable to common stock

(4) net income

(5) per common share; net income

(6) per common share; income from continuing operations before extraordinary items

(7) and capital surplus

No of Employees: 5,600

COREY STEEL CO

2800 S 61st Court, Cicero, IL 60650
Tel: (312) 242-3000
Telex: TWX 910 2291 540 corey steel

Chairman: Paul J Darling Sr
President: Paul J Darling II (and Chief Executive Officer)
Senior Executive Officers: William D Perkins (Executive VP Engineering and Operations), Robert E Vassar (VP and Assistant Secretary), Kevin A Lavery (Assistant VP and Operations Manager)

PRINCIPAL ACTIVITIES: Manufacture of steel products; steel service center
Principal Bank: Harris Trust and Savings Bank
Financial Information:

	$'000
Sales revenues	53,000

No of Employees: 220

CORNELL-DUBILIER ELECTRONICS

Wayne Interchange Plaza, Wayne, NJ 07470
Tel: (201) 256-2000

President: J R Kaplan
Senior Executive Officers: A Jenkins (Senior VP), R Breed (Senior VP), A Cavuto (VP Sales), E Read (VP Marketing)

PRINCIPAL ACTIVITIES: Manufacture of electronic equipment
Financial Information:

	$'000
Sales revenues	75,000

CORNING GLASS WORKS

Houghton Park, Corning, NY 14831
Tel: (607) 974-9000

Chairman: James R Houghton (and Chief Executive Officer); Chairman of Executive Committee: Amory Houghton Jr; Vice Chairmen: Thomas C MacAvoy, Van C Campbell (Finance and Administration)
Presidents: Richard Dulude (Electronics and Telecommunications Group), William H Hudson (Consumer and Industry Group)
Senior Executive Officers: Roger G Ackerman (Senior VP Manufacturing and Engineering Division), Forrest E Behm (Senior VP, General Manager Electrical and Electronic Products Division), James L Flynn (Senior VP and Treasurer), Kenneth W Freeman (Senior VP and Controller), William C Ughetta (Senior VP and Legal Counsel), John R Hutchins III (Senior VP Research and Development Division), James E Riesbeck (Senior VP), Conrad R Stemski (Senior VP Administration), Eric N Birch (VP), Robert C Buhrmaster (VP), Allan D Cors (VP Government Affairs), Henry F Frailey (VP Productivity Program), Norman E Garrity (VP), Susan B King (VP Corporate Communications and Consumer Affairs), Mary L Bundy (VP Manufacturing Services), David B Luther (VP Personnel), Richard C Marks (VP), Francis H Olmstead (VP, General Manager TV Products), Richard E Rahill (VP, General Manager Electronic Components), Paul J Regan Jr (VP), Richard J Sphon (VP), David N Van Allen (VP General Manager Consumer Products)

PRINCIPAL ACTIVITIES: Manufacture of a wide range of glass products for industry and the home
Principal Subsidiaries: Corning International Corpn; Corning Enterprises Inc; Corning Europe Inc (France); Corning Glas GmbH (Germany); Components Inc; Corning Canada Inc; Corning Ltd (UK); Productos Corning de Mexico SA de CV; Sovcor SA (France); Corning Brasil-Vidros Especiais Ltda (Brazil); EIVS SA (France); QVF Glastechnik GmbH (Germany); Corning France SA; Draloric Electronic GmbH (Germany); Gilford Instrument Laboratories Inc; K C Biological Inc; Metpath Inc; Corning (HK) Ltd (Hong Kong); Corning Medical GmbH (Germany); Corning Japan Inc; Corning KK (Japan); Corning Latin America/Asia Pacific Inc; Corning Medical KK (Japan); Corning SpA (Italy); Corning Trading (Sengapore) Pte Ltd; IMA Gilford Analysentechnik GmbH (Germany); Malkin Ltd (UK); Rigolleau SA (Argentina); Teddington Co Ltd (Bermuda)
Principal Bank: Citibank

Financial Information:

	Dec 31 1986
	$'000
Sales revenues	1,856,300
Net income	177,100
Earnings per share	$4.04
Shareholders equity	1,352,500

No of Employees: 30,500

CORONET INDUSTRIES, INC

Cleveland Road, Dalton, GA 30720
Tel: (404) 259-4511
Telex: WUT 543 416 coronet dto b

Chairman: M B Seretean
President: Stanley R Peszat (and Chief Executive Officer)
Senior Executive Officers: Walter J Moryl (Executive VP Finance and Treasurer), G Myers (VP Industrial Relations), E M Overby (VP and Secretary)

PRINCIPAL ACTIVITIES: Manufacture of tufted carpets and plastic goods
Parent Company: RCA Corp, New York, NY
Principal Bank: First Atlanta Corp
Financial Information:

	$'000
Sales revenues	350,000

No of Employees: 4,000

CORROON & BLACK CORPORATION

Wall Street Plaza, New York, NY 10005
Tel: (212) 363 4100

Chairman: Robert F Corroon (and Chief Executive Officer)
President: Richard M Miller (and Chief Operating Officer)
Senior Executive Officers: Frank M Hagan (Chairman Executive Committee), Joseph V Ambrose Jr (Senior VP, Secretary and Legal Counsel), Crawford A Black (Senior VP), C Jackson Blair (Senior VP, VP Administration and Human Resources), Paul T Carter (Senior VP), Stephen A Crane (Senior VP and Chief Financial Officer), Joseph O Estes (Senior VP), Donald R King (Senior VP), J Bransford Wallace (Senior VP), Jennifer B Cartwell (VP and Treasurer), Robert P Cuthbert (VP and Controller), James V Davis (VP), Marnix L Guillaume (VP International), John R Lamberson (VP), Gerald W Cusack (VP Information Systems)

PRINCIPAL ACTIVITIES: Insurance services
Principal Subsidiaries: Corroon & Black Inc; Corroon & Black of Michigan; Corroon & Black of Nashville; Corroon & Black; Corroon-Black; Powers Carpenter and Hall Inc; Relex Inc
Principal Bank: Manufacturers Hanover Trust Co
Financial Information:

	Dec 31 1985	Dec 31 1986
	$'000	$'000
Revenues	263,500	338,000
Net income	28,000	42,000

No of Employees: 3,800

CORVUS SYSTEMS, INC

160 Great Oaks Blvd, San Jose, CA 95119-1347
Tel: (408) 281-4100
Telex: 278976

Chairman: Roger Mosher
President: Lewis T Lipton (and Chief Executive Officer)
Senior Executive Officers: W G Herrick (Controller and Acting Chief Financial Officer), J D Hughes (VP and Secretary), Joseph W Rooney (Executive VP), Robert W Butche (Secretary)

PRINCIPAL ACTIVITIES: Manufacture of computer peripherals
Trade Names: Corvus, Omninet, PC-NOS
Principal Subsidiaries: Corvus Systems UK, France, Canada

Financial Information:

	May 31 1986	May 31 1987
	$'000	$'000
Sales revenues	42,137	36,053
(Loss) before taxes	(32,428)	(19,643)
Net (loss)	(32,428)	(19,780)
Common stock	63,907	66,428
Retained (deficit)	(48,032)	(67,802)
Shareholders equity (deficit)	15,875	(1,374)

No of Employees: 160

COSMAIR, INC

575 Fifth Avenue, New York, NY 10017
Tel: (212) 818-1500
Telex: ITT 421973 COS UI

Chairman: Jacques H Correze
President: Guy Peyrelongue (and Chief Executive Officer)
Senior Executive Officers: James Nixon (Executive VP), Joseph Augeri (Executive VP), Roy Benjamin (President, Retail Divisions), Rodolphe d'Ornano (Senior VP, North American Zone), Roger Dolden (VP Business Planning), Christian Boutin (Senior VP Manufacturing), John Penicnak (Senior VP, Research and Development), Dermot Flynn (VP, Human Resources), Richard Furlong (Treasurer), John Sullivan (Corporate Counsel)

PRINCIPAL ACTIVITIES: Manufacture of beauty products
Trade Names: L'Oréal, Lancôme, Biotherm. Fragrances: Ralph Lauren, Paloma Picasso, Guy Laroche, Cacharel
Parent Company: L'Oréal SA
Principal Bank: Morgan Guaranty and Trust Co
Financial Information:

	$'000
Sales revenues	730,000

No of Employees: 3,200

COSMO COMMUNICATIONS CORPORATION

16501 Northwest 16th Court, Miami, FL 33169
Tel: (305) 621 4227

Chairman: Amancio Victor Suarez (and President and Chief Executive Officer)
Senior Executive Officers: Jorge A Rodriguez (Executive VP and Secretary), Yu Wing Kin (VP Administration), Richard Franklin (VP Sales), Lim Lap Wah (VP Manufacturing)

PRINCIPAL ACTIVITIES: Manufacture of clocks, watches and consumer electronic products
Principal Bank: Chase Manhattan Bank
Financial Information:

	$'000
Sales revenues	60,000

No of Employees: 500

COSMOPOLITAN CARE CORPORATION

330 7th Avenue, New York, NY 10001
Tel: (212) 736 0700

Chairman: Ronald Berman (and President and Chief Executive Officer)
Senior Executive Officers: Joel A Klarreich (Executive VP and Legal Counsel), Robert Feldman (Senior VP), Larry Saltzman (VP Administration), Henry Lowenstein (VP Home Health Care Division), Sheldon Fox (Treasurer), Bernice Berman (Secretary)

PRINCIPAL ACTIVITIES: Supply of temporary staff
Principal Bank: National Westminster Bank
Financial Information:

	$'000
Sales revenues	94,000

No of Employees: 250

COTTER & CO

2740-52 N Clyborne Avenue, Chicago, IL 60614
Tel: (312) 975-2700
Telex: WUT 253587 cottert vvs cgo

Chairman: John M Cotter
President: Daniel A Cotter (and Chief Executive Officer)
Senior Executive Officers: Paul F Fee (Executive VP and Chief Operating Officer), Richard Lynn (VP), B Maze (VP), Edward E Lanctot (Secretary, Treasurer and Advertising Manager)

PRINCIPAL ACTIVITIES: Manufacture of garden machinery, sport and leisure goods and home hardware
Principal Subsidiaries: Cotter Acceptance Co Inc; Cotter Data Services Inc; Cotter Finance Co Inc; Warner Industrial Supply Inc; Warner True Value Hardware Inc; Wheeler Manufacturing Co
Principal Bank: Harris Trust and Savings Bank
Financial Information:

	$'000
Sales revenues	1,150,000

No of Employees: 2,500

COTY DIVISION

235 E 42nd Street, New York, NY 10017
Tel: (212) 573-3500

President: Joseph Harmon
Senior Executive Officers: Joseph Markowski (VP Marketing), William Doran (VP Research and Development), Jerry Abernathy (VP Sales)

PRINCIPAL ACTIVITIES: Manufacture of beauty products including cosmetics and perfumes
Parent Company: Pfizer Inc, New York, NY
Principal Bank: Chase Manhattan Bank
Financial Information:

	$'000
Sales revenues	100,000

No of Employees: 1,000

COUNTRY FRESH, INC

2555 Buchanan Avenue SW, Grand Rapids, MI 49508
Tel: (616) 243-0173

Chairman: J V Eberhard
President: Delton C Parks (and General Manager)
Senior Executive Officers: Robert Leppink (VP), Ronald De Young (Secretary and Treasurer)

PRINCIPAL ACTIVITIES: Manufacture of dairy products
Principal Subsidiaries: Embest Inc
Principal Bank: Old Kent Bank and Trust Co
Financial Information:

	$'000
Sales revenues	135,000

No of Employees: 300

COUNTRYMARK, INC

35 E Chestnut Street, PO Box 479, Columbus, OH 43216
Tel: (614) 225-8711

Chairman: Donald Benschneider; Vice Chairman: Clark Boatman
President: W Loren Chalfin
Senior Executive Officers: Robert Scherer (Executive VP), Steve Buckalew (VP Local Operations), William Cubbage (VP Agronomy and Supply), Dennis C Sargent (VP Administration), Gene Newsom (VP Feed and Petroleum)

PRINCIPAL ACTIVITIES: Countrymark, Inc was formed from a merger of Landmark, Inc and Ohio Farmers Grain & Supply Association. It is a farmer-owned wholesale cooperative engaged in the manufacture of agricultural supplies including fertilizers and animal feeds; processing of food products including meat and dairy products
Principal Bank: The Huntington National Bank
Financial Information:

	Aug 31 1986
	$'000
Sales revenues	834,280
Shareholders equity	55,160

No of Employees: 890

COUNTRYWIDE CREDIT INDUSTRIES INC

155 North Lake Avenue, Pasadena, CA 91101
Tel: (818) 304 8400

Chairman: David S Loeb (and President)
Senior Executive Officers: Angelo R Mozilo (Executive VP), Lee Bartlett (Senior VP), Stanford L Kurland (Senior VP and Chief Financial Officer), Ralph S Mozilo (Senior VP), Jovita B Vera (VP and Treasurer), Wayne Turkheimer (Secretary), Robert Miller (VP Marketing)

PRINCIPAL ACTIVITIES: Financial services inlcuding mortgages and loans
Principal Subsidiaries: Countrywide Acceptance Corporation; Countrywide Agency Inc; Countrywide Funding Corporation; Countrywide Securities Corporation; Countrywide Thrift & Loan
Principal Bank: Bank of America

No of Employees: 700

COURIER CORPORATION

165 Jackson Street, Lowell, MA 01852
Tel: (617) 458-6351

Chairman: James F Conway Jr (and Chief Executive Officer)
President: A French Jr (and Chief Operating Officer)
Senior Executive Officers: Robert C McCallum (Senior VP), John W Martin (Senior VP and Chief Financial Officer), Robert P Story Jr (VP and Treasurer), Peter M Folger (Controller), Donald A Taft (VP), Jas Murray Howe (Clerk and Secretary)

PRINCIPAL ACTIVITIES: Courier Corporation provides a broad range of capabilities in the printing and manufacturing of books and telephone directories. The business of Courier is conducted by the following five operating units. The Murray Printing Company of Westford, Massachusetts is a high quality manufacturer of educational, trade and scientific books. National Publishing Company in Philadelphia, Pennsylvania, prints and binds Bibles, religious books and reference texts utilizing lightweight papers. North American Directory Corporation located in Lowell, Massachusetts, prints and binds telephone subscriber directories including white and yellow pages, for three major Regional Bell Operating Companies in the Northeast and a Number of independent telephone directory customers. Alpine manufactures hardcover and softbound books primarily for educational, trade and high-technology customers. Anchor Brendon, located in the United Kingdom, provides paperback and casebound book production primarily to trade publishers
Principal Subsidiaries: The Murray Printing Company; National Publishing Company; Courier-Citizen Company; The Alpine Press Inc; North American Directory Corporation; Anchor Brendon Limited
Principal Bank: State Street Bank and Trust
Financial Information:

	Sep 28 1985	Sep 27 1986
	$'000	$'000
Sales revenues	103,686	122,517
Income before taxes	8,375	5,563
Net income	4,736	3,711
Dividends	777	812
Dividends per share	$0.35	$0.40
Earnings per share	$2.11	$1.82
Common stock	3,000	4,500
Retained earnings	35,180	38,079
Shareholders equity	30,162	29,947

No of Employees: 1,736

COURIER-JOURNAL & LOUISVILLE TIMES CO

525 W Broadway, Louisville, KY 40202
Tel: (502) 582-4011

President: George Gill (and Publisher)
Senior Executive Officers: Bernard Block (Senior VP), Donald B Towles (VP Public Affairs), Ralph Drury (VP Operations), J L VonderHarr (VP Human Resources), James D Marchal (VP Advertising), David Thomas (VP Circulation)

PRINCIPAL ACTIVITIES: Publication of newspapers
Trade Names: The Courier-Journal
Parent Company: Gannett Co, Inc

No of Employees: 1,100

COUSINS HOME FURNISHINGS INC

11230 Sorrento Valley Road, San Diego, CA 92121
Tel: (619) 452 5560

Chairman: M J McKeon (and Chief Executive Officer)
President: D P Selznick (and Chief Operating Officer)
Senior Executive Officers: Conrad E Brownlee (Secretary, Treasurer and Chief Financial Officer), Harris Blickstein (VP Merchandising), Sam R Levitz (VP Merchandising), Gary C Reif (VP Soft Furnishings and Subsidiary Officer), Razelle L Selznick (VP Product Area)

PRINCIPAL ACTIVITIES: Retailing of furniture and other home furnishing products
Principal Subsidiaries: SA Levitz Inc
Principal Bank: Wells Fargo Bank
Financial Information:

	$'000
Sales revenues	124,000

No of Employees: 1,000

COUSINS PROPERTIES INCORPORATED

2500 Windy Ridge Parkway, Suite 1600, Marietta, GA 30067
Tel: (404) 955 2200

Chairman: Thomas G Cousins (and President and Chief Executive Officer)
Senior Executive Officers: Vipin L Patel (Executive VP), Robert P Hunter Jr (Senior VP, Secretary and Legal Counsel), Peter A Tartikoff (Senior VP Finance)

PRINCIPAL ACTIVITIES: Development of property and real estate
Principal Bank: Trust Company Bank
Financial Information:

	Dec 31 1985	Dec 31 1986
	$'000	$'000
Sales revenues	38,910	52,526
Income before taxes	14,541	42,070
Net income	9,365	29,570
Dividends	2,891	3,353
Dividends per share	$0.25	$0.29
Earnings per share	0.82	$2.59
Common stock	13,491	13,491
Retained income	47,738	73,955
Shareholders equity	45,480	71,951

Principal Shareholders: Thomas G Cousins
No of Employees: 6

COVINGTON TECHNOLOGIES

2451 E Orangethorpe Avenue, Fullerton, CA 92631
Tel: (714) 879-0111

Chairman: Loran D Covington (and Chief Executive Officer)
President: Robert P Fitzpatrick (and Chief Operating Officer)
Senior Executive Officers: Donald L Lloyd (VP International Division), Barry Zimmerman (VP Housing Division)

PRINCIPAL ACTIVITIES: Construction of homes and manufacture of building materials and construction equipment
Principal Bank: Security Pacific National Bank
Financial Information:

	$'000
Sales revenues	38,000

No of Employees: 180

COWLES MEDIA CO

329 Portland Avenue, Minneapolis, MN 55415
Tel: (612) 375-7000

Chairman: David Kruidenier (and Chief Executive Officer)
President: David C Cox (and Chief Operating Officer and Treasurer)
Senior Executive Officers: Roger P Parkinson (Executive VP), James A Alcott (VP Administration), John J Grieman (VP and Controller), Hazel H Reinhardt (VP Market Development), Alan W Zaeske (VP Human Resources)

PRINCIPAL ACTIVITIES: Newspaper publishers
Principal Subsidiaries: Great Falls Tribune Co; Information Publishers Inc; Rapid City Journal Co Inc; Sentinel Publishing Co
Principal Bank: First National Bank
Financial Information:

	$'000
Sales revenues	240,000

No of Employees: 2,850

COX CABLE COMMUNICATIONS INC

1400 Lake Hearn Drive, Atlanta, GA 30319
Tel: (404) 843-5000

President: David Van Valkenburg; Vice President: Lew Davenport
Senior Executive Officers: Arthur A Dwyer (Senior VP Operations), Robert O'Leary (Senior VP Finance), Garold S Tjaden (Senior VP Engineering and Technology), Paul Waring (Senior VP Corporate Development), David C Andersen (Director Public Relations)

PRINCIPAL ACTIVITIES: Provision of telecommunication and security services
Parent Company: Cox Communications Inc, New York, NY, ultimate parent company, Cox Enterprises Inc
Financial Information:

	$'000
Sales revenues	340,000

No of Employees: 4,020

COX COMMUNICATIONS, INC

1400 Lake Hearn Drive, Atlanta, GA 30348
Tel: (404) 843-5000

Chairman of Executive Committee: Garner Anthony
President: William A Schwartz (and Chief Executive Officer)
Senior Executive Officers: Stanley G Mouse (Senior VP), Frederick R Barber Jr (VP), Alan J Bell (VP), John R Dillon (VP Finance and Chief Financial Officer)

PRINCIPAL ACTIVITIES: Operation of radio and television services; cable television
Parent Company: Cox Enterprises Inc
Principal Subsidiaries: Cox Cable Communications Inc
Principal Bank: First National Bank of Atlanta
Financial Information:

	$'000
Sales revenues	740,000

No of Employees: 8,600

COX ENTERPRISES INC

72 Marietta Street NW, Atlanta, GA 30303
Tel: (404) 572-5537

Chairman: Garner Anthony
President: William A Schwartz (and Chief Operating Officer)

Senior Executive Officers: Charles E Glover (Executive VP), Carl Gross (Senior VP and Chief Administration Officer), Richard Tatum (VP, Secretary and Treasurer), John R Dillon (VP Finance and Chief Financial Officer), Timothy W Hughes (VP Human Resources)

PRINCIPAL ACTIVITIES: Publication of newspapers; trucking services

Principal Subsidiaries: Clarendon Farms Inc; Cox AZ Publications Inc; Cox Cable Queens Inc; Cox Communications Inc; California Services Corp; Carolina Broadcasting Co; Cox Cable Communications Inc; Cablerep Inc; Commline Inc; Commline New Orleans Inc; Commline Omaha Inc; Commline Tucson Inc; Cox Cable Cedar Rapids Inc; Cox Cable Cranston/Johnson Inc; Roanoke Valley Cablevision; Video Service Co; Cox Radio Systems Inc; Indax corp; Portvision Cable Co Inc; Telesystems Corp; Trans-Video Corp; Pan-Oklahoma Corp; Bing Crosby Productions Inc; Cybertel Corp; KFI Inc; Manheim Services Corp; Miami Valley Broadcasting Corp; Midwest Services Corp; New England Auto Auction Inc; North Carolina Services Corp; Pennsylvania Services Corp; Tele-Rep Inc; Wisconsin Services Corp; WKBD Inc; WLIF Inc; WPXI Corp; WWSH Inc; Dayton Newspapers Inc; Grand Junction Newspapers Inc; Guide Newspaper Corp; Longview Newspaper Inc; Miami Daily News Inc; Palm Beach Newspapers Inc; Springfield Newspapers Inc; Sun Printing Co; TSC Express Co

Principal Bank: Texas Commerce Bank

Financial Information:

	$'000
Sales revenues	1,500,000

No of Employees: 8,000

CP NATIONAL CORPORATION

120 Montgomery Street, San Francisco, CA 94104
Tel: (415) 397 8580

Chairman: Ben W Agee (and President and Chief Executive Officer)

Senior Executive Officers: Albert H Eaton (Executive VP), Michael E Holmstrom (Executive VP and Chief Financial Officer), Donn T Wonnell (Executive VP and Chief Administrative Officer), Marvin S Litt (Senior VP, Legal Counsel and Secretary), Michael L French (Assistant VP and Controller), John C Grimm (Assistant VP Finance and Treasurer)

PRINCIPAL ACTIVITIES: Telecommunications and energy services; telephone, natural gas, water and electricity services

Principal Bank: Bank of America

Financial Information:

	Dec 31 1985
	$'000
Sales revenues	250,370
Net income	21,080

No of Employees: 2,220

CPC INTERNATIONAL INC

International Plaza, PO Box 8000, Englewood Cliffs, NJ 07632
Tel: (201) 894-4000

Chairman: James R Eiszner (and President and Chief Executive Officer)

Senior Executive Officers: Ivan A Burns (Corporate Executive VP), Wolfgang Hesse (Corporate Executive VP and President, International Consumer Products Group), Richard W Siebrasse (Corporate Executive VP and President, Best Foods Division), Clifford B Storms (VP and General Counsel), Richard P Bergeman (VP, Human Resources), William F Cody (VP and President, Cooperative Management Group, Corn Wet Milling Division), Charles Feldberg (VP, Health, Safety and Quality Assurance), Robert J Gillespie (VP and Executive VP, Best Foods Division), Delbert A Gregory (VP and Chief Liaison Officer, International Consumer Products Group), Paul E Grunder (VP, Corporate Affairs), Howard F Harris (VP, Corporate Affairs), Eric D Haueter (VP, Corporate Business Research and External Affairs), Osvaldo A Martinez (VP and President, CPC Consumer Products Division), Fred C Meendsen (VP and President, North American Region, Corn Wet Milling Divisions), Andre M Osser (VP and President, Latin American Region, Corn Wet Milling Division), John W Scott (VP, Capital Expenditures and Systems), Charles R Shoemate (VP, President, Corn Wet Milling Division), Richard A Zuniga (VP and Senior VP Administration and Finance, CPC Europe Consumer Products Division), Ronald K Moss (VP and President, CPC Europe Consumer Products Division), Konrad Schlatter (VP, Financial Planning, Reporting and Control), Angelo S Abdela (Treasurer), John B Meagher (Secretary), James E Healey (Comptroller)

PRINCIPAL ACTIVITIES: CPC International is a worldwide group of businesses, principally engaged in two major industry sectors: grocery products and corn wet milling. CPC's grocery products include soups, sauces, bouillons, mayonnaise, corn oil, peanut butter, margarine and other bread spread and cheese products, English muffins, pasta, corn starch, syrups and desserts. CPC is the world's largest corn wet miller and produces a wide range of products used by over 70 different industries. These products include corn starches, corn syrups, high fructose corn syrups and dextrose, as well as corn oil and animal feed ingredients

Trade Names: Hellmann's, Best Foods (mayonnaise and salad dressings), Mazola (corn oil), Knorr (dehydrated and canned soups, bouillons, sauces, gravies, base mixes), Mealmakers (snack meals), Knorr Aromat (seasonings), Knorr Stocki (potato products), Skippy, Lady's Choice (peanut butter), Mazola, Nucoa, Marina (margarines), Thomas' (English muffins and specialty baked goods), Sahara (pita bread), Adler, Bavaria, Quelac, Cheesy, Frischette (cheese products), Maizena, Argo, Duryea, Brown & Polson (corn starches and corn flours), Mondamin Fix, Veloutine, Maizena Express (sauce binders), Mueller's Royal, Best Foods (pastas), Karo, Golden Griddle, Old Tyme (syrups), Dextropur, Dextro-Energen, Dextrosol (quick energy products), Alsa, Lady's Choice, Majala (desserts and baking aids), Hirz (dairy products), Robertsons (seasonings and spices), Fruco (catsup, mayonnaise, canned vegetables and fruits), H-O, Knorr, Uncle Tobys (oats), Chirat (condiments, sauces, and mayonnaise), Caterplan (products and systems for the food service industry), Niagara, Argo (laundry starches), Rit (tints and dyes), Gerber (baby foods under European license from Gerber Products Company)

Principal Subsidiaries: (100% owned unless stated): United States: CPC Europe (Group) Ltd; Best Foods-Caribbean Inc; Peterson/Puritan Inc; S B Thomas Inc; C F Mueller Co; Acme Resin Corp; Amerchol Corp; Penick Corp. Canada: Canada Starch Company Inc (99.9%). Netherlands Antilles: CPC Finance NV. Europe and Africa: Knorr Holding Gesellschaft mbH (Austria); Mais-Monda SA (99.9%) (Belgium); CPC Danmark A/S (Denmark); CPC (United Kingdom) Ltd (UK); OY Suomen CPC (Finland); Société des Produits du Mais SA (99.9%); Maizena Gesellschaft mbH (Germany); Knorr (Hellas) ABEE (Greece); CPC Netherland BV (Netherlands); CPC (Ireland) Ltd (Eire); Fabbriche Riunite Amido Glucosio Destrina SpA (86.3%) (Italy); CPC Kenya Ltd (89.39%) (Kenya); CPC Maghreb SA (Morocco); CPC Norge A/S (Norway); Knorr Portuguesa-Produtos Alimentares SARL (Portugal); CPC South Africa (Pty) Ltd (South Africa); CPC Espana SA (Spain); CPC Svenska Livsmedel AB (Sweden); Knorr Zurich AG (Switzerland). Latin America: Refinerias de Maiz SAIC (Argentina); Refinacoes de Milho, Brasil Ltda (Brazil); Industrias de Maiz y Alimentos SA (Chile); Maizena SA (Colombia); Productos de Maiz y Alimentos SA (Guatemala); Almidones del Istmo SA de CV (Honduras); Productos de Maiz SA (Mexico); Alimentos y Productos de Maiz SA (95.86%) (Peru); Industrializadora de Maiz SA (Uruguay); Aliven SA (Venezuela). Asia: Clifford Love & Co Ltd (Australia); Corn Products Co (Hong Kong) Ltd (Hong Kong); CPC Japan Ltd (Japan); CPC (Malaysia) Sdn Berhad

(Malaysia); Rafhan Maize Products Co Ltd (51%) (Pakistan); California Manufacturing Co Inc (Philippines); CPC (Taiwan) Ltd (Taiwan); CPC Thailand Ltd (Thailand)

Financial Information:

	Dec 31 1985	Dec 31 1986
	$'000	$'000
Sales revenues	4,029,900	4,548,800
Income before taxes	234,200	380,900
Net income	142,000	219,200
Dividends	106,900	106,000
Dividends per share	$1.10	$1.13
Earnings per share	$1.46	$2.30
Common stock	12,200	24,400
Retained earnings	1,359,900	1,472,300
Total shareholders equity	1,371,900	956,100

No of Employees: 38,000

CPI CORPORATION

1706 Washington Avenue, St Louis, MO 63103
Tel: (314) 231 1575

Chairman: Alyn V Essman (and Chief Executive Officer); Vice Chairman: M Strauss (and Secretary)
President: Sander Coovert (and Chief Operating Officer)
Senior Executive Officers: Milford Bohm (Executive Officer), Russell Isaak (Executive VP Finance and Administration and Chief Financial Officer), Alvin G Beck (Executive VP Manufacturing), Paul Latta (Executive VP Corporate Development and Marketing), R E Arnold (Divisional President)

PRINCIPAL ACTIVITIES: Photographic services and processing
Principal Subsidiaries: Consumer Programs Inc; CPI Office Equipment and Printing Company; F J Pechman Inc
Principal Bank: Mercantile Trust Company
Financial Information:

	$'000
Sales revenues	198,295

No of Employees: 5,000

CPT CORPORATION

8100 Mitchell Road, Eden Prairie, MN 55344
Tel: (612) 937-8000
Telex: WUT 290 775 cpt corp enpe

Chairman: Dean F Scheff (and Chief Executive and Operating Officer)
Senior Executive Officers: Lawrence Bunka (Senior VP), Steven Graham (VP Sales), Ted Manakas (VP International Sales), Bruce Hurwitz (VP Engineering), Clarence Lehman (VP Research), Fred Valfer (VP Customer Services), Eugene V Dimenna (VP Procurement), Paul Moquist (VP Branch Sales), James Kaufenberg (VP and Chief Financial Officer), Elizabeth Schweizer (Treasurer), Gerald Galush (VP Manufacturing)

PRINCIPAL ACTIVITIES: Manufacture of office automation equipment
Principal Bank: First National Bank of St Paul
Financial Information:

	$'000
Sales revenues	150,000

No of Employees: 1,200

CRACKER BARREL OLD COUNTRY STORE INC

Hartmann Drive, PO Box 787, Lebanon, TN 37088-0787
Tel: (615) 444 5533

Chairman: Dan W Evins (and President and Chief Executive Officer)
Senior Executive Officers: Donald M Turner (Senior VP Operations), Mattie H Hankins (VP and Controller), Benton Van Winkle (VP and Treasurer), Jimmie D White (VP Finance and Chief Financial Officer), Evalina C Bennett (Secretary), L Ted Mason (VP Marketing), Wayne Jerkins (VP Human Resources), Kenneth L Dingler (VP Property Development), Rich Parsons (VP Merchandising)

PRINCIPAL ACTIVITIES: Restaurants
Principal Bank: The Peoples Bank
Financial Information:

	$'000
Sales revenues	67,505

No of Employees: 2,900

CRADDOCK-TERRY SHOE CORPORATION

3100 Albert Lankford Drive, Lynchburg, VA 24506
Tel: (804) 845-3411
Telex: TWX 710 87 11 504 cradterry lurg

President: G B Miller (and Chief Executive Officer)
Senior Executive Officers: R K Peters (VP Administration), Edward F Haley (VP Mail Order), R H Newman (VP Marketing), James S Barrett II (VP Sales), S P Craighill Jr (VP Sales), John W Froman (VP Sales), Malcolm K Sydnor (VP Sales), Elias Richards III (VP and Secretary), F E Thomas (Treasurer and Controller), F Rogers Vaden (VP Sales)

PRINCIPAL ACTIVITIES: Manufacture of footwear; mail order and retail sale of footwear
Parent Company: H H Holdings Inc
Financial Information:

	$'000
Sales revenues	83,000

No of Employees: 3,000

CRAIG CORPORATION

116 N Robertson Blvd, Suite 609, Los Angeles, CA 90048
Tel: (213) 659-6641
Telefax: (213) 659-9120

Chairman: Paul O Koether
President: Peter M Behrendt
Senior Executive Officers: Robert L Woolheater (VP, Secretary and Treasurer) Charles J Smith (Controller and Assistant Secretary)

PRINCIPAL ACTIVITIES: Retail supermarkets
Trade Names: Stater Bros
Principal Subsidiaries: Stater Bros Inc
Principal Bank: Bank of America
Financial Information:

	Jun 30 1986	Jun 30 1987
	$'000	$'000
Sales revenues	8,271	954,542
Net income	1,139	2,684
Earnings per share	$0.98	$1.45
Common stock	788	788
Retained income	24,758	27,442
Shareholders equity	15,599	19,432

Principal Shareholders: James J Cotter; HECCO Ventures
No of Employees: 5,600

CRANE & CO, INC

30 South Street, Dalton, MA 01226
Tel: (413) 684-2600
Telex: TWX 710 3520 124 crane co dtom

Chairman: Benjamin J Sullivan (and Chief Executive Officer)
President: Thomas H White (and Chief Operating Officer)
Senior Executive Officers: J B McInerney (VP Marketing), Stephen H Wismer (Executive VP and Treasurer)

PRINCIPAL ACTIVITIES: Manufacture of a wide range of paper; printing
Financial Information:

	$'000
Sales revenues	106,000

No of Employees: 1,025

CRANE CO

757 Third Avenue, New York, NY 10017
Tel: (212) 415-7300

Chairman: Robert S Evans (and Chief Executive Officer)
President: Edwin F Phelps (and Chief Operating Officer)
Senior Executive Officers: William C Dackis (VP Administration), B J Barnes (VP Hydro-Aire Division), Robert R Foster (VP Crane Supply Co), Ray R Baker (VP Valve Division), R K Whitley (VP Finance), William R T Crolius (VP Government Relations), Paul R Hundt (VP, Secretary and Legal Counsel)

PRINCIPAL ACTIVITIES: Holding company with interests in engineering and a range of industrial products including valves and pipe fittings, pumps, fluid handling and pollution control systems, building materials, aircraft and aerospace equipment
Principal Subsidiaries: Chempump Division; Cochrane Environmental Systems Division; Crane Supply Co; Hydro-Aire Division; Valves and Fittings Division; Huttig Sash and Door Co; Medusa Corpn; Crane Canada Inc; Crane Australia Pty Ltd; Crane Ltd (England); Crane-Deming de Mexico SA
Principal Bank: Morgan Guaranty Trust Co
Financial Information:

	Dec 31 1986
	$'000
Sales revenues	1,204,240
Net income	38,380
Earnings per share	$2.80
Shareholders equity	173,030

No of Employees: 8,000

CRANSTON PRINT WORKS COMPANY

1381 Cranston Street, Cranston, RI 02920
Tel: (401) 943-4800
Telex: WUT 927 515 cranprint crnt

Chairman: Frederic L Rockefeller (and President)
Senior Executive Officers: Richard Schein (Group VP), George W Shuster (Group VP Manufacturing), Leo G Hutchings (VP and Treasurer)

PRINCIPAL ACTIVITIES: Textile finishing and manufacture of specialty chemicals
Principal Subsidiaries: Bercen Inc; Ericson Travel Inc
Principal Bank: The Chase Manhattan Bank NA
Financial Information:

	$'000
Sales revenues	227,000

No of Employees: 2,000

CRAWFORD & COMPANY

5620 Glenridge Drive NE, Atlanta, GA 30342
Tel: (404) 256 0830

Chairman: T G Germany (and Chief Executive Officer)
President: F L Minix (and Chief Operating Officer)
Senior Executive Officers: D R Chapman (Executive VP Finance), P A Bollinger (Executive VP Service), C C Lefler (Executive VP Marketing), B C Usher (Senior VP), R P Albright (Senior VP Marketing), S F Barber (VP Information Systems), G N Cox (VP Human Resources)

PRINCIPAL ACTIVITIES: Insurance services
Principal Subsidiaries: Calesco Inc
Principal Bank: Trust Company Bank
Financial Information:

	Dec 31 1985
	$'000
Revenues	213,750
Net income	13,395

No of Employees: 4,460

CRAY RESEARCH, INC

608 Second Avenue S, Minneapolis, MN 55402
Tel: (612) 333-5889

Chairman: John A Rollwagen (and President and Chief Executive Officer); Vice Chairman: Andrew Scott
Senior Executive Officers: Lester T Davis (Executive VP), John F Carlson (Executive VP and Chief Financial Officer), Marcelo A Gumucio (Executive VP Marketing), Steve S Chen (Senior VP Development), Michael G Dickey (VP International Marketing), Paul W Dillingham Jr (VP Government Marketing), Robert H Ewald (VP Commercial Marketing), Robert A Gaertner (VP Human Resources and Communications), Bruce N Kasson (VP Marketing and Customer Operations), Michael J Lindseth (VP Finance and Treasurer), Margaret A Loftus (VP Software Development), Richard F Morris (VP Technical Operations), M Dean Roush (VP Engineering), Don F Whiting (VP Manufacturing)

PRINCIPAL ACTIVITIES: Manufacture of computers
Principal Bank: Northwestern National Bank
Financial Information:

	Dec 31 1986
	$'000
Sales revenues	596,685
Net income	124,815
Earnings per share	$3.99
Shareholders equity	441,860

No of Employees: 3,200

CRAZY EDDIE INC

2845 Coney Island Avenue, Brooklyn, NY 11235
Tel: (718) 934 0100

Chairman: Eddie Antar (and President and Chief Executive Officer)
Senior Executive Officers: Sam Antar (Executive VP), David Pardo (Executive VP), Morton Gindi (VP), David P Panoff (VP), Eddy Antar (Treasurer), Sam E Antar (Controller), Solomon E Antar (Secretary and Legal Counsel), Mitchell Antar (VP Purchasing)

PRINCIPAL ACTIVITIES: Specialty retail stores for consumer electronics and home entertainment equipment
Financial Information:

	$'000
Sales revenues	136,000

No of Employees: 1,000

CREATIVE INDUSTRIES GROUP, INC

3080 E Outer Drive, Detroit, MI 48234
Tel: (313) 366-3020
Telex: TWX 810 243 4004 creatv ind det

Chairman: Richard A Leasia
President: Verne T Koppin
Senior Executive Officers: Robert A Vandriesen (VP Finance and Administration)

PRINCIPAL ACTIVITIES: Holding company with interests in fabricated metal products and plastic fittings; commercial photography and marketing communications
Principal Subsidiaries: Creative Universal Inc
Principal Bank: Michigan National Bank of Detroit
Financial Information:

	$'000
Sales revenues	75,000

No of Employees: 1,300

CREDITHRIFT FINANCIAL CORPORATION

601 NW Second Street, Evansville, IN 47701
Tel: (812) 424-8031

Chairman: Wendell L Dixon (and President and Chief Executive Officer)

Senior Executive Officers: Louis Durfee Jr (Executive VP Operations), Arthur D Holley (Senior VP and Treasurer), Thomas E Kleist (Senior VP Data Processing), Robert P Plummer (Senior VP and Controller), H N Robinson (Senior VP Insurance), William A Rotzien (VP, Secretary and Legal Counsel), Eric H Krebs (VP Taxation)

PRINCIPAL ACTIVITIES: Financial services
Parent Company: Credithrift Financial Inc

No of Employees: 4,500

CREPACO, INC
8303 W Higgins Road, Chicago, IL 60631
Tel: (312) 693-4000
Telex: WUT 254537 crepaco cgo

Chairman: James Shannahan
President: Don Hefner
Senior Executive Officers: Tom M Nilles (Executive VP), Robert H Fisher (VP Sales), Roy Bryant (VP Engineering), William Cunnynham (VP Manufacturing), John Hersheman (VP and Comptroller), Mel Jolly (VP International), Milton Knapp (VP Research and Development and Engineering)

PRINCIPAL ACTIVITIES: Manufacture of food processing plant and refrigeration equipment
Parent Company: APV Holdings PLC, Crawley, West Sussex, UK
Principal Bank: First National Bank
Financial Information:

	$'000
Sales revenues	100,000

No of Employees: 1,500

CREST FOAM CORPORATION
100 Carol Place, Moonachie, NJ 07025
Tel: (201) 641 9030

Chairman: Karl G Lens (and Secretary and Treasurer)
President: Irving Rifkin
Senior Executive Officers: Stanley Bernstein (VP Administration)

PRINCIPAL ACTIVITIES: Manufacture of a range of plastic products including foam
Principal Bank: Barclays Bank
Financial Information:

	$'000
Sales revenues	42,915

No of Employees: 400

CRESTAR FINANCIAL CORPORATION (FORMERLY UNITED VIRGINIA BANKSHARES INC)
919 East Main Street, Richmond, VA 23219
Tel: (804) 782-5000
Telex: 782-7324

Chairman: Richard G Tilghman (and President and Chief Executive Officer); Vice Chairmen: Samuel P Cardwell, Patrick D Giblin (and Chief Financial Officer); Executive Vice Presidents: C Garland Hagen (Investment Bank), O H Parrish Jr (and Senior Credit Officer), James M Wells III
Senior Executive Officers: James D Barr (Senior VP, Controller and Treasurer), William V Bunting (Executive VP-Regional Operations), William K Butler II (President-Eastern Region), John C Clark III (Senior VP, General Counsel and Corporate Secretary), William M Ginther (Executive VP-Automated Information Services), F Edward Harris (President-Western Region), William C Harris (President-Greater Washington Region), Ellwood F Hudson (Senior VP and General Auditor), Robert N Norfleet Jr (President-Capital Region and Executive VP Corporate Banking), James C Warrick (Executive VP Administrative Services), James M Wilson III (Senior VP and Human Resources Director)

PRINCIPAL ACTIVITIES: Crestar Financial Corporation is the holding company for three subsidiary banks. Headquartered in Richmond, Virginia it serves consumers through 232 branches in Virginia, Washington, DC and Maryland, and businesses, institutions and governments throughout the Southeast United States. The Company offers a broad range of banking services including personal lines of credit, various loan and deposit instruments, trust, VISA, discount brokerage and international banking. First and second mortgage loan origination and servicing and investment advisory services are offered by the Bank's subsidiaries: Crestar Mortgage Corporation and Capitoline Investment Services Incorporated
Principal Subsidiaries: Crestar Bank (Virginia); Crestar Bank N.A. (Washington, D.C.); Crestar Bank MD; Crestar Insurance Agency Inc; Crestar Mortgage Corporation; Crestar Securities Corporation; Capitoline Investment Services Inc
Financial Information:

	Dec 31 1985	Dec 31 1986
	$'000	$'000
Income before taxes	72,427	87,073
Net income	67,595	81,927
Dividends*	20,661	28,271
Dividends per share*	$0.82	$0.92
Earnings per share	$2.65	$2.92
Common stock	66,312	134,130
Retained income	295,715	350,529
Shareholders equity	503,525	564,781
Deposits	5,956,414	6,896,462
Total assets	8,099,556	9,412,574

*common stock

No of Employees: 6,300

CRISPIN CO
800 Gessner, Houston, TX 77024-4257

Chairman: Andre A Crispin (and President)
Senior Executive Officers: D M Portugal (Executive VP), B R Dickerson (Senior VP, Secretary and General Council), J E Goodson (VP), Tom Knox (Comptroller)

PRINCIPAL ACTIVITIES: Manufacture of steel tubes and pipes, oil well equipment and earth moving machinery
Principal Bank: Bankers Trust Company
Financial Information:

	$'000
Sales revenues	100,000

No of Employees: 60

CROCKER, H S, CO, INC
1000 San Mateo Avenue, San Bruno, CA 94066
Tel: (415) 589-8100
Telex: TWX 910 37 17 132 crocker sb

Chairman: Richard N Kauffman
President: Leland Johnson
Senior Executive Officers: Peter P Passanisi (VP and General Manager Office Products), Carolyn S Scarola (VP, Secretary and Chief Financial Officer)

PRINCIPAL ACTIVITIES: Manufacture of stationery and printing supplies and the sale of office furniture
Principal Bank: Crocker National Bank
Financial Information:

	$'000
Sales revenues	100,000

No of Employees: 1,000

CROCKER NATIONAL CORPORATION
One Montgomery Street, San Francisco, CA 94104
Tel: (415) 477-3050

Chairman: Thomas R Wilcox; Vice Chairman: William L Morris; Deputy Chairman: John B M Place
President: J Hallan Dawson

Senior Executive Officers: Owen H Harper (Executive VP), Laurence H Silberman (Executive VP), Arthur B Hall (Executive VP and Chief Financial Officer), Jordan V Burkart (Senior VP and Treasurer), Jon P Christenson (Senior VP and Comptroller), Robert E Hauser (Senior VP and Secretary), G Christian Meyer (VP Investor Relations)

PRINCIPAL ACTIVITIES: Holding company for banking operations
Principal Subsidiaries: Crocker National Bank; Bishop Trust Co Ltd; Bishop Building Co Inc; Miles Crossing Ltd; Honomo Inc; CNC Insurance Agency Inc; Crocker Holdings Inc; Crocker Investment Management Corp; Crocker McAlister Equipment Leasing; Center City Travel Service Inc; Crocker Commercial Services Inc; Crocker Equipment Leasing Inc; Crocker International Investment Corp; Crocker Properties Inc
Financial Information:

	Dec 31 1985
	$'000
Net income	38,000
Shareholders equity	1,163,000
Deposits	14,981,000
Total assets	19,208,000

No of Employees: 14,500

CROFT METALS, INC
24th Street, McComb, MS 39648
Tel: (601) 684-6121

Chairman: Joseph C Bancroft (and Chief Executive Officer)
President: Donald D Raborn
Senior Executive Officers: Gerald M Abdalla (Executive VP and Legal Counsel), Virginia Waldrop (Executive VP Finance), H W Hitt Jr (Executive VP), Richard T Degler (VP Procurement)

PRINCIPAL ACTIVITIES: Manufacture of a wide range of aluminum products including hardware and building products
Principal Subsidiaries: Croft Metals Inc of NC
Principal Bank: First National Bank
Financial Information:

	$'000
Sales revenues	60,000

No of Employees: 3,000

CROMPTON & KNOWLES CORPORATION
345 Park Avenue, New York, NY 10154
Tel: (212) 754-1660

Chairman: Vincent A Calarco (and President and Chief Executive Officer)
Senior Executive Officers: William J Ferracone (VP), David S Alcorn (VP), Charles J Marsden (VP Finance and Chief Financial Officer), Marvin H Happel (VP)

PRINCIPAL ACTIVITIES: Manufacture of specialty chemicals, dyes and insecticides; manufacture of extrusion machinery for the production of rubber, plastics and wire
Principal Subsidiaries: Crompton & Knowles Acceptance Corp; Crompton & Knowles Overseas Corp; KEM Manufacturing Corp; KEM International Corp; Orlex Chemical Corp; Southern Mill CRK Production Corp
Principal Bank: The Chase Manhattan Bank NA
Financial Information:

	$'000
Sales revenues	230,000

No of Employees: 2,300

CRONUS INDUSTRIES, INC
12700 Park Central Drive, Dallas, TX 75251
Tel: (214) 386-2900

President: C A Rundell Jr
Senior Executive Officers: T C Arnett (Executive VP), Robert E Price (Executive VP), Edward H Belanger (Senior VP and Chief Financial Officer)

PRINCIPAL ACTIVITIES: Manufacture of agricultural equipment and prefabricated metal buildings and heat transfer equipment
Principal Subsidiaries: Agrequip Inc; American Buildings Co; ABC Transportation Co; Mid-West American Inc; Business Records Corp; Polymer Metals Inc; Polymer Extruded Products Inc; Southwestern Engineering Co
Principal Bank: Interfirst Bank Dallas NA
Financial Information:

	$'000
Sales revenues	277,000

No of Employees: 2,700

CROSBY, PHILIP, ASSOCIATES INC
807 West Morse Boulevard, Winter Park, FL 32789
Tel: (305) 645 1733

President: Larry N McFadin (and Chief Operating Officer)
Senior Executive Officers: James B Gunshanan (VP and Chief Financial Officer)

PRINCIPAL ACTIVITIES: Public relations and management consultancy services
Financial Information:

	$'000
Sales revenues	34,330

No of Employees: 180

CROSBY VALVE & GAGE CO
43 Kendrick Street, Wrentham, MA 02093
Tel: (617) 384-3121
Telex: WUT 92 44 43 crosbyash wram

President: R T Levis
Senior Executive Officers: W D Greenlaw (VP Engineering), M L Tiner (VP Marketing), J F Walter (VP)

PRINCIPAL ACTIVITIES: Manufacture of valves and gages
Parent Company: Moorco International Inc
Principal Bank: Industrial National Bank of Rhode Island
Financial Information:

	$'000
Sales revenues	50,000

No of Employees: 750

CROSS & TRECKER CORPORATION
505 North Woodward Avenue, Bloomfield Hills, MI 48013
Tel: (313) 644-4343

Chairman: Russell A Hedden
President: Richard T Lindgren (and Chief Executive Officer)
Senior Executive Officers: Johannes A Buiteweg (VP Law and Secretary), John J Hinnendael (VP Finance)

PRINCIPAL ACTIVITIES: Manufacture of machine tools and automated industrial equipment
Principal Subsidiaries: The Cross Co; Cross & Trecker Credit Corp; Kearney & Trecker Corp; Machine Remarketing Corp; Roberts Corp; The Warner & Swasey Co; Alliance Automation Systems Inc
Financial Information:

	Sep 30 1986	Sep 30 1987
	$'000	$'000
Sales revenues	399,301	422,200
(Loss) before taxes	(6,619)	(38,174)
Net income (loss)	189	(24,450)
Dividends	9,935	31
Dividends per share	$0.80	-
Earnings (loss) per share	$0.02	($1.97)
Common stock	12,451	12,456
Retained income	168,614	144,133
Shareholders equity	208,257	187,936

No of Employees: 4,100

CROSS, A T, CO

One Albion Road, Lincoln, RI 02865
Tel: (401) 333-1200

Chairman: Bradford R Boss (and Chief Executive Officer)
President: Russell A Boss (and Chief Operating Officer)
Senior Executive Officers: John E Buckley (Executive VP and Chief Financial Officer), Edward M Watson (Corporate Secretary), Edwin G Torrance (Assistant Secretary), Joseph F Eastman (VP Employee Relations), Lawrence R Farmer (VP Manufacturing), J John Lawler (VP International), Peter C McCarthy (VP European Manufacturing), Carl V Pergola (Corporate Controller), Gregory J Rogers (VP International Marketing), John T Ruggieri (Treasurer), Richard B Walls (VP Marketing)

PRINCIPAL ACTIVITIES: The A.T Cross Company is a major international manufacturer of fine writing instruments. These products are sold to the consumer gift market through selected jewelry, department, stationery, gift and book stores, and sold to the business gift market via a network of companies specializing in recognition programs. Cross products include 14 karat gold, sterling silver, 14 karat and 10 karat gold filled, Classic Black (R) and lustrous chrome and the new Gray by Cross ball point pens, mechanical pencils, rolling ball/porous point pens, and fountain pens. Cross also produces desk sets, featuring bases crafted from cherry, walnut, onyx, crystal and ebony. Mark Cross Inc, a wholly-owned subsidiary of the A.T. Cross Company, markets the finest quality luggage, leather goods, and other distinctive gifts for personal and business use
Principal Subsidiaries: ATX Marketing Company; ATX International Inc; A.T. Cross Export Company; A.T. Cross Export Company Limited (Virgin Islands); A.T. Cross Limited (Eire); A.T. Cross (Ireland) Limited (Eire); A.T. Cross (France) SA (France); A.T. Cross (UK) Limited (UK); A.T. Cross (España) SA (Spain); A.T. Cross Deutschland GmbH (Germany); A.T. Cross (Bermuda); A.T. Cross Company (Puerto Rico); Mark Cross Inc
Principal Bank: Fleet National Bank
Financial Information:

	Dec 31 1985	Dec 31 1986
	$'000	$'000
Sales revenues	138,792	155,327
Income before taxes	32,019	35,950
Net income	18,819	21,360
Dividends	11,638	12,902
Dividends per share	$1.41	$1.56
Earnings per share	$2.28	$2.58
Common stock class A	7,357	7,372
Common stock class B	902	902
Retained income	83,536	91,994
Shareholders equity	94,414	103,293

No of Employees: 1,530

CROSSLAND SAVINGS, FSB

211 Montague St, Brooklyn, NY 11201
Tel: (718) 780-0400
Telefax: (718) 780-0579

Chairman: Luke A Baione (and Chief Executive Officer)
President: Maurice L Reissman (and Chief Operating Officer)
Senior Executive Officers: Frank A Dellomo (Vice Chairman), Donald E White Jr (Executive VP and Chief Financial Officer), Thomas A Eschmann (Executive VP and Chief Lending Officer), Salvatore S Citrano (Executive VP and Chief Retail Officer), William A Shea (Secretary). Administrative Vice Presidents: Harry A Baierlein Jr, Ramesh C Gupta. Senior Vice Presidents: Barry M Donohue, John E Gunther, Elizabeth M Hohenester, James R Kerr, Jonathon G Matuscak, Lance S Miller, David T O'Shea, Richard J Pace, Joseph V Sabella, John P Sullivan, William J Taylor

PRINCIPAL ACTIVITIES: CrossLand Savings offers a full-scope of financial services through its coordinated companies which are managed to serve its communities nationwide in a progressive and responsive manner and to enhance stockholder value through sustained profitability. The Bank's focus is on generating quality assets, particularly real estate loans and interests, using least cost funding sources, carefully controlling operating costs and retaining and developing management talent. Lines of business extensions and geographic diversification will be emphasized as strategies to achieve these objectives
Principal Subsidiaries: CrossLand Savings, FSB of Utah; CrossLand Mortgage Corp; CrossLand Credit Corp
Principal Bank: CrossLand Savings, FSB (FDIC)
Financial Information:

	Dec 31 1985	Dec 31 1986
	$'000	$'000
Revenues	890,000	879,000
Income before taxes	163,000	119,000
Net income	148,000	101,000
Common dividends	-	1,500
Dividends per share	-	$0.40
Earnings per share	$1.18	$5.32
Common stock	14,600	14,634
Retained income	306,000	403,007
Stockholders equity	422,000	643,000
Deposits	6,971,000	6,876,000
Total assets	8,022,000	10,096,000

No of Employees: 2,900

CROWLEY FOODS, INC

145 Conklin Avenue, Binghamton, NY 13902
Tel: (607) 722-6441

Chairman: Tom Van Noort; Vice Chairman: Norman A Roberts
President: Robert W Allen (and Chief Executive Officer)
Senior Executive Officers: Martin Murgherio (VP Sales and Marketing), Herbert E Axelrod (VP), James H Bender (VP Research and Development), Stephen Einfalt Jr (VP Organisation and Planning), Timothy A Natole (VP Finance), Leonard Ingrando (VP Production), G Yanceey (VP)

PRINCIPAL ACTIVITIES: Manufacture of a wide range of dairy products
Parent Company: Wessanen USA Inc
Financial Information:

	$'000
Sales revenues	160,000

No of Employees: 700

CROWLEY MILNER & COMPANY

2301 West Lafayette Boulevard, Detroit, MI 48216
Tel: (313) 962 2400

President: Robert B Carlson (and Chief Executive Officer)
Senior Executive Officers: J Stephen Kennedy (VP Operations), Andrew J Soffell (VP Finance, Secretary and Treasurer)

PRINCIPAL ACTIVITIES: Retail stores
Principal Bank: Manufacturers National Bank of Detroit
Financial Information:

	$'000
Sales revenues	104,000

No of Employees: 1,900

CROWN AUTO INC

7550 Corporate Way, Eden Prairie, MN 55344
Tel: (612) 937 9000

President: Floyd R Adelman (and Chief Executive and Chief Operating Officer)
Senior Executive Officers: Arvin D Adelman (Executive VP and Assistant Secretary), Richard K Roderick (VP and Treasurer), Ted Manley (VP Merchandising), Israel E Krawetz (Secretary)

PRINCIPAL ACTIVITIES: Retail of motor vehicle components and supplies

Principal Bank: First National Bank of Minneapolis
Financial Information:

	$'000
Sales revenues	36,000

No of Employees: 605

CROWN BOOKS CORPORATION

3300 75th Avenue, Landover, MD 20785
Tel: (301) 731 1200

Chairmen: Herbert H Haft, Leonard, H Straus
President: Robert M Haft (and Chief Executive Officer)
Senior Executive Officers: Jose A Gonzalez (VP), Jeanne Herick (VP), Ronald M Hirschel (Secretary and Treasurer)

PRINCIPAL ACTIVITIES: Retail trade in books
Principal Bank: Riggs National Bank
Financial Information:

	$'000
Sales revenues	137,000

No of Employees: 1,320

CROWN CENTRAL PETROLEUM CORPORATION

1 North Charles, Baltimore, MD 21203
Tel: (301) 539-7400
Telex: WUT 9080 32 crowncen bal

Chairman: Henry A Rosenberg Jr (and Chief Executive Officer); Vice Chairman: George W Jandacek (and Chief Administration Officer)
President: James F Smith (and Chief Operating Officer)
Senior Executive Officers: Ted M Jackson (Senior VP and Chief Financial Officer), William R Snyder (VP Administration and Secretary), James A King (VP Supply and Transport), Francis X Jackson (VP Financial Services), Thomas L Owsley (VP Legal), J E Wheeler Jr (VP and Controller), T E Yates (VP Exploration and Production), J P Candella (VP Marketing), B A Smith (VP Human Resources)

PRINCIPAL ACTIVITIES: Manufacture of petrochemicals and petroleum products
Principal Subsidiaries: Continental American Corp; Crown Central Holding Corp; Crown Central Pipe Line Co; Crown Central Petro Foundation Co; Crown Gold Inc; Crown Nigeria Inc; Crown Oil & Gas Co; Crown Stations Inc; Crown-Rancho Pipe Line Corp; Crowncen International NV; FZ Corp; Fast Fare Inc; Fast Fare Markets of NC Inc; Fast Fare Markets of SC Inc; Kwik-Pik Realty Inc; Mr Zip Inc; Tiny Tote Inc; Zippy Mart Inc; Zippy Mart Properties Inc; International Calciners Inc; Pioneer Coal Co Inc; Sunset International Management Co; Teche Petroleum Inc; Tongue Brooks & Co Inc; Tongue Brooks (Bermuda) Ltd; Tongue Brooks Insurance Management
Principal Bank: The Chase Manhattan Bank NA
Financial Information:

	Dec 31 1985	Dec 31 1986
	$'000	$'000
Sales revenues	1,473,253	1,051,564
Net income (loss)	4,100	(20,230)
Earnings (loss) per share	$0.46	($3.66)
Shareholders equity	191,634	242,626

No of Employees: 5,640

CROWN CONTROLS CORPORATION

40 S Washington Street, New Bremen, OH 45869
Tel: (419) 629-2311
Telex: WUT 242425 crown nebn

Chairman: James F Dicke (and Treasurer)
President: James F Dicke II (and Chief Executive Officer)
Senior Executive Officers: T L Bidwell (Executive VP), Dane W Dicke (Senior VP and Secretary), James Uetrecht (VP Engineering), Craig Hirschfeld (VP Manufacturing)

PRINCIPAL ACTIVITIES: Manufacture of electrical and electronic equipment and lifting equipment
Financial Information:

	$'000
Sales revenues	120,000

No of Employees: 1,200

CROWN CORK & SEAL COMPANY, INC

9300 Ashton Road, Philadelphia, PA 19136
Tel: (215) 698-5100

Chairman: John F Connelly (and Chief Executive Officer)
President: William J Avery
Senior Executives: Henry E Butwel (Senior VP Finance), Michael J McKenna (Senior VP Sales), G Richard Belt (VP Latin America), James T Bennett (VP Manufacturing), Edward J Boyle Jr (VP Eastern Division), Cornelius W Curran (Controller), Francis X Dalton (Treasurer), Forrest K Eason (VP Southwest Division), Victoria K Flaville (Assistant Secretary), Joe A George Jr (VP Southern Division), B Douglas Goodell (VP Machinery Division), Mark W Hartman (VP Northeast Division), William R Howard (VP Manufacturing), Richard L Krzyzanowski (VP, Secretary and General Counsel), Raymond H Shinn (VP Research), Richard D Slocum (VP Western Division), Ronald R Thoma (VP Procurement and Traffic), Clinton J Waring (VP Central Division). Sales Managers: Arthur L Anagnost (Machinery-International), Joseph J Belcher (Aerosol General Manager), William J Brayer (Machinery-Domestic), Gary A Munson (Marketing), Frank E Young Jr (Machinery-Industrial). Manufacturing Directors: Harold J Abrams (Industrial Relations), Lewis W Ascah (Purchasing), Daniel J Donaghy (Industrial Engineering), Lee B Draper (Engineering), Frank J Juska (Technical Services), John M Gahan (Production Planning), Robert A Phillips (Quality Assurance). Crown Financial Corporation: Francis X Dalton (VP and Treasurer)

PRINCIPAL ACTIVITIES: The Company's business is the manufacture and sale of metal cans, crowns and closures for the building of filling, packaging; and handling machinery. These products are manufactured in 25 plants within the United States and 63 plants outside the United States and are sold through the Company's own sales organization to the food, citrus, brewing, soft drink, oil, paint, toiletries, drug, antifreeze, chemical and pet food industries
Principal Subsidiaries: USA: Crown Financial Corp and Divisions throughout the USA. Canada: Crown Cork & Seal Canada Inc. Mexico: Crown Cork De Mexico SA. Puerto Rico: Crown Cork De Puerto Rico Inc. Trinidad & Tobago: Crown Cork & Seal (West Indies) Ltd. Argentina: Crown Cork de Argentina SA. Brazil: Crown Cork do Brasil SA. Chile: Crown Cork de Chile SAI. Costa Rica: Crown Cork Centroamericana SA. Ecuador: Crown Cork del Ecuador CA. Guatemala: Crown Cork de Guatemala SA. Peru: Crown Cork del Peru SA. Colombia: Crown Litometal SA. Austria: Crown Reisinger GmbH. Belgium: Crown Cork Company (Belgium) NV; Crown Baele NV. France: Emballages-Couronne Crown Cork Company (France) SA. Holland: De Nederlandsche Kroonkurk Maatschappij Crown Cork Company (Holland) BV. Italy: Compagnia Tappi Corona SpA Crown Cork Company (Italy). Spain: Crown Metalinas SA. Switzerland: Crown Obrist AG. West Geramany: Crown Bender-Werke GmbH. Great Britain: The Crown Cork Company Ltd. Denmark: Crown Cork Co (Scandinavia) A/S. Ireland: The Irish Crown Cork Company Ltd. Portugal: Produtos Corticeiros Portugueses SARL. Ethiopia: Crown Cork Company, Ethiopia. Kenya: The Crown Cork Company (East Africa) Ltd. Mocambique: Crown Cork Company (Mocambique) Limitada. South Africa: Crown Cork Company SA (Pty) Ltd. Zaire: Crown Cork Company (Zaire) SPRL. Zambia: Crown Cork Company (Zambia) Ltd. Zimbabwe: Crown Cork Company (1958) (PVT) Ltd. Morocco: Crown Cork Company (Morocco) SA. Nigeria: The Crown Cork & Seal Company (Nigeria) Ltd; Canmakers (Nigeria) Ltd. Indonesia: PT Crown Cork & Seal Indonesia). Malaysia.

Crown Corks of Malaysia SDN BHD. Papua New Guinea: Crown Cork & Seal (PNG) Pty Ltd. Singapore: Crown Cork & Seal (Singapore) Co Ltd. Thailand: Crown Cork & Seal (Thailand) Co Ltd

Principal Bank: First Pennsylvania Bank

Financial Information:

	Dec 31 1985	Dec 31 1986
	$'000	$'000
Sales revenues	1,487,143	1,618,932
Income before taxes	127,930	148,616
Net income	71,725	79,441
Earnings per share	$6.52	$7.46
Common stock	52,665	49,781
Retained income	617,321	637,930
Shareholders equity	531,541	576,565

No of Employees: 12,403

CROWN CRAFTS INC

Edmond Street, PO Box 371, Calhoun, GA 30701
Tel: (404) 629 7941

Chairman: Philip Bernstein (and Secretary)
President: Michael H Bernstein (and Chief Executive Officer)
Senior Executive Officers: Lewis S Andrews (VP Manufacturing), P A Criscillis Jr (VP Finance and Treasurer), Rudolph J Schmatz (VP Administration), Dennis G Cochran (Controller)

PRINCIPAL ACTIVITIES: Manufacture of textiles
Principal Bank: Bankers Trust Company
Financial Information:

	$'000
Sales revenues	42,000

No of Employees: 650

CROWN ZELLERBACH CORPORATION

Rincon Annex, PO Box 3475, San Francisco, CA 94104
Tel: (415) 951-5000

Chairman: Brenton S Halsey
President: Robert C Williams
Senior Executive Officers: Harry L Fledderman (Senior VP, Secretary and Legal Counsel), A G Resnick (Senior VP), E H Grubb (Senior VP Distribution Group), D Taylor (Senior VP Public Affairs), J A Toney (Senior VP), H W Reed (Senior VP Converted Papers), E S Leopold (Senior VP Communication Papers), Larry D Busboom (VP and Controller), Richard L Ritchie (VP and Treasurer)

PRINCIPAL ACTIVITIES: Manufacture of paper and packaging products
Parent Company: James River Corp of Virginia
Financial Information:

	Dec 31 1985
	$'000
Sales revenues	3,083,000
Net (loss)	(26,800)
Shareholders equity	1,128,400

No of Employees: 16,890

CROWNAMERICA, INC

Drawer 1127, Dalton, GA 30720
Tel: (404) 278-1422

Chairman: D D Hamilton (and President)
Senior Executive Officers: E D Smith (VP), G L Hamilton (Secretary and Treasurer)

PRINCIPAL ACTIVITIES: Processing filament yarns for carpets
Principal Subsidiaries: Texture-Tex Inc; Texture-Tex (Europe) Ltd; Texture-Tex (Europe) BV
Principal Bank: Hardwick Bank & Trust Co, Dalton, GA
Financial Information:

	Aug 31 1986
	$'000
Sales revenues	87,144
Income before taxes	2,739
Net income	1,626
Dividends	374
Dividends per share	$0.325
Earnings per share	$1.41
Common stock	1,300
Retained income	11,782
Shareholders equity	15,260

No of Employees: 360

CRSS

1177 West Loop South, Suite 900, Houston, TX 77027
Tel: (713) 552 2000
Telex: 6868544 CRS UW

Chairman: Thomas A Bullock
President: Bruce W Wilkinson (and Chief Executive Officer)
Senior Executive Officers: Socrates S Christopher (Executive VP Operations), Richard L Daerr Jr (Executive VP, Chief Administrative Officer), M Glenn Hobratschk (Senior VP, Treasurer and Controller), Frank Perrone (General Counsel, Secretary)

PRINCIPAL ACTIVITIES: Consultancy services including engineering, architecture and surveying
Principal Bank: Morgan Guaranty Trust Company
Financial Information:

	June 30 1986	Jun 30 1987
	$'000	$'000
Sales revenues	357,658	332,137
Income (loss) before taxes	8,376	(40,109)
Net income (loss)	4,486	(32,401)
Dividends	1,382	1,392
Dividends per share	$0.23	$0.23
Earnings (loss) per share	$0.73	($5.27)
Common stock	6,620	6,647
Retained income	48,185	14,392
Shareholders equity	87,521	55,039

No of Employees: 2,300

CRUMP COMPANIES INC

5350 Poplar Avenue, Memphis, TN 38119
Tel: (901) 761 1550

Chairman: Sidney A Stewart Jr (and Chief Executive Officer)
President: James M Power (and Chief Operating Officer)
Senior Executive Officers: Edward B Morrow Jr (Executive VP), Gordon E Noble (Executive VP), Donald A Thomas (Executive VP), Charles H Gray III (Senior VP Finance and Chief Financial Officer), Horace W Nelson (Senior VP), Robert Smithwick Jr (Senior VP and Assistant Secretary), Frank J Huffman Jr (VP Communications)

PRINCIPAL ACTIVITIES: Insurance services
Principal Subsidiaries: Benson Insurance Agency Inc; E H Crump & Co Inc; G & M Marine Inc; E H Crump of Georgia Inc; Crump-Davis Inc; Kindler & Laucci Insurance; La Bow Haynes Co Inc; Professional Reinsurance Office; Southern American Insurance Co; Warren & Sommer Inc
Principal Bank: Midland Bank and Trust Co
Financial Information:

	$'000
Revenues	100,000

No of Employees: 1,500

CRUTCHER RESOURCES CORPORATION

PO Box 534024, Grand Prairie, TX 75053
Tel: (214) 988 8200

Chairman: Jerry E Goldress (and President and Chief Executive Officer)

Senior Executive Officers: B J Bucy (VP Administration), William B Philips (VP, Secretary and Treasurer)

PRINCIPAL ACTIVITIES: Manufacture of equipment and provision of services for the oil and gas industry
Principal Bank: First City National Bank of Houston
Financial Information:

	$'000
Sales revenues	98,000

No of Employees: 2,000

CRYOVAC DIVISION

Box 464, Duncan, SC 29334
Tel: (803) 433-2000
Telex: RCA 216 904 cryo ur

President: W B Sturgis
Senior Executive Officers: Leonard R Byrne (VP Finance), Robert P Prevost (VP Manufacturing), W S Hardin (VP Administration), R Hight (VP Sales), E L Chesnutt (VP Marketing and Business Development), A P Engelmann (VP Research and Development and Engineering)

PRINCIPAL ACTIVITIES: Manufacture of packaging products and equipment
Parent Company: W R Grace & Co, New York, NY
Financial Information:

	$'000
Sales revenues	100,000

No of Employees: 3,000

CRYSTAL BRANDS INC

1411 Broadway. New York, NY 10018
Tel: (212) 869 8900

Chairman: Richard F Kral (and Chief Executive Officer)
President: Richard A Baker
Senior Executive Officers: Gerald M Chaney (VP and Controller), Edward B Dailey (VP and Chief Financial Officer), Michael B McLearn (VP Legal Counsel and Secretary), Charles J Smith (Group VP)

PRINCIPAL ACTIVITIES: Sports clothing; costume jewelry; retail trading
Financial Information:

	$'000
Sales revenues	480,000

No of Employees: 5,570

CRYSTAL CREAM & BUTTER CO

PO Box 1313, Sacramento, CA 95806
Tel: (916) 444-7200

Chairman: Gerald Hansen
President: Donald K Hansen
Senior Executive Officers: Charles R Hills (VP Personnel and Advertising), Pete Cornacchio (VP Production)

PRINCIPAL ACTIVITIES: Manufacture, wholesale and distribution of dairy products
Principal Subsidiaries: Vitafreeze Frozen Confections
Principal Bank: Bank of America
Financial Information:

	$'000
Sales revenues	125,000

No of Employees: 380

CRYSTAL OIL CO

229 Milam Street, Box 21101, Shreveport, LA 71120
Tel: (318) 222-7791
Telex: TWX 510 973 4067 crystl shr

Chairman: Robert F Roberts
President: Joe N Averett Jr (and Chief Executive Officer)
Senior Executive Officers: Mark A Roberts (Executive VP), R D Miller (Senior VP Land and Exploration), Sam J Clinton (Senior VP Drilling and Production), Ed Bull (VP Audit and Legal), Dan Grubb (VP Exploration), James Renz (VP Accounting)

PRINCIPAL ACTIVITIES: Exploration and production of oil and gas; refining of crude oil
Principal Subsidiaries: Crystal Exploration Co; Crystal Exploration and Production Co; Crystal Program Ltd Inc
Principal Bank: Bankers Trust Company
Financial Information:

	$'000
Sales revenues	94,000

No of Employees: 220

CSX CORPORATION

901 E Cary Street One James Center, Richmond, PO Box C-32222, VA 23261
Tel: (804) 782 1400

Chairman: Hays T Watkins (and Chief Executive Officer); Vice Chairman: John T Collinson
Senior Executive Officers: Robert L Hintz (Executive VP; President and Chief Executive Officer, CSX Energy Group and CSX Properties Group), Mark G Aron (Senior VP-Law and Public Affairs), James Ermer (Senior VP-Finance), Alex J Mandl (Senior VP-Corporate Development and Administration; Chairman and Chief Executive Officer, CSX Technology Group), Josiah A Stanley Jr (Senior VP-Audit), Donald D Davis (VP-Human Resources), Carl C Hawk (VP and Corporate Secretary), Thomas E Hoppin (VP-Corporate Communications), Bruce G Lawler (VP and Controller), Woodruff M Price (VP Government Relations), William H Sparrow (VP and Treasurer), P Michael Giftos (General Counsel-Special Projects), Alan A Rudnick (General Counsel-Corporate), L Wayne Farrell (VP-Taxes)

PRINCIPAL ACTIVITIES: CSX Corporation, headquartered in Richmond, VA, is one of America's leading transportation and natural resource company. Through its rail, barge, trucking and pipeline units, the company offers a wide range of coordinated transportation services. The company also has substantial oil and gas, coal and realty interests and operates the country's premier resort hotel-The Greenbrier
Principal Subsidiaries: CSX Transportation; CSX Distribution Services; CSX Equipment; CSX Rail Transport; American Commercial Lines; Fruit Growers Express Company; Sea-Land Corporation; CSX Energy; Texas Gas Transmission Corporation; CSX Oil & Gas Corporation; CSX Technology; Lightnet; CSX Properties; CSX Realty Inc; CSX Hotels Inc; The Greenbrier; Rockresorts Inc
Financial Information:

	Dec 31 1985	Dec 31 1986
	$'000	$'000
Operating revenue	7,288,000	6,345,000
Income (loss) before taxes	(263,000)	729,000
Net income (loss)	(118,000)	418,000
Dividends	170,000	179,000
Dividends per share	$1.13	$1.16
Earnings (loss) per share	($0.78)	$2.73
Common stock	152,000	154,000
Retained income	2,741,000	2,980,000
Shareholders equity	4,595,000	4,873,000

No of Employees: 60,900

CT SUPPLY CO

41099 Boyce Road, Fremont, CA 94538
Tel: (415) 656-8800

President: H R Zetterquist
Senior Executive Officers: Joseph W Goodman (VP, Secretary and Treasurer)

PRINCIPAL ACTIVITIES: Manufacture of metal cans
Parent Company: California Canners & Growers, San Francisco, CA

Financial Information:

	$'000
Sales revenues	110,000

No of Employees: 500

C-TEC CORPORATION

46 Public Square, Box 3000, Wilkes-Barre, PA 18703
Tel: (717) 825-1100
Telefax: (717) 825-5243

Chairman: A J Sordoni III (and President and Chief Executive Officer); Vice Chairman: William B Sordoni
Senior Executive Officers: William L Moyer (Executive VP and General Counsel), William J Umphred (Senior VP Administration External Affairs and Secretary), John J Menapale (VP Human Resources), Donald P Roskos (VP Finance and Development and Treasurer)

PRINCIPAL ACTIVITIES: Telecommunications services
Principal Subsidiaries: Commonwealth Telephone Company; Lewisberry Telephone Company; Coopersburg Telephone Company; Commonwealth Cable Systems Inc; Commonwealth Cable Systems of New York Inc; ComVideo Systems Inc; Commonwealth Communications Inc; Commonwealth Information Services Company; Commonwealth Mobile Services; Business Systems Incorporated
Principal Bank: Morgan Guaranty Trust Co
Financial Information:

	Dec 31 1985	Dec 31 1986
	$'000	$'000
Sales revenues	110,875	120,723
Income before taxes	28,691	25,872
Net income	11,068	9,245
Dividends	4,266*	4,655
Dividends per share	$0.77*	$0.83
Earnings per share	$2.01*	$1.66
Common stock	5,538*	5,625
Retained income	46,383	50,973
Shareholders equity	68,961	74,911

*restated for stock split

No of Employees: 1,020

CTS CORPORATION

905 N West Blvd, Elkhart, IN 46514
Tel: (219) 293-7511
Telex: TWX 810 2942167 cts corp b elk

Chairman: George F Sommer
President: Robert D Hostetler (and Chief Executive and Administrative Officer)
Senior Executive Officers: Wayne A Beaverson (VP Corporate Development), John P Colglazier (VP), Duane H Daering (VP Human Resources), Garry B Erekson (VP and Chief Financial Officer), Charles C Smith (VP), Robert G Early (VP Sales), Willie P Ozbirn (VP Research and Development)

PRINCIPAL ACTIVITIES: Electronic components
Principal Subsidiaries: CTS Fabri-Tek Inc; CTS Printex Inc; CTS of Brownsville Inc
Principal Bank: Continental Illinois National Bank and Trust Company of Chicago
Financial Information:

	$'000
Sales revenues	262,000

No of Employees: 6,000

CUBIC CORPORATION

9333 Balboa Avenue, San Diego, CA 92123
Tel: (619) 277-6780
Telex: 188918
Telecopy: (619) 277-1878

Chairman: Walter J Zable (and President and Chief Executive Officer); Vice Chairman: Walter C Zable (and Vice President)
Senior Executive Officers: Colvin C Wellborn (Senior VP), William W Boyle (VP Finance and Treasurer), Marlyn L Hicks (VP/Corporate), Raymond L deKozan (VP/Marketing), James B Jenkins (VP/Contracts), Thomas A Baz (VP/Corporate Controller), William C Stewart Jr (VP, General Counsel and Secretary), Louis G Dameson Jr (VP/Corporate Planning), William J Thompson (VP/Development Planning)

PRINCIPAL ACTIVITIES: Cubic provides air combat training systems for the US military. This electronic system forms the heart of the Navy's Top Gun training school, and similar systems are located at Navy and Air Force installations throughout the world. Cubic has long been involved in manufacturing electronic products for the government, but its interests have widened steadily through the years. Indeed, Cubic has become a national leader in three significant market areas. They are: Defense systems; Computerized revenue collection equipment for transit, bus and toll applications; and passenger and freight elevator systems. Among the other elements of the corporate business mix is the radio communications market. Cubic produces high-reliability communications equipment for a variety of military and civilian uses, including intelligence work and critical point-to-point voice transmission and reception. Cubic is one of the country's largest regional distributors of industrial and medical gases. It also operates a large mechanized corrugated paper converting plant, and produces electro-optical products and land surveying instruments.
Principal Subsidiaries and Divisions: Cubic Defense Systems; US Elevator; Cubic Western Data; Westinghouse Cubic Limited (UK); Cubic Far East (Singapore) Pte Ltd (Singapore); Automatic Toll Systems; Cubic Communications; Cubic Data Systems; Cubic Precision Electro-Optical Division; Cubic Precision Survey Systems Division; G S Parsons Companies; Consolidated Converting Company
Principal Bank: Union Bank
Financial Information:

	Sep 30 1986	Sep 30 1987
	$'000	$'000
Sales revenues	337,802	357,569
Income before taxes	843	13,181
Net income	1,125	7,932
Dividends	3,035	2,983
Dividends per share	$0.39	$0.39
Earnings per share	0.14	$1.04
Common stock	234	234
Retained income	99,184	104,133
Shareholders equity	108,654	111,632

No of Employees: 3,700

CULBRO CORPORATION

387 Park Avenue South, New York, NY 10016-8899
Tel: (212) 5610-8700
Telex: 325896 culbro corp

Chairman: Edgar M Cullman
President: Edgar M Cullman Jr
Senior Executive Officers: William R Lewis (Executive VP Finance and Treasurer), Richard F Bonini (Senior VP), William S Brown (Senior VP), A Russ Wollen (Senior VP and General Counsel), Harvey Dashefsky (VP), Thomas G Edge (VP), Joseph Aird (Controller)

PRINCIPAL ACTIVITIES: Consumer Products:- Tobacco- Production and marketing of cigars. Distribution:- Wholesaling of tobacco products, candy, health and beauty aids and general merchandise. Consumer Finance:-Originating, servicing and reselling first mortgages in Puerto Rico, principally on single family homes. Nursery:- Growing plants which are sold principally to landscape nurseries and garden centers. Industrial Products:-Manufacture of injection molded plastics components and standard and custom designed production and packaging machinery. Land Resources:- Owner/builder/manager of industrial and commercial properties and developer of residential subdivisions on real

estate owned by the Corporation in Connecticut and Massachusetts
Trade Names: Cigars:- Ramon Allones, Partagas, Macanudo, Canaria D'Oro, Cohiba, Gold Label, Garcia y Vega, White Owl, Robt Burns, Corina, Wm Penn, Van Dyck, Tiparillo, Tijuana Smalls, Jim Burley. Disposable Lighters:-D'Jeep
Principal Subsidiaries: General Cigar Company; The Seneco Company; The Eli Witt Company; Flaks Inc; HF Inc (Puerto Rico); Imperial Nurseries; Moll Tool & Plastics Corp; Culbro Machine Systems; Culbro Land Resources Inc
Principal Bank: Manufacturers Hanover Trust Company
Financial Information:

	Dec 28 1985	Dec 27 1986
	$'000	$'000
Sales revenues	1,058,879	1,031,100
Net income	11,532	25,649
Dividends	3,384	3,426
Dividends per share	$0.80	$0.80
Earnings per share	$2.73	$6.00
Common stock	4,457	4,506
Retained income	136,826	104,049
Shareholders equity	148,658	116,522

No of Employees: 4,500

CULLEN/FROST BANKERS INC

PO Box 1600, San Antonio, TX 78296
Tel: (512) 220-4011

Chairman: Thomas C Frost (and Chief Executive Officer)
President: Robert S McClane
Senior Executive Officers: (Senior VP), Norton B Hargis (VP)

PRINCIPAL ACTIVITIES: Banking services
Principal Subsidiaries: Frost Bank of San Antonio, Texas
Financial Information:

	Sep 30 1987
	$'000
Total assets	3,042,869

No of Employees: 1,900

CULLINET SOFTWARE INC

400 Blue Hill Drive, Westwood, MA 02090
Tel: (617) 329 7700

Chairman: John T Cullinane (and Chief Executive Officer); Vice Chairman: Donald L Chapman (and President and Chief Executive Officer)
Senior Executive Officers: James A Pitts (Executive VP, Finance, Administration and Strategic Planning), David G Ireland (Senior VP Customer Support), William E Linn (Senior VP), David A Litwack (VP Product Development), Vic Morris (Senior VP International), Robert G White (VP), Edward B Stead (VP, Clerk and General Counsel), William J Drummey (VP, US Sales) Carli (Treasurer)

PRINCIPAL ACTIVITIES: Computer services including programs and software
Principal Bank: First National Bank of Boston
Financial Information:

	$'000
Sales revenues	184,000

No of Employees: 1,800

CULLUM COMPANIES, INC

14303 Inwood Road, Dallas, TX 75234
Tel: (214) 661-9700

Chairman: Charles G Cullum
President: Jack W Evans (and Chief Executive Officer)
Senior Executive Officers: J T Hairston Jr (Executive VP and Chief Operating Officer), Robert B Cullum Jr (VP), Houston E Holmes Jr (VP and Secretary), James T Stiles (VP and Chief Financial Officer)

PRINCIPAL ACTIVITIES: Management of supermarkets and other retail outlets; packaging of meat products
Principal Subsidiaries: American Community Corp TX; Cullum Development Co Inc; Gooch Packing Co Inc; Pages Drugs Inc; Pantry Food Markets Inc of CA; Tom Thumb Stores Inc
Principal Bank: Republic Bank Dallas
Financial Information:

	$'000
Sales revenues	1,170,000

No of Employees: 7,000

CULP, INC

2020 Logan Street, High Point, NC 27263
Tel: (919) 889-5161
Telex: TWX 510 9261806 culp hip

Chairman: R G Culp Jr (and Chief Executive Officer)
President: R G Culp III
Senior Executive Officers: Sharyn M Andrews (VP and Secretary), J Leonard Bagwell Jr (VP and Comptroller), H L Dunn Jr (VP), Kenneth M Ludwig (VP Personnel), F N Saxon (VP Finance)

PRINCIPAL ACTIVITIES: Manufacture of furnishing fabrics
Principal Subsidiaries: Culp of TN Inc; Culp Weaving Inc; Culp Woven Velvets Inc
Principal Bank: First Union National Bank
Financial Information:

	$'000
Sales revenues	131,000

No of Employees: 970

CUMBERLAND MILLS, INC

PO Box 189 Duvall Road, Chatsworth, GA 30705
Tel: (404) 695-7411
Telex: WUT 543 439 cumb mills ct wh

President: Robert L McEntire
Senior Executive Officers: Don L McEntire (Executive VP), Smith H McEntire (VP Shipping), Gary J Robinson (Secretary, Treasurer and Comptroller)

PRINCIPAL ACTIVITIES: Manufacture of carpets
Principal Bank: Cohutta Banking Co
Financial Information:

	$'000
Sales revenues	60,000

No of Employees: 350

CUMMINS ENGINE COMPANY, INC

Box 3005, Columbus, IN 47202-3005
Tel: (812) 377-5000

Chairman: Henry B Schacht (and Chief Executive Officer); Chairman of Executive Committee and Chairman of Finance Committee: J I Miller; Vice Chairman: Richard B Stoner
President: James A Henderson (and Chief Operating Officer)
Senior Executive Officers: John T Hackett (Executive VP and Chief Financial Officer)

PRINCIPAL ACTIVITIES: Cummins is a leading worldwide designer and manufacturer of in-line and V-type diesel engines ranging from 55 to 1800 horsepower. In addition, Cummins produces and markets a broad range of engine-related components, power systems and services worldwide.
Trade Names: CUMMINS
Principal Subsidiaries: Atlas Crankshaft Corporation; Cummins Electronics Company Inc; Cummins Financial Inc; Cummins Realty Inc; Cummins Cash and Information Services Inc; Cummins Driver Training Schools Inc; Cummins Professional Drivers Association Inc; McCord Heat Transfer Corporation; Fleetguard Inc; Holset Engineering Company Ltd; Northwest Motor Welding Inc; Onan Corporation; Comsolidated Diesel Corporation
Principal Bank: Chemical Bank

Financial Information:

	Dec 31 1985	Dec 31 1986
	$'000	$'000
Sales revenues	2,146,272	2,303,731
Income (loss) before taxes	60,953	(156,894)
Net income (loss)	50,355	(107,331)
Dividends per share	$2.20	$2.20
Earnings (loss) per share*	$5.22	($10.45)
Common stock	23,947	26,473
Retained income	547,932	417,878
Shareholders equity	711,585	770,343

*fully diluted

Number of shareholders: 5,400
No of Employees: 23,000

CUPPLES CO, MANUFACTURERS

9430 Page Street, Box 8430, St Louis, MO 63132
Tel: (314) 426-7750
Telex: TWX 910 7650914 cupples co stl

Chairman: Harold M Stuhl (and President)
Senior Executive Officers: Howard Ruweler Jr (VP), Allan S Barton (VP and Secretary)

PRINCIPAL ACTIVITIES: Manufacture of rubber goods
Principal Subsidiaries: Cupples Paper Bag Co
Principal Bank: Centerre Bank
Financial Information:

	$'000
Sales revenues	65,000

No of Employees: 500

CURRENT, INC

PO Box 2559, Colorado Springs, CO 80901
Tel: (303) 594-4100

President: Barry Nolan
Senior Executive Officers: Harry Dockwell (VP Finance), Jon Medved (VP Marketing), Bill Skea (VP Personnel), Lee Meyer (VP Production), Gary Richard (VP Management Information Systems)

PRINCIPAL ACTIVITIES: Manufacture of stationery and books; mail order sales
Parent Company: Looart Press Inc, Colorado Springs, CO
Principal Bank: First National Bank of Colorado Springs
Financial Information:

	$'000
Sales revenues	100,000

No of Employees: 1,000

CURTICE-BURNS, INC

One Lincoln First Square, Rochester, NY 14603
Tel: (716) 325-1020

Chairman: Ralph Winsor
President: David J McDonald
Senior Executive Officers: Hubert Hill (Executive VP), William Petty (Executive VP), Theodore J Holmgren (VP Marketing and Secretary), Roy A Myers (VP), W D Rice (VP Finance and Treasurer)

PRINCIPAL ACTIVITIES: Canning and freezing of a wide range of food products including fruit, vegetables, jellies, jams, preserves. sauces, dressings, meats, juices, ready prepared meals and snack products
Principal Bank: Lincoln First Bank of Rochester
Financial Information:

	$'000
Sales revenues	636,000

No of Employees: 6,065

CURTIS 1000 INC

1000 Curtis Drive SE, Smyrna, GA 30080
Tel: (404) 436-6155
Telex: TWX 810 766 4849 C1000 natl

Chairman: W J Biggers
President: C H Jones
Senior Executive Officers: Roger G Tobin (Executive VP and General Manager), Edward B Donaldson (Executive VP), W S Barentine (Executive VP), Wallace B Graves (VP Finance), O J Holloman (VP Sales), John B McKinney (VP Production), Robert W Chappell (VP KY Division), Germain J Suminski (VP Ohio Division)

PRINCIPAL ACTIVITIES: Manufacture of stationery and data processing equipment and peripherals
Parent Company: American Business Products Inc, Atlanta, GA
Principal Bank: Citizens and Southern National Bank
Financial Information:

	$'000
Sales revenues	145,000

No of Employees: 2,070

CURTISS-WRIGHT CORPORATION

1200 Wall Street W, Lyndhurst, NJ 07071
Tel: (201) 777-2900

Chairman: T R Berner (and President and Chief Executive Officer)
Senior Executive Officers: C E Ehinger (Executive VP), Richard P Sprigle (Executive VP), David Lasky (Senior VP and General Counsel)

PRINCIPAL ACTIVITIES: Manufacture of components for the aerospace and nuclear industries; manufacture of engines
Principal Subsidiaries: Metal Improvement Co; Target Rock Corpn; Canadian Curtiss-Wright Ltd (68.6%); Curtiss-Wright Flight Systems Inc; Curtiss-Wright/Marquette Inc; C W Properties Inc; Lynch Corp; M-Tron Industries Inc
Financial Information:

	$'000
Sales revenues	174,000

No of Employees: 2,030

CUTTERS EXCHANGE, INC

627 19th Avenue North, Nashville, TN 37203
Tel: (615) 329-4931
Telex: WUT 554328 cuttersexc nas

President: Arthur J Rebrovick Jr
Senior Executive Officers: A Rebrovick Jr (Executive VP and Secretary), James M Fite (VP Machinery), Norbert Ackerman (VP and Manager Atlanta), Joe Terry (Treasurer and Controller)

PRINCIPAL ACTIVITIES: Manufacture of sewing equipment and materials
Principal Bank: Third National Bank
Financial Information:

	$'000
Sales revenues	50,000

No of Employees: 450

CWC CASTINGS DIVISION

Henry Street, Muskegon, MI 49441
Tel: (616) 733-1331
Telex: TWX 510 39 44 120 cwctextron msk

President: John J Kelly
Senior Executive Officers: James B Kenny (VP Sales, Marketing and Engineering), Jed Larsen (VP Manufacturing), Donald Garbison (VP and Controller), Richard G Zidjunas (VP Industrial Relations)

PRINCIPAL ACTIVITIES: Manufacture of iron castings
Parent Company: Textron Inc, Providence, RI

Financial Information:

	$'000
Sales revenues	150,000

No of Employees: 1,300

CYCARE SYSTEMS INC

520 Dubuque Building, PO Box 1278, Dubuque, IA 52001
Tel: (319) 556 3131

Chairman: Jim H Houtz (and President)
President: James D Dyer (and Chief Operating Officer)
Senior Executive Officers: David H Koeller (VP Operations), Ronald E Gray (VP Finance, Treasurer and Secretary), James R Eley (VP Customer Service), James K Kemp (VP Sales), Joseph P Schiesl (VP), Clifford B Blake (VP), Kevin R Green (VP)

PRINCIPAL ACTIVITIES: Specialty data processing services
Principal Subsidiaries: DX Practice Management Systems
Principal Bank: First National Bank
Financial Information:

	$'000
Sales revenues	48,085

No of Employees: 540

CYCLOPS INDUSTRIES, INC

650 Washington Road, Pittsburgh, PA 15228
Tel: (412) 343-4000
Telex: 910-380-6448 cyclops HQ

Chairman: W H Knoell (and Chief Executive Officer)
President: James F Will (and Chief Operating Officer)
Senior Executive Officers: John R Ranelli (VP and Chief Financial Officer), Robert A Kushner (VP/Secretary/General Counsel), Joseph Enis (Treasurer), Robert J Tate (Assistant Secretary)

PRINCIPAL ACTIVITIES: Steel Products- including stainless, carbon, galvanized, and silicon steels, high temperature alloys, and tubular products. Nonresidential Construction-designing, manufacturing, and erecting wall, floor, and roof systems for commercial, industrial and institutional buildings
Principal Operating Units: Steel Products: Coshocton Stainless Division; Cytemp Specialty Steel Division; Detroit Strip Division; Empire-Detroit Steel Division; Sawhill Tubular Division; Tex-Tube Division; Miami Industries. Nonresidential Construction: Bowman Metal Deck Division; E G Smith Construction Products Inc; Flour City Architectural Metals Division. Steel components: MSL Stampings; Howard Industries; Flexible Metal Hose
Principal Bank: Pittsburgh National Bank
Financial Information: Pro Forma(1)

	Dec 31 1986 $'000
Sales revenues	970,543
Income before taxes	34,940
Net income	27,516
Earnings per share	$4.28
Common stock(2)	6,400

(1) company formed September 1, 1987
(2) shares outstanding in thousands

No of Employees: 7,000

CYPRUS MINERALS COMPANY

7200 South Alton Way, PO Box 3299, Englewood, CO 80155
Tel: (303) 740-5000

Chairman: John C Duncan
President: Kenneth J Barr (and Chief Executive Officer)
Senior Executive Officers: Chester B Stone Jr (Executive VP and Chief Financial Officer), Dennis C Haugh (VP and Treasurer), Gerald J Malys (VP and Corporate Controller), Philip C Wolf (General Counsel and Corporate Secretary)

PRINCIPAL ACTIVITIES: Production of coal and minerals including gold
Principal Subsidiaries: Cyprus Coal Co; Cyprus Industrial Minerals Co; Cyprus Metals Co
Principal Bank: Citibank
Financial Information:

	Dec 31 1986 $'000
Sales revenues	810,822
Net income	21,125
Earnings per share	$0.81
Shareholders equity	816,765

No of Employees: 4,730

D H HOLMES & CO LTD

See HOLMES, D H, & CO LTD

DAHLBERG INC

7731 Country Club Drive, Minneapolis, MN 55427
Tel: (612) 545 3721

Chairman: Kenneth H Dahlberg
President: Thomas M Rootness
Senior Executive Officers: Jane E Hixson (Executive VP Corporate Communications), Richard R Mass (Executive VP Operations), Norman L Blemaster (Executive VP Franchising)

PRINCIPAL ACTIVITIES: Manufacture of medical and surgical aids; electronic control systems
Principal Subsidiaries: Dahlbergs Electronics Inc
Principal Bank: National City Bank
Financial Information:

	$'000
Sales revenues	31,160

No of Employees: 400

DAIRY MART CONVENIENCE STORES INC

240 South Road, Enfield, CT 06082
Tel: (203) 745 1661

Chairman: Charles Nirenberg (and President and Chief Executive Officer)
Senior Executive Officers: Lawrence D Handler (Executive VP and Treasurer), Frank Colaccino (VP Real Estate), Mitchell J Kupperman (VP Human Resources), Steven Montgomery (VP), Janet Nirenberg (Secretary)

PRINCIPAL ACTIVITIES: Retail food stores
Principal Bank: Connecticut Bank and Trust Company
Financial Information:

	$'000
Sales revenues	292,000

No of Employees: 570

DAIRYLEA COOPERATIVE INC

831 James Street, Syracuse, NY 13203
Tel: (315) 476-9101

President: Clyde E Rutherford
Senior Executive Officers: Bob Hall (Chief Executive Officer, General Manager), Richard Smith (Administrative VP, General Counsel), Jack Atkinson (VP Sales)

PRINCIPAL ACTIVITIES: Marketing of milk and dairy products
Trade Names: Dairylea
Principal Subsidiaries: Agri-Service Agencies Inc (insurance); Hudson Valley Dairy Distributors Inc
Principal Bank: Marine Midland
Financial Information:

	Mar 31 1986 $'000	Mar 31 1987 $'000
Sales revenues	379,871	342,163*
Members equity	7,100	11,000

*Sold Metro NYC Business

No of Employees: 950

DAIRYMEN, INC

10140 Linn Station Road, Louisville, KY 40223
Tel: (502) 426-6455
Telex: WUT 204291 dairymen lvl c

Chairman: Ray Moss Tucker (and President)
Senior Executive Officers: Ben Morgan Jr (Executive VP and Chief Executive Officer), Harold Gay (Senior VP), Jim McDowell (Senior VP and Chief Operating Officer), Jim Mueller (Senior VP and Chief Financial Officer), Al Ortego (Senior VP), Warren James (VP), John Mays (VP), Tony Haynes (VP-Controller), Phil Kenney (VP), Jerry Roadcap (VP), George Jung (VP)

PRINCIPAL ACTIVITIES: Processing of milk and manufacture of dairy products
Trade Names: FLAV-O-RICH, FARMBEST, RICH & CREAMY
Principal Subsidiaries: FLAV-O-RICH, Inc
Principal Bank: Liberty National Bank
Financial Information:

	Aug 31 1987 $'000
Sales revenues	1,009,386
Net income	5,806
Shareholders equity	81,576

No of Employees: 4,600

DAIRYMENS CREAMERY ASSOCIATION

Fifth & Albany, Caldwell, ID 83605
Tel: (208) 459-3687
Telex: WUT 150094 dca dairy cwll

President: Dale S Pline
Senior Executive Officers: Jerry Jaeger (VP)

PRINCIPAL ACTIVITIES: Dairy products
Principal Bank: Idaho First National
Financial Information:

	$'000
Sales revenues	100,000

No of Employees: 140

DAIRYPAK

One Champion Plaza, Stamford, CT 06921
Tel: (203) 358-6691

Senior Executive Officers: Earle Bensing (VP and General Manager), H D Platzbecker (VP and General Manager), William C Mosgrove (VP and General Manager), John R Cumming (VP and Divisional Manager), Augustus Bachman (VP and Divisional Manager), Jim Tonore (VP and Divisional Manager)

PRINCIPAL ACTIVITIES: Manufacture of cartons for milk
Parent Company: Champion International Corporation
Financial Information:

	$'000
Sales revenues	160,000

No of Employees: 1,000

DAISY SYSTEMS CORPORATION

700 Middlefield Rd, Mountain View, CA 94039
Tel: (415) 960-0123

Chairman: Max Palevsky (and Chief Executive Officer); Vice Chairman: Stanford Kaplan
President: H C Jones Jr (and Chief Operating Officer)
Senior Executive Officers: C C McCorkle (Treasurer), D A Stamm (Executive VP), Rafael Chatav (VP), Sol Kershner (VP)

PRINCIPAL ACTIVITIES: Computer systems and software
Principal Bank: Bank of America NT & SA
Financial Information:

	$'000
Sales revenues	122,600

No of Employees: 900

DALE ELECTRONICS, INC

2064-12th Avenue, Columbus, NE 68601
Tel: (402) 564-3131
Telex: TWX 910 6268314 dale elec cbus

President: Carroll A Novicki (and Chief Executive Officer)
Senior Executive Officers: James J Holmberg (VP Legal and Secretary), Floyd Mason (VP Services), William L Gaines (Senior VP Film-Wirewound), Kenneth W Moerson (VP Finance and Chief Financial Officer)

PRINCIPAL ACTIVITIES: Electronic component manufacturing
Parent Company: Dale Holdings, Inc
Financial Information:

	$'000
Sales revenues	116,096

No of Employees: 2,974

DALGETY FOODS, INC

909 Blanco Circle, Salinas, CA 93901
Tel: (415) 956-6340
Telex: TWX 910 368 7361 dalgety sli

Chairman: Peter A Gardiner
President: A F Stuart
Senior Executive Officers: Fred B DeBon (VP Operations), Bernard M Berry (VP Finance), R K Ernest (VP Marketing)

PRINCIPAL ACTIVITIES: Freezing of fruit and vegetables
Parent Company: Dalgety Inc, San Mateo, CA
Principal Bank: Security Pacific National Bank
Financial Information:

	$'000
Sales revenues	100,000

Principal Shareholders: Dalgety PLC, London, UK
No of Employees: 1,500

DALLAS CERAMIC CO

900 E 21st, Bakersfield, CA 93301
Tel: (805) 834 6714
Telex: TWX 910 8619 167 dal-tile da

Chairman: Robert M Brittingham
President: John J LoMonaco
Senior Executive Officers: Richard W Lee (VP Sales), Forest L Bryant (VP Manufacturing), Wiley R Page (VP Transport), Charles C Nies (VP Finance, Secretary and Treasurer)

PRINCIPAL ACTIVITIES: Manufacture of ceramic floor and wall tiles
Principal Bank: Republic National Bank
Financial Information:

	$'000
Sales revenues	50,000

No of Employees: 600

DALLAS CORPORATION

6750 LBJ Freeway, Dallas, TX 75240
Tel: (214) 233-6611
Telex: 203951; A/B 203951 DAL CORP

President: Robert C Haugh
Senior Executive Officers: Brian J Bolton (Executive VP and Chief Operating Officer), Howard A Bacon (Senior VP Overhead Door Group), John C Dahl (Senior VP Vehicular Equipment Group), Verne Lockard (VP and Treasurer), Alan R Bashov (VP Human Resources), Keith W Brockman (VP-Controller), Daniel G Flohr III (VP Auditing), Joseph C Nelson (VP-General Counsel and Secretary), Andre Schwirtter (VP-Specialty Products/Commercial), Jerry H Higgins (VP Specialty Products/Residential)

PRINCIPAL ACTIVITIES: Manufacturers of doors
Trade Names: TODCO, Overhead Door
Principal Subsidiaries: The Overhead Door Co of Texas; W B McGuire Co Inc; Architectural Engineering Products Co; U E

C Manufacturing Co; Span Metals Corp; O H D Rockford; Waldon Inc; Premier Products Inc; General Aluminum Corporation; OHD Thermacore Inc; Overhead/Lodi Door Corporation

Financial Information:

	Dec 31 1985	Dec 31 1986
	$'000	$'000
Sales revenues	396,672	396,248
Income before taxes	10,585(1)	2,292
Net income	5,940(1)	1,293
Dividends	4,697	4,861
Dividends per share	$0.645	$0.66
Earnings per share	$0.82	$0.18
Common stock(2)	39,804	39,612
Retained income	72,139	68,496
Shareholders equity	111,943	108,108

(1) before losses from discontinued operations of $7,976
(2) and paid in capital

No of Employees: 4,930

DALLAS FEDERAL SAVINGS & LOAN ASSOCIATION

8333 Douglas Avenue, Dallas, TX 75225
Tel: (214) 750-5000

Chairman: Lloyd S Bowles Sr (and Chief Executive Officer); Vice Chairman: Milton H Thomas (and Chief Operating Officer)
President: Lloyd S Bowles Jr (and Chief Administrative Officer)
Senior Executive Officers: William E Livingstone (Senior Executive VP Lending), Kenneth B Drake (Executive VP Operations), Ron Green (Senior VP), Cullen Rogers (Senior VP), J Stephen Goodlett (Senior VP Loans), Sam V Akins (Senior VP Investor Public Relations), Louis Ainsworth (Senior VP), Deryl Stevenson (Senior VP Administration Services)

PRINCIPAL ACTIVITIES: Financial services
Principal Subsidiaries: Dallas Federal Development Corp
Principal Bank: Chase Manhattan Bank

No of Employees: 650

DALTON INDUSTRIES, INC

Dalton Blvd, Willoughby, OH 44094
Tel: (216) 946-4000
Telex: WUT 980 633 daltonind wiby

Chairman: Kenneth Dery (and Chief Executive Officer)
President: James Dery
Senior Executive Officers: Robert Dery (Senior VP), Edwin Young (VP Finance), H Leonard Kleinman (VP Production), Larry Preiser (VP Sales)

PRINCIPAL ACTIVITIES: Clothing manufacture
Financial Information:

	$'000
Sales revenues	50,000

No of Employees: 1,000

DAMON CORPORATION

115 Fourth Avenue, Needham Heights, MA 02194
Tel: (617) 49-0800

Chairman: Dr D I Kosowsky
President: R P Schneider (and Chief Operating Officer)
Senior Executive Officers: A B Beitchman (Senior VP and Chief Financial Officer), Marcia A Kean (VP Corporate Communications), Daniel R Cotte (VP Management Information Systems), Norman Curtis (VP Medical Instrumentation), Joseph C Isola (Senior VP Medical Services), D J Powell (Senior VP and Chief Administrative Officer), Vernan F Sherman Jr (Senior VP Finance and Treasurer), David L Steele (VP and Controller), Richard T Theken (VP Human Resources)

PRINCIPAL ACTIVITIES: Medical products and health care services; craft and hobby products
Principal Subsidiaries: Damon Biotech Inc
Principal Bank: First National Bank of Boston
Financial Information:

	Aug 31 1986
	$'000
Sales revenues	147,962
Net (loss)	(2,619)
Dividends per share	$0.20
(Loss) per share	($0.39)
Shareholders equity	57,079

No of Employees: 2,700

DAMON CREATIONS INC

16 East 34th Street, New York, NY 10016
Tel: (212) 683 2465

Chairman: David Rappaport
President: Michael Rappaport (and Chief Executive Officer)
Senior Executive Officers: Lawrence Weinstein (Senior VP and Division President), Harold Hoskins (VP Operations and Manufacturing), Richard Rappaport (VP), Frances Rappaport (Secretary)

PRINCIPAL ACTIVITIES: Manufacture of men's shirts, knitted sportswear and neckwear
Principal Bank: Bankers Trust Company
Financial Information:

	$'000
Sales revenues	44,925

No of Employees: 900

DAMSON OIL CORPORATION

366 Madison Avenue, New York, NY 10017
Tel: (212) 503-8500

Chairman: Barrie M Damson (and President)
Senior Executive Officers: Robert N Stafford (Executive VP), Monte E Wetzler (Executive VP and Chief Financial Officer), William T Ouzts (Senior VP), Allan B Ecker (Senior VP and Legal Counsel), Carole G Donlin (VP Corporate and Investor Relations), Peter R Garland (VP Processing and Marketing), Charles W Gleeson (VP Production), William T Hurn (VP Law, Oil and Gas), Robert Ross Smith (VP Information Systems), Richard J Popper (VP and Secretary), William T Van Kleef (VP and Chief Accounting Officer)

PRINCIPAL ACTIVITIES: Production of oil and gas
Principal Subsidiaries: Damson Acquisition Sub Inc; Damson Securities Corp
Principal Bank: First City National Bank of Houston
Financial Information:

	$'000
Sales revenues	89,000

No of Employees: 1,000

DAN RIVER INC

2291 Memorial Drive, Danville, VA 24543
Tel: (804) 799-7000
Telex: TWX 710 8722601 dr damv

Chairman: David W Johnston Jr (and Chief Executive Officer)
President: Lester A Hudson Jr
Senior Executive Officers: L A Goodson Jr (Senior VP Research), J C Plowden Jr (VP Corporate Planning), W J Mika (VP), Harlan H Huntley (VP, General Counsel and Secretary), Robert C Crawford (VP), Grover S Elliott (VP Finance), Curtis E Wyatt (VP), Larry W Van de Visser (VP), G J Kintz (VP), E L Wright III (VP)

PRINCIPAL ACTIVITIES: Textile manufacture
Parent Company: Dan River Holding Co
Principal Bank: Chemical Bank

Financial Information:

	$'000
Sales revenues	520,000

No of Employees: 10,000

DANA CORPORATION

PO Box 1000, Toledo, OH 43697
Tel: (419) 535-4500

Chairman: G B Mitchell (and President and Chief Executive Officer)
Senior Executive Officers: Robert E Byrket (Executive VP, Chief Administrative Officer and Chief Financial Officer), Borge R Reimer (Executive VP), Carl H Hirsch (VP Planning), Martin J Strobel (VP, Secretary and General Counsel), James E Ayers (VP and Treasurer)

PRINCIPAL ACTIVITIES: Automotive components and industrial parts
Principal Subsidiaries: Cherokee Insurance Co; Diamond Financial Holdings Inc; Diamond Savings & Loan Co; Diamond Mortgage Corp; Potomac Leasing Co; Lantex Hydraulics Inc; Ford Steel & Supply Inc; Omicron Inc; Tyrone Hydraulics Inc; Warner Electric Brake & Clutch Co; Wix Corp; Gard Corp; Summey Building Systems Inc; 30 Inc
Financial Information:

	Dec 31 1985	Dec 31 1986
	$'000	$'000
Sales revenues	3,754,440	3,695,145
Net income	165,106	85,870
Earnings per share	$2.95	$1.68
Shareholders equity	1,194,753	954,943

No of Employees: 37,300

DANAHER CORPORATION

3524 Water Street NW, Washington, DC 20007
Tel: (202) 332-1805

Chairman: Steven M Rales (and Chief Executive Officer)
Senior Executive Officers: Mitchell P Rales (Executive VP)

PRINCIPAL ACTIVITIES: Manufacture of tires and rubber products for industrial use; vinyl products for the construction industry; real estate
Principal Subsidiaries: Chicago Pneumatic Tool Co; Diversified Mortgage Investors Inc; Master Shield Inc; The Mohawk Rubber Co
Financial Information:

	Dec 31 1986
	$'000
Sales revenues	524,000
Net income	15,400
Earnings per share	$1.51
Shareholders equity	65,240

No of Employees: 2,400

DANIEL INDUSTRIES, INC

PO Box 19097, Houston, TX 77224-9097
Tel: (713) 960-1300
Telex: WUT 794 547 dan ied hou

Chairman: W A Griffin Jr (and Chief Executive Officer)
President: Ralph H Clemons Jr (and Chief Operating Officer)
Senior Executive Officers: Rex W Landry (VP), W C Clingman (VP Information Services), E E Lowe (VP), H D Morrison Jr (VP, Secretary and Treasurer), James M Sharp (VP Research)

PRINCIPAL ACTIVITIES: Gas and oil production equipment and services; valves; electronic products
Principal Subsidiaries: Daniel Bolt Co Inc; Daniel Export Sales Corp; Daniel Geophysical; Daniel Oil Tools Co; Daniel Service Inc; Daniel Valve Co; Square W Machine & Manufacturing Inc
Principal Bank: Bank of the Southwest
Financial Information:

	$'000
Sales revenues	137,570

No of Employees: 1,840

DANIS INDUSTRIES CORPORATION

2 Riverplace-Suite 400, PO Box 1510, Dayton, OH 45401
Tel: (513) 228-1225
Telex: WUT 288 084 chem inc dtn

Chairman: Benhamin G Danis Jr
President: Thomas J Danis (and Chief Operating Officer)
Senior Executive Officers: Richard R Danis (Senior VP and Chief Administration Officer)

PRINCIPAL ACTIVITIES: Civil engineering; property development; manufacture of construction products
Principal Subsidiaries: Dayton Superior Corporation
Principal Bank: Bank One, Dayton, OH
Financial Information:

	Dec 31 1985	Dec 31 1986
	$'000	$'000
Sales revenues	189,000	252,000

No of Employees: 2,200

DANISH CREAMERY ASSOCIATION

755 F Street, Fresno, CA 93706
Tel: (209) 233-5154

Chairman: Oliver Espinola; First Vice Chairman: Henry Massaro
President: Galen W Brunner (and General Manager)
Senior Executive Officers: Paul A Rollin (Secretary)

PRINCIPAL ACTIVITIES: Dairy products
Principal Subsidiaries: Challenge Dairy
Principal Bank: Security Pacific
Financial Information:

	$'000
Sales revenues	86,000

No of Employees: 95

DANLY MACHINE CORPORATION

2100 S Laramie Avenue, Chicago, IL 60650
Tel: (213) 242-1800
Telex: WUT 254 153 danmach cro

President: Richard S Cummins (and Chief Executive Officer)
Senior Executive Officers: Eugene F Finkin (Executive VP Operations), David D Lowum (VP Die Set Dales), Steven G Jones (VP and Chief Financial Officer), Frank G Leach (VP Sales and Marketing)

PRINCIPAL ACTIVITIES: Danly Machine Corporation is engaged in the manufacture of mechanical presses, automated parts-handling systems for presses and presslines, die sets, diemakers' supplies, metal-cutting machine tools, and woodworking machinery
Parent Company: Ogden Corporation, New York, NY
Financial Information:

	$'000
Sales revenues	120,000

DANNERS INC

6060 North Guion Road, PO Box 1146, Indianapolis, IN 46206
Tel: (317) 291 8011

Chairman: Mark S Danner (and President, Chief Executive Officer and Chief Operating Officer)
Senior Executive Officers: A Wallace Williams (VP Real Estate), Robert C Bolsinger (VP Finance and Treasurer), David C Danner (Secretary and VP Administration), David E Brown (VP Information Systems), Norman A Spradlin (VP 3D Operations and Secretary), Jay Banner (VP Administration and Specialty Stores)

PRINCIPAL ACTIVITIES: Operation of department stores

Principal Bank: American Fletcher National Bank
Financial Information:

	$'000
Sales revenues	171,315

No of Employees: 2,600

DARLING DELAWARE COMPANY, INC
8737 King George Drive, Dallas, TX 75235
Tel: (214) 638-2223

Chairman: Edward W Rose III
President: William A Shirley Jr
Senior Executive Officers: J O'Brien (Executive VP), J Pearson (Senior VP and Secretary), C Rolland (VP)

PRINCIPAL ACTIVITIES: Manufacture of tallow, oils and animal feedstuffs
Parent Company: Darling Holdings Inc, Dallas, TX
Principal Subsidiaries: Darling & Company Inc
Principal Bank: First National Bank of Boston
Financial Information:

	$'000
Sales revenues	250,000+

No of Employees: 1,500

DART GROUP CORPORATION
3300 75th Avenue, Landover, MD 20785
Tel: (301) 731 1200

Chairman: Herbert H Haft (and Chief Executive Officer)
President: Robert M Haft (and Chief Operating Officer and Subsidiary Officer)
Senior Executive Officers: Ben S Kovalsky (Executive VP), Adam W Talarek (Executive VP), Richard J Koll (Senior VP Finance and Administration and Chief Financial Officer), William E Bolton (VP Loss Prevention), Gloria G Haft (VP), Ronald M Hirschel (VP and Legal Counsel), Linda G Haft (VP Dart Group Financial Corp), Dennis N Weiss (VP Real Estate)

PRINCIPAL ACTIVITIES: Sale of motor vehicle components and related products
Principal Subsidiaries: Trak Auto Corporation; Trak Auto East Corporation
Principal Bank: First American Bank of Maryland
Financial Information:

	$'000
Sales revenues	98,000

No of Employees: 55

DATA CARD CORPORATION
11111 Bren Road, W Minnetonka, MN 55343
Tel: (612) 933-1223
Telex: ITT 431 00 39 data ui

Chairman: D J Ekberg (and Chief Executive Officer)
President: G R Holland (and Chief Operating Officer)
Senior Executive Officers: Charles Schmidt (VP and Chief Financial Officer)

PRINCIPAL ACTIVITIES: Manufacture of equipment for the embossing and encoding of plastic cards
Principal Subsidiaries: Laserdyne Corp
Principal Bank: The First National Bank of Saint Paul
Financial Information:

	$'000
Sales revenues	104,000

No of Employees: 1,800

DATA COM, INC
301 Lakeside Drive, Horsham, PA 19044
Tel: (215) 659-2500
Telex: WUT 510 665 5897 datacom hosm

President: M H Berliner
Senior Executive Officers: Michael Berliner (VP), Joseph Smith (VP), H D Abramson (Secretary and Treasurer)

PRINCIPAL ACTIVITIES: Stationery, paper, office products
Principal Bank: Bank of New England
Financial Information:

	$'000
Sales revenues	60,000

No of Employees: 600

DATA GENERAL CORPORATION
4400 Computer Drive, Westboro, MA 01580
Tel: (617) 366-8911

President: Edson D deCastro
Senior Executive Officers: Donald V Bateman (VP, Human Resources), William W Bentley (VP, North American Field Engineering), James P Campbell (VP, Administration), Richard A Camuso (Senior VP, Worldwide Field Engineering), Frederick P Cochrane (VP, Field Engineering, Engineering Services), Colin Crook (Senior VP, Communications Systems Group), Vahram V Erdekian (VP, North American Manufacturing Operations), Michael B Evans (VP, Chief Financial Officer), Wayne Fitzsimmons (VP, Americas/Far East), Raymond Fortune (Senior VP, International Marketing and Sales), Jacob Frank (VP, Legal), Lee Henning (VP, Central Manufacturing Services), Carl E Kaplan (Secretary), John D Kavazanjian (VP, International Manufacturing), Frank Keaney (VP, North American Sales), J David Lyons (VP, Group Marketing), Ward D MacKenzie (VP, Value Added Reseller Marketing and Development), Anthony C Nicoletti (VP, Sales Support and Planning), Herbert J Richman (Executive VP, Director), James J Ryan (VP, Information Management Group), Vahe Sarkissian (VP, Sunnyvale Division), Michael Schneider (VP, Customer Service Division), Frank Silkman (Senior VP, Manufacturing and Field Engineering), Ronald L Skates (Senior VP, Finance and Administration), Hisashi Tomino (VP; President, Nippon Data General), J Thomas West (VP, Systems Development Division)

PRINCIPAL ACTIVITIES: Data General Corporation designs, manufactures and sells general purpose computer systems and provides peripheral equipment, software, communications systems and related products and services, including training and maintenance
Principal Bank: Shawmut Bank NA of Boston
Financial Information:

	Sep 30 1986	Sep 30 1987
	$'000	$'000
Sales revenues	1,267,959	1,274,348
Income (loss) before taxes	14,118	(69,949)
Net (loss)	(28,980)	(127,078)
(Loss) per share	($1.07)	($4.71)
Common stock	268,182	302,639
Retained income	406,827	279,749
Shareholders equity	682,628	588,243

No of Employees: 16,000

DATA I/O CORPORATION
10525 Willows Road NE, C-46 Redmond, WA 98052
Tel: (206) 881-6444
Telex: ITT 471091 data i o itt

President: Lawrence L Mayhew (and Chief Executive Officer)
Senior Executive Officers: Edgar F Rampy (VP Finance and Administration, Secretary and Treasurer), Richard C Karr (VP Operations), William D Ellis (VP Product and Business Developments)

PRINCIPAL ACTIVITIES: Computer equipment and components
Principal Subsidiaries: Futurenet Corp
Principal Bank: Rainier National Bank

Financial Information:

	$'000
Sales revenues	56,000

No of Employees: 520

DATA SWITCH CORPORATION

1 Enterprise Drive, Shelton, CT 06484

Tel: (203) 926 1801

Chairman: Richard E Greene

President: Robert G Gilbertson (and Chief Executive Officer)

Senior Executive Officers: Rudolph G Morin (Senior VP Finance and Administration), Russell B Drew (Senior VP Sales and Marketing), Aldis Klavins (VP Engineering), Elvio P Del Monte (VP Manufacturing), Bo Linnell (VP Marketing), Todd M Dematteo (Secretary and Legal Counsel)

PRINCIPAL ACTIVITIES: Manufacture of switching and management systems and data processing equipment

Principal Bank: Shawmut Bank of Boston

Financial Information:

	$'000
Sales revenues	32,700

No of Employees: 330

DATA SYSTEMS GROUP

15 Main Street, Rte 520, Holmdel, NJ 07733

Tel: (201) 870-4500

Senior Executive Officers: James K Sims (Senior VP), Salvatore Alini (Group VP Development), Patrick J Zilvitis (Group VP Marketing)

PRINCIPAL ACTIVITIES: Data processing equipment

Parent Company: Perkin-Elmer Corporation, Norwalk, CT

Financial Information:

	$'000
Sales revenues	230,000

DATA-DESIGN LABORATORIES

7925 Center Avenue, PO Box 711, Cucamonga, CA 91730

Tel: (714) 987-2511

Telefax: (714) 989-7055

Chairman: Thomas C Beiseker

President: Lester Hill (and Chief Executive Officer)

Senior Executive Officers: Stephen M Andres (VP Administration), G L Milliken (VP Planning and Contracts), Milton L Sneller (Executive VP and Cheif Operations Officer), Alan R Steel (VP Finance and Treasurer), Richard G Littman (Secretary)

PRINCIPAL ACTIVITIES: Data-Design Laboratories is a diversified, high-technology corporation which operates primarily in four major business segments: Engineering Services, Electronics, Communications, and light manufacturing for commercial customers

Principal Subsidiaries: Aeroscientific Corporation; A J Electronics; Catel Telecommunications Inc; Irlandus Circuits (NI) Ltd (Northern Ireland); Sierra Precision; Siltron Illumination; DDL OMNI Engineering

Principal Bank: Bank of America National Trust and Savings Association

Financial Information:

	Jun 30 1986 $'000	Jun 30 1987 $'000
Sales revenues	67,393	74,707
Income (loss) before taxes	(2,513)	10,200
Net income (loss)	(372)	7,165
Dividends	1,555	1,572
Dividends per share	$0.24	$0.24
Earnings (loss) per share	($0.06)	$1.09
Common stock*	2,188	2,182
Retained income	26,234	31,827
Shareholders equity	33,375	36,302

*number of shares in thousands

No of Employees: 1,400

DATAPOINT CORPORATION

9725 Datapoint Drive, San Antonio, TX 78284

Tel: (512) 699-7000 (US); (44-932) 222228 (International)

Telex: US. 767300 US Data Disc SNT

Chairman: Asher B Edelman

President: Edward P Gistaro (and Chief Executive Officer)

Senior Executive Officers: Doris D Bencsik (Chief Operating Officer), Richard A Hahn (Senior VP, Americas), Stewart J Paperin (Senior VP, Finance, Chief Financial Officer), Donald J Shapiro (Senior VP, Advanced Product Development), Olaf von Bulow (Senior VP, International), Henrik Besserman (VP, Regional General Manager, International), Yvon le Roux (VP, Regional General Manager, International), William Littlejohn (VP, Technical Operations, International)

PRINCIPAL ACTIVITIES: Worldwide supplier of networked data processing and office automation

Trade Names: Registered Trademarks: ARC (Attached Resource Computer), ARCNET, DATABUS, DATAPOINT, DATAPOLL, DATASHARE, INFOSWITCH (International only), INFOSET (International only), ISX & KSX (International only), Integrated Electronic Office System, LIGHTLINK, RMS (Resource Management System). Trademarks: AIM (Associative Index Method), ARCSTAT DASP, DATASORT, ELECTRONIC MESSAGE SERVICE, INTELLIGENT NETWORK, INTELLIGENT NETWORK EXECUTIVE, INX, MINX (Multimedia Information Network Exchange), MULTILINK, PC-Intelligent Network, PRO-VISTA, SHARE, VISTA-BOARD, VISTA-FINDER, VISTA-GUIDE, VISTA-MAIL, VISTA-OFFICE, VISTA-PC, VISTA-PLAN, VISTA-SCRIPT, VISTA-SPELL I, VISTA-SPELL II, VISTA-STATION-82, VISTA-STATION-84, VISTA-VIEW, VISTA-WORD

Principal Subsidiaries: Datapoint Corporation Pty Ltd (Australia); Datapoint Belgium SA (Belgium); Datapoint do Brasil (Brazil); Canada Inc (Canada); Datapoint Deutschland Gmbh (Germany); Datapoint Oy (Finland); Datapoint Matra Informatique SA (France); Datapoint Nederland BV (Netherlands); Datapoint Italia SpA (Italy); Datapoint Corporation (NZ) Ltd (New Zealand); Datapoint Iberica SA (Spain); Datapoint Svenska AB (Sweden); Datapoint (Schweiz) AG (Switzerland); Datapoint (UK) Ltd (UK); European Headquarters: Datapoint International Ltd (UK)

Principal Bank: International: Banque Nationale de Paris, Paris

Financial Information:

	$'000
Sales revenues	520,000

No of Employees: 4,000

DATAPRODUCTS CORPORATION

6200 Canoga Avenue, Woodland Hills, CA 91365

Tel: (213) 887-8000

Telex: WUT 674734 data pro lsa

Chairman: Jack C Davis (and President and Chief Executive Officer)

Senior Executive Officers: Erwin Tomash (Chairman Executive Committee), Paul J Smith (Executive VP Printer Business),

John T Laws (Senior VP Finance), Clifford J Helms (Senior VP Advanced Technology), Paul D Weiser (Senior VP, Secretary and Counsel), Frank J McQuaid (Senior VP), John Leggat (Senior VP Corporate Development and Marketing), Clifford Jones (Senior VP Corporate Development), Gary D Bernard (Senior VP Human Resources), W Allen Gerber (Senior VP Corporate Development)

PRINCIPAL ACTIVITIES: Computer peripherals, supplies and services
Principal Subsidiaries: Dataproducts Inc; Dataproducts of New England Inc
Principal Bank: Chase Manhattan Bank
Financial Information:

	$'000
Sales revenues	354,000

No of Employees: 4,200

DATASCOPE CORPORATION

580 Winters Avenue, Paramus, NJ 07652
Tel: (201) 265 8800
Telex: TWX 710-990-6630
Telefax: (201) 265-8562

Chairman: Lawrence Saper (and President)
Senior Executive Officers: George Heller (Senior VP and Secretary), Ernst Janzen (Senior VP International), Bruce L Hanson (Executive VP Operations), Murray Pitkowsky, (VP, Finance and Treasurer), Andre Cohen (Executive VP Marketing), William H Terrell (VP Corporate Development)

PRINCIPAL ACTIVITIES: Medical device manufacturing of physiological monitors and cardiac assist systems
Principal Subsidiaries: Datascope BV; Datascope GmbH; Datascope Medical Co Ltd; Bioplex
Principal Bank: Midlantic National Bank
Financial Information:

	June 30 1986	June 30 1987
	$'000	$'000
Sales revenues	67,400	87,600
Income before taxes	5,008	10,092
Net income	3,028	5,450
Earnings per share	$0.79	$1.26
Common stock	36	42
Retained income	21,407	26,857
Shareholders equity	24,521	42,042

No of Employees: 840

DAUPHIN DEPOSIT BANK & TRUST COMPANY

PO Box 2961, Harrisburg, PA 17105
Tel: (717) 255-2121
Telex: WUT 902364 dauph dep hbg

Chairman: John D Wickert (and Chief Executive Officer)
President: William J King (and Chairman Executive Committee and Chief Operating Officer)
Senior Executive Officers: John J Fawley (Executive VP), Roderick C MacDonald (Executive VP and Chief Financial Officer), Richard E Reese (Executive VP), George D McKeon (Senior VP and Trust Officer), Kenneth M Bistline (Senior VP), Robert E Fishel (Senior VP), John E McCann (Senior VP), Robert M Spicer Jr (VP and Secretary)

PRINCIPAL ACTIVITIES: Banking
Parent Company: Dauphin Deposit Corp

No of Employees: 725

DAUPHIN DEPOSIT CORPORATION

213 Market Street, Harrisburg, PA 17105
Tel: (717) 255 2121

Chairman: John D Wickert (and Chief Executive Officer); Vice Chairman: Frederick E Huccius Jr
President: William J King (and Chief Operating Officer and Chairman of Executive Committee)
Senior Executive Officers: John J Fawley (Executive VP), Roderick C MacDonald (Executive VP and Chief Financial Officer), Edward A Klitsch (Senior VP, Treasurer and Assistant Secretary), Samuel W Bomberger (Senior VP and Auditor), Clyde E Fulton (Senior VP and Chief Investment Officer), Robert M Spicer Jr (VP, Secretary and Assistant Treasurer)

PRINCIPAL ACTIVITIES: Holding company with interests in banking
Principal Subsidiaries: Bancorp of PA Inc; Bank of PA; Dauphin Deposit Bank & Trust Co; Financial Realty Inc
Principal Bank: Dauphin Deposit Bank & Trust Co

No of Employees: 1,500

DAVIS WALKER CORPORATION

6315 Bandini Blvd, Los Angeles, CA 90040
Tel: (213) 721-6000
Telex: WUT 691 437 united intl lsa

Chairman: James L Walker (and Chief Executive Officer); Vice Chairman: James Franzen
Senior Executive Officers: Larry Valenti (VP Industrial Relations), C W Stauffer (VP Purchasing)

PRINCIPAL ACTIVITIES: Steel wire manufacture
Principal Subsidiaries: Davis Walker Steel & Wire Corp
Principal Bank: Bank of America
Financial Information:

	$'000
Sales revenues	250,000

No of Employees: 1,600

DAVIS WATER & WASTE INDUSTRIES, INC

1820 Metcalf Avenue, Thomasville, GA 31792
Tel: (912) 226-5733

Chairman: Jasper C Davis; Vice Chairman: R R Davis
President: R D White (and Chief Executive and Operating Officer)
Senior Executive Officers: Stanley O White (Secretary and Treasurer)

PRINCIPAL ACTIVITIES: Production and distribution of equipment and supplies for the water distribution and treatment industry
Trade Names: Davis-Emu, Davis Meter & Supply Company, Davco, Davis Process
Principal Subsidiaries: Taylor-Jett Co
Principal Bank: Commercial Bank
Financial Information:

	Apr 30 1986	Apr 30 1987
	$'000	$'000
Sales revenues	101,354	124,895
Income before taxes	3,291	5,051
Net income	1,666	2,650
Dividends	244	338
Dividends per share	$0.09	$0.12
Earnings per share	$0.58	$0.92
Common stock	2,875	2,876
Retained income	11,327	13,639
Shareholders equity	15,046	17,389

No of Employees: 595

DAVY MCKEE EQUIPMENT CORPORATION

441 Smithfield Street, Pittsburgh, PA 15222
Tel: (412) 562-9500
Telex: WUT 902 943 davy mckee pgh

Chairman: A G Raper
President: Keith H Hoyle

Senior Executive Officers: John M Kelman (Executive VP), D Berg (VP Mills and Auto Division), Alan Ridley (VP, E & C Division)

PRINCIPAL ACTIVITIES: Industrial plant for the manufacture of iron and steel
Parent Company: Davy Inc
Principal Bank: National Westminster Bank PLC, UK
Financial Information:

	$'000
Sales revenues	50,000

Principal Shareholders: Davy Corporation PLC, London, UK
No of Employees: 170

DAY INTERNATIONAL (FORMERLY DAYCO CORPORATION)

333 W First Street, Dayton, OH 45402
Tel: (513) 226-7000
Telex: 288219
Telefax: (513) 226-4689

Chairman: Richard J Jacob
President: Ernest F Dourlet
Senior Executive Officers: Peter J Neroni (Executive VP), David S Gutridge (Executive VP), J Lee Finger (Senior VP Operations), Nick G Crnkovich (VP and Controller), Bruce A McNiel (VP and Treasurer), Denis G Daly (VP, General Counsel and Corporate Secretary), Jack O Quamme (Senior Group VP), Donald E Ross (Group VP), Wilhelmus Waanders (Group VP), Richard O Christian (VP Global Sourcing and Strategies), John J Cook (VP Budgeting and Planning), John S Haley (VP Physical Distribution), Yale J Holt (VP Corporate Development), William H Matthews (VP Marketing), Ronald Kane (VP Management Information Systems), Ped W Phillips (VP and Director of Taxation), William K Roberts (VP Purchasing), William W Ruyle (VP Quality Control), Thomas E Ryan (VP Corporate Communications), Ralph Zimmerman (VP Benefits/Pension Management)

PRINCIPAL ACTIVITIES: Day International manufactures and distributes a wide variety of rubber and plastic parts. A large number of these parts are used as replacement items. Day International is either the leader-or a strong second-in most of its markets. Operations are organized into four segments: Industrial Products, Transportation Products, Plastic Products and Consumer Products. Industrial: Products:- industrial V-belts; hydraulic hose and industrial hose; flexible couplings; formulated rubber compounds; industrial inking and business machine rollers; printing blankets; single-ply roofing membrane; textile cots, aprons and loom supplies; latex-coated industrial fabric. Customers:- industrial distributors; chemical industry; textile industry; printing industry; petroleum and mining industries; computer and business machine manufacturers; heavy duty equipment manufacturers; appliance manufacturers; lawn and garden equipment manufacturers; agricultural equipment manufacturers; roofing system suppliers. Transportation: Products:- automotive and heavy duty V-belts; serpentine belts; V-ribbed drives; radiator hose; heater hose; power steering hose; fan clutch assemblies; transmission oil coolers; belt tensioners; seat and back cushioning; insulation and sound deadening mateials; automotive trim; molded rubber; hydraulic hose and fittings; plastic center plate liners. Customers:- major domestic and foreign automotive manufacturers; truck and heavy-duty equipment manufacturers; farm equipment manufacturers; automotive parts distributors; major oil companies; mass merchandising outlets; railroads. Plastics: Products:- plastic sheets, rods, tubes and film; graphic arts materials; engineered flexible plastic hose; formulated thermoplastic compounds; engineered plastics. Customers:-appliance industry; hospital supply houses; construction industry; petroleum and chemical industries; plastic fabricators; graphic arts industry. Consumer: Products:- Contract and designer wall coverings; sound absorbing wall systems; garden hose; safety products. Customers:- major department stores; chain, variety and mass merchandising retail outlets; hardware stores; home improvement market; architects builders and interior designers; general industrial manufacturers
Trade Names: DAYCO, DAYFLEX, DAY-FLO, DAYVENT, DURAVENT, E-Z CRIMP, PLIADUCT, GOLD LABEL, SANITAS, VICRACOUSTIC, VICRTREX, ACCU-DOT, POLY-RIB, EASY-FLEX, DAYCOLLAN (all registered trademarks)
Principal Subsidiaries: Allen Industries Inc; Cadillac Plastic & Chemical Co; L E Carpenter and Company; Colonial Rubber Works Inc; Eaglemotive Industries Inc; Eagle Die Casting
Principal Bank: Bank One, Dayton, NA
Financial Information:

	Oct 31 1986
	$'000
Sales revenues	911,002
Net income	3,120
Earnings per share	$0.39
Shareholders equity	236,250

No of Employees: 10,000

DAY-BRITE LIGHTING DIVISION

1015 S Green Street, Tupelo, MS 38801
Tel: (601) 842-7212
Telex: 533359 DAYBRITE TUP

President: Robert G Schreiner
Senior Executive Officers: J C Ramsey (Executive VP Sales/Marketing), W D Markwell (VP Finance), S J Smith (VP Operations), W W Scoville (VP Marketing), A A Dunn (VP International Sales), M L Clegg (VP Industrial Relations), E W White (VP Sales)

PRINCIPAL ACTIVITIES: Manufacture of commercial and industrial electric lighting equipment and flexible wiring systems
Parent Company: Emerson Electric Co, St Louis, MO
Financial Information: Divn of Emerson Electric Co

	$'000
Sales revenues	75,000

No of Employees: 800

DAYS INNS CORPORATION

2751 Buford Highway Northeast. Atlanta, GA 30324
Tel: (404) 329 7466

Chairman: Henry R Silverman (and Chief Executive Officer)
President: Michael A Leven (and Chief Operating Officer)
Senior Executive Officers: Frederick B Beilstein III (Executive VP and Chief Financial Officer), James E Buckman (Executive VP, Legal Counsel and Secretary), Peter J Housman II (Executive VP), Donald G Raider (Executive VP), Stephen F McLaughlin (Senior VP), John J Russell (Senior VP Operations), Julio Vazquez (Senior VP), Alan A Printer (Senior VP Marketing Support and Product Development)

PRINCIPAL ACTIVITIES: Motels and hotels
Financial Information:

	$'000
Sales revenues	73,000

No of Employees: 2,500

DAYTON HUDSON CORPORATION

777 Nicollet Mall, Minneapolis, MN 55402
Tel: (612) 370-6948

Chairman: Kenneth A Macke (and Chairman Executive Committee and Chief Executive Officer); Vice Chairman: Gerald R Gallaher (and Chief Administrative Officer)
President: Boake A Sells
Senior Executive Officers: Bruce G Allbright (Senior VP), James T Hale (Senior VP and Secretary), John F Kilmartin (Senior VP), Willard C Shull III (Senior VP Finance), Edwin H Wingate (Senior VP Personnel), Ann H Barkelew (VP), David W Beckley (VP), Susan S Boren (VP and Controller), Larry E Carlson (VP), Peter Corcoran (VP), Karol D Emmerich (VP and

Treasurer), Thomas M Etzkorn (VP), L Fred Hamacher (VP), William E Harder (VP and Assistant Secretary), Peter C Hutchinson (VP), William P Hise (Assistant Secretary)

PRINCIPAL ACTIVITIES: Dayton Hudson Corporation is a growth company focusing exclusively on retailing. At year-end, the Corporation was operating 1,206 stores in 48 states, the District of Columbia and Puerto Rico. Dayton Hudson's principal operating strategy is to provide exceptional value to the American consumer through mutiple retail formats. Retail operations are conducted by five companies, which are organized into four business segments: Target:- Target is an upscale discount store chain operating in 22 states. Target offers low prices on a broad assortment of high-quality fashion and basic hardlines and softgoods in easy-to-shop, self-service stores. Dayton Hudson Department Store Company:- The Dayton Hudson Department Store Company emphasizes fashion leadership, quality merchandise, broad selections and customer service. It operates Hudson's and Dayton's stores in seven states. Mervyn's:- Mervyn's is a highly promotional, popular priced, value-oriented department store company operating in 10 states. Mervyn's stores feature nationally branded and private-label apparel, accessories and household softgoods. Specialty Merchandisers:- Specialty merchandising operations are conducted by two multi-store companies: B Dalton Bookseller, a national bookstore chain, and Lechmere, a New England hardlines retailer

Principal Subsidiaries: Target; Mervyn's; B Dalton Booksellers; Lechmere; Dayton Hudson Department Store Company

Financial Information:

	Feb 1 1986	Feb 1 1987
	$'000	$'000
Sales revenues	8,793,400	9,300,000
Net income	283,600	255,000

No of Employees: 128,000

DAYTON POWER & LIGHT COMPANY

Courthouse Plaza Southwest, Dayton, OH 45402
Tel: (513) 224 6000

Chairman: Robert E Frazer
President: Peter H Forster (and Chief Executive Officer and Executive VP)
Senior Executive Officers: Robert E Buerger (VP and Manager Finance), Allen M Hill (VP, Treasurer and Chief Financial Officer), Carl R Morey (VP), Wilbur C Shoup (VP), Steven G Smith (VP), Paul R Anderson (Controller and Treasurer), Stephen F Koziar Jr (Secretary)

PRINCIPAL ACTIVITIES: Supply of electricity, natural gas and steam
Parent Company: DPL Inc
Financial Information:

	$'000
Sales revenues	1,000,000

No of Employees: 3,000

DAYTON-WALTHER CORPORATION

2800 E River Road, Box 1022, Dayton, OH 45401
Tel: (513) 296-3113
Telex: WUT 288 291 dy walther mrme

Chairman: Daniel Walther (and Chief Executive Officer); Vice Chairman: Eugene M Mitchell
President: Fred Walther (and Chief Operating Officer)
Senior Executive Officers: James Vance (Executive VP Finance and Law), Richard E Phillips (VP Human Resources), Thomas A Endicott (VP and General Manager Dayton Products), Jerry L Wantz (VP Dayton Sales)

PRINCIPAL ACTIVITIES: Manufacture of automobile and truck components
Principal Subsidiaries: Camden Castings Center Inc; Citation-Walther Corp

Principal Bank: Continental Illinois National Bank and Trust Company of Chicago
Financial Information:

	$'000
Sales revenues	250,000

No of Employees: 2,000

DBA SYSTEMS INC

1200 South Woody Burke Road, Melbourne, FL 32901
Tel: (305) 725 3711

Chairman: Howard N Hebert (and President and Chief Executive Officer)
Senior Executive Officers: Gerald A Nathe (Senior VP), Edward I Williams (Senior VP), Gary J Cooey (VP Administration), John N Elder (VP, Treasurer and Assistant Secretary), Jon D Guess (VP and Controller), Eugene S Cavallucci (VP, Secretary and Legal Counsel), John L Schaumann (VP Strategic Planning), Charles N Keating Jr (VP Business Development)

PRINCIPAL ACTIVITIES: Manufacture of high technology photographic equipment
Principal Subsidiaries: Logetronics Inc; Loge Compuslide Inc; Loge Dunn Instruments Inc; Loge Interpretation Systems; Loge Spatial Data Systems Inc; Loge/Robertson Inc; Photographic Corporation of America
Principal Bank: Atlantic Bank
Financial Information:

	$'000
Sales revenues	66,000

No of Employees: 820

DBS, INC

Randolph Industrial Park, Randolph, MA 02368
Tel: (617) 963-8500

Chairman: Robert Henderson
President: C W Doulton
Senior Executive Officers: R E McManus (VP Finance and Treasurer)

PRINCIPAL ACTIVITIES: Office equipment
Principal Bank: New England Merchants Bank
Financial Information:

	$'000
Sales revenues	130,000

No of Employees: 1,875

DCA FOOD INDUSTRIES, INC

919 Third Avenue, New York, NY 10022
Tel: (212) 207-2000

President: David H Lipka (and Chief Executive Officer)
Senior Executive Officers: Alvin W Russell (VP Corporate Purchasing), John Runk (VP DCA Company Division), Stanley Rock (DCA Company, Division Doco Bakeries/International), John Moyer (VP Research and Development), Paul E Benner (VP and Controller), Leonard A Fischer (VP DCA Company Division), Richard Humi (VP Golden Dipt Company)

PRINCIPAL ACTIVITIES: Manufacture of food mixes for cakes and other bakery products
Trade Names: DCA, Charles Dennery, Golden Dipt
Parent Company: Allied-Lyons North America Corp
Principal Bank: Manufacturers Hanover Trust Company
Financial Information:

	$'000
Sales revenues	150,000

Principal Shareholders: Allied-Lyons PLC, London, UK
No of Employees: 1,250

DCNY CORPORATION

58 Pine St, New York, NY 10005
Tel. (212) 248-8900

Chairman: R F Peters
President: A J Hanlon
Senior Executive Officers: D G Brodie (Executive VP), S E Pardee (Executive VP), P E Gall (Senior VP and Treasurer), R T Bird (Senior VP and Secretary), M V Dawes (Senor VP), K G Rehm (VP and Controller), Phebe C Miller (VP and Legal Counsel)

PRINCIPAL ACTIVITIES: Dealers in securities
Financial Information:

	Dec 31 1986
	$'000
Revenues	273,613
Net income	24,613
Earnings per share	$6.14
Stockholders equity	110,045
Total assets	4,867,972

No of Employees: 354

DE TOMASO INDUSTRIES, INC

107 Monmouth Street, Red Bank, NJ 07701
Tel: (201) 842-7200

Chairman: Kjell H Qvale
President: Alejandro de Tomaso
Senior Executive Officers: Catherine D Germano (Treasurer), Howard E Chase (Secretary)

PRINCIPAL ACTIVITIES: Manufacture of motor vehicles and motorcycles
Principal Subsidiaries: Maserati Automobiles Inc; Bennelli/Moto Guzzi North America
Principal Bank: Midlantic Merchants
Financial Information:

	$'000
Sales revenues	213,000

No of Employees: 3,170

DEAD RIVER GROUP OF COMPANIES

55 Broadway, Bangor, ME 04401
Tel: (207) 947-8641

Chairman: P Andrews Nixon (and President)
Senior Executive Officers: Philip H Grantham (Senior VP Planning and Development and Treasurer), John H Cox (VP Personnel and Public Affairs), Rollin F Haynes (VP Real Estate), F M McClain (VP Petroleum), George W Weiland (VP Forest Products)

PRINCIPAL ACTIVITIES: Timber industries; fuel distribution
Principal Subsidiaries: Dead River Petroleum Co; Dead River Co NH Inc; Scott Motor Transport Co
Principal Bank: Merrill Trust Company
Financial Information:

	$'000
Sales revenues	195,000

No of Employees: 930

DEAN FOODS COMPANY

3600 N River Road, Franklin Park, IL 60131
Tel: (312) 678-1680

Chairman: Kenneth J Douglas
President: Howard M Dean
Senior Executive Officers: John V Guckien, Robert F Antoine, N Dale Finch, William D Fischer, James R Greisinger, George A Muck, Thomas A Ravencroft, Wilbert E Rittmueller, Thomas L Rose, Terence J Smith, Dale I Hecox

PRINCIPAL ACTIVITIES: Purchasing, processing and distribution of dairy products and specialty food products
Trade Names: Principal Brand Name: Dean Foods. Other Trade Names: McArthur, T G Lee, Creamland, Gandy, Fieldcrest, Baskin Robbins, McCadam, Atkins, Sunflo, Hoffman House, Hart's, Bell, Price's, Gilt Edge, Reiter, St Thomas, Bowman, Peter Pipers, Heifetz, Freshlike, Veg-all, Reiter
Principal Subsidiaries: T G Lee Foods Inc; Creamland Dairies Inc; Gandy's Dairies Inc; McCadam Cheese Company Inc; Gilt Edge Farms Inc; Atkins Pickle Company Inc; Juice Services Inc; Dean Dairy Products Co; Bell Dairy Products Inc; Bowman Dairy Company Inc; Dean Milk Company Inc; DFC Transportation Co; Green Bay Food Co; Hart's Dairy Inc; Liberty Dairy; McArthur Dairy Inc; St Thomas Dairies Inc; Ryan Milk Company; Reiter Dairy Inc; Fairmont Products Inc; The Larsen Company; Elgin Blenders; Verifine Dairy Products Corporation; Amboy Specialty Foods; Price's Creameries
Principal Bank: Harris Trust & Savings
Financial Information:

	May 31 1986	May 31 1987
	$'000	$'000
Sales revenues	1,268,580	1,434,600
Income before taxes	77,656	82,794
Net income	40,723	41,067
Dividends	10,590	12,835
Dividends per share	$0.40	$0.48
Earnings per share	$1.53	$1.54
Common stock	26,693	26,769
Retained income	180,527	208,759
Shareholders equity	207,220	236,417

No of Employees: 6,900

DEAN, JIMMY, MEAT COMPANY, INC

1341 Mockingbird Lane, Dallas, TX 75247
Tel: (214) 638-1190

Chairman: Jimmy Dean
President: Duane F Getty
Senior Executive Officers: Don Guard (VP Sales and Marketing), R J Ellis (VP Technical Services), Angelo G Laros (VP and Chief Financial Officer), Charles J Boudreaux (VP, Secretary and Controller)

PRINCIPAL ACTIVITIES: Manufacture of sausages and other pork products; leather goods; restaurant interests
Parent Company: Sara Lee Corporation, Chicago, IL
Principal Bank: First City Bank of Dallas
Financial Information:

	$'000
Sales revenues	85,000

No of Employees: 350

DEB SHOPS INC

9401 Blue Grass Road, Philadelphia, PA 19114
Tel: (215) 676 6000

Chairman: Philip Rounick; Vice Chairman: Aaaron Weiner
President: Marvin Rounick (and Chief Executive Officer)
Senior Executive Officers: Warren Weiner (Executive VP, Secretary and Treasurer), Crawford Grogan (VP Display), Traci Jan Morrow (VP Operations), Leonard Reed (VP Operations), Lester E Wolser (VP Finance and Chief Financial Officer), Barry Vesotsky (VP Merchandising), Marvin Waxman (Controller), Jack A Rounick (Assistant Secretary)

PRINCIPAL ACTIVITIES: Retail trade in women's clothing through a chain of stores specializing in clothes for juniors
Principal Bank: Philadelphia National Bank
Financial Information:

	1985	1986
	$'000	$'000
Sales revenues	120,405	147,104
Income before taxes	15,274	19,705
Net income	7,850	10,350
Earnings per share	$1.04	$1.37
Shareholders equity	29,734	39,127

No of Employees: 1,300

DEC INTERNATIONAL, INC

PO Box 8050, Madison, WI 53708
Tel: (608) 222-4778
Telex: RCA 201 317 deci ur

President: H Moe
Senior Executive Officers: R Smith (VP and General Counsel), R Albrecht (VP and Secretary)

PRINCIPAL ACTIVITIES: Manufacture of dairy and food processing machinery and equipment
Principal Bank: First Wisconsin
Financial Information:

	$'000
Sales revenues	235,000

No of Employees: 830

DECATUR FEDERAL SAVINGS & LOAN ASSOCIATION

250 E Ponce De Leon Avenue, Decatur, GA 30030
Tel: (404) 371-4000

Chairman: J R Harris (and Chief Executive Officer)
President: Robert C McMahan (and Chief Operating Officer)
Senior Executive Officers: Roger T Hansen (Senior VP Administration Group), William P Wallace (Senior VP Banking Group), Peter M Lynch (Senior VP Property Group), Wilbur G Kurtz III (Senior VP), C Richard Sissom (Group VP), E P Jennings Jr (Divisional VP Marketing), Julia L Mitchell (Divisional VP and Treasurer), Donald C Williamson (Divisional VP Auditing and Internal Auditor), Larry D Simpson (Divisional VP Human Resources)

PRINCIPAL ACTIVITIES: Savings and loans
Principal Subsidiaries: Decatur Holding Co Inc; Decatur Capital Corp; DFS Services; Fairfield Mortgage Services Inc
Principal Bank: Trust Company Bank of Georgia

No of Employees: 600

DECISION INDUSTRIES CORPORATION

400 Horsham Road, Horsham, PA 19044
Tel: (215) 674-3300
Telex: WUT 831 471 decision hosm

Chairman: Richard N Schineller
President: Joseph J Ciasullo
Senior Executive Officers: Howard Bernard (Senior VP and General Counsel), John J Brennan (VP Product Planning)

PRINCIPAL ACTIVITIES: Manufacture of data processing equipment; leasing of computers
Principal Bank: Provident National Bank
Financial Information:

	$'000
Sales revenues	176,000

No of Employees: 1,200

DEERE & COMPANY

Moline, IL 61265
Tel: (309) 752-8000
Cable: DEERECO
Telex: 468514 DEFERECO MOLI

Chairman: Robert A Hanson (and Chief Executive Officer)
President: Boyd C Bartlett (and Chief Operating Officer)
Senior Executive Officers: Thomas A Gildehaus (Executive VP Corporate Staff and Administration), Hans W Becherer (Executive VP Farm Equipment and Consumer Products Worldwide), Robert W Boeke (Senior VP Components Division), Joseph W England (Senior VP Accounting-Control), L Neel Hall (Senior VP Farm Equipment and Consumer Products Division, US and Canada), Michael S Plunkett (Senior VP Engineering, Technology and Human Resources), Eugene L Schotanus (Senior VP Financial Services), David H Stowe Jr (Senior VP Industrial Equipment Division), Neil U Christenson (VP Farm Equipment and Consumer Products Marketing, US and Canada), Michael Frank (VP Managing Director-Europe, Africa and the Middle East), Billy C Harpole (VP Latin America, Australia, The Far East and Export Operations), David P Hopley (VP Engine Group), James F Lardner (VP Tractor and Component Operations), Chester K Lasell (VP Corporate Communications), John K Lawson (VP Farm Equipment and Consumer Products Manufacturing US Canada), R J Peterson (VP Aftermarket Services Farm Equipment and Consumer Products Manufacturing US and Canada), G Russell Sutherland (VP Engineering and Technology), Robert W Weeks (VP and General Counsel), Glendon D Gustafson (Comptroller), Pierre E Leroy (Treasurer), Richard G Silliman (Secretary)

PRINCIPAL ACTIVITIES: Manufacture of agricultural and horticultural machinery, construction and forestry equipment, and diesel engines and components
Trade Names: John Deere
Principal Subsidiaries: Deere Credit Services Inc; Farm Plan Corp; John Deere Finance Ltd (Canada); John Deere Leasing Co. Affiliated Companies: SLC SA Industria e Comercio (Brazil); John Deere SA de CV (Mexico); Bunton Company; John Deere Insurance; John Deere Credit Co; John Deere Technologies International, Inc
Financial Information:

	Oct 31 1985	Oct 31 1986
	$'000	$'000
Sales revenues	4,060,648	3,516,289
Net income (loss)	30,505	(229,272)
Dividends per share	$1.00	$0.875
Earnings (loss) per share	$0.45	($3.38)
Common stock	491,419	492,013
Retained income	1,877,153	1,596,995
Shareholders equity	2,258,616	1,999,277

No of Employees: 37,481

DEKALB CORPORATION

3100 Sycamore Road, De Kalb, IL 60115
Tel: (815) 758-3461
Cable: DEKALBCO
Telex: WUT 257342 dekalbco dklb

Chairman: Thomas H Roberts Jr; Vice Chairman: Charles C Roberts
President: Bruce P Bickner (and Chief Executive Officer)
Senior Executive Officers: Frank L Bauer (Senior VP), John H Witmer (VP, General Counsel and Secretary), Richard O Ryan (Group VP), John P Stafford (VP Finance and Chief Financial Officer), Alan D Skouby (VP and Controller), William D Broadhurst (Assistant Treasurer)

PRINCIPAL ACTIVITIES: Agriculture; poultry breeding stock; gas and oil exploration production and services; irrigation equipment; hybrid swine breeding sock;.hybrid seed; livestock marketing
Principal Subsidiaries: DEKALB-PFIZER GENETICS; DEKALB Swine Breeders, Inc; DEKALB Poultry Research, Inc; DEPCO, Inc; DeKalb-Petroleum Corporation; Inc; Pride Oil Well Service Co; Lindsay Manufacturing Co; DEKALB Financial Services, Inc
Financial Information:

	Aug 31 1986	Aug 31 1987
	$'000	$'000
Sales revenues	406,700	367,000
Net income (loss)	(50,700)	16,900
Dividends per share	$0.54	$0.32
Earnings (loss) per share	($4.22)	$1.41
Common stock*	11,942	11,919
Shareholders equity	317,100	332,800

*average shares outstanding-undiluted in thousands

No of Employees: 4,800

DEL E WEBB CORPORATION

See WEBB, DEL E, CORPORATION

DEL LABORATORIES, INC

565 Broad Hollow Road, Farmingdale, NY 11735
Tel: (516) 293-7070

Chairman: Martin Revson
President: Dan K Wassong (and Chief Executive Officer)
Senior Executive Officers: Charles Hinkaty (VP, President, Commerce Drug Co), Melvyn C Goldstein (VP Finance and Treasurer), William McMenemy (Group VP of Marketing, Cosmetics and Toiletries Division), Dr Harry Gordon (VP and Scientific Director), Phil Rosenzweig (VP of Manufacturing), Michael E La Rocco (VP, Materials Management), Richard Levy (Controller) , Robert Kapnek (VP Creative Services), Steve Mann (VP of Sales Chain Division), John Sweetser (VP, Manager Variety Division), Eileen Raymond (VP, Marketing Sally Hansen and La Cross Divisions), Linda Vitale (VP, Marketing Flame Glow and Quencher Division), Peter Liman (VP, Marketing Commerce Drug Division), William J Prelli (VP of Sales Commerce Drug Division), Nathanial Sabshon (VP, Finance International Division)

PRINCIPAL ACTIVITIES: Del Laboratories, Inc is a fully integrated marketing and manufacturing company, operating in four major segments of the packaged consumer products business: cosmetics, toiletries, beauty aids and proprietary pharmaceuticals. Each of the Company's marketing divisions is responsible for branded lines fitting into one of these general categories and develops its own plans and goals consistent with its operating environment and Del Laboratories' corporate objectives. Products reach the consumer through the Company's overall channels of distribution to chain and independent drug stores, mass merchandisers and supermarkets
Trade Names: Auro, Tanac, Baby Orajel, Exocaine, Propa PH, Flame Glow, La-Cross, La Salle, Nutri-Tonic, Rejuvia, Sally Hansen, Sally Hansen Hard as Nails, Quencher, Schiaparelli (all Registered Trademarks)
Principal Subsidiaries and Divisions: Commerce Drug Co Inc Division; Flame Glow Division; La-Cross Division; La Salle Laboratories Division; Nutri-Tonic Division; Rejuvia Division; Sally Hansen Division; Quencher Division; Schiaparelli Fragrances Division; Del Laboratories Inc
Financial Information:

	Dec 31 1985	Dec 31 1986
	$'000	$'000
Sales revenues	101,118	106,699
Income before taxes	6,244	5,375
Net income	3,670	3,108
Dividends	547	550
Dividends per share	$0.39	$0.3975
Earnings per share	$2.43	$2.07
Common stock	1,854	1,854
Retained earnings	27,888	30,447
Shareholders equity	29,433	31,920

No of Employees: 1,000

DEL PERO-MONDON MEAT COMPANY, INC

1109 Chestnut Street, Marysville, CA 95901
Tel: (916) 742-2311
Telex: WUT 910 537 3371 dpm mave

Chairman: Mario F Del Pero (and President and Chief Executive Officer)
Senior Executive Officers: Joel D Pero (Executive VP Corporate Sales), Donald R Buford (VP and Controller), Ronald M Fear (VP Credit and Risk Manager), Catherine Beam (VP Cost Control), Elton Correll (VP Meat Production)

PRINCIPAL ACTIVITIES: Meat and meat processing
Principal Subsidiaries: DPM of KS Inc
Principal Bank: First Interstate Bank
Financial Information:

	$'000
Sales revenues	50,000

No of Employees: 230

DELCHAMPS INC

305 Delchamps Drive, PO Box 1668, Mobile, AL 36633-1668
Tel: (205) 433 0431

Chairman: A F Delchamps Jr (and President and Chief Executive Officer); Vice Chairman: O H Delchamps Sr
Senior Executive Officers: O H Delchamps Jr (Chairman of Executive Committee), J R Delchamps (VP Real Estate), John H Holland (VP and Controller), Walter M Rhodes (VP Operations), John F Feagan (VP Finance and Planning), Annie Delchamps Moore (Treasurer), James N Giddeon (VP Merchandising), Donald Mathews (VP Distribution)

PRINCIPAL ACTIVITIES: Operation of retail food outlets
Principal Bank: First Alabama Bank
Financial Information:

	$'000
Sales revenues	630,000

No of Employees: 5,200

DELLWOOD FOODS, INC

170 Saw Mill River Road, Yonkers, NY 10701
Tel: (914) 965-4200

Chairman: Irving J Kern (and Chief Executive Officer); Vice Chairman: Seymour Hayman
President: Jacques Linker
Senior Executive Officers: Herbert Whitehead (Senior VP), Albert Steinhart (VP), Jack Schreiber (VP Manufacturing), Sidney Adler (VP Sales), J D Wasserman (Treasurer), Harvey Breier (VP Marketing)

PRINCIPAL ACTIVITIES: Manufacture of dairy products and fruit drinks
Principal Subsidiaries: Dellwood Distributors Inc; Deltown Chemurgic Corp; Farmlea-Westchester Dairy Inc; Gannon Brothers Inc; Skylab Foods Inc; Sun Dew Sales Corp
Principal Bank: Chemical Bank
Financial Information:

	$'000
Sales revenues	134,000

No of Employees: 700

DELMARVA POWER & LIGHT CO

PO Box 231, Wilmington, DE 19899
Tel: (302) 429-3011

Chairman: Nevius M Curtis (and President and Chief Executive Officer)
Senior Executive Officers: H E Cosgrove (Executive VP), H R Landon (Senior VP), H M Wakefield Jr (Senior VP), Roger D Campbell (VP, Treasurer and Chief Financial Officer), Richard H Evans (VP Corporate Communications), Thomas C Shaw (VP Production), Wayne Lyons (VP), Paul S Gerritsen (VP Regulatory Practice)

PRINCIPAL ACTIVITIES: Distribution of electricity
Principal Subsidiaries: Delmarva Capital Investments Inc; DCI Inc; Delmarva Energy Co Inc; Delmarva Industries Inc
Principal Bank: Wilmington Trust Co
Financial Information:

	Dec 31 1985	Dec 31 1986
	$'000	$'000
Sales revenues	723,000	715,000
Net income	96,600	89,000

No of Employees: 2,600

DELMED INC

Route 33 & Howell Road, Freehold, NJ 07728
Tel: (201) 431 5300

Chairman: James F Marten (and President and Chief Executive Officer)
President: Rob Schwarz
Senior Executive Officers: James O'Shea (Senior VP Sales and Marketing), Francis D John (VP Finance, Treasurer and Chief Financial Officer)

PRINCIPAL ACTIVITIES: Manufacture of medical and surgical apparatus and equipment
Principal Subsidiaries: Briggs Corporation; Home Hyperalimentation Services; Medicon Sales Corporation; Royal B Wholesale Supply; Serologicals Services Inc; Sherlof Inc
Principal Bank: Manufacturers Hanover Trust Company
Financial Information:

	$'000
Sales revenues	48,025

No of Employees: 550

DELTA AIR LINES, INC

Hartsfield Atlanta International Airport, Atlanta, GA 30320
Tel: (404) 765-2600

Chairman: R W Allen Jr (and Chief Executive Officer)
President: Hollis L Harris (and Chief Operating Officer)
Senior Executive Officers: Robert Oppenlander (Vice Chairman of the Board and Chief Financial Officer), James W Callison (Senior VP-General Counsel and Secretary), Rex McClelland (Senior VP-Operations), W Whitley Hawkins (Senior VP-Marketing), Russell H Heil (Senior VP-Personnel), D P Hetterman (Senior VP-Technical Operations), R G Caldwell (VP-Management Services), Frank S Chew (VP and Treasurer), Robert H Cowart (VP-Information Services), John P Davis (VP-Maintenance), M E Dullum (VP-Government Affairs), J D Dunn (VP-Purchasing), R Lamar Durrett (VP-Facilities and Technical Operations Administration), Julius P Gwin (VP and Comptroller), Robert S Harkey (VP-Associate General Counsel), John Hume (VP-In-Flight Service), C J May (VP-Engineering), C A Thompson (VP-Stations), Don M Adams (Assistant VP-Law), H C Alger (Assistant VP-Flight Operations), E R Bennett (Assistant VP-Internal Auditing), Robert W Coggin (Assistant VP-Marketing Development), W E Condra (Assistant VP-Information Services Applications Development), John W Cox (Assistant VP-Community Affairs), H M Johnson (Assistant VP-Employment), W B Suggs (Assistant VP-Materiel Services), Lawson Rollins (Assistant Comptroller-Revenue Accounting), Marcy McCann (Assistant VP-Reservation Sales), James Taylor (Assistant VP-Investment Management), Jenny Poole (Assistant VP-In Flight Service)

PRINCIPAL ACTIVITIES: Delta Air Lines Inc is a major trunk air carrier providing scheduled air transportation for passengers, freight and mail over a network of routes throughout the United Stated and abroad
Principal Bank: The Citizens and Southern National Bank
Financial Information:

	Jun 30 1986	Jun 30 1987
	$'000	$'000
Operating revenues	4,460,062	5,318,172
Income before taxes	3,434	447,199
Net income	47,286	263,729
Dividends	40,073	44,397
Dividends per share	$1.00	$1.00
Earnings per share	$1.18	$5.90
Common stock	120,349	145,918
Reinvested earnings	1,088,264	1,307,596
Shareholders equity	1,301,946	1,937,912

No of Employees: 39,047

DELTA DATA SYSTEMS CORPORATION

2595 Metropolitan Drive, Trevose, PA 19047
Tel: (215) 322 5400

Chairman: Robert W Cross (and Chief Executive Officer)
President: William J Rolya (and Chief Operating Officer)
Senior Executive Officers: Ephraim Gittelman (Senior VP Operations), Theodore L Gendelman (VP and Secretary), Robert A Wainer (VP Federal Systems Sales), Ronald A Martignoni (VP Accounting and Treasurer), Philip H Gallo (VP Sales and Service), John H Brillante (VP Manufacturing)

PRINCIPAL ACTIVITIES: Manufacture of electronic equipment for the computer industry
Principal Bank: American Bank and Trust Company
Financial Information:

	$'000
Sales revenues	31,000

No of Employees: 300

DELTA QUEEN STEAMBOAT COMPANY

30 Robin Street Wharf, New Orleans, LA 70130
Tel: (504) 586 0631

Chairman: Samuel Zell
President: Franklin Fried (and Chief Executive Officer)
Senior Executive Officers: Gerald Butcher (Senior VP), Joyce A Early (Senior VP, Secretary and Treasurer), Fred Martin (Senior VP)

PRINCIPAL ACTIVITIES: Overnight passenger cruise services
Parent Company: Equity Holdings
Principal Bank: Fifth Third Bank
Financial Information:

	$'000
Sales revenues	32,000

No of Employees: 300

DELTAUS CORPORATION

Interfirst Plaza Tower, 110 North College Street, Tyler, TX 75702
Tel: (214) 595 7700

Chairman: Keeting V Zeppa
President: Donald L Frankel (and Chief Financial Officer)
Senior Executive Officers: Carl E Haskett (Executive VP), T C Carlton (VP Contract Drilling), Robert L Hampton Jr (VP and Treasurer), Charles H White Jr (VP and Controller), Linda M Kerr (Secretary)

PRINCIPAL ACTIVITIES: Exploration and production of oil and natural gas
Principal Subsidiaries: Etexas Producers Gas Company; Triangle Gas Pipeline Co; Triangle Marketing Corporation
Principal Bank: Interfirst Bank
Financial Information:

	$'000
Sales revenues	72,060

No of Employees: 1,500

DELTONA CORPORATION

3250 Southwest 3rd Avenue, Miami, FL 33129
Tel: (305) 854 1111

Chairman: Roger M Bowman
President: William R Avella (and Chief Executive Officer)
Senior Executive Officers: E D Cortright Jr (Executive VP and Chief Financial Officer), J M Stackpole (Senior VP, President Deltona Marketing Corp), C E Hinkley (VP Construction and Development), R L Mehl (VP Advertising and Sales Promotion), Arnesio Milian (President Deltona Utilities Inc), D O McNelley (Treasurer and Controller), M R Garbis (Secretary and Legal Counsel)

PRINCIPAL ACTIVITIES: Management and development of property and real estate
Principal Subsidiaries: Delmarco Corp; Deltona Resorts Inc; Marco Shores Resorts Inc; Rentals of Marco Island Inc; Deltona Acceptance Corporation; Deltona Asphalt Co Inc; Deltona Broadcasting Co Inc; Deltona Equities Inc; Deltona International Inc; Deltona Lakeside Inc; Deltona Land and

Investment Corporation; Delainco lc; Deldade Inc; Delrando Inc; DLIC Inc; Deltona Marketing Corp; Florida's Mackle Brothers; Deltona Mortgage Co; Deltona Utilities Inc; Seaboard Utilities Corp; Deltona Utility Consultants Inc; Deltona-Marco Properties; Deltonas Mackle BLT Construction Co; Delonas Real Estate Services Inc; Delverde Inc; Delvero Inc; Five Points Title Services Co Inc; Five Points Insurance Services Inc; Flordia Mackle Brothers Inc; Intercoastal Properties II St Augustine; Intercoastal Properties St Augustine SHRS; Lakeshore Properties Inc; Marco Bayfront Inc; Marco Island Beachfront Inc; Marco Seaside Inc; Marco Shoreline Properties Inc; Marco Surfside Inc; Marco Tropical Properties Inc; Pelican Utility Co; Realty Services Representatives Inc; Southern Property Services Inc; Three Seasons Corporation; Deltona Corp Realty Co; Deltonas Marco Island Realty Co; United Florida Utilities Corp

Principal Bank: City Bank

Financial Information:

	$'000
Sales revenues	97,000

No of Employees: 800

DELUXE CHECK PRINTER, INC

1080 W County Road F, St Paul, MN 55112
Tel: (612) 483-7111

Chairman: Eugene R Olson
President: Harold V Haverty (and Chief Executive and Operating Officer)
Senior Executive Officers: W N Hansen (Senior VP Sales), R W Allen (Senior VP), William R Phillips (Senior VP Marketing), C M Osborne (VP Finance)

PRINCIPAL ACTIVITIES: Printing of bank forms and checks
Principal Bank: First National Bank of Saint Paul
Financial Information:

	Dec 31 1985 $'000	Dec 31 1986 $'000
Sales revenues	764,420	866,829
Net income	104,215	121,109
Earnings per share	$2.43	$1.42
Shareholders equity	354,083	413,130

No of Employees: 12,670

DENKA CHEMICAL CORPORATION

8701 Park Place Blvd, Houston, TX 77017
Tel: (713) 477-8821
Telex: TWX 910 8811 624 denka usa hou

President: Marvin Woskow
Senior Executive Officers: Marshall Kendrick (VP), Kenneth Ferguson (Treasurer), James R McGinnis (Secretary)

PRINCIPAL ACTIVITIES: Manufacture of chemicals
Principal Bank: Texas Commerce Bank of Houston
Financial Information:

	$'000
Sales revenues	80,000

No of Employees: 300

DENNISON MANUFACTURING COMPANY

300 Howard Street, Framingham, MA 01701-0344
Tel: (617) 879-0511
Telex: RCA 200211 denn ur

Chairman: Nelson S Gifford (and Chief Executive Officer); Vice Chairman: Henry R Lewis (and Chief Strategic Officer)
President: John B Gray (and Chief Operating Officer)
Senior Executive Officers: Daniel J Sullivan (VP and Chief Financial Officer), Henry R Lewis (Senior VP Research and Development), Daniel L Sullivan (VP and Controller)

PRINCIPAL ACTIVITIES: Paper and stationery manufacture; adhesive labels; marking machines; office supplies and inks
Trade Names: Carters(R), National(R), Marks-A-Lot(R), HI-LITER(R), Supra (TM), Mark III (TM), TransLiter(R), PRES-a-ply(R), Stenso(R)
Principal Subsidiaries: Dennison National Company; Dennison Monarch Systems; Dennison Manufacturing Canada; IPC Dennison Company; Dennison International Company; Dennison France; D.S. Corporation; R Ancker Jorgensen A/S; Metallised Films and Paper Ltd
Principal Bank: The First National Bank of Boston
Financial Information:

	Dec 31 1986 $'000
Sales revenues	701,059
Income before taxes	60,610
Net income	30,254
Dividends*	18,191
Dividends per share*	$1.20
Earnings per share	$1.94
Common stock	55,354
Retained income	197,375
Shareholders equity	230,959

*common stock

No of Employees: 8,000

DENNISON NATIONAL COMPANY

PO Box 791, Holyoke, MA 01041
Tel: (413) 539-9811
Telex: TWX 710 3510 589 natonal hlke

President: Ronald Feinstein
Senior Executive Officers: Joseph S Picariello (VP Manufacturing), Richard P Towne Jr (VP Human Resources), William J Heldmann (VP Finance), Thomas E Loper (VP Marketing)

PRINCIPAL ACTIVITIES: Manufacture of blank books and computer stationery
Parent Company: Dennison Manufacturing Co, Framingham, MA
Principal Bank: Bank of New England
Financial Information:

	$'000
Sales revenues	125,000

No of Employees: 1,700

DENNY'S INC

16700 Valley View Ave, La Miranda, CA 90637
Tel: (714) 739-8100

Chairman: Verne H Winchell
President: Vern O Curtis (and Chief Executive Officer)
Senior Executive Officers: John D Radebaugh (Senior VP and Chief Financial Officer), Roger K Mercier (Senior VP and Legal Counsel), David H Bixler (Senior VP Operations), Vincent A Lambiase (Senior VP), Bruce Evans (VP Operations Franchise Development), Steve F Joyce (VP Human Resources), Richard Kislowski (VP Information Services), Donald Pierce (VP, President El Pollo Division), Robert I Higgins (VP and President International Division), Terence J Wallock (VP and Legal Secretary), Carol A Campbell (VP)

PRINCIPAL ACTIVITIES: Holding company with interests in restaurants, a Mexican fast food chain, bakeries and wholesale food products
Principal Subsidiaries: CBR Development Co Inc; Dennys International Inc; El Pollo Loco; Portiontrol Foods Inc; Proficient Food Co
Principal Bank: Wells Fargo Bank
Financial Information:

	$'000
Sales revenues	1,372,000

No of Employees: 52,000

DENTSPLY INTERNATIONAL, INC
570 W College Avenue, York, PA 17405
Tel: (717) 845-7511

President: Burton C Borgelt (and Chief Executive Officer)
Senior Executive Officers: Edward J Lipawsky (Senior VP), Leslie A Jones (Senior VP), John R Behrmann (Senior VP Finance), Bernard J Beazley (Senior VP Professional Relations, Secretary and General Counsel)

PRINCIPAL ACTIVITIES: Supplier of dental equipment and supplies
Parent Company: Dentsply Holdings
Principal Bank: Chemical Bank
Financial Information:

	$'000
Sales revenues	190,000

No of Employees: 3,500

DEPOSIT GUARANTY CORPORATION
210 E Capital St, Jackson, MS 39201
Tel: (601) 354-8564

Chairman: Emerson B Robinson Jr (and Chief Executive Officer)
President: Howard L McMillan Jr (and Chief Operating Officer)
Senior Executive Officers: Warren A Hood (Executive Officer), Charles H Sewell (Executive Officer), Arlen L McDonald (Treasurer)

PRINCIPAL ACTIVITIES: Banking
Principal Subsidiaries: Deposit Guaranty National Bank; Deposit Guaranty Mortgage Co; Parking Services Inc
Principal Bank: Deposit Guaranty National Bank
Financial Information:

	Dec 31 1985 $'000
Revenues	281,000
Net income	21,700
Total assets	2,860,000

No of Employees: 10

DERBY REFINING COMPANY
PO Box 1030, Wichita, KS 67201
Tel: (316) 267-0361
Telex: TWX 910 7416 994 derby wic

Chairman: Frederick M Otto (and Chief Executive Officer)
President: Kenneth O Johnson
Senior Executive Officers: W W Mueller (Senior VP), R H Meadows (VP Supply), R E Drevo (VP Wholesale Marketing), M D Tindall (VP Marketing Services), M D Taylor (VP Retail Marketing), J C Hesser (VP Refining)

PRINCIPAL ACTIVITIES: Oil refining
Parent Company: Coastal Corporation
Financial Information:

	$'000
Sales revenues	380,000

Principal Shareholders: Coastal Corp, Houston, TX
No of Employees: 770

DES MOINES REGISTER & TRIBUNE COMPANY
715 Locust Street, Des Moines, IA 50304
Tel: (515) 284-8000

Chairman: David Kruidenier (and Chief Executive Officer)
President: Michael Gartner (and Chief Operating Officer and Editorial Chairman)
Senior Executive Officers: Gary G Gerlach (Executive VP and Publisher), James P Gannon (VP and Editor), Richard W Gilbert (VP Broadcasting), James M Kiser (VP and Associate Publisher), Glenn H Roberts (VP Research), John J Kemp (VP Human Resources), Ronald J Peterson (Chief Financial Officer)

PRINCIPAL ACTIVITIES: Newspaper publishing
Parent Company: Gannett Co Inc, Arlington, VA
Financial Information:

	$'000
Sales revenues	99,000

No of Employees: 1,700

DESIGN & MANUFACTURING CORPORATION
2000 Illinois Avenue, Connersville, IN 47331
Tel: (317) 825-3181

Chairman: Sam N Regenstrief (and Chief Executive Officer)
President: L L Burke (and Chief Operating Officer)
Senior Executive Officers: Glen G Kaufman (Executive VP Production), Gerald K Nichols (VP Production), Gary E Conklin (VP Marketing), William Yake (VP Engineering)

PRINCIPAL ACTIVITIES: Manufacture of household electrical appliances
Principal Subsidiaries: Absocold Corp; Wallace Expanding Machines Inc
Principal Bank: American Fletcher National Bank and Trust Company
Financial Information:

	$'000
Sales revenues	190,000

No of Employees: 2,000

DESIGNCRAFT INDUSTRIES INC
23 West 47th Street, New York, NY 10036
Tel: (212) 719 3960

Chairman: Sam Beckerman (and Chief Executive Officer and Treasurer)
President: Martin Steinberg (and Chief Operating Officer)
Senior Executive Officers: Frank Sebastiano (Executive VP and Chief Financial Officer), Al Hussain (Controller and Chief Accounting Officer), Murray Beckerman (Secretary)

PRINCIPAL ACTIVITIES: Manufacture of jewelry
Principal Subsidiaries: Asco Rings Inc; Baker Eichmuller Inc; Karlan & Bleicher Inc
Principal Bank: Rhode Island Hospital Trust National Bank
Financial Information:

	$'000
Sales revenues	46,000

No of Employees: 380

DESOTO, INC
1700 South Mt Prospect Road, Des Plaines, IL 60017
Tel: (312) 391-9000

Chairman: Richard R Missar (and President and Chief Executive Officer)
Senior Executive Officers: Richard J Anderson (VP-Group President, Chemical), Jay Barreiro (VP-Personnel and Industrial Relations), William L Lamey Jr (VP-Finance), Glenn F Workman (VP-Corporate Services and Purchasing), John P Harness (Controller), Robert S Kersch (Secretary), Nicholas A Vittore (Treasurer)

PRINCIPAL ACTIVITIES: DeSoto Inc is a diversified manufacturer of chemical coatings (consumer paints and industrial coatings) and specialty products (detergents and other household cleaning products, surfactants, emulsifiers, specialty chemicals)
Trade Names: DeSoto
Principal Subsidiaries: DeSoto Coatings Ltd, Canada
Principal Bank: Harris Trust and Savings Bank

Financial Information:

	Dec 31 1986 $'000
Sales revenues	413,802
Income before taxes	7,709
Net income	3,909
Dividends	6,712
Dividends per share	$1.40
Earnings per share	$0.82
Common stock	5,619
Retained income	133,828
Shareholders equity	89,542

No of Employees: 2,378

DETREX CHEMICAL INDUSTRIES, INC

400 Town Center, Suite 1100, Southfield, MI 48075
Tel: (313) 358-5800

Chairman: Arbie O Thalacker
President: Louis Schlossberg (and Chief Executive Officer)
Senior Executive Officers: Robert A Emmett (VP), C B Stockmeyer Jr (VP and Treasurer)

PRINCIPAL ACTIVITIES: Specialty chemicals; dry cleaning machines and ultrasonic equipment for hospitals and industry
Principal Subsidiaries: Elco Corp; Harvel Plastics Inc; Wayne Chemical Products Co
Principal Bank: Comerica Bank
Financial Information:

	$'000
Sales revenues	90,000

No of Employees: 600

DETROIT EDISON COMPANY

2000 Second Avenue, Detroit, MI 48226
Tel: (313) 237-8808
Telex: WUT 235 228 edison det b

Chairman: Walter J McCarthy Jr (and Chief Executive Officer); Vice Chairman: Ernest L Grove Jr (and Chief Financial Officer)
President: Charles M Heidel (and Cheif Operating Officer)
Senior Executive Officers: Leon S Cohan (Senior VP and General Counsel), Burkhard H Schneider (Group VP Division), Harry Tauber (Group VP Engineering and Construction), B Ralph Sylvia (Group VP Nuclear), Saul J Waldman (VP Public Affairs), J Philip Lenihan (VP Marketing), Jane Kay (VP Administration), Frank E Agosti (VP Nuclear Operations), Claybourne Mitchell Jr (VP Planning and Research), Willard R Holland (VP), John E Lobbia (VP Financial Services), James B Oliver (VP Employee Relations), Malcolm G Dade (VP Community and Government Affairs)

PRINCIPAL ACTIVITIES: Generation and distribution of electricity
Principal Subsidiaries: Edison Illuminating Co Detroit; Midwest Energy Resources Inc; St Clair Energy Corp; Synceco; UTS; Utility Technical Services Inc; Washtenaw Energy Corp
Principal Bank: Bankers Trust Company
Financial Information:

	Dec 31 1986 $'000
Sales revenues	2,869,284
Net income	477,095
Earnings per share	$2.58
Shareholders equity	3,246,093

No of Employees: 10,967

DETROIT FREE PRESS, INCORPORATED

321 W Lafayette, Detroit, MI 48231
Tel: (313) 222-6400
Telex: TWX 810 22 11 667 freeprsdis det

Chairman: David Lawrence Jr (and Publisher)
President: Jerome S Tilis
Senior Executive Officers: Robert J Hall (Executive VP-General Manager), Joe Stroud (Senior VP and Editor), Timothy J Kelleher (VP Employee Relations), Myron Didyk (VP Circulation), J G Teagan (VP and Treasurer), James Spaniolo (VP Human Resources)

PRINCIPAL ACTIVITIES: Publishing of newspapers
Parent Company: Knight-Ridder Inc, Miami, FL

No of Employees: 1,900

DEVELOPMENT CORPORATION OF AMERICA

2514 Hollywood Blvd, Hollywood, FL 33020
Tel: (305) 920-6600

Chairman: Alvin P Sherman
Senior Executive Officers: Irving Fishman (Senior VP), Edward Lempka (Senior VP), Pedro Diaz (VP and Treasurer), Steven I Engel (VP and Corporate Counsel), Rosalind Stanco (VP Marketing)

PRINCIPAL ACTIVITIES: Building contractors; real estate agents and land developers
Principal Subsidiaries: Boca Greens Inc; Central Park South Inc; DCA; DCA General Contracting Inc; DCA Homes Inc; DCA Realty Inc; DCA Financial Corp; DCA Homes West Inc; DCA Properties Inc; DCA Services Inc; Devco Land Corp; Florida Homes Title Insurance Agency; Gate Development Corp; Green Fever Inc; Leisure Colony Management Corp; Lucerne Lakes Golf Colony Inc; MAP Builders Inc; Niki-Lu Industries Inc; Oak Hill West Inc; Par Four Development Corp; Par One Development Corp; Par Two Development Corp; State Home Mortgage Corp; Superior Realty & Marketing Corp; Talladega Manufacturing Inc; TIC Group; Town Homes of Country Run Inc; WB Homes Inc
Principal Bank: Southeast Bank
Financial Information:

	$'000
Sales revenues	186,000

No of Employees: 870

DEVLIEG MACHINE COMPANY

Fair Street, Royal Oak, MI 48073
Tel: (313) 280-1100
Telex: WUT 230281 devlieg royl

Chairman: Charles R Devlieg
President: H A Beyer
Senior Executive Officers: D L Brown (Executive VP), J W Anderson (VP Sales), Richard A Jerue (VP Engineering), George C Green (VP Microbore Division), J A Bandfield (VP and Controller)

PRINCIPAL ACTIVITIES: Manufacture of machine tools
Principal Bank: National Bank of Detroit
Financial Information:

	$'000
Sales revenues	60,000

No of Employees: 750

DEVON APPAREL

3001 Red Lion Road, Philadelphia, PA 19114
Tel: (215) 632-8100

Chairman: Stanley Matzkin
President: Eric Matzkin
Senior Executive Officers: Donald Ochs (Senior VP), Herbert Denenberg (VP Finance), Joann Casa (VP Merchandising) Louis Krassen (VP Operations), Ario Cardillo (VP Sales/Major Accounts), Gary Sussman (VP Regional Sales)

PRINCIPAL ACTIVITIES: Manufacture of ladies' clothing
Trade Names: Devon, Lady Devon, Petite Concept, Blake, Lady Blake
Parent Company: INTERCO Incorporated
Principal Bank: Philadelphia National Bank

Financial Information:

	$'000
Sales revenues	75,000

No of Employees: 1,000

DEVRY INC

2201 West Howard Street, Evanston, IL 60202
Tel: (312) 328 8100

Chairman: Donald N Frey
President: Philip A Clement (and Chief Executive Officer)
Senior Executive Officers: Edward N Cabot (VP), Harold E Harris (VP, Treasurer and Chief Financial Officer), Casimir V Kroll (VP), Norman C Metz (VP), Harry B Overton Jr (VP), Edward M Rahill (VP), Robert R Roehrich (VP), Robert D Whitney (VP), Mary Ann Garvey (Secretary and Legal Counsel)

PRINCIPAL ACTIVITIES: Operation of training establishments for the computer industry
Principal Bank: First National Bank of Chicago
Financial Information:

	$'000
Sales revenues	148,000

No of Employees: 2,730

DEXTER CORPORATION (THE)

One Elm Street, Windsor Locks, CT 06096
Tel: (203) 627-9051
Telex: TWX 710 4200 501 dex corp wind

Chairman: David L Coffin (and Chief Executive Officer)
President: Worth Loomis
Senior Executive Officers: Harold V Fleming (Senior VP), Robert E McGill III (Senior VP Finance and Administration and Secretary), Joseph C Day (VP), Albert Paolini (VP), K G Walker (VP), Bradley J Hughes (VP and Controller), Joseph C Stokes Jr (Treasurer)

PRINCIPAL ACTIVITIES: Specialty chemical products; biotechnology products; non-wovens for industrial and medical applications
Principal Bank: Morgan Guaranty Trust Company of New York
Financial Information:

	Dec 31 1986
	$'000
Sales revenues	650,051
Income before taxes	56,503
Net income	33,635
Dividends	13,664
Dividends per share	$0.5667
Earnings per share	$1.35
Common stock	24,893
Retained income	233,772
Shareholders equity	258,843

No of Employees: 5,500

DEXTER SHOE COMPANY

Water Street, Dexter, ME 04930
Tel: (207) 924-7341

Chairman: Harold Alfond
President: Peter H Lunder
Senior Executive Officers: Joe Soltz (VP Sales), Kenneth V Moody Sr (Comptroller)

PRINCIPAL ACTIVITIES: Manufacture of footwear and footwear components
Financial Information:

	$'000
Sales revenues	150,000

No of Employees: 2,000

DI GIORGIO CORPORATION

One Maritime Plaza, San Francisco, CA 94111
Tel: (415) 765-0100
Telex: RCA 278 666 digco ur

Chairman: Peter F Scott (and President and Chief Executive Officer); Vice Chairman: Benjamin Zdatny (and Chief Operating Officer)
Senior Executive Officers: Donald E Miller (Senior VP), Norman P Adler (VP), Robert E Mellor (VP, Secretary and General Counsel)

PRINCIPAL ACTIVITIES: Production of food including meat products and fruit juices; distribution of food products, pharmaceuticals, electrical goods; manufacture of building materials
Principal Subsidiaries: Carando Inc; DG Shelter Products Co; Di Giorgio Development Corp; Ladco Laboratories Inc; Serv-a-Portion Inc; White Rose Food Corp; White Rose Dairy Corp; White Rose Frozen Food Corp; White Rose Meat Corp
Principal Bank: Bank of America
Financial Information:

	Dec 31 1985	Dec 31 1986
	$'000	$'000
Sales revenues	1,093,126	1,204,529
Net income	11,150	14,330
Earnings per share	$1.72	$1.85
Shareholders equity	118,955	158.640

No of Employees: 3,800

DIABLO SYSTEMS, INC

24500 Industrial Blvd, Hayward, CA 94545
Tel: (415) 786-5000

President: Joseph Sanchez
Senior Executive Officers: Bernard Horn (VP), Paul McIntire (VP Operations), William White (VP Business Development), Ted Charter (VP), Richard Couch (VP Personnel)

PRINCIPAL ACTIVITIES: Data processing equipment; computer software and services
Parent Company: Xerox Corporation, Stamford, CT
Financial Information:

	$'000
Sales revenues	225,000

No of Employees: 1,000

DIAGNOSTIC/RETRIEVAL SYSTEMS, INC

16 Thornton Rd, Oakland, NJ 07436
Tel: (201) 337-3800
Telex: 710-988-4191

Chairman: Leonard Newman (and Chief Executive Officer and Secretary)
President: David E Gross (and Chief Operating Officer)
Senior Executive Officers: John V Giordano (Corporate Controller), Mark S Newman (Executive VP, Chief Financial Officer), Allen P Tucker (VP, President of Precision Echo, Inc-subsidiary), Richard Ross (Assistant VP, Corporate Business Development), Patricia N Williamson (Assistant VP, Corporate Communications), John C Dale (VP, Ship Systems), Jackson Kemper Jr (VP, Government Relations), Dennis J Lanahan (VP, Washington Operations), Francis A Montenes (VP, Avionics and Instrumentation), David M Orth (VP, Business Development), Lewis F Ozimek (VP, Contracts), Jack R Williams (VP, Research and Technology, Presidnet, DRS of California, Inc-subsidiary), Werner J Christmann (VP Operations-subsidiary), Stephen K Conlisk (Controller-subsidiary), Edward K Shum (VP, Engineering-subsidiary), Grant M Wheeler (VP, Military Products), Ralph Hiteman (VP, Business Development-California Office), William Tuck (VP, Program Business-subsidiary), Theodore Augsburg (VP, Product Business-subsidiary)

PRINCIPAL ACTIVITIES: DRS Designs, manufactures and markets high-technology defense electronics products for antisubmarine warfare, intelligence and other military and industrial applications, including signal processing, video-image generation, recording and trainer systems for surface ships, helicopters, patrol planes and submarines

Trade Names: AN/SQR-17A Sonar Signal Processing System, AN/AQH-9 Mission Tape Recording System, AN/AQH-4(V)2 Recording System, RD-420B Recording System, DMED Digital Data Converter, WRR-441C Transient-free recorder, AN/AQA-7A(V) Display Enhancement, AN/AQH-7 Recording System, MK 46 Torpedo Test Tape Recorder, AN/SQR-18A (Unit 2) Signal Processing System, MASTER (Modular Acoustic Stimulator/Emulator), Periscope Image Generator, EFS-2G Discasette (R) Recorder

Principal Subsidiaries: DRS of California Inc; Precision Echo Inc

Principal Bank: Morgan Guaranty Trust Company of New York

Financial Information:

	Mar 31 1986	Mar 31 1987
	$'000	$'000
Sales revenues	35,979	53,259
Income before taxes(1)	593	5,985
Net income	1,033	3,434
Earnings per share	$0.18	$0.61
Common stock(2)	5,625	5,628
Shareholders funds	24,442	27,915

(1) benefit in 1986

(2) shares outstanding in thousands

No of Employees: 500

DIAL CORPORATION (THE)

Greyhound Tower, 111 West Clarendon, Phoenix, AZ 85077
Tel: (602) 248-2800

President: Edward J Walsh (and Chief Executive Officer)

Senior Executive Officers: William T Bennett (Executive VP Finance and Administration), George D Evans (Executive VP), William H Windham (Senior VP General Sales), A S Patti (Senior VP Operations), R L Trott (Senior VP Custom Products), Russell C Bayne (VP Employee Relations and Personnel), B M Birmingham (VP Quality Control), Ronald E Brockman (VP Purchasing), Bernard F Carpenter (VP Transport and Distribution), Allan R DeBolt (VP Specialty Markets), Thomas A DeRossett (VP Customer Development), J C Doney (VP Manufacturing and Engineering Food), R J Eriksson (VP Marketing Sales/Chemcial Specialties), M J Genualdi (VP Management Division Services), Charles H Ferry (VP National Field Sales), William C Goulding (VP Trade Relations), D L Johnson (Senior VP and Controller), L G Lemon (VP and General Counsel), William R Lindstrom (VP National Account Sales, Custom Products), P J Lustig (VP Marketing/Personal Care and Food Products), Donald E McAdams (VP Sales, Southern Region), Brendan M McGuinness (VP Sales, Eastern Region), D D Moffatt (VP Manufacturing and Engineering, Bar Soaps and Brillo), Thomas T Moore (VP Sales, Southwest Region), D J Morrison (VP Manufacturing and Engineering/Household and Laundry), Robert A Murphy (VP Sales, East Central Region), Thomas A Palmer (VP), Gus Pappademus (VP Sales, West Central Region), David I Richardson (VP Research and Development), James E Rinkel (VP Sales, Southeast Region), Neri A Phillip (VP Sales, Western Region), Fred W Thatcher (VP Sales Private Label), R S Yaffe (VP, HQ Purchasing)

PRINCIPAL ACTIVITIES: Manufacture of soaps, detergents and toiletries; household cleaning products; canned meat products; pet foods; pizza mixes; pharmaceuticals

Parent Company: The Greyhound Corporation

Financial Information:

	$'000
Sales revenues	470,000

No of Employees: 5,000

DIAMOND CRYSTAL SALT COMPANY

916 S Riverside Avenue, St Clair, MI 48079
Tel: (313) 329-2211
Telex: WUT 235 485 diam salt stcr

Chairman: Frederick S Moore; Vice Chairman: Charles D Cronenworth

President: Roy C Satchell (and Chief Executive Officer)

Senior Executive Officers: A B Graf (VP, President Salt Division), Robert B Sonnier (VP, President Packet Products Division), Walter E Fitzgerald (VP, VP M and E Salt Division), Frank N Hayes (Treasurer and Chief Financial Officer), Carl W Kucsera (VP Personnel and Industrial Relations)

PRINCIPAL ACTIVITIES: Manufacture of salt for edible purposes, for water softening and agriculture; portion controlled packets of salt

Principal Bank: Morgan Guaranty Trust Company of New York

Financial Information:

	$'000
Sales revenues	120,000

No of Employees: 1,300

DIAMOND GLASS COMPANY

First Avenue, Royersford, PA 19468
Tel: (215) 948-3400

President: Frank B Foster III

Senior Executive Officers: W G Gies (VP Production), John R Edleman (VP and Secretary), C J Kirchgessner (VP Sales), James A Butchart (VP Purchasing and Distribution), M Greenberg (VP and Treasurer)

PRINCIPAL ACTIVITIES: Manufacture of glass packaging products

Parent Company: Diamond-Bathurst Inc, Royersford, PA

Financial Information:

	$'000
Sales revenues	63,000

No of Employees: 700

DIAMOND INTERNATIONAL CORPORATION

650 Fifth Avenue, New York, NY 1001
Tel: (212) 887-0700

Chairman: William J Koslo (and President and Chief Executive Officer)

Senior Executive Officers: James C Wemyss Jr (Group VP), Roy E Baharian (VP Engineering and Purchasing), Victor Stronski (VP and General Counsel), George Pascale (VP and Secretary), Jack J Agliata (VP), Michael Barrow (VP), Ronald D Rocheleau (VP and Treasurer)

PRINCIPAL ACTIVITIES: Forestry and timber production

Parent Company: Cavenham Holdings Inc

Principal Subsidiaries: Groveton Papers Co Inc; LMF Mortgage Co Inc; Mohawk Containers Inc

Financial Information:

	$'000
Sales revenues	781,000

No of Employees: 1,800

DIAMOND SHAMROCK R&M

717 N Harwood Street, Dallas, TX 75201
Tel: (214) 922-3000

Chairman: Roger M Hemminghaus

PRINCIPAL ACTIVITIES: Oil refining and marketing

Financial Information:

	$'000
Sales revenues	1,600,000

DIAMOND-BATHURST, INC

325 Technology Drive, Malvern, PA 19355
Tel: (215) 251-0400

Chairman: Joseph E Souccar
President: F B Foster III (and Chief Executive Officer)
Senior Executive Officers: Robert A Ericsson (Senior VP, Sales and Marketing), W Glenn Gies (Senior VP, Operations), Ronald R Arrington (VP Facilities Engineering), James D Butchart (VP Materials Management), T Charles Chitwood (VP Finance), Edwin H Holt (VP Industrial Relations, Quality Control and Technical Service), Thomas E Judge (VP and Assistant to Chief Executive Officer), Carol Wardle (VP Management Information Services), Myron Greenberg (Secretary), Philip C Jackson (Treasurer)

PRINCIPAL ACTIVITIES: Manufacture of glass containers to food industry, distilled spirits industry, soft drink industry, wine industry, as well as other industries
Principal Subsidiaries: Diamond Glass Co; Diamond Glass Vienna Inc; Diamond Container General Inc; Diamond Thatcher Inc
Principal Bank: Philadelphia National Bank
Financial Information:

	Dec 31 1985	Dec 31 1986
	$'000	$'000
Sales revenues	407,504	491,806
Net income (loss)	10,995	(6,240)
Earnings (loss) per share	$1.94	($0.82)
Shareholders equity	76,784	70,218

No of Employees: 6,000

DIASONICS, INC

1708 McCarthy Blvd, Milpitas, CA 95035
Tel: (408) 946-9001

Chairman: Albert Waxman
President: Stewart Carrell (and Chief Executive and Chief Operating Officer)
Senior Executive Officers: Jerry Burke (Senior VP), Karl Rudow (Senior VP), Walter Stafford (VP Administration and Secretary), Ruediger Naumann-Etienne (VP and Chief Financial Officer), Jerry McMillin (VP), Ronald Schilling (VP), Benno Lotz (VP), Bruce Moore (VP), William Hammack (VP), Timothy R Craig (VP Corporate Relations)

PRINCIPAL ACTIVITIES: Manufacture of medical diagnostic imaging systems
Principal Subsidiaries: Diasonics Cardio Imaging Inc
Financial Information:

	$'000
Sales revenues	158,000

No of Employees: 1,300

DIBRELL BROTHERS, INC

PO Box 681, Danville, VA 24543
Tel: (804) 792-7511
Telex: 574455 DIBRELL DAIE A

Chairman: R B Bridgforth Jr (and Chief Executive Officer)
President: C B Owen Jr
Senior Executive Officers: Willie G Barker Jr (Executive VP and Chief Operating Officer), Louis N Dibrell III (Senior VP), Thomas H Faucett (Senior VP, Chief Financial Officer), James M Dail (VP and Treasurer), H Peyton Green III (Senior VP), Paul W Mengel (Senior VP), T Wayne Oakes (Senior VP), Charles A Carr Jr (VP), Peter J Dodd (VP), Jerry L Parker (VP-Controller), J Martin Scott Jr (VP), R A Lassister (VP), John O Hunnicutt III (VP-Administration and Secretary), Donald W Crane (Assistant Treasurer), Oscar W Mahan Jr (Assistant Treasurer), Darrell F Hawkins (Assistant Secretary)

PRINCIPAL ACTIVITIES: The company is principally engaged in the business of buying and processing leaf tobacco in the United States and foreign countries for sale to manufacturers of cigarettes and other tobacco products. The Company also engages in the manufacture and sale of home ice cream freezers
Principal Subsidiaries: Carolina Leaf Tobacco Company, Inc; Dibrell Brothers Tobacco Company, Inc; Dibrell Tobacco Processing Inc; Dibrell Brothers of Canada Ltd (Canada); DCFE SA (Switzerland); Dibrell Brothers GmbH (Germany); Dibrell Brothers International (PVT) Ltd (Zimbabwe); Dibrell Brothers International BV (Netherlands); Dibrell Brothers International SA (Switzerland); Dibrell Brothers UK Branch (UK); Dibrell-Kentucky, Incorporated; Jose Duran Taveras & CIA (Dominican Republic); Procesadores De Tobaco SA (Argentina); Richmond Cedar Works Manufacturing Corp; Rohtabakvergaerungs Aktiengesellschaft (West Germany); Dibrell Brothers Zimbabwe (Pvt) Ltd (Zimbabwe); TEIC SA (Switzerland); Verafumos, Comercio, Industria, Agircultura de Fumos e Cereais Ltda (Brazil). Affiliated Companies: Dibrell Carolina Far Eastern Corporation (Philippines); Dibrell Intertrade, Inc; Fumex-Exportadora de Tabacos SA (Brazil); Hanil Tobacco Export Company, Ltd (Korea); Reditab, SpA (Italy); Tobacco Export Corp of Africa (PVT) Ltd (Zimbabwe); Tobacos Norte SA (Argentina); A majority shareholder in Florimex Verwaltungsgesellschaft mbH, a major importer and exporter of fresh cut flowers worldwide
Principal Bank: First Wachovia Bank and Trust Company
Financial Information:

	Jun 30 1986	Jun 30 1987
	$'000	$'000
Sales revenues	342,168	308,094
Income (loss) before taxes*	15,362	(2,153)
Net income (loss)	11,328	(1,093)
Dividends	3,290	3,198
Dividends per share	$0.84	$0.92
Earnings (loss) per share	$2.88	($0.31)
Common stock	3,521	3,446
Retained earninigs	38,956	34,665
Shareholders equity	63,662	57,659

*and minority interests and equity in net income of investee companies

No of Employees: 4,700 worldwide

DICEON ELECTRONICS, INC

18522 Von Karman Avenue, Irvine, CA 92714
Tel: (714) 833-0870

President: R G Matthews
Senior Executive Officers: P S Jonas (Executive VP, Secretary and Chief Financial Officer), F L Hale (VP), L R Laubauch (VP), Joe Philips (VP), B Sorensen (VP)

PRINCIPAL ACTIVITIES: Electronic components
Financial Information:

	$'000
Sales revenues	55,000

No of Employees: 690

DICK, A B, COMPANY

5700 W Touhy Avenue, Chicago, IL 60648
Tel: (312) 647-8800

Chairman: David Powell (and Chief Executive Officer)
Senior Executive Officers: A H Walker (VP-General Counsel; Secretary), S V Tessitore (VP and Controller), R L Rosy (VP-Distributor Division; VP-Marketing, Reprographics Products), B Ahluwalia (VP and General Manager-International Division), H J Bode (VP), R K Harrison (VP), P K Hunt (VP-Operations), K S Levin (VP-Finance); P G Mcdonald (VP-Branch Division)

PRINCIPAL ACTIVITIES: High performance printing systems, including offset presses, platemakers, collators, supplies, and copiers
Parent Company: The General Electric Co p.l.c.
Principal Bank: The Northern Trust Company

No of Employees: 7,400

DICKEY-JOHN CORPORATION

155 Country Club Road, Box 10, Auburn, IL 62615
Tel: (217) 438 3371

Chairman: Robert C Lanphier III (and President and Chief Executive Officer)
Senior Executive Officers: James H Anson (Senior VP and Chief Operation Officer), Warren H Kelly (Senior VP, Chief Operating, Secretary and Treasurer), Richard T Holtkamp (VP Manufacturing), Lawrence L Senger (Controller)

PRINCIPAL ACTIVITIES: Manufacture of electronic measuring equipment and controls
Principal Subsidiaries: Dickey-John International Ltd; Dickey-John International Ltd (DISC); Insto Inc; Swenson Spreader Company
Principal Bank: Springfield Marine Bank
Financial Information:

	$'000
Sales revenues	42,000

No of Employees: 635

DICTAPHONE CORPORATION

120 Old Post Road, Rye, NY 10580
Tel: (914) 967-7300
Telex: TWX 710 569 1601 dictaphone nv

Chairman: Marc C Breslawsky (and President and Chief Executive Officer)
Senior Executive Officers: John E Schlactenhaufen (VP, Marketing), Frank McCarthy (VP Sales)

PRINCIPAL ACTIVITIES: Office equipment including dictating machines, multi-channel communications recording systems and telephone answering systems
Parent Company: Pitney Bowes Inc, Stamford, CT

DIDDE GRAPHIC SYSTEMS CORPORATION

1200 Graphic Arts Road, Emporia, KS 66801
Tel: (316) 342-4740
Telex: TWX 910 7401660 didde empo

Chairman: Carl Didde
President: David D Didde (and Chief Executive Officer)
Senior Executive Officers: Wiliam D Vancelette (Executive VP and Chief Operating Officer)

PRINCIPAL ACTIVITIES: Manufacture of printing machinery
Principal Bank: Continental Illinois National Bank and Trust Company of Chicago
Financial Information:

	$'000
Sales revenues	60,000

No of Employees: 550

DIE CAST DIVISION

PO Box 570, Dowagiac, MI 49047
Tel: (616) 782-8671

Senior Executive Officers: Gary Walker (General Manager), James Peters (Sales Manager), Lee Topping (Purchasing Agent), Gerald Petznick (Engineering Manager), Roger Conrad (Manufacturing Manager)

PRINCIPAL ACTIVITIES: Die casting; aluminum and zinc products
Parent Company: Sealed Power Corporation, Muskegon, MI
Principal Bank: Harris Trust Company
Financial Information:

	$'000
Sales revenues	50,000

No of Employees: 500

DIEBOLD INC

818 Mulberry Road, SE Canton, OH 44711
Tel: (216) 489-4000
Telex: TRT 196 115 diebold ctn ut

Chairman: Raymond C Koontz
President: Robert W Mahoney (and Chief Executive Officer)
Senior Executive Officers: Walter Crow (Senior VP Marketing Services), Harry E Parr Jr (Senior VP, Chief Administrative Officer and Treasurer), Robert P Barone (Senior VP Sales and Marketing), Alben Waef (VP), Robert M Yopko (Group VP Customer Services), Warren Dettinger (VP Legal and Assistant Treasurer), Charles B Scheurer (VP Employee Relations), Harry O Seitzinger (VP and Controller), Charee Francis-Vogelsang (VP and Secretary)

PRINCIPAL ACTIVITIES: Manufacture and marketing of transaction automation and physical security systems
Principal Subsidiaries: Diebold Company of Canada, Ltd
Financial Information:

	Dec 31 1986 $'000
Sales revenues	413,668
Income before taxes	56,705
Net income	34,905

No of Employees: 5,229

DIEM & WING PAPER COMPANY

824 Broadway, Cincinnati, OH 45202
Tel: (513) 721-2163
Telex: TWX 810 461273 diem & wing cin

Chairman: P A Stuhlreyer Jr
President: J B Schneider (and Chief Executive Officer)
Senior Executive Officers: F H Lesh (Senior VP), J M Troxell (VP and Manager Dayton Division), E L Michel Jr (VP and Manager Columbus Division), P A Stuhlreyer III (Secretary and Treasurer)

PRINCIPAL ACTIVITIES: Manufacture of paper
Parent Company: Ris Paper Co
Principal Bank: First National Bank of Cincinnati
Financial Information:

	$'000
Sales revenues	58,000

No of Employees: 150

DIGICON INC

3701 Kirby Drive, Suite 112, Houston, TX 77098
Tel: (713) 526 5611

Chairman: Edward R Prince Jr (and President and Chief Executive Officer)
Senior Executive Officers: Larry E Lenig Jr (Executive VP), Patrick H Poe (Senior VP), David R Steetle (Senior VP and Secretary), George A Cloudy (VP), Allan C Pogach (VP Finance and Treasurer)

PRINCIPAL ACTIVITIES: Provision of surveying services for the oil industry
Principal Subsidiaries: Bluewater Maintenance Inc; Digicon (Nigeria) Ltd; Digicon Geophysical Corporation; Digicon AK Inc; Digicon Exploration Ltd; Houston Drilling Co Inc; Digicon Marine Inc; Digicon Systems Inc; Digicon Utility Services Corp; Digisonics Inc; Geophysical Field Survey Inc; Information Products Systems; Ocean Marine Services Inc; Ocean Marine Services Partnership No1; Tensor Geophysical Service Corp
Principal Bank: RepublicBank
Financial Information:

	$'000
Sales revenues	158,730

No of Employees: 2,500

DIGITAL COMMUNICATIONS ASSOCIATES, INC

1000 Alderman Drive, Alpharetta, GA 30201
Tel: (404) 442-4000

Chairman: Bertil D Nordin
President: James F Ottinger
Senior Executive Officers: John C Bacon (VP), Craig J Huffaker (Executive VP, Secretary and Treasurer), James B Lee III (VP), Paul A Rodwick (VP), Robert J Zack (VP), John Douglas (VP), R DeLio (VP)

PRINCIPAL ACTIVITIES: DCA designs, manufactures and markets communications equipment and systems to allow transmission of data over a wide variety of transmission media. The Company's products consist of various data interfacing products for personal computers and compatible modular network processors and multiplexors
Trade Names: Netlink, System 355, System 375, IRMA, IRMAline, IRMAlette, IRMAprint, IRMAcom, IRMAvision, IRMAlink, IRMAX
Principal Subsidiaries: DCA International Inc; DCA Investment Corporation; Digital Communications Associates (Puerto Rico) Corporation
Principal Bank: Citizens and Southern National Bank
Financial Information:

	Jun 30 1986	Jun 30 1987
	$'000	$'000
Sales revenues	150,705	181,399
Net income	14,923	28,433
Earnings per share	$1.10	$1.91
Common stock	1,418	1,435
Retained income	32,978	61,411
Shareholders equity	125,154	157,296

No of Employees: 100

DIGITAL EQUIPMENT CORPORATION

146 Main Street, Maynard, MA 01754
Tel: (617) 897-5111
Telex: 94.8457

President: Kenneth H Olsen
Senior Executive Officers: Winston R Hindle Jr (Senior VP, Corporate Operations), John J Shields (Senior VP, Sales, Services, Marketing and International), John F Smith (Senior VP, Engineering, Manufacturing and Product Marketing, John L Alaxanderson (VP, Peripherals and Supplies Group), Don K Busiek (VP, Software and Educational Services and Computer Special Systems) George A Chamberlain III (VP, Manufacturing, Engineering and Marketing Finance), Henry J Crouse (VP, Group Manager), James G Cudmore (VP, Product Operations), William R Demmer (VP, Mid-Range Systems Business Group), Pier Carlo Falotti (VP, President and Chief Executive Officers-Europe), Samuel H Fuller (VP, Research), Rose Ann Giordano (VP, Consultant and Information Systems Marketing), Robert M Glorioso (VP, High Performance Systems), David W Grainger (VP, Corporate Field Service), William C Hanson (VP, Manufacturing Operations), William J Heffner (VP, Systems Software Group), Robert C Hughes (VP, Service Industry Marketing), Donato A Infante, Jr (VP, Manufacturing Information and Technology), Ilene B Jacobs (VP, and Treasurer), William R Johnson Jr (VP, Distributed Systems Engineering and Marketing), John C MacKeen (VP, Channels Marketing), Edward B McDonough (VP, GIA Operations), Kevin C Melia (VP, Manufacturing Materials and Corporate Distribution), Albert E Mullin Jr (VP Corporate Relations), James M Osterhoff (VP, Finance), Robert B Palmer (VP, Group Manager, Semiconductor Operations), Richard Poulsen (VP, General International Area), Bruce J Ryan (VP, and Corporate Controller), F Grant Saviers (VP, Storage Systems), Edward A Schwartz, (VP, General Counsel and Secretary), Godfrey S Shingles (VP, Managing Director, United Kingdom Region), Charles E Shue (VP, US Sales), John L Sims (VP, Strategic Resources), David L Stone (VP, International Engineering and Strategic Resources), William D Strecker, (VP, Product Strategy and Architecture), Harvey L Weiss (VP, US Operations and Government Systems Group), William G Whitmore (VP, Basic Industry Marketing), Richard H Yen (VP, GIA Manufacturing and Engineering), Donald P Zereski (VP, US Field Service)

PRINCIPAL ACTIVITIES: Digital Equipment Corporation is the world's leading manufacturer of networked computer systems and associated peripheral equipment, and is the leader in systems integration with its networks, communications, services and software products. The Company's products are used worldwide in a variety of applications and programs, including scientific research, computation, communications, education, data analysis, industrial control, timesharing, commercial data processing, graphic arts, word processing, personal computing, health care, instrumentation, engineering and simulation

Trade Names: Digitial Equipment Corporation; Digital; DEC

Principal Subsidiaries: Computer Insurance Company Limited (Bermuda); Digital Computer Taiwan Limited (Taiwan); Digital Equipment Aktiebolag AB (Sweden); Digital Equipment BV (Netherlands); Digital Equipment Betriebliche Altersversorgungsgesellschaft mbH (West Germany); Digital Equipment of Canada Limited-Digital Equipment du Canada Limitée (Canada); Digital Equipment Caribbean Inc (Delaware); Digital Equipment Centre Technique (Europe) SARL (France); Digital Equipment China Ltd (Delaware); Digital Equipment do Brazil Ltda (Brazil); Digital Equipment Co Limited (UK); Digital Equipment Corporation A/S (Norway); Digital Equipment Corp A/S (Denmark); Digital Equipment Corporation (Australia) Pty Ltd (Australia); Digital Equipment Corporation (Consultancy) Limited (States of Jersey); Digital Equipment Corporation Espana SA (Spain); Digital Equipment Corporation Gesellschaft mbH (Austria); Digital Equipment Corporation International (Massachusetts); Digital Equipment Corporation International (Europe) (Switzerland); Digital Equipment Corporation OY (Finland); Digital Equipment Corporation de Puerto Rico (Delaware); Digital Equipment Corporation (New Zealand) Limited (New Zealand); Digital Equipment Corporation SA (Switzerland); Digital Equipment (DEC) Limited (Israel); Digital Equipment (DEC) Technical Center (Israel); Digital Equipment Filipinas Incorporated (Philippines); Digital Equipment Finance Corporation (Delaware); Digital Equipment Foreign Sales Corporation BV (Netherlands); Digitial Equipment France (France); Digital Equipment GmbH (West Germany); Digital Equipment Hellas Ltd (Greece); Digital Equipment (Holdings) BV (Netherlands); Digital Equipment Hong Kong Limited (Hong Kong); Digital Equipment International BV (Netherlands); Digital Equipment International Betriebliche Altersversorgungsgesellschaft mbH (West Germany); Digital Equipment International GmbH (West Germany); Digital Equipment International Limited (Switzerland); Digital Equipment Ireland Limited (Eire); Digital Equipment (Malaysia) Sdn Bhd (Malaysia); Digital Equipment de Mexico SA de CV (Mexico) Digital Equipment NV/SA (Belgium); Digital Equipment Overseas Finance NV (Netherlands Antilles); Digital Equipment Panama Inc (Panama); Digital Equipment Parts Center BV (Netherlands); Digital Equipment Portugal Ltda (Portugal); Digital Equipment PRC Limited (Hong Kong); Digital Equipment SpA (Italy), Digital Equipment Scotland Limited (UK); Digital Equipment Services Inc (Delaware); Digital Equipment Singapore (PTE) Limited (Singapore); Digital Equipment Taiwan Limited (Taiwan); Digital Growth Inc (Massachusetts); Digital Incorporated (Delaware); Digital International Sales Corporation (Delaware); Digital-Natcom (Saudi Arabia); Kam Hon Development Company Limited (Hong Kong); Nihon Digital Equipment Corporation (Japan); Old Colony Insurance Limited (Bermuda); Sesam SpA (Italy)

Principal Bank: Morgan Guaranty Trust Co; Chase Manhattan Bank, Citibank

Financial Information:

	Jun 28 1986	Jun 27 1987
	$'000	$'000
Sales revenues	7,590,357	9,389,444
Income before taxes	857,529	1,688,953
Net income	617,420	1,137,435
Earnings per share	$4.81	$8.53
Common stock	128,591	130,008
Retained income	3,374,932	4,410,242
Shareholders equity	5,727,827	6,293,471

No of Employees: 110,500

DILLARD DEPARTMENT STORES

900 West Capitol, Little Rock, AR 72203
Tel: (501) 376-5200

Chairman: William T Dillard (and Chief Executive Officer); Vice Chairman: E Ray Kemp (and Chief Administration Officer)
President: William Dillard II (and Chief Operating Officer)
Senior Executive Officers: Alex Dillard (Executive VP), Mike Dillard (Executive VP), J K Jameson (VP, Secretary and Treasurer)

PRINCIPAL ACTIVITIES: Department store retailing
Principal Subsidiaries: Dillard Investment Co Inc; Construction Developers Inc
Principal Bank: Centerre Bank
Financial Information:

	Dec 31 1985	Dec 31 1986
	$'000	$'000
Sales revenues	861,600	1,851,423
Net income	66,900	74,458
Earnings per share	$2.29	$2.35
Shareholders equity	362,330	556,617

No of Employees: 18,412

DILLINGHAM CORPORATION

2 Embarcadero Center, San Francisco, CA 94111
Tel: (415) 362-1501

Chairman: L S Dillingham
President: J J Casey (and Chief Executive Officer)
Senior Executive Officers: G W Robertson (Executive VP and Chief Financial Officer), D J Johnson (Senior VP Energy), Donald K Stager (Senior VP Construction), E M Beard (VP Human Resources), J V Pollock (VP Administration), G W Muth (VP Taxes), G Gates (VP and Treasurer), S C Smith (VP and Controller)

PRINCIPAL ACTIVITIES: The company is engaged in a range of activities which include building, quarrying shipping and shipbuilding, gas and petroleum production and distribution
Principal Bank: Bankers Trust
Financial Information:

	$'000
Sales revenues	1,500,000

No of Employees: 12,000

DILLON COMPANIES, INC

700 E 30th Avenue, Hutchinson, KS 67501
Tel: (316) 663-6801
Telex: TWX 910 7401632 dillon huc

Chairman: R E Dillon Jr; Vice Chairman: R W Dillon
President: Joseph A Pichler
Senior Executive Officers: P W Dillon (Senior VP, Secretary and Treasurer), David B Dillon (VP), Paul Christensen (VP), D E Gollegos (VP), F Remar (VP), Harold Ryan (VP), R V Armstrong (VP and Controller)

PRINCIPAL ACTIVITIES: Operation of a variety of retail outlets including supermarkets, department stores and convenience stores; manufacture of frozen desserts, ice cream and milk products
Parent Company: Kroger Co, Cincinnati, OH
Principal Bank: Hutchinson National Bank
Financial Information:

	$'000
Sales revenues	3,000,000

No of Employees: 25,000

DIME SAVINGS BANK OF NEW YORK

9 DeKalb Ave, Brooklyn, NY 11201
Tel: (718) 403-7500

Chairman: Harry W Albright Jr (also Chief Executive Officer)
President: John W Sapanski (also Chief Operating Officer)
Senior Executive Officers: Paul D Colasono (Senior Executive VP and Comptroller), William A Volckhausen (Executive VP, Secretary and Counsel), James J Bolster Jr (Executive VP Finance), Arthur J Bassin (Executive VP Banking), Warren C Marquardt (Executive VP Residential Business Development), Lawrence W Peters (Executive VP Lending), John J Monaghen (Executive VP Administration Services), John T Allison (Senior VP and Auditor), Maria J Alleva (Senior VP Banking), John Bent (Senior VP Financial Research), Bernard I McDermott (Senior VP Advertising), Edward B Kramer (Senior VP Business Development), Arthur C Anderson (Senior VP and Treasurer), Joseph F Davey (Senior VP Building Operations), Robert J Murphy (Senior VP, HRD), John Pettit (Senior VP), Morley Reid (Senior VP Residential Services), Jon R Schmitt (Senior VP), Robert G Turner (Senior VP Commercial Real Estate)

PRINCIPAL ACTIVITIES: Savings bank and real estate finance
Financial Information:

	Dec 31 1986
	$'000
Net income	130,612
Stockholders equity	564,559
Deposits	6,691,224
Total assets	8,366,595

No of Employees: 3,500

DINERS CLUB INTERNATIONAL

575 Lexington Avenue, New York, NY 10043
Tel: (212) 906-2481

Senior Executive Officers: Philip Hensley (Chief Operating Officer), Richard Kampe (Executive VP Marketing), Robert Schwarze (Senior VP Sales), Steven Komar (Senior VP Finance), Richard Gross (Senior VP and General Council)

PRINCIPAL ACTIVITIES: Operation of credit card service
Parent Company: Citibank
Principal Bank: Citibank NA
Financial Information:

	$'000
Revenues	2,500,000

No of Employees: 1,350

DINNER BELL FOODS, INC

Drawer 388, Defiance, OH 43512
Tel: (419) 782-9015

Chairman: Elwood L Elberson (and President and Chief Executive Officer)
Senior Executive Officers: Terry S Elberson (Executive VP Operations), Ian F Keith (Executive VP Corporate Development), Tom Evans (VP Processed Meats), Del Gero (VP Fresh Meats), William Hohenberger (VP Procedures and Methods), John Mills (VP Corporate Accounts), Christopher Smitley (VP Finance and Treasurer), Norman Thomas (VP Technical), Karl H Weaner Jr (VP Legal)

PRINCIPAL ACTIVITIES: Distribution and sale of meat and meat products
Principal Bank: Society National Bank

Financial Information:

	$'000
Sales revenues	256,000

No of Employees: 1,500

DIONEX CORPORATION

501 Mercury Drive, Sunnyvale, CA 94086
Tel: (408) 737-0700

President: A Blaine Bowman (and Chief Executive Officer)
Senior Executive Officers: Eric J Keller (VP Finance and Administration and Chief Financial Officer), Barton Evans Jr (VP Operations), William E Rich (VP Marketing and Sales), Robert V Gunderson Jr (Secretary)

PRINCIPAL ACTIVITIES: Production of measuring and control devices for industrial and scientific use
Principal Subsidiaries: Dionex Export Corporation
Principal Bank: Bank of American National Trust and Savings Association
Financial Information:

	$'000
Sales revenues	45,000

No of Employees: 370

DIPLOMAT ELECTRONICS CORPORATION

110 Marcus Drive, Melville, NY 11747
Tel: (516) 454 6334

President: Jack Darcy (and Chief Executive Officer)
Senior Executive Officers: Laurence Garter (Executive VP and Secretary), M W Katz (VP Finance and Treasurer)

PRINCIPAL ACTIVITIES: Manufacture of electronic products
Financial Information:

	$'000
Sales revenues	104,000

No of Employees: 400

DIRECT ACTION MARKETING INC

3000 Marcus Ave, Lake Success, NY 11042
Tel: (516) 354 6333

Chairman: Howard R Katz (and Chief Executive Officer)
President: W G Gassman (and Chief Operating Officer)
Senior Executive Officers: Joseph M Esposito (Executive VP Corporate Development and Secretary), Daniel J Stone (VP Operations and Administration and Secretary), Paul D Zucker (VP Merchandising), Arthur S Goldberg (Treasurer, Chief Financial Officer and Principal Accounting Officer)

PRINCIPAL ACTIVITIES: Mail order services
Principal Bank: European American Bank
Financial Information:

	$'000
Sales revenues	40,000

No of Employees: 50

DISNEY, WALT, PRODUCTIONS

500 S Buena Vista Street, Burbank, CA 91521
Tel: (818) 840-1000
Telex: TWX 910 498 2707 disney bubk

Chairman: Michael D Eisner (and Chief Executive Officer); Vice Chairman: Roy E Disney
President: Frank G Wells (and Chief Operating Officer)
Senior Executive Officers: Gary L Wilson (Executive VP-Chief Financial Officer), Joe Shapiro (Senior VP-General Counsel), Jose M Deetjen (VP-Tax Administration and Counsel), John H Forsgren (VP-Treasurer), Arthur Levitt III (VP-Corporate Projects), Neil R McCarthy (VP-Planning and Control), Lawrence P Murphy (VP-Strategic Planning), Peter F Nolan (VP-Counsel), Erwin D Okun (VP-Corporate Communications), Joseph F Santaniello (VP-Counsel), Doris A Smith (VP-Secretary), Bruce F Johnson (Controller), Luther R Marr (VP-Stockholder Affairs)

PRINCIPAL ACTIVITIES: Production of motion pictures and television programs; operation of amusement theme parks, hotels
Principal Bank: Bank of America
Financial Information:

	Sep 30 1985	Sep 30 1986
	$'000	$'000
Sales revenues	2,015,400	2,470,900
Net income	173,500	247,300
Dividends per share	$0.30	$0.315*
Earnings per share	$1.29	$1.82
Common stock	129,400	129,400
Shareholders equity	1,184,900	1,418,700

*both 1985 and 1986 before 4-for-1 distribution

No of Employees: 30,000

DISTILLERS COMPANY LTD

41 Harbor Plaza Drive, Stamford, CT 06902
Tel: (203) 348-4444
Telex: TWX 710 47400 17 distco ltd std

Chairman: C W Greaves (and President)
Senior Executive Officers: Hugh J Kelly (Executive VP and Secretary), Richard P Chianese (Treasurer and Assistant Secretary)

PRINCIPAL ACTIVITIES: Manufacture of spirits
Parent Company: United Distillers Company plc, Edinburgh, UK
Principal Bank: Irving Trust Co
Financial Information:

	$'000
Sales revenues	150,000

No of Employees: 500

DISTRIBUCO INC

601 West Dyer Road, Box 2156, Santa Ana, CA 92707
Tel: (714) 549 8711

Chairman: William G McGaughey (and President and Chief Executive Officer)
Senior Executive Officers: Kenneth P Henderson (Senior VP), Edward L Blauvelt (VP), Lynes D Wobken (VP Finance, Treasurer and Secretary)

PRINCIPAL ACTIVITIES: Retail food outlets
Principal Bank: Wells Fargo Bank
Financial Information:

	$'000
Sales revenues	110,000

No of Employees: 230

DITTLER BROS, INC

1375 Seabord Ind Blvd, N W Atlanta, GA 30318
Tel: (404) 355-3423

Chairman: Gilbert Bachman (and Chief Executive Officer)
President: W Aaron (and Chief Operating Officer)
Senior Executive Officers: James Breen (VP), R M Hartman (VP), B Edenfield (VP Sales), W G Shockley (VP and Treasurer), G Stewart (VP Marketing Development)

PRINCIPAL ACTIVITIES: Printing of lottery tickets, and games, airline timetables, hotel directories and other specialty printing
Parent Company: Southam, Inc
Principal Subsidiaries: Production Color, Inc; Marketing Technologies Group
Principal Bank: Trust Company Bank

Financial Information:

	1987 $'000
Sales revenues	70,000
Shareholders equity	24,000

Principal Shareholders: Southam Inc
No of Employees: 700

DIVERSIFIED ENERGIES, INC

201 S Seventh St, Minneapolis, MN 55042
Tel: (612) 372-4664

Chairman: P W Kraemer
President: Albert D Etchelecu (and Chief Executive Officer)
Senior Executive Officers: S J Nelson Jr (Senior VP and Chief Financial Officer), D H Oglesby (Senior VP and Legal Counsel), J F Dyer (Senior VP), K J Whitaker (Senior VP), C D Applequist (Senior VP), J D Somrock (Senior VP), E H Swetman Jr (VP and Controller)

PRINCIPAL ACTIVITIES: Distribution of natural gas
Principal Subsidiaries: Cal Dive International Inc; E F Johnson Co; Minnegasco Inc
Financial Information:

	Dec 31 1986 $'000
Sales revenues	780,000
Net (loss)	(15,000)

No of Employees: 2,000

DIVERSIFIED INDUSTRIES, INC

101 S Hanley Rd, St Louis, MO 63105-3406

Chairman: Ben Fixman (and President)
Senior Executive Officers: Harold B Shapiro (VP Finance, Treasurer and Assistant Secretary), Richard Beldner (VP, Secretary and General Counsel), Arthur J Cohen (Controller and Assistant Secretary)

PRINCIPAL ACTIVITIES: Diversified Industries, Inc's metal trading activities are conducted domestically and internationally. The company, through its divisions and other subsidiaires, reclaims precious and semi-precious metals; is engaged in the production of specialty brass strip; marketing of structural steel; metallurgical and chemicals treatment of steel wire and rod; processing of high temperature alloys; and reclamation of various metals
Principal Subsidiaries and Divisions: Operating Divisions:- Diversified Metals Corporation; Drachman Structurals Inc; Kemco Metal Processing Corporation; Liberty Smelting Works (1962) Inc (Canada); Midwest Steel Processing Inc; Plume & Atwood Brass Mill Division; Theodore Sall Inc; United Refining & Smelting Co
Principal Bank: Mercantile Bank; Mercantile Trust Co NA
Financial Information:

	$'000
Sales revenues	157,000

No of Employees: 300

DIVERSIFIED PRODUCTS

309 Williamson Avenue, Opelika, AL 36801
Tel: (205) 749-9001

President: Cal E James
Senior Executive Officers: Raymond Pilgrim (Executive VP), Richard Jenkins (VP Finance), Jimmy Thompson (VP Sales and Marketing), Paul Chamblee (VP Manufacturing), Ira Silberman (VP Research and Development), Ira Pollack (VP Purchasing), Rick Himmer (VP Distribution and Transport), Mike Murphy (VP Personnel)

PRINCIPAL ACTIVITIES: The leading manufacturer of physical fitness and exercise equipment for use in the home
Trade Names: DP Gympac systems, DP Body Tone rowers
Parent Company: GrandMet USA Inc
Financial Information:

	$'000
Sales revenues	250,000

Principal Shareholders: Grand Metropolitan PLC, London, UK
No of Employees: 2,800

DIXICO INC

Box 225116, Dallas, TX 75265
Tel: (214) 943-7521
Telex: TWX 910 8614044 dixico inc dal

Chairman: Thomas S Williams
President: Louis T Kimple (and Chief Executive and Operating Officer)
Senior Executive Officers: R D Shook (Executive VP), R F Allen (Executive VP), Gary S Wilfert (VP Finance, Chief Financial Officer and Treasurer)

PRINCIPAL ACTIVITIES: Manufacture of plastic packaging materials
Principal Bank: Mercantile National Bank
Financial Information:

	$'000
Sales revenues	83,000

No of Employees: 600

DIXIE CARRIERS, INC

1717 St James Place, Houston, TX 77056
Tel: (713) 622-5502
Telex: TWX 910 8813702 dixie hou

Chairman: George Peterkin Jr
President: J Pine
Senior Executive Officers: R H Dale (Executive VP), Edward Gaither (VP, Secretary and Treasurer)

PRINCIPAL ACTIVITIES: Repair and maintenance of barges
Parent Company: Kirby Exploration Co Inc
Principal Bank: First City National Bank
Financial Information:

	$'000
Sales revenues	55,000

No of Employees: 300

DIXIE YARNS, INC

1100 South Watkins Street, PO Box 751, Chattanooga, TN 37401
Tel: (615) 698-2501
Telex: 462 1072 DIXIUI
Fax: (615) 629-2654; (615) 622-0261

Chairman: Daniel K Frierson (and Chief Executive Officer)
President: James C Fry (and Chief Operating Officer)
Senior Executive Officers: Morgan M Schuessler (Senior VP-Finance), L T Prigmore (VP of Organization Development), E Bryan Gibson (VP of Industrial Relations), Thomas C Robinson Jr (Secretary-Treasurer), C Rex Childers (VP President of Dixie/Ti-Caro Yarn Group), C Pat Driver (VP, President of Carpet Yarn Group), Albert G Myers III (VP, President of Threads, USA Group), John J Callaghan III (VP, President of Ti-Caro Knits Group)

PRINCIPAL ACTIVITIES: Manufacture of yarns and threads from natural and man-made fibers, some of which are further processed through mercerizing, dyeing, or bleaching; processing of yarns into knit fabrics. Four product categories: specialty yarns, industrial sewing threads, knit fabrics, and carpet and rug yarn
Principal Subsidiaries: Ti-Caro Inc; China Grove Cotton Mills Company
Principal Bank: American National Bank and Trust Company of Chattanooga, Tennessee

Financial Information:

	Dec 28 1985	Dec 27 1986
	$'000	$'000
Sales revenues	253,471	300,770
Income before taxes	12,788	21,566
Net income	7,093	13,378
Dividends(1)	1,472	2,868
Dividends per share(2)	$0.2667	$0.4958
Dividends per share(3)	$0.1000	$0.4291
Earnings per share	$1.24	$2.24
Common stock	16,234	20,653
Common stock(3)	2,207	2,207
Retained income	53,678	41,335
Shareholders equity	47,523	92,317

(1) common stock and Class B common stock
(2) common stock
(3) Class B common stock

No of Employees: 4,400

DIXIELINE LUMBER COMPANY

3250 Sports Arena Blvd, San Diego, CA 92110
Tel: (614) 224-4120

President: W S Cowling II
Senior Executive Officers: Max Robinson (VP Finance), R Gauthier (VP Sales), W Heise (VP)

PRINCIPAL ACTIVITIES: Sale of timber and timber products
Parent Company: Nortek Inc
Principal Bank: Bank of America
Financial Information:

	$'000
Sales revenues	100,000

No of Employees: 500

DIXON TICONDEROGA COMPANY

Box 3504, Beach Station, Vero Beach, FL 32960
Tel: (305) 231-3190

Chairman: David K Brewster (and Joint Chief Executive Officer)
President: Gina N Pala (and Joint Chief Executive Officer)
Senior Executive Officers: Len D Dahlberg Jr (VP)

PRINCIPAL ACTIVITIES: Holding company with interests in stationery and art materials, property development and restaurants
Principal Subsidiaries: Bryn Mawr Ocean Resorts Inc; Bryn Mawr Resorts Inc; Dixon Disc Inc; Garden State Coachways Inc; Wallace Pencil Co
Principal Bank: Citicorp
Financial Information:

	$'000
Sales revenues	74,000

No of Employees: 1,000

DOALL COMPANY

254 N Laurel Avenue, Des Plaines, IL 60016
Tel: (312) 824-1122
Telex: WUT 726 451 doallintl dsp

Chairman: P J Weber; Chairman of Executive Committee: Leighton A Wilkie; Vice Chairman: Robert J Wilkie
President: Michael L Wilkie
Senior Executive Officers: Robert H Pletch (VP and Purchasing Agent)

PRINCIPAL ACTIVITIES: Manufacture of machine tools
Principal Bank: Continental Illinois National Bank and Trust Co
Financial Information:

	$'000
Sales revenues	75,000

No of Employees: 200

DOBOY PACKAGING MACHINERY, INC

215 N Knowles Avenue, New Richmond, WI 54017
Tel: (715) 246-6511
Telex: ITT 431 0046 doby ui

President: John M Johnston
Senior Executive Officers: John Deboer (Treasurer and Comptroller), Ken Payson (General Sales Manager), Brant Short (VP Engineering)

PRINCIPAL ACTIVITIES: Manufacture of machinery for the packaging industry
Parent Company: SIG Holding USA
Principal Bank: First Bank Minneapolis
Financial Information:

	$'000
Sales revenues	30,000

No of Employees: 400

DOC OPTICS CORPORATION

19800 West Eight Mile Road, Southfield, MI 48075
Tel: (313) 354 7100

Chairman: Donald L Golden (and President)
Senior Executive Officers: Michael E Golden (VP and Secretary), Richard S Golden (VP), Thomas R Liegl (Controller), Jack L Posar (Treasurer)

PRINCIPAL ACTIVITIES: Retail stores specializing in spectacles and contact lenses
Principal Bank: Michigan National Bank
Financial Information:

	$'000
Sales revenues	41,050

No of Employees: 800

DOCUTEL/OLIVETTI CORPORATION

5615 Highpoint Drive, Irving, TX 75038
Tel: (214) 258-5400
Telex: RCA 203969 docc ur

Chairman: Giovanni Fei (and Chief Executive Officer and Financial Officer)
President: Enrico Pesatori (and Chief Operating Officer)
Senior Executive Officers: Giulio Salvi (Chief Financial Officer), Bill Cronin (VP Marketing), Rick Medeiros (VP Marketing), B J Turner (VP)

PRINCIPAL ACTIVITIES: Manufacture of automated systems for banks
Parent Company: Ing C Olivetti & Co SPA, Italy
Principal Bank: Allied Bank of Texas
Financial Information:

	$'000
Sales revenues	164,000

No of Employees: 820

DOERR ELECTRIC CORPORATION

W 57 N 14371 Doerr Way, Cedarburg, WI 53012
Tel: (414) 377-0500
Telex: WUT 26744 doerrelec cedar

Chairman: David W Grainger
President: George T Mathews
Senior Executive Officers: James P Dries (VP Engineering), James H Windsor (VP and General Manager Dayton Industries), David A Gall (VP Original Equipment Manufacturing and Sales), Jack D Carbone (VP Sales), Bernard R Berntson (VP Marketing and Engineering), Timothy W Hennessey (VP Manufacturing), Robert J Slobig (VP and Controller)

PRINCIPAL ACTIVITIES: Manufacture of electrical equipment, compressors and electric motors
Parent Company: W W Grainger Inc, Skokie, IL
Principal Bank: M & I Bank of Menominee Falls

Financial Information:

	$'000
Sales revenues	115,000

No of Employees: 1,500

DOLLAR GENERAL CORPORATION

427 Beach Street, Scottsville, KY 42164
Tel: (502) 237 5444

Chairman: Cal Turner
President: Cal Turner Jr
Senior Executive Officers: James Stephen Turner (Executive VP), Jim Barton (VP Operations), Edward J Burke (VP Finance, Secretary and Treasurer), Bobby R Carpenter (VP Administration)

PRINCIPAL ACTIVITIES: Retailing of miscellaneous goods including clothing
Principal Subsidiaries: Dolgencorp Inc
Principal Bank: First American Bank
Financial Information:

	Dec 31 1985
	$'000
Sales revenues	584,440
Net income	17,830

No of Employees: 2,000

DOMINICK INTERNATIONAL CORPORATION

90 Broad Street, New York, NY 10004
Tel: (212) 558-8800
Telex: WUT 126192 dominick nyk

Chairman: Peter M Kennedy
President: Alan A Moses
Senior Executive Officers: Robert T Neumayer (VP), Robert Lawler (VP and Treasurer), Pasquale Luongo (VP and Secretary)

PRINCIPAL ACTIVITIES: Manufacture of furniture; financial services
Principal Subsidiaries: Dominick & Dominick Inc; Dominick Investor Services Inc; Veniculum Inc; Dominick Management Corp; Drexel Heritage Furnishings Corp; Frederick Edward Inc
Principal Bank: Manufacturers Hanover Trust Co
Financial Information:

	$'000
Sales revenues	264,000

No of Employees: 5,500

DOMINION BANK, NA

201 S Jefferson Street, Roanoke, VA 24040
Tel: (703) 563-7000

Chairman: Warner L Dalhouse (and Chief Executive Officer)
President: J C Quarles (and Chief Operating Officer)
Senior Executive Officers: J R Carling (Executive VP Commercial Banking), David L Caudill (Executive VP Delivery Systems), Earl E McGuire Jr (Executive VP Retail Banking), John F Fisher (Executive VP), C Ray Bowling (Senior VP, Grundy), Thomas F Conn (Senior VP Consumer Credit Group), James E Cornett (Senior VP, Appalachia), Charles E Coudriet (Senior VP Banking Group), Ted W English (Senior VP, Grundy), Dewey R Fortune Jr (Senior VP, Grundy), Harry M Francis Jr (Senior VP, Marion), Edwin R Hale (Senior VP, Bristol), Paul W Holt (Senior VP, Bristol), Paul W Holt (Senior VP, Bristol), Clarence E Hoover (Senior VP Operations Group and Cashier), Charles N Kilgore (Senior VP, Grundy), G C Luck Jr (Senior VP, Bedford), R Morris Mahan (Senior VP), Robert W Meador (Senior VP, Lexington), Cecil R McCullar (Senior VP, Bassett), R Bruce Munro (Senior VP Community Banks Group), Howard A Payne (Senior VP, Bassett), N R Rusinko (Senior VP Real Estate Finance Group), John F Shoulders Jr (Senior VP Commercial Banking), Glenn M Stirewalt (Senior VP, Bluefield), Douglas H Vincill (Senior VP, Bristol), Charles E Warsaw II (Senior VP Retail Banking), Robert M Webb (Senior VP), Byron L Yost (Senior VP Credit Group)

PRINCIPAL ACTIVITIES: Bank
Parent Company: Dominion Bankshares Corporation

No of Employees: 770

DOMINION BANKSHARES CORPORATION

213 S Jefferson Street, Roanoke, VA 24040
Tel: (703) 563-7000

Chairman: Byron A Hicks
President: Warner N Dalhouse (and Chief Executive Officer)
Senior Executive Officers: David Caudill (Vice Chairman and Chief Operating Officer)

PRINCIPAL ACTIVITIES: Bank holding company
Principal Bank: Dominion Bank NA
Financial Information:

	Dec 31 1985	Dec 31 1986
	$'000	$'000
Income before taxes	62,512	54,917
Net income	50,495	47,321
Dividends	19,598	16,730
Dividends per common share	$0.675	$0.615
Earnings per share	$1.68	$1.66
Common stock	148,597	88,376
Retained income	156,831	184,087
Shareholders equity	395,027	335,417
Deposits	5,214,185	4,521,159
Total assets	6,761,145	5,652,081

No of Employees: 4,500

DOMINION RESOURCES, INC

One James River Plaza, PO Box 26532, Richmond, VA 23261
Tel: (804) 771-3000
Telex: (804) 771-3160 (Xerox 495)

Chairman: William W Berry (and Chief Executive Officer)
President: Jack H Ferguson (and Chief Operating Officer)
Senior Executive Officers: Thomas E Capps (Executive VP). Senior Exeuctive Officers of Virginia Electric and Power Company only: John I Oatts (Executive VP), Samuel C Brown Jr (Senior VP Corporate Technical Assessment), Robert F Hill (Senior VP Commercial Operations), Ronald H Leasburg (Senior VP Engineering and Construction), James T Rhodes (Senior VP Power Operations)

PRINCIPAL ACTIVITIES: Dominion Resources Inc (Dominion Resources), a holding company having general business powers, was organized in 1983 as a Virginia corporation. Virginia Electric and Power Company, Dominion Resources' major subsidiary, conducts electric business in most of Virginia and in parts of North Carolina and West Virginia. In its service area it sells electricity to retail customers (including governmental agencies) and, at wholesale, to rural electric cooperatives and municipalities. Virginia Natural Gas, a division of Virginia Electric and Power Company, provides gas service in the Tidewater area of Virginia
Trade Names: Virginia Power, North Carolina Power, West Virginia Power
Principal Subsidiaries: Virginia Electric and Power Company (The Power Company); Virginia Natural Gas (Division of the Power Company); Dominion Resourse Services Inc (subsidiary of Dominion Resources); Laurel Run Mining Company (subsidiary of the Power Company); Dominion Exploration Inc (subsidiary of the Power Company)
Principal Bank: United Virginia Bank; The Chase Manhattan Bank, N A

Financial Information: Consolidated figures

	Dec 31 1986
	$'000
Sales revenues	3,071,600
Net income	379,800
Earnings per share	$4.10
Shareholders equity	2,813,100

No of Employees: 13,863 Group

DONALDSON COMPANY, INC

1400 West 94th Street, Box 1299, Minneapolis, MN 55440
Tel: (612) 887-3131
Telex: WUT 290 434 don co inc mps

Chairman: William A Hodder (and President and Chief Executive Officer)
Senior Executive Officers: Robert L Findorff (Senior VP). Business Groups:- Thomas A Baden (VP Original Equipment), Edmund C Craft (VP, Aftermarket), Norman E Johnson (VP, Microfiltration and Defense Products), Alfons J Laleman (VP, International), Kenneth N Olson (Area VP, International), Jerry Phillips (VP, Corporate Development), William G Van Dyke (VP, Industrial). Worldwide Support Group:- Erland D Anderson (VP, Engineering), Ernest W Andberg (Treasurer), Raymond F Vodovnik (VP, Legal), Don Brattain (VP Finance and Administration)

PRINCIPAL ACTIVITIES: Donaldson Company, Inc, specializes in separation technology. It designs, manufactures and sells proprietary products which separate something unwanted from something wanted. Products separate particles from air, particles from smaller particles, particles from liquids, liquids from liquids. Products are designed to solve specific customer problems. They protect machines, manufacturing processes and people from contaminants, quiet noise in factories and on thoroughfares, and recapture useful raw materials. They include air filters and cleaners, hydraulic filters, liquid clarifiers, air pollution control equipment and muffler systems
Principal Subsidiaries: US Plants:- Frankfort, IN; Cresco, IA; Grinnell, IA; Oelwein, IA; Chillicothe, IA; Dixon, IL; Baldwin, WI; Stevens Point, WI; Nicholasville, KY. Overseas Affiliates - Wholly Owned Subsidiaries:-Donaldson Gesellschaft mbH (West Germany); Donaldson Europe NV (Belgium); Nippon Donaldson Ltd (Japan); Donaldson Far East Limited (Hong Kong); Donaldson France SA (France); Donaldson Air Cleaners (Pty) Limited (South Africa); Donaldson Autralasia (Pty) Ltd (Australia); Donaldson do Brasil Ltda (Brazil); Donaldson Filter Components Ltd (UK). Joint Venture:- Donaldson Micro Pore SA de CV (Mexico); Mexico DF (Mexico)
Principal Bank: Bank of Minneapolis
Financial Information:

	$'000
Sales revenues	262,000

No of Employees: 2,883

DONALDSON, LUFKIN & JENRETTE, INC

140 Broadway, New York, NY 10005
Tel: (212) 902-2000
Telex: ITT 421760 pins tk

Chairman: Richard H Jenrette; Vice Chairman: Carl B Menges
President: John S Chalsty (and Chief Executive Officer)
Senior Executive Officers: Richard S Pechter (Managing Director), Theodore P Shen (Managing Director), Anthony F Daddino (Executive VP and Chief Financial Officer)

PRINCIPAL ACTIVITIES: Financial services
Parent Company: The Equitable Life Assurance Society of the United States
Principal Subsidiaries: Donaldson, Lufkin & Jenrette Securities Corporation
Principal Bank: Citibank NA
Financial Information:

	Dec 31 1985	Dec 31 1986
	$'000	$'000
Revenues	505,354	731,524
Net income	19,000	37,500
Shareholders equity	212,862	245,987
Total assets	8,796,613	9,563,309

Principal Shareholders: Equitable Investment Corporation (effective Jan 1985)
No of Employees: 3,000

DONNELLEY, R R, & SONS COMPANY

2223 Martin Luther King Drive, Chicago, IL 60616
Tel: (312) 326-8000

Chairman: John B Schwemm; Vice Chairman: Charles C Haffner III
President: John R Walter
Senior Executive Officers: Donald M Hackbert (Executive VP, Operations), Barton L Faber (VP, Corporate Development), Robert L Hildebrand (VP, Employee Relations), Nicholas A Martellotto (Senior VP, Technology), John A Capstick (Group President, International), James R Donnelley (Group President, Financial Printing Services), Carl K Doty (Group President, Catalogs), Hubert R Gotzes (Group President, Books), Robert G Myers (Group President, Magazines), Ronald K Vickrey (Group President, Directories), James W Fletcher (Senior VP and Treasurer), Frank J Uvena (Senior VP, Law and Corporate Staffs), Gordon D Friday (VP Purchasing and Transportation), John E Hillman (VP Administration), John R Johanson (VP Manufacturing Engineering), James A Lawlor (VP Technical Center), Arthur C Prine Jr (VP Corpoate Relations), J E Treadway (VP Human Resources), William L White (Controller), David C Hart (VP and General Counsel), Richard M Sawdey (VP and Secretary)

PRINCIPAL ACTIVITIES: R R Donnelley & Sons Company is America's leader in printing and print-related services serving publishers, merchandisers, the telephone industry, financial institutions and other industries requiring substantial amounts of printing. Major products include catalogs and newspaper inserts, magazines, software manuals, directories, books and financial printing
Principal Subsidiaries: Manufacturing facilities and service centers located throught the United States and in the UK through the subsidiary Ben Johnson & Co Ltd
Financial Information:

	Dec 31 1985	Dec 31 1986
	$'000	$'000
Sales revenues	2,038,408	2,233,511
Earnings before taxes	255,887	266,562
Net income	148,414	158,268
Dividends	44,349	49,224
Dividends per share	$1.16	$1.28
Earnings per share	$3.88	$4.05
Common stock	180,916	181,916
Retained income	746,920	863,641
Shareholders equity	895,903	1,005,008

No of Employees: 17,700

DONNKENNY, INC

1411 Broadway, New York, NY 10018
Tel: (212) 730-7770
Telex: RCA 237905 donk ur

Chairman: Richard Rubin (and President and Chief Operating Officer)
Senior Executive Officers: Gustave Birnberg (Senior VP), Maarten Hemsley (VP Finance), Raymond Mabry (VP Manufacturing), Mark Hassin (VP Sales)

PRINCIPAL ACTIVITIES: Manufacture of ladies' clothing
Parent Company: Donnkenny Holding Co Inc
Principal Bank: Manufacturers Hanover Trust Co

Financial Information:

	$'000
Sales revenues	75,000

No of Employees: 2,000

DONOVAN WIRE & IRON COMPANY

805 Chicago Street, Toledo, OH 43611
Tel: (419) 726-1511
Telex: WUT 286426 donovan tol

Vice Chairman: Irwin Fruchtman
President: Leonard Fruchtman
Senior Executive Officers: Michael Fruchtman (VP), Morris Fruchtman (VP), Real P Remillard (Treasurer)

PRINCIPAL ACTIVITIES: Wholesale trade in steel and steel products
Financial Information:

	$'000
Sales revenues	120,000

No of Employees: 600

DONREY MEDIA GROUP

PO Box 1359, Fort Smith, AR 72902
Tel: (501) 785-7827

President: Donald W Reynolds
Senior Executive Officers: Fred W Smith (Executive VP)

PRINCIPAL ACTIVITIES: Printing and publishing of newspapers, advertising, radio and television broadcasting
Principal Subsidiaries: Daily World Inc; Donrey of TX Inc; Great Western Construction Co; Hawaii Tribune-Herald Ltd; Logan Publishing Co; Nevada Radio-Television Inc; Northwest AR Publishing Co; Progress-Bulletin Publishing Co; Red Bluff News Inc; Southwestern Operating Co; Southwestern Broadcasting Corp; Springdale Publishing Co Inc; Times Herald Inc; Times Publishing Co; Western Communications Inc; Northwestern AR Broadcasting TV Inc; Western Publishing Co Inc
Financial Information:

	$'000
Sales revenues	200,000

No of Employees: 4,000

DORCHESTER GAS CORPORATION

5735 Pineland Drive, Dallas, TX 75231
Tel: (214) 750-3500
Telex: TWX 910 861 4078 dorchester dal

Chairman: George S Rooker (and Chief Executive Officer); Vice Chairman: Preston A Peak
President: John R Barnes (and Chief Operating Officer)
Senior Executive Officers: William E Cornell (Executive VP), Robert K Taylor (Senior VP Exploration), James E Raley (Senior VP), C F Brady (Treasurer), J Norman Blair (VP Exploration), Bernard L Bobo (VP Coal and Minerals), Harold T Connally (VP Refining), James M Perkins Jr (VP Production Exploration)

PRINCIPAL ACTIVITIES: Exploration and production of oil, gas and coal; marketing of petroleum products
Principal Subsidiaries: Coastal Plains Inc; Air Hydraulics Inc; Dorchester Coal Co; Dorchester Enterprises Inc; Dorchester Exploration Inc; Dorchester Gas Production Co; Dorchester Refining Co; Dorchester Sea-3 Products Inc; Rosamund Phillip Drilling Co
Principal Bank: Interfirst Bank Dallas
Financial Information:

	$'000
Sales revenues	712,000

No of Employees: 1,200

DORMAN, N, & COMPANY, INC

125 Michael Drive, Syosset, NY 11791
Tel: (516) 364-1600
Telex: TWX 510 2212 161 n dorman

Chairman: Victor S Dorman
President: Avram Dorman
Senior Executive Officers: William Dorman (Executive VP), Roger Strang (VP and Chief Operating Officer), Steve Peacock (VP Marketing), Ken Dorman (VP Finance), Neil Dorman (VP Production), David Dorman (VP Manufacturing), Vince Carotenuto (VP Finance), Ken Sampson (VP Plant Management), Ned Dorman (VP), Marjorie Dorman (VP Imports)

PRINCIPAL ACTIVITIES: Manufacture of cheese
Principal Bank: Manufacturers Hanover Trust Co
Financial Information:

	$'000
Sales revenues	125,000

No of Employees: 350

DORON PRECISION SYSTEMS, INC

174 Court Street, Box 400, Binghamton, NY 13901
Tel: (607) 772-1610
Telex: 821644

Chairman: Carl J Wenzinger Jr (and President)
Senior Executive Officers: W R Price (Executive VP), Carl E Hedges (VP Personnel and Administration), Robert J Nole (Treasurer)

PRINCIPAL ACTIVITIES: Manufacture of simulation equipment for training and amusement purposes
Principal Bank: Chase Manhattan Bank NA
Financial Information:

	$'000
Sales revenues	80,000

No of Employees: 100

DORR-OLIVER, INC

Havemeyer Lane, Stamford, CT 06904
Tel: (203) 358-3200
Telex: WUI 6819019 doine uw

Chairman: A W Whitehouse Jr; Vice-Chairmen: E J Finn, J E Goodell, W P Madar, J R Miller
President: C J Barton
Senior Executive Officers: G Ehinger (Senior VP North America), A H Ford (Senior VP), R C Raynor (Senior VP International), M S Madigan (VP Finance and Treasurer)

PRINCIPAL ACTIVITIES: Manufacture of processing plant for a wide range of industries
Parent Company: Kennecott Corp
Principal Bank: The Chase Manhattan Bank NA
Financial Information:

	$'000
Sales revenues	230,000

No of Employees: 2,900

DORSEY CORPORATION

715 Market Street, Box 6339, Chattanooga, TN 37401
Tel: (615) 267-2973

Chairman: John T Pollock (and Chief Executive Officer)
President: Charles F Casey (and Chief Operating Officer)
Senior Executive Officers: Marylyn Marks (VP), David Tatum (VP and Controller), G L Collier (VP), Ladd Duryea (VP), James J Goldman (VP Finance and Treasurer)

PRINCIPAL ACTIVITIES: Manufacture of truck trailers, lifting equipment and plastic containers
Principal Subsidiaries: Dorsey Trailers, Inc; Bickfords Family Fare Inc; Dorsey Trailers Southeast Inc; Dorsey Trailers-Midwest Corp; Sewell Plastics Inc

Principal Bank: Chemical Bank
Financial Information:

	Dec 31 1985	Dec 31 1986
	$'000	$'000
Sales revenues	532,240	526,754
Net income	10,375	9,480
Earnings per share	$3.21	$1.32
Shareholders equity	79,790	74,830

No of Employees: 5,000

DORSEY TRAILERS, INC

Elba, AL 36323
Tel: (205) 897-5711

President: George L Collier
Senior Executive Officers: Roy C Belcer (VP Planning and Engineering), Joe B Devane (VP Sales)

PRINCIPAL ACTIVITIES: Manufacture of truck trailers and lifting equipment
Parent Company: Dorsey Corporation, Chattanooga, TN
Financial Information:

	$'000
Sales revenues	100,000

No of Employees: 1,000

DOSKOCIL COMPANIES INC

321 North Main Street, South Hutchinson, KS 67505
Tel: (316) 663 1005

President: Larry Doskocil (and Chief Executive Officer)
Senior Executive Officers: James W Cole (Executive VP), Orvin L Miller (Senior VP Marketing), Wendel J Strong (VP and Division President), David Moak (VP Finance and Chief Financial Officer), Erwin H Unruh (Controller and Secretary)

PRINCIPAL ACTIVITIES: Manufacture of toppings for pizzas
Principal Bank: Fourth National Bank and Trust Company
Financial Information:

	Dec 31 1985
	$'000
Sales revenues	114,940
Net income	6,080

No of Employees: 450

DOUGHTIE'S FOODS, INC

2410 Wesley Street, Portsmouth, VA 23707
Tel: (804) 393-6007

Chairman: Vernon W Mules
President: Thomas R Beeler
Senior Executive Officers: Steven C Houfek (Senior VP), Marion S Whitfield Jr (VP), Dewey A Rodgerson (VP), George D Spicer (VP and Controller), Martin Carter (VP), Charles E Smith (VP)

PRINCIPAL ACTIVITIES: Processing, distribution and sale of meat and meat products; prepared products for catering; frozen meat
Principal Subsidiaries: Doughties Barbecue of MD Inc; Dutterers of Manchester Corp
Principal Bank: United Virginia Bank
Financial Information:

	$'000
Sales revenues	52,000

No of Employees: 350

DOUGLAS & LOMASON COMPANY

24600 Hallwood Court, Farmington Hills, MI 48018
Tel: (313) 478-7800
Telex: TWX 810 2429 365 d & l ofc fmhl

Chairman: W K Lomason
President: Harry A Lomason II (and Chief Executive Officer)
Senior Executive Officers: C D Crisp (VP Manufacturing), H R Dombrowski (VP Sales), H J Kouris (VP Purchasing), James J Hoey (VP and Treasurer), B G Morelli (VP Engineering), R I Homier (VP Executive Engineering), O V Cheatham (VP Personnel)

PRINCIPAL ACTIVITIES: Manufacture of parts for motor vehicles and heavy goods vehicles; manufacture of conveying equipment and packaging
Principal Bank: National Bank of Detroit
Financial Information:

	$'000
Sales revenues	267,000

No of Employees: 3,300

DOVER CORPORATION

277 Park Avenue, New York, NY 10172
Tel: (212) 826-7160

President: G L Roubos (and Chief Executive Officer)
Senior Executive Officers: John F McNiff (VP Finance), Edward J Kata (VP), Cloyd Laporte Jr (Secretary), Alfred Suesser (Controller)

PRINCIPAL ACTIVITIES: Electronic products; manufacture of elevators; equipment for production of oil and gas; components for the aerospace industry
Trade Names: Norriseal (R)
Principal Subsidiaries: Building Industry: Dover Elevator International; Dover Elevator Systems; Hawaiian Pacific; Dover Elevator Company; Lagerquist; Miami Elevator; Sound Elevator; Dover Elevator Division (Canada); Hammond & Champness Ltd (UK). Petroleum Industry: Norris Sucker Rods; Norris-O'Bannon; Alberta Oil Tool (Canada); Norriseal Controls; Sargent-Oil Well; C Lee Cook:- Compressor Components, Manley Valve; OPW:-Industrial Division (Canada), Dover International BV, I.S.T. GmbH; Blackmer Pump. Electronic Products: Universal Instruments Corporation; Arbell Inc (Canada); Cencorp; Corpane Industries; DEK Printing Machines Ltd (UK); UIC Nordic (Sincotron) (Sweden); Soltec International BV (Netherlands); Measurement Systems; K & L Microwave:- Dielectric Laboratories, Oscillatek, Communications Techniques; Nurad Inc. Industrial & Aerospace Products: Bernard:- Weldcraft; Davenport Machine Tool; De-Sta-Co:- De-Sta-Co GmbH; Dieterich Standard; Groen:- American Metal Ware; Holmes International; Pathway Bellows; Randell; Ronningen-Petter; Rotary Lift; Sargent Industries:- Airite, Central Research Laboratories, Huntington Park, Kahr Bearing, Stillman Seal, Sweeney; Tipper Tie, Tranter inc; Waukesha Bearings:- P M E
Financial Information:

	Dec 31 1985	Dec 31 1986
	$'000	$'000
Sales revenues	1,439,548	1,439,844
Income before taxes	160,088	134,466
Net income	100,028	83,829
Dividends	30,089	31,148
Dividends per share	$0.85	$0.90
Earnings per share	$2.83	$2.42
Common stock	37,840	37,898
Retained income	644,552	677,233
Shareholders equity	625,541	627,674

No of Employees: 16,539

DOVER ELEVATOR COMPANY

PO Box 2177, Memphis, TN 38101
Tel: (601) 393-2110

Chairman: Gary L Roubos
President: Charles A Davenport
Senior Executive Officers: George E Powell (VP and Secretary), L E Hamilton (VP), Phillip Mock (Treasurer)

PRINCIPAL ACTIVITIES: Manufacture of elevators and industrial machinery

Parent Company: Dover Corporation, New York, NY
Financial Information:

	$'000
Sales revenues	50,000

No of Employees: 2,800

DOW CHEMICAL COMPANY

2030 Willard H Dow Center, Midland, MI 48674
Tel: (517) 636-1000
Telex: 227455
Telecopy: (517) 636-0922 a

Chairman: Paul F Oreffice (and President and Chief Executive Officer)
Senior Executive Officers: Hunter W Henry (Executive VP), Robert M Keil (Executive VP), Frank P Popoff (Executive VP), Joseph G Temple Jr (Executive VP), David P Sheetz (Senior VP), Keith R McKennon (Group VP), Enrique C Falla (Financial Vice President and Treasurer), Bernard B Butcher (VP), Andrew J Butler (VP), Herbert H Dow (VP), Joseph L Downey (VP), Wayne M Hancock (VP and General Counsel), Roger L Kesseler (VP and Controller), Donald A Rikard (VP), Donna J Roberts (Secretary), William C Schmidt (Assistant Controller), R William Barker (Assistant Secretary), Lois J Hoerlein (Assistant Secretary), Glenn W White (Assistant Treasurer), Howard W Burdett (Assistant Treasurer), Arnold L Johnson (Assistant Treasurer), John S Walshaw (Assistant Treasurer), Dale A Bywater (Auditor)

PRINCIPAL ACTIVITIES: The Dow Chemical Company is a diversified manufacturer of basic chemicals and plastics and specialty products and services. The sixth largest chemical company in the world in terms of sales, Dow serves a broad range of industries from its base in Midland, Michigan and six operating areas: the United States, Europe, Canada, the Pacific, Latin America and Brazil. More than 50 percent of Dow's sales are outside the United States. Dow Chemical is a principal producer for most of the products it makes including polystyrene, polyethylene, chlorine, caustic soda, vinyl chloride monomer, ethylene glycols, styrene-butadiene latexes, magnesium metal, plastic films, epoxy resins and insulation materials. The Company also has growing global businesses in human health products, agricultural chemicals and household products and plastics
Trade Names: Aspun, Calibre, Derakane, DOW, Dowanol, Dowex, Dowfax, Dowicide, Dowicil, Dowlex, Dowpon, Dowtherm, Drytech, Dursban, Ethafoam, Garlon, Generon, Lontrel, Lorsban, Magnum, MegaRad, Methocel, N-Serve, Pelaspan-Pac, Plictran, Primacor, Rovel, Saran, Saran Wrap, Separan, Starane, Styrofoam, Styron, Tandem, Telone, Tordon, Trycite, Tyril, Tyrin, Versene, Voranate, Voranol, Zetabon. Trademarks of Merrell Dow Pharmaceuticals Inc:- Cepacol, Citrucel, Lorelco, Nicorette, Novahistine, Rifadin, Rifocin, Seldane, Teldane, Triludan. Trademarks of Dow Consumer Products Inc:- DOW Bathroom Cleaner, Fantastik, Glass Plus, Handi-Wrap, Pine Magic, Spray 'n Wash, Tough Act, Vivid, Yes, Ziploc
Financial Information:

	Dec 31 1985	Dec 31 1986
	$'000	$'000
Sales revenues net	10,500,000	11,113,000
Income before taxes	30,000	1,236,000
Net income	58,000	732,000
Dividends	341,000	364,000
Dividends per share	$1.80	$1.85
Earnings per share	$0.31	$3.82
Common stock	528,000	535,000
Retained income	4,058,000	4,426,000
Shareholders equity	4,792,000	5,168,000

No of Employees: 51,300

DOW CORNING CORPORATION

Box 1767, Midland, MI 48640
Tel: (517) 496-4000
Telex: WUT 227450 dowcornco midl

President: J S Ludington
Senior Executive Officers: L A Reed (Executive VP), J K Campbell (VP), E Steinhoff (VP Finance and Chief Financial Officer)

PRINCIPAL ACTIVITIES: Manufacture of silicones
Principal Bank: Citibank NA
Financial Information:

	Dec 31 1985	Dec 31 1986
	$'000	$'000
Sales revenues	901,100	1,085,400
Net income	95,200	110,600
Shareholders equity	575,700	601,700

No of Employees: 6,190

DOW JONES & COMPANY, INC

World Financial Center, 200 Liberty Street, New York, NY 10281
Tel: (212) 416-2000
Telex: 844450 dowjones

Chairman: Warren H Phillips (and Chief Executive Officer)
President: Ray Shaw (and Chief Operating Officer)
Senior Executive Officers: William L Dunn (Executive VP), Peter R Kann (Executive VP), Kenneth L Burenga (Senior VP and Chief Financial Officer), James H Ottaway Jr (Senior VP), Frank C Breese III (VP), Robert H Schmitz (VP), Peter G Skinner (VP, Corporate General Counsel and Secretary), Sterling E Soderlind (VP/Planning), Donald L Miller (VP, Employee Relations), Dorothea Coccoli Palsho (VP, Circulation), Kevin J Roche (VP, Finance)

PRINCIPAL ACTIVITIES: Dow Jones & Company, Inc is a leading publisher of business news and information, community newspapers and textbooks
Trade Names: The Wall Street Journal, Dow Jones News Services, Dow Jones News/Retrieval, Barron's, Irwin Books
Principal Subsidiaries: Ottaway Newspapers, Inc; Richard D Irwin, Inc; American Demographics
Principal Bank: Manufacturers Hanover Trust Co
Financial Information:

	Dec 31 1985	Dec 31 1986
	$'000	$'000
Sales revenues	1,039,314	1,134,867
Income before taxes	258,460	331,323
Net income	138,600	183,362
Dividends	50,228	53,585
Dividends per share	$0.78	$0.553
Earnings per share	$2.15	$1.89
Common stock issued	65,164	97,744
Retained income	526,967	637,923
Shareholders equity	600,200	727,977

No of Employees: 7,069

DOWNEY SAVINGS & LOAN ASSOCIATION

3200 Bristol, PO Box 6000, Costa Mesa, CA 92626
Tel: (714) 549-8811

President: Maurice L McAlister
Senior Executive Officers: Gerald H McQuarrie (Chief Executive Officer/Secretary), J Morsillo (Senior VP/Treasurer), David Dutts (Senior VP), Gary R Steinberg (Senior VP/Assistant Secretary), Robert D Bly (VP), Gene Boultault (VP), Thomas R Cornish (VP), Nancy Gucciardo (VP), John Oliver (VP), William F Thurston (VP/Assistant Secretary), Richard L Wilson (VP), Jim Mizell (VP)

PRINCIPAL ACTIVITIES: California state-chartered Downey Savings attracted nationwide attention during 1986 for its innovative yet conservative financial practices and ranks today among the top 2 percent of the largest savings and loans in the United States, with assets of $2.5 billion. Downey

Savings has met its first obligation to provide for home ownership and it has pioneered investment into income-producing commercial developments. Today, Downey Savings along with its wholly-owned subsidiary, DSL Service Company, is one of the largest residential and shopping center developers in California and Arizona. A highly-diversified lending program includes the full spectrum of activities in real estate, consumer finance, personal lines of credit, debit cards and corporate banking

Principal Subsidiaries: DSL Service Co
Principal Bank: Federal Home Loan Bank of San Francisco
Financial Information:

	Dec 31 1985	Dec 31 1986
	$'000	$'000
Income before taxes*	77,451	90,267
Net income	53,378	57,155
Dividends	1,890	3,741
Dividends per share	$0.27	$0.35
Earnings per share	$5.02	$5.36
Common stock	350	350
Retained income	96,767	152,072
Shareholders equity	100,002	155,528
Savings deposits	1,929,001	2,186,847
Total assets	2,591,252	2,466,666

*and extraordinary item

No of Employees: 1,094

DOXSEE FOOD CORPORATION

8323 Pulaski Highway, Baltimore, MD 21237
Tel: (301) 686-2800
Telex: WUT 87918 doxsee food bal

Chairman: Philippe E Bieler
President: Joseph Appelbaum
Senior Executive Officers: Marvin M Klompus (Senior VP Sales), Donald E Albers (Senior VP Finance), Howard J Fischler (VP Sales)

PRINCIPAL ACTIVITIES: Manufacture of sauces and relishes
Principal Bank: First National Bank of Maryland
Financial Information:

	$'000
Sales revenues	71,000

No of Employees: 600

DPM OF KANSAS

800 E 37th Street, N Wichita, KS 67219
Tel: (316) 838-9311
Telex: TWX 910 7416 816 d p m wic

President: Meddon Moss
Senior Executive Officers: Douglas J Brown (Executive VP and General Manager), Oliver Lea (VP), James D Faulkner (Controller)

PRINCIPAL ACTIVITIES: Production of beef and processing of beef products
Parent Company: Del Pero Mondon Meat Co Inc, Marysville, CA
Principal Bank: Union National Bank
Financial Information:

	$'000
Sales revenues	70,000

No of Employees: 180

DR PEPPER COMPANY

PO Box 225086, Dallas, TX 75265
Tel: (214) 824-0331
Telex: TWX 910 8614324 finance dal

Chairman: W W Clements (and Chief Executive Officer)
President: John R Albers (and Chief Operating Officer)
Senior Executive Officers: Ira M Rosentein (Executive VP Finance and Chief Financial Officer), Nelson Bangs (VP Legal), Donald L Antle (VP Franchise), Jim Ball (VP Corporate Relations)

PRINCIPAL ACTIVITIES: Manufacture of syrups and soft drinks
Principal Bank: InterFirst Bank Dallas, NA
Financial Information:

	$'000
Sales revenues	560,000

DRAPER-KING COLE, INC

King Cole Drive, Milton, DE 19968
Tel: (302) 684-8555
Telex: WUT 46 9115 King Cole ci

Chairman: Harry Bonk
President: Will James
Senior Executive Officers: W Tappan (Senior VP and Treasurer), Joe Wolfe (Senior VP Production), Frank Newton (VP Personnel and Public Relations), Hank Bonk (VP Sales), Greg Cox (VP and Secretary)

PRINCIPAL ACTIVITIES: Freezing and canning of vegetables
Financial Information:

	$'000
Sales revenues	50,000

No of Employees: 500

DRAVO CORPORATION

One Oliver Plaza, Pittsburgh, PA 15222
Tel: (412) 566-3000
Telex: WUT 866125 dravo pgh ee

President: T F Faught Jr (and Chief Executive and Operating Officer)
Senior Executive Officers: William S Brown (Senior VP Materials Handling and Systems), Lloyd W Donnelly (Senior VP Engineering and Construction), Carl A Torbert Jr (Senior VP), W P Stewart (VP Corporate Communications), Thomas J Ward (VP, Secretary and Legal Counsel), R G Quick (VP Corporate Planning and Development), D E Snowberger (VP Administration and Real Estate), F A Joss (VP Finance and Treasurer), Joseph J Kappel (VP and Controller)

PRINCIPAL ACTIVITIES: Manufacture of industrial plant for the chemical, food, paper, coal and iron and steel industries
Principal Subsidiaries: Dravo Constructors Inc; Dravo Engineers Inc; Dravo Mechling Corp; Dravo Natural Resources Co; Dravo Basic Materials Co; Dravo Coal Co; Dravo Lime Co; Dravo Van Houten Inc; Dravo Wellman Co; Gibbs & Hill Inc; Ryan-Walsh Stevedoring Co Inc; Southern Steamship Agency Inc; Weyher/Livsey Constructors Inc
Financial Information:

	Dec 31 1985	Dec 31 1986
	$'000	$'000
Sales revenues	892,738	902,860
Net income	3,240	14,170
Earnings per share	$0.21	$0.99
Shareholders equity	199,031	210,508

No of Employees: 6,800

DRAVO NATURAL RESOURCES COMPANY

PO Box 1685, Mobile, AL 36601
Tel: (205) 438-3531

Chairman: D E Dawson Jr (and Chief Executive Officer)
President: Carl A Torbert Jr
Senior Executive Officers: Ernest F Ladd III (Executive VP), Selden S Kearns (VP and Secretary), Edward N Lennox (VP Public Affairs), A N Tenhundfeld Jr (VP Finance), Carl A Gilbert (VP), Craig Pollack (VP Business Development), H Donovan Ross (VP), Alex L Sanders (VP), James A Berneburg (VP and Legal Counsel)

PRINCIPAL ACTIVITIES: Production and sale of aggregates for the building and chemical industries and building materials
Parent Company: Dravo Corporation, Pittsburgh, PA

Financial Information:

	$'000
Sales revenues	140,000

No of Employees: 1,600

DRESHER INC

7200 South Mason, PO Box 8, Bedford Park, IL 60499
Tel: (312) 594 8900

Chairman: Barry A Merkin
President: Joseph E Geiger (and Treasurer and Secretary)
Senior Executive Officers: James Schreiber (VP Marketing), Richard A Yargus (VP Sales), James R Nolan (VP Manufacturing), Robert A Drell (VP)

PRINCIPAL ACTIVITIES: Manufacture of beds and related accessories
Principal Bank: Bank of Boston
Financial Information:

	$'000
Sales revenues	31,000

No of Employees: 360

DRESS BARN INC (THE)

88 Hamilton Avenue, Stamford, CT 06902
Tel: (203) 327 4242
Telex: (203) 359-4458

Chairman: Elliot S Jaffe (and President and Chief Executive Officer)
Senior Executive Officers: Michael Palmer (Senior VP Finance and Assistant Secretary), Roslyn S Jaffe (Secretary and Treasurer), Burt Steinberg (Senior VP), Eric Hawn (VP Stores)

PRINCIPAL ACTIVITIES: The Dress Barn, Inc. operates a chain of off-price women's apparel stores. The stores, operating principally under the name "Dress Barn", offer in-season, moderate to better quality fashion apparel. Dress Barn emphasizes department store quality merchandise, primarily with nationally recognized brand names bearing the manufacturer's label, at a substantial discount from department store prices
Trade Names: Dress Barn
Principal Banks: Connecticut Bank and Trust Company; Citizens Fidelity Bank & Trust
Financial Information:

	Jul 26 1986	Jul 25 1987
	$'000	$'000
Sales revenues	135,828	173,671
Income before taxes	17,671	24,447
Net income	9,161	12,908
Earnings per share	$0.42	$0.58
Common stock*	11,078	22,203
Retained income	21,522	34,429
Shareholders equity	26,193	39,779

*shares outstanding in thousands

Principal Shareholders: Elliot Jaffe and family (36.13%) of total shares outstanding
No of Employees: 3,000

DRESSER INDUSTRIES, INC

1600 Pacific Building, PO Box 718, Dallas, TX 75221
Tel: (214) 740-6000
Telex: TWX 910 861 4136

Chairman: John J Murphy (and President and Chief Executive Officer)
Senior Executive Officers: Bill D St John (Executive VP Administration), C M Browning (Senior VP Operations), Ralph W Ytterberg (Senior VP Operations), G H Karb (Senior VP Operations), W E Bradford (Senior VP Operations), James J Corboy (Senior VP Finance and Accounting)

PRINCIPAL ACTIVITIES: Manufacture of goods for industries involved in energy and natural resources; oil field services
Principal Trade Names: Atlas, Grinberson, Magcobar, Security, Swaco, Wayne/Clark, Pacific, Roots, Turbodyne, Waukeska, Worthington/Galion, Hough, Jeffrey, Marion, Wabco/Ashcroft, Bay State, Consolidated, De Wrance, Dresser, Hancock, Harbison-Walker, Masonelian
Principal Subsidiaries: Direlco Inc; Dresser Leasing Corp; Reliance Standard Life Insurance Co
Financial Information:

	Oct 31 1986
	$'000
Sales revenues	3,661,300
Net income	9,600
Earnings per share	$0.12
Shareholders equity	1,613,600

No of Employees: 46,200

DREW CHEMICAL CORPORATION

One Drew Chemical Plaza, Boonton, NJ 07005
Tel: (201) 263-7600
Telex: WUT 136 444 drewchems boon

President: Raymond M Burke
Senior Executive Officers: Robert E Gottlieb (Group VP Industrial Chemicals), Thomas A Cuomo (Group VP Marine and International), Cary Cappeline (VP and General Manager Industrial Chemicals USA), David R Sexsmith (VP Technical), Ralph W Giasi (VP Human Resources), Robert O'Brien (VP, Secretary and Legal Counsel), Richard Rhinesmith (VP International), Paul W Chellgren (VP), J A Brothers (VP)

PRINCIPAL ACTIVITIES: Manufacture of specialty chemicals for a range of applications including water treatment chemicals and addititives for fuel
Parent Company: Ashland Oil Inc, Ashland, KY
Principal Bank: Mellon Bank
Financial Information:

	$'000
Sales revenues	83,000

No of Employees: 1,000

DREWRY PHOTOCOLOR CORPORATION

211 South Lake Street, Burbank, CA 91502
Tel: (213) 849 7131

Chairman: William W Drewry III (and President and Chief Executive Officer and Chief Operating Officer)
Senior Executive Officers: Harold W Ellis (VP Finance), Blair Wilson (VP), Dieter Goerke (VP), Blair Wilson III (VP)

PRINCIPAL ACTIVITIES: Photographic processing
Principal Bank: Security Pacific National Bank
Financial Information:

	$'000
Sales revenues	30,000

No of Employees: 400

DREYER'S GRAND ICE CREAM, INC

5929 College Avenue, Oakland, CA 94618
Tel: (415) 652-8187

Chairman: Gary T Rogers (and Chief Executive Officer)
President: William F Cronk III
Senior Executive Officers: Paul R Woodland (VP and Chief Financial Officer), John E Thomason (VP Manufacturing), Jan L Booth (VP Marketing), Norman Lawson (VP Sales)

PRINCIPAL ACTIVITIES: Manufacture of ice cream
Principal Bank: Security Pacific National Bank
Financial Information:

	$'000
Sales revenues	103,000

No of Employees: 600

DREYFUS CORPORATION

767 Fifth Avenue, New York, NY 10153
Tel: (212) 715-6000

Chairman: Howard M Stein (and Chief Executive Officer); Vice Chairman: Julian M Smerling
President: Joseph P DiMartino (and Chief Operating Officer)
Senior Executive Officers: Herbert Elish (Senior VP), Alan M Eisner (VP and Chief Financial Officer), Daniel C Maclean (VP and General Counsel), Robert F Dubuss (VP), Monte J Gordon (VP Research), Peter Santoriello (VP)

PRINCIPAL ACTIVITIES: Financial services, security broking, investment services; insurance
Principal Subsidiaries: Dreyfus Consumer Life Insurance; Dreyfus Life Insurance Co; Dreyfus Management Inc; Dreyfus Service Corp; Major Trading Corp
Financial Information:

	1986
	$'000
Revenues	220,000
Net income	81,000

No of Employees: 560

DRIVER-HARRIS COMPANY

308 Middlesex Street, Harrison, NJ 07029
Tel: (201) 483-4800
Telex: WUT 138185 driver hson

Chairman: Frank L Driver III (and President)
Senior Executive Officers: Stanley M Babson Jr (VP, Secretary and Treasurer)

PRINCIPAL ACTIVITIES: Manufacture of rolled and drawn products for the electrical and electronic industries
Principal Subsidiaries: Driver-Harris Alloys Inc; Driver-Harris Systems Inc
Principal Bank: National Westminster Bank USA
Financial Information:

	$'000
Sales revenues	65,000

No of Employees: 500

DRUG SYSTEMS INC

111 East Wisconsin Avenue, Suite 1250, Milwaukee, WI 53202
Tel: (414) 272-5373
Telefax: (414) 271-3108

Chairman: Donald E Runge (and Treasurer)
President: Vincent W Dixon
Senior Executive Officers: Richard Y Fisher (Secretary), Mark A Zubrensky (VP Finance and Assistant Secretary), Beverly J Hanke (Assistant Secretary)

PRINCIPAL ACTIVITIES: The Company oversees the activities of its subsidiaries which are all involved in retailing
Principal Subsidiaries: Wil-Car Enterprises Inc (Portsmouth, Ohio); Economy Dry Goods Inc (South Glens Falls, New York); Pill & Puff Inc (Milwaukee, Wisconsin)
Principal Bank: Marine Bank N.A.
Financial Information:

	Mar 29 1986	Mar 31 1987
	$'000	$'000
Sales revenues	80,130	99,743
Income (loss) before taxes	(788)	3,108
Net income (loss)	(1,458)	1,769
Dividends	1,741	1,406
Dividends per share	$0.50	$0.45
Earnings (loss) per share	($0.44)	$0.56
Common stock	3,750	3,750
Retained income	780	1,143
Shareholders equity	16,207	16,570

No of Employees: 4

DRUMMOND COMPANY, INC

PO Box 10246, Birmingham, AL 35202
Tel: (205) 945-6500
Telex: 261327

President: E A Drummond; Chief Executive Officer: Gary N Drummond

PRINCIPAL ACTIVITIES: Production of coal and coal products
Trade Names: Drummond Coal, ABC Coke

No of Employees: 3,300

DSC COMMUNICATIONS CORPORATION

1000 Coit Road, Plano, TX 75075
Tel: (214) 519-3000

Chairman: James M Nolan
President: James L Donald (and Chief Executive Officer)
Senior Executive Officers: Gunnar J Korpinen (Senior VP), Gerald E Montry (Senior VP, Chief Financial Officer), Henry R Northhaft (Senior VP), Peter C Waal (VP), William R Tempest (Secretary and General Counsel), Kenneth R Vines (VP and Controller), Christian J Ornes (VP and Treasurer)

PRINCIPAL ACTIVITIES: DSC Communications Corporation designs, manufactures and markets digital switching systems and transmission products for the telecommunications industry
Principal Subsidiaries: Digital Switch Corporation; Granger Associates; Nestar Systems Inc
Principal Bank: Chase Manhattan Bank
Financial Information:

	Dec 31 1985	Dec 31 1986
	$'000	$'000
Sales revenues	287,634	303,951
Income (loss) before taxes	(64,601)	13,422
Net income(loss)	(63,308)	16,951
Earnings (loss) per share	($1.60)	$0.41
Common stock	398	410
Retained income	16,176	33,127
Shareholders equity	176,033	201,339

Number of shareholders: 6,175
No of Employees: 2,365

DSM NORTH AMERICA, INC

PO Box 1483-13, Augusta, GA 30913
Tel: (404) 823-4000

Chairman: William P Copenhaver (and President)
Senior Executive Officers: M J van Campen (VP Finance and Treasurer)

PRINCIPAL ACTIVITIES: Holding company with interests in chemicals and fertilizers
Parent Company: DSM Naamloze Vennootschap, Heerlen, Netherlands
Financial Information:

	$'000
Sales revenues	350,000

DST SYSTEMS INC

301 W 11th St., Kansas City, MO 64105
Tel: (816) 474 8520

President: Thomas A McDonnel (and Treasurer)
Senior Executive Officers: Royce D Closterman (Group VP), Kent H Flury (Group VP), David C Ostermeyers (Group VP), Richard D Stucky (Group VP), Michael A Waterford (Group VP)

PRINCIPAL ACTIVITIES: Provision of financial information services; software and data handling for mutual-fund accounts

Financial Information:

	Dec 31 1986
	$'000
Sales revenues	89,000
Net income	13,000

No of Employees: 1,000

DU PONT, E I, DE NEMOURS AND COMPANY

1007 Market Street, Wilmington, DE 19898
Tel: (302) 774-1000
Telex: 835420

Chairman: Richard E Heckert (and Chief Executive Officer)
President: Edgar S Wooland Jr (and Chief Operating Officer)
Senior Executive Officers: Chemical and Specialty Products: Agricultural Products:- J A Krol (Group VP). Medical Products:- David D Mooberry (Group VP), Hazen L Richardson (VP), E G Cook Jr (VP). Chemicals and Pigments:- Archie W Dunham (Group VP). Fabricated Products:- Bruce A Beardwood (VP). International:- Robert v.d. Luft (Group VP), W Robert Clay (VP), J A Blumberg (VP). Petrochemicals:- Robert M Aiken (Group VP), Ernest F Ruppe (VP). Electronics: Charles J Henry (Group VP). Automotive Products: John P McAndrews (Group VP). Polymer Products:- Nicholas Pappas (Group VP), J M Lipton (VP). Imaging Systems: Mark A Suwyn (Group VP). Textile Fibers:-James F Kearns (Group VP), Anthony J Cardinal (VP). Energy: Petroleum:-Constantine S Nicandros (Executive VP and President and Chief Executive Officer, Conoco Inc). Exploration and Production:- Elmer J Grivetti (Group VP-Exploration and Production, North America), J C Patterson (VP-North American Exploration), Harry C Sager (VP-North American Production), Floyd E Ellis (Group VP-Exploration and Production, International), Max G Pitcher (VP-International Exploration), William K Dietrich (VP-International Production), D John Ogren (VP and Chairman and Managing Director-Conoco (UK) Ltd). Refining, Marketing, Supply and Transportation:- Colin H Lee (Group VP), Gary W Edwards (VP-Refining and Marketing-Europe), H Kent Bowden (VP-Refining and Marketing, North America). Coal:- Bobby R Brown (Chairman and Chief Executive Officer-Consolidation Coal Company), H Douglas Dahl (Executive VP-Engineering and Exploration), Jarvis B Cecil (Executive VP-Finance and Corporate Affairs), Robert B Atwater (Executive VP-Marketing), C Wes McDonald (Executive VP-Operations). Corporate Plans:- Samuel Schwartz (Senior VP-Corporate Plans), J W Giggy (VP-Corporate Plans), Richard A Stuckey (Chief Economist). Employee Relations:- H Gordon Smyth (Senior VP). External Affairs:- John R Malloy (Senior VP). Finance:- John J Quindlen (Senior VP), Martin G Mand (VP and Comptroller), C Raeford Minix (VP and Treasurer). Legal:- John F Schmutz (Senior VP and General Counsel), William E MacIntyre (Assistant General Counsel), Howard J Rudge (Assistant General Counsel). Materials and Logistics:- W Earl Tatum (Senior VP). Pension Fund Investment:- Keith E Tucker (VP). Technology:- Alexander MacLachlan Senior VP with responsibility for:- Central Research and Development:- Howard E Simmons (VP). Engineering:- Charles D Brown (VP). Information Systems:-Raymond E Cairns Jr (VP)

PRINCIPAL ACTIVITIES: The company has eight principal business segments-Biomedical Products; Industrial and Consumer Products; Fibers; Polymer Products; Agricultural and Industrial Chemicals; Petroleum Exploration and Production; Petroleum Refining, Marketing and Transportation; and Coal. Manufacturing and selling activities of the chemical and specialty businesses are conducted principally through various industrial departments. The energy businesses are conducted through Conoco and Consolidation Coal. Other subsidiaries and affiliates also conduct manufacturing or selling activities, and some are distributors of products manufactured by the company. The company has approximately 90 major businesses selling a wide range of products to many different markets, including the energy, electronics, packaging, textile, transportation, construction, health care and agricultural markets. Business operations exist in more than 50 nations worldwide; and as a result, about 40% of consolidated revenues are derived from sales outside the United States
Trade Names: The Company has about 920 registered trademarks for its own products. These include: Dacron, Monece, Antron, Kevlar, Nomex, Cronaflow, Cromacheck, Mylar, Butacite, Teflon, Hytrel, Viton, Kapton, Glean, Oust, Ti-Pure, Freon, Velspar, Kannate, Bexloy, Vydate, Lycra, Corian
Principal Subsidiaries: Conoco; Consolidation Coal Co; DuPont Canada Inc; DuPont de Nemours (Deutschland) GmbH (Germany); DuPont de Nemours (Nederland)
Financial Information:

	Dec 31 1986	Dec 31 1987
	$'000	$'000
Sales revenues	27,148,000	30,468,000
Earnings before taxes	2,985,000	3,660,000
Net income	1,538,000	1,786,000
Dividends	744,000	*
Dividends per share	$3.05	$3.30
Earnings per share	$6.35	$7.39
Common stock	400,000	*
Reinvested earnings	8,202,000	*
Shareholders equity	13,374,000	*

*Not available until later date

No of Employees: 141,268

DUAL LITE INC

Simm Lane, Newtown, CT 06470
Tel: (203) 426 8011

President: William A Luca (and Chief Operating Officer)
Senior Executive Officers: Edward Kozek (VP International), John P Moriarty (VP Finance and Chief Financial Officer), J I Greenberg (Secretary), J R Carson (VP Marketing and Sales)

PRINCIPAL ACTIVITIES: Production of specialty lighting systems and related equipment
Principal Subsidiaries: New England Circuits Inc
Principal Bank: Bank of New England Corp
Financial Information:

	$'000
Sales revenues	37,000

No of Employees: 500

DUCHE, T M, NUT COMPANY, INC

PO Box 845, Orland, CA 95963
Tel: (916) 865-5511
Telex: TWX 910 5360 964 duche orda

President: John J Feder
Senior Executive Officers: Skip Hubbard (VP and Sales Manager), Joe Edgar (VP and Manufacturing Manager)

PRINCIPAL ACTIVITIES: Production of nuts
Principal Bank: Security Pacific National Bank
Financial Information:

	$'000
Sales revenues	75,000

No of Employees: 350

DUCOMMUN INC

611 W Sixth Street, Los Angeles, CA 90017
Tel: (213) 612-4200

Chairman: Wallace W Booth (and President and Chief Executive Officer)
Senior Executive Officers: Frederick N Bailard (Senior VP-Corporate Affairs and Secretary and General Counsel), H R Byrne (Senior VP Finance and Chief Financial Officer), Raymond Pregent (Staff Vice President), Mark Jorgensen (VP Public Relations), Stephen R Christie (Assistant Controller), James S Henehan (Assistant Treasurer), Gene M Griffith (Executive Director Human Resources), James S Heiser (Assistant General Counsel and Secretary)

PRINCIPAL ACTIVITIES: Holding company whose subsidiaries are engaged in the distribution and manufacture of electronic equipment and aerospace equipment

Principal Subsidiaries: Kierulff Electronics; MTI Systems; Ducommun Data Systems; TRI-TEC Engineering; Aerochem Inc; AHF-Ducommon; Jay-El Products Inc

Principal Bank: Security Pacific National Bank

Financial Information:

	Dec 31 1985	Dec 31 1986
	$'000	$'000
Sales revenues	417,034	455,179
(Loss) before taxes	(6,750)	(19,698)
Net (loss)	(3,263)	(19,213)
Net (loss)(1)	(19,685)	(19,213)
Dividends	2,595	1,143
Dividends per share	$0.80	$0.35
(Loss) per share	($0.98)	($5.76)
(Loss) per share(1)	($5.94)	($5.76)
Common stock(2)	3,351	3,277
Retained income	23,686	3,307
Shareholders equity	73,250	53,035

(1) Total including discontinued

(2) Shares outstanding at year end in thousands

No of Employees: 2,474

DUFF-NORTON COMPANY, INC

100 Pioneer Avenue, Charlotte, NC 28210

Tel: (704) 588-0510

Telex: WUT 575 188 duffnorton cha

Chairman: Howard B Wentz Jr

President: Lonnie P Jenkins (and Chief Executive Officer)

Senior Executive Officers: P J Stewart (VP and General Manager Hoist Division), Robert P Harbage (VP and General Manager Actuator and Fluid Power Division), Joseph F Kenney (VP Finance, Treasurer and Assistant Secretary), Claude G Carraux (VP International)

PRINCIPAL ACTIVITIES: Manufacture of lifting gear and couplings

Parent Company: Amstar Corp, New York, NY

Principal Bank: North Carolina National Bank

Financial Information:

	$'000
Sales revenues	60,000

No of Employees: 700

DUKE POWER COMPANY

422 S Church Street, Charlotte, NC 28242

Tel: (704) 373-4011

Telex: TWX 810 6210 503 duke pwr d eng

Chairman: William S Lee (and Chief Executive Officer)

President: D W Booth (and Chief Operating Officer)

Senior Executive Officers: W H Grigg (Executive VP Finance and Administration), W H Owen (Executive VP Engineering and Construction), Aubtin C Thies (Executive VP Power Operations), John D Hicks (Senior VP Public Affairs)

PRINCIPAL ACTIVITIES: Electricity supply

Financial Information:

	Dec 31 1985	Dec 31 1986
	$'000	$'000
Sales revenues	2,898,911	3,400,933
Income before taxes	764,458	846,672
Net income	376,681	409,067
Dividends	317,907	325,991
Dividends per share	$2.54	$2.64
Earnings per share	$3.72	$4.04
Common stock	101,178	101,220
Retained income	119,454	138,415
Shareholders equity	1,071,814	1,210,229

No of Employees: 20,473

DUN & BRADSTREET CORPORATION (THE)

299 Park Avenue, New York, NY 10171

Tel: (212) 593-6800

Chairman: Charles W Moritz (and Chief Executive Officer)

President: Robert E Weissman (and Chief Operating Officer)

Senior Executive Officers: Edwin A Bescherer Jr (Executive VP Finance and Chief Financial Officer), N Eugene Harden (Executive VP), John C Holt (Executive VP), David A McBride (Executive VP), James E Rutter (Executive VP), Richard F Schmidt (Executive VP Finance and Planning), Volney Taylor (Executive VP), Robert S Diamond (Senior VP Corporate Communications), George J Feeney (Senior VP Advanced Development), David Fehr (Corporate Senior VP), John J Fitzpatrick (Senior VP Human Resources Administration), Bruce A Hubler (Senior VP Management Resources Planning and Development), William G Jacobi (Senior VP Planning and Acquisitions), James K Murray Jr (Senior VP Customer Information Needs), Charles F G Raikes (Senior VP and General Counsel)

PRINCIPAL ACTIVITIES: Business information and marketing services

Principal Subsidiaries: Worldwide

Financial Information:

	Dec 31 1986	Dec 31 1987
	$'000	$'000
Sales revenues	3,113,506	3,359,164
Income before taxes	586,190	660,503
Net income	339,990	392,999
Dividends	187,897	219,725
Dividends per share*	$1.235	$1.445
Earnings per share*	$2.23	$2.58
Common stock	152,122	152,051
Retained income	1,309,237	1,451,166
Shareholders equity	1,488,830	1,663,798

*reflects 2 for 1 stock split which became effective June 10 1987

No of Employees: 60,000

DUNDEE CEMENT COMPANY

Dundee, MI 48131

Tel: (313) 529-2411

Telex: WUT 286 452 dundcmt dnde

Chairman: Erwin Maechler

President: Marc R von Wyss

Senior Executive Officers: Raymond S Chase (Senior VP Marketing), James J Woods (Senior VP Finance, Secretary and Treasurer), Steven K Griffith (Senior VP Planning), David A Smith (Senior VP Manufacturing), James C James (VP Sales Midwest Division)

PRINCIPAL ACTIVITIES: Cement production

Parent Company: Holderbank Financière Glaris Ltd, Switzerland

Principal Bank: Citibank

Financial Information:

	$'000
Sales revenues	100,000

No of Employees: 1,000

DUNDEE MILLS, INC

PO Draw E, Griffin, GA 30224
Tel: (404) 227-5581

President: John T Newton
Senior Executive Officers: R W Boyd (Senior VP), John H Cheatham Jr (VP Sales), Floyd C Newton Jr (VP and Treasurer), J H Walker III (VP Manufacturing and General Manager)

PRINCIPAL ACTIVITIES: Manufacture of towels and towelling products
Principal Bank: First National Bank of Griffin
Financial Information:

	$'000
Sales revenues	140,000

No of Employees: 2,500

DUNHAM-BUSH, INC

175 South Street, West Hartford, CT 06110
Tel: (203) 249-8671
Telex: RCA 221902 dubu ur

Chairman: Steven Cerri
President: James V Lester (and Chief Executive Officer)
Senior Executive Officers: Derek J Smith (VP Sales and Marketing), Winfred M Kirkman (VP Market Development), Robert J Perry (VP Finance, Treasurer, Controller and Assistant Secretary), Anthony M Costello (VP), Richard O'Connell (VP Administration), Sebastian J Gianni (VP Engineering)

PRINCIPAL ACTIVITIES: Manufacture of air conditioning equipment for industrial and domestic use; manufacture of heating and refrigeration equipment
Parent Company: Allied-Signal Inc
Financial Information:

	$'000
Sales revenues	100,000

No of Employees: 1,500

DUNKIN' DONUTS INC

5 Pacella Park Drive, PO Box 317, Randolph, MA 02368
Tel: (617) 961-4000

Chairman: Robert M Rosenberg (and Chief Executive Officer)
President: Thomas R Schwarz (and Chief Operating Officer)
Senior Executive Officers: Officers: Lawrence W Hantman (Senior VP-General Counsel), Richard N Hart Jr (VP and Treasurer), Bernard R Patriacca (VP and Controller), Gilbert Rosenberg (Secretary), William Rosenberg (Chairman Emeritus), David P Segal (VP-Real Estate). Dunkin'Donuts of America Inc: Vincent G Brown Jr (VP-Corporate Development), R Thomas Burger (VP-Information Services), Eugene D Cerrotti (VP-Real Estate and Franchise Development), James Dangelo (Senior VP), Irving Eison (VP-Products Marketing and Development), Sidney J Feltenstein Jr (Senior VP-Marketing), Ralph Gabellieri (Senior VP-Operations), Leonard Geller (Senior VP-International Development), Abraham Goldberg (VP-Architecture), Neil Guanci (VP Operations-Company-operated Shops), John E Hellriegel (VP-Franchised Operations), Roy Jemison (VP-Franchised Operations), Richard H Power (VP-Industrial Relations), John D Shafer Jr (Senior VP-Development), Bruce L Yates (VP-Franchised Operations). Dunkin' Ventures Corporation: Ronald E Blain (VP-Development), James Dangelo (President), Ernest V Trigilio (VP and Controller)

PRINCIPAL ACTIVITIES: World's largest Coffee and Donut Shop Chain (1,539 shops worldwide). Exclusive licensee for Chili's Grill & Bar Restaurants in New England states, upstate New York, and eastern Canada
Principal Subsidiaries: Dunkin Donuts of America Inc; Dunkin' Ventures Corporation
Principal Bank: First National Bank of Boston
Financial Information:

	Oct 26 1986 $'000	Oct 31 1987 $'000
Sales revenues	104,150	105,596
Income before taxes	23,099	24,400
Net income	12,127	13,298
Dividends	1,955	2,217
Dividends per share	$0.27	$0.31
Earnings per share	$1.63	$1.80
Common stock	7,441	73,910
Retained income	66,054	77,135
Shareholders equity	72,603	68,219

No of Employees: 2,220

DUNN PAPER COMPANY

218 Riverview Street, Port Huron, MI 48060
Tel: (313) 984-5523
Telex: TWX 810 289-2730 dunpaper pthu

President: R E Hubbard (and Chief Executive Officer)
Senior Executive Officers: Thomas E Gallagher (Executive VP and Chief Operating Officer), A H Hupp (Senior VP), J R Scohy (VP Manufacturing), Peter R Hoppe (VP Administration and Controller)

PRINCIPAL ACTIVITIES: Manufacture of a wide range of papers
Parent Company: Dennison Manufacturing Co, Framingham, MA
Financial Information:

	$'000
Sales revenues	60,000

No of Employees: 300

DUPLEX PRODUCTS INC

1947 Bethany Road, Sycamore, IL 60178
Tel: (815) 895-2101
Telex: TWX 910 6390610 duplex syc

Chairman: Lucien T Smith
President: Carl L Peterson (and Chief Executive Officer)
Senior Executive Officers: Paul J Trausch (Senior VP-Sales and Marketing), Jack L Turk (Senior VP-Manufacturing and Operations), Andrew N Peterson (VP-Finance)

PRINCIPAL ACTIVITIES: Manufacture and sale of business forms
Principal Subsidiaries: Puerto Rico Envelopes
Principal Bank: The Northern Trust
Financial Information:

	Oct 26 1985 $'000	Oct 25 1986 $'000
Sales revenues	254,101	248,355
Income before taxes	26,391	21,467
Net income	14,100	11,707
Dividends	3,436	3,972
Dividends per share	$0.45	$0.52
Earnings per share	$1.85	$1.53
Common stock	7,633	7,648
Retained income	79,850	87,585
Shareholders equity	85,943	93,635

No of Employees: 2,400

DUQUESNE LIGHT CO

One Oxford Centre, Pittsburgh, PA 15279
Tel: (412) 393-6000

Chairman: John M Arthur
President: Wesley W von Schack (and Chief Executive and Finance Officer)

Senior Executive Officers: Charles M Atkinson (Executive VP), Walter T Wardzinski (VP Legal and Corporate Communications), Earl J Woolever (VP Special Nuclear Products), Clifford N Dunn (VP Power Supply), William F Gilfillan Jr (VP Customer Services), John J Carey (VP Nuclear), Roger D Beck (VP Administrative Services)

PRINCIPAL ACTIVITIES: Electricity distribution
Principal Subsidiaries: Allegheny County Steam Heating Co
Financial Information:

	Dec 31 1985	Dec 31 1986
	$'000	$'000
Sales revenues	915,000	896,000
Net income	176,000	130,000

No of Employees: 4,700

DURA CORPORATION

PO Box 276, Southfield, MI 48037
Tel: (313) 352-5700

Chairman: Ronald A West (and Chief Executive Officer); Vice Chairmen: Marvin Novick; Ernest V Smutek
President: William J Ross (and Chief Operating Officer)
Senior Executive Officers: J H King (VP Sales and Marketing), Lawrence A Zak (VP and Chief Financial Officer), Charles S Peltz (VP)

PRINCIPAL ACTIVITIES: Manufacture of electrical equipment and other components for the automotive industry
Principal Bank: National Bank of Detroit
Financial Information:

	$'000
Sales revenues	130,000

No of Employees: 1,500

DURAKON INDUSTRIES INC

2101 North Lapeer Road, Lapeer, MI 48446
Tel: (313) 664 0850

Chairman: Michael Wayne (and Chief Executive Officer)
President: David W Wright (and Chief Operating Officer)
Senior Executive Officers: Dean McDonald (Group VP Operations), John Bambery (VP Finance, Secretary and Treasurer), Gary Ferguson (VP Marketing), Judith Grotts (VP Manufacturing)

PRINCIPAL ACTIVITIES: Manufacture of a wide range of plastic products
Principal Bank: Manufacturers National Bank
Financial Information:

	$'000
Sales revenues	50,000

No of Employees: 580

DURAMAX, INC

16025 Johnson Street, Middlefield, OH 44062
Tel: (216) 632-1611
Telex: WUT 980416 jonsonrbr mdlf

Chairman: Paul C Miller
President: P C Miller Jr (and Chief Executive Officer)
Senior Executive Officers: Ray Warner (Executive VP and Chief Operating Officer), R F Miller (VP Sales and Marketing), Guy Williams (VP Administration)

PRINCIPAL ACTIVITIES: Rubber and plastic products
Trade Names: Johnsonite Flooring Products, Duramax Marine Products
Principal Subsidiaries: Norbalt Rubber; Johnson Plastics; Johnson Rubber Co; Welter Rubber JR CA Ltd
Principal Bank: National City Bank
Financial Information:

	$'000
Sales revenues	80,000

No of Employees: 1,000

DUREZ RESINS & MOLDING MATERIALS

1080-7 Walck Road, North Tonawanda, NY 14120
Tel: (716) 696-6000
Telex: TWX 710 262 1266 durzhkr ntda a

Senior Executive Officers: George Balsam (VP and General Manager)

PRINCIPAL ACTIVITIES: Manufacture of resins
Parent Company: Occidental Chemical Corporation
Financial Information:

	$'000
Sales revenues	100,000

No of Employees: 400

DURHAM CORPORATION

2610 Wycliff Road, PO Box 27807, Raleigh, NC 27611
Tel: (919) 782 6110

Chairman: George M Womble (and President)
Senior Executive Officers: James H Pou Bailey Jr (Senior VP), Felton P Coley (Executive VP and Treasurer), Donald L Johnson (VP and Controller), Floyd E Skipper (VP and Controller), Joel A Millikan (VP Security and Assistant Secretary)

PRINCIPAL ACTIVITIES: Holding company with interests in insurance services and broadcasting
Principal Subsidiaries: Durco Agency Inc; Durham Life Broadcasting; Durham Life Insurance Company; State Capital Insurance Company
Principal Bank: Wachovia Bank and Trust Company
Financial Information:

	Dec 31 1985
	$'000
Revenues	232,280
Net income	26,135

No of Employees: 1,300

DURIRON COMPANY, INC

425 N Findlay Street, Dayton, OH 45404
Tel: (513) 226 4000
Telex: ITT 4335017 durcodtna

Chairman: H J Gazeley
President: John S Haddick (and Chief Executive Officer)
Senior Executive Officers: R D Gillaugh (Senior VP and Chief Administration Officer), John C Banas (Group VP), William M Jordan (Group VP), Robert F Fooksman (Group VP), Joe E Johnson (VP and Controller)

PRINCIPAL ACTIVITIES: Manufacture of plant for the chemical industry; compressors, valves and pumps
Principal Bank: Bank One of Dayton
Financial Information:

	$'000
Sales revenues	146,000

No of Employees: 2,200

DURO-TEST CORPORATION

2321 Kennedy Blvd, North Bergen, NJ 07047
Tel: (201) 867-7000
Telex: WUT 129 215 duro test nbgn

Chairman: Jack M Ross (and Treasurer)
President: G R McGruther (and Chief Executive Officer)
Senior Executive Officers: William M Ramaccia (VP), Marion Croom (VP Sales), Jerry Conboy (VP Administration)

PRINCIPAL ACTIVITIES: Manufacture of electric lamps
Principal Subsidiaries: Arc Ray Electric Corp; Duro-Lite Lamps Inc; Duro-Test International Corp; Jewel Electric Products Inc; Tungsten Products Corp; Luxor Lighting Products Inc
Principal Bank: Irving Trust Company

Financial Information:

	$'000
Sales revenues	68,000

No of Employees: 1,700

DURR-FILLAUER MEDICAL INC

PO Box 951, Montgomery, AL 36192

Tel: (205) 271-3512

Chairman: W A Williamson Jr (and Chief Executive Officer)

President: Charles E Adair (and Chief Operating Officer)

Senior Executive Officers: Robert E Barnes (Executive VP Business Development), M W Cotton (Executive VP Wholesale Drug), John W Durr (Executive VP Administration), Robert H Klebber (Executive VP Orthopedic), Richard L Klein (Senior VP and Chief Financial Officer), Carlton E Fillauer (VP Orthopedic Division), Michael E Miller (VP Data Processing), Charles T Gross (VP, Secretary and Treasurer)

PRINCIPAL ACTIVITIES: Distribution of medical, surgical and pharmaceutical supplies and audio-visual and verterinary products

Principal Subsidiaries: E L McConnell & Co; Source Video Distribution Co Inc

Principal Bank: AmSouth Bank

Financial Information:

	$'000
Sales revenues	427,000

No of Employees: 1,000

DWG CORPORATION

6917 Collins Ave, Miami Beach, FL 33141

Tel: (305) 866-7771

Chairman: Victor Posner (and Chief Executive Officer); Vice Chairman: Stephen Posner (and Chairman of Executive Committee)

President: Monford A Orloff (and Chief Operating Officer)

Senior Executive Officers: Russell A Bayle (Group Executive VP), V Jerome Kaplan (Group Executive VP), Donald J Glazer (Executive VP), Jack Coppersmith (Senior VP and Chief Financial Officer), Melvin Colvin (Senior VP), Raymond J Dettore (Senior VP), Bernard I Posner (Senior VP), Renée Mottram (Senior VP Administration), Walter Sieckman (Senior VP), Philip A Smalley Jr (Senior VP Human Resources), F E Autrey (VP), Edward A Christensen (VP and Secretary), Harry T Clew (VP), David Glasser (VP Textiles and Apparel), Mitchell B Gregory (VP Finance), Robert C Griffin (VP, Treasurer and Assistant Secretary), Leonard Leifert (VP), Jack Lubin (VP), John C Luby (VP)

PRINCIPAL ACTIVITIES: Trade in liquid petroleum gas; interests in the manufacture of men's shirts, cold storage warehouses and general construction

Principal Subsidiaries: National Propane Corp; Arrow Gas Co of Clovis Inc; Arrow Gas Co of Flagstaff Inc; Arrow Gas Co; Arrow Gas Co of NM; Brunswick Gas & Fuel Co; Good Housekeeping Gas Co FL; Home Gas Corp Great Barrington; NPC Leasing Corp; Southeastern Public Service Co; Blume Tree Services Inc; Graniteville Vo; Graniteville International SLS; CH Patrick & Co; Houston Oil & Gas Co Inc; Northwestern Ice Cold Storage Co; Public Gas Co; Royal Palm Ice Co; SES Electric Services Inc; Southeastern Gas Co; Tree Preservation Co Inc; Pressure Concrete Construction Co; Western Refrigerating Cold Storage; Wilson Tree Co Inc; Wright & Lopez Inc; Wright & Lopez of FL Inc; Wright Lopez AL Inc

Principal Bank: Security Pacific National Bank

Financial Information:

	Apr 30 1986 $'000
Sales revenues	1,162,360
Net (loss)	(8,610)
(Loss) per share	($0.55)
Shareholders equity	98,576

No of Employees: 16,800

DYATRON CORPORATION

210 Automation Way, PO Box 235, Birmingham, AL 35201

Tel: (205) 956-7500

Telex: 596215

Chairman: James R Forman Jr (and Secretary)

President: Charles E Rueve (and Chief Executive Officer)

Senior Executive Officers: Donald R Benson (VP, Data Processing), Donald W Birdwell (VP Financial Systems Divisions), T Ray Davis (VP, Employee Benefit Services Division), Michael L Dikeman (VP Automated Services Division), Edwina Johnson (VP, Human Resources), Roy W Myers (VP, Finance), Garry E Paddick (VP and General Manager, CARS Division), John F Lynch (Treasurer), James R Forman Jr (Secretary)

PRINCIPAL ACTIVITIES: DYATRON is a diversified computer services company providing applications software systems, hardware, and continuing systems support for the automotive, trust and banking, employee benefits, and mass mailing industries. DYATRON's services are designed to provide information management and automation for a variety of operations in DYATRON's primary markets. DYATRON offers a wide range of services with four delivery methods: on a processing services basis - customer data is processed on DYATRON's computers utilizing DYATRON's application software; on a software products basis - the customer is licensed to process data on his own mainframe computer using DYATRON's application software; on a professional services basis - special programming services utilizing DYATRON's software are performed upon request; on a turnkey basis - the customer purchases computer hardware and license applications software from DYATRON for use at the customer's location. DYATRON also provides other computer services, including computerized billing, direct mail marketing, and laser printing from its computer center at the corporate headquarters in Birmingham, Alabama

Trade Names: CARS/36-Automatic Dealership Software, OmniTrust-Trust and Securities Accounting Software, TeleTRADES-/Trade Order and Securities Control Software, OmniTRAC-Capital Activity and Income Processing Software, International Securities Processing System (ISPS)-Global Custody Accounting Software, OMNI-PLAN-Employee Benefit Plan Recordkeeping Software

Principal Bank: AmSouth Bank, N.A., Birmingham, Alabama

Financial Information:

	Dec 31 1985 $'000	Dec 31 1986 $'000
Sales revenues	40,103	33,103
Income before taxes	2,520	2,214
Net income	2,259	1,919
Earnings per share	$0.73	$0.56
Common stock	1,750	1,778
Retained (deficit)	(2,706)	(787)
Shareholders equity	7,344	9,101

No of Employees: 400

DYNALECTRON CORPORATION

1313 Dolley Madison Blvd, McLean, VA 22101

Tel: (703) 356-0480

Cable: DYNA MCLN

Telex: 89-2730

Chairman: Jorge Carnicero; Vice Chairman: Raymond J Mulligan

President: Daniel R Bannister (and Chief Executive Officer)

Senior Executive Officers: Walther Ewalt (Executive VP and Chief Operating Officer), Eugene T Blanchard (Senior VP and Chief Financial Officer), J P Schnelling (Senior VP and General Counsel)

PRINCIPAL ACTIVITIES: Technical and maintenance services in electronics, weapons and defense systems, electromechanical repairs, aerospace; and specialty contracting services, including commercial and industrial, electrical, mechanical and insulation contracting

Principal Subsidiaries: ITS International Inc; Dynalectric Co; Aneco Co; Dynamech Contractors Inc; ITS International Services GmbH; B & B Contracting and Supply Co; Dyn Construction Corp; Airtech Service Inc; Servair Inc; Hydrocarbon Research Inc; TRANS-DYN Control Systems Inc; Fuller-Austin Insulation Co; Solar Insulators Inc; Fuller-Austin of Canada Ltd; PAC ORD; Hydrocarbon Research Inc; Dynarabia Co Ltd; CFE Air Cargo Inc; Dynalectric Eastern Region; Dynalectric Western Region; ANECO Power Co; HRI Inc; Dynalectron Service Network; Sea Mobility Inc

Principal Bank: RepublicBank Dallas

Financial Information:

	Dec 31 1985	Dec 31 1986
	$'000	$'000
Sales revenues	640,347	749,067
Net income	3,291	13,112
Earnings per share*	$0.34	$1.23
Shareholders equity	103,871	128,332

*fully diluted

No of Employees: 15,200

DYNAMICS CORPORATION OF AMERICA

475 Steamboat Road, Greenwich, CT 06830

Tel: (203) 869-3211

Chairman: Andrew Lozyniak (and President); Vice Chairman: Edward J Mooney (and VP and Secretary)

Senior Executive Officers: Patrick J Dorme (VP Finance and Chief Financial Officer), Henry V Kensing (VP and General Counsel)

PRINCIPAL ACTIVITIES: Manufacture of domestic electrical equipment, agricultural equipment, generating sets, air conditioning and heating equipment

Principal Subsidiaries: International Electronic Resources Inc

Principal Bank: Chemical Bank

Financial Information:

	$'000
Sales revenues	148,000

No of Employees: 1,920

DYNAMICS RESEARCH CORPORATION

60 Concord Street, Wilmington, MA 01887

Tel: (617) 438-3900

Chairman: John S Anderegg Jr (and President)

President: Albert Rand

Senior Executive Officers: Albert Rand (Senior VP Systems), J J Bakewell (VP Metrigraphics), John L Wilkinson (VP Human Resources), Chester Ju (VP and General Manager Encoder), Nancy M Bodenstein (Director Communications)

PRINCIPAL ACTIVITIES: Provides computer-based studies and analyses supporting the effective acquisition and operation of major weapon systems

Principal Bank: Bank of New England

Financial Information:

	Dec 31 1986
	$'000
Sales revenues	75,000
Income before taxes	5,300
Net income	2,450
Earnings per share	$0.61
Common stock	42,000*
Retained income	5,000
Shareholders equity	12,300

*4 million shares at $10.50

No of Employees: 1,200

DYNAMIT NOBEL OF AMERICA, INC

10 Link Drive, Rockleigh, NJ 07647
Tel: (201) 767-1660
Telex: WUI 685 3322 us nobel rklh

President: Hans Schefer

PRINCIPAL ACTIVITIES: Manufacture of plastics and chemicals, wholesale trade in silicon components and firearms
Parent Company: Dynamit Nobel AG, Troisdorf, Germany
Financial Information:

	$'000
Sales revenues	160,000

Principal Shareholders: Friedrich Flick Industrieverwaltung KGaA, Düsseldorf-Oberkassel, Germany
No of Employees: 750

DYNASCAN CORPORATION

6460 Cortland, Chicago, IL 60635
Tel: (312) 889-8870
Telex: RCA 244332 DYNACUR
Facsimile: (312) 794-9740

Chairman: Carl Korn
President: Jerry Kalov (and Chief Executive Officer)
Senior Executive Officers: Selgene Balaban (General Manager, VP Telemotive Division), Henry J Gronski (VP), Leonard Abrahamson (VP), J Dennis Burke (VP and General Manager Cobra Consumer Products Division), Fred Hackendahl (VP Corporate Development), Orie Fritts (VP Industrial Products Group), James Twerdahl (VP, President-Marantz Company, Inc), David T Allen (VP, Chief Financial Officer, Secretary/Treasurer)

PRINCIPAL ACTIVITIES: Manufacture and marketing of consumer electronics products (CB radios, scanners, corded and cordless telephones, answering systems, radar detectors), audio and audio/video equipment, radio remote control systems for material handling equipment, and test and measurement equipment
Trade Names: Cobra, Marantz, Telemotive, B&K-Precision
Principal Subsidiaries: Marantz Company Inc; Dynascan-Asia Limited
Principal Bank: Continental Illinois National Bank and Trust Co of Chicago
Financial Information:

	Dec 31 1985	Dec 31 1986
	$'000	$'000
Sales revenues	128,084	146,800
Income before taxes	138	12,048
Net income	138	6,083
Earnings per share	$0.03	$1.28
Retained income	6,054	12,137
Shareholders equity	31,439	37,666

Number of Shareholders: 2,200
No of Employees: 691

DYNATECH CORPORATION

3 New England Executive Park, Burlington, MA 01803
Tel: (607) 272-3304
Telex: WUI 951 928 dynatech burl

Chairman: Warren M Rohsenow
President: J P Barger (and Chief Executive Officer)
Senior Executive Officers: Kenneth D Roberts (Senior VP and Treasurer), James R Turner (Group VP Scientific Instruments), William W Welsh Jr (Group VP Diagnostic Instruments), Ronald H Weatherhogg (VP Data Communications), John F Reno (Group VP Video Communications and Test Measurement), Howard M Crow (Group VP Specialty Electronics), R Claude Olier (Group VP Data Communications), Dorothy G Cooley (VP Human Resources and Industrial Relations), John A Powers (VP Corporate Development)

PRINCIPAL ACTIVITIES: Manufacture of data processing and telecommunications equipment, medical instruments and laboratory equipment
Principal Subsidiaries: Artek Systems Corp; Controlonics Corp; Dynatech Diagnostics Inc; Dynatech Frontier Corp; Dynatech Instruments Inc; Dynateck Laboratories Inc; Dynatech Data Systems; Dynatech NV Inc; Dynatech Precision Sampling Corp; Dynatech U-Z Inc; Interface Technology Inc; Telecommunications Techniques Corp; Trans-Met Engineering Inc; Tri-Med; Utah Scientific Inc
Principal Bank: The First National Bank of Boston
Financial Information:

	Mar 31 1987
	$'000
Sales revenues	305,000
Net income	23,000

No of Employees: 2,000

DYNATECH FRONTIER CORPORATION
5655 Kircher Blvd, N E Albuquerque, NM 87109
Tel: (505) 345-3611
Telex: TWX 910 989 0611 dynatech abq

President: James V Wilson
Senior Executive Officers: Jeff Wilson (Sales, Product and Production Manager), Glenn Rondeau (Purchasing Agent), James Baluenbush (Engineering Manager)

PRINCIPAL ACTIVITIES: Manufacture of measuring equipment valves and scientific instruments
Parent Company: Dynatech Corporation, Burlington, MA
Principal Bank: First National Bank of Boston
Financial Information:

	$'000
Sales revenues	70,000

No of Employees: 1,000

DYNEER CORPORATION
33 Riverside Avenue, Westport, CT 06880
Tel: (203) 226-1071
Telex: TWX 710 4572168 dyneer wept

Chairman: Harlan W Smith (and President and Chief Executive Officer)
Senior Executive Officers: James R Gerrity (Senior VP Finance and Administration), J B Perkins (VP Electronic Products Group), Charles F Greenwood (VP Human Resources)

PRINCIPAL ACTIVITIES: Manufacture of components for a wide range of vehicles; security equipment; scientific instruments
Principal Subsidiaries: Dico Co Inc; Granning Suspensions Inc; Kraftube Inc; Sensor Technology Inc; Sprengnether Instruments Inc; Spun Steel (AL) Inc; Spun Steel (MS) Inc; Tractech Inc; Mud Hog Corp
Principal Bank: The Chase Manhattan Bank NA
Financial Information:

	$'000
Sales revenues	215,100

No of Employees: 1,850

DYSAN CORPORATION
5210 Patrick Henry Drive, Santa Clara, CA 95050
Tel: (408) 988-3472
Telex: RCA 278681 dysan ur

Chairman: C N Dion
President: Bert L Zaccaria
Senior Executive Officers: John A Barber (Executive VP), Dennis T Maruyama (Executive VP), George L Farinsky (VP and Chief Financial Officer), Sam Laub (VP, Secretary and General Counsel)

PRINCIPAL ACTIVITIES: Manufacture of data processing equipment
Parent Company: Xidex Corp, Sunnyvale, CA
Financial Information:

	$'000
Sales revenues	180,000

No of Employees: 2,600

E F HOUGHTON & CO
See HOUGHTON, E F, & CO

E F HUTTON GROUP, INC
See HUTTON, E F, GROUP, INC

E I DU PONT DE NEMOURS AND COMPANY
See DU PONT, E I, DE NEMOURS AND COMPANY

E R SQUIBB & SONS, INC
See SQUIBB, E R, & SONS, INC

E STANWYCK COIL CO, INC
See STANWYCK, E, COIL CO, INC

E W SCRIPPS COMPANY INC
See SCRIPPS, E W, COMPANY INC

E&B MARINE INC
980 Gladys Court, Edison, NJ 08818
Tel: (201) 287-8100

Chairman: Gerald Bench (and President and Chief Executive Officer)
Senior Executive Officers: Debra Cassera (Executive VP, Chief Financial Officer and Treasurer), Frederick H Bond (Executive VP, Treasurer and Chief Financial Officer), Robert G Defonte (Senior VP and Secretary), Maureen Mead (VP Administration)

PRINCIPAL ACTIVITIES: Retail trade in boating supplies and accessories
Principal Subsidiaries: James Bliss & Co Inc
Financial Information:

	$'000
Sales revenues	56,400

No of Employees: 700

EAC INDUSTRIES, INC
224 S Michigan Ave, Chicago, IL 60604-2401
Tel: (312) 922-7111

Chairman: Peter B Fritzsche (and President and Chief Executive Officer)
Senior Executive Officers: Paul Fritzsche (VP and Secretary), Arthur L Goldberg (VP Finance and Treasurer)

PRINCIPAL ACTIVITIES: Manufacture of electrical machinery and hardware and parts for jet engines
Principal Bank: La Salle National Bank
Financial Information:

	$'000
Sales revenues	77,000

No of Employees: 700

EAC USA INC

73-45 Woodhaven Blvd, Glendale, NY 11385

Tel: (718) 830-7800

Chairman: Henning H Sparsoe

President: Hans Peetz-Larsen

Senior Executive Officers: Karsten Hess (Executive VP, Secretary and Chief Financial Officer),

PRINCIPAL ACTIVITIES: Manufacture and distribution of meat products; distribution of graphic arts equipment to the printing/bookbinding/pre-press markets; export/import hardwood and softwood lumber; ocean transportation

Parent Company: East Asiatic Co Ltd, Copenhagen, Denmark

Principal Subsidiaries: The East Asiatic Co de Mexico SA (Mexico); Heidelberg Eastern Inc (USA); Johnson, Walton Steamships Ltd (Canada); Plumrose Inc (Canada); Transamerican Steamship Corp (USA); The West Indian Co Ltd (St Thomas WI); EAC Graphics USA Inc; Baumfolder Corporation (USA); The East Asiatic Company (Canada) Inc (Canada);

Principal Bank: Relationships with major European Banks through New York Operations, eg: Standard Chartered; Barclays; Commerzbank; Credit Lyonnais; as well as major US Banks eg: Chemical Bank; Citibank; Manufacturers Hanover Trust Co

Financial Information:

	Dec 31 1987	Dec 31 1988*
	$'000	$'000
Sales revenues	675,000	800,00

*estimated

Principal Shareholders: The East Asiatic Company Ltd A/S (100%)

No of Employees: 2,200

EAGLE CLOTHES, INC

10 West 33rd Street, New York, NY 10001

Tel: (212) 947-6935

Chairman: Mortimer H April (and Chief Executive Officer)

President: Marvin A Blumenfeld (and Chief Operating Officer)

Senior Executive Officers: Arthur M Chase (Executive VP), Robert Kuhn (VP)

PRINCIPAL ACTIVITIES: Manufacture of clothing for men

Financial Information:

	$'000
Group sales revenues	97,000

No of Employees: 125

EAGLE-PICHER INDUSTRIES, INC

580 Walnut Street, Cincinnati, OH 45202

Tel: (513) 721-7010

Telex: WUI 6842082 eagle pich cin

Chairman: William D Atteberry

President: Thomas E Petry (and Chief Executive Officer)

Senior Executive Officers: John W Painter (Executive VP), James M Dines (Group VP), Jack D Grinton (Group VP), John E Powers (Senior VP), David N Hall (VP and Treasurer), James G Baird (VP), Charles S Dantel (VP and Secretary), Ernest H Hirsh (VP), J Rodman Nall (VP), James A Ralston (VP and Legal Counsel), Carroll D Curless (VP and Controller)

PRINCIPAL ACTIVITIES: Manufacture of mineral and non-ferrous metal compounds and electronic equipment

Principal Subsidiaries: Hillsdale Tool & Manufacturing Co

Principal Bank: First National Bank of Cincinnati

Financial Information:

	Nov 30 1986
	$'000
Sales revenues	648,337
Net income	38,808
Earnings per share	$3.80
Shareholders equity	179,476

No of Employees: 8,170

EARL SCHEIB INC

See SCHEIB, EARL, INC

EARLE M JORGENSEN COMPANY

See JORGENSEN, EARLE M, COMPANY

EARLY & DANIEL INDUSTRIES, INC

733 S Missouri St, Indianapolis, IN 46204

Tel: (317) 636-6491

Telex: WUT 272221 tidegrain ind

Chairman: Samuel M Harrell (and Chief Executive Officer)

President: Robert C Hall (and Treasurer)

Senior Executive Officers: John W Sharp (Senior VP)

PRINCIPAL ACTIVITIES: Processing and sale of grain; flour milling; manufacture of animal feedstuffs

Principal Subsidiaries: Acme Evans Co; Early & Daniel Co Inc; Tidewater Grain Co

Principal Bank: Indiana National Bank

Financial Information:

	$'000
Sales revenues	493,000

No of Employees: 250

EASCO ALUMINUM CORPORATION

State Street, Gerard, OH 4420

Tel: (216) 545-4311

Telex: TWX 8104369314 easco alu gira

President: John F Henry

Senior Executive Officers: M J Bartelmay (VP Finance)

PRINCIPAL ACTIVITIES: Manufacture of aluminum products including foil and sheet

Parent Company: Easco Corporation, Baltimore, MD

Principal Bank: Dollar Savings and Trust Co

Financial Information:

	$'000
Sales revenues	150,000

No of Employees: 750

EASCO CORPORATION

PO Box 60, Girard, OH 44420

Chairman: Richard P Sullivan (and Chief Executive Officer)

President: Robert L Swan (and Chief Operating Officer)

Senior Executive Officers: Edmund J Fick (Senior VP and Chief Financial Officer), Robert E Anderson (VP), John F Henry (VP), Melvin Merians (VP)

PRINCIPAL ACTIVITIES: Manufacture of tools and aluminum products

Principal Subsidiaries: Borden Metal Products Inc; Easco Aluminum Corp; Indiana Aluminum Extrusion Inc; Easco Hand Tools Inc; Greulich Inc; New Jersey Aluminum Co

Principal Bank: Equitable Bank

Financial Information:

	$'000
Sales revenues	541,308

No of Employees: 5,090

EAST NEW YORK SAVINGS BANK

41 W 42nd Street, New York, NY 10036

Tel: (212) 382-4770

President: Paul B Murray (and Chief Executive Officer)

Senior Executive Officers: Thomas J Wiss (Executive VP Finance), Paul W Stedman (Senior VP Mortgage), Frank Puma (Senior VP Banking), Kevin A McCoy (VP Branches), Donald C Fleming (VP Finance), Joan Schoenberger (VP Personnel)

PRINCIPAL ACTIVITIES: Banking services

Principal Bank: Savings Banks Trust Company

No of Employees: 470

EAST PENN MANUFACTURING COMPANY

Deka Road, Lyon Station, PA 19536

Tel: (215) 682-6361

Telex: TWX 510 6513297 deka lyst

President: DeLight E Breidegam Jr

Senior Executive Officers: Richard P Bowers (Executive VP Sales), Faith H Himmebreich (VP), John C Grim (Secretary, Treasurer and Comptroller)

PRINCIPAL ACTIVITIES: Manufacture of batteries and cables

Principal Subsidiaries: Federal Battery & Cable Manufacturing Co

Principal Bank: American Bank and Trust Company of Pennsylvania

Financial Information:

	$'000
Sales revenues	120,000

No of Employees: 1,400

EASTERN AIR LINES, INC

Miami International Airport, Miami, FL 33148

Tel: (305) 873-2211

Telex: ITT 441458 eastair

President: Joseph B Leonard (and Chief Operating Officer)

Senior Executive Officers: Thomas R Buttion (Senior VP Airline Operations), Jerry Cosley (Senior VP Communications), John E Hurst Jr (Senior VP Technical Support Services), Jack W Johnson (Senior VP Human Resources), Richard P Mogurno (Senior VP Legal and Secretary), Wayne A Yeoman (Senior VP Finance), Rolf S Andersen (VP and Treasurer), Dwain C Andrews (VP Employee Services), Paul C Auger (VP Marketing Programs), O F Auten (VP Field Management), Robert R Baujan (VP Treasury Administration and Treasurer), Francisco Contreras (VP Sales and Service Mexico), Kevin E Cooper (VP Maintenance), William H Dowse (VP Advertising), George R Dutton (VP Equipment and Sales Services), Camilio Fabrega (VP Panama), Joseph L Feldman (VP Sales and Service, Central Region), Alan C Gibson (VP Pilot Relations and Administration), Edwina S Gilbert (VP In-Flight Services), Edward L Green (VP Sales and Services, Northeast), Frank M Heinzmann (VP Computer and Communications Services), Harold L Holt (VP Sales and Services, Southern), Daniel S Klein (VP Strategic Planning), David B Kunstler (VP Purchasing and Contracts), John L Lillibridge (VP Facilities), George A Lyall (VP Sales and Services), Donald P Martin (VP Operations), George W McCarter (VP Atlanta), John W Nelson (VP Sales), J Robert O'Neill (VP Schedules), Leopoldo Pflucker (VP Peru), Jerry Schorr (VP Cargo Sales), Robert J Shipner (VP Flight Operations and Systems Chief Pilot), Lawrence H Siebers (VP Personnel Planning), John M Siefert (VP Sales and Services, Western), Jose I Smith (VP Financial Planning and Controller), Billy Stephens (VP Flying Operations and Safety), Juan Ucros (VP Columbia), A Russell Upshaw Jr (VP Government Affairs), Robert J Walcot (VP Reservation and Telephone Sales), Philip A Wester (VP Accounting), J Emmet Wolfe Jr (VP Operational Service Support)

PRINCIPAL ACTIVITIES: Air transportation services

Principal Bank: Chase Manhattan Bank NA

Financial Information:

	Dec 31 1985
	$'000
Sales revenues	4,815,070
Net income	6,310
Shareholders equity	260,940

No of Employees: 37,500

EASTERN COMPANY

112 Bridge Street, Naugatuck, CT 06770

Tel: (203) 729-2255

Chairman: Russell G McMillen

President: Stedman G Sweet

Senior Executive Officers: D E Whitmore Jr (VP, Secretary and Treasurer)

PRINCIPAL ACTIVITIES: Manufacture of iron and steel products

Principal Subsidiaries: Eberhard Hardware, Ltd

Principal Bank: Bank of Boston, Connecticut

Financial Information:

	Dec 31 1985	Dec 31 1986
	$'000	$'000
Sales revenues	75,435	71,675
Net income	2,597	1,823
Earnings per share	$2.37	$1.77
Retained income	14,037	13,620

No of Employees: 719

EASTERN GAS & FUEL ASSOCIATES

One Beacon Street, Boston, MA 02108

Tel: (617) 742-9200

Telex: TWX 7103210713 egfa mys bs

Chairman: William J Pruyn (and Chief Executive Officer)

President: Robert W Weinig (and Chief Operating Officer)

Senior Executive Officers: John N Philips (Chairman Executive Committee), Robert H Freeman (Executive VP Natural Resource Operations), John D Geary (Senior VP Marine), John J Bacon (Senior VP Utility), John W Hancock (Senior VP Coal), Richard C O'Brien (Senior VP Administration), H B Baldwin (VP), Michael C Cook (VP), Jesse R Mohorovic (VP), John A O'Callaghan (VP), John J Glessner (VP), James C Donnelly (VP Finance)

PRINCIPAL ACTIVITIES: Natural gas distribution, inland barge transportation

Principal Subsidiaries: Midland Enterprises Inc; Boston Gas Company; Boston Gas Co; Eastern Exploration Co; Massachusetts Liquefied Natural Gas Co; Boston Gas Products Inc; Castner Curran & Bullitt Inc; Second Sterling Corp; E G Leasing Corp; Eastern Associated Real Estate Corp; Eastern Realty Corp; Eastern Urban Services Inc; Midland Affiliated Co; Midland Enterprises Inc; Boston Tow Boat Co; Chotin Transportation Inc; Eastern Associated Terminals Co; Federal Barge; Heartland Transportation; Ohio River Co; WCM Radio Pittsburgh Inc; Omega Properties Inc; Orgulf Transport Co; Port Allen Marine Service Inc; Red Circle Transport Co; Triangle Fleet; Midland Properties Inc; Capital Marine Supply Inc; Hartley Marine Corp; Inland Water Propulsion Systems Inc; Ohio River Terminals Co; Mystic Steamship Corp; PCC Land Co Inc; Delta Properties Corp; Eastern Associated Properties Inc; North Fork Energy Corp; River Properties Corp; Western Associated Energy Corp

Principal Bank: The First National Bank of Boston

Financial Information:

	Dec 31 1985	Dec 31 1986
	$'000	$'000
Sales revenues	1,330,880	1,200,000
Net income (loss)	(37,008)	19,088
Earnings (loss) per share	($1.61)	$0.82
Shareholders equity	442,805	431,961

No of Employees: 9,800

EASTERN STAINLESS STEEL COMPANY

PO Box 1975, Baltimore, MD 21203
Tel: (301) 522-6432
Telex: WUT 8-7840 essco bal

Chairman: Richard E Gray
President: William F Dausch (and Chief Executive Officer)
Senior Executive Officers: James F Beisler (Executive VP and Chief Operating Officer), Edward F Curley (VP Purchasing), Thomas A Howley (VP Sales), Mario W Francioli (VP Industrial Relations), Edmund G Riccio (VP Operations), Joseph J Duffy (VP Finance and Chief Financial Officer)

PRINCIPAL ACTIVITIES: Manufacture of stainless steel
Parent Company: Eastmet Corporation, Cockeysville, MD
Financial Information:

	$'000
Sales revenues	230,000

No of Employees: 1,150

EASTERN UTILITIES ASSOCIATES

One Liberty Square, Boston, MA 02109
Tel: (617) 357 9590

Chairman: John F G Eichorn Jr (and Chief Executive Officer)
President: Donald G Pardus (and Treasurer and Chief Financial Officer)
Senior Executive Officers: Arthur A Hatch (VP), Robert P Tassinari (VP), Richard M Burns (Controller), William F O'Connor (Secretary)

PRINCIPAL ACTIVITIES: Distribution of electricity
Principal Subsidiaries: Blackstone Valley Electric Co; Eastern Edison Co; Montaup Electric Co; EUA Service Corp
Financial Information:

	Dec 31 1985 $'000	Dec 31 1986 $'000
Sales revenues	333,510	343,000
Net income	29,770	32,000

No of Employees: 1,100

EASTMAN GELATINE CORPORATION

227 Washington Street, Box 473, Peabody, MA 01960
Tel: (617) 531-1700

President: Frank A Butler
Senior Executive Officers: Dan T Spencer Jr (VP), Wendell W Cook (VP), Colby H Chandler (VP), Irving A Francis (Treasurer)

PRINCIPAL ACTIVITIES: Manufacture of gelatine
Parent Company: Eastman Kodak Co
Financial Information:

	$'000
Sales revenues	50,000

No of Employees: 270

EASTMAN INC

2301 E Willow Street, Long Beach, CA 90806
Tel: (213) 426-7391

President: W E Pichler
Senior Executive Officers: John Duncan (VP Marketing)

PRINCIPAL ACTIVITIES: Wholesale and retail trade in office supplies; printing
Parent Company: David Jones California Inc
Principal Bank: First Interstate Bank
Financial Information:

	$'000
Sales revenues	70,000

No of Employees: 400

EASTMAN KODAK COMPANY

343 State Street, Rochester, NY 14650
Tel: (716) 724-40000
Telex: 978481

Chairman: Colby H Chandler (and Chief Executive Officer); Vice Chairman: J Phillip Samper (and Executive Officer)
President: Kay R Whitmore (and Executive Officer)
Senior Executive Officers: Toy F Reid (Executive VP and General Manager Eastman Chemicals Division), Cecil D Quillen Jr (Senior VP and General Counsel), Paul L Smith (Senior VP), William L Sutton (Senior VP), Leo J Thomas Jr (Senior VP and General Manager Life Sciences Division)

PRINCIPAL ACTIVITIES: Photographic products; imaging systems; life sciences; chemicals
Principal Subsidiaries: Verbatim; Qualis
Principal Bank: Lincoln First Bank
Financial Information:

	Dec 31 1985 $'000	Dec 31 1986 $'000
Sales revenues	10,631,000	11,550,000
Income before taxes	530,000	598,000
Net income	332,000	374,000
Dividends	553,000	551,000
Dividends per share	$2.43	$2.44
Earnings per share	$1.46	$1.66
Common stock	621,000	622,000
Retained income	6,710,000	6,533,000
Shareholders equity	6,562,000	6,388,000

Number of Shareholders: 172,713
No of Employees: 116,185

EASTMET CORPORATION

PO Box 1975, 7700 Rolling Mill Rd, Baltimore, MD 21203
Tel: (301) 522 6200

Chairman: George R Walsh (and Chief Executive Officer)
President: William F Dausch (and Chief Operating Officer)

PRINCIPAL ACTIVITIES: Manufacture of a wide range of steel and other metal products
Principal Subsidiaries: Eastmet Industrial Products Group Inc; Aelco Foundries Inc; Belgium Foundry Corp; Harry Davies Molding Co Inc; VIP Engineered Products Corp; Zalk Josephs Fabricators Inc
Principal Bank: First National Bank of Maryland
Financial Information:

	$'000
Sales revenues	238,908

No of Employees: 1,500

EATON CORPORATION

Eaton Center, Cleveland, OH 44114
Tel: (216) 523-5000
Telex: 98-0595 etn whq clv

Chairman: James R Stover (and Chief Executive Officer)
Senior Executive Officers: S R Hardis (Vice Chairman and Chief Financial Officer), Alfred M Rankin (Vice Chairman and Chief Operating Officer), Administration), M C Baird (President-Defense and Electronics Group), W E Butler (President-Automotive Components Group), R W Gillison (President-Truck Components Group), A M Cutler (President-Industrial Group), J M Carmont (VP and Treasurer), J D Evans (VP-Human Resources), J L Forbis (VP-Strategic Planning), G L Gherlein (VP and General Counsel), B Hattox (VP and Controller), H Hubben (VP-International), J W Hushen (VP-Government Relations), W R Kiessel (VP-Manufacturing Services), R L Leach (VP-Accounting), W B Offutt (VP-Technical Management), R T Sadler (VP and Secretary), F M Wilkerson (VP-Administration), M Wright VP-Corporate Affairs)

PRINCIPAL ACTIVITIES: Manufacturer of electronic and electrical systems and components including automation systems and equipment for the control of manufacturing processes, the storage, retrieval and movement of materials, and the manufacturing and testing of semiconductors; aerospace and defense systems for electronic warfare applications, the control of waterway and air traffic, and microwave communications; capital goods components, including drives, clutches, brakes and a wide array of other components used for industrial process and power control; consumer goods components, including circuit breakers and components for appliances and power tools; and vehicle components including valves and other highly engineered engine components for passenger cars and trucks; transmissions, axles, and brakes for medium and heavy-duty trucks; and mechanical and hydrostatic transmissions and hydraulic motors for off-highway vehicles

Trade Names: AIL, AILTECH, Airflex, Char-Lynn, Cutler-Hammer, Dekoron, Dill, Dole, Durant, Dynamatic, Eaton, Felsted, Fuller, Golf Pride, Kenway, Lebow, Mears, MSC, Synflex, Tinnerman

Principal Subsidiaries: Analytical Assessments Corp; Eaton-Optimetrix Inc; Master Specialties Co; Eaton International Corp; AIL International, Inc; Cutler-Hammer Export Sales Corp; Eaton DISC Co; Yale Materials Handling Corp; Eaton Consulting Services Corp; Eaton-Kenway Inc; The Yale & Towne Co; Kenway Handling Systems Inc; Eaton I.C.S.A.; Eaton Pty Ltd; Cutler-Hammer Australia Pty Ltd; Samuel Moore Europe SA; Eaton Yale Ltd; Milner Road Enterprises Ltd; Eaton Controles Industriales SA; Eaton SA; Eaton Technologies Ltd; Eaton SpA; Eaton EST SpA; Eaton Controls SpA; Eaton Automotive SpA; Eaton Components SpA; Eaton Nova SpA; Eaton Japan Co Ltd; Eaton International Inc; Cutler-Hammer Anstalt; Condura, SA de CV; Cutler-Hammer Mexicana SA; Eaton sam; Eaton BV; Eaton Finance NV; Cutler-Hammer New Zealand Ltd; Cutler-Hammer Nigeria Ltd; Cutler-Hammer (South Africa) Ltd; Eaton Truck Components (Proprietary) Ltd; Cutler-Hammer Babelegi (Proprietary) Ltd; Kacee Ware (Empangeni) (Proprietary) Ltd; Eaton SA; Productos Eaton Livia SA; Cutler-Hammer Espanola, SA; Cutler-Hammer Svenska Aktiebolag; Eaton Ltd; Yale Materials Handling Ltd; Eaton GmbH; Yale GmbH; Cutler-Hammer Zambia Ltd; CHI Properties (Private) Ltd

Principal Bank: Bankers Trust Company

Financial Information:

	Dec 31 1986
	$'000
Sales revenues	3,811,600
Net income	137,600
Earnings per share	$4.29
Shareholders equity	1,255,600

No of Employees: 41,000

EATON-KENWAY INC

515 E 1st South, Salt Lake City, UT 84102
Tel: (801) 530-4000

President: Jules Mirabal

Senior Executive Officers: John Ryder (VP), James D Larsen (VP), Robert Tolle (VP), Lewis W Nielsen (VP), Tom Freyburg (VP Administration)

PRINCIPAL ACTIVITIES: Production of storage systems and mechanical handling equipment; manufacture of trucks

Parent Company: Eaton Corporation, Cleveland, OH

Principal Bank: Zions First National Bank

Financial Information:

	$'000
Sales revenues	100,000

No of Employees: 600

EBSCO INDUSTRIES, INC

PO Box 1943, Birmingham, AL 35201
Tel: (205) 991-6600
Telex: 78-2663

Chairman: Elton B Stephens

President: J T Stephens

Senior Executive Officers: Jack H Breard Jr (Director of Marketing)

PRINCIPAL ACTIVITIES: Recreational products and supplies for armed services, government agencies, and civilians; sheet metal and wire point-of-purchase displays; custom printed binders; printing; advertising specialties; magazine reading services; library subscription services; audio-visual furniture; steel joists and roof decking; warehousing and delivery service for textbook manufacturers; classroom teaching and learning tools for school systems; full service telemarketing capabilities; Cordell, Doll, Hedden and Rebel fishing lures; Rebel tackle boxes; billiard, carom and snooker tables and accessories; commercial carpet; custom imprinted wearables; business products and services; magazine subscription sales; real estate services

Trade Names: EBSCONET, HEDDON, REBEL, COTTON CORDELL, DOLL, VULCAN, NATIONAL, (all Registered trademarks)

Principal Subsidiaries: Bennett-EBSCO Subscription Services; CANEBSCO Subscription Services Ltd; EBSCO Investment Services Inc; Franklin Square Agency Overseas Inc; Libris-EBSCO Ltda

Principal Bank: Southtrust; AmSouth

No of Employees: 2,600

ECHLIN INC

100 Double Beach Road, Branford, CT 06405
Tel: (203) 481-5751

Chairman: Frederick J Mancheski (and President and Chief Executive Officer)

Senior Executive Officers: Daniel S Carboni (Executive VP-Engine Systems), John P Gethin (Executive VP-Brake and Clutch Systems), Richard B Patterson (VP-Finance), Edward D Toole (VP, Secretary and General Counsel), Earl F Lind (VP-Materials Management), Milton J Makoski (VP-Human Resources), Robert F Tobey (VP-Corporate Development), Richard A Wisot (Treasurer), Andrew J Mazzarella (Corporate Controller)

PRINCIPAL ACTIVITIES: Echlin is a worldwide manufacturer of top quality products used by professional mechanics and do-it-yourselfers to maintain or improve the efficiency and safety of motor vehicles. Echlin parts are used on automobiles, trucks, trailers, and buses and on off-road, industrial, farm, recreational, and residential engine powered equipment

Trade Names: Vehicle efficiency products include: Electrical and fuel system parts sold under the names NAPA Echlin, Borg-Warner, Niehoff, Whitaker, ACCEL, Auto-Tune, Ace, EPE, Sierra Supply, and Prime Line; and Clutches and other power transmission parts marketed under the names Borg-Warner, Lipe, EPE, and Quinton Hazell. Vehicle safety products include: Automotive brake system parts sold under the names NAPA United, Raybestos, and EPE; Heavy duty brake system parts offered under the names Midland, NAPA United, Grey-Rock, and Grau Girling; Controllers for electric brakes sold under the name Tekonsha; and Steering and suspension system components marketed under the name Quinton Hazell. The Company also sells lift truck parts under the name LPM; automotive and industrial motion, location, metering, and sensing devices under the name Sensor; and security access system readers and cards under the name Sensor

Principal Subsidiaries: Engine Systems Group: Ace Electric Company Inc: Automotive Controls Corp; Blackstone Manufacturing Co Inc; Echlin of Puerto Rico Inc; Echlin-Ponce Inc; Pacer Industries Inc; Pacer KS Inc; Ristance Corporation. Automotive Brake Group: Brake Parts Company; Brake Systems Inc; Buchanan Metalform Products Inc; Continental Hydraulic Hose Corp; Distex Ind Inc (Canada); Distex New Jersey Inc; Echlin Canada Inc (Canada); ITAPSA SA de CV (Mexico); Prattville Mfg Inc; Sierra Supply Company; Tekonsha Engineering Company. Heavy Duty Group-North

American Operations: Echlin Canada Inc (Canada); Lipe Corporation; Midland Brake Inc. European Group: Grau Girling GmbH (West Germany); Grau Girling Limited (UK); Lipe Limited (UK); Quinton Hazell PLC (UK, Eire, France and Italy). Distribution Group: BWD Automotive Corporation; Lift Parts Mfg Co Inc. Remanufacturing Group: BWD Automotive Corporation; EPE Inc. Southern Hemisphere Group: BWD Automotive of Puerto Rico Inc; BWD International; Echlin Australia (Pty) Ltd (Australia); Echlin do Brasil SA (Brazil); Echlin Charger Mfg Co (Pty) Ltd (South Africa); Echlin Mexicana SA de CV (Mexico); Echlin Sales/International; Echlin de Venezuela CA (Venezuela). Sensor Engineering Company

Principal Bank: First National Bank of Chicago

Financial Information:

	Aug 31 1985 $'000	Aug 31 1986 $'000
Sales revenues	771,390	901,890
Income before taxes	76,646	83,969
Net income	45,603	48,844
Dividends	17,058	20,463
Dividends per share	$0.41	$0.47
Earnings per share	$1.10	$1.11
Common stock	41,955	48,391
Retained income	190,317	218,698
Shareholders equity	289,721	423,043

Number of Shareholders: 5,743 at August 31, 1986

No of Employees: 10,900

ECKERD, JACK, CORPORATION

8333 Bryan Dairy Road, Clearwater, FL 33518

Tel: (813) 397-7461

Telex: WUT 526722 eckerd lrgo

Chairman: Stewart Turley (and Chief Executive Officer)

President: Harry Lambert

Senior Executive Officers: Leslie D Reagin III (Executive VP Store Operations), Ron Peterson (Executive VP Marketing), John W Boyle (Senior VP Finance and Administration), Curt M Neel (VP Distribution), Don L McIver (VP Real Estate), Michael Zagorac Jr (VP Public Affairs)

PRINCIPAL ACTIVITIES: Drugstores, optical stores, photofinishing services

Principal Bank: Royal Trust Bank

Financial Information:

	Jan 31 1986 $'000	Jan 31 1987 $'000
Sales revenues	2,555,589	2,566,474

No of Employees: 32,400

ECKRICH, PETER, & SONS, INC

3515 Hobson Road, Fort Wayne, IN 46805

Tel: (219) 481-2034

Telex: WUT 232422 beatrice fwa

President: Robert L Lill (and Chief Operating Officer)

Senior Executive Officers: J B Weatherspoon (VP Research and Development), Ted T Neely (VP Operations), Patrick M Ciez (VP Marketing), Donald L Menze (VP Sales), Ronald C Fuhrman (VP Administration)

PRINCIPAL ACTIVITIES: Processing of meat

Parent Company: Beatrice Companies Inc, Chicago, IL

Financial Information:

	$'000
Sales revenues	300,000

No of Employees: 2,700

ECOLAB INC

Ecolab Center, St Paul, MN 55102

Tel: (612) 293-2233

Telex: WUT 207061 el inc stp

Chairman: Pierson M Grieve (and President and Chief Executive Officer)

Senior Executive Officers: Bruce J Bentcover (Treasurer), Kenneth I Bjerk (VP-US Purchasing), Gerald K Carlson (Senior VP-International Division), Jon R Grunseth (VP-Public Affairs), John G Forsythe (Director-Corporate Tax), James M Millsap (VP-Corporate Development), S Lars Olson (VP and Controller), Richard F Rintelmann (VP-Klenzade Division), Donald R Rodel (Senior VP-US Manufacturing, Distribution and Systems), William R Rosengren (Senior VP, General Counsel and Secretary), Robert H Sayre (Senior VP-Human Resources), Allan L Schuman (Senior VP-Institutional Division), Michael E Shannon (Executive VP and Chief Financial and Administrative Officer), F William Tuominen (VP-Coporate Technology), L Jack Van Fossen (Presidnet of ChemLawn Corporation, a subsidiary)

PRINCIPAL ACTIVITIES: Ecolab Inc is a leading worldwide developer and marketer of premium institutional and residential services. Worldwide institutional services include cleaning and sanitizing products, systems and services for the lodging, food service, dairy and food processing markets. Residential services include lawn and tree and shrub care.

Trade Names: Solid Power, Scrub Free, Electrasol, Finish, Lime-A-Way, Guardian

Financial Information:

	Jun 30 1986 $'000	Jun 30 1987 $'000
Sales revenues	588,450	762,813
Income before taxes	57,858	90,361
Net income	43,686	52,220
Dividends	14,452	15,665
Dividends per share	$0.535	$0.58
Earnings per share	$1.30	$1.76
Common stock	27,272	26,857
Retained income	200,253	226,301
Shareholders equity	261,586	290,271

No of Employees: 13,104

ECOLAIRE, INC

One Country View Road, Malvern, PA 19355

Tel: (215) 647-9900

Telex: WUT 83-1395 bh ash marn

Chairman: R Wennerholm Jr (and President and Chief Executive Officer)

Senior Executive Officers: Carl G Larsen (Group VP Finance and Treasurer), L A Thaxton (Group VP), A R Brady (VP, Secretary and General Counsel), C C Morton (VP Corporate Development), O A Grieshaber (VP), F V Wolters (VP), G Grodecki (VP), C Wennerholm (VP)

PRINCIPAL ACTIVITIES: Manufacture of industrial equipment for a range of applications including capital electrical equipment and pollution control equipment

Principal Bank: Philadelphia National Bank

Financial Information:

	$'000
Sales revenues	140,000

No of Employees: 1,000

ECOLAT INC

Escolab Center, St Paul, MN 55102

Tel: (612) 293-2233

Telex: WUT 297061

Telefax: el inc stp

Chairman: Pierson M Grieve (and President and Chief Executive Officer)

Senior Executive Officers: Bruce J Bentcover (Treasurer), Kenneth I Bjert (VP-US Purchasing), Gerald K Carlson (Senior VP-International Division), Jon R Grunseth (VP-Public Affairs), John G Forsythe (Director-Corporate Tax), James M Millsap (VP-Corporate Development), S Lars Olson (VP and Controller), Richard F Rintelmann (VP-Klenzade Division)

Donald R Rodel (Senior VP-US Manufacturing, Distribution and Systems), William R Rosengren (Senior VP, General Counsel and Secretary), Robert H Sayre (Senior VP-Human Resources), Allan L Schuman (Senior VP-Institutional Division), Michael E Shannon (Executive VP and Chief Financial and Administrative Officer), F William Tuominen (VP-Coporate Technology), L Jack Van Fossen (Presidnet of ChemLawn Corporation, a subsidiary)

PRINCIPAL ACTIVITIES: Ecolan Inc is a leading worldwide developer and marketer of premium institutional and residential services. Worldwide institutional services include cleaning and sanitizing products, systems and services for the lodging, food service, diary and food processing markets. Residential services include lawn and tree and shrub care.

Trade Names: Solid Power, Scrub Free, Electrasol, Finish, Lime-A-Way, Guardian

Financial Information:

	Jun 30 1986 $'000	Jun 30 1987 $'000
Sales revenues	588,450	762,813
Income before taxes	57,858	90,361
Net income	43,686	52,220
Dividends	14,452	15,665
Dividends per share	$0.535	$0.58
Earnings per share	$1.30	$1.76
Common stock	27,272	26,857
Retained income	200,253	226,301
Shareholders equity	261,586	290,271

No of Employees: 13,104

EDGAR FABRICS

295 5th Avenue, New York, NY 10016
Tel: (212) 686-2952

President: Edgar Silberman
Senior Executive Officers: Albert Rubin (Executive VP)

PRINCIPAL ACTIVITIES: Import and export of fabrics
Principal Bank: Bankers Trust Company
Financial Information:

	$'000
Sales revenues	58,000

No of Employees: 30

EDGEWATER CORPORATION

300 College Avenue, Oakmont, PA 15139
Tel: (412) 828-4000
Telex: TWX 710 7963648 edgewater oknt

Chairman: C T Marshall
President: C E Slater
Senior Executive Officers: Robert N Peck (Secretary, Treasurer and Controller)

PRINCIPAL ACTIVITIES: Circular metal products for aircraft, industrial and transportation uses
Parent Company: Wilmington Securities, Inc
Principal Bank: Mellon Bank
Financial Information:

	$'000
Sales revenues	46,000

Principal Shareholders: Private (100%) owned
No of Employees: 600

EDISON BROTHERS STORES INC

Box 14020, St Louis, MO 63178
Tel: (314) 331-6000

Chairman: Julian I Edison
President: Bernard Edison
Senior Executive Officers: Andrew E Newman (Executive VP), Eric P Newman (Executive VP and Secretary), Martin K Sneider (Executive VP), Walter H Heinecke (VP Real Estate), M Richard Wyman (VP Corporate Development), Lewis L Pate (VP and Treasurer), Lee G Weeks (VP Finance and Controller)

PRINCIPAL ACTIVITIES: Retail trade in footwear
Principal Subsidiaries: EBS Jeans West Inc; EBS Size 5-7-9 Shops Inc; Fashion Conspiracy Inc
Principal Bank: Chase Manhattan Bank
Financial Information:

	Dec 31 1985 $'000	Dec 31 1986 $'000
Sales revenues	808,300	904,000
Net income	27,000	34,000

No of Employees: 20,300

EDNASA INTERNATIONAL, INC

2500 East T C Jester, Houston, TX 77008
Tel: (713) 868-8980

Chairman: Robin S Loh (and President and Chief Executive Officer)
Senior Executive Officers: Neil B Biggerstaff (Executive VP), Dora Loh (VP), Robby T K Loh (VP), W L Hixon Jr (Treasurer)

PRINCIPAL ACTIVITIES: Holding company with interests in oilfield equipment manufacture and the manufacture of truck trailers and sectional buildings
Principal Subsidiaries: PRE Corp; Elder International Inc; Birmingham Mfg Co Inc; Hacker-Pyramid Co; World-Wide Tec Service; Bonyx Precorp Capital Inc
Principal Bank: Citibank
Financial Information:

	$'000
Sales revenues	83,000

No of Employees: 900

EDO CORPORATION

14-04 111th Street, College Point, NY 11356
Tel: (718) 445-6000
Telex: ITT 423094 edo ui

Chairman: William R Ryan
President: Gerald Albert (and Chief Executive Officer)
Senior Executive Officers: Michael J Hegarty (VP Finance and Treasurer), Robert L Richards (VP Corporate Development)

PRINCIPAL ACTIVITIES: EDO Corporation designs and manufactures advanced electronic and specialized equipment for military, aviation, marine and industrial markets. Principal products include: sonar equipment, mine countermeasures systems and aircraft stores suspension and ejection mechanisms; piezoelectric ceramic components, acoustic, navigational and video scanning systems; and fiber-reinforced composite components for the aviation and transportation industries
Principal Subsidiaries/Divisions: Government Systems Division; Fiber Science Division; Western Division
Principal Bank: Irving Trust Company
Financial Information:

	Dec 31 1985 $'000
Sales revenues	116,152
Income before taxes	14,160
Net income	8,061
Dividends	2,043
Dividends per share	$0.27
Earnings per share	$1.01
Common stock	8,454
Retained income	37,444
Shareholders equity	58,694

No of Employees: 1,330

EDWARD A CANTOR AFFILIATED INTERESTS

See CANTOR, EDWARD A, AFFILIATED INTERESTS

EDWARD HINES LUMBER CO
See HINES, EDWARD, LUMBER CO

EDWARD KRAEMER & SONS, INC
See KRAEMER, EDWARD, & SONS, INC

EDWARD LEVY CO
See LEVY, EDWARD, CO

EDWARDS, A G, INC
1 North Jefferson Ave, St Louis, MO 63103
Tel: (314) 289-3000

Chairman: Benjamin F Edwards III (and President and Chief Executive Officer); Vice Chairman: Raymond J Kalinowski (and Treasurer)
Senior Executive Officers: Robert G Avis (Executive VP, Director of Marketing and Sales), David W Mesker (Senior VP, Director of Finance), David M Sisler (Executive VP, Director Group)

PRINCIPAL ACTIVITIES: General financial and investment services
Principal Subsidiaries: A G Edwards & Sons Inc; Sage Inc
Financial Information:

	1986 $'000
Revenues	526,000
Net income	54,000

No of Employees: 4,500

EDWIN L WIEGAND
See WIEGAND, EDWIN L,

EECO INC
1601 East Chestnut Avenue, PO Box 659, Santa Ana, CA 92701
Tel: (714) 835 6000

Chairman: Burgess Dempster; Vice Chairman: Robert B Bonney
President: Robert C Milo (and Chief Executive Officer)
Senior Executive Officers: Robert W Allen (VP Administration), A W Finamore (VP, Chief Financial Officer and Secretary), Carl Jeremias (VP, President EECO Computers Inc), John M Ludutsky (VP and Divisional Manager Video Products), Robert F Meinicke (VP and Divisional Manager Component Products Division), Edward Sidor (VP Engineering), Vincent G Smedes (VP Material and Busines Development)

PRINCIPAL ACTIVITIES: Manufacture of electronic products including computer systems for hotels; passenger service and entertainment controls for aircraft; micro-processor-based video products for use in television studios; switch products
Principal Bank: Wells Fargo Bank
Financial Information:

	Dec 31 1985 $'000
Sales revenues	54,315
Net income	1,620

No of Employees: 750

EG & G, INC
45 William Street, Wellesley, MA 02181
Tel: (617) 237-5100
Telex: TWX 310-294037

Chairman: Dean W Freed
President: John M Kucharski (and Chief Executive Officer)
Senior Executive Officers: John R Dolan (Senior VP, Finance), David J Beaubien (Senior VP), Donald M Kerr (Senior VP), Leo M Kelly (VP, General Counsel and Clerk), William T Barrett (VP), Philip C Kautt (VP), Daniel F Riley (VP), Samuel Robinovitz (VP), Louis P Valente (VP), Charles M Williams (VP), Peter H Zavattaro (VP), Richard F Murphy (VP), Donald R Peters (VP), James O Zane (VP), Richard P Delio (Controller), Peter A Broadbent (Treasurer)

PRINCIPAL ACTIVITIES: EG&G, Inc and its subsidiaries provide a variety of advanced technical and scientific products and services to commercial, industrial and governmental customers throughout the world. The Company designs and produces sophisticated electronic instruments and systems. It also manufactures specialized mechanical, electro-mechanical, and electro-optic components; conducts energy-related investigations and surveys; and is involved in biomedical research. Under Government contracts EG&G participates in engineering and site-management programs related to national defense and security, physics and space research, and nuclear and nonnuclear energy research and development
Operating Organizations: Instruments Group:- EG&G Gamma Scientific; EG&G Geometrics; EG&G Mount Sopris Instruments; EG&G Environmental Equipment; EG&G Ocean Products; EG&G Wakefield Systems; EG&G Princeton Applied Research, Princeton, NJ; EG&G Princeton Applied Research, Lawrenceville, NJ; EG&G Chandler Engineering; EG&G ORTEC; EG&G Instruments (Brazil); EG&G Instruments (Canada); EG&G Instruments (France); EG&G Instruments (Germany); ESN (Germany); EG&G Instruments (UK); Fiber Optics Systems (UK); EG&G Ireland (Eire); EG&G Instruments (Italy); Seiko EG&G (Joint Venture) (Japan); EG&G Instruments (Netherlands). Military Products Group:- EG&G Almond Instruments; EG&G Frank Hill Associates; EG&G CEA Berkleonics; EG&G Cirtech; EG&G Electronic Components; EG&G Frequency Products; EG&G Regenerative Blowers; EG&G Rotron; EG&G CINOX. Solid State Products Group:- EG&G Reticon; EG&G Photon Devices; EG&G Vactec; EG&G Reticon (Germany); EG&G Reticon (UK). Special Products Group:- EG&G Birtcher Industrial Products; EG&G Electro Optics; EG&G Torque Systems; EG&G Wakefield Components; Arno-Rotron Equipamentos Eletricos (Joint Venture) (Brazil); EG&G Electro Optics (Eire). Fluid Components Technology Group:- EG&G KT Aerofab; EG&G Sealol (Elmhurst); EG&G Pressure Science; EG&G Wright Components; EG&G Sealol (Warwick); EG&G Sealol Eagle (Joint Venture); EG&G Sealol (Cranston); EG&G Sealol (Australia); EG&G Sealol, Sarnia, Ontario (Canada); EG&G Sealol, Dorval, Quebec (Canada); EG&G Sealol, Mississauga, Ontario (Canada); EG&G Sealol, Edmonton, Alberta (Canada); Sealol-Egypt (Egypt); EG&G Sealol SARL (France); EG&G Sealol GmbH (Germany); EG&G Euroseals GmbH (Germany); EG&G Sealol Ltd (UK); Sealol Hindustan Ltd (Joint Venture) (India); EG&G Sealol (Eire); EG&G Sealol SpA (Italy); Sealol Kuwait KSC (Joint Venture) (Kuwait); Asmuss-Sealol (NZ) Ltd (Joint Venture) (New Zealand); Sealol SA (Venezuela). Testing Services Group:- EG&G Structural/Kinematics; EG&G Automotive Research. Government Systems and Services Group:- EG&G Florida, Kennedy Space Center; EG&G Idaho; EG&G Mason Research Institute; EG&G Washington Analytical Services Center; EG&G Energy Measurements; EG&G Reynolds Electrical & Engineering Co; EG&G Special Projects; EG&G Services
Principal Bank: First National Bank of Boston
Financial Information:

	Dec 28 1985 $'000	Dec 28 1986 $'000
Revenues	1,177,117	1,167,118
Income before taxes	88,565	77,298
Net income	55,708	44,897
Dividends	12,923	14,160
Dividends per share	$0.48	$0.52
Earnings per share	$2.07	$1.65
Common stock	27,431	27,431
Retained income	173,378	201,901
Shareholders equity	203,401	236,331

No of Employees: 23,000

EIL INSTRUMENTS INC
10 Loveton Circle, Sparks, MD 21152
Tel: (301) 771 4800

Chairman: Hallie P Rice (and President)

Senior Executive Officers: James W Howard (Senior VP), Patrick R O'Brien III (VP and Chief Financial Officer), Keith K Rice (VP), Samuel T Woodside (VP and General Manager), Lynn C Fay (VP), Robert O Weller (VP Marketing), Charles R Rouse (Secretary)

PRINCIPAL ACTIVITIES: Maintenance and repair of electrical and electronic instruments

Principal Subsidiaries: Conservation & Controls Inc

Principal Bank: Maryland National Bank

Financial Information:

	$'000
Sales revenues	31,000

No of Employees: 370

EL CHICO CORPORATION

12200 Stemmons, Dallas, TX 75234

Tel: (214) 241 5500

Chairman: Gilbert Cuellar Jr (and President and Chief Executive Officer)

Senior Executive Officers: James F Collins (VP, Treasurer and Chief Financial Officer), John A Cuellar (VP, Secretary and Legal Counsel), Paul W Vinyard (VP and Director Operations), Rodney Allen (VP Marketing), Robert P Flack (VP Corporate Development)

PRINCIPAL ACTIVITIES: Restaurants specializing in Mexican food

Principal Bank: Allied Lakewood Bank

Financial Information:

	$'000
Sales revenues	93,650

No of Employees: 4,630

EL PASO COMPANY

One Paul Kayser Center, El Paso, TX 79978

Tel: (915) 541-3000

Chairman: Travis H Petty (and President and Chief Executive Officer)

Senior Executive Officers: Richard S Morris Jr (Executive VP), Michael Bracy (Senior VP), Virgil R Cowart (Senior VP), W A Wise (Senior VP and Secretary), Billy B Ross (Senior VP and Controller)

PRINCIPAL ACTIVITIES: Distribution of natural gas

Parent Company: Burlington Northern Inc

Financial Information:

	$'000
Sales revenues	4,000,000

No of Employees: 8,000

EL PASO ELECTRIC CO

PO Box 982, El Paso, TX 79960

Tel: (915) 543-5711

Chairman: Erven R Wall (and President and Chief Executive Officer)

Senior Executive Officers: B E Bostic (Executive VP Finance), Charlie Mais (Senior VP), L M Downum (VP Mesilla Valley Drive), William J Johnson (VP and Controller), James P Maloney (VP), W W Royer (VP Data Processing, Treasurer and Legal Counsel), Ignacio Troncoso (VP Engineering Transmission and Development), Joseph E Wasiak (VP)

PRINCIPAL ACTIVITIES: Electricity distribution

Principal Subsidiaries: Franklin Land & Resources Inc

Principal Bank: First City National Bank of El Paso

Financial Information:

	Dec 31 1986
	$'000
Sales revenues	318,000
Net income	81,000

No of Employees: 1,100

EL PASO NATURAL GAS CO

One Paul Kayser Center, El Paso, TX 79978

Tel: (915) 541-2600

Fax: (915) 541-2544

Chairman: Travis H Petty

President: Richard S Morris (and Chief Executive Officer)

Senior Executive Officers: Walter G Henderson (Executive VP), Francis J Boyle (Senior VP, Treasurer and Chief Financial Officer), Donald J MacIver Jr (Senior VP, General Counsel and Secretary), William A Wise (Senior VP)

PRINCIPAL ACTIVITIES: Transmission of natural gas; oil and gas exploration and production

Parent Company: Ultimate Parent Company: Burlington Northern, Inc, Seattle, WA through The El Paso Company

Principal Subsidiaries: El Paso Hydrocarbons Company

Financial Information:

	Dec 31 1985
	$'000
Sales revenues	3,993,016
Income before taxes	375,894
Net income	213,213
Preferred dividends	25,320
Common dividends	100,000
Common stock	94,265
Retained income	485,255
Shareholders equity	1,069,258

No of Employees: 4,000

EL TORITO RESTAURANTS INC

2450 White Road, PO Box 19609, Irvine, CA 92714

Tel: (714) 863 6400

Chairman: J Peter Grace; Vice Chairman: Anwar Soliman

President: Larry J Cano (and Chief Executive Officer)

Senior Executive Officers: Frederick A LeFranc (Executive VP Operations), James W Stryker (Executive VP and Chief Financial Officer), Robert D Johnson (VP Finance)

PRINCIPAL ACTIVITIES: Restaurants

Financial Information:

	Dec 31 1985
	$'000
Sales revenues	318,850
Net income	10,590

No of Employees: 10,000

ELCO INDUSTRIES, INC

1111 Samuelson Road, Box 7009, Rockford, IL 67125

Tel: (815) 397-5151

Telex: TWX 910 6313420 elco ind inc

President: Jack W Packard (and Chief Executive and Operating Officer)

Senior Executive Officers: Frank A Fiorenza (Senior VP, Treasurer and Chief Financial Officer), Phil Jacoby (VP Manufacturing), Kenneth R Carlson (VP Engineering), Derek M Hasse (VP Industrial Relations)

PRINCIPAL ACTIVITIES: Metal castings and stampings; industrial fasteners

Principal Bank: The First National Bank of Chicago

Financial Information:

	$'000
Sales revenues	109,000

No of Employees: 1,400

ELCOR CORPORATION

2100 Wilco Bldg, Midland, TX 79701
Tel: (915) 685-0200

Chairman: Roy E Campbell (and President and Chief Executive Officer)
Senior Executive Officers: Richard J Rosebery (VP, Chief Financial Officer and Treasurer), William C Morrow (VP, Secretary and General Counsel), W F Ortloff (VP), H R Newson (VP), Harold K Work (VP)

PRINCIPAL ACTIVITIES: Building materials and fittings; chemical plant and other industrial plant including mining and oilfield equipment
Principal Subsidiaries: Chromium Corp; Elk Corp of America; Elk Corp of AL; Elk Corp of AR; Elk Corp of TX; Gory Associated Industries Inc; Mosley Machinery Co Inc; Ortloff Corp; Ortloff International Corp; Ortloff Minerals Services Corp; Pro-Quip Corp
Principal Bank: Republic Bank Dallas
Financial Information:

	$'000
Sales revenues	115,000

No of Employees: 900

ELDER BEERMAN STORES CORPORATION

3155 El-bee Road, Dayton, OH 45439
Tel: (513) 296 2700

Chairman: Max Gutmann (and Chief Executive Officer)
President: Charles M Waldron (and Vice Chairman and Chief Administrative Officer)
Senior Executive Officers: Herbert O Glaser (Executive VP and Division President), Kenneth R Epstein (Senior VP Administration), Rafael Furst (Senior VP and Treasurer), Bernard Gutmann (Senior VP), C Wayne Harris (Senior VP and Division President), Paul E Lazorski (Senior VP Operations), David W Lovejoy (Senior VP and Controller), Leonard Beerman Peal (VP Cost and Leased Department), Richard E Valentine (VP and Assistant Treasurer), Harry A Jensen (Secretary)

PRINCIPAL ACTIVITIES: Retail stores
Principal Subsidiaries: Bee-Gee Shoe Corp; El-Bee Charge It Corp; Margos La Mode Inc; M C Cook Wholesale Corp
Principal Bank: Bank One
Financial Information:

	$'000
Sales revenues	352,000

No of Employees: 7,000

ELDON INDUSTRIES, INC

9920 La Clenega Blvd, Inglewood, CA 90301
Tel: (213) 642-7716
Telex: WUT 691575 eldon ind hwth

President: Robert Silverstein
Senior Executive Officers: Herbert M Rome (Executive VP), James Stinnett (VP and Treasurer), Richard Agins (VP and Secretary), Robert Stephenson (VP and General Manager Ungar Division), George Carver (VP and General Manager Davson Division), Glen Church (VP, President and General Manager Eldon Office Products Division)

PRINCIPAL ACTIVITIES: Office equipment; electrical and electronic equipment
Principal Bank: Crocker National Bank
Financial Information:

	$'000
Sales revenues	66,720

No of Employees: 600

ELDORADO MOTOR CORPORATION

Box 266, Minneapolis, KS 67467
Tel: (913) 392-2171
Telex: 910 742-1430 Honorbuilt

Chairman: Robert L Stewart (and Chief Executive Officer)
President: Gregory K Stewart (and Chief Operating Officer)
Senior Executive Officers: Sheldon E Walle (Senior VP, Commercial Vehicle Division), Donald R Schwegmann (Senior VP, Industrial Operations), E Gordon Johnson (Senior VP, Finance and Administration and Chief Financial Officer)

PRINCIPAL ACTIVITIES: Manufacture of motor vehicles including recreational vehicles and commercial buses
Trade Names: ElDorado, Encore, Mirada, Prelude, Firenza, Conestoga, Falcon, Aerotech, Express, MST, Starfire, Renaissance
Principal Subsidiaries: ElDorado Motor Acceptance Corporation
Principal Bank: Bank IV
Financial Information:

	Jun 30 1985	Jun 29 1986
	$'000	$'000
Sales revenues	55,315	66,059
Net income	917	981
Earnings per share	$0.35	$0.37
Common stock	2,650	2,650

No of Employees: 700

ELECTRO NUCLEONICS INC

350 Passaic Avenue, Fairfield, NJ 07006
Tel: (201) 227 6700

Chairman: Vincent V Abajian (and Chief Executive Officer); Vice Chairman: Richard M Mandle (and VP)
President: Herbert M Appleton (and Chief Operating Officer)
Senior Executive Officers: Joseph J Cardillo (VP), Alan M Fishman (VP),Ernest Maclin (VP), Paul Plunkett (VP and Controller), Richard Abajian (Secretary and Treasurer)

PRINCIPAL ACTIVITIES: Manufacture of a range of medical and surgical instruments
Principal Bank: National Westminster Bank
Financial Information:

	$'000
Sales revenues	56,900

No of Employees: 600

ELECTRO RENT CORPORATION

3340 Ocean Park Boulevard, Suite 1000, Santa Monica, CA 90405
Tel: (213) 452 3200

Chairman: Daniel Greenber (and Chief Executive Officer)
President: William Weitzman (and Chief Financial Officer)
Senior Executive Officers: Leslie R Evans (Senior VP), Billy G Fullwood (VP Regional), Charles A Motzko (Group VP), Gary B Phillips (VP Regional), Renard Tarullo (VP and Manager, National Sales), Steven Markham (Controller), James O Pike Jr (Treasurer), Dean Wilson (Secretary), Ahmad Husasmi (VP Marketing)

PRINCIPAL ACTIVITIES: Leasing and rental services for electronic test equipment
Principal Bank: Continental Illinois National Bank and Trust Company
Financial Information:

	$'000
Sales revenues	89,900

No of Employees: 600

ELECTRO SCIENTIFIC INDUSTRIES, INC

13900 N W Science Park Drive, Portland, OR 97229
Tel: (503) 641-4141
Telex: GRT 3777927 esi vi ptl

Chairman: William D Walker (and President and Chief Executive Officer); Vice Chairman: Douglas C Strain
Senior Executive Officers: Edward Swenson (VP Engineering), Dean Finley (VP Finance and Treasurer), Mike Ellsworth (VP Systems), Wally Masters (VP Manufacturing), Jim Currier (VP Instruments), Heinrich Stenger (VP International), Clifford T Krouse (VP Passive Components)

PRINCIPAL ACTIVITIES: Electrical and electronic equipment
Principal Bank: United States National Bank
Financial Information:

	$'000
Sales revenues	84,000

No of Employees: 1,000

ELECTROMAGNETIC SCIENCES INC

125 Technology Park, Norcross, GA 30092
Tel: (404) 448 5770

President: John E Pippin
Senior Executive Officers: William F Evans (Senior VP Administration), Don T Scartz (VP Finance, Treasurer and Secretary), Thomas E Sharon (Executive VP Development), Joseph W Simon (Senior VP Research and Development)

PRINCIPAL ACTIVITIES: Manufacture of electronic equipment including semiconductors
Financial Information:

	Dec 31 1985
	$'000
Sales revenues	33,340
Net income	4,290

No of Employees: 530

ELECTRONIC ASSOCIATES INC

185 Monmouth Parkway, West Long Branch, NJ 07764
Tel: (201) 229 1100

Chairman: William R Smart
President: Robert G Finney (and Chief Executive Officer)
Senior Executive Officers: Richard K Stanislaw (VP Finance and Secretary), John J Fendrock (VP Manufacturing), Robert J Welle (VP Field Service), Otis C Wright Jr (VP Product Area)

PRINCIPAL ACTIVITIES: Manufacture of data processing equipment
Principal Bank: Midlantic National Bank
Financial Information:

	$'000
Sales revenues	33,700

No of Employees: 490

ELECTRONIC DATA SYSTEMS CORPORATION

7171 Forest Lane, Dallas, TX 75230
Tel: (214) 661-6000
Telex: WUT 791526 eds dal

Chairman: Ross Perot; Vice Chairman: Morton H Meyerson
President: Lester M Alberthal Jr (and Chief Executive Officer)
Senior Executive Officers: Paul J Chiapparone (Senior VP), Gary J Fernandes (Senior VP), William K Gayden (Senior VP), Malcolm Gudis, Jeffrey M Heller (Senior VP), Kennard F Hill (Senior VP), Dean Linderman (Senior VP), J T Walter Jr (Senior VP and Chief Financial Officer)

PRINCIPAL ACTIVITIES: Data processing equipment; computer software and services
Parent Company: General Motors Corporation
Principal Bank: Fort Worth National Bank
Financial Information:

	Dec 31 1985	Dec 31 1986
	$'000	$'000
Sales revenues	3,406,400	4,321,000
Net income	189,800	260,900
Earnings per share	$1.57	$2.13
Shareholders equity	530,600	798,300

No of Employees: 45,000

ELECTRONIC MEMORIES & MAGNETICS CORPORATION

16000 Ventura Blvd, Encino, CA 91436
Tel: (213) 995-1755
Telex: TWX 910 4951740 eleceemmag lsa

Chairman: Trude C Taylor
President: Walter D Warren (and Chief Executive Officer)
Senior Executive Officers: Raymond C Lawhon (VP Finance and Chief Financial Officer)

PRINCIPAL ACTIVITIES: Manufacture of computer components and metals, alloys and metallic oxides for manufacturers or users requiring products with specific magnetic properties
Principal Subsidiaries: Emm World Trade Corp; Severe Environment Systems Co
Principal Bank: Bank of America NT & SA
Financial Information:

	$'000
Sales revenues	87,700

No of Employees: 1,860

ELECTRONIC MODULES CORPORATION

McCormick Road, Cockeysville, MD 21030
Tel: (301) 666-3300

Chairman: Robert E Vogel (and Chief Executive Officer)
President: Ralph E Bothne (and Chief Operating Officer)
Senior Executive Officers: Donald P Aiken (Executive VP Process Control), John E Armstrong Jr (VP Marketing and Secretary), David J Houck (VP Speical Projects), Joseph Ritter (VP Operations), James Tebay (VP and Chief Financial Officer), Bruce Manthey (VP Sales)

PRINCIPAL ACTIVITIES: Manufacture of computer control systems including process control systems
Parent Company: Rexnord
Principal Bank: Mercantile Safe Deposit and Trust
Financial Information:

	$'000
Sales revenues	65,000

No of Employees: 930

ELECTRONICS CORPORATION OF AMERICA

265 Winter Street, Waltham, MA 02142
Tel: (617) 466 8000

President: Arthur G B Metcalf
Senior Executive Officers: William Eisner (Executive VP), Richard R Glendon (VP and Treasurer), Thomas J Lechner (VP Engineering), Guy W Bragdon Jr (VP Manufacturing), Stanley L Davis (VP Photoswitch Marketing), Elik I Fooks (VP Industrial Products Engineering), Peter N Renzi (VP Product Planning and Marketing), E Craig Thomson (VP and Chief Engineer), Nicholas P Fowler (VP Materials Management)

PRINCIPAL ACTIVITIES: Manufacture of a wide range of industrial controls
Principal Bank: United States Trust Company
Financial Information:

	$'000
Sales revenues	50,690

No of Employees: 980

ELECTROSOUND GROUP INC

800 Veterans Memorial Highway, Hauppauge, NY 11788
Tel: (516) 724 3700

President: Richard Projain (and Chief Executive Officer)
Senior Executive Officers: Richard Meixner (Senior VP), Ronald S Hoffman (VP Finance and Chief Financial Officer)

PRINCIPAL ACTIVITIES: Production of records and tapes
Principal Subsidiaries: Electro Sound Inc; Electrosound Group Midwest Inc; Electrsound Tape Services Inc; Monarch Record Manufacturing Corp
Principal Bank: United States Trust Company
Financial Information:

	$'000
Sales revenues	36,000

No of Employees: 550

ELECTROSPACE SYSTEMS, INC

301 East Collins Blvd, Richardson, TX 75081
Tel: (214) 470-2000
Telex: TWX 9108674768; 163-590 ESI UT

Chairman: James R Lightner (and President and Treasurer)
Senior Executive Officers: Dr Robert L Carrel (Executive VP and Secretary), Milton W Holcombe (VP Systems), Richard C Fenwick (VP Research and Development), Donald E Heitzman (VP Marketing)

PRINCIPAL ACTIVITIES: Manufacture of telecommunications and navigation equipment and defense electronics
Principal Subsidiaries: Electrotel, Inc
Principal Bank: MBank, Dallas
Financial Information:

	Feb 29 1986 $'000
Sales revenues	145,034
Income before taxes	23,249
Net income	13,377
Dividends	957
Dividends per share	$0.072(1)
Earnings per share	$0.98
Common stock (2)	13,348
Retained earnings	46,396
Shareholders equity	51,508

(1) adjusted for 25% stock split Sept 85 effected in the form of a stock dividend
(2) outstanding in thousands

No of Employees: 1,974

ELF AQUITAINE, INC

High Ridge Park, Stamford, CT 06904
Tel: (203) 968-5000

Chairman: Michael Schneider-Maunory (and President and Chief Executive Officer); Vice Chairman: Gino P Guisti (and President and Chief Executive Officer Texasgulf Inc)
Senior Executive Officers: Earl L Huntington (Senior VP and General Counsel), Michel A Rapaccioli (Senior VP and Chief Financial Officer), L Williams (VP Employee Relations and Administration), Max S Bass (Senior VP, President and Chief Executive Officer M & T Chemicals Inc), Gilbert M Portal (Senior VP, President Elf Aquitaine Petroleum), Thomas J Wright (Senior VP, President Texasgulf Chemicals)

PRINCIPAL ACTIVITIES: Oil and gas exploration and production; petrochemicals
Parent Company: Société Nationale Elf Aquitaine (SNEA), Paris, France
Principal Bank: Morgan Guaranty Trust Company
Financial Information:

	$'000
Sales revenues	3,400,000

No of Employees: 4,700

ELGIN NATIONAL INDUSTRIES, INC

120 S Riverside Plaza, Chicago, IL 60606
Tel: (312) 454-1900
Telex: WUT 253226 robshafco cgo

Chairman: Milton S Gould
President: Richard G Miller Jr (and Chief Executive Officer)
Senior Executive Officers: Elmo J Hurst (Executive VP), Robert F McDonald (VP Finance), Warren W Browning (VP, Secretary and General Counsel)

PRINCIPAL ACTIVITIES: Manufacture of watches and clocks, photographic equipment, mining equipment and equipment for the construction industry
Principal Subsidiaries: Harwood Manufacturing Co Inc; Roberts & Schaefer Co Inc; Cabell Construction Co; Centrifugal & Mechanical Industries Corp; Clinch River Corp; Langley & Morgan Corp; Darby Construction Corp; J O Lively Construction Co; Lively Manufacturing Equipment Co; Mining Controls Inc; Norris Screen & Manufacturing Inc; Tabor Machine Co
Principal Bank: First National Bank
Financial Information:

	$'000
Sales revenues	139,700

No of Employees: 1,180

ELI LILLY AND COMPANY

See LILLY, ELI, AND COMPANY

ELIXIR INDUSTRIES

17925 S Broadway, Gardena, CA 90248
Tel: (213) 321-1191
Telex: TWX 910 3467012 elixirind gdna
Telefax: (213) 323-1467

Chairman: Roland R Sahm (and Chief Executive Officer)
President: David C Whitt
Senior Executive Officers: Charles L "Roy" Maxey (Executive VP and Chief Operating Officer), Steven L Solomon (Chief Financial Officer), Leslie Moreau (Secretary)

PRINCIPAL ACTIVITIES: Manufacture of components for mobile homes and recreational motor vehicles; manufacture of building materials
Principal Subsidiaries: Club Wholesale Concepts Inc; Wholesale Membership Warehouse; Garden Insurance Companies; Insurance Co & Agency
Principal Bank: Wells Fargo Bank

Principal Shareholders: Roland R Sahm
No of Employees: 1,800

ELKAY MANUFACTURING COMPANY

2222 Camden Court, Oak Brook, IL 60521
Tel: (312) 986-8484
Telex: WUT 255106 elkay oakr

Chairman: Ronald C Katz
President: David F Craigmile
Senior Executive Officers: Paul C Sternberg (Chairman Executive Committee), Richard A Gatehouse (Group VP), Robert W Briska (Group VP), John P Edl (VP Marketing), Richard W Swain (VP Industrial Relations), Robert W Briska (VP)

PRINCIPAL ACTIVITIES: Manufacture of stainless steel products
Principal Subsidiaries: Avon-Dale Manufacturing Co Inc; Elkay Industries Sales Corp; Pioneer Ltd; Seltex Factors Corp; Skyline Ltd; Skyline Manufacturing Co Inc
Principal Bank: First National Bank of Chicago
Financial Information:

	$'000
Sales revenues	100,000

No of Employees: 1,000

ELSINORE CORPORATION

202 E Fremont St, Las Vegas, NV 89101

Tel: (702) 385-4011

President: Jeanne Hood

Senior Executive Officers: Kathryn F Serl (VP and Chief Financial Officer), Richard LeVasseur (VP), Edward Fasulo (VP)

PRINCIPAL ACTIVITIES: Operation of hotels, casinos, bars and restaurants

Principal Subsidiaries: Elsinore Finance Corp; Elsub Corp; Four Queens Inc; Hyatt Tahoe Inc

Principal Bank: Valley Bank

Financial Information:

	$'000
Sales revenues	85,000

No of Employees: 4,300

EMC INSURANCE GROUP INC

717 Mulberry Street, Des Moines, IA 50309

Tel: (515) 280 2581

Chairman: Robert B Kelley (and Chief Executive Officer and Subsidiary Officer)

President: George W Kochheiser (and Chief Operating Officer and Subsidiary Officer)

Senior Executive Officers: Thomas X Wright (Senior VP), E H Creese (VP and Treasurer), Philip T Van Ekeren (VP and Secretary)

PRINCIPAL ACTIVITIES: Insurance services

Parent Company: Employers Mutual Casualty Co

Principal Bank: Brenton National Bank of Des Moines

Financial Information:

	Dec 31 1985
	$'000
Revenues	102,240
Net income	4,930

No of Employees: 1,460

EMERSON ELECTRIC COMPANY

8000 W Florissant Avenue, St Louis, MO 63136

Tel: (314) 553-2000

Telex: RCA 209904 emel ur

Chairman: Charles F Knight (and Chief Executive Officer); Vice Chairmen: James J Kerly, Laurence L Browning Jr

President: E L Keyes Jr (and Chief Operating Officer)

Senior Executive Officers: J J Adorjan (Executive VP), James F Hardymon (Executive VP), Robert W Staley (Executive VP), Albert E Suter (Executive VP), Jan K Ver Hagen (Executive VP), William C Bousquette (Senior VP and Chief Financial Officer), Charles A Dill (Senior VP), Charles Hansen (Senior VP Law, Secretary and General Counsel), John C Rohrbaugh (Senior VP Industrial Relations), H F Faught (Group VP Technical), E L Clary (Group VP Corporate Services), Stephen P Cortinovis (VP), Robert L Cox Jr (VP and Treasurer), Peter L Gartman (VP Development), A A Gilbert (VP Manpower Development), Charles W Groennert (VP Audit Services), J R Marchiano (VP Corporate Manufacturing), Charles O Planting (VP Corporate Sales), J C Wilson (VP Finance and Controller), H John Yopp (VP Taxes)

PRINCIPAL ACTIVITIES: Electrical and electronic equipment including power equipment and process control systems

Principal Subsidiaries: Appleton Electric Co; Automatic Switch Co; Angar Scientific Co Inc; Asco Electrical Products Co; General Casting Co; A & M Ludwig Corp; Bells Foundry Inc; A Chance Co; Power Switching Equipment Inc; Computer Power Systems Corp; Electronic Navigation Industries Inc; Kay Ray Inc; Metaloy Inc; Morse Industrial Products; Ridge Tool Co; Rosemount Inc; Rosemount Office Systems Inc; Uniloc; Skil Corp; Loud-Wendel Inc; Skil Europe Corp; Sweco Inc; Therm-o-Disc Inc; Urick Foundry Co; Vacco Industries Inc; Van Gorp Corp; Western Forge Corp; Xomox Corp; Atwood & Morrill Co Inc

Principal Bank: Centerre Bank

Financial Information:

	Sep 30 1985	Sep 30 1986
	$'000	$'000
Sales revenues	4,649,200	4,952,900
Net income	401,100	408,900
Earnings per share	$5.43	$5.62
Shareholders equity	2,222,200	2,347,000

No of Employees: 58,000

EMERSON RADIO CORPORATION

One Emerson Lane, North Bergen, NJ 07047

Tel: (201) 662 2000

Telex: WUT 127603 emerson seca

Chairman: William W Lane

President: Stephen L Lane

Senior Executive Officers: Donald Dvorkin (Executive VP and Secretary), Saul Knazick (Senior VP Marketing), Harold Falix (VP Finance and Treasurer), Hachiro Masuda (VP Design), Kunio Takei (VP Far East Operations), Marino Andriani (VP Sales), Edward Beller (VP Sales Operations), Rick Bond (VP Sales), Kenneth Fournier (VP Domestic Operations), Toshinori Ishii (VP Engineering), Rudolph Malacrida (VP Management Information Systems)

PRINCIPAL ACTIVITIES: Manufacture of Hi-Fi equipment, radios and televisions

Principal Subsidiaries: Cardiac Resuscitator Corp

Principal Bank: Manufacturers Hanover Trust Company

Financial Information:

	$'000
Sales revenues	183,000

No of Employees: 550

EMERY AIR FREIGHT CORPORATION

Wilton, CT 06897

Tel: (203) 762-8601

Telex: TWX 7104793213 eaf nda wilt

Chairman: John C Emery Jr (and Chief Executive Officer)

President: Denis M McCarthy (and Chief Operating Officer)

Corporate Officers: Terence M Browne (Senior VP-Transportation), Brian D Costar (Senior VP-International), Arthur W DeMelle (Senior VP and Chief Financial Officer), Richard W Ball (VP and Treasurer), Robert R Bohannon (VP-Information Systems), Ton C M Heijmen (Senior VP-Marketing and Strategic Planning), Edward A Klein (VP-Purchasing), William A Kromberg (VP-Taxes), Robert J Conologue (VP and Controller), Daniel W Shea (Senior VP-Human Resources), Clifford J Stueck (Senior VP-North America), J Baxter Urist (VP-Marketing), Daniel J McCauley (Executive VP, Secretary and General Counsel)

PRINCIPAL ACTIVITIES: Emery Air Freight is the oldest overnight air courier and air cargo transportation system in the United States

Trade Names: Emery Worldwide

Principal Subsidiaries: Emery Customs Brokers; Emery Distribution Service; Emery Ocean Freight

Principal Bank: Manufacturers Hanover Trust Company

Financial Information:

	Dec 31 1985 $'000	Dec 31 1986 $'000
Sales revenues	875,814	887,523
Income (loss) before taxes	25,764	(18,682)
Net income (loss)	16,232	(5,440)
Dividends	9,620	7,301
Dividends per share	$0.50	$3.75
Earnings (loss) per share	$0.85	$(0.28)
Common stock	3,866	3,909
Retained income	109,948	97,207
Shareholders equity	178,604	170,797

No of Employees: 7,100

EMHART CORPORATION

426 Colt Highway, Farmington, CT 06032
Tel: (203) 678-3000

Chairman: Peter L Scott (and Chief Executive Officer); Vice Chairman: Stephen J Ruffi (and Chief Administrative Officer)
President: William C Lichtenfels (and Chief Operating Officer)
Senior Executive Officers: Achim Knust (Senior VP and Chief Financial Officer), Robert M Byrnes (Senior VP Human Resources), Ralph M Branca (VP Development), John F Budd Jr (VP External Affairs), Richard L Cote (VP and Chief Accounting Officer), Dean M Hennessy (VP and General Counsel), Leo T Hinkley Jr (VP), Walter A Jaeger (VP Manufacturing Staff), Gilbert W O'Neil (VP Investor Relations), John S Rydz (VP Technical), Royal E Cowles (VP Personnel), David W Dandro (VP Information Systems), Carl A Horne (VP and Tax Counsel), Tom Bleasdale (VP and Group President), Raymond A DeVita (VP and Group President), Thomas T Gately (VP and Group President), Fred M Hollfelder (VP and Group President), Kenneth A Josephson (VP and Group President), Robert R Quackenbush (VP and Group President)

PRINCIPAL ACTIVITIES: Manufacture of machinery for a range of industrial outlets including packaging machinery, footwear machinery and glass container manufacturing machinery; building materials, locks and other builders' hardware; components for motor vehicles
Principal Subsidiaries: Emhart Industries Inc; Dom Security Locks Inc; Emhart Hardware Sales Corp; Emhart Overseas Capital NV; Fellows Corp; Hill Refrigeration Corp; Mallory Components Sales Corp; Notifier Co; Powers Manufacturing Co; Technology Licensing Corp; Texon Inc; USM Corp; Emhart Credit Corp; HTC Corp; USM Co of Puerto Rico Inc; USM Community Realty Corp
Principal Bank: Connecticut Bank & Trust Co
Financial Information:

	Dec 31 1986 $'000
Sales revenues	2,094,300
Net (loss)	(10,200)
(Loss) per share	($0.35)
Shareholders equity	717,100

No of Employees: 30,422

EMPERY CORPORATION

10 S Leopard Road, Suite 201, Paoli, PA 19301
Tel: (215) 644-5900

President: A J Clegg
Senior Executive Officers: John C Heenan (VP Finance)

PRINCIPAL ACTIVITIES: Printing of tickets, labels, direct mail printing, business forms, computer checks, cable TV
Principal Subsidiaries: Globe Ticket & Label Company; SBF Communications Graphics; TVC Supply Company
Principal Bank: Mellon Bank
Financial Information:

	$'000
Sales revenues	53,000

No of Employees: 600

EMPIRE DISTRICT ELECTRIC COMPANY

602 Joplin Street, Joplin, MO 64801
Tel: (417) 623 4700

President: R L Lamb
Senior Executive Officers: J A Reed (Senior VP Operations), V E Brill (VP Finance), G C Hunter ()Treasurer), G A Knapp (Controller and Assistant Treasurer), H H Kost (Secretary), D A Vice (VP Transportation and Distribution), J H Weitzel (VP Production), R B Fancher (VP Corporate Services), M W McKinney (VP Customer Service)

PRINCIPAL ACTIVITIES: Supply of electricity and water
Principal Bank: First National Mercantile Bank and Trust
Financial Information:

	$'000
Sales revenues	127,000

No of Employees: 620

EMPIRE GAS CORPORATION

1700 South Jefferson Street, Lebanon, MO 65536
Tel: (417) 532 3101

Chairman: Robert W Plaster (and President and Chief Executive Officer); Vice Chairman: Harry N Forman
President: Larry D Ellison (Executive VP), Paul S Lindsey Jr (Executive VP), Martin F Dryden (Senior VP), Darrell Kays (Senior VP), Robert L Wooldridge (Senior VP), Dwight Gilpin (VP), Earl Noe (VP and Secretary), Geoen Van Derhoef (VP)

PRINCIPAL ACTIVITIES: Distribution of bottled gas
Principal Bank: Manufacturers Hanover Trust
Financial Information:

	$'000
Sales revenues	260,000

No of Employees: 1,500

EMPIRE OF AMERICA FSA

One Main Pl, Buffalo, NY 14202
Tel: (716) 845-7000

Chairman: Harlan J Swift
President: Paul A Willax (also Chief Executive Officer)
Senior Executive Officers: Daniel D Brown (Senior Executive VP), Robert S Johnson (Executive VP), Robert C Hausrath (Executive VP and Treasurer), Edwin R Sherwood (Executive VP), Kenneth Myers (Executive VP), Dennis W O'Beill (Executive VP), Jay S Doerflein (Senior VP Asset Services), Donald P Henry (Senior VP and Auditor), Gary G Berner (Senior VP Mortgage Investment), Kenneth R Fosburg (VP Commercial Mortgage Services)

PRINCIPAL ACTIVITIES: Savings and loan association
Principal Subsidiaries: Brandywine Enterprises Inc; Empire of America FSA Deland; Empire of America FSA Inc; Shelton Square Corp; Brandywine Realty Inc; William M Cadden & Co; Consumer Information Center Inc; Gallery of Homes; Intermark Consulting Services Inc; Macrotel Inc; Sherwin-Greenberg Productions Inc; Metrodata Inc; Metroteller Systems Inc; Moneyplex Inc; Pacific Thrift & Loan Co; Robshaw Realty Associates/Gallery of Homes; Shelton Square Agency Inc
Financial Information:

	Dec 31 1986 $'000
Net income	66,638
Earnings per share	$4.24
Stockholders equity	218,240
Deposits	7,352,759
Total assets	9,095,241

No of Employees: 3,840

EMPIRE OF CAROLINA INC

Daniel St, Tarboro, NC 27886
Tel: (919) 823 4111

Chairman: Maurice A Halperin (and Chief Executive Officer)
President: Barry S Halperin
Senior Executive Officers: Robert Lauck (VP Operations), Sumner Segal (VP and Treasurer), Stephen Hale (Secretary), Richard S Nugent (Controller)

PRINCIPAL ACTIVITIES: Manufacture of a range of toys and games
Principal Subsidiaries: Carolina Enterprises Inc
Principal Bank: Wachovia Bank
Financial Information:

	$'000
Sales revenues	36,760

No of Employees: 690

EMULEX CORPORATION

3545 Harbor Blvd, Box 6725, Costa Mesa, CA 92626
Tel: (714) 662-5600
Telex: WUT 183627 emulex csma

Chairman: Fred B Cox (and Chief Executive Officer)
President: Stephen W Frankel (and Chief Operating Officer)
Senior Executive Officers: Sol Zechter (VP Marketing), Michael J Lewis (VP Finance and Chief Financial Officer), William Mathrani (VP), Jim Orris (VP)

PRINCIPAL ACTIVITIES: Computer peripherals
Principal Subsidiaries: Computer Array Development Inc
Principal Bank: Security Pacific Bank
Financial Information:

	$'000
Sales revenues	103,170

No of Employees: 900

ENCORE SHOE CORPORATION

51 Wakefield Street, Rochester, NH 03867
Tel: (603) 332-8000
Telex: 910 240 3150 Zodiac

Chairman: Earl L Katz (and Treasurer)
President: James M Katz
Senior Executive Officers: Ronald A Katz (Executive VP), Albert Charette (Senior VP), Dennis Corliss (VP and Controller), Paul Duchemin (VP), John Paris (VP)

PRINCIPAL ACTIVITIES: Manufacture of footwear
Trade Names: Zodiac USA
Principal Bank: Shawmut Bank of Boston
Financial Information:

	$'000
Sales revenues	50,000

No of Employees: 800

ENCYCLOPAEDIA BRITANNICA, INC

310 S Michigan Avenue, Chicago, IL 60604
Tel: (312) 347-7000

Chairman: Robert P Gwinn
President: Peter B Norton
Senior Executive Officers: Thomas A Gies (Executive VP), Stanley D Frank (Executive VP), Patricia A Wier (VP Planning, Development and Controller), F H Figge Jr (VP and Treasurer), Raymond Majesty (VP Manufacturing), Norman L Braun (VP Public Affairs), Anthony J Migas (VP Information Services, Encyclopaedia Britannica)

PRINCIPAL ACTIVITIES: Publishing of educational books
Principal Subsidiaries: Britannica Home Library Services Inc; Encyclopaedia Britannica Holding Co Inc; Library Resources Inc; Merriam Webster Inc
Principal Bank: The First National Bank of Boston
Financial Information:

	$'000
Sales revenues	324,000

No of Employees: 2,800

ENDATA INC

501 Great Circle Road, Nashville, TN 37228
Tel: (615) 244 0244

Chairman: Douglas C Altenbern (and President and Chief Executive Officer)
Senior Executive Officers: Julius M Dziak (Executive VP), James M Felts (Senior VP), Stephen D Kane (Senior VP Administration), Douglas W Britt (Group VP), Stephen W Barkley (VP, Controller and Treasurer)

PRINCIPAL ACTIVITIES: Data processing services
Principal Bank: First American Bank of Nashville
Financial Information:

	$'000
Sales revenues	37,140

No of Employees: 570

ENDEVCO, INC

8080 N Central Expressway, Lockbox 47, Dallas, TX 75206
Tel: (214) 691-5536

Chairman: James W Bryant (and President)
Senior Executive Officers: Michael G Wright (Executive VP), Kelcy L Warren (VP), William S Leftwich (VP Finance)

PRINCIPAL ACTIVITIES: Transportation, processing and production of natural gas
Principal Subsidiaries: Mississippi Fuel Company; Cornerstone Natural Gas; Endevco Pipeline Company; Endevco Oil & Gas Company; Endevco Natural Gas Company; Endevco Producing; Endevco Industrial Gas Sales; Endevco Taft Company
Principal Banks: MBank Dallas; Citibank
Financial Information:

	Dec 31 1985	Dec 31 1986
	$'000	$'000
Sales revenues	155,287	114,319
Income before taxes	5,585	156
Net income	3,681	117
Earnings per share*	$0.77	$0.02
Common stock	6,396	20,739
Retained income	9,816	5,873
Shareholders equity	16,212	26,612

*fully diluted

No of Employees: 90

ENDICOTT JOHNSON CORPORATION

1100 E Main Street, Endicott, NY 13760
Tel: (607) 757-4000
Telex: WUT 932 412 ej corp endi

Chairman: Harold P McGowan
President: Charles C Murray (and Chief Executive Officer)
Senior Executive Officers: R E Mills (VP Instock Division), Kenneth E Mansfield (Executive VP), Frank G Figge (Executive VP Wholesale and Manufacturing), Charles F Thomas (VP Finance), Willard J Ackley (VP Instock Division), Matthew J Hastings (VP Manufacturing), Donald G Smith (VP Retail), John Raos (VP), George H Hempstead (VP)

PRINCIPAL ACTIVITIES: Manufacture of footwear
Parent Company: H M Acquisition Corp
Financial Information:

	$'000
Sales revenues	300,000

No of Employees: 5,000

ENERFAB, INC

4955 Spring Grove Avenue, Cincinnati, OH 45232
Tel: (513) 641-0500

Chairman: Dwaine Godfrey (and President)

PRINCIPAL ACTIVITIES: Manufacture of food processing equipment; nuclear spare parts sales; nuclear technical support; concrete cutting
Parent Company: Bishopric, Inc
Principal Subsidiaries: Enerfab Corporation; EMC Corporation
Principal Bank: Huntington National
Financial Information:

	$'000
Sales revenues	30,000

No of Employees: 300

ENERGAS COMPANY

PO Box 65025, Dallas, TX 75266
Tel: (214) 934 9227

Chairman: Charles K Vaughan (and President and Chief Executive Officer)
Senior Executive Officers: Jack C Gholson (Senior VP and Chief Financial Officer), Dennis S Gillmore (Senior VP), James A Enloe (General Manager Operations), Donald E James (VP and Legal Counsel), William P McKee Jr (VP Gas Supply and Industrial Sales), Charles V Mercer (VP Human Resources), Harry E Neel (VP Administration and Technical Services), Robert F Stephens (VP Corporate Services), E Gary Carter (Controller and Assistant Treasurer), Carolyn G Shaffer (Secretary)

PRINCIPAL ACTIVITIES: Transmission of natural gas
Financial Information:

	$'000
Sales revenues	287,000

No of Employees: 1,050

ENERGEN CORPORATION

2101 Sixth Avenue North, Birmingham, AL 35203
Tel: (205) 326 8100

Chairman: Rex J Lysinger (and President and Chief Executive Officer)
Senior Executive Officers: Richard J Patzke (Executive VP Finance and Treasurer), Dudley C Reynolds (VP and Secretary)

PRINCIPAL ACTIVITIES: Holding company with interests in the production and distribution of oil and natural gas
Principal Bank: SouthTrust Bank of Alabama
Financial Information:

	$'000
Sales revenues	383,000

No of Employees: 1,100

ENERGYNORTH INC

1260 Elm Street, PO Box 329, Manchester, NH 03105
Tel: (603) 625 4000

Chairman: Edward T Borer; Vice Chairman: Charles H Toll Jr
President: Howard W Kelley (and Chief Executive Officer)
Senior Executive Officers: N George Mattaini (Executive VP and Chief Administrative Officer), Donald S Inglis (Senior VP), Robert R Giordano (Senior VP), Ronald A Nichols (VP Operations), John R McLane Jr (Secretary)

PRINCIPAL ACTIVITIES: Distribution of natural gas
Principal Subsidiaries: Gas Service Inc; Manchester Gas Co
Principal Bank: Bank of New Hampshire
Financial Information:

	$'000
Sales revenues	60,500

No of Employees: 220

ENERSERV PRODUCTS, INC

777 N Eldridge, Houston, TX 77079
Tel: (713) 495 1885

Chairman: Stephen L Feinberg
President: William P Dillard (and Chief Executive Officer)
Senior Executive Officers: Thomas C Eisenbarth (VP Finance), Robert G Beckoff (VP and Treasurer)

PRINCIPAL ACTIVITIES: Oil and gas services and equipment
Principal Subsidiaries: Tubular Services Inc; Tubular Services West Inc
Principal Bank: State National Bank of El Paso
Financial Information:

	$'000
Sales revenues	30,620

No of Employees: 200

ENGELHARD CORPORATION

Menlo Park, PO Box 2901, Edison, NJ 08818-2901
Tel: (201) 632-6000

Chairman: Reuben F Richards
President: Orin R Smith (and Chief Executive Officer)
Senior Executive Officers: Cyrus H Holley (Executive VP nd Chief Operating Officer), Arthur A Dorbusch II (VP, General Counsel and Secretary), R Keith Elliott (VP, Finance and Chief Financial Officer), Harmon M Garfinkel (VP Research and Development), Fredric M Guist (VP and President of the Specialty Chemicals Division), Alan J Shaw (Controller), David M Wexler (Treasurer)

PRINCIPAL ACTIVITIES: Engelhard Corporation is a leading producer of specialty chemical and metallurgical products and processes. It operates with a global perspective, with plants, sales and service strategically located to give the Company a competitive advantage in serving its customers. The Specialty Chemicals Division is comprised of four business areas: catalysis, petroleum refining technology, performance minerals and electronic chemicals. The Specialty Metals Division conducts three closely interrelated businesses: fabricated metallurgical products, precious metals recovery and refining and precious metals dealing and management
Trade Names: ART, Dynamics, ANSILEX(R), ULTRASIV(R), HANOVIA(R), MAGNAFORMING, ULTRAWHITE(R), ARISTALOY(R), MTL-80
Principal Subsidiaries: Freeport Kaolin Company. In addition to manufacturing locations in the United States, Engelhard maintains operations in Australia, Brazil, Canada, France, Italy, Japan, Korea, Mexico, New Zealand, Switzerland, United Kingdom, Venezuela and West Germany
Financial Information:

	Dec 31 1985	Dec 31 1986
	$'000	$'000
Sales revenues	2,263,697	2,289,531
Net earnings	42,660	53,268
Earnings per share	$1.58	$1.31
Shareholders equity	512,277	561,128

No of Employees: 7,100

ENGELHARD SPECIALTY CHEMICALS DIVISION

Menlo Park, CN 40, Edison, NJ 08818
Tel: (201) 632-6000
Cable: MICOR
Telex: 13-8552 (US); 21 9984 (Int'l)

Division President: Fredric M Guist
Senior Executive Officers: Larry E Campbell (Senior VP Electronics), Martin J Connor Jr (Senior VP Finance), L Donald LaTorre (Senior VP Performance Minerals), Paul J Norris (Senior VP Catalysts)

PRINCIPAL ACTIVITIES: The Specialty Chemicals Division applies chemical technologies in working with such vital raw materials as performance minerals and precious metals to produce a wide range of products and processes. The division's leading markets include petroleum, petrochemical and chemical processing; paper, plastics and paint; electronics and environmental protection

Trade Names: Dynamics, Anisilex, Satintone, Translink, Torvex, PTX
Parent Company: Engelhard Corporation, Edison, NJ
Financial Information:

	Dec 31 1985
	$'000
Sales revenues	598,218
Operating earnings	62,075

No of Employees: 3,400

ENGELHARD SPECIALTY METALS DIVISION

Menlo Park, CN 40, Edison, NJ 08818
Tel: (201) 632-6000

President: Robert V Jeck
Senior Executive Officers: George H Scott Jr (Senior VP Metallurgical Operations), William F Lohman (Senior VP Precious Metals Management), Frederic J Hammerle (Group VP), Les C Vinney (VP Finance), Juergen F Schroeter (VP Operations, Carteret)

PRINCIPAL ACTIVITIES: Worldwide supplier of a package of services that includes custom-fabricated metal-based products, refining these products for reuse, and securing and managing precious metals. The division produces some 10,000 fabricated products-everything from brazing alloys to microwave filament, from medical implants to high-temperature thermocouples, plus a broad range of alloys and parts used in electrical switches and other devices
Parent Company: Engelhard Corporation, Edison, NJ
Financial Information:

	Dec 31 1985
	$'000
Sales revenues	1,665,479
Operating earnings	23,163

No of Employees: 2,200

ENGINEERED METAL PRODUCTS GROUP

PO Box 298, Baltimore, MD 21203
Tel: (301) 547-7420

Senior Executive Officers: L L Murray (VP and General Manager), Hugh J Blecki (VP and General Manager Piston Ring and Seal), Samuel W Koster (VP and General Manager Power Transmission Division), W C Arnold (VP and General Manager Container Machinery Division), William Carty (VP and General Manager Sprout-Waldron Division), James E Stevenson (Controller)

PRINCIPAL ACTIVITIES: Production of automobile components; industrial equipment and process equipment
Parent Company: Koppers Co Inc, Pittsburgh, PA
Financial Information:

	$'000
Sales revenues	230,000

No of Employees: 3,600

ENGINEERED SUPPORT SYSTEMS INC

1270 North Price Road, St Louis, MO 63132
Tel: (314) 993-5880

Chairman: Jerome V Labarbera
President: Michael F Shanahan (and Chief Executive Officer)
Senior Executive Officers: Gregory P Boyer (Executive VP and Secretary), John R Bartelt (VP and Controller), Ronal W Davis (VP), J Daniel Fisher (VP), Gary C Gerhardt (VP), Kenneth D Hayes (VP), Lawrence D King (VP), J Philemon Norton (VP), W Kent Pobanz (Group VP), A James Schell (VP), Marvin L Smith (Group VP), Bruce P Windesheim (VP), Timothy R Wolf (Assistant Secretary)

PRINCIPAL ACTIVITIES: Manufacture of engineered metal products
Financial Information:

	$'000
Sales revenues	50,860

No of Employees: 530

ENGINEERED SYSTEMS & DEVELOPMENT CORPORATION

600 Meridian Avenue, San Jose, CA 95126
Tel: (408) 280 5000

Chairman: Robert J Tomsich; Vice Chairman: Regis H Farrell (and Chief Executive Officer)
President: William H Price (and Chief Executive Officer)
Senior Executive Officers: Richard Heaney (Senior VP and Chief Operating Officer), Ronald D Payne (VP Administration and Secretary), Edward J Lamb (Principal Accounting Officer and Principal Financial Officer and Treasurer)

PRINCIPAL ACTIVITIES: Manufacture of specialty industrial machinery
Parent Company: Nesco Inc
Principal Subsidiaries: ESDM Corporation; Seaborn Development Inc; ESDM International Sales Corporation
Financial Information:

	Dec 31 1985
	$'000
Sales revenues	39,860
Net income	1,080

No of Employees: 220

ENGRAPH, INC

2635 Century Parkway NE, Atlanta, GA 30345
Tel: (404) 329-0332

Chairman: Leo Benatar
Senior Executive Officers: John H Dykes (VP-Finance), David E McFarlane Jr ((VP), Maurice M Richardson (VP), Basil H Ford (VP), Farrel F Potts (VP and Secretary), Dan C Tuttle (VP), Richard M Bruno (Treasurer)

PRINCIPAL ACTIVITIES: Engraph, Inc serves carefully selected market segments within the multi-billion dollar packaging materials and product identification markets. These market utilize custom manufactured, high value-added materials requiring superior capabilities in printing fabrication. The majority of packaging materials and product identification applications are sold to manufacturers and merchandisers of materials including flexible films, specialty papers, paperboard and rigid plastics
Principal Subsidiaries: Engraph is organized operationally within the business unit concept. Each unit is headed by a President/General Manager who has responsibility for profit and loss and the management of all assets used in his business unit. These units are: Flexible Packaging, Charlotte, NC; Morrill Press, Fulton, NY; Standard Cap & Seal, Atlanta, GA; Specialty Packaging, Charlotte, NC; Colonial Packaging, Atlanta, GA; Screen Art, Knoxville, TN; Creative Screen Print, Richmond, VA
Principal Bank: Trust Company Bank
Financial Information:

	Dec 31 1986
	$'000
Sales revenues	108,843
Income before taxes	5,769
Net income	2,988
Dividends	839
Dividends per share	$0.155
Earnings per share	$0.55
Common stock	18,880
Retained income	7,684
Shareholders equity	26,564

No of Employees: 1,000

ENNIS BUSINESS FORMS, INC

107 N Sherman Street, Ennis, TX 75119

Tel: (214) 875-3811

Chairman: Kenneth A McCrady (and Chief Executive Officer)

President: Robert Mitchell (and Chief Operating Officer)

Senior Executive Officers: Brewster McClure (Executive VP), Charles Ray (Executive VP Operations), Nolan Young (VP Marketing and Sales), H M Powell (VP), Harve Cathey (VP Finance, Secretary and Treasurer)

PRINCIPAL ACTIVITIES: Manufacture of business forms

Principal Subsidiaries: American Business Equipment Corp; Coast Gordon Business Forms Inc; Connolly Tool Machine Co; Mid America Business Forms Inc; Southern Business Forms Corp; Tested Advertising Techniques; Texas Tag & Specialty Co Inc

Principal Bank: Mercantile National Bank at Dallas

Financial Information:

	$'000
Sales revenues	110,600

No of Employees: 1,500

ENRON CORP.

1400 Smith Street, Houston, TX 77002

Tel: (713) 853-6161

Telex: 765443 Enron Corp

Telecopy: (713) 853-3129

Chairman: Kenneth L Lay (and Chief Executive Officer)

President: John M Seidl (and Chief Operating Officer)

Senior Executive Officers: Daniel L Dienstbier (President, Gas Pipeline Group and Executive VP of Enron Corp), Keith D Kern (Executive VP and Chief Financial Officer), Richard D Kinder (Executive VP, Law and Administration), Royston C Hughes (Senior VP, Corporate Affairs), James S Prentice (Senior VP, Administration and Human Resources), J Ronald Knorpp (Senior VP and Chief Information Officer), Ross Workman (Senior VP), E Joseph Hillings (Senior VP, Federal Government Affairs), Kathleen K Anderson (VP, Public and Investor Relations), James G Barnhart (VP, Administration), Donald H Gullquist (VP and Treasurer), Robert J Hermann (VP, Tax), David G Woytek (VP, Auditing), Luther D Snow (VP, Human Resources), Louis E Potempa (VP, Corporate Development), Earl F Trevithick (VP, Financial Planning and Controller), Gary W Orloff (VP and Associate General Counsel), Bruce N Stram (VP, Corporate Planning), James DeClue (VP Information Systems), Donald G Bledsoe (VP, Information Services), Peggy B Menchaca (VP and Corporate Secretary)

PRINCIPAL ACTIVITIES: Exploration, production and transmission of natural gas; liquid fuels; international trading in hydrocarbons; oil exploration and production; cogeneration

Principal Subsidiaries: Northern Natural Gas Co; Enron Oil and Gas Co; Northern Plains Natural Gas Co; Enron Liquid Fuels Co; Houston Pipeline Co; Transwestern Pipeline Co; Florida Gas Transmission Co

Principal Banks: Citibank; Morgan Guaranty Trust

Financial Information:

	Dec 31 1985	Dec 31 1986
	$'000	$'000
Sales revenues	9,724,253	7,590,658
Income (loss) before taxes(1)	233,989	(157,624)
Net income (loss)	(54,667)	57,663
Dividends	109,633	109,809
Dividends per share(2)	$2.48	$2.48
Earnings (loss) per share(3)	$(2.33)	$0.21
Common stock	452,452	454,043
Retained income	751,422	617,556
Shareholders equity	1,491,610	1,208,652

(1) and before extraordinary charge in 1985

(2) common stock

(3) after extraordinary charge and reflective of discontinued operations

Principal Shareholders: The Belfer Group; Employee Trustee Plan; Employee Stock Ownership Plan; American General Co

No of Employees: 7,200

ENSERCH CORPORATION

300 S St Paul Street, Dallas, TX 75201

Tel: (214) 651-8700

Telex: 732502 ENSCORPDAL

Chairman: W C McCord (and President and Chief Executive Officer)

Senior Executive Officers: William T Satterwhite (Senior VP, General Counsel and Chief Legal Officer), Sanford R Singer (Senior VP Finance and Corporate Development and Chief Financial Officer), Richard B Williams (Senior VP Administration), Benjamin A Brown (VP, Financial Relations and Analysis), Robert E Ebel (VP, International Affairs), Robert H Goodman (VP, Corporate Development and Planning), James W Hinds (VP, State Relations), Candice Shy Hooper (VP, Federal Relations), Robert E Wilber (VP, Chief Accounting Officer), Annell Costlow Rogers (Controller), Michael G Fortado (Corporate Secretary and Assistant General Counsel), Albert E Gallatin (VP and Treasurer), Keith Mond (VP Taxes). Engineering and Construction Division: John A Scarola (Senior VP), R F Albosta (VP, Business Development), William H Fraser (VP)

PRINCIPAL ACTIVITIES: ENSERCH Corporation, headquartered in Dallas, Texas, operates worldwide in diversified energy, engineering and construction activities. Initially a natural gas utility company organized in 1909, the Corporation's major businesses today include: petroleum exploration and production; natural gas transmission and distribution; engineering and construction; and oil field services

Principal Subsidiaries and Divisions: Lone Star Gas Co; Enserch Exploration Inc; Pool Co; Samson Ocean Systems Inc; Ebasco Services Inc; Enserch Alaska Services Inc; Humphreys & Glasgow Ltd; Losinger AG (50%); Dorsch Consult AG (minority owned)

Financial Information:

	Dec 31 1985	Dec 31 1986
	$'000	$'000
Sales revenues	3,391,035	2,722,821
Income (loss) before taxes	(38,956)	18,188
Net income (loss)	(38,508)	26,894
Dividends	122,482	99,894
Dividends per share	$1.60*	$1.20
Earnings (loss) per share	($1.12)	$0.17
Common stock	12,471	14,952
Retained income	343,307	272,143
Shareholders equity	1,028,002	973,393
*plus $0.17 value of distribution of Enserch Exploration Partners Ltd units		

Shareholders of record: 33,594 at December 31, 1986
No of Employees: 16,300

ENSOURCE INC
1001 Fannin Street, Houston, TX 77002
Tel: (713) 739 0200

Chairman: Paul D Meadows
President: John B Brock (and Chief Executive Officer)
Senior Executive Officers: E J Dickinson (VP Operations), Keith R Finger (VP and Treasurer), Emelio A Mattorano (VP and Controller), William Malin (VP Exploration and Assistant Secretary)

PRINCIPAL ACTIVITIES: Exploration and production of oil and natural gas
Principal Bank: Chemical Bank
Financial Information:

	$'000
Sales revenues	52,000

No of Employees: 110

ENTENMANN'S INC
1724 Fifth Avenue, Bay Shore, NY 11706
Tel: (516) 273-6000

Chairman: E Shanes; Vice Chairman: William Entenmann
President: David W Johnson (and Chief Executive Officer)
Senior Executive Officers: R D Rosenthal (Executive VP), Charles Urban (VP Manufacturing)

PRINCIPAL ACTIVITIES: Bread and bakery products
Parent Company: General Foods Corporation, White Plains, NY
Financial Information:

	$'000
Sales revenues	142,000

No of Employees: 2,500

ENTERRA CORPORATION
2 Radnor Corporate Center, 100 Matsonford Road, Radnor, PA 19087
Tel: (215) 293-9500

Chairman: Stanley P Gold
President: John A Sergovic (and Chief Operating Officer)
Senior Executive Officers: Lee Daniel (Senior VP), Donald L Meldrum (Senior VP), Winslow Whiting (Senior VP), Frederick C Bertsch III (VP Corporate Development and Chief Financial Officer), Robert J Lynch (VP Administration and Treasurer)

PRINCIPAL ACTIVITIES: Oil and gas production equipment
Principal Subsidiaries: Central Machine Inc. Enterra Instrumentation Technologies Inc; Evans Pipeline Equipment Co; Feecon Corp; Hale Fire Pump Co; Oil Field Rental Service Co Inc; Venture Chemicals Inc; Venture Innovations Inc; Whiting Oilfield Rentals Inc
Principal Bank: Philadelphia National Bank
Financial Information:

	$'000
Sales revenues	141,860

No of Employees: 1,700

ENTERTAINMENT PUBLICATIONS INC
1400 N Woodward Avenue, Birmingham, MI 48011
Tel: (313) 642 8300

Chairman: Hughes L Potiker (and President)
Senior Executive Officers: Edward A Engel (Executive VP), Sheila M Potiker (Executive VP and Secretary), James E Beyer (Treasurer), Joel Laufer (VP Marketing and Advertising)

PRINCIPAL ACTIVITIES: Publishing
Financial Information:

	$'000
Sales revenues	33,000

No of Employees: 200

ENTEX, INC
1600 Smith Street, Houston, TX 77002
Tel: (713) 654-5100
Telex: 792-768

Chairman: Jackson C Hinds (and Chief Executive Officer)
President: Gale L Galloway
Senior Executive Officers: Howard E Bell (Executive VP Distribution Operations), Thomas L Boudreaux (Executive VP, Corporate Planning and Rates), Hubert Gentry Jr (Executive VP and General Counsel), Sam J Jeffrey (Executive VP, Chief Financial Officer and Treasurer), Jimmy L Terrill (Executive VP, Pipeline Operations), Thomas B Burke (Senior VP, Personnel and Administration), W L Clayton (Senior VP, Engineering and Operations), Earl D Coleman (Senior VP, Gas Supply and Large Volume Sales), L P Jones (Senior VP, Marketing), Thomas J Lee Jr (Senior VP, Public Affairs), Ronald K Crowell (Corporate Controller and Secretary)

PRINCIPAL ACTIVITIES: Distribution of natural gas
Principal Subsidiaries: Unit Gas Transmission; Industrial Gas Supply Corp; Louisiana Unit Gas Transmission Co; Datotek Inc
Principal Bank: First City National Bank of Houston
Financial Information:

	Jun 30 1986	Jun 30 1987
	$'000	$'000
Sales revenues	799,685	744,176
Income before taxes*	64,403	78,077
Net (loss)	(84,664)	(77,362)
Dividends	30,521	23,690
Dividends per share	$1.36	$1.05
(Loss) per share	($3.77)	($3.43)
Common stock	22,538	22,601
Retained income	117,197	16,145
Shareholders equity	176,560	76,552
*operating income		

No of Employees: 3,100

ENTRE COMPUTER CENTERS INC
1951 Kidwell Drive, Vienna, VA 22180
Tel: (703) 556 0800

President: Bert I Helfinstein (and Chief Executive Officer)
Senior Executive Officers: James J Edgette (Executive VP and Secretary)

PRINCIPAL ACTIVITIES: Supply of microcomputers and related equipment through franchised retail stores
Principal Bank: Bank of Virginia
Financial Information:

	$'000
Sales revenues	235,000

No of Employees: 230

ENVIRODYNE INDUSTRIES INC

142 East Ontario Street, Tenth Floor, Chicago, IL 60611
Tel: (312) 649 0600
Telefax: (312) 649-0547

Chairman: Ronald K Linde (and President)
Senior Executive Officers: Lawrence C Henry (VP), Maxine H Linde (Secretary and Legal Counsel)

PRINCIPAL ACTIVITIES: Manufacture of a range of plastic products
Principal Subsidiaries: Viskase Corporation; Filmco Industries Inc; Clear Shield National Inc; Pure Aire Corp
Principal Bank: The Northern Trust Co, Chicago, Illinois
Financial Information:

	Dec 31 1985	Dec 31 1986
	$'000	$'000
Sales revenues	50,617	316,620
Income before taxes	8,208	26,965
Net income	7,686	17,347
Earnings per share	$0.60	$1.06
Common stock*	12,844	16,260
Retained income	16,937	34,284
Shareholders equity	23,325	81,297

*average common shares in thousands

No of Employees: 3,000

ENVIRONMENTAL ELEMENTS CORPORATION

3700 Koppers Street, Baltimore, MD 21227
Tel: (301) 368-7000
Telex: WUT 87937 enelco kop bal

Chairman: Raymond A Mason
President: Richard E Hug (and Chief Executive Officer)
Senior Executive Officers: F B Smith (Executive VP and Chief Financial Officer), John C Nichols (Senior VP Administration and Secretary), Henry C Lancaster (VP Engineering), Carl J Becker (VP Manufacturing), Curtis M Snow (VP Technical), Thomas R Schaub (VP and General Manager Air Cleaning Systems Division), Michael W Schneider (VP and General Manager Sound Control Systems Division)

PRINCIPAL ACTIVITIES: Manufacture of pollution control equipment
Principal Bank: American Security Bank
Financial Information:

	$'000
Sales revenues	100,000

No of Employees: 490

ENVIRONMENTAL SYSTEMS COMPANY

1015 Louisiana Street, Little Rock, AR 72202
Tel: (501) 376 8142

Chairman: Melvyn Bell (and Chief Executive Officer; Vice Chairman: H Clay Robinson
President: Joseph W Gillespie
Senior Executive Officers: Jack W Forrest (VP Finance, Secretary, Treasurer and Chief Financial Officer), Charles L Robertson (VP Sales and Marketing), George D Coombs (VP Engineering)

PRINCIPAL ACTIVITIES: Production of waste disposal systems
Principal Bank: MBank Dallas
Financial Information:

	$'000
Sales revenues	57,000

No of Employees: 400

EPSILON

50 Cambridge Street, Burlington, MA 01803
Tel: (617) 273 0250

Chairman: Thomas O Jones (and President)
Senior Executive Officers: Robert J Drummond (Senior VP Marketing), John E Groman (Senior VP Direct Response), Timothy F Hult (Senior VP Information Services), Brian Cahill (Controller), Robert G Romasco (VP New Business), Gene M Henderson (VP Not-for-Profit Division), Charles C Carey Jr (VP Consumer Business), Robin Riggs (VP Direct Response), Charles Harrington (VP Creative Services)

PRINCIPAL ACTIVITIES: Data processing services
Principal Subsidiaries: Master Software Corp
Principal Bank: Shawmut Bank of Boston
Financial Information:

	1987
	$'000
Sales revenues	47,210
Net income	189
Earnings per share	$0.07

No of Employees: 550

EQUATORIAL COMMUNICATIONS COMPANY

189 N Bernardo Avenue, Mountain View, CA 94043
Tel: (415) 969 9500

President: Dean T Mack (and Chief Executive Officer)
Senior Executive Officers: John C Grimm (VP and Treasurer), John L Katsaros (VP), Michael L Olson (VP), Joseph Trombadore (VP)

PRINCIPAL ACTIVITIES: Manufacture of electronic transmitting and detection equipment
Principal Bank: Bank of America
Financial Information:

	$'000
Sales revenues	56,120

No of Employees: 200

EQUIFAX INC

1600 Peachtree St NW, PO Box 4081, Atlanta, GA 30302
Tel: (404) 885-8000

Chairman: Lee Burge
President: Jeff White (and Chief Executive Officer)
Senior Executive Officers: W N Aitken (Senior VP), J A Baker (Senior VP), E T Merrigan (Senior VP), H A Phillips Jr (VP and Treasurer), Ralph N Jones (Corporate VP), W R Flory (VP), Edward D DeVaney Jr (VP and Secretary)

PRINCIPAL ACTIVITIES: Business and government information services
Principal Subsidiaries: Credit Bureau Inc; Equifax Services Inc; Acrofax Inc; Equifax Services Ltd; Elrick & Lavidge Inc; Credit Bureau Marketing Inc; Equifax Marketing Services Inc; Equifax Insurance Systems Inc
Principal Bank: Trust Company Bank of Middle Georgia
Financial Information:

	Dec 31 1985	Dec 31 1986
	$'000	$'000
Sales revenues	566,600	635,000
Net income*	22,400	26,000

*from continuing operations

No of Employees: 10,000

EQUIMARK CORPORATION

Two Oliver Plaza, Pittsburgh, PA 15222
Tel: (412) 288 5000

Chairman: Alan S Fellheimer (and President and Chief Executive Officer)
Senior Executive Officers: William H Brandeis (Executive VP and Chief Financial Officer), Michael E Jehle (Senior VP, Secretary and Legal Counsel), James M Murphy (Executive VP and General Auditor)

PRINCIPAL ACTIVITIES: Banking services
Principal Subsidiaries: Equibank

Financial Information:

	$'000
Revenues	300,000

No of Employees: 1,700

EQUIPMENT RENEWAL COMPANY

PO Box 82, Houston, TX 77001
Tel: (713) 226-5544

Chairman: Warren Harber
President: M L Lewis
Senior Executive Officers: Nolan R Riggs (VP Sales), Bill Smith (VP and Secretary), George Stewart (Treasurer)

PRINCIPAL ACTIVITIES: Oil and gas services and equipment
Parent Company: Kenai Corporation, New York, NY
Principal Bank: Mercantile National Bank at Dallas
Financial Information:

	$'000
Sales revenues	50,000

No of Employees: 300

EQUITABLE BANCORPORATION

100 S Charles St, Baltimore, MD 21201
Tel: (301) 547-4000

Chairman: Alfred Lerner
President: H Grant Hathaway (and Chief Executive Officer)
Senior Executive Officers: Joseph A Cicero (Senior VP and Treasurer), B B Lucas (VP and Secretary)

PRINCIPAL ACTIVITIES: Banking services
Financial Information:

	Dec 31 1985
	$'000
Revenues	401,000
Net income	32,600
Total assets	3,800,000

No of Employees: 2,700

EQUITABLE LIFE ASSURANCE SOCIETY OF THE UNITED STATES

1285 Avenue of the Americas, New York, NY 10019
Tel: (212) 554-1234

Chairman: Robert F Froehlke; Vice Chairmen: Harry D Garber; Richard H Jenrette (and Chief Investment Officer)
President: John B Carter (and Chief Executive Officer)
Senior Executive Officers: David H Harris (Executive VP and Chief of Staff), Robert M Hendrickson (Executive VP and Assistant to President), Glenn H Gettier (Executive VP and Chief Financial Officer), Herbert P Shyer (Executive VP and General Counsel), Ruth S Block (Executive VP Insurance Operations), Raymond B Dolan (Executive VP Agency Operations), Benjamin D Holloway (Executive VP Realty Operations), Donald R Kurtz (Executive VP Securities Operations), Gilbert M Reich (Executive VP Group Operations), Barry V Smith (Executive VP Pension Operations)

PRINCIPAL ACTIVITIES: Mutual life insurance company
Principal Subsidiaries: Bullock Balanced Shares Inc; Bullock Dividend Shares Inc; Bullock Growth Shares Inc; Bullock Tax-Free Shares Inc; Canadian Fund Inc; Equitable International Investment Corp; Alliance Capital Management Corp; Donaldson Lufkin & Jenrette Inc; Equico Capital Corp; Equico Securities Inc; Equitable Casualty Insurance Co; Equitable Investment Management Corp; Autranet Corp; Equitable Life Leasing Corp; Equitable Life Leasing Corp; Equitable Omnilease Corp; Equitable Real Estate Group Inc; Equitable Agri-Business Inc; Equitable Mortgage Resources Inc; Equitable Real Estate Investment Management Corp; Equitable Relocation Management Corp; Equitable Variable Life Insurance Co
Principal Bank: Chase Manhattan Bank
Financial Information:

	Dec 31 1985	Dec 31 1986
	$'000	$'000
Premium income	2,594,630	5,500,913
Investment income	2,744,543	2,733,134

No of Employees: 25,000

EQUITABLE OF IOWA COMPANIES

604 Locust Street, Des Moines, IA 50306
Tel: (515) 245 6911

Chairman: James W Hubbell Jr (and Chief Executive Officer)
President: K R Austin
Senior Executive Officers: Luther L Hill Jr (Executive VP and Secretary), Raymond A Speas (Executive VP), K E Westerbeck (VP and Treasurer)

PRINCIPAL ACTIVITIES: Life insurance services
Principal Subsidiaries: Equitable American Insurance Co; Equitable Investment Service; Equitable Life Insurance Co; Massachusetts Casualty Insurance Co; Tower Locust Ltd; Younkers Inc
Principal Bank: Bankers Trust Company
Financial Information:

	Dec 31 1985
	$'000
Revenues	447,340
Net income	27,900

No of Employees: 1,990

EQUITABLE RESOURCES INC

420 Boulevard of the Allies, Pittsburgh, PA 15219
Tel: (412) 471-7600

President: Donald I Moritz (and Chief Executive Officer)
Senior Executive Officers: John G Caldwell (Executive VP), John C Bertges (Senior VP Finance and Administration), F H Abrew (VP Utility Operations and Real Estate Officer), J J Ayres (VP Corporate Planning), Joseph L Giebel (VP Accounting), A A Mazzei Jr (VP and Legal Counsel), R E Daley (VP and Treasurer), Audrey C Moeller (VP and Secretary)

PRINCIPAL ACTIVITIES: Distribution of natural gas
Financial Information:

	Dec 31 1985	Dec 31 1986
	$'000	$'000
Sales revenues	473,000	455,000
Net income	55,000	54,000

No of Employees: 1,500

EQUITABLE SHIPYARDS, INC

Covington Highway, Madisonville, LA 70447
Tel: (504) 845 3556

President: Archie Dunn
Senior Executive Officers: J F Williams (VP Sales), E B Breeding (Treasurer), J J French (Secretary)

PRINCIPAL ACTIVITIES: Shipbuilding and marine engineering; oil and gas production equipment
Parent Company: Trinity Industries Inc, Dallas, TX
Principal Bank: Republic National Bank of Dallas
Financial Information:

	$'000
Sales revenues	80,000

No of Employees: 150

EQUITABLE VARIABLE LIFE INSURANCE CO

1285 Avenue of the Americas, New York, NY 10019
Tel: (212) 554-0836

Chairman: Robert Barth (and President)
Senior Executive Officers: Dave Hughes (VP Marketing Support)
PRINCIPAL ACTIVITIES: Life insurance

Parent Company: Equitable Life Assurance Society of the United States
Financial Information:

	Dec 31 1985	Dec 31 1986
	$'000	$'000
Premium income	1,065,330	1,501,921
Investment income	248,130	360,508

No of Employees: 75

EQUITEC FINANCIAL GROUP INC

7677 Oakport Street, PO Box 2470, Oakland, CA 94614
Tel: (415) 430 9900

Chairman: Marsden S Cason (and Chief Executive Officer); Vice Chairman: C Todd Conover
President: Kenneth E Nitzberg
Senior Executive Officers: Gerald G Lindquist (VP and Chief Financial Officer), Russell W McDonald (Group Senior VP), Kenneth F Siebel Jr (Group Senior VP), Susan H Kopp (VP Marketing), Vickie R Jackson (VP Personnel Affairs and Secretary)

PRINCIPAL ACTIVITIES: Financial services including securities and commodity broking
Principal Subsidiaries: Equitec Financial Controls Inc; Equitec Financial Planning; Equitec Leasing Co Inc; Equitec Properties Co; Equitec Securities Co; Equitec Savings Bank; Siebel Capital Management Inc

No of Employees: 1,100

ERB LUMBER COMPANY

375 S Eton Road, Birmingham, MI 48012
Tel: (313) 644-5300

Chairman: Fred A Erb (and President)
Senior Executive Officers: John A Theisen (Senior VP), William G Mallon (VP Finance), John M Erb (VP Operations), Harold W Bock (VP Sales), Drayton A McClelland Jr (VP Millwork), Richard Kramer (VP Personnel), William M Green (VP Retail Operations), Noel H Goulston (VP and General Merchandising Manager)

PRINCIPAL ACTIVITIES: Timber industries; lumber and construction materials
Principal Subsidiaries: E E Venture Corp; ERB Building Systems Inc; ERB Lumber Co Inc; First-Troy Corp; McClelland & Sup Coe Inc; Superior Mortgage Co
Principal Bank: Comerica
Financial Information:

	$'000
Sales revenues	150,150

No of Employees: 870

ERBAMONT NV

1266 Main Street, Stamford, CT 06902
Tel: (203) 967-4882

Chairman: Mario Schimberni
President: Alberto M Ferrari (and Chief Executive Officer)
Senior Executive Officers: G Aliprandi (VP and Controller), G A DeFarrari (VP Strategic Planning), Anthony Innamorato (VP), Robert M Stephen (VP and General Council), R C Williams (VP and Chief Financial Officer)

PRINCIPAL ACTIVITIES: Manufacture of pharmaceuticals and veterinary products; manufacture of laboratory equipment and instruments
Principal Bank: Connecticut National Bank
Financial Information:

	$'000
Sales revenues	772,400

No of Employees: 10,000

ERC INTERNATIONAL INC

3211 Jermantown Rd, Box 10107, Fairfax, VA 22030
Tel: (703) 246-0200
Telex: 903044 ERC VINA
Telefax: (703) 246-0761

Chairman: Jack E Aalseth (and Chief Executive Officer)
President: John E Gray (and Chief Operating Officer)
Senior Executive Officers: David A Karish (VP and Treasurer), George R DeVaux (VP), Mark J Elliott (VP), Harrison N Hoppes (VP), David L Parkinson (VP), Joseph G Procopio (VP), William L Sargent (VP, Secretary and Legal Counsel), Leslie W Wright (VP)

PRINCIPAL ACTIVITIES: Professional and technical services, engineering services, hazardous and toxic waste management. Consulting in defense, energy, environmental, biomedical
Trade Names: ERCI
Principal Subsidiaries: International Energy Associates Limited; D-K Associates; Westel Services Inc; EDGe Group
Principal Bank: Maryland National Bank
Financial Information:

	1985	1986
	$'000	$'000
Sales revenues	59,666	95,280
Income before taxes	6,034	7,909
Earnings(1)	3,106	4,146
Net income	2,166	337
Earnings per share(1)	$0.80	$0.98
Common stock(2)	3,900	4,200
Retained income	7,500	7,800
Shareholders equity	16,700	17,400

(1) from continuing operations
(2) number of shares in thousands

Principal Shareholders: Parson Partnership; Mass Mutual Ins Co; Wisconsin Investment Bd
No of Employees: 2,000

ERICO PRODUCTS, INC

34600 Solon Road, Cleveland, OH 44139
Tel: (216) 248-0100

Chairman: E B Neff
President: A M Kies (and Chief Executive Officer)
Senior Executive Officers: R G Smith (VP), A M Kics (VP and General Manager), W E Pritts (VP and General Manager), R B Savage (VP and General Manager), R D Church (Secretary and Treasurer)

PRINCIPAL ACTIVITIES: Metal products including screws, nuts and bolts; conveying equipment; electrical components; welding equipment
Principal Subsidiaries: Dixie Bronze Co of OH; Erico Inc; Erico Jones Co; Knight Metalcraft; Musser Manufacturing Inc; Wateredge-Uniflex Inc
Principal Bank: National City Bank
Financial Information:

	$'000
Sales revenues	82,000

No of Employees: 1,400

ERLANGER, N, BLUMGART & CO, INC

1450 Broadway, New York, NY 10018
Tel: 212 221-7100
Cable: ERBLUM NY
Telex: 125816 ERLBLUM NYK

Chairman: Girard Iason
President: John Iason
Senior Executive Officers: Nathaniel B Lang (Executive VP), Bruce Freeman (VP and Secretary), Michael Sedransk (VP), Hymen Weiner (VP), Anthony DiResta (Treasurer)

PRINCIPAL ACTIVITIES: Manufacture of textiles
Trade Names: EARL-GLO, EARL-LOOM
Principal Subsidiaries: Greenhalgh Mills Corp; Brand & Oppenheimer Inc
Principal Bank: Bankers Trust Company
Financial Information:

	Mar 31 1986	Mar 31 1987
	$'000	$'000
Sales revenues	75,307	75,997
Income before taxes	835	998
Net income	444	465
Common stock	5,000	5,000
Retained income	3,574	4,034
Shareholders equity	4,772	5,232

No of Employees: 100

ERLY INDUSTRIES, INC

10960 Wilshire Blvd, Los Angeles, CA 90024-3708
Tel: (213) 879-1480
Telex: TWX 910 3426896 ecf fa

Chairman: Gerald D Murphy (and President)
Senior Executive Officers: Frank M Feffer Jr (VP and Director, President, Chemonics Industries), Gerard P Thomas (VP, Chief Financial Officer, Secretary and Director), Bill J McFarland (VP and Director, President, Sierra Wine), Lolan M Pullen (VP), Kurt A Grey (VP), Thomas A Whitlock Jr (Corporate Controller)

PRINCIPAL ACTIVITIES: ERLY Industries is one of the largest independent rice companies in the United States and the largest independent bulk processor of wine in the US. The ERLY Sales and Marketing Company sells Colony wines and Hansen beverages. In addition to its export sales, Comet markets packaged branded rice through a joint venture, Comet American Marketing. The Company also manufactures and sells fire retardant chemicals, and provides international agribusiness consulting services
Principal Subsidiaries: Comet Rice Inc; Chemonics Industries Inc; Comet Rice of Puerto Rico Inc; Chemonics Industries (Canada) Ltd (Canada); Chemonics Scientific Ltd (Canada)
Principal Bank: Chase Manhattan Bank
Financial Information:

	Mar 31 1986	Mar 31 1987
	$'000	$'000
Sales revenues	168,007	123,023
Income (loss) before taxes	(16,917)	5,942
Net income	16,167	4,242
Earnings per share net	$5.54	$2.09
Common stock	2,667	1,944
Retained income	31,718	24,900
Shareholders equity	37,359	31,603

No of Employees: 1,200

ERO INDUSTRIES INC

5940 West Touhy Avenue, Chicago, IL 60648
Tel: (312) 647 0700

Chairman: Martin N Sandler (and Chief Executive Officer)
President: Robert J Lipsig (and Chief Operating Officer)
Senior Executive Officers: Thomas M Gasner (Executive VP Operations), Donald J Cashmere (Executive VP Sales), Gerald Gallup (Senior VP Sales), Robert Galecke (VP Sales Administration), Paul P Feder (Treasurer), Laurance P Nathan (Secretary)

PRINCIPAL ACTIVITIES: Manufacture of water skis, life jackets and sleeping bags; wholesale of water sports equipment
Principal Subsidiaries: Ben's Inc
Principal Bank: First National Bank
Financial Information:

	$'000
Sales revenues	31,220

No of Employees: 500

ESCALADE INC

817 Maxwell Avenue, Evansville, IN 47717
Tel: (812) 426 2281

President: Robert E Griffin (and Chief Executive Officer)
Senior Executive Officers: John R Wilson (Secretary, Treasurer and Chief Accounting Officer)

PRINCIPAL ACTIVITIES: Manufacture of sports goods and games equipment
Principal Subsidiaries: Indian Industries Inc; Harvard Sports Inc; Martin Yale Industries
Principal Bank: Citizens National Bank
Financial Information:

	$'000
Sales revenues	35,150

No of Employees: 400

ESCO CORPORATION

2141 N W 25th Avenue, Portland, OR 97210
Tel: (503) 228-2141

Chairman: Henry T Swigert
President: Nick Collins
Senior Executive Officers: Gene Huey (VP Finance), Bill Wamsley (VP International), Richard Ridgley (VP Production), Halle Robb (VP Industrial Service Contracts), Bill Webber (VP Sales and Marketing), Steve Pratt (VP Corporate Manufacturing)

PRINCIPAL ACTIVITIES: Metal castings; process engineering
Principal Bank: Bank of California
Financial Information:

	$'000
Sales revenues	150,000

No of Employees: 1,500

ESI INDUSTRIES INC

1304 Summit Ave, Box 846, Plano, TX 75074-8512

Chairman: Herbert M Gardner
President: Robert J Campbell (and Chief Executive Officer)
Senior Executive Officers: Omer G Kropf (Executive VP), Kenneth W Uselton (VP Finance, Treasurer and Chief Financial Officer), William J Barrett (Secretary and Assistant Treasurer)

PRINCIPAL ACTIVITIES: Manufacture of commercial vehicle bodies
Principal Bank: Manufacturers Hanover Trust
Financial Information:

	$'000
Sales revenues	48,670

No of Employees: 560

ESMARK, INC

55 E Monroe Street, Chicago, IL 60603
Tel: (312) 431-3600

Chairman: Donald P Kelly (and President and Chief Executive Officer)
Senior Executive Officers: Edward J Harrison (VP and General Counsel), Robert E Palenchar (VP Corporate Affairs and Personnel), Philip L Thomas (VP Corporate Communications), William P Carmichael (VP Taxes and Insurance), Geoffrey C Murphy (VP Finance), Michael E McDonnell (VP Corporate Development)

PRINCIPAL ACTIVITIES: Holding company whose activities include food processing, electronic equipment and specialty chemicals
Parent Company: Beatrice Companies Inc, Chicago, IL
Financial Information:

	$'000
Sales revenues	4,000,000

ESSELTE BUSINESS SYSTEMS INC

71 Clinton Road, Garden City, NY 11530

Tel: (516) 741-1477

Cable: ESSPEND

Telex: 221506 OXFIL UR

Chairman: Sven Wallgren

President: Hans Fristedt (and Chief Executive Officer)

Senior Executive Officers: John D Bardner (VP, President of Esselte Letraset Division and Director), Frederick G Chiswell (VP, President of Esselte Dymo Division and Director), Dieter A Kattge (VP and President of Esselte Meto Division), Bjorn E Saven (VP and President of Esselte Pendaflex Division), Hans T G Biorck (VP, Chief Financial Officer and Treasurer), Robert R Black (VP, General Counsel and Secretary)

PRINCIPAL ACTIVITIES: The Company is engaged primarily in the manufacture and marketing of office supplies, graphic arts supplies and retail supplies and equipment. Office supplies which are sold principally under the names Dymo(R), Pendaflex(R), Oxford(R) and Esselte, consists of a broad range of products, including suspension filing systems, loose-leaf binders and embossing tools and tapes. Graphic art supplies include the Letraset range of dry transfer lettering and symbols, the PANTONE(R) color matching system, and extruded aluminum molding and board products for the custom picture framing market. Retail supplies and equipment consist principally of hand-held price marking tools, self-adhesive labels and electronic scales, primarily marketed under the name Meto(R)

Trade Names: PENDAFLEX, DYMO, OXFORD, BOORUM & PEASE, LETRASET, METO

Parent Company: Esselte AB

Principal Subsidiaries: Esselte Pendaflex Corporation

Principal Banks: Citibank NA; Chemical Bank: Morgan Guaranty Trust Co

Financial Information:

	Dec 31 1985	Dec 31 1986
	$'000	$'000
Sales revenues	695,509	972,832
Net income	34,403	45,854
Earnings per share	$1.69	$2.24
Shareholders equity	292,452	346,249

Principal Shareholders: Esselte AB, Stockholm-Solna, Sweden

No of Employees: 10,640

ESSEX CHEMICAL CORPORATION

1401 Broad Street, Clifton, NJ 07015

Tel: (201) 273-6300

Cable: ESSEXCHEM, CLIFTON, NJ

Telex: 710-989-7045

Chairman: L J Polite Jr (and Chief Executive Officer)

Senior Executive Officers: Irwin S Zonis (Senior VP), Maurice J Kopf (Senior VP), William E Leuchten (Senior VP), Walter F Rant (VP Corporate Communications), Jack T Sandberg (VP Engineering), William Van Treuren (VP), Kenneth J Houle (VP), Robert P Beaven (VP), Michael A Appelbaum (VP and Treasurer), Robert Andrews (Controller)

PRINCIPAL ACTIVITIES: General and specialty chemicals; pharmaceuticals

Trade Names: BETASEAL, BETABRACE, BETAMATE

Principal Subsidiaries: Essex Industrial Chemicals, Inc; Essex Specialty Products, Inc; Racon, Inc; Orsynex, Inc; Pioneer Pharmaceuticals, Inc; Essex Vencap Inc

Principal Bank: Manufacturers Hanover Trust Company

Financial Information:

	Dec 31 1985	Dec 31 1986
	$'000	$'000
Sales revenues	190,049	205,624
Income before taxes	14,574	14,529
Net income	8,502	8,836
Dividends	3,191	3,492
Dividends per share	$0.54*	$0.58
Earnings per share	$1.40*	$1.44
Retained income	15,645	21,009
Shareholders equity	51,830	59,425

*adjusted to reflect the impact of stock dividends and splits

No of Employees: 1,000

ESSEX COUNTY GAS COMPANY

7 North Hunt Road, Amesbury, MA 01913

Tel: (617) 388 4000

Chairman: Charles E Billups (and President)

Senior Executive Officers: L David Vincola (Senior VP), Kenneth N Wells (Senior VP), Allen R Neale (VP Planning and Engineering), James H Hastings (Treasurer), George A Miller (VP Corporate Affairs)

PRINCIPAL ACTIVITIES: Distribution of natural gas

Principal Bank: State Street Bank and Trust Company

Financial Information:

	$'000
Sales revenues	36,000

No of Employees: 130

ESTERLINE CORPORATION

1120 Post Road, Darien, CT 06820

Tel: (203) 655-7651

Chairman: Charles H Dyson

President: Thomas P Howes (and Chief Executive Officer)

Senior Executive Officers: Theodore F Brolund (VP and Group Executive), John J Kane (VP and Group Executive), John H MacDonald (VP Finance and Treasurer), Robert D Farley (VP General Counsel and Secretary), Robert A Goldschmidt (VP and Controller), H F Doolittle (VP Corporate Development), Thomas F Gavin (VP Corporate Relations)

PRINCIPAL ACTIVITIES: Manufacture of factory automation equipment for the production of electronic circuits and fabrication of metal, and of quality control, power measurement and process instrumentation

Principal Subsidiaries: Boyar Schultz Corp; Esterline Angus Instrument Corp; Excellon Industries Corp; Tulon Inc; Federal Products Corp; A G Davis Gage & Engineering Co Inc; Hollis Automation Inc; Scientific Columbus Inc; W A Whitney Corp

Principal Bank: Manufacturers Hanover Trust Company

Financial Information:

	1985
	$'000
Sales revenues	254,252
Income before taxes*	3,213
Net income	2,163
Dividends	720
Dividends per share	$0.72
Earnings per share	$0.26
Common stock	8,466
Retained income	94,120
Shareholders equity	103,547

*includes $839,000 extraordinary item

No of Employees: 3,400

E-SYSTEMS, INC

PO Box 660248, Dallas, TX 75266-0248

Tel: (214) 661-1000

Telex: 703365 e-sys dal

Chairman: David R Tacke (and Chief Executive Officer)
President: E Gene Keiffer (and Chief Operating Officer)
Senior Executive Officers: A Lowell Lawson (Executive VP), T D Kelly (VP Finance and Chief Financial Officer), J W Russell (VP Corporate Relations), W R McClain (VP Government and International Operations)

PRINCIPAL ACTIVITIES: Manufacture of a wide range of electronic equipment for the aerospace industry
Principal Bank: Bank of America
Financial Information:

	Dec 31 1985	Dec 31 1986
	$'000	$'000
Sales revenues	926,753	1,135,072
Income before taxes	95,162	109,330
Net income	59,476	61,553
Dividends per share	$0.50	$0.50
Earnings per share	$1.95	$2.00
Shareholders equity	319,000	376,971

No of Employees: 15,000

ETHYL CORPORATION

330 South 4th Street, Richmond, VA 23219
Tel: (804) 788-5000

Chairman: Floyd D Gottwald Jr (and Chairman Executive Committee and Chief Executive Officer); Vice Chairman: Lawrence E Blanchard Jr
President: Bruce C Gottwald (and Chief Operating Officer)
Senior Executive Officers: Lloyd B Andrew Jr (Executive VP and Chief Financial Officer), C R Hailey (Senior VP Plastics), E M Harvey (Senior VP Aluminum), Roger A Moser (Senior VP Research and Development), Ray Wilkins Jr (Senior VP Petroleum Chemicals Group), A P Rowe (VP Corporate Communications), Barry B Abrahamson (VP Petroleum Additives), E Whitehead Elmore (VP, Secretary and Legal Counsel), Patrick D Fitzpatrick (VP and Controller), Gary L Ter Haar (VP Health and Environment), Arthur W Helwig (VP Corporate Planning), Louis A Mitchell (VP Purchasing and Engineering), Henry C Page Jr (VP Employee Relations), Charles B Walker (VP and Treasurer), Paul E Weimer (VP Budget), Andrew O Wikman (VP Industrial Chemicals)

PRINCIPAL ACTIVITIES: Manufacture of industrial chemicals, petrochemicals, plastic and aluminum building products. Other interests include oil and gas exploration and production and services and life and health insurance
Principal Subsidiaries: William L Bonnell Co Inc; Capitol Products Corp; Edwin Cooper & Co GmbH; Elkhorn Coal Corp; Ethyl Development Corp; Ethyl Petro Additives Inc; Ethyl Products Co; Fiberlux Inc; First Colony Life Insurance Co; American Mayflower Life Insurance Co; Hardwicke Chemical Co; Massie Tool & Mold Inc; Modern Technical Molding Inc; Nashwaak Development Co
Principal Bank: Sovran Bank
Financial Information:

	Dec 31 1986
	$'000
Sales revenues	1,579,245
Net income	177,734
Earnings per share	$1.40
Shareholders equity	941,121

No of Employees: 10,500

ETONIC INC

147 Center Street, Brockton, MA 02402
Tel: (617) 583-9100
Telex: WUT 924488 etonic brok

President: Kenneth Snyder
Senior Executive Officers: John Larsen (VP Marketing), John Taylor (VP Finance), Jos Chabot (VP Manufacturing), James Noyes (VP International Sales), Thomas Hess (VP Sales)

PRINCIPAL ACTIVITIES: Specialist footwear manufacture
Parent Company: Colgate-Palmolive Co
Principal Bank: The First National Bank of Boston
Financial Information:

	$'000
Sales revenues	70,000

No of Employees: 1,000

E'TOWN CORPORATION

600 South Avenue, PO Box 788, Westfield, NJ 07090
Tel: (201) 654 1234
Telefax: (201) 232-2719

Chairman: Robert W Kean (and Chief Executive Officer)
President: Chester A Ring III
Senior Executive Officers: Henry S Patterson II (Vice Chairman), Thomas J Cawley (Executive VP), Edward F Cash (VP-Customer Services), Frank L Critelli (Senior VP-Accounting and Rates), Henry S Patterson III (VP-Public Affairs and Human Resources), Gail P Brady (Controller), John Kerr Jr (VP-Secretary-Treasurer), Walter M Braswell (Assistant Secretary and General Attorney), Norbert Wagner (VP-Operations)

PRINCIPAL ACTIVITIES: Supply of water
Principal Subsidiaries: Mt Holly Water Company
Principal Bank: National State Bank
Financial Information:

	1985	1986
	$'000	$'000
Sales revenues	59,570	66,299
Income before taxes	13,979	15,050
Net income	6,393	6,992
Dividends per share	$2.63	$2.74
Earnings per share	$3.24	$3.49
Common stock*	1,973	2,004
Retained income	1,203	1,495
Shareholders equity	52,338	55,350
*number of shares in thousands		

No of Employees: 321

EUROPEAN AMERICAN BANKCORPORATION

10 Hanover Square, New York, NY 10015
Tel: (212) 437-4300

Chairman: Raymond J Dempsey (and President and Chief Executive Officer)
Senior Executive Officers: Rudolf P Guenzel (Executive VP), Arnold L Bartfeld (Executive VP Administration and Legal), Harold L Connell (Executive VP and Chief Financial Officer), Conrad J Gunther Jr (Executive VP Corporate Banking)

PRINCIPAL ACTIVITIES: Banking
Principal Subsidiaries: European American Bank
Principal Bank: European American Bank
Financial Information:

	Dec 31 1985	Dec 31 1986
	$'000	$'000
Net income	20,652	21,123
Shareholders equity	338,624	359,747
Deposits	4,658,606	4,539,610
Total assets	6,654,672	6,744,465

No of Employees: 3,261

EVANS & SUTHERLAND COMPUTER CORPORATION

580 Arapeen Drive, Salt Lake City, UT 84108
Tel: (801) 582-5847

Chairman: David C Evans (and President and Chief Executive Officer)
Senior Executive Officers: Rodney S Rougelot (VP) Gary E Meredith (VP), J Robert Driggs (VP and Chief Financial Officer), Richard F Leahy (VP, Secretary and Treasurer), Susan Mickelsen (VP), C Grant Schultz (Controller), Ivan E

Sutherland (Director), Peter O Crisp (Director), Henry N Christiansen (Director), Stewart Carrell (Director)

PRINCIPAL ACTIVITIES: Evans & Sutherland Computer Corporation designs, manufactures, sells and services special-purpose digital computers and software for such computers. The Company's products rely on two basic underlying technologies: (1) Creation of computer models of real-world objects, and (2) display of computer generated images of such models. Although the Company uses other technologies in the design and manufacture of its products, it believes that it has maintained a leading edge position in these two important areas

Principal Subsidiaries: Evans & Sutherland Ltd (UK); Tripos Associates

Principal Bank: Zions First National Bank

Financial Information:

	Dec 27 1985 $'000	Dec 26 1986 $'000
Sales revenues	79,588	109,264
Net income	6,191	10,877
Earnings per share	$0.72	$1.33
Shareholders equity	65,238	76,664

No of Employees: 1,200

EVANS, BOB, FARMS, INC

3776 South High Street, PO Box 07863-Station G, Columbus, OH 43207-9947

Tel: (614) 491-2225

Chairman: Daniel E Evans (and Chief Executive Officer and Secretary)

Senior Executive Officers: Lawrence E Carroll (Executive VP, Chief Operating Officer, Sausage Division), Robert S Wood (Executive VP, Chief Operating Officer, Restaurant Division), Larry C Corbin (Senior VP Operations, Restaurant Division), Keith P Bradbury (VP, Treasurer and Chief Financial Officer), David P McHolland, (Assistant Corporate Treasurer), W Joseph Griesenbrock (VP, Director of Construction, Restaurant Division), W Lowell Call (VP of Sausage Production-Bidwell, Hillsdale, and Gallipolis), Judy D Harrington (Assistant Corporate Secretary), Victor W Argobright (VP, Director of Field Operations, Restaurant Division), Richard G McLaren (VP Director of Sausage Sales), Roger D Williams (VP, Director of Marketing, Restaurant Division), Howard J Berrey (VP, Director of Real Estate, Restaurant Division), R Earl Beery, (VP of Sausage Production)

PRINCIPAL ACTIVITIES: Bob Evans Farms produces a line of 20 pork sausage products and owns and operates 185 family-style restaurants

Principal Bank: Bancohio National Bank

Financial Information:

	Apr 25 1986 $'000	Apr 24 1987 $'000
Sales revenues	262,682	327,160
Income before taxes	36,608	41,226
Net income	20,575	21,470
Dividends	5,327	6,288
Dividends per share	$0.23	$0.27
Earnings per share	$0.92	$0.95
Common stock	18,131	23,438
Retained income	47,348	62,530
Shareholders equity	127,868	159,359

No of Employees: 13,000

EVANS PRODUCTS CO

1920 E Hallandale Beach Blvd, Hallandale Beach, FL 33009

Tel: (305) 454 6446

Chairman: Victor Posner (and Chief Executive Officer); Vice Chairman: Steven Posner

President: Monford A Orloff (and Chief Operating Officer)

Senior Executive Officers: John C Felten (Executive VP, President Transport Systems and Industrial Group), William C Finkenstaedt (Executive VP, President Shelter Products Group), Maurice E Grossman (Executive VP, President Retail Group), Edward Kahn (Executive VP), Peter H Koehler (Executive VP, President Forest Fiber Products Group), Melvin R Colvin (Senior VP), Raymond Dettore (Senior VP), Walter Sieckman (Senior VP), Jerry F Colson (VP and Controller), F Edwin Denniston (VP Taxes), Leonard Leifert (VP), Renée Mottram (VP), Donald O Nellis (VP and Treasurer), Steven Hopkins (VP Corporate Relations), Tracy Posner (VP)

PRINCIPAL ACTIVITIES: Manufacture of trucks and trailers for road and rail; manufacture and sale of timber and building supplies; sale of pre-manufactured homes and trailers

Principal Subsidiaries: ATEC Industries Inc; Evans Financial Corp; Evans Transportation Co; Evans Railcar Leasing Co; Evans Tank Co; Evans Track Products & Construction Co; Evans Track-Work Leasing Co; Evans Trailer Leasing Co; Louisville NW Albany Corydon Railroad; Railway Track Work Co; Lindsley Inc; Minneapolis Electric Steel Castings; PDI Inc

Principal Bank: Philadelphia National Bank

Financial Information:

	$'000
Sales revenues	1,400,000

No of Employees: 13,000

EVANS TRANSPORTATION COMPANY

2550 Golf Road, Rolling Meadows, IL 60008

Tel: (312) 640-7000

Senior Executive Officers: C R Barney (VP and Chief Operating Officer), William M Peyton (VP), Jerry Ehrlich (VP)

PRINCIPAL ACTIVITIES: Manufacture and leasing of railroad vehicles and truck trailers; leasing

Parent Company: Evans Products Co

Principal Bank: Continental Illinois National Bank of Chicago

Financial Information:

	$'000
Sales revenues	205,000

No of Employees: 2,000

EVEREST & JENNINGS INTERNATIONAL

2310 S Sepulveda Blvd, Los Angeles, CA 90064

Tel: (213) 479-4141

Chairman: Gerald M Jennings (and President)

Senior Executive Officers: Bruce C Blickensderfer (Executive VP), C B Call (VP Operations), Richard S Hopkins (VP Finance), David D Jennings (VP)

PRINCIPAL ACTIVITIES: Processing of aluminum and non-ferrous metals; manufacture of wheelchairs and rehabilitation and medical equipment

Principal Subsidiaries: Bernic Screw Products Inc; Ev-Jen Medical Inc; Thompson-Blair Inc; Everest & Jennings Export Sales Corp; Everest & Jennings Inc; Jennings Investment Co; International Medical Equipment Corp; Metal Products Group Inc; Sigma Plating Co

Principal Bank: Security Pacific National Bank

Financial Information:

	$'000
Sales revenues	174,200

No of Employees: 3,200

EXAR CORPORATION

750 Palomar Avenue, Sunnyvale, CA 94086

Tel: (408) 732 7970

Chairman: Ken Sato

President: Nabuo Hatta

Senior Executive Officers: Ronald W Guire (VP, Chief Financial Officer and Secretary), Stephen M Robb (Manager Finance), Keizo Ueda (Controller)

PRINCIPAL ACTIVITIES: Manufacture of electronic components including semiconductors
Financial Information:

	$'000
Sales revenues	57,000

No of Employees: 540

EXCEL INDUSTRIES, INC
1120 N Main Street, Elkhart, IN 46514
Tel: (219) 264-2131

Chairman: J J Lohman (and President and Chief Executive Officer)
Senior Executive Officers: J D Burt (VP), J O Futterknecht Jr (VP), W M Gude (Secretary and Treasurer and Chief Financial Officer)

PRINCIPAL ACTIVITIES: Manufacture of vehicle windows and other components for the automotive industry
Principal Subsidiaries: Excel of Tennessee, Inc; Excel Industries of Florida, Inc; Machine-Rite Products, Inc; Excel Metalcraft Ltd; Belvedere Corporation; Excel of California, Inc; Excel Manufacturing of Kentucky Inc; Urethane Technology Inc
Principal Bank: Ameritrust Company National Association
Financial Information:

	Dec 31 1985	Dec 31 1986
	$'000	$'000
Sales revenues	92,159	148,202
Income before taxes	4,382	7,854
Net income	2,537	4,024
Dividends	1,266(1)	1,496(2)
Dividends per share(3)	$0.29	$0.32
Earnings per share(3)	$0.63	$0.85
Shareholders equity	13,411	33,698
(1) and 10% stock		
(2) and 5-for-4 split		
(3) adjusted for splits and stock dividends		

Principal Shareholders: Ford Motor Co, Inc (40%)
No of Employees: 2,000

EX-CELL-O CORPORATION
2855 Coolidge, Troy, MI 48084
Tel: (313) 637-1230

Chairman: E Paul Casey (and President and Chief Executive Officer)
Senior Executive Officers: Seymour S Feuer (Executive VP), E Earl Fleck (Group VP), Otto Kern (Group VP), Derek Plummer (Group VP), Walter B Fisher (VP and Controller), J William Lenz (VP), Alan D MacDonald (VP, Secretary and General Counsel), Richard A McWhirter (VP), Thomas J Stuart (VP and Treasurer), Terry W Wilson (VP), Henry E Gajewski (Assistant VP), John G Turner (Assistant VP), Jack A Stone (Assistant Treasurer), Walter E Vashak Jr (Assistant Secretary)

PRINCIPAL ACTIVITIES: Ex-Cell-O is engaged in the manufacture and sale of a wide variety of products primarily for industry. For financial reporting purposes, Ex-Cell-O has organized its business into four industry segments and a category comprised of several smaller business segments which is treated as a fifth industry segment. The segments are as follows: Industrial Equipment, Automotive Components, Aerospace, Ordnance and Specialty Products
Trade Names: Pure-Pak, FlexCenter
Parent Company: Textron Inc
Principal Subsidiaries: Ex-Cell-O Credit Corporation; Ace Industries Inc; Atlantic Aerospace Inc
Principal Bank: National Bank of Detroit

Financial Information:

	$'000
Sales revenues	1,140,000

No of Employees: 15,100

EXCELLON INDUSTRIES
23915 Garnier Street, Torrance, CA 90509
Tel: (213) 325-8000

President: John Pomeroy (and Chief Executive Officer)
Senior Executive Officers: Earnest Barnett (VP and Treasurer), Richard Crow (VP Marketing), James Henshall (VP Engineering), Clifford Graves (VP Manufacturing), Robert Weil (VP and Controller)

PRINCIPAL ACTIVITIES: Manufacture of machine tools
Parent Company: Esterline Corporation, Darien, CT
Principal Bank: Manufacturers Hanover Trust Co
Financial Information:

	$'000
Sales revenues	60,000

No of Employees: 900

EXCHANGE INTERNATIONAL CORPORATION
120 South LaSalle Street, Chicago, IL 60603
Tel: (312) 781 8000
Cable: EXCHANBANK
Telex: 25-3454

Chairman: Ira J Kaufman (and Chief Executive Officer); Deputy Chairman: John Rau
President: Norman Bobins
Senior Executive Officers: Charles S Bishop Jr (Executive VP), Thomas C Heagy (Executive VP), Walter M Macur (Executive VP), Michael A Murray (Executive VP), M Hill Hammock (Executive VP), Jack P Katz (Senior Credit Officer), Theodore E Schultz (First VP and Treasurer), Kent L Suarez (First VP and Auditor), Robert Dunn Glick (Secretary)

PRINCIPAL ACTIVITIES: Banking
Principal Subsidiaries: Exchange National Bank of Chicago
Financial Information:

	Dec 31 1986
	$'000
Revenues	170,216
Income before	21,842
Net income	10,154
Dividends	379
Dividends per share	$0.05
Earnings per share	$1.10
Common stock	10,603
Retained income	47,103
Stockholders equity	108,788
Deposits	1,411,818
Total assets	1,921,180

No of Employees: 820

EXECUTIVE LIFE INSURANCE CO
9777 Wilshire Blvd, Beverly Hills, CA 90212
Tel: (213) 273-4202

Chairman: Fred Carr (and President)
Senior Executive Officers: Cheryl A Wada (Executive VP and Chief Operating Officer), William J Adams (Senior VP), Merle A Horst (Senior VP, Chief Financial Officer and Treasurer), Joe E Suske (Senior VP Sales), Gary R Schulte (Senior VP Marketing)

PRINCIPAL ACTIVITIES: Insurance
Parent Company: First Executive Corporation, Beverly Hills, CA (92%)
Principal Bank: Security Pacific National Bank

Financial Information:

	Dec 31 1985	Dec 31 1986
	$'000	$'000
Premium income	1,365,688	1,615,782
Investment income	574,244	800,593

No of Employees: 800

EXECUTONE, INC

2 Jericho Plaza, Jericho, NY 11753
Tel: (516) 681-4000

President: William Y O'Connor
Senior Executive Officers: Robert A Barone (VP Distribution Services), Martin Gelerman (VP Personnel and Administration Services), James W Holland (VP Communications), Joseph P Holohan (VP Legal and Assistant Secretary), William A Jacobson (VP Marketing), John B Millard (VP Engineering), John T O'Kane (VP Management Information Services), Gerald P Paris (VP Finance)

PRINCIPAL ACTIVITIES: Manufacture of communications equipment
Parent Company: Contel Corporation, Atlanta, GA
Principal Bank: Manufacturers Hanover Trust Co
Financial Information:

	$'000
Sales revenues	180,000

No of Employees: 1,500

EXPOSAIC INDUSTRIES, INC

1373 Boggs Drive, Mount Airy, NC 27030
Tel: (919) 786-2141

Chairman: Howard O Woltz Jr (and President)
Senior Executive Officers: Thomas J Cumby (Executive VP Arch Division), Kenneth W Leonard (VP Administration), Gary D Kniskern (Secretary and Treasurer)

PRINCIPAL ACTIVITIES: Exposiac Industries, Inc. is one of the largest wire manufacturers in the United States, producing welded wire reinforcement, high carbon wire, industrial wire, and nails. The wire products are used in the construction, furniture, bedding, automative, and appliance industries. The Company is also a major manufacturer of architectural precast and structural prestressed concrete products.
Principal Subsidiaries: (100% owned unless stated): Intersteel Corporation; Rappahannock Wire Co; Exposaic Wire Co; Federal Nail Mfg Co (80%)
Principal Bank: First Union Bank, Charlotte, NC
Financial Information:

	Sep 30 1986	Sep 30 1987
	$'000	$'000
Sales revenues	100,416	178,607
Income before taxes	7,118	6,397
Net income	3,773	4,729
Dividends	556	584
Dividends per share	$0.22	$0.23
Earnings per share*	$1.37	$1.58
Common stock	4,632	5,107
Retained income	12,519	12,956
Shareholders equity	20,005	24,202

*fully diluted

No of Employees: 1,145

EXTEL CORPORATION

4000 Commercial Avenue, Northbrook, IL 60062
Tel: (312) 291-2500
Telex: WUT 724398 extel nbrk

Chairman: Kenneth R Anderson (and President)
Senior Executive Officers: Rao Ashok (Senior VP Marketing), John M Connolly (Senior VP Finance and Treasurer), Daniel C Wonak (VP Engineering), Spencer Heynis (VP Manufacturing), James G Johnson (VP), Lawrence A Hagemann (VP)

PRINCIPAL ACTIVITIES: Manufacture of equipment for the telecommunications industry
Parent Company: Northern Engineering Industries PLC, Newcastle-on-Tyne, UK
Principal Bank: Continental Illinois National Bank and Trust Co
Financial Information:

	$'000
Sales revenues	40,000

No of Employees: 400

EXXON CORPORATION

1251 Avenue of the Americas, New York, NY 10020-1198
Tel: (212) 333-6900

Chairman: Lawrence G Rawl (and Chief Executive Officer)
President: L R Raymond
Senior Executive Officers: J F Bennett (Senior VP), J G Clarke (Senior VP), D M Cox (Senior VP), M E J O'Loughlin (Senior VP), L R Raymond (Senior VP), R H Beresford (VP-Petroleum Products), R N Dolph (VP),Richard E Faggioli (VP and Secretary), C M Harrison (VP-Producing), E C Holmer (VP), R M Ingram (VP), W D Kruger (VP), R J Kruizenga (VP-Corporate Planning), R S Lombard (VP and General Counsel), G B McCullough (VP-Employee Relations), T J McDonagh (VP-Medicine and Environmental Health), Randall Meyer (VP), A L Monroe (VP and Controller), W B Nobles (VP-Communications and Computer Sciences), F M Perkins (VP-Gas), E A Robinson (VP and Treasurer), R A Schroder (VP and General Tax Counsel), D E Smiley (VP-Washington Office), Stephen Stamas (VP-Public Affairs), R A Winslow (VP)

PRINCIPAL ACTIVITIES: Divisions and affiliated companies of Exxon Corporation operate in the United States and over 80 other countries. Their principal business is energy, involving exploration for and production of crude oil and natural gas, manufacturing of petroleum products and transportation and sale of crude oil, natural gas and petroleum products; exploration for and mining and sale of coal and fabrication of nuclear fuel. Exxon Chemical Company is a major manufacturer and marketer of petrochemicals. Exxon is also engaged in exploration for and mining of minerals other than coal. Reliance Electric Company, an affiliate, manufactures, markets and services a broad line of industrial equipment. Exxon conducts extensive research programs in support of these businesses and provides capital to innovative new ventures, some of which are not related to these businesses
Principal Subsidiaries: Divisions of Exxon Corporation: Exxon International Company; Exxon Chemical Company; Exxon Minerals Company; Esso Middle East; Exxon Company, USA; Exxon Enterprises. Affiliated Companies: Exxon Research and Engineering Company; Esso Exploration Inc; Esso Eastern Inc; Imperial Oil Ltd; Reliance Electric Company; Esso Europe Inc; Exxon Production Research Company; Esso Inter-America Inc
Financial Information:

	Dec 31 1986
	$'000
Revenues	69,888,000
Net income	5,360,000
Earnings per share	$7.42
Shareholders equity	32,012,000

No of Employees: 150,000

EXXON PIPELINE CO

800 Bell Avenue, Houston, TX 77002
Tel: (713) 656-4364

President: L D Wooddy Jr
Senior Executive Officers: J C Stone (VP Operations), J I Finch (VP Administration, Treasurer and Controller)

PRINCIPAL ACTIVITIES: Crude oil and petroleum pipeline operations
Parent Company: Exxon Corporation, New York, NY

Financial Information:

	Dec 31 1985
	$'000
Sales revenues	977,915
Net income	361,570
Shareholders equity	254,031

No of Employees: 752

E-Z-EM INC

7 Portland Avenue, Westbury, NY 11590
Tel: (516) 333 8230

Chairman: Howard S Stern (and President and Chief Executive Officer)
Senior Executive Officers: George P Carden (VP International Sales Marketing), Edward D Cohen (VP Domestic Sales and Marketing), Franklin R Greene (VP Manufacturing), Joseph A Rüna (VP Research and Development), Arthur L Zimmer (VP New Projects), W Philip Van Kirk (Secretary)

PRINCIPAL ACTIVITIES: Manufacture of medical equipment
Principal Bank: National Westminster Bank
Financial Information:

	$'000
Sales revenues	40,000

No of Employees: 400

F L SMIDTH & CO

See SMIDTH, F L, & CO

F W WOOLWORTH CO

See WOOLWORTH, F W, CO

FAB INDUSTRIES, INC

200 Madison Avenue, New York, NY 10016
Tel: (212) 279-9000

Chairman: Samson Bitensky (and President)
Senior Executive Officers: Howard A Soren (VP Finance and Administration)

PRINCIPAL ACTIVITIES: Manufacture of knitted fabrics
Principal Bank: Citibank
Financial Information:

	Nov 30 1986
	$'000
Sales revenues	121,782
Income before taxes	16,770
Net income	10,726
Dividends	2,179
Dividends per share	$0.60
Earnings per share	$2.95
Common stock	2,950
Shareholders equity	79,408

No of Employees: 1,500

FABERGE INCORPORATED

725 Fifth Avenue, New York, NY 10022
Tel: (212) 735-9300

Chairman: Daniel J Manella (and Chief Executive Officer)
Senior Executive Officers: Kenneth Leccesse (Executive VP Sales, Chief Financial Officer and Secretary)

PRINCIPAL ACTIVITIES: Manufacture of clothing, fragrances and toiletries; Licensing of trademarks
Trade Names: "McGregor", "Botany 500", Bert Pultizer, Billy the Kid, Anvil, Coat Tails, Fabergé, Brut, Aquanet, Babe
Parent Company: McGregor Holding Corp

Financial Information:

	Jan 31 1986	Jan 31 1987
	$'000	$'000
Sales revenues	482,900	554,600
Income before taxes	33,900	49,200
Net income	16,700	25,900
Common stock	61,900	61,900
Retained income	30,100	51,300
Shareholders equity	90,600	112,000

No of Employees: 6,600

FABRIC WHOLESALERS INC

2035 Northeast 181st Avenue, Portland, OR 97230
Tel: (503) 666 4511

President: Tony J Bosboom (and Chief Executive Officer)
Senior Executive Officers: William E Maher (Senior VP Real Estate), Jeffrey D Boyd (VP Finance), Judy Bennett (VP Advertising), Ray Cantu (VP Store Installations), Ron Hamilton (VP Retail Sales), Ron Westcott (VP Purchasing), Jacques B Nichols (Treasurer and Secretary)

PRINCIPAL ACTIVITIES: Retail trade in sewing and needlework supplies
Principal Bank: US National Bank
Financial Information:

	$'000
Sales revenues	48,000

No of Employees: 1,400

FABRI-CENTERS OF AMERICA INC

23550 Commerce Park Road, Beachwood, OH 44122
Tel: (216) 464 2500

Chairman: Martin Rosskamm
President: Alan Rosskamm (and Chief Executive Officer)
Senior Executive Officers: Brian Burton (Executive VP, Chief Financial Officer and Chief Operating Officer), Michael Feuer (Senior VP Marketing, Advertising and Corporate Communications), Travis Ballew (VP Merchandising), Roger Lytle (VP Personnel), Barry Sands (VP Corporate Planning), John Stec (VP Real Estate), Gordon Williams (VP Store Operations), Alma Zimmerman (VP), Justin Zimmerman (Senior VP), Betty Rosskamm (Secretary and Treasurer)

PRINCIPAL ACTIVITIES: Retail trade in sewing machines, fabrics and notions
Principal Bank: AmeriTrust Company
Financial Information:

	$'000
Sales revenues	233,000

No of Employees: 7,000

FABSTEEL COMPANY

PO Box 688, Hwy 80E, Waskam, TX 75692
Tel: (214) 687 3325

Chairman: Fletcher T Thomsen (and President)
Senior Executive Officers: Robert E Burnley (Executive VP), William S Oliver (Senior VP), A W Kinnard (VP Sales), Glynn Tompkins (VP Purchasing), John Whitaker (VP Engineering), Margaret J Black (VP and Secretary)

PRINCIPAL ACTIVITIES: Metal fabrication
Principal Subsidiaries: Fabsteel Co LA; Fabsteel of Texarkana
Principal Bank: Interfirst Bank
Financial Information:

	$'000
Sales revenues	50,000

No of Employees: 500

FACET ENTERPRISES, INC

6100 S Yale Avenue, Tulsa, OK 74136
Tel: (918) 492-1800
Telex: 820717

President: James R Malone (and Chief Executive Officer)
Senior Executive Officers: Clyde Wyant (Executive VP), Richard C Brinckerhoff (VP), Alan H Spicer (VP), Vincent J Riley (VP), James D Murphy (VP), Patrick B Burns (VP), Robert A Geweniger (VP), Charles S Chapel (Secretary)

PRINCIPAL ACTIVITIES: Manufacturer and marketer of Purolator name-brand automotive filters and private label automotive filters, filtration products, transportation components, wellhead equipment and motion control products sold to industrial and commercial users as well as distributors mainly in the United States and Europe
Trade Names: "POSITORK"(R) Starter Drives, Purolator(R), Zenith Carburetors(R)
Principal Subsidiaries: Purolator Products Inc; Facet Automotive Filter Company; Facet Aerospace Products Company; Woods Energy Products Company; Quantek
Principal Bank: Bank of Oklahoma, Tulsa NA
Financial Information:

	Sep 30 1985	Sep 30 1986
	$'000	$'000
Sales revenues	165,721	171,854
Income before taxes	1,280	2,760
Net income	1,222	2,527
Earnings per share	$0.40	$0.82
Common stock	3,018	3,108
Retained (deficit)	(9,079)	(6,705)
Shareholders equity	40,738	44,118

No of Employees: 3,600

FAG BEARINGS CORPORATION

Hamilton Avenue, Stamford, CT 06904
Tel: (203) 327-1960

Chairman: G Schafer
President: M C Frowein
Senior Executive Officers: Gerald K Dankelson (VP Manufacturing), Larry E Wilson (VP Marketing), Walter P Wieland (VP Engineering), Gino DiTomaso (VP Finance and Comptroller), A M Raffaele (VP Human Resources)

PRINCIPAL ACTIVITIES: Manufacture of ballbearings
Parent Company: FAG Kugelfischer Georg Schäfer & Co, Schweinfurt, Germany
Principal Bank: Morgan Guaranty
Financial Information:

	$'000
Sales revenues	93,000

No of Employees: 640

FAIR LANES INC

1112 North Rolling Road, Baltimore, MD 21228
Tel: (301) 788 6300

Chairman: Archibald E MacKay; Vice Chairman: David P Gordon
President: Walter J Hall
Senior Executive Officers: Stephen P Freidberg (Executive VP and Chief Operating Officer), James J Fogarty (VP Administration), Gerald J Stank (VP, Treasurer and Chief Financial Officer), Phillip E McKenna (Controller), Marc J Lipchin (Legal Counsel and Assistant Secretary), Edward E Obstler (Secretary), Timothy L McManus (VP Planning)

PRINCIPAL ACTIVITIES: Bowling alleys and bowling equipment
Principal Subsidiaries: English Co; International Bowl Equipment Supplies; Sportland-Durham Bowl Lanes
Principal Bank: Maryland National Bank
Financial Information:

	$'000
Sales revenues	93,000

No of Employees: 5,500

FAIRCHILD CAMERA & INSTRUMENT CORPORATION

464 Ellis Street, Mountain View, CA 94042
Tel: (415) 962-5011

President: Thomas C Roberts (and Chief Executive Officer)
Senior Executive Officers: N Stone (VP, General Counsel, Secretary and Treasurer), T A Longo (VP Microsystems Group), Donald Brooks (VP), T Ley (VP Technical)

PRINCIPAL ACTIVITIES: Electronic equipment; telecommunications and photographic equipment
Parent Company: Schlumberger Ltd, New York, NY
Principal Bank: The Bank of New York
Financial Information:

	$'000
Sales revenues	534,000

No of Employees: 21,300

FAIRCHILD INDUSTRIES INC

300 W Service Rd, Box 10803, Chantilly, VA 22021
Tel: (703) 478-5800

Chairman: Emanuel Fthenakis (and President and Chief Executive Officer)
Senior Executive Officers: James R Wilson (Executive VP and Chief Financial Officer), Charles B Husick (Senior VP Corporate Planning and Evaluation), John J McDonnell (Senior VP and Legal Counsel), Philip Schneider (Senior VP and Group Executive Communications and Electronics), John W Townsend Jr (Senior VP and Group Executive Aerospace), Rodney L Woodworth (Senior VP and Group Executive Commercial/Industrial), Harold Gruen (VP, President Fairchild Communication Networks & Services Co), Hal Howes (VP Government Relations), John W Sandford (VP, President Fairchild Republic Co), Gordon A Smith (VP, President Aerospace Products Division), Robert J Terry (VP and Tax Counsel), Thomas Turner (VP Marketing), Richard G Orr (VP, President Fairchild Industrial Products Co), James M Schell (VP and Treasurer), John D Jackson (VP and Secretary), James P Allen (VP and Controller)

PRINCIPAL ACTIVITIES: Aircraft building and the manufacture of aerospace equipment and components; satellite communications systems
Principal Subsidiaries: American Satellite Corp; Fairchild Aircraft Corp; Fairchild General Aero Inc; Sat-Air Inc; Fairchild Communication Networks & Services Co; Fairchild Communications Products Co; Fairchild Credit Corp; Fairchild Data Corp; Fairchild Industrial Products Co; Fairchild Precision Fabrication Center; Fairchild Space Communications Co; Space Communications Co; Insouth Microsystems Inc
Principal Bank: Bankers Trust Company
Financial Information:

	Dec 31 1985	Dec 31 1986
	$'000	$'000
Sales revenues	917,293	967,300
Net (loss)	(167,095)	(9,962)
Shareholders equity	45,396	28,873

No of Employees: 12,700

FAIRFIELD COMMUNITIES INC

PO Box 3375, 2800 Cantrell Road, Little Rock, AR 72202
Tel: (501) 664-6000

Chairman: C Randolph Warner (and President and Chief Executive Officer); Vice Chairman: Robert L Callender

Senior Executive Officers: A H Adams III (Executive VP), Robert L Boone (Senior VP Corporate Development), Vincent W Dean (Senior VP Fairfield Homes Group), Terry L Flora (Senior VP and General Counsel), Joe T Gunter (Senior VP and Special Counsel), William J Hoag (Senior VP Marketing and Advertising), John W McConnell (Senior VP, Treasurer and Chief Financial Officer), Jerry C Spearman (Senior VP Resort Community Group), Robert W Howeth (VP), James F Mackley (VP Sales), David F Marano (VP Corporate Planning), Pamela K Szedelyi (VP Resort Operations), Paul C Watson (VP Loan Administration), W Richard Young (VP and Controller), James F Zecchini (VP Operations Control)

PRINCIPAL ACTIVITIES: Building and management of residential property for retirement and holiday purposes
Principal Subsidiaries: Fairfield Acceptance Corp; Fairfield Harbour Inc; Fairfield Mortgage Corp; Fairfield Pagosa Inc; Imperial Life Insurance Co
Principal Bank: First National Bank of Boston
Financial Information:

	$'000
Sales revenues	270,000

No of Employees: 3,000

FAIRMONT FINANCIAL INC
4111 West Alameda Avenue, Burbank, CA 91505
Tel: (818) 843 0755

Chairman: Joseph G Havlick (and President); Vice Chairman: Sydney M Irmas
Senior Executive Officers: Stanley Brown (Executive VP), Lee W Spitler Jr (Senior VP), Thomas G Bernard (Chief Financial Officer and Treasurer), Tanna P Handley (Secretary), Trude A Tsujimoto (Secretary and Legal Counsel)

PRINCIPAL ACTIVITIES: Insurance services
Principal Subsidiaries: Fairmont Insurance Co; Fairmont Leasing Corp
Principal Bank: Union Bank
Financial Information:

	Dec 31 1985 $'000
Revenues	78,750
Net income	5,140

No of Employees: 420

FALCON JET CORPORATION
Teterboro Airport, Teterboro, NJ 07608
Tel: (201) 288-5300
Telex: WUT 642187 fjcterm ttbr

Chairman: Serge Dassault
President: Frank W Wisekal
Senior Executive Officers: Roy E Bergstrom (Senior VP Marketing), Gerard Meyer (Senior VP Customer Support), F T Brown (Senior VP and General Manager Little Rock), J M Young (VP Finance and Administration)

PRINCIPAL ACTIVITIES: Aircraft manufacture
Trade Names: Falcon Jet
Parent Company: Avions Marcel Dassault-Breguet Aviation
Principal Bank: Citibank
Financial Information:

	$'000
Sales revenues	205,000

No of Employees: 1,000

FALCON PRODUCTS INC
9387 Dielman Industrial Drive, Saint Louis, MO 63132
Tel: (314) 991 9200

Chairman: Franklin A Jacobs (and President)
Senior Executive Officers: Robert L Rosenfeld Jr (VP Finance), Donald Maitland (Secretary), Joseph Horvath (Senior VP Manufacturing)

PRINCIPAL ACTIVITIES: Manufacture of furniture
Principal Bank: Marine Midland Bank
Financial Information:

	$'000
Sales revenues	31,000

No of Employees: 800

FALLS DAIRY CO
Jim Falls, WI 54748
Tel: (715) 382-4113

President: Ervin Purdeu
Senior Executive Officers: B Axness (Controller)

PRINCIPAL ACTIVITIES: Dairy Products
Parent Company: DEC International Inc
Principal Bank: First Wisconsin Bank
Financial Information:

	$'000
Sales revenues	120,000

No of Employees: 200

FALSTAFF BREWING CORPORATION
312 W 8th Street, Vancouver, WA 98660
Tel: (206) 695-3381

Chairman: Lutz Issleib (and President and Chief Executive Officer)
Senior Executive Officers: Gary Damveld (VP Sales), Marvin Bowerman (VP), John Schiess (Secretary and Treasurer)

PRINCIPAL ACTIVITIES: Brewing
Financial Information:

	$'000
Sales revenues	52,530

No of Employees: 270

FAMILIAN CORPORATION
7651 Woodman Avenue, Van Nuys, CA 91402
Tel: (213) 786-9720

Chairman: Leonard Shapiro
President: Bernard J Shapiro
Senior Executive Officers: Leonard D Gross (Chief Financial Officer and Treasurer)

PRINCIPAL ACTIVITIES: Manufacture of valves, fittings, plastic and metal tubing for plumbing
Principal Subsidiaries: Custom Pipe & Coupling Corp; Familian Pipe & Supply Co; Familian Sierra Craft Inc; Kelly Pipe Co Inc; MG Coupling Co
Principal Bank: Bank of America
Financial Information:

	$'000
Sales revenues	280,000

No of Employees: 1,000

FAMILY CIRCLE, INC
488 Madison Avenue, New York, NY 10022
Tel: (212) 593-8000

Chairman: William H Davis; Vice Chairman: William T Kerr
President: Arthur Hettich
Senior Executive Officers: David L Gorham (Senior VP), Benjamin Handelman (Senior VP), Michael E Ryan (Senior VP), Thomas C Redd (VP Advertising Sales), Richard H Steinman (VP Finance), Vito Colaprico (VP Production), John A Pfriender (VP Promotions), Robert L Neary (VP), James Fraguela (VP Advertising and Sales), Lawrence Kane (VP), Jesse Iverson (VP Circulation), Susan Baron (VP), David P F Hess (VP), James W Wall (VP)

PRINCIPAL ACTIVITIES: Publishing of magazines
Parent Company: New York Times Company, New York, NY
Principal Bank: Chemical Bank

Financial Information:

	$'000
Sales revenues	115,000

No of Employees: 450

FAMILY DOLLAR STORES INC

PO Box 25800, 10401 Old Monroe Road, Charlotte, NC 28105
Tel: (704) 847 6961

Chairman: Leon Levine (and Chief Executive Officer)
President: Lewis E Levine
Senior Executive Officers: George R Mahoney Jr (Senior VP, Legal Counsel and Secretary), James A Seagraves (Senior VP Store Operations), Stephen G Simms (Senior VP Real Estate and Construction), David J Krause (VP Finance), Richard H Griner (VP Distribution and Transportation), Robert S Parker (VP Coss Prevention), Albert S Rorie (VP Data Processing), Douglas B Sullivan (VP Real Estate), Philip W Thompson (VP Store Operations), Norman B Weizer (VP Store Operations)

PRINCIPAL ACTIVITIES: Retail variety stores
Principal Bank: NCNB National Bank
Financial Information:

	1986 $'000
Sales revenues	488,000
Net income	31,000

No of Employees: 6,000

FAMOUS RESTAURANTS INC

4725 North Scottsdale Road, Suite 350, Scottsdale, AZ 85251
Tel: (602) 990 1123

Chairman: Dennis B Mullen (and President and Chief Executive Officer)
Senior Executive Officers: Doyle R Judd (VP, Chief Financial Officer, Secretary and Treasurer), Dan Anderson (VP Operations), Geoffrey R Zinke (VP Research and Development)

PRINCIPAL ACTIVITIES: Restaurant chain; seafood and Mexican specialities
Principal Bank: First Interstate Bank
Financial Information:

	$'000
Sales revenues	50,660

No of Employees: 2,600

FANNY FARMER CANDY SHOPS, INC

20 Harvard Mill Square, Wakefield, MA 01880
Tel: (617) 245-0300
Telex: WUT 923485 wkfd
Telefax: (617) 245-7972

President: B Millet (and Chief Executive Officer)
Senior Executive Officers: A Graham (VP Finance and Secretary), B Mastrodicasa (VP Manufacturing), S Kahn (VP Shops), N Connelly (VP Merchandise and Marketing)

PRINCIPAL ACTIVITIES: Manufacture and retail of candy
Parent Company: Midial, France
Principal Subsidiaries: Fannie Farmer Cookbook
Principal Bank: Bank of New England
Financial Information:

	$'000
Sales revenues	50,000

No of Employees: 2,000

FANSTEEL INC

One Tantalum Place, North Chicago, IL 60064
Tel: (312) 689-4900
Telex: TWX 910 235 1577 fansteel n c

Chairman: Keith R Garrity (and Chief Executive Officer)
President: Arthur J Wagner Jr (and Chief Operating Officer)
Senior Executive Officers: Howard J Kerr (VP and General Manager), Robert W McGinnis (VP Corporate Planning and Operations Analysis), Conrad L Brown (VP and General Manager Metals Division), Stanley W Lindroth (VP and Chief Financial Officer), James G Duggan (VP and General Counsel), John B Lambert (VP Technical)

PRINCIPAL ACTIVITIES: Steel industry; metal fabrication; manufacture of machine tools
Financial Information:

	$'000
Sales revenues	208,000

No of Employees: 2,000

FAR WEST FINANCIAL CORPORATION

4001 MacArthur Blvd, Newport Beach, CA 92660
Tel: (714) 833-8585

Chairman: William Belzberg
President: David E Blackford (and Chief Executive Officer)
Senior Executive Officers: Charles H Green (Executive VP, Chief Financial Officer and Treasurer), Kurt C Kemper (Senior VP, Legal Counsel and Secretary), Alexander L Popof (Senior VP), Julia Leah Greenfield (VP and Assistant Secretary), Edward V Lyon (VP and Controller)

PRINCIPAL ACTIVITIES: Financial services including savings and loans; finance for the construction industry and second mortgages
Principal Subsidiaries: Beneficial Service Co; Far West Savings & Loan Association; Farwest Financial Insurance Agency
Principal Bank: Crocker Bank
Financial Information:

	Dec 31 1985 $'000	Dec 31 1986 $'000
Net income	16,054	23,158
Earnings per share	$2.63	$3.01
Shareholders equity	81,352	142,657
Deposits	-	2,119,008
Total assets	2,425,985	3,030,281

No of Employees: 525

FARAH MANUFACTURING CO, INC

8889 Gateway Blvd W, El Paso, TX 79925
Tel: (915) 593-4444

Chairman: William F Farah (and President and Chief Executive Officer)
President: James C Farah (and Chief Operating Officer)
Senior Executive Officers: Richard L Jaeger (Chairman Executive Committee, Chief Financial Officer and Treasurer), Robert N Farah (Senior VP International), Charles E Pollock (Senior VP Sales), Richard W Myers (Senior VP Operations), Carlos Ortiz (VP Personnel), Thaddeus D Lepkowski (VP Information Services), Franz A Maccarone (VP Advertising), Douglas A Pontious (VP Inventory Management), James C Swaim (VP Finance), Jack R Green (VP and Secretary)

PRINCIPAL ACTIVITIES: Manufacture of outerwear
Principal Subsidiaries: Farah International Inc; Farah Sales Corp; Value Slacks Inc
Principal Bank: InterFirst Bank Dallas
Financial Information:

	$'000
Sales revenues	322,350

No of Employees: 5,800

FARLEY INDUSTRIES

233 South Wacker Drive, 6300 Sears Tower, Chicago, IL 60606
Tel: (312) 876-1724

Chairman: William F Farley (and President and Chief Executive Officer)
Senior Executive Officers: Richard Cion (Executive VP and Chief Financial Officer), William K Hall (Executive VP and Chief

Operating Officer), William H Vaba (Executive VP Administration and Operations and Secretary), Robert J Meier (VP Treasurer and Controller), Kevin S Moore (VP Mergers and Acquisitions)

PRINCIPAL ACTIVITIES: Manufacture of textiles, clothing, footwear and automobile and industrial products

Trade Names: Fruit of the Loom, BVD, Dan Post Boots, Dingo Boots, Acme Boots

Principal Subsidiaries: Anaheim Citrus Products Co Inc; ConDiesel Mobile Equipment; Doehler-Jarvis; Farley Apparel Inc; Acme Boot Co Inc; Fruit of the Loom Inc; General Battery Corp; Magnus; Southern Screw; Tool & Engineering

Principal Bank: Bankers Trust Co

Financial Information:

	Dec 31 1986
	$'000
Sales revenues	1,246,400
Net income	12,100

FARM & HOME SAVINGS ASSOCIATION

221 W Cherry, Nevada, MO 64772
Tel: (417) 667-3333
Telefax: (417) 667-9502

Chairman: Howard L Terry (Director only, not an employee)

President: Donald F Roby (also Chief Executive Officer and a Director)

Senior Executive Officers: Bernard J Figiel (Senior Executive VP), Charles A Fisher (Senior Executive VP), David A Todd II (Senior Executive VP), R Wagner Love (Executive VP), Jerry Forrester (Executive VP and Chief Financial Officer), John Horseman (Executive VP), Joan McFarland (Administrative VP), Francis G Clark (Senior VP), Bruce Lynn (Senior VP), Roy A Johnson (Senior VP), James L Carney (Senior VP), L L Weaver (Senior VP), Joe Johnson (Senior VP and Manager), Fred W Wilmot (Senior VP Loan), Mickey Brown (Senior VP and Manager), James Besher (Senior VP and Manager), Gerald Orman (Senior VP), John Vieth (Senior VP and Manager), Harry Gilbert (VP and Treasurer), Jack Eiffert (VP and Secretary)

PRINCIPAL ACTIVITIES: Financial services including loans and savings

Principal Subsidiaries: Caltrop Corporation

Principal Bank: Federal Home Loan Bank

Financial Information:

	Dec 31 1985	Dec 31 1986
	$'000	$'000
Revenues	295,638	299,649
Income before taxes	20,646	33,138
Net income	13,771	21,739
Dividends	-	3,479
Dividends per share	-	$0.50
Earnings per share	$1.95	$3.07
Common stock	6,921	6,985
Retained income	103,750	122,133
Shareholders equity	183,415	202,697
Deposits	2,499,504	2,590,606
Total assets	2,800,891	3,301,007

No of Employees: 724

FARM CREDIT BANKS OF BALTIMORE

14114 York Road, Sparks, MD 21152
Tel: (301) 628-5500

Chairman: Harold B Short

President: Gene L Swackhamer

Senior Executive Officers: J H Settle (Executive VP), C F Dickson (Senior VP Audit and Review), Richard A Chaffinch (Senior VP Credit and Operations), Donald L Shiflet (Senior VP Corporate Services)

PRINCIPAL ACTIVITIES: Financial services to the agricultural industry

No of Employees: 800

FARM FRESH INC

3487 Investors Road, PO Box 1289, Norfolk, VA 23501
Tel: (804) 853 7461

Chairman: David Furman; Assistant Chairman: H L Kanter (and Secretary and Legal Counsel)

President: Eugene Walter

Senior Executive Officers: Gerald J Reuss (Executive VP), Martin B Berry (VP Merchandising), Larry W Dobrinsky (VP and Treasurer), Kent A Little (VP Real Estate), Herbert D Watson Jr (VP and Controller)

PRINCIPAL ACTIVITIES: Retail food stores

Principal Bank: United Virginia Bank

Financial Information:

	$'000
Sales revenues	439,210

No of Employees: 5,000

FARM HOUSE FOODS CORPORATION

111 E Wisconsin, Suite 1900, Milwaukee, WI 53202
Tel: (414) 271-5050

Chairman: Donald E Runge (and President and Chief Executive Officer)

Senior Executive Officers: Dale D Drewek (Executive VP and Chief Financial Officer), Gordon McKay (VP and Chief Financial Officer), James D Nowatzky (VP Drugs), Gary R Placek (VP Finance and Treasurer)

PRINCIPAL ACTIVITIES: Wholesalers of food and confectionery; pharmaceutical retailers

Principal Subsidiaries: Don-Lou Artesian Wells Ltd; Drug Systems Inc; F/H Industries Corp; Fairbank Farms Inc; FH Financial Corp; Bankit Financial Corp; Ben Kozloff Inc; Pan-Am Seafood Ltd; Worcester Quality Foods Inc

Principal Bank: First National of Minneapolis

Financial Information:

	$'000
Sales revenues	1,520,000

No of Employees: 1,400

FARMER BROS CO

20333 s Normandie Avenue, Torrance, CA 90509
Tel: (213) 775-2451

Chairman: Roy F Farmer (and President)

Senior Executive Officers: Roy E Farmer (VP Administration), Belmont Beattie (VP Sales), Guenter W Berger (VP Manufacturing), David W Uhley (Secretary), John E Simmons (Treasurer)

PRINCIPAL ACTIVITIES: Processing and sale of coffee to hotels and restaurants; manufacture of coffee making equipment

Principal Bank: First Interstate Bank of California

Financial Information:

	Jun 30 1986
	$'000
Sales revenues	207,568
Income before taxes	11,641
Net income	6,349
Dividends per share	$0.90
Earnings per share	$3.30
Common stock	1,926
Shareholders equity	85,890

Principal Shareholders: Roy F Farmer; Catherine E Crowe

No of Employees: 1,177

FARMERS GROUP INC

4680 Wilshire Blvd, Los Angeles, CA 90010
Tel: (213) 932-3200

Chairman: Leo E Denlea Jr (and Chief Executive Officer and Chief Operating Officer)

Senior Executive Officers: Robert R McClintick, Darell F Norris, Charles L Schultz

PRINCIPAL ACTIVITIES: Holding company with interests in insurance

Trade Names: Farmers Insurance Group of Companies

Principal Bank: Bank of America

Financial Information:

	Dec 31 1985	Dec 31 1986
	$'000	$'000
Revenues	992,903	1,119,922
Income before taxes	312,936	369,720
Net income	184,649	213,470
Dividends	59,775	68,932
Dividends per share	$0.88	$1.00
Earnings per share	$2.72	$3.09
Common stock*	34,440	68,991
Retained income	966,674	1,111,212
Shareholders equity	1,237,536	1,398,294

*reflects stock split in the form of a 100% stock dividend June, 1986

No of Employees: 15,506

FARMERS PETROLEUM COOPERATIVE, INC

7373 West Saginaw, Box 30960, Lansing, MI 48909
Tel: (517) 323-7000

President: Elton R Smith

Senior Executive Officers: Richard T Krueger (Executive VP), John Laurie (VP), Matthew S Butzin (Treasurer)

PRINCIPAL ACTIVITIES: Oil services and products; automobile components

Principal Bank: Bank of Lansing

Financial Information:

	$'000
Sales revenues	52,000

No of Employees: 140

FARMERS UNION CENTRAL EXCHANGE, INC CENEX

PO Box 64089, St Paul, MN 55164-0089
Tel: (612) 451-5151

Chairman: Edward Melby; Vice Chairmen: Dixie Lee Riddle, Elroy Webster

President: Darrell Moseson

Senior Executive Officers: Noel K Estenson (Senior VP Petroleum and Finance), David Johnson (Senior VP Operations), Joel Blake (VP Petroleum), Richard Siderius (VP Marketing), Jerry Hahn (VP Corporate Finance), Paul Rhein (VP Agri-Products), Charles Habergarten (VP and Legal Counsel), Richard Baldwin (VP Human Resources), Stan Lehman (VP Feed and Seed), Maurice Miller (VP Corporate Planning)

PRINCIPAL ACTIVITIES: Integrated petroleum company and wholesale distributor of agricultural supplies, principally petroleum, fertilizer, agchemicals, feed and seed

Trade Names: CENEX

Principal Subsidiaries: CENEX AG Inc; CENEX Inc; Full Circle Inc; Pax Co Inc

Principal Bank: First National Bank of St Paul

Financial Information:

	Sep 30 1985	Sep 30 1986
	$'000	$'000
Sales revenues	1,375,813	1,220,181
Shareholders equity	300,547	283,246

No of Employees: 2,830

FARMLAND INDUSTRIES, INC

3315 N Oak Trafficway, Kansas City, MO 64116
Tel: (816) 459-6000

Chairman: Francis B Gwin; Vice Chairman: Robert McDowell

President: Kenneth A Nielsen (and Chief Executive Officer)

Senior Executive Officers: Robert E Johanson (Executive VP), Robert N Wakefield (Executive VP Foods and Feed), Garvin E Matthiesen (Executive VP Fertilizer and Petroleum Operations), Earl L Knauss (Financial VP and Treasurer)

PRINCIPAL ACTIVITIES: Manufacture of agricultural supplies, petroleum and oils; trade in food products and grain

Principal Subsidiaries: Co-operative Finance Association Inc; Cooperative Service Co; Far-Mar-Co Inc; Farmers Chemical Co; Farmland Foods Inc; Farmland Securities Co

Financial Information:

	Aug 31 1986
	$'000
Sales revenues	2,690,096
Shareholders equity	313,258

No of Employees: 7,400

FARR CO

2301 Rosecrans Avenue, El Segundo, CA 90245
Tel: (213) 772-5221

Chairman: Richard S Farr; Vice Chairman: M S Farr (and Secretary)

President: Allan B Foy (and Chief Executive and Operating Officer)

Senior Executive Officers: Jack D Carr (VP and Chief Financial Officer), J Michael Burke (VP), James R Burnett (VP Manufacturing), Matthew J Pastell (VP)

PRINCIPAL ACTIVITIES: Farr Company's basic business is the control of contaminants in air, gas and liquids. The Company is engaged in the design, development, manufacture, sales and service of filters and filtration systems. These products are used for a wide variety of applications including heating, ventilating and air-conditioning systems, process manufacturers, nuclear power plants, diesel-powered trucks, railroad locomotives, construction and mining equipment and gas turbines. Noise abatement equipment and systems used primarily for gas turbine applications are also engineered, manufactured and sold. Products are available as standard items or may be custom engineered. They range in size and complexity from a small throwaway air filter to large systems with a single component module weighing in excess of fifty tons. Products are sold throughout the world. Sales are through direct company salesmen, manufacturer's representatives, distributors and foreign licensees

Principal Subsidiaries: Farr Inc (Canada); Farr Filtration Ltd (UK); Farr Company SA (Belgium)

Principal Bank: Security Pacific National Bank

Financial Information:

	Dec 28 1985	Jan 31 1987
	$'000	$'000
Sales revenues	55,236	60,078
Income before taxes	5,869	4,248
Net income	3,224	2,256
Dividends	540	647
Dividends per share	$0.24	$0.24
Earnings per share	$1.15*	$0.80
Common stock	2,311	2,890
Retained income	10,759	12,368
Shareholders equity	21,188	22,942

*Restated for 5:4 stock split June 1986

No of Employees: 831

FARREL COMPANY

Ansonia, CT 06401
Tel: (203) 734-3331
Telex: WUT 963 498 farrel ans

President: F J McFarland Jr
Senior Executive Officers: A W Sampson (VP and General Manager General Machine Division), W A Rapetski (VP and General Manager Polymer Processing Machinery Division), R D Schuman (VP and General Manager Manufacturing Division), W K Shepherd (VP Marketing), F J McFarland (VP Finance and Administration)

PRINCIPAL ACTIVITIES: Manufacture of industrial plant; rubber and plastics processing equipment; machine tools
Parent Company: Emhart Corporation
Financial Information:

	$'000
Sales revenues	80,000

No of Employees: 900

FASCO INDUSTRIES, INC

601 N Federal Hwy, Boca Raton, FL 33432
Tel: (305) 368-0600

Chairman: James F Callahan
President: Frank W Mack (and Chief Executive Officer)
Senior Executive Officers: Roderic B Karpen (Senior VP Motor Division), Richard E Fetter (VP Finance), B L Lakin (VP Engineering Motor Division), David G Wilson (VP Consumer Division), James A Bennett (VP Ozark Motor Plant), Morris D Castleberry (VP Cassville Motor Plant), Glen H Sherer (VP Eldon Motor Plant), Owens J Binnette (VP Sales Motor Division), John F Golen (VP Human Resources)

PRINCIPAL ACTIVITIES: Manufacture of motors, controls and ventilation equipment
Parent Company: Hawker Siddeley Group PLC, London, UK
Principal Bank: Marine Midland Bank
Financial Information:

	$'000
Sales revenues	237,000

No of Employees: 4,700

FAY, LESLIE, COMPANIES

1400 Broadway, New York, NY 10018
Tel: (212) 221-4000
Telex: RCA 237 211 fay ur

President: John J Pomerantz
Senior Executive Officers: Walter I Leiter (Executive VP), Alan Golub (Senior VP), Paul F Polishan (Controller)

PRINCIPAL ACTIVITIES: Clothing manufacture
Principal Bank: Manufacturers Hanover Trust Company
Financial Information:

	$'000
Sales revenues	550,000

No of Employees: 2,800

FAY'S DRUG CO INC

7245 Henry Clay Boulevard, Liverpool, NY 13088
Tel: (315) 451 8000

Chairman: Henry A Panasci Jr (and Chief Executive Officer)
President: Daniel A Herrmann (and Chief Operating Officer)
Senior Executive Officers: Peter E Rhodes (Executive VP and Chief Financial Officer), John A Kogut (Senior VP), Paul T Anderson (VP and Controller), Warren D Wolfson (VP, Legal Counsel and Secretary), Allan R Travis (VP Advertising), Michael F Winahradsky (VP Distribution), David H Panasci (VP Corporate Development), James F Poole Jr (VP Planning), Raymond J Ryan (VP Real Estate), James B Miller (VP Personnel), Bruce R Berg (VP Store Operations), John A Kuznia (VP Information Systems), Gillian H McAuliffe (VP Consumer Affairs)

PRINCIPAL ACTIVITIES: Retail trade in drugs and pharmaceutical products
Principal Bank: Merchants National Bank
Financial Information:

	$'000
Sales revenues	445,000

No of Employees: 3,400

FEDDERS CORPORATION

158 Highway 206, PO Box 265, Peapack, NJ 07977
Tel: (201) 234-2100
Telex: 6858027 Feddair

Chairman: Salvatore Giordano; Vice Chairman: Salvatore Giordano Jr (and Chief Financial Officer)
President: Richard D Tyler (and Chief Operating Officer)
Senior Executive Officers: Joseph Giordano (Senior VP, Director), Howard S Modlin (Director and Secretary), Clarence R Moll (Director), C A Keen (VP and Treasurer), Robert W Nelson (Controller)

PRINCIPAL ACTIVITIES: Room air conditioning
Trade Names: Fedders, Airtemp, Climatrol, Climatrol By Fedders, Tempair
Principal Subsidiaries: Fedders USA; Fedders Air Conditioning USA
Principal Bank: PNB; Citibank
Financial Information:

	Dec 31 1985(1)	Dec 31 1986(1)
	$'000	$'000
Sales revenues	77,502	94,429
Income before taxes	2,930	5,477
Net income(2)	2,838	5,330
Dividends(3)	626	1,245
Dividends(4)	123	384
Dividends per share(3)	$0.060	$0.130
Dividends per share(4)	$0.036	$0.117
Earnings per share	$0.22	$0.41
Common stock	9,380	9,890
Class B stock	3,335	3,257
Retained deficit	(92,351)	(6,446)
Shareholders equity (deficit)	(5,792)	8,310(5)

(1) restated for NYCOR spin off Jan 1987
(2) from continuing operations
(3) Common stock
(4) Class B Stock
(5) $55.1m at Jun 30 1987

No of Employees: 700

FEDERAL EXPRESS CORPORATION

2990 Airways Blvd, Memphis, TN 38194
Tel: (901) 369-3600

Chairman: Frederick W Smith (and President and Chief Executive Officer)

Senior Executive Officers: James L Barksdale (Executive VP and Chief Operating Officer), David C Anderson (Senior VP and Chief Financial Officer), Thomas R Oliver (Senior VP Marketing and Customer Services), Brian E Pecon (Senior VP International Operations), James R Riedmeyer (Senior VP Line Haul Operations), Charles D Winston (Senior VP Electronic Products), James A Perkins (Senior VP Personnel), Theodore L Weise (Senior VP Bus Service Centers), Fred Manske (Senior VP Group Operations), John C Miller (Senior VP Logistics), Kenneth R Masterson (Senior VP and Legal Counsel), Patrick R Greenish (VP International Telecommunications), Carl R Williams (VP Electronic Products Marketing), W Jack Roberts (VP and Controller)

PRINCIPAL ACTIVITIES: Express air transportation services for packages
Principal Bank: First National Bank of Chicago
Financial Information:

	May 31 1986
	$'000
Sales revenues	2,606,210
Net income	131,839
Earnings per share	$2.64
Shareholders equity	1,091,714

No of Employees: 33,990

FEDERAL HOME LOAN BANK OF NEW YORK

One World Trade Center, New York, NY 10048
Tel: (212) 432-2000
Telex: TWX 710 581 3806 fhlb ny

Chairman: Lois L Evans; Vice Chairman: Edward Mallaney
President: Brian D Dittenhafer
Senior Executive Officers: Lorenzo Munoz Franco (Chairman Executive Committee), Angelo A Vigna (Executive VP Agency Functions), LeRoy D Brubaker (Senior VP Finance and Treasurer), Philip J Bailey (Senior VP Demand Deposit Accounts Services), Joseph DeFarrari Jr (Senior VP Bank Operations), Dean Schultz (Senior VP and Legal Counsel), Leigh W Allard (VP Human Resources), William J Durbin (VP Supervision), Linda Mercurio Swan (VP Industry Development), Harold J Fletcher (VP Business Information)

PRINCIPAL ACTIVITIES: Banking services

No of Employees: 500

FEDERAL NATIONAL MORTGAGE ASSOCIATION

3900 Wisconsin Avenue NW, Washington, DC 20016
Tel: (202) 537-7000
Telex: WUT 892 500 fnma wsh

Chairman: David O Maxwell (and Chief Executive Officer)
President: Roger E Birk (and Chief Operating Officer)
Senior Executive Officers: Caryl S Bernstein (Executive VP, Secretary and General Counsel), Bruce C McMillen (Executive VP and Chief Financial Officer), Michael A Smilow (Executive VP-Mortgage Operations), Dale P Riordan (Executive VP-Administration and Corporate Relations), Samuel A Alward (Executive VP-Technology), Edward J Pinto (Executive VP and Chairman-Credit Policy Committee)

PRINCIPAL ACTIVITIES: Financial services including mortgages
Financial Information:

	Dec 31 1985	Dec 31 1986
	$'000	$'000
Revenues	10,342,000	10,540,000
Net income	37,000	183,000
Earnings per share	$0.52	$2.46
Shareholders equity	1,342,000	1,593,000
Total assets	99,087,000	100,406,000

No of Employees: 2,000

FEDERAL PAPER BOARD COMPANY, INC

75 Chestnut Ridge Road, Montvale, NJ 07645
Tel: (201) 391-1776
Telex: 858675 FEDERAL

President: John R Kennedy Jr (and Chief Executive Officer)
Senior Executive Officers: Quentin J Kennedy (Executive VP and Secretary), Paul R Kinsey (Senior VP, Manufacturing, Forest Products and Recycled Division), Robert D Baldwin (Senior VP, Marketing, Forest Products and Recyled Division), B W Bowie (Senior VP, Packaging and Printing Division)

PRINCIPAL ACTIVITIES: Manufacturing of pulp and paper products and packaging supplies
Principal Bank: Morgan Guaranty Trust Company
Financial Information:

	Dec 31 1985	Dec 31 1986
	$'000	$'000
Sales revenues	783,927	948,560
Income before taxes	17,896	67,135
Net income	11,196	18,410(1)
Dividends (2)	13,452	16,680
Dividends per share (3)	$0.70	$0.70
Earnings per share (4)	$0.53	$0.81(5)
Common stock	65,283	78,287
Retained income	112,073	113,908
Shareholders equity	273,974	337,852

(1) after extraordinary charge of $15,125 pre-tax
(2) common stock
(3) assuming full dilution
(4) $5.00 par value
(5) after extraordinary charge of $1.88 per share

No of Employees: 5,700

FEDERAL SCREW WORKS

535 Griswold, 2400 Buhl Bldg, Detroit, MI 48226-3602
Tel: (313) 963 2323

Chairman: W T Zurschmiede Jr (and Chief Executive Officer)
President: Hugh G Harness (and Chief Operating Officer)
Senior Executive Officers: M Quick (Senior VP), Mack Quick (Senior VP), John M O'Brien (VP and General Manager), William L Short (VP and General Manager), F D Tennent (Senior VP, Secretary and Treasurer), Arthur E Velthoven (VP), Raymond R White Jr (VP and General Manager), Gerald R Smith (Controller)

PRINCIPAL ACTIVITIES: Manufacture of a wide range of metal fasteners including screws, nuts, bolts and rivets
Principal Bank: National Bank of Detroit
Financial Information:

	$'000
Sales revenues	52,000

No of Employees: 520

FEDERAL SIGNAL CORPORATION

1415 W 22nd Street, Oak Brook, IL 60521-9945
Tel: (312) 954-2000

Chairman: Karl F Hoenecke (and Chief Executive Officer)
President: Joseph J Ross (and Chief Operating Officer)
Senior Executive Officers: Charles R Campbell (Senior VP and Chief Financial Officer), James W Morrall (VP Corporate Services), Robert W Racic (VP and Treasurer), Kim A Wehrenberg (VP, General Counsel and Secretary), Richard L Ritz (Controller), Vicki L Casmere (Assistant Secretary and Corporate Attorney)

PRINCIPAL ACTIVITIES: Federal Signal Corporation, founded in 1901, is a diversified NYSE-listed company comprised of four major groups: Signal, Sign, Tool and Vehicle. Principal products include sirens, emergency lights, fire alarm systems, security and parking control systems, signs, fire trucks, street sweepers, special vehicle chassis, precision punches and cutting tools

Principal Divisions and Subsidiaries: Signal Group: Signal Products Division; Federal Construction Products; CMI Inc; Federal APD Incorporated; The Autocall Division. Sign Group: Federal Sign; F.E.D. Products. Tool Group: Dayton Progress Corporation; Bassett Rotary Tool Company; Jamestown Perforators Inc. Vehicle Group: Elgin Sweeper Company; Emergency One Inc; Federal Motors

Financial Information:

	Dec 31 1985	Dec 31 1986
	$'000	$'000
Sales revenues	278,300	283,500
Income before taxes	16,300	20,500
Net income	11,700	11,800
Dividends	6,650	6,863
Dividends per share	$0.80	$0.80
Earnings per share	$1.41	$1.37
Common stock	8,527	8,664
Retained income	19,167	23,606
Shareholders equity	91,071	102,362

No of Employees: 3,388

FEDERAL-MOGUL CORPORATION

PO Box 1966, Detroit, MI 48235

Tel: (313) 354-7700

Chairman: Thomas F Russell (and Chief Executive Officer)

President: William C Adams (and Chief Operating Officer)

Senior Executive Officers: Robert W Hague (Senior VP, Chief Financial Officer and Secretary), Dennis J Gormley (Executive VP), John F Peyton (Senior VP and Group Executive Components-International), Robert W Denning (VP and Group Executive Materials Processing Group), James M Eastman (VP-Employee Relations), H George Faulkner (VP and Group Executive Huck Manufacturing), David K Leak (VP Materials Management and Technical Systems), Roy E Parrott (VP and Group Executive Federal-Mogul Components Group), Richard M Szary (VP and Group Executive General Products Group). Other Management: Larry A Edwards (VP and Controller), Philip H Embury (Assistant Secretary), Thomas J English (Director-Information Resources Management F-M Service), Leonard Gay (VP and Treasurer), Charles B Grant (VP Corporate Development), Fred J Musone (VP and General Manager Federal-Mogul Service), Raymond P Peck (Senior VP Customer Relations), Philip Tomkinson (President-Federal-Mogul World Trade), Walter P Work Jr (Director-Organizational Planning and Executive Resources), James J Zamoyski (Assistant Treasurer)

PRINCIPAL ACTIVITIES: The principal products sold by Federal-Mogul Corporation and its subsidiaries are grouped into three industry segments-vehicle and machinery components, fastening systems and materials processing products. The first industry segment, vehicle and machinery components, includes ball and roller bearings, engine and transmission products (engine bearings, pistons, bushings and washers), sealing devices (oil seals, O-rings and other specialty seals), Sinta Forge (R) parts, automotive fuel pumps and related systems, lighting and safety components. Fastening, systems comprise the second segment and include fasteners, installation tools and power sources. Materials processing products is the third segment and is composed of metal, concrete, masonry and specialty cutting tools, air bearing spindles and circuit board drills

Financial Information:

	Dec 31 1985	Dec 31 1986
	$'000	$'000
Sales revenues	895,483	941,612
Income before taxes*	102,373	17,788
Net income	51,973	3,606
Dividends	20,515	20,547
Dividends per share	$1.54	$1.60
Earnings per share	$3.89	$0.28
Common stock	67,687	67,711
Retained income	294,310	277,369
Shareholders equity	339,272	320,470

*and extraordinary loss

No of Employees: 14,011

FEDERATED DEPARTMENT STORES, INC

Seven W Seventh Street, Cincinnati, OH 45202

Tel: (513) 579-7000

Chairman: Howard Goldfeder (and Chief Executive Officer); Vice Chairmen: Norman S Matthews, Donald J Stone, Will M Storey, John W Burden III

Senior Executive Officers: Bernard S Klayf (Executive VP), Eugene Rappeport (Senior VP), James B Selonick (Senior VP), Phyllis S Sewell (Senior VP), Thomas G Cody (Senior VP), Russell S Davis (Senior VP), Avner M Parat (Senior VP Human Resources), James M Leahy (VP and Treasurer), Boris Auerbach (VP and Secretary), Jack Brown (VP and Controller)

PRINCIPAL ACTIVITIES: Operation of department stores; retail grocery products

Principal Subsidiaries: Federated Acceptance Corp; Federated Stores Realty Inc

Principal Bank: Central Trust Co

Financial Information:

	Dec 31 1985	Dec 31 1986
	$'000	$'000
Sales revenues	9,978,027	10,512,425
Net income	286,626	288,000
Earnings per share	$2.98	$2.97
Shareholders equity	2,707,268	2,662,554

No of Employees: 133,000

FEDERATED GROUP INC

5655 East Union Pacific Avenue, City of Commerce, CA 90022

Tel: (213) 728 5100

Chairman: Wilfred Schwartz (and Chief Executive Officer)

President: Keith L Powell (and Chief Operating Officer)

Senior Executive Officers: Merrill Lyons (Senior VP Finance and Corporate Planning, Treasurer and Secretary), Michael A Pastore (Senior VP Sales and Merchandising), Joseph H Blaustein (VP Advertising and Sales), Martin R Jacob (VP Purchasing)

PRINCIPAL ACTIVITIES: Retail trade through a chain of stores specializing in home entertainment and consumer electronic products

Principal Bank: Security Pacific National Bank

Financial Information:

	$'000
Sales revenues	363,650

No of Employees: 1,000

FEDERATED GUARANTY CORPORATION

2108 East South Boulevard, PO Box 11000, Montgomery, AL 36198

Tel: (205) 288 3900

Chairman: Goodwin L Myrick (and President)

Senior Executive Officers: B Phil Richardson (Executive VP Operations), Boyd Christenberry (Executive VP Marketing), Jimmy Azar (Senior VP Planning), Young J Boozer (Senior VP), Marcia P Martin (Senior VP Personnel), Emory McKinney

(Senior VP Life Operations), Mayme Arkinson (VP Life Accounting), Kerry Lashlee (VP), Ken Nelson (VP Actuary), Donald Price (VP Finance), J T Salmon (Secretary and Legal Counsel), C Lee Ellis (VP Investments), Tommy Wright (VP Marketing)

PRINCIPAL ACTIVITIES: Life insurance
Principal Subsidiaries: Federated Guaranty Insurance Co; Federated Guaranty Life Insurance
Principal Bank: First Alabama Bank
Financial Information:

	Dec 31 1985
	$'000
Revenues	43,870
Net income	10,260

No of Employees: 390

FEDERATED PUBLICATIONS, INC
155 W Van Buren Street, Battle Creek, MI 49016
Tel: (616) 964-7161

Senior Executive Officers: Larry F Miller (Treasurer), Thomas L Chapple (Secretary), Theodore H Sondag (Sales Manager), John F Newman (Sales Manager), Gerald Rhea Jr (Sales Manager), Howard Sutherland (Sales Manager)

PRINCIPAL ACTIVITIES: Publishing newspapers
Parent Company: Gannett Co Inc, Rochester, NY
Financial Information:

	$'000
Sales revenues	90,000

No of Employees: 1,400

FELLOWES MANUFACTURING COMPANY
1789 Norwood Avenue, Itasca, IL 60103
Tel: (312) 893-1600
Telex: 210 264

Chairman: John Fellowes
President: James Fellowes
Senior Executive Officers: James Colwell, Clinton Bull, Robert Moore

PRINCIPAL ACTIVITIES: Manufacturer of office products, home organizer products and home/office products
Trade Names: ART-FOLIO, BB MONOGRAM, BANKERS BOX, BANKERS BOX & DESIGN, BONUS, CONVERT-A-TRAY, COPY-FRAME IT'S MORE THAN A COPYHOLDER, DATA-PAK, FLAT/STOR, FOLDER-MATE, HIGH-STAK, LIBERTY, STAXTONSTEEL, STAX-SORTER, STAX-TAB, STOR/DRAWER, SYSTEMATIC, TANDEM, HIGH-STAK, LIBERTY BINDERS & STRING BINDERS, R-KIVE, STAXONSTEEL, LIBERTY BINDERS & STRING BINDERS, LIBERTY BOXES, LIBERTY COPYHOLDERS, LIBERTY SHELVING, MAGIC BINDING POSTS, NEAT IDEAS, POLYLOCK, R-KIVE, R-KIVE II (Indemnity Agreement), ROLL/STOR, SIMPLIMATIC
Principal Bank: Continental Illinois National Bank & Trust Co
Financial Information:

	$'000
Sales revenues	70,000

No of Employees: 700

FELLOWS CORPORATION
Precision Drive, PO Box 851, Springfield, VT 05156
Tel: (802) 886-8333
Telex: 710-227-1701

President: Joseph W Smith
Senior Executive Officers: Carl Easler (Manager Finance and Administration), Donald G Chabot (VP Marketing), Robert S Boekhout (VP Manufacturing), Henry Swierczynski (VP Engineering)

PRINCIPAL ACTIVITIES: Manufacture of gear cutting machine tools
Principal Subsidiaries: J & L Metrology Company Inc
Financial Information:

	$'000
Sales revenues	50,000

No of Employees: 425

FELMONT OIL CORPORATION
6 East 43rd Street, New York, NY 10017
Tel: (212) 867-2211

Chairman: Lynn Walker (and President)
Senior Executive Officers: Randall K Walker (Senior VP), Richard A Mills (VP), Dominick J Golio (VP), Raymond A Keeney (VP and Secretary)

PRINCIPAL ACTIVITIES: Production of oil and gas; manufacture of petrochemicals; management of real estate
Parent Company: Homestake Mining Company, San Francisco, CA
Principal Bank: The Bank of New York
Financial Information:

	$'000
Sales revenues	60,000

No of Employees: 100

FENIX & SCISSON, INC
1401 S Boulder, Tulsa, OK 74119
Tel: (918) 560-5000

Chairman: S E Scisson
President: Fred Scharf
Senior Executive Officers: Kermit Allen (Senior VP), Charles S Dunn (Senior VP), D L Lockwood (Senior VP), Robert Lange (VP), A L Sowards (VP), Tom Costello (VP and Treasurer)

PRINCIPAL ACTIVITIES: Civil engineering; steel foundry products
Principal Subsidiaries: Fenix & Scisson International Inc; Fenson Oil & Gas Co; Love Process Engineering Inc; Missouri Steel Castings Co Inc
Principal Bank: Bank of Oklahoma
Financial Information:

	$'000
Sales revenues	35,000

No of Employees: 700

FERRO CORPORATION
One Erieview Plaza, Cleveland, OH 44114
Tel: (216) 641-8580

President: Adolph Posnick (and Chief Executive Officer)
Senior Executive Officers: A C Bersticker (Executive VP Operations), Clyde A MacFie (Executive VP Finance and Administration), Frank A Carragher (Group VP Chemicals), James F Lochridge (Group VP Coatings, Colors and Electronic Materials), R C Lynham (Group VP Ceramics), Werner F Bush (Senior VP International), John W Slaton (Senior VP Corporate Development), Hector R Ortino (VP Finance), Edward D Grant Jr (VP Grant Chemical), R V Harrington (VP Research), Philip A Contreras (VP and Legal Counsel), John V Goodger (VP and Treasurer), David B Woodbury (VP Human Resources)

PRINCIPAL ACTIVITIES: Manufacture of chemicals, dyes, coating materials and ceramics
Financial Information:

	Dec 31 1986
	$'000
Sales revenues	725,241
Net income	24,082
Earnings per share	$1.20
Shareholders equity	223,297

No of Employees: 8,020

FERRO MANUFACTURING CORPORATION

2100 N Woodward Ave, Bloomfield Hills, MI 48013-2748
Tel: (313) 352 7300

President: Dale J Offenbecher
Senior Executive Officers: Rick Kendall (VP Operations), Dave Rucinski (VP Sales), J E Stewart (VP), John B Davies (VP Finance, Secretary and Treasurer), Joseph Pickles (VP Research)

PRINCIPAL ACTIVITIES: Manufacture of parts and equipment for the motor and aerospace industries
Parent Company: Johnson Controls Inc
Financial Information:

	$'000
Sales revenues	112,000

No of Employees: 2,000

FERROFLUIDICS CORPORATION

40 Simon Street, Nashua, NH 03061
Tel: (603) 883 9800
Telex: Easylink 62934044
Telefax: (603) 883-2308

Chairman: Ronald Moskowitz (and President)
Senior Executive Officers: Frank Bloom (Executive VP), Frank Bloom (Executive VP), Robert Cauto (Assistant Treasurer and Assistant Clerk), Carl Muscari (VP Division), Kuldip Raj (VP), Juergen Zinsstag (VP Europe), Leonard Guida (Treasurer), Robert Couto (Assistant Treasurer), Maurice Zilber (Clerk)

PRINCIPAL ACTIVITIES: Ferrofluidics Corporation is a transnational Company employing advanced technologies to create innovative products for rapidly expanding strategic markets. Currently, the primary business of the Company is the worldwide marketing of proprietary products based on its expertise and world leadership in magnetic fluid technology to the computer peripheral, semiconductor and other growth industries
Trade Names: Ferrofluidic (R), Ferro-Sound (R), Ferrometic (R)
Principal Subsidiaries: Spin Technology Corporation; Ferrofluidics GmbH (Germany); AF Technologies Ltd (UK); Spin Technology Ltd (UK); Ferrofluidics Ltd (UK); Ferrofluidics SARL (France)
Principal Bank: Fleet National Bank
Financial Information:

	Jun 30 1986 $'000	Jun 30 1987 $'000
Net sales and revenues	28,184	34,600
Income (loss) before taxes	(1,513)	18,169
Net income (loss)	(1,512)	12,085
Earnings (loss) per share*	($0.13)	$0.90
Common stock	13	14
Retained income (deficit)	(1,199)	10,886
Shareholders equity	25,025	35,843

*assuming no dilution

No of Employees: 327

FIATALLIS NORTH AMERICA, INC

245 E North Avenue, Carol Stream, IL 60188
Tel: (312) 653-1000
Telex: WUT 722 454 falcon casm a

Chairman: Giovanni Germano
President: Robert L Green
Senior Executive Officers: Louis T Bland Jr (VP Human Resources), William R Ligon (VP Manufacturing), Willard R Hildebrand (VP Marketing)

PRINCIPAL ACTIVITIES: Manufacture of construction plant
Parent Company: Fiat SpA
Principal Bank: Bank of America
Financial Information:

	$'000
Sales revenues	300,000

Principal Shareholders: Fiat SpA, Torino, Italy
No of Employees: 1,000

FIBERITE CORPORATION

501-559 W 3rd Street, Winona, MN 55987
Tel: (507) 454-3611
Telex: TWX 910 565 2270

Senior Executive Officers: Thomas A Brand (Senior VP and General Manager West Coast), William A Laurie (Senior VP and General Manager), Herbert Barge (VP Manufacturing)

PRINCIPAL ACTIVITIES: Manufacture of plastics and plastic products
Parent Company: ICI American Holdings Inc
Principal Bank: Continental Illinois National Bank and Trust Company
Financial Information:

	$'000
Sales revenues	120,000

No of Employees: 1,000

FIDATA CORPORATION

67 Broad Street, New York, NY 10004
Tel: (212) 530 2400

Chairman: William M Siegel
President: Michael H Mindlin
Senior Executive Officers: Donald J McLellan (Executive VP, Chief Financial Officer and Treasurer), Leopold S Rassnick (Executive VP, Legal Counsel and Secretary), Joseph Sansone (Executive VP Systems and Information Processing), David Williams (Senior VP), William Peters (VP Sales and Marketing), James M Wright (VP Auditing), Peter A Kase (VP and Controller)

PRINCIPAL ACTIVITIES: Securities and commodity broking; data processing
Principal Subsidiaries: Bradford Securities Processing Services; Fidata Brokerage Inc; Fidata Securities Management Inc; Fidata Securities Services Inc; Fidata Services Inc; Fidata Systems Inc; Fidata Trust Company California; Fidata Trust Company Massachusetts; Fidata Trust Company New York
Principal Bank: Bradford Trust Co
Financial Information:

	$'000
Sales revenues	123,580

No of Employees: 3,100

FIDELCOR, INC

Broad & Walnut Streets, Philadelphia, PA 19109
Tel: (215) 985-6000
Telex: 834480

Chairman: Joseph A Gallagher; Vice Chairmen: Bernard J Morgan (and Chief Operating Officer); F Robert Dieter
President: Harold W Poke (and Chief Executive Officer)
Senior Executive Officers: John B Bartlett (Executive VP Administration and Secretary), Richard W Billings (Executive VP Loan Administration), Anthony Edgar (Executive VP Financial Management) Jean-Pierre G Galy (Executive VP International), Rosemarie B Greco (Executive VP Community Banking), Robert E Keith (Executive VP Corporate Banking), Gerald R Pacella (Executive VP Operations), Jonathan J Palmer (Executive VP Marketing Automation), Frederick H Pennekamp (Executive VP Treasury), William H Sayre (Executive VP Credit Audit), J Roger Williams Jr (Executive VP Legal)

PRINCIPAL ACTIVITIES: Banking
Principal Subsidiaries: Fidelity Bank

Financial Information:

	Dec 31 1985	Dec 31 1986
	$'000	$'000
Net income	45,551*	92,267
Earnings per share	$3.82	$3.95
Shareholders equity	328,304	694,364
Deposits	5,226,685	9,026,105
Total assets	6,760,455	11,391,725

*reflects extraordinary item of ($2,654)

No of Employees: 5,680

FIDELITY BANK

Broad & Walnut Streets, Philadelphia, PA 19109
Tel: (215) 985-6000
Telex: 834480 FIDELPHA PHA A

Chairman: Howard W Pote (and Chief Executive Officer)
President: Bernard J Morgan (and Chief Operating Officer)
Senior Executive Officers: John B Bartlett (Executive VP and Secretary), Rosemarie B Greco (Executive VP), Robert Keith (Executive VP), Richard W Billings (Executive VP), William H Sayre (Executive VP), Jonathan J Palmer (Executive VP), Gerald Pacella (Executive VP), Frederick Pennekamp (Executive VP and Treasurer), Frank J Noonan (Senior VP and Controller)

PRINCIPAL ACTIVITIES: Banking
Parent Company: Fidelcor Inc, Philadelphia, PA (100%)
Principal Bank: Bankers Trust Co

No of Employees: 2,590

FIDELITY NATIONAL FINANCIAL CORPORATION

440 Riverside Mall, Box 3597, Baton Rouge, LA 70801
Tel: (504) 381-2000

Chairman: Donald F Gerald (and Chief Executive Officer)
President: John G Munsell (and Chairman of Executive Committee)

PRINCIPAL ACTIVITIES: Banking
Principal Subsidiaries: Fidelity National Bank

No of Employees: 800

FIELD PACKING COMPANY

PO Box 766, Owensboro, KY 42301
Tel: (502) 926-2324

President: Josiah Ryland
Senior Executive Officers: Keith Luedke (VP Sales)

PRINCIPAL ACTIVITIES: Meat packaging
Principal Bank: Owensboro National Bank
Financial Information:

	$'000
Sales revenues	70,000

No of Employees: 500

FIELDCREST CANNON, INC

326 E Stadium Drive, Eden, NC 27288
Tel: (919) 627-3000

Chairman: Joseph B Ely II (and Chief Executive Officer); Vice Chairman: Francis X Larkin
President: Charles G Horn
Senior Executive Officers: W Randle Mitchell Jr (Executive VP and Chief Financial Officer), K William Fraser Jr (Senior VP), Larry W Owen (Senior VP), W Giles Hunnings Jr (VP), Chris L Kametches (VP), Edward J C Molitor (VP), Osborne L Raines (VP), William O Stone (VP), M Kenneth Doss (General Counsel and Secretary), Thomas R Staab (Controller), Lawrence L Mann (Treasurer), Mary E Wilson (Assistant Secretary)

PRINCIPAL ACTIVITIES: Company designs, manufactures and markets a broad range of household textile products consisting of blankets, automatic blankets, towels, sheets, bedspreads, comforters, quilted bedspreads, kitchen products, bath rugs and woven and tufted carpet and rugs
Trade Names: Fieldcrest, Cannon, St Marys, Karastan, Bigelow-Sanford
Principal Subsidiaries: Cannon Mills Company (purchased Jan 30 1986); Bigelow-Sanford (purchased Dec 18 1986)
Principal Bank: Bank of Boston
Financial Information:

	Dec 31 1985	Dec 31 1986
	$'000	$'000
Sales revenues	586,092	1,083,236
Income before taxes	22,682	31,689
Net income	13,062	17,389
Dividends	4,866	4,693
Dividends per share	$0.63	$0.57
Earnings per share	$1.68	$2.11
Common stock authorized(1)	11,000(2)	25,000
Common stock issued(1)	7,801(2)	5,956
Common stock Class B(1)(3)	-	15,000
Common stock Class B(4)	-	4,260
Retained income	138,040	150,736
Shareholders equity	181,163	269,389

(1) number of shares in thousands
(2) restated for 2 for 1 stock split
(3) authorized
(4) issued

Principal Shareholders: Amoskeag Co
No of Employees: 23,207

FIFTH THIRD BANCORP

38 Fountain Square Plaza, Cincinnati, OH 45263
Tel: (513) 579-5300

President: Clement L Buenger (and Chief Executive Officer)
Senior Executive Officers: Ronald A Dauwe (Executive VP), George A Schaefer Jr (Executive VP), N Beverly Tucker Jr (Executive VP and Treasurer)

PRINCIPAL ACTIVITIES: Banking services
Principal Subsidiaries: Bank of Russellville; Farmers Bank; Fayette County Bank; Fifth Third Bank; Fifth Third Bank of Miami Valley; First National Bank; Peoples National Bank
Principal Bank: Fifth Third Bank
Financial Information:

	Dec 31 1985	Dec 31 1986
	$'000	$'000
Revenues	296,000	325,000
Net income	44,200	55,000

No of Employees: 2,000

FIGGIE INTERNATIONAL

1000 Virginia Center Pkway, Richmond, VA 23295
Tel: (804) 264-5600

Chairman: H E Figgie Jr (and President and Chief Executive Officer)
Senior Executive Officers: J W Tardiff (Senior VP and Controller), Luther A Harthun (Senior VP), W G Gilmore (Senior VP), G O Haglund (Group VP), C C Rieger Jr (Group VP), J W Partridge (Group VP), S L Charlton (Group VP), Joseph J Skadra (VP and Controller)

PRINCIPAL ACTIVITIES: Holding company with interests in fire prevention and fire fighting equipment
Principal Subsidiaries: Figgie Systems Mgt Group Inc; Figgie Acceptance Corp

Financial Information:

	Dec 31 1985 $'000	Dec 31 1986 $'000
Sales revenues	803,410	919,818
Net income	29,240	42,426
Earnings per share	$5.03	$6.31
Shareholders equity	218,420	292,766

No of Employees: 15,970

FINALCO GROUP INC

8200 Greensboro Drive, McLean, VA 22102
Tel: (703) 790 0970

Chairman: Jon J Prager (and Chief Executive Officer)
President: Lee B Burnett
Senior Executive Officers: Terry J Billingsley (Executive VP), Paul M Finfer (Executive VP), Edward J Larese (Executive VP and Chief Financial Officer), Charles Duggan (VP Finance and Treasurer), Ellen M Kirsh (Secretary and Legal Counsel)

PRINCIPAL ACTIVITIES: Leasing of a wide range of equipment including vehicles, aircraft and computers
Principal Subsidiaries: FAC Leasing Inc; FEP Investors Inc; Finalco Aircraft Leasing Inc; Finalco Capital Corp; Financial Municipal Leasing Inc; Finalco Realty Inc; Finalco Management Corp; Finalco Inc; Finalco Fleet Services Inc; Finalco Financial Services Inc; Finalco Exploration and Development Inc; Finalco Equipment Corp
Principal Bank: Sovran Bank
Financial Information:

	$'000
Sales revenues	76,540

No of Employees: 200

FINANCIAL CORPORATION OF AMERICA

18401 Von Karman Avenue, Irvine, CA 92715
Tel: (714) 553-6900

Chairman: William J Popejoy (and President)
Senior Executive Officers: Michael Durkin (Executive VP-Lending), Victor Indiek (Executive VP-Finance), Kenneth Krause (Executive VP-Administration), Donald Royer (Executive VP-Legal and General Counsel)

PRINCIPAL ACTIVITIES: The origination and management of loans secured by various types of real property, through its principal operating subsidiary American Savings and Loan Association
Principal Subsidiaries: American Savings and Loan Association; FCA American Mortgage Corporation; FCA Mortgage Corporation; FCA Asset Management Company
Financial Information:

	Dec 31 1986 $'000
Revenues	3,330,773
Income before taxes	101,982
Net income	95,369
Earnings per share	$2.18
Common stock	19,460
Retained (deficit)	(320,819)
Shareholders equity	313,893
Deposits	16,929,388
Total assets	33,952,994

FINANCIAL CORPORATION OF SANTA BARBARA

PO Box 1109, Santa Barbara, CA 93102
Tel: (805) 682-2300

Chairman: Philip R Brinkerhoff (and President and Chief Executive Officer); Vice Chairman: David L Tilton
Senior Executive Officers: Arthur B Hall (Chief Financial Officer, Executive VP), Glen H Carter (Executive VP), Michael D Schley (Senior VP and Secretary)

PRINCIPAL ACTIVITIES: Holding Company with interest in savings and loan
Principal Subsidiaries: Santa Barbara Savings & Loan Association
Principal Bank: Bank of America
Financial Information:

	Dec 31 1986 $'000	Dec 31 1987 $'000
Income before taxes	30,564	3,485
Net income	19,088	2,770
Common dividends	-	446
Preferred dividends	1,141	283
Dividends per common share	-	$0.075
Dividends per pref share	$8.7274	$0.54575
Earnings per share	$3.16	$0.39
Common stock	5,715	6,053
Retained income	7,556	8,968
Shareholders equity	38,651	41,859
Deposits	2,005,337	2,251,918
Total assets	4,557,952	5,347,087

No of Employees: 850

FINANCIAL NATIONAL BANCSHARES COMPANY

6 Fountain Square Plaza, Elgin, IL 60120
Tel: (312) 697 1100

Chairman: William E Redeker
President: Wilber G Smith (and Chief Executive Officer and Subsidiary Officer)
Senior Executive Officers: John W Modaff (Executive VP), F Thomas Michels (Executive VP), John M Eshelman (VP, Secretary and Assistant Treasurer), James L Duewel (VP and Treasurer), John D Hubbard (VP Marketing), Thomas Johannesen (VP), Mary T Ross (VP Audit)

PRINCIPAL ACTIVITIES: Banking
Principal Subsidiaries: First National Bank; Larkin Bank
Principal Bank: First National Bank of Elgin

No of Employees: 230

FINCH, PRUYN & CO, INC

1 Glen Street, Glens Falls, NY 12801
Tel: (518) 793-2541
Telex: WUT 145 497 finchp ruyn glf

Chairman: Richard J Carota (and President and Chief Executive Officer)
Senior Executive Officers: Peter J Bruno (Executive VP), John R Buchanan (VP Sales), Daniel J Gleason (VP Manufacturing), John A Shaffer (VP and Treasurer), Roger S Hague (VP and Secretary), John A Sheldon (VP Purchasing)

PRINCIPAL ACTIVITIES: Publishing and printing and paper processing
Financial Information:

	$'000
Sales revenues	160,000

No of Employees: 860

FINDLEY ADHESIVES, INC

11320 Watertown Plank Rd, Wauwatosa, WI 53228
Tel: (414) 774-2250

Chairman: Ralph Findley; Vice Chairman: Kenneth Findley Sr
President: Edward Mahoney
Senior Executive Officers: Roger Carr (VP Research and Development), Thomas Walsh (VP South Division), David Jackson (VP Sales and Marketing), Thomas B Weis (VP Finance), William Hanson (VP West Division), Ivan E Welborn (VP Manufacturing)

PRINCIPAL ACTIVITIES: Manufacture of industrial adhesives
Principal Bank: M & I Marshall and Ilsley Bank

Financial Information:

	$'000
Sales revenues	90,000

No of Employees: 360

FINNIGAN CORPORATION

355 River Oaks Pkwy, San Jose, CA 95134
Tel: (408) 946-4848

Chairman: T Z Chu (and President); Vice Chairman: Robert E Finnigan (and Senior VP)
Senior Executive Officers: John Hearn (Executive VP), James T Lindstrom (VP, Chief Financial Officer and Treasurer), Edward J McGonagle (VP Information and Administration Systems), Philip L Warren (VP Field Operations), Ernst Weber (VP Bremen Operations)

PRINCIPAL ACTIVITIES: Analytical instrument systems-mass spectrometers
Principal Subsidiaries: Finnigan International Sales Inc; Finnigan Mat (NV) Inc; Finnigan Mat International Sales Inc; Finnigan Properties Inc
Principal Bank: Union Bank
Financial Information:

	$'000
Sales revenues	80,600

No of Employees: 950

FIREMAN'S FUND CORPORATION

77 San Marin Drive, Novato, CA 94998
Tel: (415) 899-2000

Chairman: John J Byrne (and Chief Executive Officer)
President: William M McCormick
Senior Executive Officers: Joseph W Brown Jr (Executive VP and Chief Financial Officer), Howard L Clark (Executive VP Investments), Borell Kirschen (Executive VP and General Counsel), Francis W Benedict (Senior VP and Secretary), Robert T Maro (Senior VP and Treasurer)

PRINCIPAL ACTIVITIES: Insurance and diversified financial services
Principal Subsidiaries: Fireman's Fund Insurance Company; Fireman's Fund Insurance Company of Texas
Financial Information:

	Dec 31 1985 $'000	Dec 31 1986 $'000
Revenues	3,350,000	3,699,000
Net income (loss)	(44,000)	228,000
Earnings per share	-	$3.45
Shareholders equity	1,344,000	1,560,000

No of Employees: 12,700

FIRESTONE TIRE & RUBBER CO (THE)

1200 Firestone Parkway, Akron, OH 44317
Tel: (216) 379-7000
Telex: 986431

Chairman: John J Nevin
President: Albert E Suter
Senior Executive Officers: Jay H Rosenson (Vice Chairman), J Robert Anderson (Senior VP and Chief Financial Officer), James H Bolender (VP and Controller), Thomas M Forman (VP and General Counsel), Laurance T Burden (VP, Management Information), Roy Gilbert (VP, Treasurer and Strategic Planning), Donald L Groninger (VP, Human Resources), George W Aucott (President World Tire Group)

PRINCIPAL ACTIVITIES: Firestone is a multinational organization whose principal business since its founding has been the development, manufacture and sale of a broad line of tires for most types of vehicles. The Company is one of the five largest tire manufacturers in the world and is also a major supplier of automotive maintenance and repair services with thousands of independent dealers and approximately 1,500 Company-operated tire and automotive service centers in the United States. In addition to the sale of tires, these outlets offer a wide range of automotive maintenance and repair services. Firestone is also an important domestic producer of synthetic rubber, molded rubber products, single-ply rubber roofing systems and air springs
Trade Names: Firestone Tires, Dayton Tires, Road King Tires, Rubberguard Roofing, MasterCare Service Centers
Principal Subsidiaries: Firestone de la Argentina SAIC; Industria de Pneumaticos Firestone SA (Brazil); Firestone Canada, Inc; Firestone France SA; Firestone Italia SpA; Firestone UK Limited; CA Firestone Venezolana; Firestone Hispania
Financial Information:

	Oct 31 1985 $'000	Oct 31 1986 $'000
Sales revenues	3,602,000	3,501,000
Income (loss) before taxes	(27,000)	119,000
Net income	3,000	85,000
Dividends	34,000	31,000
Dividends per share	$0.80	$0.80
Earnings per share	$0.06	$2.16
Common stock	41,092	39,052
Retained income	1,364,000	1,418,000
Shareholders equity	1,163,000	1,167,000

No of Employees: 59,900

FIRST ALABAMA BANCSHARES INC

PO Box 1448, Montgomery, AL 36102
Tel: (205) 832-8450

Chairman: Willard L Hurley (and Chief Executive Officer); Vice Chairman: Richard D Horsley (and Chief Financial Officer)
Senior Executive Officers: Robert P Houston (Executive VP and Controller), Gordon B Trulock (Executive VP Loan Administration), Sam F Malone (Executive VP Investments), Delmar F Epton (Executive VP Operations Group)

PRINCIPAL ACTIVITIES: Bank holding company; subsidiaries are engaged in banking and financial services and insurance
Principal Subsidiaries: First Alabama Bank
Principal Bank: First Alabama Bank
Financial Information:

	Dec 31 1985 $'000	Dec 31 1986 $'000
Income before taxes	62,665	68,030
Net income	51,089	54,078
Dividends	17,299	20,235
Dividends per share	$1.12	$0.64
Earnings per share	$3.31	$1.67
Common stock	19,859	20,872
Retained income	231,133	267,379
Shareholders equity	341,507	387,420
Deposits	3,021,928	3,721,365
Total assets	3,684,056	4,396,627

No of Employees: 3,782 (FTE)

FIRST AMARILLO BANCORPORATION INC

PO Box 1331, Amarillo, TX 79180
Tel: (806) 379 5321
Telex: 738417
Telefax: (806) 378-1841; (806) 374-1151

President: Don Powell (and Chief Executive Officer)
Senior Executive Officers: Carter B Kelly (VP and Secretary), Jack Hall (Chief Accounting Officer and Assistant Secretary), H Joe Horn (Chief Financial Officer and Treasurer), Jim Wilhite (Assistant Secretary), Tess Walters (Assistant Treasurer), Margaret Chandler (Auditor)

PRINCIPAL ACTIVITIES: Banking
Principal Subsidiaries: The First National Bank of Amarillo; First Bank of Amarillo; First Amarillo Mortgage Company
Principal Bank: First National Bank of Amarillo

Financial Information:

	Dec 31 1985	Dec 31 1986
	$'000	$'000
(Loss) before taxes	(17,938)	(24,850)
Net (loss)	(17,665)	(24,850)
Dividends	297	-
Dividends per share	$0.10	-
(Loss) per share	($5.98)	($8.49)
Common stock	2,947	2,955
Retained income (deficit)	9,948	(14,902)
Stockholders equity	43,950	15,890
Deposits	757,065	714,533
Total assets	948,937	915,930

No of Employees: 570

FIRST AMERICAN BANK OF VIRGINIA

1970 Chain Bridge Road, McLean, VA 22102

Tel: (703) 821-7777

Chairman: Milton L Drewer Jr (and President and Chief Executive Officer; Vice Chairman: E Guy Ridgely

Senior Executive Officers: Eric W Erdossy (Executive VP Administration), William J Fauver (Executive VP Loans), Donald W Lee (Executive VP Finance/Operations), Daniel J Vaughan (Senior VP Credit Administration), James R Ayres III (Senior VP), Paul Moore (Senior VP Operations), Lena F Talbert (Senior VP and General Auditor), Jeremiah Manning (Senior VP Finance and Treasurer), Charles H Avent (Senior VP Consumer Loans), Robert H Hawthorne (Senior VP Commercial Banking), Donald F Tattee (Senior VP Corporate Planning), Maristeve Bradley (Senior VP Marketing), Gary L Clark (Senior VP Real Estate), Bonnie Carter (VP Personnel)

PRINCIPAL ACTIVITIES: First American Bank of Virginia serves 18 communities in Northern Virginia, Hampton Roads, Loudoun Country and the Shenandoah Valley. Headquartered in McLean, the bank has 96 offices and assets of more than $2 billion. It is the largest bank in the rapidly growing Northern Virginia market and by far the leading bank serving the businesses of that region. First American offers a complete portfolio of banking products for both businesses and individuals. Its legal lending authority is one of the largest in the mid-Atlantic states. As a member of First American Bankshares, the bank has affiliates in Washington, DC, Maryland, New York and Tennessee, whose services and lending capability are available when customers require them. Through that network, it is uniquely positioned to serve businesses with interstate or international banking needs. First American Bankshares, a $5.7 billion multi-state holding company, owned 84 percent of the shares of the Bank at year-end

Parent Company: First American Bankshares, Washington, DC

Financial Information:

	Dec 31 1985
	$'000
Income before taxes	28,409
Net income	21,190
Dividends	5,673
Dividends per share	$1.20
Earnings per share	$4.48
Common stock	47,275
Surplus	18,779
Retained income	73,013
Shareholders equity	139,067
Deposits	2,062,640
Total assets	2,377,497

No of Employees: 1,250

FIRST AMERICAN BANKSHARES, INC

First American Bank Building, 15th and H Streets NW, Washington, DC 20005

Tel: (202) 383-1400

Telex: 904228 FR AM BKSH WSH

Chairman: Clark M Clifford; Vice Chairman: Stuart Symington

President: Robert G Stevens (and Chief Executive Officer)

Senior Executive Officers: Jack W Beddow (Executive VP and Secretary), Robert J King (Senior VP and Director of Audits), William S Ringler (Senior VP), A Vincent Scoffone (Senior VP and Treasurer), Anthony Torentinos (Senior VP and Director of Human Resources)

PRINCIPAL ACTIVITIES: Banking

Trade Names: First American Bank; Money Exchange

Parent Company: First American Corporation

Principal Subsidiaries: First American Bank of Virginia; First American Bank NA; First American Bank of Maryland; First American Bank of New York; Valley Fidelity Bank and Trust Company; Eastern Shore National Bank; First American Data Services Inc

Principal Bank: First American Bank, NA

Financial Information:

	Dec 31 1985	Dec 31 1986
	$'000	$'000
Income before taxes	58,416	38,530
Net income	41,100	30,417
Dividends	9,000	9,000
Retained income	209,025	176,925
Shareholders equity	418,522	341,422
Deposits	5,917,510	4,820,662
Total assets	7,209,709	5,725,786

No of Employees: 4,548

FIRST AMERICAN CORPORATION

First American Center, Nashville, TN 37237

Tel: (615) 748-2100

Chairman: Kenneth L Roberts (and Chief Executive Officer); Vice Chairman: F G Cavin Jr

President: Andrew G Higgins (and Chief Operating Officer)

Senior Executive Officers: C R Bobo (Executive VP Senior Lending Officer), Neil L Cunningham (Executive VP Public Affairs), John C Fox (Executive VP Finance and Administration and Chief Financial Officer), M H Hamilton (Assistant to the Chairman), John W Logan (Executive VP-Asset/Liability), Willis R Rhodes (Executive VP Operations and Information Services), James D Catington (Executive VP Trust and Investment), Jay Y Phillips (Senior VP Planning and Marketing), John W Smithwick (Executive VP Human Resources), E C Stone (Executive VP Corporate Planning), Jack F Stringham (Senior VP, Secretary and General Counsel), Alex P Waddell IV (Senior VP and Treasurer)

PRINCIPAL ACTIVITIES: Banking

Principal Bank: First American National Bank of Nashville

Financial Information: *

	Dec 31 1985 $'000	Dec 31 1986 $'000
Income before taxes	54,020	68,377
Net income	43,691	53,294
Dividends	14,698	18,561
Dividends per share	$0.87	$0.99
Earnings per share	$2.44	$2.79
Common stock	118,867	175,333
Retained income	187,927	222,246
Shareholders equity	313,393	397,579
Deposits	4,157,787	4,676,966
Total assets	5,212,920	5,950,777

*Amounts have not been restated for pooling of interests with the $65 million FPB Corporation and its wholly owned subsidiary, First & Peoples National Bank of Gallatin, Tennessee, which was consummated on April 1 1987. EPS as restated would amount to $2.77 for 1986

No of Employees: 3,600

FIRST AMERICAN FINANCIAL CORPORATION

114 East Fifth Street, Santa Ana, CA 92701
Tel: (714) 558-3211
Telefax: (714) 541-6372

Chairman: D P Kennedy (and President)
Senior Executive Officers: J H Derloshon (VP and Chief Financial Officer), William G Zaenglein Jr (Secretary and Legal Counsel), Parker Kennedy (Executive VP)

PRINCIPAL ACTIVITIES: Holding company with interests in title insurance and trust business
Principal Subsidiaries: First American Title Insurance Company
Principal Bank: First Interstate Bank
Financial Information:

	1985 $'000	1986 $'000
Revenues	268,350	377,533
Income before taxes	24,835	55,923
Net income	14,040	27,328
Dividends	1,928	2,447
Dividends per share	$0.76	$0.90
Earnings per share	$5.54	$10.57
Common stock	2,543	2,747
Retained income	62,259	87,140
Shareholders equity	94,094	128,985

No of Employees: 6,054

FIRST BANCORPORATION OF OHIO

106 S Main Street, Akron, OH 44308
Tel: (216) 384-8000
Telex: 986-398

President: Howard L Flood (and Chief Executive Officer)
Senior Executive Officers: P D Shanafelt (Senior Executive VP and Chief Operating Officer), Daniel Waldron (Senior VP), Wm A Flickinger (Executive VP/Treasurer), J L Jennings (Senior VP), Dean E Krauter (Senior VP), Robert E Lawrence (Senior VP and Auditor), Terry E Patton (Senior VP/Secretary), David B Jones (Executive VP), Bill F Nash (Executive VP), C Donald Bramley (Executive VP), Lawrence A McGrath (Senior VP)

PRINCIPAL ACTIVITIES: Banking
Principal Subsidiaries: First National Bank of Ohio; Elyria Savings & Trust National Bank; The Old Phoenix National Bank of Medina; FBOH Credit Life Insurance Company
Principal Bank: First National Bank of Ohio
Financial Information:

	Dec 31 1985 $'000	Dec 31 1986 $'000
Income before taxes	27,904	35,619
Net income	27,475	31,385
Dividends	9,464	11,118
Dividends per share	$0.95*	$1.03
Earnings per share	$2.55*	$2.89
Common stock	36,076	36,179
Retained income	124,583	144,850
Shareholders equity	196,882	217,460
Deposits	2,068,532	2,164,832
Total assets	2,403,735	2,477,313

*restated for stock dividends 1985-86

No of Employees: 2,800

FIRST BANK SYSTEM INC

1200 First Bank Place East, Minneapolis, MN 55402
Tel: (612) 370-5100

Chairman: D H Ankeny (and Chief Executive Officer)
President: Dennis E Evans (and Chief Operating Officer)
Senior Executive Officers: Darrell G Knudson (Vice Chairman), Richard W Schoenke (Vice Chairman), Gerald B Fischer (Executive VP and Chief Financial Officer), John L Gigerich (Executive VP and Chief Information Officer), Gerald A Kraut (Executive VP), Mark W Sheffert (Executive VP), Richard L Shepley (Executive VP), M Claire Canavan (Senior VP), John R Danielson (Senior VP), Garrett R Hegel (Senior VP and Controller), David G Herzer (Senior VP), Jim Hetland (Senior VP), Howard W Moody (Senior VP), Frank E Porter (Senior VP, Secretary and General Counsel), John Taylor (Senior VP), James E Ulland (Senior VP), Glen Walters (Senior VP)

PRINCIPAL ACTIVITIES: Bank holding company. First Bank System, Inc is the 15th largest bank holding company in the United States comprised of First Bank Minneapolis, First Bank Saint Paul and 63 other banks and trust companies, with 137 banking offices in Minnesota, North Dakota, South Dakota, Montana, Washington and Wisconsin. The company also provides financial services through a number of domestic and international subsidiaries and offices. These services include trust, international banking, commercial and agricultural finance, capital markets, investment management, data processing, insurance brokerage, leasing, mortgage banking, venture capital, merchant banking and brokerage services
Principal Subsidiaries: Metropolitan Division: Money Center Banks:-Minneapolis: First Bank Minneapolis with branches in New York (NY) and Milwaukee (WI), UK, Cayman Islands, West Indies, Spain; CMB Investment Counselors; FBS Merchant Banking Group; First Asset Management; Matrix Leasing International, Inc; W Ross Campbell Co. Saint Paul: First Bank Saint Paul with a branch in Bahamas. Other Metropolitan Division Banks: First Bank Lake, Minneapolis; First Bank Plymouth; First Bank Northtown, Blaine; First Bank Burnsville; First Bank Edina; First Bank Southdale, Edina; First Bank Hopkins; First Bank Robbinsdale; First Bank Grand, Saint Paul; First Bank East, Saint Paul; First Bank Security, Saint Paul; First Bank White Bear Lake. Other Metropolitan Division Subsidiaries: FBS Business Finance Corporation; FBS Leasing; FBS Mortgage Corporation (Commercial). Regional Division: First Banks throughout Minnesota, North Dakota, South Dakota, Montana, Washington and FBS Agricultural Credit Corporation in Iowa. Financial Services Division: FBS Brokerage Services, Inc; FBS Insurance; FBS Mortgage Corporation (Residential). Other Operating Subsidiaries: FBS Information Services; FBS Properties Management, Inc; FBS Venture Capital Company; FBS Capital Markets Group; FBS Capital Markets Ltd; FBS Capital Markets Funding Inc. Wisconsin Division: First Bank (NA), LaCrosse, Milwaukee. Trust and Investment Management Division: First Trust Company Inc, St Paul

Principal Bank: First Bank Minneapolis; First Bank Saint Paul
Financial Information:

	Dec 31 1985	Dec 31 1986
	$'000	$'000
Income before taxes	194,974	177,297
Net income	166,781	202,921
Dividends*	44,153	51,904
Dividends per share*	$0.80	$0.91
Earnings per share-primary	$2.84	$3.42
Common stock	77,710	78,455
Retained income	1,111,501	1,255,780
Shareholders equity	1,239,678	1,416,583
Deposits	16,039,194	16,260,609
Total assets	25,484,355	28,011,495

*common stock

Number of Shareholders: 12,825
No of Employees: 9,970

FIRST BANKERS CORP OF FLORIDA

PO Box T, Pompano Beach, FL 33061
Tel: (305) 941-2810

Chairman: Frank L McGinn
President: M G Sanchez (and Chief Executive Officer)
Senior Executive Officers: Arthur E Kavanagh (Executive VP and Treasurer), Edward J Mangan (Executive VP), H Eugene Nace (Executive VP), Roger M Bruce Jr (Senior VP), John M Burford (Senior VP), J Norman Coleman (Senior VP), Paul D Lockard (Senior VP), Jose G Tamblyn (Senior VP)

PRINCIPAL ACTIVITIES: Banking
Principal Subsidiaries: First Bankers Data Corp; First Bankers Management Group Inc; First Bankers NA; First Bankers Service Corp
Financial Information:

$'000

No of Employees: 60

FIRST BOSTON INC

Park Avenue Plaza, New York, NY 10055
Tel: (212) 909-2000

Chairman: Alvin V Shoemaker; Vice Chairman: John M Hennessy
President: Peter Buchanan (and Chief Executive Officer)
Senior Executive Officers: George L Shinn (Chairman (Executive Committee), Michael G Zeiss (VP and Secretary), Morgan C Brown III (VP and Assistant Secretary)

PRINCIPAL ACTIVITIES: Holding company whose subsidiaries are engaged in financial services operations
Principal Subsidiaries: First Boston Corp; First Boston International Ltd; First Boston Securities Corp; First Boston Asset Management Corp; First Boston Capital Group Inc; First Boston Research & Development Corp
Principal Bank: Citibank
Financial Information:

	Dec 31 1985	Dec 31 1986
	$'000	$'000
Revenues	888,290	1,309,765
Net income	130,297	180,555
Earnings per share	$4.29	$5.14
Shareholders equity	703,820	958,780
Total assets	45,531,110	48,618,206

No of Employees: 4,493

FIRST CAPITAL CORPORATION

PO Box 291, Jackson, MS 39205
Tel: (601) 354-5111

Chairman: Frank R Day (and Chief Executive Officer)
President: Richard D Chotard
Senior Executive Officers: Clyde B Edwards Jr (Executive VP), R R Swittenberg (Executive VP), John B Tullos (Secretary and Treasurer)

PRINCIPAL ACTIVITIES: Banking services
Principal Subsidiaries: First Building Corp; First National Bank; First Service Corp
Principal Bank: First National Bank
Financial Information:

	Dec 31 1985
	$'000
Revenues	205,000
Net income	21,000
Total assets	2,300,000

No of Employees: 1,400

FIRST CHEMICAL CORPORATION

700 N Street, Jackson, MS 39201
Tel: (601) 969-0217

Chairman: James K Williams
President: O E Wall
Senior Executive Officers: R B Barker (VP), H D Gillilard (Treasurer)

PRINCIPAL ACTIVITIES: Manufacture of chemicals
Parent Company: First Mississippi Corporation, Jackson, MS
Principal Bank: First National Bank of Jackson County
Financial Information:

	$'000
Sales revenues	79,000

No of Employees: 140

FIRST CHICAGO CORPORATION

One First National Plaza, Chicago, IL 60670
Tel: (312) 732-4000
Cable: National
Telex: 4330253 FNBCUI

Chairman: Barry F Sullivan (and Chief Executive Officer)
President: Richard L Thomas
Senior Executive Officers: William J McDonough, Burton R Abrahams, M James Alef Jr, James E Annable, Kenneth G Arnesen, J Stephen Baine, John W Ballantine, Scott E Bates, William E Bennett, George C Bergland, James D Best, L Gene Beube, Gary P Brinson, Martin M Bronstein, Clark Burrus, F Gerald Byrne, John A Canning Jr, James J Carey, Leonard Caronia, Kent P Dauten, Alan F Delp, Stephen C Diamond, David P Earle III, Marion R Foote, Lawrence E Fox, A D Frazier Jr, Richard C Gallagher, Mark T Garrigus, Donald B Gibbins, John E Gilchrist, Richard J Gilgan, Earl W Glazier Jr, Donald Glickman, Emile S Godfrey, Sherman I Goldberg, Donna R Green, William J Hagenah, Jean D Hamilton, Stephen L Harris, Richard C Hartnack, David M Harvey, John B Haseltine, Paul C Hennessy, William R Hinchman, Thomas H Hodges, Donald R Hollis, Carol A Holmes, Jacqueline A Hurlbutt, Michael S Kessler, Norma S Lauder, William S Lear, Benjamin F Lenhardt Jr, Michael R Leyden, Daniel A Lupiani, Scott P Marks, Arthur J Massolo, Paul M McGonagle, G Edward Means, Anthony K Metta, M Peter Miller, William E Moeller, Charles H Montgomery, Perry Moore, Leo F Mullin, Angelo Papa, David J Paulus, Charles J Petre, William J Roberts, James Y Robertson, Robert A Rosholt, Barry M Sabloff, Gordon J Sapstead, Ian L Schmiegelow, D John Stavropoulos, Page W Stockwell, Geoffrey L Stringer, L Britt Swofford, Jeffrey P Tassani, J Mikesell Thomas, Michael E Tobin, E Neal Trogdon, Francois Van Reephinghen, David J Vitale, James P Wallace III, James S Winn Jr, Richard L Wood

PRINCIPAL ACTIVITIES: Banking
Principal Subsidiaries: The First National Bank of Chicago; American National; Bank of Chicago

Financial Information:

	Jun 30 1987
	$'000
(Loss) before taxes	(718,387)
Net (loss)	(698,287)
Common dividends	20,965
Dividends per share-annual	$1.50
(Loss) per share	($12.74)
Common stock	280,968
Retained earnings	139,760
Shareholders equity	1,692,316
Deposits	30,534,858
Total assets	41,664,759

No of Employees: 13,900

FIRST CITY BANCORPORATION OF TEXAS, INC

1001 Main Street, Houston, TX 77002
Tel: (713) 658-6873

Senior Chairman: J A Elkins Jr (and Chief Executive Officer); Chairman: Daniel C Arnold (and President)
Senior Executive Officers: Roland L Burrows (Executive VP Human Resource Facilities and Interbank Services), W L Medford (Executive VP Finance), Betty S Peabody (Executive VP), Larry L Snaufer (Executive VP), Hugh J Barrett (Senior VP Technical Planning and Co-ordination), Robert W Brown (Senior VP and Auditor), Joe J Fulmer (Senior VP Human Resources), Charles W Hinton (Senior VP Human Resources), Theodore H Howe (Senior VP Human Resources), Robert R Robertson Jr (Senior VP Audit and Credit Administration), P L Sampson (Senior VP and Secretary), Vernon Scott (Senior VP Bank Co-ordination), Roy A Skoba (Senior VP Marketing), Jack L Whitt (Senior VP Bank Co-ordination), James E Day (VP Public Relations)

PRINCIPAL ACTIVITIES: Banking
Principal Subsidiaries: Central Park Bank; Financial Center Inc; First Bank & Trust Co; First City Bank; First City National Bank; First City Energy Finance Co; First City Financial Corp; First City Leasing Corp; First City Services Co; First Security Finance Systems Inc; First Financial Advisors Inc; Graham National Bank
Principal Bank: First City National Bank of Houston
Financial Information:

	Dec 31 1985	Dec 31 1986
	$'000	$'000
Net income (loss)	41,811	(401,962)
Earnings (loss) per share	$0.75	($12.70)
Shareholders equity	974,000	560,959
Deposits	12,902,685	11,045,079
Total assets	16,819,100	13,681,179

No of Employees: 7,612

FIRST CITY INDUSTRIES INC

8383 Wilshire Boulevard, Suite 800, Beverly Hills, CA 90211
Tel: (213) 852-0499

Chairman: William Belzberg (and President and Chief Executive Officer)
Senior Executive Officers: Robert B Friedman (Senior VP), John C Crum (Senior VP, Secretary, Treasurer and Chief Financial Officer)

PRINCIPAL ACTIVITIES: Production of electrical building supplies, domestic electrical appliances, garment fasteners, door locks; property development
Trade Names: NuTone, Hamilton Beach, Scovill, Yale
Principal Subsidiaries: First City Properties Inc; Scovill Inc; Hamilton Beach Inc; NuTone inc; Scovill Apparel Fasteners Inc; Yale Security Inc
Principal Bank: Security Pacific National Bank

Financial Information:

	Dec 31 1986
	$'000
Sales revenues	637,808
Net (loss)	(9,501)
(Loss) per share	($1.54)
Shareholders equity	91,494

FIRST CITY NATIONAL BANK OF HOUSTON

1001 Main Street, Houston, TX 77002
Tel: (713) 658-6011

Chairman: Ernest Deal (and Chief Executive Officer); Chairman of Executive Committee: Nat S Rogers; Vice Chairmen: Grover Ellis, Thomas K Matthews II
President: Fred L Bollerer
Senior Executive Officers: John O Bullington (Executive VP Commercial), George W Grosz (Executive VP), Fred D Herring (Executive VP Retail), Robert C Howard (Executive VP International), Michael D Williams (Executive VP Operations), Randall E Meyer (Executive VP Special Industries), Al J Newman (Executive VP Credit), Robert D Wagner Jr (Executive VP Energy), F T Webster (Executive VP Petroleum and Minerals)

PRINCIPAL ACTIVITIES: Banking
Parent Company: First City Bancorporation of Texas Inc

No of Employees: 2,000

FIRST COLONIAL BANKSHARES CORPORATION

5825 West Belmont Avenue, Chicago, IL 60634
Tel: (312) 237 4242

Chairman: Paul C Johnson (and President and Chief Executive Officer)
Senior Executive Officers: William R Duquaine (Executive VP), Robert F Sherman (Executive VP), Thomas J Maier (Senior VP, Chief Financial Officer and Secretary), Hubert F Messe (VP), Walter A Krolski (VP Marketing), James P Trunck (VP), Marlene Katsion (VP), Robert Dodro (VP), Richard Slehofer (Controller)

PRINCIPAL ACTIVITIES: Banking services
Principal Bank: American National Bank and Trust Company
Financial Information:

	Dec 31 1985
	$'000
Revenues	50,150
Net income	5,280

No of Employees: 300

FIRST COLUMBIA FINANCIAL CORPORATION

5850 S Ulster Circle, Englewood, CO 80111
Tel: (303) 773-3444

Chairman: Bob R Baker (and President)
Senior Executive Officers: Larry A Olsen (Senior Executive VP, President of Columbia Savings), Thomas J Brennan (Senior Executive VP of the Company and Columbia Savings), Charles I Thompson (Executive VP and Chief Financial Officer of the Company and Columbia Savings), Jerry G Percy (Senior VP, Secretary and General Counsel of the Company and Columbia Savings), Gary J Nesmith (Executive VP and Chief Lending Officer of Columbia Savings), Ronald L Johnson (Senior VP-Retail Banking of Columbia Savings), Joseph H Kremer (Senior VP-Marketing and Corporate Relations of Columbia Savings), Terence W Kucharski (Senior VP-Administration of Columbia Savings), Dennis R LaVigne (Senior VP Investments of Columbia Savings), Nicholas M Schmidt (President of Colrad Development Corporation)

PRINCIPAL ACTIVITIES: First Columbia Financial Corporation is a Colorado holding company with assets of $2.7 billion at

December 31 1986 whose principal subsidiary is engaged in the savings and loan business

Principal Subsidiaries: Columbia Savings, A Federal Savings and Loan Assocation; Colrad Development Corporation; Columbia Insurance Service, Inc; Columbia Capital Corporation

Principal Bank: United Bank

Financial Information:

	Dec 31 1985	Dec 31 1986
	$'000	$'000
Total revenues	278,026	276,205
(Loss) before taxes*	(7,433)	(39,849)
Net (loss)	(5,806)	(14,254)
(Loss) per share	($2.34)	($5.69)
Common stock	30,445	30,762
Retained income (deficit)	5,833	(8,421)
Shareholders equity	36,003	22,066
Deposits	1,795,826	1,650,724
Total assets	2,439,340	2,696,460

*from continuing operations

Principal Shareholders: First Eagle Fund NV and Arnhold and S Bleichroeder, Inc (9.6%); Cameo Partners (9.5%); Research to Prevent Blindness, Inc (8.8%); CHC Investment Co (7.3%); Lew R Wasserman MCA INC (7.1%)

No of Employees: 600

FIRST COMMERCE BANCSHARES INC

NBC Center, 13th and O Streets, Lincoln, NE 68508

Tel: (402) 472 4110

Chairman: James Stuart Jr (and President and Chief Executive Officer)

Senior Executive Officers: Hugh Hansen (Executive VP), Thomas E Henning (Executive VP), John Sable (Senior VP Finance and Secretary), Joan K Cromwell (VP and Senior Auditor), Donald D Kinley (VP and Assistant Treasurer)

PRINCIPAL ACTIVITIES: First Commerce Bancshares Inc is a multi-bank holding company organized as a Nebraska corporation. The Corporation's primary business is the ownership and management of six commercial bank subsidiaries and three industrial loan and investment company subsidiaries. These subsidiaries provide a comprehensive range of trust, commercial consumer, correspondent and mortgage banking services. The Corporation provides computer services to banks throughout Nebraska and surrounding states through its subsidiary, NBC Computer Services Corporation. NBC Computer Services Corporation presently has four computer centers in Nebraska and one in Denver. The company is geographically located throughout Nebraska with a market presence in nearly every major city of the state, including Lincoln, Grand Island, Hastings, Kearney, West Point, Columbus, North Platte and Scottsbluff

Principal Subsidiaries: National Bank of Commerce Trust and Savings Association, Lincoln; City National Bank and Trust Company, Hastings; First National Bank and Trust Company, Kearney; Overland National Bank, Grand Island; North Platte National Bank, North Platte; First National Bank, West Point; Commerce Savings Lincoln Inc; Commerce Savings Scottsbluff Inc; Commerce Savings Columbus Inc; NBC Computer Services Corporation

Financial Information:

	Dec 31 1985	Dec 31 1986
	$'000	$'000
Revenues	109,183	105,333
Income before taxes	7,857	6,403
Net income	5,762	5,198
Dividends	593	760
Dividends per share	$0.12	$0.25
Earnings per share	$1.90	$1.71
Common stock	3,083	3,085
Retained income	46,072	50,510
Shareholders equity	65,417	69,873
Deposits	717,867	744,064
Total assets	900,987	919,251

No of Employees: 851

FIRST COMMERCE CORP LOUISIANA

210 Baronne Street, New Orleans, LA 70112

Tel: (504) 561 1371

Chairman: William E Trotter III

President: Ian Arnof (and Chief Executive Officer)

Senior Executive Officers: Jack W Parker (Treasurer and Chief Financial Officer)

PRINCIPAL ACTIVITIES: Holding company with interests in banking

Principal Subsidiaries: First National Bank of Commerce

Financial Information:

	Dec 31 1985
	$'000
Revenues	311,990
Net income	22,370

No of Employees: 2,690

FIRST COMMERCIAL CORPORATION

Capitol & Broadway, Little Rock, AR 72201

Tel: (501) 371-7000

Chairman: B F Vinson (and Chief Executive Officer); Vice Chairmen: James R Cobb (and Executive VP)

President: Barnett Grace

Senior Executive Officers: W H Bowen (Chairman Executive Committee), David Wilcox (Treasurer)

PRINCIPAL ACTIVITIES: Banking

Principal Subsidiaries: First Commercial Bank; First Commercial Mortgage Co; First National Bank

Financial Information:

	Dec 31 1985
	$'000
Revenues	126,016
Net income	10,418

FIRST COMMMUNITY BANCORP INC

124 North Water Street, PO Box 4900, Rockford, IL 61110

Tel: (815) 962 3003

Chairman: Howard E Bell

President: Richard R Bastian III

Senior Executive Officers: Donald H Pratt (Senior VP), Richard S Peterson (Senior VP and Secretary), Gregory A Abbott (VP), Jerry A Lecklider (VP, Controller and Treasurer)

PRINCIPAL ACTIVITIES: Holding company with interests in banking

Principal Subsidiaries: First Bank; First Bank of Loves Park; First COmmunity National Bank; First National Bank & Trust Co; Guaranty National Bank

Principal Bank: First National Bank and Trust Co

Financial Information:

	Dec 31 1985
	$'000
Revenues	50,170
Net income	4,280

No of Employees: 300

FIRST DATA MANAGEMENT COMPANY INC

120 North Robinson Street, PO Box 25189, Oklahoma City, OK 73125
Tel: (405) 232 6600

Chairman: Gary D Bunch (and President)
Senior Executive Officers: William P Adams (Executive VP), Ethan R Norris (Executive VP), Richard N Garman (VP and Chief Financial Officer)

PRINCIPAL ACTIVITIES: Computer services
Principal Bank: First National Bank
Financial Information:

	$'000
Sales revenues	36,220

No of Employees: 370

FIRST DISTRICT ASSOCIATION

216 W Commercial Street, Litchfield, MN 55355
Tel: (612) 693-3236

President: M H Lenzmeier
Senior Executive Officers: Bill Dropik (VP), Donald Slinden (Treasurer)

PRINCIPAL ACTIVITIES: Manufacture of dairy products
Principal Bank: First State Bank
Financial Information:

	$'000
Sales revenues	120,000

No of Employees: 180

FIRST EASTERN CORPORATION PENNSYLVANIA

11 W Market Street, Wilkes-Barre, PA 18768
Tel: (717) 826-4623
Telex: TWX 510 6582824 few first wlb

Chairman: Richard M Ross Jr (and President and Chief Executive Officer)
President: William R Mainwaring
Senior Executive Officers: William R Mainwaring (Executive VP), Jos F McKeown (Executive VP), Bernard F Slusarz (Senior VP), Thomas Peeler III (Senior VP), Robert P Richardson (Senior VP), Emerino J Marchetti (Senior VP)

PRINCIPAL ACTIVITIES: Banking
Principal Bank: Fidelity Bank
Financial Information:

	Dec 31 1985
	$'000
Revenues	139,200
Net income	13,270

No of Employees: 1,000

FIRST EMPIRE STATE CORPORATION

One M&T Plaza, Buffalo, NY 14240
Tel: (716) 842 5445

Chairman: Robert G Wilmers (and President and Chief Executive Officer)
Senior Executive Officers: James L Vardon (Executive VP and Chief Financial Officer), Dennis C Smith (VP), Richard A Lammert (Legal Counsel and Secretary)

PRINCIPAL ACTIVITIES: Financial services including mortgages and loans
Principal Subsidiaries: First National Bank; Manufacturers and Traders Trust Co
No of Employees: 2,090

FIRST EXECUTIVE CORPORATION

11444 West Olympic Blvd, Los Angeles, CA 90064
Tel: (213) 312-1000

Chairman: Fred Carr (and President and Chief Executive Officer)
Senior Executive Officers: William J Adams (VP, General Counsel and Secretary), Merle A Horst (VP and Chief Financial Officer), Russell J Lasher (VP and Treasurer), Cheryl A Wada (VP)

PRINCIPAL ACTIVITIES: Insurance services including life insurance and annuities
Principal Subsidiaries: (100% owned unless stated): Executive Life Insurance Co; Executive Life Insurance Co of New York (96%)
Principal Bank: Security Pacific National Bank
Financial Information:

	1986
	$'000
Revenues	3,600,000
Net income	141,000

No of Employees: 600

FIRST FARWEST CORPORATION

400 Southwest Sixth Avenue, Portland, OR 97204
Tel: (503) 224 7740

Chairman: Forrest W Simmons (and Chief Executive Officer)
President: Don K Lloyd
Senior Executive Officers: William C Bittick Jr (Secretary and Treasurer), Ronald T Delude (VP Finance)

PRINCIPAL ACTIVITIES: Life insurance
Principal Subsidiaries: National Hospital Association; First Farwest Life Insurance Co; Farwest American Assurance Co
Principal Bank: United States National Bank
Financial Information:

	Dec 31 1985
	$'000
Revenues	132,740
Net income	1,380

No of Employees: 325

FIRST FEDERAL OF MICHIGAN

1001 Woodward, Detroit, MI 48226
Tel: (313) 965-1400

Chairman: James A Aliber (and Chief Executive Officer); Vice Chairman: Donald H Mitzel
President: C Gene Harling (and Chief Operating Officer)
Senior Executive Officers: Michael T Welsh (Senior VP and Secretary), Richard Platt (Senior VP Marketing), Ronald A Sinclair (Senior VP Mortgage), William A Hoffhines (Senior VP), Eric H Truhol (Senior VP Personnel), Richard W Neu (Senior VP and Chief Financial Officer)

PRINCIPAL ACTIVITIES: Banking and financial services including loans and savings
Principal Subsidiaries: 1001 Holding Inc; Bay Savings Bank; 1001 Services Inc
Principal Bank: National Bank of Detroit
Financial Information:

	Dec 31 1985	Dec 31 1986
	$'000	$'000
Net income	55,680	73,023
Earnings per share	$5.31	$6.58
Shareholders equity	292,082	361,622
Deposits	-	5,047,913
Total assets	10,195,908	11,271,916

No of Employees: 2,214

FIRST FEDERAL SAVINGS & LOAN ASSOCIATION CHARLESTON

34 Broad Street, Charleston, SC 29401
Tel: (803) 724 0800

President: Robert L Cale (and Chief Executive Officer)
Senior Executive Officers: A Thomas Hood (Executive VP), A L Hutchinson Jr (Executive VP), Malcolm M Erwin Jr (Senior VP), John L Ott Jr (Senior VP)

PRINCIPAL ACTIVITIES: Financial services including savings and loans
Principal Bank: Federal Reserve Bank
Financial Information:

	Dec 31 1985
	$'000
Revenues	68,840
Net income	4,160

No of Employees: 290

FIRST FEDERAL SAVINGS & LOAN ASSOCIATION OF AUSTIN

200 East Tenth Street, Austin, TX 78701
Tel: (512) 476 8301

Chairman: Charles F Herring (and Chief Executive Officer)
President: Joe E Simpson (and Chief Operating Officer)
Senior Executive Officers: James E Stafford (Executive VP), Bobbie Lou Clark (Senior VP), Robert E Rhoades (Senior VP), T J Sandridge (Senior VP), Charles C Shierlow (Senior VP and Secretary), Alfred Staehely (Senior VP), Richard N Waite Jr (Senior VP), Philip Breland (Senior VP Commercial Lending)

PRINCIPAL ACTIVITIES: Financial services including savings and loans
Principal Subsidiaries: First Service Corp
Principal Bank: Texas Commerce Bank

No of Employees: 400

FIRST FEDERAL SAVINGS & LOAN ASSOCIATION OF SOUTH CAROLINA

301 College St, Greenville, SC 29602
Tel: (803) 271-7222

Chairman: H Ray Davis (and Chief Executive Officer)
President: Luther C Boliek (and Chief Operating Officer)
Senior Executive Officers: Thomas M Creech (Executive VP, Purchasing, Advertising and Marketing), James League (Executive VP and Mortgage Group Manager), Mason G Alexander (Executive VP and Retail Banking Group Manager), Milton E Futch (Executive VP, Chief Financial Officer), Jerry Chapman (President of Real Estate Group)

PRINCIPAL ACTIVITIES: Savings, loans and financial services
Principal Subsidiaries: Academy Mortgage Corporation; The First Real Estate Group Inc; Palisades Group Inc
Financial Information:

	Jun 30 1986	Jun 30 1987
	$'000	$'000
Income before taxes	5,199	10,798
Net income	5,179	7,775
Earnings per share	$1.68	$1.82
Common stock	4,215	4,227
Retained income	34,537	42,312
Shareholders equity	71,415	79,309
Deposits	1,427,189	1,463,451
Total assets	1,873,311	1,899,360

No of Employees: 1,125

FIRST FEDERAL SAVINGS BANK OF ARIZONA

3003 North Central Avenue, Phoenix, AZ 85012
Tel: (602) 248-4221

Chairman: Gene E Rice (and President and Chief Executive Officer)

Senior Executive Officers: George E Leonard (Executive VP), Ernest F Modzelewski (Executive VP), Robba Benjamin (Senior VP), Delbert R Ellis (Senior VP), Michael Feeney (Senior VP), Gary W Hickel (Senior VP), Gary R Javitch (Senior VP and Treasurer), Norman E Rahan (Senior VP), Michael J Boland (Senior VP), Phillip D Wilson (Senior VP), Carroll Roarty (Senior VP), Kenneth A McLemore (VP and Controller), William P Inman (Corporate Secretary and Counsel)

PRINCIPAL ACTIVITIES: First Federal is principally engaged in the business of attracting deposits from the general public and using such deposits, together with borrowings, proceeds of loan sales and other funds, to originate and purchase real estate loans, mortgage-backed securities and other investments. Loans are also originated and purchased for portfolio and for sale by First Federal's mortgage banking subsidiary, First Service Mortgage Corporation. Through First Service Corporation and its real estate joint ventures, First Federal is also significantly engaged in real estate development activities

Principal Subsidiaries: First Service Mortgage Corporation; First Service Insurance Corporation; First Service Life Insurance Corporation; First Service Franchising Inc; First Service Corporation; First Service Investment Corporation; First Service Securities Corporation; First Service Management Corporation

Principal Bank: FHLB of San Francisco

No of Employees: 1,471

FIRST FEDERAL SAVINGS BANK OF CALIFORNIA

401 Wilshire Boulevard, Santa Monica, CA 90401

Tel: (213) 458 3011

Chairman: William S Mortensen (and Chief Executive Officer)

President: Gerald R Johnson (and Chief Operating Officer)

Senior Executive Officers: Babette E Heimbuch (Executive VP, Treasurer and Chief Financial Officer), Martin B Gottlieb (Senior VP), Valdemar G Mellgren III (Senior VP)

PRINCIPAL ACTIVITIES: Banking

Principal Subsidiaries: Oceanside Insurance Agency Inc; Santa Monica Capital Group; Seaside Financial Corp

Principal Bank: Union Bank

Financial Information:

	Dec 31 1985
	$'000
Revenues	136,100
Net income	10,120

No of Employees: 320

FIRST FIDELITY BANCORPORATION

550 Broad Street, Newark, NJ 07102

Tel: (201) 565-3200

Chairman: Robert R Ferguson (and President and Chief Executive Officer); Chairman of Executive Committee: W P Stillman; Vice Chairmen: Elwood F Kirkman

Senior Executive Officers: Edward D Knapp (Senior Executive VP), William P Tuggle III (Executive VP)

PRINCIPAL ACTIVITIES: Banking

Principal Bank: First Fidelity Bank, N.A., New Jersey

Financial Information:

	Dec 31 1986 (12 mths) $'000	Jun 30 1987 (6 mths) $'000
Income before taxes	132,292	18,490
Net income	119,543	24,477
Commomn dividends	43,597	23,447
Preferred dividends	8,117	3,810
Dividends per common share	$1.62	$0.84
Earnings per share(1)	$4.12	$0.74
Earnings per share(2)	$3.95	N/A(3)
Common stock	173,271	175,143
Retained income	439,559	436,779
Shareholders equity	890,397	893,303
Deposits	12,054,723	11,324,041
Total assets	15,170,304	15,367,698

(1) primary
(2) fully diluted
(3) N/A-Not Applicable-Anti-Dilutive

No of Employees: 9,900

FIRST FINANCIAL BANCORP OHIO

108 South Main Street, Monroe, OH 45050
Tel: (513) 867 4700

President: Richard J Fitton (and Chief Executive Officer)
Senior Executive Officers: William G Rutherford (VP), Carlos E Watkins (VP and Treasurer), Richard Weinman (VP and Secretary)

PRINCIPAL ACTIVITIES: Banking services
Principal Bank: First National Bank
Financial Information:

	Dec 31 1985 $'000
Revenues	74,690
Net income	8,430

No of Employees: 640

FIRST FINANCIAL MANAGEMENT CORPORATION

3 Corporate Square, Suite 700, Atlanta, GA 30329
Tel: (404) 321 0120

Chairman: Patrick H Thomas (and President and Chief Executive Officer)
Senior Executive Officers: M Tarlton Pittard (Executive VP, Treasurer, Chief Financial Officer and Secretary), Clarence L Coleman (Executive VP Service), Harold H Kinney (Senior VP), T J Manus (Senior VP), Norman E Marwitz Jr (Group Executive VP), Harlan F Seymour (VP), H L Miller (VP and Auditor), R E Johnston (VP Human Resources)

PRINCIPAL ACTIVITIES: Information processing services
Principal Bank: First Georgia Bank
Financial Information:

	$'000
Sales revenues	52,400

No of Employees: 840

FIRST FINANCIAL SAVINGS & LOAN ASSOCIATION

100 First Financial Plaza, Stevens Point, WI 54481
Tel: (715) 341 0400

Chairman: Ralph R Steven (and Chief Executive Officer)
President: John C Seramur (and Chief Operating Officer)
Senior Executive Officers: Bruce R Buss (VP, Treasurer and Chief Financial Officer), Paul C Kehrer (Secretary)

PRINCIPAL ACTIVITIES: Financial services including savings and loans
Financial Information:

	Dec 31 1985 $'000
Revenues	242,170

No of Employees: 1,220

FIRST FLORIDA BANKS INC

111 Madison St, PO Box 1810, Tampa, FL 33601
Tel: (813) 224-1455

Chairman: Bronson A Thayer (and Chief Executive Officer); Vice Chairman: J C Wulbern
President: D L Murphy
Senior Executive Officers: John H Boyet (Executive VP), F A DiMarco (Executive VP and Secretary), W H Thompson (Executive VP and Treasurer), J W Warren (Executive VP), F L Groves Jr (Executive VP Consumer Lending), J M Kelly (Executive VP Trust Services), F M Roebuck (Executive VP Bond Department)

PRINCIPAL ACTIVITIES: Banking
Principal Subsidiaries: First Florida Bank, NA; First Financial Properties Inc; First Florida Bank St Petersburg Branch
Financial Information:

	Dec 31 1985 $'000	Dec 31 1986 $'000
Net income	47,972	47,152
Earnings per share	$3.04	$2.97
Shareholders equity	274,115	315,845
Deposits	3,271,240	4,043,714
Total assets	4,026,340	4,845,177

Principal Shareholders: 7 L Corporation (36%)
No of Employees: 3,513

FIRST HAWAIIAN, INC

165 South King Street, Honolulu, HI 96813
Tel: (808) 525-7000
Telex: 7430070

Chairman: John D Bellinger (and President and Chief Executive Officer)
Senior Executive Officers: Hugh R Pingree (Executive VP), Walter A Dods Jr (Executive VP), John A Hoag (Executive VP), Philip H Ching (VP), Howard H Karr (VP and Treasurer), Donald G Horner (VP), Herbert E Wolff (VP and Secretary)

PRINCIPAL ACTIVITIES: Banking, financing, leasing and consumer financing
Principal Subsidiaries: First Hawaiian Bank; First Hawaiian Overseas Corp; FHB Properties Inc; First Hawaiian Creditcorp, Inc (Formerly Hawaii Thrift & Loan Inc); First Hawaiian Leasing; FHI International Inc
Principal Bank: First Hawaiian Bank
Financial Information:

	Dec 31 1985 $'000	Dec 31 1986 $'000
Revenues	298,119	311,411
Income before taxes	34,389	34,106
Net income	27,155	30,750
Dividends	9,708	11,381
Dividends per share	$0.725	$0.85
Earnings per share	$2.03	$2.30
Common stock	33,570	67,140
Retained income	107,864	93,663
Shareholders equity	167,993	187,260
Deposits	2,760,542	3,099,803
Total assets	3,241,510	3,609,853

No of Employees: 2,201 (worldwide)

FIRST ILLINOIS CORPORATION

800 Davis Street, Evanstown, IL 60204
Tel: (312) 866 5500

Chairman: Howard B Silverman (and President and Chief Executive Officer)

Senior Executive Officers: James A Doyle (VP), Bruce N Duff (VP), Michael J Fitzgerald (VP and Auditor), Robert A Lennox Jr (VP), Bruce I McPhee (VP and Assistant Secretary), Howard I Kain (Treasurer and Secrertary), Michael D Stronberg (Secretary and Legal Counsel)

PRINCIPAL ACTIVITIES: Banking

Principal Subsidiaries: First Illinois Bank NA

Principal Bank: Continental Illinois National Bank

Financial Information:

	Dec 31 1985
	$'000
Revenues	99,250
Net income	9,800

No of Employees: 450

FIRST INDIANA FEDERAL SAVINGS BANK

One North Pennsylvania Street, Indianapolis, IN 46204

Tel: (317) 269 1200

Chairman: Robert H McKinney

President: Owen B Melton Jr

Senior Executive Officers: Larry M Campbell (Senior VP), David L Gray (Senior VP and Treasurer), Timothy J O'Neill Jr (Senior VP), R Douglas Sylvester (Senior VP Loans), David A Lindsey (Senior VP Marketing), James D Cunliffe (VP Personnel)

PRINCIPAL ACTIVITIES: Banking services

No of Employees: 270

FIRST INTERSTATE BANCORP

707 Wilshire Blvd, PO Box 54068, Los Angeles, CA 90017

Tel: (213) 614-3001

Cable: FIBANCORP, Los Angeles

Telex: 674421

Chairman: Joseph J Pinola (and Chief Executive Officer); Vice Chairman: George E Rothell

President: Edward M Carson

Senior Executive Officers: William J Bogaard (Executive VP), James F Burns Jr (Executive VP Finance), Don M Griffith (Executive VP), Gerald L Shott (Executive VP)

PRINCIPAL ACTIVITIES: Banking

Principal Subsidiaries: Subsidiary Banks: First Interstate Bank of:-California, Los Angeles; Oregon NA, Portland; Arizona NA, Phoenix; Oklahoma City, Oklahoma; Nevada NA, Reno; Denver NA, Colorado; Washington NA, Seattle; Utah NA, Salt Lake City; Idaho NA, Boise; Albuquerque, New Mexico; Casper NA, Wyoming; Fort Collins NA, Colorado; Lea County, New Mexico; Santa Fe NA, New Mexico; Englewood NA, Colorado; Kalispell NA, Montana; Roswell, New Mexico; Great Falls, Montana; Laramie NA, Wyoming; Gallup, New Mexico; Riverton NA, Wyoming; Glacier County, Montana; Bancard Company NA, Los Angeles

Financial Information:

	Dec 31 1985	Dec 31 1986
	$'000	$'000
Income before taxes	379,458	425,334
Net income	313,058	337,934
Dividends-common stock	107,123	120,433
Dividends-preferred	11,633	2,906
Dividends per common share	$2.26	$2.62
Dividends per pref share	$2.375	$2.375
Earnings per share(1)	$6.84	$7.19
Earnings per share(2)	$6.64	$7.13
Common stock (3)	43,503	47,015
Common stock (4)	87,006	94,029
Preferred stock	120,510	2,453
Capital surplus	534,938	671,916
Retained income	1,771,658	1,991,351
Shareholders equity	2,514,112	2,759,749
Deposits	35,554,486	39,457,006
Total assets	48,991,038	55,421,736

(1) primary
(2) fully diluted
(3) shares outstanding in thousands
(4) par value $2 a share

No of Employees: 36,552

FIRST INTERSTATE BANK OF UTAH, N.A.

175 S Main Street, Salt Lake City, UT 84111
Tel: (801) 350-7000

Chairman: Leon G Harmon (and President and Chief Executive Officer)

Senior Executive Officers: Richard W Kieffer (Executive VP Retail Banking), Robert J Ward (Executive VP Commercial Banking), Michael D Fowler (Senior VP Finance), George L Moosman (Senior VP), Robert H Owens (Senior VP Loan Administration), A B Simmons (Senior VP Marketing), John Gisler (VP Administration), D M Watkins (VP Branch Administration)

PRINCIPAL ACTIVITIES: Banking

Parent Company: First Interstate Bancorp, Los Angeles, CA

No of Employees: 850

FIRST INTERSTATE CORPORATION OF ALASKA

716 West Fourth Avenue, Anchorage, AK 99501
Tel: (907) 276 7200

Chairman: A B Swalling

President: R J Miller Jr (and Chief Executive Officer)

Senior Executive Officers: Tony J Swartz (Senior VP), Charles L Whitney (Secretary and Treasurer), Frank M Reed Sr (Senior VP Community Affairs), James E Pratt (Senior VP Mortgage Banking), Mona Kammermeyer (VP Central Operations), Michael L Longlet (VP Data Processing), Kenneth J Czajkowski (VP and Chief Financial Officer), Michael D Hook (VP Commercial Real Estate), Brigitte H Selden (VP Commercial Real Estate Loan), Jerry Siedschlag (VP Commercial Real Estate Loan), Paul M Kapansky (VP Residential Construction), Sharron S Matson (VP Residential Lending), Ann Herring (VP Branch Operations)

PRINCIPAL ACTIVITIES: Banking

Financial Information:

	Dec 31 1985
	$'000
Revenues	48,160
Net income	4,060

No of Employees: 295

FIRST INTERSTATE CORPORATION OF WISCONSIN

636 Wisconsin Avenue, Sheboygan, WI 53081
Tel: (414) 459 2000

Chairman: Richard D Pauls (and Subisidary Officer)
President: David C Beck (and Chief Executive Officer)
Senior Executive Officers: G L Beiersdorf (Executive VP), Robert F Quasius (Executive VP), J Frederic Ruf (Executive VP), Herbert G Weber (Executive VP, Chief Financial Officer, Secretary and Treasurer)

PRINCIPAL ACTIVITIES: Banking
Principal Subsidiaries: First Interstate Bank of Wisconsin; First Interstate Bank
Financial Information:

	Dec 31 1985
	$'000
Revenues	116,600
Net income	9,010

No of Employees: 1,020

FIRST INTERSTATE OF IOWA INC

900 First Interstate Bank Bldg, Locust & 6th Avenue, Des Moines, IA 50309
Tel: (515) 245 7230

Chairman: Kenneth M Myers (and Chief Executive Officer)
President: Oliver H Hagen (and Chief Operating Officer)
Senior Executive Officers: James B Fogt (Executive VP and Treasurer), Howard R Harris III (Senior VP and Chief Financial Officer), Daniel J Fliger (VP and Secretary), Patrick E McNerney (VP Administration), Marcene A Oberholtz (Auditor), Robert A Shelquist (Controller)

PRINCIPAL ACTIVITIES: Holding company with interests in banking
Principal Subsidiaries: First Interstate Bank; Plaza State Bank; United Central Bank & Trust Company
Principal Bank: United Central Bank
Financial Information:

	Dec 31 1985
	$'000
Revenues	112,595

No of Employees: 30

FIRST JERSEY NATIONAL CORPORATION

2 Montgomery Street, Jersey City, NJ 07302
Tel: (201) 547-7000

Chairman: Thomas J Stanton Jr (and Chief Executive Officer); Vice Chairman: Herman H Suenholz
President: W Richard Hazen (and Chief Administration Officer)
Senior Executive Officers: Donald A Morrow (Executive VP Operations), James X Kilbridge (Executive VP, Secretary and General Counsel), Ensley A Tower (Executive VP Administration), Ronald J Chanda (Senior VP Human Resources), Joseph R Donofrio (Senior VP Marketing), Donald J Coleman (Senior VP and Chief Finance Officer), Edmund D Ferri (Senior VP and Auditor), Richard Schuetz (Senior VP Operations), Michael B Tucker (Senior VP and Assistant Legal Counsel)

PRINCIPAL ACTIVITIES: Banking services
Principal Subsidiaries: First Jersey National Bank; First Jersey National Bank South
Principal Bank: Chemical Bank
Financial Information:

	Dec 31 1985	Dec 31 1986
	$'000	$'000
Revenues	338,400	404,000
Net income	30,000	35,000

No of Employees: 3,140

FIRST KENTUCKY NATIONAL CORPORATION

101 South Fifith Street, Louisville, KY 40202
Tel: (502) 581 4498
Telex: 6842090
Telefax: (502) 581-5359

Chairman: A Stevens Miles
President: Morton Boyd
Senior Executive Officers: Charles D Barnes (Executive VP Administration), Roger M Dalton (Senior VP), Holland N McTyeire IV (Senior VP Investments), Gail W Pohn (General Counsel and Secretary), Joseph E Ryan (Senior VP and Auditor), George B Wombwell (Chief Financial Officer and Treasurer)

PRINCIPAL ACTIVITIES: Holding company with interests in banking
Principal Subsidiaries: First Kentucky Company; First Kentucky Investment Advisors; First Kentucky Trust Company; First National Bank; First National Bank, Louisville; National Processing Company Inc; Third National Bank; Central Bank & Trust; Commerce National Bank; American National Bank; Mutual Trust Bank
Principal Bank: First National Bank
Financial Information:

	Dec 31 1985	Dec 31 1986
	$'000	$'000
Income before taxes	50,076	53,381
Net income	43,654	50,061
Dividends	14,730	17,757
Dividends per share	$0.69	$0.82
Earnings per share	$2.04	$2.31
Common stock	8,620	8,720
Retained income	213,633	246,165
Stockholders equity	268,816	303,495
Deposits	3,214,972	3,657,002
Total assets	4,387,017	5,128,486

No of Employees: 474

FIRST LINCOLN FINANCIAL CORPORATION

2735 E Camelbuck Rd, Phoenix, AZ 85016
Tel: (602) 957-7170

President: Judy Wisher
Senior Executive Officers: Andre A Niebling (VP and Treasurer), James Grogan (VP, Secretary and General Council), Paul R Mehlhorn (VP and Chief Financial Officer)

PRINCIPAL ACTIVITIES: Holding company with interests in a wide range of financial services
Parent Company: American Continental Corporation, Phoenix, AZ
Principal Bank: Union Bank, Los Angeles

No of Employees: 350

FIRST MARYLAND BANCORP

25 S Charles Street, Baltimore, MD 21201
Tel: (301) 244-4000
Cable: FIRST BANK
Telex: 87-600

Chairman of the Board: Jeremiah E Casey
President: Charles W Cole Jr (and Chief Executive Officer)
Senior Executive Officers: Robert W Schaefer (Executive VP), William T Murray III (Executive VP), Frederick M Meier Jr (Executive VP), Joseph E Peters (Executive VP), Gerald H Spivey (Senior VP and Treasurer), Carroll S Jackson (Senior VP and Secretary)

PRINCIPAL ACTIVITIES: Banking services
Trade Names: First Maryland Bancorp
Principal Subsidiaries: First National Bank of Maryland; First Maryland Brokerage Corporation; First Omni Bank N.A.; First Maryland Cheque Corporation; First Maryland Credit Corporation; First Maryland Holdings Corporation; First Maryland Leasecorp; First Maryland International Banking

Corporation; First Manufactured Housing Credit Corporation; First Maryland Life Insurance Company; First Maryland Mortgage Corporation; First Carolina Financial Corp

Financial Information:

	Dec 31 1985 $'000	Dec 31 1986 $'000
Net income	28,280	36,054
Earnings per share	$2.23	$2.68
Shareholders equity	279,994	319,630
Deposits	3,177,348	3,906,087
Total assets	4,493,068	5,487,202

No of Employees: 4,077

FIRST MICHIGAN BANK CORPORATION

101 East Main Street, PO Box 300, Zeeland, MI 49464
Tel: (616) 396 9000

Chairman: Randall M Decker
President: David M Ondersma (and Chief Executive Officer)
Senior Executive Officers: Dale N Kaper (Treasurer and VP Finance), Benjamin A Smith III (Senior VP Investments), James E Hoffman (VP Marketing), Albert Gustafson (VP Auditing), Evelyn E Vork (VP Human Resources)

PRINCIPAL ACTIVITIES: Savings bank services
Principal Subsidiaries: First Community Bank; FMB First Michigan Bank; FMB Michigan Bank Metro NA; FMB Lumbermans Bank; FMB-First Michigan Bank; FMB-Oceans Bank
Principal Bank: First National Bank

No of Employees: 630

FIRST MIDWEST BANCORP INC

1230 E Diehl Road, Naperville, IL 60566
Tel: (312) 357 3500

Chairman: C D Oberwartmann (and Chief Executive Officer); Vice Chairman: Andrew B Barber
President: Robert P O'Meara (and Chief Operating Officer)
Senior Executive Officers: Nicholas J Horner (VP Administration), Donald J Swistowicz (VP and Chief Financial Officer), Todd C Johnson (Secretary and Assistant Controller), Keith D Neaderhiser (VP Investments)

PRINCIPAL ACTIVITIES: Banking and investment services
Principal Subsidiaries: First Midwest Capital Corporation
Principal Bank: First National Bank
Financial Information:

	Dec 31 1985 $'000
Revenues	143,000
Net income	9,100

No of Employees: 50

FIRST MISSISSIPPI CORPORATION

700 North Street, Box 1249, Jackson, MS 39215-1249
Tel: (601) 948-7550
Telex: 810-966-2738 First Miss C

Chairman: LeRoy P Percy
President: J Kelley Williams (and Chief Executive Officer)
Senior Executive Officers: Charles M McAuley (Group VP), R Michael Summerford (VP), Charles R Gibson (VP), James B Lange (Secretary/Treasurer), Alfred L Price (General Counsel)

PRINCIPAL ACTIVITIES: First Mississippi Corporation is a diversified resource company with emerging interests in technology development and application. Established operations include: fertilizer production and marketing; production and marketing of industrial chemicals; exploration, development, and production of oil and natural gas; and mining and marketing of coal. New and emerging interests include: development, manufacture and marketing of computer peripherals; production and marketing of specialty chemicals; minerals exploration; commercial development of thermal plasma technology; research in biotechnology; manufacture and marketing of ceramic refractory products
Principal Subsidiaries: (100% owned unless stated): FEC Marketing, Inc; Maxadyne Corporation (82%); First Chemical Corporation; First DeSoto Corporation; First Energy Corporation; FRM, Inc; FRM Minerals, Inc; Imperial Technology, Inc; Plasma Energy Corporation; Pyramid Mining, Inc; Steel Casting Engineering, Ltd (80%). 50% Joint Ventures: Ammonia Products; FRM Agricultural Sciences Partnership (51%); Triad Chemical
Principal Bank: Chase Manhattan
Financial Information:

	Jun 30 1985 $'000	Jun 30 1986 $'000
Sales revenues	273,185	268,898
Income (loss) before taxes	23,703	(57,800)
Net income (loss)	19,139	(28,110)
Dividends	4,876	4,729
Dividends per share	$0.24	$0.24
Earnings (loss) per share	$0.94	($1.42)
Common stock*	20,443	19,828
Retained income	170,981	138,142
Shareholders equity	180,787	142,070

*weighted average shares outstanding

No of Employees: 731 Group

FIRST NATIONAL BANCORP

111 Green Street NE, PO Box 937, Gainesville, GA 30501
Tel: (404) 535 5500

Chairman: J M McRae (and Chief Executive Officer)
President: Richard L Shockley
Senior Executive Officers: Peter D Miller (Executive VP and Chief Financial Officer), C Talmadge Garrison (Secretary and Treasurer)

PRINCIPAL ACTIVITIES: Holding company with interests in banking and financial services
Principal Subsidiaries: First National Bank; Granite City Bank; First National Bank of Habersham; Bank of Clayton; Bank of Banks; First National Bank of White County; First National Bank of Jackson County; Bank of Toccoa; First State Bank of Gilmer County
Financial Information:

	Dec 31 1986 $'000	Dec 31 1987 $'000
Income before taxes	13,097	17,083
Net income	12,297	14,601
Dividends per share	$0.345	$0.41
Earnings per share	$1.68	$1.90
Common stock	46,216	47,291
Retained income	31,901	44,955
Stockholders equity	78,116	92,246
Deposits	793,632	885,000
Total assets	916,873	1,050,000

*estimated

No of Employees: 625

FIRST NATIONAL BANK & TRUST CO OF OKLAHOMA CITY

120 North Robinson, Oklahoma City, OK 73125
Tel: (405) 272-4000

Chairman: Charles A Vose; Vice Chairmen: Charles A Vose Jr, Ken Townsend
President: William A Dick
Senior Executive Officers: Edward G Alexander (Executive VP), Larry A Evans (Executive VP), Joe T Schockley Jr (Senior VP and Chief Financial Officer), John P Sherry (Senior VP and Legal Counsel), Gerald Cornelison (Senior VP and Cashier)

PRINCIPAL ACTIVITIES: Banking

Parent Company: First Oklahoma Bancorporation Inc, Oklahoma City, OK
Principal Bank: First National Bank and Trust Co

No of Employees: 900

FIRST NATIONAL BANK OF BOSTON (THE)

100 Federal Street, Boston, MA 02110
Tel: (617) 434-2200
Cable: BOSTONBANK BOSTON
Telex: 940581; ITT 4996527 BOSTONBK BSN

Chairman: W L Brown
President: Ira Stepanian (and Chief Executive Officer)
Senior Executive Officers: L K Fish (Executive VP), C K Gifford (Executive VP), A L McKinnon (Executive VP), C W Miller (Executive VP), E G Morris III (Executive VP), P C Read (Executive VP)

PRINCIPAL ACTIVITIES: Banking
Parent Company: Bank of Boston Corporation, Boston, MA
Principal Subsidiaries: Banking Subsidiaries: The First National Bank of Boston (Mass); Casco Northern Bank, N.A. (Maine); Colonial Bank (Conn); Rhode Island Hospital Trust National Bank (RI)
Principal Bank: The First National Bank of Boston
Financial Information:

	Dec 31 1985	Dec 31 1986
	$'000	$'000
Income before taxes	289,500	368,395
Net income	173,800	232,764
Common dividends	48,000	55,076
Dividends per share*	$0.82	$0.91
Earnings per share*	$2.82	$3.69
Common stock	208,628	208,436
Retained income	971,450	1,135,665
Shareholders equity	1,474,590	1,769,000
Deposits	19,214,060	21,725,000
Total assets	28,296,340	34,045,000

*adjusted to reflect two-for-one stock split in March 1986; three-for-two stock split declared in November 1986 in the form of a dividend payable in January 1987

No of Employees: 20,000

FIRST NATIONAL CINCINNATI CORPORATION

425 Walnut Street, Cincinnati, OH 45201
Tel: (513) 632-4000

Chairman: Oliver W Waddell (and Chief Executive Officer)
President: Mark P Johnson
Senior Executive Officers: Samuel M Cassidy (Executive VP), Gust J Totlis (VP and Chief Financial Officer)

PRINCIPAL ACTIVITIES: Banking services
Financial Information:

	Dec 31 1986
	$'000
Revenues	386,000
Net income	40,000

No of Employees: 1,860

FIRST NATIONAL SUPERMARKETS INC

17000 Rockside Rd, Maple Heights, OH 44137
Tel: (216) 587-7100

Chairman: Richard J Bogomolny (and Chief Executive Officer)
President: Robert T Samuels (and Chief Operating Officer)
Senior Executive Officers: John A Shields (Senior VP, President Ohio Division), Bruce Weitz (Senior VP, President Eastern Division), Kenneth S Betuker (Senior VP, Chief Financial and Administration Officer), Frank L McDonald (Group VP Labor Management Affairs), Frank H Burke (VP, Secretary and Legal Counsel), George F McPhilips (VP Real Estate)

PRINCIPAL ACTIVITIES: Retail supermarkets

Parent Company: FNS Holding Co Inc

Principal Bank: AmeriTrust Co

Financial Information:

	Dec 31 1985	Dec 31 1986
	$'000	$'000
Sales revenues	1,450,000	1,495,000

No of Employees: 15,000

FIRST NATIONWIDE FINANCIAL CORPORATION

700 Market Street, San Francisco, CA 94102

Tel: (415) 772-1400

Chairman: Anthony M Frank (and Chief Executive Officer); Vice Chairman: John L Carr (and General Counsel)

President: Robert E Lackovic

Senior Executive Officers: Robert T Barnum (Executive VP Chief Financial Officer), Tor D Folkedal (Executive VP Information Systems), R E Small (Executive VP Loan Division), William C Walbrecher Jr (Executive VP Retail Banking Division). Senior Vice Presidents: Robert F Anderson (Residential Lending Director), Donald R Ansbro (Treasurer), J Thomas Byrom (Budget and Profits Planning Director), Don R Coots (Secondary Marketing Director), Evelyn S Dilsaver (Bank Controller), John B Goeglein (Major Loans and Investments Director California South), James V Harbison (Major Loans and Investments Director), Nicholas J Imparato (Strategic Operations Director), Paul J Jullien (Real Estate Management Director), Leonard Kaiser (Eastern Area Manager Retail Banking Division), Lee G Kirkpatrick (Western Area Manager), B Ashley Latteri (Human Resources Director), Donald P Lubell (Bank General Counsel), Carolyn K MacKenzie (Marketing Director), Hal N Mayer (Southern Area Manager Retail Banking Division), Neil F M McKay (FNFC Controller), J Leslie Oakley (Major Loans Director), Larry Padilla (Loan Service Director), Robert Pawelski (Internal Audit Director), Don Sarno (Real Estate Development Director), A C Schoultz III (Facilities Management and Administrative Services Director), Allen E Vickers (Acquisitions and Mergers), Paul D Weinberg (Corporate Planning and Development Director). Other Officers and Operating Executives: David Bretoi (President Beverley Hills Savings Management Consignment Program), Hugh Hayman (Executive VP Chief Operating Officer First Nationwide Network), James J Overby (President TranSouth Financial Corporation), R W Veerkamp (Chairman FNS Corporate Funding, Inc)

PRINCIPAL ACTIVITIES: First Nationwide Financial Corporation's principal business is the ownership of First Nationwide Bank, a federal savings bank providing savings, checking, investments, consumer loans, real estate mortgages and other financial services to more than a million American individuals and familes. First Nationwide Bank is the nation's seventh largest savings institution, with assets of over $15 billion and 253 branch offices in eight states: California, Colorado, Florida, Hawaii, Kentucky, Missouri, New York and Ohio.

Parent Company: Ford Motor Company (effective December 16 1985)

Principal Subsidiaries: TranSouth Financial; The First Nationwide Network

Principal Bank: Bank of America

Financial Information:

	Dec 31 1985	Dec 31 1986
	$'000	$'000
Revenues	1,261,936	1,381,118
Net income	70,780	101,787
Retained income	4,160	105,947
Shareholders equity	499,013	600,800
Deposits	8,797,922	11,111,194
Total assets	11,592,853	15,247,523

No of Employees: 4,400

FIRST NH BANKS INC

1000 Elm Street, Manchester, NH 03101

Tel: (603) 668 5020

President: Frank O Buhl (and Chief Executive Officer)

Senior Executive Officers: Elliott Bendrihem (Senior VP Finance and Secretary), Robert C Matheson (Senior VP Operations), Raymond G Schwedhelm (Senior VP Marketing), John W Bullard (VP Treasurer and Controller), Edward H Lee (VP Operations), Donald E Padfield (VP Marketing), Joseph DeAngelis (VP Human Resources), Richard C Keith (VP Investments)

PRINCIPAL ACTIVITIES: Holding company with interests in banking and a wide range of financial acitivites

Principal Subsidiaries: Bedford Bank; Concord National Bank; First NH Bank; First NH Bank of Lebanon; First NH Mortgage Corporation; Granite State National Bank; Laconia Peoples Bank and Trust Company; Merchants National Bank; Plymouth Guaranty Savings Bank; White Mountain National Bank; Wolfeboro National Bank

Principal Bank: Merchants National Bank

Financial Information:

	Dec 31 1985
	$'000
Revenues	139,000
Net income	15,120

No of Employees: 1,110

FIRST OF AMERICA BANK CORPORATION

108 E Michigan Avenue, Kalamazoo, MI 49007

Tel: (616) 383-9000

Telefax: (616) 383-9283

Chairman: Daniel R Smith (and Chief Executive Officer); Vice Chairman: Richard D Klein

President: Richard F Chormann (and Chief Operating Officer)

Senior Executive Officers: George S Nugent (Executive VP), Thomas W Lambert (Senior VP, Funds Management), Dean R Williams (Senior VP, Chief Financial Officer and Treasurer), David B Wirt (Senior VP), John B Rapp (Senior VP, Trust and Secretary to the Board), Mervin D Burtis (Senior VP-Audit and Loan Review)

PRINCIPAL ACTIVITIES: Banking

Principal Subsidiaries: As of August 1 1987: 49 Banks, 10 affiliated companies

Principal Bank: First of America Bank, Michigan, N.A. (Kalamazoo)

Financial Information:

	Dec 31 1986 (12 mths)	Jun 30 1987 (6 mths)
	$'000	$'000
Income before taxes	62,975	43,016
Net income	52,904	33,763
Common dividends	13,295	7,806
Preferred dividends(1)	5,281	8,634
Dividends per common share	$1.50	$0.80
Earnings per common share	$5.47	$2.58
Common stock and surplus	168,569	198,539
Retained income	174,606	191,929
Shareholders equity(2)	517,096	601,245
Deposits	6,927,313	7,340,534
Total assets	7,869,918	8,402,485

(1) preferred/preference
(2) includes non redeemable preferred/preference stock

No of Employees: 6,838

FIRST OF AMERICA BANK-DETROIT, N.A,

645 Griswold, Detroit, MI 48226
Tel: (313) 965-1900
Cable: FIRST AMBK
Telex: ITT 4320025 FRSTAMERBK-DET

Chairman: Robert D Krestel (and President and Chief Executive Officer)
President: J M Berry
Senior Executive Officers: Loren D Allston (Executive VP and Cashier), Robert P Feeser (Executive VP), Robert E Nye (Senior VP Investment), Thomas L Leto (Senior VP Commercial Banking), Donald G Walker (Senior VP International), Willis A Hicks (Senior VP Operations), Allen W Hagadon (Senior VP Real Estate), R W Shauman (Senior VP Trust Division)

PRINCIPAL ACTIVITIES: Banking
Parent Company: First of America Bank Corporation, Kalamazoo, MI
Financial Information:

	Dec 31 1985
	$'000
Net income	7,373
Shareholders equity	60,320
Deposits	885,499
Total assets	1,063,280

No of Employees: 900

FIRST OHIO BANCSHARES INC

606 Madison Avenue, Toledo, OH 43604
Tel: (419) 259 6960

Chairman: Philip L LeBoutillier
President: Charles L McKelvy (and Chief Executive Officer)
Senior Executive Officers: Robert C Freeman (VP), John T Rogers (VP), Thomas O Messinger (Treasurer), Glenn N Raitz (Secretary), James P Silk (General Counsel)

PRINCIPAL ACTIVITIES: Banking services
Principal Subsidiaries: First National Bank; First Ohio Bancshares Realty
Financial Information:

	Dec 31 1985
	$'000
Revenues	78,570
Net income	10,600

No of Employees: 670

FIRST PENNSYLVANIA CORPORATION

Centre Square, Philadelphia, PA 19101
Tel: (215) 786-5000
Telefax: (215) 786-8899

Chairman: George A Butler (and Chief Executive Officer)

President: Frank E Reed (and Chief Operating Officer)
Senior Executive Officers: John J Brine (Senior Executive VP and Chief Financial Officer), Leslie R Butler (Senior Executive VP and Chief Administrative Officer), Cameron S Clark (Executive VP), Stuart T Saunders Jr (Executive VP), Steven R Garfinkel (Executive VP, Controller and Treasurer), John P Britt (Executive VP), Leonard A Caldwell (Executive VP), Cameron S Clark (Executive VP), Richard F Di Lorenzo (Executive VP), Joseph T Drennan (Executive VP)

PRINCIPAL ACTIVITIES: Banking
Principal Subsidiaries: First Pennsylvania Bank (Del); First Pennsylvania Investments Co; Centre Square Investments Group
Principal Bank: First Pennsylvania Bank N.A.
Financial Information:

	Dec 31 1985 $'000	Dec 31 1986 $'000
Net interest and other revenue	220,483	232,888
Income before taxes	27,562	36,625
Net income	27,562	36,265
Preferred dividends	19,586	20,917
Earnings per share	$0.35	$0.68
Common stock	23,163	23,409
Retained income	15,230	34,776
Shareholders equity	343,590	463,813
Deposits	3,861,910	3,998,842
Total assets	5,652,398	5,887,589

No of Employees: 3,616

FIRST RAILROAD & BANKING COMPANY OF GEORGIA

699 Broad Street, Augusta, GA 30913
Tel: (404) 823 2753

Chairman: Charles B Presley (and Chief Executive Officer)
President: Walton K Nussbaum (and Chief Operating Officer)
Senior Executive Officers: C Alex Spivey (Executive VP), Charles D Walker (Executive VP), C Dexter Jordan Jr (Senior VP and Secretary), Jerry Murrell (Senior VP Loan Review), W Mitchell Denning (Controller), R Stephens Pannill (Senior VP Investments), Steven V Hall (VP), Larry Pridemore (VP), Donald Y Sharp (VP)

PRINCIPAL ACTIVITIES: Holding company with interests in a wide range of banking services
Principal Subsidiaries: Bank of Dalton; Bank of Screven County; Capitol Finance Group Inc; Amity Life Insurance Company; Capital Credit Plan of NC Inc; Capitol Credit Plan of TN Inc; Capitol Premium Plan Inc; Central Bank of Georgia; Commercial Bank; Commercial Bank and Trust Company; Farmers & Merchants Bank; First Financial Management; First Georgia Bank; First National Bank; Georgia Railroad Bank & Trust Company; Savannah Bank & Trust COmpany
Principal Bank: Georgia Railroad Bank & Trust Company
Financial Information:

	Dec 31 1985 $'000
Revenues	424,630
Net income	40,335

No of Employees: 4,080

FIRST REPUBLICBANK CORPORATION

Pacific at Ervay Streets, Dallas, TX 75201
Tel: (214) 922-5031
Telex: 73358

Chairman: Gerald W Fronterhouse (and President and Chief Executive Officer); Vice Chairmen: Harvey R Mitchell, Joseph R Musolino, Charles Pistor, Ronald G Steinhart
Managing Directors: John D Dienes (Corporate Banking Group), John H Falb Jr (Multinational Banking Group), Eugene C Fiedorek (Energy Banking Group), W Gordon Hobgood Jr (Trust Services), Raleigh Hortenstine III (Funds Management Group), Robert B Lane (General Banking Group), Jerry McElhatton (Operations Group), John T Stuart III (Real Estate Banking Group). Executive Directors: Samuel J Atkins III (Energy Banking Group), Joe M Bailey (General Banking Group), Thomas G Barksdale (General Banking Group), Joe B Fortson III (Real Estate Banking Group), James W Lake (Operations Group), William C Nelson (General Banking Group), Robert T Rork (General Banking Group)
Senior Executives: Roger A Dunn (Executive VP Human Resources), James R Erwin (Chairman Credit Policy), Thomas E Foster (Executive VP Credit Policy-Real Estate), Hugh G Holcomb (Executive VP Audit/Credit Review), Edward R McPherson (Executive VP and Chief Financial Officer), R Brooks Wimberly (President Republic of Texas Properties Company), Joseph C Bowles (Director Public Affairs), Lee Drain (Senior VP and Secretary), Kathy B Guy (Senior VP Legal)

PRINCIPAL ACTIVITIES: Commercial and consumer banking; mortgage lending; money orders and travelers checks; personal and corporate trust management
Trade Names: First RepublicBank
Principal Subsidiaries: Affiliate Banks: First RepublicBank Dallas, NA; First RepublicBank Oak Cliff; First RepublicBank Park Cities; First RepublicBank Greenville Avenue; First RepublicBank North Dallas, NA; First RepublicBank Irving; First RepublicBank Carrollton; First RepublicBank Garland, NA; First RepublicBank Las Colinas; First RepublicBank Plano, NA; First RepublicBank Denison, NA; First RepublicBank Richardson; First RepublicBank Grand Prairie, NA; First RepublicBank Dallas East, NA; First RepublicBank Pleasant Grove; First RepublicBank Greenville, NA; First RepublicBank Paris; First RepublicBank Forney; First RepublicBank Preston North, NA; First RepublicBank DFW Freeport, NA; First RepublicBank Hutchins; First RepublicBank Fort Worth, NA; First RepublicBank Midland, NA; First RepublicBank Tyler, NA; First RepublicBank Lubbock, NA; First RepublicBank Wichita Falls, NA; First RepublicBank Ridglea; First Republic Bank Lufkin; First RepublicBank Abilene, NA; First RepublicBank El Paso, NA; First RepublicBank Fort Worth East, NA; First RepublicBank University Drive; First RepublicBank Odessa, NA; First RepublicBank Mineral Wells, NA; First RepublicBank Mt Pleasant, NA; First RepublicBank Brownwood, NA; First RepublicBank Stephenville, NA; First RepublicBank Cleburne, NA; First RepublicBank Henderson, NA; First RepublicBank Gateway, NA; First RepublicBank South Fort Worth; First RepublicBank River Oaks; First RepublicBank Richland, NA; First RepublicBank SW Arlington, NA; First RepublicBank Chelmont, NA; InterFirst Bank Brownwood; First RepublicBank South Abilene; First RepublicBank Houston, NA; First RepublicBank Fannin; First RepublicBank Galveston, NA; First RepublicBank Conroe, NA; First RepublicBank Spring Branch; First RepublicBank Jefferson County; First RepublicBank Jefferson County; First RepublicBank San Felipe, NA; First RepublicBank SW Houston, NA; First RepublicBank Nassau Bay, NA; First RepublicBank East Houston; First RepublicBank Pasadena; First RepublicBank Post Oak; First RepublicBank Greenspoint; First RepublicBank Tomball; First RepublicBank Baytown; First RepublicBank Nederland; First RepublicBank Braes Bayou, NA; First RepublicBank Richmond, NA; First Republic Bank Kingwood, NA; First RepublicBank Eldridge, NA; First RepublicBank Austin, NA; First RepublicBank San Antonio NA; National Bank of Fort Sam Houston; First RepublicBank Waco, NA; First RepublicBank Harlingen, NA; First RepublicBank Corsicana, NA; First RepublicBank Victoria; First RepublicBank Temple, NA; First RepublicBank Alamo Heights, NA; First RepublicBank Lake Air, NA; First RepublicBank NW San Antonio, NA; First RepublicBank South Austin; First RepublicBank Oak Hill, NA; First RepublicBank Ennis, NA; First RepublicBank A & M; First RepublicBank NW Austin, NA; First RepublicBank Clifton; First RepublicBank Northern Hills; First RepublicBank Hillsboro; First

RepublicBank Westlake, NA; First RepublicBank Countryside, NA; First RepublicBank Williamson County, NA; First Republic Bank Universal City, NA; First RepublicBank Malakoff; First RepublicBank SW Temple, NA; First RepublicBank North Austin, NA; RepublicBank Delaware; InterFirst Bank Delaware

Principal Bank: First RepublicBank Dallas, NA

Financial Information:

	Dec 31 1985	Dec 31 1986
	$'000	$'000
Income before taxes	160,396	379
Net income	140,179	53,969
Dividends	44,924	45,007
Dividends per share	$1.64	$1.64
Earnings per share*	$4.72	$1.65
Common stock	137,131	137,291
Retained income	715,090	715,585
Shareholders equity	1,220,328	1,221,320
Deposits	15,764,377	15,997,462
Total assets	23,205,593	20,944,300

*primary

No of Employees: 15,300

FIRST SAVINGS ASSOCIATION OF WISCONSIN

250 E Wisconsin, Milwaukee, WI 53202

Tel: (414) 278-1000

Chairman: Robert S Brown (and President and Chief Executive Officer)

Senior Executive Officers: Thomas A Drew (Executive VP, Chief Financial Officer and Treasurer), Philip J Hesselbein (Executive VP), Selma Criucllo (Senior VP), Robert J Muth (Senior VP), Gregory P Julian (Senior VP)

PRINCIPAL ACTIVITIES: Savings bank

No of Employees: 897

FIRST SECURITY CORPORATION

PO Box 30006, Salt Lake City, UT 84130

Tel: (801) 350-50000

Chairman: Spencer F Eccles (and President and Chief Executive Officer)

Senior Executive Officers: George L Denton Jr (Executive VP Manager, Investments Division), Elmer D Tucker (Executive VP Chief Financial Officer, Financial Division), Jerry F Hill (Senior VP Chief Auditor), Dr Kelly K Matthews (Senior VP and Economist), Richard C Seastrand (Senior VP Investments Division), David R Wilson (Senior VP Investments Division), Thomas F Hawkes (VP and Treasurer), Leslie F Paskett (VP and Tax Officer), Scott C Ulbrich (VP Manager, Asset and Liability Management Department), Gary R Vance (VP and Comptroller), Alonzo W Watson Jr (Secretary)

PRINCIPAL ACTIVITIES: Holding company whose subsidiaries are engaged in banking

Banking Subsidiaries: First Security Bank of Idaho, NA; First Security Bank of Utah, NA; First Security State Bank; First Security Bank of Rock Springs, Wyoming. Non Banking Subsidiaries: First Security Realty Services Corporation; First Security Realty Services (West); First Security Leasing Company; First Security Financial; First Security Investment Services Inc; First Security Investment Management, Inc; First Security Discount Brokerage Inc; First Security Insurance, Inc; First Security Life Insurance Company of Texas; First Security Realtor; First Security Cheque Corporation; First Security Service Company; First Security Computer Center Inc

Principal Bank: First Security Bank of Utah, NA

Financial Information:

	Dec 31 1985	Dec 31 1986
	$'000	$'000
Net income	19,033	5,093
Earnings per share	$1.56	$0.41
Shareholders equity	356,856	351,219
Deposits	3,831,148	3,923,672
Total assets	5,293,620	5,079,578

No of Employees: 4,315

FIRST TENNESSEE NATIONAL CORPORATION

165 Madison Avenue, Memphis, TN 38103

Tel: (901) 523-4444

Chairman: Ronald Terry (and Chief Executive Officer)

President: John Dulin

Senior Executive Officers: Charles B Dudley III (Executive VP, Transactions and Information, Group Manager), J Kenneth Glass (Executive VP, Retail Banking, Group Manager) John C Kelley Jr (Executive VP, Business and Institutions, Group Manager), George P Lewis (Executive VP, Money Management, Group Manager), Lee Welch (Executive VP, General Counsel), Susan Schmidt Bies (Executive VP, Chief Financial Officer), M List Underwood, Jr (Senior VP, Controller), Sarah L Meyerrose (VP and Treasurer), Roderick A White (Senior VP and Auditor), G Robert Vezina (Senior VP and Personnel Division Manager)

PRINCIPAL ACTIVITIES: Holding company with interests in banking

Principal Bank: First Tennessee Bank National Association

Financial Information:

	Dec 31 1985	Dec 31 1986
	$'000	$'000
Income before taxes	38,942	55,094
Net income	39,682	49,164
Dividends	14,875	15,707
Dividends per share	$1.09	$1.13
Earnings per share	$2.68	$3.30
Common stock	38,071	38,133
Retained income	195,318	227,284
Shareholders equity	281,404	315,356
Deposits	3,989,228	4,369,475
Total assets	5,365,216	5,685,550

No of Employees: 4,182

FIRST UNION CORPORATION

First Union Plaza, Charlotte, NC 28288

Tel: (704) 374-6565

Chairman: Edward E Crutchfield Jr (and Chief Executive Officer); Vice Chairmen: Theodore B Sumner Jr, B J Walker

President: Ben J Craig

Senior Executive Officers: Max A Harris (Executive VP and Chief Financial Officer) B D Allen (Executive VP), Marion A Cowell Jr (Senior VP, Secretary and General Counsel), J Robert Lee (Senior VP and Treasurer), Thomas P Rideout (Senior VP)

PRINCIPAL ACTIVITIES: Financial services

Principal Subsidiaries: Cameron-Brown Co; Fairfax Corp; First Union Mortgage Corp; Commercial Research Inc; Dis-Com Securities Inc; First Card Corp; First Computer Services Inc; First National Bank & Trust Co; First Union Financial Corp; First Union National Bank; Carolina Finance Co; First Union Commercial Corp; First Union Futures Corp; First Union International Banking Corp; General Financial Agency Inc; General Financial Life Insurance Co; Salem Securities; Tryon Management Inc

Financial Information:

	Dec 31 1985	Dec 31 1986
	$'000	$'000
Net income	173,624	274,347
Earnings per share	$2.16	$2.53
Shareholders equity	1,063,864	1,602,479
Deposits	9,885,309	17,003,549
Total assets	16,567,276	26,820,240

No of Employees: 19,266

FIRST VALLEY CORPORATION

One Bethlehem Plaza, Bethleham, PA 18018
Tel: (215) 865-8411
Telefax: (215) 865-8678

Chairman: John R Howell
President: Robert K Gicking
Senior Executive Officers: Frederick P Banyard (Executive VP, Treasurer and Secretary), Donald B Jennings (Executive VP), Timothy J McDonald (Executive VP), James M O'Brien (Senior VP), Michael J Foster (VP and Controller)

PRINCIPAL ACTIVITIES: Holding company with interests in banking
Principal Subsidiaries: First Valley Bank
Principal Bank: Mellon Bank
Financial Information:

	Dec 31 1985	Dec 31 1986
	$'000	$'000
Income before taxes	12,722	16,197
Net income	12,607	14,763
Dividends	3,052	4,442
Dividends per share	$0.525	$0.70
Earnings per share	$2.21	$2.40
Common stock*	5,977	6,242
Retained income	36,804	47,125
Stockholders equity	86,154	101,925
Deposits	987,022	1,049,948
Total assets	1,215,818	1,279,095
*shares outstanding in thousands		

No of Employees: 825

FIRST VIRGINIA BANKS INC

6400 Arlington Boulevard, Falls Church, VA 22046
Tel: (703) 241 4000

Chairman: Robert H Zalokar (and Chief Executive Officer)
President: Paul H Geithner Jr (and Chief Administration Officer)
Senior Executive Officers: Harry W Allen (Senior VP and Secretary), Hugh L Campbell (Senior VP), Charles R Cash (Senior VP and Regional Officer), Barry J Fitzpatrick (Senior VP), Henry Howard Hicks Jr (Senior VP and Regional Officer), Ronald Locke (Senior VP and Treasurer), A Paul Lanzillotta (Senior VP Service), Shirley C Beavers Jr (Senior VP), Richard F Bowman (VP and Controller), James S Talley (VP), Larry P Watson (VP and Marketing Director), Thomas P Jennings (Legal Counsel), Robert R Ambrogi (VP Engineering), John L Bowles (VP Investments), Guy G Harper III (VP Personnel Affairs), Melodye M Tomlin (VP and General Auditor), Richard H Irwin (VP Functional Area), James B Pask (VP Real Estate)

PRINCIPAL ACTIVITIES: Holding company with interests in banking and a wide range of financial and investment services
Principal Subsidiaries: Arlington Mortgage Company Inc; Eastern Operations Centre Inc; First General Insurance Agency Inc; First VA Bank; First VA Bank Central; First VA Bank Commonwealth; First VA Bank Northern Neck; First VA Bank of Augusta; First VA Bank of the Southwest; First VA Bank of Tidewater; First VA Bank Roanoke-West; First VA Bank South; First VA Bank South Central; First VA Bank; First General Morgage Company Inc; First VA Bank-Highlands; First VA Bank-Colonial; First VA Bank-Eastern Shore; First VA Bank-Franklin County; First VA Bank-Highlands; First VA Bank-Planters; First VA Bank-Shenandoah Valley; First VA Services Inc; Northern Operations Center Inc; Southwest Operations Center Inc
Principal Bank: First Virginia Bank
Financial Information:

	Dec 31 1985
	$'000
Revenues	356,155
Net income	40,020

No of Employees: 3,800

FIRST WACHOVIA CORPORATION

301 N Main Street, Winston-Salem, NC 27101
Tel: (919) 748-5000

Chairman: Thomas R Williams
President: John G Medlin Jr
Senior Executive Officers: L M Baker Jr (Executive VP), Thomas E Boland (Executive VP), David L Cotterill (Executive VP), J Scott Cramer (Executive VP), Paul D Hill (Executive VP), John F McNair III (Executive VP), D Raymond Riddle (Executive VP), H Jack Runnion (Executive VP), Hans W Wanders (Executive VP), Graham P Dozier III (Comptroller)

PRINCIPAL ACTIVITIES: First Wachovia Corporation was formed on December 5th 1985 by a merger of Wachovia Corporation and First Atlanta Corporation and is a bank holding company
Principal Bank: Wachovia Bank & Trust Co
Financial Information:

	Dec 31 1985	Dec 31 1986
	$'000	$'000
Net income	187,680	193,780
Earnings per share	$3.51	$3.59
Shareholders equity	1,033,694	1,177,429
Deposits	12,674,943	13,780,612
Total assets	17,706,535	18,689,550

No of Employees: 12,890

FIRST WESTERN FINANCIAL CORPORATION

2700 W Sahara Avenue, Las Vegas, NV 89102
Tel: (702) 871-2000

Chairman: Frank E Scott (and Chief Executive Officer); Vice Chairman: R G Taylor
President: John H Brebbia
Senior Executive Officers: H B Francis (VP and Treasurer), Raymond J Gregor (VP), Regina Larsen (VP and Secretary)

PRINCIPAL ACTIVITIES: Holding company with interests in savings and loans, real estate investment, data processing services for race and sportsbook operators, advertising
Principal Bank: Valley Bank
Financial Information:

	Dec 31 1985
	$'000
Revenues	120,700
Net income	812

No of Employees: 290

FIRST WISCONSIN CORPORATION

777 E Wisconsin Avenue, Milwaukee, WI 53202
Tel: (414) 765-4321

Chairman: Hal C Kuehl (and Chief Executive Officer)
President: Gary B Rafn (and Chief Operating Officer)
Senior Executive Officers: Ronald A Bero (Senior VP), William H Risch (Senior VP Finance and Treasurer), Chris M Bauer (Senior VP), Howard H Hopwood III (Senior VP and Legal Counsel), Louis B Giese (First VP), Fred Wittkowske (First VP), James R Blackman (First VP), John T Franey (First VP), Larry A Greves (First VP), Errol G Hohmann (First VP), William J Schulz (First VP, Secretary and Deputy Counsel)

PRINCIPAL ACTIVITIES: Banking

Principal Subsidiaries: Elaneo Investment Services Inc; First WI Bank; First WI Bank of Mayfair; First WI Bank of West Green Bay, First WI Development Corp; First WI Insurance Services Corp; First WI Mortgage Co; First WI National Bank; First WI Community Investment Corp; First WI Export Credit Ltd; First WI Financial Corp; First WI International Bank; First WI Leasing Corp; Foremost Properties of WI Inc; Chicago Steel Corp; Marshall WI Co Inc; First WI National Bank; First WI Northwestern National Bank; First WI Trust Co; First Insurance Management Inc; RE Services Inc

Principal Bank: First Wisconsin National Bank of Milwaukee

Financial Information:

	Dec 31 1985	Dec 31 1986
	$'000	$'000
Net income	39,599	52,694
Earnings per share	$2.10	$2.53
Shareholders equity	375,168	466,806
Deposits	5,126,000	5,666,903
Total assets	6,477,324	7,090,197

No of Employees: 5,373

FIRSTIER INC

1700 Farnam St, Omaha, NE 68102
Tel: (402) 348 7906

Chairman: John D Woods (and Chief Executive Officer)
President: William C Smith (and Chief Operating Officer and Subsidiary Officer)
Senior Executive Officers: Howard H Moldenhauer (VP and Secretary)

PRINCIPAL ACTIVITIES: Holding company with intersts in the provision of financial services

Principal Subsidiaries: First National Bank and Trust Company; Firstier Mortgage Company; FirsTier Bank Omaha; FirsTier Bank NA Lincoln

Principal Bank: Omaha National Bank

Financial Information:

	Dec 31 1985
	$'000
Revenues	243,200
Net income	14,285

No of Employees: 1,500

FIRSTSOUTH, FA

121 West Sixth Ave, PO Box 5900, Pine Bluff, AR 71611
Tel: (501) 541-8500

Chairman: Del L Brannon
President: Roderick D Reed (and Chief Executive Officer)
Senior Executive Officers: William K Bruton (Executive VP Operations), Tad Lowrey (Executive VP and Chief Financial Officer)

PRINCIPAL ACTIVITIES: FirstSouth is a statewide full service financial institution with 46 offices in 35 cities in Arkansas. The Association is primarily engaged in the business of obtaining funds in the form of deposits and borrowings and investing these funds in loans on residential and other real properties, mortgage-backed securities, money market securities, commercial loans and consumer loans. FirstSouth has significantly increased its non-interest income in recent years through increased emphasis on commercial and residential real estate lending, acquisition and sale of loan portfolios, mortgage banking activities and other service activities which generate fee income

Trade Names: FirstSouth Fed S & L

Principal Subsidiaries: FirstSouth Capital Corporation

Principal Bank: FHLB of Dallas

No of Employees: 480

FISCHBACH CORPORATION

485 Lexington Avenue, New York, NY 10017
Tel: (212) 986-4100

Chairman: Victor Posner
President: A R Manville (and Chief Executive Officer)
Senior Executive Officers: John W Snow (Executive VP Construction), E A Wilinski (Executive VP Administration), J Littman (Senior VP), Robert J Niehaus (Senior VP), John P Bigda (VP, Secretary and Legal Counsel), Harvey Hennes (VP and Controller), M R Appel (Treasurer)

PRINCIPAL ACTIVITIES: Electrical engineering contractors

Principal Subsidiaries: W A Chester Inc; Electricon Inc; Fischbach & Moore Inc; Corbin-Dykes Electric Co; John Miller Electric Co; Fischbach & Moore International Corp; W Heath & Co; Mercury Co of Norwood Inc; Moran Co; Nacon Corp; Associated Mechanical Contractors Inc; Natkin & Co; Charter Page Inc; Johansen Co; Natkin Service Co; Power Systems Inc

Principal Bank: Chase Manhattan Bank

Financial Information:

	Sep 30 1985	Sep 30 1986
	$'000	$'000
Sales revenues	1,039,046	1,318,162
Net (loss)	(10,447)	(29,222)
(Loss) per share	($2.69)	($7.47)
Shareholders equity	161,852	132,630

No of Employees: 13,000

FISCHER & PORTER CO

125 E County Line Road, Warminster, PA 18974
Tel: (215) 674-6000
Cable: FISHPORT
Telex: 173127 FISHPORT WSTR

Chairman: Jay H Tolson (and President)
Senior Executive Officers: Geoffrey H Sayer (Executive VP), David J Nessim (Executive VP), Laurence P Finnegan Jr (Senior VP Finance and Chief Financial Officer), Edward A France Jr (Senior VP), Hubert A Riester (Senior VP)

PRINCIPAL ACTIVITIES: Process control instrumentation and systems

Principal Subsidiaries: 13 international subsidiaries of which 10 are in Europe

Principal Bank: Mellon Bank

Financial Information:

	Dec 31 1985	Dec 31 1986
	$'000	$'000
Sales revenues	170,500	177,000
Income before taxes	9,000	7,000
Net income	5,000	2,400
Dividends	5% stock	5% stock
Earnings per share	$1,11	$0.46
Common stock	4,172	3,790
Retained income	21,621	20,549
Shareholders equity	60,725	69,374

Principal Shareholders: Publicly held. Stock traded on AMEX
No of Employees: 2,650

FISCHER PACKING CO

Box 35640, Louisville, KY 40232
Tel: (502) 893-3611

President: Miller Owings
Senior Executive Officers: Vincent Cotter (Treasurer), Reef Ivey (Secretary), Robert J Brumley (Controller), Raymond Haley (Data Processing Manager), Louis Gueltzow (Sales Manager)

PRINCIPAL ACTIVITIES: Meat production and processing

Parent Company: Wilson Foods Corporation, Oklahoma City, OK

Principal Bank: Stockyard's Bank

Financial Information:

	$'000
Sales revenues	140,000

No of Employees: 850

FISHER CONTROLS INTERNATIONAL, INC

8000 Maryland Avenue, Clayton, MO 63105
Tel: (314) 694-9900
Telex: 442-383

Chairman: Robert E Flynn (and Chief Executive Officer)
President: Arthur L French (and Chief Operating Officer)
Senior Executive Officers: Hans Gerresheim (VP and Managing Director-Sunvic), Roland Robichaud (Group VP, Process Instrumentation and Group VP, Measurement Instrumentation), Larry W Solley (Group VP Support Services), James W Teegarden (Group VP Final Control Systems), Claes Huttman (Group VP Worldwide Sales), Mel M O'Donnell (VP and Area Director Asia-Pacific), Stanley R Pylipow (Seior VP and Chief Financial Officer), Dennis J Green (VP and General Counsel), N F Hamilton (Director, Finance-Europe), James G Bloch (VP and Controller), M A Maley (VP and Treasurer), Joe S Maloney (Director, Planning and Business Development), Bill C Nicoll (VP, Information Management), James G Thorne (VP, Human Resources), James C Elias (Director, Human Resources MI and Sunvic), S P Keck (Personnel Representative), J P Ryan (Director, Human Resources Management Development), Gary L DeVet (Director, Human Resources FCS and Support Services), Kamel Boustany (President, Permea Inc)

PRINCIPAL ACTIVITIES: The largest manufacturer of automatic control valves and regulators in the world. A major producer of measurement and control room instrumentation among worldwide suppliers. Fisher Controls provide control products and services, worldwide, to all industries requiring the control of liquids and gases. A listing of the major industries served by Fisher would include:- Chemical Processing; Refining; Oil and Gas Production; Power; Pulp and Paper; Food and Beverage; Pharmaceuticals and Biotech; Mining and Metals Processing
Trade Names: POSI-SEAL
Parent Company: Monsanto Company, St Louis, MO
Principal Subsidiaries: Posi-Seal
Financial Information:

	Dec 31 1985	Dec 31 1986
	$'000	$'000
Sales revenues	652,000	645,000
Net income (loss)	34,000	(66,000)

No of Employees: 9,000

FISHER FOODS INC

5300 Richmond Road, Bedford Heights, OH 44146
Tel: (216) 292 7000

Chairman: Carl H Lindner (and Chief Executive Officer)
President: Robert L Hayden (and Chief Operating Officer)
Senior Executive Officers: Robert R Gerber (Senior VP and Chief Financial Officer), James E Evans (VP and Secretary), Gregory Mays (Controller)

PRINCIPAL ACTIVITIES: Retail outlets; sale of general merchandise including food
Principal Subsidiaries: Jax Inc
Principal Bank: Society National Bank
Financial Information:

	$'000
Sales revenues	495,000

No of Employees: 4,000

FISHER MILLS INC

3235 16th Ave SW, Seattle, WA 98134
Tel: (206) 622-4430
Telex: TWX 910 444 2170

Chairman: Ken Fisher
President: J L Cook (and Chief Executive Officer)
Senior Executive Officers: C E Bowden (VP Export), Glenn Gabbert (VP Operations), George H Grimes (VP Sales), Matt Biwer (VP Feed Sales), Terry Barrans (VP Finance)

PRINCIPAL ACTIVITIES: Flour milling and production of animal feedstuffs
Parent Company: Fisher Companies Inc
Principal Bank: Seattle First National Bank
Financial Information:

	$'000
Sales revenues	50,000

No of Employees: 200

FISHER-PRICE TOYS

606 Girard Avenue, East Aurora, NY 14052
Tel: (716) 687-3000

President: R B Sampsell
Senior Executive Officers: Charles S Riter (VP Research and Development), David B Fisher (VP Juvenile Products), James R Tindall (VP US Toys and Canada), JoAnne G Jackson (VP and Controller), Mary A Lambertsen (VP Personnel), James T Lasky (VP Information Services), Michael S Krause (VP Operations), Thomas A Oller (VP Product Design), Sandra R Danon (VP Marketing)

PRINCIPAL ACTIVITIES: Manufacture of toys and games
Parent Company: Quaker Oats Company, Chicago, IL
Financial Information:

	$'000
Sales revenues	422,000

No of Employees: 6,000 (domestic and overseas)

FITCHBURG GAS & ELECTRIC LIGHT COMPANY

120 Royall Street, Canton, MA 02021
Tel: (617) 828 8660

Chairman: Charles H Tenney II (and Chief Executive Officer)
President: Frank L Childs
Senior Executive Officers: Peter J Stulgis (VP and Treasurer), Lawrence T Gingrow Jr (VP), Allen R Damren (Controller)

PRINCIPAL ACTIVITIES: Supply of gas and electricity
Principal Bank: First National Bank of Boston
Financial Information:

	Dec 31 1985
	$'000
Sales revenues	54,000

No of Employees: 125

FLAMBEAU CORPORATION

801 Lynn Avenue, Baraboo, WI 53913
Tel: (608) 356-5551
Telex: TWX 910 280 2644 flambeau babo

Chairman: W R Sauey (and Chief Executive Officer)
President: Craig L Sauey (and Chief Operating Officer)
Senior Executive Officers: Harold R Siekert (VP Finance), Leroy W Mason (VP)

PRINCIPAL ACTIVITIES: Manufacture of household goods, sports equipment, plastics and toys
Trade Names: Principal
Principal Bank: First Wisconsin National Bank of Milwaukee
Financial Information:

	$'000
Sales revenues	50,000

Principal Shareholders: W R Sauey; Craig Sauey; Eric Sauey; Todd Sauey; Jason Sauey
No of Employees: 1,000

FLANIGAN'S ENTERPRISES INC

16565 Northwest 15th Avenue, Miami, FL 33169
Tel: (305) 624 9681

Chairman: Joseph G Flanigan (and Chief Executive Officer); Vice Chairman: Walter L McManus Sr
President: Stephen L Bobersky
Senior Executive Officers: Mary C Reymann (VP Finance and Secretary), Jeffrey D Kastner (Assistant Secretary), Charles Kuhn (VP Retail Package Operation), Michael K Larrison (VP Retail Lounge Operation)

PRINCIPAL ACTIVITIES: Sale of liquor through a chain of stores; recreational interests include private clubs, discotheques and cocktail lounges
Financial Information:

	$'000
Sales revenues	55,000

No of Employees: 905

FLAV-O-RICH,INC

10140 Linn Station Road, Louisville, KY 40223
Tel: (502) 426-6455

President: Jerry Conerly
Senior Executive Officers: Ben F Morgan Jr (Executive VP and Chief Executive Officer), Jim Mueller (Senior VP Finance), Jim McDowell (Senior VP), Bruce Ellison (VP), Phil Kenney (VP)

PRINCIPAL ACTIVITIES: Dairy products; fruit products
Parent Company: Dairyman Inc, Louisville, KY
Principal Bank: Citizens Fidelity Bank
Financial Information:

	$'000
Sales revenues	460,000

No of Employees: 3,660

FLEET, C B, CO, INC

4615 Murray Place, Lynchburg, VA 24506
Tel: (804) 528-4000
Telex: TWX 710 8711 501 cb fleet lurb

President: Brian Duffy
Senior Executive Officers: William R Chambers (Chief Executive Officer), S B Cox (VP Materials and Administration Services), G M Hricz (VP Manufacturing)

PRINCIPAL ACTIVITIES: Manufacture of health and beauty products and pharmaceuticals
Principal Bank: United Virginia Bank
Financial Information:

	$'000
Sales revenues	70,000

No of Employees: 370

FLEET FINANCIAL GROUP INC

50 Kennedy Plaza, Providence, RI 02903
Tel: (401) 278-5800

Chairman: J T Murray (and President and Chief Executive Officer)
Senior Executive Officers: James J Preble (Vice-Chairman), William C Bullock Jr (Executive VP), Robert L Mushkin (Executive VP), Charles W Carey (Executive VP, Chairman Credit Policy), William C Mutterperl (VP, Secretary and General Counsel), John W Flynn (Executive VP and Chief Financial Officer), Robert J Higgins (VP), H J Sarles (Executive VP), Thomas J Skala (VP)

PRINCIPAL ACTIVITIES: Banking
Principal Bank: Fleet National Bank
Financial Information:

	Dec 31 1985(1) $'000	Dec 31 1986(1) $'000
Income before taxes	143,353	187,347
Net income	105,353	136,744
Dividends declared	26,569	38,143
Cash dividends(2)	8,122	3,860
Dividends per share(3)	$0.675	$0.74
Earnings per share primary(3)	$2.06	$2.58
Common stock(4)	227,136	237,563
Retained income	388,654	483,091
Shareholders equity	665,790	770,654
Deposits	5,694,979	6,713,681
Total assets	9,322,434	11,690,346

(1) All financial information has been restated to reflect the acquisitions of First Connecticut Bancorp and Merrill Bankshares in March of 1986. These acquisitions were accounted for as pooling-of-interests
(2) declared by acquired banks prior to merger
(3) common share information has been restated to reflect the two-for-one stock split distributed to stockholders of record at March 15 1987
(4) par and surplus

No of Employees: 8,410

FLEETWOOD ENTERPRISES, INC

3125 Myers Street, Riverside, CA 92523
Tel: (714) 351-3500

Chairman: John C Crean (and Chief Executive Officer); Vice Chairman: William W Weide
President: Glenn F Kummer (and Chief Operating Officer)
Senior Executive Officers: Boyd R Plowman (Senior VP Finance), Jon A Nard (VP Housing Group), Lawrence F Pittroff (VP Administration), Elden L Smith (VP Recreational Vehicle Group), William H Lear (VP, Secretary and General Counsel), Paul M Bingham (VP and Controller)

PRINCIPAL ACTIVITIES: Sectional buildings, motor homes and travel trailers
Principal Subsidiaries: Armada Industries Inc; Hauser Lake Lumber Operations Inc; Avion Coach Corp; Continental Lumber Products Inc; FEI Corp; Flordevco Co Inc; Fleetwood Canada Ltd (Canada); Fleetwood Holidays Inc; Fleetwood Homes Inc; Fleetwood International Inc; Fleetwood Motor Homes Inc; Fleetwood Travel Trailers Inc; Gold Shield Fiberglass Inc
Principal Bank: Bank of America
Financial Information:

	Apr 30 1986 $'000
Sales revenues	1,218,359
Net income	39,345
Earnings per share	$1.69
Shareholders equity	288,344

No of Employees: 10,000

FLEMING COMPANIES, INC

Box 26647, Oklahoma City, OK 73126
Tel: (405) 840-7200

Chairman: R D Harrison (and Chief Executive Officer)
President: E D Werries (and Chief Operating Officer)

Senior Executive Officers: Glenn E Mealman (Executive VP), Harry A Perry II (Executive VP), James D Sweeney (Executive VP), Richard D Williams (Executive VP)

PRINCIPAL ACTIVITIES: Wholesale distributors of groceries, cosmetics, toiletries, hardware and other general merchandise; manufacture of bakery products; foodservice products
Principal Bank: Morgan Guaranty Trust
Financial Information:

	Dec 31 1985 $'000	Dec 27 1986 $'000
Sales revenues	7,094,991	7,652,624
Income before taxes	-	70,388
Net income	60,082	39,315
Dividends	-	21,880
Dividends per share	-	$1.00
Earnings per share	$2.87	$1.80
Shareholders equity	446,894	472,732

No of Employees: 15,880

FLETCHER OIL & REFINING CO
24721 S Main, Carson, CA 90744
Tel: (213) 775-3731
Telex: TWX 910 3457451 forco crsn

President: R G Fletcher
Senior Executive Officers: E L McDaniels (Executive VP), D S Fletcher (VP), W D Fletcher (Treasurer)

PRINCIPAL ACTIVITIES: Production of liquid fuel and industrial gases
Principal Bank: Security Pacific National Bank
Financial Information:

	$'000
Sales revenues	200,000

FLEXSTEEL INDUSTRIES, INC
Brunswick Ind Block, Dubuque, IA 52001
Tel: (319) 556-7730

Chairman: Frank H Bertsch
President: Jack B Crahan
Senior Executive Officers: Herbert L Hughes (VP Finance and Secretary), J R Richardson (VP Marketing), Bruce Lauritsen (VP Sales), Edward J Monaghan (VP Manufacturing)

PRINCIPAL ACTIVITIES: Manufacture of furniture
Principal Bank: American Trust and Savings Bank
Financial Information:

	Jun 30 1986 $'000	Jun 30 1987 $'000
Sales revenues	138,590	156,473
Income before taxes	9,710	12,798
Net income	5,313	6,682
Dividends	2,304	2,306
Dividends per share	$0.48	$0.48
Earnings per share	$1.23	$1.39
Common stock	4,803	4,813
Retained income	48,263	52,639
Shareholders equity	53,626	57,978

No of Employees: 2,400

FLICKINGER GROUP
609 Dingens St, Box 68, Buffalo, NY 14240
Tel: (716) 892 8900

Chairman: Jerry D Metcalf and Chief Executive Officer)
President: D Clark Ogle (and Chief Operating Officer)
Senior Executive Officers: Rudolph A Comchoc (Executive VP South East Division Operations), Larry W Kordisch (Executive VP Finance and Chief Financial Officer), James A Demme (Executive VP Operations, Northern), Burt P Flickinger Jr (Senior VP Government Relations), William E Payne (Senior VP Sales and Merchandising), Brian J Keller Sr (Senior VP, Legal Counsel and Secretary), Peter B Flickinger (VP Research and Special Projects), Thomas R Flickinger (VP Purchasing), William K Houseknecht (VP Labor Relations), Tony Anthony (VP Sales Development), John A Patrick (VP Information Systems), Kenneth H Johnson (VP Real Estate and Engineering), Paul A Barone (VP Food Services), J Kenneth Deault (VP Jamestown Division), Clarence Johnson (VP Elmira Division), Stan A Erikson (VP Advertising and Sales Promotion), T Kapron (VP Wholesaling and Transportation), Richard A Ilgenfritz (VP, PA & S Small Co W/O Sub), Gerald J Bogacz (VP), John H Kimberlin (VP)

PRINCIPAL ACTIVITIES: Wholesale distribution of dairy foods, meat and frozen foods
Parent Company: Scrivner Inc
Principal Bank: Liberty National Bank
Financial Information:

	$'000
Sales revenues	1,500,000

No of Employees: 7,000

FLIGHTSAFETY INTERNATIONAL INC
Marine Air Terminal, Laguardia Airport, Flushing, NY 11371
Tel: (718) 565 4100

Chairman: Albert L Ueltschi (and President and Chief Executive Officer)
Senior Executive Officers: Bruce N Whitman (Executive VP), Elmer G Gleske (VP Government Affairs), James T Ueltschi (VP and Treasurer), Kenneth W Motschwiller (Controller), Peter M Mullen (Secretary), James S Waugh (VP Marketing)

PRINCIPAL ACTIVITIES: Training services for business and naval pilots
Principal Bank: Chase Manhattan Bank
Financial Information:

	Dec 31 1986 $'000
Sales revenues	101,000
Net income	29,000

No of Employees: 1,600

FLINT INDUSTRIES, INC
1624 West 21st Street, Tulsa, OK 73101
Tel: (918) 587-8451

Chairman: C W Flint Jr
President: Paul K Lackey Jr
Senior Executive Officers: Anne S Li (VP Administration)

PRINCIPAL ACTIVITIES: Oil and gas industry service equipment and services; general contractors; manufacture of electronic components
Principal Subsidiaries: Flint Engineering & Construction Co; Flintco Inc; Gordos Corp; Gordos International Corp; Gordos AK Inc; Oakridge Builders Inc
Principal Bank: First National Bank of Tulsa
Financial Information:

	$'000
Sales revenues	195,000

No of Employees: 3,500

FLINTCO
1624 W 21st Street, Tulsa, OK 74101
Tel: (918) 587-8451

President: W F Herren (and Chief Executive Officer)
Senior Executive Officers: Nolan R Hatcher (Senior VP Construction), Ata Y Elauf (VP Construction), Tom E Maxwell (VP Finance, Secretary and Treasurer), J R Nevins (VP Estimating)

PRINCIPAL ACTIVITIES: Construction industry; trade in timber products and building materials
Parent Company: Flint Industries Inc, Tulsa, OK
Principal Bank: First National Bank

Financial Information:

	$'000
Sales revenues	70,000

No of Employees: 300

FLOATING POINT SYSTEMS, INC

PO Box 23489, Portland, OR 97223
Tel: (503) 641-3151
Telex: 360470 FLOATPOIN BEAV

Chairman: Milton R Smith (and Chief Executive Officer)
President: George P O'Leary (and Chief Operating Officer)
Senior Executive Officers: James T Richardson (VP Finance and Administration), Lance H Johnson (VP Product Development), Roy T Houston (VP Operations)

PRINCIPAL ACTIVITIES: Manufacture of special purpose computers
Principal Bank: United States National Bank of Oregon
Financial Information:

	Oct 31 1985	Oct 31 1986
	$'000	$'000
Sales revenues	126,568	88,579
Income (loss) before taxes	19,697	(25,038)
Net income (loss)	14,379	(14,272)
Earnings (loss) per share	$1.75	($1.67)
Shareholders equity	107,090	100,732

No of Employees: 800

FLORAFAX INTERNATIONAL, INC

PO Box 45745, Tulsa, OK 74145
Tel: (918) 622-8415
Telex: WUT 492 478 florefax tul

Chairman: Joseph S Chalfont
President: Floyd Cox Jr (and Chief Executive Officer)
Senior Executive Officers: Ronald W Fore (VP and Secretary), G William Matthews (VP, Treasurer and Chief Financial Officer), Jay Radcliff (VP Sales), Herschel Workman (VP)

PRINCIPAL ACTIVITIES: Production and sale of flowers and floral arrangements; flowers sent by wire worldwide
Principal Subsidiaries: Eddan Inc; Florafax Spirits By Wire; Garden Path Imports Inc
Principal Bank: Bank of Oklahoma
Financial Information:

	$'000
Sales revenues	46,250

No of Employees: 400

FLORASYNTH, INC

410 East 62 Street, New York, NY 10021
Tel: (212) 371-7700
Telex: WUI 620426 flora 620426

Chairman: Jack N Friedman (and President)
Senior Executive Officers: Richard Coleman (Executive VP), Joseph H Fein (VP, Treasurer and Purchasing Agent), Kenneth L Rugg (VP Fragrance Division), Michael F Mann (Secretary and Chief Financial Officer)

PRINCIPAL ACTIVITIES: Manufacture of essences and extracts for coloring, flavoring and perfume production
Principal Bank: Bankers Trust Company
Financial Information:

	$'000
Sales revenues	100,000

No of Employees: 900

FLORIDA EAST COAST INDUSTRIES INC

1 Malaga Street, St Augustine, FL 32084
Tel: (904) 829 3421

Chairman: Winfred L Thornton (and President and Chief Executive Officer)
Senior Executive Officers: William E Durham Jr (VP), Raymond W Wyckoff (VP), Carl F Zellers Jr (VP and Secretary), Neal T Smith (Treasurer), Richard J Yastrzemski (Controller), Charles B Evans (Legal Counsel)

PRINCIPAL ACTIVITIES: Railroad services
Parent Company: St Joe Paper Company
Principal Subsidiaries: Florida East Coast Railway Company
Principal Bank: Florida National Bank
Financial Information:

	Dec 31 1986
	$'000
Sales revenues	130,000
Net income	31,000

No of Employees: 1,470

FLORIDA FEDERAL SAVINGS AND LOAN ASSOCIATION

Central Avenue at Fourth Street, St Petersburg, FL 33701
Tel: (813) 893-1131

Chairman: Eric Stattin (and Chief Executive Officer); Vice Chairman: Raleigh W Greene (and Legal Counsel)
Senior Executive Officers: Eugene L Williams Jr (Senior Executive VP and Secretary), Thomas V Ogletree (Executive VP and Treasurer), Steve Hudson (Executive VP), Richard Allen (Executive VP)

PRINCIPAL ACTIVITIES: Financial services
Principal Subsidiaries: Florida First Service Corp; Sundial Group Inc
Financial Information:

	Jun 30 1985	Jun 30 1986
	$'000	$'000
Net income (loss)	2,097	(65,461)
Earnings (loss) per share	$0.22	($6.99)
Shareholders equity	290,407	224,882
Deposits	-	3,432,526
Total assets	4,782,813	5,192,036

No of Employees: 1,686

FLORIDA HYDROCARBONS CO

Rte 1, Box 83, Brooker, FL 32622
Tel: (904) 485-1222

Chairman: T W Rollins
President: W J Smith
Senior Executive Officers: J R Knorpp (Executive VP and Chief Financial and Administration Officer), W V Morgan (Executive VP), W H Gillett (Senior VP and General Manager), Richard D Kinder (VP, General Counsel and Assistant Secretary), Dennis S Shea (VP Finance and Accounting and Treasurer), Albert R Aiken (VP), Robert E King (VP)

PRINCIPAL ACTIVITIES: Industrial gases
Parent Company: Continental Resources Co, Houston, TX
Principal Bank: Barnett Bank of Orlando/Winter Park
Financial Information:

	$'000
Sales revenues	50,000

Principal Shareholders: Continental Group Inc, Stamford, CT
No of Employees: 30

FLORIDA MINING & MATERIALS CORPORATION

PO Box 23965, Tampa, FL 33630
Tel: (813) 933-6711

President: Thomas E Bronson (and Chief Executive Officer)
Senior Executive Officers: Fred W Cohrs (VP Cement), John P Roebuck (VP Concrete Sales), T M Kaney (VP Concrete Products), R M Coleman (VP Aggregates)

PRINCIPAL ACTIVITIES: Concrete products; quarrying
Parent Company: Moore McCormack Resources Inc, Stamford, CT

Principal Bank: Exchange National Bank of Tampa
Financial Information:

	$'000
Sales revenues	150,000

No of Employees: 1,800

FLORIDA NATIONAL BANKS OF FLORIDA, INC

214 Hogan Street, Jacksonville, FL 32201
Tel: (904) 359-5111

Chairman: John D Uible (and Chief Executive Officer)
President: E B Bower (and Chief Operating Officer)
Senior Executive Officers: James E Linkenauger (Executive VP and Chief Financial Officer), Robert M Ulsch (Executive VP and Chief Administration Officer)

PRINCIPAL ACTIVITIES: Holding company with interests in banking
Principal Subsidiaries: Florida National Bank; Kingsley Bank
Principal Bank: Florida National Bank
Financial Information:

	Dec 31 1985	Dec 31 1986
	$'000	$'000
Net income	88,649	34,389
Earnings per share	$7.13	$1.30
Shareholders equity	383,013	430,571
Deposits	4,990,929	5,816,445
Total assets	5,980,814	6,876,822

No of Employees: 4,739

FLORIDA PROGRESS CORPORATION

270 First Ave S, St Petersburg, FL 33701
Tel: (813) 895-1705

Chairman: Andrew H Hines Jr (and President and Chief Executive Officer)
Senior Executive Officers: Clarence W McKee Jr (Executive VP), S A Brandimore (Executive VP and General Counsel), Allen J Keesler Jr (Group VP), Lee H Scott (Group VP), Gus A Stauros (Group VP)

PRINCIPAL ACTIVITIES: Holding company with interests in electricity supply and coal distribution; business and commercial services
Principal Subsidiaries: Better Business Systems Inc; Better Business Farms Inc; Better Computer Supplies Inc; Cavalier Packaging Corp; Computer Supply Mart Inc; H & D Packaging Inc; Electric Fuels Corp; Florida Power Corp; Progress Equities Inc; Progress Financial Services Inc; Talquin Corp; Hunnicutt Equities Inc
Principal Bank: Florida National Bank
Financial Information:

	Dec 31 1986
	$'000
Sales revenues	1,900,000
Net income	181,000

No of Employees: 7,000

FLORIDA PUBLIC UTILITIES COMPANY

401 South Dixie Highway, West Palm Beach, FL 33402
Tel: (305) 832 2461

Chairman: Edward J Patterson (and Chief Executive Officer and Chief Financial Officer)
President: Franklin C Cressman
Senior Executive Officers: Robert L Terry (Chairman of Executive Committee), Gordon O Jerauld (Senior VP), B L Demmon (VP), E T Neun (VP and Treasurer), M K Hall (Secretary)

PRINCIPAL ACTIVITIES: Supply of electricity, water and gas
Principal Subsidiaries: Flo-Gas Corporation
Principal Bank: Florida National Bank

Financial Information:

	Dec 31 1985
	$'000
Sales revenues	57,735
Net income	1,105

No of Employees: 290

FLORIDA ROCK INDUSTRIES, INC

155 E 21st Street, Jacksonville, FL 32206
Tel: (904) 355-1781

Chairman: Thompson S Baker
President: Edward L Baker
Senior Executive Officers: S R Hays (VP Concrete Group), C J Shepherdson Sr (VP Concrete Group), John D Baker II (VP Aggregate Group), Ruggles B Carlson (VP Finance and Treasurer), Paul E Knollman Jr (VP Administration)

PRINCIPAL ACTIVITIES: Mining and quarrying; concrete products
Financial Information:

	Sep 30 1985	Sep 30 1986
	$'000	$'000
Sales revenues	247,312	258,948
Income before taxes	33,849	36,862
Net income	21,192	21,726
Cash dividends	3,158	4,118
Dividends per share cash	$0.35	$0.45
Earnings per share	$2.33	$2.36
Common stock	903	927
Retained income	117,537	88,712
Shareholders equity	126,580	100,871

No of Employees: 2,008

FLORIDA STEEL CORPORATION

Box 23328, Tampa, FL 33630
Tel: (813) 251-8811
Telex: 52-731 FLA STEEL TA

Chairman: Edward L Flom (and Chief Executive Officer)
President: Thomas G Creed (and Chief Operating Officer)
Senior Executive Officers: J C Hogue (VP Employee Relations), J D Haney (Group VP Fabricated Reinforcing Steel Products), R R Boswell (VP Steel Mills), A D Gres (VP, Secretary, Treasurer and Chief Financial Officer)

PRINCIPAL ACTIVITIES: Production and fabrication of steel
Principal Subsidiaries: Atlas Steel & Wire Corporation; Stafford Rail Products Inc
Principal Bank: AmeriTrust Company
Financial Information:

	Sep 30 1986
	$'000
Sales revenues	319,324
Income before taxes	28,363
Net income	15,393
Dividends	3,548
Dividends per share	$0.59
Earnings per share	$2.56
Common stock*	6,022
Retained income	98,088
Shareholders equity	108,048

*number of shares in thousands

Principal Shareholders: Listed New York Stock Exchange
No of Employees: 2,300

FLOW GENERAL INC

7655 Old Springhouse Road, McLean, VA 22102
Tel: (703) 893-5915
Telex: 440543 FGI UI
Telefax: (703) 356-0774

Chairman: Grant C Ehrlich (and Chairman Executive Committee)
President: Robert E Wengler (and Chief Executive Officer)

Senior Executive Officers: Harris W Seed (Assistant Secretary), Charles R McCarthy Jr (General Counsel and Assistant Secretary), Philip R Pietras (Acting Chief Financial Officer)

PRINCIPAL ACTIVITIES: Research and analysis services; biomedical products; electronics and software products

Principal Subsidiaries: General Research Corporation; SWL Inc; Moseley Associates Inc; Semifab Inc; Flow Laboratories Inc; Flow Laboratories Australia (Pty) Ltd (Australia); Flow Laboratories NV/SA Belgium); Flow Laboratories SA (France); Gruppo Flow SpA (Italy); Flow Laboratories Japan Co Ltd (Japan); Amstelstad BV (Netherlands); Flow Laboratories Ltd (UK); Flow Laboratories AG (Switzerland); Flow Laboratories GmbH (West Germany)

Principal Bank: Philadelphia National Bank

Financial Information:

	Jun 30 1986	Jun 30 1987
	$'000	$'000
Sales revenues	165,029	208,392
Income before taxes*	906	1,419
Net income	24	318
Earnings per share	-	$0.03
Common stock	881	885
Retained (deficit)	(26,970)	(26,668)
Shareholders equity	46,096	50,602

*and extraordinary item

Principal Shareholders: G David Frankel (6.8%); Dimensional Fund Advisors Inc (5.7%)

No of Employees: 2,263

FLOWERS INDUSTRIES, INC

US Highway 19 S, PO Box 1338, Thomasville, GA 31792

Tel: (912) 226-9110

Chairman: Amos R McMullian (and Chairman Executive Committee and Chief Executive Officer); Vice Chairman: Frederick E Cooper

President: Heeth Varnedoe III (Executive VP)

Senior Executive Officers: Heeth Varnedoe III (Executive VP), C M Wood III (Senior VP and Chief Financial Officer), Robert P Crozer (VP)

PRINCIPAL ACTIVITIES: Flowers Industries is a specialty foods company which serves regional and national markets with a variety of branded food products, including fresh and frozen breads, buns and specialty rolls; sweet and salted snacks; and frozen specialty vegetables, fruits, cakes and pies

Trade Names: Nature's Own, Cobblestone Mill, Beebo, Flowers

Principal Bank: Wachovia Bank and Trust Company

Financial Information:

	Jun 28 1986	Jun 27 1987
	$'000	$'000
Sales revenues	698,394	797,196
Income before taxes	53,660	48,213
Net income	29,531	27,645
Ordinary dividends	10,911	12,796
Dividends per ord share	$0.47	$0.55
Earnings per share*	$1.25	$1.18
Common stock	14,754	14,754
Retained income	140,007	154,938
Shareholders equity	161,842	177,747

*fully diluted

No of Employees: 10,000

FLUKE, JOHN, MFG CO, INC

6920 Seaway Blvd, Box C 9090, Everett, WA 98203

Tel: (206) 342-6300

Chairman: John M Fluke Jr (and Chef Executive Officer)

President: George M Winn (and Chief Operating Officer)

Senior Executive Officers: Everts L Johns (VP and Treasurer), Jerome A Froland (VP and General Manager), William R Hoffman (VP), Fred R Hume (VP Technical and Planning), Richard W Van Saun (VP and General Manager), John R Smith (VP and Corporate Controller), George O Trickell (VP Personnel and Employee Relations), Ronald R Wambolt (VP)

PRINCIPAL ACTIVITIES: Electronic equipment including measuring and testing instruments

Principal Subsidiaries: J Fluke CCI Sales Group; Fluke International Corp; Fluke Export Sales Corp; Fluke International Sales Corp; Instrument Specialists Sales Group Inc; J Fluke SBM Sales Group

Principal Bank: Peoples National Bank of Washington

Financial Information:

	$'000
Sales revenues	216,560

No of Employees: 2,860

FLUOR CORPORATION

3333 Michelson Drive, Irvine, CA 92730

Tel: (714) 975-2000

Chairmen: David S Tappan Jr (and Chief Executive Officer); Vice Chairman: B Mickel

President: John A Wright (and Chief Operating Officer)

Senior Executive Officers: N A Peterson (Senior VP and Secretary), P J Trimble (Senior VP Law and Tax), C J Bradley (VP Human Resources and Administration), J R Byron (VP Government Relations), L N Fisher (VP Corporate Law), J R Fluor II (VP Corporate Relations), W M Hofacre (VP and Controller), W J Holleman (VP Tax), R D Paul (VP Finance and Operations Evaluation), J O Rollans (VP Corporate Communications), W D Trammell (VP Project Finance), D R Copley (VP and Treasurer)

PRINCIPAL ACTIVITIES: Civil engineering and construction; mining and quarrying

Principal Subsidiaries: Fluor Drilling Services Inc; Fluor Engineering & Construction Group Inc; Daniel International Corp; Daniel Construction Co International; Fluor Constructors Inc; Fluor Engineers Inc; Fluor Technology Inc; Fluor Oil & Gas Corp; St Joe Minerals Corp; St Joe International Corp

Principal Bank: California Canadian Bank

Financial Information:

	Oct 31 1985	Oct 31 1986
	$'000	$'000
Sales revenues	4,168,444	4,678,660
Net (loss)	(633,324)	(60,440)
(Loss) per share	($8.01)	($0.76)
Shareholders equity	1,033,904	950,240

No of Employees: 26,958

FLUORCARBON COMPANY

27611 LaPaz Road, Laguna Niguel, CA 92656

Tel: (714) 831-5350

Telex: TWX 910-595-2552

Chairman: Peter Churm; Vice Chairman: George L Angle

President: J M Hagan

Senior Executive Officers: Monty A Houdeshell (VP and Chief Financial Officer), William M Joslin (VP), Lonnie J Wimberly (VP), Michael L Craddock (VP), Larry K Hanson (VP), Terry A Noonan (VP)

PRINCIPAL ACTIVITIES: Plastics and plastic products; rubber and rubber goods; electronic components; cables and wires; pumps, valves and compressors

Principal Bank: Security Pacific National Bank

Financial Information:

	Jan 31 1986 $'000	Jan 31 1987 $'000
Sales revenues	103,957	97,782
Income before taxes	11,070	8,256
Net income	6,111	4,046
Dividends per share	$0.26	$0.28
Earnings per share	$1.40	$0.93
Common stock	8,645	8,681
Retained income	32,120	34,959
Shareholders equity	40,765	43,640

Number of Shareholders: 4,800 shareholders on record
No of Employees: 1,800

FMC CORPORATION

200 E Randolph Drive, Chicago, IL 60601
Tel: (312) 861-6000
Telex: 429459 FMCH Q UI

Chairman: Robert H Malott (and Chief Executive Officer)
President: Raymond C Tower (and Chief Operating Officer)
Senior Executive Officers: Arthur D Lyons (VP-Finance), W J Kirby (VP-Administration), P J Head (VP-General Counsel)

PRINCIPAL ACTIVITIES: Agricultural chemicals; specialty chemicals; defense systems; specialized machinery
Principal Subsidiaries: Foret SA; FMC Gold Company; FMC Wyoming Corp; Lithium Corporation of America
Financial Information:

	Dec 31 1985 $'000	Dec 31 1986 $'000
Sales revenues	3,260,847	3,002,746
Income before taxes	269,077	192,585
Net income	196,553	152,529
Dividends	57,571	14,428
Earnings per share	$1.30	$1.62
Retained income (deficit)	1,440,204	(454,933)
Shareholders equity (deficit)	1,123,100	(506,602)

No of Employees: 24,996

FME CORPORATION

30955 Huntwood Ave, Hayward, CA 94544
Tel: (415) 489-6800

Chairman: Jacques Vandamme
President: Robert J Goldmann (and Chief Executive Officer)
Senior Executive Officers: Joseph P Balsama (VP Operations), Paul D Sharps (VP Marketing), John Hughes (VP Engineering), Steven B McElfresh (VP Human Resources and Secretary)

PRINCIPAL ACTIVITIES: Postal machinery and equipment
Parent Company: Compagnie Générale d'Électricité, France
Principal Bank: Bank of America
Financial Information:

	$'000
Sales revenues	60,000

No of Employees: 1,200

FMI FINANCIAL CORPORATION

1 East Fourth Street, Cincinnati, OH 45202
Tel: (513) 579 2177

Chairman: Harper Sibley Jr (and President)
Senior Executive Officers: Keith E Lindner (Executive VP), Christopher B Hewett (VP and Legal Counsel), Kenneth A Luban (VP and Secretary), Fred J Runk (VP and Treasurer)

PRINCIPAL ACTIVITIES: Insurance services including casualty and property insurance; real estate development
Principal Bank: Provident Bank
Financial Information:

	$'000
Revenues	110,000

No of Employees: 300

FOOD LION INC

PO Box 1330, Harrison Rd, Salisbury, NC 28145-1330
Tel: (704) 633-8250
Telex: (810) 6240 336

Chairman: Ralph W Ketner
President: Tom E Smith (and Chief Executive Officer)
Senior Executive Officers: Jerry W Helms (Chief Operating Officer and Senior VP Operations), Brian P Woolf (Chief Financial Officer and VP Finance and Secretary)

PRINCIPAL ACTIVITIES: Supermarkets
Principal Bank: Wachovia Bank & Trust
Financial Information:

	Dec 31 1985 $'000	Jan 31 1987 $'000
Sales revenues	1,865,632	2,406,582
Income before taxes	89,185	122,923
Net income	47,585	61,823
Dividends	4,523	5,700
Dividends per share	$0.028	$0.036
Earnings per share	$0.30	$0.39
Common stock	26,614	80,255
Retained income	174,691	184,143
Shareholders equity	207,379	264,864

No of Employees: 24,624

FOODARAMA SUPERMARKETS INC

303 West Main Street, PO Box 592, Freehold, NJ 07728
Tel: (201) 462 4700

Chairman: Joseph J Saker (and President)
Senior Executive Officers: Sidney Cohen (Senior VP Administration and Assistant Secretary), Richard Saker (Senior VP and Chief Operating Officer), Joseph C Troilo (Senior VP Finance and Assistant Treasurer), Robert V Condon (Senior VP Sales and Merchandising), John J McAteer (Senior VP Employee Relations and Personnel Affairs), Mary S Saker (Treasurer)

PRINCIPAL ACTIVITIES: Holding company with interests in grocery stores and drug stores
Principal Subsidiaries: New Linden Price Rite Inc; Regal Drugs Inc; Shop Rite Drugs Inc; Shop Rite of Malverne Inc; Shop Rite of Reading Inc; Shop Wise of CT Inc; Shop Wise Supermarket of PA
Principal Bank: National Bank of North America
Financial Information:

	$'000
Sales revenues	441,050

No of Employees: 4,250

FOODWAYS NATIONAL, INC

PO Box 41, Boise, ID 83707
Tel: (208) 383-6700

President: G D Herrick
Senior Executive Officers: S D Wiley (VP), F E Osborne (VP and Treasurer)

PRINCIPAL ACTIVITIES: Manufacture of frozen food products including ready-meals and desserts
Parent Company: H J Heinz Co, Pittsburgh, PA
Principal Bank: First Security Bank of Idaho
Financial Information:

	$'000
Sales revenues	140,000

No of Employees: 440

FOOTE & DAVIES INC

3101 McCall Drive, Doraville, GA 30340
Tel: (404) 451-4511

Chairman: Frank E Kutcher Jr (and President)
Senior Executive Officers: Alvan A Herring (Senior VP Administration and Finance), Bill Traub (VP) Sales), Keith

Pierce (VP Manufacturing), Robert Smith (VP Materials), Robert Lindsay (VP A.C.T.), Bruce Thompson (General Counsel)

PRINCIPAL ACTIVITIES: Printing
Trade Names: Foote & Davies/Atlanta, Foote & Davies/Lincoln
Principal Subsidiaries: Mid-America Webpress; Atlanta Color Concepts
Principal Bank: Bank South-Atlanta
Financial Information:

	$'000
Sales revenues	200,000

Principal Shareholders: Management
No of Employees: 1,500

FOOTE, CONE & BELDING COMMUNICATIONS, INC

401 N Michigan Ave, Chicago, IL 60611
Tel: (312) 467-9200

Chairman: Norman W Brown (and Chief Executive Officer); Vice Chairman: Stanley H Katz
President: Abbott C Jones (and Chief Operating Officer)
Senior Executive Officers: Allan Wilson Jr (Executive VP and Chief Financial Officer)

PRINCIPAL ACTIVITIES: Advertising and public relations services
Principal Subsidiaries: Albert Frank-Guenther Law Inc; Carl Byoir & Associates Inc; Mediacom Communications Training; Deutsch Shea & Evans; FCB Advertising Inc; FCB International Inc; Foote Cone & Belding Advertising Inc; Foote Cone & Belding-Honig Inc; Lewis Gilman & Kynett Inc; Wahlstrom & Co Inc
Principal Bank: First National Bank of Chicago
Financial Information:

	$'000
Sales revenues	287,000

No of Employees: 5,800

FOOTE MINERAL COMPANY

Rte 100, Exton, PA 19341
Tel: (215) 363-6500

Chairman: Richard B Leather
President: Thomas A Williams (and Chief Executive Officer)
Senior Executive Officers: Frank E Hurley (VP and General Manager, Ferroalloys Division), Richard N Jacobson (VP and General Manager, Chemicals and Minerals Division), Peter B Thomas (VP Industrial Relations)

PRINCIPAL ACTIVITIES: Foote is one of the principal suppliers of lithium products in the world and is also an important domestic producer of ferroalloys. Foote's lithium products come from solar evaporation of brines in Nevada, from spodumene ore from an open-pit mine in North Carolina and from a new solar evaporation system in Chile that went on stream in 1984
Parent Company: Newmont Mining Corporation, New York, NY (87.5%)
Financial Information:

	$'000
Sales revenues	126,700

No of Employees: 1,175

FOOT-JOY, INC

144 Field Street, Brockton, MA 02403
Tel: (617) 586-2233

Chairman: Richard N Tarlow
President: James Boosales
Senior Executive Officers: William E Tarlow (Executive VP), Keith Johnson (VP Finance), Eckhard Knoepke (VP Operations), James R Ireland (VP Promotions), J E Conathan (VP Product Development), Patrick O'Grady (VP Sales), Mary J Kenney (VP Personnel), Thomas Nachmann (VP Marketing and International), Paul Kasimatis (VP Marketing), Elizabeth Webster (VP Marketing), Jerry Daly (VP Marketing)

PRINCIPAL ACTIVITIES: Manufacture of leisure and sporting footwear
Parent Company: General Mills Inc, Minneapolis, MN
Principal Bank: First National Bank of Boston
Financial Information:

	$'000
Sales revenues	70,000

No of Employees: 425

FOR BETTER LIVING INC

33049-C Calle Aviador, San Juan Capistrano, CA 92675
Tel: (714) 831 9600

Chairman: F G Fabian Jr (and President)
Senior Executive Officers: Walter B Hahne (VP), Frank Ciotti (VP Finance, Secretary and Subsidiary Officer), William J Nolan III (Controller and Assistant Secretary)

PRINCIPAL ACTIVITIES: Production of building materials and fittings
Principal Subsidiaries: Associated Concrete Products; Associated Plastics Inc; MCG Industries; Surfer Publications; US Radiator Corporation
Principal Bank: Wells Fargo Bank
Financial Information:

	$'000
Sales revenues	47,065

No of Employees: 460

FORD MOTOR CO

The American Road, Dearborn, MI 48121
Tel: (313) 322-3000

Chairman: Donald E Petersen (and Chief Executive Officer); Vice Chairman: William C Ford
President: Harold A Poling (and Chief Operating Officer)
Senior Executive Officers: Philip E Benton Jr (Executive VP Diversified Products Operation), John A Betti (Executive VP Technical Affairs), Allan D Gilmour (Executive VP and Chief Financial Officer), Louis R Ross (Executive VP Ford North American Auto Operation), David N McCammon (VP and Controller), James K Bakken (VP Operations Support Services), Lionel M Chicoine (VP Purchase and Supply), James W Ford (VP), Stuart M Frey (VP Car Product Development), Edward E Hagenlocker (VP and General Manager Truck Operations), L Lindsey Halstead (VP Latin American Auto Operations), William J Hayden (VP Manufacturing, Ford Co of Europe Inc), Walter Hayes (VP, Vice Chairman Ford Co of Europe Inc), Frederick Z Herr (VP Engineering and Manufacturing), Donald F Kopka (VP Design), Louis E Lataif (VP Sales Operations), Mervyn H Manning (VP, President Ford Asia-Pacific Inc), John P McTague (VP Research), Robert F Moglia (VP and General Manager Ford Tractor Operations), Henry R Nolte Jr (VP and Legal Counsel), Peter J Pestillo (VP Employees and External Affairs), Helen O Petrauskas (VP Environmental and Safety Engineering), Donald B Rassier (VP, President Ford Aerospace and Communications Corp), Robert L Rewey Jr (VP and General Manager Ford Division), William E Scollard (VP Manufacturing Operations), David W Scott (VP Public Affairs), Will Scott (VP Governmental Relations), Stanley A Seneker (VP and Treasurer), Wayne H Smithey (VP Washington Affairs), Alexander J Trotman (VP, President Ford Co of Europe Inc), Lewis C Veraldi (VP and General Manager Lincoln-Mercury Division), Kenneth Whipple (VP, Chairman Ford Co of Europe Inc), Edson P Williams (VP, Ford Diversified Products Operation)

PRINCIPAL ACTIVITIES: Manufacture of motor vehicles; heavy duty vehicles; agricultural vehicles

Principal Subsidiaries: Dearborn Capital Corp; Dearborn Inn Co; Dearborn Marine Inc; Environ Inc; Eveleth Taconite Co; Ford Aerospace Communications Inc; Ford Aerospace & Communications Overseas Inc; Ford Aerospace Satellite Services Corp; Logistic Services Corp; Ford Communications Inc; Ford Direct Markets Inc; Ford Electronics & Refrigeration Corp; Ford Export Corp; Ford International Services Corp; Ford Leasing Development Co; Cardinal Redevelopment Corp; Ford Motor Dealership Facilities Co; Ford Microelectronics Inc; Ford Motor Credit Co; American Road Equity Corp; Ford Financial Services Inc; American Road Insurance Co; Ford Life Insurance Co; Vista Insurance Co; Vista Life Insurance Co; American Road Services Co; Ford Auto Club Inc; Ford Consumer Credit Co; Ford Consumer Discount Co; Ford Motor Credit Co International; Ford Motor Credit Co of IA; Ford Motor Land Development Co; Detroit Downtown Development Corp; Ford Motor Properties Inc; Ford Colo Properties Inc; Greenfield Properties Inc; Renaissance Retail Shop Inc; Ford Products Co; Fordson Coal Co Inc; Ghia Inc; Lincoln Motor Co Inc; Parker Chemical Co; Parklane Insurance Co; Predelivery Service Corp; Rouge Steel Co; Sunglass Products Inc; 3000 Schaefer Road Co

Principal Bank: Philadelphia National Bank

Financial Information:

	Dec 31 1985	Dec 31 1986
	$'000	$'000
Sales revenues	52,774,400	62,715,800
Net income	2,515,400	3,285,100
Earnings per share	$13.63	$12.32
Shareholders equity	12,268,600	14,859,500

No of Employees: 369,300

FORD MOTOR CREDIT CO

American Road, Dearborn, MI 48121

Tel: (313) 322-3000

Chairman: James W Ford

President: William E Odom

Senior Executive Officers: Richard L Fenstermacher (Executive VP North American Auto Finance Operations), James G Duff (Executive VP Insurance and Special Finance Operations), Robert D Warner (Executive VP Overseas Operations), Richard C Bentley (VP Finance), Wayland F Blood (VP and Treasurer), George V Brown III (VP Strategic and Diversification Planning), George L Faistenhammer (VP Personnel and Organisation), Joseph P Henley (VP Western US Operations), Alfred F LaBarge (VP Diversified Financial Operations), Leo C Larkin (VP Insurance Operations), Stefan M Poth (VP Business Planning), Vincent J Radzik (VP Eastern US and Canadian Operations), Andrew J Salmon (VP Latin American and Asia Pacific Credit Operations), Ramon A Von Drehle (VP Legal), Robert Svoboda (VP European Credit Operations)

PRINCIPAL ACTIVITIES: Automotive finance; insurance

Parent Company: Ford Motor Co, Dearborn, MI

Financial Information:

	$'000
Revenues	3,200,000

No of Employees: 5,507

FOREMOST CORPORATION OF AMERICA

5800 Foremost Drive Southeast, PO Box 2450, Grand Rapids, MI 49501

Tel: (616) 942 3233

Chairman: Edward J Frey

President: Richard L Antonini (and Chief Executive Officer)

Senior Executive Officers: Richard L Heroux (VP), Robert J Shipman (VP), Russell G DeYoung (Controller), Betty A Mohr (Auditor), F Robert Woudstra (Treasurer), Paul D Yared (Legal Counsel)

PRINCIPAL ACTIVITIES: Insurance services; finance and loan facilities

Principal Subsidiaries: Access Controls Systems Ltd; Centennial Park Hotel Corporation; Foremost Home Brokers Inc; Foremost Insurance Company; Foremost Financial Services; Minnehoma Life Insurance Company; Foremost Guaranty Corporation; Mach V Aviation Insurance Managers; Minnehoma Insurance Company; Adesco Inc; Foremost Life Insurance Company

Principal Bank: Union Bank and Trust Company

Financial Information:

	Dec 31 1985
	$'000
Revenues	461,005
Net income	23,290

No of Employees: 1,800

FOREST CITY ENTERPRISES, INC

10800 Brookpark Rd, Cleveland, OH 44130

Tel: (216) 267-1200

Chairman: Max Ratner; Vice Chairmen: Samuel H Miller (and Chief Operating Officer), Nathan Shafran

President: Albert Ratner (and Chief Executive Officer)

Senior Executive Officers: Alan S Ellett (Executive VP), Charles A Ratner (Executive VP), Thomas G Smith (Senior VP and Chief Financial Officer), Gilles A E Stucker (Senior VP Finance), William M Warren (Senior VP and General Counsel), Helen F Morgan (VP, Secretary and Treasurer), D Layton McCown (VP and Corporate Controller), Albert L Reisenfeld (Associate General Counsel)

PRINCIPAL ACTIVITIES: Forest City Enterprises, Inc is a major real estate company which is vertically integrated and comprised of three main groups: Investment Real Estate Group; Land Development and Merchant Building Group; and Specialty Retailing Group

Principal Subsidiaries and Divisions: Forest City Apartment Management Division; Forest City Commercial Management Division; Forest City Dillon Inc; Forest City Land Division-Sunrise Land Co; Forest City Rental Properties Corporation; Forest City Trading Group Inc

Principal Bank: AmeriTrust Company N.A.

Financial Information:

	Jan 31 1986	Jan 31 1987
	$'000	$'000
Total revenues	230,013	251,444
Net income	7,444	13,061
Dividends	2,151	2,151
Dividends per Class A share	$0.30	$0.30
Dividends per Class B share	$0.24	$0.24
Earnings per share	$0.94	$1.64
Common stock class A	1,351	1,352
Common stock class B	1,298	1,297
Retained income	60,527	71,437
Shareholders equity	70,405	81,315

No of Employees: 2,400

FOREST OIL CORPORATION

950-17th St, 1500 Colorado National Bldg, Denver, CO 80202

Tel: (303) 629-1916

Chairman: Clayton G Dorn (and Chief Executive Officer)

President: David F Dorn (and Chairman of Executive Committee)

Senior Executive Officers: Herbert J Warner (Executive VP), Everado Goyanes (VP Finance and Treasurer), John C Dorn (Regional VP), Richard B Dorn (Regional VP), William F Higie (VP, Secretary and Legal Counsel), Jack D Riggs (VP and Regional Manager), Richard L Coons (VP and Regional Manager), Paul L Keyes (VP Exploration), W Jeffrey Burford (VP Administration), Edwin J Gilbert (VP Production), Dale F Dorn (VP), William L Dorn (VP), John F Dorn (VP)

PRINCIPAL ACTIVITIES: Natural gas and crude oil exploration and production

Principal Subsidiaries: Forest Energy Inc; Forest Exploration Inc; Forest Land & Royalty Exploration Inc; Forest

Management Inc; Forest Oil of Canada Ltd; Forest Petroleum UK Ltd
Principal Bank: Chase Manhattan Bank
Financial Information:

	$'000
Sales revenues	134,850

No of Employees: 500

FOREST PRODUCTS DIVISION

PO Drawer 1164, Orangeburg, SC 29116
Tel: (803) 534-4420

Senior Executive Officers: Gerald Freeman (Corporate VP and General Manager Forest Products), C P Dempsey (Divisional VP and General Manager Solid Wood Products), Edward Lee (General Manager Wood Procurement), Thomas Clonts (General Manager Woodlands), Michael Vickio (Comptroller)

PRINCIPAL ACTIVITIES: Timber industry
Parent Company: Stone Container Corporation, Chicago, IL
Principal Bank: Citizens and Southern Bank
Financial Information:

	$'000
Sales revenues	200,000

No of Employees: 750

FORESTON COAL INTERNATIONAL INC

468 Park Avenue S, New York, NY 10016
Tel: (212) 481-1020
Telex: ITT 420 197 coal ui

Chairman: Meyer Sabsevitz; Vice Chairman: Arnold L Sabin (and Secretary and Treasurer)
President: Herbert Kobin (and Chief Executive Officer)
Senior Executive Officers: Siegmund Kupferberg (Executive VP), Gerard McEvoy (VP), Stephen C Miller (Second VP), Theodore Sohnen (Second VP)

PRINCIPAL ACTIVITIES: Export of coal and coal products
Parent Company: Foreston Securities Corp
Principal Bank: The Chase Manhattan Bank NA
Financial Information:

	$'000
Sales revenues	76,000

No of Employees: 40

FORT HOWARD PAPER CO

1919 S Broadway, Box 19130, Green Bay, WI 54307
Tel: (414) 435-8821

Chairman: Paul J Schierl (and Chief Executive Officer)
President: Donald H DeMeuse
Senior Executive Officers: James J Schoshinski (Executive VP), Kathleen J Hempel (Executive VP), R James Alexey (Executive VP, President Maryland Cup Corp), Leon H Freischmidt (VP), George F Hartmann Jr (VP), James W Nellen (VP and Secretary), Timothy J Twomey (VP), Jeffrey P Eves (VP), Gerald O Patterson (VP), John F Rowley (VP)

PRINCIPAL ACTIVITIES: Paper products; packaging
Principal Subsidiaries: Maryland Cup Corp
Financial Information:

	Dec 31 1985 $'000	Dec 31 1986 $'000
Sales revenues	1,363,292	1,549,290
Net income	157,010	146,391
Earnings per share	-	$2.18
Shareholders equity	1,115,225	1,202,918

No of Employees: 13,900

FORT WORTH DIVISION

Grant's Lane, Fort Worth, TX 76101
Tel: (817) 777-2000

Senior Executive Officers: H F Rogers (VP and General Manager), T S Webb (VP, F-16 Programs), D B Scheideman (VP Contracts), E E Hatchett (VP Finance), R Krueger (VP Logistics and Support), C N White (VP Operations), D J Wheaton (VP Marketing), N E Day (VP Materials), D J Talley (VP Quality Assurance), C A Anderson (VP Engineering), D R Kent (VP, ATF), G L Davis (VP, F-111), W C Dietz (VP Special Projects), D M Hancock (VP, F-16 International), D S Zummer (VP Industrial Relations), D H Huckaby (VP Cen Center)

PRINCIPAL ACTIVITIES: Components and equipment for fighter aircraft
Parent Company: General Dynamics Corp, St Louis, MO
Principal Bank: FortWorth National Bank
Financial Information:

	$'000
Sales revenues	2,000,000

No of Employees: 17,000

FORTUNE FINANCIAL GROUP INC

2120 U.S. 19 South, Clearwater, FL 33546-6802
Tel: (813) 538-1000

Chairman: J B Sweger (and President and Chief Executive Officer); Vice Chairman: L R Hammock
Senior Executive Officers: Rausey W Mason (Executive VP), Leon H Hammock (VP and Treasurer), Martin W Gladysz (Senior VP Finance and Chief Financial Officer)

PRINCIPAL ACTIVITIES: Holding company with interests in financial services including savings and loans
Principal Subsidiaries: Fortune Savings Bank
Financial Information:

	Sep 30 1985 $'000	Sep 30 1986 $'000
Revenues	206,225	224,700
Income before taxes	9,943	13,839
Net income	8,045	12,179
Earnings per share	$2.62	$3.03
Common stock*	3,187	4,685
Retained income	50,261	62,440
Shareholders equity	88,790	133,821
Deposits	1,323,477	1,429,448
Total assets	2,060,410	2,320,336

*number of shares in thousands

No of Employees: 816

FORTUNE SYSTEMS CORPORATION

101 Twin Dolphin Drive, Redwood City, CA 94065
Tel: (415) 595-8444

Chairman: James S Campbell (and President and Chief Executive Officer)
Senior Executive Officers: Robert A Davis (Executive VP), Robert J Ruebel (Senior VP Marketing), LeRoy C Cochran (VP and Chief Financial Officer), Richard Blaschke (VP Software Engineering), Victor W Maxted (VP Hardware Engineering), James F Ferenz (VP Manufacturing)

PRINCIPAL ACTIVITIES: Hardware and software for desk top computer systems
Principal Bank: Brobeck, Phleger and Harrison
Financial Information:

	$'000
Sales revenues	47,500

No of Employees: 500

FORUM GROUP INC

8900 Keystone Crossing, Suite 1200, Indianapolis, IN 46240
Tel: (317) 846 0700

Chairman: J Fred Risk
President: O U Mutz (and Chief Executive Officer)

Senior Executive Officers: Fred S Klipsch (Executive VP and Chief Operating Officer), John W Swann (Executive VP), Lewis F Wood Jr (Executive VP), Bruce R Karr (Senior VP, Legal Counsel and Secretary), Paul A Shivley (Senior VP, Treasurer and Chief Financial Officer), Wayne S Tush (VP and Controller)

PRINCIPAL ACTIVITIES: Nursing services
Financial Information:

	$'000
Sales revenues	177,200

No of Employees: 4,000

FOSTER, L B, CO

415 Holiday Drive, Pittsburgh, PA 15220
Tel: (412) 928-3400

Chairman: E C Mabbs (and Chief Executive Officer and President)
Senior Executive Officers: M Porter (Chairman Executive Committee), J C Frueh (Senior VP Finance and Planning), H R Gordon (VP), B S Mars (VP), T A Upchurch (VP and Treasurer)

PRINCIPAL ACTIVITIES: Oil production equipment; steel fabrication; railroad equipment
Principal Subsidiaries: Hydro Ash Corp
Principal Bank: Mellon Bank
Financial Information:

	$'000
Sales revenues	339,230

No of Employees: 1,250

FOSTER WHEELER CORPORATION

Perryville Corporate Park, Clinton, NJ 08809-4000
Tel: (201) 730-4000
Cable: REWOPERRYVILLE

Chairman: William C Reynolds Jr
President: Louis E Azzato (and Chief Executive VP)
Senior Executive Officers: Arthur H Hansen (Executive VP Equipment Operations), Ernest L Daman (Senior VP Research), N W Atwater (Executive VP), Harold E Kennedy (Senior VP and General Counsel)

PRINCIPAL ACTIVITIES: Design, engineering, construction and manufacture of plants for power generation and the oil, chemical and pharmaceutical industries; industrial equipment; real estate
Principal Subsidiaries: World Headquarters (Clinton, NJ); Engineering Offices (Clinton, NJ); Research Center (Livingston, NJ). Manufacturing Plants (Dansville, NY; St Catherines, Ontario, Canada; Hartlepool, UK). International Operations: Australia:- Foster Wheeler Australia Pty Ltd. Canada:- Foster Wheeler Ltd; SNC/FW Ltd. UK:- Foster Wheeler Ltd; Foster Wheeler Energy Ltd; Foster Wheeler Petroleum Development Ltd; Foster Wheeler Power Products Ltd; Foster Wheeler World Services Ltd; FW Management Operations (UK) Ltd. France:- Société Foster Wheeler Française; World Services France SA. Italy:- Foster Wheeler Italiana SpA; Foster Wheeler World Services SpA. Saudi Arabia:- Foster Wheeler Saudi Arabia Company Ltd; Foster Wheeler Middle East Services Inc. Spain:- Foster Wheeler Agro Development Company Ltd; Foster Wheeler Iberia SA; Generadores De Vapor Foster Wheeler SA. Switzerland:- Foster Wheeler Trading Company AG. Turkey:-Birlesik Insaat Ve Muhendislik AS (BIMAS). Venezuela:- Foster Wheeler Venezolana CA. USA:- Belco Pollution Control Corporation; Carbogel Inc; Conergics Corporation; Foster Wheeler Constructors Inc; Enviresponse Inc; Forney Engineering Company; Foster Wheeler Development Corporation; FW Energy Applications Inc; Foster Wheeler Energy Corporation; Foster Wheeler International Corporation; Foster Wheeler Power Systems Inc; Foster Wheeler Real Estate Development Corp; Foster Wheeler USA Corporation; Foster Wheeler World Services Corporation; FW Management Operations Ltd (USA); Glitsch Inc; Thermacote Welco Company; Ullrich Copper Inc
Principal Bank: Chemical Bank
Financial Information:

	Dec 31 1985	Dec 31 1986
	$'000	$'000
Sales revenues	1,227,758	1,295,175
Income before taxes	28,473	35,275
Net income	26,019	28,027
Dividends per share	$0.44	$0.44
Earnings per share	$0.76	0.81
Common stock*	-	34,483
Shareholders equity	408,000	433,469
*number of shares in thousands		

No of Employees: 14,000

FOSTER-FORBES GLASS CO

E Charles Street, Marion, IN 46952
Tel: (317) 668-1200

President: Herbert H Thompson
Senior Executive Officers: Steven J Friesen (Divisional Senior VP Marketing and Asset Management), William Grant (Divisional Senior VP Manufacturing), Harold E Friemuth (Divisional VP Sales), Richard M Deneau (Divisional Controller)

PRINCIPAL ACTIVITIES: Manufacture of glass containers
Parent Company: National Can Corporation
Financial Information:

	$'000
Sales revenues	90,000

No of Employees: 3,000

FOTOMAT CORPORATION

205 9th Street, St Petersburg, FL 33701
Tel: (813) 823-2027

Chairman: Shigeru Suzuki (and Chief Executive Officer)
President: John R Chase (and Chief Operating Officer)
Senior Executive Officers: Bill Kirkman, Michael H Alden (VP, Secretary and General Counsel), Shinji Arat (VP Technical Development), Robert E Nemecek (VP Human Resources), Larry Pyles (VP, President Portrait World), Dan N Daniel (VP West Const), Thomas A Meyer (VP Marketing, Dealer Division), William J Meyer (VP Marketing, Dealer Division), John R Gross (VP and Controller), James Fischer (VP Corporate Development)

PRINCIPAL ACTIVITIES: Photographic supplies and photofinishing laboratories
Parent Company: Konishiroku Photo Industry Co Ltd
Financial Information:

	$'000
Sales revenues	180,000

No of Employees: 8,000

FOURCO GLASS DIVISION

PO Box 890, Clarksburg, WV 26301
Tel: (304) 739-4355

Chairman: R D Hubbard
President: Wayne Basler
Senior Executive Officers: Larry Kaufman (VP Sales), Roger Kennedy (VP Marketing), Fred Cason (Secretary and Treasurer)

PRINCIPAL ACTIVITIES: Manufacture of glass
Parent Company: AFG Industries Inc, Kingsport, TN
Principal Bank: Bank of Tennessee

Financial Information:

	$'000
Sales revenues	50,000

No of Employees: 650

FOUR-PHASE SYSTEMS, INC

10700 N DeAnza Blvd, Cupertino, CA 95014
Tel: (408) 255-0900

President: Howard A Thraikill
Senior Executive Officers: Wes Thrash (Senior Group VP), Edgar Vance Jr (Senior VP), James Risher (Senior VP Marketing), George Needham (Senior VP Operations), F Anthony Yates (Senior VP Indirect Sales), Tom Little (VP 4000 Product Line), Wayne Sennett (VP 2000/6000 Product Line), Daniel E Halloran (VP Human and Physical Resources), Steve Beason (VP Quality and Productivity), Ray L Harter (VP Distributor Sales), David Barnay (VP Finance), Jerry Thom (VP National Sales), B G Starkey (VP Eastern Region Sales), Curtis Abel (VP Federal Region Sales), Ronald Reynolds (VP Western Region Sales), Ronald McClanahan (VP Field Engineering), Jerzy Skibinski (VP Development), Robert Dunham (VP Development), Martin Cohen (VP Marketing Administration), Peter Cook (VP Systems Architecture)

PRINCIPAL ACTIVITIES: Data processing equipment
Parent Company: Motorola Inc, Schaumburg, IL
Principal Bank: Bank of America
Financial Information:

	$'000
Sales revenues	230,000

No of Employees: 4,500

FOURTH FINANCIAL CORPORATION

100 N Broadway, PO Box 4, Wichita, KS 67201
Tel: (316) 261-4444
Telefax: (316) 261-4515

Chairman: Jordan L Haines; Vice Chairman: Thomas R Clevenger
President: Frank A Lowman
Senior Executive Officers: Robert W Asmann (Executive VP), Ronald L Baldwin (Executive VP), Robert M Smith Jr (Executive VP), Kurt D Watson (Executive VP), John C Maloney (Senior VP, Secretary and General Counsel), David L Strohm (Treasurer)

PRINCIPAL ACTIVITIES: Banking services
Trade Names: NASDAQ Symbol: FRTH
Principal Subsidiaries: Ten Commercial Bank subsidiaries
Principal Bank: Bank IV Wichita, N.A.
Financial Information:

	Dec 31 1986	Dec 31 1986
	$'000	$'000
Revenues	204,203	248,467
Income before taxes	20,965	26,760
Net income	25,775	30,466
Dividends	8,133	11,782
Dividends per share	$0.70	$0.88
Earnings per share*	$2.07	$2.28
Common stock	61,139	67,592
Retained income	51,976	68,937
Shareholders funds	167,625	205,359
Deposits	1,963,068	2,140,452
Total assets	2,565,788	2,644,438

*fully diluted

Principal Shareholders: William T Kemper; Dwane L Wallace
No of Employees: 1,532

FOX PHOTO INC

8750 Tesoro Drive, San Antonio, TX 78286
Tel: (512) 828 9111
Telex: WUT 767453

Chairman: Carl D Newton Jr
President: Carl D Newton III
Senior Executive Officers: John L Brack Jr (Senior VP, Chief Financial Officer, Assistant Secretary and Treasurer), Pat LeMay Burr (Senior VP), Richard M Finkbeiner (Senior VP and Controller), Gary Greenberg (Senior VP), Michael J Kelly (Senior VP), Don Harman (Senior VP Dealer Division), Glynn Bloomquist (Senior VP Product Division), Ted deBuhr (Senior VP Retail Division), Thomas J McEvoy (Senior VP Management Information Systems Finance)

PRINCIPAL ACTIVITIES: Photographic processing services
Principal Bank: Texas Commerce Bank
Financial Information:

	$'000
Sales revenues	185,000

No of Employees: 4,500

FOXBORO COMPANY

38 Neponset Avenue, Foxboro, MA 02035
Tel: (617) 543-8750

Chairman: Earle W Pitt (and Chief Executive Officer)
President: Gary K Willis
Senior Executive Officers: Gerald F Morris (VP and Treasurer), Howard L Osler (VP, Secretary and Controller)

PRINCIPAL ACTIVITIES: Industrial control equipment
Principal Subsidiaries: Foxboro Intertrade Inc; Foxboro Trading Inc; Foxboro/ICT Inc; Foxboro/Jordan Inc; Octek Inc
Principal Bank: The First National Bank of Boston
Financial Information:

	Dec 31 1985	Dec 31 1986
	$'000	$'000
Sales revenues	572,175	543,986
Net income (loss)	(34,154)	9,272
Earnings per share	-	$0.75
Shareholders equity	259,910	274,785

No of Employees: 8,750

FOXMEYER CORPORATION

2821 S Parker Rd, Aurora, CO 80014
Tel: (303) 695-0884

Chairman: William Y Tauscher (and President)
Senior Executive Officers: Richard H Bard (Executive VP Secretary, President of FoxMeyer Drug Company), Robert H Dyer (Senior VP-Data Processing, Executive of Foxmeyer Drug Company), Robert C Kuntzendorf (Senior VP-Operations, Executive VP of FoxMeyer Drug Company, President of Fox Trucking Company, Inc), John M Walz (Senior VP-Marketing, Executive VP of FoxMeyer Drug Company), Darwin K Naccarato (VP and Controller, Senior VP of all subsidiary companies), Daniel L Shimer (VP and Treasurer), Joseph G Gschwendtner (VP-Credit and Financial Services)

PRINCIPAL ACTIVITIES: FoxMeyer Corporation is the third largest and the fastest growing drug wholesaler in the United States. FoxMeyer distributes a full line of pharmaceuticals and other items typically found in retail drugstores. Products are supplied to independently owned drugstores, hospitals and the pharmacy operations of mass merchandisers and food stores. Value added support products and services are provided through the Company's Health Mart (R) retail franchise program, Promotional Services group, the Computer Products group, the Hospital Supply divisions and Fox Trucking Company.
Parent Company: National Intergroup, Inc
Principal Subsidiaries: FoxMeyer Drug Company; FoxMeyer-TBL, Inc; Ben Franklin Stores Inc
Principal Bank: Citibank
Financial Information:

	$'000
Sales revenues	725,000

No of Employees: 1,100

FPA CORPORATION

2501 Palm-Aire Drive North, Pompano Beach, FL 33069
Tel: (305) 972 3300

Chairman: Marvin Orleans (and Chief Executive Officer)
President: Thor P Amlie (and Chief Operating Officer)
Senior Executive Officers: Norman J Greenough (Senior VP and Treasurer), Graham A Bayliss (Senior VP and Real Estate Director, Florida), Jeffrey P Orleans (Senior VP), Robert W Brant (VP and Controller), T W Gell (VP and Secretary), Delano B Purscell (VP and Real Estate Director, Philadelphia Area), Benjamin Weinstock (VP)

PRINCIPAL ACTIVITIES: Development of property and real estate
Principal Bank: Chase Manhattan Bank
Financial Information:

	$'000
Sales revenues	81,200

No of Employees: 1,040

FPL GROUP, INC

PO Box 08801, North Palm Beach, FL 33408-8801
Tel: (305) 694-6300
Telefax: (305) 694-6385

Chairman: Marshall McDonald (and President and Chief Executive Officer)
Senior Executive Officers: R J Gardner (VP), J L Howard (VP-Chief Financial Officer), Astrid E Pfeiffer (Secretary), R R Sears (Treasurer), Dilek Samil (Assistant Treasurer), G M Konecsny (Assistant Treasurer), J E Moore (Assistant Secretary)

PRINCIPAL ACTIVITIES: Energy, financial and real estate services
Principal Subsidiaries: Florida Power & Light Company; Colonial Penn Group, Inc; FPL Group Capital Inc; Praxis Group Inc; Telesat Cablevision Inc; FPL Qualtec Inc; Alandco Inc; FPL Energy Srvices Inc
Principal Bank: Southeast, Miami, FL
Financial Information:

	Dec 31 1985	Dec 31 1986
	$'000	$'000
Sales revenues	4,348,827	4,091,504
Income before taxes	699,015	681,479
Net income	372,254	365,411
Dividends	231,800	254,260
Dividends per share	$1.94	$2.02
Earnings per share	$3.11	$2.90
Common stock at par	1,210	1,300
Retained income	1,154,985	1,266,136
Shareholders equity	2,588,446	2,988,939

Shareholders of record: 71,496
No of Employees: 18,700

FRANK B HALL & CO INC

See HALL, FRANK B, & CO INC

FRANKLIN ELECTRIC CO, INC

400 E Spring Street, Bluffton, IN 46714
Tel: (219) 824-2900

Chairman: August L Streater
President: William H Lawson (and Chief Executive Officer)
Senior Executive Officers: William A Garvey (VP International Operations), John B Lindsay (VP Marketing and Sales), L E Staak (VP and General Manager Fractional Motor Division), Dean W Pfister (VP Finance, Secretary and Treasurer)

PRINCIPAL ACTIVITIES: Electrical motors; packaging machinery for the food industry
Principal Subsidiaries: Franklin Electric Subsidiary Inc
Principal Bank: Lincoln National Bank
Financial Information:

	$'000
Sales revenues	179,300

No of Employees: 3,000

FRANKLIN LIFE INSURANCE CO

Franklin Square, Springfield, IL 62713
Tel: (217) 528-2011

Chairman: William J Alley (and President and Chief Executive Officer)
Senior Executive Officers: Howard C Humphrey (VP and Chief Operating Officer), Chas Becker Jr (Senior VP Corporate Relations), Arthur C Cragoe (Senior VP and Actuary), Frederick H Stone (Senior VP, Secretary and General Counsel), John C Watson (Senior VP Marketing), Keith R Wright (Senior VP Finance)

PRINCIPAL ACTIVITIES: Life insurance company
Parent Company: American Brands
Principal Bank: Morgan Guaranty Trust
Financial Information:

	Dec 31 1985	Dec 31 1986
	$'000	$'000
Premium income	429,130	448,035
Investment income	270,030	292,198

No of Employees: 4,219

FRANKLIN RESOURCES INC

155 Bovet Road, San Mateo, CA 94402
Tel: (415) 570 3000

President: Charles B Johnson (and Chief Executive Officer)
Senior Executive Officers: Rupert H Johnson Jr (Senior VP and Assistant Secretary), Kenneth L Koskella (Senior VP), Roger M Loar (Senior VP, Treasurer and Chief Financial Officer), Harmon E Burns (Senior VP Legal, Administration and Secretary)

PRINCIPAL ACTIVITIES: Investment services; gas and oil drilling
Principal Subsidiaries: FS Capital Group; Franklin Administrative Services; Franklin Agency Inc; Franklin Asset Management Systems; Franklin Distributors Inc; Franklin Energy Corporation; Franklin Management Inc; Franklin Trust Company
Principal Bank: Bank of America
Financial Information:

	$'000
Sales revenues	63,340

No of Employees: 630

FRANTZ MANUFACTURING COMPANY

301 West Third Street, Sterling, IL 61081
Tel: (815) 625 0163

Chairman: H B Musgrove (and President and Chief Executive Officer)
Senior Executive Officers: D A Corzett (VP Marketing Door Division), R E Stumpff (VP Manufacturing Door Division), J R McCormick (Treasurer), E L Froeliger (Secretary and Controller)

PRINCIPAL ACTIVITIES: Manufacture of garage doors in steel, wood and fiberglass; carbon steel balls
Principal Bank: First National Bank
Financial Information:

	$'000
Sales revenues	48,460

No of Employees: 600

FRED MEYER INC

See MEYER, FRED, INC

FREDERICKS OF HOLLYWOOD INC

6608 Hollywood Boulevard, Los Angeles, CA 90028
Tel: (213) 466 5151

Chairman: George W Townson (and Chief Executive Officer)
Senior Executive Officers: L Colleen Menerey (VP Finance, Chief Financial Officer, Treasurer and Assistant Secretary), Morton R Field (Secretary), Marshall F Coil (VP Engineering)

PRINCIPAL ACTIVITIES: Retailing of women's clothing
Principal Bank: Security Pacific National Bank
Financial Information:

	$'000
Sales revenues	45,500

No of Employees: 1,000

FREEDOM SAVINGS & LOAN ASSOCIATION

222 N Dale Mabry Hwy, Tampa, FL 33630
Tel: (813) 870-5000

Chairman: Robert M Klinger (and President and Chief Executive Officer)
Senior Executive Officers: Ronald E Zajack (Executive VP), Wm J McVeigh III (Senior VP Operations), C L Schuler (Treasurer and Chief Financial Officer)

PRINCIPAL ACTIVITIES: Financial services including savings and loans
Principal Subsidiaries: Freedom Mortgage Co; Independence Investment Co; Liberty Title Co; Sunbay Corp of FL
Principal Bank: Irving Trust Company

No of Employees: 1,200

FREEMAN CHEMICAL CORPORATION

222 E Main Street, Port Washington, WI 53074
Tel: (414) 284-5541

President: George H MacDonald
Senior Executive Officers: R C Ross (VP and General Manager), Robert J Winters (VP Sales), Glenn R Svoboda (VP Research and Development), Russell L Cerk (VP Manufacturing), Fred W Ziegenhagen (Secretary and Treasurer)

PRINCIPAL ACTIVITIES: Plastics materials; synthetic rubber
Parent Company: H H Robertson Co, Pittsburgh, PA
Principal Bank: M and I Marshall & Ilsley Bank
Financial Information:

	$'000
Sales revenues	66,000

No of Employees: 300

FREEMAN SHOE CO

Mill Street, Beloit, WI 53511
Tel: (608) 365-6665

President: Sid Sharpstein
Senior Executive Officers: Bruce Polcek (Executive VP), D E Desing (Executive VP Finance and Administration), Geo McDorman (VP Manufacturing)

PRINCIPAL ACTIVITIES: Freeman is one of the country's leading men's brands. The line is comprised of medium-to-higher quality dress and casual footwear, supplemented by a group of updated styles for slightly younger men. Freeman Free-Flex dress shoes are created for customers who demand superior comfort. This division also markets Bill Blass */Capezio designer lines which are distributed to better department and specialty stores. *Under License
Parent Company: United States Shoe Corporation
Principal Bank: First Wisconsin Milwaukee Bank
Financial Information:

	$'000
Sales revenues	150,000

No of Employees: 3,000

FREEPORT-MCMORAN INC

200 Park Avenue, New York, NY 10166
Tel: (212) 578-9200

Chairman: James R Moffett (and Chief Executive Officer); Vice Chairman: Nils S Kindwall (and Chief Financial Officer and Chief Administrative Officer)
President: Milton H Ward
Senior Executive Officers: Benno C Schmidt (Chairman Executive Committee), Louis A Clinton (Senior VP and Treasurer), Edward C Stebbins (Senior VP and General Counsel), Ronald Grossman (Senior VP and Controller), Ernest E Howard III (Senior VP), Albert E Rothwell (Senior VP), W Russell King (VP), Rene L Latiolais (VP), Charles B Murphy Jr (VP Corporate Environmental Department), Thomas L Vandegrift (VP Human Resources)

PRINCIPAL ACTIVITIES: Gas exploration and production; mining and quarrying
Financial Information:

	Dec 31 1986 $'000
Sales revenues	629,700
Net income	25,700
Earnings per share	$0.38
Shareholders equity	610,744

No of Employees: 5,500

FREMONT GENERAL CORPORATION

1633 26th Street, Santa Monica, CA 90404
Tel: (213) 315-5500
Telex: 592 653 FREMONT LSA

Chairman: Lee E McIntyre
President: James A McIntyre (and Chief Executive Officer)
Senior Executive Officers: David L McIntyre (Executive VP, President and Chief Executive Officer of Fremont Insurance Group), James R McNiel (Executive VP, Treasurer and Chief Financial Officer), E J Lieber (Secretary and General Counsel),

PRINCIPAL ACTIVITIES: Fremont General Corporation is a holding company headquartered in Santa Monica, California and is engaged through subsidiaries in financial service businesses. Additionally, Fremont underwrites certain lines of property and casualty insurance of which it is in the process of divesting
Principal Subsidiaries and Affiliates: Financial Services:- Commercial Bankers Life Insurance Company; Commonwealth Financial Corporation
Principal Bank: Bank of America
Financial Information:

	Dec 31 1985 $'000	Dec 31 1986 $'000
Premium income	43,658	41,215
Investment income	26,554	23,502
Income before taxes*	14,514	18,309
Net income (loss)	89,543	(22,989)
Dividends	5,176	5,053
Dividends per share	$0.48	$0.48
Earnings (loss) per share	$8.30	($2.18)
Common stock	10,783	10,526
Retained income	160,336	132,294
Shareholders equity	222,174	187,500

*and discontinued operations and extraordinary items

No of Employees: 1,300

FRIEDMAN INDUSTRIES INC

4001 Homestead Road, Houston, TX 77028
Tel: (713) 672 9433

Chairman: Jack Friedman (and Chief Executive Officer)
President: Harold Friedman (and Chief Operating Officer)
Senior Executive Officers: Ronald Burgerson (VP), William Crow (VP), Ted Henderson (VP), Jerry Starnes (VP Sales), Leo

Daniel (VP Engineering), Benny Harper (Treasurer), Randol Kemper (Secretary)

PRINCIPAL ACTIVITIES: Metal fabrication; steel production; blast furnaces

Principal Bank: Capital Bank

Financial Information:

	$'000
Sales revenues	48,000

No of Employees: 80

FRIGITRONICS, INC

770 River Road, Shelton, CT 06484

Tel: (203) 929-6321

President: Ralph E Crump (and Treasurer)

Senior Executive Officers: Lawrence E Dorner (VP Finance)

PRINCIPAL ACTIVITIES: Medical and surgical equipment and opthalmic products

Principal Subsidiaries: Angel Engineering Corp; Benson Optical Co Inc; Bisman Optical Laboratories Inc; C C Caldwell Opticians Inc; Ostertag Optical Services of IA Inc; Ostertag Opticians of KY Inc; Parsons Optical Service Inc; Criss Optical Manufacturing Co Inc; Precision-Cosmet Co Inc; Custom Contact Lens Co Inc; FCL Laboratories Inc; Stereo Optical Co Inc

Principal Bank: First National Bank of Minneapolis

Financial Information:

	$'000
Sales revenues	129,000

No of Employees: 2,550

FRIONA INDUSTRIES, INC

PO Box 8210, Amarillo, TX 79114

Tel: (806) 359 4511

President: Dennis Farley (and Chief Executive Officer)

Senior Executive Officers: Charles H Hughes (VP Finance and Secretary), Robert L Bliss (VP Custom Cattle Feeding), Robert C White (VP), Jack Hamil (VP)

PRINCIPAL ACTIVITIES: Livestock and animal feeds; meat products

Principal Subsidiaries: Friona Agricultural Credit Corp; Village Meats Inc

Principal Bank: Friona State Bank

Financial Information:

	$'000
Sales revenues	274,350

No of Employees: 500

FRISCH'S RESTAURANTS INC

2800 Gilbert Avenue, Cincinnati, OH 45206

Tel: (513) 961 2660

Telefax: (513) 559-5160

Chairman: Jack C Maier (and President)

Senior Executive Officers: Marvin G Fields (Senior VP Operations), Louis J Ullman (Senior VP Finance), Carl V Goodin (VP Administration), Joseph L Yowell (VP Property Development)

PRINCIPAL ACTIVITIES: Restaurants; franchising; motels

Trade Names: Big Boy, Roy Rogers, Prime 'N Wine, Quality Hotels

Principal Bank: First National Bank

Financial Information:

	1987
	$'000
Sales revenues	139,822
Income before taxes	5,245
Net income	2,823
Dividends	1,058
Dividends per share	$0.22
Earnings per share	$0.58
Common stock	4,729
Retained income	20,009
Shareholders equity	43,703

No of Employees: 6,000

FRITO-LAY, INC

Frito-Lay Tower, Dallas, TX 75235

Tel: (214) 351-7000

Chairman: Willard C Korn (and President and Chief Executive Officer and Chief Operating Officer)

Senior Executive Officers: John W Ewing (Senior VP Employee Relations), Ronald R Kranzow (VP Legal), Kirtman C Anton (VP Finance), W Leo Kiely III (Senior VP Sales and Marketing), James H O'Neal (VP Manufacturing), Ronald R Kranzow (VP Legal), D D Heard (VP Research and Development), Kirtman C Anton (VP Finance), T A Fassburg (VP Public Affairs), Joseph Hanson (VP and Comptroller)

PRINCIPAL ACTIVITIES: Snack foods including potato chips, corn chips and cookies

Trade Names: O'Grady's, Cheese Dips, Doritos, Fritos, Ruffles, Grandma's, Rich & Chewy

Parent Company: PepsiCo Inc, New York, NY

Principal Bank: InterFirst Bank

Financial Information:

	$'000
Sales revenues	1,000,000

No of Employees: 28,000

FRITZI OF CALIFORNIA MFG CORPORATION

199 First Street, San Francisco, CA 94105

Tel: (415) 986-4133

President: Valli D Benesch

PRINCIPAL ACTIVITIES: Manufacture of sports and leisure clothes for women

Trade Names: Fritzi, You Babes, You Babes II

Financial Information:

	$'000
Sales revenues	73,000

No of Employees: 480

FROEDTERT MALT CORPORATION

PO Box 712, Milwaukee, WI 53201

Tel: (414) 671-1166

Telex: TWX 910 262 3333 froedtert mil

President: R B Welch

Senior Executive Officers: Joseph S Englert (Executive VP Marketing), James T Klein (Executive VP Operations), F A Barney (VP Sales), Lee W Holland (VP Sales), James R Schindhelm (VP and Controller), Henry Kneuer (VP Matting)

PRINCIPAL ACTIVITIES: Manufacture of malt for the brewing, distilling and food industries

Parent Company: Harvest States Cooperatives

Financial Information:

	$'000
Sales revenues	60,000

No of Employees: 300

FROZEN FOOD EXPRESS INDUSTRIES INC

318 Cadiz Street, Dallas, TX 75207

Tel: (214) 428 7661

Chairman: Stoney M Stubbs Jr (and President and Chief Executive Officer); Vice Chairmen: Stoney M Stubbs, Edgar O Weller

Senior Executive Officers: Charles G Robertson (Executive VP) Robert Marquette Jr (Senior VP)

PRINCIPAL ACTIVITIES: Freight services

Principal Subsidiaries: Conwell Corporation; FFE Transportation Services Inc; W&B Refrigeration Service Company

Principal Bank: MBank Dallas

Financial Information:

	Dec 31 1985 $'000	Dec 31 1986 $'000
Sales revenues	86,916	91,195
Income (loss) before taxes	(630)	1,287
Net income	1,157	1,055
Dividends	333	93
Dividends per share	$0.25	$0.07
Earnings per share	$0.88	$0.80
Common stock	2,746	2,592
Retained income	18,899	19,441
Shareholders equity	18,796	19,105

Number of Shareholders: 983

No of Employees: 440

FRUEHAUF CORPORATION

10900 Harper Avenue, PO Box 33238, Detroit, MI 48213

Tel: (313) 267-1000

Telex: 235351

Chairman: Robert D Rowan (and Chief Executive Officer)

President: T Neal Combs (and Chief Administrative and Financial Officer)

Senior Executive Officers: Robert G Siefert (President and Chief Executive Officer Kelsey-Hayes Company), Richard F Darke (VP, General Counsel and Secretary), Howard O Emorey (VP and Treasurer), Edward J Hayes (Executive VP and Senior Technical Advisor to the Chairman), Charles P Jacoby (VP-Marketing), Arnold P McIlwain (Executive VP-Maritime Operations), Michael W Parres (VP-Industrial Relations), Adolph T Silverstein (VP and Controller). Fruehauf Trailer Operations: Leon Alexander (President and Chief Executive Officer Trailer Operations), James W Barber (VP-Operations), Richard S Glazer (VP-General Manager Liquid and Bulk Tank Division), Joseph Mack II (VP International and President-Fruehauf International Limited), Thomas N Nanos (VP-Financing Affairs), Stanley J Thompson Jr (VP-Sales and Marketing), Al M Van Steenkiste (VP and Controller), Robert E Beers (VP-Manufacturing), Jean Gaschard (President-Fruehauf Europe Inc), Gerald E Hart (VP-Intermodal), Robert T Hawkins (VP-Marketing), Donald H Hayes (VP-Material and Transportation), Richard D Kendall (VP-Sales Administration), Bobby W Legg (VP-Information Services), James M McGraw (VP-Finance-Fruehauf International Ltd), Frank J Miller (VP-Reliability and Quality Assurance), Robert B Schwartz (VP-Engineering), W Richard Smith (VP-Communications), K M Stanley (VP-Used Trailers), Gary W Washburn (VP Marketing - Hobbs Regional VP-Southwest Region), Peter F Wytka (VP-Engineering and Manufacturing-Fruehauf International Ltd), William P Carozza (Regional VP-Canadian Region), Joseph J Plevel (Regional VP-Central Region), G Edwin Smith II (Regional VP-Northeast Region), Charles M Tedesco (Regional VP-North Central Region), Quinn D Thomas (Regional VP-Mid-Atlantic Region), Carl Phillipoff (General Manager-Government Services Division). Automotive Operations Kelsey-Hayes Company: Robert G Siefert (President and Chief Executive Officer), John J Garber (VP and Controller), Alex Jackson III (President-Aerospace Group), John P Kenny (VP-Information Systems), Arthur A Kowalski (VP-International), William H Shinn (President-Heavy Duty Group), Robert W Sullivan (VP-Research and Development), John E Utley (President-Automotive Group). Maritime Operations Jacksonville Shipyards Inc: Arnold P McIlwain (President and Chief Executive Officer), Elmer L Ahlwardt (VP-Mayport Division), Lawrence Brown (VP-Operations Commercial Division), Richard G Seitz (VP-Engineering Jacksonville). Paceco, Inc: Robert D Teece (President and Chief Executive Officer), Robert A Spoerl (VP-Operations), George J Thompson (VP-Technical Director)

PRINCIPAL ACTIVITIES: Fruehauf Corporation manufactures, sells, distributes and services transportation-related equipment and components in three primary industry segments: truck-trailers, automotive and maritime. Products manufactured: More than 325 standard models of truck-trailers, containers and container chassis. Brakes, wheels, electronic sensors and other components for passenger automobiles, light duty trucks, heavy duty trucks, agricultural vehicles, recreational vehicles and industrial vehicles. Container handling cranes and other cargo-handling equipment used at ports and railyards around the world. Services include: Service of truck-trailers. Service of ships of all sizes

Trade Names: Fruehauf, Kelsey-Hayes, Paceco-Portainer (R), Transtainer (R), Shipstainer (R), Pro-Par-axles, suspensions, brakes, tires, batteries

Principal Subsidiaries and Divisions: Fruehauf Trailer Operations; Hobbs; Liquid & Bulk Tank Division; Kelsey-Hayes Company (Subsidiary, wholly-owned); Jacksonville Shipyards Inc; Paceco Inc; Fruehauf International Ltd

Principal Bank: Registrar & Transfer Agent:- National Bank of Detroit

Financial Information: (1)

	Dec 31 1986(2) $'000	Dec 31 1986(3) $'000
Sales revenues	2,365,000	-
(Loss) before extra items	(88,000)	-
Net (loss)	(60,900)	-
Accumulated (deficit)	-	(20,306)
Common shareholders equity	-	38,188

(1) A new Corporation ("New Fruehauf" or "Successor") was formed on June 24, 1986, to facilitate the acquisition of the old Fruehauf Corporation ("Old Fruehauf" or "Predecessor") which was treated for accounting purposes as a purchase as of December 31, 1986

(2) The Predecessor

(3) The Successor

No of Employees: 26,100

FRUIT GROWERS SUPPLY CO

14130 Riverside Drive, Sherman Oaks, CA 91423

Tel: (818) 986-6480

Chairman: Ralph E Bodine; Vice Chairmen: Max L Cardey, Thomas N Dungan, Paul J Leavens

President: Timothy J Lindgren

Senior Executive Officers: Paul E Rooney (VP Northern Operations), Fielding D Thompson (VP Supplies), Michael A Ensey (VP Administration, Secretary and Treasurer), Fred R Kruse (VP Finance)

PRINCIPAL ACTIVITIES: Manufacture of packing containers for fruit growers

Principal Subsidiaries: Standard Lumber Co Inc

Principal Bank: Security Pacific National Bank

Financial Information:

	$'000
Sales revenues	96,300

No of Employees: 250

FRYE COPYSYSTEMS

2205 Bell Avenue, Des Moines, IA 50321

Tel: (515) 246-2300

Telex: 478397 Frye Copy DMS

President: Russell W Dohrmann

Senior Executive Officers: Paul Hess (VP Operations), Floyd R Stewart (VP Sales)

PRINCIPAL ACTIVITIES: Designer, manufacturer and marketer of imaging technology for computer supplies industry in addition to being the leader in the sale of carbon paper and other one-time imaging products

Trade Names: Frye Copsystems

Parent Company: Allied Signal Inc

No of Employees: 1,500

FULLER BRUSH CO

Westport Addition, Box 729, Great Bend, KS 67530

Tel: (316) 792-1711

President: Leonard Dualap

Senior Executive Officers: Richard E Benner (Executive VP), Russ Imler (Senior VP), Roy Johnson (Chief Financial Officer)

PRINCIPAL ACTIVITIES: Manufacture of brushes, beauty products, chemicals and cleaning equipment

Parent Company: Sara Lee Corporation, Chicago, IL

Principal Bank: Security State Bank

Financial Information:

	$'000
Sales revenues	100,000

No of Employees: 1,800

FULLER CO

2040 Avenue C, Bethlehem, PA 18017

Tel: (215) 264-6011

Telex: WUT 847 443 fullerco caga

Chairman: K A Krick

President: E D Gates

Senior Executive Officers: E L Decker (Senior VP International), R G Schlauch (Senior VP Sales), J Warshawsky (Senior VP Products Division), J A Alogna (VP and Secretary), D A Nepereney (VP Project Division)

PRINCIPAL ACTIVITIES: Manufacture of plant and equipment for the chemical, mineral and cement industry; manufacture of pollution control equipment

Parent Company: GATX Corporation, Chicago, IL

Financial Information:

	$'000
Sales revenues	250,000

No of Employees: 1,500

FULLER, H B, COMPANY

2400 Kasota Avenue, St Paul, MN 55108

Tel: (612) 645-3401

Telex: 431-0055

Chairman: E L Andersen

President: A L Andersen (and Chief Executive Officer)

Senior Executive Officers: Walter Kissling (Senior VP), Robert Odom (Senior VP), Paul Johnson (Senior VP Administration and Secretary), Vartkes Ehramjian (Senior VP, Treasurer and Chief Financial Officer)

PRINCIPAL ACTIVITIES: Manufacture of a wide range of chemical products including paints, inks, adhesives and disinfectants

Principal Subsidiaries: Kativo Chemical Industries SA; H B Fuller GmbH; H B Fuller Austria Ges mbH

Principal Bank: First National Bank of St Paul

Financial Information:

	Nov 30 1986
	$'000
Sales revenues	528,483
Income before taxes	33,839
Net income	18,922
Dividends	3,279
Dividends per share	$0.35
Earnings per share	$2.00
Common stock	9,367
Retained income	115,023
Shareholders equity	135,479

No of Employees: 4,500

FULLERTON INDUSTRIES, INC

3000 Shermer Road, Northbrook, IL 60062

Tel: (312) 291-2400

Telex: WUT 724459 ful metcs nbrk

Chairman: Kenneth K Riskind; Chairman of Executive Committee: Phillip A Riskind

Senior Executive Officers: Donald J Riskind (Executive VP), Joseph L Marzullo (Controller)

PRINCIPAL ACTIVITIES: Manufacture of steel and non-ferrous metal products; metal service center

Principal Subsidiaries: Fullerton Metals Co; Fultran Inc

Financial Information:

	$'000
Sales revenues	120,000

No of Employees: 300

FUQUA INDUSTRIES, INC

4900 Georgia-Pacific Center, Atlanta, GA 30303

Tel: (404) 658-9000

Chairman: J B Fuqua

President: Lawrence P Klamon

Senior Executive Officers: Dooley E Culbertson (Executive VP), James M Bahin (VP-Finance), Samuel W Norwood III (VP-Corporate Development), Barney L Goldberg (Group VP-Sporting Goods), Colin W Brown (VP and General Counsel), Mildred H Hutcheson (VP-Legal Services), John C McCune (VP-Operations), John F Bartels (VP-Controller), James R Foster (VP-Treasurer), William D Dodge (VP-Insurance), James M Adamovitz (Assistant VP-Director of Taxes)

PRINCIPAL ACTIVITIES: Fuqua Industries, Inc is a diversified manufacturing, distribution and service company with four principal areas of business: lawn and garden, photofinishing, sporting goods and financial services

Trade Names: Snapper, Colorcraft, Ajay, Hutch, Vitamaster, Georgia Federal, First Family

Principal Subsidiaries: Ajay Enterprises Corporation; Colorcraft Corporation; Fuqua World Trade Corporation; Hutch Sporting Goods, Inc; Nelson Recreation Products, Inc; Snapper Power Equipment Division; Weather-Rite, Inc; Willow Hosiery Company, Inc; Georgia Federal Bank

Principal Bank: Chemical Bank

Financial Information:

	Dec 31 1986 $'000
Sales revenues	701,194
Income before taxes(1)	78,524
Net income(1)	46,873
Dividends	4,388
Dividends per share(1)	$0.22
Earnings per share (1)(2)	$2.20
Common stock (3)	20,037
Retained earnings	206,223
Shareholders equity	246,434

(1) continuing operations
(2) fully diluted
(3) number of shares in thousands

No of Employees: 12,000

FUR VAULT INC

360 W 31st St, New York, NY 10001
Tel: (212) 736 8620

Chairman: Fred P Schwartz (and President)
Senior Executive Officers: Harold Schwartz (Executive VP), Allen Soifer (VP and Secretary), Jack Balsam (Treasurer and Assistant Secretary), Stuart Schwartz (Director Merchandising)

PRINCIPAL ACTIVITIES: Retail trade in furs
Principal Bank: Chase Manhattan Bank
Financial Information:

	$'000
Sales revenues	68,000

No of Employees: 300

FURNAS ELECTRIC CO

1000 McKee Street, Batavia, IL 60510
Tel: (312) 879-6000
Telex: WUT 720458 furnas bvai

Chairman: Richard W Hansen (and President)
Senior Executive Officers: G R Nary (Executive VP and Controller), J M O'Rourke (Executive VP Marketing), M E Johnson (VP Finance and Treasurer), R C Trumpy (VP Manufacturing), T F Caughlin (VP Industrial Relations), R Doty (VP Sales), Dennis L Walstad (VP Engineering)

PRINCIPAL ACTIVITIES: Manufacture of electric controls and other electrical and electronic equipment
Principal Bank: Harris Bank and Trust Co
Financial Information:

	$'000
Sales revenues	80,000

No of Employees: 1,200

FUTORIAN CORPORATION

666 Lake Shore Drive, Chicago, IL 60611
Tel: (312) 642-5604

Chairman: Stanley I Landgraf
President: William S Richman
Senior Executive Officers: Leslie E Sumner (Executive VP Operations), Bernard Horowitz (Executive VP Marketing and Sales), Fred Atkinson (VP Marketing), Nathan Shapiro (VP Sales), Gary W Parker (VP and Controller)

PRINCIPAL ACTIVITIES: Manufacture of a range of furniture
Parent Company: Mohasco Corporation, Amsterdam, NY
Financial Information:

	$'000
Sales revenues	100,000

No of Employees: 3,200

G H BASS & CO

See BASS, G H, & CO

G HEILEMAN BREWING CO, INC

See HEILEMAN, G, BREWING CO, INC

G O CARLSON INC

See CARLSON, G O, INC

G&K SERVICES INC

400 S County Rd 18, Shelard Plaza S, Suite 475, Minneapolis, MN 55426
Tel: (612) 546 7440

Chairman: Richard Fink (and President)
Senior Executive Officers: William Hope (VP), Stephen Labelle (Secretary and Treasurer)

PRINCIPAL ACTIVITIES: Provision of laundry and dry cleaning services; linen and garment rental
Principal Subsidiaries: Service Inc
Principal Bank: North Western National Bank of Minneapolis
Financial Information:

	$'000
Sales revenues	63,830

No of Employees: 1,000

GA TECHNOLOGIES INC

10955 John Jay Hopkins Drive, San Diego, CA 92138
Tel: (619) 455-3000
Telex: WUT 695065 ga tech

President: Kerry A Dance
Senior Executive Officers: N E Carey (VP), R A Dean (VP), H C House (VP)

PRINCIPAL ACTIVITIES: Commercial testing laboratories in the fields of energy and nuclear power
Parent Company: Chevron USA Inc
Principal Bank: Bank of America
Financial Information:

	$'000
Sales revenues	150,000

No of Employees: 1,900

GAF CORPORATION

1361 Alps Road, Wayne, NJ 07470
Tel: (201) 628-3000
Telex: ITT 420945
Telefax: gafc ui

Chairman: Samuel J Heyman (and Chief Executive Officer); Vice Chairman: James T Sherwin (and Chief Administrative Officer)
Senior Executive Officers: Irving Kagan (Senior VP, General Counsel and Secretary), Salvatore Bellini (VP and Controller), Carl R Eckardt (Executive VP) John A Brennan (Senior VP and President, Building Materials Division), Gerald Whitmore (VP Human Resources), Bernard L Kapell (VP Taxes), Matthew L Gooby (VP, Management Information Services), Joel A Asen (VP, Treasury and Business Development)

PRINCIPAL ACTIVITIES: Manufacture of specialty chemicals; manufacture of building materials
Principal Bank: Marine Midland Bank

Financial Information:

	Dec 31 1985 $'000	Dec 31 1986 $'000
Sales revenues	731,962	753,774
Income before taxes	87,474	125,476
Net income	77,581	293,161
Dividends	3,370	3,540
Dividends per share	$0.20	$0.10
Earnings per share	$2.25*	$8.08
Common stock	34,848	35,508
Retained income	229,586	519,207
Shareholders equity	298,153	601,498

*adjusted for stock split (2 for 1) in 1986

No of Employees: 4,300

GALAXY CARPET MILLS, INC

850 Arthur Avenue, Elk Grove Village, IL 60007
Tel: (312) 593-0555
Telex: 54-3456

Chairman: Irwin H Harvey
President: Alvin B Bush
Senior Executive Officers: Charles A Bramlett (Executive VP, Director of Manufacturing), B T Mosteller (Senior VP, Manufacturing, Planning and Operations), Robert A Izard (Senior VP, International Sales), Fran Brantley (Senior VP, Director of Marketing), Larry D Reed (VP, Finance and Administration), Myron H Lurie (VP Distribution), Philip Steinway (VP Sales), Dewey French (VP Marketing), Frank McMurtry (VP Western Division), Donald J Savon (VP Eastern Division)

PRINCIPAL ACTIVITIES: Carpet manufacture
Trade Names: Galaxy, Nautilus
Principal Subsidiaries: Galaxy International, Inc
Principal Bank: Continental Illinois National Bank & Trust Company of Chicago
Financial Information:

	$'000
Sales revenues	195,310

No of Employees: 2,000

GALLAGHER, ARTHUR J, AND COMPANY

10 Gould Center, Golf Road, Rolling Meadows, IL 60008
Tel: (312) 640 8500

President: Robert E Gallagher (and Chief Executive Officer)
Senior Executive Officers: John P Gallagher (Executive VP and Secretary), J Patrick Gallagher (VP Operations), Walter F McClure (VP), Michael J Cloherty (VP Finance and Treasurer), Richard Kieffer (VP Information Services)

PRINCIPAL ACTIVITIES: Insurance broking services
Principal Subsidiaries: Price McDermott & Associates; UIC Ltd
Principal Bank: Harris Trust and Savings Bank
Financial Information:

	$'000
Revenues	81,570

No of Employees: 1,160

GALOOB, LEWIS, TOYS INC

500 Forbes Boulevard South, San Francisco, CA 94080
Tel: (415) 952 1678

Chairman: Barbara Frankel (and Treasurer)
President: David Galoob (and Chief Executive Officer)
Senior Executive Officers: Robert Galoob (Executive VP and Chief Operating Officer), Saul Jodel (Senior VP Marketing), Dennis McGill (Chief Financial Officer), Linda Schneidman (Secretary)

PRINCIPAL ACTIVITIES: Manufacture of toys

Financial Information:

	$'000
Sales revenues	90,000

No of Employees: 100

GALVESTON-HOUSTON CO

4900 Woodway, Houston, TX 77056
Tel: (713) 966-2500
Telex: TWX 910 881 1505 gal hou co hou

Chairman: Nathan M Avery (and Chief Executive Officer)
Senior Executive Officers: David O Rodrigue (Senior VP and Chief Financial Officer), W Todd Bratton (Senior VP Operations), Betty P McClure (Secretary), Dennis G Berryhill (Director of Human Resources), Robert A Mahlstedt (Director of Marketing)

PRINCIPAL ACTIVITIES: The Company and its subsidiaries manufacture and market products to a diversity of energy and non-energy related industries. The Company's business activities comprise two distinct segments, which are (1) the mining and construction equipment segment and (2) the energy and industrial equipment segment. The Company's mining and construction equipment segment manufactures and markets certain proprietary original equipment and replacement wear parts for the mining, construction and other earth-moving industries. These include wear parts such as teeth, rippers, end buckets, blade savers and adapters, as well as specially-designed buckets for excavators and backhoes. The energy and industrial equipment segment manufactures valve actuators and specially-cast or fabricated products used principally in oil and gas production, pipeline and processing operations. Valve actuators and certain cast and fabricated products, however, are also used in many other industrial or commercial operations. These include marine, municipal water/waste, chemical, pharmaceutical, nuclear power generation and food/beverage.
Principal Subsidiaries and Divisions: GH-Bettis; GH-Bettis Actuators and Controls Ltd (UK); GH DeSoto Mining; GH-Hensley; GH-Hensley Bucket Division
Principal Bank: Allied Bank of Texas
Financial Information:

	Dec 31 1985 $'000	Dec 31 1986 $'000
Net revenues	45,894	46,617
Net (loss)	(25,089)	(19,613)
(Loss) per share	($4.47)	($3.80)
Shareholders equity (deficit)	18,195	(3,433)

No of Employees: 560

GAMBLE-SKOGMO, INC

833 S/d/St, Broken Bow, NE 68822
Tel: (308) 872 2862

Chairman: Stanford C Sigoliff (and President and Chief Executive Officer)
Senior Executive Officers: Wilhelm A Mallory (Senior VP and Treasurer), James V Tatenhouse (Senior VP), Anthony J Swiss (Senior VP), James Castleberry (VP), Robert Fenton (VP), G G Valentine (VP), Michael Jamieson (VP and Assistant Controller), Paul Hyberg (VP), Seymour Strasberg (VP), Ronald Strongwater (VP)

PRINCIPAL ACTIVITIES: Retail trading through department stores, drug stores, variety stores, clothes and furniture stores
Parent Company: Wickes Companies Inc, Santa Monica, CA
Financial Information:

	$'000
Sales revenues	1,500,000

No of Employees: 17,000

GAMLEN CHEMICAL CO
121 S Maple Avenue, South San Francisco, CA 94080
Tel: (415) 873-1750
Telex: WUI 677039 gamlen ssf

President: Richard M Klein
Senior Executive Officers: W M Langhart (VP Operations and President Gamlen Far East), J A Nolet (Manager Marine Sales), D Dent (Manager Industrial Sales), B D Ancheta (Manager Equipment), Ezat Zahrai (President Gamlen Europe)

PRINCIPAL ACTIVITIES: Manufacture of specialty chemicals; pollution control equipment
Principal Bank: Morgan Guaranty Trust
Financial Information:

	$'000
Sales revenues	50,000

No of Employees: 500

GANG-NAIL SYSTEMS INC
PO Box 59-2037 AMF, Miami, FL 33159
Tel: (305) 696-0930
Telex: 264236 GANG UR
Fax: 305-693-2563

President: Carlos S Rionda (and Chief Executive Officer)
Senior Executive Officers: J M Casper (Senior VP International and Chief Financial Officer), Jerry Huxell (VP Manufacturing), Dave Covington (VP Marketing), R E Harris (VP Pacific Basin)

PRINCIPAL ACTIVITIES: Metal connector plates, principally for engineered timber structures and laminated veneer lumber
Parent Company: Redland PLC, Reigate, Surrey, UK (78.2%)
Principal Bank: Southeast First National Bank of Miami
Financial Information:

	$'000
Sales revenues	76,400

No of Employees: 700

GANNETT CO, INC
1000 Wilson Blvd, Arlington, VA 22209
Tel: (716) 546-8600; (703) 276-5900
Telex: WUT 978471 gannett co roc

Chairman: Allen H Neuharth; Vice Chairman: Douglas H McCorkindale (and Chief Financial and Legal Officer)
President: John J Curley (and Chief Operating Officer)
Senior Executive Officers: Cathleen P Black (Executive VP), John C Quinn (Executive VP), Madelyn P Jennings (Senior VP), William J Keating (Senior VP), Louis A Weil III (Senior VP), Peter B Hickey (VP), Larry F Miller (VP and Controler), John B Jaske (VP Labor Relations), Jimmy L Thomas (VP and Treasurer), Thomas L Cahpple (VP and Secretary), Lawrence B Sackett (VP), Charles L Overby (VP), Susan V Watson (VP Investor Relations)

PRINCIPAL ACTIVITIES: A diversified information company with interests in newspaper publishing, radio and television broadcasting and advertising
Principal Subsidiaries: Bulletin Co; California Newspapers Inc; Cape Publications Inc; Seminole Citizen News Inc; Citizen Publishing Co; Tucson Newspapers Inc; Coffeyville Publishing Co Inc; Combined Communications Corp; Combined Communications Corp OK; Gannett MA Broadcasting Inc; Gannett Outdoor Co Inc of NJ; Gannett Outdoor Co North CA Inc; Gannett Outdoor Co of AZ; Eller Electric Sign Co; Gannett Outdoor Co of CT; Gannett Outdoor Sales Co Inc; Globe Broadcasting Co Inc; KPNX Broadcasting Co; Pacific & Southern Co; Eleven Fifty Corp; PIA Merchandising Co; Tennessean Newspapers Inc; Newspaper Printing Corp; Tennessee Continental Corp; Des Moines Register & Tribune Co; Western Sun Inc; El Paso Times Inc; Newspaper Printing Corp; Newspaper Realty Corp; Eller Outdoor Advertising Co; Equitable Publishing Co; Federated Publications Inc; Gannett Media Sales Inc; Gannett News Service Inc; Gannett Newscope Subsidiary Inc; Gannett Offset Inc; Gannett Pacific Corp; Hawaii Newspaper Agency Inc; Gannett Productions Inc; Ministage Inc; Gannett Satellite Information Network Inc; Fair Press Inc; Newspaper Production Co; Sturgis Journal Inc; Gannett Supply Corp; Gannett Edmonton Corp; Gannett Tel-Sel Inc; Louis Harris Associates Inc; National Research Center of the Arts Inc; Huntington Publishing Co; Jackson Sun Inc; Knoxville Journal Corp; McClure Newspapers Inc; Mississippi Publishers Corp; New Mexican Inc; News Press Publishing Co; Northwestern Publishing Co; Oklahoma Press Publishing Inc; Palladium Publishing Corp; Pensacola News-Journal Inc; Rockford Newspapers Inc; Salem County Sampler Inc; Southland Publishing Co; Speidel Newspapers Inc; Fort Collins Newspapers Inc; Fremont Newspapers Inc; Press Citizen Co; Reno Newspapers Inc; Salinas Newspapers Inc; Sioux Falls Newspapers Inc; St Cloud Newspapers Inc; Stockton Newspapers Inc; Visalia Newspapers Inc; Springfield Newspapers Inc; Statesman-Journal Co; Sun Co San Bernadino CA Inc; Times Herald Co
Principal Bank: Chase Lincoln First Bank
Financial Information:

	Dec 31 1985 $'000	Dec 31 1986 $'000
Sales revenues	2,151,605	2,801,497
Net income	253,277	276,404
Earnings per share	-	$1.71
Shareholders equity	1,275,213	1,433,781

No of Employees: 26,000

GANNETT, GUY, PUBLISHING CO
PO Box 1460, Portland, ME 04104
Tel: (207) 775-5811

President: John Di Matteo
Senior Executive Officers: Mrs Jean G Hawley (Publicity), John H Gannett (VP), George F Marshall Jr (VP), James E Baker (VP and Treasurer)

PRINCIPAL ACTIVITIES: Publication of newspapers
Principal Bank: Casco Bank and Trust Co
Financial Information:

	$'000
Sales revenues	50,000

No of Employees: 1,000

GAP INC (THE)
900 Cherry Avenue, San Bruno, CA 94066
Tel: (415) 4400

Chairman: Donald G Fisher (and President and Chief Executive Officer)
Senior Executive Officers: Millard S Drexler (Executive VP Merchandising), Alan E Zimtbaum (Senior VP and Chief Financial Officer), John P Carver (Senior VP Human Resources), Edward A Strobin (Senior VP), Dexter C Tight (Senior VP and Secretary), Steven B Kaplan (VP Real Estate), Frances A Ziemniak (VP Finance), Harry J Lindner (Treasurer)

PRINCIPAL ACTIVITIES: Stores chain for the sale of men's clothing and accessories
Principal Bank: Crocker National Bank
Financial Information:

	1985 $'000
Sales revenues	848,000

No of Employees: 11,000

GARAN, INC
350 Fifth Avenue, New York, NY 10001
Tel: (212) 563-2000
Telex: WUT 124144 garan nyk

Chairman: Seymour Lichtenstein (and Chief Executive Officer)
President: Jerald Kamiel (and Chief Operating Officer)
Senior Executive Officers: Perry Mullen (VP Manufacturing), William J Wilson (VP Administration)

PRINCIPAL ACTIVITIES: Manufacture of sportswear, trousers and children's clothing
Principal Bank: Manufacturers Hanover Trust Co
Financial Information:

	$'000
Sales revenues	138,200

No of Employees: 4,500

GARDEN STATE PAPER CO, INC
600 E Broad Street, Richmond, VA 23219
Tel: (804) 649-6671

Chairman: Richard B Scudder
President: Basil Snider Jr
Senior Executive Officers: Richard C Crane (Executive VP Sales), Richard E Franklin (VP Sales), Gustavo Valdez (VP International Operations), James L Burke (Executive VP and General Manager Eastern Region), Royce Adair (General Manager Western Region), Milo Jensen (VP Industrial Relations)

PRINCIPAL ACTIVITIES: Production and sale of newsprint paper
Parent Company: Media General Inc, Richmond, VA
Principal Bank: United Virginia Bank
Financial Information:

	$'000
Sales revenues	175,000

No of Employees: 750

GARDENAMERICA CORPORATION
401 Grand Avenue, Suite 400, Oakland, CA 94610
Tel: (415) 839 5511

Chairman: James S Fetherston (and President and Chief Executive Officer)
Senior Executive Officers: Richard W Kraber (VP, Chief Financial Officer and Treasurer), J Marty O Donohue (VP), Edmund R Manwell (Secretary)

PRINCIPAL ACTIVITIES: Agricultural chemicals and pesticides
Financial Information:

	$'000
Sales revenues	37,590

No of Employees: 750

GARDINIER BIG RIVER INC
US Hwy 41 S, Box 3269, Tampa, FL 33601
Tel: (813) 677-9111
Telex: WUT 52666 gardinier tpa

Chairman: Francois Gardinier; Vice Chairman: Jean Constantin (and Chief Executive Officer)
Presidents: Christien Gardinier, Pearce Nelson

PRINCIPAL ACTIVITIES: Manufacture of a wide range of chemicals and fertilizers
Financial Information:

	$'000
Sales revenues	178,000

No of Employees: 1,300

GATE CITY STEEL CORPORATION
PO Box 14022, Omaha, NE 68114
Tel: (402) 399-9905
Telex: TWX 9106220288 gcs oma

Chairman: S L Cate (and President)
Senior Executive Officers: R D Tucker (Senior VP), G D Allie (Senior VP), G L Crouch (VP Finance, Secretary and Treasurer), D Kavalec (VP Human Resources), R Calek (VP)

PRINCIPAL ACTIVITIES: Wholesale trade in steel and steel products
Parent Company: NVCO Holdings Inc
Financial Information:

	$'000
Sales revenues	100,000

No of Employees: 850

GATES CORPORATION (THE)
900 South Broadway, Denver, CO 80209
Tel: (303) 744-1911
Telex: ITT 4322026 gates rbr dvr

Chairman: C C Gates; Vice Chairman: H B Duke
President: D E Miller (and Chief Operating Officer)
Senior Executive Officers: J D Maxwell (Group VP), J M Riess (Group VP), T J Gibson (Executive VP), Robert H Shiley (President Gates Energy Products)

PRINCIPAL ACTIVITIES: Manufacture of industrial rubber products, batteries and formed fiber products
Principal Subsidiaries: The Gates Rubber Company; Gates Energy Products Inc; Gates Formed-Fibre Products Inc
Principal Bank: United Bank of Denver
Financial Information:

	$'000
Sales revenues	1,091,000

Principal Shareholders: Privately owned. Ownership is within the Gates family
No of Employees: 13,000

GATES LEARJET CORPORATION
PO Box 11186, Tucson, AZ 85734
Tel: (602) 746-5100
Telex: 683-5032 LEAR UW; 666408 LEAR MKTG TUC; 497-5083 LEAR UI

Chairman: Charles C Gates
President: James B Taylor (and Chief Executive Officer)
President: Bermar S Stillwell
Senior Executive Officers: Donald J O'Mara (Executive VP and Chief Operating Officer), Robert P Anderson (President, Combs Gates-Denver Inc), Michael K Lowry (Treasurer and Chief Financial Officer), Dennis H Coley (Assistant Treasurer and Corporate Controller), William J Patrigo (Secretary and General Counsel), William G Edgar (Corporate VP, Government Relations), William G Robinson (Corporate VP, Public Affairs), William A Boettger (VP and General Manager, Commercial Aircraft), Robert C Williams (VP General Sales Manager), Edward R Miller (VP Human Resources), Donald J Grommesh (Engineering and Quality Assurance), Ralph W Lloyd (VP Marketing Services), Michael I Berger (VP Resale Marketing), Dr Richard M Mooney (VP and General Manager, Aerospace Division)

PRINCIPAL ACTIVITIES: Manufacture of business jets for commercial and military customers in both domestic and international markets; operate six fixed base aircraft service facilities in the continental US; customer service and refurbishment of aircraft, and provider of logistical support to the US Air Force fleet of C-21A (Learjets) aircraft and support to Air National Guard C-21A aircraft
Trade Names: Learjet
Parent Company: Gates Learjet stock is traded on the American Stock Exchange. Gates Corporation of Denver, Colorado owns 64.8% of the company's 12,100,208 shares outstanding, but presently is in the process of selling this stock to a partnership formed by Integrated Acquisition Inc, a wholly ownes subsidiary of Integrated Resources, Inc of New York, and the management of Learjet. This transacton is expected to be completed in September, 1987.
Principal Subsidiaries: Combs-Gates Denver Inc; Combs-Gates Arapahoe (Denver); Combs-Gates Indianapolis; Combs-Gates Palm Springs; Combs-Gates Florida (Fort Lauderdale); Combs-Gates Bradley (Windsor Locks, CT); Gates Learjet Aircraft Services Corporation (GLASCO), Wichita, KS.
Manufacturing Facilities: Tucson, AZ and Wichita, KS

Financial Information:

	Dec 31 1986
	$'000
Sales revenues	259,045
Net (loss)	(21,720)

No of Employees: 2,317

GATEWAY INDUSTRIES, INC

17512 Carriage Way Drive, Hazel Crest, IL 60429
Tel: (312) 957-4400
Telex: 910 221 1936

Chairman: Jerry Ganz (and Chief Executive Officer)
President: Frank J Frick
Senior Executive Officers: Edward L Barcus (VP Engineering), Jackson E Flynn (VP Material Control), Clark R House (VP Quality Control), Ronald Massow (VP Midwest Operations), William K Conway (VP Western Operations)

PRINCIPAL ACTIVITIES: Manufacture of safety belts for motor vehicles
Principal Bank: Continental Illinois National Bank and Trust Co of Chicago
Financial Information:

	$'000
Sales revenues	53,000

No of Employees: 1,000

GATX CORPORATION

120 S Riverside Plaza, Chicago, IL 60606
Tel: (312) 621-6200
Telex: 25-4502

Chairman: James J Glasser (and Chief Executive Officer)
President: J Warren Samborn (and Chief Operating Officer)
Senior Executive Officers: John F Chlebowski Jr (VP Finance and Chief Financial Officer), Roland I Finkelman (VP Human Resources), Paul A Heinen (VP, Secretary and General Counsel), Frederick B Ollet III (Treasurer), Ralph L O'Hara (Controller)

PRINCIPAL ACTIVITIES: Holding company with interests in the transportation and storage of bulk products; leasing of railcars and financial services; Great Lakes shipping
Principal Subsidiaries: General American Transportation Corporation; GATX Terminals Corpn; GATX Financial Services Inc; American Steamship Co
Financial Information:

	Dec 31 1985	Dec 31 1986
	$'000	$'000
Sales revenues	554,500	533,100
Income (loss) before taxes	(7,900)	24,000
Net income (loss)	(45,500)	28,700
Dividends	19,500	15,900
Dividends per common share	$1.20	$1.35
Earnings (loss) per share	($3.80)	$2.40
Common stock	8,900	6,500
Retained income	221,200	151,800
Shareholders equity	379,200	211,000

No of Employees: 1,900

GCA CORPORATION

Seven Shattuck Road, Andover, MA 01810
Tel: (617) 975-0000
Telex: 92-3350 GCA HQTRS BFRD

Chairman: Richard P Rifenburgh (and President and Chief Executive Officer)
Senior Executive Officers: James E Gallagher (Senior VP-International and Government Affairs), Ephraim Radner (Senior VP-Finance and Administration, Treasurer), Philip H Chaffee (VP and Controller), Warren R Davidson (VP-Corporate Relations), Griffith L Resor III (VP-Corporate Technology), Michael L Sandler (VP-Human Resources), Dr Leonard M Seale (VP), Peter J Simone (VP), Dennis E Wisnosky (VP), Roger M Barzun (Secretary and General Counsel)

PRINCIPAL ACTIVITIES: GCA Corporation designs and manufactures automated capital equipment used in the production of advanced integrated circuits; computer-integrated factory automation products, including hardware and software systems used to automate production processes and facilities; and precision optical lenses for industrial applications. GCA also manufactures and markets laboratory instruments and equipment and performs hazardous waste research under contract with Federal, State and local agencies in the United States
Trade Names: Products that help produce integrated circuits: DSW Wafer Stepper (R) (exposure system), Wafertrac (R) (process system), Waferetch (dry etch system), Photorepeater (R) (mask making system). Products used in automating manufcturing processes or facilities: XR (R) (robot gantry system), CIMROC (R) (robot control system), CIMCELL (cell control system), CIMNET (networking system), AUTOSORT (R) (wafer flatness analyzer)
Principal Subsidiaries: GCA International Operations; GCS Manufacturing Operations; GCA Service Co
Principal Bank: Bank of New England
Financial Information:

	$'000
Sales revenues	156,484

No of Employees: 3,400

GEARHART INDUSTRIES, INC

1100 Everman Road, Fort Worth, TX 76101
Tel: (817) 293-1300
Telex: WUI 6829 058 glarh uw

Chairman: Marvin Gearhart (and President and Chief Executive Officer)
Senior Executive Officers: Robert E Bailey (Executive VP and Chief Financial Officer), R Dean Caswell (VP and Legal Counsel)

PRINCIPAL ACTIVITIES: Manufacture of equipment for the exploration of oil and gas
Principal Subsidiaries: Drilling Information Service Co; Gearhart Finance NV; Gearhart Industries Asia Inc; Gearhart Asia SA; M E Gearhart Holdings; Gearhart Middle East SA; Gearhart NS Holdings Inc; Gearhart WA Holdings; Gearhart West Africa SA; Go International South America SA; Mineral Logging Systems Inc
Principal Bank: The First National Bank of Chicago
Financial Information:

	$'000
Sales revenues	450,000

No of Employees: 1,000

GEHL CO

143 Water Street, West Bend, WI 53095
Tel: (414) 334-9461
Telex: WUT 26701 gehlco wben

Chairman: Joseph J Zadra
President: Bernard L Nielsen (and Chief Executive Officer)
Senior Executive Officers: John W Gehl (VP Corporate Development), Joseph J Ecker (VP Marketing), Richard J Semler (VP Data Processing), J J Givens (VP Manufacturing), Kenneth F Kaplan (Treasurer and Corporate Controller), Edward J Robinson (VP Product Engineering and Research), Michael J Mulcahy (VP, General Counsel and Secretary), Arthur D Lastofka (VP Human Resources)

PRINCIPAL ACTIVITIES: Manufacture of agricultural and industrial equipment
Principal Subsidiaries: Hedlund-Martin, Inc
Principal Bank: Marine Bank NA

No of Employees: 800

GEICO CORPORATION

Geico Plaza, Washington, DC 20076

Tel: (301) 986-3000

Chairman: William B Snyder (and President and Chief Executive Officer)

Senior Executive Officers: Louis A Simpson (Vice Chairman of the Board), Donald K Smith (Senior VP), W A Sparks Jr (Senior VP)

PRINCIPAL ACTIVITIES: Insurance and financial services

Principal Subsidiaries: Government Employees Insurance Company; GEICO Indemnity Company; Criterion Casualty Company; GEICO General Insurance Company; Garden State Life Insurance Company; GEICO Annuity and Insurance Company; Resolute Group, Inc; Government Employees Financial Corporation

Principal Bank: Riggs National Bank

Financial Information:

	Dec 31 1985	Dec 31 1986
	$'000	$'000
Revenues	1,219,408	1,429,863
Premium income	1,078,042	1,294,688
Investment income	118,312	118,301
Income before taxes	68,147	136,480
Net income	170,579	217,742
Dividends	18	19
Dividends per share	$1.00	$1.08
Earnings per share(1)	$9.25	$12.61
Common stock(2)	215,481	220,598
Retained income	609,273	808,549
Shareholders equity	515,636	623,997

(1) net income

(2) including paid in surplus, excluding treasury stock

Principal Shareholders: Berkshire Hathaway, Inc

No of Employees: 5,391

GELCO CORPORATION

One Gelco Drive, Eden Prairie, MN 55344

Tel: (612) 828-1000

Chairman: N B Grossman (and Chief Executive Officer)

President: Andrew C Grossman (and Chief Operating Officer)

Senior Executive Officers: Michael J Morris (Executive VP), Richard W McFerran (Executive VP and Chief Financial Officer), O B Kinney (Executive VP), Kevin R Mitchell (Senior VP and Chief Administrative Officer), Elin A Schomaker (VP Communications), Harry Meadows (VP and Controller), Emerson P Greenberg (VP Real Estate and Facilities), Donald R Herbert (Senior VP, General Counsel and Secretary), Harold R Lefty (VP Taxes), Rubin Lewis (Chairman and Chief Executive Officer, Gelco CTI Container Services), Jeffrey S Werner (VP and Treasurer), Charles D DeVine (VP Human Resources), John Riener (President, Gelco Travel Management Services), J Daniel Morrissey (President, Gelco Payment Systems) Robert W Ward (President and Chief Executive Officer, Gelco Fleet Management Services)

PRINCIPAL ACTIVITIES: Rental and leasing of truck and automobile fleets

Principal Bank: Manufacturers Hanover Trust Co

Financial Information:

	Jul 31 1986 (12 mths)	Apr 30 1987 (9 mths)
	$'000	$'000
Sales revenues	1,016,391	736,122
Income before taxes	29,163	31,373
Net income (loss)	(6,408)	9,945
Dividends(1)	7,671	-
Dividends per share(1)	$0.56	-
(Loss) per share(1)	($0.47)	($0.11)
Common shares(2)	13,685	7,114
Shareholders equity	214,830	218,070

(1) common stock

(2) outstanding

No of Employees: 6,724

GELMAN SCIENCES INC

600 South Wagner Road, Box 1448 Ann Arbor, MI 48106
Tel: (313) 665-0651
Telex: 810 223 6036
Telefax: (313) 761-1208

Chairman: Charles Gelman (and President)
Senior Executive Officers: James C Marshall (Senior VP Operations), Jon Ehrmann (Chief Financial Officer), William Emhiser (VP and Division President), Robert Grano (VP International)

PRINCIPAL ACTIVITIES: Manufacture of laboratory equipment including fluid and air filtration equipment and electrophoresis instrumentation
Trade Names: Polypure, Chemvent, Acrodisk, Suporvac
Financial Information:

	Jul 31 1986	Jul 31 1987
	$'000	$'000
Sales revenues	50,164	53,201
Income (loss) before taxes	(838)	924
Net income (loss)	(686)	413

No of Employees: 600

GELMART INDUSTRIES, INC

20-20 129th Street, College Point, NY 11356
Tel: (718) 961-9400
Telex: ITT 426916 gelmart

Chairman: Albert Nasser; Vice Chairman: Jack Nasser
President: Morris Nasser
Senior Executive Officers: Ezra Dayan (VP Bra & Hosiery), Joseph Levy (VP Childrens)

PRINCIPAL ACTIVITIES: Manufacture of underwear, knitted goods and children's clothing
Principal Bank: Manufacturers Hanover Trust
Financial Information:

	$'000
Sales revenues	50,000

No of Employees: 10,000

GEMCRAFT INC

9494 Southwest Freeway, Houston, TX 77074
Tel: (713) 995 2500

Chairman: Jerome R Hutchins (and Chief Executive Officer)
President: G Russell Hutchins
Senior Executive Officers: Lawrence P Mosher (Executive Officer and Subsidiary Officer), J Larry Sorsby (Executive Officer), Andrew M Zdobylak (Executive Officer and Subsidiary Officer), Frank L Romero (Executive VP), James R Adair (Senior VP), Sheldon M Blazar (Senior VP), Diane O Sauder (VP), Robert I Solomon (VP), James R Streetman (VP), Michael J Thibodeaux (VP, Legal Counsel and Secretary), Eugene K Rowehl (Controller and Chief Financial Officer)

PRINCIPAL ACTIVITIES: General construction and civil engineering

Principal Subsidiaries: Mortgage Banque Inc; Gemcraft Homes Inc
Principal Bank: Texas Commerce Bank
Financial Information:

	$'000
Sales revenues	216,000

No of Employees: 800

GENCORP INC

One General Street, Akron, OH 44329
Tel: (216) 798-3000

Chairman: M G O'Neil; Chairman of Finance Committee; John O'Neil
President: A William Reynolds (and Chief Executive Officer)
Senior Executive Officers: Samuel Salem (Group VP), D M Stevart (VP and Treasurer), J L Heckel (VP), R L Malcolm (VP), Steven G Ellis (VP Communications), Charles R Ennis (VP and Legal Counsel), G W Meader (VP and Chief Financial Officer), David L Harbert (VP and Controller), G H Neal (VP), S O'Neill (VP), C N Nye (VP)

PRINCIPAL ACTIVITIES: Manufacture of electronic equipment for the aerospace industry, plastic products and tires; broadcasting; bottling of soft drinks
Principal Subsidiaries: Aerojet General; Diversitech General; General Tire; RKO General; Abilene General Tire Co; Aerojet Electro Systems Co; Aerojet Liquid Rocket Co; Aerojet Ordnance Co; Aerojet Strategic Propulsion Co; Aerojet Tactical Systems Co; Chemical Construction Corp; Cordova Chemical Co of MI; Graver Energy Systems Inc; TNS Inc; Bruin General Tire Inc; Coastal General Tire Supply Co; General Tire International Co; General Tire Service Inc; General Tire Service of Houston Inc; Nevison General Tire Service Inc; Cardinal Bottling Co Inc; Consolidated Bottling Co; Pepsi Cola Bottling Co Brookville Inc; Performance Properties Inc; RKO Bottlers of Bryan Inc; RKO Bottlers of Fort Wayne Inc; RKO Bottlers of Lima Inc; RKO Radio Network Inc; RKO Radio Sales Inc; RKO Tape Corp; Southern Lights Inc; Youngblood General Tire Inc
Financial Information:

	Nov 30 1985	Nov 30 1986
	$'000	$'000
Sales revenues	3,020,750	3,099,000
Net income	75,210	130,000
Earnings per share	$3.43	$5.82
Shareholders equity	950,516	1,048,000

No of Employees: 28,000

GENENTECH INC

460 Point San Bruno Blvd, S San Francisco, CA 94080
Tel: (415) 266-1000

Chairman: Thomas J Perkins
President: G Kirk Raab (and Chief Operating Officer)
Senior Executive Officers: Robert A Swanson (Chief Executive Officer), Herbert W Boyer (VP), Brian C Cunningham (VP and General Counsel), Shirley L Clayton VP and Treasurer), James M Gower (VP Pharmaceutical Marketing), Thomas D Kiley (VP Corporate Affairs), Reinaldo F Gomez (VP Process Services), William W Higgins (VP), Mark B Hirsch (VP), Paul F Hohenschuh (VP Biochemical Manufacturing), Louis J Lavigne Jr (VP and Controller), David W Martin Jr (VP Research), Richard D Ring (VP Quality Assurance), Michael J Ross (VP Development), William D Young (VP Manufacturing and Process Sciences)

PRINCIPAL ACTIVITIES: Manufacture of pharmaceuticals; laboratories; biotechnology
Principal Bank: Bank of America
Financial Information:

	$'000
Sales revenues	127,000

No of Employees: 1,000

GENERAL AMERICAN LIFE INSURANCE CO

700 Market Street, St Louis, MO 63101
Tel: (314) 231-1700

Chairman: H Edwin Trusheim (and President and Chief Executive Officer)
Senior Executive Officers: Dean E Williams (Executive VP Group), James C McIntyre (Executive VP Individual), Leonard M Rubenstein (VP and Treasurer), Warren A Goodenough (VP Public Relations), Frederick M Siegfried (VP Group Sales), Robert J Banstetter (VP and Legal Counsel), Robert C Orton (VP Sales), John W Barber (VP and Controller), Thomas R McPherron (VP Individual Actuarial Administration and Services), A Greig Woodring (VP Reinsurance), Donald L Smith (VP Mortgage Loan and Real Estate), Roy R Dressel (VP Administration Services), Michael P Ingrassia (VP Group Operations), E Thomas Hughes (VP Group General Markets), George T Lacy (VP Group Field Sales), Philip A Schorr (VP Product Management), Carl E Anderson (VP New Ventures), Rowland Ricketts (VP Individual New Business and Claims) Sales)

PRINCIPAL ACTIVITIES: Mutual life insurance company
Principal Subsidiaries: General American Holding Co; Consultec Inc; Genelco Inc; General American Investment Management Co; Walnut Street Securities Inc; General American Insurance Co; General American Life Annuity Co
Principal Bank: Centerre Bank
Financial Information:

	Dec 31 1985	Dec 31 1986
	$'000	$'000
Premium income	1,084,064	1,208,038
Investment income	271,446	308,301

No of Employees: 3,880

GENERAL AUTOMATION, INC

1045, S East Street, Box 4883, Anaheim, CA 92803
Tel: (714) 778-4800
Telex: WUT 685513 gai ank

Chairman: L N Mackenzie
President: Donald G Heitt (Computer Division)
Senior Executive Officers: Robert Bohn (VP Engineering), Rene Caron (VP Sales and Marketing), James C Tung (VP Business Planning), B Marshall (VP Manufacturing), John D Murray (VP Finance and Treasurer)

PRINCIPAL ACTIVITIES: Manufacture of computers and automated systems
Principal Subsidiaries: Consolidated Technology International Inc; National Power Technology Inc
Principal Bank: Crocker National Bank
Financial Information:

	$'000
Sales revenues	75,500

No of Employees: 1,000

GENERAL BANCSHARES CORPORATION

720 Olive Street, PO Box 118, St Louis, MO 63166
Tel: (314) 241 3600

Chairman: Jack W Minton
President: Kenneth Poslasky
Senior Executive Officers: Fred W Fangmann (Executive VP), Donald W Moriarty (Senior VP), Thomas E Arey (VP)

PRINCIPAL ACTIVITIES: Holding company with interests in banking
Principal Subsidiaries: Ashmore State Bank; Bank of Benton; Bank of Zeigler; Central Bank of Clayton; Charleston National Bank; Commercial and Industrial Bank; First National Bank; General Bank; Illinois State Bank; Security Bank & Trust Company
Principal Bank: General Bank

Financial Information:

	Dec 31 1985
	$'000
Revenues	203,000
Net income	1,430

No of Employees: 1,585

GENERAL BATTERY CORPORATION

PO Box 1262, Reading, PA 19603
Tel: (215) 378-0500
Telex: TWX 510 6510 478 gbc corp rdg

Chairman: J W Horton (and Chief Executive Officer)
Senior Executive Officers: P M Ehlerman (Senior VP Administration), Robert P Restrepo (Senior VP), Philip A Noznesky (VP National Account Sales), Thomas J Reilly (VP Sales and Marketing), John A Bitler (VP Environmental Resources), John N Cullen (VP Industrial Products Group), John A Harmyk (VP Manufacturing SLI), Raymond T O'Brien (VP Management Information Systems), Robert F Schmitt (VP Human Resources), Peter P Pellicano (VP and Controller)

PRINCIPAL ACTIVITIES: Manufacture of batteries for motor vehicles and for industrial use; lead smelting and refining
Parent Company: Northwest Industries Inc, Chicago, IL
Principal Bank: Philadelphia National Bank
Financial Information:

	$'000
Sales revenues	275,000

No of Employees: 3,000

GENERAL BINDING CORPORATION

One GBC Plaza, Northbrook, IL 60062
Tel: (312) 272-3700
Telex: RCA 210 122 gbc ur

Chairman: William N Lane III; Chairman of Executive Committee: Warren R Rothwell
President: Rudolph Grua (and Chief Executive Officer)
Senior Executive Officers: Govi C Reddy (Senior VP Operations), Joseph J LaPorte (VP Corporate Relations), George M Durkin (VP Domestic Sales), Walter M Hebb (VP Market Development), Edward J McNulty (VP and Chief Financial Officer), Elliott L Smith (Senior VP International), Steve Rubin (VP, Secretary and General Counsel), John A Janes (VP Dealer Sales), John A Lindroth (Senior VP Sales)

PRINCIPAL ACTIVITIES: Manufacture of binding systems, laminating systems, paper shredders and specialized printing machinery
Principal Subsidiaries: Domestic: US Ring Binder Corp; Webtron Corp
Principal Bank: Harris Trust and Savings Bank
Financial Information:

	Dec 31 1985	Dec 31 1986
	$'000	$'000
Sales revenues	174,624	200,001
Income (1)	6,878	11,197
Net income	3,606	6,030
Dividends	1,815	1,933
Dividends per share	$0.37	$0.40
Earnings per share	$0.74	$1.25
Common stock (2)	4,903	4,830
Retained income	69,035	73,132
Shareholders equity	67,511	71,516

(1) from continuing operations before taxes and extraordinary item
(2) average number of shares oustanding in thousands

No of Employees: 3,049

GENERAL CINEMA CORPORATION

27 Boylston Street, PO Box 1000, Chestnut Hill, MA 02167
Tel: (617) 232-8200
Telex: (710) 331-1480

Chairman: Richard A Smith (and Chief Executive Officer)
President: Robert J Tarr Jr (and Chief Operating Officer)
Senior Executive Officers: J Atwood Ives (Vice Chairman and Chief Financial Officer), Samuel Frankenheim (Senior VP and General Counsel), Thomas C Colbert (VP-Human Resources), Paul R Del Rossi (VP), Bert J Einloth III (VP), James C Moodey (VP-Treasurer), A Anthony Trauber (VP-Controller), Emmanuel Kurland (Secretary)

PRINCIPAL ACTIVITIES: General Cinema's two primary businesses are soft drink bottling and motion picture exhibition. The Company's Beverage Division is the largest independent Pepsi-Cola bottler in the country and a major bottler of Dr Pepper, 7-Up and Sunkist products. The Theatre Division operates the nation's largest theatre circuit, primarily multiscreen units in or near regional shopping centers
Principal Subsidiaries: GCC Beverages, Inc; GCC Theatres, Inc
Principal Bank: The First National Bank of Boston
Financial Information:

	Oct 31 1986
	$'000
Sales revenues	1,012,167
Net income	125,820
Earnings per share	$3.43
Shareholders equity	494,395

No of Employees: 12,000

GENERAL CRUSHED STONE COMPANY

Box 321, Rte 115, Easton, PA 18042
Tel: (215) 253-4271

Chairman: F C Moore
President: Bernard E Elmer (and General Manager)
Senior Executive Officers: Thomas H Barry (VP and Area Manager New York), James R Carr (VP and General Manager Pennsylvania), E W Purdy Jr (VP and Controller)

PRINCIPAL ACTIVITIES: Stone quarrying and mining of sand and gravel; manufacture of paving stones and construction materials
Parent Company: Koppers Co Inc, Pittsburgh, PA
Principal Bank: Mellon Bank of Pittsburgh
Financial Information:

	$'000
Sales revenues	98,000

No of Employees: 900

GENERAL DATACOMM INDUSTRIES, INC

Rte 63, Middlebury, CT 06762-1299
Tel: (203) 574-1118
Telex: 643 357 Gen Data C MDDY (Int'l); TWX 710 474 0027 Gendata MDDY (Domestic)

Chairman: Charles P Johnson (and Chief Executive Officer)
President: John C Taylor (and Chief Operating Officer)
Senior Executive Officers: Frederick R Cronin (VP Technology), William S Lawrence (VP Finance), Robert S Smith (VP Corporate Planning), James R Arcara (VP Corporate Operations), Dennis J Nesler (Treasurer), Howard S Modlin (Secretary), Hugh J Tremblay (VP Sales), Arthur R Braun (VP Engineering), Paul W DeLacey (VP Operations), Roger E Grinstead (VP Human Resources)

PRINCIPAL ACTIVITIES: Manufacture of data-communications systems
Principal Subsidiaries: DataComm Leasing Corporation; DataComm Rental Corporation; DataComm Service Corporation; General DataComm Inc; General DataComm Ltd; General DataComm International Corporation; General DataComm Systems Inc; General DataComm Limited; General

DataComm Foreign Sales Corporation; GDC Realty, Inc; GDC Naugatuck, Inc
Principal Bank: First Pennsylvania Bank and Trust Co
Financial Information:

	$'000
Sales revenues	182,000

No of Employees: 2,630

GENERAL DEFENSE CORP

3350 Whiteford Rd, York, PA 17402
Tel: (717) 755-0755

Chairman: Harry D Clarke Jr; Chairman of Executive Committee: Ralph R Ehrman
President: Robert A Zummo (and Chief Operating Officer)
Senior Executive Officers: Donald W Royston (Senior VP), James A Wild (VP and Controller), Daniel J Burchstead (VP and Treasurer)

PRINCIPAL ACTIVITIES: Manufacture of armaments and defense equipment; manufacture of parts for jet engines
Parent Company: Clabir Corp
Principal Subsidiaries: ABA Electromechanical System Corp; ABA Industries Inc; Hamilton Technology Inc
Principal Bank: Citibank NA
Financial Information:

	$'000
Sales revenues	240,000

No of Employees: 2,440

GENERAL DEVELOPMENT CORPORATION

111 South Bayshore Drive, Miami, FL 33131
Tel: (305) 350 1200

Chairman: David F Brown
President: Robert F Ehrling
Senior Executive Officers: C C Crump (Senior VP Special Projects), Tore T Debella (Senior VP Marketing), Harold W Fenno (Senior VP Finance), William H McQuillan (Senior VP Housing Operations), Gerard P Mozian (Senior VP Planning and Finance), Jack G O'Neal (Senior VP Homesite Development), Gordon J Pfersich (Senior VP Land Operations), Arlene A Polifroni (Senior VP, GDV Financial), Stuart S Wylie (Senior VP Commercial Operations), Saul J Sack (VP and Legal Counsel), Gerald A Stilwell (VP and Treasurer), Joseph P Zdon (VP and Controller)

PRINCIPAL ACTIVITIES: Management and development of real estate
Principal Bank: Citibank
Financial Information:

	$'000
Sales revenues	346,600

No of Employees: 4,000

GENERAL DEVICES INC

207 East Main Street, PO Box 667, Norristown, PA 19404
Tel: (215) 272 4477

Chairman: Thedore A Raymond (and President and Chief Executive Officer)
Senior Executive Officers: James R Braun (VP and Controller), James E Meneses (VP, Legal Counsel and Secretary), Francis W Bishop (Treasurer)

PRINCIPAL ACTIVITIES: Provision of temporary personnel services; computer consultants
Principal Subsidiaries: MRG Search and Placement Inc; Timesavers Inc; Worldwide Computer Services
Principal Bank: Philadelphia National Bank
Financial Information:

	$'000
Sales revenues	66,130

No of Employees: 1,300

GENERAL DYNAMICS CORPORATION

Pierre Laclede Center, St Louis, MO 63105
Tel: (314) 889-8200
Cable: GENDYN
Telex: 6841036

Chairman: Stanley C Pace (and Chief Executive Officer)
President: Oliver C Boileau
Senior Executive Officers: Herbert F Rogers (Executive VP Aerospace), Lester Crown (Executive VP, Chairman Material Service Corporation), Standley H Hoch (Executive VP Finance), James R Mellor (Executive VP Marine, Land Systems and International), Russell W Meyer Jr (Executive VP, Chairman Cessna Aircraft Company), Melville R Barlow (VP General Manager, Electronics), Leonard F Buchanan (VP-Advanced Engineering and Business Development), James J Cunnane (VP and Controller), Robert H Duesenberg (VP and General Counsel), B Edward Ewing (VP-Operations and Production Engineering), William H Mullins (VP-Government Relations), Gary S Grimes (VP), Alan M Lovelace (VP General Manager, Space Systems), John P Maguire (VP and Secretary), John E McSweeny (VP General Manager, Convair), Arch H Rambeau (VP-Human Resources), Charles A Anderson (VP General Manager, Fort Worth), Sterling V Starr (VP General Manager, Pomona), Fritz G Tovar (VP General Manager, Electric Boat), Robert W Truxell (VP General Manager, Land Systems), C Robert Stoker (VP and Treasurer), Frederick S Wood (VP-Contracts, Pricing and International Offset), Ralph E Hawes (VP General Manger, Valley Systems)

PRINCIPAL ACTIVITIES: Manufacture of military and commercial aircraft and submarines; electronic systems; armored vehicles; strategic systems; guided missiles; space launch systems; Computer Out Microfilm; production of coal and lime
Principal Subsidiaries and Divisions: Divisions:- Convair Division; Data Systems Division; Electric Boat Division; Electronics Division; Fort Worth Division; Land Systems Division; Pomona Division; Space Systems Division; Valley Systems Division. Subsidiaries:- American Overseas Marine Corporation; Cessna Aircraft Company; Freeman United Coal Mining Co; General Dynamics Services Company; Marblehead Lime Co; Material Service Corporation
Financial Information:

	Dec 31 1985 $'000	Dec 31 1986 $'000
Sales revenues net	7,952,300	8,892,000
Income before taxes	635,600	197,600
Net income (loss)	383,300	(52,500)
Dividends	42,300	42,700
Dividends per share	$1.00	$1.00
Earnings (loss) per share	$9.05	($1.23)
Common stock	55,400	55,400
Retained income	1,981,600	1,885,000
Shareholders equity	1,335,800	1,264,400

No of Employees: 106,001

GENERAL ELECTRIC CO

3135 Easton Tpke, Fairfield, CT 06431
Tel: (203) 373-2211

Chairman: John F Welch Jr (and Chief Executive Officer)
Corporate Executive Officers: Lawrence A Bossidy (Vice Chairman and Executive Officer), Edward E Hood Jr (Vice Chairman and Executive Officer), Michael D Lockhart (Corporate Executive Office VP), Charles V Sheehan (Corporate Executive Office VP), Dennis D Dammerman (Senior VP Finance), Frank P Doyle (Senior VP Corporate Relations), Jack O Peiffer (Senior VP Executive Management Staff), Walter A Scholotterbeck (Senior VP General Counsel and Secretary), Roland W Schmitt (Senior VP Corporate Research and Development)

PRINCIPAL ACTIVITIES: GE has identified 15 major businesses that are leaders in their markets today. These are grouped into three circles-core, high technology and services-surrounded by three support operations. Core Businesses:- lighting, major appliance, motor, turbine, transportation and construction equipment. High-Technology Businesses:- GE's high-tech businesses are medical systems, aerospace, materials and industrial electronics. Services Businesses:- GE has four major services businesses: financial, construction and engineering, nuclear and information. Support Operations:- the semi conductor business, petroleum subsidiary and trading company help support the drive for world leadership by the fifteen major businesses
Trade Names: General Electric, GE, Lexan, Valox, Noryl, Ultem, Hotpoint
Principal Subsidiaries: General Electric Financial Services Inc; Ladd Petroleum Corporation; General Electric Information Services Company; General Electric (USA) China Company Ltd; Aircraft Services Corp; Atlantic Plant Maintenance Corp; General Electric Real Estate Equities Corp; General Electric Credit Corp; GECC Financial Corp; GECC HI Leasing Corp; Auto & Equipment Leasing Corp of HI; General Electric Credit Corp GA; General Electric Credit AT Lease; General Electric Mortgage Corp; General Electric Railcar Services Corp; General Electric Mortgage Insurance Co; General Electric Mortgage Insurance Corp; Puritan Insurance Co; Monogram General Insurance Agency; Monogram Reinsurance Agency; Monogram Reinsurance Corp; Puritan Life Insurance Co; General Electric Environment Co; Software International Corp; General Electric Property Management Co; General Electric Technical Services Co; General Electric Venture Capital Corp; Ladd Petroleum Corp; Ladd Exploration Co
Principal Bank: Bank of New England
Financial Information:

	Dec 31 1986 $'000
Sales revenues	35,211,000
Net income	2,492,000
Earnings per share	$5.46
Shareholders equity	15,109,000

No of Employees: 241,000 USA, 330,000 worldwide

GENERAL ELECTRIC CREDIT CORPORATION

570 Lexington Avenue, New York, NY 10022
Tel: (212) 750-3131

Chairman: John F Welch Jr; Vice Chairmen: Edward E Hood Jr, Lawrence A Bossidy, John W Stanger
President: Gary C Wendt (and Chief Executive Officer)
Senior Executive Officers: Michael S Blum (VP), James R Bunt (VP and Controller), Leo A Halloran (Senior VP Finance), Daniel L Hale (Senior VP), Burton J Kloster Jr (Senior VP, Secretary and Legal Counsel), Bernard P Long (Senior VP), J H Ozanne (Senior VP), Geoffrey R Norman (VP and Treasurer)

PRINCIPAL ACTIVITIES: Financial services and insurance
Parent Company: General Electric Company, Fairfield, CT
Financial Information:

	$'000
Revenues	1,524,000

No of Employees: 6,800

GENERAL ELECTRIC ENVIRONMENTAL SERVICES, INC

200 N Seventh Street, Lebanon, PA 17042
Tel: (717) 272-2001

President: James Guerts
Senior Executive Officers: Bob Stype (VP Industrial Marketing), William N Gentile (VP Project Operations), Bill Langan (VP Product Services), Dennis Galli (VP Finance), Ab Saleem (VP Marketing and Technical), James Santora (VP Employee Relations), Ed Lowe (VP Utility Marketing)

PRINCIPAL ACTIVITIES: Manufacture of pollution control equipment
Parent Company: General Electric Company, Fairfield, CT
Financial Information:

	$'000
Sales revenues	150,000

No of Employees: 400

GENERAL FELT INDUSTRIES, INC

Park 80 Plaza West-One, Saddle Brook, NJ 07662
Tel: (201) 843-0900
Telex: TWX 710 990 5481 gen felt sark

Chairmen: Marshall S Cogan (and Chief Executive Officer)
President: Rocco A Barbieri (and Chief Operating Officer)
Senior Executive Officers: Robert T Howard (VP Sales West Coast Division), James B Liddle (VP Sales Central Division), Donald Howell (VP Sales Eastern Division), Robert V Condon Jr (VP Finance), Terry Kall (VP Marketing), John J Byrne (VP Manufacturing), Peter Cohen (VP Materials and Administration), Robert Harzog (VP Industrial Relations), Barry Zimmerman (VP Product Management and Technical Services)

PRINCIPAL ACTIVITIES: Manufacture of carpets, furniture and furnishing textiles and supplies
Principal Bank: Manufacturers Hanover Trust Co
Financial Information:

	$'000
Sales revenues	427,000

No of Employees: 3,500

GENERAL FOODS CORPORATION

250 North Street, White Plains, NY 10625
Tel: (914) 335-2500

Chairman: James L Ferguson
President: Phillip L Smith (and Chief Executive Officer)
Senior Executive Officers: Irwin Engelman (Executive VP and Chief Financial Officer), Jerry M Hiegel (Executive VP, President and Chief Executive Officer Oscar Mayer), Robert L Seelert (Executive VP Coffee and Food Services), Ervin R Shames (Executive VP, President International Operations), Peter J DeLuca (Senior VP), Andrew J Schroder (Senior VP Administration), Adolph S Clausi (Senior VP and Chief Research Officer), John M Keenan (Group VP, President General Foods Europe), Robert Sansome (Group VP Sales, Information Management, Purchasing and Distribution), James C Tappan (Group VP Development and Corporate Marketing), Lee A Archer Jr (VP Urban Affairs), C Richard Blundell (VP Personnel), Charles J Bowen (VP General Manager Meals Division), Thomas F Duesley (VP, Group VP Oscar Meyer), Richard D Finucane (VP Health Services), Harold A Golle (VP and Group Executive, Operations), Enrique J Guardia (VP Technical Research), Anthony Hass (VP External Development), Gabrielle J Hermann (VP Consumer Affairs), Sylvester T Hinkes (VP, General Manager Hag GFAG), Thomas J Hoeppner (VP and Controller), David F Hurwitt (VP, General Manager Breakfast Foods Division), David W Johnson (VP, President and Chief Executive Officer Entenmann's Inc), Paul J Keating (VP Green Coffee Operations), Robert A Klath (VP Planning), William H Korab (VP and General Manager Beverage Division), Philip A Korn (VP and Group Executive Purchasing and Distribution), Brian G Laragh (VP, President Cheese Division), James W McVey (VP, President Oscar Meyer Foods Corp), F Kent Mitchel (VP Marketing Staffs), Stephen B Morris (VP, General Manager Maxwell House Division), Lloyd A Nelson (VP Sales), Alan R Plassche (VP, President, Food Service Products Division), Raymond C Schaub (VP Tax), Edward A Schefer (VP Information Services), Jack H Scott (VP, President General Foods Inc, Canada), Douglas A Smith (VP, President General Foods Latin America), David E Soffe (VP, Area Director Northern Europe), Joseph B Tharp (VP), Raymond G Viault

(VP General Manager Desserts Division), Gerald D Wollert (VP, President General Foods Asia/Pacific)

PRINCIPAL ACTIVITIES: Manufacture of a wide range of food products including frozen food, cereal products, sauces, coffee, chocolate, beverages, sausages and other meat products, bakery products and cheese

Parent Company: Philip Morris Companies

Principal Subsidiaries: Entenmanns Inc; Entenmanns Bakery of FL Inc; Entenmanns Frozen Foods Inc; Oroweat Foods Co; Thos Garroway Ltd; General Foods Credit Corp; General Foods Capital Corp; GF Hag Vertriebs & Marketing Corp; Hudson Commercial Corp; General Foods Trading Co; Maxwell House Inc; Oscar Meyer Foods Corp; Oscar Meyer & Co Inc; Peacock Foods Inc; Ronzoni Foods Corp; Otto Roth & Co Inc; Moonachie Sales Co Inc

Financial Information:

	$'000
Sales revenues	9,000,000

No of Employees: 52,000

GENERAL HOMES CORPORATION

7322 Southwest Freeway, Houston, TX 77074

Tel: (713) 270-4177

Chairman: Jeffrey P Payson (and President and Chief Executive Officer); Vice Chairman: J W Olafson

Senior Executive Officers: W Donald Parr (Executive VP and Chief Financial Officer), Samuel H Yager Jr (Executive VP and Secretary), J C Alexander (VP and Treasurer), S H Evans (VP and Controller), J P DeGeorge (VP), T M Hartzell (VP)

PRINCIPAL ACTIVITIES: Building of single family homes

Financial Information:

	$'000
Sales revenues	350,200

No of Employees: 620

GENERAL HOST CORPORATION

22 Gate House Road, Stamford, CT 06904

Tel: (203) 357-9900

Chairman: Harris J Ashton (and President and Chief Executive Officer)

Senior Executive Officers: William F Downey (Secretary), James C Hull (VP and Controller), Richard G Kuhbach (General Counsel), Daniel J Gilmartin (Director of Planning), Walter B Rogers (Director of Corporate Communications)

PRINCIPAL ACTIVITIES: General Host Corporation is a specialty retailer of nursery and craft products and a manufacturer of salt products

Trade Names: Frank's Nursery & Crafts, Flower Time, Mini-Cube, Solar Cube

Principal Subsidiaries: Frank's Nursery & Crafts Inc; Flower Time Inc; American Salt Company

Principal Bank: Manufacturers Hanover Trust Company

Financial Information:

	Jan 27 1986(1)	Jan 31 1987
	$'000	$'000
Sales revenues	347,107	-
(Loss) before taxes	(10,698)(2)	-
Net income	-	4,674
Dividends per share	-	$0.225
(Loss) per share	($0.41)(2)	-
Shareholders equity	-	202,765

(1) restated to reclassify All American Gourmet and Hickory Farms results to discontinued operations

(2) includes gain from settling accumulated benefits under a retirement plan, amounting to $13,900 before income taxes and $5,880 or $0.23 per share

GENERAL HOUSEWARES CORPORATION

Six Suburban Avenue, Box 10265, Stamford, CT 06904
Tel: (203) 325-4141

Chairman: John H Muller Jr (and President)
Senior Executive Officers: Paul A Saxton (Executive VP), Philip H Dallow (VP Finance and Treasurer), Charles D Adams (VP)

PRINCIPAL ACTIVITIES: Manufacture of home hardware, household linens and giftware
Principal Bank: Chemical Bank
Financial Information:

	Dec 31 1985	Dec 31 1986
	$'000	$'000
Sales revenues	74,003	75,208
Income (loss) before taxes	(5,300)	1,610
Net income (loss)	(2,756)	966
Dividends	559	565
Dividends per share	$0.24	$0.24
Earnings (loss) per share	($1.18)	$0.41
Common stock	788	791
Retained income	16,673	17,074
Shareholders equity	25,018	25,626

No of Employees: 1,000

GENERAL INDUSTRIES CO

Olive & Taylor Streets, Elyria, OH 44036
Tel: (216) 323-3136
Telex: TWX 810 4242 109 gen in elyria

President: Fred Ouweleen
Senior Executive Officers: J Byzinski (VP Plastics Division), D E Elbert (VP Motors Division), J M Callihan (VP Marketing), K L Allsop (VP and Treasurer), Milan A Bendik (VP Personnel), J M Lynam (VP), R Rossi (VP Marketing Electric Comp Division)

PRINCIPAL ACTIVITIES: Manufacture of electric motors and plastic products
Parent Company: Walco National Corporation, New York, NY
Principal Bank: Mellon Bank NA
Financial Information:

	$'000
Sales revenues	85,000

No of Employees: 1,000

GENERAL INSTRUMENT CORPORATION

767 Fifth Avenue, New York, NY 10153
Tel: (212) 207-6200

Chairman: Frank G Hickey (and Chief Executive and Operating Officer)
Senior Executive Officers: Rein Narma (Executive VP Corporate Development) George E Safiol (Executive VP Operations), John A DeVries (Senior VP), Frederick Shuh (Senior VP), Christopher F Sutphin (Senior VP Components Group),

Gerard G Johnson (VP Finance and Chief Financial Officer), Stephen A Davidson (VP Personnel and Organisation), Roger L Heffernan (VP Manufacturing), Richard M Hoffman (VP, Secretary and Legal Counsel), Edward R Kearney (VP Investor Relations and Communications), Cornelius F Sullivan (VP Risk Management and Customs), Thomas C DeFazio (VP and Controller), Lemuel Tarshils (VP Corporate Technology)

PRINCIPAL ACTIVITIES: Manufacture of electronic equipment and components and data processing equipment

Principal Subsidiaries: American Totalisator Corp; American Totalisator Systems Inc; American Totalisator Co; Century III Electronics (International) Inc; Century Management Corp; Cinema Races Inc; Energy Management Corp; General Instrument Cable TV Services Inc; General Instrument Remittance Products Inc; General Instrument International Corp; General Instrument Overseas Corp; Northern Scientific Laboratories Inc; Sytek Inc; Tocom Inc; Tocom Financial Corp

Principal Bank: Bankers Trust Company

Financial Information:

	Feb 28 1986	Feb 28 1987
	$'000	$'000
Sales revenues	841,845	788,000
Net income (loss)	(66,543)	18,000

No of Employees: 13,600

GENERAL LATEX & CHEMICAL CORPORATION

666 Main Street, Cambridge, MA 02139

Tel: (617) 864-7750

Telex: TWX 710 320 1354 genlatex cam

Chairman: Robert W MacPherson (and Treasurer)

President: William H Jefferson

PRINCIPAL ACTIVITIES: Manufacture of synthetic rubber and related chemicals, urethane and vinyl products and adhesives

Principal Subsidiaries: General Latex Chemical Corp; General Latex Chemical Corp OH

Principal Bank: State Street Bank & Trust Co

Financial Information:

	$'000
Sales revenues	88,000

No of Employees: 260

GENERAL MILLS, INC

Number One General Mills Blvd, Minneapolis, MN 55440

Tel: (612) 540-2311

Chairman: H B Atwater Jr (and Chief Officer); Vice Chairman: F C Blodgett

President: Mark H Willes

Senior Executive Officers: Paul L Parker (Executive VP and Chief Administration Officer), Mark H Willes (Executive VP and Chief Financial Officer), Walter R Barry Jr (Executive VP), Michael J Boyle (Executive VP), James G Fifield (Executive VP), Joe R Lee (Executive VP), Stephen M Rothschild (Executive VP), Dean Belbas (VP Corporate Communications)

PRINCIPAL ACTIVITIES: Processing and marketing of a wide range of food products including dessert mixes, cereal products, yogurt, snacks, seafood and frozen fish, family restaurants

Financial Information:

	May 31 1986	May 31 1987
	$'000	$'000
Sales revenues	4,586,600	5,189,300
Income before taxes	323,600	433,200
Net income	183,500	222,000
Dividends per share	$1.13	$1.25
Earnings per share	$2.06	$2.50
Common stock(1)	89,200	88,700
Retained income	812,900	924,100
Shareholders equity(2)	$1.61	$8.28

(1) number of shares in thousands

(2) per share

No of Employees: 65,619

GENERAL MOTORS ACCEPTANCE CORPORATION

3044 W Grand Blvd, Detroit, MI 48202

Tel: (313) 556-5000

Chairman: Robert F Murphy (and Chairman of Executive Committee)

President: Raymond F McCarthy

Senior Executive Officers: G T Patton Jr (Executive VP Administration), Gordon R Samardich (Executive VP Operations), Norman Christman (VP Finance), Charles A Krauss (VP Public Affairs and Advertising)

PRINCIPAL ACTIVITIES: Installment sale finance, leasing and insurance

Trade Names: GMAC Financial

Parent Company: General Motors Corporation, Detroit, MI

Principal Subsidiaries: GMC Leasing Corp; GMAC Commercial Corp; GMAC Mortgage Corp; Motor Insurance Corpn; Banque de Credit General Motors (France); General Motors Acceptance Corpn (Australia); General Motors Acceptance Corpn of Canada Ltd; General Motors Acceptance Corpn Colombia SA (Colombia); General Motors Acceptance Corpn Continental (Belgium, Denmark and Sweden); General Motors Acceptance Corpn International (Japan); General Motors Acceptance Corpn Italia SpA (Italy); General Motors Acceptance Corpn de Mexico SA; General Motors Acceptance Corpn Nederland NV (Netherlands); General Motors Acceptance Corpn (NZ) Ltd (New Zealand); General Motors Acceptance Corpn South America (Venezuela); General Motors Acceptance Corpn Suisse SA (Switzerland); General Motors Acceptance Corpn (UK) Ltd; General Motors Austria Beteiligungsgeselschaft mbH; GMAC Comercial Automotriz Chile SA; GMAC Espana SA de Financiacion (Spain); GMAC Overseas Finance Corpn NV (Netherlands Antilles); Opel Kredit Bank GmbH (W Germany)

Financial Information:

	Dec 31 1985
	$'000
Sales revenues	9,755,800
Income before taxes	1,764,200
Net income	1,021,000
Dividends	100,000
Dividends per share	$4.62
Earnings per share	$47.16
Common stock	2,165,000
Retained income	2,981,800
Shareholders equity	5,146,800

Principal Shareholders: General Motors Corporation (100%)

No of Employees: 14,300

GENERAL MOTORS CORPORATION

3044 W Grand Boulevard, Detroit, MI 48202

Tel: (313) 556-5000

Chairman: *Roger B Smith (and Chief Executive Officer), Vice Chairman: *Donald J Attwood

President: *Robert C Stempel (and Chairman of Executive Committee and Chief Operating Officer)
Senior Executive Officers: *F A Smith (Executive VP Finance), *Lloyd E Reuss (Executive VP-North American Passenger Car Operations), *Elmer W Johnson (Executive VP-Operating, Public Affairs, Legal Staffs), Marina v N Whitman (VP and Group Executive), John W McNulty (VP Public Relations), *Members of Executive Committee

PRINCIPAL ACTIVITIES: Manufacture of motor vehicles and components; railroad equipment; aircraft engines and components and aerospace equipment
Trade Names: Chevrolet, Pontiac, Oldsmobile, Buick, Cadillac, GMC Truck
Principal Subsidiaries: New United Motor Manufacturing Ltd; Electronic Data Systems Corporation; Applied Intelligent Systems Inc; Automatix Inc; Diffracto Ltd; Robotic Vision Systems Inc; View Engineering Inc; Hughes Aircraft Co
Financial Information:

	Dec 31 1985	Dec 31 1986
	$'000	$'000
Sales revenues	96,372,000	102,813,700
Income before taxes	-	1,460,300
Net income	3,999,000	2,944,700
Dividends	-	10,800
Dividends per share(1)	$5.00	$5.00
Dividends per share(2)	-	$0.40
Dividends per share(3)	-	$0.60
Earnings per share(1)	$12.28	$8.21
Earnings per share(2)	-	$136.2
Earnings per share(3)	-	$190.000
Retained income	22,606,600	25,551,300
Shareholders equity	-	30,678,000

(1) common stock
(2) class E
(3) class H

No of Employees: 876,000

GENERAL NUTRITION
921 Penn Avenue, Pittsburgh, PA 15222
Tel: (412) 288-4600

Chairman: Jerry D Horn (and President and Chief Executive and Chief Operating Officer)
Senior Executive Officers: C A Koempel (Executive VP and Treasurer), William E Watts (Senior VP), P Robert Dunn (Senior VP), Kern L Gillette (VP), Rodney Hamilton (VP) John Stebbins (VP), David Walsh (VP)

PRINCIPAL ACTIVITIES: Manufacture of health foods, vitamins and mineral supplements; manufacture of cosmetics and personal care products
Principal Subsidiaries: Pioneer Specialty Foods Inc; Shakarian Realty Inc
Principal Bank: Mellon Bank
Financial Information:

	$'000
Sales revenues	370,000

No of Employees: 6,500

GENERAL PHYSICS CORPORATION
10650 Hickory Ridge Road, Columbia, MD 21044
Tel: (301) 964 6000

Chairman: Robert W Deutsch (and President and Chief Executive Officer)
Senior Executive Officers: Frank A Andrews (Senior VP Science), David L Thames (Senior VP), John H Beakes (Group President), Roger E Klose (VP), William A Kuhlman (Group President), David R Roth (Group President), Alan P Tattersall (VP), Clyde H VanLandingham (VP), John W Whitney (VP, Chief Administration Officer, Assistant Secretary and Assistant Treasurer), Frank F Seecchia (Secretary)

PRINCIPAL ACTIVITIES: Training services for the power industry; electrical engineering consultants
Parent Company: Seven Oaks Corporation
Principal Bank: Equitable Bank
Financial Information:

	$'000
Sales revenues	66,540

No of Employees: 1,250

GENERAL PORTLAND INC
1281 N Central Expwy, Dallas, TX 75243
Tel: (214) 934-7100

Chairman: James B Lendrum
President: B P Collomb (and Chief Executive Officer)
Senior Executive Officers: F W Koester (Executive VP), Henry C Boecker (Senior VP), B S Dryburgh (Senior VP and General Manager Texas Region), E L Guitton (Senior VP), David S Fields (VP, Secretary and Treasurer), G A Mercier (VP Strategic Planning), T W Tatum (VP Employee Relations), J P Cloiseau (VP and Treasurer), J L Hurt (VP and General Manager California Region), L D Smith Jr (VP and General Manager Citadel Division), E H Sundquist (VP and General Manager Florida Division), H L Youngblood (VP and General Manager Peninsular Division), J C Poole (VP and Assistant General Manager Texas Region), J F Sautin (VP Texas Operations), J R Beasley (VP Texas Marketing), J W Collier (VP Texas Distribution), J R Moran (VP Texas Aggregates), J E Scott (VP and General Manager Victor Division), G L White (VP and General Manager Whitehall Division), H Lavigne (VP and General Manager NE Region-New England), A W Cadotte (VP and General Manager NE Region-New York)

PRINCIPAL ACTIVITIES: Manufacture and sale of cement and concrete
Parent Company: LaFarge Corp
Principal Bank: RepublicBank Dallas
Financial Information:

	$'000
Sales revenues	420,000

No of Employees: 2,000

GENERAL PUBLIC UTILITIES CORPORATION
100 Interpace Pkwy, Parsippany, NJ 07054
Tel: (201) 263-6500

Chairman: John F O'Leary (and Chief Executive Officer)
President: Herman M Dieckamp (and Chief Operating Officer)
Senior Executive Officers: John G Graham (VP and Chief Financial Officer), Michael P Morrell (Treasurer), F Allen Donofrio (Comptroller), Grace Wade (Secretary)

PRINCIPAL ACTIVITIES: Holding company whose subsidiaries are involved in the generation and supply of electricity
Principal Subsidiaries: Jersey Central Power and Light Co; Pennsylvania Electric Co; Metropolitan Edison Co; GPU Service Corp; GPU Nuclear Corp
Financial Information:

	Dec 31 1985	Dec 31 1986
	$'000	$'000
Sales revenues	2,869,509	2,787,077
Net income	117,106	205,247
Dividends per share	-	$0.15*
Earnings per share	$1.86	$3.26
Common stock	157,159	157,159
Retained income	663,718	867,223
Shareholders equity	1,584,379	1,786,139

*Payable August 28 1987

No of Employees: 13,934

GENERAL RE CORPORATION
Financial Center, PO Box 10351, Stamford, CT 06904
Tel: (203) 328-5000

Chairman: F W Munson (and Chief Executive Officer)

President: R E Furguson (and Chief Operating Officer)
Senior Executive Officers: J C Etling (Senior VP and Group Executive), R O Shepler (Senior VP and Group Executive), Ronald G Anderson (VP Finance), E F Rondepierre (VP, General Counsel and Secretary), J S Wilbourn (VP Investment), P W Ness (VP International), M R Zucchini (VP Administration)

PRINCIPAL ACTIVITIES: Holding company with interests in insurance, reinsurance and financial services
Principal Subsidiaries: Herbert Clough Inc; General Re Holdings Inc; General Re Services Inc; General Reinsurance Corp; Elm Street Corp; General Reassurance Corp; Farfield Life Insurance Co; Genstar Indemnity Co; GRC Realty Corp; North Star Reinsurance Corp; North Star Syndicate Inc; United States Aviation Underwriters Inc; Aerospace Management Services Inc
Principal Bank: Bank of New York
Financial Information:

	Dec 31 1985	Dec 31 1986
	$'000	$'000
Revenues	2,123,000	3,175,200
Net income	135,800	328,700
Earnings per share	$2.90	$3.22
Shareholders equity	1,794,200	2,413,100

No of Employees: 2,332

GENERAL REFRACTORIES COMPANY

225 City Avenue, Bala-Cynwyd, PA 19004
Tel: (215) 667-7900
Telex: WUT 834 334 grefco bc yn

Chairman: Raymond G Perelman (and President and Chief Executive Officer)
Senior Executive Officers: Jeffrey E Perelman (Executive VP Operations), Richard S Funk (VP and Secretary), Joseph M Mulvaney (VP Personnel), John P Kotona (VP, Treasurer, Chief Financial and Accounting Officer), Karl F Miller (VP Corporate Development)

PRINCIPAL ACTIVITIES: Manufacture of heat resistant and insulating products for industry and the building trade
Principal Subsidiaries: American Refractories Co; Grefco Inc; Chemrock Corp; Chemrock Corp; Mapleton Development Inc
Principal Bank: Mellon Bank NA
Financial Information:

	$'000
Sales revenues	316,000

No of Employees: 4,540

GENERAL SHALE PRODUCTS CORPORATION

3209 N Roan Street, Box 3547, Johnson City, TN 37601
Tel: (615) 282-4661

Chairman: George C Sells (and Chief Executive Officer); Vice Chairman: Sam R Sells II
President: W E Hawkins Jr
Senior Executive Officers: William L DeBoard (VP Personnel), Joseph F Edwards (VP Engineering), H H Underwood (VP Sales), James L Perkins (VP and Treasurer), Philip Garland (VP Manufacturing), Walter Banyas (VP Real Estate)

PRINCIPAL ACTIVITIES: Manufacture of cement and bricks, sand and gravel and lighweight aggregates
Parent Company: Marley Plc, UK
Principal Bank: First American Bank NA
Financial Information:

	$'000
Sales revenues	82,600

No of Employees: 1,100

GENERAL SIGNAL CORPORATION

High Ridge Park, PO Box 10010, Stamford, CT 06904
Tel: (203) 357-8800
Telex: TWX 710 474 3386 gsc std

Chairman: David T Kimball (and Chief Executive Officer)
Senior Executive Officers: Theodore J Wiedemann (Senior VP and Chief Financial Officer), Joel S Friedman (Senior VP-Operations), John E Halter (Senior VP-Operations), Peter A Laing (Senior VP-Operations), Michael R Jacqmin (VP and Treasurer), J Robert Hipps (VP and Controller), Erwin Kantor (VP-Taxes), George Falconer (VP-Human Resources), Nino J Fernandez (VP-Investor Relations), Edward C Prellwitz (VP-Planning), Edgar J Smith Jr (VP, General Counsel and Secretary)

PRINCIPAL ACTIVITIES: General Signal Corporation is a leader in instrumentation and control technology for semiconductor production, telecommunications, industrial automation, energy management and rail transportation
Principal Subsidiaries: Operating Units: Process Controls: Aurora Pump; BIF; Blue M Electric; Ceilcote; DeZurik; Kinney Vacuum; L&N Instruments; L&N International; L&N Systems; Lindberg; Marsh Instrument; Metallurgical Products; Mixing Equipment Company; Stock Equipment Company. Technology Industries: Advanced Mechanization, Inc; Axel Electronics; Circuits Processing Apparatus; Dielectric Communications; Drytek; Henschel; Karkar Electronics; Kayex; Semiconductor Systems, Inc; Tau-Tron; Telecommunication Technology, Inc; Telenex; Ultratech-Stepper; Xynetics. Electrical Controls: Dowzer Electric; Edwards; GS Electric; Hevi-Duty Electric; Nelson Electric; O-Z/Gedney; Sola Electric. Transportation Controls: Dynapower/Stratopower; General Railway Signal; Metal Forge; New York Air Brake
Principal Bank: Marine Midland Bank NA
Financial Information:

	Dec 31 1985	Dec 31 1986
	$'000	$'000
Sales revenues	1,800,878	1,583,368
Income before taxes	80,189	117,547
Net income	49,267	74,622
Dividends	51,868	51,735
Dividends per share	$1.80	$1.80
Earnings per share	$1.72	$2.60
Common stock	40,436	40,527
Retained income	689,436	712,323
Shareholders equity	903,989	927,354

No of Employees: 20,180

GENERAL TELEPHONE COMPANY OF CALIFORNIA

1 GTE Place, Thousand Oaks, CA 91362
Tel: (805) 372 6000

President: David E Anderson
Senior Executive Officers: E Robert Wellman (Executive VP Operations), Richard M Cahill (VP, Group Officer and Secretary), Robert L Giffin (VP Finance), J J Casey (VP Customer Services), B B Heiler (VP Marketing), E E Wilson (VP Network Engineering and Construction), William D Griffith (VP Government Affairs), S C Herzberger (VP), Richard L Schaulin (VP Human Resources), J J Parrish (VP Public Affairs), George W Blake (VP and Area Manager Northern), Harold R Nelms (VP and Area Manager Southern), Bernard B Heiler (VP Marketing), Karen S Shaw (VP Customer Relations), Charles M Hanna (VP Information Management), Charles J O'Rourke (Treasurer and Assistant Secretary), William D Wilson (Controller)

PRINCIPAL ACTIVITIES: Operation of telephone services
Parent Company: GTE Corporation
Financial Information:

	$'000
Sales revenues	2,600,000

No of Employees: 25,000

GENESCO INC

Genesco Park, Nashville, TN 37202
Tel: (615) 367-7000
Cable: GENCORP Nashville
Telex: Nashville, Tennessee 554405 Genesco NAS

Chairman: William S Wire II (and President and Chief Executive Officer)
Senior Executive Officers: Larry B Shelton (Executive VP), William Dragon Jr (Executive VP), James S Gulmi (VP Finance, Treasurer and Chief Financial Officer), Richard L Daniels (VP), James O'Brien (VP-Human Resources), Robert E Brosky (Controller and Chief Accounting Officer), William C O'Connor (VP-Law and Corporate Secretary)

PRINCIPAL ACTIVITIES: Manufacture of footwear and clothing
Trade Names: Johnston & Murphy, Jarman, Laredo, Wrangler, Charm Step, Easy Street, Mitre, Greif, Kilgour French & Stanbury, Lanvin of Paris, Chaps by Ralph Lauren, Polo University Club by Ralph Lauren, Phoenix, Colours by Alexander Julian, Donald Brooks and Perry Eills
Principal Subsidiaries: Genesco Financial Corp
Principal Bank: First American Bank, Nashville, Tennessee
Financial Information:

	Jan 31 1986	Jan 31 1987
	$'000	$'000
Sales revenues	514,589	538,486
Income (loss) before taxes	15,220	(29,834)
Net income (loss)	20,426	(33,929)
Earnings (loss) per share(1)	$1.20	($2.39)
Earnings (loss) per share(2)	$1.14	($2.39)
Common stock(3)	15,174	15,099
Retained (deficit)	(18,235)	(38,661)
Shareholders equity	110,619	82,657

(1) primary
(2) fully diluted
(3) number of shares in thousands

No of Employees: 6,700

GENESEE BREWING CO INC

445 St Paul Street, Rochester, NY 14605
Tel: (716) 546-1030
Telex: WUT 978 234 genesee roc

Chairman: John L Wehle (and Chief Executive Officer)
President: John L Wehle Jr (and Chief Operating Officer)
Senior Executive Officers: John D Reifenrath (Senior VP Marketing), John T Janssen (VP Finance), C C Geminn (VP Production), Donald A York (VP Sales), Hugh T Crossin (VP Marketing and Planning), J M Dennee (VP Materials)

PRINCIPAL ACTIVITIES: Brewing of beer
Principal Bank: Marine Midland Bank
Financial Information:

	$'000
Sales revenues	142,000

No of Employees: 880

GENEVE CAPITAL GROUP INC

96 Cumming Point Road, Stamford, CT 06902
Tel: (203) 358-8000

Chairman: Edward Netter (and Chief Executive Officer); Vice Chairman: Vincent R Serrecchia
President: F P Zoch III (and Chief Operating Officer)
Senior Executive Officers: Ronald Strackbein (VP), Robert G Donnalley Jr (VP), Fred S Eichler (VP and Chief Financial Officer)

PRINCIPAL ACTIVITIES: Financial services
Parent Company: Geneve Corp
Principal Subsidiaries: Independence Holding Co; South Atlantic Financial Corp; Southern Life & Health; Standard Security Life
Principal Banks: Chase Manhattan Bank; Continental Illinois
Financial Information:

	Dec 31 1985
	$'000
Revenues	134,712
Income before taxes	11,522
Net income	12,760
Dividends	2,602
Dividends per share	$0.10
Earnings per share	$6.96
Common stock	1,057
Retained income	58,122
Shareholders equity	87,263

No of Employees: 1,250

GENISCO TECHNOLOGY CORPORATION

18435 Susana Road, Rancho Dominguez, CA 90221
Tel: (213) 537 4750

Chairman: Robert B Phinizy (and President and Chief Executive Officer)
Senior Executive Officers: Phillip G Halamandaris (Executive VP and Chief Operating Officer), William R Esser (VP and President Electric Division), Robert J Gray (VP, President Genisco Computers Corp), Robert Haro (VP, President Memory Products Division), Peter J Snow (VP and Division President), John A Calfas (Secretary)

PRINCIPAL ACTIVITIES: Manufacture of computer components including accelerometers, transducers and indicator lights; electromagnetic interference testing; computer peripherals, graphic display terminals
Principal Bank: Bank of America
Financial Information:

	$'000
Sales revenues	36,470

No of Employees: 510

GENOVA INC

7034 East Court Street, Davison, MI 48423
Tel: (313) 744 4500

Chairman: Robert F Williams
President: Robert M Williams (and Treasurer and Chief Executive Officer)
Senior Executive Officers: Dwight P Van Steenkiste (Senior VP)

PRINCIPAL ACTIVITIES: Manufacture of plastic pipes, tubes and related products
Principal Subsidiaries: Genova-Indiana Inc; Genova-Minnesota Inc; Genova-Pennsylvania Inc; Wiltic Chemical Manufacturing Company Inc
Principal Bank: National Bank
Financial Information:

	$'000
Sales revenues	50,000

No of Employees: 360

GENOVESE DRUG STORES INC

80 Marcus Drive, Melville, NY 11747
Tel: (516) 420 1900

Chairman: Leonard Genovese (and President)
Senior Executive Officers: Herbert J Kett (Senior VP), Jerome Stengel (VP and Treasurer), Albert Wilent (VP), Donald W Gross (VP and Secretary), Alan Patrick (VP), Dominick Lettieri (VP Management Information Systems), Ralph Resildo (VP), Raymond Resildo (VP), J Robert McCarthy (VP)

PRINCIPAL ACTIVITIES: Drug stores chain
Principal Subsidiaries: Living Color Inc
Principal Bank: Citibank
Financial Information:

	$'000
Sales revenues	233,150

No of Employees: 2,400

GENRAD, INC

300 Baker Avenue, Concord, MA 01742
Tel: (617) 369-4400
Telex: WUT 951 037 genrad a werd

President: William R Thurston (and Chief Executive Officer)
Senior Executive Officers: Richard G Rogers (Executive VP and Chief Operating Officer), Charles E Peters (Senior VP, Treasurer and Chief Financial Officer), Harold T McAleer (Senior VP), Robert E Anderson (Group VP), Joseph Z Rivlin (Group VP), John R Held (VP Sales and Service), S Russel Craig (VP), Constantine J Lahanas (VP Corporate Development), Eric L Mudama (VP), Richard C Tippett (VP)

PRINCIPAL ACTIVITIES: Manufacture of electronic equipment including testing equipment
Principal Bank: New England Merchants Bank of Boston
Financial Information:

	$'000
Sales revenues	220,000

No of Employees: 2,800

GENSCO, INC

PO Box 67, Uvalde, TX 78801
Tel: (512) 278-5666
Telex: WUT 767397 gensco uval

President: C F Schwab
Senior Executive Officers: Bill McWhorter (VP Pipe Distribution), Walter M Stage (VP Pipe Finishing), Richard C Fenton (Secretary and Treasurer)

PRINCIPAL ACTIVITIES: Distribution of steel pipe and operation of metal service center
Parent Company: 1600 Corporation
Principal Bank: First City National
Financial Information:

	$'000
Sales revenues	200,000

No of Employees: 450

GENUINE PARTS COMPANY

2999 Circle 75 Pkwy, Atlanta, GA 30339
Tel: (404) 953-1700

Chairman: Wilton Looney (and Chief Executive Officer); Vice Chairman: Earl Dolive
President: Larry L Prince
Senior Executive Officers: Edward M Jones (Executive VP), John Scalley (Executive VP), William Valentine (Senior VP-Sales), Robert Breci (Group VP), James Prince (Group VP), Jerry Nix (VP Finance), Louis Rice Jr (Senior VP Personnel)

PRINCIPAL ACTIVITIES: Manufacture and wholesale trade of parts for the automotive industry
Trade Names: NAPA
Principal Subsidiaries: Motion Industries Inc; S P Richards Company; Balkamp Inc; Genuine Parts Holding Ltd
Principal Bank: Trust Company Bank
Financial Information:

	Dec 31 1985 $'000	Dec 31 1986 $'000
Sales revenues	2,332,480	2,394,072
Income before taxes	-	240,565
Net income	126,240	121,553
Dividends	-	16,963
Dividends per share	-	$1.51
Earnings per share	$2.34	$2.28
Common stock	-	54,354
Retained income	-	717,777
Shareholders equity	729,230	758,493

No of Employees: 13,906

GEO A HORMEL & CO

See HORMEL, GEO A, & CO

GEO INTERNATIONAL CORPORATION

1 Landmark Square, Stamford, CT 06901
Tel: (203) 964-1955
Telex: WUT 643820 geomstamfrd std

Chairman: John E McConnaughy (and Chief Executive Officer)
President: Anthony J Giglio (and Chief Operating Officer)
Senior Executive Officers: Ernest G Alldredge (Executive VP), William J Garry (VP Finance and Controller), Nedd McArthur (VP Communications and Marketing Services), William P Constantini (VP and General Counsel), Douglas J Hansen (VP and Treasurer), Al J Betley (VP Benefits Administration), F D Rogers (VP Acquisitions), Norman L Graham (VP)

PRINCIPAL ACTIVITIES: Exploration for oil and gas; provision of equipment and services for the oil industry; operation of quality control services
Principal Subsidiaries: Geo Cactus Pipe & Supply Co; Geo Cactus Wellhead Equipment; Geo Churchill Inc; Geo Condor Inc; Geo Drilling Fluids Inc; Geo Reliability Services; Geo Seismic Services; Geo Vann Inc; Magnaflux Corp; Magnaflux Surface Conditioner Corp
Principal Bank: Bank of New York
Financial Information:

	$'000
Sales revenues	244,000

No of Employees: 3,800

GEORGE BANTA COMPANY, INC

See BANTA, GEORGE, COMPANY, INC

GEORGE KOCH SON, INC

See KOCH, GEORGE, SON, INC

GEORGE WASHINGTON CORPORATION

8059 Arlington Expressway, Jacksonville, FL 32211
Tel: (904) 725 8231

Chairman: John H Wilbur (and President and Subsidiary Officer)
Senior Executive Officers: Michael J Davoli (Executive VP and Subsidiary Officer), Robert J Lamb (VP and Subsidiary Officer), Frank E Clark Jr (Secretary and Treasurer)

PRINCIPAL ACTIVITIES: Holding company with interests in a wide range of insurance services
Principal Subsidiaries: George Washington Life Insurance Company
Principal Bank: Barnett Bank
Financial Information:

$'000

No of Employees: 200

GEORGETOWN INDUSTRIES INC

1901 Roxborough Rd, Charlotte, NC 28211
Tel: (704) 366-6901

Chairman: Roger R Regelbrugge
Senior Executive Officers: Gary L Anderson (VP Finance), Albert E Crabtree (VP Administration)

PRINCIPAL ACTIVITIES: Manufacture of steel rods and bars and wire products
Principal Subsidiaries: Georgetown Steel Corp
Principal Bank: National Bank of North Carolina
Financial Information:

	$'000
Sales revenues	170,000

No of Employees: 900

GEORGIA FEDERAL BANK, FSB

20 Marietta Street NW, Atlanta, GA 30303
Tel: (404) 588-2600

Chairman: John B Zellars
President: Richard D Jackson (and Chief Executive Officer)

Senior Executive Officers: Don B Stout (Senior Executive VP and Chief Operating Officer), Charles Clark (Executive VP Banking), Joe F Ferguson (Senior VP Branch Operations), Dale E Johnson (Senior VP and Chief Financial Officer), Wyatt E Johnson (Senior VP Lending), C W Marlow (Senior VP Administration)

PRINCIPAL ACTIVITIES: Banking services
Principal Subsidiaries: First Family Financial Services Inc
Financial Information:

	Dec 31 1985
	$'000
Revenues	313,705
Net income	20,064
Earnings per share	$2.54
Shareholders equity	172,172
Total assets	2,787,018

No of Employees: 1,600

GEORGIA KRAFT CO

PO Box 1551, Rome, GA 30161
Tel: (404) 291-6920

Chairman: E M Karter
President: C G Ames
Senior Executive Officers: J G Lee (Executive VP), A D Correll (VP), B J Lancashire (VP), R E Dean (VP Human Resources), S R Schwartz (VP Administration), T A Owens (VP Wood Operations)

PRINCIPAL ACTIVITIES: Manufacture and sale of paperboard
Parent Companies: Inland Container Corp; The Mead Corporation
Principal Bank: First National Bank of Chicago
Financial Information:

	Dec 31 1985	Dec 31 1986
	$'000	$'000
Sales revenues	557,030	557,428
Net income	31,764	27,578
Shareholders equity	383,326	410,904

No of Employees: 3,100

GEORGIA MARBLE CO

2575 Cumberland Pkwy N.W, Atlanta, GA 30339
Tel: (404) 432-0131
Telex: WUT 549599 ga marble atl

President: A L Gay
Senior Executive Officers: Joe B Cordell (VP), William T Aycock (VP), E G Hartleb (VP), W H Runge Jr (VP), Milton Hamrick (VP), John Cline (VP), E M Monger (VP and Controller)

PRINCIPAL ACTIVITIES: Production of various kinds of stone including marble, granite and limestone
Parent Company: Jim Walter Corporation, Tampa, FL
Principal Bank: The First National Bank of Chicago
Financial Information:

	$'000
Sales revenues	95,000

No of Employees: 1,000

GEORGIA POWER COMPANY

333 Piedmont Avenue Northeast, Atlanta, GA 30308
Tel: (404) 526 6526

Chairman: Robert W Scherer (and Chief Executive Officer)
President: James H Miller Jr
Senior Executive Officers: H Grady Baker Jr (Executive VP and General Manager), Elmer B Harris (Executive VP), Warren Y Jobe (Executive VP and Chief Financial Officer), J A Gantt (Senior VP Divisional Operations), R E Conway (Senior VP Nuclear Power), G F Head (Senior VP Fossil and Hydro Power), J C Casuey (Senior VP Administration Services), J C Hemby Jr (Senior VP), J P O'Reilly (Senior VP Nuclear Operations), R E Scott (Senior VP Economic Services)

PRINCIPAL ACTIVITIES: Supply of electricity

Parent Company: Southern Company

Principal Bank: Citizens & Southern National Bank

Financial Information:

	$'000
Sales revenues	3,444,300

No of Employees: 15,000

GEORGIA-PACIFIC CORPORATION

133 Peachtree Street NE, Atlanta, GA 30303

Tel: (404) 521-4000

Telex: 804600

Chairman: T Marshall Hahn Jr (and Chief Executive Officer)

President: Harold Airington (and Chief Operating Officer as of Jan 2 1988)

Senior Executive Officers: Ronald P Hogan (Executive VP-Building Products as of Jan 2 1988), Davis K Mortensen (Executive VP-Building Products Manufacturing), Conrad Schweitzer (Executive VP-Pulp and Paper), James C Van Meter (Executive VP and Chief Financial Officer), J Kermit Birchfield Jr (Senior VP-Legal and Governmental Affairs), George A MacConnell (Senior VP-Distribution Division), Daniel A Martinez (Senior VP-Pulp and Paper Manufacturing), Carroll T Tolar (Senior VP-Engineering), Glenn E Wilson (Senior VP-Gypsum and Roofing Division), Maurice W Kring (Group VP-Tissue, Pulp and Paperboard), J Wayne Amy (VP-Distribution Division, Southwest Region), Joseph J Armetta (VP-Distribution Division, Midwest Region), David S Dimling (VP-Printing Paper Division), Willie L Duke (VP-Eastern Wood Products Manufacturing Division), Diane Durgin (VP-Law and Secretary), Donald L Glass (VP-Roofing Division), Stephen K Jackson (VP-Distribution Division Marketing and Advertising), Joseph H Joiner (VP-Controller and Information Resources), John F McGovern (VP-Finance), Dennis D Melstrom (VP-Pulp and Paper Information Resources), Thomas F Mitchell (VP-Government Affairs), Dewey L Mobley (VP-Western Wood Products Manufacturing Division), Allan J Nadeau (VP-Northern Pulp and Paper Division), Kelly E Powell Jr (VP-Distribution Division, Western Region), John F Rasor (VP-Mid-Continent Wood Products Manufacturing Division), David W Reynolds (VP-Human Resources), Robert A Starling (VP-Distribution Division, Southeast Region), Marion L Talmadge (VP-Executive Affairs), James R Taylor (VP-Chemical Division), Douglas A Thom (VP-Packaging Division), Michael A Vidan (VP-Wood Products Sales Division), Michael B Wilson (VP-Sales and Marketing Consumer and Commercial Paper Products), Wayne I Tamblyn (Treasurer)

PRINCIPAL ACTIVITIES: Georgia-Pacific Corporation is a major manufacturer and wholesale distributor of building products, pulp, paper, packaging and related chemicals. Georgia-Pacific is one of the nation's largest manufacturers of building products. Much of the success of G-P's building products business is attributed to the 141-branch Distribution Division, the industry's most extensive, which serves every major metropolitan area in the United States. The company entered the pulp and paper business 30 years ago at Toledo, Oregon, when it built a kraft pulp and paper mill. Since then, Georgia-Pacific has become a national presence with facilities across the US manufacturing pulp, printing and writing paper, tissue, linerboard and corrugated containers
Principal Bank: Bank of America

Financial Information:

	Dec 31 1985	Dec 31 1986
	$'000	$'000
Sales revenues	6,716,000	7,223,000
Income before taxes(1)	309,000	485,000
Net income	187,000	296,000
Dividends	94,000	97,000
Dividends per share	$0.80	$0.85
Earnings per share(2)	$1.61	$2.64
Common stock	83,000	86,000
Retained income	1,114,000	1,304,000
Shareholders equity	2,147,000	2,452,000

(1) before extraordinary item
(2) fully diluted

No of Employees: 39,000

GERBER PLUMBING FIXTURES CORPORATION

4656 W Touhy Avenue, Chicago, IL 60646
Tel: (312) 675-6570

Chairman: Harriet G Lewis (and President)
Senior Executive Officers: Maurice L Lewis (Executive VP), Alan G Lewis (VP Sales), Robert C Luker (VP and Treasurer)

PRINCIPAL ACTIVITIES: Manufacture of plumbing supplies
Principal Bank: Harris Trust and Savings Bank
Financial Information:

	1987
	$'000
Sales revenues	70,000

No of Employees: 1,000

GERBER PRODUCTS CO

445 State Street, Fremont, MI 49412
Tel: (616) 928-2000

Chairman: David W Johnson (and Chief Executive Officer and President)
Senior Executive Officers: Gerald F Britt (Executive VP Admin and Service Companies Group), Robert L Johnston (Executive VP, General Manager-Gerber Products Division), Kenneth B Peirce (Executive VP, General Counsel and General Manager-Apparel Group)

PRINCIPAL ACTIVITIES: Manufacture of food, clothing, toys, furniture and equipment for babies
Principal Subsidiaries: Gerber (Canada) Inc; G & M Finishing Inc; Kent Inc; Centrury Originals; Gerber Products Company of Puerto Rico Inc; Gerber Life Insurance Co; Productos Gerber De Centroamerica SA (Costa Rica); Gerber Children's Centers Inc; Walter W Moyer Co; Gerber Family Services Inc; Geradco Associates Inc; C W Transport Inc; Century Products Inc; Okla Homer Smith Furniture Manufacturing Co Inc; Bilt Rite Juvenile Products Inc; Atlanta Novelty Inc; Weather Tamer Inc; Buster Brown Apparel Inc; Bates Childrenswears Co; Palo Alto Educational Systems Inc; Soft Care Apparel Inc
Financial Information:

	Mar 31 1987
	$'000
Sales revenues	917,320
Income before taxes	922,605
Dividends	26,575
Dividends per share	$1.32
Earnings per share	$1.42

No of Employees: 15,872

GERBER SCIENTIFIC INC

83 Gerber Road W, South Windsor, CT 06074
Tel: (203) 644-1551

President: H J Gerber
Senior Executive Officers: David J Logan (Senior VP Engineering), Robert J Moore (Senior VP Operations and Marketing), George M Gentile (Senior VP and Treasurer), Stanley Leven (Senior VP), Robert Lipira (Public Relations Director)

PRINCIPAL ACTIVITIES: Manufacture of computer aided design and computer aided manufacturing systems for the electronics, apparel, luggage, aerospace, automotive, printing, signmaking, graphic arts and engraving industries
Principal Subsidiaries: Beta Engineering and Development Ltd (35%); Gerbert Garment Technology Inc; Gerber Scientific UK Ltd; Gerber Scientific Europe SA; Gerber Scientific Exporting Inc; The Gerber Scientific Instrument Company GmbH; Gerber Scientific Leasing Inc; Gerber Systems Technology (80%); Gerber Scientific Instrument Co; Gerber Scientific Products Inc; Gerber Scientific France SARL; Gerber Scientific Scandinavia AB: Gerber Systems Technology International Inc; Gerber Systems Technology GmbH; Gerber Camsco Inc
Financial Information:

	Apr 30 1987
	$'000
Sales revenues	223,854
Net income	21,057
Earnings per share	$1.21

No of Employees: 1,650

GERIATRIC & MEDICAL CENTERS INC

63rd and Walnut Streets, Philadelphia, PA 19139
Tel: (215) 476 2250

Chairman: Daniel Veloric (and President and Chief Executive Officer)
Senior Executive Officers: Robert F Carfagno (VP Finance and Chief Financial Officer), Esther Ponnocks (VP Patient Services and Education), Gary Veloric (Treasurer), Ramon R Obod (Secretary)

PRINCIPAL ACTIVITIES: Provision of medical and health care services including retirement centers and nursing homes
Principal Bank: First Pennsylvania Bank
Financial Information:

	$'000
Sales revenues	75,000

No of Employees: 3,405

GESTETNER CORPORATION

Gestetner Park, Yonkers, NY 10703
Tel: (914) 968-6666
Telex: WUT 131578 gestetner yks

President: Hector Wiltshire (and Chief Executive Officer)
Senior Executive Officers: Ian J Cumming (VP and Secretary), E G Vollmer (VP Finance and Treasurer)

PRINCIPAL ACTIVITIES: Sale and distribution of reprographic equipment
Parent Company: Gestetner Holdings (USA) Ltd
Principal Bank: Bank of New York
Financial Information:

	$'000
Sales revenues	80,000

No of Employees: 1,100

GETTY OIL CO

3810 Wilshire Blvd, Los Angeles, CA 90010
Tel: (213) 739-2100
Telex: ITT 4720164 getty

Chairman: S R Petersen (and Chief Executive Officer)
Senior Executive Officers: Jack D Jones (Group VP), Victor E Bartlett (VP), Thomas A Differ (VP), S W Evey (VP), Don F Carlos (VP), Moody Covey (VP), John C Linehan (Controller)

PRINCIPAL ACTIVITIES: Exploration, production and sale of petroleum
Parent Company: Texaco Inc, White Plains, NY

Financial Information:

	$'000
Sales revenues	12,300,000

No of Employees: 1,000

GETTY PETROLEUM CORPORATION

175 Sunnyside Boulevard, Plainview, NY 11803
Tel: (516) 576 9500

President: Leo Liebowitz (and Chief Executive Officer)
Senior Executive Officers: Milton Safenowitz (Executive VP), Alvin Smith (Senior VP), Stephen P Salzman (VP and Secretary), John J Fitteron (Senior VP Finance), Milton Cooper (VP), George E De Forest (VP Real Estate), Samuel M Jones (VP and Legal Counsel), Herbert Wechsler (VP Marketing), Lorenzo Cinque (Treasurer)

PRINCIPAL ACTIVITIES: Gasoline and related products
Principal Bank: Chemical Bank
Financial Information:

	$'000
Sales revenues	1,300,000

No of Employees: 1,700

GF CORPORATION

4944 Belmont Avenue, Youngstown, OH 44501
Tel: (216) 759-8888

Chairman: Ronald R Anderson (and President and Chief Executive Officer)
Senior Executive Officers: John C Amer (VP, Secretary and Treasurer), Robert R Austin (VP Operations), Charles R Culhane (VP Manufacturing), Charles J Saylor (VP Marketing), Ronald W Myers (Controller), Ronald W Ogrodnik (VP Human Resources)

PRINCIPAL ACTIVITIES: Manufacture of a wide range of office furniture
Principal Subsidiaries: GF Furniture Systems Inc; Crenlo Inc
Principal Bank: Bank One
Financial Information:

	$'000
Sales revenues	134,513

No of Employees: 1,500

GIANT FOOD INC

PO Box 1804, Washington, DC 20013
Tel: (301) 341-4100

Chairman: *Israel Cohen (and President and Chief Executive Officer)
Senior Executive Officers: *David B Sykes (Senior VP Finance, Secretary and Treasurer), *Alvin Dobbin (Senior VP-Operations), *David N Freedman (Senior VP-Corporate Facilities), *Pete L Manos (Senior VP-Food Operations), *David W Rutstein (Senior VP-General Counsel), Michael J Bush (VP-Real Estate), Ronald A Cooke (VP-Store Operations) Terry A Gans (VP-Advertising and Sales Promotion), George W Hannis Jr (VP-Dairy, Delicatessen, Meat, and Seafood Operations), M Davis Herriman (VP-Grocery Operations), David A Larson (VP-Manufacturing), Albert J Lechert Jr (VP-Construction), Odonna Mathews (VP-Consumer Affairs), *Roger D Olson (VP-Labor Relations and Personnel), Stephen L Oseroff (VP-Shopping Centers), Emanuel Richman (VP-Pharmacy Operations), Barry F Scher (VP-Public Affairs), *Robert W Schoening (VP-Data Processing), Alan Swoff (VP-Frozen Food Operations), *Samuel E Thurston (VP-Distribution), Arthur D Koch (Assistant Secretary), Albert Reinach (Controller), *Members of the Management Committee

PRINCIPAL ACTIVITIES: Giant Food Inc was incorporated in Delaware in 1935 and, together with its subsidiaries, operates a chain of 141 supermarkets selling, at retail, food and general merchandise in Washington, DC, Maryland and Virginia. Of the Company's 141 supermarkets, one of which is a gourmet store, 98 are in the Washington, DC metropolitan area; 36 are in or near Baltimore, Maryland and others are in Fredericksburg, Warrenton, and Charlottesville, Virginia; Salisbury, Annapolis and Frederick, Maryland. The Company operates pharmacies in 87 of its supermarkets and one freestanding drug store
Principal Subsidiaries: Giant DC Inc; Giant of Maryland Inc; Giant of Virginia Inc; Giant of Salisbury Inc; Warex-Jessup Inc; Giant Construction Co Inc; GFS Realty Inc; Landover Wholesale Tobacco Corp; Bursil Inc; LECO Inc
Principal Bank: The National Bank of Washington
Financial Information:

	Feb 22 1986 (52 wks) $'000	Feb 28 1987 (53 wks) $'000
Sales revenues	2,247,218	2,528,492
Income before taxes	102,595	93,266
Net income	57,003	46,453
Dividends	14,990	18,011
Dividends per share	$0.50	$0.60
Earnings per share	$1.90	$1.55
Common stock	30,128	30,128
Retained income	240,249	268,691
Shareholders equity	271,319	299,926

No of Employees: 22,800

GIANT GROUP LIMITED

Highway 453, PO Box 218, Harleyville, SC 29448
Tel: (803) 496 7880
Telefax: (803) 496-5071

Chairman: Burt Sugarman (and President and Chief Executive Officer)
Senior Executive Officers: Roblee B Martin (Senior VP), Terry Kinder (VP, Chief Financial Officer, Secretary and Treasurer)

PRINCIPAL ACTIVITIES: Production of cement; resource recovery
Principal Subsidiaries: Giant Cement Company; Keystone Cement Company
Principal Bank: North Carolina National Bank
Financial Information:

	Dec 31 1985 $'000	Dec 31 1986 $'000
Gross sales	78,394	89,990
Net sales	69,499	81,329
Income before taxes	4,018	23,541
Net income	3,876	21,398*
Earnings per share primary	$0.89	$5.47
Common stock	3,286	4,331
Retained income	6,965	27,886
Shareholders equity	30,021	60,281

*includes extraordinary credit of $6,762,00, $1.77 per share for reduction of income taxes by net operating loss cary forwards

Principal Shareholders: Burt Sugarman
No of Employees: 500

GIBBONS CO

1111 Brickyard Road, Salt Lake City, UT 84110
Tel: (801) 486-2411

Chairman: P M Gibbons (and President and Chief Executive Officer)
Senior Executive Officers: E M Carter (Executive VP), W A Gibbons (Secretary and Treasurer), Jerry L Palmer (Comptroller)

PRINCIPAL ACTIVITIES: Holding company with interests in building and construction and the manufacture of building materials including ready mixed concrete, sand and gravel

Principal Subsidiaries: Gibbons & Reed Co; Circle G Inc; Gibbons Realty Co; Pavement Planning Co
Financial Information:

	$'000
Sales revenues	70,000

No of Employees: 3,000

GIBRALTAR FINANCIAL CORPORATION

9111 Wilshire Blvd, Beverly Hills, CA 90213
Tel: (213) 278-8720

Chairman: Herbert J Young (and President); Chairman of Executive Committee; Jay Janis
Senior Executive Officers: John R Williamson (VP Finance, Secretary and Treasurer), Jerome Nussbaum (Executive VP)

PRINCIPAL ACTIVITIES: Holding company with interests in financial services including savings and loans
Principal Subsidiaries: GFC Insurance Services Inc; GFC Securities Corp; Gibraltar Savings Corp; First Gibraltar Mortgatge Corp; Gibraltar Money Center Inc
Principal Bank: Crocker National Bank
Financial Information:

	Dec 31 1986 $'000
Net income	49,077
Earnings per share	$2.66
Shareholders equity	331,101
Deposits	6,001,205
Total assets	12,248,615

No of Employees: 2,416

GIBRALTAR SAVINGS ASSOCIATION

13401 N Freeway, Houston, TX 77060
Tel: (713) 872-3100
Fax: (713) 872-0016

Chairman: E M Lallinger; Chief Executive Officer: J Livingston Kosberg
Senior Executive Officers: M J B Brookner (Executive VP and Chief Financial Officer), John Averett (President Mortgage Banking Group), R B Stowell (Executive VP), L J Flynne (Senior VP, Secretary and Controller), M L Mayer (Senior VP and Treasurer)

PRINCIPAL ACTIVITIES: Financial services including loans and savings
Parent Company: First Texas Gibraltar Financial Corporation of Delaware
Principal Subsidiaries: Houston Imperial Corporation; GSA/UMC Inc
Principal Bank: InterFirst Bank

Principal Shareholders: First Texas Gibraltar Financial Corporation
No of Employees: 1,057

GIBRALTAR STEEL CORPORATION

2545 Walden Avenue, Buffalo, NY 14225
Tel: (716) 684-1020
Telex: WUT 646215 gibraltar chee

Chairman: Dr Kenneth E Lipke
President: Brian Lipke
Senior Executive Officers: Walter T Erazmus (VP Finance), Joseph A Rosenecker (VP Sales), Carl P Spezio (VP Operations)

PRINCIPAL ACTIVITIES: Manufacturer of steel strapping, cold rolled strip steel converter and service center
Principal Bank: Chase Manhattan
Financial Information:

	$'000
Sales revenues	110,000

Principal Shareholders: Dr Kenneth E Lipke
No of Employees: 400

GIBSON GREETINGS INC

2100 Section Road, Cincinnati, OH 45237
Tel: (513) 841-6600
Telex: 214606

President: T M Cooney (and Chief Executive Officer)
Senior Executive Officers: W M Langford (VP and Secretary), L R Jalenak Jr (VP), D R Taub (VP), W A Cavanaugh (VP), B F Cook (VP), J H Johnson (Treasurer and Controller)

PRINCIPAL ACTIVITIES: Manufacture of stationery products including giftwrap and greetings cards
Parent Company: Bankers Trust Co
Principal Subsidiaries: Gibson Greetings Cards Inc
Principal Bank: Bankers Trust Co
Financial Information:

	$'000
Sales revenues	328,800

No of Employees: 4,000

GIBSON-HOMANS CO

1755 Enterprise Pkwy, Twinsburg, OH 44087
Tel: (216) 425-3255
Telex: WUT 980 206 gh co clv

Chairman: Eric S Wormser; Vice Chairman: Edwin J Hull Jr
President: Douglas E Bryant (and Chief Executive Officer)
Senior Executive Officers: James J Abel (Senior VP Finance), Andy Strachan (Senior VP Marketing), R Brian Tillyer (VP Technical), Alan Stickler (VP Fosroc Division)

PRINCIPAL ACTIVITIES: Manufacture of protective materials for coating roofs, floors and walls
Parent Company: Foseco Minsep Inc
Principal Bank: National City Bank, Cleveland
Financial Information:

	$'000
Sales revenues	68,000

Principal Shareholders: Foseco Minsep PLC, Birmingham, UK
No of Employees: 380

GIFFORD-HILL & COMPANY, INC

300 E John Carpenter Freeway, Irving, TX 75062
Tel: (214) 258-7000

Chairman: John R Hill Jr (and Chief Executive Officer)
President: Thomas B Howard Jr (and Chief Operating Officer)
Senior Executive Officers: R G Turner (Executive VP and Chief Financial Officer), Royce W Montgomery (VP and Secretary), Leon D Allard (VP and General Manager Concrete and Concrete Products Division), E A Decker (VP and General Manager Chemical Division), Dennis P Foster (VP and General Manager Construction Materials), R L Serpan (VP and General Manager Riverside Division), R A Beadle (VP Administration), Allen C Perry (VP) Management Information Systems), Kenneth H Cole (VP Marketing Construction Materials), C P Fontaine (VP Marketing), Bruce Tompkins (VP Cement Division), W T Rush (VP Aggregate)

PRINCIPAL ACTIVITIES: Manufacture of stone products for the construction industry; cement; ready mixed concrete; concrete pipes
Principal Subsidiaries: Amcord Inc; Gifford-Hill American Inc; GHA Lock Joint Inc; Gifco Properties Inc; Gifco Development Co; First Employees Insurance Co; Servetex Materials Co; Gifford-Hill Cement Co of Texas; Texas Concrete Works Inc; G F H Financial Services Corp; Gifford-Hill International Ltd; Picon Transportation Inc; Gifford-Hill Ag Development Ltd; York Manufacturing; Magnum Minerals Inc; Gifford-Hill Cement Co; Gifford-Hill Cement Co of South Carolina; ConAgg Transportation Inc
Principal Bank: InterFirst Bank, Dallas

Financial Information:

	$'000
Sales revenues	435,000

No of Employees: 3,200

GILBERT ASSOCIATES, INC

PO Box 1498, Reading, PA 19603
Tel: (215) 775-2600
Cable: GILASOC
Telex: 836-431

Chairman: Alexander F Smith (and President and Chief Executive Officer)
Senior Executive Officers: James R Itin (VP and Chief Financial Officer), Michael L Alexander (VP), Gregory W Johnson (VP Human Resources), Maurice D James (Treasurer), Robert J Johnson (General Counsel), George L Ball (Controller), Elizabeth J Rutter (Secretary)

PRINCIPAL ACTIVITIES: Engineering consultants, communications equipment, simulation systems
Principal Subsidiaries: Gilbert/Commonwealth, Inc; Gilbert/Commonwealth International, Inc; Gilbert Services Inc; United Energy Services Corporation; Autodynamics, Inc; GAI-Tronics Corporation
Principal Bank: Meridian Bank
Financial Information:

	Jan 3 1986 $'000	Jan 2 1987 $'000
Sales revenues	232,345	235,741
Income before taxes	64,015(1)	19,763(4)
Net income	24,490(2)	9,819(5)
Dividends	4,748	4,529
Dividends per share	$1.70	$1.70
Earnings per share	$8.77(3)	$3.69(6)
Common stock	2,876	2,876
Retained income	77,855	83,145
Shareholders equity	113,818	117,023

(1)(2)(3)(4)(5)(6) include the following effect of non-recurring items
(1) income before taxes $49.571m
(2) net income $17.733m
(3) earnings per share $6.35
(4) income before taxes $4.484m
(5) net income $2.349m
(6) earnings per share $0.88

No of Employees: 3,306

GILBERT PAPER CO

430 Ahnaip Street, Menasha, WI 54952
Tel: (414) 722-7721
Telex: TWX 910 2731 213 gilbert mnsh

President: Patricia B Robinson
Senior Executive Officers: George R Browner Jr (VP Marketing), George W Ruth (VP Operations), Preston L Melton (VP Administration), Carolyn L Paine (Controller)

PRINCIPAL ACTIVITIES: Manufacture of specialized papers
Parent Company: Mead Corporation, Dayton, OH
Financial Information:

	$'000
Sales revenues	55,000

No of Employees: 350

GILLETTE CO

Prudential Tower Building, Boston, MA 02199
Tel: (617) 421-7000

Chairman: Colman M Mockler Jr (and Chief Executive Officer); Vice Chairman: Alfred M Zeien
President: Joseph F Turley (and Chief Operating Officer)
Senior Executive Officers: Rodney S Mills (Executive VP Gillette International), Derwyn F Phillips (Executive VP Gillette North America), Lorne R Waxlax (Executive VP Diversified Operations), Joseph E Mullaney (Senior VP Legal), Thomas F Skelly (Senior VP Finance), Samuel N Schell (Senior VP Diversified Companies), John B Bush Jr (VP Research and Development), David A Fausch (VP Corporate Public Relations), Paul N Fruitt (VP Corporate Planning), Robert P Giovacchini (VP Corporate Product Integrity), Milton L Glass (VP and Treasurer), Michael C Hawley (VP Operations Services), Gaston R Levy (VP, Group General Manager, Latin American Group), Anthony S Lucas (VP and Controller), William J McMorrow (VP, Administration), Robert E Ray (VP, New Business Development), William J Ryan (VP and President Personal Care Division), Robert F Sama (VP and Tax Counsel), Frederick H Stephens Jr (VP Business Relations), Robert H Stier Jr (VP Program Management), John W Symons (VP and Group General Manager, Gillette Europe)

PRINCIPAL ACTIVITIES: The Gillette Company, founded in 1901, is an international consumer products firm engaged in the development, manufacture and sale of a wide range of products for personal care or use. Major lines include blades and razors, toiletries and cosmetics, writing instruments and office products, Braun electric shavers and small appliances and Oral-B oral care products

Trade Names: AAPRI (Facial Scrub, Replenishing Creme and Replenishing Lotion), ACCU-POINT (Rolling Ball Pens), AD MATE (Pens), ADORN (Hair Preparations), ANSWER (Toiletries), ARISTA (Hair Preparations), ARRAY (Hair Preparations), ATRA (Pivoting Head Razors and Blades), ATRA PLUS (Pivoting Head Razor and Blades), BARE ELEGANCE (Body Shampoo), BEHAVE (Hair Preparations), BIG BODY (Perm Rods), BOBBI (Home Permanent), BODY FLOWERS (Body Spray), BRUSH PLUS (Shaving System), BRUSH UP (Denture Cleanser), CLEAR BENEFIT (Hair Prepartions), CLEAR DIFFERENCE (Hair Setting Gel), CURL FREE (Curl Relaxer), CURVE 'N BODY (Perm Rods), DAISY (Disposable Lady's Shaver), DEEP MAGIC (Cleansing Lotions and Moisturizers), DIPPITY DO (Setting Gels), DRIVE (Anti-Perspirants and After Shave), DRY IDEA (Anti-Perspirant), DUNE (Deodorant), EARTH BORN (Shampoo), EL MARKO (Markers), EPIC (Pen), EPIC (Toiletries), ERASER MATE (Pens and Refills), FEEL FREE (Deodorant), FINGER PINKIES (Hand Cleaners), FLAIR (Porous Point and Plastic Point Pens), FOAMY (Shave Preparations), FOHO FOR OILY HAIR ONLY (Shampoo and Rinse), FOOT GUARD (Deodorant), FREE 'N EASY (Shampoo), GILLETTE SUPER-SPEED (Razor), GILLETTE (Shave Creams, Blades, Razors), GILLETTE BLUE BLADES (Blades), GILLETTE SUPER BLUE BLADES (Blades), GOOD NEWS! (Twin Blade Disposable Razors and Toiletries), GYRO (Shave Cream), HAPPY FACE (Cleansing Lotion), HARDHEAD FLAIR (Plastic Tip Pens), HEADS UP (Hair Grooms), HEART (Shampoo), HOLD AND CLEAN (Hair Prepartions), HOT LINER (Pens), JUST FOR COPIES)Opaquing Fluid), JUST WHISTLE (Twin Blade Self-Adjusting Razor), LEMON UP (Shampoo and Creme Rinse), LIQUID PAPER (Correction Fluids and Typewriter Correction Film), LOOK OF NATURE (Setting Gel), MALIBU (Pens and Pen and Pencil Sets), MARINER'S (Skin Lotion), MINK DIFFERENCE (Hair Spray and Shampoo), MISTAKE OUT (Correction Fluid), MY ISLANDS (Women's Cologne), OFF-HAND (Cleaning Towels), PAPER MATE (Ball Point Pens, Fountain Pens, Pencils and Refills), PAPERCREME (Fingertip Moistener), PEN & INK (Correction Fluid), PLATINUM-PLUS (Blades), POWERPOINT (Ball Point Pens and Refills), PROBAK JR (Blades), PROFILE (Pens and Pen and Pencil Sets), PROM (Home Permanent, Hand Lotion and Shampoo), QUICKSILVER FLAIR (Pens), RALLY (Pens), RIGHT GUARD (Deodorants and Anti-Perspirants), ROLLER PERM (Home Permanent), ROLLERSTICK (Rolling Ball Pen), SILKIENCE (Shampoos, Conditioners and Hair Sprays), SILVER CURL (Home Permanent), SOFT & DRI (Anti-Perspirants), SOFT

TOUCH (Toiletries), SPIN (Curlers), S.T. DUPONT (Writing Instruments, Watches, Clocks, Cigarette Lights, Personal Leather Goods, Scarfs and Ties), STATIC (After Shave), SWIVEL (Disposable Pivoting Head Razor), TAME (Hair Preparations), TECH-RAZOR (Razor and Blades), THE DRY LOOK (Hair Control), THE HOT ONE (Shave Cream), THE KNACK (Razor), TIP TONI (Home Permanent), TONETTE (Children's Home Permanent), TONI LIGHTWAVES (Home Permanent), TONI SILKWAVE (Home Permanent), TRAC II (Razor, Blades and Shave Creams), TRINITY (Anti-Perspirants), VALET AUTO-STROP (Blades), WHITE RAIN (Hair Preparations), WIDGET (Scraper and Cutter), WRITE BROS. (Retractable and Stick Pens), X-HYDRA (Anti-Perspirants)

Principal Subsidiaries: Compañia Gillette de Argentina (Argentina); Gillette (Australia) Pty Limited (Australia), Braun AG (Germany)-Its subsidiaries: Braun Argentina SA (Argentina); Braun Electric Austria Ges mbH (Austria); Braun do Brasil & Cia (Brazil); Braun Canada Ltd/Ltée (Canada); Braun Española SA (Spain); Braun Electric Finska AB (Finland); Braun Electric France SA (France); Braun Ireland Ltd (Eire); Braun Italia Srl (Italy); Braun Japan KK (Japan); Braun Electric Nederland BV (Netherlands); Braun Electric (UK) Ltd (UK). Gillette do Brasil Inc and Rio Manufacturing Company (Brazil)-Partners in: Gillette do Brasil & Cia (Brazil)-Its subsidiary: Gillette de Amazônia SA (Brazil). Gillette Canada Inc (Canada); Gillette de Colombia SA (Colombia); Colton Development Inc; Colton Gulf Coast Inc; Colton East Inc; Colton North Central Inc; Colton West Inc; Gillette Capital Corporation-Its Subsidiaries: Jafra Cosmetics Inc; Oral-B Laboratories Inc-Its subsidiaries: Oral-B Laboratories Limited (UK); Oral-B Laboratories Pty Limited (Australia). Gillette Deutschland GmbH (Germany); Gillette Direct Response Group Inc; Gillette Española SA (Spain); Gillette Foreign Sales Corporation Limited (Jamaica); Gillette France (99.9%) (France); Compañia Giva SA-Its subsidiary: Comañia Gillette de Venezuela SA (Venezuela). Compañia Interamericana Gillette SA (Panama); Inter-Nile Manufacturing Company SAE (70%) (Egypt); Gillette Italy SpA (Italy); Gillette (Japan) Inc (Japan); Liquid Paper Corporation; Gillette de Mexico Inc and Mexico Manufacturing Company-Partners in: Gillette de México y Cia de CV (Mexico). Misco Inc; Optimum View Inc; Gillette Overseas Finance Corporation NV (Netherlands Antilles); Gillette Overseas Receivables Corporation NV (Netherlands Antilles); Gillette del Peru Inc and Lima Manufacturing Company-Partners in: Gillette del Peru SC (Peru). Gillette (Philippines) Inc (Philippines); Gillette South Africa Limited (South Africa); S T Dupont (95.5%) (France); Gillette (Switzerland) AG (Switzerland); Gillette Industries Limited (UK)-Its subsidiaries: Gillette UK Limited (UK); Jafra Cosmetics International Limited (UK)
Principal Bank: Bank of Boston
Financial Information:

	Dec 31 1985	Dec 31 1986
	$'000	$'000
Sales revenues	2,400,000	2,818,300
Net income	159,900	15,800
Earnings per share	$5.18	$0.25
Shareholders equity	898,300	460,800

No of Employees: 31,400

GILMAN, MARTY, , INC

Gilman, CT 06336
Tel: (203) 889-7334

President: Shirley J Gilman (and Treasurer)
Senior Executive Officers: Neil Gilman (VP and Secretary)

PRINCIPAL ACTIVITIES: Manufacture of sports equipment
Principal Bank: United Bank and Trust Co
Financial Information:

	$'000
Sales revenues	450,000

No of Employees: 00

GILSTER MARY LEE CO

1037 State Street, Chester, IL 62233
Tel: (618) 826-2361
Telex: 510 520 0084

Chairman: Wm H Welge
President: Donald E Welge
Senior Executive Officers: Michael W Welge (Executive VP, Secretary, Treasurer and Comptroller), Delbert Dethrow (VP), Albert Lindner (VP), Ron Tretter (VP)

PRINCIPAL ACTIVITIES: Manufacture of food mixes and cereal products
Parent Company: Mary Lee Packaging
Principal Bank: Buena Vista National Bank
Financial Information:

	$'000
Sales revenues	150,000

No of Employees: 1,400

GILTSPUR NORTH AMERICA, INC

4616 Henry Street, Pittsburgh, PA 15213
Tel: (412) 621-3700
Telex: TWX 710 6642 040 giltspur pgh

Chairman: R O Cadwalader (UK)
President: Q H Douden
Senior Executive Officers: B F Miller (Secretary and Comptroller)

PRINCIPAL ACTIVITIES: Holding company with interests in the manufacture of fabricated products and exhibition displays
Parent Company: Giltspur Ltd, UK
Principal Subsidiaries: Giltspur Expo Industries, Inc
Principal Bank: Mellon Bank NA
Financial Information:

	$'000
Sales revenues	61,000

No of Employees: 600

GIT INDUSTRIES, INC

345 Hudson Street, New York, NY 10014
Tel: (212) 741-8500

Chairman: R M Cohen; Vice Chairman: Stanley Kreitman
President: Morris Weissman
Senior Executive Officers: J T Gorman, (Executive VP), Walter M Hoft (VP Finance)

PRINCIPAL ACTIVITIES: Recycling of rubber; printing, including stock and bond certificates and commercial printing
Principal Bank: Manufacturers Hanover Trust Co
Financial Information:

	$'000
Sales revenues	94,000

No of Employees: 1,200

GIUMARRA VINEYARDS CORPORATION

PO Bin 1969, Bakersfield, CA 93303
Tel: (805) 366-5511

Chairman: Joe Giumarra
President: Sal Giumarra
Senior Executive Officers: Al Giumarra (VP), Robert L Corsaro (VP), Ted Jablonski (Chief Financial Officer)

PRINCIPAL ACTIVITIES: Viticulture; wine shipping
Financial Information:

	$'000
Sales revenues	50,000

No of Employees: 2,000

GK TECHNOLOGIES INC

500 W Putnam Avenue, Greenwich, CT 06830
Tel: (200) 620 5000

President: Alfred Martinelli (and Chief Executive Officer)

Senior Executive Officers: Herbert Winokor (Senior Executive VP), Edward Kosnik (Executive VP and Chief Financial Officer), Ernest Varalli (Senior VP and Controller), Francis Kareken (Senior VP and Secretary)

PRINCIPAL ACTIVITIES: Manufcture of electrical and electronic components and cable and wire products

Parent Company: Penn Central Corp

Principal Bank: Irving Trust Company

Financial Information:

	$'000
Sales revenues	1,350,000

No of Employees: 23,000

GLADIEUX REFINERY INC

4133 New Haven Avenue, Fort Wayne, IN 46803

Tel: (219) 423-4477

Telex: TWX 810 3321 563 gladieux fwa

President: James M Gladieux (and Chief Executive Officer and Treasurer)

Senior Executive Officers: Michael J Gladieux (VP and Secretary), William C Hittie (VP and Treasurer)

PRINCIPAL ACTIVITIES: Refining of crude oil

Principal Bank: Manufacturers Hanover Trust Company

Financial Information:

	$'000
Sales revenues	190,000

No of Employees: 300

GLATFELTER, P H, CO

228 S Main Street, Spring Grove, PA 17362

Tel: (717) 225-4711

Chairman: P H Glatfelter III

President: T C Norris (and Chief Executive Officer)

Senior Executive Officers: M A Johnson II (Executive VP, Treasurer and Chief Financial Officer), R W Wand (VP Administration), R H Boyer (VP Sales), S L Cozzens (Secretary and Assistant Treasurer), D F Grady (Comptroller and Assistant Secretary)

PRINCIPAL ACTIVITIES: P H Glatfelter Company, headquartered in Spring Grove, Pennsylvania, is a manufacturer of printing, writing, and technical specialty papers at paper mills located in Spring Grove, Pennsylvania and in Neenah, Wisconsin. The Company's products are marketed in most parts of the United States either through wholesale paper merchants and brokers or direct to customers. The Spring Grove facility has, for many years, been an integrated paper manufacturer, producing a substantial part of its fiber requirements from wood. The Neenah mill utilizes recycled high grade wastepapers as its principal raw material. In 1986, about 13% of the total fiber required by the Company was in the form of virgin wood pulp purchased from others. The Glatfelter Pulp Wood Company, a wholly-owned subsidiary, is responsible for woodlands management and procurement of pulpwood from Company-owned land and from independent sources.

Principal Subsidiaries: The Glatfelter Pulp Wood Company

Principal Bank: Provident National Bank

Financial Information:

	Dec 31 1985 $'000	Dec 31 1986 $'000
Sales revenues	277,114	284,832
Income before taxes	71,715	78,173
Net income	39,731	41,474
Dividends*	11,638	12,451
Dividends per share*	$0.455	$0.50
Earnings per share	$1.55	$1.66
Common stock	11,323	271
Retained income	221,916	250,927
Shareholders equity	240,757	250,562

*common stock

No of Employees: 1,700

GLEASON CORPORATION

30 Corporate Woods, PO Box 22856, Rochester, NY 14692
Tel: (716) 272-6000
Telex: 6715107
Fax: (716) 272-6099

Chairman: James S Gleason (and President and Chief Executive Officer)
Senior Executive Officers: Derrell S Lynch (Senior VP Finance and Administration), John B Kodweis (VP Human Resources), James E Thomas (Corporate Controller), Edward C Berlinski (Treasurer), Richard C Hellwig (Assistant Treasurer), Morton A Polster (Secretary, Corporate Counsel), Ralph E Harper (Assistant Secretary, Assistant Corporate Counsel)

PRINCIPAL ACTIVITIES: Manufacture of machine tools
Principal Subsidiaries: Gleason Works Ltd (UK); Gleason Stuttgart (Germany); Gleason Works SA (Belgium); Alliance Tool Corporation; Pennsylvania Pressed Metals Inc; Hackett Precision Co; Gleason Milano (Italy)
Principal Bank: Lincoln First Bank of Rochester
Financial Information:

	Dec 31 1985 $'000	Dec 31 1986 $'000
Sales revenues	228,641	252,185
Income before taxes	2,398	174
Net income	782	347
Earnings per share	$0.14	$0.06
Common stock	5,699	5,726
Retained income	83,069	83,416
Shareholders equity	92,775	94,118

No of Employees: 3,400

GLENDALE FEDERAL SAVINGS & LOAN ASSOCIATION

700 N Brand Blvd, Glendale, CA 91203
Tel: (818) 500-2000

Chairman: Raymond D Edwards (and Chief Executive Officer)
President: Norman M Coulson
Senior Executive Officers: Frank P DePaul (Senior Executive VP), David T Hansen (Senior Executive VP, Financial Services), Keith P Russell (Senior Executive VP)

PRINCIPAL ACTIVITIES: Financial services including savings, loans and mortgage finance
Parent Company: Glenfed Inc

No of Employees: 4,560

GLEN-GERY CORPORATION

1166 Spring Street, PO Box 7001, Wyomissing, PA 19610-6001
Tel: (215) 374-4011
Telex: WUT 902257 glen gery rdg

Chairman: Paul C Hyde-Thompson
President: Richard G Boxall (and Chief Executive Officer)
Senior Executive Officers: Robert D Beverforden (VP Marketing), Romuald W Tymczak (VP Production), Lawson Booker (VP Human Resources), Steve Matsick (VP Finance

and Treasurer), Benjamin Riggs (VP and General Manager), William Peckham (VP and General Manger)

PRINCIPAL ACTIVITIES: Manufacture of bricks and building blocks
Parent Company: Ibstock Johnsen, UK
Principal Bank: Hamilton Bank
Financial Information:

	$'000
Sales revenues	80,000

No of Employees: 1,000

GLENMORE DISTILLERIES CO

Citizens Plaza, Louisville, KY 40202
Tel: (502) 589-0130

Chairman: James Thompson (and President and Chief Executive Officer); Vice Chairmen: Robert M Nash, Joseph B Woodlief
Senior Executive Officers: Tom Reynolds Jr (Executive VP Sales, Sales Administrations and Marketing), Phillip Newman III (1st VP Manufacturing), Keith E Davis (1st VP and Treasurer), Leslie Matson (1st VP Operating Services), Richard S Young (1st VP Sales), Paul R Kirn (VP), James E Lynch (VP Marketing)

PRINCIPAL ACTIVITIES: Manufacture of wines and spirits; wine importers
Principal Subsidiaries: Corbett Canyon Vineyards; Foreign Vintages Inc; Glenmore International Inc; Mr Boston Distiller Corp; Viking Distillery Inc
Principal Bank: Citizens Fidelity Bank
Financial Information:

	$'000
Sales revenues	107,600

No of Employees: 520

GLENSHAW GLASS CO, INC

1101 William Flinn Hwy, Glenshaw, PA 15116
Tel: (412) 961-0200

Chairman: George W Meyer Jr (and Chief Executive Officer)
President: Howard D Caulfield Jr
Senior Executive Officers: Gunter G Rohland (VP Sales and Marketing), Edward M Pierson (VP Finance)

PRINCIPAL ACTIVITIES: Manufacture of glass containers
Principal Bank: Union National Bank
Financial Information:

	$'000
Sales revenues	80,000

No of Employees: 700

GLITSCH, INC

4900 Singleton Blvd, Dallas, TX 75212
Tel: (214) 631-3841
Telex: WUT 73329 glitsch dal

Chairman: R C McKelvy
President: M Acerra
Senior Executive Officers: E McGree (VP Industrial Relations), L A Venincasa (VP Sales), Bob Hill (VP Engineering and Manufacturing), G K Chen (VP Process and Research and Development), R Norton (Secretary and Treasurer)

PRINCIPAL ACTIVITIES: Manufacture of equipment for the petroleum and chemical industries
Parent Company: Foster Wheeler Corp
Principal Bank: Republic National Bank
Financial Information:

	$'000
Sales revenues	150,000

No of Employees: 500

GLOBAL MARINE, INC

777 North Eldridge Road, Houston, TX 77079
Tel: (713) 596-5100

Chairman: C R Luigs (and President and Chief Executive Officer)
Senior Executive Officers: Jerry C Martin (Senior VP and Chief Finance Officer), John G Ryan (Senior VP, Legal Counsel and Secretary), Robert E Sleet Jr (VP and Treasurer), David A Herasimchuk (VP Market Development), James C Schmitz (VP Tax and Government Affairs)

PRINCIPAL ACTIVITIES: Exploration and production of natural gas and oil; marine engineering
Principal Subsidiaries: Applied Drilling Technology Inc; Challenger Minerals Inc; Del Mar Oil & Gas (UK) Ltd; Global Marine Adriatic Inc; Global Marine Baltic Inc; Global Marine Bismarck Sea Inc; Global Marine BV; Global Marine Deepwater Drilling Inc; Global Marine Australia Inc; Global Marine West Africa Inc; Global Marine Development Inc; Global Marine Drilling Co; Global Marine Caribbean Inc; Global Marine Drilling Services; Global Marine Nautilus Inc; Global Marine North Sea Inc; Global Marine (Malaysia) SDN
Principal Bank: Bank of America
Financial Information:

	$'000
Sales revenues	380,000

No of Employees: 2,700

GLOBAL NATURAL RESOURCES INC

5300 Memorial Drive, Suite 900, Houston, TX 77007
Tel: (713) 880 5464

President: John R Dempsey (and Chief Executive Officer)
Senior Executive Officers: Mhare M Peschel (VP, Secretary and Treasurer), Walter E Belt Jr (VP Land), Gary L Trotter (VP Operations)

PRINCIPAL ACTIVITIES: Production of oil and natural gas
Financial Information:

	$'000
Sales revenues	50,000

No of Employees: 60

GLOBE GLASS & MIRROR CO

1880 W Fullerton Avenue, Chicago, IL 60614
Tel: (312) 278-6900

President: Joseph Kellman
Senior Executive Officers: Ed Cheskis (Executive VP), Gladys Lazar (VP)

PRINCIPAL ACTIVITIES: Manufacture of glass and glass products
Principal Subsidiaries: Continental Illinois National Bank and Trust Co
Financial Information:

	$'000
Sales revenues	60,000

No of Employees: 800

GLOBE NEWSPAPER CO

135 Wm T Morrissey Blvd, Boston, MA 02107
Tel: (617) 929-2000

Chairman: Wm O Taylor; Vice Chairman; John P Guiggio
President: Richard O Ockerbloom
Senior Executive Officers: David Stanger (Senior VP and General Manager), Millard G Owen (VP Sales and Marketing), Arthur F Kingsbury (VP, Treasurer and Chief Financial Officer)

PRINCIPAL ACTIVITIES: Publication of newspapers
Parent Company: Affiliated Publications Inc, Boston, MA
Principal Bank: State Street Bank and Trust Company

Financial Information:

	$'000
Sales revenues	250,000

No of Employees: 1,850

GODCHAUX-HENDERSON SUGAR CO, INC

PO Box 5308, Denver, CO 80217
Tel: (303) 534-1930
Telex: TWX 810 950658 godhen I resvv

President: Douglas Hunt (and Chief Executive Officer)
Senior Executive Officers: Ramon Luzarraga Jr (VP Cane Sugar Manufacturing), Calvin A Rousse (VP Engineering and Development)

PRINCIPAL ACTIVITIES: Sugar refining
Parent Company: Great Western Sugar Company, Denver, CO
Financial Information:

	$'000
Sales revenues	268,000

Principal Shareholders: Hunt International Resources Corporation, Dallas, TX

GODFREY COMPANY

1200 West Sunset Drive, Waukesha, WI 53187
Tel: (414) 542 9311

Chairman: Robert F Norris (and Chairman Executive Committee)
President: James H DeWees (and Chief Executive and Chief Operating Officer)
Senior Executive Officers: Allen C Gehrke (Senior VP), Rodger G Scott (Senior VP), Michael J George (VP, Chief Financial Officer and Treasurer), Douglas R Barth (VP Wholesale Operations), Edward T O'Donnell (VP and Controller), Rodney E Vaughan (VP Merchandising), Kenneth F Wilkinson (VP Meats)

PRINCIPAL ACTIVITIES: Operation of retail outlets selling wide range of goods including groceries, drugs and hardware
Principal Subsidiaries: Artesian Farms Inc; Ball Motor Service Inc; Crestwood Bakery Inc; Hub City Foods Inc; Jay's of Waukesha Inc; Sentry Drugs Inc; Sentry Markets Inc; Store Equipment Inc; Sunrise Wholesale Inc
Principal Bank: First WI National Bank
Financial Information:

	$'000
Sales revenues	601,800

No of Employees: 2,500

GOLD FIELDS AMERICAN CORPORATION

230 Park Avenue, New York, NY 10169
Tel: (212) 880-5100
Telex: WUI 620858 azcon

Chairman: Rudolph I Agnew; Vice Chairman: J H Wood (and Chief Executive Officer)
Senior Executive Officers: Vincent A Filippone (Executive VP), Edward Virshup (VP Tax), Joseph E Davis (VP Finance)

PRINCIPAL ACTIVITIES: Manufacture of steel products including heavy equipment for oil exploration; processing of scrap metal; mining of precious metals
Parent Company: Consolidated Gold Fields PLC, London, UK
Principal Bank: Morgan Guaranty Trust Co
Financial Information:

	$'000
Sales revenues	430,000

No of Employees: 20

GOLD FIELDS AMERICAN INDUSTRIES, INC

230 Park Avenue, New York, NY 10017
Tel: (212) 880-5250

Chairman: J H Wood; Vice Chairman: C Spence
President: R A Secrist
Senior Executive Officers: V A Filippone (VP Legal and Administration), W M Kelly (VP Operations)

PRINCIPAL ACTIVITIES: Manufacture of steel and steel products
Principal Bank: Morgan Guaranty Trust Co
Financial Information:

	$'000
Sales revenues	300,000

Principal Shareholders: Consolidated Gold Fields PLC, London, UK
No of Employees: 2,500

GOLD KIST INC

244 Perimeter Center Pkwy NE, Atlanta, GA 30346
Tel: (404) 393-5000
Telex: WUT 708404 goldkist a atl

Chairman: Holmes Neel; Chairman of Management Executive Committee: W W Gaston (and Chief Executive Officer)
President: D W Sands
Senior Executive Officers: Harold O Chitwood (Executive Group VP), Gaylord O Coan (Executive Group VP), Michael A Stimpert (Group VP), Lester F Schanke (VP Retail Operations), Peter J Gibbons (VP Finance), W A Epperson (VP Human Resources), Paul G Brower (VP Communications), Jean Rice (VP Public Relations and Advertising), Jack L Lawing (VP Law and Secretary), Jerry Stewart (VP Marketing Poultry Group), Kenneth N Whitmire (VP Operations Poultry Group), Jack K Hogan (VP Administration), Allen Merritt (VP Fertilizer and Chemical Division), Ray Lollar (VP Information Services), John McLaughlin (VP Feed and Animal Health Division)

PRINCIPAL ACTIVITIES: Cooperative organisation with interests in the manufacture of fertilizers and insecticides; production of nuts, eggs, meat, grain products and animal feeds
Principal Subsidiaries: Agra Trade Financing Inc; Agri International Inc; Agratech Seeds Inc; Golden Poultry Co Inc; Luker Engineering Fabricating Corp; Agvestments Inc
Principal Bank: Columbia Bank for Cooperatives
Financial Information:

	Jun 30 1986 $'000
Sales revenues	1,394,877
Shareholders equity	133,849

No of Employees: 8,790

GOLD KIST PEANUTS

PO Box 2210, Atlanta, GA 30301
Tel: (404) 393-5469

Chairman: William W Gaston (and Chief Executive Officer)
President: D W Sands (and Chief Operating Officer)
Senior Executive Officers: Michael A Stimpert (Group VP)

PRINCIPAL ACTIVITIES: Production of peanuts and peanut products
Parent Company: Gold Kist Inc, Atlanta, GA
Financial Information:

	$'000
Sales revenues	56,000

No of Employees: 250

GOLDEN DIPT CO

12813 Flushing Meadow Drive, St Louis, MO 63131
Tel: (314) 821-3113
Telex: TWX 9107601403 goldendipt stl

President: Richard J Hurni (and General Manager)
Senior Executive Officers: Lige Jessup (VP Sales, Processor Division), Jim O'Leary (VP Sales), Steven E Dyvig (VP Sales, Grocery Products Division), James M Kragenbring (VP Sales, Foodservice/Institutional), Dale J Ewalt (VP Operations), Bernard E Woltering (Divisional Comptroller)

PRINCIPAL ACTIVITIES: Manufacture of bakery products
Parent Company: DCA Food Industries Inc
Financial Information:

	$'000
Sales revenues	80,000

No of Employees: 300

GOLDEN EAGLE REFINING CO

707 Wilshire Blvd, Los Angeles, CA 90017
Tel: (213) 624-7841
Telex: WUT 688475 goldenegl lsa

President: David Bacigalupo
Senior Executive Officers: Murray Covert (VP Refinery Sales and Supply), Tom Sloan (Treasurer)

PRINCIPAL ACTIVITIES: Manufacture of petroleum products
Parent Company: American Ultramar Ltd, New York, NY
Principal Bank: Union Bank
Financial Information:

	$'000
Sales revenues	225,000

Principal Shareholders: Ultramar PLC, London, UK
No of Employees: 70

GOLDEN ENTERPRISES INC

2101 Magnolia Avenue, Birmingham, AL 35205
Tel: (205) 326-6101

Chairman: Sloan Y Bashinsky (and Chief Executive Officer)
President: J Wallace Nall
Senior Executive Officers: John H Shannon (VP, Secretary and Controller)

PRINCIPAL ACTIVITIES: Manufacture of a wide range of snack products including popcorn, peanuts and potato chips; also interests in advertising and the manufacture of nuts, bolts and screws
Trade Names: Golden Flake
Principal Subsidiaries: Golden Flake Snack Foods, Inc; Steel City Bolt & Screw, Inc; Nall & Associates, Inc
Principal Bank: AmSouth Bank, N.A.
Financial Information:

	$'000
Sales revenues	117,000

No of Employees: 1,580

GOLDEN NUGGET, INC

129 E Fremont St, Las Vegas, NV 89101
Tel: (702) 385-7111

Chairman: Stephen A Wynn (and President and Chief Executive Officer)
Senior Executive Officers: Barry A Shier (Executive VP Hotel Operations), Clyde T Turner (Executive VP, Chief Financial Officer and Treasurer), Shannon L Bybee (Senior VP), Douglas G Pool (VP Finance), Kenneth R Wynn (VP Design and Construction, and Secretary), Bruce A Levin (VP and Legal Counsel), James Powers (VP Corporate Security), George Thompson (VP Slot Operations and Special Projects), James G Burns Jr (VP Information Systems), James E Pettis (VP Risk Management)

PRINCIPAL ACTIVITIES: Operation of hotels, restaurants and casinos
Principal Subsidiaries: Atlandia Design & Furnishings Inc; GNLV Corp; GNOC Corp; Golden Nugget (Asia) Ltd; Leisure Time Tours Inc; SCB Development Co Inc; Tyoh Advertising Inc
Principal Bank: Valley Bank of Nevada
Financial Information:

	$'000
Sales revenues	382,000

No of Employees: 5,500

GOLDEN STATE FOODS CORPORATION

639 57th Ave, Box 1448, City of Industry, CA 91749
Tel: (213) 686 0347

President: James E Williams (and Chief Executive Officer)
Senior Executive Officers: Jerry L Gilomen (Senior Executive VP), James R McMaster (Executive VP), Robert O McMaster (Senior VP), Gene L Olson (VP Finance and Secretary)

PRINCIPAL ACTIVITIES: Meat processing; distribution of food products to the catering trade
Principal Bank: Bank of America
Financial Information:

	$'000
Sales revenues	540,000

No of Employees: 1,200

GOLDEN SUN FEEDS, INC

PO Box 517, Estherville, IA 51334
Tel: (712) 362-3551

Chairman: Donald Slotkin
President: Robert L Hammond
Senior Executive Officers: Marvin Rohlf (VP Research and Nutrition), Harold C Hauber (VP Sales and Marketing), Bruce Scott (VP Purchasing), Maurice Show (VP Operations and Chief Engineer), John Ball (Controller)

PRINCIPAL ACTIVITIES: Manufacture of animal feedstuffs
Parent Company: John Morrell & Co Inc, Winnetka, IL
Principal Bank: United Central Bank of Estherville
Financial Information:

	$'000
Sales revenues	75,000

Principal Shareholders: United Brands Company, New York, NY
No of Employees: 300

GOLDEN WEST FINANCIAL CORPORATION

1901 Harrison St, Oakland, CA 94612
Tel: (415) 446-6000

Chairman: Herbert M Sandler
President: Marion O Sandler
Senior Executive Officers: James T Judd (Executive VP), J L Helvey (Senior VP Finance), Russell W Kettell (Executive VP), Richard A Crane (VP and Secretary), David C Welch (Senior VP and Treasurer)

PRINCIPAL ACTIVITIES: Holding company with interests in loans and savings
Principal Bank: Union Bank
Financial Information:

	Dec 31 1985	Dec 31 1986
	$'000	$'000
Revenues	1,384,525	1,358,947
Net income	160,040	183,808
Earnings per share	$5.14	$5.89
Shareholders equity	472,102	651,170
Total assets	12,129,556	12,435,350

No of Employees: 2,600

GOLDEN WEST HOMES

1308 Wakeham Avenue, Santa Ana, CA 92705
Tel: (714) 835-4200

Chairman: William Lyon
President: Harry Karsten Jr (and Chief Executive Officer)
Senior Executive Officers: Lawrence E Wessel (VP, Chief Financial Officer and Secretary), William R Oakes (VP Operations)

PRINCIPAL ACTIVITIES: Manufacture of sectional buildings
Principal Bank: Bank of America

Financial Information:

	$'000
Sales revenues	72,000

No of Employees: 909

GOOCH PACKING CO

800 Almond Street, Abilene, TX 79604

Tel: (915) 673-8223

President: Jim Garrison

Senior Executive Officers: Blaine Badenstein (VP Operations), Ray Schwertner (VP Finance), Robert W Morford (VP and Secretary)

PRINCIPAL ACTIVITIES: Packaging of meat products and wholesale trade in frozen foods

Parent Company: Cullum Companies Inc, Dallas, TX

Principal Bank: Citizens National Bank

Financial Information:

	$'000
Sales revenues	100,000

No of Employees: 400

GOODALL RUBBER COMPANY

572 Whitehead Raod, Trenton, NJ 08604

Tel: (609) 587-4000

Telex: WUT 843 432 goodall hq trn

Chairman: Rune Andersson

President: Claes Svensson (and Chief Executive Officer)

Senior Executive Officers: A J Rosso (Treasurer), R L Brictson (VP), P D Smith (VP, General Counsel and Secretary)

PRINCIPAL ACTIVITIES: Manufacture of rubber goods including boots, clothing, belting, hose and packaging; plastic goods including industrial goods and pipe

Parent Company: Trelleborg AB, Trelleborg, Sweden

Principal Subsidiaries: Rubberhide Co, Inc; Goodall Rubber Co of Canada; Goodall Transportation Company

Principal Bank: New Jersey National Bank

Financial Information:

	$'000
Sales revenues	92,000

No of Employees: 1,000

GOODRICH, B F, COMPANY (THE)

3925 Embassy Parkway, Akron, OH 44313

Tel: (216) 374-2000

Chairman: John D Ong (and Chief Executive Officer)

President: Leigh Carter (and Chief Operating Officer)

Senior Corporate Management: D Lee Tobler (Executive VP and Chief Financial Officer), Donald G Barger Jr (VP and Controller), Matthew J Battista (VP Administrative and Management Information Services), Nicholas J Calise (Secretary), C William Gray (VP, Human Resources), Jon V Heider (VP and General Counsel), Robert A Macmillan (VP and Treasurer), George K Sherwood (VP, Tax Administration)

PRINCIPAL ACTIVITIES: Manufacture of plastics, specialty chemicals, aerospace and defense products and other polymer-based products for commercial, consumer, industrial and construction applications

Financial Information:

	Dec 31 1985	Dec 31 1986
	$'000	$'000
Sales revenues	3,200,500	2,553,300
Income (loss) before taxes	(292,000)	63,000
Net income (loss)	(354,600)	32,700
Dividends	36,700	37,400
Dividends per share*	$1.56	$1.56
Earnings (loss) per share	($15.79)	$1.32
Common stock	118,800	118,800
Retained income	351,800	347,100
Shareholders equity	690,100	814,700

*common stock

No of Employees: 11,914

GOODY PRODUCTS, INC

969 Newark Turnpike, Kearny, NJ 07032

Tel: (201) 997-3000

Cable: Celcomb Krny

TWX: Goody Krny 710-995-4795

Chairman: Leonard Goodman (and President)

Senior Executive Officers: Robert Z Rothstein (Executive VP), Marvin Katz (VP, General Counsel, Secretary), Hiram Silverman (VP, Finance and Treasurer), Robert Spittel (VP, Sales), Earl Holden (VP, Manufacturing Operations), Stanley Goldberg (VP, Warehousing and Distribution)

PRINCIPAL ACTIVITIES: Goody Products, Inc is primarily engaged in the design, manufacture and sale of a wide variety of hair care accessories under the "Goody" trademark. The Company produces barrettes, ponytail holders, combs, brushes and rollers. The Company's products are used by women of all ages for styling and decorating their hair. Goody Products is generally recognised as the leading hair accessories company in the world. Opti-Ray, Inc, a subsidiary of Goody, markets a complete line of sunglasses

Trade Names: Goody, Opti-Ray, Duray, Opti-Ray Coppertone Sunglasses

Principal Subsidiaries: Opti-Ray; Duray; Southeastern Box; Goody Canada Ltd; Ace Comb

Principal Bank: First National Bank of Boston

Financial Information:

	Dec 31 1985	Dec 31 1986
	$'000	$'000
Sales revenues	133,500	163,668
Income before taxes	10,116	14,982
Net income	5,813	6,435
Dividends	1,461	1,966
Dividends per share	$0.233	$0.306
Earnings per share	$0.93	$1.00
Common stock*	6,249	6,404
Retained income	55,568	60,037
Shareholders equity	61,635	66,883

*number of shares in thousands

No of Employees: 3,100

GOODYEAR TIRE & RUBBER COMPANY

1144 E Market Street, Akron, OH 44316

Tel: (216) 796-2121

Chairman: Robert E Mercer (and Chief Executive Officer); Vice Chairman: Ib Thomsen

President: Tom H Barrett (and Chief Operating Officer)

Senior Executive Officers: James R Glass (Executive VP Finance and Planning), Jacques R Sardas (Executive VP President International), James A Bailey (Executive VP Tire Division, President North American Tire Operations), F V Prus (Executive VP Research and Development), Westi Hansen (Executive VP General Products), Stanley J Mihelick (Executive VP Corporate Manufacturing), R W Milk (Executive VP Materials Management), Frank R Tully (VP Industrial Relations), Earl W Dahl (VP Product Quality and Safety),

George S Lenox (VP Advertising), Fredrick S Myers (VP, Secretary and Legal Counsel), Dennis E Dick (VP General Products Research and Development), Hoyt M Wells (VP Domestic General Products Manufacturing), Frederick J Kovac (VP Tire Development), Richard A Davies (VP Tire and Textile Manufacturing), Nissim Calderon (VP Research), Oren G Shaffer (VP and Treasurer), James E McDonald (VP and Comptroller), Richard G Pruett Jr (VP OE Sales), Joseph C Graden (VP Manufacturing, International), Robert M Hehir (VP Government Environmental Safety, Health Assurance Programs), William R Miller (VP Government Relations), Stanley C Rose (VP Merchandise Distribution and Controller), Douglas F Hill (VP OE Tire Sales), James W Barnett (VP Tire Sales and Marketing), William L Newkirk (VP Public Relations)

PRINCIPAL ACTIVITIES: Manufacture of rubber prodcuts including tires, aircraft components and footwear components; synthetic rubber products, chemicals and plastics

Principal Subsidiaries: Celeron Corporation; Celeron Oil & Gas Co Inc; Lig Chemical Co; Mid LA Gas Co; Cosmoflex Inc; Goodyear Aerospace Corp; Air Treads Inc; Goodyear Atomic Corp; Goodyear Farms Inc; Litchfield Park Service Co; Goodyear Financial Corp; Goodyear International Corp; Goodyear International Export Corp; Goodyear International Finance Corp; Goodyear Rubber Plantations Co; Goodyear Western Hemispheres Corp; Hose Coupling Manufacturing Co; Lee Tire & Rubber Co; Litchfield Park Properties Inc; Motor Wheel Corp; Reneer Films Corp

Financial Information:

	Dec 31 1985	Dec 31 1986
	$'000	$'000
Sales revenues	9,896,700	10,327,700
Net income	412,400	124,100
Earnings per share	$3.84	$1.16
Shareholders equity	-	3,002,600

No of Employees: 133,115

GORDON JEWELRY CORPORATION

820 Fannin Street, Houston, TX 77002
Tel: (713) 222 8080

Co-Chairman: Aron S Gordon, Harry B Gordon; Vice Chairman: W Lowry Barfield (and Chief Financial Officer and Secretary)

President: Daniel P Gordon

Senior Executive Officers: James C Gordon (Executive VP and Chief Operating Officer), Vincent Ambriola (Senior VP Information Systems), Douglas B Gordon (Senior VP Corporate Development), Larry T Hampton (Senior VP and Director Human Resources), Stanley J Hoffman (Senior VP Administration), William R Leighton (Senior VP Finance, Treasurer and Controller), Leonard R Schneider (Senior VP Real Estate), Joe F Williams (VP Store Design and Construction), Robert A Miller Jr (VP Store Systems and Administration)

PRINCIPAL ACTIVITIES: Manufacture of jewelry; operation of jewelry retail outlets

Principal Subsidiaries: Alltex Data Center Inc; Citizens Jewelry Inc; Consolidated Wholesale and Discount Inc; D P Paul Jewelers Company of NC; Daniels Jewelry Company of AZ; Feders Jewelry Company Inc Bassett; Feders Jewelry Inc; Globe Distributors Inc Cocoa; Gordon Importing Company Inc; Gordon Jewelry Company of AR; Gordon Jewelry Company of TX Inc; Gordon Jewelry Corporation FL; Gordon Realty Corporation; Gordon-Chandler Jewelry Inc; Gordons Jewelers Inc; Gordons Jewelry Company Dallas; Gordons Jewelry Company in Village Center; Gordons Jewelry Company of Baytown; Gordons Jewelry Company of Monroe; Gordons Jewelry Panama PLZ; Gordons-Eastern Hills Mall Inc; Gulf Coast Jewelry Specialty Company Mobile; J Herbert Hall Company Inc; Hamilton Wholesale Jewelry Company; R Harris & Company Inc; Hordon-Cielo Vista Mall Inc; Jaccard & King Jewelry Company; Jaccards Raleigh Springs Inc; Jaccards Springfield Inc; Jewelry of New Orleans Inc; Lawtons Hollywood Inc; Lawtons Jewelry Company Inc; Lawtons Tampa Inc; Linz Brothers Inc; Mermod Jaccard King Jewelry KNS; Mermod Jaccard King Jewelry NE; Mermod Jaccard King Jewelry OH; National Alts Life Insurance Company; Oskamp-Nolting Company Inc; D P Paul-Eastland Mall Inc; D P Paul Jewelers Inc; D P Paul Jewelry Company Inc; Rost Jewelry Company Inc; Southern Realty Corporation; Southwestern Wholesale Jewelry Inc; Star Engraving Company; B H Stief Jewelry Company Inc; J J Sweeney Jewelry Company Inc; Traditional Jewelers of America; United Bescar Jewelers Distributing; United General Products Knox Inc; United Jewelers & Distributors; United Jewelers & Distributors LA; United Jewelers Distribution House; United Jewelers and Distributors Baytown; United St Petersburg Inc; United-Voss Road Inc; Universal Service Bureau Inc

Principal Bank: Texas Commerce Bank

Financial Information:

	$'000
Sales revenues	502,000

No of Employees: 6,100

GORMAN-RUPP CO

305 Bowman Street, Box 1217, Mansfield, OH 44901
Tel: (419) 755-1011
Telex: WUT 987422 gormanrupp mfl

President: James C Gorman (and Chief Executive Officer)

Senior Executive Officers: K J Bargahiser (VP), Kenneth E Dudley (Treasurer), Jeffrey S Gorman (Corporate Secretary)

PRINCIPAL ACTIVITIES: Manufacture of pumping equipment

Principal Subsidiaries: Gorman-Rupp of Canada Ltd; Gorman-Rupp International Company

Principal Bank: Bank One of Mansfield

Financial Information:

	Dec 31 1986
	$'000
Sales revenues	65,274
Income before taxes	8,218
Net income	4,397
Dividends	3,151
Dividends per share	$0.80
Earnings per share	$1.12
Common stock	5,203
Retained income	40,736
Shareholders equity	45,330

No of Employees: 740

GOSHEN RUBBER CO, INC

1525 S 10th, Goshen, IN 46526
Tel: (219) 533-1111
Telex: TWX 8102900992 goshrubber

Chairman: William J Johnson

President: William P Johnson (and Treasurer)

Senior Executive Officers: Carroll D Hobson (Senior VP Manufacturing and Engineering), Robert Alexander (VP Finance), L F Yann (VP Industrial Relations), John P Gilleese (VP Sales), Richard Robbins (VP Materials), Edward S Johnson (VP Canadian Operations), LaMar D Malone (VP Product Development)

PRINCIPAL ACTIVITIES: Manufacture of molded rubber products

Principal Subsidiaries: GNC Corp; GRN Corp; GSH Corp; Simmons Mold & Machine Inc

Principal Bank: Salem Bank

Financial Information:

	$'000
Sales revenues	60,000

No of Employees: 700

GOTTSCHALKS INC

860 Fulton Mall, Fresno, CA 93721

Tel: (209) 485-1111

Telefax: (209) 266-5238

Chairman: Joseph W Levy (and Chief Executive Officer)

President: Gerald H Blum (and Chief Operating Officer and Secretary)

Senior Executive Officers: Gary L Gladding (VP Merchandising), Robert E Lawson (VP and Chief Financial Officer), Jack B Moody (VP Advertising), Michael J Schmidt (VP Stores), Diane F Wilson (VP Personnel)

PRINCIPAL ACTIVITIES: Department store trading

Principal Bank: Wells Fargo

Financial Information:

	Jan 31 1986	Jan 31 1987
	$'000	$'000
Sales revenues	112,785	125,924*
Income before taxes	5,863	7,912
Net income	3,005	4,021
Earnings per share	$0.55	$0.57
Common stock	5,500	7,091
Retained income	3,005	4,021
Shareholders equity	10,861	29,605

*Sales Jan 31 1988 $156,224,000

No of Employees: 2,300

GOULD COMPUTER SYSTEMS INC

6901 W Sunrise Blvd, Fort Lauderdale, FL 33313

Tel: (305) 587-2900

Telex: TWX 510 9559821

President: C S James

Senior Executive Officers: Gerald E Rodts (VP Marketing and Sales), L Harwood (VP Operations), S Dinkes (VP Finance), R C Baker (VP Development), W Ward (VP Advanced Development), D Squires (VP Human Resources), J Wright (VP International Operations)

PRINCIPAL ACTIVITIES: Manufacture of mini-computers

Parent Company: Gould Inc, Rolling Meadows, Inc

Principal Bank: Southeast First National Bank of Miami

Financial Information:

	$'000
Sales revenues	130,000

No of Employees: 2,300

GOULD INC

10 Gould Center, Rolling Meadows, IL 60008

Tel: (312) 640-4000

Chairman: James F McDonald (and Chief Executive Officer);

Senior Executive Officers: Harry A Caunter (Executive VP-Defense Systems), C David Ferguson (Executive VP-Materials and Components), C Shelton James (Executive VP-Information Systems), John E Jones (Executive VP-Instrumentation and Automation Systems), Charles M Brennan III (Senior VP-Chief Financial Officer and Treasurer), Richard L Williams III (Senior VP-Administration and General Counsel), Robert M Penn (Group VP-Semiconductore), Peter R Strong (Group VP-Test and Measurement), James E Forrest (VP-Strategic Planning), Jerry W Gaskin (VP and Controller), Nancy R Jack (VP and Secretary), Patrick L Rickard (VP), George W Welsh (VP-Corporate Development), Arnold W Frees (VP-Corporate Communications)

PRINCIPAL ACTIVITIES: Manufacture of data processing equipment; medical and scientific instruments; aerospace equipment and components; defense systems

Financial Information:

	Dec 31 1985*	Dec 31 1986*
	$'000	$'000
Sales revenues	923,200	908,800
Income (loss) before taxes	(82,800)	57,100
Net income (loss)	(102,400)	34,600
Dividends per share	$0.68	$0.34
Earnings (loss) per share	($2.29)	$0.77
Common stock	44,300	44,500
Shareholders equity	674,000	557,700

*continuing operations

No of Employees: 10,600

GOULD PAPER CORPORATION

315 Park Ave S, Street, New York, NY 10010

Tel: (212) 505-1000

Telex: 422 636

Chairman: Harry E Gould Jr (and President)

Senior Executive Officers: Robert I Anderson (Executive VP Sales), D J Lala (Executive VP), Peter J Gould (Senior VP), Richard Irwin (Senior VP Sales and General Manager Publishing, Papers Division), Rudolph J Sanson (VP, Secretary and Treasurer)

PRINCIPAL ACTIVITIES: Manufacture of paper; manufacture of agricultural machinery

Principal Subsidiaries: Ingalls Manufacturing Inc; McNair Manufacturing Inc; Samuel Porritt & Co; Weiss Manufacturing Inc

Principal Bank: Chemical Bank

Financial Information:

	$'000
Sales revenues	130,000

No of Employees: 300

GOULDS PUMPS, INC

240 Fall Street, Seneca Falls, NY 13148

Tel: (315) 568-2811

Telex: 256401 SEFS UR

Chairman: Robert L Tarnow

President: Stephen V Ardia

Senior Executive Officers: Eugene B Bradshaw (VP, Secretary and General Counsel), H R Lemcke (Group VP, Water Technologies), C J Connell (Group VP, Industrial Products), J M Morphy (VP, Chief Financial Officer), Linda L Polcaro (Corporate Treasurer), R F Landers (Director Human Resource), R W Montembeault (General Manager PRO Shops), A H Stuhlreyer (VP, General Manager Water Systems Division), F J Zonarich (VP Sales, Industrial Products Group), J K Kilbane (VP Industrial Operations), J A Nelson (VP Water Technologies Group/Corporate Communications)

PRINCIPAL ACTIVITIES: Designing, manufacturing and servicing pumps for industrial, agricultural, commercial and consumer markets.

Trade Names: Goulds Pumps Inc, Morris Pump Division, Goyne Pump Division, Gaso Pumps, Perma-Base (TM) (Bedplate), SumpThing (TM) (Submersible water pump)

Principal Subsidiaries: Gaso Pumps Inc; Goulds Pumps (Philippines) Inc (Philippines); Goulds Pumps Canada Inc (Canada)

Principal Bank: Citibank NA

Financial Information:

	Dec 31 1986 $'000
Sales revenues	356,226
Income before taxes	23,407
Net income	16,815
Dividends	13,563
Dividends per share	$0.76
Earnings per share	$0.96
Common stock	18,283
Retained income	117,616
Shareholders equity	138,178

No of Employees: 3,600

GOVERNMENT SYSTEMS SECTOR

PO Box 37, Melbourne, FL 32902
Tel: (305) 727-4000

Senior Executive Officers: F J Lewis (Senior VP and Sector Group Executive), C J Herbert (VP and General Manager, Government Information Services Division), J Rosa (VP and General Manager Government Electronic Systems Division), J C Robertson (VP Manufacturing Operations, J C Hunt (Controller)

PRINCIPAL ACTIVITIES: Data processing equipment; computer software and services; electronic equipment; telecommunications
Parent Company: Harris Corporation, Melbourne, FL
Principal Bank: National City Bank
Financial Information:

	$'000
Sales revenues	280,000

No of Employees: 4,000

GRABER INDUSTRIES

Graber Plaza, Middleton, WI 53562
Tel: (608) 836-1011

President: James M Sheridan (and Chief Executive Officer)
Senior Executive Officers: R A Branflick (VP Finance), J E Cole (VP Marketing), Kent Anderson (VP Operations), F R Nichols (VP Sales)

PRINCIPAL ACTIVITIES: Manufacture of blinds (horizontal and vertical), drapery hardware and shades for windows
Parent Company: Springs Industries Inc, Fort Mill, SC
Financial Information:

	$'000
Sales revenues	85,000

No of Employees: 1,400

GRACE, W R, & CO

1114 Avenue of the Americas, New York, NY 10036
Tel: (212) 819-5500

Chairman: J P Grace (and Chief Executive Officer); Vice Chairmen: Charles H Erhart Jr (and Chief Administration Officer), D W Robbins Jr (and Chairman Executive Committee)
President: Carl N Graf (and Chief Operating Officer)
Senior Executive Officers: J P Bolduc (Executive VP and Chief Financial Officer), Albert E Eustis (Executive VP, Secretary and Legal Counsel), Francis J Brennan (Senior VP Staff and Treasurer)

PRINCIPAL ACTIVITIES: Manufacture of chemicals; mining; oil and gas production
Principal Subsidiaries: Amargosa Pipeline Corp; American Breeders SV Canada Corp; Axial Basin Ranch Co; Baker & Taylor GmbH; Baker & Taylor of CA Ltd; Bartow Chemical Products Co; Beckett Golf Club Inc; Berman Catalog Sales Inc; Berry Gas Co; Booker Drilling Co Inc; Borg Holding AG; Coalgrace Inc; H-G Coal Co; Davison Specialty Chemical Co; Daylin-Summit Inc; DDI Realty Inc; Del Taco Corp; Devcoa Inc; Diners Rendezvous Inc; Drilling Mud Co; Drys Inc; Dunbee-Elm Ltd; Duncan Lagnese & Associates Inc; Ecarg Inc; Ecotrol Inc; Elm-Dundee Inc; Emabond Inc; Emerson & Cuming Inc; Envases Industriales y Comerciales SA; Federation Chemicals Ltd; G/R of PA Inc; GHL Management Inc; Joe Gilbert Restaurants Inc; Gilbert/Robinson Inc; Gloucester New Communities Co; Grace & Co Central America; Grace Communications Inc; Grace Drilling Co; Grace Industrial Chemicals Co; Grace Oil Corp (Italy); Grace Oxo-Alcohols Inc; Grace Petroleum Corp; Petrodyne Ltd; Grace Petroleum Libya Inc; Grace Restaurant Co; El Torito Restaurants Inc; W R Grace Capital Corp; W R Grace Land Corp; W R Grace Properties Inc; Gracoal Inc; Hand Realty Corp; Hand Realty Properties Inc; Handy Dan Hardware Inc; Handy Dan HM Improvement Center; Thrift Builders Supply Inc; Hanover Square Co; Hayden Gulch West Coal Co; Homco International Inc; Houlihans Inc; Invertol SA de CV; Jefferson 4740 Corp; Jojos Restaurants Inc; KC Stadium Concession Inc; Killam T Elson Associates Inc; Killam-Dearborn Environmental Engineers Inc; LCS Beverage Co Inc; Leaf Confections Ltd; Leaf Sales (Confectionery) Ltd; Leather Battle No1 Inc; Liquor Lounges Inc; LKS Enterprises Inc; MB Distributing Co Inc; Mays Restaurants Inc; Midwest Restaurants Inc; Neville Coal Sales Co; New American Restaurant Corp; Offshore Fisheries Inc; Oklahoma Nitrogen Co; One Hundred West of St Louis Inc; One Hundred West Inc; Paramont Coal Co; Paramont Minerals Corp, Penn 4743 Corp; Petit IV Corp; Petit IV Ltd; Plaza III Restaurant Corp; Process Evaluation & Development Corp; Rapoca Energy Co; Red Steer Inc; Rent-It Inc; Restaurant Supply Inc; J B Robinson Jewelers Inc; S & H Beverage Co Inc; Seven Hanover Square Corp; Sheplers Inc; Southern Oil Resin & Fiberglass Inc; ST Services; Stan Trans Inc; Standard Transpipe (VA) Inc; Standard Transpipe Corp; Stopover Restaurants Inc; Terry Eagle Coal Co; Topfgucker Restaurant GmbH München; Woolwich Sewer Co Inc; Woolwich Water Co Inc
Principal Bank: Citizens National Bank Independence KS
Financial Information:

	Dec 31 1985 $'000	Dec 31 1986 $'000
Sales revenues	7,260,100	6,808,300
Net income	146,900	472,300
Earnings per share	$2.82	$11.25
Shareholders equity	2,404,500	1,308,600

No of Employees: 116,900

GRACO INC

4050 Olson Memorial Highway, PO Box 1441, Minneapolis, MN 55440
Tel: (612) 623-6000

Chairman: David A Koch
President: Walter E Weyler
Senior Executive Officers: Roy Richardson (VP, Human Resources and Corporate Development), Roger King (VP, Treasurer), George Aristides (VP, Operations), Barry Calhoon (VP, International Operations), Mark Christopher (VP, Finishing), Robert Hasse (VP-Commercial), John Heller (VP-Far East Operations), Ralph Todd (VP, US Sales), Norman Fender (President, Graco Robotics, Inc), Bruce McFadden (VP, Fluid Handling)

PRINCIPAL ACTIVITIES: Graco designs, manufactures and markets quality-engineered equipment and systems to meet worldwide users' needs for efficiently moving and applying fluids and semi-solid materials
Trade Names: GRACO
Principal Subsidiaries: Graco Canada Inc (Canada); Graco France SA (France); Graco GmbH (Germany); Graco Hong Kong Ltd (Hong Kong); Graco Norge AS (Norway) (1); Graco Pumps Scandinavia AB (Sweden); Graco Robotics, Inc; Graco Srl (Italy); Graco UK Ltd (UK); Lockwood Technical, Inc (99%); Nihon Gray KK (Japan); Soprea SA (France) (2): (1) Owned by Graco Geneva SA; (2) Owned by Graco France SA

Financial Information:

	Dec 31 1985	Dec 31 1986
	$'000	$'000
Sales revenues	208,325	225,071
Income before taxes	20,761	26,996
Net income	10,761	14,296
Dividends	2,765	3,284
Dividends per share	$0.44	$0.52
Earnings per share	$1.84	$2.38
Common stock	5,815	5,964
Retained income	75,034	64,019
Shareholders equity	78,893	90,404

No of Employees: 2,000

GRAHAM CORPORATION

20 Florence Avenue, Batavia, NY 14020
Tel: (716) 343-2216

Chairman: F D Berkeley (and Chief Executive Officer)
President: C G Driver
Senior Executive Officers: A L Snyder (VP Finance)

PRINCIPAL ACTIVITIES: Manufacture of industrial equipment including pumps, heat transfer equipment and process equipment
Principal Subsidiaries: Heat Transfer Ltd; Graham Process Equipment Ltd (UK); Graham Manufacturing Ltd (UK); Graham Precision Pumps Ltd (UK); Heat Transfer Ltd (UK); Graham Manufacturing Company; L and A Engineering and Equipment Inc
Principal Bank: Norstar NA, Buffalo, NY
Financial Information:

	Dec 31 1986
	$'000
Sales revenues	54,211
Net (loss)	(1,186)
(Loss) per share	($1.21)
Common stock	98
Retained income	8,098
Shareholders equity	8,344

Principal Shareholders: F D Berkeley
No of Employees: 852

GRAIN PROCESSING CORPORATION

1600 Oregon Street, Muscatine, IA 52761
Tel: (319) 264-4211
Telex: WUT 468497 gp corp musc

Chairman: R C Kautz
President: J H Kent
Senior Executive Officers: C J Lewis (Executive VP Corporate Research and Development), Robert E Miller (Senior VP), R G Rohwer (Senior VP), R L Koll (Senior VP), D J Kolar (Senior VP Finance), William B Trent Jr (VP Personnel Administration)

PRINCIPAL ACTIVITIES: Distilling; milling; cereal products; chemicals
Principal Bank: Central State Bank
Financial Information:

	$'000
Sales revenues	202,000

No of Employees: 900

GRAINGER, W W, INC

5500 W Howard Street, Skokie, IL 60077
Tel: (312) 982-9000
Telex: 910-223-3651 GRAINGER NILES
Telefax: (312) 647-6995

Chairman: David W Grainger; Vice Chairman: Jere D Fluno
President: Wiley N Caldwell
Senior Executive Officers: James M Baisley (VP and Gneral Counsel), Lee J Flory (VP and Secretary), Donald E Bielinski (VP and Controller), Neal Ormond III (VP Human Resources), Richard D Quast (VP Real Estate), Edward C Bender (VP Information Services), David K Barth (VP Planning and Development), Robert D Pappano (VP and Treasurer)

PRINCIPAL ACTIVITIES: Nationwide distributor of electrical, mechanical and other products to the industrial and commercial markets
Principal Subsidiaries: Dayton Electric Manufacturing Co; Grainger FSC Inc
Principal Banks: Continental Illinois National Bank and Trust Company of Chicago; The Northern Trust Company
Financial Information:

	Dec 31 1985	Dec 31 1986
	$'000	$'000
Sales revenues	1,091,590	1,159,595
Income before taxes	132,553	140,656
Net income	71,775	86,112
Dividends	19,222	20,549
Dividends per share	$0.665	$0.71
Earnings per share	$2.47	$2.96
Common stock	28,919	28,897
Retained income	459,301	520,582
Shareholders equity	518,234	582,091

No of Employees: 5,578

GRAND AUTO INC

7200 Edgewater Drive, Oakland, CA 94621
Tel: (415) 568 6500

Chairman: Irving E Krantzman (and President and Chief Executive Officer); Vice Chairman: Max M Brown (and Senior Executive VP)
Senior Executive Officers: John F Goodsell (Executive VP and Chief Executive Officer), Earl L Eastin (Super G), R J Micheletti (VP Industrial Relations and Personnel Affairs), Donald J Nickols (VP Operations), Ellington Owensby (VP Construction), Gary D Hill (VP and Chief Financial Officer), Bruce J Levitin (VP Store Operations), Daniel C Santo (VP Tires, Batteries and Operations), Robert L Seymour (VP Merchandising), R N Stefan (Secretary)

PRINCIPAL ACTIVITIES: Supply of auto accessories and parts, tools, batteries and tires
Principal Bank: Bank of America
Financial Information:

	$'000
Sales revenues	167,660

No of Employees: 2,140

GRAND TRUNK CORPORATION

131 W Lafayette Blvd, Detroit, MI 48226
Tel: (313) 962-2260

Chairman: J M Leclair
President: J H Burdakin
Senior Executive Officers: P E Tatro (VP Finance), R E Lawless (VP), K Baird (Secretary), J E Shepherd (Treasurer)

PRINCIPAL ACTIVITIES: Holding company whose subsidiaries are engaged in railroad transportation services
Principal Subsidiaries: Central Vermont Railway Inc; Grand Truck Western Railroad Co; Duluth Winnipeg & Pacific Railway Co
Financial Information:

	Dec 31 1985	Dec 31 1986
	$'000	$'000
Sales revenues	404,920	382,498
Net income (loss)	13,340	(11,841)
Shareholders equity	307,790	295,946

No of Employees: 4,580

GRAND UNION CO

100 Broadway, Elmwood Park, NJ 07407
Tel: (201) 794-2000
Telex: TWX 7109882201 granuco epat

Chairman: Floyd Hall (and Chief Executive Officer)
President: Joseph J McCaig (and Chief Operating Officer)
Senior Executive Officers: Henry T Johnson (Executive VP and Chief Administration Officer), William A Louttit (Executive VP Merchandising), James E Herlihy (Executive VP and Chief Financial Officer), Louis Sherwood (Senior VP Development), William Reffett (Senior VP Administration Services), James L Zahner (Senior VP Management Information Systems and Logistics), Henry S Addison (VP Carolina Region), Kenneth R Baum (VP and Controller), Jack Calderone (VP Meat Merchandising), Roger W Kennedy (VP and Treasurer), Michael J Larkin (VP NY Region), Charles Barrett (VP Labor Relations), Brooke D Lennon (VP), Richard J Mawker (VP), Buck Jones (VP Services Departments), Anthony P Misasi (VP), Robert E Mohel (VP Product Development and Quality Control), Robert J Saba (VP), Bryan Springthorpe (VP), Craig C Sturken (VP)

PRINCIPAL ACTIVITIES: Food retailing
Trade Names: Grand Union, Big Star, Basic Foods Warehouse
Parent Company: Cavenham Holdings, Inc
Principal Bank: First National Bank of New Jersey
Financial Information:

	$'000
Sales revenues	2,530,000

Principal Shareholders: Générale Occidentale, Paris, France
No of Employees: 31,000

GRANDMET CONSUMER PRODUCTS INC

100 Paragon Drive, Montvale, NJ 07645
Tel: (201) 573-4000

Chairman: Walter D Scott
President: Jonathan W Old Jr (and Chief Executive Officer)
Senior Executive Officers: Thomas M Gaffey Jr (Senior VP and Chief Financial Officer), Roger W Hooker (Senior VP General Counsel and Secretary), James G Adams (VP Strategic Planning and Development), John E Curley (VP Taxes), Harry F Dawley (VP Employee Relations), Braxton E Barrett Jr (VP and Controller)

PRINCIPAL ACTIVITIES: GrandMet Consumer Products Inc is engaged through subsidiary companies in retailing eyecare products and services and manufacturing pet foods and soft drinks
Parent Company: Grand Metropolitan PLC, London, UK
Principal Subsidiaries: Pearle Health Servics Inc; ALPO Petfoods Inc; Atlantic Soft Drink Company; Pepsi Cola San Joaquin Bottling Company Company
Principal Bank: Morgan Guaranty Trust Company
Financial Information:

	1986	1987
	$'000	$'000
Sales revenues	622,800	635,000
Trading profit	58,800	67,800

No of Employees: 30,400

GRANGER ASSOCIATES

3101 Scott Blvd, Santa Clara, CA 95051
Tel: (408) 727-3101
Telex: TWX 910373 1291 granger snta

President: Henry R Nothaft

PRINCIPAL ACTIVITIES: Manufacture of telecommunications equipment
Parent Company: DSC Communications Corporation
Principal Bank: Bank of California
Financial Information:

	$'000
Sales revenues	71,300

No of Employees: 000

GRANITEVILLE CO

Graniteville, SC 29829
Tel: (803) 663-7231
Telex: WUT 545435 gvl co grvt

Chairman: Victor Posner (and Chief Executive Officer); Vice Chairman: Steven Posner
Senior Executive Officers: John L Barnes Jr (Executive VP), Joseph E Bresnahan (Senior VP Operations), W E Johnson (VP Administration), Thomas A Tantillo (VP Dyeing and Finishing), R J Fisher (VP Manufacturing), A N Thompson (VP Yarn Sales)

PRINCIPAL ACTIVITIES: Textile manufacture
Parent Company: Southeastern Public Services Company, Miami, FL
Principal Bank: Citizens and Southern National Bank
Financial Information:

	$'000
Sales revenues	255,000

Principal Shareholders: DWG Corporation, Miami, FL
No of Employees: 4,300

GRANNY GOOSE FOODS INC

930 98th Avenue, Oakland, CA 94603
Tel: (415) 635-5400
Telex: WUT 337752 granny oak

President: Wesley Felton
Senior Executive Officer: Linn Green (VP Operations), Dave Divine (VP Finance), Jim Clizbe (VP Marketing)

PRINCIPAL ACTIVITIES: Manufacture of snack products
Parent Company: GF Industries Inc
Principal Bank: Crocker National Bank
Financial Information:

	$'000
Sales revenues	50,000

No of Employees: 700

GRANT INDUSTRIES INC

High Street, West Nyack, NY 10994
Tel: (914) 358-4400

Chairman: Harvey R Blau
Senior Executive Officers: Mark E Berman (VP Finance and Treasurer), Peter Caruso (VP Manufacturing), Joseph T DelVecchio (VP Industrial Operations), Eugene F Dumesnil (VP Commercial Sales)

PRINCIPAL ACTIVITIES: Manufacture of hardware products
Principal Bank: Barclays Bank of New York
Financial Information:

	$'000
Sales revenues	49,300

No of Employees: 850

GRANT OIL TOOL CO

2042 E Vernon Avenue, Los Angeles, CA 90058
Tel: (213) 232-8161
Telex: WUT 673653 grant oil lsa

President: R E Masters
Senior Executive Officers: G T Carter (VP Sales), A A Sylvester (VP Finance), M Audirsh (VP International Sales)

PRINCIPAL ACTIVITIES: Manufacture of oilfield equipment
Parent Company: Masco Corporation, Taylor, MI
Principal Bank: National Bank of Detroit
Financial Information:

	$'000
Sales revenues	50,000

No of Employees: 400

GRANT SOUTHERN IRON & METAL

9100 John Kronk Avenue, Detroit, MI 48210
Tel: (313) 582-2910
Telex: TWX 810 221 6901 grant-south-im

Chairman: Marvin H Goldman
President: Irving Goldman
Senior Executive Officers: John Morissey (Executive VP), Robert Webber (VP Sales), Earl Grant (Secretary and Treasurer)

PRINCIPAL ACTIVITIES: Iron and steel processing
Principal Bank: First of America
Financial Information:

	$'000
Sales revenues	50,000

No of Employees: 90

GRANTREE CORPORATION

2501 SW First Avenue, PO Box 3210, Portland, OR 97201
Tel: (503) 223 1161

Chairman: Walker M Treece (and Chief Executive Officer)
President: Gary A Kisling (and Chief Operating Officer)
Senior Executive Officers: Zolman M Cohen (VP Rental Operations), Gerdon Fahland (VP Marketing), William A Norris (VP Finance and Treasurer), J Franklin Cable (Secretary)

PRINCIPAL ACTIVITIES: Holding company with interests in the sale, lease and hire of new and second-hand furniture
Principal Subsidiaries: Grantree Furniture Rental and Sales Corporation; Grantree Furniture Rental Corporation; Multiform Enterprises Inc
Principal Bank: First Interstate Bank
Financial Information:

	$'000
Sales revenues	91,100

No of Employees: 1,205

GRAPHIC CONTROLS CORPORATION

PO Box 1271, Buffalo, NY 14240
Tel: (716) 853-7500
Telex: RCA 200902 grap ur

President: Donald P Quinlan (and Chief Executive Officer)
Senior Executive Officers: Lyman K Randall (VP Industrial Products Division), Robert A Evans (VP Medical Products Division), Larry R Drake (VP Human Resources), William C Gates (Secretary, Treasurer and Chief Financial Officer)

PRINCIPAL ACTIVITIES: Manufacture of printing and recording equipment and paper processing; disposable medical products; plotter supplies, industrial and medical recording charts, disposable pens, coated/thermal/facsimile paper and disposable medical supplies
Principal Bank: Marine Midland Bank-Western
Financial Information:

	$'000
Sales revenues	150,000

No of Employees: 1,800

GRAPHIC INDUSTRIES, INC

2155 Monroe Drive NE, Atlanta, GA 30324
Tel: (404) 874-3327

Chairman: Mark C Pope III (and President)
Senior Executive Officers: J L Smith (Executive VP), Mark C Pope IV (VP), E E Miller (VP Finance, Secretary and Treasurer)

PRINCIPAL ACTIVITIES: Printing
Principal Subsidiaries: Heritage Press Inc
Principal Bank: Citizens and Southern National
Financial Information:

	$'000
Sales revenues	130,400

No of Employees: 1,800

GRAPHIC SCANNING CORPORATION

329 Alfred Avenue, Teaneck, NJ 07666
Tel: (201) 837 5100

Chairman: Joel R Packer (and Chief Executive Officer)
President: William S Wheatley Jr (and Treasurer)
Senior Executive Officers: Alfred K Ganschow (VP Operations), Richard Sherwin (VP Marketing), Ronald P Vicari (VP Engineering), Edward R Busch (VP and Secretary), Robert Slodowitz (VP Corporate and Financial Development)

PRINCIPAL ACTIVITIES: Provision of telephone and telecommunications services
Principal Subsidiaries: Spectrum Communications Electrical; Switchco Inc; Time & Space Processing Inc; US Paging Inc; Richard L Vega Associates Inc
Principal Bank: Chemical Bank
Financial Information:

	$'000
Sales revenues	120,000

No of Employees: 800

GRAY COMMUNICATIONS SYSTEMS INC

PO Box 3130, Albany, GA 31708
Tel: (912) 883-0154

Chairman: James H Gray (and President)
Senior Executive Officers: Raymond E Carow (Executive VP), Ray H Holloway (VP, WJHG-TV Inc, Panama City), Perley E Eppley Sr (VP, Gray Communications Consultants Inc), Richard D Carson (Controller), Barbara Jones (Treasurer), Dorothy A Zimmerman (Secretary)

PRINCIPAL ACTIVITIES: Supply of electronic parts for audio-visual equipment; publishing; television broadcasting
Principal Subsidiaries: Albany Herald Publishing Company; Gray Communications Consultants Inc; Gray Transportation Company Inc; KTVE Inc; WALB-TV Inc; WJHG-TV Inc
Principal Bank: Bank of the South
Financial Information:

	$'000
Sales revenues	43,650

No of Employees: 530

GREAT AMERICAN CORPORATION

1 American Place, Suite 940, Baton Rouge, LA 70825
Tel: (504) 346 6002

Chairman: Huey J Wilson (and Chief Executive)
Senior Executive Officers: W J Noel Jr (Executive VP, Chief Operating Officer), J Ray Heil (Senior VP Commercial Lending), Charles Bradley (Senior VP Retail Credit), Charles Chiasson (Senior VP Management Information Services), C A Altazan Jr (VP Administration Services), V Jackson Carney III (VP and Manager Regional Banking), Wolfe G Decker (VP Credit Policy and Review), Irwin L Felpts Jr (VP and Manager Investments), Herbert R Hassell (VP and Manager Trusts), Hal Hinchliffe (VP and Manager Real Estate Lending), James LaBauve (VP Data Processing), Raymond L Raines (Chief Financial Officer)

PRINCIPAL ACTIVITIES: Provision of a wide range of banking and financial services
Principal Subsidiaries: Ambank Financial Services Corporation; Ambank Mortgage Company; American Bank & Trust Company; American Branch Building Corporation; American Holding Corporation; American Investment and Management Corporation
Principal Bank: American Bank & Trust Company

No of Employees: 720

GREAT AMERICAN FEDERAL SAVINGS & LOAN ASSOCIATION

1001 Lake Street, Oak Park, IL 60301
Tel: (312) 383-5000

Chairman: John L Domeier (and President and Managing Officer)
Senior Executive Officers: James D O'Malley (VP and Secretary), William C Eldridge (VP), Richard Klancer (VP), John Evans (VP), Ralph R Bellon (VP and Treasurer)

PRINCIPAL ACTIVITIES: Banking

No of Employees: 350

GREAT AMERICAN FIRST SAVINGS BANK

600 B Street, San Diego, CA 92183
Tel: (619) 231-1885
Telex: 750352 GRT AMER FEDUD

Chairman: Gordon C Luce (and Chief Executive Officer); Vice Chairman: Lorna H Mills
President: James C Schmidt (and Managing Officer)
Senior Executive Officers: William S Chapman (Senior Executive VP), Roger K Lindland (Senior Executive VP), Barry I Newman (Senior Executive VP), Marc W Sandstrom (Senior Executive VP), Rodney P Tompkins (Executive VP), William D Hinz (Executive VP), James A Krzeminski (Senior First VP), F Raymond Silliman (Senior First VP), Jan M Strode (Senior First VP), Marilyn R Allen (First VP), Ronald G Arehart (First VP), Robert F Atherton (First VP), Thomas H Detrick (First VP), John R Faires (First VP), Richard J Gannon (First VP), Russell J Grisanti (First VP), June N Hendershot (First VP), Richard H Keyes (First VP), Ray B Lancaster (First VP), Darwin D Olsen (First VP), Robert C Reif (First VP), David C Safina (First VP), Douglas F Sawyer (First VP), Donald J Schiffer (First VP), Charles Shryock (First VP), Eugene W Traverso (First VP), Ronald J Wade (First VP)

PRINCIPAL ACTIVITIES: Great American First Savings Bank is a $13.1 billion, publicly held savings bank headquartered in San Diego, California. Founded in 1885, Great American has 180 deposit offices and 157 automatic teller machines throughout California and Arizona, and 13 mortgage banking offices in seven Western and Sunbelt states. It operates under a California state charter, is a member of the Federal Home Loan Bank System, and carries Federal Savings and Loan Insurance Corporation coverage for its accounts. The company offers a variety of deposit and investment products; financial and insurnace services; and real estate, business and consumer loans, It also is an active participant in the secondary loan market.
Principal Subsidiaries: (Wholly-owned): Great American First Savings Bank of Arizona; Great American Development Co; Franklin & Assoc; California General Mortgage Service Inc; Great American Mortgage Corp; GRAM Finance N.V.; Great American Asset Management Co

Financial Information: (1)(2)(3)

	Dec 31 1985 $'000	Dec 31 1986 $'000
Income before taxes	70,713	154,837
Net income(4)	45,666	93,745
Dividends	5,759	8,332
Dividends per share	$0.46	$0.38
Primary earnings per share	$3.65	$4.18
Earnings per share(4)(5)	$3.50	$3.52
Common stock	12,575	22,696
Retained earnings	232,457	330,138
Shareholders equity	385,896	545,096
Deposits	5,891,416	5,877,414
Total assets	8,211,046	13,064,815

(1) on March 21 1986 Great American acquired Home Federal Savings & Loan, Tucson, Arizona. Home Federal had total assets of $2.4 billion
(2) on May 7 1986 Great American acquired Los Angeles Federal Savings Bank using the pooling of interests method of accounting. Los Angeles Federal had total assets of $745 million
(3) on March 9 1987 Great American acquired First Security Savings & Loan, Grand Junction, Colorado. First Security had total assets of $53 million
(4) after extraordinary item
(5) fully diluted

Principal Shareholders: Forstmann-Leff Associates; Wedbush Corporation; Miller Anderson Sherrard
No of Employees: 3,227

GREAT AMERICAN INDUSTRIES, INC

300 Plaza Drive, Binghamton, NY 13903
Tel: (607) 729-3475

Chairman: Burton I Koffman (and President)
Senior Executive Officers: Milton Koffman (Executive VP Real Estate, Secretary and Treasurer), Leo P Serowik (VP Finance), Richard Koffman (VP)

PRINCIPAL ACTIVITIES: Manufacture of rubber goods including foam products, underwater equipment and diving suits; electro mechanical products
Parent Company: PLC Enterprises Inc
Principal Subsidiaries: GAI Real Estate and Development Corporation; Parkway Fabricators; Rubatex Corporation; Tech-Aero Foam Products Inc; Chenango Industries Inc; IAG Corporation; Paeco Industries Inc; Great American Minerals Corporation
Financial Information:

	$'000
Sales revenues	237,600

No of Employees: 2,770

GREAT AMERICAN RECREATION INC

PO Box 848, McAfee, NJ 07428
Tel: (201) 827 2000

Chairman: Gene W Mulvihill
President: John Renna
Senior Executive Officers: Edward Kelley (VP), Roger W Scott (VP and Treasurer), Debra Evers (Secretary)

PRINCIPAL ACTIVITIES: Provision of leisure and recreational services including an action park and ski area
Parent Company: First Fidelity Bank

Financial Information:

	$'000
Sales revenues	38,500

No of Employees: 1,500

GREAT ATLANTIC & PACIFIC TEA COMPANY, INC

2 Paragon Drive, Montvale, NJ 07645
Tel: (201) 573-9700

Chairman: James Wood (and Chief Executive Officer); Vice Chairmen: James W Rowe (and Chief Administration Officer), Eckart C Siess (International Operations)
President: P L Sherwood
Senior Executive Officers: Alan C Goulding (Senior Executive VP and Chief Operations Officer), Martin H Kern (Executive VP Merchandising and Distribution), Joseph H McCarthy (Executive VP Store Operations), Vito A Cardace (Senior VP Finance and Chief Financial Officer), Peter O'Gorman (Senior VP Development), J Paul Stilwell (Senior VP, President Family Center), Ivan K Szathmary (Senior VP, IAS Manufacturing and Distrtibution), Robert Gulrich (Senior VP and Legal Counsel), Thomas L Barrette (VP Human Resources), Randall A Bostwick (VP Supermarket Services Corp), Peter R Brooker (VP Planning and Secretary), James B Burmeister (VP Southeast Group), Timothy J Courtney (VP Taxation), O C Cook (VP Perishables), Julian J DiFore (VP, President Super Fresh Food Markets), Donald B Dobson (VP Southern Group), R Paul Gallant (VP, President Compass Foods), Peter R Lavoy (VP Grocery), Frank X Leonard (VP Real Estate), H Nelson Lewis (VP Retail Operations Services), James B Madden (VP Mid-Atlantic Group), Edward C Mossop (VP, Chairman, A&P Canada), Joseph P Quirk (VP Labor Relations), Gregory K Raven (VP and Treasurer), Michael J Rourke (VP Communications/Corporate Affairs), John D Ryder (VP Marketing), John C Sherrard (VP Special Assistant US Store Operations), Caryle Sherwin (VP, President US A&P Michigan Operations), William G Spearman (VP, President and Chief Executive Officer Kohl's), Robert W Toomey (VP Distribution), Burton J Weinbaum (VP Northeast Group), George Graham (VP Merchandising Metro Group), Michael Larkin (VP Store Operations Metro Group), William J Vitulli (VP Community/Government Relations)

PRINCIPAL ACTIVITIES: Retailing of food products
Principal Bank: Chemical Bank
Financial Information:

	Feb 28 1986 $'000
Sales revenues	6,615,422
Net income	88,290
Earnings per share	$2.33
Shareholders equity	668,688

No of Employees: 53,000

GREAT DANE TRAILERS, INC

PO Box 67, Savannah, GA 31402
Tel: (912) 232-4471
Telex: WUT 546467 gtdane pts sav

President: Harvey Granger Jr (and Chief Executive Officer)
Senior Executive Officers: Henry T Skipper Jr (Executive VP Marketing), Victor L Johnson (Senior VP Materials), Fred T Mote (Senior VP Operations), Christopher F Hammond III (VP Sales), Jimmy R Phillips (VP Manufacturing), John Storz (VP Engineering), E Oscar Wright (VP Branch Operations), R Dan Hartley (VP Distribution and Direct Sales), Daniel J O'Connor (VP and Controller), Thor Egede-Nissen (VP Industrial Relations), Lon Stull (VP Management and Information Systems)

PRINCIPAL ACTIVITIES: Production of truck trailers
Parent Company: International Controls Corporation
Principal Bank: Citizen and Southern Bank

Financial Information:

	$'000
Sales revenues	400,000

No of Employees: 3,000

GREAT LAKES BANCORP, A FEDERAL SAVINGS BANK

401 E Liberty Street, Ann Arbor, MI 48107
Tel: (313) 769-8300

Chairman: Roy E Weber (and President and Chief Executive Officer)
Senior Executive Officers: William Lawrence (Executive VP and Secretary), Hans W Maier (Executive VP), Robert J Delonis (Executive VP and Chief Financial Officer), Dennis Pearsall (Executive VP)

PRINCIPAL ACTIVITIES: Banking and financial services
Principal Subsidiaries: Great Lakes Bancorp, A Federal Savings has 57 branches
Principal Bank: Chase Manhattan, NA
Financial Information:

	Dec 31 1985 $'000	Dec 31 1986 $'000
Income before taxes (1)	19,242	32,638
Net income	12,356	22,234
Dividends (2)	759	1,368
Dividends per share	$0.20	$0.35
Earnings per share	$3.21	$5.67
Common stock (3)	35,427	35,935
Retained income	55,016	75,882
Shareholders equity	90,443	111,817
Deposits	1,621,714	1,698,117
Total assets	2,404,019	2,691,390

(1) and extraordinary items
(2) cash
(3) and paid in capital

No of Employees: 1000

GREAT LAKES CARBON CORPORATION

320 Old Briarcliff Road, Briarcliff Manor, NY 10510
Tel: (914) 941 7800
Telex: TWX 7105814805 glc nyk

Chairman: William E Flaherty; Vice Chairmen: Ira P Barsky, John P Sachs (and Chief Executive Officer)
President: Harry N Walters (and Chief Operating Officer)
Senior Executive Officers: James H Davis (Senior VP Operations and Technical), Ronald J Statile (VP Finance and Treasurer), Michael A Wrotniak Jr (Senior VP Marketing), I William Gazda (VP Technical), Peter M Hoffman (VP Human Resources), James D McKenzie (VP, Secretary and Legal Counsel), Gary A Waytena (VP and Business Manager Electrodes), Mack P Whittaker (VP and Business Manager Calcinated Coke), W Carlton Wood (VP Operations)

PRINCIPAL ACTIVITIES: Trade in ores, minerals and chemicals; manufacture of carbon and graphite products including electrodes and anodes and petroleum coke
Parent Company: Horsehead Industries Inc
Principal Bank: Mellon Bank
Financial Information:

	$'000
Sales revenues	350,000

No of Employees: 1,500

GREAT LAKES CHEMICAL CORPORATION

PO Box 2200, West Lafeyette, IN 47906
Tel: (317) 463-2511
Telex: 279428

President: Emerson Kampen (and Chief Executive Officer)
Senior Executive Officers: Allen W Smith (Group VP), William G McGuire (Senior VP), Bob G Tibbetts (Senior VP), William P Blake (VP, Specialty and Flame Retardants), Lowell C

Horwedel (VP), Robert T Jeffares (VP, Finance and Chief Financial Officer), John S Little (VP, Corporate Technology), Robert B McDonald (VP, Engineering), Wayne R Merriman (VP, International Operations), Norman L Ritter (Secretary and Treasurer), Frank H Wheeler (VP)

PRINCIPAL ACTIVITIES: Manufacture of: Bromine and brominated compounds; flame retardants; fire extinguishing agents; agricultural chemicals and fumigants; oil field chemicals; water treatment chemicals; and specialty intermediates
Principal Subsidiaries: E/M Corporation; Enzyme Technology Corp; Great Lakes Chemical (Europe) Ltd; Hydrotech Chemical Corp; Inland Specialty Chemicals; Oilfield Service Corp of America; WIL Research Laboratories
Principal Bank: Chemical Bank
Financial Information:

	$'000
Sales revenues	277,000

No of Employees: 1,700

GREAT LAKES INTERNATIONAL, INC

2122 York Rd, Oak Brook, IL 60521
Tel: (312) 920-3000

Chairman: John A Downs
President: William L Colnon (and Chief Executive Officer)
Senior Executive Officers: Frederick R Hazard (Executive VP), Robert W Muller (VP and Treasurer), A F Zeman Jr (VP), R L Jackson (VP), V G Hussin (VP), P R Dickinson (VP and Secretary)

PRINCIPAL ACTIVITIES: Marine engineering and river and harbor construction and dredging
Principal Subsidiaries: Henry Du Bois Sous Co; Great Lakes Dredge & Dock Co; North American Trailing Co Inc
Principal Bank: Continental Illinois National Bank & Trust Co
Financial Information:

	$'000
Sales revenues	157,760

No of Employees: 1,230

GREAT NORTHERN NEKOOSA CORPORATION

75 Prospect Street, Box 9309, Stamford, CT 06904
Tel: (203) 359-4000

Chairman: William R Laidig (and President and Chief Executive Officer)
Senior Executive Officers: Emery E Allain (Executive VP), Robert F Barlett (VP), James G Crump (VP), William Laimbeer (VP), Victor F Mattson (VP), Arnold M Nemirow (VP), Francis G Walker (VP), Joseph F O'Handley (VP, General Counsel and Secretary), Philip Cannella (Treasurer), James G Carr (Controller)

PRINCIPAL ACTIVITIES: Great Northern Nekoosa Corporation is a major producer of pulp and paper, with a capacity of 4,000,000 tons a year. Pulp and paper manufacturing, corrugated box manufacturing, paper distribution and envelope manufacturing account for about 95 percent of sales. The Company is also in the lumber and plywood business. In pulp and paper, concentration is on four product lines: business papers, containerboard, newspaper publishing and groundwood printing papers and market pulp. The Company is a leading US producer of paper for the office copier and a leading supplier of containerboard to independent corrugated box makers. The Company has the only newsprint mill in New England and is a major US producer of bleached kraft market pulp
Principal Subsidiaries: Chattahoochee Industrial Railroad; F A Marsden Ltd (UK): GNN Foreign Sales Corporation (US Virgin Islands); Great Northern Properties Inc; Great Southern Properties Inc; Industria Panamena de Papel SA (50%) (Panama); Marplex Products Company Inc; Nekoosa Packaging Corporation; Nekoosa Papers Inc; Mail-Well Envelope Company; Butler Paper Company; Wisco Envelope Company Inc; Leaf River Corporation; Leaf River Forest Products Inc; Old Augusta Railroad Company
Financial Information:

	Dec 31 1985	Dec 31 1986
	$'000	$'000
Sales revenues	1,934,000	2,039,200
Income before taxes	68,200	146,500
Net income	46,200	85,300
Dividends	38,200	41,300
Dividends per share	$1.52	$1.57
Earnings per share	$1.78	$3.20
Common stock	126,300	133,300
Retained income	766,000	810,000
Shareholders equity	962,900	1,054,400

No of Employees: 14,000

GREAT PLAINS SUPPLY COMPANY

1667 N Snelling Avenue, St Paul, MN 55165
Tel: (612) 631-4600

Chairman: Donald F Giffey; 1st Vice Chairman: Philip Testerman; 2nd Vice Chairman: Gerald Redlin
President: Allen D Hanson
Senior Executive Officers: Karl Butzer (Group VP Farm Supply), Edward Ellison (Secretary and Treasurer)

PRINCIPAL ACTIVITIES: Construction materials and fittings; sectional buildings
Parent Company: Harvest States Cooperatives
Principal Bank: National City Bank of Mineapolis
Financial Information:

	$'000
Sales revenues	80,000

No of Employees: 400

GREAT SOUTHERN FEDERAL SAVINGS BANK

132 East Broughton Street, Savannah, GA 31401
Tel: (912) 944 6200

Chairman: N Carson Branan
President: Peter S Knox III (and Chief Executive Officer)
Senior Executive Officers: G T Stump (Executive VP), J O Baker (Senior VP and Treasurer), J D Gardner (Senior VP, Legal Counsel and Secretary), E C Allen (Senior VP), A B Pace Jr (Senior VP), A H Wilson (Senior VP), N B Wright (Senior VP), R L Ashcraft (First VP), H O Dicks (First VP), T R Hamilton (First VP), R E Monroe (First VP), S Ann Taylor (First VP), R P Weller (First VP), S J Henry (First VP and General Auditor)

PRINCIPAL ACTIVITIES: Banking
Principal Subsidiaries: Great Southern Mortgage Corp
Financial Information:

	Dec 31 1985
	$'000
Revenues	116,130

No of Employees: 530

GREAT WESTERN BANK & TRUST

4041 N Central, Phoenix, AZ 85001
Tel: (602) 264-7441

Chairman: J S Lowry; Vice Chairman: Allen L Rosenberg
Senior Executive Officers: Robert Franko (Executive VP Retail Banking), Charles Syburg (Executive VP Corporate Banking), Nancy McCort (VP and Chief Financial Officer), Michael Kinnison (VP Northern Region Branch Administration), Dennis Smith (VP Central Region Branch Administration), James Cosbey (VP Southern Region Branch Administration), James C Adamany (VP Commercial Finance), Jeffrey Stern (VP Retail Credit/Loan Operations), James Latta (VP Commercial Credit), Elfriede Conrad (VP, Cashier and Controller), Herbert Machol

(VP Audit), Walter Enger (VP Compliance), Phillip E Kerce (Group VP)

PRINCIPAL ACTIVITIES: Banking
Parent Company: GWB Holding Co
Principal Bank: Valley National Bank

No of Employees: 750

GREAT WESTERN FINANCIAL CORPORATION

8484 Wilshire Blvd, Beverly Hills, CA 90211
Tel: (213) 852-3411

Chairman: James F Montgomery (and Chief Executive Officer); Vice Chairman: Stuart Davis
President: John F Maher (and Chief Operating Officer)
Senior Executive Officers: Executive Management Committee: J Lance Erikson (Executive VP, Secretary and General Counsel), Carl F Geuther (Executive VP and Chief Financial Officer), Firmin A Gryp (Executive VP), Edward R Hoffman (Executive VP and President Real Estate Services Division), Glendon E Johnson (President, Insurance Division), Anthony C La Scala (Executive VP and President, Retail Banking Division), William J Marschalk (Executive VP and President, Planning and Administration Division), M M Pappas (President, Consumer Finance Group)

PRINCIPAL ACTIVITIES: General financial services; savings and loans; retail banking and finance for real estate, mortgage banking, consumer finance
Principal Subsidiaries: Great Western Bank; Great Western Real Estate; Insurance Agency; GWF Securities Corporation; California Reconveyance Company; Blazer Financial Services; Great Western Financial Services; Advantage Direct; GWF Mortgage Corporation; City Finance Company
Principal Bank: Great Western Bank, A Federal Savings Bank
Financial Information:

	Dec 31 1985 $'000	Dec 31 1986 $'000
Revenues	3,404,248	3,850,396
Income before taxes	335,402	512,528
Net income	201,702	307,228
Dividends	37,725	49,178
Dividends per share	$0.94	$0.46
Earnings per share	$5.02	$2.87
Common stock	40,145	112,737
Retained income	863,580	1,142,969
Shareholders equity	1,197,090	1,626,592
Deposits	17,593,910	18,726,905
Total assets	25,471,349	28,363,832

Number of shareholders: 23,572
No of Employees: 11,909

GREAT WESTERN SAVINGS (A FEDERAL SAVINGS & LOAN ASSOCIATION)

8484 Wilshire Blvd, Beverly Hills, CA 90211
Tel: (213) 852-3400
Telex: TWX 910 4902561 gws bbhl

Chairman: James F Montgomery (and Chief Executive Officer)
President: Robert B Holmes (and Chief Operating Officer)
Senior Executive Officers: Stuart Davis (Chairman Executive Committee), Firmin A Gryp (Executive VP Real Estate Development), Edward R Hoffman (Executive VP Real Estate Services Division), Anthony C La Scala (Executive VP Retail Banking and Customer Services Division), William J Marschalk (Executive VP Finance and Administration Division), Mark L Lipson (Executive VP, Chief Operations Officer Retail Banking and Customer Services), Bertill A Gustafson (Senior VP and Controller), R Phillip Altman (Senior VP Branch Operations), E A Crane (Senior VP Service Operations), E S Lyons (Senior VP Mortgage Banking), Charles A Riach (Senior VP Major Loans), Jerry E Weeks (Senior VP Loan Coordination), Joe M Jackson (Senior VP Systems and Data Processing), Jerome W Johnson (Senior VP Operations Analysis), Paul O Maier (Senior VP Branch Premises), Monroe Morgan (Senior VP Investor Relations), Jerry Oflock (Senior VP Consumer Lending), Michael J Palko (Senior VP Tax Administration), James D Sage (Senior VP and Chief Counsel), Richard Terzian (Senior VP and Treasurer), A T Lombardi (Senior VP Personnel), Frederick H Robins (Senior VP Real Estate), J Lance Erikson (Senior VP and Secretary), C Harrison Newman (Senior VP Florida Loan Department), Lester M Wintz (Senior VP Marketing)

PRINCIPAL ACTIVITIES: Banking services including savings and loans
Parent Company: Great Western Financial Corporation, Beverly Hills, CA
Principal Bank: Union Bank

No of Employees: 6,700

GREAT WESTERN SUGAR EXPORT CO

1530 16th Street, Denver, CO 80202
Tel: (303) 893-4600

President: Douglas Hunt
Senior Executive Officers: Larry Hoehn (Senior VP Agriculture), James Mark (Senior VP Sales and Marketing), Kenneth Hoff (VP Sugar Beet Manufacturing), Gene Sciba (VP Industrial Sales)

PRINCIPAL ACTIVITIES: Sugar beet refining and sugar distribution
Parent Company: Great Lakes Sugar Co
Principal Bank: IntraWest Bank of Denver
Financial Information:

	$'000
Sales revenues	760,000

No of Employees: 1,220

GREATER NEW YORK SAVINGS BANK

One Penn Plaza, New York, NY 10119
Tel: (212) 613-4000

Chairman: Frank Wille (and Chief Executive Officer)
Senior Executive Officers: Gerard C Keegan (Executive VP), Charles J Ohlig (Executive VP), Charles Heebner (Executive VP), Michael J Henchy (Senior VP), Allan E Matson (Senior VP), Philip T Spies (VP and Auditor)

PRINCIPAL ACTIVITIES: Banking
Principal Bank: Manufacturers Hanover Trust

No of Employees: 700

GREDE FOUNDRIES, INC

9898 W Bluemound Road, Milwaukee, WI 53226
Tel: (414) 257-3600

Chairman: Burleigh E Jacobs Jr; Vice Chairman: Wm J Grede
Senior Executive Officers: Walter S Davis (VP Legal), Jack Steele (VP Marketing), W S Irvine (VP Steel), H H Robinson (VP Gray Iron), Bruce Jacobs (VP Wichita Operation), J Allread (VP Engineering and Reedsburg Operation), James T Williams (VP Environmental Affairs), N J Goller (VP and Chief Financial Officer), Stew Davis (VP Industrial Relations), P E Sohlden (VP Manufacturing Services)

PRINCIPAL ACTIVITIES: Cast metal products
Principal Bank: M & I Marshall & Ilsley Bank
Financial Information:

	$'000
Sales revenues	110,000

No of Employees: 2,500

GREEN, A P, REFRACTORIES CO

Green Blvd, Mexico, MO 65265
Tel: (314) 473-3626
Cable: "GREENCO"
Telex: 447411

President: P J O'Bryan (and Chief Executive Officer)
Senior Executive Officers: P F Hummer (Senior VP), H R Copeland (Senior VP and Secretary), M C Aitken (VP Sales and Installation) D G Binder (VP and Treasurer), D Y Hagan (VP International Marketing), J Maunder (VP Manufacturing), O Hunter Jr (VP Research)

PRINCIPAL ACTIVITIES: Manufacture of refractory products
Parent Company: United States Gypsum Co, Chicago, IL
Principal Bank: Mercantile Trust Company
Financial Information:

	$'000
Sales revenues	150,000
Shareholders equity	60,000

No of Employees: 1,500

GREEN BAY PACKAGING INC

PO Box 19017, Green Bay, WI 54307
Tel: (414) 433-5311

Chairman: George F Kress
President: James F Kress
Senior Executive Officers: Roger P Hoffman (Executive VP Mill Operations), Fred J Wakeman (Executive VP Converting Operations), Leo N Crowley (Executive VP Planning and Administration), Donald F Kress (Senior VP), William R Nelson (VP Corporate Research and Development), John D L Droege (VP Industrial Relations), J C Dellinger (VP Southern Woodlands), S Lawrence Mayer (VP Administration Services, Converting Operations), William R Olson (VP Manufacturing Services, Converting Operations)

PRINCIPAL ACTIVITIES: Manufacture of containerboard products, folding cartons, coated papers, kraft paper, corrugating medium
Principal Subsidiaries: Arkansas Kraft Corp; Little Rock & Western Railway Corp; Arkansas Kraft Export Corp; Pinecrest Lumber Co
Principal Bank: Marshall & Ilsley Bank
Financial Information:

	$'000
Sales revenues	250,000

No of Employees: 1,900

GREEN GIANT CO

200 S 6th Street, Minneapolis, MN 55402
Tel: (612) 330-4966
Telex: TWX 9105783771

Chairman: William H Spoor
President: John M Stafford (and Chief Executive Officer)
Senior Executive Officers: Kent Larson (VP Frozen), D A Osell (VP Diversified)

PRINCIPAL ACTIVITIES: Production of canned and frozen vegetables
Trade Names: Registered Trademarks: Le Sueur, B'n B, Green Giant Harvest Fresh
Parent Company: The Pillsbury Company, Minneapolis, MN
Financial Information:

	1985
	$'000
Sales revenues	486,000

No of Employees: 6,600

GREEN MOUNTAIN POWER CORPORATION

25 Green Mountain Drive, PO Box 850, South Burlington, VT 05402
Tel: (802) 864 5731

Chairman: Thomas P Salmon (Chairman of the Board, Former Governor of Vermont)
President: J V Cleary Jr (and Chief Executive Officer and Chairman of the Executive Committee)
Senior Executive Officers: D F Graf (Assistant to the President), D G Hyde (Executive VP), A N Terreri (Senior VP), B F Brault (VP Operations and Engineering), Glen J Purcell (Controller), E M Norse (VP Finance and Chief Financial Officer), C L Dutton (VP, Legal Counsel and Secretary), T Boucher (Assistant VP Planning), T V O'Connor (VP, Consumer Services, Marketing, MIS), S C Terry (Assistant VP, Corporate Relations)

PRINCIPAL ACTIVITIES: Supply of electricity
Principal Bank: Chase Manhattan; Marine Midland
Financial Information:

	1986
	$'000
Sales revenues	113,116
Income before taxes(1)	20,914
Net income	9,540
Dividends(2)	8,042
Dividends per share	$1.78
Earnings per share	$2.45
Total shareholders equity	62,975

(1) operating
(2) balance for common

No of Employees: 370

GREEN RIVER STEEL CORPORATION

PO Box 1190, Owensboro, KY 42302
Tel: (502) 926-4400
Telex: TWX 8105363705 obo gr steel

President: G A Hulse
Senior Executive Officers: E E Belfiglio (VP Sales), T E Riney (VP Finance), R W Goetz (VP Operations)

PRINCIPAL ACTIVITIES: Steel industry
Parent Company: Athlone Industries Inc, Parsippany, NJ
Principal Bank: Manufacturers Hanover Trust
Financial Information:

	$'000
Sales revenues	100,000

No of Employees: 700

GREEN TREE ACCEPTANCE INC

1100 Amhoist Tower, 345 St Peter Street, St Paul, MN 55102
Tel: (612) 293 3400

Chairman: Harold W Greenwood Jr
President: Lawrence M Coss (and Chief Executive Officer)
Senior Executive Officers: Gary P Mills (Senior VP Regional Operations), Alan J Roers (VP and Secretary), Kenneth R Wilson (VP), Abdul Rajput (VP)

PRINCIPAL ACTIVITIES: Provision of a range of financial services including finance for mobile homes
Principal Bank: First National Bank of Minneapolis
Financial Information:

	$'000
Revenues	173,000

No of Employees: 800

GREENMAN BROS INC

105 Price Parkway, Farmingdale, NY 11735
Tel: (516) 293 5300

Chairman: Bernard Greenman (and Chief Executive Officer), Vice Chairman: Stanley Greenman (and Chief Executive Officer and Secretary)
President: Stewart Katz
Senior Executive Officers: David Yankey (VP Finance and Assistant Secretary), Jerry Cohen (Treasurer)

PRINCIPAL ACTIVITIES: Wholesale and retail trade in recreational goods and toys
Principal Subsidiaries: Associated Sales Agency Inc; Playland Toy Stores Inc; Watson Triangle Co Inc; Watson Triangle Co; Zippel Martin Co Inc

Principal Bank: Manufacturers Hanover Trust Co
Financial Information:

	$'000
Sales revenues	218,000

No of Employees: 1,000

GREENVILLE STEEL CAR CO

Greenville, PA 16125
Tel: (412) 588-7000

Chairman: Marshall Berkman
President: K R Hittle
Senior Executive Officers: R L Johnson (VP Finance), T J Fortunato (VP Manufacturing)

PRINCIPAL ACTIVITIES: Manufacture and leasing of railroad vehicles
Parent Company: Ampco-Pittsburgh Corporation, Pittsburgh, PA
Principal Bank: First Boston Bank
Financial Information:

	$'000
Sales revenues	100,000

No of Employees: 800

GREENWOOD MILLS

PO Box 1017, Greenwood, SC 29646
Tel: (803) 229-2571
Telex: TWX 8102842366 grwdmlll grwd sc

Chairman: J C Self Jr
President: W M Self
Senior Executive Officers: K E Young (VP Finance), Wayne Justinson (VP, Secretary and General Counsel), J W Davis (VP Real Estate), R F Hawthorne (VP Finishing), W L Roark (VP Engineering), E W Roberts (VP Manufacturing), H E Munnerlyn (VP Sales), L W McCalin (VP Greige Manufacturing)

PRINCIPAL ACTIVITIES: Manufacture of natural and synthetic textile products
Financial Information:

	$'000
Sales revenues	300,000

No of Employees: 7,500

GREER HYDRAULICS, INC

6500 E Slauson Ave, City of Commerce, CA 90040
Tel: (213) 725 0110

President: Les T Hansen
Senior Executive Officers: D Miller (Sales Manager)

PRINCIPAL ACTIVITIES: Hydraulic equipment and accumulators
Parent Company: Fairchild Industries Inc
Principal Bank: Security Pacific National Bank
Financial Information:

	$'000
Sales revenues	50,000

No of Employees: 200

GREFCO, INC

3435 Lomita Blvd, Torrance, CA 90505
Tel: (213) 517-0700
Telex: 664266

President: J F Lang
Senior Executive Officers: J E Perelman (VP and Treasurer), D S Costello (VP and Secretary), C J Vogelsang (VP Operations), D L Ruff (VP Sales and Marketing), M J Mirliss (VP Technical), R F McGuffin (Assistant Secretary and Treasurer), I R Rule (VP and Controller)

PRINCIPAL ACTIVITIES: Manufacture of filter aids and fillers
Trade Names: Dicalite, Dicaperl, Permalite
Parent Company: General Refractories Co, Bala-Cynwyd, PA
Principal Subsidiaries: Chemrock; Dicalite Corp; Dicalite Europe Nord
Principal Bank: First Interstate Bank

No of Employees: 800

GREIF BROS CORPORATION

621 Pennsylvania Avenue, Delaware, OH 43015
Tel: (614) 363-1271

Chairman: John C Dempsey (and Chief Executive Officer)
President: John P Berg
Senior Executive Officers: Elmer A Reitz (Executive VP), Allan Hull (VP, Director and General Counsel), Matthew J Hickey III (Director), Robert C Macauley (Director), Lloyd D Baker (VP), Michael M Bixby (VP), Edward M Bobula (VP and Director of Industrial Relations), William C Boyd (VP), Herbert L Carpenter Jr (VP), Edward L Dean (VP), Thomas A Dubbe (VP), Robert A Dubois (VP), William F Flanigan (VP), Harry R Gardner (VP), Harrison C Golway Jr (VP), C J Guilbeau (VP), William H Gushard (VP-National Accounts Sales and Technical Service), C Leon Howard (VP), Doris J Hyre (VP), Ralph A Kelley (VP), Dennis J Kuhn (VP), Hadley W Saathoff (VP), Alvis H Snipes (VP), Edward L Stanford (VP), Russell J Rehark (Treasurer), Arthur H Rubow (Secretary), John P Conroy (Assistant Secretary), Vincent M Henry (National Sales Manager, Plastics Division), Richard E Gerstner (General Manager, Steel Drum Operations, East Coast Division), Kenneth W Ferguson (General Manager of Sales, Corrugated Operations, Bettis Division), E Alton Skinner (General Manager, Steel Drum Operations, Raible Division), Michael J Gasser (Controller), Philip R Metzger (Assistant Controller and Assistant Treasurer)

PRINCIPAL ACTIVITIES: The Company operates over 100 locations in 29 states of the United States and in 3 provinces of Canada and manufactures principally bulk shipping containers such as fibre drums, steel drums, corrugated containers, multiwall bags and plastic containers
Principal Subsidiaries: Down River International Inc; Greif Board Corporation; Michigan Packaging Company; Soterra Incorporated; Greif Containers Inc (Canada)
Financial Information:

	Oct 31 1985 $'000	Oct 31 1986 $'000
Sales revenues	310,067	315,550
Income before taxes	42,232	34,153
Net income	23,632	18,953
Dividends Class A	3,100	3,059
Dividends Class B	6,096	5,867
Dividends per share Class A	$0.56	$0.56
Dividends per share Class B	$0.82	$0.82
Earnings per share Class A	$1.68	$1.36
Earnings per share Class B	$1.94	$1.62
Capital stock*	9,034	9,034
Retained income	192,303	195,054
Shareholders equity	198,743	201,228

*without par value

No of Employees: 3,650

GREINER ENGINEERING INC

300 East Carpenter Freeway, Suite 1210, Irving, TX 75062
Tel: (214) 258 6208

Chairman: Thomas H Lenagh
President: Frank T Callahan (and Chief Executive Officer)
Senior Executive Officers: Robert Costello (VP and Secretary), Michael J Kozlowski (VP, Treasurer and Chief Financial Officer), Joseph M Bolton (VP)

PRINCIPAL ACTIVITIES: Provision of a range of engineering services including surveying and architectural services
Principal Subsidiaries: Daverman Associates Inc; Genge Aerial Surveys; Greiner Engineering Sciences; Meurer-Serafini & Meurer Inc; SP Group/West
Principal Bank: Lloyds Bank

Financial Information:

	$'000
Sales revenues	68,200

No of Employees: 1,100

GREY ADVERTISING, INC

777 Third Ave, New York, NY 10017

Tel: (212) 546-2000

Chairman: Edward H Meyer (and President and Chief Executive Officer)

Senior Executive Officers: Alan B Fendrick (Executive VP, Secretary and Treasurer)

PRINCIPAL ACTIVITIES: Advertising

Principal Subsidiaries: Com-Step Inc; Crescendo Productions Inc; Grey & Davis Inc; Grey Conahay & Lyon Inc; Grey Direct Marketing Group Inc; Grey Medical Advertising Inc; Grey-North Inc; Lexington Broadcast Services Corp Inc; Market Horizons Inc; Statter Inc

Principal Bank: Chase Manhattan Bank

Financial Information:

	$'000
Sales revenues	227,000

No of Employees: 2,200

GREYHOUND CORPORATION (THE)

Greyhound Tower, Phoenix, AZ 85077

Tel: (602) 248-4000

Chairman: John W Teets (and President and Chief Executive Officer)

Senior Executive Officers: Corporate Staff Officers: Ermo S Bartoletti (VP-Internal Auditing), James T Corcoran (VP-Government Affairs), Armen Ervanian (VP-Real Estate), Ralph A Korn (VP-Insurance), F Edward Lake (VP-Finance), L Gene Lemon (VP and General Counsel), Lawrence F Lamb (VP-Public Relations and General Counsel), Leo S McDonald (VP-Convention Services), John W Meredith (VP-Corporate Planning), Harry S Oakes (VP-Office and Information Systems), Richard C Stephan (VP-Controller), Robert A Lang (VP-Human Resources), Richard B Zoller (VP-Investments), Frederick G Emerson (Secretary), Ronald G Nelson (Treaurer)

PRINCIPAL ACTIVITIES: Diversified holding company with interests in consumer products, financial services, transportation, manufacturing and consumer and business services

Principal Subsidiaries: The Dial Corp; Armour International Company; Greyhound Lines of Canada Inc (Canada); Texas, New Mexico and Oklahoma Coaches Inc; Vermont Transit Company Inc; Brewster Transport Company Ltd (Canada); Greyhound Food Management Inc; Glacier Park Inc; Restaura SA (Belgium); Greyhound Financial and Leasing Corporation AG (Switzerland); Greyhound Financial Corp; Travelers Express Company Inc; Verex Corporation; Motor Coach Ltd (Canada); Motor Coach Industries Inc; Transportation Manufacturing Corporation; Universal Coach Parts Inc; Consultants and Designers Inc; Greyhound Exhibitgroup Inc; Greyhound Exposition Services Inc; MCI Acceptance Corporation; Aircraft Service International Inc; Greyhound Leisure Services Inc; Premier Cruise Lines Ltd, Jetsave

Financial Information:

	Dec 31 1985	Dec 31 1986
	$'000	$'000
Sales revenues	2,352,276	2,454,206
Income before taxes	114,817	72,682
Net income	114,214	188,805
Dividends	60,820	59,849
Dividends per share	$1.26	$1.32
Earnings per share(1)	$2.36	$4.18
Common stock(2)	72,832	72,832
Shares-issued	48,554	48,554
Shares-outstanding	39,466	46,423
Average shares(3)	47,933	44,884
Retained income	794,994	920,426
Shareholders equity	1,130,692	1,027,488

(1) common and equivalents
(2) $1.50 par value
(3) of common and equivalents

No of Employees: 35,400

GRI CORPORATION

65 East Southwater Street, Chicago, IL 60601
Tel: (312) 977 3700

Chairman: David R Rubin (and Chief Executive Officer)
President: Anthony P DeNunzio (and Chief Operating Officer)
Senior Executive Officers: Anthony C Brown (Executive VP Marketing), Joseph J Basgall (VP), Lawrence I Hollins (VP), Thomas Rehwald (VP Finance, Secretary and Treasurer), Richard P DiStasio

PRINCIPAL ACTIVITIES: Mail order trading in packaged goods, cosmetics and toiletries and stainless steel flatware
Trade Names: World of Beauty, S.A.V.E.
Principal Bank: LaSalle/ABN
Financial Information:

	Nov 30 1985	Nov 30 1986
	$'000	$'000
Sales revenues	81,237	74,008
Income before taxes	1,893	1,744
Net income (loss)	(5,673)	1,251
Net earnings (loss) per share	($2.59)	$0.56
Common stock	281	239
Retained income	10,157	11,386
Shareholders equity	9,974	11,286

No of Employees: 400

GRIEF COMPANIES

939 Marcon Road, Allentown, PA 18001
Tel: (215) 266-2200

Chairman: Larry B Shelton
President: Norman Fryman
Senior Executive Officers: David Pergola (VP Marketing), Bill Stewmetz (VP Merchandising), Robert Dilgard (VP Finance and Administration), Phil Looby (Executive VP Manufacturing and Operations), Roland Plojing (VP Design), Terry Smith (VP Human Resources)

PRINCIPAL ACTIVITIES: Clothing manufacture
Parent Company: Genesco Inc, Nashville, TN
Financial Information:

	Jan 31 1986	Jan 31 1987
	$'000	$'000
Sales revenues	94,873	93,354
(Loss) before taxes	(12,631)	(2,882)
Net (loss)	(12,631)	(2,882)

No of Employees: 1,900

GRIFFIN & BRAND OF MCALLEN INC

4702 N 23rd Street, McAllen, TX 78501
Tel: (512) 682-6181
Telex: WUT 700044 trophy mca

Chairman: Othal E Brand
President: Wayne A Showers
Senior Executive Officers: Mike Gower (VP Sales), James Ferrell (VP Mexico), Onas D Brand (Secretary and Treasurer)

PRINCIPAL ACTIVITIES: Growers and processers of fruits and vegetables; fresh and frozen products
Principal Subsidiaries: Griffin & Brand Inc
Principal Bank: First National Bank
Financial Information:

	$'000
Sales revenues	75,000

No of Employees: 1,000

GRINNELL FIRE PROTECTION SYSTEMS COMPANY, INC

10 Dorrance Street, Providence, RI 02903
Tel: (401) 456-5600
Telex: WUT 927553 grinnellmkt pud

President: L Dennis Kozlowski
Senior Executive Officers: A Beck (Executive VP), J H Peck (VP Southern Region), J S Pepi (VP Research and Development), J T Gard (VP), R E Mead (VP Finance and Treasurer), D P Brownell (VP and General Manager Alarm, Detection and Corporate Marketing), J S Pepi (VP Research and Development), B J Doherty (VP, Secretary and Legal Counsel)

PRINCIPAL ACTIVITIES: Manufacture of fire protection equipment including sprinklers and detection and alarm systems
Parent Company: Tyco Laboratories Inc, Exeter, NH
Financial Information:

	$'000
Sales revenues	200,000

No of Employees: 3,500

GRISWOLD RUBBER COMPANY, INC

PO Box 638, Moosup, CT 06354
Tel: (203) 564-3321

Chairman: Mark J O'Friel (and Treasurer)
President: Lawrence V Sarni (and General Manager)
Senior Executive Officers: Nebbie P Joseph (VP Marketing)

PRINCIPAL ACTIVITIES: Manufacture of foam rubber
Principal Bank: The Connecticut Bank & Trust Company
Financial Information:

	$'000
Sales revenues	60,000

No of Employees: 75

GROCERS BAKING CO

210 28th St SE, Grand Rapids, MI 49508
Tel: (616) 245-9127

Chairman: Parker T Feldpausch; Vice Chairman: Pat Quinn
President: Vincent S Callaghan (and General Manager)
Senior Executive Officers: Jerry Veldkamp (VP Sales), Dale E Kris (VP Finance), Gene Bast (VP Operations)

PRINCIPAL ACTIVITIES: Manufacture of bread and bakery products
Principal Subsidiaries: April Hill Inc; Jackco Enterprises Inc
Principal Bank: Comerica Bank-Kentwood, NA
Financial Information:

	$'000
Sales revenues	50,000

No of Employees: 600

GROLIER INC

Sherman Turnpike, Danbury, CT 06816
Tel: (203) 797-3500
Cable: GROLIER DURY
Telex: 969641

Chairman: Robert B Clarke (and President and Chief Executive Officer)
Senior Executive Officers: A J Reinhart (Executive VP), Howard B Graham (Senior VP Marketing and Product Development), Geoffrey Kerr (VP Planning), E L Marino (VP), Richard G Webb (VP Finance and Treasurer), Edward J Gildea (Secretary-Corporate Counsel)

PRINCIPAL ACTIVITIES: Publishing including educational books and educational material
Principal Subsidiaries: Federated Credit Corp; Franklin Watts Inc; Grolier Credit Services Inc; Grolier Educational Corp; Scarecrow Press Inc; Grolier Electronic Publishing Inc; Grolier Enterprises Inc; Grolier International Inc; Publishers World Trade Corp; Grolier Reading Programs Inc; Grolier Telemarketing Inc; Grolier Year Book Inc; Lexicon Publications Inc; New Grolier Interstate Inc
Principal Bank: Chase Manhattan Bank
Financial Information:

	$'000
Sales revenues	296,065

No of Employees: 7,200

GROVE MANUFACTURING CO

PO Box 21, Shady Grove, PA 17256
Tel: (717) 597-8121
Telex: 84 2308 grove mfg shgr

Chairman: J M Benchoff (and Chief Executive Officer)
Senior Executive Officers: Charles A Warner (Executive VP), Gary W Spickler (Senior VP Manufacturing Operations), John D Marshall (Senior VP Finance), Eugene C Gardenhour (Senior VP Engineering), Ray E Kane (VP Materials), Gene E Kessler (VP Customer Services), J Kirk Smith (VP International Marketing), Joseph A Shull (VP Domestic Marketing), Rodney C Benchoff (VP Administration)

PRINCIPAL ACTIVITIES: Manufacture of construction plant and mechanical handling equipment
Parent Company: Kidde Inc, Saddle Brook, NJ
Financial Information:

	$'000
Sales revenues	450,000

No of Employees: 3,000

GROW GROUP INC

200 Park Avenue, New York, NY 10166
Tel: (212) 599-4400

President: Russell Banks (and Chief Executive Officer)
Senior Executive Officers: John F Gleason (Executive VP), Leslie D Stott (Group VP, Automotive), J Robert Desjardins (Group VP, Trade Sales), Joseph M Quinn (Group VP, Marine and Corrosion Control), David J Magid (Group VP, Consumer), Bernard T Hanley (VP, Finance), Edward A Smolinski (VP and Treasurer), Grant McLennan (VP, Consumer Marketing), W Horton Russell (VP, Manufacturing, Safety, Health and Environment), Teresa A McCaslin (Director of Human Resources), Frank V Esser (Controller), Lloyd Frank (Secretary). Assistant Secretaries: Evelyn Charney (Shareholder Relations), Judith Krupka (Group Insurance), Richard Holcombe (Corporate Risk Manager), James E Feeney, Catherine Lemon

PRINCIPAL ACTIVITIES: Manufacture of coatings, paints, solvents and thinners for industrial, marine and domestic markets; household cleaning products; food processing systems
Trade Names: Alumigrip, Awlgrip, Awl-Fair Epoxy Trowelable Fairing Compound, Alumigard Primer, Hydro-Shur, Uni-Grip, Color-Key Program, Deuflex, Devran, Devprep, Prufcoat Pre-Prime Sealer, GrowPak, Like Magic, Trewax, Enviro-Spray, Thermaljet, Golden Roast, Like Magic Mist & Feed
Principal Subsidiaries: Automotive and Industrial Group:- Automotive Division, Grow Group, Inc, Troy, Michigan,

Detroit, Michigan, Baton Rouge, Louisiana, Cerritos, California; Grow Chemical Europe, NV (Belgium); Grow AG (Switzerland); US Paint Division, Grow Group, Inc. Trade Sales Group: Devoe & Raynolds Co, Division of Grow Group, Inc; Ameritone Paint Corporation; Harris & Devoe Paints Corp (Puerto Rico); Bennett Paint Corp. Marine and Corrosion Control Group: Devoe Marine Coatings Co, Division of Grow Group, Inc; Napko Corporation; Devoe Marine Coatings of Canada, Ltd (Canada); Devoe Coatings, BV (Netherlands); Grow AG (Swtizerland); Devoe Prufcoat, Division of Grow Group, Inc. Consumer Group: Cello Corp; Cello Puerto Rico Corp (Puerto Rico); Cello West; Trewax; Tewax Company of Canada, Inc (Canada); Grow Consumer Products, Inc; National Aerosol Products Company; Reply-O-Letter Company, Inc. Grow Ventures Corporation: Enviro-Spray Systems, Inc; Grow-Group-Enviro-Spray Systems Belgium NV (Belgium); Enviro-Spray Canada Inc (Joint Venture) (Canada); Thermaljet, Ltd; Grow Food Processing Corporation; Growlane Foods (Joint Venture)

Principal Bank: Chemical Bank

Financial Information:

	$'000
Sales revenues	274,850

No of Employees: 2,100

GROWMARK, INC

1701 Towanda Avenue, Bloomington, IL 61701
Tel: (309) 557-2111
Telex: TWX 510352 1998 growmark blmg

Chairman: O G Webb; Vice Chairmen: Howard D Poulson, Daryle L Stonier

Senior Executive Officers: Kenneth P Baer (Executive VP and Chief Executive Officer), Ros W Gilfillan (Senior VP), T E Mulligan (Senior VP Finance), Earl Grossmann (Group VP Supply), Marvin Weisert (VP Marketing), Stanley Nielsen (VP Distribution), George R Niebur (VP Field Services), John McCleranthan (VP Grain Operations), Norman T Jones (VP Corporate Services)

PRINCIPAL ACTIVITIES: Manufacture of fertilizers and animal feedstuffs

Principal Subsidiaries: Illinois Co-op Future Co

Principal Bank: First National Bank of Chicago

Financial Information:

	$'000
Sales revenues	1,750,000

No of Employees: 6,400

GRUBB & ELLIS CO

One Montgomery St, Crocker Center-West Tower, San Francisco, CA 94104
Tel: (415) 956-1990

Chairman: Harold A Ellis Jr (and President and Chief Executive Officer)

Senior Executive Officers: Emmett R DeMoss Jr (Executive VP and Chief Operating Officer), Donald L McGee (Senior VP, Secretary and Legal Counsel), Joseph F Hamilton (Senior VP and Chief Financial Officer)

PRINCIPAL ACTIVITIES: Property management; residential relocation services; mortgage broking

Principal Bank: Bank of America

Financial Information:

	$'000
Sales revenues	254,660

No of Employees: 6,000

GRUMA CORPORATION

2343 Saybrook Avenue, City of Commerce, CA 90040
Tel: (213) 722-8790

President: E Livas

Senior Executive Officers: Ray Fernandez (VP Finance)

PRINCIPAL ACTIVITIES: Milling; food and beverage plant

Principal Bank: Security Pacific Bank

Financial Information:

	$'000
Sales revenues	70,000

No of Employees: 1,000

GRUMMAN CORPORATION

1111 Stewart Avenue, Bethpage, NY 11714
Tel: (516) 575-0574

Chairman: John C Bierwirth (and Chief Executive Officer)

President: John O'Brien (and Chief Operating Officer)

Senior Executive Officers: George E R Kinnear II (Senior VP Washington), Robert W Bradshaw (VP and Secretary), George L Brown (VP Washington Relations and EEO), Natale P Busi (VP and Controller), John J Carroll (VP Community Relations), Dean G Cassell (VP Product Integrity and Environmental Protection), Howard J Dunn Jr (VP Auditor), Thomas L Genovese (VP and Legal Counsel), W B Jones (VP Public Affairs), Steven Dely (VP and Assistant to President), Richard A Scheuing (VP Corporate Research Center), David L Walsh (VP Marketing)

PRINCIPAL ACTIVITIES: Holding company with interests in the manufacture of aircraft and aerospace equipment; motor vehicles manufacture; leasing; data processing equipment, software and services

Principal Subsidiaries: Grumman Internatinoal Inc; Grumman Aerospace Corporation; Grumman Allied Industries Inc; Grumman Data Systems Corporation; Paumanock Development Corporation; Grumman Ohio Corporation; Grumman Credit Corporation; Grumman Houston Corp; Grumman St Augustine Corp; Grumman Technical Services Corp; Grumman Emergency Products Inc; Grumman CTEC Inc; Grumman Data Information Services Inc; Systematic Associates Inc; ISI Systems Inc

Principal Bank: Citibank

Financial Information:

	Dec 31 1986 $'000
Sales revenues	3,440,125
Net income	78,690
Earnings per share	$2.32
Shareholders equity	721,975

No of Employees: 32,000

GRUNAU CO, INC

307 W Layton Avenue, Milwaukee, WI 53207
Tel: (414) 769-5400
Telex: TWX 910262 1180 grunau mil

Chairman: Gary P Grunau

Senior Executive Officers: John Dragisic (Executive VP), Thomas A Anderson (VP Finance), Ted Angelo (VP), Michael Foley (VP Florida Division), Oscar Kornblum (VP), Thomas Bohlmann (VP), Edward Pendzich (VP), Wayne Van Alstyne (VP)

PRINCIPAL ACTIVITIES: Heating, ventilation and plumbing contractors

Parent Company: Grucon Corp

Principal Bank: M & I Marshall & Ilsley

Financial Information:

	$'000
Sales revenues	80,000

No of Employees: 1,200

GRUNTAL FINANCIAL CORPORATION

14 Wall Street, New York, NY 10004
Tel: (212) 267 8800

Chairman: Frederick M Stern; Vice Chairman: William M Lendman

President: Howard Silverman (and Chief Executive Officer)

Senior Executive Officers: Edward E Bao (Executive VP Administration and Operations), Albert M Hartig (Executive VP, Treasurer and Secretary), Sandra Rudel (Executive VP), Norbert L Grunwald (Senior VP), Barry Richter (Senior VP), James L Spingarn (Senior VP)

PRINCIPAL ACTIVITIES: Provision of financial services including dealing in securities

Principal Subsidiaries: Regional Clearing Corp

Principal Bank: Irving Trust Co

Financial Information:

	$'000
Revenues	200,000

No of Employees: 1,340

GTE COMMUNICATIONS SYSTEMS CORPORATION

2500 W Utopia Road, Phoenix, AZ 85027

Tel: (602) 582-7000

Telex: TWX 910 9500176 gte auto z phx

President: Jack M Kirker

Senior Executive Officers: Kenneth N Fromm (VP Human Resources), Roger B Ray (VP Finance), William S Martin (VP Strategic Planning), P R Harrington (VP Research and Development), M L Keith (VP GTE Sales)

PRINCIPAL ACTIVITIES: Manufacture of telecommunications systems

Parent Company: GTE Corporation, Stamford, CT

Financial Information:

	$'000
Sales revenues	200,000

No of Employees: 5,000

GTE CORPORATION

One Stamford Forum, Stamford, CT 06904

Tel: (203) 965-2000

Telex: 4750071

Chairman: Theodore F Brophy

President: James L Johnson

Senior Executive Officers: James L Broadhead (President, Telephone Operations), Bruce Carswell (Senior VP Human Resources), Charles R Lee (Senior VP Finance), Allan L Rayfield (President, Products and Systems), Edward C Schmults (Senior VP and General Counsel), Timothy P Murphy (VP Investor Relations)

PRINCIPAL ACTIVITIES: Telecommunications, lighting products, and precision materials and electronic equipment

Trade Names: SYLVANIA

Principal Subsidiaries: GTE Products of Connecticut Corporation; GTE Government Systems Corporation; GTE Communications Systems Corporation; GTE Products Corporation; GTE Laboratories Inc; GTE International Inc; GTE Sylvania Licht GmbH (Germany); GTE Spacenet Corporation; GTE Valeron Corporation; Anglo-Canadian Telephone Company (Canada) (86.39%); British Columbia Telephone Company (50.38%) (Canada); Microtel Limited (Canada); Canadian Telephones and Supplies Limited (Canada); Quebec-Telephone (50.56%) (Canada); Dominion Directory Company Limited (Canada); GTE Florida; GTE North; GTE South; GTE Southwest; GTE California; GTE Alaska; Hawaiian Telephone Company; GTE Directories Corporation; GTE Data Services Inc; GTE Finance Corporation; GTE Global Corporation (USA Virgin Islands); GTE Investment Management Corporation; GTE Mobilnet Inc; GTE Realty Corporation; GTE Reinsurance Company Ltd (Bermuda); GTE Service Corporation; GTE Shareholders Services Inc; GTE Telecom; US Sprint

Financial Information:

	Dec 31 1985 $'000	Dec 31 1986 $'000
Sales revenues	14,372,000	15,111,528
Income (loss) before taxes	(162,386)	2,090,611
Net income (loss)	(161,091)	1,184,312
Dividends per share	$2.08	$2.20
Earnings (loss) per share	($0.63)	$3.53
Common stock	312,455	326,309
Shareholders equity	7,055,609	7,885,274

Number of shareholders: 424,000

No of Employees: 160,000

GTE DIRECTORIES CORPORATION

West Airfield Dr, Box 619810, D/FW Airport, TX 75261

Tel: (214) 453 7000

President: Thomas F Lysaught

Senior Executive Officers: Anthony J Knight (VP Domestic), Douglas T Mullen (VP Production and Services), W D McFaddin (VP International), Ann P Delo (VP Human Resources), Peter L Green (VP Administration and Treasurer), Paul W Schlake (VP and Controller), Donald B Cotton (VP Information Management), Paul J Willis (VP National Marketing Services)

PRINCIPAL ACTIVITIES: Production of telephone directories

Parent Company: GTE Corporation, Stamford, CT

Principal Bank: First National Bank of Chicago

Financial Information:

	$'000
Sales revenues	711,000

No of Employees: 4,300

GTE INTERNATIONAL INC

One Stamford Forum, Stamford, CT 06904

Tel: (203) 965-2000

President: Robert J Gressens

Senior Executive Officers: Edward C Schmults (Senior VP and General Counsel), Nicholas B Tournillon (VP and Treasurer), Marianne Drost (Secretary)

PRINCIPAL ACTIVITIES: Manufacture of telecommunications and electrical equipment

Parent Company: GTE Corporation, Stamford, CT

Financial Information:

	$'000
Sales revenues	860,000

GTE PRODUCTS CORPORATION

One Stamford Forum, Stamford, CT 06904

Tel: (203) 865-2000

President: Dean T Langford

Senior Executive Officers: Claude A Burleson (VP Taxes), J A Lincoln (VP and General Counsel), Stuart M Kleinfelter (VP Operations Service), Timothy P Murphy (VP Finance), Robert P Hausmann (VP Human Resources), George M Shahian (VP Business Development and Planning), Allan T Wang (VP and Controller), Vincent R D'Allesandro (VP Public Affairs), Richard P de la Chapelle (VP Engineering and Manufacturing)

PRINCIPAL ACTIVITIES: Manufacture of lighting equipment and telecommunications equipment

Parent Company: GTE Corporation, Stamford CT

Financial Information:

	$'000
Sales revenues	1,900,000

No of Employees: 28,000

GTECH CORPORATION

101 Dyer Street, Providence, RI 02903

Tel: (401) 273 7700

Chairman: Robert K Stern

President: Guy B Snowden (and Chief Executive Officer)
Senior Executive Officers: Victor Markowicz (Executive VP and Secretary), William G Gerber (VP and Contract Control Officer), Donald C McCauley (VP Finance, VP Administration, Treasurer and Chief Financial Officer), Leonard G Morrissey Jr (VP Marketing), Paul R Nock (VP Production), Donald L Stanford (VP Advanced Development)

PRINCIPAL ACTIVITIES: Provision of computer services for betting including on-line lottery systems
Principal Bank: First National Bank of Boston
Financial Information:

	$'000
Sales revenues	81,000

No of Employees: 500

GUARANTEE ELECTRICAL CO

3405 Bent Avenue, St Louis, MO 63116
Tel: (314) 772-5400
Telex: TWX 9107612108 gecpstlouis

Chairman: Charles W Oertli
President: Fred G Oertli
Senior Executive Officers: Fred J Oertli (Chairman Executive Committee), Joseph D Brumm (Executive VP and Treasurer), Otis H Hettich (VP Construction), G E Kirk (VP Estimating), Roger Stammer (VP Illinois), D D Metcalfe (VP Marketing), Myron Bernard (VP Geco Engineering)

PRINCIPAL ACTIVITIES: Electrical engineering contractors; construction materials and fittings
Principal Bank: Mercantile Bank and Trust Company
Financial Information:

	$'000
Sales revenues	55,000

No of Employees: 850

GUARANTEE FINANCIAL CORPORATION OF CALIFORNIA

1177 Fulton Mall, Fresno, CA 93721
Tel: (201) 268-8111

Chairman: Lewis S Eaton (and Chief Executive Officer)
President: Ed L Hickman (and Chief Operating Officer); John J McMenimon (GESCO Corp)
Senior Executive Officers: John P Dickey (Executive VP), Mildred Huddlestone (Executive VP), Peter J Savarino (Executive VP and Treasurer), Katharine Chrisman (Executive VP Consumer Banking), Warren Houston (Executive VP Marketing), Richard A Nichols (Executive VP and Secretary), David H Adams (Senior VP Finance), William L Eaton (Senior VP Auditor), Larry Nystom (Senior VP), Philip M Girard (VP Property Management), Ronald L Fitzgerald (VP and Controller), Charles R Yeats (VP Corporate Systems), Jack Armistead (VP General Service Purchasing)

PRINCIPAL ACTIVITIES: Financial services
Principal Subsidiaries: Guarantee Financial Real Estate; Guarantee Financial Services; Guarantee Savings; GESCO Corp
Principal Bank: Bank of America
Financial Information:

	Dec 31 1985 $'000	Dec 31 1986 $'000
Net income	14,131	8,042
Earnings per share	$2.32	$1.31
Shareholders equity	79,604	86,419
Deposits	-	2,167,143
Total assets	2,860,230	2,874,138

No of Employees: 1,696

GUARANTY NATIONAL CORPORATION

100 Inverness Terrace East, PO Box 3329, Englewood, CO 80155
Tel: (303) 790-8200

Chairman: Alan R Gruber; Vice Chairman: Abraham L Berenbeim
President: Roger B Ware (and Chief Executive Officer)
Senior Executive Officers: Fred T Roberts (Senior VP Claims), James B Schallett (Senior VP Personal Lines), Bobby Maes (Senior VP Underwriting), Michael Pautler (Senior VP, Treasurer and Chief Financial Officer), Richard D Rock (VP), Larry G Dick (Secretary)

PRINCIPAL ACTIVITIES: Property and casualty insurance
Principal Bank: United Bank of Denver
Financial Information:

	$'000
Revenues	89,450

No of Employees: 240

GUARDIAN INDUSTRIES CORPORATION

43043 W Nine Mile Road, Northville, MI 48167
Tel: (313) 349-6700

President: William M Davidson (and Chief Executive Officer)
Senior Executive Officers: Thomas F Gaffney (Executive VP), Russell J Ebeid (Group VP), William F Black (Group VP), William E Morrow (Group VP), John P Ory (Group VP), Jeffrey A Knight (VP and Chief Financial Officer), Ralph J Gerson (VP Government and International Affairs), Murray J Yudin (VP National Sales), Alton K Brown (VP Western Region), Barney H Hertzberg (VP Marketing), Norman Shulman (VP Flat Glass Sales), Richard Alonzo (VP Engineering)

PRINCIPAL ACTIVITIES: Glass and glass products; photographic products and photofinishing services
Principal Subsidiaries: Guardian Industries Distribution Center Inc; Consulting Services Inc; GIC Financial Services Corporation; GIC Equipment Leasing Company; GIC Leasing Services Inc; Permaglass Industries Ltd; Permaglass Ltd (50.2%); Guardian Glass Company; Guardian Disc Corporation; Glass Guard Industries Inc; Sitelines Inc; Fast Foto Inc; Guardian Photo Inc; Luxguard SA (70%); Pennsylvania Float Glass Inc
Principal Bank: Michigan National Bank of Detroit
Financial Information:

	$'000
Sales revenues	470,000

No of Employees: 4,200

GUARDIAN LIFE INSURANCE CO OF AMERICA

201 Park Avenue S, New York, NY 10003
Tel: (212) 598-8000
Telex: 014-65-401

Chairman: John C Angle
President: Arthur V Ferrara
Senior Executive Officers: Joseph D Sargent (Senior VP Life Insurance), Peter L Hutchings (Executive VP and Chief Financial Officer) (Executive VP Group Insurance), Edward K Kane (Senior VP and General Counsel), Henry B Spencer (Senior VP Investments), Franklin E Sorrentino (VP Health Insurance), John M Smith (Senior VP Equity Products), Herbert N Grolnick (Secretary), John J Pallotta Jr (Senior VP Group Insurance), Thomas Kabele (VP and Corporate Actuary)

PRINCIPAL ACTIVITIES: Mutual life and health insurance company
Trade Names: The Guardian
Principal Subsidiaries: Guardian Investment and Annuity Corporation; Guardian Investor Services Corporation
Principal Bank: Chemical Bank

Financial Information:

	Dec 31 1985	Dec 31 1986
	$'000	$'000
Premium income	1,769,400	1,657,861
Investment income	268,733	289,759
Income before taxes(1)	144,442	91,701
Income (loss) before taxes	31,230	(21,264)
Net income (loss)	17,415	(9,681)
Dividends(2)	113,212	112,965
Surplus	223,292	388,925
Total assets	3,172,289	3,691,576

(1) and dividends
(2) to policy holders

No of Employees: 3,500

GUARDSMAN CHEMICALS INC

PO Box 1521, Grand Rapids, MI 49501
Tel: (616) 957-2600
Telex: TWX 8102736968 guardsman gdr

President: Keith C Vander Hyde (and Chief Executive Officer)
Senior Executive Officers: Kenneth Gilchrist (Executive VP), Joe Knoll (Executive VP), Lester P Kragt (VP Finance and Treasurer), Chuck Bennett (VP Coatings)

PRINCIPAL ACTIVITIES: Manufacture of paints, varnishes and enamels, packaging and fabricated metal products
Principal Bank: Old Kent Bank and Trust Company
Financial Information:

	$'000
Sales revenues	87,500

No of Employees: 770

GUERDON INDUSTRIES, INC

3773 Cherry Creek No. Drive, Denver, CO 80209
Tel: (303) 355-6100

Chairman: J Frederick Huckvale (and President and Chief Executive Officer)
Senior Executive Officers: Tom Wilson (Executive VP), Douglas Bonnette (VP-Finance), Ray Malone (VP-Legal)

PRINCIPAL ACTIVITIES: Manufacture of manufactured homes and sectional buildings
Trade Names: Magnolia, Embassy, Great Lakes
Parent Company: Huckvale Acquisition, Inc, Los Angeles, CA
Principal Subsidiaries: Magnolia Homes, Inc
Principal Bank: Bank of America
Financial Information:

	$'000
Sales revenues	150,000

Principal Shareholders: Huckvale Acquisition, Inc, Los Angeles, CA
No of Employees: 1,600

GUILFORD INDUSTRIES, INC

Oak Street, Guilford, ME 04443
Tel: (207) 876-3331

Chairman: H K Cummings
President: Leonard Saulter
Senior Executive Officers: H K Melvin (Secretary and Treasurer)

PRINCIPAL ACTIVITIES: Manufacture of natural and synthetic fabrics for furnishing
Principal Bank: Bank of New England
Financial Information:

	$'000
Sales Revenues	65,820

No of Employees: 1,300

GUILFORD MILLS, INC

4925 W Market Street, Greensboro, NC 27402
Tel: (919) 292-7550

Chairman: Charles A Hayes (and Chief Executive Officer); Vice Chairman: Maurice Fishman (and Senior VP)
President: George Greenberg
Senior Executive Officers: Norman C Weisbecker (Executive VP Marketing), Paul R McGarr (VP Finance, Treasurer and Secretary), Bernard Fleisher (VP Manufacturing), Stan Mackney (VP Sales), Leonard Naider (VP Sales)

PRINCIPAL ACTIVITIES: Manufacture of knitted fabrics
Principal Subsidiaries: Guilford International Inc; Guilford Kapwood Inc
Principal Bank: The First National Bank of Boston
Financial Information:

	$'000
Sales revenues	356,521

No of Employees: 2,200

GULF CHEMICAL & METALLURGICAL CO

202 Midway Road, Freeport, TX 77541
Tel: (409) 233-7882
Telex: WUT 765456 gulfchem tecy

President: E B King
Senior Executive Officers: Wilson R Barnes (VP Research and Development), Keith R Dean (VP and General Manager)

PRINCIPAL ACTIVITIES: Manufacture of non ferrous metal and chemicals
Principal Bank: The Chase Manhattan Bank
Financial Information:

	$'000
Sales revenues	50,000

No of Employees: 300

GULF RESOURCES & CHEMICAL CORPORATION

1100 Milam Building, Houston, TX 77002
Tel: (713) 658-0471
Telex: WUT 775482 gulf res hou

Chairman: Robert G Boulton (and Chairman Executive Committee); Vice Chairman: Seymour Graubard (and Vice Chairman Executive Committee)
President: Donald E McCuaig (and Chief Executive Officer)
Senior Executive Officers: Gene M Baker (VP), Donald M Rose (VP and Controller), Lawrence R Mehl (VP, Secretary and General Counsel)

PRINCIPAL ACTIVITIES: A diversified company with interests in the exploitation of natural resources including oil and gas, coal, minerals and salt
Principal Subsidiaries: C & K Coal Co; Cambria Coal Co; Reade Mining Co Inc; Charter Coal Corp; GRC Mining Co; Shannon Coal Co Inc; GRC Coal Co; Great Salt Lake Mineral & Chemical Co; Industrial Mineral Ventures Co; Lithium Corp of America; Pend Oreille Oil & Gas Co; Pintlar Corp
Principal Bank: Citibank
Financial Information:

	$'000
Sales revenues	155,800

No of Employees: 2,400

GULF STATES ASPHALT CO, INC

601 Jefferson Avenue, Houston, TX 77002
Tel: (713) 651-1507

Chairman: Reba H Bramble
President: Orin A Sharp
Senior Executive Officers: L J Spillane Jr (VP Operations), Luis Pena (VP and Controller)

PRINCIPAL ACTIVITIES: Manufacture of asphalt
Principal Bank: First City National Bank of Houston

Financial Information:

	$'000
Sales revenues	50,000

No of Employees: 250

GULF STATES UTILITIES CO

285 Liberty Avenue, Beaumont, TX 77701
Tel: (409) 838-6631

Chairman: E Linn Draper (and Chief Executive Officer)
President: Norman R Lee (and Principal Operating Officer)
Senior Executive Officers: Edward M Loggins Jr (Senior Executive VP), Joseph E Bondurant (Executive VP), J L Donnelly (Executive VP), Wm J Cahill (Senior VP), James R Aldridge (VP Human Resources), William F Barksdale (VP Technical Services), James R Deddens (VP), A F Gabrielle (VP), Charles D Glass (VP Texas Operations), C J Hebert (VP Finance), Wm J Jefferson (VP Rates and Regional Affairs), George J McCollough (VP Fuels, Materials and Projects), Fred C Repper (VP Public Affairs), Edward J Serwan (VP Production), Aubrey D Sprawls (VP Consumer Services), S L Stelly (VP Louisiana Operations), J G Weigand (VP Administration), Bobby J Willis (VP and Controller), Jasper F Worthy (VP General Services)

PRINCIPAL ACTIVITIES: Distribution of electricity and natural gas
Principal Subsidiaries: Varibus Corporation; Prudential Drilling Company; Gulf States Overseas Finance NV (Netherlands Antilles)
Financial Information:

	Dec 31 1985	Dec 31 1986
	$'000	$'000
Sales revenues	1,858,436	1,478,388
Net income	265,499	244,981
Earnings per share	$2.10	$1.71
Shareholders equity	-	2,048,672

No of Employees: 5,000

GULFSTREAM AEROSPACE CORPORATION

Travis Field, Savannah, GA 31402
Tel: (912) 964-3000
Telex: WUT 546470 gulfam sav

Chairman: Allen E Paulson (and President and Chief Executive Officer)
Senior Executive Officers: James L Bradbury (Senior VP Finance and Administration), John C Stellman (VP Corporate Planning)

PRINCIPAL ACTIVITIES: Holding company with interests in the manufacture and sale of aircraft
Parent Company: Chrysler Corp
Principal Subsidiaries: GAC Aircraft Company
Principal Bank: First National Bank of Chicago
Financial Information:

	$'000
Sales revenues	601,600

No of Employees: 3,550

GULFSTREAM AEROSPACE CORPORATION, COMMANDER DIVISION

PO Box 22500, Oklahoma City, OK 73123-1500

Chairman: Allen E Paulson (and President)
Senior Executive Officers: Bill M Humes (VP Operations), Thomas R Merry (VP Finance), Robert H Cooper (VP Marketing)

PRINCIPAL ACTIVITIES: Manufacture of aircraft
Parent Company: Gulfstream Aerospace Corporation, Savannah, GA
Financial Information:

	$'000
Sales revenues	70,000

No of Employees: 900

GULFSTREAM LAND & DEVELOPMENT CORPORATION

The Gulfstream Building, 8751 West Broward Boulevard, Plantation, FL 33324
Tel: (305) 472 4200

President: Jack H Chambers (and Chief Executive Officer)
Senior Executive Officers: John Laguardia (Senior VP, Chief Financial Officer and Treasurer), Stuart H Reich (Senior VP), J Larry Rutherford (Senior VP)

PRINCIPAL ACTIVITIES: Property development
Principal Subsidiaries: American Housing & Development Corp; Argyle Homes Inc; Bel-Air Home Inc; Bel-Aire West Inc; Brandon Construction Co Inc; Bel-Aire Realty Inc; Current Builders Inc; Du-Lay Utility Co; Grange Properties Inc; Gulfstream Bentbrook Inc; Gulfstream Central Inc; Gulfstream Homes Inc; Gulfstream Jacaranda Associates Inc; Gulfstream Utility Co; Jacaranda Country Club Inc; Jacaranda Nursery Inc; Jacaranda West Country Club; Lake of the Woods Inc; Lakes Inc; Mays Landing Gulfstream Inc; Clover Gulfstream Inc; Seminole Utility Co Inc; Robert L Turchin Inc; Venice Gardens Utility Corp; Winter Springs Development Corp; Tuscawilla Country Club Inc
Principal Bank: Pan American Bank
Financial Information:

	$'000
Sales revenues	141,300

No of Employees: 900

GULF+WESTERN INC

One Gulf+Western Plaza, New York, NY 10023-7780
Tel: (212) 337-8000
Cable: gulfwestin nyk
Telex: 12-7961 G AND W NYK

Chairman: Martin S Davis (and Chief Executive Officer)
Corporate Officers: Reece A Overcash Jr (Senior Executive VP, President, G+W Financial Services), Michael S Hope (Executive VP and Chief Financial Officer), Donald Oresman (Executive VP General Counsel and Secretary), Edgar W Levin (Senior VP-Planning), Lawrence E Levinson (Senior VP-Government Relations), Eugene I Meyers (Senior VP and Senior Tax Counsel), William F Ashcroft (VP-Human Resources), Peter A Butler (VP-Insurance and National Purchasing), Earl H Doppelt (VP and Deputy General Counsel), Rudolph L Hertlein (VP-Internal Audit and Special Projects), Raymond M Nowak (VP-Accounting and Systems), James E Parent (VP-Financial and Investor Relations), Jerry Sherman (VP-Corporate Communications), Edward T Weaver (VP; President, Gulf+Western Foundation), Lewis S White (VP and Treasurer)

PRINCIPAL ACTIVITIES: Gulf+Western has operations in financial services, publishing and information services and entertainment

Principal Subsidiaries: Associates Corporation of North America; Simon & Schuster Inc; Paramount Pictures Corporation; Madison Square Garden Corporation; Famous Players Ltd; Mann Theatres
Principal Bank: Manufacturers Hanover Trust Company

Financial Information:

	Oct 31 1985(1) $'000	Oct 31 1986 $'000
Sales revenues (2)	3,320,700	3,781,100
Income before taxes (3)	235,200	386,300
Net income(3)(4)	151,600	228,700
Net earnings	247,800	267,400
Dividends	63,900	56,400
Dividends per share	$0.90	$0.90
Earnings per share(3)	$3.51	$3.66
Net earnings per share	$3.51	$4.28
Common stock	62,300	61,700
Retained income	1,196,500	1,363,700
Shareholders equity	1,737,700	1,902,100

(1) In December 1985 Gulf+Western changed its fiscal year-end from July 31 to October 31. The financial information reflects this change
(2) includes revenues of unconsolidated financial subsidiary of $1,459.9 and $1,687.3 for fiscal 1985 and 1986 respectively
(3) from continuing operations
(4) before extraordinary items

No of Employees: 19,300

GULL INC

395 Oser Avenue, Smithtown, NY 11787
Tel: (516) 231 3737

Chairman: Peter D D'Agrosa (and Chief Executive Officer and Treasurer)
President: Lawrence Perry (and Chief Operating Officer)
Senior Executive Officers: Sebastian F Digiacomo (Senior VP and Secretary), Martin Horowitz (Senior VP), Robert Connolly (VP Marketing Gull Resource Management Systems), Angelo M DePietto (VP and General Manager Gull Resource Management Systems), George S Gilliland (VP and General Manager), Robert S Hultmark (VP Marketing and Corporate Communications), John J Lombardi (VP Product Integrity), Alan Rosenblum (VP Technical Services Gull Resource Management Systems), Stanley Shatunoff (VP Business Development), Stanley R Sporn (VP Engineering), Irvin E Van Sickle (VP Customer Support), Gerald F Wood (VP Operations), Samuel P Shaw (Assistant Secretary)

PRINCIPAL ACTIVITIES: Manufacture of control and measurement equipment for military and commercial aircraft
Principal Bank: Manufacturers Hanover Trust Co
Financial Information:

	$'000
Sales revenues	62,000

No of Employees: 1,000

GULTON INDUSTRIES, INC

212 Durham Ave, Metuchen, NJ 08840-1740
Tel: (609) 452-1811

Chairman: E Maclin Roby (and President and Chief Executive Officer)
Senior Executive Officers: Philip Garnick (VP), Ronald J Klammer (VP), R Diane Mickle (VP-Administration), Robert D Pabs (VP), Robert H Tansor (VP-Finance), Robert G Thesing (VP), Edward W Whaley (VP), Henry Hirschmann (Treasurer), Robert L Pelz (Chairman of the Executive Committee, Secretary), Lee C Lund (Assistant Secretary), Richard P Streicher (Assistant Secretary)

PRINCIPAL ACTIVITIES: Gulton Industries is an electronic instrument and transducer manufacturing company with operations concentrated in four business sectors: audio, defense, graphic display and industrial
Trade Names: Electro-Voice (EV), Tapco, T2 C2, Luminator
Parent Company: Mark IV Industries Inc
Principal Subsidiaries and Divisions: Audio:- Electro-Voice Inc. Defense:-Data Systems Division; Engineered Magnetics Division; Servonic Division. Graphic Display:- Graphic Instruments Division. Industrial:- Femco Division; Luminator Division; West Division (UK)
Principal Bank: Morgan Guaranty Trust Co of NY
Financial Information:

	$'000
Sales revenues	148,000

No of Employees: 2,490

GUY F ATKINSON CO OF CALIFORNIA

See ATKINSON, GUY F, CO OF CALIFORNIA

GUY GANNETT PUBLISHING CO

See GANNETT, GUY, PUBLISHING CO

GWC CORPORATION

3219 Philadelphia Pike, Claymount, DE 19703
Tel: (302) 798-3883

Chairman: Jerome Monod
President: Allen E Rosenberg (and Chief Executive Officer)
Senior Executive Officers: Lewis R Masotti (Senior VP), R S Dugan (VP), Joseph V Boyle (Controller), Frank L Fitzpatrick (Treasurer), James L Kilsdonk (Secretary)

PRINCIPAL ACTIVITIES: Water supply
Principal Subsidiaries: General Waterworks Corp; Clearview Water Supply Co; Merchanicsburg Water Cop; Toms River Water Co Inc; Wakefield Co; Wrightsville Water Supply Co
Financial Information:

	$'000
Sales revenues	82,000

No of Employees: 700

H & R BLOCK INC

See BLOCK, H & R, INC

H B FULLER COMPANY

See FULLER, H B, COMPANY

H F AHMANSON & CO

See AHMANSON, H F, & CO

H H BROWN SHOE CO

See BROWN, H H, SHOE CO

H H KEIM COMPANY, LTD

See KEIM, H H, COMPANY, LTD

H H ROBERTSON COMPANY

See ROBERTSON, H H, COMPANY

H J HEINZ CO

See HEINZ, H J, CO

H K PORTER COMPANY, INC

See PORTER, H K, COMPANY, INC

H P HOOD INC

See HOOD, H P, INC

H S CROCKER CO, INC

See CROCKER, H S, CO, INC

H T HACKNEY CO

See HACKNEY, H T, CO

HACH COMPANY

57th Street and Lindbergh Parkway, Loveland, CO 80537
Tel: (303) 669 3050

Chairman: Clifford C Hach (and Chief Executive Officer); Vice Chairman: Kathryn C Hach (and President)
Senior Executive Officers: Franz L Zupan (Senior VP and Treasurer), Michael Buck (VP Product Development), R Dan Gerber (VP) Jerry Churchill (VP Domestic Sales and Marketing), Bruce Hach (VP Instrument Operations and Human Relations), Loel Sirouy (VP Instrument Operations), Robert O Case (Secretary)

PRINCIPAL ACTIVITIES: Manufacture of scientific and precision engineering products and instruments
Principal Bank: First National Bank
Financial Information:

	$'000
Sales revenues	37,400

No of Employees: 600

HACKNEY, H T, CO

300 Fidelity Building, Knoxville, TN 37901
Tel: (615) 546-1291

Chairman: William B Sansom
President: B E France
Senior Executive Officers: George T Williamson (Senior VP), W L Marks (VP), Julie M Benson (VP), Boyd K Jarnagin (VP), Byrl Logan (VP), G M Grinstead (Assistant VP and Controller)

PRINCIPAL ACTIVITIES: Wholesale trade in groceries, distribution of sanitary products and equipment and industrial equipment
Principal Subsidiaries: Brinks Inc; Installation Service Co; United States Trucking Corp; Transervice Lease Corp; Carolina Oil & Gas Co; Dale Sanitary Supply Co; Hackney Carolina Co; Hackney Jellico Co; Haywood Grocery Co; Jellico Grocery Co; Park Oil Co; Pride Markets Inc; Testoil Co; Tri-State Wholesale Inc
Principal Bank: First American National Bank
Financial Information:

	$'000
Sales revenues	113,000

No of Employees: 700

HADCO CORPORATION

10 Manor Pkway, Salem, NH 03079
Tel: (603) 898-8000

Chairman: H H Irvine II (and Chief Executive Officer); Vice Chairman: M E Needham Jr
President: J E Kropper (and Chief Operating Officer)
Senior Executive Officers: A E Lietz (VP), R P DeRego (VP), D J Pucci (VP), J R Schaefer (VP), D R Schofield (VP), W P Meehan (VP and Chief Financial Officer)

PRINCIPAL ACTIVITIES: Hadco Corporation, along with its wholly-owned subsidiaries, is a leading independent manufacturer of high density multilayer and two-sided printed circuits used in the computer, communications and other electronic equipoment industries
Principal Subsidiaries: Qualitron Corporation; Circuit Image Industries, Inc. Joint Venture: S A Comelim
Principal Bank: First National Bank of Boston
Financial Information:

	$'000
Sales revenues	92,000

No of Employees: 1,350

HADSON CORPORATION

101 Park Avenue, Suite 1400, Oklahoma City, OK 73102
Tel: (405) 275 9531

Chairman: T K Hendrick
President: Stephen W Houghton (and Chief Executive Officer)
Senior Executive Officers: H W Peace II (Executive VP), John W Cooke Jr (VP), Vinod K Dar (VP), G Curt Harris (VP), William C Rankin Jr (VP and Controller), Terry L Toole (VP Finance and Treasurer), J Michael Adcock (Legal Counsel and Secretary)

PRINCIPAL ACTIVITIES: Exploration and production of oil and natural gas
Principal Bank: Harris Trust and Savings Bank
Financial Information:

	$'000
Sales revenues	117,700

No of Employees: 110

HAGGAR CO

6113 Lemmon Avenue, Dallas, TX 75209
Tel: (214) 352-8481
Telex: TWX 9108614303 haggar slx dal

Chairman: Edmond R Haggar
President: Joseph M Haggar Jr
Senior Executive Officers: Jack S Smith (President Manufacturing), Sylvan Landau (President RSJ Division), E R Haggar Jr (President Haggar Womens Wear), J M Haggar III (President Haggar Mens Wear)

PRINCIPAL ACTIVITIES: Wholesale trade in slacks for men
Principal Bank: First National Bank in Dallas
Financial Information:

	$'000
Sales revenues	220,000

No of Employees: 6,500

HAL INC

1164 Bishop St, Box 30008, Honolulu, HI 96820
Tel: (808) 836-7365

President: P J Finazzo (and Chief Operating Officer)
Senior Executive Officers: R A Anzai (VP Treasurer and Controller), J A Sonoda (VP and Secretary)

PRINCIPAL ACTIVITIES: Holding company whose interests include transportation of passengers, cargo and mail on routes connecting the six main islands of Hawaii; airport services
Principal Subsidiaries: Hawaiian Airlines Inc
Financial Information:

	Dec 31 1986 $'000
Sales revenues	225,010
Net income	3,433
Earnings per share	$1.83
Shareholders equity	22,112

No of Employees: 2,343

HALL, FRANK B, & CO INC

549 Pleasantville Road, Briarcliff Manor, NY 10510
Tel: (914) 769-9200
Telex: WUT 996505 hallcoy brff

Chairman: John F McCaffrey (and Chief Executive Officer); Vice Chairmen: William C Bartholomay, Henry E Froebel, C Colby Hewitt Jr
President: Peter T Pruitt (and Chief Operating Officer)
Senior Executive Officers: Saul P Steinberg (Chairman Executive Committee), George E Bello (Chairman Audit Committee), Peter L Keane (Chairman Compensation Committee), Walter E Danielewski (Executive VP), Holmes Harden (Executive VP and Chief Financial Officer), George E Corde (Executive VP Marketing Services), James M Schlomann (Senior VP and Controller), William R Dolan (Senior VP, Secretary and Legal Counsel), Joseph E Johnson (Senior VP Market Relations), John Addeo (Senior VP and Treasurer), Carlton E Wade (Senior VP Information Services), Delle J Brinkerhoff (VP Personnel), Arthur F Blum (VP

National Corporate Services), Edward P Hollingsworth (VP Education and Training), Richard Williams (VP Information Services), David Woods (VP Public Relations)

PRINCIPAL ACTIVITIES: Insurance broking and financial services
Principal Subsidiaries: Adjustco Inc; Frank B Hall & Co of CA Inc; Frank B Hall & Co of IL; Frank B Hall & Co of NY Inc; Frank B Hall & Co Overseas Inc; Frank B Hall Underwriters Inc; Insurers Service Corp; Union Indemnity Insurance Co NY; Universal Relocation Insurance Services Inc
Principal Bank: The Bank of New York
Financial Information:

	Dec 31 1985
	$'000
Revenues	417,406
Net (loss)	(22,452)
(Loss) per share	($1.92)
Shareholders equity	101,600

No of Employees: 7,000

HALL, W F, PRINTING CO

One Pierce Place, Itasca, IL 60143

President: E C Nytko
Senior Executive Officers: J A DeLorey (Executive VP Operations), R Johnson (Senior VP Sales and Marketing), Preston Powell (VP Sales), H A Haave (VP Manufacturing Service), R L Epstein (VP and Secretary), L F Schmidt (VP Treasurer and Assistant Secretary)

PRINCIPAL ACTIVITIES: Printing and binding of paper backed books and magazines
Parent Company: Mobil Corporation
Principal Bank: Harris Trust Bank
Financial Information:

	$'000
Sales revenues	200,000

No of Employees: 3,600

HALLIBURTON CO

3600 Lincoln Plaza, 500 N Akard St, Dallas, TX 75201
Tel: (214) 978-2600

President: Thomas H Cruikshank (and Chief Executive Officer)
Senior Executive Officers: Dale P Jones (Executive VP-Oil Field Services), Lester L Coleman (Executive VP Finance and Corporate Development), Guy T Marcus (VP-Investor Relations), Robert M Kennedy (VP-Legal), James R Flow (Controller), C Robert Fielder (Treasurer), Susan S Keith (Secretary); Don P Woosley (VP-Corporate Development)

PRINCIPAL ACTIVITIES: Halliburton Company is one of the world's larger and more diversified oil field services and engineering/construction organizations. The oil field services group is a major provider of products and services, both onshore and offshore, to the exploration and production segments of the petroleum industry. Industrial engineering/construction services are performed for the petroleum industry, public utilities and general industry. Services include the design, construction and maintenance of industrial facilities. Marine engineering/construction services are performed predominantly for the petroleum industry. These services include the design, fabrication and installation of offshore structures and pipelines. Approximately three-fourths of revenues and about 90 percent of operating income are derived from services to, including construction for, the petroleum industry. Generally, 30 percent of revenues and 40 percent of operating income come from international sales and services. The Company also is engaged in the property, casualty and life insurance businesses
Principal Subsidiaries and Divisions: Oil Field Services and Products:-Halliburton Services Division: Otis Engineering Corporation; Welex Division; Halliburton Resource Management Division; Vann Systems Division; Halliburton International Inc; Jet Research Center Inc; FreightMaster Division. Engineering and Construction Services:- Brown and Root Inc; Brown and Root USA Inc; Brown and Root International Inc; Taylor International Inc; NUS Corporation; Mid-Valley Inc; Brown and Root Development Inc. Insurance Services:- Highlands Insurance Company; Life Insurance Company of the Southwest; Health Economics Corporation
Financial Information:

	Dec 31 1985	Dec 31 1986
	$'000	$'000
Sales revenues	4,778,695	3,509,439
Net income (loss)	(339,276)(1)	515,214(2)
Dividends	195,561	127,434
Dividends per share	$1.80	$1.20
(Loss) per share	($3.12)(1)	($4.85)
Common stock	297,172	297,629
Retained income	2,764,705	2,122,057
Shareholders equity	2,857,854	2,150,172

(1) Results reflect special after-tax charges totalling $563.0 million or $5.18 per share. Special charges related to settlement of the South Texas Nuclear Project litigation ($368.0 million or $3.39 per share) and the write-down of marine engineering/construction assets ($195.0 million or $1.79 per share)
(2) Results reflect after-tax write-down of assets totalling $488.7 million

No of Employees: 64,955

HALLIDAY LITHOGRAPH CORPORATION

Circuit Street, West Hanover, MA 02339
Tel: (617) 826-8385
Telex: WUT 951689 halliday hvms

Senior Executive Officers: John A Baird (VP and Divisional Manager), Abe M Brauner (Controller)

PRINCIPAL ACTIVITIES: Printing of books
Parent Company: Arcata Corporation, San Francisco, CA
Financial Information:

	$'000
Sales revenues	40,000

No of Employees: 800

HALLMARK CARDS INC

2501 McGee Trafficway, Kansas City, MO 64141
Tel: (816) 274-5111
Telex: WUI 6841027 hallmark ksc

Chairman: Donald J Hall; Vice Chairman: David H Hughes
President: Irvine O Hockaday (and Chief Executive Officer)
Senior Executive Officers: Robert L Stark (Senior VP Social Expressions Group), John F Collins (VP Management Information Systems), Glenn Davis (VP Order Distribution), Charles J Egan (VP, Secretary and Legal Counsel), Homer C Evans (VP Hallmark Cards Product Division), William S Gorman (VP Graphic Services), Charles W Hucker (VP Public Affairs and Communications), Tom Johnston (VP Hallmark Specialty Products Division), Lanny Julian (VP Hallmark Sales), Chuck Koester (VP Corporate Finance and Treasury), Lowell J Mayone (VP Personnel and Services), Greg McMonigle (VP Operations), Robert D Payne (VP Manufacturing), Clark Randall (VP Product Innovation), Jim Roud (VP Social Expression Group Finance), Walter M Ulin (VP Planning and Development), Kenneth West (VP Technical Development and Graphics Production), Robert Firnhaber (President Ambassador Cards), William Hall (President Hal

Family Foundation), Stanley Hamilton (President International), Robert Kipp (President Crown Center Redevelopment Corp)

PRINCIPAL ACTIVITIES: Manufacture of a wide range of greetings cards

Principal Subsidiaries: Binney & Smith Inc; Charles D Burns Co Inc; Crown Center Redevelopment Corp; American Food Service Enterprises Inc; Graphics International Inc; Hallmark Marketing Corp; Evenson Card Shops Inc; Halls Merchandising Inc; Litho-Krome Co; Trifari Krussman & Fishel Inc

Principal Bank: Morgan Guaranty Trust Co

Financial Information:

	$'000
Sales revenues	1,500,000

No of Employees: 20,000

HALSTEAD INDUSTRIES INC

W New Castle Street, Zelienople, PA 16063

Tel: (412) 452-9400

Telex: TWX 510 462 1430 hmp zel

Chairman: Byron Halstead (and Chief Executive Officer)

President: William B Halstead

Senior Executive Officers: James D Lawson (Chief Operating Officer), Fred E Halstead (Senior VP Engineering), William E Rapp Jr (Senior VP), Charles F Hohmann Jr (VP, Secretary and Treasurer)

PRINCIPAL ACTIVITIES: Manufacture of copper tubes and parts for refrigeration equipment

Principal Bank: Mellon Bank

Financial Information:

	$'000
Sales revenues	174,000

No of Employees: 1,750

HAMBURGER HAMLETS INC

14156 Magnolia Blvd; Chemenois, CA 91423

Tel: (818) 995-7333

Chairman: Marilyn Lewis (and Secretary and Treasurer)

President: Harry Lewis

Senior Executive Officers: Vernon R Boyce (VP), Paul M Brockman (VP and Chief Financial Officer)

PRINCIPAL ACTIVITIES: Restaurant chain

Principal Bank: Union Bank

Financial Information:

	$'000
Sales revenues	38,000

No of Employees: 1,300

HAMILTON OIL CORPORATION

1560 Broadway, Suite 2000, Denver, CO 80202

Tel: (303) 863-3000

Telecopier: (303) 839-1024

Telex: 45-881 HABROSOIL DVR

Chairman: Fredric C Hamilton (and President)

Senior Executive Officers: P David Mantor (Senior Executive VP), Jay A Precourt (Senior Executive VP), A J Miller (Executive VP Finance and Treasurer)

PRINCIPAL ACTIVITIES: Exploration for, and production of oil and natural gas

Principal Subsidiaries and Affiliates: Hamilton Brothers Petroleum Corp; Tejas Gas Corp

Financial Information:

	Dec 31 1985	Dec 31 1986
	$'000	$'000
Sales revenues	275,209	273,986
Income before taxes	49,477	20,746
Net income	26,452	11,007
Dividends per common share	$0.10	$0.05
Earnings per share	$0.95	$0.35
Common shares outstanding	25,435	25,404
Shareholders equity	288,117	294,729

No of Employees: 130 (367 including affiliates)

HAMILTON TECHNOLOGY INC

101-121 N Queen Street, Lancaster, PA 17604

Tel: (717) 299-2581

Chairman: H D Clarke Jr

President: R A Zummo (and Chief Executive Officer)

Senior Executive Officers: S S Lesher (Treasurer and Controller)

PRINCIPAL ACTIVITIES: Manufacture of fuzes and timers for explosive devices

Financial Information:

	$'000
Sales revenues	55,000

No of Employees: 660

HAMMERMILL PAPER CO

PO Box 10050, Erie, PA 16533

Tel: (814) 456-8811

Chairman: Donald S Leslie Jr

President: W Craig McClelland (and Chief Executive Officer)

Senior Executive Officers: Robert J Kilgore (Senior VP and Secretary), James S Stolley (Senior VP), Douglas C Wright Jr (Senior VP Finance), Donald P Boyd (VP), Richard M Ludwig (VP), Richard A Reeves (VP)

PRINCIPAL ACTIVITIES: Manufacture of an extensive range of papers and paper products

Principal Subsidiaries: Harbor Pulp and Paper Co (33%); American Lumber International; Endbehr Corp; Hammermill Export Corp; Rohner Corp

Financial Information:

	$'000
Sales revenues	1,876,914

No of Employees: 13,000

HAMPTON INDUSTRIES, INC

PO Box 614, Kinston, NC 28501

Tel: (919) 527-8011

Chairman: David Fuchs (and Chief Executive Officer)

President: Sol Schechter

Senior Executive Officers: Paul Chused (VP), Martin Camnitz (VP Manufacturing), Robert J Stiehl Jr (VP Finance)

PRINCIPAL ACTIVITIES: Manufacture of clothing

Principal Subsidiaries: Samsons Manufacturing Corp; Kinston Shirt Company Inc; Kinston Die Cutting Corp; Kinston Paper Box Co Inc; Prep Shirt Inc; Hampco Apparel Inc; Samsons Inc; Hampton Shirt Co Inc; Snow Hill Apparel Co Inc; Hamptex Inc

Principal Bank: Wachovia Bank and Trust Co

Financial Information:

	$'000
Sales revenues	157,000

No of Employees: 2,750

HANCOCK BANK

Gulfport, MS 39501

Tel: (601) 868-4716

Telex: TWX 5109988 393 hancock bk gup

President: Leo W Seal Jr (and Chief Executive Officer)
Senior Executive Officers: Walter C Hinkle Jr (Executive VP Branch Administration), George A Scholoegel (Executive VP Operations Administration), Charles A Webb Jr (Executive VP Loan Administration), Theresa M Johnson (Executive VP, PMP Division), T Moreno Jones (Executive VP, PMP Division), C E Hutchins Jr (Senior VP Corporate and Business Loan Division), James C Nicholson (Senior VP Personal and Consumer Loan Division)

PRINCIPAL ACTIVITIES: Banking
Parent Company: Hancock Holding Co
Principal Bank: Whitney National Bank

No of Employees: 560

HANCOCK, JOHN, MUTUAL LIFE INSURANCE COMPANY

John Hancock Place, Boston, MA 02117
Tel: (617) 421-6000
Telex: TWX 710 321 66 88 hamulife bsn

Chairman: John G McElwee (and Chief Exeuctive Officer)
President: E J Morton (and Chief Operating Officer)
Senior Executive Officers: Horace R Baker Jr (Executive VP), William L Boyan (Executive VP Corporate Operations), Stephen L Brown (Executive VP Finance Operations), Bertram N Pike (Executive VP Group Operations), John C Scully (Executive VP Individual Operations), Nancy E Concannon (Senior VP), Frank S Irish (Senior VP), Foster L Aborn (Senior VP Financial Services), John Q Adams (Senior VP Bond and Corporate Finance), Howard D Allen (Senior VP Individual), Peter B Carbone (Senior VP District Agency), H Alfred Colby (Senior VP Information Services), Herbert F Gold (Senior VP), Paul F Harrington (Senior VP Marketing), William E Leary (Senior VP Marketing RE), John T Longmoore (Senior VP Individual Equity Pensions), Robert D Lowden (Senior VP Actuarial), Terence P McKenna (Senior VP Marketing), Henry D Shaw (Senior VP Underwriting and Issue), Gordon W Thomas (Senior VP Group Marketing), Raeburn B Hathaway Jr (Senior VP Investment Operations), Barry L Shemin (Senior VP Group Services), John V Sullivan (Senior VP Controller)

PRINCIPAL ACTIVITIES: Life insurance
Principal Subsidiaries: John Hancock Property Casualty Holding Co; Hanseco Insurance Co; John Hancock Reinsurance Co; Unigard Security Insurance Co; Unigard Inc; Unigard Indemnity Co Inc; Unigard Insurance Co; Unigard Service Corp; Unigard Service Corp of CA; John Hancock Subsidiaries Inc; John Hancock Advisers Inc; John Hancock Capital Corp; John Hancock Distributors Inc; John Hancock Financial Access Inc; John Hancock Financial Services Inc; John Hancock Realty Services Corp; John Hancock Venture Capital Management Inc; Independence Investment Associates Inc; Profesco Corp; Anthony Tucker Holding Corp; Hancock/Dikewood Services Inc
Principal Bank: The First National Bank of Boston
Financial Information:

	Dec 31 1985	Dec 31 1986
	$'000	$'000
Premium income	2,351,140	4,173,912
Investment income	1,443,128	1,406,348

No of Employees: 18,306

HANDI KUP CO

240 Tamal Vista Blvd, Corte Madera, CA 94925
Tel: (415) 927-0800
Telex: TWX 910 384 2002 h-k eng ctmr

President: Peter J Hunt
Senior Executive Officers: Joseph P Hunt (Executive VP), Douglas M Bell (VP Engineering), Carl Magnuson (VP Finance), Thomas Woods (VP Sales), James Uhlman VP Marketing)

PRINCIPAL ACTIVITIES: Manufacture of disposable cups and containers
Parent Company: Fiberplastics Inc
Principal Bank: Union Bank
Financial Information:

	$'000
Sales revenues	54,000

No of Employees: 830

HANDLEMAN COMPANY

500 Kirts Boulevard, PO Box 7045 Troy, MI 48084-7045
Tel: (313) 362-4400

Chairman: David Handleman (and Chief Executive Officer)
President: Frank M Hennessey (and Chief Operating Officer)
Senior Executive Officers: James E Powers (Executive VP), (VP), Lawrence R Hicks (VP), Richard D Sadlon (VP), Stephen Salsberg (VP), Stephen Strome (VP)

PRINCIPAL ACTIVITIES: Wholesale trade in records, cassette tapes, compact discs, video cassettes, home computer software and books
Principal Bank: National Bank of Detroit
Financial Information:

	$'000
Sales revenues	460,400

No of Employees: 2,200

HANDSCHY INDUSTRIES INC

120 25th Ave., Bellwood, IL 60104
Tel: (312) 547-7500

Chairman: E H Friesendorf (and Chief Executive Officer)
President: John P McMahon (and Chief Operating Officer)
Senior Executive Officers: W S Bradfield (Senior VP Marketing and Sales), William J LaSarre (VP Administration), R H Thorburn (Treasurer and Controller), Fred L Skimel (VP Operations)

PRINCIPAL ACTIVITIES: Manufacture of inks and chemicals for the printing industry, wrapping paper and plastic packaging materials
Principal Subsidiaries: Handschy Industries Ltd; Pak-Well Paper Products Co; St Clair Manufacturing Corp
Principal Bank: First National Bank of Chicago
Financial Information:

	$'000
Sales revenues	59,000

No of Employees: 600

HANDY & HARMAN

850 Third Avenue, New York, NY 10022
Tel: (212) 752-3400
Telex: ITT 4222751 hnh ui

Chairman: R N Daniel (and President and Chief Executive and Operating Officer)
Senior Executive Officers: R M Thompson (Group VP), P G Deuchler (Group VP), S B Mudd (VP, Treasurer and Chief Financial Officer)

PRINCIPAL ACTIVITIES: Manufacture of a wide range of metals and metal products including precious metals
Principal Subsidiaries: American Chemical & Refining Co; Bigelow Components Corp; Brunner Engineering and Manufacturing Inc; Camdel Metals Corp; Conn-Form Corp; Continental Industries Inc; Daniel Radiator Corp; Form Tool & Manufacturing Co; Greenback Industries Inc; Handy & Harman Electronic Materials Corp; Handy & Harman Tube Co Inc; Indiana Tube Corp; Industrial Heat Exchange Manufacturing Corp; Lucas-Milhaupt Inc; Maryland Specialty Wire Inc; Merit Plastics Inc; Midway Tool & Manufacturing Co; New Industrial Techniques Inc; O & M Manufacturing Co; Pennsylvania Wire Rpe Corp; Platina Laboratories Inc; Rathbone Corp; Rigby-Maryland (Stainless) Ltd (UK); Handy &

Harman of Canada Ltd; US Auto Radiator Manufacturing Corp

Principal Bank: Chase Manhattan Bank

Financial Information:

	Dec 31 1985	Dec 31 1986
	$'000	$'000
Sales revenues	556,706	558,917
Income (loss) before taxes	8,126	(15,993)
Net income (loss)	6,306	(8,843)
Dividends	9,108	9,126
Dividends per share	-	$0.66
Earnings (loss) per share	$0.46	($0.64)
Retained income	115,292	97,323
Shareholders equity	131,740	114,907

No of Employees: 5,680

HANDYMAN CORPORATION

6666 Convoy Court, San Diego, CA 92111

Tel: (619) 560 6666

Chairman: B A Edison

President: Harvey W Rosen (and Chief Executive Officer)

Senior Executive Officers: William E Tilburg (Executive VP and Treasurer), Thomas P Vertetis (Executive VP), Philip Finkel (Senior VP), Alan D Miller (Senior VP, Chief Financial Officer and Secretary)

PRINCIPAL ACTIVITIES: Supply of wood and other building materials

Financial Information:

	$'000
Sales revenues	228,105

No of Employees: 3,500

HANNA, M A, COMPANY

100 Erieview Plaza, Cleveland, OH 44114

Tel: (216) 589-4000

Telex: WUT 980582 hanna mng clv

Chairman: Martin D Walker (and Chief Executive Officer)

President: Carl E Nickels Jr (and Chief Operating Officer)

Senior Executive Officers: James E Courtney (Executive VP), Sooi P Chong (VP, Technical Services), Peter M Earl (VP, Ore Sales), William P Holmes (VP, Finance and Chief Financial Officer), John S Pyke Jr (VP and Secretary), Gail A Siler (VP, Energy Resources), Wilfred J Tremblay (VP, Taxes), Thomas H Wilson (VP, Human Resouces and Industrial Relations), Garth W Henry (VP and Comptroller), L C Van Hoeven Jr (Treasurer)

PRINCIPAL ACTIVITIES: M A Hanna Company is comprised of three major business segments: Polymer products; Minerals and metals; Energy resources and services

Principal Subsidiaries: (100% owned unless stated): Iron Ore:- Iron Ore Company of Canada (26%) (Canada). Coal:- Colowyo Coal Company (50%); Terry Eagle Coal Company. Silicon:- Cerro Matoso SA (5.1%); Coastal Mining Group; Exploraciones y Explotaciones Mineras Izabel SA (Exmibal) (20%) (Guatemala); Hanna Silicon; Siskon Corporation. Oil and Gas:- Hanna Hamilton Holdings Company; Hanna Petroleum Company; Midland SouthWest Corporation (99%). Polymer Products:- Burton Rubber Processing Inc; Allied Color Industries Inc; Day International Corp; Avecor Inc

Principal Bank: National City Bank

Financial Information:

	Dec 31 1985	Dec 31 1986
	$'000	$'000
Total revenues	230,975	197,816
Net (loss)	(115,214)	(104,515)
Dividends	4,524	4,524
Dividends per share	$0.40	$0.40
(Loss) per share net	$(10.19)	($9.38)
Common stock	11,347	11,310
Retained income	199,480	88,853
Shareholders equity	313,892	275,055

No of Employees: 4,070

HANNAFORD BROTHERS COMPANY

145 Pleasant Hill Road, Scarborough, ME 04074

Tel: (207) 883 2911

Chairman: James L Moody Jr (and Chief Executive Officer)

President: Hugh G Farrington (and Chief Operating Officer)

Senior Executive Officers: Walter J Salmon (Chairman Executive Committee), R W Hoyt (Senior VP), R T Perry (Senior VP), John J Russell (Senior VP and Treasurer), Virgil E Beane (VP Wholesale and Transport), Norman E Brackett (VP Management Services), A F Carville (VP Technical Services), Robert E Dunton (VP Wellby Division), K M Greenleaf (VP Human Resources), J J Jermann (VP Merchandising), E F Johnson (VP Government Relations), Larry A Plotkin (VP Corporate Development)

PRINCIPAL ACTIVITIES: Wholesale and retail of a wide range of food products and pharmaceuticals

Principal Subsidiaries: Cottles Shop 'N Save Inc; Gays Super Markets Inc; Hampden Food Stores Inc; Hanbro Inc; Martin Foods of South Burlington Inc; Sampson Supermarkets Inc; Shop Rite Supermarkets Inc; South Paris Shop 'N Save Inc

Principal Bank: Maine National Bank

Financial Information:

	$'000
Sales revenues	899,000

No of Employees: 7,000

HANOVER BRANDS, INC

RD3 Route 116, PO Box 334, Hanover, PA 17331

Tel: (717) 632-6000

Telex: 840-401 HBI HNVR

Chairman: Alan R Warehime (and President and Chief Executive Officer)

Senior Executive Officers: Cyril T Noel (VP Finance), Keith V Cousin (VP)

PRINCIPAL ACTIVITIES: Processing, canning and freezing of food including fruit and vegetables; snack products

Trade Names: Hanover, Myers, Phillips, Gibbs

Principal Subsidiaries: Consumers Packing Co; Eastern Freeze-Dry Corp; Tri-Co Foods Corp; Sunwise Corp; Alimentos Congelados Monte Bello, SA

Principal Bank: Farmers Bank and Trust Company

Financial Information:

	$'000
Sales revenues	100,000

No of Employees: 1,800

HANOVER INSURANCE COMPANIES

440 Lincoln Street, Worcester, MA 01605

Tel: (617) 853-7200

Chairman: Frederick Fedeli

President: William J O'Brien (and Chief Executive Officer)

Senior Executive Officers: Joseph D Duffy (VP), J E Sutton (VP and Secretary), John A Ritacco (Treasurer)

PRINCIPAL ACTIVITIES: Insurance and financial services

Financial Information:

	Dec 31 1985 $'000	Dec 31 1986 $'000
Revenues	897,700	1,162,135
Net income	23,317	96,962
Earnings per share	$2.27	$9.41
Shareholders equity	-	448,486

No of Employees: 2,764

HANSON INDUSTRIES NORTH AMERICA INC

100 Wood Avenue S, Iselin, NJ 08830
Tel: (201) 549-7050
Telex: WUT 844403 hanson isln

Chairman: Sir Gordon White
President: David H Clarke
Senior Executive Officers: Edward H Collins (VP Public Relations), H E Hanson (VP), George Hempstead III (VP and Secretary), John G Roos (VP and Comptroller)

PRINCIPAL ACTIVITIES: Manufacture of textile machinery and textiles, furniture, machine and garden tools, building materials
Parent Company: Hanson Trust PLC, London, UK
Principal Bank: Chemical Bank
Financial Information:

	Dec 31 1985 $'000	Dec 31 1986 $'000
Sales revenues	2,289,830	3,768,541
Net income	110,950	103,062
Shareholders equity	-	1,694,688

No of Employees: 37,000

HARBISON-FISCHER MFG CO

901 N Crowley Road, PO Box 2477, Fort Worth, TX 76101
Tel: (817) 297-2211

Chairman: Charles K Fischer (and President)
Senior Executive Officers: James A Burns (Executive VP), G W Stowe (VP Manufacturing and Production), Roy John Bracken (VP Finance), Don L Burum (VP Sales), Lewis F Filewood Jr (VP Personnel and Insurance), William L Cook Jr (VP Marketing Services)

PRINCIPAL ACTIVITIES: Manufacture of pumps and equipment for the oil industry
Principal Bank: First National Bank of Fort Worth
Financial Information:

	$'000
Sales revenues	85,000

No of Employees: 700

HARCOURT BRACE JOVANOVICH, INC

Orlando, FL 32887
Tel: (305) 345-2000

Chairman: William Jovanovich (and President and Chief Executive Officer); Vice Chairman: Robert L Edgell
Senior Executive Officers: Ralph D Caulo (Executive VP), Peter Jovanovich (Executive VP), Jack O Snyder (Executive VP), James Barsky (Senior VP), Margaret M McQuillan (Senior VP and Secretary), J W Brandner (Senior VP and Treasurer), Jack B Chertok (VP), Julian P Muller (VP), Ernest G Godyn (VP), Richard Udell (VP and Counsel), Eric L Brown (VP), Marsha Carow (VP), Leanna A Landsmann (VP), B Anne Papantonio (VP), Bill M Barnett (VP), Robert A Richards (VP)

PRINCIPAL ACTIVITIES: Publication of books and journals
Principal Subsidiaries: Academic Press Inc; Crafacon Inc; Johnson Reprint Corp; Beckleg-Cardy Co; Channel 10 Inc; Coronado Publishers Inc; Davidson Printing Co; Drake Beam Morin Inc; Grune & Stratton Inc; HBJ Real Properties Corp; Harcourt Brace Jovanovich Legal Proof Publishers Inc; Harvest Insurance Agency Inc; Harvest Life Insurance Co; Harvest Publishing Co; HBJ Media Systems Corp; Health Careers Academy Inc; History Book Club Inc; Instructor Publications Inc; Law & Business Inc; Legal Times of WA Inc; Miller Comprehensive CPA Review Inc; Nebraska Farmer Co; Psychological Corp; MSRD Inc; John M Riehle Inc; Knox Lent & Tucker Inc; Gary Wood Associates Inc; Sea World Inc; Sea World of FL Inc; F&C of Orlando Inc; Selective Programs Inc
Principal Bank: Morgan Guaranty Trust Co
Financial Information:

	Dec 31 1985 $'000	Dec 31 1986 $'000
Sales revenues	818,909	968,555
Net income	50,550	7,480
Common stock	$18.14	$1.91
Shareholders equity	-	531,477

No of Employees: 10,750

HARDEE'S FOOD SYSTEMS, INC

1233 N Church Street, Rocky Mount, NC 27801
Tel: (919) 977-2000
Telex: 824760 FFMRYMOUF

Chairman: Jack A Laughery (and Chief Executive Officer)
President: William E Prather Jr (and Chief Operating Officer)
Senior Executive Officers: Gerald McGinnis (Executive VP-Restaurant Development), Jesse M Harrington III (Senior VP and Treasurer), Breen O Condon (Senior VP, General Counsel, Secretary), Gerald L Richards (Senior VP-Operations Services), Gary Langstaff (Executive VP-Marketing), Donald R Mucci (Senior VP-Franchising), John C Wilson (Senior VP-Chief Financial Officer), Thomas H Sparks (Senior VP-Personnel), Hugh Todd Jr (President-FFM Division); Paul R Lovin Jr (Executive VP-Operations); Gene G Arnold (Senior VP-Training)

PRINCIPAL ACTIVITIES: Operation of restaurants and production of convenience food
Trade Names: Hardee's
Parent Company: Imasco Limited, Montreal, Quebec, Canada
Principal Subsidiaries: Fast Food Merchandisers, Inc
Principal Bank: First Union National Bank
Financial Information:

	Mar 31 1986 $'000	Mar 31 1987 $'000
Sales revenues	1,088,858	1,197,387
Income before taxes	51,966	67,804
Net income	27,542	30,911
Shareholders equity	92,237	116,748

No of Employees: 35,000

HARDWARE WHOLESALERS INC

Nelson Rd, Fort Wayne, IN 46803
Tel: (219) 749-8531

Chairman: Kenneth Gartland; Vice Chairman: Max Haggesman
President: Don Wolf (and Chief Executive Officer)
Senior Executive Officers: Michael McClelland (Senior VP)

PRINCIPAL ACTIVITIES: Wholesale trade in home hardware, plumbing supplies and building materials, electrical goods
Principal Bank: Fort Wayne National Bank
Financial Information:

	Jun 30 1987 $'000
Sales revenues	831,000

No of Employees: 680

HARDWICK STOVE CO

240 Edwards St.SE, Cleveland, TN 37311
Tel: (615) 479-4561
Telex: WUT 558454 har stove cend

Chairman: Dan Krumm
President: Fred E Zeller

Senior Executive Officers: Richard J Roza (VP Marketing), Coleman Sawyer (VP Manufacturing), Jack H Scruggs (VP and Controller), Doyle D Rogers (VP Administration)

PRINCIPAL ACTIVITIES: Manufacture of gas and electric stoves and microwave ovens
Parent Company: Maytag Company, Newton, IA
Principal Bank: American National Bank and Trust Company
Financial Information:

	$'000
Sales revenues	70,000

No of Employees: 1,000

HARLAN ELECTRIC CO

24000 Telegraph Croad, Southfield, MI 48034
Tel: (313) 353-8660

Chairman: John M Harlan (and President)
Senior Executive Officers: Blinn B Rush (Executive VP), Richard Miller (VP Construction), William L Patterson (VP Piping Division), Richard Cline (VP), James B Murphy (VP), G W Lowenstein (Treasurer)

PRINCIPAL ACTIVITIES: Electrical and pipeline engineering
Principal Subsidiaries: Cogitate Inc; Cybertrol Inc; Power Piping Co; Sturgeon Electric Co; Titan Electric Co Inc
Principal Bank: Manufacturers National Bank of Detroit
Financial Information:

	$'000
Sales revenues	100,000

No of Employees: 1,900

HARLAND, JOHN H, CO

2939 Miller Road, Decatur, GA 30032
Tel: (404) 981-9460

Chairman: J William Robinson (and Chief Executive Officer)
President: Robert R Woodson
Senior Executive Officers: John A Conant (Senior VP), James E Hooper (Senior VP), I W Lang (Senior VP and Secretary), A C Baxter III (Senior VP), Donald K Voshall (VP), Vickie Weyland (VP Personnel)

PRINCIPAL ACTIVITIES: Check printers
Principal Subsidiaries: South Carolina Harland Co Inc; Ohio Harland Co; Florida Harland Co Inc; Virginia Harland Co Inc; Tennessee Harland Co Inc; John H Harland Co of Puerto Rico; National Safe Corpo; J William Co
Financial Information:

	$'000
Sales revenues	266,000

No of Employees: 3,700

HARLEY-DAVIDSON MOTOR CO, INC

3700 W Juneau Avenue, Milwaukee, WI 53201
Tel: (414) 342-4680
Telex: TWX 910 26 23 013 hardav mil

Chairman: Vaughn L Beals (and Chief Executive Officer)
Senior Executive Officers: J L Bleustein (VP Engineering), T Gelb (VP Manufacturing), C Sartalis (VP and Secretary), J H Paterson (VP Marketing), Richard F Teerlink (VP and Chief Financial Officer), Mark Tuttle (VP Engineering), T Hoelter (VP and Legal Counsel), P L Profumo (VP Program Management), D Lickerman (VP International)

PRINCIPAL ACTIVITIES: Manufacture of motorcycles
Principal Bank: First Wisconsin National Bank
Financial Information:

	$'000
Sales revenues	287,000

No of Employees: 2,300

HARNISCHFEGER INDUSTRIES

13400 Bishops Lane, Brookfield, WI 53005
Tel: (414) 671-4400

Chairman: William W Goessell (and Chief Executive Officer)
President: Jeffery T Grade (and Chief Operating Officer)
Senior Executive Officers: F J Fagan (Senior VP Mining Equipment), John P Moran (Senior VP and Group Executive), John R Teitgen (Senior VP, Secretary and Legal Counsel), Richard W Schulze (Senior VP Personnel, Industrial and Public Relations), C P Cousland (Senior VP Marketing), Francis M Corby Jr (Senior VP Finance and Chief Financial Officer), James C Benjamin (VP and Controller), James H Kaufman (VP, P&H World Services)

PRINCIPAL ACTIVITIES: Manufacture of cranes and lifting equipment; mining equipment and excavators
Principal Subsidiaries: Harnischfeger Engineers Inc; Harnischfeger Credit Corp; Harnischfeger Export Corp; Harnischfeger World Services Corp; Conrol Logic Inc; Cranetex Inc
Principal Bank: First WI National Bank
Financial Information:

	Oct 31 1986 $'000
Sales revenues	829,958
Net income	1,310
(Loss) per share	($1.14)
Shareholders equity	212,207

No of Employees: 4,000

HARPER & ROW PUBLISHERS, INC

10 E 53rd Street, New York, NY 10022
Tel: (212) 207-7000
Telex: WUI 62501 harrow 62501

Chairman: Brooks Thomas (and President and Chief Executive Officer)
Senior Executive Officers: Norman Pomerance (Group VP General Books Group), Edward L Burlingame (VP Trade Division), Howard S Aksen (VP College Division), Clayton E Carlson (VP Harper & Row San Francisco), Elizabeth Gordon (VP Junior Books Group), William G Baker (VP and Comptroller), Edward A Miller (VP and Legal Counsel), M S Wyeth Jr (VP and Executive Editor Trade Division), Norman L Cannon (VP Investor Relations and Treasurer), Chester S Logan (VP Personnel), Nak Young Choung (VP International Division), Eugene A Clarke (VP Manufacturing Services)

PRINCIPAL ACTIVITIES: Publishing
Principal Subsidiaries: Basic Books Inc; Ballinger Publishing Co; J B Lippincott Co; Editora Harper & Row do Brasil Ltda (Brazil); Harper & Row (Australasia) Pty Ltd (Australia); Harper & Row Ltd (UK); Harper & Row Latinoamericana (Harla) SA de CV (Mexico); Harper & Row, Publishers, Asia PTC Ltd (Singapore)
Financial Information:

	$'000
Sales revenues	201,400

No of Employees: 1,800

HARPER GROUP

260 Townsend Street, San Francisco, CA 94107
Tel: (415) 978 0600

Chairman: John H Robinson (and President)
Senior Executive Officers: M R Collins (Senior VP and Secretary), Joseph H Healy (VP), Kenneth Turnham (VP), Michael P Williams (VP)

PRINCIPAL ACTIVITIES: Freight forwarding in the fields of airfreight and ocean freight forwarding; customs brokerage
Principal Subsidiaries: Binford Insurance Company; Circle Airfreight Corporation; Jet Urban Renewal Corporation; Harper Robinson & Company; Harper Shipping Company; J R

Michels Inc; Pacific Intermodal Corporation; Western Navigation Corporation
Principal Bank: Bank of America
Financial Information:

	$'000
Sales revenues	175,000

No of Employees: 1,725

HARRIS BANKCORP, INC

111 W Monroe Street, PO Box 755, Chicago, IL 60690
Tel: (312) 461-2121
Telex: 206569

Chairman: B Kenneth West (and Chief Executive Officer)
President: Philip A Delaney
Senior Executive Officers: Richard L McAuliffe (Executive VP and Treasurer)

PRINCIPAL ACTIVITIES: Bank holding company
Parent Company: Bankmont Financial Corp
Principal Subsidiaries: Bank Subsidiaries: Harris Trust and Savings Bank; First National Bank and Trust Company of Barrington (1); Harris Bank Glencoe-Northbrook, N.A.; Harris Bank Hinsdale, N.A.; Harris Bank Naperville; Harris Bank Roselle; Harris Bank Argo; Harris Bank Wilmette, N.A.; Harris Bank Winnetka, NA. Non-Bank Subsidiaries: Harris Trust Company of Arizona; Harris Trust Company of Florida; Harris Trust Company of New York; Bank of Montreal Trust Company; Harris Trust Company of California; Harriscorp Finance, Inc; Harris Futures Corporation; Derivative Markets Management, Inc; Harris Brokerage Services, Inc (2); (1) Effective October 1 1987 the name will become Harris Bank Barrington, N.A. (2) Effective April 1 1987 this subsidiary became a subsidiary of Harris Bankcorp rather than Harris Trust and Savings Bank
Principal Bank: Harris Trust and Savings Bank
Financial Information:

	Dec 31 1985	Dec 31 1986
	$'000	$'000
Income before taxes	69,586	64,583
Net income	57,510	68,167
Earnings per share	$8.63	$10.22
Common stock-par	53,340	53,340
Retained income	364,545	432,712
Shareholders equity	621,782	689,949
Deposits	6,841,346	7,600,616
Total assets	9,245,095	10,277,701

Principal Shareholders: Bankmont Financial Corp
No of Employees: 4,893

HARRIS CORPORATION

1025 W NASA Boulevard, Melbourne, FL 32919
Tel: (305) 727-9100
Telex: 803719 HRSCORP MELB (WU); 441936 HARRIS HQ MELB (ITT); 5109596010 HARISCPNB MELB (TWX)

Chairman: Joseph A Boyd
President: John T Hartley (and Chief Executive Officer)
Senior Executive Officers: James R Oyler (Senior VP-Senior Executive, Information Systems Sector), John T Hartley (Acting Senior VP-Sector Executive, Lanier Business Products), Jon E Cornell (Senior VP-Sector Executive-Semiconductor Sector), Frank J Lewis (Senior VP-Sector Executive, Government Systems Sector), Guy W Numann (Senior VP-Sector Executive, Communications Sector), Bryan R Roub (Senior VP Finance), Robert E Sullivan (Senior VP-Administration), Fayette Brown (VP Corporate Development), Ricardo A Diaz (VP, Manufacturing Programs), Nick E Heldreth (VP-Human Resources), John A Hubner (VP, Controller), Herbert N McCauley (VP, Information Management), Raymond J Oglethorpe (VP, Marketing), Donald F Wright (VP, General Counsel), David S Wasserman (VP-Taxes), Robert W Fay (Treasurer), O W Hudson (Secretary)

PRINCIPAL ACTIVITIES: Products: The company provides a wide range of standard and custom products for both the commercial and government segments of the information technology market: 1. Products for Processing Information: Super-minicomputers, engineering workstations, interactive terminals, distributed data processing systems, business computers, personal computers, multifunction workstations, word processing systems, dictating equipment, local area networks, supervisory control systems, composition equipment and copying products. 2. Products for Communicating Information: Digital telephone switches, private branch exchanges, business telephone key stations, satellite communications systems, microwave radios, packet-switched networks, lightwave systems, radio and TV broadcast equipment, studio automation systems, long and short range radios, auxiliary telephone products, private communication networks and network support services. 3. Microelectronic Products: Integrated circuits based on CMOS (complementary metal oxide semiconductor), dielectric isolation, GaAs (gallium arsenide), and radiation hardening technologies. These products, for both analog and digital applications, include memory, logic, data conversion, telecommunication and microprocessor circuits
Principal Brand Names or Trade Names: Harris, Harris/Lanier, Lanier, Farinon, Dracon, Scicards
Principal Bank: The AmeriTrust Company (Transfer Agent and Registrar)
Financial Information:

	Jun 30 1986	Jun 30 1987
	$'000	$'000
Sales revenues	2,216,636	2,078,964
Income before taxes	60,716	122,398
Net income	59,609	84,502
Dividends	35,450	36,379
Dividends per share	$0.88	$0.88
Earnings per share	$1.48	$2.05
Common stock*	40,255	41,206
Retained income	727,516	776,078
Shareholders equity	900,841	984,271

*outstanding in thousands

No of Employees: 25,000

HARRIS DIGITAL TELEPHONE SYSTEMS

1 Digital Drive, Novato, CA 94947
Tel: (415) 472-2500

Senior Executive Officers: William J Adams (VP and General Manager), Peter Killens (VP Production), Ron Kliewer (VP Sales and Marketing), Paul Thompson (VP Engineering)

PRINCIPAL ACTIVITIES: Manufacture of electronic equipment for the telecommunications industry
Parent Company: Harris Corporation, Melbourne, FL
Principal Bank: First National Bank
Financial Information:

	$'000
Sales revenues	50,000

No of Employees: 700

HARRIS FARMS, INC

Rte 1, Box 420, Coalinga, CA 93210
Tel: (209) 884-2477

President: John C Harris
Senior Executive Officers: David Wood (VP Cattle Division), Donald Devine (VP Finance), William P Smoyer (VP Development and Corporate Personnel and Real Estate Officer)

PRINCIPAL ACTIVITIES: Cotton growing, cattle farming and beef production; operation of restaurants and service stations; breeding of horses
Principal Subsidiaries: H & H Cotton Ginning Inc; Harris Feeding Co Inc; Harris Ranch Beef Co; Harris Ranch Cattle Co; Harris Leasing Co; Harris-Idaho Inc

Principal Bank: Bank of America
Financial Information:

	$'000
Sales revenues	200,000

No of Employees: 700

HARRIS GRAPHICS CORPORATION

200 Seminole Avenue, Melbourne, FL 32901
Tel: (305) 676-9400

Chairman: Merle H Banta (and Chief Executive Officer)
Senior Executive Officers: B P O'Donnell (President Harris Graphics International Sales), H P S Silber (President Webb Press Division), W A Whitescarrer (President Bindery and Forms), P Niggli (President Webb Press Europe), James E Pruitt (Executive VP), John Shuey (Senior VP Finance and Administration), Wayne R Rockenbach (VP and Controller)

PRINCIPAL ACTIVITIES: Manufacture of printing machinery
Parent Company: A M International Inc
Principal Bank: Manufcturers Hanover Trust Company
Financial Information:

	$'000
Sales revenues	496,140

No of Employees: 4,200

HARRIS PINE MILLS

2203 S W Court, Pendleton, OR 97801
Tel: (503) 276-1421

Chairman: Neal C Wilson; Vice Chairman: Kenneth Emmerson
President: Eldon N Spady
Senior Executive Officers: Ray Watson (VP), Clyde Iverson (VP), Timothy E Enders (Secretary and Treasurer)

PRINCIPAL ACTIVITIES: Production of timber and manufacture of furniture
Financial Information:

	$'000
Sales revenues	60,000

No of Employees: 2,500

HARRIS RANCH BEEF CO

16277 S McCall Avenue, Selma, CA 93662
Tel: (209) 896-3081

President: John Harris
Senior Executive Officers: Roger Hall (VP and General Manager)

PRINCIPAL ACTIVITIES: Beef production
Parent Company: Harris Farms Inc, Coalinga, CA
Principal Bank: Bank of America
Financial Information:

	$'000
Sales revenues	153,000

No of Employees: 350

HARRIS TRUST & SAVINGS BANK

PO Box 755, Chicago, IL 60690
Tel: (312) 461-2121
Telex: 206569

Chairman: B Kenneth West (and Chief Executive Officer)
President: Philip A Delaney
Senior Executive Officers: Richard C Caldwell (Executive VP Trust Department), Rolland S Carlson (Executive VP Operations Department), Charles H Davis (Executive VP Credit Administration), David S Finch (Executive VP Investment Department), Donald S Hunt (Executive VP Affiliate Bank Management), Richard L McAuliffe (Executive VP Financial Administration), Ben T Nelson (Executive VP Banking Department), John A Civright (Executive VP Banking Department), John L Stephens (Executive VP Public and Employee Relations)

PRINCIPAL ACTIVITIES: Banking
Parent Company: Harris Bankcorp, Inc
Principal Subsidiaries: Harris Building Services Corporation; Harris Brokerage Services, Inc (1); Harriscorp Leasing, Inc; Harris Trading Advisory Corporation; Harris Bank International Corporation; (1) Effective April 1 1987 this subsidiary became a subsidiary of Harris Bankcorp rather than Harris Trust and Savings Bank.
Financial Information:

	Dec 31 1985	Dec 31 1986
	$'000	$'000
Income before taxes	57,499	45,563
Net income	45,666	50,913
Common stock-par	100,000	100,000
Retained income	182,150	214,813
Shareholders equity	463,900	514,813
Deposits	5,534,960	6,096,175
Total assets	7,628,656	8,458,533

Principal Shareholders: Harris Bankcorp, Inc
No of Employees: 3,848

HARRISBURG, INC

PO Box 2108, Houston, TX 77252
Tel: (713) 943-8390

Chairman: T C Davis
President: George J Merrick
Senior Executive Officers: Hugh H Foster (Executive VP and General Manager), Marvin P Zoch (Senior VP), Darryl G Stegemoller (VP Domestic Sales), W E Strittmatter (Secretary and Treasurer)

PRINCIPAL ACTIVITIES: Manufacture of equipment for the oil industry
Parent Company: Ken Davis Industries International Inc
Financial Information:

	$'000
Sales revenues	50,000

No of Employees: 180

HARSCO CORPORATION

PO Box 8888, Camp Hill, PA 17011
Tel: (717) 763-7064
Telefax: (717) 763-6424

Chairman: Jeffrey J Burdge
President: Malcom W Gambill (also Chief Executive Officer)
Senior Executive Officers: Jerome D Brady (Senior VP-Operations), Ralph P Cordes (Senior VP-Operations), Gerald F Gilbert Jr (Senior VP-Corporate Secretary), George F Rezich (Senior VP-Finance), Derek C Hathaway (Senior VP-Operations), LeRoy W Brick (VP and Controller), Roger Snodgrass (VP-Employee Relations), Robert A Haynos (VP-Public Affairs), William J Kelly Jr (VP-Taxes), Louis J Sheehan (Treasurer), Paul C Coppock (Assistant Secretary and Genera Counsel)

PRINCIPAL ACTIVITIES: Selected defense systems; steel mill specialty support services; construction products; gas control and containment; engineered/fabricated metal products
Trade Names: BMY (defense), HECKETT (mill services), PATENT (construction)
Principal Divisions: Defense Group:- Tracked Vehicles, Defence Systems, Wheeled Vehicles - BMY. Industrial Services and Building Products:- CAN-TEX Industries; Heckett; Kinnear; Patent Scaffolding; Reed Minerals. Engineered Products:- Astro; Capitol Manufacturing; Fairmont Railway Motors; IKG Industries; Patterson-Kelley; Plant City Steel; Sherwood
Principal Bank: The Chase Manhattan Bank, NA

Financial Information:

	Dec 31 1985	Dec 31 1986
	$'000	$'000
Sales revenues	1,261,193	1,130,253
Income before taxes	107,929	81,603
Net income	60,458	49,613
Dividends (1)	25,952	27,903
Dividends per share(1)	$0.87	$0.94
Earnings per share	$2.03	$1.67
Common stock(2)	29,811	29,764
Shareholders equity	467,687	473,393

(1) declared

(2) number of shares in thousands

No of Employees: 11,800

HARSHAW/FILTROL PARTNERSHIP

30100 Chagrin Blvd, Cleveland, OH 44124

Tel: (216) 292-9232

Telex: TRT 196137

President: Howard M Nelson

Senior Executive Officers: J B Hobby (VP), H R Garner (VP), E T Nesselroade (VP), J H Fisher (VP), R L Jeansonne (VP), P Grosso (VP)

PRINCIPAL ACTIVITIES: Specialty chemicals, pigments, crystals and electronics, metal finishing processes and equipment, catalysts

Principal Bank: Mellon Bank

Financial Information:

	$'000
Sales revenues	300,000

Principal Shareholders: Kaiser Aluminum & Chemical Corp; Chevron Corp

No of Employees: 2,500

HARTE-HANKS COMMUNICATIONS, INC

PO Box 269, San Antonio, TX 78291

Tel: (512) 344-8000

Chairman: Houston H Harte; Chairman of the Executive Committee: Andrew B Shelton

President: Robert G Marbut (and Chief Executive Officer)

Senior Executive Officers: Larry D Franklin (Executive VP and Chief Operating Officer), Donald R Crews (Senior VP and Secretary), Charles H Everill (Senior VP), William G Moll (Senior VP), Tucker Sutherland (Senior VP), Harry J Buckel (VP), Craig Combest (VP), Richard M Hochhauser (VP), John C Ginn (VP), Bill R Gulledge (VP Information Services), A L Hall (VP Tax), James W Hopson (VP), James D Lonergan (VP), Richard D Mandt (VP), Frank Puckett Jr (VP), T D Sherwin Jr (VP), Stephen W Sullivan (VP), Stephen L Thompson (VP), Gary G Weik (VP), John T Williams (VP)

PRINCIPAL ACTIVITIES: Publication of newspapers and broadcasting

Principal Bank: Interfirst Bank

Financial Information:

	$'000
Sales revenues	550,000

No of Employees: 4,220

HARTFORD NATIONAL CORPORATION

777 Main Street, Hartford, CT 06115

Tel: (203) 728-2000

Chairman: Joel B Alvord (and Chief Executive Officer)

Senior Executive Officers: Gunnar S Overstrom Jr (Executive VP and Chief Financial Officer), Raymond A Guenter (VP and Secretary)

PRINCIPAL ACTIVITIES: Holding company with interests in financial services

Principal Subsidiaries: Connecticut National Bank; Hartford Trust Co of NY

Principal Bank: Connecticut National Bank

Financial Information:

	Dec 31 1985	Dec 31 1986
	$'000	$'000
Net income	80,360	114,000
Earnings per share	$4.15	$2.90
Shareholders equity	515,652	761,462
Deposits	6,649,023	10,778,917
Total assets	8,342,637	13,879,294

No of Employees: 7,570

HARTFORD STEAM BOILER INSPECTION AND INSURANCE CO

1 State Street, hartford, CT 06102

Tel: (203) 722 1866

President: Wilson Wilde (and Chief Executive Officer)

Senior Executive Officers: Kenneth J Kelly (Senior VP, Secretary and Legal Counsel), T Skipwith Lewis (Senior VP Engineering), Donald K Wilson Jr (Senior VP Marketing, BO Administration), William Zindel (Senior VP Insurance), Robert W Trainer (VP, Treasurer and Chief Financial Officer)

PRINCIPAL ACTIVITIES: Engineering, insurance, surveying and architecture services

Principal Subsidiaries: Radian Corporation

Principal Bank: Connecticut National Bank

Financial Information:

	$'000
Sales revenues	387,000

No of Employees: 2,900

HARTMARX CORPORATION

101 N Wacker Drive, Chicago, IL 60606

Tel: (312) 372-6300

Cable: WU 254725

Telex: 6871283

Chairman: John R Meinart (and Chief Administrative Officer); Vice Chairman: Harvey A Weinberg (and Chief Executive Officer)

President: Elbert O Hand (and Chief Operating Officer)

Senior Executive Officers: Jerome Dorf (Senior VP and Chief Financial Officer), Frank A Brenner (VP Marketing Services), James E Condon (VP and Treasurer), Carey M Stein (VP, Secretary and General Counsel), Glenn R Morgan (VP and Controller), Ralph Kaufmann (VP-International Licensing), Guy W Gunzberg (VP-Information Systems), Sherman D Rosen (VP-Human Resources)

PRINCIPAL ACTIVITIES: Manufacture of clothing; retail trade in clothing

Trade Names: Hart Schaffner & Marx, Hickey Freeman, Kuppenheimer, Pierre Cardin, Austin Reed, Christian Dior, Sansabelt, etc

Principal Subsidiaries: Hart Schaffner & Marx, Hickey Freeman, Jaymar Ruby, Hartmarx Specialty Stores, Kuppenheimer, Country Miss

Principal Bank: The First National Bank of Chicago

Financial Information:

	Nov 30 1985 $'000	Nov 30 1986 $'000
Sales revenues	1,109,537	1,053,011
Income before taxes	81,250	47,525
Net income	42,660	24,775
Dividends	16,044	18,565
Dividends per share	$0.853	$0.903
Earnings per share*	$2.10	$1.20
Common stock	26,253	46,349
Retained income	306,159	312,369
Shareholders equity	332,412	358,718

*adjusted for split

No of Employees: 22,000

HARTSVILLE OIL MILL

829 S Fifth Street, Hartsville, SC 29550
Tel: (803) 332-3526

President: Edgar H Lawton Jr (and Treasurer)
Senior Executive Officers: Joseph J Lawton (VP and Secretary), R A Koppein (VP Sales)

PRINCIPAL ACTIVITIES: Production of cottonseed oil
Financial Information:

	$'000
Sales revenues	50,000

No of Employees: 160

HARTZELL CORPORATION

2515 Wabash, St Paul, MN 55114
Tel: (612) 642-2880

Chairman: Thomas Hartzell (and President)
Senior Executive Officers: Robert B Hartzell (Secretary and Treasurer), Robert Berg (Personnel Director), Erling N Anderson (Credit Manager)

PRINCIPAL ACTIVITIES: Manufacture of metal castings, hardware for doors and windows, plastic products and electronic equipment and components
Principal Subsidiaries: Component Sales Inc; Sunn Musical Equipment Co; Wright Products Inc
Principal Bank: Northwestern National Bank of Minneapolis
Financial Information:

	$'000
Sales revenues	65,000

No of Employees: 800

HARVARD INDUSTRIES, INC

4321 Semple Avenue, St Louis, MO 63120
Tel: (314) 382-5590

President: W D Hurley
Senior Executive Officers: J J Gagliardi (VP Finance and Chief Financial Officer), S D Colman (VP), B M Abrams (VP, Secretary and Legal Counsel)

PRINCIPAL ACTIVITIES: Manufacture of furniture, armaments and electronic equipment
Principal Bank: Citicorp
Financial Information:

	$'000
Sales revenues	205,870

No of Employees: 3,500

HARVEST STATES COOPERATIVES

1667 N Snelling Avenue, St Paul, MN 55165
Tel: (612) 646-9433

Chairman: Donald F Giffey; 1st Vice Chairman: Philip Testerman; 2nd Vice Chairman: Gerald G Redlin
President: Allen D Hanson
Senior Executive Officers: Harvey S Kaner (Senior VP), T F Baker (Senior VP Finance), George J Boos (Senior VP Manufacturing), Garry Pistori (Senior VP), R B Welch (Senior VP Manufacturing), Karl Butzer (Group VP Farm Supply), R A Pavek (Group VP Country and Grain Operations), Merritt E Petersen (Group VP Food and Oilseed Processing), Russell J Eichman (VP Transport)

PRINCIPAL ACTIVITIES: Cooperative for the marketing and distribution of farm products
Principal Bank: St Paul Bank for Cooperatives
Financial Information:

	$'000
Sales revenues	2,450,000

No of Employees: 2,800

HARVEY HUBBELL, INC

584 Derby-Milford Road, Orange, CT 06477
Tel: (203) 789-1100

President: Fred R Dusto (and Chief Executive Officer)
Senior Executive Officers: G J Ratcliffe Jr (Executive VP), Gerald E Martin (Group VP), Vincent R Petrecca (Group VP), H B Rowell Jr (Group VP Manufacturing), V L Carissimi (VP Engineering), C J Linski (VP Manufacturing), D G McNamara (VP Control Accounting), Vincent J Meads (VP International), R M Search (VP), E C Corner (VP Manager Industrial Controls Division), D A Gresh (VP Manager Wiring Device Division), J A O'Neill (VP Manager Hermetic Rfgn Division), Richard H Montague Jr (VP), Douglas E Winters (VP), J E Britt (VP Manufacturing Division)

PRINCIPAL ACTIVITIES: Manufacture of electrical equipment
Principal Subsidiaries: Harvey Hubbell of Canada Inc (Canada); Harvey Hubbell Ltd UK); Kerite Co; Ohio Brass Co; Raco Inc
Principal Bank: City Trust Co
Financial Information:

	$'000
Sales revenues	521,140

No of Employees: 5,770

HASBRO INC

1027 Newport Avenue, Pawtucket, RI 02861
Tel: (401) 726-4100

Chairman: Stephen Hassenfeld
President: Alan G Hassenfeld
Senior Executive Officers: Carole L Anderson (Senior VP), Christopher P Dona (Senior VP), Lawrence H Bernstein (Senior VP), George A Dunsay (Senior VP), Hugh C Maxwell (Senior VP), Anthony J Parkinson (Senior VP Corporate Development International), Stephen A Schwartz (Senior VP), Richard S Thompson (Senior VP), Alfred J Verrechia (Senior VP Finance), George R Ditomassi (Group VP), William J Daly (VP Industrial Relations), Sylvia Hassenfeld (VP Corporate Affairs), William Lansing (VP International Marketing), Leonard Engle (VP Purchasing), Brian S Prodger (VP Far Eastern Operations), Donald M Robbins (VP, Secretary and Legal Counsel), John E Sterling (VP Engineering), Philip H Waldoks (VP Corporate Legal Affairs)

PRINCIPAL ACTIVITIES: Manufacture of toys
Principal Subsidiaries: Aviva Hasbro Inc; Aviva Hasbro (International) Ltd (Hong Kong); Tomee Tippee Playskool Inc; Hasbro Industries (Canada) Ltd; Hasbro Industries (UK) Ltd; Romper Room Enterprises Inc; Playskool Inc; Milton Bradley GmbH (Germany); Milton Bradley Ltd (UK); Milton Bradley Canada Inc (Canada); M B France SA (France); M B Italy SRL (Italy); M B International BV (Netherlands); M B Belgium SA (Belgium); M B Espana SA (Spain); Milton Bradley (NZ) Ltd (New Zealand); Milton Bradley Australia Pty Ltd (Australia); Hasbro Bradley (Far East) Limited (Hong Kong); Hasbro Toy; Milton Bradley Games
Principal Bank: First National Bank of Boston

Financial Information:

	Dec 31 1986
	$'000
Sales revenues	1,329,631
Net income	99,159
Earnings per share	$1.71
Shareholders equity	580,272

No of Employees: 7,000

HASTINGS MANUFACTURING CO

300 N Hanover Street, Hastings, MI 49058
Tel: (616) 945-2491

President: Stephen I Johnson
Senior Executive Officers: R H Wallin (VP Sales), Dale Koop (VP and Chief Engineer), Andrew F Johnson (Treasurer)

PRINCIPAL ACTIVITIES: Manufacture of engine components and filters
Principal Subsidiaries: Hastings Inc (Canada), Douglas Corp
Principal Bank: National Bank of Detroit
Financial Information:

	$'000
Sales revenues	62,600

No of Employees: 700

HATFIELD QUALITY MEATS, INC

2700 Funks Road, Hatfield, PA 19440
Tel: (215) 368-2500
Telex: WUT 846334 htfld pak hald

President: John W Clemens
Senior Executive Officers: Clair W Clemens (Executive VP), Kenneth W Clemens (VP Processed/Smoked Meats), J Kenneth Jones (VP Finance and Secretary/Treasurer), Jacob L Clemmer (VP Marketing/Sales), Richard L Clemens (VP Fresh Pork/Rendering), Philip A Clemens (VP Human Resources)

PRINCIPAL ACTIVITIES: Meat processing
Principal Bank: Continental Bank of Norristown
Financial Information:

	$'000
Sales revenues	192,000

No of Employees: 850

HATHAWAY, C F, CO

10 Water Street, Waterville, ME 04901
Tel: (207) 873-4241
Telex: TWX 710 2291234 hathaway wtels

President: E B Wilson
Senior Executive Officers: Alton Laliberte (Executive VP Operations), Edward A Locklin (Executive VP Finance and Administration), Stanley Kaufman (Chairman Dior Shirts Unit), Anthony Chillemi (President Stern Merritt Unit), George Ackerman (President, Chaps by Ralph Lauren Unit), George Petersen (President Destino Unit), Joseph Visconti (President Hathaway Unit), William Bell (President Albert Nipon Unit)

PRINCIPAL ACTIVITIES: Manufacture of men's clothing and accessories
Parent Company: Warnaco Inc, Bridgeport, CT
Financial Information:

	$'000
Sales revenues	127,000

No of Employees: 1,700

HATHAWAY CORPORATION

350 Interlocken Pkwy, Broomfield, CO 80022
Tel: (303) 450-1500

Chairman: Eugene E Prince (and President and Chief Executive Officer); Vice Chairman: A J Hintze
Senior Executive Officers: James A Bright (VP Product Development), Richard D Smith (VP Finance, Secretary, Treasurer and Chief Financial Officer), E J Westback (VP and General Manager)

PRINCIPAL ACTIVITIES: Products for the measurement of electrical and electronic systems
Principal Subsidiaries: Acoustic Emission Technology Corporation; Computer Optical Products Inc; Data Capture Technology; First Centennial Leasing Corporation; Systems Northwest Inc
Principal Bank: Colorado National Bank of Denver
Financial Information:

	$'000
Sales revenues	36,500

No of Employees: 610

HAUSERMAN, INC

5711 Grant Avenue, Cleveland, OH 44105
Tel: (216) 883-1400

Chairman: Wm F Hauserman
President: John M Burke (and Chief Executive Officer)
Senior Executive Officers: A H Dillemuth (VP), L J Buttitta (VP), D A Chiodo (VP), K B Erickson (VP), J A Tanis (VP), J M Palmer (VP), A J Haueisen (Secretary)

PRINCIPAL ACTIVITIES: Hauserman, Inc through SunarHauserman, is a leading designer and supplier of furniture, textiles, systems and movable walls for integrated office interiors in North America. Hauserman Limited in Korea produces movable walls and furniture systems for far eastern markets. Sunar Ltd, sourcing, manufacturing and marketing a full line of furniture products in the United Kingdom
Principal Subsidiaries: SunarHauserman; Sunar Ltd; SunarHauserman Asia Ltd; Hauserman Ltd
Principal Bank: Society National Bank of Cleveland
Financial Information:

	Jun 30 1985	Jun 30 1986
	$'000	$'000
Sales revenues	144,154	140,318
Income before taxes	4,704	5,259
Net income	5,426	3,602
Dividends	943	1,112
Dividends per share	$0.40	$0.45
Earnings per share	$2.29	$1.53
Stated capital	5,014	5,373
Retained income	31,838	34,328
Shareholders equity	28,796	33,325

No of Employees: 1,900

HAVERTY FURNITURE COMPANIES INC

866 West Peachtree Street NW, Atlanta, GA 30308
Tel: (404) 881 1911

Chairman: Rawson Haverty (and Chief Executive Officer)
President: Frank S McGaughey Jr (and Chief Operating Officer)
Senior Executive Officers: Leonard O Gay (Executive VP, Treasurer and Chief Financial Officer), John E Slater Jr (VP), Clarence H Smith (VP and General Manager Regional), James E Smith (VP Real Estate and Insurance Division), Daniel E Walters (VP Credits and Collections), Hugh G Wells Jr (VP and Assistant Treasurer), Roger P Whitaker (VP), Dan C Bryant (Controller), Christine M Jones (Secretary)

PRINCIPAL ACTIVITIES: Furniture retail stores
Principal Bank: Bank South
Financial Information:

	$'000
Sales revenues	196,000

No of Employees: 1,780

HAWKEYE BANCORPORATION

6th Floor First Building, 319 7th Street, Des Moines, IA 50307
Tel: (515) 284 1930

President: Paul D Dunlap (and Chief Executive Officer)
Senior Executive Officers: Robert W Murray (Executive VP and Treasurer), Stephan L Jones (Senior VP), Lewis L Lowe (Senior VP), Donald R Runger (Senior VP), John T Seitz (VP and Legal Counsel), William Hayen (VP Auditing), Michael B Smith (VP and Controller), James R Bullard (VP Loans)

PRINCIPAL ACTIVITIES: Holding company with interests in banking
Principal Subsidiaries: Citizens National Bank; Commercial State Bank; First National Bank; Hawkeye Bancorp Computer Services; Hawkeye Bank and Trust Company; Hawkeye Capital Bank and Trust; Hawkeye Insurance Services; Hawkeye Investment Management; Hawkeye Mortgage Company; Hawkeye State Bank; Hawkeye-Ankeny Bank and Trust; Houghton State Bank; Inman Realty; Jasper County Savings Bank; Lake City State Bank; Lyon County State Bank; National Bank of Washington; Onawa State Bank; Pella National Bank; State Bank; State Bank and Trust Company; State Bank of Allison; Tipton State Bank; United State Bank; Wauken State Bank
Financial Information:

	Dec 31 1985 $'000
Revenues	219,250

No of Employees: 1,600

HAWORTH INDUSTRIES INC
One Haworth Center, Holland, MI 49423
Tel: (616) 392-5961
Telex: TWX 810 2926154 haworth hola

Chairman: Gerard W Haworth
President: Richard G Haworth
Senior Executive Officers: James E Stonick (Executive VP Finance), Jerry Johanneson (Executive VP Marketing and Sales), William A Sikkel (Senior VP Major Accounts), Dennis C Dombush (VP Finance), Alan Keith (VP Manufacturing), David McLeod (VP Venture Group), Alvin Alders (VP Production and Engineering), Richard Codel (VP International Operations), John Amell (VP Material and Logistics Management), Judith Thomas (VP Human Resources)

PRINCIPAL ACTIVITIES: Manufacture of dividers and furniture for offices
Principal Subsidiaries: Haworth Inc
Principal Bank: First National Bank of Chicago
Financial Information:

	$'000
Sales revenues	270,000

No of Employees: 2,200

HAWTHORN MELLODY, INC
1827 Walden Office Square, Schaumburg, IL 60195
Tel: (312) 397-1200

President: J E Spielman Jr
Senior Executive Officers: Edmund Ellis (VP), Harley Mickelson (VP), Walter R Woodbury (VP), Thomas B Bohlender (VP), Joseph Niemasz (Secretary and Treasurer)

PRINCIPAL ACTIVITIES: Manufacture and sale of ice cream and dairy products
Principal Bank: First Citizens Bank of Wisconsin
Financial Information:

	$'000
Sales revenues	190,000

No of Employees: 1,000

HAWTHORNE FINANCIAL CORPORATION
13001 South Hawthorne Boulevard, Hawthorne, CA 90250
Tel: (213) 973-1000

Chairman: Cecil O Garton
President: Vernon D Herbst (and General Manager)
Senior Executive Officers: C P Briggs (VP and Secretary), Douglas J Herbst (Treasurer and Subsidiary Officer)

PRINCIPAL ACTIVITIES: Holding company with interests in savings and loan services
Principal Subsidiaries: Hawthorne Savings and Loan Association
Principal Bank: Crocker National Bank
Financial Information:

	Dec 31 1985 $'000
Sales revenues	68,790

HAYDEN PUBLISHING CO
10 Mulholland Drive, Hasbrouck Heights, NJ 07604
Tel: (201) 393-6000

President: J S Mullholland Jr (and Treasurer)
Senior Executive Officers: John Wade (VP Finance and Administration), Bond Blake (VP), Don Huber (VP), Stacy Bearse (VP), Robert Lydon (VP), Chuck Houpt (VP)

PRINCIPAL ACTIVITIES: Publication of specialist magazines and books of technical interest
Principal Bank: United Jersey Bank
Financial Information:

	$'000
Sales revenues	72,000

No of Employees: 400

HAYES INTERNATIONAL CORPORATION
PO Box 2287, Birmingham, AL 35201
Tel: (205) 592-0011
Telex: TWX 810 7333687 haves bham

Chairman: Willis C Hagan Jr
President: Michael E Howarth Jr (and Chief Executive Officer)
Senior Executive Officers: Charles D Brown (VP Targets Division), T J Robinson (VP Birmingham Division), L Nalley III (Chief Financial Officer and Controller), Donald E Bush (VP Dotham Division)

PRINCIPAL ACTIVITIES: Maintenance of aircraft for commercial airlines and the armed forces; manufacture of aerial target equipment
Parent Company: Pace Industries Inc
Principal Bank: Citibank NA
Financial Information:

	$'000
Sales revenues	140,000

No of Employees: 3,500

HAYES-ALBION CORPORATION
2701 N Dettman Road, Jackson, MI 49201
Tel: (517) 782-9421

Chairman: Charles E Drury
President: John Whiting (and Chief Executive Officer)
Senior Executive Officers: George E Hammell (Senior VP), R L Zach (VP Cast Products Group), Robert J Negri (VP and Treasurer), Nancy L Bayer (VP and Secretary)

PRINCIPAL ACTIVITIES: Manufacture of metal castings, automotive parts, hardware, window frames, wheels, pulleys and pumps
Principal Bank: National Bank of Detroit
Financial Information:

	$'000
Sales revenues	226,500

No of Employees: 2,700

HAYWARD INDUSTRIES, INC
900 Fairmount Avenue, Elizabeth, NJ 07207
Tel: (201) 351-5400

Chairman: Oscar Davis (and President)

Senior Executive Officers: Richard E Garbee (Senior VP, Secretary and Treasurer), Sidney A Lewis (Senior VP), William E Treene (Senior VP), Hachy Horasan (VP Manufacturing), Albert Lemer (VP Finance), Harold Paitchell (VP Engineering), George Williams (VP Sales)

PRINCIPAL ACTIVITIES: Manufacture of valves and filters for swimming pools and industry
Principal Subsidiaries: Hayward Pool Products Inc
Financial Information:

	$'000
Sales revenues	100,000

No of Employees: 600

HAZELTINE CORPORATION

Greenlawn, NY 11740
Tel: (516) 261-7000
Cable: neutrodyne
Telex: 96-7800 Greenlawn NY

Chairman: Sal J Nuzzo
President: Merle L Engle (and Chief Executive Officer)
Senior Executive Officers: Frederick C Brehm (Senior VP), Joseph R Colarusso (Executive VP), Randolph H Cope Jr (Senior VP), Raymond J Hoehn (Senior VP), David E Kern (Senior VP and Chief Financial Officer), Robert F Normandin (Senior VP), James W Evans (VP Community and Public Relations)

PRINCIPAL ACTIVITIES: Manufacture of electronic equipment for the armed forces including C3I and ASW; microwave landing systems
Parent Company: Emerson Electric Co
Principal Subsidiaries: Hazeltine Research Inc

No of Employees: 2,400

HAZLETON LABORATORIES CORPORATION

9200 Leesburg Turnpike, Vienna, VA 22180
Tel: (703) 893 5400

Chairman: Kirby L Cramer
President: Donald P Nielsen (and Chief Operating Officer)
Senior Executive Officers: Roy M Dagnall (VP), Bruce J Hegstad (VP), James R Larkin (VP), Cyrus C Lippman (VP), Lewis E S Parker (VP), Carl C Schwan (VP, Secretary and Treasurer), Marshall Steinberg (VP), David A Valerio (VP)

PRINCIPAL ACTIVITIES: Biological research services
Principal Subsidiaries: Hazleton Laboratories American Inc
Principal Bank: Sovran Bank
Financial Information:

	$'000
Sales revenues	56,000

No of Employees: 1,600

HBO & COMPANY

301 Perimeter Center North, Atlanta, GA 30346
Tel: (404) 393 6000

Chairman: Walter S Huff
President: James V Napier (and Chief Executive Officer)
Senior Executive Officers: John Kerr (Executive VP), Joseph G Bleser (VP, Controller, Chief Operating Officer and Assistant Secretary), Ed H Bowman Jr (VP Marketing), King M Deets (VP), Larry G Gerdes (VP and Chief Operating Officer), Thomas H Muller (VP, Chief Financial Officer, Secretary and Treasurer), Darrell H Young (VP Research and Development), John Blend (VP Eastern), Donald B Graham (VP Western)

PRINCIPAL ACTIVITIES: Computer systems for hospitals
Principal Bank: Continental Illinois National Bank and Trust Company

Financial Information:

	$'000
Net income	20,845

No of Employees: 600

HCC INDUSTRIES

16311 Ventura Boulevard, Suite 1180, Encino, CA 91436
Tel: (818) 995 4131

Chairman: Jack Goldfarb (and Chief Executive Officer); Vice Chairman: Michael Pelta
President: Andrew Goldfarb (and Chief Operating Officer)
Senior Executive Officers: Alan W Wong (Chief Financial Officer), Fredric Horowitz (Secretary)

PRINCIPAL ACTIVITIES: Manufacture of electronic components including connection devices, electromechanical and other types of transducers for a wide range of industries including military and space electronics and oil and gas industries; power conversion components for use in computers, telecommunications and other electronic equipment
Principal Bank: Wells Fargo Bank
Financial Information:

	$'000
Sales revenues	40,000

No of Employees: 900

HEALTH EXTENSION SERVICES INC

6900 Jericho Turnpike, Syosset, NY 11753
Tel: (516) 364 2500

President: Martin Weissman
Senior Executive Officers: Israel Cohen (Executive VP), Allen H Fisher (VP Finance and Secretary), Harvey H Schaffler (VP Marketing and Business Development)

PRINCIPAL ACTIVITIES: Healthcare facilities
Principal Subsidiaries: Professional Care Inc; Professional Care Properties Corporation
Financial Information:

	$'000
Sales revenues	55,800

No of Employees: 500

HEALTHAMERICA CORPORATION

3310 West End Avenue, Nashville, TN 37203
Tel: (615) 385 7300

Chairman: Philip N Bredesen (and President and Chief Executive Officer)
Senior Executive Officers: John E Gillmore (Executive VP and Legal Counsel), Joseph P WIlliams (Executive VP and Chief Financial Officer), John H Austin (VP, Managing Director and Director of Medicine), R R Herrick (VP), F A Logue (VP), W P Melling (VP), M A Raesenger (VP), S I Seringer (VP), Kenneth D Den Besten (VP Finance and Treasurer), Mary V Anderson (Secretary and Assistant Legal Counsel), Steven D Stedman (Controller and Chief Accounting Officer)

PRINCIPAL ACTIVITIES: Non-residential healthcare services
Financial Information:

	$'000
Sales revenues	650,000

No of Employees: 4,000

HEALTHCARE INTERNATIONAL INC

9737 Great Hills Trail, Austin, TX 78759
Tel: (512) 346 4300

Chairman: James L Fariss Jr
President: David L Whelan
Senior Executive Officers: ELliott H Weir Jr (Executive VP, Secretary and Treasurer), Jean P Smith (Senior VP), Dan G Fariss (VP), Michael P Heeley (VP), Brent W Jorgeson (VP), J Mack Nunn (VP and Controller), Stan D Pinder (VP), Frank T

Rafferty (VP), John T Scully (VP), Robert G Wallace (VP), Deborah H Frankovich (VP and Treasurer)

PRINCIPAL ACTIVITIES: Operation of hospitals

Financial Information:

	$'000
Sales revenues	152,810

No of Employees: 3,030

HEALTHCARE SERVICES OF AMERICA INC

2000 Southbridge Parkway, Suite 200, Birmingham, AL 35209

Tel: (205) 879 8970

President: Charles A Speir (and Chief Executive Officer)

Senior Executive Officers: Thomas M Rodgers Jr (Senior Executive VP Finance and Chief Financial Officer), Kerry G Teel (Senior Executive VP), Joseph W Curtin Jr (Executive VP Human Resources and Development), Carl M Holden Jr (Executive VP), Thomas P Millea (Senior VP), Arthur P Bolton III (VP and Legal Counsel), Morris S Strickland (Controller)

PRINCIPAL ACTIVITIES: Operation of hospitals

Financial Information:

	$'000
Sales revenues	53,000

No of Employees: 1,275

HEALTHCARE USA INC

701 South Parker Street, Orange, CA 92668

Tel: (714) 633 5420

Chairman: Harlan W Loomas (and President and Chief Executive Officer)

President: William C Scott (and Chief Operating Officer)

Senior Executive Officers: Larry L Fredericksen (Executive VP, Chief Financial Officer and Treasurer), Michael E Henry (Senior VP and Division President), M Donald Kowitz (Senior VP and Division President)

PRINCIPAL ACTIVITIES: Healthcare for out patients

Principal Bank: Bank of America

Financial Information:

	$'000
Sales revenues	183,000

No of Employees: 2,100

HEALTHCO INTERNATIONAL, INC

25 Stuart Street, Boston, MA 02116

Tel: (617) 423-02116

Telex: 948036

Telefax: (617) 423-6220

Chairman: Marvin M Cyker (and Chief Executive Officer)

President: Michael Cyker

Senior Executive Officers: Robert E Daggett (VP, Information Services), Raymond R Doherty (Senior VP, Finance and Operational Controls, Assistant Secretary), Harvey W Eaton (VP, Personnel and Benefits Administration), Frederick L Haggerty (VP, Marketing), Eugene G Hay (VP, Controller), Yves Lambert (VP, Canadian Operations), Joel Lewin (Secretary Healthco International, Inc Partner; Snyder, Tepper & Comen (Attorneys), Boston), Arthur P Souza (VP, Treasurer)

PRINCIPAL ACTIVITIES: Distribution of dental equipment and supplies

Principal Bank: First National Bank of Boston

Financial Information:

	Dec 28 1985	Dec 27 1986
	$'000	$'000
Sales revenues	307,040	349,211
Income before taxes	15,086	31,557
Net income	8,312	23,491
Earnings per share*	$1.48	$3.48
Common stock	301	303
Retained income	35,661	59,152
Shareholders equity	93,048	117,250

*fully diluted

Principal Shareholders: J P Morgan & Co Inc; Nicholas Company Inc; Citibank NA; Marvin M Cyher

No of Employees: 2,700

HEALTHDYNE INC

2250 Northwest Pkwy, Marietta, GA 30067

Tel: (404) 955-9555

Telex: TWX 8107634715

Chairman: Peter H Petit (and Chief Executive Officer)

President: Jeffrey D Koepsell

Senior Executive Officers: J T Dewberry (Executive VP)

PRINCIPAL ACTIVITIES: Manufacture of medical equipment including incubators and infant monitoring devices; provision of home health care services

Principal Bank: Citizens and Southern Bank

Financial Information:

	$'000
Sales revenues	120,900

No of Employees: 1,400

HEART FEDERAL SAVINGS & LOAN ASSOCIATION

648 Lincoln Way, Auburn, CA 95603

Tel: (916) 823-7283

Directors: Stuart R Foster (and Chief Executive Officer)

Senior Executives: Albert M French (Senior VP), Lewis R Gale III (Senior VP, Chief Financial Officer and Treasurer), Obie K Ladd (Senior VP), Gerald L Rodgers (Senior VP), Donald R Walker (Senior VP), Joyce E Keane (Secretary)

PRINCIPAL ACTIVITIES: Savings and loans

Principal Subsidiaries: Heart of CA Corporation

Principal Bank: Federal Home Loan Bank

No of Employees: 315

HEAT CONTROLLER, INC

1900 Wellworth Avenue, Jackson, MI 49203

Tel: (517) 787-2100

Telex: TWX 8102531919 heatcontrol jkn

Chairman: J A Knight (and President)

Senior Executive Officers: E D Sayles (VP Marketing), E A Bako (Treasurer)

PRINCIPAL ACTIVITIES: Manufacture of air conditioning and heating equipment

Principal Bank: National Bank of Detroit

Financial Information:

	$'000
Sales revenues	50,000

No of Employees: 120

HEBREW NATIONAL KOSHER FOODS, INC

600 Food Center Dr, Bronx, NY 10474

Tel: (212) 842 5000

President: Isidore Pines

Senior Executive Officers: Martin Silver (Executive VP), Werner Fontein (VP Marketing), E Schwarzman (VP Purchasing), Lee Miller (VP Technical Services), Jonathan Bernstein (VP

Finance), Harvey Potkin (VP Distribution), J DiPrima (VP Engineering)
PRINCIPAL ACTIVITIES: Kosher meat and other Kosher food products
Principal Bank: Manufacturers Hanover Trust Company
Financial Information:

	$'000
Sales revenues	100,000

No of Employees: 800

HECHINGER COMPANY
3500 Pennsy Drive, Landover, MD 20785
Tel: (301) 341 1000

Chairmen: John W Hechinger Sr, Richard England
President: John W Hechinger
Senior Executive Officers: Stephen E Bachand (Executive VP), Philip J Mansfield (Executive VP), Catherine S Russell (Senior VP Human Resources), Sally A Courtney (VP and General Manager Merchandising), Joan S England (VP Sales Promotion), S Ross Hechinger (VP Distribution), W Clark McClelland (VP Finance, Treasurer and Secretary), Richard L Ponton (VP and Director Merchandise), Joanne Barrett (VP and Divisional Merchandise Manager), Jerry Brase (VP and Divisional Merchandise Manager), Robert DeMarco (VP Management Information Systems), George Kelly (VP and Divisional Merchandise Manager), Jack McGrath (VP and Regional Manager)
PRINCIPAL ACTIVITIES: Retail trade in hardware and DIY materials
Principal Bank: American Security Bank
Financial Information:

	$'000
Sales revenues	588,000

No of Employees: 7,500

HECK'S INC
Hub Industrial Park, McJunkin Road, PO Box 158, Nitro, WV 25143
Tel: (304) 755 8331

Chairman: Russell L Isaacs (and Chief Executive Officer and Chief Financial Officer); Vice Chairman: Ray O Darnall
President: Theodore W Kazleman
Senior Executive Officers: R A Chambers (Senior VP Corporate Information Systems), James V Doss (Senior VP Merchandising), R L Frady (Senior VP Operations), Thomas A Weaver (Senior VP and Comptroller), R A Petryszak (Treasurer), H G Shaffer Jr (Secretary)
PRINCIPAL ACTIVITIES: Retail outlets selling wide range of goods including clothing, hardware, toys and jewelry
Principal Subsidiaries: Federal Wholesale Company; Harris & Frank Inc; M & W Distributors Inc
Principal Bank: Charleston National Bank
Financial Information:

	$'000
Sales revenues	523,335

No of Employees: 6,700

HECLA MINING CO
6500 Mineral Drive, Box C-8000, Coeur D'Alene, ID 83814-1931
Tel: (208) 769-4100

Chairman: Arthur Brown (and President and Chief Executive Officer)
Senior Executive Officers: W J Grismer (Senior VP), Elmer Bierly (VP), Gene Ealy (VP), Robert Wallace (VP)
PRINCIPAL ACTIVITIES: Mining and processing of gold, silver, lead, zinc and other non-ferrous metals; major producer of specialty ball clay and volcanic scoria
Principal Subsidiaries: Kentucky-Tennessee Clay Co; Colorado Aggregate Company
Principal Bank: Chase
Financial Information:

	Dec 31 1985	Dec 31 1986
	$'000	$'000
Sales revenues	82,600	62,000
(Loss) before taxes	(8,700)	(23,300)
Net (loss)	(4,200)	(21,200)
Dividends per share	$0.20	$0.05
Common stock	26,974	26,970
Shareholders equity	143,800	118,200

No of Employees: 700

HEEKIN CAN INC
11310 Cornell Park Drive, Cincinnati, OH 45242
Tel: (513) 489-3200

Chairman: H E Uehlein
President: J A Haas
Senior Executive Officers: K M Dickson (VP Purchasing), D P Hull (VP Manufacturing), E R Jackson (VP Research), P H Schwartz (VP Finance), L R Sheppard (VP Industrial Relations), G E Tierney (VP Sales), R A Hummel (Controller, Treasurer and Secretary)
PRINCIPAL ACTIVITIES: Manufacture of metal packaging products
Principal Bank: First National of Cincinnati
Financial Information:

	$'000
Net sales	221,814

No of Employees: 1,100

HEI CORPORATION
7676 Woodway, Suite 112, Houston, TX 77063
Tel: (713) 780 7802

Chairman: George G Alexander (and Chief Executive Officer)
President: Robert C Hux (and Chief Operating Officer)
Senior Executive Officers: J Russell Denson (Executive VP), R Pringle Ramsey (Executive VP and Chief Financial Officer), Thomas R Rice (Executive VP Division), Richard H Shafer (VP, Secretary and Treasurer)
PRINCIPAL ACTIVITIES: Operation of hospitals
Financial Information:

	$'000
Sales revenues	81,600

No of Employees: 1,400

HEIL CO
3000 W Montana Street, Milwaukee, WI 53201
Tel: (414) 647-3333
Telex: ITT 4311041 heilco mil

Chairman: Joseph F Heil Jr
President: Richard J Fridl
Senior Executive Officers: Lawrence Gray (Executive VP), William H Nehrkorn (VP Secretary and General Counsel), Rolland A Cross (VP and Controller)
PRINCIPAL ACTIVITIES: Manufacture of truck bodies, refuse collection equipment, mechanical handling equipment and hoists
Principal Subsidiaries: Heil Rotomold Inc (Phoenix, AZ); Heil FSC Inc (Milwaukee, WI); Hillend Environmental Industry Ltd (Dunfermline, Scotland)
Principal Bank: First Wisconsin National Bank of Milwaukee
Financial Information:

	1986
	$'000
Sales revenues	130,000
Income before taxes	10,815
Net income	5,886

No of Employees: 1,000

HEILEMAN, G, BREWING CO, INC

100 Harborview Plaza, La Crosse, WI 54601
Tel: (608) 785-1000
Telex: WUT 293414 heileman lcr

Chairman: Russell G Cleary (and President and Chief Executive Officer)
Senior Executive Officers: John S Isherwood (Senior Executive VP Operations), John S Pedace (Executive VP Marketing), John D Glenn (Executive VP Operations), Ronald W Rizzo (Executive VP Sales), Peter J O'Sullivan (VP Purchasing), John P Barrett (VP Commodities), Ralph E Horn (VP Administration), Ronald J Drout (VP Brand Management Central Sales Division), Thomas J Myers (VP Brand Management Eastern Sales Division), Daniel J Schmid Jr (VP and Controller), James G Martin (VP Marketing Western Sales Region), Sydney A Marcus (VP Advertising Eastern Region), James P Legat (VP Brand Management), Randy J Smith (VP and Legal Counsel)

PRINCIPAL ACTIVITIES: Production of beer
Principal Subsidiaries: Machine Products Company; G Heileman Baking Company; Nesco Sigsn Corp; Lone Star Brewing Company Inc
Principal Bank: Northwestern National Bank
Financial Information:

	Dec 31 1985	Dec 31 1986
	$'000	$'000
Sales revenues	1,169,230	1,173,786
Net income	43,300	48,300
Earnings per share	$1.65	$1.83
Shareholders equity	298,150	335,850

No of Employees: 6,300

HEILIG-MEYERS COMPANY

3228 West Cary Street, Richmond, VA 23221
Tel: (804) 359-9171

Chairman: William C DeRush (and Chief Executive Officer)
President: Troy A Peery Jr (and Chief Financial Officer)
Senior Executive Officers: Douglas M Adams (Senior VP Corporate Planning and Management Information Systems), R H Beam (Senior VP Operations Western Region), William J Dieter (Senior VP Accounting, Controller and Chief Accounting Officer), R Gene Laughter (Senior VP Advertising), James Riddle (Senior VP Merchandising), Lloyd C King (Senior Regional VP), James A McCoy (Senior VP Finance), Ronald M Ragland (VP)

PRINCIPAL ACTIVITIES: Retailing of household furniture
Principal Subsidiaries: Augusta Furniture Company Inc; Heilig Meyers Company of Virginia; Heilig-Meyers Company of South Carolina Inc; Heilig-Meyers Company of West Virginia; Heilig-Meyers of North Carolina; Heilig-Meyers Company of Georgia; Rhodes-Day-Elledge Inc; Thornton Furniture Company Inc; Thornton Vaughan Inc
Principal Bank: United VA Bank
Financial Information:

	$'000
Sales revenues	182,000

No of Employees: 1,600

HEINICKE INSTRUMENTS COMPANY

3000 Taft Street, Hollywood, FL 33021
Tel: (305) 987 6101

Chairman: Chester A Warner (and President and Chief Executive Officer)
Senior Executive Officers: Thomas S Irwin (VP, Treasurer and Chief Financial Officer), Julie A Shumpert (Secretary)

PRINCIPAL ACTIVITIES: Manufacture of scientific equipment; aircraft components
Principal Subsidiaries: Hotpack Corporation; National Appliance Company
Principal Bank: NCNB National Bank
Financial Information:

	$'000
Sales revenues	32,000

No of Employees: 400

HEIN-WERNER CORPORATION

1005 Perkins Avenue, Waukesha, WI 53186
Tel: (414) 542 6611

President: J L Dindorf (and Chief Executive Officer)
Senior Executive Officers: R D Liegel (Senior VP), Michael J Koons (VP Industrial Affairs and Personnel Affairs), T E Walsh (VP Finance, Treasurer and Assistant Secretary), Gerald Pfeiffer (VP and General Manager Auto Division)

PRINCIPAL ACTIVITIES: Production of equipment for processing of metals; industrial tools; hydraulic equipment
Principal Subsidiaries: Kansas-Jack Inc
Principal Bank: First WI National Bank
Financial Information:

	$'000
Sales revenues	51,000

No of Employees: 400

HEINZ, H J, CO

600 Grant Street, Pittsburgh, PA 15230
Tel: (412) 237-5757

Chairman: Anthony J F O'Reilly (and President and Chief Executive Officer)
Senior Executive Officers: Albert Lippert (Chairman Weight Watchers International), Paul I Corddry (Senior VP), R D Finlay (Senior VP Corporate Development), Karl Von Der Heyden (Senior VP Finance and Chief Financial Officer), S D Willey (Senior VP, Secretary and General Counsel), Joseph J Bogdanovich (Senior VP), J Wray Connolly (Senior VP), Richard B Patton (Senior VP)

PRINCIPAL ACTIVITIES: Food processing; canned food products
Principal Subsidiaries: H J Heinz Company of Canada Ltd; H J Heinz Company Ltd (UK); H J Heinz Company Australia Ltd (Australia); Plasmon Dietetici Alimentari SpA (Italy); Star-Kist Foods Inc; Star-Kist Caribe Inc (Puerto Rico); Star-Kist Samoa Inc (Samoa); Ore-Ida Foods Inc; The Hubinger Company; Weight Watchers International Inc; Star-Kist International SA (Panama); Gagliardi Bros Inc; The Stanley Wine Company Pty Ltd (Australia); Epicurean Foods and Beverages Pty Ltd (Australia); Galco Food Products Ltd (Canada); Caribbean Restaurants Inc (Puerto Rico); Alimentos Heinz CA (Venezuela); W Darlington and Sons Ltd (UK); Country Kitchen Foods Ltd (UK); H J Heinz BV (Netherlands); H J Heinz Sarl (France); Industrias de Alimentacoa Ltda (Portugal); Foodways National Inc; Star-Kist Canada Inc; Ets Paul Paulet (France); Heinz Japan Ltd; Liven International SpA (Italy); Fratelli Sperlari SpA (Italy); Olivine Industries (Pte) Limited (Zimbabwe); Montrose Canned Foods Ltd (UK); SA HJ Heinz Central Europe NV (Belgium); Nadler-Werke GmbH (Germany); H J Heinz GmbH (Germany); Somycel SA (France); Johma Holding International BV (Netherlands); Heinz-UFE Ltd (China); Frutsi Alimenticia SA (Brazil); Seoul-Heinz Ltd (Korea)
Financial Information:

	Apr 30 1986	Apr 30 1987
	$'000	$'000
Sales revenues	4,366,177	4,639,486
Income befores taxes	499,328	564,576
Net income	301,734	338,506
Dividends	117,351	132,278
Dividends per share	$0.875	$1.005
Earnings per share	$2.20	$2.47
Retained income	1,380,425	1,564,581
Shareholders equity	1,360,007	1,392,949
Total assets	2,837,364	3,364,197

No of Employees: 48,987

HEINZ USA

1062 Progress Street, Pittsburgh, PA 15212
Tel: (412) 237-5757
Telex: WUT 812333 hjh hoe pgh

President: J W Connolly
Senior Executive Officers: C L Roberts (VP Processed Foods), W V Costello (VP Sales), R H Wamhoff (VP Logistics), W L Springer (VP Finance and Miscellaneous), W R Johnson (VP Consumer Products Marketing)

PRINCIPAL ACTIVITIES: Canned food products
Parent Company: H J Heinz Co
Principal Bank: Mellon Bank
Financial Information:

	$'000
Sales revenues	700,000

No of Employees: 5,000

HEIST, C H, CORPORATION

810 North Belcher Road, Clearwater, FL 33575
Tel: (813) 461 5656

Chairman: Willard F Foster (and Chief Executive Officer)
President: Charles H Heist (and Chief Operating Officer)
Senior Executive Officers: Frank Trotter (VP Operations), Richard J O'Neil (VP Finance), John L Rowley (Treasurer), Isador Snitzer (Secretary), W David Foster (VP Marketing and Sales)

PRINCIPAL ACTIVITIES: Cleaning services including sand blasting and high pressure water cleaning
Principal Bank: Manufacturers Traders Trust Company
Financial Information:

	$'000
Sales revenues	41,000

No of Employees: 1,100

HELDOR INDUSTRIES, INC

One Cory Road, Morristown, NJ 07960
Tel: (201) 898-9445

Chairman: Robert Ellington (and Chief Executive Officer); Vice Chairmen: John De Elorza (and Chairman Executive Committee), Thomas H Mahon Jr, Donald Gough
President: John F Zaccaro (and Chief Operating Officer)
Senior Executive Officers: Calvin R Patterson Jr (VP Finance)

PRINCIPAL ACTIVITIES: Swimming pools and equipment
Principal Subsidiaries: Richardson Industries Inc; Kratz Laboratories Inc
Principal Bank: Wells Fargo
Financial Information:

	$'000
Sales revenues	91,700

HELENE CURTIS INDUSTRIES, INC

325 N Wells Street, Chicago, IL 60610
Tel: (312) 661-0222
Cable: HELECURT CHICAGO
Telex: 210301 HELECURT

Chairman: Gerald Gidwitz; Vice Chairman: Joseph L Gidwitz, Si R Wynn
President: Ronald J Gidwitz
Senior Executive Officers: Charles G Cooper (Executive) VP), Michael Goldman (Senior VP), Eugene Zeffren (VP Research Division), Gilbert P Smith (Senior VP, President Consumer Products Division), Robert Sack (VP), Rees Orland (VP, President Professional Division), Jack L Calahro (VP), Lewis D Duberman (VP, Chief Financial Officer), Robert L Grey (Treasurer), Roy A Wentz (Secretary)

PRINCIPAL ACTIVITIES: Cosmetics and beauty products
Trade Names: Suave, Finesse, Atune, Salon Selectives, Quantum, Moisture Quotient, LaForme
Principal Subsidiaries: Helene Curtis Inc; Helene Curtis Ltd Ltee (Canada); Helene Curtis (Europa) BV (Netherlands); Loma Holdings Inc; Economy Beauty Supply Company; HC Enterprises Inc (Japan); Helene Curtis Japan Inc (Japan); Beauty Incorporated Pty Ltd (Australia); Spencer L Ayrey Ltd (New Zealand)
Principal Bank: Harris Trust and Savings Bank
Financial Information:

	Feb 28 1986	Feb 28 1987
	$'000	$'000
Sales revenues	360,754	400,082
Income befores taxes	17,167	20,435
Net income	8,927	10,269
Dividends per share	-	$0.30
Earnings per share	$2.44	$2.80
Common stock*	3,669	3,668
Retained income	62,999	72,286
Shareholders equity	67,286	77,408
*number of shares outstanding in thousands		

No of Employees: 2,300

HELIX TECHNOLOGY CORPORATION

Kelvin Park, 204 Second Avenue, Waltham, MA 02254
Tel: (617) 890 9292

Chairman: Frank P Gabron (and President and Chief Executive Officer)
Senior Executive Officers: Robert E Blakelock (Senior VP, Chief Financial Officer and Secretary), Robert J Lepofsky (Senior VP and Chief Operationg Officer), Stanley D Piekos (Controller), Bruce T Wright (VP Human Resources)

PRINCIPAL ACTIVITIES: Manufacture of refrigerators and cryogenic vacuum pumps
Principal Bank: First National Bank of Boston
Financial Information:

	$'000
Sales revenues	49,140

No of Employees: 445

HELM RESOURCES INC

2 Hammarskjold Plaza, New York, NY 10017
Tel: (212) 355 7788

Chairman: Herbert M Pearlman (and President and Chief Executive Officer)
Senior Executive Officers: David S Lawi (Executive VP and Secretary), Walter M Craig Jr (VP and Legal Counsel), Daniel T Murphy (VP and Chief Financial Officer), Joseph J Farley (VP Marketing and Engineering)

PRINCIPAL ACTIVITIES: Manufacture of agricultural machinery
Principal Subsidiaries: Bamberger Polymers Inc; Intersystems Inc; Parsons Manufacturing Inc; Teletrak Advanced Technology; Triangle Geophysical Company
Financial Information:

	$'000
Sales revenues	95,310

No of Employees: 225

HELMERICH & PAYNE, INC

Utica at 21st, Tulsa, OK 74114
Tel: (918) 742-5531

Chairman: W H Helmerich
President: Hans Helmerich
Senior Executive Officers: W R Horkey (Senior VP), Allen S Braumiller (VP, Exploration), George S Dotson (VP, President of Helmerich & Payne International Drilling Co), Leon C Gavras (VP and General Counsel), Geoffrey Hibner (VP, Finance), Ray Marsh (VP, Drilling), Tim Johnson (President of Natural Gas Odorizing, Inc), Steven R Shaw (VP, Production), Carl Young III (VP, Human Resources), Robert G Gambrell (Treasurer)

PRINCIPAL ACTIVITIES: Helmerich & Payne, Inc is a diversified, energy-oriented company enaged in contract drilling, oil and gas exploration and production, chemicals manufacturing, and real estate development and management. The Company also holds substantial equity investments in several other publicly-owned corporations
Principal Subsidiaries: Helmerich & Payne International Drilling Co; Natural Gas Odorizing, Inc; Helmerich & Payne Properties, Inc
Principal Bank: First National Bank and Trust Company, Tulsa, OK
Financial Information:

	Sep 30 1986 $'000	Sep 30 1987 $'000
Revenues	160,368	153,915
Income before taxes	2,589	32,117
Net income	7,025	22,016
Dividends	8,819	9,433
Dividends per share	$0.36	$0.38
Earnings per share	$0.28	$0.91
Common stock	2,677	2,677
Retained earnings	394,526	407,109
Shareholders equity	408,185	420,833

Principal Shareholders: Cadijan Helmerich Patterson (5.394%); W H Helmerich III (5.05%)
No of Employees: 1,026

HENLEY GROUP, INC (THE)

11255 North Torrey Pines Road, La Jolla, CA 92037
Tel: (619) 455-9494
Telex: 182800 SIGCO LJLA

Chairman: Michael D Dingman (and Managing Director-Chief Executive Officer)
President: Paul M Montrone (and Managing Director)
Senior Executive Officers: Managing Directors: Michael D Dingman, Paul M Montrone, Robert J Barone, Paul X Bouzan, William V Buccella, Harold W Buirkle, Clifford T Dirkes, Harold S Eastman, Daniel E Hilder, Paul M Meister, William J Rauch, Christopher J Reinhard, Norman R Ritter, Richard R Russell, Walter D Sanborn III, Ronald I Simon, Marc I Stern, David L Summers, Mark A Underberg, Dale L Ziegler

PRINCIPAL ACTIVITIES: The Henley Group, Inc was formed in December 1985 by Allied-Signal Inc for the purpose of effecting the distribution of Henley's common stock to the shareholders of Allied-Signal. Such distribution was completed on May 27, 1986. Henley's operations currently consist of a group of diversified businesses, the activities of which are conducted primarily through four major operating segments and several unconsolidated businesses. Henley's business objective is to increase the profitability of its businesses and the return on its other assets to enhance their value to stockholders. Henley seeks to achieve this objective by improving the operating results of its existing businesses, by acquiring businesses that are complementary to its operations as a whole and by engaging in various other transactions, including divestitures, joint ventures, public offerings and partial or total spin-offs of its existing businesses. Henley seeks to build its asset base through greater cash flow, prudent investment in product development and undervalued assets, and transactions to reposition its operating entities in business structures and add value to the whole. Henley expects to make significant acquisitions if it identifies businesses it believes are undervalued or will complement its operations as a whole. In addition, Henley from time to time acquires securities of publicly traded companies that Henley determines to be attractive investment opportunities
Trade Names: Henley has registered and unregistered trademarks for some of its products. The principal trademarks are in Fisher Group, General Chemical and the Manufacturng Group. Some of the more significant trademarks include Blastrac, Combos and Prestolite
Principal Subsidiaries: The Major operating subsidiaries of the Company are: Fisher Scientific Group Inc; Wheelabrator Technologies Inc; General Chemical; The M W Kellogg Company and various manufacturing entities. Unconsolidated entities include: Signal Capital Corporation; Signal Landmark Properties Inc; Equilease Corporation
Principal Bank: Mellon Bank, N.A.
Financial Information:

	Dec 31 1985 $'000	Dec 31 1986 $'000
Sales revenues	1,826,000	3,172,000
(Loss) before taxes	(87,000)	(440,000)
Net (loss)	(66,000)	(426,000)
(Loss) per share	-	($5.33)
Common stock*	-	109,486
Retained income (deficit)	-	(426,000)
Shareholders equity	2,622,000	3,364,000

*number of shares outstanding in thousands

No of Employees: 22,400

HENREDON FURNITURE INDUSTRIES, INC

Morganton, NC 28655
Tel: (704) 437-5261
Telex: WUT 572302 henredon mtgn

President: William E Smith
Senior Executive Officers: B B Isaacs (Secretary and Treasurer)

PRINCIPAL ACTIVITIES: Manufacture of household furniture
Parent Company: Masco Corp
Principal Bank: Wachovia Bank Trust Company
Financial Information:

	Mar 31 1986 $'000
Sales revenues	127,407
Net income	10,846

No of Employees: 2,400

HERCULES INCORPORATED

Hercules Plaza, Wilmington, DE 19894
Tel: (302) 594-5000

Chairman: David S Hollingsworth
President: Fred L Buckner
Senior Executive Officers: A B Engebretsen (Corporate VP and Chief Financial Officer), S M Turk (VP and General Counsel)

PRINCIPAL ACTIVITIES: Diversified international chemical company
Principal Subsidiaries: Hercules Inc has over 40 major subsidiary companies
Financial Information:

	Dec 31 1986 $'000
Sales revenues	2,615,100
Income befores taxes	203,636
Net income	226,733
Dividends	93,816
Dividends per share	$1.72
Earnings per share	$4.02
Common stock	48,500
Shareholders equity	1,703,151

No of Employees: 24,262

HERITAGE COMMUNICATIONS INC

2195 Ingersoll Avenue, Des Moines, IA 50312
Tel: (515) 246 1440

Chairman: James M Hoak
President: James M Hoak Jr
Senior Executive Officers: James S Cownie (Executive VP), David J Lundquist (Senior VP Finance), David N Walthall (Senior VP), Russell W Calkins III (VP Corporate

Development), Wayne Kern (VP and Secretary), Arlan Van Roekel (Treasurer and Controller)

PRINCIPAL ACTIVITIES: Cable television and advertising services
Principal Subsidiaries: Da-Lite Screen Company Inc; Shaw-Barton Inc; Braun-Brumfield Inc; Oravisual Company Inc; Welt Safe-Lock Inc
Principal Bank: Citibank
Financial Information:

	$'000
Sales revenues	157,375

No of Employees: 3,000

HERITAGE FINANCIAL CORPORATION

500 Forest Avenue, Richmond, VA 23229
Tel: (804) 282 8100

Chairman: Jay M Weinberg
President: E Mason Cockrell Jr (and Chief Executive Officer)
Senior Executive Officers: Gerald A Aust (Senior VP and Chief Administration Officer), Richard H Hamlin (Treasurer and Secretary)

PRINCIPAL ACTIVITIES: Savings and loans
Principal Subsidiaries: Heritage Savings and Loan Association
Principal Bank: The Federal Home Loan Bank

No of Employees: 160

HERMAN, JOSEPH M, SHOE CO

5 Cambridge Center, Cambridge, MA 02142
Tel: (617) 491-8800

President: Charles W Holmes
Senior Executive Officers: James F Famulare (VP Sales)

PRINCIPAL ACTIVITIES: Manufacture of heavy duty and leisure footwear
Parent Company: Stride Rite Corporation, Cambridge, MA
Principal Bank: First National Bank of Boston
Financial Information:

	$'000
Sales revenues	50,000

No of Employees: 350

HERMAN MILLER, INC

See MILLER, HERMAN, , INC

HERMAN'S SPORTING GOODS INC

2 Germak Drive, Cateret, NJ 07008
Tel: (201) 541 1550

Chairman: Peter Grace; Vice Chairman: Edward H Tutun
President: John L Sisk
Senior Executive Officers: Jack A Smith (Executive VP and Chief Operating Officer), George R Mrkonic (Senior VP and Chief Financial Officer), John V Chow (VP Management Information Services), James Didieo (VP South East Territory), Lawrence Levine (VP Personnel), Edward J Marino (VP North East Territory), Arnold Sedel (VP Mid West Territory), Norman Thier (VP Merchandising Hard Lines), Robert Timinski (VP Merchandising Soft Lines)

PRINCIPAL ACTIVITIES: Retail of sports goods and bicycles
Parent Company: Dee Corporation PLC
Principal Bank: Citibank
Financial Information:

	$'000
Sales revenues	420,345

No of Employees: 5,000

HERRUD & CO

2000 Oak Industrial Drive NE, Grand Rapids, MI 49505
Tel: (616) 774-0711
Telex: WUT 226339 herrud gdr

Senior Executive Officers: Donald Braam (Senior VP Operations), Gilbert Schroeter (Controller)

PRINCIPAL ACTIVITIES: Meat and meat products; wholesale distribution
Parent Company: Thorn Apple Valley Inc, Southfield, MI
Principal Bank: Old Kent Bank and Trust Company
Financial Information:

	$'000
Sales revenues	80,000

No of Employees: 500

HERSHEY FOODS CORPORATION

PO Box 814, Hershey, PA 17033
Tel: (717) 534-4000

Chairman: Richard A Zimmerman (and Chief Executive Officer)
President: Kenneth L Wolfe (and Chief Operating Officer)
Senior Executive Officers: Ogden C Johnson (Senior VP), Michael F Pasquale (VP Finance and Chief Financial Officer), Kenneth L Bowers (VP Corporate Communications), William P Noyes (VP Human Resources), Charles E Duroni (VP and General Counsel), William F Suhring (VP Corporate Development), Barry L Zoumas (VP Science and Technical), William Lehr Jr (VP and Secretary)

PRINCIPAL ACTIVITIES: Manufacture of chocolate confectionery and pasta; restaurants
Principal Subsidiaries: Cory Food Services Inc; Friendly Ice Cream Corp; Hershey Canada Inc (Canada); Hershey International Inc
Principal Bank: Citibank
Financial Information:

	Dec 31 1985 $'000	Dec 31 1986 $'000
Sales revenues	2,035,250	2,169,614
Net income	112,230	132,764
Earnings per share	$3.58	$1.42
Shareholders equity	-	727,941

No of Employees: 15,240

HESSTON CORPORATION

420 W Lincoln Blvd, Hesston, KS 67062
Tel: (316) 327-4000
Telex: TWX 910 740 1921 hesstonex hest

Chairman: Lyle E Yost
President: Mario Chessa (and Chief Executive and Chief Operating Officer)
Senior Executive Officers: Richard F Hrdlicka (Senior VP, Secretary and General Counsel), Guido Orru (VP Finance, Treasurer and Chief Financial Officer), James D Gaeddert (VP Sales), Fred Scharer (Executive VP and General Manager Woods Division), Renato Iodice (Executive VP Industrial)

PRINCIPAL ACTIVITIES: Manufacture of agricultural machinery
Parent Company: Fiat SpA, Torino, Italy
Principal Banks: Chemical Bank, New York; Citibank, New York
Financial Information:

	$'000
Sales revenues	157,512

No of Employees: 1,297

HEWLETT-PACKARD CO

3000 Hanover Street, Palo Alto, CA 94304
Tel: (415) 857-1501

Chairman: David Packard; Vice Chairman: William R Hewlett
President: John D Young (and Chief Executive Officer)
Senior Executive Officers: Richard C Alberding (Executive VP), John L Doyle (Executive VP), Dean O Morton (Executive VP and Chief Operating Officer), William E Terry (Executive VP), Douglas C Chance (Senior VP and General Manager Information Systems Group), Alfred P Oliverio (Senior VP Major Accounts Marketing), Lewis E Platt (Senior VP

Manufacturing Medical and Analytical Systems), Richard W Anderson (VP and General Manager Microwave and Communications Group), James L Arthur (VP US Field Operations), Alan D Bickell (VP Intercontinental Operations), Joes S Birnbaum (VP Hewlett-Packard Laboratories), S T Jack Brigham III (VP Administration and Legal Counsel), Harold E Edmonson (VP Corporate Manufacturing), Richard A Hackborn (VP and General Manager Peripherals Group), Benjamin L Holmes (VP and General Manager Medical Group), Franco Mariotti (VP European Operations), William G Parzybok Jr (VP and General Manager Design Systems Group), Charles W Richion (VP, US Field Operations), Robert P Wayman (VP and Chief Financial Officer), Cyril I Yansouni (VP and General Manager Personal Computer Group)

PRINCIPAL ACTIVITIES: Manufacture of electronic instruments and equipment; data processing equipment
Principal Bank: Crocker National Bank
Financial Information:

	Oct 31 1985	Oct 31 1986
	$'000	$'000
Sales revenues	6,605,000	7,102,000
Net income	489,000	516,000
Earnings per share	$1.91	$2.02
Shareholders equity	3,982,000	4,374,000

No of Employees: 80,000

HEXCEL CORPORATION

650 California Street, San Francisco, CA 94108
Tel: (415) 828-4200
Telefax: (415) 391-3318

Chairman: Harvie M Merrill
President: Robert L Witt (and Chief Executive Officer)
Senior Executive Officers: James D Neff (Senior VP Engineered and Structural Products), James D Otis (Senior VP International and Specialty Products), Fred G Beyerlein (VP Resins and Chemicals Division), D Thomas Divird (VP and Chief Financial Officer), John F O'Flaherty (VP, Chief Counsel and Secretary), Robert A Penezic (VP Administrative Operations), Christopher J Ward (Treasurer), David M Wong (Controller)

PRINCIPAL ACTIVITIES: Hexcel Corporation is an international developer and manufacturer of honeycomb, advanced fiber composites, and specialty chemicals and resins used in the aerospace, space and defense, naval, transportation, general industrial and other markets
Principal Bank: Wells Fargo
Financial Information:

	Dec 31 1986	Dec 31 1987
	$'000	$'000
Sales revenues	290,383	349,184
Income before taxes	16,695	21,648
Net income	7,031	12,869
Dividends	2,672	2,667
Dividends per share	$0.60	$0.60
Earnings per share	$2.28	$2.87
Common stock	46,566	54,759
Retained income	46,371	56,573
Shareholders equity	93,010	114,456

No of Employees: 3,200+

HIBERNIA CORPORATION

PO Box 61540, New Orleans, LA 70161
Tel: (504) 586-5552

Chairman: Martin C Miler (and President and Chief Executive Officer)
Senior Executive Officers: Donald J Nalty (Executive VP), Richard A McNeece (VP Finance)

PRINCIPAL ACTIVITIES: Banking services
Principal Subsidiaries: Hibernia National Bank
Principal Bank: The Hibernia National Bank
Financial Information:

	Dec 31 1985	Dec 31 1986
	$'000	$'000
Revenues	242,000	364,000
Net income	24,300	35,000

No of Employees: 1,200

HIGH INDUSTRIES INC

1905 Old Phila Pike, Box 1526, Lancaster, PA 17603
Tel: (717) 299-5211

Chairman: S Dale High (and President)
Senior Executive Officers: Calvin G High (Senior VP), Thomas C Kile (VP Finance), Walter J Kissel (VP Administration)

PRINCIPAL ACTIVITIES: Structural metal work and construction; precast/prestressed concrete; real estate development and management
Principal Bank: Core States Bank
Financial Information:

	Dec 31 1987
	$'000
Sales revenues	200,000

No of Employees: 1,700

HIGH STEEL STRUCTURES, INC

1911 Old Phila Pike, Lancaster, PA 17604
Tel: (717) 299-5211

President: Calvin G High
Senior Exectutive Officers: S D High (Executive VP), Daniel E Barto (VP), Bradford D Mills (VP Sales), Bradford D Mills (VP Sales), Thomas C Kile (Secretary and Treasurer)

PRINCIPAL ACTIVITIES: Metal construction components
Parent Company: High Industries Inc, Lancaster, PA
Principal Bank: Hamilton Bank
Financial Information:

	$'000
Sales revenues	70,000

No of Employees: 600

HIGH VOLTAGE ENGINEERING CORPORATION

South Bedford Street, Burlington, MA 01803
Tel: (617) 272-1313
Telex: TWX 7103320848 hi volt burl

Chairman: Pascal Levesque (and President and Chief Executive Officer)
Senior Executive Officers: Robert O Svensson (VP and Treasurer), Gordon R Hamilton Jr (VP Industrial Relations), William J Flanagan Jr (VP, Corporate), Donald R Reilly (General Counsel and Clerk), Irene A Doyle (Assistant Clerk)

PRINCIPAL ACTIVITIES: Through its diversification, High Voltage Engineering Corporation manufactures a spectrum of products in the areas of industrial instrumentation, electrical components and specialty plastics for industrial and medical applications. High Voltage has achieved leadership in a number of specialized markets, often providing a single industry with complementary products through its related divisions and subsidiaries. The strategy of augmenting internal growth with carefully selected acquisitions continues to enable High Voltage to capitalize on opportunities as they develop in the rapidly evolving world of high-tech industrializaton.
Principal Subsidiaries: Anacon/Waters Division; Anacon (Instruments) Ltd (UK); Anderson Power Products Company; Beam Parts Division; Berger; Halmar Electronics Inc; HIVEC BV; Judd Wire Division; Datcon Instrument Co; General Eastern Instruments Co; Uniforce Electronics Co; Carbolon Division; Specialty Connector Company Inc; Culver-Stearns Manufacturing Company
Principal Bank: BayBank Harvard Trust Company

Financial Information:

	Dec 28 1985	Dec 27 1986
	$'000	$'000
Sales revenues	83,756	98,011
Income before taxes	11,589	8,561
Net income	5,809	3,128
Dividends	880	858
Dividends per share	$0.17	$0.17
Earnings per share	$1.12	$0.62
Common stock	6,224	6,224
Retained income	45,833	48,103
Shareholders equity	56,498	59,971

No of Employees: 1,516

HIGHLAND SUPERSTORES, INC

909 Sheldon Rd, Plymouth, MI 48170
Tel: (313) 451-3200
Telefax: (313) 451-3200 X3336

Chairman: David S Mondry (and Chief Executive Officer)
President: Eugene P Mondry (and Chief Operating Officer)
Senior Executive Officers: Ira S Mondry (Executive VP), Yale Levin (Senior VP Finance), Louis Bernucca (VP-Merchandising), William O'Brien (VP-Operations), Paul Ruggerillo (VP-General Manager Midwest Division), Richard A Brouwer (VP-General Manager Southwest Division), Donald S Wysocki (VP-General Manager Central Division)

PRINCIPAL ACTIVITIES: Retail consumer electronics and appliances
Trade Names: Retail Stores-Highland Superstores, Highland Appliance
Principal Bank: National Bank of Detroit
Financial Information:

	Jan 31 1986	Jan 31 1987
	$'000	$'000
Sales revenues	520,527	656,456
Income before taxes	41,271	36,112
Net income	23,602	20,214
Earnings per share	$1.36	$1.11
Common stock	52,986	52,997
Retained income	40,883	61,097
Shareholders equity	93,869	114,094

No of Employees: 4,250

HILLENBRAND INDUSTRIES, INC

Hwy 46, Batesville, IN 47006
Tel: (812) 934-7000
Cable: HILLROM
Telex: WUT 272284 hillenbrd batb

Chairman: Daniel A Hillenbrand (and Chief Executive Officer)
President: W August Hillenbrand (and Chief Operating Officer)
Senior Executive Officers: Lonnie M Smith (Senior Executive VP), Thomas E Brewer (Senior VP Finance), Robert C Smith (VP Investor Relations), George Brinkmoeller (VP Corporate Services), F K Koepcke (VP, Secretary and General Counsel), David Robertson (VP Human Resources)

PRINCIPAL ACTIVITIES: Hospital furniture, burial caskets, high security locks, luggage, wound care therapy and pre-arranged funeral insurance
Trade Names: HILL-ROM, MEDECO, BATESVILLE, AMERICAN TOURISTER, CLINITRON, FORETHOUGHT, FLEXICARE
Principal Subsidiaries: Batesville Casket Co; Hill-Rom Company; American Tourister, Inc; SSI Medical Services, Inc; Medeco Security Locks Inc; The Forethought Group
Principal Bank: American Fletcher National Bank

Financial Information:

	Nov 30 1985	Nov 30 1986
	$'000	$'000
Sales revenues	507,613	641,067
Income before taxes	61,740	99,956
Net income	32,834	50,523
Dividends	10,492	10,857
Dividends per share	$0.27	$0.28
Earnings per share	$0.85	$1.30
Common stock*	19,437	38,057
Retained income	265,321	304,987
Shareholders equity	257,609	290,914
*number of shares in thousands		

No of Employees: 6,900

HILLERICH & BRADSBY CO

PO Box 35700, Louisville, KY 40232
Tel: (502) 585-5226
Telex: 756396 H&B LVL UD

Chairman: John A Hillerich III (and President)
Senior Executive Officers: B W Becker (Executive VP and Secretary), Jerome D Martin (VP Marketing), Richard G Sawyer (VP Sales) Hubert B Roberts Jr (VP Manufacturing), Donald F Hess (VP Purchasing), Billy B Williams (VP Advertising), Harold Fisher (Treasurer)

PRINCIPAL ACTIVITIES: Sporting and leisure equipment
Trade Names: Powerbilt (R), Golf, Louisville Slugger (R), Baseball/Softball, Louisville Hocket (R)
Principal Subsidiaries: H&B of Canada; Larimar & Norton
Principal Bank: First National Bank of Louisville
Financial Information:

	$'000
Sales revenues	50,000

Principal Shareholders: Family
No of Employees: 700

HILLS BROS COFFEE, INC

2 Harrison Street, San Francisco, CA 94105
Tel: (415) 546-4600
Telex: ITT 470248 hbci ui

Chairman: P J Miller
President: N E Dean
Senior Executive Officers: F L Doar (Executive VP), Richard L Thompson (VP Commodities), Sherman W Nelson (VP Operations), Robert J Otto (VP Sales), Ken L Broz (VP Food Services), Barry M Reis (VP Marketing), Norwin T Coahran (VP Finance, Secretary and Treasurer), William E Sweeney (VP Private Label Sales)

PRINCIPAL ACTIVITIES: Coffee and coffee products
Parent Company: Nestle Holdings Inc
Principal Bank: Citicorp Industrial Credit
Financial Information:

	$'000
Sales revenues	350,000

Principal Shareholders: Nestlé SA, Vevey, Switzerland
No of Employees: 750

HILLS STORES COMPANY

15 Dan Road, Canton, MA 02021
Tel: (617) 821-1000
Telex: 172127
Telefax: (617) 821-1000

President: Stephen A Goldberger
Senior Executive Officers: John C Brouillard (Senior VP-Finance and Administration), Stephen A Feldman (VP-Treasurer), John G Reen (VP-Controller)

PRINCIPAL ACTIVITIES: Retailing; department stores
Parent Company: Hill Department Stores, Inc

Principal Subsidiaries: Hills Stores Company
Principal Bank: Bankers Trust Co
Financial Information:

	Jan 25 1986	Jan 31 1987
	$'000	$'000
Sales revenues	163,560	1,343,102
Income (loss) before taxes	(15,298)	(7,122)
Net (loss)	(15,298)	(7,402)
Common stock	10	10
Retained (deficit)	(21,736)	(50,737)
Shareholders (deficit)	(13,503)	(41,959)

No of Employees: 12,000 full time; 8,000 part-time

HILTON HOTELS CORPORATION

9880 Wilshire Blvd, Beverley Hills, CA 90210
Tel: (213) 278-4321
Telex: WUT 698344 hltn htls bvhl

Chairman: Barron Hilton (and President and Chief Executive Officer); Vice Chairman: William H Edwards
Senior Executive Officers: Gregory R Dillon (Executive VP Corporate Property), John V Giovenco (Executive VP Finance), John T Fitzgerald (Executive VP Operations Nevada Division), Carl T Mottek (Executive VP Operations, President Hilton Hotels Division), Earl Mcdonough (Senior VP Hawaiin Region), Arthur A Surin (Senior VP Eastern Region), James F Sheerin (Senior VP Central Region), Joseph F Frederick Jr (Senior VP Human Resources), Eric M Hilton (Senior VP Real Estate Development, International and Southwestern Region), Peter J Kleiser (Senior VP Food and Beverage), James C Collins (Senior VP Marketing), James L Philon (Senior VP Real Estate and Development), James R Galbraith (Senior VP Corporate Affairs), Lloyd S Farwell (Senior VP Franchising and Development), Robert F Eiseman (Senior VP Purchasing), Hilmar A Rosenast (Senior VP Western), Maurice J Scanlon (Senior VP, Treasurer and Chief Financial Officer), Dennis C Gomes (Senior BP Casino Operations), Salvatore F Guarino (Senior VP Development and Acquisitions), Steve Krithis (VP and Corporate Comptroller), William C Lebo Jr (Senior VP and Legal Counsel), Jorgen H Hansen (Senior VP Southern Region), Joseph P Smyth (Senior VP Marketing)

PRINCIPAL ACTIVITIES: Hotels
Principal Bank: First National Bank
Financial Information:

	Dec 31 1985	Dec 31 1986
	$'000	$'000
Sales revenues	684,417	740,366
Net income	100,163	97,839
Earnings per share	$4.03	$3.92
Shareholders equity	651,446	707,352

No of Employees: 34,000

HINDERLITER INDUSTRIES, INC

PO Box 35505, Tulsa, OK 74153-0505
Tel: (918) 494-0992
Telex: WUT 79-6098
Telecopier: (918) 494-0238

Chairman: John L Robertson (and Chief Executive Officer)
President: Richard H Hughes (and Chief Operating Officer)
Senior Executive Officers: Donald S Lockhart (Executive VP), Dan F Witt (Senior VP), Stuart P Honeybone (VP Marketing), Michael A Lasley (VP Management Information Systems), Jimmy C Strong (VP Personnel)

PRINCIPAL ACTIVITIES: Manufacture of building materials, pumps and compressors and components for the automobile industry
Parent Company: Equidyne Industries Inc
Principal Bank: First National Bank of Oklahoma City
Financial Information:

	$'000
Sales revenues	66,400

No of Employees: 600

HINES, EDWARD, LUMBER CO

200 South Michigan Ave, Chicago, IL 60604
Tel: (312) 294-2000

Chairman: Howell H Howard
President: Edward P Hines (and Chief Executive Officer)
Senior Executive Officers: Paul R Leak (Senior VP and Chief Financial Officer), William M Archibald (Senior VP), John P Vetter (Senior VP Marketing), Curt W Powell (Senior VP Home Centers), Ernest F Michael (VP Skokie Wholesale Manager), Edward W Stein (VP Wholesale Warehouse)

PRINCIPAL ACTIVITIES: Manufacture and sale of lumber and other building materials
Principal Subsidiaries: E Hines Lumber Co Inc; Edward Hines Lumber Co of OR
Principal Bank: First National Bank
Financial Information:

	$'000
Sales revenues	280,000

No of Employees: 1,140

HI-SHEAR INDUSTRIES INC

3333 New Hyde Park Road, North Hills, NY 11042
Tel: (516) 627-8600
Telex: 510-223-0644 MICWOOD NHRK

Chairman: David A Wingate (and Chief Executive Officer)
President: Anthony E Mirti (and Chief Operating Officer)
Senior Executive Officers: S Gerard Benford (VP and Chief Financial Officer), Harold L Bernstein (Secretary and General Counsel), Victor J Galgano (Treasurer and Controller)

PRINCIPAL ACTIVITIES: Hi-Shear Industries Inc is engaged primarily in manufacture and sale of high technology products for the aerospace and defense markets through its two segments: (1) Aerospace fastening systems and (2) Space and defense ordnance systems
Trade Names: Registered Trademarks: Hi-Lok/Hi-Tigue, Hi-Torque, Hi-Set, Hi-Safe, Hi-Lite. Trade Mark: Blind Bolts
Principal Subsidiaries: Hi-Shear Corporation; Hi-Shear Technology Corporation; Hi-Shear Fasteners Europe Ltd
Principal Bank: Banks Trust Company
Financial Information:

	$'000
Net sales and revenues	60,000

Principal Shareholders: David A Wingate (approx. 25%)
No of Employees: 740

HITCHCOCK INDUSTRIES, INC

8701 Harriet Avenue South, Bloomington, MN 55420
Tel: (612) 887-7800
Telex: 29-0486 HITCHCOCK MPS

Chairman: Gregory T Hitchcock
Preident: Timothy R Hitchcock (and Chief Executive Officer)

PRINCIPAL ACTIVITIES: Non-ferrous metal castings
Principal Bank: Norwest Bank Minneapolis
Financial Information:

	$'000
Sales revenues	50,000

No of Employees: 750

HITCHINER MANUFACTURING CO

PO Box 232, Milford, NH 03055
Tel: (603) 673-03055
Telex: TWX 7103661863 hitchiner

Chairman: John H Morison

President: Nicholas Babich (and Chief Executive Officer)
Senior Executive Officers: Edward M Broad (VP International), G D Chandley (VP Technical), R E Cummings (VP Sales and Marketing), John S Noga (VP Finance and Administration)

PRINCIPAL ACTIVITIES: Ferrous and non-ferrous metal castings
Principal Bank: The First National Bank of Boston
Financial Information:

	$'000
Sales revenues	60,000

No of Employees: 1,300

HITCO

840 Newport Ctr Drive, Newport Beach, CA 92715
Tel: (714) 720-9300
Telex: TWX 9103466326

President: H T Cusic
Senior Executive Officers: G E Bezar (VP Finance and Treasurer), C W Eads (VP, President Fabricated Composites Division), J C Chang (VP, President Materials Division)

PRINCIPAL ACTIVITIES: Manufacture of industrial fasteners and aerospace equipment; coated fabrics
Parent Company: Owens-Corning Fiberglas Corp
Financial Information:

	$'000
Sales revenues	170,000

No of Employees: 2,000

HMO AMERICA INC

540 North Lasalle Street, Chicago, IL 60610
Tel: (312) 751 7500

President: Robert J Weinstein
Senior Executive Officers: Charles Kelly (Executive VP), Gerald Brown (Senior VP), David Citron (VP), James Terrig (VP), Arthur Adelman (Secretary and Treasurer)

PRINCIPAL ACTIVITIES: Health care services including out patient care facilities
Principal Bank: Northern Trust Company
Financial Information:

	$'000
Revenues	61,010

No of Employees: 260

HOBART BROTHERS CO

Hobart Square, Troy, OH 45373
Tel: (513) 332-4000
Telex: WUT 288265 hobroco tryo
Telefax: (513) 339-5648

Chairman: William H Hobart (and Chief Executive Officer)
President: P Kim Packard (and Chief Operating Officer)
Senior Executive Officers: J H Rasbach (VP Finance and Treasurer), Dennis Custance (VP Welding Equipment Division), Terry Lefever (VP Filler Metals Division), Chet Woodman (VP Advanced Welding Division), Roger Williams (VP Power Systems Division), Jon Lang (VP Administration)

PRINCIPAL ACTIVITIES: Arc welding power sources and filler metals, robotics, industrial battery chargers, aircraft ground power equipment, power conversion systems
Principal Bank: First National Bank
Financial Information:

	$'000
Sales revenues-over	150,000

Principal Shareholders: Private ownership
No of Employees: 1,500

HOBBS TRAILERS

4800 Blue Mound Road, Fort Worth, TX 76101
Tel: (817) 625-2181

Senior Executive Officers: E E Baker (VP Sales), Jim Barber (VP and General Manager), Bob Legg (Controller)

PRINCIPAL ACTIVITIES: Manufacture of truck trailers
Parent Company: Fruehauf Corporation, Detroit, MI
Principal Bank: Texas American Bank
Financial Information:

	$'000
Sales revenues	163,000

No of Employees: 1,360

HOECHST CELANESE CORPORATION

Routes 202-206 N, Somerville, NJ 08876
Tel: (201) 231-2000

Chairman: Dieter zur Loye; Vice Chairman: Richard M Clarke
President: Dr Ernie H Drew (and Chief Executive Officer)
Senior Executive Officers: Harry Benz (Executive VP and Chief Financial Officer), Dr Hubert E Huckel (President of the Life Sciences Unit), Harry Bartley (President of Chemical Group), James J Bigham (President of Hoechst Celanese Advanced Technology), John A Fennie (President of Hoechst Celanese Specialty Operations), Gerald Elden (President of Textile Fibers, Corporate VP), J Douglas Libbys (President of, Film and Fiber Intermediates, Corporate VP), Joseph H Patterson (President, Industrial Fibers, Corporate VP), Alban W Schuele (VP, Quality and Communications), William B Harris (VP and Treasurer), Thomas C Bohrer (President, Specialty Products, Corporate VP), Dr Heinz K Hofmeister (Corporate VP, Director, President, Specialty Chemicals)

PRINCIPAL ACTIVITIES: Hoechst Celanese Corporation is the largest subsidiary of the Hoechst Group worldwide which operates 467 companies in 140 nations. Hoechst Celanese produces a wide range of products-pharmaceuticals, diagnostic agents, fibers, plastics, film, information technology and chemicals-used to meet such basic human needs as food, clothing, shelter, and health. These products respond to demands of modern society in the areas of communications, transportation, security, leisure, energy, information transfer, technology, and life enrichment.
Trade Names: Trevira (R), AZ Photoresist, Hostphan (R), Hostaform (R), Genotherm (R), ENCO (R), Hostalen (R), Celgard (R), Lasix (R), Trental (R), PBI (R), Celcon (R), Celanese Nylon 6/6 (R), Celanex (R), Sanwet (R), Durel (R), Vectra (R), Celebrate!
Parent Company: Hoechst AG, Frankfurt/Main, Germany
Principal Subsidiaries: Hoechst-Roussel Pharmacueticals Inc; Hoechst-Roussel Agri-Vet Company; Cape Industries; Virginia Chemicals Inc; Corporate Class Software; Celanese Research Company; Celanese Canada Inc (Canada)
Financial Information:

	Sep 30 1987 (9 mths) $'000
Sales revenues	3,150,000

No of Employees: 23,000

HOEGANAES CORPORATION

River Road & Taylor's Lane, Riverton, NJ 08077
Tel: (609) 829-2220
Telex: TWX 7109410521 hoeganes riv

President: Ian A White
Senior Executive Officers: William Michael (VP Marketing), P Ulf Gummerson (VP Research and Development), John Mutschler (VP Manufacturing), John Brunkhorst (Treasurer, Assistant Secretary and Controller), Grant L Johnson (Secretary)

PRINCIPAL ACTIVITIES: Manufacture of ferrous and non-ferrous metal powders
Parent Company: The Interlake Corporation

Financial Information:

	$'000
Sales revenues	112,000

No of Employees: 500

HOFFMAN BROS PACKING CO, INC

2731 S Soto Street, Los Angeles, CA 90023
Tel: (213) 264-1181
Telex: WUT 674459 hoffpkgco lsa

President: Julius Hoffman
Senior Executive Officers: Irwin Diamond (Executive VP, Secretary and Treasurer)

PRINCIPAL ACTIVITIES: Meat and meat processing
Parent Company: Hofpaco Inc
Principal Bank: Bank of America
Financial Information:

	$'000
Sales revenues	80.000

No of Employees: 300

HOFMANN INDUSTRIES, INC

Sinking Spring, PA 19608
Tel: (215) 678-8051

Chairman: Vincent D Hofmann
President: Bernard M Hofmann (Operations)
Senior Executive Officers: Richard H Schreck (Executive VP), Gerald W Eddinger (VP Sales), Martin J Hofmann (VP Manufacturing), Preston E Rohrbaugh (Secretary and Treasurer)

PRINCIPAL ACTIVITIES: Manufacture of steel tube; castings; mechanical handling equipment
Principal Subsidiaries: Bonus-Bilt Inc; Marjon Inc; HI Products; Bonus-Bilt East Inc
Principal Bank: Hamilton Bank
Financial Information:

	$'000
Sales revenues	53,000

No of Employees: 650

HOLBROOK CO, INC

350 Fifth Avenue, New York, NY 10118
Tel: (212) 760-1575

President: Marvin Lord
Senior Executive Officers: Leonard Wolfson (Executive VP Marketing), Erle Norton (VP Manufacturing), John McNames (VP Finance and Administration)

PRINCIPAL ACTIVITIES: Manufacture of men's clothing
Parent Company: Oxford Industries Inc
Financial Information:

	$'000
Sales revenues	100,000

No of Employees: 100

HOLIDAY CORPORATION

1023 Cherry Road, Memphis, TN 38117
Tel: (901) 762 8600

Chairman: Michael D Rose (and Chief Executive Officer)
President: Richard J Goeglein (and Chief Operating Officer)
Senior Executive Officers: Stephen F Bollenbach (Senior VP and Chief Financial Officer), D Michael Meeks (Senior VP Development), Ben C Peternell (Senior VP Human Resources), Richard T Ashman (VP), Neil Barnhart (VP), Robert L Brannon (VP), Thomas H Brettschneider (VP Real Estate), E James House Jr (VP and Treasurer), Robert W Jannins (VP Project Finance), Duane E Knapp (VP), J W McAllister (VP), Richard L Nauman (VP), Craig H Norville (VP and Legal Counsel), Daniel H Philip (VP), Charles G Pinkowski (VP), Timothy V Williams (VP and Controller)

PRINCIPAL ACTIVITIES: Operation of chain of hotels and gambling establishments
Trade Names: Holidex II, Holiday Inn Crowne Plaza, Embassy Suites, Hampton Inn, Residence Inn
Principal Subsidiaries: Holiday Inns Inc; Embassy Suites Inc
Principal Bank: Citibank
Financial Information:

	Dec 31 1986
	$'000
Sales revenues	1,647,788
Net income	103,370
Earnings per share	$4.15
Shareholders equity	638,733

HOLLINGSWORTH & VOSE CO

112 Washington Street, East Walpole, MA 02032
Tel: (617) 668-0295
Telex: WUT 924470 novoco wpol

President: Gordon W Moran
Senior Executive Officers: H R O'Donnell (VP), H W Mason (VP Manufacturing), David R Smith (VP Engineering), D W Phillips (VP Industrial Relations), Stoughton L Ellsworth (VP Sales), Howard P Whittle (Treasurer and Clerk)

PRINCIPAL ACTIVITIES: Production of specialty papers
Principal Bank: Brown Brothers Harriman and Company
Financial Information:

	$'000
Sales revenues	75,000

No of Employees: 590

HOLLY CORPORATION

2600 Maxus Energy Tower, 717N Harwood St, Dallas, TX 75201
Tel: (214) 979-0210
Telex: 730550

Chairman: Lamar Norsworthy (and Chief Executive Officer)
President: E I Parsons
Senior Executive Officers: Refining: Jack P Reid (Executive VP, Refining), William J Gray (Senior VP, Marketing and Supply), Gordon R Bussey (VP, Marketing), W Truett Lloyd (VP Supply and Transportation), Mike Mirbagheri (VP International Crude Oil and Refined Products), Dewie O Stevenson (VP, Manufacturing), Corporate and Financial: Henry L Stern (Senior VP, General Counsel and Secretary), James W Robertson (VP and Treasurer), Henry A Teichholz (Controller)

PRINCIPAL ACTIVITIES: Refining and marketing of petroleum products
Principal Subsidiaries: Navajo Refining Company
Financial Information:

	Jul 31 1986	Jul 31 1987
	$'000	$'000
Net sales	348,552	281,581
Income before taxes	29,281	3,241
Net income	15,125	1,022
Dividends	227	-
Dividends per share	$0.038	-
Net earnings per share	$3.16	$0.25
Common stock	43	43
Retained income	19,843	20,865
Shareholders equity	21,391	22,824

No of Employees: 344

HOLLY FARMS CORPORATION

PO Box 17236, Memphis, TN 38187
Tel: (901) 761-3610

Chairman: Lewis K McKee
President: R Lee Taylor II (and Chief Executive Officer)
Senior Executive Officers: W F Bailey (VP), John T Stout (VP), Elbert L Thomas Jr (VP), James H Thompson (Secretary-Treasurer)

PRINCIPAL ACTIVITIES: Holly Farms Corporation is a diversified foods company, producing a variety of high quality, branded food products sold in the retail and food service markets
Principal Subsidiaries: Holly Farms Foods Inc; Holly Farms Food Service Inc; National By-Products Inc; Dixie Portland Flour Mills Inc; The White Lily Foods Company; Rustco Products Company; Globe Products Company Inc; Diana Fruit Preserving Company Inc; Harker's Inc; Henry House Inc; Quik-to-Fix Food Products Inc
Principal Bank: Morgan Guaranty Trust Co
Financial Information:

	May 31 1986	May 30 1987
	$'000	$'000
Sales revenues	1,230,572	1,419,635
Income before taxes	63,764	141,716
Net income	36,657	71,689
Dividends	16,023	18,397
Dividends per share	$0.98	$1.11
Earnings per share*	$2.24	$4.31
Common stock	200,570	213,596
Retained income	71,736	125,028
Shareholders equity	266,551	343,171

*primary

No of Employees: 11,000

HOLLY SUGAR CORPORATION

Holly Sugar Bldg, Colorado Springs, CO 80903
Tel: (303) 471-0123

Chairman: Michael S Buchsbaum; Vice Chairmen: J E Rich (and Chief Operating Officer), Dennis O'Rourke
President: Charles Azaro (and Chief Executive Officer)
Senior Executive Officers: John Evans (Senior VP, Secretary and General Counsel), Roger W Hill (Senior VP Agricultural), Donald P Berra (Senior VP Sales), William O Ludwig (Senior VP Finance and Chief Financial Officer), Lloyd L Neville (Senior VP Operations), John A Richmond (VP Technical Services), Louis Garcia (VP), Wm Johannsen (VP), A L Sharp (VP)

PRINCIPAL ACTIVITIES: Sugar refining
Principal Subsidiaries: Holly Export Corp
Principal Bank: National Westminster
Financial Information:

	Mar 31 1987
	$'000
Sales revenues	265,385
Income before taxes	8,232
Net income	4,718
Dividends per share	$1.00
Earnings per share	$4.21
Retained income	77,765
Shareholders equity	64,776

No of Employees: 950

HOLMES, D H, & CO LTD

819 Canal Street, New Orleans, LA 70112
Tel: (504) 561 6611

Chairman: T Robert Fidler
President: Donald W Johnston (and Chief Executive Officer)
Senior Executive Officers: Robert L Karem (Executive VP and Chief Administrative Officer), James E Ammon (Senior VP Finance), Robert G Morgan (Senior VP Personnel Affairs and Operations), L Richard Roussel (Senior VP Real Estate and Merchandising), Paul R Falter (VP, Treasurer and Controller), E Stewart Maunsell II (VP and Assistant Secretary), Jay F Hebert (VP Public Relations), Charles Ennis (VP and General Merchandise Manager Hardlines), Kenneth DeZwaan (VP and Senior Station Manager Baton Rouge), John N Kuchler (VP and Senior Station Manager), Raymond E Weidenbacher (VP and Senior Station Manager), Elizabeth Tahir (VP and General Merchandise Manager Ready to Wear Accessories), Steve Wall (VP and General Merchandise Manager Men's and Small Wear), Ann Strug (VP and General Merchandise Manager Sportswear, Lingerie and Children), George W Dodge (Secretary)

PRINCIPAL ACTIVITIES: Department stores
Principal Subsidiaries: D H Holmes Baton Rouge; D H Holmes Credit Corporation; D H Holmes Realty Inc
Principal Bank: First National Bank of Chicago
Financial Information:

	$'000
Sales revenues	272,000

No of Employees: 5,600

HOME BENEFICIAL CORPORATION

3901 West Broad Street, Richmond, VA 23230
Tel: (804) 358 8431

Chairman: R W Wiltshire (and President)
Senior Executive Officers: R W Wiltshire Jr (Executive VP), H D Garnett (VP and Controller), C M Glenn Jr (VP and Treasurer), G T Richardson (VP), Lynwood W Richardson (VP), J M Wiltshire Jr (VP), W B Wiltshire (VP), W V Collins (Secretary), W G Hancock (Legal Counsel)

PRINCIPAL ACTIVITIES: Holding company with interests in a wide range of insurance services
Principal Subsidiaries: Home Beneficial Life Insurance Co
Principal Bank: Sovran Bank
Financial Information:

	Dec 31 1985	Dec 31 1986
	$'000	$'000
Revenues	181,900	188,000
Investment income	43,070	44,000

No of Employees: 1,400

HOME DEPOT INC

2727 Paces Ferry Road, Atlanta, GA 30339
Tel: (404) 433-8211

Chairman: Bernard Marcus (and Chief Executive Officer and Secretary)
President: Arthur M Blank (and Chief Operating Officer)
Senior Executive Officers: William Kelley (Executive VP), Ronald M Brill (Senior VP, Chief Financial Officer and Treasurer), Nathan Morton (Senior VP Operations), E Dennis Ross (Senior VP Management Information Systems), William Harris Sr (VP Corporate Development)

PRINCIPAL ACTIVITIES: The Home Depot, Inc. operates retail "warehouse" stores selling a wide assortment of building materials and home improvement products primarily to the "do-it-yourself" and home remodeling markets. Stores are clustered in the Atlanta, Orlando, Tampa Bay, Jacksonville, Southern Florida, Phoenix, Tucson, Houston, Los Angeles, San Diego, San Francisco Bay, New Orleans and Dallas/Ft Worth markets, as well as individual stores in Baton Rouge, Shreveport and Mobile
Principal Bank: Security Pacific National Bank
Financial Information:

	Feb 2 1986	Feb 1 1987
	$'000	$'000
Sales revenues net	700,729	1,011,462
Income before taxes	11,619	47,073
Net income	8,219	23,873
Earnings per share	$0.33	$0.99
Common stock	1,258	1,419
Retained income	38,934	62,807
Shareholders equity	89,092	163,042

No of Employees: 9,900

HOME FEDERAL BANK OF FLORIDA

1901 Central Ave, St Petersburg, FL 33713
Tel: (813) 823-1111

Chairman: Rusell L Stewart

President: Alfred T May (and Chief Executive Officer)

Senior Executive Officers: Robert L Carr (Executive VP, Lending), David M Coffin (Senior VP, Finance), Peter J Blank (Senior VP Marketing), Alan C Brown (Senior VP Operations), Van Neely (Senior VP Administration), Robert L Heinchon (Senior VP Commercial Lending), Charles L Amerman (Senior VP Corporate Banking)

PRINCIPAL ACTIVITIES: Banking services

No of Employees: 530

HOME FEDERAL SAVINGS & LOAN ASSOCIATION OF SAN DIEGO

625 Broadway, Suite 1400, San Diego, CA 92101

Tel: (619) 699-8000

Chairman: Kim Fletcher (and Chief Executive Officer)

President: Robert Adelizzi

Senior Executive Officers: Chuck Taylor (Director/Strategic Planning), William Nichol (Executive VP, Chief Financial Officer), William Mayer (Chief Accounting Officer), John J Roach (Executive VP, Chief Lending Officer), James E Stutz (Chief Operating Officer/Consumer Banking), Mike McCook (President/Horne Capital Development Group), Bill Kinter (Chief Marketing Officer)

PRINCIPAL ACTIVITIES: Financial services

Principal Subsidiaries: Home Capital Corp; Home Federal Trust; Home Fed Insurance Services; Home Fed Credit Corporation; Charles K Fletcher Insurance Agency Inc.

Principal Bank: Bank of America

Financial Information:

	Dec 31 1985	Dec 31 1986
	$'000	$'000
Revenues	1,111,841	1,241,980
Income before taxes	117,175	161,465
Net income	72,786	103,358
Dividends per share(1)	$0.20	$0.20(2)
Earnings per share	$3.53	$4.62
Common stock(3)	-	20,900
Retained income	372,817	472,002
Shareholders equity	698,380	801,069
Deposits	7,426,584	8,562,059
Total assets	10,018,646	12,074,620

(1) annually

(2) $0.05 quarterly

(3) shares outstanding in thousands

Number of Shareholders: 6,800

No of Employees: 3,856

HOME FEDERAL SAVINGS & LOAN ASSOCIATION OF TUCSON

PO Box 2871, Tucson, AZ 85702

Tel: (602) 623-7771

Chairman: Thomas C Weir (and Chief Executive Officer)

President: William D Hinz (Chief Operating Officer)

Senior Executive Officers: Kenneth H Herman (Senior Executive VP), Frederick R McGill (Executive VP), Leon Goodman (Executive VP), Carol M Martel (Senior VP and Treasurer)

PRINCIPAL ACTIVITIES: Savings and loan association

Principal Subsidiaries: First State Service Corp; Title Guaranty of AZ

Principal Bank: Arizona Bank

Financial Information:

	Dec 31 1985
	$'000
Sales revenues	249,044
Net income	16,558
Earnings per share	$5.68
Shareholders equity	80,617
Total assets	2,371,183

No of Employees: 583

HOME GROUP INC

59 Maiden Lane, New York, NY 10038

Tel: (212) 530 7000

Chairman: Marshall Manley (and Chief Executive Officer)

Senior Executive Officers: T Bowring Woodbury II (Executive VP), Jack R Plaxe (Senior VP, Chief Financial Officer and Treasurer)

PRINCIPAL ACTIVITIES: Insurance services

Financial Information:

	Dec 31 1986
	$'000
Revenues	2,193,700
Net income	178,700
Earnings per share	$4.59
Shareholders equity	812,800

No of Employees: 7,800

HOME LIFE INSURANCE CO OF NEW YORK

253 Broadway, New York, NY 10007

Tel: (212) 306-2000

Telex: WUT 12070 home life nyk

President: Kenneth C Nichols

Senior Executive Officers: Robert Casper (Executive VP), Jon O Stufflebeem (Senior VP Group), Gary Laughinghouse (Senior VP Information Services), John A Fabian (Senior VP Investments), Larry R Pike (Senior VP Underwriting), William R Bock Jr (Senior VP Personnel and Secretary), John Meyerholz (Senior VP Law), Edward Ludlum (Senior VP Pensions), James Hetherington (VP Actuary), Jerry Cohen (VP Bond and Short Term Investments), John Ericson (VP and Controller)

PRINCIPAL ACTIVITIES: Life insurance

Principal Subsidiaries: Home Life Financial Services In; Home Life Financial Assurance Corp; Orange State Life and Health Insurance Co

No of Employees: 2,642

HOME OWNERS FEDERAL SAVINGS AND LOAN ASSOCIATION

21 Milk Street, Boston, MA 02109

Tel: (617) 482 0630

Chairman: B D Grossman

President: Albert H Holgerson Jr (and Chief Executive Officer)

Senior Executive Officers: Constance F Armstrong (First VP), H H Kombliet (Senior VP), Phyllis M Penta (First VP), Jonathan W Randall (First VP and Treasurer), Lenore S Treiman (First VP), Kevin J McGillicuddy (Executive VP and Chief Financial Officer), Fredrick W Biel (Senior VP), Philip H Brady (Senior VP), Richard A M Lyon (Senior VP), Ruth C Treanor (Secretary)

PRINCIPAL ACTIVITIES: Savings and loans

Principal Subsidiaries: Knutson Mortgage and Finance

Financial Information:

	$'000
Sales revenues	149,000

No of Employees: 300

HOME SAVINGS OF AMERICA, A FEDERAL SAVINGS & LOAN ASSOCIATION

1001 Commerce Drive, Irwindale, CA 91706

Tel: (818) 960 6311

Chairman: Richard H Deihl

President: Mario Antoci

Senior Executive Officers: Robert Jacobson (Executive VP), Warren Androus (Executive VP), Michael Brent (Executive VP Real Estate), Charles Seale (Executive VP)

PRINCIPAL ACTIVITIES: Savings and loans

Parent Company: H F Ahmanson & Co

Principal Bank: Union Bank

No of Employees: 6,000

HOMECRAFTERS WAREHOUSE INC

1 Perimeter Park South, PO Box 10084, Birmingham, AL 35243

Tel: (205) 972 8500

Chairman: Georges A Hanzi (and President and Chief Executive Officer)

Senior Executive Officers: A J Block Jr (VP Real Estate and Assistant Secretary), Richard M Shepperd (VP and Chief Financial Officer), Talmadge A Payton (Controller)

PRINCIPAL ACTIVITIES: Wholesale and retail supply of building materials

Financial Information:

	$'000
Sales revenues	90,000

No of Employees: 730

HOMESTAKE MINING CO

650 California St, San Francisco, CA 94108

Tel: (415) 981-8150

Chairman: Harry M Conger (and Chief Executive Officer)

President: DAvid K Fagin (and Chief Operating officer)

Senior Executive Officers: William A Humphrey (Executive VP Operations and Engineering), Lynn Walker (Executive VP, Oil and Gas), Kenneth S Canfield (VP, Commercial), Lee A Graber (VP, Corporate Development), Rex Guinivere (VP, Engineering), Richard R Hinkel (VP, Human Resources), William G Langston (VP, General Counsel and Assistant Secretary), Robert A Reveles (VP, Government Affairs), Richard W Stumbo Jr (VP Finance and Chief Financial Officer), Jonathan J Williams (Treasurer and Secretary), Robert L Watson (Controller), Vincent Schioppo (Assistant Secretary and Assistant Treasurer)

PRINCIPAL ACTIVITIES: Homestake Mining Company is one of the largest gold producers in the United States and one of the largest in the western world outside South Africa. The Company operates two of the largest gold mines in the US: the Homestake mine in South Dakota, which has operated for 109 years, and the McLaughlin mine in northern California, which began operation in 1985. Homestake also produces and markets refined lead metal and silver, and concentrates of uranium and zinc and conducts continuing exploration for new mineral sources, with primary emphasis on precious metals. In addition, the Company has substantial interests in oil and natural gas exploration, development and production through its wholly-owned Felmont Oil Corporation subsidiary

Principal Subsidiaries: Felmont Oil Corporation; Homestake Mining Company of California; Homestake Australia Limited; Homestake Gold Limited; Homestake International Minerals Ltd; Homestake Lead Company of Missouri; Homestake Nevada Corporation

Financial Information:

	Dec 31 1985	Dec 31 1986
	$'000	$'000
Total revenues	343,171	347,664
Income before taxes	12,513	25,529
Net income	23,296	22,576
Dividends	9,875	9,716
Dividends per share	$0.20	$0.20
Earnings per share	$0.47	$0.46
Common stock	49,440	49,511
Retained income	410,953	423,813
Shareholders equity	567,314	554,388

No of Employees: 2,038

HOMESTEAD FINANCIAL CORPORATION

1777 Murchison Drive, Burlingame, CA 94010

Tel: (415) 692-1432

Chairman: Lawrence Weissberg (and President)

Senior Executive Officers: Britt Evans (Executive VP), John P Halicky (Senior VP, Treasurer), G Eric Lonquist (Senior VP, General Counsel and Secretary), Willis Newton (VP, Controller)

PRINCIPAL ACTIVITIES: Financial services; interests in real estate development and mortgage banking

Principal Subsidiaries: Homestead Savings, A Federal Savings and Loan Association

Principal Bank: Bank of America

Financial Information:

	Dec 31 1985	Dec 31 1986
	$'000	$'000
Income before taxes*	25,576	61,339
Net income	15,093	29,445
Dividends	1,753	2,193
Dividends per share	$0.40	$0.40
Earnings per share	$1.31	$2.51
Common stock	20,800	20,854
Retained income	72,253	99,505
Shareholders equity	90,763	118,067
Deposits	2,348,822	2,538,168
Total assets	4,692,446	5,492,380

*and extraordinary items

No of Employees: 1,000

HON INDUSTRIES INC

414 E 3rd Street, Muscatine, IA 52761

Tel: (319) 264-7400

Telex: TWX 468552 hon co musc

Chairman: S M Howe (and President); Vice Chairman: R H Stanley

Senior Executive Officers: R M Derry (Senior VP), John W Axel (VP Finance)

PRINCIPAL ACTIVITIES: Manufacture of office furniture and storage equipment, mechanical handling equipment and factory built fireplaces

Trade Names: HON, Murphy-Miller, Hiebert, Corry Jamestown, Holga, Prime-Mover, Heatilator, Arrow Woodstove, Firelite, ANYWHERE CHAIR, Ring King, Data Defender, Sound-write

Principal Subsidiaries: The Hon Company; Rishel; Corry Hiebert Corporation; Heatilator Inc; The Prime-Mover Co; Ring King Visibles Inc

Principal Banks: Northern Trust Company; Morgan Guaranty

Financial Information:

	Dec 28 1985	Jan 3 1987
	$'000	$'000
Sales revenues	473,292	503,575
Income before taxes	50,047	56,466
Net income	26,024	29,254
Dividends	6,422	6,569
Dividends per share	$0.60	$0.64
Earnings per share	$2.43	$2.85
Common stock	10,402	10,181
Retained income	110,413	126,150
Shareholders equity	120,913	136,336

No of Employees: 5,806

HONEYWELL INC

Honeywell Plaza, Minneapolis, MN 55408
Tel: (612) 870-5200
Telex: 290651 HYWLAMAIN MPS

Chairman: Edson W Spencer
President: James J Renier (and Chief Executive Officer)
Senior Executive Officers: David R Bergerson (VP and General Counsel), Michael R Bonsignore (President, International), Fosten A Boyle (VP, Corporate Human Resources), Richard J Boyle (Corporate VP, Marketing and Business Development), Joe E Chenoweth (President, Home and Building Automation and Control), Gerald P Dinneen (VP, Science and Technology), Dean M Fjelstul (Treasurer), William W George (President, Space and Aviation Systems), James J Grierson (VP, Finance), Clint O Larson (Corporate VP, Operations), William H Mackey (VP and Controller), Louis E Navin (VP and Chief Financial and Administrative Officer), Sigurd Ueland Jr (VP and Secretary), Warde F Wheaton (President Defense and Marine Systems),

PRINCIPAL ACTIVITIES: Honeywell is organized into five businesses: 1.Home and Building Automation and Control business: Systems and Services for commercial and residential buildings. 2.Defense and Marine Systems business: comprises Defense Systems Group and Marine Systems Group. Designs, develops and manufactures sophisticated materials for three US military services and commercial customers. 3.Space and Aviation Systems Business: comprises Space Systems Group, Sperry Commercial Flight Systems Group and Military Avionics Group. Designs, develops and manufactures sophisticated materials for NASA and commercial customers and US military. 4.Industrial Automation and Control: combines Industrial Systems Group, Components Group and Information Systems operations. Research and development and manufacturing of industrial products from sensors to integrated process control systems. 5.International business: markets and distributes control systems, control products and aerospace and defense products and services throughout the world.
Principal Bank: Stock transfer agent-registrars: Norwest Bank Minneapolis, NA
Financial Information:

	Dec 31 1986	Dec 31 1987
	$'000	$'000
Sales revenues	5,378,200	6,679,300
Income before taxes	39,800	411,900
Net income (loss)	(398,100)	253,700
Dividends per share	$2.00	$2.025
Earnings (loss) per share net	($8.83)	$5.75
Common stock	71,100	71,000
Retained earnings	1,599,200	1,763,600
Shareholders equity	2,221,200	2,245,300

No of Employees: 78,881 worldwide

HOOD, H P, INC

500 Rutherford Avenue, Boston, MA 02129
Tel: (617) 242 0600

Chairman: John Talmage
President: Leonard M Wilson (and Chief Executive Officer)
Senior Executive Officers: Richard W Garrett (VP and Treasurer), Richard J Emberly (Senior VP Development)

PRINCIPAL ACTIVITIES: Dairy products including milk and cheese, ice cream and other frozen food products; citrus fruit products
Parent Company: Agway Inc, Syracuse, NY
Principal Bank: Springfield Bank
Financial Information:

	$'000
Sales revenues	560,000

No of Employees: 2,260

HOOPER HOLMES INC

170 Mount Airy Road, Basking Ridge, NY 07920
Tel: (201) 766 5000

Chairman: Frederick D King; Vice Chairman: Frank J Schwindler
President: James M McNamee (and Chief Executive Officer)
Senior Executive Officers: Forest D Ferguson (Executive VP), William T Breed (Senior VP), John H McDowall (Senior VP), G Earle Wight (Senior VP), Linda L Woodward (Senior VP), Raymond A Sinclair (VP), Robert William Jewett (Secretary and Legal Counsel), Michael J Lafrance (Chief Financial Officer and Treasurer)

PRINCIPAL ACTIVITIES: Business information and direct mail marketing services; health care
Principal Bank: Midlantic National Bank
Financial Information:

	$'000
Sales revenues	55,370

No of Employees: 4,420

HOOVER COMPANY (THE)

101 Maple Street East, North Canton, OH 44720
Tel: (216) 499-9200

Chairman: Merle R Rawson (and President and Chief Executive Officer)
Senior Executive Officers: The Hoover Company:- Merle R Rawson (Chairman-President and Chief Executive Officer), Joseph R Cutinella (Executive VP), Robert J Elsaesser (Executive VP), Dallas B Barnhouse (Senior VP-Finance and Secretary), Frank E Vaughn Jr (Senior VP-US Operations), Jerry M Harroff (VP-US Manufacturing and Engineering), Eugene O Hatfield (VP-Marketing), William H Ray (VP-Administrative Services), George E Volkmann (VP-Taxes), Clarence B Lozaw (Treasurer and Assistant Secretary), Lyle A Carr (Controller US Operations). Hoover Worldwide Corporation:- Merle R Rawson (Chairman and Chief Executive Officer), Joseph R Cutinella (President and Chief Operating Officer), Robert J Elsaesser (VP), Peter R Goode (Senior VP-Finance), Dallas B Barnhouse (Senior VP-Finance), Calvert V Batton (VP-Administration), Ray W Gillman (VP-Public Affairs), Harry Hill (VP), Melvin H Ripple (VP-Engineering), George E Volkmann (VP-Financial Services), William H Wells (VP-Manufacturing), Clarence B Lozaw (Treasurer and Assistant Secretary), Peter M Foradas (Controller), Ronald K Bennington (Secretary), Riley W Marrell (Assistant VP)

PRINCIPAL ACTIVITIES: The principal products manufactured by the Company and its subsidiaries include vacuum cleaners, carpet shampooers and floor polishers, laundry equipment and other small electrical household appliances. These appliances are sold through dealers and distributors. The company has about 40,000 sales outlets in the United States and about 110,000 sales outlets worldwide
Trade Names: Hoover, Concept Two, Help-Mate, Sensotronic, Powerplus, Dustette, Crystaljet, Turbopower, Compact, Spirit
Parent Company: Chicago Pacific Corp
Principal Subsidiaries: Hoover PLC (UK) which owns the following subsidiaries: Hoover (Australia) Pty Ltd (Australia);

Meadowbank Properties Pty Ltd (Australia); Hoover Ges mbh (Austria); Hoover El-Udstyr Aps (Igselect Aps) (Denmark); Hoover Oy (Finland); Hoover (NZ) Ltd (New Zealand); Hoover Norsk AS (Norway); Hoover Electrica Portuguesa Ltda (Portugal); Hoover SA Pty Ltd (South Africa) whichs the following subsidiaries: Hoover Properties Pty Ltd (South Africa); Hoover (Zimbabwe) (Pte) Ltd (Zimbabwe); Hoover Espanola SA (Spain); Svenska Hoover A/B (Sweden); Readylink Limited (UK). Hoover (Holland) BV which owns the following subsidiaries: L'Etablissement Hoover SA (Belgium); S A Hoover (France); Hoove: GmbH (Germany); De Hoover Handemaatschappij BV (Netherlands); Hoover Italianca Societa Per Azioni (Italy); Hoover Apparate AG (Switzerland). Hoover Worldwide Corporation; Hoover Comercial Ltda (Brazil); Hoover Canada Inc (Canada); Hoover Industrial y Comercial SA (Colombia); Hoover Mexicana SA de CV (Mexico); Hoover Export Corporation; Juver Industrial SA de CV

Principal Bank: Society Bank of Eastern Ohio
Financial Information:

	$'000
Sales revenues	680,000

No of Employees: 15,005

HOOVER UNIVERSAL, INC

PO Box 591, Milwaukee, WI 53201
Tel: (414) 228 1200

Chairman: Fred L Brengel (and Chief Executive Officer); Vice Chairman: J F Daly
President: James H Keyes (and Chief Operating Officer)
Senior Executive Officers: W L Rootham (Executive VP and Chief Financial Officer), John M Barth (VP), Dave Bigler (VP), Eugene Goodson (VP), Robert Gustine (VP), George T Jacobi (VP), William P Killian (VP), Joseph W Lewis (VP), Frank M Sterner (VP), Richard D Wilson (VP), Milton C Zilis (VP)

PRINCIPAL ACTIVITIES: Manufacture of automobile and aerospace components and seating; materials handling equipment; furniture components
Parent Company: Johnson Controls Inc
Principal Subsidiaries: Hoover Ball and Bearing Company (Canada) Ltd (Canada); Hoover Ball and Bearing Company (UK) Ltd (UK); American Welding and Manufacturing Company; Construgioni Meccaniche SpA (Italy)
Principal Bank: National Bank of Detroit
Financial Information:

	$'000
Sales revenues	850,000

No of Employees: 8,000

HOOVER-NSK BEARING COMPANY

25 Hanes Drive, Wayne, NJ 07470
Tel: (201) 696 2351
Telex: WUT 230442

Chairman: M Hasegawa; Vice Chairman: T Sekiya
President: Bruce R Paxton
Senior Executive Officers: Patrick D Burke (VP Marketing), Ron Hurley (VP Manufacturing), Charles L Steiner (VP Materials), Takayuki R Kawai (Secretary-Treasurer)

PRINCIPAL ACTIVITIES: Manufacture of ball and roller bearings
Principal Bank: National Bank of Detroit
Financial Information:

	$'000
Sales revenues	65,000

No of Employees: 800

HOPPER, INC

301 Espee Street, Bakersfield, CA 93303
Tel: (805) 861-7000
Telex: TWX 910327 1125

President: V D Hopper
Senior Executive Officers: Frank Hopper III (VP), Harold F Clifton (VP, Secretary and Treasurer)

PRINCIPAL ACTIVITIES: Oil and gas production equipment; industrial plant; power tools
Principal Bank: Bank of America
Financial Information:

	$'000
Sales revenues	70,000

No of Employees: 640

HORACE W LONGACRE INC

See LONGACRE, HORACE W, INC

HORIZON AIR INDUSTRIES INC

1221 South 188th Street, PO Box 48309, Seattle, WA 98148
Tel: (206) 241 6757

Chairman: Milton G Kuolt II (and President and Chief Executive Officer)
Senior Executive Officers: George D Bagley (Senior VP Operations), Melvyn R Kays (Senior VP Finance and Administration), William F Peare (Senior VP Marketing and Products Services), Donald W Streun (Senior VP Planning and Product Development), William S Ayer (VP Strategic Planning), Kenneth L Hobby (VP Maintenance), John R Kuolt (VP Sales and Marketing), Dianna M Maul (VP Stations), B Stephen Fortenberry (VP Flight Operations), Larry A Numato (VP and Controller), Arthur E Thomas (Legal Counsel and Secretary)

PRINCIPAL ACTIVITIES: Regional air transportation services
Principal Bank: Seattle First National Bank
Financial Information:

	$'000
Sales revenues	69,000

No of Employees: 915

HORIZON BANCORP NEW JERSEY

225 South St, Morristown, NJ 07960
Tel: (201) 539-7700

Chairman: Roger B Etherington; Vice Chairman: Joseph F Lord Jr
President: William J Shepherd (and Chief Executive Officer)
Senior Executive Officers: Ira Geschwint (Executive VP Finance and Treasurer), James S Little (Senior VP, General Counsel and Secretary), John T McAuley (Senior VP Data Processing), Raymond W Widmer (Senior VP Personnel), Harold S Thomson (VP Investments), Florence I Fahner (VP Accounting), James C Angus (VP Loan Review), Thomas J Beirne (VP and Auditor), John A Hendricks (VP Investor Relations)

PRINCIPAL ACTIVITIES: Banking services
Financial Information:

	Dec 31 1985	Dec 31 1986
	$'000	$'000
Revenues	309,000	330,000
Net income	30,600	33,000

No of Employees: 2,700

HORIZON INDUSTRIES, INC

South Industrial Blvd, Calhoun, GA 30701
Tel: (404) 629-7721
Telex: WUT 804367 horizon clhn

Chairman: P R Spirer (and Chief Executive Officer)
President: Ralph J Boe (and Chief Operating Officer)
Senior Executive Officers: D L Fink (VP and Secretary)

PRINCIPAL ACTIVITIES: Production of carpets
Principal Bank: First National Bank of Atlanta

Financial Information:

	$'000
Sales revenues	184,000

No of Employees: 1,800

HORMEL, GEO A, & CO

501 16th Avenue NE, Austin, MN 55912
Tel: (507) 437-5611

Chairman: Richard L Knowlton (and President and Chief Executive Officer)
Senior Executive Officers: Raymond Asp (Executive VP), Charles D Nyberg (Senior VP, Secretary and Legal Counsel), Stanley Kerber (Senior VP), Robert Thatcher (Senior VP and Treasurer), James A Silbaugh (Group VP), William R Hunter (Group VP), Don J Hodapp (Group VP), David A Larson (VP), James Dinicola (VP), Marvin Moes (VP), James N Rieth (VP), Richard Schlange (VP and Controller), Alan Krejci (Director Public Relations)

PRINCIPAL ACTIVITIES: Meat processing
Principal Subsidiaries: Algona Food Engineering Company (90%); Hormel International Corp; Farm Fresh Catfish Company Inc
Principal Bank: First National Bank Minneapolis
Financial Information:

	Oct 31 1985 $'000	Oct 31 1986 $'000
Sales revenues	1,502,235	1,960,237
Net income	38,618	39,079
Earnings per share	$2.01	$2.03
Shareholders equity	311,605	339,925

No of Employees: 7,000

HORN & HARDART CO

101 Convention Center Drive, Las Vegas, NV 89109
Tel: (702) 369-9500

Chairman: Barry W Florescue (and President)
Senior Executive Officers: Robert F Byrnes (Senior Executive VP and Secretary), Munir Saltoun (Executive VP and Chief Financial Officer), Franklin I Levy (Executive VP Real Estate), William J Fitzgerald (Executive VP, President Hanover House Industries), Michael P Sherman (VP, Secretary and Legal Counsel), Wayne P Garten (VP and Controller)

PRINCIPAL ACTIVITIES: Mail order services; food service products; restaurant interests
Principal Bank: Chemical Bank
Financial Information:

	$'000
Sales revenues	360,000

No of Employees: 8,300

HORTEX INC

PO Box 9817, El Paso, TX 79988
Tel: (915) 545-4000

Chairman: Dan Manella (and President and Chief Executive Officer); Vice Chairman: J C Keith
Senior Executive Officers: Thomas J Ahmann (Executive VP Finance and Chief Financial Officer)

PRINCIPAL ACTIVITIES: Manufacture of jeans and pants
Parent Company: BTK Industries, Inc
Principal Bank: Manufcturers Hanover Trust
Financial Information:

	$'000
Sales revenues	100,000

No of Employees: 1,300

HOSPITAL CORPORATION OF AMERICA

One Park Plaza, Nashville, TN 37202
Tel: (615) 327-9551

Chairman: Thomas F Frist (and Chief Executive Officer); Chairman Executive Committee: Donald S McNaughton; Vice Chairman: David J Williamson Jr
President: R Clayton McWhorter (and Chief Operating Officer)
Senior Executive Officers: Charles N Martin Jr (Executive VP Marketing and Development), John H Tobin Jr (Executive VP Operations), H E Adams III (Senior VP International), Samuel H Howard (Senior VP Government Affairs), Donald W Fish (Senior VP and Secretary), C Richard Gaston (Senior VP Administration), Joseph C Hutts Jr (Senior VP Health Plans), S Douglas Smith (Senior VP Management Contracts), Roger E Mick (Senior VP Finance and Chief Financial Officer), Joseph L DiLorenzo (Senior VP Operations), James S Main (Senior VP Operations)

PRINCIPAL ACTIVITIES: Ownership and management of hospitals
Principal Bank: Chase Manhattan Bank
Financial Information:

	Dec 31 1985 $'000	Dec 31 1986 $'000
Sales revenues	4,151,715	4,665,592
Net income	338,614	174,644
Earnings per share	$3.75	$2.08
Shareholders equity	2,092,133	2,015,383

No of Employees: 89,000

HOUDAILLE, INDUSTRIES, INC

One Financial Plaza, Fort Lauderdale, FL 33394
Tel: (305) 764-4141

Chairman: Jerome Kohlberg Jr
President: Phillip A O'Reilly (and Chief Executive Officer)
Senior Executive Officers: John Latona (VP and Secretary), Charles M Bischoff (VP and Controller), Donald N Boyce (VP Finance and Group Executive), G J Pomar Jr (VP), Kenneth L Slawson (VP and Group Executive), Arthur L Knight Jr (VP and Group Executive), Harry Tankus (VP and Group Executive), John A Johns (VP and Group Executive)

PRINCIPAL ACTIVITIES: Manufacture of industrial equipment including pumping equipment and machine tools
Financial Information:

	$'000
Sales revenues	650,000

No of Employees: 10,000

HOUGHTON, E F, & CO

Madison & Van Buren Avenue, Valley Forge, PA 19482
Tel: (215) 666-4000
Telex: TWX 510 6604158
Telefax: houghton ph

Chairman: W F MacDonald Jr (and President)
Senior Executive Officers: C F Kalmbach (VP Purchasing), B A Schuck (VP Manufacturing), H J Fastrich (VP Sales), B M Robin (VP Technology), T G Kauffman (Secretary and Treasurer)

PRINCIPAL ACTIVITIES: Manufacture of specialty chemicals
Financial Information:

	Dec 31 1985 $'000	Dec 31 1986 $'000
Sales revenues	109,000	115,000
Income before taxes	8,738	11,893
Net income	4,147	6,822
Dividends	1,094	1,012
Dividends per share	$1.65	$1.70
Earnings per share	$6.23	$11.23
Common stock	660	567
Retained income	52,503	58,301
Shareholders equity	36,058	33,740

No of Employees: 800

HOUGHTON MIFFLIN COMPANY
One Beacon Street, Boston, MA 02108
Tel: (617) 725-5000
Cable: HOUGHTON
Telex: WUT 940959 houghton bsn

Chairman: Harold T Miller (and President and Chief Executive Officer); Vice Chairman: Richard B Gladstone
President: Richard W Young
Senior Executive Officers: George W Breitkreuz (Executive VP Finance), David R Replogle (Executive VP), Robert Janas (Executive VP), William H Berman (Executive VP), Marjorie C Dyer (Senior VP), Austin G Olney (Senior VP), Richard T Bueschel (Senior VP), John E Baack (Senior VP), John P Schram (Senior VP), Nader F Darehshori (Senior VP), Damaris Ames (Senior VP, Publisher), James Evans (VP and Treasurer), Pierre B Balliett (VP), George L Hall (VP and Controller)

PRINCIPAL ACTIVITIES: Publishing
Principal Subsidiaries: Houghton Mifflin Canada Ltd (Canada); Ticknor and Fields Inc; The Riverside Publishing Company
Principal Bank: Bank of Boston
Financial Information:

	Dec 31 1985 $'000	Dec 31 1986 $'000
Sales revenues	277,526	321,347
Income before taxes	32,508	39,916
Net income	18,920	22,612
Dividends per share*	$0.49	$0.535
Earnings per share*	$1.37	$1.61
Common stock*	7,379	14,759
Shareholders equity	138,760	154,253

*share and per share amounts reflect a two-for-one stock split distributed on Sep 10 1986

No of Employees: 2,003

HOUSE OF FABRICS INC
13400 Riverside Drive, Sherman Oaks, CA 91423
Tel: (818) 995 7000

Chairman: Barney Sofro
President: Gary L Larkins (and Chief Executive Officer)
Senior Executive Officers: Donald R Ardemagni (Senior VP Purchasing), L J Bowen (VP Notions), Gary A Bunch (VP Sewing Machine Operations), Edward L Chow (VP Data Processing), Larry R Eames (VP Marketing), James R Hartwig (VP Store Operations), Wm James Heaton (VP Finance, VP Advertising and Chief Financial Officer, Edwin F Johnson (VP Construction), Marvin S Maltzman (VP, Legal Counsel and Secretary), Russell M Meppen (Controller), Bill M Smith (VP Building and Warehousing), John A Sofro (VP Fabric Buying), F Douglas Trovato (VP Fabric Buying), Aurora Stewart (Treasurer and Assistant Secretary), James C Webb (VP Real Estate)

PRINCIPAL ACTIVITIES: Retail of textile piece goods and related accessories and equipment
Principal Subsidiaries: House of Fabrics SC; Sofro Fabrics Inc
Principal Bank: Bank of America Trust and Savings Association
Financial Information:

	$'000
Sales revenues	286,750

No of Employees: 9,700

HOUSEHOLD INTERNATIONAL, INC
2700 Sanders Road, Prospect Heights, IL 60070
Tel: (312) 564-5000
Telex: WUT 254336 hfc ha cgo

Chairman: Donald C Clark (and President and Chief Executive Officer)
Senior Executive Officers: J R Hull (Senior VP and General Counsel), Edward A Wiegner (Senior VP and Chief Financial Officer), James L McCormick (Senior VP Government and Public Affairs), James D Pinkerton (Senior VP Administration and Secretary), Gaylen N Larson (Group VP and Controller)

PRINCIPAL ACTIVITIES: Holding company with interests in financial services, insurance and manufacturing
Principal Subsidiaries: Household Financial Services; Household Manufacturing
Financial Information:

	Dec 31 1985 $'000	Dec 31 1986 $'000
Sales revenues	2,356,900	2,740,500
Income before taxes	232,100	162,000
Net income	210,900	208,600
Dividends(1)	114,500	91,400
Dividends per share	$1,78	$1.84
Earnings per share	$3.65	$4.48
Common stock(2)	51,300	40,600
Retained income	1,482,800	1,521,500
Shareholders equity	1,630,900	1,161,600

(1) common and preferred
(2) number of shares in thousands

No of Employees: 20,000

HOUSEHOLD MANUFACTURING, INC
2700 Sanders Road, Prospect Heights, IL 60070
Tel: (312) 564-3910

President: Gary G Dillon
Senior Executive Officers: Scott G Arbuckle (Executive VP), Terence J McCarthy (Executive VP), Richard C Osborne (Executive VP), W E Chandler (VP and Chief Financial Officer), Robin G Munden (VP, General Counsel and Secretary), Jack C Hoffman (VP)

PRINCIPAL ACTIVITIES: Building materials; process engineering; machine tools; heating and ventilation equipment; motor vehicle components
Parent Company: Household International, Inc, Prospect Heights, IL
Principal Bank: Manufacturers National Bank of Detroit
Financial Information:

	Dec 31 1985 $'000	Dec 31 1986 $'000
Sales revenues	899,830	910,345
Net income (loss)	50,100	(42,833)
Shareholders equity	-	325,572

No of Employees: 10,800

HOUSTON INDUSTRIES INC
P O Box 4567, Houston, TX 77210
Tel: (713) 629 3000

President: D D Jordan (and Chief Executive Officer)
Senior Executive Officers: H R Dean (Executive VP and Chief Financial Officer), Donald Sykora (VP), H R Kelly (VP, Legal Counsel and Secretary)

PRINCIPAL ACTIVITIES: Electricity supply; production of oil and gas; coal supply
Principal Subsidiaries: Houston Lighting and Power Co; Primary Fuels Inc; Utility Fuels Inc
Principal Bank: Texas Commerce Bank
Financial Information:

	Dec 31 1985 $'000	Dec 31 1986 $'000
Sales revenues	4,061,812	3,535,968
Net income	464,394	424,935
Earnings per share	$4.42	$3.81
Shareholders equity	-	3,102,627

No of Employees: 11,900

HOVNANIAN ENTERPRISES INC

10 Highway 35, PO Box 500, Red Bank, NJ 07701
Tel: (201) 747 7800

Chairman: Kevork S Hovnanian (and President)

Senior Executive Officers: John J Schimpf (Senior VP), Frank J Steinitz (Senior VP, K Hovnanian Properties of Florida Inc), George P Yankowich (Senior VP, K Hovnanian Companies of NJ Inc), Paul W Buchanan (VP and Controller), Gary M Levine (VP, K Hovnanian Investment Properties Inc), Timothy P Mason (VP, Administration), Tavit O Najarian (President Najarian & Associates Inc), Robert E Scott Jr (President R E Scott Mortgage Co)

PRINCIPAL ACTIVITIES: Construction of domestic and industrial building projects; management of real estate

Principal Subsidiaries: Hovnanian Companies Inc; K Hovnanian Companies of Florida; Najarian & Associates Inc; R E Scott Mortgage Company

Principal Bank: Midlantic National Bank

Financial Information:

	$'000
Sales revenues	278,000

No of Employees: 500

HOWARD BANCORP

111 Main Street, Burlington, VT 05402
Tel: (802) 658 1010

President: Harry R Mitiguy

Senior Executive Officers: John P Spencer (VP and Treasurer)

PRINCIPAL ACTIVITIES: Banking

Financial Information:

	Dec 31 1985
	$'000
Revenues	53,340
Net income	3,720

No of Employees: 475

HOWARD PAPER MILLS, INC

115 Columbia Street, Dayton, OH 4445407
Tel: (513) 224-1211
Telex: TWX 810 4591936 how dy

Chairman: Ward D Harrison

President: Lou N Mehr

Senior Executive Officers: Bradis Arnett (Executive VP and Treasurer), Robert C Finley (VP Marketing), Justin H McCarthy Jr (VP Sales), Charles H Swain (VP Engineering)

PRINCIPAL ACTIVITIES: Paper manufacture

Principal Bank: Union Commerce Bank

Financial Information:

	$'000
Sales revenues	100,000

No of Employees: 800

HOWARD SAVINGS BANK

768 Broad St, Newark, NJ 07101
Tel: (201) 430-2000

Chairman: Donald F McCormack (and Chief Executive Officer)

President: Leo J Rogers Jr

Senior Executive Officers: Donald J Stevenson (Executive VP), Joseph G Wojak (Executive VP and Chief Financial Officer)

PRINCIPAL ACTIVITIES: Banking

Financial Information:

	Dec 31 1985	Dec 31 1986
	$'000	$'000
Net income	16,024	24,049
Earnings per share	$1.47	$1.20
Shareholders equity	236,620	256,059
Deposits	-	3,704,461
Total assets	3,656,405	4,294,392

No of Employees: 1,402

HOWE RICHARDSON COMPANY

4421 N Church Avenue, Tampa, FL 33614
Tel: (813) 877 3082

Presidents: A A Toivonen (HCR International) F M Campiglia (HR United States of America)

Senior Executive Officers: J W Aquadro (VP Industrial/Vehicular), E D Wilcox (VP Packaging/Bulk Products), T J Stasiak (VP), R L Ohlweiler (VP), C B McGouch (VP)

PRINCIPAL ACTIVITIES: Manufacture of weighing and measuring equipment

Principal Bank: Security Pacific National Bank

Financial Information:

	$'000
Sales revenues	70,000

No of Employees: 1,200

HOWELL CORPORATION

1010 Lamar Building, Houston, TX 77002
Tel: (713) 658-4000
Telex: TWX 910881 1658 howell hoy

Chairman: Paul N Howell (and Chief Executive Officer)

President: Steven K Howell

Senior Executive Officers: John J Innes (VP), Paul W Funkhouser (VP), Joe A Salkeld (VP and Chief Financial Officer)

PRINCIPAL ACTIVITIES: Exploration and production of oil, gas and coal; oil refining

Principal Subsidiaries: Lake Coal Co Inc; Howell Hydrocarbons Inc; Howell Crude Oil Co; Howell Petroleum Corp; Fayette Oilfield Services Inc

Principal Bank: Continental Illinois National Bank and Trust Co

Financial Information:

	$'000
Sales revenues	107,000

No of Employees: 260

HOWELL INDUSTRIES INC

17515 West Nine Mile Road, Suite 650, Southfield, MI 48075
Tel: (313) 424 8220

Chairman: Herbert Freedland (and President)

Senior Executive Officers: Henry Kowaleski (VP), Cyril Moscow (Secretary), Morton Schiff (Treasurer)

PRINCIPAL ACTIVITIES: Metal stampings for automobile industry

Principal Bank: National Bank of Detroit

Financial Information:

	$'000
Sales revenues	38,500

No of Employees: 320

HOWES LEATHER CO INC

1 Batterymarch Park, Quincy, MA 02169
Tel: (617) 770-3900
Telex: WUT 921839 howes bsn

President: Barry Getto

Senior Executive Officers: Leo Ganoe (VP Manufacturing), Joseph McHugh (Treasurer)

PRINCIPAL ACTIVITIES: Manufacture of leather
Principal Bank: Bank of Boston
Financial Information:

	$'000
Sales revenues	50,000

No of Employees: 400

HOWMEDICA, INC

235 E 42nd Street, New York, NY 10017
Tel: (212) 697-5656
Telex: TWX 710581 3749 howmedica nyk

Chairman: Theodore W Eckels
President: Edward Bessey (and Chief Executive Officer)
Senior Executive Officers: Russell B Whitman (Senior VP), David Fitzgerald (Senior VP), Paul T Kerins (VP Personnel), Richard L Myerson (VP Research and Development)

PRINCIPAL ACTIVITIES: Manufacture of medical equipment and instruments
Parent Company: Pfizer Inc, New York, NY
Principal Bank: Chase Manhattan Bank
Financial Information:

	$'000
Sales revenues	300,000

No of Employees: 4,300

HOWMET TURBINE COMPONENTS CORPORATION

475 Steamboat Road, Greenwich, CT 06830
Tel: (203) 661-4600
Telex: RCA 221 9 ptcg ur33

Chairman: Robert F Ellsworth
President: Joseph Mallardi (and Chief Executive Officer)
Senior Executive Officers: David Squier (Senior VP), Rex D Eberly (Senior VP), Joseph P O'Brien (VP Finance), Roland A Paul (VP and Secretary)

PRINCIPAL ACTIVITIES: Manufacture of turbine engine components
Parent Company: Pechiney, Paris, France
Principal Bank: Chase Manhattan Bank
Financial Information:

	$'000
Sales revenues	795,000

No of Employees: 11,798

HPM CORPORATION

820 Marion Road, Mt Gilead, OH 43338
Tel: (419) 946-0222
Telex: WUT 987 426 hpm corp mtgd

President: R T Studer
Senior Executive Officers: Thomas G Bishop (VP Sales), R Akialis (VP Manufacturing), W T Flickinger (VP Engineering), W Ahrens (Treasurer)

PRINCIPAL ACTIVITIES: Manufacture of machinery and equipment for plastics molding and metal casting
Principal Bank: Cleveland Bank and Trust Co
Financial Information:

	$'000
Sales revenues	50,000

No of Employees: 850

HR TEXTRON INC

25200 W Rye Canyon Road, Valencia, CA 91355
Tel: (805) 259-4030
Telex: TWX 910 336 1438 hydra resrch

Chairman: S X Garcia
President: Peter Gandell (and Chief Executive Officer)
Senior Executive Officers: Louis A Drazin (VP Corporate Marketing), David T Stewart (Senior VP HR Division), Robert A Smith (Senior VP PTI Division), Craig Johansen (VP Marketing), Ronald E Trapp (VP Administration)

PRINCIPAL ACTIVITIES: Servoactuation systems and associated electronic controllers for flight control and motion controls for aircraft, missiles, spacecraft, armored vehicles, automatic test equipment. Filters and modules for filtration of fluid systems. Fuel valves/systems and stored energy systems
Parent Company: Textron Inc, Providence, RI
Financial Information:

	$'000
Sales revenues	160,000

No of Employees: 1,800

HRT INDUSTRIES, INC

2525 Military Avenue, Los Angeles, CA 90064
Tel: (213) 824-5800

Chairman: Steven J Green (and President and Chief Executive Officer)
Senior Executive Officers: Jeffrey J Buresh (Senior VP, Secretary and Chief Financial Officer)

PRINCIPAL ACTIVITIES: Retail stores; manufacture of clothing
Parent Company: McCrory Corp
Principal Subsidiaries: Karl's Shoe Stores Ltd; Jody-Tootique
Principal Bank: First Interstate Bank of California
Financial Information:

	$'000
Sales revenues	444,000

No of Employees: 3,000

HUBBARD MILLING CO

424 N Front Street, Mankato, MN 56001
Tel: (507) 625-1882
Telex: TWX 910 5652448 huboo mako

Chairman: Ogden P Confer (and Chief Executive Officer)
President: Harry Lusk
Senior Executive Officers: Richard P Confer (Executive VP), Denis Daly (Group VP), Jerry Corley (VP and Manager, Feed), Ogden W Confer (VP and Secretary)

PRINCIPAL ACTIVITIES: Manufacture of flour, animal feeds and poultry products
Principal Bank: The First National Bank of Minneapolis
Financial Information:

	$'000
Sales revenues	175,000

No of Employees: 1,200

HUBBELL INC

584 Derby Milford Road, Orange, CT 06477
Tel: (203) 789-1100

President: Fred R Dusto (and Chief Executive Officer)
Senior Executive Officers: Gerald E Martin (Executive VP Operations), G J Ratcliffe Jr (Executive VP Administration), Richard H Montague (Group VP), Vincent R Petrecca (Group VP), Harry B Rowell Jr (Group VP), Roger M Search (VP Personnel), David G McNamara (VP Accounting and Controls)

PRINCIPAL ACTIVITIES: Manufacture of electrical and electronic equipment including telecommunications
Principal Subsidiaries: The Kerite Co; Killark Electric Manufacturing Co; The Ohio Brass Co; Raco Inc
Principal Bank: Manufacturers Hanover Trust Co
Financial Information:

	$'000
Sales revenues	559,000

No of Employees: 5,770

HUBCO INC
3100 Bergenline Avenue, Union City, NJ 07087
Tel: (201) 348 2300

Chairman: James C McClave
President: John T Clark (and Subsidiary Officer)
Senior Executive Officers: Henry Schroeder (VP and Secretary), Charles R Dovico (Treasurer)

PRINCIPAL ACTIVITIES: Banking
Principal Bank: Hudson United Bank
Financial Information:

	$'000

No of Employees: 355

HUBER, J M, CORPORATION
Thornall Street, Edison, NJ 08818
Tel: (201) 549-8600
Telex: WUT 138733 j m huber mepk

President: Michael W Huber
Senior Executive Officers: Peter C Huber (Group VP Finance, Administration, Oil and Gas), George Schenk (Group VP Clay, Calcium Carbonate, Chemical Division), Rolf C Margenau (Group VP Ink, Carbon Black and Equipment Divisions), W J Ryan (VP Finance and Controller), P M Rowe (VP Administration), J A Rogers (VP Clay), J C Waggoner (VP Carbon Black), D C Semonite (VP Timber and Minerals), J H Becker (VP Chemicals), J F Rives (VP Equipment), Robert B Black (VP Calcium Carbonate), David B Martin (VP Oil and Gas)

PRINCIPAL ACTIVITIES: Production of oil and gas; manufacture of chemicals, inks, pigments, carbon black and equipment for the oil industry
Principal Bank: Chase Manhattan Bank
Financial Information:

	$'000
Sales revenues	470,000

No of Employees: 3,000

HUCK MANUFACTURING CO
PO Box 19590, Irvine, CA 92713
Tel: (714) 851-9801
Telex: WUT 683306 huck mfg irin

President: H George Faulkner
Senior Executive Officers: Robert S Levine (VP and General Manager International Division), Mervin F Mull (VP and General Manager, Waco Division), Edward F Gowen (VP and General Manager, Los Angeles Division), Roy Taylor (VP and Controller), Fred P Luvisi (VP Corporate Planning and Administration), Joseph Phillips (VP Technical Development)

PRINCIPAL ACTIVITIES: Manufacture of industrial fasteners
Parent Company: Federal-Mogul Corporation, Southfield, MI
Principal Bank: National Bank of Detroit
Financial Information:

	$'000
Sales revenues	89,000

No of Employees: 1,000

HUDSON FOODS INC
Hudson Road and 13th Street, Rogers, AR 72757
Tel: (501) 636 1100

Chairman: James T Hudson (and Chief Executive Officer)
President: Michael J Hudson
Senior Executive Officers: Gary L Anderson (VP), John M Hoyt Jr (VP), Charles B Jurgensmeyer (Chief Financial Officer, VP, Secretary and Treasurer)

PRINCIPAL ACTIVITIES: Turkey processing
Financial Information:

	$'000
Sales revenues	184,600

No of Employees: 2,200

HUDSON GENERAL CORPORATION
111 Great Neck Road, Great Neck, NY 11021
Tel: (516) 487-8610

Chairman: Jay B Langner
President: Alan J Stearn
Senior Executive Officers: Katie F Goldberg (Secretary), Michael Rubin (VP, Treasurer and Chief Financial Officer), Noah E Rockowitz (VP and Legal Counsel)

PRINCIPAL ACTIVITIES: Airports and related services
Principal Subsidiaries: Hudson Aviation Services Inc; Hudson Aviation Services Inc CA; Hudson Aviation Services Inc DE; Hudson Kohala Inc; Hudson Stretch Car Corporation
Principal Bank: First National Bank
Financial Information:

	$'000
Sales revenues	67,000

No of Employees: 2,200

HUFFY CORPORATION
7701 Byers Road, Miamisburg, OH 45342
Tel: (513) 866-6251
Telex: ITT 4333041 huffy msbg

Chairman: Harry A Shaw; Vice Chairman: Stuart Northrop (and Chairman of Executive Committee)
President: Richard L Molen (and Chief Operating Officer)
Senior Executive Officers: W A Huffman (VP Marketing), Barry T Ryan (VP and Treasurer), Robert R Wieland (VP, Secretary and Legal Counsel), James K Lane (VP Technical)

PRINCIPAL ACTIVITIES: Manufacture of bicycles and sports equipment
Principal Subsidiaries: Raleigh Cycle Co of America; Huffy Bicycle Division; YLC Enterprises Inc; Sporting Goods Division; Gerico Inc
Principal Bank: Security Pacific National Bank
Financial Information:

	$'000
Sales revenues	264,000

No of Employees: 3,100

HUGHES AIRCRAFT CO
PO Box 45066, Los Angeles, CA 90045
Tel: (213) 568-7200

Chairman: Albert D Wheelon (and Chief Executive Officer)
Senior Executive Officers: Malcolm R Currie (Executive VP), Albert D Wheelon (Executive VP), M T Smith (Senior VP Finance and Chief Financial Officer), P P Alder (Senior VP), C B Shull (Senior VP)

PRINCIPAL ACTIVITIES: Manufacture of weapons systems, guided missile defense systems, anti-submarine equipment, radar equipment, data processing equipment
Parent Company: General Motors Corporation
Financial Information:

	$'000
Sales revenues	10,400,000

No of Employees: 80,000

HUGHES SUPPLY, INC
521 W Central Blvd, PO Box 2273, Orlando, FL 32802
Tel: (305) 841-4710

Chairman: Harry C Hughes
President: David H Hughes (and Chief Executive Officer)
Senior Executive Officers: John E Young (Executive VP), J Holland (VP Plumbing Sales), Robert McGinnis (VP Electrical

Sales), Stephen Sopp (VP Finance and Treasurer), Stewart Hall (VP Credit), Russell V Hughes (VP), Vincent S Hughes (VP), William C Weir III (VP and General Manager)

PRINCIPAL ACTIVITIES: Manufacture of electrical and plumbing equipment and supplies
Principal Subsidiaries: Southern Lighting Manufacturing Co
Principal Bank: Sun Bank NA
Financial Information:

	$'000
Sales revenues	325,000

No of Employees: 1,460

HUGHES TOOL COMPANY

6500 Texas Commerce Tower, Houston, TX 77002
Tel: (713) 222-0686

Chairman: William A Kistler Jr (and President and Chief Executive Officer)
Senior Executive Officers: E C Broun Jr (Executive VP), Calvin D Sholtess (Executive VP), Scott R Willis (Senior VP Finance and Treasurer), J W Stewart ((VP Legal and Secretary), I C Kerridge Jr (VP Stockholder Relations), R E Sternenberg (VP), J M Tidwell (VP)

PRINCIPAL ACTIVITIES: Manufacture of drilling equipment for the oil and gas industry
Principal Bank: Texas Commerce Bank
Financial Information:

	Dec 31 1986
	$'000
Sales revenues	806,070
Net (loss)	(475,849)
(Loss) per share	$(8.50)
Shareholders equity	444,709

No of Employees: 12,900

HUMANA INC

PO Box 1438, Louisville, KY 40201
Tel: (502) 561-2000

Chairman: David A Jones (and Chief Executive Officer); Chairman of Executive Committee: William T Young
President: Wendell Cherry (and Chief Operating Officer)
Senior Executive Officers: Carl F Pollard (Senior Executive VP), William C Ballard Jr (Executive VP), Thomas J Flynn (Executive VP), Jack Clark (Executive VP), Paul A Gross (Executive VP), Wayne T Smith (Executive VP), James D Bohanon (Senior VP), Randolph G Brown (Senior VP), H Linden McLellan (Senior VP), Gary W Metcalf (Senior VP), H Herbert Phillips (Senior VP), Fred Pirman (Senior VP Information Systems), F David Rollo (Senior VP), David G Anderson (VP and Treasurer), Michael A Hendricks (VP Real Estate)

PRINCIPAL ACTIVITIES: Operation of hospitals
Principal Bank: The First National Bank of Boston
Financial Information:

	Aug 31 1985	Aug 31 1986
	$'000	$'000
Sales revenues	2,188,610	2,600,000
Net income	216,220	54,452
Earnings per share	$2.19	$0.56
Shareholders equity	902,850	896,358

No of Employees: 42,000

HUNT INTERNATIONAL RESOURCES CORPORATION

3600 First International Building, Dallas, TX 75221
Tel: (214) 747 7011

Chairman: N B Hunt; Vice Chairman: W H Hunt
President: Douglas Hunt
Senior Executive Officers: James R Parish (VP Finance), Thomas M Maney (VP and Secretary)

PRINCIPAL ACTIVITIES: Sugar production; restaurants; land development and exploration of natural resources
Financial Information:

	$'000
Sales revenues	450,000

No of Employees: 4,000

HUNT, J B, TRANSPORT SERVICES INC

Highway 71 North, Lowell, AR 72745
Tel: (501) 659-8800
Telefax: (501) 659-8320

Chairman: J B Hunt
President: Kirk Thompson (and Chief Operating Officer and Chief Executive Officer)
Senior Executive Officers: Paul R Bergant (Executive VP Marketing), Bruce Jones (VP Finance and Chief Financial Officer), Johnelle Hunt (Secretary and Treasurer), Bob Ralston (VP Maintenance), Paul James (VP Operations), Steve Palmer (VP Human Resources)

PRINCIPAL ACTIVITIES: J B Hunt is an irregular route, common carrier transporting general commodities throughout the 48 contiguous states
Principal Subsidiaries: J B Hunt Transport Inc
Principal Bank: First Chicago Bank
Financial Information:

	Dec 31 1985	Dec 31 1986
	$'000	$'000
Sales revenues	131,475	203,786
Income before taxes	25,524	22,603
Net income	16,314	14,141
Dividends	2,316	2,823
Dividends per share	$0.10	$0.12
Earnings per share net	$0.70	$1.05
Common stock	120	240
Retained income	39,668	61,583
Shareholders equity	76,801	98,967

No of Employees: 3,623

HUNT MANUFACTURING CO

230 S Broad Street, Philadelphia, PA 19102
Tel: (215) 732-770

Chairman: George E Bartol III; Vice Chairman: Ronald J Naples (and President and Chief Executive Officer)
Senior Executive Officers: Rudolph M Peins Jr (Senior VP Finance and Administration), Robert B Fritsch (VP), Donald J Polak (VP), W E Precious (VP International Sales), K H Morsman (VP Marketing)

PRINCIPAL ACTIVITIES: Manufacture of office equipment and furniture
Principal Subsidiaries: (100% owned unless stated): Hunt World Trade Corp; Hunt Holdings Inc; Productos Hunt Mexico (49%)
Principal Bank: Mellon Bank (East)
Financial Information:

	$'000
Sales revenues	112,000

No of Employees: 1,000

HUNT OIL COMPANY

1401 Elm Street, Suite 2900, Dallas, TX 75202
Tel: (214) 744-7911
Telex: ITT 4630124; WU 730239

Chairman: Ray L Hunt
President: Gary T Hurford
Senior Executive Officers: George Cunyus (Senior VP), James B Jennings (Senior VP)

PRINCIPAL ACTIVITIES: Gas and oil exploration and production; oil refining and distribution; farming and ranching
Parent Company: Hunt Consolidated, Inc

Principal Subsidiaries: Yemen Hunt Oil Company; Hunt Refining Company
Principal Bank: First National Bank of Dallas

HUNT, PHILIP A, CHEMICAL CORPORATION

Roosevelt Place, Palisades Park, NJ 07650
Tel: (201) 977-6000
Telex: 710 991 9620

Chairman: Alfred T Blomquist Jr (and Chief Executive Officer)
President: Robert T Zetena
Senior Executive Officers: Harold L Berkowitz (Senior VP Operations), Donald J Fiete (Senior VP and Chief Financial Officer), James M O'Connor (Senior VP Research and Development)

PRINCIPAL ACTIVITIES: Manufacture of specialty chemicals for the photographic industry
Parent Company: Olin Corporation, Stamford, CT
Principal Bank: Citibank
Financial Information:

	$'000
Sales revenues	120,000

No of Employees: 980

HUNTER ENGINEERING COMPANY

11250 Hunter Drive, Bridgeton, MO 63044
Tel: (314) 731-3020
Telex: WUT 442 454 heco stl

Chairman: Lee Hunter
President: Stephen F Brauer
Senior Executive Officers: Donald J Mattingly (VP Administration and Secretary), E Gerards (VP Manufacturing), David Smith (VP Marketing), H P Degreen (VP National Accounts), John Braver (VP Training and Services)

PRINCIPAL ACTIVITIES: Manufacture of industrial equipment for use in automotive industry
Principal Bank: Centerre Bank
Financial Information:

	$'000
Sales revenues	60,000

No of Employees: 440

HUNTINGTON BANCSHARES, INCORPORATED

41 S High Street, Columbus, OH 43287
Tel: (614) 476-8300
Telex: 245475 HuntingtonCol

Chairman: Frank Wobst
President: Zuheir Sofia
Senior Executive Officers: John T Williams (President-The Huntington Mortgage Co), T Carl Alderman (President, The Huntington National Bank), George S Brookes (President, Northern Ohio Region, The Huntington National Bank), Lloyd D Peele (President, Central Ohio Region, The Huntington National Bank), J Virgil Early Jr (President, The Huntington Trust Company, NA), Ralph K Frasier (General Counsel and Secretary), Ralph H Lockwood (President, The Huntington Service Company), William J Williams (Chairman, The Huntington National Bank), Donald J Stuhldreher (President, The Huntington Company), Gregory C Sheridan (President, Huntington Bancshares, Indiana Inc), Merwin Greyson Jr (President, Huntington Bancshares Kentucky Inc), Charles S Kassab (Chairman, Huntington Bancshares Michigan Inc)

PRINCIPAL ACTIVITIES: Huntington offers a complete commercial and retail banking organization through 200 banking offices located in Ohio, Indiana, Kentucky and Michigan. International banking services are maintained through the headquarters office in Columbus and a branch located in the Cayman Islands. Additionally, the Company's subsidiaries engage in trust and investment services, mortgage banking, and other related activities

Principal Subsidiaries: The Huntington National Bank; The Huntington Leasing Co; The Huntington Mortgage Company; The Huntington Company; Scioto Life Insurance Co; Huntington Bancshares Indiana Inc; Huntington Bancshares Kentucky Inc; Huntington Bancshares Michigan Inc; The Huntington Service company; The Huntington Trust Company NA
Principal Bank: The Huntington National Bank
Financial Information:

	Dec 31 1985	Dec 31 1986
	$'000	$'000
Income before taxes	69,951	82,575
Net income	54,066	64,691
Dividends (1)	18,846	20,745
Dividends per share	$0.75	$0.80
Earnings per share (2)	$2.26	$2.59
Common stock (3)	20,243	24,855
Retained income	35,160	43,946
Shareholders equity (4)	399,618	470,995
Deposits (4)	4,990,129	5,952,839
Total assets (4)	6,514,502	7,717,915

(1) includes preferred stock
(2) fully diluted
(3) shares outstanding end of year
(4) end of year

No of Employees: 4,855 (full-time equivalents)

HUNT-WESSON FOODS, INC

1645 W Valencia Drive, PO Box 3h, Fullerton, CA 92633
Tel: (714) 680-1000
Telex: ITT 4722066 bw intl flt

President: Frederick B Rentschler (and CHief Executive Officer)
Senior Executive Officers: Robert J Crosson (Executive VP), J F Stollsteimer (Executive VP), Donald D Rohdy (Senior VP)

PRINCIPAL ACTIVITIES: Production of canned fruit and vegetables, edible oils and fats
Parent Company: Esmark Inc, through Norton Simon Inc, New York, NY
Financial Information:

	$'000
Sales revenues	940,000

Principal Shareholders: BCI Holdings
No of Employees: 6,000

HURCO COMPANIES INC

6460 Saguaro Court, Indianapolis, IN 46268
Tel: (317) 293 5309

Chairman: E Keith Moore
President: Gary M Neal (and Chief Executive Officer)
Senior Executive Officers: Michael K Campbell (VP Finance), Frank E Gary (VP Marketing and Sales), Joe H Loudenback (VP Manufacturing), Gerald C Michael (VP Product Development), Jack E Moore (VP Administration)

PRINCIPAL ACTIVITIES: Manufacture of equipment for processing and fabrication of metals
Principal Subsidiaries: Dynapath Systems Inc
Principal Bank: Merchants National Bank
Financial Information:

	$'000
Sales revenues	46,000

No of Employees: 440

HUTCHINSON TECHNOLOGY INC

40 West Highland Park, Hutchinson, MN 55350
Tel: (612) 587 3797

Chairman: Jeffrey W Green (and Chief Executive Officer)
President: Wayne M Fortun (and Chief Operating Officer)
Senior Executive Officers: John A Ingleman (VP and Treasurer), Richard B Solum (Secretary)

PRINCIPAL ACTIVITIES: Manufacture of computer peripheral and defense electronic equipment
Principal Bank: Norwest Bank
Financial Information:

	$'000
Sales revenues	47,000

No of Employees: 1,000

HUTTIG SASH & DOOR COMPANY

14500 S Forty Outer Drive, Chesterfield, MO 63017
Tel: (314) 878-2222

President: Stuart P Wells
Senior Executive Officers: Geroge E Kessel (VP and Treasurer), Duane R Duff (VP), R D Sutton (VP Sales), L M Johnston (VP), F J Schweitzer (VP), H Jackson Anstedt (VP)

PRINCIPAL ACTIVITIES: Building materials and fittings including windows and doors
Parent Company: Crane Co
Principal Bank: Centerre Bank
Financial Information:

	$'000
Sales revenues	240,000

No of Employees: 1,600

HUTTON, E F, GROUP, INC

1 Battery Park Plaza, New York, NY 10004
Tel: (212) 742-5000

Chairman: Robert P Rittereiser (and Chief Executive Officer); Vice Chairmen: W R Wigley Jr, Peter M Detwiler
Senior Executive Officers: Gordon B Crary Jr (Executive VP), Norman M Epstein (Executive VP), Stephen J Friedman (Executive VP and Legal Counsel), Michael T Judd (Executive VP), John Latshaw (Executive VP), Edward J Lill (Executive VP and Chief Financial Officer), Richard S Locke (Executive VP), W J Lopp II (Executive VP), Jerome H Miller (Executive VP), Scott Pierce (Executive VP)

PRINCIPAL ACTIVITIES: Holding company with interests in banking and other financial services
Principal Subsidiaries: E F Hutton & Co Inc; E F Hutton Insurance Group Inc; E F Hutton Credit Corp
Principal Bank: Bank of America
Financial Information:

	Dec 31 1985	Dec 31 1986
	$'000	$'000
Revenues	3,205,186	3,504,927
Net income (loss)	43,685	(90,286)
Earnings (loss) per share	$1.63	($2.90)
Shareholders equity	809,988	733,484

No of Employees: 14,200

HYDE ATHLETIC INDUSTRIES INC

Centennial Industrial Park, Centennial Drive, Peabody, MA 01961
Tel: (617) 532 9000

Chairman: Leonard R Fisher (and Chief Executive Officer)
President: John H Fisher (and Chief Operating Officer)
Senior Executive Officers: David L Landay (Executive VP Operations), Hal DeWaltoff (VP Sales and Marketing), O J Simpson (VP Promotions), Charles A Gottesman (Treasurer), Joel A Kozol (Clerk)

PRINCIPAL ACTIVITIES: Manufacture of athletic shoes
Principal Bank: Shawmut Bank of Boston
Financial Information:

	$'000
Sales revenues	57,500

No of Employees: 300

HYDRAULIC COMPANY

835 Main Street, Bridgeport, CT 06601
Tel: (203) 367 6621

President: William S Warner (and Chief Executive Officer)
Senior Executive Officers: Jack E McGregor (Executive VP), Joseph J Murphy (Executive VP, Treasurer and Chief Financial Officer), Raymond C Smedberg (Executive VP), Anthony M MacLeod (VP and Legal Counsel), Martha W Bodurtha (Assistant Secretary), Janes M Hansen (Assistant Treasurer), Russell B Hintz (Controller)

PRINCIPAL ACTIVITIES: Holding company with interests in water supply and development of real estate
Principal Subsidiaries: Bridgeport Hydraulic Company; Main Street South Corporation; Timco Inc
Principal Bank: Connecticut National Bank
Financial Information:

	Dec 31 1986
	$'000
Sales revenues	63,727
Income before taxes	17,437
Net income	9,224
Dividends	5,883
Dividends per share	$1.46
Earnings per share	$2.17
Common stock*	4,238
Retained income	22,300
Shareholders equity	65,498

*number of shares in thousands

No of Employees: 410

HYDRIL COMPANY

PO Box 60458, 3300 North Belt East, Houston, TX 77205
Tel: (713) 449-2000
Telex: 168905 hydril csd hou

Chairman: Richard C Seaver
President: John B Griffiths
Senior Executive Officers: John F Hall (VP and Secretary), Larry B Wilber (Controller), Dennis W Winter (Treasurer), Charles Robinson (Assistant Treasurer)

PRINCIPAL ACTIVITIES: Oil and gas services and equipment
Principal Subsidiaries: Hydril Canadian Company Ltd; Hydril UK Ltd; Hydril Private Ltd; Hydril SA de CV; Hydril Africa Company; Hydril SpA (inactive); Hydril SA Company
Principal Banks: Security Pacific National Bank; Texas Commerce Bank NA
Financial Information:

	$'000
Sales revenues	200,000

No of Employees: 1,000

HYGIENE INDUSTRIES

295 Fifth Avenue, New York, NY 10016
Tel: (212) 689-6300

President: Noel Levine
Senior Executive Officers: H C V Lanen (Executive VP), Richard A Guggenheimer (Senior VP), Donald Stevens (VP Corporate Finance), Richard Silberman (VP Finance), Murray Mandel (VP Purchasing)

PRINCIPAL ACTIVITIES: Manufacture of table linen and bathroom accessories
Parent Company: Associated Products Inc
Principal Bank: Manufacturers Hanover Trust
Financial Information:

	$'000
Sales revenues	50,000

No of Employees: 1,000

HYGRADE FOOD PRODUCTS CORPORATION

PO Box 4771, Detroit, MI 48219
Tel: (313) 355-1100

Chairman: Newton Glekel (and Chief Executive Officer)
President: D C Riley (and Chief Operating Officer)
Senior Executive Officers: Frank Kirk (VP), John Harrington (VP), Carl Gylfe (VP Advertising), Rocco Minghine (VP Finance)

PRINCIPAL ACTIVITIES: Meat products; livestock feeds; fertilizers
Parent Company: Hanson Industries Inc
Principal Bank: Manufacturers National Bank of Detroit
Financial Information:

	$'000
Sales revenues	280,000

Principal Shareholders: Hanson Trust PLC, London, UK
No of Employees: 1,200

HYPLAINS DRESSED BEEF, INC

PO Box 539, Dodge City, KS 67801
Tel: (316) 227-7135

President: Sam V Davis
Senior Executive Officers: Ruth Davis (Secretary and Treasurer)

PRINCIPAL ACTIVITIES: Meat and meat processing
Principal Bank: First National Bank of Oklahoma City
Financial Information:

	$'000
Sales revenues	250,000

No of Employees: 230

HYPONEX CORPORATION

2013 S Anthony Blvd, Fort Wayne, IN 46803
Tel: (219) 422-6511

Chairman: Robert Rosenkranz
President: Donald A Sherman (and Chief Financial Officer)
Senior Executive Officers: Robert M Webb (VP Operations), Joseph Diogardi (VP Marketing)

PRINCIPAL ACTIVITIES: Agricultural and horticultural products
Principal Bank: Manufacturers Hanover Trust Company
Financial Information:

	$'000
Sales revenues	92,000

No of Employees: 530

HYSOL DIVISION

15051 E Don Julian Road, City of Industry, CA 91749
Tel: (213) 968-6511
Telex: TWX 910584 1342 hysol cal coid

President: Mike Devaney (Aerospace and Industrial Products Division); Ron Benham (Electronic Chemicals Division)
Senior Executive Officers: Cataldo Ciadella (Senior VP), Allen C Sheals (VP and General Manager Liquid Products), Charles Sharp (VP and Comptroller), Jeffery McClellan (VP and General Manager Aerospace Products), Charles Call (VP and General Manager Industrial Products)

PRINCIPAL ACTIVITIES: Manufacture of adhesives and resins
Parent Company: Dexter Corporation, Windsor Locks, CT
Principal Bank: Bank of America
Financial Information:

	$'000
Sales revenues	56,000

No of Employees: 310

HYSTER COMPANY

PO Box 2902, Portland, OR 97208
Tel: (503) 280-7000
Cable: Hyster Portlandore
Telex: 18-5999; 18-5904 hysterco ptl
Fax Transceiver: (503) 280-7326

Chairman: William H Kilkenny
President: J Phillip Frazier
Senior Executive Officers: Bergen I Bull (VP of Corporate Administration, General Counsel and Secretary), Jack P Greer (VP Sales of U.S.I.D.), Roger A Jensen (Controller), Ronald J Leptich (VP Engineering), David M Pollock (VP Managing Director, Hyster Europe Limited), James V Rose (Senior VP General Manager of U.S.I.D.), John M Scott (VP Tresurer), E Ned Snow (VP Corporate Manufacturing), James B Stewart (VP Finance), Herman Stoopman (VP Manufacturing, Hyster Europe), Robert D Strawser (President, Construction Equipment Division)

PRINCIPAL ACTIVITIES: Manufacture of fork lift trucks and construction equipment
Parent Company: Esco Corporation
Principal Bank: Morgan Guaranty Trust Company of New York

No of Employees: 4,690

I S JOSEPH COMPANY, INC

See JOSEPH, I S, COMPANY, INC

IA HOLDINGS CORPORATION

PO Box 8, Concordville, PA 19331
Tel: (215) 459-3136

Chairman: Charles A Ernst Jr; Vice Chairman: William W Gibb (and Chairman of Executive Committee)
President: George B Searle (and Chief Executive Officer)
Senior Executive Officers: Laurent J Lavigne (VP), Harry W Merz Jr (VP), Donald E Alford (Secretary and Treasurer)

PRINCIPAL ACTIVITIES: Manufacture of concrete paving materials; construction of airports and highways
Principal Subsidiaries: IA Construction Corporation
Principal Bank: Dauphin Deposit Bank & Trust
Financial Information:

	$'000
Sales revenues	65,000

No of Employees: 800

IBP, INC

Dakota City, NE 68731
Tel: (402) 494-2061

Chairman: Robert L Peterson (and President and Chief Executive Officer)
Senior Executive Officers: Perry V Haines (Executive VP), Maurice L McGill (Executive VP Finance and Administration), Russell A Walker (Senior VP Cattle Procurement), Troy C Calhoun (Group VP Engineering and Construction), David J LaFleur (Group VP Production), David C Layhee (Group VP Sales and Marketing), Daniel Foley (Group VP Human Resources), Lonnie O Grigsby (VP, Secretary and Legal Counsel), Kenneth W Browning (VP Hides), Richard L Bond (VP Boxed Beef Sales), George Spencer (VP Public Affairs), Kenneth L Rose (VP Transport)

PRINCIPAL ACTIVITIES: Meat production and meat packaging
Parent Company: Occidental Petroleum Corporation, Los Angeles, CA
Financial Information:

	$'000
Sales revenues	7,000,000

No of Employees: 12,300

IC INDUSTRIES, INC

One Illinois Center, Chicago, IL 60601
Tel: (312) 565-3000

Chairman: William B Johnson (and Chief Executive Officer)
President: Boyd F Schenk (and Chief Operating Officer)
Senior Executive Officers: Robert F Stewart (Senior Executive VP), John P Fagan (Executive VP Finance), Robert S Kirby (Executive VP Administration), Wendell W Larsen (Senior VP Corporate Affairs), Frank T Westover (Senior VP and Controller), Ronald A Wright (Senior VP Human Resources), Gary A Lee (VP Government Affairs), Wence F Cerne (VP Real Estate), J Robert Copper (VP Corporate Planning and Development), John F Palmer (VP Taxes), Alexander R Lehmann (VP Investor Relations), Charles H Connolly (VP Corporate Communications), Paul M O'Hara (VP Corporate Finance), Ralph J Switzer (VP and Treasurer), Richard D Neece (VP Financial Systems)

PRINCIPAL ACTIVITIES: Holding company with interests in the manufacture and bottling of soft-drinks; manufacture of automotive components; food products including dairy products, canned meat, seafood and bakery products; railroad transportation and real estate
Principal Subsidiaries: Pet Inc; Pepsi-Cola General Bottlers Inc; Midas International Corporation; Hussmann Corporation; Abex Corporation; Illinois Central Gulf Railroad; Pneumo Corporation
Principal Bank: Continental Illinois National Bank and Trust Co
Financial Information:

	Dec 31 1985	Dec 31 1986
	$'000	$'000
Sales revenues	5,292,100	4,439,400
Net income (loss)	162,800	(136,700)
Earnings (loss) per share	$3.04	($1.24)
Shareholders equity	1,638,600	1,528,400

No of Employees: 43,050

ICC INDUSTRIES, INC

720 Fifth Avenue, New York, NY 10019
Tel: (212) 903-1700
Telex: WUT 127787 icc trade nyk

Chairman: John G Farber
President: John L Oram
Senior Executive Officers: Robert C Podewils (Executive VP)

PRINCIPAL ACTIVITIES: Manufacture and sale of chemicals
Principal Bank: Marine Midland Bank
Financial Information:

	$'000
Sales revenues	300,000

No of Employees: 1,800

ICH CORPORATION

4211 Norbourne Blvd, Louisville, KY 40207
Tel: (502) 897-1861

Chairman: Robert T Shaw (and Chief Executive Officer)
President: John W Gardiner (and Chief Operating Officer)
Senior Executive Officers: C Fred Rice (Senior Executive VP Marketing and Real Estate), James R Kerber (Executive VP Insurance Operations), Phillip E Allen (Executive VP and General Counsel), Thomas J Brophy (Executive VP Insurance Operations), Webster H Hurley (Executive VP Insurance Operations), Marvin H Meyerson (Executive VP Insurance Operations), Barth T Murphy (Executive VP Insurance Operations),John T Hull (Senior VP and Treasurer), Paul Carmody (Senior VP and Chief Actuary), Lee G Baker (Senior VP and Chief Operating Officer), Steven B Bing (Senior VP Corporate Relations), Paul W Janus (Senior VP and Chief Actuary), W Sherman Lay (Senior VP), Gregory J Palmquist (Senior VP), Jack A Zimmer (Senior VP and Chief Financial Officer), Weldon Kern (VP)

PRINCIPAL ACTIVITIES: Insurance services including health and life
Principal Bank: MBank Dallas
Financial Information:

	$'000
Revenues	1,515,000

No of Employees: 4,000

ICN PHARMACEUTICALS INC

3300 Hyland Avenue, Costa Mesa, CA 92626
Tel: (714) 545 0100

Chairman: Milan Panic (and President and Chief Executive Officer)
Senior Executive Officers: Adam Jerney (Executive VP Operations), Jack Sholl (Senior VP, Public Relations), John Giordani (Senior VP Finance, Chief Financial Officer), Cari Matthews (VP General Council), Weldon B Jolley (VP R & D), Roland K Robins (VP), Roberts A Smith (VP), Bill A MacDonald (Senior VP Tax and Corporate Development and Corporate Development)

PRINCIPAL ACTIVITIES: Manufcture of pharmaceutical products
Principal Subsidiaries: ICN Biomedicals Inc; SPI Pharmaceuticals Inc; Viratex Inc
Principal Bank: Bank of America National Trust & Savings Association
Financial Information:

	1985	1986
	$'000	$'000
Sales revenues	62,780	102,770
Income (loss) before taxes	(18,280)	9,420
Net income (loss)	(20,450)	13,440
Earnings (loss) per share	($2.10)	$0.81
Common stock	10,790	19,753
Retained (deficit)	(30,790)	(16,770)
Shareholders equity	141,260	181,920

No of Employees: 1,600

ICO, INC

One Ridgmar Center, 6500 W Freeway Suite 320, Forth Worth, TX 76116
Tel: (817) 735-1331

Chairman: Bobby L Payne
President: Alan H Bush
Senior Executive Officers: Norman D Pool (Executive VP), Stephen D Houk (VP and Treasurer)

PRINCIPAL ACTIVITIES: Maintenance and repair of equipment for the oil industry
Principal Subsidiaries: Platte Rental Tools Co; Buck's Straightening Inc; UTS of Corpis Christi Inc; Pipeliners Inc; American Shotpeening Inc; Platte Rod and Pipe Co
Principal Bank: First City Bank of Dallas
Financial Information:

	Sep 30 1985	Sep 30 1986
	$'000	$'000
Sales revenues	60,007	38,219
(Loss) before taxes	(7,060)	(21,942)
Net (loss)	(4,998)	(21,283)
(Loss) per share	$(0.93)	($3.94)
Common stock	10,264	10,264
Retained income (deficit)	4,698	(16,585)
Shareholders equity (deficit)	16,963	(4,281)

No of Employees: 400

IDAHO FIRST NATIONAL BANK

101 South Capitol Blvd, PO Box 8247, Boise, ID 83733
Tel: (208) 383-7000
Telex: 368431 idalfirstbk bse

Chairman: Daniel Nelson
President: Robert Lane (and Chief Executive Officer)

Senior Executive Officers: V D Blickenstaff (Executive VP Asset and Liability Management), Donn A Miller (Senior VP), Thomas F Ripke Jr (Senior VP)

PRINCIPAL ACTIVITIES: Banking services
Parent Company: Moore Financial Group Inc (100%)
Principal Subsidiaries: Western Loan Corporation
Financial Information:

	Dec 31 1986	Dec 31 1987
	$'000	$'000
Income before taxes	14,682	36,672
Net income	13,836	25,768
Shareholders equity	175,902	190,670
Deposits	2,220,140	2,169,385
Total assets	2,727,789	2,838,795

No of Employees: 1,500

IDAHO POWER CO

PO Box 70, Boise, ID 83707
Tel: (208) 383-2200

Chairman: James E Bruce
President: Robert J O'Connor (and Chief Executive Officer)
Senior Executive Officers: Thomas A Spofford (Executive VP and Chief Operating Officer), Robert F Klumpp (Senior VP Finance), Logan E Lanham (Senior VP), L G Teply (VP Engineering), W W Anderson (VP Human Resources), C E Bissell (VP Power Plant Construction and Operation), Daniel K Bowers (VP and Treasurer), L R Gumoe (VP Divisional Operations), D D Hammond (VP and Controller), Paul L Jauregui (VP, Secretary and Legal Counsel), J W Marshall (VP Planning, Resources and Rates)

PRINCIPAL ACTIVITIES: Distribution of electricity
Principal Bank: Morgan Guaranty Trust Co
Financial Information:

	$'000
Sales revenues	409,000

No of Employees: 1,600

IDC SERVICES INC

303 East Ohio Street, Chicago, IL 60611
Tel: (312) 943 7500

Chairman: Charles C Townsend
President: Lawrence J Berkowitz
Senior Executive Officers: Martin B Robins (VP and Secretary)

PRINCIPAL ACTIVITIES: Business services including accounting and auditing; public relations
Principal Bank: American National Bank and Trust Company
Financial Information:

	$'000
Sales revenues	42,125

No of Employees: 500

IDEAL BASIC INDUSTRIES, INC

950 Seventeenth Street, Denver, CO 80202
Tel: (303) 623-5661

Chairman: Thomas E Bronson (and President and Chief Executive Officer)
Senior Executive Officers: Fred W Cohrs (Executive VP), Paavo T Tuominen (Senior VP)

PRINCIPAL ACTIVITIES: Manufacture of cement
Principal Subsidiaries: Louisana-Nevada Transit Co; Graysonia, Nashville & Ashdown Railroad Co; Ideal Development Corp; Kevaland Texas Corp; Kevaland Corp; Belmont Bay Investing Corp; Thorstenberg Materials Corp Inc; Ideal Cement Co (BC) Ltd; Braswell Concrete Products Inc; Braswell Industries Inc; Braswell Sand & Gravel Co Inc; Potash Resources Inc; Southern Cement Transport Inc; Ideal Dominicana
Principal Bank: North Carolina National Bank-Charlotte, NC

Financial Information:

	Dec 31 1985	Dec 31 1986
	$'000	$'000
Sales revenues	269,280	252,304
(Loss) before taxes	(390,683)	(21,408)
Net income (loss)	(513,622)	45,436
Earnings (loss) per share	($37.55)	$2.64
Common stock*	13,835	17,188
Retained (deficit)	(294,987)	(249,551)
Shareholders equity (deficit)	(146,910)	23,480

*average number of shares outstanding

Principal Shareholders: Holdernam Inc (68.2%); Philip F Anschutz (18%)
No of Employees: 1,517

IDEAL ELECTRIC COMPANY

330 East First Street, Mansfield, OH 44903
Tel: (419) 522-3611
Telex: 98-4710 Ideal Elec

President: Robert A Baynton
Senior Executive Officers: Lanny R Clark (VP International Sales, Field Service), Kenneth R Gerhardstein (VP Marketing), Robert G Currier (Manager Personnel), William S Logan (Chief Financial Officer)

PRINCIPAL ACTIVITIES: Manufacturer of large electric motors, generators and related switchgear 1,000 to 10,000 KW and 1,000 to 10,000 HP and larger
Parent Company: United Technologies, Hartford, CT; Carrier Corp, Syracuse, NY
Principal Bank: Mellon Bank
Financial Information:

	$'000
Sales revenues	50,000

No of Employees: 400

IDLE WILD FOODS, INC

256 Franklin Street, Worcester, MA 01604
Tel: (617) 757-7761

Directors: Ezra Zilkha, Anthony Geller
President: Anthony Geller
Senior Executive Officers: William Reeder (VP), Herbert Daitch (Chief Financial Officer), Rodney White (Treasurer), Roger Johnson (Secretary)

PRINCIPAL ACTIVITIES: Holding company with interests in meat and other food products; trucking; cattle feeding
Parent Company: Union Holdings, Inc
Principal Subsidiaries: National Beef Packing Company (Division); National Carriers Inc; Supreme Feeders (Division); Idle Wild Farm Incorporated
Financial Information:

	Aug 31 1985	Aug 31 1986
	$'000	$'000
Sales revenues	921,950	979,181

Principal Shareholders: Union Holdings, Inc (100%)
No of Employees: 2,700

IDS FINANCIAL CORPORATION

IDS Tower 10, Minneapolis, MN 55440
Tel: (612) 372-3131

President: Harvey Golub (and Chief Executive Officer)
Senior Executive Officers: Peter J Anderson (Senior Vp), Douglas M Baker (Senior VP), Karl J Breyer (Senior VP), Theodore H Busboom (Senior VP), William H Dudley (Executive VP), David R Hubers (Senior VP), John F Kelly (Senior VP), James A Mitchell (Senior VP), R Reed Saunders, Frank L Skillern Jr (Senior VP), John R Thomas (Senior VP), Richard R Weller (Senior VP), John J Wilke (Senior VP)

PRINCIPAL ACTIVITIES: IDS Financial Corporation is a leader in the financial planning field. More than 6,000 well-trained representatives offer individuals and businesses sound financial plans and the products and services to fulfill those plans. Among its many offerings are investment certificates, mutual funds, life insurance, annuities, unit investment trusts, individual retirement accounts, limited partnerships, and management and fiduciary services for pension and employee benefit plans

Trade Names: IDS

Parent Company: American Express Company

Principal Subsidiaries: IDS Life Insurance Company; IDS Financial Services Inc; Advisory Bank & Trust Company; IDS Management Corporation; IDS Property Casualty Insurance Company; IDS Certificate Company

Financial Information:

	Dec 31 1985	Dec 31 1986
	$'000	$'000
Revenues	2,200,579	2,394,914
Income before taxes	108,499	140,010
Net income	76,102	96,316
Retained income	108,675	142,269
Shareholders equity	921,449	955,151
Total assets owned	8,601,180	10,206,221
Total assets managed	15,557,000	19,978,000

Principal Shareholders: American Express Company

No of Employees: 2,800

IDS LIFE INSURANCE COMPANY

IDS Tower, Minneapolis, MN 55402

Tel: (612) 372-3131

Chairman: James A Mitchell (and President)

Senior Executive Officers: Earlon L Milbrath (Executive VP Operations), Richard W Kling (Executive VP Product Management), Rogert P Husenmoller (VP Intercorporate Development), Gerald D Johnson (VP Underwriting), John F Kelly (VP Sales), Paul F Kolkman (VP Finance), William H Dudley (VP), Jerald R Hoeft (VP, Treasurer and Controller), Ryan R Larson (VP Annuity and Group Product Development), Richard N Latzer (VP Investments), William F Nuessle (VP and Medical Director), Richard J O'Brien (VP, Secretary and Legal Counsel), Cathy H Waldhauser (VP, Corporate Actuary, Planning and Analysis)

PRINCIPAL ACTIVITIES: Insurance

Parent Company: American Express

Financial Information:

	Dec 31 1985	Dec 31 1986
	$'000	$'000
Premium income	1,438,520	1,213,298
Investment income	482,623	580,540

Principal Shareholders: American Express Company, New York, NY

No of Employees: 6,170

IFINT-CR INC

375 Park Ave, New York, NY 10022

Tel: (212) 421-9700

President: Alberto Cribiore

Senior Executive Officers: Andrea Geisser (Senior VP)

PRINCIPAL ACTIVITIES: Manufacture of motor vehicle bodies and components

Principal Subsidiaries: CR Industries; Moog Automotive Inc; Moog Canada Ltd; Rolero Inc; DJT Realty Co; Precision Universal Voint Corp; Precision Overseas Corp

Principal Bank: Chase Manhattan Bank

No of Employees: 1,200

ILC INDUSTRIES, INC

Airport Intl Plaza, Bohemia, NY 11716

Tel: (516) 567-5600

Telex: 510 2287324

Chairman: Leonard C Lane

Senior Executive Officers: Anthony W Trapani (Chief Executive Officer), Stuart H Aarons (Secretary)

PRINCIPAL ACTIVITIES: Manufacture of electronic equipment

Principal Bank: Barclays Bank of New York

Financial Information:

	$'000
Sales revenues	95,000

No of Employees: 1,600

ILLINOIS CENTRAL GULF RAILROAD COMPANY

233 N Michigan Avenue, Chicago, IL 60601

Tel: (312) 565-1600

Telex: TWX 910221 0951 icg rr cgo

Chairman: Harry J Bruce (and Chief Executive Officer)

President: James E Martin (and Chief Operating Officer)

Senior Executive Officers: D D Hagestad (Senior VP Marketing), A F Reardon (Senior VP Law), Glenn E Konker (Senior VP and Chief Financial Officer), W G Bumpus (Senior VP Operations), G G Hester (VP and Chief Transportation Officer), R A Irvine (VP Real Estate), J C Taylor (VP Communications and Computer Services), G S Stuckey (VP), D R Montgomery (VP and Comptroller), R P Bessette (VP Corporate Planning), G F Mohan (VP Market Development and Pricing), J H Curtis (VP Intermodal), R L Rushing (VP Sales), R J Neubauer (VP Coal)

PRINCIPAL ACTIVITIES: Operation of railroad services

Parent Company: IC Industries Inc, Chicago, IL

Principal Bank: Continental Illinois National Bank and Trust Co

Financial Information:

	Dec 31 1985	Dec 31 1986
	$'000	$'000
Sales revenues	1,026,493	715,462
Net income (loss)	29,968	(171,674)
Shareholders equity	661,717	339,265

No of Employees: 5,870

ILLINOIS CEREAL MILLS, INC

616 S Jefferson Street, Paris, IL 61944

Tel: (217) 465 5331

Chairman: W F Wiggins

President: Joseph W Hasler

Senior Executive Officers: James Buchanan (VP Grain), T A Russell (Secretary and Treasurer)

PRINCIPAL ACTIVITIES: Corn milling; grits

Principal Subsidiaries: Evans Milling Co Inc; Gurleys Inc; ICM Grain Co

Principal Bank: Harris Trust and Savings Bank

Financial Information:

	$'000
Sales revenues	90,000

No of Employees: 400

ILLINOIS MARINE BANCORP INC

105 S York Street, Elmhurst, IL 60126

Tel: (312) 834 2100

Chairman: Alben F Bates Jr

President: Frank C Rathje (and Chief Executive Officer)

Senior Executive Officers: Loren J Clark (Senior VP, Treasurer and Chief Financial Officer), James W Giffin (Senior VP), Robert D Sorenson (VP Operations), Michael Welgat (VP Trusts)

PRINCIPAL ACTIVITIES: Holding company with interests in banking
Principal Subsidiaries: Illinois Marine Bank
Principal Bank: Illinois Marine Bank
Financial Information:

	Dec 31 1985
	$'000
Revenues	44,870
Net income	3,060

No of Employees: 350

ILLINOIS POWER COMPANY

500 South 27th Street, Decatur, IL 62525
Tel: (217) 424-6600
Fax: (217) 424-6978

Chairman: Wendell J Kelley (and President)
Senior Executive Officers: William C Gerstner (Executive VP), Charles W Wells (Executive VP), Larry D Haab (Executive VP), William E Warren (Senior VP)

PRINCIPAL ACTIVITIES: Illinois Power Company is a public utility engaged primarily in the generation, transmission, distribution and sale of electric energy and the distribution and sale of natural gas in the state of Illinois
Principal Subsidiaries: IP Gas Supply Company; Illinois Power Fuel Company; IPF (Illinois Power Finance) Company NV
Principal Bank: Continental Illinois National Bank and Trust Company of Chicago
Financial Information:

	Dec 31 1985	Dec 31 1986
	$'000	$'000
Sales revenues	1,167,364	1,183,865
Net income before taxes	325,174	368,094
Net income	239,999	292,721
Dividends declared	191,796	207,956
Dividends per common share	$2.64	$2.64
Earnings per share	$3.48	$3.98
Common stock	1,140,531	1,210,686
Retained income	398,755	481,192
Shareholders equity	1,940,457	2,203,049

No of Employees: 4,600

ILLINOIS TOOL WORKS, INC

8501 W Higgins Road, Chicago, IL 60631
Tel: (312) 693-3040
Telex: ITT 4330353 illi corp cgo

Chairman: John D Nichols (and President and Chief Executive Officer); Chairman of Executive Committee: Harold B Smith Jr; Vice Chairman: J Thomas Schank
Senior Executive Officers: H R Crowther (Executive VP President, Plastiglide and Extruded Products), W J Farrell (Executive VP President, Specialty Mechanical and Chemical Products), Robert G Rettig (Executive VP President, Packaging Systems and Instrument Group), Steve A Stefan (Executive VP President, Industrial Components and Medical Products), Arthur M Wright (VP, Secretary and Legal Counsel), William S Gemmell (VP and Controller), Thomas W Buckman (VP Patents and Technical), David B Smith (VP and Treasurer), Stephen J Kaye (VP Corporate Communications), Michael H Hudson (VP Public Affairs), Sidney H Paige (VP Human Resources)

PRINCIPAL ACTIVITIES: Manufacture of electronic products, fasteners and tools, plastic products for packaging and chemical products
Principal Bank: The Northern Trust Company
Financial Information:

	Dec 31 1985	Dec 31 1986
	$'000	$'000
Sales revenues	596,130	961,077
Net income	31,550	79,583
Earnings per share	$1.25	$3.11
Shareholders equity	403,440	476,550

No of Employees: 7,300

IMC MAGNETICS CORPORATION

100 Jericho Quadrangle, Jericho, NY 11753
Tel: (516) 938-0800
Telex: TWX 510221 212 imc mag jrco

President: Fenimore Fisher (and Chief Executive Officer)
Senior Executive Officers: Richard Hofmann (Executive VP Aerospace Products, Eugene J Egan (VP Sales), Anthony J Gambale (VP Manufcturing), Anthony J Puglisi (VP Finance and Treasurer)

PRINCIPAL ACTIVITIES: Manufacture of fans, blowers, electrical and mechanical engineering equipment; valves, pumps, generators
Principal Bank: European American Bank
Financial Information:

	$'000
Sales revenues	58,000

No of Employees: 1,200

IMO DELAVAL INC

3450 Princeton Pike, Lawrenceville, NJ 08648
Tel: (609) 896-7600
Telex: 84-3333 DELAVAL LWRV

Chairman: W J Holcombe (and President and Chief Executive Officer)
Senior Executive Officers: P Garnick (Executive VP), J J Carr (Executive VP), Stephen F Agocs (VP and Secretary), D Neukranz (VP), R G Rittmann (VP and Treasurer and Chief Financial Officer)

PRINCIPAL ACTIVITIES: Production of valves, pumps and compressors; power equipment; industrial engines; process control equipment
Principal Bank: Philadelphia National Bank
Financial Information:

	Dec 31 1985	Dec 31 1986
	$'000	$'000
Sales revenues	384,700	358,414
Income (loss) before taxes	12,038	(10,580)
Net income (loss)	8,000	(10,986)
Dividends	8,000	-
Earnings (loss) per share	$1.10	($1.51)
Common stock	7,500	7,291
Retained income	178,863	167,877
Shareholders equity	205,399	197,579

No of Employees: 3,700

IMPERIAL BANCORP

Imperial Bank Bldg, 9920 Sth Lan Cienege Boulevard, Inglewood, CA 90301
Tel: (213) 417 5600

Chairman: George M Eltinge; Vice Chairman: George L Graziadio Jr (and President)
Senior Executive Officers: H Wayne Snavely (Executive VP and Chief Administration Officer), Norman P Creighton (1st Senior VP), Richard M Baker (Secretary and Legal Counsel)

PRINCIPAL ACTIVITIES: Banking
Principal Subsidiaries: Imperial Bank; Imperial Credit Corp; Imperial Management Inc; Imperial Plan; Imperial Trust Co; Imperial Ventures; Imperial Bank Realty Co; Imperial Thrift Loan Association
Principal Bank: Imperial Bank

Financial Information:

	Dec 31 1985
	$'000
Revenues	146,515
Net income	2,700

No of Employees: 900

IMPERIAL CORPORATION OF AMERICA

8787 Complex Drive, San Diego, CA 92123
Tel: (619) 292-6300

Chairman: Victor N Goulet
President: Kenneth J Thygerson (and Chief Executive Officer)
Senior Executive Officers: Stephen G Haines (Executive VP and Chief Administration Officer), Kevin E Villani (Executive VP and Chief Financial Officer), Earyle D Woodard (Executive VP and Treasurer), Richard M Geller (Executive VP), John M Robbins (Executive VP), William W Haynor (Senior VP), John M Kucey (Senior VP), Gary Palmer (Senior VP Corporate Finance and Treasury), Vernon A Nelson (VP and Controller), Claudia Thornton (VP), Lyle W Olson (VP), Richard B Vazquez (VP), Joseph A Zerwekh (VP, Secretary and Legal Counsel)

PRINCIPAL ACTIVITIES: Holding company with interests in financial services including savings and loans, real estate
Principal Bank: Bank of America
Financial Information:

	Dec 31 1985	Dec 31 1986
	$'000	$'000
Net income (loss)	(16,450)	50,340
Earnings (loss) per share	($1.16)	$3.55
Shareholders equity	175,688	226,313
Deposits	-	6,063,147
Total assets	8,046,970	9,597,240

No of Employees: 3,000

IMPERIAL INDUSTRIES, INC

15105 NW 77th Ave, Miami Lakes, FL 33014
Tel: (305) 557-2525

Chairman: Eugene C Ferri Jr (and President)
Senior Executive Officers: Daniel N Sherrick (Executive VP), Howard L Ehler Jr (VP)

PRINCIPAL ACTIVITIES: Holding company with interests in building supplies, electrical equipment and hardware
Principal Bank: Atlantic National Bank
Financial Information:

	$'000
Sales revenues	46,000

No of Employees: 150

IMPERIAL SUGAR COMPANY

PO Box 9, Sugar Land, TX 77478
Tel: (713) 491-9181
Telex: WUT 762659 impusugco sugl

Chairman: I H Kempner III (and Chairman of Executive Committee)
President: R C Hanna (and Chief Executive Officer)
Senior Executive Officers: A M Bartolo (Executive VP), W A Little (VP Sales), James R Skiles (VP Distribution), R E Henderson (VP Secretary and Treasurer)

PRINCIPAL ACTIVITIES: Sugar refining
Principal Bank: United States National Bank
Financial Information:

	$'000
Sales revenues	250,000

No of Employees: 630

IMS INTERNATIONAL, INC

800 Third Avenue, New York, NY 10022
Tel: (212) 371-2310
Cable: Imsglobe
Telex: 62923308

Chairman: Thomas J Russell Jr
President: Robert Louis-Dreyfus (and Chief Executive Officer)
Senior Executive Officers: Andrew L Clark (Chairman Emeritus), Dennis A Calvanese (Senior VP), Martin Steinmeyer (Senior VP, President, Communications Division), Christian Tourres (Senior VP President, Market Research Division), David A West (Senior VP), Hans Biedermann (VP), Hans Fischer (VP), Elisa Menicatti (VP), Serge Okun (VP), Brian Simpkin (VP), Norman Taylor (VP), Charles T Scott (Controller), John A Scott (Secretary and General Counsel), Andrea Pascual (Assistant Secretary)

PRINCIPAL ACTIVITIES: Market Research:- The Market Research Division is the Company's main line of business and provides information services and data base publishing oriented to marketing and general management in the health and personal care industries. Communications:- The Communications Division publishes or distributes a number of products and services primarily in the medical publishing and communications business. The Division also produces some professional and trade publications.
Principal Subsidiaries: IMS America Ltd; Institut Remy Genton Sarl (France); Pipeline Reseach Inc
Financial Information:

	Dec 31 1985	Dec 31 1986
	$'000	$'000
Sales revenues	272,394	375,543
Income before taxes	48,340	63,659
Net income	30,099	38,562
Dividends	3,297	5,262
Dividends per share	$0.085	$0.13
Earnings per share*	$0.71	$0.90
Common stock	204	410
Retained earnings	116,006	148,941
Shareholders equity	118,323	162,055

*fully diluted

No of Employees: 3,000

INACOMP COMPUTER CENTERS INC

1800 West Maple Road, Troy, MI 48084
Tel: (313) 649-5580

Chairman: Joseph T Inatome (and Executive VP)
President: Rick Inatome (and Chief Executive Officer)
Senior Executive Officers: Gerald B Blouch (Chief Financial Officer), Peter D Lytle (Controller), Ronald E McComas (VP-Operations), Michael M Ampe (President Michigan Region), Stephen L Cleary (Corporate Counsel), William Cumming (President Illinois Region), David R Dukes (President Florida and Georgia Region), Kemp C Gillis Sr (VP-Inacomp Financial Services Inc), Walter Kelly (VP-Human Relations), Luc Serriere (VP/General Manager California Region), Russell W Smith (President Inacomp Catalogue Marketing Inc), Richard Stopa (VP-Franchising Inacomp America Inc)

PRINCIPAL ACTIVITIES: Inacomp Computer Centers, Inc and its subsidiaries market microcomputer systems and related products and services
Principal Subsidiaries: Inacomp America Inc*; Inacomp Computer Centers of California Inc*; Inacomp Computer Centers of Georgia Inc*; ICC of Florida Inc*; ICC of Illinois Inc*; Inacomp Computer Centers of Michigan Inc*; Inacomp Financial Services Inc*, *Conducts business under the "Inacomp Computer Centers" name
Principal Bank: National Bank of Detroit

Financial Information:

	Aug 2 1986 $'000	Aug 1 1987 $'000
Total revenue	158,410	187,821
Income before taxes	1,833	4,933
Net income	1,025	2,420
Earnings per share net	$0.20	$0.45
Common stock	258	348
Retained income	4,945	7,365
Shareholders equity	16,039	32,201

No of Employees: 800

INCO ALLOYS INTERNATIONAL, INC

Huntington, WV 25720
Tel: (304) 696-2150

President: William F Bissett
Senior Executive Officers: John O Allen (Executive VP), Donald E DeBord (VP Materials), R R Bissett (VP Sales), John H Tundermann (VP Technology), John R Roche (Treasurer)

PRINCIPAL ACTIVITIES: Manufacture of nickel products and alloys
Parent Company: Inco United States Inc
Principal Bank: Morgan Guaranty Trust Co
Financial Information:

	$'000
Sales revenues	250,000

No of Employees: 3,000

INCOM INTERNATIONAL INC

415 Holiday Drive, Pittsburgh, PA 15220
Tel: (412) 928-3232

President: Richard H Allen (and Chief Executive Officer)
Senior Executive Officers: Paul L Soske (Treasurer and Chief Financial Officer), Richard D Erickson (President and Chief Operating Officer Power Transmission Group), Brian Lewis (President and Chief Operating Officer Controls Group)

PRINCIPAL ACTIVITIES: Manufacture and sale of power transmission equipment and mechanical controls
Parent Company: IFINT-Incom Inc
Principal Divisions: Boston Gear; Acme Chain; Heim; Fincor; Morse Controls; Controlex/Eanco; Morse Controls Ltd
Principal Bank: Mellon Bank, NA
Financial Information:

	$'000
Sales revenues	202,000

No of Employees: 2,900

INDEPENDENCE BANCORP INC

Corporate Center, North Fifth Street, PO Box 67, Perkasie, PA 18944
Tel: (215) 257 2402

Chairman: D Patrick M Robinson; Vice Chairman: Monroe W Long
President: R Roy Hager (and Chief Executive Officer)
Senior Executive Officers: Josseph P Abromitis (Senior VP Operations and Information Services), David L Astheimer (Senior VP Finance, Treasurer and Principal Financial Officer), Frederick E Schea (Controller, Assistant Treasurer and Principal Accounting Officer), J Lawrence Grim Jr (Legal Counsel), Feryl L Spanninger (Secretary), E Douglas Adams (Senior VP Special Projects and Assistant Secretary), Charlotte W Podowski (Senior VP Human Resources)

PRINCIPAL ACTIVITIES: Holding company with interests in banking
Principal Subsidiaries: Cheltenham Bank; Union Bank & Trust Co of Eastern PA
Principal Bank: Bucks County Bank & Trust Co

No of Employees: 1,000

INDEPENDENCE HOLDING COMPANY

96 Cummings Point Road, Stamford, CT 06902
Tel: (203) 358 8000

Chairman: Frank J Hermann (and Chief Executive Officer); Vice Chairman: Edward Netter
Senior Executive Officers: David E Anderson (Executive VP), Bernard M Croghan (Executive (VP), Bruce Crystal (VP), Roy T K Thung (Treasurer and Chief Financial Officer)

PRINCIPAL ACTIVITIES: Operation and management of non-residential properties
Principal Bank: Fleet National Bank
Financial Information:

	$'000
Sales revenues	85,000

No of Employees: 350

INDEPENDENT INSURANCE GROUP INC

One Independent Drive, Jacksonville, FL 32276
Tel: (904) 358 5151

Chairman: Wilford C Lyon Jr (and Chief Executive Officer)
President: Jacob F Bryan IV
Senior Executive Officers: Wilford C Lyon Sr (First VP), J Alex Howard (VP and Secretary), Boyd E Lyon (VP, Treasurer and Chief Financial Officer)

PRINCIPAL ACTIVITIES: Life insurance services
Principal Subsidiaries: Independent Life Accident Insurance Co
Principal Bank: Flordia First National Bank
Financial Information:

	$'000
Revenues	426,750

No of Employees: 5,500

INDIAN HEAD BANKS INC

One Indian Head Plaza, Nashua, NH 03060
Tel: (603) 880 5000

Chairman: James E Chandler
President: Hollis E Harrington Jr (and Chief Executive Officer)
Senior Executive Officers: Robert P Keller (Executive VP, Treasurer and Secretary), Donald E Bossi (Senior VP and Director Special Projects and Marketing), Bradford F Alden (Senior VP Customer Service), Bruce N Johnstone (Loan Policy and Administration), Arthur L Barrett Jr (VP Business Development), Arthur H Dyer (VP Investment), Alan J Cieto (VP and Controller), James C Real (VP Consumer Financial Services), Donald R Brabant (VP Consumer Financial Services), Ilene McCune (VP Human Resources), Clarke R Chandler (VP Auditing)

PRINCIPAL ACTIVITIES: Banking
Principal Subsidiaries: Indian Head Bank & Trust Co; Indian Head Data Services Inc; Indian Head National Bank
Principal Bank: Bank of New England

No of Employees: 100

INDIANA & MICHIGAN ELECTRIC CO

One Summit Square, PO Box 60, Fort Wayne, IN 46801
Tel: (219) 425 2111

Chairman: W S White Jr (and Chief Executive Officer)
President: William A Black (and Chief Operating Officer)
Senior Executive Officers: Jack F Stark (Senior VP), Milton P Alexich (VP), William N D'Onofrio (VP), Richard E Disbrow (VP), John E Dolan (VP), A Joseph Dowd (VP), Richard F Hering (VP), Gerald P Maloney (VP), Richard C Menge (VP), Joseph H Vipperman (VP), Peter J DeMaria (Treasurer), John R Burton (Secretary)

PRINCIPAL ACTIVITIES: Generation and distribution of electricity
Parent Company: American Electric Power Company Inc

Financial Information:

	$'000
Sales revenues	1,059,900

No of Employees: 3,000

INDIANA FARM BUREAU CO-OPERATIVE ASSN, INC

120 E Market Street, Indianapolis, IN 46204
Tel: (317) 631-8361
Telex: TWX 810 3413 17 f b coop indp

President: Charles Kerber
Senior Executive Officers: Philip French (Executive VP), Russell White (VP), C G Mitchener (Treasurer)

PRINCIPAL ACTIVITIES: Co-operative for the distribution of farm produce and supplies; manufacture of animal feed and fertilizers
Principal Bank: The Indiana National Bank
Financial Information:

	Aug 31 1985	Aug 31 1986
	$'000	$'000
Sales revenues	1,185,830	892,453

No of Employees: 950

INDIANA GAS CO INC

1630 North Meridian Street, Indianapolis, IN 46202
Tel: (317) 926 3351

Chairman: Duane M Amundson (and Chief Executive Officer)
President: Lawrence A Ferger (and Chief Operating Officer)
Senior Executive Officers: Robert D Stegner (Senior VP Operations and Engineering), Christopher M Crawford (VP Administration), William R Mullis (VP Operations), Jack L Diley (Controller), Niel C Ellerbrook (VP Finance and Chief Financial Officer), R Lewis Squires (Treasurer), Julian G Piercefield (Secretary), Paul T Baker (VP Marketing and Government Affairs), Wendell L Thaler (VP Engineering), Anthony E Ard (VP Public Affairs)

PRINCIPAL ACTIVITIES: Distribution of natural gas
Parent Company: Indiana Energy Inc
Principal Subsidiaries: IGC Energy Inc; Ohio River Pipeline Corp
Principal Bank: Merchants National Bank & Trust
Financial Information:

	$'000
Sales revenues	420,000

No of Employees: 1,150

INDIANA NATIONAL CORPORATION

One Indiana Square, Indianapolis, IN 46266
Tel: (317) 266-6000

Chairman: Thomas P Miller (and Chief Executive Officer); Vice Chairman: Andrew J Paine Jr
President: David W Givens
Senior Executive Officers: J Frederic Wiese Jr (Executive VP), Percy N Clark (Executive VP), Steven J Schenck (VP and Chief Financial Officer), John H Fry (Senior VP), James J Kommann (Senior VP), Lloyd C Lyons (Senior VP), Gary K McWilliams (Senior VP), Robert E Schneider (Senior VP, Legal Counsel and Secretary), Frank A Shackelford (Senior VP), John R Walsh (Senior VP)

PRINCIPAL ACTIVITIES: Bank holding company
Principal Subsidiaries: Indiana National Bank (100%)
Financial Information:

	Dec 31 1985	Dec 31 1986
	$'000	$'000
Net income	32,100	43,008
Earnings per share	$3.35	$3.49
Shareholders equity	263,460	333,957
Deposits	3,361,860	3,815,917
Total assets	4,391,470	5,106,296

No of Employees: 2,917

INDIANAPOLIS WATER COMPANY

1220 Waterway Boulevard, Indianapolis, IN 46202
Tel: (317) 639 1501

President: Dale B Luther (and Chief Executive Officer)
Senior Executive Officers: Robert J Becker (Executive VP Operations), Michael G Hinkle (Senior VP and Treasurer), Stephen G Lyons (Senior VP Engineering), Joseph R Broyles (Senior VP), Joseph W Jordan (Secretary), J Darrell Bakken (VP Engineering), Paul K Doane (VP Distribution), Kenneth N Giffin (VP Human Resources and Consumer Relations), David S Probst (VP Customer Service)

PRINCIPAL ACTIVITIES: Water supply
Parent Company: IWC Resources Corp
Principal Subsidiaries: Compucom Development Corp
Principal Bank: Merchants National Bank
Financial Information:

	$'000
Sales revenues	44,500

No of Employees: 350

INDUCTOTHERM INDUSTRIES INC

10 Indel Avenue, Rancocas, NJ 08073
Tel: (609) 267-9000
Telex: TWX 6851048

President: Henry M Rowan Jr
Senior Executive Officers: Robert Hotchkin (Treasurer)

PRINCIPAL ACTIVITIES: Manufacture of industrial furnaces
Principal Subsidiaries: Magnetic Metals Corporation
Principal Bank: Provident National Bank
Financial Information:

	$'000
Sales revenues	240,000

No of Employees: 2,700

INDUSTRIAL ACOUSTICS COMPANY, INC

1160 Commerce Avenue, Bronx, NY 10462
Tel: (212) 931-8000
Telex: WUT 125880 i a c nyk

Chairman: Martin Hirschorn (and President)
Senior Executive Officers: Frederic M Oran (Executive VP), Arnold W Kanarek (Senior VP and Secretary), John M Handley (Senior VP Marketing), Morton I Schiff (VP Sales), Kirit K Kapadia (VP Finance), Ellis E Singer (VP Sales), Robert E Schmitt (VP Sales), James Morgan (VP Research and Development), Sy Wasserman (VP Engineering), Henry Lauro (VP Manufacturing), William E Fry (VP Sales), Jasjit T Ahluvalia (VP Management Information Services)

PRINCIPAL ACTIVITIES: Manufacture of noise control and other pollution control equipment
Principal Subsidiaries: Argo of PA Inc
Principal Bank: Irving Trust Company
Financial Information:

	$'000
Sales revenues	57,780

No of Employees: 550

INEXCO OIL COMPANY

Republicbank Center, 700 Louisiana Street, Suite 2100, Houston, TX 77002
Tel: (713) 546 3500

President: Erving Wolf (and Chief Executive Officer)
Senior Executive Officers: Coles S Tinkler (Executive VP), Michael J August (VP Finance), Edmund A Giese Jr (Treasurer), William N Shaefer (Controller), Robert L Zieve (VP Exploration), Arthur S Berner (VP Public Relations, Secretary and Legal Counsel), William G Goodwin (VP Land), N A Prince (VP Production)

PRINCIPAL ACTIVITIES: Exploration and production of oil and natural gas
Parent Company: Louisiana Land & Exploration Co
Principal Subsidiaries: Inexco Energy Co Canada Ltd; Inexco Gas Transmission Co; Inexco Mining Co; Inexco Securities Co; Wilson Brothers Drilling Co; Wilson Brothers Corp
Principal Bank: Texas Commerce Bank
Financial Information:

	$'000
Sales revenues	145,000

No of Employees: 790

INFLIGHT SERVICES INC
485 Madison Avenue, New York, NY 10022
Tel: (212) 751 1800

Chairman: James P Hassett (and President and Chief Executive Officer)
Senior Executive Officers: Anthony Latessa (Senior VP Operations), Robert J Brooks (Senior VP Marketing), John J Wills (VP, Treasurer and Chief Financial Officer), John G McMahan (VP Media), Peter H Honnegger (VP Sales)

PRINCIPAL ACTIVITIES: Provision of equipment leasing services; supply of movies for aircraft and offshore installations
Principal Bank: Chase Manhattan Bank
Financial Information:

	$'000
Sales revenues	40,000

No of Employees: 300

INFORMATICS GENERAL CORPORATION
21031 Ventura Blvd, Suite 800, Woodland Hills, CA 91364
Tel: (818) 887-9040

Chairman: Walter F Bauer (and Chief Executive Officer)
President: Bruce T Coleman (and Chief Operating Officer)
Senior Executive Officers: Richard C Lemons (Executive VP), Jeannette Meier Zacker (VP, Secretary and Legal Counsel)

PRINCIPAL ACTIVITIES: Development and marketing of software; data processing services
Principal Bank: Bankers Trust Co
Financial Information:

	$'000
Sales revenues	190,000

No of Employees: 2,600

INFORMATION HANDLING SERVICES
15 Inverness Way E, Englewood, CO 80150
Tel: (303) 790-0600
Telex: ITT 4322083 ihs ui

President: Michael J Timbers
Senior Executive Officers: Robert Jordan (Executive VP Sales, Marketing and Product Management), L Christopher Meyer (VP Finance), Michael Biery (Senior VP Human Resources and Administration Services), Rudy Rutelionis (Senior VP Product Development), Bernie Michalek (VP Marketing), Art Salmons (VP Manufacturing), Robert Wing (VP International Sales)

PRINCIPAL ACTIVITIES: Publishing and information services
Parent Company: TBG NV
Principal Bank: The Central Bank and Trust Company
Financial Information:

	$'000
Sales revenues	50,000

No of Employees: 1,000

INFORMATION RESOURCES INC
150 North Clinton Street, Chicago, IL 60606
Tel: (312) 726 1221

Chairman: John Malec; Vice Chairman: Gerald Eskin
President: Gian Fulgoni (and Chief Executive Officer)
Senior Executive Officers: Steven C Page (Executive VP, Chief Financial Officer, Secretary and Treasurer)

PRINCIPAL ACTIVITIES: Development of computerized data bases; software
Principal Bank: Harris Trust and Savings Bank
Financial Information:

	Dec 31 1985	Dec 31 1986
	$'000	$'000
Sales revenues	75,060	94,000
Net income	8,730	10,000

No of Employees: 1,000

INFOTRON SYSTEMS CORPORATION
9 North Olney Avenue, Cherry Hill Industrial Center, Cherry Hill, NJ 08003
Tel: (609) 424-9400
Telex: 7109401247
Fax: (609) 424-6461

Chairman: Robert E Purcell
President: James C Hahn (and Chief Executive Officer)
Senior Executive Officers: Gerald Rhoades (Executive VP, Chief Operating Officer and Treasurer), David P Barnhill (Senior VP of Finance and Chief Financial Officer), Clarence Barnes (VP of Business Development), Robert J Bauer (VP of Corporate Development), Richard T Mullen (VP of Technical Services), Norman San Soucie (VP of Manufacturing), Steven Stuart (VP of Marketing), David Morris (VP of Engineering), Robert D Francis (VP of Sales)

PRINCIPAL ACTIVITIES: Infotron designs, manufactures, markets and services a wide range of data communications equipment, utilized in both private and public data communications networks. Its principal products include data multiplexers, modems, intelligent switching systems and network concentrators
Principal Subsidiaries: Infotron Systems Limited (UK); Infotron Canada Limited (Canada); Infotron Puerto Rico, Inc (Puerto Rico)
Financial Information:

	Dec 31 1985	Dec 31 1986
	$'000	$'000
Sales revenues	72,199	81,049
Income (loss) before taxes	4,450	(4,503)
Net income (loss)	3,703	(2,335)
Earnings (loss) per share	$0.72	($0.45)
Common stock	52	52
Retained income	26,643	24,308
Shareholders equity	61,959	59,955

No of Employees: 1,000

INGALLS SHIPBUILDING, INC, DIVISION OF LITTON INDUSTRIES, INC
1000 W River Road, Box 149, Pascagoula, MS 39568
Tel: (601) 935-1122
Telex: TWX 510990 3051 lamps purch ms

President: G J St Pe' (and Senior VP Litton Industries Inc)
Senior Executive Officers: W P Keene (VP Operations), Mark Farnum (VP Programs Management), J R Lindgren (VP Engineering), E B Robbins (VP Administration), D F Knecht (VP Industrial Public Relations)

PRINCIPAL ACTIVITIES: Shipbuilding and repair
Parent Company: Litton Industries Inc, Beverly Hills, CA
Financial Information:

	$'000
Sales revenues	1,193,000

Principal Shareholders: Litton Industries Inc, Beverly Hills, CA
No of Employees: 12,000

INGERSOLL-RAND COMPANY

200 Chestnut Ridge Road, Woodcliff Lake, NJ 07675
Tel: (201) 573-0123

Chairman: Thomas A Holmes (and President and Chief Executive Officer); Vice Chairman: Clyde H Folley (and Chief Financial Officer)
Senior Executive Officers: James E Perrella (Executive VP), Richard D Wendeborn (Executive VP), William J Armstrong (VP and Treasurer), Thomas E Bennett (VP), Frank A DelleCave (VP), M William Grant (VP), Frederick W Hadfield (VP), Robert D Krumme (VP and General Counsel), Thomas E McBride (VP and Comptroller), William G Mulligan (VP), Robert G Ripston (VP), Francesco Rosati (VP), Gerald E Swimmer (VP), Robert T Boyd (Secretary), Sidney W Templeton (Assistant Secretary)

PRINCIPAL ACTIVITIES: Manufacturing of a wide range of mechanical engineering equipment including drilling equipment, pumps, compressors and machinery for the paper industry
Principal Subsidiaries: Ingersoll-Rand Financial Corporation
Principal Bank: Chase Manhattan Bank NA
Financial Information:

	Dec 31 1985	Dec 31 1986
	$'000	$'000
Sales revenues	2,637,421	2,799,481
Income before taxes(1)	132,681	154,334
Net income	79,581	93,974
Dividends	56,137	56,367
Dividends per common share	$2.60	$2.60
Dividends per pref share	$2.35	$2.35
Earnings per share(2)	$3.78	$4.43
Common stock	39,784	40,107
Retained income	964,866	1,002,473
Shareholders equity	1,031,960	1,178,365

(1) and extraordinary item
(2) fully diluted

No of Employees: 29,857

INGRAM INDUSTRIES INC

4304 Harding Rd, Nashville, TN 37210
Telex: WUT 554419 ingram nas

President: E Bronson Ingram
Senior Executive Officers: Philip Maurice Pfeffer (Executive VP), John M Donnelly Jr (Executive VP), Thomas L Lunn (VP and Treasurer), Michael L Goldblatt (VP and Secretary), R E Claverie (VP and Controller)

PRINCIPAL ACTIVITIES: Distribution of software for personal computers; interests in barge transportation, oilfield drilling equipment and the production of oil and coal
Financial Information:

	$'000
Sales revenues	750,000

No of Employees: 1,700

INGREDIENT TECHNOLOGY CORPORATION

10 Pelham Pkwy, Box 505, Pelham Manor, NY 10803
Tel: (914) 738-4446

President: Rudolf Eberstadt Jr (and Chief Executive Officer)
Senior Executive Officers: James M Harrison (VP, Secretary and Treasurer), J Carey Hutchison (VP), R Dale McDowell (VP), J Ted Theriault (VP), Allan P Howell (VP), David G Mohr (VP), J E Salomon (VP), William P Shevis (Controller)

PRINCIPAL ACTIVITIES: Manufacture of sugar products, baking supplies and flavorings
Principal Subsidiaries: Archibald & Kendall Inc; Beaver Home Products Inc; Breddo-Food Products Corp Inc; Grandma Food Products Inc (Canada); Neumann-Buslee and Wolfe Inc
Principal Bank: Bankers Trust Company
Financial Information:

	$'000
Sales revenues	93,000

No of Employees: 500

INLAND CONTAINER CORPORATION

151 N Delaware, Indianapolis, IN 46206
Tel: (317) 262-0222
Telex: 810 341 3112

Chairman: Ben J Lancashire (and President and Chief Executive Officer)
Senior Executive Officers: J E Cory (Senior VP), R B Morse (Senior VP), E B Ciotti (Senior VP), William A Long (Group VP), W E Babin (Group VP), Joseph M Areddy (VP Public Affairs), David J Harrison (VP Employee Relations and Staff Services)

PRINCIPAL ACTIVITIES: Manufacture of containers for shipping and and other solid fiber and corrugated boxes
Parent Company: Temple-Inland Inc
Principal Subsidiaries: Anderson Box Company
Principal Bank: The Indiana National Bank
Financial Information:

	$'000
Sales revenues	750,000

No of Employees: 5,500

INLAND DIVISION

PO Box 1224, Dayton, OH 45401
Tel: (513) 267-5000

Senior Executive Officers: Ross M Haun (General Manager), D G Schafer (Division Comptroller), C A Anderson (Personnel Director), D R Levering (Development Director), A H Billis (Materials Management Director), R J McCuen (General Manufacturing Manager)

PRINCIPAL ACTIVITIES: Manufacture of components for motor vehicles
Parent Company: General Motors Corporation, Detroit, MI
Principal Bank: Bank One
Financial Information:

	$'000
Sales revenues	900,000

No of Employees: 19,000

INLAND STEEL INDUSTRIES, INC

30 West Monroe Street, Chicago, IL 60603
Tel: (312) 346-0300

Chairman: Frank W Luerssen (and Chief Executive Officer)
President: Robert J Darnall (and Chief Operating Officer)
Senior Executive Officers: O Robert Nottelmann (Senior VP), David B Anderson (VP, Corporate Planning and General Counsel), Theodore A Myers (VP, Finance), Jay E Dittus (Treasurer), Thomas L Gleason (Comptroller), Clark L Wagner (Secretary and Assistant General Counsel), Stephen R Wilson (Assistant Treasurer)

PRINCIPAL ACTIVITIES: Inland Steel Industries, Inc is a holding company whose principal activities, which are conducted by wholly owned subsidiaries, are centered in the following two business segments: Integrated Steel Operations: The Indiana Harbor Works of Inland Steel Company located in East Chicago, Indiana, manufactures four principal lines of products: sheets, bars, plates and structurals. Wholly and jointly owned sources in the US and Canada furnish most of the iron ore, and limestone required for steelmaking. The Company maintains its own Great Lakes carriers and railroad hopper cars for the transportation of raw materials. Steel product and process research is conducted at the Inland Steel Research Laboratories in East Chicago. Steel Service Center Operations: Inland Steel Industries, Inc has two service center subsidiaries-Joseph T Ryerson & Son, Inc and

J M Tull Metals Company, Inc. Ryerson is the nation's largest materials service center organization with 26 full-service plants in major cities of the US. It is headquartered in Chicago. J M Tull, which was acquired in May 1986, is based in Norcross, Georgia, near Atlanta. Tull operates 10 service centers and two processing facilities in the south-eastern portion of the US

Principal Subsidiaries: Joseph T Ryerson & Son Inc; J M Tull Metals Co, Inc

Financial Information:

	Dec 31 1985	Dec 31 1986
	$'000	$'000
Sales revenues	2,998,400	3,173,200
Net income (loss)	(178,400)	19,300
Dividends(1)	17,300	7,800
Dividends per common share	$0.375	-
Income (loss) per share	($7.37)	$0.40
Common stock(2)	25,266	28,479
Shareholders equity	958,400	1,067,700

(1) common and preferred
(2) average number of shares in thousands

No of Employees: 22,668

INMED CORPORATION

3030 B Holcomb Ridge Road, Norcross, GA 30071
Tel: (404) 446 3004

President: Roland Petersen-Frey
Senior Executive Officers: Gregory D Alexander (Controller and Secretary), Dan J Cuddy (VP Finance)

PRINCIPAL ACTIVITIES: Manufacture of surgical and medical equipment and supplies including catheters
Principal Bank: Trust Company Bank
Financial Information:

	$'000
Sales revenues	34,000

No of Employees: 1,060

INSILCO CORPORATION

1000 Research Parkway, Meriden, CT 06450
Tel: (203) 634-2000
Telex: (203) 634-2022

Chairman: Donald J Harper (and President and Chief Executive Officer)
Senior Executive Officers: John A McLendon (Executive VP and Chief Operating Officer), George E Peterson Jr (VP, General Counsel), William E Baer (VP), Gregory B Howey (Executive VP-Administration and Planning), Henry L DyKema (VP-Finance), John C Scott (VP), Malcolm S Todt (VP and Treasurer), John J Weber (VP and Controller), Herbert F Kahler (VP), Randolph B Marston (VP President, Taylor Publishing Company). Subsidiary Presidents: High Technology Supplier Sector:- Ving Paulson (Basic Industries), Peter J Meehan (Computer Circuitry Group Inc), Hugh Arnold (Signal Transformer Co, Inc), Gilbert H Boas (Stewart Stamping Corporation), Barry W Clark (Steel Parts Corporation), C Bari Saunders (Thermal Components, Inc), John W Clark (Valentec International Corporation). Specialty Consumer Products Sector:-Richard Cornwall (Miles Homes Companies), Frederick J Betz (Nationwide Homes, Inc), Donald H Gels (Red Devil Company), Robert M Sinclair (Sinclair Paint Company), Randolph B Marston (Taylor Publishing Company), Robert W Burton (Rolodex Corporation), William A Luca (Dual-Lite, Inc)

PRINCIPAL ACTIVITIES: Suppliers to High Technology Sector: metal parts machining mainly for mainframe computer drives; specialized wire harnesses, coaxial cable and external cable assemblies for the computer industry; design and manufacture of transformers; small precision parts from metal strip, wire and plastic that link components for the electronics industry, manufacturer of battery operated emergency lighting equipment and systems, steel parts including metal automobile parts, high volume precision stamping, finishing and assembly; heat exchange products; metal cartridges, cartridge link belts and projectiles for the defense industry. Specialty Consumer Products Sector: supply of pre-cut homes to do-it-yourself builder; supply of modular housing; manufacture of consumer and industrial paint products; publishing; desk top and rotary files, list finders and paper punches
Trade Names: Label Express, Rolodex, Type Vision, Index Vision
Principal Subsidiaries: Basic Industries; Computer Circuitry Group; Signal Transformer; Stewart Stamping; Steel Parts; Thermal Components; Valentec International; Miles Homes; Nationwide Homes; Red Devil Paints Company; Sinclair Paint; Taylor Publishing; Rolodex Corporation; Dual-Lite Inc
Principal Bank: Morgan Guaranty Trust Company of New York; Citibank, NA; Canadian Imperial Bank of Commerce Trust Company
Financial Information:

	Dec 31 1985	Dec 31 1986
	$'000	$'000
Sales revenues	811,780	745,059
Income before taxes (1)	56,811	47,221
Net income	26,119	33,345
Dividends	19,230	20,035
Dividends per share (2)	$0.95	$0.95
Earnings per share (2)	$1.37	$1.66
Common stock	20,263	21,357
Retained income	102,257	95,690
Shareholders equity	314,815	330,560

(1) From continuing operations
(2) Adjusted to give effect to 5% stock dividends

No of Employees: 7,800

INSPIRATION CONSOLIDATED COPPER COMPANY

8655 E Via De Ventura (G-350), Scottsdale, AZ 85258
Tel: (602) 998-0888
Telex: 261-756

Chairman: John J Ellis (and President and Chief Executive Officer)
Senior Executive Officers: Jacob Timmers (Senior VP Operations), Robert A Prescott (VP and General Manager), Robert F Morison (VP Finance and Administration and Secretary)

PRINCIPAL ACTIVITIES: Copper mining and processing and manufacture of copper products
Parent Company: Inspiration Resources Corporation, New York, NY
Principal Bank: First Interstate Bank of Arizona
Financial Information:

	$'000
Sales revenues	171,000

No of Employees: 900

INSPIRATION RESOURCES CORPORATION

250 Park Avenue, New York, NY 10177
Tel: (212) 503-3100
Telex: 291533 (IRCUR)

Chairman: Reuben F Richards (and President)
Senior Executive Officers: Richard S Davis (Senior VP, General Counsel), Adrian M Doull (Senior VP, Group Executive), William H Frank (Senior VP, CFO), J Blair Howkins (Senior VP, Group Executive), Clifford H R DuPree (Corporate Secretary, Assistant General Counsel), John H Melville (Treasurer), M Brian O'Shaughnessy (Senior VP, Marketing), Evert T Bron (VP, Technical), Kenneth C Brown (VP, Planning

and Development), Angelo R Peluso (VP, Human Resources), Michael B Smith (VP, Finance)

PRINCIPAL ACTIVITIES: A diversified natural resources and energy company with interests in agricultural products and services, nonferrous and precious metals, petroleum, venture capital and coal

Principal Subsidiaries: Inspiration Consolidated Copper Company; Hudson Bay Mining and Smelting Co Ltd; Terra International, Inc; Inspiration Coal, Inc; Inspiration Mines, Inc; Danville Resources, Inc; Madison Resources, Inc

Principal Bank: Chemical Bank

Financial Information:

	Dec 31 1986
	$'000
Sales revenues	1,098,835
Net income	37,846
Earnings per share	$0.59
Shareholders equity	316,523

No of Employees: 6,700

INSTRON CORPORATION

100 Royall Street, Canton, MA 02021
Tel: (617) 828-2500
Telex: 924434

Chairman: Harold Hindman (and Chief Execuitve Officer)
President: Salvatore J Vinciguerra (and Chief Operating Officer)
Senior Executive Officers: George S Burr (Vice-Chairman of the Board), Andre P Sampou (VP and General Manager, Western Hemisphere), Donald R Meltzer (VP of Finance and Treasurer), John H Griffiths (VP-Corporate Technical Director, Ian M MacGregor (VP and Managing Director of Instron Limited)

PRINCIPAL ACTIVITIES: Instron develops, manufactures, markets and services materials testing instruments, systems and accessories for assessing the physical and mechanical characteristics of materials. The Company's products are used principally in research and development and quality control applications to test the strength, elasticity and other properties of materials such as plastics, metals, rubbers and textiles. Instron offers a comprehensive range of materials testing instruments. In the worldwide market for these instruments, Instron is the leading producer of static (electromechanical) instruments and is one of the three leading producers of dynamic (servohydraulic) instruments. Static instruments typically stretch or compress the material being tested at a user-selected, constant speed. These instruments measure precisely the force being applied and the resulting deformation of the material. Dynamic products use a hydraulic actuator to apply the test force instead of the screw drive system used in static products. Because the actuator allows a test to be repeated with great rapidity, dynamic instruments can simulate quickly the stretching compressing, twisting or bending effects of using a material over a long period of time. Instron's products are typically assembled from a number of standard modules and accessories, selected and configured for the customer's specific application. Additional modules or accessories may be purchased at a later date. All new instruments are microprocessor based, and the more complex instruments have the ability to interface with minicomputers and microcomputers which enhance control of the test and analysis of test data

Trade Names: INSTRON

Principal Subsidiaries: Instron Ltd (UK); Instron International (UK); Instron SA (France); Instron Pty Ltd (Australia); Instron Canada Ltd (Canada); Instron Asia Ltd (Japan); Instron Japan Company Ltd (Japan); Equipamentos Cientificos Instron Ltda (Brazil)

Principal Bank: First National Bank of Boston

Financial Information:

	Dec 31 1985	Dec 31 1986
	$'000	$'000
Sales revenues	78,917	87,384
Income before taxes	7,099	8,288
Net income	4,279	4,664
Dividends	589	692
Dividends per share	$0.099	$0.115
Earnings per share	$0.69	$0.75
Common stock	6,002	6,020
Retained income	22,073	26,045
Shareholders equity	23,795	28,213

No of Employees: 1,000

INSTRUMENT SYSTEMS CORPORATION

100 Jericho Quadrangle, Jericho, NY 11753
Tel: (516) 938-5544

Chairman: Harvey R Blau (and Chief Executive Officer)
President: Robert Balemian (and Chief Operating Officer)
Senior Executive Officers: H Fleming (VP), Myron Levy (VP), Susan E Reilly (Secretary)

PRINCIPAL ACTIVITIES: Manufacture of electronic equipment and household furnishings and hardware

Principal Subsidiaries: Buildex Inc; Instrument Management Corp; Lightron Corp; Markstone Manufacture Co; SKG Realty Corp; Telephonics Corp

Principal Bank: National Westminster Bank USA

Financial Information:

	$'000
Sales revenues	180,000

No of Employees: 1,600

INSTRUMENTATION LABORATORY, INC

113 Hartwell Avenue, Lexington, MA 02173
Tel: (617) 861-0710
Telex: RCA 2000159 spillx ur

Chairman: Thomas A Rosse
President: Fred Feldman
Senior Executive Officers: Norman R Robertson (VP Finance), Lawrence Harding (VP Administration), Philip Spergel (VP Corporate Quality Assurance), Lawrence Cohen (VP International)

PRINCIPAL ACTIVITIES: Manufacture of medical instruments

Trade Names: I.L.

Parent Company: The Henley Group Inc

Principal Subsidiaries: In Italy, UK, Germany, Hong Kong, Netherlands, Austria

Principal Bank: Bank of Boston

Financial Information:

	$'000
Sales revenues	123,000

No of Employees: 2,600

INTECOM, INC

601 Intecom Drive, Allen, TX 75002
Tel: (214) 727-9141
Telex: 269188 INTCM UR

Chairman: C M Bowen (and Chief Executive Officer)
President: Erik T Ringkjob (and Chief Operating Officer)
Senior Executive Officers: Bill L Collinsworth (Senior VP Operations), Thomas B Cannon (VP Engineering), Richard L Henander (Senior VP Finance), Tom W Kemp (VP Sales), Terry L Marksberry (VP Field and Support Operations), Lee C Thomas (VP Product Marketing), Ralph J Thornton Jr (VP Administration), Ralph A Walch (VP and Controller)

PRINCIPAL ACTIVITIES: Manufacture of communications equipment

Parent Company: Wang Laboratories Inc

Principal Bank: M Bank Dallas

Financial Information:

	$'000
Sales revenues	123,565

Principal Shareholders: Exxon, Wang Labs
No of Employees: 1,291

INTEGRATED DEVICE TECHNOLOGY INC

3236 Scott Boulevard, Santa Clara, CA 95051
Tel: (408 727 6116

President: D John Carey (and Chief Executive Officer)
Senior Executive Officers: Luc O Bauer (VP and Division Manager), Maurice C Chidlow (VP and Chief Operating Officer), Norman Godinho (VP and Secretary), Leonard C Perham (VP and Division Manager), Joseph F Santandrea (VP and Division Manager), Jay R Zerfoss (Secretary), George F Hwang (VP Engineering)

PRINCIPAL ACTIVITIES: Manufacture of electronic products including semiconductors
Principal Bank: Security Pacific National Bank
Financial Information:

	$'000
Sales revenues	58,000

No of Employees: 580

INTEGRATED RESOURCES INC

666 Third Avenue, New York, NY 10017
Tel: (212) 551-6000

Chairman: Selig A Zises (and Chief Executive Officer)
President: Arthur P Goldberg (and Chief Operating Officer)
Senior Executive Officers: William Adair (Senior Executive VP), Richard Ader (Senior Executive VP), Jay Chazanoff (Senior Executive VP), Joel M Pashcow (Senior Executive VP), Philip H Cohen (Executive VP Finance and Chief Financial Officer)

PRINCIPAL ACTIVITIES: Financial services including security broking and dealing
Principal Bank: Mellon Bank
Financial Information:

	Dec 31 1985	Dec 31 1986
	$'000	$'000
Revenues	440,025	832,879
Net income	49,812	18,048
Earnings (loss) per share	$2.04	($1.73)
Shareholders equity	462,460	505,711
Total assets	1,283,198	5,136,668

No of Employees: 3,200

INTEGRATED SOFTWARE SYSTEMS CORPORATION

10505 Sorrento Valley Road, San Diego, CA 92121
Tel: (619) 452 0170

Chairman: Peter Preuss (and Chief Executive Officer)
President: Meldon Gafner
Senior Executive Officers: Anders Winberg (Senior VP), Carl Zeiger (Senior VP and Chief Financial Officer), Richard E Brown (VP), Louise B Courtier (VP), Friederich Schaaf (VP)

PRINCIPAL ACTIVITIES: Computer related services and software
Financial Information:

	$'000
Sales revenues	40,370

No of Employees: 350

INTEGRITY FINANCIAL GROUP INC

Mack Centre II, Mack Centre Drive, Paramus, NJ 07652
Tel: (201) 262 9320

Chairman: Christian C Yegen (and President and Chief Executive Officer)
Senior Executive Officers: Robert W Stubbs (Executive VP), John W Nolan (Senior VP and Treasurer), Joel H Schleifstein (VP and Controller), Irving Silber (Senior VP Finance and Treasurer), Irwin S Markowitz (Secretary aand Legal Counsel), Betty Louise Smith (VP Human Resources)

PRINCIPAL ACTIVITIES: Provision of a range of insurance services
Parent Company: Yegen Holdings Corporation
Principal Bank: Continental Illinois National Bank and Trust Company
Financial Information:

	Dec 31 1985
	$'000
Revenues	124,070

No of Employees: 400

INTEL CORPORATION

3065 Bowers Avenue, Santa Clara, CA 95051
Tel: (408) 987-8080

Chairman: Andrew S Grove (and Chief Executive Officer; Vice Chairman: Robert E Noyce; Chairman of Executive Committee: Arthur Rock
Senior Executive Officers: Jack C Carsten (Senior VP and General Manager ASIC Components), Edward L Gelbach (Senior VP Corporate Sales), Lawrence R Hootnick (Senior VP Corporate Marketing and Sales), Leslie L Vadasz (Senior VP Systems Group), Craig Barrett (VP Components Technical and Manufacturing Group), Richard D Boucher (VP), Frank Gill (VP Administration Group), David L House (VP Microcomputer Group), Willard Kaufman (VP Components Quality and Reliability), Eugene J Flath (VP), William Lattin (VP Corporate Strategic Staff), Gerhard H Parker (VP Technical Development), Robert Reed (VP Finance), George H Schneer (VP Memory Components), Keith Thomson (VP Systems Group), R Whittier (VP Marketing), Thomas J Dunlap Jr (Secretary and General Counsel)

PRINCIPAL ACTIVITIES: Manufacture of components for computers and other electronic equipment
Principal Bank: Wells Fargo Bank NA
Financial Information:

	Dec 31 1985	Dec 31 1986
	$'000	$'000
Sales revenues	1,364,980	1,265,011
Net income (loss)	1,570	(173,165)
Earnings (loss) per share	$0.01	($1.48)
Shareholders equity	1,421,480	1,275,227

No of Employees: 19,300

INTELLIGENT SYSTEMS MASTER, LP

4355 Shackleford Road, Norcross, GA 30093
Tel: (404) 381-2900
Fax: (404) 381-2808

Chairman: J Leland Strange (and President)
Senior Executive Officers: John E McCormick, Francis A Marks, Bonnie L Herron

PRINCIPAL ACTIVITIES: Intelligent Systems designs, manufactures and markets enhancement products for personal computers, small business accounting software, and portable computers
Trade Names: Quadboard, Quadram, Video-7, Quad Emst, Peachtree Software, Back to Basics, Quad EGA, HX-12, HX-9/9E, Datavue, Snap 1+1, Spark
Principal Subsidiaries: Quadram Corporation; Princeton Graphic Systems Inc; Peachtree Software Inc; Datavue Corporation; Video Seven
Principal Bank: C & S National Bank; First National Bank of Atlanta

Financial Information:

	Dec 31 1985	Dec 31 1986
	$'000	$'000
Sales revenues	101,651	138,675
Income (loss) before taxes	(17,040)	3,796
Net income (loss)	(8,277)	5,604
Earnings (loss) per share	($0.75)	$0.50
Common stock	564	-
Retained income	20,499	-
Partners capital	47,733	43,956

Principal Shareholders: J Leland Strange (11%)
No of Employees: 502

INTER-AMERICAN DEVELOPMENT BANK

808 17th Street NW, Washington, DC 20577
Tel: (202) 634-8000
Telex: ITT 440124 idba ui

President: Antonio Ortiz Mena
Senior Executive Officers: Michael E Curtin (Executive VP), Henry J Costanzo (Financial Manager)

PRINCIPAL ACTIVITIES: Banking services
Principal Subsidiaries: Inter-American Investment Corp (Argentina); Institute for Latin American Integration (Argentina)

Principal Shareholders: United States Government (34.54%); Brazilian Government (11.9%); Argentinian Government (11.9%)
No of Employees: 1,960

INTERBAKE FOODS, INC

PO Box 27487, Richmond, VA 23261
Tel: (804) 257-7497

Chairman: Douglas J McMullen (and Chief Executive Officer)
President: Charles J Maurer (and Chief Operating Officer)
Senior Executive Officers: Erwin T Hadorn (Senior VP Purchasing), R P Jones (VP Finance), Frank P Sterrett (VP Distribution)

PRINCIPAL ACTIVITIES: Manufacture of cookies
Parent Company: George Weston Inc
Principal Bank: First and Merchants National Bank
Financial Information:

	$'000
Sales revenues	100,000

Principal Shareholders: George Weston Holdings Ltd, London, UK
No of Employees: 1,500

INTERCO INC

101 South Hanley Rd, St Louis, MO 63102
Tel: (314) 863-1100

Chairman: Harvey Saligman (and Chief Executive Officer); Vice Chairman: Ronald L Aylward
President: Harry M Krogh (and Chief Operating Officer)
Senior Executive Officers: Eugene F Smith (Senior VP Finance), Nathan S Ancell (VP), Stanley M Cohen (VP), J Carl Powers (VP), Charles J Rothschild Jr (VP)

PRINCIPAL ACTIVITIES: Manufacture of clothing, footwear and furnishings; retail stores
Financial Information:

	$'000
Sales revenues	2,500,000

No of Employees: 46,000

INTERCONTINENTAL LIFE CORPORATION

40 Parker Road, Elizabeth, NJ 07208
Tel: (201) 351 1400

Chairman: Roy F Mitte (and President and Chief Executive Officer)
Senior Executive Officers: James M Grace (VP and Treasurer)

PRINCIPAL ACTIVITIES: Provision of life insurance services
Principal Subsidiaries: Intercontinental Life Insurance Co
Principal Bank: First National State Bank of New Jersey
Financial Information:

	$'000
Revenues	34,000

No of Employees: 100

INTERCRAFT INDUSTRIES CORPORATION

10 South Riverside Plaza, Chicago, IL 60606
Tel: (312) 930-2500
Telex: 25 3079
Telefax: (312) 454 1312

Chairman: Philip Spertus (and Chief Executive Officer); Chairman of Executive Committee: Herman Spertus
President: Trevor Redmayne (and Chief Operating Officer)
Senior Executive Officers: Thomas M Pyra (Treasurer)

PRINCIPAL ACTIVITIES: Manufacture of picture frames
Principal Subsidiaries: IIC Ltd (UK); Intercraft (Canada)
Principal Bank: Harris Trust and Savings Bank
Financial Information:

	$'000
Sales revenues	130,000

Principal Shareholders: Private company controlled by Spertus Family
No of Employees: 2,000

INTERFACE FLOORING SYSTEMS, INC

Orchard Hill Road, Box 1503, La Grange, GA 30241
Tel: (404) 882-1891
Telex: WUT 540 450 cpts intl laga

President: R C Anderson
Senior Executive Officers: D H Lee (VP, Secretary and Treasurer), J H Kyle (VP), D E Russell (VP), Grant Todd (VP)

PRINCIPAL ACTIVITIES: Holding company with interests in the manufacture of flooring materials including carpets and carpet tiles
Financial Information:

	$'000
Sales revenues	123,000

No of Employees: 940

INTERFIRST BANK DALLAS, NA

PO Box 83000, Dallas, TX 75283
Tel: (214) 744-8000
Telex: WUT 73353 firstnatl dal

Chairman: Robert H Stewart III (and Chief Executive Officer); Vice Chairmen: Edward A Townsend (and Chief Financial Officer), Richard M Hart
President: Harvey R Mitchell
Senior Executive Officers: James A Brickley (Chairman Aset/Liablility Management Committee), James R Erwin (Chairman Credit Policy Committee), Alan D Brown (Executive VP US Corporate Banking), Daniel H Chapman (Executive VP Dallas Corporate Banking), Larry L Helm (Executive VP Energy Division), W G Hobgood (Executive VP Trust Division), J R Hudspeth (Executive VP International), William G Kelley (Executive VP Credit Administration), A Earl Ladd (Executive VP Investment), Richard B LaSance (Executive VP Special Credits), William C Nelson (Executive VP Personal Financial Services), Timothy T Sidley (Executve VP Global Funding), A G Wallace (Executive VP Real Estate), Robert C Ammons (Senior VP Human Resources Group), L Eldon Miller (Senior VP and Cashier), William W Sullivan (Senior VP Controllers Group), Marilyn J Szech (Senior VP Financial Management)

PRINCIPAL ACTIVITIES: Bank
Parent Company: InterFirst Corporation, Dallas, TX

No of Employees: 2,000

INTERFIRST BANK FORT WORTH, NA

1 Burnett Plaza, Fort Worth, TX 76102
Tel: (817) 390-6161
Telex: 758260

Chairman: James R Perry
President: Jeffrey K Wentworth
Senior Executive Officers: William R Biggs (Executive VP and Chief Financial Officer), Leland C Clemons (Executive VP Personal Financial Services), Bruce A Duncan (Executive VP and Chief Credit Officer), Sam L Gill (Executive VP Administration Services), Don Jancosek (Executive VP Trust and Investment Management), Allen Sanders (Executive VP Credit Administration), James W Jones (Executive VP Real Estate), D Richard Andrews (Senior VP Human Resources), W P Cranz Jr (Senior VP Financial Services Marketing), Gerald Hartman Jr (Senior VP Real Estate Management), Billy Ray Henson (Senior VP Mineral Property Management), Charles W Lasater (Senior VP General Banking), Greg Murphy (Senior VP Special Credit), James R Redfearn (Senior VP InterFirst Investment Managemnt), Robert E Scott (Senior VP Accounts Administration Services)

PRINCIPAL ACTIVITIES: Bank
Parent Company: InterFirst Corporation, Dallas, TX

No of Employees: 640

INTERFIRST BANK HOUSTON, NA

PO Box 2555, Houston, TX 77001
Tel: (713) 652-6211
Telex: WUT 762800 intfstbk hou a

Chairman: Joe M Bailey (and Chief Executive Officer)
President: Robert B Sale Jr
Senior Executive Officers: William C Lee (Executive VP Financial Division and Chief Financial Officer), K T Arnoult (Executive VP Special Credits), Britt D Davis (Executive VP and Senior Trust Officer), C B Robertson (Executive VP Credit Administration), Eduardo Aguirre Jr (Senior VP Multi-National Group), Ron McKesson (Senior VP Personal Financial Services Group), Karen J Cole (Senior VP Corporate Services Group and Trust Officer), George Hamilton (Senior VP Corporate Services Group), Mark B Ferris (Senior VP Personal Services Group and Trust Officer), Frank King (Senior VP Personal Services Group), Paul S Lindholm Jr (Senior VP Houston Corporate Group), Steven G Lea (Senior VP Special Credit Group), Mark C Kirk (Senior VP Special Credit Group), John T Kopriva (Senior VP Human Resources), Claude R Markham (Senior VP Financial Institutions Group), John H Hall (Senior VP Real Estate), Gregory Sprawka (Senior VP and Controller), Terrie G Elkins (Senior VP Real Estate), Ben W Tabor (Senior VP Loan Operations), C John Thompson (Senior VP Energy Group), Earl M Worstell (Senior VP Petroleum Management Group), Don Stubbe (Senior VP Investment and Funds Management)

PRINCIPAL ACTIVITIES: Bank
Parent Company: InterFirst Corporation, Dallas, TX

No of Employees: 750

INTERFIRST CORPORATION

901 Main Street, Dallas, TX 75202
Tel: (214) 977-3333

Chairman: Robert H Stewart III (and Chief Executive Officer)
President: Ronald G Steinhart (and Chief Operating Officer)
Senior Executive Officers: George H Kilpatrick (Executive VP), Paul L Hill (Chief Financial Officer), John W Beeman (Secretary and Treasurer)

PRINCIPAL ACTIVITIES: Financial services
Financial Information:

	Dec 31 1985	Dec 31 1986
	$'000	$'000
Net income (loss)	61,100	(326,500)
Earnings (loss) per share	$0.91	($4.86)
Shareholders equity	1,181,000	844,000
Deposits	17,504,000	14,878,000
Total assets	22,071,000	17,986,000

No of Employees: 8,636

INTERGRAPH CORPORATION

One Madison Industrial Park, Huntsville, AL 35807
Tel: (205) 772-2000

Chairman: James W Meadlock (and President)
Senior Executive Officers: Roland E Brown (Executive VP and Secretary), Nancy B Meadlock (Executive VP), Keith H Schonrock Jr (Executive VP), James F Taylor Jr (Executive VP), John M Thorington Jr (Executive VP), Robert E Thurber (Executive VP), Allan B Wilson (Executive VP), William D Zarecor (Executive VP)

PRINCIPAL ACTIVITIES: Manufacture of computer graphics systems
Principal Bank: Birmingham Trust National Bank
Financial Information:

	Dec 31 1986
	$'000
Sales revenues	605,737
Net income	70,362
Earnings per share	$1.26
Shareholders equity	496,157

No of Employees: 5,600

INTERLAKE, INC

2015 Spring Road, Oak Brook, IL 60521
Tel: (312) 986-6600
Telex: WUT 254287 interlake oakr

Chairman: Frederick C Langenberg (and Chief Executive Officer)
President: Edward Hopkins (and Chief Operating Officer)
Senior Executive Officers: Grant L Johnson (Senior VP and General counsel), W Robert Reum (VP-Finance and Chief Financial Officer), H Harry Henderson (VP-Marketing and Public Affairs), Raymond T Anderson (Treasurer), David R Downs (VP-Human Resources), Ian R MacLeod (Secretary), Richard I Polanek (Controller)

PRINCIPAL ACTIVITIES: The Interlake Corporation is a technology driven internatonal manufacturer, supplying engineered materials and handling/packaging systems, We create improved values for customers and shareholders.
Principal Subsidiaries: Aerospace Components: Arwood Corporation; Chem-tronics Inc. Powdered Metals: Hoeganaes Corporation. International: Dexion Ltd (UK); Acme Gerrard Ltd (UK); Dexion Australia Pty Ltd (Australia); SA Dexion-Redirack NV (Belgium); Dexion GmbH (Germany). Material Handling Systems: Interlake Material Handling; Redirack Ltd. Packaging Systems: Interlake Packaging Corporation; Acme Strapping Inc (Canada)

Financial Information:

	Dec 29 1985	Dec 28 1986
	$'000	$'000
Sales revenues	635,327	736,009
Income before taxes	51,652	60,740
Net income(1)	28,181	32,555
Dividends	14,470	14,873
Dividends per share(2)	$1.30	$1.30
Earnings per share(3)	$2.53	$2.85
Common stock	126,229	88,202
Retained income	305,133	191,338
Shareholders equity(3)	351,753	250,362

(1) includes results of Acme Steel Company until June 23 1986
(2) restated for two-for-one stock split
(3) after the spin-off of Acme Steel Company of $131.5m or $11.42 per share

No of Employees: 9,000

INTERMARK, INC

PO Box 1149, La Jolla, CA 92038
Tel: (619) 459-3841

President: Charles R Scott
Senior Executive Officers: Frank C Alexander (VP and Chief Financial Officer), Mitchell R Woodbury (VP and Secretary), Vernon A LoForti (VP and Controller)

PRINCIPAL ACTIVITIES: Manufacture of parts for the automotive industry including wheels; manufacture of ambulances; manufacture and sale of nursery and sporting goods; printing
Principal Subsidiaries: Goldenwest Graphics; Graphic Arts Center Inc; Arts & Crafts Press Inc; Franklin Press; Dynamark Inc; Keystone Products; Appliance Industries Inc; Superior Trans-Med; Muson Sporting Goods
Principal Bank: First Interstate Bank
Financial Information:

	$'000
Sales revenues	520,000

No of Employees: 6,950

INTERMATIC INC

Intermatic Plaza, Spring Grove, IL 60081
Tel: (815) 675-2321
Telex: 25265

Chairman: James C Miller (and Chief Executive Officer)
President: Leon E Vinyard
Senior Executive Officers: William E Morrison (VP Administration), Robert C Bedford (VP Sales), John L Halka (VP Manufacturing), L E Larsen (VP Finance), Edward F Condon Jr (VP Engineering), Donald J Ferguson (VP Marketing)

PRINCIPAL ACTIVITIES: Manufacture of electrical switches, timers and controls
Principal Bank: The Northern Trust Company
Financial Information:

	$'000
Sales revenues	60,000

No of Employees: 1,100

INTERMEDICS, INC

PO Box 4400, Angleton, TX 77515
Tel: (409) 233-8611
Telex: WUT 794707 intrmedcs aglt

Chairman: Richard A Gilleland (and President and Chief Executive Officer)
Senior Executive Officers: Peter G Dorflinger (VP Legal and Corporate Secretary), Bruce K Bennett (VP Manufacturing), James A Kenton (VP and Chief Financial Officer), Richard O Martin (VP Scientific Affairs), Theodore J Swift (VP Corporate Relations)

PRINCIPAL ACTIVITIES: Intermedics, Inc. manufactures and markets such biomedical products as cardiac pacemakers and pacemaker leads, mechanical heart valve components, orthopedic implants and dental and oral surgery biomaterials
Principal Subsidiaries: Intermedicas International Inc; CarboMedics Inc; Intermedics Orthopedics Inc; Calcitek Inc; Intermedics Pacemakers Inc; Inermedics SA (Switzerland)
Principal Bank: Citibank
Financial Information:

	Nov 3 1985	Nov 2 1986
	$'000	$'000
Sales revenues	164,901	178,308
(Loss) before taxes	(20,670)	(16,513)
Net income (loss)	(20,046)	6,159
Earnings (loss) per share	($1.95)	$0.57
Common stock	1,028	1,030
Retained income	32,631	38,790
Shareholders equity	73,152	81,530

No of Employees: 1,500

INTERMET CORPORATION

2849 Paces Ferry Road, Suite 700, Atlanta, GA 30339
Tel: (404) 436 1102

Chairman: George W Mathews Jr; Vice Chairman: Carl I Gable
President: Alvin W Singleton
Senior Executive Officers: A Wayne Hardy (VP), Wallace Day (VP), D L Jean (VP), Robert W Orr (Controller), John D Ernst (Secretary and Treasurer)

PRINCIPAL ACTIVITIES: Manufacture of iron
Financial Information:

	$'000
Sales revenues	265,370

No of Employees: 3,480

INTERMETRICS INC

733 Concord Avenue, Cambridge, MA 02138
Tel: (617) 661 1840

Chairman: John E Miller
President: Joseph A Saponaro (and Chief Executive and Operating Officer)
Senior Executive Officers: Frederick H Martin (VP Corporate Development), Nicholas A Pettinella (VP Finance, Chief Financial Officer and Treasurer)

PRINCIPAL ACTIVITIES: Provision of computer related services and software
Principal Subsidiaries: Intermetrics International Inc; Intermetrics Securities Inc
Principal Bank: State Street Bank & Trust Company
Financial Information:

	$'000
Sales revenues	43,000

No of Employees: 560

INTERNATIONAL AIR SERVICE COMPANY, LTD

1710 Gilbreth Road, Burlingame, CA 94010
Tel: (415) 692-8670
Telex: WUT 331346 iasco b brgm

Chairman: James C Jack Jr (and President)
Senior Executive Officers: Richard W Jack (Senior VP), Leslie M Kratter (Senior VP)

PRINCIPAL ACTIVITIES: General aviation consultancy and training services; air freight transportation services

Financial Information:

	$'000
Sales revenues	60,000

No of Employees: 500

INTERNATIONAL ALUMINUM CORPORATION

767 Monterey Pass Road, Monterey Park, CA 91754
Tel: (213) 264-1670
Telex: WUT 677606 intalum mypk

Chairman: Cornelius C Vanderstar
President: John P Cunningham
Senior Executive Officers: Hugh E Curran (VP Sales), Ronald Rudy (VP Manufacturing), David C Treinen (VP Finance and Secretary)

PRINCIPAL ACTIVITIES: Holding company with interests in the manufacture of glass and aluminum products especially for the building industry
Principal Bank: City National Bank
Financial Information:

	$'000
Sales revenues	150,000

No of Employees: 2,000

INTERNATIONAL BANKNOTE COMPANY

230 Park Avenue, New York, NY 10169
Tel: (212) 697-6600

President: Edward H Weitzen
Senior Executive Officers: Annabelle W Model (Executive VP and Secretary), Eugene Jonas (VP and Treasurer), Gerhard A Henning (VP)

PRINCIPAL ACTIVITIES: Specialist printing; engraving and plate printing of security documents and currency
Principal Subsidiaries: American Banknote Company; Bradbury, Wilkinson plc; Globe Ticket Company; American Banknote-Security Systems Inc
Principal Bank: Mellon Bank
Financial Information:

	Dec 31 1985	Dec 31 1986
	$'000	$'000
Sales revenues	143,658	86,313
Income before taxes	1,909	11,225
Net income	1,629	9,651
Earnings per share	$0.09	$0.56
Common stock*	16,904	16,739
Retained (deficit)	(20,711)	(11,060)
Shareholders equity	21,730	41,794

*number of shares in thousands

No of Employees: 2,300

INTERNATIONAL BUSINESS MACHINES CORPORATION

IBM

Old Orchard Road, Armonk, NY 10504
Tel: (914) 765-1900

Chairman: John R Opel; Vice Chairman: Paul J Rizzio
President: John F Akers (and Chief Executive Officer)
Senior Executive Officers: C Michael Armstrong (Senior VP and Group Executvie), George B Beitzel (Senior VP), Kaspar V Cassani (Senior VP), Ralph E Gomory (Senior VP), Nicholas de B Katzenbach (Senior VP and General Counsel), Allen J Krowe (Senior VP Finance and Planning), Jack D Kuehler (Senior VP and Group Executive), Ralph A Pfeiffer Jr (Senior VP), Dean P Phypers (Senior VP), Clarence B Rogers Jr (Senior VP and Group Executive), George H Conrades (VP and Group Executive), Frank A Metz Jr (VP and Group Executive), John E Bertram (VP), Charles P Biggar (VP), James A Bitoni (VP), Charles E Branscomb (VP), Lewis M Branscomb (VP), Walton E Burdick (VP), Ronald F Casella (VP), Carl J Conti (VP), Vincent N Cook (VP), Edward M Davis (VP), Wallace C Doud (VP), Robert B Dunlop (VP), William W Eggleston (VP), Philip D Estridge (VP), Donato A Evangelista (VP), P Martin Foley (VP), James J Forese (VP and Controller), Richard T Gerstner (VP), Victor J Goldberg (VP), William O Grabe (VP), Lewis W Gray (VP), Paul J Kofmehl (VP), Terry R Lautenbach (VP), Thomas M Liptak (VP), Paul R Low (VP), Edward E Lucente (VP), Victor R Macdonald (VP), Marvin L Mann (VP), James E Manning (VP), David E McKinney (VP), Charles E McKittrick Jr (VP), M Kenneth Oshman (VP), Theodore C Papes Jr (VP), Stephen B Schwartz (VP), Patrick A Toole (VP), H Mitchell Watson Jr (VP), John F Williams (VP), John H Grady (Secretary), Jon W Rotenstreich (Treasurer), Robert E Bonchick (Assistant Controller), J William Scruggs (Assistant Controller), John H Stewart (Assistant Controller), Thomas C Irwin (Assistant Secretary), Sidney Handler (Assistant Treasurer), Bruce E Langton (Assistant Treasurer)

PRINCIPAL ACTIVITIES: IBM's operations are primarily in the field of information-handling systems, equipment and services to solve the increasingly complex problems of business, government, science, space exploration, defense, education, medicine and many other areas of human activity. IBM's products include information processing products and systems, program products, telecommunications systems, information distributors, office systems, typewriters, copiers, educational and testing materials and related supplies and services. Most products are both leased and sold through IBM's worldwide marketing organizations. Selected products are marketed and distributed through authorized dealers and remarketers
Principal Subsidiaries: Divisions: Information Systems and Communications Group:- Communication Products Division; Entry Systems Division. Information Systems and Products Group:- Information Products Division; System Products Division. Information Systems and Technology Group:- Data Systems Division; General Products Division; General Technology Division; Systems Technology Division. Information Systems Group:- National Accounts Division; National Distribution Division; National Marketing Division; National Service Division. Other Divisions:- Federal Systems Division; Real Estate and Construction Division; Research Division. Subsidiaries: IBM Credit Corporation; IBM Instruments, Inc; ROLM Corporation; Science Research Associates, Inc; IBM World Trade Americas/Far East Corporation (With a territory extending across four continents, this subsidiary is responsible for IBM operations in 46 countries, including Australia, Brazil, Canada, China and Japan); IBM World Trade Europe/Middle East/Africa Corporation (Through its subsidiary, IBM Europe, located in Paris, it is responsible for IBM operations in 83 countries); IBM World Trade Corporation
Financial Information:

	Dec 31 1986
	$'000
Gross income	51,250,000
Net earnings	4,789,000
Earnings per share	$7.81
Shareholders equity	34,374,000

No of Employees: 394,930

INTERNATIONAL CLINICAL LABORATORIES INC

5 Park Plaza, Nashville, TN 37203
Tel: (615) 327 1025

Chairman: Harold E Resinger
President: William C O'Neil (and Chief Executive Officer)
Senior Executive Officers: Michael L Jeub (Executive VP, Chief Financial Officer and Secretary), Lowell B Foster (President ICL East), Bert H Hood (President ICL West), H Michael Finley (VP Finance), Harry G Browne (Treasurer)

PRINCIPAL ACTIVITIES: Clinical laboratories for testing services
Principal Bank: Third National Bank
Financial Information:

	$'000
Sales revenues	144,000

No of Employees: 3,000

INTERNATIONAL CONTROLS CORP

5499 N Federal Hwy, PO Box 3010, Boca Raton, FL 33431
Tel: (305) 997-7400

Chairman: Uzi Zucker
President: Arthur M Goldberg (and Chief Executive Officer)
Senior Executive Officers: Jay H Harris (Executive VP-Operations and Chief Operating Officer), J Kenneth Looloian (Executive VP-Administration and Finance), John J Delucca (Senior VP-Finance), George L Hebert (VP and Treasurer), William C Ragals Jr (VP Secretary and General Counsel), Thomas W Horan (Controller)

PRINCIPAL ACTIVITIES: International Controls Corp (ICC) is a diversified engineering and manufacturing company and distributor of liquefied petroleum gas (LPG). Through its subsidiaries, ICC manufactures truck trailers; designs, manufactures and supplies products for the aerospace/defense markets; and distributes and sells liquefied petroleum gas
Principal Subsidiaries and Divisions: Great Dane Trailers Inc; Tropigas International Corp; All American Engineering Company; Intercontinental Manufacturing Company Inc; Elektro/Metall Export GmbH (Germany); EEMCO Division; Tech Systems Corp
Principal Bank: Colonial Bank
Financial Information:

	Dec 31 1985	Dec 31 1986
	$'000	$'000
Sales revenues	141,683	736,829
Income before taxes	12,747	13,436
Net income (loss)	7,461	(6,879)
Dividends	1,514	1,772
Dividends per share	$0.45	$0.50
Earnings (loss) per share*	$2.17	($2.01)
Common stock	421	421
Retained income	33,455	24,804
Shareholders equity	59,246	59,166

*fully diluted

No of Employees: 1,800

INTERNATIONAL DAIRY QUEEN, INC

PO Box 35286, Minneapolis, MN 55435
Tel: (612) 830-0200
Telex: 910-576-3449 IDQ COS BLTN

Chairman: John W Mooty
President: Harris Cooper
Senior Executive Officers: Gordon F Huber (Executive VP), Glenn H Mueffelmann (Executive VP), Frank L Heit (Executive VP and Treasurer), Edward A Watson (Executive VP), David M Bond (Controller and Assistant Treasurer), Mark S Broin (VP-Information Services/Administrative Services), Edward P Gherity (VP-Purchasing and Distribution), Michael J Leary (VP-Mix, Manufactured Novelties and Research and Development), Shrin Murthy (VP-Facilities), Herman E Nelson (VP-Law), Gary H See (VP-Marketing), Gilbert N Stemmerman (VP-Franchise Operations), Signe M Studer (VP-Administration/Human Resources Development), Michael P Sullivan (Vice Chairman of the Board of Directors and Secretary and a Director), Walter S Tellegen (VP-Franchise Operations), William R von Hassel (VP-Special Projects)

PRINCIPAL ACTIVITIES: The "Dairy Queen" system is comprised of more than 4,800 "Dairy Queen" and "Dairy Queen Brazier" stores located in the United States, Canada and 13 other countries. IDQ is one of the world's largest retailers of fast food and frozen dairy dessert items.
Trade Names: "Dairy Queen", "Brazier", "Queen's Choice", "Blizzard"
Principal Subsidiaries: American Dairy Queen Corp; Dairy Queen Canada, Inc; Dairy Queen Japan (Co) Ltd; Golden Skillett International, Inc
Principal Bank: Norwest Bank Minneapolis, NA
Financial Information:

	$'000
Revenues	159,000

No of Employees: 450 (330, plus 120 corporate store employees)

INTERNATIONAL FLAVORS & FRAGRANCES, INC

521 W 57th Street, New York, NY 10019
Tel: (212) 765-5500
Telex: WUT 126307 iff nyk

Chairman: Eugene P Grisanti (and Chief Executive Officer)
Senior Executive Officers: Bernard Chant (Senior VP), Harry Fields (Senior VP), Ronald D Anderson (VP), Ronald S Fenn (VP), John M Jarvis (Senior VP), Hugh R Kirkpatrick (VP), Lewis G Lynch Jr (VP), Rudolf Merz (VP), Joel P Pearlstein (VP), Gordon V Phillips (VP), Hendrik C van Baaren (VP), John P Winandy (VP and Treasurer)

PRINCIPAL ACTIVITIES: Manufacture of perfumes, flavorings and other specialty chemicals
Principal Subsidiaries: IFF Trading Company BV; IFF Essencias e Fragrancias Ltda; PT Essence Indonesia; Sabores y Fragrancias SA; Irish Flavours and Fragrances Ltd; Alva Insurance Limited; Kepp Concentrates Inc; IFF Export Inc
Principal Bank: Citibank
Financial Information:

	Dec 31 1986
	$'000
Sales revenues	620,679
Net income	85,683
Earnings per share	$2.29
Shareholders equity	521,475

No of Employees: 3,700

INTERNATIONAL GAME TECHNOLOGY

520 S Rock Blvd, Reno, NV 89502
Tel: (702) 323-5060
Telex: TWX 910 3957014 igt rno

Chairman: Charles Mathewson
President: W S Redd (and Chief Executive Officer)
Senior Executive Officers: P D Dickinson (VP), Clarence Thiesen (VP Finance and Treasurer), R Fedor (VP), R D Pike (VP, Secretary and Legal Counsel), R Irvine (VP)

PRINCIPAL ACTIVITIES: Manufacture of video games and other entertainment equipment
Principal Bank: First Interstate Bank
Financial Information:

	$'000
Sales revenues	56,600

No of Employees: 900

INTERNATIONAL HYDRON CORPORATION

185 Crossways Park Drive, Woodbury, NY 11797
Tel: (516) 364 1700

Chairman: Jerome I Feldman
President: Martin M Pollak (and Chief Executive Officer)
Senior Executive Officers: Edward J Hopkins (VP), Kevin H P MacGiffin (VP), Judy A Palatella (VP), David L Rawlings (VP), Paul V Rossi (VP, Chief Financial Officer, Secretary and Treasurer)

PRINCIPAL ACTIVITIES: Manufacture of soft contact lenses and related lens care solutions and products
Parent Company: National Patent Development Corporation
Principal Bank: National Westminster Bank
Financial Information:

	$'000
Sales revenues	53,000

No of Employees: 1,500

INTERNATIONAL KING'S TABLE INC

1500 Valley River Drive, Suite 300, Eugene, OR 97401
Tel: (503) 686 8030

Chairman: Roger W Houmes (and Chief Executive Officer)
Senior Executive Officers: Jack N Clark (VP Operations), Stephen A Wendell (VP Finance and Treasurer), Kenneth Sherman (Secretary)

PRINCIPAL ACTIVITIES: Restaurant chain
Principal Subsidiaries: Oh Susannah's Inc; King's Enterprises Inc
Principal Bank: United States National Bank
Financial Information:

	$'000
Sales revenues	85,000

No of Employees: 2,550

INTERNATIONAL LEASE FINANCE CORPORATION

84484 Wilshire Boulevard, Suite 850, Beverly Hills, CA 90211
Tel: (213) 658 7871

Chairman: Leslie L Gonda (and Chief Executive Officer)
President: Steven F Udvar-Hazy
Senior Executive Officers: Louis L Gonda (Executive VP and Secretary), V Anthony Carbonar (VP), Kenneth D Taylor (VP), Alan H Lund (VP Finance and Treasurer)

PRINCIPAL ACTIVITIES: Operation of aircraft leasing services
Principal Subsidiaries: Interlease Management Corp; Interlease Trading Corp
Principal Bank: Bank of America National Trust and Savings Association
Financial Information:

	$'000
Sales revenues	80,000

No of Employees: 10

INTERNATIONAL METALS & MACHINES, INC

2200 E Devon Avenue, Des Plaines, IL 60018
Tel: (312) 297-0808

Chairman: George McKewen (and President)
Senior Executive Officers: Barry J Carroll (VP), Denis Carroll (VP), Carlos Tiernon (VP), Richard J Anderson (Secretary and Controller)

PRINCIPAL ACTIVITIES: Production of industrial plant, handling equipment, control equipment, wire products, mining equipment, candy manufacturing plant, printing machinery
Parent Company: CRL Inc
Principal Bank: First National Bank of Chicago
Financial Information:

	$'000
Sales revenues	200,000

No of Employees: 2,200

INTERNATIONAL MINERALS & CHEMICAL CORPORATION

2315 Sanders Road, Northbrook, IL 60062
Tel: (312) 564-8600
Telex: 206-313

Chairman: R A Lenon
President: G D Kennedy (and Chief Executive Officer)
Senior Executive Officers: B B Turner (Senior VP, President, Fertilizer Group), K J Burns Jr (VP and General Counsel), N Bruns Jr (VP, Secretary and Assoc. General Counsel), D L Feaker (VP and Treasurer), I David Paley (VP, President, Industry Group), D E Phillips (VP, President, Animal Products Group), J F Sonderegger (VP and Controller), J M Stapleton (VP, Organization and Human Resources)

PRINCIPAL ACTIVITIES: International Minerals & Chemical Corporation, traded on the New York Stock Exchange, is the world's largest private-enterprise producer of two basic plant nutrients, phosphate and potash, and a manufacturer of the third, nitrogen. The Company is also the largest producer of phosphate and potassium animal nutrients and growth-promoting implants for cattle and feedlot lambs, and produces feed additives and supplements for livestock and poultry, and poultry vaccines. Other businesses include petroleum coke, ferroalloys, foundry products, industrial minerals, chemicals and energy products
Trade Names: Fertilizer Group:- Rainbow Premium Fertilizers, Sul-Po-Mag (sulphate of potash, magnesia). Animal Products Group:- BIOFOS (mono/dicalcium phosphate), DYNAFOS (di/monocalcium phosphate), LIQUIFOS (phosphoric acid), MONOFOS (monoammonium phosphate), MULTIFOS (tricalcium phosphate), Dyna-K (potassium), Dynamate (double sulphate of potash, magnesia), Baciferm (zinc bacitracin), Animate (flavor enhancer), RALGRO (growth-promoting implant). Industry Group:- TRIMET (pentaglycerol), TURFACE (soil amendment), ZORB-ALL (floor absorbent), TRAKSHUN (mineral traction aid), CUSTOMIX (foundry mineral), CLAYCALC (foundry software), DIXIE BOND (Southern bentonite), BLACK HILLS (Western bentonite), OLIFLUX (mineral agent), ENVIROMAT (fabric/bentonite liner), GREEN LIGHTNING (mineral blasting agent)
Principal Subsidiaries: Sterwin Laboratories, Inc; IMC Exploration Company; Overseas Marine Services, Inc; IMC Productos Minerais Y Quim (Brazil); IMC (Canada) Ltd (Canada); IMC de Mexico SA (Mexico)
Principal Bank: The First National Bank of Chicago (transfer agent and dividend disbursing agent)
Financial Information:

	$'000
Sales revenues	1,200,000

No of Employees: 8,700

INTERNATIONAL MULTIFOODS CORPORATION

Multifoods Tower, Box 2942, Minneapolis, MN 55402
Tel: (612) 340-3300
Telex: WUT 192114 im mps

Chairman: Andre Gillet (and Chief Executive Officer)
President: Robert M Howard
Senior Executive Officers: Jack E Mayne (Group VP Agri-Industrial Operations), Paul J Quinn (Group VP Non-US Operations), Frank T Madden (VP Human Resources), K Marvin Eberts Jr (VP Finance and Chief Financial Officer), Logan R Brown (VP, President Robin Hood Multifoods Inc), Paul A Taylor (VP Information Services), James H Beardsley Jr (VP and General Manager Consumer Products Division), James R Stolle (VP and General Manager Grain), Thomas P Brennan (VP, Secretary and Legal Counsel), John E Sampson (VP Planning and Development)

PRINCIPAL ACTIVITIES: Milling of flour; animal feedstuffs; bakery mixes; meat products; restaurant interests
Principal Subsidiaries: (100% owned unless stated): C C Credit Corp; DANCA International Corp; Fabrico Inc (81%); Food Enterprises Inc (80%); Mister Donut of America Inc; Robin Hood Multifoods Inc; Boston Sea Party Restaurants Inc; Multifoods Export Sales Corp; Multifoods Transportation Inc; Eastern Nankin Express Ltd; VSA Inc
Principal Bank: First National Bank of Minneapolis

Financial Information:

	Feb 28 1986
	$'000
Sales revenues	1,355,378
Net income	24,939
Earnings per share	$3.04
Shareholders equity	227,524

No of Employees: 9,400

INTERNATIONAL ORE & FERTILIZER CORPORATION

1230 Avenue of the Americas, New York, NY 10020
Tel: (212) 586-7800
Cable: INTERORE
Telex: 177166 interore nyk

Chairman: B D Cooper
Senior Executive Officers: M J Hartman (Senior VP), L S Herz (Senior VP), R H A Tonino (Treasurer), M J Kennedy (VP and General Counsel)

PRINCIPAL ACTIVITIES: Trading of fertilizers and metals
Parent Company: Occidental Chemical Corporation, Dallas, TX
Principal Subsidiaries: Interore Trading Ltd
Principal Bank: Manufacturers Hanover Trust

Principal Shareholders: Occidental Petroleum Corporation, Los Angeles, CA
No of Employees: 70

INTERNATIONAL PACKINGS CORPORATION

Ragged Mountain Hwy, Bristol, NH 03222
Tel: (603) 744-2281
Telex: TWX 510 2981140 ipc bristol

President: Dale F Hirschy
Senior Executive Officers: Harold E Adams Jr (VP Sales), Arthur H Ginn (VP Engineering), Joseph T McGrath (VP Manufacturing), William C Hoyt (VP Finance)

PRINCIPAL ACTIVITIES: Manufacture of rubber products including seals
Parent Company: Carl Freudenberg Co
Principal Bank: State Street Bank & Trust Co
Financial Information:

	$'000
Sales revenues	100,000

Principal Shareholders: Freudenberg & Co, Weinheim, Germany
No of Employees: 2,100

INTERNATIONAL PAINT COMPANY, INC

PO Box, 386, Union, NJ 07083
Tel: (201) 686-1300

Chairman: Thomas M Reinhardt
President: John P Merrill Jr
Senior Executive Officers: James Dale (Executive VP and Chief Operating Officer), James M Drubel (VP Manufacturing), Ferris Van Dien (VP Finance and Controller), Francis B Hurst (VP), James H Leonhard (VP)

PRINCIPAL ACTIVITIES: Production of specialty paints for marine purposes; industrial maintenance paints and coatings
Parent Company: Courtaulds plc
Principal Bank: Manufacturers Hanover Trust Company
Financial Information:

	$'000
Sales revenues	85,000

No of Employees: 500

INTERNATIONAL PAPER COMPANY

77 W 45th Street, New York, NY 10036
Tel: (212) 536-6000

Chairman: John A Georges (and Chief Executive Officer)
President: Paul H O'Neill
Senior Executive Officers: Victor Casebolt (Senior VP), Ely Gonick (Senior VP), Richard M Harris (Senior VP), David I Wang (Senior VP), Dana G Mead (VP and Group Executive), John T Dillon (VP and Group Executive), Marc F Wray (VP and Group Executive), Frank P Hart (VP), James P Melican Jr (VP and Legal Counsel), Robert A Moore Jr (VP), John M Nevin (VP), John L O'Brien Jr (VP), David W Oskin (VP), William R Pollert (VP), Richard M Smith (VP)

PRINCIPAL ACTIVITIES: Manufacture of pulp and paper and related products
Financial Information:

	Dec 31 1985	Dec 31 1986
	$'000	$'000
Sales revenues	4,502,000	5,501,000
Net income	133,000	305,000
Earnings per share	$2.16	$5.79
Shareholders equity	3,195,000	3,664,000

No of Employees: 31,900

INTERNATIONAL PROTEINS CORPORATION

123 Fairfield Road, Fairfield, NJ 07006
Tel: (201) 227-2710
Telex: TRT 178010 mapco ffld
Telecopier: (201) 227-6533

Chairman: Pierre J Petrou (and President); Chairman Executive Committee: David H Clarke
Senior Executive Officers: Celia Meilan (Executive VP), Gilbert A Read (VP), James E Kelly (VP, Finance), J Eric Hanson (Senior VP)

PRINCIPAL ACTIVITIES: Fish processing; manufacture of fish meal and oils; frozen shrimp
Principal Subsidiaries: Pan American Seafood Inc
Principal Bank: Citicorp Industrial Credit Inc
Financial Information:

	Dec 31 1985	Dec 31 1986
	$'000	$'000
Sales revenues	98,338	95,031
Income before taxes	947	2,136
Net income	778	1,302
Earnings per share	$0.37	$0.62
Common stock	2,091	2,091
Retained income	4,491	5,793
Shareholders equity	15,626	16,971

Principal Shareholders: Pierre J Petrou; Celia Meilan; David H Clarke
No of Employees: 1,100

INTERNATIONAL RECTIFIER CORPORATION

233 Kansas St, El Segundo, CA 90245
Tel: (213) 772 2000

Chairman: Eric Lidow (and President)
Senior Executive Officers: George H Krause (Executive VP Finance and Treasurer), Robert J Mueller (Executive VP Marketing), Gerald A Koris (VP, Secretary and Legal Counsel), Richard D Farrer (VP Planning and Shareholder Relations)

PRINCIPAL ACTIVITIES: Electrical equipment; production of pharmaceuticals
Principal Subsidiaries: (100% owned unless stated): International Rectifier Canada Ltd (Canada); Rectificadores Internacionales SA; International Rectifier Company (Great Britain) Ltd (UK); International Rectifier Corp Italiana SpA (Italy); International Rectifier Corp (Japan) Ltd (11%) (Japan); Rachelle Laboratories Inc; BV Diode Laboratorium voor Electronentechniek; International Rectifier GmbH (Germany); Ruttonsha-International Rectifier Private Ltd (34%)
Principal Bank: Security Pacific National Bank

Financial Information:

	$'000
Sales revenues	136,800

No of Employees: 2,150

INTERNATIONAL SHIPHOLDING CORPORATION

650 Poydras Street, New Orleans, LA 70130
Tel: (504) 529 5461

Chairman: Niels W Johnsen
President: Erik F Johnsen
Senior Executive Officers: Harold Grehan Jr (VP), G L Ferguson (Controller), Stanley E Morrison (Treasurer), George Denegre (Secretary)

PRINCIPAL ACTIVITIES: Shipping
Principal Bank: Chase Manhattan Bank
Financial Information:

	$'000
Sales revenues	153,470

No of Employees: 370

INTERNATIONAL SIGNAL & CONTROL GROUP

3750 Electronics Way, PO Box 3040, Lancaster, PA 17604
Tel: (717) 285-3113
Telex: 150186 ISCINTL UT

Chairman: James H Guerin (and President)
Directors: Sir David Checketts (European Director), Carl H Dreyer (Administrative Director), John Fox (Non-Executive Director), John Heywood (Non-Executive Director), R Clyde Ivy (Executive Director), Joseph H Zilligen (Finance Director)

PRINCIPAL ACTIVITIES: Manufacture of electronic systems and components, telecommunication systems and equipment, defense equipment, radar systems, space propulsion and electronic systems
Principal Bank: Barclays Bank PLC; Standard Chartered Bank
Financial Information:

	Mar 31 1986	Mar 31 1987
	$'000	$'000
Sales revenues	444,300	590,562
Income before taxes	46,500	56,808
Net income	29,100	36,808
Dividends	4,100	6,148
Dividends per share	$0.030	$0.036
Earnings per share	$0.213	$0.228
Common stock*	13,600	17,076
Retained income	79,500	102,941
Shareholders equity	186,600	320,553

*par value

No of Employees: 1,600

INTERNATIONAL TECHNOLOGY CORPORATION

23456 Hawthorne Boulevard, Suite 220, Torrance, CA 90505
Tel: (213) 378 9933

Chairman: Murray H Hutchison (and Chief Executive Officer)
President: William D King (and Chief Operating Officer)
Senior Executive Officers: Paul T Kaufmann (Executive VP), David J D'Appolonia (Senior VP), Sung K Lee (Senior VP), John T Schofield (Senior VP), Joseph C Mendel (Chief Financial Officer and Treasurer), Bernard L Simonsen (Secretary and VP Administration), Kenneth E Honeycutt (VP Engineering), John H Hutchison (VP Facilities and Equipment), David L Bauer (VP Environmental Affairs), Richard D Harris (VP Human Resources), John O'Shea (VP and Controller)

PRINCIPAL ACTIVITIES: Disposal of hazardous waste; environmental services
Principal Bank: Continental Illinois National Bank

Financial Information:

	$'000
Sales revenues	208,000

No of Employees: 2,240

INTERNATIONAL THOROUGHBRED BREEDERS INC

202 Abbington Drive, East Windsor, NJ 08520
Tel: (609) 443 6111

Chairman: Robert E Brennan
President: Kerry B Fitzpatrick (and Chief Executive Officer and Chief Financial Officer)
Senior Executive Officers: Robert J Quigley (VP), William H Warner (Treasurer), Arthur Winkler (Secretary)

PRINCIPAL ACTIVITIES: Breeding of throughbred horses; operation of racetracks and insurance services
Principal Subsidiaries: Colonial Racing Club Inc; Garden State Race Track Inc; Olde English Equine Insurance Agency; Philadelphia Turf Club Inc
Principal Bank: First Fidelity Bank
Financial Information:

	$'000
Sales revenues	49,000

No of Employees: 1,500

INTERPUBLIC GROUP OF COMPANIES, INC

1271 Avenue of the Americas, New York, NY 10020
Tel: (212) 399-8000

Chairman: Philip H Geier Jr (and Chief Executive Officer); Vice Chairman: Peter H Dailey
President: J D McNamara
Senior Executive Officers: Eugene P Beard (Executive VP Finance), Edward A Garba (Senior VP and Treasurer), Henry Strock (Senior VP and Controller), Enrique A Tejerina (Senior VP), C K Kroeber (Senior VP), Edwin A Kiernan Jr (Senior VP, General Counsel and Secretary), Charles A Mittelstadt (Senior VP), Michael J Kelly (VP and Deputy Controller), Monroe S Singer (VP and Assistant Secretary), William S Keating (VP), Vincent P Lubrano (VP Tax Planning and Administration), Thomas J Volpe (VP Financial Operations)

PRINCIPAL ACTIVITIES: Advertising and public relations
Principal Bank: Chase Manhattan Bank
Financial Information:

	Dec 31 1985	Dec 31 1986
	$'000	$'000
Sales revenues	668,455	797,166
Net income	36,557	41,051
Earnings per share	$1.67	$1.87
Shareholders equity	207,820	242,889

No of Employees: 12,600

INTER-REGIONAL FINANCIAL GROUP INC

100 Dain Tower, Minneapolis, MN 55402
Tel: (612) 371 7750

Chairman: Richard D McFarland (and Chief Executive Officer)
President: Irving Weiser
Senior Executive Officers: Richard A Schroeder (Senor VP, Chief Financial Officer and Treasurer)

PRINCIPAL ACTIVITIES: Provision of a range of financial services including security broking
Principal Subsidiaries: Dain Bosworth Inc; Dain Corp; IFG Information Services Inc; Investment Advisers Inc; Midwest Life Insurance Co; Rauscher Pierce Refsnes Inc
Principal Bank: First Minneapolis Bank
Financial Information:

	Dec 31 1985
	$'000
Sales revenues	256,580

No of Employees: 2,200

INTERROYAL CORPORATION
Community Ave, Plainfield, CT 06374
Tel: (203) 564 3341

Chairman: Alexander A Dadourian
President: Haig Dadourian
Senior Executive Officers: Poozant Piranian (Treasurer)

PRINCIPAL ACTIVITIES: Institutional and commercial furniture and fittings
Principal Bank: Chase Manhattan Bank
Financial Information:

	$'000
Sales revenues	30,000

No of Employees: 500

INTERSIL, INC
10710 N Tantau Avenue, Cupertino, CA 95014
Tel: (408) 996-5000
Telex: TWX 910 3380533 intrslint cpto

President: James E Dykes (and Chief Executive Officer)
Senior Executive Officers: R Paul Gupta (Senior VP and General Manager), H L Jensen (VP), Stephen L Pletcher (VP Marketing and Sales), Murray E Swedenborg (VP Finance and Administration)

PRINCIPAL ACTIVITIES: Electronic equipment and components and computer components
Parent Company: General Electric Co
Financial Information:

	$'000
Sales revenues	167,000

No of Employees: 4,000

INTERSTATE BAKERIES CORPORATION
PO Box 1627, Kansas City, MO 64141
Tel: (816) 561-6600

Chairman: Howard Berkowitz
President: Robert W Hatch (and Chief Executive Officer)
Senior Executive Officers: Ronald A Bevacqua (Executive VP and Chief Financial Officer), Leo E LaFauce (Executive VP), Thomas J Ratcliff (Executive VP), Paul E Yarick (VP and Treasurer), R D O'Connor (VP), Ray S Sutton (VP, Secretary and General Counsel)

PRINCIPAL ACTIVITIES: Bakery products including bread and cakes
Principal Subsidiaries: Interstate Brands Corporation
Principal Bank: First National Bank of Boston
Financial Information:

	May 31 1986 $'000
Sales revenues	708,483
Net income	15,332
Earnings per share	$2.95
Shareholders equity	86,642

No of Employees: 11,200

INTERSTATE CONTAINER CORPORATION
Grace & Meade, Reading, PA 19611
Tel: (215) 839 7795

President: Melvin Bricker

PRINCIPAL ACTIVITIES: Paper and board packaging materials
Principal Bank: Hamilton Bank
Financial Information:

	$'000
Sales revenues	60,000

No of Employees: 1,000

INTERSTATE DROP FORGE COMPANY
4051 N 27th Street, Milwaukee, WI 53216
Tel: (414) 444-0911

Chairman: Franklyn Esenberg (and Chief Executive Officer)
President: L F Schuetz (and Chief Operating Officer)
Senior Executive Officers: J R Phillips (VP and Treasurer), William Bryant (VP), James Mitchell (President Interstate Southwest Division)

PRINCIPAL ACTIVITIES: Metal castings and forgings
Principal Bank: M & I Marshall & Isley Bank
Financial Information:

	$'000
Sales revenues	50,000

No of Employees: 650

INTERSTATE POWER COMPANY
1000 Main Street, Dubuque, IA 52001
Tel: (319) 582 5421

Chairman: D H Buswell (and President, Chairman of Executive Committee) and Chief Executive Officer)
Senior Executive Officers: W H Stoppelmoor (Executive VP and VP Administration), G L Kopischke (VP Operations), D E Hamill (VP Budget and Government Affairs), W C Troy (Controller), L Schreiber (Secretary and Treasurer), D G Schroeder (VP Planning), D J Carlson (VP Production and Operations), A D Cordes (VP Distribution Administration)

PRINCIPAL ACTIVITIES: Supply of electricity
Financial Information:

	$'000
Sales revenues	300,000

No of Employees: 970

INTERSTATE RESTAURANT SUPPLY COMPANY, INC
901 E 31st Street, Los Angeles, CA 90011
Tel: (213) 232-4141

Chairman: Sidney Horowitz
President: Steve Horowitz (and Chief Executive Officer)
Senior Executive Officers: E D Lawrence (Executive VP Operations), Harold Horowitz (Senior VP Food Purchasing), Jim Matsumura (Senior VP Non-Food Purchasing), Irving Goldman (Senior VP Government Sales), William Howards (Senior VP Executive Sales), Morton Stone (VP Executive Sales), John Diaz (VP Distribution and Manufacturing), George Vernon (VP and General Manager Construction and Design), Robert Lloyd (VP and Comptroller), Harold Nelson (VP Credit Department)

PRINCIPAL ACTIVITIES: Wholesale distribution of food and equipment for restaurants and institutions
Parent Company: Rykoff-Sexton Inc
Principal Bank: Bank of America
Financial Information:

	$'000
Sales revenues	90,000

No of Employees: 370

INTERSTATE SECURITIES INC
2700 NCNB Plaza, Charlotte, NC 28280
Tel: (704) 379 9000

Chairman: Parks H Dalton (and Chief Executive Officer)
President: J Craighill Redwine (and Chief Operating Officer)
Senior Executive Officers: Edward C Ruff (VP and Treasurer), Glen R Shipway (VP), Michael D Hearn (Secretary)

PRINCIPAL ACTIVITIES: Provision of financial services including securities and commodity broking
Financial Information:

	$'000
Revenues	97,000

No of Employees: 940

INTERSTATE STEEL COMPANY

421 Touhy Avenue, Des Plaines, IL 60018
Tel: (312) 827-5151
Telex: WUT 282512 interstate dsp

Chairman: Howard R Conant
President: David S Soble
Senior Executive Officers: Dennis B Kildare (VP Sales), Raymond E Kivi (VP Purchasing), Dennis Breit (VP Operations), Arthur Karowski (Controller)

PRINCIPAL ACTIVITIES: Steel industry
Principal Bank: Continental Illinois National Bank and Trust Company of Chicago
Financial Information:

	$'000
Sales revenues	95,000

No of Employees: 250

INTER-TEL INC

6505 W Williams Fields Road, Chandler, AZ 85224
Tel: (602) 961 9000

Chairman: Steven G Mihaylo (and President and Chief Executive Officer)
Senior Executive Officers: Gary G Arnold (Senior VP and Chief Financial Officer), Maurice H Esperseth (Senior VP Administration, Operations and Research and Development), Morton J Wichansky (Senior VP Sales and Marketing), Craig W Rauchle (VP Regional), Barry E Wichansky (VP Regional), Edward O McHenry (Treasurer), Jayne S Campbell (VP Sales and Marketing), Thomas C Parise (VP Sales), Thomas N Peiffer Jr (VP Engineering)

PRINCIPAL ACTIVITIES: Supply of telephone equipment
Principal Subsidiaries: Inter-Tel COmmunications; Inter-Tel Equipment Inc; Intel-Tel Midwest Inc; Intel-Tel/NJ; TCI Industries Inc
Principal Bank: First Interstate Bank of Arizona
Financial Information:

	$'000
Sales revenues	38,000

No of Employees: 300

INTERTHERM INC

10820 Sunset Office Drive, St Louis, MO 63127
Tel: (314) 822-9600
Telex: 910 761 1007

Chairman: George W Hoddy; Vice Chairman: Gerald F Brown
President: Bernard Duchinsky (and Chief Executive Officer)
Senior Executive Officers: John Smith (Executive VP Administration and Treasurer), Joe Voypick (VP Operations), Harold Fleit (VP Marketing), Rafath Ali (VP Engineering), John Oxley (VP Manufacturing)

PRINCIPAL ACTIVITIES: Heating and ventilation equipment
Parent Company: Nortek Inc
Principal Bank: Centerre Bank
Financial Information:

	$'000
Sales revenues	88,000

No of Employees: 600

INTERTRANS CORPORATION

8505 Freeport Parkway, Suite 360, Irving, TX 75063
Tel: (214) 258-4888

Chairman: Sam N Wilson (and President)
Senior Executive Officers: David M Thomas (VP, Secretary and Controller)

PRINCIPAL ACTIVITIES: Operation of freight forwarding services
Financial Information:

	$'000
Sales revenues	26,000

No of Employees: 200

INTEXT, INC

Oak & Pawnee Sts, Scranton, PA 18515
Tel: (717) 342-7701

Chairman: H D Bright
President: Ronald N Tapper
Senior Executive Officers: David R Crowther (Senior VP), Jerome W Cwiertnia (VP Finance), Jeffrey A Brill (VP), Leonard Gingerella (VP)

PRINCIPAL ACTIVITIES: Operation of vocational schools; publishing of textbooks
Parent Company: National Education Corporation
Financial Information:

	$'000
Sales revenues	67,000

No of Employees: 300

INTRAWEST FINANCIAL CORPORATION

633 Seventeenth Street, Terminal Annex Box 5605, Denver, CO 80202
Tel: (303 293 2000

Chairman: Robert G Boucher (and President and Chief Executive Officer)
Senior Executive Officers: Clayton G Mammel (Executive VP), John A Giannakos (Senior VP and Controller), Clark E Weaver (Senior VP and Secretary), David W Witte (Senior VP, Treasurer and Assistant Secretary), Susan K Koonsman (VP Human Resources), Douglas F Ward (VP Examination and Chief Auditor), G Spencer Kesson (VP Corporate Insurance), Wesley H Sargent (VP Marketing), Ralph A Adams (VP and Senior Credit Manager), Fell L Stubbs (VP Affiliates Liaison)

PRINCIPAL ACTIVITIES: Holding company with interests in banking
Principal Bank: Intrawest Bank of Southglenn
Financial Information:

	Dec 31 1985
	$'000
Revenues	138,060
Net income	5,380

No of Employees: 1,090

INVACARE CORPORATION

899 Cleveland St, Elyria, OH 44036
Tel: (216) 329 6000

Chairman: A M Mixon III (and President and Chief Executive Officer)
Senior Executive Officers: E P Nalley (Senior VP International), J B Richey (Senior VP Engineering), M L Tabickman (VP Respiratory Products), Gary A Howell (VP Human Resources), Jay P Auwerter Jr (Chief Financial Officer)

PRINCIPAL ACTIVITIES: Manufacture of invalid care products and rehabilitation equipment
Principal Subsidiaries: Mobilite Corp
Principal Bank: National City Bank
Financial Information:

	$'000
Sales revenues	100,000

No of Employees: 1,200

INVESTORS HERITAGE LIFE INSURANCE COMPANY

200 Cpital Avenue, PO Box 717, Frankfort, KY 40601
Tel: (502) 223 2361

Chairman: Harry Lee Waterfield (and Chief Executive Officer)

President: Harry Lee Waterfield II (and Chief Operating Officer)
Senior Executive Officers: Raymond L Carr (VP Administration), Howard L Graham (VP Corporate Services), N Douglas Hippe (VP Actuary), Nancy W Walton (VP Underwriting), John Simmons (VP Credit Life), Donald R Philpot (VP Ordinary Life), Joe R Johnson (Treasurer and Assistant General Counsel), James D Milich (VP Service)

PRINCIPAL ACTIVITIES: Life insurance
Parent Company: Kentucky Investors Inc
Principal Bank: Farmers Bank and Capital Trust Company
Financial Information:

	Dec 31 1985
	$'000
Revenues	49,100
Net income	1,720

No of Employees: 150

IOMEGA CORPORATION
1281 E Main St., Stamford, CT 06902
Tel: (203) 359 9858

Chairman: D J Dunn
President: G P Fusco (and Chief Executive Officer)
Senior Executive Officers: E K Dahill (Corporate Development and Planning), D G Norton (VP Advanced Technical and Product Development), R J Linton (VP Quality), S D McVay (VP Marketing and Sales), L E Olson (VP Manufacturing), A J Radman Jr (VP Corporate Development), T Mark Morley (VP Finance and Chief Financial Officer)

PRINCIPAL ACTIVITIES: Manufacture of computer disk drives
Financial Information:

	$'000
Sales revenues	117,000

No of Employees: 1,200

IONICS, INC
65 Grove Street, Watertown, MA 02172
Tel: (617) 926-2500
Telex: ITT 4430022 ionics wtwn

Chairman: Averell E Daniell
President: Arthur L Goldstein
Senior Executive Officers: William E Katz (Executive VP Water Systems), Carl J McCurdy (Executive VP Bridgeville), Walter J Polens (VP Household Water Conditioning Sales), Herman A Zenk (VP Nuclear and Custom Fabrication Sales), Wayne A McRae (VP), Thomas A Kirkman (VP), T G Papastavros (VP Operations), Kachig Kachdurian (VP International, Water Systems), William B Jaconelli (VP Food and Chemicals), Edgardo J Parsi (VP Research and Development), Harry S Melikian (VP, Treasurer and Chief Financial Officer)

PRINCIPAL ACTIVITIES: Pollution control products
Principal Subsidiaries: (100% owned unless stated): General Ionics Inc; Ionics Italiana SpA (Italy); Italba Spa (58.2%) (Italy)
Principal Bank: The First National Bank of Boston
Financial Information:

	$'000
Sales revenues	69,000

No of Employees: 675

IOWA ELECTRIC LIGHT & POWER COMPANY
Tower, Cedar Rapids, IA 52401
Tel: (319) 398 4411

Chairman: Lee Liu (and President and Chief Executive Officer)
Senior Executive Officers: James M Davidson (Senior VP), Larry D Root (Senior VP Operations and Production), J B Rehnstrom (Senior VP Finance and Secretary), Samuel J Tuthill (Senior VP Technical Services), Robert J Kucharski (VP and Treasurer), Thomas J Pitner (VP and Legal Counsel), Virgil J Schmidt (VP Marketing), Robert J Latham (VP Corporate Affairs and Planning)

PRINCIPAL ACTIVITIES: Supply of electricity and gas
Parent Company: IE Industries Inc
Principal Subsidiaries: Cedar Rapids and Iowa City Railway; Industrial Energy Applications Inc; Iowa Land & Building Co
Principal Bank: Merchants National Bank
Financial Information:

	$'000
Sales revenues	453,260

No of Employees: 1,600

IOWA ILLINOIS GAS & ELECTRIC CO
206 E Second St, Davenport, IA 52803
Tel: (319) 326-7273

Chairman: Barry C O'Brien (and President and Chief Executive Officer)
Senior Executive Officers: Donald H Shaw (VP Finance), John J Daniel (VP Operations), W T Green (VP Public Relations and Marketing), Edward J Hartman (VP and General Counsel), Karl H Schafer (VP Power Production and Systems Operation), Stephen E Shelton (VP Engineering and Energy Planning), William T Green (VP Public Relations and Marketing), H R Poe (VP and Comptroller)

PRINCIPAL ACTIVITIES: Distribution of electricity and natural gas
Principal Bank: First National Bank of Chicago
Financial Information:

	$'000
Sales revenues	538,000

No of Employees: 1,500

IOWA MANUFACTURING COMPANY
916 Sixteenth Street NE, Cedar Rapids, IA 52402
Tel: (319) 363 3511
Telex: WUT 464475 iowa mfg b cdr

Chairman: Joseph Loufek
President: Ronald W Dunmire (and Chief Executive Officer)
Senior Executive Officers: Vernon L Schrimper (Executive VP Operations), Robert E Copping (VP Finance, Secretary and Treasurer), Weldon Thalacker (VP Sales)

PRINCIPAL ACTIVITIES: Quarrying and mining equipment
Parent Company: Raytheon Co, Lexington, MA
Principal Bank: Merchants National Bank
Financial Information:

	$'000
Sales revenues	100,000

No of Employees: 1,200

IOWA POWER & LIGHT COMPANY
666 Grand Avenue, PO Box 657, Des Moines, IA 50303
Tel: (515) 281 2900

Chairman: M W Putney
Senior Executive Officers: E L Birdsall (Senior VP Iowa Generation), L K Vorbrich (Senior VP Iowa Power), J P Glahn (VP Finance), Eugene E Young (VP Marketing), L R Homback (VP Area Operations), R E Jorgensen (VP Purchasing), D K Hamerlinck (VP Public Affairs)

PRINCIPAL ACTIVITIES: Supply of electricity and gas
Parent Company: Iowa Resources Inc
Financial Information:

	$'000
Sales revenues	323,000

No of Employees: 1,320

IOWA RESOURCES INC
666 Grand Avenue, PO Box 657, Des Moines, IA 50303
Tel: (515) 281 2900

Chairman: Mark W Putney (and President and Chief Executive Officer)

Senior Executive Officers: L K Vorbrich (VP and Legal Counsel), J P Glahn (Senior VP Finance and Treasurer)

PRINCIPAL ACTIVITIES: Supply of gas and electricity

Principal Subsidiaries: Enercor Inc; Enserco Inc; Iowa Computer Resources Inc; Iowa Gas Co; Iowa Power and Light Co; Middlewood Inc; Redlands Inc; Unitrain Inc

Principal Bank: Norwest Bank of Des Moines

Financial Information:

	$'000
Sales revenues	336,000

No of Employees: 1,500

IOWA SOUTHERN UTILITIES COMPANY

300 Sheridan Avenue, Centerville, IA 52544

Tel: (515) 437 4400

Chairman: C R S Anderson (and President and Chief Executive Officer)

Senior Executive Officers: Gordon F Cooper (Senior VP), Leo J Crow (Senior VP, Treasurer, Chief Financial Officer and Chief Accounting Officer), Robert K Harbour (VP), David A Little (VP), Thomas M Cox (Controller), S W Southwick (Secretary and Legal Counsel)

PRINCIPAL ACTIVITIES: Supply of gas and electricity

Principal Subsidiaries: Sidco Inc; Sirco Inc; Southern Iowa Manufacturing Co

Principal Bank: Irving Trust Co

Financial Information:

	$'000
Sales revenues	140,120

No of Employees: 550

IPALCO ENTERPRISES INC

PO Box 1595B, Indianapolis, IN 46206

Tel: (317) 261-8261

Chairman: Zane G Todd (and President)

Senior Executive Officers: John R Hodowal (VP and Treasurer), John D Wilson (Controller), Marcus E Woods (Secretary and General Counsel), John R Brehm (Assistant Secretary and Assistant Treasurer)

PRINCIPAL ACTIVITIES: IPALCO Enterprises is a holding company which indirectly conducts business through its two subsidiaries, Indianapolis Power & Light Co (IPL) and Mid America Capital Resources, Inc (mid-America). IPL is engaged primarily in the generation, transmission, distribution and sale of electric energy. Mid-America is the holding company for IPALCO Enterprises' non-utility operations

Principal Subsidiaries: Indianapolis Power & Light Company; Mid-America Capital Resources Inc

Principal Bank: Merchants National Bank & Trust Co; Manufacturers Hanover Trust Co

Financial Information:

	Dec 31 1985	Dec 31 1986
	$'000	$'000
Sales revenues	471,225	512,446
Income before taxes	112,634	200,377
Net income(1)	70,906	122,723
Dividends	56,666	57,074
Dividends per share(2)	$1.52	$1.52
Earnings per share(2)	$1.91	$3.27
Common stock	375,261	375,261
Retained income	177,001	242,650
Shareholders funds(3)	553,625	619,274

(1) includes $48,684,000 gain, $1.30 per share on sale of non-utility assets in 1986

(2) reflects two-for-one common stock split in 1986

(3) includes premium on 4% cumulative preferred stock of subsidiary

Number of Shareholders: 26,324
No of Employees: 2,292

IPCO CORPORATION

1025 Westchester Ave, White Plains, NY 10604
Tel: (914) 682-4500
Telex: 996575

Chairman: Robert S Savin (and Chief Executive Officer)
President: Charles V Linfante (and Chief Financial Officer)
Senior Executive Officers: Howard M Landa (VP Secretary and General Counsel), David L Brody (VP), Bernard Weissman (VP)

PRINCIPAL ACTIVITIES: Manufacture and wholesale trade in disposable paper products, medical and dental supplies and retailer of optical eyewear
Trade Names: Sterling Optical, Whitestone Products, Whaledent Int'l
Principal Bank: Chemical Bank
Financial Information:

	Jun 30 1986	Jun 30 1987
	$'000	$'000
Sales revenues	194,870	210,550
Income (loss) before taxes	9,767	(207)
Net income (loss)	5,881	(1,608)
Dividends	1,902	1,864
Dividends per share	$0.36	$0.36
Earnings (loss) per share	$1.10	($0.30)
Common stock	5,294	5,207
Retained income	50,637	47,165
Shareholders equity	66,499	62,002

No of Employees: 3,660

IPM TECHNOLOGY, INC

6851 W Imperial Hwy, Los Angeles, CA 90045
Tel: (213) 646-2994

President: Seymour Kahn
Senior Executive Officers: Robert S Goldstein (Executive VP), Randy Aser (Secretary and Treasurer)

PRINCIPAL ACTIVITIES: Manufacture of electronic equipment for the aviation industry
Principal Subsidiaries: (100% owned unless stated): Workman Electronic Products Inc; Mercury Service Inc; Mercury Refueling Inc; Crew Transit Inc; Madison and Wall Inc; IPM Industries Inc; MCM Oil Company (54%)
Principal Bank: Wells Fargo

Financial Information:

	$'000
Sales revenues	77,000

No of Employees: 900

IROQUOIS BRANDS LTD

41 W Putnam Avenue, PO Box 2000, Greenwich, CT 06836-2000
Tel: (203) 622-9000

Chairman: Terence J Fox (and Chief Executive Officer and President)
Senior Executive Officers: Joseph H Sweeney (Senior VP and Treasurer), Kyle Alexander (Senior VP and Secretary), Edward J Duer (VP and Controller)

PRINCIPAL ACTIVITIES: Vitamin and pharmaceutical products
Principal Subsidiaries: Leeds-Dixon Laboratories Inc; Chase Chemical Company; Pharmacaps Inc
Principal Bank: Bankers Trust Company
Financial Information:

	Dec 31 1985	Dec 31 1986
	$'000	$'000
Sales revenues	62,893	71,701
(Loss) before taxes	(4,445)	(4,245)
Net income	19	3,103
Earnings per share net	$0.02	$3.31
Common stock	899	673
Retained income	5,782	2,971
Shareholders equity	13,113	8,500

No of Employees: 600

IRVIN INDUSTRIES, INC

630 Fifth Avenue, New York, NY 10111
Tel: (212) 977-2500
Telex: WUI 661248 irvnyk

Chairman: H K Blumberg
President: Stephen M Gordon (and Chief Executive Officer)
Senior Executive Officers: W E Brennan (Executive VP Auto), R W Rhoads (VP Controller), M Bombacci (VP Europe), M Lobanoff (VP Business Development), G Eastley (VP Aerospace), T Montroy (VP Aerospace), J Swannigan (VP Aerospace)

PRINCIPAL ACTIVITIES: Manufacture of motor vehicle components; aeronautical systems
Parent Company: Halle & Stieglitz Inc, New York, NY
Principal Bank: Manufacturers Hanover Trust Company
Financial Information:

	$'000
Sales revenues	113,000

No of Employees: 2,230

IRVING BANK CORPORATION

One Wall Street, New York, NY 10005
Tel: (212) 635-7942
Cable: IRVINGBANK, NEW YORK
Telex: RCA-232241; WUI-62832; ITT-420268; TRT-177612

Chairman: Joseph A Rice (and Chief Executive Officer)
President: Samuel F Chevalier
Senior Executive Officers: John J Houseman (Executive VP), Peter C Palmieri (Executive VP), William C Bennett (Senior VP), Daniel J Keane (Senior VP), John F McIlwain (Senior VP), Joseph J Tenicki (Senior VP IBCI), William R Hamcke (Treasurer), Eliot N Vestner Jr (General Counsel and Secretary), Thomas J Mastro (VP)

PRINCIPAL ACTIVITIES: Banking
Trade Names: Irving Bank Corporation
Principal Subsidiaries: Irving Trust Company
Principal Bank: Irving Trust Company
Financial Information:

	Dec 31 1985	Dec 31 1986
	$'000	$'000
Net income	115,979	128,107
Earnings per share	$6.14	$6.83
Shareholders equity	955,926	1,052,347
Deposits	14,026,275	15,327,955
Total assets	21,650,661	24,232,521

No of Employees: 10,200

IRVING TANNING COMPANY (DELAWARE)

Main Street, Hartland, ME 04934
Tel: (207) 938-4491
Telex: WUT 950019 irving htld

President: Richard C Larochelle
Senior Executive Officers: Clarence J Ostalkiewicz (Executive VP and Treasurer), Walter Sauer (VP), Carl J Simon (VP and Secretary)

PRINCIPAL ACTIVITIES: Leather tanning and manufacture of leather goods including clothing and footwear components
Parent Company: Vista Resources Inc, New York, NY
Principal Bank: Manufcturers Hanover Trust Company
Financial Information:

	$'000
Sales revenues	60,000

No of Employees: 650

IRWIN UNION CORPORATION

500 Washington Street, Columbus, IN 47201
Tel: (812) 372 1020

Chairman: John A Nash (and President); Chairman of Executive Committee: Irwin Miller
Senior Executive Officers: Thomas D Washburn (Senior VP and Chief Financial Officer), Robert S Kaspar (VP and Controller), Matthew F Souza (VP and Secretary), Timothy L Murphy (VP and Treasurer), Dorothy J Jones (VP)

PRINCIPAL ACTIVITIES: Banking
Principal Subsidiaries: Inland Mortgage Corp; Irwin Union Bank & Trust Co; White River Capital Corp
Principal Bank: Irwin Union Bank & Trust Co
Financial Information:

	Dec 31 1985
	$'000
Revenues	37,330
Net income	2,190

No of Employees: 345

ISC SYSTEMS CORPORATION

E 901 Second Avenue, Box TAF-C8, Spokane, WA 99220
Tel: (509) 536-4014

Chairman: Ted C DeMerritt (and Chief Executive Officer)
President: John Lindeblad (and Chief Operating Officer)
Senior Executive Officers: Harold L Covert (Executive VP Operations), David M Stoner (Executive VP Marketing), Bruce C McGilaway (Senior VP Corporate Sales), J M Lekstrum (VP International Operations), Glen Cavanaugh (VP Marketing Support), Charles Furniss (VP Human Resources), Jerry Griffin (VP Field Services), Allen Hardin (VP Central Region), Ron Mason (VP Eastern Division), Geoffrey W Packwood (VP Development), Brady Rackley (VP Southern Region), Bernard D Reilley (VP Information Systems), Frank Wypychowski (VP Operational Programs)

PRINCIPAL ACTIVITIES: Electronic data processing equipment
Principal Bank: Seattle First National Bank
Financial Information:

	$'000
Sales revenues	166,000

No of Employees: 370

ISC WINES OF CALIFORNIA, INC

490 Second Street, San Francisco, CA 94107
Tel: (415) 541-9463

President: Richard N McCombs (and Chief Executive Officer)
Senior Executive Officers: Joseph A Lasky (VP-General Counsel/Secretary), Richard E Moyer (VP-Marketing), Ralph A Ward (VP-Operations), Edmund A Rossi Jr (VP-Winemaker), William D Reading (VP Sales-West), Gregory J Mauloff (VP Sales-East), Tim T Turner (VP Finance), William S Widman (VP Systems and Administration)

PRINCIPAL ACTIVITIES: Producer and marketer of wine, sparkling wine, brandy, vermouth, sweet wines
Trade Names: Colony, Lejon, Jacques Boney, Petri, G & D
Parent Company: Allied Grape Growers
Principal Bank: Union Bank; BT Commercial Corporation

No of Employees: 200

ISRAEL DISCOUNT BANK LTD

511 Fifth Avenue, New York, NY 10017
Tel: (212) 551-8500
Telex: ITT 420250 idb ui

Chairman: Raphael Recanati (and Managing Director)
Senior Executive Officers: A Kahana (Executive VP), D N Recanati (Senior VP and Comptroller), Haim Bar-Ziv (Senior VP), Benjamin Berger (Senior VP), Edmond Eskanazi (Senior VP), Leonard Greer (Senior VP), Gary Leeds (Senior VP), William J Roberts (Senior VP)

PRINCIPAL ACTIVITIES: Banking services
Parent Company: IDB Bankholding Corp Ltd
Principal Subsidiaries: Israel Discount Bank of New York (82%)

No of Employees: 6,100

ISS-INTERNATIONAL SERVICE SYSTEM, INC

1430 Broadway, New York, NY 10018
Tel: (212) 382 9800

Chairman: Paul Andreassen
President: James N Perry (and Chief Executive Officer)
Senior Executive Officers: Ronald Goins (Executive VP New York Group), Henrik Slipsager (Executive VP and Chief Operating Officer), Michael L Dudas (Senior VP Finance), Stanley J Gross (Senior VP), Bernard Young (1st VP Labor Relations), Robert E Atkins Jr (VP, Secretary and Legal Counsel), Gabriel A Gelber (VP), Irwin Arden (VP Atlantic Group), Robert Byrne (VP Midwest Group), Jan Kaupas (VP Southwest Group), Edward W Owens Jr (VP New England Group), Anthony Pisano (VP Energy Group)

PRINCIPAL ACTIVITIES: Cleaning and maintenance services
Parent Company: ISS-International Service System A/S, Charlottenlund, Denmark (62.58%)
Principal Bank: PRIVATbanken A/S
Financial Information:

	$'000
Sales revenues	137,000

No of Employees: 8,000

ITEL CORPORATION

55 San Francisco St, San Francisco, CA 94133
Tel: (415) 984-4000

Chairman: Samuel Zell (and President and Chief Executive Officer)
Senior Executive Officers: Elliott Steinberg (VP and Legal Counsel)

PRINCIPAL ACTIVITIES: Leasing of cargo containers and capital equipment
Principal Bank: Union Bank
Financial Information:

	$'000
Sales revenues	108,000

No of Employees: 900

ITT BUSINESS COMMUNICATIONS CORPORATION

300 E Park Drive, Harrisburg, PA 17111
Tel: (717) 564-4343
Telex: 842358

President: Howard A Laffler
Senior Executive Officers: Harry J Walten (VP Services), B H Tucker (VP, Secretary and General Counsel)

PRINCIPAL ACTIVITIES: Manufacture of telecommunications equipment
Parent Company: ITT Telecom Products Corporation, Raleigh, NC
Principal Bank: Dauphin Deposit Trust Company
Financial Information:

	$'000
Sales revenues	100,000

Principal Shareholders: ITT Corporation, New York, NY
No of Employees: 1,400

ITT CONSUMER FINANCIAL CORPORATION

400 S County Road 18, Minneapolis, MN 55426
Tel: (612) 540-0800

President: Thomas E Wilshire (and Chief Executive Officer)
Senior Executive Officers: Gladwin M Born (Senior VP), Paul B Fleckenstein (Senior VP Planning), James D Fowler Jr (Senior VP Administration), Clarence E Polzin (Senior VP Loan Administration), Richard A Schultz (Senior VP), Joseph F McCarthy (Senior VP Governmental Affairs), John E Thomas (Senior VP, Secretary and General Counsel), Ronald O Walters (Senior VP), Charles C Pratt (Senior VP), Roger L Shipp (Senior VP and Controller)

PRINCIPAL ACTIVITIES: Financial services
Parent Company: ITT Financial Corporation, St Louis, MO
Financial Information:

	$'000
Revenues	3,300,000

Principal Shareholders: ITT Corporation, New York, NY
No of Employees: 4,500

ITT CORPORATION

320 Park Avenue, New York, NY 10022
Tel: (212) 752-6000
Cable: Intelco New York
Telex: 420760 ITTHUI

Chairman: Rand Araskog (and Chairman Executive Committee, and Chief Executive Officer), Vice Chairmen: DeRoy C Thomas, M Cabell Woodward (and Chief Financial Officer)
President: Edmund M Carpenter
Senior Executive Officers: Howard J Aibel (Executive VP and General Counsel), Daniel P Weadock (Executive VP), Juan C Cappello (Senior VP)

PRINCIPAL ACTIVITIES: Interests in defense equipment, aerospace equipment, automotive components, electrical products, information services, finance and insurance services, Sheraton hotels, pulp and forest products and 37% interest in Alcatel NV, the world's largest telecommunications manufacturing company

Financial Information:

	Dec 31 1987 $'000
Sales revenues	19,500,000
Net income	1,002,000
Dividends per share	$1.25
Earnings per share	$6.76

No of Employees: 125,000

ITT COURIER TERMINAL SYSTEMS, INC

2406-TS 24th Street, Phoenix, AZ 85034

Chairman: Frederick W Gibbs
President: D E Lemon (and Chief Executive Officer)
Senior Executive Officers: Philip P Krumb (VP, Treasurer and Comptroller), F G Beldsoe (VP Quality Control), Robert T Basserman (VP and Secretary), Jack Milligan (VP), Donald W Baal (VP Manufacturing), George Colliat (VP Engineering), David Sedgwick (VP Marketing, West), Daniel F Lundy (VP), Robert McKeon (VP)

PRINCIPAL ACTIVITIES: Manufacture, sale and leasing of computer peripherals and point of sale systems
Parent Company: ITT Corporation, New York, NY
Principal Bank: Valley National Bank
Financial Information:

	$'000
Sales revenues	90,000

No of Employees: 1,800

ITT GRINNELL CORPORATION

260 W Exchange Street, Providence, RI 02901
Tel: (401) 831-7000
Telex: TWX 710 3818796 grnlintop pvd

Chairman: James D Fleming; Vice Chairman: Clarence H Rison
President: Daniel P Nugent (and Chief Executive Officer)
Senior Executive Officers: Harry W Wilcox Jr (Senior VP and President Industrial and Construction Division), James B Coyle Jr (Senior VP Operations), James R McMenamin (VP International), D D McKenney (VP, Secretary and Legal Counsel), Thomas W Cook (VP and President US Manufacturing and Supply), Dale J Waterhouse (VP and General Manager Manufacturing, US and Canada), George H Goodman (VP and General Manager Columbia PA), Harry C Hall (VP Administration), James E Bergold (VP Finance), Thomas A Jones (VP and President Engineered Piping Products), Paul T Paben (VP and President Canadian Manufacturing and Supply), Paul V Shea (VP and President Marketing), Jack L Huss (VP, President The Valve Co and General Manager), Raymond E Miller (VP, President Engineering Piping Products Group and General Manager), Richard T Howard (President Paul N Howard Co), Paul Milman (VP and Executive VP Engineering Piping Products Group)

PRINCIPAL ACTIVITIES: Manufacture of pipes, valves and fittings; metal foundries; plumbers' supplies
Parent Company: ITT Holdings Inc, New York, NY
Financial Information:

	$'000
Sales revenues	1,000,000

Principal Shareholders: ITT Corporation, New York, NY
No of Employees: 7,000

ITT HIGBIE MANUFACTURING COMPANY

4th & Water Sts, Rochester, MI 48063
Tel: (313) 651-5300
Telex: TWX 810 2321592 hgbiemfg roch

President: Ralph A Iorio
Senior Executive Officers: C J Clemens (VP Sales), Gerald W Cross (VP Finance, Secretary and Treasurer), R Liddicoat (VP Employee and Industrial Relations)

PRINCIPAL ACTIVITIES: Manufacture of steel pipes and tubes
Parent Company: ITT Corporation, New York, NY
Principal Bank: National Bank of Rochester
Financial Information:

	$'000
Sales revenues	50,000

No of Employees: 1,100

ITT INDUSTRIAL CREDIT COMPANY

1400 N Central Life Tower, St Paul, MN 55164
Tel: (612) 227-0011

Chairman: Melvin Brown
Senior Executive Officers: Robert J Osbeck (Senior VP Equipment Finance), Richard A Bobb (Senior VP Marketing), John F Kelly (VP and Secretary)

PRINCIPAL ACTIVITIES: Financial services
Parent Company: ITT Financial Corporation through ITT Diversified Credit Corporation, St Louis, MO
Principal Bank: Northwestern National Bank of St Paul
Financial Information:

	$'000
Revenues	500,000

Principal Shareholders: ITT Corporation, New York, NY
No of Employees: 300

ITT PHILLIPS DRILL DIVISION

US 12 & Liberty Trail, Michigan City, IN 46360
Tel: (219) 874-4217
Telex: WUT 258488 redhead a mci

President: John Knapp (and General Manager)
Senior Executive Officers: James Ham (VP Marketing), Dale Donnalley (VP Manufacturing), R Taschler (Comptroller)

PRINCIPAL ACTIVITIES: Manufacture of machine tools, hand tools, building materials and concrete anchoring devices for the construction industry
Parent Company: ITT Corporation, New York, NY
Principal Bank: Citizens Bank of Michigan City
Financial Information:

	$'000
Sales revenues	50,000

No of Employees: 400

ITT RAYONIER, INC

1177 Summer Street, Stamford, CT 06904
Tel: (203) 348-7000
Telex: ITT 4750024 itt ray ui

Chairman: Ronald M Gross (and President and Chief Executive Officer)
Senior Executive Officers: Stanley Barton (Senior VP Technical and Quality), James B Dykes (Senior VP Pulp Products Manager), William S Berry (Senior VP Land Forest Resources), W Lee Nutter (Senior VP Forest Products Operations), Carl W Peacock (Senior VP Administration), Samuel A Everitt (VP and Treasurer)

PRINCIPAL ACTIVITIES: Lumber and wood products, paper pulp, mining interests, chemicals
Parent Company: ITT Holdings Inc, New York, NY
Financial Information:

	$'000
Sales revenues	565,000

Principal Shareholders: ITT Corporation, New York, NY
No of Employees: 5,000

ITT THOMPSON INDUSTRIES

PO Box 2460, Southfield, MI 48037-2460
Tel: (313) 353-2400
Telex: TWX 810 2244950 thompson sofd

President: Desmond J Toal

Senior Executive Officers: C J Register (VP Operations), J J Klein (Comptroller)

PRINCIPAL ACTIVITIES: Manufacture of motor vehicle components
Parent Company: ITT Corporation, New York, NY
Principal Bank: Detroit Bank and Trust
Financial Information:

	$'000
Sales revenues	100,000

No of Employees: 1,400

IU INTERNATIONAL CORPORATION
1105 N Market Street, Wilmington, DE 19801
Tel: (302) 571-5000

Chairman: John G Christy (and Chief Executive Officer)
President: William H Waltrip (and Chief Operating Officer)
Senior Executive Officers: Robert W Wolcott Jr (Executive VP), Laurent J Remillard (Senior VP and Chief Financial Officer), W Allen Doane (Group VP Distribution), John B Bowron (Group VP Truck Load Transportation), Anna Mae Papso (VP and Controller), H Beatty Chadwick (VP, Secretary and Legal Counsel), Douglas L Cox (VP and Treasurer)

PRINCIPAL ACTIVITIES: Holding company with interests in transportation; agriculture and the manufacture of food products including sugar and coffee; mineral mining; commodity trading and real estate
Principal Subsidiaries: IU International Management Corp
Principal Bank: Morgan Guaranty Bank
Financial Information:

	Dec 31 1985	Dec 31 1986
	$'000	$'000
Sales revenues	1,941,775	1,455,391
Net income (loss)	(175,531)	88,354
Earnings (loss) per share	($6.43)	$3.22
Shareholders equity	160,453	244,925

No of Employees: 14,000

IVAC CORPORATION
10300 Campus Point Drive, San Diego, CA 92121
Tel: (619) 456-7000
Telex: TWX 910 3371273 ivacserv sdg

Chairman: Eugene L Step
President: Arthur J Benvenuto
Senior Executive Officers: Thomas K Bowie (Senior VP), Dale Hornback (VP Finance), Richard M Mirando (VP Sales), K B Parker (VP Research and Development), Fred Schramm (VP Manufacturing)

PRINCIPAL ACTIVITIES: Electronic medical and surgical equipment and instruments
Parent Company: Eli Lilly & Co, Indianapolis, IN
Principal Bank: Union Bank
Financial Information:

	$'000
Sales revenues	100,000

No of Employees: 1,700

IVY CORPORATION
PO Box 15633, Houston, TX 77020
Tel: (713) 674-8431

President: J S Burns
Senior Executive Officers: J G Wilking (Treasurer)

PRINCIPAL ACTIVITIES: Concrete products; quarrying products
Parent Company: Koppers Corporation, Pittsburgh, PA
Principal Bank: Mellon Bank
Financial Information:

	$'000
Sales revenues	65,000

No of Employees: 400

J & J CORRUGATED BOX CORPORATION
350 N Main Street, Fall River, MA 02721
Tel: (617) 679-2151
Telex: WUT 927774 jjhdqs friv

Chairman: Edwin A Jaffe (and Treasurer)
President: Robert L Jaffe
Senior Executive Officers: Morin A Handell (Executive VP), Carleton L Duvall (VP Finance), W D Hensley (VP Sales)

PRINCIPAL ACTIVITIES: Manufacture of packaging materials
Principal Bank: Trust Company Bank
Financial Information:

	$'000
Sales revenues	100,000

No of Employees: 650

J B HUNT TRANSPORT SERVICES INC
See HUNT, J B, TRANSPORT SERVICES INC

J C PENNEY COMPANY, INC
See PENNEY, J C, COMPANY, INC

J F JELENKO & CO
See JELENKO, J F, & CO

J HENRY SCHRODER BANK & TRUST CO
See SCHRODER, J HENRY, BANK & TRUST CO

J I CASE COMPANY
See CASE, J I, COMPANY

J I CASE WAUSAU PLANT
See CASE, J I, WAUSAU PLANT

J L CLARK MFG CO
See CLARK, J L, MFG CO

J M HUBER CORPORATION
See HUBER, J M, CORPORATION

J M SMUCKER CO
See SMUCKER, J M, CO

J P MORGAN AND COMPANY INCORPORATED
See MORGAN, J P, AND COMPANY INCORPORATED

J P STEVENS & CO, INC
See STEVENS, J P, & CO, INC

J W MAYS INC
See MAYS, J W, INC

JACK ECKERD CORPORATION
See ECKERD, JACK, CORPORATION

JACK WINTER INC
See WINTER, JACK, INC

JACKSON NATIONAL LIFE INSURANCE COMPANY
5901 Executive Drive, Leasing, MI 48910
Tel: (517) 394-3400

Chairman: A J Pasant (and President)
Senior Executive Officers: James H Pasant (Senor VP Administration and Assistant Secretary), Larry C Jordan (VP and Treasurer), William Gray (VP Corporate Relations), Thomas J Meyer (VP and Legal Counsel), John A Isaac (VP Underwriting), Thomas M Pasant (General Manager Regional), Robert A Fritts (VP Actuary), Malcolm J Sutherland (Secretary), Joseph Yacullo (VP Resources and

Development), Frank Deyoung (VP Planning and Human Resources), Beryl Timmerman (VP Business Development)

PRINCIPAL ACTIVITIES: Life insurance
Principal Subsidiaries: Jackson National Life Insurance Co of Texas
Principal Bank: Bank of Lansing
Financial Information:

	$'000
Revenues	686,270

No of Employees: 520

JACOBS ENGINEERING GROUP INC

251 South Lake Avenue, Pasadena, CA 91101
Tel: (213) 681-3781

Chairman: Joseph J Jacobs (and President and Chief Executive Officer)
Senior Executive Officers: Gary L Allison (Executive VP), Noel G Watson (Executive VP), James E Berkley (Group VP Central Region), William R Kerler (Senior VP Marketing), Robert J Shapiro (Senior VP), Richard J Slater (Senior VP Marketing), John W Prosser Jr (Senior VP Finance and Administration and Treasurer), Andrew V Reznack (Group VP Western Region), G L Stevenson (Group VP Field Operations), Paul E Stucker (Group VP Field Operations), Nazzim G Thawerbhoy (Controller), Robert M Barton (Secretary)

PRINCIPAL ACTIVITIES: Chemical and constructional engineering
Principal Subsidiaries: Jacobs Constructors Inc; Jacobs Constructors of California Inc; Jacobs Service Co; J E Meritt Constructors Inc; Ohio Atlas Construction Co Inc; Pace Company Consultants and Engineers; Pace International Inc; Southern Instruments Inc; UMC of Louisiana Inc; Zellers-Williams Inc
Principal Bank: Wells Fargo Bank
Financial Information:

	$'000
Sales revenues	220,000

No of Employees: 1,600

JACOBSON GROUP

One Mark Road, Kenilworth, NJ 07033
Tel: (201) 686-0200
Telex: 138699

Chairman: Harvey Jacobson
Senior Executive Officers: Charles Sundstrom (Executive VP), Richard Baubles (VP Research and Development), E G Fattell (VP)

PRINCIPAL ACTIVITIES: Manufacture of fasteners
Principal Bank: Citibank NA
Financial Information:

	$'000
Sales revenues	70,000

No of Employees: 400

JACUZZI, INC

11511 New Benton Hwy, Little Rock, AR 72209
Tel: (501) 455-1234
Telex: WUT 536446 jacuzzi a lrk

President: Raymond E Horan
Senior Executive Officers: Hugh H Shull Jr (VP)

PRINCIPAL ACTIVITIES: Manufacture of pumps, equipment for swimming pools and whirlpool baths
Parent Company: Kidde Inc
Principal Bank: First Commercial Bank
Financial Information:

	$'000
Sales revenues	117,000

No of Employees: 1,400

JAMES RIVER CORPORATION

PO Box 2218, Tredegar Street, Richmond, VA 23217
Tel: (804) 644-5411
Telex: 827316

Chairman: Brenton S Halsey
President: Robert C Williams
Senior Executive Officers: Judd H Alexander (Executive VP Pkg), James E Rogers (Senior VP Group Executive, Specialty Papers), Charles M Foster (Senior VP, Group Executive, Dixie Products), Ernest S Leopold (Senior VP, Group Executive, Communication Papers), Ronald L Singer (Senior VP, Group Executive, Towel and Tissue), David J McKittrick (Senior VP, Group Executive Finance, Transportation and Risk, Chief Financial Officer), Lawrence S Morrow (Senior VP, Group Executive Human Resources), E Lee Showalter (Senior VP, Group Executive Corporate Development), Ronald B Estridge (Senior VP, Group Executive Technology), Robert J Sherry (Senior VP, Employee and Public Relations), Benjamin A Thorp (Senior VP, Engineering)

PRINCIPAL ACTIVITIES: James River Corporation, Headquartered on the banks of the James River in Richmond, Virginia, is an integrated producer of pulp, paper and converted paper and plastic products. Through its subsidiaries, the Company processes basic raw materials - wood, woodpulp, synthetic fibers and plastic resins - into finished products such as towel and tissue papers, disposable food and beverage service items and folding cartons, as well as a wide array of communication papers and specialty industrial and packaging papers
Trade Names: Northern, Aurora, Vanity Fair, Brawny, Gala, Bolt, Marathon, Nibroc, Dorsette, Dixie, Papermaid, Dixie/Marathon, Maratuff Curtis printing papers, Polyweb, Airtex, Spill Mate, Nice'n Soft, Marina, Chiffon, Zee, Rollmastr, Natural Touch, Linensoft, Humboldt, Soft Plus, Signature, Crown, Kowtowls, Envoy, Signature, Safe-t-Gard, Crown Proco, Crown Safetex, Towlsaver, Towelmastr, Aqua Quilt, Shopmastr, Marawipe, (Registered Trade Names)
Principal Subsidiaries: COMMUNICATION PAPERS BUSINESS:- Business Papers Group. Premium Printing Papers Group: Richmond Converting Division, GB Papers (UK), Curtis Mills Division. Printing Papers Group. Groundwood Specialty Papers Group. Northeast Group: Paper Division, Pulp Division, James River-Marathon Ltd (Canada), Solka Floc Division, Woodlands Division. Northwest Group: Camas Mill, Wauna Mill. DIXIE PRODUCTS BUSINESS:- Handi-Kup Division. Canada Cup Division. PACKAGING BUSINESS:- Flexible Packaging Group. Advanced Films Division. Flexible Packaging Division. Coated Products Division. CZ Inks Division. Paperboard Packaging Group. SPECIALTY PAPERS BUSINESS:- Filtration & Custom Papers Group: James River-Fitchburg Division, Riegel Custom Products Division, Filtration Products Division. Graphics Group: Custom & Imaging Division, Decorative Products Division, Design Products Division, Premoid Division, Smith & McLaurin Ltd (UK). Specialty Industrial Papers Group: James River-Massachusetts Papermaking Division, James River-Otis Division, James River-Pepperell Division. Specialty Packaging Papers Group: KVP/Dunn Paper Division, KVP Paper Division, Dunn Paper Division. Parchment Division, Service Products Division, HP Smith Division, Riegel Packaging Papers Division. TOWEL & TISSUE BUSINESS:- Food Service Specialties Division, Gorham Absorbent Products. Nonwovens Division. TECHNICAL & ENGINEERING:- Canada Cup Research, Development & Engineering Plant, Corporate Engineering, Dixie Products Engineering, Environmental Services, Filtration Products Technical Laboratory, Graphics Research & Development, Mechanical Design Engineering, Nonwovens Research & Development, Packaging Research & Development, Neenah Technical Center, Technical Services Group. TRANSPORTATION:- Berlin Mills Railroad, Meridan & Bigbee Railroad, Riverside Transportation Headquarters, Western Transportation Company
Principal Bank: Sovran Bank, NA

Financial Information:

	Apr 30 1985	Apr 26 1986
	$'000	$'000
Sales revenues	2,492,009	4,479,001
Income before taxes	170,923	356,281
Net income	101,351	169,864
Dividends-total	18,400	36,413
Dividends per share (1)	$0.37	0.40
Earnings per share	$1.93	$2.03
Common stock	2,905	8,235
Retained income	269,133	478,243
Shareholders equity (2)	678,600	1,854,096

(1) annual rate
(2) preferred income and common shareholders equity

No of Employees: 35,455

JAMES RIVER CORPORATION-RIEGEL DIVISION

Frenchtown Road, Milford, NJ 08848
Tel: (201) 995-2411

Senior Executive Officers: Frederick T Dalrymple (VP General Manager), Orrin B Clifford (VP Marketing and Sales)

PRINCIPAL ACTIVITIES: Manufacture of specialty papers including packaging papers
Parent Company: James River Corporation, Richmond, VA
Principal Bank: Morgan Guaranty Trust Co of New York
Financial Information:

	$'000
Sales revenues*	70,000

* Riegel Division only

No of Employees: 800

JAMESBURY CORPORATION

640 Lincoln Street, Worcester, MA 01605
Tel: (617) 852-0200
Telex: WUT 920448 jamesbury worc

President: Howard G Freeman
Senior Executive Officers: William W Rawstron (VP Engineering), Joaquim S Ribeiro (VP and Chief Financial Officer), Daniel L DeSantis (VP and Chief Operating Officer), Joseph F Paparella (VP Corporate Sales and International)

PRINCIPAL ACTIVITIES: Manufacture of valves and process control equipment
Parent Company: Combustion Engineering Inc
Principal Bank: Bank of New England
Financial Information:

	$'000
Sales revenues	84,000

No of Employees: 1,000

JAMESWAY CORPORATION

40 Hartz Way, Secaucus, NJ 07094
Tel: (201) 330-6000

Chairman: Herbert Fisher (and Chief Executive Officer)
President: Arlie G Lazarus (and Chief Operating Officer)
Senior Executive Officers: Barry Rockland (Senior VP Finance and Chief Financial Officer), Kevin Regan (Senior VP), Joseph Radecki (Senior VP), John Stanhope (Senior VP), Eric Zorn (Senior VP Administration), Arnold Dunn (Treasurer), Gary Kauffman (Controller), Murray Kaplan (VP Advertising), Victor Scire (VP Sales), Howard J Blaugrund (Secretary), Alfred Petrillo (VP Planning and Engineering), Kenneth Simon (VP Industrial Development), Gerald R Fitzgerald (VP Personnel), Monroe J Simon (VP Human Resources), Andrew Loconti (VP Real Estate), Gary Boetes (VP Merchandising), Joe Ettore (VP Merchandising), Angelo Bianco (VP Merchandising), Tom Kiley (VP Merchandising), Jack Cotroeo (VP Distribution), David Owens (VP Management Information Systems)

PRINCIPAL ACTIVITIES: Operation of department stores
Principal Subsidiaries: Hardware Distributors Inc; Horizon Advertising Agency
Principal Bank: Marine Midland Bank
Financial Information:

	$'000
Sales revenues	523,000

No of Employees: 7,000

JANITROL AERO DIVISION

4200 Surface Road, Columbus, OH 43228
Tel: (614) 276-3561
Telex: TWX 810 482 1622 janitrol div

Senior Executive Officers: J L Witham (General Manager), Mark Karrenbauer (Personnel Director), Jim Cole (Purchasing Agent), P N Levesque (Engineering Manager), C R Hollinger (Director Operations), E E Schwarz (Director Marketing)

PRINCIPAL ACTIVITIES: Manufacture of components for the aerospace industry and pollution control equipment
Parent Company: Midland-Ross Corp, Cleveland, OH
Financial Information:

	$'000
Sales revenues	60,000

No of Employees: 500

JANTZEN, INC

PO Box 3001, Portland, OR 97208
Tel: (503) 238-5000
Telex: WUT 360572 jantzen a ptl

Presidents: Jerome M Pool (and Chief Executive Officer), Robert E Ludeman (Men's Division), Al Zindel (Misses Division)
Senior Executive Officers: J R Titsworth (VP Administration and Personnel), Dennis Maloney (VP Sales Men's Division), Doug Gibson (VP Sales Misses Division), Ray Tuleya (VP Finance and Treasurer), Robert S Lawrence (VP International), Rog Knutson (VP Manufacturing Misses Division), Dick Rockstad (VP Manufacturing Mens Division), Bob Rodkey (VP Merchandising Mens Division), Bart Blout (VP Merchandising Misses Division)

PRINCIPAL ACTIVITIES: Manufacture of swimwear and casual clothing for men and women; manufacture of swimming accessories including beach bags and towels and swim caps
Parent Company: Blue Bell Inc, Greensboro, NC
Principal Bank: First Interstate Bank of Oregon
Financial Information:

	$'000
Sales revenues	170,000

No of Employees: 4,000

JAS I MILLER TOBACCO CO

See MILLER, JAS I, TOBACCO CO

JB'S RESTAURANTS INC

1010 West 2610 South, Salt Lake City, UT 84119
Tel: (801) 974 4300

Chairman: Jack M Broberg
President: Clark D Jones (and Chief Executive Officer)
Senior Executive Officers: Paul W Warner (Senior VP Service), Richard B Huntington (Senior VP Development), Joe L Logan (VP), David J Asay (VP Marketing), Van L Dalton (VP Maintenance), Dan J Harrison (VP Training), Frank C I Hsu (VP Administration), Michael S Madsen (VP Operations, Big Boy), Robert S Merritt (VP Finance), Wallace E Broberg Sr (Secretary)

PRINCIPAL ACTIVITIES: Restaurant chain operating under the names JB's Big Boy, Bob's Big Boy, The Old City Jail Restaurants, The Suntowner and Apple Butter Farms
Principal Bank: Zions First National Bank

Financial Information:

	$'000
Sales revenues	96,000

No of Employees: 5,500

JEFFBOAT, INC

1030 E Market Street, Jeffersonville, IN 47130

Tel: (812) 288-0100

Telex: WUT 204130 jeffboat jeve

President: R W Greene III

Senior Executive Officers: Kent Hoffmeister (Executive VP and General Manager), Ken Peters (Senior VP Finance), Wayne P LaGrange (VP Production), W T Toutant (VP Engineering), Leo R Toupin (VP Industrial Relations), K J Funk (VP Sales), F J Haendiges (VP and Treasurer)

PRINCIPAL ACTIVITIES: Marine engineering

Parent Company: American Commercial Barge Lines Inc

Principal Bank: Chase Manhattan Bank

Financial Information:

	$'000
Sales revenues	60,000

No of Employees: 700

JEFFERIES GROUP INC

445 South Fugueroa Street, Suite 3300, Los Angeles, CA 90071

Tel: (213) 624 3333

Chairman: Boyd L Jefferies (and Chief Executive Officer)

President: Frank E Baxter (and Chief Operating Officer)

Senior Executive Officers: Alan D Browning (Executive VP and Chief Administration Officer), Raymond L Killian Jr (Executive VP), Barry M Taylor (Executive VP), James L Owens (VP, Treasurer and Chief Financial Officer), Jerry M Gluck (Secretary)

PRINCIPAL ACTIVITIES: Financial services including dealing in securities

Principal Bank: First Interstate Bank

Financial Information:

	$'000
Revenues	137,880

JEFFERSON BANKSHARES, INC

PO Box 711, 123 East Main Street, Charlottesville, VA 22902

Tel: (804) 972-1100

Chairman of Board: H Hiter Harris Jr

President: Hovey S Dabney (and Chief Executive Officer)

Senior Executive Officers: George A Bull (Executive VP and Treasurer), Robert P Hodous (Senior VP and Secretary), Walter A Pace Jr (Senior VP), Donald W Fulton Jr (VP-Investor Relations), O Kenton McCartney (VP)

PRINCIPAL ACTIVITIES: Jefferson Bankshares, Inc is a holding company for Jefferson National Bank and 4 non-bank subsidiaries with headquarters in Charlottesville, Virginia. Jefferson National Bank operates 76 offices and 19 automated teller locations throughout Virginia

Principal Subsidiaries: Jefferson National Bank; Jefferson Data Services Inc; Jefferson Properties Inc; Jefferson Financial Management Inc; Charter Insurance Managers Inc

Principal Bank: Jefferson National Bank

Financial Information:

	Dec 31 1985	Dec 31 1986
	$'000	$'000
Income before taxes	15,889	16,448
Net income	12,063	12,245
Dividends	4,479	4,903
Dividends per share	$1.07	$1.12
Earnings per share	$2.63	$2.66
Common stock*	3,062	4,609
Retained income	58,008	65,225
Stockholders equity	91,902	99,679
Deposits	1,005,853	1,090,279
Total assets	1,155,376	1,254,726

*number of shares in thousands

No of Employees: 919 Full Time; 115 Part Time

JEFFERSON SMURFIT CORPORATION

400 George Street, Alton, IL 62002

Tel: (618) 463-6300

Chairman: Michael W J Smurfit (and Chief Executive Officer); Deputy Chairmen: P A Smurfit, D F Smurfit

Senior Executive Officers: Michael R J Pettigrew (Secretary), Howard E Kilroy (Chief Operations Director), Robert D Holmes (Chief Financial Officer)

PRINCIPAL ACTIVITIES: Manufacture of packaging products

Parent Company: Jefferson Smurfit Group Ltd, Dublin, Ireland (79%)

Principal Bank: Continental Illinois National Bank and Trust Co

Financial Information:

	Dec 31 1985	Dec 31 1986
	$'000	$'000
Sales revenues	630,425	1,044,313
Net income	16,826	28,003
Earnings per share	$1.75	$1.46
Shareholders equity	125,230	141,852

No of Employees: 11,650

JEFFERSON-PILOT CORPORATION

101 N Elm Street, Greensboro, NC 27420

Tel: (919) 378-2011

President: William R Soles

Senior Executive Officers: William E Blackwell (Senior VP Corporate Development), Charles R Andrews Sr (VP Corporate Communications), Thomas Fee (VP and Treasurer), Richard W Herbin (VP Corporate Planning), Kenneth P Hinsdale (VP), Robert H Koonts (VP and Associate Legal Counsel), Charles G Powell Jr (VP and Legal Counsel), Louis C Stephens Jr (VP), John T Warmath Jr (VP)

PRINCIPAL ACTIVITIES: Holding company with interests in insurance, newspaper publishing and television and radio broadcasting

Principal Bank: National Bank of NC Charlotte

Financial Information:

	$'000
Sales revenues	1,000,000

No of Employees: 5,150

JEFFREY MARTIN, INC

See MARTIN, JEFFREY, , INC

JEFFRIES BANKNOTE COMPANY

1330 W Pico Blvd, Los Angeles, CA 90015

Tel: (213) 742-8888

Telex: WUT 194944 jeffriesbn sa

President: Hugh J McDonald

Senior Executive Officers: Robert K Wilcox (Executive VP), Harvey B Stern (Senior VP and Chief Financial Officer), John K Barnett (VP Production)

PRINCIPAL ACTIVITIES: Financial printing services
Parent Company: Chas P Young Co
Principal Bank: Bank of America
Financial Information:

	$'000
Sales revenues	70,000

No of Employees: 500

JELD-WEN, INC
3303 Lakeport Blvd, Klamath Falls, OR 97601
Tel: (503) 882-3451

President: Richard L Wendt (and Treasurer)
Senior Executive Officers: Larry V Wetter (Executive VP and Secretary), William B Early (VP), T S Schnormeier (VP)

PRINCIPAL ACTIVITIES: Manufacture of wooden window frames and doors
Principal Bank: First Interstate Bank
Financial Information:

	$'000
Sales revenues	100,000

No of Employees: 1,500

JELENKO, J F, & CO
99 Business Park Drive, Armonk, NY 10504
Tel: (914) 273-8600
Telex: TRT 177951 jelko ut

President: Ronald J Leavesley
Senior Executive Officers: Arnold Aaron (VP), John Condon (VP and Comptroller)

PRINCIPAL ACTIVITIES: Manufacture of dental products
Parent Company: Pennwalt Corp, Philadelphia, PA
Principal Bank: Citibank NA
Financial Information:

	$'000
Sales revenues	85,000

No of Employees: 250

JENNIE-O FOODS, INC
2505 Willmar Avenue SW, Willmar, MN 56201
Tel: (612) 235-2622
Telex: TWX 910 5782644 jennie o wlar a

Chairman: Earl B Olson
President: Charles B Olson
Senior Executive Officers: Donald H Handahl (VP Administration), Roger K Giese (VP Finance), Jim Richardson (VP Sales and Marketing), Jeff Olson (VP Retail Sales), Ralph W Hixon (VP Sales), John Jeffords (VP Production)

PRINCIPAL ACTIVITIES: Fresh and frozen poultry and poultry products
Principal Bank: First Bank of St Paul
Financial Information:

	$'000
Sales revenues	140,000

No of Employees: 1,600

JERRICO, INC
101 Jerrico Drive, Lexington, KY 40511
Tel: (606) 268-5211

Chairman: Warren W Rosenthal; Vice Chairman: David S Weil (and Senior VP)
President: John E Tobe (and Chief Executive Officer)
Senior Executive Officers: Theodore J Papit (Executive VP Operations), Christian Onden (Executive VP), Anthony M Lavely (Executive VP Marketing), William E Anderson II (Senior VP, Secretary and Legal Counsel), Ron Cegnar (Senior VP Procurement and Technical Services), William Connery (Senior VP Operations LJS Eastern Division), Bruce C Cotton (Senior VP Public Affairs), L A Gornto (Senior VP Finance, Treasurer and Chief Financial Officer)

PRINCIPAL ACTIVITIES: Operation of restaurants; supply of catering equipment; advertising interests
Principal Bank: Citibank
Financial Information:

	$'000
Sales revenues	562,000

No of Employees: 16,000

JERVIS B WEBB COMPANY
See WEBB, JERVIS B, COMPANY

JESSOP STEEL COMPANY
500 Green Street, Washington, PA 15301
Tel: (412) 222-4000
Telex: TWX 510 690 8545 jessop wash pa

President: Guy F McCracken
Senior Executive Officers: R T Orie (Executive VP Operations), R E Bailey (VP Technical Services), E J Houser (VP Purchasing and Traffic), C R Moulton (VP Commercial), A J Morack (VP and Treasurer)

PRINCIPAL ACTIVITIES: Manufacture of steel and specialty metals including tool steels and stainless steels
Parent Company: Athlone Industries Inc, Parsippany, NJ
Principal Subsidiaries: Jessop Steel of California
Principal Bank: Manufacturers Hanover Trust Co
Financial Information:

	$'000
Sales revenues	105,000

No of Employees: 780

JET AMERICA AIRLINES INC
3521 East Spring Street, Long Beach, CA 90806
Tel: (213) 492 6000

Chairman: J Thomas Talbot
President: Donald C Rhoades (and Chief Executive Officer)
Senior Executive Officers: John F Rhoades (VP Operations), John R Severson (VP and Chief Financial Officer), George L Chelius (VP, Secretary and Legal Counsel)

PRINCIPAL ACTIVITIES: Operation of airline services
Financial Information:

	$'000
Sales revenues	101,980

No of Employees: 300

JETRONIC INDUSTRIES INC
Main & Cotton Streets, Philadelphia, PA 19127
Tel: (215) 482 7660

Chairman: Daniel R Kursman (and President and Treasurer)
Senior Executive Officers: Garth E Bower (Group VP), Jerome I Kursman (VP and Secretary), Peter J Kursman (VP), Leonard W Pietrzak (VP Finance)

PRINCIPAL ACTIVITIES: Retail trade in furniture; manufacture of a range of electronic products
Principal Subsidiaries: Harry Levin Inc; Matthews Ross Corp
Principal Bank: Central Pennsylvania National Bank
Financial Information:

	$'000
Sales revenues	51,000

No of Employees: 550

JEWEL COMPANIES, INC
5725 N East River Road, Chicago, IL 60631
Tel: (312) 693-6000

President: Thomas H Sunday (and Secretary and Legal Counsel)

Senior Executive Officers: Scott Bergeson (Executive VP), Ralph E Davis (Executive VP), Clifford R Johnson (Executive VP Real Estate and Construction), John L Benner (VP and Controller), Charles E McClellan (VP Taxes), Jacob J Schnur (VP)

PRINCIPAL ACTIVITIES: Operation of retail stores including supermarkets and a drug store
Parent Company: American Stores Co
Financial Information:

	$'000
Sales revenues	5,700,000

No of Employees: 60,000

JEWELCOR INC

72 N Franklin Street, Wilkes-Barre, PA 18773
Tel: (717) 824-8761

President: Seymour Holtzman (and Chief Executive Officer)
Senior Executive Officers: Frank P Cuscela (Executive VP and Secretary), Joseph F Litchman (Senior VP, Chief Financial Officer and Treasurer), Raymond Perlman (Senior VP Jewelry Division), Leonard Walker (VP, RE and FAC), Earl Zimbler (VP Marketing)

PRINCIPAL ACTIVITIES: Manufacture and sale of jewelry; printing; restaurant and leisure interests
Principal Subsidiaries: (100% owned unless stated): Jewelcor Jewelers and Distributors Inc; Jewelcor Travel Services Inc; Jewel Diamond Setters Inc; Circus Playhouse Inc; Catalog Showroom Realty Inc; Gruen Industries Inc (58.9%); Robert Tabakow Inc
Principal Bank: Chemical Bank
Financial Information:

	$'000
Sales revenues	252,000

No of Employees: 1,700

JIM WALTER CORPORATION

See WALTER, JIM, CORPORATION

JIM WALTER RESOURCES, INC

See WALTER, JIM, RESOURCES, INC

JIMMY DEAN MEAT COMPANY, INC

See DEAN, JIMMY, MEAT COMPANY, INC

JLG INDUSTRIES INC

JLG Drive, McConnellsburg, PA 17233
Tel: (717) 485 5161

Chairman: John L Grove (and President)
President: Stephen R Cecil (Executive VP and General Manager), Paul K Shockey (Executive VP and Assistant Secretary), Charles H Diller Jr (VP Finance and Treasurer), Millard A Ullman (Secretary), Thomas N Nelson (VP Marketing), Rao G Bollimpalli (VP Engineering), Raymond F Tremly (VP Manufacturing), Ernest J Merz (VP Corporate Assurance), Samuel Swope (VP Human Resources)

PRINCIPAL ACTIVITIES: Manufacture of lifting equipment including cranes and aerial work platforms and hoists
Principal Bank: First National Bank of Maryland
Financial Information:

	$'000
Sales revenues	50,000

No of Employees: 700

JOAN OF ARC COMPANY

2231 W Altorfer Drive, Peoria, IL 61614
Tel: (309) 692-1020
Telex: TWX 910 652 4291 joan of arc peo

President: William R DeTroye
Senior Executive Officers: Robert H Truitt (Chief Executive Officer), William J Regan (Executive VP and Secretary), Larry Day (VP Finance and Treasurer), John Slevin (VP Sales and Marketing)

PRINCIPAL ACTIVITIES: Processing of vegetables; products include asparagus, corn and beans
Principal Bank: The Northern Trust Company
Financial Information:

	$'000
Sales revenues	88,000

No of Employees: 500

JOANNA WESTERN MILLS COMPANY

2141 S Jefferson Street, Chicago, IL 60616
Tel: (312) 226-3232
Telex: WUT 281029 joanna cgo

Chairman: Henry Regnery
President: Frederick C Meyers
Senior Executive Officers: Richard N Greisch (VP Finance and Treasurer), David R Meyers (VP Manufacturing, Sales and Marketing), T L Robinson (VP) Marketing and Sales Computer Products)

PRINCIPAL ACTIVITIES: Manufacture of window shutters and shades; hardware for drapes; plastic film and coated fabrics
Principal Bank: Harris Trust and Savings Bank
Financial Information:

	$'000
Sales revenues	130,000

No of Employees: 1,400

JOHN BLAIR COMPANY

See BLAIR, JOHN, COMPANY

JOHN BROWN INC

See BROWN, JOHN, INC

JOHN E CAIN CO

See CAIN, JOHN E, CO

JOHN FLUKE MFG CO, INC

See FLUKE, JOHN, MFG CO, INC

JOHN H HARLAND CO

See HARLAND, JOHN H, CO

JOHN HANCOCK MUTUAL LIFE INSURANCE COMPANY

See HANCOCK, JOHN, MUTUAL LIFE INSURANCE COMPANY

JOHN MORRELL & CO

See MORRELL, JOHN, & CO

JOHN O BUTLER CO

See BUTLER, JOHN O, CO

JOHN WILEY & SONS, INC

See WILEY, JOHN, & SONS, INC

JOHNSON & JOHNSON

One Johnson & Johnson Plaza, New Brunswick, NJ 08933
Tel: (201) 524-0400
Telex: 219 837 JJ HQ UR

Chairman: James E Burke (and Chief Executive Officer)
President: David R Clare (and Chairman, Executive Committee)
Senior Executive Officers: J Taylor Woodward III (Secretary), Robert E Campbell (Vice Chairman, Executive Committee), Stuart A Christie (VP, Operations, Technology and Development), David E Collins (Vice Chairman of the Board, Executive Committee), Victor J Dankis (Executive Committee), Lawrence G Foster (VP, Public Relations), George S Frazza (General Counsel), Robert Z Gussin, Ph.D. (VP, Science and

Technology), John J Heldrich (VP, Administration Executive Committee), Andrew J Markey (Treasurer), Ralph S Larsen (Vice Chairman, Executive Committee), John C Walcott (VP, Finance Executive Committee), Verne M Williaman (Executive Committee), Robert N Wilson (Vice Chairman, Executive Committee). Company Group Chairmen: John E Avery Jr, Jack Bowman, Philip E Carne, William Dearstyne Jr, Pierre J Dupasquier, Edward J Hartnett, Paul A J Janssen MD, Thomas M Lane, Ronald R Morris, Giorgio Petronio, Raymond P Regimbal, Thomas E Taylor, James R Utaski, Bert Van Deun

PRINCIPAL ACTIVITIES: Johnson & Johnson is the world's leading health care company with 165 companies located in 53 countries. Products include fabrics, hospital and surgical products including instruments, equipment, disposables, products for opthalmic microsurgery, pharmaceuticals, consumer baby products, dental supplies for orthodontic, preventive and restorative work, cough/cold preparations, prescription drugs, diagnostic systems for clinics and research laboratories, contraceptives, products for feminine hygiene, disposable surgical packs, gowns and surgical specialty products for use in major operating procedures, soft contact lenses, products for laser surgery, edible natural protein sausage casings

Principal Subsidiaries: Originating Companies:- Chicopee; Codman & Shurtleff Inc; Critikon Inc; Devro; Ethicon Inc; Iolab Corporation; Janssen Pharmaceutica Inc; The Johnson & Johnson Baby Products Company; Johnson & Johnson Cardiovascular; The Johnson & Johnson Dental Care; Johnson & Johnson Hospital Services; Johnson & Johnson Ultrasound; McNeil Consumer Products Company; McNeil Pharmaceutical; Ortho Diagnostic Systems Inc; Ortho Pharmaceutical Corporation; Personal Products; Surgikos Inc; Vistakon Inc; Johnson & Johnson Health Care; Johnson & Johnson Health Management Inc; Johnson & Johnson Orthopaedics; Johnson & Johnson Patient Care; LifeScan Inc; Noramco Inc; Windsor Minerals Inc

Financial Information:

	1985	1986
	$'000	$'000
Sales revenues	6,421,300	7,002,900
Net income	613,700	329,500
Dividends	233,200	244,700
Dividends per share	$1.28	$1.37
Earnings per share	$3.36	$1.85
Common stock*	182,900	178,400
Shareholders equity	3,350,900	2,824,200

*average shares outstanding in thousands

No of Employees: 77,100

JOHNSON, A, & COMPANY, INC

110 E 59th Street, New York, NY 10022
Tel: (212) 758-3200
Telex: ITT 428894 johnson

Chairman: Antonio A Johnson
President: John W Priesing (and Chief Executive Officer)
Senior Executive Officers: G P Souther (VP), Geoffrey T Magrath (VP Finance and Corporate Treasurer), T Grant John (VP)

PRINCIPAL ACTIVITIES: Petroleum refining; equipment for the treatment of waste water; manufacture of stainless steel and titanium; production of hydraulic motors and propellers
Principal Bank: Citibank
Financial Information:

	$'000
Sales revenues	1,000,000

No of Employees: 1,200

JOHNSON CONTROLS, INC

5757 N Green Bay Avenue, Milwaukee, WI 53201
Tel: (414) 228-1200
Telex: TWX 910 262 3084

Chairman: F L Brengal (and Chief Executive Officer); Vice Chairman: J F Daley
President: J H Keyes (and Chief Operating Officer)
Senior Executive Officers: W L Rootham (Executive VP and Chief Financial Officer), G T Jacobi (VP), R D Wilson (VP), F M Sterner (VP), M C Zilis (VP), J W Lewis (VP), J M Barth (VP), D A Bigler (VP), R E Goodson (VP), R D Gustine (VP), William P Killian (VP)

PRINCIPAL ACTIVITIES: Industrial control equipment; process engineering; motor vehicle batteries; automotive seating; plastic containers; plastics blowmolding machines
Principal Subsidiaries: Hoover Universal Inc; Johnson Controls International Inc; G-U Export Inc; JCI Automotive Enterprises, Inc
Principal Bank: First Wisconsin National Bank of Milwaukee
Financial Information:

	Sep 30 1985	Sep 30 1986
	$'000	$'000
Sales revenues	1,787,049	2,639,376
Income before taxes	142,130	174,397
Net income	78,290	95,926
Dividends(1)	31,702	44,147
Dividends per share(2)	$1.86	$2.00
Earnings per share	$4.80	$4.71
Common stock-par	9,356	3,157
Retained income	305,642	357,421
Shareholders equity	765,331	828,841

(1) Common and Preferred
(2) Common Shareholders

No of Employees: 26,200

JOHNSON MATTHEY INVESTMENTS, INC

PO Box 733, Valley Forge, PA 19482-0733
Tel: (215) 971-3000
Telefax: (215) 971-3051

Chairman: C Eugene Anderson; Vice Chairman: Joseph A Stevenson
President: Kenneth E Dubuc
Senior Executive Officers: Daryl Perkins (VP Gold and Silver Refining), Edward F Gilhooly (Associate General Counsel and Secretary), William J Quindlen (VP, Catalytic Systems), John Kutzler (Treasurer), Robert Cannon (Controller), David W R Wright (Assistant Secretary), Dr George McGuire (VP Research and Engineering), Edward J Grosso (VP, Corporate Planning and Development), Daniel M Miller (VP, General Counsel and Assistant Secretary)

PRINCIPAL ACTIVITIES: Johnson Matthey PLC are specialists in advanced materials and precious metals technology. Principal activities include the manufacture of catalysts and pollution control systems; speciality chemicals, pharmaceutical compounds and intermediates, electronic materials, components and equipment; the refining, marketing and fabrication of precious metals; and the production of pigments, ceramic colours and transfers. The Johnson Matthey group has just over 7,000 employees in 24 countries
Parent Company: Johnson Matthey PLC, London, UK
Principal Bank: Girard Bank

Principal Shareholders: Johnson Matthey PLC

JOHNSON PRODUCTS CO INC

8522 South Lafayette Avenue, Chicago, IL 60620
Tel: (312) 483 4100
Cable: JPCINT
Telex: 254-377
Telefax: (312) 962-5741

Chairman: George E Johnson (and President)

Senior Executive Officers: Dorothy McConner (Executive VP and Secretary), Marilynn J Cason (VP International), Danny O Clarke (VP Finance and Chief Financial Officer), Tehsel S Dhaliwal (VP Operations), Joan B Johnson (Treasurer), Gregory J Andrews (Executive VP and General Manager), Eric G Johnson (Senior VP Corporate Sales)

PRINCIPAL ACTIVITIES: Johnson Products Co, Inc manufactures and markets personal care products for the retail and professional markets in the US and overseas. Its main product lines include hair relaxers, conditioners, dressings, shampoos and cosmetics

Trade Names: Ultra Sheen, Ultra Sheen's Precise, Classy Curl, Ultra Star, Gentle-Treatment, Afro-Sheen, Ultra Sheen 2, Bantu

Principal Subsidiaries: Kovado Inc; Johnson Products Export Sales Inc; Johnson Products Co (UK) Ltd; Mellow Touch Laboratories Inc; Celex Corporation; Ultra Sheen Beauty Boutique Inc

Principal Bank: Independence Bank of Chicago

Financial Information:

	Aug 31 1986	Aug 31 1987
	$'000	$'000
Sales revenues	29,811	31,641
Income (loss) before taxes	(1,730)	1,130
Net income (loss)	(1,983)	1,234
Earnings (loss) per share	($0.50)	$0.31
Common stock	2,027	2,027
Retained income	8,849	10,083
Shareholders equity	11,150	12,378

Principal Shareholders: George E and Joan B Johnson

No of Employees: 285

JOHNSON WAX ASSOCIATES, INC

4041 N Main Street, Racine, WI 53403

Tel: (414) 631-2207

Telex: WUT 264429 jon wax rcn

President: Terence S Malone

Senior Executive Officers: Paul N Herrmann (VP Administration and Control)

PRINCIPAL ACTIVITIES: Manufacture of products for the leisure industry

Parent Company: S C Johnson & Son Inc

Principal Bank: Heritage Bank and Trust Company

Financial Information:

	$'000
Sales revenues	150,000

No of Employees: 1,300

JOHNSTON INDUSTRIES INC

111 Crossways Park West, Woodbury, NY 11797

Tel: (516) 921 1500

Chairman: David L Chandler (and President and Chief Executive Officer);

Senior Executive Officers: Samuel S Herkovitz (VP, Secretary and Treasurer)

PRINCIPAL ACTIVITIES: Wholesale trade in motor vehicle components

Principal Subsidiaries: Johnston Group Inc; Opp & Micolas Mills Inc; Southern Phenix Textiles Inc; Wales Manufacturing Co Inc

Principal Bank: European American Bank

Financial Information:

	$'000
Sales revenues	118,000

No of Employees: 1,900

JOHNSTON PUMP & GENERAL VALVE COMPANIES

1775 E Allen Avenue, Glendora, CA 91740

Tel: (714) 599-2351

Telex: TWX 910 584 1873 johnston glda

President: W J Blood

Senior Executive Officers: J Rasmussen (VP Finance), H A Greutink (VP Technical), P Giacobbi (VP Engineering), R Mytinger (VP Marketing), A Arace (VP Marketing), T J Fitzgerald (VP Industrial Relations), M Zaki (VP International Sales)

PRINCIPAL ACTIVITIES: Manufacture of pumps and valves

Parent Company: Aerojet-General Corporation-Ultimate Parent Company-Gencorp

Financial Information:

	$'000
Sales revenues	70,000

No of Employees: 450

JOHNSTOWN AMERICAN COMPANIES

5775 A Peachtree Dunwoody Road, Suite 300, Atlanta, GA 30342

Tel: (404) 252 8780

Chairman: John Lie-Nielsen (and President and Chief Executive Officer)

Senior Executive Officers: David V John (Executive VP and Chief Financial Officer), Tom McCauley (Executive VP, President Johnstown Mortgage Co), William B Hamilton (Senior VP Property Management)

PRINCIPAL ACTIVITIES: Real estate and property management services

Principal Subsidiaries: American Realty Partners Ltd

Principal Bank: Trust Company Bank

Financial Information:

	$'000
Sales revenues	86,000

No of Employees: 5,500

JONATHAN LOGAN INC

See LOGAN, JONATHAN, INC

JONES & LAUGHLIN STEEL, INC

1701 Wm Flynn Hwy, Pittsburgh, PA 15223

Tel: (412) 227-4000

Telex: TWX 710 664 4463

Chairman: R A Hay

Senior Executive Officers: J F Powers (VP and Treasurer)

PRINCIPAL ACTIVITIES: Steel industry; production of oilfield equipment

Parent Company: LTV Corp, Dallas, TX

Principal Subsidiaries: Monongahela Connecting Railroad Co; Aliquippa & Southern Railroad Co; Cuyahoga Valley Railway Co; Midland Terminal Co; Mahoning Valley Railroad Co; Olga Coal Co; Youngstown Mines Corp; Dearborn Leasing Co Inc; Jones & Laughlin Ore Mining Co

Financial Information:

	$'000
Sales revenues	3,300,000

No of Employees: 19,000

JONES & VINING INC

166 Forbes Road, Braintree, MA 02184

Tel: (617) 848 7310

President: Sven A Vaule Jr (and Chief Executive Officer)

Senior Executive Officers: Eugene J Zurio (Executive VP), Joseph A Iredale (Senior VP), Robert C Iredale (Senior VP), Edwin C Deschamps (VP Finance and VP Administration), Wallace A King (Treasurer), William C Sawyer (Secretary)

PRINCIPAL ACTIVITIES: Manufacture of a range of plastic products
Principal Bank: State Street Bank & Trust Company
Financial Information:

	$'000
Sales revenues	41,400

No of Employees: 680

JORGENSEN, EARLE M, COMPANY
10700 Alameda Street, Lynwood, CA 90262
Tel: (213) 567-1122

Chairman: Earle M Jorgensen
President: John W Jorgensen
Senior Executive Officers: S M Robinson (Senior VP Finance), J F Watkins (Senior VP Administration), L R Terry (Senior VP Marketing), W J Shaw (VP and Treasurer), P Densmore (VP and Controller), R J Haas (VP and Secretary)

PRINCIPAL ACTIVITIES: Distributor and processor of steel and aluminum. Steel producer and manufacturer of heavy steel, aluminum and other non-ferrous forgings
Trade Names: Earle M Jorgensen Company for parent and all subsidiaries
Principal Subsidiaries: Jorgensen Steel Company; Alloy Steels Inc; Wm G Wetherall Co; EMJ Company of New England
Principal Bank: Security Pacific National Bank
Financial Information:

	Dec 31 1985	Dec 31 1986
	$'000	$'000
Sales revenues	297,442	285,171
Income (loss) before taxes	15,075	(28,248)
Net income (loss)	9,351	(14,812)*
Dividends	6,334	6,314
Dividends per share	$1.00	$1.00
Earnings (loss) per share	$1.48	($2.35)
Common stock	7,101	7,101
Retained income	160,365	139,239
Shareholders equity	164,884	144,003

*The company charged 1986 income an amount of $22,440,000 as a "provision for asset impairment" of plant equipment and inventories connected with serving the depressed energy industry. ($20,800,000 of this amount was for plant and equipment)

No of Employees: 1,662

JOSEPH E SEAGRAM & SONS, INC
See SEAGRAM, JOSEPH E, & SONS, INC

JOSEPH, I S, COMPANY, INC
777 Grain Exchange Bldg, Minneapolis, MN 55415
Tel: (612) 338-8431
Telex: WUT 290615 iskosephco mps

Chairman: Burton M Joseph
President: Robert D Anderson
Senior Executive Officers: David J Hopkins (Senior VP Processing), A P McMaster (Senor VP), Dana X Marshall (VP Finance), Charles McInerney (VP)

PRINCIPAL ACTIVITIES: Shipping and wholesale trade in grain and animal feedstuffs
Principal Bank: Northwestern National Bank of Minneapolis
Financial Information:

	$'000
Sales revenues	350,000

No of Employees: 120

JOSEPH M HERMAN SHOE CO
See HERMAN, JOSEPH M, SHOE CO

JOSEPHSON INTERNATIONAL INC
40 West 57th Street, New York, NY 10019
Tel: (212) 556 5600

Chairman: Marvin Josephson (and President and Chief Executive Officer); Vice Chairman: Ralph S Mann
Senior Executive Officers: Michael Cooperman (VP, Chief Financial Officer and Treasurer), Ronald T Peters (Secretary), Jim Wiatt (Subsidiary Officer)

PRINCIPAL ACTIVITIES: Josephson International Inc Owns: International Creative Management, Inc (ICM) one of the two largest talent and literary agencies in the world, representing over 2,600 active clients; ICM Artists Ltd, a leading manager of classical music and dance artists; and Impresario, presenting major cultural and entertainment attractions; Josephson Office Products, the largest office planning, design and furnishings group in the country; and Robert Keeshan Associates, Inc, which holds the rights to the Captain Kangaroo Television Programs
Principal Subsidiaries: ICM Artists Ltd; International Creative Management Inc; Josephson Office Planning Design Furniture; General Office Products Co;Inventory Networking Inc; United Business Interiiors; Robert Keeshan Associates Inc; Rucker-Fuller Co;Southwest Business Interiors; Wilson Business Products
Principal Bank: Chase Manhattan Bank
Financial Information:

	Jun 30 1986	Jun 20 1987
	$'000	$'000
Sales revenues	236,629	235,128
Income (loss) before taxes	(4,688)	5,256
Net income	6,962	21,883
Earnings per share net	$1.44	$4.61
Common stock	367	372
Retained income	8,132	30,015
Shareholders equity	17,477	35,096

No of Employees: 1,290

JOSLYN CORPORATION
30 South Wacker Drive, Chicago, IL 60606
Tel: (312) 454-2900
Telex: TWX 910 221 4220

Chairman: Donald B Hamister (and Chief Executive Officer)
President: Richard A Kruk (and Chief Operating Officer)
Senior Executive Officers: Alwyn A Desouza (Group VP), Roland E Mattson (VP), Raymond E Micheletti (VP and General Manager), Lawrence G Wolski (VP, Treasurer and Chief Financial Officer), James T Staulcup (VP and General Manager Hardware Division)

PRINCIPAL ACTIVITIES: Electrical distribution telecommunications equipment and defense equipment
Principal Subsidiaries: Joslyn Defense Systems Inc; Joslyn Clark Controls Inc; Joslyn Industries Canada Ltd
Principal Bank: The First National Bank of Chicago
Financial Information:

	$'000
Sales revenues	161,514

No of Employees: 1,700

JOSTENS, INC
5501 Norman Center Drive, Minneapolis, MN 55437
Tel: (612) 830-3300

Chairman: H William Lurton (and Chief Executive Officer); Vice Chairman: John W Stodder
President: Robert W Leslie (and Chief Operating Officer)
Senior Executive Officers: Don C Lein (Executive VP Finance and Administration and Secretary), Robert L Pope (Executive

VP, Scholastic, Printing and Publishing, Artex, Canada), Gary L Buckmiller (Senior VP Education Division)

PRINCIPAL ACTIVITIES: Jewelry, clothing and stationery for academic use including class rings, gowns and caps, diplomas and graduation announcements; yearbooks; custom-imprinted activewear; customized sales and service awards; student photography packages; athletic awards; computer-based educational products and services

Principal Divisions: Scholastic Division; Printing & Publishing Division; Recognition Division; Artex Division; Prescription Learning Corporation; Jostens Canada Ltd

Principal Bank: First Bank Minneapolis

Financial Information:

	Jun 30 1986	Jun 30 1987
	$'000	$'000
Sales revenues	449,117	505,151
Income before taxes(1)	65,096	65,887
Net income	40,315	44,712
Dividends	18,451	17,169
Dividends per share	$0.44	$0.48
Earnings per share(1)	$0.80	$0.93
Common stock(2)	20,727	35,828
Retained income	169,829	91,020
Shareholders equity	192,947	112,892

(1) continuing operations
(2) number of shares in thousands

No of Employees: 7,000 plus 1,200 independent sales representatives

JOURNAL COMMUNICATIONS

333 W State Street, Milwaukee, WI 53203
Tel: (414) 224-2000

Chairman: Thomas J McCollow
President: Warren J Heyse
Senior Executive Officers: Robert A Kahlor (Executive VP, President Newspapers Inc), Steven J Smith (Senior VP, President WTMJ Inc), Roger Perry (Senior VP, Chairman Perry Printing), Donald J Massa (Senior VP and Treasurer), Robert C James (Senior VP, President Midwestern Relay), Thomas Karavakis (Senior VP, President ADD, Inc), Joseph Bower (VP, President MJE Corp), Jack E Knake (VP Corporate Communications)

PRINCIPAL ACTIVITIES: Publishing of newspapers and shopping papers; radio and television broadcasting; commercial printing services; telecommunications services

Principal Subsidiaries: Journal/Sentinel Inc; WTMJ Inc; Perry Printing Corp; Midwestern Relay Co; Add Inc; MJE Corp

Principal Bank: First Wisconsin National Bank

Principal Shareholders: 2,450 employees

No of Employees: 3,650

JOVAN, INC

980 N Michigan Avenue, Chicago, IL 60611
Tel: (312) 951-7000
Telex: WUT 25 4472 jovaninc cgo

President: Richard E Meyer
Senior Executive Officers: Barry E Shipp (Executive VP), Joseph P Forkish (Senior VP and General Manager), Ken Cawthorne (VP Finance and Treasurer), Neil Rocklin (VP Sales), William Hughes (VP Operations), Russell Williams (VP Engineering), Rod Heckman (VP Export), Bruce Cowgill (VP Marketing), Charles Pomles (VP Package Development)

PRINCIPAL ACTIVITIES: Perfumes, toiletries and cosmetic products

Parent Company: Beecham Group PLC, UK

Principal Bank: American National Bank

Financial Information:

	$'000
Sales revenues	100,000

No of Employees: 1,000

JOY MANUFACTURING COMPANY

301 Grant Street, Pittsburgh, PA 15219
Tel: (412) 562-4500

Chairman: A William Calder (and President and Chief Executive Officer)
Senior Executive Officers: James W Wilcock (Chairman Executive Committee), A F Atwood (VP Finance), A M Hess (VP Petroleum Equipment Group), P D Castenholz (VP Process Equipment Group), R M Morford (VP Environmental Systems Group), J R Glansdor (VP Human Resources), R D Jordan (VP Labor Relations), William Galese (VP General Products Group), C L Harper (VP, WKM Division), E F Minter (VP Industrial Compressor Group), J J Bellas (VP and Treasurer), J A Chokey (VP and Legal Counsel), F M Corby Jr (VP and Controller)

PRINCIPAL ACTIVITIES: Manufacture of machinery for the coal mining industry and the oil and gas industry; air pollution control equipment; compressors

Principal Subsidiaries: Joy Finance Co; Ozone Industries Inc; T&L Supply Inc

Principal Bank: Mellon Bank

Financial Information:

	Sep 30 1985	Sep 30 1986
	$'000	$'000
Sales revenues	800,180	692,755
Net income (loss)	14,670	(83,884)
Earnings (loss) per share	-	($4.73)
Shareholders equity	-	314,527

No of Employees: 7,000

JOYCE BEVERAGES, INC

Joyce Road, New Rochelle, NY 10802
Tel: (914) 632-7060

Chairman: John M Joyce
President: Sydney P Mudd
Senior Executive Officers: Robert J Pritchard (VP and Treasurer), William J Colliar (VP and Secretary), Thomas P Joyce (VP), John M Joyce III (VP), Timothy J Joyce (VP), Shaun Higgins (VP)

PRINCIPAL ACTIVITIES: Bottling of non-alcoholic beverages

Principal Bank: Lincoln First Bank

Financial Information:

	$'000
Sales revenues	200,000

No of Employees: 1,600

JP INDUSTRIES, INC

325 Eisenhower Parkway, Ann Arbor, MI 48104
Tel: (313) 663-6749
Telex: 8102232419

Chairman: John Psarouthakis (and President)
Senior Executive Officers: John L Menson, Gareth L Reed, Mike Nistal

PRINCIPAL ACTIVITIES: The operations of the Company are divided into the following industry segments: Plumbing Products: the Company manufactures and sells single-handled and two-handled faucets, wastes, drains and strainers, as well as stamped and forged brass and stainless steel trim parts. These products are sold for new construction and replacement purposes in residential, commercial, institutional and industrial buildings. Transportation Components: the Company manufactures and sells cams, camshafts and stamped and forged components for the automotive, aviation, farm equipment, marine, railroad and

truck industries. These products are sold to the replacement parts markets, as well as to the original equipment manufacturers
Trade Names: Briggs, JPI Plumbing Products, Spin-N-Grin, Weyburn-Bartel
Principal Subsidiaries: American Metalcraft Company; Precision Cold Forged Products; Weyburn-Bartel Group: Grand Haven MI, Elstead (UK), Hamburg (Germany). JPI Plumbing Products Company; Garvin; Guarantee Specialties Inc; Briggs Inc
Principal Bank: National Bank of Detroit
Financial Information:

	$'000
Sales revenues	133,000

No of Employees: 2,000

JSJ CORPORATION

700 Robbins Road, Box 687, Grand Haven, MI 49417
Tel: (616) 842-6350

Chairman: Paul A Johnson (and Treasurer)
President: F M Johnson (and Chief Executive Officer)
Senior Executive Officers: Michael Silver (VP Finance)

PRINCIPAL ACTIVITIES: Metal castings; plastics; machine tools; data processing services
Principal Bank: Pacesetter Bank & Trust West
Financial Information:

	$'000
Sales revenues	90,000

No of Employees: 1,400

JUDY BOND INC

See BOND, JUDY, INC

JUDY'S INC

7710 Haskell Avenue, Van Nuys, CA 91406
Tel: (213) 873 6200

Chairman: Lawrence Israel (and Treasurer)
President: Marcia Israel (and Chief Executive Officer)
Senior Executive Officers: Ron Goldstein (VP Operations), Ben Sumner (VP Finance and Secretary)

PRINCIPAL ACTIVITIES: Retail trade in ladies' fashions through a chain of "Judy's" stores; retail of men's apparel through "G.Hq" stores
Principal Bank: Bank of America
Financial Information:

	Jan 31 1986	Jan 31 1987
	$'000	$'000
Sales revenues	56,729	58,717
Income before taxes	2,014	837
Net income	1,170	426
Dividends	272	272
Dividends per share	$0.06	$0.06
Earnings per share	$0.26	$0.09
Common stock	4,113	4,108
Retained income	12,054	12,208
Shareholders equity	16,167	16,316

Principal Shareholders: M & L Israel
No of Employees: 1,100

JUMPING-JACKS SHOES INC

100 Fifth Street, Monett, MO 65708
Tel: (417) 235 3122

Chairman: John C McPhee (and President)
Senior Executive Officers: Gerald A McCaffrey (Executive VP and General Manager), Charles E Hinkle (VP Administration and Treasurer), John E Schaeffer (Secretary), James H Schumacher (VP Sales), Rose Mary Lobato (VP Retail), Donald Mills (VP Style)

PRINCIPAL ACTIVITIES: Manufacture of footwear
Principal Bank: Bank of America
Financial Information:

	$'000
Sales revenues	42,000

No of Employees: 1,000

JUNO LIGHTING INC

2001 South Mt Prospect Road, PO Box 5065, Des Plaines, IL 60017-5065
Tel: (312) 827 9880
Telefax: (312) 827-2925

President: Robert S Fremont (and Treasurer)
Senior Executive Officers: George J Bilek (Controller), Julius Lewis (Secretary), Ronald McCarthy (VP Sales), Thomas W Tomsovic (VP Operations)

PRINCIPAL ACTIVITIES: Manufacture of track and recessed lighting products
Trade Names: Juno Trac-Master (R), Juno Down-Lites (R)
Principal Bank: American National Bank
Financial Information:

	Nov 30 1985	Nov 30 1986
	$'000	$'000
Sales revenues	37,167	42,756
Income before taxes	12,268	14,136
Net income	6,339	7,461
Earnings per share*	$1.39	$1.63
Common stock	46	46
Retained income	19,192	26,653
Shareholders equity	22,061	29,418

*after adjusting for a 2-for-1 stock split in the form of a stock dividend declared in April, 1985

No of Employees: 400

JUPITER INDUSTRIES, INC

400 E Randolph Street, Chicago, IL 60601
Tel: (312) 527-2000

Chairman: Jerrold Wexler
President: Edward W Ross
Senior Executive Officers: Philip Rootberg (VP Corporate Development), Elmer R Bruksch (VP), Fredric P Dunne (VP and Treasurer), C H Jamison (VP), J I Kidd (VP), Ira A Kipnis (VP), Jerry Margolis (VP), James V Scattergood (VP)

PRINCIPAL ACTIVITIES: The Company has interests in trucking, construction, natural gas distribution, air conditioning and bakery products
Principal Bank: Continental Bank
Financial Information:

	$'000
Sales revenues	260,000

No of Employees: 2,500

JUSTIN BOOT COMPANY

PO Box 548, Fort Worth, TX 76101
Tel: (817) 332-4385
Telex: 925300 JUSTIN BOOT

Chairman: John Justin
President: J T Dickenson (and Chief Operating Officer)
Senior Executive Officers: Gary Liggett (VP and Controller), Frank Scivetti (VP Sales)

PRINCIPAL ACTIVITIES: Manufacture of footwear and leather goods
Parent Company: Justin Industries Inc
Principal Bank: Texas American Bank/Fort Worth

Financial Information:

	1985 $'000	1986 $'000
Sales revenues	75,000	75,000
Income before taxes	3,200	4,200
Net income	1,900	2,200
Shareholders equity	14,000	16,000

No of Employees: 1,150

JUSTIN INDUSTRIES, INC

2821 W 7th Street, Fort Worth, TX 76101
Tel: (817) 336-5125

Chairman: John S Justin Jr (and Chief Executive Officer)
President: Ernest Blank (and Chief Operating Officer)
Senior Executive Officers: Edward L Stout Jr (VP Brick), J T Dickenson (VP Boots), Jon M Bennett (VP Personnel), David E Houseman (VP Finance and Chief Financial Officer), Richard J Savitz (Vice President and Controller)

PRINCIPAL ACTIVITIES: Production of building materials; sale and service of John Deere earthmoving equipment; manufacture of footwear and leather goods; publishing of books
Principal Bank: Texas American Bank
Financial Information:

	$'000
Sales revenues	296,990

No of Employees: 4,275

JWT GROUP, INC

466 Lexington Avenue, New York, NY 10017
Tel: (212) 210-7000
Telex: 425-769

Chairman: Don Johnston (and Chief Executive Officer)
Senior Executive Officers: Hugh P Connell (Executive VP and Secretary), Glen A Dell (Executive VP-Finance and Administration)

PRINCIPAL ACTIVITIES: Advertising, public relations and market research
Principal Subsidiaries: J Walter Thompson Company; Hill and Knowton, Inc; Lord, Geller, Federico, Einstein, Inc; MRB Group, Inc
Principal Bank: Irving Trust Co
Financial Information:

	$'000
Sales revenues	559,042

Principal Shareholders: Institution own approximately (60%); Directors and Officers own approximately (2.2%)
No of Employees: 9,500

K MART CORPORATION

3100 W Big Beaver Rd, Troy, MI 48084
Tel: (313) 643-1000

Chairman: Bernard M Fauber (and Chief Executive Officer); Vice Chairman: Samuel G Leftwich
President: Joseph E Antonini (and Chief Operating Officer)
Senior Executive Officers: Robert E Dewar (Chairman of the Executive and Finance Committees), Larry M Parkin (Executive VP, US K mart Stores), Joseph R Thomas (Executive VP, Chief Administrative Officer), Roger E Davis (Senior VP, General Counsel and Secretary), Richard S Miller (Senior VP, Store Operations), Thomas H Nigolian (Senior VP, General Merchandise), Bernard E Thomas (Senior VP, Corporate Personnel), Edward C Andrews (VP, Midwestern Region), David M Carlson (VP, Corporate Information Systems), Ronald R Dejaeghere (VP, Store Planning and Design), Gerald R Fletcher (VP), Helen C Lefler (VP and Treasurer), Robert C McAllister (VP, Southern Region), Glen R Mielki (VP, Southwestern Region), James L Moser (VP, Merchandise Systems Coordinator), Thomas F Murasky (VP and Chief Financial Officer), Anthony N Palizzi (VP, Associate General Counsel and Assistant Secretary), Arthur E Riley (VP, Eastern Region), Michael L Skiles (VP, Corporate Facilities), Glenn B Smith (VP, President of K mart Apparel Corp), A Robert Stevenson (VP, Government and Public Relations), David P Walling (VP, Corporate Accounting and Reporting), Thomas W Watkins (VP, Western Region), Michael G Wellman (VP, Corporate Planning), Richard O Williams VP, Central Region)

PRINCIPAL ACTIVITIES: K mart Corporation is the world's second-largest retailer. The Company is composed of two separate business groups: the principal general-merchandise group and the newer specialty retail group. At January 28 1987 the company employed over 320,000 people and operated 2,342 general merchandise stores and 1,440 specialty stores. General merchandise stores in the United States, Canada and Puerto Rico include: 2,204 K mart discount department stores; 116 Kresge variety stores; 22 Jupiter limited-line discount stores. The specialty retail group includes: Waldenbooks Company, Inc, one of the nations's largest retail bookstore chains, operating 994 stores in all 50 states; Pay Less Drug Stores Northwest, Inc operating a chain of 196 super drug stores, 14 Wonder World stores and eight Key Drug stores in the western United States; Builders Square, Inc operating 86 warehouse home improvement centers in 16 states across the country; Bargain Harold's consisting of 134 stores across Canada and eight in the United states featuring deep discounts on special purchase merchandise. In addition, the company has important equity interests in: The Meldisco subsidiaries of the Melville Corporation operating footwear departments in domestic K mart stores; Coles Myer Ltd, the largest retailer in Australia
Principal Subsidiaries: K mart Canada Limited (Canada); K mart Apparel Corporation; Waldenbooks Company Inc; Builders Square Inc; Pay Less Drug Stores; Northwest Inc
Financial Information:

	Jan 29 1985 $'000	Jan 28 1986 $'000
Sales revenues	22,035,000	23,812,000
Income before taxes	757,000	1,028,000
Net income	221,000	582,000
Dividends	176,000	193,000
Dividends per share	$0.92	$1.00
Earnings per share	$1.15	$2.90
Common stock issued	31,000	259,000
Shareholders equity	3,273,000	3,939,000

No of Employees: 320,000

KAHLER CORPORATION

20 Second Avenue Southwest, Rochester, MN 55902
Tel: (507) 282 2581

President: Harold W Milner (and Chief Executive Officer)
Senior Executive Officers: Kevin L Molloy (Senior VP Operations), Jeffrey L Coy (Senior VP Marketing), Jean H Freeman (VP and Secretary), James E Hinrichs (VP Accounting), Steven R Stenhaug (Treasurer), Paul R Tieskoetter (Controller), Paul E Coats (VP Engineering and Energy)

PRINCIPAL ACTIVITIES: Holding company with interests in hotels and motels; laundry services; rental of formal wear
Principal Subsidiaries: Hospitality Growth Services; Kahler Green Oaks Inn Inc; Lakeview of Rochester Inc; Lawlers Inc; Andersons Formal Wear Inc
Principal Bank: First National Bank
Financial Information:

	$'000
Sales revenues	46,630

No of Employees: 1,400

KAHN'S & CO

3241 Spring Grove Avenue, Cincinnati, OH 45225
Tel: (513) 541-4000

President: Robert L Huber
Senior Executive Officers: William A Maxwell (VP), William Geoppinger (VP), James D Schloss (VP), Milton J Schloss Jr (VP), Lucien Royse (VP), Raymond C Wissel (Treasurer and Chief Financial Officer)

PRINCIPAL ACTIVITIES: Meat processing and the manufacture of meat products including sausages and prepared meats; by-products including hides
Parent Company: Sara Lee Corporation
Financial Information:

	$'000
Sales revenues	100,000

No of Employees: 1,000

KAIBAB INDUSTRIES

4602 E Thomas Road, Phoenix, AZ 85018
Tel: (602) 840-9670

Chairman: A M Whiting (and President)
Senior Executive Officers: James S Whitney (Executive VP), Jim T Gotcher (Executive VP), E J Whiting (Senior VP), Richard A Fletcher (VP Finance), R B Whiting (VP), William M Cassel (VP)

PRINCIPAL ACTIVITIES: Timber industries; wholesale trade in building materials and gasoline
Principal Bank: Valley National Bank
Financial Information:

	$'000
Sales revenues	200,000

No of Employees: 925

KAISER AEROSPACE & ELECTRONICS CORPORATION

300 Lakeside Drive, Oakland, CA 94612
Tel: (415) 835-5554

President: H J Smead
Senior Executive Officers: Edward Durbin (Senior VP), W W Sidney (VP), H J Hill (VP), R S Carlson (VP)

PRINCIPAL ACTIVITIES: Aerospace equipment and components
Parent Company: K Systems Inc
Principal Bank: Bank of America
Financial Information:

	$'000
Sales revenues	200,000

No of Employees: 2,000

KAISER ALUMINUM & CHEMICAL CORPORATION

300 Lakeside Drive, Oakland, CA 94612
Tel: (415) 271-3300

Chairman: Cornell C Maier (and Chief Executive Officer)
President: A S Hutchcraft Jr (and Chief Operating Officer)
Senior Executive Officers: Jesse D Erickson (Senior VP), Howard M Nelson (Senior VP), Edward M Quinnan (VP and Chief Financial Officer), John R Cady (V), Robert E Cole (VP), Wayne C Gunderson (VP), John A Moore (VP and Secretary), David L Perry (VP and Legal Counsel), Timothy F Preece (VP), James E Sparkman (VP), C M Hines (VP and Controller)

PRINCIPAL ACTIVITIES: Production of aluminum and chemicals including agricultural and industrial chemicals; interests in oil and gas, refractories, real estate and international trading
Principal Subsidiaries: Queensland Alumina Ltd; Boyne Smelters Ltd, Australia; Aluminium Bahrain; Phenix Aluminium SA, Belgium; Kaiser Aluminum & Chemical of Canada Ltd, Canada; Kaiser Aluminium Europe Inc, Germany; Volta Aluminium Co Ltd, Ghana; Hindustan Aluminium Corpo, India; Alumina Partners of Jamaica; Kaiser Jamaica Bauxite Co, Jamaica; Nyffeler Conti AG, Switzerland; Anglesey Aluminium Ltd, UK
Principal Bank: Branch Bank & Trust Co Wilson NC
Financial Information:

	Dec 31 1985 $'000	Dec 31 1986 $'000
Sales revenues	2,701,700	2,233,500
Net income (loss)	(186,500)	158,268
Dividends per share	-	$4.05
Shareholders equity	-	1,005,008

No of Employees: 13,450

KAISER CEMENT CORPORATION

300 Lakeside Drive, Oakland, CA 94612
Tel: (415) 271-2000
Telex: 470382 KAISER CMNT UI

Chairman: Walter Ousterman Jr (and President and Chief Executive Officer)
Senior Executive Officers: John F Burns (Executive VP, Finance and Administration, and Treasurer), John H Wimberly (Executive VP, Operations, and Chief Operating Officer), Myron E Bernstein (VP, Industrial Relations), Elmer L Erwin (VP, Manufacturing and Distribution), David B Hunn (VP, Investor Relations and Public Affairs), Bob J Murphy (VP, Sales), Thomas R O'Connor (VP, Corporate Marketing and Sales Planning), Edward E Taggart (VP and General Manager, International Operations), Carl R Pagter (VP, Secretary and General Counsel), Wayne D Marquart (Controller), Donna M Anderson (Assistant Secretary), Melissa A Youngman (Assistant Treasurer), Frederick A Nelson (General Manager, Northern California Region), Kimball P McCloud (General Manager, Southwest Region), James S McGahey (General Manager, Northwest Region), Donald W Henning (General Manager, Texas Region)

PRINCIPAL ACTIVITIES: Kaiser Cement is the largest cement producer in the Western United States
Trade Names: Registered Trademarks: Permanente, Longhorn, Kaiser
Principal Subsidiaries: Texas Radymix; Southwest Materials Inc. International Affiliates: P T Semen Cibinong (Indonesia); Orient Trading Corporation (Japan); Micronesia Cement Co Inc (CNMI)
Principal Bank: Bank of America
Financial Information:

	$'000
Sales revenues	248,000

No of Employees: 1,100

KAISER STEEL CORPORATION

9400 Cherry Avenue, Fontana, CA 92335
Tel: (714) 350-5199

Chairman: M H Rial (and Chief Executive Officer); Vice Chairman: C S McNeil
Senior Executive Officers: K L Gibson (VP Corporate Development), M E Stewart (Senior VP), M G Yeagley (Senior VP), A W Mullin (VP and Chief Financial Officer), C A Bradford (VP and Treasurer), R W Gambino (VP)

PRINCIPAL ACTIVITIES: Metal castings; metal fabrication
Principal Subsidiaries: Kaiser Steel Tubing Inc; Myers Drum Company; Industrial Molding Corporation; Kaiser Coal Corporation; Kaiser International Corporation; Kaiser Coal Corporation of Colorado
Principal Bank: Bank of America
Financial Information:

	$'000
Group sales revenues	220,400

Principal Shareholders: J A Frates Investor Group, Tulsa
No of Employees: 1,600

KAL KAN FOODS, INC

3386 E 44th Street, Vernon, CA 90058
Tel: (213) 587-2727
Telex: ITT 4720301 klıf la

President: John Barrow
Senior Executive Officers: Robert Gould (VP Services and Finance), John Bridgeman (VP Administration), John Bridges (VP Operations), A Poe (VP Marketing), Neil Commerford (VP Research and Development)

PRINCIPAL ACTIVITIES: Manufacture of pet foods
Principal Bank: Union Bank
Financial Information:

	$'000
Sales revenues	250,000

No of Employees: 1,000

KALAMA CHEMICAL, INC

1110 Bank of California Center, Seattle, WA 98164
Tel: (206) 682-7890
Telex: TWX 9104442294 KALCHEM SEA

Chairman: Ted W Palmer
President: Robert A Kirchner
Senior Executive Officers: L C Macomber (VP Administration and Secretary), James H Harris (VP Marketing), Wayne H Ostermiller (VP Manufacturing), Jarl L Opgrande (VP Engineering), John P Fairman (VP Finance)

PRINCIPAL ACTIVITIES: Production of industrial chemicals
Principal Bank: U.S. National Bank, Portland
Financial Information:

	$'000
Sales revenues	45,559

No of Employees: 250

KAMAN CORPORATION

Blue Hills Avenue, Bloomfield, CT 06002
Tel: (203) 243-8311
Telex: WUT 99326 kamanacft blcn

Chairman: Charles H Kaman (and President)
Senior Executive Officers: Harvey S Levenson (Senior VP and Chief Financial Officer), Fred L Smith (Senior VP), Glenn M Messemer (VP), William P Desautelle (Treasurer), Robert M Garneau (Controller), J S Murtha (Secretary)

PRINCIPAL ACTIVITIES: Industrial equipment distribution
Principal Subsidiaries: Kaman Diversified Technologies Corp; Kaman Aerospace Corp; Kamatics Corp; Kaman Aerospace International Corp; Kaman Aircraft Services Corp; Electromagnetic Launch Research Inc; Kaman Sciences Corp; Kaman Instrumentation Corp; AirKaman of Jacksonville, Inc; Kaman Bearing & Supply Corp; Kaman Bearing & Supply Corp; Kaman Bearing & Supply, Ltd (Canada); Kaman Music Corp; C Bruno & Son, Inc; Coast Wholesale Music Co; Ovation Instruments, Inc; Kaman Music International Corp
Principal Bank: Connecticut National Bank
Financial Information:

	Dec 31 1986 $'000
Sales revenues	587,820
Net income	20,256
Earnings per share	$11.86
Shareholders equity	136,802

No of Employees: 5,000

KANEB SERVICES, INC

14141 Southwest Freeway, Sugar Land, TX 77478
Tel: (713) 490-5000

Chairman: James R Whatley
President: Michael G Shoup
Senior Executive Officers: Robert E Rose (Executive VP and Chief Operating Officer), G C Bankston (Executive VP Exploration), Jack D Strube (Senior VP and Controller), Carroll M Selby (Senior VP-Finance and Administration)

PRINCIPAL ACTIVITIES: Oil and gas services; oil and gas production
Principal Subsidiaries: Diamond M Company; Kaneb Energy Partners Ltd; Kaneb Pipe Line Company
Principal Bank: First City National Bank
Financial Information:

	$'000
Sales revenues	178,789

No of Employees: 1,600

KANE-MILLER CORPORATION

555 White Plains Road, Tarrytown, NY 10591
Tel: (914) 631-6900

Chairman: Daniel Kane
President: Stanley B Kane (and Secretary)
Senior Executive Officers: Harold Oelbaum (Executive VP), Arnold S Bloom (VP and General Counsel), James R Morris (VP Engineering),

PRINCIPAL ACTIVITIES: Meat packaging and food products including margarine, vegetable oils, dairy products, canned vegetables, wine
Principal Bank: The Bank of New York
Financial Information:

	$'000
Sales revenues	760,000

No of Employees: 2,800

KANSAS CITY LIFE INSURANCE COMPANY

3520 Broadway, Kansas City, MO 64111
Tel: (816) 753 7000

Chairman: Joseph R Bixby (and President); Vice Chairman: W E Bixby
Senior Executive Officers: David D Dysart (Executive VP), H Marshall Chatfield (Senior VP and Secretary), Francis P Lemery (Senior VP and Actuary), John D Petrie (Senior VP), Richard L Finn (Senior VP Finance), Donald H Fromm (Senior VP Marketing), John K Koetting (VP and Controller), C John Malacarne (VP and Legal Counsel), Dennis M Gaffney (VP Administration), Wayne K Hein (VP Operational Services), Eugene Bova (VP Selection), W T Tidwell (VP Marketing Administration), Robert Carson (VP Marketing Administration), R Philip Bixby (VP), Michael J Sanders (VP Computer and Information Services), Michael P Horton (VP Group), Bill Sears (VP Insurance Services)

PRINCIPAL ACTIVITIES: Life insurance
Principal Subsidiaries: Armour Life Insurance Co; Sunset Life Insurance of America
Principal Bank: Commerce Bank
Financial Information:

	$'000
Revenues	252,340

No of Employees: 650

KANSAS CITY POWER & LIGHT COMPANY

1330 Baltimore Avenue, Kansas City, MO 64105
Tel: (816) 471-5275
Telefax: (816) 556-2924

Chairman: Arthur J Doyle (and Chief Executive Officer)
President: A Drue Jennings
Senior Executive Officers: J Robert Miller (Executive VP-Operations and Chief Operating Officer), Louis C Rasmussen (Executive VP-Finance and Chief Financial Officer), Samuel P Cowley (Senior VP-Corporate Affairs, Secretary and Chief Legal Officer), J Michael Evans (Senior VP-Systems Operations)

PRINCIPAL ACTIVITIES: Kansas City Power & Light Company is a medium-size electric utility which generates and distributes electricity to about 390,000 electric customers in a 4,700-square-mile area located in all or portions of 23 counties in Western Missouri and Eastern Kansas

Principal Subsidiaries: WYMO Fuels Inc; Wolf Creek Nuclear Operating Corporation; Utility Fuel Company; Red Hill Coal Company; KCPL Fuel Trust
Principal Bank: Commerce Bank of Kansas City, N.A.
Financial Information:

	Dec 31 1985	Dec 31 1986
	$'000	$'000
Sales revenues	596,621	664,870
Income before taxes	277,572	237,698
Net income	155,121	106,458
Preference dividends	21,722	19,383
Common dividends	71,181	64,669
Dividends per common share	$2.36	$2.09
Earnings per share	$4.41	$2.80
Common stock	449,262	449,697
Retained income	384,353	406,759
Shareholders funds	838,394	860,252

No of Employees: 3,039 (Excludes or includes data related to employees allocated to or from jointly-owned power stations, as of December 31 1986)

KANSAS CITY SOUTHERN INDUSTRIES, INC

114 W 11th Street, Kansas City, MO 64105
Tel: (816) 556-0303

Chairman: William N Deramus III (and Chief Executive Officer)
President: Landon H Rowland (and Chief Operating Officer)
Senior Executive Officers: M F McClain (Senior VP Marketing), Robert E Zimmerman (Senior VP Law), Donald L Graf (Senior VP Finance and Chief Financial Officer), Thomas A Giltner (VP and Comptroller), J L Deveney (VP Personnel), James E Judge (VP Corporate Systems), P S Brown (VP Government Affairs), Richard P Bruening (VP and Legal Counsel), Walter W Howland (VP Taxes), Albert P Mauro (VP and Secretary), H H Salisbury (VP Public Affairs)

PRINCIPAL ACTIVITIES: Holding company with interests in railroad operations, real estate, finance and insurance, fabricated metal products and automotive components
Principal Bank: Chemical Bank
Financial Information:

	Dec 31 1985	Dec 31 1986
	$'000	$'000
Sales revenues	474,583	481,507
Net income(loss)	49,850	(42,242)
Earnings (loss) per share	$4.92	($4.33)
Shareholders equity	437,659	354,800

No of Employees: 4,750

KANSAS GAS AND ELECTRIC COMPANY

201 North Market, Wichita, KS 67202
Tel: (316) 261-6611
Telex: 910-741-0001

Chairman: Wilson K Cadman (and President)
Senior Executive Officers: Kent R Brown (Group VP), Richard M Haden (Group VP), James Haines (Group VP), Robert L Rives (Group VP), James T Clark (VP-Accounting), Ralph B Foster (VP-General Counsel), Glenn L Koester (VP-Nuclear), William B Moore (VP Finance), E D Prothro (Controller and Assistant Secretary), W R Whitmer (Treasurer), Richard D Terrill (Secretary and Attorney), W R Whitmer (Treasurer), Verna L Ridgeway (Assistant VP-Consumer Affairs), Jack Skelton (Assistant Controller), K F Klassen (Assistant Treasurer) Joe R Gibbens (Assistant Secretary)

PRINCIPAL ACTIVITIES: The Company is an electric utility engaged in the generation, distribution and sale of electricity in the southeastern portion of the State of Kansas, including the Wichita metropolitan area. At December 31 1986, electric service was being rendered at retail to 247,687 customers and at wholesale to 27 communities and 12 other electric utilities. The Company owns no gas properties.
Principal Bank: Morgan Guarantee Trust of New York
Financial Information:

	Dec 31 1985	Dec 31 1986
	$'000	$'000
Sales revenues	410,786	496,340
Income before taxes	136,543	145,361
Net income	97,732	67,885
Dividends	80	50
Dividends per share	$2.065	$1.225
Earnings per share	$2.13	$1.44
Common stock*	39,118	40,753
Retained income	5	2
Shareholders equity	814	823
*average shares in thousands		

No of Employees: At December 31, 1986, the Company had 2,410 employees. Effective January 1, 1987, 1,157 of these employees transferred to the newly formed Wolf Creek Nuclear Generating Corporation. KG&E remains a part owner of the assets of Wolf Creek

KANSAS POWER & LIGHT COMPANY

818 Kansas Avenue, Topeka, KS 66612
Tel: (913) 296 6300

Chairman: David S Black (and Chief Executive Officer)
President: Leland R Nicholson (and Chief Operating Officer)
Senior Executive Officers: William E Brown (Senior VP Division), Ronald C Kuether (Senior VP Operations), Vernon E Percell (Senior VP Operations), Ned A Vahldieck (Senior VP Marketing and Supply), Norman E Jackson (VP Regional), Richard D Lagree (VP Regional), John F Nichols (VP Regional), Robert F Riordan (VP Administration), Stanley E Wingate (VP Regional), Jerry D Courington (Controller), Steven L Kitchen (VP Finance and VP Accounting), Ferdinand G Meyer (Treasurer and Assistant Secretary), Rebecca R Tilden (Secretary), James W Ingram (VP Marketing), Michael Blumenfeld (VP Corporate Affairs), A W Woellhof (VP Human Resources and Services), M L Brunton (VP Production)

PRINCIPAL ACTIVITIES: Distribution of natural gas
Financial Information:

	$'000
Sales revenues	1,200,000

No of Employees: 4,510

KAPLAN INDUSTRIES, INC

Box 427, Bartow, FL 33830
Tel: (813) 533-0685
Telex: (Easylink) 62879906

Chairman: Donald Kaplan (and Chief Executive Officer and Treasurer)
President: John Kaplan (and Chief Operating Officer)
Senior Executive Officers: Tom Mondello (VP Operations), James W Beasley Jr (Secretary)

PRINCIPAL ACTIVITIES: Meat processing and packaging
Principal Subsidiaries: Diamond Meats Inc
Principal Bank: Citrus and Chemical Bank
Financial Information:

	Dec 31 1985	Dec 31 1986
	$'000	$'000
Sales revenues	61,093	69,783
Income (loss) before taxes	(1,184)	514
Net income (loss)	(1,184)	405
Earnings (loss) per share	($0.15)	$0.05
Common stock	79	79
Retained (deficit)	(1,138)	(733)
Shareholders equity	2,351	2,756

No of Employees: 236

KARCHER, CARL, ENTERPRISES INC

1200 North Harbor Boulevard, Anaheim, CA 92801
Tel: (714) 774 5706

Chairman: Carl M Karcher (and Chief Executive Officer)
President: Donald F Karcher (and Chief Operating Officer)
Senior Executive Officers: Loren C Pannier (Group VP Finance and Administration), George R Cloward (VP and Controller), Donald E Glenn (VP), Raymond J Perry (VP), Robert W Wisely (VP Marketing), Frank J Karcher (VP Real Estate), Paul J Mitchell (VP Corporate Affairs), Thomas C Pine (VP Real Estate)

PRINCIPAL ACTIVITIES: Operation of "Carl's Jr" chain of fast food restaurants
Principal Bank: First Interstate Bank of California
Financial Information:

	$'000
Sales revenues	321,000

No of Employees: 14,500 (including part-time)

KARP, L, & SONS, INC

1301 Estes Avenue, Elk Grove Village, IL 60007
Tel: (312) 593-5700

President: J L Karp
Senior Executive Officers: W Goldman (VP Finance), D Snyder (VP Sales), E Day (VP), W Rock (VP), Jack Waldron (VP)

PRINCIPAL ACTIVITIES: Manufcture of supplies for the food industry including flavorings and products for the bakery industry
Principal Bank: American National Bank
Financial Information:

	$'000
Sales revenues	70,000

No of Employees: 300

KASLE STEEL CORPORATION

4343 Wyoming Avenue, Dearborn, MI 48216
Tel: (313) 943-2500

Chairman: Leonard Kasle
President: Roger H Kasle
Senior Executive Officers: Ben Jones (Vice Chairman and Treasurer), Reginald Campbell (VP Marketing), Roger Kasle (Secretary), STephen Kasle (VP Administration)

PRINCIPAL ACTIVITIES: Steel industry; aluminum fabrication
Principal Subsidiaries: Kasle Steel of Canada Ltd
Principal Bank: Manufacturers National Bank
Financial Information:

	$'000
Sales revenues	160,000

No of Employees: 350

KASLER CORPORATION

PO Box 387, San Bernardino, CA 92402
Tel: (714) 884-4811

Chairman: R E Kasler (and Chief Executive Officer)
President: E Robert Ferguson (and Chief Operating Officer)
Senior Executive Officers: Dean F Gordinier (Senior VP), George R Pache (VP, Treasurer and Chief Financial Officer), John L Cowan (VP Administration), J Robert Varshay (VP Estimating), Edward D Hughes (VP and Secretary), Homer E Holmes (VP)

PRINCIPAL ACTIVITIES: Civil engineering contractors
Principal Bank: Bank of America
Financial Information:

	$'000
Sales revenues	132,450

No of Employees: 900

KATY INDUSTRIES, INC

853 Dundee Avenue, Elgin, IL 60120
Tel: (312) 379-1121

Chairman: Wallace E Carroll (and Chief Executive Officer)
President: Jacob Saliba
Senior Executive Officers: Harold E Miller (Executive VP Industrial Operations), Charles W Sahlman (Executive VP Consumer Operations), Phil Alspach (Group VP), Gerald N Goldberger (VP Operations), William H Murphy (VP Finance, Treasurer and Controller), James T McGuire (VP and Secretary)

PRINCIPAL ACTIVITIES: Holding company with diversified interests in machinery for the chemical, food and packaging industries; electrical equipment including aircraft navigational equipment, testing and gaging instruments; oil and gas exploration and oilfield equipment manufacture; transportation of freight by railroad
Principal Bank: First National Bank of Chicago
Financial Information:

	Dec 31 1986 $'000
Sales revenues	420,494
Net (loss)	(9,799)
(Loss) per share	($1.90)
Shareholders equity	117,373

No of Employees: 5,650

KAUFMAN & BROAD, INC

11601 Wilshire Blvd, Los Angeles, CA 90025
Tel: (213) 312-5000

Chairman: Eli Broad (and President and Chief Executive Officer)
Senior Executive Officers: Norman J Metcalfe (Executive VP and Chief Financial Officer), Bruce Karatz (Executive VP), Robert R Saltzman (Executive VP), Donald R Boulanger (Senior VP Investments), Jana W Greer (VP Public Affairs), Kenneth L Cohen (VP), Scott L Robinson (VP), Susan Harris (Secretary and Corporate Counsel),

PRINCIPAL ACTIVITIES: Life insurance/financial services; homebuilding; mortgage financing; manufactured housing
Principal Subsidiaries: Kaufman and Broad Home Corporation (92.6%); Sun Life Insurance Co of America; Anchor National Life Insurance Co; Anchor National Financial Services; Kaufman and Broad Home Systems
Principal Bank: Security Pacific National Bank
Financial Information:

	Nov 30 1985 $'000	Nov 30 1986 $'000
Sales revenues	921,433	1,137,690
Premium income	324,649	284,165
Investment income	176,347	309,799
Income before taxes	48,951	78,664
Net income	38,891	44,164
Cash dividends	12,030	12,607
Dividends per share(1)	$0.27	$0.33
Dividends per share(2)	$0.12	$0.30
Earnings per share(3)	$1.87	$2.20
Common stock(4)	12,009	16,050
Common stock(2)	4,152	4,847
Retained income	144,968	176,525
Shareholders equity	280,774	326,299
Total assets	2,200,577	4,375,418

(1) Common stock
(2) Class B stock
(3) Primary
(4) Common

No of Employees: 2,500

KAWASHO INTERNATIONAL (USA)

299 Park Avenue, New York, NY 10171
Tel: (212) 371-0990
Telex: WUT 126755 kawasho nyk

President: Y Watanabe
Senior Executive Officers: H Fujimura (VP), H Kume (VP), K Igi (VP), H Sihara, T Terewaza (VP)

PRINCIPAL ACTIVITIES: Trading in steel

Principal Bank: Baiichkangyo Bank
Financial Information:

	$'000
Sales revenues	230,000

No of Employees: 30

KAY CORPORATION

320 King Street, Alexandria, VA 22314
Tel: (703) 683-3800

President: Anthonie C van Ekris (and Chief Executive Officer)
Senior Executive Officers: Arie Nugteren (Executive VP, President International Trade Division), Russell E Diaz (VP, Controller and Principal Accounting Officer), Murray Ackerman (VP and Treasurer)

PRINCIPAL ACTIVITIES: Wholesale and retail jewelry; wholesale trade in a wide range of goods including groceries, drugstore supplies, electrical goods and chemicals; commodity trading
Principal Bank: Bankers Trust Co
Financial Information:

	Dec 31 1985 $'000	Dec 31 1986 $'000
Sales revenues	666,342	809,643
Net income	14,010	13,326
Earnings per share	$2.76	$2.64
Shareholders equity	49,980	34,591

No of Employees: 730

KAY JEWELERS INC

320 King Street, Alexandria, VA 22314
Tel: (703) 683 3800

Chairman: Anthonie C Van Ekris (and Chief Executive Officer)
President: Michael R Lavington (and Chief Operating Officer)
Senior Executive Officers: Joe Bernstein (Senior VP), Harry Braverman (Senior VP), John Rambo (Senior VP), John C Belknap (VP), Roldan Fernandez (VP and Chief Financial Officer), William Heide (VP), John F Kosik (VP and Secretary), Frank Schmidt (VP), Harold Schlackman (VP), William T Sharp (VP)

PRINCIPAL ACTIVITIES: Retailing of jewelry
Parent Company: Kay Corporation, Alexandria, VA
Financial Information:

	$'000
Sales revenues	230,390

No of Employees: 3,210

KAYDON CORPORATION

2860 McCracken Street, Muskegon, MI 49443
Tel: (616) 755-3741
Telex: 228436

Chairman: G W Bailey
President: R A Shantz (and Treasurer)
Senior Executive Officers: J R Hays (VP and Controller), W C Wolffis (VP and Secretary)

PRINCIPAL ACTIVITIES: Industrial equipment components; motor vehicle components
Principal Bank: Continental Illinois National Bank & Trust Co
Financial Information:

	$'000
Sales revenues	84,830

No of Employees: 920

KAYPRO CORPORATION

533 Stevens Avenue, Solana Beach, CA 92075
Tel: (619) 418-4300

Chairman: A F Kay (and President and Chief Financial Officer)
President: D A Kay
Senior Executive Officers: A M Kay (VP), John F Purner (VP)

PRINCIPAL ACTIVITIES: Manufacture of data processing equipment
Financial Information:

	$'000
Sales revenues	75,000

No of Employees: 600

KDI CORPORATION

5721 Dragon Way, Cincinnati, OH 45227
Tel: (513) 272-1421
Telex: TWX 8104612299 kdi corp hdgrs

President: Louis W Matthey (and Chief Executive Officer)
Senior Executive Officers: William C Gamble (Executive VP), Kenneth L Byrne (VP Legal), Theodore W Miller (VP Industrial Relations), F E Pfingstag (VP and Treasurer), Donald J Scheidler (VP), Victor J Camardo (VP Finance and Controller)

PRINCIPAL ACTIVITIES: Supply of swimming pools, fittings and equipment; electrical and electronic products; ordnance; plastic products
Principal Bank: First National Bank of Cincinnati
Financial Information:

	$'000
Sales revenues	260,000

No of Employees: 3,600

KEANE, INC

10 City Square, Boston, MA 02129
Tel: (617) 241-9200

Chairman: John F Keane (and President)
Senior Executive Officers: Ray E Becker (VP), Wallace A Cataldo (VP), Philip J Harkins (VP), Raymond W Paris (VP)

PRINCIPAL ACTIVITIES: Keane, Inc operates via two divisions: The Information Services Division (ISD) provides management and technical skills to large companies for the development and implementation of business application software. KeaMed Hospital Systems offers a complete family of "Worry-Free Software" (TM) for hospitals, including financial, patient care and ancillary department applications. KeaMed markets its products in cooperation with the IBM and Wang sales organizations
Trade Names: "Worry-Free Software" (TM) for hospitals; "Productivity Management" (TM) - an internally developed project management approach that is the subject of a book published by Prentice-Hall. Project Manager Development Program (PMDP) - a unique training program, tailored to the needs and norms of client organizations
Principal Subsidiaries: Access Associates Inc; Data Skills Inc
Principal Bank: Bank of Boston, Boston, MA
Financial Information:

	Dec 31 1985 $'000	Dec 31 1986 $'000
Sales revenues	39,701	40,396
Income before taxes	1,152	8
Net income	766	283
Dividends	178	90
Dividends per share	$0.13	$0.03
Earnings per share	$0.55	$0.21
Common stock	1,344	1,379
Retained income	5,074	5,267
Shareholders equity	6,560	6,970

No of Employees: 747

KEARNEY-NATIONAL INC

Two Continental Towers, Suite 400, 1701 Golf Rd, Rolling Mdws, IL 60008
Tel: (312) 593-6046
Telex: 5101003780 KEARNEY NATL

Chairman: Robert R Dyson (and Chief Executive Officer)
President: James A Jaffe (and Chief Operating Officer)

Senior Executive Officers: James F Zboyovsky (Group VP), Joseph L Aurichio (Senior VP Finance, Chief Financial Officer and, Secretary), Ronald W Keipper (VP)

PRINCIPAL ACTIVITIES: Electronic and electrical equipment; electrical power distribution equipment
Trade Names: Kearney; Wabash
Principal Subsidiaries: Kearney; Wabash, Inc
Principal Bank: Manufacturers Hanover Trust
Financial Information:

	$'000
Sales revenues	140,783

No of Employees: 2,200

KEEBLER COMPANY

One Hollow Tree Lane, Elmhurst, IL 60126
Tel: (312) 833-2900
Telex: 910-254-0167

President: Thomas M Garvin (and Chief Executive Officer)
Senior Executive Officers: D R Splithoff (Senior VP Retail Sales), Thomas J Finn (Senior VP Purchasing), C A Gerber (Senior VP Finance and Administration), W T Hanna (Senior VP Biscuit Marketing), Jack J Simoneau (Senior VP Manufacturing), Charles L Shemely (Senior VP)

PRINCIPAL ACTIVITIES: Snack products, cookies and other bakery products
Parent Company: United Biscuits (Holdings) plc, Isleworth, Middlesex, UK
Principal Bank: The Northern Trust Company; InterFirst Bank in Dallas
Financial Information:

	1984/85	1985/86
	$'000	$'000
Sales revenues	988,600	1,005,100
Trading profit	43,200	48,600

Principal Shareholders: United Biscuits (Holdings) plc
No of Employees: 8,250

KEELER BRASS COMPANY

955 Godfrey Avenue, SW, Grand Rapids, MI 49503
Tel: (616) 247-4000
Telex: WUT 226469 keeler br gdr

Chairman: E A Madenski
President: A S Nemy
Senior Executive Officers: Y N El-Masry (VP Engineering), J E Sheline (VP Materials), Theodore F Smith (VP Furniture Hardware Sales), W D Pate (Controller)

PRINCIPAL ACTIVITIES: Manufacture of hardware including components for furniture and motor vehicles
Parent Company: Babcock Keeler Corp
Financial Information:

	$'000
Sales revenues	140,000

No of Employees: 2,800

KEENE CORPORATION

200 Park Avenue, New York, NY 10166
Tel: (212) 557-1900
Telex: WUT 126434 keene corp nyk

Chairman: Glenn W Bailey
President: Eugene A Cafiero
Senior Executive Officers: David Conway (VP Administration), Howard A Mileaf (VP and Secretary), P Roger Byer (VP Finance), Gordon D Olson (VP Manufacturing)

PRINCIPAL ACTIVITIES: Lighting equipment; industrial equipment including bearings
Parent Company: Bairnco Corporation, New York, NY
Financial Information:

	$'000
Sales revenues	136,000

No of Employees: 1,500

KEIM, H H, COMPANY, LTD

PO Drawer 338, Nampa, ID 83651
Tel: (208) 466-2478

Chairman: Kenneth B Keim
President: S G Keim (and Treasurer)
Senior Executive Officers: Richard V Keim Jr (VP and General Manager), Donald S Keim (Secretary)

PRINCIPAL ACTIVITIES: Meat and meat processing
Principal Bank: First Interstate Bank
Financial Information:

	$'000
Sales revenues	60,000

No of Employees: 145

KEITHLEY INSTRUMENTS INC

28775 Aurora Road, Cleveland, OH 44139
Tel: (216) 248 0400

Chairman: Joseph F Keithley
President: Thomas G Brick (and Chief Executive Officer)
Senior Executive Officers: Gregory R Bigadza (VP), Noel E Morgan (VP), Ronald M Rebner (VP, Controller and Treasurer), Terrence E Sheridan (VP), Joseph P Keithley (VP Corporate Marketing), Hermann Hamm (VP Europe), Bruce Griswold (Secretary)

PRINCIPAL ACTIVITIES: Manufacture of instruments for the electrical industry
Principal Bank: AmeriTrust Co
Financial Information:

	$'000
Sales revenues	47,090

No of Employees: 480

KELLER INDUSTRIES, INC

18000 State Road 9, Miami, FL 33162
Tel: (305) 651-7100
Telex: WUT 512340 kellex mia

Chairman: Dugald Fletcher
President: Bruce A Keller
Senior Executive Officers: Robert M Connors (Senior VP and Treasurer), Henry A Keller Jr (VP and Secretary), Fred Phillips (VP Manufacturing), Sam Bamman (VP Sales and Marketing), Alan Mendal (VP Purchasing)

PRINCIPAL ACTIVITIES: Manufacture of aluminum products including doors and windows
Parent Company: Keller Holdings Inc
Principal Bank: Union Bank
Financial Information:

	$'000
Sales revenues	170,000

No of Employees: 3,000

KELLOGG COMPANY

235 Porter Street, Box 3423, Battle Creek, MI 49016
Tel: (616) 966-2000

Chairman: William E LaMothe (and Chief Executive Officer); Vice Chairmen: Robert L Nichols, Paul J Kehoe
President: Gerald D Robinson (and Chief Operating Officer)
Senior Executive Officers: Arnold G Langbo (Executive VP, President Kellogg International), Horst W Schroeder (Executive VP, President Kellogg Co NA), G E Costley (Executive VP US Subsidiaries, Chairman Mrs Smith's Frozen Foods Co), Scott R Campbell (Senior VP, Legal Counsel and Secretary), Daryl R Schaller (Senior VP Corporate Science

and Technology), Louis R Somers (Senior VP Finance), Donald J Brett (VP Corporate Information Technology), Ross Buckland (VP European Operations), Fred C Buhler (VP Corporate Development), Robert L Burrows (VP Materials Planning), William A Camstra (VP Latin American Operations), Robert L Creviston (VP Employee Relations), George A Franklin (VP Government Relations), Rosalyn Franta (VP Quality and Nutrition), John R Hinton (VP and Treasurer), Paul A Humiston (VP Corporate Technology), Thomas A Knowlton (VP, President Kellogg Salada Canada Inc), Richard J Lilly (VP Travel Services), Stephen D McCurry (VP Food Research), Stanley W Ruis (VP and Controller), Joseph M Stewart (VP Public Affairs)

PRINCIPAL ACTIVITIES: Manufacture of a wide range of food products including cereals, prepared meat products, sauces, pickles and dressings, frozen foods, tea, coffee and snack foods
Principal Bank: Harris Trust and Savings Bank
Financial Information:

	Dec 31 1985 $'000	Dec 31 1986 $'000
Sales revenues	2,930,100	3,340,700
Net income	281,100	318,900
Earnings per share	$2.28	$2.58
Shareholders equity	-	898,400

No of Employees: 17,080

KELLWOOD COMPANY

600 Kellwood Parkway, St Louis, MO 63178
Tel: (314) 576-3100
Telex: 193104 KWBSTL

Chairman: Fred W Wenzel
President: William J McKenna (Chief Executive Officer)
Senior Executive Officers: Bud Berman (VP), Joseph P Collins (VP), James C Jacobsen (VP-Finance and Treasurer), Eugene D Johnson (VP), Robert A Maddocks (VP, Secretary and General Counsel), Gene W Slagle (VP), Lawrence E Hummel (Controller)

PRINCIPAL ACTIVITIES: Kellwood Company is an international manufacturer and marketer of apparel and home fashions. Kellwood also operates Ashley's Outlet Stores which sell overruns and seconds of apparel, home fashions and recreational products
Trade Names: Denver, Cascade Blues, Weekenders, Laser Beams, Junior Collections, Cape Cod Matchmate, Cricket Lane, The American Collection Ltd
Principal Subsidiaries: Ashley's The Outlet Store, Inc; Cape Cod-Cricket Lane, Inc; Kellwood Asia Limited; Kellwood Haiti SA; Smart Shirts Limited; Smart Shirts (Lanka) Limited; Tri-W Corporation
Principal Bank: Continental Illinois National Bank and Trust Company of Chicago
Financial Information:

	Apr 30 1985 $'000	Apr 30 1986 $'000
Sales revenues	588,531	572,961
Net income	15,510	19,162
Earnings per share	$5.06	$3.03
Shareholders equity	95,988	130,715

*exclusive Treasury Stock

No of Employees: 16,000 worldwide

KELLY SERVICES, INC

999 West Big Beaver Rd, Troy, MI 48084
Tel: (313) 362-4444

Chairman: William R Kelly
President: Terence E Adderley
Senior Executive Officers: Angelo A Agnello (Executive VP), Thomas Anton (Executive VP), Patrick F Brady (Senior VP), Harley R Ferguson (Senior VP), Carolyn Fryar (Senior VP), Gerald F Jorissen (Senior VP), Gene L Knapp (Senior VP), Stanley A Mills Jr (Senior VP), James F Peil (Senior VP), Robert F Stoner (Senior VP Finance)

PRINCIPAL ACTIVITIES: Temporary help services for a wide range of applications including home health, nursing, office, industrial and marketing
Principal Bank: National Bank of Detroit
Financial Information:

	Dec 31 1985 $'000	Dec 31 1986 $'000
Sales revenues	876,437	1,033,560
Net income	32,615	36,436
Earnings per share	$2.01	$2.27
Shareholders equity	-	147,883

No of Employees: 43,000

KELLY-MOORE PAINT COMPANY, INC

987 Commercial Street, San Carlos, CA 94070
Tel: (415) 592-8337

Chairman: William E Moore
President: Joseph P Cristiano
Senior Executive Officers: Svend A Stubb (VP Manufacturing), John M DeLong (VP Paint Store Operations), Frank L Skaggs (VP Sales), Eric H Swanson (VP Subsidiary Operations), John W Bacigalupo (Secretary and Treasurer)

PRINCIPAL ACTIVITIES: Manufacture of paint; retail trade in paint and hardware goods
Principal Bank: Golden State Sanwa Bank
Financial Information:

	$'000
Sales revenues	140,000

No of Employees: 1,300

KELSEY-HAYES COMPANY

38481 Huron River Drive, Romulus, MI 48174
Tel: (313) 941-2000
Telex: WUI 6877039 kel sayhay romu

Presidents: Robert G Siefert (and Chief Executive Officer), William H Shinn (Heavy Duty Group)
Senior Executive Officers: Robert G Flagan (VP), T Neal Combs (VP and Secretary), Robert W Sullivan (VP Research and Development), Arthur A Kowalski (VP Marketing and International Auto Group), Frank P Coyer Jr (VP), Edward J Hayes (VP), A Jackson (VP), John E Utley (VP), Michael W Parres (VP), John J Garber (VP and Controller)

PRINCIPAL ACTIVITIES: Manufacture of components for the aerospace and automotive industries
Parent Company: Fruehauf Corporation
Principal Bank: Manufacturers Bank of Detroit
Financial Information:

	$'000
Sales revenues	865,000

No of Employees: 10,000

KEMPER CORPORATION

Kemper Center, Long Grove, IL 60049
Tel: (312) 540-2000

Chairman: Joseph E Luecke (and President and Chief Executive Officer)
Senior Executive Officers: Thomas R Anderson (Executive VP), Donald R Clark (Executive VP), Rudolf F Landolt (Executive VP), Gerald L Maatman (VP)

PRINCIPAL ACTIVITIES: Property casualty insurance; reinsurance; life insurance; investment services
Principal Subsidiaries: (100% owned unless stated): American Motorists Insurance Company; Economy Fire & Casualty Company; Federal Kemper Insurance Company; Iowa Kemper Insurance Company; Sequoia Insurance Company; National Auto Insurance Company; Kemper Reinsurance Co; Federal Kemper Life Assurance Co; Kemper Investors Life Insurance

Co; Kemper Financial Services, Inc; Bateman Eichler, Hill Richards, Inc; Boettcher Investment Corporation (80%); Loewi Financial Companies, Ltd; Prescott Ball & Turben, Inc (80%)
Financial Information:

	Dec 31 1986 $'000
Revenues	3,329,897
Net income	201,110
Operating income per share	$3.40
Shareholders equity	1,423,530

No of Employees: 17,000

KEMPER INVESTORS LIFE INSURANCE COMPANY

120 S La Salle Street, Chicago, IL 60603
Tel: (312) 781-1121

Chairman: T R Anderson (and Chief Executive Officer)
President: Charles M Kierscht
Senior Executive Officers: Paul R Knapp (Senior VP and Treasurer and Chief Financial Officer), W R Buecking (Senior VP), R A Redeker (Senior VP), H R Schaad (Senior VP), G P Wilson (Senior VP)

PRINCIPAL ACTIVITIES: Life insurance
Parent Company: Kemper Corporation, Long Grove, IL
Principal Bank: Harris Trust and Savings Bank
Financial Information:

	Dec 31 1985 $'000	Dec 31 1986 $'000
Premium income	498,033	485,854
Investment income	244,530	261,401

No of Employees: 200

KENNAMETAL, INC

1 Lloyd Avenue, Latrobe, PA 15650
Tel: (412) 539-5000
Telex: TWX 510 468 7277 kenna lobe

Chairman: Alex G McKenna
President: Quentin C McKenna (and Chief Executive Officer)
Senior Executive Officers: R E Morgan (VP Operations), John L Pollock (VP and Chief Financial Officer), Robert N Eslyn (VP and General Manager), David B Arnold (VP International Group), Richard C Hendricks (VP and General Manager), George W Roland (VP Technical), Thomas J McGuigan (VP Human Resources), John W Turko (VP Management Information Systems), William C Weaver (VP and Treasurer)

PRINCIPAL ACTIVITIES: Manufacture of hard metals for the tool industry
Principal Subsidiaries: Kennametal Australia Pty Ltd; Kennametal GmbH (Germany); Kennametal Holdings Limited (UK); Kennametal International SA (Panama); Kennametal Limited (Canada); Kennametal France SA (France); Kennametal Belgium SA (Belgium); Kennametal Nederland BV (Netherlands); Kennametal South Africa (Pty) Ltd (South Africa); Kennametal Tool Systems Singapore Private Limited; Kenroc Tools Inc (Canada); AC Wickman Limited (Canada); Erickson Tool Company; Bristol Erickson Limited (UK); Kennametal Foreign Sales Corporation (Barbados)
Principal Bank: Mellon Bank NA
Financial Information:

	$'000
Sales revenues	340,000

No of Employees: 5,500

KENNER PARKER TOYS INC

50 Dunham Road, Beverly, MA 01915
Tel: (617) 927 7600

Chairman: E R Kinney
President: Ronald J Jackson (and Chief Executive Officer)
Senior Executive Officers: Rodney V Campbell (Senior VP), Bruce J Oravec (Senior VP and Legal Counsel), G Neal Ryland (Senior VP, Chief Financial Officer and Treasurer),

PRINCIPAL ACTIVITIES: Manufacture of toys and sports equipment
Financial Information:

	Dec 31 1986 $'000
Sales revenues	502,776
Net income	24,911
Earnings per share	$1.90
Shareholders equity	199,704

No of Employees: 3,400

KENNER PRODUCTS COMPANY

1014 Vine Street, Cincinnati, OH 45202
Tel: (513) 579-4000

President: David Mauer (and Chief Executive Officer)
Senior Executive Officers: Andrew Holland (Senior VP Engineering), Pete Kelly (Senior VP Sales), G L Kleven (Senior VP Finance and Controller), John Tamashasky (Senior VP Personnel), Louis Gioia (VP Marketing), John Luchas (VP Services)

PRINCIPAL ACTIVITIES: Manufacture of toys
Parent Company: General Mills Inc
Financial Information:

	$'000
Sales revenues	250,000

No of Employees: 2,000

KENNEY MANUFACTURING COMPANY

1000 Jefferson Blvd, Warwick, RI 02887
Tel: (401) 739-2200
Telex: WUT 927714 kenneymfg wrwk

Chairman: George M Kenney
President: G D Kenney
Senior Executive Officers: David Homer (VP Marketing), John J Tuohy (Secretary, Treasurer and Comptroller)

PRINCIPAL ACTIVITIES: Manufacture of blinds and fittings for drapes
Principal Bank: Fleet National Bank of Rhode Island
Financial Information:

	$'000
Sales revenues	95,000

No of Employees: 30

KENRICH CORPORATION

24 River Road, Bogota, NJ 07603
Tel: (212) 421-6400

President: Hermann Rogge
Senior Executive Officers: James Goldstein (Executive VP), Martin Wright (VP and Treasurer)

PRINCIPAL ACTIVITIES: Manufacture of cables and wires; interests in real estate and financial services
Principal Subsidiaries: Laribee Wire, Inc
Principal Bank: Marine Midland Bank
Financial Information:

	$'000
Sales revenues	85,000

No of Employees: 450

KENT H LANDSBERG CO

See LANDSBERG, KENT H, CO

KENTUCKY CENTRAL LIFE INSURANCE COMPANY

Kincaid Towers, Lexington, KY 40507
Tel: (606) 253 5111

Chairman: W E Burnett Jr (and President)
Senior Executive Officers: W L Gunn (Senior VP, Secretary and Treasurer), R D Preston (Senior VP Corporate Development), W G Rehfuss (Senior VP Administration) W T Tozer (Senior VP Product and Risk Management), E W Yates Jr (Senior VP and Counsel), D M Baker (VP New Business), L A Barbee (Policy Owners Services), R E Casher (VP Career Agency Sales), Richard E Epps (VP Executive Marketing), F L Foltz (VP Group Sales), C H Forbush Jr (VP Investment), W G Franklin (VP Consumer Savings Sales), L R Gordon (VP Marketing Services), B J Harris (VP and Controller), C Honaker Jr (VP Policy Benefits), Kenneth W Jackson Jr (VP Underwriting), T Moss (VP Management Information Systems), J F Rampulla (VP Mortgage Loans), T W Robinson (VP Tax), Don C Ross Jr (VP Legal), Lawrence J Samartin (VP Executive Marketing), Paul K Sewell (VP Executive Marketing), P), E A Winiarczyk (VP Administration Services), M Z Zeidler (VP Personnel)

PRINCIPAL ACTIVITIES: Life insurance
Principal Subsidiaries: Mid-Central Investment Co Inc; Bluegrass Broadcasting Co Inc; Kentucky Central Television; Voice of Columbus Inc; Voice of Savannah Inc; WHOO Radio Inc; WVLK Radio Inc; Brevard Grove Inc; Kentucky Casualty Insurance Co; Kentucky Central Insurance Co; Kentucky Finance Co Inc; Kentucky National Insurance
Principal Bank: Central Bank & Trust Company
Financial Information:

	Dec 31 1985
	$'000
Revenues	291,100
Net income	25,420

No of Employees: 1,370

KENTUCKY UTILITIES COMPANY

One Quality Street, Lexington, KY 40507
Tel: (606) 255 1461

President: William B Bechanan (and Chief Executive Officer)
Senior Executive Officers: Milton H Lewis (Senior VP Engineering, Operations and Construction), John T Newton (Senior VP Accounting, Rates and Finance), Lynwood Schrader (Senior VP Customer Services, Information and Field Administration), R M Hewett (VP Rates and Contracts), Owen H Lewis (VP Field Administration and Franchises), J W Spurrier III (VP Public Affairs), Michael R Whitley (VP and Secretary), C Fred Davis (Controller), William N English (Treasurer)

PRINCIPAL ACTIVITIES: Electricity supply
Principal Subsidiaries: Old Dominion Power Co Inc
Principal Bank: First National Bank
Financial Information:

	Dec 31 1985	Dec 31 1986
	$'000	$'000
Sales revenues	538,040	551,000
Net income	65,600	54,000

No of Employees: 2,000

KERN FOODS, INC

13000 E Temple Avenue, City of Industry, CA 91749
Tel: (213) 962-5111
Telex: TWX 910 584 1810

President: Charles E Kern
Senior Executive Officers: J Nakai (VP), James G Karsatos (VP Finance and Administration), Richard Kern (VP Marketing), Bill M Snyder (VP Manufacturing)

PRINCIPAL ACTIVITIES: Manufacture of fruit products including juices, jellies and preserves; manufacture of sauces and soft drinks
Principal Bank: Wells Fargo Bank
Financial Information:

	$'000
Sales revenues	175,000

No of Employees: 1,400

KERR GLASS MANUFACTURING CORPORATION

501 S Shatto Place, Los Angeles, CA 90020
Tel: (213) 487-3250
Telex: TWX 910 321 3318 kerr execb lsa

Chairman: Roger W Norian (and President and Chief Executive Officer)
Senior Executive Officers: D Gordon Strickland (Senior VP Finance and Chief Financial Officer), V J Brennan (VP and General Manager Packaging Products), Oscar N Byrd (VP Sales), Richard Morse (VP Employee Relations), Albert W Recher (VP and Controller), Robert S Reeves (VP and General Manager), Louis L Ramband (VP Planning)

PRINCIPAL ACTIVITIES: Manufacture of glass and plastic containers
Principal Bank: Security Pacific National Bank
Financial Information:

	$'000
Sales revenues	252,000

No of Employees: 3,000

KERR-MCGEE CORPORATION

PO Box 25861, Oklahoma City, OK 73125
Tel: (405) 270-1313
Telex: 747-128

Chairman: Frank A McPherson (and Chief Executive Officer
President: Jere W McKenny (and Chief Operating Officer)
Senior Executive Officers: John C Linehan (Senior VP and Chief Financial Officer), Ray A Freels (Senior VP), W Loy Johnson (Senior VP), Tom J McDaniel (Senior VP), James G Randolph (Senior VP), Paul D Romano (Senior VP), Thomas B Stephens (VP and Treasurer)

PRINCIPAL ACTIVITIES: Exploration for, and production of crude oil and natural gas; petroleum refining and marketing; manufacture of industrial chemicals; offshore contract drilling and uranium processing
Principal Subsidiaries: Kerr-McGee Refining Corporation; Kerr-McGee Chemical Corporation; Quivira Mining Company; Kerr-McGee Coal Corporation; Transworld Drilling Company; Transworld Drilling Company Limited; Kerr-McGee Oil (UK) PLC; Sequoyah Fuels Corporation; Cato Oil and Grease Company; Triangle Refineries Inc; Southwestern Refining Company Inc; Sunningdale Oils Limited; Transocean Drilling Company Limited (51%)
Principal Banks: Morgan Guaranty Trust Co of New York; Citibank; The First National Bank of Chicago
Financial Information:

	Dec 31 1985	Dec 31 1986
	$'000	$'000
Sales revenues	3,345,000	2,535,000
Income (loss) before taxes	272,000	(486,000)
Net income (loss)	137,000	(292,000)
Dividends	58,000	53,000
Dividends per share	$1.10	$1.10
Earnings (loss) per share	$2.62	($6.01)
Common stock	53,000	53,000
Retained income	1,538,000	1,192,000
Shareholders equity	1,722,000	1,338,000

No of Employees: 7,373

KETCHUM & CO INC

One Selleck St, Norwalk, CT 06855
Tel: (203) 853 1090

Chairman: Harold M Altshul (and Chief Executive Officer)
President: Robert J Edinger (and Chief Operating Officer)

Senior Executive Officers: W Phil Gibson (VP), Stephen J Young (Treasurer and Chief Financial Officer), Stuart Z Krinsly (Secretary and Legal Counsel)

PRINCIPAL ACTIVITIES: Manufacture of drugs
Principal Subsidiaries: Bio Products Inc; Ketchum Distributors Inc; Ketchum Laboratories Inc; Dietic Vitamins Inc; Steri Med Co Inc; Ketchum Marketing Services Inc
Financial Information:

	$'000
Sales revenues	304,080

No of Employees: 450

KEUFFEL & ESSER COMPANY

Ford Road, Rockaway, NJ 07866
Tel: (201) 525-9005
Telex: WUT 136425 k & e a mwn

President: William L Bordages
Senior Executive Officers: Mark A Rapp (VP)

PRINCIPAL ACTIVITIES: Manufacture of drafting materials, repographic equipment
Parent Company: Azon Corporation
Financial Information:

	Dec 31 1986
	$'000
Sales revenues	66,745
Income before taxes	6,531
Net income	6,531
Earnings per share	$0.66
Common stock	4,451
Retained (deficit)	(42,598)
Shareholders (deficit)	(24,502)

Principal Shareholders: Azon Corp
No of Employees: 400

KEWAUNEE SCIENTIFIC CORPORATION

1144 Wilmette Ave, Wilmette, IL 60091
Tel: (312) 251-7100
Telefax: (312) 251-7100

President: William M Bartlett (and Chief Executive Officer)
Senior Executive Officers: James J Habschmidt (VP Finance and Chief Financial Officer), J Scott Adams (VP and President of SEAMARK), Daniel S Miller (President of Laboratory Division)

PRINCIPAL ACTIVITIES: Manufacture of fittings and equipment for laboratories
Trade Names: Flex-Tech, Sturdi-lite, J.M. Products, Kewaunee, SEAMARK
Principal Subsidiaries: SEAMAK
Principal Bank: North Carolina National Bank
Financial Information:

	Apr 30 1986	Apr 30 1987
	$'000	$'000
Sales revenues	58,707	59,450
(Loss) before taxes	(3,100)	(11,266)
Net (loss)	(800)	(7,735)
Dividends	1,126	990
Dividends per share	$0.44	$0.275
(Loss) per share	($0.31)	($3.01)
Common stock	6,550	6,550
Retained income	19,267	10,542
Shareholders equity	25,594	17,022

No of Employees: 820

KEY CENTURION BANCSHARES INC

Virginia & Capitol Sts, PO Box 1113, Charleston, WV 25324
Tel: (304) 526 4303

Chairman: Marshall T Reynolds; Vice Chairman: Theodore A Platz Jr
President: A Michael Perry (and Chief Financial Officer)
Senior Executive Officers: L Thomas Bulla (Senior VP), Carl R Daniel Jr (Senior VP), Charles C Lanham (Senior VP), Charles F Dodrill (VP), Albert J Dye (VP), Max Saunders (VP), L A Starke (VP), Raymond J Scites (Treasurer), Edsel R Burns (Secretary and Chief Financial Officer)

PRINCIPAL ACTIVITIES: Holding company with interests in banking
Financial Information:

	Dec 31 1985
	$'000
Revenues	60,970
Net income	6,800

No of Employees: 1,000

KEY COMPANY

1020 East Wendover Avenue, Greensboro, NC 27405
Tel: (919) 273 2521

President: W Griswold Smith
Senior Executive Officers: Edward J Chase (Executive VP Operations), Francis M Tivnan Jr (Subsidiary Officer), Henry S Zalkin (VP Finance, Assistant Secretary and Treasurer), John M May (Secretary), Jean I Eades (Assistant Secretary), Doreen U Hodge (Assistant Secretary)

PRINCIPAL ACTIVITIES: House building
Principal Subsidiaries: First Southern Leasing Ltd
Principal Bank: First Union National Bank
Financial Information:

	$'000
Sales revenues	32,100

KEY INTERNATIONAL INC

24175 Northwestern Hwy, Southfield, MI 48075
Tel: (313) 353-0790

Chairman: Barney Keywell
President: J D Tauber (and Chief Executive Officer)
Senior Executive Officers: L M Kaspers (VP), W J Wottowa (VP), J C Rose (VP), D C Benoit (VP), K A Dishell (Treasurer)

PRINCIPAL ACTIVITIES: Manufacture of steel, metal fasteners and plastic products; recycling of metal
Principal Subsidiaries: Key International Mfg Inc; Superior Mold Builders, Inc
Financial Information:

	$'000
Sales revenues	170,000

No of Employees: 1,000

KEY PHARMACEUTICALS, INC

4400 Biscayne Boulevard, Miami, FL 33137
Tel: (305) 578 5800
Telex: WUT 808 235 keypharm mmia

Chairman: Phillip Frost
President: Michael Jaharis Jr (and Chief Executive Officer)
Senior Executive Officers: Daniel M Bell (Senior VP), Robert Baldini (Senior VP), David Cohen (VP), A F Gant (VP), Ronald Tuttle (VP), Allyn Golub (VP), Robert Moran (VP), David L Weinberg (VP and Treasurer)

PRINCIPAL ACTIVITIES: Manufacture of pharmaceuticals
Parent Company: Schering-Plough Corp
Principal Subsidiaries: Transmedix Laboratories Inc; Sonoptics Corporation; Mediquip Corporation; Chester A Baker Laboratories Inc; John Cummins Pharmaceutical Company Inc; Key International Inc; Key Pharmaceuticals Export Company Inc
Principal Bank: Southeast First National Bank of Miami
Financial Information:

	$'000
Sales revenues	152,000

No of Employees: 1,200

KEY TRONIC CORPORATION

N 4424 Sullivan, Spokane, WA 99216
Tel: (509) 928-8000
Telefax: 509-928-3851

Chairman: Lewis G Zirkle (and President and Chief Executive Officer)
President: Donald J Meyers
Senior Executive Officers: Randall M Pierson (Senior VP-Sales and Marketing), Charles A Reilly (VP, Chief Financial Officer and Treasurer), Howard G Sachs (Senior VP-Technology), William L Boyle (VP-Materials), Alan S Dernbach (Director of Finance and Controller), James H Dickson (Director of CIS and Personnel), Bruce E Foreman (VP-Printed Circuit Boards), Per A Larsen (VP-Spokane Industrial Park), David L Powers (General Counsel and Secretary), Edward L Sonderman (Director of Engineering), Thomas L Stewart (Director of Cheney Facility)

PRINCIPAL ACTIVITIES: Manufacturing of input devices for the data entry and word processor market
Principal Subsidiaries: KT Services, Inc; KT FSC; Key Tronic Taiwan Corporation; Key Tronic Europe Ltd; KT Servcices Ltd; KTI Ltd
Principal Bank: Rainier National Bank
Financial Information:

	Jun 30 1986	Jun 30 1987
	$'000	$'000
Sales revenues	111,655	107,636
Income before taxes	841	1,086
Net income	561	524
Earnings per share	$0.06	$0.06
Common stock	38,789	38,306
Retained income	26,831	28,007
Shareholders equity	65,620	66,313

No of Employees: 2,000

KEYCORP

One Keycorp Plaza, Box 88, Albany, NY 12201-0088
Tel: (518) 447-3273

President: Victor J Riley Jr (and Chief Executive Officer)
Senior Executive Officers: R W Bouchard (Executive VP), A J Brown Jr (Executive VP), C M Carlson (Executive VP and Treasurer), A G Espe (Executive VP), R J Frank (Executive VP), J M Lang (Executive VP), C D McGary (Executive VP), J P McNulty (Senior VP), J P Menzies (Senior VP), B E Tofte (Senior VP), A J Volkenant (Executive VP), F J Ward (Executive VP)

PRINCIPAL ACTIVITIES: Banking - financial services
Trade Names: KEYCORP
Principal Subsidiaries: New York Subsidiaries:- Key Bank NA, Albany; Key Bank of Central New York, Syracuse; Key Bank of Northern New York NA, Watertown; Key Bank of Southeastern New York NA, Chester; Key Bank of Western New York NA, Buffalo; Key Bank of Long Island, Sayville; Key Trust Company, Albany; Key Mortgage Funding, Inc, Albany; Key Services Corporation, Albany; Key Venture Capital Corp, Albany; Key Financial Services Inc, Albany; Key Advisory Services Inc, Albany. Florida Subsidiary:- Key Trust Company of Florida NA, Orlando. Maine Subsidiaries:-Key Bank of Central Maine, Augusta; Key Bank of Southern Maine, Portland; Key Bank of Northern Maine, Presque Isle; Key Bank of Eastern Maine, Bangor. Alaska Subsidiaries:- Alaska Pacific Bank, Anchorage; First National Bank of Fairbanks, Fairbanks; Alaska Pacific Mortgage Company, Anchorage; Alaska Pacific Trust Company, Anchorage; Alaska Pacific Investment Company, Anchorage. Oregon Subsidiary:- Key Bank of Oregon, Woodburn. Other Subsidiaries:- Key Capital Corp, Wellesley Hills, MA; Key Bank Life Insurance Ltd, Albany, New York; All Coast Financial, Inc. San Diego, California; Howe and Rusling Inc, Rochester, New York; Key Bank USA NA, Albany, New York
Principal Bank: Key Bank NA
Financial Information: Consolidated

	Dec 31 1985	Dec 31 1986
	$'000	$'000
Income before taxes	79,992	98,766
Net income	68,407	82,190
Dividends*	27,257	31,530
Dividends per share	$0.87	$1.00
Earnings per share	$2.61	$2.93
Common stock	126,140	143,821
Retained income	217,871	268,531
Shareholders equity	479,424	618,514
Deposits	7,390,982	5,725,326
Total assets	7,122,181	9,072,750

No of Employees: 10,000

KEYES FIBRE COMPANY

3003 Summer Street, Stamford, CT 06905
Tel: (203) 357-9100
Telex: TWX 710 4743 102 keyes std

President: M W Rast
Senior Executive Officers: William A Largent (Senior VP Sales and Marketing), Ralph H Field (Senior VP Operations), Phillip J Pierucci (Senior VP Operations), Eivind P Rynning (VP Licensees and Affiliates), H W Ehrler (VP Finance and Treasurer), Walter J Heissenbuttel (VP Personnel and Industrial Relations), Thomas E Gestrich (VP Manufacturing), John T Sutton (VP Technical Services), J I Morris (VP Purchasing and Distribution)

PRINCIPAL ACTIVITIES: Manufacture of paper and polystyrene packaging products for the food industry
Parent Company: Royal Packaging Industries Van Leer BV, Netherlands
Principal Bank: The First National Bank of Boston
Financial Information:

	$'000
Sales revenues	242,000

No of Employees: 3,000

KEYSTONE CAMERA PRODUCTS CORPORATION

468 Getty Avenue, Clifton, NJ 07015
Tel: (201) 546 2800

Chairman: Mark Auerbach (and President and Chief Executive Officer)
Senior Executive Officers: Arnold Baum (VP, Secretary and Legal Counsel), Stanley S Binder (VP and Treasurer), Richard S Rosenfeld (VP and Controller),

PRINCIPAL ACTIVITIES: Manufacture of photographic equipment
Principal Subsidiaries: Atlantic Utilities Corp; Atlantic Gas Corp; Keystone Camera Corp
Principal Bank: United Jersey Bank
Financial Information:

	$'000
Sales revenues	31,930

No of Employees: 670

KEYSTONE CARBON COMPANY

State Street, St Marys, PA 15857
Tel: (814) 781-1591
Telex: WUT 914 517 keystonecbm smy

President: Richard J Reuscher (and Treasurer)
Senior Executive Officers: Everett D Shea Jr (VP Sales), William E Reuscher (VP Industrial Relations), Eugene Gleixner (VP Engineering and Research), Robert B Reuscher (VP Operations)

PRINCIPAL ACTIVITIES: Manufacture of powder metal products and electrical components for temperature control
Principal Bank: Deposit National Bank

Financial Information:

	$'000
Sales revenues	80,000

No of Employees: 1,250

KEYSTONE CONSOLIDATED INDUSTRIES, INC

4835 LBJ Freeway, Dallas, TX 75234
Tel: (214) 458-0028

Chairman: J W Tucker Jr (and Chief Executive Officer)
President: Nicholas R Owens (and Chief Operating Officer)
Senior Executive Officers: Stephen K Emery (Treasurer and Controller), Sandra K Myers (Secretary), Charles W Holzwarth (President, National Metal Crafters), Ralph P End (Corporate Counsel)

PRINCIPAL ACTIVITIES: Manufacture of steel and wire and a wide range of metal products including hardware and fasteners
Principal Subsidiaries: Keystone Steel and Wire Company; National Metalcrafters Inc; Keystone Holdings Inc; Waterloo Metal Stampings Limited; Tornillas Especiales de Mexico SA (Mexico); Keystone American Insurance Company; KISC Limited; Broderick & Bascom Rope Co
Financial Information:

	$'000
Sales revenues	198,000

No of Employees: 5,000

KEYSTONE FINANCIAL INC

1330 South Atherton, PO Box 4, State College, PA 16804
Tel: (814) 234 5195

Chairman: J B McMurtie
President: John R Beyer (and Chief Executive Officer)
Senior Executive Officers: Donald L Beaver (VP and Director Administration), Mark L Pulaski (VP, Treasurer and Chief Financial Officer), Ben G Rooke (VP, Legal Counsel and Secretary), B E Moyer (VP)

PRINCIPAL ACTIVITIES: Banking
Principal Subsidiaries: Mid-State Bank and Trust Co; Mid-State Investment Corporation; NCB Bank; Northern Central Bank; Northern Central Life Insurance Co
Financial Information:

	Dec 31 1985
	$'000
Revenues	141,310
Net income	13,055

No of Employees: 1,040

KEYSTONE FOODS CORPORATION

931 Haverford Road, Bryn Mawr, PA 19010
Tel: (215) 527-1920

Chairman: Herbert Lotman (and President)
Senior Executive Officers: A Joe Benjamin (Senior VP Finance), Edward B Fink Jr (Group VP), Hector A Coats (VP), Bernard Cooper (VP) Edward L Silverberg (VP), John S Grabowski (VP and Treasurer), John F Conway (VP and Controller)

PRINCIPAL ACTIVITIES: Manufacture of frozen meat products; distribution of food and catering supplies to restaurants
Parent Company: New Key Inc
Principal Bank: First Pennsylvania Bank
Financial Information:

	$'000
Sales revenues	420,000

No of Employees: 2,000

KEYSTONE HERITAGE GROUP INC

555 Willow Street, Lebanon, PA 17042
Tel: (717) 274 6800
Telefax: (717) 274-6912

Chairman: Elvin H Spitler
President: Albert B Murry (and Chief Executive Officer and Subsidiary Officer)
Senior Executive Officers: Richard C Bordner (Subsidiary Officer), Calvin L Cassel Jr (Subsidiary Officer), Larry H Eberly (Subsidiary Officer), Michael H Firestine (Subsidiary Officer), J Martin Dell (Subsidiary Officer), Salvador A Miller (Subsidiary Officer), Elvin H Spitler (VP and Subsidiary Officer), Erwin K Wenner (Subsidiary Officer), Kurt A Phillips (Treasurer and Subsidiary Officer), Lance M Frehafer (Secretary and Subsidiary Officer)

PRINCIPAL ACTIVITIES: Banking
Principal Subsidiaries: Lebanon Valley National Bank; Keystone Heritage Life Insurance Company
Financial Information:

	Dec 31 1986
	$'000
Income before taxes	3,339
Net income	3,414
Dividends	1,239
Dividends per share	$0.75
Earnings per share	$2.07
Common stock	18,197
Retained income	10,950
Shareholders equity	29,147
Deposits	301,957
Total assets	347,939

No of Employees: 100

KEYSTONE INTERNATIONAL, INC

9600 W Gulf Bank Drive, Houston, TX 77240
Tel: (713) 466-1176
Telex: 166423 KIIUT

Chairman: Ray A LeBlanc (and Chief Executive Officer)
President: Malcolm D Clark
Senior Executive Officers: W W Patterson (Executive VP and Chief Financial Officer), Don S Cook (VP and Corporate Controller)

PRINCIPAL ACTIVITIES: Keystone's primary business is designing, manufacturing and marketing in the United States and various other countries certain specialized industrial products used primarily to control the flow of liquids, solids and gases
Trade Names: Keystone, Drum Owen, TMI, AGCO, Yarway
Principal Subsidiaries: Keystone Valve (Canada) Limited (Canada); Keystone Valve (Europa) BV (Netherlands); Keystone Valve (Korea) Limited (Korea) (90%); Keystone Pacific Pty Ltd (Australia); Keystone Valve (UK) Limited (UK); Valvulas Keystone de Mexico SA (Mexico); Keystone/Drum-Owen Valve Company; Texas Microsystems Inc; Keystone do Brasil Ltda (Brasil); Keystone Sales Inc; Keystone Japan Ltd (Japan); Keystone Ball Valve Ltd (UK); Keystone Southeast Asia Pty Ltd (Singapore); Keystone Valve Middle East Inc; West Gulf Holdings Inc; Keystone Valve Hong Kong Ltd (Hong Kong); Keystone Saudi Inc; Anderson, Greenwood & Co; Anderson-Greenwood USA Inc; Instrumentation Products Inc; Prince Valve Inc; Anderson-Greenwood Canada Ltd (Canada); AGEX BV (Netherlands); Anderson-Greenwood International Inc; Belgravians Limited (UK); Unicell Limited (UK); Unit Controls Limited (UK); Anderson Greenwood (UK) Limited (UK); Establissements Sarasin et Cie SA (France); Unit Controls Nederland BV (Netherlands); Anderson-Greenwood Overseas Ltd (Cayman Islands); Anderson-Greenwood Middle East (United Arab Emirates); LuMac Inc; The Rutherford Company Inc; A-G Casualty Ltd (British Virgin Islands); West Holdings Inc; Anderson-Greenwood Aviation Corp; Yarway Corporation; Tech/Serv Corporation; BriskHeat Corporation; YWHC Inc; KMW Corporation; Yarway Ltd (UK); Yarway Canada Inc (Canada); Yarway do Brasil Ltda (Brasil); Société Industrielle des Charmilles SA (France); Yarway Europa BV (Netherlands); Yarway Australia Pty Ltd (Australia); HP Valves BV (Netherlands). Unconsolidated Joint Ventures

of the Company: Anderson Greenwood (Australia) Pty Ltd (40%) (Australia); Gadelius Yarway Corporation (49%) (Japan)
Principal Bank: MBank Houston
Financial Information:

	Dec 31 1985 $'000	Dec 31 1986 $'000
Sales revenues	194,868	244,984
Income before taxes	36,198	22,316
Net income	20,097	12,608
Dividends	10,262	11,600
Dividends per share	$0.46	$0.48
Earnings per share	$0.77	$0.51
Common stock	25,998	26,760
Retained income	63,503	46,337
Shareholders equity	132,012	127,283

No of Employees: 2,800

KEYSTONE STEEL & WIRE COMPANY

7000 S W Adams Street, Peoria, IL 61641
Tel: (309) 697-7020
Telex: TWX 910 65201 35 keystone peo

President: Nicholas R Owens

PRINCIPAL ACTIVITIES: Manufacture of wire
Parent Company: Keystone Consolidated Industries Inc, Dallas, TX
Financial Information:

	$'000
Sales revenues	100,000

No of Employees: 1,350

KFC CORPORATION

PO Box 32070, Louisville, KY 40232
Tel: (502) 456-8300

Chairman: *Richard P Mayer (and Chief Executive Officer)
Presidents: *Don E Doyle (KFC-USA), *Steven V Fellingham (KFC International)
Senior Executive Officers: *Donald E Parkinson (Executive VP, Home Delivery Group), *Michael J McGraw (Executive VP, Worldwide Service), William B Evans (Senior VP, Franchising and Franchise Service), Richard D Maloney (Senior VP, Retail Operations), *Frederic Reynolds (Senior VP, Finance and Control and Chief Financial Officer), *Olden C Lee (Senior VP, Human Resources), *Roger Kramer (VP, Strategic Planning), Gregg M Reynolds (VP, Public Affairs), *Members of the Executive Committee

PRINCIPAL ACTIVITIES: With some 6,600 restaurants owned or franchised in 57 countries, Kentucky Fried Chicken is the world's second largest chain of quick services restaurants. There are 4,728 Kentucky Fried Chicken restaurants in the United States (3,491 franchised and 1,237 company-owned units). There are 1,855 company-owned and franchised quick service restaurants operating in 56 other countries (676 company-owned, 1,179 owned by franchisees). The seven largest overseas markets are Australia, Japan, New Zealand, Great Britain, Puerto Rico, and Mexico. (In addition, 759 stores are operated in Canada by an independent company. On July 29, 1987 KFC Corp., purchased the trademarks and franchising rights in Canada, subject to government approvals)
Trade Names: Kentucky Fried Chicken
Parent Company: PepsiCo Inc, Purchase, New York
Financial Information:

	Dec 31 1985 $'000	Dec 31 1986 $'000
Sales revenues	3,000,000	3,500,000

No of Employees: 115,000 (Worldwide)

KIDDE CONSUMER DURABLES CORP

2 Bala Plaza, Bala Cynwyd, PA 19004
Tel: (215) 668-2227
Telex: 845165

President: Jerome H Feig
Senior Executive Officers: David P Herbster (Executive VP and Treasurer)

PRINCIPAL ACTIVITIES: Manufacture of household products including cookware and electric appliances, clocks, home cleaning systems, plastic housewares, whirlpool baths, spas and pumps, lighting fixtures and architectural lighting products, diecast miniature vehicle toys, archery and fitness equipment, golf clubs and pool tables
Trade Names: Farberware, Spartus, Rexair, Tucker, Jacuzzi, Progress, Spaulding, Kim, Ertl, Bear, Universal, PGA, Valley
Parent Company: Kidde Inc, Saddle Brook, NJ
Principal Bank: Union National Bank
Financial Information:

	$'000
Sales revenues	450,000

No of Employees: 6,500

KIDDE, INC

Park 80 West - Plaza Two, Box 5555, Saddle Brook, NJ 07662
Tel: (201) 368-9000
Telex: 134-251 Kidde Sark

Chairman: Fred R Sullivan (and President)
Senior Executive Officers: Leonard T Riccardo (Executive VP), David R Ficca (Vice Chairman and Executive VP). Senior Vice Presidents: Richard P Barnitt (Controller), Hugh H Shull Jr (Secretary), S Harrison Dogole, Leonard T Riccardo. Vice Presidents: Harvey S Ekenstierna, Vincent S DeLorenzo, John L Kidde, Francis V Lloyd, William B McBride (Treasurer), Charles L Prothero, Kevin M Sheridan, Louis J Tedeschi

PRINCIPAL ACTIVITIES: Kidde, Inc is a broadly diversified multinational company whose more than 100 operating units are concentrated in three major groups; Consumer and Recreation; Safety, Security and Protection and Industrial and Commercial. Among the quality lines of consumer and recreation products are Progress lighting fixtures, Farberware cookware and electric appliances, Spartus clocks, Rexair home cleaning systems, Tucker plastic housewares, Jacuzzi whirlpool baths, spas and pumps, Whiteway and Kim architectural lighting products, Ertl diecast miniature vehicle toys, Bear archery and Universal physical conditioning equipment, PGA golf clubs and balls and Valley pool tables. Kidde's many well-known lines of safety, security and protection equipment are Kidde and Fenwal fire protection; as well as Globe Security uniformed guard services. Leading products in the industrial and commercial area include Weber aircraft interior equipment, Jade robotics and semi-conductor industry products, Craig electronic equipment shelters, Garden State automotive leather, Theurer truck trailers and New Jersey Office Supply, Bayless, Scott Rice and Ross-Martin office equipment, supplies and forms
Parent Company: Hanson Trust PLC, UK (from August 5th 1987)
Financial Information:

	Dec 31 1985 $'000	Dec 31 1986 $'000
Sales revenues	2,164,812	2,356,212
Income before taxes	83,591	91,526
Net income	72,245	25,170
Dividends common shares	25,360	25,593
Dividends per share	$1.20	$1.20
Earnings per share net*	$3.31	$1.08
Common stock	26,567	26,707
Retained income	474,780	475,158
Shareholders equity	721,359	722,659

*primary

No of Employees: 38,000

KIMBALL INTERNATIONAL, INC

1600 Royal Street, Jasper, IN 47546
Tel: (812) 482-1600

Chairman: Thomas L Habig (and Chief Executive Officer); Assistant to Chairman: Arnold F Habig
President: Douglas A Habig
Senior Executive Officers: Maurice R Kuper (Senior Executive VP and Chief Operations Officer, Assistant Secretary), John B Habig (Senior Executive VP, Consumer Products Production), James C Thyen (Senior Executive VP, Finance and Administration, Treasurer), John T Thyen (Senior Executive VP, Marketing), H E Thyen (Executive VP, Secretary), Anthony P Habig (Executive VP, International Division)

PRINCIPAL ACTIVITIES: Manufacture business and home furnishings, electronics, pianos and organs, timber products including lumber, plywood and veneer
Principal Subsidiaries: Manufacturing and Service Operations: Consumer Products: Kimball Office Furniture Co; Artec; Kimball Upholstered Products; National Office Furniture Co; National Healthcare Co; Office Furniture Distribution Centers; Office Furniture Showrooms; Kimball Piano & Organ; Kimball Piano Division; Kimball Music Center and Wilking Music; Kimball Furniture Reproductions Inc. Electronics; Kimball Electronics Inc; Batesville American Mfg Co; McAllen-American Corporation. Contract: The Jasper Corporation and Cabinet Division; Kimball Hospitality Furniture Inc; Heritage Hills; Jasper Plastics; ToolPro. Raw Materials/Ply-Products: Lafayette Manufacturing Co; Lafayette Sawmill Division; Dale-Wood Manufacturing; Indiana Hardwoods; Cloverport Sawmill Division; Greensburg Mfg Co; West Jefferson Wood Products Inc; Jasper Laminates; Evansville Veneer & Lumber Co; Chandler Veneers; The Jasper-American Mfg Co. International: Herrburger Brooks PLC (UK); Kimball Europe Ltd (UK); Kimball World Inc; L Bösendorfer Klavierfabrik AG (Austria); Kimco SA (Mexico). Services: Corporate Headquarters and Annex; Property Management Division; Research & Development Division; Machine & Equipment Division; Energy Center; Kimball International Transit Inc; HRJ Automotive Service; Education Center and Showroom; Tech Center.
Principal Bank: The Indiana National Bank
Financial Information:

	Jun 30 1986	Jun 30 1987
	$'000	$'000
Sales revenues	394,092	477,081
Income before taxes	46,188	58,974
Net income	26,056	29,854
Dividends	6,192	6,851
Dividends per share	$0.585	$0.65
Earnings per share	$2.44	$2.81
Common stock	6,723	6,723
Retained income	173,285	196,153
Shareholders equity	178,852	201,223

No of Employees: 7,440

KIMBALL OFFICE FURNITURE COMPANY

Route 60, Borden, IN 47106
Tel: (812) 967-2041

Chairman: Thomas L Habig (and Chief Executive Officer); Assistant to Chairman: Arnold F Habig (and Chief Executive Officer)
President: Douglas A Habig
Senior Executive Officers: John B Habig (Senior Executive VP Keyboard), James C Thyen (Senior Executive VP and Treasurer), Maurice Kuper (Senior Executive VP and Chief Operating Officer), Herbert E Thyen (Executive VP and Secretary), John C Ackerman (Executive VP Ply-Products Division), James A Birk (Executive VP Keyboard Sales), Gary Critser (Executive VP and Comptroller), Roman B Oser (Executive VP Raw Materials), Herman F Dekemper (Executive VP Contract), Anthony B Habig (Executive VP International), Ronald J Thyen (Executive VP Officer Furniture Division), John T Thyen (Executive VP Office Furniture Sales), Randall Weales (Executive VP Keyboard Division), Victor A Geiger (VP International Sales), Guy Hurst (VP Product Planning), Louis Korff (VP), Robert Kreilein (VP), Kenneth R Lampert (VP Marketing Development), John Wotte (VP Keyboard Sales), Matthew A Slaats (VP Research and Development), William Wells (VP)

PRINCIPAL ACTIVITIES: Manufacture and sale of office furniture
Parent Company: Kimball International Inc, Jasper, IN
Principal Bank: The Indiana National Bank
Financial Information:

	$'000
Sales revenues	80,000

No of Employees: 600

KIMBALL PIANO & ORGAN COMPANY

1549 Royal Street, Jasper, IN 4756
Tel: (812) 482-1600

Chairman: Thomas L Habig (and Chief Executive Officer); Assistant to Chairman: Arnold F Habig (and Chief Executive Officer)
President: Douglas A Habig
Senior Executive Officers: John B Habig (Senior Executive VP Keyboard), Maurice R Kuper (Senior Executive VP and Chief Operating Officer), James C Thyen (Senior Executive VP and Treasurer), Herbert E Thyen (Executive VP and Secretary), Anthony P Habig (Executive VP International)

PRINCIPAL ACTIVITIES: Manufacture of pianos and electronic organs
Parent Company: Kimball International Inc, Jasper, IN
Principal Bank: The Indiana National Bank
Financial Information:

	$'000
Sales Revenues	50,000

No of Employees: 400

KIMBERLY-CLARK CORPORATION

PO Box 619100, Dallas-Fort Worth Airport Station, Dallas, TX 75261
Tel: (214) 830-1200

Chairman: Darwin E Smith (and Chief Executive Officer); Vice Chairmen: Marvin F Gade, Robert C Ernest; Donald R Hibbert (and Treasurer and Chief Financial Officer)
Senior Executive Officers: Walter H Drew (Executive VP), James G Grosklaus (Executive VP), Peter N Larson (Executive VP), Richard H Sonnentag (Executive VP), O George Everbach (Senior VP and General Counsel), Terrence L Murray (Senior VP, Chief Accounting and Control Officer and Controller), Brendan M O'Neill (Senior VP), Wayne R Sanders (Senior VP), Donald M Crook (VP and Secretary), Nick D Hansen (VP and Tax Counsel), Anthony W Gamron (VP and Treasurer), William W Wicks (VP)

PRINCIPAL ACTIVITIES: Manufacture of paper and paper products including consumer disposables, health care products and specialty paper products
Principal Bank: Citibank
Financial Information:

	Dec 31 1985	Dec 31 1986
	$'000	$'000
Sales revenues	4,072,900	4,303,100
Net income	267,100	269,400
Earnings per share	$5.84	$5.87
Shareholders equity	1,743,900	1,919,900

No of Employees: 36,648

KINCAID FURNITURE COMPANY, INC

PO Box 605, Hudson, NC 28638
Tel: (704) 728-3261

Chairman: J W Kincaid
President: Steven M Kincaid
Senior Executive Officers: Ben H Kincaid (VP Purchasing), James A Kincaid (VP Traffic), Thomas M Robbins (VP Transport), Leo Kahn (VP Sales and Advertising), John M Harwell (VP Finance and Administration)

PRINCIPAL ACTIVITIES: Manufacture of furniture
Principal Bank: The Northwestern Bank
Financial Information:

	Jan 31 1987
	$'000
Sales revenues	74,606
Income before taxes	5,346
Net income	2,701
Earnings per share	$0.80
Common stock	4,567
Retained income	14,029
Shareholders equity	23,982

No of Employees: 1,300

KINDER CARE LEARNING CENTERS INC
2400 Presidents Drive, Montgomery, AL 36116
Tel: (205) 277 5090

Chairman: Perry Mendel (and Chief Executive Officer)
President: Richard J Grassgreen (and Chief Operating Officer)
Senior Executive Officers: Edward H Gibson (Executive VP Administration and Human Resources), Jack A Hanchow (Senior VP Development), Robert Hartley (VP Marketing), Ann Muscari (VP Communications), Eddie O Nabors (VP Finance and Treasurer), Laurene Smith (VP Research and Development), Joel C Sockwell (VP Administration), Franklin Eugene Montgomery (VP Operations)

PRINCIPAL ACTIVITIES: Kindergarten facilities
Principal Bank: Chemical Bank
Financial Information:

	1986
	$'000
Sales revenues	231,000
Net income	33,000

No of Employees: 10,000

KING FIFTH WHEEL COMPANY
Box 68 Mountaintop, PA 18707
Tel: (717) 474-6371
Telex: TWX 510 658 3304 king fifth

President: Robert E Dunham
Senior Executive Officers: Donald Symanski (VP), R J Ballard (VP), John Rowlands (Secretary), John Marks (Comptroller, Assistant Secretary and Treasurer)

PRINCIPAL ACTIVITIES: Manufacture of welded products
Parent Company: TI Group plc
Principal Bank: Provident National Bank
Financial Information:

	$'000
Sales revenues	50,000

No of Employees: 480

KING RADIO CORPORATION
400 N Rogers Road, Olathe, KS 66062
Tel: (913) 782-0400
Telex: 4-2299

Chairman: Edward J King Jr
President: R T Cox
Senior Executive Officers: R C Christie (VP Marketing), R S Dunn (VP Operations), C J Weltsch (VP Finance), Kevin J Growney (VP Material), Bernard L Glover (VP General Aviation Sales), James V Stothard (VP International Marketing), Gary Burrell (VP Engineering)

PRINCIPAL ACTIVITIES: Manufacture of electronic equipment for navigation and communications for the aircraft industry
Parent Company: Bendix Corp
Principal Bank: United Missouri Bank
Financial Information:

	$'000
Sales revenues	87,000

No of Employees: 2,100

KING WORLD PRODUCTIONS INC
480 Morris Avenue, Summit, NJ 07901
Tel: (201) 522 0100

Chairman: Roger King
President: Michael King (and Chief Executive Officer)
Senior Executive Officers: Karen Rabe ((VP and Secretary)

PRINCIPAL ACTIVITIES: Television program and feature film distributors
Financial Information:

	$'000
Sales revenues	81,000

No of Employees: 80

KING-SEELEY THERMOS COMPANY
2700 Sanders Road, Prospect Heights, IL 60070
Tel: (312) 564-3910

President: G Dillon (and Chief Executive Officer)
Senior Executive Officers: S Arbuckle (Executive VP), T McCarthy (Executive VP), R Osborne (Executive VP), W E Chandler (Senior VP and Chief Financial Officer), R Munden (VP and Secretary), J C Hoffmann (VP and Chief Financial Officer)

PRINCIPAL ACTIVITIES: Manufacture of cast iron products, leisure and outdoor cooking equipment, vacuum containers, water cooling products and ice making machines
Parent Company: Household Manufacturing Inc-Ultimate Parent Company-Household International Inc
Principal Bank: Manufacturers National Bank of Detroit
Financial Information:

	$'000
Sales revenues	334,000

No of Employees: 3,800

KINGSPORT PRESS, INC
Press Street, Kingsport, TN 37662
Tel: (615) 246-7131
Telex: WUT 553414 kpt presskst

Senior Executive Officers: Luther M Odom (VP and General Manager), Dean J Dietrich (VP and Secretary), Jerry W Allee (VP and New York Sales Manager) Christopher G Mumford (Treasurer)

PRINCIPAL ACTIVITIES: Printing of books and manufacture of ringbinders
Parent Company: Arcata Corporation, San Francisco, CA
Financial Information:

	$'000
Sales revenues	120,000

No of Employees: 3,300

KINNEY SYSTEM, INC
60 Madison Avenue, New York, NY 10010
Tel: (212) 889 4444

Chairman: Andrew Heine
President: Lewis Weinstein
Senior Executive Officers: Daniel J Stark (Executive VP), Saul P Schwartz (Executive VP), Richard L Levinson (Senior VP), Shelley Boxer (Senior VP, Treasurer, Chief Financial Officer), Edward P Katz (VP), James J Milioti (VP), Robert A Rapuano (VP and Assistant Secretary)

PRINCIPAL ACTIVITIES: Parking facilities
Trade Names: Kinney System, Inc; The Katz Parking System, Inc; SPS Group
Parent Company: Cromwell Group Inc
Principal Bank: Manufacturers Hanover Trust
Financial Information:

	$'000
Sales revenues	85,000

No of Employees: 1,600

KIPLINGER WASHINGTON EDITORS, INC

1729 H Street NW, Washington, DC 20006
Tel: (202) 887-6400

Chairman: Austin H Kiplinger (and President)
Senior Executive Officers: James O Mayo (Executive VP and Secretary), Knight A Kiplinger (VP and Publisher, Editor-in-Chief Changing Times Magazine), Corbin M Wilkes (VP Finance), Rozella O Flick (Treasurer)

PRINCIPAL ACTIVITIES: Publication of magazines
Principal Bank: The Riggs National Bank of Washington
Financial Information:

	$'000
Sales revenues	56,000

No of Employees: 600

KIRBY BUILDING SYSTEMS, INC

PO Box 140700, Nashville, TN 37210
Tel: (615) 889-0020

President: George F King (and President and Chief Executive Officer)
Senior Executive Officers: R W Osgood (VP Finance and Administration), J Walter Lewis (VP Technical and Customer Services), Robert R Jones (VP Sales and Marketing), E S Polak (VP Operations), Jay C Pence (VP Purchasing)

PRINCIPAL ACTIVITIES: Manufacture of structural steel
Principal Bank: Commerce Union Bank
Financial Information:

	$'000
Sales revenues	40,000

No of Employees: 300

KIRBY EXPLORATION COMPANY, INC

1717 St James Place, Suite 500, Houston, TX 77056
Tel: (713) 629-9370
Telex: 1-9108813702

Chairman: Robert G Stone Jr
President: George A Peterkin Jr
Senior Executive Officers: Myron H Newman (VP, Treasurer and Assistant Secretary), Henry Gilchrist (Secretary). Subsidiary Senior Executives: Patrick W Kelly (President of Kirby Exploration Company of Texas), James C Laird (VP and Treasurer of Kirby Exploration Company of Texas), Joseph H Pyne (President of Dixie Carriers Inc), Robert H Dale Jr (Senior VP Dixie Carriers, Inc), Edward Gaither (VP Secretary and Treasurer-Dixie Carriers, Inc), Adrian Ortiz (President, Universal Insurance Company), John Lipscomb (President, The Mariner Reinsurance Company Limited)

PRINCIPAL ACTIVITIES: Kirby Exploration Company, Inc, headquartered in Houston, Texas, is a diversified corporation that, through its subsidiaries, is engaged in the acquisition, exploration and development of oil and gas properties, the transportation and towage of freight by barge, writing property insurance and reinsurance. The Company's oil and gas activities are conducted primarily in the Southwest and Gulf Coast inland area and offshore Texas and Louisiana. The Company's transportation and towage of freight activities are conducted primarily in the regions of the Gulf of Mexico, the Gulf Intracoastal Waterway and the Mississippi River and its insurance activities are conducted primarily in Puerto Rico and London
Principal Subsidiaries: Kirby Exploration Company of Texas; Dixie Carriers, inc; Universal Insurance Company of Puerto Rico
Principal Bank: MBank Houston
Financial Information:

	Dec 31 1985	Dec 31 1986
	$'000	$'000
Sales revenues	76,461	64,147
Income (loss) before taxes	2,094	(26,833)
Net income (loss)	2,613	(26,417)
Earnings (loss) per share	$0.11	($1.10)
Common stock	23,994	24,093
Retained (deficit)	(12,468)	(38,885)
Shareholders equity	73,430	46,369

Number of Shareholders: 4,800
No of Employees: 521

KIRBY FOREST INDUSTRIES, INC

600 Jefferson, Houston, TX 77002
Tel: (713) 652-5400
Telex: ITT 4620186 kirby fi hou

President: J E Stevens
Senior Executive Officers: J R Wood (VP Resources), C W Ratliff (Assistant to President), A A Horton (Secretary and Treasurer)

PRINCIPAL ACTIVITIES: Manufacture of timber products including lumber, plywood, particle board and other building materials
Parent Company: Santa Fe Southern Pacific Corporation thru Santa Fe Industries Inc
Principal Bank: First City Bank of Houston
Financial Information:

	$'000
Sales revenues	150,000

No of Employees: 1,600

KIRKWOOD INDUSTRIES, INC

4855 W 130th Street, Cleveland, OH 44135
Tel: (216) 267-6200
Telex: WUT 980630 kirkwood chv

Chairman: William P Kirkwood
President: Richard Klym
Senior Executive Officers: Earl V Cochran (VP Sales), Richard E Hojnacki (VP Finance)

PRINCIPAL ACTIVITIES: Manufacture of electrical and electronic equipment
Principal Subsidiaries: Kirkwood Commutator Company
Principal Bank: National City Bank
Financial Information:

	$'000
Sales revenues	50,000

No of Employees: 1,000

KIRSCH COMPANY

309 N Prospect Street, Sturgis, MI 49091
Tel: (616) 651-0211
Telex: TWX 510 3989260 kirsch stur

President: Robert A Addison
Senior Executive Officers: William P Hagenbuch (VP Manufacturing), J A Ford (VP Marketing), M G Scheske (VP Finance)

PRINCIPAL ACTIVITIES: Manufacture of rails and fittings for drapes
Parent Company: Cooper Industries Inc, Houston, TX
Principal Bank: Texas Commerce Bank

Financial Information:

	$'000
Sales revenues	170,000

No of Employees: 3,000

KIT MANUFACTURING COMPANY

PO Box 848, 530 East Wardlow Road, Long Beach, CA 90807
Tel: (213) 595 7451

Chairman: Dan Pocapalla (and President and Chief Executive Officer); Vice Chairman: Arnold J Romeyn (and VP and Treasurer)
Senior Executive Officers: Marylyce A Faldetta (Secretary), Dale J Gonzalez (VP Finance), Matthew S Pulizzi (VP Customer Service), Arnold J Romeyn (VP and Treasurer)

PRINCIPAL ACTIVITIES: Manufacture of recreational vehicles including travel trailers; manufactured housing
Principal Bank: First Interestate Bank of California
Financial Information:

	$'000
Sales revenues	50,500

No of Employees: 610

KIWI BRANDS INC

Rte 662 N, Douglassville, PA 19518
Tel: (215) 385-3061
Telex: TWX 710 6530 140 niki doug

President: Edward L Collier
Senior Executive Officers: Arthur J DiFuria (VP Finance), Steven P Stanbrudic (VP Sales)

PRINCIPAL ACTIVITIES: Manufacture of shoe polish and household cleaning materials
Trade Names: Kiwi
Parent Company: Sara Lee Corp
Principal Bank: Philadelphia National Bank
Financial Information:

	$'000
Sales revenues	85,000

No of Employees: 300

KLA INSTRUMENTS CORPORATION

2051 Mission College Boulevard, Santa Clara, CA 95052
Tel: (408) 988 6100

Chairman: Robert R Anderson (and Executive VP, Chief Operating Officer and Assistant Secretary)
President: Kenneth Levy (and Chief Executive Officer)
Senior Executive Officers: Robert J Boehlke (Senior VP and General Manager), Kenneth L Schroeder (Senior VP and General Manager), Paul Sandland (VP Development), Robert M Walsh (VP and Treasurer), Kate Ludeman (VP), John Mathews (VP), Paul E Kreutz (Secretary)

PRINCIPAL ACTIVITIES: Manufacture of automation equipment
Principal Bank: Bank of America
Financial Information:

	$'000
Sales revenues	83,000

No of Employees: 400

KLEINERT'S INC

120 W Germantown Pike, Suite 100, Plymouth Meeting, PA 19462-1420

Chairman: Jack Brier (and Chief Executive Officer)
President: Victor J Montemayor (and Subsidiary Officer)
Senior Executive Officers: Bernard M Borish (Secretary), Joseph J Connors (Treasurer and Chief Financial Officer), Marvin Grossman (Subsidiary Officer)

PRINCIPAL ACTIVITIES: Manufacture of children's clothing, sanitary garments, bathing caps and dress shields
Principal Subsidiaries: Kleinert's Inc of Alabama
Principal Bank: Philadelphia National Bank
Financial Information:

	$'000
Sales revenues	41,170

No of Employees: 1,000

KN ENERGY INC

12055 West 2nd Place, PO Box 15265, Lakewood, CO 80215
Tel: (303) 989 1740

Chairman: J Robert Wilson (and President and Chief Executive Officer)
Chairman of the Executive Committee: Thomas Creigh Jr
Senior Executive Officers: Larry D Hall (Executive VP Service), Robert C McHugh (Senior VP, Legal Counsel and Secretary), Roger L Bruton (Subsidiary Officer), Judith A Aden (Treasurer), E Wayne Lundhagen (VP Accounting), James A Miller (VP Finance and Administration), B Neal Hanson (VP Production), S D Whiteman Jr (VP Distribution), Frank T Zitzso (VP Energy), Howard R Frederickson (VP Acquisitions)

PRINCIPAL ACTIVITIES: Distribution of natural gas; exploration and production of oil, natural gas, minerals including coal and uranium
Principal Subsidiaries: Excelsior Oil Corp; Midlands Transportation Co; North Central Energy Co; Northern Gas Co; Northern Mountain Gas Co; Northern Utilities Inc; Plains Production Co; Slurco Corp; Western Alfalfa Corp; Western Gas Corp; Western Oil Corp; Wyoming Fuel Co
Principal Bank: Northern Trust Co
Financial Information:

	$'000
Sales revenues	420,270

No of Employees: 1,740

KNAPE & VOGT MANUFACTURING COMPANY

2700 Oak Industrial Drive NE, Grand Rapids, MI 49505
Tel: (616) 459-3311
Telex: WUT 226317 knapevogt gdr

President: Raymond E Knape
Senior Executive Officers: David M Zoch (VP Sales), Walter Knauss (VP Production), Robert J Bowman (VP Corporate Development and Secretary), Richard C Simkins (VP Finance)

PRINCIPAL ACTIVITIES: Manufacture of hardware supplies for the building trade and household hardware products
Principal Bank: Old Kent Bank and Trust Company
Financial Information:

	Jun 30 1986	Jun 30 1987
	$'000	$'000
Sales revenues	74,444	84,733
Income before taxes	8,463	8,271
Net income	4,825	4,346
Dividends	1,943	1,998
Dividends per common share	$0.500	$0.522
Dividends per Class B share	$0.500	$0.492
Earnings per share	$1.24	$1.10
Common stock*	3,923	4,007
Shareholders equity	39,201	43,339
*shares outstanding in thousands		

No of Employees: 1,117

KNAPP SHOES INC

One Knapp Centre, Brockton, MA 02401
Tel: (617) 588-9000

President: John J Schlueter (and Treasurer and Clerk)
Senior Executive Officers: John B Foye (VP Manufacturing), John G Clayton (VP Retailing)

PRINCIPAL ACTIVITIES: Manufacture of footwear and retail trade in clothing and footwear; mail order sales

Principal Bank: Shawmut Bank of Boston
Financial Information:

	$'000
Sales revenues	100,000

No of Employees: 1,800

KNIGHT-RIDDER INC
1 Herald Plaza, Miami, FL 33101
Tel: (305) 376-3800

Chairman: Alvah H Chapman Jr (and Chief Executive Officer)
Presidents: James K Batten, P Anthony Ridder (Newspaper Division)
Senior Executive Officers: Robert F Singleton (Senior VP Finance), Larry Jinks (Senior VP), Marvin B Berenblum (Senior VP Personnel), C W Baker (Group VP), W H Harwell Jr (Group VP), Donald A Nizen (VP Circulation), Edward T Parmelee (VP Marketing), David K Ray (VP), Daniel H Ridder (VP), Ralph S Roth (VP Production), Ann Wrenn King (VP and Treasurer)

PRINCIPAL ACTIVITIES: Publication of newspapers; information services; television broadcasting and cable TV interests
Principal Bank: Manufacturers Hanover Trust Co
Financial Information:

	Dec 31 1986
	$'000
Sales revenues	1,910,650
Net income	140,039
Earnings per share	$2.41
Shareholders equity	815,982

No of Employees: 22,200

KNOGO CORPORATION
350 Wireless Boulevard, Hauppauge, NY 11788
Tel: (516) 232-2100
Telex: 6852166/716852166
Telefax: (516) 232-2124

President: Arthur J Minasy
Senior Executive Officers: Frederick Cicchetti (VP), Michael N Cooper (VP Engineering), James R Dellomo (VP Finance and Treasurer), Michael F Trentacosti (VP Operations), Tom A Nicolette (VP and General Manager Knogo North America), Peter J Mundy (Corporate Controller), Neil A Smith (VP International)

PRINCIPAL ACTIVITIES: Manufacture of electronic security equipment
European Headquarters: Knogo SA, Mons, Belgium. World Headquarters: Knogo Corporation, Hauppauge, NY
Principal Bank: Chemical Bank
Financial Information:

	Feb 28 1986	Feb 28 1987
	$'000	$'000
Sales revenues	36,006	49,021
Income before taxes	7,349	10,819
Net income	5,803	8,547
Earnings per share	$1.19	$1.25
Shareholders equity	80,654	97,504

No of Employees: 597 worldwide

KNOLL INTERNATIONAL INC
Water Street, East Greenville, PA 18041
Tel: (215) 679 7991
Telex: WUT 127 997 knollet ny

Chairmen: M S Cogan (and Chief Executive Officer); S C Swid (and Chief Executive Officer)
President: L R Ryan (and Chief Operating Officer)
Senior Executive Officers: Mel Silver (Senior VP), A D Sager (Senior VP), Lewis Singer (Senior VP), F M Pope (VP and Controller), R A Barbieri (VP, Secretary and Treasurer), W H Oler (VP), Robert V Condon Jr (VP)

PRINCIPAL ACTIVITIES: Manufacture of furniture
Parent Company: General Felt Industries Inc
Principal Subsidiaries: Knoll Overseas Ltd
Financial Information:

	$'000
Sales revenues	203,000

No of Employees: 2,300

KNOUSE FOODS COOPERATIVE, INC
Peach Glen, PA 17306
Tel: (717) 677-8181
Telex: TWX 510 650 2270 knouse pgin

President: Dean L Carey
Senior Executive Officers: M E Weiser (VP), John A Leeti (VP and Treasurer), Kenneth E Guise (VP Marketing)

PRINCIPAL ACTIVITIES: Manufacture of fruit products
Financial Information:

	$'000
Sales revenues	160,000

No of Employees: 1,500

KNUDSEN FOODS, INC
Box 2335 Terminal Annex, Los Angeles, CA 90051
Tel: (213) 744-7000

Chairman: Dee R Bangerter (and Chief Executive Officer); Co Chairman: David F Greenawalt (and President and Chief Operating Officer); Vice Chairman: Fallen A Meyer
Senior Executive Officers: John C Thompson (Senior VP Sales and Marketing), Richard Van Wagenen (VP Finance), Frank Bernier (VP Manufacturing), Jack Markin (VP Distribution Systems and Administration), Brian R Thompson (VP and Treasurer), Michael A Piraino (VP and Controller)

PRINCIPAL ACTIVITIES: Manufacture of dairy products and food extracts and essences; operation of retail stores and fast food outlets
Parent Company: Winn Enterprises Inc, Fullerton, CA
Principal Subsidiaries: Knudsen Corporation
Principal Bank: Wells Fargo Bank
Financial Information:

	$'000
Sales revenues	480,000

No of Employees: 2,000

KOCH, GEORGE, SON, INC
10 S 11th Street, Evansville, IN 47744
Tel: (812) 426-9600
Telex: TWX 810 3530527 geokochson evs

Chairman: Robert L Koch
President: Robert L Koch II
Senior Executive Officers: James H Muehlbauer (Executive VP), L J Koch Jr (VP and Treasurer), Clarence H Arbeiter (VP Industrial Relations), Jess Gregory (VP Air Conditioning), James C Oskins (Assistant Secretary)

PRINCIPAL ACTIVITIES: Manufacture of a wide range of industrial equipment including paint spraying systems, portable buildings, refrigeration, heating and air conditioning equipment, conveyors and ovens, brass and glass furniture
Principal Subsidiaries: Gibbs Aluminium Diecasting Corp; National Sealant and Adhesives Inc; Brake Supply Co Inc; Uniseal Rubber Products Inc
Principal Bank: Citizens National Bank
Financial Information:

	$'000
Sales revenues	180,000
Shareholders equity	65,000

No of Employees: 900

KOGER COMPANY

3986 Boulevard Center Drive, Jacksonville, FL 32207
Tel: (904) 396 4817

Chairman: Ira M Koger (and Chief Executive Officer); Vice Chairman: S D Stoneburner (and Chief Financial Officer)
President: W F E Kienast (and Chief Operating Officer)
Senior Executive Officers: Robert N Bridger (Senior VP Development), Irvin H Davis (Senior VP Finance), Henry Fisher (Senior VP Finance), Wade L Hampton (Senior VP Marketing), Murray A Lewis (Senior VP Operations), Allen R Ranson (Senior VP Accounting)
PRINCIPAL ACTIVITIES: Management of real estate
Principal Bank: First Union Bank
Financial Information:

	$'000
Sales revenues	39,600

No of Employees: 80

KOH-I-NOOR RAPIDOGRAPH, INC

100 North Street, PO Box 68, Bloomsbury, NJ 08804
Tel: (201) 479-4124
Telex: 6858126 KIN NJ
Facsimile: (201) 479-4285

Chairman: Karl H Ditze
President: Michael Barthe
Senior Executive Officers: Robert H Lasater (Senior VP), Frederick D Clauser (Treasurer and Managing Director), John P Leuenberger (VP, Research and Development), Edward A Murray (VP, Sales), John Landis (VP, Manufacturing), John N Wollman (Assistant Treasurer), Fred Clauser (Secretary), Christie Miller (Assistant Secretary)
PRINCIPAL ACTIVITIES: Manufacturer of engineering and drafting supplies, technical fountain pens, drawing inks, leads, holders, pencils and art materials, also cosmetics
Trade Names: KOH-I-NOOR, RAPIDOGRAPH, rotring
Parent Company: Rotring, Hamburg, West Germany
Principal Subsidiaries: Cosmolab Inc; Koh-I-Noor Radpidograph Inc (Canada)
Principal Banks: Horizon Bank; Third National Bank; Schroders International Bank; Hypo Bank
Financial Information:

	1986
	$'000
Sales revenues	80,000

No of Employees: 800

KOLLMORGEN CORPORATION

10 Mill Pond Lane, Simsbury, CT 06070-2429

Chairman: Robert L Swiggett; Vice Chairmen: Allan M Doyle Jr (and Chief Financial Officer), George P Stephan
President: James E Swiggett (and Chief Executive Officer)
Senior Executive Officers: Donald S Fischer (VP), Edwin M Felske (VP and Chief Accounting Officer), Jack R Walnes (VP), Robert N Williams (VP Corporate Development)
PRINCIPAL ACTIVITIES: Manufacture of electrical and electronic equipment; generators, electric motors, electrical machinery; optical electronic instruments including artillery directors and submarine periscopes
Principal Subsidiaries: Crystal Specialties Inc; IMD Properties Inc; Kollmorgen Overseas Corp; Kollmorgen Technologies Corp; PCK Elastomerics Inc; Photocircuits Atlanta Inc; Proto-Power Corp; Questec Enterprises Inc; 31 Sea Cliff Avenue Corp; Kollmorgen AG (Switzerland); Kollmorgen Foreign Sales Corp (Virgin Islands); Kollmorgen International Finance NV (Netherlands Antilles); Kollmorgen (Ireland) Ltd (Eire); Kollmorgen (UK) Ltd (UK): Société Anonyme Artus (France)
Principal Bank: Morgan Guaranty Trust Co
Financial Information:

	$'000
Sales revenues	311,000

No of Employees: 5,000

KOLLSMAN INSTRUMENT CO

220 Daniel Webster Hwy S, Merrimack, NH 03054
Tel: (603) 889-2500
Telex: WUT 943537 kollsman merr

Senior Executive Officers: Fred L Gagnon (VP and General Manager), Joseph C Allwarden (VP Marketing), Dino G Geretti (VP Finance and Controller), Chris Smith (VP Procurement), Charles F Richmond (VP Contracts and Marketing), Rolf Pagel (VP Industrial Relations), Arian Dzerouch (VP Operations)
PRINCIPAL ACTIVITIES: Manufacture of instruments and equipment for the aviation industry
Parent Company: Sun Chemical Corp
Principal Bank: North Carolina National Bank
Financial Information:

	$'000
Sales revenues	180,000

No of Employees: 2,300

KOOMEY INC

800 Koomey Road, Brookshire, TX 77423
Tel: (713) 391 1000
Telex: WUT 795265 koomey co hou

Chairman: Bjarne Skeie
President: B A Stangeland
Senior Executive Officers: Owystein Jahren (VP)
PRINCIPAL ACTIVITIES: Manufacture of equipment for the oil industry
Principal Bank: First City National Bank of Houston
Financial Information:

	$'000
Sales revenues	25,000

No of Employees: 320

KOPPERS CO, INC

Koppers Building, Pittsburgh, PA 15219
Tel: (412) 227-2000
Telex: TRT 199116 koppers pgh

Chairman: C R Rullin (and Chief Executive Officer)
President: G C Tenley
Senior Executive Officers: B G Bartley (Executive VP), L L Murray (VP Technology Services and Business Development), D H Cuozzo (VP Legal Services, General Counsel and Secretary), T M St Clair (VP, Treasurer and Chief Financial Officer), J R Beidler (VP Communications Group), C P Dorsey (VP Executive Dept), R R Wingard (VP Administration Services Group), Dr D J McGraw (VP Science and Technology)
PRINCIPAL ACTIVITIES: Manufacture of a wide range of materials for the construction industry including road making aggregates, ready-mixed concrete, wood preserving chemicals and insulation materials; construction and engineering services
Principal Subsidiaries: Thiem Corporation; The General Crushed Stone Co; Sully-Miller Contracting Co

Financial Information:

	Dec 31 1985	Dec 31 1986
	$'000	$'000
Sales revenues	1,400,200	1,396,400
Income (loss) before taxes	(30,000)	63,200
Net income (loss)	(106,200)	74,100
Common dividends	22,859	22,875
Dividends per common share	$0.80	$0.80
Earnings (loss) per share net	($3.72)	$2.59
Common stock	35,764	37,359
Retained income	239,761	289,836
Shareholders equity	435,050	479,100

No of Employees: 11,000

KORODY-COLYER CORPORATION

112 N Avalon Blvd, Wilmington, CA 90744
Tel: (213) 830-0330
Telex: WUT 677 296 korodiesl wiln

President: Gabor M Korody
Senior Executive Officers: John E Colyer (Executive VP), Joseph W Reynolds (VP Administration)

PRINCIPAL ACTIVITIES: Manufacture of components for diesel engines
Principal Bank: Union Bank
Financial Information:

	$'000
Sales revenues	55,000

No of Employees: 400

KRACO ENTERPRISES INC

505 E Euclid, Compton, CA 90224
Tel: (213) 774-2550
Telex: TWX 910 3467748 kraco cmtn

Chairman: Maurice H Kraines
President: Lawrence M Kraines
Senior Executive Officers: John M Shapiro (Senior VP), Bob Brocoff (Senior VP Finance), Steve Kraines (Senior VP Sales), Yasuko Kraines (VP International Operations), Mark Boone (VP Auto Division), Gary Hodge (VP Consumer Electronics Division), Ken Balch (VP Sales and Operations)

PRINCIPAL ACTIVITIES: Manufacture of electrical and electronic equipment for the consumer market including stereo equipment, CB equipment and telephones and rubber mats for vehicles
Principal Bank: Union Bank
Financial Information:

	$'000
Sales revenues	150,000

No of Employees: 700

KRAEMER, EDWARD, & SONS, INC

One Plainview Road, Plain, WI 53577
Tel: (608) 546-2311
Telex: WUT 265 457 kraemer plan

President: Rudolph L Kraemer (and Treasurer)
Senior Executive Officers: Victor A Kraemer (VP and Secretary), John Olsen (VP Finance)

PRINCIPAL ACTIVITIES: Civil engineering and construction
Principal Bank: Bank of Spring Green
Financial Information:

	$'000
Sales revenues	60,000

No of Employees: 650

KRAFT, INC

Kraft Court, Glenview, IL 60025
Tel: (312) 998-2000
Cable: KRAFT INC GLVW
Telex: 724320

Chairman: John M Richman (and Chief Executive Officer)
President: Michael A Miles (and Chief Operating Officer)
Senior Executive Officers: Gary P Coughlan (Senior VP and Chief Financial Officer), William W Crawford (Senior VP, General Counsel and Secretary), J Bruce Harreld (Senior VP-Strategy and Development and President, Venture Group), Mardie P MacKimm (Senior VP-Corporate Communications), John J Tucker (Senior VP-Human Resources), Daryl D Boddicker (Group VP-President, Operations and Technology), Joseph P Durrett (Group VP-President, Sales and Sales Operations), Thomas Herskovits (Group VP-President, Dairy Group), C Robert Kidder (Group VP-President, Duracell), Miles L Marsh (Group VP-President, International Group), Robert S Morrison (Group VP-President, Refrigerated Products Group), R Dean Nelson (Group VP-President, Foodservice Group), Rick Avery (Group VP-President, Industrial Foods Group), Eric C Strobel (Group VP-President, Grocery Products Group), Joel D Weiner (Senior VP-Corporate Marketing, Group VP President, Sales and Sales Operations), John L Carl (VP and Controller), Donald W Carlin (VP and Associate General Counsel)

PRINCIPAL ACTIVITIES: Kraft is a multinational food and consumer products company
Trade Names: Kraft, Philadelphia Brand, Velveeta, Cracker Barrel, Cheez Whiz, Miracle Whip, Parkay, Lender's, Celestial Seasonings, Tombstone, Breakstone's, Breyers, Frusen Glädjé, Light n'Lively, Sealtest, Knudsen, Foremost, Duracell, Durabeam
Principal Subsidiaries: Refrigerated Products Group; Grocery Products Group; Venture Group; International Group (subsidiaries in Australia, Belgium, Canada, Denmark, Eire, Germany, Italy, Mexico, Panama, The Philippines, Spain, UK and Venezuela); Dairy Group; Foodservice Group; Industrial Foods Group; Duracell Inc
Financial Information:

	Dec 28 1985	Dec 27 1986
	$'000	$'000
Sales revenues	7,919,500	8,742,200
Income before taxes	719,500	709,000
Net income	466,100	413,200
Dividends	219,000	234,000
Dividends per share	$1.52	$1.68
Earnings per share	$3.22	$2.93
Common stock*	164,700	164,700
Retained earnings	3,191,800	2,810,900
Shareholders equity	2,880,200	1,798,000

*$1.00 par value

No of Employees: 51,300

KRELITZ INDUSTRIES INC

900 North 3rd Street, Minneapolis, MN 55401
Tel: (612) 339 7401

Chairman: Philip J Krelitz (and Treasurer)
President: Barry M Krelitz (and Assistant Treasurer)
Senior Executive Officers: Dennis J Allingham (VP Finance)

PRINCIPAL ACTIVITIES: Wholesale trade in pharmaceuticals, cosmetics and medical and surgical equipment
Principal Subsidiaries: James Phillips Co; Therapac Inc
Principal Bank: Norwest Bank
Financial Information:

	Dec 31 1985
	$'000
Sales revenues	140,445
Net income	105

No of Employees: 220

KROGER CO

1014 Vine Street, Cincinnati, OH 45201
Tel: (513) 762-4000

Chairman: Lyle Everingham (and Chief Executive Officer)

Senior Executive Officers: David A Burt (Senior VP), Ray E Dillon Jr (Chairman of the Board Dillon Companies Inc), Richard W Dillon (Vice Chairman of the Board Dillon Companies Inc), Walter R Dryden (Senior VP), Donald F Dufek (Group VP), Jack G Hudson (Group VP), Lorrence T Kellar (Group VP), Richard M Koster (Executive VP), George A Leonard (VP and General Counsel), Thomas E Murphy (Group VP), Joseph A Pichler (President and Chief Operating Officer), William J Sinkula (Group VP and Secretary), Lawrence M Turner (VP and Treasurer)

PRINCIPAL ACTIVITIES: Operation of supermarkets and the manufacture of food products including canned fruit and vegetables, bakery products and dairy products

Financial Information:

	Dec 31 1985	Dec 31 1986
	$'000	$'000
Sales revenues	15,966,620	17,122,518
Income before taxes	276,981	95,614
Net income	180,750	51,493
Common dividends	88,353	89,428
Dividends per share	$1.00	$1.025
Earnings per share	$2.05	$0.55
Common stock	396,387	409,953
Retained income	980,003	938,752
Shareholders equity	1,188,670	1,154,771

No of Employees: 178,150

KROY INC

PO Box C4300, Scottsdale, AZ 85260
Tel: (602) 948-2222

Chairman: Donald W Gustafson; Vice Chairman: Andrew A Kole (and Chief Executive Officer)
President: Errol W Bartine (and Chief Operating Officer)
Senior Executive Officers: James P Fitzpatrick (VP Finance and Treasurer), Randall E Grant (VP Business Development), Victor Srimushnam (VP Corporate Planning)

PRINCIPAL ACTIVITIES: Manufacture of lettering equipment
Principal Bank: First Interstate Bank of Arizona
Financial Information:

	$'000
Sales revenues	66,000

No of Employees: 700

KRUEGER, W A, CO

7301 East Helm Drive, Scottsdale, AZ 85260
Tel: (602) 948-5650

Chairman: Jack W Fowler (and President and Chief Executive Officer)
Senior Executive Officers: Jack B Sandler (Executive VP and Chief Operating Officer), Jerome M Cotter (Senior VP), James H Lacy (VP Book Sales), John D Netsel (VP)

PRINCIPAL ACTIVITIES: Printing services
Principal Bank: M & I Marshall and Ilsley Bank
Financial Information:

	$'000
Sales revenues	288,000

No of Employees: 2,500

K-TRON INTERNATIONAL INC

Routes 55 and 553, Suite D 360, Pitman, NJ 08071
Tel: (609) 589 0500

Chairman: Leo C Beebe (and Chief Executive Officer)
Senior Executive Officers: Kenneth W Bullivant (Senior VP and Chief Technical Officer), John C Tucker (VP, Chief Financial Officer and Treasurer), Edward Goodwin (VP and General Manager K-Tron Corp), Alan R Sukoneck (Controller and Assistant Secretary)

PRINCIPAL ACTIVITIES: Manufacture of weighing and measuring instruments for industrial use
Principal Subsidiaries: K-Tron; K-Tron Corp
Principal Bank: First Interstate Bank
Financial Information:

	$'000
Sales revenues	31,600

No of Employees: 300

KUHLMAN CORPORATION

2565 W Maple Road, Troy, MI 48084
Tel: (313) 649-9300

Chairman: Arthur Kaufmann
President: D O Dulude (and Chief Executive and Operating Officer)
Senior Executive Officers: Kuhlman Fluehr (VP Corporate Relations), William J MacAdam (VP), Richard W Spicka (VP Finance) Richard A Walker (VP, General Counsel and Secretary)

PRINCIPAL ACTIVITIES: Kuhlman Corporation, consisting of three divisions and six subsidiaries, is organized into two main groups: The Electrical Group manufactures distribution power and instrument transformers marketed primarily to utility, industrial and commercial users of electric energy. The Plastic and Metal Products Group includes Bronson Plastics, Borse Plastic Products and Kuhlman Plastics of Canada, which manufacture high quality, blow molded plastic products. Principal markets include the automotive, truck, appliance, computer and office equipment, furniture, construction, leisure products and other industries. Quality Spring Products Division and Emtex manufacture custom springs and spring assemblies and stampings. Kuhlman International is a subsidiary engaged in the coordination and marketing of the Company's international ventures and activities
Principal Subsidiaries: Emtec Inc; Associated Engineering Co; Bronson Specialties Inc; Borse Plastic Products Corp; Quality Spring Products; Kuhlman International
Principal Bank: Manufacturers National Bank of Detroit
Financial Information:

	Dec 31 1985	Dec 31 1986
	$'000	$'000
Sales revenues	152,910	147,457
Income (loss) before taxes	8,331	(119)
Net income	6,345	193
Dividends	1,956	1,972
Dividends per share	$0.40	$0.40
Earnings per share net	$1.27	$0.04
Common stock	4,942	4,942
Retained income	37,305	35,526
Shareholders equity	45,552	43,501

No of Employees: 1,449

KULICKE & SOFFA INDUSTRIES, INC

2101 Blair Mill Road, Willow Grove, PA 19090
Tel: (215) 784-6000
Telex: TWX 510 665 7929 KULSOF WGVE

Chairman: C S Kulicke; Vice Chairman: Albert Soffa
President: Donald Van Luvanee (and Chief Operating Officer)
Senior Executive Officers: Max Bycer (VP), Morton Perchick (VP), Dan Kahan (Senior VP), Edwin Clarke (VP), Mark Klug (Senior VP), Ueli Meili (VP), Graham Yeldon (VP)

PRINCIPAL ACTIVITIES: Manufacture of machinery for the electrical manufacturing industry
Principal Bank: Continental Bank

Financial Information:

	Sep 30 1985	Sep 30 1986
	$'000	$'000
Sales revenues	125,102	64,771
(Loss) before taxes	(5,829)	(9,237)
Net (loss)	(489)	(7,445)
Dividends	893	-
Dividends per share	$0.12	-
(Loss) per share	($0.07)	($0.99)
Shareholders equity	48,137	40,473

No of Employees: 1,138

KUSAN, INC

Seven Maryland Farms, Brentwood, TN 37027

Tel: (615) 373-4000

President: Reynold Nebel (and Chief Executive Officer)

Senior Executive Officers: C W Lockwood (Executive VP and Chief Financial Officer), John W Foltz (VP and Comptroller), R T Applegate (VP and Treasurer), John P Mikulak (VP Marketing), L P Brittain Jr (VP Development), John P Miller (VP Human Resources), Donald Gallagher (VP Purchasing), W L McKeithan (VP Planning)

PRINCIPAL ACTIVITIES: Manufacture of plastics and building products including custom-molded plastic industrial products such as vinyl siding, shutters, wood-framed windows and doors; fiber glass pipe; and toys. The markets for these products include the automotive, electronics, appliances, oil, chemical and home improvement industries and toy and game businesses

Trade Names: BeXor (Plastic sheet)

Parent Company: KAC Inc

Principal Subsidiaries: Fiber Glass Systems Inc; Mastic Corporation

Financial Information:

	$'000
Sales revenues	330,000

No of Employees: 3,200

KYSOR INDUSTRIAL CORPORATION

One Madison Avenue, Cadillac, MI 49601

Tel: (616) 775-4645

Telex: TWX 810 291 3355 kysor centra

Chairman: Raymond A Weigel

President: George R Kempton (and Chief Executive Officer)

Senior Executive Officers: Clayton C Jesweak (Senior VP, Secretary and Treasurer), Michio Inakage (VP Kysor Japan), Stuart C Wright (VP Human Resources), Timothy D Peterson (VP Marketing and International), David Crooks (VP), Thomas P Forrestal (Group VP)

PRINCIPAL ACTIVITIES: Manufacture of heating, air conditioning and temperature control equipment, and truck trailer landing gears and safety fuel tanks for the heavy-duty truck and RV industries; and commercial refrigerated display cases

Principal Subsidiaries: Kysor of Byron; Kysor of Cadillac; Kysor Worldwide Corp; Michigan Fleet Equipment; Warren-Sherer; Kysor Industries SA (Belgium); Kysor Industrial (UK); Dynair Ltd; Austin Transportation

Principal Banks: Old Kent Bank and Trust Co; National Bank of Detroit

Financial Information:

	Dec 31 1985
	$'000
Sales revenues	144,037
Income before taxes	18,174
Net income	9,714
Dividends	2,591
Dividends per share	$0.84
Earnings per share	$3.05
Common stock	3,158
Retained income	52,592
Shareholders equity	53,497

Principal Shareholders: Kysor ESOD
No of Employees: 1,538

L B FOSTER CO
See FOSTER, L B, CO

L E MYERS COMPANY GROUP
See MYERS, L E, COMPANY GROUP

L G BALFOUR COMPANY, INC
See BALFOUR, L G, COMPANY, INC

L KARP & SONS, INC
See KARP, L, & SONS, INC

L LURIA AND SON, INC
See LURIA, L, AND SON, INC

L S STARRETT CO
See STARRETT, L S, CO

LA PETITE ACADEMY INC
PO Box 26610, Kansas City, MO 64196
Tel: (816) 474-4750

Chairman: Robert F Brozman
President: Jack L Brozman (and Treasurer)
Senior Executive Officers: Robert A Rodriguez (Executive VP), David J Anglewicz (VP), Molly M McCarthy (VP), Delia Maloney (VP), Barry Huffman (Secretary), Paul J Vadovicky (Controller)

PRINCIPAL ACTIVITIES: Pre-school education and child care
Principal Bank: Centerre Bank of Kansas City MO, N.A.
Financial Information:

	Dec 31 1985	Dec 31 1986
	$'000	$'000
Revenues	82,725	104,625
Income before taxes*	8,817	13,701
Net income	5,424	7,512
Earnings per share	$0.38	$0.48
Common stock	1,180	1,578
Retained income	12,673	19,782
Shareholders equity	40,342	48,023

* and extraordinary item

No of Employees: 8,000

LA QUINTA MOTOR INNS INC
La Quinta Plaza, 10010 San Pedro, PO Box 32064, San Antonio, TX 78216
Tel: (512) 366 6000

Chairman: Sam Barshop (and President and Chief Executive Officer)
Senior Executive Officers: David B Daviss (Executive VP and Chief Operating Officer), Robert R Moore (Executive VP and Chief Development Officer, Francis P Bassaillon (Senior VP Administration and Treasurer), Jerry N Wiggins (Senior VP Operations), Walter J Biegler (Senior VP Finance), Robert S Noyes (Senior VP Quality Control), Roland B Bliss (VP Operations, West), Alan L Tallis (VP and General Counsel), J Knox Huff (VP Operations, East), Charles F Hamlett Jr (VP

Data Processing), Michael A Nosil (VP Personnel), William VandenBosch (VP Design Management and Chief Architect), William F Waechter (VP and Controller), Bruce Walker (VP Marketing), Allen I Bassuk (VP Taxes and Insurance), Tom Neilon (VP Real Estate), Thomas G Gruide (VP Internal Audit), Dan Mallum (VP Property Services), Norman S Davis (Secretary)

PRINCIPAL ACTIVITIES: Motels
Principal Bank: First National Bank
Financial Information:

	$'000
Sales revenues	160,000

No of Employees: 4,700

LABARGE, INC

707 N 2nd Street, St Louis, MO 63102
Tel: (314) 231-5960
Telex: 756703

Chairman: Pierre L LaBarge Jr (Chief Executive Officer)
President: Craig E LaBarge (Chief Operating Officer)
Senior Executive Officers: Edward J Nestor Jr (Senior VP Administration and Secretary), J C Kunn Jr (VP), Edward A O'Brien (VP), William J Maender (VP-Finance), Colleen P Clements (Public Relations Director)

PRINCIPAL ACTIVITIES: LaBarge, Inc (LB-AMEX) is comprised of one business, LaBarge Electronics is a manufacturer of sophisticated electronic systems and devices and complex interconnect assemblies for the defense/aerospace, computer, and telecommunications industries
Principal Divisions: LaBarge Electronics
Principal Bank: Mercantile Bank N.A.
Financial Information:

	Jun 30 1986 $'000	Jun 30 1987 $'000
Sales revenues	63,187	55,759
Income (loss) before taxes	(3,846)	58,840
Net income (loss)	(24,816)	6,769
Earnings (loss) per share	($3.68)	$0.59
Common stock	1,778	3,464
Retained (deficit)	(16,256)	(10,244)
Shareholders equity (deficit)	(13,534)	9,433

No of Employees: 1,200

LACLEDE GAS COMPANY

720 Olive Street, St Louis, MO 63101
Tel: (314) 342 0500

Chairman: Lee M Liberman (and President)
Senior Executive Officers: Donald A Novatny (Senior VP Office Director and Marketing), Robert C Jaudes (Senior VP Finance), H Elliott Jr (VP Administration), David L Gardner (VP, Secretary and Treasurer), D L Godiner (VP and Legal Counsel), G F Smith (VP and Controller), L R Bannister (VP Marketing), C M Rainey (VP Personnel and Industrial Relations), M E McMillan (VP Human Resources)

PRINCIPAL ACTIVITIES: Natural gas supply
Financial Information:

	$'000
Sales revenues	617,110

No of Employees: 2,050

LACLEDE STEEL CO

Equitable Building, St Louis, MO 63102
Tel: (314) 425-1400

Chairman: John B McKinney (and President and Chief Executive Officer)
Senior Executive Officers: Michael H Lane (VP, Secretary and Treasurer), A P Mueller (VP), J W Hebenstreit (VP)

PRINCIPAL ACTIVITIES: Steel industry
Parent Company: Ivaco Inc, Canada
Principal Bank: Centerre Bank NA
Financial Information:

	Dec 31 1986 $'000
Sales revenues	236,575
Income before taxes	7,201
Net income	4,021
Dividends	676
Dividends per share	$0.25
Earnings per share	$1.49
Common stock	54,082
Retained income	30,889
Shareholders equity	85,218

No of Employees: 1,850

LADD FURNITURE INC

One Plaza Center, Box HP3, High Point, NC 27261-1500
Tel: (919) 889-0333

Chairman: Don A Hunziker (and Chief Executive Officer)
President: O W Fenn Jr (and Chief Operating Officer)
Senior Executive Officers: Richard R Allen (Executive VP, Chief Financial Officer, Secretary and Treasurer), David C Ogren (VP), John N Foster Jr (VP), Gerald R Grubbs (VP), Robert B Spivey (VP), Oliver S Etheridge (VP), Lloyd M Rowe (VP), S L Parsley Jr (VP)

PRINCIPAL ACTIVITIES: Manufacture of residential furniture, marketed to residential customers and to contract markets (hotels, motels, etc)
Principal Subsidiaries: American Drew; American of Martinsville; Barclay Furniture; Clayton-Marcus Furniture; Daystrom Furniture; Lea Industries; Lea Lumber & Plywood Co; LADD Transportation
Financial Information:

	Dec 31 1985 (52 wks) $'000	Jan 3 1987 (53 wks) $'000
Sales revenues	247,467	298,238
Income before taxes	34,348	42,438
Net income	18,448	22,190
Dividends	2,585	3,356
Dividends per share	$0.135	$0.175
Earnings per share	$0.96	$1.16
Common stock(1)	958	1,923
Common stock(2)	19,160	19,232
Retained income(3)	43,001	61,835
Shareholders equity	64,407	83,616

(1) par value year end
(2) number of shares in thousands
(3) year end

Principal Shareholders: Officers and Directors own (40%) of common stock
No of Employees: 6,720

LAFARGE CORPORATION

12801 N Central Exp, Suite 1700, Box 361, Dallas, TX 75221
Tel: (214) 934-7400

Chairman: John D Redfern; Vice Chairman: Bertrand Collomb (and Chief Executive Officer)
President: Robert W Murdoch (and Chief Operating Officer)
Senior Executive Officers: Louis G Munin (Executive VP and Chief Financial Officer), R Gary Gentles (Senior VP and President-Northeastern Region), Fred W Koester (Senior VP and President-Southern Region), David F G Lovett (Senior VP and President-Construction Materials Group), J Richard Maze (Senior VP and President-Western Region), John M Piecuch (Senior VP and President-Great Lakes Region), Bruce S Dryburgh (Senior VP and Senior Vice President-Corporate Planning and Strategy), Jean-Louis Nicolas (Senior VP and Senior Vice President-Corporate Technical Services), Thomas W Tatum (Senior VP and Senior Vice President-Human

Resources), Jean-Pierre Cloiseau (VP & Treasurer), Tom C Hardy Jr (Corporate Secretary), Larry J Waisanen (VP and Controller), Philip A Millington (Assistant Controller), Majorie K Farris (Assistant Treasurer and Assistant Secretary), David S Fields (Assistant Treasurer and Assistant Secretary), James E Elliott (Assistant Treasurer and Assistant Secretary), Jeffery W Henson (Assistant Treasurer and Assistant Secretary), Clement J Leslie (Assistant Treasurer and Assistant Secretary), Alain Fredette (Assistant Secretary)

PRINCIPAL ACTIVITIES: Manufacture of cement and construction materials; waste recovery and disposal

Financial Information:

	Dec 31 1985	Dec 31 1986
	$'000	$'000
Sales revenues	944,524	963,799
Income before taxes	41,483	58,610
Net income	14,138	25,955
Dividends*	7,415	7,870
Dividends per share*	$0.20	$0.20
Earnings per share	$0.31	$0.58
Preferred stock	6,603	9,003
Retained income	111,344	126,119
Shareholders equity	377,119	491,085

*common equity interests

No of Employees: 6,000

LAIDLAW INDUSTRIES INC

340 Arlington Hts, Arlington Hts, IL 60005-4516

Chairman: Michael G Degroote
President: Douglas R Gowland
Senior Executive Officers: J Edward Fixari (Executive VP), Ivan R Cairns (VP, Legal Counsel and Secretary), Leslie W Haworth (VP and Treasurer), Jack M Tomlinson (VP and Legal Counsel)

PRINCIPAL ACTIVITIES: Waste disposal
Financial Information:

	$'000
Sales revenues	156,070

No of Employees: 1,160

LAKE SHORE, INC

Kingsford, MI 49801
Tel: (906) 774-1500
Telex: TWX 8102784843 lk shore im

Chairman: J T Malsack
President: Carmen Guide Jr (and Chief Executive Officer)
Senior Executive Officers: E Coughlin (VP Marine), R Lehmann (VP Mining), R Shuman (VP Manufacturing), R A Dickman (Secretary and Treasurer)

PRINCIPAL ACTIVITIES: Manufacture of industrial equipment including mining machinery and construction equipment
Principal Bank: Huntington National Bank
Financial Information:

	$'000
Sales revenues	90,000

No of Employees: 650

LAKE TO LAKE DAIRY COOPERATIVE

2000 S 10th Street, Manitowoc, WI 54220
Tel: (414) 684-3343

President: John Siegmund
Senior Executive Officers: Lawrie Kull (Chief Operating Officer), Fred Fisher (Secretary and Treasurer), William Hertler (Controller), Fran Cobian (Public Relations Director)

PRINCIPAL ACTIVITIES: Manufacture and sale of dairy products
Parent Company: Land O'Lakes Inc

Financial Information:

	$'000
Sales revenues	150,000

No of Employees: 350

LAKE VIEW TRUST & SAVINGS BANK

3201 N Ashland Avenue, Chicago, IL 60657
Tel: (312) 525-2180
Telex: WUI 6871156 lakeview cgo

Chairman: William N Lane III
President: Richard G Wacker (and Chief Executive Officer and Cashier)
Senior Executive Officers: R K Alger (Senior VP Loans), Raymond W Kinzie (Senior VP), Michael T McGrogan (VP Real Estate Loans), James C Lytle (VP Business Development), Donald A Roubitchek (VP Finance), Martin F Quinn (VP Personnel), Patrick A Witowski (VP Commercial Loans), Robert D Rybka (VP Operations), Frank L Dwojacki (VP Consumer Loans)

PRINCIPAL ACTIVITIES: Financial services

No of Employees: 280

LAM RESEARCH CORPORATION

47655 Warm Springs Boulevard, Fremont, CA 94539
Tel: (415) 659 0200

Chairman: Roger D Emerick (and President and Chief Executive Officer); Vice Chairman: D K Lam (and VP and Secretary)
Senior Executive Officers: Carl A Kountz (Senior VP Operations), Stev Y Muto (VP Operations), Thomas J Nicoletti (VP Finance and Administration, Chief Financial Officer and Secretary), Thomas J Voehl (VP Sales and Marketing), Raymond L Degner (VP Design), Steven P Deornellas (VP Engineering)

PRINCIPAL ACTIVITIES: Design and manufacture of systems for the manufacture of very large scale integrated circuits
Principal Bank: First Interstate Bank
Financial Information:

	$'000
Sales revenues	34,000

No of Employees: 290

LAMA, TONY, CO INC

1137 Tony Lama Street, El Paso, TX 79915
Tel: (915) 778-8311

Chairman: Anthony B Lama Jr (and Chief Financial Officer)
President: Louis R Lama
Senior Executive Officers: V E Hosey (Chief Executive Officer and Executive VP), Joseph H Lama Jr (VP Purchasing), Armando Romero (VP Advertising), Rudolph E Lama (VP Industrial Relations), Teresa L Bean (VP, Secretary, Treasurer and Controller)

PRINCIPAL ACTIVITIES: Manufacture of leather goods including cowboy boots
Principal Bank: El Paso National Bank
Financial Information:

	$'000
Sales revenues	70,000

No of Employees: 1,200

LAMAR LIFE CORPORATION

317 East Capitol Street, Jackson, MS 39201
Tel: (601) 949 3100

Chairman: Jack P Dean
President: Michael T McRee
Senior Executive Officers: Dan M Swain Jr (VP and Controller), T O Burris Jr (VP and Secretary)

PRINCIPAL ACTIVITIES: Life insurance
Principal Bank: Trustmark National Bank

Financial Information:

	Dec 31 1985
	$'000
Revenues	92,960
Net income	12,240

LAMAUR INC

5601 East River Road, Fridley, MN 55432
Tel: (612) 571-1234

Chairman: Maurice L Spiegel
President: Richard G Spiegel
Senior Executive Officers: James A Brooks (VP Professional Sales), Harold K Rosenbaum (VP Contract Packaging), John W Soranno (Senior VP, Consumer Products Division), Wallace R Johnson (VP, Finance and Treasurer), Mike Madalo (VP Operations)

PRINCIPAL ACTIVITIES: Manufacture of hair preparations and personal grooming products
Trade Names: STYLE, PERMA SOFT, NUCLEIC A, ION, BODY PLUS, NATURAL MAN, NATURAL WOMAN, NEW ERA, ORGANICORE, ICS, VITA E, APPLE PECTIN
Principal Bank: Norwest Midland
Financial Information:

	$'000
Sales revenues	117,000

No of Employees: 517

LAMB TECHNICON CORPORATION

5663 E 9 Mile Road, Warren, MI 48091
Tel: (313) 536-3535

Chairman: Jonathan K Rye (and Chief Executive Officer)
Senior Executive Officers: William Bournias (Executive VP), J T Graham (VP Systems Engineering), Carlo Clavenna (VP), James Bowers (VP Sales), Art Kusner (VP Purchasing), E Kidder Meade (VP Finance), James Baker (VP Engineering), John Borseth (VP Sales and Marketing), J Konkel (VP Engineering), Mitchell Malicki (VP Sales)

PRINCIPAL ACTIVITIES: Manufacture of industrial machinery, machine tools and automation equipment
Principal Bank: National Bank of Detroit
Financial Information:

	$'000
Sales revenues	340,000

No of Employees: 2,000

LAMB WESTON, INC

6000 S W Hampton Street, Portland, OR 97223
Tel: (503) 639-8612
Telex: TWX 910 4588796 lamb west ptl

President: Robert S Conroy
Senior Executive Officers: William F Clyde (Senior VP), Daniel A Curry (Senior VP and General Counsel), William F Miller (Senior VP), Regis R Muller (Senior VP), R H Beale (VP), Coy F Baugh (VP and Treasurer), Thomas L Braje (VP), Howard E Cicon (VP), D A Daugherty (VP and Assistant Secretary), Stephen R Rummel (VP Finance), John K Geist (VP), R P Hill (VP), Charleen K Ikeda (VP and Assistant Secretary), Samuel J Lowman (VP), W W Phillips Jr (VP), R O Randolph (VP), Edward L Russell Jr (VP), Lawrence L Shipp (VP), Ronald R Sloan (VP), J N Standerfer (VP)

PRINCIPAL ACTIVITIES: Manufacture of fruit and vegetable products; frozen foods
Parent Company: Amfac Foods Inc-Ultimate Parent Company-Amfac Inc
Financial Information:

	$'000
Sales revenues	150,000

No of Employees: 3,000

LAMSON & SESSIONS CO (THE)

25701 Science Park Drive, Cleveland, OH 44122
Tel: (216) 464-3400
Telex: 650258-8863 MCI

Chairman: Russel B Every (and President and Chief Executive Officer)
Senior Executive Officers: Walter L Johnson (Executive VP Transportation Equipment Products), Charles E Allen (VP Industrial Relations), Gene F Budd (Senior VP Finance, Administration and Treasurer), Raymond H Heller (VP Development), Thomas M Kostelnik (VP and Controller), Alan L Miller (VP and Secretary), Melvin W Johnson (VP Engineering)

PRINCIPAL ACTIVITIES: Leading domestic producer of a broad line of thermoplastic conduit, ducts, fittings, enclosures and accessories used primarily in electrical applications and manufacture and sale of a variety of fabricated and machined metal components and parts that are sold primarily to domestic markets for use by original equipment manufacturers in the transportation equipment industry.
Principal Subsidiaries: The Youngstown Steel Door Co; Camel Co Ltd; Lamson & Sessions GmbH (97%) (Germany); Langeskov Motrikfabrik A/S (97%); The Carlon Company; Thyrocon Controls Corporation; Thyrocon Controls Corporation of Canada Limited (Canada)
Principal Bank: Bank One, Cleveland, NA
Financial Information:

	Dec 31 1985	Dec 31 1986
	$'000	$'000
Sales revenues	132,255	129,453
Income (loss) before taxes	2,315	(2,002)
Net income (loss)	13,935	(7,303)
Dividends	293	-
Dividends per share	$0.05	-
Earnings (loss) per share	$1.85	($1.25)
Shareholders equity	26,500	20,087

No of Employees: 2,206

LANCASTER COLONY CORPORATION

37 W Broad Street, Columbus, OH 43215
Tel: (614) 224-7141

Chairman: J J Gerlach (and Secretary)
President: J B Gerlach
Senior Executive Officers: John B Gerlach (Executive VP), F W Batsch (VP), D J Zuver (VP), M S Halpern (VP), Theodore A Lazar (VP), Jack W Kennedy (Treasurer)

PRINCIPAL ACTIVITIES: Manufacturer and marketer of automotive (retail aftermarket and original equipment manufacturers), specialty foods (retail and food service) and housewares (glassware: consumer, commercial, florist and industrial; and candles)
Trade Names: Automotive: Rubber Queen, Dee Zee, Pro Tecta, Line-A-Bed; Specialty Foods: Marzetti, Pfeiffer, Moutain Top; Housewares: Indiana, Tiara, Colony, Fostoria
Principal Subsidiaries: Bartlett-Collins Company; Dee Zee Inc; Indiana Glass Company, Lancaster Glass Corporation; Pretty Products Inc; T Marzetti Company
Financial Information:

	Jun 30 1986	Jun 30 1987
	$'000	$'000
Sales revenues	456,835	429,558
Income before taxes	8,610	33,290
Net income	4,774	17,225
Dividends	5,767	7,207
Dividends per share	$0.57	$0.64
Earnings per share	$0.41	$1.46
Common stock	27,594	26,658
Retained income	92,595	100,769
Shareholders equity	120,209	127,707

No of Employees: 4,400

LANCE, INC

8600 South Blvd, Charlotte, NC 28210
Tel: (704) 554-1421
Telex: WUT 802026 lance inc cha

Chairman: A F Sloan (and Chief Executive Officer)
President: C J Buchanan
Senior Executive Officers: J W Disher (Executive VP), J S Moore (VP Marketing), J S Howell (VP Finance), W E Royal (VP), G R Melvin (VP Manufacturing), P H Gwynn III (VP)

PRINCIPAL ACTIVITIES: Manufacture of peanut products, bakery products and confectionery
Principal Subsidiaries: Midwest Biscuit Co; Nutrition Pak Corp
Principal Bank: North Carolina National Bank
Financial Information:

	Dec 31 1985	Dec 31 1986
	$'000	$'000
Sales revenues	355,200	367,000
Net income	33,300	36,000
*number of shares		

No of Employees: 5,360

LAND O'LAKES, INC

4001 Lexington Avenue N, Arden Hills, MN 55126
Tel: (612) 481-2222
Telex: TWX 910 5633 663 loldstr ardh

Chairman: Claire Sandness; 1st Vice Chairman: William Kerkvliet; 2nd Vice Chairman: Eldon Netz
President: Ralph Hofstad
Senior Executive Officers: Vern Moore (Senior VP Corporate Services), John Rebane (Senior VP), Jack Martin (VP), Richard Fogg (Group VP), Duane Halverson (Group VP), John Gherty (Group VP), Ron Ostby (VP Finance and Chief Financial Officer)

PRINCIPAL ACTIVITIES: Agricultural services; manufacture of food products including poultry products, dairy products, edible fats
Principal Bank: St Paul Bank for Cooperatives
Financial Information:

	Dec 31 1985	Dec 31 1986
	$'000	$'000
Sales revenues	2,267,150	2,215,123

Principal Shareholders: Farmer-owned cooperative
No of Employees: 7,200

LANDIS & GYR INC

First Stamford Place, Stamford, CT 06902
Tel: (203) 323-0707

Chairman: Ernest Hotz
President: W James Bell
Senior Executive Officers: Joseph C Dolan (VP and Treasurer), Garrett B Wall III (VP and Secretary)

PRINCIPAL ACTIVITIES: Holding company with interests in computer control systems, switches, electric meters
Parent Company: Landis & Gyr AG, Switzerland
Principal Subsidiaries: Landis & Gyr Metering Inc

No of Employees: 1,350

LANDMARK BANCSHARES CORPORATION

10 South Brentwood Boulevard, Clayton, MO 63105
Tel: (314) 889 9500

Chairman: S Lee Kling (and Chief Executive Officer); Vice Chairman: Charles W Sunderman, Harvey A Friedman
Presidents: John E Brock (and Chief Operating Officer), Gerald W Schoor (Banking Operations)
Senior Executive Officers: Leon Neuman (Executive VP), Fred H Eller (Senior VP), Mary L De Hahn (VP Customer Relations), Roy W Fischer Jr (VP Investment), Michael W Forster (VP, Legal Counsel and Secretary), Paul E Gerson (VP and Controller), Michael E Thaman (VP, Treasurer and Chief Financial Officer)

PRINCIPAL ACTIVITIES: Banking
Principal Subsidiaries: Landmark Bank; Landmark KCI Bank; Landmark Services Corporation; Landmark St Louis Bank
Principal Bank: Landmark Bank
Financial Information:

	Dec 31 1985
	$'000
Revenues	98,930
Net income	6,160

No of Employees: 470

LANDMARK BANKING CORPORATION OF FLORIDA

One Financial Plaza, Box 5367, Fort Lauderdale, FL 33310
Tel: (305) 765-2275

Chairman: Joseph J Tuohy (and Chief Executive Officer)
President: Richard W Sherman (and Chief Operating Officer)
Senior Executive Officers: Thomas V Ogeltree (Senior VP Finance)

PRINCIPAL ACTIVITIES: Banking

No of Employees: 2,850

LANDMARK COMMUNICATIONS, INC

150 W Brambleton Avenue, Norfolk, VA 23501
Tel: (804) 446-2000

Chairman: Frank Batten
President: Richard F Barry III
Senior Executive Officers: J W Diederich (Executive VP), Conrad M Hall (Executive VP), Louis F Ryan (VP and Secretary), James D Wagner (Treasurer)

PRINCIPAL ACTIVITIES: Publication of newspapers; printing; broadcasting services and cable television
Principal Bank: Sovran Bank
Financial Information:

	$'000
Sales revenues	100,000

No of Employees: 3,300

LANDMARK LAND COMPANY INC

100 Clock Tower Place, Suite 200, Carmel, CA 93923
Tel: (408) 625 4060

Chairman: Gerald G Barton (and President, Chief Executive Officer and Subsidiary Officer)
Senior Executive Officers: Ernest O Vossler (Senior VP), Joe W Walser Jr (Senior VP), Taylor Casey (VP), D Kaye Chandler (VP), D Scott Cone (VP), Hugh Edgman (VP and Assistant Secretary), Gary R Kerney (VP), Joe Olree (VP), Barbara Royse (VP and Assistant Secretary), Lee Schmidt (VP), Richard L Singleton (VP, Treasurer, Chief Financial Officer and Subsidiary Officer), Louis A Spagna (VP and Assistant Secretary), John F Taylor (VP), Bill D Thompson (VP), Phillip D Tomlinson (VP), William W Vaughan III (VP, Legal Counsel and Assistant Secretary), Andrew R Vossler (VP), Terry Wilcox (VP), Lawrence J Woodard (VP), Karla Ambler (Assistant Secretary), Lowery Bea Roselle (Secretary), Leoda Willis (Assistant Secretary)

PRINCIPAL ACTIVITIES: Holding company with interests in finance, building supplies, construction and property development
Principal Subsidiaries: Clock Tower Place Investment Limited; Dixie Escrow Company Inc; Dixie Savings and Loan Association; Landmark Land Development Corporation; Landmark Land Company of CA Inc; Carmel Valley Ranch Inc; Mission Hills Company; Landmark Land Company of LA Inc; Landmark Land Company of OK Inc; Dixiensurance Agency Inc; Hotel Resort Management Limited; La Quinta Air Services Inc; Landmark Financial Services; Landmark Title

Agency Inc; Landmark Title Insurance Company; LML Construction Company; LML Mission Hills Corporation; LML Real Estate Company Inc; Mission Hills Real Estate Company; Unique Colf Concepts Inc
Principal Bank: J Henry Schroeder Bank and Trust
Financial Information:

	$'000
Sales revenues	227,640

No of Employees: 1,600

LANDMARK SAVINGS ASSOCIATION
335 Fifth Avenue, Pittsburgh, PA 15222
Tel: (412) 471-9800

Chairman: Richard E Knapp
President: J Richard Eshleman (and Chief Executive Officer)
Senior Executive Officers: John A Forbes (Executive VP and Chief Real Estate Officer), Timothy K Zimmerman (Senior VP and Chief Financial Officer), James G Caliendo (Senior VP Community Banking and Marketing), Thomas J Finnegan III (Senior VP Mortgage Banking), Mildred Thomas (Senior VP Human Resources), Rebecca A Jackson (VP and Controller), David K Schoyer (VP, Secretary and Counsel)

PRINCIPAL ACTIVITIES: Financial services
Principal Bank: Pittsburgh National Bank

No of Employees: 370

LANDSBERG, KENT H, CO
1640 S Greenwood Avenue, Montebello, CA 90640
Tel: (213) 726-7776

Chairman: Kent H Landsberg
President: Eugene Shelton
Senior Executive Officers: Michael Wald (VP), Joseph Giller (VP), Charles Reynolds (VP), Tom Pusheck (VP), Robert Hart (VP), Seth Landsberg (VP), C W Dodds (VP and Treasurer)

PRINCIPAL ACTIVITIES: Manufacture of paper and packaging products
Parent Company: Sunclipse Inc
Principal Bank: United California Bank
Financial Information:

	$'000
Sales revenues	60,000

No of Employees: 650

LANE CO, INC
Altavista, VA 24517
Tel: (804) 369-5641
Telex: WUT 829436 thelaneco alvi

Chairman: Bernard B Lane
President: R S Moore
Senior Executive Officers: William A Thornhill (Senior VP), Alvin E Bland (VP), Hugh M Boyer (VP), Gary G Ash (VP), Lee S Booth Jr (VP), Richard T Johnson (VP), R R Ramey (VP), Edward O Shelton (VP), Glenn S Thomas (VP), Donald H Tucker (VP), K Scott Tyler Jr (VP), Jasper S Worley (VP), R L Short (Treasurer)

PRINCIPAL ACTIVITIES: Manufacture of furniture for homes and offices
Principal Bank: Wachovia Bank & Trust Co
Financial Information:

	$'000
Sales revenues	321,650

No of Employees: 6,100

LANGDALE CO
Madison Highway, Box 1088, Valdosta, GA 31601
Tel: (912) 242-7450

Chairman: Harley Langdale Jr; Vice Chairman: John W Langdale
President: J L Respess
Senior Executive Officers: W P Langdale (Senior VP), Randy Cooper (VP Administration and Secretary), John J Langdale (VP Lands), G W Street (VP Marketing), R H Langdale (VP Engineering), J W Langdale Jr (VP Forests), Delores M Parrish (Treasurer)

PRINCIPAL ACTIVITIES: Manufacture of timber products
Principal Bank: The Citizens and Southern National Bank
Financial Information:

	$'000
Sales revenues	52,000

No of Employees: 540

LANGSTON DIVISION
111 Woodcrest Road, Cherry Hill, NJ 08034
Tel: (609) 795-7100
Telex: WUT 845368 langston chil

President: L B Tipson
Senior Executive Officers: E Downey (VP Finance), D H Whitman (VP Engineering), R E Slaugenhoupt (VP Personnel), W J Burns (VP Manufacturing), D F Zuhlke (VP Domestic Sales), M Hoysted (VP International Sales)

PRINCIPAL ACTIVITIES: Manufacture of machinery for the packaging industry
Parent Company: Molins Machine Co Inc
Principal Bank: Bank of New Jersey
Financial Information:

	$'000
Sales revenues	50,000

No of Employees: 500

LANZ, INC
8680 Hayden Place, Culver City, CA 90230
Tel: (213) 558-0200
Telex: TWX 910 340 7069 lanz culv

Chairman: Werner G Scharff (and Secretary and Treasurer)
President: Peter M Scharff
Senior Executive Officers: Robert Fiddler (Executive VP), Joel Pancer (Senior VP), Louis Hamai (VP and General Manager), Alexis Scharff (VP Retail)

PRINCIPAL ACTIVITIES: Manufacture of clothing
Principal Bank: Union Bank
Financial Information:

	$'000
Sales revenues	50,000

No of Employees: 570

LAREDO NATIONAL BANK
PO Drawer 59, Laredo, TX 78040
Tel: (512) 723-1151

Chairman: Max A Mandel
President: Gary G Jacobs (and Chief Executive Officer)
Senior Executive Officers: Jack Avigael (Executive VP), Javier Garza (Executive VP), Sam H Liesman (Executive VP), Alberto H Magnon Jr (Executive VP), Toribio J Saucedo (Executive VP and Chief Financial Officer), C E Whitworth (Executive VP), A B Barrera (Senior VP and Senior Trust Officer), Joaquim G Cigarroa III (Senior VP), Richard N Hansen (Senior VP), J Patrick Hearn (Senior VP and Cashier), Duane L Lewis (Senior VP), Edward R Leyendecker Jr (Senior VP), James E Moore (Senior VP), Adelina M Guzman (First VP), John V Puig (First VP), Abraham Ramon (First VP)

PRINCIPAL ACTIVITIES: Bank
Parent Company: Laredo National Bankshares Inc
Principal Bank: RepublicBank Dallas
No of Employees: 370

LARIBEE WIRE, INC

777 Third Avenue, New York, NY 10017
Tel: (212) 421-6400

Chairman: Hermann Rogge (and President)
Senior Executive Officers: Manuel L Ramos (VP Administration), Aaron Kraut (VP Manufacturing), Martin Wright (VP Finance), Anthony L Spina (VP Marketing), J T Simmons (VP Manufacturing), Jordan N Wright (VP Marketing)

PRINCIPAL ACTIVITIES: Manufacture of copper wire
Parent Company: Kenrich Corporation
Principal Bank: Marine Midland Bank
Financial Information:

	$'000
Sales revenues	63,000

No of Employees: 540

LARSEN CO (THE)

PO Box 19027, Green Bay, WI 54307-9027
Tel: (414) 435-5301

President: Quentin F Willems (and Chief Executive Officer)
Senior Executive Officers: Donald F Larsen (Senior VP/Sales), Roger W Huibregtse (Senior VP/Operations), James W Jackson (VP/Distribution), Edward F Mattick (VP/Engineering), Raymond A Page (VP/Frozen Sales), Donald P Qualmann (VP/Raw Product Procurement), James D Wagner (VP/Finance and Treasurer), Abbott E Wilson (VP/Marketing), Gerald W Berger (Secretary), Ronald J Uutala (Controller and Assistant Secretary), Elizabeth K Morse (Administrative Assistant to the President)

PRINCIPAL ACTIVITIES: The Company is engaged principally in the business of processing and marketing canned and frozen vegetables
Trade Names: FRESHLIKE, VEG-ALL, LARSEN
Principal Bank: Harris Trust
Financial Information:

	$'000
Revenues	170,000

No of Employees: 750

LAUHOFF GRAIN COMPANY

PO Box 571, Danville, IL 61832
Tel: (217) 442-1800
Telex: TWX 910 244 1453 lauhoffgrain

Chairman: John E Klein; Vice Chairman: John R Phillips
President: Richard T Pittelkow
Senior Executive Officers: Murray H Warschauer (VP and Secretary), Charles H Butler (VP), William J Cotter (VP), John M Crawford (VP), Paul R Lange (VP), James H Rutledge (VP), Dale W Salonen (VP), Alvin C Scheeter (VP), Marvin J Woods (VP), Marvin F Sobtka (Treasurer and Controller)

PRINCIPAL ACTIVITIES: Milling of corn and manufacture of soybean products including edible oil
Parent Company: Bunge Corporation, New York, NY
Financial Information:

	$'000
Sales revenues	400,000

No of Employees: 650

LAURA SCUDDER'S, INC

1525 N Raymond Avenue, Anaheim, CA 92801
Tel: (714) 772-5151

President: Joseph W Halligan
Senior Executive Officers: Frank Martin (Senior VP Marketing), James Katzenstein (VP Manufacturing and Operations), David Lattanzio (VP Finance)

PRINCIPAL ACTIVITIES: Manufacture of snack food products and peanut butter

Financial Information:

	$'000
Sales revenues	100,000

No of Employees: 1,200

LAWSON PRODUCTS, INC

1666 E Touhy Ave, Des Plaines, IL 60018
Tel: (312) 827-9666

Chairman: Daniel J Meyo (and Chief Executive Officer)
President: Bernard P Kalish (and Chief Operating Officer)
Senior Executive Officers: Peter G Smith (Executive VP Operations), Louis Carrol (Executive VP Sales), Jerome Shaffer (Treasurer), Joseph Pawlick (Controller)

PRINCIPAL ACTIVITIES: Wholesale trade in a wide range of products including hardware, automotive repair, welding supplies equipment and industrial maintainence repair supplies
Principal Subsidiaries: Lawson Products Inc (DE); Cronatron Welding Systems Inc (NJ); Cronatron Welding Systems Inc (GA); Drummond American Corporation; Lawson Products Inc (CA); Lawson Products Inc (TX); Lawson Products Inc (NJ); Lawson Products Inc (GA); Lawson Products Inc (Canada)
Principal Bank: Exchange National Bank of Chicago
Financial Information:

	Dec 31 1985 $'000
Sales revenues	127,561
Income before taxes	24,754
Net income	13,192
Dividends*	2,022
Dividends per share*	$0.30
Earnings per share	$1.93
Common stock	7,539
Retained income	79,965
Shareholders equity	60,714

*declared

Principal Shareholders: Sidney L Port; Bette Port
No of Employees: 600

LAWTER INTERNATIONAL INC

990 Skokie Blvd, Northbrook, IL 60062
Tel: (312) 498-4700
Telex: WUT 724488 lawt int nbrk

Chairman: Daniel J Terra (and President)
President: Richard D Nordman (and Chief Operating Officer)
Senior Executive Officers: Richard A Hacker (Senior VP), Ludwig P Horn (VP), Hermann Mueller (VP), James A Campbell (VP)

PRINCIPAL ACTIVITIES: Manufacture of inks, resins and pigments
Principal Subsidiaries: Virkotype International Corp; Lawter (Canada) Ltd; Lawter SA of Belgium; Lawter Ltd (UK); Lawter GmbH (Germany); Lawter Products BV (Eire); Lawter International (Australasia) Pty Ltd
Principal Bank: First National Bank of Chicago
Financial Information:

	$'000
Sales revenues	96,770

No of Employees: 340

LA-Z-BOY CHAIR CO

1284 North Telegraph Road, Monroe, MI 48161
Tel: (313) 242-1444
Easylink: 62806276
Fax: (313) 241-4422

Chairman: C T Knabusch (and President)
Senior Executive Officers: F H Jackson (VP Finance), E J Shoemaker (Vice Chairman and Executive VP Engineering), G M Hardy (Secretary and Treasurer), L G Stevens (VP Manufacturing), P H Norton (Senior VP Sales and Marketing)

PRINCIPAL ACTIVITIES: La-Z-Boy is a leading manufacturer of residential motion furniture including the world's best-known reclining chairs. The Company also produces sofas, sleep sofas, swivel rockers and modular seating
Trade Names: Recliner-Rocker, La-Z-Rocker, La-Z-Sleeper, La-Z-Sofa, Reclina-Way, Sofette, La-Z-Lounger, Reclina-Rest, Signature II, Motion-Modular
Principal Subsidiaries: La-Z-Boy Canada Limited; La-Z-Boy Ad Co; Burris Industries Inc; RoseJohnson Inc
Principal Bank: Monroe Bank and Trust Company
Financial Information:

	Apr 26 1986 $'000	Apr 25 1987 $'000
Sales revenues	341,656	419,991
Income before taxes	41,759	44,947
Net income	23,010	24,664
Dividends	6,413	7,130
Dividends per share	$1.40	$1.55
Earnings per share	$5.02	$5.36
Common stock	4,660	4,660
Retained income	122,335	138,932
Shareholders equity	148,716	166,731

No of Employees: 6,650

LDBRINKMAN CORPORATION

2123 Sidney Baker Street, Kerrville, TX 78028
Tel: (512) 896-5111

Chairman: Lloyd D Brinkman (and President and Chief Executive Officer)
Senior Executive Officers: Byron Smith (Executive VP), William Wade (Executive VP), Steve L Webster (VP Information Services)

PRINCIPAL ACTIVITIES: Marketing of flooring materials; manufacture of mobile and sectional homes; retail of specialty food products
Principal Bank: Mercantile Bank of Dallas
Financial Information:

	$'000
Sales revenues	260,000

No of Employees: 1,300

LE ROY INDUSTRIES INC

7921 E Main Road, Le Roy, NY 14482
Tel: (716) 768-6242
Telex: TWX 510 244 3730

Chairman: Carol G Mosher
President: James W Blair Jr (and Chief Executive Officer)
Senior Executive Officers: James E Cuddeback (Executive VP Operations), J D Hare (VP), Matthew G Roberts Jr (VP Sales), Dennis T Byrne (Treasurer)

PRINCIPAL ACTIVITIES: Manufacture of components for the automotive industry
Principal Subsidiaries: York Merit Products Inc
Principal Bank: M & T Bank
Financial Information:

	$'000
Sales revenues	50,000

No of Employees: 500

LEAR PETROLEUM CORPORATION

950 One Energy Square, 4925 Greenville Avenue, Dallas, TX 75206
Tel: (214) 363 6085

Chairman: Max W Woodard
President: Joseph T Williams (Chief Executive Officer)
Senior Executive Officers: Don H Edgington (Senior VP Exploration and Production), Gordon D Mowl (Senior VP Finance and Administration), H Monroe Helm III (VP Investor Relations), Joe E Lanier (VP Information Services), Randall B Wilson (VP Secretary and General Counsel)

PRINCIPAL ACTIVITIES: Exploration, production and distribution of oil and natural gas
Principal Subsidiaries: Lear Petroleum Exploration Inc; LPC Energy Inc; Producers Gas Co
Principal Bank: Manufacturers Hanover Trust Company
Financial Information:

	$'000
Sales revenues	426,600

No of Employees: 300

LEAR SIEGLER, INC

2850 Ocean Park Blvd, Santa Monica, CA 90405
Tel: (213) 452-6000

Chairman: Norman A Barkeley (and President and Chief Executive Officer); Chairman of Executive Committee: Robert T Campion
Senior Executive Officers: Robert U Grant (Senior VP Corporate Development), David J Louks (Senior VP and Controller), Ronald V Paolucci (Senior VP), Charles F Pitts (Senior VP Administration), James N Thayer (Senior VP Finance), Laurence A Thompson (Senior VP), Robert A Loebl (VP Corporate Planning), Elmar Klotz (VP Aerospace Group), Kenneth L Way (VP Auto Group), Barry Rodgers (VP Industrial/Recreational), Paul V Smith (VP Materials Handling), Kenneth A Ruck (VP Commercial Products), Larry R De Jarnett (VP Information Systems), Albert F Myers (VP Purchasing), Stephen D Natcher (VP, Secretary and General Counsel), Robert J Wyma (VP Aircraft Group), Ronald C Buehner (VP Management Services), Jerry H Burnett (VP and Corporate Auditor), Harvey A Marsh (VP and Assistant Controller)

PRINCIPAL ACTIVITIES: Manufacture of equipment for the aerospace industry and components for the automotive industry; mechanical handling equipment
Principal Bank: Security National Bank
Financial Information:

	Jun 30 1986 $'000
Sales revenues	2,464,127
Net income	55,510
Earnings per share	$3.02
Shareholders equity	626,892

No of Employees: 29,725

LEARONAL, INC

272 Buffalo Avenue, Freeport, NY 11520
Tel: (516) 868-8800
Telex: 221684; 221729; 967786
Facsimile: 516/868-8824; 8825

Chairman: Barnet D Ostrow
President: Ronald F Ostrow (and Chief Operating Officer)
Senior Executive Officers: Fred I Nobel (Executive VP and Secretary), Daniel Glassman (VP Finance and Treasurer), Richard Kessler (VP)

PRINCIPAL ACTIVITIES: Specialty chemicals and electro-plating equipment
Principal Subsidiaries: (100% owned unless stated): Lea-Ronal (UK) Ltd (93%); Lea-Ronal Pacific Corp; Lea-Ronal AG (92.7%); Lea-Ronal Export Sales Inc; Lea-Ronal GmbH; Lea Ronal France
Principal Bank: National Westminster Bank USA
Financial Information:

	$'000
Sales revenues	105,000

No of Employees: 335

LEASEWAY TRANSPORTATION CORPORATION

3700 Park East Drive, Beachwood, OH 44122
Tel: (216) 464-3300

Chairman: Gerald C McDonough (and Chief Executive Officer)
President: John C Dannemiller (and Chief Operating Officer)
Senior Executive Officers: Robert K Healey (Executive VP Controlled Transport Systems), Richard A Damsel (Senior VP Finance and Chief Financial Officer), Robert V Delaney (Senior VP and Chief Planning Officer), Peter E Smith (Senior VP Information Systems), Alex M Warren Jr (Senior VP Administration), Richard J Sykora (VP, Controller and Principal Accounting Officer), Mark Jones (VP Marketing), Robert T Peterson (VP), Raymond J Rehor (VP Taxes)

PRINCIPAL ACTIVITIES: Holding company with interests in leasing, trucking and warehousing
Principal Bank: Society National Bank
Financial Information:

	Dec 31 1985	Dec 31 1986
	$'000	$'000
Sales revenues	1,503,848	1,484,669
Net income	62,451	50,791
Earnings per share	$5.29	$2.55
Shareholders equity	341,056	269,890

No of Employees: 20,000

LECHMERE INC
275 Mildwood Street, Woburn, MA 01801
Tel: (617) 935-8320

Chairman: George Scala (and President and Chief Executive Officer)
Senior Executive Officers: Dennis Chantland (Executive VP Administration and Finance), James Kelly (VP Store), George Earley (VP Distribution), Paul Chaddock (VP Personnel)

PRINCIPAL ACTIVITIES: Department store retailing
Parent Company: Dayton-Hudson Corporation, Minneapolis, MN
Financial Information:

	$'000
Sales revenues	230,000

No of Employees: 2,500

LEE APPAREL COMPANY, INC
9001 W 67th Street, Merriam, KS 66202
Tel: (913) 384-4000
Telex: RCA 209531 laemo ur

Chairman: L R Pugh
President: M G Winne
Senior Executive Officers: R C Lamm (Senior VP and Secretary), R S Stec (VP Merchandising), T L Lay (Senior VP Business Development and Planning), A F Ahnemann (VP Industrial Relations), P C Bhatt (VP Engineering), A W Hughes (VP Management Information Systems), J G Hughes (VP Distribution), B F Kominick (VP Private Lable), A A Kussman (VP Operational Planning), G P McDonald (VP Production, Planning and Scheduling), T A Lancaster (VP Marketing), H D McKemy (VP), T E Lair (VP Manufacturing), R S Mangini (VP Sales), C J Persing (VP Procurement), G L Smith (VP Business Development)

PRINCIPAL ACTIVITIES: Manufacture of clothing
Parent Company: V F Corporation, Reading, PA
Principal Bank: United Missouri Bank
Financial Information:

	$'000
Sales revenues	418,000

No of Employees: 10,100

LEE DATA CORPORATION
7075 Flying Cloud Drive, Minneapolis, MN 55344
Tel: (612) 828-0300
Telex: 910-576-1690

Chairman: John M Lee (and Chief Executive Officer)
President: Charles Askanas (and Chief Operating Officer)
Senior Executive Officers: Duane S Carlson (Executive VP, Secretary), Edwin G McMullen (Senior VP Corporate Development), James A Vellenga (Group VP, International), Wayne A Zuehlke (VP Corporate Controller and Treasurer), John F Roy (Group VP, Bell Operating Company Division), Scott D Whittenburg (Group VP, Operations), Robert D Gordon (Senior VP, Chief Financial Officer)

PRINCIPAL ACTIVITIES: Lee Data Corporation designs, manufactures, markets and services display terminal systems for use with large-scale IBM or IBM-compatible computers. Display systems from Lee Data are fully compatible with IBM's 3270 display terminal line, but also provide unique connectivity to most other suppliers' data processing equipment. Lee Data is an industry leader in the area of concurrent, multi-host communications using the unique windowing and interconnection capabilities of its terminal systems. Lee Data's multi-functional displays can be used for such applications as data entry and retrieval, financial spreadsheet analysis, programming, word processing and personal computing. Lee Data also provides protocol converters as well as networking systems for interconnecting PCs
Trade Names: Registered Trademarks:- All-In-One, LDC, Lee Data. Trade Marks:- LANMASTER, Coax Eliminator, QuickLink, Open Window
Principal Subsidiaries: Leedata Canada, Inc; Lee Data Far East Ltd; Lee Data Export Ltd. Division: Lee Data Texas Corporation
Principal Bank: First Bank of St Paul
Financial Information:

	Mar 31 1986	Mar 31 1987
	$'000	$'000
Sales revenues	93,068	114,525
Income before taxes	7,829	10,054
Net income	2,098	5,581
Earnings per share	$0.15	$0.39
Common stock	703	708
Additional paid-in capital	57,115	57,497
Retained income	31,637	37,363
Number of equity	89,495	95,568

Number of Shareholders: 2,427
No of Employees: 1,075

LEE ENTERPRISES, INC
130 E 2nd Street, Davenport, IA 52801
Tel: (319) 383-2202

President: Lloyd G Schermer (and Chief Executive Officer)
Senior Executive Officers: Richard B Belkin (VP), Ronald L Rickman (VP), Robert D Ross (VP), Wayne E Schile (VP), Larry J Siegel (VP), John S Stemlar (VP and Treasurer)

PRINCIPAL ACTIVITIES: Publication of newspapers and broadcasting
Principal Subsidiaries: Lee Publishers Group Inc
Principal Bank: Continental Illinois National Bank and Trust Co
Financial Information:

	Sep 30 1986
	$'000
Sales revenues	213,000
Net income	33,000

No of Employees: 3,000

LEEDS & NORTHRUP CO
Sumneytown Pike, North Wales, PA 19454
Tel: (215) 643-2000
Telex: WUT 846192 leednth nwal a

President: George J Demos
Senior Executive Officers: Robert D Eisenhardt Jr (Group Executive, General Signal and Unit President-Instruments), A C Martin (Unit President International), John P Puckett (United President-Systems), D F Fish (VP-Employee Relations),

Stephen Loidl Jr (VP Finance and Treasurer), W C Wiley (VP Corporate Resources)

PRINCIPAL ACTIVITIES: Manufacture of electrical and electronic instruments and process control systems
Parent Company: General Signal Corporation, Stamford, CT
Principal Bank: First Pennsylvania Bank
Financial Information:

	$'000
Sales revenues	300,000

No of Employees: 4,500

LEES CARPETS & BURLINGTON HOUSE CARPETS

Valley Forge Corporate Center, King of Prussia, PA 19406
Tel: (215) 666-7770

Presidents: David Polley (Lees Carpets), Don Moroh (Burlington House Carpets)
Senior Executive Officers: Curtis C Deardorff (Executive VP Administration), Robert Barnes (Group VP Manufacturing), Bernard Egerter (Senior VP Commercial Carpet Sales), John E Collier (VP Operations), Robert O Barrett (VP Sales), Walter O Stokes (VP Sales), James Harper (Public Relations Manager)

PRINCIPAL ACTIVITIES: Manufacture of woven and tufted carpets
Parent Company: Burlington Industries Inc
Financial Information:

	$'000
Sales revenues	200,000

No of Employees: 3,000

LEGG MASON INC

7 East Redwood Street, Baltimore, MD 21202
Tel: (301) 539 3400

Chairman: Raymond A Mason (and President); Vice Chairman: John F Curley Jr (and Chief Administrative Officer)
Senior Executive Officers: Edmund J Cashman Jr (Senior Executive VP), James W Brinkley (Senior Executive VP Sales and Marketing), Richard J Himelfarb (Executive VP Investments), Charles A Bacigalupo (Senior VP and Secretary), Harry M Ford Jr (Senior VP), Philip O Rogers (Senior VP), F Barry Bilson (VP and Controller), Horace M Lowman Jr (VP and Treasurer)

PRINCIPAL ACTIVITIES: Dealers in securities and investments
Principal Bank: First National Bank of Maryland
Financial Information:

	$'000
Revenues	112,000

No of Employees: 1,000

LEGGETT & PLATT, INCORPORATED

1 Leggett Road, Carthage, MO 64836
Tel: (417) 358-8131
Telex: 910 777 7902 L&P CTGE

Chairman: Harry M Cornell Jr
President: Felix E Wright
Senior Executive Officers: Duane W Potter (Senior VP-President Bedding Components Group), William J Distler (VP- Executive VP Eastern Group), Richard P Fanning (VP-President Western Group), C Richard Gamble (VP-Executive VP Eastern Group), Roger D Gladden (VP-President Commercial Products Group), Michael A Glauber (VP, Finance and Treasurer), David S Haffner (VP, President Furniture Components Group), Gary C Hertweck (Controller), Larry Higgins (VP-President International Division), Jerry H Hudkins (VP-President Wire Group), Robert A Jefferies Jr (VP-General Counsel and Secretary), Jay W Sanders (VP-Director Marketing and Sales, Bedding Components), Sanford E Strickland (VP-Business Development), Wayne R Wickstrom (VP-Director Marketing and Sales, Furniture Components)

PRINCIPAL ACTIVITIES: Manufacture and marketing of components used by companies making bedding and furniture for homes, offices and institutions
Trade Names: Lectro-LOK, Mira-Coil (Continuous Coil), Mira-Foam, Flotura-Lok, Plus 2, Hinge-flex, Kay Arc, Wall Hugger, Motion Lounger, Adjusta-Magic, Cyclo-Index
Financial Information:

	Dec 31 1985	Dec 31 1986
	$'000	$'000
Sales revenues	500,660	585,686
Income before taxes(1)	45,121	58,138
Net income	26,469	34,575
Dividends	4,519	6,456
Dividends per share	$0.333	$0.40
Earnings per share(2)	$1.80	$2.07
Earnings per share(3)	$1.68	$2.03
Common stock	16,321	16,512
Retained income	129,040	151,864
Shareholders equity	166,361	183,106

(1)from continuing operations
(2)primary
(3)fully diluted

No of Employees: 6,700

LEHIGH PRESS, INC

7001 North Park Drive, Pennsauken, NJ 08109
Tel: (609) 665-5200

Chairman: J D DePaul (and President and Chief Executive and Operating Officer); Vice Chairman: William O Krenkler
Senior Executive Officers: James R Lentz (Executive VP Sales), M E Rosenblum (Executive VP Administration), Marie K White (VP, Secretary and Assistant to Chairman), William S Goldstein (VP and Assistant to President), William F Love (VP Finance)

PRINCIPAL ACTIVITIES: Printing services
Principal Subsidiaries: Lehigh/Steck-Warlick Inc; Lehigh Special Products Inc; C Albert Sauter Co Inc
Principal Bank: Philadelphia National Bank
Financial Information:

	Dec 31 1985
	$'000
Sales revenues	124,365
Income before taxes	8,824
Net income	5,359
Dividends	654
Dividends per share	$0.40
Earnings per share	$3.25
Common stock	216
Retained income	30,164
Shareholders equity	34,387

No of Employees: 1,000

LEHIGH STECK WARLICK, INC

1515 Round Table Drive, Dallas, TX 75247
Tel: (214) 988-1799

Chairman: John DePaul (and President and Chief Executive Officer); Vice Chairman: William Kremkler
President: William Kremkler
Senior Executive Officers: William F Love (Treasurer), Marie K White (Secretary)

PRINCIPAL ACTIVITIES: Printing services
Parent Company: Lehigh Press Inc, Pennsauken, NJ
Principal Bank: Fidelity Bank of Philadelphia
Financial Information:

	$'000
Sales revenues	75,000

No of Employees: 300

LEHIGH STRUCTURAL STEEL CO

One Allen Street, Allentown, PA 18105
Tel: (215) 434-5221

President: R L Mullen
Senior Executive Officers: J C Klein (VP Operations), D J Lonergan (VP Tower Sales), Richard Marshall (VP Engineering), Walter W Toth (VP Finance and Treasurer), W J Dooley (VP Structural Sales)

PRINCIPAL ACTIVITIES: Steel fabricators; manufacture of structural steel; galvanizing
Principal Subsidiaries: Lehigh-Lancaster Inc; Utilities Service Co
Principal Bank: First National Bank of Allentown
Financial Information:

	$'000
Sales revenues	50,000

No of Employees: 600

LEHIGH VALLEY INDUSTRIES INC

200 East 42nd Street, New York, NY 10017
Tel: (212) 867 0300

Chairman: Howard Lazar (and Chief Executive Officer); Vice Chairman: Burton T Fried (and Legal Counsel)
President: Salvatore J Zizza (and Chief Financial Officer and Principal Accounting Officer)
Senior Executive Officers: Ronald L Bern (Senior VP), Albert J Savage Jr (Subsidiary Officer), Charles D Etgen (Assistant Treasurer and Secretary)

PRINCIPAL ACTIVITIES: Manufacture of metal castings; production of shoes
Principal Subsidiaries: Dori Shoe Company Inc; Mobile Pulley Machine Works Inc; Riverside Manufacturing Inc
Principal Bank: National Bank
Financial Information:

	$'000
Sales revenues	50,270

No of Employees: 600

LEINER, P, NUTRITIONAL PRODUCTS CORPORATION

1845 West 205th Street, Torrance, CA 90501
Tel: (213) 328 9610

Chairman: Michael Leiner (and Chief Executive Officer)
President: David Brubaker
Senior Executive Officers: Kevin Lanigan (VP Operations and Secretary), Laurel Winston (VP, Chief Financial Officer and Treasurer), Gale Bensussen (VP Marketing and Products Development), Robert Kaminski (VP Sales), Carl Short (Senior VP Marketing), Bob Poey (VP Quality Control and Product Development)

PRINCIPAL ACTIVITIES: Manufacture of food supplements, vitamins and bodycare products
Principal Bank: Wells Fargo Bank
Financial Information:

	$'000
Sales revenues	54,000

No of Employees: 200

LEISURE & TECHNOLOGY INC

12233 West Olympic Boulevard, Los Angeles, CA 90064
Tel: (213) 826 1000

Chairman: Michael L Tenzer (and President and Chief Executive Officer)
Senior Executive Officers: Michael S Linsk (Senior VP), John A Kilduff (Senior VP, Chief Financial Officer, Secretary and Treasurer), Jerry Falcon (VP, President Midwest Division), Anthony Garruto (VP, Controller and Chief Accounting Officer), Eric Levin (VP and President NJ Division), Jim Osborne (VP and President Southeast Division)

PRINCIPAL ACTIVITIES: Planning and operation of recreational and retirement communities
Principal Bank: Morgan Guaranty Trust Co
Financial Information:

	$'000
Sales revenues	90,000

No of Employees: 400

LENNAR CORPORATION

770 Northwest 107 Ave, Miami, FL 33172
Tel: (305) 559-4000

Chairman: Leonard Miller (and President); Chairman Executive Committee: Robert C Cole (and Secretary and General Counsel)
Senior Executive Officers: Irving Bolotin (Senior VP), Allan J Pekor (VP Finance), Marshall Ames (VP), Sherman J Kronick (VP)

PRINCIPAL ACTIVITIES: Building contractors and property development
Principal Bank: Citibank
Financial Information:

	$'000
Sales revenues	230,900

No of Employees: 690

LENOX CHINA, INC

Tilton Road, Pomona, NJ 08240
Tel: (609) 965-0177
Telex: TWX 510 6885800 lenox pmna

President: Harold H Goucher
Senior Executive Officers: William R Miller (Senior VP Manufacturing), J B Chiles (VP Finance), Safford P Sweatt (VP Marketing), Robert J Sullivan (VP Advertising and Promotions)

PRINCIPAL ACTIVITIES: Manufacture of china and jewelry
Parent Company: Lenox Inc, Ultimate Holding Company Brown-Forman Distillers Corporation
Principal Bank: Citibank NA
Financial Information:

	$'000
Sales revenues	69,000

No of Employees: 4,000

LENOX, INC

3190 Princeton Pike, Lawrenceville, NJ 08648
Tel: 609 896-2800
Telex: TWX 510 6859 331 lenox inc trn

Chairman: John S Chamberlin (and Chief Executive Officer)
President: Frank E Grzelecki (and Chief Operating Officer)
Senior Executive Officers: E L Laforge (Group VP), A M Bylin (Group VP), J B Chiles (VP Finance), S F Lichtenstein (VP and Secretary), G A Mays (VP and Controller)

PRINCIPAL ACTIVITIES: Manufacture of a wide range of consumer products including tableware, glassware, jewelry, toiletries, soap, and luggage
Parent Company: Brown-Forman Distillers Corporation, Louisville, KY
Principal Bank: Citibank NA
Financial Information:

	$'000
Sales revenues	275,000

No of Employees: 5,000

LESCO INC

20005 Lake Road, Rocky River, OH 44116
Tel: (216) 333 9250

Chairman: James I FitzGibbon (and Chief Executive Officer)
President: Robert F Burkhardt

Senior Executive Officers: Arthur Wick (VP), James A Fink (VP), Herbert Cole (VP), Ronald Smith (VP), Phillip Gardner (VP), Daniel G Dunstan (Secretary and Treasurer)

PRINCIPAL ACTIVITIES: Manufacture specialty chemicals including fertilizers; seed and equipment for golf courses and lawn care
Principal Bank: National City Bank
Financial Information:

	$'000
Sales revenues	53,000

No of Employees: 350

LESHNER CORPORATION
1010 Eaton Avenue, PO Box 179, Hamilton, OH 45012
Tel: (513) 868-3500
Telex: WUT 214514 leshner ham

President: Mark Petricoff
Senior Executive Officers: Georgiana S Thompson (VP Sales, Secretary and Treasurer), Allan Selig (Assistant VP Works)

PRINCIPAL ACTIVITIES: Manufacture of household linens and blankets
Principal Bank: First National Bank and Trust Company
Financial Information:

	$'000
Sales revenues	70,000

No of Employees: 490

LESLIE FAY COMPANIES
See FAY, LESLIE, COMPANIES

LETTS INDUSTRIES, INC
1111 Bellevue Avenue, Detroit, MI 48207
Tel: (313) 579-1100
Telex: GRT 3750007 letts

President: Chuck Letts
Senior Executive Officers: Charles Van Dusen (Treasurer)

PRINCIPAL ACTIVITIES: Metal fabrication; metal treatment; motor vehicle components and mining machinery
Principal Bank: National Bank of Detroit
Financial Information:

	$'000
Sales revenues	50,000

No of Employees: 270

LEUCADIA NATIONAL CORPORATION
315 Park Avenue South, New York, NY 10010
Tel: (212) 460 1900

Chairman: Ian M Cumming
President: Joseph S Steinberg
Senior Executive Officers: Thomas E Mara (Executive VP), P Douglas Campbell (VP and Treasurer), David Cumming (VP), Norman P Kiken (VP and Controller), Richard G Petitt (VP), Ruth Klindtworth (Secretary and Assistant VP Administration)

PRINCIPAL ACTIVITIES: Holding company with interests in real estate and consumer finance
Principal Subsidiaries: Leucadia Inc
Principal Bank: Manufacturers Hanover Trust Co
Financial Information:

	Dec 31 1985 $'000
Revenues	292,300
Net income	25,850

No of Employees: 30

LEVER BROTHERS COMPANY
390 Park Avenue, New York, NY 10022
Tel: (212) 688-6000
Telex: RCA 234023 lev ur

Chairman: Gordon K Stevens (and Chief Executive Officer)
Senior Executive Officers: Gerard V Batti (Divisional VP Marketing), Richard A Warren (Divisional VP Distribution), Ronald C Smith (Divisional VP Data Services), Manfred Stach (VP, Financial Services), Frank H Healey (VP, Research), John R Cookson (VP, President Household Division), Wayne K Nelson (VP, President Personal Products Division), A Cline Butler (VP, President Foods Division), Walter M Volpi (VP, Secretary and General Counsel), P Edward Bohlender (VP, Personnel)

PRINCIPAL ACTIVITIES: Manufacture of soaps and detergents; oils and fats
Parent Company: Unilever NV, Rotterdam, Netherlands
Financial Information:

	Dec 31 1985 $'000	Dec 31 1986 $'000
Sales revenues	2,099,348	2,474,609
Net (loss)	(38,530)	(18,584)
Shareholders equity	194,218	150,889

No of Employees: 4,920

LEVI STRAUSS & CO
1155 Battery Street, San Francisco, CA 94120
Tel: (415) 544-6000
Telex: GRT 3717253 sf ol

Chairman: Peter E Haas
President: Robert D Haas (and Chief Executive and Operating Officer)
Senior Executive Officers: Walter A Haas Jr (Chairman Executive Committee), Thomas J Bauch (Senior VP and General Counsel), George B James (Senior VP and Chief Financial Officer), David K Lelewer (Senior VP), Peter L Thigpen (Senior VP, President Levi & Strauss USA), Thomas W Tusher (Senior VP, President Levi Strauss International), Harry H Cohn (VP, President Menswear Division, Levi Strauss USA), Katherine B Durgin (VP and Secretary), Robert H Dunn (VP), Rita M Guiney (VP Corporate Affairs), Ira S Hirschfield (VP), Leo P Isotalo (VP, President Battery Street Enterprises), Thomas M Kasten (VP, President Jeanswear Division Levi Strauss USA), James A McDermott (VP, Senior VP Marketing Levi Strauss USA), Richard D Murphy (VP and Controller), David D Smith (VP and Treasurer), Lee C Smith (VP, Executive VP Group I, Levi Strauss International)

PRINCIPAL ACTIVITIES: Manufacture of clothing
Trade Names: Crocker National Bank
Principal Bank: Crocker National Bank
Financial Information:

	$'000
Sales revenues	2,500,000

No of Employees: 37,000

LEVINSON STEEL CO
799 Castle Shannon Blvd, Pittsburgh, PA 15234
Tel: (412) 571-2000

Chairman: Aaron P Levinson
President: Edwin Z Schuman
Senior Executive Officers: Calvin L Levinson (Senior VP and Treasurer), Leo B Lieberman (VP and General Manager Steel Service Center)

PRINCIPAL ACTIVITIES: Steel and aluminum fabrication; steel service center
Financial Information:

	$'000
Sales revenues	60,000

No of Employees: 160

LEVITON MANUFACTURING CO
59-25 Little Neck Pkwy, Little Neck, NY 11362
Tel: (718) 229-4040
Telex: TWX 710 582 4893 leviton nyk

Chairman: Jack Amsterdam (and Treasurer)
President: Harold Leviton
Senior Executive Officers: Harvey Kram (VP Operations), Ralph D Biasi (VP Finance), James Pearse (VP Engineering), Steven Sokolow (VP Administration and Secretary), Donald Hendler (VP Distribution), Robert Upton (VP), Thomas Blumberg (VP Marketing)

PRINCIPAL ACTIVITIES: Electrical equipment
Financial Information:

	$'000
Sales revenues	50,000

No of Employees: 5,000

LEVITT CORPORATION

7777 Glades Road, Suite 410, Boca Raton, FL 33434
Tel: (305) 482 5100

Chairman: Elliott M Wiener (and President and Chief Executive Officer)
Senior Executive Officers: Rafael A Torrens Jr (Senior VP Operations), Harvey P Rafofsky (Senior VP Sales and Marketing), Nat Greenberg (Senior VP Construction), Joseph J Lamendola (VP Finance, Chief Financial Officer and Treasurer), Harry Sleek (VP Finance), Alfred G West (Secretary)

PRINCIPAL ACTIVITIES: Building and construction
Parent Company: Starrett Housing Corporation
Principal Bank: Manufacturers Hanover Trust Co
Financial Information:

	$'000
Sales revenues	73,010

No of Employees: 340

LEVY, CHAS, CIRCULATING CO

1200 N Branch Street, Chicago, IL 60622
Tel: (312) 440-4400
Telex: WUT 270 114 clcc trans cgo

Chairman: Charles Levy; Vice Chairman: Barbara Kipper
President: David Moscow
Senior Executive Officers: Peter Cook (Senior VP), H P Davidson (VP and General Manager), Glenn Greene (VP Administration and Controller), Charles Lynch (VP Transportation), Frank Tiano (VP Norbran Leasing)

PRINCIPAL ACTIVITIES: Wholesale distribution of books and magazines; interests in the leasing of trucks and trucking services
Principal Bank: American National Bank and Trust Company of Chicago
Financial Information:

	$'000
Sales revenues	160,000

No of Employees: 1,000

LEVY, EDWARD, CO

8800 Dix Avenue, Detroit, MI 48209
Tel: (313) 843-7200

President: Edward C Levy Jr (and Treasurer)
Senior Executive Officers: J J Stone (VP and Secretary), Robert Carson (VP), J J Broderick (VP)

PRINCIPAL ACTIVITIES: Manufacture of building materials including ready mix concrete and paving mixtures
Principal Bank: Manufacturers Bank
Financial Information:

	$'000
Sales revenues	100,000

No of Employees: 800

LEWIS GALOOB TOYS INC

See GALOOB, LEWIS, TOYS INC

LEWIS, PALMER G, COMPANY INC

525 C Street Northwest, Auburn, WA 98071
Tel: (206) 941 2600

Chairman: John N Anderson (and Chief Executive Officer)
President: Richard E Lundgren
Senior Executive Officers: Gilbert R Halley (Secretary, Treasurer and Chief Financial Officer)

PRINCIPAL ACTIVITIES: Supply of building materials and components including lumber, wallboards, plywood, roofing, insulation, nails, windows and doors
Principal Bank: Seattle First National Bank
Financial Information:

	$'000
Sales revenues	140,770

No of Employees: 400

LFE CORPORATION

55 Green Street, Clinton, MA 01510
Tel: (617) 835-1000
Telex: TWX 710 3471 734 lfe corp clit

Chairman: Sal H Alfiero
President: Lee M Faulkner (and Chief Operating Officer)
Senior Executive Officers: Ronald A Riggs (Senior VP and General Manager Fluid Controls), Charles N Davis (VP and General Manager Traffic Control), Thomas P Graham (VP Finance), E M Fraser (VP, Secretary and General Counsel), Clement R Arrison (VP), William P Montague (VP), John J Byrne (VP)

PRINCIPAL ACTIVITIES: Industrial control instrumentation; fluid, traffic and process control equipment; environmental control equipment; heating and ventilation plant; civil engineering consultants
Parent Company: Mark IV Industries Inc
Principal Subsidiaries: Anderson-Nichols & Co Inc; Interstate Highway Sign Co
Principal Bank: The First National Bank of Boston
Financial Information:

	$'000
Sales revenues	76,000

No of Employees: 1,370

LIBBY, MCNEILL & LIBBY, INC

200 S Michigan Avenue, Chicago, IL 60604
Tel: (312) 341-4111
Telex: TWX 910 221 6063 libbys cgo

President: Leonard P Judy
Senior Executive Officers: James W Stevenson (Senior VP Business Development and Administration), Walter J Barry (VP and National Sales Manager), D S Loveless (VP Distribution Services), W Cuff (VP Special Foods), W W Keightley (VP, Treasurer and Controller), J B Cox (VP Operations), R W Fleming (VP Finance and Planning), G D James (VP Grocery Products)

PRINCIPAL ACTIVITIES: Production of fruit juices
Parent Company: Nestle SA, Vevey, Switzerland
Principal Bank: The First National Bank of Chicago
Financial Information:

	$'000
Sales revenues	265,000

No of Employees: 800

LIBCO CORPORATION

625 N Michigan Avenue, Chicago, IL 60611
Tel: (312) 677-7400

Chairman: Clyde W Engle (and Secretary)
President: George S Contarsy (and Treasurer)

PRINCIPAL ACTIVITIES: Diversified company with interests in the manufacture of household appliances, the leasing of medical equipment and linen supply
Principal Bank: American National Bank
Financial Information:

	$'000
Sales revenues	50,000

No of Employees: 500

LIBERTY CORPORATION (THE)

Wade Hampton Blvd, Greenville, SC 29602
Tel: (803) 268-8111
Telex: 8032681470

Chairman: Francis M Hipp (and Chairman Executive Committee)
President: W Hayne Hipp (and Chief Executive Officer)
Senior Executive Officers: Martha G Williams (VP, General Counsel and Secretary), Barry L Edwards (VP and Treasurer), A James Pollard (Controller)

PRINCIPAL ACTIVITIES: Insurance services; broadcasting; real estate interests
Principal Subsidiaries: Liberty Life Insurance Company
Principal Bank: South Carolina National Bank
Financial Information:

	Dec 31 1985	Dec 31 1986
	$'000	$'000
Revenues	354,500	381,000
Net income	24,000	28,000

No of Employees: 2,630

LIBERTY GLASS CO

1000 N Mission, Sapulpa, OK 74066
Tel: (918) 224-1440

Chairman: Fulton Collins (and President)
Senior Executive Officers: James A Bolin (Executive VP Manufacturing), David L Beyer (VP and Controller), Wills Young (VP Sales)

PRINCIPAL ACTIVITIES: Glass manufacture; glass packaging products
Principal Bank: American National Bank & Trust Co
Financial Information:

	$'000
Sales revenues	50,000

No of Employees: 450

LIBERTY HOMES, INC

PO Box 35, Goshen, IN 46526
Tel: (219) 533-0431

President: Edward J Hussey
Senior Executive Officers: Ben G Finley (Executive VP), Lester Molnar (VP), Michael F Hussey (VP Finance and Secretary)

PRINCIPAL ACTIVITIES: Manufacture of mobile homes
Principal Bank: Mid West Commerce Banking Company
Financial Information:

	$'000
Sales revenues	92,620

No of Employees: 1,000

LIBERTY NATIONAL BANCORP INC

PO Box 32500, Louisville, KY 40232
Tel: (502) 566-2000
Telex: WUT 204359 libertynat lvl

Chairman: Frank B Hower Jr (and Chief Executive Officer)
President: Joseph W Phelps
Senior Executive Officers: Malcolm B Chancey Jr (Executive VP and Cashier), James T Crain Jr (Executive VP Trust), Ted R Frith (Executive VP Marketing), R K Guillaume (Executive VP Corporate Banking), Robert G Scherer (Executive VP Trust), Albert B Schnell (Executive VP Operations), Jack H Shipman (Executive VP Retail Banking), Hugh M Shwab III (Executive VP Leasing and Insurance), John Y Van Bibber (Executive VP Commercial Mortgage), H Scott Davis Jr (Executive VP, Treasury and Money Management), Carl R Page (Secretary), Carl E Weigel (Treasurer)

PRINCIPAL ACTIVITIES: Banking
Principal Subsidiaries: Liberty National Bank & Trust Co of Louisville; Banker's Investment Group Inc; Citizens State Bank (Owensboro, KY); Fort Thomas-Bellevue Bank (Fort Thomas KY); Kentucky Bank & Trust Company (Madisonville, KY); Liberty Bank & Trust Co of Indiana (Corydon, IN); LNB Life Insurance Co; Liberty National Leasing Co
Financial Information:

	Dec 31 1985	Dec 31 1986
	$'000	$'000
Income before taxes	18,915	21,341
Net income	18,290	22,671
Dividends	4,507	5,567
Dividends per share*	$0.52	$0.57
Earnings per share	$1.97	$2.14
Common stock	67,877	82,735
Retained income	70,454	87,321
Shareholders equity	138,331	170,056
Deposits	1,710,924	2,066,463
Total assets	2;213,435	2,600,091

*fully diluted

Principal Shareholders: American Life and Accident Insurance Company of Kentucky (5.24%); Nancy L Ray (5.29%); Liberty National Bank and Trust Company of Louisville (21.31%); The Liverty Thrift Plan and The Liberty Employee Stock Ownership Plan (7.6%); All Directors and Officers of Liberty as a Group (26 in number) (11.69%); All Directors Emeriti, Directors, Officers and certain Employees of Liberty and the Banks as a Group (26.82%)
No of Employees: 1,661

LIBERTY NATIONAL BANK & TRUST CO OF OKLAHOMA CITY

100 Broadway, Oklahoma City, OK 73102
Tel: (405) 231-6000

Senior Chairman: J W McLean; Chairman: William M Bell; Vice Chairman: W Kenneth Bonds
President: Fred M Moses
Senior Executive Officers: Kenneth R Brown (Executive VP Investment Services), James W Bruce Jr (Executive VP and Secretary), D Dewayne Davidson (Executive VP), William P Dowling (Executive VP), Robert A Gregory (Executive VP Banking), Dale Schroeder (Executive VP Operations), Willis J Wheat (Executive VP Marketing), Jack E White (Executive VP Trust), J Terry Aimone (Senior VP Natural Resources), Donald E Balaban (Senior VP Trust Services), John H Brown (Senior VP Trust Services), Melvin E Burch (Senior VP Trust Services), Ben R Byers (Senior VP Trust Services), Robert L Brown (Senior VP Corporate Planning and Development), Gary Burton (Senior VP Retail Banking), Perry W Duncan (Senior VP Residential Lending), John Eickman (Senior VP Construction Development Lending), Alan H Kraft (Senior VP Commercial Banking), Harry E DeBee (Senior VP International Division), Harvey Dowdy (Senior VP Retail Banking), Mischa Gorkuscha (Senior VP Corporate Planning and Development), George H Hammonds (Senior VP and Controller), C A Hartwig (Senior VP Human Resources), James A Jennings (Senior VP Legal), David Jensen (Senior VP Investment and Money Market Services), Charles Johnson (Senior VP and Investment Officer), Klaholt P Kimker (Senior VP Income Property Lending), Claudine Long (Senior VP Administration), Leland C Nelson (Senior VP and Cashier), W Jeffrey Pickrye (Senior VP Commercial Banking), Dale Randolph (Senior VP Data), Edward T O'Leary (Senior VP Special Asset Group), Dennis R Olsta (Senior VP Trust Services), Stephen D Plunk (Senior VP Loan Administration), Jake Riley (Senior VP Trust Services), Rodney F Saunders (Senior VP Construction and

Development Lending), Paul E Scott (Senior VP Commercial Banking, Metro), William N Shafer Jr (Senior VP Data Services), L W Smith (Senior VP Data Services), Dick Soergel (Senior VP Investment and Money Market), Jim Sullivan (Senior VP Purchasing), David L Sutter (Senior VP Construction and Development Lending), Louis F Trost Jr (Senior VP Professional and Executive), Marvin M Wensel (Senior VP Liberty Property Management Co), Gary D Wilhite (Senior VP Servicing and Accounting, Liberty Mortgage Co)

PRINCIPAL ACTIVITIES: Banking
Parent Company: Banks of Mid-America Inc

No of Employees: 1,140

LIBERTY NATIONAL LIFE INSURANCE CO

2001 Third Avenue S, Birmingham, AL 35233
Tel: (205) 325-2722

Chairman: R K Richey
President: John S P Samford (and Chief Executive Officer)
Senior Executive Officers: Frank P Samford Jr (Chairman Executive Committee), William H Ray Jr (Executive VP Finance and Treasurer), R M Foster (Executive VP Marketing), William R Dean (Executive VP and Chief Actuary), William C Barcliff (Senior BP and General Counsel), J Stephen Beckman (Executive VP), John W Lovin Jr (Execuitve VP Administration), Harry W Mims (Senior VP Insurance Administration), J H Powell (Senior VP Personnel), James L Mayton Jr (VP and Controller), Jack V Brown (VP Field Management), Charles T Clayton Jr (VP Brokerage and General Agencies), Robert H Dobbs (VP Administration Services), Vurl E Duce (VP Agency), James W Ethridge (VP Underwriting), D Lawrence Faulkner (VP and Treasurer), Jack D Wells (VP Marketing Services), Dan T Head (VP Agency), Mary E Hester (VP Underwriting), Kenneth N Johnson (VP Information Services), Jack A Kelley Jr (VP and Actuary), Michael J Klyce (VP Securities), Anthony L McWhorter (VP and Actuary), John W Miller (VP Agency), H Hicks Moore (VP Agency), Murray W Smith (VP Marketing Services), Howard R Vaughan (VP Government Relations), James B White (VP and Director Field Training), Donald G Yates (VP and Actuary), James B Adams (VP Agency), Charles P Cope (VP Agency), Murray H Armstrong (VP Claims), W N Ray (VP and Assistant General Counsel)

PRINCIPAL ACTIVITIES: Life insurance
Parent Company: Torchmark Corporation

No of Employees: 4,700

LIEBERMAN ENTERPRISES INC

9549 Penn Avenue South, Minneapolis, MN 55431
Tel: (612) 887 5300

Chairman: David J M Lieberman
President: Harold M Okinow
Senior Executive Officers: Stephen E Lieberman (Executive VP and Secretary), Richard K Moerbitz (VP Operations), Robert W Pockrandt (VP), Gerald R Rowe (VP), Dennis M Sinclair (VP), Sylvester M Vanyo (VP), Sanford J Goldberg (VP Finance and Treasurer), D L Borgendale (VP), James A Hanke (VP Sales), J L Minor (VP)

PRINCIPAL ACTIVITIES: Distribution of records, cassette tapes and musical supplies
Financial Information:

	$'000
Sales revenues	195,000

No of Employees: 1,000

LIEBERT CORPORATION

1050 Dearborn Drive, Columbus, OH 43229
Tel: (614) 888-0246
Telex: WUI 687 4616 liebert wogn

Chairman: Larry L Liebert (and Chief Executive Officer)
President: Daniel C Brower (and Chief Operating Officer)
Senior Executive Officers: Daniel T Zallanta (VP Manufacturing), John Carey (VP Production), Dale A Donovan (VP), James C Bresnahan (VP Finance), Fred Lancia (VP Research and Development), Kenneth E Reynard (VP Accounting), William J Mrukowski (VP Worldwide Marketing), Paul E McKnight (VP Personnel), Edward K Feeney (VP Corporate Planning)

PRINCIPAL ACTIVITIES: Industrial and environmental control equipment
Principal Bank: Bank Ohio National Bank
Financial Information:

	$'000
Sales revenues	272,000

No of Employees: 1,800

LIEN, PETE, & SONS, INC

PO Box 440, Rapid City, SD 57709
Tel: (605) 342-7224

Chairman: Bruce H Lien (and Secretary)
President: Charles H Lien (and Treasurer)
Senior Executive Officers: Edwin Hubbeling (Senior VP), Paul Haerr (Senior VP), Robert J Schurger (VP and Manager), Pete Birrenkott (VP Sales), William Reuter (VP Operations)

PRINCIPAL ACTIVITIES: Production of limestone materials, aggregates, concrete, ready mixed concrete; oil exploration and production
Principal Subsidiaries: Western Production Co
Principal Bank: First Bank of South Dakota
Financial Information:

	$'000
Sales revenues	50,000

No of Employees: 400

LIFE INVESTORS INC

4333 Edgewood Rd NE, Cedar Rapids, IA 52499
Tel: (319) 398-8511

Chairman: Thomas M Collins
President: Robert D Ray (and Chief Executive Officer)
Senior Executive Officers: Arthur L Christoffersen (Executive VP), Edwin L Ingraham (Executive VP and Treasurer), Donald I Shepard (Executive VP), Ronald F Mosher (Senior VP and Chief Financial Officer), George R Lambert (Senior VP, Secretary and General Counsel), Perry B Lewis (Senior VP Corporate Administration)

PRINCIPAL ACTIVITIES: Insurance services including life and health insurance
Principal Bankers: Merchants National Bank
Financial Information:

	Dec 31 1986
	$'000
Revenues	1,000,000
Net income	433,000

No of Employees: 1,300

LIFESTYLE RESTAURANTS INC

401 Park Avenue South, New York, NY 10016
Tel: (212) 696 7700

Chairman: Laurence Ellman (and President); Vice Chairman: Norman M Kramer
Senior Executive Officers: Ronald Colello (Executive VP Operations), Robert G Everett (Executive VP and Chief Financial Officer), Lewis R Cohen (Senior VP and Secretary), Kenneth N Bracken (VP Franchising), Alan A Lanigan (VP Marketing), Marvin M Shore (VP and Treasurer), Edmund O'Heron (VP Operational Services)

PRINCIPAL ACTIVITIES: Restaurant chain
Principal Bank: Bank Leumi Trust Co of New York

Financial Information:

	$'000
Sales revenues	77,500

No of Employees: 3,600

LIGHTRON CORPORATION

100 Jericho Quadrangle, Jericho, NY 11753
Tel: (516) 938-5544

President: Myron Levy
Senior Executive Officers: Allen R Kaden (VP Operations and Comptroller)

PRINCIPAL ACTIVITIES: Furniture and furnishings, refrigeration hardware, beverage dispensing equipment
Parent Company: Instrument Systems Corporation, Jericho, NY
Principal Subsidiaries: Crown Novelty Works Corp; Standard Keil Industries Inc
Principal Bank: Barclays Bank of New York
Financial Information:

	$'000
Sales revenues	60,000

No of Employees: 1,200

LILLY, ELI, AND COMPANY

307 E McCarty Street, Indianapolis, IN 46285
Tel: (317) 261-2000
Telex: 276051 INDI

Chairman: Richard D Wood (and President and Chief Executive Officer)
Senior Executive Officers: A J Carnaghi (VP, Production Operations and Distribution Operation), Dr T L Emmick (VP, Biochemical Production and Development Division), J C Cook Jr (VP, Production Planning and Corporate Services), E G Davis (VP, Corporate Affairs), Dr Irving S Johnson (VP, Lilly Research Labs), E W Lange (Group VP, Marketing Planning and Development), E P Roberts (President, Elanco Products Division), Dr J G Whitney (VP, Lilly Research Labs), E M Cavalier (Group VP, Sales), M Cave (VP, Industrial Relations), (will retire 6/88; then replaced by S A Stitle), S A Taurel (President, Eli Lilly International Corporation), Dr M Perelman (Executive VP, President, Lilly Research Labs), V D Bryson (Executive VP Alanco Products, Medical Instrument Systems Division, Production Planning and Corporate Services, Corporate Affairs), Dr E B Herr Jr (Executive VP, Lilly Research Labs), E L Step (Executive VP, President, Pharmaceutical Division), J M Cornelius (VP Finance and Chief Financial Officer), Richard A Warne (VP and Controller), C H Bradley Jr (VP and General Counsel)

PRINCIPAL ACTIVITIES: Pharmaceuticals, animal health products, agricultural chemicals
Principal Subsidiaries: Cardiac Pacemakers Inc; IVAC Corporation; Physio-Control Corporation; Advanced Cardiovascular Systems Inc; Hybritech; Elanco Products Division
Financial Information:

	Dec 31 1985	Dec 31 1986
	$'000	$'000
Sales revenues	3,270,600	3,720,400
Income before taxes	796,600	876,300
Net income	517,600	558,200
Dividends	224,900	250,900
Dividends per share	$1.60	$1.80
Earnings per share	$3.69	$4.01
Common stock	91,300	91,400
Retained income	2,740,600	3,041,200
Shareholders equity	2,387,700	2,739,600

No of Employees: 29,100

LILLY INDUSTRIAL COATINGS, INC

546 Abbott Street, Indianapolis, IN 46225
Tel: (317) 634-8512

Chairman: J R Pickering (and President and Chief Executive Officer)
Senior Executive Officers: W I Longsworth Jr (VP and Manager Memphis, TN), M E Evans (VP and Manager Montebello, CA), Joseph V Borland (VP and Manager Paulsboro, NJ), Thomas P Kelly (VP and Manager Templeton, MA), Robert S Bailey (VP), P James Stokes (VP Finance and Secretary)

PRINCIPAL ACTIVITIES: Manufacture of paints and resins
Principal Subsidiaries: Alamatex, Inc; Lilly Coatings (Far East) Ltd
Principal Bank: The Indiana National Bank
Financial Information:

	$'000
Sales revenues	145,189

No of Employees: 1,012

LILY-TULIP, INC

PO Box 1808, 209 Seventh Street, Augusta, GA 30903
Tel: (404) 823-5459

Chairman: A J Dunlap (and President)
Senior Executive Officers: A P Witt (VP and Chief Financial Officer), J P Murtagh (VP), J J O'Brien (VP)

PRINCIPAL ACTIVITIES: Manufacture of paper and foam cups, paper plates, foam labels and plastic carriers
Trade Names: Lily, Trophy (R) cups, Plasti-Shield (R) labels, Foam-A-Round (R) labels, Contour-Pak (R) carriers
Principal Subsidiaries: Lily Cups, Inc (Canada)
Principal Bank: Continental Illinois National Bank; Bankers Trust Co (NY); First National Bank of Atlanta
Financial Information:

	$'000
Sales revenues	319,510

No of Employees: 3,200

LIMITED, INC (THE)

One Limited Parkway, Columbus, OH 43230
Tel: (614) 475-4000

Chairman: Leslie H Wexner (and President); Vice Chairman: Robert H Morosky
Senior Executive Officers: Thomas G Hopkins (Executive VP), David T Kollat (Executive VP), A Donald Bird (VP), Jerald Dick (VP), Kenneth B Gillman (VP and Controller), Charles W Hinson (VP), Timothy B Lyons (VP)

PRINCIPAL ACTIVITIES: Retail trade in women's apparel
Principal Bank: Bank One
Financial Information:

	Dec 31 1985	Dec 31 1986
	$'000	$'000
Sales revenues	2,387,110	3,142,696
Net income	145,317	227,780
Earnings per share	$1.20	$1.21
Shareholders equity	404,075	781,542

No of Employees: 34,900

LIN BROADCASTING CORPORATION

1370 Avenue of the Americas, New York, NY 10019
Tel: (212) 765-1902

Chairman: Donald A Pels (and President and Chief Executive Officer)
Senior Executive Officers: E B Byrne (Group VP Television), Harold N Spitz (VP), Barrett H Geoghegan (VP), Ronald E Graiff (VP Engineering), Arnold S Blauweiss (VP Finance), David M Naseman (VP, Secretary and General Counsel), Michael Plouf (VP Corporate Development and Treasurer), Frank A O'Neil (VP), Robert S Cecil (Group VP Cellular), Daniel B Stokes (VP and Controller)

PRINCIPAL ACTIVITIES: Television broadcasting; cellular telephone services; publishing

Financial Information:

	Dec 31 1985 $'000	Dec 31 1986 $'000
Sales revenues	141,718	195,340
Income before taxes	61,873	67,562
Net income*	32,287	39,982
Earnings per share	$0.63	$0.72
Common stock	152,811	157,952
Retained income	172,291	238,531
Shareholders equity	314,814	386,039

*continuing operations

No of Employees: 950

LINCOLN DIVISION

1 Lincoln Way, St Louis, MO 63120
Tel: (314) 679-4200

President: Thomas L Glover
Senior Executive Officers: Kenneth P Lockwood (Chief Financial Officer), E J Lane (VP Marketing)

PRINCIPAL ACTIVITIES: Industrial lubrication equipment
Parent Company: Pentair Corporation
Principal Bank: Commerce Manchester
Financial Information:

	$'000
Sales revenues	100,000

No of Employees: 1,600

LINCOLN ELECTRIC CO

22801 St Clair Avenue, Cleveland, OH 44117
Tel: (216) 481-8100
Telex: WUT 985 471 lincoln eucd

Chairman: William Irrgang (and Chief Executive Officer)
President: George Willis
Senior Executive Officers: D N Manross (VP), W I Miskoe (VP), D F Hastings (VP), A S Patnik (VP), L R Bauman (VP), J Gonzalez (VP), T Ashton (VP), R F Young (VP), Harry Carlson (VP)

PRINCIPAL ACTIVITIES: Electric welding apparatus; generating equipment; industrial engines
Principal Bank: AmeriTrust
Financial Information:

	$'000
Sales revenues	350,000

No of Employees: 2,400

LINCOLN FINANCIAL CORPORATION

116 East Berry Street, PO Box 960, Fort Wayne, IN 46801
Tel: (219) 423 6111

Chairman: Robert J Delaney Jr (and President and Chief Executive Officer)
Senior Executive Officers: Donald L Felten (VP Trust Services), Joseph L Fritzsche (VP Administration), John P McBride (VP Affiliates Services), Randolph F Williams (VP Corporate Development), Alvin R Moll Jr (Treasurer and Assistant Secretary)

PRINCIPAL ACTIVITIES: Banking
Principal Subsidiaries: Lincoln National Bank and Trust Company
Principal Bank: Lincoln National Bank & Trust Co
Financial Information:

	Dec 31 1985 $'000
Revenues	87,750
Net income	7,190

No of Employees: 510

LINCOLN FIRST BANKS INC

One Lincoln First Square, Rochester, NY 14603
Tel: (716) 258-5058

Chairman: Alexander D Hargrave
President: William Balderston III (and Chief Executive Officer)
Senior Executive Officers: Wesley C Tallman (Senior Executive VP), Louis A Langie Jr (Executive VP), William A Wilson (Executive VP), Mark B Grier (Senior VP and Treasurer), Robert J Maggs Jr (Senior VP, Secretary and General Counsel), Kevin M Considine (Senior VP)

PRINCIPAL ACTIVITIES: Banking services
Principal Bank: Lincoln First Bank

No of Employees: 3,286

LINCOLN NATIONAL CORPORATION

1300 South Clinton Street, Fort Wayne, IN 46801
Tel: (219) 427-2000
Telex: WUT 232672 inl ins fwa

President: Ian M Rolland
Senior Executive Officers: David D Allen (Executive VP), P Kenneth Dunsire (Executive VP), Jack D Hunter (Executive VP), Richard S Robertson (Executive VP), Robert W Crispin (Executive VP), Michael Marchese (Senior VP), Max A Roesler (VP and Treasurer)

PRINCIPAL ACTIVITIES: Insurance holding company
Principal Subsidiaries: Lincoln National Life Insurance Company; American States Insurance Companies; Cannon Assurance Limited; Security Connecticut Life Insurance Company; First Penn-Pacific Life Insurance Company
Principal Bank: Lincoln National Bank & Trust
Financial Information:

	Dec 31 1985 $'000	Dec 31 1986 $'000
Premium income	3,813,024	4,622,099
Investment income	1,005,625	1,191,861
Income before taxes	266,084	303,883
Net income	214,278	284,392
Dividends	89,229	99,597
Dividends per share	$1.88	$2.04
Earnings per share	$4.89	$6.12
Common stock	55,159	55,334
Retained income	1,604,885	1,786,472
Shareholders equity	2,004,634	2,196,594

No of Employees: 14,003

LINCOLN NATIONAL LIFE INSURANCE COMPANY

1300 S Clinton Street, Fort Wayne, IN 46801
Tel: (219) 427-2000
Telex: WUT 232672 inl ins fwa

Chairman: Ian M Rolland (and President)
Senior Executive Officers: P Kenneth Dunsire (Executive VP), Howard E Steele (Executive VP), Thomas M West (Executive VP), Stephen H Berkey (Senior VP), William Lawson (Senior VP), Harlan K Holly (Senior VP), Jon A Boscia (Senior VP), William K Tyler (Senior VP), Jack D Hunter (Executive VP and General Counsel), David D Allen (Executive VP Data Processing), C Lawrence Edris (Senior VP), Michael Marchese (Senior VP), Donald C Chambers (VP), Max A Roesler (VP and Treasurer)

PRINCIPAL ACTIVITIES: Life insurance
Parent Company: Lincoln National Corporation, Fort Wayne, IN
Principal Subsidiaries: Lincoln National Pension Insurance Company; Health Win Insurance Company; Lincoln National Health & Casualty Insurance Company; Employers Health Insurance Company
Principal Bank: Lincoln National Bank & Trust

Financial Information:

	Dec 31 1985 $'000	Dec 31 1986 $'000
Premium income	1,705,259	1,500,004
Investment income	327,564	328,410
Income before taxes	229,978	87,200
Net income	171,729	127,712
Dividends	228,100	170,000
Dividends per share	$22.81	$17.00
Earnings per share	$17.17	$12.77
Common stock	25,000	25,000
Retained income	594,775	552,487
Shareholders equity	629,936	686,990

Principal Shareholders: Lincoln National Corporation (100%)
No of Employees: 4,436

LINCOLN NATIONAL PENSION INSURANCE CO

1300 S Clinton St, Box 1110, Fort Wayne, IN 46801
Tel: (219) 427-2000
Telex: 232 672
Telefax: (219) 427-2525

President: Robert W Crispin
Senior Executive Officers: Jack D Hunter (Executive VP), Thomas M West (Executive VP), Jon A Boscia (Senior VP), William K Tyler (Senior VP), Michael Marchase Jr (Senior VP), Kenneth J Clark (VP), Max A Roesler (VP and Treasurer)

PRINCIPAL ACTIVITIES: Pension and retirement plans and annuities
Parent Company: Lincoln National Life Insurance Co; ultimate parent company-Lincoln National Corporation
Financial Information:

	Dec 31 1985 $'000	Dec 31 1986 $'000
Premium income	172,826	174,198
Investment income	334,779	425,091
Income before taxes	23,603	35,636
Operating income	14,177	23,630
Net income	16,227	34,370
Common stock	2,000	2,000
Paid in surplus	64,500	64,500
Retained income	55,820	90,190
Shareholders equity	122,045	156,690

No of Employees: 295

LINCOLN SAVINGS BANK

200 Park Avenue, New York, NY 10166
Tel: (212) 972-9500
Telex: WUI 667 222 lsh 667 222

Chairman: Alton G Marshall (and President and Chief Executive Officer)
Senior Executive Officers: Louis L Rosenberg (Chairman Executive Committee), Milton F Gidge (Executive VP), Harold A Jones (Senior VP Banking), Jeffrey M Zwirn (Senior VP and Treasurer), Anthony P Marino (Senior VP and Mortgage Officer), Richard P Gonzales (VP, EDP Operation), Gerard J Jones (VP), Lawrence Morace (VP), Alfred A Porzio (VP and Comptroller), Harvey B Singer (VP), Jack P Wu (VP Banking Operations), John J Reilly (VP and Auditor), Joseph S Antonio (VP Life Insurance), Patricia Carucci (VP Personnel)

PRINCIPAL ACTIVITIES: Banking
Principal Bank: Manufacturers Hanover Trust Company

No of Employees: 700

LINCOLN TELECOMMUNICATIONS CO

1440 M Street, Lincoln, NE 68508
Tel: (402) 474-2211

Chairman: Thomas C Woods Jr (and Chief Executive Officer)
President: James E Geist (and Chief Operating Officer)
Senior Executive Officers: Laurence A Connealy (VP Administration and Controller), Michael J Tavlin (VP, Treasurer and Secretary), Thomas C Woods III (VP), Frank H Hilsabeck (VP), James W Strand (VP)

PRINCIPAL ACTIVITIES: Telecommunications services and equipment
Principal Subsidiaries: The Lincoln Telephone and Telegraph Company
Principal Bank: Harris Trust and Savings Bank, Chicago, Illinois
Financial Information:

	Dec 31 1985 $'000	Dec 31 1986 $'000
Sales revenues	145,372	159,425
Income before taxes	24,895	32,728
Net income	15,150	18,963
Dividends	9,127	9,127
Dividends per share	$2,20	$2.20
Earnings per share*	$3.50	$4.42
Common stock	116,533	125,099

*primary

No of Employees: 1,860

LINDBERG CORPORATION

8600 W Bryn Mawr Avenue, Chicago, IL 60631
Tel: (312) 693-2021
Telex: 910-221-5701 LINDBERG CGO

Chairman: George H Bodeen (and President and Chief Executive Officer)
Senior Executive Officers: F J Waldeck (Executive VP), Bruce J Biemeck (VP and Controller), R W Gilliland (VP)

PRINCIPAL ACTIVITIES: Heat treatment of metals
Financial Information:

	Dec 31 1985 $'000
Sales revenues	69,433
Income before taxes	2,342
Net income	1,527
Dividends	845
Dividends per share	$0.16
Earnings per share	$0.29
Common stock	14,183
Retained income	9,399
Shareholders equity	23,765

No of Employees: 1,060

LINDSAY MANUFACTURING COMPANY

Box 156, Lindsay, NE 68644
Tel: (402) 428-2131

President: Gary D Parker
Senior Executive Officers: Bruce Karsk (VP Finance), Cliff Loseke (VP Manufacturing), Charlie Meis (VP Engineering), Ed Enriquez (VP International), Bob Snoozy (VP Marketing)

PRINCIPAL ACTIVITIES: Production of irrigation equipment
Parent Company: De Kalb AgResearch Inc, De Kalb, IL
Principal Bank: First National Bank
Financial Information:

	$'000
Sales revenues	100,000

No of Employees: 500

LINDSAY OLIVE GROWERS

PO Box 278, Lindsay, CA 93247
Tel: (209) 562-5121
Telex: TWX 910 541 2443 linoliv trflsy

Chairman: R R McLain; Vice Chairmen: Willard Turek, Clifton Paregien Jr
President: Robert D Rossio
Senior Executive Officers: Edward F Brennan (Executive VP), Jerry Sullivan (VP Operations), Ray L Scott (VP Field

Operations), F A Davey (VP Administration and Secretary), W J Osterbauer (VP Finance and Treasurer), Eric M Boyle (VP Marketing)

PRINCIPAL ACTIVITIES: Olive products including canned olives and sauces
Principal Bank: Sacramento Bank for Cooperatives
Financial Information:

	$'000
Sales revenues	55,000

No of Employees: 500

LINEAR CORPORATION

2055 Corte Del Nogal, Carlsbad, CA 92009
Tel: (619) 438 7000
Telex: 910-528-6519
Telefax: (619) 438-7043

Chairman: Joe Davis
President: Andrew Smalz (and Chief Executive Officer)
Senior Executive Officers: Terry Holdt (President-Linear Security), George Lippert (Executive VP), Stephen Schorr (VP Finance and Chief Financial Officer), Carl Minton (Secretary)

PRINCIPAL ACTIVITIES: Electronic and infra-red security devices, home hardware, security services
Principal Subsidiaries: Colorado Electro Optics Inc; Moore-O-Matic Inc; Security Sciences Corporation of America
Principal Bank: Wells Fargo
Financial Information:

	May 31 1986	May 31 1987
	$'000	$'000
Sales revenues	41,502	56,292
Income (loss) before taxes	(1,314)	3,781
Net income (loss)	(433)	2,830
Earnings per share	($0.14)	($0.94)
Common stock*	3,000	3,040
Retained income	9,565	12,395
Shareholders equity	18,185	21,263

*number of shares in thousands

Principal Shareholders: Inter Active Tehcnologies Inc
No of Employees: 887 full time

LINEAR FILMS INC

4920 South 48th West Avenue, Tulsa, OK 74157
Tel: (918) 446 1651

President: William E Baab
Senior Executive Officers: Michael J Baab (Executive VP), Thomas R Ackley (VP), John A Cerny (VP), Gerald E Milton (VP and Treasurer), Jack R Smith (VP), Patrick W Waddel (Secretary)

PRINCIPAL ACTIVITIES: Rubber and plastic products
Financial Information:

	$'000
Sales revenues	34,000

No of Employees: 250

LINN-CORRIHER CORPORATION

Landis, NC 28088
Tel: (704) 857-1121

Chairman: Alex R McAslan
President: H Alton Conner
Senior Executive Officers: William J Rouse (VP Administration), Harold W Buchanan (VP Manufacturing), Ricky J Bullard (VP Sales)

PRINCIPAL ACTIVITIES: Textile spinning
Parent Company: Dominion Textile Inc
Principal Bank: North Carolina National Bank
Financial Information:

	$'000
Sales revenues	70,000

No of Employees: 1,000

LIONEL CORPORATION

441 Lexington Avenue, New York, NY 10017
Tel: (212) 818-0630

Chairman: Michael J Vastola (and President, Chief Executive Officer, Chief Financial Officer and Treasurer)
Senior Executive Officers: George A Padgett (Senior VP, Secretary and General Counsel), Marvin J Katz (Senior VP), Louis P Mongeluzzi (Assistant Secretary), Robert F Armweg (Assistant Controller)

PRINCIPAL ACTIVITIES: Lionel has emerged from reorganization as a reconstituted force in toy specialty retailing. The Company, through its subsidiary Lionel Leisure, Inc, operates 66 toy supermarkets under the names Lionel Kiddie City, Lionel Playworld and Lionel Toy Warehouse in 15 states. The Company also receives royalties under a license agreement with Lionel Trains, Inc Covering the manufacture and sale of "Lionel" trains and other toys
Principal Subsidiaries: Lionel Leisure, Inc
Principal Bank: Manufacturers Hanover Trust Co
Financial Information:

	Jan 25 1986	Jan 31 1987
	$'000	$'000
Sales revenues	246,076	282,667
Income before taxes	3,723	10,707
Net income	39,588	8,664
Earnings per share net	$4.74	$0.65
Common stock	1,367	1,367
Retained income	3,843	12,508
Shareholders equity	66,765	75,987

No of Employees: 2,500

LIPTON, THOMAS J, , INC

800 Sylvan Avenue, Englewood Cliffs, NJ 07632
Tel: (201) 567-8000
Telex: WUT 135421 lipton egwd

President: H M Tibbetts (and Chief Executive Officer)
Senior Executive Officers: D W von Arx (Executive VP General Management Group), E Feliciotti (Senior VP Science and Technology), C B Fuller (Senior VP Operations and Finance), J N Byrne (Senior VP Corporate Development), J W Riehm (Senior VP, Secretary and Assistant to President), J Benson (Senior VP Marketing), G B Boycks (VP Beverages), D J Carroll (VP Corporate Relations), C J Tagliabue (VP Engineering and Packaging Development), W K Godfrey (VP Personnel), H N Graham (VP Research and Product Development), R J Hlavacek (VP Quality Assurance), E Ladendorff (VP Marketing Support), J McPeak (VP Financial Administration), E L Qualls (VP and General Manager Broker Products/Special Markets), J Reid (VP Operations), D W St Clair (VP and General Counsel), A L Franke (VP Food Division), R E Livingston (VP Sales Division)

PRINCIPAL ACTIVITIES: Tea, pasta, dressings and seasonings, soups, ice cream
Parent Company: Unilever NV, Rotterdam, Netherlands
Financial Information:

	Dec 31 1985	Dec 31 1986
	$'000	$'000
Sales revenues	1,269,770	1,303,194
Net income	80,426	91,458
Shareholders equity	460,796	517,350

No of Employees: 5,230

LIQUI-BOX CORPORATION

PO Box 494, Worthington, OH 43085
Tel: (614) 888-9280
Telex: WUT 245 430 liqui box wogn

Chairman: Samuel B Davis (and Chief Executive Officer and Treasurer)
Senior Executive Officers: C J Bond (Senior VP), Robert S Hamilton (Executive VP), Peter Linn (VP Finance and Administration), John M Wolotschaj (VP Sales and Marketing)

PRINCIPAL ACTIVITIES: Packaging products
Principal Bank: Huntington National Bank
Financial Information:

	Mar 31 1986	Mar 31 1987
	$'000	$'000
Sales revenues	63,860	70,667
Net income	4,619	6,042

No of Employees: 480

LIQUID AIR CORPORATION

One Embarcadero Center, San Francisco, CA 94111
Tel: (415) 765-4500
Telex: ITT 470876 liquid air sfo

Chairman: J Delorme; Vice Chairmen: P A Salbaing, Jacques G Maisonrouge, M V Breber
President: T E Slattery (and Chief Executive Officer)
Senior Executive Officers: R A Johnson (Executive VP and Chief Operations Officer), M J Bignolas (Executive VP, President Industrial Gases Division), Thaddeus Pylko (VP), Claude Salama (VP), W J Sheridan (VP)

PRINCIPAL ACTIVITIES: Production of industrial gases; medical gases; underwater diving equipment and life support equipment; welding equipment and products
Trade Names: Aqua Lung
Parent Company: L'Air Liquide, Paris, France
Principal Subsidiaries: USD Corporation; Cardox Corporation; Oxigenio do Brazil SA
Principal Bank: Royal Bank of Canada
Financial Information:

	Dec 31 1985	Dec 31 1986
	$'000	$'000
Sales revenues	543,040	570,565
Net income	31,753	34,680
Earnings per share	$2.42	$2.42
Shareholders equity	261,196	275,644

No of Employees: 4,380

LITHIUM CORPORATION OF AMERICA

449 N Cox Road, Gastonia, NC 28054
Tel: (704) 867-8371
Telex: WUT 575 253 lithcoa gana

President: Harold J Andrews
Senior Executive Officers: R L Nielsen (VP Chemical Manufacturing), G J Orazem (VP Marketing and Commercial Development), J B Holman (VP Mining), H E Ridgeway (VP Finance), G E Foltz (VP Technical), R W Barnes (VP Sales)

PRINCIPAL ACTIVITIES: Specialty chemicals; ore mining
Parent Company: FMC Corporation
Financial Information:

	$'000
Sales revenues	86,000

No of Employees: 700

LITHONIA LIGHTING DIVISION

PO Box A, Conyers, GA 30207
Tel: (404) 922-9000
Telex: WUT 804274 lithonia cony

President: J H McClung
Senior Executive Officers: H O Gailey (VP Fluorescent), R W Bowman (VP High Intensity), E Haar (VP Emergency Lighting), C J Darnell (VP Information Services), G W Vanderwater (VP Finance and Administration), R Lee (VP Marketing), C R Bryant (VP Sales), J T Mogan (VP Research and Development)

PRINCIPAL ACTIVITIES: Light fittings and lighting equipment
Parent Company: National Service Industries Inc, Atlanta, GA
Principal Bank: First National Bank of Atlanta
Financial Information:

	$'000
Sales revenues	500,000

No of Employees: 4,500

LITTLE, ARTHUR D, INC

Acorn Park, Cambridge, MA 02140
Tel: (617) 864 5770

Chairman: John F Magee
President: Charles R Lamantia (and Chief Operating Officer)
Senior Executive Officers: Samuel C Fleming (Senior VP), Richard E Heitman (Senior VP), Theodore P Heuchling (Senior VP), Ashok S Kalelkar (Senior VP), Albert J Kelley (Senior VP), John M Ketteringham (Senior VP), William F O'Neil (Senior VP and Chief Financial Officer), Louis M Rambo (Senior VP), Harland A Riker Jr (Senior VP), Alfred E Wechsler (Senior VP), D Reid Weedon Jr (Senior VP), John R White (Senior VP)

PRINCIPAL ACTIVITIES: Provision of public relations and management consultancy services
Principal Bank: First National Bank of Boston
Financial Information:

	$'000
Sales revenues	230,000

No of Employees: 2,600

LITTON INDUSTRIES, INC

360 N Crescent Drive, Beverly Hills, CA 90210
Tel: (213) 859-5000
Telex: 67-4991

Chairman: Fred W O'Green
President: Orion L Hoch (and Chief Executive Officer)
Senior Executive Officers: Joseph T Casey (Executive VP Financial Affairs), Joseph F Caligiuri (Executive VP Advanced Electronic Systems), M H Dingman Jr (Senior VP Resource Exploration Group), Wayne L Grosvenor (Senior VP and Controller), Roland O Peterson (Senior VP Components Group), Gerald F St Pé (Senior VP Marine Engineering)

PRINCIPAL ACTIVITIES: Diversified company with interests in advanced electronics including data processing equipment, laser systems, navigation and telecommunications equipment; electrical and electronic products including components, industrial automation systems including mechanical handling equipment, machine tools and hand tools; marine engineering; resource exploration for oil and gas
Financial Information:

	Jul 31 1986	Jul 31 1987
	$'000	$'000
Sales revenues	4,521,005	4,419,689
Income before taxes	128,027	249,033
Net income	71,137	138,112
Earnings per share	$2.52	-
Common stock	27,200	26,600
Retained income	543,948	-
Shareholders equity	1,019,896	-

Principal Shareholders: Teledyne Inc (approx 28%)
No of Employees: 51,000

LIVINGSTON-GRAHAM, INC

16080 E Arrow Hwy, Irwindale, CA 91706
Tel: (213) 9600-5471

President: David D Davis

Senior Executive Officers: A R Dyck (Executive VP), John K Thomas (VP Marketing)

PRINCIPAL ACTIVITIES: Mining; production of building materials
Parent Company: Symons Corp
Principal Bank: Bank of America
Financial Information:

	$'000
Sales revenues	60,000

No of Employees: 350

LIZ CLAIBORNE, INC
See CLAIBORNE,, LIZ, INC

LJN TOYS LTD
200 Fifth Avenue, New York, NY 10010
Tel: (212) 243-6565

Chairman: D C Yeh
President: Jack Friedman (and Chief Executive Officer)
Senior Executive Officers: S J Drell (Executive VP and Chief Operations Officer), P Y Kwan (Executive VP), J J Mason (Senior VP), J S Schopick (VP Finance and Controller), Murray Bass (VP)

PRINCIPAL ACTIVITIES: Production and retailing of toys
Parent Company: MCA Inc
Financial Information:

	$'000
Sales revenues	78,000

No of Employoes: 90

LLC CORPORATION
4835 LBJ Freeway, Suite 300, Dallas, TX 75244
Tel: (214) 386 4110

Chairman: Harold C Simmons
President: Hugh C Shurtleff (and Chief Executive Officer and Treasurer)
Senior Executive Officers: Charles N Hyslop (VP), William L Wortman (VP, Treasurer and Assistant Secretary), Harold M Curdy (Controller), Carolyn L Glazener (Secretary)

PRINCIPAL ACTIVITIES: Restaurants; manufacture of wire mesh and hardware
Principal Subsidiaries: Beacon Agency Inc; Liberty Financial Management Company; Liberty Loan Corp MI; Sybra Inc; J W Management Company; Sybsidiary Inc; Morris Plan Company; Morris Plan Company Inc; Oklahoma Morris Plan Company
Principal Bank: MBank Dallas
Financial Information:

	$'000
Sales revenues	112,000

No of Employees: 3,580

LLOYD'S ELECTRONICS, INC
180 Raritan Center Parkway, Edison, NJ 08818
Tel: (201) 225-2030
Telex: 844-562 LLOYTRA-EDIN

Chairman: Manuel Luis del Valle; Vice Chairman: Alfred P O'Hara
President: G Rosell (and Chief Executive Officer)
Senior Executive Officers: J Kirshner (Senior VP Sales), Gene Rissetto (VP Far East Operations), Sol Rosenberg (VP Far East Operations)

PRINCIPAL ACTIVITIES: Design, importation and marketing of consumer electronics products
Trade Names: LLOYD'S
Parent Company: Bacardi Corporation
Principal Bank: First National Bank of Boston
Financial Information:

	$'000
Sales revenues	85,000

No of Employees: 100

LOCKHEED CORPORATION
255 North Hollywood Way, PO Box 551, Burbank, CA 91520
Tel: (818) 847-6121
Telex: 67208

Chairman: Lawrence O Kitchen (and Chief Executive Officer)
President: Robert A Fuhrman (and Chief Operating Officer and Group President-Missile, Space and Electronic Systems)
Senior Executive Officers: Vincent N Marafino (Executive VP-Chief Financial and Administrative Officer), Robert B Ormsby Jr (Group President-Aeronautical Systems), Lawrence A Smith (Group President-Marine Systems), Richard W Taylor (Group President-Information Systems), Robert H Wertheim (Senior VP-Science and Engineering), Louis J Barnard (VP-Human Resources), Harold T Bowling (VP-Corporate Development), Clayton H Chisum (VP-Information and Administrative Services), Richard K Cook (VP-Washington Area), H David Crowther (VP-Corporate Communications), Dale D Daniels (VP-Operations), Charles de Bedts (VP-Marketing), Russell H Hopps (VP-Engineering), Anthony G Van Schaick (VP and Treasurer), Robert H Northcutt Jr (VP and Controller), Robert C Johnson (VP Contracts and Administration), James J Ryan (VP-Secretary and Assistant General Counsel), Joseph G Twomey (VP and General Counsel), A Gene Otsea (Assistant Treasurer), Sam F Pearce (Assistant Secretary)

PRINCIPAL ACTIVITIES: Lockheed's primary businesses embrace research, development and production of products and systems for aerospace and defense. Programs for the US government accounted for 85 percent of the company's 1984 sales. Sales to foreign governments represented 10 percent. Commercial customers worldwide accounted for five percent. Lockheed's 16 operating companies are aligned into four groups representing major lines of business. The Missiles, Space and Electronics Systems Group produces military and civilian space systems and satellites, strategic fleet ballistic missiles, and tactical defense and communications systems, in addition to providing technical management services for the US space program, the Department of Defense and other government agencies. The Aeronautical Systems Group builds special mission and high performance aircraft and systems for military and civilian operations. In its aerospace support work, Lockheed designs and performs aircraft modifications, maintains military and commercial aircraft at domestic and overseas bases and provides related logistics and other support services. The Marine Systems Group builds and repairs ships and conducts advanced marine research and development, primarily for the US Navy. The Information Systems Group develops and markets specialized computer software and services
Principal Subsidiaries: Lockheed Corporation International; Lockheed Finance Corporation. Missiles, Space and Electronics Systems Group:-Lockheed Electronics Company Inc; Lockheed Engineering and Management Services Company Inc; Lockheed Missiles & Space Company Inc; Lockheed Space Operations Company. Aeronautical Systems Group:- Lockheed Advanced Aeronautics Company; Lockheed Air Terminal Inc; Lockheed Aircraft International AG (Saudi Arabia); Lockheed Aircraft Service Company; Lockheed-California Company; Lockheed Georgia Company. Marine Systems Group:- Advanced Marine Systems; Lockheed Shipbuilding Company. Information Systems Group:- Cadam Inc; Datacom Systems Corporation; Dialog Information Services Inc; Lockheed Dataplan Inc
Principal Bank: Bank of America; Banker's Trust; City Bank; The Chase Manhatten Bank; Manufacturers' Hanover Bank; Security Pacific National Bank

Financial Information:

	Dec 30 1986
	$'000
Sales revenues	10,273,000
Net income	408,000
Earnings per share	$6.18
Shareholders equity	1,866,000

No of Employees: 84,900

LOCKHEED SHIPBUILDING CO

2929 16th Avenue SW, Seattle, WA 98134
Tel: (206) 292-5656
Telex: WUT 320 328 lscc sea

Chairman: L A Smith (and President)
President: J R Santosuosso
Senior Executive Officers: L E Houk (VP Finance and Treasurer), J P Hayes (VP Human Resources), D F Tellman (VP Operations and Ship Repair), M E Young (VP Business Development)

PRINCIPAL ACTIVITIES: Ship design, systems engineering and construction; ship overhaul and repair; integrated logistics support
Parent Company: Lockheed Corporation, Burbank, CA
Principal Bank: First Interstate Bank of Washington
Financial Information:

	$'000
Sales revenues	160,000

No of Employees: 1,600

LOCKWOOD CORPORATION

PO Box 160, Gering, NE 69341
Tel: (308) 436-5051
Telex: WUT 484454 lockwood geri

Chairman: C H McCall
President: Lewis S Armstrong
Senior Executive Officers: G L Johnson (VP Finance), Norman H Walton (VP Manufacturing), George Olsen (VP Sales), Les Jones (VP Engineering)

PRINCIPAL ACTIVITIES: Agricultural machinery and equipment and irrigation systems
Parent Company: McCall Industries Inc
Principal Bank: Gering National Bank & Trust Co
Financial Information:

	$'000
Sales revenues	60,000

No of Employees: 600

LOCTITE CORPORATION

705 N Mountain Road, Newington, CT 06111
Tel: (203) 278-1280
Telex: WUT 99348 loctitect newi

Chairman: Kenneth W Butterworth (and President and Chief Executive Officer)
Senior Executive Officers: Theodore F Patlovich (Senior VP, President Loctite International), David Freeman (Senior VP, President Loctite North America), Robert L Aller (VP-Finance and Treasurer), Eugene F Miller (Secretary and General Counsel), Western A Todd (Director-Corporate Communications)

PRINCIPAL ACTIVITIES: Manufacture of adhesive and sealant products
Trade Names: Loctite, Permatex, Duro (all registered trademarks)
Financial Information:

	Jun 30 1986	Jun 30 1987
	$'000	$'000
Sales revenues	266,788	337,802
Income before taxes	34,035	45,363
Net income	23,173	30,665
Dividends	7,417	8,540
Dividends per share	$0.82	$0.94
Earnings per share	$2.56	$3.38
Common stock	12,207	14,175
Retained income	147,610	167,748
Shareholders equity	153,560	181,723

Principal Shareholders: Henkel of America (26.3%)
No of Employees: 3,151

LOEWS CORPORATION

666 Fifth Avenue, New York, NY 10103
Tel: (212) 841-1000
Telex: TRT 177812 loe ut

Chairman: Laurence A Tisch (and Chief Executive Officer)
Senior Executive Officers: James S Tisch (Executive VP), Barry Hirsch (Senior VP, Secretary and General Counsel), Roy E Posner (Senior VP-Chief Financial Officer), Robert J Hausman (VP; Chairman, Loews Hotels), Kenneth Abrams (VP, Personnel), Herbert C Hoffmann (VP-Operations Planning; Chief Operating Officer, Bulova), Andrew Tisch (VP-Strategic Planning; President, Bulova), John G Malino (VP-Real Estate), Stuart B Opotowsky (VP-Tax), Guy A Kwan (Controller), Charles G Sposato Jr (Treasurer), William E Duffy (Assistant Treasurer), Gary W Garson (Assistant Secretary and Deputy General Counsel), Ross A Miller (Assistant Treasurer)

PRINCIPAL ACTIVITIES: Diversified holding company with interests including tobacco, hotel management insurance (property, casualty and life), watches and other timing devices
Trade Names: Lorillard (Tobacco); Loews Hotels (Hotel Management); CNA Insurance; Bulova (Watches)
Principal Subsidiaries: Lorillard, Inc; CNA Financial Corp; Loew Hotels Holding Corporation; Bulova Watch Company Inc
Financial Information:

	Dec 31 1985	Dec 31 1986
	$'000	$'000
Revenues	6,700,270	8,625,988
Income before taxes	605,938	601,275
Net income	588,975	545,503
Dividends	244,510	81,503
Dividends per share	$3.00	$1.00
Earnings per share	$7.23	$6.69
Common stock	81,503	81,503
Retained income	2,235,180	2,699,180
Shareholders equity	2,442,241	2,916,624

Principal Shareholders: Laurence A Tisch (11.88%); Preston R Tisch (11.88%)
No of Employees: 21,900

LOF PLASTICS INC

1150 Stephenson Hwy, Box 3230, Troy, MI 48007
Tel: (313) 583-2020
Telex: TWX 810 232 1640 lof trmi

Chairman: H M Selland (and President)
Senior Executive Officers: E W Ribolin (Executive VP Laminated Products Group), D R Allen (Executive VP Molded Products Group), D R Vosburg (VP Finance and Secretary), J R Saunders (VP Manufacturing Administration), J H McFarland (VP Corporate Development), W J Smallwood (VP Human Resources), D R Decker (VP Planning and Management Information Systems)

PRINCIPAL ACTIVITIES: Plastic products for a variety of applications including automotive components, radio and television components and laminates for furniture

Parent Company: Trinova Corporation
Principal Bank: Continental Illinois National Bank and Trust Company of Chicago
Financial Information:

	$'000
Sales revenues	200,000

No of Employees: 2,200

LOGAN, JONATHAN, INC

50 Terminal Road, Secaucus, NJ 07094
Tel: (201) 867-9350

Chairman: Richard J Schwartz (and Chief Executive Officer)
President: Ron Casolotti
Senior Executive Officers: David Keery (VP)

PRINCIPAL ACTIVITIES: Manufacture of clothing
Trade Names: United Merchants & Manufacturers Inc
Principal Bank: Citibank
Financial Information:

	$'000
Sales revenues	383,000

No of Employees: 2,000

LOGICON, INC

3701 Skypark Drive, Torrance, CA 90505
Tel: (213) 373-0220

President: John R Woodhull (and Chief Executive Officer)
Senior Executive Officers: James D Hogan (Senior VP Technical), Robert G Walden (Senior VP Finance and Administration), James P Brown (VP Corporate Development), Frank T Cummings (VP Strategic and Information Systems Division), E T Richmond (VP Operational Systems Division), Richard J McGrath (VP Tactical and Training Systems Division), Hugh E Beatty (VP Marketing), Donald L Farr (VP), Albert L Latter (VP President Research and Development Associates), Ralph L Webster (VP and Controller), James E Dalton (VP and President RDA Associates)

PRINCIPAL ACTIVITIES: Electronic equipment; high-technology electronics and services for industry and government
Principal Bank: First Interstate Bank
Financial Information:

	$'000
Sales revenues	168,000

No of Employees: 2,000

LOMAS & NETTLETON FINANCIAL CORPORATION

2001 Bryan Tower, Box 655644, Dallas, TX 75265
Tel: (214) 746-7111

Chairman: Jess T Hay (and Chief Executive Officer); Vice Chairman: Albert N Rohnstedt
President: Ted Enloe
Senior Executive Officers: Lanelle Latendresse (Executive VP), John F Sexton (Executive VP Finance), Gary White (Senior VP and Controller), Henry Hortenstine (Senior VP Data Services), Bradley S Buttermore (VP Controller), Ned R Harris (VP Insurance), Cloressa Hill (VP), M Robert Roofner (VP Taxes), James N Sabin (VP Legal), Charles Werner (VP Human Resources)

PRINCIPAL ACTIVITIES: Financial services
Principal Bank: Mercantile National Bank at Dallas
Financial Information:

	1986
	$'000
Revenues	420,000
Net income	54,000

No of Employees: 3,080

LONE STAR INDUSTRIES, INC

One Greenwich Plaza, Box 5050, Greenwich, CT 06836

Tel: (203) 661-3100

Chairman: James E Stewart (and Chief Executive Officer); Vice Chairman: Robert W Hutton (International Operations)

President: William M Troutman (and Chief Operating Officer)

Senior Executive Officers: Carmine J Muratore (Executive VP Staff), Jerome Bennett (Senior VP and Chief Financial Officer), Ronald L Blick (Senior VP Domestic Operations), John J Martin (Senior VP, General Counsel and Secretary), Allen R Potts (Senior VP, Chairman Southeast Region), James B Baines (VP, President Southeast Region), Roger J Campbell (VP Cement Operations), James T Cleven (VP Management Information Services), James T Davis (VP Real Estate Operations), Gordon A Fox (VP and Controller), Conrad J Gordon (VP and Controller), John J Graham (VP, President North Central Region), Joseph A Hogan (VP, President New York Trap Rock Corp), Gerald F Hyde (VP Personnel), Wallace G Irmscher (VP Sales), Dennis M Kash (VP Special Projects), Billy F Manning (VP, President Southwest Region), Michael W Puckett (VP Operations Control), F Eugene Purcell (VP Special Projects Division), M Michael Reid (VP Manufacturing and Construction Services), Usher T Winslett Jr (VP International Operations)

PRINCIPAL ACTIVITIES: Production of cement and building materials

Principal Bank: First City Bank Dallas

Financial Information:

	Dec 31 1985	Dec 31 1986
	$'000	$'000
Sales revenues	871,763	883,415
Net income	58,316	117,400
Earnings per share	$3.02	$7.01
Shareholders equity	558,147	631,900

No of Employees: 6,670

LONG ISLAND LIGHTING COMPANY

175 East Old Country Road, Hicksville, NY 11801

Tel: (516) 933-4590

Telefax: (516) 933-2760

Chairman: William J Catacosinos (and Chief Executive Officer)

President: Russell C Youngdahl (and Chief Operating Officer)

Senior Executive Officers: James W Dye Jr (Executive VP), Matthew C Cordaro (Senior VP, Operations and Engineering), Anthony F Earley Jr (General Counsel), George J Sideris (Senior VP Finance). Vice Presidents: Lynne D Abraham (Public Affairs), Ralph T Brandifino (Finance), James T Flynn (Fossil Production), Ira L Freilicher (Corporate Affairs), Robert X Kelleher (Human Resources), Jay R Kessler (Gas Operations), John D Leonard (Nuclear), Adam M Madsen (Corporate Planning), Brian R McCaffrey (Administration), William J Museler (Electric Operations), John J Russell (Community Affairs), John A Weismantle (Research, Development and Corporate Studies), Walter F Wilm Jr (Customer Relations), William G Schiffmacher (Engineering). John J Kearney Jr (Secretary), Herbert M Leiman (Assistant Secretary), Edward W Eacker (Treasurer), Michael Czumak (Controller), Francis M Walsh (General Claims Attorney), Arthur N Pietrow (Assistant VP, Computer Services), Stanley S Skorupski Jr (Assistant VP, Nuclear Operations)

PRINCIPAL ACTIVITIES: Supply of gas and electricity

Financial Information:

	Dec 31 1985	Dec 31 1986
	$'000	$'000
Sales revenues	2,050,340	1,977,121
Operating income	388,140	387,077
Net income	524,288	316,675
Income for common stock	440,563	236,864
Earnings per share	$3.97	$2.28
Common stock*	110,842	111,085

*average shares outstanding

No of Employees: 6,300

LONGACRE, HORACE W, INC

Route 113, Franconia, PA 18924
Tel: (215) 723-4335
Telex: TWX 510 661 6007 longacre frac

Chairman: Horace W Longacre
President: Kenneth A Longacre
Senior Executive Officers: Henry W Longacre (Senior VP), Paul L Seaman (Treasurer)

PRINCIPAL ACTIVITIES: Poultry processing
Financial Information:

	$'000
Sales revenues	120,000

No of Employees: 650

LONG-AIRDOX COMPANY

227 W Maple Avenue, PO Box 331, Oak Hill, WV 25901
Tel: (304) 469-3301
Telex: TWX 710 938 1632 LONGAROX OKHL

President: William E Meador
Senior Executive Officers: Carl L Remington (Executive VP-Administration), D C Torre (Senior VP-International), L E Harding (VP-Engineering)

PRINCIPAL ACTIVITIES: Manufacture and marketing of coal mining equipment. Major product lines are:- conveyors, belt and chain; continuous haulage systems for mining and tunnelling; feeders and feeder-breakers; drills-face and roof; personnel carriers; dusters; auger miners; LADCO compressed air systems to promote free flow of stored materials; AIRDOX ultra high pressure air blasting systems; carbide typped drilling and breaking tools
Trade Names: "Lo-Rope" Conveyor Structure, "Lo-Frame" Conveyor Structure, "Full Dimension Continuous Haulage Systems", LADCO Bulk Breaker Systems, ROSCO, RHINO and HIPPO Feeder-Breakers
Parent Company: The Marmon Group Inc
Financial Information:

	$'000
Sales revenues	50-75,000

No of Employees: 400-450

LONGS DRUGSTORES INC

141 N Civic Drive, PO Box 5222, Walnut Creek, CA 94596
Tel: (415) 937-1170

Chairman: J M Long
President: Robert M Long (and Chief Executive Officer)
Senior Executive Officers: R A Scott (Executive VP), R A Plomgren (Senior VP Development), S D Roath (Senior VP Marketing), D Madsen (VP Finance), L C Anderson (VP Personnel), M Baird (VP), R W Boyd (VP Professional Affairs), B M Brandon (VP), W G Combs (VP Administration and Treasurer), D G DeShane (VP), G A Duey (VP), D D England (VP), V H Howe (VP), O D Jones (VP Real Estate and Secretary), P E Paz (VP Merchandising and Sales Development), T R Sweeney (VP), R W Vienop (VP), D R Wilson (VP)

PRINCIPAL ACTIVITIES: Retail drugstores
Principal Bankers: Bank of America
Financial Information:

	Dec 31 1986
	$'000
Sales revenues	1,635,442
Net income	38,594
Earnings per share	$1.78
Shareholders equity	290,444

No of Employees: 12,000

LONGVIEW FIBRE CO

PO Box 639, Longview, WA 98632
Tel: (206) 425-1550
Telex: ESL550173 LGVWFIBER LGVW (Easy Link)

Chairman: R P Wollenberg (and President)
Senior Executive Officers: G E Schwartz (Executive VP), R E Wertheimer (Executive VP)

PRINCIPAL ACTIVITIES: Sale of logs and manufacturing kraft paper, containerboard, shipping containers and paper bags
Trade Names: Longfibre Kraft
Principal Bank: Rainier National Bank
Financial Information:

	Oct 31 1985	Oct 31 1986
	$'000	$'000
Sales revenues	459,058	487,685
Income before taxes	26,018	48,984
Net income	22,418	33,484
Dividends	14,212	15,543
Dividends per share	$1.28	$1.40
Earnings per share	$2.02	$3.02
Common stock	109,298	109,298
Retained income	158,492	176,433
Shareholders equity	215,815	233,711

No of Employees: 3,300

LONGYEAR COMPANY

925 Delaware Street SE, Minneapolis, MN 55414
Tel: (612) 331-1331
Telex: WUT 290331 longyr hqgq ur

President: Donald F Chisholm
Senior Executive Officers: C Lamorie (VP Finance), C J Bavage (VP), J J Doolin (VP), H Hansen (VP), V L Merriman (VP), P D Sears (VP)

PRINCIPAL ACTIVITIES: Mining services and equipment
Parent Company: Boart International Limited
Principal Bank: The First National Bank of Minneapolis
Financial Information:

	$'000
Sales revenues	134,000

No of Employees: 1,350

LORAIN PRODUCTS

1122 F Street, Lorain, OH 44052
Tel: (216) 288-1122
Telex: TWX 810 4262130 lorain prod

Senior Executive Officers: Walter M Miller (VP and General Manager)

PRINCIPAL ACTIVITIES: Telecommunications equipment
Parent Company: Reliance Electric Company
Financial Information:

	$'000
Sales revenues	100,000

No of Employees: 1,300

LORAL CORPORATION

600 Third Avenue, New York, NY 10016
Tel: (212) 697-1105
Telex: WUT 644 018 loral hq nyk

Chairman: Bernard L Schwartz (and Chief Executive Officer)

President: Frank C Lanza (and Chief Operating Officer)
Senior Executive Officers: Harry Emerzian (Group VP, Microwave-West Coast), Michael P DeBlasio (Senior VP, Finance), Robert W Clark (VP and President Loral Systems Group, Akron, OH), Jack Davis (VP and President, Loral Optical Systems), Stephen L Jackson (VP, Administration), Robert V LaPenta (VP and Controller), Arthur J O'Connor (VP, Corporate Communications), Michael B Targoff (VP, General Counsel and Secretary), Robert F Welte (VP, Yonkers, NY and President, Loral Electronic Systems), Lisa F Stein (Assistant Corporate Secretary), Gerard E Dorsey (Treasurer), Harold Penn (Assistant Treasurer), Bertram Bell (Assistant VP and Secretary and Counsel of Loral Systems Group)

PRINCIPAL ACTIVITIES: Defense electronic equipment; telecommunications equipment; warfare systems; systems and components for airborne and shipboard self protection, antisubmarine warfare, command, control and communications (C3), radar reconnaissance, simulation for military training
Principal Subsidiaries and Divisions: Loral Electronic Systems; Loral Defense Systems-Akron; Loral Defense Systems-Arizona; Loral Electro-Optical Systems; Rolm Mil-Spec Computers; Loral Randtron Systems; Loral Data Systems/Conic; Loral Instrumentation; Loral Information Display Systems; Loral Hycor; Narda Microwave-New York; Narda-Western Operations; Frequency Sources; Frequency West; Wavecom; Loral Aircraft Braking Systems; Loral Engineered Fabrics; Loral Terracom; Loral American Beryllium; Loral International
Principal Bank: Manufacturers Hanover Trust Company
Financial Information:

	Mar 31 1986	Mar 31 1987(1)
	$'000	$'000
Sales revenues	663,818	690,043
Income before taxes	91,218	98,728
Net income	52,993	57,460
Dividends	12,005	13,869
Dividends per share	$0.51	$0.58
Earnings per share(2)	$2.21	$2.35
Common stock	5,967	6,048
Retained income	315,183	367,808
Shareholders equity	309,346	362,899

(1) these figures do not reflect the acquisition of Goodyear Aerospace Corporation, completed March 13, 1987
(2) primary

No of Employees: 13,500

LORILLARD

666 5th Avenue, New York, NY 10103
Tel: (212) 841-8500
Telex: WUT 126258 lorillard nyk

President: J R Ave (and Chief Executive Officer)
Senior Executive Officers: Alexander W Spears (Executive VP Operations and Research), Richard H Orcutt (Senior VP Sales), Dewey R Tedder (Senior VP Leaf and Support Services), Arthur J Stevens (Senior VP and General Counsel), M A Peterson (Senior VP Financial Administration), Tom H Mau (Senior VP Advertising), Roger P Edwards (VP Manufacturing), Frederick J Schultz (VP Research and Development), Sara R Ridgway (VP Public Relations), J R Cherry (VP, Deputy General Counsel), J P Mastandrea (VP Sales), L Gordon (VP Trade Development)

PRINCIPAL ACTIVITIES: Tobacco products
Trade Names: Kent, Old Gold, True, Triumph, Newport, Max, Satin
Parent Company: Loew's Corporation, New York, NY
Financial Information:

	Dec 31 1986
	$'000
Sales revenues	1,567,882

No of Employees: 6,000

LORIMAR TELEPICTURES CORPORATION

3970 Overland Avenue, Culver City, CA 90232-3783
Tel: (213) 202-2000

Chairman: Merv Adelson (and Chief Executive Officer)
Office of the President: Michael Garin, Dick Robertson, David E Salzman, Michael Jay Solomon
Senior Executive Officers: J Anthony Young (Executive VP and Chief Financial Officer), Barbara S Brogliatti (Senior VP Worldwide Corporate Communications), Robert Giovannetone (Senior VP Corporate Financial Planning), Jerry Gottlieb (Senior VP), Art Loomis (Senior VP and Treasurer), Michael Meltzer (Senior VP and Controller), Stephen Ross (Senior VP and Legal Counsel), Mary McCarthy (Senior VP Corporate Development), Ellen Bailey (VP Public Affairs), Stephen Davidson (VP Corporate Finance), Burt Vaupen (VP Administration), Carol J Henry (VP Investor Relations), Marie McKellar (VP and Secretary)

PRINCIPAL ACTIVITIES: Production and distribution of TV movies, series and feature films
Principal Bank: City National Bank
Financial Information:

	1986
	$'000
Sales revenues	766,000
Net (loss)	(37,000)

No of Employees: 640

LOS ANGELES NUT HOUSE

737 Terminal Street, Los Angeles, CA 90021
Tel: (213) 623-2541

President: Edward Gendel
Senior Executive Officers: Burt Gold (VP Purchasing)

PRINCIPAL ACTIVITIES: Confectionery; fruit products; nuts and snack foods
Parent Company: MEI Corporation, Minneapolis, MN
Principal Bank: First Interstate Bank
Financial Information:

	$'000
Sales revenues	70,000

No of Employees: 350

LOS ANGELES TIMES

Times Mirror Square, Los Angeles, CA 90053
Tel: (213) 972-5000
Telex: ITT 472 0079 la times lsa

President: Donald F Wright (and Chief Operating Officer)
Senior Executive Officers: Tom Johnson (Publisher and Chief Executive Officer), William F Thomas (Editor and Executive VP), Vance Stickell (Executive VP Marketing), James D Boswell (VP Employee and Public Relations), Larry Strutton (VP Operations), James B Shaffer (VP and Chief Financial Officer), William A Niese (VP and General Counsel)

PRINCIPAL ACTIVITIES: Publishing of "The Los Angeles Times" Newspaper
Parent Company: The Times Mirror Company
Financial Information:

	$'000
Sales revenues	700,000

No of Employees: 8,000

LOTUS DEVELOPMENT CORPORATION

55 Cambridge Parkway, Cambridge, MA 02142
Tel: (615) 577 8500

Chairman: Jim P Manzi (and President and Chief Executive Officer)
Senior Executive Officers: Robert P Schechter (Senior VP Finance and Operations and Chief Financial Officer), Charles J Digate (Senior VP Analytic Software Group), Thomas Limberg (VP, Secretary and Legal Counsel), Stephen J Crummey (VP International Sales and Service), Michael E Kolowich (VP Graphics, Text and Information Management), Edward J Belove (VP Research and Development), Frank Ingari (VP Corporate Marketing and Business Development), David Tarrant (VP New Ventures), Harry Andersen (Controller)

PRINCIPAL ACTIVITIES: The Company and its subsidiaries are engaged primarily in the development, production and marketing of business productivity software and information services for personal computers
Principal Bank: State Street Bank & Trust Co
Financial Information:

	Dec 31 1986	Dec 31 1987
	$'000	$'000
Sales revenues	282,864	395,595
Income before taxes	71,030	102,918
Net income	48,300	72,043
Earnings per share	$1.03	$1.58
Common stock	526	546
Retained income	135,317	207,360
Shareholders equity	114,593	202,046

No of Employees: 900

LOU ANA FOODS, INC

PO Box 591, Opelousas, LA 70570
Tel: (318) 948-6561
Telex: WUT 586645 laf opls

Chairman: Theodore G Schad Jr (and President and Chief Executive Officer)
Senior Executive Officers: Donald W Haight (Executive VP), Warren D Barnes (VP Production), James W Boswell (VP Sales), Ray B Stroup Jr (VP Retail Sales), Don R Gulley (VP Distribution and Purchasing), Arthur K House (VP Commodity Operations), R Leon Ross (VP Food Services and Concession Sales)

PRINCIPAL ACTIVITIES: Refining of a range of vegetable oils
Parent Company: Lou Ana Industries Inc
Principal Bank: Continental Illinois National Bank and Trust Company
Financial Information:

	$'000
Sales revenues	100,000

No of Employees: 170

LOUISIANA GENERAL SERVICES INC

1233 Westbank Expressway, Harvey, LA 70058
Tel: (504) 367 7000

Chairman: James W Swenson (and President and Chief Executive Officer)
Senior Executive Officers: Richard A Faust Jr (VP, Legal Counsel and Secretary), Charles Fernandez Jr (VP Data Processing), David A Hanrath (VP Human Resources), Thomas O Porteous Jr (VP, Chief Financial Officer and Treasurer)

PRINCIPAL ACTIVITIES: Holding company with interests in the supply of natural gas; oil and gas exploration
Principal Subsidiaries: LGS Concord Corporation; LGS Exploration Inc; LGS Pipeline Inc; LGS Intrastate Inc; LGS Natural Gas Company; Louisiana Gas Service Company
Principal Bank: Hibernia National Bank
Financial Information:

	$'000
Sales revenues	176,000

No of Employees: 640

LOUISIANA LAND & EXPLORATION CO (THE)

PO Box 60350, New Orleans, LA 70160
Tel: (504) 566-6500
Telex: 584478

Chairman: E L Williamson (and Chief Executive Officer)
President: H L Steward (and Chief Operating Officer)
Senior Executive Officers: Richard A Bachmann (Executive VP Finance and Administration and Chief Financial Officer), Jack V Eumont (Senior VP), Donald P Mitchell (Senior VP), David E Sibley (Senior VP), John F Greene (Executive VP Exploration and Production)

PRINCIPAL ACTIVITIES: Exploration for and production of oil and gas
Principal Subsidiaries: Candex Development Ltd; CL & E Corporation; Jacintoport Corporation; Kalua Koi Corporation; LL & E Australia Inc (Australia); LL & E Canada Limited (Canada); LL & E Colombia Inc (Colombia); LL & E Egypt Inc (Egypt); LL & E Espana Inc (Spain); LL & E (Europe-Africa-Middle East) Inc; LL & E Inc; LL & E Indonesia (Cilacap) Inc (Indonesia); LL & E Indonesia (Southwest Java) Inc (Indonesia); LL & E International Inc; LL & E International Finance NV (Netherlands Antilles); LL & E Gas Marketing Inc; LL & E (Netherlands) Inc (Netherlands); LL & E Netherlands Petroleum Company (Netherlands); LL & E Overseas Petroleum Ltd; LL & E Peru Inc (Peru); LL & E Petroleum Marketing Inc; LL & E Petroleum Resources International Inc; LL & E Pipeline Corporation; LL & E Suez Inc; LL & E Trinidad (Block 1) Inc (Trinidad); LL & E Tunisia Inc (Tunisia); LL & E (UK) Inc (UK); Molakai California Ltd
Financial Information:

	Dec 31 1985	Dec 31 1986
	$'000	$'000
Sales revenues	1,147,100	779,100
(Loss) before taxes	(6,000)	(54,900)
Net income (loss)	10,400	(20,600)
Dividends	27,700	29,100
Dividends per share	$1.00	$1.00
Earnings (loss) per share	$0.38	($0.71)
Common stock	5,700	5,700
Additional paid in capital	66,200	40,700
Retained earnings	825,500	775,800
Less treasury stock	(330,900)	(218,100)
Total shareholders equity	566,500	604,100

No of Employees: 850

LOUISIANA-PACIFIC CORPORATION

111 S W Fifth Avenue, Portland, OR 97204
Tel: (503) 221-0800

Chairman: Harry A Merlo (and President)
Senior Executive Officers: Lee C Simpson (VP Operations), John C Hart (VP Finance and Treasurer), Robert D Becknal (Director, Taxes and Internal Audit), Robert E Erickson (Assistant Treasurer), Larry Campbell (Director, Corporate Communications), William L Hebert (Controller-Finance), Vern H Talcott (General Counsel), Dr C Edward Taylor (Corporate Energy and Environmental Manager), Randy E Vandehey (Controller-Operations), Montel W Work (Director, Aviation)

PRINCIPAL ACTIVITIES: Louisiana-Pacific's principal business is growing and harvesting trees and turning them into a variety of wood products including lumber, hardwood and softwood plywood, particleboard, hardboard, medium density fiberboard, Waferwood and mouldings, as well as pulp, paperboard and corrugated packaging. Manufacture of Pabco high temperature industrial insulation, Weather-Seal wood and aluminum windows and doors and printing plates. Products are used throughout the world in home-building, manufacturing and other commercial and industrial activities
Trade Names: Waferwood, Pabco, Weather-Seal
Principal Subsidiaries: Fibreboard Corporation; Louisiana-Pacific International Inc. Divisions: Western Division; Container Products Division; Northern Division; Ketchikan Division;

Northstar Division; Pabco Insulation Division; Southern Division; Weather-Seal Division

Financial Information:

	Dec 31 1985	Dec 31 1986
	$'000	$'000
Sales revenues	1,260,920	1,506,200
Net income	25,500	64,910
Earnings per share	$0.70	$1.77
Shareholders equity	775,290	944,220

No of Employees: 13,000

LOUISVILLE BEDDING CO

10400 Bunsen Way, Louisville, KY 40299
Tel: (502) 491-3370
Telex: WUT 213 293 lvlbedco lvl

Chairman: Jas R Hartsock
President: John M Minihan (and Chief Executive Officer)
Senior Executive Officers: Kenneth A King (Executive VP), Charles J Lohman (Senior VP), Frank A Preston (VP), Christian F Rapp (VP Finance and Secretary and Treasurer), Ronald Benson (VP)

PRINCIPAL ACTIVITIES: Textiles for household use
Trade Names: Louisville Bedding Co, Reed Handicrafts, Quiltcraft
Principal Bank: Liberty National Bank and Trust Company
Financial Information:

	Sep 30 1985	Sep 30 1986
	$'000	$'000
Sales revenues	66,121	65,095
Income before taxes	1,717	1,438
Net income	856	713
Dividends	372	372
Dividends per share	$0.60	$0.60
Earnings per share	$1.38	$1.15
Common stock	620	620
Retained income	7,014	7,355
Shareholders equity	10,304	10,644

No of Employees: 883

LOUISVILLE GAS & ELECTRIC CO

PO Box 32010, Louisville, KY 4032
Tel: (502) 566-4011

President: Robert L Royer (and Chief Executive Officer)
Senior Executive Officers: Peter Ronald (Senior VP Finance), William W Hancock (Senior VP Administration and Secretary), Robert C Somers (Senior VP Operations), John Hart Jr (VP Rates and Economic Research), Plummer C Smither Jr (VP Human Resources), C G Uligian (VP Management Services), Frank L Wilkerson (VP Corporate Planning and Accounting), Fred Wright (VP Customer Affairs)

PRINCIPAL ACTIVITIES: Distribution of electricity and natural gas
Principal Bankers: Citizens Fidelity Bank & Trust Co
Financial Information:

	Dec 31 1986
	$'000
Sales revenues	660,000
Net income	64,000

No of Employees: 3,700

LOUVERDRAPE, INC

1100 Colorado Avenue, Santa Monica, CA 90401
Tel: (213) 450-6100
Telex: TWX 910 343 6446 louvrdrap nrcs

President: J R Leth (and General Manager)
Senior Executive Officers: William L Skinner (VP Sales), George Ebert (VP Materials), Ernie Kochis (VP Manufacturing), Richard Bissell (VP Marketing)

PRINCIPAL ACTIVITIES: Manufacture of window blinds, folding doors
Parent Company: Beatrice Companies Inc, Chicago, IL
Principal Bank: First National Bank of Chicago
Financial Information:

	$'000
Sales revenues	60,000

No of Employees: 650

LOWES COMPANIES INC

PO Box 1111, North Wilkesboro, NC 28656
Tel: (919) 651-4000
Telex: (919) 651-4766

Chairman: Robert L Strickland
President: Leonard G Herring (and Chief Executive Officer)
Senior Executive Officers: Dwight E Pardue (Senior Executive VP-Real Estate), Wendell R Emerine (Executive VP), Harry B Underwood II (Senior VP-Finance, Chief Financial Officer and Treasurer)

PRINCIPAL ACTIVITIES: Wholesale and retail trade in building materials, plumbing supplies, hardware, electrical goods and floor coverings
Principal Bank: First Union National Bank
Financial Information:

	Jan 31 1986	Jan 31 1987
	$'000	$'000
Sales revenues	2,072,569	2,283,480
Net income	59,714	52,219
Earnings per share	$1.64	$1.34
Shareholders equity	407,373	540,534

No of Employees: 14,783

LOWY ENTERPRISES

4001 N King Hwy, St Louis, MO 63115
Tel: (314) 383-2055

Chairman: Steve Lowy (and President and Chief Executive Officer)
Senior Executive Officers: Norman Gibbs (Executive VP), Frank Schveninger (Vice President), Frank Klaus (Comptroller)

PRINCIPAL ACTIVITIES: Floor covering products
Principal Subsidiaries: Blue Ridge Carpet Mills Flooring Distributors
Principal Banks: The Boatmen's National Bank of St Louis; Centerre Bank, St Louis; C+S Bank, Atlanta
Financial Information:

	Jun 30 1986	Jun 30 1987
	$'000	$'000
Sales revenues	63,218	68,000
Income before taxes	1,800	2,950
Net income	724	1,600
Earnings per share	$2.50	$6.03
Common stock	291	265
Retained income	14,267	16,600
Shareholders equity	17,309	19,100

Principal Shareholders: Steve Lowy
No of Employees: 450

LOZIER CORPORATION

4401 N 21st Street, Omaha, NE 68110
Tel: (402) 541-5000

Chairman: Allan G Lozier
President: Lee E Shultz
Senior Executive Officers: Wayne Moeller (VP Marketing and Sales), James E Sedlacek (VP Production), Dennis Monaghan (VP Administration)

PRINCIPAL ACTIVITIES: Store shelving and fittings
Principal Bank: Omaha National Bank

Financial Information:

	$'000
Sales revenues	100,000

No of Employees: 200

LSB INDUSTRIES, INC

16 S Penn, Oklahoma City, OK 73107
Tel: (405) 235-4546
Telex: ITT 747-157
Fax: (405) 235-5067

Chairman: Jack E Golsen (and President)
Senior Executive Officers: David R Goss (Senior VP Operations), Tony M Shelby (Senior VP Finance), Irwin H Steinhorn (Senior VP and General Counsel), Jim D Jones (VP and Controller)

PRINCIPAL ACTIVITIES: (1) Manufacture and sale of air handling and heat pump products for use in commercial and residential air conditioning and heating systems. (2) Manufacture and sale of chemical products and (3) Industrial products, including bearings and machine tools
Principal Subsidiaries: L & S Bearing Co; Techniform Corp; Summit Machine Tool Manufacturing Corp; Hart Industrial Supply Co; Hercules Energy Manufacturing Corp; California Heat Pump Co; International Environmental Manufacturing Co; Friedrich Climate Master Inc; El-Dorado Chemical Co; Summit Machinery Co
Principal Banks: Philadelphia National; Wells Fargo
Financial Information:

	Dec 31 1985	Dec 31 1986
	$'000	$'000
Sales revenues	149,439	169,057
Net income (loss)	(16,629)	2,837
Earnings (loss) per share	($3.37)	$0.47
Shareholders equity	6,031	26,383

No of Employees: 1,300

LSI LOGIC CORPORATION

1551 McCarthy Blvd, Milpitas, CA 95035
Tel: (408) 433-8000
Telex: WUT 171641 lsi log mpts

Chairman: Wilfred J Corrigan (and Chief Executive Officer)
President: George Wells (and Chief Operating Officer)
Senior Executive Officers: Robert N Blair (President, LSI Logic Europe Limited), Mitchell D Bohn (President, LSI Logic Corporation of Canada, Inc), Keiske K Yawata (President, LSI Logic KK), William J O'Meara (VP, Chief Marketing Officer), Robert M Walker (VP, Chief Engineering Officer), Murray L McLachlan (VP, Chief Development Officer), D Scott Mercer (VP, Chief Financial Officer), Norman W Chanoski (VP, R & QA/Military Operations), Perry G Constantine (VP, Marketing, LSI Logic Corporation of Canada, Inc), Conrad J Dell'Oca (VP, Research and Development), Bruce L Entin (VP Corporate Communications), Raymond M Fritz (VP and Controller), Cyril F Hannon (VP, Components and Technology), James S Koford (VP, Software and Computer Services), Ven L Lee (VP, Engineering Services), Keith R Lobo (VP, Advanced Silicon and Software Products), Lewis C Wallbridge (VP, Industrial Relations), A Travis White (VP, Assembly, Test and Packaging), Joseph M Zelayeta (VP, Wafer Manufacturing Operations)

PRINCIPAL ACTIVITIES: LSI Logic Corporation is the leading designer and manufacturer of HCMOS application-specific integrated circuits (ASIC). Using proprietary software, customers computer-customize ASICs for unique applications in the fields of electronic data processing military/aerospace and telecommunications as well as other emerging industries. HCMOS is a high performance processing technology involving complementary metal oxide semiconductors
Trade Names: Registered Trademark (R): LDS. Trademarks (TM): ASMC, Application Specific Module Compiler, bASIC, bASIC Capture, bASIC Designer, BSIM, Channel-Free, Compacted Array, Custom Structured Array, FSIM, Gigacell, LDEL, LDIS, Logic Integrator, LSIM, LSED, LVER, MACGEN, MDE, Megacell Compiler, Micro Array, Micro bASIC, Modular Design Environment, MSIM, RAMGEN, ROMGEN, Silicon Integrator, Structured Array, Structured Cell, System Integrator, ZSIM
Principal Subsidiaries: Affiliated Companies: LSI Logic Europe Limited (UK); LSI Logic KK (Japan); LSI Logic Corporation (Canada)
Principal Bank: Bank of America
Financial Information:

	Dec 31 1985	Dec 31 1986
	$'000	$'000
Sales revenues	140,000	194,300
Income before taxes	15,386	8,535
Net income	10,114	3,855
Earnings per share	$0.26	$0.10
Common stock	191,759	196,380
Retained income	32,444	36,299
Shareholders equity	372,456	451,404

No of Employees: 2,125

LSI-CERTIFIED BRAKES

Stewarts Lane, Danville, KY 40422
Tel: (606) 236-8224

President: J R Schmeltzer
Senior Executive Officers: D White (VP Finance), E Riftshmiter (VP Marketing), R Weishart (VP Operations)

PRINCIPAL ACTIVITIES: Production of motor vehicle components
Parent Company: Lear Siegler Inc
Financial Information:

	$'000
Sales revenues	60,000

No of Employees: 800

LTV AEROSPACE & DEFENSE CO

Box 225907, Dallas, TX 75265
Tel: (214) 266-2011

President: Robert L Kirk (and Chief Executive Officer)
Senior Executive Officers: Ed F Cvetko (Senior VP), P A Greco (Senior VP), Robert N Parker (Senior VP), Billie M Smith (Senior VP), John J Welch (Senior VP), Robert B Corlett (VP Human Resources), H M Fish (VP International), D R Hagler (VP and Group Counsel), Jay E Hawley (VP Finance)

PRINCIPAL ACTIVITIES: Aerospace equipment and components including commercial and military aircraft, missiles and launch vehicles for the space program
Parent Company: LTV Corporation, Dallas, TX
Financial Information:

	$'000
Sales revenues	700,000

No of Employees: 10,000

LTV CORPORATION (THE)

2001 Ross Avenue, Box 225003, Dallas, TX 75265-5003
Tel: (214) 746-7711

Chairman: Raymond A Hay (and Chief Executive Officer)
Senior Executive Officers: James J Paulos (Executive VP), G Emmett Smith (Senior VP, General Counsel and Secretary), Julian Scheer (Senior VP-Corporate Affairs), Walter E Meyer (Senior VP-Personnel), James F Powers (Senior VP-Chief Financial Officer), Sheldon M Lambert (Senior VP-Corporate Planning), Lee A Drake (Group VP, President and Chief Executive LTV Energy Products Company), David H Hoag (Group VP, President and Chief Executive LTV Steel Company, Inc), Robert L Kirk (Group VP, President and Chief Executive LTV Aerospace and Defense Company), Robert L Guyett (VP and Controller), John W Johnson (VP-Advertising), John K Meagher (VP-Government Relations)

PRINCIPAL ACTIVITIES: The LTV Corporation is a diversified operating company involved in steel, aerospace/defense and energy products. The company is a primary supplier of steel products to the automotive, appliance and construction industries; missiles, aircraft components, tactical wheeled vehicles and electronics to the defense and commercial aerospace markets; and tubular products, oil field supplies and drilling and production equipment to the petroleum industry
Principal Subsidiaries: LTV Steel Company; LTV Aerospace and Defense Company; LTV Energy Products Company
Principal Bank: Mellon Bank
Financial Information:

	Dec 31 1985 $'000	Dec 31 1986 $'000
Sales revenues	8,198,800	7,271,400
(Loss) before taxes	(769,700)	(3,251,600)
(Loss) per share net	($8.94)	($35.41)
Shareholders equity (deficit)	652,200	(2,558,900)

No of Employees: 56,800

LTX CORPORATION

LTX Park at University Avenue, Westwood, MA 02090
Tel: (617) 329-7550
Telex: TWX 710 348 6626 csupt wood

Chairman: Graham C C Miller (and President)
Senior Executive Officers: Roger W Blethen (VP Sales and Support), Richard Boltrus (VP Operations), James Healy (VP), John Arcari (Chief Financial Officer)

PRINCIPAL ACTIVITIES: Manufacture of electronic testing equipment
Principal Subsidiaries: Trillium Corporation; LTX Japan Co Ltd; LTX (Europe) Ltd
Principal Bank: State Street Bank and Trust Company
Financial Information:

	Jul 31 1986 $'000
Sales revenues	95,400
(Loss) before taxes	(18,873)
Net (loss)	(12,662)
(Loss) per share	($1.40)
Stock	467
Paid in capital	48,707
Retained income	9,888
Shareholders equity	58,595

No of Employees: 1,120

LUBRIZOL CORPORATION

29400 Lakeland Blvd, Wickliffe, OH 44092
Tel: (216) 943-4200
Telex: ITT 4332033 hubrizol wick

Chairman: Lester E Coleman (and Chief Executive Officer)
President: W G Bares
Senior Executive Officers: Philip L Krug (Executive VP), Roger Y Hsu (Senior VP Law), W D Manning (Senior VP Sales and Marketing), R W Scher (Senior VP Manufacturing), W A Snell (Senior VP Sales), W T Beargie (Group VP Finance), Jean-Pol Arzul (VP), G R Hill (VP Research and Development), D L Murfin (VP), Douglas W Richardson (VP)

PRINCIPAL ACTIVITIES: Specialty chemicals including fuel additives and industrial chemicals
Principal Bank: National City Bank
Financial Information:

	Dec 31 1985 $'000	Dec 31 1986 $'000
Sales revenues	903,403	976,780
Net income	60,224	78,185
Earnings per share	$1.49	$1.97
Shareholders equity	519,300	572,679

No of Employees: 5,200

LUBY'S CAFETERIAS INC

2211 Northeast Loop 410, PO Box 33069, San Antonio, TX 78265
Tel: (512) 654 9000

Chairman: George H Wenglein
President: John B Lahourcade (and Chief Executive Officer)
Senior Executive Officers: Ralph Erben (Executive VP and Chief Operating Officer), Alvin B Beal (Senior VP Property Development), Herbert D Knight (Senior VP Unit Operations), John E Curtis Jr (VP and Controller), Dawes Bodell (VP and Treasurer), William E Robson (VP Food Services), Vernon E Schrader (VP Marketing), Don M Goudge (VP Equipment), Paul H Gowen (VP Construction), Davis W Simpson (VP Management Personnel), James R Hale (Secretary)

PRINCIPAL ACTIVITIES: Restaurants and catering
Principal Bank: InterFirst Bank San Antonio
Financial Information:

	1986 $'000
Sales revenues	215,000
Net income	22,000

No of Employees: 5,930

LUCKY STORES INC

6300 Clark Avenue, Dublin, CA 94568
Tel: (415) 833-6000

Chairman: John M Lillie
President: Lawrence A Del Santo (and Chief Executive Officer)
Senior Executive Officers: Edgar H Grubb (Senior VP and Chief Financial Officer), Leon Roush (Senior VP)

PRINCIPAL ACTIVITIES: Operation of a chain of retail food stores
Trade Names: Lucky, Kash N'Karry
Principal Bank: Bank of America
Financial Information:

	Jan 31 1986 $'000	Jan 31 1987 $'000
Sales revenues	9,382,280	6,440,871
Income before taxes	148,061	101,791
Net income	86,526	225,940
Dividends	59,130	44,671
Dividends per share	$1.16	$0.87
Earnings per share	$1.67	$4.47*
Common stock	261,821	2,903
Retained income	374,541	269,186
Shareholders equity	636,362	272,089

*continuing operations $0.97

No of Employees: 64,000

LUDLOW CORPORATION

2 Tyco Park, Exeter, NH. 03833
Tel: (603) 778-1500
Telefax: (603) 778-9151

President: John C Armacost
Senior Executive Officers: Dale B Smith (VP Finance and Chief Financial Officer), G Kevin Hynes (VP Marketing and Business Development), Fred Florio (VP Industrial Relations), William King (VP Manufacturing)

PRINCIPAL ACTIVITIES: Manufacture of specialty papers and packaging materials
Parent Company: Tyco Laboratories Inc, Exeter, NH
Principal Divisions: Laminating and Coating Division (Homer, LA); Flexible Packaging Division (Mt Vernon, OH); Technical Papers Division (Chicopee, MA and W Springfield, MA); Twitchell (Dothan, AL); Accurate Forming (Hamburg, NJ)
Principal Bank: Mellon Bank

Financial Information:

	May 31 1986	May 31 1987
	$'000	$'000
Sales revenues	171,041	172,822
Income before taxes	19,783	13,098
Net income	10,470	8,506
Common stock	22,774	22,090
Retained income	41,182	51,171
Shareholders equity	75,440	85,246

No of Employees: 1,600

LUFKIN INDUSTRIES, INC

601 S Raquet, Lufkin, TX 75902

Tel: (409) 637-5555

Telex: TWX 910 880 4201 lufkinind lufn

President: F B Stevenson (and Chief Executive Officer)

Senior Executive Officers: H J Green (VP), J R Partridge (VP), E G Pittman (VP), J E Riggs (VP), W W Trout Jr (VP), M A Penn (VP), C J Haley Jr (Secretary and Treasurer)

PRINCIPAL ACTIVITIES: Oil and gas services and equipment

Principal Bank: First City National Bank of Lufkin

Financial Information:

	$'000
Sales revenues	242,000

No of Employees: 2,600

LUKENS INC

50 South First Avenue, Coatesville, PA 19320

Tel: (215) 383-2000

Telefax: (215) 383-2616

Chairman: Frederick M Myers

President: W R Wilson (and Chief Executive Officer)

Senior Executive Officers: Arthur H Aronson (Senior VP; President and Chief Operating Officer, Lukens Steel Company Division), John R Bartholdson (Senior VP-Finance, Lukens Inc), Albert W Eastburn Jr (Senior VP-Manufacturing Services and Planning, Lukens Inc), Dennis M Oates (VP and Controller, Lukens Inc), James F Mulligan (VP-Law and Corporate Affairs, Corporate Secretary, Lukens Inc), Fred G Peil (VP; President of Flex-O-Lite Inc), Robert Schaal (VP; Products Group)

PRINCIPAL ACTIVITIES: Lukens, Inc provides diverse products and services to the industrial, energy, transportation, construction and defense markets. Lukens' companies supply plate steel and plate products, materials-handling equipment and supplies, glass beads and highway safety products, pipe-coating and cathodic protection services and specialized railway truck engineering services

Trade Names: Lukens Steel Company, Canadian Lukens, ENCOAT, Flex-O-Lite, Cathodic Protection Services, GSI Engineering, Gruendler Crusher, Ludlow-Saylor, Simplicity Engineering

Principal Subsidiaries: Lukens Steel Company; Flex-O-Lite Inc ; Lukens Development Company; CSI Engineering; Canadian Lukens Limited

Principal Banks: Provident National Bank-Philadelphia; Pittsburgh National Bank-Pittsburgh; Philadelphia National Bank-Philadelphia; Marine Midland Bank-New York, NY

Financial Information:

	Dec 28 1985	Dec 27 1986
	$'000	$'000
Sales revenues	422,480	405,297
Income (loss) before taxes	(9,515)	18,130
Net income (loss)	(4,189)	8,774
Dividends	2,450	2,429
Dividends per share	$0.48	$0.48
Earnings (loss) per share	$(0.82)	$1.72
Common stock	3,180	3,455
Earnings invested	119,606	125,951
Shareholders equity	115,190	129,428

No of Employees: 3,570

LUMEX INC

100 Spence Street, Bay Shore, NY 11706

Tel: (516) 273 2200

Chairman: Charles E Murcott (and President)

Senior Executive Officers: Laurence N Cohen (VP and Division President), David Hillery (VP and Division President), Robert McNally (VP Finance, Secretary and Treasurer)

PRINCIPAL ACTIVITIES: Medical equipment for physical rehabilitation, sports medicine, physical fitness, patient and geriatric care

Principal Bank: Citibank

Financial Information:

	$'000
Sales revenues	58,470

No of Employees: 960

LUNDY ELECTRONICS AND SYSTEMS INC

1 Robert Lane, Glen Head, NY 11545

Tel: (516) 671 9000

President: Edward J Mulvey (and Chief Executive Officer)

Senior Executive Officers: David Seltzer (Executive VP and Treasurer), Morgan E Death (VP), Joseph E Duquette (VP), James E Henning (VP), Robert M Tripp (VP), Rose Clayton (Secretary)

PRINCIPAL ACTIVITIES: Data processing equipment

Principal Bank: Barclays Bank of New York

Financial Information:

	$'000
Sales revenues	43,000.

No of Employees: 600

LUNKENHEIMER CO

Beekman Street & Waverly Avenue, Cincinnati, OH 45214

Tel: (513) 244 5230

Telex: WUT 214471 lunken cin

President: J S Mikovich (and General Manager)

Senior Executive Officers: David Hunter (Executive VP Marketing), James Sheline (Executive VP), Ronald Pandolfi (VP New Product Development)

PRINCIPAL ACTIVITIES: Manufacture of industrial valves

Parent Company: Condec Corporation

Financial Information:

	$'000
Sales revenues	60,000

No of Employees: 700

LURIA, L, AND SON, INC

5770 Miami Lakes Drive, Miami Lakes, FL 33014

Tel: (305) 557 9000

Telex: 6811378

Telefax: (305) 825-3711

Chairman: Leonard Luria (and President, Chief Executive Officer and Treasurer)

Senior Executive Officers: Peter P Luria (Executive VP), John M Mann (VP Finance and Chief Financial Officer), Gloria Luria (Secretary), Henry S Luria (VP Corporate Development), Gary Y Holtzman (Senior VP of Store Operations), Neil Mergler (VP Advertising and Marketing), Joan Reece (VP Jewelry Merchandising), Jeffrey Bayer (VP General Merchandise), Russell Hutchings (VP Real Estate)

PRINCIPAL ACTIVITIES: L Luria & Son Inc is Florida's, as well as one of the nation's leading specialty retailers. The Company currently operates thirty-nine stores within the Florida retail market, each offering a wide assortment of quality jewelry and nationally advertised brand name giftware, housewares and electronics
Trade Names: Luria's
Principal Bank: The Citizens & Southern National Bank of Ft Lauderdale
Financial Information:

	Feb 1 1986	Jan 31 1987
	$'000	$'000
Sales revenues	108,591	172,379
Income before taxes	8,625	7,919
Net income	4,578	4,580
Earnings per share	$0.84	$0.83
Common stock	55	36
Retained income	38,769	43,349
Shareholders equity	57,296	61,994

No of Employees: 2,260

LUSKIN'S INC
7540 Washington Boulevard, Baltimore, MD 21227
Tel: (301) 799 9000

Chairman: Jack Luskin (and Chief Executive Officer)
President: Cary A Luskin (and Chief Operating Officer)
Senior Executive Officers: Kevin E Luskin (VP and Secretary), William F Love Jr (Treasurer)

PRINCIPAL ACTIVITIES: Retail of domestic electrical appliances, televisions and audio equipment
Principal Bank: Maryland National Bank
Financial Information:

	$'000
Sales revenues	109,830

No of Employees: 500

LYDALL, INC
One Colonial Road, Manchester, CT 06040
Tel: (203) 646-1233
Telex: TWX 710 427 2654 lydall manh

Chairman: Millard H Pryor Jr
President: David W Clark Jr
Senior Executive Officers: John E Sundman (VP Finance and Treasurer), Richard C Conner (VP), Leonard R Jaskol (VP), Carole F Butenas (Secretary)

PRINCIPAL ACTIVITIES: Manufacture of specialty fiber materials and engineered and fiber components
Principal Bank: Connecticut National Bank and Trust Company
Financial Information:

	Dec 31 1985	Dec 31 1986
	$'000	$'000
Sales revenues	104,645	113,183
Income before taxes	7,057	3,502
Net income	4,205	2,499
Earnings per share	$1.45	$0.87
Retained income	25,718	28,084
Shareholders equity	38,636	39,496

No of Employees: 1,160

LYNCH COMMUNICATION SYSTEMS INC
204 Edison Way, Reno, NV 89520
Tel: (702) 786-4020

Chairman: E F Dertinger (and Chief Executive Officer)
President: James H Vogt (and Chief Operating Officer)
Senior Executive Officers: R S Boreri (VP), James B Sanders (VP, Secretary and Treasurer)

PRINCIPAL ACTIVITIES: Telecommunications apparatus
Principal Subsidiaries: Lynch/Reno Transcom Electronics Inc; Transcom Electronics Manufacturing Ltd (Canada); Lynch Circuits Inc
Principal Bank: The Bank of California
Financial Information:

	$'000
Sales revenues	58,770

No of Employees: 1,140

LYNDEN, INC
PO Box 3757, Seattle, WA 98124
Tel: (206) 241-8778
Telex: 882805 LYNDEN UD

Chairman: Henry Jansen
President: James H Jansen
Senior Executive Officers: Richard A Korpela (Senior VP, Secretary and Treasurer)

PRINCIPAL ACTIVITIES: Trucking services; interests in barge transportation
Principal Subsidiaries: Lynden Transport, Inc; LTI, Inc; Lynden Air Freight, Inc; Alaska Marine Lines, Inc; Alaska West Express, Inc; Knik Construction Co, Inc; Dairy Express, Inc; Bering Marine Corporation; Bowhead Equipment Company
Principal Bank: Rainier National Bank
Financial Information:

	Dec 31 1985	Dec 31 1986
	$'000	$'000
Sales revenues	109,667	116,851
Income before taxes	3,783	1,407
Net income	2,318	788
Earnings per share	$1.92	$0.68
Common stock	1,210	1,163
Retained income	31,207	31,995
Shareholders equity	33,289	34,077

No of Employees: 811

LYNES INC
8787 Tally Ho Street, Houston, TX 77061
Tel: (713) 943-0170
Telex: WUI 6868052 lynes mfg hou

President: J T Lembcke
Senior Executive Officers: D E Farmer (VP Engineering), D A Lawson (VP Marketing), W A Guthrie (VP Finance)

PRINCIPAL ACTIVITIES: Oil field machinery and equipment
Parent Company: Baker International Corporation, Orange, CA
Principal Bank: Texas Commerce Bank
Financial Information:

	$'000
Sales revenues	55,000

No of Employees: 850

LYON METAL PRODUCTS, INC
PO Box 671, Aurora, IL 60507
Tel: (312) 892-8941

Chairman: R P Washington (and Chief Executive Officer)
President: B K Chamberlain (and Chief Operating Officer)
Senior Executive Officers: W G Gosselin (Executive VP), D E Anderson (VP Human Resources), James T Lindstrom (Director Communications)

PRINCIPAL ACTIVITIES: Metal shelves, store fittings and furniture
Principal Bank: The Merchants National Bank of Aurora

Financial Information:

	$'000
Sales revenues	59,000

No of Employees: 600

LYPHOMED INC

2020 Ruby Street, Melrose Park, IL 60160
Tel: (312) 345 6170

Chairman: John N Kapoor (and President and Chief Executive Officer)
Senior Executive Officers: Richard R Wieland (Senior VP, Chief Financial Officer, Secretary and Treasurer), Charles S J Insalaco (VP Operations), Robert J Sullivan (Controller, Assistant Secretary and Assistant Treasurer), Jeffrey M Yordon (VP Sales and Marketing), Neil Surwara (VP Functional Area)

PRINCIPAL ACTIVITIES: Manufacture of pharmaceuticals for critical care
Principal Bank: Harris Trust & Savings Bank
Financial Information:

	Dec 31 1986
	$'000
Sales revenues	129,000
Net income	16,000

No of Employees: 450

M A HANNA COMPANY

See HANNA, M A, COMPANY

M/A-COM INC

7 New England Executive Park, Burlington, MA 01803
Tel: (617) 272-9600

Chairman: Irving J Helman; Vice Chairmen: John Puente (and Executive VP), Frank Drendel (and Executive VP)
Senior Executive Officers: Frank Brand (Executive VP, Chief Executive and Chief Operating Officer), Thomas F Burke (Executive VP Finance, Secretary and Treasurer), Hugh E Bradshaw (Senior VP), Joseph C Bothwell Jr (Senior VP), James F Bunker (Senior VP)

PRINCIPAL ACTIVITIES: Manufacture of electronic equipment including communications equipment, microwave equipment, semi-conductors and integrated circuits
Principal Bank: The First National Bank of Boston
Financial Information:

	Sep 30 1986
	$'000
Sales revenues	886,132
Net income	8,800
Earnings per share	$0.20
Shareholders equity	453,853

No of Employees: 11,800

M&T CHEMICALS INC

One Woodbridge Center, Woodbridge, NJ 07095
Tel: (201) 499-0200
Cable: MANTCHEMS-RAILWAY, NJ
Telex: 642-853 mt chem hq ud

Chairman: M S Maunoury
President: M S Bass (and Chief Executive Officer)
Senior Executive Officers: J G Kaplan (Executive VP Operations and Chief Operating Officer), B B Stranz (Senior VP Development), W H Brewster (VP), A P Deluca (VP), D R Hanlon (VP), W M Kraus (VP), J de Boer (VP), Gordon Andrews (VP), M M Besso (VP), P C Chapin (VP and General Manager), J D Litow (VP and Controller)

PRINCIPAL ACTIVITIES: Production of industrial chemicals
Trade Names: BioMet, Certincoat, Durastrength, Photomet, Metclad, Thermoguard, Thermolite, Ultrox
Parent Company: Elf Aquitaine
Principal Subsidiaries: M&T Chemicals Pty Ltd (Australia); M&T Produtos Quimicos Ltda (Brazil); M&T Chemicals Ltd (Canada); M&T Waldberg SA (France); M&T Chimie SA (France); M&T Industries Ltd (Hong Kong); M&T Japan Ltd (Japan); M&T Chemicals BV (Netherlands); M&T Chemicals Ltd (New Zealand); M&T Chemicals Ltd (UK); M&T Chemicals GmbH (Germany)
Financial Information:

	$'000
Sales revenues	283,000

No of Employees: 1,700

MAC ARTHUR CO

2400 Wycliff Street, St Paul, MN 55114
Tel: (612) 646-2773

Chairman: Richard C Lockwood (and Chief Executive Officer); Chairman of Executive Committee: John G Ordway
President: Jerry S Szeicbat
Senior Executive Officers: Clyde A Rhodes Jr (VP Finance), Richard G Stahl (Secretary and Treasurer)

PRINCIPAL ACTIVITIES: Manufacture of insulation materials for the building industry
Principal Bank: First Security Bank
Financial Information:

	$'000
Sales revenues	85,000

No of Employees: 270

MAC TOOLS, INC

PO Box 370, Washington C H, OH 43160
Tel: (614) 335-4112

President: John E Campbell (and General Manager)
Senior Executive Officers: Bill Robertson (VP Sales), David Gamble (VP Marketing), Ken Holliday (VP Manufacturing), Ken Allen (VP Engineering), Matthew Bronson (Controller)

PRINCIPAL ACTIVITIES: Manufacture of mechanics' tools for the aircraft and motor vehicle industries
Parent Company: Stanley Works, New Britain, CT
Principal Bank: The Huntington National Bank of Columbus

No of Employees: 1,500

MACANDREWS & FORBES GROUP, INC

36 East 63rd Street, New York, NY 10021
Tel: (212) 688-9000

Chairman: Ronald O Perelman (and Chief Executive Officer); Vice Chairman: Howard Gittis
President: Bruce Slovin
Senior Executive Officers: Robert T Carlton (Senior Executive VP and Chief Financial Officer), Meyer Laskin (Executive VP), Norman J Ginstling (VP), Frederick W McNabb Jr (VP and Secretary), Carl T Tsang (VP and Controller)

PRINCIPAL ACTIVITIES: Manufacture and sale of jewelry and confectionery; motion picture production; processing of film
Principal Subsidiaries: MacAndrews & Forbes Co; Wilbur Chocolate Co Inc; Technicolor Inc
Principal Bank: Chase Manhattan Bank NA
Financial Information:

	$'000
Sales revenues	340,000

No of Employees: 2,250

MACDERMID INC

50 Brookside Road, Waterbury, CT 06708
Tel: (203) 575-5700

Chairman: Harold Leever
President: Arthur J Lovetere (and Treasurer and Chief Executive Officer)

Senior Executive Officers: Charles T Cobb (Executive VP Electronics), John J Grunwald (VP Research), William P Innes (VP Metal Finishing), Carl E Landon (VP Administration), William T Lee (VP European Operations), Donald J Montfort (VP Metal Finishing Sales), Reginald H Post (VP Manufacturing), Michael A Pfaff (VP Electronics)

PRINCIPAL ACTIVITIES: Manufacture of chemicals for industrial machinery
Principal Bank: Colonial Bank and Trust
Financial Information:

	$'000
Sales revenues	95,000

No of Employees: 560

MACGREGOR SPORTING GOODS INC
25 East Union Avenue, East Rutherford, NJ 07073
Tel: (201) 935 6300

Chairman: Frederic H Brooks (and Chief Executive Officer); Vice Chairman: Martin A Rosenfeld
President: Herbert A Rosenfeld (and Chief Operating Officer and Secretary)
Senior Executive Officers: Henry M Dubrow (VP Finance and Assistant Secretary), Saul Neidell (VP Product Development), Zachery A Weintraub (Treasurer)

PRINCIPAL ACTIVITIES: Manufacture of a wide range of sports equipment
Principal Bank: Security Pacific Bank
Financial Information:

	$'000
Sales revenues	62,800

No of Employees: 1,500

MACK TRUCKS, INC
Box M, 2100 Mack Blvd, Allentown, PA 18105
Tel: (215) 439-3011
Telex: 847429 WORLDWIDE ATW

Chairman: John B Curcio (and President)
Senior Executive Officers: Fred J Kerber (Senior Executive VP Resource Management), Louis J LaFontaine (Executive VP Administration), Walter C Meck (Executive VP Finance), Joseph P Rossetti (Executive VP Marketing), Robert F Zalokar (Executive VP Product and Engineering), John J Costa (VP Manufacturing), J Anthony Donaldson (VP, General Counsel and Secretary), Paul C Ritter (Senior VP Sales), Charles J Browne (VP and Controller), Earl W Brunner (VP Fleet Sales and Product Planning), Gary D Johnson (VP Canadian Operations), Richard F Murphy (VP Marketing Distribution), David J Smith (VP and Treasurer)

PRINCIPAL ACTIVITIES: Manufacturer of heavy duty diesel trucks
Trade Names: MACK TRUCKS
Principal Subsidiaries: Mack Canada, Inc; Mack Trucks Australia Pty, Ltd; Mack Financial Corporation
Principal Bank: Bankers Trust Co
Financial Information:

	Dec 31 1985 $'000	Dec 31 1986 $'000
Sales revenues	2,063,312	1,711,844
(Loss) before taxes	(61,753)	(24,761)
Net (loss)	(59,216)	(30,569)
(Loss) per share	($2.07)	($1.06)
Common stock	366,713	334,550
Retained income	181,136	149,710
Shareholders equity	535,811	470,482

Principal Shareholders: Regie Nationale des Usines Renault (42%)
No of Employees: 10,942

MACKLANBURG-DUNCAN CO
4041 N Santa Fe, Oklahoma City, OK 73125
Tel: (405) 528-4411

Chairman: N J Hulsey (and Chief Executive Officer)
President: R L Gaugler
Senior Executive Officers: D B Horan (Senior VP Finance, Secretary and Treasurer), Pat Flores (Senior VP Operations), Ed LeBlanc (Senior VP Sales and Marketing), U S Conner (VP), David J Lyon (VP), Vernon L McKenzie (VP Employee Relations), William J O'Hare (VP), Darwin Frankum (VP), Carl Hancuff (VP), William Bowlware (VP Manufacturing and Engineering), Hoyt Gatiis (VP Distribution)

PRINCIPAL ACTIVITIES: Manufacture of building supplies
Principal Bank: Liberty National Bank
Financial Information:

	$'000
Sales revenues	92,000

No of Employees: 1,100

MACMILLAN, INC
866 Third Avenue, New York, NY 10022
Tel: (212) 935-2000

Chairman: Edward P Evans (and Chief Executive Officer)
President: William F Reilly (and Chief Operating Officer)
Senior Executive Officers: Philip E Hoversten (VP and Chief Financial Officer), Dale R Bauer (VP), George Philips (VP), Beverly C Chell (VP, General Counsel, and Secretary), William H Houghton (VP), John D Limpitlaw (VP), William A Naughton (VP), Eleanor P Vreeland (VP), Douglas E Moran (Controller), Richard F Marangelo (Treasurer), Edward A Friedland (Assistant Secretary)

PRINCIPAL ACTIVITIES: Book publishing and printing; educational textbooks and encyclopedias as well as school supplies; foreign language courses and tapes, office skills instruction and technical training; retailing
Principal Subsidiaries and Divisions: Publishing: School Division; Glencoe Division; College Division; Professional Books Division; Trade Division; Mass Market Division; Que Corporation; Howard W Sams & Co; Macmillan Software Company. Information Services: Standard Rate & Data Service; Directory Division; The Michie Company; Intertec Publishing; Direct Marketing Division; Business Mailers; Healthcare Information Division. Instruction: Berlitz; Katharine Gibbs Schools; Technical School Division. Home Learning and Reference Materials: Encyclopedia Division. GUMP'S
Financial Information:

	Dec 31 1985 $'000	Dec 31 1986 $'000
Sales revenues	676,949	817,797
Income before taxes	82,624	103,795
Net income	45,400	59,526
Dividends	11,999	13,459
Dividends per share	$0.5375	$0.60
Earnings per share	$2.07	$2.59
Common stock	184,255	193,451
Retained income	73,220	114,904
Shareholders equity	245,955	297,795

No of Employees: 8,600

MACMILLAN RING-FREE OIL CO, INC
90 Park Avenue, New York, NY 10016
Tel: (212) 867-0250
Telex: WUT 127052 newrfco nyk a

Chairman: Kevin C Foster (and President)
Senior Executive Officers: Jesse Taub (Senior VP and Secretary), Barbara Pauline (VP)

PRINCIPAL ACTIVITIES: Manufacture of liquid fuels and lubricating products
Principal Bank: M Bank, Dallas, TX

Financial Information:

	Dec 31 1985	Dec 31 1986
	$'000	$'000
Sales revenues	169,567	95,752
Net (loss)	(463)	(3,823)
Common stock*	2,670	2,674
Shareholders equity	7,624	3,858

*outstanding in thousands

No of Employees: 125

MACY, R H, & CO, INC

151 W 34th Street, New York, NY 10001
Tel: (212) 560-3600

Chairman: Edward S Finkelstein (and Chief Executive Officer)
President: Mark S Handler (and Chief Operating Officer)
Senior Executive Officers: Arthur E Reiner (Chairman Macy's New York), Robert N Friedman (Chairman Bamberger's), Harold D Kahn (Chairman Macy's California), Herbert Friedman (Chairman Davison's), Gertrude G Michelson (Senior VP External Affairs), Theodore M Ronick (Senior VP Corporate Buying), James O York (Senior VP Planning and Development and President R H Macy Property Division), A David Brown (Senior VP Personnel and Labor Relations), Donald Eugene (Senior VP Financial Administration and Control), Marvin Fenster (Senior VP, Secretary and Special Counsel), Herbert M Hellman (Senior VP and General Counsel), Nat Kurtz (Senior VP Taxes), Michael W Stemen (Senior VP Store Planning, Design and Construction), Richard A Wall (Senior VP Special Projects)

PRINCIPAL ACTIVITIES: Retail stores
Financial Information:

	$'000
Sales revenues	4,650,000

No of Employees: 57,000

MADISON DAIRY PRODUCE CO

1018 E Washington Avenue, Madison, WI 53701
Tel: (608) 256-5561
Telex: WUT 590 569 madison dairy

Chairman: Frederick C Steinhauer (and President)
Senior Executive Officers: Chuck Steinhauer (Executive VP), Gary Steinhauer (Secretary and Treasurer)

PRINCIPAL ACTIVITIES: Manufacture of dairy products
Principal Bank: Bank of Middleton
Financial Information:

	$'000
Sales revenues	60,000

No of Employees: 30

MADISON GAS AND ELECTRIC COMPANY

PO Box 1231, Madison, WI 53701
Tel: (608) 252 7964

Chairman: Donald J Helfrecht (and President and Chief Executive Officer)
Senior Executive Officers: Frank C Vondrasek (Executive VP), Gerald A Wilson (Senior VP), Kent M Barlow (VP), Richard M Lawrence (VP), David C Mebane (VP and General Counsel), G Howard Phipps (VP and Treasurer), Terrence J Schuh (VP)

PRINCIPAL ACTIVITIES: Supply of natural gas and electricity
Principal Bank: First Wisconsin National Bank
Financial Information:

	$'000
Sales revenues	224,000

No of Employees: 730

MAGNA GROUP INC

19 Public Square, Belleville, IL 62220
Tel: (618) 234 0020

Chairman: William S Badgley (and President); Vice Chairmen: G Thomas Andes, Harry E Cruncleton
Senior Executive Officers: George R Klann (VP, Chief Financial Officer and Controller), Lowel G Burger (Secretary and Treasurer)

PRINCIPAL ACTIVITIES: Banking
Principal Bank: Mercantile Trust
Financial Information:

	$'000
Revenues	118,650

No of Employees: 1,000

MAGNAFLUX CORPORATION

7300 W Lawrence Avenue, Chicago, IL 60656
Tel: (312) 867-8000

Chairman: E G Alldredge
President: K Diecker
Senior Executive Officers: J J Flaherty (VP Marketing and Sales), John J Flaherty (VP Engineering and Research), John Grimley (VP Manufacturing), Kenneth Sniegowski (Controller)

PRINCIPAL ACTIVITIES: Manufacture of a wide range of testing equipment
Parent Company: GEO International Corporation, Stamford, CT
Financial Information:

	$'000
Sales revenues	50,000

No of Employees: 600

MAGNAVOX GOVERNMENT & INDUSTRIAL ELECTRONICS COMPANY

1313 Production Road, Fort Wayne, IN 46808
Tel: (219) 429-6000
Telex: WUT 592056 magnavox

Chairman: James T Smith (and President and Chief Executive Officer)
Senior Executive Officers: Brant W Hill (Senior VP), James R Loomis (Senior VP), Arthur P Stern (Senior VP), Samuel H Newnam (VP Purchasing), Anthony B Hausfeld (VP and Treasurer), Charles E Hively (VP and Controller), King K Culp (VP), John McKenna (VP Administration)

PRINCIPAL ACTIVITIES: Manufacture of electronic equipment for military applications including signalling and communications equipment
Parent Company: North American Philips Corp
Principal Bank: Citibank
Financial Information:

	$'000
Sales revenues	500,000

No of Employees: 6,600

MAGNETIC METALS CORPORATION

Hayes Avenue at 21st Street, Camden, NJ 08105
Tel: (609) 964-7842
Telex: TWX 710 8917 054 magmetal cam

Chairman: H M Rowan Jr
President: Herbert D Risley
Senior Executive Officers: James E Hasson (VP and General Manager), G B Finke (VP Technology)

PRINCIPAL ACTIVITIES: Manufacture of specialized metals and metal products; industrial equipment
Parent Company: Inductotherm Industries Inc, Rancocas, NJ
Principal Bank: Heritage Bank
Financial Information:

	$'000
Sales revenues	50,000

No of Employees: 440

MAIDENFORM, INC

90 Park Avenue, New York, NY 10016
Tel: (212) 953-1400

President: Beatrice Coleman
Senior Executive Officers: David C Masket (Executive VP), Abraham P Kanner (Senior VP Finance and Treasurer), Robert Brawer (Senior VP and Assistant Secretary), Henry C Heppen (Senior VP and Secretary), Alan Lesk (Senior VP National Sales), Jerry H Rodman (VP Manufacturing), S Edward Kantrowitz (VP Advertising), Morris Komblatt (VP Marketing Management), Irwin Bernstein (VP Planning and Administration), James Mogan (VP National Sales), Jerome M Pruden (VP Licensing)

PRINCIPAL ACTIVITIES: Manufacture of underwear and nightwear
Financial Information:

	$'000
Sales revenues	100,000

MAINE NATIONAL CORPORATION

400 Congress Street, Portland, ME 04101
Tel: (207) 775-1000
Telex: WUT 94 44 54 bac 41 39 por

President: W D Verrill Jr (and Chief Executive Officer)
Senior Executive Officers: V K Wilson Jr (Executive VP), Wayne C McGarvey (Senior VP Planning and Finance), Wallace G Soule Jr (Senior VP, Secretary and Cashier), William B Kirkpatrick (Senior VP Sales and Loan Administration), Samuel A Ladd III (Senior VP Sales Administration)

PRINCIPAL ACTIVITIES: Banking
Parent Company: Bank of New England Corp
Principal Subsidiaries: Maine National Bank

No of Employees: 800

MAINE PUBLIC SERVICE COMPANY

209 State Street, Presque Isle, ME 04769
Tel: (207) 768 5811

Chairman: Ralph A Brown
President: G Melvin Hovey (and Chief Executive Officer)
Senior Executive Officers: Paul R Cariani (VP Finance and Treasurer), Stephen A Johnson (Secretary and General Counsel), Frederick C Bustard (VP Engineering and Operations)

PRINCIPAL ACTIVITIES: Supply of electricity
Principal Bank: Manufacturers Hanover Trust Company
Financial Information:

	$'000
Sales revenues	40,000

No of Employees: 160

MAINZER MINTON CO INC

48 W 38th Street, New York, NY 10018
Tel: (212) 944-3630
Telex: RCA 238950 main ur

Chairman: James H Michelman (and President)
Senior Executive Officers: Murray Steyer (Executive VP and Treasurer), Arthur Fried (Senior VP Marketing), Jack Shevrin (Senior VP Sales), Morton Samen (VP), Joel Hoffman (VP), Mel Weinfeld (VP)

PRINCIPAL ACTIVITIES: Manufacture of fabrics
Principal Bank: Manufacturers Hanover Trust
Financial Information:

	$'000
Sales revenues	55,000

No of Employees: 30

MAKITA USA, INC

12950 E Alondra Blvd, Cerritos, CA 90701
Tel: (213) 926-8775
Telex: WUT 691630 makitausa nrwk

Chairman: Kanichi Kamiya
President: Noris Hattori
Senior Executive Officers: Harry Suzuki (Corporate VP), Mark Kato (Secretary and Treasurer)

PRINCIPAL ACTIVITIES: Manufacture of hand tools and electric power tools
Trade Names: MAKITA
Parent Company: Makita Electric Works Ltd
Principal Subsidiaries: Makita Corporation of America Ltd
Principal Bank: The Sumitomo Bank of California
Financial Information:

	$'000
Sales revenues	144,000

Principal Shareholders: Makita Electric Works Ltd, Japan
No of Employees: 500

MALLINCKRODT INC

675 McDonnell Blvd, St Louis, MO 63134
Tel: (314) 895-2000
Telex: WUT 44 72 45 malinkrodt stl

President: Raymond F Bentele (and Chief Executive Officer)
Senior Executive Officers: John L Ufheil (Executive VP and Chief Operating Officer), William D Phillips (Senior VP), Mack G Nichols (VP and Group Executive), Carl R Holman (VP and Group Executive), Walter W Thulin (VP and Group Executive), William B Stone (VP and Controller), Roger A Hebrank (VP), Richard E Kelly (VP), Donald G Sillies (VP), Raymond M Asher (VP and Secretary)

PRINCIPAL ACTIVITIES: Manufacture of specialty chemicals, health care products, fragrances and food flavorings
Parent Company: International Minerals & Chemical Corp
Financial Information:

	$'000
Sales revenues	513,000

No of Employees: 4,900

MALNOVE INC

13134 F Street, Omaha, NE 68137
Tel: (402) 330-1100
Telex: 910 662 0776

Chairman: Paul Malnove (and President and Treasurer)
Senior Executive Officers: James Cantrell (VP Finance), Tim Barger (VP Sales Administration)

PRINCIPAL ACTIVITIES: Manufacture of packaging products and packaging machinery
Principal Bank: Norwest Bank Omaha NA
Financial Information:

	$'000
Sales revenues	50,000

No of Employees: 400

MALONE & HYDE, INC

3030 Poplar Avenue, Memphis, TN 38111
Tel: (901) 325 4200

Chairman: Joseph R Hyde III (and President and Chief Executive Officer)
Senior Executive Officers: Peter Formanek (Executive VP Specialty Retailing), John E Moll (Executive VP Wholesale Food Distribution), Andrew Clarkson (Senior VP Finance and Administration and Chief Financial Officer), J L Crain Jr (VP and Secretary), Lawrence L Crane Jr (VP), Robert A Sandifer (VP), Robert F Harris (VP), Robert J Hunt (VP), Don Lasseter (VP), J M Robinson (VP)

PRINCIPAL ACTIVITIES: Wholesale and retail trade in food including meat, frozen foods, dairy products and groceries; wholesale and retail trade in automotive products, drugs and sports equipment
Principal Bank: First Tennessee Bank NA
Financial Information:

	$'000
Sales revenues	3,100,000

No of Employees: 13,000

MALRITE COMMUNICATIONS GROUP INC
1200 Statler Office Tower, Cleveland, OH 44115
Tel: (216) 781 3010

Chairman: Milton Maltz (and Chief Executive Officer)
Senior Executive Officers: John G Rosenwald (Executive VP and Division President), John C Chaffee Jr (Senior VP and Division President), Kevan A Fight (VP Finance and Chief Financial Officer), John R Wilson (Treasurer and Chief Accounting Officer), John M Schohl (Secretary and Assistant General Counsel), Tom L Bracanovich (VP Engineering), Jim Wood (VP Radio Programs)

PRINCIPAL ACTIVITIES: Radio and TV broadcasting services
Principal Bank: Society Bank
Financial Information:

	$'000
Sales revenues	83,000

No of Employees: 650

MANAGEMENT SCIENCE AMERICA, INC
3445 Peachtree Rd NE, Atlanta, GA 30326
Tel: (404) 239-2000
Telex: 549638

Chairman: John P Imlay
President: William P Graves
Senior Executive Officers: Donald L House (Executive VP), Dennis V Vohs (Executive VP), R Douglas MacIntyre (Senior VP), Larry L Smart (Senior VP), William J Laney (VP and Chief Financial Officer)

PRINCIPAL ACTIVITIES: Production of computer software
Financial Information:

	Dec 31 1985	Dec 31 1986
	$'000	$'000
Sales revenues	151,661	193,449
Income before taxes(1)	10,554	36,142
Net income(1)	6,860	18,741
Earnings per share	$0.39	$1.03
Common stock(2)	17,745	18,144
Retained income	42,732	61,473
Shareholders equity	130,403	151,929

(1) continuing operations
(2) shares outstanding

No of Employees: 2,641

MANGOOD CORPORATION
155 Wicks St., Grayslake, IL 60030
Tel: (312) 223 4801

Chairman: Stanley Tulchin; Vice Chairman: Marvin B Levine
President: Regis A Vey (and Chief Executive Officer)
Senior Executive Officers: John L Westermann III (VP Finance and Treasurer), Charles E Heckman (VP and Controller), Layton C Merriam (President Howe Richardson Inc), Phillip W Trueman (Managing Director Chronos Richardson Ltd), Wolfgang Wagner (Managing Director Chronos Richardson GmbH)

PRINCIPAL ACTIVITIES: Manufacture of electronic measuring and weighing equipment; process control systems
Principal Subsidiaries: Mangood Ltd; Railweight Ltd; Streeter Richardson Division (NJ); Streeter Richardson Division (IL); Howe Richardson Inc; Mangood International Inc; Chronos Richardson GmbH; Chronos Richardson SA Chronos Richardson SpA; Chronos Richardson Ltd
Financial Information:

	$'000
Sales revenues	60,620

No of Employees: 1,120

MANHATTAN INDUSTRIES, INC
1271 Avenue of the Americas, New York, NY 10020
Tel: (212) 265-3700

Chairman: Laurence C Leeds Jr (and Chief Executive Officer); Chairman of Executive Committee: Donald H Kallman (and Vice Chairman, Executive VP and General Counsel)
President: Nicholas P Di Paolo (and Chief Operating Officer)
Senior Executive Officers: Zachary Solomon (Senior VP Marketing), Bruce P Fogwell (VP Advertising and Public Relations), Samuel M Miller (VP, Secretary, Treasurer and Controller)

PRINCIPAL ACTIVITIES: Manufacture and retail of clothing for men and women
Principal Bank: Manufacturers Hanover Trust Co
Financial Information:

	Jan 31 1986
	$'000
Sales revenues	471,550

No of Employees: 5,200

MANHATTAN NATIONAL CORPORATION
111 West 57th Street, NY 10019
Tel: (212) 484 9300

Chairman: Thomas E Lovejoy III; Vice Chairman: Wilmot F Wheeler Jr
President: Michael J Morrisey (and Chief Operating Officer)
Senior Executive Officers: L John Achenbach II (Executive VP), William J Flynn (Executive VP), Alfred B Tenreiro (Executive VP), Andrew Corselli (VP, Secretary and General Counsel), Charles R Fitzpatrick (Chief Financial Officer)

PRINCIPAL ACTIVITIES: Provision of life insurance services
Principal Subsidiaries: Manhattan Life Insurance Company; Manhattan National Life Insurance Company
Principal Bank: Chemical Bank
Financial Information:

	$'000
Revenues	311,770

MANITOWOC COMPANY, INC (THE)
500 S 16th Street, Manitowoc, WI 54220
Tel: (414) 684-6621
Telex: RCA TELEX NO: 29-7863 MANCO UR

Chairman: J D West
President: P R Helm
Senior Executive Officers: Frank Stevens (VP and General Counsel), R A Becker (President of Manitowoc Equipment Works Division of The Manitowoc Company, Inc)

PRINCIPAL ACTIVITIES: The Manitowoc Company, Inc, a Wisconsin corporation, organized in 1902, and its subsidiaries, are principally engaged (a) in the design and manufacture of cranes and excavators which are used by the utility, petroleum exploration and production, mining, construction and other industries, (b) in the operation of a shipyard in Sturgeon Bay, Wisconsin, for marine vessel construction and repair, (c) in the design and manufacture of commercial ice cube making machines for the food service and lodging industries, and (d) in the design and manufacture of other products, including log debarking equipment
Trade Names: Manitowoc
Principal Subsidiaries: Wholly-Owned Subsidiaries of Parent:- Bay Shipbuilding Corp; Manitex Inc; Manitowoc Europe BV (Netherlands); Manitowoc-Forsythe Corp; Manitowoc International Corp (Delaware); Manitowoc International Corp

(Nevada); Manitowoc Shipbuilding, Inc; North Central Crane & Excavator Sales Corp. Wholly-Owned Subsidiaries of Manitowoc Europe BV:- Manitowoc (UK) Limited (UK); Manitowoc AG (Switzerland); Manitowoc France SA (France)

Principal Banks: The Northern Trust Company; Continental Bank; Morgan Guaranty Trust Company; Associated Manitowoc Bank

Financial Information:

	$'000
Sales revenues	145,000

No of Employees: 2,300

MANOR CARE INC

10750 Columbia Pike, Silver Spring, MD 20901

Tel: (301) 681-9400

Telefax: (301) 681-9400 ext 4291

Chairman: Stewart Bainum Jr (and Chief Executive Officer); Vice Chairman: Stewart Bainum

President: C Arnold Renschler (and Chief Operating Officer)

Senior Executive Officers: Weldon Humphries (Senior VP Real Estate and Development), James A MacLutcheon (Senior VP Finance and Treasurer), Raymond G Murphy (Senior VP Administration), James H Rempe (Senior VP General Counsel and Secretary)

PRINCIPAL ACTIVITIES: Manor Healthcare Corp is a premier provider of long-term care services operating nursing centers nationwide. It also operates an acute care hospital, assisted living units and pharmacy outlets. Quality Inns International, Inc franchises and manages hotels for others while Quality Inns, Inc owns, leases and operates hotels and resorts. The hotels are located in 48 states, Canada, Mexico, Europe, the United Kingdom, Australia and New Zealand

Trade Names: Quality Inn, Comfort Inn, Clarion

Principal Subsidiaries: Manor Healthcare Corp; Quality Inns Inc; Quality Inns International Inc

Financial Information:

	May 31 1986	May 31 1987
	$'000	$'000
Total revenues	482,518	501,761
Income before taxes	68,441	75,839
Net income	39,278	39,102
Dividends	4,523	5,036
Dividends per share	$0.11	$0.13
Earnings per share	$0.96	$0.98
Common stock par	4,028	4,034
Retained income	116,572	150,638
Shareholders equity	173,234	203,275

No of Employees: 18,000

MANPOWER INC (FORMERLY PARKER PEN CO)

5301 North Ironwood Place, Milwaukee, WI 53217

Tel: (414) 961-1000

President: Mitchell S Fromstein (and Chief Executive Officer)

Senior Executive Officers: Gilbert Palay (Executive VP), Milton B Berland (Senior VP Finance, Treasurer and Assistant Secretary), James A Fromstein (Senior VP International Marketing), Joel W Biller (Senior VP International Corporate Affairs), Robert E Collins (VP and Secretary), Walter G Kozlowsky (VP, General Counsel and Assistant Secretary), David E Zolewski (VP and Controller International Division), William L Bates (VP, US Administration Services), Edward P Drudge Jr (VP, US Operations), Richard J Gallagher (VP, US National Accounts), Terry A Hueneke (VP, US Marketing and Business Development), Douglas H Krueger (VP, US Field Management Services), Joel B Miller (VP, US Corporate Development), L J Rasmussen (VP, US Finance), Richard E Schryver (VP, US Data Management and Systems)

PRINCIPAL ACTIVITIES: Provision of temporary staff for a wide range of professions and activities

Principal Bank: First National Bank of Chicago

Financial Information:

	Feb 28 1986
	$'000
Sales revenues	979,086
Net (loss)	(29,351)
(Loss) per share	($1.67)
Shareholders equity	83,934

No of Employees: 3,500

MANUFACTURED HOMES INC

PO Box 24549, 3410 Healy Drive, Winston-Salem, NC 27103

Tel: (919) 768 9890

Chairman: R M Sauls (and President)

Senior Executive Officers: Robert L Berner (Executive VP), Lloyd G Stinson (VP and Chief Financial Officer), Harrison R Laramore (VP Sales), James E Tinkler (VP), Wayne F Sloop (VP and Controller)

PRINCIPAL ACTIVITIES: Sale of modular homes

Principal Bank: Southern National Bank

Financial Information:

	$'000
Sales revenues	79,525

No of Employees: 600

MANUFACTURERS HANOVER CORPORATION

270 Park Avenue, New York, NY 10017

Tel: (212) 286-6000

Chairman: John F McGillicuddy (and Chief Executive Officer); Vice Chairmen: John J Evans, Edward A Farley

President: John R Torell III

Senior Executive Officers: Douglas E Ebert (Sector Executive VP), Albert R Gamper (Sector Executive VP), Donald G McCouch (Sector Executive VP), Donald H McCree (Sector Executive VP), Edward D Miller (Sector Executive VP), Peter J Tobin (Executive VP and Chief Financial Officer), Ernest D Stein (Executive VP and General Counsel), Charles V Austin (Senior VP), Eugene M McQuade (Senior VP and Controller)

PRINCIPAL ACTIVITIES: Manufacturers Hanover Corporation is a bank holding company which was organized under the laws of the State of Delaware in 1968. On April 28 1969, the Corporation acquired all the outstanding capital stock of Manufacturers Hanover Trust Company a banking corporation organized under the laws of the State of New York. In addition to Manufacturers Hanover, the Corporation has investments in other companies which make available a variety of banking and related financial services. Manufacturers Hanover operates domestically through a network of 213 branches in New York City, its surrounding counties and upstate New York, and through a number of specialized departments. Internationally, it operates through its New York City headquaters, its network of Edge Act offices headquartered in Miami, its International Banking Facility in New York, overseas branches and a network of representative offices, subsidiary and affiliated banks and financial service institutions. Manufacturers Hanover provides a complete range of retail banking services to individuals and small and medium-size businesses

Principal Subsidiaries: Manufacturers Hanover Trust Company, CIT

Principal Bank: Manufacturers Hanover Trust Company

Financial Information: Consolidated figures

	Dec 31 1985	Dec 31 1986
	$'000	$'000
Income before taxes(1)	597,209	443,370
Net income(2)	407,475	377,189
Dividends-Common Stock	131,040	134,896
Dividends-Preferred Stock	66,697	46,660
Dividends per common share	$3.21	$3.25
Earnings per share(1)	$8.38	$8.80
Common stock	310,082	315,127
Undivided profits	1,884,770	2,079,849
Shareholders equity	3,547,389	3,766,354
Deposits	46,261,146	45,544,277
Total assets	76,525,769	74,397,389

(1) before extraordinary items

(2) after extraordinary items

No of Employees: 32,218

MANUFACTURERS NATIONAL CORPORATION

100 Renaissance Center, Detroit, MI 48243

Tel: (313) 222-4000

Telex: 235808/235796

Chairman: Dean E Richardson (and President)

Senior Executive Officers: John T Cannis (Senior VP, Administration), John G Bascom (Senior VP Community Banking West), Thomas J Conway (Senior VP, Wholesale Administration), Thomas B Craigie Jr (VP, Senior Corporate Services Officer), Thomas D Ogden (VP, Senior Officer Michigan Corp Division), David C White (First VP National Division), Joseph J Buttigieg III (First VP, Administration), Jerry A Lamb (VP, Senior Officer Wholesale Administration), Edward J Miller (First VP, Community Banking East), David L Littmann (VP, Senior Economist Economics), Lawrence J Hemmen (Senior VP Operations Administration), Donald G Hooper (First VP Retail Marketing), Richard W Heiss (Senior VP and Senior Trust Officer Private Banking), Patrick M McQueen (Senior VP Consumer Loans), Antonio Forcellini (First VP Private Banking), Thomas K Fisher (First VP, Community Banking North), Gerald T Berry (First VP, Mortgage), Don B Dean (Senior VP Administration), Robert R Schoonbeck (Senior VP, Senior Trust Officer Trust Pension), Thaddeus J Winiarski (Senior VP, Loan Control Officer), Michael D Taschner (VP and Government Relations Officer), Robert A Herdoiza (Executive VP, International), Alan R Goldman (Senior VP Bank Investments), Ronald S Plaine (First VP Bank Investments), Joseph A Mazur (Senior VP, Controller), Donald D Staver (VP and Senior Corporate Officer), Alastair Carlyle (Executive VP, Administration), Vernon W Pietila (Senior VP, Auditor), John M Ryan (Senior VP, Personnel Director), Thomas H Alberts (VP and Senior Marketing Officer Marketing), Michael T Maurer (VP, Public Relations)

PRINCIPAL ACTIVITIES: Foreign exchange dealing; leasing; mortgage financing; portfolio management; private banking; consumer corporate banking

Principal Subsidiaries: Manufacturers National Bank of Grand Rapids; Manufacturers Bank of Lansing; Manufacturers Bank of Saline; Manufacturers Trust Company of Florida; Manufacturers Bank-Wilmington

Principal Bank: Manufacturers National Bank of Detroit

Financial Information:

	Dec 31 1985	Dec 31 1986
	$'000	$'000
Income before taxes	54,801	78,388
Net income	50,026	60,009
Dividends	11,883	15,252
Dividends per share	$1.12	$1.34
Earnings per share	$4.72	$5.27
Common stock	107,179	115,077
Retained income	218,499	263,497
Shareholders equity	374,666	450,917
Deposits	5,483,795	6,159,383
Total assets	6,980,430	8,110,207

No of Employees: over 4,400

MANVILLE CORPORATION

PO Box 5108, Denver, CO 80217

Tel: (303) 978-2000

Chairman: George C Dillon

President: W Thomas Stephens (and Chief Executive Officer)

Senior Executive Officers: G Earl Parker (Executive VP Law and Corporate Communications), S R Heath Jr (Executive VP Finance and Administration), Alfred B Gough (Senior VP Operations Manville Specialty Products), Harry W Sherman (Senior VP Operations Manville Forest Products), William A Sells (Senior VP Operations Manville Fiber Glass), Chester J Sulewski (Senior VP Production and Technical), James F Beasley (Senior VP Finance), John H Svensen (VP), Richard B Von Wald (VP and Corporate Counsel), Donald L Ferguson (VP Corporate Relations), Robert E Cole (VP Executive Department), Samuel B Hartung (VP Administration), Roger H Bengtson (VP), William B Reitze (VP, HS and E), Frederick E Schlachter (VP)

PRINCIPAL ACTIVITIES: Holding company with interests in forest products, fiber glass products and other building supplies

Principal Bank: Morgan Guaranty Trust Co

Financial Information:

	Dec 31 1985	Dec 31 1986
	$'000	S'000
Sales revenues	1,880,050	1,920,262
Net income (loss)	(45,067)	81,228
Earnings per share	-	$2.34
Shareholders equity	878,230	973,943

No of Employees: 21,000

MAPCO INC

1800 S Baltimore Avenue, Tulsa, OK 74119

Tel: (918) 581-1800

President: J E Barnes (and Chief Executive Officer)

Senior Executive Officers: Robert M Howe (Chief Operating Officer), S F Isaacs (Senior VP Transport), W J Hart (Senior VP Petroleum), C G McConnell (Senior VP MAPCO Products), D S Leslie (VP Public Affairs and Assistant to President), J W Craft III (Senior VP Coal)

PRINCIPAL ACTIVITIES: Production and distribution of oil, gas and coal

Principal Bank: Harris Trust and Savings Bank

Financial Information:

	Sep 30 1986 (9 mths) $'000	Sep 30 1987 (9 mths) $'000
Sales revenues	1,183,219	1,160,200
Income before taxes	108,213	72,113
Net income	59,438	45,100
Dividends per share	$0.75	$0.75
Earnings per share	$2.72	$2.14
Common stock	30,908	30,948
Retained income	675,161	704,417
Shareholders equity	489,564	504,458

No of Employees: 5,200

MARANTZ COMPANY INC

20525 Nordhoff Street, Chatsworth, CA 91311
Tel: (818) 998 9333

Chairman: Joseph S Tushinsky (and Chief Executive Officer)
President: Fred C Tushinsky (and Chief Operating Officer and Secretary)
Senior Executive Officers: William Morris (Senior VP Finance, Administration, Chief Financial Officer, Treasurer and Assistant Secretary), Harvey A Schneider (Senior VP Marketing and Sales)

PRINCIPAL ACTIVITIES: Manufacture and sale of audio home entertainment products; electronic piano reproducing systems; pre-recorded cassette tapes and picture books
Trade Names: Pianocorder, Tele-Story, Story Teller
Principal Subsidiaries: Rentabeta International; Superscope Tape Duplicating Products
Principal Bank: Foothill Capital Corporation
Financial Information:

	$'000
Sales revenues	49,960

No of Employees: 160

MARATHON ELECTRIC MANUFACTURING CORPORATION

100 E Randolph Street, Wausau, WI 54401
Tel: (715) 675-3311
Telex: 260175 ME WAU
Fax: (715) 675-6361

Chairman: San W Orr Jr (and Secretary)
President: Russell S Hale (and Chief Executive Officer)
Senior Executive Officers: Charles J Bayer (VP and General Manager, Marathon Special Products Corp), Billy D Dodson (VP, Finance and Corporate Services and Treasurer), David L Eisenreich (VP, Administration), Hugh D Reardon (VP, Quality Assurance), Gary L Schurter (VP, Engineering), James L Feighery (VP, Manufacturing), Marvin R Lilley (VP, Materials), Raymond C Kacvinsky (VP, Sales and Marketing, Motors)

PRINCIPAL ACTIVITIES: Manufacture and sale of electric motors and generators which meet NEMA standards and serve many industries. Sales are made to OEM's, distributors, and through representatives, as well as through our own field sales force located nationwide
Trade Names: Blue Chip Motors, 629 Line Series, Magna-One Generator, Magna-Mite Generator, MagnaMax Generator
Principal Subsidiaries: Marathon Special Products Corporation; Lima Electric Co Inc
Principal Bank: M & I Marshall & Ilsley Bank

No of Employees: 2,000 (Including Subsidiaries)

MARATHON LETOURNEAU CO

Longview, TX 75657
Tel: (214) 753-4411
Telex: 730371

Presidents: John B Allison (Gulf Marine), Clyde H Wilson (Marine), Paul E Glaske (Longview)
Senior Executive Officers: Francis J Fair (VP Gulf Marine), Thomas M McCoy (VP Gulf Marine), Donald Cross (VP Marine), Walter J Beall (VP Marine), Lynn R Helberg (VP and Controller Marine), Gerald E Whitehurst (Senior VP Longview), Dwight Baker (VP Longview), Charles H Bellatti (VP Longview), Jack E Davis (VP Longview), Ronald G Glass (VP Longview), Dan W Jones (VP Longview), Bart W McCoy (VP Longview), Bill Nolen (VP Longview), Bobby G Wallace (VP Longview)

PRINCIPAL ACTIVITIES: Heavy lifting machinery and construction equipment
Parent Company: Marathon Manufacturing Co Inc, Ultimate Holding Company-Penn Central Corporation
Principal Bank: First City National Bank
Financial Information:

	$'000
Sales revenues	61,000

MARATHON MANUFACTURING CO

600 Jefferson Bldg, Houston, TX 77002
Tel: (713) 659-7444
Telex: 77002

President: Ray R Seegmiller (and Chief Executive Officer)
Senior Executive Officers: Leonel Alejandro (VP), Roland B Gray (VP), Roger J Klatt (VP Finance), Clyde H Wilson (VP), George H Morris (VP), William K Trimble (VP), Ernest C English Jr (VP and Controller)

PRINCIPAL ACTIVITIES: Manufacture of a wide range of industrial equipment for the oil and gas, mining and materials handling industries; interests in electronics and telecommunications and leasing
Parent Company: Penn Central Corporation, Greenwich, CT
Principal Bank: First City National Bank of Houston
Financial Information:

	$'000
Sales revenues	365,000

No of Employees: 3,000

MARATHON OFFICE SUPPLY INC

10323 Santa Monica Blvd, Suite D, Los Angeles, CA 90025
Tel: (213) 557-2708

Chairman: Walter Kornbluh (and President)
Senior Executive Officers: Kathryn Mariano (VP), Stanley W Singer (VP), Dennis Cook (Secretary)

PRINCIPAL ACTIVITIES: Distribution of office supplies
Principal Bankers: Lloyds Bank of California
Financial Information:

	$'000
Sales revenues	50,000

No of Employees: 240

MARATHON OIL COMPANY

539 S Main Street, Findlay, OH 455840
Tel: (419) 422-2121
Telex: ITT 4332075 maratoil fly

President: W E Swales
Senior Executive Officers: E A Graham (Executive VP Finance and Administration), V G Beghini (Senior VP Exploration and Production), J H Brannigan (VP Research), R T Chamblin (VP International Production), R D Cooley (VP Finance), C P Giardini (VP Domestic Production), R E Clements (VP Engineering and Technical), W E Lewellen (VP Pittsburgh)

PRINCIPAL ACTIVITIES: Exploration for, and production of oil
Parent Company: USX Corporation, Pittsburgh, PA
Financial Information:

	$'000
Sales revenues	10,500,000

No of Employees: 6,000

MARCADE GROUP INC

1372 Broadway, New York City, NY 10018
Tel: (212) 944-0877

Chairmen: Robert K Lifton (and Assistant Secretary); Howard L Weingrow (and Assistant Secretary)
President: Charles S Ramat (and Secretary)
Senior Executive Officers: John Kuehn (Senior VP Finance and Administration and Assistant Secretary)

PRINCIPAL ACTIVITIES: The Marcade Group Inc under its wholly owned subsidiaries Marlene Industries and Booth Bay, Ltd manufactures a wide variety of women's clothing
Principal Subsidiaries: Marlene Industries; Booth Bay Ltd
Financial Information:

	Feb 1 1986 (53 wks) $'000	Jan 31 1987 (52 wks) $'000
Sales revenues	69,084	72,286
Income (loss) before taxes(1)	(6,669)	526
Net income (loss)	(10,511)	15,119
Earnings (loss) per share(2)	($1.13)	$1.12
Common stock	954	954
Retained (deficit)	(18,963)	(3,844)
Shareholders equity (deficit)	(14,922)	3,588

(1) and extraordinary credits
(2) fully diluted

No of Employees: 4,400

MARCUS CORPORATION

212 W Wisconsin Ave, Milwaukee, WI 53203
Tel: (414) 272-6020

Chairman: Ben Marcus (and Chief Executive Officer)
President: Stephen H Marcus (and Chief Operating Officer and Treasurer)
Senior Executive Officers: Robin Irwin (Secretary)

PRINCIPAL ACTIVITIES: Operation of motels, hotels, restaurants, a bowling alley and motion picture theaters
Trade Names: Budgetel Inns, Marco Big Boy, Kentucky Fried Chicken, Captains, PFister Hotel, Marc Plaza Hotel
Principal Bank: Marine
Financial Information:

	May 31 1986 $'000	May 31 1987 $'000
Sales revenues	141,076	151,386
Income before taxes	14,449	14,808
Net income	8,719	8,078
Dividends	1,526	1,608
Dividends per share	$0.20	$0.22
Earnings per share	$1.13	$1.05
Common stock	7,892	7,891
Retained income	54,319	60,789
Shareholders equity	76,328	82,952

No of Employees: 8,000

MARINE CONSTRUCTION & DESIGN CO

2300 W Commodore Way, Seattle, WA 98199
Tel: (206) 285-3200
Telex: ITT 471038 marco sea

Chairman: Peter G Schmidt (and President)
Senior Executive Officers: Robert F Allen (Executive VP), Charles R Hart (Senior VP), Paul A Gilliland (Senior VP), Dale E Alberda (Treasurer and Controller)

PRINCIPAL ACTIVITIES: Holding company with interests in boat building
Principal Bank: Sea First Bank
Financial Information:

	$'000
Sales revenues	100,000

No of Employees: 2,000

MARINE CORP ILLINOIS

East Old State Capitol Plaza, Springfield, IL 62701
Tel: (217) 525 9600

Chairman: Willard Bunn Jr (and Chief Executive Officer)
President: Willard Bunn III (and Chief Operating Officer)
Senior Executive Officers: William R Enlow (VP, Secretary and General Counsel), John E Staudt (VP Finance and Treasurer)

PRINCIPAL ACTIVITIES: Holding company with interests in financial services
Principal Bank: Marine Bank of Springfield
Financial Information:

	Dec 31 1985 $'000
Revenues	84,100
Net income	5,050

No of Employees: 550

MARINE CORPORATION

111 E Wisconsin Ave, PO Box 481, Milwaukee, WI 53201
Tel: (414) 765-3000

Chairman: George R Slater (and Chief Executive Officer); Vice Chairman: William J Morrissey (Investor Relations Office, Acquisitions)
President: Daniel J Gannon (and Chief Operating Officer)
Senior Executive Officers: Ronald C Baldwin (Senior VP Corporate Group), Frederick L Cullen (Senior VP Waukesha Group), James W Eyster (Group Senior VP), Leila Fraser (Senior VP Marketing), Norman A Jacobs (Senior VP Consumer and Trust Group), James C LaVelle (Senior VP Credit Services Group), Alex J Pollock (Senior VP Finance Group), Jon R Schumacher (Senior VP Southern Wisconsin Group), Jon H Stowe (Senior VP Financial Institutions and International Group), Otto H Wirth (Senior VP Northern Wisconsin Group), Thomas G Boyer (VP and General Counsel), John P Hickey Jr (VP Personnel), Jerome L Hochgurtel (VP and Auditor), Timothy L King (VP and Controller), William A Reed (VP and Treasurer)

PRINCIPAL ACTIVITIES: Banking services
Financial Information:

	Dec 31 1985 $'000
Revenues	356,000
Net income	26,600
Total assets	3,720,000

No of Employees: 4,000

MARINE MIDLAND BANKS, INC

One Marine Midland Center, Buffalo, NY 14203
Tel: (716) 843-2424

Chairman: John R Petty (and Chief Executive Officer); Vice Chairman: Thomas F Donovan
Senior Executive Officers: Martin T Birmingham (Regional President), Charles M Mitschow (Regional President), Robert E Wehrle (Regional President), Richard C Keller (Senior Executive VP), W J Tozer Jr (Senior Executive VP), Arthur B Ziegler (Senior Executive VP), Edward H Brode (Executive VP and Chief Financial Officer), Walter W Brown (Senior VP and Controller)

PRINCIPAL ACTIVITIES: Banking
Parent Company: Marine Midland Banks Inc
Financial Information:

	Dec 31 1985 $'000	Dec 31 1986 $'000
Net income	125,119	144,944
Earnings per share	$6.06	$7.19
Deposits	16,593,427	17,418,418
Total assets	23,385,612	24,789,596

Principal Shareholders: Hong Kong & Shanghai Banking Corp (52%)
No of Employees: 12,300

MARINE TRANSPORT LINES INC

150 Meadowland Parkway, Secaucus, NJ 07094
Tel: (201) 330 0200

Chairman: Louis J Conti
President: Bruce E Kahler (and Chief Executive Officer)
Senior Executive Officers: Henry A Downing (Executive VP), Ian Parker (Executive VP), Ira A Bird (VP Finance), Sundar K Sundaresan (VP), Michael C Berkowitz (VP Marketing)

PRINCIPAL ACTIVITIES: Operation of shipping services
Principal Bank: Citibank
Financial Information:

	$'000
Sales revenues	70,000

No of Employees: 200

MARINETTE MARINE CORPORATION

Ely Street, Marinette, WI 54143
Tel: (715) 735-9341
Telex: TWX 910 2701388 marmarine mant

Chairman: Roger H Derusha (and President)
Senior Executive Officers: Robert J Derusha (Executive VP), John A Booker (VP Manufacturing), Larry A Bowsher (VP Contract Administration), William J Keller (VP Engineering), Harold H Krider (VP Finance), Donald J Meyer (VP Materials), Joe E Mott (VP Programs), Gordon Wicklund (VP Employee Relations)

PRINCIPAL ACTIVITIES: Shipbuilding
Principal Bank: First Wisconsin National Bank of Milwaukee
Financial Information:

	$'000
Sales revenues	50,000

No of Employees: 840

MARION LABORATORIES, INC

PO Box 9627, Kansas City, MO 64134
Tel: (816) 966-5000

Chairman: Ewing M Kauffman
President: Fred W Lyons Jr (and Chief Executive Officer)
Senior Executive Officers: James E McGraw (Senior Executive VP and Chief Operating Officer), Michael E Herman (Executive VP and Chief Financial Officer), D B Cotterman (Senior VP Operations/Systems), Alfred A Mannino (VP Corporate Affairs), Harley L Tennison (Senior VP Marketing)

PRINCIPAL ACTIVITIES: Manufacture of pharmaceuticals
Principal Bank: Commerce Bank of Kansas City
Financial Information:

	Jun 30 1987 $'000
Sales revenues	597,420
Income before taxes	173,804
Net income	96,898
Dividends per share	$0.145
Earnings per share	$0.61
Common stock*	158,601
Retained income	95,968
Shareholders equity	303,574

*number of shares

No of Employees: 3,000

MARK CONTROLS CORPORATION

5202 Old Orchard Road, Skokie, IL 60077
Tel: (312) 470-8585
Telex: 72-4353

Chairman: Gary E MacDougal (and President and Chief Executive Officer); Vice Chairman: Harvey W Branigar Jr
Senior Executive Officers: William E Bendix (Group VP), Arne R Salvesen (President-Marpac and President-Clayton Mark), Thomas C Mattick (VP Finance and Secretary), John J Grad (VP), Michael P Nicholas (Executive VP Sales and Marketing-Flow Control Group)

PRINCIPAL ACTIVITIES: Building management and control systems for both new and existing nonresidential buildings, and valves and related flow control products for the petroleum, chemical process, petrochemical and power industries
Principal Subsidiaries: Mark Controls Ltd; Mark Controls International Corp; Powers Regulator Company International; Powers JVA Company; Mark Controls GmbH; Mark Valves SA; Rodyne Ltd; Mark Control Systems Corp
Principal Bank: Continental Illinois National Bank and Trust Co
Financial Information:

	Dec 31 1985 $'000
Sales revenues	278,954
Income before taxes	3,910
Net income	2,710
Dividends	2,308
Common dividends per share	$0.32
Preferred dividends per share	$1.20
Earnings per share*	$0.43
Common stock	4,263
Retained income	32,985
Shareholders equity	49,532

*common

No of Employees: 3,302

MARK IV INDUSTRIES INC

501 John James Audubon Parkway, Box 450, Amherst, NY 14228
Tel: (716) 689 4972

Chairman: Sal H Alfiero
President: Clement R Arrison
Senior Executive Officers: William P Montague (VP), John J Byrne (Treasurer and Controller), Gerald S Lippes (Secretary)

PRINCIPAL ACTIVITIES: Manufacture of industrial seals, plastic plugs and child resistant caps for medicine bottles
Principal Subsidiaries: LFE Corp
Principal Bankers: Manufacturers Hanover Trust Co
Financial Information:

	$'000
Sales revenues	39,000

No of Employees: 450

MARK TWAIN BANCSHARES INC

8820 Ladue Road, St Louis, MO 63124
Tel: (314) 727 1000

Chairman: Adam Aronson; Vice Chairman: Robert J Baudendistel, Alvin Siteman
President: John Dubinsky (and Chief Operating Officer)
Senior Executive Officers: Peter F Benoist (Executive VP and Division President), Robert C Butler (Executive VP), Anthony L Guerrerio (Senior VP), Walter W Pinnel (Senior VP), Carl A Wattenberg Jr (VP, Secretary and General Counsel), Keith Miller (VP Finance), Robert W Holle (Treasurer and Assistant Secretary)

PRINCIPAL ACTIVITIES: Banking
Principal Bank: Centerre Bank

No of Employees: 730

MARKEM CORPORATION

150 Congress Street, Keene, NH 03431
Tel: (603) 352-1130
Telex: TWX 710 366 1800 Markemusa keen

Chairman: Joseph A Baute (and Chief Executive Officer)

President: Thomas P Putnam (and Treasurer)
Senior Executive Officers: Jeffrey J Lomax (Senior VP), Phillip Faulkner (VP), George M Rossiter (VP)

PRINCIPAL ACTIVITIES: Manufacture of printing equipment
Principal Bank: Bank of Boston
Financial Information:

	$'000
Sales revenues	85,000

No of Employees: 1,200

MARKET FACTS INC

676 North St Clair, Chicago, IL 60611
Tel: (312) 280 9100

Chairman: David K Hardin
President: Verne B Churchill (and Chief Executive Officer)
Senior Executive Officers: Gregory J Spagna (Chief Operating Officer), Richard B Ross (Executive VP), Glenn W Schmidt (Executive VP, Assistant Secretary and Assistant Treasurer), Robert S Kaufman (VP, Treasurer and Assistant Secretary), Wesley S Walton (Secretary)

PRINCIPAL ACTIVITIES: Provision of public relations and management consultancy services; market research
Principal Bank: Harris Trust and Savings Bank
Financial Information:

	$'000
Sales revenues	37,770

No of Employees: 630

MARLEY CO

1900 Johnson Drive, Kansas City, KS 66205
Tel: (913) 362-5440
Telex: WUI 6711030 mrley uw

Chairman: Robert L McFadin
President: Robert J Dineen (and Chief Executive Officer)
Senior Executive Officers: Neil E Holmes (VP and Controller), R F Wrobel (VP Administration), Errol P Mitlyng (VP Finance and Treasurer), Robert A Pitcel (VP Taxes), Jack A Mozur (VP Corporate Communications)

PRINCIPAL ACTIVITIES: Manufacture of a wide range of water treatment equipment including heaters, condensers and pumps
Principal Bank: First National Bank of Kansas City
Financial Information:

	$'000
Sales revenues	470,000

No of Employees: 5,000

MARLEY-WYLAIN CO

1900 Johnson Drive, Kansas City, KS 66205
Tel: (913) 362-5440

Chairman: Robert L McFadin (and President and Chief Executive Officer)
President: R J Dineen
Senior Executive Officers: Errol P Metlyng (VP and Treasurer)

PRINCIPAL ACTIVITIES: Manufacture of pumps and equipment for heating and ventilation; manufacture of metal products and sectional buildings
Parent Company: Marley Co, Kansas City, KS
Principal Bank: First National Bank of Kansas City
Financial Information:

	$'000
Sales revenues	320,000

No of Employees: 1,600

MARLIN FIREARMS CO

100 Kenna Drive, North Haven, CT 06473
Tel: (203) 239-5621

President: Frank Kenna
Senior Executive Officers: Stephen Schramm (VP and General Manager), E E Oberst (Secretary and General Counsel)

PRINCIPAL ACTIVITIES: Manufacture of guns
Principal Bank: The Connecticut Bank and Trust Co
Financial Information:

	$'000
Sales revenues	55,000

No of Employees: 650

MARMON GROUP, INC (THE)

39 S LaSalle Street, Chicago, IL 60603
Tel: (312) 372-9500
Telex: 253112

Chairman: Jay A Pritzker
President: Robert A Pritzker
Senior Executive Officers: Robert C Gluth (Executive VP), Sidney H Bonser (Executive VP), L William Emmert (VP), Norman C Gustafson (VP Taxes), Gerald T Shannon (VP)

PRINCIPAL ACTIVITIES: Marmon's principal activities include manufacture and marketing of industrial materials and components, industrial, mining, agricultural, institutional and commercial equipment and automotive building and consumer products; building and leasing of railway tank and freight cars; engineering and fabrication of water and industrial fluids treatment systems; mining and processing of non-ferrous metals and international metals trading; international marketing, distribution and manufacturing services; rental of electronic equipment, mobile crane and LP gas storage facilities; consumer credit information and telecommunication services

Principal Subsidiaries: The Marmon Group Inc:- Accutronics; Aluminum Forge Co; Amarillo Gear Co; American Box Co; American Safety Equipment Corp; Cerro Conduit Co; Cerro Copper Products Co; Cerro Metal Products; Cerro Sales Corp; Cerro Wire & Cable Co Inc; Darling Store Fixtures; Detroit Steel Products; Fenestra Corp; Fontaine Truck Equipment Co; Hammond Organ Co; Inter-City Suspension Parts; Jamesway Co; Long-Airdox Co; Marlok Co; Marmon/Keystone Corp; Marmon Transmotive; McRobert Springs; Micro-Aire Surgical Instruments Inc; Midwest Foundry Co; Penn Aluminum International; Perfection Hy-Test Co; The Rockbestos Co; Triangle Auto Spring Co; Wells Lamont Corp. The Marmon Group Ltd (UK):- A.S.E. UK Ltd; Cerro Metals (UK) Ltd; Colson Castors (Europe) Ltd; Hammond Organ (UK) Ltd; Kangol Wear Ltd; Pikrose & Company Ltd; Procor (UK); Rail Car Services Ltd; Rochester Instrument Systems Ltd. Affiliated Companies:- Austins Marmon Ltd; Compania Minera Raura SA; Explosivos SA; Fundicion de Metales Bera del Peru SA; Indeco Peruana SA; Industrias Metalicas Sudamericanas Ltda; Metalurgica Peruana SA; Reductores de Mexico SA; Refractarios Peruanos SA; Southern Peru Copper Corp. Marmon Industrial Corporation:- Atlas Bolt & Screw Co; Ecodyne Corp; The Getz Corp; The Graver Co; Ecodyne Ltd; Graver Chemical Division; Graver Water Division; Unitech Division; Industrias Ecodyne SA; Leasametric Inc; Lithcote Co; MRM Co; New Century Freight Traffic Association Inc; Phoenix Forging Co; Procor LPG Storage Division; Procor Rail Car Division; Procor Sulphur Services Division; Procrane Inc; Robertson-Whitehouse; Rochester Instrument Systems Inc; Solidstate Controls Inc; Trans Union Credit Information Co; Union Tank Car Co; WCTU Railway Co. The Colson Group Inc:- Colson Caster Corp; Colson Casters Ltd; Colson Equipment Inc. Marmon Industries Inc:- Huron Steel Co; Webb Division. The RegO Group Inc:-Anderson Copper and Brass Co; RegO Co. Other Marmon Companies:- MTS Inc; Meyer Material Co; Miles Metal Co
Principal Bank: Security Pacific National Bank

Financial Information:

	Dec 31 1985
	$'000
Sales revenues	1,623,232
Net income	54,340
Shareholders equity	413,863

No of Employees: 17,800

MARRIOTT CORPORATION

Marriott Drive, Washington, DC 20058
Tel: (301) 897-9000
Telex: 89597 MARMSGCTR BHDA

Chairman: J Willard Marriott Jr (and President and Chief Executive Officer)
Senior Executive Officers: Daniel J Altobello (Executive VP), Francis W Cash (Executive VP), John H Dasburg (Executive VP and Chief Financial Officer), Frederic V Malek (Executive VP and President, Marriott Hotels and Resorts), Richard E Marriott (Vice Chairman and Executive VP)

PRINCIPAL ACTIVITIES: Company operations include: full service hotels and resorts; moderate price hotels; other lodging-related businesses-including all-suite, compact and economy hotels, vacation ownership resorts and lifecare retirement communities; contract food services-including food service management for businesses and industries, health care and educational indtitutions, airline catering, and airport terminal food, beverage and merchandise operations; and fast food, family and turnpike restaurants operated under various national brand names
Trade Names: Marriott Hotels and Resorts, Courtyard by Marriott, Marriott Suites, Host International, Big Boy family restaurants, Roy Rogers fast food restaurants, Hot Shoppe cafeterias and retaurants
Principal Bank: Riggs National Bank of Washington, D.C.
Financial Information:

	Dec 31 1985	Dec 31 1986
	$'000	$'000
Sales revenues	4,241,700	5,266,500
Income before taxes	295,700	360,200
Net income	167,400	191,700
Dividends	14,800	17,800
Dividends per share	$0.113	$0.136
Earnings per share	$1.24	$1.40
Common stock*	130,994	130,606
Retained income	775,000	948,900
Shareholders equity	848,500	991,000
*outstanding shares in thousands		

No of Employees: 200,000

MARS STORES INC

689 Spring Street, North Dighton, MA 02746
Tel: (617) 822 1500

Chairman: Matthew Tatelbaum; Vice Chairman: Samuel Katz
President: Paul J Kwasnik (and Chief Executive Officer)
Senior Executive Officers: Benjamin Lederman (VP), David Filipels (VP Finance and Treasurer)

PRINCIPAL ACTIVITIES: Department stores
Principal Bank: Shawmut Bank of Boston
Financial Information:

	$'000
Sales revenues	110,000

No of Employees: 1,530

MARSH & MCLENNAN

1221 Avenue of the Americas, New York, NY 10020
Tel: (212) 997-2000

Chairman: Frank J Tasco; Chairman of Executive Committee: John M Regan Jr
President: A J C Smith
Senior Executive Officers: Frank J Borelli (Senior VP and Chief Financial Officer), Edward O Cole (VP), Larry M Cains (VP and Controller), Douglas C Davis (VP Audit and Control), John E McCauley (VP Taxes), Gregory F Van Gundy (General Counsel and Secretary)

PRINCIPAL ACTIVITIES: Insurance brokers
Principal Bankers: Morgan Guaranty Trust Co
Financial Information:

	Dec 31 1986
	$'000
Premium income	1,804,100
Net income	243,200
Earnings per share	$3.30
Shareholders equity	638,700
Total assets	1,476,600

No of Employees: 20,000

MARSH SUPERMARKETS INC

Yorktown, IN 47396
Tel: (317) 759 8101

Chairman: William P Givens
President: Don E Marsh (and Chief Executive Officer)
Senior Executive Officers: P Lawrence Butt (VP, General Counsel and Secretary), Porter Eckerty (VP Operations), C Alan Marsh (Subsidiary Officer), William L Marsh (VP and General Manager Property Management), Ronald R Walicki (VP and Divisional Manager), John S Hayford (VP Finance and Treasurer), Donald M Rix (VP Merchandising), Kenneth D Kelly (VP), John W Laboda (VP Information Services), David M Redden (VP Personnel)

PRINCIPAL ACTIVITIES: Supermarkets
Principal Bank: Indiana National Bank
Financial Information:

	Mar 31 1986	Mar 31 1987
	$'000	$'000
Sales revenues	718,506	772,241
Income before taxes	9,369	11,351
Net income	6,933	6,695
Dividends	1,849	1,971
Dividends per share	$0.34	$0.39
Earnings per share	$1.15	$1.32
Common stock	15,712	16,002
Retained income	38,648	43,382
Shareholders equity	45,479	50,637

No of Employees: 8,800

MARSHALL & ILSLEY CORPORATION

770 North Water St, Milwaukee, WI 53201
Tel: (414) 765-7801

Chairman: John A Puelicher (and President and Chief Executive Officer)
Senior Executive Officers: G H Gunnlaugsson (VP), D J Kuester (VP), A N Renner (VP Administration), M J Revane (VP Trusts), J B Wigdale (VP Administration), G D Strelow (VP Personnel)

PRINCIPAL ACTIVITIES: Banking
Principal Bank: M & I Marshall & Ilsley Bank
Financial Information:

	Dec 31 1985	Dec 31 1986
	$'000	$'000
Net income	42,950	55,018
Earnings per share	$2.66	$2.95
Shareholders equity	290,785	351,915
Deposits	3,589,843	4,331,830
Total assets	4,741,013	6,000,935

No of Employees: 4,800

MARSHALL INDUSTRIES

9674 Telstar Ave, El Monte, CA 91731
Tel: (818) 442-7204

Chairman: Gordon S Marshall (and President, Chief Executive Officer and Chief Operating Officer)
Senior Executive Officers: David O Zertuche (VP Finance and Chief Financial Officer), William J Smith (VP Sales), George Tarnawsky (VP Marketing), Peter B Heric (VP Management Information Services), Carl R Sittman (VP Facilities)

PRINCIPAL ACTIVITIES: Supplies for the electronics industry including connectors, wires and semiconductors
Trade Names: Marshall Claude Michael; Marshall Kinatechnics
Principal Bank: Security Pacific National Bank
Financial Information:

	$'000
Sales revenues	245,000

Principal Shareholders: Gordon S Marshall
No of Employees: 1,100

MARTIN INDUSTRIES, INC

PO Box 128, Florence, AL 35630
Tel: (205) 767-0330

Chairman: C A Martin; Vice Chairmen: F H Martin, W H Martin Jr
President: W H Martin III (and Chief Executive Officer)
Senior Executive Officers: Emerson Priest (Executive VP), B G Hughey (VP Operations), A R Tomlinson III (VP Administration and Secretary), Jack Townsend (VP Sales), James W Truitt (VP Finance and Treasurer)

PRINCIPAL ACTIVITIES: Manufacture of domestic heaters, dehumidifiers and heat pumps
Trade Names: Martin, King, Ashley, Aspen
Principal Bank: A M South Bank
Financial Information:

	$'000
Sales revenues	60,000

No of Employees: 1,000

MARTIN, JEFFREY, , INC

410 Clermont Terrace, Union, NJ 07083
Tel: (201) 687-4000
Telex: RCA 219304 jmi ur

Chairman: Martin Himmel (and President)
Senior Executive Officers: J M Schocket (Executive VP), Franke P Diprima (Executive VP and Chief Operating Officer), Joseph Amari (VP Treasurer and Controller), Robert Varian (VP), J M Appel (VP), Sidney Zucker (VP), Harriet Himmel (VP)

PRINCIPAL ACTIVITIES: Manufacture of medicines and beauty products
Principal Bank: National State Bank
Financial Information:

	$'000
Sales revenues	66,000

No of Employees: 160

MARTIN MARIETTA CORPORATION

6801 Rockledge Drive, Bethesda, MD 20817
Tel: (301) 897-6000

Chairman: Thomas G Pownell (and Chief Executive Officer)
President: Norman R Augustine (and Chief Operating Officer)
Senior Executive Officers: David C Dressler (Senior VP), Caleb B Hurtt (Senior VP), Marcus C Bennett (VP Finance), William E Benso (VP), K K Bigelow (VP), J Peter Dunston (VP), William B Harwood (VP), Bobby F Leonard (VP), Melvin A McCubbin (VP and Chief Financial Officer), Frank H Menaker Jr (VP and General Counsel), Dan A Peterson (VP), Robert J Polutchko (VP), Robert W Powell Jr (VP and Treasurer), Philip H Sendel (VP), Peter B Teets (VP), A Thomas Young (VP)

PRINCIPAL ACTIVITIES: Manufacture of equipment for the aerospace industry; defense systems
Principal Bank: Morgan Guaranty Trust Co of New York
Financial Information:

	Dec 31 1985	Dec 31 1986
	$'000	$'000
Sales revenues	4,410,064	4,752,537
Net income	249,390	202,344
Earnings per share	$4.36	$3.67
Shareholders equity	707,960	843,376

No of Employees: 65,000

MARTIN PROCESSING INC

PO Box 5068, Martinsville, VA 24115
Tel: (703) 629 1711

Chairman: William F Franck
President: R Keith Smith
Senior Executive Officers: Donald C Martin (Executive VP), Ronald W Martin (VP), Albert K Scriven Jr (VP), Alan Taylor (VP), Stephen A Briley (Treasurer), Martha J Wagner (Secretary)

PRINCIPAL ACTIVITIES: Manufacture of specialty polyester products including films for solar control and decorative uses; processing and dyeing of carpet yarn
Principal Bank: NCNB National Bank of North Carolina
Financial Information:

	$'000
Sales revenues	51,035

No of Employees: 1,000

MARTY GILMAN, INC

See GILMAN, MARTY, , INC

MARWAIS STEEL CO

700 Larkspur Landing Circle, Larkspur, CA 94939
Tel: (415) 461-3912
Telex: WUT 171099 marwais lark

Chairman: Marshall I Wais (and President)
Senior Executive Officers: Marshall I Wais Jr (Executive VP), Peter Wais (VP Commercial), C D A Coch (Comptroller)

PRINCIPAL ACTIVITIES: Coating of metals; manufacture of protective shelters
Principal Bank: Crocker National Bank
Financial Information:

	$'000
Sales revenues	75,000

No of Employees: 200

MARY KAY COSMETICS, INC

8787 Stemmons Freeway, Dallas, TX 75247
Tel: (214) 630-8787

Chairman: Mary Kay Ash
President: Richard R Rogers
Senior Executive Officers: Gerald M Allen (VP, Administration), Monty C Barber (VP, Secretary), Myra O Barker Ph D (VP, Research and Product Development), Richard C Bartlett (VP, Marketing), Timothy M Byrd (VP, Controller), Lawrence G Cox (VP, Treasurer), G Lowrence Hodge (VP, Manufacturing Operations), Patrick E Howard (VP, Manufacturing Group), John P Rochon (VP, Finance)

PRINCIPAL ACTIVITIES: Mary Kay Cosmetics Inc, is engaged in the production and marketing of cosmetics and skin care products.
Trade Marks and Registered Trade Names: Acapella(R), Alameda & Ampersand(R), Angelfire(R), Applause(R), Avenir(R), Beaker and Flower Design(R), Beauty Blotter(R), Brisante, Business in a Book(R), Calais(R), Candor, Challenger, Color Awareness, Cosmetic Creations(R), Cross Fire(R), Day Radiance(R), Exquisite(R), Eye Logo(R), Face Fashion(R), Facets(R), Fashion Forecast(R), Genji(R), Glamour Adventure(R), Great Fashion(R), Great Fashion Forecast(R), Intrigue(R), K Logo(R), Laredo(R), Lead Times(R), Magic

Masque(R), Mary Kay Logo(R), Mary Kay(R), Mary Kay Newsline(R), Mary Kay Rose(R), Mesquite (chose to register TAMERISK), MK Design(R), Mr K(R), Palatino(R), Personal Touch(R), Quattro, Raz(R), Sakari, Season's Best, Shinji, Silverton(R), Souvenir(R), Sun Veil(R), Tamerisk(R), That's the Beauty of Mary Kay(R), The Cosmetic That's More Than a Cover-up(R), TLC and Heart Logo(R), Try Before You Buy, Voyage(R)
Parent Company: Mary Kay Corporation
Principal Subsidiaries: Mary Kay Cosmetics SA (Argentina); Mary Kay Cosmetics Pty Ltd (Australia); Mary Kay Cosmetics Ltd (Canada); Business Travel Management Inc
Principal Bank: Bank of New York
Financial Information:

	Dec 31 1985	Dec 31 1986
	$'000	$'000
Sales revenues	248,970	255,016
Income (loss) before taxes*	46,346	(31,966)
Net income (loss)	19,520	(33,262)
Dividends	2,576	9,378
Common stock	100	100
Retained income	49,319	6,477
Shareholders equity	137,883	95,041

*and extraordinary item

No of Employees: 1,089 USA, 176 abroad

MARYLAND CUP CORPORATION

Owings Mills, MD 21117
Tel: (301) 363-1111
Telex: TWX 710 862 0855 mccc opr bal

Chairman: Paul J Schierl
President: James Alexy
Senior Executive Officers: Milton C Borenstein (Executive VP and Treasurer), Arnold Shapiro (Senior VP), Edward Shapiro (VP), Herbert Chernis (VP), Eugene Foreman (VP and Secretary), Morton C Gilden (VP)

PRINCIPAL ACTIVITIES: Manufacture of paper and plastic cups, plates and containers, drinking straws, ice cream wafers and cones
Parent Company: Fort Howard Paper Co, Green Bay, WI
Financial Information:

	$'000
Sales revenues	655,000

No of Employees: 10,000

MASCO CORPORATION

21001 Van Born Road, Taylor, MI 48180
Tel: (313) 274-7400

Chairman: Richard A Manoogian (and Chief Executive Officer)
President: Wayne B Lyon
Senior Executive Officers: Gerald Bright (VP, General Counsel and Secretary), David A Doran (VP, Taxes), John R Leekley (VP, Corporate Counsel), Richard G Mosteller (Senior VP, Finance), John C Nicholls Jr (Treasurer), Robert B Rodowski (VP, Controller), Samuel Valenti III (VP, Investments), David G Wesenberg (VP, Human Resources), Brian P Campbell (Director of Business Development), Frederick L Copeland (Group VP), Sam A Cracchiolo (Director of Corporate Development), Charles Janjikian (Group President), Raymond F Kennedy (Group President), Allan J Krauss (Group VP), Hans-Georg Mangold (VP, International Europe), Peter J Pirsch (Group President), Phillip D Pryne (Group President)

PRINCIPAL ACTIVITIES: Masco Corporation manufactures building and home improvement products, home furnishings and other specialty consumer products
Trade Names: Acqua Glass, Delta, Merillat, Baldwin, Henredon, Drexel, Weiser Lock
Principal Subsidiaries: Aqua Glass; Merillat; Baldwin; Henredon Furniture; Drexl Heritage Furnishings; Brass-Craft Mfg Co
Principal Banks: Morgan Guaranty, New York; National Bank of Detroit
Financial Information:

	Dec 31 1985	Dec 31 1986
	$'000	$'000
Sales revenues	1,153,960	1,452,010
Income before taxes	268,780	330,910
Net income	164,480	203,420
Dividends	35,860	49,630
Dividends per share	$0.29	$0.34
Earnings per share	$1.28	$1.56
Common stock	64,370	130,860
Retained income	832,420	986,420
Shareholders equity	978,970	1,159,070

No of Employees: 22,900

MASCO INDUSTRIES, INC

21001 Van Born Road, Taylor, MI 48180
Tel: (313) 274-7405

Chairman: Richard A Manoogian (and Chief Executive Officer)
President: Erwin H Billig
Senior Executive Officers: Hans R Beisch (Group President), James W Hook (Group President), James J Sigouin (VP Finance and Treasurer), Michael J Vogel (Group President), Timothy Wadhams (Controller)

PRINCIPAL ACTIVITIES: Masco Industries manufactures custom engineered and other commercial and specialty industrial products
Trade Names: Atlas Door, Acme Steel, Taylor Building Products
Principal Subsidiaries: Flo-Con; Braun Engineering; Rieke Corp; Acme Steel; C & C
Principal Bank: National Bank of Detroit
Financial Information:

	Dec 31 1985	Dec 31 1986
	$'000	$'000
Sales revenues	599,080	712,260
Income before taxes	46,800	51,740
Net income	2,900	9,390
Earnings per share	$0.15	$0.83
Common stock	18,400	36,800
Retained income	26,700	32,930
Shareholders equity	105,760	335,530

No of Employees: 15,800

MASLAND, C H, & SONS

Box 40, Springs Road, Carlisle, PA 17013
Tel: (717) 249-1866

Chairman: Frank E Masland III
President: Beryl C Gardner (and Chief Executive Officer)
Senior Executive Officers: Charles H Masland III (VP Research), Daniel L Masland (VP Auto Purchasing and Development), Michael L Clymin (VP Diversification), Edmund C Peach Jr (VP and General Manager Floorcovering Products), William J Branch (VP and General Manager Auto Products), John H Bowers (Secretary and Treasurer)

PRINCIPAL ACTIVITIES: Manufacture of carpets
Financial Information:

	$'000
Sales revenues	199,200

No of Employees: 2,000

MASON & HANGER-SILAS MASON CO

200 West Vine Street, Lexington, KY 40507
Tel: (606) 252-4421
Telex: WUT 382 947 masonhanger

Chairman: Robert L Telford
President: Robert B Jewell
Senior Executive Officers: D E Heffelbower (Executive VP Operations), L L Snedden (Executive VP Engineering), D R Dunham (Senior VP Defense Activities), John C Custer (Senior VP International), R L Holmberg (VP Iowa Facility), C

R Poole Jr (VP Pantex Facility), J M Higgins (VP Cornhusker Facility)
PRINCIPAL ACTIVITIES: Management services and engineering consultancy; manufacture of computer related products and ammunition
Principal Bank: Chemical Bank
Financial Information:

	$'000
Sales revenues	180,000

No of Employees: 4,400

MASONITE CORPORATION

One South Wacker Drive, Chicago, IL 60606
Tel: (312) 750-0900
Telex: TWX 510 100 7138 masonite cgo

President: Anthony J Falvo Jr (and Chief Executive Officer)
Senior Executive Officers: Richard H Fleming (VP Finance and Chief Financial Officer and Treasurer), Kenneth J Giacomino (Controller), Kenneth M Hepler (VP, Wood Fiber Division), Edward A Markus Jr (VP, Secretary and General Counsel), Timothy A McGagin (Group VP, Furniture Components), James U Morrison (Group VP, Hardboard), Jack R Mulholland (VP Engineering and International), Howard A Spalt (VP, Research and Development), John F Carlson (Assistant Treasurer), Vincent P Flood (Assistant Secretary)

PRINCIPAL ACTIVITIES: Manufacture of timber products for the building industry
Parent Company: USG Corporation
Principal Bank: Continental Illinois National Bank
Financial Information:

	Dec 31 1986 $'000
Sales revenues	492,118
Income before taxes	29,401
Net income	13,819
Common stock	246,331
Retained income	104,201
Shareholders equity	344,306

No of Employees: 7,000

MASSACHUSETTS COMPUTER CORPORATION

1 Technology Park, Westford, MA 01886
Tel: (617) 692 6200

Chairman: Daniel S Gregory
President: August P Klein (and Chief Executive Officer)
Senior Executive Officers: Daniel M Murray (VP International), Robert B Schmidt (VP Finance and Treasurer), Gary J Bowen (VP Sales), Douglas M Rowan (VP Marketing), Lorrin G Gale (VP Engineering), Richard A Phillips (VP Manufacturing), Allan L Wallack (VP Business Development)

PRINCIPAL ACTIVITIES: Manufacture of electronic computer products
Financial Information:

	$'000
Sales revenues	45,000

No of Employees: 540

MASSACHUSETTS MUTUAL LIFE INSURANCE COMPANY

1295 State Street, Springfield, MA 01111
Tel: (413) 788-8411

Chairman: James R Martin
President: William J Clark
Senior Executive Officers: David J Blackwell, Richard G Dooley, John M Naughton, C Norman Peacor, A Peter Quinn Jr, Seymour Sternberg, Thomas B Wheeler

PRINCIPAL ACTIVITIES: Mass Mutual sells and services traditional and non-traditional forms of life and disability insurance, tax qualified retirement plans, annuities and equity products through its Individual Product Line. The Company offers a broad portfolio of group life and health benefit funding options and health care cost containment through its Group Life and Health Product Line. Mass Mutual is a major US provider of investment and benefit services to retirement plan sponsors through its Group Pension Product Line
Principal Subsidiaries: MML Bay State Life Insurance Company; MML Life Insurance Company; MML Pension Insurance Company; MML Syndicate Inc; MML Investors Services Inc; MML Realty Management Corporation
Financial Information:

	Dec 31 1986 $'000
Premium income	2,487,919
Investment income	1,338,391
Total assets	18,027,848

No of Employees: 8,500

MASSEY-FERGUSON INC

1901 Bell Avenue, Des Moines, IA 50315
Tel: (515) 247-2011
Telex: WUT 478 413 masferg dms a

Chairman: A A Thornbrough
President: John H Ruth (and Chief Executive Officer)
Senior Executive Officers: E D Ludlow (VP Administration and Legal), Barry Sullivan (Treasurer)

PRINCIPAL ACTIVITIES: Manufacture of machinery for the agricultural and construction industries
Parent Company: Varity Corporation
Principal Bank: Continental Illinois National Bank & Trust Co of Chicago
Financial Information:

	$'000
Sales revenues	1,600,000

No of Employees: 4,500

MASTER LOCK COMPANY

2600 N 32nd Street, Milwaukee, WI 53210
Tel: (414) 444-2800
Telex: 2 69444

President: George F Villwock (and Chief Executive Officer)
Senior Executive Officers: Earl G Stintzi (VP Manufacutring), Peter U Jung (VP Marketing and Sales), Ralph A Mirsberger (VP and Controller)

PRINCIPAL ACTIVITIES: The world's largest padlock manufacturer, producer of keyed and combination padlocks, locker locks and locking accessories marketed through hardware outlets, home centers, volume retailers, locksmiths, as well as to industry, schools and institutions
Trade Names: Master Locks
Parent Company: American Brands Inc, New York, NY
Principal Subsidiaries: Dexter Lock
Principal Bank: First Wisconsin Milwaukee
Financial Information:

	1986 $'000
Sales revenues	128,225

No of Employees: 1,250

MATERIAL SCIENCES CORPORATION

2300 East Pratt Boulevard, Elk Grove Village, IL 60007
Tel: (312) 439-8270

Chairman: William N Guthrie (and Chief Executive Officer)
Senior Executive Officers: William R Beattie (Director, VP Finance and Secretary), Frank J Lazowski (VP-Human Resources)

PRINCIPAL ACTIVITIES: Material Sciences Corporation was founded in 1971 to develop and commercialize advanced materials technologies for emerging and growth markets. Through its subsidiaries, the company utilizes coil-coating, metallizing, electroplating and composite technologies to produce coated, laminated and composite materials through continuous processes. The company intends, through internal development and acquisitions, to diversify further into the advanced coated-materials technologies of metallizing, coating and laminating thin, polymeric films; to expand its geographic base and market share in coil-coated sheet-metal materials, including structural composites; and to maintain its leadership position in providing corrosion-resistant sheet steel to automotive and other industries

Principal Subsidiaries: Pre Finish Metals Incorporated; Scharr Industries Inc; Deposition Technology Inc

Financial Information:

	Feb 28 1986	Feb 28 1987
	$'000	$'000
Sales revenues	113,704	126,270
Income before taxes	21,065	7,872
Net income	10,708	6,480
Earnings per share(1)	$2.10	$1.25
Earnings per share(2)	$2.08	$1.22
Common stock	102	103
Retained income	28,264	34,744
Shareholders equity	37,004	44,263

(1) primary
(2) fully diluted

No of Employees: 490

MATERIALS RESEARCH CORPORATION

Orangeburg, NY 10962
Tel: (914) 359-4200
Telex: 221862
Telefax: (914) 425-6075

Chairman: Sheldon Weinig (and President and Chief Executive Officer)
Senior Executive Officers: Garrett E Pierce (Executive VP and Treasurer), N Jakobs (VP), T S Catalano (VP), D Yorke (VP), M Lipton (VP), F Shinneman (VP)

PRINCIPAL ACTIVITIES: MRC provides technically innovative products used in thin film technology. Thin films, the core of our technology, are typically several millionths of an inch thick. They are layers of highly characterized metals or sophisticated alloys and compounds which are used in the production of semiconductor and hybrid integrated circuits, computer memory disks and an increasing array of new products. The Company develops and manufactures high technology consumable materials from which these films are made, high performance ceramic substrates on which hybrid integrated circuits are deposited and sputtering and plasma etching equipment for thin film fabrication. We market these products to the semiconductor, telecommunications and computer industries on a worldwide basis

Principal Subsidiaries: Materials Research Ltd (UK); Materials Research GmbH (Germany); Materials Research SA (France); Materials Research Srl (Italy); MRC Export Corp; NIHON MRC Co Ltd (Japan)

Principal Bank: Chase Manhattan Bank

Financial Information:

	Nov 2 1986	Oct 31 1987
	$'000	$'000
Sales revenues	89,095	97,977
(Loss) before taxes	(12,274)	(1,894)
Net (loss)	(10,117)	(1,964)
Dividends	370	-
Dividends per share	$0.09	-
(Loss) per share net	($2.46)	($0.47)
Common stock	4,142	4,142
Retained income	5,053	3,089
Shareholders equity	32,312	30,759

No of Employees: 550

MATRIX CORPORATION

One Ramland Road, Orangeburg, NY 10962
Tel: (914) 365-0190

Chairman: Peter Harvey
President: Franklin G Bishop (and Chief Executive Officer)
Senior Executive Officers: Ivan Volent (VP), Elliot Schick (VP and Treasurer), M Kochman (VP and Assistant Secretary), Michael Druckman (VP)

PRINCIPAL ACTIVITIES: Manufacture of electrical and electronic equipment including communications, computer and radio and television equipment, medical equipment including X-ray equipment, photographic equipment

Principal Subsidiaries: Industrial Communications Co; Matrix Instruments Inc; Matrix Instruments Service Corp; Instrument Leasing Corp; Matrix Instrument Export Corp; Multi-Track Magnetics Inc; Vas Corp; VAS Digital Inc; VAS Internation Corp; Digital Optics Corp

Principal Bank: Continental Illinois National Bank and Trust Co

Financial Information:

	$'000
Sales revenues	93,000

No of Employees: 850

MATRIX SCIENCE CORPORATION

455 Maple Avenue, Torrance, CA 90503
Tel: (213) 328-0271
Telex: TRT 188147 matrix trnc

Chairman: Joseph S O'Flaherty (and Chief Executive Officer)
President: Ronald Hammond
Senior Executive Officers: John MacQueen (Senior VP Operations and Secretary), Thomas Fleming (VP Finance), William Mattingly (VP Engineering), Thomas Maher (VP Reliability), Anthony Westcot (VP Marketing)

PRINCIPAL ACTIVITIES: Manufacture of electrical equipment

Principal Bank: First Interstate Bank

Financial Information:

	$'000
Sales revenues	80,000

No of Employees: 1,000

MATSUSHITA ELECTRIC CORPORATION OF AMERICA

One Panasonic Way, Secaucus, NJ 07094
Tel: (201) 348-7000

Chairman: Masaharu Matsushita
President: Kyoshi Seki (and Chief Executive Officer)
Senior Executive Officers: Toru Doi (VP Finance and Accounting), Ira Perlman (VP Administration), Seth Waller (VP Legal and Secretary), Kaoru Nagao (VP Corporate Planning)

PRINCIPAL ACTIVITIES: Electrical and electronic equipment for the consumer market, industry and telecommunications

Parent Company: Matsushita Electric Industrial Co Ltd (Japan)

Financial Information:

	$'000
Sales revenues	3,700,000

No of Employees: 8,000

MATTEL INC

5150 Rosecrans Avenue, Hawthorne, CA 90250
Tel: (213) 978-5150

Chairman: John W Amerman (and Chief Executive Officer)
President: Glenn A Hastings
Senior Executive Officers: Jill E Barad (Executive VP), Raymond W Ferris (Executive VP and Chief Financial Officer), Loren H Hildebrand (Executive VP), Joseph F Morrison Jr (Executive VP Marketing), Gary L Schwander (Executive VP), Judith A Shackleford (Executive VP), Richard W Caslow (Senior VP Orient Operations), Leonard Croft (Senior VP International), Sam S Djujic (Senior VP Domestic Operations), Donald W

Howell (Senior VP Asia/Pacific Region), William P Johns (Senior VP Systems and Product Planning), Steven A Nelson (Senior VP Design and Development), Timothy P Reames Sr (Senior VP, Secretary and General Counsel), Lindsay F Williams (Senior VP International), Spencer C Boise (VP Corporate Affairs), Ben J Little (VP and Treasurer), Jerry E Neal (VP and Corporate Control)

PRINCIPAL ACTIVITIES: Manufacture of toys
Principal Bank: Bank of America
Financial Information:

	Jan 31 1986 $'000
Sales revenues	1,058,702
Net (loss)	(951)
(Loss) per share	($0.20)
Shareholders equity	152,372

No of Employees: 20,000

MATTHEW BENDER & CO
See BENDER, MATTHEW, & CO

MATTHEWS INTERNATIONAL CORPORATION
PO Box 4999, Pittsburgh, PA 15206
Tel: (412) 363-2500

President: William M Hauber (and Chief Executive Officer)
Senior Executive Officers: Donald Edwards (Executive VP and Chief Administration Officer), James L Parker (VP and Secretary), Robert T Bustebo (VP), Thomas N Kennedy (VP and Treasurer), David J DeCarlo (VP)

PRINCIPAL ACTIVITIES: Manufacture of lettering equipment and products
Principal Bank: Mellon Bank
Financial Information:

	$'000
Sales revenues	73,000

No of Employees: 1,260

MAUI LAND & PINEAPPLE CO, INC
PO Box 187, Kahului, Maui, HI 96732
Tel: (808) 877-3351
Telex: 910 350 2258

Chairman: Colin C Cameron (and President)
Senior Executive Officers: Joseph W Hartley Jr (Executive VP Operations), Paul J Meyer (Executive VP Finance), Dennis K Iwasaka (Secretary and Treasurer)

PRINCIPAL ACTIVITIES: Growing and canning of pineapple; development of resort facilities on the island of Maui including restaurants, hotels and condominiums
Principal Subsidiaries: Maui Pineapple Co Ltd; Kapalua Land Co Ltd
Principal Bank: Bank of Hawaii
Financial Information:

	$'000
Sales revenues	108,000

No of Employees: 2,520

MAX FACTOR & CO
1655 N McCadden Place, Hollywood, CA 90028
Tel: (213) 856-6000
Telex: WUT 559673 mirage

President: Paul Masturgo (US Division)
Senior Executive Officers: Lin Stinson (Executive VP US Sales), Art De Gasteno (Senior VP Packaging Design), Cheryl Scott Daniels (VP Frangrance), Sharon Le Van (VP Cosmetics), Carol Walters (VP Public Relations)

PRINCIPAL ACTIVITIES: Manufacture of beauty products including cosmetics and fragrances
Parent Company: Norton Simon Inc, Ultimate Holding Company-Beatrice Companies Inc
Principal Subsidiaries: Almay Inc; Stephen Burrows Fragrance Inc; Halston Fragrances Inc; Parfums Corday Inc
Financial Information:

	$'000
Sales revenues	520,000

No of Employees: 9,000

MAXCO INC
PO Box 22218, Lansing, MI 48909-2218
Tel: (517) 484-1414

Chairman: Max A Coon (and President)
Senior Executive Officers: Vincent Shunsky (Treasurer), Eric L Cross (Secretary)

PRINCIPAL ACTIVITIES: Manufacture of welding equipment, plastic products and materials handling machinery; wholesale trade in paint and paper products
Principal Subsidiaries: Pak-Sak Industries
Principal Bank: Detroit Bank and Trust
Financial Information:

	$'000
Sales revenues	67,000

No of Employees: 700

MAXICARE HEALTH PLANS INC
5200 West-Century Boulevard, Los Angeles, CA 90045
Tel: (213) 568-9000

Chairman: Fred W Wasserman (and Chief Executive Officer)
President: Pamela K Anderson (and Chief Operating Officer)
Senior Executive Officers: David M Hallis (Senior VP Marketing), Alan Bloom (Secretary and General Counsel), Randall S Anderson (VP Operations), Stephen R Casey (VP Government Relations), John E Christensen (Treasurer), Horace Clark (VP Management Information Systems), Perry Cohen (VP Pharmacy Services), Mark Hanrahan (VP Market Development), Frank Matricardi (VP Planning), Kathleen Sage (VP Human Resources), John Shehorn (VP Facility Development), Samuel L Westover (VP and Chief Financial Officer), Karl Wichser (VP Administrative Services), Thomas Williams (VP Development), Gerald Zaid (VP Medical Affairs)

PRINCIPAL ACTIVITIES: Operation of health maintenance systems
Principal Subsidiaries: Maxicare Life and Health Insurance Co; Pritikin Programs Inc; Maxicare Indiana Inc; Mexicare Texas Inc; Maxicare Utah Inc; Maxicare Medical Centers Inc; Maxi-Lomita Pharmacy; Maxicare Health Plan of Missouri Inc
Financial Information:

	Dec 31 1986 $'000
Sales revenues	914,400
Net income	4,297
Earnings per share	$0.13
Shareholders equity	227,786

No of Employees: 7,000

MAXTOR CORPORATION
211 River Oaks Parkway, San Jose, CA 95134
Tel: (408) 432 1700

Chairman: James M McCoy
President: George Scalise
Senior Executive Officers: Jack S Swartz (Senior VP), William J Dobbin (Senior VP, Finance and Administration), Steven P Kitrosser (Executive VP, Operations), Mike Kowalski (VP, Finance and Administration), John Levinson (VP, Strategic Planning), Mike Warner (VP, Engineering), Leon Malmed (VP, Disk Drive Products)

PRINCIPAL ACTIVITIES: Manufacturing high capacity Winchester and optical data storage products

Principal Subsidiaries: U.S. Design Corporation; Storage Dimensions Corporation
Financial Information:

	Mar 31 1986	Mar 31 1987
	$'000	$'000
Sales revenues	85,155	175,299
Income before taxes	12,004	36,944
Net income	10,682	26,337
Earnings per share	$0.78	$1.39
Common stock	147	182
Retained income (deficit)	24,177	(2,160)
Shareholders equity	101,563	43,333

No of Employees: 2,000

MAXUS ENERGY CORPORATION

Diamond Shamrock Tower, 717 North Harwood Street, Dallas, TX 75201
Tel: (214) 922-2000

Chairmen: W H Bricker, C L Blackburn (also President)
Senior Executive Officers: J T Fretthold (Secretary)

PRINCIPAL ACTIVITIES: Exploration, production, processing and sale of oil and gas
Principal Subsidiaries: Diamond Shamrock Exploration Co; Diamond Shamrock Refining & Marketing Co; Diamond Shamrock Coal Co; Diamond Shamrock Offshore Partners
Financial Information:

	31.12.86
	$'000
Sales revenues	2,514,000
(Loss) before taxes	(116,000)
(Loss) per share	($0.6)

MAXWELL LABORATORIES INC

8888 Balboa Avenue, San Diego, CA 92123
Tel: (619) 279 5100

Chairman: Alan C Kolb (and Chief Executive Officer)
President: Monson H Hayes Jr (and Chief Operating Officer)
Senior Executive Officers: Michael Montgomery (Senior VP), Floyd R Graham (VP), Donald R Grine (VP), Kedar D Pyatt Jr (VP), Joseph A Sevigny (VP), Andrew R Wilson (VP), Sean M Maloy (VP Finance and Chief Financial Officer), Karl M Samuelian (Secretary)

PRINCIPAL ACTIVITIES: Manufacture of high voltage pulse power systems and components for scientific, commercial and defense applications; pollution control equipment
Principal Bank: Lloyds Bank of California
Financial Information:

	$'000
Sales revenues	47,000

No of Employees: 650

MAY DEPARTMENT STORES COMPANY (THE)

611 Olive Street, St Louis, MO 63101
Tel: (314) 342-6300

Chairman: David C Farrell (and Chief Executive Officer)
President: Thomas A Hays
Senior Executive Officers: Richard L Battram (Vice Chairman), Lawrence E Honig (Vice Chairman), Jerome T Loeb (Vice Chairman and Chief Financial Officer), Louis J Garr Jr (Executive VP and General Counsel), R Dean Wolfe (Executive VP, Real Estate), John F Danahy (Senior VP, Data Processing), Douglas J Giles (Senior VP, Human Resources), James F Harner (Senior VP, Customer Service and Operations), Lonny J Jay (Senior VP, Planning and Reporting), Charles B Luber (Senior VP, Real Estate), J Kent McHose (Senior VP, Control), James Abrams (VP, Corporate Communications), Robert B Aldridge (VP, Shortage Control and Security), George A Alexander (VP, Credit), Gene E Bauer (VP, Executive Recruiting), James R Bodemuller (VP, Merchandise Information Systems), Richard A Brickson (VP, Secretary and Counsel), Michael C Canarios (VP, Planning and Analysis), William M Goddard (VP, Risk Management and Insurance), Frank D Gunter (VP, Taxes), Laurence M Hellman (VP, Merchandise Research), Mark E Hood (VP, Accounting and Reporting), Jan R Kniffen (VP, Treasurer), Dennis M Lee (VP, Executive Development), Robert L McDowell (VP, Corporate Development), Barry S Silver (VP, Audit), Ruth A Streit (VP, Compensation and Benefits), Henry A Wagner (VP, EDP Systems Development), John E White (VP, Merchandise Distribution), Frank J Williams Jr (VP, Public Affairs and Counsel)

PRINCIPAL ACTIVITIES: Retail stores including department stores, shopping centers, discount stores and self-service shoe stores
Trade Names: NYSE-(MA), Daily Newspapers (MayDS)
Principal Subsidiaries and Divisions: Lord & Taylor, 12 states; May Co, California; Hecht's, Washington, DC; J W Robinson's, Los Angeles; Famous-Barr Co, St Louis; Kaufmann's, Pittsburgh; L S Ayres, Indianapolis; G Fox, Hartford; May Co, Cleveland; May D&F, Denver; Meier & Frank, Portland, OR; Sibley's Rochester, NY; O'Neil's, Akron; Goldwaters, Scottsdale; Hahne's, New Jersey; May Cohens, Jacksonville; Caldor, 9 states; Venture, 7 states; Volume Shoe, 42 states; Loehmann's, 29 states; May Centers, Inc, 9 states; May Merchandising Corporation; May Department Stores International; May Design & Construction Company
Principal Bank: Centerre Trust Co (Transfer Agent and Registrar)
Financial Information:

	Feb 1 1986	Jan 31 1987
	$'000	$'000
Revenues*	9,542,000	10,376,000
Income before taxes	647,000	668,000
Net income	347,000	381,000
Dividends	124,000	131,000
Dividends per share	$0.92	$1.02
Earnings per share	$2.20	$2.44
Common stock	122,000	153,000
Retained income	2,049,000	2,263,000
Shareholders equity	2,421,000	2,595,000

*Net retail sales and rental revenues

No of Employees: 151,000

MAYER, OSCAR, FOODS CORPORATION

PO Box 7188, Madison, WI 53707
Tel: (608) 241-3311
Telex: 26 5468

Chairman: Jerry M Hiegel (and Chief Executive Officer)
President: James W McVey
Senior Executive Officers: Peter J DeLuca (Senior VP), Ralph H Johnson (Senior VP), Walter S Brager (Group VP Operations and Engineering), Thomas F Duesler (Group VP Marketing), Eugene E Jarrel (Group VP International), Alan G Becker (Group VP Operations), Ronald S Kelley (Group VP Operations), Bjorn J Thompson (Group VP Technical Services), Raymond G Winburn (Group VP Operations), Robert C Lowes (Group VP, Treasurer and Chief Financial Officer), Lowell E Brower (VP Business Development Asia/Pacific), Francis L Campanile (VP Business Development Europe), Harry F Clew (VP and Managing Director Prima), Alan C Dieter (VP and Plant Manager), Albert L Frommeyer (VP and Plant Manager), Gary Karp (VP and General Manager Food Services), Roger D Kinson (VP and Plant Manager), John I Lillie (VP and General Manager Claussen Operation), Phyllis A Lovrien (VP Consumer Affairs), Harold F Mayer (VP Corporate Mateirals), Patrick J Luby (VP and Corporate Economist), Roman A Meier (VP and Plant Manager), Donald E Peterson (VP Management Information Services), Hal G Smith (VP and Plant Manager), Paul G Roehrig (VP Research and Development), Thomas J Ryan (VP, Secretary and Chief

Legal Counsel), Lee N Scheele (VP Strategic Planning and Corporate Development), John E Spohn (VP and Plant Manager), Richard J Waldrop (VP Engineering), C David Harkness (VP and Plant Manager)

PRINCIPAL ACTIVITIES: Meat production and processing
Parent Company: General Foods Corporation, White Plains, NY
Financial Information:

	$'000
Sales revenues	1,770,000

No of Employees: 14,500

MAYFAIR SUPER MARKETS INC

681 Newark Avenue, Elizabeth, NJ 07208
Tel: (201) 352 6400

Chairman: Stanley P Kaufelt (and President and Chief Executive Officer)
President: Anthony R Petrillo (and Chief Operating Officer)
Senior Executive Officers: Michael Shapiro (Senior VP Finance, Administration, Treasurer and Chief Financial Officer), Jacqueline K Keller (VP Marketing and Communications), Robert Behrens (VP Production), Richard Cantalino (VP Engineering), Paul Cona (VP Corporate Affairs)

PRINCIPAL ACTIVITIES: Retail food stores
Principal Bank: Midlantic National Bank
Financial Information:

	$'000
Sales revenues	360,000

No of Employees: 3,600

MAYFLOWER CORP INC

9998 N Michigan Road, Carmel, IN 46032
Tel: (317) 875-1000
Telex: 910 9977043

Chairman: John B Smith (and President and Chief Executive Officer)
Senior Executive Officers: Gary L Light (Executive VP), Richard L Russell (Executive VP), Michael L Smith (Executive VP), Patrick F Carr (Senior VP Finance and Treasurer), Harold R Elliot Jr (Senior VP Corporate Affairs), Ted A Helkema (Senior VP Administration), Robert H Irvin (Senior VP and Secretary), Dennis C Norman (Senior VP Management Information Systems), Kenneth R Richman (Senior VP Warehouse Division), Donald K Sears (Senior VP Special Transport Systems Division), Elizabeth O Stevens (Senior VP Corporate Communications), Donald H Warner (Senior VP Household Goods Division), Daniel E Yates (Senior VP)

PRINCIPAL ACTIVITIES: Holding company with interests in long distance trucking and storage
Principal Bank: American Fletcher National Bank
Financial Information:

	Dec 31 1985	Dec 31 1986
	$'000	$'000
Sales revenues	619,264	705,796
Net income	14,653	3,527
Shareholders equity	87,092	29,331

No of Employees: 2,200

MAYS, J W, INC

510 Fulton Street, Brooklyn, NY 11201
Tel: (718) 624 7400

Chairman: Max L Shulman
President: Lloyd J Shulman (and Senior VP)
Senior Executive Officers: Alex Slobodin (Executive VP and Treasurer), Richard D'Amura (Senior VP), Ward Lyke (VP), Salvatore Cappuzzo (Secretary)

PRINCIPAL ACTIVITIES: Department store trading
Principal Bank: Republic National Bank of New York
Financial Information:

	$'000
Sales revenues	81,000

No of Employees: 1,300

MAYTAG CO

One Dependability Square, Newton, IA 50208
Tel: (515) 792-7000

Chairman: D J Krumm (and President and Chief Executive Officer)
Senior Executive Officers: R L Nunn (VP Marketing), C W Creagan (VP Labor Relations), Leonard A Hadley (VP Corporate Planning), John C Mellinger (VP Research and Development), J A Schiller (VP and Chief Financial Officer), Jay R Storey (VP Personnel), R J Hoover (Public Relations Director), S O Swanger (VP Manufacturing), D C Byers (Secretary and General Counsel), E J Bennett (Assistant Secretary and Assistant General Counsel)

PRINCIPAL ACTIVITIES: Manufacture of domestic electrical appliances
Principal Subsidiaries: The Maytag Co Ltd; Maytag International Co; Hardwick Stove Co; Jenn-Air Co; Jenn Industries
Principal Bank: Harris Trust and Savings Bank
Financial Information:

	Dec 31 1985	Dec 31 1986
	$'000	$'000
Sales revenues	683,721	1,838,465
Net income	71,840	111,205
Earnings per share	$2.65*	$2.57
Shareholders equity	285,321	550,639

*earnings per share restated to reflect 12/30/85 stock split

No of Employees: 4,930

MAYVILLE METAL PRODUCTS, A DIVISION OF CONNELL LIMITED PARTNERSHIP

First & Highland, Mayville, WI 53050
Tel: (414) 387-3000

Chairman: William Connell
President: Raymond Biegler
Senior Executive Officers: R Gould (VP Operations), L R Huser (VP of Sales and Marketing), D Hickle (Director Engineering), M Malesevich (Controller)

PRINCIPAL ACTIVITIES: Manufacture of precision fabricated metal components and electro/mechanical assembly to the information processing, computer and telecommunications equipment industries
Parent Company: Connell Limited Partnership, Boston, MA
Principal Bank: Bank of Boston
Financial Information:

	$'000
Sales Revenues	50,000

Principal Shareholders: William Connell
No of Employees: 550

MBANK EL PASO, N A

One State National Plaza, PO Box 1072, El Paso, TX 79958
Tel: (915) 532-9922

Chairman: H M Daugherty Jr (and Chief Executive Officer); Vice Chairman: Martin Kern (and Chief Financial Officer)
President: Henry Ellis (and Chief Credit Officer)
Senior Executive Officers: Bailey Greenberry (Executive VP Planning and Analysis), E C Houghton (Executive VP Marketing Services), Morrison Smith (Executive VP Commercial Banking), Dahl Marshall (Senior VP and Senior Trust Officer), Robert D Spear (Senior VP and Controller), Gene Rook (Senior VP Commercial Loans), Robert E Dymsza (Senior VP Investment), Donald J O'Neill (Senior VP Commercial Banking), Steve Curl (Senior VP Commercial

Loans), Donald Shuffstall (Senior VP International Department)

PRINCIPAL ACTIVITIES: Bank
Parent Company: MCorp, Dallas, TX (100%)

No of Employees: 500

MBANK HOUSTON, N A

910 Travis Street, Houston, TX 77002
Tel: (713) 751 6100
Telex: WUT 762613 mbank hou

Chairman: C Richard Vermillion Jr (and Chief Executive Officer); Vice Chariman: Lynn H Miller (Administration)
President: J Thomas Hudgins (and Chief Banking Officer)
Senior Executive Officers: John T Cater (Chairman of Executive Committee), Barry L Allen (Executive VP Affiliates Banking Group), Barrett Burns (Executive VP Credit Policy Group), Stephen D Chipman (Executive VP Individual Banking Group), John T Cooney (Executive VP Trust Group), Arthur R Gralla Jr (Executive VP Energy Group), Walter B Hendrick (Executive VP Real Estate Group), Ben B McAndrew (Executive VP Corporate Banking Group), Charles V Rainwater (Executive VP Treasury Group), John D Sasiadek (Executive VP Operations Group), Richard D Cutsinger (Senior VP and Chief Financial Officer)

PRINCIPAL ACTIVITIES: Bank
Parent Company: MCorp

No of Employees: 1,000

MBI BUSINESS CENTRES INC

1201 Seven Locks Road, Rockville, MD 20854
Tel: (301) 279 0551

Chairman: Avner Parnes (and Chief Executive Officer)
President: Armen A Manoogian (and Chief Operating Officer)
Senior Executive Officers: Ralph B Wagner (Executive VP), Robert J Guerra (Senior VP), Allen A Ashforth (VP), Kenneth K Cleeland (VP, Chief Financial Officer and Treasurer), Edward F Golderer (VP), Russell R Stepke (Secretary)

PRINCIPAL ACTIVITIES: Retail stores for microcomputers and associated products and services
Principal Bank: Maryland National Bank
Financial Information:

	$'000
Sales revenues	95,730

No of Employees: 480

MCA INC

100 Universal City Plaza, Universal City, CA 91608
Tel: (818) 777-1000
Telex: 67-7053

Chairman: Lew R Wasserman (and Chief Executive Officer)
President: Sidney Jay Sheinberg (and Chief Operating Officer)
Senior Executive Officers: Thomas Wertheimer (Executive VP), Irving Azoff (VP, President Music Entertainment Group), Richard E Baker (VP and Controller), Robert B Braswell (VP, Corporate Contributions), J Eugene Brog (VP, Chairman-Spencer Gifts), James N Fiedler (VP, President-Discovision Associates-a joint venture), Lawrence P Fraiberg (VP, President-MCA Broadcasting Group), Eugene F Giaquinto (VP, President-MCA Home Entertainment Group), Harold M Haas (VP and Treasurer, Chief Financial Officer), Robert D Hadl (VP, VP-Universal City Studios, Senior Legal Executive), Robert A Harris (VP, President-MCA Television Group), Gareth Hughes (VP), Peter Israel (VP, Chairman-The Putnam Publishing Group), Stuart K Mandel (VP, Director of Industrial Relations), Donald Menchel (VP, President-MCA TV), Stanley Newman (VP, President-Consumer Products Group), Charles S Paul (VP, President-MCA Enterprises), Thomas Pollock (VP, Chairman-Motion Picture Group), Alvin Rush (VP, Chairman-MCA Television Group), Michael Samuel (VP and Secretary), George Smith (VP, General Tax Counsel), Lawrence D Spungin (VP, President-MCA Development), Jay S Stein (VP, President-MCA Recreation Services Group), Dennis F Dallara (Assistant Controller), Richard C Schiller (Assistant Secretary), Christine R Hanson (Assistant Secretary)

PRINCIPAL ACTIVITIES: MCA Inc is a diversified international company engaged in production and distribution of theatrical, "non-theatrical", television and home video product; operation of a tour of the Company's motion picture studio; licensing of merchandising rights and film property publishing rights; manufacture and distribution of recorded music, music publishing, concert and sports merchandising, personal management and other music entertainment activities; retailing and mail order of gift merchandise; book publishing; development and marketing of toy products; recreation services; and real estate development. The Company has a substantial investment in a corporation primarily engaged in theatrical exhibition of motion pictures in the United States and Canada. On April 3 1987, the Company entered the television broadcast business with the acquisition of WOR-TV in Secaucus, New Jersey
Principal Subsidiaries: Berkley Publishing Corporation; Charter Communications Inc; Cinema International Corporation NV (49%) (Netherlands); Coward-McCann Inc; Duchess Music Corporation; Facility Merchandising Inc; Family Line Inc; Front Line Management Co; Grand Toys Ltd (Canada); Grosset & Dunlap Inc; Jove Publications Inc; Leeds Music Corporation; LJN Toys Ltd; LJN Toys (Hong Kong) Limited (Hong Kong); MCA Artists (England) Ltd (UK); MCA Broadcasting Inc; MCA Cable Services Inc; MCA Canada Ltd (Canada); MCA Concerts Inc; MCA Distributing Corporation; MCA Enterprises Inc; MCA Filmes Do Brasil Ltda (Brazil); MCA Home Video Inc; MCA International BV (Netherlands); MCA Music Ltd (UK); MCA Radio Network Inc; MCA Records Inc; MCA Television Ltd; MCA Videodisc Inc; Merchandising Corporation of America Inc; Miller International Schallplatten GmbH (Germany); Richard Marek, Publishers Inc; Spencer Gifts Inc; The Putnam Publishing Group Inc; Universal City Consultants Ltd; Universal City Property Management Company; Universal City Studios Inc; Universal Film Exchanges Inc; Universal International Films Inc; Universal Pay Television Inc; Walter Lantz Productions Inc; Yosemite Park and Curry Co. Additionally, various subsidiaries do business under the following names: The Putnam Publishing Group, The Berkley Publishing Group, G.P. Putnam's Sons, Perigee Books, Philomel Books, MCA Publishing Rights, The Putnam Young Readers Group, Unicity Music, Musicor Music, MCA Home Entertainment, MCA Manufacturing, MCA Development Company, MCA Music Publishing, MCA Publishing, Coral Records, Decca Records, Kapp Records, Full Moon Records, Lankershim Advertisng, MCA Records International, MCA Special Markets, Songbird Records, Uni Records, Encore Programs, MCA TV, MCA TV Enterprises, MCA TV International, EMKA, United World Films, MCA Recreation Services, MCA/Universal, The Corner Store, Universal Amphitheatre, Universal Education and Visual Arts, Universal Pictures, Universal Pictures Distribution, Universal Pictures Marketing, Universal Pictures Production, Universal Studios Tour, Universal Facilities Rentals, Universal Television, Universal Classics, Universal Studios, Womp's, Womp's Restaurant Bar & Grill, Universal Station, Universal City Florida, 10 UCP Associates, Beautiful Beginnings, Intrigue, Rings 'N Things, Spencer Gifts, Sunset House, A2Z The Best of Everything, Dreamz, Spencer Data Processing Systems, MCA Videocassette, Discovision Associates, and Yosemite Sierra Services Company
Principal Banks: Bank of America; Crocker National Bank; First National Bank of Chicago; National Westminster Bank; Security Pacific Bank

Financial Information:

	Dec 31 1985 $'000	Dec 31 1986 $'000
Sales revenues	2,098,525	2,441,374
Income before taxes	208,259	203,704
Net income	149,959	155,204
Dividends	45,346	52,657
Dividends per share	$0.61	$0.68
Earnings per share	$2.02	$2.02
Common stock	248,851	451,013
Retained income	1,154,339	1,256,886
Shareholders equity	1,400,761	1,582,394

No of Employees: 16,000

MCA RECORDS, INC

70 Universal City Plaza, Universal City, CA 91608
Tel: (818) 508-4000

Chairman: Irving Azoff
President: Myron Roth
Senior Executive Officers: James Bowen (Executive VP, President Nashville Division), Richard Palmese (Executive VP Marketing and Promotions), Jheryl Busby (Senior VP), Bruce Hinton (Senior VP Nashville), Zachary I Horowitz (Senior VP), Steve Meyer (Senior VP), Steve Moir (Senior VP), Larry Solters (Senior VP)

PRINCIPAL ACTIVITIES: Manufacture of records and tapes
Parent Company: MCA Inc
Principal Bank: Bank of America
Financial Information:

	$'000
Sales revenues	308,000

No of Employees: 1,150

MCC POWERS

2942 MacArthur Boulevard, Northbrook, IL 60062
Tel: (312) 272-9555
Telex: WUT 724 357 mcc powers sko

President: John Grad
Senior Executive Officers: Tom Carlin (VP Product Operations), Leon White (VP Sales and Field Operations), Dale Mercer (VP International)

PRINCIPAL ACTIVITIES: Management services for the energy industry
Parent Company: Mark Controls Corp
Principal Bank: Citibank
Financial Information:

	$'000
Sales revenues	172,000

No of Employees: 2,300

MCCALL PUBLISHING CO

230 Park Avenue, New York, NY 10169
Tel: (212) 551-9500

Chairman: Allen M Turner
President: Raymond Eyes (and Publisher)
Senior Executive Officers: Robert Stein (Executive VP and Editor), Andrew Dempsey (VP), Lowell Logan (VP), Vivian Cadden (VP), Larry Galchen (VP Circulation)

PRINCIPAL ACTIVITIES: Publication of magazines
Principal Bank: National Bank of North America
Financial Information:

	$'000
Sales revenues	100,000

No of Employees: 250

MCCONWAY & TORLEY CORPORATION

109 40th Street, Pittsburgh, PA 15201
Tel: (412) 682-4700

Chairman: Richard E Bowe
President: Buddy F Bell (and Chief Executive Officer)
Senior Executive Officers: Joseph F Kahl (VP Sales and Marketing), R Sleeman (VP Manufacturing), Bryan G Deschamps (Treasurer)

PRINCIPAL ACTIVITIES: Manufacture of cast steel products including couplings for the railroad industry
Parent Company: Ellicott Machine Corporation, Baltimore, MD
Principal Bank: Mellon National Bank
Financial Information:

	$'000
Sales revenues	50,000

No of Employees: 400

MCCORMICK & CO, INC

11350 McCormick Road, Hunt Valley, MD 21031
Tel: (301) 667-7301
Panafax: 301-667-7462
Telex: 87410 87410

Chairman: Charles P McCormick (and Chief Executive Officer)
President: Hillsman V Wilson (and Chief Operating Officer)
Senior Executive Officers: Michael A Cipollaro (VP and Managing Director International Group), Donald W Dick Jr (VP and General Manager Consumer Products Group), John W Felton (VP Corporate Communications), Leonard O Gerber (VP Finance and Chief Financial Officer), Richard L Hall (VP-Science and Technology), James J Harrison Jr (VP, Secretary and General Counsel), James A Hooker (VP-Controller), H Donald Jeter (VP-Manufacturing), Thomas B McCord (VP and Treasurer), Charles P McCormick Jr (VP-Packaging Group), Robert M McFadden (VP-Administration), Thomas T Miller (VP-Procurement), Carroll D Nordhoff (VP-HR), Bailey A Thomas (VP-Food Service and Industrial Groups), John P Thompson (VP-Management Information Resources), W Gordon Yates (VP)

PRINCIPAL ACTIVITIES: Manufacture of a wide range of food products including seasonings, flavourings, spices, pickles, dressings and frozen foods, dehydrated fruit and vegetables, popcorn; manufacture of plastic containers and food processing plant
Principal Subsidiaries: (100% owned unless stated): Food and Packaging Operations: USA: Consolidated Operating Units:- Food Service Division; Gilroy Foods, Incorporated; Golden West Foods, Inc; Grocery Products Division; International Division; McCormick-Stange Flavor Division; Setco, Inc; Tubed Products, Inc. Affiliate: Sesame Products, Inc (50%). Real Estate Operations: Unconsolidated Subsidiary:- McCormick Properties, Inc; Huntington Realty Interests, Ltd; McCormick Construction Company, Inc. Outside USA: Consolidated Operating Units:- Botanicus Pte Ltd (Singapore); McCormick do Brasil, S.A. (76%) (Brazil); Club House Foods Inc (Canada); McCormick de Centro America, S.A. (El Salvador); McCormick de Venezuela C.A. (Venezuela); McCormick Foods Australia Pty Ltd (Australia); McCormick GmbH (West Germany); McCormick S.A. (Switzerland); Paterson Jenks plc (UK); McCormick Foods (UK) Limited (UK); Stange Canada, Inc (Canada). Affiliates:-McCormick de Mexico, SA de CV (50%) (Mexico); McCormick-Lion Ltd (49%) (Japan); Stange (Japan) KK (50%) (Japan)
Principal Bank: Chase Manhattan Bank
Financial Information:

	Nov 30 1985 $'000	Nov 30 1986 $'000
Sales revenues	873,000	975,727
Net income	27,800	29,739
Earnings per share	$2.27	$2.46
Shareholders equity	261,100	271,616

No of Employees: 7,460

MCCREARY TIRE & RUBBER CO

Box 749, Indiana, PA 15701

Tel: (412) 357-6600

Telex: TWX 510 4685 140 McCreary inna

Chairman: Harry C McCreary

President: D D Mateer (and Chief Executive Officer)

Senior Executive Officers: Thomas E Anthony (VP Marketing), Robert J Ianarelli (VP Manufacturing), L L Fulton (Treasurer and Controller)

PRINCIPAL ACTIVITIES: Manufacture of tires and industrial rubber products and plastic products

Principal Bank: Marine Midland Bank

Financial Information:

	$'000
Sales revenues	30,000

No of Employees: 300

MCDERMOTT INTERNATIONAL INC

1010 Common Street, New Orleans, LA 70112

Tel: (504) 587-5400

Chairman: J E Cunningham (and Chief Executive Officer)

President: Robert E Howson (and Chief Operating Officer, McDermott Marine Construction and Babcock & Wilcox, Chief Operating Officer, McDermott Int'l Trading Co Inc)

Senior Executive Officers: John A Lynott (Executive VP and Chief Financial and Administrative Officer), Walter M Vannoy (Vice Chairman of the Board), F C Allen Jr (VP and General Counsel, and Corporate Secretary), C F Kraus (VP, Tax Administration), E A Robidoux (VP and Controller), R A Jolliff (Treasurer), N E Mezey (President, McDermott International Investments Co, Inc), G A Stoddart (VP, Financial Relations), R E Woolbert (VP, Employee and Public Relations), G F Ellis (VP, Government Operations), W L Higgins (VP and Group Executive, Marine Construction, North and South America and West Africa Operations), R J Machen (VP and Group Executive, Marine Construction, Middle East, Southeast Area and Europe Operations), J J Stewart (VP and Group Executive, B&W Power Generation), J P Eckert (VP and Group Executive, B&W, Defense and Nuclear Power), M A Keyes (VP and Group Executive, B&W, Industrial Products and Service), K C Thyssen (President, McDermott Int'l Trading Co Inc)

PRINCIPAL ACTIVITIES: McDermott International operates in four business segments: Marine Construction Services performs activities for the oil and gas industry for offshore development drilling and for the production and transportation of oil and gas on a world-wide basis. Power Generation Systems and Equipment principally serves the electric utility industry and the US Government. Engineered Materials produces metal tubular products for mechanical and pressure applications, and insulating products for a variety of industries. Trading comprises the world-wide trading, engineering and construction operations of Coutinho, Caro & Co KGaA (West Germany) as well as other trading services of International

Parent Company: McDermott International, Inc, Panama

Principal Subsidiaries: McDermott International Investments Co, Inc and its subsidiaries; McDermott Incorporated and its subsidiaries; The Babcock and Wilcox Company and its subsidiaries

Financial Information:

	Mar 31 1986 $'000	Mar 31 1987 $'000
Revenues	3,109,239	3,289,322
Income before taxes	32,611	93,434
Net income (loss)	59,089	(102,421)
Dividends	66,533	66,586
Dividends per share	$1.80	$1.80
Earnings (loss) per share	$1.84	($3.46)
Common stock*	36,974	37,053
Retained income	885,436	716,429
Shareholders equity	1,204,373	1,035,275
*number of shares in thousands		

No of Employees: 29,000

MCDONALD, A Y, INDUSTRIES, INC

4800 Chavenelle Road, Dubuque, IA 52001
Tel: (319) 583-7311
Cable: AYMCD DUBUQUE, IOWA USA
Telex: 43-9020 AYMCD DUQU
Fax: (319) 588-0720

Chairman: J M McDonald III (and President and Chief Executive Officer)
Senior Executive Officers: J B McDonald (Senior VP and Corporate Secretary), L J Sherman (Senior VP Corporate Finance)

PRINCIPAL ACTIVITIES: Manufacturers water service products, gas valves and fittings, petroleum handling equipment, pumps and water systems, and solar-powered water pumping systems. Wholesale and retail distributors of plumbing, heating, cooling, lighting, kitchen and industrial supplies and equipment
Principal Subsidiaries: A Y McDonald Mfg Co; A Y McDonald Supply Co Inc; Brock-McVey Company
Principal Bank: First National Bank of Chicago
Financial Information:

	$'000
Sales revenues	90,000

No of Employees: 730

MCDONALD AND COMPANY INVESTMENTS INC

2100 Central National Bank Building, Cleveland, OH 44114
Tel: (216) 443 2300

Chairman: Willard E Carmel (and Subsidiary Officer)
President: Thomas M O'Donnell
Senior Executive Officers: K David Keady (Executive VP), John E Kohl (Executive VP and Secretary), Dean G Lauritzen (Executive VP), John F O'Brien (Executive VP), James V Pease (Executive VP), Robert A Perrier (Executive VP), William B Summers (Executive VP), Edward L Tobol (Executive VP and Chief Financial and Administration Officer)

PRINCIPAL ACTIVITIES: Provision of a wide range of financial services including investment banking and security broking
Principal Subsidiaries: McDonald & Company Securities Inc
Principal Bank: Central National Bank of Cleveland
Financial Information:

	$'000
Revenues	68,000

No of Employees: 440

MCDONALD DAIRY CO

PO Box 469, Flint, MI 48501
Tel: (313) 232-9193

Senior Executive Officers: Dan Schummer (General Manager)

PRINCIPAL ACTIVITIES: Manufacture of a range of dairy products
Parent Company: Michigan Milk Producers Association

Principal Bank: Citizens Commercial and Savings Bank
Financial Information:

	$'000
Sales revenues	100,000

No of Employees: 400

MCDONALD'S CORPORATION

One McDonald Plaza, Oak Brook, IL 60521
Tel: (312) 575-3000
Cable: c/o McDONALD'S PLAZA-OAK BROOK, IL 60525
Telex: 254751 McD OAK R B

Chairman: Fred L Turner
President: Michael R Quinlan (and Chief Executive Officer)
Senior Executive Officers: Gerald Newman (Senior Executive VP and Chief Accounting Officer), Edward H Rensi (Chief Operations Officer, President and Chief Operating Officer-McDonald's U.S.A.), Paul D Schrage (Senior Executive VP, Chief Marketing Officer), Jack M Greenberg (Executive VP and Chief Financial Officer), Donald P Horwitz (Executive VP-Law and Secretary)

PRINCIPAL ACTIVITIES: Quick service restaurants
Financial Information:

	Dec 31 1985	Dec 31 1986
	$'000	$'000
Total revenues	3,760,860	4,240,166
Income before taxes	782,239	848,125
Net income	433,039	479,725
Common stock dividends	75,819	82,519
Dividends per common share*	$0.39	$0.43
Earnings per common share*	$2.22	$2.48
Common stock*	23,062	23,075
Retained earnings	2,499,448	2,893,156
Shareholders equity	2,244,818	2,506,457

*restated for stock splits

No of Employees: 159,000

MCDONNELL DOUGLAS CORPORATION

PO Box 516, St Louis, MO 63166
Tel: (314) 232-0232

Chairman: Sanford N McDonnell (and Chief Executive Officer)
President: John F McDonnell (and Chief Operating Officer)
Senior Executive Officers: R C Little (Corporate VP, Aerospace Group Executive), J E Worsham (Corporate VP, Aerospace Group Executive), J J Causley (Corporate VP, Information Systems Group Executive Officer), J H MacDonald (Corporate VP, Human Resources), J T Sant (Corporate VP, General Counsel), J S McDonnell III (Corporate VP), D Malvern (Corporate VP), G J Meyer (Corporate VP, Communications), Jerry G Brown (VP, Finance), Robert L Harmon (VP, Civic Affairs)

PRINCIPAL ACTIVITIES: Manufacture of aircraft and components; manufacture of electronic and aerospace equipment; computers
Principal Subsidiaries: McDonnell Douglas Finance Corpn; Douglas Aircraft Co; McDonnell Aircraft Co; McDonnell Douglas Astonautics Co; Hughes Helicopters Inc
Financial Information:

	Dec 31 1985	Dec 31 1986
	$'000	$'000
Sales revenues	11,477,700	12,660,600
Income before taxes	541,300	462,200
Net income	345,700	277,500
Dividends	74,000	84,300
Dividends per share	$1.84	$2.08
Earnings per share	$8.60	$6.86
Common stock	40,300	40,600
Retained income	2,195,300	2,388,500
Shareholders equity	2,634,600	2,844,800

No of Employees: 105,696

MCDOWELL ENTERPRISES INC

301 Plus Park Boulevard, Nashville, TN 37217
Tel: (615) 366 4141

Chairman: H B Horner
President: James E Poole (and Chief Executive Officer)
Senior Executive Officers: Charles H Warfield Jr (VP Administration and Secretary), Charles R Honeycutt (VP Contracts and Purchasing), W Gerald Smalling (VP Finance and Chief Financial Officer)

PRINCIPAL ACTIVITIES: Civil engineering and road construction
Principal Bank: Third National Bank
Financial Information:

	$'000
Sales revenues	51,880

No of Employees: 700

MCFADDIN VENTURES INC

1900 Yorktown, Suite 100, Houston, TX 77056
Tel: (713) 871 0212

Chairman: Lance C McFaddin (and President and Chief Executive Officer)
Senior Executive Officers: Theodore M Heesch (Executive VP Development), Gary A Connolly (Senior VP Group), Ross Stewart (Senior VP Administration, Secretary and Treasurer), Michael E Kohy (Controller)

PRINCIPAL ACTIVITIES: Operation and management of bars; supply of alcoholic beverages and food
Principal Bank: InterFirst Bank
Financial Information:

	$'000
Sales revenues	65,890

No of Employees: 1,500

MCGILL MANUFACTURING CO, INC

909 N Lafayette Street, Valparaiso, IN 46383
Tel: (219) 465-2200
Telex: WUT 258 446 McGill valp

Chairman: James C McGill (and President and Chief Executive Officer)
Senior Executive Officers: James S Eason (Executive VP and Chief Operating Officer), Seth H Moseley (Senior VP Industrial Relations), James A Rader (VP Engineering Bearing Division), Phillip Bain (VP Marketing Electrical Division), Ronald E Kozlowski (VP and General Manager Electrical Division), Arnold Brown (VP and General Manager Bearing Division), Walter Ailes (VP, Treasurer and Secretary), James R Heffernan (VP Manufacturing Bearing Division), Charles V Martin (VP Sales Bearing), Detlef Rathman (VP Plant Manager Bearing Division)

PRINCIPAL ACTIVITIES: Manufacture of bearings and electrical equipment
Principal Bank: Continental Illinois National Bank and Trust Co
Financial Information:

	$'000
Sales revenues	82,000

No of Employees: 1,236

MCGRAW-EDISON POWER SYSTEMS DIVISION

PO Box 2850, Pittsburgh, PA 15230
Tel: (412) 777-3200
Telex: TWX 710 793 3611

Chairman: Robert Cizik
President: E Jeney
Senior Executive Officers: Robert W Heiden (VP Finance), William F Oberschelp (VP Marketing and Planning), D J DiFilippo (VP Distribution Apparatus), R B Kalich (VP Power and Switching Apparatus)

PRINCIPAL ACTIVITIES: Manufacture of a wide range of electrical equipment; power distribution equipment

Parent Company: Cooper Industries Inc

Financial Information:

	$'000
Sales revenues	400,000

No of Employees: 5,200

MCGRAW-HILL, INC

1221 Avenue of the Americas, New York, NY 10020

Tel: (212) 512-2000

Telex: 12-7960 (MCGRAWH NYK)

Chairman: Harold W McGraw Jr

President: Joseph L Dionne (and Chief Executive Officer)

Senior Executive Officers: Walter D Serwatka (Executive VP and Chief Financial Officer), Thomas J Sullivan (Executive VP, Administration), Donald L Fruehling (Executive VP, Publishing Operations), Howard D Hosbach (Executive VP, Operations), Robert N Landes (Executive VP, Secretary and General Counsel), Frank J Kaufman (Senior VP, Taxes), Gerard M Orent (Senior VP, Operating Services), Mary A Cooper (Senior VP, Corporate Affairs and Senior VP, Executive Assistant to the President), William W Mauritz (Senior VP, Human Resources), Robert J Bahash (Senior VP, Corporate Financial Operations), Ralph R Schulz (Senior VP, Editorial), Robert M Thompson (VP and Controller), Frank Penglase (Senior VP, Treasury Operations), Donald S Rubin (VP, Public Affairs), William P Giglio (VP, Washington Affairs), Joan L Muessen (VP, Human Resources Administration), Walter F Whitt (VP, Staffing and Development), Robert W Stahl (VP, Facilities Management), Kurt D Steele (VP, Associate General Counsel and Assistant Secretary), Herbert Cytryn (VP, Corporate Creative Services), Bernard C Koval (VP, Employee Benefits), Sheldon F Asen (VP, Manufacturing), Albert J Hanson (Regional VP, Hightstown, NJ), Robert M Wilhemy (Regional VP, Lexington, Mass), Paul Jenkinson (Director Corporate Administration, UK-Maidenhead, England)

PRINCIPAL ACTIVITIES: McGraw-Hill is one of the world's leading corporations in information and communication. McGraw-Hill provides information in virtually every medium: magazines, newsletters and newswires; books, learning systems and training programs; software, on-line data bases and real-time electronic feed; film, videotape and audio cassettes; information systems and broadcasting

Principal Subsidiaries: Data Resources Inc; Data Resources Europe Inc (DRI Europe); Datapro Services SA (Switzerland); The Monchik-Weber Corporation; Standard & Poor's Corporation; Standard & Poor's Compustat Services Inc; Standard & Poor's Securities Inc; Standard & Poor's International SA (Belgium); Editora McGraw-Hill de Portugal Ltda; Editorial McGraw-Hill Latinoamericana SA; Libros McGraw-Hill de Mexico SA de c v; McGraw-Hill Book Company Australia Pty Limited; McGraw-Hill Book Company New Zealand Limited; McGraw-Hill Book Company GmbH (Germany); McGraw-Hill Holdings (UK) Limited; McGraw-Hill Book Company UK Ltd; McGraw-Hill International Publications Co Ltd; McGraw-Hill International Training Systems UK Ltd; DRI Europe Ltd; McGraw-Hill Information Systems Co of Canada Ltd; McGraw-Hill Book Kabushiki Kaisha (Japan); McGraw-Hill Ryerson Ltd (Canada); Nueva Editoral Interamerica SA de CV (Mexico)

Principal Bank: Manufacturers Hanover Trust

Financial Information:

	Dec 31 1985 $'000	Dec 31 1986 $'000
Sales revenues	1,491,208	1,576,834
Income befores taxes	284,327	295,779
Net income	147,404	154,009
Dividends	71	77
Dividends per share*	$1.40	$1.52
Earnings per share*	$2.92	$3.04
Common stock	50,541	50,651
Retained income	705,093	782,348
Shareholders equity	776,674	861,418

*common stock

No of Employees: 15,232

MCI COMMUNICATIONS CORPORATION

1133 Nineteenth St NW, Washington, DC 20036
Tel: (202) 872-1600
Telex: 64613

Chairman: Vernon O Wright (and Chief Executive Officer)
President: Bert C Roberts (and Chief Operating Officer)
Senior Executive Officers: William E Conway (Senior VP and Chief Financial Officer), Kenneth A Cox (Senior VP), Howard C Crane (Senior VP Corporate Affairs)

PRINCIPAL ACTIVITIES: Telecommunications services
Principal Subsidiaries: MCI Digital Information Services; MCI International; Western Union International; MCI Airsignal, Inc
Principal Bank: First National Bank of Chicago
Financial Information:

	Dec 31 1985 $'000	Dec 31 1986 $'000
Sales revenues	2,542,271	3,592,000
Net income (loss)	139,611	(450,000)
Earnings (loss) per share	$0.48	($1.63)
Shareholders equity	1,318,008	1,262,000

No of Employees: 13,660

MCKEE BAKING CO

Apison Pike, Collegedale, TN 37315
Tel: (615) 396-9151

Chairman: O D McKee
President: Ellsworth McKee
Senior Executive Officers: Jack C McKee (Executive VP), John A Phillips (Senior VP Sales), J L Parks (VP Engineering), Charles Wilson (Treasurer)

PRINCIPAL ACTIVITIES: Bakery products
Principal Bank: Pioneer Bank
Financial Information:

	$'000
Sales revenues	150,000

No of Employees: 1,500

MCKESSON CORPORATION

One Post Street, San Francisco, CA 94104
Tel: (415) 983-8300
Cable: FOREMINT
Telex: 170712 McKesson SFO
Telefax: (415) 893-7160

Chairman: Neil E Harlan
President: Thomas W Field Jr (and Chief Executive Officer)
Senior Executive Officers: John Wheaton (Executive VP-Administration), Rex Malson (Executive VP-Operations), Kenneth C Hicken (Executive VP Operations), Marvin L Krasnansky (VP Corporate Relations), Alan J Seelenfreund (Executive VP and Chief Financial Officer)

PRINCIPAL ACTIVITIES: Distributor of pharmaceuticals, health and beauty aids, wines and spirits, bottled water, office supplies, household goods and a broad variety of other non-food products

Trade and Product Names: Alhambra, Aqua-Vend, Armor All, Ballantine's "21" Brands, Canadian Rich and Rare, Chartreuse, Crystal, Economost, Emmets, Folonari, Liquore Galliano, Martin's V.V.O., Mohawk, Mount Gay, Nordik Wolf Light, Paul Cheneau, PCS, PDS, Pharmaserv, Rene Junot, Rosegarden, Scriptrac, Sparkletts, St Pauli Girl, SunMark, Tawn, Valu-Rite, Zee Medical, Clean Start, Great Valu, Medalist, Valu-Star
Principal Subsidiaries: McKesson Drug Company; Spectro Industries, Inc; Rawson Drug & Sundry Corporation; 3PM, Inc; Valu-Rite Pharmacies; McKesson Veterinary Services Company; Zee Medical Products Company, Inc; McKesson Wine & Spirits Co; McKesson Water Division; "21" Brands, Inc; Carlton Importing Company; Galliano International; Mohawk Liqueur Corporation; Mosswood Wine Company; McKesson Office Products; Armor All Products; Pharmaceutical Card System, Inc; Garrett-Hewitt International, Inc; McKesson International; Mass Merchandisers Inc; McKesson Home Health Care
Principal Bank: Bank of America
Financial Information:

	Mar 31 1986	Mar 31 1987
	$'000	$'000
Sales revenues	5,665,700	6,671,600
Income before taxes	144,000	172,900
Net income	77,900	89,700
Dividends per share	$1.20	$1.26
Earnings per share	$1.84	$1.95
Shareholders equity	695,800	762,200

No of Employees: 17,000

MCLEAN INDUSTRIES, INC
660 Madison Avenue, Suite 602, New York, NY 10021
Tel: (212) 593-3325

President: Malcolm P McLean
Senior Executive Officers: Malcolm P McLean Jr (VP), Allen L Stevens (VP and Treasurer), Kevin J Baxley (Secretary), John D McCown Jr (Assistant Treasurer)

PRINCIPAL ACTIVITIES: Holding company whose four principal subsidiaries are engaged in freight transportation, residential real estate and undeveloped rural real estate
Principal Subsidiaries: United States Lines Inc; United States Lines (SA) Inc; Purcell Co Inc; First Colony Farms Inc
Principal Bank: Citibank NA
Financial Information:

	Dec 31 1986
	$'000
Total revenues	896,995
Net (loss)	(248,773)

MCM CORPORATION
Box 12317, 1001 Wade Avenue, Raleigh, NC 27605
Tel: (919) 834 0751

Chairman: Jack H Quaritius (and President and Chief Executive Officer)
Senior Executive Officers: Ericson Berg (Executive VP), George E King (Executive VP), Ernest C Steele (Executive VP), Jon M Livers (Executive VP Property and Casualty), Jeffrey C Paige (Senior VP Information Services), Stephen L Stephano (Senior VP and Chief Financial Officer), Lou J Davis (VP Human Resources), Henry E Fredericks (VP and Treasurer), Lowell E Miller (VP Controller and Assistant Secretary), Hugh R Owen (VP and Secretary)

PRINCIPAL ACTIVITIES: Provision of a wide range of insurance services
Principal Bank: Wachovia Bank and Trust Company
Financial Information:

	$'000
Revenues	199,620

No of Employees: 690

MCNALLY PITTSBURG INC
100 N Pine Street, Pittsburg, KS 66762
Tel: (316) 231-3000

Chairman: Edward T McNally
President: George E Nettels Jr
Senior Executive Officers: Lyle H Laughlin (VP and General Manager Kansas Division), Joseph E Keller (VP Manufacturing), C E Packard (VP Sales), J H Florence (VP Finance)

PRINCIPAL ACTIVITIES: Manufacture of equipment for the coal industry; conveyors; steel
Principal Bank: Commercial Bank of Kansas City
Financial Information:

	$'000
Sales revenues	250,000

No of Employees: 2,000

MCNEIL CORPORATION
666 W Market Street, Akron, OH 44303
Tel: (216) 434-6000

Chairman: R A Michelson (and Chief Executive Officer)
President: Glenn H Meadows (and Chief Operating Officer)
Senior Executive Officers: John A McKay (Group VP), Robert J Botzum (VP Personnel), J R Hadnett (VP Finance and Treasurer), Terry R Hollister (VP Legal and Secretary)

PRINCIPAL ACTIVITIES: Manufacture of a wide range of industrial equipment including pumps, materials handling and lifting machinery and lubricating equipment; air conditioning and heating equipment
Principal Subsidiaries: Lincoln Canada Ltd; Cleveland Crane & Engineering Co; F E Myers Co; F E Myers (Canada) Ltd; Lincoln GmbH (Germany)
Principal Bank: AmeriTrust Co
Financial Information:

	$'000
Sales revenues	178,430

No of Employees: 2,100

MCO HOLDINGS, INC
10880 Wilshire Blvd, Los Angeles, CA 90024
Tel: (213) 474-6264

Chairman: Charles E Hurwitz (and Chief Executive Officer); Vice Chairmen: Joseph L Hegener, Barry Munitz
President: William C Leone
Senior Executive Officers: James V Iaco Jr (VP Finance and Treasurer), Howard J Bressler (VP, Secretary and General Counsel), Paul N Schwartz (VP)

PRINCIPAL ACTIVITIES: The company has interests in the development of real estate; exploration for, and production of oil and gas; natural gas supply; the manufacture of paper patterns for dressmaking
Principal Subsidiaries: MCO Properties Inc; MCO Resources Inc; Simplicity Pattern Co Inc (38.7%)
Principal Bank: First Interstate Bank of California
Financial Information:

	$'000
Sales revenues	113,000

No of Employees: 600

MCO RESOURCES INC
MCO Plaza, 5718 Westheimer, Houston, TX 77057
Tel: (713) 953 7777

Chairman: George Kozmetsky
President: Aurelio Madrazo
Senior Executive Officers: Larry M Smith (VP, General Manager Operations), Byron L Wade (VP, Secretary and General Counsel), Michael F Loy (VP Finance, Treasurer and Assistant Secretary), Victor D Obadiah (VP Corporate Services)

PRINCIPAL ACTIVITIES: Exploration and production of petroleum and natural gas
Principal Subsidiaries: MCOR Oil Exploration Inc; MCOR Oil and Gas Corporation; MCR Exploration Limited; MCR Geothermal Corporation
Principal Bank: First Interstate Bank of California
Financial Information:

	$'000
Sales revenues	59,000

No of Employees: 155

MCORP

PO Box 225415, Dallas, TX 75265
Tel: (214) 698-5000

Chairman: Gene H Bishop (and Chief Executive Officer); Vice Chairmen: Karl T Butz Jr, Charles E McMahen
President: John T Cater (and Chief Operating Officer)
Senior Executive Officers: Peter B Bartholow (Managing Director Planning and Finance), B L Ball Jr (Managing Director Forth Worth), George L Clark (Managing Director Dallas), H M Daugherty Jr (Managing Director El Paso), John H Garner (Managing Director Corpus Christi), J T Hudgins (Managing Director Houston), William J Renfro (Managing Director Austin)

PRINCIPAL ACTIVITIES: Banking and financial services
Principal Bank: Mercantile National Bank at Dallas
Financial Information:

	Dec 31 1985	Dec 31 1986
	$'000	$'000
Net income (loss)	132,370	(82,000)
Earnings (loss) per share	$3.02	($2.21)
Shareholders equity	-	1,146,000
Deposits	17,583,420	17,492,000
Total assets	22,586,270	21,887,000

No of Employees: 8,470

MCQUAY INC

13600 Industrial Park Blvd, Minneapolis, MN 55441
Tel: (612) 553-5330
Telex: WUT 290 421 McQuay ploh a

Chairman: James B Hoaglund (and Chief Executive Officer)
President: Eugene M Booker (and Chief Operating Officer)
Senior Executive Officers: Sidney D Johnston (Senior VP Planning and Administration), Robert L Jenkins (VP and General Manager Components Division), Thomas J Nicoski (VP and General Manager Specialty Products Division), G H Touw (VP and General Manager Energy Systems Division), Walter H Robilliard (VP and Treasurer), L Lee Runzheimer (VP and Controller), Dorothy A Sorensen (VP and Secretary), B L Bailey (VP Human Resources), Charles J Tamborino (VP and General Manager Air Conditioning Division), Thomas C Butterbrodt (VP and General Manager Berlin Foundry Division)

PRINCIPAL ACTIVITIES: Manufacture of a wide range of heating, refrigeration and air conditioning equipment
Parent Company: Snyder General Corp
Principal Bank: Northwestern National Bank
Financial Information:

	$'000
Sales revenues	229,000

No of Employees: 3,500

MCQUAY-NORRIS, INC

2320 Marconi Avenue, St Louis, MO 63110
Tel: (314) 776-4800
Telex: TWX 910 7610 493 mcqn oem stl

President: Daniel J Hesske
Senior Executive Officers: Dennis B Clark (VP Sales), J K Fasick (Controller)

PRINCIPAL ACTIVITIES: Manufacture of engine components and automotive parts
Parent Company: AB SKF, Göteborg, Sweden
Principal Bank: Mercantile Trust Co
Financial Information:

	$'000
Sales revenues	85,000

No of Employees: 1,800

MCWANE INC

23 Inverness City Parkway, Birmingham, AL 35243
Tel: (205) 322-3521

Chairman: J R McWane
President: J J McMahon Jr (and Secretary and Treasurer)
Senior Executive Officers: L A Nolan (Divisional General Manager McWane Pipe Division), James R McWane Jr (Divisional General Manager Empire Coke Division), J M Bushnell (Divisional General Manager Pacific States Division), C G Matlock (Divisional General Manager Atlantic States Division), J P Duke (Divisional General Manager Simsco Division)

PRINCIPAL ACTIVITIES: Manufacture of cast iron products; coke production
Principal Bank: The First National Bank of Birmingham
Financial Information:

	$'000
Sales revenues	350,000

No of Employees: 3,000

MDC HOLDINGS INC

3600 S Yosemite St, Denver, CO 80237
Tel: (303) 773-1100

Chairman: Larry A Mizel; Senior Vice Chairman: Emil Hecht; Vice Chairman: Michael A Feiner (and Chief Executive Officer)
President: David D Mandarich (and Chief Operating Officer)
Senior Executive Officers: Steven M Mizel (Senior VP), Marshall A Abrahams (VP and Secretary), Michael H Feinstein (VP Finance and Treasurer)

PRINCIPAL ACTIVITIES: Construction and financing of housing; real estate development
Principal Bank: First Interstate Bank of Denver
Financial Information:

	Dec 31 1986
	$'000
Sales revenues	674,564
Net income	35,722
Earnings per share	$1.81
Shareholders equity	218,868

No of Employees: 1,217

MDU RESOURCES GROUP INC

400 North Fourth Street, Bismarck, ND 58501
Tel: (701) 222 7900
Telefax: (701) 222 7606

Chairman: John A Schuchart (and President and Chief Executive Officer)
Senior Executive Officers: Harold J Mellen Jr (Senior VP Finance and Chief Financial Officer), Robert E Wood (VP), Joseph R Maichel (Division President), John F Renner (Controller and Chief Accounting Officer), Thomas A Winter (Treasurer and Assistant Secretary), Lester H Loble II (General Counsel and Secretary), John F Stewart (VP Communications)

PRINCIPAL ACTIVITIES: Distribution and transmission of natural gas and electricity, coal mining, and net proceeds ownership of oil and gas production
Principal Subsidiaries: Williston Basin Interstate Pipeline Company; Knife River Coal Mining Company; Fidelity Oil Company

Principal Bank: Citibank
Financial Information:

	Dec 31 1986
	$'000
Sales revenues	363,515
Income before taxes	60,900
Net income	37,883
Dividends	24,530
Dividends per share	$1.39
Earnings per share	$1.90
Common stock and premium	136,712
Retained income	113,000
Shareholders equity	249,712

No of Employees: 1,972

MEAD CONTAINERS DIVISION

950 W Marietta Street NW, Atlanta, GA 30302
Tel: (404) 897 2100

President: David C Stevens
Senior Executive Officers: Timothy L Campbell (Senior VP), Jay H Hayes (VP National Sales), Keith G Rasmussen (VP, HR)

PRINCIPAL ACTIVITIES: Manufacture of shipping containers
Parent Company: Mead Corporation, Dayton, OH
Financial Information:

	$'000
Sales revenues	240,000

No of Employees: 1,500

MEAD CORPORATION

Courthouse Plaza NE, Dayton, OH 45463
Tel: (513) 222-6323

Chairman: Burnell S Roberts (and Chief Executive Officer)
President: Steven C Mason (and Chief Operating Officer)
Senior Executive Officers: Ronald P Carzoli (Senior VP, Human Resources), A D Correll Jr (Senior VP, Forest Products), William A Enouen (Senior VP and Chief Financial Officer), John W Herbert (Senior VP, Consumer, Distribution and Specialty), Gerald D Rapp (Senior VP Legal and General Counsel), John W Herbert (Group VP Consumer and Distribution), James Van Vleck (Senior VP International), Elias M Karter (VP, Manfuacturing and Technology). Officers: Ronald F Budzik (VP, Government Affairs), Sidney G Hawkes (VP, Washington Affairs), Dudley P Kircher (VP, Corporate Communications), John K Langenbahn (VP, Information Resources), Wallace O Nugent (VP, Marketing and Supply), Charles W Spalding (VP, Research and Development), William D Ticknor III (VP, Woodlands), A Kurt Renick (Controller), Robert E Miller (Treasurer), George J Maly Jr (Secretary and Associate General Counsel), Charles N Shane Jr (Associate General Counsel), Gregory S DeWolfe (Assistant General Counsel and Assistant Secretary), Lorraine J Francis (Assistant Secretary), Gerald W Bialka (Assistant Treasurer), Fred C Houck (Assistant Treasurer), L H Rogero Jr (Assistant Controller), Eric A Copeland Jr (Director of Audits), Joseph I Hitter (Director of Taxation). Division Heads: Samuel S Benedict (President, Publishing Paper), Clayton E Burke (President, Paperboard Products), John E Franz (President, Distribution Division), Francis J Guiliano (President and Chief Executive Officer, Ampad Corporation), Thomas H Johnson (President, Paperboard Division), Charles W Joiner Jr (President, Mead Imaging), David L Klausmeyer (President, Specialty Paper), John C McCurrach (President, Mead Products), Gary W Pichon (President, Gilbert Paper), Jack W Simpson (President, Mead Data Central Inc), P Carter Smith (President, Mead Packaging), J Hans Stausboll (President, Mead Pulp Sales Inc), David C Stevens (President, Mead Containers), Jerome F Tatar (President, Fine Paper)

PRINCIPAL ACTIVITIES: Paper: Coated and uncoated printing papers, carbonless copy paper, bond papers, saturating papers, technical papers. Packaging and Paperboards: Coated natural kraft paperboard, kraft linerboard corrugating medium board, bleached paperboard, multiple packaging, shipping containers, paperboard specialties. Pulp and Wood Products: Bleached softwood and hardwood pulp; spruce, pine and fir, dimension lumber; hardwood lumber; plywood.
Principal Bank: Bankers Trust Company
Financial Information:

	Dec 31 1985	Dec 31 1986
	$'000	$'000
Sales revenues	2,740,400	3,217,700
Income before taxes	145,200	225,800
Net income	93,500	36,300
Dividends	37,200	37,500
Dividends per share	$1.20	$1.20
Earnings per share	$3.02	$1.16
Common stock	185,300	186,800
Retained income	780,400	779,200
Shareholders equity	1,033,600	1,058,900

No of Employees: 20,600

MEAD PACKAGING DIVISION

950 W Marietta Street NW, Atlanta, GA 30302
Tel: (404) 875-2711
Telex: TWX 810 751 3383 mead pkg a atl

President: P C Smith
Senior Executive Officers: Harold L Smith (VP Administration and Control), Reginald Bradford (VP Beverages Sales), Robert D Sparrow (VP Human Resources), Charles R House (VP International), Charles N Maynard (VP Manufacturing), Thomas H Mozley (VP Merchandising), Harold L Marquis (VP Legal), George B Hood (VP Systems Packaging), Dick Rossetti (VP Soft Drinks)

PRINCIPAL ACTIVITIES: Manufacture of packaging products; manufacture and leasing of packaging machinery
Parent Company: Mead Corporation, Dayton, OH
Principal Bank: The First National Bank of Atlanta
Financial Information:

	$'000
Sales revenues	300,000

No of Employees: 2,500

MEAD PUBLISHING PAPER DIVISION

PO Box 757, Escanaba, MI 49829
Tel: (906) 786-1660

President: Samuel S Benedict
Senior Executive Officers: William R O'Donnell (VP Marketing), Timothy J Morgan (VP Administration), Gary L Butryn (VP Manufacturing), William F Houghton (VP Sales)

PRINCIPAL ACTIVITIES: Manufacture of paper and pulp
Financial Information:

	$'000
Sales revenues	300,000

No of Employees: 1,450

MEADOWDALE FOODS, INC

8711 Meadowdale, Detroit, MI 48228
Tel: (313) 943-3300
Telefax: (313) 943-3332

Chairman: David K Page (and Chief Executive Officer)
President: Lon D Makanoff (and Chief Operating Officer)
Senior Executive Officers: Joseph Mocnik (Senior VP-Retail), Desmond DeFigueiredo (Senior VP-Information Systems), Donald R Gapp (VP-Controller), David McQueen (VP-Retail Store Operations), Larry J Rasmussen (VP-Real Estate/Store Development), Dennis M Siedlaczek (VP-Wholesale Warehousing), Lloyd Silberman (VP-Administration and Treasurer), Edward Sudzina (VP-Wholesale Sales and Merchandising)

PRINCIPAL ACTIVITIES: Supermarkets, drugstores; wholesale trade in food

Trade Names: Great Scott!, Family Discount Drugs, Abner Wolf Distributors
Financial Information:

	$'000
Sales Revenues	480,000

No of Employees: 2,200 approx

MEASUREX CORPORATION

One Results Way, Cupertino, CA 95014
Tel: (408) 255-1500

President: David A Bossen (and Chief Executive Officer)
Senior Executive Officers: John C Gingerich (Executive VP), Jerome Raffel (Senior VP Operations), Robert McAdams Jr (Senior VP Finance), Doris S Bossen (VP Corporate Communications), Phillip E Peterson (VP Personnel), William H Moore (VP Measurex Systems Inc), Thomas King (VP Engineering), Glenn R Wienkoop (VP Corporate Development), John J Burke (VP, US Sales and Services)

PRINCIPAL ACTIVITIES: Manufacture of computerised process control equipment
Principal Bank: Bank of America
Financial Information:

	$'000
Sales revenues	193,000

No of Employees: 2,300

MECHANICAL TECHNOLOGY INC

968 Albany-Shaker Road, Latham, NY 12110
Tel: (518) 785-2211
Telex: TWX 710 4438150 mti latm

Chairman: Harry Apkarian (and Chief Executive Officer and General Manager)
President: Richard K Schmidt (and Chief Operating Officer)
Senior Executive Officers: J Brad Perkins (Group VP), John Recupero (Treasurer)

PRINCIPAL ACTIVITIES: Manufacture of electrical measuring equipment, turbines and compressors, electro-dynamic reliability testing systems, servo hydraulic vibration testing systems, missile launchers, transponders, automotive trim
Trade Names: Fotonic Sensor (TM), Accumeasure (TM) System; Leading Edge (TM) Systems; Hydrosil (TM) Bearings
Principal Subsidiaries: Turbonetics Inc; Ling Electronics Inc; St Clair Metal Products Corp; United Telecontrol Electronics
Principal Banks: Chase Lincoln; National Bank of Detroit
Financial Information:

	Sep 30 1986
	$'000
Sales revenues	66,257
Net income	2,614
Earnings per share	$0.74
Common stock*	3,578
Shareholders equity	23,709

*number of shares in thousands

No of Employees: 870

MEDALIST INDUSTRIES INC

10218 N Port Washington Road, Mequon, WI 53092
Tel: (414) 241-8500

Chairman of Executive Committee: Alvin J Korth
President: Peter A Fischer (and Chief Executive and Operating Officer)
Senior Executive Officers: Robert L Van Dinter (VP), Raymond M Volp (VP), James L Sievert (VP and Treasurer)

PRINCIPAL ACTIVITIES: Manufacture of sports clothing and equipment, machinery for woodworking and concrete production, fasteners, cast iron products and industrial engines
Principal Bank: Harris Bank and Trust Company
Financial Information:

	$'000
Sales revenues	127,000

No of Employees: 1,640

MEDCO CONTAINMENT SERVICES INC

491 Edward H Ross Drive, Elmwood Park, NJ 07407
Tel: (201) 794-7000

Chairman: Martin J Wygod (and President and Chief Executive Officer)
Senior Executive Officers: James V Manning (Executive VP, Treasurer and Secretary), Leonard Schatzberg (Executive VP), Max Hand (Senior VP), Frederick Klein (Senior VP), Gary J Sekulski (Senior VP), Paul C Suthern (Senior VP)

PRINCIPAL ACTIVITIES: Mail order services for prescription drugs
Financial Information:

	$'000
Sales revenues	136,000

No of Employees: 360

MEDFORD CORPORATION

PO Box 550, Medford, OR 97501
Tel: (503) 773-7491
Telex: TWX 510 757 0612 medcorp mef

Chairman: Michael A Snetzer (and President and Chief Executive Officer)
Senior Executive Officers: Ted J Bauer, (VP-Medite Division), Robert E Kellso (VP-Timber Operations), L W Newbry (VP), Ronald C Parker (VP-Finance and Treasurer), Henry Snow (VP-Information Systems), Donna L Little (Corporate Secretary)

PRINCIPAL ACTIVITIES: Sawmill products including lumber, fiberboard and plywood; forestry
Parent Company: Amalgamated Sugar Co
Principal Bank: United States National Bank of Oregon
Financial Information:

	$'000
Sales revenues	180,000

No of Employees: 1,200

MEDIA GENERAL, INC

333 E Grace Street, Richmond, VA 23219
Tel: (804) 649-6000

Chairman: David T Bryan; Vice Chairmen: Alan S Donnahoe, J Stewart Bryan III (and Executive VP)
President: James S Evans (and Chief Executive Officer)
Senior Executive Officers: Gerald W Estes (Senior VP), James A Linen IV (Senior VP), David L Jordan (VP), J C Barden (VP and Chief Financial Officer), James L Dillon (VP)

PRINCIPAL ACTIVITIES: Holding company with interests in publishing, printing and broadcasting
Principal Bank: United Virginia Bank
Financial Information:

	Dec 31 1985	Dec 31 1986
	$'000	$'000
Sales revenues	578,560	634,627
Net income	32,820	17,107
Earnings per share	$4.61	$1.20
Shareholders equity	305,350	314,459

No of Employees: 5,500

MEDICAL CARE INTERNATIONAL INC

15110 Dallas Parkway, Suite 600, Dallas, TX 75248
Tel: (214) 490 3190

Chairman: William B Stanberry Jr
President: Donald E Steen

Senior Executive Officers: Emmett E Moore (Executive VP and Chief Financial Officer), William H Wilcox (Senior VP), E Timothy Geary (VP Development), Richard D Pence (VP Operations), Sue H Shelley (VP Operations), Edward D Stack (VP Acquisitions) Jonathan R Bond (Treasurer), John K Carlyle (Controller)

PRINCIPAL ACTIVITIES: Provision of medical services including ambulatory surgical centers
Principal Bank: MBank Dallas
Financial Information:

	$'000
Sales revenues	35,000

No of Employees: 650

MEDICAL ECONOMICS CO INC

680 Kinderkamack Road, Oradell, NJ 07649
Tel: (201) 262-3030
Telex: WUT 135093 medec orad

President: Thomas J McGill (and Chief Executive Officer)
Senior Executive Officers: Jack E Angel (Senior VP), Howard C Clutterbuck (Senior VP), Stuart J Horton (Senior VP), Stephen J Sorkenn (Senior VP and Secretary), Edward R Barnhart (VP), Jeffrey M Fass (VP), James H Jenkins (VP), William J Reynolds (VP), Lewis A Scaliti (VP)

PRINCIPAL ACTIVITIES: Publishing
Trade Names: Magazines & Journals: Contemporary Ob/Gyn, Contemporary Pediatrics, Diagnosis, Drug Topics, Home Care Economics, HPN-Hospital Purchasing News, Medical Economics, Medical Economics for Surgeons, MLO/Medical Laboratory Observer, MLP/Medical Laboratory Products, MPS-Medical Product Sales, Patient Care, PR-Professional Representative, RN, TNH-Today's Nursing Home, Veterinary Economics, Veterinary Medicine. Directories/References: CLR/Clinical Laboratory Reference, Drug Topics Red Book, Drug Topics Red Book Update, Medical Device Register: (MedSpec, Product SOS, Catalog Library Service, Distributor Profiles, Supplier Hotlist), Nursing Opportunities, PDR-Physicians' Desk Reference (R), PDR For Nonprescription Drugs (R), PDR For Ophthalmology (R), Veterinary Pharmaceuticals & Biologicals. Electronic Services: PDR Direct Access, PDR On-line, Red Book Data Base Services. Newsletters: Addictions Alert, Advanced Clinical Updates, AIDS Alert, Back Pain Monitor, Clinical Cardiology Alert, Clinical Laser Monthly, Clinical Oncology Alert, Contraceptive Technology Update, Convenience Care Update, Diagnostic Testing Alert, Drug Testing Success, Drug Utilization Review, Emergency Medicine Reports, Employee Health & Fitness, Home Care Economics, Hospital Admitting Monthly, Hospital Employee Health, Hospital Home Health, Hospital Infection Control, Hospital Peer Review, Hospital Risk Management, Infectious Disease Alert, Internal Medicine Alert, Medical Ethics Advisor, Neurology Alert, Ob/Gyn Clinical Alert, Physician's Marketing, Prospective Payment Survival, Same-Day Surgery, Surgery Alert. Other: Medical Economics Books, MEDECommunications Custom Communications Programs, Health Bulletin, National & International Conferences Programs, Mailing Lists-Health Care Professionals
Parent Company: International Thomson Business Press
Principal Subsidiaries/Divisions: American Health Consultants Inc; Medical Device Register Inc; McKnight Medical Communications; Veterinary Medicine Publishing Co

No of Employees: 450

MEDICARE-GLASER CORPORATION

2320 Schuetz Road, St Louis, MO 63146
Tel: (314) 569 1100

Chairman: Harlan Steinbaum (and President)
Senior Executive Officers: Stuart L Bascomb (Executive VP and Treasurer), Louis F Glaser (Executive VP), G Richard Coates (VP, Secretary and Controller)

PRINCIPAL ACTIVITIES: Pharmacies and retail outlets
Principal Bank: Mercantile Bank
Financial Information:

	$'000
Sales revenues	82,000

No of Employees: 1,150

MEDIQ INCORPORATED

One Mediq Plaza, Pennsauken, NJ 08110
Tel: (609) 665-9300

Chairman: Bernard B Rotko MD
President: Bernard J Korman
Senior Executive Officers: Lionel Felzer (Senior VP-Finance, Treasurer), Donald M Gleklen (Senior VP, Corporate Development and Administration), Robert E Mathews (Senior VP), Ian Berg (VP), Allen S Braverman (VP), Harvey J Comita (VP), Norman H Martin (VP), Ralph W Pries (VP), Eugene M Schloss Jr (Secretary)

PRINCIPAL ACTIVITIES: MEDIQ provides a broad spectrum of quality, cost-effective services to more than 2,000 hospitals, 700 nursing homes and to the general public. To acute care facilities, MEDIQ provides management and consulting, design and development and data processing and telecommunications consulting services. MEDIQ also offers shared diagnostic services and leases and rents medical equipment. To long term care clients, MEDIQ offers management and consulting, mobile x-ray, pharmaceutical, transportation, data processing and telecommunications services. To physicians and hospitals, MEDIQ designs, manages, equips and finances freestanding imaging and other outpatient centers. To pharmaceutical manufacturers, MEDIQ provides a one-sources facility for designing, printing manufacturing and assembling all packaging components. To the general public, MEDIQ offers full-service vision and orthodontic centers, in addition to renting specialized medical equipment for home service use
Trade Names: MEDIQ Mobile Services, MEDIQ/PRN Life Support Services, CompuHealth, Swank Optical, Copelco Leasing
Principal Subsidiaries: Pan Optics; Western States Optical; Packaging Coordinators Inc; MDM Services Inc; MEDIQ Mobile Services Inc; MEDIC/PRN Life Support Services Inc; MEDIQ Mobile X-Ray Services Inc; Triage Ambulance & Transportation; Suburban Medical Services Inc; Computer Health Corporation; Copelco Leasing Corporation; Copelco Leverage Leasing Corp; Aid Pack Inc; Harrisburg Healthcare Inc; MDM Services Inc; Medifac Inc; Mental Health Management Inc
Principal Bank: Mellon Bank (East)
Financial Information:

	Sep 30 1986 $'000	Sep 30 1987 $'000
Sales revenues	159,409	258,323
Income before taxes	11,781	15,945
Net income	7,466	9,092
Dividends	1,744	2,186
Dividends per share(1)	$0.015	$0.018
Dividends per share(2)	$0.025	$0.030
Earnings per share	$0.33	$0.36
Common stock	13,598	17,127
Retained income	29,114	36,020
Shareholders equity	71,441	78,224

(1) Preferred
(2) Common

No of Employees: 3,600

MEDLINE INDUSTRIES

1 Medline Place, Northbrook, IL 60060
Tel: (312) 949 5500

Chairman: James S Mills (and Chief Executive Officer)
President: Jon Mills (and Chief Operating Officer)

Senior Executive Officers: Allan E Levin (VP Marketing and Sales and Secretary), Courtland P Larkin (VP), Dennis McGongal (VP), Noel Sterling (VP), Steve Redford (VP), Frank Resnick (VP), Ed Becker (VP), Stan Fisher (Treasurer)

PRINCIPAL ACTIVITIES: Manufacture and distribution of medical supplies; hospital planning and design
Principal Bank: American National Bank & Trust Co
Financial Information:

	$'000
Sales revenues	75,000

No of Employees: 750

MEDTRONIC, INC

3055 Old Hwy Eight, PO Box 1453, Minneapolis, MN 55440
Tel: (612) 574-4000

Chairman: Winston R Wallin (and President and Chief Executive Officer)
Senior Executive Officers: Gerard C Planchon (Executive VP), Donald R Stone (Senior VP), John P Pfouts (VP and Chief Financial Officer), Richard L Fast (VP), John A Meslow (VP), Richard Sauter (VP), Raymond J Dittrich (VP, Secretary and General Counsel)

PRINCIPAL ACTIVITIES: Manufacture of electrical medical and surgical equipment
Principal Subsidiaries: Medtronic Blood Systems Inc; Med Rel Inc; International Medical Corp
Principal Bank: Northwestern National Bank of Minneapolis
Financial Information:

	$'000
Sales revenues	502,000

No of Employees: 4,950

MEDUSA CORPORATION

Lee & Monticello Blvd, Cleveland Heights, OH 44118
Tel: (216) 371-4000

Chairman: Edwin F Phelps
President: Daniel E Somes
Senior Executive Officers: Phillip W Gutmann (Senior VP), R Kenneth Whitley (VP), Brien Bammel (VP and Controller)

PRINCIPAL ACTIVITIES: Manufacture of cement; mining of aggregates for road construction and maintenance; manufacture of safety equipment for highways
Parent Company: Crane Company, New York, NY
Principal Subsidiaries: Cement Transit Co; Crescent Stone Co; James H Drew Corp; Medusa Aggregates Co; The Thomasville Stone & Lime Co
Financial Information:

	$'000
Sales revenues	138,000

MEENAN OIL CO, INC

6800 Jericho Turnpike, Syosset, NY 11791
Tel: (516) 364-9030

Chairman: Wm F Kenny III (and President)
Senior Executive Officers: Paul A Vermylen Jr (VP, Finance), Stanley R Orczyk (VP, Operations)

PRINCIPAL ACTIVITIES: Retail and wholesale distribution of home heating oil and related services and products
Trade Names: Meenan, Burke, Effron, Love, Young, Jesse Terry
Principal Subsidiaries: Burke Fuel & Heat; Effron Fuel; Jesse Terry Co; Young Supply Co; Petrolube Inc
Principal Bank: Chemical Bank
Financial Information: Figures for first full year

	$'000
Sales revenues	225,000

No of Employees: 750

MEI DIVERSIFIED INC

90 S Sixth Street, Minneapolis, MN 55402
Tel: (612) 339-8853

Chairman: Carl R Pohlad; Vice Chairman: Paul R Christen
President: D E Benson
Senior Executive Officers: Philip N Hughes (Senior VP), James A Lee (VP Finance), Lyle C Kasprick (VP)

PRINCIPAL ACTIVITIES: Bottling of non-alcoholic beverages; manufacture of snack foods and candy
Parent Company: Pepsi Co Inc
Principal Bank: First National Bank of St Paul
Financial Information:

	Dec 31 1985
	$'000
Sales revenues	808,270
Net income	37,680
Earnings per share	$2.23
Shareholders equity	234,810

No of Employees: 5,200

MELLON BANK CORPORATION

Mellon Bank Center, 500 Grant St, Pittsburgh, PA 15258
Tel: (412) 234-5000

Chairman: Frank V Cahouet (and Chief Executive Officer); Vice Chairmen: Elmer G Grant, G C Lantzsch (and Treasurer), Edward A Montgomery Jr, Norman M Steere, Richard H Daniel
President: George T Farrell

PRINCIPAL ACTIVITIES: Banking
Financial Information:

	Dec 31 1985	Dec 31 1986
	$'000	$'000
Net income	201,700	183,253
Earnings per share	$7.44	$6.20
Shareholders equity	1,637,180	1,818,982
Deposits	18,582,630	21,647,152
Total assets	33,406,200	34,499,370

No of Employees: 19,800

MELPAR DIVISION

7700 Arlington Blvd, Falls Church, VA 22046
Tel: (703) 560-5000

Senior Executive Officers: Talbot S Huff (VP and General Manager), S M Warren (VP Advanced Development), Donald R Gibbs (VP Finance), Charles E Isbell (VP Engineering)

PRINCIPAL ACTIVITIES: Research and development of electronic warfare products
Parent Company: E-Systems Inc, Dallas, TX
Principal Bank: Philadelphia National Bank
Financial Information:

	$'000
Sales revenues	60,000

No of Employees: 2,000

MELROE COMPANY

112 N University Drive, Fargo, ND 58102
Tel: (701) 293-3220

President: Robert N Spolum (and General Manager)
Senior Executive Officers: James Kertz (VP Marketing), James P Strand (VP Manufacturing), Carman Lynnes (VP Engineering), James G Brust (VP Industrial Sales), Jack R Wilson (VP Agricultural Sales), R H Robel (VP International Marketing), Loel Stanaway (Controller)

PRINCIPAL ACTIVITIES: Manufacture of lifting and loading vehicles for agriculture and industry
Parent Company: Clark Equipment Co, Buchanan, MI
Principal Bank: Continental Illinois National Bank and Trust Co

Financial Information:

	$'000
Sales revenues	200,000

No of Employees: 1,000

MELVILLE CORPORATION

3000 Westchester Avenue, Harrison, NY 10528
Tel: (914) 253-8000

Chairman: Stanley P Goldstein (and Chief Executive Officer); Vice Chairman: Kenneth K Berland (and Chief Financial Officer)
Senior Executive Officers: Richard L Anderson (Executive VP), Robert Kuhn (Executive VP), E S Fitzgibbons (VP), Michael Friedheim (VP), Larry A McVey (VP), Frank H Brenton (VP), Ira H Peterman (VP), Harvey Rosenthal (VP), Howard Kaufman (VP), A N Stricker (VP), Arthur V Richards (Secretary)

PRINCIPAL ACTIVITIES: Retail trade in footwear, clothing, beauty products, household linens and toys
Principal Bank: Bankers Trust Co New York
Financial Information:

	Dec 31 1985	Dec 31 1986
	$'000	$'000
Sales revenues	4,805,380	5,262,364
Net income	210,812	238,332
Earnings per share	$3.90	$4.40
Shareholders equity	1,102,205	1,263,004

No of Employees: 80,400

MEM CO, INC

Union Street Extension, Northvale, NJ 07647
Tel: (201) 767-0100

Chairman: Stephen H Mayer
President: Gay A Mayer (and Chief Operating Officer)
Senior Executive Officers: Robert G Burch (Executive VP), Roy W Stogner (VP), Robert O Hurry (VP and Treasurer), Robert Grossman (VP Operations), Harvey Chanler (VP Advertising)

PRINCIPAL ACTIVITIES: Manufacture of toiletry products, packaging and plastics; operation of a mail order house
Principal Subsidiaries: Marton Freres Inc; English Leather Inc; Lebanon Packaging Corp; MEM Co (Canada) Ltd; MEM International Ltd; Tom Fields Ltd; GEM Estates Ltd; Victor of Milano Ltd; Tom Fields (UK) Ltd
Principal Bank: United Jersey Bank
Financial Information:

	$'000
Sales revenues	76,000

No of Employees: 800

MEMOREX CORPORATION

San Tomas at Central Expressway, Santa Clara, CA 95052
Tel: (408) 987-1000
Telex: 346 442

Chairman: Clarence W Spangle (and Chief Executive Officer)
Senior Executive Officers: James C Castle (Executive VP), Frank J Sordello (VP Technology), Michael C Haltom (VP Corporate Development and Finance), Lars Turndal (VP, President Memorex International), Foster A Markolf (VP Legal, Secretary and General Counsel), John J Mitcham (VP, President Communication Group), Thomas S Stevens (VP, President Media Products Group), Frank C Buckley (VP Original Equipment Manufacturing, Storage Equipment), Robert P Berry (VP, US Storage System Sales and Services), Larry M Chamberlin (VP Human Resources), Wade F Meyercord (VP, President Storage Equipment Manufacturing and Development Group), Clyde J Johnston (VP, President Memorex Finance Co), C Al Conover (VP Planning and Program Management Storage Equipment)

PRINCIPAL ACTIVITIES: Manufacture of information storage equipment including large disk drives, tape drives, rigid disks and solid state storage devices; communications products including terminals, controllers and printers; media products-tapes and flexible disks
Parent Company: Unisys Corporation
Principal Bank: Bank of America
Financial Information:

	$'000
Sales revenues	720,000

No of Employees: 11,100

MENNEL MILLING CO

128 W Crocker Street, Fostoria, OH 44830
Tel: (419) 435-8151
Telex: WUT 286049 mennel fora

Chairman: Donald M Mennel
President: Donald L Mennel
Senior Executive Officers: J S Meier (VP By Products and Assistant Secretary), Robert E Tindall (VP Traffic), J W Mennel (VP Sales)

PRINCIPAL ACTIVITIES: Flour milling and production of animal feeds
Financial Information:

	$'000
Sales revenues	60,000

No of Employees: 250

MENNEN COMPANY

Morristown, NJ 07960
Tel: (201) 631-9000
Telex: WUT 136 312 mennen mwn

Chairman: L D Horne (and Chief Executive Officer); Vice Chairman: G J Mennen
Presidents: Harold Danenberg (and Chief Operating Officer), Jack Hughes (US), Peter Diemand (International)
Senior Executive Officers: Leonard J Sichel (Executive VP and Chief Financial Officer), Francis B Henry (Senior VP and Secretary), Coleman de Hegedus (VP International Area I), George Ross (VP International Area II), Eusebio S Parapar (VP International Area III), Hans Kellner (VP International Operations), S O Wagner (VP Operations), Robert Suffis (VP Science and Technology), M Marcus (VP Human Resources), Dominic J LaRosa (VP Marketing), Bill Boswell (VP Sales), William C Scalia (VP and Treasurer)

PRINCIPAL ACTIVITIES: Manufacture of toiletry and beauty products
Principal Bank: Citibank NA
Financial Information:

	$'000
Sales revenues	100,000

No of Employees: 850

MENTOR GRAPHICS CORPORATION

8500 SW Creekside Place, Beaverton, OR 97005
Tel: (503) 626 7000

President: Thomas H Bruggere (and Chief Executive Officer)
Senior Executive Officers: Ning Nan (Executive VP), Gerard Langeler (Executive VP and Chief Operating Officer), Colin C Kidd (Senior VP), Michael F Boswarth (VP and Subsidiary Officer), Frank S Delia (VP, General Counsel and Secretary), Thomas J Fretz (VP Operations), Brian C Henry (VP and Chief Financial Officer), Alberto Jimenez (VP and Divisional Manager), David C Moffenbeier (VP International), John C Carveth (Treasurer and Assistant Secretary), Berkeley T Merchant (VP Manufacturing), Richard J Anderson (VP Human Resources), Michael Feuer (VP)

PRINCIPAL ACTIVITIES: Manufacture of data processing equipment and computers

Financial Information:

	$'000
Sales revenues	174,000

No of Employees: 780

MERCANTILE BANCORPORATION INC

Mercantile Tower, St Louis, MO 63166
Tel: (314) 425-2525
Telex: ITT 431-2015; Western Union 44-23-00

Chairman: Donald E Lasater (and Chief Executive Officer)
Senior Executive Officers: Neal J Farrell (Vice Chairman of the Board), Ralph W Babb Jr (Executive VP and Chief Financial Officer), John H Obermann (Executive VP), D Bruce Adamson (Senior VP), Leigh A Doxsee (Senior VP), Thomas M Metzger (Senior VP), John Q Vye (Senior VP), D J Miller Jr (Senior VP), Michael T Normile (Senior VP and Treasurer), J Richard Skouby (Secretary), Arthur G Heise (Auditor)

PRINCIPAL ACTIVITIES: Mercantile Bancorporation Inc is a $5.94 billion asset regional multi-bank holding company providing complete banking and related financial services primarily in the 8th and 10th United States Federal Reserve Districts, through a network of affiliated banks in the state of Missouri. Mercantile's lead bank is the 132-year-old Mercantile Bank NA in St Louis, which has total assets of $3,726,462,000. Mercantile's other affiliate banks have combined total assets of $2,346,839,000. Services include commercial, retail, correspondent and international banking, corporate and personal trust management and bond investment and underwriting activities
Principal Subsidiaries: Marcantile Bank NA; Mercantile Bank of Kansas City; First National Mercantile Bank and Trust Company; Mercantile Bank of Springfield; Mercantile Bank of Poplar Bluff; Mercantile Bank of Farmington; Franklin County Mercantile Bank; Mercantile Bank of St Charles County; Mercantile Bank of Eldon; High Ridge Mercantile Bank; Trenton National Mercantile Bank; Cape Mercantile Bank and Trust Company; Alton Mercantile Bank NA; Bethalto Mercantile Bank NA; First National Mercantile Bank of Monett; Mercantile Bank of Memphis; Sedalia Mercantile Bank & Trust Company; Home Trust Mercantile Bank; Shelbina Mercantile Bank; Mercantile First National Bank of Doniphan; Mercantile First County Bank NA; Salisbury Mercantile Bank; Washington County Mercantile Bank; Farmers Mercantile Bank; Mercantile Wright County Bank; Mercantile Bank of Sikeston; The First National Mercantile Bank of Montgomery City; Mercantile Bank of Table Rock Lake; Mercantile Bank of Willow Springs; Rozier Mercantile Bank; Mercantile Bank of Macon; McDonald County Mercantile Bank; Mercantile Bank of Miller. Off-Shore Branch-Mercantile Bank NA (Grand Cayman, BWI). Mexican Representative Office-Mercantile Bank NA (Mexico)
Principal Bank: Mercantile Bank NA
Financial Information:

	Dec 31 1986 (12 mths) $'000	Jun 30 1987 (6 mths) $'000
Income (loss) before taxes	64,338	(53,687)
Net income (loss)	55,584	(25,923)
Dividends	75,125	11,173
Dividends per share	$1.40	$0.70
Earnings (loss) per share	$3.49	($1.62)
Common stock	79,701	79,831
Retained earnings	327,090	290,163
Shareholders equity	469,075	432,534
Deposits	5,186,148	5,272,932
Total assets	6,725,802	6,618,039

Number of shareholders: 11,109
No of Employees: 4,579

MERCANTILE BANKSHARES CORPORATION

Two Hopkins Plaza, PO Box 1477, Baltimore, MD 21203
Tel: (301) 237-5900

Chairman: H Furlong Baldwin (and Chief Executive Officer); Vice Chairman: Douglas W Dodge
President: John H Mosner Jr
Senior Executive Officers: Charles C McGuire (VP and Treasurer), John A O'Connor Jr (Secretary), Lawrence H Ey (Auditor)

PRINCIPAL ACTIVITIES: Banking services
Principal Bankers: Mercantile Safe Deposit & Trust Company
Financial Information:

	Dec 31 1985 $'000	Dec 31 1986 $'000
Income before taxes	58,983	65,166
Net income	36,729	39,467
Dividends	11,000	12,540
Dividends per share	$0.87	$0.99
Earnings per share	$2.90	$3.12
Common stock	26,753	26,753
Retained income	174,041	200,968
Shareholders equity	248,593	277,094
Deposits	2,171,776	2,566,331
Total assets	2,567,560	3,054,747

No of Employees: 2,500

MERCANTILE STORES CO, INC

1100 North Market Street, Wilmington, DE 19801
Tel: (302) 575-1816
Cable: MERSTORE

Chairman: Leon F Winbigler (and Chief Executive Officer); Chairman of Executive Committee: Harold W Jockers
President: James C Lovell
Senior Executive Officers: LeRoy J Sheldon (VP Operations), Edward J Sharkey (VP Real Estate), William A Heineman (VP and Treasurer), William A Carr (Controller), Dennis F Murphy (Secretary)

PRINCIPAL ACTIVITIES: Mercantile Stores Company, Inc is engaged in general merchandise department store retailing. The Company operates seventy nine department stores, all located in the continental United States. A subsidiary, Mercantile Stores Company Inc (NY), maintains central buying and administrative offices in New York City. The stores are operated under twelve different chain names which are familiar to their clientele within the regions in which the stores are located
Principal Bank: Citibank NA
Financial Information:

	Jan 31 1986 $'000	Jan 31 1987 $'000
Sales revenues	1,880,039	2,028,202
Income before taxes	196,448	216,200
Net income	102,448	111,065
Dividends	18,791	21,371
Dividends per share	$0.51*	$0.58
Earnings per share	$2.78*	$3.01
Common stock	5,404	5,404
Retained income	666,534	756,228
Shareholders equity	678,034	767,728

*restated for 2.5 for 1 stock split paid June 1987

No of Employees: 20,000

MERCANTILE TRUST CO, N A

8th & Locust Street, Mercantile Tower, St Louis, MO 63101
Tel: (314) 425-2525
Telex: ITT 4312023 merintl stl d

Chairman: Donald E Lasater; Vice Chairman: Robert O Blomquist
President: Neal J Farrell (and Chief Executive Officer)
Senior Executive Officers: Ralph W Babb Jr (Executive VP and Chief Financial Officer), Robert L Bergmann (Executive VP Data Processing and Operations), Robert J Carroll Jr (Executive VP Corporate Banking), Walter F Gray (Executive

VP Trust), J D Huber (Executive VP), Michael Graves (Senior VP International)

PRINCIPAL ACTIVITIES: Bank
Parent Company: Mercantile Bancorporation Inc, St Louis, MO
Principal Bank: Mercantile Trust Company

No of Employees: 2,000

MERCHANTS BANCORP INC

702 Hamilton Mall, Allentown, PA 18101
Tel: (215) 821 7339

Chairman: Carl J Feichtel (and Chief Executive Officer)
President: John G Kelly
Senior Executive Officers: Lamar M Steigerwalt (Senior VP and Treasurer), Eugene T Sobol (VP Finance and Controller), Robert W Capkovic (Secretary)

PRINCIPAL ACTIVITIES: Banking
Financial Information:

	Dec 31 1985
	$'000
Revenues	176,100
Net income	21,580

No of Employees: 700

MERCHANTS BANCSHARES INC

123 Church Street, Burlington, VT 05401
Tel: (802) 658 3400

President: Dudley H Davis (and Chief Executive Officer and Subsidiary Officer)
Senior Executive Officers: Frederick R McGibney (Treasurer and Subsidiary Officer), Parnell C Kirby (Secretary)

PRINCIPAL ACTIVITIES: Banking
Financial Information:

	Dec 31 1985
	$'000
Revenues	44,350
Net income	4,840

No of Employees: 400

MERCHANTS CO

PO Box 1351, Hattiesburg, MS 39401
Tel: (601) 583-4351

Chairman: F M Tatum
President: G R Hall
Senior Executive Officers: R S Thompson (VP), Donald Suber (VP Grocery House Division), D R Carter (Controller & Treasurer)

PRINCIPAL ACTIVITIES: Manufacture of food products and processing of meat; wholesale trade
Principal Bank: Citizens Bank of Hattiesburg
Financial Information:

	$'000
Sales revenues	40,000

No of Employees: 200

MERCHANTS NATIONAL BANK OF MOBILE

106 St Francis Street, Mobile, AL 36622
Tel: (205) 690-1212
Telex: 505528

Chairman: Carl E Jones Jr (and President and Chief Executive Officer)
Senior Executive Officers: Clarence C Keller (Executive VP), Roger J Geil (Executive VP), William B Inge Jr (Executive VP), Thomas M Hinds (Executive VP), Sam L Armistead (Senior VP), Melvin R Coxwell (Senior VP)

PRINCIPAL ACTIVITIES: Banking
Parent Company: First Alabama Bancshares Inc, Montgomery, AL

No of Employees: 750

MERCHANTS NATIONAL CORPORATION

One Merchants Plaza, Indianapolis, IN 46255
Tel: (317) 267-7000

Chairman: Otto N Frenzel III; Vice Chairman: Donald W Tanselle
President: James D Masey (and Chief Operating Officer)
Senior Executive Officers: Robert L Fesler (Executive VP, Chief Financial Officer and Treasurer), James D Madigan (Executive VP Subsidiary Banks), Randall D Rogers (Executive VP Real Estate Finance Group), Dan C Whitmore (Executive VP Operations), Donald J Hatke (Senior VP Subsidiary Banks), Christian F Lipkaman (Senior VP Marketing), Clifford B Spears (Senior VP Human Resources), Bruce A Wooldridge (Senior VP Loan Co-ordination)

PRINCIPAL ACTIVITIES: Banking services
Principal Bankers: Merchants National Bank & Trust Co
Financial Information:

	Dec 31 1985
	$'000
Revenues	264,000
Net income	17,300
Total assets	2,580,000

No of Employees: 1,500

MERCK & CO, INC

PO Box 2000, Rahway, NJ 07065
Tel: (201) 574-4000

Chairman: P Roy Vagelos (and President and Chief Executive Officer)
Senior Executive Officers: John E Lyons (Executive VP), Robert L Banse (Senior VP and General Counsel), A E Cohen (Senior VP), Robert F Hendrickson (Senior VP Manufacturing and Technical), Jerry T Jackson (Senior VP Human Health Marketing), Howard F Powers (Senior VP, President Specialty Chemical and Environmental Products), Albert D Angel (VP Public Affairs), Robert A Ingram (VP Government Relations), Alfred P Smith (VP and Treasurer), Francis H Spiegel Jr (VP Finance), Walter R Trosin (VP Human Resources), William B Van Buren (VP and Secretary), Edgar H Philbrick (VP Planning and Development), Steven M Darien (VP Employee Relations)

PRINCIPAL ACTIVITIES: Manufacture of specialty chemicals, pharmaceuticals and veterinary products; biotechnology; water treatment chemicals
Principal Subsidiaries: Merck Sharp & Dohme; Merck Sharp & Dohme International; Merck Sharp & Dohme Research Laboratories; MSD AGVET Division; Hubbard Farms Inc; Merck Chemical Manufacturing Division; Baltimore Aircoil Co Inc; Calgon Corpn; Kelco Division
Principal Bank: Morgan Guaranty Trust Co
Financial Information:

	Dec 31 1985	Dec 31 1986
	$'000	$'000
Sales revenues	3,547,500	4,128,900
Net income	540,000	675,700
Earnings per share	$7.58	$4.85
Shareholders equity	2,634,000	2,569,100

No of Employees: 30,900

MERCURY GENERAL CORPORATION

5900 Wilshire Boulevard, Los Angeles, CA 90036
Tel: (213) 937 1060

Chairman: George Joseph (and President and Chief Operating Officer)
Senior Executive Officers: Cooper Blanton (Executive VP), Robert S Frieson (VP), Donna J Moore (VP and Controller), Bruce E Norman (VP), Keith L Parket (VP and Chief Financial Officer), Judy A Walters (Secretary)

PRINCIPAL ACTIVITIES: Automobile insurance services
Financial Information:

	Dec 31 1985
	$'000
Revenues	145,000
Net income	13,050

No of Employees: 550

MERCURY SAVINGS & LOAN ASSOCIATION

7812 Edinger Avenue, Huntington Beach, CA 92647
Tel: (714) 842-9333

Chairman: Leonard Shane (and President and Managing Officer); Vice Chairman: Edward Nusser
President: William A Shane (and Chief Operating Officer)
Senior Executive Officers: Gerald Berens (Senior Executive VP Loans), Ed Span (Senior Executive VP), Ronald Hansen (Senior Executive VP), William A Shane (Senior Executive VP), Melvin Kapson (Executive VP Administration Services), James Rech (Executive VP), Charles Allen (Executive VP Loan Administration), William Morris (Executive VP Real Estate), Richard E Koelling (Executive VP Internal Audit), Jerome Zamos (Executive VP and General Counsel), Edwin J Richardson (VP Finance), Mickey Greenberg (VP Marketing)

PRINCIPAL ACTIVITIES: Financial services including savings and loans
Principal Bank: Security Pacific National Bank
Financial Information:

	Dec 31 1985
	$'000
Revenues	237,110
Net income	11,072
Earnings per share	$2.25
Shareholders equity	45,609
Total assets	2,154,834

No of Employees: 1,000

MEREDITH CORPORATION

1716 Locust Street, Des Moines, IA 50336
Tel: (515) 284-3000

Chairman: E T Meredith III
Presidents: Robert A Burnett (and Chief Executive Officer), Allen L Sabbag (Real Estate Group), Jack D Rehm (Publishing Group), William C McReynolds (Broadcasting Group)
Senior Executive Officers: Neil Kuehn (VP Product Development), Walter A Voss (VP), Donald L Arnold (VP Corporate Relations), William H Straw (VP Finance), Gerald D Thornton (VP Administration Services), Thomas G Fisher (VP and General Council)

PRINCIPAL ACTIVITIES: Publishing, printing and broadcasting; real estate services
Principal Subsidiaries: Mer Print Co; San Joaquin Communications Corp; Meredith International Ltd; Meredith Relocation Corp; Meredith Mortgage Corp; Sail Publications Inc; Meredith Video Publishing Corp; Better Homes and Gardens Insurance Agency Inc; Better Homes and Gardens Security Inc
Principal Bank: Iowa-Des Moines National Bank
Financial Information:

	Jun 30 1986
	$'000
Sales revenues	533,376
Net income	47,218
Earnings per share	$4.98
Shareholders equity	304,077

No of Employees: 2,980

MERICO INC

1820 N Josey Lane, Carrollton, TX 75006
Tel: (214) 242-6502
Telex: TWX 910 8609517 merico carn

President: Joe Ausere
Senior Executive Officers: Luis Alpizar (VP), Jerry Collins (VP), Waldon Calamia (VP), J D Hayes (VP), Barry Homer (VP), Gary Kennedy (VP), Mike Kleypas (VP), Glenn Ward (VP), R A Loughmiller (VP), Joe Lancaster (VP), Fred B Lanham (VP), Roger Sommer (VP), F Lynn Surber (VP), Rick Witherspoon (VP), T E Mason (Treasurer)

PRINCIPAL ACTIVITIES: Manufacture of bakery goods
Parent Company: Campbell Taggart Inc
Principal Bank: InterFirst Bank Dallas
Financial Information:

	$'000
Sales revenues	450,000

No of Employees: 3,000

MERIDIAN BANKCORP INC

35 North Sixth Street, Reading, PA 19603
Tel: (215) 320-2000
Telex: 173003 MERIDAN BK PHA

Chairman: Harold F Still Jr
President: Samuel A McCullough (and Chief Executive Officer)
Senior Executive Officers: Ezekiel S Ketchum, Russell J Kunkel, Terry L Troupe, Robert C Williams, Richard P Hoverter

PRINCIPAL ACTIVITIES: Banking and financial services
Trade Names: Meridian Bancorp, Inc
Principal Subsidiaries: Meridian Bank; Meridian Title Insurance Company; Meridian Properties, Inc; Meridian Asset Management Inc; Meridian Investment Company; Meridian Trust Company; DBS Discount Brokerage Services Inc; Meridian Capital Corp; Meridian Funding Corp; Meridian Life Insurance Company; Meridian Mortgage Corporation; American Title Insurance Company; Meridian Acceptance Corporation; The First National Bank of Pike County
Principal Bank: Meridian Bankcorp, Inc
Financial Information:

	Dec 31 1986
	$'000
Income before taxes	71,203
Net income	69,100
Common dividends	24,413
Dividends per common share	$0.93
Earnings per share(1)	$2.48
Earnings per share (2)	$2.34
Common stock	133,820
Preferred stock	42,174
Retained income	223,845
Shareholders equity	494,944
Deposits	5,453,125
Total assets	6,801,115

(1) primary
(2) fully-diluted

Principal Shareholders: 60% Individuals, 40% Institutions, Delaware Management Company, Meridan Bancorp-Employee Plans etc
No of Employees: 5,500

MERILLAT INDUSTRIES, INC

PO Box 1946, Adrian, MI 49221
Tel: (517) 263-0771

President: Orville D Merillat
Senior Executive Officers: Richard D Merillat (Executive VP), John D Thurman (VP Finance and Treasurer), Robert L Meyers (VP Industrial Relations), Duane A Bingel (VP Marketing)

PRINCIPAL ACTIVITIES: Manufacture of fitments for kitchens
Parent Company: Masco Corporation
Principal Bank: Commercial Savings Bank

Financial Information:

	$'000
Sales revenues	118,000

No of Employees: 1,700

MERITOR FINANCIAL GROUP (FORMERLY PSFS)

12 S Twelfth St, Philadelphia, PA 19107
Tel: (215) 636-6000

Chairman: Frederick S Hammer (and Chief Executive Officer)

PRINCIPAL ACTIVITIES: Holding company with interests in banking including savings
Principal Subsidiaries: Philadelphia Saving Fund Society
Financial Information:

	Dec 31 1986
	$'000
Net income	22,900
Shareholders equity	970,171
Deposits	12,676,100
Total assets	18,447,272

No of Employees: 5,662

MERLE NORMAN COSMETICS, INC

9130 Bellanca Avenue, Los Angeles, CA 90045
Tel: (213) 641-3000
Telex: WUT 664637 mernor cosm lsa

Chairman: J B Nethercutt (and Chief Executive Officer)
President: Gary Hollister
Senior Executive Officers: Richard Nolind (Executive VP), Robert Dressler (Senior VP Research and Development), Randall L Herrel (Senior VP Finance, and Chief Financial Officer), Melvin Baker (VP Operations), Steve Islander (VP Distribution), Kittie Lawrence (VP Training and Education), Gene Morris (VP Advertising), Tom Smith (VP Purchasing)

PRINCIPAL ACTIVITIES: Manufacture of beauty products
Principal Bank: Union Bank
Financial Information:

	$'000
Sales revenues	90,000

No of Employees: 700

MERRILL CORPORATION

1731 University Avenue, St Paul, MN 55104
Tel: (612) 646 4501

Chairman: Kenneth F Merrill
President: John W Castro (and Chief Executive Officer)
Senior Executive Officers: Rick R Atterbury (VP), Phillip J Bifulk (VP), John B McCain (VP, Chief Financial Officer and Treasurer), Robert F Nienhouse (VP), Richard G Lareau (Secretary)

PRINCIPAL ACTIVITIES: Commercial printing
Financial Information:

	$'000
Sales revenues	38,560

No of Employees: 360

MERRILL LYNCH & CO, INC

165 Broadway, New York, NY 10080
Tel: (212) 637-7455

Chairman: William A Schreyer (and Chief Executive Officer)
President: D P Tully
Senior Executive Officers: Michael von Clemm (Executive VP), Stephen L Hammerman (Executive VP, Chief Administration Officer and General Counsel), Courtney F Jones (Executive VP, Treasurer and Chief Financial Officer), Jerome P Kenney (Executive VP), DuWayne J Peterson (Executive VP), Charles H Ross Jr (Executive VP), John L Steffens

PRINCIPAL ACTIVITIES: Holding company with interests in finance and investment, management consultancy, insurance and real estate
Financial Information:

	Dec 31 1986
	$'000
Revenues	9,606,349
Net income	454,349
Earnings per share	$4.30
Shareholders equity	2,875,514
Total assets	53,013,471

No of Employees: 47,900

MERRY-GO-ROUND ENTERPRISES INC

1220 East Joppa Road, Towson, MD 21204
Tel: (301) 828-1000

Chairman: Harold Goldsmith
President: Michael D Sullivan
Senior Executive Officers: Isaac Kaufman (Senior VP, Chief Financial Officer), Paul Levine (VP Store Operations), Stuart Lucas (VP-Merchandising), Ken Rodriguez (VP-Merchandising), George Kucin (VP-Merchandising), Frank Peters (VP/Controller), Marvin Rice (VP-Construction and Design), Lou Heyman (VP-Warehousing), Wayne Schuchart (VP MIS), Barrie Wood (VP-Real Estate)

PRINCIPAL ACTIVITIES: Specialty retailer of contemporary fashion for young men and women. At the end of fiscal year 1987, the Company operated 388 stores in 32 states. As of October 1987, the Company operated 415 stores in 32 states
Trade Names: Merry-Go-Round, The Go-Round, DJ's Fashion Center For Men, Cignal, Merry-Go-Round Kids, Attivo (Store Trade Names)
Principal Bank: Signet
Financial Information:

	Jan 31 1986	Jan 2 1987
	$'000	$'000
Sales revenues	164,119	207,483
Income before taxes	13,453	14,664
Net income	7,285	7,485
Earnings per share	$1.15	$1.18

No of Employees: 4,300

MERTZ, INC

PO Box 150, Ponca City, OK 74602
Tel: (405) 762-5646
Telex: WUT 748553 mertz inc ponc

President: Don Mertz
Senior Executive Officers: Forrest Mertz (VP, Secretary and Treasurer), Larry Williamson (Assistant to President), Pete Caldwell (Sales Manager)

PRINCIPAL ACTIVITIES: Manufacture of vibrating and drilling equipment and metal products
Principal Bank: First National Bank and Trust Co
Financial Information:

	$'000
Sales revenues	30,000

No of Employees: 170

MESA PETROLEUM CO

One Mesa Square, PO Box 20029, Amarillo, TX 79189
Tel: (806) 378-1000

Chairman: T Boone Pickens Jr (and Chief Executive Officer)
President: David H Batchelder (and Chief Operating Officer)
Senior Executive Officers: Sidney L Tassin (VP Finance), Andrew P Craig (VP, Treasurer and Secretary)

PRINCIPAL ACTIVITIES: Oil and gas exploration and production

Financial Information:

	$'000
Sales revenues	363,000

No of Employees: 660

METALS DIVISION

PO Box 7588, Birmingham, AL 35223
Tel: (205) 877-3661
Telex: 810 733 4455

President: R S Weatherly Jr
Senior Executive Officers: W L Germain (Executive VP and General Manager), R C Cooper (VP Manufacturing), T J LaRose (VP), D A Nebergall (VP)

PRINCIPAL ACTIVITIES: Scrap metal processing
Parent Company: Vulcan Materials Co
Financial Information:

	$'000
Sales revenues	250,000

No of Employees: 1,300

METCO INC

1101 Prospect Avenue, Westbury, NY 11590
Tel: (516) 334-1300
Telex: TWX 910 3506876 metco inc

Chairman: F F Freund (and President and Chief Executive Officer)
Senior Executive Officers: K E Davis (Senior VP Materials and Surface Technical Group), Thomas R Fisher (VP and General Manager), Thomas R Klein (Controller)

PRINCIPAL ACTIVITIES: Manufacture of steam cleaning equipment
Parent Company: Perkin-Elmer Corporation, Norwalk, CT
Principal Bank: Manufacturers Hanover Trust Co
Financial Information:

	$'000
Sales revenues	102,000

No of Employees: 800

METHODE ELECTRONICS INC

7447 W Wilson Avenue, Chicago, IL 60656
Tel: (312) 867-9600
Telex: TWX 910 2212 468 methode cgo

President: William J McGinley
Senior Executive Officers: Michael G Andre (Executive VP Interconnect Products Group), William T Jensen (Executive VP), D Stalzer (Executive VP West Coast and Instruments Operations), Kevin Hayes (VP and Treasurer), Arnold A Brevick (VP Electrical Products Division), William T Dwyer (VP Technical Components Co), John L Glasser (VP Eastern Operations), Jerry Kirchenbaum (VP Trace Laboratories), Ronald Lesky (VP Backplane Division), James Robinson (VP Trace Instruments)

PRINCIPAL ACTIVITIES: Manufacture of electronic equipment and components
Principal Subsidiaries: Methode of California Inc
Principal Bank: Continental Illinois National Bank & Trust Co of Chicago
Financial Information:

	$'000
Sales revenues	96,000

No of Employees: 1,600

METRO AIRLINES INC

PO Box 612626, DFW Airport, Irving, TX 75261-2626
Tel: (214) 929-3400
Telex: 76-2558 METRO FLT DFW
Telefax: (214) 929-3444

Chairman: Edmond A Henderson (and Chief Executive Officer)
President: J L Seaborn (and Chief Operating Officer)
Senior Executive Officers: James A Ceresa (VP Finance, Secretary and Treasurer), Arlene J Dean (Staff Senior VP-Human Resources), Edward B Harrison (Staff VP-Pricing and Scheduling), Harry E Johnson (Staff VP-Maintenance), Fred H Junek (Staff VP-Flight Operations), Brian K Miller (Corporate Controller)

PRINCIPAL ACTIVITIES: Metro Airlines, Inc, a holding company for five wholly-owned operating subsidiaries, is one of the largest and oldest regional airlines in the United States. The Company primarily serves as a feeder network for travelers to connect with domestic and international carriers at its hub airports, Dallas/Fort Worth International Airport, Atlanta Hartsfield International Airport, and Luis Munoz Marin International Airport in San Juan, Puerto Rico. Metro provides regularly scheduled air service to 49 airports in 13 southwestern and southeastern states and the Caribbean as of August 31, 1987. At Dallas/Fort Worth Metro operates as American Eagle in affiliation with American Airlines, Inc and identifies its flights by American's designator code. Through recent acquisitions Metro has become the exclusive American Eagle carrier at Dallas/Fort Worth. At Atlanta and San Juan, the Company is affiliated with Eastern Air Lines, Inc, operates as Eastern Metro Express and identifies its flights by Eastern's designator code. American and Eastern currently carry more passengers to and from Dallas/Fort Worth and San Juan, respectively, than any other airline, and Eastern currently carries the second-highest number of passengers to and from Atlanta. Based on the number of passengers boarded in 1986, Atlanta and Dallas/Fort Worth are the second and fourth largest airports in the United States, respectively
Trade Names: American Eagle, Eastern Metro Express
Principal Subsidiaries: Metroflight, Inc; Metro Express, Inc; Aviation Associates, Inc; Chaparral Airlines, Inc; Metro Express II, Inc; Metro Leasing, Inc
Principal Bank: MBank Dallas, N.A.
Financial Information:

	Apr 30 1986	Apr 30 1987
	$'000	$'000
Sales revenues	87,830	120,301
Income before taxes	2,812	5,856
Net income	3,411	4,067
Earnings per share	$0.60	$0.66
Common stock	411	618
Additional paid in capital	8,331	8,298
Retained income	11,684	15,611
Shareholders equity	20,426	24,527

No of Employees: 1,800

METROMAIL CORPORATION

901 W Bond St, Lincoln, NE 68521
Tel: (402) 475-4591

Chairman: Don E Ackerman
President: William L Howe (and Chief Operating Officer)
Senior Executive Officers: Reginald C Troncone (Executive VP, Treasurer and Secretary), J D McQuaid (Executive VP), L G Aliano (Senior VP), Ralph Cuca (Senior VP), H C Garrett (Senior VP), John A Glascott (Senior VP Sales), Neill D Ingerslew (Senior VP Operations), R K Sher (Senior VP)

PRINCIPAL ACTIVITIES: Compilation of specialized mailing lists
Financial Information:

	$'000
Sales revenues	75,000

No of Employees: 1,300

METROMEDIA, INC

1 Harmon Plaza, Secaucus, NJ 07094
Tel: (201) 348-3244

Chairman: John W Kluge (and President and Chief Executive Officer)

Senior Executive Officers: George H Duncan (Senior VP Operations), Stuart Subotnick (Senior VP Finance), Ross Bennett (Senior VP Broadcasting), Stanley T Landow (Senior VP and Controller), Kenneth Cohen (VP Labor Relations), Thomas J Dougherty (VP Regulatory Affairs), Ira J Goldstein (VP and General Counsel), Robert A Maresca (VP and Treasurer)

PRINCIPAL ACTIVITIES: Broadcasting, advertising and telecommunications
Principal Bank: Manufacturers Hanover Trust Co
Financial Information:

	$'000
Sales revenues	356,000

No of Employees: 6,000

METROPOLITAN FEDERAL SAVINGS AND LOAN ASSOCIATION

215 N Fifth Street, Fargo, ND 58108
Tel: (701) 293-2600
Telex: 910 333 3179

Chairman: G L Lawrence (and Chief Executive Officer)
President: E W Moats (and Chief Operating Officer)
Senior Executive Officers: E W Graham III (Executive VP), M D Mitchell (Senior VP and Secretary), T H Webber III (Senior VP and Treasurer), J C Armistead Jr (Senior VP), D M Emerson (Senior VP), P W Elam (Senior VP), H W Fitzpatrick (Senior VP), M H Herbert (Senior VP), L R Travis (Senior VP), Martha W Wallace (Senior VP), J S Tanner (Senior VP)

PRINCIPAL ACTIVITIES: Savings and loan association
Principal Bank: Federal Home Loan Bank

No of Employees: 450

METROPOLITAN FINANCIAL CORP N DAKOTA

1600 Radisson Tower, Fargo, ND 58108
Tel: (701) 293 2600

Chairman: Norman M Jones (and Chief Executive Officer)
President: William O Nilles (and Chief Operating Officer)
Senior Executive Officers: Gary W Dietz (Executive VP), Ronald L Hanson (Executive VP), Maurice H Jones Jr (Executive VP), Charles D Kalil (Executive VP), Gordon A Everson (Senior VP), DAvid A Lysne (Senior VP), Douglas C Oksendahl (Senior VP), John E Pugh (Senior VP), Anton A Renner (Treasurer)

PRINCIPAL ACTIVITIES: Financial services including savings and loans

No of Employees: 570

METROPOLITAN LIFE INSURANCE CO

1 Madison Avenue, New York, NY 10010
Tel: (212) 578-2211
Telex: RCA 236756 group ur

Chairman: Robert G Schwartz; Vice Chairman: Philip Briggs, J Pierre Mauser
President: John J Creedon (and Chief Executive Officer)
Senior Executive Officers: Stewart G Nagler (Senior Executive VP), Ted Athanassiades (Executive VP), Robert E Chappell Jr (Executive VP), Glen E Coverdale (Executive VP), John D Moynahan Jr (Executive VP), Donald A Odell (Executive VP), William G Poortvliet (Executive VP)

PRINCIPAL ACTIVITIES: Insurance, including life and health, and pensions and related services
Principal Subsidiaries: Insurance: MetLife Security Insurance Companies; Metropolitan Insurance and Annuity Co; Metropolitan Property and Liability Insurance Co; Metropolitan Reinsurance Co; Metropolitan Tower Life Insurance Co. Noninsurance: Century 21 Real Estate Corp; Corporate Health Strategies Inc; Cross & Brown Co; Farmers National Co; MetFirst Financial Co; MetLife Capital Corp; MetLife Capital Credit Corp; MetLife HealthCare Management Corp; MetLife-State Street Investment Services Inc; Metmor Financial Inc; State Street Research & Management Co. Canadian Operations: Future Focus Health Systems Ltd; Metropolitan Insurance Co; Metropolitan Life Insurance Co of Canada; Morguard Group Ltd. European Operations: Albany Life Assurance Co Ltd; Metropolitan Reinsurance Co (UK)
Financial Information:

	Dec 31 1985	Dec 31 1986
	$'000	$'000
Premium income	11,960,000	12,149,000
Investment income	6,321,000	6,706,000
Income before taxes	329,000	173,000
Net income	170,000	236,000
Dividends	1,608,000	1,496,000
Retained income	170,000	236,000
Total assets	76,494,000	81,581,000

No of Employees: 33,000

METZ BAKING CO

1014 Nebraska, Sioux City, IA 51102
Tel: (712) 255-7611

Chairman: William C Metz; Vice Chairman: William H Metz
President: H J Metz
Senior Executive Officers: Bob Henchal (Senior VP Production), Frank D Gruenzner (VP Sales), Joe Holt (VP Procurement), Marlin M Lessmann (VP, Secretary and Legal Counsel), Dick Harrison (VP Transport), William K Stoneburg (VP and Treasurer)

PRINCIPAL ACTIVITIES: Bread and other bakery products
Financial Information:

	$'000
Sales revenues	100,000

No of Employees: 2,500

METZ METALLURGICAL CORPORATION

3900 S Clinton Avenue, South Plainfield, NJ 07080
Tel: (201) 561-1100
Telex: TWX 710 9979 524 metz sopd

Chairman: W P Metz (and President and Treasurer)
President: Michael Metz
Senior Executive Officers: E P Becker (Executive VP), Ruth M Metz (VP and Secretary), David Berry (VP), Ralph P Tremo

PRINCIPAL ACTIVITIES: Manufacture of precious metal products
Principal Bank: First National Bank of New Jersey
Financial Information:

	$'000
Sales revenues	250,000

No of Employees: 200

MEYER, FRED, INC

3800 S E 22nd, Portland, OR 97202
Tel: (503) 232-8844

Chairman: Oran B Robertson (and Chief Executive Officer)
President: Cyril K Green (and Chief Operating Officer)
Senior Executive Officers: C Dale Warman (Executive VP Marketing), Kenneth Thrasher (VP Finance and Secretary), Gary L Baker (Senior VP Human Resources), Larry Ofstedahl (Senior VP Food), Mary F Sammons (Senior VP Soft Goods), Donald E Tripp (Senior VP), Gordon Deeds (Senior VP)

PRINCIPAL ACTIVITIES: Fred Meyer, Inc is a leading regional retailer of a wide range of general merchandise, food, apparel and home improvement products. The company operates 93 stores in 34 markets in six Western states: Oregon, Washington, Utah, Idaho, Alaska and Montana. Stores average 103,000 square feet in up to eleven individualised departments, emphasizing one-stop shopping for items of everyday use

Principal Subsidiaries: B&B Stores Inc; CB&S Advert Agency Inc; Distribution Trucking Company; Grand Central Inc; Roundup Co; Natur Glo; Fred Meyer of Alaska Inc
Principal Bank: Continental Illinois National Bank
Financial Information:

	Feb 1 1986	Jan 31 1987
	$'000	$'000
Sales revenues	1,583,796	1,688,208
Income before taxes*	32,467	45,415
Net income	19,467	22,535
Earnings per share	$1.06	$1.08
Common stock	167	217
Retained income	46,026	68,561
Shareholders equity	93,395	186,692

*and extraordinary items

Principal Shareholders: Kohlberg, Kravis, Roberts & Co
No of Employees: 16,000

MEYERS PARKING SYSTEM INC

330 W 42nd Street, New York, NY 10036
Tel: (212) 947 9888

Chairman: Leo R Fink (and Chief Executive Officer); Vice Chairman: Robert Schlageter
President: Senior Aronson
Senior Executive Officers: Marvin E Eglin (Executive VP), Shelley M Boxer (VP and Treasurer), Roger A Gerber (VP, Secretary and Legal Counsel), Arnold Klauber (VP), Anthony J Policella (VP), Susan Goldberg (VP), Marvin Schlusberg (Controller)

PRINCIPAL ACTIVITIES: Operation of car parking facilities; maintenance of elevators
Principal Bank: Bankers Trust Company
Financial Information:

	$'000
Sales revenues	67,550

No of Employees: 1,500

MFC SERVICES (AAL)

US Hwy 51 N, Madison, MS 39110
Tel: (601) 856-2400

Chairman: W S Pearce; Vice Chairman: Ray Bass
President: Jerry L Harpole (and General Manager)
Senior Executive Officers: Robert A Filgo (Executive VP and Assistant General Manager), W Robert Sharman (Senior VP Operations), John A Gaston (Senior VP and Treasurer)

PRINCIPAL ACTIVITIES: Wholesale trade in agricultural supplies
Principal Bank: New Orleans Bank for Cooperatives
Financial Information:

	$'000
Sales revenues	190,000

No of Employees: 650

MGM GRAND HOTELS, INC

3645 Las Vegas Blvd S, Las Vegas, NV 89109
Tel: (702) 739-4848

Chairman: Alvin Benedict (and Chief Executive Officer)
President: Bernard J Rothkopf (and Chief Operating Officer)
Senior Executive Officers: Joseph Esposito (Executive VP), Bernard Segelin (VP and Secretary)

PRINCIPAL ACTIVITIES: Operation of the MGM Grand Hotel-Las Vegas and the MGM Grand Hotel-Reno and casinos
Principal Bank: First Interstate Bank of NV
Financial Information:

	$'000
Sales revenues	333,000

No of Employees: 7,900

MGM/UA ENTERTAINMENT CO

10202 W Washington Blvd, Culver City, CA 90230
Tel: (213) 558-5000

Chairman: Alan Ladd Jr (and President and Chief Executive Officer)
Senior Executive Officers: Burton J Morrison (Executive VP Finance), Jay M Behling (Senior VP and Controller), Karla Davidson (Senior VP and General Counsel), Frank I Davis (Senior VP Business Affairs), Benjamin B Kahane (Senior VP Industrial Relations), Roger L Mayer (Senior VP Studio Administration), Raymond T Bernett (VP Taxes), Andrew B Benson (VP Internal Audit), William C Bevins Jr (VP and Treasurer), George Brenner (VP Management Information Systems), James Gentilcore (VP, Controller District Accounting), Martha Mikita (VP, Controller Corporate Accounting), Arthur E Rockwell (VP Corporate Relations), Harold E Samboy (VP Financial Services), Arnold Shupack (VP Facilities), Sally Suchil (VP and Secretary), David C Terrasi (VP Employment Benefits), Kenneth A Wagner (VP Controller Production Accounting)

PRINCIPAL ACTIVITIES: Production of motion pictures and television programs
Parent Company: Turner Broadcasting System Inc
Principal Bank: Bank of America
Financial Information:

	$'000
Sales revenues	707,000

No of Employees: 2,700

MIAMI CAREY CORPORATION

203 Garver Road, Monroe, OH 45050
Tel: (513) 539-8441
Telex: WUT 241301 miami carey

Chairman: Robert Meltzer
President: Gordy E Loftin
Senior Executive Officers: Michael J Scorti (Executive VP)

PRINCIPAL ACTIVITIES: Manufacture of bathroom equipment
Parent Company: Jim Walter Corporation
Principal Bank: First Third Bank
Financial Information:

	$'000
Sales revenues	50,000

No of Employees: 590

MIAMI MARGARINE CO

5226 Vine Street, Cincinnati, OH 45217
Tel: (513) 242-2310
Telex: WUT 241 383 miami marg cin

Chairman: James K Heidrich Jr
President: Robert O Clark
Senior Executive Officers: Paul C Riordan (Secretary and Treasurer), D Goodman (Sales Manager), David Fisher (Purchasing Director)

PRINCIPAL ACTIVITIES: Manufacture of margarine
Principal Bank: The Fifth Third Bank
Financial Information:

	$'000
Sales revenues	40,000

No of Employees: 210

MICHAEL BAKER CORPORATION

See BAKER, MICHAEL, CORPORATION

MICHAELS STORES INC

Box 612566, DFW, TX 75261-2566
Tel: (214) 580-8242
Telefax: (214) 580-1345

Chairman: Sam Wyly
President: B B Tuley (and Chief Executive Officer)

Senior Executive Officers: James R Kelly (Senior VP Operations), J Eugene Stubbs (Senior VP Finance and Administration), R Richard Fontaine (Senior VP Marketing), Joel H Mathis (VP Administration)

PRINCIPAL ACTIVITIES: Michaels Stores, Inc owns and operates a chain of specialty retail stores featuring creative products for the home. Michaels stores offer a wide selection of competitively priced picture framing materials and services, silk and dried flowers and related floral items, needlework and other arts and craft items, greeting cards and party supplies, hobby kits, and related supplies
Principal Bank: First Republic, Dallas, Texas
Financial Information:

	Dec 29 1985	Feb 1 1987
	$'000	$'000
Sales revenues	76,197	115,904
Income before taxes	2,759	6,641
Net income	1,484	3,336
Earnings per share	$0.19	$0.35
Common stock	933	958
Retained income	3,724	7,061
Shareholders equity	23,598	28,227

Principal Shareholders: Sam Wyly; Charles Wyly
No of Employees: 2,000

MICHIGAN CONSOLIDATED GAS COMPANY
500 Griswold Street, Detroit, MI 48226
Tel: (313) 965 2430

Chairman: Alfred R Glancy III (and Chief Executive Officer); Vice Chairman: William K McCrackin (and Chief Financial Officer)
President: Stephen E Ewing (and Chief Operating Officer)
Senior Executive Officers: John J Feeheley (Senior VP Government Affairs), Patrick J Scullion (Senior VP Marketing and Distribution), William L Johnson (VP Distribution Operations), Edward H Klersy Jr (VP Corporate Information), Gilbert L Lavey (VP and Controller), Benson Manlove (VP Administration), Carol A Meyers (VP Personnel), Marc M Mozhan (VP Federal Regulation), Stanley A Surowiec (VP Gas Acquisition, Supply and Storage), Kenneth W Thompson (VP Federal Affairs), David P Vanote (VP and General Counsel), John E Vonrosen (VP Customer Services), Richard W Zemmin (VP Public Affairs)

PRINCIPAL ACTIVITIES: Supply of natural gas
Parent Company: Primark Corporation
Financial Information:

	$'000
Sales revenues	1,845,755

No of Employees: 3,680

MICHIGAN ENERGY RESOURCES COMPANY
899 South Telegraph Road, Monroe, MI 48161
Tel: (313) 242 5210

Chairman: William L Matheson (and President and Chief Executive Officer); Vice Chairman: Paul L Schreur
Senior Executive Officers: William F Braeuninger (VP, Secretary and General Counsel), James G Miller (VP), Lawrence A Mills (VP Finance), Stephen F Mumblow (VP), Michael E Hertling (Controller)

PRINCIPAL ACTIVITIES: Supply of natural gas
Principal Bank: Morgan Guaranty Trust Co
Financial Information:

	$'000
Sales revenues	161,440

No of Employees: 435

MICHIGAN GENERAL CORPORATION
Park 80 W, Plaza One, Saddle Brook, NJ 07002
Tel: (201) 368 1212

Chairman: Ralph J Shapiro (and Chairman of Executive Committee)
President: Rocco A Barbieri (and Chief Executive Officer)
Senior Executive Officers: Paul Barrett (VP, General Counsel and Secretary), Peter S Dye (VP Corporate Development), Frederick Marcus (VP), Alfred Von Stein (VP, Treasurer and Chief Financial Officer), William A Fager (Controller)

PRINCIPAL ACTIVITIES: Manufacture and sale of building supplies; retail stores; manpower services
Principal Bank: First City Bank of Dallas
Financial Information:

	$'000
Sales revenues	440,000

No of Employees: 3,800

MICHIGAN MILK PRODUCERS ASSOCIATION
26300 Northwestern, Southfield, MI 48219
Tel: (313) 354-9780

President: Elwood Kirkpatrick
Senior Executive Officers: Carl Kline (VP), Velmar Green (Treasurer)

PRINCIPAL ACTIVITIES: Milk production
Principal Bank: National Bank of Detroit
Financial Information:

	Sep 30 1985	Sep 30 1986
	$'000	$'000
Sales revenues	517,110	431,590

No of Employees: 740

MICHIGAN NATIONAL BANK
124 W Allegan Street, Lansing, MI 48901
Tel: (517) 377-3111

Vice Chairman: Paul C Souder
Senior Executive Officers: Alden G Walters (Executive VP Loan Administration and Commercial Services), Herbert K Peterson (Executive VP), Hugh M Wright (Senior VP), Daniel R Edward (Senior VP Depositor Accounts and Data Processing), Arthur W Noren (Senior VP Depositor Accounts and Data Processing), Felix L Fliss (Senior VP Loan Administration and Commercial Services), Ray Bauer (Senior VP Oklahoma Loan Officer), Howard P Stoddard (Senior VP Marketing Northern Region), Richard H Jones (Senior VP Battle Creek), Otwell J Derr (Senior VP Charlotte), John B Baum (Senior VP Grand Rapids), Robert J Van Zanten (Senior VP Grand Rapids), William M Walworth (Senior VP), Daniel B McFadden (Senior VP Marshall), Gerald A Barber (Senior VP Saginaw), Robert D Sznewajs (Senior VP Michigan Bankard), Thomas C Robberson (Senior VP Trust Division)

PRINCIPAL ACTIVITIES: Banking services
Parent Company: Michigan National Corporation, Bloomfields Hills, MI

No of Employees: 2,300

MICHIGAN NATIONAL BANK OF DETROIT
22595 W S Mile Road, Detroit, MI 48219
Tel: (313) 255-6800

Chairman: Robert J Mylod (Michigan National Corp); Vice Chairman: Fred J Romanoff (Michigan National Corp)
President: Andrew R Brodhun
Senior Executive Officers: Gerald J DeVore (Executive VP Michigan National Corp), Richard C Webb (Executive VP), David R Buckler (Senior VP Finance and Controller), Patrick R Crosson (Senior VP Bank Operations), Mark B Dillon (Senior VP Retail Banking), John Gerec (Senior VP Consumer Lending), Edward M Klusowski (Senior VP Mortgage), Leonard M Matz (Senior VP Funds Management), M Richard Olson (Senior VP Trust), Robert C Scott (Senior VP Executive Administration), W David Tull (Senior VP Corporate Banking),

Thomas J Wagner (Senior VP Corporate Banking), Hugh M Wright (Senior VP)

PRINCIPAL ACTIVITIES: Banking
Parent Company: Michigan National Corporation, Bloomfield Hills, MI
Principal Bank: Irving Trust Company

No of Employees: 1,700

MICHIGAN NATIONAL CORPORATION

PO Box 589, Bloomfield Hills, MI 48013
Tel: (313) 642-9001
Telex: TWX 910 333 4425 mich natl co mi

Chairman: Robert J Mylod (and President and Chief Executive Officer)
Senior Executive Officers: Eric D Booth (Executive VP), K Larry Hastie (Executive VP), Peter K Thomsen (Executive VP), Donald E Entwistle (Senior VP), Farris G Kalil (Senior VP), Alan Nelson (Senior VP), Alden G Walters (Senior VP), Richard Strichartz (VP, Secretary and General Counsel), Barbara K Baker (VP), Robert R Denton (VP), Gerald J DeVore (VP Real Estate), H Perry Driggs Jr (VP and Treasurer), Robert D Sznewajs (VP), B Matt Morris III (VP Audit), Kenneth A DiLaura (VP and Controller)

PRINCIPAL ACTIVITIES: Banking
Principal Bank: Michigan National Bank
Financial Information:

	Dec 31 1985	Dec 31 1986
	$'000	$'000
Net income	34,427	52,220
Earnings per share	$2.64	$3.59
Shareholders equity	408,560	462,157
Deposits	6,328,180	6,759,164
Total assets	7,251,730	7,672,215

No of Employees: 6,500

MICKELBERRY CORPORATION

405 Park Ave, New York, NY 10022
Tel: (212) 832-0303

Chairman: James C Marlas (and Chief Executive Officer); Chairman of Executive Committee: Franklin D Roosevelt Jr
President: Richard J Diamond (and Chief Operating Officer)
Senior Executive Officers: George Kane (VP Finance and Secretary)

PRINCIPAL ACTIVITIES: Advertising and printing of advertising material
Principal Bank: Citibank
Financial Information:

	$'000
Sales revenues	132,000

No of Employees: 1,380

MICOM SYSTEMS, INC

4100 Los Angeles Avenue, Box 8100, Simi Valley, CA 93062
Tel: (805) 583-8600
Telex: TWX 910 49 44 910 micom sys lsa

Chairman: William A Norred
President: Roger L Evans
Senior Executive Officers: Christopher G Kenber (Corporate VP Marketing Operations), Michael E Barker (Corporate VP and President MICOM-Interlan, Inc), Robert A Weaver (VP Finance and Administration, Secretary and Treasurer), Alexander Saunders (Corporate VP and President MICOM Technologies), Joseph A Fields (Corporate VP Manufacturing), Roger D Shober (Corporate VP and President Sales Division)

PRINCIPAL ACTIVITIES: Manufacture of computer based data communications equipment
Trade Names: Registered Trademarks:- DIALNET 3000, INSTANET, INSTAMUX 470, INSTATRUNK 480, INSTALINK 460, INSTANET 6000, MICOM, MICOM BOX, INSTANET 6600 (refers to the product). Other Registered Trademarks:- BLACK BOX (refers to the Catalog-No Products), BLACK BOX and logo (refers to products), Black Box logo only (refers to products and catalogs), WIDGET (refers to products), WIDGET World (refers to catalogs). Trademark Registration Applied For (but not yet approved):- FEATUREPAK, BLACK BOX (for services)
Principal Subsidiaries: MICOM-Borer Ltd; MICOM Caribe, Inc; MICOM-Interlan, Inc; Black Box Corporation
Principal Bank: Bank of America
Financial Information:

	Mar 31 1986	Mar 31 1987
	$'000	$'000
Sales revenues	189,900	197,600
Income before taxes	12,000	15,300
Net income	10,100	11,600
Earnings per share	$0.57	$0.66
Common stock	74,800	76,100
Retained income	81,000	92,600
Shareholders equity	157,200	171,300

No of Employees: 2,032

MICRO D, INC

2801 S Yale, Santa Ana, CA 92704
Tel: (714) 540-4781

Chairman: Linwood A Lacy Jr (and Chief Executive Officer)
President: Harold L Clark (and Chief Operating Officer)
Senior Executive Officers: Godfred Otuteye (Senior VP and Chief Financial Officer), Carol Miltner (VP Sales), Bruce Frederickson (VP Marketing), John Winkelhaus (VP Sales Services), Bruce Martin (VP Purchasing), Michael Kelly (VP MIS), Steven Weinberg (VP Technical Products Division), Wayne Ortenburger (Secretary and Director Internal Audit)

PRINCIPAL ACTIVITIES: Micro D, Inc is one of the largest independent wholesale distributors of microcomputer software, hardware, peripherals and accessories in the United States. The company serves thousands of retailers with a broad-line inventory of approximately 3,800 products from over 250 manufacturers. Micro D offers credit financing to qualified dealers and is able to ensure rapid product delivery through a nationwide chain of warehouse locations
Principal Bank: Union Bank
Financial Information:

	Oct 31 1985	Dec 31 1986
	(14 mths)	(12 mths)
	$'000	$'000
Sales revenues	119,836	221,419
Income (loss) before taxes	(4,495)	4,646
Net income (loss)	(3,122)	3,012
Earnings (loss) per share	($0.47)	$0.44
Common stock	67,061	67,061
Retained earnings (deficit)	(139)	2,874
Shareholders equity	26,389	29,402

Principal Shareholders: Ingram Distribution Group Inc
No of Employees: 248

MICRODOT INC

20 S Clark Street, Chicago, IL 60603
Tel: (312) 899-1925

President: Richard P Strubel (and Chief Executive Officer)
Senior Executive Officers: John C Roberson (Executive VP), John S Vanecko (VP, Secretary and Controller), Dianne H Blanco (VP Planning), James S Lewis (President Valley Mould Division), Bernard G Rethore (President Microdot Industries Division)

PRINCIPAL ACTIVITIES: Manufacture of connectors and moulds for ingot casting
Principal Bank: Continental Bank of Chicago

Financial Information:

	$'000
Sales revenues	375,000

No of Employees: 4,500

MICROGRAPHICS SYSTEMS DIVISION
520 Logue Avenue, Mountain View, CA 94043
Tel: (415) 965-3700
Telex: 348301

Chairman: C E Exley (and President)
Senior Executive Officers: Romano R Durini (General Manager), John Phillips (Director Finance and Administration), Keith Ebeling (Director Marketing), Ray Mayer (Director Operations)

PRINCIPAL ACTIVITIES: Manufacture of a comprehensive line of Computer Output Microfiche recorders, duplicators and readers
Parent Company: NCR Corporation, Dayton, OH
Financial Information:

	$'000
Sales revenues	70,000

No of Employees: 300

MICRON TECHNOLOGY INC
2805 E Columbia Road, Boise, ID 83706
Tel: (208) 383-4000
Telex: 910 970 5973 micron bse

Chairman: J L Parkinson
President: J A Benitez
Senior Executive Officers: J W Garrett (VP), T M Trent (VP), R W Chance (VP), L A Gill (Treasurer), L L Grant (Legal Counsel)

PRINCIPAL ACTIVITIES: Manufacture of semiconductor memory components, electronic camera products, add-on memory boards, and burn-in and test oven, and PC memory expansion products
Trade Names: AMBYX (Trademark), Burn-in and Test System, MicronEye Camera, Idetix Camera
Principal Bank: Idaho First National Bank
Financial Information:

	Sep 3 1986	Sep 3 1987
	$'000	$'000
Sales revenues	48,865	91,187
(Loss) before taxes	(33,941)	(22,933)
Net (loss)	(33,941)	(22,933)
(Loss) per share	($1.75)	($0.94)
Common stock	2,226	2,581
Retained (deficit)	(14,716)	(37,649)
Shareholders equity	79,079	72,576

No of Employees: 1,600

MICROPOLIS CORPORATION
21123 Nordhoff Street, Chatsworth, CA 91311
Tel: (818) 709-3300
Telex: 651486 MICROPLS CHCA

Chairman: Stuart P Mabon (and President and Chief Executive Officer)
Senior Executive Officers: Chester Baffs (VP-Marketing and Sales), Ericson M Dunstan (VP-Corporate Engineering), Dundas I Flaherty (VP-Finance and Chief Financial Officer), Constance J Friedman (VP-Human Resources), Edwin P Heacox (VP-Operations), Sidney T Schell (VP-Product Development), Michael W Warner (VP-Engineering), Eugene F Hovanec (Controller)

PRINCIPAL ACTIVITIES: Micropolis designs and manufactures high performance disk drives and markets these drives to original equipment manufacturers (OEM's). The Company's principal products are 5.25 inch and 8 inch Winchester drives with high capacity, fast access and low lifetime cost
Trade Names: 1320 Series high-performance 85 megabyte 5.25 Winchester disk drives, 1350 Series high-performance 170 megabyte 5.25 Winchester disk drives
Principal Subsidiaries: Micropolis Incorporated; Micropolis GmbH
Principal Bank: First Interstate Bank of California
Financial Information:

	$'000
Sales revenues	213,000

No of Employees: 611

MICROPRO INTERNATIONAL CORPORATION
33 San Pablo Avenue, San Rafael, CA 94903
Tel: (415) 499 1200

Chairman: Leon Williams (and President and Chief Executive Officer)
Senior Executive Officers: William G Crowell (VP), David K Izuka (Controller), E Ric Giardina (Legal Counsel and Secretary)

PRINCIPAL ACTIVITIES: Provision of computer software and related services
Principal Bank: Bank of America
Financial Information:

	$'000
Sales revenues	42,650

No of Employees: 290

MICROSEMI CORPORATION
2830 South Fairview Street, Santa Ana, CA 92704
Tel: (714) 979 8220

Chairman: Richard L Geiger (and Treasurer)
President: Philip Frey Jr (and Chief Executive Officer)
Senior Executive Officers: David Socksen (VP Finance), George Sandera (VP Engineering), Richard R Sandburg (Secretary)

PRINCIPAL ACTIVITIES: Manufacture of components for electronic equipment including diodes, glass rectifiers and hybrid circuits; telecommunications equipment
Principal Bank: Security Pacific National Bank
Financial Information:

	$'000
Sales revenues	35,000

No of Employees: 1,120

MICROSOFT CORPORATION
16011 NE 36th St, Redmond, WA 98073
Tel: (206) 882 8080

Chairman: William H Gates III (and Chief Executive Officer)
President: J A Shirley
Senior Executive Officers: Steven A Ballmer (VP), Ida S Cole (VP), Francis J Gaudette (VP and Chief Financial Officer), James W Harris (VP), Thomas M Lopez (VP), William H Neukom (VP), Scott D Oki (VP), Jean D Richardson (VP), Gerald A Ruttenburg (VP)

PRINCIPAL ACTIVITIES: Computer services including software
Financial Information:

	$'000
Sales revenues	198,000

No of Employees: 1,000

MID AMERICA BANCORP
500 West Broadway, Louisville, KY 40202
Tel: (502) 562 5439

Chairman: Samuel H Klein (and Chief Executive Officer)
President: Bertram W Klein
Senior Executive Officers: Orson P Oliver (Legal Counsel), Stanley L Atlas (Executive VP), Thomas L Weber (Executive VP)

PRINCIPAL ACTIVITIES: Banking

Financial Information:

	Dec 31 1985
	$'000
Revenues	66,130
Net income	6,505

No of Employees: 370

MID AMERICA INDUSTRIES INC

900 Rogers Avenue, Fort Smith, AR 72901
Tel: (501) 785 1461

Chairman: John M Yantis
President: Marshall L Yantis (and Chief Executive Officer)
Senior Executive Officers: S Birnie Harper (Executive VP and Chief Operating Officer), Roscoe E Thompson (Senior VP Administration and Real Estate Officer), Robert A Holder (Stores), John B Fanning (VP Wholesale), Merril J Howard (VP Personnel), Thomas A King (Treasurer), Sid W Lawrence (Controller), Peggy J S Hambrick (Legal), Birnie N Pryor (VP Marketing), Michael L Schluterman (VP Investments)

PRINCIPAL ACTIVITIES: Wholesale supply of motor vehicle components
Principal Bank: Merchants National Bank
Financial Information:

	$'000
Sales revenues	92,900

No of Employees: 820

MID STATE FEDERAL SAVINGS AND LOAN ASSOCIATION

3300 SW 34th Avenue, Suite 101, Ocala, FL 32670
Tel: (904) 732 9977

Chairman: W Elton Clemmons
President: R M Dunwoody (and Chief Executive Officer)
Senior Executive Officers: A B Tucker (Executive VP and Treasurer), Anthony C Copozzi (Financial VP), Nathan C Gilman (Financial VP), Michael P Hill (Financial VP), John P McKeever (Financial VP and Legal Counsel), Winston M Needham (VP and Assistant Secretary), Frederick J Sitzberger (VP and Controller)

PRINCIPAL ACTIVITIES: Financial Services including savings and loans
Financial Information:

	Dec 31 1985
	$'000
Revenues	70,155
Net income	1,630

No of Employees: 330

MID-AMERICA DAIRYMEN, INC

PO Box 1837, Springfield, MO 65805
Tel: (417) 865-9641
Telex: TWX 910 7754745 midamer dpo sp

President: Ivan Stickler
Senior Executive Officers: Gary Hanman (Executive VP and General Manager), Edward Nierman (VP), Glenn Freese (VP), Albert Bos (VP), Walter E Stemler (VP), Harry C Burger (VP), Maynard Lang (VP), Robert Pedersen (VP), James Reeves (VP and General Manager Northern Operations), M O Hedeman (VP and General Manager Western Operations), W H Johnson (VP and General Manager Southern Operations), William A Phipps (VP and General Manager Eastern Operations)

PRINCIPAL ACTIVITIES: Manufacture of dairy products
Principal Bank: St Louis Bank for Cooperatives

Financial Information:

	Dec 31 1985	Dec 31 1986
	$'000	$'000
Sales revenues	1,344,280	1,420,321
Shareholders equity	-	126,272

No of Employees: 3,000

MIDAS INTERNATIONAL CORPORATION

225 N Michigan, Chicago, IL 60601
Tel: (312) 565-7500
Telex: WUT 270 251 midas a cgo

President: John R Moore (and Chief Executive Officer)
Senior Executive Officers: Robert M Bailey (VP and Secretary), R L Barclay (VP and Controller), Russell J Richards (VP Franchise Operations), Terrence E Reynolds (VP Auto Manufacturing), Brian W Burhoe (VP Human Resources), A W Johnstone (VP International)

PRINCIPAL ACTIVITIES: Manufacture of spare parts for motor vehicles
Parent Company: IC Industries Inc
Financial Information:

	$'000
Sales revenues	300,000

No of Employees: 2,700

MIDCON CORPORATION

701E 22nd St, Lombard, IL 60148
Tel: (312) 691-2500

Chairman: O C Davis (and Chief Executive Officer); Vice Chairmen: George L Morrow; Joseph M Wells
President: W C Terpstra (and Chief Operating Officer)
Senior Executive Officers: J S Davis (Executive VP), P J Gasparac (VP and Chief Financial Officer), R E Hodge (Senior VP), R R MacNicholas (Senior VP), P E Goldstein (VP and General Counsel), J R Angell (VP), G R Bartlett (VP), R B Casriel (VP and Treasurer), C R Eberst Jr (VP), J E Ebright (VP, Controller and Chief Accounting Officer), M W Ehlers (VP), P C Hebner (VP), R F Pasteris (VP), J L Pelletier (VP), J R Templeton (VP)

PRINCIPAL ACTIVITIES: Transmission of natural gas; oil extraction; coal mining
Parent Company: Occidental Petroleum Corp
Principal Bank: Harris Trust & Savings Bank
Financial Information:

	$'000
Sales revenues	4,000,000

No of Employees: 8,370

MID-CONTINENT SYSTEMS, INC

310 Mid-Continent Plaza, West Memphis, AR 72301
Tel: (501) 735-4295
Telex: TWX 910 350 1795 midcontinent

Chairman: D G Seago Jr (and Chief Executive and Financial Officer)
Senior Executive Officers: Larry W Seago (Executive VP), Tom W Lawhorn (Executive VP Refined Products), Joe E Gurley (Executive VP Marketing, Fleet Services), Gerald G Gunter (VP Corporate Administration), Marvin Shoemake (VP Real Estate)

PRINCIPAL ACTIVITIES: Distribution and sale of oil and gas; oil refining; interests in timber and hotels
Principal Bank: Citicorp
Financial Information:

	$'000
Sales revenues	57,000

No of Employees: 700

MIDDLE SOUTH UTILITIES, INC

225 Baronne Street, New Orleans, LA 70112
Tel: (504) 529-5262

Chairman: Edwin A Lupberger (and President)
Senior Executive Officers: William Cavanaugh III (Senior VP), Jack King (Senior VP), Jerry Jackson (Senior VP), H Stuart Bell (Treasurer), D E Stapp (Secretary)

PRINCIPAL ACTIVITIES: Electricity supply
Principal Subsidiaries: Arkansas Power & Light; Louisiana Power & Light; Mississippi Power & Light; New Orleans Public Service; System Energy Resources
Principal Banks: Manufacturers Hanover; Citibank
Financial Information:

	Dec 31 1985	Dec 31 1986
	$'000	$'000
Sales revenues	3,238,459	3,485,912
Operating income	716,051	1,162,245
Net income	400,991	451,302
Dividends	175,128	-
Dividends per share	$0.89	-
Earnings per share	$2.01	$2.21
Common stock	1,022,905	1,022,905
Retained income	1,316,388	1,765,632
Shareholders equity	3,907,159	3,354,426

No of Employees: 13,640

MIDLAND COMPANY

111 East Fourth Street, Cincinatti, OH 45202
Tel: (513) 721 3777

Chairman: J P Hayden Jr
President: William F Plettner
Senior Executive Officers: Michael J Conaton (Executive VP and Chief Financial Officer), Edmund M Garber (VP), Robert W Hayden (VP), John R LaBar (VP and Secretary), Grant Owings (VP and Legal Counsel), Thomas J Rohs (VP), John I Von Lehman (Treasurer and Chief Accounting Officer)

PRINCIPAL ACTIVITIES: Holding company with interests in insurance, financial services and river transportation
Financial Information:

	$'000
Revenues	110,100

No of Employees: 600

MIDLAND-ROSS CORPORATION

20600 Chagrin Blvd, Cleveland, OH 44122
Tel: (216) 491-8400

Chairman: Harry J Bolwell (and Chief Executive Officer); Vice Chairman: Edward C Gendron
Senior Executive Officers: H G Carlson (Executive VP Electronics/Electrical), R H Hollinger (Executive VP Aerospace), A Launois (Executive VP Thermal Systems), Judson E Smith (Senior VP), David S Wasserman (Senior VP), Frank N Fittipaldi (VP and Secretary), David S Wasserman (Senior VP Taxes), D M Pasco (VP Human Resources), James D Jung (VP and Treasurer), Kenneth A Saban (VP Corporate Communications), Donald F Kimmel (VP International),

PRINCIPAL ACTIVITIES: Manufacture of heat treatment equipment for the paper and steel industries; metal castings; aerospace equipment; electronic components; pollution control equipment; pneumatic equipment and valves
Principal Bank: National City Bank
Financial Information:

	$'000
Sales revenues	715,000

No of Employees: 9,200

MIDLANTIC CORPORATION

Metro Park Plaza, Box 600, Edison, NJ 08818
Tel: (201) 321-8000

Chairman: Robert Van Buren (and Chief Executive Officer)
President: Roy T Peraino
Senior Executive Officers: Frank P Garnevicus (Executive VP and Treasurer), Richard C Rishel (Executive VP), David E Sparks (Executive VP), Frank E Lawatsch Jr (Senior VP, Secretary and General Counsel), R R Lockhart (Senior VP and Auditor), John E Homestead (VP)

PRINCIPAL ACTIVITIES: Banking
Principal Subsidiaries: Midlantic Banks Inc Subsidiaries:- Midlantic National Bank; Midlantic National Bank/North; Midlantic National Bank/South; Midlantic National Bank/Merchants; Midlantic National Bank/Sussex & Merchants; Midlantic National Bank/Union Trust. Continental Bancorp, Inc Subsidiaries: Continental Bank; United Penn Bank; The York Bank and Trust Company
Principal Bank: Midlantic National Bank
Financial Information:

	Dec 31 1985	Dec 31 1986
	$'000	$'000
Income before taxes	177,749	188,708
Net income	141,643	147,534
Cash dividends	43,846	48,704
Dividends per share(1)	$1.18	$1.30
Earnings per share(2)	$3.95	$3.92
Common stock	107,367	107,943
Retained income	422,692	521,522
Shareholders equity	893,125	996,573
Deposits	12,111,768	13,542,207
Total assets	15,072,853	17,184,802

(1) Represents historical amount of Midlantic Banks Inc
(2) Fully diluted

Number of Shareholders: 31,510
No of Employees: 10,715

MIDWAY AIRLINES INC

5959 South Cicero Avenue, Chicago, IL 60638
Tel: (312) 838 0001

Chairman: David R Hinson (and Chief Executive Officer)
Senior Executive Officers: Jeffrey H Erickson (Executive VP and Manager Operations), Robert L Smith (VP Operations), Paul H Tate (VP Advertising and Controller), Alfred S Altschul (VP Finance and Chief Financial Officer), David B Armstrong (VP Legal and Secretary), Lois A Gallo (VP), R Lawrence Hughes (VP Marketing), Edwin A Leiser (VP Maintenance and Engineering), Bruce R LeMar (VP Personnel), Richard E Pfennig (VP and General Manager Midway Airlines 1984 Inc), Paul H Tate (VP Administration and Controller)

PRINCIPAL ACTIVITIES: Air transportation services
Principal Bank: First National Bank
Financial Information:

	Dec 31 1986
	$'000
Sales revenues	261,365
Net income	9,030
Earnings per share	$0.87
Shareholders equity	55,614

No of Employees: 1,950

MIDWEST COMMERCE CORPORATION

121 West Franklin Street, PO Box 1686, Elkhart, IN 46515
Tel: (219) 294 6621

Chairman: Jon S Armstrong
President: Terrence D Brennan
Senior Executive Officers: G Richard Nisbeth (VP Administration), T N Ertel (Secretary)

PRINCIPAL ACTIVITIES: Banking; insurance; leasing; data processing services
Parent Company: NBD Bancorp Inc
Financial Information:

	Dec 31 1985
	$'000
Revenues	69,820
Net income	5,550

No of Employees: 485

MID-WEST CONVEYOR CO, INC

450 E Donovan Road, Kansas City, KS 66115
Tel: (913) 321-5700
Telex: WUT 42533 murestconv ksck

Chairman: Joseph P Forte (and President and Chief Executive Officer)
Senior Executive Officers: B Graves (Executive VP and General Manager), James Alexander (Senior VP Sales and Secretary), Robert Clark (VP Sales), P Houlne (VP Bulk Handling), B Diehl (VP Operations), D Krohn (VP and Controller), S Vohra (VP Business Development), D Strietzel (VP ITG Sales), T Napiecek (VP Government Sales), J Van Zon (VP Engineering)

PRINCIPAL ACTIVITIES: Manufacture of mechanical handling machinery and conveyors
Parent Company: Conergics Corp
Principal Bank: Commercial National Bank
Financial Information:

	$'000
Sales revenues	80,000

No of Employees: 1,000

MIDWEST CORPORATION

Union Building, Box 271, Charleston, WV 25321
Tel: (304) 343-8874
Telex: TWX 910 3500020 midwest corp

President: Sam Silverstein
Senior Executive Officers: Stanley Silverstein (VP), Jack McClung (VP), Jerry Thompson (VP Finance)

PRINCIPAL ACTIVITIES: Wholesale trade in communications equipment; retail interests; manufacture and sale of railroad equipment including track equipment and rails
Parent Company: UNR Industries, Chicago, IL
Principal Bank: National Bank of Commerce
Financial Information:

	$'000
Sales revenues	40,000

No of Employees: 280

MIDWEST ENERGY COMPANY

401 Douglas Street, PO Box 1348, Sioux City, IA 51102
Tel: (712) 277 7400
Telefax: (712) 277-7761

Chairman: Russell E Christiansen (and President and Chief Executive Officer)
Senior Executive Officers: R C Engle (Senior VP), G J Harward (Senior VP and Chief Financial Officer), B A Wharton (Senior VP and Corporate Secretary), P D Ehm (Senior VP of Principal Subsidiary), C A Ellwanger (Senior VP of Principal Subsidiary)

PRINCIPAL ACTIVITIES: Holding company with major interests in electric and natural gas utility operations and additional investments in diversified businesses
Principal Subsidiaries: Iowa Public Service Company Midwest; Capital Group Inc
Principal Bank: Morgan Guaranty Trust Company of New York
Financial Information:

	Dec 31 1985	Dec 31 1986
	$'000	$'000
Sales revenues	388,060	592,591
Income before taxes	58,670	61,885
Net income	30,654	34,780
Dividends	29,470	31,399
Dividends per share	$1.370	$1.455
Earnings per share	$1.42	$1.61
Common stock(1)	21,518	21,580
Retained income	79,674	83,055
Shareholders equity	257,661	260,766

(1) average shares outstanding in thousands
(2) total common equity

No of Employees: 2,180

MIDWEST FINANCIAL GROUP INC

301 Southwest Adams Street, Peoria, IL 61631
Tel: (309) 655 5500

Chairman: Walter J Charlton
President: Leonard B Marshall Jr (and Chief Executive Officer)
Senior Executive Officers: Donald Houk (Executive VP and Treasurer), Dale P Arnold (VP Marketing), Barbara J Duryea (VP and Controller), David R Leitch (VP Public Relations), Sandra M Traicoff (VP and Secretary), Harlan A White (VP)

PRINCIPAL ACTIVITIES: Holding company with interests in banking
Principal Bank: Commercial National Bank of Peoria
Financial Information:

	Dec 31 1985
	$'000
Revenues	227,785

No of Employees: 1,000

MIDWEST SOLVENTS COMPANY, INC

1300 Main Street, Atchison, KS 66002
Tel: (913) 367-1480

Chairman: C L Cray Jr
President: Ladd Seaberg
Senior Executive Officers: J M Carrigan (1st VP and Secretary), Philip M Wolters (VP Sales Gluten and Feed), Raymond L Miller (VP Traffic), Tommy J Monk (VP Marketing Feed), Howard W Hinton (VP Industrial Alcohol), Jerry Lasater (VP Marketing Wheat Starch), Robert G Booe (Treasurer), Tom Herriage (Advertising and Press)

PRINCIPAL ACTIVITIES: Manufacture of alcohol, spirits and cereal products
Principal Bank: Exchange National Bank
Financial Information:

	$'000
Sales revenues	70,000

No of Employees: 300

MILES HOMES

4700 Nathan Lane, Minneapolis, MN 55442
Tel: (612) 553-8300

President: Herbert F Kahler (and Chief Executive Officer)
Senior Executive Officers: Charles W Blome (Senior VP), Richard L Parry (Senior VP), Walter B Roberts Jr (Senior VP), Cosiman J Burzyusk (VP Consumer Relations), E E Orwale (VP Legal), Stu Goldberg (VP Sales), Gunther J Stern (VP Production)

PRINCIPAL ACTIVITIES: Manufacture of sectional homes
Parent Company: Insilco Corp
Principal Bank: Norwest Bank

Financial Information:

	$'000
Sales revenues	50,000

No of Employees: 350

MILES INC

1127 Myrtle Street, Elkhart, IN 46515
Tel: (219) 264-8111
Telex: 258450

Chairman: Konrad M Weis
President: Klaus H Risse (and Chief Executive Officer)
Senior Executive Officers: Karl H Voepel (Executive VP), Wilhelm F Schaeffler (Executive VP), Horst K Wallrabe (Executive VP), Roger G Stoll (Executive VP), Horst Meyer (Executive VP), Klaus E Seeger (Executive VP), Stephen M Reim (VP), John W Howell (VP), Franz Wenzel (VP)

PRINCIPAL ACTIVITIES: Manufacture of pharmaceuticals, medical instruments, plasma fractions, citric acid, industrial enzymes, household cleaning products, and over-the-counter medicines
Trade Names: Alka-Seltzer, One-A-Day and Flinstones vitamins, S.O.S cleaning products, Ames diagnostics
Parent Company: Bayer USA Inc, Pittsburgh, PA
Financial Information:

	Dec 31 1985	Dec 31 1986
	$'000	$'000
Sales revenues	1,177,473	1,225,400
Income before taxes	34,100	48,400
Net income	20,167	28,950
Retained income	98,359	112,309
Shareholders equity	504,713	529,055

No of Employees: 11,557

MILGRAY ELECTRONICS, INC

77 Schmitt Boulevard, Farmingdale, NY 11735
Tel: (516) 420-9800
TWX: (510) 225-3673
Telex: 82934 MILGRAYEL
Telefax: (516) 752-9870

Chairman: Herbert S Davidson (and President)
Senior Executive Officers: Richard Hyman (Executive VP), John Tortorici (VP Finance), Gary Adams (Regional VP), Darren O'Donnell (VP Marketing), Steven Sokoloff (VP Marketing), Elliott Stevens (Regional VP), Thomas Woolf (Regional VP)

PRINCIPAL ACTIVITIES: Distributor mainly of electronic components produced by a large number of manufacturers consisting principally of semi-conductors, electromechanical devices (principally relays and electronic hardware) and passive components
Trade Names: ACDC, Augat, Babcock, Beckman, Birnbach Wire, Cermetek, Corning, Dallas Semiconductor, Delevan, Deutsch, Elco Connectors, Etri, Fujitsu, General Electric, General Instrument, Hitachi, Intersil, Logic Devices, Master Specialties, Micro Power Systems, Mitsubishi, Murata/Erie, NEC, Printed Circuits Int'l, RCA, Sealectro, SGS Semiconductor, Sharp, Silicon General, Siliconix, Standard Microsystems, Teledyne Relays, Toshiba, Varo
Principal Subsidiaries: Milgray Electronics Inc; Milgray/Atlanta; Milgray/Chicago; Milgray/Cleveland; Milgray/Connecticut; Milgray/Dallas; Milgray/Delaware Valley; Milgray/Florida; Milgray/International (in Farmingdale NY, UK and Germany); Milgray/Kansas City; Milgray/New England; Milgray/New York; Milgray/Upstate New York; Milgray/Washington; Birnbach Company; Milgray/Toronto; Milgray Electronics/PR Inc
Principal Bank: Manufacturers Hanover Trust Company

Financial Information:

	Dec 31 1985	Dec 31 1986
	$'000	$'000
Sales revenues	57,533	62,004
Income before taxes	932	209
Net income	616	176
Earnings per share	$0.79	$0.23
Common stock	200	200
Retained income	10,395	10,571
Shareholders equity	10,572	10,747

No of Employees: 300

MILLER & CO

55 E Monroe Street, Chicago, IL 60603
Tel: (312) 372-1500
Telex: WUT 280219 miller & com cgo

Chairman: Roger U Engel
President: A Gordon Gledhill
Senior Executive Officers: Karl J Weber (VP), John D Openshaw (VP Finance and Administration), Donald B Marsh (VP Technical Development)

PRINCIPAL ACTIVITIES: Manufacture of metals and coke
Parent Company: Stinnes Corp
Principal Bank: Citibank
Financial Information:

	$'000
Sales revenues	90,000

No of Employees: 90

MILLER BREWING COMPANY

3939 West State Street, Milwaukee, WI 53208
Tel: (414) 931-2000

Chairman: John A Murphy (and President of Philip Morris Companies Inc)
President: William K Howell (and Chief Executive Officer)
Senior Executive Officers: Warren H Dunn (Senior VP Administration), Leonard J Goldstein (Senior VP Sales), Allen A Schumer (Senior VP Operations), Billy R Apple (VP Plant Operations), Dr Vincent S Bavisotto (VP Brewing and Research), Rodney J Blucher (VP National Retail Sales), Alan G Easton (VP Corporate Affairs), Leonard H Jacob (VP Information Systems), Raymond E Jones Jr (VP General Counsel and Secretary), Thomas A Koehler (VP Field Sales), Paul R Mollomo (VP Purchasing), George D Riemer (VP Personnel and Industrial Relations), William A Saupe (VP International), Ronald R Strain (VP Controller and Treasurer), Georgy L Tarala (VP Engineering), Robert A Toledo (VP Brand Management), William G Schmus (Associate General Council, Assistant Secretary), Daniel P Dockery (Assistant General Council, Assistant Secretary)

PRINCIPAL ACTIVITIES: Miller Brewing Company is a wholly owned subsidiary of Philip Morris Companies Incorporated. Principal beer brands include Miller High Life, Miller Lite, Lowenbrau, Miller Genuine Draft, Magnum, Meister Brau and Milwaukee's Best
Parent Company: Philip Morris Inc, New York, NY
Principal Subsidiaries: Breweries: Miller Brewing Company (Milwaukee WI); Miller Brewing Company (Albany, GA); Miller Brewing Company (Fort Worth, TX); Miller Brewing Company (Irwindale, CA); Miller Brewing Company (Trenton, OH); Miller Brewing Company (Eden, NC); Miller Brewing Company (Fulton, NY). Container Divisions: Central New York Bottle Company (Auburn, NY); Fulton Container Division (Fulton, NY); Reidsville Container Division (Reidsville, NC); Fort Worth Container Division (Fort Worth, TX); Milwaukee Container Division (Milwaukee, WI); Moultrie Container Division (Moultrie, GA). Branch Operations: Crescent Distributing Company (Harahan, LA). Miller Brands, Inc (Portland, OR); Miller Brands, Inc (Kent, WA); Miller Brands Inc (Fort Myers, FL); Miller Distributing of Oklahoma, Inc (Oklahoma City, OK); Miller Brands of Oklahoma, Inc (Tulsa, Oklahoma)

Principal Bank: Marshall and Ilsey Bank
Financial Information:

	$'000
Sales revenues	3,054,000

No of Employees: 9,700

MILLER CO

99 Center Street, Meriden, CT 06451
Tel: (203) 235-4474
Telex: WUT 99 4489 millerco meri

Chairman: B G Tremaine
President: B G Tremaine Jr
Senior Executive Officers: D D Rode (Senior VP Human Resources), Robert P Sweeney (Secretary and Treasurer), R E Liepold (President Lighting Division), N R Ferency (VP Lighting Division), B G Tremaine III (VP and General Manager Mill Division)

PRINCIPAL ACTIVITIES: Manufacture of lighting products and metal coil and strip
Principal Bank: AmeriTrust Company
Financial Information:

	$'000
Sales revenues	50,000

No of Employees: 500

MILLER ELECTRIC MFG CO

718 S Bounds Street, Appleton, WI 54911
Tel: (414) 734-9821
Telex: TWX 910 350 7392 miller elec

President: Elizabeth Miller
Senior Executive Officers: Margaret Miller Gilson (Senior Executive VP), F C Okada (Executive VP Administration, Secretary and Treasurer), D J Corrigall (VP Engineering), R L Geissbuhler (VP Domestic Sales), F J Grist (VP Research), T M Lally (VP), T A Martin (VP Materials), A C Mulder (Corporate VP), R M Erbland (VP International Sales), W B Wieckert (VP Finance and Controller)

PRINCIPAL ACTIVITIES: Manufacture of welding equipment and generators
Principal Bank: Valley Bank
Financial Information:

	$'000
Sales revenues	150,000

No of Employees: 1,500

MILLER, HERMAN, , INC

8500 Byron Road, Zeeland, MI 49464
Tel: 616 772-3300
Telex: TWX 810 2926133 hermillerzee

Chairman: Max O De Pree (and Chief Executive Officer)
President: Edward R Simon Jr (and Chief Operating Officer)
Senior Executive Officers: Richard H Ruch (Senior VP and Chief Financial Officer)

PRINCIPAL ACTIVITIES: Manufacture of furniture for institutions and offices
Principal Bank: First Michigan Bank and Trust
Financial Information:

	May 31 1986 $'000	May 31 1987 $'000
Sales revenues	531,640	573,520
Income before taxes	66,518	62,265
Net income	37,818	33,265
Dividends	10,805	10,800
Dividends per share	$0.44	$0.44
Earnings per share	$1.53	$1.35
Retained income	141,541	164,006
Shareholders equity	192,101	212,467

No of Employees: 4,050

MILLER, JAS I, TOBACCO CO

2201 Regency Road, Wilson, NC 27893
Tel: (919) 237-1106

Chairman: A Winniett Peters
President: Harvey B Ruffin
Senior Executive Officers: F M Lynch III (VP), W H Feetham (VP), Graham D Evans (VP), E C Dilda (VP), Raymond J Geiger (Secretary and Treasurer)

PRINCIPAL ACTIVITIES: Tobacco processing and wholesale tobacco products
Parent Company: Standard Commercial Tobacco Co Inc
Principal Bank: North Carolina National Bank
Financial Information:

	1986 $'000
Sales revenues	110,000
Income before taxes	8,110
Net income	4,988
Dividends*	18
Dividends per share*	$9.00
Common stock	993
Retained income	19,386
Shareholders equity	21,367

*Pfd STK

Principal Shareholders: Standard Commercial Corp
No of Employees: 500

MILLER PRINTING EQUIPMENT CORPORATION

1101 Reedsdale Street, Pittsburgh, PA 15233
Tel: (412) 237-7500
Telex: WUT 315 139 miller print

President: J K Martin
Senior Executive Officers: G R Weber (VP Finance), D E Fuerst (Manufacturing Manager), John H Conwell Jr (Material Manager)

PRINCIPAL ACTIVITIES: Manufacture of printing machinery
Principal Bank: Mellon Bank
Financial Information:

	$'000
Sales revenues	60,000

No of Employees: 400

MILLIPORE CORPORATION

80 Ashby Road, Bedford, MA 01730
Tel: (617) 275-9200
Telex: 4430066 MILLIPR UI

Chairman: John A Gilmartin (and Chief Executive Officer)
Senior Executive Officers: William L Shippey, Geoffrey Nunes, Douglas A Berthiaume, James L Dwyer, Adrian R Reti, David B Lawrence

PRINCIPAL ACTIVITIES: Manufacturers fluid analysis and purification products for the industrial, University/Government and health care markets
Trade Names: Major Products (Including Trade Marks):- DURAPORE (membrane disc filter), FLUOROPORE (membrane disc filter), IVEX (filter unit), MILLEX (filter unit), MILLI-Q (water system), MILLI-RO (water system), FLUOROGARD (cartridge filter), KILOPREP (process chromotography system), MILLICELL (culture plate insert), MILLIDISK (cartridge filter), MILLISTAK (filter unit), MILLITITER (filtration system), MINITAN (ultrafiltration system), PROTSTAK (filtration module), DURAPAK (liquid coated GC packing), PREPAK (500NH2, CN, SILICA, C18 cartridge), SEP-PAK (C18, silica, florisil, alumina cartridges), ACCELL (ion exchange media), DELTA PREP (3000 preparative liquid chromatography system), EXPERT (multi-instrument software), NOVA-PAK (C18, CN, phenyl column), PICO.TAG (amino acid analysis system), WAVS (waters

automated valve station), WISP (waters intelligent sample processor)
Principal Subsidiaries: Principal Facilities: Millipore Products Division (Bedford, MA); Waters Chromatography Division (Milford, MA); Waters Chromatography Division (Taunton, MA); Millipore Products Division (Jaffrey, NH)
Principal Bank: First National Bank of Boston
Financial Information:

	Dec 31 1986
	$'000
Sales revenues	443,092
Net income	39,064
Earnings per share	$1.40
Shareholders equity	289,647

No of Employees: 4,215

MILLMASTER ONYX GROUP, INC

99 Park Avenue, New York, NY 10016
Tel: (212) 687-2757

Chairman: Robert J Milano (and President and Chief Executive Officer)
Senior Executive Officers: Sidney Beinfest (VP Technology), Dennis A Sadlowski (VP and Secretary)

PRINCIPAL ACTIVITIES: Manufacture of chemicals, specialty chemicals, printing inks and detergents
Principal Bank: First Jersey National Bank
Financial Information:

	$'000
Sales revenues	160,000

No of Employees: 950

MILNOT CO

120 W St John Street, Litchfield, IL 62056
Tel: (217) 324-2146

President: William Adams
Senior Executive Officers: W F Hilton (VP and Assistant Secretary), R Hajicek (VP Sales and Marketing)

PRINCIPAL ACTIVITIES: Manufacture of dairy products and canned foods including meat and milk
Parent Company: Canteen Corporation-Ultimate Holding Company-Trans World Corporation
Financial Information:

	$'000
Sales revenues	50,000

No of Employees: 150

MILPRINT, INC

4200 N Holton Street, Milwaukee, WI 53201
Tel: (414) 332-5800
Telex: TWX 910 2623158 milprint mil

President: Richard Bromley (and Treasurer)
Senior Executive Officers: Thomas K Rosselet (Executive VP and Secretary), Paul Verbeten (Director of Sales), Karen Cverko (Director of Sales), Gerald S Binder (VP International Division)

PRINCIPAL ACTIVITIES: Manufacture of packaging products
Trade Names: Milcote TM, KLing SeAL, Candy Lam
Principal Bank: First Wisconsin Bank of Wisconsin
Financial Information:

	$'000
Sales revenues	60,000+

No of Employees: 500

MILTON BRADLEY CO

443 Shaker Road, East Long Meadow, MA 01028
Tel: (413) 525-6411
Telex: WUT 955316 milbradco spm

Senior Executive Officers: George R Ditomassi Jr (Chief Operating Officer), Stanley Stryzempek (Senior VP Finance)

PRINCIPAL ACTIVITIES: Manufacture of a wide range of toys and games for leisure and educational purposes
Parent Company: Hasbro Inc
Financial Information:

	$'000
Sales revenues	337,000

No of Employees: 5,100

MILTON ROY CO

PO Box 12169, St Petersburg, FL 33733
Tel: (813) 823-4444

Chairman: Richard E Schmidt (and President and Chief Executive Officer)
Senior Executive Officers: H R Smith (VP), Darrell N Clark (VP), J C Degremont (VP International), W Barry Gilbert (VP), C E Liggans (VP Administration), Stephen G Matthews (VP), John L West (VP), John M McNamara (VP, Secretary and Treasurer), J Ronald Moore (VP and Controller)

PRINCIPAL ACTIVITIES: Manufacture of laboratory equipment, pumps and valves
Principal Bank: Wachovia Bank and Trust Co
Financial Information:

	$'000
Sales revenues	98,000

No of Employees: 1,460

MILTOPE GROUP INC

733 3rd Avenue, New York, NY 10017
Tel: (212) 661 6343

Chairman: Inman E McElvy
President: R Pandolfi
Senior Executive Officers: Bryan Birch (Senior VP), Frederick J Buckholtz Jr (VP), Frederick S Korb (VP), W W Whinna (VP Finance and Treasurer), Leonard Gubar (Secretary)

PRINCIPAL ACTIVITIES: Manufacture of electronic equipment for the computer industry
Financial Information:

	$'000
Sales revenues	61,000

No of Employees: 700

MINE SAFETY APPLIANCES COMPANY

600 Penn Center Boulevard, Pittsburgh, PA 15235
Tel: (412) 273-5000
Telex: 812-453

Chairman: J T Ryan Jr
President: Eugene W Merry
Senior Executive Officers: J W Carville (VP and Treasurer), D E Crean (VP), J T Ryan III (VP), L N Short Jr (VP and President, MSA International), F Tepper (VP)

PRINCIPAL ACTIVITIES: The primary business of MSA is the manufacture and sale of products designed to safeguard the health and safety of workers throughout the world. Principal products include respiratory protective equipment, head protection, eye and face protection, hearing protectors, safety belts and clothing, industrial emergency care products, mining safety equipment, workplace filters, monitoring instruments and heart pacemaker power cells. Many of these products have wide application for worker protection in industries including manufacturing, mining, public utilities, chemicals, petroleum, construction and transportation as well as fire, police and governmental activities. Other products include boron-based and similar specialty chemicals, gas mantles, liquid metal hardware and thermal batteries
Trade Names: Operating Trade Name:- MSA
Principal Subsidiaries: United States: Callery Chemical; Catalyst Research; MSA Research. Europe: Auergesellschaft GmbH

(Germany); MSA (Britain) Limited (UK); MSA Espanola SA (Spain); MSA de France (France); MSA Italiana SpA (Italy); MSA Nederland BV (Netherlands); MSA (Switzerland) Ltd (Switzerland); Schonholzer AG (Switzerland); AB Tegma (Sweden). Other: Mine Safety Appliances Limited (India); MSA (Africa) (Pty) Limited (South Africa); MSA (Aust) Pty Limited (Australia); MSA do Brasil Ltda (Brazil); MSA Canada (Canada); MSA de Chile Ltda (Chile); MSA Export Limited (Barbados); MSA Japan Ltd (Japan); MSA de Mexico SA (Mexico); MSA del Peru (Peru); MSA S E Asia Pte Ltd (Singapore); MSA Zambia Limited (Zambia); MSA Zimbabwe (Pvt) Limited (Zimbabwe)

Principal Bank: Mellon National Bank; Pittsburgh National Bank

Financial Information:

	$'000
Sales revenues	393,000

No of Employees: 7,000

MINISCRIBE CORPORATION

1871 Lefthand Circle, Longmont, CO 80501

Tel: (303) 651-6000

President: Gerald W Goodman

Senior Executive Officers: D B Pearie (VP Finance, Secretary and Treasurer), D J Resnik (VP), R J Garter (VP), Joseph C Consoli (VP and Chief Financial Officer)

PRINCIPAL ACTIVITIES: Manufacture of Winchester disk drives for microcomputers

Financial Information:

	$'000
Sales revenues	114,000

No of Employees: 1,700

MINNESOTA MUTUAL LIFE INSURANCE CO

400 N Robert Street, St Paul, MN 55101

Tel: (612) 298-3500

Telex: TWX 910 380 1545 minn mutual

Chairman: Coleman Bloomfield (and President and Chief Executive Officer)

Senior Executive Officers: Joseph Bird (Senior VP and Treasurer), Richard A Engen (Senior VP), Robert E Hunstad (Senior VP), Robert J Hasling (VP and Secretary)

PRINCIPAL ACTIVITIES: Life insurance

Principal Subsidiaries: MIMLIC Asset Management; MIMLIC Sales Corporation; Personal Finance Company

Principal Bank: The First National Bank of St Paul

Financial Information:

	Dec 31 1985	Dec 31 1986
	$'000	$'000
Premium income	749,726	816,990
Investment income	250,543	280,121

No of Employees: 1,400

MINNESOTA POWER & LIGHT CO

30 W Superior St, Duluth, MN 55802

Tel: (218) 722-2641

Chairman: Jack F Rowe (and Chief Executive Officer)

President: Arend J Sandbulte (and Chief Operating Officer)

Senior Executive Officers: Robert J Marchetti (Senior VP Power Supply and Engineering), Robert D Edwards (VP Finance and Chief Financial Officer), Raymond G Erickson (VP Public Affairs), James R Habicht (VP, Secretary and General Counsel), Robert M Miller (VP Customer Operations), Gerald B Ostroski (VP Information and Planning), C M Reichert (VP Administration), Ritter J Humphrey (VP Systems Engineering and Operations), Bert T Phillips (VP Power Supply)

PRINCIPAL ACTIVITIES: Distribution of electricity

Principal Bankers: Northwest Bank

Financial Information:

	Dec 31 1985	Dec 31 1986
	$'000	$'000
Sales revenues	413,000	395,000
Net income	69,400	76,000

No of Employees: 1,800

MINNESOTA RUBBER CO

3630 Wooddale Avenue, Minneapolis, MN 55416

Tel: (612) 927-1400

Telex: WUT 882211 mrc corp ud

Chairman: Robert W Carlson Jr (and Chief Executive Officer)

President: James Lande

Senior Executive Officers: Gerald Mitchell (VP Manufacturing), Alan Fero (VP Quality Assurance), Gary West (VP Sales), Robert C Dye (VP Finance), Floyd Vincent (VP Human Resources), Tony Braga (Advertising and Marketing)

PRINCIPAL ACTIVITIES: Manufacture of rubber and plastic products; manufacture of aluminum products

Parent Company: Quadion Corporation

Principal Bank: The First National Bank of Minneapolis

Financial Information:

	$'000
Sales revenues	80,000

No of Employees: 1,600

MINNETONKA INC

Jonathan Industrial Park, Peavey Road, Chaska, MN 55318

Tel: (612) 448-4181

Telex: 290357 Minnetonka UD

Chairman: Robert R Taylor (and President)

Senior Executive Officers: Robert W Hebeisen (VP and Treasurer), Grant L Wood (VP and General Manager-Group 1, President-Village Bath Products Inc), Ronald L Whipperman (VP-Operations, General Manager-Group IV), Richard E Reever (VP-Research and Development), Jerome J Jenko (VP, Secretary and General Counsel), Robert R Burns (President-Calvin Klein Cosmetics Corporation), Robert E Thiner (Corporate Controller)

PRINCIPAL ACTIVITIES: Manufacture and distribution of personal care products

Trade Names: Softsoap, Check Up, Calvin Klein, Obsession, Village Bath Products, Claire Burke, Rogert & Gallet, L'Homme, Country Diary, Institute Swiss and Davron

Principal Bank: First National Bank of St Paul

Financial Information:

	$'000
Sales revenues net	124,000

No of Employees: 600

MINSTAR INC

1215 Marshall Street NE, Minneapolis, MN 55413

Tel: (612) 379-1800

Chairman: Irwin L Jacobs (and Chief Executive Officer)

President: W J Mahanes

Senior Executive Officers: Richard E Karkow (Senior VP Finance), James B Farrell (VP and Secretary)

PRINCIPAL ACTIVITIES: Long distance trucking; other interests include boat building; manufacture of snowmobiles; manufacture of clothing and rubber products

Principal Subsidiaries: AMF Inc

Principal Bank: Norwest Bank Minneapolis

Financial Information:

	Dec 31 1985	Dec 31 1986
	$'000	$'000
Sales revenues	1,253,116	1,156,362
Net income	30,784	738
Earnings per share	$1.90	$0.04
Shareholders equity	233,650	235,174

No of Employees: 4,000

MIRRO CORPORATION

1512 Washington Street, Manitowoc, WI 54220
Tel: (414) 684-4421
Telex: TWX 910 260 3501 mirrocorp

Chairman: Daniel C Ferguson
President: Leonard S Raskin
Senior Executive Officers: Harold F Higgins (VP Manufacturing), William Frieder (VP Merchandise), Vincent J Pasquale (VP Sales), Darrell J Olson (VP Personnel), William R Frederick (VP Finance and Treasurer)

PRINCIPAL ACTIVITIES: Manufacture of aluminum cookware and aluminum extruded products
Parent Company: Newell Companies Inc, Freeport, IL
Principal Bank: First Wisconsin National Bank
Financial Information:

	$'000
Sales revenues	90,000

No of Employees: 1,200

MISCHER CORPORATION

2727 N Loop West, Suite 200, Houston, TX 77008
Tel: (713) 869 7800

Chairman: Walter M Mischer (and Chief Executive Officer)
President: Walter M Mischer Jr (and Chief Operating Officer)
Senior Executive Officers: Herbert G Tigner (Senior VP), James C Box (VP), Majane Martin (VP and Controller), George Ruhlen (VP), Carl J Stephens (Executive VP), C Ronald Blankenship (Executive VP Finance, Secretary and Treasurer)

PRINCIPAL ACTIVITIES: Wholesale trade in heating and air conditioning equipment and household appliances; interests in civil engineering and real estate
Principal Bank: First City National Bank
Financial Information:

	$'000
Sales revenues	83,000

No of Employees: 1,000

MISSION INSURANCE GROUP INC

2600 Wilshire Blvd, Los Angeles, CA 90057
Tel: (213) 381-6811
Telex: WUT 698 308 mission iv Lsa

Chairman: Carl H Lindner
President: Ray D Johnson (and Chief Executive Officer)
Senior Executive Officers: W A Greenup (Senior VP), John L Shedd (VP and Chief Financial Officer), L G Becker (VP, Secretary and General Counsel)

PRINCIPAL ACTIVITIES: Insurance services including property and casualty insurance
Principal Bank: United California Bank
Financial Information:

	$'000
Revenues	440,000

No of Employees: 2,000

MISSISSIPPI CHEMICAL CORPORATION

PO Box 388, Yazoo City, MS 39194
Tel: (601) 746-4131

Chairman: Leroy Percy
President: Tom C Parry
Senior Executive Officers: David W Arnold (Senior VP Engineering), W F Hawkins (Senior VP Finance), Donald A McGraw (Senior VP Sales and Distribution), John R Phillips (Senior VP Special Consultant), A M Feland (Vice Chairman of Board), Paul Lacy (VP Energy), James M Gambrell (VP Operations), A B Sherling (VP and General Manager Yazoo City Plant), M L Brown (VP Research and Development), Thomas K Tidsdale (VP Corporate Services), Robert E Jones (Associate General Council), Gene A Triggs (VP Governmental Affairs), Rosalyn B Glascoe (Assistant Secretary)

PRINCIPAL ACTIVITIES: Maufacture and distribution of chemical fertilizers
Trade Names: MCC
Principal Subsidiaries: Triad Chemical (50%) (Joint Venture)
Principal Bank: Deposit Guaranty National Bank
Financial Information:

	$'000
Sales revenues	226,000

No of Employees: 790

MISSOURI FARMERS ASSOCIATION, INC

615 Locust, Columbia, MO 65201
Tel: (314) 874-5111
Telex: 910 760 1448

Chairman: William Stouffer; Vice Chairman: David Wissbaun
President: B L Frew
Senior Executive Officers: David Jobe (VP Operations), Don Copenhaver (VP Retail Distribution Operations), Joe Powell (VP Manufacturing), Janice Schuerman (VP Corporate Services), Lowell Morse (VP Traffic), Bob Rothwell (VP Finance), Janice Sherman (VP Communications)

PRINCIPAL ACTIVITIES: Growing, manufacture and distribution of seeds, fertilizers and animal feedstuffs; supply of agricultural equipment
Principal Bank: St Louis Bank for Cooperatives
Financial Information:

	$'000
Sales revenues	830,000

No of Employees: 1,400

MISSOURI PUBLIC SERVICE COMPANY

10700 East M-350 Highway, Kansas City, MO 64138
Tel: (816) 737 9331

Chairman: Avis G Tucker
President: William I Owen (and Chief Executive Officer)
Senior Executive Officers: John R Baker (Senior VP), Jackson E Barry (VP), James E Franklin (VP), Richard C Green Jr (Executive VP), James J Sage (VP), Dennis A Sieg (VP), James W Stephens (Senior VP), Dale J Wolf (VP and Treasurer)

PRINCIPAL ACTIVITIES: Supply of electricity and other services
Financial Information:

	$'000
Sales revenues	234,000

No of Employees: 915

MISSOURI-KANSAS-TEXAS RAILROAD CO

Katy Bldg, Dallas, TX 75202
Tel: (214) 651-6706

Chairman: Reginald N Whitman (and Chief Executive Officer)
President: Harold L Gastler (and Chief Operating Officer)
Senior Executive Officers: Karl R Ziebarth (Executive VP Finance), Billy R Bishop (VP), Harold O Brandt (VP Real Estate and Industrial Development), Harry T Dimmerman (VP Traffic), William L Dorcy (VP Accounting), V Raye Reynolds (VP Property Management), Martin F Rister (VP Mechanical), Thomas F Steiniger (VP Marketing), Thomas G Todd (VP Operations), William H Zeidel (VP Administration)

PRINCIPAL ACTIVITIES: Railroad services

Parent Company: Katy Industries Inc
Financial Information:

	Dec 31 1986
	$'000
Sales revenues	236,021
Net income	25,001
Earnings per share	$12.81

No of Employees: 2,317

MITCHELL ENERGY & DEVELOPMENT CORPORATION

PO Box 4000, 2001 Timberloch Place, The Woodlands, TX 77387-4000
Tel: (713) 363-5500
Telex: 775889 MEDC WDLD

Chairman: George P Mitchell (and President and Chief Executive Officer)
Senior Executive Officers: Bernard F Clark (Vice Chairman), F D Covey (President-Exploration and Production Division, Corporate Senior VP), Philip S Smith (President-Administration and Financial Division, Corporate Senior VP and Chief Financial Officer), Morris D Thompson Jr (Senior VP), Bruce M Withers Jr (President-Transmission and Processing Division, Corporate Senior VP), Paul W Wommack (Senior VP, Secretary and General Counsel)

PRINCIPAL ACTIVITIES: Mitchell Energy & Development Corp is a large petroleum independent with real estate interests. Based in Texas, the Company engages in energy-related activities throughout the nation, although its primary area of operation is in North Texas. The Company is also a major real estate developer in the Houston-Galveston area. Operations include gas and oil exploration and production; oil field equipment supply; contract drilling; gas processing, gathering and transmission; and real estate development
Principal Subsidiaries: Mitchell Energy Corporation and its subsidiaries:-Liquid Energy Corporation, Mitchell Energy Production Corp, MND Drilling Corporation, Oilworld Supply Company, Southwestern Gas Pipeline Inc. Mitchell Development Corporation of the Southwest and its subsidiary:- The Woodlands Corporation
Principal Bank: M-Bank Houston NA; Manufacturers Hanover Trust Company, New York
Financial Information:

	Jan 31 1986
	$'000
Sales revenues	843,925
Net income	48,233
Earnings per share	$1.01
Shareholders equity	575,756

MITE CORPORATION

446 Blake Street, New Haven, CT 06515
Tel: (203) 387-2572
Telex: 963 419

Chairman: Robert J Blinken
President: Leo J Brancato
Senior Executive Officers: William Ryan (VP), Stewart Hampton (VP Public and Industrial Relations), Marcel J Lamy (VP and Controller), Richard R Swanson (VP)

PRINCIPAL ACTIVITIES: Manufacture of a range of industrial equipment including fasteners, valves and spindles
Parent Company: Emhart Corp
Principal Subsidiaries: Whitnon Manufacturing Co; MITE International Sales Corp; Heli-Coil Canada Inc (Canada)
Principal Bank: National Bank of North America
Financial Information:

	$'000
Sales revenues	86,000

No of Employees: 1,030

MITSUBISHI AIRCRAFT INTERNATIONAL, INC

Mathis Field, Box 3848, San Angelo, TX 76902
Tel: (915) 942 4200
Telex: WUT 791637 mai intl dal

President: Nobuo Hayashi
Senior Executive Officers: M Diabo (Executive VP Operations), George M Zieres Jr (VP Operations), Borge Boeskov (VP Marketing), C W Cole (VP International Sales), Ichiro Okada (Treasurer)

PRINCIPAL ACTIVITIES: Manufacture of aircraft
Financial Information:

	$'000
Sales revenues	150,000

No of Employees: 600

MITSUI MANUFACTURERS BANK

135 E Ninth Street, Los Angeles, CA 90015
Tel: (213) 688-8100
Telex: WUT 674184 mitman bk lsa a

Chairman: Kenichi Kamiya; Acting Chairman: Taizo Nakamura
President: Leonard Weil (and Chief Executive Officer); Deputy President: Yutaro Hayashi (and Chief Operating Officer)
Senior Executive Officers: Bruce E Fane (Executive VP), Naruo Otsubo (Executive VP), Charles Soloman (Executive VP), Charles D Baillie (Senior VP Credit Administration), Allen S Berg (Senior VP San Fernando Valley and Hollywood), J Neal Churchill (Senior VP Loan Adjustment), Allen H Court (Senior VP Orange County Office), Jay M David (Senior VP, Secretary and General Counsel), Frank Fratto (Senior VP Textile Division), Minoru Fukushima (Senior VP Loan Administration), Michael J Henniger (Senior VP Personnel), Ronald B Hicks (Senior VP Commercial Loans), Michael L Ingraham (Senior VP Investments), William J LaBelle (Senior VP Operations), Donald B Marts (Senior VP Commercial Loans) Tsuneo Masumoto (Senior VP Little Tokyo Office), Charles E McLaughlin (Senior VP San Jose Office), James R O'Brien (Senior VP San Diego Office), Yuji Okada (Senior VP Loan Administration), Yoshikazu Omata (Senior VP Commercial Loans), Claude J Rumph (Senior VP Corporate Headquarters), S Price Scott Jr (Senior VP Real Estate Loans), Howard P Smith (Senior VP Commercial Loans), Richard G Stebbins (Senior VP Instalment Loans), Hiroshi Toyozumi (Senior VP San Francisco Office), James L Wheeler (Senior VP Beverly Hills Office), Charles K Williamson (Senior VP Commercial Loans)

PRINCIPAL ACTIVITIES: Banking and financial services
Parent Company: Mitsui Bank

No of Employees: 1,000

MNC FINANCIAL, INC

PO Box 987, Baltimore, MD 21203
Tel: (301) 244-1940

Chairman: Alan P Hoblitzell Jr (and Chief Executive Officer); Vice Chairman: William H Daiger Jr
President: Daniel J Callahan III
Senior Executive Officers: Harry F Wright Jr (Executive VP and Chief Financial Officer), Edward J Stark (VP and Secretary), David L Spilman (VP, Treasurer and Chief Accounting Officer), George B P Ward Jr (VP and Assistant Secretary), Arthur D Gilbert (VP and Assistant Treasurer)

PRINCIPAL ACTIVITIES: MNC Financial (formerly Maryland National Corporation) is a bank holding company which owns the capital stock of three nationally chartered commercial banks including Maryland National Bank and American Security Bank, which provide a full range of commercial, consumer and fiduciary bank services, and Maryland Bank, NA, which conducts a nationwide consumer lending program, principally credit card loans. The Corporation also owns six principal non-bank subsidiaries which are engaged in such financially related activities as commercial collaterilized lending, equipment leasing, mortgage banking, real estate financing, consumer lending, credit related insurance and investment counseling

Principal Subsidiaries: Maryland National Bank; American Security Bank; Maryland Bank NA; Maryland National Credit Corporation; Maryland National Leasing Corporation; Maryland National Mortgage Corporation; National Personal Finance Corporation

Principal Banks: Maryland National Bank; American Security Bank

Financial Information:

	Dec 31 1985	Dec 31 1986
	$'000	$'000
Income before taxes	122,195	157,592
Net income	98,427	122,788
Dividends	28,452	33,046
Dividends per share	$0.95	$1.15
Earnings per share	$3.60	$4.35
Common stock	68,503	69,773
Retained income	525,513	613,049
Shareholders equity	713,606	818,055
Deposits	8,224,907	9,907,858
Total assets	11,946,130	14,170,406

No of Employees: 7,500

MOBAY CORPORATION

Mobay Road, Pittsburgh, PA 15205
Tel: (412) 777-2000

Chairman: K M Weis (and President); Vice Chairman: K H Risse

President: N H Prater (and Chief Executive Officer)

Senior Executive Officers: G D Mueller (Executive VP), H G Kraetzer (Executive VP), R L White (Executive VP), W E Becker (Group VP), H W Machatzke (Group VP), H L Noble (Group VP), H K Wehner (Group VP)

PRINCIPAL ACTIVITIES: Manufacture of and marketing of chemical products

Parent Company: Bayer AG, Leverkusen, Germany

Financial Information:

	Dec 31 1986
	$'000
Sales revenues	1,710,000
Net income	150,000

No of Employees: 6,495

MOBIL CORPORATION

150 East 42nd Street, New York, NY 10017-5666
Tel: (212) 883-4242

Chairman: Allen E Murray (and President, Chief Executive Officer and Chairman of the Executive Committee); Vice Chairmen: Richard F Tucker, James Q Riordan

Senior Executive Officers: Rex D Adams (VP), Andrew L Gaboriault (VP), Lucio A Noto (VP), Herbert Schmertz (VP), Robert G Weeks (VP), Dede Thompson Bartlett (Secretary), J Edward Fowler (General Counsel), R Hartwell Gardner (Treasurer), Philip W Matos (Controller)

PRINCIPAL ACTIVITIES: In 1986, Mobil Corporation was the second largest US oil company. It consists of one of the world's largest petroleum operations and a growth-orientated chemical business. It also owns a land-development company and a major retailing operation in the United States. Mobil companies do business in more than 100 countries

Trade Names: Mobil, Baggies, Hefty, Kordite

Principal Subsidiaries: Mobil Oil Corporation; Mobil Chemical Company; Mobil Land Development Corporation; Montgomery Ward & Co Incorporated

Financial Information:

	Dec 31 1985	Dec 31 1986
	$'000	$'000
Total revenues	60,609,000	49,865,000
Net income	1,040,000	1,407,000
Dividends	898,000	898,000
Dividends per share	$2.20	$2.20
Earnings per share	$2.55	$3.45
Common stock	858,000	860,000
Retained earnings	14,539,000	15,048,000
Shareholders equity	14,089,000	15,239,000

No of Employees: 127,400

MOBIL OIL CORPORATION

150 East 42nd Street, New York, NY 10017-5666
Tel: (212) 883-4242

Chairman: Allen E Murray (and Chief Executive Officer and Chairman of the Executive Committee)

President: Richard F Tucker (and Vice Chairman of the Executive Committee and Chief Operating Officer)

Senior Executive Officers: P J Hoenmans (Executive VP), W E MacDonald (Executive VP), E A Renna (Executive VP), J Q Riordan (Executive VP), R D Adams (VP), W A Bork (VP), J V D'Ambrisi (VP), N N Farr (VP), A L Gaboriault (VP), R R Graves (VP), J P Keehan (VP), L A Noto (VP), Herbert Schmertz (VP), R O Swanson (VP), R G Weeks (VP)

PRINCIPAL ACTIVITIES: Mobil Oil conducts an integrated petroleum business in the United States. It has many affiliates throughout the world-separately incorporated and independently operated-that are engaged in petroleum operations. Mobil Oil and some of its affiliates also engage in the manufacture and marketing of chemicals

Trade Names: Mobil

Parent Company: Mobil Corporation

Principal Subsidiaries: Mobil Alaska Pipeline Company; Mobil Oil Credit Corporation

Financial Information:

	Dec 31 1985
	$'000
Total revenues	51,423,000
Net income	1,969,000
Shareholders equity	13,669,000

No of Employees: 71,300 worldwide

MOBILE COMMUNICATIONS CORP OF AMERICA

1500 Capital Towers, Jackson, MS 39201
Tel: (601) 969 1200

Chairman: John N Palmer (and President and Chief Executive Officer)

Senior Executive Officers: Salvatore J Albano (VP), Jai P Bhagat (VP Engineering), Jere T Little (VP), Caroll D McHenry (VP Marketing), Ernest A Oswalt (VP Technical Systems), Rainer Sautermeister (Executive VP), Richard T Weatherholt (VP Finance), Arnold L Young (VP Treasurer), Elizabeth B Vicker (Controller and Assistant Secretary), Victor C Rasier II (Secretary)

PRINCIPAL ACTIVITIES: Communications services including cellular telephone systems and independent paging services

Principal Subsidiaries: American Cellular Telephone Corp; Tel-Page Corp

Principal Bank: Deposit Guaranty National Bank

Financial Information:

	$'000
Sales revenues	71,000

No of Employees: 1,340

MOBILE GAS SERVICE CORPORATION

2828 Dauphin Street, Mobile, AL 36606
Tel: (205) 470 2700

Chairman: William J Hearin
President: Walter L Hovell
Senior Executive Officers: Kenneth H Dean (Executive VP), John D McAlister (VP and Treasurer), J H Castle (VP Sales), Frederick R Crawford (VP Gas Supply), George M Yon (VP Operations), Charles L Dyas (VP Personnel), Sam M Johnston Jr (Secretary)

PRINCIPAL ACTIVITIES: Supply of natural gas
Principal Bank: First National Bank
Financial Information:

	$'000
Sales revenues	58,000

No of Employees: 240

MOBILE HOME INDUSTRIES INC

2032 Thomasville Rd, Tallahassee, FL 32316
Tel: (904) 224 5111

Chairman: Fred O Drake Jr (and President and Chief Executive Officer)
Senior Executive Officers: Robert B Johnson (VP and Secretary and Chief Financial Officer), David J McLaurin (Executive VP), E D Wilkinson (VP), James E Tinkler (VP Finance)

PRINCIPAL ACTIVITIES: Sale of mobile homes
Principal Bank: Southeast Bank
Financial Information:

	$'000
Sales revenues	71,000

No of Employees: 445

MOBILE PREMIX CONCRETE, INC

PO 5183 TA, Denver, CO 80217
Tel: (303) 534-3165

Chairman: Burton C Boothby (and Treasurer)
President: Howard J Bozarth Jr
Senior Executive Officers: Dennis L Carter (Executive VP), Donald E Yale (Executive VP Finance and Secretary)

PRINCIPAL ACTIVITIES: Production of ready mixed concrete and other concrete products
Parent Company: MPM Inc
Principal Bank: United Bank of Denver
Financial Information:

	$'000
Sales revenues	60,000

No of Employees: 500

MODERN MAID FOOD PRODUCTS, INC

200 Garden City Plaza, Garden City, NY 11530
Tel: (516) 877-1000

Chairman: Peter A Gardiner
President: Emmet P O'Sullivan (and Chief Executive Officer)
Senior Executive Officers: Jim Gallam (VP Food Services Sales), George E Bure (VP Manufacturing), George Marinos (VP Finance, Chief Financial Officer and Secretary), Douglas Cox (VP Operations Planning), Neil J Trager (VP Quality Control)

PRINCIPAL ACTIVITIES: Manufacture of premixes and food coatings
Parent Company: Dalgety PLC, UK
Principal Bank: First and Merchants National Bank
Financial Information:

	$'000
Sales revenues	50,000

No of Employees: 450

MODERN WELDING CO, INC

2880 New Hartford Road, Owensboro, KY 42301
Tel: (502) 685-4404
Telex: TWX 810 5363710 modernweld owe

Chairman: John A Reisz (and Chief Executive Officer); Vice Chairman: E K Barnard
President: John W Jones
Senior Executive Officers: Martin E Knott (1st VP Sales), Haskell Pedigo (Senior VP and Manager), Morris Weaver (VP and Manager), Larry Chapman (VP and Manager), James Jones (Secretary and Treasurer), Ernest Sutherlin (VP, Burlington Plant and Manager), Bob Bartlett (VP, Fresno Plant), Victor Q Shirley (VP and Manager), Douglas Farmer (VP and Manager), Dave Graham (VP and Manager), George Kauffeld (VP and Manager), Terry Webb (VP Supply Division), Leland C Jones (VP Purchasing)

PRINCIPAL ACTIVITIES: Manufacture of fabricated steel products, structural steel and tanks
Principal Bank: The Owensboro National Bank
Financial Information:

	$'000
Sales revenues	60,000

No of Employees: 700

MODINE MANUFACTURING CO

1500 DeKoven Avenue, Racine, WI 53401
Tel: (414) 636-1200
Telex: 26 4447 modine rcn

President: E E Richter (and Chief Executive Officer)
Senior Executive Officers: F W Jones (Executive VP), A F Simpson (Executive VP), B K Jacob (Group VP), R T Savage (Group VP)

PRINCIPAL ACTIVITIES: Development, manufacture, sales and distribution of heat-transfer products to the automotive aftermarket, original equipment manufacturers, and nonresidential-building markets
Trade Names: BETA-WELD, ALFUSE, ALBRAZE, etc
Principal Bank: M & I Marshall and Ilsley Bank
Financial Information:

	Mar 31 1986 $'000	Mar 31 1987 $'000
Sales revenues	312,017	349,027
Income before taxes	39,031	37,529
Net income	20,506	19,646
Dividends	5,111	5,606
Dividends per share(1)	$0.68	$0.76
Earnings per share	$2.67	$2.61
Common stock(2)	7,667	7,525
Retained income	104,989	117,468
Shareholders equity	124,786	131,413

(1) annual
(2) average common and common stock equivalent shares outstanding in thousands. August 17 1987 is the pay date for a 2-for-1 stock split in the form of a 100% stock dividend

No of Employees: 4,000

MODULAR COMPUTER SYSTEMS, INC

1650 W McNab Road, Fort Lauderdale, FL 33309
Tel: (305) 974-1380
Telex: 510 956 9414 mod comp ftl

Chairman: Gabriel A Rosica (and President and Chief Executive and Operating Officer)
Senior Executive Officers: Kendrick A Estey (VP Operations and Customer Services), Frederick E Baxter (VP Finance), Harold Koplow (VP Research and Development), L David Osborne (VP Sales and Marketing)

PRINCIPAL ACTIVITIES: Manufacture of computer systems
Parent Company: AEG Aktiengesellschaft
Principal Bank: First National Bank of Boston

Financial Information:

	$'000
Sales revenues	69,000

No of Employees: 900

MODULINE INTERNATIONAL, INC

205 College Street SE, Lacey, WA 98503
Tel: (206) 491-1130

Chairman: Leonard C Merta (and President)
Senior Executive Officers: Max A McCaslin (VP), Robert A Raney (Treasurer)

PRINCIPAL ACTIVITIES: Manufacture and sale of modular buildings and mobile homes
Principal Bank: First Interstate Bank
Financial Information:

	$'000
Sales revenues	34,000

No of Employees: 500

MOEBIUS PRINTING CO

300 N Jefferson Street, Milwaukee, WI 53202
Tel: (414) 276-5311

President: Howard E Moebius
Senior Executive Officers: Lee Cookle (Executive VP and Treasurer), Kenneth D Moebius (VP and Secretary), Alfred Schlecht (VP Administration), Robert Wolff (VP Sales and Marketing)

PRINCIPAL ACTIVITIES: Printing services
Financial Information:

	$'000
Sales revenues	60,000

No of Employees: 450

MOHASCO CORPORATION

4401 Fair Lakes Court, Fairfax, VA 22033
Tel: (703) 908-8000

Chairman: Herbert J Broner (and President and Chief Executive Officer)
Senior Executive Officers: Charles M Egan (Executive VP), David L Kolb (Executive VP), Robert W Overholtzer (VP Finance and Chief Financial Officer), Joseph P Lamb (VP Human Resources), Joseph P Flanagan (General Counsel and Secretary), Albert F Smith (Treasurer)

PRINCIPAL ACTIVITIES: Manufacture of furniture and carpets and rental of furniture
Principal Subsidiaries: Mohasco Upholstered Furniture Corp; Super Sagless Corp; Chromcraft Corp; Choice Seats Corp; International Supply Co Inc; Peters-Revington Corp; Mohasco International NV; Cort Furniture Rental Corp; Mohasco Carpet Corp
Principal Bank: Manufacturers Hanover
Financial Information:

	Dec 31 1986 $'000	Dec 31 1987 $'000
Sales revenues	757,710	806,906
Income before taxes	33,952	41,368
Net income	15,835	12,672
Dividends	3,125	3,584
Dividends per common share*	$0.2266	$0.26
Earnings per share*	$1.15	$0.92
Retained income	179,675	182,414
Shareholders equity	226,563	229,011

*three for two stock split declared in August 1986 and August 1987

No of Employees: 10,647

MOHAWK DATA SCIENCES CORPORATION

7 Century Drive, Parsippany, NY 07054
Tel: (201) 540-9080
Telex: 136365 mds papy

Chairman: Asher B Edelman; Chairman of Executive Committee: Ralph H O'Brien
President: Matthew E Tutino (and Chief Executive Officer)
Senior Executive Officers: R W Bell (Executive VP and Chief Financial Officer), William J Mann (Executive VP), F M Gallagher (Senior VP and Chief Financial Officer), Robert J Hingre (Senior VP), Herbert G Price (Senior VP Technical Planning), F W Stamper (Senior VP Product Strategy), John C Walters (Senior VP Legal and Secretary), Tayne M Elam (VP), Stuart Goldsmith (VP Corporate Planning and Development), Kenneth E James (VP Human Resources), Robert E Sundius (VP Quality Assurance), Joseph R Brooks (VP, Senior VP Finance and Administration MDS Quantel Division), Vincent L Tofany (VP, President MDS Dek Division), Guido Fischler (VP Europe/Africa Marketing Group)

PRINCIPAL ACTIVITIES: Manufacture of data processing equipment
Principal Bank: The First National Bank of Boston
Financial Information:

	$'000
Sales revenues	363,000

No of Employees: 4,150

MOHAWK RUBBER CO (THE)

3560 West Market St, Akron, OH 44313
Tel: (216) 666-8177
Telex: TWX 810 4372356 mohawk hdsn

Chairman: Henry M Fawcett
President: William T Ernst
Senior Executive Officers: Terry C Hill (Senior VP and Chief Financial Officer), Terence F Deane (VP Tire Operations and Corporate Affairs), Hugh C Feguson (VP Sales Industrial Products Group), Russel L Mulvey (VP Sales Tire Division), M Teri Lynch (Controller)

PRINCIPAL ACTIVITIES: Manufacture of rubber products, tires, tread rubber and metal automobile air conditioning components
Parent Company: Danaher Corporation
Principal Bank: Society National Bank
Financial Information:

	$'000
Sales revenues	261,000

No of Employees: 2,180

MOLEX INCORPORATED

2222 Wellington Court, Lisle, IL 60532
Tel: (312) 969-4550
Telex: TWX 910 380 3020 molex il

Chairman: John H Krehbiel
President: John H Krehbiel Jr
Senior Executive Officers: Frederick A Krehbiel (Executive VP), Ronald L Schubel (VP), Kerry M Krafthefer (VP), Ronald H Canaday (VP), John C Psaltis (VP and Treasurer), Louis A Hecht (Corporate Secretary and General Counsel), J J King (VP), Werner W Fichtner (VP)

PRINCIPAL ACTIVITIES: Molex is a recognized leader in electronic interconnection systems, planar cable, control panels, and application tooling. The Company currently produces over 25,000 products at 37 manufacturing plants on 6 continents
Trade Marks: Molex*, MX*, Inconect*, Edgecon*, Claspon*, Wafercon*, Postcon*, Transkon, Pinsetter*, KK*, Boss*, Complus, IDT, Molex-A-Matic*, Lo-Pro, Zipcon, Soldercon, Crimpcon*, Dualcon, Jet-Flecs*, MX-50, C-Grid, Zifcon, Qik-Flecs, SPOX, Trifurcon, TM-40, Polyshield, SEMCONN, and C-Grid S/L. *Registered trademarks of Molex Incorporated

Principal Subsidiaries: Molex International, Inc; Molex US Inc
Principal Bank: American National Bank
Financial Information:

	Jun 30 1986	Jun 30 1987
	$'000	$'000
Sales revenues	291,913	386,759
Income before taxes	53,586	75,754
Net income	32,039	43,416
Dividends	608	767
Dividends per share	$0.02	$0.03
Earnings per share	$1.27	$1.72
Common stock	1,008	1,268
Retained income	218,617	261,012
Shareholders equity	254,610	315,802

Principal Shareholders: J H Krehbiel; J H Krehbiel Jr; F A Krehbiel
No of Employees: 4,962

MOLINS MACHINE CO, INC

3900 Caroline Avenue, Richmond, VA 23222
Tel: (804) 329-9081
Telex: WUT 827431 molinismo rch

Chairman: Christopher G Ross
Division Presidents: C E Robbins Jr, David E North
Senior Executive Officers: Alan C Palmer (VP Operations), Leo P Maynes (VP and Controller), Edward Downey (VP and Controller)

PRINCIPAL ACTIVITIES: Manufacture of machines for the paper and tobacco industries
Parent Company: Molins Overseas Holdings Ltd
Principal Bank: Sovran Bank
Financial Information:

	$'000
Sales revenues	70,000

No of Employees: 900

MOLYCORP, INC

PO Box 54945, Los Angeles, CA 90054
Tel: (213) 977-6525

President: Thomas B Sleeman
Senior Executive Officers: R G Dewey (VP Domestic Exploration and Mining), W N Warhol (VP Manufacturing), T A Wilson (VP Marketing), W R Moran (VP Foreign Exploration)

PRINCIPAL ACTIVITIES: Mining and processing of minerals
Parent Company: Unocal Corporation through Union Oil Company of CA
Financial Information:

	$'000
Sales revenues	70,000

No of Employees: 880

MONARCH CAPITAL CORPORATION

One Financial Plaza, Springfield, MA 01102
Tel: (413) 781-3000
Telex: TWX 910 3500 224 s gula

Chairman: Benjamin F Jones
President: Gordon N Oakes Jr (and Chief Executive Officer)
Senior Executive Officers: James M Durham (VP and Treasurer), George W Siguler (Executive VP)

PRINCIPAL ACTIVITIES: Insurance and financial services
Principal Subsidiaries: Monarch Life Insurance Company; Springfield Life Insurance Company, Inc; First Variable Life Insurance Company; Monarch Investment Management Corporation; 3 Real Estate Companies; Monarch Resources, Inc; Monarch Systems Group; Monarch Direct, Inc
Principal Bank: BayBank Valley Trust Company

Financial Information:

	$'000
Revenues	1,400,000

No of Employees: 1,843

MONARCH MACHINE TOOL CO

615 N Oak Street, Sidney, OH 45365
Tel: (513) 492-4111
Telex: 2888281 monarlath sdye

Chairman: Kermit T Kuck (and Chief Executive Officer)
Senior Executive Officers: N V Gusching (VP Engineering), Charles R Bradlee (VP and Manager Stamco Division), D E Lundeen (VP and Manager Cortland Division)

PRINCIPAL ACTIVITIES: Manufacture of machine tools
Principal Subsidiaries: Monarch Werkzeugmaschinen GmbH (Germany); Stamco UK Ltd (UK); Dean Smith & Grace Ltd (UK); Monarch Machine Tool Export Company Inc
Financial Information:

	$'000
Sales revenues	79,000

No of Employees: 1,000

MONARCH MARKING SYSTEMS, INC

PO Box 608, Dayton, OH 45401
Tel: (513) 865-2123
Telex: 28 8284

Chairman: Elton R Vogel
Senior Executive Officers: Kenneth F Schuba (VP Finance), Thomas P Derby (VP Manufacturing), James W Tschantz (VP Marketing), Rudolph J Klein (VP Systems Development)

PRINCIPAL ACTIVITIES: Manufacture of marking equipment and price tags and printing machinery
Parent Company: Pitney Bowes Inc, Stamford, CT
Principal Bank: First National Bank
Financial Information:

	$'000
Sales revenues	180,000

No of Employees: 2,000

MONAT CAPITAL CORPORATION

4646 Rowanoak Parkway, Kansas City, MO 64112
Tel: (816) 931 7500

President: R M Shteamer
Senior Executive Officers: Frank C Plas (Executive VP and Chief Financial Officer), Michael B Schteamer (Secretary)

PRINCIPAL ACTIVITIES: Insurance services
Financial Information:

	Dec 31 1985
	$'000
Revenues	43,490
Net income	730

No of Employees: 70

MONEY MANAGEMENT CORPORATION

1000 East 80th Place, Merrillville, IN 46410
Tel: (219) 738 6283

Chairman: Raymond E Daly III
President: F J Backe
Senior Executive Officers: D H Brubeck (VP), Larry T Gerzema (Executive VP), Sarah R Glass (VP and Treasurer), Michael L McMillan (Auditor), Robert A Lucas (Secretary)

PRINCIPAL ACTIVITIES: Banking
Principal Bank: LaSalle National Bank

Financial Information:

	Dec 31 1985
	S'000
Revenues	35,290
Net income	2,780

No of Employees: 235

MONFORT OF COLORADO, INC

1930 AA Street, Box G, Greeley, CO 80632
Tel: (303) 353-2311
Telex: WUT 450155 monfortpg grel

Chairman: Roland L Mapelli (and Senior VP)
President: Kenneth Monfort (and Chief Executive Officer)
Senior Executive Officers: Richard L Monfort (Executive VP and Chief Operating Officer), A D Davis (Group VP Engineering, Purchasing and Construction), James E Leonard (Group VP Beef Processing), Donald D Mueller (Group VP Financial Services and Lamb Operations), Michael L Sanem (Group VP Beef Slaughter, By Products), Gene Meakins (VP Industrial and Public Relations)

PRINCIPAL ACTIVITIES: Meat production and processing; by products including hides and pet food
Parent Company: ConAgra
Principal Bank: First Interstate Bank
Financial Information:

	Aug 31 1985	Aug 31 1986
	$'000	$'000
Sales revenues	1,462,770	1,576,979
Net income	14,500	25,145
Earnings per share	$3.31	$5.84
Shareholders equity	91,970	114,021

No of Employees: 4,500

MONOGRAM INDUSTRIES, INC

50 Kennedy Plaza, Providence, RI 02903
Tel: (401) 751-1600

Chairman: Ralph R Papitto
President: Richard L Bready
Senior Executive Officers: Mort A Maurer (VP), Almon C Hall (VP and Controller), Richard J Harris (VP and Treasurer), John R Potter (VP and Secretary)

PRINCIPAL ACTIVITIES: Manufacture of electrical equipment, metal goods and sanitary ware; interests in real estate
Parent Company: Nortek Inc, Cranston, RI
Financial Information:

	$'000
Sales revenues	180,000

MONOLITHIC MEMORIES, INC

2175 Mission College Blvd, Santa Clara, CA 95054-1592
Tel: (408) 970-9700
Telex: 62883897ESLUD
Fax: 910 338 2226

Chairman: Zeev Drori
President: Irwin Federman
Senior Executive Officers: Michael J Callahan (Executive VP and Chief Operating Officer), John C Bolger (VP, Finance), Larry W Sonsini (Secretary), James M Eustice (Treasurer)

PRINCIPAL ACTIVITIES: Leading producers of proprietary semi-custom and standard high-performance, large-scale-integration (LSI) logic and memory circuits
Trade Names: Monolithic Memories, Inc, MMI, MMI (logo)
Principal Subsidiaries: Monolithic Memories (France) SARL; Monolithic Memories GmbH; MMI Integrated Circuits (Singapore); MMI-Japan KK; Monolithic Memories Ltd; Monolithic Memories Malaysia Sdn.Bhd.
Principal Bank: Security Pacific National Bank; The First National Bank of Boston; Chase Manhattan Bank

Financial Information:

	$'000
Sales revenues	178,000

No of Employees: 3,700 worldwide

MONSANTO COMPANY

800 N Lindbergh Blvd, St Louis, MO 63167
Tel: (314) 694-1000

Chairman: Richard J Mahoney (and Chief Executive Officer)
President: Earle H Harbison Jr (and Chief Operating Officer)
Senior Executive Officers: Nicholas L Reding (Executive VP), Robert L Berra (Senior VP Administration), Harold J Corbett (Senior VP Environment, Safety and Health), Dr Howard A Schneiderman (Senior VP Research and Development), Francis A Stroble (Senior VP and Chief Financial Officer), Richard W Duesenberg (Senior VP, Secretary and General Counsel), Thomas L Gossage (Group VP), Robert G Potter (Group VP), Earl N Brasfield (VP), Leonard A Cohn (VP Information Systems Department), Stewart D Daniels (VP and Managing Director Asia-Pacific), Dr S Allen Heininger (VP Resource Planning), John F Hussey (VP Public Affairs), Martin J Kallen (VP and Managing Director Europe-Africa), Thomas H Lafferre (VP), Richard A Overton (VP Tax), James H Senger (VP Environmental Policy Staff), David L Sliney (VP) Lawrence B Skatoff (VP and Controller), B Clare Harris (VP and Treasurer), Robert L Walter (VP and Managing Director Latin America)

PRINCIPAL ACTIVITIES: The Monsanto Company is skilled in researching, manufacturing and marketing more than 1,000 products, including chemical and agricultural products, man-made fibers, electronic materials, health care, process controls, fabricated products, and oil and gas. Monsanto has investments in 164 manufacturing plants, offshore oil and gas exploration sites, laboratories and technical centers in 27 countries, and conducts business in more than 100 countries
Trade Names: Roundup, Richochet, Sting, Rodeo, Lasso, Lasso Micro-Tech, Limit, Alimet, MHA, Quantum, Wear-Dated, Ultron, Santroprene, Lustran ABS, SAN, Cadon, Saflex, Prism, Cycle-Safe, Cloud Nine, AstroTurf, Hydraway, Ecopac, ProVox
Principal Subsidiaries: HybriTech Seed International Inc; Continental Pharma SA (Belgium); Fisher Controls International Inc; Monsanto Oil Company
Financial Information:

	Dec 31 1986
	$'000
Sales revenues	6,879,000
Net income	433,000
Earnings per share net	$5.55
Shareholders equity	3,781,000

No of Employees: 50,754

MONSANTO ENVIRO-CHEM SYSTEMS, INC

Corporate Square Office Park, St Louis, MO 63178
Tel: (314) 694-1000

Chairman: D L Chapman (and President)
Senior Executive Officers: G H Crozier (VP), J A Werner III (VP), D R Bounds (VP)

PRINCIPAL ACTIVITIES: Manufacture of chemical plant
Trade Names: Ecopac
Parent Company: Monsanto Company, St Louis, MO
Financial Information:

	$'000
Sales revenues	100,000

No of Employees: 250

MONTANA POWER CO

40 E Broadway, Butte, MT 59701-9334
Tel: (406) 723-5421

Chairman: W Paul Schmechel (and Chief Executive Officer); Vice Chairman: J J Burke
President: D M Leuschen
Senior Executive Officers: F V Woy (Executive VP Finance), R J Labrie (Executive VP Engineering and Technical), D T Berube (VP Colstrip Project Division), John Carl (VP and Secretary), J F Doran (VP Economic Requirements), R P Gannon (VP and General Counsel), C J Gilder (VP Administration), D A Johnson (VP Gas Operations), C D Regan (VP Consumer Services and Conservation), W A Russell (VP and Chief Operating Officer), W C Verbael (VP Accounting and Finance)

PRINCIPAL ACTIVITIES: Distribution of electricity and natural gas
Principal Bankers: Citibank
Financial Information:

	$'000
Sales revenues	447,000

No of Employees: 3,500

MONTGOMERY WARD & CO, INC

Montgomery Ward Plaza, Chicago, IL 60671
Tel: (312) 467-2000

President: Bernard F Brennan
Senior Executive Officers: Robert C Carr (Executive VP Finance), Douglas A Fields (Executive VP, Administration), William J McCarthy (Executive VP Store Operations), Bernard W Andrews (Executive VP Merchandising), Richard Bergel (Senior VP Logistics), Richard Jennings (Senior VP Merchandise Presentation Development), J Burke Gelling (Senior VP Stores), John J McGivern (Senior VP and General Merchandise Manager), John A Daynard (Senior VP Marketing), Dominic M Mangone (Senior VP Corporate Planning), Robert A Kasenter (VP Human Resources), Glen DuBois (VP Store Operations), Spencer H Heine (VP, Secretary and General Counsel), Donald E Norman (VP Management Information Systems), Richard C Scheidt (VP Labor Relations), Mal Pavik (VP and Territorial Manager Eastern), Richard Exline (VP and Territorial Manager North Central), William Dane (VP and Territorial Manager South Central), Daniel Darr (VP and Territorial Manager Northwest), William Herrmann (VP and Territorial Manager Southern CA), Peter Jensen (VP and Territorial Manager Southwest), Joseph A Sarnowski (VP and Treasurer), Robert Schoeberl (VP Auto and Recreation/Leisure), Steven Peterson (VP and Director, Merchandise Manager Home and Home Care), Warrn E Flick (VP and Divisional Merchandise Manager Women's Apparel and Accessories), Edwin G Pohlmann (VP Merchandise Planning and Control), Jerome C Jordan (VP and Controller), Vernon B Kenny (VP Credit), Thomas Cato (VP Distribution)

PRINCIPAL ACTIVITIES: Montgomery Ward & Co, Inc is one of the nation's largest retail merchandising organizations. Montgomery Ward operates a chain 315 retail stores, including six new specialty stores
Parent Company: Mobil Corporation
Financial Information:

	Dec 25 1985	Dec 31 1986
	$'000	$'000
Total net sales	5,388,000	4,383,000
Net income (loss)	(298,000)	110,000
Shareholders equity	1,420,000	1,456,000

No of Employees: 56,300

MONUMENTAL CORPORATION

1111 North Charles Street, Baltimore, MD 21201
Tel: (301) 685 2900

Chairman: Leslie B Disharoon (and President and Chief Executive Officer)
Senior Executive Officers: B Larry Jenkins (Executive VP), William N Sanders (Executive VP), Semmes G Walsh (Executive VP Corporate Growth and Finance), Robert J McGraw (Senior VP and Treasurer), Ronald M Nagler (Senior VP Investments), Larry J Brown (VP and Secretary), John E Harring (VP Sales), Frank S Piff (VP Development), Donald W Chamberlain (VP Investment)

PRINCIPAL ACTIVITIES: Holding company whose subsidiaries are engaged in insurance
Parent Company: Aegon NV, Netherlands
Principal Subsidiaries: Monumental Life Insurance Company
Principal Bank: Equitable Bank
Financial Information:

	Dec 31 1985
	$'000
Revenues	245,375
Net income	11,740

No of Employees: 1,885

MONY FINANCIAL SERVICES

Mutual Life Insurance Co of New York (MONY) and its subsidiaries

1740 Broadway, New York, NY 10019
Tel: (212) 708-2000

Chairman: James A Attwood (and President and Chief Executive Officer)
Senior Executive Officers: Gray C Castle (Executive VP), Robert L Lindsay (Executive VP), Gordon E Perry (Executive VP), Albert J Schiff (Executive VP), Floyd L Smith (Executive VP), Walter B Bancroft (Senior VP), Michael J Drabb (Senior VP), Rita K Farrelly (Senior VP), Weaver H Gaines Jr (Senior VP), Neal M Jewell (Senior VP), Matthew M Lind (Senior VP), F Allen Spooner (Senior VP), Peter S Stutts (Senior VP), Norcross Teel Jr (Senior VP), John J Whittle (Senior VP)

PRINCIPAL ACTIVITIES: MONY Financial Services is principally engaged in the business of writing life insurance and related products and providing a variety of financial services
Trade Names: The Mutual Life Insurance Company of New York; MONY; MONY Financial Services; MONY Enterprise
Principal Subsidiaries: MONY has five direct wholly-owned subsidiaries: MONY Life Insurance Company of America; MONY Legacy Life Insurance Company; MONY Pension Insurance Corporation; MONY Life Insurance Company of Canada and MONYCO, Inc. MONYCO is a holding company whcih has 18 wholly-owned financial service subsidiaries
Principal Banks: Citibank; Chase Manhattan; Chase Lincoln Bank; Morgan Guaranty Trust Co; Chemical Bank; Bankers Trust Co
Financial Information:

	Dec 31 1985	Dec 31 1986
	$'000	$'000
Premium income	2,387,160	3,167,039
Investment income	967,671	1,083,199
Net income*	325,509	295,812
Dividends	289,540	295,245
Surplus income	508,170	508,737
Surplus and MSVR	630,992	724,043

*before dividends

No of Employees: 8,960

MOOG INC

East Aurora, NY 14052
Tel: (716) 652-2000
Telex: WUT 91399 moogsales eara

President: William C Moog
Senior Executive Officers: Robert T Brady (Division President Aerospace Controls Group), John Burgess (VP, Divisional President Carleton Group), Daniel C Clark (Division President Industrial Controls Group), Herald D Bidlack (Division President International Controls Group), Robert R Banta (VP Finance), Kenneth D Garnjost (VP), Robert Maskrey (VP), William J Thayer (VP), J C Green (VP)

PRINCIPAL ACTIVITIES: Manufacture of controls, valves and machine tools

Principal Subsidiaries: (100% owned unless stated): Moog GmbH; Moog SARL; Moog of Japan Ltd (90%); Moog do Brasil Controles Ltda; Moog Controls Ltd; Moog DISC Ltd; Moog Industrial Controls Corp; Moog Italiana SRL; Moog Norden AB; Moog Australia Pty Ltd; Moog Ltd; Moog Controls Corp
Principal Bank: MarineMidland Bank-Western
Financial Information:

	$'000
Sales revenues	240,000

No of Employees: 3,000

MOORE & MUNGER INC

292 Pequot Avenue, Southport, CT 06430
Tel: (203) 259-7272

Chairman: David A Rosow (and President)
Senior Executive Officers: Victor C Braun (VP), Wayne G Granquist (VP and General Counsel)

PRINCIPAL ACTIVITIES: Manufacture of waxes, clays and petrochemical products; oil refining; interests in oil exploration and ski resorts
Principal Bank: Morgan Guaranty Trust Company
Financial Information:

	$'000
Sales revenues	190,000

No of Employees: 540

MOORE FINANCIAL GROUP INC

101 S Capitol Blvd, PO Box 8247, Boise, ID 83733
Tel: (208) 383-7000

Chairman: Daniel R Nelson (and Chief Executive Officer)
President: D Michael Jones
Senior Executive Officers: V Dale Blickenstaff (Vice Chairman), Scott M Hayes (VP and Chief Financial Officer), Dwight V Board (VP, Secretary and General Counsel), John W Crim (VP and Treasurer)

PRINCIPAL ACTIVITIES: Banking services
Principal Subsidiaries: Idaho First National Bank; Continental Bank; Oregon First Bank; Moore Financial Services; Moore Trust Company
Financial Information:

	Dec 31 1987
	$'000
Income before taxes	23,378
Net income	16,906
Dividends per share	$1.20
Earnings per share	$2.25
Common stock*	7,500
Shareholders equity	220,390
Deposits	2,673,423
Total assets	3,519,327

*weighted average shares outstanding in thousands

No of Employees: 2,600

MOORE MCCORMACK RESOURCES, INC

One Landmark Square, Stamford, CT 06901-2685
Tel: (203) 358-2200

Chairman: Paul R Tregurtha (and President and Chief Executive Officer)
Senior Executive Officers: Donald Beck (VP-Administration), Richard D Kline (VP), Douglas B Otten (VP), Paul J Evanson (Executive VP), Robert A Hurwich (VP, Secretary and General Counsel), Laurence W Ehrhardt (Treasurer), Robert M Brody (Controller), Betty G Graham (Assistant Controller), Andrew P Langlois (Assistant Controller),

PRINCIPAL ACTIVITIES: Moore McCormack produces cement, concrete products and aggregates, primarily in the Southeastern United States, and is engaged in oil and gas exploration and production
Principal Subsidiaries: Moore McCormack Cement Inc; Moore McCormack Energy Inc
Financial Information:

	Dec 31 1985	Dec 31 1986
	$'000	$'000
Sales revenues	325,930	334,148
Income (loss) before taxes	22,919	(47,970)
Net income (loss)	21,231	(116,485)
Common dividends	9,105	6,852
Preferred dividends	5,150	4,900
Dividends per common share	$1.04	$0.78
Earnings (loss) per share	$1.84	($13.80)*
Common stock	27,372	27,372
Retained income	329,896	201,659
Shareholders equity	389,942	263,190

*a valuation charge in oil and gas reduced net income by $36.7 million, or $4.18 per share

No of Employees: 2,900

MOORE MEDICAL CORPORATION

PO Box 3070, New Britain, CT 06050
Tel: (203) 225 2225

President: Jerald K Rome
Senior Executive Officers: Mark E Karp (Senior VP), Herbert M Walter (VP Operations), Alan L Fier (VP Finance), Joseph Greenberger (Secretary)

PRINCIPAL ACTIVITIES: Supply of pharmaceutical products
Financial Information:

	$'000
Sales revenues	148,000

No of Employees: 260

MOORE PRODUCTS CO

Sumneytown Pike, Spring House, PA 19477
Tel: (215) 646-7400
Telex: 83-4378 MOOREPROD SHSE

Chairman: Edwin G Rorke (and Chief Executive Officer)
President: William B Moore (and Chief Operating Officer)
Senior Executive Officers: William J Young (VP Finance), Hugh S Wilson (VP International Operations), George W Tall (VP Sales), Robert B Adams (VP Engineering), Richard J Faber (VP Manufacturing), Edward J Curry (VP, Director Corporate Planning)

PRINCIPAL ACTIVITIES: Moore Products Co develops, manufactures and sells electronic and pneumatic industrial instrumentation and systems for process control in such industries as chemical, petrochemical, pulp and paper, iron and steel, petroleum, and others. The Company also custom designs and builds automatic machines for dimensional measurement of mass-produced parts in the automotive, bearing and other high volume precision manufacturing industries
Trade Names: VertiGage (Process Indicators), SYNCRO (Process Control Instrumentation), SSPH (Fluidic Valves), MYCRO (Distributed Control Systems), DATA GAGE (Machines for statistical process control)
Principal Subsidiaries: Moore Products Co (UK) Ltd (UK); Moore Instruments Ltd/Ltee (Canada); Moore Products Co BV (Netherlands); Moore Products de Mexico SA de CV (Mexico); Moore Products Co (Italia) SRL (Italy)
Principal Bank: Mellon Bank (East) N.A.

Financial Information:

	Dec 31 1985	Dec 31 1986
	$'000	$'000
Sales revenues	71,680	79,769
Income before taxes	4,793	8,638
Net income	3,074	4,710
Dividends	1,829	1,829
Dividends per common share	$0.88	$0.88
Earnings per share primary	$1.48	$2.27
Common stock	2,070	2,083
Retained income	39,462	42,343
Shareholders equity	42,992	46,411

No of Employees: USA: 981, Worldwide: 1,156

MOR-FLO INDUSTRIES, INC

18450 S Miles Road, Cleveland, OH 44128
Tel: (216) 663-7300

President: Walter L Abt (and Chief Executive Officer)
Senior Executive Officers: A R Abt (Executive VP), Alfred E Badal (VP Finance and Treasurer), Julian Gawiser (VP), Gary Kaufman (VP Marketing), Robert A Discenzo (VP), Henry J Moore (VP Engineering), E T Taylor II (VP engineering), Bernard I Grossman (VP and Western General Manager), Robert J Montgomery (VP), Jerry Polster (VP Corporate Development), Henry Schneps (VP Data Processing), Bernard J Brown (VP), C Richard McAfee (VP), Geoffrey Stein (VP), Lynn Rogers (VP)

PRINCIPAL ACTIVITIES: Manufacture of a wide range of water heaters
Principal Bank: AmeriTrust Company
Financial Information:

	$'000
Sales revenues	206,000

No of Employees: 1,700

MORGAN CONSTRUCTION CO

15 Belmont Street, Worcester, MA 01605
Tel: (617) 755-6111
Telex: TWX 910 3507701 morgan const

Chairman: Paul S Morgan
President: Philip R Morgan
Senior Executive Officers: Richard Brannaman (Senior VP Operations), Daniel M Morgan (Senior VP Rolling Mill Sales and Marketing), Peter S Morgan (VP Administration), John W Bergen (VP and Treasurer), Daniel Borda (VP Services), Homer E MacNutt Jr (VP Manufacturing Operations), Gavin D Roberson (VP Human Resources), L S Salter (VP Morgoil Bearings), Scott Sargent (VP and Controller), Edward W Randall (VP Purchasing), Budd Carlin (VP Wire Drawing Machinery)

PRINCIPAL ACTIVITIES: Manufacture of equipment for the steel industry
Principal Bank: Citibank
Financial Information:

	$'000
Sales revenues	50,000

No of Employees: 650

MORGAN GUARANTY TRUST CO OF NEW YORK

23 Wall Street, New York, NY 10015
Tel: (212) 483-2323
Telex: ITT 420230 mgt ui

Chairman: Lewis T Preston; Chairman of Executive Committee: Dennis Weatherstone; Vice Chairmen: Boris S Berkovitch, John E Ruffle, Rodney B Wagner (Credit Policy Committee)

President: Robert V Lindsay

Senior Executive Officers: William E Pike (Chairman Credit Policy Committee), Donald B Riefler (Chairman Sources and Uses Fund Committee), A B Brackenridge (Executive VP), James T Flynn (Executive VP), David L Hopkins Jr (Executive VP), Roberto G Mendoza (Executive VP), Peter B Smith (Executive VP), John W Spurdle Jr (Executive VP), John M Stadter Jr (Executive VP), Robert G Engel (Executive VP and Treasurer)

PRINCIPAL ACTIVITIES: Banking

Parent Company: J P Morgan & Co Inc

No of Employees: 9,460

MORGAN, J P, AND COMPANY INCORPORATED

23 Wall Street, NY 10015

Tel: (212) 483-2323

Telex: 420230 MGT UI

Chairman: Lewis T Preston

President: Robert V Lindsay

Senior Executive Officers: Dennis Weatherstone (Director; Chairman of the Executive Committee), Boris S Berkovitch (Director; Vice Chairman of the Board), John M Stadter Jr (Executive VP), James T Flynn (Executive VP), John F Ruffle (Treasurer Executive VP and Chief Financial Officer), Peter B Smith (Executive VP), William E Pike (Chairman, Credit Policy Committee), Donald B Riefler (Chairman, Sources and Uses of Funds Committee), A Kendall Raine Jr (Senior VP), Richard Delbridge (Comptroller), J James Lewis (Senior VP and Comptroller), Donald R Brunner (Senior VP and Treasurer), Penelope A Flugger (Senior VP and Auditor), Edmund P Rogers III (Secretary)

PRINCIPAL ACTIVITIES: Commercial banking activities; investment banking and trading activities; trust and agency services

Trade Names: Morgan Guaranty Trust Company of New York

Principal Subsidiaries: Subsidiaries of J P Morgan:- Bank: Morgan Guaranty Trust Company of New York; Morgan Bank (Delaware) (USA and Cayman Islands). Nonbank: J P Morgan Investment Management Inc; Morgan Community Development Corporation; Morgan Futures Corporation (USA, UK and Singapore); J P Morgan Leasefunding Corp; Morgan Holdings Corp; Morgan Capital Corporation; J P Morgan International Finance NV (Netherlands Antilles); J P Morgan International Capital NV (Netherlands Antilles); Morgan Portfolio Corp; Morgan Data Services Inc; Morgan Trust Company of Florida NA; Morgan Trust Company of The Bahamas Ltd (Bahamas); Morgan Guaranty International Bank (Cayman) Ltd (Cayman Islands); Morgan Fonciere Cayman Islands (Cayman Islands); Morgan Realty Corporation. Subsidiaries of Morgan Guaranty:- J P Morgan Interfunding Corp; Morprop Inc; Morgan Guaranty International Finance Corp; Morgan Guaranty International Bank (USA and Bahamas). Subsidiaries of Morgan Guaranty International Finance Corporation:- AUC Holdings Limited (67.5%) (Australia); J P Morgan Overseas Capital Corp; J P Morgan (Suisse) SA (Switzerland); J P Morgan Investment Management Pacific Ltd (Hong Kong); Morgan Bank of Canada (Canada); Morgan Bank Nederland NV (Netherlands); Morgan & Cie SA (France); Morgan Guaranty GmbH (Germany); Morgan Guaranty Ltd (UK, Hong Kong and Japan); Morgan Guaranty (Switzerland) Ltd (Switzerland); Morgan Guaranty SAE (Spain); Morgan Guaranty Finance Ltd (Bermuda); Morgan Guaranty Pacific Ltd (Singapore); Morgan International Finance (Italy) SpA (Italy); N V Morgan Finance (Belgium) SA (Belgium)

Principal Bank: Morgan Guaranty Trust Company of New York

Financial Information:

	Dec 31 1986
	$'000
Net income	872,500
Earnings per share	$4.74
Shareholders equity	5,130,000
Deposits	42,960,000
Total assets	76,039,000

No of Employees: 14,518

MORGAN KEEGAN INC

50 Front Street, Memphis, TN 38103
Tel: (901) 524 4100

Chairman: Allen B Morgan Jr (and Chief Executive Officer); Vice Chairman: John W Stokes Jr
President: William W Deupree Jr
Senior Executive Officers: Joseph C Weller (Executive VP and Treasurer), Richard A McStay (Executive VP), Robert D Gooch Jr (Senior VP and Secretary), L Jack Powell (Senior VP Syndicate), Franklin P Allen (Senior VP Fixed Income), David Ramsey (Senior VP Corporate Finance)

PRINCIPAL ACTIVITIES: Provision of a range of financial services
Principal Bank: First Tennessee Bank
Financial Information:

	$'000
Revenues	51,000

No of Employees: 475

MORGAN PACKING CO, INC

Austin, IN 47102
Tel: (812) 794-1170
Telex: WUT 217436 mpc asin

Chairman: I H Morgan
President: J S Morgan
Senior Executive Officers: James Reynolds (Executive VP), Culver Field (VP Marketing), Donald Craig (VP Sales), Burt Turner (VP Production)

PRINCIPAL ACTIVITIES: Canning and packaging of vegetables
Principal Bank: Austin State Bank
Financial Information:

	$'000
Sales revenues	50,000

No of Employees: 400

MORGAN PRODUCTS LTD

601 Oregon Street, PO Box 2446, Oshkosh, WI 54903
Tel: (414) 235 7170

Chairman: F J Hawley, Jr
President: George T Brophy (and Chief Executive Officer)
Senior Executive Officers: J Phillipe Latreille (VP), Michael A Lupo (Executive VP, Chief Financial Officer and Secretary), Robert L Slagle (VP), Robert L Watts (VP), R E Parker (VP)

PRINCIPAL ACTIVITIES: Timber building components
Financial Information:

	$'000
Sales revenues	120,000

No of Employees: 1,600

MORGAN STANLEY GROUP INC

1251 Avenue of the Americas, New York, NY 10020
Tel: (212) 703 4000
Telex: 620131
Telefax: (212) 703-6503

Chairman: S Parker Gilbert
President: Richard B Fisher
Senior Executive Officers: Bryan J Walsh (Treasurer), Ned R Sachs (Secretary and Legal Counsel)

PRINCIPAL ACTIVITIES: Provision of financial services including investment banking and brokerage
Principal Subsidiaries: Morgan Stanley & Co Incorporated
Principal Bank: Morgan Guaranty
Financial Information:

	Dec 31 1986	Dec 31 1987
	$'000	$'000
Revenues	2,463,484	3,147,909
Income before taxes	322,516	364,265
Net income	201,250	230,944
Dividends per share	$0.35	$0.80
Earnings per share	$8.42	$8.99
Common stock	24,877	24,864
Retained income	473,406	680,313
Shareholders equity	797,571	1,137,426
Total assets	29,190,361	29,662,615

No of Employees: 6,521

MORRELL, JOHN, & CO

191 Waukegan Road, Northfield, IL 60093
Tel: (312) 441-4800
Telefax: (312) 441-4340

President: Donald Slotkin
Senior Executive Officers: A E Nash (Executive VP), D L Hough (Senior VP), D D Dannen (Senior VP), A S Mikelburg (Senior VP), J M Hurley (Executive VP), R W Gass (Senior VP, General Counsel and Secretary), R A Dearth Jr (Senior VP, CFO and Treasurer)

PRINCIPAL ACTIVITIES: Meat packing and processing
Trade Names: Rath Black Hawk and others
Parent Company: United Brands Co (100%)
Principal Subsidiaries: Saratoga Specialties; Roberts & Oake Inc
Principal Bank: First National Bank of Chicago
Financial Information:

	Dec 31 1985	Dec 31 1986
	(9 mths)	(12 mths)
	$'000	$'000
Sales revenues	1,239,000	1,874,000

No of Employees: 6,500

MORRISON INC

4721 Morrison Drive, Mobile, AL 36625
Tel: (205) 344 3000

Chairman: E E Bishop (and Chief Executive Officer), Vice Chairman: Arthur R Outlaw
President: S E Beall III (and Chief Operating Officer)
Senior Executive Officers: R D McClenagan Jr (Senior VP Division), R K Stoll (Senior VP Division), J L Lambert (Senior VP Finance and Administration), Larry E Davis (Senior VP Cafeterias), Joseph B Byrum (Senior VP Management Services, R A McGeoch (Senior VP Corporate Planning and Investor Relations), Philip G Hunt (Senior VP, Secretary and General Counsel), R H Wetmore (Senior VP Human Resources), Paul Freeman Jr (VP and Treasurer), J R Mothershead (VP and Controller), W G Cole Jr (VP, Assistant General Counsel and Assistant Secretary)

PRINCIPAL ACTIVITIES: Restaurants and catering services
Principal Bank: Am South Bank
Financial Information:

	$'000
Sales revenues	522,000

No of Employees: 18,000

MORRISON-KNUDSEN CO, INC

One Morrison-Knudsen Plaza, Boise, ID 83729
Tel: (208) 345-5000
Telex: 368439

Chairman: W J Deasey (and Chief Executive Officer)
President: G W Gilfillan (and Chief Operating Officer)

Senior Executive Officers: J L Beto (VP Administration), Samuel H Crossland (VP Secretary), H R Finn (VP Financial Affairs), K W Smith (VP, Secretary and General Counsel)

PRINCIPAL ACTIVITIES: Civil engineering and construction, coal mining and ship building
Parent Company: Morrison-Knudsen Corp
Principal Subsidiaries: Astoria Oil Services Inc; Broadway Insurance Company Inc; Emkay Development Company Inc; M-K Railroad Equipment Leasing Company Inc; Morrison Knudsen Engenharia SA; Morrison-Knudson Forest Products Company Inc; Morrison-Knudsen of Arabia Inc; Morrison-Knudsen Technologies Inc; National Steel and Shipbuilding Co; Northern Construction Company Ltd; Morrison-Knudsen Engineers Inc; Morrison-Knudsen International Company Inc; The HK Ferguson Company
Financial Information:

	Dec 31 1985 $'000	Dec 31 1986 $'000
Sales revenues	2,082,796	2,083,191
Net income	41,546	39,411
Earnings per share	$3.85	$3.60
Shareholders equity	392,543	423,642

No of Employees: 15,660

MORSE CUTTING TOOLS
163 Pleasant Street, Box F-923, New Bedford, MA 02742
Tel: (617) 994-9611
Telex: TWX 710 3441186 morse tool nbe

President: William E Sweetman
Senior Executive Officers: William E Green Jr (VP Marketing), Thomas L Sheehan (VP Manufacturing), Thomas A Holden (VP Engineering), J F Dee (Controller)

PRINCIPAL ACTIVITIES: Manufacture of cutting tools and drills
Parent Company: Gulf & Western Manufacturing Company
Principal Bank: Trust Company Bank
Financial Information:

	$'000
Sales revenues	50,000

No of Employees: 500

MORSE SHOE, INC
555 Turnpike Street, Canton, MA 02021
Tel: (617) 828-9300
Telex: TRT 174125 morse shoe ctn

Chairman: Manuel Rosenberg (and President and Chief Executive Officer)
Senior Executive Officers: Jerome Zimmerman (Chairman Finance Committee), Thomas J Galligan III (Senior VP, Chief Financial Officer and Treasurer), James Best (VP Merchandise Control), Richard Bowen (VP Operations and Administration), Kenneth C Cummins (VP, Secretary and General Counsel), Daniel L Goldberg (VP Merchandise Planning), Charles F Messina (VP Personnel and Employee Relations), Herbert Rosenberg (VP and General Merchandise Manager, Leased Division), Marvin G Schwartz (VP and Comptroller), Norman M Weiser (VP Management Information Systems)

PRINCIPAL ACTIVITIES: Manufacture of shoes; wholesale and retail trade in shoes
Principal Subsidiaries: Isabela Shoe Corp; Lowell Shoe Inc; Morse Shoe (Canada) Ltd; Morse Shoe International Inc
Principal Bank: The First National Bank of Boston
Financial Information:

	$'000
Sales revenues	541,000

No of Employees: 5,600

MORTGAGE CORPORATION OF AMERICA
17071 West Dixie Hwy, North Miami Beach, FL 33160
Tel: (305) 947-7888

Chairman: Benedict A Silverman
President: Terry A Murphy
Senior Executive Officers: Allan Frank (Senior VP)

PRINCIPAL ACTIVITIES: Financial services
Principal Bank: First American Bank of Dade County
Financial Information:

	$'000
Revenues	800,000

No of Employees: 15

MORTON SALT DIVISION
110 N Wacker Drive, Chicago, IL 60606
Tel: (312) 621-5200
Telex: TWX 910 2215520 morton chgo

President: W H Johnston Jr
Senior Executive Officers: L H Kreisel (VP Operations), W W Becky II (VP Finance and Controller), R L Pierobon (VP Manufacturing), J C Hedley (VP Employee Relations), J F Poe (VP Sales), R P Buschmann (VP Legal)

PRINCIPAL ACTIVITIES: Manufacture of salt for highways, agriculture and consumers
Parent Company: Morton Thiokol Inc
Principal Bank: First National Bank of Chicago
Financial Information:

	$'000
Sales revenues	365,000

No of Employees: 3,400

MORTON THIOKOL, INC
110 N Wacker Drive, Chicago, IL 60606
Tel: (312) 621-5200
Telex: WUT 254433 morton cgo

Chairman: Charles S Locke (and Chief Executive Officer)
President: Robert C Hyndman (and Chief Operating Officer)
Senior Executive Officers: William E Johnston Jr (Group VP Salt), John R Bowen (VP Finance), U E Garrison (VP Aerospace), Robert B Gerrie (VP Legal Affairs), Perry R Grace (VP Management Information and Services), S J Stewart (VP Specialty Chemicals), Thomas S Russell (VP Corporate Development and Strategic Planning), Hugh C Marx (VP Human Resources), James A Robertson (VP)

PRINCIPAL ACTIVITIES: Manufacture of specialty chemicals, salt, high-technology propulsion equipment and ordnance systems for the US Government
Principal Subsidiaries: Bee Chemical Company; The Canadian Salt Co Ltd; Morton Bahamas Ltd
Principal Bank: The First National Bank of Chicago
Financial Information:

	Jun 30 1986 $'000
Sales revenues	1,949,900
Net income	132,900
Earnings per share	$2.80
Shareholders equity	821,900

No of Employees: 17,900

MOSELEY HOLDING CORP
60 State Street, Boston, MA 02109
Tel: (617) 367-2400

Chairman: Howard G Berg (and Co-Chief Executive Officer); Chairman Executive Committee: Frederick S Moseley III; Vice Chairman: Hikmat S Nashashibi
President: Stephen Parker (and Co-Chief Executive Officer)
Senior Executive Officers: James W Wolitarsky (Executive VP and Chief Financial Officer)

PRINCIPAL ACTIVITIES: Holding company with interests in financial services including portfolio management, security broking and dealing

No of Employees: 950

MOSHER STEEL CO

3910 Washington Avenue, Houston, TX 77007
Tel: (713) 861-8181
Telex: WUT 762545 mosher hou

Chief Executive Officer: Oscar W Stewart
Senior Executive Officers: John T Sanford (Executive VP), V H Thompson Jr (VP)

PRINCIPAL ACTIVITIES: Manufacture of structural steel
Parent Company: Trinity Industries Inc
Financial Information:

	$'000
Sales revenues	60,000

Principal Shareholders: Mosher Steel Co is a division of Trinity Industries Inc
No of Employees: 1,000

MOSINEE PAPER CORPORATION

1244 Kronenwetter Drive, Mosinee, WI 54455-9099
Tel: (715) 693-4470
Telex: WUT 290363 mosineepa mosi (Pulp and Paper Division)
Fax: (715) 693-4083

Chairman: Sam W Orr Jr
President: James L Kemerling (and Chief Executive Officer)
Senior Executive Officers: Daniel G Briner (VP Finance, Secretary and Treasurer), R W Bruce (VP and General Manager Sorg Paper Company-wholly owned subsidiary), Thomas C Potter (Divisional VP and General Manager Pulp and Paper), Jack Broeren (Divisional VP and General Manager Bay West Paper), James Stelow (Divisional VP and General Manager Converted Products), Kevin Hogan (Divisional VP and General Manager Green Bay Plastics)

PRINCIPAL ACTIVITIES: Manufacture of pulp, paper and plastics
Principal Subsidiaries: The Sorg Paper Company
Principal Bank: M & I Marshall & Ilsley Bank
Financial Information:

	Dec 31 1985	Dec 31 1986
	$'000	$'000
Sales revenues	187,724	195,453
Income before taxes	14,392	8,653
Net income	8,912	4,678
Dividends declared	1,922	2,072
Dividends per share(1)	$0.24	$0.26
Earnings per share(1)	$1.15	$0.60
Common stock(2)	5,140	7,697
Retained income	43,133	37,130
Shareholders equity	65,006	67,457

(1) The per share data restated for 3 for 2 stock split in the form of a 50:1 stock dividend paid May 22 1986
(2) Number of shares in thousands

Principal Shareholders: Descendants of A P Woodson and Family, Wasau, WI
No of Employees: 1,400

MOTHER'S CAKE & COOKIE CO

810 81st Avenue, Oakland, CA 94621
Tel: (415) 569-2323
Telex: WUT 176745 mothers oak

Chairman: A Martin
President: Michel Laverne
Senior Executive Officers: Robert A Curran (VP Sales), Mark Bernel (VP Manufacturing), H Walsh (VP Finance and Secretary)

PRINCIPAL ACTIVITIES: Manufacture of cakes and cookies
Principal Bank: Bank of California
Financial Information:

	$'000
Sales revenues	90,000

No of Employees: 800

MOTHER'S COOKIE CO

2287 Ralph Avenue, Louisville, KY 40216
Tel: (502) 448-1730
Telex: TWX 810 535 2769 mthrcookie lvl

President: James F Yowell
Senior Executive Officers: Bill Bayers (VP Sales), H V Morris (VP Sales and Marketing)

PRINCIPAL ACTIVITIES: Manufacture of cookies
Parent Company: Beatrice Companies Inc
Principal Bank: Continental Bank and Trust Company
Financial Information:

	$'000
Sales revenues	40,000

No of Employees: 400

MOTION INDUSTRIES, INC

741 Alton Road, Birmingham, AL 35210
Tel: (205) 956-1122

President: Michael S Gaffney
Senior Executive Officers: C Thomas Fowler (Senior VP), George Kalafut (Senior VP), Ralph C Bolton (VP), R C Burmester (VP), James L Clark (VP), Jerry R Dean (VP), Frank J McPharlin (VP), Thomas S Robertshaw (VP), William J Stevens (VP Personnel), G Harold Dunaway (VP Finance and Treasurer), Ralph Buntyn (VP)

PRINCIPAL ACTIVITIES: Industrial replacement parts and automotive components
Parent Company: Genuine Parts Co, Atlanta, GA
Principal Bank: Amsouth Bank of Birmingham
Financial Information:

	$'000
Sales revenues	400,000

No of Employees: 2,000

MOTOR CLUB OF AMERICA

484 Central Avenue, Newark, NJ 07107
Tel: (201) 733 1234

Chairman: William Green
President: David Green
Senior Executive Officers: Samuel Green (Senior Executive VP), Robert S Fried (Senior VP), Robert A Green (Senior VP), Henry M Carlson (VP), Joseph M Dijulio (VP), Thomas Fastiggi (VP), Stephen A Gilbert (VP and Assistant Legal Counsel), William Irwin (VP), George B Meyers (VP), Carmen Molinari (VP), Charles J Pelosi (VP), Joseph Roznoy (VP), Peter Violette (VP), Ernest Zito (VP), Norma Rodriguez (Finance), Doris Greeley (Secretary)

PRINCIPAL ACTIVITIES: Insurance
Financial Information:

	$'000
Revenues	43,000

No of Employees: 240

MOTOR WHEEL CORPORATION

4000 Collins Road, Lansing, MI 48910
Tel: (517) 337-5700
Telex: TWX 810 2510791 mtrwhly lns ud

Chairman: Robert E Mercer

President: Joseph C Overbeck
Senior Executive Officers: John R Kinstler (VP Engineering), James R Glass (VP), Alton N McCotter (VP Sales and Marketing), Frederick S Myers (VP), Richard W Tuley (VP Finance), Glen D Friedrichsen (VP Manufacturing), D C Pearson (Director Public Relations)

PRINCIPAL ACTIVITIES: Manufacture of wheels and other automotive components
Parent Company: Goodyear Tire & Rubber Company, Akron, OH
Principal Bank: National Bank of Detroit
Financial Information:

	$'000
Sales revenues	380,000

No of Employees: 3,300

MOTOROLA, INC

1303 E Algonquin Road, Schaumburg, IL 60196
Tel: (312) 397-5000
Telex: TWX 910 6934078 moc schaum

Chairman: Robert W Galvin; Vice Chairman: William J Weisz (and Chief Executive Officer)
President: John F Mitchell (and Chief Operating Officer)
Senior Executive Officers: Steven L Levy (Executive VP and General Manager, Japanese Operations), Levy Katzir (Senior VP and General Manager, New Enterprises), Donald R Jones (Executive VP and Chief Financial Officer), David W Hickie (Senior VP and Assistant Chief Financial Officer), Richard H Weise (Senior VP and General Counsel), Kenneth J Johnson (Corporate VP and Controller), H Richard Klotz (Corporate VP and Director of Taxes), Victor R Kopidlansky (Corporate VP and Assistant General Counsel), Carl E Lindholm (Executive VP, International Operations), C Travis Marshall (Senior VP and Motorola Director of Government Relations), George M C Fisher (Senior Executive VP and Deputy to the Chief Executive Office), Gary L Tooker (Senior Executive VP and Chief Corporate Staff Officer)

PRINCIPAL ACTIVITIES: Motorola, Inc is one of the world's leading manufacturers of electronic equipment, systems and components produced for both United States and international markets. Motorola products include two-way radios, pagers, cellular radiotelephones and other forms of electronic communications systems, semiconductors, defense and aerospace electronics, automotive and industrial electronic equipment, data communications and information processing and handling equipment. Motorola is one of the few end-equipment manufacturers that can draw on expertise in both semiconductor technology and government electronics
Principal Groups, Divisions and Organizations: Communications Sector -Groups and Divisions: Communcations Distribution Group:- Commercial Markets Division; Distribution Service Group; National Markets Division; Special Markets Division; State and Local Government Markets Division. Communications International Group:- European Division. Communications Manufacturing Group:- Components Division. Land Mobile Products Group:-Fixed Products Division; Land Mobile Systems Division; Mobile Products Division; Portable Products Division. Paging Products Division; Data Products Division. Semiconductor Products Sector- Groups and Divisions: Discrete and Special Technologies Group:- Low-frequency Power Transistor/Thyristor Products Division; RF and Optoelectronic Products Division; Small Signal and Sensor Products Division; Zener/Rectifier Products Division. Integrated Circuits Wafer Manufacturing Group:- Bipolar Wafer Processing Division; MOS Wafer Processing Division. International Semiconductor Group:- Asia Pacific Semiconductor Products Division. European Semiconductor Group:- Discrete and Analog Products Division (France); Logic, ASIC and Microsystems Products Division (Germany); MOS Memory and Microprocessor Division (UK). Microprocessor Products Group. Standard Logic and Analog IC Group:- Bipolar Analog IC Division; Bipolar Logic and Memory IC Division; MOS Logic and Analog IC Division. Application Specific Integrated Circuits Division. Assembly Manufacturing and Equipment. Engineering Division. MOS Memory Division. Information Systems Group-Organizations:- Codex; Universal Data Systems; International. Government Electronics Group-Organizations: Communications Division; Tactical Electronics Division; Aerospace Operations; Radar Operations. Automotive and Industrial Electronics Group-Organizations: Automotive Electronics; Electronic Appliance Controls; International.
Principal Bank: Harris Trust and Savings Bank
Financial Information:

	Dec 31 1985 $'000	Dec 31 1986 $'000
Sales revenues	5,443,000	5,888,000
Income before taxes	45,000	265,000
Net income	72,000	194,000
Dividends	76,000	82,000
Dividends per share	$0.64	$0.64
Earnings per share	$0.61	$1.53
Common stock	358,000	385,000
Retained income	1,444,000	1,552,000
Shareholders equity	2,284,000	2,754,000

No of Employees: 94,400

MOTT'S SUPER MARKETS INC

59-63 Leggett Street, East Hartford, CT 06108
Tel: (203) 289 3301

Chairman: Joseph P Mott (and Chief Executive Officer); Vice Chairman: Lewis Ellish
President: Barry P Baskind (and Chief Operating Officer)
Senior Executive Officers: Richard Neff (Executive VP, Director Operations), Stanley M Baskind (Executive VP Finance and Treasurer), Sylvia Gottlieb (Executive VP and Secretary), Steven D Goldberg (Executive VP Store Operations), Peter Casasanta (Senior VP Marketing), Graham W Waddill (VP and Controller), Richard Z Cohen (VP Sales and Merchandising)

PRINCIPAL ACTIVITIES: Retail food stores
Principal Bank: Connecticut Bank and Trust Company
Financial Information:

	$'000
Sales revenues	290,000

No of Employees: 2,680

MOUNT VERNON MILLS, INC

Daniel Building, Greenville, SC 29602
Tel: (803) 233-4151

Chairman: Robert B Pamplin Sr (and Chief Executive Officer); Vice Chairman: Robert B Pamplin Jr
President: Joseph L Jennings Jr (and Chief Operating Officer)
Senior Executive Officers: R L King Jr (Executive VP), C R Mabry (VP Manufacturing), David C Meek (VP and Treasurer), J Edward Thomas Jr (VP and Secretary), J H Greer (VP), D L Harrison (VP)

PRINCIPAL ACTIVITIES: Manufacture of cotton and man made fabrics
Parent Company: R B Pamplin Corp, Portland, OR
Principal Bank: Wachovia Bank and Trust Company
Financial Information:

	$'000
Sales revenues	400,000

No of Employees: 7,000

MOUNTAIRE CORPORATION

204 E 4th St., Box 5726, Little Rock, AR 72119
Tel: (501) 372 6524

President: Ronald M Cameron
Senior Executive Officers: Mike Lofton (VP Finance and Treasurer), Dee Ann Brannon (VP and Secretary)

PRINCIPAL ACTIVITIES: Meat processing
Principal Bank: First American National Bank
Financial Information:

	$'000
Sales revenues	100,000

No of Employees: 1,000

MOVIE STAR, INC
392 Fifth Avenue, New York, NY 10018
Tel: (212) 563-3000
Telex: ITT 421789 movstar 421789

Chairman: Irwin Goldberger (and President)
Senior Executive Officers: Neil S Rothfeld (Executive VP, Secretary and Treasurer), Enrico Vanani (VP Sales), Frank D'Amato (VP Production), Gary Goldberger (VP), Michael Goldberk (VP Purchasing), Russell Ladner (VP Manufacturing), Betty Krayosky (VP)

PRINCIPAL ACTIVITIES: Manufacture of clothing
Principal Subsidiaries: Fabrica Michael Inc; Virginia Garment Company Inc; Fabrica Avrameto Inc
Principal Bank: The Chase Manhattan Bank NA
Financial Information:

	$'000
Sales revenues	77,000

No of Employees: 1,950

MOXIE INDUSTRIES, INC
2211 E Orangewood Avenue, Anaheim, CA 92806
Tel: (714) 634-4000

Chairman: Reinold M Fries
President: Joseph A Sasenick (and Chief Executive Officer)
Senior Executive Officers: David H Gretton (Treasurer)

PRINCIPAL ACTIVITIES: Manufacture of vitamins and beverages and ingredients for the food industry
Principal Bank: Chase Manhattan Bank
Financial Information:

	$'000
Sales revenues	39,000

No of Employees: 250

MOYER, WALTER W, COMPANY, INC
400 W Main Street, Ephrata, PA 17522
Tel: (717) 733-2261

Chairman: Carl G Smith
President: Notley J Butler
Senior Executive Officers: Bob R Sears (VP Marketing), James L DeForest (VP Operations), Clair L Wolf (VP Planning), Dennis J Rupp (Comptroller/Treasurer)

PRINCIPAL ACTIVITIES: Manufacture of women's and children's clothing
Parent Company: Gerber Products Company, Fremont, MI
Principal Bank: Hamilton Bank
Financial Information:

	$'000
Sales revenues	50,000

No of Employees: 1,000

MR GASKET COMPANY
8700 Brookpark Road, Brooklyn Heights, OH 44129
Tel: (216) 398 8300

President: Joe Hrudka (and Chief Executive Officer)
Senior Executive Officers: Howard B Gardner (Executive VP), Tom Hrudka (Executive VP Operations), John A Scafidi (VP), Richard A Luff (VP Finance, Treasurer and Chief Financial Officer), Clayton G Leroux (Legal Counsel and Secretary)

PRINCIPAL ACTIVITIES: Manufacture of automotive components including engine parts, suspension and clutches
Parent Company: American Industries Inc
Financial Information:

	$'000
Sales revenues	118,000

No of Employees: 1,360

MR STEAK INC
5100 Race Court, Denver, CO 80216
Tel: (303) 292 3070

Chairman: Randall L Pike (and President and Chief Executive Officer)
Senior Executive Officers: Robert W Hite (VP, Secretary and Legal Counsel), James P Russo (VP Franchising), Robert L Stein (VP Marketing), Dale D Thompson (VP Sales)

PRINCIPAL ACTIVITIES: Franchising of restaurants; restaurant services
Principal Bank: First National Bank
Financial Information:

	$'000
Sales revenues	34,000

No of Employees: 260

MRFY CORPORATION
2323 Terminal Road, St Paul, MN 55113
Tel: (612) 633 7911

Chairman: Edward L Murphy Jr (and President)
Senior Executive Officers: Kevin S Murphy (VP Finance and Secretary)

PRINCIPAL ACTIVITIES: Trucking services
Principal Bank: First National Bank of St Paul
Financial Information:

	$'000
Sales revenues	82,120

No of Employees: 1,000

MSI DATA CORPORATION
340 Fischer Avenue, Costa Mesa, CA 92627
Tel: (714) 549-6000
Telex: TWX 910 5951719 msi csm

Chairman: William J Bowers
President: Charles S Strauch (and Chief Executive Officer)
Senior Executive Officers: Charles E Butler (VP Marketing), Herb Espeland (VP Operations), Joseph R Falvey (VP Sales), H H Simeroth (VP Engineering),

PRINCIPAL ACTIVITIES: Manufacture of data processing equipment, software and services
Principal Subsidiaries: MSI Data International; MSI France SRL; MSI Data GmbH; MSI Data Italia srl; MSI Data Ltd; MSI Switzerland; MSI Australia Pty Ltd
Principal Bank: Bank of America
Financial Information:

	$'000
Sales revenues	56,000

No of Employees: 800

MSL INDUSTRIES, INC
7373 N Lincoln Avenue, Lincolnwood, IL 60646
Tel: (312) 777-3300

Chairman: David C Stuege (and President and Chief Executive Officer)
Senior Executive Officers: Jamie C Gibson (Senior VP), Nancy J Nykaza (VP and Secretary), Lee Bookman (VP), James W Harris (VP), Rex A McClure (VP), August F DeLuca (VP Finance)

PRINCIPAL ACTIVITIES: Manufacture of industrial fasteners, motors and structural steel
Parent Company: Alleghany Corporation, New York, NY
Principal Bank: American National Bank & Trust Company of Chicago

Financial Information:

	$'000
Sales revenues	164,000

No of Employees: 1,500

MTS SYSTEMS CORPORATION

1400 Technology Drive, Eden Prairie, MN 55344
Tel: (612) 937-4000
Fax: (612) 937-4515
Telex: WUT 382005 mts systems

Chairman: George N Butzow
President: Donald M Sullivan (and Chief Executive Officer)
Senior Executive Officers: Marshall L Carpenter (VP and Treasurer), Richard Clarke (VP), George I Doering (VP), Milan L Sebek (VP), Keith D Zell (VP), William T Dolan (Secretary), J Howell Owens (VP)

PRINCIPAL ACTIVITIES: MTS Systems Corporation provides computer-based systems and software for analyzing the durability of materials, products and structures and for automating production processes. Decision makers in science and industry throughout the world use MTS technologies to advance product design, improve product quality and reduce production costs
Principal Subsidiaries: MTS Systems (Hong Kong) Inc; MTS Testing Systems (Canada) Ltd; MTS Systems GmbH (Germany); MTS Systems France; MTS (Japan) Ltd; MTS Limited (UK); MTS Systems SRL (Italy); MTS International Ltd (West Indies); MTS Systems Norden AB (Sweden); MTS Vektronics Corporation; MTS Sistemas do Brasil Ltda; MTS Systems (China) Limited
Principal Bank: First National Bank of St Paul
Financial Information:

	Sep 30 1985	Sep 30 1986
	$'000	$'000
Sales revenues	95,879	109,842
Income before taxes	7,709	12,080
Net income	5,025	6,914
Dividends	651	725
Dividends per share	$0.24	$0.26
Earnings per share	$1.19*	$1.58*
Common stock	1,028*	1,068*
Retained income	35,568	41,757
Shareholders equity	40,314	48,805

*restated for a 3-for-2 stock split in February 1987

No of Employees: 1,161

MUELLER CO

500 W Eldorado Street, Decatur, IL 62522
Tel: (217) 423-4471
Telex: WUI 6871470 mueller

Chairman: Edward D Powers (and Chief Executive Officer)
President: Fred C Ausnehmer (and Chief Operating Officer)
Senior Executive Officers: George Pearse (Group VP), Marvin A Brown (Group VP), John A Helfrich (VP Personnel), A M Yurko (VP Finance)

PRINCIPAL ACTIVITIES: Gas and water distribution products including valves
Principal Bank: Morgan Guaranty Trust Co
Financial Information:

	$'000
Sales revenues	120,000

No of Employees: 2,200

MUELLER, PAUL, COMPANY

1600 West Phelps Street, PO Box 828, Springfield, MO 65801
Tel: (417) 831-3000
Telex: 43-6427 MUE SPG
Telefax: (417) 831-3528

Chairman: Paul Mueller

President: Daniel C Manna

Senior Executive Officers: Ronald P Tappan (Executive VP-Marketing), Donald E Golik (VP-Finance), Larry R Pointelin (VP-Manufacturing), Larry R Rathbun (VP-Engineering)

PRINCIPAL ACTIVITIES: Paul Mueller Company specializes in the manufacture of stainless steel tanks and related processing equipment. Products include dairy farm equipment; food, dairy, meat and poultry processing equipment; beer, wine and beverage equipment; and chemical, pharmaceutical and industrial equipment. All qualifying export sales are handled through its wholly owned subsidiary, Mueller International Sales Corporation

Principal Subsidiaries: Mueller International Sales Corporation (100%); Mueller Europa BV (100%) (Netherlands)

Principal Bank: Commerce Bank of Kansas City; Centerre Bank of St Louis

Financial Information:

	Dec 31 1985	Dec 31 1986
	$'000	$'000
Sales revenues	56,428	51,869
Income (loss) before taxes	2,375	(339)
Net income (loss)	870	(1,420)
Dividends	1,986	1,986
Dividends per share	$1.70	$1.70
Earnings (loss) per share	($1.22)	$0.75
Common stock*	1,168	1,168
Retained income	30,317	26,912
Shareholders equity	33,026	29,716

*number of shares in thousands

Number of Shareholders: 500

No of Employees: 841

MULTIBANK FINANCIAL CORP

100 Rustcraft Road, Dedham, MA 02026

Tel: (617) 461 1820

Telefax: (617) 461-5579

Chairman: David B Lynch (and Chief Executive Officer)

President: Selwyn I Atherton (and Chief Operating Officer)

Senior Executive Officers: Paul M Diesel (Executive Officer and Subsidiary Officer), Richard B Collins (Executive Officer and Subsidiary Officer), Forrest R Cook Jr (Executive Officer and Subsidiary Officer), Bruce S Mackilligan (Executive Officer and Subsidiary Officer), Leon J Pyzik Jr (Executive Officer and Subsidiary Officer), Gary P Scarafoni (Executive Officer and Subsidiary Officer), Herman H Hipson (Senior VP Operations and Information Systems), Peter F Russo (Senior VP, Treasurer and Chief Financial Officer), Robert M Goodreau (VP), Hammond G Reed (VP), Richard T Frederics (VP Auditing), O Frank Belanger (VP), Alan R Schwalm (VP Investment), Lesley M Beszterczey (VP), Alan B Neville (VP), John R Riemer (VP)

PRINCIPAL ACTIVITIES: Banking

Trade Names: Multibank

Principal Subsidiaries: Durfee Attleboro Bank; The Falmouth National Bank; First Agricultural Bank; Mechanics Bank; Multibank National of Western Mass; South Shore Bank; Multibank International

Principal Bank: Citibank

Financial Information:

	Dec 31 1986 (12 mths) $'000	Sep 30 1987 (9 mths) $'000
Revenues	227,193	172,838
Income before taxes	23,244	23,761
Net income	16,655	14,965
Dividends	4,234	3,673
Dividends per share	$0.49	$0.39
Earnings per share	$1.95	$1.61
Common stock	55,286	59,267
Retained income	147,211	170,133
Shareholders equity	2,029,088	2,122,248
Deposits	2,360,678	2,545,325

No of Employees: 1,629

MULTIMEDIA, INC

305 S Main Street, PO Box 1688, Greenville, SC 29602
Tel: (803) 298-4373

Chairman: Wilson C Wearn
President: Walter E Bartlett (and Chief Executive Officer)
Senior Executive Officers: Thelma M Anderson (Assistant Secretary), Donald J Barhyte (Treasurer, Chief Financial Officer; President, Multimedia Newspaper Co), Alfred F Burgess (Secretary), Donald L Dahlman (VP), David L Freeman (Assistant Secretary), Robert E Hamby Jr (VP, Finance), George D Hayes Jr (Assistant Treasurer), James T Lynagh (VP; President, Multimedia Broadcasting Co), Thomas L Magaha (Controller), Elizabeth S Mills (VP, Corporate Communications), Donald D Sbarra (VP; President, Multimedia Cablevision Co), Peter A Lund (VP, President, Multimedia Entertainment Co)

PRINCIPAL ACTIVITIES: Multimedia, Inc is a media communications company with corporate headquarters located in Greenville, South Carolina. Multimedia's four divisions publish 14 daily and 33 non-daily newspapers; own and operate five television and eight radio broadcasting stations; operate more than 100 cable franchises in four states, and produce and syndicate quality television programming including the Phil Donahue and Sally Jessy Raphael Shows
Principal Subsidiaries & Divisions: Multimedia Broadcasting Company; Multimedia Entertainment Company; Multimedia Newspaper Company; Multimedia Cablevision Company
Principal Bank: Wachovia Bank & Trust
Financial Information:

	Dec 31 1985 $'000	Dec 31 1986 $'000
Sales revenues	336,271	371,799
Income before taxes	47,918	2,439
Net income (loss)	21,638	(4,661)
Dividends	8,251	-
Dividends per share	$0.495	-
Earnings (loss) per share net	$1.40	($0.42)
Common stock	1,100	1,101
Retained (deficit)	(686,626)	(691,287)
Shareholders (deficit)	(576,399)	(580,134)

No of Employees: 3,100

MUNFORD, INC

1860-74 Peachtree Road NW, Atlanta, GA 30309
Tel: (404) 352-6641
Telex: 4953545 MUN UI

Chairman: Dillard Munford (and Chief Executive Officer)
President: Russell C Fellows (and Chief Operating Officer)
Senior Executive Officers: James M Carroll (Executive VP Finance and Secretary), H E Lambert (VP, Corporate Counsel and Assistant Secretary), J W Hardin (VP and Treasurer), Jay E Rubel (VP Administration), Fred J Mershad (President, World Bazaar Division), John A Popple (President, Leewards Creative Crafts Inc)

PRINCIPAL ACTIVITIES: Munford, Inc is a specialty retailer, which includes convenience food stores, gasoline outlets, import home decorative stores and craft and art stores
Trade Names: Majik Market, World Bazaar, Leewards Craft Bazaar
Principal Subsidiaries: ATL Inc; City Ice Delivery Company; FCF Inc; Jacksons Minit Markets Inc; KPM Inc; Asian Arts Inc (40%); On Yun Trading Compay Ltd; United Refrigerated Services Inc (45.7%); TMM Inc; Leewards Creative Crafts Inc
Principal Bank: Citizens & Southern Trust Company Bank
Financial Information:

	Jan 2 1986 $'000	Jan 1 1987 $'000
Sales revenues	456,562	459,501
Income before taxes	7,322	301
Net income	5,532	1,641
Dividends	2,071	2,052
Dividends per share	$0.54	$0.54
Earnings per share	$1.40	$0.42
Common stock	4,163	4,218
Retained income	34,742	34,351
Shareholders equity	52,392	52,788

Principal Shareholders: Fiduciary Management, Inc; Dillard Munford; Dimensional Fund Advisors; Paragon Assoc & Paragon Assoc II
No of Employees: 8,500

MUNSINGWEAR, INC

724 N First Street, Minneapolis, MN 55401
Tel: (612) 340--4700
Telex: ITT 4310065 munsinginc mps

President: George K Hansen (and Chief Executive Officer)
Senior Executive Officers: Robert G Higginbotham (VP), Michael Kagan (VP)

PRINCIPAL ACTIVITIES: Clothing manufacture
Principal Bank: Norwest Bank Minneapolis
Financial Information:

	$'000
Sales revenues	114,250

No of Employees: 2,470

MURCO, INC

11 11th Street, Plainwell, MI 49080
Tel: (616) 685-6886
Telex: WUT 224479 murco plwl

Chairman: Paul J Murray (and President)
Senior Executive Officers: Phil Verduce (VP Sales), James Hatch (VP Operations), Sharon Hollingshead (Management Information Systems Manager)

PRINCIPAL ACTIVITIES: Production of meat packing plant
Principal Bank: Manufacturers National Bank
Financial Information:

	$'000
Sales revenues	175,000

No of Employees: 450

MURPHY OIL CORPORATION

200 Peach Street, El Dorado, AR 71730
Tel: (501) 862-6411
Telex: 536210 MURPHOIL ELDO; TWX 910 720 7865 MURPHYOIL ELDO

Chairman: C H Murphy Jr
President: Robert J Sweeney
Senior Executive Officers: Jack W McNutt (Executive VP), Jerry W Watkins (VP and General Counsel), George E Breazeal (Controller), B David Richardson (Treasurer)

PRINCIPAL ACTIVITIES: Murphy Oil Corporation, operating as a holding company, is the corporate parent of the consolidated group of companies which conduct the various businesses of the Murphy enterprise, worldwide. Exploration and Production:- During 1986 various subsidiary companies were engaged in onshore and offshore exploration activities in 13 countries. Crude oil, condensate and natural gas liquids are produced in the USA, Canada, UK North Sea, Gabon, Egypt and Spain. Natural gas is produced in the USA, Canada the UK North Sea and Spain. Refining, Marketing and Transportation:- Murphy Oil USA, Inc, wholly owned, has two refineries in the USA and Murco Petroleum Limited, also 100 percent owned, shares ownership in a refinery in the UK. Refined products are sold in retail and wholesale markets in the USA and Western Europe. Contract Drilling:-Contract drilling for oil and gas is a major diversification conducted by Ocean Drilling & Exploration Company (ODECO), a 61 percent owned subsidiary which owns and operates one of the world's largest fleets of offshore drilling barges. A wholly owned subsidiary of ODECO provides underwater services to the petroleum industry, worldwide. Farm and Timber: Wholly owned Deltic Farm & Timber Co Inc is engaged in farm, timber and lumber manufacturing operations, primarily in Arkansas and North Louisiana

Trade Names: "Spur"-United States, "Murco", "EP"-United Kingdom

Principal Subsidiaries: (100% owned unless stated): Murphy Oil USA Inc; Murphy Eastern Oil Company (UK); Deltic Farm & Timber Co Inc; Murphy Oil Company Ltd (77%); Ocean Drilling & Exploration Company (61%); Murphy Petroleum Ltd (UK); Murco Petroleum Ltd (UK); Murphy Oil Trading Co (Eastern)

Principal Bank: Chemical Bank

Financial Information:

	Dec 31 1985	Dec 31 1986
	$'000	$'000
Total revenues	2,223,343	1,369,817
Income (loss)(1)	313,815	(350,092)(2)
Net income (loss)	79,704	(194,750)(3)
Dividends	35,441	33,766
Dividends per share	$1.00	$1.00
Earnings (loss) per share	$2.25	($5.76)(3)
Common stock	37,742	37,742
Retained income	940,788	712,272(3)
Shareholders equity	1,014,391	776,686(3)

(1) from continuing operations before taxes and minority interests

(2) after $387,163 provision for write-down in stated value of certain assets

(3) effect of write-down in assets, after taxes and minority interests on net income was $228,760, $6.77 a share

No of Employees: 4,012

MURRAY OHIO MANUFACTURING CO

PO Box 268, Brentwood, TN 37027
Tel: (615) 373-6500
Telex: TWX 810 3711029 murray o nhul

Chairman: William M Hannon
President: R W Sappenfield (and Chief Executive Officer)
Senior Executive Officers: J M Barr (Executive VP Sales and Marketing), R G Hash (Senior VP Sales), C E Goss (VP Finance), William N Scott (VP Engineering), Clark Rutledge (VP Purchasing), D D Lay (VP Corporate Information Systems), Larry J Heard (VP Personnel)

PRINCIPAL ACTIVITIES: Manufacture of bicycles and garden equipment
Principal Bank: Third National Bank
Financial Information:

	$'000
Sales revenues	387,600

No of Employees: 3,000

MUSSELMAN'S MFP ENTERPRISES, INC

PO Box K, Biglerville, PA 17307
Tel: (717) 677-7111
Telex: TWX 510 6503509

Chairman: Mark T Concannon Sr
President: Mark T Concannon Jr
Senior Executive Officers: W P Mahler (VP and General Manager), Louis S James (Treasurer)

PRINCIPAL ACTIVITIES: Apple products including juices, pie fillings and apple sauce
Principal Bank: American Bank
Financial Information:

	$'000
Sales revenues	62,000

MUTUAL BENEFIT LIFE INSURANCE CO

520 Broad Street, Newark, NJ 07101
Tel: (201) 481-8000
Telex: WUT 501939 mut bnet life

Chairman: Robert V Van Fossan (and Chief Executive Officer)
President: Frank E Sullivan
Senior Executive Officers: W P Stillman (Chairman Executive Committee), Ted D Simmons (Executive VP), John Henry E Kates (Executive VP Individual Insurance), Robert W Kopchains (Senior VP Real Estate Investment), J E Helsing (Senior VP and Chief Operating Officer), Guy C Bosetti (VP and General Counsel), Charles G McCraig (VP Data Processing), W G Michael Farrell (VP Venture Capital), Donald E Hagemann (VP Capital Markets), Robert Davidow (VP Pensions), Edward Mekeel (VP and Comptroller), Betty Lee Hagerty (VP Public Affairs), Kenneth M Donaldson (VP Personnel)

PRINCIPAL ACTIVITIES: Life insurance
Principal Bank: First National State Bank
Financial Information:

	Dec 31 1985	Dec 31 1986
	$'000	$'000
Premium income	1,422,616	1,634,881
Investment income	826,573	891,052

No of Employees: 4,130

MUTUAL OF AMERICA LIFE

666 Fifth Ave, New York, NY 10103
Tel: (212) 399-1600

Chairman: William J Flynn (and Chief Executive Officer)
President: Dwight K Bartlett III
Senior Executive Officers: Manfred Altstadt (Senior VP and Treasurer)

PRINCIPAL ACTIVITIES: Life insurance
Principal Bank: Bank of New York
Financial Information:

	Dec 31 1985	Dec 31 1986
	$'000	$'000
Premium income	326,332	421,085
Investment income	225,109	256,796
Total assets	2,887,590	3,435,530

No of Employees: 650

MUTUAL OF OMAHA INSURANCE CO

Mutual of Omaha Plaza, Omaha, NE 68175
Tel: (402) 342-7600

Chairman: V J Skutt; Vice Chairmen: Thomas J Skutt (and Chief Executive Officer), Hugh V Plunkett Jr
President: John D Minton (and Chief Operating Officer)
Senior Executive Officers: Thomas Child (Senior Executive VP and Chief Agent Canadian Operations), M Thomas Crummer (Senior Executive VP and Chief Investment Officer), Donald J Goaley (Senior Executive VP Internal Operations), John W

Weekly (Senior Executive VP Computer Data Services and Group Insurance), Conrad S Young (Senior Executive VP)

PRINCIPAL ACTIVITIES: Insurance services
Principal Subsidiaries: Companion Life Insurance Co; Kirkpatrick, Pettis, Smith, Polian Inc; Mutual of Omaha Fund Management Co; Omaha Financial Life Insurance Co; Omaha Property and Casualty Co; Tele-Trip Co; United of Omaha Life Insurance Co; United World Life Insurance Co

MYERS DRUM COMPANY

6549 San Pablo Avenue, Oakland, CA 94662
Tel: (415) 652-6847

President: K J Reidy
Senior Executive Officers: C H Black (Executive VP), T J Hunt (VP and Treasurer), L K Whitaker (VP and Secretary), J Brignano (VP and Controller)

PRINCIPAL ACTIVITIES: Manufacture of steel drums and steel containers
Parent Company: Kaiser Steel Corporation, Fontana, CA
Principal Bank: Bank of America
Financial Information:

	$'000
Sales revenues	53,000

No of Employees: 660

MYERS INDUSTRIES, INC

1293 S Main Street, Akron, OH 44301
Tel: (216) 253-5592
Telex: WUT 986321 myers ind akr

Chairman: Louis S Myers
President: Stephen E Myers (and Chief Executive Officer)
Senior Executive Officers: Milton I Wiskind (Senior VP), Gregory J Stodnick (VP and Treasurer)

PRINCIPAL ACTIVITIES: Manufacture of rubber automotive parts
Principal Subsidiaries: Akro-Mills Inc; Patch Rubber Company; Elrick Industries; J C Heintz Co; Myers Tire Supply Inc; Myers Tire Supply (Canada) Inc; Bert Schwarz S & H Inc; Myers Tire Supply Inc; Myers Industries International Inc; Myers-Wadsworth; Midland Tire Supply Inc
Principal Bank: Society National Bank
Financial Information:

	$'000
Sales revenues	85,000

No of Employees: 780

MYERS, L E, COMPANY GROUP

1010 Jorie Boulevard, Oak Brook, IL 60521
Tel: (312) 325 4666

Chairman: Leo A Grant (and President and Chief Executive Officer)
Senior Executive Officers: Byron D Nelson (Senior VP, Secretary and Legal Counsel), Elliott C Robbins (Senior VP, Treasurer and Chief Financial Officer), Peter W Youngwerth (Senior VP), Marcy A Chapman (VP and Controller), Ralph H Morgan (VP Equipment)

PRINCIPAL ACTIVITIES: Pipeline and power line engineering and construction
Principal Subsidiaries: L E Myers Company; Grisson & Johnson Inc; Lemco Construction Inc; Lemco Engineers Inc
Principal Bank: First National Bank
Financial Information:

	$'000
Sales revenues	114,310

No of Employees: 260

MYLAN LABORATORIES INC

130 Seventh Street, Pittsburgh, PA 15222
Tel: (412) 232-0100

Chairman: Roy McKnight (and Chief Executive Officer)
President: Milan Puskar
Senior Executive Officers: Frank Beber (VP Finance), Dana G Barnett (VP Operations), C B Todd (VP)

PRINCIPAL ACTIVITIES: Manufacture of pharmaceuticals
Principal Bank: Equibank
Financial Information:

	$'000
Sales revenues	95,000

No of Employees: 230

N DORMAN & COMPANY, INC

See DORMAN, N, & COMPANY, INC

N ERLANGER BLUMGART & CO, INC

See ERLANGER, N, BLUMGART & CO, INC

NACCO INDUSTRIES INC

12500 Shaker Blvd, Cleveland, OH 44120
Tel: (216) 752-1000

Chairman: Otes Bennett Jr
President: Ward Smith (and Chief Executive Officer)
Senior Executive Officers: John R Cook (VP Finance and Administration), Robert S Hawekotte (VP and Treasurer), Thomas A Koza (VP, Secretary and General Counsel)

PRINCIPAL ACTIVITIES: Holding company with interests in coal mining and the mining of lignite
Financial Information:

	Dec 31 1986 $'000
Sales revenues	584,034
Net income	33,342
Earnings per share	$3.48
Shareholders equity	181,982

NA-CHURS, INC

421 Leader Street, Marion, OH 43302
Tel: (614) 382-5701
Telex: 8104871776

President: John D Kelly
Senior Executive Officers: Louis F Nemeth (VP Finance), Orville E Gaffney (VP Sales)

PRINCIPAL ACTIVITIES: Manufacture of fertilizers
Parent Company: CanWest Investment Corp
Principal Bank: Continental Illinois National Bank and Trust Co
Financial Information:

	$'000
Sales revenues	40,000

No of Employees: 300

NAFCO FINANCIAL GROUP, INC

5801 Pelican Bay Blvd, Naples, FL 33940
Tel: (813) 597-1611

Chairman: D B zumFelde (and President and Chief Executive Officer)
Senior Executive Officers: J M Holmes (VP and Treasurer)

PRINCIPAL ACTIVITIES: Financial services including savings and loans
Principal Subsidiaries: Naples Federal Savings and Loan Association; The Mueller Company; NAFCO Equipment Corporation; Trust Company of Naples. Subsidiaries of Naples Federal: Horizon Appraisal Services Inc; Naples Financial Services Inc; NAFCO Financial Leasing Corporation; NFS Mortgage Corporation; Naples Investment Services Inc
Principal Bank: Naples Federal Savings & Loan Association

Financial Information:

	Sep 30 1986	Sep 30 1987
	$'000	$'000
Income before taxes	5,161	7,040
Net income	1,986	4,170
Dividends	2,921	3,026
Dividends per share	$0.86	$0.89
Earnings per share	$0.59	$1.23
Common stock	31	34
Retained income*	7,767	3,196
Shareholders equity	53,876	54,478
Deposit accounts	1,103,196	1,226,748
Total assets	1,369,868	1,585,190

*Substantially restricted

Principal Shareholders: NAFCO Financial Group Inc Tax Credit Employee Stock Ownership Plan (25%); NAFCO Financial Group Inc Employee Stock Ownership Plan (6.9%); NAFCO Financial Group Inc Pension Plan (0.3%); NAFCO Financial Group Inc Employee Thrift Plan (1.6%); Naples Federal Savings and Loan Association Employee Stock Ownership Plan (1.5%); Delaware Management Company Inc (9.2%); Drexel Burnham Lambert Group Inc (6.9%); The Travelers Companies (6.3%); Dimensional Fund Advisors Inc (5.7%)
No of Employees: 688

NALCO CHEMICAL CO

One Nalco Center, Naperville, IL 60566-1024
Tel: (312) 961-9500
Cable: NALCO-NAPERVILLE
Telex: 3734846 NALCOINTL UB

Chairman: W H Clark Jr (and President and Chief Executive Officer)
Senior Executive Officers: D E Jackson (Executive VP), F V Paine (Executive VP), K V Davis (Executive VP), E J Mooney (Group VP), W S Weeber (Group VP), C A Smith (Group VP), R M Bloom (Senior VP Finance and Chief Financial Officer)

PRINCIPAL ACTIVITIES: Manufacture of a wide range of chemicals
Principal Subsidiaries: (100% owned unless stated): Domestic: Adco Products Inc; Chicago Chemical Co; Circuit Services-W R Hatch Corporation; Day-Glo Color Corporation; Nalco Foreign Sales Corporation; Nalco International Sales Company; Nalco Leasing Corporation; Nalco Resources Investment Company; Penray Company; "X" Laboratories Inc; US Packaging Inc; Visco Products Company. Foreign: Deutsche Nalco-Chemie GmbH (Germany); Nalco Capital Corporation AG (Switzerland); Nalco Chemical AB (Sweden); Nalco Chemical BV (Netherlands); Nalco Chemical Company (Philippines) Inc (Philippines); Nalco Chemical Gesellschaft mbH (Austria); Nalco Chemical (HK) Limited (Hong Kong); Nalco de Venezuela CA (Venezuela); Nalco Espanola SA (Spain); Nalco Europe SARL (France); Nalco France SARL (France); Nalco Hellas SA (Greece); Nalco Italiana SpA (Italy); Nalco Japan Company Ltd (Japan); Nalco Limited (UK); Nalco Productos Quimicos de Chile Limitada (80%) (Chile); Nalco Productos Quimicos Limitada (Brazil); Nalco Saudi Co Ltd (60%) (Saudi Arabia); Nalquimica SA (Argentina); Nalquimica del Ecuador SA (Ecuador); Quimica Nalco de Colombia SA (Colombia); Suomen Nalco Oy (Finland)
Financial Information:

	Dec 31 1985	Dec 31 1986
	$'000	$'000
Sales revenues	736,074	682,330
Income before taxes	108,295	121,834
Net income	63,672	73,332
Dividends	47,094	46,960
Dividends per share	$1.20	$1.20
Earnings per share	$1.62	$1.87
Common stock	15,054	15,054
Retained income	441,327	424,749
Shareholders equity	407,470	384,238

No of Employees: 4,868

NALLEY'S FINE FOODS

3303 S 35th Street, Tacoma, WA 98411
Tel: (206) 383-1621
Telex: WUT 327415 nalleys tac

President: J W Petty (and Chief Executive Officer)
Senior Executive Officers: Robert T Sutich (Senior VP), J R McEntee (VP Manufacturing), Larry Hile (VP Distribution), Richard S Meyer (VP Technical Services), R Mulholland (VP Finance), Robert M O'Connor (VP and General Manager Food Services), Thomas C Tussing (VP Marketing), Helen Whatmough (VP Administration)

PRINCIPAL ACTIVITIES: Snack food products including potato chips, salad dressings, canned meats
Parent Company: Curtice-Burns Inc
Financial Information:

	$'000
Sales revenues	132,000

No of Employees: 800

NANTUCKET INDUSTRIES INC

105 Madison Avenue, New York, NY 10016
Tel: (212) 889-5656

Chairman: George J Gold (and Chief Executive Officer and Treasurer)
President: Donald D Gold (and Secretary)
Senior Executive Officers: Drewry F Wofford (VP Operations), Theresa M Bohrenberger (VP), Richard Tretler (VP Finance)

PRINCIPAL ACTIVITIES: Manufacture of underwear and panty hose
Principal Subsidiaries: Nantucket Hosiery Mills
Principal Bankers: Manufacturers Hanover Trust Co
Financial Information:

	Mar 1 1986	Feb 27 1987
	$'000	$'000
Sales revenues	50,164	51,515
Income (loss) before taxes	3,427	(3,011)
Net income (loss)	1,890	(1,695)
Earnings (loss) per share	$0.69	($0.63)
Retained income	4,739	3,044
Shareholders equity	13,742	11,598

No of Employees: 950

NAPCO INTERNATIONAL INC

1600 Second Street South, Hopkins, MN 55343
Tel: (612) 931 2400

Chairman: Gary B Rappaport (and Chief Executive Officer)
President: Henri M Jacob
Senior Executive Officers: Edwin S Arganoff (Group VP), Edward S Chesen (Group VP), Patrick J C Higgins (Group VP), Edward E Grosmann (Senior VP), Richard A Marcus (Senior VP, Secretary and Legal Counsel), Abdel A Attia (VP), Wallace W Doble (VP), Jack Horowitz (VP), Richard H Leibo (VP), Donald J Millar (VP), Gregory C Anderson (Controller, Assistant Secretary and Chief Financial Officer)

PRINCIPAL ACTIVITIES: Supply of communications, construction, transportation, medical and industrial equipment to governments and government agencies
Financial Information:

	$'000
Sales revenues	41,480

No of Employees: 165

NARCO MEDICAL SERVICE

455 Pennsylvania Avenue, Fort Washington, PA 19034
Tel: (215) 641-5800
Telex: 846112

Chairman: E R Garfield
Senior Executive Officers: Michael F Doyle (VP Finance and Chief Financial Officer), James J Tuite (Treasurer)

PRINCIPAL ACTIVITIES: Manufacture of medical equipment and instruments
Parent Company: Healthdyne Inc
Principal Bank: Girard Bank
Financial Information:

	$'000
Sales revenues	72,000

No of Employees: 1,000

NASCO INTERNATIONAL, INC

901 Janesville Avenue, Fort Atkinson, WI 53538
Tel: (414) 563-2446
Telex: WUT 265476 nasco int ftan

President: Arthur W Nesbitt (and Chief Executive Officer)
Senior Executive Officers: Carl G Dobratz (Executive VP, Secretary and Treasurer), Robert G Donnalley Jr (VP), Ronald G Strackbein (VP, Charles Lubochinski (VP), Steven B Lapin (VP and Assistant Secretary)

PRINCIPAL ACTIVITIES: Manufacture and distribution of agricultural and educational products; operation of mail order service
Parent Company: Geneve Corp
Principal Bank: Continental Illinois National Bank and Trust Company
Financial Information:

	$'000
Sales revenues	118,000

No of Employees: 1,050

NASH-FINCH COMPANY

3381 Gorham Avenue, Minneapolis, MN 55426
Tel: (612) 929-0371
Telex: TWX 910 5763146 nashfinch mpls

Chairman: Harold B Finch (and Chief Executive Officer)
President: Russell N Mammel (and Chief Operating Officer)
Senior Executive Officers: J O Rodysill (Senior VP), Norman R Soland (Secretary), Robert F Nash (Treasurer)

PRINCIPAL ACTIVITIES: Wholesale and retail trade in a range of foods including fruit and vegetables, groceries and bakery products; wholesale distribution of beauty aids
Trade Names: Sun Mart, Metoo, Cliftons, Piggly Wiggly, Jack & Jill, Food Pride, Warehouse Market, Food Bonanza Market, Praire Market, Econofoods, Family Thrift Center
Principal Subsidiaries: Nash DeCamp Company; GTL Trucklines Inc; N-F Properties Inc; McLean Wholesale Grocery Co Inc; Merchants Finance Co; Piggly Wiggly Northland Corp; Peerys Super Market Inc; S C Shannon Company; Valley Cash & Carry Inc; Thomas & Howard Company of Rocky Mount Inc; Thomas and Howard of Hickory Inc; Virginia Foods of Bluefield Inc
Principal Banks: Northwestern National Bank of Minneapolis; First National Bank of Minneapolis
Financial Information:

	Dec 28 1985	Jan 3 1987
	$'000	$'000
Sales revenues	1,323,294	1,573,716
Income before taxes	22,026	26,012
Net income	12,006	13,834
Dividends	5,100	5,332
Dividends per share	$1.00	$1.04
Earnings per share	$2.36	$2.70
Common stock	6,917	10,301
Retained income	100,467	108,968
Shareholders equity	107,384	116,416

No of Employees: 5,500

NASHUA CORPORATION

44 Franklin Street, Nashua, NH 03061
Tel: (603) 880-2323
Telex: RCA 294120 nash ur

President: Charles E Clough (and Chief Executive Officer)
Senior Executive Officers: John T Montesi (VP Research and Development and Real Estate), William Luke (VP Finance, Treasurer and Chief Financial Officer), Joseph R Kershaw (VP Human Resources), John G Barnes (VP Coated Products Group), Eric N Birch (VP Office Systems and Supplies), William W Teeple (VP Computer Products and Secretary)

PRINCIPAL ACTIVITIES: Manufacture of office equipment and supplies and computer products
Principal Bank: Manufacturers Hanover Trust Co
Financial Information:

	Dec 31 1985	Dec 31 1986
	$'000	$'000
Sales revenues	621,560	704,221
Net income	16,420	20,635
Earnings per share	$3.46	$2.13
Shareholders equity	146,250	174,701

No of Employees: 5,280

NATIONAL BANCORP OF ALASKA INC

PO Box 100600, Anchorage, AK 99510
Tel: (907) 276 1132

Chairman: Edward B Rasmusson
President: Robert P Gray
Senior Executive Officers: Kathleen Knowles (Treasurer), B W Williams (Controller and Subsidiary Officer), Bennett D Black (Secretary)

PRINCIPAL ACTIVITIES: Banking
Financial Information:

	Dec 31 1985
	$'000
Revenues	125,180
Net income	19,460

No of Employees: 870

NATIONAL BANCSHARES CORPORATION OF TEXAS

PO Box 121, San Antonio, TX 78291
Tel: (512) 225-2511

Chairman: Richard W Calvert (and Chief Executive Officer)
President: Mark M Johnson (and Chief Operating Officer)
Senior Executive Officers: Robert H Seal (Senior VP), Michael G Sweeney (Senior VP and Senior Lending Officer), Robert G Harris (Executive VP, Chief Financial Officer and Secretary), Thomas S Newman (Senior VP-Asset Review), Andrew D Hiduke (Senior VP-Human Resources), Pradeep K Bhargava (Senior VP-Corporate Planning), Robert E Orr (Executive VP-Member Bank Administration), James B Forehand (Senior VP-Administrative Services), Daniel S Shook (General Auditor)

PRINCIPAL ACTIVITIES: Banking
Trade Names: NBCT
Principal Subsidiaries: NBC Bank-San Antonio, N.A.; NBC Bank-Heights
Principal Bank: NBC Bank-San Antonio, N.A.

Financial Information:

	Dec 31 1985 $'000	Dec 31 1986 $'000
Revenues	306,544	294,995
Income (loss) before taxes	28,787	(44,607)
Net income (loss)	26,815	(32,079)
Dividends	8,077	7,909
Dividends per share	$0.74	$0.685
Earnings (loss) per share(1)	$2.27	($2.72)
Earnings (loss) per share(2)	$2.18	($2.72)
Common stock	58,995	59,014
Retained income	96,431	56,365
Shareholders equity	211,094	171,107
Deposits	2,668,575	2,948,913
Total assets	3,028,786	3,340,169

(1) Primary
(2) Fully diluted

Principal Shareholders: A Fayed
No of Employees: 2,000

NATIONAL BY-PRODUCTS, INC

1020 Locust Street, PO Box 615, Des Moines, IA 50303
Tel: (515) 288-2166

Chairman: R J Fleming
President: C D Carlson (and Chief Executive Officer)
Senior Executive Officers: Paul M Bohlig (Treasurer)

PRINCIPAL ACTIVITIES: Manufacture of animal by-products including tallow and hides
Parent Company: Federal Co, Memphis, TN
Principal Bank: Bankers Trust Company
Financial Information:

	$'000
Sales revenues	117,000

No of Employees: 900

NATIONAL CITY BANCORPORATION

75 South Fifth Street, Minneapolis, NM 55402
Tel: (612) 340 3183

Chairman: Lowell W Andreas (and Chief Executive Officer)
President: James H Hearon III (and Chief Operating Officer and Subsidiary Officer)
Senior Executive Officers: David L Andreas (Senior VP), Thomas J Freed (Secretary and Controller)

PRINCIPAL ACTIVITIES: Banking
Principal Subsidiaries: National City Bank of Minneapolis
Principal Bank: National City Bank of Minneapolis
Financial Information:

	Dec 31 1985 $'000
Revenues	53,190
Net income	1,596

No of Employees: 320

NATIONAL CITY CORPORATION

1900 East Ninth Street, Cleveland, OH 44114
Tel: (216) 575-2000
Telex: 212537 NCB UR

Chairman: Julian L McCall (and Chief Executive)
President: J Robert Killpack
Senior Executive Officers: Eric C Andrews (Executive VP Operations), Edward B Brandon (Executive VP), Gene F Carpenter (Executive VP Credit Administration), David A Daberko (Executive VP), Charles W Hall (Executive VP Investments), Theodore W Jones (Executive VP General Counsel and Secretary), William R Robertson (Executive VP Financial), Willis I Else (Senior VP Operations), Thomas W Owen (Senior VP General Auditor), Patrick D Walsh (Senior VP Data Processing), Thomas A Richlovsky (VP Treasurer)

PRINCIPAL ACTIVITIES: National City Corporation, a $14.1 billion bank holding company, is headquartered in Cleveland, Ohio. Its principal banking subsidiaries include National City Bank, Cleveland, BancOhio National Bank, Columbus and banks in Akron, Dayton and Toledo. Several other banks serve cities and towns throughout Ohio. The Corporation's banks and 10 other subsidiaries are also engaged in venture capital, small business investment, mortgage banking, leasing, credit card processing and other financial and fiduciary activities
Principal Subsidiaries: National City Bank, Cleveland; BancOhio National Bank, Columbus; National City Bank, Akron; First National Bank, Dayton; Ohio Citizens Bank, Toldeo; First National Bank, Ashland; Citizens National Bank, Bryan; National City Bank, Northeast; National City Bank, Marion; National City Bank, Norwalk; Third National Bank, Sandusky; BancOhio Mortgage Company; BancOhio Leasing Company; W Lyman Case & Company; National City Capital Corporation; National City Venture Corporation; National City Credit Corporation; National City Community Development Corporation; National City Life Insurance Company; National City Trust Company; Plaza Trust Company
Financial Information:

	Dec 31 1985 $'000	Dec 31 1986 $'000
Net income	108,447	134,953
Earnings per share	$3.03	$3.44
Shareholders equity	736,827	880,390
Deposits	9,448,398	10,427,356
Total assets	12,505,476	14,107,259

No of Employees: 9,013

NATIONAL COMMERCE BANCORPORATION

One Commerce Square, Memphis, TN 38150
Tel: (901) 523 3242

Chairman: Bruce E Campbell Jr (and Chief Executive Officer)
Senior Executive Officers: Walter B Howell Jr (VP)

PRINCIPAL ACTIVITIES: Banking
Principal Subsidiaries: Commerce Capital Management Inc; National Bank of Commerce; Commerce General Corporation Commerce McGehee Mortgage Inc; National Commerce Life Insurance Company
Financial Information:

	Dec 31 1985 $'000
Revenues	119,100
Net income	11,260

No of Employees: 325

NATIONAL COMPUTER SYSTEMS, INC

11000 Prairie Lakes Drive, Eden Prairie, MN 55344
Tel: (612) 829-3000
Telex: 192126 NCS EDNA

Chairman: Charles W Oswald
President: David C Malmberg
Senior Executive Officers: Robert J Korkowski (VP-Finance and Chief Financial Officer), Richard L Poss (VP-Organization and Management Development)

PRINCIPAL ACTIVITIES: NCS manufactures and markets automated information management products and services to help solve customers' information gathering, data entry, analysis and report generation needs. NCS' products include optical mark readers, scannable documents, specialized information systems, proprietary software, data processing and assessment services and related supplies and services
Principal Subsidiaries: NCS Learning Corporation; Commonwealth Leasing Corporation
Principal Bank: Norwest Bank Minneapolis, NA

Financial Information:

	Jan 31 1986	Jan 31 1987
	$'000	$'000
Sales revenues	215,800	262,100
Income before taxes	24,500	28,100
Net income	15,200	15,800
Dividends	2,200	3,100
Dividends per share	$0.13	$0.17
Earnings per share	$0.89	$0.84
Common stock	514	568
Retained income	44,700	57,400
Shareholders equity	76,200	116,100

No of Employees: 1,800

NATIONAL CONTROLS INC

2320 Airport Boulevard, Santa Rosa, CA 95401

Tel: (707) 527 5555

Chairman: Linus G Schwartz

President: Ronald W Sykes (and Chief Executive Officer)

Senior Executive Officers: Gary W Leopold (VP Finance and Treasurer), Albert M Kovanis Jr (Secretary and Controller), Gene I Katz (VP Engineering), David B Shepard (VP Manufacturing)

PRINCIPAL ACTIVITIES: Manufacture of electric scales and weighing equipment

Financial Information:

	$'000
Sales revenues	40,230

No of Employees: 590

NATIONAL CONVENIENCE STORES INCORPORATED

100 Waugh Drive, Houston, TX 77007

Tel: (713) 863-2200

President: V H Van Horn (and Chief Executive Officer)

Senior Executive Officers: J C Brewster (Senior VP-Finance and Chief Financial Officer), Craig K Calton (VP-Marketing), William K Elwood (VP-Systems), A J Gallerano (VP-General Counsel and Secretary), Michael C Kearney (VP and Treasurer), Patricia A Raybon (VP-Internal Audit), Charles T Spear (VP-Stores), Raymond P Springer (VP and Controller), R C Wortham (VP-Real Estate), Jerry M Comstock Jr (Regional VP)

PRINCIPAL ACTIVITIES: National Convenience Stores Incorporated and its consolidated subsidiaries operated 950 specialty convenience stores in six Sunbelt states, primarily under the name Stop N Go, at June 30, 1987. Over (70%) of the Company's stores are located in Texas, and the balance are in California, Nevada, Tennessee, Florida and Georgia. The stores sell fast food, alcoholic and non-alcoholic beverages, tobacco products, groceries, health and beauty aids and other non-food items. Approximately (76%) of the Company's stores are equipped with self-serve gasoline dispensing facilities. The Company believes that it is one of the largest operators of convenience stores in its market areas

Trade Names: Neighborstores (R)

Principal Subsidiaries: Kempco Petroleum Company

Financial Information:

	Jun 30 1986	Jun 30 1987
	$'000	$'000
Sales revenues	949,874	828,044
Income (loss) before taxes	4,152	(9,898)
Net income (loss)	3,582	(5,445)
Dividends	8,312	8,183
Dividends per share	$0.36	$0.36
Earnings (loss) per share	$0.15	($0.24)
Common stock	9,911	9,963
Retained income	37,999	24,371
Shareholders equity	89,509	73,511

No of Employees: 6,800

NATIONAL COOPERATIVE REFINERY ASSOCIATION

PO Box 1404, McPherson, KS 67460

Tel: (316) 241-2340

Telex: WUT 129194 nat conv favw

Chairman: Ralph Hofstad

President: Larry E Williams (and Chief Executive Officer)

Senior Executive Officers: R G Hall (VP Finance), Fred J Pierce (VP Refining), Ronald A Berke (VP Supply and Transport), Richard N Walker (VP Exploration and Production), Ronald G Schaumburg (VP Human Resources)

PRINCIPAL ACTIVITIES: Refining of petroleum; oil exploration operations

Principal Subsidiaries: Clear Creek Inc; Petroleum Resources Corp

Principal Bank: Mellon National Bank and Trust Company

Financial Information:

	Jun 30 1986	Jun 30 1987
	$'000	$'000
Sales revenues	715,900	544,977

No of Employees: 570

NATIONAL CORPORATION FOR HOUSING PARTNERSHIPS

1133 15th Street NW, Washington, DC 20005

Tel: (202) 857-5700

Telex: WUT 887243 mkgt wash

Chairman: George M Brady Jr

President: J Roderick Heller III (and Chief Executive Officer)

Senior Executive Officers: William D Comings Jr (Executive VP Multifamily Development), G L Crump (Executive VP Corporate Planning), Robert L Tracy (Executive VP Multifamily Development), David B Low (Executive VP Finance and Treasurer), D Terrence MacHamer (Executive VP Development), Larry W Asbury (Senior VP Property Management), James M Cluett (Senior VP Joint Ventures), Kersy B Dastur (Senior VP), Linda G Davenport (Senior VP, General Counsel and Secretary), Anthony J D'Ermes (Senior VP Human Resources/Administration), Conrad E Egan (Senior VP Ownership Services), Richard V McCracken (Senior VP Equity Sales), Kenneth Becker (VP Development), Michael Bowman (VP), Joan Frenz (VP), Thomas J Gorman (VP Property Management), Christopher B Hanback (VP, Deputy General Counsel and Assistant Secretary), Mark D Hasencamp (VP), John Koczela (VP), Lisa Kilker (VP), Sammie Lowery (VP Asset Management), Michael D Noonan (VP, Deputy General Counsel and Assistant Secretary), William E Papaj (VP, Associate General Counsel and Assistant Secretary), Richard M Powell (VP Equity Sales), Joseph P Stefan (VP), Raymond R Wojack (VP Property Management)

PRINCIPAL ACTIVITIES: Building contractors; real estate managers and agents; financial services

Parent Company: NHP Inc

Principal Bank: The Riggs National Bank of Washington

N

Financial Information:

	$'000
Revenues	700,000

No of Employees: 460

NATIONAL DISTILLERS & CHEMICAL CORPORATION

99 Park Avenue, New York, NY 10016
Tel: (212) 949-5000
Telex: Domestic-968158 NAT DIST NY; International-177136 NDC UT

Chairman: John Hoyt Stookey
Senior Executive Officers: Douglas L Allen (Executive, VP, President NDCC Chemical Group), Mark J Anton (Executive VP, Chairman and President, Suburban Propane), Francis L Brophy (Senior VP, Chief Financial Officer), Robert T Betz (VP, General Manager Emery Chemicals), F Donald Brigham (VP, Treasurer and Assistant Secretary), H Weston Clarke Jr (VP, Human Resources), Roger W Hill Jr (VP, Pension Fund Investments), Salvatore G Pastore (VP, General Manager Suburban Propane), John F Salisbury (VP, General Counsel and Secretary), James F Schorr (VP, President USI Chemicals Co), Richard A Tilghman (VP, Corporate Relations), Richard G Williams (VP, Planning), Pierre Van assche (Controller), George M Kuhn (Assistant Controller), James M Stio (Assistant Controller), Edward J Zurawski (Assistant Controller), Kevin T McIver (Assistant Secretary), Linda J Pavony (Assistant Secretary), John D Rice (Assistant Secretary), Frank Baio (Assistant Treasurer), Brian T Fearn (Assistant Treasurer)

PRINCIPAL ACTIVITIES: National Distillers and Chemical Corporation is primarily engaged in the production of petrochemical products: polyethylene resins, industrial alcohol, acetic acid and vinyl acetate; oleochemicals: specialty chemicals; marketing and distribution of propane
Trade Names: Chemicals and Plastics: USI, EVAL(R), FILMEX(R), PETROTHENE(R), MELTHENE (R), MICROTHENE(R), NORCHEM(R), NORKOOL(R), NORPROP(R), NORTECH(R), NORTUFF(R), PETROTHENE XL(R), PLEXAR(R), SPECTRATHENE(R), ULTRATHENE(R), VYNATHENE(R). Chemicals: EMERY, EMPOL, EMERSOL, EMEROX, EMTALL, PLASTOLEIN, EMGARD, FRIGIDGO, EMEREST, EMSORB, EMRITE, EMERSIST, EMERSAL, EMERY, TRYCOL, TRYDET, TRYFAC, TRYLOX, TRYMEEN, EMERLUBE, EMERSTAT, EMERSOFT, EMERZONE, LANTROL, LANFRAX, EMERWAX, LANOQUAT, NIMLESTEROL, ETHOXYGEL, ETHOXYOL, EMERESSENCE, FIR BALSAM, CHAMOL, PRIVETONE, EMERCIDE, EMERDRI
Associated Companies: National Helium Corporation; RMI Company; Quimic SA de CV (Mexico)
Principal Bank: Morgan Guaranty Trust Company of New York

Financial Information:

	Dec 31 1985(1)	Dec 31 1986
	$'000	$'000
Sales revenues	1,615,900	1,729,600
Income (2)	58,500	55,100
Net income	77,200	75,600
Common dividends	66,600	67,200
Dividends per common share	$2.20	$2.20
Earnings per share (2)	$1.66	$1.54
Earnings per share (3)	$0.62	$0.67
Common stock (4)	30,390	30,712
Shareholders equity	905,300	912,400

(1) restated to reflect the spirits and wines segment as a discontinued operation
(2) from continuing operations
(3) from discontinued operations
(4) shares outstanding in thousands

No of Employees: 10,930

NATIONAL EDUCATION CORPORATION

4361 Birch Street, Newport Beach, CA 92660
Tel: (714) 546-7360

Chairman: John J McNaughton
President: H D Bright (and Chief Executive Officer)
Senior Executive Officers: Jerry W Cwiertnia (Executive VP), Wallace O Laub (Executive VP Marketing), Jeffrey A Brill (VP, Secretary and General Counsel), Robert E Dowdell (VP, President, Education Centers), Michael W Mersch (VP, Finance Chief Financial Officer), Keith K Ogata (Treasurer), Jack C Polley (VP, Corporate Communications), Ronald N Tapper (VP, President DELTAK Training Corp), Christine A Tarantola (Corporate Controller)

PRINCIPAL ACTIVITIES: National Education Corporation is the nation's largest training company, with the industry's broadest range of educational and training services. It offers vocational training through company-operated education centers and through home study, provides training programs for business and publishes supplemental materials used in elementary, secondary and adult education
Principal Subsidiaries: National Education Centers Inc; DELTAK Training Corp; International Correspondence Schools Inc; Steck-Vaughn Company
Principal Bank: Bank of America
Financial Information:

	Dec 31 1985	Dec 31 1986
	$'000	$'000
Sales revenues	183,082	247,250
Income before taxes	20,596	24,100
Net income	12,477	14,984
Earnings per share*	$0.85	$1.00
Common stock	1,903	1,952
Retained income	34,373	49,268
Shareholders equity	64,062	79,722

*fully diluted

No of Employees: 4,780

NATIONAL FORGE CO

Irvine, PA 16329
Tel: (814) 563-7522
Telex: TWX 510 695 2650 matlforge pa

Chairman: Robert O Wilder (and Chief Executive Officer); Vice Chairman: John H Morse (and Chief Financial Officer and Secretary)
President: George H Wells (and Chief Operating Officer)
Senior Executive Officers: Robert Fulton (Executive VP Advanced Materials Group), Charles Olsen (General Manager

Irvine Components Division), William E Erickson (VP, General Manager Crankshaft Division), Steven Yodoff (General Manager Erie Components Division), Richard Pike (General Manager Materials Division), John G Koedel (VP and Treasurer)

PRINCIPAL ACTIVITIES: Manufacture of finish machined forged steel products
Principal Subsidiaries: Industrial Materials Technology Inc
Principal Bank: Mellon Bank
Financial Information:

	Dec 29 1985	Dec 28 1986
	$'000	$,000
Sales revenues	110,785	90,677

Principal Shareholders: Privately held
No of Employees: 1,100

NATIONAL FRUIT PRODUCTS CO, INC

PO Box 2040, Winchester, VA 22601
Tel: (703) 662-3401
Telex: TWX 710 833 0782 nfpc winr

Chairman: Frank Armstrong Jr
President: Frank Armstrong III
Senior Executive Officers: E T McBirney (VP Marketing and Sales), V R Strader Jr (VP and Treasurer), Verlis E Miller (VP Manufacturing)

PRINCIPAL ACTIVITIES: Manufacture of fruit products including juices and canned fruit
Financial Information:

	$'000
Sales revenues	50,000

No of Employees: 500

NATIONAL FUEL GAS CO

30 Rockefeller Plaza, New York, NY 10112
Tel: (212) 541-7533

President: Louis R Reif (and Chief Executive Officer)
Senior Executive Officers: Bernard J Kennedy (Executive VP and General Counsel), Philip C Ackerman (VP Finance)

PRINCIPAL ACTIVITIES: Holding company with interests in the exploration for, and production of natural gas; natural gas supply
Principal Bank: Chase Manhattan Bank
Financial Information:

	$'000
Sales revenues	906,000

No of Employees: 3,400

NATIONAL GAS AND OIL COMPANY

1500 Granville Road, Newark, OH 43055
Tel: (614) 344 2102

Chairman: J W Straker (and Chief Executive Officer)
President: D E Lane (and Chief Operating Officer)
Senior Executive Officers: Richard W Dallas (VP and Chief Engineer), John B Denison (VP and Secretary), M A Russell (VP and Treasurer), Kim A Watkins (Controller), Patrick J McGonagle (Legal Counsel)

PRINCIPAL ACTIVITIES: Supply of natural gas
Principal Subsidiaries: National Energy Service Company; National Gas and Oil Corporation; National Production Corporation
Principal Bank: BancOhio National Bank
Financial Information:

	$'000
Sales revenues	46,390

No of Employees: 140

NATIONAL GUARDIAN CORPORATION

777 W Putnam Avenue, Greenwich, CT 06830
Tel: (203) 561-3500

Chairman: William R Berkley; Vice Chairman: Frank C Cole
President: George V Flagg
Senior Executive Officers: Dennis M Stern (Executive VP, Legal Counsel and Secretary), Robert H Baxter (Senior VP Guard Operations), James J Jackson (Senior VP Alarm Operations), Jeffrey P Ahrenstein (Chief Accounting Officer, Controller and Assistant Treasurer), Andrew M Bursky (Chief Financial Officer, Treasurer and Assistant Secretary)

PRINCIPAL ACTIVITIES: Security systems and protective services
Principal Bank: Chemical Bank
Financial Information:

	$'000
Sales revenues	64,385

No of Employees: 3,350

NATIONAL GYPSUM CO

4500 Lincoln Plaza, Dallas, TX 75201-3318
Tel: (214) 740-4500
Telex: TRT 163195 natgypint dal

Chairman: John P Hayes (and Chief Executive Officer); Vice Chairman: John M Thompson
President: Bernard L Kasriel (and Chief Operating Officer)
Senior Executive Officers: Joseph A Keller (Senior VP Science and Technology), John P Burrall (VP and Controller), James C Quinly (VP International Operations), Axel H Swanson III (VP Finance and Treasurer), David F Byrne (VP Human Resources), Paul T Even (Assistant Treasurer), Edward W Fordyce Jr (VP and General Counsel), John L Genung (VP Corporate Development and Secretary), Edward A Porter (VP)

PRINCIPAL ACTIVITIES: National Gypsum Company is an integrated, diversified manufacturer and supplier of products and services used worldwide in building and construction. The Company engages in the manufacture, sale and distribution of a broad and strategically important spectrum of high-quality products including gypsum wallboard, predecorated wallboard and wallboard systems; glazed, unglazed ceramic mosaic and quarry tiles; and provides design, engineering and construction services
Parent Company: Aancor Holdings Inc (from May 1 1986)
Principal Subsidiaries: American Olean Tile Co; The Austin Co; Gold Bond Building Products Division
Principal Bank: Banque Paribas, Dallas, TX
Financial Information:

	Dec 31 1985*	Dec 31 1986*
	$'000	$'000
Net sales	1,300,000	1,300,000
Net earnings	55,300	-

*The Company's financial results, other than net sales, are not readily comparable to prior periods because of a substantial increase in interest expense and the depreciation and amortization of acquisition-related items

Principal Shareholders: Private Company
No of Employees: 10,000

NATIONAL HARDGOODS DISTRIBUTORS INC

365 Washington Street, Stoughton, MA 02072
Tel: (614) 341 1810

President: Sheldon M Woolf
Senior Executive Officers: Jerry L Goad (VP and General Manager), Arthur M Kagan (VP and Treasurer), Earl L Woolf

(VP Administration and Corporate Development), Douglas M Cohen (VP Finance)

PRINCIPAL ACTIVITIES: Operation of hardware stores
Principal Subsidiaries: NHD Realty Inc; NHD of RI Inc; Resnicks of MA Inc
Principal Bank: Citizens Bank Providence RI
Financial Information:

	$'000
Sales revenues	27,000

No of Employees: 500

NATIONAL HEALTH CORPORATION

814 South Church Street, Murfreesboro, TN 37130
Tel: (615) 896 5921

Chairman: Carl E Adams
President: W Andrew Adams
Senior Executive Officers: Robert G Adams (Senior VP), Ernest G Burgess III (Senior VP Operations), Richard F LaRoche Jr (Senior VP, Secretary and Legal Counsel), Donald K Daniel (VP and Controller), James O Keathley (VP)

PRINCIPAL ACTIVITIES: Provision of nursing care and related facilities
Financial Information:

	1985	1986
	$'000	$'000
Sales revenues	75,550	87,238
Net income	7,790	6,062

No of Employees: 7,000

NATIONAL HOME PRODUCTS, INC

2525 Main Place Tower, Buffalo, NY 14202
Tel: (716) 854-8070
Telex: TWX 710 522 1829 national buf

Chairman: F S Berg (and President and Chief Executive Officer)
Senior Executive Officers: William E Mooar (VP Finance and Treasurer)

PRINCIPAL ACTIVITIES: Manufacture of snack foods; furniture in kits
Principal Bank: Centerre Bank
Financial Information:

	$'000
Sales revenues	90,000

No of Employees: 1,200

NATIONAL HOMES CORPORATION

Earl & Wallace, Lafayette, IN 47902
Tel: (317) 448-2000
Telex: TWX 810 342 1886 nhc laf

Chairman: Frank P Flynn Jr; Chairman of Executive Committee: Charles A Winding
President: David R Price (and Chief Executive Officer)
Senior Executive Officers: Wilmer R Files (Executive VP), J F Harless (Executive VP Marketing), G W Price (VP), Edmund M Wasmuth (Treasurer)

PRINCIPAL ACTIVITIES: Manufacture of sectional homes
Principal Subsidiaries: NRC Inc
Principal Bank: First National Bank of Chicago
Financial Information:

	$'000
Sales revenues	70,000

No of Employees: 800

NATIONAL INTERGROUP, INC

20 Stanwix Street, Pittsburgh, PA 15222
Tel: (412) 394-4100
Telex: WUT 866122 nat stl pgh

Chairman: Howard M Love (and Chief Executive Officer); Vice Chairman: Richard S Smith
President: James E Haas (and Chief Operating Officer)
Senior Executive Officers: Fred E Tucker (Senior VP Public Affairs), Benno A Bernt (VP and Chief Financial Officer), Larry J Pilon (VP Human Resources), Thomas J Mavor (VP Administration and Management Services), William Rodgers Jr (VP, Secretary and General Counsel), John A Rosicky (VP and Controller)

PRINCIPAL ACTIVITIES: Holding company with interests in steel, aluminum, oil, mining, financial services and wholesale drug distribution
Principal Bank: Citibank
Financial Information:

	Dec 31 1985	Dec 31 1986
	$'000	$'000
Sales revenues	2,370,350	4,166,294
Net (loss)	(15,230)	(88,451)
Earnings (loss) per share	-	($4.50)
Shareholders equity	911,583	763,023

No of Employees: 7,000

NATIONAL INVESTORS LIFE

Second & Broadway, Little Rock, AR 72203
Tel: (501) 376-3261

Chairman: Tony T Dechant
Directors: Sherman M Jenson (and Chief Executive Officer)

PRINCIPAL ACTIVITIES: Life insurance
Financial Information:

	Dec 31 1986
	$'000
Premium income	382
Investment income	148,989

No of Employees: 65

NATIONAL LIFE INSURANCE CO

National Life Drive, Montpelier, VT 05604
Tel: (802) 229-3333
Telex: WUT 954 623 nlico mont

Chairman: Richard I Fricke (and Chief Executive Officer); Vice Chairmen: Richard J Borda, Ronald E Bishop, John H Harding
President: Frederic H Bertrand (and Chief Operating Officer)
Senior Executive Officers: James B Antell (Senior VP Marketing), Robert D MacLennan (Senior VP Financial Operations and Treasurer), Claude J Trudel (Senior VP Planning), William V Boyd (Senior VP Information Systems), William L Cassidy (Senior VP Home Office Services), Keniston P Merrill (Senior VP Common Stocks), Ronald J Majewicz (VP Auditing), Ralph T Heath (VP Mortgage and Real Estate Investment), Beverly B Bagalio (VP Pension), Richard J Geisler (VP Product Implementation), L James L Rivers (VP Automation Support), Philip A Ware (VP Product Development), Michael J Sheehy (VP Marketable Fixed Income Securities), Theodore N von Wallmenich (VP and Chief Actuary), Mark J Levesque (VP Information Systems), William R Schillhammer Jr (VP Media Director), Brian Vachon (VP Communications), Edward S Blackwell (VP Fixed Income Securities), Robert J Ricketts (VP Agency), Alden Guild (VP and General Counsel), Orland F Smith Jr (VP Human Resources and Administration), Thomas H MacLeay (VP and Controller), William L Wagner Jr (VP New Business)

PRINCIPAL ACTIVITIES: Life insurance
Principal Bank: Rhode Island Hospital Trust National Bank
Financial Information:

	Dec 31 1985	Dec 31 1986
	$'000	$'000
Premium income	430,107	488,273
Investment income	205,444	215,625

No of Employees: 3,600

NATIONAL LUMBER AND SUPPLY INC
17102 New Hope Street, Fountain Valley, CA 92708
Tel: (714) 751 3970

Chairman: Sol Jaffee
President: Melvin Jaffee (and Chief Executive Officer)
Senior Executive Officers: Jordan C Silverberg (Executive VP), V J Carnevale (VP, Chief Financial Officer and Treasurer), Craig R Schumacher (VP Operations), Richard C Sturt (VP Administration and Secretary)

PRINCIPAL ACTIVITIES: Discount stores for home improvement products
Principal Bank: Bank of America NT & SA
Financial Information:

	$'000
Sales revenues	136,000

No of Employees: 1,300

NATIONAL MANUFACTURING CO
One First Avenue, Sterling, IL 61081
Tel: (815) 625-1320
Telex: WUT 206902 natl mfg ster

Chairman: Joseph H Bittorf
President: Keith W Benson Jr
Senior Executive Officers: M M Benson (VP Purchasing), J L Hay (VP Finance and Treasurer), J D Bittorf (VP Manufacturing and Secretary), J W McConnell (VP Marketing), L M Stolmeier (VP Sales)

PRINCIPAL ACTIVITIES: Manufacture of door fittings
Principal Bank: Continental Illinois National Bank
Financial Information:

	$'000
Sales revenues	50,000

No of Employees: 600

NATIONAL MARINE SERVICE, INC
1750 Brentwood Blvd, St Louis, MO 63144
Tel: (314) 968-2700
Telex: TWX 910 7601652 natmarines tl

Chairman: C J Gauthier; Vice Chairman: T L Fisher
President: G H Fornell
Senior Executive Officers: T K Babington (VP and Secretary), D D Baringer (VP), C H Walters (VP)

PRINCIPAL ACTIVITIES: Shipping and marine engineering
Parent Company: Nicor Inc, Naperville, IL
Principal Bank: Manufacturers Hanover Trust Company
Financial Information:

	$'000
Sales revenues	80,000

No of Employees: 700

NATIONAL MEDICAL CARE INC
1601 Trapelo Road, Waltham, MA 02154
Tel: (617) 466-9850
Telex: TWX 710 3211419 natlmedcare

Chairman: Constantine L Hampers (and Chief Executive Officer)
Senior Executive Officers: Edmund G Lowrie (Senior VP), Samuel J Scialabba (Senior VP), A Miles Nogelo (VP and Chief Financial Officer), Robert W Armstrong III (VP and Controller), Timothy I McFeeley (VP and Secretary), Robert K Maloney (VP), Ernestine Lowrie (VP), William D Whitaker (VP)

PRINCIPAL ACTIVITIES: Health care services and supplies
Principal Bank: The First National Bank of Boston
Financial Information:

	$'000
Sales revenues	330,000

No of Employees: 5,000

NATIONAL MEDICAL ENTERPRISES, INC
11620 Wilshire Boulevard, Los Angeles, CA 90025
Tel: (213) 479-5526
Telex: 664389 NMEUSA LSA

Chairman: Richard K Earmer (and Chief Executive Officer)
President: Leonard Cohen (and Chief Operating Officer)
Senior Executive Officers: John C Bedrosian (Senior Executive VP), Daniel R Baty (Executive VP), Peter deWetter (Executive VP), Taylor R Jenson (Executive VP and Chief Financial Officer), James P Livingston (Executive VP), Maris Andersons (Senior VP and Treasurer), Marcus E Powers (Senior VP and General Counsel), Gerald L Stevens (Senior VP), Sidney F Tyler Jr (Senior VP), Scott M Brown (VP and Secretary)

PRINCIPAL ACTIVITIES: National Medical Enterprises (NME) owns, operates and manages approximately 500 facilities in all fields of patient care: acute care, rehabilitation, psychiatric and chemical dependency treatment, long term care and home care. NME also provides comprehensive services to health care providers across the United States and overseas. Among the world's largest health care companies, NME has been the most diversified since its founding in 1969. Today, the company represents a complete health care system, as demonstrated in its medical campuses that provide all forms of community health services and facilities at one site - all planned, constructed and operated by collaborating NME subsidiaries. A typical campus includes acute care, rehabilitation, psychiatric and convalescent hospitals; related outpatient services; medical office buildings; a pharmacy; and home care supplies and services. The NME International Group extends all services of the company to health care providers in other countries. Currently NME owns two operating hospitals in the United Kingdom, has two more under construction and manages a fifth. In Singapore, NME owns and operates 485-bed Mount Elizabeth Hospital and in Kuala Lumpur NME operates by contract the new Subang Jaya Medical Centre
Principal Subsidiaries: NME Hospitals Inc; Rehab Hospital Services Corporation; Psychiatric Institutes of America; The Hillhaven Corporation; National Medical Homecare; Cadem Corporation; Stolte Inc; CuraCare. Other subsidiaries specialize in hospital office systems, equipment leasing services, purchasing and specialized patient services such as hemodialysis and occupational health care
Principal Bank: Manufacturers Hanover Trust Company
Financial Information:

	May 31 1986 $'000
Sales revenues	2,962,000
Net income	85,000
Earnings per share	$1.08
Shareholders equity	1,010,000

No of Employees: 72,000

NATIONAL METAL CRAFTERS
4500 Kishwaukee St., Box 7005, Rockford, IL 61125
Tel: (815) 962-7100

Chairman: Charles W Holzwarth (and President)
Senior Executive Officers: Donald L Schultz (VP)

PRINCIPAL ACTIVITIES: Manufacture of metal fasteners
Parent Company: Keystone Consolidated Industries Inc
Financial Information:

	$'000
Sales revenues	50,000

No of Employees: 750

NATIONAL MICRONETICS INC
5600 Kearney Mesa Road, San Diego, CA 92111
Tel: (914) 338-0333
Fax: (914) 338-0377

Chairman: Charles J Lawson Jr (and Chief Executive Officer)

President: Eric W Markrud (and Chief Financial Officer)
Senior Executive Officers: Jan V Peer (Executive VP), Robert C Ristagno (VP and Corporate Controller), Joseph R Sequenzin (VP), Tugrul Yasar (VP)

PRINCIPAL ACTIVITIES: Manufacture of computer products (magnetic recording heads for computer disc drives)
Principal Banks: Wells Fargo; Chemical Bank
Financial Information:

	Jun 30 1986	Jun 30 1987
	$'000	$'000
Sales revenues	36,332	35,385
(Loss) before taxes*	(9,121)	(3,074)
Net (loss)	(7,152)	(1,585)
(Loss) per share	($0.99)	($0.33)
Common stock	918	933
Retained (deficit)	(38,616)	(40,201)
Shareholders equity	10,078	8,855

*and discontinued operations

Principal Shareholders: Polaroid (10%)
No of Employees: 600

NATIONAL MINE SERVICE COMPANY
PO Box 310, Indiana, PA 15701-0310
Tel: (412) 349 7100
Telex: TWX 710 6642012 nmsc pgh

Chairman: J M Little
President: Herbert F Gerhard (and Chief Executive Officer)
Senior Executive Officers: Thomas J DeWitt (VP and General Manager Hydraulics), J G La Forte (VP and General Manager Distribution), John D Weagraff (VP Finance and Controller), Samuel D Scott (VP Personnel Administration and Systems)

PRINCIPAL ACTIVITIES: Manufacture of machinery for the mining industry
Parent Company: Anderson Strathclyde plc, UK
Principal Subsidiaries: National Mine Service (Canada) Ltd; International Mine Service Co
Principal Bank: Pittsburgh National Bank
Financial Information:

	$'000
Sales revenues	62,000

No of Employees: 500

NATIONAL OATS CO, INC
1515 H Avenue NE, Cedar Rapids, IA 52402
Tel: (319) 364-9161
Telex: WUT 46 4440 natl oats cdr

President: W F Hanser (and Chief Executive Officer)
Senior Executive Officers: Nevin Mederith (VP Marketing), C S Vermeersch (VP Finance and Secretary), G Busha (VP Manufacturing)

PRINCIPAL ACTIVITIES: Manufacture of cereal products
Parent Company: Curtice Burns Inc
Financial Information:

	$'000
Sales revenues	50,000

No of Employees: 350

NATIONAL PATENT DEVELOPMENT CORPORATION
9 West 57th St, New York, NY 10019
Tel: (212) 826-8500

Chairman: Jess Larson
President: Jerome I Feldman (and Chief Executive Officer)
Senior Executive Officers: Martin M Pollak (Executive VP and Treasurer), David A Rapaport (Senior VP and Secretary), William Lester (Group VP), Mark Adams (VP Corporate Development), Scott N Greenberg (VP Finance), Samuel Ronel (VP Research and Development), Charles M Rosenfeld (VP Employee Relations)

PRINCIPAL ACTIVITIES: Manufacture of optical and medical equipment
Principal Bank: Marine Midland Bank
Financial Information:

	$'000
Sales revenues	128,000

No of Employees: 2,400

NATIONAL PENN BANCSHARES INC
Philadelphia and Reading Avenues, Boyertown, PA 19512
Tel: (215) 367 6001

President: James K Boyer (and Subsidiary Officer)
Senior Executive Officers: Lawrence T Jilk Jr (Executive VP and Subsidiary Officer), Wayne R Weidener (Treasurer) Sandra L Spayd (Secretary)

PRINCIPAL ACTIVITIES: Banking
Principal Bank: National Bank of Boyertown

No of Employees: 240

NATIONAL PIZZA COMPANY
720 W 20th Street, Pittsburg, KS 66762
Tel: (316) 231-3390
Telefax: (316) 231-1188

Chairman: O Gene Bicknell (and Chief Executive Officer)
President: Gordon W Elliott (and Chief Executive Officer)
Senior Executive Officers: J J Fitzsimmons (VP, Chief Financial Officer, and Assistant Secretary), John B Towner (Secretary)

PRINCIPAL ACTIVITIES: The Company is the largest Pizza Hut franchisee in the world and operates 248 Pizza Hut restaurants and delivery units in thirteen states
Trade Names: Pizza Hut
Principal Banks: Bank of Oklahoma; First Republic, Continental Illinois
Financial Information:

	Mar 31 1986	Mar 31 1987
	$'000	$'000
Sales revenues	68,064	96,479
Income before taxes	10,187	13,787
Net income	5,784	7,387
Earnings per share	$0.70	$0.88
Common stock	82	82
Retained income	16,187	15,854
Shareholders equity	26,095	26,369

Principal Shareholders: Gene Bicknell (65%); MacKay-Shields Financial Corporation (5.3%); Gordon W Elliott (4.7%); All directors and executive officers as a group (75.1%)
No of Employees: 5,200

NATIONAL PRESTO INDUSTRIES, INC
Eau Claire, WI 54701
Tel: (715) 839-2121
Telex: TWX 910 2821630 natl presto

Chairman: Melvin S Cohen
President: Joseph H Berney
Senior Executive Officers: Francis C Sorrentino (Executive VP), Gilbert L Braun (VP Engineering), Maryjo R Cohen (Treasurer), James F Bartl (Secretary)

PRINCIPAL ACTIVITIES: Manufacture of domestic electrical appliances and ammunition
Trade Names: Presto (R), PopCorn Now (R), AboveAll, FryDaddy (R), FryBaby (R), GranPappy (R), DiamondCoat (R), Control Master (R), Liddle Griddle (R), SilverStone (R), KitchenKettle, CutUp, High'N Dry, "sweep of heat".
Principal Subsidiaries: Presto Manufacturing Co; Presto Products Manufacturing Co; Canton Manufacturing Co; National Holding Investment Co; National Defense Corp; Century Leasing and Liquidating Inc; Presto Export Ltd
Principal Bank: First Wisconsin National Bank

Financial Information:

	$'000
Sales revenues	96,396

No of Employees: 1,100

NATIONAL PRODUCTION SYSTEMS

9100 S Norwalk Blvd, Los Nietos, CA 90606
Tel: (213) 699-0931

President: David A Higbee
Senior Executive Officers: Dale E Gilbert (Plant Manager), Richard L McCarter (Plant Controller), F P O'Brien (Marketing Manager)

PRINCIPAL ACTIVITIES: Manufacture of machinery and equipment for the oil industry
Parent Company: National Supply Co
Financial Information:

	$'000
Sales revenues	80,000

No of Employees: 200

NATIONAL ROLLING MILLS CO

Morehall Road, Malvern, PA 19355
Tel: (215) 644-6700

President: John H McCoy
Senior Executive Officers: Richard Ryan (VP Acoustical Sales), Thomas F Kilcullen Jr (VP and Treasurer), James A Fisher (VP Steel Sales), Donald Kimmel (VP Personnel), Michael J Civitello (VP Steel Manufacturing), Robert Hogan (VP Acoustical Manufacturing)

PRINCIPAL ACTIVITIES: Steel processing and suspension systems for acoustical ceilings
Parent Company: Worthington Industries, Columbus, OH
Principal Bank: Philadelphia National Bank
Financial Information:

	$'000
Sales revenues	70,000

No of Employees: 650

NATIONAL SANITARY SUPPLY CO

13217 S Figueroa, Los Angeles, CA 90061
Tel: (213) 770-1970
Telex: WUT 506276 nat san supply

Chairman: Albert B Rubin
President: Robert B Garber (and Treasurer)
Senior Executive Officers: Charles Lane (Executive VP Purchasing), Thomas Lane (VP, Secretary and Comptroller)

PRINCIPAL ACTIVITIES: Manufacture of soaps and detergents
Parent Company: Chemed Corp
Principal Bank: Security Pacific National Bank
Financial Information:

	$'000
Sales revenues	50,000

No of Employees: 450

NATIONAL SEMICONDUCTOR CORPORATION

2900 Semiconductor Drive, Santa Clara, CA 95051
Tel: (408) 721-5000
Telex: TWX 910 3399 240 nscsbns snta a

Chairman: Peter J Sprague
President: Charles E Sporck
Senior Executive Officers: David Martin (Executive VP), James Smaha (Executive VP), J Philip Russell (VP and Controller)

PRINCIPAL ACTIVITIES: Manufacture of semiconductors and data processing equipment
Principal Bank: Bank of America
Financial Information:

	May 31 1985 $'000	May 31 1986 $'000
Sales revenues	1,787,500	1,478,100
Net income (loss)	43,200	(91,500)
Earnings (loss) per share	$0.48	($1.10)
Shareholders equity	681,200	717,000

No of Employees: 38,000

NATIONAL SEMICONDUCTOR DATACHECKER/DTS CORP

124 Acton Street, Maynard, MA 01754
Tel: (617) 897-3221

President: Johnny M Humphreys
Senior Executive Officers: Larry A Penattori (VP Finance and Administration), Mark A Parrish Jr (VP Marketing and Sales), Rudolf Friessnig (VP Marketing), Klaus Hushke (VP International Operations), Phil Ahlfeldt (VP Sales), Edward H Sonn (VP), Robert D O'Brien (VP and Controller), Ray Irvine (VP Engineering)

PRINCIPAL ACTIVITIES: Manufacture of cash registers
Parent Company: National Semiconductor Corporation, New York, NY
Principal Bank: Bank of New England
Financial Information:

	$'000
Sales revenues	90,000

No of Employees: 2,300

NATIONAL SERVICE INDUSTRIES, INC

1180 Peachtree Street NE, Atlanta, GA 30309
Tel: (404) 892-2400

Chairman: Erwin Zaban (and Chief Executive Officer)
President: Sidney Kirschner (and Chief Operating Officer)
Senior Executive Officers: Robert H Creviston (Senior VP and Chief Financial Officer), David Levy (Senior VP and Secretary), James A Schroeder (Group VP), Don W Hubble (Group VP), Henry R Dressel (VP Taxes)

PRINCIPAL ACTIVITIES: Manufacture of a wide range of products which include furniture, electrical products, protective gloves, chemicals and stationery; operation of a linen supply service
Principal Bank: The First National Bank of Atlanta
Financial Information:

	Aug 31 1986 $'000
Sales revenues	1,282,922
Net income	71,341
Earnings per share	$2.17
Shareholders equity	462,907

No of Employees: 18,700

NATIONAL STANDARD COMPANY

1618 Terminal Road, Niles, MI 49120
Tel: (616) 683 8100

Chairman: Gerald H Frieling Jr (and President and Chief Executive Officer)
Senior Executive Officers: Norman J Birch (Group VP), Richard A Crawford (Group VP), John A Johnson (VP Division), D Gilmore MacNeill (VP Administration), Michael B Savitska (VP Division), William D Grafer (Treasurer and Controller), Rene J VanSteelandt (VP Division, Legal Counsel and Secretary), Charles J Ebeling (VP Research and Development and Engineering), Thomas I Rodhouse (VP Product Area)

PRINCIPAL ACTIVITIES: Manufacture of cables and wires
Principal Subsidiaries: Strip Steel Inc; National Standard Co of Canada Ltd; National Standard Co Ltd (UK); National Standard Co (SA) (Pty) Ltd (South Africa)

Financial Information:

	$'000
Sales revenues	247,440

No of Employees: 2,870

NATIONAL STARCH AND CHEMICAL CORPORATION

10 Finderne Avenue, Bridgwater, NJ 08807
Tel: (201) 685-5000
Telex: TWX 710 480 9272 nsc b wtr

Chairman: Wallace K Grubman (and Chief Executive Officer); Chairman of Executive Committee: Donald D Pascal; Chairman of Finance Committee: Frank K Greenwall
President: Nicholas G Marotta (and Chief Operating Officer)
Senior Executive Officers: A G Battaglia (Group VP), Daniel F Peck (Group VP), Robert B Albert (VP Finance and Chief Financial Officer), Herbert J Baumgarten (VP and Secretary), Robert B Hennessy (VP Human Resources), Frank V Caccavo (VP), Irwin Cohen (VP), Robert A DeWolfe (VP), James A Kennedy (VP), Alexander J McCarthy (VP), Leslie B Moberly (VP), William H Stone (VP), Thomas F Walsh (VP)

PRINCIPAL ACTIVITIES: Manufacture of starch and a range of specialty chemicals
Parent Company: Unilever NV, Netherlands
Financial Information:

	Dec 31 1985	Dec 31 1986
	$'000	$'000
Sales revenues	880,570	1,063,644
Net income	66,010	71,806
Shareholders equity	375,200	402,905

No of Employees: 5,700

NATIONAL STEEL & SHIPBUILDING CO

Harbor Drive & 28th Street, San Diego, CA 92138
Tel: (619) 696-7000
Telex: WUI 6971 004 nasc uw

Chairman: W J Deasy
President: R H Vortmann (and Chief Executive Officer)
Senior Executive Officers: A W Lutter Jr (Senior VP Marketing and Business Affairs), F W Hallett (VP Finance, Treasurer and Controller), R D Jacobs (VP Business Affairs and Secretary), D A Spanninga (Senior VP), J Tucker (VP Engineering), Jim Scott (VP Materials), S French (VP Repair)

PRINCIPAL ACTIVITIES: Shipbuilding and shiprepairing
Parent Company: Morrison-Knudsen Co Inc, Boise, ID
Principal Bank: Bank of America
Financial Information:

	$'000
Sales revenues	300,000

No of Employees: 3,000

NATIONAL TWIST DRILL & TOOL CO

341 Industrial Drive, Lexington, SC 29072
Tel: (313) 651-9531

President: W Lazich
Senior Executive Officers: Louis A Mitzelfeld (VP Manufacturing), C Kremser (VP Marketing), Roger H Griffis (VP Finance)

PRINCIPAL ACTIVITIES: Manufacture of cutting tools and drills
Parent Company: Regal-Beloit Corporation
Principal Bank: National Bank of Detroit
Financial Information:

	$'000
Sales revenues	60,000

No of Employees: 1,000

NATIONAL UNION ELECTRIC CORPORATION

1201 E Bell Street, Bloomington, IL 61701
Tel: (309) 828-2367

Chairman: Robert P Dole (and President)
Senior Executive Officers: L W Kenney (VP Finance and Treasurer)

PRINCIPAL ACTIVITIES: Manufacture of domestic electrical appliances and air conditioning equipment
Parent Company: Electroloux Group AB, Sweden
Principal Bank: Continental Illinois National Bank and Trust Co
Financial Information:

	$'000
Sales revenues	300,000

No of Employees: 3,300

NATIONAL VALVE & MFG CO

701 Alpha Drive, Pittsburgh, PA 15238
Tel: (412) 963-8200
Telex: TWX 710 6642 024 navcobasic pgh

Chairman: William T Solomon; Vice Chairman: Henry E Haller Jr
President: William C Biddle
Senior Executive Officers: Joseph P Buczkowski (Senior VP), John A Krill (Senior VP), Clyde F Stone (Senior VP), Ralph L Trew (Secretary and Treasurer)

PRINCIPAL ACTIVITIES: Design, manufacture and erection of industrial piping and piping for the energy industry
Principal Bank: Mellon Bank
Financial Information:

	$'000
Sales revenues	64,000

No of Employees: 550

NATIONAL WESTERN LIFE INSURANCE COMPANY

850 East Anderson Lane, Austin, TX 78776
Tel: (512) 836 1010

Chairman: Robert L Moody (and Chief Executive Officer)
President: Harry L Edwards (and Chief Operating Officer)
Senior Executive Officers: Robert R Johnson (Executive VP Administration), Richard C Andrews (VP Employee Benefits), Charles Baley (VP Data Processing), Richard L Boswell (VP and Actuary), Robert L Busby III (VP and Controller), David G Caldwell (VP and Legal Counsel), Richard M Edwards (VP International), Jose M Galano (VP International), James V Robinson (VP and Secretary), John R Howard (VP Finance and Treasurer), Andrew M Hansen (VP Marketing), Weldon K Huffman (VP Systems Management and Assistant Secretary), Ralph K Schmitz (VP Sales), Larry D White (VP), James A Kincl (VP Business Development), Bobby Laughlin (VP), Charles D Milos (VP) Investment Analysis), James R Naiser (VP Systems Development), Harold L Ponder (VP Risk Selection)

PRINCIPAL ACTIVITIES: Life insurance
Principal Bank: First City National Bank of Austin
Financial Information:

	$'000
Revenues	230,530

No of Employees: 200

NATIONAL WESTMINSTER BANK USA

175 Water Street, New York, NY 10038
Tel: (212) 623-4000
Telex: RCA 2323 69

Chairman: William T Knowles (and Chief Executive Officer)
President: Robert F Wallace (and Chief Operating Officer)
Senior Executive Officers: John Gale (Senior Executive VP and Chief Administration Officer), James Alban-Davies (Executive VP International Management and Administration), Craig S Bartlett Jr (Executive VP), Robert G Chapman Jr (Executive VP), Burt R Clark (Executive VP), Brendon Dugan (Executive VP, US Administration Group), Robert W Keeler (Executive VP Operations Group), Carl W Klemme (Executive VP

Administration), Paul C Krench (Executive VP Regional Group Administration), Edward McDougal (Executive VP Human Resources, Group Staff), L Douglas O'Brien (Executive VP Community Banking, Group Administration), John A Petts (Executive VP Corporate Planning Group), Allan C Schreiber (Executive VP New York City Administration)

PRINCIPAL ACTIVITIES: Banking
Parent Company: National Westminster Bank Plc, UK
Financial Information:

	Dec 31 1985	Dec 31 1986
	$'000	$'000
Net income	54,575	67,673
Shareholders equity	-	621,044
Deposits	7,910,161	8,784,311
Total assets	9,796,328	11,080,016

No of Employees: 4,700

NATIONAL WIRE PRODUCTS CORPORATION

Fischer Road & Penna RR, Baltimore, MD 21222
Tel: (301) 477-1700
Telex: WUT 87955 nat wire bal

Chairman: Ray C Faust (and President)
Senior Executive Officers: G A Seling (Executive VP Finance, Secretary and Treasurer), Ross French (VP Commercial), Ray C Faust Jr (VP Operations), Frank Burns (VP Finance)

PRINCIPAL ACTIVITIES: Manufacture of wire products for concrete reinforcement and masonry reinforcement
Parent Company: Ivaco Inc
Principal Bank: Maryland National Bank
Financial Information:

	$'000
Sales revenues	90,000

No of Employees: 650

NATIONWIDE LIFE INSURANCE CO

One Nationwide Plaza, Columbus, OH 43216
Tel: (614) 227-7111

Chairman: John E Fisher (and Chief Executive Officer)
President: John L Marakas
Senior Executive Officers: Peter F Frenzer (Executive VP), Jack A Baughn (Senior VP), Edmond Coughlin (Senior VP), Ohmer O Crowell (Senior VP), Harvey S Galloway Jr (Senior VP and Chief Actuary), Gordon E McCutchan (Senior VP and General Counsel), D Richard McFerson (Senior VP Finance), Robert H Ourant (Senior VP Corporate Services), Raymond L Wilson (Senior VP Life and Health Operations), G W Woodard (VP and Treaurer)

PRINCIPAL ACTIVITIES: Life insurance
Parent Company: Nationwide Corp
Principal Bank: Bank One Columbus
Financial Information:

	Dec 31 1985	Dec 31 1986
	$'000	$'000
Premium income	827,970	1,013,129
Investment income	320,530	386,565

No of Employees: 7,400

NATURE'S BOUNTY INC

90 Orville Drive, Bohemia, NY 11716
Tel: (515) 567 9500

Chairman: Arthur Rudolph (and President)
Senior Executive Officers: Harvey Kamil (Executive VP and Secretary), Aram Garabedian (Senior VP), Michael C Duban (VP and Legal Counsel), Dominic Liberato (Treasurer), Irwin Wolin (VP Marketing), Abraham H Kleinman (VP Manufacturing), James E Taylor (VP Production)

PRINCIPAL ACTIVITIES: Production of chemicals for food industry; vitamin supplements; cosmetic preparations
Financial Information:

	$'000
Sales revenues	40,000

No of Employees: 450

NATURE'S SUNSHINE PRODUCTS INC

1655 North Main Street, PO Box 1000, Spanish Fork, UT 84660
Tel: (801) 798 9861

Chairman: Kristine F Hughes
President: Kerry O Asay
Senior Executive Officers: Richard S Hughes (Senior VP), Kim S Asay (VP), Brent F Ashworth (VP, Secretary and Legal Counsel), Vaugh R Erickson (VP and Treasurer), Eugene L Hughes (VP Purchasing), Joseph A Speirs (VP)

PRINCIPAL ACTIVITIES: Manufacture of medicinal preparations
Financial Information:

	$'000
Sales revenues	29,000

No of Employees: 200

NAUGLES INC

2932 East Nutwood Avenue, Fullerton, CA 92634
Tel: (714) 532 0700

Chairman: F Wayne Withers (and Chief Executive Officer); Vice Chairman: Richard N Naugle
President: Richard Birmingham
Senior Executive Officers: Jim Ken Masuda (Executive VP), John A Fisher (VP Operations), Jeff Naugle (VP Operations), Anita J Bent (Controller and Assistant Treasurer)

PRINCIPAL ACTIVITIES: Operation and management of restaurants
Parent Company: Collins Foods International Inc
Principal Bank: Lloyds Bank of California
Financial Information:

	$'000
Sales revenues	126,000

No of Employees: 5,500

NAVISTAR INTERNATIONAL (FORMERLY INTERNATIONAL HARVESTER CO)

401 N Michigan Avenue, Chicago, IL 60611
Tel: (312) 836-2000

Chairman: Donald D Lennox (and Chief Executive Officer); Vice Chairmen: James C Cotting (and Chief Financial Officer)
President: Neil A Springer (and Chief Operating Officer)
Senior Executive Officers: Roxanne J Decyk (Senior VP Corporate Relations), Robert I Morrison (VP and Controller), Robert C Lannert (VP and Treasurer), John J Bongiorno (VP Financial Services), Michael Clayton (VP Corporate Planning), Gary E Dewel (VP Materials Management), Dean P Stanley (VP Engineering), John R Horne (VP and General Manager Engine and Foundry)

PRINCIPAL ACTIVITIES: Manufacture of agricultural machinery and heavy-duty vehicles
Financial Information:

	Oct 31 1986
	$'000
Sales revenues	3,356,534
Net income	1,739

No of Employees: 16,840

NBD BANCORP, INC

611 Woodward Avenue, Detroit, MI 48226
Tel: (313) 225-1000
Telex: ITT 4320060 NATIONBKDET

Chairman: Charles T Fisher III (and President)

Senior Executive Officers: Richard H Cummings (Senior Vice Chairman), Verne G Istock (Vice Chairman), Thomas H Jeffs II (Vice Chairman)

PRINCIPAL ACTIVITIES: NBD Bancorp Inc, the largest bank holding company in the State of Michigan, is a diversified financial services provider. In the 14 years since the holding company was formed, it has grown to 19 domestic banks in key Michigan markets and 17 non-bank subsidiaries, encompassing finance, mortgage, insurance, trust, leasing and venture capital. Its principal subsidiary, National Bank of Detroit, is the largest bank in Michigan, Ohio and Indiana. NBD operates branch offices in London, Frankfurt and Tokyo, a Canadian-chartered commercial bank headquartered in Toronto, a consumer credit processing company and has financial affiliates in Australia, the Far East and South America. Among the largest financial institutions in the United States, NBD Bankcorp offers a broad array of financial services to corporate, retail and trust customers across the country and around the world.
Principal Subsidiaries: Bank Subsidiaries:- National Bank of Detroit and its subsidiares, International Bank of Detroit and National Bank of Detroit, Canada; NBD Alpena Bank; NBD Ann Arbor NA; NBD Cadillac Bank; NBD Commerce Bank, Lansing; NBD Dearborn Bank NA; NBD Evart Bank NA; NBD F&M Bank NA; NBD Grand Valley Bank NA; NBD Monroe County Bank; NBD Northwest Bank NA; NBD Port Huron Bank NA; NBD Portage Bank; NBD Roscommon Bank; NBD Saginaw; NBD Sandusky Bank; NBD Troy Bank NA; *Community State Bank of Fowlerville; *Genesee Merchants Bank & Trust Co; *Peoples State Bank of Caro; Pontiac State Bank. Non-Bank Subsidiaries:- Computer Communications of America; Corporate Funding Inc; Michigan Capital and Service Inc; NBD Building Company; NBD Business Finance Inc; NBD Delaware Bank; NBD Equity Corp; NBD Financial Services of Florida Inc; NBD Financial Services of Michigan Inc; NBD Insurance Agency Inc; NBD Insurance Company; NBD Leasing Company; NBD Management Corp; NBD Mortgage Company; NBD Service Corp; NBD Trust Company of Florida NA; Safe Deposit Company of Michigan; *United Michigan Mortgage Co, *Subsidiary of United Michigan Corporation affiliated with NBD Bancorp in 1985
Principal Bank: National Bank of Detroit
Financial Information:

	Dec 31 1986 $'000
Net income	145,805
Earnings per share	$3.87
Shareholders equity	1,158,007
Deposits	15,011,323
Total assets	21,176,031

No of Employees: 7,092

NBI INC

3450 Mitchell Lane, Boulder, CO 80301
Tel: (303) 444-5710
Telex: 216159 (NBI UR)

President: T S Kavanagh
Senior Executive Officers: Bernard A Cohen (VP), Charles L Dumas (VP), Richard N LaBarbera (VP), David Klein (Executive VP), Donald A Oliverio (VP), Ernest T Pope (VP), Robert K Reid (VP), Jesse A Simmons (VP, Treasurer, Secretary), Douglas G Swartz (VP)

PRINCIPAL ACTIVITIES: Design, develop, manufacture, sell, and service and support customer systems, in addition to buying office products and selling to end users
Principal Subsidiaries: NBI's The Office Place Inc; Yukon Office Supply Inc; Yukon Office Supply of Hawaii Inc; Yukon Office Supply of Washington Inc; Yukon Paper Distributors Inc; NBI Office Supplies of Washington Inc; Peninsula Office Supply Inc; Commercial Office Products Co; Integrated Solutions Inc; NBI Systems Inc; NBI France Inc; NBI International Inc; NBI Virgin Islands Inc; NBI GmbH; NBI SA; NBI Limited; NBI Canada Inc
Principal Bank: Bank of America
Financial Information:

	Jun 30 1987 $'000
Sales revenues	278,255
Net (loss)	(5,405)
(Loss) per share	($0.63)
Retained income	40,732
Shareholders equity	91,177

No of Employees: 3,145

NCH CORPORATION

2727 Chemsearch Blvd, Irving, TX 75062
Tel: (214) 438-0211
Telex: 311422

Chairman: Lester A Levy; Chairman of Executive Committee: Milton P Levy Jr
President: Irvin L Levy
Senior Executive Officers: Earl Nicholson (VP), James H Stone (VP Operations), Allen Piassick (VP and Treasurer)

PRINCIPAL ACTIVITIES: Manufacture of chemicals including industrial cleaning chemicals; metal products
Principal Subsidiaries: (100% owned unless stated): NCH Philippines Inc (65%); National Chemsearch SA (51%); NCH Venezuela SA (51%); Membership Services Inc; American Display Inc; LSP Specialty Products Co; American Allsafe Co; Allsafe Products of Canada Ltd; Allsafe AG; Proquicheme-Produtos Quimicos Industrias Lda (60%); LCH Colombia SA (70%); NCH Ecuador SA (85%)
Principal Bank: First National Bank
Financial Information:

	$'000
Sales revenues	348,000

No of Employees: 7,730

NCNB CORPORATION

One NCNB Plaza, Charlotte, NC 28255
Tel: (704) 374-5000

Chairman: Hugh L McColl Jr; Vice Chairman: James W Thompson
President: Francis B Kemp
Senior Executive Officers: Timothy P Hartman (Corporate Executive VP Chief Financial Officer), James M Berry (Corporate Executive VP Corporate and International Banking), James H Hance (Executive VP Finance), Charles L Cooley (Executive VP Personnel), Frank L Gentry (Senior VP Planning), J W Kiser (Senior VP and Secretary), C D Lohri (Senior VP Auditing), Russell J Page (Senior VP Corporate Communications)

PRINCIPAL ACTIVITIES: Banking
Financial Information:

	Dec 31 1985 $'000	Dec 31 1986 $'000
Net income	164,490	198,765
Earnings per share*	$2.30	$2.53
Deposits	13,950,398	18,519,315
Total assets	19,754,317	27,472,434

*restated for 2-for-1 stock split November 20 1986

No of Employees: 12,107 (full time)

NCR CORPORATION

1700 S Patterson Blvd, Dayton, OH 45479
Tel: (513) 445-5000
Telex: 28-8093

Chairman: Charles E Exley Jr (and President)

Senior Executive Officers: William F Buster (Executive VP), Donald J Herman (Executive VP), R Elton White (Executive VP), Gilbert P Williamson (Executive VP)

PRINCIPAL ACTIVITIES: Business information processing systems for worldwide markets. Generally, NCR products can be grouped according to the following categories:- General purpose computer systems, which range from small business systems to large mainframe processors. Industry - specific workstations for retail, financial, manufacturing and other markets. General purpose workstations which include personal computers and data entry/inquiry workstations. Data communications products and systems. Office automation products and systems. Semiconductor products business forms and supplies

Trade Names: NCR WorkSaver, NCR Tower

Principal Subsidiaries: NCR Comten; Applied Digital Data Systems

Principal Bank: Bank of Boston, Boston, MA

Financial Information:

	Dec 31 1985	Dec 31 1986
	$'000	$'000
Revenues	4,317,166	4,881,641
Income before taxes	562,816	619,724
Net income	315,216	336,524
Dividends	86,760	88,545
Dividends per share	$0.88	$0.92
Earnings per share	$3.15	$3.42
Common stock	544,125	544,125
Retained income	2,200,522	2,443,192
Shareholders equity	2,318,360	2,396,332

No of Employees: 62,000 worldwide

NEC AMERICA, INC

532 Broad Hollow Road, Melville, NY 11747

Tel: (516) 752-9700

President: Ko Muroga (and Chief Executive Officer)

Senior Executive Officers: Robert C Miller (Executive VP), Kazamasu Yoneyama (Senior VP Administration), Ryoji Tamura (Senior VP), Itsumi Iwasaki (VP Finance), Satoshi Nakaichi (VP and Secretary)

PRINCIPAL ACTIVITIES: Manufacture of telecommunications and computer equipment

Parent Company: NEC Corporation, Japan

Principal Bank: The Sumitomo Bank

Financial Information:

	$'000
Sales revenues	815,000

No of Employees: 1,400

NEENAH FOUNDRY CO

3121 Brooks Avenue, Neenah, WI 54956

Tel: (414) 725-7000

Telex: WUT 262739 neemah fdry nea

Chairman: E W Aylward (and President)

Senior Executive Officers: R Warren (VP Sales and Marketing), J P Keating (VP Manufcaturing), R G Hathaway (VP Industrial Relations), T R Franklin (VP Finance and Treasurer), Fred C Hathaway (VP Administration and Secretary), Warren E Wilson (VP Production Operations)

PRINCIPAL ACTIVITIES: Manufacture of cast iron products

Financial Information:

	$'000
Sales revenues	90,000

No of Employees: 1,300

NELSON INDUSTRIES, INC

Box 428, Stoughton, WI 53589

Tel: (608) 873-4373

Telex: WUT 265433 nelsonind sthn

President: Rockne G Flowers

Senior Executive Officers: Glenn J LaZotte (VP), Stephen J Dickmann (Secretary), Larry Eriksson (VP Research)

PRINCIPAL ACTIVITIES: Manufacture of silencers and other motor vehicles components

Principal Bank: M & I Bank of Madison

Financial Information:

	$'000
Sales revenues	56,000

No of Employees: 1,150

NELSON, THOMAS, INC

Nelson Place & Elm Hill Pike, Nashville, TN 37214

Tel: (615) 889-9000

Chairman: Sam Moore (and President)

Senior Executive Officers: Robert J Niebel (Executive VP), Thomas Harris (Senior VP and Secretary), Bernard Deefer (VP Marketing), Joe Powers (VP), Wayne Mayo (VP Data Processing), Charles Z Moore (VP)

PRINCIPAL ACTIVITIES: Publishing

Principal Bank: Third National Bank

Financial Information:

	$'000
Sales revenues	71,000

No of Employees: 700

NEPTUNE INTERNATIONAL CORPORATION

4360 Chamblee-Dunwoody Rd, Suite 410, Atlanta, GA 30341

Tel: (404) 458-8111

Telex: RCA 261317 neptu ur

President: William F Shepard

Senior Executive Officers: Richard I York (VP Human Resources), Frank Madonia (VP), Bruce M Wicinski (VP and Controller)

PRINCIPAL ACTIVITIES: Manufacture of water, industrial and petroleum meters including development of the new central meter reading system which enables gas, water and electric meters to be read electronically from a central location

Parent Company: Schlumberger Ltd, New York, NY

Principal Bank: Morgan Guaranty

Financial Information:

	$'000
Sales revenues	85,000

No of Employees: 950

NERCO INC

111 SW Columbia, Portland, OR 97201

Tel: (503) 796-6600

Telecopier: (503) 241-2819

President: Gerard K Drummond

Senior Executive Officers: Charles C Adams (VP), Lawrence E Heiner (VP), Ellworth P Ingraham (VP), William W Lyons (VP), Roy R Watts (VP), Mary H Oldshue (Treasurer), Martin V Quinn (Controller)

PRINCIPAL ACTIVITIES: Mining of coal and precious metals, and exploration and development of minerals, precious metals, and oil and gas, as well as industrial materials

Parent Company: PacifiCorp, Portland, OR

Principal Subsidiaries: NERCO Coal Corp; NERCO Minerals Company; NERCO Oil & Gas Inc; NERCO Advanced Materials Inc

Financial Information:

	Dec 31 1985	Dec 31 1986
	$'000	$'000
Sales revenues	533,900	594,700
Income before taxes	40,400	89,300
Net income	39,400	57,500
Dividends	21,200	21,200
Dividends per share	$0.64	$0.64
Earnings per share	$1.19	$1.73
Common stock*	33,200	33,200
Retained income	61,900	98,200
Shareholders equity	269,700	306,000

*average number of shares outstanding in thousands

Principal Shareholders: PacifiCorp
No of Employees: 2,144

NES, INC
3003 Wakefield Drive, Carpentersville, IL 60110
Tel: (312) 426-5900

Chairman: Robert A Martin (and President)
Senior Executive Officers: William Cunningham (VP Sales), M A Morton (VP Finance), C H Thomas (VP Engineering), J T Grant (VP Manufacturing), T C Hanson (VP Marketing)

PRINCIPAL ACTIVITIES: Manufacture of electronic controls for process equipment
Principal Bank: First National Bank
Financial Information:

	$'000
Sales revenues	740,000

No of Employees: 1,650

NESTLE FOODS CORPORATION
100 Bloomingdale Road, White Plains, NY 10605
Tel: (914) 682-6000
Telex: TWX 710 5681325 nestle whp

Chairman: James M Biggar
President: C A MacDonald (and Chief Executive Officer)
Senior Executive Officers: S D Blair (Senior VP), C K Buckley (VP), L T Davidson (VP), P Kamber (Senior VP), A Kish, A Kull (VP), M T Loughran (VP and Controller), B E Gensamer (Senior VP), E L Sinclair (VP and Treasurer), J F Donlan (VP and Secretary), Robert V Richards (VP), P D Reidy (VP), J Willard (VP)

PRINCIPAL ACTIVITIES: Manufacture of coffee, tea, instant chocolate drinks, chocolate and confectionery, cheese and butter, yoghurt and chilled desserts, infant cereals and baby foods, soups, seasonings, prepared dishes and frozen foods
Parent Company: Nestlé SA, Vevey, Switzerland
Financial Information:

	$'000
Sales revenues	1,000,000

No of Employees: 6,000

NETWORK SYSTEMS CORPORATION
7600 Boone Avenue North, Minneapolis, MN 55428
Tel: (612) 424 4888
Telex: 201678
Telefax: (612) 424-2853

Chairman: James E Thornton
President: Lyle D Altman (and Chief Executive Officer)
Senior Executive Officers: Richard A Fisher (VP Finance and Treasurer), Malcolm Reid (Secretary and Legal Counsel), Mahlon L Moore (VP Marketing), James W Checco (VP Product Engineering), Donald Humphrey (VP New Product Design), Gerald R Olson (VP Operations), Gary S Christensen (VP Development)

PRINCIPAL ACTIVITIES: Data communications services; networking of mainframe computers
Trade Names: HYPERCHANNEL, NETEX, HYPERBUS
Principal Bank: Norwest Bank Minneapolis NA
Financial Information:

	Dec 31 1985	Dec 31 1986
	$'000	$'000
Sales revenues	90,080	108,792
Income before taxes	30,004	31,307
Net income	17,050	18,007
Earnings per share	$0.59	$0.62
Common stock*	29,091	29,042
Retained income	51,245	69,252
Shareholders equity	150,442	170,530

*number of shares in thousands

No of Employees: 1,000

NEUTROGENA CORPORATION
5755 W 9th Street, Los Angeles, CA 90045
Tel: (213) 642-1150
Telex: WUT 181 914 neutrogena lsa

President: Lloyd E Cotsen (and Chief Executive Officer)
Senior Executive Officers: Bruce Kanter (VP and Chief Financial Officer), Dasha Lewin (VP, Secretary and Treasurer), Harry Wurmbrand (VP-Operations), Christian Bardin (President-International)

PRINCIPAL ACTIVITIES: Manufacture of soap and other skin-care products for sensitive skin
Principal Subsidiaries: Neutrogena SARL (Paris, France); Neutrogena (UK) Ltd (London, UK)
Financial Information:

	Oct 31 1986
	$'000
Sales revenues	96,023
Income before taxes	16,437
Net income	8,126
Dividends	Annual
Dividends per share	$0.12
Earnings per share	$0.86
Common stock	9,486,099
Shareholders equity	26,433,000

Principal Shareholders: L E Cotsen Trust
No of Employees: 444

NEVADA NATIONAL BANCORPORATION
P O Box 11500, Reno, NV 89550
Tel: (702) 785 6590

Chairman: William E Martin (and President)
Senior Executive Officers: John Woodworth (Senior VP and Real Estate Officer), Lynwood M Read (VP and Treasurer), Shelle K Grim (Secretary)

PRINCIPAL ACTIVITIES: Banking
Principal Subsidiaries: Nevada National Bank
Financial Information:

	Dec 31 1985
	$'000
Revenues	67,690
Net income	750

No of Employees: 550

NEVADA POWER COMPANY
6226 West Sahara Avenue, Las Vegas, NV 89102
Tel: (702) 367 5000

Chairman: Conrad L Ryan
President: Charles A Lenzie
Senior Executive Officers: C Keith Grant (Senior VP Operations), William G McGarry (Senior VP Customer Services and Communications), John W Arlidge (VP Resource Planning), Connell Marsden (VP Rates and Regulation), M Gene Matteucci (VP, Secretary and Legal Counsel), John C McCarthy (VP Administration Services), Raymond M McNeill

(VP Personnel), Gordon F Smith (VP Transport and Distribution), Charlie F Vaughn (VP Generation), William E Littler (Treasurer), David L Sloan (VP Finance)

PRINCIPAL ACTIVITIES: Supply of electricity
Principal Bank: First Interstate Bank of Nevada
Financial Information:

	$'000
Sales revenues	383,000

No of Employees: 1,390

NEVADA SAVINGS & LOAN ASSOCIATION

PO Box 2191, Las Vegas, NV 89101
Tel: (702) 385-2222

Chairman: Sherman Miller
President: Kenny C Guinn (and Chief Executive Officer)
Senior Executive Officers: David H Rogers (Senior Executive VP and Chief Operating Officer), Ted Paul Comfort (Executive VP and Chief Loan Officer), Charles Rogers (Executive VP), Charles E Dixon (Senior VP Administration Services), Derek Crook (Senior VP Appraisal), Michael Hennessey (Senior VP Northern Division), James Kochnick (Senior VP Marketing), Jacqueline Ashely (VP Loan Services), Charles C Bishop (VP Savings), Kathleen Ferguson (VP Personnel), Joseph Marcella (VP Management Information Services), Ralph Hillman (VP Construction Operations), Tom Schalk (VP Audit), David Youngberg (VP Savings, North Division), Estelle C Skalla (Secretary)

PRINCIPAL ACTIVITIES: Savings and loans
Principal Subsidiaries: First Nevada Corporation
Principal Bank: Valley Bank of Nevada

No of Employees: 450

NEW ENGLAND BUSINESS SERVICE, INC

500 Main Street, Groton, MA 01471
Tel: (617) 448-6111

Chairman: Jay R Rhoads Jr
President: Richard H Rhoads
Senior Executive Officers: Bartley H Colder (Senior VP Operations), Charles E McLatchy (VP Administration), Russell V Corsini Jr (VP Finance), Nancy J Wilber (VP-General Manager NEBS Business Forms), L Kent Lineback (VP-General Manager NEBS Computer Forms), Christopher H Corbett (VP-General Manager NEBS Fulfillment Division), Paul F Robinson (Treasurer and Secretary)

PRINCIPAL ACTIVITIES: Printing of a wide range of business forms
Trade Names: NEBS
Principal Subsidiaries: NEBS Business Forms Ltd (Canada); Devoke; Sycom Inc
Principal Bank: First National Bank of Boston
Financial Information:

	Jun 27 1986	Jun 26 1987
	$'000	$'000
Sales revenues	176,034	188,416
Income before taxes	33,104	37,287
Net income	16,893	19,130
Dividends	4,947	7,539
Dividends per share	$0.29	$0.44
Earnings per share	$0.99	$1.12
Common stock	8,582	17,310
Retained income	59,194	64,878
Shareholders equity	68,990	83,340

Principal Shareholders: Jay R Rhoads Jr; Yeager Wood & Mars; Boston Company
No of Employees: 1,870

NEW ENGLAND ELECTRIC SYSTEM

25 Research Drive, Westborough, MA 01582
Tel: (617) 366-9011

Chairman: Joan T Bok
President: Samuel P Huntington (and Chief Executive Officer)
Senior Executive Officers: John F Kaslow (Executive VP and Chief Operating Officer)

PRINCIPAL ACTIVITIES: Supply of electricity
Principal Bankers: First National Bank of Boston
Financial Information:

	$'000
Sales revenues	1,400,000

No of Employees: 5,000

NEW ENGLAND MUTUAL LIFE INSURANCE CO, THE,

501 Boylston Street, Boston, MA 02117
Tel: (617) 578-2000
Telex: TWX 710 3216749 nemlico bsn

Chairman: Edward E Phillips (and Chief Executive Officer)
President: John A Fibiger (and Chief Operating Officer)
Senior Executive Officers: Robert A Shafto (Executive VP), Ralph F Verni (Executive VP Finance), Michael I Brown (Senior VP Information, Management Services), J S Caras (Senior VP Marketing), Gordon D MacKay (Senior VP Public Affairs and Public Relations), John E Rodgers (Senior VP, Investment Administration), Hamilton Coolidge (Senior VP, Mortgage), Daniel Toran (Senior VP, Agencies), Edward C Hall (Senior VP, Client Services), Herbert F Clark (Senior VP, Group Insurance)

PRINCIPAL ACTIVITIES: Life insurance and financial services
Principal Subsidiaries: New England Securities Corp; New England Financial Advisors; Copley Real Estate Advisors; Back Bay Advisors; Loomis, Sayles and Co Inc; Connecticut National Life Insurance Co
Principal Bank: Bank of New England
Financial Information:

	Dec 31 1985	Dec 31 1986
	$'000	$'000
Premium income	2,316,400	2,793,600
Investment income	931,300	1,032,900
Income before taxes	3,300,000	4,084,400
Net income	247,600	425,600
Dividends	227,000	248,100
Retained income	20,600	177,500

No of Employees: 10,567

NEW HAMPSHIRE BALL BEARINGS, INC

Rte 202, Peterborough, NH 03458
Tel: (603) 924-3311
Telex: TWX 710 364 1805

Chairman: Emil J Karkut
President: Jerry G Calvin
Senior Executive Officers: Jack E Langridge (VP), Gary C Yomantas (VP), Charles H Trumbo (VP), Michael R Samide (VP and Treasurer)

PRINCIPAL ACTIVITIES: Manufacture of ball bearings, rod end and spherical bearings, and tube/duct assemblies
Parent Company: Minebea Co Ltd, Tokyo, Japan
Financial Information:

	$'000
Sales revenues	150,000

Principal Shareholders: Parent company via its subsidiary, NMB (USA)
No of Employees: 1,500

NEW HAMPSHIRE SAVINGS BANK CORPORATION

27 North State Street, Concord, NH 03301
Tel: (603) 224 7711

Chairman: John R Hardie
President: Robert E Dustin (and Treasurer)

Senior Executive Officers: David H Rogers (Executive VP and Secretary), Stephen J Gilhooly (Chief Financial Officer), Philip B Emma (VP Financial), Bruce E Macey (VP Personnel)

PRINCIPAL ACTIVITIES: Banking

No of Employees: 340

NEW JERSEY NATIONAL CORPORATION

CN-1, Pennington, NJ 08534
Tel: (609) 771 5700

Chairman: John H Walther (and Chief Executive Officer)
President: John D Wallace

PRINCIPAL ACTIVITIES: Holding company with interests in banking
Principal Subsidiaries: New Jersey National Bank

No of Employees: 5

NEW JERSEY RESOURCES CORPORATION

1415 Wyckoff Road, Wall, NJ 07719
Tel: (201) 938 1000

Chairman: J S Abrams
President: James T Dolan Jr (and Chief Executive Officer)
Senior Executive Officers: Thomas B Toohey (Executive VP, Chief Financial Officer and Treasurer), James M Bollerman (Senior VP and Assistant to the President), Oletta J Harden (VP and Secretary)

PRINCIPAL ACTIVITIES: Supply of natural gas
Principal Subsidiaries: Commercial Realty and Resources Corporation; New Jersey Natural Gas Company; New Jersey Natural Resources Company
Principal Bank: Midlantic National Bank
Financial Information:

	$'000
Sales revenues	283,000

No of Employees: 630

NEW PROCESS COMPANY

220 Hickory Street, Warren, PA 16366
Tel: (814) 723 3600

President: Murray K McComas
Senior Executive Officers: Alan J Blair (Executive VP), Robert W Blair (VP and Secretary), Giles W Schutte (VP and Treasurer), John H Carter (VP Merchandising), John A Losher (VP Advertising), Steven M Blair (VP Order Handling), Blair T Smoulder (VP Planning), Robert D Crowley (VP Product Area), Robert B Dietsch (VP Product Area and Assistant Secretary), C Wayne Kipple (VP Product Area), Michael J Samargya (VP Data Processing)

PRINCIPAL ACTIVITIES: Mail order services
Financial Information:

	Dec 31 1985 $'000	Dec 31 1986 $'000
Sales revenues	329,717	359,609
Income before taxes	38,579	35,740
Net income	19,170	17,695
Dividends	11,783	11,056
Dividends per share	$1.25	$1.18
Earnings per share	$2.03	$1.89
Common stock	420	420
Retained income	80,620	87,259
Shareholders equity	75,962	81,246

No of Employees: 1,900

NEW PROCESS STEEL CORPORATION

5800 Westview Drive, Houston, TX 77055
Tel: (713) 686-9631
Telex: TWX 910 88169 37 newsprocesb hou

President: Eugene R Fant
Senior Executive Officers: Phil O Kelley (Executive VP and Chief Financial Officer), Robert L Proch (Executive VP Operations), David R Schunick (VP), Doyle Clements (VP), Jimmy C Kollaja (VP and Controller), Wade Rice (VP Credit)

PRINCIPAL ACTIVITIES: Processing of steel
Parent Company: E R Fant Inc
Principal Bank: Allied Bank of Texas
Financial Information:

	$'000
Sales revenues	90,000

No of Employees: 200

NEW WORLD PICTURES INC

1440 South Sepulveda Boulevard, Los Angeles, CA 90025
Tel: (213) 444 8100
Telex: WUT 664 937 new world lsa

Chairmen: Robert Rehme (and Chief Executive Officer), Harry E Sloan (Assistant Secretary)
President: Roger A Burlage (and Chief Operating Officer)
Senior Executives: Peter R Bierstedt (Executive VP and Legal Counsel), Paul Culberg (Executive VP and General Manager), Jon Feltheimer (Executive VP), Paul S Almond (Senior VP), Gerald Ament (Senior VP), Albert T Linton (Senior VP and Chief Financial Officer), Elliot Slutzky (Senior VP), Roy Cox (VP)

PRINCIPAL ACTIVITIES: Production of motion pictures
Financial Information:

	$'000
Sales revenues	106,570

No of Employees: 240

NEW YORK LIFE INSURANCE & ANNUITY CORPORATION

51 Madison Ave, New York, NY 10010

Chairman: Donald K Ross; Vice Chairman: George A W Bundschuh
President: Jacob B Underhill
Senior Executive Officers: William H Creamer III (Senior VP), Richard M Kernan Jr (Senior VP), Malcolm MacKay (Senior VP), Leif Rode (Senior VP and General Auditor), Stephen N Steinig (Senior VP), Nora M Beattie (VP and Actuary), William B Birdsall (VP), Bruce J Davey (VP and Treasurer)

PRINCIPAL ACTIVITIES: Health, life and accident insurance; annuities
Parent Company: New York Life Insurance Co
Financial Information:

	Dec 31 1985 $'000	Dec 31 1986 $'000
Premium income	1,286,830	1,489,552
Investment income	389,940	483,440

No of Employees: 18,300

NEW YORK LIFE INSURANCE CO

51 Madison Avenue, New York, NY 10010
Tel: (212) 576-7000
Telex: WUT 126287 nylic nyk

Chairman: Donald L Ross; Vice Chairman: George A Bundschuh, Harry G Hohn
President: Jacob B Underhill
Senior Executive Officers: William E Keiter (Executive VP), John H Stimpson (Executive VP), Walter Shur (Executive VP), John T DeBardeleben (Executive VP), Roberta A Shields (Senior VP and Controller), Harold K Herzog (Senior VP Real Estate), Alice T Kane (Senior VP and General Counsel), Edward G Wendt Jr (Senior VP), Michael J McLaughlin (Senior VP Information Systems and Services), Herbert L Cheskis (Senior VP), Jerald R Hinrichs (Senior VP Marketing), Malcolm KacKay (Senior VP), Kenneth R O'Brien (Senior VP Pensions), Stephen N Steinig (Senior VP), Lee M Gammill Jr (Senior VP

Industrial Life), William F Yelverton (Senior VP Industrial Health), Walter C Weissinger Jr (Senior VP), Robin B Welch (Senior VP Industrial Policy Services), Mark Crowley (Senior VP), Richard M Kernan Jr (Senior VP Investment), William H Creamer III (Senior VP), Walter E Hossfeld Jr (Senior VP Canada), Edward C Walsh (Senior VP)

PRINCIPAL ACTIVITIES: Life insurance

Principal Subsidiaries: New York Life Insurance & Annuity

Financial Information:

	Dec 31 1985	Dec 31 1986
	$'000	$'000
Premium income	3,830,010	3,477,186
Investment income	2,236,880	2,412,632

No of Employees: 18,300

NEW YORK MARINE AND GENERAL INSURANCE COMPANY

100 Park Avenue, New York, NY 10017

Tel: (212) 953 0580

Chairman: John N Blackman (and President and Chief Executive Officer)

Senior Executive Officers: John N Blackman Jr (Executive VP), Mark W Blackman (Executive VP), Jean H Goulding (VP), Anthony J Kuczinski (VP and Chief Operating Officer), Charles A Mitchell (VP), David G Castell (Treasurer), Brice Leon (Assistant Secretary), Marjorie J Phillips (Secretary)

PRINCIPAL ACTIVITIES: Insurance services

Principal Bank: Chemical Bank

NEW YORK STATE ELECTRIC & GAS CORPORATION

PO Box 287, Ithaca, NY 14851

Tel: (607) 729-2551

Chairman: Wells P Allen Jr (and Chief Executive Officer); Chairman: Executive Committee: Charles F Kennedy

President: James A Carrigg (and Chief Operating Officer)

Senior Executive Officers: Robert B Mackenzie (Executive VP Operations and Engineering), R A Jacobson (Senior VP Corporate), Eugene E Forrest (Senior VP Administration), Allen E Knight (Senior VP Generation), Orlin W Darrach (VP Marketing Services), J A Ackerman (VP Area Administration), John D Scott (VP Finance), M J Turkovic (VP Purchasing), R W Page (VP Personnel), Jack H Roskoz (VP Public Affairs), B M Rider (VP Electrical Engineering), R A Perine (VP Gas Operations), V W Rider (VP Plant Operation and Engineering), F X Carney (VP Research and Development), M F Felo Jr (VP and Treasurer)

PRINCIPAL ACTIVITIES: Supply of electricity and natural gas

Principal Bankers: Chase Manhattan Bank

Financial Information:

	Dec 31 1986
	$'000
Sales revenues	1,277,284
Net income	228,494
Earnings per share	$3.86
Shareholders equity	1,558,462

No of Employees: 4,400

NEW YORK TIMES COMPANY (THE)

229 W 43rd Street, New York, NY 10036

Tel: (212) 556-1234

Telex: ITT 420401 NYK TIMES; WESTERN UNION 62291 NYK TIMES; RCA 224734 NYK TIMES

Chairman: Arthur Ochs Sulzberger

President: Walter E Mattson

Senior Executive Officers: Michael E Ryan (Senior VP), Benjamin Handelman (Senior VP), David L Gorham (Chief Financial Officer), Denise K Fletcher (Treasurer), Leslie Martenborough (Director, Personnel), Solomon B Watson IV (Secretary), Laura J Corwin (Assistant Secretary), Denise K Fletcher (Treasurer), Richard G Thomas (Assistant Treasurer), Frank R Gatti (Corporate Controller, Principal Accounting Officer), Andrew Fenster (Assistant Corporate Controller), Katharine P Darrow (General Counsel), Gordon Medenica (Director of Planning), Nancy Nielsen (Corporate Relations Director), Marjorie W Longley (Public Affairs Director), Thomas H Nied (Director of Taxation), Jack Hayon (Internal Audit Director), Stephen A O Golden (Director of Forest Products)

PRINCIPAL ACTIVITIES: The Company has classified its business into the following segments and equity interests: Newspapers: The New York Times, a newspaper of general circulation with readership in New York City, its suburbs and throughout the US, 35 smaller-city newspapers principally in the southeast, a news service and a features syndicate. In 1987, three new Southeastern newspapers were acquired. Magazines: Cruising World, Family Circle, Golf Digest, Golf World (Great Britain), Child, Decorating, Remodelling, Southern Travel, Snow Country and Tennis. Broadcasting/Cable TV: WREG-TV, Memphis, Tenn., KFSM-TV, Fort Smith, Ark., WHNT-TV, Huntsville, Ala., WQXR AM/FM radio, New York, NY and NYT Cable TV, southern New Jersey. In 1985, two additional television stations have been acquired; one in the "Quad Cities" area of Illinois and Iowa and the other in the Wilkes Bonne/Scranton area of Pennsylvania. Associated Companies: Equity interests in three Canadian newsprint companies - Donohue Malbaie Inc (35%); Gaspesia Pulp and Paper Company Ltd (49%); and Spruce Falls Power and Paper Company Limited (49.5%); Madison Paper Industries (a partnership); and International Herald Tribune SA (33%). The three Canadian newsprint companies and the partnership supply the major portion of the annual paper requirements for production of The New York Times

Principal Subsidiaries: Newspapers:- The New York Times; The New York Times Syndication Sales Corp; The New York Times Co Regional Newspaper Group; Avon Park Sun; The Banner Independent; Claiborne Progress; The Comet; The Daily Corinthian; Daily News; Daily World; The Dispatch; Gainesville Sun; The Golden Gate Eagle; The Harlan Daily Enterprise; Houma Daily Courier; Lake City Reporter; The Ledger; Leesburg/Commercial; Lenoir News-Topic; Marco Island Eagle; The Messenger; The News-Leader; Ocala Star-Banner; The Palatka Daily News; The Sarasota Herald-Tribune; The Sebring News; State Gazette; Times Daily; The Times-News; Wilmington Morning Star; York County Coast Star. Magazines:- The New York Times Co Magazine Group; Retail Magazine Marketing Company; Cruising World; Family Circle; Golf Digest; Golf World (UK); Tennis. Broadcasting/Cable TV:- The New York Times Co Broadcasting Group; KFSM-TV; WHNT-TV; WQXR AM/FM; WREG-TV; NYT Cable TV. Associated Companies: Donohue Malbaie Inc (Canada); Gaspesia Pulp and Paper Company Ltd (Canada); International Herald Tribune (France); Madison Paper Industries; Spruce Falls Power and Paper Company Limited (Canada)

Principal Bank: Morgan Guaranty Trust Company

Financial Information:

	Dec 31 1985 $'000	Dec 31 1986 $'000
Sales revenues	1,393,772	1,564,663
Income before taxes (1)	193,472	236,081
Net income	116,318	132,227
Common dividends	23,357	26,878
Dividends per share	$0.29	$0.33
Earnings per share	$1.45	$1.63
Common stock (2)	3,815	8,155
Common stock (3)	231	45
Retained income	525,129	632,180
Shareholders equity	538,363	707,423

(1) and equity in earnings from associated Companies
(2) Class A
(3) Class B

No of Employees: 10,000

NEW YORKER MAGAZINE, INC

25 W 43rd Street, New York, NY 10036
Tel: (212) 840-3800
Telex: RCA 236799 nyker ur

Chairman: Peter F Fleischmann
President: Steven T Fiorio (and Publisher)
Senior Executive Officers: Jonathan E Newhouse (Executive VP), Milton Greenstein (VP), Sam R Spoto (VP), Stuart Jason (VP and Comptroller), Elaine M Matteo (Secretary and Treasurer)

PRINCIPAL ACTIVITIES: Publishing of the "New Yorker" Magazine
Principal Bank: Morgan Guaranty Trust Co
Financial Information:

	$'000
Sales revenues	81,000

No of Employees: 400

NEWARK BOXBOARD CO

57 Freeman Street, Newark, NJ 07105
Tel: (201) 589-6853

President: George A Oechsle
Senior Executive Officers: Edward K Mullen (Executiv VP), James Hoover (VP), William D Harbor (VP and Chief Financial Officer), Richard R Meagher (VP Marketing)

PRINCIPAL ACTIVITIES: Production of paperboard
Parent Company: Newark Group Inc
Principal Bank: Fidelity Union Bank
Financial Information:

	$'000
Sales revenues	90,000

No of Employees: 600

NEWBERY ENERGY CORPORATION

1414 West Broadway, Suite A210, Tempe, AZ 85282
Tel: (602) 966 6234

Chairman: W W Arbogast; Vice Chairman: Ralph E Herman (and Chief Executive Officer)
President: Robert S Mies
Senior Executive Officers: Robert H Davis (Executive VP), Homer R Gilchrist (Secretary and Treasurer)

PRINCIPAL ACTIVITIES: Construction and pipeline engineering; electrical installations
Principal Subsidiaries: CHR-Newbery; Interect Constructors Inc; Newburg Electric Corporation; Newbury Industrial Inc; Newbery Oil and Gas Inc; Newbury-State Inc; Newcon-Aire Inc; Nexco Corporation; Spectrum Electrical Constructors Inc; State West Inc
Principal Bank: United Bank of AZ
Financial Information:

	$'000
Sales revenues	72,000

No of Employees: 730

NEWCENTURY BANK CORPORATION

108 W School St, Frankenmuth, MI 48734
Tel: (517) 652 3283

Chairman: Franklin Rittmueller (and President and Chief Executive Officer)
Senior Executive Officers: Thomas O Steinbauer (Executive VP and Chief Operating Officer), James L Richardson (VP and Treasurer)

PRINCIPAL ACTIVITIES: Banking

No of Employees: 120

NEWCOR, INC

3270 W Big Beaver Rod, Troy, MI 48084
Tel: (313) 643-7730
Telex: WUT 235 423 newcor trml

Chairman: William F Mitchell (and Chief Executive Officer)
President: Richard A Smith (and Chief Operating Officer)
Senior Executive Officers: Kenneth B Hollidge Jr (VP), Lawrence P Nolta (VP), Robert N Goltz (VP), Neil C Wester (VP Finance and Chief Financial Officer), Albert S Pramuk (Treasurer)

PRINCIPAL ACTIVITIES: Manufacture of welding machinery and cutting equipment, machine tools and precision machined components
Principal Subsidiaries: Eonic Inc; Newcor Canada Ltd; Newcor Machine Tool Co
Principal Bank: Manufacturers Bank
Financial Information:

	Oct 31 1986 $'000
Sales revenues	105,667
Net (loss)	(1,998)
Dividends	900
Dividends per share	$0.32
(Loss) per share	($0.71)
Retained income	13,393

No of Employees: 656

NEWELL CO.

29 East Stephenson St, Freeport, IL 61032
Tel: (815) 235-4171
Telex: TWX 910 6420923 newell co frpt

Chairman: William R Cuthbert; Vice Chairman: Daniel C Ferguson (and Chief Executive Officer)
Presidents: William P Sovey (and Chief Operating Officer), Robert F Gilbert (Newell Operating Companies)
Senior Executive Officers: William T Alldredge (VP Finance), W K Doppstadt (VP Personnel Relations), Donald L Krause (VP and Controller), Clarence R Davenport (Treasurer), Roland E Knecht (VP Administrative Services and Corporate Secretary), Robert P Maher (VP Corporate Information Services), Shirley K Martin (Assistant Corporate Secretary), Byron H Stebbins (VP Trade Development)

PRINCIPAL ACTIVITIES: The only business of Newell is marketing high-volume, do-it-yourself hardware/housewares consumer products
Trade Names: BernzOmatic, Boye, Bulldog, Counselor, Dorfile, EZ Paintr, Foley, Mirro, Newell, Surefire, Wrights
Principal Subsidiaries and Divisions: Domestic Operations:- BernzOmatic Corporation; Boye Needle Company; Bulldog Company; Dorfile Company; Counselor Company; EZ Paintr Corporation; Foley Company; Mirro Corporation; Newell Window Furnishings Co; Wm E Wright Co. Distribution Centers:- Dayton, NJ; Omaha, NE; Sparks Nevada. Canadian Companies:- Androck Company; Bulldog Products;

BernzOmatic Company; Counselor Products Company; EZ Paintr Canada; Newell Window Furnishings Company; Wm E Wright. Export Operations:- Newell International Company
Principal Bank: Transfer Agent and Registrar: Morgan Shareholder Services Trust Company
Financial Information:

	Dec 31 1985	Dec 31 1986
	$'000	$'000
Sales revenues	350,045	401,357
Income before taxes	32,833	44,920
Net income	18,854	24,009
Dividends(1)	4,520	7,867
Dividends per share(1)	$0.525	$0.735
Earnings per share(2)	$2.09	$2.17
Common stock	8,649	11,455
Retained income	81,385	96,925
Shareholders equity	120,089	198,009

(1) common stock
(2) primary

No of Employees: 4,500

NEWHALL REFINING CO, INC

22674 N Clampitt Road, Newhall, CA 91321
Tel: (805) 259-2660

President: E J Barnes
Senior Executive Officers: K T Kenny (VP Marketing), Hans J Mangold (VP Manufacturing), Edward J Babineau Jr (Treasurer)

PRINCIPAL ACTIVITIES: Oil refining and production of gasoline, jet fuel and fuel oil
Parent Company: Pauley Petroleum Inc, Los Angeles, CA
Principal Bank: Security Pacific Bank
Financial Information:

	$'000
Sales revenues	60,000

No of Employees: 100

NEWMARK & LEWIS INC

595 South Broadway, Hicksville, NY 11802
Tel: (516) 681 6900

Chairman: Warren G Hyman (and Secretary)
President: Richard D Lewis (and Treasurer)
Senior Executive Officers: William J Hoh (VP), Peter H Lewis (VP), Michael J Marks (VP), Richard G Shorey (VP)

PRINCIPAL ACTIVITIES: Retail trade in domestic appliances, home entertainment equipment and consumer electronics
Principal Bank: Citibank NA
Financial Information:

	$'000
Sales revenues	142,000

No of Employees: 700

NEWMONT MINING CORPORATION

200 Park Avenue, New York, NY 10166
Tel: (212) 953-6900

Chairman: Gordon R Parker (and Chief Executive Officer)
Senior Executive Officers: Richard B Leather (Executive VP and General Counsel), T Peter Philip (Senior VP), Robert F Boyce (VP, Taxes), Peter J Crescenzo (VP, Engineering), Edward P Fontaine (Senior VP, Finance and Chief Financial Officer), Leonard Harris (VP, Metallurgical Operations), James F Hill (VP, Corporate Relations), Robert J Miller (VP, Exploration), Christopher S Hardesty (VP and Treasurer), Roger C Adams (Secretary), Timothy J Schmitt (VP and Controller), John R Parry (Senior VP), E Paul Mortimer (VP, Development), Graham M Clark Jr (VP, Western General Counsel), Jack Gordon (VP), John H Johnson Jr (VP), Ronald J Vance (VP, Marketing), Charles G Freeman (Assistant VP, Exploration), Vernon E Stedronsky (Assistant VP, Engineering), Kevin Moore (Assistant Controller), Owen R O'Neill (Assistant Controller), Paul L Maroni (Assistant Treasurer), David A Peters (Assistant Secretary), H David Potter (Assistant Secretary)

PRINCIPAL ACTIVITIES: Newmont Mining Corporation is a leading natural resource company engaged in exploration for, operation and management of precious metal mining, hydrocarbon energy and minerals properties
Principal Subsidiaries: Gold:- Newmont Gold Company (90.1%); Newmont Australia Ltd (75%) (Australia). Nonferrous Metals:- Newmont Mines Ltd (Canada); Resurrection Mining Company; Palabora Mining Company Ltd (28.6%) (South Africa); O'okiep Copper Company (40.2%) (South Africa); Tsumeb Corporation Ltd (32.6%) (Namibia). Energy:-Newmont Oil Company (North America, Europe, Far East); Peabody Holding Company, Inc (49.97%). Other Interests:- Chile); Sherritt Gordon Mines Ltd (33.6%). Investments:-Highveld Steel and Vanadium Corporation Ltd (10.3%) (South Africa); Southern Peru Copper Corporation (10.7%) (Peru) E.I.du Pont de Nemours and Company (2.5%); Fluor Corporation (1.1%); International Minerals & Chemical Corp (0.5%); Magma Copper Company
Financial Information:

	Dec 31 1985	Dec 31 1986
	$'000	$'000
Sales revenues	249,173	380,781
Income (loss) before taxes*	(24,984)	114,642
Net income (loss)	(34,850)	74,219
Dividends	30,323	30,372
Dividends per share	$1.00	$1.00
Earnings (loss) per share	($1.15)	$2.44
Common stock	30,363	30,412
Retained income	1,037,183	1,080,223
Shareholders equity	1,404,131	1,451,874

*and extraordinary item

Principal Shareholders: Consolidated Guld Fields PLC (49.9%)

NEWPARK RESOURCES, INC

2900 Ridgelake Drive, Metairie, LA 70002
Tel: (504) 838-8222

Chairman: John J Graham
President: James D Cole (and Chief Executive Officer)
Senior Executive Officers: Frank T King (Executive VP), Roger N McMennamy (VP Finance, Secretary and Treasurer)

PRINCIPAL ACTIVITIES: Tools and supplies for the oil industry; operation of services for the oil industry; marine repair, barge cleaning and construction
Principal Subsidiaries: SOLOCO Inc; Newpark Wellhead Services Inc; Newpark Pipe & Supply Inc; Guillory Tank Trucj Service Inc; Newpark Waste Treatment Systems Inc; Newpark Shipbuilding & Repair Inc; Newpark Industrial Services Inc
Principal Bank: Manufacturers Hanover Trust Co
Financial Information:

	$'000
Sales revenues	164,284

No of Employees: 800

NEWPORT CORPORATION

18235 Mount Baldy Circle, Fountain Valley, CA 92708
Tel: (714) 963 9811

Chairman: Erwin Tomash
President: Milton M T Chang (and Chief Executive Officer)
Senior Executive Officers: Robert C Hewitt (VP, Secretary and Treasurer), Tony Hsu (VP Marketing), Thomas A Galantowicz (VP), Dennis C Terry (VP Special Projects), Aaron Gara (VP), Dean T Hodges (VP Sales and Marketing)

PRINCIPAL ACTIVITIES: Manufacture of optical, laser and electro-optic equipment
Principal Bank: First Interstate Bank of California

Financial Information:

	Jul 31 1986	Jul 31 1987
	$'000	$'000
Sales revenues	40,774	44,559
Income before taxes	11,746	9,300
Net income	6,269	4,794
Dividends	563	565
Dividends per share	$0.06	$0.06
Earnings per share	$0.67	$0.51
Common stock	3,286	3,302
Retained income	33,179	37,408
Shareholders equity	64,254	69,125

No of Employees: 341

NEWPORT ELECTRIC CORPORATION

12 Turner Road, Middletown, RI 02840
Tel: (401) 847 4480

Chairman: Richard B Sheffield
President: Elliott G Whitney (and General Manager)
Senior Executive Officers: Frank S Ceglarski (VP Operations and Engineering), Larry D Settle (VP Finance and Treasurer), L Eugene Rankin Jr (Secretary)

PRINCIPAL ACTIVITIES: Supply of electricity
Principal Bank: Connecticut Bank and Trust Company
Financial Information:

	$'000
Sales revenues	41,480

No of Employees: 120

NEWPORT NEWS SHIPBUILDING AND DRY DOCK CO

4101 Washington Avenue, Newport News, VA 23607
Tel: (804) 380-2000
Telex: WUT 823453 nnshpbldg npns

President: Edward J Campbell (and Chief Executive Officer)
Senior Executive Officers: Carl E Whitman (Senior VP and General Counsel), W R Phillips Jr (Senior VP Engineering), James E Turner Jr (Senior VP Overhaul and Ship Repair), Richard Broad (VP), Julian F Cox Jr (VP), William P Fricks (VP), Jack A Garrow (VP), John E Graham (VP), Herbert J Lanese (VP), William H Smith (VP), Lloyd R Sorenson Jr (VP), Y B Williams Jr (VP)

PRINCIPAL ACTIVITIES: Shipbuilding and ship repairing; manufacture of equipment for the nuclear power industry and specialized machinery
Parent Company: Tenneco Inc, Houston, TX
Financial Information:

	$'000
Sales revenues	1,800,000

No of Employees: 29,000

NEWS AMERICA PUBLISHING INC

210 South Street, New York, NY 10002
Tel: (212) 349-5000
Telex: WUT 559862 nap dittrich

Chairman: K Rupert Murdoch (and Chief Exeuctive Officer)
President: Donald D Kummerfeld (and Chief Operating Offcier)
Senior Executive Officers: Richard A Sarazen (Executive VP), Ian Rae (Senior VP), E G Viles (VP Newspapers), Raymond A Dittrick (VP Production), John Bender (VP, General Counsel and Secretary)

PRINCIPAL ACTIVITIES: Publishing of magazines and newspapers
Parent Company: The News Corporation Ltd, Australia
Principal Bank: First National Bank of Boston
Financial Information:

	$'000
Sales revenues	350,000

No of Employees: 3,500

NEWSWEEK, INC

444 Madison Avenue, New York, NY 10022
Tel: (212) 350-4000
Cable: NEWSWEEK NEW YORK
Telex: WUT 126143; WUI 620364; ITT 420395; RCA 234011

President: Christopher M Little
Senior Executive Officers: Gerard Smith (Publisher), Howard W Smith (Executive VP), Peter Luffman (President International Division), Richard Smith (Editor-in-Chief), Diana M Daniels (VP and General Counsel), Angelo Rivello (VP, Manufacturing), Sidney R Ferenc (VP, Finance), Harold Shain (VP, Circulation), Arthur Karlan (VP, Assoc Pub)

PRINCIPAL ACTIVITIES: Publishing of magazines:- Newsweek-a weekly news magazine published in New York City. Newsweek has a 1987 rate base of 3,050,000. It ranks first among the nation's leading newsweeklies in terms of advertising pages and second in circulation. Newsweek publishes 58 geographic and demographic editions. It maintains 10 U.S. and 17 foreign news bureaus and has 17 regional and overseas advertising sales offices. The magazine is printed at 4 U.S. sites and in Ontario, Canada. Newsweek International-an English-language news magazine published in New York City and circulated throughout the world. For 1987, Newsweek International has rate bases of 310,000 for its Atlantic edition, 325,000 for its Pacific edition (including 125,000 for the Bulletin with Newsweek, Australia's largest newsweekly) and 55,000 for its Latin America edition. Newsweek International maintains sales offices in 2 U.S. and 10 foreign cities. It is printed in Zurich, Tokyo, Hong Kong and Hollywood, Florida. Newsweek Japan (Newsweek Nihon Ban)-the first Japanese-language newsweekly, with an average weekly circulation of 120,000. It is produced with TBS-Britannica, which translates and publishes the magazine. Newsweek also publishes Travel & Leisure/Asia, a monthly magazine for the Asian market with editorial copy supplied by American Express Publishing Corporation. T&L Asia has a circulation rate base of 110,000 and is printed in Hong Kong
Trade Names: Newsweek, Newsweek International, Newsweek Japan (Newsweek Nihon Ban)
Parent Company: The Washington Post Company
Principal Bank: The Chase Manhattan Bank
Financial Information:

	Dec 31 1985	Dec 29 1986
	$'000	$'000
Sales revenues	326,053	320,924

Principal Shareholders: The Washington Post Company
No of Employees: 1,500

NEXUS INDUSTRIES INC

570 S Miami Street, Wabash, IN 46992
Tel: (219) 563-8302

Chairman: William B Hensley (and Chief Executive Officer)
President: Dan P Cooke (and Chief Operating Officer)

PRINCIPAL ACTIVITIES: Production of custom imprinted sports clothing
Principal Subsidiaries: Shirt Shed Inc
Principal Bank: Security Pacific Bank
Financial Information:

	$'000
Sales revenues	286,000

No of Employees: 250

NI INDUSTRIES INC

One Golden Shore, Long Beach, CA 90802
Tel: (213) 435-6676

Chairman: H J Meany (and President)
President: Hans Beisch (and Chief Operating Officer)
Senior Executive Officers: B M Feldman (VP Industrial Relations), D L Hirsch Jr (VP and Senior Counsel), J J Kimes

(VP Administration and Controller), A R Owens Jr (VP), R J Shaffer (VP, General Counsel and Secretary)

PRINCIPAL ACTIVITIES: Manufacture of motor vehicle components; hardware including door furniture and faucets; household electrical equipment including microwave ovens; vitreous china bathroom fixtures
Trade Names: Waste King, Thermador, Artistic Brass
Parent Company: Nimas Corp
Principal Bank: Security Pacific National Bank
Financial Information:

	$'000
Sales revenues	550,000

No of Employees: 6,000

NIAGARA MOHAWK POWER CORPORATION
300 Erie Blvd W, Syracuse, NY 13202
Tel: (315) 474-1511
Telex: TWX 710 5410484 niagara syr

Chairman: John G Haehl Jr (and Chief Executive Officer)
President: William J Donlon
Senior Executive Officers: John M Endries (Senior VP), Anthony J Buratta (Senior VP), John P Hennessey (Senior VP), Charles V Mangan (Senior VP), John W Powers (Senior VP and Treasurer), Michael P Ramalli (Senior VP)

PRINCIPAL ACTIVITIES: Supply of gas and electricity
Principal Subsidiaries: Hydra-Co Enterprises Inc; N M Uranium Inc; Opinac Investments Ltd (Canada); Beebee Island Corp; Moreau Manufacturing Corp
Financial Information:

	Dec 31 1985 $'000	Dec 31 1986 $'000
Sales revenues	2,694,940	2,660,319
Net income	411,430	397,865
Dividends	252,218	264,312
Dividends per share	$2.08	$2.06
Earnings per share	$2.88	$2.71
Common stock	126,928	127,141
Retained income	842,115	921,851
Shareholders equity	2,778,620	2,861,491

No of Employees: 11,400

NIAGARA OF WISCONSIN PAPER CORPORATION
PO Box 5, Niagara, WI 54151
Tel: (715) 251-3151
Telex: 260373 niagara niag

Chairman: D E Nugent
President: Thomas J Thomsen
Senior Executive Officers: Thomas Murphy (Controller)

PRINCIPAL ACTIVITIES: Manufacture of paper including coated paper
Parent Company: Pentair Inc, St Paul, MN
Principal Bank: First National Bank
Financial Information:

	$'000
Sales revenues	190,000

No of Employees: 700

NIBCO INC
500 Simpson Avenue, Elkhart, IN 46515
Tel: (219) 295 3000
Telex: 276151 NIBCO INTL EKR

Chairman: Lee Martin
President: James Hostetler
Senior Executive Officers: Rex Martin (Executive VP), James Pullen (VP-Administration), Brad Hahn (VP-Marketing), William O'Hagan (VP-Manufacturing, Plumbing Products), Bob Krok (VP-Chemtrol Division), James Goza (VP-Finance), Tom Smith (VP-Manufacturing, Industrial Valves)

PRINCIPAL ACTIVITIES: Manufacturing of copper and plastic fittings, washerless faucets, plumbing valves and industrial valves (bronze, iron, steel and plastic)

NICHOLS, S E, INC
275 Seventh Avenue, New York, NY 10001
Tel: (212) 206 9400

Chairman: Manfred Brecker (and Chief Executive Officer)
President: Kenneth A Davis (and Chief Operating Officer)
Senior Executive Officers: Joseph Keller (Executive VP Development), Erich Metzger (Executive VP and Secretary), Edwin Denenberg (Senior VP Merchandising), Herbert Kaltbaum (Senior VP Merchandising), Maarten D Hemsley (Senior VP Finance, Treasurer and Chief Financial Officer), Joseph Keller Jr (Senior VP Store Operations), Marcie B Davis (VP Human Resources), Philip J Frank (VP Advertising), Joseph H Klein (VP, Secretary and Corporate Planning), Lester Levy (VP), Lee Lobelson (VP Advertising)

PRINCIPAL ACTIVITIES: Department stores
Principal Subsidiaries: Nichols Elmira Concessions; Nichols Lebanon Corporation
Principal Bank: Mellon Bank
Financial Information:

	$'000
Sales revenues	309,970

No of Employees: 3,800

NICHOLS-HOMESHIELD, INC
1470 N Farnsworth Avenue, Aurora, IL 60507
Tel: (312) 851-5430
Telex: TWX 910 2381705 nichols stci

Chairman: Daniel B Stuart
President: J M Morris (and Chief Executive Officer)
Senior Executive Officers: F W Adkins (VP), M E Johnson (VP), M L Nuzzo (VP)

PRINCIPAL ACTIVITIES: Manufacture of aluminum products including building products, wire and coils
Principal Bank: Continental Illinois National Bank & Trust Company of Chicago
Financial Information:

	$'000
Sales revenues	90,000

No of Employees: 900

NICOLET INSTRUMENT CORPORATION
5225 Verona Road, Madison, WI 53711
Tel: (608) 271-3333
Telex: TWX 910 2862528 nycscary msn

President: John B Krauss (and Chief Executive Officer)
Senior Executive Officers: Robert E Penrod (Group VP), Arthur F Smith (Group VP), Keith Brue (VP and Treasurer), Joseph Royere (VP, President Nicolet Computer Graphics Division), Hiroshi Bando (VP, Manager Nicolet Japan Corp), Richard J Cushing (VP, President Nicolet Analytical), Robert L Olsen (VP, President Nicolet Biomedical), Gregory B Johnson (VP International Operations)

PRINCIPAL ACTIVITIES: Manufacture of engineering and scientific instruments; electronic computing equipment
Principal Bank: M & I Bank of Madison
Financial Information:

	$'000
Sales revenues	114,000

No of Employees: 1,000

NICOR INC
1700 West Ferry Rd, PO Box 200, Naperville, IL 60566-0200
Tel: (312) 242-4470
Telex: 9106510071 NICOR INC NPVL

Chairman: Richard G Cline (and President and Chief Executive Officer)
Senior Executive Officers: Thomas L Fisher (VP Operations), John C Flowers (VP Human Resources), John J Lannon (VP Finance), Kathleen L Halloran (Secretary and Controller), D W Lohrentz (Treasurer)

PRINCIPAL ACTIVITIES: NICOR is a diversified holding company engaged in the purchase, storage, distribution, transportation and sale of natural gas; oil and gas exploration and production; gas gathering and marketing; offshore marine support to the oil and gas industry; and containerized liner shipping
Principal Subsidiaries: Northern Illinois Gas Company; NICOR Exploration Company; Reliance Pipeline Company; Tropical Shipping and Construction Co Ltd; NICOR Marine Inc
Principal Bankers: The Northern Trust company, Chicago, IL
Financial Information:

	Dec 31 1985	Dec 31 1986
	$'000	$'000
Sales revenues	2,128,799	1,806,921
Income before taxes(1)	26,509	132,939
Net income(1)	11,396	79,961
Total income (loss)	(152,059)	183,146
Dividends(2)	85,150	53,278
Dividends(3)	6,540	5,827
Dividends per share(2)	$3.04	$1.80
Earnings per share(1)	$0.17	$2.52
Earnings (loss) per share(4)	($5.69)	$6.01
Common stock(5)	28,202	29,645
Retained earnings(6)	-	124,225
Shareholders equity	371,245	525,419

(1) continuing operations
(2) common
(3) preferred and preference
(4) total earnings
(5) outstanding at year end in thousands
(6) NICOR charged the Dec 31 1985 deficit in retained earnings against paid-in capital

No of Employees: 4,100

NIEDERMEYER-MARTIN CO

PO Box 3768, Portland, OR 97208
Tel: (503) 287-2411
Telex: WUT 151323 niedo ptl

President: E C Niedermayer
Senior Executive Officers: T J Niedermayer (Executive VP) Stephen V Nava (VP International Sales)

PRINCIPAL ACTIVITIES: Forest products including building materials, plywood and lumber
Principal Bank: First Interstate Bank of Oregon
Financial Information:

	$'000
Sales revenues	50,000

No of Employees: 120

NIELSEN, A C, CO

Nielsen Plaza, Northbrook, IL 60062
Tel: (312) 498-6300
Telex: WUT 206466 niel nrbk

Chairman: H Burk (and Chief Executive Officer)
President: N E Hardin
Senior Executive Officers: James D Lyons (Executive VP MR Management), K J Burghardt (Executive VP NEO Management), R B Moran (Executive VP NCH), Richard W Vipond (Executive VP Marketing), W N Fleischman (VP Administration and Real Estate), James W Carter Jr (VP and General Counsel), Philip R Nielsen (VP Corporate Planning and Development), L G Honeywell (VP Finance)

PRINCIPAL ACTIVITIES: General business consultants; market research and consumer information
Parent Company: The Dun & Bradstreet Corporation, New York, NY
Principal Bank: Harris Trust and Savings Bank
Financial Information:

	$'000
Sales revenues	680,000

No of Employees: 21,570

NIKE, INC

3900 S W Murray Blvd, Beaverton, OR 97005
Tel: (503) 641-6453
Telex: TWX 910 333 9969 nike ud

Chairman: Philip H Knight (and President and Chief Executive Officer); Vice Chairman: William J Bowerman
Senior Executive Officers: Delbert J Hayes (Executive VP), David Chang (VP), Neil Goldschmidt (VP), James Manns (VP), Robert L Mueller (VP), Ronald E Nelson (VP), George E Porter (VP Finance), Robert Strasser (VP), Richard H Werschkul (VP), Dale N Wahl (Treasurer)

PRINCIPAL ACTIVITIES: Manufacture of sports shoes and clothing
Principal Bank: Seattle First National Bank
Financial Information:

	May 31 1985	May 31 1986
	$'000	$'000
Sales revenues	946,370	1,069,222
Net income	10,270	59,211
Earnings per share	$0.27	$1.55
Shareholders equity	271,970	316,846

No of Employees: 3,400

NIXDORF COMPUTER CORPORATION

168 Middlesex Tpke, Burlington, MA 01803
Tel: (617) 273-0480
Telex: TWX 710 3321263 nixdorf z burl

Chairman: Heinz Nixdorf; Vice Chairman: Klaus Luft
President: Michael Anderson
Senior Executive Officers: Robert J Nicewicz (Senior VP), James Addlesberger (VP Sales), William Kehrig (VP Manufacturing), John Clifford (VP Finance), Rudolf O Ploue (VP Legal)

PRINCIPAL ACTIVITIES: Production of electronic computing equipment
Parent Company: Nixdorf Computer AG, Paderborn, Germany
Principal Bank: First National Bank of Chicago
Financial Information:

	$'000
Sales revenues	150,000

No of Employees: 2,000

NL INDUSTRIES, INC

1230 Avenue of the America, New York, NY 10020
Tel: (212) 621-9400
Telex: WUT 128212 nli nyk

Chairman: Theodore C Rogers (and President and Chief Executive Officer)
Senior Executive Officers: Fred W Montanari (Executive VP Chemicals and Metals), John R Slowik (Executive VP), Ilan Kaufthal (Senior VP Finance), Robert E Brooker Jr (VP), James A Heely (VP and Controller), Robert J Hurley (VP and General Counsel), Michael L Moore (VP), Jean-Pierre De Vleeschouwer (VP), William H Welch (VP)

PRINCIPAL ACTIVITIES: Manufacture of equipment and operation of services for the oil industry

Financial Information:

	Dec 31 1985	Dec 31 1986
	$'000	$'000
Sales revenues	1,422,995	1,283,203
Net income (loss)	21,530	(324,195)
Earnings (loss) per share	-	($5.80)
Shareholders equity	785,560	356,890

No of Employees: 12,330

NLT CORPORATION

National Life Center, Nashville, TN 37203
Tel: (615) 749-1000

Chairman: Harold S Hook (and Chief Executive Officer); Vice Chairman: H J Bremermann Jr
President: Michael J Poulos
Senior Executive Officers: Neil M Anderson (Executive VP), Nicholas R Rasmussen (Senior VP and Treasurer), Carroll D Shanks (Senior VP)

PRINCIPAL ACTIVITIES: The company has interests in insurance, financial services and real estate

No of Employees: 10,180

NOBIL SHOE CO

1100 E Main Street, Endicott, NY 13760
Tel: (607) 757-4000

President: James H Webster
Senior Executive Officers: George H Hempstead (VP), Kenneth E Mansfield (VP), Charles F Thomas (VP Finance and Treasurer)

PRINCIPAL ACTIVITIES: Retailing of footwear and accessories
Parent Company: Endicott Johnson Corporation
Financial Information:

	$'000
Sales revenues	50,000

No of Employees: 1,500

NOBLE AFFILIATES, INC

333 W Main, PO Box 1967, Ardmore, OK 73402
Tel: (405) 226 1900

Chairman: Sam Noble
President: Robert L Kelley (and Chief Executive Officer)
Senior Executive Officers: William D Dickson (VP Finance and Treasurer)

PRINCIPAL ACTIVITIES: Exploration for and production of oil and natural gas
Principal Subsidiaries: Noble Drilling Corporation; Samedan Oil Corp
Financial Information:

	$'000
Sales revenues	123,000

No of Employees: 1,600

NOLAND COMPANY

2700 Warwick Boulevard, Newport News, VA 23607
Tel: (804) 928-9000
Telex: (804) 244-9817

Chairman: Lloyd U Noland III
President: Carl Watson
Senior Executive Officers: L B Blackmon (VP Manager Merchandising Electrical), Frank L Brewer (VP Manager Merchandising Industrial and Machine Tool), William T Smith (Director, Human Resources), William G Ovoiman (Director, Purchases), A W Granzow (VP, Manager Merchandising Air Conditioning and Refrigeration), John E Gullett (VP, Corporate Communications), Charles A Harvey (VP, Corporate Data), Arthur P Henderson Jr (VP Finance), Don G Hurley (VP, Manager Merchandising Plumbing and Heating)

PRINCIPAL ACTIVITIES: Wholesale supply of ventilation, heating, plumbing and refrigeration products, electrical supplies, well drilling equipment and machine tools
Principal Bank: Crestar Bank
Financial Information:

	Dec 31 1985	Dec 31 1986
	$'000	$'000
Sales revenues	380,913	426,489
Income before taxes	10,996	12,259
Net income	6,457	6,303
Dividends	1,382	1,458
Dividends per share	$0.37	$0.39
Earnings per share	$1.74	$1.70
Common stock	38,273	38,273
Retained income	41,692	46,537
Shareholders equity	79,965	84,810

NORD RESOURCES CORPORATION

8111 Timberlodge Trail, Dayton, OH 45459
Tel: (513) 433 6307

Chairman: Edgar F Cruft (and Chief Executive Officer)
President: Richard L Steinberger (and Secretary)
Senior Executive Officers: Terence H Lang (Senior VP Finance and Treasurer)

PRINCIPAL ACTIVITIES: Mineral exploration and mining
Principal Subsidiaries: Nord Kaolin Corporation; Nord Manatee Limited; Sierra Rutile Limited
Principal Bank: Continental Illinois National Bank and Trust Company
Financial Information:

	$'000
Sales revenues	60,030

No of Employees: 1,000

NORDA INC

140 Rte 10, East Hanover, NJ 07936
Tel: (201) 887-5600
Telex: WUI 685 3095 norda

Chairman: Elena D Benedict
President: Louis J Amaducci (and Chief Executive Officer)
Senior Executive Officers: Robert L Amaducci (Executive VP), Richard A Piemonte (VP Corporate Affairs), John M Colyer (VP)

PRINCIPAL ACTIVITIES: Production of specialty chemicals including fragrance chemicals and flavorings
Principal Bank: Irving Trust Co
Financial Information:

	$'000
Sales revenues	56,000

No of Employees: 350

NORDSON CORPORATION

28601 Clemens Road, Westlake, OH 44145
Tel: (216) 892 1580
Telex: WUT 243 436 nordson d amhr

Chairman: Eric T Nord
President: William P Madar (and Chief Executive Officer)
Senior Executive Officers: Robert E Thayer (President Packaging and Assembly Division), Donald J McLane VP, FED Division), Richard E Klein (VP Engineering), Fred C Erler (VP Human Resources), Drexel R Bunch (VP Quality and Supply), Thomas L Moorhead (VP Law), Toshiro Akasaki (VP Japanese Operations), James C Doughman (Director Public Affairs)

PRINCIPAL ACTIVITIES: Production of industrial coating equipment and packaging machinery
Principal Bank: Society National Bank

Financial Information:

	$'000
Sales revenues	140,000

No of Employees: 1,680

NORDSTROM INC

1501 Fifth Avenue, Seattle, WA 98101
Tel: (206) 628-2111

Co Chairmen: Bruce A Nordstrom, John N Nordstrom
President: James F Nordstrom
Senior Executive Officers: John A McMillan (Executive VP), Robert E Bender (Senior VP), John Goesling (Senior VP, Treasurer and Chief Financial Officer), R Gary Baughn (VP), Dale Crichton (VP), Cindy Demme (VP), Barden Erickson (VP), Darrel Hume (VP), Paul Hunter (VP), Jack Irving (VP), Galen Jefferson (VP), Gail Lessler (VP), Bob Nunn (VP), Suzanne Patneaude (VP), Elizabeth Sanders (VP), Malinda Walderhang (VP)

PRINCIPAL ACTIVITIES: Retail trade in apparel for men, women and children; shoe retailing
Principal Bankers: First Interstate Bank of Washington
Financial Information:

	Dec 31 1986 $'000
Sales revenues	1,629,918
Net income	72,939
Earnings per share	$1.82
Shareholders equity	451,196

No of Employees: 17,800

NORFOLK SHIPBUILDING & DRYDOCK CORPORATION

PO Box 2100, Norfolk, VA 23501-2100
Tel: (804) 545-3551
Telex: WUT 823613 norshipco nfk

Chairman: John L Roper III (and Chief Executive Officer)
President: Charles H Eure Jr (and Chief Operating Officer)
Senior Executive Officers: G H Curtis III (VP Engineering), W D Payne (Executive VP Production), C E Agnese (Senior VP Estimating), E L Carlyle (VP Finance and Treasurer)

PRINCIPAL ACTIVITIES: Shipbuilding and shiprepairing
Trade Names: NORSHIPCO
Principal Subsidiaries: Norshipco Financial Corporation; Marepcon Corporation-International; The Flagship Group, Ltd; CISERV Norfolk, Inc
Principal Bank: Crestar, Norfolk, VA
Financial Information:

	Dec 31 1985 $'000	Dec 31 1986 $'000
Sales revenues	154,400	176,000
Income before taxes	5,300	513
Net income	3,000	436
Retained income	50,000	49,400
Shareholders equity	52,700	52,100

No of Employees: 2,800

NORFOLK SOUTHERN CORPORATION

One Commercial Place, Box 3609, Norfolk, VA 23514
Tel: (804) 629-2600
Telex: TWX 910 350 1949 norfsou hq

Chairman: Arnold B McKinnon (and Chief Executive Officer)
President: Harold H Hall (and Chief Operating Officer)
Senior Executive Officers: John L Jones (Executive VP Administration), D Henry Watts (Executive VP Marketing), John S Shannon (Executive VP Law), John R Turbyfill (Executive VP Finance), Edward B Burwell (President Southern Railway), Richard F Dunlap (President Norfolk & Western Railway), Edward T Breathitt Jr (Senior VP Public Affairs), Hobart L Scott Jr (Senior VP and Chief Mechanical Officer), Walter W Simpson (Senior VP and Chief Engineer), William B Bales (VP Coal and Ore Traffic), R Alan Brogan (VP Material Management), Robert E L deButts (VP Real Estate and Industrial Development), Gerald C Durand (VP Management Information Services), David R Goode (VP Tax), Samuel D Guy (VP Sales), Jean Jones (VP Sepcial Projects), Thomas H Kerwin (VP and Treasurer), Edward G Kreyling Jr (VP Marketing Services), Joseph R Neikirk (VP Personnel and Labor Relations), L I Prillaman Jr (VP Accounting), Magda A Ratajski (VP Public Relations), James L Tapley (VP and Washington Counsel), Donald M Tolmie (VP and General Counsel), Rodney M White (VP and Assistant to Chairman and Chief Executive Officer)

PRINCIPAL ACTIVITIES: Holding company with interests in the operation of railroads
Principal Bank: Sovran Bank
Financial Information:

	Dec 31 1985 $'000	Dec 31 1986 $'000
Sales revenues	3,825,080	4,076,407
Net income	500,230	518,688
Earnings per share	$2.65	$2.74
Shareholders equity	4,761,504	5,070,751

No of Employees: 38,300

NORGREN, C A, CO

5400 S Delaware, Littleton, CO 80120
Tel: (303) 794-2611
FAX: 303/798-4856
Telex: WUT 45541 norgrenco litl

Chairman: T A Lamb
President: George C Loury (and Chief Executive Officer)
Senior Executive Officers: Pat Maley (VP Marketing), Richard N Bailey (VP Engineering), William J Wolsky (VP Manufacturing), Robert A Felt (VP, Treasurer and Secretary), Donald McMahon (VP Administration)

PRINCIPAL ACTIVITIES: Manufacture of valves, filters and lubricators
Trade Names: Norgren
Parent Company: IMI plc, Birmingham, UK
Principal Bank: United Bank of Denver
Financial Information:

	$'000
Sales revenues	50,000

No of Employees: 700

NORSTAN INC

2905 Northwest Boulevard, Minneapolis, MN 55441
Tel: (612) 553 3200

Chairman: Sidney R Cohen; Vice Chairman: Richard Cohen (and VP and Treasurer)
President: Paul Baszucki (and Chief Operating Officer)
Senior Executive Officers: Roger Van Beusekom (VP Finance), Winston E Munson (Secretary)

PRINCIPAL ACTIVITIES: Manufacture of electronic equipment and components
Principal Subsidiaries: Norstan Communication Systems; Norstan Financial Corporation; Norstan Information Systems Inc; Summit Gear Inc
Principal Bank: Norwest Bank Minneapolis
Financial Information:

	$'000
Sales revenues	54,380

No of Employees: 400

NORSTAR BANKCORP INC

Norstar Building, 1450 Western Avenue, Albany, NY 12203
Tel: (518) 447-4043

Chairman: Peter D Kiernan (and President); Vice Chairmen: Robert J Donough, Frank H Odell

Senior Executive Officers: Eugene T Mann (Executive VP), John B Robinson Jr (Executive VP), Robert H Sloan (Executive VP), Barry Brandt (VP Corporate Communications), David M DeFazio (VP), James J McAssey (VP), Harry P Meislahn (VP, Secretary and General Counsel), Stephen T Wilson (VP and Auditor), Richard J Heller (VP, Treasurer and Chief Financial Officer)

PRINCIPAL ACTIVITIES: Holding company with interests in banking and financial services
Principal Bank: Norstar Bank of Upstate New York
Financial Information:

	Dec 31 1985	Dec 31 1986
	$'000	$'000
Net income	93,005	104,830
Earnings per share	$2.54	$2.87
Shareholders equity	692,560	763,864
Deposits	7,350,950	9,009,416
Total assets	8,998,270	11,132,015

No of Employees: 8,680

NORTEK INC

50 Kennedy Plaza, Providence, RI 02903
Tel: (401) 751-1600

Chairman: Ralph R Papitto (and Chief Executive Officer)
President: Richard L Bready (and Chief Operating and Finance Officer)
Senior Executive Officers: Lloyd E Brumley (VP Operations and Controller), Eric W Dehmel (VP Employee Relations and Administration), Bruce E Fleming (VP Corporate Development), Frank P Ganzer (VP Group Operations), Almon C Hall (VP and Controller), Richard J Harris (VP and Treasurer), George O Neumann (VP Group Operations), John R Potter (VP and Secretary), William J Wind (VP Group Operations)

PRINCIPAL ACTIVITIES: Manufacture of building products, electrical products, textiles and metal goods
Principal Bank: Manufacturers Hanover Trust Co
Financial Information:

	Dec 31 1985	Dec 31 1986
	$'000	$'000
Sales revenues	603,370	962,765
Net income	17,600	29,000
Earnings per share	$2.03	$2.00
Shareholders equity	177,790	240,829

No of Employees: 6,480

NORTH AMERICAN BIOLOGICALS INC

16500 Northwest 15th Avenue, Miami, FL 33169
Tel: (305) 625 5303

Chairman: Thomas Halasz (and Chief Executive Officer)
President: David J Gury (and Chief Operating Officer)
Senior Executive Officers: Stephen W Weston (Chief Financial Officer, VP Finance and Treasurer), Morris C Brown (Secretary)

PRINCIPAL ACTIVITIES: Manufacture of biological and clinical diagnostic products; plasma
Principal Bank: Barnett Bank of South Florida
Financial Information:

	$'000
Sales revenues	34,000

No of Employees: 500

NORTH AMERICAN COAL CORPORATION

12800 Shaker Blvd, Cleveland, OH 44120
Tel: (216) 752-1000

Chairman: Otes Bennett (and Chief Executive Officer)
President: Harry L Washburn
Senior Executive Officers: Robert E Murray (Executive VP), Herschell A Cashion (VP Sales), John R Cook (VP Finance and Administration), Robert S Hawekotte (VP and Treasurer), Clifford R Miercort (VP), Thomas A Koza (VP, Secretary and General Counsel)

PRINCIPAL ACTIVITIES: Coal mining
Parent Company: NACCO Industries Inc
Principal Bank: The AmeriTrust Company
Financial Information:

	$'000
Sales revenues	542,000

No of Employees: 3,000

NORTH AMERICAN PHILIPS CORPORATION

100 E 42nd Street, New York, NY 10017
Tel: (212) 697-3600

Chairman: Cees Bruynes (and President)
Senior Executive Officers: Richard A Daunoras (Executive VP and Chief Financial Officer), Frank Hopkins (Executive VP), Edward L Klein (Executive VP), Stephen C Tumminello Jr (Executive VP), Winfred van Hoff (Executive VP), R T Cavanagh (Senior VP), Daniel F Minahan (Senior VP), James S Cole (VP and Controller), Wallace E J Collins (VP, Secretary and General Counsel), Stanley I Cundey Jr (VP and Treasurer), Arthur J Dojan (VP), Charles F Dransfield (VP), Bruce D Bengston (VP), Charles E Ferguson (VP), Larry J French (VP), Paul Friedlander (VP), Patrick J Greaney (VP), Donald L Hamilton (VP), John C Messerschmitt (VP), Albert A Ruttner (VP)

PRINCIPAL ACTIVITIES: Manufacture of electronic equipment and household electrical goods; electro-medical equipment
Principal Bank: The Bank of New York
Financial Information:

	Dec 31 1985	Dec 31 1986
	$'000	$'000
Sales revenues	4,395,210	4,531,640
Net income	81,540	68,520
Earnings per share	$2.82	$2.36
Shareholders equity	1,050,600	1,096,229

No of Employees: 58,760

NORTH AMERICAN PHILIPS LIGHTING CORPORATION

1 Westinghouse Plaza, Bloomfield, NJ 07003
Tel: (201) 429-3000
Telex: RCA 219369 lamp ur

President: Alan K Hegedus
Senior Executive Officers: Francis H Olmstead Jr (Executive VP), R E Cappalli (VP Sales), J J Briody (VP Sales), W V Attardi (VP Marketing), F H Olmstead (VP Marketing), D A Giordano (VP Industrial Relations)

PRINCIPAL ACTIVITIES: Manufacture of lighting equipment
Parent Company: North American Philips Corporation
Financial Information:

	$'000
Sales revenues	600,000

No of Employees: 8,000

NORTH AMERICAN REFRACTORIES CO

Hanna Bldg, E 14th & Euclid, Cleveland, OH 68101
Tel: (216) 348-5000
Telex: TWX 810 4218 108 alcanf dv

President: Edmund S Wright
Senior Executive Officers: R F Whitford (VP Engineering), H P Berry (VP Finance), R C Crosson (VP Marketing), J B Polson (VP Operations)

PRINCIPAL ACTIVITIES: Production of cement and bricks
Parent Company: Kirtland Capital Corporation
Principal Bank: National City Bank

Financial Information:

	$'000
Sales revenues	100,000

No of Employees: 1,000

NORTH AMERICAN SAVINGS ASSOCIATION

125th & South 71 Highway, Grandview, MO 64030
Tel: (816) 765 2200

Chairman: Robert F Hoefer (and Chief Executive Officer)
President: Frank M Pruett
Senior Executive Officers: Donald B Coleman (Senior Executive VP and Chief Financial Officer), Michael R Hoefer (Executive VP), Kurt W Lutz (Senior VP), Joseph A Huppe (VP), Edwin L Stimpson (VP),

PRINCIPAL ACTIVITIES: Financial services including savings and loans
Principal Subsidiaries: Nor-Am Service Corporation; Premium Financing Specialists

No of Employees: 170

NORTH ATLANTIC INDUSTRIES INC

60 Plant Avenue, Hauppauge, NY 11788
Tel: (516) 582 6500

President: Malcom D Widenor
Senior Executive Officers: Walter Lipkin (Senior VP, Treasurer and Secretary), R A Carlson (VP and Division President), B R Clare (VP), J S Truesdell (VP Industrial Relations)

PRINCIPAL ACTIVITIES: Manufacture of laser and dot matrix printers, peripheral products, and other equipment for military operations
Principal Bank: Barclays Bank of New York
Financial Information:

	$'000
Sales revenues	32,000

No of Employees: 470

NORTH CAROLINA FEDERAL SAVINGS & LOAN ASSOCIATION

PO Box 668000, Charlotte, NC 28266
Tel: (704) 847 1344

President: J Graham Harwood
Senior Executive Officers: Richard A Harper (Executive VP), T Kevin Walsh (Executive VP, Treasurer and Chief Financial Officer), Wade H McSwain Jr (Senior VP), Renée E Hatley (Senior VP), James A Coates (Subsidiary Officer), Sherrill Williams (VP)

PRINCIPAL ACTIVITIES: Provision of financial services including savings and loans
Principal Bank: Federal Reserve Bank of Richmond

No of Employees: 275

NORTH CAROLINA NATURAL GAS CORPORATION

150 Rowan Street, Fayetteville, NC 28302
Tel: (919) 483 0315

Chairman: Frank Barrigan Jr (and President)
Senior Executive Officers: Calvin B Wells (Executive VP), William G Hill (Senior VP), Arthur P Gnann Jr (Senior VP), Cecil C Dew (VP and Treasurer), Jerald A Teele (VP), Donald W McCoy (Secretary)

PRINCIPAL ACTIVITIES: Supply of natural gas
Principal Bank: First Union National Bank of North Carolina
Financial Information:

	$'000
Sales revenues	164,000

No of Employees: 440

NORTH DAKOTA MILL ELEVATOR ASSOCIATION

1823 Mill Road, Grand Forks, ND 58201
Tel: (701) 795-7000
Telex: TWX 910 6738383 nd mill gfks

Senior Executive Officers: Sam Kuhl (General Manager), Ben Hennesy (Assistant General Manager)

PRINCIPAL ACTIVITIES: Flour milling and related services
Principal Bank: Bank of North Dakota
Financial Information:

	$'000
Sales revenues	60,000

No of Employees: 145

NORTH FORK BANCORPORATION INC

245 Love Lane, Mattituck, NY 11952
Tel: (516) 298 8366

Chairman: John Adam Kanas (and President); Vice Chairman: Irving L Price Jr
Senior Executive Officers: Frank A Anderson (Senior VP and Secretary), Marilyn E Boehl (VP Administration and Assistant Secretary), Charles W Wright (VP and Treasurer)

PRINCIPAL ACTIVITIES: Banking
Principal Subsidiaries: Acudata Service Corporation; North Fork Bank and Trust Company; North Fork Leasing Corporation
Financial Information:

	1985 $'000
Revenues	37,750
Net income	5,620

No of Employees: 300

NORTH STAR CONCRETE CO

Mound Avenue & Poplar Street, Mankato, MN 56001
Tel: (507) 625-1802

Chairman: Paul W Radichel (and Secretary)
President: William D Radichel
Senior Executive Officers: Myron L Mohr (Executive VP and Treasurer), James Borseth (VP), Bill Malcenf (VP)

PRINCIPAL ACTIVITIES: Production of concrete
Principal Bank: North Western National Bank
Financial Information:

	$'000
Sales revenues	70,000

No of Employees: 750

NORTHEAST BANCORP INC

Church & Elm St., New Haven, CT 06510
Tel: (203) 348-6211

Chairman: Frank J Kugler Jr (and Chief Executive Officer); Vice Chairman: Kenneth A Randall
Senior Executive Officers: George R Kaburek (Senior VP and Chief Financial Officer), Peter V Young (Senior VP), David A Della-Bitta (VP), Joseph A Gozzo (VP), Leo G Kleine (VP), Edward G Williams (VP)

PRINCIPAL ACTIVITIES: Banking services
Financial Information:

	Dec 31 1986 $'000
Revenues	267,000
Net income	35,000

No of Employees: 1,600

NORTHEAST SAVINGS, FA

50 State Street, Hartford, CT 06103
Tel: (203) 280-1000
Fax: (203) 280-1199

Chairman: Kent Dixon (and President and Chief Executive Officer); Vice Chairman: Wallace M Campbell

Senior Executive Officers: Howard G Carpenter Jr (Senior Executive VP, General Counsel and Corporate Secretary)

PRINCIPAL ACTIVITIES: Financial services including savings and loans

Financial Information:

	Mar 31 1986	Mar 31 1987
	$'000	$'000
Income before taxes	37,804	35,706
Net income	37,804	33,276
Preferred dividends	1,600	3,622
Earnings per share(1)	$7.07	$5.58
Earnings per share(2)	$5.93	$3.77
Common stock(3)	51	52
Retained income	105,458	135,112
Shareholders equity	222,195	316,660
Deposits	3,186,573	3,713,968
Total assets	5,075,023	6,264,657

(1) primary
(2) fully diluted
(3) $1.00 par value

No of Employees: 1,565

NORTHEAST UTILITIES

PO Box 270, Hartford, CT 06141-0270
Tel: (203) 665-5000

Chairman: William B Ellis (and President and Chief Executive Officer)

Senior Executive Officers: Bernard M Fox (VP and Chief Financial Officer)

PRINCIPAL ACTIVITIES: Supply of gas and electricity

Principal Subsidiaries: The Connecticut Light and Power Company; Western Massachusetts Electric Company; Holyoke Water Power Company

Principal Bank: Hartford National Bank

Financial Information:

	Dec 31 1985	Dec 31 1986
	$'000	$'000
Sales revenues	2,081,021	2,032,117
Net income	288,541	300,894
Earnings per share	$2.72	$2.78
Shareholders equity	1,738,871	1,884,145

No of Employees: 9,132

NORTHERN AIR FREIGHT INC

330-120th Ave NE, PO Box 6969, Bellevue, WA 98008
Tel: (206) 646-7171
Telex: 261759 (RCA) Answerback: NAF NSC; 4979607 (ITT) Answerback: NAF NSC
Telefax: (206) 646-7188

Chairman: John E Whalen (and President and Chief Executive Officer)

Senior Executive Officers: John S Diefendorf (Chief Operating Officer), Malcolm J Montague (VP-Finance and Secretary-Treasurer). Regional Vice Presidents: Philip E Cranmer (VP-Alaska/Hawaii Region), Anthony V Fiacchino (VP-Northeast Region), David Kratochvil (VP-Midwest Region), Henry G McDonnell (VP-Northwest Region), Gerald C Nichols (VP-Southeast Region), Marcos G Figueroa (VP-Southwest Region). Corporate Staff: David L Greenshields (VP-Pricing/Claims), William W LaMothe (VP-International), Charles R Nelson (VP-Operations), Michael J Schuller (VP-Sales and Marketing), Robert A Warren (VP-Far East)

PRINCIPAL ACTIVITIES: Air freight forwarding

Trade Names: MAX I, MAX II, FREIGHT MISER

Principal Subsidiaries: Northern Consolidators Inc

Principal Bank: Rainier National Bank, Seattle

Financial Information:

	Dec 31 1985	Dec 31 1986
	$'000	$'000
Sales revenues	55,155	58,827
Income before taxes	780	1,009
Net income	476	536
Earnings per share net	$0.26	$0.29
Common stock	18	18
Retained income	3,940	4,477
Shareholders equity	6,429	6,965

Principal Shareholders: John Whalen; State Farm Ins; Quest Advisory Group

No of Employees: 510

NORTHERN FIBRE PRODUCTS CO

50 W Third Street, Holland, MI 49423
Tel: (616) 396-3528
Telex: TWX 810 2926 158 nf p hlnd ud

Senior Executive Officers: D F Sallee (VP)

PRINCIPAL ACTIVITIES: Manufacture of motor vehicle trim

Parent Company: Sheller-Globe Corp

Principal Bank: National Bank of Detroit

Financial Information:

	$'000
Sales revenues	50,000

No of Employees: 500

NORTHERN GAS PRODUCTS CO

2223 Dodge Street, Omaha, NE 68101
Tel: (402) 348-5000

President: H L Hawks

Senior Executive Officers: L E Bauer (Senior VP), J R Empson (VP Administration), D W Ryser (VP), L H Kaiser (VP), S M Sawtell (VP), J G Scoville (VP), H F Matheson (VP Finance), F J Duffy (VP)

PRINCIPAL ACTIVITIES: Extraction and sale of liquid natural gas

Parent Company: Internorth Inc

Financial Information:

	$'000
Sales revenues	235,000

No of Employees: 400

NORTHERN INDIANA PUBLIC SERVICE CO

5265 Hohman Avenue, Hammond, IN 46320
Tel: (219) 853-5200
Telex: TWX 910 6963886 nip sco hmd

Chairman: Edmund A Schroer (and President and Chief Executive Officer)

Senior Executive Officers: Jack Stine (Executive VP and Chief Operating Officer), John W Dunn (Senior VP and General Manager, Energy Distribution), Glen E LaVine (Treasurer)

PRINCIPAL ACTIVITIES: Gas and electricity supply

Principal Subsidiaries: Shore Line Shops Incorporated; NIPSCO Exploration Company Inc; NIPSCO Fuel Company Inc; NIPSCO Energy Services Inc

Principal Bank: Continental Illinois National Bank & Trust Company of Chicago

Financial Information:

	Dec 31 1985	Dec 31 1986
	$'000	$'000
Revenues	1,908,503	1,626,127
Income before taxes	269,442	233,670(1)
Net income (loss)(2)	107,141	(14,117)(3)
Extraordinary loss	94,843(4)	-
Net income (loss)	12,298	(14,117)
Dividends	83,354	-
Dividends per share	$1.56	-
Earnings (loss) per share(2)	$1.10	($0.57)
Extraordinary (loss)	($1.33)(4)	-
(Loss) per average share	($0.23)	($0.57)
Common stock	974,172	858,418
Retained income	28,642	104,294
Shareholders equity	1,002,814	962,712

(1) excludes income taxes related to satisfaction of Carbon County Coal contract dispute of $91,687,000
(2) before extraordinary item
(3) the 1986 loss included a charge of $193,645,000 ($101,958,000 after taxes) relating to satisfaction of the Carbon County Coal dispute
(4) extraordinary loss related to Bailly N1 plant abandonment-net of income taxes

Principal Shareholders: Depositories
No of Employees: 5,695

NORTHERN PETROCHEMICAL CO

2223 Dodge Street, Omaha, NE 68102
Tel: (402) 633-5628
Telex: TWX 910 622 0328

Chairman: S F Segnar; Vice Chairman: G L Severa
President: W R Beasley
Senior Executive Officers: H J Hyatt (Executive VP Marketing), W J Monahan (Senior VP National Accounts), L H Kaiser (VP and Treasurer), R L Lienemann (VP Administration), S J MacEachen (VP), D R Overholt (VP), S J MacEachen (VP), D R Overholt (VP), J S Prentice (VP), S M Sawtell (VP and Secretary), R E Taylor (VP)

PRINCIPAL ACTIVITIES: Production of petrochemicals, synthetic resins and plastics
Parent Company: Internorth Inc
Financial Information:

	$'000
Sales revenues	330,000

No of Employees: 1,300

NORTHERN STATES POWER CO (MN)

414 Nicollet Mall, Minneapolis, MN 55401
Tel: (612) 330-5500
Fax: 330-2900

Chairman: Donald W McCarthy
President: James J Howard (and Chief Executive Officer)
Senior Executive Officers: Roland Jensen (Senior VP-Power Supply), Harry W Spell (Senior VP Finance and Chief Financial Officer), J A Cascalenda (VP Public Affairs)

PRINCIPAL ACTIVITIES: Supply of gas, electricity and steam; telecommunications services

Financial Information:

	Dec 31 1986
	$'000
Sales revenues	1,781,630
Net income	206,882
Preferred dividends	13,539
Common dividends	116,641
Dividends per share	$1.865
Earnings per share	$3.09
Common stock	512,019
Retained income	788,697
Common stock equity	1,300,716

No of Employees: 7,515

NORTHERN TRUST CORPORATION

50 S La Salle Street, Chicago, IL 60675
Tel: (312) 630-6000

Chairman: Weston R Christopherson; Vice Chairman: Robert F Reusché
President: David W Fox (and Chief Operating Officer)
Senior Executive Officers: Robert G Dederick (Executive VP), Van R Gathany (Executive VP), Clyde W Reighard (Executive VP), John S Sutfin (Executive VP and Chief Financial Officer), John H Robinson (Senior VP and Controller), Perry R Pero (Executive VP), John B Snyder (Executive VP and General Counsel/Secretary), David L Eddy (Senior VP and Treasurer)

PRINCIPAL ACTIVITIES: Banking
Principal Subsidiaries: Northern Trust Company
Financial Information:

	Dec 31 1985	Dec 31 1986
	$'000	$'000
Income before taxes	34,943	60,632
Net income	34,133	52,290
Preferred dividends	3,347	2,981
Common dividends	13,509	13,708
Dividends per common share	$0.9066	$0.9166
Earnings per share	$2.07	$3.24
Common equity(1)	371,038	408,543
Shareholders equity(2)	406,038	496,043
Deposits	5,032,241	6,207,109
Total assets	7,500,172	9,090,107

(1) at December 31
(2) including preferred

No of Employees: 4,895

NORTHFIELD CHEESE CO

375 Chestnut, Northvale, NJ 07648
Tel: (201) 767-8010
Telex: WUT 642371 norcheese nval

Chairman: Daniel Kane
President: Mark O Robbins
Senior Executive Officers: Laurence Needleman (Executive VP), Charles Leister (VP Mid Atlantic Region)

PRINCIPAL ACTIVITIES: Production of cheese
Parent Company: Kane-Miller Corp
Principal Bank: The Bank of New York
Financial Information:

	$'000
Sales revenues	60,000

No of Employees: 150

NORTHLAND ALUMINUM PRODUCTS, INC

Hwy7 at 100, Minneapolis, MN 55416
Tel: (612) 920-2888

Chairman: H D Dalquist Sr (and Chief Executive Officer)
President: H D Dalquist III
Senior Executive Officers: Don Mathiowetz (Controller)

PRINCIPAL ACTIVITIES: Manufacture of cooking and catering eqiupment

Trade Names: Nordic Ware
Principal Bank: First Bank
Financial Information:

	$'000
Sales revenues	65,000

No of Employees: 500

NORTHROP CORPORATION

1840 Century Park E, Los Angeles, CA 90067
Tel: (213) 553-6262
Telex: WUT 181 861 northr a hurth

Chairman: Thomas W Jones (and Chief Executive Officer); Vice Chairman: Frank W Lynch
President: Kent Kresa (and Chief Operating Officer)
Senior Executive Officers: Donald A Hicks (Senior VP Marketing), William M Elliott (Senior VP), William G McGagh (Senior VP Finance), Welko E Gasich (Senior VP), Stanley Ebner (Senior VP), David N Ferguson (Group VP)

PRINCIPAL ACTIVITIES: Production of aircraft and aerospace equipment and components; electronics systems; advanced weaponry systems
Principal Subsidiaries: Northrop Services Inc; Northrop Worldwide Aircraft Services Inc
Principal Bank: The Chase Manhattan Bank
Financial Information:

	Dec 31 1985	Dec 31 1986
	$'000	$'000
Sales revenues	5,056,600	5,608,400
Income before taxes	348,100	49,500
Net income	214,400	41,200
Dividends	55,600	55,800
Dividends per share	$1.20	$1.20
Earnings per share	$4.63	$0.89
Common stock	161,600	176,800
Retained income	755,500	740,900
Shareholders equity	899,600	898,700

No of Employees: 46,800

NORTHWEST AIRLINES, INC

NWA Inc

Minneapolis-St Paul International Airport, St Paul, MN 55111
Tel: (612) 726-2111
Telex: WUT 297 024 nwair stp a

Chairman: Steven G Rothmeier (and Chief Executive Officer)
President: John F Horn (and Chief Operating Officer)
Senior Executive Officers: James A Abbott (Vice Chairman and General Counsel), Benjamin G Griggs Jr (Executive VP-Operations), T J Koors (Executive VP-Customer Serivces), E B Magary (Executive VP-Marketing), John A Edwardson (Executive VP-Finance), William C Wren (VP-Public Relations)

PRINCIPAL ACTIVITIES: Air transportation services
Principal Subsidiaries: Northwest Airlines; NATCO; Mainline Travel Inc
Financial Information:

	Dec 31 1986	Dec 31 1986
	$'000	$'000
Sales revenues	2,655,490	3,589,174
Net income	73,120	76,941
Earnings per share	$3.18	$3.26
Shareholders equity	947,000	1,105,916

No of Employees: 34,080

NORTHWEST CHEMCO, INC

6300 Sears Tower, Chicago, IL 60606
Tel: (312) 876-7000

Chairman: Ben W Heineman (and President)
Senior Executive Officers: Bernard Firestone (VP and Treasurer), Brendan M O'Neill (VP Finance)

PRINCIPAL ACTIVITIES: Manufacture of industrial and agricultural chemicals
Parent Company: Northwest Industries Inc
Financial Information:

	$'000
Sales revenues	215,000

No of Employees: 1,600

NORTHWEST NATURAL GAS COMPANY

220 NW Second Avenue, One Pacific Square, Portland, OR 97209
Tel: (503) 226 4211

Chairman: Ronald T Miller
President: Robert L Ridgley (and Chief Executive Officer and Chairman Executive Committee)
Senior Executive Officers: Joseph R Smith (Senior VP Operations), Bruce R DeBolt (VP Legal and Corporate Development), Dwayne L Foley (VP Gas Supply), William L Gibbs (VP Operations), John K Lobdell (VP Corporate Communications) Michael S McCoy (VP), Wesley E Radford (VP Finance, Treasurer and Assistant Secretary), James J Vistica (Controller and Assistant Treasurer), C J Rue (Secretary), Patric D Dignan (VP Marketing), Paul L Hathaway (Senior VP Corporate Development and Human Resources), Donald J Miller (VP Corporate Planning and Business Development), G Richard Weaver (VP Human Resources)

PRINCIPAL ACTIVITIES: Supply of natural gas
Principal Subsidiaries: Biogas Technology Inc; Oregon Natural Gas Development; Pacific Square Corporation
Principal Bank: Bankers Trust Co
Financial Information:

	$'000
Sales revenues	412,160

No of Employees: 1,240

NORTHWEST PAPER DIVISION

Avenue C & Arch, Cloquet, MN 55720
Tel: (218) 879-2300
Telex: TWX 910 561 2111

Senior Executive Officers: Edwin F Erickson (VP and General Manager), Patrick R Nortah (Divisional VP Marketing), Arnold C Oss Jr (Divisional VP Sales), Archie D Chelseth (Divisional Public Relations Manager)

PRINCIPAL ACTIVITIES: Manufacture of paper; printing
Parent Company: Potlatch Corporation, San Francisco, CA
Financial Information:

	$'000
Sales revenues	280,000

No of Employees: 1,800

NORTHWEST PIPELINE CORPORATION

295 Chipeta Way, Salt Lake City, UT 84108
Tel: (801) 583 8800

Chairman: V T Jones (and Chief Executive Officer)
President: R W Keener (and Chief Operating Officer)
Senior Executive Officers: H F Assmus (Senior VP), T J Hausler (VP), J R Herbster (VP), L A Hightower (VP), L C Randolph (VP), J Douglas Whisenant (VP, Controller and Chief Accounting Officer)

PRINCIPAL ACTIVITIES: Supply of natural gas
Parent Company: Northwest Energy Company
Financial Information:

	$'000
Sales revenues	1,138,980

No of Employees: 900

NORTHWESTERN MUTUAL LIFE INSURANCE CO (THE)

720 E Wisconsin Avenue, Milwaukee, WI 53202

Tel: 1-414-271-1444

President: Donald J Schuenke (and Chief Executive Officer)

Senior Executive Officers: Peter W Bruce (Senior VP, General Counsel and Secretary), Robert O Carboni (VP Communications), Robert E Carlson (Executive VP), Gordon C Davidson (Senior VP, Securities), James W Ehrenstrom (VP, Human Resources), James D Ericson (Executive VP), Edward A Flitz (VP, Information Systems), Richard L Hall (VP-Individual Product Marketing), Madonna M Hostetter (VP-New Business), Francis J Kosednar (VP, Administrative Services), Kenneth J Lafferty (VP, Group and Pension Marketing), Gary E Long (VP and Controller), James C McDonald (VP, Assistant to the President), James J Murphy (VP and Chief Actuary), Robert W Ninneman (Senior VP, Operations), James F Reiskytl (VP-Tax and Financial Planning), Frank H Rice FSA (VP, Policy Benefits), Frederic H Sweet (VP), Dennis Tamcsin (Senior VP, Agencies), Walter J Wojcik (Senior VP, Corporate Planning), Richard W Wright (Executive VP), Edward J Zore (Senior VP and Treasurer), Donald L Mellish (VP Field Financial Services), Mason G Ross (VP Real Estate), Leonard F Stecklein (VP Policyowner Services)

PRINCIPAL ACTIVITIES: The Northwestern Mutual Life Insurance Co is the 10th largest life insurance firm in the US, with assets of more than $16 billion. In addition to life insurance, the company offers disability insurance and a variety of fixed-dollar and variable annuities

Trade Names: Northwestern Mutual Life

Financial Information:

	Dec 31 1985	Dec 31 1986
	$'000	$'000
Premium income	2,484,600	2,979,900
Investment income	1,331,100	1,441,400

No of Employees: 2,400

NORTHWESTERN NATIONAL LIFE INSURANCE CO

20 Washington Avenue S, Minneapolis, MN 55440

Tel: (612) 372-5432

Telex: WUT 29 06 45 nwnatllife mps

Chairman: John E Pearson (and Chief Executive Officer)

President: John G Turner (and Chief Operating Officer)

Senior Executive Officers: Don D Henyan (Executive VP Group), Philip A Larson (Executive VP Individual Insurance), R Michael Conley (Senior VP, Group Customer Division), John H Flittie (Senior VP and Chief Financial Officer), David W Haskin (Senior VP, Corporate Resources), Royce N Sanner (Senior VP, General Counsel and Secretary), Steven W Wishart (Senior VP, Investments and Pensions)

PRINCIPAL ACTIVITIES: Insurance services

Principal Subsidiaries: North Atlantic Life Insurance Company; Northern Life Insurance Company; NWNL General Insurance Company; NWNL Management Corporation; NWNL Reinsurance Company; Washington Square Capital, Inc; NWNL Life Assurance Company; NWNL Benefits Corporation

Financial Information:

	Dec 31 1985	Dec 31 1986
	$'000	$'000
Premium income	1,427,632	1,367,573
Investment income	295,120	340,643
Income before taxes	35,061	67,120
Operating income	25,984	48,472
Dividends*	7,472	8,684
Dividends per share*	$0.80	$0.845
Operating earnings per share*	$2.02	$3.33
Common stock*	11,675	13,975
Retained income*	225,761	265,549
Shareholders equity*	282,027	371,786

*stock department only

No of Employees: 2,945 and 14,042 agents under contract

NORTHWESTERN PUBLIC SERVICE COMPANY

Third Street and Dakota Avenue South, Huron, SD 57350
Tel: (605) 352 8411

Chairman: A D Schmidt (and Chief Executive Officer)
President: R A Wilkens (and Chief Operating Officer)
Senior Executive Officers: R N Graham (VP Operations), R E Heimlich (VP Operations), E H Dickol (VP Finance and Treasurer), D A Larson (Controller), E E Hoyt (Senior VP Legal, Secretary and Assistant Treasurer), A M Lau (VP Corporate Services), I J Strommen (Assistant VP)

PRINCIPAL ACTIVITIES: Supply of electricity and natural gas
Principal Bank: Chase Manhattan Bank
Financial Information:

	$'000
Sales revenues	125,990

No of Employees: 470

NORTHWESTERN STEEL & WIRE CO

121 Wallace Street, Sterling, IL 61081
Tel: (815) 625-2500
Telex: TWX 910 6423894 nws & w stly

Chairman: Peter W Dillon
President: Robert M Wilthew (and Chief Executive Officer)
Senior Executive Officers: C H Biermann (VP), Edward G Maris (VP Finance, Secretary and Treasurer), Robert W Martin (VP), Tom L Galanis (VP), Michael J Mullen (VP)

PRINCIPAL ACTIVITIES: Manufacture of fabricated wire products and structural steel
Principal Bank: American National Bank and Trust Company of Chicago
Financial Information:

	Jul 31 1986	Jul 31 1987
	$'000	$'000
Sales revenues	356,165	397,429
Income before taxes	6,101	10,322
Net income	6,101	10,322
Dividends	-	1,502
Dividends per share	-	$0.20
Earnings per share	$0.81	$1.38
Common stock	38,505	38,505
Retained income	119,517	128,337
Shareholders equity	158,022	166,842

No of Employees: 2,800

NORTON CO

120 Front Street, Worcester, MA 01608-1446
Tel: (617) 795-5000
Telex: 920-428; TWX: 710-340-1126

Chairman: Donald R Melville (and Chief Executive Officer)
President: John M Nelson (and Chief Operating Officer)

Senior Executive Officers: Bernard F Meyer (Group VP-Engineering Materials), Michael F Mee (VP Finance and Chief Financial Officer)

PRINCIPAL ACTIVITIES: Norton Company, with more than 100 years' experience in materials engineering, is the world's leading manufacturer of abrasives, and produces technologically advanced ceramics, plastics, and products used in chemical processing, Through joint ventures, it is a leading supplier of performance drilling products and services for the energy industry

Principal Bank: First National Bank of Boston

Financial Information:

	Dec 31 1985	Dec 31 1986
	$'000	$'000
Sales revenues	1,193,000	1,107,100
(Loss) before taxes	(177,500)	(13,800)
Net (loss)	(129,800)	(33,100)
Dividends per share	$2.00	$2.00
(Loss) per share	($1.63)	($6.50)
Common stock*	20,000	20,400
Retained income	330,100	256,300
Shareholders equity	499,100	453,100
*number of shares in thousands		

No of Employees: 15,000

NORTON SIMON, INC

114 Avenue of the Americas, New York, NY 10036
Tel: (212) 704-0744
Telex: TRT 177350 nosim ut

Chairman: James L Dutt (and President and Chief Executive Officer)

Senior Executive Officers: James A Johnson (VP Finance), Chance Bahadur (VP)

PRINCIPAL ACTIVITIES: Diversified company with interests in the manufacture and sale of cosmetics and perfumes; car rental and leasing services; the manufacture of ladies' apparel; food products including edible oils and fats; canned fruit and vegetables and the manufacture of cans; printing including magazines and dress patterns; advertising

Parent Company: BCI Holdings Corp

Principal Subsidiaries: Max Factor & Co; Avis Inc; Halston Enterprises Inc; Hunk Foods & Industries Inc; Hunt-Wesson Foods Inc; McCall Pattern Co; Norton Simon Communications; Norton Simon International; Southern Cotton Co Inc; United Can Co

Financial Information:

	$'000
Sales revenues	3,000,000

No of Employees: 35,000

NORWEST BANK OMAHA, NA

1919 Douglas Street, Omaha, NE 68103
Tel: (402) 536-2000

Chairman: James R Campbell

President: John R Cochran (and Chief Operating Officer)

Senior Executive Officers: G W O'Keefe (Executive VP), Jon A Lindhjem (Executive VP and Chief Financial Officer), Edward Kohout (Senior VP), Paul D Kadavy (Senior VP), Jack Shafer (Senior VP), Robert E Dahl (Senior VP), David R Michael (Senior VP)

PRINCIPAL ACTIVITIES: Banking

Parent Company: Norwest Corporation

No of Employees: 355

NORWEST CORPORATION

1200 Peavey Bldg, Minneapolis, MN 55479
Tel: (612) 372-8268

Chairman: Lloyd P Johnson (and Chief Executive Officer); Vice Chairmen: Richard M Kovacevick (and Chief Operating Officer Banking Group); Richard S Levitt (and Chief Operating Officer Specialized Finance Group)

Senior Executive Officers: Kenneth R Murray (Executive VP), Brian R Phillips (Executive VP), Pierce R Smith (Senior VP and Treasurer), Stanley S Stroup (Senior VP, Secretary and General Counsel), John T Thornton (Senior VP and Controller), John E Allerson (VP, Treasurer and Assistant Controller), J Daniel Vandermark (VP)

PRINCIPAL ACTIVITIES: Holding company with interests in banking

Principal Bank: Norwest Bank

Financial Information:

	Dec 31 1985	Dec 31 1986
	$'000	$'000
Income before taxes	107,600	121,700
Earnings per share	$3.20	$3.64
Shareholders equity	1,219,300	1,303,500
Deposits	14,336,800	14,099,800
Total assets	21,418,600	21,539,400

No of Employees: 15,300

NORWEST FINANCIAL, INC

206 8th Street, Des Moines, IA 50309
Tel: (515) 243-2131

Chairman: Richard S Levitt

President: Richard J Brinkman

Senior Executive Officers: Robert H Cox (Senior VP), H R Evans (Senior VP), Donald C Carano (Senior VP), David C Wood (Senior VP and Secretary), Dennis E Young (Senior VP and Treasurer), James R Berens (VP and General Counsel), Marylee Lankamer (VP), Alfred Z Winick (VP)

PRINCIPAL ACTIVITIES: Financial services; leasing; life insurance and data services

Parent Company: Norwest Financial Services Inc-Ultimate Holding Company-Norwest Corporation

Principal Bank: Continental Illinois National Bank & Trust of Chicago

No of Employees: 3,170

NOVELL INC

1170 North Industrial Park Drive, Orem, UT 84057
Tel: (801) 226 8202

Chairman: Raymond J Noorda (and President and Chief Executive Officer)

Senior Executive Officers: Harry J Armstrong (VP), G Craig Burton (VP), Judith A Clark (VP), Ronald S Eliason (VP and Treasurer), David P Owen (VP), Kelly H Spencer (VP), L Craig Taylor (VP), David R Bradford (Secretary)

PRINCIPAL ACTIVITIES: Manufacture of data processing and computer products

Financial Information:

	$'000
Sales revenues	82,000

No of Employees: 300

NOVO CORPORATION

1075 Central Park Avenue, Scarsdale, NY 10583
Tel: (914) 472-2252

President: Walter E Bronston (and Chief Executive Officer)

Senior Executive Officers: William I Wunderlich (Executive VP, Treasurer and Chief Financial Officer), Martin J Kabcenell (VP and Secretary)

PRINCIPAL ACTIVITIES: Holding company with interests in data processing and services, paint manufacture and the manufacture of windows

Principal Bank: Carteret Savings Bank

Financial Information:

	$'000
Sales revenues	53,000

No of Employees: 570

NOXELL CORPORATION

11050 Yor Road, Hunt Valley, MD 21030
Tel: (301) 628-7300
Telex: ITT 4991165 noxell

Chairman: G Lloyd Bunting Jr (and Chief Executive Officer)
President: Marvin L Hathaway (and Chief Operating Officer)
Senior Executive Officers: Sears W Ingraham (Executive VP International), Hugh G Arnold (Senior VP International), F J Harrison (Senior VP Marketing), Eugune H Levering (Senior VP Sales), James H Matson (Senior VP Manufacturing), Donald S Arning (VP Purchasing), Franklin J Kneller (VP International), Robert W Lindsay (VP and Secretary), Robert W Pierce (VP Finance), Peter M Troup (VP Cover Girl Cosmetics)

PRINCIPAL ACTIVITIES: Manufacture of cosmetics and skin creams; household cleaning products
Trade Names: Cover Girl
Principal Bank: Maryland National Bank
Financial Information:

	$'000
Sales revenues	439,000

No of Employees: 1,650

NS & T BANKSHARES INC

15th Street & New York Avenue NW, Washington, DC 20005
Tel: (202) 383-8000
Telex: TWX 710 822 9376 ns and t bank wsh

Chairman: John J Mason (and Chief Executive Officer); Vice Chairman: William C Harris
Senior Executive Officers: Stephen C Asheroff (Executive VP Real Estate Finance Division),Peter R Boyd (Executive VP Retail Group), William J Lewis (Executive VP Trust), Peter F Nostrand (Executive VP Commercial Group), James M Wells III (Executive VP Banking Group), James D Barr (Senior VP and Controller), John C Clark III (Senior VP and Legal Counsel), Lewis B Flinn Jr (Senior VP and Secretary), C Garland Hagen (Senior VP and Treasurer)

PRINCIPAL ACTIVITIES: Banking
Parent Company: United Virginia Bankshares Inc
Principal Subsidiaries: NS & T Bank, NA

No of Employees: 600

NU MED INC

16633 Ventura Boulevard, 13th Floor, Encino, CA 91436
Tel: (818) 990 2000
Telefax: (818) 902-2256

Chairman: Maurice Lewitt (and Chief Executive Officer)
President: Kenneth E Rappaport (and Chief Operating Officer)
Senior Executive Officers: William N Hartauer (Executive VP Corporate Financing and Investor Relations), Liston A Witherill (Senior VP), John D Porterfield (Senior VP), Yoram Dor (Executive VP Finance), Stephen A Bowles (Executive VP Operations), Carol Schardt (VP and Assistant Secretary), Leon Lewitt (Secretary), Stuart Bruck (VP Marketing), William Satt (VP), Scott Delanty (Treasurer)

PRINCIPAL ACTIVITIES: Acute care hospitals, psychiatric hospitals and health care facilities
Principal Subsidiaries: National Healthcare Review; Nu-Med Hospitals Inc (owner of acute care facilities); Nu-Med Management; Nursing Services International; Professional Medical Recovery; Home X-Ray Service of America; Nu-Med Clinics; Nu-Med Psychiatric Inc (owner of psychiatric facilities)
Principal Bank: U.S. Bank
Financial Information:

	Apr 30 1986	Apr 30 1987
	$'000	$'000
Sales revenues	315,307	391,762
Income before taxes	3,119	8,362
Net income	2,019	4,360
Dividends(1)	833	668
Earnings per share	$0.12	$0.37
Common stock(2)	52,693	29,787
Retained income	13,484	17,176
Shareholders equity	70,824	51,338

(1) on preferred stock
(2) including additional paid-in capital

NUCLEAR DATA, INC

500 Park Blvd, Itasca, IL 60143
Tel: (312) 773-0200

President: Richard J Sandberg (and Chief Executive Officer)
Senior Executive Officers: Harold E Tellefsen (Senior VP), C S Havens (VP Finance), Raymond C Master (Senior VP Instrumentation Division), Gerald W Gaughran (VP Engineering, Executive VP and General Manager Instrumentation Division), Albert E Puhlman (President Metropolitan Circuits Inc)

PRINCIPAL ACTIVITIES: Manufacture of data processing equipment; computer software and services; electronic equipment
Principal Subsidiaries: Metropolitan Circuits Inc of Cal; Metropolitan Circuits Inc of Ill; Metropolitan Circuits Inc of NJ; Nuclear Data GmbH (Germany); Nuclear Data (UK); Nuclear Data Instruments AB (Sweden); Nuclear Data Instrumentation; ASTA/Advanced Science and Technology Associates
Principal Bank: Continental Illinois National Bank and Trust Company of Chicago
Financial Information:

	$'000
Sales revenues	53,000

No of Employees: 840

NUCLEAR METALS INC

2229 Main Street, Concord, MA 01742
Tel: (617) 369 5410
Telex: TWX 710-347-1056
Telefax: (617) 263-8884

Chairman: George J Matthews
President: Wilson B Tuffin (and Treasurer)
Senior Executive Officers: Paul Loewenstein (VP), R Bruce MacKay (VP Operations), Thomas A Wooters (Financial), George A Clattenburg (VP Engineering), Alden R Gilman (VP Health and Safety), Robert Quinn (VP Sales)

PRINCIPAL ACTIVITIES: Nuclear Metals Inc utilizes over 40 years of sophisticated metallurgical technology in the development and manufacture of unique metal products for a broad range of applications. Products include depleted uranium penetrators used for armor piercing ammunition by each branch of the US armed forces, and spherical REP powders used in aerospace, medical, photocopier and specialty areas. NMI also produces specialty products consisting of depleted uranium components for commercial applications, extruded beryllium tubing and dissimilar metal transition joints for aerospace applications, braze rings for a reactor application, and high temperature bearing steel used in aircraft engines
Principal Subsidiaries: Carolina Metals Inc

Financial Information:

	Sep 30 1986	Sep 30 1987
	$'000	$'000
Sales revenues	41,770	42,395
Income (loss) before taxes	5,617	(3,019)
Net income (loss)	2,782	(1,567)
Earnings (loss) per share	$1.03	($0.58)
Common stock	271	271
Retained earnings	25,936	24,369
Shareholders equity	42,198	40,632

No of Employees: 569

NUCOR CORPORATION

4425 Randolph Road, Charlotte, NC 28211
Tel: (704) 366-7000
Telex: WUT 572411 n u e cha

Chairman: F Kenneth Iverson (and Chief Executive Officer)
President: Hugh D Aycock
Senior Executive Officers: Samuel Siegel (VP Finance), Hasting M Crapse (VP and General Manager Vulcraft Alabama Division), John A Doherty (VP and General Manager Nucor Steel Nebraska Division), James W Cunningham (VP and General Manager Research Chemicals Division), William J Kontor (VP and General Manager Nucor Steel Texas Division), Donald N Holloway (VP and General Manager Vulcraft Nebraska Division), Larry A Roos (VP and General Manager Vulcraft Texas Division), Richard L Havekost (VP and General Manager Vulcraft South Carolina Division), Keith E Busse (VP and General Manager Vulcraft Indiana Division), Wilburn G Manuel (VP and General Manager Nucor Steel Utah Division), John D Correnti (VP and General Manager Vulcraft Utah Division)

PRINCIPAL ACTIVITIES: Steel industry
Financial Information:

	Dec 31 1985	Dec 31 1986
	$'000	$'000
Sales revenues	758,500	755,229
Net income	58,480	46,439
Earnings per share	$4.11	$2.17
Shareholders equity	357,500	383,699

No of Employees: 3,900

NUI CORPORATION

11011 Route 22, PO Box 6060, Bridgewater, NJ 08807
Tel: (201) 685 3900

Chairman: John Keane (and President and Chief Executive Officer)
Senior Executive Officers: Joseph P Coughlin (Senior VP Finance and Administration and Treasurer), Russell Fleming Jr (Legal Counsel), James W Christmas (VP Planning)

PRINCIPAL ACTIVITIES: Supply of natural gas
Principal Subsidiaries: Elizabethtown Gas Company; Enercorp; Enercorp Resources; Lenape Resources Corporation; National Computer Utility Company; National Enerdrill Corporation; National Energy Leasing Company; Utility Propane Corporation
Principal Bank: Citibank
Financial Information:

	$'000
Sales revenues	340,000

No of Employees: 1,160

NUMERICA FINANCIAL CORPORATION

1000 Elm Street, Manchester, NH 03101
Tel: (603) 624 2424

Chairman: John J Reilly Jr
President: Ralph E Jensen (and Chief Executive Officer)
Senior Executive Officers: Richard C Ducharme (Executive VP), Carol Themelis (Senior VP), Thomas Boucher (VP and Treasurer), Richard Campbell (VP), Shawn Kelly (VP), Laura Monica (VP)

PRINCIPAL ACTIVITIES: Banking
Financial Information:

	Dec 31 1985
	$'000
Revenues	88,700
Net income	6,270

No of Employees: 500

NUNN-BUSH SHOE CO

PO Box 2047, Milwaukee, WI 53201
Tel: (414) 374-8900
Telex: 910 262 1101
Telefax: (414) 374-6088

Chairman: Thomas W Florsheim; Vice Chairman: Robert Feitler
President: Peter Grossman
Senior Executive Officers: Thomas O McArdle (VP), Michael Melser (VP), Roland L Keuler (Secretary and Treasurer)

PRINCIPAL ACTIVITIES: Manufacture and retail of men's footwear
Trade Names: Nunn-Bush, Brass Boot, Standard Shoes, Morgan Hayes
Parent Company: Weyenberg Shoe Manufacturing Company
Principal Subsidiaries: House of Advertising Inc
Principal Bank: Marine Bank N.A.
Financial Information:

	Dec 31 1985	Dec 31 1986
	$'000	$'000
Sales revenues	73,530	66,113
Income before taxes	3,165	958
Net income	1,705	598
Dividends	-	6,000
Common stock	800	800
Retained income	16,131	10,729*
Shareholders equity	16,931	11,529

*$6,000,000 dividend to parent

Principal Shareholders: Wholly owned subsidiary of Weyenberg Shoe Mfg Co
No of Employees: 600

NUTRI SYSTEM INC

2655 Philmont Ave, Huntingdon Va, PA 19006
Tel: (215) 947-9700

Chairman: Harold Katz
President: A Donald McCulloch Jr (and Chief Executive Officer)
Senior Executive Officers: Norman Amster (VP), Robert Katz (VP and Secretary), Philip Voluck (VP)

PRINCIPAL ACTIVITIES: Slimming centers
Parent Company: Diversified Services Group
Principal Subsidiaries: GMFC Inc; Morris Fox Associates Inc
Principal Bank: Mellon Bank (East)
Financial Information:

	$'000
Sales revenues	101,250

No of Employees: 4,000

NVF COMPANY

Yorklyn Road, Yorklyn, DE 19736
Tel: (302) 239-5281
Telex: RCA 291747 nvf ur

Chairman: Victor Posner (and President and Chief Executive Officer); Vice Chairman: Steven Posner (and Chairman of Executive Committee)
Senior Executive Officers: Walter Sieckman (Group Executive VP), Russell S Davis Jr (Executive VP and Chief Operating Officer), Melvin R Colvin (Senior VP), Jack Coppersmith (Senior VP), Raymond J Dettore (Senior VP), Renee Mottram

(Senior VP), Bernard I Posner (Senior VP), Philip A Samlley Jr (Senior VP Personnel and Organisation), Harry T Clew (VP), Mitchell V Gregory (VP), Robert C Griffin (VP, Treasurer and Assistant Secretary), Leonard Leifert (VP), William N Merchant (VP Finance), Tracy Posner (VP and Assistant Secretary)

PRINCIPAL ACTIVITIES: Manufacture of specialty papers and plastics
Principal Bank: Manufacturers Hanover Trust Company
Financial Information:

	Dec 31 1986
	$'000
Sales revenues	1,100,000

No of Employees: 9,000

NYCOR INC

158 Highway 206, PO Box 502, Peapack, NJ 07977
Tel: (201) 781-5400

Chairman: Salvatore Giordano; Vice Chairman: Salvatore Giordano Jr
President: William J Brennan (and Treasurer)
Senior Executive Officers: Joseph Giordano (Senior VP), S A Muscarnera (Senior VP, General Counsel and Secretary), Robert L Laurent Jr (Controller), John K McFee (VP, President of Rotorex Company), G Nino Palescandolo (VP, Chairman, NYCOR International Business Development Company), Anthony Currerei (VP, NYCOR International Business Development Company)

PRINCIPAL ACTIVITIES: NYCOR, Inc, which until January 27 1987, was a subsidiary of Fedders Corporation, is now a separate public company comprising two operating units, Rotorex Company and FEDCO Automotive Components Company. Rotorex Company, headquartered in Frederick, Maryland, produces hermetic rotary compressors for the air conditioning, refrigeration and related industries. FEDCO Automotive Components Company, headquartered in Buffalo, New York, produces heater cores, and radiators, primarily for the automotive aftermarket
Principal Subsidiaries: Rotorex Company; FEDCO Automotive Components Company
Financial Information:

	Dec 31 1985	Dec 31 1986
	$'000	$'000
Sales Revenues	47,640	49,866
Income before taxes	2,278	3,129
Net income	2,180	3,089
Earnings per share	$0.36	$0.23
Common stock	1	1
Retained (deficit)	(94,914)	(91,825)
Stockholders (deficit)	(8,373)	(5,284)

NYNEX CORPORATION

335 Madison Ave, New York, NY 10017
Tel: (212) 370-7400

Chairman: Delbert C Staley (and Chief Executive Officer); Vice Chairmen: William G Burns, William Ferguson
Senior Executive Officers: Robert J Eckenrode (Executive VP), James E Hennessy (Executive VP Marketing and Technology), Raymond F Burke (VP and General Counsel), Grace J Fippinger (VP, Secretary and Treasurer), Arthur J Keenan (VP and Comptroller), R Bruce Pulling (VP Human Resources), Donald J Sacco (VP Corporate Markting), Ivan G Seidenberg (VP External Affairs), Casimir S Skrzypczak (VP Science and Technology)

PRINCIPAL ACTIVITIES: NYNEX Corporation provides information products and systems to a diverse base of customers regionally, nationally, and internationally. Through New England Telephone and New York Telephone, we provide quality communications services to the Northeast portion of the United States. Our other companies offer cellular mobile telephone service, market information systems and products, publish directories and other publications, and purchase equipment and services. We also provide credit financing, real estate consulting and development, and international marketing and consulting services
Principal Subsidiaries: New York Telephone; New England Telephone; NYNEX Business Information Systems; NYNEX Information Resources; NYNEX Information Solutions Group; NYNEX Materiel Enterprises; NYNEX Mobile Communications; NYNEX Properties Company; NYNEX Credit Company
Financial Information:

	Dec 31 1985	Dec 31 1986
	$'000	$'000
Revenues	10,314,000	11,342,000
Income before taxes	1,891,100	2,105,000
Net income	1,095,300	1,215,300
Dividends	647,000	704,700
Dividends per share	$3.20	$3.48
Earnings per share	$5.42	$6.01
Common stock	101,100	202,700
Retained income	2,473,300	2,889,000
Shareholders equity	8,348,800	8,868,400

No of Employees: 90,200

NYPRO INC

101 Union Street, Clinton, MA 01510
Tel: (617) 365-9721
Telex: TWX 910 3503393 nypro esl clit

Chairman: Gordon B Lankton (and President)
Senior Executive Officers: Wiley L Easley (Senior VP), Nicholas Aznoian (VP Finance), John Weeks (VP Sales), William Flynn (VP Administration), Eugene Jones (VP Engineering)

PRINCIPAL ACTIVITIES: Manufacture of plastics and plastic products
Principal Bank: State Street Bank & Trust Co
Financial Information:

	$'000
Sales revenues	55,000

No of Employees: 1,000

O C TANNER CO

See TANNER, O C, CO

O M SCOTT & SONS COMPANY

See SCOTT, O M, & SONS COMPANY

OAK HILL SPORTSWEAR CORPORATION

1411 Broadway, New York, NY 10018
Tel: (212) 354-0444
Telex: TWX 710 5815397 oak hill nyk

Chairman: Arthur L Asch (and Chief Executive Officer)
President: Joseph DeClemente
Senior Executive Officers: Martin Jacobson (VP and Chief Financial Officer)

PRINCIPAL ACTIVITIES: Manufacture of women's clothing and sportswear
Principal Bank: Bankers Trust Company
Financial Information:

	$'000
Sales revenues	100,000

No of Employees: 1,000

OAK INDUSTRIES INC

:16935 W Bernardo Drive, Rancho Bernardo, CA 92127
Tel: (619) 485-9300
Telex: WUT 697973 oak ind sdg

Chairman: E L McNeely (and Chief Executive Officer)
Senior Executive Officers: M A Houdeshell (Executive VP and Chief Financial Officer), S A Larson (VP Human Resources), S J Miller (VP General Counsel and Corporate Secretary), D A Hathaway (Assistant Corporate Secretary and Senior Attorney)

PRINCIPAL ACTIVITIES: Communications equipment; electronic components; appliance controls; railbed track maintenance equipment
Trade Names: OAK, NORDBERG, SIGMA
Principal Subsidiaries: Oak Communications Inc
Principal Bank: The First National Bank of Chicago
Financial Information:

	Dec 31 1985 $'000	Dec 31 1986 $'000
Sales revenues	153,116	151,743
(Loss) before taxes	(49,334)	(27,588)
Net income (loss)	(37,576)	34,665
Earnings (loss) per share	($1.54)	$1.01
Common stock	33,902	72,195
Retained (deficit)	(264,014)	(203,796)
Shareholders equity	24,442	59,420

No of Employees: 4,000

OAKITE PRODUCTS, INC
50 Valley Road, Berkeley Heights, NJ 07922
Tel: (201) 464-6900
Telex: TWX 710 9845459 oakite inc bkts

Chairman: Charles F Rell (and Chief Executive Officer)
President: Kenneth P Mitchel (and Chief Operating Officer)
Senior Executive Officers: Christian T Knoeller (Senior VP), Oke I Johnson (Group VP), Edward H Wallner (VP Manufacturing), Fred A Schnitzler (VP Sales)

PRINCIPAL ACTIVITIES: Manufacture of cleaning products and operation of cleaning services
Principal Subsidiaries: Solventol Chemical Products Inc; Oakite Products of Canada Ltd; Claire Manufacturing Co; Sprayway Inc; Reilly-Whiteman Inc
Principal Bank: Chase Manhattan Bank
Financial Information:

	$'000
Sales revenues	80,700

No of Employees: 891

OAKWOOD HOMES CORPORATION
2225 South Holden Road, Greensboro, NC 27407
Tel: (919) 292-7061

Chairman: Ralph L Darling
President: Nicholas J St George (and Chief Executive Officer)
Senior Executive Officers: Robert D Harvey Sr (VP), Wayne E Patterson (VP Sales), S G Steifel Jr (VP, Secretary, Treasurer and Chief Financial Officer)

PRINCIPAL ACTIVITIES: Site development and construction and maintenance of mobile homes
Principal Subsidiaries: Oakwood Mobile Homes Inc; Homes by Fisher Inc; Oakwood Land Development Corp; Homes by Oakwood; Oakwood Acceptance Corp
Principal Bank: First Union Bank
Financial Information:

	$'000
Sales revenues	94,000

No of Employees: 1,000

O'BRIEN CORPORATION (THE)
450 Grand Avenue, South San Francisco, CA 94080
Tel: (415) 761-2300

President: Jerome J Crowley Jr
Senior Executive Officers: Edward P Daly (VP), Philip T Newton (VP and Secretary), Albert E Cash (VP), Robert T Stahmer (VP), Rusell Robison (VP), William Rosenthal (VP)

PRINCIPAL ACTIVITIES: Manufacture of paints and industrial coatings
Trade Names: Fuller-O'Brien, Nason, Nap Gard
Principal Subsidiaries: Fuller-O'Brien Corporation; Fuller-O'Brien International Sales Corporation; Surety Pacific Insurance Co
Principal Bank: First Interstate Bank of CA
Financial Information:

	$'000
Sales revenues	150,000

Principal Shareholders: The O'Brien Family
No of Employees: 1,100

OCCIDENTAL CHEMICAL CORPORATION
800 Connecticut Ave, Norwalk, CT 06854
Tel: (203) 854-3800

Chairman: R R Irani (and Chief Executive Officer)
President: J R Hirl (and Chief Operating Officer)
Senior Executive Officers: A W Lopez (Executive VP Agricultural Products), J F Riordan (Executive VP Industrial Chemicals), C F Hazzard (Senior VP Administration), F H Romanelli (Senior VP, Planning and Development), S W Schaeffer (Senior VP, PVC Products), M Concha (VP International), R Rajaji (VP Finance and Controller), T L Jennings (VP Corporate Environmental Affairs), G King (VP Research and Development), M J Ruddick (VP Legal and Environmental Affairs)

PRINCIPAL ACTIVITIES: Manufacture of specialty and industrial chemicals, agricultural chemcials, animal feedstuffs, plastics and synthetic resins
Parent Company: Occidental Petroleum Corporation, Los Angeles, CA
Financial Information:

	$'000
Sales revenues	2,000,000

No of Employees: 10,000

OCCIDENTAL PETROLEUM CORPORATION
10889 Wilshire Blvd, Los Angeles, CA 90024
Tel: (213) 879-1700
Telex: WUT 673389 OXYPETE LSA

Chairman: Armand Hammer (and Chief Executive Officer)
President: Ray R Irani (and Chief Operating Officer)
Senior Executive Officers: O C Davis (Executive VP), John J Dorgan (Executive VP and Chief Financial Officer), Paul C Hebner (Executive VP and Secretary), David A Hentschel (Executive VP), J R Hirl (Executive VP), Dale R Laurance (Executive VP Operations), Angelo Leparulo (Executive VP), David R Martin (Executive VP), William F McSweeney (Executive VP), Sylvester O Ogden (Executive VP), Robert L Peterson (Executive VP), Gerald M Stern (Executive VP and Senior General Counsel), Norman D Alexander (VP Corporate Affairs)

PRINCIPAL ACTIVITIES: Oil and gas exploration and production; transportation of natural gas; coal mining; industrial chemicals and plastics; agricultural chemicals, fertilizers and the processing of meat
Principal Subsidiaries: Occidental International Corp; Occidental International Exploration & Production Co; Occidental Oil & Gas Corp; Occidental International Oil Inc; Occidental Chemical Corp; Occidental Agricultural Products Inc; IBP Inc; Cities Service Co; Island Creek Coal Co; MidCon Corp
Financial Information:

	Dec 31 1985 $'000	Dec 31 1986 $'000
Sales revenues	15,643,914	16,028,519
Income before taxes	1,576,550	528,228
Net income	696,003	181,064
Dividends	258,317	373,573
Dividends per share	$2.50	$2.50
Earnings per share	$4.49	$0.72
Common stock	22,203	32,942
Retained income	1,342,648	1,047,034
Shareholders equity	3,281,021	4,308,341

No of Employees: 51,000

OCEAN DRILLING & EXPLORATION CO

1600 Canal St, New Orleans, LA 70161
Tel: (504) 561-2811
Telex: 58-4124

President: Hugh J Kelly (and Chief Executive Officer)
Senior Executive Officers: James L Kilpatrick (Executive VP). Contract Drilling: Enoch L Dawkins (VP, Marketing), W J Wilkinson (VP Operations). Design and Engineering: Dr Terry D Petty (VP). Oil and Gas: Herbert E Price (VP, Oil and Gas Production), Stephen C Hurley (VP, Oil and Gas Exploration). Diving (Sub Sea International Inc): Herbert G Newbury (Chairman of the Board and President). Finance and Administration: Richard E Roberson Jr (VP, Finance), Odie F Vaughan (VP of Taxes and Treasurer), Steven A Cossé (General Counsel), Tucker H Couvillon III (Corporate Secretary), Ronald W Herman (Controller)

PRINCIPAL ACTIVITIES: Offshore drilling operations for gas and oil
Trade Names: ODECO
Parent Company: Murphy Oil Corp
Principal Subsidiaries: Sub Sea International, Inc
Principal Bank: Whitney National Bank, New Orleans
Financial Information:

	Dec 31 1985	Dec 31 1986
	$'000	$'000
Total revenues	648,404	364,443
Income (loss) before taxes	139,848	(310,726)
Net income (loss)	33,694	(262,747)
Dividends	51,628	5,145
Dividends per share	$1.00	$0.10
Earnings (loss) per share	$0.65	($5.10)
Common stock	25,992	25,992
Retained income	675,718	407,826
Shareholders equity	839,502	578,975

Principal Shareholders: Murphy Oil Corp
No of Employees: 3,000

OCEAN SPRAY CRANBERRIES, INC

225 Water Street, Plymouth, MA 02360
Tel: (617) 747-1000
Telex: ITT 4997702 ocspray plth

Chairman: Stuart Pedersen; Vice Chairman: William Atwood
President: Harol Thorkilsen (and Chief Executive Officer)
Senior Executive Officers: Patrick M McCarthy (Group VP), Alvin E Wanthal (Group VP and Chief Financial Officer), John S Llewellyn Jr (Senior VP), Curtis L Collison Jr (VP Communications), Kenneth J Beeby (VP General Counsel and Secretary), S Woodworth Chittick (VP Corporate Planning and Business Development), A MacIsaac (VP Logistics), Michael Shae (VP and Controller), James E Tillotson (VP Technical Research and Development), Thomas Wagner (VP Manufacturing)

PRINCIPAL ACTIVITIES: Manufacture of concentrated and frozen fruit juices, fresh fruit products and cranberry sauce
Financial Information:

	Aug 31 1986
	$'000
Sales revenues	624,381
Shareholders equity	131,239

No of Employees: 1,780

OCEANEERING INTERNATIONAL INC

16001 Park Ten Place, Suite 600, Houston, TX 77084
Tel: (713) 578 8868

Chairman: Michael D Hughes
President: John Rossman Huff (and Chief Executive Officer)
Senior Executive Officers: Louis L Tapscott (Executive VP Operations), Michael D John (Senior VP Asia-Pacific), John T Johnson (Senior VP Sales), Paul E Gillen (VP International), Stephen Halburn (VP), Edward A Lowe (VP Americas), Stanley E Rauhut (VP and Legal Counsel), Joseph W Walker (VP Middle East), E Warren Bennett Jr (Treasurer), James H Haddox (VP Finance), Jim R Lock (Controller), Victor A Allum (Senior VP), F Richard Frisbie (VP Underwater Technology)

PRINCIPAL ACTIVITIES: Operation of a wide range of marine construction and surveying services
Principal Subsidiaries: Steadfast Marine Inc; Underwater Technology Services Inc; Woodward Clyde Oceaneering
Principal Bank: Morgan Guaranty Trust
Financial Information:

	$'000
Sales revenues	120,000

No of Employees: 1,820

OCILLA INDUSTRIES, INC

Hwy 129 N, Box 587, Ocilla, GA 31774
Tel: (912) 468-7464

Chairman: Elijah Waldron (and President)
Senior Executive Officers: Howard R Katz (Executive VP), Harry V Maccarrone (VP and Treasurer), Charles E Lott (VP Marketing),

PRINCIPAL ACTIVITIES: Manufacture of modular housing; real estate
Principal Bank: Citibank
Financial Information:

	$'000
Sales revenues	99,000

No of Employees: 900

ODETICS INC

1515 South Manchester Avenue, Anaheim, CA 92802
Tel: (714) 774 5000

Chairman: Joel Slutzky (and Chief Executive Officer)
President: Crandall Goodmundson
Senior Executive Officers: Jerry Muench (VP and Secretary), Eugene T Juengel (VP Finance and Treasurer), David E Lewis (VP Production), Gordon Schulz (VP Mechanical Engineering), James Welch (VP Electric Engineering)

PRINCIPAL ACTIVITIES: Production of electronic audio-visual equipment
Principal Subsidiaries: Kode Inc
Principal Bank: Bank of America
Financial Information:

	$'000
Sales revenues	33,000

No of Employees: 450

O'DONNELL-USEN FISHERIES CORPORATION

255 Northern Avenue, Boston, MA 02110
Tel: (617) 542-2700
Telex: WUT 940303 usenco bsn

Chairman: Irving Usen
President: Gerald Ajemian
Senior Executive Officers: Arnold S Wolf (Executive VP), Herbert Buckman (VP Production)

PRINCIPAL ACTIVITIES: Fish and fish processing
Principal Bank: Bank of New England
Financial Information:

	$'000
Sales revenues	75,000

No of Employees: 680

OEA INC

34501 East Quincy Avenue, PO Box 10488, Denver, CO 80210
Tel: (303) 693 1248

Chairman: Ahmed D Kafadar (and Chief Executive Officer)
President: Charles B Kafadar (and Chief Operating Officer)

Senior Executive Officers: John E Banko (Senior VP, Chief Financial Officer, Secretary and Treasurer), John M Cuthbert (VP Engineering), Nuri Y Olver (VP)

PRINCIPAL ACTIVITIES: Manufacture of aircraft components; defense equipment including missile and aeronautical technology
Principal Subsidiaries: Explosive Technology Inc; Aerotest Operations Inc; Pyronetics Devices Inc
Principal Bank: Northern Trust Company
Financial Information:

	$'000
Sales revenues	34,000

No of Employees: 465

OERLIKON MOTCH CORPORATION

1250 E 222nd Street, Cleveland, OH 44117
Tel: (216) 486-3600
Telex: TWX 810 4218169 Motchmerry ud

President: Klaus Eberius (and Chief Executive Officer)
Senior Executive Officers: Richard N Legan (VP and General Manager Machine Tool Group), Stanley Lenox (VP Jet Stream Systems Co), Robert J Mayer (VP and Controller)

PRINCIPAL ACTIVITIES: Manufacture of machine tools
Parent Company: Oerlikon-Buhrle Holding Ltd, Zurich, Switzerland
Principal Subsidiaries: Cone Blanchard Machine Company; Upton Bradeen & James Ltd (Canada)
Principal Bank: Central National Bank of Cleveland
Financial Information:

	$'000
Sales revenues	80,500

No of Employees: 500

OFFICIAL INDUSTRIES, INC

100 Perkins Avenue, Brockton, MA 02403
Tel: (617) 583-5000

Chairman: Joseph P Tyrrell
President: Paul I Kleven (and Chief Executive Officer)
Senior Executive Officers: William E Strong (VP, Secretary and Treasurer)

PRINCIPAL ACTIVITIES: Manufacture of footwear; retail trade in clothing for men, women and children, furniture and household furnishings; wholesale trade in timber products and building materials; distribution of television of tapes and films
Principal Subsidiaries: New Ideal Stores Inc
Principal Bank: Fleet National Bank
Financial Information:

	$'000
Sales revenues	51,000

No of Employees: 1,000

OFFSHORE LOGISTICS INC

900 East University Avenue, PO Box 5-C, Lafayette, LA 70505
Tel: (318) 233 1221

President: James B Clement
Senior Executive Officers: George M Small (VP, Controller and Treasurer), William Bright (VP and General Manager), G D Cook (VP)

PRINCIPAL ACTIVITIES: Charter transport services for offshore installations; helicopters and ships
Principal Subsidiaries: Air Logistics of AK Inc; Heliflight Systems Inc, Offfshore Realty Inc
Principal Bank: Morgan Guaranty
Financial Information:

	$'000
Sales revenues	110,000

No of Employees: 1,200

OGDEN CORPORATION

277 Park Avenue, New York, NY 10172
Tel: (212) 754-4000

Chairman: Ralph E Ablon
President: Donald A Krenz
Senior Executive Officers: James M Russo (Senior VP, Chief Financial Officer and Treasurer), Robert E Curry Jr (Senior VP and General Counsel), Constantine G Caras (VP), Burton J Carbino (VP-Risk Management), Robert M DiGia (VP and Controller), Salvatore S Ferrara (VP-Taxes), Maria P Monet (VP), Kathleen Ritch (VP and Secretary), Philip F Ruppel (VP-Corporate Relations), David L Sokol (VP), George Tremblay (VP-Compensation and Benefits

PRINCIPAL ACTIVITIES: Ogden consists of three major activity areas; Services, Marine and Modular Construction and Products. Services include building and plant maintenance, aviation fueling and ground handling services and engineering services; food and beverage services to sports, entertainment, travel and industrial markets; food and housekeeping services to offshore oil and gas drilling rigs and logistical support services to remote industrial campsites; security and risk analysis services; the operation of four racetracks and the provision of complete facility management; and the design, construction, maintenance and management of refuse-fueled power plants. Marine and Modular Construction designs, builds, modernizes and repairs oceangoing vessels, non-oceangoing craft, offshore structures and drilling vessels; and builds modular units for oil exploration and production, chemical and processing plants and hydroelectric facilities. The Industrial Products area consists of ferrous scrap operations and secondary aluminum activities, the engineering and construction of special-purpose railroad cars, the custom fabrication of metal components and cabinetry equipment, the design and manufacture of heat transfer and similar equipment, primarily for the electric utility and process industries, and the manufacture of precision-built machine tools and accessories. Food Products processes and markets a broad line of branded specialty food products
Trade Names: Food Products:- Progresso: Italian-style foods; Las Palmas: Mexican-style foods; Hain: Health foods; Hollywood: Natural foods
Principal Subsidiaries: Ogden Allied Services Inc; Ogden Projects, Inc; Ogden Food Products, Inc
Principal Bank: Chase Manhattan Bank
Financial Information:

	Dec 31 1986 $'000
Sales revenues	1,046,689
Net income	119,562
Earnings per share	$6.15
Shareholders equity	395,781

No of Employees: 38,008

OGILVY GROUP INC (THE)

2 East 48th St, New York, NY 10017
Tel: (212) 907-3400

Chairman: William E Phillips (and Chief Executive Officer); Vice Chairmen: Michael J Ball; James Benson; Kenneth Roman
Senior Executive Officers: John P Gill (Secretary and Treasurer)

PRINCIPAL ACTIVITIES: Advertising and public relations services
Principal Bank: Morgan Guaranty Trust Co of New York
Financial Information:

	$'000
Sales revenues	560,500

No of Employees: 8,700

OGLEBAY NORTON COMPANY

1100 Superior Avenue, Cleveland, OH 44114
Tel: (216) 861-3300
Telex: WUT 517238 ogle petro ca

Chairman: Courtney Burton; Vice Chairman: Fred R White Jr
President: Renold D Thompson (and Chief Executive Officer)
Senior Executive Officers: R T Greene Jr (VP Iron Ore Operations), Frank A Castle (VP), A F Bradfish (VP Coal Operations), Marcus A Hyre (VP Ore Sales), Richard J Kessler (VP Finance), John L Selis (VP Administration-Law)

PRINCIPAL ACTIVITIES: Coal mining, iron ore and silica sand and perlite mining; transportation of ores on the Great Lakes; manufacture of metal castings and refractories
Principal Bank: Central National Bank
Financial Information:

	Dec 31 1985	Dec 31 1986
	$'000	$'000
Sales revenues	159,052	130,777
Net income (loss)	6,418	(1,608)

No of Employees: 1,775

OHIO ART COMPANY
PO Box 111, Bryan, OH 43506
Tel: (419) 636 3141

Chairman: W C Killgallon
President: William C Killgallon Jr
Senior Executive Officers: M L Kilgallon (Senior VP Marketing), N O Mayers (VP International), W H Martins (VP Finance and Administration), L F Koerber Jr (Secretary), C G Dahl (VP), J Sito (VP Manufacturing), L T Wilson (VP Products Development)

PRINCIPAL ACTIVITIES: Manufacture of toys and games
Principal Subsidiaries: Ohio Art Company Canada Limited; Strydel Inc; Trinc Company
Principal Bank: First National
Financial Information:

	$'000
Sales revenues	34,200

No of Employees: 550

OHIO BANCORP
801 Dollar Bank Building, Youngstown, OH 44503
Tel: (216) 744 2093

Chairman: D W McGowan (and President); Vice Chairman: Paul J Thomas
Senior Executive Officers: T R Hollern (VP), Carl A Nunziato (Secretary)

PRINCIPAL ACTIVITIES: Holding company with interests in banking
Principal Subsidiaries: Dollar Savings Trust Company

No of Employees: 500

OHIO CASUALTY CORPORATION
136 N Third Street, Hamilton, OH 45025
Tel: (513) 867-3000
Telex: TWX 810 4628279 ohio cas ham

Chairman: John G Sloneker (and Chief Executive Officer)
President: Joseph L Marcum
Senior Executive Officers: William L Woodall (Senior VP and Secretary), Barry S Porter (Treasurer)

PRINCIPAL ACTIVITIES: Insurance including casualty, property, fire, marine and life; financial services
Financial Information:

	Dec 31 1985	Dec 31 1986
	$'000	$'000
Revenues	1,165,990	1,415,268
Net income	44,080	102,714
Earnings per share	$3.91	$4.54
Shareholders equity	539,009	606,002
Total assets	2,112,753	2,475,392

No of Employees: 5,700

OHIO DECORATIVE PRODUCTS, INC
220 S Elizabeth, Spencerville, OH 45887
Tel: (419) 647-4191

President: Charles Moeller
Senior Executive Officers: Richard Moeller (VP), Lowell Powell (Secretary and Treasurer)

PRINCIPAL ACTIVITIES: Manufacture of metal and synthetic rubber building materials and fittings
Financial Information:

	$'000
Sales revenues	100,000

No of Employees: 1,200

OHIO EDISON CO
76 S Main Street, Akron, OH 44308
Tel: (216) 384-5100

President: Justin T Rogers Jr (and Chief Executive Officer)
Senior Executive Officers: D W Tschappat (Executive VP and Chief Operating Officer), V A Owoc (Executive VP and Chief Financial Officer), Lynn Firestone (Senior VP Engineering), D R Gundry (Senior VP Divisional Operations), R J McWhorter (Senior VP Production), R D Best (VP Marketing), H P Burg (VP Finance), F E Derry (VP Communications), J A Gill (VP Administration), J D Wilson (VP Rate), R J Spetrino (VP and General Counsel)

PRINCIPAL ACTIVITIES: Supply of electricity
Principal Subsidiaries: Pennsylvania Power Co; Edison Finance NV
Principal Bank: Chase Manhattan Bank
Financial Information:

	Dec 31 1985	Dec 31 1986
	$'000	$'000
Sales revenues	1,754,750	1,741,900
Net income	379,685	410,828
Earnings per share	$2.45	$2.47
Shareholders equity	2,660,190	2,955,374

No of Employees: 7,500

OHIO FERRO-ALLOYS CORPORATION
PO Box 8228, Canton, OH 44711
Tel: (216) 492-5110
Telex: WUT 241044 ohio ferro ctn

Chairman: Ronald L Cunningham
President: Ronald M Cunningham (and Chief Executive Officer)
Senior Executive Officers: R N McClure (Senior VP), C E Schott (VP), D Matter (VP)

PRINCIPAL ACTIVITIES: Manufacture of electro-metallurgical products
Principal Bank: Central Trust Co
Financial Information:

	$'000
Sales revenues	68,550

No of Employees: 890

OHIO MATTRESS CO
1300 East 9th Street, Cleveland, OH 44114
Tel: (216) 522-1310

Chairman: Ernest M Wuliger (and Chief Executive Officer)
President: Ronald E Trzcinski (and Chief Operating Officer)
Senior Executive Officers: Sam F Smith (Senior VP), William J McDade (VP Industrial Relations), Thomas L Smudz (VP Finance and Treasurer)

PRINCIPAL ACTIVITIES: Components for the manufacture of mattresses
Principal Subsidiaries: OMT Corp; Jack Ward Mattress Inc; Monterey Manufacturing Co; The Stearns & Foster Co; Ohio Mattress Co (Houston, TX); Ohio Mattress Co (Randolph,

MA); Ohio Mattress Co (Tucker, GA); Ohio Mattress Co (Fort Worth, TX); Woodstuff Manufacturing Inc
Principal Bank: National City Bank Cleveland
Financial Information:

	$'000
Sales revenues	267,000

No of Employees: 2,395

OIL DRI CORP OF AMERICA

520 North Michigan Avenue, Chicago, IL 60611
Tel: (312) 321 1515

President: Richard M Jaffee
Senior Executive Officers: Robert D Jaffee (Executive VP), Elwyn J Allbritton (VP Operations), Norman B Gershon (VP Europe), V R Roskam (VP Division), Bruce H Sone (VP Division), R David Morris (VP Finance), Richard Pietrowski (Treasurer), Albert L Swendlik (Secretary), Richard V Hardin (VP Sales and Marketing), Richard A Chapman (VP Production), Dennis E Peterson (VP Distribution)

PRINCIPAL ACTIVITIES: Mining and processing of minerals and earths
Principal Subsidiaries: Oil-Dri Corp of GA; Oil-Dri Production Company Inc MS; Oil-Dri West
Principal Bank: Harris Trust and Savings Bank
Financial Information:

	$'000
Sales revenues	46,550

No of Employees: 400

OILGEAR COMPANY

2300 South 51st Street, Milwaukee, WI 53219
Tel: (414) 327 1700

President: Carl L Gosewehr (and Chief Executive Officer)
Senior Executive Officers: Thomas M Healy (VP), Otto F Klieve (VP Engineering), David A Zuege (VP Finance and Secretary)

PRINCIPAL ACTIVITIES: Production of pumps, valves and compressors
Principal Subsidiaries: Petrodyne Corporation
Principal Bank: Marshall and Ilsley Bank
Financial Information:

	$'000
Sales revenues	41,000

No of Employees: 850

OKLAHOMA GAS & ELECTRIC CO

PO Box 321, Oklahoma City, OK 73101
Tel: (405) 272-3000

Chairman: James G Harlow Jr (and President and Chief Executive Officer)
Senior Executive Officers: P J Ryan (Executive VP Finance), B G Bunce (Senior VP and Controller), W O Coleman (Senior VP Region Management), J T Gilliam (VP and Arkansas Region Manager), H Leon Grover (VP and Western Region Manager), V M Hines (VP Operations), Richard C Day (VP Marketing), George L Gibbons (VP Production)

PRINCIPAL ACTIVITIES: Distribution of electricity and natural gas
Principal Bankers: First National Bank & Trust Co
Financial Information:

	$'000
Sales revenues	1,100,000

No of Employees: 4,100

OKLAHOMA PUBLISHING CO

500 N Broadway, Box 25125, Oklahoma City, OK 73125
Tel: (405) 232-3311
Telex: WUT 883662 opubco okc ud

President: Edward L Gaylord
Senior Executive Officers: Howard J Nicks (VP), Thelma F Gaylord (VP), Glenn M Stinchcomb (Treasurer)

PRINCIPAL ACTIVITIES: Publishing of newspapers
Principal Bank: First National Bank & Trust Co
Financial Information:

	$'000
Sales revenues	350,000

No of Employees: 4,000

OKONITE COMPANY

PO Box 340, Ramsey, NJ 07446
Tel: (201) 825-0300
Telex: TWX 710 9881017 okonite ramsey

Chairman: Victor A Viggiano (and President and Chief Executive Officer)
Senior Executive Officers: Alfred C Coppola (Executive VP), Jack S Lasky (VP Research), Robert T Brennan (VP Finance), Donald F Schwamb (VP Operations), Robert W Ryan (VP Manufacturing), Donald C Huber (VP Advertising), Jeffry H Kittross (VP and Secretary), Edwin C Moen (VP)

PRINCIPAL ACTIVITIES: Manufacture of cables and wires
Principal Bank: Bank of America
Financial Information:

	$'000
Sales revenues	200,000

No of Employees: 1,700

OLD EL PASO MOUNTAIN PASS CANNING

1200 N Main Street, Anthony, TX 88021
Tel: (915) 886-3951

Senior Executive Officers: R A Kersey (Director Manufacturing and Operations)

PRINCIPAL ACTIVITIES: Production of canned Mexican foods
Parent Company: Pet Incorporated
Principal Bank: Texas Commerce Bank of El Paso
Financial Information:

	$'000
Sales revenues	100,000

No of Employees: 550

OLD KENT BANK & TRUST CO

One Vandenberg Center, Grand Rapids, MI 49503
Tel: (616) 774-5440
Telex: 226 373 OLDKENT

Chairman: Richard M Gillett
President: John C Canepa (and Chief Executive Officer)
Senior Executive Officers: Ralph Garlick (Executive VP Corporate Banking), Robert L Sadler (Executive VP), James Wynsma (Executive VP Trust Administration), Martin J Allen Jr (Senior VP Marketing), Philip H Battershall (Senior VP Loan Review), Thomas Bobrowski (Senior VP), Charles W Jennings Jr (Senior VP Personnel), James La Fleur (Senior VP Trust Investment), David A Radius (Senior VP Administration Services), B P Sherwood III (Senior VP Bank Affiliate Administration), William L Waanders (Senior VP and Controllers), William C Whitney (Senior VP Finance), Thomas D Wisnom (Senior VP Bank Affiliate Administration)

PRINCIPAL ACTIVITIES: Banking and finance
Parent Company: Old Kent Financial Corporation

No of Employees: 1,215

OLD KENT FINANCIAL CORPORATION

One Vandenberg Center, Grand Rapids, MI 49503
Tel: (616) 774-5000

Chairman: Richard M Gillett
President: John C Canepa (and Chief Executive Officer)
Senior Executive Officers: Robert L Sadler (Executive VP), B P Sherwood III (Executive VP, Secretary and Treasurer),

Thomas D Wisnom (Executive VP), Martin J Allen Jr (Senior VP), William L Waanders (Senior VP and Chief Financial Officer), William C Whitney (Senior VP)

PRINCIPAL ACTIVITIES: Banking
Principal Subsidiaries: Old Kent Bank & Trust Company
Principal Bank: Old Kent Bank & Trust Company
Financial Information:

	Dec 31 1985	Dec 31 1986
	$'000	$'000
Net income	49,414	60,585
Earnings per share	$3.82	$2.71
Shareholders equity	306,896	393,844
Deposits	3,634,290	4,863,209
Total assets	4,323,290	5,582,276

No of Employees: 3,000

OLD NATIONAL BANCORP

420 Main Street, Evansville, IN 47708
Tel: (812) 464 1200

Chairman: Dan W Mitchell (and Chief Executive Officer)
President: Richard A Schlottman
Senior Executive Officers: John N Royse (Senior VP), Laurence A Dennis (Treasurer and Subsidiary Officer), Steve H Parker (VP Finance)

PRINCIPAL ACTIVITIES: Banking
Principal Subsidiaries: Bancshares Mortgage Company; Cascade Escrow Company Inc; First National Bank; Old National Bank; Compass Group Inc; ONB Securities Inc; Old Nat Credit Corp; Old National Financial SV Inc; Old National Leasing Co

No of Employees: 570

OLD NATIONAL BANCORPORATION

1230 Old National Bank Building, Spokane, WA 99201
Tel: (509) 456 3491

Chairman: David A Clack (and Chief Executive Officer)
President: D Michael Jones
Senior Executive Officers: Terrance J Dobson (VP), Steven P Erwin (VP and Treasurer), Bryan C Grineau (VP Operations Review), T Andy Ike (VP and Assistant Treasurer), James L Lemery (VP Operations Research), JoAnn G Matthiesen (VP Public Relations), David A McLeod (VP), Robert L Magnuson (Secretary)

PRINCIPAL ACTIVITIES: Banking
Principal Bank: Old National Bank

No of Employees: 1,600

OLD REPUBLIC INTERNATIONAL CORPORATION

307 N Michigan Avenue, Chicago, IL 60601
Tel: (312) 346-8100

Chairman: William R Stover (and Chief Executive Officer)
President: A C Zucaro (and Chief Financial Officer)
Senior Executive Officers: C J McConville (Senior VP)

PRINCIPAL ACTIVITIES: Holding company with interests in insurance and finance
Principal Bank: The Northern Trust Company
Financial Information:

	Dec 31 1985	Dec 31 1986
	$'000	$'000
Revenues	889,000	1,143,500
Investment income	23,500	67,700
Earnings per share	$1.20	$3.55
Shareholders equity	381,200	426,700

No of Employees: 4,700

OLD STONE CORPORATION

150 S Main St, Providence, RI 02903
Tel: (401) 278-2000

President: Theodore W Barnes (and Chief Executive Officer)
Senior Executive Officers: Winfield W Major (Executive VP, Secretary and General Counsel), Joseph F Murphy (Executive VP Credit and Operations), James V Rosati (Executive VP), David L Savoie (Executive VP), Janet M Scacciotti (Executive VP), Dennis E Stark (Executive VP), John R Treat (Executive VP), Stephen M Bessette (Senior VP), J Scott Burns (VP) (Executive VP)

PRINCIPAL ACTIVITIES: Banking
Principal Bank: Old Stone Bank
Financial Information:

	Dec 31 1985	Dec 31 1986
	$'000	$'000
Net income	23,825	29,051
Earnings per share	$4.10	$3.32
Shareholders equity	140,567	184,527
Deposits	-	2,690,056
Total assets	3,704,633	3,876,453

No of Employees: 2,009

OLGA COMPANY

7915 Haskell Avenue, Van Nuys, CA 91409
Tel: (818) 782-7568
Telex: WUT 651328 olga co van

President: Jeffrey W Paul
Senior Executive Officers: John Semrad (Senior VP Sales), Stan Marshall (VP Manufacturing), Harold Ecklund (Senior VP Merchandising), Christina Johnson (VP Design), Niccolette Sohl (VP Finance), Catherine Drummond (VP Merchandising-Olga), Gerald Cohen (VP Advertising), Roger Telsey (Chief Financial Officer)

PRINCIPAL ACTIVITIES: Manufacture of women's underwear
Trade Names: Olga, Olga's Christina
Parent Company: Warnaco Inc, Bridgeport, CT
Principal Bank: Bank of America
Financial Information:

	$'000
Sales revenues	80,000

No of Employees: 1,700

OLIN CORPORATION

120 Long Ridge Road, Stamford, CT 06904
Tel: (203) 356-2000
Telex: ITT 4750119 olin ui

Chairman: John W Johnstone Jr (and President and Chief Executive Officer)
Senior Executive Officers: Richard R Berry (Executive VP), Thomas J Berardino (Senior VP), Joseph M Gaffney (Senior VP Corporate Planning and Development), Sigurd D Medhus (Senior VP and Senior Finance Officer), Edward B Pollak (Senior BP International Operations), Alfred T Blomquist (VP, President and Chief Executive Officer Olin Hunt Specialty Products Inc), John F Dembeck (VP and Treasurer), Donald W Griffin (VP, President Winchester Group), James G Hascall (VP, President Brass Group), Richard Hiendlmayr (VP), E McIntosh Cover (VP and General Counsel), James A Riggs (VP and Comptroller), George S Sutherland (VP, Chairman and Chief Executive Officer Rockor Inc), John S Swartley (VP, President Water Products and Services Division), Richard N Williams (VP Human Resources and Administration), Robert L Yohe (VP, President Chemicals Group)

PRINCIPAL ACTIVITIES: Manufacture of aerospace and defense products, electronics and water systems

Financial Information:

	Dec 31 1985 $'000	Dec 31 1986 $'000
Sales revenues	1,890,910	1,707,261
Net income (loss)	(165,350)	75,226
Earnings per share	-	$3.36
Shareholders equity	686,530	654,048

No of Employees: 14,900

OLSON FARMS, INC

13400 Riverside Drive, Sherman Oaks, CA 91423
Tel: (213) 995-1238

Chairman: John W Buffington (and President and Chief Executive Officer)
Senior Executive Officers: Eino A Haulley (VP Finance), Jonathan M Berge (VP and General Counsel)

PRINCIPAL ACTIVITIES: Production, wholesale and distribution of eggs; manufacture of foam packaging products for eggs, fruit and meat
Principal Bank: Bank of America
Financial Information:

	$'000
Sales revenues	147,000

No of Employees: 1,200

OLSTEN CORPORATION

One Merrick Avenue, The Olsten Building, Westbury, NY 11590
Tel: (516) 832 8200

Chairman: William Olsten (and Chief Executive Officer)
President: Frank N Liguori (and Chief Operating Officer)
Senior Executive Officers: Stuart Olsten (Executive VP), Patricia L Morse (Senior VP), Laurin L Laderoute Jr (VP, Secretary and Legal Counsel), Robert J Vitamante (Treasurer and Controller)

PRINCIPAL ACTIVITIES: Supply of temporary personnel; health care
Trade Names: Olsten Services; Olsten Health Care Services
Principal Bank: Chase Manhattan Bank
Financial Information:

	Dec 31 1985 $'000	Dec 31 1986 $'000
Sales revenues	262,850	313,480
Income before taxes	13,970	17,125
Net income	7,325	9,265
Dividends	1,300	1,630
Dividends per share	$0.16	$0.20
Earnings per share	$0.90	$1.13
Common stock	813	815
Retained income	30,805	38,440
Shareholders equity	42,350	50,190

No of Employees: 145,840

OMI CORP

280 Park Avenue, New York, NY 10017
Tel: (212) 949 4500

Chairman: Michael Klebanoff
President: Jack Goldstein (and Chief Executive Officer)
Senior Executive Officers: Richard T Du Moulin (Executive VP), Stanley S Unger (Executive VP), W F Kirkpatrick (VP), Desmond F Mann (VP), Charles N Tammara (VP, Treasurer and Secretary)

PRINCIPAL ACTIVITIES: Operation of shipping lines
Financial Information:

	$'000
Sales revenues	189,000

No of Employees: 700

OMNICARE INC

1300 Fountain Square South, Cincinatti, OH 45202
Tel: (513) 762 6666

Chairman: Edward L Hutton
President: Joel F Gemunder
Senior Executive Officers: Kenneth W Chesterman (Executive VP), James C Wigginton (Executive VP), Judi K O'Steen (VP Finance and Treasurer), Cheryl D Hodges (VP Corporate Relations), Larry P Rapp (Controller), Kevin J McNamara (Secretary)

PRINCIPAL ACTIVITIES: Provision of medical services; manufacture of medical and surgical supplies and pharmaceuticals
Principal Subsidiaries: Greene and Kellogg Inc; HPI Healthcare Services Inc; Inspiron Corp; Unidisco Inc; Veritex Corp
Principal Bank: Fifth Third Bank
Financial Information:

	S'000
Sales revenues	193,000

No of Employees: 2,090

OMNICOM GROUP INC

909 Third Avenue, New York, NY 10022
Tel: (212) 935-5660
Telex: 428245 OMNI UI
Telefax: (212) 758-8106

President: Allen Rosenshine (and Chief Executive Officer)
Senior Executive Officers: Raymond E McGovern (Secretary and General Counsel), James A Cannon (Comptroller), Jack Kraushaar (Director of Corporate Services), Barry E Loughrane (Chairman, Chief Executive Officer of Diversified Agency Services Group), Norman W Campbell (Chairman, Chief Executive Officer of BBDO Worldwide), Willi Schalk (President, Chief Operating Officer of BBDO Worldwide), Keith L Reinhard (Chairman, Chief Executive Officer of DDB Needham Worldwide), John L Bernbach (President, Chief Operating Officer of DDB Needham Worldwide), Joseph R Daly (Chairman, Executive Committee of DDB Needham Worldwide)

PRINCIPAL ACTIVITIES: Omnicom Group Inc is the company formed as a result of the merger of BBDO International, Doyle Dane Bernbach Group and Needham Harper Worldwide. The business of Omnicom companies is marketing communications, principally consumer and business media advertising, with capacity to provide the full complement of integrated collateral services necessary to meet the most sophisticated marketing needs, whether local or global. Worldwide billings come from a wide range of product and service categories representing practically every marketing-oriented classification of industry
Principal Subsidiaries: BBDO Worldwide; DDB Needham Worldwide; Tracy Locke; Doremus Porter Novelli
Principal Bank: Chase Manhattan Bank NA; Marine Midland Bank
Financial Information:

	Dec 31 1985 $'000	Dec 31 1986 $'000
Sales Revenues	673,403	753,527
Income before taxes	63,079	22,113
Net income (loss)	30,142	(4,077)
Dividends	19,458	21,674
Dividends per share	$0.82	$0.887
Earnings (loss) per share	$1.27	($0.17)
Common stock	12,576	12,761
Retained income	145,144	119,393
Shareholders equity	187,775	174,305

No of Employees: 9,846 Worldwide 6,296 USA

ONE BANCORP (THE)

PO Box 1280, Portland, ME 04101
Tel: (207) 871 1111

Chairman: Frederick W Pape Jr
President: Robert R Masterton (and Chief Executive Officer)
Senior Executive Officers: Francis E McFarland (Executive VP and Chief Financial Officer), Robert J Jolicoeur (Senior VP), Allen F Betz (Treasurer), William E Saufley (Secretary)

PRINCIPAL ACTIVITIES: Banking
Principal Bank: Maine Savings Bank

No of Employees: 600

ONE VALLEY BANCORP OF WEST VIRGINIA INC

1 Valley Sq, Summers & Lee Streets, PO Box 1793, Charleston, WV 25326
Tel: (304) 348 7000

President: Robert F Baronner (and Chief Executive Officer)
Senior Executive Officers: Phyllis H Arnold (Senior VP), David A King (Senior VP), Laurence G Jones (Treasurer and Chief Financial Officer), Carl E Little (Senior VP), J Holmes Morrison (Senior VP), James L Whytsell (Senior VP Data Processing Services), Frederick G Lauer (VP), Frederick H Belden Jr (Secretary)

PRINCIPAL ACTIVITIES: Banking
Principal Subsidiaries: Bank of St Albans; Citizens National Bank; Kanawha Valley Bank NA; Mercer County Bank; Security Bank
Principal Bank: Kanawha Valley Bank

No of Employees: 860

ONEIDA LTD

Kenwood Station, Oneida, NY 13421
Tel: (315) 361-3636

Chairman: John L Marcellus Jr (and President and Chief Executive Officer)
Senior Executive Officers: Robert E Sanderson (Vice Chairman of the Board), Harold C Lilholt (VP, Finance and Treasurer), James R Colway (Senior VP, Advertising), William D Matthews (Senior VP, Secretary and General Counsel), Walter A Stewart (Senior VP, Manufacturing and Engineering), John L Hatcher (VP, Corporate Planning Administration), Francis C Mangione (VP, Human Resources), Glenn B Kelsey (VP and Corporate Controller)

PRINCIPAL ACTIVITIES: The world's largest maker of fine quality consumer tableware. Interests in institutional and industrial market segments. Through its Camden Wire subsidiary Oneida also participates in the transportation, electronic, appliance, building and energy industries
Trade Names: ONEIDA, COMMUNITY, HEIRLOOM, ROGERS, WEBSTER WILCOX, BUFFALO CHINA, DJ
Principal Subsidiaries: Oneida Silversmiths Division; Oneida Canada Ltd (Canada); Oneida Tableware Group (UK); Oneida Mexicana SA (Mexico); Buffalo China Inc; DJ Tableware Inc; Camden Wire Co Inc
Principal Bank: Lincoln First Bank Rochester
Financial Information:

	$'000
Sales revenues	252,000

No of Employees: 3,855

ONEITA INDUSTRIES INC

Conifer St, Andrews, SC 29510
Tel: (803) 264-5223

Chairman: Harvey R Blau
President: F Richard Redden Jr
Senior Executive Officers: A Rebit (Executive VP Sales), Robert Balemian (VP, President Instrument Systems Corp), W H Boyd (VP and Controller), K M McAleer (VP Operations)

PRINCIPAL ACTIVITIES: Manufacture of knitted clothing
Parent Company: Instrument Systems Corp
Principal Bank: Trust Company of Georgia
Financial Information:

	$'000
Sales revenues	60,000

No of Employees: 2,000

ONEOK INC

100 W Fifth St, Tulsa, OK 74103
Tel: (918) 588-7000

Chairman: J D Scott (and President and Chief Executive Officer)
Senior Executive Officers: J R Mosteller (President-Oklahoma Natural Gas Company-ONG Transmission Company), B M Van Meter (President-Energy Companies of ONEOK), P A Wimpey (Senior VP and Chief Financial Officer and Treasurer), N E Duckworth (VP, Secretary, and Assistant Treasurer)

PRINCIPAL ACTIVITIES: Natural gas public utility, distribution and transmission; exploration for, and production of oil and natural gas; gas liquids extraction; contract well drilling, etc
Trade Names: Oklahoma Natural Gas Co; ONG Transmission Co; Energy Cos of ONEOK
Principal Subsidiaries/Divisions: Divisions: Oklahoma Natural Gas Company; ONG Transmission Company; Energy Companies of ONEOK. Subsidiaries: Caney River Transmission Company; ONG Red Oak Transmission Company; ONG Sayre Storage Company; ONG Western, Inc; Thermal Systems, Inc; TransTex Pipeline Company; ONEOK Drilling Company; ONEOK Exploration Company; ONEOK Leasing Company; ONEOK Parking Company; ONEOK Products Company; ONEOK Resources Company
Principal Bank: Bank of Oklahoma, NA, Tulsa, OK
Financial Information:

	Aug 31 1985(1)	Aug 31 1986
	$'000	$'000
Sales revenues	1,049,116	736,776
Income before taxes	60,915	64,727
Net income	34,500	34,460
Dividends(2)	34,301	35,505
Dividends per share(3)	$2.56	$2.56
Earnings per share(3)	$2.57	$2.48
Common stock	199,393	208,162
Retained income	134,171	133,126
Shareholders equity(2)	342,564	350,288

(1) restated for a change to the successful-efforts method of accounting for oil and gas producing activities
(2) common and preferred
(3) common

Principal Shareholders: Thrift Plan for Employees of ONEOK Inc, Common (5.46%), Preferred (6.71%); Sidney Paxton, Preferred (12.11%)
No of Employees: 2,256

OPELIKA MANUFACTURING CORPORATION

361 W Chestnut Street, Chicago, IL 60610
Tel: (312) 664-8300
Telex: TWX 910 2212625 m snower cgo

President: Lee N Mortenson (and Chief Executive Officer)
Senior Executive Officers: Cecil Eggert (VP), Norman Raven (Secretary, Treasurer and Director Materials Management)

PRINCIPAL ACTIVITIES: Manufacture of clothing and household linen; manufacture of machinery for the textile industry
Principal Bank: The First National Bank of Chicago
Financial Information:

	$'000
Sales revenues	63,000

No of Employees: 1,930

OPEN AIR MARKETS INC

1187 Azalea Garden Road, Norfolk, VA 23502
Tel: (804) 855 6011

President: Joseph A Vita Jr (and Chief Executive Officer)
Senior Executive Officers: Gary W Rosso (Secretary)

PRINCIPAL ACTIVITIES: Retail food outlets
Financial Information:

	$'000
Sales revenues	197,000

No of Employees: 3,250

OPP AND MICOLAS MILLS, INC

PO Box 70, 1800 Cummins Avenue, Opp, AL 36467
Tel: (205) 493-3531 (Alabama); (212) 398-9850 (New York Sales Office)
Telex: 710-581-5398 OPPMICOLASNY

Chairman: Austin List (President-Textile Division)
President: G Ray Jeffcoat
Senior Executive Officers: Philip Stanley (VP and General Manager), F Ferrell Walton (VP and Assistant Secretary), V J Rizzo (VP-Sales)

PRINCIPAL ACTIVITIES: Manufacturer of textile greige goods of 100% cotton and polyester/cotton blends of the following constructions:- Bull Denim, Drill, Duck, Clean Osnaburgs, Part Waste Osnaburgs, Sheetings, Twills, Polyester Blends
Parent Company: Johnston Industries Inc
Principal Bank: Southtrust Bank of Covington County NA
Financial Information:

	Jun 30 1986	Jun 30 1987
	$'000	$'000
Sales revenues	49,116	58,380

No of Employees: 934

OPTICAL COATING LABORATORY, INC

2789 Northpoint Pkwy, Santa Rosa, CA 95407
Tel: (707) 545-6440
Telex: ITT 4996530 ocli i saro

Chairman: Rolf F Illsley (and Chief Executive and Operating Officer)
Senior Executive Officers: Danforth Joslyn (Executive VP), John McCullough (Senior VP), G E Michel (VP Corporate Services), Joseph H Apfel (VP Research), R Russel Austin (VP), Joseph F Cussen (VP), Robert M Gelber (VP), Williams G Gittins (VP), James W Seeser (VP), Gilbert L Whissen (VP Finance and Treasurer)

PRINCIPAL ACTIVITIES: Manufacture of optical equipment and scientific instruments
Principal Bank: Bank of America
Financial Information:

	$'000
Sales revenues	59,000

No of Employees: 1,190

OPTICAL RADIATION CORPORATION

1300 Optical Drive, Azusa, CA 91702
Tel: (818) 969 3344

Chairman: Richard D Wood (and President)
Senior Executive Officers: John N Wilkinson (Senior VP and Secretary), Horst Funfstuck (Group VP), Michael Furillo (Group VP), R Richard Geatty (Group VP), Richard J McMullen (VP and Treasurer),

PRINCIPAL ACTIVITIES: Manufacture of ophthalmic products and optical components for industry, science and medicine
Principal Bank: First Business Bank
Financial Information:

	$'000
Sales revenues	97,000

No of Employees: 500

ORANGE & ROCKLAND UTILITIES INC

1 Blue Hill Plaza, Pearl River, NY 10965
Tel: (914) 352 6000

Chairman: James F Smith (and Chief Executive Officer)
President: Thomas A Griffin Jr (and Chief Operating Officer)
Senior Executive Officers: Patrick J Chambers Jr (Senior VP and Chief Financial Officer), Victor J Blanchet Jr (VP), Frank E Fischer (VP), Thomas A Folchi (VP and Controller), Raymond J Richardson (VP), Linda Winikow (VP Human Resources), Robert J McBennett (Treasurer), L Mario Di Valentino (Assistant Treasurer)

PRINCIPAL ACTIVITIES: Supply of electricity and gas
Principal Subsidiaries: Clove Development Corporation; O & R Development Inc; O & R Energy Development Inc; Pike County Light and Power Co Inc; Pike County Light and Power Co; Rockland Electric Co
Principal Bank: Marine Midland Bank
Financial Information:

	$'000
Sales revenues	475,000

No of Employees: 1,660

ORANGE CO, INC

PO Box 127, Lake Hamilton, FL 33851
Tel: (813) 439-1585

Chairman: Randon A Samuelson (and Chief Executive Officer)
President: Larry W Montanus (and Chief Operating Officer)
Senior Executive Officers: Joseph Souza (Chief Financial Officer)

PRINCIPAL ACTIVITIES: Production and processing of oranges; distribution of fresh fruit and the manufacture of fresh and frozen concentrated orange juice
Principal Subsidiaries: Orange-co of Florida Inc
Financial Information:

	$'000
Sales revenues	63,600

No of Employees: 600

ORBANCO FINANCIAL SERVICES CORPORATION

1001 S W 5th Avenue, PO Box 1110, Portland, OR 97207
Tel: (503) 222-7960

Chairman: Craig Courtemanche
President: Francis J O'Connor (and Chief Executive Officer)
Senior Executive Officers: Graham C Bryce (Senior VP and Chief Financial Officer), Leroy C Livermore (VP and Controller), Loretta Johnson (Director Investor Relations)

PRINCIPAL ACTIVITIES: Banking and financial services
Principal Bank: Wells Fargo Bank
Financial Information:

	$'000
Revenues	162,506

No of Employees: 1,310

ORCOMATIC INC

Ohio Avenue, Norwich, CT 06360
Tel: (203) 886-2451
Telex: TWX 710 4329078 orcomatic nowh

Chairman: Thomas E Petry
President: Lawrence H Smith
Senior Executive Officers: Karl W Engstrom (VP Sales), Robert A Simalchik (VP Manufacturing), J J Loughery (VP and Controller)

PRINCIPAL ACTIVITIES: Manufacture of rubber goods
Trade Names: Orcomatic, Orthane, Ortex
Parent Company: Eagle-Picher Industries Inc
Principal Bank: First National Bank of Ashland

Financial Information:

	Dec 31 1986
	$'000
Sales revenues	648,337
Income before taxes	69,108
Net income	38,808
Dividends	105,000
Dividends per share	$1.04
Earnings per share	$3.80
Common stock	10,668
Retained income	131,978
Shareholders equity	179,476

No of Employees: 7,900

OREGON METALLURGICAL CORPORATION

530 West 34th Avenue, PO Box 580, Albany, OR 97321
Tel: (503) 926 4281

Chairman: Howard T Cusic
President: Frank Caputo (and Chief Executive Officer)
Senior Executive Officers: Donald G Symonds (Controller), Douglas Blair (VP Sales), Donald G Symonds (Controller), Orval N Thompson (Secretary, Treasurer and Legal Counsel)

PRINCIPAL ACTIVITIES: Production of ingots, castings and bars of zirconium and titanium
Parent Company: Owens-Corning Fiberglas Corp
Principal Bank: First National Bank of Oregon
Financial Information:

	$'000
Sales revenues	52,860

No of Employees: 360

OREGON STEEL MILLS DIVISION

14400 N Rivergate Blvd, Portland, OR 97208
Tel: (503) 286-9651
Telex: TWX 910 4641549 ore steel ptl

Chairman: C L Emerson
President: T B Boklund (and Chief Executive Officer)
Senior Executive Officers: V N Fulton (VP Finance and Treasurer), M Long (Controller), Robert Mansshardt (VP Marketing), Robert J Sikora (VP Manufacturing), Malcolm G Putman (VP Industrial Relations)

PRINCIPAL ACTIVITIES: Manufacture of steel plate
Parent Company: Gilmore Steel Corporation
Principal Banks: Bank of America; First Interstate Bank of Oregon
Financial Information:

	$'000
Sales revenues	100,000

Principal Shareholders: Company Employee Stock Ownership Plan
No of Employees: 450

ORE-IDA FOODS CO, INC

PO Box 10, Boise, ID 83707
Tel: (208) 383-6100
Telex: TWX 910 9705951 ore ida bse

President: Gerald D Herrick
Senior Executive Officers: F E Osborne (VP Finance), Pete Helming (VP Operations), Lee Bondurant (VP Logistics), Geoffrey Supko (VP Sales and Marketing), John Catey (VP Procurement), Donald E Masterson Jr (VP Human Resources)

PRINCIPAL ACTIVITIES: Manufacture of frozen foods including pizzas, vegetables and bakery products
Parent Company: H J Heinz Co, Pittsburgh, PA
Financial Information:

	$'000
Sales revenues	500,000

No of Employees: 4,200

ORIOLE HOMES CORPORATION

1151 NW 24th Street, Pompano Beach, FL 33064
Tel: (305) 972 7660

Chairman: Richard D Levy (and Chief Executive Officer); Vice Chairman: E E Hubshman
President: Mark A Levy (and Chief Operating Officer)
Senior Executive Officers: Antonio Nunez (Senior VP and Treasurer), Rudolph M Potesta (VP Plumbing), Stephen B Tolces (VP Commercial Division), Eugene H Berns (VP Sales and Marketing), James R Clowney (VP Land Development), George C Wiesman (VP Architecture and Design), Harry A Levy (Secretary)

PRINCIPAL ACTIVITIES: Property development and construction
Principal Bank: Florida National Bank
Financial Information:

	$'000
Sales revenues	74,230

No of Employees: 290

ORION CAPITAL CORPORATION

30 Rockefeller Plaza, New York, NY 10112
Tel: (212) 541-4646

Chairman: Alan R Gruber (and Chief Executive Officer)
President: Edward J Hobbs (and Chief Operating Officer)
Senior Executive Officers: Salvatore J Cali (VP), Leo J Coleman (VP), William H Crandell (VP), David A Ferrante (VP), Peter B Hawes (VP), Ronald C Licata (VP), Michael P Maloney (VP, Secretary and General Counsel), John T Narton (VP), Vincent T Papa (VP and Treasurer), Warren R Petersen (VP), Louis H Roushon Jr (VP), David W Searfoss (VP and Controller), Raymond J Schuyler (VP Investment), George H Slack (VP)

PRINCIPAL ACTIVITIES: Diversified company with interests in insurance and financial services
Financial Information:

	$'000
Revenues	528,690

No of Employees: 2,000

ORION PICTURES CORPORATION

711 Fifth Avenue, New York, NY 10022
Tel: (212) 758 5100

Chairman: Arthur B Krim
President: Eric P Pleskow (and Chief Executive Officer)
Senior Executive Officers: William Bernstein (Executive VP), Morris Medavoy (Executive VP), Leonard B Pack (Senior VP, General Counsel and Secretary), Robert P Schwartz (Senior VP Administration), Melvin F Woods (Senior VP and Chief Financial Officer), Kimberle Aronzon (VP Business Affairs, Home Entertainment), Michael Barlow (VP Production), Rochel Blachman (VP Business Affairs), Robert N Fried (VP Production), Joel Grossman (VP, Controller and Chief Accounting Officer), John L Martin (VP Production Finance West Coast), Jonathan Sheinberg (VP Production), Eric Shonz (VP Production Finance East Coast), Wendy Smith Stover (VP Administration)

PRINCIPAL ACTIVITIES: The production, distribution and financing of motion pictures and television programs
Principal Bank: First National Bank of Boston
Financial Information:

	$'000
Sales revenues	198,000

No of Employees: 550

ORION RESEARCH INC

840 Memorial Drive, Cambridge, MA 02139
Tel: (617) 864 5400

Chairman: Richard D Condon
President: Alexander Jenkins III (and Chief Executive Officer)

Senior Executive Officers: James D Wiltshire (VP Operations), Peter W Smith (VP Finance and Treasurer), Susan F Stewart (Legal Counsel), Albert Diggens (VP Marketing), Howard J Langejans (VP Sales), Bernard Stein (VP Product Development), James W Ross (VP Research)

PRINCIPAL ACTIVITIES: Manufacture of a wide range of instruments for industrial measurement and control
Principal Subsidiaries: Orion Resdel Corporation; Orion Scientific Instruments Corporation
Principal Bank: The First National Bank of Boston
Financial Information:

	$'000
Sales revenues	33,000

No of Employees: 485

ORMAND INDUSTRIES INC

15530 East Salt Lake Avenue, City of Industry, CA 91744
Tel: (818) 968 9301

Chairman: Jarrell D Ormand (and President and Chief Executive Officer)
Senior Executive Officers: R Allen Hicks (Executive VP Finance, Secretary and Treasurer), James F Ormand (VP)

PRINCIPAL ACTIVITIES: Manufacture of metal containers
Principal Subsidiaries: General Can Co Inc; Gencan Inc
Principal Bank: MBank Dallas
Financial Information:

	$'000
Sales revenues	35,670

No of Employees: 110

ORTNER FREIGHT CAR, DIVISION AVONDALE INDUSTRIES INC

5300 Dupont Circle, Milford, OH 45150
Tel: (513) 248-0300
Telex: WUT 857650 ortner cin

President: John Lowry
Senior Executive Officers: Thomas L Dunham (Director Finance), Robert C Ortner Jr (Director Sales)

PRINCIPAL ACTIVITIES: Ortner Freight Car of Cincinnati, Ohio, engineers and builds various types of specialized railroad freight cars. Design include Ortner's patented Rapid Discharge and other special-purpose cars used to transport bulk products such as coal, construction aggregates, ores, chemicals, and wood chips. The company's major customers include railroads, utilities, and mining companies
Trade Names: Rapid Discharge
Parent Company: Avondale Industries, Inc, Boston, MA
Financial Information:

	$'000
Sales revenues	50,000

No of Employees: 400

OSCAR MAYER FOODS CORPORATION

See MAYER, OSCAR, FOODS CORPORATION

OSHKOSH B'GOSH, INC

112 Otter Avenue, Oshkosh, WI 54901
Tel: (414) 231-8800
Telex: WUT 857424 oshkosh b gosh

President: Charles F Hyde
Senior Executive Officers: Thomas R Wyman (Executive VP), W P Jacobsen (VP and Treasurer), John F Beckman (VP Sales), A S Giordano (VP Manufacturing), Douglas W Hyde (VP Merchandising)

PRINCIPAL ACTIVITIES: Manufacture of clothing particularly childrenswear
Principal Bank: First Wisconsin Bank
Financial Information:

	$'000
Sales revenues	198,000

No of Employees: 3,500

OSHKOSH TRUCK CORPORATION

2307 Oregon Street, PO Box 2566, Oshkosh, WI 54903-2566
Tel: (414) 235-9150
Telex: WUT 260197 osh truck corp

Chairman: John P Mosling; Vice Chairman: Stephen P Mosling (and Executive VP)
President: John P Carroll
Senior Executive Officers: V Preston Grove (VP-Government Affairs), Charles J Hulsbosch (VP-Finance and Treasurer), Daniel J Koenings (VP-Materials), J Peter Mosling Jr (VP-Administration and Corporate Communications), Frederick S Murley (VP-Engineering), W Thatcher Peterson (VP-Employee Resources), Ted L Zimmerman (VP-Manufacturing), Ronald P Ziebell (VP-Defense Products), Charles R Walker (Assistant Treasurer and Controller), Timothy M Dempsey (Corporate Secretary)

PRINCIPAL ACTIVITIES: Oshkosh Truck Corporation manufactures a broad range of specialized heavy duty, all wheel drive vehicles for on/off highway applications. Oshkosh trucks are built in low to medium production volumes. They are engineered for market niches where a unique, innovative design will meet a purchaser's requirements for use in specific, usually adverse operating conditions. Vehicles are sold world wide to defense, municipal and commercial markets
Financial Information:

	Sep 30 1986 $'000	Sep 30 1987 $'000
Sales revenues	399,844	403,901
Income before taxes	49,599	47,622
Net income	24,824	25,811
Class A dividends	79	117
Class B dividends	1,712	2,568
Dividends per Class A share	$0.175	$0.26
Dividends per Class B share	$0.20	$0.30
Earnings per share	$2.76	$2.87
Class A common stock	4	4
Class B common stock	86	86
Retained income	72,561	95,687
Shareholders equity	80,052	103,178

No of Employees: 1,700

OSHMAN'S SPORTING GOODS INC

2302 Maxwell Lane, Houston, TX 77023
Tel: (713) 928 3171

Chairman: Jeanette Oshman Efron; Vice Chairman: Alvin L Lubetkin (and Chairman of Executive Committe and Chief Executive Officer)
President: Marvin Aronowitz (and Chief Operating Officer)
Senior Executive Officers: Joe D Nanny (Senior VP Operations), Charles Rosemond (Senior VP Operations), Richard L Bockhart (VP, Treasurer and Assistant Secretary), Glen B Boyd (VP Merchandise), Edward R Carlin (VP, Chief Financial Officer and Assistant Secretary), Michael B Karchmer (VP), Allan Lisse (VP Information Systems), Edgar H Regan (VP Merchandise), A Lynn Boerner (Controller)

PRINCIPAL ACTIVITIES: Retail of a wide variety of sports equipment and clothing
Principal Subsidiaries: Abercrombie & Fitch Co; Oshman Athletic Goods; Oshman J S Co Inc
Principal Bank: M Bank
Financial Information:

	$'000
Sales revenues	312,000

No of Employees: 3,100

OSMOSE WOOD PRESERVING CO OF AMERICA, INC

980 Ellicott Street, Buffalo, NY 14209
Tel: (716) 882-5905
Telex: WUT 91328 osmosewood buf

President: John L Surdam
Senior Executive Officers: John W Storer (VP Executive), Paul A Goydan (VP), William S McNamara (VP Research), Ronald J Orlowski (VP Administration and Treasurer), James R Spengler (VP), John W Storer (VP)

PRINCIPAL ACTIVITIES: Manufacture of wood preserving products; operation of wood treatment services
Principal Bank: Manufacturers and Traders Trust Company
Financial Information:

	$'000
Sales revenues	80,000

No of Employees: 500

O'SULLIVAN CORPORATION

1944 Valley Avenue, Box 3510, Winchester, VA 22601
Tel: (703) 667-6666
TWX: 710-8330-0733
Telefax: (703) 667-3351

Chairman: Arthur H Bryant II (Chief Executive Officer)
President: James T Holland (and Chief Operating Officer)
Senior Executive Officers: R C Westfall (VP Research), T T Lewandowski (VP), Phillip S Griffin (VP), Bruce Dawson (VP), B J Manno (VP), Anthony A Barone (VP and Secretary), John S Campbell (VP), James L Tremoulis (VP), D L Holton (VP), C Bryant Nickerson (Treasurer)

PRINCIPAL ACTIVITIES: Manufacture of plastic products including automotive parts
Principal Bank: United Virginia Bank/National
Financial Information:

	Dec 31 1985 $'000	Dec 31 1986 $'000
Sales revenues	145,005	164,491
Net income	11,081	9,080
Dividends per share	$0.31	$0.32
Earnings per share	$1.10	$0.90
Retained income	39,949	43,278
Shareholders equity	51,246	57,130

No of Employees: 2,000

OTTAWAY NEWSPAPERS, INC

PO Box 401, Campbell Hall, NY 10916
Tel: (914) 294-8181

Chairman: James H Ottaway Jr
President: John S Goodreds
Senior Executive Officers: D J Clifford (VP Operations), Richard A Myers (VP Operations), Stephen W Ryder (VP Operations), Peter G Stone (VP Finance and Law and Treasurer), Gerald T Tache (VP Operations), A N Romm (VP News), J D Hitchman (VP Production)

PRINCIPAL ACTIVITIES: Publication of newspapers; printing services
Parent Company: Dow Jones & Co Inc, New York, NY
Principal Bank: Bankers Trust Company
Financial Information:

	$'000
Sales revenues	200,000

No of Employees: 2,400

OTTER TAIL POWER COMPANY

215 South Cascade Street, Fergus Falls, MN 56537
Tel: (218) 739 8200

Chairman: Robert M Bigwood
President: John C MacFarlane (and Chief Executive Officer)
Senior Executive Officers: Dennis R Emmen (Senior VP Finance), Royal Berstler (VP Division), William A Giesen (VP Division), Donald F Vraspir (VP Operations and Engineering), Jay D Myster (VP Legal), Gary O Cranston (VP), Richard W Muehlhausen (VP Corporate Services), Andrew E Anderson (Controller)

PRINCIPAL ACTIVITIES: Supply of electricity
Principal Subsidiaries: Minnesota Dakota Generating Co
Principal Bank: First National Bank
Financial Information:

	$'000
Sales revenues	175,455

No of Employees: 850

OUTBOARD MARINE CORPORATION

100 Sea Horse Drive, Waukegan, IL 60085
Tel: (312) 689-6200

Chairman: Charles D Strang (and Chief Executive Officer)
President: James C Chapman
Senior Executive Officers: Sherwood L Richardson (VP-Finance), Thomas J Beeler (VP and General Counsel), Beat J Jenni (VP-International Operations), Herbert A Jespersen (Manager, OMC Lincoln), David F Myers (VP-Marine Products), Michael M Potter (VP-Manager, OMC Parts and Accessories), Edgar Rose (VP-Marine Engineering and Research), Edward J Schroedter (VP-Industrial Relations), Wayne E Jones (Controller-Financial Planning), Keith A Pope (Treasurer), Hugh B Thomas (Secretary), Samuel J Winett (Controller-Operations), R Warren Comstock (Assistant Secretary)

PRINCIPAL ACTIVITIES: The Company is the world's largest producer of outboard motors with manufacturing facilities in six countries and distribution in nearly every nation of the free world. The company also produces power mowers, industrial vehicles and turf care equipment for the maintenance of large tracts of grass such as golf courses
Trade Names: Evinrude, Johnson, OMC Drive Systems, OMC stern drives, OMC Sea Drive, Lawn-Boy, Ryan, Cushman, Ryan
Principal Subsidiaries: Outboard Marine Asia Ltd; Outboard Marine International SA, Hong Kong; Outboard Marine Australia Pty Ltd, Australia; Outboard Marine Belgium, Belgium; Outboard Marine Corporation of Canada Ltd, Canada; Outboard Marine International Inc, USA; Outboard Marine de Mexico SA de CV, Mexico
Principal Bank: Continental Bank & Trust Co
Financial Information:

	Sep 30 1986 $'000
Sales revenues	971,828
Net income	14,339
Earnings per share	$0.85
Shareholders equity	392,478

No of Employees: 9,540

OVAKO STEEL, INC

22 Waterville Road, PO 745, Avon, CT 06001
Tel: (203) 677-4423
Telex: 295185

Chairman: John H Greenaway
President: Anders Teneback
Senior Executive Officers: Edward Krazia (Treasurer)

PRINCIPAL ACTIVITIES: Manufacture of steel wire, bars, and tubing
Parent Company: Ovako Steel AB, Stockholm, Sweden
Financial Information:

	$'000
Sales revenues	60,000

No of Employees: 50

OVALTINE PRODUCTS, INC

1 Ovaltine Court, Villa Park, IL 60181
Tel: (312) 530-6600
Telex: TWX 910 2540162 ovaltine vipk

Chairman: Pierre Lansel
Senior Executive Officers: Ramon Maher (Senior VP Manufacturing), W L Schmidt (VP Distribution), Charles Perreault (VP Marketing), C E Boehm (VP Sales), W A Rohmann (VP Industrial Relations), F E Stuhlmann (Comptroller)

PRINCIPAL ACTIVITIES: Manufacture of Ovaltine Malted Food Drink, snack foods and dietetic products
Parent Company: Sandoz United States Inc-Ultimate Holding Company-Sandoz Ltd, Basle, Switzerland
Principal Bank: Oak Brook Bank
Financial Information:

	$'000
Sales revenues	50,000

No of Employees: 250

OVERLAND EXPRESS INC

1631 West Thompson Road, Box 7025, Indianapolis, IN 46207
Tel: (317) 787 4300

Chairman: William F Hagerman (and President and Chief Executive Officer)
President: Frank Andrasik (and Chief Operating Officer)
Senior Executive Officers: B J Callen (VP), Charles Craig (VP), Ronald J Ludwig (VP), Ray R Murray (VP), Charles E Juntunen (VP Finance and Chief Financial Officer), Dennis H Bowman (Secretary)

PRINCIPAL ACTIVITIES: Long distance freight transportation services
Principal Bank: First National Bank of Minneapolis
Financial Information:

	$'000
Sales revenues	96,160

No of Employees: 1,335

OVERNITE TRANSPORTATION CO

1000 Semmes Avenue, Richmond, VA 23224
Tel: (804) 231-8000

Chairman: Harwood Cochrane (and Chief Executive Officer)
President: A W Duke Jr
Senior Executive Officers: Roy S Cayton (Executive VP), J R Farish (Senior VP Pricing and Marketing), William F Koch (Senior VP), A L Branham (VP Insurance and Personnel), Edward N Bromley (VP and Secretary), Bobby W Edwards (VP Safety), J Paul Heaton (VP Operations), Marvin McCurry (VP Maintenance), B L Whitener (VP Marketing), Harvey L Ramos (VP and Treasurer), John Burton (VP Pricing), Donald Sebastian (VP Claims)

PRINCIPAL ACTIVITIES: Warehousing and transportation of freight by common carrier
Principal Bank: United Virginia Bank
Financial Information:

	$'000
Sales revenues	470,330

No of Employees: 8,700

OVERSEAS SHIPHOLDING GROUP INC

1114 Avenue of the Americas, New York, NY 10036
Tel: (212) 869 1222

Chairman: Raphael Recanati
President: Morton P Hyman
Senior Executive Officers: Morris Feder (Senior VP), Milton R Kliger (Senior VP, Treasurer and Controller), Jack Goldstein (VP), Peter P Long (VP Corporate Relations), Robert N Cowen (Secretary)

PRINCIPAL ACTIVITIES: Shipping services including tankers and dry bulk cargo carriers
Principal Bank: Chase Manhattan Bank
Financial Information:

	$'000
Sales revenues	292,000

No of Employees: 1,920

OWATONNA TOOL CO

Owatonna, MN 55060
Tel: (507) 451-5310

Chairman: R W Kaplan
President: Dale A Johnson
Senior Executive Officers: K C Kaplan (VP and Director Manufacturing), C N Hough (VP Marketing), Larry Stordahl (VP Planning and Operations), Donald H Johnson (Secretary, Treasurer and Controller), Harvey West (Advertising Manager)

PRINCIPAL ACTIVITIES: Manufacture of hydraulic machinery, maintenance tools and machine tools
Parent Company: Sealed Power Corp
Principal Subsidiaries: Truth Inc; Burroughs Tool & Equipment Corp; Twin Tool Inc; Tri/Mark Corp; Twin Tool Inc
Financial Information:

	$'000
Sales revenues	110,000

No of Employees: 1,950

OWENS & MINOR INC

2727 Enterprise Parkway, Richmond, VA 23229
Tel: (804) 747-9794

Chairman: G Gilmer Minor Jr
President: G Gilmer Minor III
Senior Executive Officers: Thomas E Coulbourn (Executive VP, Chief Operating Officer and Chief Financial Officer), Philip M Minor (Vice Chairman), W Frank Fife (Senior VP), Robert E Anderson III, W Howard Bush (VP Drug), Henry A Berling (VP Medical), Lester L Jones (VP DP), Richard Ciofani (VP Finance)

PRINCIPAL ACTIVITIES: Ownes & Minor Inc is a wholesale distributor of medical and surgical supplies to hospitals, nursing homes and physicians and of pharmaceutical and other products to retail drugstores and hospital pharmacies. Medical and surgical supplies are distributed in the Mid-Atlantic, Southeastern and South Central portions of the United States and pharmaceutical and other products are sold in Virginia, North Carolina, the District of Columbia and Florida. The company also packages generic and branded pharmaceuticals for use in hospitals, outpatient clinics, nursing homes and in the home health care environment
Trade Names: PANDAC
Principal Bank: Sovran Bank NA
Financial Information:

	$'000
Sales revenues	367,300

No of Employees: 820

OWENS-CORNING FIBERGLAS CORPORATION

Fiberglas Tower, Toledo, OH 43659
Tel: (419) 248-8000
Telex: WUT 286494 fiberglas tol

Chairman: William W Boeschenstein (and President and Chief Executive Officer); Vice Chairman: Richard W Muzzy
Senior Executive Officers: Guy O Mabry (Executive VP), Max O Weber (Senior VP, President Construction Products Group), William W Colville (Senior VP Law, Secretary), Howard T Cusic (Senior VP), Paul V Daverio (Senior VP), Robert C Doban (Senior VP Science and Technology), Lewis W Saxby (Senior VP), Joseph E Doherty (VP Marketing Communications), John E Gates (VP Industrial Relations),

Charles C Gifford Jr (VP Personnel Relations), Frank E Glover (VP Management Information Systems), C Peter Hauck (VP and Controller), Robert D Heddens (VP Corporate Purchases and Transportation), Harry G Kaminer (VP and Treasurer), Gilbert Soors (Director International Finance/Assistant Treasurer), Bradford C Oelman (VP Corporate Relations)

PRINCIPAL ACTIVITIES: Owens-Corning develops and markets materials that provide improved performance, lowered costs, and new market opportunities for its customers. We serve a broad range of industries as the world's leading manufacturer of glass fiber materials and a major producer of polyester resins. The company operates in three units, with many of its products trademarked Fiberglas: The Construction Products Group manufactures and sells insulation and roofing products for residential, commercial and industrial construction and remodeling. We also produce specialty asphalts and corrosion-resistant underground petroleum storage tanks. Owens-Corning has established solid franchises for these businesses through brand identification and customer support programs. The Industrial Materials Operating Division produces reinforcements, yarns, and resins for industries such as transportation, marine, aerospace, energy, appliance and electronics. Through aggressive technical and marketing support, Owens-Corning has opened up markets for its products as replacements for traditional materials. Our International operations manufacture and sell reinforcements, yarns and insulation products outside the United States through subsidiaries and affiliates. We also produce products domestically for export to enhance our position overseas.

Trade Names: Fiberglas

Financial Information:

	Dec 31 1985 $'000	Dec 31 1986 $'000
Sales revenues	3,304,959	3,644,410
Income before taxes	167,451	18,268
Net income	131,212	15,643
Dividends	41,571	31,419
Dividends per share	$1.40	$1.05
Earnings per share	$4.42	$0.49
Common stock	129,851	253,032
Retained income (deficit)	804,329	(1,266,970)
Shareholders equity (deficit)	944,683	(1,025,196)

No of Employees: 27,700

OWENS-ILLINOIS, INC

One Seagate, Toledo, OH 43666
Tel: (419) 247-5000
Telex: WUT 556 339 oilpb

Chairman: Robert J Lanigan (and Chief Executive Officer)
President: Joseph H Lemieux (and Chief Operating Officer)
Senior Executive Officers: William Laimbeer (Executive VP and President Diversified Operations), Richard L Berry (Senior VP External Affairs and Administration), Jerome A Bohland (Senior VP Finance), William J Graham (Senior VP West), Laurence W Hecht (Senior VP Corporate Development), Bill B Jones (Chairman and Chief Executive Officer Health Care and Retirement Corp), David A Ward (Senior VP Law and Human Resources and Secretary), Louis T Alesi (VP and General Manager Libbey Glass Division), Gunther R Berger (VP, Chairman Board of Management Gerresheim, Germany), Charles G Depew (VP Government Relations), Lester B Garton Jr (VP and General Manager Worldwide Glass Container Operation), Ronald J Glick (VP and General Manager Forest Products Division), John L Hodges (VP Manufacturing Glass Container Division), John D Lebold (VP and General Manager Converting Operations Forest Products Division), H Randell Litten (VP Marketing International Operations), Robert H Little (VP International), Richard W Lock (VP, Treasurer and Assistant Chief Financial Officer, Donald E McHugh (VP Human Resources), Paul A Ormond (VP, President and Chief Operating Officer Health Care and Retirement Corp), Clarence L Perry (VP Marketing Consumer and Specialty Glass), Charles H Pietsch (VP Sales and Marketing Glass Container Division), W Joseph Riley (VP and General Manager Kimble Division), Thomas C Theiler (VP and General Manager Primary Operations Forest Products Division), Danile J Toth (VP and General Manager Consol Services Division), R Scott Trumbull (VP and General Manager Plastic Products Division), Charles L Weir (VP and General Closure Division) Thomas R Weiss (VP Communications)

PRINCIPAL ACTIVITIES: Manufacture of a wide range of containers made of glass, plastic, paper, wood and metal; manufacture of glass products for household, industrial and laboratory uses

Financial Information:

	Dec 31 1985 $'000	Dec 31 1986 $'000
Sales revenues	3,673,700	3,641,800
Net income	156,100	179,200
Earnings per share	$5.23	$2.96
Shareholders equity	1,564,000	1,677,100

No of Employees: 44,050

OXFORD CHEMICALS INC

5001 Peachtree Industrial Blvd, Chamblee, GA 30366
Tel: (404) 452-1100
Telex: TWX 810 757152 oxford cham

President: Jack Kirkham (and Chief Executive Officer)
Senior Executive Officers: M A Feffer (Executive VP Finance), John C Tremonti (Executive VP Sales), Eugene Schaffstall (VP Technology)

PRINCIPAL ACTIVITIES: Manufacture of a wide range of chemicals including agricultural chemicals, disinfectants, toiletries and cleaning products

Parent Company: Diversey World Holdings Inc
Principal Bank: Citizens and Southern National Bank of Atlanta
Financial Information:

	$'000
Sales revenues	45,000

No of Employees: 900

OXFORD INDUSTRIES, INC

222 Piedmont Avenue NE, Atlanta, GA 30308
Tel: (404) 659-2424
Telex: ITT 4611013 oxford atl

Chairman: J H Lanier (and President and Chief Executive Officer)
Senior Executive Officers: John M Hall (Group VP), Fraser L Hunter (Group VP), Knowlton J O'Reilly (Group VP), Grady M Jackson (VP Human Resources), John P Hunter Jr (VP Research Development), R W Lee Jr (VP Finance and Administration)

PRINCIPAL ACTIVITIES: Manufacture of clothing
Principal Subsidiaries: Oxford Apparel Inc; Oxford Products (Far East) Ltd; Camisas Bahia Kino SA de CV; Merox Apparel International Ltd
Principal Bank: Trust Company Bank
Financial Information:

	May 31 1986 $'000
Sales revenues	533,581
Net income	10,304
Earnings per share	$0.93
Shareholders equity	128,746

No of Employees: 11,360

O-Z/GEDNEY CO

Main Street, Terryville, CT 06786
Tel: (203) 584-0571
Telex: TWX 710 454 2844 gedney tery
Fax: (203) 584-9560

President: M J Cheshire
Senior Executive Officers: T P McDonald (Director of Sales), B Bradley (VP Operations)

PRINCIPAL ACTIVITIES: Manufacture of electrical conduit and cable fittings and enclosures
Registered Trademarks: O-Z/GEDNEY, OZ, GEDNEY, OZ/G, Ground-Tite, FIRE-SEAL, GRIP-TITE, EASY WIRE
Parent Company: General Signal Corp, Stamford, CT
Principal Subsidiaries: Nelson, Edwards, Sola, Hevi-Duty, Dowzer
Principal Banks: Chase Manhattan; Marine Midland
Financial Information:

	$'000
Sales revenues	50,000

No of Employees: 700

P H GLATFELTER CO
See GLATFELTER, P H, CO

P LEINER NUTRITIONAL PRODUCTS CORPORATION
See LEINER, P, NUTRITIONAL PRODUCTS CORPORATION

PABST BREWING CO
1000 N Market Street, PO Box 766, Milwaukee, WI 53201
Tel: 414 347-7300
Telex: TWX 910 3506993 pabst brewing

Chairman: Thomas M McGowen Jr
Senior Executive Officers: William G Bowen (VP Administration and Planning), John J Culhane (VP), A J Dooley (VP and Controller), Philip D Israel (VP Quality Assurance), Richard J Ratcheson (VP Advertising), R C Werle (VP Sales)

PRINCIPAL ACTIVITIES: Brewing; production of ale, beer, malt, animal feed supplements and corn grits
Principal Bank: First Wisconsin Bank
Financial Information:

	$'000
Sales revenues	752,000

No of Employees: 3,400

PACCAR INC
777 106th Avenue NE, Bellevue, WA 98004
Tel: (206) 455-7400
Telex: WUI 683 8005

Chairman: Charles M Pigott (and Chief Executive Officer)
President: Joseph M Dunn
Senior Executive Officers: D J Hovind (Executive VP), J A Chantrey (Senior VP), Robert W Dickey (Senior VP), Leonard A Haba (Senior VP), R A Johnsen (Treasurer)

PRINCIPAL ACTIVITIES: Manufacture of heavy vehicles, including trucks and military vehicles; construction equipment and mining machinery; forged and cast metal products
Financial Information:

	Dec 31 1985	Dec 31 1986
	$'000	$'000
Sales revenues	1,893,184	1,795,633
Net income	72,920	54,283
Earnings per share	$4.02	$3.02
Shareholders equity	714,640	726,969

No of Employees: 8,323

PACE INDUSTRIES, INC
350 Park Ave, New York, NY 10022
Tel: (212) 735-8800

Chairman: James W Willcock (and Chief Executive Officers)
Senior Executive Officers: Gerald S Armstrong (Executive VP), David A Zackrison (VP, Controller and Secretary), Michael Chu (VP Finance)

PRINCIPAL ACTIVITIES: Manufacture of water heating and air conditioning equipment; other interests include the production of telephone directories and magazines, the manufacture of plastic and steel containers for shipping
Principal Subsidiaries: World Color Press Inc
Financial Information:

	$'000
Sales Revenues	2,000,000

No of Employees: 20,000

PACESETTER CORPORATION
4343 S 9th Street, Omaha, NE 68127
Tel: (402) 331-9400

Chairman: Phillip G Schrager (and Chief Executive Officer)
President: Harley D Schrager (and Chief Operating Officer)
Senior Executive Officers: James W Russell (VP Marketing), Lynn D Anthony (VP Manufacturing)

PRINCIPAL ACTIVITIES: Manufacture of windows and doors, patio covers and awnings
Principal Bank: First National Bank of Omaha
Financial Information:

	$'000
Sales revenues	60,000

No of Employees: 1,250

PACIFIC FIRST FINANCIAL CORPORATION
PO Box 1257, 1145 Broadway, Tacoma, WA 98401
Tel: (206) 383-2511

Chairman: *Jerry E Pohlman (and President and Chief Executive Officer)
Senior Executive Officers: *George L Johnson (Executive VP-Finance and Chief Financial Officer), *Robert D McIntosh (Executive VP-Real Estate Group), *Theodore M Johnson Jr (Executive VP-Corporate Control Group, Corporate Secretary and General Counsel), Richard D Stan (Senior VP-Corporate Development, President Pacific First Securities Ltd), *Gary L Johnson (Senior VP-Branch Banking Administration), *Member of the Executive Committee

PRINCIPAL ACTIVITIES: Pacific First Financial Corporation, parent to Pacific First Federal Savings Bank, Pacific First Securities, Ltd and Pacific First Mortgage Corporation has 58 financial services offices in the major markets throughout Washington, Oregon, California and five other Western states. Through its various financial affiliates, the company provides consumer, mortgage, commercial and income property loans as well as savings, checking, insurance investment and securities brokerage services. Pacific First Federal is the largest federally chartered savings bank headquartered in the State of Washington

Principal Subsidiaries: Pacific First Federal Savings Bank; Pacific First Mortgage Corporation; Pacific First Securities, Ltd; Pacific First Investor Services, Ltd; Pacific First Leasing; Pacific First Investment Services, Inc; Pacific First Real Estate, Inc; Trans-Columbia Corporation; Trans-Columbia II Corporation; Builders Mortgage Corporation; Atlantic Investment Company; Pacific Loan Agency; Pacific Mortgage & Investment Company; Pacific Mortgage & Insurance Company; Pacific First Financial Insurance Services, Inc

Financial Information:

	Dec 31 1985	Dec 31 1986
	$'000	$'000
Income (loss) before taxes	(9,863)	41,411
Net income (loss)	(9,849)	23,469
Dividends per share	-	$0.10*
Earnings (loss) per share	($1.32)	$3.14
Common stock	7,480	7,487
Retained earnings	77,055	99,655
Shareholders equity	183,658	207,352
Deposits	1,886,036	2,096,648
Total assets	3,359,893	4,097,364

*quarterly

Principal Shareholders: none over 5%
No of Employees: 1,333

PACIFIC GAMBLE ROBINSON CO

10829 NE 68th Street, Kirkland, WA 98033
Tel: (206) 828-6200

President: Douglas S Gamble (and Chief Executive Officer)
Senior Executive Officers: Donald P Gamble Jr (VP), E W Sandygren (VP and Secretary), John L Knutson (Treasurer)

PRINCIPAL ACTIVITIES: Wholesale and retail trade in groceries, fruit, vegetables and frozen foods; supermarkets; interests in trucking, truck leasing, wholesale building materials and paper
Principal Bank: First National Bank of Minneapolis
Financial Information:

	$'000
Sales revenues	782,547

No of Employees: 4,700

PACIFIC GAS & ELECTRIC CO

77 Beale Street, San Francisco, CA 94106
Tel: (415) 781-4211
Telex: TWX 910 3726587 pac g & e go sf

Chairman: Richard A Clarke (and Chief Executive Officer); Vice Chairman: Stanley T Skinner
President: George A Maneatis
Senior Executive Officers: John A Sproul (Executive VP), Ellis B Langley (Senior VP), M Willrich (Senior VP)

PRINCIPAL ACTIVITIES: Gas, water and electricity supply
Principal Subsidiaries: Pacific Gas Transmission Company; Alberta & Southern Gas Co Ltd
Financial Information:

	Dec 31 1985	Dec 31 1986
	$'000	$'000
Sales revenues	8,430,981	7,816,661
Net income	1,030,805	1,081,223
Dividends per share	$1.84	$1.92
Earnings per share	$2.65	$2.60
Common stock*	326,838	355,937
Retained income	2,610,512	2,855,748
Shareholders equity	5,443,546	7,015,728

*weighted average shares outstanding in thousands

No of Employees: 29,200

PACIFIC LIGHTING CORPORATION

801 S Grand Avenue, Los Angeles, CA 90017
Tel: (213) 895-500
Telex: TWX 910 321 3946 pac lght lsa

Chairman: Paul A Miller (and Chief Executive Officer)
President: James R Ukropina
Senior Executive Officers: Lloyd A Levitin (Executive VP), Willis B Wood Jr (Executive VP)

PRINCIPAL ACTIVITIES: Oil and gas exploration and production; natural gas distribution; retailing
Principal Subsidiaries: Southern California Gas Company; Pacific Lighting Oil and Gas Company; Thrifty Corporation
Principal Bank: Wells Fargo Bank
Financial Information:

	Dec 31 1986	Dec 31 1987
	$'000	$'000
Sales revenues	5,323,757	5,339,310
Income before taxes(1)	122,539	396,826
Income(2)	59,781	224,614
Gain on sale(3)	23,824	18,554
Net income	83,605	251,168
Preferred dividends	5,906	5,906
Common dividends	179,714	206,020
Dividends per share	$3.48	$3.48
Income per share(1)	$0.93	$3.69
Income per share(2)	$0.41	$0.45
Net income per share	$1.34	$4.14
Common stock	855,139	874,914
Retained income	736,091	775,025
Shareholders equity	1,657,440	1,721,739

(1) From continuing operations
(2) From discontinued operations
(3) Less income taxes of $28,456

No of Employees: 27,928

PACIFIC LUMBER & SHIPPING CO

3131 Raimer Bank Tower, Seattle, WA 98111
Tel: (206) 682-7262
Telex: RCA 277123 pls ur

President: Charles L Spence
Senior Executive Officers: Robert L Spence (Executive VP), Gerald C Strand (VP Export Sales), Larry Lundberg (Treasurer), Thomas C Spence (Secretary)

PRINCIPAL ACTIVITIES: Timber production and export
Principal Bank: Pacific National Bank of Washington
Financial Information:

	$'000
Sales revenues	156,000

No of Employees: 460

PACIFIC LUMBER CO

PO Box 7406, San Francisco, CA 94120
Tel: (415) 421-3000
Telex: WUT 314 042 palco sfhqfol

Chairman: Robert B Hoover; Chairman of Executive Committee: Edward M Carpenter
President: Gene G Elam (and Chief Executive Officer)
Senior Executive Officers: John A Campbell (Executive VP), Thomas B Malarkey Jr (Executive VP), George J Martin (Executive VP), Edward W Beck (VP, Secretary and General Counsel), Vincent C Garner (VP Finance and Treasurer), Robert E Giusti (VP), Robert C Halvorsen (VP and Controller)

PRINCIPAL ACTIVITIES: Timber products including plywood and lumber; welding equipment and industrial equipment; pumps
Parent Company: Maxxam Group Inc
Principal Subsidiaries: Yosuba Farms; Palco Industries Inc; Canadian Cylinder Co Ltd; Coyne Co; Cyclomatic Industries Inc; Palco International Corp; Palco Welding Products of Canada Ltd; Tweco Products Inc; Victor Equipment Co
Principal Bank: Crocker National Bank
Financial Information:

	$'000
Sales revenues	280,750

No of Employees: 4,000

PACIFIC MUTUAL LIFE INSURANCE CO

700 Newport Center Drive, Newport Beach, CA 92660

Tel: (714) 640-3011

Telex: TWX 910 5961376 pacmu ins npbh

Chairman: Walter B Gerken (and Chief Executive Officer)

President: Harry G Bubb (and Chief Operating Officer)

Senior Executive Officers: William Cunningham (Executive VP Pension Investment Operations), Thomas C Sutton (Executive VP Individual Operations), Gerald W Kimmerle (Executive VP Group Insurance), William L Ferris (Senior VP Group Employment Benefit Operations), Stephen T O'Hare (Senior VP Human Resources and Corporate Services), Harold T Joanning (Senior VP and Treasurer), Joseph A Thomas (Senior VP and General Counsel), Glenn L Hammer Jr (VP Realty Account Management), Carl A Mayer Jr (VP Asset Management), Clement B Penrose (VP and Corporate Actuary)

PRINCIPAL ACTIVITIES: Life insurance

Principal Bank: First Interstate Bank

Financial Information:

	Dec 31 1985	Dec 31 1986
	$'000	$'000
Premium income	1,296,280	1,457,421
Investment income	365,040	438,057

No of Employees: 2,825

PACIFIC RESOURCES INC

PO Box 3379, Honolulu, HI 96842

Tel: (808) 547-3111

Telex: ITT 0292

Chairman: Robert G Reed III (and President and Chief Executive Officer)

Senior Executive Officers: Charles L Dunlap (Executive VP), Robert F Loughridge (Senior VP), Richard F Hall (VP, Federal Affairs), Howard J Lee (VP), Melvin M Nakamura (VP, Human Resources), Maurice V Pagella (VP, Financial Planning and Analysis), Mario A Roberti (VP and General Counsel), Andrea L Simpson (VP Corporate Communications), George C Slain (VP and Treasurer), Fidencio M Mares (VP, Administration), F David Hoffman (Secretary), Winona L Kataoka (Assistant Secretary), Richard J Lau (Controller), Gilbert S Mendelson (Assistant Controller), Paul L Takenaka (Assistant Treasurer)

PRINCIPAL ACTIVITIES: Pacific Resources, Incorporated is a rapidly-growing, independent energy company strategically located in the mid-Pacific. With its headquarters in Honolulu, Hawaii, PRI purchases, transports, processes, sells, trades and distributes energy products in Hawaii, the US, West Coast, Asia and the South Pacific. Its major source of revenue is the sale of petroleum products refined from crude oil purchased from several sources throughout the world. Its Hawaiian Independent Refinery, Inc located near Honolulu has a capacity of 67,900 barrels per day. PRI is also a distributor of utility and nonutility gas to commercial and domestic customers throughout the State of Hawaii. It operates a synthetic natural gas plant adjacent to its refinery and distributes purchased propane gas. PRI also sells alternative energy products such as solar, submetering and cogeneration systems

Trade Names: Gas Express (gasoline brand)

Principal Subsidiaries: Hawaiian Independent Refinery, Inc; Gasco, Inc; Enerco, Inc; PRI Energy Systems, Inc; PRI South Pacific Inc, Pacific Resources Terminals, Inc; PRI International, Inc; Gas Express (Promana, Inc)

Financial Information:

	Dec 31 1985	Dec 31 1986
	$'000	$'000
Sales revenues	1,367,738	816,138
Income before taxes	33,737	51,040
Net income	18,162	27,783
Earnings (loss) per share	($0.21)	$1.42
Common stock*	14,291	16,062
Shareholders equity	154,661	199,404

*average shares outstanding in thousands

No of Employees: 861

PACIFIC SCIENTIFIC CO

1350 S State College Blvd, Anaheim, CA 92803

Tel: (714) 535-8141

Telex: WUT 655 421 psco anh

Chairman: Harry R Goff

President: Edgar S Brower (and Chief Executive Officer)

Senior Executive Officers: Richard V Plat (Senior VP Finance and Administration and Secretary), Douglas D Fockler (VP), Joseph J Sacco Jr (VP), Charles A Collins (VP), Robert J DalPonte (VP), William L Nothwang (Controller), Peer A Swan (Treasurer)

PRINCIPAL ACTIVITIES: Instruments and Components: Near-infrared electro-optical instruments to determine composition of various materials; electro-optical instruments for measuring color and other appearance qualities in the visible spectrum; electro-optical instruments to measure size and distribution of particles in fluids, air and powders; welded and formed metal bellows, mechanical seals. Advanced Technology Group: Aircraft restraint systems, electro-mechanical flight control components, hydraulic actuators; mechanical shock arrestors, kinetic energy restraints and dampers; fire detection and suppression systems, high pressure vessels, pneumatic actuators; pyrotechnic-actuated ordnance devices; pyrotechnic devices, cable and harness assemblies; fire detection and suppression systems; AC and DC generators, electro-mechanical actuators. Motors and Controls: Low inertia, permanent magnet DC and brushless motors; electronic motor controllers

Principal Bank: First Interstate Bank California

Financial Information:

	Dec 27 1985	Dec 26 1986
	$'000	$'000
Total revenues	89,832	88,992
Income before taxes	8,205	3,680
Net income	5,699	2,840
Dividends	2,156	2,196
Dividends per share	$0.40	$0.40
Earnings per share	$1.05	$0.52
Common stock	5,420	5,500
Retained income	48,407	49,051
Shareholders equity	57,463	58,650

No of Employees: 1,800

PACIFIC SMELTING CO

22219 S Western Avenue, Torrance, CA 90501

Tel: (213) 328-4811

Telex: WUT 687 471 pacsmelt trnc

Chairman: Frank H Osborn

President: David M Carlile

Senior Executive Officers: William Lamers (VP Industrial Relations) David F Schwartz (VP and General Manager Memphis Plant), Charles A Tourville (VP and Treasurer)

PRINCIPAL ACTIVITIES: Manufacture of zinc products

Parent Company: Australian Mining & Smelting Ltd

Principal Bank: Bank of America

Financial Information:

	$'000
Sales revenues	40,000

No of Employees: 150

PACIFIC TELECOM INC

805 Broadway, PO Box 9901, Vancouver, WA 98668
Tel: (206) 696 0983

Chairman: A M Gleason
President: Charles E Robinson (and Chief Executive Officer)
Senior Executive Officers: Dennis W Elliott (Executive VP), Charles E Peterson (Executive VP Operations), James P Best (Senior VP and Controller), Vern K Dunham (Senior VP Group Relations), Robert W Bunke (VP), Edward R Geiger (VP Administration), Brian M Wirkkala (VP and Treasurer), B Charles Russell (VP Engineering), James C Warwick (VP Planning), Charles Kegley Jr (VP Industrial Relations), John E McGill (VP Government and Secretary)

PRINCIPAL ACTIVITIES: Telecommunications services, electricity supply, resource development and mining
Parent Company: Pacificorp
Principal Bank: Seattle-First National Bank
Financial Information:

	$'000
Sales revenues	489,000

No of Employees: 3,420

PACIFIC TELESIS GROUP

Pacific Telesis Center, 130 Kearny St, San Francisco, CA 94105
Tel: (415) 882-8000

Chairman: D E Guinn (and Chief Executive Officer); Vice Chairmen: T J Saenger, J E Hulse (and Chief Financial Officer)
President: S L Ginn (and Chief Operating Officer)
Senior Executive Officers: B W Dial (Executive VP), R V R Dalenberg (Executive VP and General Counsel), A C Latno Jr (Executive VP), R C Blanz (Executive VP), J R Moberg (Executive VP)

PRINCIPAL ACTIVITIES: Telephone and telecommunications services
Trade Names: (1) PAC - New York, Pacific, Midwest, (2) Pacific Telesis -London, Switzerland, (3) PacTel - Newspaper stock tables
Principal Subsidiaries: PacTel Cullular; PacTel Paging; Multicom; Pacific Bell; Nevada Bell; Pacific Bell Director; PacTel InfoSystems; Pacific Telesis International; PacTel Properties; PacTel Finance; PacTel Spectrum Services
Financial Information:

	Dec 31 1985 $'000	Dec 31 1986 $'000
Sales revenues	8,498,600	8,977,300
Income before taxes	1,739,000	1,979,000
Net income	929,100	1,079,400
Dividends	594,100	654,100
Dividends per share*	$1.43	$1.52
Earnings per share*	$2.27	$2.51
Common stock	429,412	430,550
Retained income	2,241,900	2,663,300
Shareholders equity	7,317,000	7,753,300

*common share data reflect two-for-one stock split March 25 1987

Number of shareholders: 1.2 million
No of Employees: 74,937

PACIFIC TIN CONSOLIDATED CORPORATION

280 Park Avenue, New York, NY 10017
Tel: (212) 557 2020

Chairman: Peter O Lawson-Johnston; Vice Chairman: Carroll P Rogers Jr
President: Harry a Durney (and Chief Executive Officer)
Senior Executive Officers: Donald Shanks (VP and Treasurer), Harry H Weiss (VP and Secretary)

PRINCIPAL ACTIVITIES: Production of minerals including tin
Principal Subsidiaries: Feldspar Corporation; Pyron Corporation
Principal Bank: Bank of New York
Financial Information:

	$'000
Sales revenues	36,000

No of Employees: 270

PACIFIC WESTERN BANCSHARES

333 West Santa Clara Street, San Jose, CA 95113
Tel: (408) 244 1700

Chairman: Philip R Boyce (and Chief Executive Officer)
President: James R Kenny
Senior Executive Officers: James R Barranti (Executive VP), Joseph D Arrigo (Senior VP Business Development), Eugene E Blakeslee (Chief Financial Officer and Treasurer), Richard M Pitagora (Secretary and Legal Counsel)

PRINCIPAL ACTIVITIES: Banking
Principal Bank: First Interstate Bank of California

No of Employees: 345

PACIFICARE HEALTH SYSTEMS INC

5400 Orange Avenue, Suite 220, Cypress, CA 90630
Tel: (714) 952 1121

Chairman: Samuel J Tibbitts; Vice Chairman: Frank F McDougall
President: Terry Hartshorn (and Chief Executive Officer)
Senior Executive Officers: Alan Hoops (Senior VP and Secretary), Richard Lipeles (Senior VP), John Siefker (Senior VP and Chief Financial Officer), Ronald Young (Treasurer)

PRINCIPAL ACTIVITIES: Insurance services including healthcare
Financial Information:

	$'000
Revenues	90,000

No of Employees: 240

PACIFICORP

851 S W Sixth Avenue, Portland, OR 97204
Tel: (503) 243-5190
Telecopier: (503) 243-4224
Telex: TWX 910-464-1594

Chairman: Don C Frisbee (and Chief Executive Officer-PacifiCorp)
President: A M Gleason (PacifiCorp)
Senior Executive Officers: PacifiCorp:- Gayle L Veber (Senior VP and Chief Financial Officer), Robert F Lanz (VP and Treasurer), Stan M Marks (VP), Steven F Rafoth (VP), Sally A Nofziger (Corporate Secretary). Pacific Power Officers: Electric Operations:- David F Bolender (President), Robert W Moench (Executive VP), Robert M Smith (Senior VP), Rodney M Boucher (VP), F Richard Brown (VP), M Wayne Goin (VP), John Melnichuk (VP), James F Pienovi (VP), Frederic D Reed (VP), William D Robertson Jr (VP), J M Samper (VP), Lee D Weislogel (VP), Larry A Olson (Treasurer), James T Watson (Controller)

PRINCIPAL ACTIVITIES: Electric, telecommunications, minerals and mining
Principal Subsidiaries: NERCO Inc; Pacific Telecom Inc; Northwest Acceptance Corporation

Financial Information:

	Dec 31 1986 $'000
Sales revenues	2,066,900
Net income	250,900
Earnings per share	$3.45
Common shareholders equity	1,835,400

No of Employees: 10,620

PACKAGING CORPORATION OF AMERICA

1603 Orrington Avenue, Evanston, IL 60204
Tel: (312) 492-5713

Chairman: A T McInnes
President: M R Haymon (and Chief Executive Officer)
Senior Executive Officers: G U Bayly (VP Paperboard Products), W H Swissheim (Senior VP Containerboard Products), L Lovell (VP Molded Fibre), R D Harlow (Senior VP)

PRINCIPAL ACTIVITIES: Manufacture of packaging products
Parent Company: Tenneco Inc, Houston, TX
Financial Information:

	$'000
Sales revenues	1,100,000

Principal Shareholders: Tenneco
No of Employees: 8,000

PACKAGING SYSTEMS CORPORATION

275 North Middletown Road, Pearl River, NY 10965
Tel: (914) 735 9200

Chairman: Leon Hershaft
President: Arthur Hershaft (and Chief Executive Officer)
Senior Executive Officers: Fred Hershaft (VP), Bruce E Hagen (Secretary and Treasurer)

PRINCIPAL ACTIVITIES: Manufacture of labels, tags and plastic packaging
Principal Bank: First National Bank of Boston
Financial Information:

	$'000
Sales revenues	38,560

No of Employees: 550

PACKERLAND PACKING CO, INC

PO Box 1184, Green Bay, WI 54305
Tel: (414) 468-4000
Telex: WUT 263459 packerland grb

Chairman: George N Gillett (and President)
Senior Executive Officers: David F Backer (Executive VP Finance, Secretary and Treasurer), Charles McCarthy (Executive VP Sales), Edward W Karrels (VP and Assistant Secretary)

PRINCIPAL ACTIVITIES: Meat production
Financial Information:

	$'000
Sales revenues	500,000

No of Employees: 1,000

PACO PHARMACEUTICAL SERVICES INC

1200 Paco Way, Lakewood, NJ 08701
Tel: (201) 367 9000

Chairman: Alfred Schechter (and Chief Executive Officer)
President: Russell R Haines (and Chief Operating Officer)
Senior Executive Officers: Joseph Berger (VP and Treasurer), Glenn M Feit (Secretary and Legal Counsel), John J Braithwaite (VP Sales)

PRINCIPAL ACTIVITIES: Manufacture of pharmaceuticals
Financial Information:

	$'000
Sales revenues	39,810

No of Employees: 875

PACWEST BANCORP

1211 Southwest Fifth Avenue, 300 Pacwest Center, Portland, OR 97204
Tel: (503) 790 7501

Chairman: Robert W Franz (and Chief Executive Officer)
President: Stephen K Foster
Senior Executive Officers: James J Atkinson (Senior VP), Terry Tracy (Chief Financial Officer, VP Finance, Treasurer and Assistant Secretary), William N Savage (VP Marketing and Planning), J Lynn Jones (VP Investments), Robert L Price (VP Credit Review)

PRINCIPAL ACTIVITIES: Banking and financial services
Principal Subsidiaries: First National Bank; Hood River County Bank; Pacific Western Bank; Associated Computer Services
Principal Bank: Pacific Western Bank

No of Employees: 30

PAINE WEBBER GROUP INC

140 Broadway, New York, NY 10005
Tel: (212) 437-2121

Chairman: Donald B Marron (and President and Chief Executive Officer)
Senior Executive Officers: Richard P Campbell Jr (Executive VP and Chief Financial Officer), Charles T Peterson (Executive VP and Treasurer), Sam S Miller (Senior VP, Secretary and General Counsel)

PRINCIPAL ACTIVITIES: Holding company with interests in financial services
Financial Information:

	Sep 30 1985 $'000	Sep 30 1986 $'000
Revenues	1,885,076	2,384,720
Net income	33,824	71,599
Earnings per share	$1.70	$2.51
Shareholders equity	431,410	633,365

No of Employees: 12,000

PALCO INDUSTRIES, INC

500 Washington Street, San Francisco, CA 94111
Tel: (415) 421-3000

President: William L Leon (and Chief Executive Officer)
Senior Executive Officers: George Martin (Executive VP), Robert E Giusti (VP), V C Garner (VP and Treasurer), Robert Halvorsen (VP and Controller), John A Miller (VP and General Counsel)

PRINCIPAL ACTIVITIES: Manufacture of welding equipment and supplies
Parent Company: Pacific Lumber Co
Principal Bank: Crocker Bank
Financial Information:

	$'000
Sales revenues	200,000

No of Employees: 2,000

PALL CORPORATION

30 Sea Cliff Avenue, Glen Cove, NY 11542
Tel: (516) 671-4000
Telex: 968855

Chairman: Dr David B Pall; Vice Chairman: Abraham Krasnoff (and Chief Executive Officer)
President: Maurice G Hardy (and Chief Operating Officer)
Senior Executive Officers: Henry Petronis (Executive VP), Mark Kachur (Senior VP), Erwin Kirnbauer (Senior VP), Sidney

Krakauer (Senior VP), Donald G E Nicholls (Senior VP), Nicholas Nickolaus (Senior VP), Stanley Wernick (Senior VP and Treasurer), Derek T D Williams (Senior VP), Joseph Campolong (Senior VP), Peter Deegan (Senior VP), Eric Krasnoff (Senior VP), John Miller (Senior VP), Arnie Weiner (Senior VP), Peter Schwartzman (Secretary), Charles A Wolowitz (Controller)

PRINCIPAL ACTIVITIES: Pall Corporation is the world leader in sophisticated fluid clarification. Pall filters, gas dryers, air cleaners and oil purifiers are used to remove contaminants (solid, liquid and gaseous) from liquids and gases in a very broad range of applications and markets. In a growing number of systems, Pall filters are used to collect or recirculate useful particles such as catalysts and in a few to collect a product such as penicillin. Oxygen concentration and purification is a new field for Pall as is monoclonal antibody immobilization

Trade Names: BIODYNE, CARDIOPLEGIA PLUS, CENTRISEP, CENTURY, CHEMINERT, CONSERVE, EC-PLUS, EMFLON, EPOCEL, GASKLEEN, GF, GF PLUS, HEAT-LES, HDC, MAX-PRO, N66, PALLCELL, PALLSCOPE, PERMAKLEEN, PMF, PMM, POSIDYNE, PRE-BYPASS PLUS, PROFILE, RIGIMESH, ROTOLOK, SCF, SEALKLEEN, SUPER CHEMINERT, ULTIPOR, DFA, PTM, Kleen-change, Disc-Flo, Profile RFN, Profile-Plus, Polyester Profile, Deltadyne, DSLK, HSLK, N66 Posidyne, Emflon Super-Cheminert, Emflon DFA, Mini-Gaskleen, Fluorodyne Super Etch, PSS, S Series PSS, Supramesh, Surfamax, Performax, Ultipor II, Strata-Trol, SABER, Flood Guard, Amloc, Pallmatic, Immunodyne, Set Saver, LoProdyne, Silent Monitor, Filtrett, Membra-Pad, Extended Life Disposables

Principal Subsidiaries: Pall Ultrafine Filtration Corp; Pall Process Filtration Corp; Pall Porous Metals Filter Corp; Pall Well Technology Corp; Aircraft Porous Media, Inc; Pall Land and Marine Corp; Mectron Industries, Inc; Pall Industrial Hydraulics Corp; Pall Biomedical Products Corp; Pall Europe Ltd; Pall Canada Ltd; Nihon Pall Ltd; Pallflex Products Inc

Principal Bank: Citibank, NA

Financial Information:

	Aug 3 1985	Aug 2 1986
	$'000	$'000
Sales revenues	275,918	332,041
Income before taxes	46,599	54,579
Net income	34,254	40,942
Dividends declared	8,323	10,005
Dividends per share	$0.31	$0.37
Earnings per share	$1.26	$1.50
Common stock	4,538	6,885
Retained income	171,245	202,182
Shareholders equity	172,877	221,399

No of Employees: 4,800

PALM BEACH INCORPORATED

400 Pine Street, Cincinnati, OH 45202
Tel: (513) 241-4260
Telex: 84247

Chairman: M John O'Donoghue
President: Alfred P Fuoco (and Chief Executive Officer)
Senior Executive Officers: William B Anneken (Executive VP Finance), Jay Shaw (Corporate Group President Men's Wear), Lawrence W Ward (Executive VP Administration), William E Beebe (Treasurer), Paul W Bridge Jr (Controller), Thomas C Roedersheimer (VP and Corporate Credit Manager), Walter L Landergan Jr (Secretary)

PRINCIPAL ACTIVITIES: Palm Beach designs, markets and manufactures apparel for men, women and boys, including tailored clothing, sportswear, outerwear and dress furnishings

Trade Names: Palm Beach's major brand names include Palm Beech(R), Evan-Picone(R), Blassport(R), John Weitz, Calvin(R), Austin Hill(R), Haspel(R), William Barry(R), Eagle Shirtmakers(R), Gant(R)

Parent Company: Palm Beach Holdings, Inc

Principal Subsidiaries: Decker Corporation; Eaglewear, Inc; Eagle Shirtmakers, Inc; Eagle Youthwear, Inc; Gant Corporation; Hunter Haig of New Haven, Inc; Palm Beach Company and its subsidiaries-Adler Pants Co, Inc, Calvin Clothing Corporation, Evan-Picone for Men, Inc, Jane & Linda Sportswear Company, Tailored Skirts Company, Trent Clothing Company, Palm Beach International Sales Corporation; Palm Sport Limited (Hong Kong); Tropic Formals Inc, Ltd; William Barry Company, Inc

Principal Bank: Manufacturers Hanover Trust Company

Financial Information:

	Dec 31 1985	Jan 3 1987
	$'000	$'000
Sales revenues	419,065	394,238
Income (loss) before taxes	9,606	(6,464)
Net income (loss)	5,279	(5,973)
Dividends	3,349	-
Dividends per share	$0.90	-
Common stock (deficiency)	8,155	(2,163)

Principal Shareholders: Palm Beach Holdings, Inc (Privately held company)

No of Employees: 5,700

PALMER G LEWIS COMPANY INC

See LEWIS, PALMER G, COMPANY INC

PAN AM CORPORATION

PAN AM Building, 200 Park Avenue, New York, NY 10166
Tel: (212) 880-1234

Chairman: C Edward Acker (and Chief Executive Officer)
Senior Executive Officers: Martin R Shugrue Jr (Vice Chairman), John M Lindsey (Senior VP, Legal and Corporate Affairs), C J David Davies (VP and Treasurer), Eugene A Ulrich (VP and Controller), Roger A Cooke (Secretary)

PRINCIPAL ACTIVITIES: Holding company whose subsidiaries are engaged in international air travel and related contract services

Principal Subsidiaries: Pan American World Airways Inc; Pan Am World Services Inc

Financial Information:

	Dec 31 1985	Dec 31 1986
	$'000	$'000
Total operating revenues	3,474,547	3,038,995
Income (loss) before taxes	55,992	(465,296)
Net income (loss)	51,750	(462,814)
Earnings (loss) per share	$0.45	($3.42)
Common stock	33,420	34,390
Retained (deficit)	(321,431)	(784,245)
Shareholders equity	448,950	8,763

No of Employees: 21,500

PAN PACIFIC FISHERIES

338 Cannery Street, Terminal Island, CA 90731
Tel: (213) 833-3564
Telex: TWX 910 3457466 panpac fsh-term

Chairman: Richard O R Bowling (and President)
Senior Executive Officers: John Bridget (VP Operations), James Crilly (Sales Manager), Harold Long (Treasurer)

PRINCIPAL ACTIVITIES: Fish processing and canning; products include canned tuna fish and pet foods

Parent Company: CHB Foods Inc, San Pedro, CA

Principal Bank: Bank of America

Financial Information:

	$'000
Sales revenues	130,000

No of Employees: 1,500

PANCHO'S MEXICAN BUFFET INC

3500 Noble Avenue, Fort Worth, TX 76111
Tel: (817) 831 0081

Chairman: Jesse Arrambide
President: Hollis Taylor (and Chief Executive Officer)
Senior Executive Officers: Charles W Askew (Executive VP and Chief Operating Officer), Platt L Allen Jr (VP, Treasurer and Chief Financial Officer), Jesse Arambide III (VP Operations), Gary Bessent (VP Operations), John Bosquez (VP Operations), Jerry Box (VP Operations, Planning and Control), Samuel L Carlson (VP Administration and Secretary), Jim Conner (VP Construction), David J Dixon (VP Human Resources), John Hill (VP Operations), Julio Nieves (VP Operations), James K Richhart (VP Purchasing and Distribution), Arthur G Taylor (VP Operations), Jackie Vinson (VP Marketing)

PRINCIPAL ACTIVITIES: Restaurants
Principal Bank: Texas American Bank/Fort Worth NA
Financial Information:

	$'000
Sales revenues	36,000

No of Employees: 2,000

PANDICK, INC

345 Hudson Street, New York, NY 10014
Tel: (212) 741-5555
Telex: WUT 855777 pandick ct

Chairman: Edward G Green (and Chief Executive Officer)
President: Anthony K Moulton (and Chief Operating Officer)
Senior Executive Officers: Frank J Garippa (Executive VP and Chief Marketing Officer), Chilton B Greer (Executive VP), Garry L Pote (Executive VP), John P O'Connor (Senior VP and Chief Financial Officer), Daniel B Burns (Senior VP), Thomas M Woodward (Senior VP Administration)

PRINCIPAL ACTIVITIES: Financial printing services
Principal Subsidiaries: Pandick Technologies Inc; Pandick Press International Finance NV
Principal Bank: US Trust Co
Financial Information:

	$'000
Sales revenues	166,250

No of Employees: 1,800

PANEX INDUSTRIES INC

477 Madison Avenue, New York, NY 10022
Tel: (212) 688-9277

Chairman: Daniel Rosenbloom
President: Andreas Gal (and Chief Executive Officer)
Senior Executive Officers: Gerson Banner (Senior VP), Sandra Shaffer (Secretary and Treasurer)

PRINCIPAL ACTIVITIES: Manufacture of clothing and buttons
Principal Bank: Irving Trust
Financial Information:

	$'000
Sales revenues	65,000

No of Employees: 1,200

PANHANDLE EASTERN CORPORATION

3000 Bissonnet, Houston, TX 77005
Tel: (713) 664-3401
Telex: 794667 Trunkline Hou

Chairman: Richard L O'Shields
President: Robert D Hunsucker (and Chief Executive Officer)
Senior Executive Officers: Kenneth E Kalen (Group VP), Thomas B Irwin (Senior VP, Finance), Charles E Lasseter (Senior VP, Controller), Vernon D Rigdon (Senior VP and Treasurer), John A Sieger (VP, General Counsel, Cyril J Smith (VP and Secretary), John F Schomaker (VP), Herbert E Schulze (VP), Stanford A Wallace (VP)

PRINCIPAL ACTIVITIES: Panhandle Eastern Corporation is a publicly owned holding company whose subsidiaries are primarily engaged in the transmission and sale of natural gas in interstate commerce
Principal Subsidiaries: Panhandle Eastern Pipe Line Company; Trunkline Gas Company; Trunkline LNG Company; Pan Border Gas Company;
Principal Bank: Manufacturers Hanover Trust Company
Financial Information:

	Dec 31 1985 $'000	Dec 31 1986 $'000
Sales revenues	2,250,102	2,589,994
Income (loss) before taxes*	(702,022)	197,810
Net income (loss)*	(403,515)	101,845
Dividends	107,379	101,340
Dividends per share	$2.225	$2.30
Earnings (loss) per share*	($8.23)	$2.31
Common stock	52,406	44,764
Retained income	128,898	1,212,952
Shareholders equity	991,761	1,695,925

*continuing operations

No of Employees: 6,100

PANNILL KNITTING CO INC

Cleveland & Water, Martinsville, VA 24112
Tel: (703) 638-8841
Telex: WUT 829346 pannill mavl

President: J D Decker
Senior Executive Officers: J R Brown (Treasurer), F M Lacy Jr (Secretary)

PRINCIPAL ACTIVITIES: Manufacture of knitted clothing
Financial Information:

	$'000
Sales revenues	191,500

No of Employees: 3,000

PANSOPHIC SYSTEMS INC

709 Enterprise Drive, Oak Brook, IL 60521
Tel: (312) 572-6000

Chairman: David J Eskra (and Chief Executive Officer)
President: William G Nelson IV (and Chief Operating Officer)
Senior Executive Officers: Jeffrey F Carr (Senior VP and General Manager, Applications Products), James R Gagnard (Senior VP and General Manager, Systems Life Cycle Products), James A Hodges Jr (Senior VP, Finance & Administration and Chief Financial Officer), Michael Bappert (VP and Treasurer), Joseph E Broderick (VP Sales, Systems Life Cycle Products), M Denis Connaghan (VP, Telon Products), James E Dvorak (VP and Controller), Dr E James Emerson (VP, Technology), Theodore M Ewing (VP and Managing Director, European Operations), Robert F Fortelka (VP, Productivity Products), Robert F Kuhne (VP and General Manager, Productivity Products), John G McAughtry (VP, International), Anthony J Paoni (VP, Library Management Products), Robert R Payne (VP Sales, Graphics Products), Douglas R Percy (VP Sales, Productivity Products), Arthur R Roldan (VP, Application Products), Vincent A Sanchez (VP, Corporate Marketing), James B Treleaven (VP and General Manager, Graphics Products), David A Hart (Secretary and General Counsel)

PRINCIPAL ACTIVITIES: Pansophic Systems, Incorporated designs, develops, markets and supports a broad range of packaged software products for IBM and IBM compatible mainframe computers, IBM System/3X minicomputers, IBM microcomputers and other mini and microcomputers including principally those of DEC and Data General. Pansophic's market-oriented software solutions enable users in commerce and industry, government and academia to realize the full benefits of their computer hardware in their day-to-day operations. Products include retrieval systems, library control, on-line applications development, applications, decision support and graphics

Trade Names: Telon, Panvalet, Library Control Systems, Easytrieve Plus, Gener/ol, D-Pict, Pansophic Manufacturing/38
Principal Subsidiaries: Pansophic Systems Australasia Pty Ltd (Australia); Pansophic Systems Europe Inc (Belgium); Pansophic Sistemas de Computadores Ltd (Brazil); Pansophic Systems of Canada Ltd (Canada); Pansophic Systems of Europe Ltd (UK); Pansophic Systems France SARL; Pansophic Systems Italia SRL; Pansophic Systems AB (Sweden); Pansophic Systems Europe Inc (Netherlands); Pansophic Systems UK Ltd (UK); Pansophic Systems GmbH (Germany)
Principal Bank: First National Bank of Chicago
Financial Information:

	Apr 30 1986	Apr 30 1987
	$'000	$'000
Sales revenues	84,237	114,625
Income before taxes	21,287	25,145
Net income	14,161	16,761
Dividends	-	1,063
Dividends per share	-	$0.06
Earnings per share	$0.81	$0.95
Common stock	17,836	17,836
Retained income	48,446	64,145
Shareholders equity	90,984	110,151

No of Employees: 1,100

PANTASOTE INC

PO Box 1800, Greenwich, CT 06830
Tel: (203) 661-0400
Telex: WUT 821432 partasote grc

Chairman: Henry W Wyman; Vice Chairmen: Harry A Russell (and Technical Director), Ralph M Wymen
President: Ted Damon (and Chief Executive Officer)
Senior Executive Officers: James L Grubbs (VP Finance and Treasurer), John E Ertel (VP Manufacturing), Robert E Turner (VP), Barbara K Eisenberg (VP and Secretary)

PRINCIPAL ACTIVITIES: Manufacture of rubber and plastic products
Principal Bank: Citibank
Financial Information:

	$'000
Sales revenues	132,800

No of Employees: 2,360

PANTRY PRIDE ENTERPRISES INC

6500 North Andrews Avenue, Fort Lauderdale, FL 3309
Tel: (305) 771 8300

Chairman: Grant C Gentry (and Chief Executive Officer)
President: Roger Glassini (and Chief Operating Officer)
Senior Executive Officers: Michael Mandelblatt (Executive VP and Chief Financial Officer), Daniel E Josephs (Executive VP Marketing), Henry H Graham (Senior VP and Treasurer), Darrell Stiffler Jr (Senior VP Industrial Relations), Thomas Ballezzi (VP Asset Disposition), Alex Cuesta Jr (VP Loss Prevention), Howard F Gordon (VP, Secretary and Legal Counsel), Marvin Kushner (VP Maintenance), Robert L McGrath (VP), Henry L Morris (VP Store Systems), John W Ruffin Jr (VP General Merchandise), Karl Siemon (VP Real Estate), John G Stebbins (VP Sales and Advertising)

PRINCIPAL ACTIVITIES: Supermarkets
Parent Company: Revlon Group Inc
Principal Subsidiaries: Pantry Pride Inc; Golden Banana Inc; Twin Packing Company Inc
Principal Bank: Chemical Bank
Financial Information:

	$'000
Sales revenues	950,000

No of Employees: 7,500

PAPERCRAFT CORPORATION

Papercraft Park, Pittsburgh, PA 15238
Tel: (412) 362-8000
Telex: WUT 866550 papercraft pgh

Chairman: Joseph M Katz; Vice Chairman: Hyman I Katz
President: Marshall P Katz (and Chief Executive and Operating Officer)
Senior Executive Officers: Howard Goldman (Senior VP, Treasurer and Chief Financial Officer), Jerry N Graf (VP)

PRINCIPAL ACTIVITIES: Manufacture of cards, wrapping paper and related products
Parent Company: Papercraft Holding Corp
Principal Subsidiaries: Le Page's Inc; American Universal Inc; Knomark Inc; Kim Color Corp; Modern Orthopedic Appliance Co Inc; Bath & Dreyfuss of California; American Technical Industries Inc
Principal Bank: Pittsburgh National Bank
Financial Information:

	$'000
Sales revenues	175,000

No of Employees: 2,500

PAR TECHNOLOGY CORPORATION

Par Technology Park, 220 Seneca Turnpike, New Hartford, NY 13413-1191
Tel: (315) 738-0600; (315) 336-8400

Chairman: Dr John W Sammon Jr (and President)
Senior Executive Officers: Charles A Constantino (Executive VP), A K Patterson (VP and Treasurer), Gregory T Cortese (VP and General Counsel), Ronald J Casciano (Corporate Controller)

PRINCIPAL ACTIVITIES: Manufacture of data processing equipment and software for restaurant systems, government and defense technology
Principal Subsidiaries and Divisions: Restaurant Systems:- PAR Microsystems Corp; Transaction Control Industries Inc. Government Systems and Services:- Par Government Systems Corp; Rome Research Corporation
Financial Information:

	Dec 31 1985	Dec 31 1986
	$'000	$'000
Total revenues	70,759	72,745
Income before taxes	12,643	8,833
Net income	8,098	5,460
Earnings per share	$1.06	$0.71
Common stock	11,397	11,971
Retained income	28,970	34,430
Shareholders equity	40,359	46,177

No of Employees: 900

PARADYNE CORPORATION

8550 Ulmerton Road, PO Box 2826, Largo, FL 34294
Tel: (813) 530 2000

Chairman: Robert S Wiggins (and President and Chief Executive Officer)
Senior Executive Officers: Jerry T Kendall (Executive VP and Chief Operating Officer), Frederick T Melberg (Executive VP and Chief Corporate Staff Officer), Cletus L Gardenhour (Senior VP and General Manager Division), F William Siegrist (Senior VP General Manager Division), George B Pressly (Senior VP Quality Control), Peter A Guglielmi (VP and Treasurer), James L Slattery (VP, Secretary and Legal Counsel)

PRINCIPAL ACTIVITIES: Manufacture of data processing equipment and related products
Principal Subsidiaries: Ark Electronic Products Inc; Solid State Circuits Inc
Principal Bank: NCNB National Bank

Financial Information:

	$'000
Sales revenues	252,530

No of Employees: 3,750

PARAMOUNT PACKAGING CORPORATION

202 Oak Avenue, Chalfont, PA 18914
Tel: (215) 822-2911
Telex: WUT 846149 para pak cfnt

Chairman: Theodore Isen
President: Harold Isen
Senior Executive Officers: Irvin Isen (Executive VP), Alan Isen (Senior VP and Secretary), Michael Jurist (VP), John Carr (VP), Joseph Moi (VP), Frank Gallagher (Treasurer and Controller)

PRINCIPAL ACTIVITIES: Manufacture of packaging products
Principal Subsidiaries: Cellu-Pak Converters Inc; Paramount Packaging Corp (Tenn & Tex)
Financial Information:

	$'000
Sales revenues	56,000

No of Employees: 530

PARAMOUNT PICTURES CORPORATION

1 Gulf + Western Plaza, New York, NY 10023
Tel: (212) 333-4128
Telex: WUT 127 985 g & w nyk b

Chairman: Frank Mancuso (and Chief Executive Officer)
Senior Executive Officers: A Robert Pisano (Executive VP and General Counsel), Patrick B Purcell (Executive VP Finance and Administration), Richard Zimbert (Executive VP), Andrew Cavanaugh (Senior VP Administration), Andrew Evans (Senior VP Finance), Warren Ferriter (Senior VP Management Information Systems), Stephen Koppekin (Senior VP Labor Relations), Paul Springer (Senior VP and Chief Resident Counsel), Joshua Wattles (Senior VP and Deputy General Counsel), Alan Bailey (VP and Treasurer), Allen Gottlieb (VP Contract Accounting), Jon J Gould (VP Corporate Communications), Sherry Harris (VP Human Resources), Steven J Kowaliw (VP Finance Planning), Gary Naiman (VP Management Information Systems West Coast), Richard Schonland Jr (VP Labor Relations), Steve Taylor (VP and Controller), Edith Tolkin (VP Rights and Acquisitions), Robert Zolan (VP Systems Planning)

PRINCIPAL ACTIVITIES: Entertainment services; production of motion pictures and television programs
Parent Company: Gulf + Western Industries Inc
Financial Information:

	$'000
Sales revenues	100,000

No of Employees: 3,600

PARISIAN INC

1101 North 26th Street, Birmingham, AL 35234
Tel: (205) 251 1300

Chairman: Emil C Hess
President: Donald E Hess
Senior Executive Officers: Harold L Abrons (Executive VP, Secretary and Treasurer), D Warren Bailey (Senior VP Finance), Tom R Amerman (Senior VP Personnel Affairs), Jim W Adams (VP), Howard R Finkelstein (VP and General Manager), John W Parrott (VP Operations), Sandra K Purvis (VP and General Manager), Gary A Smith (VP and Controller)

PRINCIPAL ACTIVITIES: Retail trade in clothing
Principal Bank: First National Bank of Birmingham
Financial Information:

	$'000
Sales revenues	184,385

No of Employees: 4,300

PARK COMMUNICATIONS INC

Terrace Hill, Ithaca, NY 14850
Tel: (607) 272 9020

Chairman: Roy H Park (and Chief Executive Officer)
President: Richard W Gilbert (and Chief Operating Officer)
Senior Executive Officers: Wright M Thomas (Senior VP, Treasurer and Assistant Secretary), Gary R Bolton (VP Television), William L Fowler (VP Radio), Robert J Rossi (VP Newspapers), Randel N Stair (VP, Controller and Assistant Secretary), Dorothy D Park (Secretary)

PRINCIPAL ACTIVITIES: Television and radio services; publishing of newspapers
Principal Subsidiaries: Park Newspaper Inc; Park Newspapers Northeast Oklahoma; Park Newspapers of Lumberton
Principal Bank: Wachovia Bank and Trust Company
Financial Information:

	$'000
Sales revenues	137,000

No of Employees: 1,800

PARK ELECTROCHEMICAL CORP

5 Dakota Drive, Lake Success, NY 11042
Tel: (516) 354-4100
Telex: WUT 960-131 park grnk
Telefax: (516) 354-4128

Chairman: Jerry Shore (and President and Chief Executive Officer)
Senior Executive Officers: Stanley H Randall (VP), Harry Linzer (VP and Secretary), E Philip Smoot (VP), Joseph A Gemmo (Treasurer), Alan Levine (Controller)

PRINCIPAL ACTIVITIES: Manufacture of telecommunications and consumer electronics equipment; copper clad circuit materials for computer applications; cast products and hardware for plumbing, military and industrial uses; decorative aluminum trim products for the automotive, cosmetic, household appliance and personal care industries
Principal Subsidiaries: Hallmark Nameplate Inc; New England Laminates Co Inc; Nelco Products Inc (California); Nelco Products Inc (Arizona); New England Laminates (UK) Ltd (UK); Grand Rapids Die Casting Corp; Dielectric Polymers Inc; Zin-Plas Corp; StemSearch Corp; Nelco SA (France); Nelco Products Pte Ltd (Singapore)
Principal Bank: The Chase Manhattan Bank
Financial Information:

	Mar 2 1986	Mar 1 1987
	$'000	$'000
Sales revenues	87,786	102,777
Income before taxes	6,758	8,063
Net income	4,380	5,885
Dividends	309	619
Dividends per share	$0.06	$0.12
Earnings per share(1)	$0.85	$1.14
Earnings per share(2)	$0.85	$1.08
Common stock	515	516
Retained income	28,640	33,906
Shareholders equity	46,798	52,870

(1) primary
(2) fully diluted

No of Employees: 900

PARKDALE MILLS, INC

1630 W Garrison Blvd, Gastonia, NC 28053
Tel: (704) 864-8761
Telex: WUT 802 104 parkdale gana

President: W D Kimbrell (and Director Fiber Procurement)
Senior Executive Officers: Arthur R Newcombe (VP Sales), Kenneth Pruitt (VP Manufacturing), George B Blomquist (VP Lexington Division), W M Ledbetter (Treasurer and Controller)

PRINCIPAL ACTIVITIES: Cotton production
Principal Bank: First Union National Bank of North Carolina

Financial Information:

	$'000
Sales revenues	115,000

No of Employees: 1,500

PARKER DRILLING CO

Parker Building, Eight East Third St, Tulsa, OK 74103
Tel: (918) 585-8221
Telex: 497403 PARCO TUL

Chairman: Robert L Parker (and Chief Executive Officer)
President: Robert L Parker Jr (and Chief Operating Officer)
Senior Executive Officers: R Michael Still (Senior VP and Chief Financial Officer), James W Linn (Senior VP, Operations)

PRINCIPAL ACTIVITIES: Drilling for oil and gas; supply of oilfield equipment; gas gathering and transmission
Trade Names: Parco, OIME
Principal Subsidiaries: OIME Inc; Parker Valve Co; Parker Kinetic Designs; Perry Gas Companies
Principal Bank: Manufacturers Hanover
Financial Information:

	Aug 31 1986 $'000
Sales revenues	196,225
(Loss) before taxes	(67,660)
Net (loss)	(70,839)
Dividends	2,112
Dividends per share	$0.07
(Loss) per share	($2.41)

No of Employees: 1,353

PARKER HANNIFIN CORPORATION

17325 Euclid Avenue, Cleveland, OH 44112-1290
Tel: (216) 531-3000
Cable: PARKERHANN CLEVELAND
Telex: 980636

Chairman: Patrick S Parker; Chairman of Executive Committee: Richard Bertea
President: Paul G Schloemer (and Chief Executive Officer)
Senior Executive Officers: Frederick A Downey (Executive VP Finance and Administration), Dennis W Sullivan (Executive VP and Chief Operating Executive, Industrial and Automotive Aftermarket), Robert C Barnd (VP, President, International), Jack E Chappell (VP), Duane E Collins (VP, President, Fluid Connectors), James P Mockler (VP, President, Fluidpower), Robert H Rau (VP, President, Aerospace), John L Hanson (VP Human Resources), Dr Zdenek J Lansky (VP Technical Director), Joseph D Whiteman (VP, General Counsel and Secretary), Harold C Gueritey Jr (Controller), Wallace C Young (Treasurer)

PRINCIPAL ACTIVITIES: Parker is a leading producer of motion-control components and systems for industrial, automotive, aviation, space and marine markets
Principal Subsidiaries: Operating Groups: Parker Bertea Aerospace Group; Automotive Aftermarket Group; Biomedical Group; Fluid Connectors Group; Fluid Connectors Group-Europe (UK); Fluidpower Group; Fluidpower Group-Europe; Intercontinental East Group; Intercontinental West Group; Parker Nichols Group; Refrigeration Components Group; Seal Group; Seal Group-Europe. International Operations: Argentina: Parker Hannifin Argentina SAIC. Australia: Parker Hannifin (Australia) (Pty) Ltd; Schrader Bellows (Australia) Pty Ltd. Austria: Parker Hannifin NMF GmbH; Ermeto Armaturen GmbH. Belgium: Parker Hannifin NVSA; Schrader Bellows NV. Brazil: Parker Hannifin do Brasil: Schrader Bellows Industria e Commercio Ltda. Denmark: Parker Hannifin Danmark A/S. England: Schrader Bellows Ltd; Cylinder, Pneumatic & Industrial Hydraulic Products; Filter; Fluid Connector Products; Parker Hannifin (UK) Ltd; Seal Products. Finland: Oy Parker Hannifin (Finland). France: Parker Hannifin RAK SA. Germany: Fluidpower Products; Parker Hannifin NMF GmbH Control Systems Division; Parker Hannifin NMF GmbH; Schrader Bellows GmbH; FluidConnector Products Parker Fluid Verbindungstelle GmbH. Parker-Ermeto GmbH; Seal Products; Parker Pradifa GmbH. Italy: Parker Hannifin SpA. Japan: Parker Hannifin Japan Ltd; Schrader Bellows Co Ltd. Netherlands: Parker Hannifin BV; Schrader Bellows BV. New Zealand: Parker Hannifin (NZ) Ltd. Norway: Parker Hannifin A/S. Scotland: Alenco North Sea; Parker Hannifin (UK) Ltd. Singapore: Parker Hannifin Singapore Pte Ltd. South Africa: Parker Hannifin (Africa) (Pty) Ltd. Spain: Parker Hannifin Espana SA. Sweden: Parker Hannifin (Sweden) AB. Pan American Division (Miami FL)
Principal Bank: AmeriTrust Company
Financial Information:

	Jun 30 1986 $'000	Jun 30 1987 $'000
Sales revenues	1,730,248	1,876,556
Net income	88,187	85,178
Earnings per share	$1.98	$1.88
Shareholders equity	672,186	751,568

No of Employees: 26,500

PARK-OHIO INDUSTRIES, INC

20600 Chagrin Blvd, Cleveland, OH 44122
Tel: (216) 991-9700

Chairman: R S Sheetz (and Chief Executive Officer)
Senior Executive Officers: James B Kirkhoff (Group VP and Secretary), D G Van Sickle (Group VP), Robert T Bourg (VP and President Bennett Container and Structural Division), G D Pfaffman (VP, President Tocco Inc), Joseph P Rattigan (VP and Treasurer)

PRINCIPAL ACTIVITIES: Manufacture of a wide range of industrial products including containers, forged metals, heating equipment and rubber goods; production of oil and gas
Principal Bank: AmeriTrust Company
Financial Information:

	$'000
Sales revenues	186,000

No of Employees: 1,750

PARSONS & WHITTEMORE INC

666 Third Avenue, New York, NY 10017
Tel: (212) 972-2000

Chairman: C C Landegger
President: A L Schwartz (and Chief Executive Officer)
Senior Executive Officers: Lena Landegger (VP), S J Napolitano (VP Finance, Treasurer and Secretary)

PRINCIPAL ACTIVITIES: Manufacture of pulp and the construction and operation of pulp and paper mills
Principal Bank: The Bank of New York
Financial Information:

	$'000
Sales revenues	400,000

No of Employees: 1,400

PARSONS CORPORATION

100 W Walnut Street, Pasadena, CA 91124
Tel: (818) 440-2000
Telex: WUT 675 336 parsons psd a

Chairman: William E Leonhard (and Chief Executive Officer)
President: Otha C Roddey
Senior Executive Officers: Thomas L Langford (Senior VP Finance and Treasurer), Joseph K Bratton (Senior VP Government Liaison), Robert M Davidson (Executive VP New Development), Dorn S Dicker (VP Corporate Relations), Gary L Stone (VP, General Counsel and Secretary)

PRINCIPAL ACTIVITIES: Civil engineering and construction
Principal Subsidiaries: Parsons Constructors Inc; The Ralph M Parsons Co; De Leuw, Cather & Co; S.I.P. Engineering Inc;

Engineering-Science Inc; The C.T. Main Corporation; Barton-Aschman Associates, Inc; Harland Bartholemew & Associates, Inc; Parsons Municipal Services, Inc; Parsons Water Resources, Inc; Parsons Construction Services, Inc
Principal Bank: Bank of America
Financial Information:

	1985	1986
	$'000	$'000
Sales revenues	772,928	821,220

No of Employees: 7,000

PASCOE BUILDING SYSTEMS INC

PO Box 7186, Columbus, GA 31908
Tel: (404) 324 3562

Chairman: Edwin Shulz
President: Talmage Rogers Jr
Senior Executive Officers: D Benstead (VP Sales and Marketing), John Grot (VP and General Manager)

PRINCIPAL ACTIVITIES: Manufacture of a range of metal buildings
Parent Company: Amcord Inc
Principal Bank: Security Pacific National Bank
Financial Information:

	$'000
Sales revenues	60,000

No of Employees: 300

PASQUALE FOOD CO

19 West Oxmoor Road, Birmingham, AL 35209
Tel: (205) 942-3371

Chairman: Neal L Andrews Jr
President: Lester Nuby Jr
Senior Executive Officers: John Sanford (Senior VP), Ron Gall (VP and Manager Cincinnati Plant), Charlie Mudd (President Wholesale Pizza Company), H E Nims (Chief Financial Officer)

PRINCIPAL ACTIVITIES: Manufacture of food products including meat and bakery products; wholesale and retail pizzas; fast food restaurants
Principal Bank: Am South
Financial Information:

	$'000
Sales revenues	66,000

No of Employees: 450

PASSPORT TRAVEL INC

6340 Glenwood, Cloverleaf Building, Overland Park, KS 66202
Tel: (913) 677 7777

President: Leonard S Hershman
Senior Executive Officers: Michael R Phenix (VP Finance and Treasurer), Phillip A Kusnetzky (Secretary)

PRINCIPAL ACTIVITIES: Travel and tourism services
Principal Bank: Merchants Bank
Financial Information:

	$'000
Sales revenues	30,000

No of Employees: 100

PATRICK INDUSTRIES, INC

1800 South 14th Street, Elkhart, IN 46514
Tel: (219) 294-7511
Telefax: (219) 522-5213

Chairman: Mervin D Lung (and President)
Senior Executive Officers: Thomas G Baer (VP Operations), Harold Wyland (National Sales Manager), Keith V Kankel (Secretary, Treasurer and VP Finance)

PRINCIPAL ACTIVITIES: Manufacture of a wide range of boards and panels for the building industry; wholesale trade in plywood and lumber
Principal Bank: Midwest Commerce Banking Company
Financial Information:

	Dec 31 1985	Dec 31 1986
	$'000	$'00C
Sales revenues	122,105	120,773
Income before taxes	2,146	2,300
Net income	1,317	1,255
Earnings per share	$0.67	$0.95
Common stock	6,066	9,647
Retained income	4,452	4,346
Shareholders equity	10,512	13,987

No of Employees: 600

PATRIOT BANCORPORATION, NA

57 Franklin Street, Boston, MA 02110
Tel: (617) 451-9100

Chairman: Allyn Levy (and Chief Executive Officer); Vice Chairmen: James R White, Bernard Solomon
President: Thomas R Heaslip
Senior Executive Officers: Leo R Breitman (Executive VP), William H Fitzgerald (Executive VP and Chief Financial Officer)

PRINCIPAL ACTIVITIES: Banking services
Parent Company: The Conifer Group
Principal Subsidiaries: Patriot Bank, NA
Principal Bank: First National Bank

No of Employees: 360

PATTERSON DENTAL CO

1100 E 80 Street, Minneapolis, MN 55420
Tel: (612) 854-2881
Telex: WUT 290948 patterson bltn

President: Peter L Frechette (and Chief Executive Officer)
Senior Executive Officers: Guy F Bradley (VP), Ronald E Ezerski (VP Finance and Treasurer), Guenther Than (VP), Andrew G Whitehead (VP Marketing)

PRINCIPAL ACTIVITIES: Manufacture of equipment and supplies for dentistry
Parent Company: Ultimate Holding Company-The Beatrice Companies Inc, Chicago, IL
Principal Bank: Sun First National Bank of Orlando
Financial Information:

	$'000
Sales revenues	160,000

No of Employees: 1,570

PATTERSON FROZEN FOODS, INC

PO Box 114, Patterson, CA 95363
Tel: (209) 892-2611
Telex: TWX 510 7663301 patterson patt

Chairman: Mario Ielmini
President: John Ielmini
Senior Executive Officers: Angelo Ielmini (Executive VP), Olaf H Raven (VP Administration and Finance and Secretary), Bud Ingebretsen (VP Operations), Bill Rembold (VP Sales)

PRINCIPAL ACTIVITIES: Freezing of fruit and vegetables
Principal Bank: Bank of America
Financial Information:

	$'000
Sales revenues	60,000

No of Employees: 800

PATTERSON-KELLEY CO

East Stroudsburg, PA 18301
Tel: (717) 421-7500
Telex: RCA 244 611; WUT 84-7313

President: William D Etzweiler

Senior Executive Officers: Richard J Smith (VP Sales), Thomas Hornkohl (VP Operations), Ronald J Kologe (Controller), Robert S Muth (Advertising Manager)

PRINCIPAL ACTIVITIES: Manufacturer of water heating equipment; mixers, dryers, fractionation internals, air-air heat exchangers, corrosion-resistant linings, metal fabrication
Parent Company: Harsco Corp
Principal Bank: Morgan Guaranty Trust Company of New York

No of Employees: 450

PAUL HARRIS STORES INC

6003 Guion Road, Indianapolis, IN 46268
Tel: (317) 293 3900

Chairman: Gerald Paul (and Chief Executive Officer)
President: Davis R Bomberger
Senior Executive Officers: E J Galm (Senior VP Finance and Treasurer), William L Lawrence Jr (Secretary and Controller), Rex Steffey (VP Planning and Distribution), Howard Barnett (VP Real Estate), R E Frankel (VP Merchandising, Construction and Administration), Cynthia Harriss (VP Merchandising), Jerry Preis (VP Merchandising), Helen Price (VP Product Area), Richard Smithson (VP Merchandising)

PRINCIPAL ACTIVITIES: Retail trade in women's clothing
Principal Subsidiaries: Classic Advertising Inc; PH Trucking Inc; Paul Harris of Virginia Inc
Principal Bank: Merchants National Bank
Financial Information:

	$'000
Sales revenues	125,860

No of Employees: 2,700

PAUL MUELLER COMPANY

See MUELLER, PAUL, COMPANY

PAUL REVERE CORPORATION

See REVERE, PAUL, CORPORATION

PAULEY PETROLEUM, INC

10000 Santa Monica Blvd, Los Angeles, CA 90067
Tel: (213) 879-5000

Chairman: William R Pagen (and President and Chief Executive Officer)
Senior Executive Officers: Edward J Babineau Jr (VP Treasurer and Controller), A W Stilley (VP and Secretary)

PRINCIPAL ACTIVITIES: Exploration for, and production of oil and natural gas
Principal Bank: Continental Illinois National Bank & Trust Co
Financial Information:

	$'000
Sales revenues	199,000

No of Employees: 190

PAWNEE INDUSTRIES INC

101 South Ridge Road, Wichita, KS 67209
Tel: (316) 722 7212

Chairman: Burton C Person (and President)
Senior Executive Officers: Michael D McLain (Treasurer, Controller and Assistant Secretary)

PRINCIPAL ACTIVITIES: Manufacture of a range of plastic products
Financial Information:

	$'000
Sales revenues	47,000

No of Employees: 330

PAYCHEX, INC

911 Panorama Trail South, Rochester, NY 14625-0397
Tel: (716) 385-6666

Chairman: B Thomas Golisano (and Chief Executive Officer)
President: Wesley C Tallman (and Chief Operating Officer)
Senior Executive Officers: J Robert Sebo (VP Operations), G Thomas Clark (Secretary, Treasurer and VP Finance)

PRINCIPAL ACTIVITIES: Provides automated payroll service for small to medium size businesses in 60 locations throughout the United Stated
Principal Bank: Chemical Bank
Financial Information:

	May 31 1986	May 31 1987
	$'000	$'000
Sales revenues	50,704	63,891
Income before taxes	7,774	10,247
Net income	4,169	5,124
Earnings per share	$0.49	$0.60
Common stock	86	87
Retained income	10,864	15,927
Shareholders equity	18,616	23,985

No of Employees: 1,400

PAYCO AMERICAN CORPORATION

180 North Executive Drive, Brookfield, WI 53005
Tel: (414) 784 9035

Chairman: Richard L Horn
President: Dennis G Punches
Senior Executive Officers: Joseph T Treleven (Executive VP and Secretary), Joseph G Krakora (VP Administration), Neal R Sparby (VP Operations), Alvin W Keeley (VP Marketing), William W Kagel (VP Production), James R Bohmann (VP Finance and Treasurer)

PRINCIPAL ACTIVITIES: Financial credit information and debt collection services
Principal Subsidiaries: Finance System of Milwaukee; NAS Creditors Service Inc; National Account Systems; Payco General American Credits; Payco of Wisconsin; University Accounting Service
Principal Bank: First Bank
Financial Information:

	$'000
Sales revenues	64,000

No of Employees: 2,000

PAYLESS CASHWAYS, INC

One Pershing Sq, PO Box 466, Kansas City, MO 64141
Tel: (816) 234-6000

Chairman: David Stanley (and Chief Executive Officer)
President: Larry P Kunz (and Chief Operating Officer)
Senior Executive Officers: Stanley K Boyd (Senior VP Stores), John Breedlove (Senior VP Merchandising), Richard E Hemer (Senior VP Development), Larry Koeppen (Senior VP Operations and Systems), Stephen A Lightstone (VP Finance), Dale Pond (Senior VP Marketing), Susan Stanton (Senior VP Administration and Corporate Planning), James A Bryan (VP Distribution and Transport), Mike Didier (VP Facility Development), John P Fischer (VP Western Region), Linda French (VP, Secretary and General Counsel), Michael T Largent (VP Midwestern Region), James A Lavender (VP Merchandise), Kristan R Maynard (VP Eastern Region), James C Neustadt (VP Advertising), David O'Halloran (VP and Controller), Bradley T Talley (VP Management Information Systems), Roger L Weverka (VP Southern Region), John Woodfill (VP and Treasurer)

PRINCIPAL ACTIVITIES: Wholesale and retail trading in building materials and lumber
Principal Bank: RepublicBank Dallas

Financial Information:

	Nov 30 1986
	$'000
Sales revenues	1,525,648
Net income	42,352
Earnings per share	$1.22
Shareholders equity	369,818

No of Employees: 13,700

PAY'N PAK STORES INC
1209 South Central, Kent, WA 98032
Tel: (206) 854 5450

Chairman: David J Heerensperger (and Chief Executive Officer); Vice Chairman: Marshall J Weigel
President: Jerry L Marlow (and Chief Operating Officer)
Senior Executive Officers: Monte A Leen (Executive VP), Peter W Gallina (Senior VP), Fred R Brotherton (VP and Controller), Barbara I Collett (VP), Victor W Crosswhite (VP Purchasing), Marvin C Iverson (VP), Calvin E Karbowski (VP Distribution), Herbert E McCleary (VP), Paul B Morris (VP), George E Smith (VP Functional Area), Douglas G Southern (VP Finance, Secretary and Treasurer), Steven C Unash (VP)

PRINCIPAL ACTIVITIES: Retail supply of home improvement, plumbing and building products
Principal Bank: Old National Bank of Washington
Financial Information:

	$'000
Sales revenues	333,780

No of Employees: 1,607

PAY'N SAVE CORPORATION
4045 Delridge Way SW, Seattle, WA 98146
Tel: (206) 938 6500

Chairman: William Zimmerman
President: M A Culver (and Chief Executive Officer)
Senior Executive Officers: K S Galvin (VP, Secretary and Treasurer)

PRINCIPAL ACTIVITIES: Retail stores
Principal Bank: Citibank
Financial Information:

	$'000
Sales revenues	1,700,000

No of Employees: 11,500

PBI INDUSTRIES
Union Bank Building, Pittsburgh, PA 15222
Tel: (412) 471-7500
Telex: WUT 866 343 pbi ind roch

Chairman: George E Klingelhofer; Vice Chairman: David B Hughes
President: L M Huizenga
Senior Executive Officers: F P Cava (VP Personnel), D J Froelich (Treasurer), D P Phillips (Controller), D C Kamaras (Senior VP), R C Barrett (VP Sales)

PRINCIPAL ACTIVITIES: Production of structural steel and building of steel structures; steel service centres
Principal Bank: Mellon Bank
Financial Information:

	$'000
Sales revenues	70,000

No of Employees: 450

PCA INTERNATIONAL INC
801 Crestdale Avenue, Matthews, NC 28105
Tel: (704) 847 8011

President: Ronald A Norelli
Senior Executive Officers: John D Hardman (Executive VP, Secretary and Chief Financial Officer)

PRINCIPAL ACTIVITIES: Photographic services
Principal Bank: Wachovia Bank and Trust Company
Financial Information:

	$'000
Sales revenues	167,000

No of Employees: 4,000

PEACHTREE WINDOWS & DOORS, INC
PO Box 5700, Norcross, GA 30091
Tel: (404) 497-2000

Chairman: James R Hewell Jr
President: C B Jennings Jr
Senior Executive Officers: Ray C Starnes (VP Materials), Michael Hillmeyer (VP Manufacturing), Richard Andrews (VP Sales), Bruce Morine (VP Finance), Bernie Governale (VP Products), Ansel D Greenway (VP Controller)

PRINCIPAL ACTIVITIES: Manufacture of doors and windows
Parent Company: Indal Limited
Principal Bank: The Citizens and Southern National Bank
Financial Information:

	$'000
Sales revenues	200,000

No of Employees: 2,000

PEARL BREWING CO
312 Pearl Pkwy, San Antonio, TX 78215
Tel: (512) 226-0231
Telex: TWX 910 8711103 pearl snt

Chairman: Paul Kalmanovitz
President: Lutz E Issleib
Senior Executive Officers: Robert E Anderson (VP Industrial Relations), Barry L Harris (VP Planning and Control), Harry McEldowney (VP Marketing), Carl Mullen (VP), John Schiess (VP Finance)

PRINCIPAL ACTIVITIES: Brewing of beer
Parent Company: General Brewing Co
Principal Bank: First Seattle Bank
Financial Information:

	$'000
Sales revenues	100,000

No of Employees: 500

PEASE INDUSTRIES, INC
7100 Dixie Hwy, Fairfield, OH 15014
Tel: (513) 870-3600
Telex: 332019

President: David H Pease Jr (and Chief Executive Officer)
Senior Executive Officers: Henry C Seasholes (VP Marketing), Leonard W Cavens (Executive VP Sales and Marketing), John E Landis (Secretary and Treasurer)

PRINCIPAL ACTIVITIES: Manufacture of doors and shutters
Trade Names: EVER-STRAIT
Principal Bank: Central Trust Company
Financial Information:

	Dec 31 1985	Dec 31 1986
	$'000	$'000
Sales revenues	48,000	53,000

No of Employees: 350

PEAVEY COMPANY
730 Second Avenue S, Minneapolis, MN 55402
Tel: (612) 370-7500
Telex: WUT 530754 pv hq trs mps

President: Thomas M Racciatti

PRINCIPAL ACTIVITIES: Retail trade in fabrics and food; trade in agricultural supplies, grain, building materials and lumber
Parent Company: ConAgra Inc, Omaha, NE
Principal Bank: Northwestern National Bank of Minneapolis

Financial Information:

	$'000
Sales revenues	820,000

No of Employees: 5,500

PEERLESS PUMP

1200 Sycamore Street, Montebello, CA 90640
Tel: (213) 726-1232
Telex: WUT 674156 peerpump mblo

President: Emile J Assaf
Senior Executive Officers: Robert Garrett (VP Manufacturing), Arthur R Huber (VP Purchasing), D L Engel (Treasurer and Chief Financial Officer)

PRINCIPAL ACTIVITIES: Manufacture of pumps
Parent Company: TBG Inc
Financial Information:

	$'000
Sales revenues	80,000

No of Employees: 1,500

PEERLESS TUBE COMPANY

58-76 Locust Avenue, Bloomfield, NJ 07003
Tel: (201) 743 5100

President: William G Remington
Senior Executive Officers: Kenneth T Fultro (VP Sales), Thomas J Lynch Jr (VP Finance), Richard W Potts (VP Manufacturing), Frederic Remington Jr (VP Engineering)

PRINCIPAL ACTIVITIES: Manufacture of plastic tubes, aluminum tubes and aerosol cans
Principal Bank: Midlantic National Bank
Financial Information:

	$'000
Sales revenues	46,500

No of Employees: 780

PENDLETON WOOLEN MILLS INC

218 SW Jefferson, PO Box 1691, Portland, OR 97207
Tel: (503) 226-4801
Telex: TWX 910 464 1598 pend wool ptld

Chairman: B H Bishop (and Treasurer)
President: C M Bishop Jr
Senior Executive Officers: R C Bishop III (Secretary)

PRINCIPAL ACTIVITIES: Manufacture of woolen textiles, clothing and blankets
Principal Bank: US National Bank of Oregon
Financial Information:

	$'000
Sales revenues	90,000

No of Employees: 2,000

PENGO INDUSTRIES, INC

1400 Everman Road, Fort Worth, TX 76140
Tel: (817) 293-7110
Telex: TRT 170 467 pengo ftw

President: Richard L Frank
Senior Executive Officers: Truett Akin (VP Wireline), Chester Bogle (VP), David King (VP Engineering), Wayne Mercer (VP, Secretary and Attorney), Jerry Oden (VP Oil Tool), James Robertson (VP Administration)

PRINCIPAL ACTIVITIES: Manufacture of equipment for the oil industry
Principal Bank: First National Bank of Fort Worth
Financial Information:

	$'000
Sales revenues	37,000

No of Employees: 500

PENICK & FORD, LTD

1001 First Street SW, Cedar Rapids, IA 52404
Tel: (319) 398-3700
Telex: TWX 910 525 1338 pen ford cdr

President: C M Widmer
Senior Executive Officers: G D Huebner (VP Marketing), K W Kirby (VP Technical), Curtis P Lindley (VP), Robert L Fisher (Treasurer)

PRINCIPAL ACTIVITIES: Processing of corn and potatoes, production of feedstuffs and starch
Parent Company: Penwest Ltd
Principal Bank: Merchants National Bank of Cedar Rapids
Financial Information:

	$'000
Sales revenues	60,000

No of Employees: 200

PENN CENTRAL CORPORATION

500 W Putnam Avenue, Greenwich, CT 06836
Tel: (203) 629-5000
Telex: 62928756

Chairman: Carl H Lindner (and Chief Executive Officer)
Senior Executive Officers: Herbert S Winokur Jr (Senior Executive VP), Edward F Kosnik (Executive VP and Chief Financial Officer), Francis A Kareken (Senior VP), Ernest R Varalli (Senior VP and Controller)

PRINCIPAL ACTIVITIES: Manufacture of products and operation of services for the electronics, telecommunications, defense and energy industries
Principal Bank: The Philadelphia National Bank
Financial Information:

	Dec 31 1985	Dec 31 1986
	$'000	$'000
Sales revenues	2,527,300	2,387,900
Net income	110,800	154,200
Earnings per share	$2.76	$3.85
Shareholders equity	1,825,900	2,092,200

No of Employees: 31,000

PENN DAIRIES, INC

1801 Hempstead Road, Lancaster, PA 17604
Tel: (717) 394-5601

Chairman: John F Garber (and President)
Senior Executive Officers: Nancy L Frankhouser (VP Human Resources and Corporate Communications), Denis J Keaveny (VP Finance and Treasurer), Michael E Osborne (VP and General Manager Dairy Division), Harold S Butz Jr (VP and General Manager Bulk Dairy Division and Secretary), Floyd N Simpson (VP and General Manager Stores Division)

PRINCIPAL ACTIVITIES: Production of milk and dairy products
Financial Information:

	$'000
Sales revenues	119,300

No of Employees: 1,000

PENN ENGINEERING & MFG CORPORATION

PO Box 1000, Danboro, PA 18916
Tel: (215) 766-8853
Fax: (215) 766-0143

Chairman: K Arent Swanstrom (and Chief Executive Officer)
President: Kenneth A Swanstrom (and Chief Operating Officer)
Senior Executive Officers: Richard B Ernest (VP), John Segraves (VP Sales), Philip M Hall (VP Manufacturing), Mark W Simon (VP Finance, Treasurer and Controller)

PRINCIPAL ACTIVITIES: Manufacture of metal fasteners, electric motors, generators and metalworking machinery
Principal Subsidiaries: P E M International Ltd
Principal Bank: Industrial Valley Bank and Trust Company

Financial Information:

	$'000
Sales revenues	43,361

No of Employees: 522

PENN FUEL GAS, INC

55 S 3rd Street, Oxford, PA 19363
Tel: (215) 932-2000

Chairman: John H Ware III (and President)
Senior Executive Officers: George Failey (Executive VP), John H Van Dorpe (VP Utility Operations), William E Horner (VP Petroleum Operations and Sales Manager), F W Sullivan (VP, Secretary and Treasurer)

PRINCIPAL ACTIVITIES: Holding company with interests in the distribution of natural gas
Principal Bank: First Pennsylvania Bank
Financial Information:

	$'000
Sales revenues	80,000

No of Employees: 300

PENN MUTUAL LIFE INSURANCE CO

Independence Square, Philadelphia, PA 19172
Tel: (215) 629-0600
Telex: WUT 757739 pennmut pha

Chairman: Frank K Tarbox
President: John E Tait (and Chief Executive Officer)
Senior Executive Officers: James W Bryant (Senior VP and Chief Investment Officer), Charles J Doerner (General Auditor), Donna D Holton (Senior VP), Joseph J Horvath (Senior VP and General Counsel), Richard J Pinola (Executive VP Insurance and Pension Business, Marketing), Thomas E Stiles (Senior VP and Chief Financial Officer), Richard R Yoder (Executive VP, Administration)

PRINCIPAL ACTIVITIES: Life insurance
Financial Information:

	Dec 31 1986
	$'000
Premium income	510,892
Investment income*	279,515
Dividends	90,493
Total assets	3,800,000

*less expenses

No of Employees: 2,700

PENN TRAFFIC CO

319 Washington Street, Johnstown, PA 15907
Tel: (814) 536-4411

Chairman: Gary Hirsch
President: Guido Malacarne (and Chief Executive Officer)
Senior Executive Officers: Robert Allen (VP Dairy Division), Raymond J Heath (VP Riverside), John M Kriak (VP, Secretary and Treasurer), Richard P Reading (VP Quality Markets)

PRINCIPAL ACTIVITIES: Retail trade in food and dairy products through supermarket outlets; manufacture of dairy products including ice cream and cottage cheese
Trade Names: Riverside Markets, Quality Markets, U-Save Markets, Sani-Dairy
Principal Subsidiaries: Dairy Dell Quality Markets Inc; Sunrise Properties Inc; R M Markets of Indiana
Principal Banks: United States National Bank in Johnstown; First Banks, Minneapolis, MN

Financial Information:

	Jan 1 1987
	$'000
Sales revenues	547,991
Income before taxes	13,920
Net income	7,300
Dividends	2,737
Dividends per share	$0.66
Earnings per share	$1.76
Common stock	4,226
Retained income	58,095
Shareholders equity	62,321

Principal Shareholders: RAC Partners, Inc
No of Employees: 4,600

PENN VIRGINIA CORPORATION

2500 Fidelity Building, Philadelphia, PA 19109
Tel: (215) 545-6600

Chairman: E B Leisenring Jr (and Chief Executive Officer)
President: John A Shober
Senior Executive Officers: William F Hahn (Senior VP), Richard M Klingaman (Senior VP), Ronald Naftal (VP), H K Nelson (VP), Peter H Dershimer (Treasurer)

PRINCIPAL ACTIVITIES: Leasing of land in connection with coal mining; mining of minerals; manufacture of mining equipment, feeders and conveyors
Principal Bank: The Fidelity Bank
Financial Information:

	$'000
Sales revenues	87,700

No of Employees: 600

PENNBANCORP

Pennbank Center, Titusville, PA 16354
Tel: (814) 827-2751

Chairman: Joseph S Harvey
President: William F Roemer (and Chief Executive Officer)
Senior Executive Officers: Charles R Skillington (Executive VP), Leonard M Carroll (VP and Treasurer), David K Stuart (Senior VP Banking Services First Seneca Bank), Edward R Trbovich (Senior VP Operations Department Pennbank), George T Forssell Jr (VP, General Counsel and Secretary)

PRINCIPAL ACTIVITIES: Banking services
Financial Information:

	$'000
Revenues	313,000

No of Employees: 1,800

PENNEX PRODUCTS CO

Eastern & Pennex Drive, Verona, PA 15147
Tel: (412) 828-2900

President: Martin Sachnoff
Senior Executive Officers: Mort Rezak (Executive VP), Irvin Friedland (VP), Harold Mendlowitz (VP), Bruce Sachnoff (VP, Secretary and Treasurer)

PRINCIPAL ACTIVITIES: Manufacture of pharmaceuticals and beauty products
Financial Information:

	$'000
Sales revenues-over	60,000

No of Employees: 625

PENNEY, J C, COMPANY, INC

1301 Avenue of the Americas, New York, NY 10019
Tel: (212) 857-4321
Telex: RCA 234142 j c pc ur

Chairman: William R Howell (and Chief Executive Officer); Vice Chairmen: Robert B Gill, David F Muller (and Chief Operating Officer)
President: David F Miller
Senior Executive Officers: Ralph B Henderson (Executive VP), Thomas J Lyons (Executive VP), A Scott Frahlich (Executive VP and Director of Stores), W Barger Tygart (Executive VP and Director of Merchandise), Rodney M Birkins (Senior VP), Charles R Lotter (Senior VP and Secretary), Richard T Erickson (Senior VP), Robert E Northam (Senior VP), William R Johnson (VP Public Affairs and Communications)

PRINCIPAL ACTIVITIES: JC Penney is a major retailer, with stores in all 50 states, Puerto Rico, and Belgium. The dominant portion of the Company's business consists of providing merchandise and services to consumers through stores, including catalog operations. The Company markets family apparel, home furnishings, leisure lines, drug store merchandise, and insurance
Trade Names: J C Penney
Financial Information:

	Jan 31 1986 $'000	Jan 31 1987 $'000
Sales revenues	13,747,000	14,740,000
Net income	386,000	497,000
Earnings per share	$5.31	$7.06
Retained income	3,122,000	3,379,000

No of Employees: 177,000

PENNSYLVANIA ENGINEERING CORPORATION

32nd Street & A.V.R.R., Pittsburgh, PA 15201
Tel: (412) 288-6800
Telex: WUT 866618 pec pgh

Chairman: Victor Posner (and President and Chief Executive Officer); Deputy Vice Chairman: Austin J Paddock
Senior Executive Officers: Walter Sieckman (Group Executive VP and Chief Operating Officer), Bernard I Posner (Senior VP), Jack Coppersmith (Senior VP and Chief Financial Officer), Philip A Smalley Jr (Senior VP Human Resources), Renée Mottram (Senior VP Administration and Assistant Secretary), Melvin R Colvin (Senior VP), Raymond J Dettore (Senior VP), Henry L Bolch (Group VP Finance), Robert Trbovich (Group VP), Mitchell V Gregory (VP), Robert C Griffin (VP, Treasurer and Assistant Secretary), Tracy Posner (VP and Assistant Secretary), Malvin G Sander (VP Law and Administration)

PRINCIPAL ACTIVITIES: Manufacture of plant and equipment for steelmaking; metal fabrication
Principal Bank: Manufacturers Hanover Trust Co
Financial Information:

	$'000
Sales revenues	116,500

No of Employees: 1,500

PENNSYLVANIA ENTERPRISES INC

Wilks-Barre Center, 39 Public Square, Wilks-Barre, PA 18711
Tel: (717) 829 8600

Chairman: Robert J Keating
President: Robert L Jones (and Chief Executive Officer)
Senior Executive Officers: Paul E Henderson (VP Operations), John F Kell Jr (VP and Controller), Robert J McBride (Treasurer), Robert Anthony (Secretary and Assistant Treasurer), Leslie M Ward (VP Energy, Marketing and Engineering), Harry E Dowling (VP Consumer Affairs), Gerald S Allen (Senior VP)

PRINCIPAL ACTIVITIES: Supply of natural gas and water services
Principal Subsidiaries: Pennsylvania Energy Resources; Pennsylvania Gas and Water Company
Principal Bank: Manufacturers Hanover Trust Company

Financial Information:

	Dec 31 1985 $'000	Dec 31 1986 $'000
Sales revenues	232,033	214,540
Income before taxes	27,221	21,786
Net income	13,243	10,846
Dividends	5,847	5,889
Dividends per share	$2.20	$2.20
Earnings per share	$4.98	$4.05
Common stock	26,715	26,857
Retained income	68,018	72,975
Shareholders equity	102,143	107,629

No of Employees: 984

PENNSYLVANIA NATIONAL FINANCIAL CORPORATION

1002 North Seventh Street, Harrisburg, PA 17102
Tel: (717) 233 6464

Chairman: Carl L Campbell (and President and Chief Executive Officer); Vice Chairman: Darwin S Harter
Senior Executive Officers: Richard E Fehr Jr (Secretary and Treasurer)

PRINCIPAL ACTIVITIES: Banking
Financial Information:

	$'000
Revenues	51,720

No of Employees: 380

PENNSYLVANIA POWER & LIGHT CO

Two N Ninth Street, Allentown, PA 18101
Tel: (215) 770-5151
Telex: TWX 510 65 11004 ppl procur atw

President: Robert K Campbell (and Chief Executive Officer)
Senior Executive Officers: Merlin F Hertzog (Executive VP Corporate Services), John T Kauffman (Executive VP Operations), Bruce D Kenyon (Senior VP Nuclear), Leon L Nonemaker (Senior VP Divisional Operations), Charles E Russoli (Senior VP Finance), John R Biggar (VP Finance), Gennaro D Caliendo (VP and General Counsel), Robert S Gombos (VP Human Resource and Development), Charles J Green (VP Harrisburg Division), William F Hecht (VP Systems Power), Harold W Keiser (VP Nuclear Operations), John P Kierzowski (VP and Treasurer), Carl R Maio (VP LeHigh Division), Grayson E McNair (VP Marketing and Customer Services), Edward M Nagel (VP and Secretary), Herbert D Nash Jr (VP Central Division), Clair W Noll (VP Procurement and Computer Services), John E Roth (VP Northern Division), John H Saeger (VP Susquehanna Division), Edwin H Seidel (VP Engineering and Construction), Brent S Shunk (VP Lancaster Division), George F Vanderslice (VP and Comptroller), William R White (VP Power Production)

PRINCIPAL ACTIVITIES: Electricity supply
Principal Bank: First PA Bank Philadelphia
Financial Information:

	Dec 31 1985 $'000	Dec 31 1986 $'000
Sales revenues	1,976,502	2,188,925
Net income	290,613	300,108
Earnings per share	$2.68	$3.10
Shareholders equity	2,137,075	2,147,024

No of Employees: 8,430

PENNWALT CORPORATION

Three Parkway, Philadelphia, PA 19102
Tel: 215 587-7000
Telex: ITT 476 1065 pennwalt

Chairman: Edwin E Tuttle (and Chief Executive Officer)
President: Seymour S Preston III
Senior Executive Officers: George Reath Jr (Senior VP, Secretary and Chief Counsel), Harry C Mandell, Jr (Senior

VP-Chemicals), Martin M Schwartzberg (Senior VP-Chemicals), Bernard C Shea (Senior VP-Pharmaceuticals), Quentin M White (Senior VP-Equipment), Anthony P Fortino (Senior VP-Personnel), Emil J Mikity (Senior VP-Treasury and Investor Relations), Raymond L Ralston (Senior VP-Controller), William B Tuemmler (Senior VP-Technical Director)

PRINCIPAL ACTIVITIES: Manufacture of an extensive range of chemicals including organic, inorganic specialty chemicals and pharmaceuticals; precision equipment

Principal Bank: Mellon Bank (East)

Financial Information:

	Dec 31 1985	Dec 31 1986
	$'000	$'000
Sales revenues	1,022,439	1,107,564
Income before taxes	13,323	82,786
Net income (loss)	(19,721)	51,947
Dividends	25,154	22,324
Dividends per share	$2.20	$2.20
Earnings (loss) per share net	($2.80)	$3.64
Common stock	12,855	12,946
Retained income	273,997	287,057
Shareholders equity	344,163	374,463

No of Employees: 9,600

PENNZOIL COMPANY

PO Box 2967, Houston, TX 77252
Tel: (713) 546-4000
Telex: WUT 762170 pennzoil hou b

Chairman: J H Liedtke (and Chief Executive Officer)

President: Richard J Howe (and Chief Operating Officer)

Senior Executive Officers: David S Holland (Group VP Oil and Gas Operations), N J Luke (Group VP Accounting), P L Manning (Group VP Communications), Robert Semrad (Group VP Sulphur), Frank A Turner (Group VP Manufacturing and Marketing), Clifton H Fridge (Senior VP Accounting and Controller), James L Pate (Senior VP Finance and Treasurer)

PRINCIPAL ACTIVITIES: Exploration, production and distribution of oil and gas; mining of precious metals, sulphur, potash and molybdenum

Principal Bank: Mellon Bank

Financial Information:

	Dec 31 1985	Dec 31 1986
	$'000	$'000
Sales revenues	2,238,710	1,782,177
Net income	113,204	45,443
Earnings per share	$2.20	$0.72
Shareholders equity	752,850	695,339

No of Employees: 8,300

PENRIL CORPORATION

5520 Randolph Road, Rockville, MD 20852
Tel: (301) 881-8151
Telex: TWX 710-828-0522 pnrl ur

President: Alva T Bonda (and Chief Executive Officer)

Senior Executive Officers: Harry O Christenson (Executive VP Finance and Chief Operating Officer), David L Johnson (VP and General Manager Data Communications Division), Charles C Zwingman Jr (VP Administration and Corporate Secretary), Gloria Ehrlich (Assistant Corporate Secretary), Frank S DiGirolamo (VP and President, Epicure Products Inc), Rod Georgiu (General Manager Alltest Division), Vito L Greco (General Manager Electro-Metrics Division), John D Phillips (VP and General Manager Technipower Division), Warren J Hess (VP and President, Triplett Electrical Instrument Corporation), Thomas J McLoughlin (President, Concord Systems Inc), Robert H Nichols (President, Network Products Inc)

PRINCIPAL ACTIVITIES: Penril Corporation designs, develops and markets, through its divisions and subsidiaries, diversified lines of high technology electronic equipment and audio electronic equipment

Subsidiaries and Divisions: Data Communications Division; Network Products Inc; Network Products Ltd (UK); Electro-Metrics Division; Epicure Products Inc; Concord Systems Inc; Altec Co Ltd (Japan); Concord Japan Co Ltd (Japan); Technipower Division; Penril Technical SA (Switzerland); Triplett Electrical Instrument Corp; Alltest Division; Data Tech Division; Triplett De Mexico SA (Mexico)

Principal Bank: The Riggs National Bank of Washington, DC

Financial Information:

	$'000
Sales revenues	74,000

No of Employees: 1,170

PENTAIR, INC

1700 West Highway 36, St Paul, MN 55113
Tel: (612) 636-7920
Telex: WUT 59 5687 pentair hq ud

Chairman: D Eugene Nugent (and Chief Executive Officer)

President: Sankey A Johnson (and Chief Operating Officer)

Senior Executive Officers: John H Grunewald (Chief Financial Officer, Secretary), Allan J Kolles (VP, Human Resources), Richard F Jost (VP, Industrial Relations), Roy T Rueb (VP, Treasurer), Robert V Touchette (VP Specialty Papers Group), James H Frank (VP Corporate Development), Mark T Schroepfer (Corporate Controller), John I Depew (VP, Materials Management, Paper Group), Robert D Kopisch (Director, Operations Analysis, Paper Group), Gary J Burwell (Director, Internal Audit), W F (Duke) Fuehrer (Director, Organization Development), Ronald D Lindberg (Director, Compensation and Benefits)

PRINCIPAL ACTIVITIES: Pentair, Inc completed 21 years of business in 1987. The company operates through seven wholly owned subsidiaries which make paper, portable electric tools, woodworking machinery, lubricating products and systems and water pumps

Principal Subsidiaries: Delta International Machinery Corporation; Flambeau Paper Corporation; Miami Paper Corporation; Niagara of Wisconsin Paper Corporation; Port Huron Paper Corporation; Porter-Cable Corporation; F E Myers and Lincoln, a Division of McNeil (Ohio) Corporation

Principal Bank: The First National Bank of St Paul

Financial Information:

	Dec 31 1985	Dec 31 1986
	$'000	$'000
Sales revenues	534,198	623,876
Income before taxes	28,697	24,612
Net income	20,058	15,228
Dividends	5,565	5,719
Dividends per share	$0.68	$0.69
Earnings per share primary	$2.32	$1.76
Earnings per share diluted	$2.23	$1.70
Common stock	1,303	1,441
Retained income	93,128	77,199
Shareholders equity	134,555	145,386

No of Employees: 7,000

PENWEST LIMITED

411 108th Avenue Northeast, Suite 300, Bellevue, WA 98004
Tel: (206) 462 6000

Chairman: Curtis P Lindley

President: Tod R Hamachek (and Chief Executive Officer)

Senior Executive Officers: Ronald B Vogel (VP and General Manager), Dale C Leman (VP Finance), Franklin E Olsen Jr (VP Employee Relations), H Thomas Reed (VP)

PRINCIPAL ACTIVITIES: Production of malt, sweeteners and starch; brewing

Principal Bank: Rainier Bank

Financial Information:

	$'000
Sales revenues	146,140

No of Employees: 500

PEOPLE EXPRESS AIRLINES, INC

North Terminal, Newark International Airport, Newark, NJ 07114
Tel: (201) 901-2935

Chairman: Donald C Burr (and Chief Executive Officer)
Senior Executive Officers: R J McAdoo (Chief Financial Officer), Gil Roberts (Chief Operating Officer)

PRINCIPAL ACTIVITIES: Passenger airline services
Financial Information:

	$'000
Sales revenues	977,864

No of Employees: 3,960

PEOPLES BANCORPORATION

1414 4th Avenue, PO Box 720, Seattle, WA 98111
Tel: (206) 344-2300

Chairman: Joshua Green III (and Chief Executive Officer)
Senior Executive Officers: Elmer M Anderson (Executive VP), Charles E Riley (Executive VP), Leo M Riley (Executive VP, Secretary and Treasurer)

PRINCIPAL ACTIVITIES: Banking services
Financial Information:

	Dec 31 1985
	$'000
Revenues	255,000
Net income	14,300
Total assets	2,380,000

No of Employees: 2,400

PEOPLE'S BANCORPORATION NORTH CAROLINA

130 South Franklin Street, Rocky Mount, NC 27801
Tel: (919) 977 4811

Chairman: Robert R Mauldin (and Chief Executive Officer)
Senior Executive Officers: R Branson Hobbs (Executive VP, Group Officer and Secretary), H Kel Landis Jr (Executive VP, Group Officer and Treasurer), Michael S Patterson (Executive VP and Group Officer), C Fred Clark (Senior VP), Charles R Gowin (Senior VP), T W Harris (Senior VP Investments)

PRINCIPAL ACTIVITIES: Holding Company with interests in banking

No of Employees: 920

PEOPLES ENERGY CORPORATION

122 S Michigan Avenue, Chicago, IL 60603
Tel: (312) 431-4000

Chairman: Eugene A Tracy (and President)
President: Louis C Baldacci Jr (and Chief Operating Officer)
Senior Executive Officers: Bruce Hasch (Executive VP), Richard E Terry (Executive VP), Donald G Holm (VP, Secretary and Treasurer), James Hinchliff (VP and General Counsel), Masao Igasaki Jr (VP and Controller)

PRINCIPAL ACTIVITIES: Distribution of natural gas
Principal Bankers: Harris Trust & Savings Bank
Financial Information:

	$'000
Sales revenues	1,500,000

No of Employees: 3,500

PEP BOYS (MANNY MOE & JACK)

3111 W Allegheny Avenue, Philadelphia, PA 19132
Tel: (215) 229-9000

Chairman: Benjamin Strauss (and President)
President: Mitchell G Leibovitz
Senior Executive Officers: Charles J Chase (Executive VP), Scott I Rosen (Executive VP), Michael J Holden (VP Finance)

PRINCIPAL ACTIVITIES: Operation of a chain of auto parts stores
Principal Bankers: Philadelphia National Bank
Financial Information:

	$'000
Sales revenues	486,000

No of Employees: 4,400

PEPCOM INDUSTRIES, INC

Roosevelt Field, Garden City, NY 11530
Tel: (516) 741-8300

Chairman: Keizo Saji
President: Harry M Hersh
Senior Executive Officers: James A Pash (Executive VP, Secretary and Treasurer), Allen Fleischer (VP), Thomas R Grant (VP)

PRINCIPAL ACTIVITIES: Manufacture of soft drinks
Parent Company: Suntory International Corporation
Principal Bank: First Union National Bank
Financial Information:

	$'000
Sales revenues	110,000

No of Employees: 900

PEPSICO, INC

Anderson Hill Road, Purchase, NY 10577
Tel: (914) 253-2000
Telex: 62848 PepsiCo62848UW

Chairman: D Wayne Calloway (and Chief Executive Officer)
President: Michael H Jordan
Senior Executive Officers: Robert G Dettmer (Executive VP and Chief Financial Officer), Peter A Bassi (VP), Robert L Carleton (VP and Controller), Donovan R Christopherson (VP and Treasurer), James H Ditkoff (VP), Peter D Houchin (VP and Deputy Treasurer), J Roger King (VP), Edward V Lahey Jr (VP, General Counsel and Secretary), Joseph F McCann (VP), John J Flaherty (General Auditor), James J Fitzsimmons (Assistant Controller), Gary M Stone (Assistant Controller), Lawrence F Dickie (Assistant Secretary), Claudia E Morf (Assistant Treasurer)

PRINCIPAL ACTIVITIES: PepsiCo, Inc is a worldwide consumer products and services company. Through its divisions and subsidiaries, both domestic and international, PepsiCo operates in three major business segments: beverages, food products and food service. It also is actively involved in sporting goods. PepsiCo has achieved a leadership position in each of these line of business. Beverages: Through Pepsi-Cola USA, the Pepsi-Cola Bottling Group and Pepsi-Cola International, PepsiCo manufactures and markets Pepsi-Cola and its allied brands. Every day more then 200 million servings of Pepsi-Cola products are enjoyed by millions of people around the world. Food Products: Frito-Lay, PepsiCo's domestic snack food company, produces the nation's best selling line of salty snacks, in addition to a growing variety of packaged cookies. PepsiCo Foods International sells numerous snack food products in 10 foreign markets. Food Service: Across the United States and in a rapidly increasing number of international markets, Pizza Hut and Taco Bell restaurants-leaders in their segments of the restaurant industry-serve more than 14 million customers a week. La Petite Boulangerie is a front runner in the growth area of specialty bread bakeries. Sporting Goods: Wilson Sporting Goods has established a worldwide reputation as the leading multi-line manufacturer of fine athletic equipment and accessories for individual and team sports

Trade Names: Pepsi-Cola, Diet Pepsi, Pepsi Free, Slice, Pepsi Light, Lay's Doritos, Fritos, Tostitos, Chee.tos, Ruffles, Personal Pan Pizza, Priazzo Pizza, Taco Salad, The Works
Principal Subsidiaries: Pepsi-Cola USA; Pepsi-Cola Bottling Group; Pepsi-Cola International; Frito-Lay, Inc; PepsiCo Foods International; Pizza Hut, Inc; Taco Bell Corp; La Petite Boulangerie; Kentucky Fried Chicken Corp
Principal Bank: Manufacturers Hanover Trust Co
Financial Information:

	Dec 31 1986
	$'000
Sales revenues	9,290,800
Net income	457,500
Earnings per share	$1.75
Shareholders equity	2,059,400

No of Employees: 150,000

PEPSI-COLA GENERAL BOTTLERS, INC

1745 N Kolmar Avenue, Chicago, IL 60639
Tel: (312) 342-9800

President: R W Selleck (and Chief Executive Officer)
Senior Executive Officers: G F Herkes (Executive VP and Secretary), G A McGuire (Group VP), M A Nehring (Group VP), A M Olsen (Senior VP Engineering and Technical Services), W L Benson (VP and General Manager Peoria), C P Dellorts (VP Munster), C G Faas (VP and General Manager Danville), L B Hafenbriedel (VP Manufacturing), C G Lund (VP and General Manager Cincinnati), W H Miller (VP Transportation), J R Mynatt (VP and General Manager Chicago), G R Noack (VP and General Manager Beloit), R K Poduch (VP and General Manager Louisville), O F Shipton (VP and Controller), C E Sinks (VP and General Manager Des Moines), E A Stange (VP and General Manager Springfield), J L Thomas (VP and General Manager Evansville)

PRINCIPAL ACTIVITIES: Bottling of non-alcoholic drinks
Parent Company: IC Industries Inc through IC Products Co
Principal Bank: Harris Trust and Savings Bank
Financial Information:

	$'000
Sales revenues	413,000

No of Employees: 3,050

PERDUE FARMS INC

PO Box 1537, Salisbury, MD 21801
Tel: (301) 543-3000

Chairman: Franklin P Perdue; Vice Chairman: Donald W Mabe (and President)
Senior Executive Officers: Sewell L Spedden Jr (Senior VP Feed, Grain and Transportation), Pelham B Lawrence (VP Finance)

PRINCIPAL ACTIVITIES: Production and processing of poultry and related products; processing of soybeans
Principal Bank: Philadelphia National Bank
Financial Information:

	$'000
Sales revenues	820,000

No of Employees: 11,000

PERGAMON HOLDING CORPORATION

Fairview Park, Elmsford, NY 10523
Tel: (914) 592-7700
Telex: WUT 137328 pergamon emfd

Chairman: Robert Maxwell (UK)
President: Laszlo Straka
Senior Executive Officers: S J Aboff (Executive VP), Edward Gray (Executive VP), Robert Miranda (Executive VP), Otto Rapp (Executive VP)

PRINCIPAL ACTIVITIES: Holding company with interests in the printing and publication of books and magazines
Principal Subsidiaries: Pergamon Press Inc
Financial Information:

	$'000
Sales revenues	650,000

No of Employees: 9,500

PERINI CORPORATION

73 Mt Wayte Avenue, Framingham, MA 01701
Tel: (617) 875-6171
Telex: WUT 948470 percon fmh

Chairman: David B Perini (and President and Chief Executive Officer); Chairman of Executive Committee: Joseph R Perini (and Vice Chairman of the Board and Senior VP International)
Senior Executive Officers: James M Markert (Senior VP Finance and Administration), Thomas E Dailey (President, Construction Group), Thomas A Steele (Senior VP, Real Estate), John E Chiaverini (Senior VP Special Projects), Irving R Huie (Senior VP, Heavy Construction)

PRINCIPAL ACTIVITIES: Building and construction, property development and coal mining
Principal Subsidiaries: R E Dailey & Co; Marvian Construction Company
Financial Information:

	Dec 31 1985	Dec 31 1986
	$'000	$'000
Sales revenues*	810,072	801,493
Net income (loss)	(17,932)	5,043
Dividends per share	$0.80	$0.80
Earnings (loss) per share	($5.64)	$1.56
Common stock	3,181	3,240
Shareholders equity	82,180	86,220

*from continuing operations

No of Employees: 1,000

PERKIN-ELMER CORPORATION

Main Avenue, Norwalk, CT 06856
Tel: (203) 762-1000
Telex: WUI 681 9014 perkin nlk

Chairman: Horace G McDonnell (and Chief Executive Officer); Chairman of Executive Committee: John S Scott
President: Gaynor N Kelley (and Chief Operating Officer)
Senior Executive Officers: Mercade A Kramer Jr (Senior VP), Kenneth E Davis (Senior VP), Charles E Minihan (Senior VP), Michael D Moore (Senior VP), Ronald G Anderson (VP), C Wendell Bergere Jr (VP, Secretary and General Counsel), Julianne A Grace (VP Administration), David A Huchital (VP), Richard C Schultz (VP and Comptroller)

PRINCIPAL ACTIVITIES: Manufacture of optical and analytical instruments; aviation instruments and missile systems; data processing equipment
Principal Bank: Citibank
Financial Information:

	Jul 31 1986
	$'000
Sales revenues	1,290,558
Net income	72,572
Earnings per share	$1.61
Shareholders equity	705,748

No of Employees: 15,500

PERKINS ENGINES, INC

32500 Van Born Road, Wayne, MI 48184
Tel: (313) 595-9600
Telex: WUT 234 002 perkeng wane

Chairman: J F Devaney (and Chief Executive Officer)
President: R L Howsman
Senior Executive Officers: K T J Hart (VP Service and Parts)

PRINCIPAL ACTIVITIES: Manufacture of diesel engines for a range of applications including agricultural and industrial vehicles
Parent Company: Massey Ferguson Inc
Principal Bank: National Bank of Detroit
Financial Information:

	$'000
Sales revenues	75,000

No of Employees: 250

PERPETUAL SAVINGS BANK, FSB
8200 Greensboro Drive, McLean, VA 22314
Tel: (703) 838-6000
Telefax: (703) 838-6127

Chairman: Thomas Owen (and Chief Executive Officer)
President: Ross Towne
Senior Executive Officers: Joseph Cicero (Chief Financial Officer), Jay Barr (Treasurer)

PRINCIPAL ACTIVITIES: Savings, loans and financial services
Principal Subsidiaries: Perpetual Mortgage Services; Perpetual Real Estate; Reilly Mortgage Group
Financial Information:

	Oct 31 1985	Oct 31 1986
	$'000	$'000
Net income	21,120	20,629
Shareholders equity	236,785	256,059
Deposits	-	3,105.930
Total assets	4,072,525	4,349,333

No of Employees: 1,450

PERRIGO COMPANY
117 Water Street, Allegan, MI 49101
Tel: (616) 673-8451

Chairman: William C Swaney (and Chief Executive Officer)
President: Michael Jandernoa
Senior Executive Officers: Ralph Klingenmeyer (VP Operations), Michael Brown (VP Technical Affairs), Dick Hansen (VP Finance), Robert Izzo (VP Sales and Marketing)

PRINCIPAL ACTIVITIES: Manufacture of medicines, vitamins and beauty products
Parent Company: Grow Group Inc
Principal Bank: Old Kent Bank
Financial Information:

	$'000
Sales revenues	100,000

No of Employees: 1,000

PERRY DRUG STORES INC
5400 Perry Drive, PO Box 1957, Pontiac, MI 48056
Tel: (313) 334 1300

Chairman· Jack A Robinson (and Chief Executive Officer)
President: Donald Fox (and Chief Operating Officer)
Senior Executive Officers: Alvin M Wander (Executive VP, Principal Financial Officer and Principal Accounting Officer), Robert A Berlow (VP, Legal Counsel and Secretary), Robert W Ruwoldt (VP Advertising), Gene Swink (VP Distribution), John P Frazzini (VP Management Information Systems), Mickey H Kole (Senior VP Merchandising and Division President), David W Peterson (VP Merchandising), Frederick C Seely (Senior VP Real Estate), Robert A Shapiro (VP Medical)

PRINCIPAL ACTIVITIES: Operation of retail drug stores, grocery and auto parts stores
Principal Subsidiaries: Auto Works Inc; Bloomlytical Procedures Inc; Comfort Care; FAS Auto Woeks Inc; FAS Auto Works of Columbus Inc; FAS Auto Works of MO Inc; Flint Medical; Perry Comprehensive Pharmacy Service; Perry Distributors Inc; Perry Drugs Company; Price AL Inc
Principal Bank: Michigan National Bank
Financial Information:

	$'000
Sales revenues	522,000

No of Employees: 6,900

PERRY PRINTING CORPORATION
240 W Madison Street, Waterloo, WI 53594
Tel: (414) 478-3551

Chairman: Roger L Perry
President: Frank A Twiss Jr
Senior Executive Officers: Lloyd A Ratcliff (Senior VP Production), Wayne W Oleson (Senior VP Finance and Treasurer), Craig Hutchison (Senior VP Marketing), Jack Laning (VP Web Sales), Dan Meyer (VP Employee Relations), Howard Nelson (VP and Controller), Albert Schaller (VP Customer Services)

PRINCIPAL ACTIVITIES: Printing of magazines
Parent Company: The Journal Co Inc, Milwaukee, MI
Principal Bank: M & I Marshall and Ilsley Bank
Financial Information:

	$'000
Sales revenues	115,000

No of Employees: 1,300

PERVEL INDUSTRIES, INC
Plainfield, CT 06374
Tel: (203) 564-2741
Telex: WUT 966 450 pervelind pfel

President: Arnold R Ganz
Senior Executive Officers: John D Kirby (VP and Treasurer), V H Weiss (VP Technology), Frank E Wilson (VP Manufacturing)

PRINCIPAL ACTIVITIES: Manufacture of vinyl products including film and foam, coated wallcoverings and fabrics
Parent Company: Bemis Company Inc, Minneapolis, MN
Financial Information:

	$'000
Sales revenues	60,000

No of Employees: 800

PET INCORPORATED
400 South Fourth Street, PO Box 392, St Louis, MO 63166
Tel: (314) 621-5400

Chairman: Boyd F Schenk
President: Ray Morris (and Chief Executive Officer)
Senior Executive Officers: John E Mackey (President, Specialty Group), Raymond N Felitto (President, Frozen and Bakery Group), A James Matson (President, Grocery Group), Larry D Umlauf (President, International Group), Thomas R Pellett (Senior VP and Chief Financial Officer), John C Elbin (VP, Strategic Planning), Thomas E Killeen (VP, Human Resources), Anthony C Knizel (VP, Controller and Assistant Treasurer), James W Nixon (VP and President, Whitman's Chocolates Division), William F Sutter (VP, General Counsel and Secretary), Leon P Ullensvang (VP, Corporate Affairs), Patrick G Wesley (Treasurer and Assistant Secretary), Robert C Drury (VP Management Information Services)

PRINCIPAL ACTIVITIES: Pet Incorporated today is a specialty foods manufacturer whose varied brands and businesses touch the lives of families around the world. Pet continues to keep pace with rapidly changing trends in the food idustry with products and services positioned in five major areas: Grocery Group; Specialty Group; Frozen and Bakery Group; International Group; and Pet Food Service
Parent Company: IC Industries
Principal Subsidiaries: Old El Paso, Underwood, Pet, Ac'cent, Sego, B & M, Progresso, Hain, Hollywood, Los Palmos, Golden Key, Dairymate, Compliment, Heartland, Sell's, Friend's, Richardson & Robbins, Pancho Villa, Sa-son, El Caldero, Evans, Downyflake, Roman Meal, Pet-Ritz,

Whitman's Sampler, Bisler Packaging, Aunt Fanny's, Pecan Twirls, St Louis Lithographing, McGrew Color Graphics, Puritan, Sween'N Low, Nu-Salt, Diablitos, Salsa de Diablitos, Shippam's, Peck's, ARSA, Estrella, Primo, Executive Chef, Montini

Financial Information:

	1986
	$'000
Sales revenues	966,000
Operating income	125,400

No of Employees: 7,400

PETE LIEN & SONS, INC
See LIEN, PETE, & SONS, INC

PETER COOPER CORPORATIONS
See COOPER, PETER, CORPORATIONS

PETER ECKRICH & SONS, INC
See ECKRICH, PETER, & SONS, INC

PETER PAN SEAFOODS, INC
1000 Denny Building, Seattle, WA 98121
Tel: (206) 624-4344
Telex: WUT 328422 premiersfh sea

President: W G Saletic
Senior Executive Officers: W J Clemmens (VP Sales), D M Rawlinson (VP Manufacturing), L V Guffey (VP Manufacturing), G R Greenwood (VP Finance), B R Thiemens (VP Purchasing)

PRINCIPAL ACTIVITIES: Freezing and canning of seafood
Parent Company: Nichiro Gyogyo Kaisha Ltd
Principal Bank: Seattle First National Bank
Financial Information:

	$'000
Sales revenues	90,000

No of Employees: 950

PETERSON BUILDERS, INC
101 Pennsylvania Street, Sturgeon Bay, WI 54235
Tel: (414) 743-5574
Telex: WUT 263423 peterson sgb

President: Ellsworth L Peterson
Senior Executive Officers: Ed Propsom (VP Operations), F J Peterson II (VP Facilities), Thomas O Kerley (VP Materials), Jack Soderlund (VP Administration), Ray Alfson (VP Finance)

PRINCIPAL ACTIVITIES: Building and repair of ships and boats in aluminum, wood, steel and fiberglass in sizes up to 300 feet
Trade Names: PBI
Principal Bank: Bank of Sturgeon Bay

No of Employees: 950

PETRIE STORES CORPORATION
70 Enterprise Avenue, Secaucus, NJ 07094
Tel: (201) 866-3600

Chairman: Milton J Petrie (and President and Chief Executive Officer); Vice Chairman: Hilda K Gerstein
Senior Executive Officers: Peter A Left (Senior VP, Secretary and Chief Financial Officer), Nancy Barrett (Senior VP), Edward Citro (Senior VP), Beverly Evans (Senior VP), Jay Galin (Senior VP and President G & G Shops Inc), Umberto Gallo (Senior VP), Robert Lind (Senior VP), Daniel Maresca (Senior VP), Samuel D Polese (Senior VP), Dorothy F Stern (Senior VP Merchandising), Jean Roberts (Senior VP Store Operations)

PRINCIPAL ACTIVITIES: Retail trade in women's clothing
Principal Bankers: Chase Manhattan Bank
Financial Information:

	$'000
Sales revenues	1,200,000

No of Employees: 15,000

PETROLEUM EQUIPMENT TOOLS CO PETCO
11000 Richmond Avenue, Suite 600, Houston, TX 77042
Tel: (713) 953 1141
Telex: 762247 PETCO HOU
Telefax: (713) 953-1568

Chairman: David M Johnson (and President)
Senior Executive Officers: Robert E Warner (Executive VP, Secretary and Treasurer)

PRINCIPAL ACTIVITIES: Petroleum Equipment Tools Co (PETCO) rents quality drill pipe and fishing and rental tools for drilling and workover operations in the oil and gas industry in the United States. Southeast Asia and the North Sea. The Company also provides skilled and experienced operators to its customers in conjunction with its fishing tools
Trade Names: PETCO
Principal Bank: First City National Bank of Houston
Financial Information:

	Dec 31 1985	Dec 31 1986
	$'000	$'000
Sales revenues	66,261	29,314
(Loss) before taxes	(16,216)	(29,698)
Net (loss)	(9,942)	(22,038)
(Loss) per share	($0.95)	($2.11)
Common stock	5,238	5,238
Retained income	35,418	13,380
Shareholders equity	74,493	52,760

No of Employees: 300

PETROLEUM HELICOPTERS INC
PO Box 23502, 5728 Jefferson Highway, New Orleans, LA 70123
Tel: (504) 7336790

Chairman: Robert L Suggs (and Chief Executive Officer); Vice Chairman: Maurice M Bayon
President: Frank W Lee (and Chief Operating Officer)
Senior Executive Officers: Vernon Albert (VP, Chief Pilot), Richard Bricknell (VP), Carl Dougherty (VP and General Manager), James Michel (VP Personnel), Harold Summers (VP Maintenance), John La Plante (Secretary and Treasurer)

PRINCIPAL ACTIVITIES: Operation of air transport services
Principal Subsidiaries: Evangeline Airmotive Inc; International Helicopter Transportation; Petroleum Helicopters de Bolivia
Principal Bank: Whitney National Bank
Financial Information:

	$'000
Sales revenues	186,000

No of Employees: 2,740

PETRO-LEWIS CORPORATION
717 Seventeenth Street, Denver, CO 80201
Tel: (303) 294-1000

Chairman: Jerome A Lewis (and Chief Executive Officer)
President: David A Frawley (and Chief Operating Officer)
Senior Executive Officers: Tom B Martinez (Senior VP and Chief Administrative Officer), G Bruce Williams (Senior VP Operations), Lon McCain (Senior VP and Chief Financial Officer)

PRINCIPAL ACTIVITIES: Production of oil and gas
Principal Subsidiaries: Petro-Lewis Funds, Inc
Principal Bank: Den Norske Creditbank

Financial Information:

	$'000
Sales revenues	233,000

No of Employees: 500

PETROLITE CORPORATION

100 N Broadway, St Louis, MO 63102
Tel: (314) 241-8370
Telex: WUT 44899 petrolite stl

Chairman: Ellis L Brown
President: M D Ingram (and Chief Executive and Operating Officer)
Senior Executive Officers: Herbert F Eggerding Jr (Executive VP Finance and Administration), R R Hirsch (Senior VP and Secretary), J T Badgett (VP Administration), W E Nasser (VP Petrolite Special Polymers Group), Claeburn Nix (VP Petrolite Oil Field Chemicals Group), J S Titone (VP Petrolite Industrial Chemicals Group), R G Tonkyn (VP Research and Development and Technical Services), R E Werley (VP Purchasing and Traffic), James M Zemenick (VP and Controller)

PRINCIPAL ACTIVITIES: Manufacture of specialty chemicals and waxes; industrial processing systems
Principal Bank: The Boatmen's National Bank of St Louis
Financial Information:

	$'000
Sales revenues	280,000

No of Employees: 2,100

PETRO-TEX CHEMICAL CORPORATION

8600 Park Place, Houston, TX 77017
Tel: (713) 477-9211

Chairman: R S Cunningham
President: H R Bowers
Senior Executive Officers: T W Bartlett (VP Finance), W H Taylor (VP Sales)

PRINCIPAL ACTIVITIES: Manufacture of petrochemicals
Parent Company: Tenneco Inc through Tenneco Corporation
Financial Information:

	$'000
Sales revenues	300,000

No of Employees: 500

PETTIBONE CORPORATION

2700 River Road, Suite 302, Des Plaines, IL 60018-4199
Tel: (312) 390-7840
Telex: 6871484 (PETTIN)
Telefax: (312) 390-3445

Chairman: Robert A Podesta
President: Larry C Klumpp
Senior Executive Officers: R J Palmer (Executive VP and Chief Financial Officer), Robert E Spencer (Executive VP), Douglas A Johnson (Secretary), Ralph G Whedon (Treasurer)

PRINCIPAL ACTIVITIES: Manufacture of materials handling equipment, construction plant, rock crushing machinery, industrial machinery, cast steel products and railroad track equipment
Trade Names: Barko, Universal
Principal Subsidiaries: (100% owned unless stated): Domestic: Barko Hydraulics Inc; Pettibone Credit Corporation; Pettibone International Sales Corporation; Pettibone Michigan Corporation; Pettibone Ohio Corporation; Pettibone Texas Corporation; Pettibone Tiffin Corporation; The Universal Engineering Corporation. Foreign: Pettibone de Mexico SA de CV (98.5%) (Mexico)
Principal Bank: The First National Bank of Chicago
Financial Information:

	Mar 31 1986	Mar 31 1987
	$'000	$'000
Sales revenues	97,549	92,624
Net income (loss)	(52,465)	2,928
Earnings (loss) per share	($18.83)	$1.05
Common stock	3,190	32
Retained (deficit)	(97,341)	(94,413)
Shareholders equity	(61,875)	(59,124)

No of Employees: 835

PFIZER INC

235 E 42nd Street, New York, NY 10017
Tel: (212) 573-2323
Cable: PFIZERSUB NY
Telex: 420440

Chairman: Edmund T Pratt Jr (and Chief Executive Officer)
President: Gerald D Laubach Ph.D.
Senior Executive Officers: Donald E Kolowsky (VP; President-Pfizer Chemical Products), Edward C Bessey (VP; President-Pfizer Hospital Products), Barry M Bloom (VP; President-Central Research), C L Clemente (VP-General Counsel and Secretary), Stephen R Conafay (VP-Government Relations), Thomas J Connors (VP; Executive VP, Operations-Pfizer International subsidiaries), Bruce Ellig (VP-Personnel), John E Jefferis (VP-Licensing and Development), Philmore H Friedman (VP-Taxes), Joseph F Harmon (VP; President-Pfizer Consumer Products), Roland M Hendrickson (VP; President-Pfizer Agricultural Products), Barry MacTaggart (VP; Chairman and President-Pfizer International Subsidiaries), Henry A McKinnell (VP-Corporate Strategic Planning), John C Mesloh (Controller), Paul S Miller (VP-General Counsel), James W Murray (Treasurer), Robert Neimeth (VP; Executive VP-Pfizer International Subsidiaries), M William Roche (VP; Executive VP-Pfizer International Subsidiaries), Robert L Shafer (VP-Public Affairs and Government Relations), William C Steere Jr (VP; President-Pfizer Pharmaceutical Products), Dean R Thacker (VP; President-Pfizer Materials Science Products), Peter G Tombros (VP; Executive VP-Pfizer Pharmaceutical Products), Jean-Paul Vallès (VP-Finance)

PRINCIPAL ACTIVITIES: Pfizer Inc is a worldwide research-based company with businesses in health care, agriculture, specialty chemicals, materials science and consumer products
Trade Names: The following are among the trademarks used by Pfizer Inc and its subsidiaries: Bacacil, Carduran, Cefobid, Diabinese, Feldene, Glucotrol, Minipress, Navane, Procardia, Sinequan, Spectrobid, Sulperazon, Unasyn, Vagistat, Vibramycin, Convexo-Concave, Force 2, Hydroflex, Infusaid Implantable Pump, Infutrol 7000, IV 7000, Monostrut, PCA Total Knee, PCA Total Hip, Pleur-evac, PolyHesive, Soft and Secure, Banminth, Mecadox, Paratect, Pathozone, Rumatel, Terramycin, Terramycin/LA, Mono-Line, Q-Vibe, Barbasol, Ben-Gay, Ben-Gay Sports-Balm, Ben-Gay Sports-Gel, Desitin, Lady Stetson, Stetson, Unisom, Unisom Dual Relief, Visine
Principal Subsidiaries: Major Operating Units:- Pfizer Pharmaceutical Products: Pfizer Laboratories; Roerig. Pfizer International. Pfizer Hospital Products: American Medical Systems Inc; Angiomedics Incorporated; Deknatel; Howmedica Inc; Shiley Incorporated; Shiley Infusaid Inc; Valleylab Inc United. Pfizer Agricultural Products. Pfizer Chemical Products. Pfizer Materials Science Products: Minerals, Pigments and Metals: Quigley Company Inc. Pfizer Consumer Products: Coty; Leeming/Pacquin. Pfizer International Bank
Principal Bank: The Chase Manhattan Bank

Financial Information:

	Dec 31 1985	Dec 31 1986
	$'000	$'000
Sales revenues	4,024,500	4,476,000
Income before taxes*	881,400	964,900
Net income	579,700	660,000
Dividends	241,200	269,700
Dividends per share	$1.48	$1.64
Earnings per share	$3.44	$3.90
Common stock	16,400	16,500
Retained income	2,543,400	2,933,700
Shareholders equity	2,927,300	3,415,200

*and minority interests

No of Employees: 40,000

PHARMACIA INC

800 Centennial Avenue, Piscataway, NJ 08854
Tel: (201) 457-8000
Telex: WUI 6858 125 pharfc

Chairman: Erik Danielsson (Sweden)
President: Magnus Moliteus
Senior Executive Officers: Richard L Easterday (Executive VP), Ken Morrow (Executive VP), William Murphy (VP), Carl-Erik Sjoberg (Secretary)

PRINCIPAL ACTIVITIES: Manufacture of pharmaceutical products, chemicals and laboratory equipment
Parent Company: Pharmacia AB, Uppsala, Sweden
Principal Bank: Fidelity Union Bank
Financial Information:

	$'000
Sales revenues	135,000

No of Employees: 800

PHELPS DODGE CORPORATION

300 Park Avenue, New York, NY 10022
Tel: (212) 940-6400
Telex: TWX 710 5812 142 pd traffic nyk

Chairman: G Robert Durham (and Chief Executive Officer)
Senior Executive Officers: Walter S Ainsworth (Senior VP), Leonard R Judd (Senior VP), Richard W Pendleton Jr (Senior VP), Patrick J Ryan (Senior VP), Douglas C Yearly (Senior VP), Charles S Burns (VP Government Relations), Michael P Cangemi (VP), John V Coulter (VP), Edson L Foster (VP), Arthur E Himebaugh (VP and General Manager Western Operations), Matthew P Scanlon (VP), Roger C Smith (VP Finance)

PRINCIPAL ACTIVITIES: Mining, smelting and refining of copper; wire drawing and copper fabrication; refining of precious metals
Principal Bank: Manufacturers Hanover Trust Co
Financial Information:

	Dec 31 1985	Dec 31 1986
	$'000	$'000
Sales revenues	886,640	845,941
Net income	29,500	61,400
Earnings per share	-	$1.79
Shareholders equity	891,060	934,866

No of Employees: 6,430

PHELPS INC

420 Sixth Ave, Greeley, CA 80632
Tel: (303) 353-7000

President: Robert G Tointon (and Chief Executive Officer)
Senior Executive Officers: Robert A Ruyle (VP and Secretary), James M Murdoch (VP Finance and Treasurer)

PRINCIPAL ACTIVITIES: Building and construction industry; institutional and commercial
Principal Subsidiaries: Southern Steel Co; Clearwater Constructors Inc; Phelps Hensel Construction Co; Rocky Mountain Prestress Inc
Financial Information:

	$'000
Sales Revenues	400,000

No of Employees: 1,200

PHEOLL MANUFACTURING CO

5700 W Roosevelt Road, Chicago, IL 60650
Tel: (312) 261-0300
Telex: TWX 910 2215312 pheoll mfg cgo

Chairman: S C Adamek (and Chief Executive Officer)
President: Robert Brown
Senior Executive Officers: C Bersch (VP Sales), T Bishop (VP Manufacturing), F Chandler (VP Sales)

PRINCIPAL ACTIVITIES: Manufacture of metal industrial fasteners
Parent Company: Allied Products Corporation
Principal Bank: Continental Illinois National Bank and Trust Company
Financial Information:

	$'000
Sales revenues	213,000

No of Employees: 300

PHH GROUP, INC

11333 McCormick Road, Hunt Valley, MD 21031
Tel: (301) 667-4000

Chairman: Jerome W Geckle (and Chief Executive Officer)
President: Robert D Kunisch (and Chief Operating Officer)
Senior Executive Officers: A S Penn (Executive VP), Frank J Schmieder (Executive VP), Phillip W Taff (Senior VP and Chief Financial Officer), Duncan H Cocroft (VP and Treasurer), John T Connor Jr (VP and General Counsel), Donald V Freiert Jr (VP and Controller), Edwin F Miller (VP and Secretary)

PRINCIPAL ACTIVITIES: Management of vehicle fleets, car and vehicle leasing, aircraft leasing and relocation on behalf of corporate clients
Principal Subsidiaries: Peterson, Howell and Heather Inc; Homequity Inc; NTS Inc; The Fantus Co Inc; Executive Air Fleet Corpn; PHH Aviation Systems Inc; Peterson, Howell & Heather Canada Inc; PHH International Ltd (UK)
Principal Bank: Maryland National Bank
Financial Information:

	$'000
Sales revenues	1,400,000

No of Employees: 3,170

PHILADELPHIA & READING CORPORATION

100 W Tenth Street, Wilmington, DE 19801
Tel: (302) 658-7581

President: Ben W Heineman
Senior Executive Officers: Bernard Firestone (Senior VP and Treasurer), Brendan M O'Neill (VP Finance), R J Hill (Secretary)

PRINCIPAL ACTIVITIES: Holding company with interests in clothing, shoes, electrical products and steel fabrication
Parent Company: Northwest Industries Inc, Chicago, IL

PHILADELPHIA ELECTRIC CO

2301 Market Street, Philadelphia, PA 19101
Tel: (215) 841-4000
Telex: WUT 831605 peco pha

Chairman: James L Everett (and Chief Executive Officer)
President: John H Austin Jr (and Chief Operating Officer)
Senior Executive Officers: Vincent S Boyer (Senior VP Nuclear Power), Richard G Gilmore (Senior VP and Chief Finance Officer), Edward G Bauer Jr (VP), Clifford Brenner (VP

Corporate Communications), Thomas W Coppock (VP Electricity Transmission and Distribution), Shields L Daltroff (VP Electricity Production), Charles L Fritz (VP Personnel and Industrial Relations), Raymond F Holman (VP General Administration), John S Kemper (VP Engineering and Research), William B Morlok (VP Communication Operations), Philip G Mulligan (VP Gas Operations), A Lewis Parry Jr (VP Purchasing and General Services), Morton W Rimerman (VP Finance and Accounting), Raymond C Williams (VP Rates)

PRINCIPAL ACTIVITIES: Electricity and natural gas supply
Principal Bank: Philadelphia National Bank
Financial Information:

	Dec 31 1985	Dec 31 1986
	$'000	$'000
Sales revenues	3,013,704	3,090,869
Net income	525,300	566,320
Earnings per share	$2.56	$2.60
Shareholders equity	3,765,520	4,066,353

No of Employees: 10,440

PHILADELPHIA GEAR CORPORATION

King of Prussia, PA 19406
Tel: (215) 265-3000
Telex: WUI 6851044 pgcpa

Chairman: Russell C Ball Jr
President: Thomas F Hayes
Senior Executive Officers: H O Kron (Executive VP), Jack M Hamilton (VP Industrial Gearing), Edgar B Melton (VP Mixers Division), James C Gabrellas (VP Administration and Finance)

PRINCIPAL ACTIVITIES: Manufacture of gears
Parent Company: American Manufacturing Corp
Financial Information:

	$'000
Sales revenues	66,000

No of Employees: 1,800

PHILADELPHIA NATIONAL BANK

Broad & Chestnut St, Philadelphia, PA 19101
Tel: (215) 629-3100
Telex: 275294 PNBI UR
Fax: (215) 629-2605

Chairman: Frederick Heldring (and President)
Senior Executive Officers: Charles L Coltman (Executive VP Corporate and Institutional Banking), Paul G Finegan (Executive VP Trust Services), Joseph K Gordon (Executive VP and Chief Counsel), A G Heebner (Executive VP Economist), George D Norton (Executive VP and Cashier), Ernest B Smith (Executive VP Specialized Banking), Robert D Spencer (Executive VP Regional Banking), Clifford R Gillam Jr (Senior VP and Secretary), Albert W Mandia (Senior VP and Comptroller), John M Hoing (VP and Treasurer), Michael A Varzally (VP and General Auditor)

PRINCIPAL ACTIVITIES: Banking services
Parent Company: CoreStates Financial Corporation (100%)

No of Employees: 6,517

PHILADELPHIA SUBURBAN CORPORATION

762 Lancaster Avenue, Bryn Mawr, PA 19019
Tel: (215) 527 8000

Chairman: John W Boyer Jr (and President)
Senior Executive Officers: John A Condon (Group VP), Earl H Graham (Group VP Water Services), John J Manion (Executive VP), David R Wilson (VP and Treasurer)

PRINCIPAL ACTIVITIES: Supply of water, construction and engineering services
Principal Subsidiaries: Controlled Coatings; Digital Systems Inc; Fire Control Inc; Gulf Carolina Coatings Inc; Hinchman Company, Leavesley-McCollum Corporation; Oilfield/Leed Rental Service Company; Penn-Del Sprinkler Company Inc; Philadelphia Suburban Water Company; Tumaround Main Supply Company Inc; Utility Management Services
Principal Bank: Provident National Bank
Financial Information:

	$'000
Sales revenues	82,680

No of Employees: 740

PHILIP A HUNT CHEMICAL CORPORATION

See HUNT, PHILIP A, CHEMICAL CORPORATION

PHILIP CROSBY ASSOCIATES INC

See CROSBY, PHILIP, ASSOCIATES INC

PHILIP MORRIS, INC

120 Park Avenue, New York, NY 10017
Tel: (212) 880-5000
Telex: RCA 233 546 pmi ur

Chairman: Hamish Maxwell (and Chief Executive Officer); Vice Chairmen: Hugh Cullman, James L Ferguson (and Chairman of the Executive Committee, General Foods Corporation)
President: John A Murphy (and Chief Operating Officer)
Senior Executive Officers: Thomas F Ahrensfeld (Senior VP and General Counsel), R Nelson Beane (VP and Controller), Eugene J T Flanagan (VP, Secretary and Associate General Counsel), Ehud Houminer (VP, Planning), George R Lewis (VP and Treasurer), William J O'Connor (VP, Administration and Human Resources), Stanley S Scott (VP, Director of Corporate Affairs), Hans G Storr (VP and Chief Financial Officer), Alexander Holtzman (Associate General Counsel), James T Breedlove (Assistant Secretary), Patricia A Malzacher (Assistant Secretary). Staff Vice Presidents: Bruce S Brown, Gene A Knorr, F Robert Kurimsky, William C Smiy, William K Transue

PRINCIPAL ACTIVITIES: Manufacture of an extensive range of products including tobacco, soft drinks, beer, fruit products, paper products and packaging; interests in real estate and land development, finance and insurance
Principal Subsidiaries: Philip Morris USA; Philip Morris International; General Foods Corporation; Miller Brewing Company; Philip Morris Credit Corporation; Mission Viejo Realty Group Inc
Principal Bank: Citibank NA
Financial Information:

	Dec 31 1985	Dec 31 1986
	$'000	$'000
Operating revenues	15,964,000	25,409,000
Income before taxes	2,329,000	2,811,000
Net income	1,255,000	1,478,000
Dividends	479,000	590,000
Dividends per share	$2.00	$2.475
Earnings per share	$5.24	$6.20
Common stock	119,000	240,000
Retained income	4,456,000	5,344,000
Shareholders equity	4,737,000	5,655,000

No of Employees: 111,000

PHILIPP BROTHERS CHEMICALS,INC

One Parker Plaza, Fort Lee, NJ 07024
Tel: (201) 944-6020
Cable: PHIBROCHEM FORTLEENEWJERSEY
Telex: RCA 277820 PBC UR; WU 710-991-0289 PHBCHM UD
Fax: (201) 944-7911

President: C H Bendheim (and Treasurer)
Senior Executive Officers: Morris Bock (Executive VP Purchasing and Secretary), J C Bendheim (Executive VP/Chief Operating Officer)

PRINCIPAL ACTIVITIES: Manufacture of chemicals for industry and agriculture
Principal Bank: Manufacturers Hanover Trust Company

Financial Information:

	$'000
Sales revenues	150,000

No of Employees: 650

PHILIPS INDUSTRIES INC

4801 Springfield Street, Dayton, OH 45401
Tel: (513) 253-7171
Telex: TWX 810 459 1971

Chairman: Jesse Philips
President: Robert H Brethen (and Chief Executive Officer)
Senior Executive Officers: Joseph W Deering (Executive VP Operations), Harry Skilten (Executive VP), Neal Baileys (VP Personnel and Industrial Relations), Robert F Berrey (VP and General Counsel), James R Collins (VP and General Manager Ventline Division), George F Loving (VP and Controller), David Palmisano (VP and General Manager Conaire Division), Leonard W Reardon (VP Finance), Chris Smith (VP and General Manager J & J Register)

PRINCIPAL ACTIVITIES: Manufacture of windows and doors for homes and vehicles; manufacture of plastic products
Principal Bank: Bank One Dayton
Financial Information:

	Mar 31 1986	Mar 31 1987
	$'000	$'000
Sales revenues	538,332	593,000
Net income	29,769	33,000

No of Employees: 5,800

PHILLIPS & JACOBS, INC

Fox Street & Roberts Avenue, Philadelphia, PA 19129
Tel: (215) 221-8800
Telex: WUT 902 612 philjacobs pha

Chairman: Philip J Baur Jr
President: James F Mullan
Senior Executive Officers: Joseph F Duden (Executive VP), John M Pettine (Treasurer)

PRINCIPAL ACTIVITIES: Wholesale distribution of chemicals and graphic arts materials
Parent Company: Tasty Baking Company, Philadelphia, PA
Principal Bank: Fidelity Bank
Financial Information:

	$'000
Sales revenues	60,000

No of Employees: 200

PHILLIPS PETROLEUM COMPANY

16 A3 Phillips Building, Bartlesville, OK 74004
Tel: (918) 661-6600

Chairman: C J Silas (and Chief Executive Officer)
President: Glenn A Cox (and Chief Operating Officer)
Senior Executive Officers: L M Rickards (Executive VP), R G Wallace (Executive VP), R E Bonnell (Senior VP Finance), William G Paul (Senior VP and General Counsel). K L Smalley (Senior VP), B M Thompson (Senior VP), C L Bowerman (VP Marketing Petroleum Products), J Thomas Boyd (VP Public Affairs), C F Cook (VP Research and Development), J W O'Toole (VP and General Tax Officer), Richard I Robinson (VP Refining), Ray G Steiner (VP Supply and Transportation), D J Tippeconnic (VP Human Resources and Services), J Bryan Whitworth (VP Government Relations), James A Kelly (Comptroller), J J Mulva (Treasurer), L E Burnham (General Auditor), G C Meese (Secretary), L F Francis (Assistant General Tax Officer), D L Cone (Assistant Secretary), Terry B Nance (Assistant Secretary)

PRINCIPAL ACTIVITIES: Phillips is engaged in petroleum exploration and production on a worldwide basis, and petroleum refining and marketing in the United States. The company produces and distributes chemicals in the United States and overseas. The company's operating activities are organized in three groups: exploration and production, gas and gas liquids and petroleum products and chemicals
Principal Subsidiaries: Applied Automation Inc: Phillips 66 Company; Phillips 66 Natural Gas Company; Phillips Driscopipe Inc; Phillips Fibers Corpn; NV Phillips Petroleum Chemicals SA; Phillips Petroleum Co Europe-Africa; Phillips Petroleum Co Norway; Phillips Pipe Line Co; Phillips Puerto Rico Core Inc; Philtankers Inc; Provesta Corporation
Financial Information:

	Dec 31 1985	Dec 31 1986
	$'000	$'000
Total revenues	15,800,000	10,015,000
Income before taxes	1,953,000	692,000
Net income	418,000	228,000
Dividends	542,000	159,000
Dividends per common share	$0.95	$0.70
Earnings per share net	$1.44*	$0.89
Common stock par value	311,000	311,000
Retained income	2,507,000	2,479,000
Shareholders equity	1,644,000	1,724,000

*adjusted for three-for-one stock split in the form of a 200 percent common stock dividend effective May 31 1985

No of Employees: 21,800

PHILLIPS-VAN HEUSEN CORPORATION

1290 Avenue of the Americas, New York, NY 10016
Tel: (212) 541-5200
Telex: RCA 236642 pvh ur

Chairman: Seymour J Phillips
President: Lawrence S Phillips (and Chief Executive Officer)
Senior Executive Officers: Robert F Reilly (Executive VP), A Bongiovi (VP, Secretary and Controller), Walter Zambrovitz (VP Data Processing), Bert G Cox (VP), Michael L Frenkel (VP), Bruce J Klatsky (VP), Murray Weinberg (VP)

PRINCIPAL ACTIVITIES: Manufacture of clothing
Principal Bank: Bankers Trust Company of New York
Financial Information:

	$'000
Sales revenues	550,000

No of Employees: 7,700

PHOENIX MUTUAL LIFE INSURANCE CO

One American Row, Hartford, CT 06115
Tel: (203) 275-5000
Telex: WUT 516915 phoenixmutlife

Chairman: John Gummere (and Chief Executive Officer)
President: Robert W Fiondella
Senior Executive Officers: Philip R Reynolds (Executive VP), Hugh B Campbell Jr (Executive VP), James G Gray Jr (Senior VP, Corporate Finance), Philip R McLoughlin (Executive VP and General Counsel), Charles J Paydos (Executive VP), Terence N Towry (Senior VP)

PRINCIPAL ACTIVITIES: Insurance
Principal Subsidiaries: Phoenix American Life Insurance Company; Phoenix General Insurance Company
Principal Bank: Conneticut Bank & Trust

Financial Information:

	Dec 31 1985	Dec 31 1986
	$'000	$'000
Premium income	713,969	756,984
Investment income	299,539	312,479
Income before taxes(1)	149,974	162,679
Net income(2)	12,638	6,265
Dividends	136,379	147,517

(1) and dividends
(2) after FIT and dividends

No of Employees: 3,420

PHOENIX STEEL CORPORATION

Claymont, DE 19703
Tel: (302) 798-1411
Telex: TWX 510 6660 195 phnix clay

Chairman: Eugene D Hug (and President and Chief Executive Officer)
Senior Executive Officers: E C Alcantara (Executive VP Claymont Division), Vincent J Pongia (VP Operations Phoenixville), Gerald Q Miller (VP Administration), Louis A Fort (Secretary, Treasurer and Chief Financial Officer)

PRINCIPAL ACTIVITIES: Manufacture of steel plate and pipe
Principal Bank: Bank of America
Financial Information:

	$'000
Sales revenues	112,000

No of Employees: 1,000

PIC 'N' SAVE CORPORATION

2430 East Del Amo Boulevard, Carson, CA 90749
Tel: (213) 537 9220

Chairman: Lewis B Merrifield III (and Chief Executive Officer)
President: Arthur Frankel
Senior Executive Officers: Arthur Borie (Executive VP and Chief Operating Officer), Bill M Thomas (Executive VP and Chief Financial Officer) Richard A Frankel (VP and General Manager Merchandising), Kenneth Johnson (VP Store Operations), Raymond L Kugel (Assistant Secretary and Controller), Sheldon S McLusky (VP Distribution and Warehousing), Martin Tepper (VP and Merchandise Manager)

PRINCIPAL ACTIVITIES: Retail stores
Principal Subsidiaries: Pic 'N' Save of Arizona Inc, Pic 'N' Save of California Inc; Pic 'N' Save of New Mexico Inc; Pic 'N' Save of Nevada Inc; Pic 'N' Save of Utah Inc; Pic 'N' Save of Texas Inc; West Coast Liquidators Inc
Principal Bank: Wells Fargo Bank
Financial Information:

	$'000
Sales revenues	303,000

No of Employees: 2,700

PICCADILLY CAFETERIAS INC

PO Box 2467, Baton Rouge, LA 70821
Tel: (504) 293 9440

Chairman: O Q Quick
President: James C Malmberg (and Chief Executive Officer)
Senior Executive Officers: James W Bennett (Executive VP, Treasurer and Chief Financial Officer), James E Durham Jr (Executive VP), Robert W Powell Jr (Executive VP), William B Schwarting (Executive VP), Malcolm T Stein Jr (Executive VP)

PRINCIPAL ACTIVITIES: Restaurants and catering services
Principal Subsidiaries: Institutional Equipment and Interiors
Principal Bank: Fidelity National Bank
Financial Information:

	$'000
Sales revenues	186,800

No of Employees: 5,500

PICKANDS MATHER & CO

1100 Superior Avenue, Cleveland, OH 44114
Tel: (216) 694-5700

President: Robert McInnes (and Chief Executive Officer)
Senior Executive Officers: Henry P Whaley (Group VP), Jay T Ansberry (VP-Administration), Ralph E Berger (VP and Controller), Robert W Biggs (VP and Treasurer), George N Chandler II (VP-Ore and Coal Sales), John O Greenwood (VP-Marine), Scott B Hayes (Senior VP-Coke and Metal Sales), Thomas J Manthey (VP-Public Affairs), Sam R Zickel (VP-Alloy Sales), Neil P Rackliffe (Assistant VP-Ore Sales), James L Tenley (Assistant VP and General Manager-Coal Operations), Frank L Hartman (General Counsel), Robert L Oldenburg (Secretary and Assistant General Counsel), John F Gribben (Assistant Treasurer), Thomas J Burke (Assistant Controller-Financial Reporting), G Bruce Weir (Assistant Controller-Financial Planning)

PRINCIPAL ACTIVITIES: Iron ore mining and processing; coal mining
Parent Company: Moore McCormack Resources Inc, Stamford, CT
Financial Information:

	$'000
Sales revenues	150,000

No of Employees: 7,000

PIEDMONT AVIATION, INC

4001 North Liberty Street, PO Box 2720, Winston-Salem, NC 27156
Tel: (919) 767-5100
Telex: ALWSL 806438

President: William R Howard (and Chief Executive Officer)
Senior Executive Officers: Gordon M Bethune (Senior VP-Operations), Joseph F Healy Jr (Senior VP-Legal Affairs and Secretary), W Howard Mackinnon (Senior VP-Finance and Treasurer), J Leonard Martin (Senior VP-Passenger Services), William G McGee (Senior VP-Marketing), Wilbur A Blackmon (VP-Station Properties and Leases), Howard M Cartwright (VP-Maintenance and Engineering), Joe H Culler (VP-General Aviation), Audree F Long (VP, Controller and Assistant Secretary), Joseph B Wilson (VP-Employee Relations), James E Bradley (Assistant VP-Industrial Relations), Samuel K Carter (Assistant VP-Computer and Communications Services), Alan J Schneider (Assistant Secretary), A James Carter (Assistant Treasurer), Forest G Bates (Assistant Controller), Jack G Walker (Assistant Controller)

PRINCIPAL ACTIVITIES: Piedmont Aviation Inc, is the parent company of Piedmont Airlines and Piedmont General Aviation of Winston-Salem, NC; Henson Airlines of Salisbury, MD; Aviation Supply Corporation of Atlanta, GA; and Air Service Inc of Greensboro, NC. Piedmont Airlines, the largest division, is a full service, transcontinental air carrier serving more than 95 cities in 26 states and the District of Columbia
Trade Names: Piedmont Airlines, Henson Aviation, AVSCO
Principal Subsidiaries: Primary Divisions: Piedmont Airlines; General Aviation Group. Subsidiaries: Henson Aviation (60%); AVSCO (Aviation Supply Corporation); Air Services Inc
Principal Bank: Wachovia Bank & Trust Co NA
Financial Information:

	Dec 31 1986
	$'000
Sales revenues	1,865,473
Net income	72,363
Earnings per share	$3.48
Total shareholders equity	783,888

No of Employees: 20,800

PIEDMONT BANKGROUP INC

PO Box 4751, Church & Ellsworth Streets, Martinsville, VA 24112
Tel: (703) 632 2971

Chairman: Irving M Groves Jr (and President and Chief Executive Officer)
Senior Executive Officers: R Bruce Valley (Senior VP and Senior Administrative Officer)

PRINCIPAL ACTIVITIES: Banking
Principal Subsidiaries: Piedmont Trust Bank Inc

No of Employees: 270

PIEDMONT MANAGEMENT COMPANY INC

99 John Street, New York, NY 10038
Tel: (212) 732 5210

Chairman: R R Richardson
President: Robert M DeMichele (and Chief Executive Officer)
Senior Executive Officers: Peter J Palenzona (VP, Treasurer and Secretary)

PRINCIPAL ACTIVITIES: Financial services including insurance
Principal Subsidiaries: Lexington Management Corporation; Reinsurance Corp of New York
Principal Bank: Morgan Guaranty Trust Company of New York
Financial Information:

	$'000
Revenues	81,700

No of Employees: 135

PIEDMONT NATURAL GAS COMPANY INC

1915 Rexford Road, Charlotte, NC 28211
Tel: (704) 364 3120

Chairman: John H Maxheim (and President and Chief Executive Officer)
Senior Executive Officers: Everette C Hinson (Senior VP Finance), Wilton L Parr (Senior VP Marketing), Nancy G Brinning (VP and Secretary), Ted C Coble (VP, Treasurer and Assistant Secretary), J William Denny (VP Nashville Division), Eugene L Manning (VP Operations), John H Paylor Jr (VP), Barry L Guy (Controller), W R Pritchard Jr (VP Information Systems), Bartlett C Winkler (VP Sales), F Arnold Jenkins (VP Distribution), Ware F Schiefer (VP Transportation and Resources), William L Lindner (VP Technology)

PRINCIPAL ACTIVITIES: Supply of natural gas
Principal Subsidiaries: Mansfield Carbon Products Company; Nashville Gas Company; Piedmont Exploration Company Inc; PNG Energy Company; PNG Exploration Company
Principal Bank: Wachovia Bank and Trust Company
Financial Information:

	$'000
Sales revenues	406,000

No of Employees: 1,620

PIER 1 INC

2520 West Freeway, Fort Worth, TX 76102
Tel: (817) 878 8000

Chairman: Luther A Henderson
President: Clark A Johnson
Senior Executive Officers: Tom Christopher (Senior VP Operations), Robert G Herndon (Senior VP and Chief Financial Officer), Marvin J Girouard (Senior VP Merchandising), David O Martin (VP, Treasurer and Secretary), William N Strassburger (VP and Controller)

PRINCIPAL ACTIVITIES: Retail trade in horticultural supplies and gardening equipment
Financial Information:

	$'000
Sales revenues	191,100

No of Employees: 3,400

PIERCE, S S, CO INC

74 Seneca Street, Dundee, NY 14837
Tel: (607) 243-7171
Telex: 510 582 4577

Chairman: Arthur S Wolcott (and Chief Executive Officer)
President: Julius G Kayser
Senior Executive Officers: Frederick W Leick (Executive VP), D P Naeye (Executive VP), Ricke A Kress (VP Research and Development), Samuel K Wolcott (VP Engineering), Daniel L Sprissler (VP, Secretary and Treasurer), R J Vautour (VP Information Services)

PRINCIPAL ACTIVITIES: Processing of fruit and vegetables; bottled canned and frozen fruit and vegetables; interests in wholesale wines and spirits and textile converting
Principal Bank: Liberty National Bank and Trust Company
Financial Information:

	$'000
Sales revenues	434,800

No of Employees: 3,560

PILGRIM INDUSTRIES INC

PO Box 93, S Texas Street, Pittsburg, TX 75686
Tel: (214) 856-3612
Telex: WUT 735 471 pi inc pibg

Chairman: Lonnie A Pilgrim
President: Bob Hendrix
Senior Executive Officers: James Miner (Senior VP), Clifford E Butler (Senior VP Finance), Mickey Bradshaw (VP)

PRINCIPAL ACTIVITIES: Manufacture of meat processing plant; production of animal feed
Principal Bank: First State Bank
Financial Information:

	$'000
Sales revenues	150,000

No of Employees: 1,200

PILLIOD CABINET CO

105 Woodland Avenue, Swanton, OH 43558
Tel: (419) 826-3540
Telex: TWX 810 490 2351 pilliod swtn

Chairman: George L Pilliod
President: Peter P Pilliod
Senior Executive Officers: John St John (Executive VP), Walter E Hable (Senior VP), Gary Wolson (VP National Accounts), David L Paper (VP Operations), William J Pilliod (VP Finance)

PRINCIPAL ACTIVITIES: Manufacture of furniture
Principal Bank: First National Bank of Toledo
Financial Information:

	$'000
Sales revenues	85,000

No of Employees: 1,300

PILLSBURY CO (THE)

200 South Sixth Street, Minneapolis, MN 55402
Tel: (612) 330-4966

Chairman: John M Stafford (and President and Chief Executive Officer)
Senior Executive Officers: Edward Stringer (Executive VP, General Counsel, Corporate Secretary and Chief Administrative Officer), Roger Hendrick (Chief Financial Officer and Executive VP), Jerry Levin (Executive VP, Corporate Development and Treasurer)

PRINCIPAL ACTIVITIES: The Pillsbury Company is a leading manufacturer of consumer packaged foods including dessert mixes; canned and frozen vegetables; refrigerated breads, rolls and biscuits; frozen pizza; frozen fish and super-premium ice cream. In addition, the Company has become the largest diversified restaurant operator in the world, setting

industry standards for quality, service and value in the fast-food, casual-dining and dinnerhouse markets
Trade Names: Pillsbury, Green Giant, Le Sueur, Hungry Jack, Totino's, Van de Kamp's, Häagen-Dazs, Green's, Hammonds, Gringoire-Brossard, Erasco, Milani, Mac'Ma, Toaster Strudel, Milk Break, Fox Deluxe, B'n B, Poppin' Fresh, BEST, Jack Rabbit, Burger King, Steak and Ale, Bennigan's, Godfather's Pizza, Luther's, The Chart House, Moxie's, Bay Street, Quik Wok, The Whopper and many others
Principal Subsidiaries: The Häagen-Dazs Co Inc; The Häagen-Dazs Shoppe Co Inc; Burger King Corporation; S & A Restaurant Corp; Totino's Finer Foods; Stead & Ale Restaurants Inc; Green Giant Company; Van de Kamp's; Diversified Inc
Financial Information:

	May 31 1986
	$'000
Sales revenues	5,847,900
Net income	208,100
Earnings per share	$4.77
Shareholders equity	1,314,200

No of Employees: 92,900 worldwide

PINCUS BROS, INC

Independence Mall East, Philadelphia, PA 19106
Tel: (215) 922-4900

President: David Pincus (and Secretary and Treasurer)

PRINCIPAL ACTIVITIES: Manufacture of men's apparel
Principal Bank: The Philadelphia National Bank
Financial Information:

	$'000
Sales revenues	60,000

No of Employees: 1,300

PIONEER CORPORATION

PO Box 511, Amarillo, TX 79163
Tel: (806) 373-6054
Telex: TWX 910 8984 108 pioneer ama

Chairman: Laurence R Jones Jr; Vice Chairman: E S Morris (and Senior VP)
President: C D Culver (and Chief Executive Officer)
Senior Executive Officers: Jerry L Hopson (VP and General Counsel), R W Lee (VP Finance and Treasurer), Joseph W Maples Jr (VP)

PRINCIPAL ACTIVITIES: Exploration and production of gas and oil; mineral extraction; supply of oilfield services and equipment; natural gas transmission
Principal Bank: Morgan Guaranty Trust Co
Financial Information:

	$'000
Sales revenues	388,000

No of Employees: 1,500

PIONEER GROUP INC

60 State Street, Boston, MA 02109
Tel: (617) 742 7825

President: John F Cogan Jr
Senior Executive Officers: P A Mullare (Executive VP), James L Spencer (Executive VP and Division President), Frank M Polestra (VP), Albert L Runge (VP and Treasurer), Joseph P Barri (Secretary)

PRINCIPAL ACTIVITIES: Financial investment services
Principal Subsidiaries: Pioneer Fund Inc; Pioneer II Inc; Pioneering Management Corporation
Principal Bank: State Street Bank and Trust
Financial Information:

	$'000
Revenues	33,600

No of Employees: 90

PIONEER HI-BRED INTERNATIONAL, INC

700 Capital Square, 400 Locust, Des Moines, IA 50309
Tel: (515) 245-3500
Telex: ITT 4991456 pioseed dms

Chairman: Thomas N Urban (and President)
Senior Executive Officers: Charles S Johnson (VP Finance), Carrol D Bolen (VP), Donald N Duvick (VP Plant Breeding Division), Suri Sehgal (VP, President Pioneer Overseas Corporation), Edward T Shonsey (VP Administration)

PRINCIPAL ACTIVITIES: Agricultural seed supplies and services
Principal Bank: Northern Trust Co
Financial Information:

	Aug 31 1986
	$'000
Sales revenues	884,726
Net income	73,753
Earnings per share	$2.31
Shareholders equity	510,609

No of Employees: 5,000

PIONEER SAVINGS BANK

5770 Roosevelt Boulevard, Clearwater, FL 33520
Tel: (813) 530 7600

Chairman: William E Nodine (and Chief Executive Officer); Vice Chairman: Edward A Proefke Sr
President: J Blair Culpepper
Senior Executive Officers: Charles W Hall (Senior VP Finance), James B Lannon (Senior VP Real Estate), Parker J Stafford (Senior VP Banking)

PRINCIPAL ACTIVITIES: Banking services; interests in real estate
Principal Bank: Sun Bank

No of Employees: 700

PIONEER STANDARD ELECTRONICS INC

4800 E 131st Street, Cleveland, OH 44105
Tel: (216) 587-3600

Chairman: Preston Heller Jr (and Chief Executive Officer)
President: James L Bayman (and Chief Operating Officer)
Senior Executive Officers: Lawrence R Cowin Jr (VP Finance and Treasurer)

PRINCIPAL ACTIVITIES: Distributor of electronic components and computer products
Principal Bank: AmeriTrust Co
Financial Information:

	Mar 31 1986	Mar 31 1987
	$'000	$'000
Sales revenues	186,805	212,234
Income (loss) before taxes*	(1,079)	3,129
Net income (loss)*	(465)	1,849
Dividends	648	648
Dividends per share	$0.12	$0.12
Earnings (loss) per share*	($0.08)	$0.34
Common stock	5,402	5,402
Retained income	22,691	22,505
Shareholders equity	29,419	29,232

*continuing operations

No of Employees: 837

PIONEER SYSTEMS INC

Hale Road, Pioneer Industrial Park, Manchester, CT 06040
Tel: (203) 644 1581

Chairman: Alan H Greenstadt (and President and Chief Executive Officer); Vice Chairman: Miles Rubin
Senior Executive Officers: Douglas K Smith (Executive VP), William T Hyland (VP Finance and Treasurer), Robert B Di Paola (Secretary)

PRINCIPAL ACTIVITIES: Manufacture of specialty textile products
Principal Subsidiaries: Kennedy Carter Corporation; Pioneer International Corporation; Flight Designs Inc; Pioneer Parachute Company Inc; Pioneer Recovery Systems Inc; Putnam-Gellman Corporation; Applikay Textile Process Corporation; Putnam-Herzel Finishing Company Inc; Vogart Crafts Corporation; Craftint Corporation; Diane Inc; Kugel Company Inc; Trio 3 Inc; Vogart Company Inc
Principal Bank: Chemical Bank
Financial Information:

	$'000
Sales revenues	34,000

No of Employees: 1,300

PIPER AIRCRAFT CORPORATION

2926 Piper Drive, Vero Beach, FL 32960
Tel: (305) 567 4361

Chairman: Robert T Campion (and Chairman Executive Committee)
President: Robert J Wyma (and Chief Executive Officer)
Senior Executive Officers: Robert D Dickerson (Executive VP and Chief Operating Officer), Vincent J Montuoro (Senior VP), Dudley C Phillips (Senior VP), Alfred J Koontz Jr (Senior VP Finance), Norman A Barkeley (VP), Morgan C Brown III (VP and Secretary), Marion J Dees Jr (VP Engineering), Harry M Graham (VP Special Projects), C Raymond Johnson (VP Airline Division), George W Mabey (VP Personnel), John S McCollom (VP Special Projects), Stephen D Natcher (VP), A W Newman (VP Marketing and Sales), Donald R Schort Jr (VP), Robert L Smith (VP and General Manager Lakeland), James N Thayer (VP)

PRINCIPAL ACTIVITIES: Manufacture of aircraft and aircraft components
Parent Company: Bangor Punta Corporation-Ultimate holding company-Lear Siegler Inc
Financial Information:

	$'000
Sales revenues	234,000

No of Employees: 3,200

PIPER INDUSTRIES, INC

5485 Beltline Road, Dallas, TX 75240
Tel: (214) 458 7595

President: Paul P Piper Jr
Senior Executive Officers: Bobby F Sammons (Executive VP and Secretary)

PRINCIPAL ACTIVITIES: Sheet metal work; manufacture of agricultural equipment; plastic products
Principal Bank: National Bank of Commerce
Financial Information:

	$'000
Sales revenues	55,000

No of Employees: 850

PIPER JAFFRAY INC

Piper Jaffray Tower, 222 South 9th Street, Minneapolis, MN 55402
Tel: (612) 342 6000

Chairman: Harry C Piper
President: William H Ellis (and Chief Operating Officer)
Senior Executive Officers: Addison L Piper (Chief Executive Officer), Harold J Bloom (Executive VP and Controller), Stanley R Cowle (Executive VP), David P Crosby (Managing Director), Dan L Lastovich (Managing Director), DeLos V Steenson (Managing Director), Richard J Stream (Managing Director), Gary M Petrucci (Senior VP), Walter E Pratt (Senior VP, Secretary and Treasurer), Fred A Sirianni (Senior VP), John R Winsor (Senior VP)

PRINCIPAL ACTIVITIES: Financial investment services
Principal Subsidiaries: Comprehensive Tax Management Inc; The Piper Capital Group Inc; Piper Jaffray & Hopwood Inc; PJH Commodities Inc
Principal Bank: First National Bank
Financial Information:

	$'000
Revenues	159,000

No of Employees: 1,600

PITNEY BOWES INC

World Headquarters, Stamford, CT 06926-0700
Tel: (203) 356-5000
Telex: WUT 643867 pitbow std

Chairman: George B Harvey (and President and Chief Executive Officer)
Senior Executive Officers: James L Bast (President, Pitney Bowes Business Systems), Hiro R Hiranandani (President, Pitney Bowes Business Systems-International), Marc C Breslawsky (President and Chief Executive Officer, Dictaphone Corp), Carmine F Adimando (VP, Finance and Administration), Carole F St Mark (VP Corporate Planning and Development), Guy L Fougere (VP, Corporate Engineering and Technology), Thomas F McGarry (VP Corporate Communications), Elton R Vogel (President, Pitney Bowes Business Supplies), Harry W Neinstedt (President, Pitney Baves Financial Services)

PRINCIPAL ACTIVITIES: Pitney Bowes is a multinational business equipment, supplies and financial services company, which develops and supplies, mailing, shipping, copying, voice processing, facsimile, and retail systems, along with business forms and supplies, and equipment leasing
Principal Subsidiaries: Pitney Bowes Business Systems-International; Pitney Bowes Austria GesmbH; Pitney Bowes of Canada Ltd; Pitney Bowes Oy (Finland); Pitney Bowes Germany GmbH; Dodwell Pitney Bowes KK (Japan); Pitney Bowes Sweden AB; Pitney Bowes Switzerland AG; Pitney Bowes PLC (UK); Pitney Bowes Business Supplies; Monarch Marking Systems Inc; Monarch Marking Systems Australia Pty Ltd; Pitney Bowes Facsimile Systems; Monarch Marking Systems Ltd (Canada); Monarch Marking System de Mexico SA de CV; Pitney Bowes Marking Systems Ltd (UK); Wheeler Group Inc; Pitney Bowes Credit Corpn; PB Leasing Ltd (UK); Dictaphone Corpn; Dictaphone Canada Ltd; Dictaphone International AG (Switzerland); Dictaphone Co Ltd (UK); Data Documents SA (Belgium); Data Documents Inc; Pitney Bowes Financial Services; Pitney Bowes of Canada-Leasing Division; Dictating Systems; Monarch Marking (SEA) Pte Ltd (Singapore); Pitney Bowes France SA (France); Data Documents Systems; Adrema Leasing Corpn (Germany); Data Documents BV (Netherlands); Colonial Pacific Leasing
Principal Bank: Chase Manhattan Bank
Financial Information:

	Dec 31 1985	Dec 31 1986
	$'000	$'000
Sales revenues	1,815,808	1,986,686
Income before taxes	163,025	201,659
Net income	141,694	166,039
Dividends	46,904	51,487
Dividends per share	$0.60	$0.66
Earnings per share	$1.90	$2.12
Common stock	79,127	79,225
Shareholders equity	802,847	912,921

No of Employees: 29,166

PITT-DES MOINES, INC

Neville Island, Pittsburgh, PA 15225
Tel: (412) 331-3000
Cable: PITTDEMOIN
Telex: 866-434

Chairman: W R Jackson Sr

President: W R Jackson Jr
Senior Executive Officers: L E Anderson Jr (VP Technical Development), R D Northcutt (VP Operations), R A Byers (VP Finance), E Halecky (VP Service Centers), John C Murphy (VP Engineering)

PRINCIPAL ACTIVITIES: Construction of specialty storage systems; civil engineering; aerospace equipment; steel service centers
Principal Subsidiaries: PDM International Ltd; Hydrostorage; Pittsburgh-Des Moines Corporation; PDM Strocal, Inc
Principal Bank: Mellon Bank
Financial Information:

	$'000
Sales revenues	233,600

No of Employees: 1,776

PITTSBURGH CORNING CORPORATION

800 Presque Isle Drive, Pittsburgh, PA 15239
Tel: (412) 327-6100
Telex: TWX 510 468 5520 pgh corning pg

President: John L Baldwin
Senior Executive Officers: J G Chase (VP Sales and Marketing), C A Francik (VP Manufacturing), R C McPherson (VP Human Resources), John H Price Jr (VP Finance), J H Coleman (Advertising Manager)

PRINCIPAL ACTIVITIES: Manufacture of glass products
Parent Company: PPG Industries Inc; Corning Glass Works
Principal Bank: Lloyds Bank International
Financial Information:

	$'000
Sales revenues	60,000

No of Employees: 1,150

PITTSTON COMPANY

One Pickwick Plaza, Greenwich, CT 06830
Tel: (203) 622-0900
Telex: ITT 421129 pco ui

Chairman: Paul W Douglas (and President and Chief Executive Officer)
Senior Executive Officers: Nicholas T Camicia (Chairman Finance Committee), Joseph C Farrell (Executive VP Coal), David L Marshall (Executive VP Finance, Administration and Corporate Strategy), Robert D Duke (Senior VP and General Counsel), Williams E Furlong (VP and Treasurer), Frank T Lennon (VP Corporate Administration), Jack D McDaniel (VP Corporate Development), Jonathan M Sturman (VP Analysis and Planning)

PRINCIPAL ACTIVITIES: Mining; freight forwarding by air; security transportation services; vehicle leasing
Principal Bank: Morgan Guaranty Trust Company of New York
Financial Information:

	Dec 31 1985 $'000	Dec 31 1986 $'000
Sales revenues	1,250,800	1,189,949
Net income	277	10,016
Earnings per share	$0.01	$0.27
Shareholders equity		500,685

No of Employees: 12,600

PITTWAY CORPORATION

333 Skokie Blvd, Northbrook, IL 60062
Tel: (312) 498-1260

Chairman: King W Harris (and Chief Executive Officer); Vice Chairman: Leo A Guthart
Senior Executive Officers: Irving B Harris (Chairman Executive Committee), George Barr (VP), Maurice Coleman (VP), Nathan Verger (VP), Ervin J LeCoque Jr (VP), Howard L Isenberg (VP), Thomas L Dempsey (VP), Sal F Marino (VP), Fred Conforti (VP), Carl A Siebel (VP), Paul R Gauvreau (VP Finance)

PRINCIPAL ACTIVITIES: Manufacture of security and safety equipment including burglar alarms and fire and smoke detectors; publishing of periodicals; plastics and plastic products; aerosol valves; property and real estate
Parent Company: Standard Shares Inc
Principal Subsidiaries: Alarm Device Mfg Co; Barr Co; Sequist Valve Co; Penton/Industrial Publishing Co; BRK Electronics
Principal Bank: Continental Illinois National Bank and Trust Company of Chicago
Financial Information:

	Dec 31 1985 $'000	Dec 31 1986 $'000
Sales revenues	541,310	585,738
Net income	31,117	27,608
Earnings per share	$6.78	$6.02
Shareholders equity	260,271	282,206

No of Employees: 6,900

PIZZA INN, INC

2930 Stemmons Fwy, PO Box 660193, Dallas, TX 75222
Tel: (214) 638-7250

Chairman: F J Spillman (and President)
Senior Executive Officers: R D Phillips (Executive VP Finance), Gayle G Cannon (VP, Secretary and General Counsel), William Curley (VP Franchise), Bill G Daily (VP Real Estate and Construction), Roger Goertz (VP Advertising), Mike Goodfellow (VP Management and Planning), Robert A McComas (VP Personnel), Linda H Sleeper (VP and Treasurer), Joseph J Wesner (VP and Controller), George W Wragg (VP Distribution)

PRINCIPAL ACTIVITIES: Operation of pizza restaurants
Principal Bank: MBank
Financial Information:

	$'000
Sales revenues	199,000

No of Employees: 6,000

PLANNING RESEARCH CORPORATION

1500 Planning Research One, McLean, VA 22102
Tel: (703) 556-1000
Cable: PLNRESCORP
Telex: 248372

Chairman: John M Toups (and Chief Executive Officer)
President: Wayne Shelton (and Chief Operating Officer)
Senior Executive Officers: Richard D Brown (VP Finance)

PRINCIPAL ACTIVITIES: Technology-based professional services firm specializing in systems integration
Principal Bank: Morgan Guaranty Trust Co of New York
Financial Information:

	$'000
Sales revenues	372,000

No of Employees: 7,000

PLANTERS CORPORATION

131 North Church Street, Nash County, Rocky Mount, NC 27801
Tel: (919) 977 8211

Chairman: James B Powers (and Chief Executive Officer)
President: J Richard Futrell Jr
Senior Executive Officers: William W Eskird Jr (Executive VP Loan Administrator and Investment), Frank L Pattillo (Executive VP), W Douglas Starr (Executive VP Marketing, Human Resources and Strategic Planning), Cheryl G Ayers (Assistant VP and Assistant Secretary)

PRINCIPAL ACTIVITIES: Banking

Financial Information:

	Dec 31 1985
	$'000
Revenues	68,160
Net income	6,270

No of Employees: 700

PLANTRONICS, INC

1762 Technology Drive, San Jose, CA 95110
Tel: (408) 998-8388

President: Neil J Hynes (and Chief Executive Officer)
Senior Executive Officers: Thomas A Blinn (Senior VP), Carlos Garner (VP Manufacturing Operations), Robert Lee (VP Personnel), Thomas W Stuart (VP, Controller and Real Estate Officer), John Tymoczko Jr (VP)

PRINCIPAL ACTIVITIES: Manufacture of telecommunications equipment including telephone and telex equipment and radio and television broadcasting equipment
Principal Subsidiaries: Plantronics/Santa Cruz; Kentrox Industries; Zehntel Inc; Fredricks Electronics Corp; Wilcom Products Inc
Principal Bank: First Interstate Bank
Financial Information:

	1986
	$'000
Sales revenues	99,580

No of Employees: 1,500

PLASTI-LINE INC

623 East Emory Road, PO Box 5066, Knoxville, TN 37928
Tel: (615) 938 1511

Chairman: Nicholas H Carlozzi
President: James R Martin
Senior Executive Officers: John J Cioffi (Senior VP Marketing), Ted V Christensen (VP Sales), Bryan J Collier (VP Finance), William E Grove (VP Operations), Charles F Ramsay (VP Engineering), Edward L Schmidt (VP Sales)

PRINCIPAL ACTIVITIES: Manufacture and installation of a range of illuminated plastic signs
Principal Bank: First American National Bank of Knoxville
Financial Information:

	$'000
Sales revenues	39,300

No of Employees: 570

PLASTRONIC ENGINEERING CO, INC

35 Walnut Street, Haverhill, MA 01830
Tel: (617) 372-7703

President: Raymond A De Nuccio
Senior Executive Officers: James R Mignanelli (VP)

PRINCIPAL ACTIVITIES: Thermosett compression and transfer molders of plastic shells, cases and hybrids for the electronic and allied industries
Trade Names: PECO
Principal Bank: Arlington Trust Company
Financial Information:

	$'000
Sales revenues	500,000

No of Employees: 20

PLAYBOY ENTERPRISES, INC

919 N Michigan Avenue, Chicago, IL 60611
Tel: (312) 751-8000
Telex: 190166 PLY BY UT

Chairman: Hugh M Hefner (and Chief Executive Officer)
President: Christie Hefner (and Vice Chairman and Chief Operating Officer)
Corporate Officers: Richard S Rosenzweig (Executive VP, Office of the Chairman), James P Radtke (Senior VP, Chief Financial Officer), John A Scott (Senior VP, and Publishing Group President), Howard Shapiro (Senior VP, Law and Administration, and General Counsel), A William Stokkan (Senior VP, and Licensing and Merchandising Group President), Dale C Gordon (VP, Secretary and Associate General Counsel), Robyn L Radomski (VP, Corporate Communications and Public Affairs), Russell A Ringl (VP, Human Resources), Thomas W Aubin (Corporate Controller), Rebecca S Maskey (Treasurer)

PRINCIPAL ACTIVITIES: Publisher of magazine and newsstand specials, produces video programming for pay television and home video; merchandises Playboy's Rabbit Head Design and other trademarks through product, magazine and club licensing; publishes catalogs as part of its direct marketing operation
Trade Names: Playboy, Playmate, Rabbit Head Design
Principal Subsidiaries: Boarts International Inc; Playboy Clubs International Inc; Playboy Video Corporation; Licensing Unlimited Inc; Playboy Sales Inc
Principal Bank: American National Bank and Trust Company of Chicago
Financial Information:

	Jun 30 1987
	$'000
Sales revenues	161,767
Income before taxes	11,076
Net income	11,117
Earnings per share	$1.18
Retained income	13,969
Shareholders equity	31,348

No of Employees: 600

PLENUM PUBLISHING CORPORATION

233 Spring Street, New York, NY 10013
Tel: (212) 620 8000
Cable: PLENUMCORP
Telex: 421139

Chairman: Martin E Tash (and President)
Senior Executive Officers: Mark Shaw (Executive VP), Ghanshyam A Patel (Treasurer and Chief Financial Officer), Bernard Bressler (Secretary), John Matzka (VP and Managing Editor), Harry Allcock (VP, IFI/Plenum Data Corporation and VP, Career Placement Registry Inc), Marshall Lebowitz (VP JS Canner & Company Inc), Carol Bischoff (Assistant VP and Managing Editor, Plenum Press Journals), John Hwang (Assistant VP and Managing Editor, Consultants Bureau Journals)

PRINCIPAL ACTIVITIES: Publishing of specialty scientific books and periodicals
Principal Subsidiaries: Da Capo Press Inc; IFI/Plenum Data Corporation; J S Canner and Company Inc
Principal Bank: Bank of New York
Financial Information:

	Dec 31 1985	Dec 31 1986
	$'000	$'000
Sales revenues	36,824	38,063
Income before taxes	15,889	19,000
Net income	10,039	12,235
Dividends	2,212	2,403
Dividends per share	$0.96	$1.04
Earnings per share	$1.74	$2.12
Common stock	251	578
Retained income	23,839	29,374
Shareholders equity	23,898	33,741

No of Employees: 310

PLIBRICO CO

1800 N Kingsbury Street, Chicago, IL 60614
Tel: (312) 549-7014
Telex: TWX 910 2215220 plibrico co

Chairman: Wm A Schaefer
President: Robert W Schaefer
Senior Executive Officers: Robert E Fisher (Executive VP, USA), Robert G Schultz (VP Purchasing and Secretary)

PRINCIPAL ACTIVITIES: Manufacture of heavy industrial plant
Principal Bank: The First National Bank of Chicago
Financial Information:

	$'000
Sales revenues	150,000

No of Employees: 200

PLUM CREEK TIMBER COMPANY, INC

PO Box 160, Columbia Falls, MT 59912
Tel: (406) 892-2141

President: D D Leland (and Chief Executive Officer)
Senior Executive Officers: Rick Holley (VP Finance and Planning), N J Kirkmire (VP Corporate Affairs), K W Kroschel (VP Law), Gary Tucker (VP Forest Products)

PRINCIPAL ACTIVITIES: Timber industries; production of building materials including particleboard and plywood
Parent Company: Burlington Northern Inc, Seattle, WA
Financial Information:

	$'000
Sales revenues	170,000

No of Employees: 1,650

PLUMLEY RUBBER CO

100 Plumley Drive, Paris, TN 38242
Tel: (901) 642-5582
Telex: TWX 810 5955560 plumley rubber

Chairman: Harold J Plumley
President: Richard Plumley
Senior Executive Officers: James Bergman (VP Auto Sales and Marketing), Robert Bertouille (VP Consumer Products), Robert Rogers (VP Administration), Priscilla Lemons (VP Industrial Relations), Len McClearn (VP Quality Assurance and Purchasing), Stephen Plumley (VP Research and Development), William Plumley (VP and Treasurer)

PRINCIPAL ACTIVITIES: Production of rubber and rubber goods including hose, tubing and automotive products; plastic products
Principal Bank: Citizens Fidelity Bank
Financial Information:

	$'000
Sales revenues	40,000

No of Employees: 900

PLUSWOOD INC

PO Box 2248, Oshkosh, WI 54903
Tel: (414) 235-0440
Telex: TWX 910 266 1058 pluswood osh

President: F L Boschwitz
Senior Executive Officers: L Rochlin (VP), A Boschwitz (Secretary and Treasurer)

PRINCIPAL ACTIVITIES: Lumber and wood products; building materials
Principal Bank: Harris Trust and Savings Bank
Financial Information:

	$'000
Sales revenues	120,000

No of Employees: 350

PLY-GEM INDUSTRIES, INC

919 Third Avenue, New York, NY 10022
Tel: (212) 832-1550
Telex: PLYGEM 668356 UM

Chairman: Jeffrey J Silverman (and President)
Senior Executive Officers: Herbert Dodskin (Executive VP), Peter Hewitt (VP), Stanford Zeisel (Secretary/Treasurer)

PRINCIPAL ACTIVITIES: Major products include specialty woods, plywood wall paneling, fire-retardant plywood and lumber, laminated particleboard, vinyl siding, insulated replacement windows and vacuum cleaner bags
Principal Subsidiaries: Studley Paper Co Inc; Air Filters Inc; Ply-Gem Manufacturing Division; Goldenberg Plywood and Lumber Co; Goldenhill Wood Products Inc; Allied Plywood Corp; Hoover Treater Wood Products; Great Lakes Window Inc; Vaciform Inc; 42 locations throughout the United States and Canada
Principal Bank: Chase Manhattan Bank
Financial Information:

	Dec 31 1985 $'000	Dec 31 1986 $'000
Sales revenues	166,477	226,436
Income before taxes	5,720	12,744
Net income	3,536	8,146
Dividends	563	919
Dividends per share	$0.1066	$0.12
Earnings per share	$0.56	$0.85
Common stock	1,849	2,781
Retained income	19,145	26,372
Shareholders equity	44,842	87,734

No of Employees: 1,500

PLYMOUTH RUBBER CO, INC

Revere Street, Canton, MA 02021
Tel: (617) 828-0220
Telex: RCA 200128 plyrub ur

President: Maurice J Hamilburg (and Treasurer and Chief Executive Officer)
Senior Executive Officers: Joseph D Hamilburg (VP), Duane E Wheeler (VP Finance), Sheldon Leppo (VP Research and Development), F D DiGiovine (VP Manufacturing), John E O'Brien (VP Vinyl Films), Alan I Eisenberg (VP Marketing), Michael A Halperson (VP Consumer Products), Joel A Kozol (Clerk and Secretary)

PRINCIPAL ACTIVITIES: Manufacture of rubber and plastic products including rubber and vinyl coated fabrics, cable insulation products, rubber bands and plastic sheet, high specification PVC films for laminating and electrical applications
Trade Names: PLYMOUTH/BISHOP
Principal Bank: The First National Bank of Boston
Financial Information:

	Nov 30 1985 $'000	Nov 29 1986 $'000
Sales revenues	52,007	48,404
(Loss)*	(348)	(1,861)
Net (loss)	(503)	-
(Loss) per share	($0.30)	($1.12)
Common stock	8,307	8,307
Retained (deficit)	(1,643)	(3,500)
Shareholders equity	6,658	4,798

*from continuing operations

No of Employees: 365

PLYWOOD PANELS INC

100 Napoleon Avenue, New Orleans, LA 70175
Tel: (504) 899-5691
Telex: RCA 266044 discurd ur

Chairman: J D Prince
President: L R Haan

Senior Executive Officers: J N Haynie (Executive VP), J L Sullivan (VP and Treasurer), J C Roark (VP Sales)

PRINCIPAL ACTIVITIES: Timber products particularly plywood wall panels
Principal Bank: Wells Fargo National Association
Financial Information:

	$'000
Sales revenues	60,000

No of Employees: 200

PNC FINANCIAL CORP
5th & Wood Streets, Pittsburgh, PA 15265
Tel: (412) 355-2666
Telex: 866533 FIRSTBANKPGH

Chairman: Roger S Hillas
President: Thomas H O'Brien
Senior Executive Officers: J David Grissom (Vice Chairman), Edward P Junker III (Vice Chairman), Robert C Milsom (Vice Chairman), David L Tressler Sr (Vice Chairman), Marlyn E Carle (Senior VP and Controller), Daniel F Gillis (Senior VP, Human Resources), Walter E Gregg Jr (Senior VP and Chief Regulatory Counsel), W Lee Hoskins (Senior VP and Chief Economist), William J Johns (Senior VP, Management Information and Reporting), David J King (Senior VP and Chief Financial Officer), Allan C Kirkman (Senior VP and Chief Planning Officer), Joseph J Nelson (Senior VP and Director of Taxes), James F O'Day (Senior VP, Governmental Affairs), Joseph A Richardson Jr (Senior VP, General Counsel and Secretary), Marlin W Stumpff (Senior VP and General Auditor), Charles J Thayer (Senior VP and Treasurer), Patricia D Yoder (Senior VP, Corporate Affairs)

PRINCIPAL ACTIVITIES: Commercial, retail and international banking. Trust and investment advisory services. Mortgage banking
Principal Subsidiaries: Banking:- Pittsburgh National Bank; Provident National Bank; Citizens Fidelity Corporation; Louisville, KY; Marine Bank; Northeastern Bank of Pennsylvania; The Hershey Bank; PNC National Bank. Non-banking:- Provident National Investment Corp; PNC Funding Corp; PINACO Inc; Pittsburgh National Life Insurance Company; PNC Trust Company of Florida NA; PNC International Finance NV; PNC Commercial Corp
Principal Bank: Pittsburgh National
Financial Information:

	Dec 31 1985 $'000	Dec 31 1986 $'000
Income before taxes	285,652	333,473
Net income	228,831	286,307
Dividends-common	73,070	86,997
Dividends per share	$1.28	$1.47
Earnings per share(1)	$3.63	$4.44
Earnings per share(2)	$3.44	$4.19
Common stock	308,689	329,155
Retained income	917,673	1,130,262
Shareholders equity	1,395,732	1,693,605
Deposits	14,633,907	17,610,572
Total assets	22,760,745	26,936,055

(1) primary
(2) fully diluted

No of Employees: 11,381

PNEUMO ABEX CORPORATION
Prudential Tower, Boston, MA 02199
Tel: (617) 375-1200
Telex: 6817526 PNMOABX

President: Norman J Ryker (and Chief Executive Officer)
Senior Executive Officers: Charles J Moisen (Senior VP and Chief Financial Officer), Christoph L Hoffmann (Senior VP)

PRINCIPAL ACTIVITIES: Manufacture of landing gear and flight controls for the aircraft industry; friction braking materials for vehicles
Parent Company: IC Industries
Principal Subsidiaries: Cleveland Pneumatic Co
Principal Bank: AmeriTrust Co
Financial Information:

	$'000
Sales revenues	900,500
Operating income	118,100

No of Employees: 9,500

PO FOLKS, INC
PO Box 17406, 435 Metroplex Drive, Nashville, TN 37217
Tel: (615) 366-0900

Chairman: R B Davenport III
President: Clyde E Culp III (and Chief Executive Officer)
Senior Executive Officers: D D Bartel (VP), R D Kirstien (VP), Bruce McGlinchey (VP), Harvey Rothstein (VP), Walter J Spear (VP and Treasurer)

PRINCIPAL ACTIVITIES: Restaurants
Principal Bank: Third National Bank in Nashville
Financial Information:

	$'000
Sales revenues	142,600

No of Employees: 5,800

POGO PRODUCING COMPANY
600 Travis Street, PO Box 61289, Houston, TX 77002
Tel: (713) 651 4300

Chairman: William C Liedtke Jr (and Chief Executive Officer)
President: William E Gipson (and Chief Operating Officer)
Senior Executive Officers: Bill D Holland (Executive VP), W M Brumley Jr (Senior VP Administration and Accounting), Lawrence A Turner (Senior VP Operations), Paul G Van Wagenen (Senior VP and Legal Counsel), John B Carter Jr (Senior VP Finance), James C Kempner (Senior VP Corporate Development and Treasurer), Hunter L Martin (VP and Secretary), Thomas E Hart (Controller)

PRINCIPAL ACTIVITIES: Oil and gas exploration and production
Principal Bank: Chemical Bank
Financial Information:

	$'000
Sales revenues	240,300

No of Employees: 190

POLAROID CORPORATION
549 Technology Square, Cambridge, MA 02139
Tel: (617) 577-2000
Telex: RCA 200083 pol ur

Chairman: William J McCune Jr
President: I MacAllister Booth (and Chief Executive Officer)
Senior Executive Officers: Sheldon A Buckler (Executive VP, Director of Technical and Industrial Photography), Milton S Dietz (Senior VP, Strategic Planning and Corporate Development), Peter O Kliem (Senior VP and Director of Research and Engineering), Harvey H Thayer (Senior VP Finance), Owen J Gaffney (Group VP, Magnetics), Joseph J McLaughlin (Group VP, Worldwide Marketing), William J O'Neill Jr (Group VP, Consumer Photography), Gerald A Sudbey (Group VP, Worldwide Manufacturing), Edward R Bedrosian (VP and Treasurer), Lee C Brewer (VP, International Marketing Operations), Robert M Delahunt (VP, Worldwide Industrial Marketing), Richard F deLima (VP and Secretary), Peter K Eichorn (VP, North American Marketing Operations), George H Fernald Jr (VP, Diversified Business Development), John T Harlor (VP Corporate Personnel), Christopher C Ingraham (VP, Corporate Materials Management and Corporate Systems), Hugh R MacKenzie (VP, Engineering), Harold S Page (VP, Director of Quality

Assurance), Julius Silver (VP and Chairman of the Executive Committee), Graham M Brown, Jr (Controller), Gerald R Dicker (Assistant Secretary), Edward M Safran (Assistant Treasurer), LLoyd D Taylor (Senior Research Fellow)

PRINCIPAL ACTIVITIES: Polaroid Corporation designs, manufactures, and markets worldwide a variety of products primarily in instant image recording fields. These include instant photographic cameras and films, magnetic media, light polarizing filters and lenses, and diversified chemical, optical and commercial products. The principal products of the Company are used in amateur and professional photography, industry, science, medicine and education

Financial Information:

	Dec 31 1985	Dec 31 1986
	$'000	$'000
Sales revenues net	1,295,200	1,629,200
Income before taxes	40,200	135,200
Net income	36,900	103,500
Dividends	31,000	31,000
Dividends per share	$1.00	$1.00
Earnings per share	$1.19	$3.34
Common stock	32,900	32,900
Retained income	814,200	886,700
Shareholders equity	922,200	994,700

No of Employees: 14,765 (including approx 1,900 worldwide temporary employees)

POLICY MANAGEMENT SYSTEMS CORPORATION

One PMS Center, PO Box 10, Blythewood, SC 29016
Tel: (803) 735 4000

Chairman: G Larry Wilson (and President)
Senior Executive Officers: David T Bailey (Executive VP Systems Services), Charles E Callahan (Senior VP Information Network Services), Donald A Coggiola (Executive VP Marketing), Robert L Gresham (Executive VP Operations and Secretary), Robert A Sizemore (Executive VP Insurance Services)

PRINCIPAL ACTIVITIES: Computer services including programs and software
Principal Bank: South Carolina National Bank
Financial Information:

	$'000
Sales revenues	151,000

No of Employees: 1,500

POLK, R L, & CO

431 Howard Street, Detroit, MI 48231
Tel: (313) 961-9470
Telex: WUT 235781 rl polk det

Chairman: Charles A Wollenzin Jr
President: John M O'Hara (and Chief Executive Officer)
Senior Executive Officers: B A Bates Jr (Executive VP Finance and Administration), Stephen R Polk (Executive VP Operations), J C Cirrincoine (VP and General Manager Motor Statistical Division), John P Heil (VP), John K Johnson (VP Marketing Services Division), D E McKenzie Jr (VP Purchasing), R D Monforton (VP and General Manager Directory Division), William T Stumb (VP and General Manager Bank Services Division)

PRINCIPAL ACTIVITIES: Publishing
Principal Bank: National Bank of Detroit
Financial Information:

	$'000
Sales revenues	170,000

No of Employees: 5,300

POLYCAST TECHNOLOGY CORPORATION

69 Southfield Avenue, Stamford, CT 06902
Tel: (203) 327 6010

Chairman: Howard R Curd
President: Richard J Schneider (and Chief Executive Officer)
Senior Executive Officers: Richard L Garthwaite (VP), Frank B Kaplan (VP and Treasurer), Mario Taracena (VP), C W Cox (Secretary)

PRINCIPAL ACTIVITIES: Manufacture of plastic products including cell cast acrylic sheet
Principal Bank: Chemical Bank
Financial Information:

	$'000
Sales revenues	55,000

No of Employees: 550

POLYCHROME CORPORATION

On the Hudson, Yonkers, NY 10702
Tel: (914) 965-8800

President: Joseph L Piot (and Chief Executive Officer)
Senior Executive Officers: Simon Chu (Senior VP), Stanley P Eysmann (Senior VP), Enrique Levy (Senior VP), Gerald Mahoney (Senior VP Finance and Administration), Donald O Wheeler (Senior VP Sales), Ronald E Muzzillo (VP Sales and Marketing), William H Saltzman (VP, Assistant Secretary and Director Legal Department), Patrick J Walsh (VP Finance and Chief Financial Officer)

PRINCIPAL ACTIVITIES: Specialty chemicals for printing and photographic industry; photographic and copying equipment
Parent Company: Dic American Inc
Principal Bank: Chemical Bank
Financial Information:

	$'000
Sales revenues	202,000

No of Employees: 1,850

POLYSIUS CORPORATION

180 Interstate North, Atlanta, GA 30339
Tel: (404) 955-3660
Telex: WUT 542 850 polat atl

President: Roger M Scovil
Senior Executive Officers: Gerd A Schroth (VP Marketing), A Penninger (Treasurer, Manager, Finance and Administration)

PRINCIPAL ACTIVITIES: Manufacture of machinery and equipment for the cement industry
Parent Company: Krupp Polysius AG, Beckum-Neubeckum, Germany
Principal Bank: Chase Manhattan Bank
Financial Information:

	$'000
Sales revenues	92,000

Principal Shareholders: Fried Krupp GmbH, Essen, Germany
No of Employees: 100

PONDEROSA INC

PO Box 578, Dayton, OH 45401
Tel: (513) 890 6400

Chairman: Gerald S Office Jr (and President and Chief Executive Officer)
Senior Executive Officers: W R Menzel (Executive VP), R C Lawson II (Senior VP and Chief Accounting Officer), J R Mohr (Senior VP and Legal Counsel), J E Thompson (Senior VP and Chief Financial Officer), R T Griffin (VP Administration Services), M J Lawless (VP Corporate Planning), H W Miller (VP Management Information Services), Dale R Ridenour (Treasurer)

PRINCIPAL ACTIVITIES: Restaurants and catering services
Principal Subsidiaries: Casa Lupita Restaurants Inc; ESI Meats Inc; Scottys Hamburger Systems Inc
Principal Bank: Ameritrust Company

Financial Information:

	$'000
Sales revenues	490,000

No of Employees: 26,000

POPE & TALBOT, INC

1500 S W 1st Avenue, Portland, OR 97201
Tel: (503) 228-9161
Telex: WUT 360216 potalbot ptl

Chairman: Peter T Pope (and Chief Executive Officer)
President: R S Mason (and Chief Operating Officer)
Senior Executive Officers: George Reinbacher (Group VP Tissue Products), Michael Flannery (Group VP Wood Products), William G Frohmayer (Group VP Fiber Products), Carlos M Lamadrid (Senior VP Finance)

PRINCIPAL ACTIVITIES: Production of lumber, chips and logs; manufacture of market pulp and tissue paper
Principal Subsidiaries: Pope & Talbot Ltd; Pope & Talbot Pulp; Pope & Talbot Wis Inc; Penn Timber Inc
Principal Bank: US National of Oregon
Financial Information:

	Dec 31 1985	Dec 31 1986
	$'000	$'000
Sales revenues	325,203	310,228
Income before taxes	7,733	21,143
Net income	6,648	15,815
Dividends	4,796	4,803
Dividends per share	$0.80	$0.80
Earnings per share	$0.55	$1.32
Common stock(1)(2)	11,990	12,010
Retained income	98,464	109,476
Shareholders equity	102,602	113,986

(1) number of shares in thousands
(2) adjusted for a 2-for-1 stock split in May 1987

No of Employees: 2,200

POPE, EVANS & ROBBINS INC

49 W 37th Street, New York, NY 10018
Tel: (212) 921-4306

President: Joseph E Robbins
Senior Executive Officers: Harry Rabinowitz (Executive VP Finance, Secretary and Treasurer)

PRINCIPAL ACTIVITIES: Production of protective fabrics and clothing
Principal Subsidiaries: (100% owned unless stated): Pope Combustion Systems Inc; PER Buying Co Inc; Putnam Mills Corp; Fluidized Combustion Co (50%); De Rotchild Knitwear Inc
Principal Bank: Citibank
Financial Information:

	$'000
Sales revenues	62,000

No of Employees: 400

POPSICLE INDUSTRIES, INC

110 Rte 4, Englewood, NJ 07631
Tel: (201) 567-8500

President: Rupert A Walters (and Chief Executive Officer)
Senior Executive Officers: James C Hardek (Executive VP Finance), Yuval Ashkenazi (VP Research and Development), William R Breakley (VP Business Development), Paul Gane (VP Manufacturing), Paul Kadin (VP Marketing), Alan Von Kreuter (VP Engineering)

PRINCIPAL ACTIVITIES: Production of ice cream and other frozen confections
Parent Company: Sara Lee Corporation, Chicago, IL
Financial Information:

	$'000
Sales revenues	50,000

No of Employees: 200

POPULAR BANCSHARES CORPORATION

100 East Flagler Street, Miani, FL 33131
Tel: (305) 579 3000

Chairman: Jose L Carrion (and Chief Executive Officer and President)
Senior Executive Officers: Joanne Brown (Senior VP and Assistant Secretary), Justo Legido (Senior VP and Treasurer)

PRINCIPAL ACTIVITIES: Holding company with interests in banking
Principal Subsidiaries: Bank of Miami
Principal Bank: Bank of Miami

No of Employees: 350

POREX TECHNOLOGIES CORPORATION

1900 Pollit Drive, Fairlawn, NJ 07410
Tel: (201) 794 9010

Chairman: Martin J Wygod (and President and Chief Executive Officer)
Senior Executive Officers: James V Manning (Executive VP Finance and Administration, Treasurer and Secretary), Frank J Failla Jr (VP), Ray E Hannah (VP Operations and Assistant Secretary), Victor Marrero (VP and Treasurer)

PRINCIPAL ACTIVITIES: Manufacture of plastic products including porous plastic products
Principal Bank: US Trust Company of New York
Financial Information:

	$'000
Sales revenues	106,000

No of Employees: 980

PORT HURON PAPER CO

1660 Thomas Street, Port Huron, MI 48060
Tel: (313) 982-0191
Telex: TWX 8102316098

President: James W Winn (and Chief Executive Officer)
Senior Executive Officers: Egil Afshim (VP Detroit Mill), Richard P Cole (VP Marketing), Edward R Gryff (VP Port Huron Mill), C D Hoy (VP Finance)

PRINCIPAL ACTIVITIES: Production of paper and stationery
Parent Company: Pentair Inc, St Paul, MN
Principal Bank: Continental Illinois National Bank and Trust Company of Chicago
Financial Information:

	$'000
Sales revenues	125,000

No of Employees: 800

PORTA SYSTEMS CORPORATION

575 Underhill Boulevard, Syosset, NY 11791
Tel: (516) 364-9300
Telex: 14-3173 PORTASYS SYET
Telefax: (516) 682-4655

Chairman: Paul V Deluca (and Chief Executive Officer)
President: Vincent F Santulli (and Chief Operating Officer)
Senior Executive Officers: Garet M Romeo (Executive VP), William V Carney (Senior VP and Secretary), Jane M Jozefek (VP, Legal Counsel and Assistant Secretary), Giovanni Magistrali (VP Operations), Eladio G Rodriguez (VP International), Daniel J Fleming (Controller), Michael A Tancredi (VP Finance and Treasurer), Warren Marcus (VP Production), John J Gazzo (VP Research and Development), Daniel G Romeo (VP Marketing)

PRINCIPAL ACTIVITIES: Manufacture of telecommunications equipment
Principal Bank: Chemical Bank
Financial Information:

	Dec 31 1985	Dec 31 1986
	$'000	$'000
Sales revenues	40,520	40,709
Net income	2,841	2,500
Earnings per share	$0.52	$0.46
Common stock	55	55
Retained income	14,274	16,775
Shareholders equity	21,717	24,146

No of Employees: 550

PORTEC, INC

300 Windsor Drive, Oak Brook, IL 60521
Tel: (312) 920-4600
Telex: WUT 590334 rpd oakr

Chairman: Thomas Guendel (and Chief Executive Officer)
President: David H Abbott (and Chief Operating Officer)
Senior Executive Officers: Gary L Bjarnson (Senior VP Finance), Manfred D Haiderer (Senior VP), Ralph J Kindl (Senior VP), Albeon G Anderson Jr (VP), J S Cooper (VP), Nancy A Dedert (VP), James C Horton (VP and Secretary)

PRINCIPAL ACTIVITIES: Manufacture of railroad vehicles and equipment; shipbuilding; heavy industrial plant; lifts and conveyors
Principal Subsidiaries: Portec Ltd (Canada); Portec Lease Corp
Principal Bank: Continental Illinois National Bank and Trust Company of Chicago
Financial Information:

	$'000
Sales revenues	118,000

No of Employees: 1,230

PORTER, H K, COMPANY, INC

Porter Building, Pittsburgh, PA 15219
Tel: (412) 391-1800

Chairman: Keith R Garrity (and President and Chief Executive Officer)
Senior Executive Officers: T M Evans (Chairman Executive Committee), Andrew D Patton (Executive VP Operations), Charles V Emory (VP and Chief Financial Officer), Carmin D Dannible (VP Operations Analysis), Lawrence E Moncrief (VP and General Counsel)

PRINCIPAL ACTIVITIES: Manufacture of hose and belting; electrical machinery; generators; industrial engines
Principal Subsidiaries: Garland Way Advertising Inc; PW Kuil; Missouri Portland Cement Company; H K Porter Co (Great Britain) Ltd; H K Porter Co (Nederland) NV
Financial Information:

	$'000
Sales revenues	140,000

No of Employees: 2,000

PORTER PAINT CO

400 S 13th Street, Louisville, KY 40201
Tel: (502) 588-9200
Telex: WUT 204279 porterpt lvl b

Chairman: James H Davis (and Chief Executive Officer)
President: Robert E Champagne (and Chief Operating Officer)
Senior Executive Officers: W R Niblock (VP Corporate Development and Corporate Secretary), L T Horton (VP-Trade Sales), Steven L Schmidt (VP-Coatings), R E Moore (VP Manufacturing and Distribution), Robert B York (VP-Finance)

PRINCIPAL ACTIVITIES: Manufacture of paint and industrial coatings
Trade Names: Tarset, Zinclock, Glyptex, Hythane, Winter Cure
Principal Subsidiaries: Consumer's Paint Factory; Porter Corrosion Control Services
Principal Bank: Citizens Fidelity Bank & Trust Co Louisville
Financial Information:

	1986	1987
	$'000	$'000
Sales revenues	108,000	120,000

No of Employees: 950

PORTLAND GENERAL ELECTRIC CO

121 SW Salmon St, Portland, OR 97204
Tel: (503) 226-8333

Chairman: Robert H Short (and Chief Executive Officer)
President: William J Linblad
Senior Executive Officers: James W Durham (Senior VP, General Counsel and Secretary), Ken L Harrison (Senior VP and Chief Financial Officer), Charles L Heinrich (Senior VP), W K Davis (VP), R E Dyer (VP), Charles Goodwin (VP), C D Hobbs (VP Finance and Planning), Wayne A Huddleston (VP and Secretary), W June (VP), H Luedemann Jr (VP), E K Stepp (VP), F D Wieden (VP), B D Withers (VP), J N Woodcock (VP and Treasurer)

PRINCIPAL ACTIVITIES: Electricity distribution
Parent Company: Portland General Corporation
Financial Information:

	$'000
Sales revenues	760,000

No of Employees: 3,100

PORTS OF CALL INC

2121 Valencia Street, Denver, CO 80220
Tel: (303) 321 6767

President: R Larry Turrill (and Chief Executive Officer)
Senior Executive Officers: Penne T Steidl (Secretary, Treasurer and Controller)

PRINCIPAL ACTIVITIES: Travel club air transportation services
Financial Information:

	$'000
Sales revenues	33,000

No of Employees: 125

POST CORPORATION

306 W Washington Street, Appleton, WI 54911
Tel: (414) 733-4411

President: V I Minahan
Senior Executive Officers: David L Nelson (Executive VP and Chief Financial Officer), John B Torinus (VP), Elmo W Reed (VP)

PRINCIPAL ACTIVITIES: Publishing; television and radio broadcasting services; printing
Principal Bank: First Wisconsin National Bank of Milwaukee
Financial Information:

	$'000
Sales revenues	95,000

No of Employees: 1,000

POTASH CO OF AMERICA

1120 Anton Post Rd, Datien, CT 06820
Tel: (203) 655-4420

President: Peter S Jack
Senior Executive Officers: A V Mracek (VP Production), H J Ripperger (VP Sales), Jack Morrison (Comptroller)

PRINCIPAL ACTIVITIES: Mining and processing of potash for agricultural and industrial use
Parent Company: Rio Algom Ltd

Financial Information:

	$'000
Sales revenues	100,000

No of Employees: 600

POTLATCH CORPORATION

PO Box 3591, San Francisco, CA 94119
Tel: (415) 947-5500
Panafax: (415) 576-8840

Chairman: Richard B Madden (and Chief Executive Officer)
Senior Executive Officers: George C Cheek (Senior VP Public Affairs), John M Richards (Executive VP Finance), Richard N Congreve (Group VP), Richard V Warner (Group VP)

PRINCIPAL ACTIVITIES: Forestry and timber products; manufacture of paper and paper products; building materials
Principal Subsidiaries: Brown & Kauffman Inc; Transcentury Properties Inc; Clearwater Commodity Corp; Duluth & Northeastern Railroad Co; The Prescott & Northwestern Railroad Co; Warren and Saline River Railroad Co; Wood Briquettes Inc; St Maries River Railroad Co
Financial Information:

	Dec 31 1985	Dec 31 1986
	$'000	$'000
Sales revenues	950,323	976,373
Income before taxes	55,259	107,568
Net income	37,669	69,943
Dividends	23,664	21,055
Dividends per share	$1.56	$1.59
Earnings per share	$2.19	$4.98
Common stock	15,406	15,406
Retained income	465,785	507,107
Shareholders equity	473,220	574,566

No of Employees: 7,840

POTOMAC ELECTRIC POWER COMPANY

1900 Pennsylvania Avenue NW, Washington, DC 20068
Tel: (202) 872-2000
Telex: 910 240 9297 PEPCO WSH UQ

Chairman: W Reid Thompson (and Chief Executive Officer); Vice Chairman: H Lowell Davis (and Chief Financial Officer)
President: Edward F Mitchell (and Chief Operating Officer)
Senior Executive Officers: Peter H Benziger (Senior VP Generation), Paul Dragoumis (Senior VP Strategic Services), Alan G Kirk II (Senior VP, General Counsel and Secretary)

PRINCIPAL ACTIVITIES: Potomac Electric Power Company (PEPCO) is engaged in the generation, transmission, distribution and sale of electric energy in the Washington, D.C. metropolitan area. PEPCO's retail service territory includes the District of Columbia and major portions of Montgomery and Prince George's counties in suburban Maryland. The area served at retail covers approximately 640 square miles and has a population of approximately 1.8 million. PEPCO also sells electricity, at wholesale, to the Southern Maryland Electric Cooperative, Inc (SMECO), which distributes electricity in Calvert, Charles, Prince George's and St. Mary's counties in southern Maryland, an area covering 1,150 square miles. Approximately 56% of PEPCO's revenues are derived from Maryland (including sales of electricity to SMECO), and 44% from the District of Columbia. About 27% of PEPCO's revenues are derived from residential customers, 67% from sales to commercial and governmental customers and 6% from sales at wholesale. Approximately 15% and 3% of revenues are derived from sales to the United States and District of Columbia governments, respectively. PEPCO's unique service territory, with virtually no heavy industry, benefits from low unemployment, a stable economy, and job growth in the services, high technology, communications and retail trade sectors. The Washington metropolitan area is one of the nation's major markets as reflected in key measures of educational achievement and affluence. All these indicators contribute to continued economic stability and future growth in the PEPCO service territory
Trade Names: PEPCO
Principal Subsidiaries: Potomac Capital Investment Corporation Subsidiaries of Potomac Capital Investment Corporation: Potomac Capital Preferred Corporation; Potomac Capital Joint Leasing Corporation; Potomac Capital Markets Corporation; Potomac Capital Leasing Corporation; Potomac Capital Sales Corporation; Potomac Capital Development Corporation; PCI Energy Corporation; Aircraft International Management Company. PEPCO Enterprises, Inc. Subsidiary of PEPCO Enterprises Inc: Energy Use Management Corporation
Principal Bankers: American Security Bank, N.A.; Chase Manhattan Bank, N.A.; First American Bank, N.A.; The Riggs National Bank of Washington, D.C.
Financial Information:

	Dec 31 1985	Dec 31 1986
	$'000	$'000
Sales revenues	1,315,669	1,370,542
Income tax expense	146,105	155,909
Net income	183,618	227,733(1)
Common stock dividends	101,783	111,121
Dividends per share	$1.08	$1.18(2)
Earnings per share	$1.79	$2.29(1)(2)
Common stock(3)	94,399	94,429(2)
Retained income	425,751	529,485
Shareholders equity	1,007,567	1,118,455

(1) Includes in 1986 an extraordinary gain of $21,680,000 (23 cents per share) on sale of Virginia Service territory, net of income taxes of $19,758,000
(2) Data for 1985 and 1986 are restated to reflect the two-for-one stock split which became effective May 4 1987
(3) Number of shares outstanding in thousands

No of Employees: 5,500

POTT INDUSTRIES INC

1 Mercantile Center, St Louis, MO 63101
Tel: (314) 231-5525
Telex: WUT 447799 pott ind stl

President: Richard P Conerly (and Chief Executive Officer)
Senior Executive Officers: Kenneth B Schaefer (Senior VP Finance), John P Fechter (VP), Dwight W Miller (VP and General Counsel), William P Kauffmann (VP and Controller)

PRINCIPAL ACTIVITIES: River and canal transportation services; shipbuilding; marine engineering and related services
Parent Company: Enron Corporation
Principal Bank: Mercantile Trust Company
Financial Information:

	$'000
Sales revenues	400,000

No of Employees: 3,400

POTTERS INDUSTRIES, INC

377 Rte 17, Hasbrouck Heights, NJ 07604
Tel: (201) 288-4700
Telex: 219054; 133447

President: William C Combs
Vice Presidents: Gerald P Balcar (Corporate Development), Adrien J Dujacquier (European Operations), Timothy H O'Leary (International), Charles A Schneider (Domestic

Operations), Carroll F Schneider (Technical), Walter T Grainger (Manufacturing)

PRINCIPAL ACTIVITIES: Manufacture and sale of high performance glass spheres for industrial and highway safety applications. Uses range from reflective highway markings, metal improvement, reinforced plastics and oil well production to medical sciences and critical instrumentation in a wide divergence of fields. Also manufacture metal coated particles for the electronics industry, carrier material for dry paper copying, and decorative beads and flakes

Trade Names: Registered Trademarks:- SPHERIGLASS, CONDUCT-O-FIL. Trademarks:- CRYSTALFIL, BALLOTINI, SPHERI-LUBE, SPHERI-GLIDE, GUARDIAN, Visibeads

Parent Company: PQ Corporation, Valley Forge, Pennsylvania

Principal Subsidiaries: Potters-Ballotini Ltd (UK); Potters-Ballotini S.A. (France); Potters-Ballotini GMBH (Germany); Potters Industrial Ltda (Brazil); Ballotini Panamericana S.A. (Mexico); Potters Industries Pty Ltd (Australia); Toshiba-Ballotini Co Ltd (Japan); Canasphere Industries (Canada); Potters Industries Ltd (Canada)

Principal Bank: National Community Bank

Principal Shareholders: PQ Corporation

No of Employees: 518

POUGHKEEPSIE SAVINGS BANK FSB

21 Market Street, Poughkeepsie, NY 12601

Tel: (914) 431-6200

Chairman: Maurice E Kinkade (and President and Chief Executive Officer)

Senior Executive Officers: J Michael Feeks (President Community Bank Group), Richard D Silverman (Executive VP and Chief Financial Officer), George L Harvey (Senior VP), Neil S Lang (Senior VP), Peter M Olympia Jr (Senior VP), Andrea J Simon (Senior VP), Lazaro V Arango (VP), Roksolana L Geramita (VP), Grant R Lewis Jr (VP), Richard J Malena (VP), Bruce W Wagner (VP)

PRINCIPAL ACTIVITIES: Banking services

Principal Subsidiaries: Florida Fidelity Financial Inc; Highland Savings & Loan Corporation; Investors Discount Corporation; Plural Realty Inc; PSB Access Systems Inc; PSB Associates Inc; Market Street Mortgage Corp; First State Savings & Loan; Farmers Federal Savings & Loan

Financial Information:

	Dec 31 1986 $'000	Dec 31 1987 $'000
Income before taxes	13,328	16,380
Net income	7,928	9,251
Dividends per share	-	$0.30
Earnings per share	$2.02	$2.38
Common stock*	3,919	3,894
Shareholders equity	97,406	98,656
Deposits	750,153	808,788
Net loans	1,045,789	1,434,991
Total assets	1,205,875	1,621,956
*average shares outstanding in thousands		

No of Employees: 500

POWELL INDUSTRIES, INC

PO Box 12818, Houston, TX 77217

Tel: (713) 944-6900

Telex: 775165

Chairman: Thomas W Powell (and President and Chief Executive Office)

Senior Executive Officers: Robert L Mitchell (VP, Secretary/Treasurer), Neal T Hare (Assistant Secretary)

PRINCIPAL ACTIVITIES: Design, manufactures and packages electrical generation, distribution, control and protection systems

Principal Subsidiaries: Powell Electrical Mfg Co; Powell Process Systems, Inc; Unibus, Inc; Delta-Unibus Corp; US Turbine Corp; Raintight Corporation

Principal Bank: Texas Commerce Bank

Financial Information:

	Oct 31 1985 $'000	Oct 31 1986 $'000
Sales revenues	65,601	78,697
(Loss) before taxes	(6,633)	(1,659)
Net (loss)	(2,607)	(928)
(Loss) per share	($0.26)	($0.09)
Common stock*	10,204	10,204
Retained income	17,589	16,661
Shareholders equity	20,594	19,666
*shares outstanding in thousands		

No of Employees: 532

POWER PIPING CO

829 Beaver Avenue, Pittsburgh, PA 15233

Tel: (412) 323-6200

Telex: 86 6449 power piping pgh

Chairman: William R Patterson (and President)

Senior Executive Officers: William J Hoegel (VP), B C Hargett (Secretary and Treasurer)

PRINCIPAL ACTIVITIES: Manufacture of fabricated pipe and pipe fittings; erection of high pressure and steam piping systems

Parent Company: Harlan Electric Company, Southfield, MI

Principal Bank: Pittsburgh National Bank

Financial Information:

	$'000
Sales revenues	50,000

No of Employees: 600

POWER TEST CORPORATION

175 Sunnyside Blvd, Plainview, NY 11803

Tel: (516) 576-9500

President: Leo Liebowitz

Senior Executive Officers: Milton Safenowitz (Executive VP and Secretary), Louis Cohen (VP), Milton Cooper (VP)

PRINCIPAL ACTIVITIES: Wholesale and retail petroleum

Financial Information:

	$'000
Sales revenues	153,000

No of Employees: 3,500

POWERS CHEMCO INC

Charles Street, Glen Cove, NY 11542

Tel: (516) 676-4000

Chairman: Charles A Powers Jr (and Executive VP)

President: J D Maxwell Jr (and Treasurer)

Senior Executive Officers: A J Powers III (Senior VP Finance), William J Streeter (Senior VP), Frank T Powers III (VP), Michael S Powers (VP)

PRINCIPAL ACTIVITIES: Manufacture of hospital X-ray and graphic arts films, chemicals and supplies; camera equipment

Principal Bank: European American Bank

Financial Information:

	$'000
Sales revenues	160,000

No of Employees: 1,000

PPG INDUSTRIES, INC

One PPG Place, Pittsburgh, PA 15272

Tel: (412) 434-3131

Telex: ITT 4423039 ppgcempgh

Chairman: Vincent A Sarni (and Chief Executive Officer); Vice Chairman: Frank V Breeze
President: Edward J Slack (and Chief Operating Officer)
Senior Executive Officers: L Blaine Boswell (VP-International), Robert D Duncan (VP-Glass Group), Eugene B Mosier (VP-Coatings and Resins Group), Richard M Rompala (VP-Chemicals Group), Edward F Voboril (VP-Biomedical Systems Division), John J Horgan (VP-Corporate Development)

PRINCIPAL ACTIVITIES: Production of flat and specialty glass; fiber glass; chemicals; coatings and resins; medical electronic systems
Financial Information:

	Dec 31 1985	Dec 31 1986
	$'000	$'000
Sales revenues	4,346,000	4,687,000
Income before taxes	537,000	553,000
Net income	303,000	316,000
Dividends	110,100	111,800
Dividends per share	$0.82	$0.94
Earnings per share	$2.27	$2.26
Common stock	133,400	118,900
Shareholders equity	1,705,000	1,978,000

No of Employees: 37,500

PQ CORPORATION
PO Box 840, Valley Forge, PA 19482
Tel: (215) 293-7200
Telex: ITT 4942917 nasi vf ui

Chairman: George P Keeley
President: Paul R Staley (and Chief Executive Officer)
Senior Executive Officers: Dale J Shimer (Executive VP), Michael R Imbriani (VP and Treasurer), Richard W Kelso (VP Plant Operations), Richard W Lynch (VP), John R McLaughlin (VP), Henry F Whalen (VP), James D McDonald (VP Staff Operations), George C Schweiker (VP Research and Development)

PRINCIPAL ACTIVITIES: Production of industrial chemicals; glass products
Financial Information:

	$'000
Sales revenues	200,000

No of Employees: 1,300

PRAIRIE FARMS DAIRY, INC
PO Box 499, Carlinville, IL 62626
Tel: (217) 854-3171

Chairman: Melvin Schweizer
Senior Executive Officers: Fletcher A Gourley (Executive VP and Chief Operating Officer), Harry Dressler Jr (VP), Lawrence Dietz (Treasurer)

PRINCIPAL ACTIVITIES: Manufacture of dairy products including milk, butter, cream cottage cheese and ice cream; wholesale trade in dairy products
Principal Bank: The Carlinville National Bank
Financial Information:

	$'000
Sales revenues	300,000

No of Employees: 1,200

PRATT & LAMBERT, INC
PO Box 22, Buffalo, NY 14240
Tel: (716) 873-6000
Telefax: (716) 873-2722

Chairman: R D Stevens Jr
President: J J Castiglia
Senior Executive Officers: J R Boldt (VP Finance, Treasurer and Secretary), W F Bensman (VP), D W Smith (VP), G J Willis (Assistant Treasurer), L D Hoerner (Assistant Secretary), R W Adams (President-Paint Division), F H Fitch (President-Pierce & Stevens Chemical Corp), A E Floyd (President-Southern Coatings Inc), W L Huettel (President-United Paint Co), W A Steele (President-Industrial Coatings Division), T Cutler (President-Miracle Adhesives Corp)

PRINCIPAL ACTIVITIES: Manufacture of paints, chemical coatings and adhesives
Trade Names: Accolade, Vapex, Aqua Royal, Aqua Satin, Permalize, Tonetic, Effecto, Cellu-tone, Style Hide, Calibrated Colors, M L Campbell, Pro-Hide Plus, Tech-gard, Miracure, Redi-Quik, Vinyl-Stik, Barge, Foamcoat, Hybond, Crimpbond, Latiseal, Miralane, Fabulon, Mansion House, Versa-Kote, Masterline, Show Coat, Flexhard, Galvicon, Fulton, Poly-Epoxy, Dura-Pox Epoxy, Chemtec Zinc Rich Primers, Master PRO, TEN YEAR House Paint, Vitralon, Jet-Glo, Enflex III, Acry GLo, Mono Pac, The Paint Place, Aqua-Gloss, Poly-Glo, UPL-500, Country Color, 60 Semi Gloss, Lumber Lock, Multi-Purpose Flooring and Carpet Adhesive, Panel, Foam and Construction Adhesive, Artificial Grass and Carpet Adhesive, DSA-20 DryWall Adhesive, MA-5005 Multi-Purpose Ceramic Tile Adhesive, MA-200 Ceramic Wall Tile Adhesive, Multi-Purpose Thin-Set Plus, D-618 High Velocity Duct Sealer and Eagle Bond Flooring Adhesive are registered or pending trademarks of Pratt & Lambert Inc and its subsidiaries, Pierce & Stevens Chemical Corp, Southern Coatings Inc, Miracle Adhesives Corporation and United Paint Company
Principal Subsidiaries: Pierce & Stevens Chemical Corp; Southern Coatings Inc; Miracle Adhesives Corporation; United Paint Co
Principal Bank: Citibank; Manufacturers & Traders Trust Co
Financial Information:

	Dec 31 1985	Dec 31 1986
	$'000	$'000
Sales revenues	184,734	193,857
Income before taxes	11,467	15,045
Net income	6,212	8,237
Dividends	1,917	2,085
Dividends per share	$0.667	$0.720
Earnings per share	$2.10	$2.76
Common stock	3,986	3,953
Retained income	39,247	45,399
Shareholders equity	35,367	41,964

No of Employees: 1,624

PRATT HOTEL CORPORATION
4099 McEwen, Suite 800, Dallas, TX 75244
Tel: (214) 386 9777

President: William Weidener (and Chief Operating Officer)
Senior Executive Officers: William D Pratt (Executive VP, Legal Counsel and Secretary)

PRINCIPAL ACTIVITIES: Management of hotels and real estate
Principal Bank: Texas American Bank
Financial Information:

	$'000
Sales revenues	213,000

No of Employees: 5,190

PRATT READ CORPORATION
Main Street, Ivoryton, CT 06442
Tel: (203) 767 8282

Chairman: Peter H Comstock
President: Harwood B Comstock (and Chief Executive Officer)
Senior Executive Officers: Gerald B Levasseur (Controller), Charles A Ruhe (Secretary and Treasurer)

PRINCIPAL ACTIVITIES: Production of a range of hardware supplies for industrial use including control devices and tools; musical instruments
Principal Subsidiaries: Allen-Rogers Corporation; Altron Inc; Sohmer & Co Inc
Principal Bank: Colonial Bank

Financial Information:

	$'000
Sales revenues	36,000

No of Employees: 950

PRE CORPORATION

2500 E TC Jester St, Houston, TX 77088
Tel: (713) 868-8980

Chairman: Robin S Loh (and President)
Senior Executive Officers: Gary Jennings (VP), Ed L Tyer (VP), Wm Hixon (Treasurer)

PRINCIPAL ACTIVITIES: Oil and gas services and equipment; modular buildings; truck trailers
Principal Bank: Citibank
Financial Information:

	$'000
Sales revenues	30,000

No of Employees: 1,400

PRECISION CASTPARTS CORPORATION

4600 SE Harney Drive, Portland, OR 97206
Tel: (503) 777-3881
Telex: 360 992 Pre Cast MUIK

Chairman: Edward H Cooley (and Chief Executive Officer)
President: William C McCormick (and Chief Operating Officer)
Senior Executive Officers: John E Ceserani (VP and General Manager, Titanium Business Operation), J William Crawford (Senior VP Marketing), Gary A Lane (VP and General Manager, Small Structurals Business Operation), William D Larsson (VP Finance), Roy M Marvin (VP Administration, Secretary and Treasurer), Corwin G Matthews (VP Human Resources), Randy B Turner (VP and General Manager, Large Structurals Business Operation), Peter G Waite (Executive VP, Airfoils)

PRINCIPAL ACTIVITIES: Metal castings for the aerospace industry and for compressors and pumps; metal cast products for bone replacement and repair in surgery
Principal Subsidiaries: PCC Airfoils Inc; Precision Castparts Corp UK Ltd; Precision Castparts Corp-France SA; PCC Exports Inc
Principal Bank: First Interstate Bank of Oregon
Financial Information:

	Mar 31 1986	Mar 31 1987
	$'000	$'000
Sales revenues	192,382	326,252
Income before taxes	16,625	39,416
Net income	9,339	21,208
Dividends	717	975
Dividends per share*	$0.05	$0.07
Earnings per share*	$0.62	$1.35
Common stock	7,490	15,232
Retained income	39,233	51,956
Shareholders equity	64,052	88,539

*restated to reflect stock splits declared through March 31 1987

Principal Shareholders: Edward H Cooley
No of Employees: 5,372

PREFORMED LINE PRODUCTS CO

660 Beta Drive, Mayfield Village, OH 44143
Tel: (216) 461-5200
Telex: WUT 980 407 preformed hdhs

President: Jon R Ruhlman
Senior Executive Officers: Wallace Adler (VP Domestic Operations), W F Corkran (VP International Operations), Carl W Gregory (VP Finance), David P Arnold (VP Marketing), Max A Lekson (VP), E J Pleszko (VP Corporate Planning), William T Hoppe (VP Manufacturing), J C Poffenberger (VP Research)

PRINCIPAL ACTIVITIES: Manufacture of apparatus for electricity transmission
Principal Bank: National City Bank
Financial Information:

	$'000
Sales revenues	78,000

No of Employees: 500

PREMARK INTERNATIONAL INC

2211 Sanders Rd, Northbrook, IL 60062
Tel: (312) 498-8000

Chairman: Warren L Bats (and Chief Executive Officer)
Senior Executive Officers: John M Costigan (Senior VP and General Counsel), Elmer M Davis (Group VP), Augustine J English (Group VP), Robert M Fisher (Group VP), William L Jackson (Group VP), Ralph Wilson Jr (Group VP), L John Fletcher (VP and Assistant (General Counsel), Robert W Hoaglund (VP Auditing), John T Kelly (VP, Secretary and Assistant General Counsel), Michael H Moskow (VP Strategy and Business Development), Wallace J Nichols (VP Compensation and Administration Services), Becky W Osterberg (VP Communications), James E Rose Jr (VP Taxes), Robert R Schuldt (VP Management Development), Ian J A Scott (VP Information Systems), David S Simon (VP and Treasurer), Paul B Van Sickle (VP and Controller)

PRINCIPAL ACTIVITIES: Manufacture of plastic products, adhesives, electrical household goods and sports equipment
Trade Names: Tupperware
Financial Information:

	Dec 31 1986
	$'000
Sales revenues	1,959,000
Net (loss)	(98,300)
(Loss) per share	($2.87)
Shareholders equity	580,300

No of Employees: 22,000

PREMIER BANCORP, INC

451 Florida St, PO Box 1511, Baton Rouge, LA 70821
Tel: (504) 389-4206
Telex: 3439074

Chairman: J Hugh Watson
President: Charles W McCoy (and Chief Executive Officer)
Senior Executive Officers: J Noland Singletary (Senior VP and Secretary), Robert C Sutton (Senior VP), L Biff Mately (Senior VP), Nancy M Richmond (Senior VP and Treasurer)

PRINCIPAL ACTIVITIES: Bank holding company
Trade Names: PRBC
Principal Subsidiaries: (all 100% owned): Louisiana National Bank of Baton Rouge; First National Bank of Shreveport; Ouachita National Bank in Monroe; State National Bank of New Iberia; Raceland Bank & Trust Company of Raceland; Gulf National Bank at Lake Charles; Guaranty Bank and Trust Company of Lafayette; Terrebonne Bank & Trust Company of Houma; Premier Mortgage Company; Premier Securities Corporation; Premier Investment Advisors Inc
Financial Information:

	Dec 31 1985	Dec 31 1986
	$'000	$'000
Income (loss) before taxes	24,845	(38,383)
Net income (loss)	27,515	(6,318)
Dividends	14,653	13,292
Dividends per share	$0.64	$0.54
Earnings (loss) per share	$1.20	($0.26)
Common stock	115,896	123,294
Retained income	174,120	154,510
Shareholders equity	311,667	319,833
Deposits	3,565,512	4,046,520
Total assets	4,293,602	4,740,502

No of Employees: 3,248

UNITED STATES OF AMERICA

PREMIER FINANCIAL SERVICES INC

27 West Main Street, Suite 101, Freeport, IL 61032
Tel: (815) 235 7141

Chairman: Harold L Fenton
President: Richard L Geach
Senior Executive Officers: David L Murray (Executive VP)

PRINCIPAL ACTIVITIES: Holding company with interests in banking
Principal Subsidiaries: Citizens Bank & Trust Company; Wagners Insurance Agency Inc; City Bank & Trust Company; First National Bank; First National Bank Freeport; Premier Data Services Inc; Premier TR Services Inc; Lincolnway Bank; Mount Carroll National Bank; Polo National Bank
Principal Bank: First National Bank
Financial Information:

	Dec 31 1985
	$'000
Revenues	37,535
Net income	1,475

No of Employees: 300

PREMIER INDUSTRIAL CORPORATION

4500 Euclid Avenue, Cleveland, OH 44103
Tel: (216) 391-8300

Chairman: Morton L Mandel; Vice Chairman: Robert Warren
President: William M Hamilton
Senior Executive Officers: Jack A Mandel (Finance Committee Chairman), Joseph C Mandel (Executive Committee Chairman), Philip S Sims (Executive VP and Treasurer). William H Barnes (VP), Denis M Bohm (VP), David R Eva (VP), Grant C Grinnell (VP and Secretary), Bruce W Johnson (Executive VP), J Robert McCabe (VP), Denis A Moore (Senior VP), Phillip Vander Pol (VP and Controller), Michael D James (VP)

PRINCIPAL ACTIVITIES: Premier is a broad line distributor of electronic components used in the production and maintenance of equipment, a supplier of maintenance products for industrial, commercial and institutional applications and a manufacturer of high performance fire-fighting accessories
Principal Subsidiaries: (100% owned): Premier Energy Corporation; United States Oil Company; D-A Lubricant Company Inc; Premier Industrial Export Corporation; Premier Industrial Corporation (Indiana); Newark Electronics Corporation; Premierco Service Corporation; PIC Corporation; MCM Electronics Inc; Premier Foreign Sales Corporation Inc (Virgin Islands); Premier Fastener Ltd (Canada); Certanium BV (Netherlands); Premier Industrial Holland BV (Netherlands); Premier Industrial Belgium SA (Belgium); Premier Industrial (UK) Ltd (UK); Premier de Venezuela CA (Venezuela); NV Certanium Services SA (Belgium); Premier Industrial France SARL (France); Certanium Deutschland GmbH (Germany)
Financial Information:

	May 31 1986	May 31 1987
	$'000	$'000
Sales revenues	435,040	459,000
Earnings before taxes	71,743	81,421
Net earnings	41,377	48,280
Dividends	11,219	12,418
Dividends per share	$0.38	$0.42
Earnings per share	$1.40	$1.63
Common stock	29,629	29,660
Retained earnings	218,775	253,793
Shareholders equity	239,622	266,888

No of Employees: 3,800

PREMIX, INC

Rt 20 and Harmon Road, North Kingsville, OH 44068
Tel: (216) 224-2181
Telex: TWX 8104272929

Chairman: George H Kaull (and Chief Executive Officer)
President: Herb B Ailes (and Chief Operating Officer)
Senior Executive Officers: Ford M Davy (Senior VP), Frank Bradish (VP and Technical Director), David J Clavadetscher (VP Marketing), David Randall (VP Manufacturing), Wilbur Shenk (VP Sales), E Terry Warren (Treasurer)

PRINCIPAL ACTIVITIES: Manufacture of plastics and plastic products for domestic and industrial purposes
Principal Bank: Ameritrust Co
Financial Information:

	$'000
Sales revenues	60,000

No of Employees: 800

PRENTICE-HALL, INC

Englewood Cliffs, NJ 07632
Tel: (201) 592-2000
Telex: WUT 384956 printicehal nj

Chairman: Frank J Dunnigan (and Chairman Executive Committee)
Senior Executive Officers: David P Amerman (Group VP), Edward B Hutton Jr (Group VP), Robert C Martin (Group VP), Michael C Bangs (VP Information Technology)

PRINCIPAL ACTIVITIES: Publishing including books and educational material
Parent Company: Gulf & Western Inc
Financial Information:

	$'000
Sales revenues	448,000

No of Employees: 5,600

PRESCOLITE INC

1251 Doolittle Drive, San Leandro, CA 94577
Tel: (415) 562-3500
Telex: GRT 3718843 presco snlo

President: B J Garet
Senior Executive Officers: Vincent F Monte (VP Finance), John H Oswald (VP Manufacturing)

PRINCIPAL ACTIVITIES: Manufacture of domestic, industrial, commercial and automobile lighting equipment and components
Parent Company: Hanson Industries North America
Principal Bank: Chemical Bank
Financial Information:

	$'000
Sales revenues	80,000

No of Employees: 950

PRESENT COMPANY INC

3042 Ridge Road West, Rochester, NY 14626
Tel: (716) 227 0700

Chairman: Gordon S Present
President: James R Present (and Chief Executive Officer)
Senior Executive Officers: Beryl M Present (Senior VP and Secretary), Robert E Meagher (Senior VP and Assistant Secretary), Norman Kramer (VP), Paul J Miller (Controller)

PRINCIPAL ACTIVITIES: Retail stores; sale of yachts
Principal Subsidiaries: Present Yachts Inc
Principal Bank: Chemical Bank
Financial Information:

	$'000
Sales revenues	48,000

No of Employees: 200

PRESIDENTIAL LIFE CORPORATION

69 Lydecker Street, Nyack, NY 10960
Tel: (914) 358 2300

President: Herbert Kurz

Senior Executive Officers: Charles Fausel (Treasurer), Callman Gottesman (Secretary)

PRINCIPAL ACTIVITIES: Insurance services
Principal Bank: Marine Midland Bank
Financial Information:

	Dec 31 1985
	$'000
Revenues	201,570
Net income	13,215

PRESTO PRODUCTS, INC

Box 2399, Appleton, WI 54913
Tel: (414) 739-9471
Telex: WUT 887187 presto app ud

Chairman: John E Lynch
President: Lawrence Wirth
Senior Executive Officers: Jerome Reich (Executive VP and Chief Executive Officer), Frank H Heckrodt (Senior VP), Gary Howard (VP Finance), James K Spanbauer (VP Administration)

PRINCIPAL ACTIVITIES: Manufacture of plastic packaging and wrapping products including containers for food, stretch wrap film and plastic cutlery
Parent Company: Coca-Cola Company, Atlanta, GA
Principal Bank: Valley Bank
Financial Information:

	$'000
Sales revenues	135,000

No of Employees: 1,300

PRESTON CORPORATION

151 Easton Boulevard, Preston, MD 21655
Tel: 1-301-673-7151

Chairman: William B Potter (and President)
Senior Executive Officers: J Sean Callahan (Senior VP-Finance), Bruce A Kennedy (Senior VP Marketing), Billy G Terrell (Senior VP-Operations), William E Lyons (Secretary and Treasurer)

PRINCIPAL ACTIVITIES: Transportation of freight for manufacturers, wholesalers and retailers
Principal Subsidiaries: Preston Trucking Company Inc; Pioneer Transport Systems Inc; Bowie Hall Trucking Inc; Reeves Transportation Company; Smalley Transportation Company; Saia Motor Freight Line Inc
Principal Bank: Maryland National Bank, Baltimore, Maryland
Financial Information:

	Dec 31 1985	Dec 31 1986
	$'000	$'000
Sales revenues	349,966	418,943
Income before taxes	5,284	14,432
Net income	4,297	7,263
Cash dividends paid	2,849	2,879
Dividends per share	$0.50	$0.50
Earnings per share*	$0.75	$1.22
Common stock	5,759	5,759
Retained income	78,260	82,644
Shareholders equity	101,811	106,195

*fully diluted

No of Employees: 7,933

PREWAY INC

1430 2nd Street N, Wisconsin Rapids, WI 54494
Tel: (715) 423-1100
Telex: TWX 510 377443 preway wira

Chairman: James W Egan (and President and Chief Executive Officer)
Senior Executive Officers: Charles Gibbons (VP Engineering), Marvin J Machon (VP Purchasing), Michael J McLaughlin (VP Finance), John Reisbeck (VP Marketing), Samue A Rizzo (VP), Tom S Ellis (Secretary and Treasurer)

PRINCIPAL ACTIVITIES: Manufacture of heating equipment
Principal Bank: Continental Illinois National Bank & Trust Company of Chicago
Financial Information:

	$'000
Sales revenues	129,300

No of Employees: 1,200

PRIAM CORPORATION

20 W Montague Expwy, San Jose, CA 95134
Tel: (408) 946-4600
Telex: TWX 910 3508618 pIriam corp ca

Chairman: William J Schroeder (and Chief Executive Officer)
President: Joe T Booker (and Chief Operating Officer)
Senior Executive Officers: James W Adkisson (Executive VP), A A Wilson (Executive VP), D S Dury (VP and Chief Financial Officer), Norman Hayes (VP), Richard Garlick (VP), J B Smith (VP), B T Taniguchi (VP), R P Lawrence (VP), G P Klein (VP)

PRINCIPAL ACTIVITIES: Manufacture of Winchester disc drives and other disc drives up to 158M bytes capacity
Principal Bank: First National Bank of Boston
Financial Information:

	$'000
Sales revenues	105,000

No of Employees: 880

PRICE BROTHERS COMPANY

367 W 2nd Street, Dayton, OH 45402
Tel: (513) 226-8700
Telex: WUT 241683 price bro dtn

Chairman: Gayle B Price Jr (and Chief Executive Officer); Vice Chairman: Harry S Price Jr (and Chairman Finance Committee)
President: Emerson W Heisler (and Chief Operating Officer)
Senior Executive Officers: Donald N Lorenz (VP Finance), J W Back (VP Utility Systems Division), James S Clift (VP Pressure Pipe Division), Richard H Rogers (VP International and General Counsel), Lee Byers (VP Administration), Lee E Stockton (VP Technology), Bradley W Evers (Secretary and Corporate Counsel)

PRINCIPAL ACTIVITIES: Manufacture of concrete sewer and pressure pipe, wire reinforcing mesh, fiber glass products, machinery
Principal Subsidiaries: McClean-Anderson; Price Brothers-Composites
Financial Information:

	$'000
Sales revenues	150,000

No of Employees: 1,500

PRICE CO

PO Box 85466, San Diego, CA 92138
Tel: (619) 581-4600

Chairman: Sol Price
President: R E Price (and Chief Executive Officer)
Senior Executive Officers: Richard M Libenson (Executive VP and Chief Operating Officer), Giles H Bateman (Executive VP and Chief Financial Officer), Theodore Wallace (Executive VP Operations)

PRINCIPAL ACTIVITIES: General merchandisers to businesses and selected retail customers for household goods, catering supplies, food, wines and spirits, hardware, automobile products, soft goods, candy, cigarettes, electronics, furniture, appliances
Trade Names: PRICE CLUB
Principal Bank: First Interstate Bank

Financial Information:

	Aug 31 1985	Aug 31 1986
	$'000	$'000
Sales revenues	1,833,972	2,590,319
Income before taxes	90,656	116,036
Net income	45,963	58,900
Earnings per share	$1.01	$1.25
Common stock	4,569	4,885
Retained earnings	105,171	164,078
Shareholders equity	161,291	301,701

No of Employees: 9,000

PRICE, T ROWE, ASSOCIATES INC

100 East Pratt Street, Baltimore, MD 21202
Tel: (301) 547 2000

President: George J Collins (and Chief Executive Officer)
Senior Executive Officers: Carter O Hoffman (Senior VP), Thomas H Braodus Jr (VP), L Gordon Croft (VP), Albert C Hubbard Jr (VP), Edward J Mathias (VP), James S Riepe (VP), George A Roche (VP and Chief Financial Officer), Charles H Salisbury Jr (VP), Edward A Taber III (VP), M David Testa (VP), Alvin M Younger Jr (VP Secretary and Treasurer), Peter J D Gordon (VP), Henry H Hopkins (VP)

PRINCIPAL ACTIVITIES: Provision of financial services including investment advice and dealing in securities
Principal Subsidiaries: Rowe Price-Fleming International Inc; T Rowe Price Investment Services Inc; T Rowe Price Trust Company Inc
Principal Bank: First National Bank of Maryland
Financial Information:

	1986
	$'000
Sales revenues	108,087
Income before taxes(1)	30,795
Net income	14,791
Dividends	1,455
Dividends per share	$0.21
Earnings per share	$2.00
Common stock(2)	1,429
Retained earnings	39,098
Shareholders equity	41,031

(1) and minority interests
(2) 7,143,076 shares at $0.20

No of Employees: 717

PRIMARK CORPORATION

8251 Greenboro Drive, McLean, VA 22102
Tel: (703) 790-7600

Chairman: R W Stewart (and President and Chief Executive Officer)
Senior Executive Officers: S H Curran (VP and Controller), J M Parker (VP), K W Thompson (VP), R W Zemimin (VP)

PRINCIPAL ACTIVITIES: The company has interests in the production and distribution of natural gas; finance and investment; leasing; communications services
Financial Information:

	$'000
Sales revenues	1,600,000
Net income	54,000

No of Employees: 5,200

PRIME COMPUTER, INC

Prime Park, Natick, MA 01760
Tel: (617) 655-8000
Telex: TWX 7103460396 prmexss ntik

Chairman: David J Dunn
President: Joe M Henson (and Chief Executive Officer)
Senior Executive Officers: Gale R Aguilar (VP Corporate Business Development and Strategy), Richard L Ballantyne (VP, General Counsel and Secretary), Lawrence M Bornstein (VP Human Resources), W L Brubaker (VP Sales), D Cheesman (VP International Development), David J Collard (VP Finance, Chief Financial Officer and Treasurer), Paul R Fones (VP Hardware Development), Mel Friedman (VP Manufacturing and Services), Richard B Goldman (VP and Controller), Leonard F Halio (VP Small Systems Business Group), Stephen C Kiely (VP Systems Marketing and Development), Marvin G Kirby (VP Domestic Sales), Andrew C Knowles III (VP, CAD/CAM Work Stations and Terminals), John T Maske (VP Corporate Operations and Programs), Donald A Newman (VP Corporate Communications), William F O'Neill (VP Systems Marketing Development Operations and Custom Systems), Richard B Snyder (VP Software Development), William J Stella (VP International Resources), Richard L Williams (VP International Marketing Operations)

PRINCIPAL ACTIVITIES: Manufacture of data processing equipment including minicomputers
Principal Bank: Citibank
Financial Information:

	Dec 31 1985	Dec 31 1986
	$'000	$'000
Sales revenues	769,673	860,173
Net income	57,782	46,925
Earnings per share	$1.20	$0.97
Shareholders equity	383,300	437,830

No of Employees: 8,120

PRIME MOTOR INNS INC

700 Route 46 East, PO Box 2700, Fairfield, NJ 07006
Tel: (201) 882 1010

Chairman: Peter E Simon (and President and Chief Executive Officer); Vice Chairman: Melvin S Taub (and Senior Executive VP and Chief Operating Officer and General Counsel)
Senior Executive Officers: Samuel Brodie (Executive VP), Herbert Kay (Senior VP), David L Barsky (VP), Michael Clarke (VP), J B Gurkoff (VP), Howard D Kahan (VP), David A Simon (VP), Joel A Simon (VP), Brian Kilduff (VP Finance), Joseph Mazzo (VP)

PRINCIPAL ACTIVITIES: Management of motels on franchise basis with Ramada, Sheraton, Holiday Inns, Howard Johnson, Hilton and Days Inc
Principal Subsidiaries: Prime Construction Co; Prime Management Co Inc
Principal Bank: Morgan Guaranty Trust Company
Financial Information:

	$'000
Sales revenues	290,000

No of Employees: 4,500

PRIME PACKING CO, INC

4170 S Union Avenue, Chicago, IL 60609
Tel: (312) 247-6060

Chairman: William E Kentor (and President)
Senior Executive Officers: Roger Maina (VP and Product Manager)

PRINCIPAL ACTIVITIES: Meat and meat processing
Parent Company: Servbest Foods Inc
Principal Bank: Continental Illinois National Bank & Trust Company of Chicago
Financial Information:

	$'000
Sales revenues	80,000

No of Employees: 60

PRIME TANNING CO, INC

Sullivan Street, Berwick, ME 03901
Tel: (207) 698-1100
Telex: WUT 944494 primetan berc

Chairman: Leonard W Kaplan (and Treasurer)

President: Richard H Goldberg
Senior Executive Officers: Samuel Rubin (Executive VP), Kenneth Purdy (Executive VP), Ralph J Amabile Jr (VP Sales)

PRINCIPAL ACTIVITIES: Tanning and finishing of leather
Principal Bank: First National Bank of Boston
Financial Information:

	$'000
Sales revenues	75,000

No of Employees: 550

PRIMEX PLASTICS CORPORATION

65 River Drive, Garfield, NJ 07026
Tel: (201) 778-7055

Chairman: John F Farber (and President and Chief Executive Officer)
Senior Executive Officers: Paul J Bertsch (Executive VP), Murray Aibinder (Executive VP), Fred A Amiano (VP)

PRINCIPAL ACTIVITIES: Manufacture of plastic products including sheets and rolls
Parent Company: ICC Industries Inc, New York, NY
Principal Bank: First Fidelity Bank
Financial Information:

	Dec 31 1985	Dec 31 1986
	$'000	$'000
Sales revenues	60,000	80,000

No of Employees: 500

PRINCE CO, INC

Prince Avenue, Lowell, MA 01853
Tel: (617) 458-4111
Telex: 947434

Chairman: Joseph Pellegrino
President: Joseph P Pellegrino
Senior Executive Officers: Armand Giarusso (Senior VP Finance), Mario Gianmini (VP Production)

PRINCIPAL ACTIVITIES: Manufacture of pasta, sauces, prepared foods; packaging cartons
Principal Bank: Union National Bank
Financial Information:

	$'000
Sales revenues	200,000

No of Employees: 800

PRINCE GARDNER CO

6245 Lemay Ferry Road, St Louis, MO 63129
Tel: (314) 487-3100
Telex: WUT 447374 princegrd stl

President: Dennis K Beardall
Senior Executive Officers: V Arnold (VP Production), Ralph L Ryman (VP Sales), Arthur N Ehlert (Senior VP Finance), John Slavinsky (VP Inventory Management)

PRINCIPAL ACTIVITIES: Manufacture of leather bags, belts and accessories
Parent Company: Swank Inc
Principal Bank: Chase Manhattan Bank
Financial Information:

	$'000
Sales revenues	50,000

No of Employees: 1,500

PRINCIPAL MUTUAL LIFE INSURANCE CO (A MEMBER OF THE PRINCIPAL FINANCIAL

711 High Street, Des Moines, IA 50309
Tel: (515) 247-5111
Telex: WUT 478491 blco dms

Chairman: John R Taylor (and Chief Executive Officer); Vice Chairman: Robert E Larson
President: G David Hurd
Senior Executive Officers: Don Carter (Executive VP), Roy Ehrle (Executive VP), Ray Crabtree (Senior VP Casualty), John Elken (Senior VP-Corporate Planning), Ted Hutchison (Senior VP, Counsel and Secretary), Dave Kauf (Senior VP-Corporate Development), Ron Keller (Senior VP-Group Claim), Charles E Rohm (Senior VP), Walter J Walsh (VP-Corporate Relations)

PRINCIPAL ACTIVITIES: Group and individual insurance; pension and profit sharing; financial services
Trade Names: The Principal Financial Group
Principal Subsidiaries: Principal Casualty Insurance Company; Principal National Life Insurance Company; Value Investors Inc
Financial Information:

	Dec 31 1985*	Dec 31 1986*
	$'000	$'000
Premium income	3,069,000	3,153,000
Investment income	1,255,000	1,392,000
Income before taxes	230,000	114,000
Net income	110,000	65,000
Total assets	14,927,000	16,994,000

*Amounts are for Principle Mutual Life Insurance Company, flagship company of the Principal Financial Group

No of Employees: 8,820

PRINTRONIX INC

17500 Cartwright Road, Irvine, CA 92713
Tel: (714) 863-1900
Telex: (910) 595-2535

Chairman: Robert A Kleist (and President)
Senior Executive Officers: Jack A Andersen (Senior VP, Domestic Marketing), Michael G de Nicola (Senior VP and General Manager, Matrix Line Printer Division), Melvin Litvin (President, Data Printer Corporation), David W Mayne (Senior VP, Corporate Development), Melvin Posin (Senior VP, World Trade), John H Weaver (Chairman, Anadex Inc), John R Weaver (President, Anadex Inc), Robert A Kleist (Chief Financial Officer)

PRINCIPAL ACTIVITIES: Printronix, Inc designs, manufactures and markets a comprehensive line of printers for use with mircrocomputers, minicomputers and main frame computer systems. These products are designed primarily to meet business applications that require hard copy, multi-part forms produced by impact printing and 8.50" x 11" cut sheet output produced by non-impact laser printing
Trade Names: Printronix. Stock Symbol: PTNX
Principal Subsidiaries: Matrix Line Printer Division; Printonix de Mexico SA (Mexico); Printronix-Singapore; Spares Division; Customer Service Division; Anadex Inc; Anadex (Hong Kong); Printronix, Europe (Belgium); Printronix Nederland BV (Netherlands); Printronix GmbH (Germany); Printronix France; Anadex Ltd (UK); Laser Printer Division; Printronix Latinoamericana, Sa de CV (Mexico)
Principal Bank: Wells Fargo Bank
Financial Information:

	$'000
Sales revenues	132,000

No of Employees: 1,300

PRITCHARD CORPORATION (THE)

8205 W 108th Terr, Overland Park, KS 66210
Tel: (913) 661-6000

Chairman: D D Dixon
President: J E Nobles
Senior Executive Officers: R S Leland (VP Sales), J V Lupo (VP Operations), G F Cockrell (Secretary and Treasurer)

PRINCIPAL ACTIVITIES: Manufacture of power equipment; chemical plant; oil and gas services and equipment

Parent Company: Black & Veatch International
Principal Bank: Centerre Bank

No of Employees: 200

PROCESS SYSTEMS INTERNATIONAL, INC

PO Box 956, Tyler, TX 75710
Tel: (214) 597-0311

Chairman: Issam M Fares; Vice Chairman: L W Heiligbrodt
President: Carl E Bochow (and Chief Executive Officer)
Senior Executive Officers: Harris G Napier (VP), John Latta (VP Finance)

PRINCIPAL ACTIVITIES: Manufacture of chemical plant; equipment for oil and petrochemical processing; food processing plant; steel fabrication
Principal Bank: Manufacturers Hanover Trust
Financial Information:

	$'000
Sales revenues	52,000

No of Employees: 250

PROCTER & GAMBLE COMPANY (THE)

One Procter & Gamble Plaza, Cincinnati, OH 45202
Tel: (513) 983-1100

Chairman: John G Smale; Vice Chairmen: Edwin L Artzt (and President Procter & Gamble International), Thomas Laco
President: John E Pepper
Senior Executive Officers: W Wallace Abbott (Senior VP), Robert E Cannon (Group VP), Gerald V Dirvin (Group VP), Harald Einsmann (Group VP), Albert E Harris (Senior VP), Malcolm Jozoff (Group VP), Powell McHenry (Senior VP and General Counsel), James W Nethercott (Senior VP), Samih A Sherif (Group VP), David S Swanson (Senior VP), Harry Tecklenburg (Senior VP), Wahib N Zaki (Senior VP), Wolfgang C Berndt (Group VP), Benjamin L Bethell (VP-Manufacturing, Engineering and Purchases, Europe), Robert T Blanchard (VP-Beverage Division), Charles D Broaddus (VP-Research), Charles C Carroll (VP-Bar Soap and Household Cleaning Products Division), William O Coleman (VP-Special Projects), William B Connell (VP-Beauty Care Division), T Marshall Courtney (VP-Cellulose and Specialties Division), Stephen P Donovan (Group VP), Edwin H Eaton Jr (VP and Treasurer), Stona J Fitch (VP-Manufacturing, US), George M Gibson (VP and Comptroller), B Jurgen Hintz (Group VP), Charles A Lieppe (VP-Health and Personal Care Division), Lawrence D Milligan (VP-Sales, Europe), Richard R Nicolosi (VP-Paper Products Division), Geoffrey Place (VP-Research and Development), Louis A Pritchett (VP-Sales), Samuel H Pruett (VP-Personnel), R Marvin Womack (VP-Purchases), Michael J Allen (VP-Disposables and Beverages-Europe), J Richard Andre (VP-Research and Development), Gary E Booth (VP-Research and Development), Gordon F Brunner (VP-Research and Development), Bruce L Byrnes (VP-Packaged Soap and Detergent Division), Larry G Dare (VP-Southern Europe), Richard M Glover (VP-Engineering), Durk I Jager (VP-Japan), Jorge P Montoya (VP-Latin America), Ashley L Ford (Secretary), Richard N Adams (Assistant Treasurer), Joseph R Lawhead (Assistant Treasurer), Carl P Slater (Assistant Treasurer), Robert R Bidwell (Assistant Secretary), John J Cummins (Assistant Secretary), Rita M Neago (Assistant Secretary), Richard C Witte (Assistant Secretary)

PRINCIPAL ACTIVITIES: Laundry and cleaning products: detergents, fabric softeners, cleaners, cleansers. Personal care products: bar soaps, skin care products, toothpastes, mouthwash, deodorants, shampoos, paper tissue products, disposable diapers, pharmaceuticals. Food products: shortenings, oils, baking mixes, peanut butter, potato chips, coffee, soft drinks, tea, citrus products, cookies. Other: cellulose pulp, chemicals, animal feed ingredients
Trade Names: Laundry and Cleaning Products:- All Fabric Bleach: Biz. Dishwashing Detergents: Cascade, Dawn, Ivory Liquid, Joy. Fabric Softeners: Bounce, Downy. Detergents/Soaps: Bold, Cheer, Dash, Dreft, Era, Gain, Ivory Snow, Liquid Tide, Oxydol, Solo, Tide. Personal Care Products:- Analgesics: Encaprin, Norwich Aspirin. Bar Soaps: Camay, Coast, Ivory, Kirk's, Lava, Safeguard, Zest. Decongestant/Expectorant: Head & Chest. Deodorants/Anti-Perspirants: Secret, Sure. Disposable Diapers: Luvs, Pampers. Disposable Incontinent Briefs: Attends. Feminine Protection Products: Always. Hair Conditioners: Ivory, Lilt. Hand & Body Lotion: Wondra. Home Permanent: Lilt. Liquid Soap: Liquid Ivory Soap. Mouthwash: Scope. Oral Antiseptic/Anesthetic: Chloraseptic. Paper Tissue Products: Banner, Charmin, Puffs, White Cloud. Paper Towel: Bounty. Prescription Drugs & Physician-Selected Products: Buprenex, Dantrium, Didronel, Entex, Comhist, Macrodantin, Vivonex. Shampoos: Head & Shoulders, Ivory, Lilt, Pert, Prell. Vidal Sassoon, Pantene. Stomach Remedy: Pepto-Bismol. Toothpastes: Crest, Gleem. Food Products:-Citrus Hill Select, Crisco, Crisco Oil, Crush, Duncan Hines, Duncan Hines Chocolate Chip Cookies, Duncan Hines Creamy Frosting, Folgers, Hires Root Beer, Instant Folgers, Instant High Point, Jif, Pringle's, Puritan Oil, Sun-drop, Tender Leaf. Skin Care Products: Oil of Olay. Cough and Cold Medicines: Vicks. Gastrointestinal Products: Metamucil, Pepto-Bismol
Principal Subsidiaries: Citrus Hill Manufacturing Co; The Buckeye Cellulose Corp; The Buckeye Oilseed Products Co; Disprocon, SA de CV (49%) (Mexico); Crush International Inc; Crush International (Overseas) Ltd (Eire); Crush Industria de Concentrados Ltda (Brazil); Inter-American Orange Crush Co; Promotora de Bienes y Valores SA de CV (Mexico); Crush Mexicana S de RL de CV (Mexico); Sacoma SA (Argentina); Deterperu SA (Peru); Fabricas de Aceite San Jacinto Ltda SA (Peru); The Folger Coffee Co; Hines-Park Foods Inc; Jetco Chemicals Inc; Laboratorio Geka SAC (Chile); Norwich Eaton Pharmaceuticals Inc; Eaton Laboratories Inc; Norwich Overseas Inc; NV Norwich Eaton SA (Benelux); Norwich de Venezuela CA (Venezuela); Norwich Eaton (Hellas) Commercial and Industrial SA (Greece); Norwich Eaton Ltd (UK); Norwich Eaton Pharmaceuticals Pty Ltd (Australia); Norwich Eaton Philippines Inc (Philippines); Norwich Eaton SA de CV (Mexico); Norwich Colombiana SA (Colombia); Norwich Pharmacal Company del Peru (Peru); RohmPharma GmbH (50%) (Germany); Rohm Pharma GmbH (60%) (Austria); P&G Consultoria E Servicos Ltda (Brazil); Procter & Gamble Aktiebolag (Sweden); Procter & Gamble AG (Switzerland); Detergent Products AG (Switzerland); Modern Industries Company-Jeddah (51%) (Saudi Arabia); Modern Industries Company-Dammam (49%) (Saudi Arabia); Modern Products Company-Jeddah (50%) (Saudi Arabia); Moroccan Modern Industries (50%) (Morocco); Procter & Gamble España SA (Spain); Procter & Gamble Hellas AE (Chemical Industries) (Greece); Procter & Gamble Vertriebsgesellschaft mbH (Austria); The Procter & Gamble Manufacturing Company of Lebanon SAL (Lebanon); Societe Immobilière Les Colombettes SA (Switzerland); Procter & Gamble Benelux (Belgium); Procter & Gamble European Technical Center (Belgium); Procter & Gamble Far East Inc; Modern Home Products Ltd (51%) (Taiwan); Procter & Gamble France (France); Procter & Gamble GmbH (Germany); Rolf H Dittmeyer GmbH (Germany); Euro-Juice GmbH (Germany); HELIX Spedition-und Lagerei GmbH (Germany); Dittmeyer France SA (France); Euro-Juice SC (Spain) (Parnership); Dittmeyer NV (Netherlands); Procter & Gamble Inc (Canada); Crush Canada Inc (Canada); Procter & Gamble International Finance NV (Netherlands Antilles); Procter & Gamble Italia SpA (Italy); Procter & Gamble Ltd (UK); Procter & Gamble (NTC) Ltd (UK): Procter & Gamble de Mexico SA de CV (Mexico); Procter & Gamble Productions Inc; Procter & Gamble OY (Finland); Procter & Gamble Philippines Inc (Phillipines); Progam Realty and Development Corp (40%) (Philippines); Procter & Gamble de Venezuela CA (Venezuela); Splendid SpA (Italy); Sycamore Investment Co; The Procter & Gamble Commercial Co; The Procter & Gamble Distributing Co; The Procter & Gamble Manufacutring Co; The D H Food Co; The Procter & Gamble Paper Products Co; The Procter &

Gamble Special Products Co; Richardson-Vicks Inc (and subsidiaries); H&PC Products Inc and a number of inactive subsidiaries
Principal Bank: The Morgan Guaranty Trust Co of New York
Financial Information:

	Jun 30 1986	1Jun 30 1987
	$'000	$'000
Sales revenues	15,439,000	17,000,000
Income before taxes	1,175,000	617,000
Net income	709,000	327,000
Dividends	440,000	455,000
Dividends per share	$2.625	$2.70
Earnings per share	$4.20	$1.87
Common stock	167,800	168,600
Additional paid in capital	374,000	427,000
Currency translation*	(158,000)	(26,000)
Retained income	5,320,000	5,170,000
Shareholders equity	5,954,000	5,990,000

*adjustments

No of Employees: 76,100 worldwide

PRODUCERS COTTON OIL CO

2907 S Maple Avenue, Fresno, CA 93725
Tel: (209) 442-4400
Telex: WUT 355495 prod fso

President: G B Brewer (and Chief Executive Officer)
Senior Executive Officers: G R Stevens (VP Field Services), C R Bell (VP), S K Evans (VP), Sidney B Cox (VP Administration)

PRINCIPAL ACTIVITIES: Farming; cotton ginning and production of cottonseed oil
Parent Company: Bangor Punta Corp-Ultimate Parent Company-Lear Siegler Inc
Principal Bank: Bank of America
Financial Information:

	$'000
Sales revenues	100,000

No of Employees: 1,500

PRODUCERS RICE MILL INC

N Anna Street, PO Box 461, Stuttgart, AR 72160
Tel: (501) 673-4444
Telex: WUT 536455 producers stgt

Chairman: Charles Hammans; Vice Chairman: Gary Sebree
President: Ronald Baily
Senior Executive Officers: Marvin Baden (Executive VP), Keith Glover (Secretary and Treasurer)

PRINCIPAL ACTIVITIES: Processing of rice
Principal Bank: St Louis Bank for Co-ops
Financial Information:

	$'000
Sales revenues	100,000

No of Employees: 300

PRODUCTION OPERATORS CORPORATION

11302 Tanner Road, PO Box 40262, Houston, TX 77240
Tel: (713) 466 0980

Chairman: Carl W Knobloch Jr
President: William C Pickard (and Chief Executive Officer)
Senior Executive Officers: Kenneth W Glover (Senior VP Operations), W W Tubbs (Senior VP, Secretary and Legal Counsel), Ralph E Wilgus (VP and Treasurer)

PRINCIPAL ACTIVITIES: Services for the exploration and production of oil and gas
Principal Subsidiaries: Production Operators Inc; Kamlok Inc; KAC Pipeline Inc; Transmission Systems Inc; Xtra Energy Corporation

Financial Information:

	$'000
Sales revenues	54,000

No of Employees: 350

PRODUCTS RESEARCH & CHEMICAL CORPORATION

5430 San Fernando Road, Glendale, CA 91203
Tel: (818) 240-2060
Telex: WUT 888718 proreco rdl

Chairman: George Gregory (and Chief Executive Officer)
President: Dean M Willard (and Chief Operating Officer)
Senior Executive Officers: Stephen J Thomas (Senior Executive VP), William Calfas (Senior VP and General Counsel), Irvin P Seegman (Senior VP), Richard A Cude (VP), Joseph J Giordano (VP), Jack W Hutt (VP), Jeffrey Young (VP Finance and Secretary)

PRINCIPAL ACTIVITIES: Manufacture of synthetic rubber polymer coatings, adhesives and sealants for insulation, fluid containment and environmental protection
Principal Subsidiaries: Chem-Electro Research Inc; Pre-Cast Inc; Specialty Products Distributing Co; International Polymer Corp; Products Research and Chemical Corp International; PRC International Inc; PRC Holding Co Ltd (Canada); PRC Canada Inc; PRC Distributing Co; Proreco de Mexico SA (Mexico)
Principal Bank: Security Pacific National Bank
Financial Information:

	$'000
Sales revenues	83,000

No of Employees: 600

PROFIT SYSTEMS, INC

80 W Sunrise Highway, PO Box 388, Valley Stream, NY 11582
Tel: (516) 791-1551

Chairman: Harvey E Pittluck
Senior Executive Officers: Dennis A Bakal (VP Operations)

PRINCIPAL ACTIVITIES: Freight forwarding by air
Principal Bank: Chemical Bank
Financial Information:

	$'000
Sales revenues	120,000

No of Employees: 780

PROGRAMABLE CONTROL DIVISION

York & Haverhill Street, Andover, MA 01810
Tel: (617) 475-4700
Telex: 947402

President: Bruce Rusch (and General Manager)
Senior Executive Officers: John A Blaeser (Executive VP), Peter Alberico (VP Finance), John Joslin (VP Engineering), Stephen Mader (VP Marketing), Richard Balmas (VP Quality Control), Albert Libbey (VP Business Development)

PRINCIPAL ACTIVITIES: Production of electronic control and communications equipment
Parent Company: Gould Inc, Rolling Meadows, IL
Principal Bank: The First National Bank of Boston
Financial Information:

	$'000
Sales revenues	66,000

No of Employees: 1,200

PROGRESSIVE CORPORATION (THE)

6300 Wilson Mills Road, Mayfield Village, OH 44143
Tel: (216) 461 5000

Chairman: Peter B Lewis (and President, Chief Executive Officer and Subsidiary Officer)

Senior Executive Officers: Robert L Moore (Senior VP and Subsidiary Officer), William P Cadden (Division President), Stephen J Leaman (Division President), Bruce W Marlow (Division President), Jerry T Shroat (Division President), Daniel L Lewis (Treasurer), Thomas V Perretti (Senior VP), Norton W Rose (Senior VP), Rex S Wolf (Senior VP)

PRINCIPAL ACTIVITIES: Insurance holding company

Principal Subsidiaries: Progressive Casualty Insurance Co; Classic Insurance Co; Progressive American Life Insurance; Progressive American Insurance Co; Progressive Gulf Insurance Co; Progressive Northern Insurance Co; Progressive Northwestern Insurance Co; Progressive Preferred Insurance Co; Progressive Southeastern Insurance Co; Progressive Specialty Insurance Co; United Financial Casualty Co

Principal Bank: National City Bank

Financial Information:

	1985
	$'000
Revenues	456,505
Net income	35,640

No of Employees: 5,500

PROLER INTERNATIONAL CORPORATION

7501 Wallisville Road, Houston, TX 77020
Tel: (713) 675-2281
Telex: TWX 9108813667 proler ho

Chairman: Herman Proler (and Chief Executive Officer and Secretary)

President: Robert L Nueller (and Chief Operating Officer)

Senior Officer: Ken Sandow (Treasurer). Other Officers: Murray P Mangum (VP), Stephen Basarab (VP), Monty Parker (VP), Tom Bodman (VP), Warner Mize (VP)

PRINCIPAL ACTIVITIES: Processing of scrap metal; steel service centers

Principal Subsidiaries: Prolerized Steel Corp (75%); Proleride Transport Systems Inc; MRI Corp. Principal Joint Operations: Hugo-Neu-Proler Company; Maru Shipping Company Inc; Point Comfort Venture; Prolerized Chicago Corporation; Prolerized New England Company; Prolerized Schiabo-Neu Company

Principal Bank: Texas Commerce Bank

Financial Information:

	Jan 31 1986	Jan 31 1987
	$'000	$'000
Sales revenues	117,086	85,757
(Loss) before taxes	(9,061)	(410)
Net income (loss)	(4,162)	518
Dividends	2,196	2,196
Dividends per share	$1.40	$1.40
Earnings (loss) per share	($2.65)	$0.33
Common stock	1,777	1,777
Retained income	76,022	74,344
Shareholders equity	74,525	72,846

No of Employees: 350

PROTECTIVE LIFE CORPORATION

2801 Highway 280 South, Birmingham, AL 35223
Tel: (205) 879 9230

Chairman: William J Rushton III (and Chief Executive Officer)

President: Drayton Nabers Jr (and Chief Operating Officer)

Senior Executive Officers: Thomas K Pennington (Executive VP), Louis C Henderson Jr (Senior VP Operations), A S Williams III (Senior VP and Treasurer), Ryburn H Bailey (VP, Secretary and Legal Counsel), Danny Campbell (VP Corporate Systems), Randy Lowery (VP and Actuary), William R Phillippi (VP Administration), David W Whitehurst (VP and Controller)

PRINCIPAL ACTIVITIES: Life insurance

Principal Subsidiaries: Protective Life Insurance Co; American Foundation Life Insurance Co; United Founders Life Insurance

Principal Bank: AmSouth Bank

Financial Information:

	Dec 31 1985
	$'000
Revenues	289,120
Net income	24,675

No of Employees: 1,100

PROVIDENCE ENERGY CORPORATION

100 Weybosset Street, Providence, RI 02903
Tel: (401) 272 5040

Chairman: Louis R Hampton (and Chief Executive Officer)

President: William S Lalonde (and Chief Operating Officer)

Senior Executive Officers: Thomas F Army (VP Marketing), Robert J Ferranty (Senior VP), George A Battey (VP and Secretary), Paul E Lemont (VP), John J Natalizia (VP), Robert W Owens (VP and Treasurer)

PRINCIPAL ACTIVITIES: Supply of natural gas

Principal Subsidiaries: Providence Gas Company

Principal Bank: Rhode Island Hospital Trust National Bank

Financial Information:

	$'000
Sales revenues	160,000

No of Employees: 275

PROVIDENCE JOURNAL CO

75 Fountain Street, Providence, RI 02902
Tel: (401) 277-7000
Telex: WUT 509317 providencejor

Chairman Emeritus: John C A Watkins; Chairman and Publisher: Michael P Metcalf

President: Stephen Hamblett

Senior Executive Officers: Charles N Mock (Senior VP Personnel), Robert L Wolf (Senior VP Finance), Charles M Hauser (VP and Executive Editor), Jack C Clifford (VP Broadcasting)

PRINCIPAL ACTIVITIES: Publishing of newspapers, radio and television broadcasting; printing

Principal Bank: Chase Manhattan Bank

Financial Information:

	$'000
Sales revenues	433,000

No of Employees: 3,700

PROVIDENT BANCORP INC

1 East 4th Street, Cincinnati, OH 45202
Tel: (513) 579 2000

Chairman: James A Markley Jr (and President)

President: Allen L David (and Chief Executive Officer)

Senior Executive Officers: Philip R Myers (Senior Executive VP), George L Ballou II (VP), T James Berry (Treasurer), Amor C Emmert (VP), Jerry R Steffey (VP), Leslie C Nomeland (Secretary and Legal Counsel)

PRINCIPAL ACTIVITIES: Banking

Principal Subsidiaries: Midwest Bank & Trust Co; Provident Bank

Principal Bank: The Provident Bank

Financial Information:

	Dec 31 1985
	$'000
Revenues	128,420
Net income	8,580

No of Employees: 960

PROVIDENT LIFE AND ACCIDENT INSURANCE COMPANY OF AMERICA

Fountain Square, Chattanooga, TN 37402
Tel: (615) 755-1011
Telex: WUT 558425 provlife cta b

Chairman: H Carey Hanlin (and Chief Executive Officer)
President: Winston W Walker (and Chief Operating Officer)
Senior Executive Officers: Thomas C Hardy (Executive VP and Chief Financial Officer), Richard Park (Treasurer and VP, Financial Controls), Charles R Griffith (Senior VP), Patrick J Harverty (Senior VP)

PRINCIPAL ACTIVITIES: Life, health and accident insurance
Trade Names: Provident Companies
Principal Subsidiaries: Provident National Assurance Co; Provident Life & Casualty Co Inc
Principal Bank: American National Bank & Trust Co
Financial Information:

	Dec 31 1985	Dec 31 1986
	$'000	$'000
Premium income	1,170,790	1,337,032
Investment income	455,598	613,294
Income before taxes	163,780	125,409
Net income	124,971	146,798
Dividends per share	$0.875	$0.82
Earnings per share	$2.89	$2.15
Common stock	39,376	39,378
Retained income	843,566	959,713
Shareholders equity	897,552	1,009,056

No of Employees: 5,900

PROVIDENT MUTUAL LIFE INSURANCE CO OF PHILADELPHIA

1600 Market Street, Phildelphia, PA 19103
Tel: (215) 636-5000

Chairman: John A Miller (and Chief Executive Officer)
President: Lester J Rowell Jr (and Chief Operating Officer)
Senior Executive Officers: John T Unipan (Executive VP), Arnold A Dicke (Senior VP), Robert J Gibbons (Senior VP), Stanley R Reber (Senior VP), Gerald B Beam (Senior VP Corporate), Guy H Edwards (VP)

PRINCIPAL ACTIVITIES: Life insurance company
Principal Subsidiaries: W H Newbold's Son & Co Inc; Continental American Life Insurance Co; PML Securities Co; Washington Square Life Insurance Co
Financial Information:

	Dec 31 1985	Dec 31 1986
	$'000	$'000
Premium income	411,770	499,979
Investment income	199,444	191,516
Net income	603,286	699,420
Total assets	2,840,000	3,030,000

No of Employees: 1,100 employees; 1,300 sales agents

PRUDENTIAL FELDCO INC

63-15 Traffic Street, Ridgewood, NY 11385
Tel: (718) 386-9000

President: Alan Hodes
Senior Executive Officers: Michael Greenberg (VP), Jack Hodes (Purchasing Agent)

PRINCIPAL ACTIVITIES: Production of paper and paper products for schools
Principal Bank: Continental Illinois National Bank & Trust Company of Chicago
Financial Information:

	$'000
Sales revenues	50,000

No of Employees: 600

PRUDENTIAL FINANCIAL SERVICES CORPORATION

127 East 3300 South, Salt Lake City, UT 84115
Tel: (801) 467 0501

Chairman: Gene Donovan (and Chief Executive Officer)
President: Kent W Larsen (and Chief Operating Officer)
Senior Executive Officers: Richard L Shanaman (Senior Executive VP and Chief Operating Officer), John A Adams (Executive VP), John B Martensen (Executive VP) Larry R Stevens (Executive VP)

PRINCIPAL ACTIVITIES: Financial services including savings and loans
Principal Subsidiaries: Prudential Capital Group; Prudential Development Co; Prudential Federal Savings and Loans Association
Financial Information:

	$'000
Revenues	85,000

No of Employees: 80

PRUDENTIAL INSURANCE COMPANY OF AMERICA (THE)

Prudential Plaza, Newark, NJ 07101
Tel: (201) 877-6000
Telex: WUT 138942 prudential nwk

Chairman: Robert C Winters (and Chief Executive Officer); Vice Chairman: Garnett L Keith Jr (and Chief Investment Officer)
President: Joseph J Melone
Senior Executive Officers: George L Ball (Chairman and Chief Executive Officer, Prudential Capital and Investment Services Inc), A Douglas Murch (Executive VP), Richard G Merrill (Executive VP). Senior Officers: Robert E Riley (Executive VP, Prudential Investment Corp), Lesley R Ralson (President, Group Operations), Pellegrino P Porraro (Executive VP, Individual Insurance), James W Stevens (Executive VP, Prudential Investment Corp), Ronald D Barbaro (President, Canadian Operations), James T Barton (President, Prudential-Bache Securities Inc), William M Bethke (President and Chief Executive Officer, Prudential Affiliated Investors), Arthur H Burton Jr (President, North Central Operations), Joseph F Dunn (Senior VP, District Agencies), James E Clark (President, Western Operations), William D Clowney (President, Eastern Operations), James E Dwane (President, Prudential Reinsurance Company), William S Field (Chairman, Prudential Venture Capital Management, Inc), James R Gillen (Senior VP and General Counsel Law Department), Eugene B Heimberg (Senior VP, Investment Services), Robert P Hill (Senior VP and Actuary Actuarial and Product Development Department), William P Link (Senior VP, Human Resources), Malcolm D MacKinnon (Senior VP, Information Systems), Kenneth E MacWilliams (Chairman, Prudential Capital, Inc), Eugene M O'Hara (Senior VP and Comptroller Comptroller's Department), Clarence F Pease (Senior VP, Ordinary Agencies), Scott Pierce (Chairman and Chief Executive Officer, The Prudential Asset Management Company), I Edward Price (Senior VP and Corporate Acutary Corporate Actuarial Department), Rodney W Reynolds (Senior Managing Director, Capital Markets Group), William H Tremayne (Senior VP, Public Affairs), Robert F Welsh (Senior VP, Individual Insurance Systems and Administration), Clifford H Whitcomb (President, Prudential Property and Casualty Company), Edward D Zinbarg (Senior Managing Director, Prudential Equity Management Associates), Martha Clark Briley (VP and Treasurer), Dorothy K Light (VP and Secretary)

PRINCIPAL ACTIVITIES: Insurance and other financial services
Principal Subsidiaries: (all wholly owned); Prudential Capital Inc; The Prudential Asset Management Company Inc; Prudential Capital and Investment Services Inc; Prudential Property and Casualty Insurance Company; Prudential Reinsurance Company; Prudential Venture Capital Management Company; Sony Prudential Life Insurance Company; The Prudential

Investment Corp; Pruco Life Insurance Company; The Prudential Mortgage Capital Co Inc; The Prudential Property Company; Prudential-Bache Securities Inc; Prudential Health Care Plan Inc; Prudential Real Estate Affiliates

Financial Information:

	Dec 31 1985	Dec 31 1986
	$'000	$'000
Premium income	17,234,000	18,123,000
Investment income	6,820,000	7,645,000
Total assets	115,728,000	134,484,000

No of Employees: 85,500

PRYOR CORPORATION

222 William St, Bensenville, IL 60106
Tel: (312) 860-3100

President: Lee Pryor
Senior Executive Officers: Mike Simpson (VP), Thomas R Hoppensteadt (VP and (Treasurer)

PRINCIPAL ACTIVITIES: Computer tape, disk packs, cartridges and cassettes
Parent Company: Pryor Computer Industries Inc
Financial Information:

	$'000
Sales revenues	50,000

No of Employees: 350

PS GROUP (FORMERLY PSA, INC)

3225 N Harbor Drive, San Diego, CA 92101
Tel: (714) 574-2100

Chairman: John P Guerin
President: Paul C Barkley (and Chief Executive Officer)
Senior Executive Officers: George M Shortley (Senior VP Finance), Morton Rible (VP Legal), Lawrence A Guske (VP)

PRINCIPAL ACTIVITIES: Holding company with interests in airline services in six Western states through Pacific Southwest Airlines; aircraft leasing and engine overhaul services
Principal Bank: Bank of America
Financial Information:

	Dec 31 1986
	$'000
Sales revenues	895,423
Net (loss)	(13,930)
(Loss) per share	($2.25)
Shareholders equity	212,282

No of Employees: 5,590

PT COMPONENTS INC

7545 Rockville Road, PO Box 802, Indianapolis, IN 46206
Tel: (317) 273 5500

President: G Ronald Morris (and Chief Executive Officer)
Senior Executive Officers: Jerry D Pierick (Senior VP Finance and Administration), R W Rogers (Senior VP Franchise), Clarence L Griffin (VP Division), James W Landers (VP Division), James J Mitchell (VP Division), M Timothy Yonker (VP Division), Robert E Swinehart (VP Corporate Development and Assistant Secretary), Ronald G Statz (VP Human Resources and Employee Relations), John P McEwen (Assistant Treasurer), Thomas C Yedlick (Controller)

PRINCIPAL ACTIVITIES: Manufacture of industrial transmission equipment
Financial Information:

	$'000
Sales revenues	204,000

No of Employees: 2,840

PUBCO CORPORATION

3830 Kelley Avenue, Cleveland, OH 44114-4534
Tel: (216) 881-5300

Chairman: Maurice Saltzman
President: Robert H Kanner (and Chief Executive Officer)
Senior Executive Officers: George H Hahn (Executive VP and Chief Executive Officer), Stephen R Kalette (VP, Assistant Secretary and Legal Counsel), Anthony M Potelicki (Controller and Treasurer), Henry W Pohl (Chief Financial Officer)

PRINCIPAL ACTIVITIES: Printing services
Parent Company: Buckeye Business Products Inc
Financial Information:

	$'000
Sales revenues	45,970

No of Employees: 1,500

PUBLIC SERVICE CO OF INDIANA, INC

1000 E Main Street, Plainfield, IN 46168
Tel: (317) 839-9611

Chairman: Hugh A Barker (and Chief Executive Officer)
President: Darrell W Menscer (and Chief Operating Officer)
Senior Executive Officers: Jon D Noland (Senior VP), W E George (Senior VP), Vernley R Rehnstrom (Senior VP), Seth W Shields (Senior VP), Larry E Thomas (Senior VP), Duejean C Garrett (VP and General Counsel), W J Hebble (VP), Gerald Hofmockel (VP), Harold L Isaacs (VP), F Dale Justis (VP), Danny L Littell (VP), John P Masselink (VP), Joseph W Messick Jr (VP), Dale W Osborn (VP), Michael M Sample (VP), Richard P Stein (VP), Richard E Willis (VP)

PRINCIPAL ACTIVITIES: Supply of electricity
Principal Bank: Chase Manhattan Bank
Financial Information:

	$'000
Sales revenues	1,000,000

No of Employees: 4,000

PUBLIC SERVICE CO OF NEW HAMPSHIRE

1000 Elm St, Manchester, NH 03105
Tel: (603) 669-4000

President: Robert J Harrison (and Chief Executive Officer)
Senior Executive Officers: John C Duffett (Executive VP and Chief Operating Officer), William B Derrickson (Senior VP Nuclear Energy), Roy G Barbour (VP Engineering and Real Estate), Charles E Bayless (VP Finance), George Branscombe (VP and Treasurer), D Pierre G Cameron Jr (VP and General Counsel), John P Edwards (VP Public Affairs), William T Frain Jr (VP Accounting and Rates), Warren A Harvey (VP Production), Ralph S Johnson (VP Power Planning and Supply), Wendell P Johnson (VP Nuclear Production), James L Nevins (VP Employee Relations and Divisional Operations), Robert A Parks (VP Management Information Services), George S Thomas (VP Nuclear Production)

PRINCIPAL ACTIVITIES: Electricity supply
Principal Bankers: First National Bank of Boston
Financial Information:

	$'000
Sales revenues	520,000

No of Employees: 2,300

PUBLIC SERVICE CO OF NEW MEXICO

1650 University Boulevard, Albuquerque, NM 87102
Tel: (505) 848-2700

Chairman: J D Geist (and President)
Presidents: J P Bundrant (and Chief Operating Officer Electric Operations); J T Ackerman (and Chief Operating Officer Gas Operations)
Senior Executive Officers: W M Eglinton (Senior VP Electric Operations), J B J Mulcock (Senior VP Corporate Affairs and Secretary), A J Robison (Senior VP and Chief Financial Officer), R B Rountree (Senior VP), J L Wilkins (Senior VP Power Supply, Electric), W C Wygant (Senior VP Administration, Electric), D A Blackwell (VP Finance and

Planning, Gas), D A James (VP Marketing, Rates and Regulatory Affairs, Gas), B D Lackey (VP and Controller), M H Lambert (VP Gas Supply), M A McDonald (VP Human Resources and Support Services, Electric), R F Mershon (VP Divisional Operations), J K Murphy (VP Regulatory and Business Policy), H O Pocock (VP Human Resources and Administration Support, Gas), L W Reynolds Jr (VP and Treasurer), J E Sterba (VP Management, Electric)

PRINCIPAL ACTIVITIES: Distribution of electricity and natural gas
Principal Bankers: Irving Trust Company
Financial Information:

	$'000
Sales revenues	698,000

No of Employees: 3,000

PUBLIC SERVICE COMPANY OF COLORADO

550 15th St, Denver, CO 80202
Tel: (303) 571-7511

Chairman: Richard F Walker
President: Delwin D Hock (and Chief Operating Officer)
Senior Executive Officers: Bryant O'Donnell (Executive VP and General Counsel), Clark B Ewald (Senior VP Customers), James N Bumpus (Senior VP Finance and Administration)

PRINCIPAL ACTIVITIES: Supply of electricity and natural gas
Financial Information:

	Dec 31 1985	Dec 31 1986
	$'000	$'000
Sales revenues	1,747,483	1,657,863
Net income	110,693	123,821
Dividends per share	$2.00	$2.00
Earnings per share	$1.81	$2.06*
Common stock	707,429	708,548
Retained income	190,257	92,428
Shareholders equity	897,686	800,976

*before extraordinary item

No of Employees: 6,100

PUBLIC SERVICE COMPANY OF NORTH CAROLINA INC

400 Cox Road, PO Box 1398, Gastonia, NC 28053
Tel: (704) 864 6731

Chairman: Charles E Zeigler (and President)
Senior Executive Officers: Frank M Creel (Senior VP), G Edgar Dabbs Jr (Senior VP Central and Western Operations), C Marshall Dickey (Senior VP), E L Flanagan Jr (Senior VP and Treasurer), H Jack Knox (Senior VP), Robert A Linn (Senior VP Administration and Services and Secretary), Joseph F Noon (Senior VP), Robert T Watkins (Senior VP), John W Brown (VP), Thomas R Kirkland (VP), Robert T Knox (VP Microcomputer Systems Applications), Jerry W Richardson (VP), Wilma D Ridly (VP and Assistant Treasurer), Allen J Schock (VP), Robert D Voigt (VP and Controller)

PRINCIPAL ACTIVITIES: Supply of natural gas
Principal Bank: First Union National Bank
Financial Information:

	$'000
Sales revenues	215,000

No of Employees: 960

PUBLIC SERVICE ENTERPRISE GROUP INC

80 Park Plaza, Newark, NJ 07101
Tel: (201) 430-7000
Telex: TWX 710 9954442 pseg tels nwk

Chairman: E James Ferland (and President and Chief Executive Officer)
Senior Executive Officers: Everett L Morris (Senior Executive VP), Frederick W Schneider (Executive VP-Operations), Frederick R DeSanti (Senior VP-Customer Operations), Robert W Lockwood (Senior VP-Administration), Stephen A Mallard (Senior VP-Planning and Research), Donald A Anderson (VP-Information Systems), Lawrence R Codey (VP and Corporate Rate Counsel), Pierre R H Landrieu (VP-Engineering and Construction), John Maddocks (VP-Public Affairs), Charles E Maginn Jr (VP-Human Resources), Wallace A Maginn (VP and Treasurer), Winthrop E Mange Jr (VP-Corporate Services), Corbin A McNeill Jr (VP-Nuclear), Parker C Peterman (VP and Comptroller), Louis L Rizzi (VP-Customer and Marketing Services), William Saller (VP-Governmental Affairs), R Edwin Selover (VP and General Counsel), Robert S Smith (VP and Secretary), Robert F Steinke (VP-Fuel Supply), Rudolph D Stys (VP-Transmission and Distribution), Richard A Uderitz (VP-Production). Public Service Enterprise Group Incorporated: E James Ferland (Chairman of the Board, President and Chief Executive Officer), Everett L Morris (Vice President), Frederick W Schneider (Vice President), Wallace A Maginn (Treasurer), Parker C Peterman (Comptroller), Robert S Smith (Secretary)

PRINCIPAL ACTIVITIES: Holding company whose subsidiaries are engaged in the generation, transmission, distribution and sale of electric energy and in the production, transmission, and distribution of natural or manufactured gas in New Jersey; the development of cogeneration and alternative energy production facilities
Principal Subsidiaries: Public Service Electric and Gas Company; Energy Development Corporation; Public Service Resources Corporation
Principal Bank: First Fidelity Bank
Financial Information:

	Dec 31 1985	Dec 31 1986
	$'000	$'000
Operating revenues	4,428,341	4,498,416
Operating income before taxes	637,769	677,284
Net income	399,632	378,463
Common dividend	346,803	390,289
Dividends per share	$2.81	$2.93
Earnings per share	$3.27	$2.84
Common stock	2,535,687	2,632,662
Retained income	1,013,285	993,836
Common equity	3,548,972	3,626,498

(1) common and preferred

No of Employees: 13,723

PUBLICKER INDUSTRIES INC

777 W Putnam Avenue, Greenwich, CT 06830
Tel: (203) 531-4500
Telex: WUT 516286 publicker ind

Chairman: Harry I Freund; Vice Chairmen: Jay S Goldsmith, Norman Kaplan
President: David L Herman (and Chief Executive Officer)
Senior Executive Officers: John A Antonaccio (Senior VP), W B Kopp (Senior VP), Morton R Shapiro (Senior VP), John Kellett (VP), Richard H Friedman (VP Finance), Gerald M Tierney Jr (VP and Secretary)

PRINCIPAL ACTIVITIES: Production of alcoholic drinks and industrial alcohol; animal feedstuffs; industrial chemicals; contract packaging
Principal Subsidiaries: Continental Distilling Corp; Inver House Distillers Ltd (UK); Publicker Chemical Corp; Publicker International Inc; Thermice Corp
Financial Information:

	$'000
Sales revenues	35,300

No of Employees: 900

PUBLISHERS PAPER CO

419 Main Street, Oregon City, OR 97045
Tel: (503) 656-5211

President: G M Ross

Senior Executive Officers: F E Woods (VP Pulp and Paper), H N Moon (VP, Treasurer and Controller)

PRINCIPAL ACTIVITIES: Production of paper and wood products
Parent Company: The Times Mirror Company, Los Angeles, CA
Financial Information:

	$'000
Sales revenues	300,000

No of Employees: 2,300

PUBLIX SUPER MARKETS INC

2040 George Jenkins Blvd, Lakeland, FL 33802
Tel: (813) 688-1188

Chairman: George W Jenkins
President: Mark C Hollis
Senior Executive Officers: J Lamar Blanton (VP Meat Operations), Lenton Brunson (VP Purchasing), Eugene Dampier (VP Contruction and Maintenance), George C Forsythe (VP Jacksonville Division), William M Hollis (VP), Charles H Jenkins Jr (VP Real Estate), Howard Jenkins (VP Research), Charles Lane (VP Lakeland Division), Clemon Newsome (VP Southeast Coast Division), Daniel M Risener (VP Information Systems), E H Ruth (VP Personnel), Lawrence Sapp (VP Warehousing and Distribution), R William Schroter (VP Advertising and Marketing), Edward T Shivers (VP Insurance and Safety), Eugene Succow (VP Bakery Operations)

PRINCIPAL ACTIVITIES: Food retailing
Principal Bank: Peoples Bank of Lakeland
Financial Information:

	Dec 31 1985	Dec 31 1986
	$'000	$'000
Sales revenues	3,445,520	3,760,453
Net income	71,830	84,308
Earnings per share	$1.47	$1.72
Shareholders equity	482,114	559,503

No of Employees: 40,100

PUGET SOUND BANCORP

1119 Pacific Avenue, Tacoma, WA 98402
Tel: (206) 593 3600

Chairman: W W Philip (and Chief Executive Officer)
President: Robert Weber
Senior Executive Officers: G C Lange (Executive VP), Lazarus Politakis (Executive VP), D G Vandenheuvel (Executive VP and Chief Financial Officer), Jonathan Fine (VP and Treasurer), J L Maxwell (VP and Counsel)

PRINCIPAL ACTIVITIES: Banking
Financial Information:

	$'000
Revenues	335,000
Net income	37,000

No of Employees: 1,750

PUGET SOUND POWER & LIGHT CO

Puget Power Building, Bellevue, WA 98009
Tel: (206) 454-6363

President: John W Ellis (and Chief Executive Officer)
Senior Executive Officers: R R Sonstelie (Executive VP Finance), D H Knight (Senior VP Office of President), R V Myers (Senior VP Operations), M M Ryan (Senior VP Administration), E A Andrews (VP Division and Customer Services), R G Bailey (VP Power Supply, Loads and Resources), B Dochnahl (VP Human Resources), R P Ernst (VP Corporate Planning), W J Finnegan (VP Engineering), D A Krause (VP Finance and Investor Relations and Treasurer), N L McReynolds (VP Corporate Relations and Communications), R E Olson (VP Finance), R H Swartzell (VP Budget and Operations Planning), G B Swofford (VP Rates and Customer Programs)

PRINCIPAL ACTIVITIES: Electricity supply
Principal Bankers: Seattle First National Bank
Financial Information:

	$'000
Sales revenues	715,000
Net income	88,000

No of Employees: 2,400

PULASKI FURNITURE CORPORATION

Box 1371, Pulaski, VA 24301
Tel: (703) 980-7330

President: B C Wampler (and Chief Executive Officer)
Senior Executive Officers: W R Kennedy (Executive VP Manufacturing), T G Wampler (VP and Secretary), James H Kelly (VP), Randolph V Chrisley (VP Sales), Ira S Crawford (VP), Jason A Gibbs (Treasurer)

PRINCIPAL ACTIVITIES: Production of household furniture
Principal Bank: Sovran Bank
Financial Information:

	$'000
Sales revenues	74,000

No of Employees: 1,400

PULITZER PUBLISHING CO

900 N Tucker Blvd, St Louis, MO 63101
Tel: (314) 622-7000
Telefax: (314) 622-7408

Chairman: Joseph Pulitzer Jr; Vice Chairman: Glenn A Christopher
President: Michael E Pulitzer
Senior Executive Officers: Ken Elkins (Senior VP-Broadcasting), Ronald H Ridgway (Senior VP-Finance), Nicholas G Penniman IV (Senior VP-Newspaper Operations), R Jeffrey Edwards (Treasurer)

PRINCIPAL ACTIVITIES: Publishing of newspapers; television and radio broadcasting
Principal Subsidiaries: KOAT Television Inc; WGAL-TV Inc; Phoenix Broadcasting Inc; Star Publishing Company; Lerner Newspapers Inc; Pulitzer Community Newspapers Inc; WLKY-TV; WPTA-TV; WXII-TV; WYFF-TV; KETV Television Inc
Principal Bank: Mercantile Bank
Financial Information:

	1986
	$'000
Sales revenues	329,115
Income before taxes	34,768
Net income	16,443
Dividends	3,508
Dividends per share	$0.202
Earnings per share	$1.22
Common stock	1,867
Retained income	145,554
Shareholders equity	6,726

Principal Shareholders: Joseph Pulitzer, Jr; Michael E Pulitzer; David E Moore
No of Employees: 3,234 Full Time; 805 Part Time

PULLMAN COMPANY (THE)

182 Nassau St, Princeton, NJ 08540
Tel: (609) 683-1770
Telex: 881646 PULLMAN TRNUD

Chairman: Thomas M Begel (and President and Chief Executive Officer); Vice Chairman: James R Shepley
Senior Executive Officers: Andrew M Massimilla (Executive VP and Chief Operating Officer), Anthony J Garcia (Senior VP and Chief Financial Officer), William D Sivitz (Senior VP and General Counsel), Joseph E Cox (VP and Treasurer), Ronald

H Glasshoff (VP and Controller), Robert P Rowe (Group VP), Ralph E Stewart (Group VP), Peyton H Houston (Secretary)

PRINCIPAL ACTIVITIES: Pullman is a Fortune 500 manufacturing company serving selected industrial, commercial, defense and municipal markets. It is a leading maker of truck trailers, aircraft seating, food service equipment, weapons-system components, refuse disposal equipment and fluid-handling systems

Financial Information:

	Sep 30 1985	Sep 30 1986
	$'000	$'000
Sales revenues	305,259	534,104
Income before taxes	17,331	27,098
Net income	14,090	16,174
Dividends	-	4,853
Dividends per share	-	$0.12
Earnings per share	$0.64	$0.40
Common stock	2,111	4,068
Retained (deficit)	(30,654)	(19,333)
Shareholders equity	32,606	163,195

No of Employees: 5,500

PULTE HOME CORPORATION

6400 Farmington Road, W Bloomfield, MI 48033
Tel: (313) 661-1500

Chairman: James Grosfeld (and Chief Executive Officer)
President: Robert K Burgess
Senior Executive Officers: William J Pulte (Chairman of the Executive Committee), Richard C Staky (Senior VP and Chief Financial Officer), David Ebling (VP and Controller), James H Waldrop (VP)

PRINCIPAL ACTIVITIES: Civil engineering and construction of domestic buildings; real estate development
Principal Bank: National Bank of Detroit
Financial Information:

	Dec 31 1985	Dec 31 1986
	$'000	$'000
Sales revenues	773,280	836,939
Net income	23,706	20,738
Earnings per share	$0.90	$0.79
Shareholders equity	169,350	188,180

No of Employees: 1,500

PUNTA GORDA ISLES INC

1625 West Marion Avenue, Punta Gorda, FL 33950
Tel: (813) 637 3881

Chairman: Andrew S Love Jr
President: James J O'Connor III (and Chief Executive Officer)
Senior Executive Officers: Paula F McQueen (VP, Secretary and Treasurer), Richard Farrell (VP), Geoffrey L Lorah (Assistant Secretary-Treasurer)

PRINCIPAL ACTIVITIES: Construction of residential property and community developer
Principal Subsidiaries: Burnt Store Marina Inc; Gulf Coast Credit Corporation; Punta Gorda Developers Inc; Twin County Utilities Co Inc; Burnt Store Utilities Inc; Deep Creek Utilities Inc
Principal Bank: Naples Federal
Financial Information:

	Dec 31 1985	Dec 31 1986
	$'000	$'000
Sales revenues	32,758	28,404
Income (loss) before taxes	(14,007)	2,966
Net income (loss)	(12,090)	2,966
Earnings (loss) per share	($4.30)	$1.02
Common stock	332	332
Retained (deficit)	(12,037)	(9,071)

No of Employees: 146

PURITAN-BENNETT CORPORATION

9401 Indian Creek Pkwy, Overland Park, KS 66225
Tel: (913) 649-0444
Telex: WUT 314517 pur ben corp

Chairman: B A Dole Jr (and President and Chief Executive Officer)
Senior Executive Officers: John L Brown (VP, General Manager, Bennett Division), Robert S Grimes (VP, General Manager, Bennett Group), Burrell C Johnson (VP, General Manager Aero Systems Division) C Johnson (VP), M E Butts (VP), John H Morrow (VP, General Manager, Puritan Division), John F Sweeney (VP, General Manager, Boston Division), Lee A Robbins (Chief Financial Officer)

PRINCIPAL ACTIVITIES: Manufacture of medical gases and industrial gases; medical and surgical instruments, orthopedic and surgical prosthetics and appliances
Principal Bank: Commerce Bank of Kansas City
Financial Information:

	$'000
Sales revenues	124,000

No of Employees: 1,740

PURITY CHEESE COMPANY

PO Box 660037, Dallas, TX 75266
Tel: (214) 450-6151

Senior Executive Officers: Frank Higgins (VP and General Manager Dairy Products), Dave Levits (VP Sales and Marketing)

PRINCIPAL ACTIVITIES: Manufacture of cheese and meat products
Parent Company: Anderson Clayton & Co
Principal Bank: Republic National Bank
Financial Information:

	$'000
Sales revenues	75,000

No of Employees: 400

PUROLATOR COURIER CORPORATION

131 Morristown Road, Basking Ridge, NJ 07920
Tel: (201) 953-6400

Chairman: Nicholas F Brady
President: C Howard Hardesty Jr (and Chief Executive Officer)
Senior Executive Officers: Frederick H Cook (Chairman of Executive Committee), Arthur N Demelle (Executive VP Finance), W Thomas Margetts (Senior VP Human Resources), Donald F Mayer (Senior VP Operations), David R Paridy (Senior VP Auto Products), Thomas J Whyte (Senior VP and General Counsel), James W Wilson (Senior VP International)

PRINCIPAL ACTIVITIES: Collection and delivery by air and land of urgent materials, interests in automotive components and filters
Principal Subsidiaries: Purolator Auto and Industrial Products; Purolator Products Inc; Purolator Services Inc; Stant Inc
Principal Bank: Fidelity Union Bank
Financial Information:

	Dec 31 1986
	$'000
Sales revenues	841,434
Net (loss)	(57,643)
(Loss) per share	($7.54)
Shareholders equity	121,031

No of Employees: 19,500

PYRO ENERGY CORPORATION

653 South Hebron Avenue, Evansville, IN 47715
Tel: (812) 473 8600

Chairman: Charles W Schulties (and President and Chief Executive Officer)

Senior Executive Officers: Harvey Fenster (Executive VP), Leland Franz (VP Oil and Gas), Charles H Arbaugh (Secretary and Legal Counsel)

PRINCIPAL ACTIVITIES: Coal mining and oil and gas exploration and drilling
Principal Bank: Morgan Guaranty Bank and Trust Company
Financial Information:

	$'000
Sales revenues	130,000

No of Employees: 1,000

QMS INC
1 Magnum Pass, Mobile, AL 36618
Tel: (205) 633 4300

Chairman: James L Busby (and President)
Senior Executive Officers: Jack R Altherr (Executive VP Finance and Administration and Treasurer), Arthur K Hyzer (Executive VP Product Development and Marketing), Michael C Dow (Senior VP Sales and Technical Services), N L Hanks (Senior VP), Donald L Parker (Senior VP Technology), R H Kennedy (VP), R W Smith (VP), L J Watt (VP), G William Speer (Secretary)

PRINCIPAL ACTIVITIES: Manufacture of electronic equipment for the computing industry
Financial Information:

	$'000
Sales revenues	48,000

No of Employees: 280

QST INDUSTRIES, INC
231 S Jefferson, Chicago, IL 60606
Tel: (312) 930-9400
Telex: RCA 210018 gst cgo

President: Ely Lionheart
Senior Executive Officers: Thomas Danch (VP), Craig Reagor (VP), Sidney Bloom (Secretary and Treasurer)

PRINCIPAL ACTIVITIES: Convertor of pocketing linings and manufacturer of Ban Rol, waistbands, bindings and elastics
Trade Names: Quick Service Textiles, Ban Rol Company, Samuel Harbor Sons, Atlantic Bias Products, Standard Bias Binding, Dallas Bias Products
Principal Bank: Mid-City National Bank
Financial Information:

	$'000
Sales revenues	150,000
Shareholders equity-over	30,000

No of Employees: 200

QUADREX CORPORATION
1700 Dell Avenue, Campbell, CA 95008
Tel: (408) 866 4510

Chairman: Sherman Naymark
President: Robert T Bruce (and Chief Executive Officer)
Senior Executive Officers: Russell J Hammer (VP), Arthur Marquardt (VP), Stanford Springel (Chief Financial Officer)

PRINCIPAL ACTIVITIES: Provision of consultancy services in the fields of engineering, architecture and surveying
Principal Subsidiaries: Nevada Inspection Services Inc; Quadrex Computer Systems Inc; Quadrex Energy Services Corporation; Quadrex HPS Inc; Quadrex International Corporation
Principal Bank: Bank of America National Trust & Savings Association
Financial Information:

	$'000
Sales revenues	55,000

No of Employees: 640

QUAKER CHEMICAL CORPORATION
Elm & Lee Streets, Conshohocken, PA 19428
Tel: (215) 828-4250
Telefax: (215) 685-1093

Chairman: Peter A Benoliel (and President and Chief Executive Officer)
Senior Executive Officers: E Robert Aemisegger (VP-International Operations), Donald E Boswell (VP-Research and Development), Ira R Dolich (VP-Corporate Technology), Anthony F Esposito (VP-Sales), William L Fennimore (VP-Marketing), William G Hamilton (Treasurer), George L Nowicki (VP-Domestic Operations), Karl H Spaeth (VP and Corporate Secretary), Joseph F Spanier (Corporate Controller), George M Zapp (Group VP)

PRINCIPAL ACTIVITIES: Manufacture of industrial and specialty chemicals
Trade Names: FERROCOTE (R), MICROCUT (R), MICROGRIND (R), QUACAST (R), KUT (R), QUAKER QUASOL (R), QUAKER QUAKEROL (R), QUINTOLUBRIC (R), QWENE (R), QWERL (R), TINNOL (R), and many others
Principal Subsidiaries and Divisions: (100% owned unless stated): Quaker Chemical Corporation; QuakerChem Canada Ltd (Canada); Quaker Computer Solutions Inc; Overdale Corp; Selby Battersby & Co; Quaker Petroleum Chemicals Company; Gulf Coast Division; Mid-Continent Division; Permian Division; Western Division; Quaker Chemical (Holland) BV (Netherlands); Quaker Chemical Ltd (UK); Quaker Chimica Italiana SpA (Italy); Quaker Chemical (Australasia) Pty Ltd (51%) (Australia); Nippon Quaker Chemical Ltd (50%) (Japan); Quaker Quimica Española SA (50%) (Spain); Quaker Commercial Chemicals (Pty) Ltd (50%) (South Africa); TecniQuimia Mexicana SA de CV (40%) (Mexico)
Principal Bank: Philadelphia National Bank
Financial Information:

	Dec 31 1985 $'000	Dec 31 1986 $'000
Sales revenues	122,745	128,059
Income before taxes	12,872	14,103
Net income	7,580	8,530
Dividends	2,703	2,957
Dividends per share	$40.39	$0.44
Earnings per share	$1.09	$1.26
Common stock	6,960	6,970
Retained income	55,096	60,669
Shareholders equity	59,200	66,654

Number of Shareholders: 900
No of Employees: 929

QUAKER OATS CO
Merchandise Mart Plaza, Chicago, IL 60654
Tel: (312) 222-77111
Telex: GRT 3733252 quaker oat cgo

Chairman: William D Smithburg (and Chief Executive Officer)
President: Frank J Morgan (and Chief Operating Officer)
Senior Executive Officers: Douglas W Mills (Executive VP Diversified Grocery Products), Paul E Price (Executive VP International Grocery Products), Hedric E Rhodes (Executive VP US Foods), R B Sampsell (Executive VP, President Fisher Price Division), Michael J Callahan (Senior VP Finance), Luther C McKinney (Senior VP Law), David R Nogle (Senior VP, US Grocery Products Services), Lawrence M Baytos (VP Human Resources), Ronald T Brzezinski (VP Information Systems), John H Calhoun (VP and Associate General Corporate Counsel), Leland R Chalmers (VP Tax), James F Doyle (VP Latin America), Joseph G Egan (VP and Special Counsel), Jon K Grant (VP, President Quaker Oats of Canada), R Thomas Howell Jr (VP and General Corporate Counsel), Richard D Jaquith (VP and Treasurer), Russell L Jones (VP, President Food Service Division), Deborah E Kelley (VP Corporate Affairs), Richard E Kozitka (VP Corporate Administration Services), Philip A Marineau (VP,

President Grocery Specialties Division), W Thomas Phillips (VP Corporate Programs), Jose A Rodriguez (VP Europe), Thomas F Roeser (VP Government Relations), William C Trotter (VP Science and Technology), Terry G Westbrook (VP Business Development and Corporate Planning), Donald G Wittmer (VP and Controller), George J Yapp (VP Pet Foods)

PRINCIPAL ACTIVITIES: Manufacture of food products including cereals, popcorn, frozen fruit and vegetables, canned meats, vegetable oil, frozen fruit juice, pet food, Fisher-Price toys; mail order house, retail interests
Principal Subsidiaries: Fisher Price Division; Adcom Inc; Ardmore Farms Inc; Jos A Bank Clothiers Inc; Eyelab Inc; Quality Operations Inc; Brookstone Co Inc; Wolf Brand Products Inc; Stokely-Van Camp Inc
Principal Bank: Northern Trust Co
Financial Information:

	Jun 30 1986
	$'000
Sales revenues	3,670,700
Net income	179,600
Earnings per share	$4.35
Shareholders equity	831,100

No of Employees: 30,000

QUAKER STATE CORPORATION

255 Elm Street, Oil City, PA 16301
Tel: (814) 676-7676
Telex: TWX 5106926863 quasta oil oc

Chairman: Quentin E Wood (and Chief Executive Officer)
President: Roger A Markle (and Chief Operating Officer)
Senior Executive Officers: James D Berry III (Executive VP), Walter B Cook (Executive VP)

PRINCIPAL ACTIVITIES: Oil refining and marketing of petroleum; coal mining
Trade Names: Quaker State; Truck-Lite; Quaker State Minit-Lube
Principal Subsidiaries: Heritage Insurance Group; The Helen Mining Corp; Truck-Lite Co Inc; Quaker State Inc (Canada); The Valley Camp Coal Co; Quaker State Minit-Lube Inc; Valley Camp Inc; Great Lakes Coal and Dock Co
Financial Information:

	Dec 31 1985	Dec 31 1986
	$'000	$'000
Sales revenues	974,251	899,065
Income before taxes	81,592	89,888
Net income	45,892	50,288
Dividends	19,439	21,418
Dividends per share	$0.85	$0.85
Earnings per share	$1.91	$2.01
Common stock*	23,979	24,993
Retained income	274,163	302,368
Shareholders equity	311,864	390,661
*number of shares in thousands		

No of Employees: 6,000

QUALITY MILLS, INC

US Highway 52 South, Mount Airy, NC 27030
Tel: (919) 789-6161
Telex: TWX 510 9225059 quality mtay

Chairman: John E Woltz (and Chief Executive Officer)
President: Jack D Grooms (and Treasurer)
Senior Executive Officers: Howard O Woltz Jr (VP), Jack A Loftis (VP Operations), Ronald A Ellis (VP Employee Relations and Administration), J E Woltz (VP Marketing), Kenneth L James (VP Merchandising), Joe C Glover (VP Contract Sales), W Ronald Wagenseil (VP Sales), William M Glenn (Secretary and Controller)

PRINCIPAL ACTIVITIES: Manufacture of clothing
Principal Bank: First Union National Bank
Financial Information:

	$'000
Sales revenues	48,641

No of Employees: 1,400

QUANEX CORPORATION

1900 West Loop S, Houston, TX 77027
Tel: (713) 961-4600
Telex: TWX 910 8815000 quanex hou

President: Carl E Pfeiffer (and Chief Executive Officer)
Senior Executive Officers: Robert C Snyder (Executive VP and Chief Operating Officer), Robert V Kelly Jr (VP), W M Rose (VP and Chief Financial Officer), J C Hill (VP), J K Peery (VP), J D Tracy (Secretary)

PRINCIPAL ACTIVITIES: Manufacture of steel bars and tubing, titanium and super alloy forgings and mill products, and oil field tubing
Principal Subsidiaries: Viking Metallurgical Corp; LaSalle Steel Co
Principal Bank: Manufacturers National Bank of Detroit
Financial Information:

	Oct 31 1985	Oct 31 1986
	$'000	$'000
Sales revenues	296,974	324,835
Income (loss) before taxes	4,320	(23,143)
Net income (loss)	10,121	(19,943)
Earnings (loss) per share	$0.89	($1.63)
Common stock	61,281	61,281
Retained income	44,073	24,130
Shareholders equity	110,707	90,764

Number of Shareholders: 5,808
No of Employees: 1,834

QUANTUM CORPORATION

1804 McCarthy Blvd, Milpitas, CA 95035
Tel: (408) 262-1100
Telex: TWX 910 3382203 quantum mpts

President: J L Patterson (and Chief Executive Officer)
Senior Executive Officers: David B Pratt (Senior VP and Chief Executive Officer), Arthur P Geffon (VP Engineering), J T Rogers Jr (VP, Secretary and Treasurer), Joe Shepela (VP Human Resources), R P Taylor (VP Manufacturing), J G Watson (VP Sales and Marketing)

PRINCIPAL ACTIVITIES: Manufacture of Winchester disc drives
Financial Information:

	$'000
Sales revenues	120,000

No of Employees: 700

QUAREX INDUSTRIES INC

4705 Metropolitan Avenue, Ridgewood, NY 11385
Tel: (718) 821 0011

Chairman: George Gamaldi (and President and Chief Executive Officer)
Senior Executive Officers: Frank Castellana (Executive VP), Joseph Castellana (VP and Secretary)

PRINCIPAL ACTIVITIES: Meat wholesaling
Principal Bank: European American Bank & Trust Co
Financial Information:

	$'000
Sales revenues	136,455

No of Employees: 575

QUESTAR CORPORATION

180 E First S Street, PO Box 11150, Salt Lake City, UT 84147
Tel: (801) 534-5000

Chairman: R D Cash (and President and Chief Executive Officer)

Senior Executive Officers: Clyde M Heiner (Senior VP Corporate Development), R L Cox (VP Public Affairs), W F Edwards (VP and Chief Financial Officer), R G Groussman (VP and General Counsel), C C Holbrook (VP and Secretary), N R Potter (VP Planning and Information Services)

PRINCIPAL ACTIVITIES: Holding company with interests in the exploration and production of oil and gas and the distribution of natural gas in Utah and Wyoming; manufacture of bricks and roofing tiles

Financial Information:

	$'000
Sales revenues	528,000

No of Employees: 2,900

QUESTECH INC

QuesTech Building, 6858 Old Dominion Drive, McLean, VA 22101
Tel: (703) 556 8666
Telefax: (703) 056-8666

Chairman: John L McLucas
President: William L Mayo (and Chief Executive Officer)
Senior Executive Officers: William E Bigler Jr (Executive VP/Finance and Administration, Secretary and Treasurer), Vincent L Salvatori (Executive VP/Government Affairs), Oscar E Hayes (Executive VP/Business Development), Jerome M Raffel (Executive VP/Technical Operations)

PRINCIPAL ACTIVITIES: Provision of a wide range of professional, scientific and engineering services to government and industry in the fields of national security, aeronautics, energy and industrial modernization
Principal Subsidiaries: DHR Inc; Dynamic Engineering Incorporated; Engineering Resources Inc; Quest Research Corporation; American Defense Systems Inc; QuesTech Ventures Inc; QuesTech North American Limited; QuesTech Nord Americain Limitée
Principal Bank: Riggs National Bank
Financial Information:

	Dec 31 1985(1)	Dec 31 1986
	$'000	$'000
Sales revenues	42,868	47,507
Income before taxes(2)	1,453	2,095
Net income	857	195
Earnings per share	$0.56	$0.13
Shareholders equity	7,213	7,408

(1) restated
(2) from continuing

No of Employees: 1,000

QUICK & REILLY GROUP INC

120 Wall Street, New York, NY 10005
Tel: (212) 943 8686

Chairman: Leslie C Quick Jr (and Chief Executive Officer)
President: L C Quick III (and Chief Operating Officer and Treasurer)
Senior Executive Officers: Alexander Benisatto (VP), Arlene B Fryer (VP and Secretary), Peter Quick (VP), T C Quick (VP)

PRINCIPAL ACTIVITIES: Financial services including security investment advice
Principal Subsidiaries: Quick & Reilly Inc; Q & R Clearing Corporation
Principal Bank: Chemical Bank
Financial Information:

	$'000
Revenues	73,000

No of Employees: 460

QUIXOTE CORPORATION

1 East Wacker Drive, Chicago, IL 60601
Tel: (312) 467-6755
Telex: 253368

Chairman: Philip E Rollhaus (and President)
Senior Executive Officers: Myron R Shain (Executive VP Finance and Treasurer), Dennis W Powers (Executive VP-Operations), James H Devries (VP and Secretary), George D Ebersole (President, Energy Absorption Systems Inc), Eric W Strom (VP and General Manager, Spin-Cast Plastics), Edward H Kight (President, Stenograph Corporation), Reginald O Parker (President, Amtel Systems Corporation), Ram Reddy Nomula (President, Laser Video Inc), John L Bishop (Chairman and Chief Executive Officer, Ocean Scientific Inc), Andrew W Perry (President, Ocean Scientific Inc)

PRINCIPAL ACTIVITIES: Designing, manufacturing and marketing energy-absorbing highway crash cushions; supplier of machine shorthand equipment to the court reporting profession; design and sale of computer-aided transcription systems and proprietary message-management systems; produce Compact Discs, laser videodiscs and CD-ROM data discs; develop and manufacture medical diagnostic equipment; and engaged in research for a whole-blood substitute for emergency and other medical applications
Trade Names: G-R-E-A-T(R), Hex-Foam (TM) Sandwich System, Hi-Dro(R) System, Alpha 1000(TM) TMA, Energite(R), Sentre (TM), Trend (TM) (highway crash cushion products). Mini-Chem, Micro-Chem, Chem-Stat, Immuno-Wash (medical diagnostic equipment). Laser Master (TM) (videodisc product). DataWriter(R) (transcription machine). RapidWriter(R) (high-speed entry system)
Principal Subsidiaries: Energy Absorption Systems Inc; Spin-Cast Plastics Inc; Stenograph Corporation; Laser Video Inc; Ocean Scientific Inc
Principal Bank: Continental Illinois National Bank and Trust, Chicago, IL
Financial Information:

	Jun 30 1986	Jun 30 1987
	$'000	$'000
Sales revenues	45,238	57,217
Income (loss) before taxes	3,035	(3,583)
Net income (loss)	1,952	(2,193)
Earnings (loss) per share	$0.27	($0.28)
Common stock*	7,307	7,741
Retained income	11,772	9,579
Shareholders equity	26,128	34,360

*average number of common and common equivalent shares outstanding in thousands

No of Employees: 740

QUOTRON SYSTEMS, INC

5454 Beethoven Street, PO Box 66914, Los Angeles, CA 90066
Tel: (213) 827-4600
Telex: 652455 LSA

Chairman: Milton E Mohr (and President and Chief Executive Officer)
Senior Executive Officers: Bruce B Jackson (Executive VP-Engineering and Manufacturing), George F Kabouchy (VP-Systems, Operations and Programs), George H Levine (VP-Marketing and Corporate Secretary), Daniel G Sadler (Chief Financial Officer and Treasurer), Nikki Parker (VP-Industrial Relations and Assistant Corporate Secretary), Pier L Rossi (VP-Engineering), Donald L Stevens (VP-Customer Engineering), Alexander F Wood (VP-International Operations), William M Simpson (President-Securities Industry Software)

PRINCIPAL ACTIVITIES: Quotron is a leading US financial information services company providing on-line real-time security and commodity market information, data processing and communications services. The Company also designs and assembles its own computers and equipment and develops its own software used in providing its services to customers
Parent Company: Citicorp Banking Corporation

Principal Subsidiaries: Quotron Systems International Inc; Securities Industry Software Corp
Principal Bank: Citicorp

Principal Shareholders: As of September 16 1986, the Company is wholly owned by Citicorp Banking Corporation?
No of Employees: 2,464

R & G SLOANE MANUFACTURING
See SLOANE, R & G, MANUFACTURING

R G BARRY CORPORATION
See BARRY, R G, CORPORATION

R H MACY & CO, INC
See MACY, R H, & CO, INC

R J REYNOLDS TOBACCO CO
See REYNOLDS, R J, TOBACCO CO

R L POLK & CO
See POLK, R L, & CO

R P SCHERER CORPORATION
See SCHERER, R P, CORPORATION

R R DONNELLEY & SONS COMPANY
See DONNELLEY, R R, & SONS COMPANY

RACAL CORPORATION (THE)
1800 Corporate Blvd NW, Boca Raton, FL 33431
Tel: (305) 997-9554 (N American HQ); (212) 687-5040 (New York Corp Communications Center)
Telex: ITT 429899 racal-milgo FTL (N American HQ); TWX 710-581-6586 (New York Corp Communications Center)

President: David C Elsbury
Senior Executive Officers: Edward Bleckner Jr (Executive VP, Corporate Administration), Raymond G Lewis (Senior VP), David H Zirkle (Executive VP and Chief Financial Officer)

PRINCIPAL ACTIVITIES: Production of electronic equipment
Trade Names: Racal-Milgo, Racal-Vadic, Racal Communications, Racal Marine, Racal Survey, Racal-Redac, Racal-Dana, Racal-Recorders, Racal Airstream, Racal Avionics, Racal-Chubb, Racal-Decca, Racal Design Services, Racal-Guardall, National Foam
Parent Company: Racal Electronics PLC, UK
Principal Subsidiaries: USA:- Racal-Milgo; Racal Vadic; Racal Communications Inc; Racal-Dana Instruments Inc; Racal Recorders Inc; Racal Marine Inc; Racal Survey Inc; Racal-Redac Inc; Racal-Chubb Inc; Racal Avionics Inc; Racal Airstream Inc; Racal Design Services Inc; Racal-Guardall Inc; National Foam System Inc. Canada:- Racal (Canada) Limited, Racal-Decca Canada Inc; Racal-Chubb Canada Limited
Principal Bank: Continental Illinois National Bank & Trust Company of Chicago

Principal Shareholders: Racal Electronics PLC
No of Employees: 5,000

RACON INC
PO Box 198, 6040 S Ridge Road, Wichita, KS 67201
Tel: (316) 524-3245
Telex: TWX 910 741 6811 racon inc

Chairman: L J Polite Jr
President: Maurice J Knopf (and Chief Executive Officer)
Senior Executive Officers: Marshall R Turner (VP Operations), Corky J Knock (VP Marketing), Michael J Schlapp (VP Production Manager), J R Buss (Secretary and Treasurer), Lynn M Nelson (Controller)

PRINCIPAL ACTIVITIES: Manufacture of industrial gases
Parent Company: Essex Chemical Corporation, Clifton, NJ
Principal Bank: Fourth National Bank & Trust Co
Financial Information:

	$'000
Sales revenues	50,000

No of Employees: 50

RADIATION SYSTEMS INC
1501 Moran Road, Sterling, VA 22170
Tel: (703) 450-5680
Telex: 89-9156
Telefax: (703) 450-4706

Chairman: R E Thomas (and Treasurer)
President: H Gruen
Senior Executive Officers: J H Arnold Jr (Senior VP), M D Shoemeke (VP), H A Siegel (VP and Legal Counsel), Y V Vondrich (VP), R A Maginnis (VP Finance), A M Stutzman (Secretary), R W Patton (VP)

PRINCIPAL ACTIVITIES: Production of detection and transmission antenna equipment for defense, broadcasting and aircraft guidance systems
Principal Divisions: Satcom Technologies Inc; Universal Antennas; Mark Antennas; Satellite Network Antennas
Principal Bank: First National Bank of Maryland
Financial Information:

	Jun 30 1987
	$'000
Sales revenues	43,812
Income before taxes	5,299
Net income	3,115
Earnings per share	$0.56
Common stock*	27,542
Retained income	24,278
Shareholders equity	51,051

*and paid-in capital

No of Employees: 410

RADIATOR SPECIALTY CO
1400 W Independence Blvd, Charlotte, NC 28234
Tel: (704) 377-6555

Chairman: Herman Blumenthal
President: Alan Blumenthal
Senior Executive Officers: Jerry Dannecker (VP and General Manager), J F Laseter (VP and Treasurer), Frank Greenspan (Divisional VP Technical), Terry G Stokes (Divisional VP Sales), M T Cory (Divisional VP Rubber Manufacturing), Robert D Bezek (Divisional VP Sales), James A Rubendall (Divisional VP Management Information Services)

PRINCIPAL ACTIVITIES: Manufacture of chemical and rubber products for automobiles; plumbers' fittings and hardware
Principal Bank: North Carolina National Bank
Financial Information:

	$'000
Sales revenues	90,000

No of Employees: 800

RADICE CORPORATION
600 Corporate Drive, Fort Lauderdale, FL 33334
Tel: (305) 493 5003

Chairman: Robert C Radice (and President and Chief Executive Officer); Vice Chairman: Charles F Radice (and Executive VP and Secretary)
Senior Executive Officers: Lawrence W Schoch (Senior VP, Chief Operating Officer and Treasurer), A George Ciampi (VP Division), Morton J Gurdin (VP Division), O Don Lauher (VP and Controller), George A Dale (VP Finance), Helene M Whalen (Assistant Secretary), Imri Ereg (VP Architecture)

PRINCIPAL ACTIVITIES: Management and development of real estate
Principal Subsidiaries: American Community Systems Inc
Principal Bank: BancBoston

Financial Information:

	$'000
Sales revenues	120,000

No of Employees: 390

RAGEN CORPORATION

9 Porete Avenue, North Arlington, NJ 07032
Tel: (201) 997 1000

Chairman: I L Lopata (and Chief Executive Officer)
President: E E Lopata
Senior Executive Officers: John DeVivo (Production Manager), L Esposito (Production Manager), D Friedman (Sales Manager and Chief Engineer), Hans Kobin (production Engineer, Norman A Lopata (Sales Manager), Tad Ratkowski (Purchasing Agent), Roland Stojanow (Traffic Manager), Alexander C Tomkins Jr (Secretary and Treasurer), T Vida (Production Manager)

PRINCIPAL ACTIVITIES: Production of specialty electronic equipment and components; instruments for the aviation industry
Principal Subsidiaries: Microtronics Corporation; Ragen Data Systems Inc
Principal Bank: CitiBank
Financial Information:

	$'000
Sales revenues	33,000

No of Employees: 520

RAINIER BANCORPORATION

PO Box 3966, Seattle, WA 98124
Tel: (206) 621-4111
Telefax: (206) 621-4895

Chairman: John D Mangels (and Chief Executive Officer); Chairman of the Executive Committee: G Robert Truex Jr
President: Jon M Christoffersen
Senior Executive Officers: Gordon F Givens (Senior VP and Senior Credit Officer), Bruce A Koppe (Secretary), Ronald H Mead (Senior VP and Treasurer), Stacia A Stratton (VP and Chief Credit Examiner), Joe O Swain (VP and General Auditor), M Ward Hughes (Assistant Treasurer and Assistant Secretary), Kathleen P Marks (Assistant Secretary)

PRINCIPAL ACTIVITIES: Banking and financial services
Principal Subsidiaries: Rainier National Bank; Rainier International Bank; Rainier Bank International; Rainier Leasing Inc; Rainier Bank Alaska, NA; Rainier Mortgage Co; Rainier Bank Oregon, NA; United Bank, A Savings Bank; Rainier Brokerage Services Inc
Principal Bank: Rainier National Bank
Financial Information:

	Dec 31 1985	Dec 31 1986
	$'000	$'000
Income before taxes	84,642	92,170
Net income	68,251	75,035
Dividends	19,953	22,118
Dividends per share	$1.00	$1.08
Earnings per share	$3.21	$3.44
Common stock	53,880	55,362
Retained income	483,734	547,247
Shareholders equity	537,614	602,609
Deposits	6,301,551	7,159,752
Total assets	8,874,490	9,822,881

No of Employees: 5,693

RAINIER NATIONAL BANK

1301 5th Avenue, PO Box 3966, Seattle, WA 98124
Tel: (206) 621-4111
Telex: Incoming Domestic (ITT) 4740137; Incoming Foreign (ITT) 4740135; Incoming and Outgoing (Western Union) 152485

Chairman: John D Mangels
President: Jon M Christoffersen
Senior Executive Officers: Richard W Brandt (Executive VP, Administration), David J Carey (Executive VP), Charles R Chadwick (Executive VP, Corporate Banking), John F Cockburn (Executive VP, Business Development), Michael J Cole (Executive VP, Chief Financial Officer-Rainier Bank), James D Cullen (Executive VP, Corporate Banking), Gordon F Givens (Executive VP, Senior Credit Officer), David I Williams (Executive VP, Branch Banking), Stanley D Savage (Executive VP, Asset and Liability Management), W Thomas Porter Jr (Executive VP, Capital Management), William L Schaumberg (Executive VP), Robert J Svare (Executive VP), Bruce A Koppe (Senior VP, Secretary and General Counsel), Donald B Summers (Senior VP, Personnel)

PRINCIPAL ACTIVITIES: Banking and financial services
Trade Names: Registered trademarks: Rainier, RainierBank, Rainier BankMachine
Parent Company: Rainier Bancorporation, Seattle, WA
Principal Subsidiaries: Rainier Bank International; Rainier International Bank; Rainier Leasing, Inc
Financial Information:

	Dec 31 1985	Dec 31 1986
	$'000	$'000
Income before taxes	72,743	84,409
Net income	60,099	68,521
Dividends	17,470	21,525
Capital stock	100,000	100,000
Undivided profits	202,991	253,366
Shareholders equity	406,664	459,314
Deposits	5,782,121	6,299,070
Total assets	7,755,210	8,273,203

No of Employees: 4,950

RALSTON PURINA CO

Checkerboard Square, St Louis, MO 63164
Tel: (314) 982-1000
Telex: WUT 447620 ralston stl

Chairman: William P Stiritz (and President and Chief Executive Officer)
Senior Executive Officers: P H Hatfield (Group VP), W M Jones (Group VP), W H Lacey (Group VP), E J Cordes (Senior VP), A J Reimers (Senior VP), J W Brown (VP, Chairman and Chief Executive Officer Continental Baking Co), F J Cornwell (VP), James R Elsesser (VP and Treasurer), J W Goodall (VP, President Foodmaker), W P McGinnis (VP), J R Micheletto (VP), J P Mulcahey (VP), J M Neville (VP and General Counsel)

PRINCIPAL ACTIVITIES: Manufacture of crackers, cookies, cereals, canned fish, pet foods, soybean products
Principal Subsidiaries: (100% owned unless stated): Duquesne-Purina SA (68%); Ralston Purina Overseas Finance NV
Financial Information:

	Sep 30 1985	Sep 30 1986
	$'000	$'000
Sales revenues	5,863,900	5,514,600
Net income	256,400	388,700
Earnings per share	$3.15	$5.79
Shareholders equity	924,500	3,664,000

No of Employees: 70,400

RAMADA INNS, INC

3838 E Van Buren Street, Phoenix, AZ 85008
Tel: (602) 273-4000
Telex: ITT 4725019 ramadaexof phx

Chairman: Richard Snell (and President and Chief Executive Officer)
Senior Executive Officers: Jerry R Manion (Executive VP Hotels), Thomas E Martin (Executive VP Finance), Paul E Rubeli (Executive VP Gaming), A W Gus Boss (Senior VP Systems Development), Robert Haddock (Senior VP Corporate Development), Jose L Torres (Senior VP US Hotel Operations), Nelson W Armstrong (VP Administration),

Thomas W Davidson (VP Human Resources), Ellis Landeau (VP and Treasurer), Jim Perry (VP and Controller), David M Thompson (VP Corporate Communications)

PRINCIPAL ACTIVITIES: Operation of hotels, bars, casinos and restaurants
Principal Bank: Bank of New England
Financial Information:

	Dec 31 1986
	$'000
Sales revenues	661,684
Net income	10,275
Earnings per share	$0.27
Shareholders equity	301,532

No of Employees: 18,600

RAMSET FASTENING SYSTEMS

Shamrock Street, East Alton, IL 62024
Tel: (618) 258 3387

Senior Executive Officers: R J Crown (Manufacturing Manager), Dave Heminger (General Manager), M A Killian (Personnel Director), Don Van Allman (Director Marketing and Product Development)

PRINCIPAL ACTIVITIES: Manufacture of industrial fasteners; manufacture of machine tools
Parent Company: Olin Corp
Financial Information:

	$'000
Sales revenues	120,000

RAMTEK CORPORATION

2211 Lawson Lane, Santa Clara, CA 95050
Tel: (408) 988 2211

Chairman: Charles E McEwan (and President and Chief Executive Officer)
Senior Executive Officers: Thomas J Adams (Executive VP, Chief Financial Officer and Treasurer), Peter Cassady (VP Marketing), Stephen V Cope (VP Engineering), Anthony Glinskas (VP Sales), Michael Gordon (VP Software Development), Joseph G Morris (VP Division), Wilbur Sattler (VP Operations), James A Swanson (VP, Legal Counsel and Secretary), G William Theriault (VP and Controller)

PRINCIPAL ACTIVITIES: Manufacture of computer graphic displays
Principal Bank: Bank of America
Financial Information:

	$'000
Sales revenues	44,000

No of Employees: 500

RANCO INC

555 Metro Pl N, Dublin, OH 43017
Tel: (614) 764-3733
Telex: TWX 810 339 2028 ranco hdq dboh

Chairman: Richard J Grosh (and Chief Executive Officer)
President: William A Chapman (and Chief Operating Officer)
Senior Executive Officers: Henry A Baker (Executive VP International), Randolph B Robert (Executive VP and Chief Financial and Administrative Officer), R R Womack (Executive VP Business Development)

PRINCIPAL ACTIVITIES: Manufacture of valves and automatic control devices; electrical and electronic components
Principal Subsidiaries: Ranco Controls Canada Ltd (Canada); Aparecchi di Controllo Ranco Srl (Italy); Ranco Italian Controls Inc (Italy); Deutsche Ranco GmbH (Germany); Ranco Europe Ltd (UK); Bodmin Precision Components Ltd (UK); Ranco Controls Ltd (UK); Ranco France SA (France); Ranco de Mexico; Electronic Controls Corp (Mexico); Teccor Electronics Inc
Principal Bank: BancOhio National Bank
Financial Information:

	$'000
Sales revenues	169,000

No of Employees: 4,900

RAND MCNALLY & COMPANY

8255 N Central Park Avenue, Skokie, IL 60076
Tel: (312) 673-9100
Telex: RCA 210041 rmcn ur

Chairman: Andrew McNally III
President: Andrew McNally IV; William W Meacham (Rand McNally Map Distributing Co); Thomas J Breen (DocuSystems Group); John C Warson (Rand McNally Book Manufacturing Co); Roger G Wildermuth (Publishing Group)
Senior Executive Officers: William J Bold (Executive VP and Secretary), Paul R Alms (VP Book Manufacturing Group), Chris J Arvetis (VP Carto-Art), John S Bakalar (VP Finance and Treasurer), Richard A Chase (VP Indianapolis Plant), Richard Clouse (VP Book Manufacturing Sales), Daniel W Dais (VP Book Manufacturing Sales), Dennis R DeCock (VP Education), Arthur DuBois (VP Map Division), Donald F Helm (VP Industrial Relations), James B Kauffman (VP Publishing Group), Irwin List (VP Purchasing), Edward C McNally (VP Finance Publishing Division), Norman J Merwise (VP Sales, Publishing Group), Donald V Pickett (VP Versailles Plant), John P Ryan (VP Ticket), Frank Sadorf (VP Information Systems), Douglas J Snow (VP Book Manufacturing Sales), Patrick J Sottile (VP DocuSystems Sales), J Robert Stanik (VP Publishing Group Sales), Russell L Voisin (VP International)

PRINCIPAL ACTIVITIES: Printing services; book publishing
Principal Bank: First National Bank of Chicago
Financial Information:

	$'000
Sales revenues	200,000

No of Employees: 3,000

RANDALL STORES, INC

1705 N Main, Mitchell, SD 57301
Tel: (605) 996-7511

Chairman: Ronald F Randall (and President)
Senior Executive Officers: Robert W McCardle (VP Public Relations)

PRINCIPAL ACTIVITIES: Retail trade in groceries; restaurant interests; manufacture and bottling of soft drinks; recreational services including operation of a bowling alley
Principal Bank: Commercial Trust & Savings Bank
Financial Information:

	$'000
Sales revenues	300,000

No of Employees: 2,700

RANGAIRE CORPORATION

501 S Wilhite Street, Box 177, Cleburne, TX 76031
Tel: (817) 645-9111

Chairman: R E Roberts (and Chief Executive Officer)
President: J M Hill (and Chief Operating Officer)
Senior Executive Officers: Vernon A Beene (Executive VP-Manufacturing), William B Cadenhead (Executive VP-Construction), Leon O Bowen Jr (VP-Engineering Services), J W Browder (VP-Marketing), Benny G Falcon (VP-National Sales Manager), F W McCorkle (Secretary), Robert F Stewart (Treasurer), J L Thompson (Operations Manager-Texas Lime), C Doris Rasnick (Assistant Secretary)

PRINCIPAL ACTIVITIES: Rangaire Corporation is a diversified company whose manufactured products are (a) Purchased by consumers, and (b) Utilized in residential and commercial construction and remodeling. Manufactured products include fluorescent lighting fixtures, range hoods, compact freezers and refrigerators and Magnawave(R) induction cooktops.

Rangaire is also a major producer in Texas, Arkansas, Pennsylvania and Virginia of limestone, quicklime and hydrated lime, which are used primarily in chemical and steel production, water treatment and construction. The company also quarries limestone in Arkansas for a major chemical producer. Rangaire is one of the major general contractors in the Dallas-Fort Worth area.

Trade Names: Vistalite, Frost Queen, Gro-Master, Twister, Magnawave, Sensi-Touch, Ranger, Batesville Marble, Rangaire (all registered trademarks)

Principal Subsidiaries: Lime Operations: Texas Lime Company; Arkansas Lime Company; Virginia Lime Company; Corson Lime Company. Manufacturing Operations: Rangaire-Cleburne; Itasca. Construction Operations: Cadenhead-Rangaire, Inc

Principal Bank: M Bank Dallas

Financial Information:

	Jul 31 1985 $'000	Jul 31 1986 $'000
Sales revenues	76,969	79,941
Income before taxes*	2,717	3,187
Net income	1,244	2,338
Dividends	913	923
Dividends per share	$0.23	$0.24
Earnings per share	$0.31	$0.60
Common stock	386	401
Retained income	16,534	16,687
Shareholders equity	30,910	32,320

*and extraordinary item

Principal Shareholders: R E Roberts and ESOP Plan

No of Employees: 938

RANSBURG CORPORATION

3939 W 56th Street, Indianapolis, IN 46208

Tel: (317) 298-5000

Telex: RCA 209150 rans ur

Chairman: Don J Kacek (and President and Chief Executive Officer)

Senior Executive Officers: Jon D Noel (Executive VP, Treasurer and Chief Financial Officer), C T Duncan (Group Senior VP Marketing), Milo E Friesen (Senior VP R&D), Duane Rohlfing (VP Human Resources and Public Relations), Charles W Walton (VP, Senior Counsel and Secretary), Thomas W Eggleston (VP and General Counsel)

PRINCIPAL ACTIVITIES: Manufacture of advanced technology equipment for special segments of the factory automation market

Principal Banks: Indiana National Bank; Harris Trust and Savings Bank

Financial Information:

	Nov 30 1985 $'000	Nov 30 1986 $'000
Sales revenues	200,413	217,396
Income before taxes	11,801	3,119
Net income (loss)	6,406	(3,304)
Dividends	5,714	5,781
Dividends per share	$0.72	$0.72
Earnings (loss) per share	$0.81	$($0.41)
Common stock	1,192	1,208
Retained income	52,391	43,306
Shareholders equity	90,081	86,881

No of Employees: 2,100

RAPID-AMERICAN CORPORATION

888 Seventh Avenue, New York, NY 10106

Tel: (212) 399-4500

Telex: WUT 971 749 rpdamercor nyk

Chairman: M Riklis (and President and Chief Executive Officer); Vice Chairman: Harold S Divine

Senior Executive Officers: Charles L Jarvie (Executive VP), Daniel J Manella (Executive VP), Peter Thorner (Executive VP and Chief Financial Officer), Stephen L Pister (Senior VP), Marcia Riklis (VP), Paul Weiner (VP and Treasurer)

PRINCIPAL ACTIVITIES: Retail variety chain stores; apparel manufacture; production and sale of wines and spirits

Parent Company: Rapid-American Holding Corp

Principal Subsidiaries: (100% owned unless stated): Schenley Industries Inc; McCrory Corp; Viewtop Corp; McGregor Corp (53.8%); Rapid Distribution Service Inc; Rapid Typographics Co Inc; Schenley Medical Imaging Inc

Principal Bank: Chemical Bank

Financial Information:

	Dec 31 1986 $'000
Sales revenues	1,893,500
Net (loss)	(20,471)
Shareholders equity	81,700

No of Employees: 40,000

RAPISTAN DIVISION

507 Plymouth Avenue NE, Grand Rapids, MI 49505

Tel: (616) 451-6200

Telex: WUT 226310 rapistan gdr

President: William R Michaels

Senior Executive Officers: Thomas Horning (VP Manufacturing), Stephen O'Neill (VP Marketing), Michael Tilton (VP Finance and Administration and Real Estate Officer), Peter P Walsh (VP Engineering)

PRINCIPAL ACTIVITIES: Manufacture of mechanical handling equipment and conveying equipment

Parent Company: Lear Siegler Inc, Santa Monica, CA

Principal Bank: Chase Manhattan Bank

Financial Information:

	$'000
Sales revenues	150,000

No of Employees: 900

RATH PACKING CO

Elm & Sycamore Streets, Waterloo, IA 50703

Tel: (319) 235-8900

Telex: TWX 9105251281 rath wloo

Chairman: Robert D Fulton

President: Lyle D Taylor (and Chief Executive Officer)

Senior Executive Officers: Wallace E Rath (Senior VP), Lyle Mowery (VP Finance), John R DeGroot (VP), William C Tobias (VP and Chief Operating Officer), Richard W Cray (VP Marketing), LeRoy H Grittmann (VP)

PRINCIPAL ACTIVITIES: Meat and meat processing

Financial Information:

	$'000
Sales revenues	425,000

No of Employees: 3,100

RAVEN INDUSTRIES INC

205 East Sixth Street, Sioux Falls, SD 57117

Tel: (605) 336 2750

Chairman: Conrad J Holgaard

President: David A Christensen (and Chief Executive Officer)

Senior Executive Officers: Ronald M Moquist (Executive VP), James A Winker (VP Division), Arnold J Thue (VP Finance and Treasurer), Joseph J Kaliszewski (Secretary), Gary L Conradi (VP Corporate Services)

PRINCIPAL ACTIVITIES: Manufacture of hot air sport balloons' plastic covers, high altitude balloons; electronic control and monitoring equipment

Principal Bank: Norwest Bank South Dakota NA

Financial Information:

	$'000
Sales revenues	42,000

No of Employees: 800

RAX RESTAURANTS INC

1266 Dublin Road, Columbus, OH 43215
Tel: (614) 486 3669

Chairman: J Pat Ross (and Chief Executive Officer); Vice Chairmen: A Grant Bowen (and Chief Financial Officer), Jules L Garel (and Legal Counsel and Secretary)
President: Larry R Ritter (and Chief Operating Officer)
Senior Executive Officers: Daniel J Corrigan (Executive VP Marketing), Edwin L Ourant (Executive VP Operations), David R Bluestone (VP Operations), William J Dolan (VP Operations), Kenneth A Jones (VP and Controller), G Michael Link (VP Operational Planning), Robert W Bafundo (VP Purchasing and Administration), Gary L Schulte (VP Real Estate)

PRINCIPAL ACTIVITIES: Fast food restaurants
Principal Bank: Bank One Columbus NA
Financial Information:

	$'000
Sales revenues	113,000

No of Employees: 5,000

RAYBRO ELECTRIC SUPPLIES, INC

907 Ellamae Street, Tampa, FL 33602
Tel: (813) 229-1291

President: Troy A Brown Jr
Senior Executive Officers: Charles A Brown (Executive VP), William T Brown (VP Marketing), Gene Halsex (VP Operations), Syd Hardie (VP Purchasing), Anne Summeral (Advertising)

PRINCIPAL ACTIVITIES: Domestic electrical appliances, lighting fixtures and other electrical products; generators
Principal Bank: The Exchange National Bank of Tampa
Financial Information:

	$'000
Sales revenues	108,000

No of Employees: 400

RAYCHEM CORPORATION

300 Constitution Drive, Menlo Park, CA 94025-1164
Tel: (415) 361-3333
Telex: WUT 176506 raychem mnpk

Chairman: Paul M Cook (and Chief Executive Officer)
President: Robert M Halperin (and Chief Operating Officer)
Senior Executive Officers: Robert J Saldich (Senior VP), William A Berry (VP and Chief Administrative Officer), Gerald R Delaney (VP), Michael T Everett (VP, Secretary and Chief Legal Officer), Frederick M Grafton (VP), Thomas S Huseby (VP), Edward A Keible Jr (VP), William E Mitchell (VP), Joachim H Ohme (VP), Harry O Postlewait (VP), James B Spradling (VP), David D Taft, Raymond J Sims, Francis J Lunger

PRINCIPAL ACTIVITIES: Raychem Corporation, founded to develop commercial applications for radiation chemistry, is a broadly based materials science company serving international markets. Raychem develops and supplies high-performance products for the aerospace, automotive, construction, electronics, electrical power, process and telecommunications industries
Trade Names: DuraSeal, ElectroLoss, ElectroMelt, EZF, Ferex, FOSC 100, GelTek, HTT, HWAT, I2S, IceStop, Jointek, PedCap, PELL, PolySwitch, PowerSleeve, Rayaten, Rayblock, Raysulate, Rayvolve, SECO, SolderSleeve, SPEC 55, Stilan, TermSeal, ThermoRail, Tinel-Lock, TRAC, TraceCalc, TraceTek, XAGA, XTV
Principal Bank: Bank of America
Financial Information:

	Jun 30 1986	Jun 30 1987
	$'000	$'000
Sales revenues	797,632	944,434
Income before taxes	65,490	100,821
Net income	48,790	73,599
Common dividends	4,547	4,767
Dividends per common share	$0.44	$0.44
Earnings per share net	$4.65	$6.74
Common stock	163,440	11,044
Retained income	326,840	395,622
Shareholders equity	452,464	570,946

No of Employees: 9,899

RAYGO, INC

9401 85th Avenue North, Minneapolis, MN 55440
Tel: (612) 425-4100
Telex: ITT 4310014 raygobn

Chairman: Charles J Mencel (and Chief Executive Officer)
Senior Executive Officers: Robert Schwingler (VP Raygo Manufacturing Company), Fernand Copie (VP), Steve Spann (VP Sales)

PRINCIPAL ACTIVITIES: Manufacture of earth moving equipment and other construction machinery
Principal Bank: First St Paul Bank & Trust
Financial Information:

	$'000
Sales revenues	35,000

No of Employees: 200

RAYMARK CORPORATION

100 Oakview Drive, Trumbull, CT 06611
Tel: (203) 371-0101
Telex: WUT 964264 ramark trum

Chairman: David A Wingate
President: Craig R Smith (and Chief Executive Officer)
Senior Executive Officers: Albert A Canosa (VP and Corporate Controller), Robert L Cleveland Jr (VP and General Manager, Dry Clutch and Brake Business), Harry D Day (VP, Secretary and General Counsel), John D Kutzler (VP and Treasurer), James J Ryan (VP, Human Resources)

PRINCIPAL ACTIVITIES: Raymark Corporation, through its operating subsidiary, Raymark Industries, Inc, is a multinational manufacturer and marketer of energy absorption and transmission products and custom engineered materials. Raymark products are used in the automotive, farm machinery, truck and bus, earth-moving, construction equipment, appliance, mining, petrochemical, aerospace and energy industries
Trade Names: Raybstos, Raybestos-Manhattan
Parent Company: Raytech Corp
Principal Subsidiaries: Raymark Industries (Canada) Inc (Canada); Raymark Industries Inc; R/M Disc Inc; Raybestos Manhattan GmbH & Co (Germany); Raybestos Manhattan Europe Inc; Naja Inc; R/M Inc
Financial Information:

	$'000
Sales revenues	112,419

No of Employees: 1,600

RAYMOND CORPORATION

N Canal Street, Greene, NY 13778
Tel: (607) 656-2311

Chairman: George G Raymond Jr (and Chief Executive Officer)
President: William R Webber (and Chief Operating Officer)
Senior Executive Officers: Stephen S Raymond (Executive VP), Margaret Gallaher (VP Marketing), Robert Lilley (VP Operations), John E Mott (VP), Rocco Nenarella (VP Research and Development)

PRINCIPAL ACTIVITIES: Manufacture of hoists and industrial cranes; mechanical handling equipment; interests in finance, leasing and rental services
Principal Bank: Marine Midland Bank
Financial Information:

	$'000
Sales revenues	113,000

No of Employees: 1,070

RAYMOND ENGINEERING INC

217 Smith Street, Middletown, CT 06457
Tel: (203) 632 1000

President: Hugh L Cox (and Chief Executive Officer)
Senior Executive Officers: John H Bickford (VP), R M Duffy (VP), Charles M Saltsman Jr (VP), David C Schilke (VP), Donald Bidwell (VP, Secretary and Treasurer)

PRINCIPAL ACTIVITIES: Manufacture of a range of weapons systems controllers based on microprocessors; manufacture of weapons components
Principal Bank: United Bank and Trust Company
Financial Information:

	$'000
Sales revenues	51,575

No of Employees: 600

RAYMOND INTERNATIONAL INC

2801 Post Oak Blvd, P O Box 27456, Houston, TX 77227
Tel: (713) 623 1500

Chairman: Henry F Lemieux (and Chief Executive Officer)
President: R Nelson Crews (and Chief Operating Officer)
Senior Executive Officers: G W Holman Jr (Executive VP), Jerry D Davis (Senior VP and Secretary), F R Mason (Senior VP Finance and Treasurer), Pat H Moore (Senior VP Sales and Marketing), Joseph F Fiorenza (VP Corporate Auditor), Gerald H Johnson (VP Finance), L R Larsen (VP Corporate Planning and Development), D R Martin (VP Tax)

PRINCIPAL ACTIVITIES: General contractors; civil engineering and construction
Principal Bank: Morgan Guaranty Trust Co of New York
Financial Information:

	$'000
Sales revenues	1,640,000

No of Employees: 5,000

RAYOVAC CORPORATION

601 Rayovac Drive, Madison, WI 53711
Tel: (608) 275-4560
Telex: 190428 ray o vac mds

Chairman: Thomas F Pyle
Senior Executive Officers: Raymond L Balfour (VP and Secretary), Trygve Lonnebotn (Senior VP Operations), Roger Warren (Executive VP Consumer Products), Judith D Pyle (Vice Chairman and Senior VP), Marketing), Marvin G Seigert (Senior VP and Chief Financial Officer), Gary E Wilson (VP Sales), Glynn M Rossa (VP and Treasurer)

PRINCIPAL ACTIVITIES: Production of dry cell batteries and lighting equipment
Principal Bank: First Chicago
Financial Information:

	$'000
Sales revenues	253,000

Principal Shareholders: T Pyle & Officers
No of Employees: 2,000

RAYTHEON CO

141 Spring Street, Lexington, MA 02173
Tel: (617) 862-6600
Cable: RAYTHEONEX
Telex: WUT 880 385 ratbur

Chairman: Thomas L Phillips (and Chief Executive Officer)
President: R Gene Shelley
Senior Executive Officers: Philip A Phalon (Senior VP Corporate Marketing), Joseph F Shea (Senior VP Engineering), Walter H Palmer (VP Public Relations)

PRINCIPAL ACTIVITIES: Manufacture of weapons and defense systems, electrical and electronic equipment; aircraft; domestic appliances; telecommunications; industry services; construction equipment; educational publishers
Principal Subsidiaries: Beech Aircraft. Appliances: Amana; Caloric; Speed Queen. Industry Services: Badger; Seismograph Services; United Engineers & Constructors; Yeargin Construction. Construction Equipment: Cedarapids; El-Jay. Publishing: D G Heath. European Firms: Cossor Electronics; Data Logic; Electrical Installations; Lacroix & Kress; Klasing; Sterling Greengate Cable; Transistor AG. Also: New Japan Radio
Principal Bank: The First National Bank of Boston
Financial Information:

	Dec 31 1985	Dec 31 1986
	$'000	$'000
Sales revenues	6,408,540	7,308,000
Net income	375,905	393,200
Dividends per share	$1.60	$1.75
Earnings per share	$4.60	$5.10
Shareholders equity	1,928,982	1,954,600

No of Employees: 76,400

RB & W CORPORATION

5970 Heisley Road, Mentor, OH 44060
Tel: (216) 357-1200

Chairman: J J Lohrman (and Chief Executive Officer)
President: S Molnar
Senior Executive Officers: A A Arena (VP Distribution Division and General Manager), D R Lockwood (VP International Division), K M Holcomb (VP Human Resources), Boyd O Murdock (Chief Financial Officer)

PRINCIPAL ACTIVITIES: Manufacture of metal industrial fasteners
Principal Subsidiaries: Lamson & Sessions of Canada Ltd
Principal Bank: National City Bank
Financial Information:

	Dec 31 1985	Dec 31 1986
	$'000	$'000
Sales revenues	154,400	158,829
Income before taxes	5,751	2,544
Net income	8,711	2,070
Dividends	-	342
Dividends per share	-	$0.075
Earnings per share	$1.89	$0.43
Shareholders equity	35,354	37,770

No of Employees: 1,484

RB INDUSTRIES, INC

1801 Century Park E, Los Angeles, CA 90067
Tel: (213) 553-3655

President: Verle L Rice
Senior Executive Officers: A T Bowker (Treasurer), Joyce M Rice (Secretary)

PRINCIPAL ACTIVITIES: Furniture manufacture and retail
Principal Subsidiaries: Laurel Development Co; R B Furniture Inc; R B Creative Systems Inc
Principal Bank: Midland Bank
Financial Information:

	$'000
Sales revenues	117,000

No of Employees: 1,260

RCA CORPORATION

30 Rockefeller Plaza, New York, NY 10020

Tel: (212) 621-6000

Telex: 222010

Chairman: Thornton F Bradshaw

President: Robert R Frederick (and Chief Executive and Operating Officer)

Senior Executive Officers: Richard W Miller (Executive VP), Eugene F Murphy (Executive VP), J D Rittenhouse (Executive VP), James M Alic (Group VP Corporate Planning), Jack K Sauter (Group VP), C A Schmidt (Group VP), John A Rolls (Senior VP Finance and Chief Financial Officer), Edward L Scanlon (Senior VP), P E Weight (Senior VP Corporate Planning), John M Bermingham (VP and Deputy General Attorney), D I Brenner (VP and Controller), D Joseph Donahue (VP and General Manager Consumer Electronics), A D Gordon (VP), B J Heidtke (VP and Treasurer), Robert S Pepper (VP and General Manager Solid State Division), R H Pollak (VP), John Regan (VP Patent Operations), Thomas B Ross (VP Corporate Communications), Ray Scherer (VP Washington), J J Tietjen (VP), William M Webster (VP Labor)

PRINCIPAL ACTIVITIES: Manufacture of electronic equipment; telecommunications and defense equipment; radio and television broadcasting; truck and automobile leasing; home entertainment goods

Parent Company: General Electric Co

Financial Information:

	$'000
Sales revenues	8,970,000

No of Employees: 87,000

REA CONSTRUCTION CO

521 E Morehead Street, Charlotte, NC 28231

Tel: (704) 373-1331

Chairman: Norman D Wilhelm (and President)

Senior Executive Officers: Fred F Parolari (Executive VP), William C Proctor (VP Equipment), Rufus E Dalton (VP Virginia), Carey K Tate (VP Raleigh), John W Copeland III (VP Charlotte), Marion V Baker (Secretary), James M Ferrell (Treasurer and Controller)

PRINCIPAL ACTIVITIES: Civil engineering and construction

Parent Company: Jones Group Inc

Principal Bank: First Union National Bank of North Carolina

Financial Information:

	$'000
Sales revenues	75,000

No of Employees: 795

READING & BATES CORPORATION

2200 Mid-Continent Tower, Tulsa, OK 74103

Tel: (918) 583 8521

Chairman: J W Bates Jr (and Chief Executive Officer)

President: D K McIntosh (and Chief Operating Officer)

Senior Executive Officers: J E Andrew (Senior VP), Bill M Burks (Senior VP), E W Crowe (Senior VP), M A Overall (Senior VP, Chief Financial Officer and Chief Administrative Officer), R A Tappmeyer (Senior VP), R G Lemons (VP and Controller), Dickson M Saunders (Secretary), T A Sims (VP Human Resources)

PRINCIPAL ACTIVITIES: Exploration and production of oil and gas; coal mining

Principal Subsidiaries: Reading & Bates Coal Company; Belva Coal Company; Belva Coal Company Inc; Golden Oak Mining Company Inc; Reading & Bates Construction Company; Reading & Bates Development Company; Reading & Bates Drilling Company; Reading & Bates Petroleum Company; Reading & Bates Exploration Company

Principal Bank: First National Bank

Financial Information:

	$'000
Sales revenues	234,000

No of Employees: 2,080

REAGENT CHEMICAL & RESEARCH, INC

124 River Road, Middlesex, NJ 08846

Tel: (201) 469-0100

Telex: TWX 710 4804266 reag-care msex

Chairman: Thomas J Skeuse (and President)

Senior Executive Officers: Robert H Dallas (Executive VP, Secretary and Treasurer), Evert J Talbot (VP Sales), Alvie S Whatley (VP Transportation)

PRINCIPAL ACTIVITIES: Production of industrial chemicals

Principal Bank: Bankers Trust Company

Financial Information:

	$'000
Sales revenues	65,000

No of Employees: 300

RECO INDUSTRIES, INC

PO Box 25189, Richmond, VA 23260

Tel: (804) 644-2611

Telex: WUT 827 474 recg rch

Chairman: Frank G Louthan Jr (and Chief Executive Officer)

President: Harry N Upson

Senior Executive Officers: Robert C Courain Jr (VP Finance), Grayson Harding (VP Engineering), W S Point Jr (VP Sales), Jerry L Dawson (VP), A E Upton Jr (VP), J A Hagan III (VP), Richard A Miller (VP), Victor Addotta (VP), Andrew Bowden (VP), W D Miller (VP)

PRINCIPAL ACTIVITIES: Fabrication of metal tanks and containers; plate work, pipes and tubes; heat exchangers

Principal Bank: United Virginia Bank

Financial Information:

	$'000
Sales revenues	55,000

No of Employees: 870

RECOGNITION EQUIPMENT INC

PO Box 660204, Dallas, TX 75266

Tel: (214) 579-6000

Telex: 275247 REIIUR

Chairman: William G Moore, Jr (and Chief Executive Officer)

Senior Executive Officers: Israel Sheinberg (Executive VP), Thomas A Loose (Senior VP), Phil Colquhoun (VP), George A O'Brien (VP and Chief Financial Officer), Robert W Reedy (VP), James P Donoho (VP), John C Hall (VP)

PRINCIPAL ACTIVITIES: Supplier of data capture systems which make human readable and bar coded information ready for a computer to process

Principal Subsidiaries: Recognition Equipment Incorporated is a multi-national company with subsidiaries throughout Western Europe and the Pacific Basin

Principal Bank: InterFirst Bank Dallas

Financial Information:

	Oct 31 1985	Oct 31 1986
	$'000	$'000
Sales revenues	163,147	241,795
Income before taxes	6,516	14,973
Net income	4,316	10,539
Earnings per share(1)	$0.41	$0.90
Earnings per share(2)	$0.44	$1.06
Common stock(3)	9,713	9.969
Common stock(4)	9,766	9,909
Retained income	5,456	15,995
Shareholders equity	98,807	115,882

(1) primary-before extraordinary
(2) primary-net income
(3) primary weighted average shares in thousands
(4) actual shares outstanding in thousands

No of Employees: 3,000

RECTICEL FOAM CORPORATION

Boyd at Darlington Road, PO Box 369, LaPorte, IN 46350
Tel: (219) 326-7977
Telex: 23-3125

Chairman: M Delefortrie
President: G W Polet (and Chief Executive Officer)
Senior Executive Officers: J H van Dijk (Senior VP and Treasurer), J Duronsoy (Senior VP), R J van Wachem (VP and General Manager)

PRINCIPAL ACTIVITIES: Manufacture of plastic and plastic foam
Parent Company: Gechem SA, Brussels, Belgium
Principal Bank: European American Bank & Trust Co
Financial Information:

	$'000
Sales revenues	100,000

No of Employees: 1,000

RED WING CO, INC

196 Newton Street, Fredonia, NY 14063
Tel: (716) 672-4321
Telex: TWX 510 2462 194 red wing frdi

President: Douglas Manly
Senior Executive Officers: Robert Luber (VP Finance), W G Gaffney (VP Operations)

PRINCIPAL ACTIVITIES: Production of sauces, relishes and dressings; fruit products including fruit juice and frozen fruit
Principal Bank: Northern Trust Company
Financial Information:

	$'000
Sales revenues	65,000

No of Employees: 450

REDKEN LABORATORIES, INC

6625 Variel Avenue, Canoga Park, CA 91303
Tel: (213) 992-2700
Telex: WUT 691338 redkenlab cnpk

Chairman: John E Meehan (and President and Chief Executive Officer)
Senior Executive Officers: Ron Marconet (Senior VP Operations), Lee Quaintance (Senior VP Administration), David Cannell (Group VP), David L Auchterlonie (VP Finance), Robert C Bushman (VP Sales), James W Griffiths (VP Human Relations), Arnold Kranz (VP Marketing), Cary Newman (VP Manufacturing), Bill Peplow (VP), D J Pekin (VP Legal)

PRINCIPAL ACTIVITIES: Manufacture of hair conditioning products for men and women, skin care preparations and cosmetics, hair colorants and fragrances
Trade Names: Redken, RK, Redken pH plus, Redken/Lapinal, Pique
Principal Bank: Union Bank
Financial Information:

	$'000
Sales revenues	108,600

No of Employees: 930

REDMAN INDUSTRIES INC

2550 Walnut Hill Lane, Dallas, TX 75229
Tel: (214) 353-3600
Telex: TWX 910 864497 redman dal

Chairman: James E Redman (and President and Chief Executive Officer)
Senior Executive Officers: Fred Babb (VP Administration), M Brian Healy (VP Finance)

PRINCIPAL ACTIVITIES: Production of pre-fabricated housing; building materials and fittings; mobile homes
Principal Subsidiaries: Redman Homes Inc; Redman Building Products Inc; Timber Tech Inc; Gallatin Aluminum Products Company Inc; Redman International Inc
Principal Bank: Mercantile National Bank at Dallas
Financial Information:

	$'000
Sales revenues	342,000

No of Employees: 4,000

REEBOK INTERNATIONAL LTD

500 Bodwell Street Extension, Avon, MA 02322
Tel: (617) 580-1600

Chairman: Paul Fireman (and Chief Executive Officer)
Senior Executive Officers: James Barclay (Executive VP), Paul R Duncan (Senior VP Finance, Treasurer and Chief Financial Officer), Sharon Cohen (VP Corporate Communications), Stephen J Encarnacao (VP Marketing), Steven Liggett (VP Design and Research), Angel Martinez (VP Business Development), Robert Meers (VP Sales), Sheldon W Rothman (VP and Treasurer)

PRINCIPAL ACTIVITIES: Manufacture of a wide variety of athletic footwear
Financial Information:

	$'000
Sales revenues	919,000
Net income	132,000

No of Employees: 640

REECE CORPORATION

200 Prospect Street, Waltham, MA 02254
Tel: (617) 894 9220

Chairman: John B Reece
President: Peter J Abate (and Chief Executive Officer)
Senior Executive Officers: Donald Blom Jr (VP and Treasurer), Leonard J Egan (VP Planning and Human Resources), Michael R Richards (VP Marketing)

PRINCIPAL ACTIVITIES: Production of specialty machinery and equipment for manufacture of clothing
Principal Subsidiaries: Reece International Corporation
Principal Bank: First National Bank
Financial Information:

	$'000
Sales revenues	45,930

No of Employees: 680

REED & BARTON CORPORATION

144 W Britannia Street, Taunton, MA 02780
Tel: (617) 824-6611
Telex: WUT 753535 reedbartn taun

Chairman: Sinclair Weeks Jr (and President and Chief Executive Officer)
Senior Executive Officers: Richard R Gillespie (Senior VP Marketing), Henry C Gill Jr (Senior VP Manufacturing), William H Dykstra (Senior VP Finance), Bryce H Blair (VP Sales), A La Chapelle (VP Sales), C Greene (VP Production)

PRINCIPAL ACTIVITIES: Production of silver plated, sterling silver, pewter and stainless steel holloware and flatware; jewelry
Principal Bank: The First National Bank of Boston
Financial Information:

	$'000
Sales revenues	60-70,000

No of Employees: 750

REED HOLDINGS INC

275 Washington St., Newton, MA 02158
Tel: (617) 964 3030
Telex: WUT 951078 reed bsn

Senior Executive Officers: Saul Goldweitz (Executive VP), Ronald G Segel (VP Finance)

PRINCIPAL ACTIVITIES: Holding company with interests in paper products including wallpaper, publishing of industrial journals and the organising of trade exhibitions
Parent Company: Reed International PLC, London, UK
Principal Bank: Citibank
Financial Information:

	$'000
Sales revenues	500,000

No of Employees: 5,000

REED NATIONAL CORPORATION

260 N Elm Street, Westfield, MA 01085
Tel: (413) 568-9571
Telex: WUT 948531 reed sser

President: John E Reed
Senior Executive Officers: S B Reed (Executive VP), E H Burk (Senior VP Manufacturing), Dennis Strom (VP Engineering), C W Sawtelle (VP Marketing), E F Bridgman (VP Marketing), James Rugg (VP and Treasurer)

PRINCIPAL ACTIVITIES: Manufacture of heating, ventilation and air-conditioning equipment
Principal Bank: Valley Bank and Trust Company
Financial Information:

	$'000
Sales revenues	50,000

No of Employees: 850

REED TOOL COMPANY

6501 Navigation Blvd, Houston, TX 77011
Tel: (713) 924-5200
Telex: TWX 910 881 1605 reedbit hou

President: Roman E Boruta (and Chief Executive Officer)
Senior Executive Officers: John C MacFarlane (VP and Chief Financial Officer), Richard L Cruse (VP Marketing), Charles L Sorrentino (VP Manufacturing), Dewey A Thiessen (VP Engineering)

PRINCIPAL ACTIVITIES: Manufacture of mining and oilfield equipment
Parent Company: Baker International Corp through Baker Drilling Equipment Co
Principal Bank: First City National Bank of Houston
Financial Information:

	$'000
Sales revenues	150,000

No of Employees: 1,300

REEVES COMMUNICATIONS CORPORATION

708 Third Avenue, New York, NY 10017
Tel: (212) 573-8600

Chairman: Marvin H Green (and President and Chief Executive Officer)

Senior Executive Officers: Merrill Grant (Executive VP), Theodore Schlissel (Executive VP), William A Wetzel (Executive VP), Renichi Ishii (Senior VP), Allen Mandel (Senior VP and Chief Financial Officer), Robert E Trivers (Senior VP, Treasurer and Secretary), Lee S Bartlett (VP, Webster F Golinken (VP), James Hartzer (VP), Mart Lachman (VP), Patrick Lemarchand (VP), Robert Winkler (VP)

PRINCIPAL ACTIVITIES: Mail order services in leisure goods and reference books; production and distribution of motion pictures; production of films for corporate and institutional clients and communication and marketing services

Principal Bank: Chase Manhattan Bank

Financial Information:

	$'000
Sales revenues	73,000

No of Employees: 1,700

REFINED SUGARS INC

One Federal Street, Yonkers, NY 10702
Tel: (914) 963-2400
Telex: TWX 710 541 1574 flosweetb yks

Chairman: John C Mitchell

President: Paul J Mirsky

Senior Executive Officers: Samuel I Edelman (Executive VP), David W Graham (VP Sales and Marketing), William R Davies (VP Operations), Peter J Harding (VP Purchasing)

PRINCIPAL ACTIVITIES: Sugar refining

Parent Company: Tate & Lyle PLC, London, UK

Principal Bank: Bankers Trust Company

Financial Information:

	$'000
Sales revenues	300,000

No of Employees: 500

REFLECTONE INC

5125 Tampa West Boulevard, Tampa, FL 33614
Tel: (813) 885 7481

Chairman: John B Mowell (and Chief Executive Officer)

President: John D McIntosh (Acting President and Executive Vice President)

Senior Executive Officers: Paul E Malagari (VP-Stimulator Engineering), Thomas L Telesca (VP-Operational Planning/Control), Joseph L Andreani (VP-New Business Programs), William M Faust (VP-Human Resources and Security), Richard W Welshhans (VP and Treasurer), Sherrill R Allen (Secretary), Williams S Jacobs (Assistant Secretary)

PRINCIPAL ACTIVITIES: Reflectone, a high technology company, produces flight and non-flight simulators and sophisticated electronic training systems. Products include flight simulators for fixed-wing aircraft and helicopters and non-flight training equipment for other man-machine systems. Through its Training Systems subsidiary, the Company provides a full range of flight and ground school training for commercial customers and the military

Principal Bank: Southeast Bank

Financial Information:

	Mar 31 1986	Mar 31 1987
	$'000	$'000
Sales revenues	49,424	48,025
Income (loss) before taxes	2,431	(2,325)
Net income (loss)	305	(2,195)
Earnings (loss) per share	$0.21	($1.54)
Common stock	12,715	12,885
Retained income	5,191	2,996
Shareholders equity	17,906	15,881

No of Employees: 620

REGAL WARE, INC

Kewaskum, WI 53040
Tel: (414) 626-2121

Chairman: Lowell N Peterson
President: James D Reigle
Senior Executive Officers: William Crooker (Senior VP Manufacturing), Robert S Zarling (Senior VP Sales and Marketing), Allen C Koepke (VP Finance, Treasurer and Real Estate Officer), James Moran (VP Human Resources), Jeffrey A Reigle (VP Sales and Secretary), Wayne Remmell (VP Corporate Engineering), Patrick Twohig (VP),

PRINCIPAL ACTIVITIES: Manufacture of household cookware in stainless steel and aluminum; household electrical goods; giftware
Principal Bank: First Wisconsin National Bank of Milwaukee
Financial Information:

	$'000
Sales revenues	150,000

No of Employees: 1,500

REGAL-BELOIT CORPORATION

5330 E Rockton Rd, PO Box 38, South Beloit, IL 61080
Tel: (815) 389-1920
Telex: TWX 910 3501134 regal blt sblt

Chairman: James L Packard (and James L Packard (and Chief Executive Officer)
Senior Executive Officers: Henry W Knueppel (Executive VP-Operations), Gerald J Berres (VP and Secretary), Robert C Burress (VP and Treasurer), Dennis M Conerton (Corporate Controller)

PRINCIPAL ACTIVITIES: Production of perishable cutting tools and power transmission components
Trade Names: Super Tuf-Cut, Regal Premium, Regal Gold, Flexaline, Century XL
Principal Banks: First National Bank & Trust Company; Brown Bros Harriman; M & I Marshall & Ilsley Bank (Milwaukee, WI)
Financial Information:

	Dec 31 1985	Dec 31 1986
	$'000	$'000
Sales revenues	55,431	78,069
Income before taxes	6,436	10,329
Net income	3,405	5,396
Dividends	1,922	2,142
Dividends per share	$0.60	$0.60
Earnings per share	$1.06	$1.55
Common stock	8,119	18,613
Retained income	16,106	19,360
Shareholders equity	24,225	37,775

No of Employees: 1,779

REGENCY ELECTRONICS, INC

7707 Records Street, Indianapolis, IN 46226
Tel: (317) 545-4282

Chairman: Joseph E Boone (and President and Chief Executive Officer)
Senior Executive Officers: Charles A Merriman (VP Corporate Development), Ronald C Patton (VP), Roger R Priami (VP), Steven L Wilkening (Treasurer)

PRINCIPAL ACTIVITIES: Manufacture of telecommunications equipment including radio and television transmission and receiving apparatus; manufacture of detection equipment
Principal Bank: Merchants National Bank & Trust Company
Financial Information:

	$'000
Sales revenues	92,000

No of Employees: 1,700

REGENSTEINER PUBLISHING ENTERPRISES, INC

1224 W Van Buren Street, Chicago, IL 60607
Tel: (312) 666-4200

Chairman: Fred W Glazer
Senior Executive Officers: John Winter (Executive VP), William J Glazer (VP), Thomas Winter (VP)

PRINCIPAL ACTIVITIES: Publishing and information services; printing
Principal Bank: The First National Bank of Chicago
Financial Information:

	$'000
Sales revenues	70,000

No of Employees: 550

REGINA COMPANY INC

313 Regina Avenue, Rahway, NJ 07065
Tel: (201) 381 1000

Chairman: David D Sheelen (and President); Vice Chairman: James A Flynn (and VP and Treasurer)
Senior Executive Officers: John Gerbeth (VP and Secretary), Edward D Haino (VP), Michael P McHugh (VP and Chief Financial Officer), Samuel Rogers (VP Research and Development)

PRINCIPAL ACTIVITIES: Manufacture of cleaning equipment including floor polishers and vacuum cleaners
Principal Bank: Marine Midland Bank
Financial Information:

	$'000
Sales revenues	67,700

No of Employees: 650

REGIS CORPORATION

5000 Normandale Road, Edina, MN 55436
Tel: (612) 929 6776

Chairman: Myron Kunin (and President)
Senior Executive Officers: Peter A Fudurich (Executive VP and Secretary), Frank Evangelist (Treasurer and Assistant Secretary), William Sipkins (VP Sales), Christopher A Fox (VP Real Estate), Ernest S Halpern (VP Personnel Affairs)

PRINCIPAL ACTIVITIES: Hair care and styling salons
Principal Bank: National City Bank
Financial Information:

	$'000
Sales revenues	135,000

No of Employees: 7,500

REICHHOLD CHEMICALS, INC

525 N Broadway, White Plains, NY 10603
Tel: (914) 682-5700
Telex: TWX 710 5680328 rci trans whp

Chairman: C R Powell (and President and Chief Executive Officer)
Senior Executive Officers: D I Barton (Executive VP), Thomas R Mitchell (Executive VP), Jay R Olson (Executive VP and Chief Financial Officer), Paul E Dixon (VP), D E Pogue (VP Human Resources), Eugene A Stevenson (Corporate Communications Director)

PRINCIPAL ACTIVITIES: Manufacture of specialty chemicals for a range of industries and synthetic resins for industrial coatings
Principal Subsidiaries: Reichold Limited; Swift Adhesives
Principal Bank: National Bank of Detroit
Financial Information:

	Dec 31 1986
	$'000
Sales revenues	765,588
Income before taxes	15,859
Dividends	5,944
Dividends per share	$0.80
Earnings per share	$2.13
Shareholders equity	196,087

Number of shareholders: 6,757
No of Employees: 3,958

REILY, WM B, & CO

PO Box 60296, New Orleans, LA 70160
Tel: (504) 524-6131
Telex: TWX 8109515127 wb reily a nln

President: William B Reily III
Senior Executive Officers: William B Burkenroad Jr (VP), James R Leach Jr (VP and Treasurer), Robert D Reily (VP)

PRINCIPAL ACTIVITIES: Production of tea, coffee, sauces, relishes and edible oils
Principal Bank: Whitney National Bank
Financial Information:

	$'000
Sales revenues	100,000

No of Employees: 800

RELIANCE ELECTRIC CO

29325 Chagrin Blvd, Cleveland, OH 44122
Tel: (216) 266-7000
Telex: TWX 810 4218183 relhqhq ppke

Chairman: H Virgil Sherrill
President: John C Morley (and Chief Executive Officer)
Senior Executive Officers: J H Portwood (VP and Secretary), E Scott Dalton (VP), K C Moore Jr (VP, Treasurer and Controller), Leon J Hendrix Jr (VP Operations), Dudley P Sheffler (VP Operations), P J Tsivitse (VP Operations)

PRINCIPAL ACTIVITIES: Manufacture of industrial a-c and d-c motors and controls, mechanical power transmission products, weighing and scale products and systems, and specialty telecommunications products
Principal Subsidiaries: Reliance Electric Industrial Corp; Toledo Scale Corp; Reliance Comm-Tec
Principal Bank: Wells Fargo N.A.
Financial Information:

	Dec 31 1985	Dec 31 1986*
	$'000	$'000
Sales revenues	1,366,100	1,409,000
Income before taxes	23,600	53,400
Net income	13,200	30,400
Shareholders equity	971,100	824,900

*in 1985 and 1986 Reliance was a wholly owned affiliate of Exxon Corporation

No of Employees: 17,000

RELIANCE GROUP HOLDINGS, INC

55 E 52nd Street, New York, NY 10055
Tel: (212) 909-1100
Telex: GRT 3766610 rgh nyk

Chairman: Saul P Steinberg (and Chief Executive Officer)
President: Robert M Steinberg (and Chief Operating Officer)
Senior Executive Officers: George E Bello (Executive VP and Controller), Lowell C Freiberg (Senior VP), Frederick A Jackson (Senior VP), Henry A Lambert (Senior VP Real Estate), Michael J Blake (Senior VP Taxes), Fred M Schriever (Senior VP), Henry R Silverman (Senior VP Business Development), Bruce L Sokoloff (Senior VP Administration), Howard E Steinberg (Senior VP), Martin J Brill (VP Internal Audit), William D Dobbins (VP Communications), Blair C Fenserstock (VP, Assistant General Counsel and Assistant Secretary), Peter J Houseman II (VP and Controller), Philip S Sherman (VP and Group Controller)

PRINCIPAL ACTIVITIES: The company has interests in insurance services; property development and management services, management consulting and public relations
Principal Bank: Continental Illinois National Bank and Trust Company of Chicago
Financial Information:

	Dec 31 1985	Dec 31 1986
	$'000	$'000
Sales revenues	2,517,250	3,225,749
Net income	43,353	62,991
Earnings per share	-	$0.50
Shareholders equity	243,640	441,058

No of Employees: 8,500

RELIANCE UNIVERSAL INC

1930 Bishop Lane, Louisville, KY 40218
Tel: (502) 459-9110
Telex: WUT 204 353 reliance lvl

President: Charles J Fisher (and Chief Executive Officer)
Senior Executive Officers: B J Smith (Group VP), Patrick L Vaughn (VP Finance, Treasurer and Chief Financial Officer), Gerald Painchaud (VP), Herb A Champlin (VP and General Manager), William J Rutledge (VP Corporate Operations Services), Gary L Fulk (VP and General Manager), Martin B Price (VP Research and Product Development)

PRINCIPAL ACTIVITIES: Manufacture of paints, varnishes and enamels
Parent Company: Tyler Corporation, Dallas, TX
Financial Information:

	$'000
Sales revenues	213,000

No of Employees: 1,400

RENT A CENTER INC

9920 East Harry Street, Wichita, KS 67207
Tel: (316) 689 4100

Chairman: W F Barton; Vice Chairman: Gene Haggestad
President: Walter E Gates
Senior Executive Officers: Robert D Taylor (Senior VP Finance, Secretary and Treasurer), Samuel E Moyers (Senior VP Marketing), P David Egan (VP and Legal Counsel), Richard L Eckert (VP Merchandising), T B Heatherly (VP)

PRINCIPAL ACTIVITIES: Supply and leasing of domestic electrical equipment including radios and television sets
Principal Subsidiaries: Rent A Center of America Inc
Principal Bank: Fourth National Bank
Financial Information:

	$'000
Sales revenues	90,000

No of Employees: 750

REPUBLIC AIRLINES, INC

7500 Airline Drive, Minneapolis, MN 55450
Tel: (612) 726-7411
Telex: 910-576-2697

Chairman: Daniel F May (and President and Chief Executive Officer)
Senior Executive Officers: Gramer D Foster (Senior VP-Operations), A B Magary (Senior VP-Marketing), Henry W Barkhausen (VP and Treasurer), Arnold J Crossman (VP-

Marketing Systems), Paul C Jasinski (VP, General Counsel and Assistant Secretary), W Thomas Lagow (VP-Marketing Planning), Gary H Lantner (VP and Secretary), Lee R Mitchell (VP-Computer and Communications Service), Bruce R Nobles (VP-Customer Service), R Terrence Rendleman (VP-Maintenance and Engineering), Paul E Schoellhamer (VP-Government Affairs, Republic Airlines, Inc, Washington, DC), Raymond W Sellwood (VP-Flight), Michael D Meyer (Controller), Walter E Nielsen (Assistant Treasurer), Joseph W Ettel (Assistant General Counsel and Assistant Secretary), Gloria B Olsen (Assistant General Counsel and Assistant Secretary), Ralph Strangis (Assistant Secretary Kaplan, Strangis & Kaplan, Minneapolis, MN)

PRINCIPAL ACTIVITIES: Public air transportation
Parent Company: NWA Inc
Principal Bank: Norwest Bank Minneapolis NA; Citibank NA
Financial Information:

	$'000
Operating revenues	1,730,000

No of Employees: 14,000

REPUBLIC AUTOMOTIVE PARTS, INC

500 Wilson Pike Circle, Suite 115, PO Box 2088, Brentwood, TN 37024
Tel: (615) 373-2050

Chairman: Edgar R Berner
President: Keith M Thompson (and Chief Executive Officer)
Senior Executive Officers: Donald B Hauk (Executive VP and Chief Financial Officer)

PRINCIPAL ACTIVITIES: Wholesale and retail distributors of automotive parts, accessories and supplies
Principal Bank: Manufacturers National Bank of Detroit
Financial Information:

	Dec 31 1986 $'000
Sales revenues	101,435
(Loss) before taxes	(5,944)
Net (loss)	(3,338)
(Loss) per share	($1.18)
Shareholders equity	26,015

No of Employees: 900

REPUBLIC GYPSUM COMPANY

PO Box 750, Dallas, TX 75221
Tel: (214) 272 0441

Chairman: Phil Simpson (and President and Chief Executive Officer)
Senior Executive Officers: Paul R Brown (VP Manufacturing Paperboard), B Joe Harris (VP Sales), Mike Ireland (VP Finance), William C Petty (VP Manufacturing), Henry B Weis III (VP Human Resources)

PRINCIPAL ACTIVITIES: Processing of gypsum; manufacture of paperboard and gypsum wallboard
Principal Bank: Republic Bank
Financial Information:

	$'000
Sales revenues	56,620

No of Employees: 490

REPUBLIC HEALTH CORPORATION

14951 Dallas Parkway, Suite 1100, Dallas, TX 75240
Tel: (214) 851 3100

Chairman: LeRoy A Pesch Vice Chairman: Jack R Anderson
President: J E Buncher (and Chief Executive Officer)
Senior Executive Officers: James W McAtee (Executive VP and Chief Financial Officer), D R Hill (Senior VP Operations), R R Patterson (Senior VP Operations), David VanDenwater (Senior VP and Treasurer), J G Vandevender (Senior VP Operations), J H Johnson (VP, Legal Counsel and Secretary)

PRINCIPAL ACTIVITIES: Provision of a wide range of healthcare services including hospitals, psychiatric centers and drug abuse facilities; nursing services
Principal Bank: Security Pacific National Bank
Financial Information:

	$'000
Sales revenues	539,900

No of Employees: 10,000

REPUBLIC NEW YORK CORPORATION

452 Fifth Avenue, New York, NY 10018
Tel: (212) 930-6000
Cable: BLICBANK
Telex: RCA 234-967

Chairman: Walter H Weiner (and Chief Executive Officer); Vice Chairmen: Cyril S Dwek, Ernest Ginsberg, Dov C Schlein, Jacques Tawil
President: Jeffrey C Keil
Senior Executive Officers: Louis Moskowitz (Chairman Executive Committee), Thomas Robards (Executive VP Finance and Treasurer), William F Rosenblum Jr (Senior VP, Deputy General Counsel and Corporate Secretary), John A Kaberle Jr (Executive VP and Comptroller)

PRINCIPAL ACTIVITIES: Holding company with banking interests
Principal Subsidiaries: Republic Factors Corp
Principal Bank: Republic National Bank of New York
Financial Information:

	Dec 31 1985 $'000	Dec 31 1986 $'000
Income before taxes	146,190	166,046
Net income	122,069	135,560
Dividends	28,299	31,167
Dividends per share	$1.09	$1.12
Earnings per share	$3.98	$4.44
Common stock	86,368	139,688
Retained income	409,111	501,021
Shareholders equity	908,953	1,136,034
Deposits	9,729,221	10,797,367
Total assets	15,323,510	17,464,897

Principal Shareholders: Edmond J Safra
No of Employees: 2,850

RESEARCH-COTTRELL, INC

PO Box 1500, Somerville, NJ 08876
Tel: (201) 685-4000
Telex: RCA 219882 rcin ur

Chairman: Peter J Gianacakes (and Chief Executive Officer)
Senior Executive Officers: Jeremiah P Cronin (Senior VP Finance), Joseph Feldstein (VP and Secretary), Harvey J Goldman (VP Project Development and Finance), Robert J Hatala (VP Information Management), Edward J O'Dowd (VP Human Resources), John A Stella (VP and Treasurer), Alan B Walker (VP Technical Ventures)

PRINCIPAL ACTIVITIES: Manufacture of pollution control devices; engineering consultants; oilfield equipment and services
Principal Subsidiaries: Custodis-Hamon Constructors Inc; Custodis-Hamon Canada Inc; Flex-Kleen Corp; Metcalf & Eddy Inc; PAMCO USA; M & E Pacific; PAMCO Ltd; Power Quip Engineering Inc; Rental Tools Inc; Production Rentals Inc; KVB Inc; Research-Cottrell (Canada) Ltd; Research-Cottrell (Belgium) SA; Research Cottrell (Germany) GmbH
Financial Information:

	$'000
Sales revenues	392,500

No of Employees: 2,100

RESER'S FINE FOODS INC

15570 SW Jenkins Road, PO Box 8, Beaverton, OR 97075
Tel: (503) 643 6431

President: Alvin L Reser
Senior Executive Officers: Norman D Price (VP), Darrell G Vandehey (VP)

PRINCIPAL ACTIVITIES: Food processing
Financial Information:

	$'000
Sales revenues	24,000

No of Employees: 200

RESINE DIVISION

29 Fuller Street, Leominster, MA 01453
Tel: (617) 537-9901
Telex: TWX 710 347 1924 polysar leom

Senior Executive Officers: Ian Cheyne (Manager), Ken Hall (Controller), Faj Magfood (Marketing Manager), Paul Stahlberg (Sales Manager)

PRINCIPAL ACTIVITIES: Polystyrene products
Parent Company: Polysar Ltd, Canada
Financial Information:

	$'000
Sales revenues	60,000

No of Employees: 170

RESORTS INTERNATIONAL, INC

915 NE 125th St, North Miami, FL 33161
Tel: (305) 891-2500

Chairman: Donald J Trump
President: I G Davis (and Chief Executive Officer)
Senior Executive Officers: Matthew B Kearney (VP-Finance and Chief Financial Officer), H Steven Norton (Executive VP), Robert Peloguin (Executive VP), John Donnelly (VP-Legal), David Bowden (VP-Controller), Thomas O'Donnell (Treasurer)

PRINCIPAL ACTIVITIES: Casinos and resort operations; real estate; airline interests; security services
Principal Subsidiaries: Domestic: Chalk's International Airlines Inc; International Intelligence Inc; International Suppliers Inc; Intertel Consultants Inc; Lectrolarm Custom Systems Inc; Paradise Island Vacations Inc; Resorts International Airlines Inc; Resorts International Financing Inc; Resorts International Hotel Inc; Resorts International Inc of New Jersey; Resorts Representation International Inc; Resorts Tours Inc; Steeplechase Transport and Parking Inc; Trams Atlantic
Financial Information:

	Dec 31 1986
	$'000
Sales revenues	468,017
(Loss) before taxes	(43,944)
Net (loss)	(30,644)
(Loss) per share	($4.76)
Common stock class A	5,679
Common stock class B	752
Retained income	226,761
Shareholders equity	102,711

No of Employees: 7,500

RESOURCES CONSERVATION CO

3101 NE Northup Way, Bellevue, WA 98004
Tel: (206) 828-2400
Telex: 350166 RCC SEA

President: John E Andrew
Senior Executive Officers: Russell C Vandenberg (VP Brine Concentrator Division), Paul S McGough (VP B.E.S.T. TM Division)

PRINCIPAL ACTIVITIES: Industrial and hazardous waste treatment systems and technology development
Parent Company: The Reading & Bates Corporation
Principal Bank: Morgan Bank
Financial Information:

	$'000
Sales revenues	20,000

No of Employees: 50

RESTAURANT ASSOCIATES INDUSTRIES, INC

1540 Broadway, New York, NY 10036
Tel: (212) 997-1400

Chairman: Martin Brody (and Chief Executive Officer)
President: Max Pine (and Chief Operating Officer)
Senior Executive Officers: S L Klepper (Executive VP and General Counsel), Daniel P Andrus (Senior VP), James M Beltrame (Senior VP Advertising), Bernard H Green (Senior VP), Nick Valenti (Senior VP), Franklin Gasgall (VP Real Estate)

PRINCIPAL ACTIVITIES: Restaurant operations, hotel management, newsstands
Principal Bank: Citibank
Financial Information:

	$'000
Sales revenues	164,000

No of Employees: 3,700

RESTAURANT MANAGEMENT SERVICES INC

4848 Mercer University Drive, Macon, GA 31210
Tel: (912) 474 5633

Chairman: Robert M Sinclair (and Chief Executive Officer)
President: William C Marstellar (and Chief Operating Officer)
Senior Executive Officers: Thomas K Clark (VP and Director Division), Regis F Helbling (VP and Director Division), Ronald K Shields (VP and Director Division), James Weber (VP Operations), Charles B Gaulding (VP Finance, Secretary and Treasurer)

PRINCIPAL ACTIVITIES: Management of restaurants and catering services
Financial Information:

	$'000
Sales revenues	35,000

No of Employees: 1,700

REVCO D S, INC

1925 Enterprise Pkwy, Twinsburg, OH 44087
Tel: (216) 425-9811
Telex: WUT 985516 revco twbg

Chairman: Sidney Dworkin (and President and Chief Executive Officer); Vice Chairman: Henry H Gray
President: William B Edwards (and Chief Operating Officer)
Senior Executive Officers: R C Hudson (Executive VP), Marc Dworkin (Executive VP), Marvin Solganik (Senior VP Real Estate), Albert Sebok (Senior VP Store Operations), Martin Zeiger (Senior VP, Secretary and General Counsel), Harold Bardon (VP and Controller), Howard G Bieber (VP Distribution), Elliot F Dworkin (VP Purchasing), Stephen P Gruber (VP Taxes), Daniel Horwitz (VP Merchandising), John P Kern (VP Professional Operations), H Scott Leeseberg (VP Systems), Frank D Petruno (VP Security), Paul Shellabarger (VP Operations), Jerry Wasserman (VP Third Party Programs), Martin Zeiger (VP, Secretary and General Counsel)

PRINCIPAL ACTIVITIES: Operation of general stores and drug stores; manufacture of pharmaceuticals; wood partitions and metal shelving
Principal Bank: AmeriTrust Co

Financial Information:

	May 31 1986
	$'000
Sales revenues	2,743,178
Dividends	56,900
Earnings per share	$1.72
Shareholders equity	392,530

No of Employees: 26,000

REVERE COPPER & BRASS, INC

High Ridge Park, Box 10327, Stamford, CT 06904
Tel: (203) 358 5300
Telex: TWX 710 581 2510 revere nyk

Chairman: Hugh H Williamson III (and President and Chief Executive Officer)
Senior Executive Officers: Ralph L Veals (Senior VP and Chief Financial Officer), Joe J Campbell (VP), Francis X Cavanagh (VP), Joseph H Groeger (VP), Frank E Haas (VP), Berney W Magneson (VP), Robert M Payne (VP Aluminum), R Rentsch (VP), J W Wick (VP)

PRINCIPAL ACTIVITIES: Non-ferrous metal fabrication
Principal Bank: Irving Trust Company
Financial Information:

	$'000
Sales revenues	459,000

No of Employees: 3,500

REVERE, PAUL, CORPORATION

40 Westminster St, Providence, RI 02903
Tel: (401) 421-2800

Chairman: Robert P Bauman
President: Donald K Farrar
Senior Executive Officers: John H Budd (VP), Glenn K Currie (VP), Dennis G Little (VP)

PRINCIPAL ACTIVITIES: Holding company with interests in insurance and financial services
Parent Company: Textron Inc
Principal Bank: Morgan Guaranty Trust Company of New York
Financial Information:

	$'000
Revenues	900,000

No of Employees: 13,400 (including subsidiaries)

REVERE SUGAR CORPORATION

280 Richards Street, Brooklyn, NY 11231
Tel: (718) 403-3400
Telex: WUT 126 489 rev sug corp nyk

Chairman: Antonio O Floirendo (and Chief Executive Officer); Vice Chairman: Louis T Merriam Jr
President: George F Mulford Jr (and Chief Operating Officer)
Senior Executive Officers: Antonio M Lagdameo (VP), Kenneth W Robinson (VP Marketing), Louis E Mahoney III, Orlando Camejo (VP Raw Sugar), Frederick Bruder (VP Technical Services), Diosdado C Ordonez (VP Administration and Secretary), Le Roy Gross (VP), James T Gebhard (VP and Treasurer)

PRINCIPAL ACTIVITIES: Sugar refining
Principal Bank: Bankers Trust Company
Financial Information:

	$'000
Sales revenues	200,000

No of Employees: 400

REVLON GROUP, INC

555 SW 12th Avenue, Pomparo Beach, FL 33069
Tel: (305) 785-4334

Chairman: Ronald O Perelman (and Chief Executive Officer); Vice Chairman: Howard Gittis; Chairman of Executive Committee: Bruce Slovin
President: Sol Levine
Senior Executive Officers: Duane K Miller (Executive VP), Robert W Armstrong (Senior VP), Jay I Bennett (Senior VP Personnel), Irving J Bottner (Senior VP), Stanley B Desson (VP), Gloria S Markfield (VP and Treasurer), Wade H Nichols III (VP and Secretary), Paul R Shackford (VP and Controller), Roger Shelley (VP), Henry Simon (VP)

PRINCIPAL ACTIVITIES: Manufacture of cosmetics and toiletries; fragrances; manufacture of pharmaceuticals and laboratory equipment; hard and soft contact lenses
Principal Subsidiaries: Amandaco Inc; Devon Stores Inc; El Dorado Sales Inc; FF Financial Corp; J M Fields Inc; Fixtures & Equipment Leasing, Food Fair Anne Arundel Inc; Food Fair West Baltimore Inc; Footwear Services Inc; The Gillette Co (Associate Co); Golden Banana Inc; Herco Inc; Hills Supermarkets Inc; Ideal Shoe Co; Idealco Inc; Mark Distribution Corp; Maryland Milk Co; Max Factor & Co; MSPA Inc; Mary Quant Cosmetics Inc; Newcorp Supermarkets Inc; PPE Realty Inc; Pantry Pride Enterprises Inc; Pantry Pride No 3 Salisbury Inc; Realmart Inc; Revlon Inc; Balmain Perfumes Inc; Barnes-Hind Inc; Bill Blass Inc; Coburn Optical Industries Inc; Etherea Inc; Lewis-Howe Co Inc; Meloy Laboratories Inc: National Health Laboratories Inc; Norell Perfumes Inc; Plasma Alliance Inc; The Princess Marcella Borghese Inc; Revlon Development Corp; Revlon of Hawaii Inc; Revlon International Corp; Revlon Government Sales Inc; Revlon Comissary Sales Inc; Revlon-Realistic Professional Products Inc; Revlon Research Center Inc; Charles Revson Inc; Roux Laboratories Inc; Sel-Lect Kent Corp; Sunshine Milk Co Inc; Supermarket Display Corp; Trojan Transportation Inc; Tulip Packaging Corp; Twin Packing Co
Financial Information:

	$'000
Sales revenues	1,700,000

No of Employees: 35,000

REXHAM CORPORATION

7315 Pineville/Matthews Road, Box 2528, Charlotte, NC 28211
Tel: (704) 541-2800

President: Scott C Lea
Senior Executive Officers: Keith F Kennedy (Senior VP Law), Thomas McVerry (VP Finance), Charles C Brown (VP), E B Frech (VP Aaron L Jestice (VP), Thomas M Little (VP), W B Wall III (VP)

PRINCIPAL ACTIVITIES: Manufacture of packaging products and packaging machinery
Principal Subsidiaries: Laminex Inc; Rexham International Inc; Rexham (UK) Ltd; Schiller Industries Inc
Financial Information:

	$'000
Sales revenues	213,000

No of Employees: 2,400

REXNORD INC

350 N Sunny Slope, Brookfield, WI 53005
Tel: (414) 797-6900
Telex: WUT 26727 rexnord wmil; TWX 910/262-3405
Fax: 414/797-5543

Chairman: Donald Taylor; Vice Chairman: Rene Charvillat (and Chief Executive Officer)
President: John P Calhoun (and Chief Operating Officer)
Senior Executive Officers: Michael T Alcox (VP and Chief Financial Officer), Robert M MacQueen (VP-Human Resources), Ronald L De Camp (Controller), Warren Persavich (Treasurer), Ben Prescott (VP), Charles R Roy (VP Finance and Administration, Secretary)

PRINCIPAL ACTIVITIES: Rexnord serves the world's markets with mechanical and electronic industrial components, process controls and systems, specialty fasteners, molded plastic components and specialty chemicals. The company also produces equipment for wastewater treatment, and equipment to meet other specialized industrial needs. Rexnord is headquartered in the Milwaukee area and employs approximately 11,200 people in 42 North American plants and 22 overseas facilities
Trade Names: Camloc (fastener, latches and inserts), Cartriseal (mechanical seals), Contech (building sealants, adhesives and admixtures), Delron (panel inserts), Envirex (industrial and municipal water and wastewater treatment equipment), Fife (automated web guiding systems), InstaRead (bar code scanners), Nordbak (resin system and abrasion resistant materials), Nordberg (mining equipment), PFT (anaerobic digestion equipment), PSI (aerospace bearings), Rexnord (automated process controls and systems), Rex (mechanical power transmission components and conveying equipment; water and wastewater treatment equipment), Rosan (aerospace fasteners and hydraulic fittings), Shafer (aerospace bearings), Sonneborn (concrete treatments, sealants, waterproofing, coatings), Tano (marine control systems), Thomas (flexible disc couplings), Tridair (aerospace fasteners)
Parent Company: Banner Industries, Inc (as of April 30 1987)
Financial Information:

	Oct 31 1985	Oct 31 1986
	$'000	$'000
Sales revenues	682,794	669,756
Net income (loss)	36,155	(103,773)
Dividends per share	$0.43	$0.44
Earnings (loss) per share	$1.57	($4.14)
Common stock(1)	24,877	25,075(2)

(1) number of shares outstanding in thousands
(2) as at November 30 1986

No of Employees: 11,200

REYNOLDS & REYNOLDS COMPANY

15 S Ludlow St, Dayton, OH 45402
Tel: (513) 443-2000
Telex: WUT 288248 rey dtn ud

Chairman: Terry D Carder (and President and Chief Executive Officer)
Senior Executive Officers: Richard H Grant Jr (Chairman Steering Committee), Robert C Nevin (Executive VP), Arnold N Cantrell (Group VP Research and Technical Ventures), Ronald M Harwith (VP Professional Services), Frank Labosco Jr (VP Corporate Services), Dale L Medford (VP Finance and Chief Financial Officer)

PRINCIPAL ACTIVITIES: Manufacture of data processing equipment; data processing services; printing of business forms
Principal Bank: Bank One
Financial Information:

	$'000
Sales revenues	404,000

No of Employees: 3,700

REYNOLDS METALS CO

6601 Broad Street Road, Richmond, VA 23261
Tel: (804) 281-2000
Telex: 827-348

Chairman: David P Reynolds
President: William O Bourke
Senior Executive Officers: Richard G Holder (Executive VP), R Bern Crowl (Executive VP and Chief Financial Officer)

PRINCIPAL ACTIVITIES: Reynolds Metals Co is a major worldwide, vertically integrated aluminum producer. Reynolds produces alumina; primary and reclaimed aluminum; aluminum sheet, plate and extrusions; and hundreds of finished products, such as aluminum cans, flexible packaging, Reynolds Wrap household foil and other consumer products, building products, solar hot water heating systems and electrical wire and cable
Trade Names: Reynolds Wrap household aluminum foil
Financial Information:

	Dec 31 1985	Dec 31 1986
	$'000	$'000
Sales net	3,415,600	3,638,900
Income (loss) before taxes	(358,100)	186,700
Net income (loss)	(291,600)	191,800
Dividends per share	$1.00	$1.00
Earnings (loss) per share	($13.65)	$8.18
Common stock (1)	21,788	22,001
Retained income (2)	753,700	911,300
Shareholders equity	1,151,700	1,342,000

(1) average shares outstanding in thousands
(2) at year end

No of Employees: 26,000

REYNOLDS, R J, TOBACCO CO

Winston-Salem, NC 27102
Tel: (919) 777-5000
Telex: TWX 510 931350 rjr cent wsl b

Chairman: Edward A Horrigan Jr
President: Gerald H Long (and Chief Executive Officer)
Senior Executive Officers: F H Christopher Jr (Executive VP), Robert A Emken (Executive VP Finance), R Angiuoli (Executive VP Sales), R A Kampe (Executive VP Marketing), Robert DiMarco (Senior VP Research and Development), W E Ainsworth Jr (VP Government Relations), Ronald B Beasley (VP Sales Operations), Robert E Clements (VP Leaf), Joseph P Dempster (VP Materials Management), William C Donovan (VP Information Resources), David B Fisher (VP Public Relations), Yancey W Ford Jr (VP Field Sales), John J Gangloff (VP Finance and Chief Financial Officer), Robert R Gordon Jr (VP Personnel), Lawrence W Hall Jr (VP Marketing DEvelopment), William M Hildebolt (VP Research and Development), Wayne W Juchatz (VP, Secretary and General Counsel), Gerald W McKenna (VP Marketing Planning), Ellen N Monahan (VP Planning), David P Sheets (VP and Comptroller), Charles E Snyder (VP Production), Timothy J Sullivan (VP Trade Relations), John R Trulove (VP Distribution), Douglas D Walker (VP Engineering), John T Winebrenner (VP Brand Management)

PRINCIPAL ACTIVITIES: Manufacture of tobacco products including four of the top ten cigarette brands in the United States
Trade Names: Winston, Salem, Camel, Vantage, More, Now, Doral, Century, Ritz
Parent Company: RJR Nabisco
Financial Information:

	$'000
Sales revenues	8,100,000

No of Employees: 14,600

RHEEM MANUFACTURING CO

350 Park Ave, New York, NY 10022
Tel: (212) 735-8900

President: Robert B Gilbert
Senior Executive Officers: Benjamin F Cake (VP Containers), Daniel H Brown (VP, Secretary and General Counsel), Daniel B Dawley (VP Refrigeration Products), Donald F Foster (VP Air Conditioning), William E Fahey (VP Water Heaters), Daniel B Lepri (VP and Controller), Joseph S Fisher (VP Industrial Relations)

PRINCIPAL ACTIVITIES: Manufacture of cargo containers; steel and plastic fabrications; heating, air-conditioning and ventilation equipment

Parent Company: Pace Industries Inc
Principal Subsidiaries: Hayes International Corp; Alma Plastics Co; Rheem International Inc
Principal Bank: Bank of America
Financial Information:

	$'000
Sales revenues	800-900,000

No of Employees: 6,000

RHODES INC

4370 Peachtree Road NE, Atlanta, GA 30319
Tel: (404) 264 4600

Chairman: J Mack Robinson (and Chief Executive Officer); Vice Chairman: Samuel Hudgins
President: Irwin L Lowenstein
Senior Executive Officers: Ronald D Philips (Executive VP Operations), Joseph A Daniels (Senior VP Finance and Treasurer), Robert A Diproua (Controller), William E Anderson (Secretary and Legal Counsel)

PRINCIPAL ACTIVITIES: Retail trade in furniture; management of real estate
Principal Subsidiaries: Rhodes Credit Corporation
Principal Bank: First National Bank
Financial Information:

	$'000
Sales revenues	197,000

No of Employees: 2,000

RHÔNE-POULENC INC

52 Vanderbilt Avenue, New York, NY 10017
Tel: (212) 883-1260
Telex: WUT 127 336 rhodia nyk

Chairman: S Tchuruk (and Chief Executive Officer)
Senior Executive Officers: V E De Felice (Senior VP and General Counsel), P Langlois (VP Finance and Administration and Treasurer), J P Marx (Chief Operating Officer)

PRINCIPAL ACTIVITIES: Production of fertilizers and pesticides; specialty chemicals; photographic equipment
Parent Company: Rhône-Poulenc SA, France
Principal Bank: Chase Manhattan Bank
Financial Information:

	$'000
Sales revenues	300,000

No of Employees: 1,400

RIBLET PRODUCTS CORPORATION

1003 Industrial Pkwy, Elkhart, IN 46515
Tel: (219) 522-0995

Chairman: Ernest J Nagy (and President)
Senior Executive Officers: David T Miller (VP Finance), William Riblet (VP)

PRINCIPAL ACTIVITIES: Manufacture of steel and plastic construction materials
Principal Bank: St Joseph National Bank
Financial Information:

	$'000
Sales revenues	106,000

No of Employees: 1,250

RICELAND FOODS, INC

2120 Park Avenue, Stuttgart, AR 72160
Tel: (501) 673-5500
Telex: TWX 910 720648 ricelandr stgt

Chairman: Stewart E Jessup; Vice Chairman: Tommy Hillman
President: R E Bell (and Chief Executive Officer)
Senior Executive Officers: David W Bickerstaff (VP Commodity Operations), Carl W Brothers (VP Rice Marketing), L H Dodson (VP Oil Refining), Charles A Gunnell (VP Finance, Secretary and Treasurer), D Michael Owens (VP, P/T Operations and Engineering), W Cary Parker (VP Food Marketing), Dorothy Seidenshcwartz (VP Soy Processing), James K Smith (VP Commodity Marketing)

PRINCIPAL ACTIVITIES: Manufacture of soybean products
Principal Bank: First National Bank
Financial Information:

	Aug 31 1986
	$'000
Sales revenues	532,300
Net income	23,800
Shareholders equity	131,400

No of Employees: 1,650

RICH PRODUCTS CORPORATION

1145 Niagara Street, Buffalo, NY 14213
Tel: (716) 878-8000
Telex: TWX 710 5221840 rich prod buf a

Chairman: Robert E Rich Sr
President: Robert E Rich Jr
Senior Executive Officers: Herbert R Kusche (Executive VP and Treasurer), Marvin Kahn (VP Research and Development), William E Meyers (VP Management Services and Data Processing), Joseph C Robida (VP Non-Dairy), Edward Ryan (VP Personnel), John E Schaible III (VP Production Bakery), John W Sheele (VP Finance), Donald Torgersen (VP Sales and Marketing)

PRINCIPAL ACTIVITIES: Manufacture of frozen food products and prepared dishes
Principal Subsidiaries: L K Baker & Co; Rich-Seapak Corp
Principal Bank: Marine Midland Bank
Financial Information:

	$'000
Sales revenues	535,000

No of Employees: 3,000

RICHARDSON ELECTRONICS LTD

40W267 Keslinger Road, LaFox, IL 60147
Tel: (312) 232-6400
Toll-Free: 800-323-1770
Telex: 283461
Telefax: (312) 232-1071

Chairman: Edward J Richardson (and Chief Executive Officer)
President: Arnie Allen (and Cheif Operating Officer)
Senior Executive Officers: Dennis R Gandy (Executive VP), David Gilden (VP), Joel Levine (VP), Leonard R Prange (VP and Chief Financial Officer), Maureen Sublett (Investor Relations Manager), Leonard W Novin (VP Sales), Eugene F Loeb (VP Engineering), George W Snyder (VP, General Manager of Manufacturing)

PRINCIPAL ACTIVITIES: Leading international distributor and manufacturer of electron tubes and power semiconductors
Trade Names: REL
Principal Subsidiaries: National Electronics Inc; CeCo Communications; RF Gain Ltd; Richardson Electronics (Europe) Ltd; Richardson Electronics France SARL; GEB Electronics (Italy); Richardson Electronics (UK)
Principal Bank: Continental Illinois National Bank and Trust Co
Financial Information:

	May 31 1986	May 31 1987
	$'000	$'000
Sales revenues	75,501	101,216
Income before taxes	10,164	14,484
Net income	6,064	8,209
Earnings per share	$0.75	$0.82
Common stock	8,087	9,998
Retained income	27,180	35,389
Shareholders equity	58,761	67,130

Number of Shareholders: 804
No of Employees: 580

RICHARDSON-VICKS INC

Ten Westport Road, Wilton, CT 06897
Tel: (203) 834-5000
Telex: RCA 221910 rvi ur

Chairman: Smith Richardson Jr
President: John S Scott
Senior Executive Officers: William I Bergman (Executive VP), John R Markley (Executive VP), Louis P Mattis (Executive VP), Ivan Husovsky (Senior VP), John D Breslin (VP Manufacturing), Donald E Hibbard (VP and Controller), John O Green (VP, Secretary and Senior Counsel), Donald E Hibbard (VP and Controller), Nick Holloway Jr (VP Personnel), Frederic D Lamb (VP and General Counsel), Joseph R Levee (VP Tax), Thomas M McGuire (VP Corporate Planning), Joseph G McIntyre Jr (VP and Treasurer), Thomas L Pettibone (VP Information Resources)

PRINCIPAL ACTIVITIES: Manufacture of health and beauty products, medical instruments, nutrition products and home care products
Principal Subsidiaries: J J Baker Chemical Co; Baker Instruments Corp; Vidal Sassoon Inc
Principal Bank: Morgan Guaranty Trust Co of New York
Financial Information:

	$'000
Sales revenues	1,280,000

No of Employees: 10,900

RICHMOND TANK CAR COMPANY

1700 West Loop South, Suite 1500, Houston, TX 77027
Tel: (713) 877 8040

Chairman: John W Adams
President: Gilbert C Osnos
Senior Executive Officers: Lewis E Ball II (VP and Treasurer), Thomas J Schwager (Controller)

PRINCIPAL ACTIVITIES: Manufacture of railroad freight trucks and tanks
Principal Subsidiaries: Dardanelle Russellville Railroad Co; Richmond Carbon-Alloy Co; Richmond Leasing Co; Richmond-Lox Equipment Co; Alloy Crafts Co; QC Services Inc
Principal Bank: Bank Southwest
Financial Information:

	$'000
Sales revenues	31,000

No of Employees: 400

RICH-SEAPAK CORPORATION

PO Box 667, St Simons Island, GA 31522
Tel: (912) 638-5000

Chairman: Robert E Rich Sr
President: H J Cofer Jr (and Chief Executive Officer)
Senior Executive Officers: Earl L Swicord (Senior VP and Secretary), Robert E Rich Jr (VP and Assistant Secretary), Darrell Cellers (VP Food Service Sales), James K Bankston (VP Military Sales), Randall Johnson (Treasurer)

PRINCIPAL ACTIVITIES: Freezing of seafoods
Parent Company: Rich Products Corporation, Buffalo, NY
Principal Bank: Trust Company Bank
Financial Information:

	$'000
Sales revenues	75,000

No of Employees: 300

RICHTON INTERNATIONAL CORPORATION

1345 Avenue of the Americas, New York, NY 10105
Tel: (212) 765 6480
Telex: 620030 RIC NYK

Chairman: Franc M Ricciardi (and President, Chief Executive Officer and Treasurer)
Senior Executive Officers: John C Farinick (Senior VP and Assistant to President), Cornelius F Griffin (VP and Chief Financial Officer), Marshall E Bernstein (Secretary)

PRINCIPAL ACTIVITIES: Manufacture of a wide range of costume jewelry
Trade Names: Vendome, Oscar de la Renta, Marvella, Corocraft
Principal Subsidiaries: Coro (Canada) Inc; Richton International Limited; Richton Jewelry Inc
Principal Bank: Manufacturers Hanover Commercial Corporation
Financial Information:

	Apr 30 1986	Apr 30 1987
	$'000	$'000
Sales revenues net	38,085	38,058
Income before taxes	4,058	1,775
Net income (loss)	1,884	(2,250)
Earnings (loss) per share	$0.90	($0.81)
Common stock	264	275
Retained income (deficit)	643	(1,607)
Shareholders equity	15,082	13,415

No of Employees: 950

RIDGEWOOD SAVINGS BANK

Myrtle & Forest Avenue, Ridgewood, NY 11385
Tel: (718) 240-4800

Chairman: James E McCartney (and Chief Executive Officer)
President: William A McKenna Jr (and Chief Operating Officer)
Senior Executive Officers: Kenneth C Camelo (VP Senior Mortgage), Conrad W Menz (VP and Treasurer), Adolf J Vrba (VP Mortgage), Jack B Peters (VP Operations), Robert A Ross (VP and Secretary), Henry Fortman (VP and Comptroller)

PRINCIPAL ACTIVITIES: Savings bank
Principal Bank: Manufacturers Hanover Trust Company

No of Employees: 360

RIEGEL TEXTILE CORPORATION

PO Box 3478, Greenville, SC 29602-3478
Tel: (803) 242-6050

Chairman: R B Pamplin (and Chief Executive Officer); Vice Chairmen: J L Jennings, R B Pamplin Jr (and Assistant Secretary)
President: R W Chastian (and Chief Operating Officer)
Senior Executive Officers: J H Greer (VP Personnel and Public Relations), D L Harrison (VP Purchasing), D J Stevens (VP)

PRINCIPAL ACTIVITIES: Manufacture of a range of textiles for clothing and furnishing
Parent Company: Mount Vernon Mills Inc
Principal Subsidiaries: Fries Textile Co; Riegel Fiber Corp; Smith & Waters Inc; Rothchilds Co; Rieser International Corp
Principal Bank: Manufacturers Hanover Trust
Financial Information:

	$'000
Sales revenues	436,000

No of Employees: 6,000

RIGGS NATIONAL CORPORATION

1503 Pennsylvania Avenue NW, Washington, DC 20005
Tel: (202) 835-6000
Telex: ITT 440 103 rigg sbk

Chairman: J L Allbritton (and Chief Executive Officer); Vice Chairman: T W Wren (and President)
Senior Executive Officers: Paul Kurgan (Secretary), J E O'Neill (Treasurer)

PRINCIPAL ACTIVITIES: Holding company with interests in banking
Principal Subsidiaries: Riggs National Bank of Washington, DC

Financial Information:

	Dec 31 1985	Dec 31 1986
	$'000	$'000
Net income	30,975	35,623
Earnings per share	$2.59	$2.65
Shareholders equity	-	333,435
Deposits	4,293,370	4,988,877
Total assets	5,434,020	6,253,385

No of Employees: 1,990

RING SCREW WORKS

31550 Stephenson Hwy, Madison Heights, MI 48071
Tel: (313) 583-6620

Chairman: Charles R O'Brien Jr (and President)
Senior Executive Officers: Lewis C Johnstone (VP Manufacturing), David F Crowley (Treasurer)

PRINCIPAL ACTIVITIES: Manufacture of bolts and screws
Principal Bank: Commerica
Financial Information:

	$'000
Sales revenues	65,000

No of Employees: 300

RINKER MATERIALS CORPORATION

PO Drawer K, West Palm Beach, FL 33402
Tel: (305) 8333-555
Telex: WUT 513400 rinker wpb

Chairman: M E Rinker Sr (and President)
Presidents: K H Watson (Materials Division)
Senior Executive Officers: J E Carpenter (VP Equipment), J F Jackson (VP and Secretary), R A Krause (VP Finance and Treasurer), J J Rinker (VP Aggregate Division), A L Spessard (VP Cement Division)

PRINCIPAL ACTIVITIES: Manufacture of a range of building materials including ready mixed concrete, cement and aggregates
Principal Bank: Sun Bank NA
Financial Information:

	$'000
Sales revenues	300,000

No of Employees: 2,000

RIO GRANDE INDUSTRIES, INC

1515 Arapahoe Street, Denver, CO 80217
Tel: (303) 595-2254

Chairman: William J Holtman (and President and Chief Executive Officer)
Senior Executive Officers: J B Love (VP), Maxim E Ehrlich (VP, Secretary and Treasurer), Samuel R Freeman (VP)

PRINCIPAL ACTIVITIES: Holding company with interests in trucking, railroad freight transportation, property and real estate
Parent Company: Anschutz Corp
Principal Subsidiaries: The Denver & Rio Grande Western Railroad Company; Rio Grande Motor Way Inc; Leavell Development Company
Financial Information:

	$'000
Sales revenues	54,000

No of Employees: 3,000

RISDON CORPORATION

One Risdon Street, Naugatuck, CT 06770
Tel: (203) 729-8231
Telex: WUT 962 485 risdon natk

President: Joseph A Zimmermann (and Chief Executive Officer)
Senior Executive Officers: Thomas J Dunleavy (Senior VP Packaging), Leonard A Rich (VP Finance and Treasurer), Jerome C Mackey (VP Industrial Relations), Robert O Barberi (VP and Secretary), John F Feeley (VP and Group Executive)

PRINCIPAL ACTIVITIES: Manufacture of metal and plastic packaging products for a range of applications
Parent Company: Metal Box America Inc
Principal Bank: Citibank NA
Financial Information:

	$'000
Sales revenues	140,000

No of Employees: 2,000

RITE AID CORP

Trindle & Railroad, Shiremanstown, PA 17011
Tel: (717) 761-2633

Chairman: Alex Grass (and President)
Senior Executive Officers: Heinz Boldes (Senior VP), Franklin Brown (Senior VP), Martin Grass (Senior VP), Timothy Noonan (Senior VP), Duane Ruble (Senior VP), Alex Schamroth (Senior VP), Joseph Skaggs (Senior VP Circus World, Toy Store Division), Larry Stern (Senior VP Circus World), William Allen (VP), Stuart Becker (VP), Frank Bergonzi (VP and Controller), Martin Binder (VP), Don Brabants (VP, ADAP), Robert F Brown (VP and Treasurer), Robert Buhrig (VP Security), F Edward Chappell (VP Real Estate), David L Dalton (VP), Howard Diener (VP), Michael Flaherty (VP), Brian Glass (VP Store Planning), Roger Grass (VP), James Krahulec (VP Government Region), Walter McCahan (VP Administration), Ronald A Miller (VP Distribution), Joseph Rosen (VP), Sidney R Rubin (VP Circus World), Charles J Slane (VP and Secretary), Robert Souder (VP Personnel), John Valvano (VP)

PRINCIPAL ACTIVITIES: Drugstores
Principal Bankers: Morgan Guaranty Trust Co of New York
Financial Information:

	Mar 31 1986	31 Mar 1987
	$'000	$'000
Sales revenues	1,591,000	1,800,000
Net income	62,550	78,000

No of Employees: 17,080

RIVAL MANUFACTURING CO

36th and Bennington, Kansas City, MO 64129
Tel: (816) 861-1000
Telex: 42-4126

Chairman: Charles W Rootes (and President)
Senior Executive Officers: Thomas K Manning (Executive VP/Sales), William J Tweed (VP/Operations), Louis K White (VP/Materials), Gerald L Wasleski (VP/Finance)

PRINCIPAL ACTIVITIES: Manufactures and distributes a broad line of portable electric appliances and other housewares, most of which are used in home food preparation, along with portable electric heaters marketed under the TITAN name
Trade Names: RIVAL, TITAN, CROCK-POT
Parent Company: Rival Holdings, Inc
Principal Subsidiaries: Rival Manufacturing Co of Canada Ltd; Magic Hostess Company; Bennington Properties Inc (formerly GLO-International Corporation); Waverly Products Co; Waverly Products Company Ltd
Principal Bank: Commerce Bank of Kansas City
Financial Information:

	Jun 30 1986*	Jun 30 1987
	$'000	$'000
Sales revenues	92,553	92,781
Income before taxes	532	4,928
Net income (loss)	(146)	2,045
Common stock	10	10
Retained (deficit)	(1,615)	(290)
Shareholders equity	(1,101)	(56)

*pro-forma

No of Employees: 1,600

RIVER CEMENT CO
12700 Southfork Road, St Louis, MO 63128
Tel: (314) 849-6980

Chairman: Ezio Testore
President: James J Sievers
Senior Executive Officers: James D Foreman (Executive VP), John L McDaniel Jr (VP, Secretary and Treasurer), Richard J Wagner (Controller)

PRINCIPAL ACTIVITIES: Manufacture of cement
Parent Company: RC Cement Co Inc
Principal Bank: Boatmen's National Bank of St Louis
Financial Information:

	$'000
Sales revenues	60,000

No of Employees: 300

RIVER FOREST BANCORP
River Forest State Bank Building, 7727 Lake St, River Forest, IL 60305
Tel: (312) 771 2500

Chairman: J C Glickman
President: R J Glickman (and Subsidiary Officer)
Senior Executive Officers: R M Heskett (Executive VP), Edward J Wehmer (Senior VP), R H Meade (Secretary and Treasurer)

PRINCIPAL ACTIVITIES: Holding company with interests in banking
Principal Subsidiaries: River Forest State Bank and Trust Co
Principal Bank: River Forest State Bank
Financial Information:

	Dec 31 1985 $'000
Revenues	44,615
Net income	6,820

No of Employees: 205

RIVER OAKS INDUSTRIES, INC
31 Inverness Center Parkway, Birmingham, AL 35243
Tel: (205) 991 1015

Chairman: Charles F DeGroot
President: Don Morring (and Chief Executive and Chief Operating Officer)
Senior Executive Officers: H Jack Callaway (VP and Treasurer), Robert M Yeager II (Secretary)

PRINCIPAL ACTIVITIES: Manufacture and sale of a range of mobile homes
Principal Subsidiaries: River Oaks Homes Inc
Principal Bank: Third National Bank
Financial Information:

	$'000
Sales revenues	112,000

No of Employees: 670

RIVERSIDE FURNITURE CORPORATION
1400 South 6th Street, Fort Smith, AR 72901
Tel: (501) 785-6000

Chairman: Herman J Udouj
President: Richard J Udouj (and Chief Executive Officer)
Senior Executive Officers: Dan J Butler (Senior VP Marketing), David H Dixon (Senior VP Administration), Howard J Spradlin (Senior VP Manufacturing), E R Carskadden (VP and Regional Sales Manager Midwest), Jim Marshall (VP and Regional Sales Manager Northeast), Jerry Orler (VP Upholstery Sales), A G Patterson (VP Sales), James W Perry (VP and Regional Sales Manager West), Bill R Phillips (VP and Regional Sales Manager Southwest), Eugene R Rapley (VP and General Sales Manager)

PRINCIPAL ACTIVITIES: Manufacture of furniture
Parent Company: Arkansas Best Corp, Fort Smith, AR
Principal Bank: Citibank
Financial Information:

	$'000
Sales revenues	81,000

No of Employees: 1,200

RIVERSIDE MFG CO
Riverside Drive, Moultrie, GA 31768
Tel: (912) 985-5210
Telex: WUT 547628 riverside mlt

President: W J Vereen (and Chief Executive Officer and Treasurer)
Senior Executive Officers: Harvey B Vereen (VP), George W Sears Jr (Secretary)

PRINCIPAL ACTIVITIES: Manufacture of clothing
Financial Information:

	$'000
Sales revenues	50,000

RIVERSIDE/TERRA CORPORATION
871 Ridge Way Loop Road, Memphis, TN 38119
Tel: (901) 761-5150

President: Paul D Foster
Senior Executive Officers: Charles Nevaril (VP)

PRINCIPAL ACTIVITIES: Manufacture of chemicals for agricultural uses
Parent Company: Terra International Inc
Principal Bank: Security National Bank
Financial Information:

	$'000
Sales revenues	186,000

No of Employees: 420

RJ FINANCIAL CORPORATION
1400 66th Street North, St Petersburg, FL 33710
Tel: (813) 344 8200

President: Thomas A James (and Chief Executive Officer)
Senior Executive Officers: Francis S Godbold (Executive VP), Robert F Shuck (Executive VP), Richard K Reiss (Senior VP Finance), L A Silver (VP Investor Relations), J P Julien (Controller), Lynn S Pippenger (Secretary and Treasurer)

PRINCIPAL ACTIVITIES: Financial services including dealing in securities
Principal Bank: Southeast Bank
Financial Information:

	1985 $'000
Revenues	85,710
Net income	4,685

No of Employees: 2,000

RJR NABISCO, INC
RJR World Headquarters Bldg, Reynolds Blvd, Winston-Salem, NC 27102
Tel: (919) 773-2000

Chairman: J Tylee Wilson (and Chief Executive Officer); Vice Chairman: Edward A Horrigan Jr
President: F Ross Johnson (and Chief Executive Officer)
Senior Executive Officers: Gerald H Long (Senior Executive VP), James O Welch Jr (Senior Executive VP), Robert J Carbonell (Executive VP), Harold L Henderson (Executive VP and General Counsel), Edward J Robinson (Senior VP, Finance and Chief Financial Officer), Harrison M Bains (Senior VP and Treasurer), Andrew S Barrett (Senior VP, Corporate Personnel), Marshall B Bass (Senior VP, Corporate Affairs), Paul C Bergson (Senior VP, Government Relations), Paul J Bott (Senior VP, Business Planning and Development), Walter G Dunnington Jr (Senior VP and Deputy General Counsel), Michael M Masterpool (Senior VP, Corporate Public

Relations), Walter N Coleman (VP and General Auditor), C Dennis Durden (VP and Assistant to the President and Chief Executive Officer), Andrew P Hines (VP and Controller), John A Maselli (VP, Corporate Research and Development), Ward M Miller Jr (VP, Associate General Counsel and Secretary), J Thomas Pearson (VP, Taxation)

PRINCIPAL ACTIVITIES: R J Reynolds Industries, Inc is among the world's leading consumer products businesses. Through its principal operating subsidiaries, the corporation has major interests in foods and tobacco products

Trade Names: R J Reynolds Tobacco USA: Cigarette Brands: Camel, Century, Doral, More, NOW, Ritz, Salem, Vantage, Winston. R J Reynolds Tobacco International Inc: International Brands: Camel, Winston, Salem, More, Vantage. Key National Brands: Europe: Reyno, M, Time. UK: Dorchester. Belgium/Luxembourg: St Michel. West Germany: Overstolz. Eastern Europe: Gold Coast. Canada: Export "A", Macdonald Select, Macdonald Special. Brazil: Mustang, River, Tempo, Vila Rica, LS, Chancellor, Century. Ecuador: Doral Suave, Full Speed, King. Nabisco Brands Inc: USA: Cookies: Almost Home Cookies, Bakers Bonus Cookies, Barnum's Animals Crackers, Biscos Cookies, Bugs Bunny Graham Cookies, Cameo Creme Sandwich, Chips Ahoy! Chocolate Chip Cookies, Chips'n More Chocolate Chip Cookies; Cookie Break Sandwich Cookies; Cookies'n Fudge Cookies, Giggles Sandwich Cookies; Hey Day Fudge, Carmel and Peanut Bars, Ideal Chocolate and Peanut Bars, Lorna Doone Shortbread, Mallomars Chocolate Cakes, Mystic Mint Sandwich Cookies, Nabisco Brown Edge Wafers, Nabisco Chocolate Chip Snaps, Nabisco Chocolate Grahams, Nabisco Chocolate Pinwheels Cakes, Nabisco Chocolate Snaps, Nabisco Devil's Food Cakes, Nabisco Famous Chocolate Wafers, Nabisco Famous Cookie Assortment, Nabisco Imported Danish Cookies, Nabisco Marshmallow Puffs, Nabisco Marshmallow Sandwich, Nabisco Marshmallow Twirls Fudge Cakes, Nabisco Old Fashion Ginger Snaps, Nabisco Pecan Shortbread Cookies, Nabisco Pure Chocolate Middles, National Arrowroot Biscuit, Newtons Fruit Chewy Cookies, Nilla Wafers, Nutter Butter Peanut Butter Cookies, Oreo Chocolate Sandwich Cookies, Pantry Molasses Cookies, Social Tea Biscuits. Crackers: Better Blue Cheese, Cheddars, Nacho, Cheddar and Bacon and Swiss Snack Thins Crackers, Cheese Nips Crackers, Cheese Tid-Bit Crackers, Chicken In A Biskit Flavored Crackers, Crown Pilot Crackers, Dandy Soup and Oyster Crackers, Doo Dads Snacks, Escort Crackers, Great Crisps! Snacks, Holland Rusk Instant Toast, Honey Maid Graham Crackers, Meal Mates Sesame Bread Wafers, Nabisco Bacon Flavored Crackers, Nabisco Cinnamon Treats, Nabisco Cracker Meal, Nabisco Graham Crackers, Nabisco Graham Cracker Crumbs, Nabisco Zweiback, Oysterettes Soup & Oyster Crackers, Premium Crackers, Ritz Crackers, Royal Lunch Milk Crackers, Sea Rounds Crackers, Sociables Crackers, Triscuit Wafers, Twigs Sesame and Cheese Snack Sticks, Uneeda Biscuits, Vegetable Thins Flavored Crackers, Waverly Crackers, Wheatsworth Stone Ground Wheat Crackers, Wheat Thins Snack Crackers. Other Biscuit Products: Comet Cones, Cups and Sugar Cones, Easy Cheese Pasteurized Processed Cheese Spreads, Mister Salty Pretzels, NAB Packs, Toastettes Toaster Pastries. Confectionery & Snack Products: Baby Ruth Candies, Beechies Chewing Gum, Beech-Nut Chewing Gum, Bonkers! Fruit Candy, Bubble Yum Bubble Gum, Butterfinger Candies, Care* Free Sugarless Gum, Charleston Chew! Candies, Fruit Stripe Gum, Junior Mints, Life Savers Roll Candy and Lollipops, Merckens Chocolate, Nabisco Bridge Mix, Nabisco Chocolate Covered Peanuts, Nabisco Chocolate Covered Raisins, Nabisco Chocolate Stars, Pearson Specialty Candy, Planters Nuts, Planters Old Fashioned Candy, Planters Peanut Bar, Planters Snacks, Pom Poms Caramels, Sugar Babies Caramels, Sugar Daddy Caramel Pops and Nuggets, Sugar Free Breath Savers Mints. Grocery Products: A1 Steak Sauce, Blue Bonnet Margarines, Brer Rabbit Molasses and Syrups, Chun King Oriental Canned Foods, College Inn Broths and Heat & Serve Entrees, Cream of Wheat and Cream of Rice Cereals, Davis Baking Powder, Del Monte Canned Vegetables and No Salt Added Vegetables, Del Monte Tomato Products and No Salt Added Tomato Products, Del Monte Canned Fruits and Lite Canned Fruits, Del Monte Dried Fruits, Del Monte Fruit Snacks, Del Monte Pickles and Pickle Products, Del Monte Fruit Cup, Del Monte Pudding Cup, Del Monte Sardines in Tomato Sauce, Dromedary Dates, Pimentos, Cake Mixes and Date Nut Roll, Egg Beaters Cholesterol-Free 99% Real Egg Product, Escoffier Sauces, Fleischmann's Margarines, Grey Poupon Dijon Mustards, Milk-Bone Brand Dog Biscuits, Milk-Bone Brand Butcher Bones Dog Snacks, My*T* Fine Puddings and Pie Fillings, Nabisco Fruit Wheats Cereal, Nabisco 100% Bran, Nabisco Shredded Wheat, Toasted Wheat & Raisins, Shredded Wheat'n Bran Cereals, Ortega Mexican Foods, Regina Cooking Wines and Wine Vinegars, Royal Gelatins, Puddings and No Bake Desserts, Spoon Size Shredded Wheat, Steak Supreme Steak Sauce, Team Flakes, Vermont Maid Syrup, Wright's Natural Hickory Seasoning. Beverages: Del Monte Blends Juice Drinks, Del Monte Juices, Juice Drinks and Nectars, Hawaiian Punch Beverages, Snap-E-Tom Tomato and Chile Cocktail. Ice Cream and Frozen Confections: Life Savers Flavor Pops, Oreo Cookies'n Cream Ice Cream*, Oreo Cookies'n Cream on a Stick*, Oreo Cookies'n Cream Sandwich*. International Brands: Del Monte, Nabisco, Planters, Ritz, Royal. Key National Brands: Canada: Aylmer Canned Fruits and Vegetables, Aylmer Soups, Blue Bonnet Margarines, Bubble Yum and Care*Free Gums, Chipits Baking Chips, Christie Cookies, Crackers and Snacks, Cream of Wheat Cereals, Dad's Cookies, David Cookies, Del Monte Canned Fruits and Vegetables, Del Monte Beverages, Del Monte and Aylmer Tomato Products, Del Monte Pudding Cups, Dickson's Club and Melrose Food Service Coffees, Fleischmann's Margarines, Life Savers Roll Candy, Lowney Candy Bars, Magic Baking Powder, Milk-Bone Brand Dog Biscuits, Moirs Boxed Chocolates, Nabisco Cereals, Peek Freans Biscuits, Planters Nuts, Royal Desserts. Continental Europe: Ardilla Pasta and Cannelloni, Ati Herb Teas, Catari Pizza Mixes, Chipster Potato Snacks, Crackers Gourmand, Cremerinos Biscuits and Wafers, Del Monte Catsup, Del Monte Canned Fruits, Del Monte Canned Vegetables and No Salt Added Vegetables, Del Monte Dried Fruits, Del Monte Fruit Juices and Nectars, Del Monte Tomato Products, Feuillete Snack Crackers, Miniquiche Crackers, Minizza Snack Crackers, Moulin de Jacobert Frozen Pastries, Oro Sweet Biscuits, Oxford Biscuits, Parisienne Pastry Cake, Pepito Chocolate-Covered Sweet Biscuits, Petits Coeurs Sweet Biscuits, Planters Snack Products, Premium Saltine Crackers, Riera-Marsa Dry Baby Foods, Flour Mixes and Instant Mashed Potatoes, Ritz Crackers, Royal Desserts, Gelatins and Cake Mixes. Asia/Pacific: Chicken In A Biskit Flavored Crackers, Chips Ahoy! Chocolate Chip Cookies, Chip Star Fabricated Potato Chips, Corn Diggers Snacks, Del Monte Banana Ketchup, Del Monte Beverages, Del Monte Canned Fruits, Del Monte Canned Vegetables, Del Monte Dried Fruits, Del Monte Tomato Products, Del Monte Vinegar, Minties Candies, Parfait Soft Cake, Picola Crepe Cookies, Planters Nuts and Snack Products, Premium Saltine Crackers, Ritz Crackers, Royal Brand Products, Rum Slice Biscuits, Vita Brits Cereal, Weeties Cereal. Latin America: Aurora Dessert Products, Bubble Yum Bubble Gum, Cameo Cream Sandwich Cookies, Del Monte Beverages, Del Monte Catsup, Del Monte Canned Fruits, Del Monte Canned Vegetables and No Salt Added Vegetables, Del Monte Dried Fruits, Del Monte Fruit Juices and Nectars, Del Monte Marmalades and Jams, Del Monte Mexican Peppers, Del Monte Pickles and Olives, Del Monte Pudding Cups, Del Monte Tomato Products, Fleischmann's Baking Products, Gamesa Biscuits and Pasta, Glorida Powdered Milk, Hawaiian Punch Beverages, Life Savers Roll Candy, Oreo Chocolate Sandwich Cookies, Planters Nuts and Snack Products, Pommys Delicatessen Products, Ritz Crackers, Royal Baking Products, Royal Desserts and Drink Powders, Royalina Drink

Powders, Sabueso Dog Biscuits, Sorbetto Sugar Wafers, Sultana Soda Crackers. Middle East: Del Monte Canned Fruits, Del Monte Canned Vegetables, Planters Nuts and Snack Products. UK: Bendicks Confectionery, Big D Nuts, Del Monte Canned Fruits, Del Monte Canned Vegetables and No Salt Added Vegetables, Del Monte Dried Fruits, Del Monte Fruit Juices, Del Monte Tomato Products, Hovis Crackers and Digestive Biscuits, Huntley & Palmer's Biscuits, Island Blends Fruit Juices, Jacob's Club Countline, Nabisco Shredded Wheat Cereal, Peek Freans Biscuits, Planters Nuts and Snack Products, Ritz Crackers, Royal Desserts, Gelatins and Cake Mixes, Shreddies Cereal, Smiths Crisps and Snack Products, Tea Time Sweet Biscuits, Trio Countlines, Biscuits, Mallows and Crackers, Walkers Crisps Snack Products. Del Monte Tropical Fruit Company: USA: Del Monte Fresh Bananas, Pineapples and Papayas. Canada, Europe, Asia/Pacific, Middle East: Del Monte Fresh Bananas and Pineapples

Principal Subsidiaries: Nabisco Brands, Inc; R J Reynolds Tobacco Company which includes R J Reynolds Tobacco USA and R J Reynolds Tobacco International; Nabisco Brands Inc which includes Nabisco Brands USA, International Nabisco Brands and Nabisco Brands Ltd (Canada); Del Monte Tropical Fruit Company; Kentucky Fried Chicken Corporation, RJR Archer, Inc

Financial Information:

	Dec 31 1985 $'000	Dec 31 1986 $'000
Sales revenues net	12,388,000	15,978,000
Income before taxes	1,789,000	1,917,000
Net income	1,001,000	1,064,000
Dividends*	357,000	378,000
Dividends per share*	$1.41	$1.51
Earnings per share*	$3.60	$3.83
Common stock net	247,000	236,000
Retained income	4,357,000	4,832,000
Shareholders equity	4,796,000	5,312,000

*common stock

No of Employees: 124,617

RKO GENERAL, INC

1440 Broadway, New York, NY 10018
Tel: (212) 764-7000
Telex: TWX 710 5814 386 rko wor ny

Chairman: Thomas F O'Neil (and Chief Executive Officer); Vice Chairmen: Hubert J DeLynn (and Chairman of Executive Committee), Frank Shakespeare

President: Shane O'Neil (and Chief Operating Officer)

Senior Executive Officers: Henry V Greene (Senior VP), Arnold Kaufman (Senior VP), C R Manby (Senior VP), John T Cahill (VP), Charles A Carrature (VP), John Howard Carter (VP), Eugene J Caser (VP), Steven Ellis (VP Corporate Communications), John B Fitzgerald (VP and Controller), Kenneth R Frankl (VP, Secretary and General Counsel), Jerry R Lyman (VP Government Relations), Lloyd D Ruth (VP), Jeffrey Ruthizer (VP Employee Relations and Administration), Henry P Sabatell (VP and Treasurer), Pat A Servodidio (VP Television), John J Spencer (VP), Robert J Williamson (VP Radio)

PRINCIPAL ACTIVITIES: Television and radio broadcasting; pay television; television program and motion picture production; bottling of non-alcoholic drinks; operation of air transportation and hotel services

Parent Company: Gencorp Inc

Principal Bank: Chase Manhattan Bank

Financial Information:

	$'000
Sales revenues	256,000

No of Employees: 8,650

RLC CORPORATION

One Rollins Plaza, Wilmington, DE 19803
Tel: (302) 479-2700

Chairman: John W Rollins (and Chief Executive Officer)

President: John W Rollins Jr (and Chief Operating Officer)

Senior Executive Officers: John C Peet Jr (VP, General Counsel and Secretary), Patrick J Bagley (VP and Treasurer)

PRINCIPAL ACTIVITIES: Trucking; leasing and rental of trucks

Financial Information:

	Sep 30 1985 $'000	Sep 30 1986 $'000
Sales revenues	382,472	419,519
Income before taxes	4,336	17,462
Net income	6,020	13,366
Dividends	3,630	3,633
Dividends per share	$0.20	$0.20
Earnings per share	$0.33	$0.73
Common stock	17,947	18,040
Retained income	23,049	23,382
Shareholders equity	109,241	119,390

No of Employees: 4,000

RLI CORPORATION

9025 North Lindberg Drive, Peoria, IL 61615
Tel: (309) 692 1000

Chairman: Gerald D Stephens (and President and Chief Executive Officer)

Senior Executive Officers: R Robert Leventry (Executive VP Operations), B Bruce Phillips (Senior VP Marketing and Sales), Evelyn Corral (VP), Jonathan E Michael (VP Finance and Chief Financial Officer), Carol R Newman (Secretary and Legal Counsel)

PRINCIPAL ACTIVITIES: Insurance including accident and health, property and liability

Principal Bank: Jefferson Trust and Savings Bank of Peoria

Financial Information:

	Dec 31 1985 $'000
Revenues	69,215
Net income	4,320

No of Employees: 200

RMI COMPANY

1000 Warren Avenue, Niles, OH 44446
Tel: (216) 652-9951
Telex: WUT 241054 rmi co nies

President: L F Gieg Jr

Senior Executive Officers: P D Weiskopf (VP and Comptroller), Warren D Jensen (VP Personnel), Stan R Seagle (VP Research and Technical Development), John H Odle (VP Commercial), William J McCarthy (VP Operations), R J Genardy (VP Engineering), R E Rohrabaugh (VP Technical and Quality Control)

PRINCIPAL ACTIVITIES: Steel works, blast furnaces, titanium, metal powders, associated chemicals

Parent Company: USX Corp

Principal Bank: Central National Bank

Financial Information:

	$'000
Sales revenues	175,000

No of Employees: 1,750

ROADWAY SERVICES, INC

1077 Gorge Blvd, Akron, OH 44309
Tel: (216) 384-1717

Chairman: Joseph M Clapp (and Chief Executive Officer); Vice Chairman: Richard W Hoss (Transport Services)

Senior Executive Officers: R D Carlson (VP and Controller), William F Klug (VP), A C Snelson (VP), Douglas A Wilson (VP and Secretary)

PRINCIPAL ACTIVITIES: Holding company with interests in trucking services

Principal Bank: Bank One of Akron
Financial Information:

	Dec 31 1985	Dec 31 1986
	$'000	$'000
Sales revenues	1,579,830	1,717,491
Net income	75,910	76,466
Earnings per share	$1.90	$1.91
Shareholders equity	613,840	654,235

No of Employees: 23,000

ROANOKE ELECTRIC STEEL CORPORATION
102 Westside Blvd, Roanoke, VA 24017
Tel: (703) 342-1831

Chairman: William M Meador
President: Donald G Smith (and Chief Executive Officer and Treasurer)
Senior Executive Officers: Donald R Higgins (VP Sales), Thomas J Crawford (Secretary), John E Morris (Comptroller and Assistant Treasurer)

PRINCIPAL ACTIVITIES: Steel industry
Principal Bank: First National Exchange
Financial Information:

	Oct 31 1986
	$'000
Sales revenues	122,000
Net income	5,194
Dividends per share	$0.55
Common stock	3,500
Shareholders equity	38,800

No of Employees: 590

ROBBINS & MYERS, INC
1400 Kettering Tower, Dayton, OH 45402
Tel: (513) 222-2610

Chairman: Maynard H Murch IV
President: Daniel W Duval (and Chief Executive Officer)
Senior Executive Officers: George M Walker III (VP and Chief Financial Officer), Alan E Cockrell (President, Fluids Handling Division), James F Howlett (President, Motor and Control Systems Division), Hugh E Becker (Director Human Resources)

PRINCIPAL ACTIVITIES: Robbins & Myers, Inc is a technology-based industrial products company with plants in the United States, Canada and Europe. The Fluids Handling Division manufactures and markets Moyno and Ramoy progressing cavity pumps and Moyno RKL pinch valves for the environmental, energy, chemical, pulp and paper, food and petroleum industries; and Moyno Down-Hole oil well pumps and hydraulic drilling motor components for the oil recovery industry. The Motor and Control Systems Division manufactures and markets Robbins & Myers specialty AC electric motors and gearmotors for business and computer equipment and light industrial markets; and Electro-Craft high technology DC motors, servosystems and optical encoders for office and computer peripheral applications, automated machine tools, robots and other industrial applications
Trade Names: Registered trademarks: Moyno, Ramoy
Principal Subsidiaries: Electro-Craft Corp; Electro-Craft Ltd (UK)
Principal Bank: Bank Ohio
Financial Information:

	Aug 31 1985	Aug 31 1986
	$'000	$'000
Sales revenues	115,173	95,715
Income (loss) before taxes*	1,609	(7,443)
Net (loss)	(3,687)	(8,804)
Loss per share net	($1.55)	($3.13)
Common stock	15,874	15,912
Retained income	24,765	15,962
Shareholders equity	40,640	31,874

*from continuing operations

ROBEL BEEF PACKERS, INC
PO Box 430, St Cloud, MN 56301
Tel: (612) 251-8484
Telex: TWX 910 5783794 robel inc sclo

Chairman: Robert J Hubbell
President: Elliott G Belzer
Senior Executive Officers: Rich E Weilliver (VP and Treasurer), Israel Krawetz (Secretary)

PRINCIPAL ACTIVITIES: Slaughterhouses; packaging of beef
Principal Bank: The First National Bank of Minneapolis
Financial Information:

	$'000
Sales revenues	81,000

No of Employees: 220

ROBERT BRUCE INC
See BRUCE, ROBERT, INC

ROBERTS & PORTER, INC
860 Thomas Drive, Bensenville, IL 60106-1627
Tel: (312) 860-1411

Chairman: Andrew Galet
President: John E Preschlack (and Chief Executive Officer)
Senior Executive Officers: James Slife (VP Finance and Secretary), Louis De Salvatore (VP West Coast), Alfred Lake (VP New England), Frank Lenahan (VP Supplies), Charles Weinholzer (VP and General Manager Ink)

PRINCIPAL ACTIVITIES: Manufacture of chemicals, photographic equipment and printing ink
Principal Bank: Citibank
Financial Information:

	$'000
Sales revenues	46,000

No of Employees: 200

ROBERTS DAIRY CO
2901 Cummings Street, Omaha, NE 68131
Tel: (402) 344-4321

Chairman: Leonard Southwell
President: Ron Richardson (and General Manager)
Senior Executive Officers: Larry Kochen (General Sales Manager), Marshall Green (General Plant Manager), Ted Fisher (Data Processing Manager)

PRINCIPAL ACTIVITIES: Wholesale and retail trade in dairy products including milk, cheese, butter, ice cream and frozen desserts
Parent Company: Joint Venture: Prairie Farms Dairy Inc, Carlinville, IL-Managing Partner + Mid-America Dairymen Inc, Springfield, MO
Financial Information:

	$'000
Sales revenues	130,000

ROBERTSHAW CONTROLS CO
1701 Byrd Avenue, PO Box 26544, Richmond, VA 23261
Tel: (804) 281-0774
Telex: 710-956-0121

Chairman: David P Reynolds
President: Ralph S Thomas
Senior Executive Officers: Dean R Dennis (Executive VP and Chief Operating Officer), Joseph A Howell Jr (Senior VP and General Counsel), H N Robinson (VP and Controller), Robert W Pendergast (VP, Financial and Public Relations and Mergers and Acquisitions), George R Martin (Treasurer), Robert E Sweaney (Secretary)

PRINCIPAL ACTIVITIES: Producer of automatic controls and control systems for homes, commercial buildings, industry and transportation

Trade Names: Autostat, Minute Minder, Infinite Control, Unitrol, Mini Gard, Burner with a Brain, Level Lance
Principal Subsidiaries: Robertshaw Controls Canada Inc; Controles Robertshaw do Brasil SA; Robertshaw Controls (Australia) Pty; Robertshaw Orient Ltd; Robertshaw Europa BV; Robertshaw Korea Ltd
Principal Bank: Central Fidelity Bank NA
Financial Information:

	$'000
Sales revenues	412,830

No of Employees: 7,920

ROBERTSON, H H, COMPANY

Two Gateway Center, Pittsburgh, PA 15222
Tel: (412) 281-3200
Telex: TWX 710 6644 284 hhr pgh

Chairman: Jack Hatcher (and President and Chief Executive Officer)
Senior Executive Officers: J W Viehman (VP Finance and Treasurer), Leonard L Crewse (VP and Controller), Frank H Roland (Senior VP Administration), James R Douglass (Senior VP, General Counsel and Secretary)

PRINCIPAL ACTIVITIES: Manufacture of building materials
Principal Subsidiaries: Freeman Chemical Corporation
Principal Banks: Mellon Bank, N.A.; Pittsburgh National Bank
Financial Information:

	Dec 31 1985	Dec 31 1986
	$'000	$'000
Sales revenues	614,249	554,175
Loss before taxes	(56,546)	(39,646)
Net (loss)	(31,987)	(41,843)
Dividends	6,925	225
Dividends per share	$1.20	-
Loss per share	($5.77)	($7.36)
Common stock	5,623	5,922
Retained income	115,900	72,969
Shareholders equity	127,117	91,063

Principal Shareholders: First City Capital Corporation
No of Employees: 6,406

ROBESON INDUSTRIES CORPORATION

49 Windsor Avenue, Mineola, NY 11501
Tel: (516) 741 0420

Chairman: Harold Weiss (and President)
Senior Executive Officers: Irwin L Septimus (Executive VP), Jack Beckering (VP Engineering), Timothy R Bennington (VP Manufacturing), William J Carfagno (VP Sales), Lawrence Ferguson (VP Sales), Ronald Jarush (VP Marketing), Eric S Matlin (Treasurer), Evelyn Pakarow (Secretary)

PRINCIPAL ACTIVITIES: Manufacture of domestic electrical equipment including coffee makers, corn poppers, electric fans and heaters, hand mixers and can openers
Principal Bank: Chemical Bank
Financial Information:

	$'000
Sales revenues	46,000

No of Employees: 430

ROBINS, A H, COMPANY, INC

1407 Cummings Drive, PO Box 26609, Richmond, VA 23261-6609
Tel: (804) 257-2000
Cable: ROBINCO
Telex: 82-8317 ROBINCO RCH

Chairman: E Claiborne Robins
President: E Claiborne Robins Jr (and Chief Executive Officer)
Senior Executive Officers: Charles E Hart (Executive VP), Robert G Watts (Executive VP), Philip H Anns (Senior VP Corporate Government Relations), John L Burke (Senior VP Consumer Products Division), Daniel E French (Senior VP Operations Division), H Arvid Johnson (Senior VP, General Counsel and Secretary), Carl D Lunsford (Senior VP Research and Development Division), Robert S Murphey (Senior VP New Business Development), G E R Stiles (Senior VP, Chief Financial Officer), John C Gordon (VP Administrative Services, and Assistant Secretary), Howard L Hall Jr (VP Administration Division), Norman D Schellenger (VP Pharmaceutical Division), John D Taylor (VP Public Affairs), H Carlton Townes (VP and Controller), David T Davis (VP and Treasurer), David E Jones (VP Special Products Division and Corporate Planning and Development), Dr Richard R McCracken (VP, Personnel), Thomas R Ransom (VP, Information Services-EDP), David A Mefford (Assistant VP, Good Manufacturing Practices), G William King (Assistant VP Corporate Licensing), Fletcher B Owen Jr (Assistant VP Medical Services)

PRINCIPAL ACTIVITIES: Manufacture of pharmaceuticals and health care products
Trade Names: Registered Trademarks:- Allbee, Bio-Cox, Caron, Chap Stick, Dimetane, Dimetapp, Donnagel, Dopram, Exerdop, Extentabs, Micro-K, Extencaps, Phenaphen, Q-3000, Q-4000, Quinidex, Quiniday Extencaps, Reglan, Robaxin, Robinul, Robitussin, Robitussin Night Relief, Rug Patrol, Sergeant's, SUNBLOCK 15, Tenex, Viokase Z-BEC
Principal Subsidiaries: Domestic Subsidiaries:- Agri-Bio Corp; A H Robins International Company; A H Robins Manufacturing Company; Elkins-Sinn, Inc; Eurand America Inc; Lee Laboratories, Inc; Mil-Mor Media, Inc; Quinton Instrument Company; US Clinical Products, Inc; Viobin Corporation. Foreign Subsidiaries:- Canada: A H Robins Canada Inc. Latin American Area- A H Robins International, SA (Colombia); Instituto Médico Técnico Sanicol, SA (Colombia); Industrial Santa Agape, SA (Guatemala); A H Robins de Mexico, SA de CV (Mexico); Laboratorios Ergos, SA (Venezuela). European Area:- A H Robins Company Ltd (UK); Eurand France SA (France); Laboratoires Martinet SA (France); Medipha SA (France); Parfums Caron SA (France); Eurand Italia SpA (Italy); Eurand International Srl (Italy); Lode BV (Netherlands); A H Robins Farmacéutica, SA (Spain); Eurand Espanola, SA (Spain); Diffucap-Eurand SA (Switzerland); Eurand Microencapsulation SA (Switzerland); A H Robins (Suisse) GmbH (Switzerland); Georg A Brenner Arzneimittel-Fabrik GmbH (West Germany); Kytta-Werk Sauter GmbH (West Germany); E Scheurich Pharmwerk GmbH (West Germany). Middle East and Africa Area:- A H Robins International Company (Greece); A H Robins International Company (Iran); A H Robins (Iran) Company (Iran). Far East Area:- A H Robins Pty Limited (Australia); A H Robins International Company (Taiwan); A H Robins International Company (Hong Kong); A H Robins International Company (Japan); A H Robins-Showa Co Ltd (Japan); American Drug Corporation (Japan); A H Robins (Philippines) Company, Inc (Philippines)
Principal Bank: Central Fidelity Bank
Financial Information:

	Dec 31 1985	Dec 31 1986
	$'000	$'000
Sales revenues	706,134	789,895
Income before taxes	117,185	154,672
Net income	75,814	81,796
Earnings per share	$2.53	$3.38
Common stock*	24,289	24,175
Retained income (loss)	(104,477)	53,133
Shareholders equity (deficit)	(47,149)	49,049

*average shares outstanding in thousands

No of Employees: 6,400

ROBINSON NUGENT, INC

800 E 8th Street, New Albany, IN 47150
Tel: (812) 945-0211
Telex: TWX 810 540 4082 robnu na

Chairman: James W Robinson
President: James C Jones

Senior Executive Officers: Larry W Burke (Executive VP), Clifford G Boggs (VP Finance), Don J Fleming (VP Marketing), David W Swanson (VP Manufacturing)

PRINCIPAL ACTIVITIES: Manufacture of electronic equipment
Principal Subsidiaries: RE-AL Inc; Cablelink Inc; Robinson Nugent Inc, Texas
Principal Bank: Mutual Trust Bank and Deposit Company
Financial Information:

	$'000
Sales revenues	49,000

No of Employees: 650

ROBINTECH, INC

2024 West St, Annapolis, MD 21401
Tel: (301) 841-5577

Chairman: Bradford G Corbett (and Chief Executive Officer); Vice Chairman: Edwin S Elgin
Senior Executive Officers: Patrick Madormo (VP Sales), John I Geary (VP), C E Rupel (Treasurer and Chief Financial Officer)

PRINCIPAL ACTIVITIES: Manufacture of plastic pipe; manufacture of machinery for the plastics industry
Principal Subsidiaries: Plastiline Inc
Principal Bank: Continental Illinois National Bank
Financial Information:

	$'000
Sales revenues	103,000

No of Employees: 1,400

ROCHESTER & PITTSBURGH COAL CO

655 Church, Indiana, PA 15701
Tel: (412) 349-5800

Chairman: Charles J Potter
President: W G Kegel (and Chief Executive Officer)
Senior Executive Officers: Peter Iselin (VP Finance and Secretary), Eugene H Jones (VP Operations), George M Evans (VP and Treasurer), W Joseph Engler Jr (VP and General Counsel), F J Ucciardi (VP Administration)

PRINCIPAL ACTIVITIES: Bituminous coal products
Principal Subsidiaries: Helvetia Coal Co; Iselin Preparation; Jeffco Inc; DSB Co; Maud Mining Co; Kent Coal Mining Co; Keystone Coal Mining Corp; Subco Inc; Allegheny Highlands Realty Co; Cowanshannock Coal Co Inc; Ropit Inc; Young Township Coal Co Inc; United Eastern Coal Sales Corp; Rogers Fuel Corp; White Star Coal Inc; Westco Coal Co; Avonmore Coal Co; Avonmore Mining Co
Principal Bank: Manufacturers Hanover Trust Co
Financial Information:

	Dec 31 1986
	$'000
Sales revenues	420,217
Net income	18,564
Earnings per share	$7.78
Shareholders equity	150,871

No of Employees: 3,675

ROCHESTER GAS & ELECTRIC CORP

89 E Avenue, Rochester, NY 14649
Tel: (716) 546-2700

Chairman: Paul W Briggs (and Chief Executive Officer)
President: Keith W Amish (and Chief Operating Officer)
Senior Executive Officers: Francis E Drake Jr (Chairman of Executive and Finance Committees), Henry G Saddock (Executive VP), (Senior VP), Mario Silvestrone (Senior VP Corporate Services), John E Arthur (VP Engineering and Construction), Joseph J Hartman (VP Gas and Transport), Robert C Henderson (VP Rates and Controller), Roger W Kober (VP Electricity and Steam Production), David K Laniak (VP Corporate Planning), John W Oberlies (VP Public Affairs), Richard J Rudman (VP Electricity Transmission and Distribution)

PRINCIPAL ACTIVITIES: Distribution of electricity and natural gas
Financial Information:

	$'000
Sales revenues	749,000

No of Employees: 2,600

ROCHESTER TELEPHONE CORPORATION

100 Midtown Plaza, Rochester, NY 14646
Tel: (716) 423 7150

President: Alan C Hasselwander (and Chief Executive Officer)
Senior Executive Officers: Ronald L Bittner (VP Operations), Jeremiah T Carr (VP Business Marketing), William Hughes (VP and General Manager Telephone Subs), David C Mitchell (VP Finance and Corporate Development, Secretary and Treasurer), John H Cline (President RCI), Richard E Sayers, (President Rotelcom)

PRINCIPAL ACTIVITIES: Telecommunications services
Principal Subsidiaries: Highland Telephone Co; RCI Corporation; Rotelcom Inc; Sylvan Lake Telephone Co Inc
Principal Bank: Lincoln First Bank
Financial Information:

	Dec 31 1985
	$'000
Sales revenues	401,000

No of Employees: 2,880

ROCK ISLAND REFINING CORPORATION

PO Box 68007, Indianapolis, IN 46268
Tel: (317) 872-3200
Telex: WUT 29307 rock i rfg ind

Chairman: L E Kincannon
President: William E Huff
Senior Executive Officers: F W Grube (Executive VP), John P Hofer (VP Finance)

PRINCIPAL ACTIVITIES: Crude oil refining
Principal Bank: Chase Manhattan Bank
Financial Information:

	$'000
Sales revenues	400,000

No of Employees: 250

ROCKAWAY CORPORATION

2001 US Hwy. 46, Parsippany, NJ 07054
Tel: (201) 335 1126

President: John J Cahill (and Chief Executive Officer)
Senior Executive Officers: Robert A Jania (Controller), Robert H Whitehead (Treasurer), Thomas J Bitar (Secretary and Legal Counsel)

PRINCIPAL ACTIVITIES: Manufacture of machinery and equipment for the woodworking industry; food processing plant
Principal Subsidiaries: Better Packages Inc; Caddy Corporation of America; IMS Leasing Inc
Principal Bank: Chemical Bank
Financial Information:

	$'000
Sales revenues	52,000

No of Employees: 500

ROCKBESTOS COMPANY

285 Nicoll, New Haven, CT 06510
Telex: WUT 855546 rockbestos

President: Robert A Pritzker

Senior Executive Officers: Donald F Bafundo (VP Finance), R C Gluth (VP), W S Ragowski (Secretary), G T Shannon (VP), Richard Thayer (VP and General Manager)

PRINCIPAL ACTIVITIES: Manufacture of wires, cables and controls
Parent Company: The Marmon Group Inc
Financial Information:

	$'000
Sales revenues	33,000

No of Employees: 500

ROCKCOR INC

11441 Willows Road NE, Redmond, WA 98052
Tel: (206) 885-5000

Chairman: George S Sutherland (and Chief Executive Officer)
President: B F Beckleman (and Chief Operating Officer)
Senior Executive Officers: Robert G Sanderson (VP Finance and Treasurer), Kevin P Teismann (VP and Secretary)

PRINCIPAL ACTIVITIES: Manufacture of computer based equipment and software for military applications; nuclear radiation simulation and analysis; rocket engines and propellant gas generators; aircraft electronic equipment; telecommunication fault monitoring equipment; power plants; oil and gas industry services
Parent Company: Olin Corp
Principal Subsidiaries: (100% owned unless stated): Physics International Co; Rocket Research Co; Pacific Electro Dynamics Inc; Larse Corp; Trans Energy Systems Inc (50%); Petroleum Technology Corp; Ravenna & Arsenal Inc; Pisces International BV
Principal Bank: Seattle-First National Bank
Financial Information:

	$'000
Sales revenues	91,000

No of Employees: 1,300

ROCKFORD PRODUCTS

707 Harrison Avenue, Rockford, IL 61101
Tel: (815) 397-6000
Telex: TWX 910 6313411 rkfd prods rkd

President: R Ray Wood
Senior Executive Officers: Harold W Naill (Executive VP Manufacturing), Dennis J Schaer (VP Finance, Secretary/Treasurer), Thomas E Johnson (VP Marketing/Sales), Richard L Goff (Group VP), Richard C Giesen (VP Employee Relations)

PRINCIPAL ACTIVITIES: Manufacture of metal industrial fasteners
Principal Bank: Amcore Bank N.A., Rockford
Financial Information:

	Oct 31 1986 $'000
Sales revenues	75,100

Principal Shareholders: ESOP Corporation
No of Employees: 840

ROCK-TENN CO

504 Thrasher Street, Norcross, GA 30071
Tel: (404) 448-2193

Chairman: A W Brown (and Chief Executive Officer)
President: Bradley Currey Jr (and Chief Operating Officer)
Senior Executive Officers: Jay Shuster (Senior VP, Secretary, Treasurer and Controller), Joel S Burch (VP Administration), Donald L Crossley (President Folding Carton Division), David E Dreibelbis (President Recycle Division), David C Nicholson (Controller), James F Parker (President Corrugated Box and Partition Division), W D Griffin Jr (President Mill Division), James L Walden (President Mill Division)

PRINCIPAL ACTIVITIES: Manufacture of paperboard containers, solid-fibre partitions and corrugated boxes from recycled paperboard
Principal Bank: Trust Company of Georgia
Financial Information:

	$'000
Sales revenues	250,000

No of Employees: 2,500

ROCKWELL INTERNATIONAL CORPORATION

600 Grant Street, Pittsburgh, PA 15219
Tel: (412) 565-2000
Telex: TWX 710 6644 355 rockwell pgh

Chairman: Robert Anderson (and Chief Executive Officer)
President: Donald R Beall (and Chief Operating Officer)
Senior Executive Officers: Martin D Walker (Executive VP), Robert L Cattoi (Senior VP), Robert A dePalma (Senior VP and Chief Financial Officer), Richard W Foxen (Senior VP Strategic Management and International), Charles H Harff (Senior VP and Secretary), Bastian Hello (Senior VP and President North American Aircraft Operations), Edward A Loeser (Senior VP Operations), Samuel Petok (Senior VP Communications), John J Roscia (Senior VP, Assistant to Chairman and Chief Executive Officer), Kent M Black (VP President Commercial Electronics Operations), Jerome A Earley (VP Corporate Development), Sam F Iacobellis (VP, President and B-IB Program Manager N A Aircraft Operation), George W Jeffs (VP, President North American Space Operation), Richard R Mau (VP), Arthur P Ronan (VP, President Automotive Operations), C R Vennel Jr (VP Human Resources), Donald J Yockey (VP, President Defense Electronics Operations)

PRINCIPAL ACTIVITIES: Manufacture of equipment for the defense electronics, automotive and aerospace industries
Principal Bank: Branch Bank & Trust Co
Financial Information:

	Sep 30 1985 $'000	Sep 30 1986 $'000
Sales revenues	11,337,600	12,295,700
Net income	595,300	611,200
Earnings per share	$4.00	$4.12
Shareholders equity	2,948,300	3,162,100

No of Employees: 123,266

ROCKWOOD HOLDING CO

118 W Main Street, Somerset, PA 15501
Tel: (814) 443-1471

President: W A Thomas
Senior Executive Officers: Richard T Misitano (VP Finance), P T Dwyer (Treasurer)

PRINCIPAL ACTIVITIES: Holding company with interests in insurance and leasing services, the printing industry and the energy industry
Principal Bank: Johnstown Bank and Trust Company
Financial Information:

	$'000
Premium income	167,000

No of Employees: 520

ROCKY MOUNT UNDERGARMENT CO., INC.

1536 Boone Street, PO Box 1280, Rocky Mount, NC 27802
Tel: (919) 446 6161
Telefax: (919) 442-4412

Chairman: Kimberly Dunton
President: Herbert Greenberg
Senior Executive Officers: Murray Rothblatt (Executive VP), Gilbert J Samuels (Senior VP), Charles Kralick (VP Finance), Julian Roodberg (VP)

PRINCIPAL ACTIVITIES: Manufacture of ladies', men's and children's under garments
Trade Names: Generation Two, Blossoms, Stretchmates, Rockymount
Principal Bank: Planters Bank
Financial Information:

	1986
	$'000
Sales revenues*	40,997
(Loss) before taxes	(3,330)
Net (loss)	(2,408)
(Loss) per share	($0.82)
Common stock	6,515
Retained income	2,340
Shareholders equity	8,855

*estimated sales for 1987 $39.4 million

No of Employees: 1,250

ROCKY MOUNTAIN BANK NOTE CO

PO Box 17727, Denver, CO 80217
Tel: (303) 233-8080
Telex: WUT 75 6543 rmbn cmw dvr

Chairman: Russell Scott Jr
President: John Holman
Senior Executive Officers: Karen Kitzmiller (Secretary and Treasurer)

PRINCIPAL ACTIVITIES: Printing of stationery for banks and commerce
Parent Company: Romo Corp
Principal Bank: United Bank of Denver
Financial Information:

	$'000
Income before taxes	85,000

No of Employees: 1,700

RODMAN & RENSHAW CAPITAL GROUP INC

120 South Lasalle Street, Chicago, IL 60603
Tel: (312) 977 7800

Chairman: Ira J Kaufman
President: Bruce J Young
Senior Executive Officers: Thomas V Hendricks (Senior VP, Secretary and Treasurer)

PRINCIPAL ACTIVITIES: Holding company with interests in security dealing
Principal Subsidiaries: Rodman & Renshaw Inc
Financial Information:

	$'000
Revenues	32,000

No of Employees: 200

ROEGELEIN COMPANY

1700 S Brazos, San Antonio, TX 78206
Tel: (512) 225-2631
Telex: TWX 910 8711153 roegelein

President: Wayne D Wendell
Senior Executive Officers: Shawn Bremmell (VP), Gary Christensen (VP Operations), Donald Galvin (VP, Secretary and Treasurer), Ralph Grinde (VP), James Nester (VP Sales), Donald Rae (VP)

PRINCIPAL ACTIVITIES: Processing of meat
Parent Company: Roegelein Enterprises Inc
Principal Bank: Republic Bank of San Antonio
Financial Information:

	$'000
Sales revenues	77,000

No of Employees: 500

ROGERS CABLESYSTEMS OF AMERICA INC

415 N Main Avenue, San Antonio, TX 78293
Tel: (512) 222 9912

Chairman: Edward S Rogers (and Chief Executive Officer); Vice Chairmen: Philip B Lind, Colin D Watson (and Chief Operating Officer)
President: D E Friesen
Senior Executive Officers: Bruce D Day (VP and Treasurer), Nicholas F Hamilton-Piercy (VP), W Wayne Howard (VP and Controller), Barry A Ross (VP), Graham W Savage (VP), M Kevin Shea (VP)

PRINCIPAL ACTIVITIES: Telecommunications services
Financial Information:

	$'000
Sales revenues	50,000

No of Employees: 840

ROGERS CORPORATION

1 Technology Drive, Rogers, CT 06263
Tel: (203) 774-9605
Telex: 710 448 0047 rogers rogers

President: Norman L Greenman (and Chief Executive Officer)
Senior Executive Officers: Richard C Berry (Senior VP-Technology), Harry H Birkenruth (Senior VP-Polymer Products Group), Paul L Anderson (VP Sales), Stuart J Safft (VP-Finance), A David Chesmer (VP Manufacturing), H A Raphaelson (Controller), Robert M Soffer (Treasurer), David M Elwood (Clerk)

PRINCIPAL ACTIVITIES: Rogers' present business has its roots in the use of polymer technology to develop problem solving materials, primarily for the electronics industry. Of 1986 total sales, 62% was comprised of Interconnection Products with polymeric products accounting for the other 38%. In short Rogers' principal activity is applying polymer chemistry and process technology to fill the needs of electronics and other selected industrial markets for engineered materials and components
Trade Names: Interconnection Products:- MEKTRON(R), Q/PAC(R), MICRO/Q(R), MINI/BUS(R), RT/duroid(R), R/flex(R), BEND/flex(R). Polymer Products:-NITROPHYL(R), ENDUR(R), ENVEX(R), PORON(R), PORON R/bak(R)
Principal Subsidiaries: Rogers Mexicana SA de CV; Rogers Japan, Inc; Mektron NV; Mektron Circuit Systems Ltd; Mektron France SA; Mektron GmbH
Principal Bank: Connecticut National Bank, Hartford, Connecticut
Financial Information:

	Dec 31 1985	Dec 31 1986
	$'000	$'000
Sales revenues	125,299	128,777
Income (loss) before taxes	(933)	2,591
Net income	772	2,327
Dividends	353	356
Dividends per share	$0.12	$0.12
Earnings per share	$0.26	$0.78
Common stock issued	2,958	2,969
Retained income	25,529	27,500
Shareholders equity	44,401	47,831

No of Employees: 2,500

ROHM AND HAAS COMPANY

Independence Mall West, Philadelphia, PA 19105
Tel: (215) 592-3000
Telex: 845-247

Chairman: Vincent L Gregory Jr (and Chief Executive Officer); Vice Chairman: J Lawrence Wilson
President: John P Mulroney (and Chief Operating Officer)
Senior Executive Officers: John J Doyle Jr (VP), Donald C Garaventi (VP), Allen M Levantin (VP), Robert E Naylor Jr (Group VP), Richard G Peterson (VP), Fred W Shaffer (VP,

Chief Financial Officer and Controller), John T Subak (Group VP and General Counsel), Samuel J Talucci (VP), Basil A Vassiliou (VP), John A Weaver (VP), Lawrence E Westkaemper (VP), Karen W McDonie (Secretary), Angus F Smith (Treasurer), William E Lambert (Assistant Secretary), Leslie A Shearman (Assistant Controller), David A Stitely (Assistant Controller), Theodore J Suess III (Assistant Treasurer)

PRINCIPAL ACTIVITIES: Manufacture of polymers, resins and monomers; plastics; industrial chemicals; agricultural chemicals; micromedic systems; polyester resin

Trade Names: Acrysol, Amberlite, Amberlyst, Ambersep, Blazer, Dithane, Duolite, Goal, Kathon, Kelthane, Paraloid, Plexiglas, Polyset, Primal, Rhoplex, Robond, Ropaque, Stam, Systhane

Principal Subsidiaries: USA: Electro-Materials Corp of America; Hydranautics; Plaskon Electronic Materials Inc; Rohm and Haas Bayport Inc; Rohm and Haas California Inc; Rohm and Haas Capital Corporation; Rohm and Haas Connecticut Inc; Rohm and Haas Credit Corporation; Rohm and Haas Delaware Inc; Rohm and Haas Delaware Valley Inc; Rohm and Haas Finance Company; Rohm and Haas Kentucky Inc; Rohm and Haas Latin America Inc; Rohm and Haas Science Inc; Rohm and Haas Tennessee Inc; Rohm and Haas Texas Inc; Romicon Inc; Southern Resin and Chemical Company; Supelco Inc. Outside the USA: Duolite International SA (France); Laboratorios Quimico Industriales SA (Costa Rica); Maquiladora General de Matamoros SA de CV (Mexico); Pitar Chemicals Co Ltd (Bermuda); Plakson Electronic Materials Ltd (Bermuda); Rohm and Haas Australia Pty Ltd (Australia); Rohm and Haas Bermuda Ltd (Bermuda); Rohm and Haas Brasil Ltda (Brazil); Rohm and Haas Canada Inc (Canada); Rohm and Haas Colombia SA (Colombia); Rohm and Haas Centro America SA (Costa Rica); Rohm and Haas Deutschland GmbH (Germany); Rohm and Haas Espana SA (Spain); Rohm and Haas Foreign Sales Corp (US Virgin Islands); Rohm and Haas France SA (France); Rohm and Haas Italia SpA (Italy); Rohm and Haas Japan KK (Japan); Rohm and Haas Mexico SA de CV (Mexico); Rohm and Haas New Zealand Ltd (New Zealand); Rohm and Haas Nordiska AB (Sweden); Rohm and Haas Philippines Inc (Philippines); Rohm and Haas (UK) Ltd (UK). Affiliates: Akril (48.5%) (Turkey); Japan Acrylic Chemical Co Ltd (47.5%) (Japan); Modipon Limited (37%) (India); Polytribo Inc (60%); Quimica Trepic SA de CV (40%) (Mexico); Shipley Company (30%); Tokyo Organic Chemical Industries Limited (50%) (Japan); Yugocryl (49%) (Yugoslavia)

Financial Information:

	Dec 31 1985	Dec 31 1986
	$'000	$'000
Sales revenues	2,051,000	2,067,000
Income before taxes	227,000	219,000
Net income	141,000	138,000
Dividends	49,000	54,000
Dividends per share	$0.70*	$0.78
Earnings per share	$2.01*	$2.01
Common stock	197,000*	197,000
Retained income	838,000	922,000
Shareholders equity	936,000	1,002,000

*restated to reflect three-for-one stock split of June 1986

No of Employees: 11,911

ROHR INDUSTRIES, INC

PO Box 878, Chula Vista, CA 92012-0878
Tel: (619) 691-4111
Telex: 69-5038

Chairman: H W Todd (and Chief Executive Officer and President); Vice Chairman: G Don Smith

Senior Executive Officers: P E Brunton (Senior VP, Finance, Chief Financial Officer and Treasurer), Robert H Goldsmith (Senior VP, Operations), John W Sandford (Senior VP, Programs and Technology), Richard W Madsen (Corporate Counsel and Secretary), William Billingslea Jr (Assistant Corporate Counsel and Assistant Secretary), Peter Colston (VP, Customer Support), Robert G Daly (VP, Manufacturing Riverside), John R Johnson (VP, Manufacturing), G A (Bud) Wetzler (VP, Management Information Systems), Alek A Mikolajczak (VP, Engineering), Jack Y Peckenpaugh (VP, Material), Donald M Purdy (VP, V2500/CFM56-5 Programs), Lawrence G Rogna (VP, Industrial Relations), Jean-Pierre Rouziere (President and Director General-Rohr France), N James Wilson (VP, Quality and Product Assurance), Keith Gentry (VP, Space Products Division)

PRINCIPAL ACTIVITIES: Rohr is an aerospace systems designer and manufacturer, producing components for commercial, military and business aircraft. The company also machines rocket motor casings for the Space Shuttle and Titan booster. Main products include nacelles, thrust reversers, engineering services, noise suppression systems and non-rotating engine components

Financial Information:

	Jul 31 1986	Jul 31 1987
	$'000	$'000
Sales revenues	626,124	663,406
Income before taxes	77,718	44,599
Net income	47,318	26,899
Earnings per share(1)	$0.68	$0.40
Earnings per share(2)	$2.70	$1.53
Shareholders equity	312,731	345,768

(1) primary
(2) fully diluted

No of Employees: 10,000

ROHTSTEIN CORPORATION

PO Box 2129, Woburn, MA 01888
Tel: (617) 935-8300
Telex: WUT 949466 rohtstein wobn

President: Steven A Rohtstein

Senior Executive Officers: Gene Cohen (VP Merchandising), Donald Samuels (VP Finance)

PRINCIPAL ACTIVITIES: Bakery products

Principal Bank: Shawmut Bank

Financial Information:

	$'000
Sales revenues	70,000

No of Employees: 130

ROLLINS ENVIRONMENTAL SERVICES INC

1 Rollins Plaza, Wilmington, DE 19803
Tel: (302) 479 2700

Chairman: Darrell M Trent (and President and Chief Executive Officer); Vice Chairmen: William B Philipbar Jr, John W Rollins Jr

Senior Executive Officers: R C Gregory (VP and Director Technology), J D Neel (VP), John C Peet Jr (VP, Legal Counsel and Secretary), R W Yennerell (Treasurer and Controller)

PRINCIPAL ACTIVITIES: Industrial chemical waste disposal services

Principal Subsidiaries: Rollins Environmental Services of Lousiana; Rollins Environmental Services (Louisiana); Rollins Environmental Services (New Jersey); Rollins Environmental Services (Texas)

Principal Bank: Continental Bank

Financial Information:

	$'000
Sales revenues	137,000

No of Employees: 460

ROLLINS, INC

2170 Piedmont Road NE, Atlanta, GA 30324
Tel: (404) 873-2355
Telex: WUT 550086 rollins inc ga

Chairman: O W Rollins (and Chief Executive Officer); Senior Vice Chairman: R R Rollins
President: Gary W Rollins (and Chief Operating Officer)
Senior Executive Officers: H T Crow (VP Public Relations and Secretary), James R Hicks Jr (VP, Treasurer and Assistant Secretary)

PRINCIPAL ACTIVITIES: Broadcasting; installation of security equipment and air conditioning equipment; operation of pest control services
Financial Information:

	$'000
Sales revenues	308,000

No of Employees: 7,000

ROLM CORPORATION

4900 Old Ironsides Drive, Santa Clara, CA 95050
Tel: (408) 986-1000

President: M K Oshman (and Chief Executive Officer)
Senior Executive Officers: Leo J Chamberlain (Executive VP), Robert R Maxfield (Executive VP Business Development Group), Jack W Blumenstein (VP), Anthony V Carollo Jr (VP Business Communications Group), Robert K Dahl (VP Finance and Chief Financial Officer), William G Friedman (VP Western Region), James M Kasson (VP Research and Development), J Geoffrey Kirsch (VP Eastern Region), Walter Loewenstern Jr (VP), Wayne J Mehl (VP and General Manager Telecommunications), John J Mitcham (VP Operations Group), Richard M Moley (VP International and Business Development Group), Dennis D Paboojian (VP Systems Development Group), George C Platt (VP Central Region), Wolfgang H Schwartz (VP and General Manager International Telecommunications Division), Oliver R Stanfield (VP Financial Planning and Analysis and Treasurer), Stanley E Tennold (VP Military-Specialty Computer Division)

PRINCIPAL ACTIVITIES: Manufacture of computers and computerized products for business and military uses
Parent Company: International Business Machines Corp
Principal Bank: Bank of America
Financial Information:

	$'000
Sales revenues	660,000

No of Employees: 8,940

ROLSCREEN COMPANY

102 Main Street, Pella, IA 50129
Tel: (515) 628-1000
Telex: WUT 478459 rolscreen pela

Chairman: Joan Farver
President: J W Bevis (and Chief Executive Officer)
Senior Executive Officers: Michael Adams (VP Marketing), Hilliard Keeney (VP Manufcturing), Marlyn G Klimotra (VP Sales), Herbert G Lienburger (VP Finance)

PRINCIPAL ACTIVITIES: Manufacture of doors and windows including aluminum and wooden windows and wooden and glass sliding doors and partitions
Principal Bank: United Central Bank of Des Moines
Financial Information:

	$'000
Sales revenues	150,000

No of Employees: 2,000

RONSON CORPORATION

Corporate Park III, Campus Drive, Somerset, NJ 08876
Tel: (201) 469-8300

President: Louis V Aronson II (and Chief Executive Officer)
Senior Executive Officers: Erwin M Ganz (Executive VP Operations), Robert A Aronson (VP Finance and Treasurer), F E Colgan (Controller), A Lester Granet (Secretary and Assistant Treasurer), Richard E Fuller (VP Hydraulics and Aerospace)

PRINCIPAL ACTIVITIES: Manufacture of cigarette lighters and related products; components for the aviation industry; operation of air charter services
Principal Subsidiaries: Ronson Aviation Inc; Ronson Hydraulic Units NC Corporation; Ronson Metals Corporation; Ronson Packaging Corporation
Principal Bank: First Fidelity Bank
Financial Information:

	$'000
Sales revenues	31,930

No of Employees: 400

ROONEY, PACE GROUP INC

11 Broadway, New York, NY 10004
Tel: (212) 908 7700

Chairman: Randolph K Pace (and President)
President: Donald Erenberg
Senior Executive Officers: Bernard Notas (Chief Financial Officer), Arnold J Weinberg (Legal Counsel and Secretary)

PRINCIPAL ACTIVITIES: Financial services including dealing in securities
Financial Information:

	$'000
Sales revenues	49,000

No of Employees: 280

ROPAK CORPORATION

660 South State College Boulevard, Fullerton, CA 92631
Tel: (714) 870-9757
Telefax: (714) 447-3871

Chairman: Wiliam H Roper (and Chief Executive Officer)
President: Robert E Roper
Senior Executive Officers: James R Connell (VP Marketing), C Richard Roper (VP and Secretary), Ronald Wm Cameron (VP Finance), James R Dobell (VP Manufacturing), Steve Thomson (VP Development)

PRINCIPAL ACTIVITIES: Ropak Corporation is a leading multinational maker of plastic packaging and handling products for foods, coatings and a variety of industrial and agricultural uses. The Company has nine plants in the United States, Canada and Japan
Trade Names: "ROPAK", "ROCAN", "QUALITI-PAK"
Principal Subsidiaries: Ropak West (Division of Ropak Corp); Ropak Central Inc; Ropak Atlantic Inc; Ropak Northwest Inc; Ropak Southwest Inc; Ropak Capilano Ltd; Ropak Pan-Am Ltd; Tokyo Kaken Company Ltd; Ropak Nippon Ltd
Principal Bank: Sanwa Bank of California
Financial Information:

	Dec 31 1985	Dec 31 1986
	$'000	$'000
Sales revenues	32,230	47,600
Income before taxes	2,352	2,447
Net income	1,380	1,003
Earnings per share	$0.79	$0.79
Common stock	11,118	11,230
Retained income	1,380	1,003
Shareholders equity	13,868	15,121

Principal Shareholders: Executive Officers and directors as a group (36.4%); Elvere Roper and William H Roper, Trustees under Roper Family Trust Agreement (5.9%); Massachusetts Mutual Life Insurance Company (5.1%); MassMutual Corporate Investors (5.2%)
No of Employees: 500+

ROPER CORPORATION

1905 W Court Street, Kankakee, IL 60901
Tel: (815) 937-6000
Telex: WUT 358 547 roper corp

Chairman: Charles M Hoover
President: Robert E Cook (and Chief Executive Officer)
Senior Executive Officers: Harry L Grumish (Executive VP), H Wayne Harris (VP Sales and Marketing), Dennis D Shrewsbury (Treasurer and Comptroller)

PRINCIPAL ACTIVITIES: Manufacture of electric and gas ovens and ranges and microwave ovens, garden tractors and mowers, hardware products
Principal Subsidiaries: Micro-mex SA (Mexico); Roper Canada Ltd; Wadsworth Control Systems Inc (79%)
Principal Bank: Continental Illinois National Bank and Trust Company
Financial Information:

	Jul 31 1986
	$'000
Sales revenues	613,506
Net income	14,498
Earnings per share	$2.73
Shareholders equity	70,835

No of Employees: 5,000

RORER GROUP INC

500 Virginia Drive, Fort Washington, PA 19034
Tel: (215) 628-6541

Chairman: Robert E Cawthorn (and Chief Executive Officer)
President: Brian H Dovey
Senior Executive Officers: John W Eckman (Chairman of Executive Committee), Joseph E Smith (Executive VP, US), Richard P Storm (Executive VP International), James R Tretter (Executive VP Research and Development), William H Rorer III (Senior VP), John B Bartlett (VP, Secretary and General Counsel), William E Bliss (VP Licensing), Robert I Kriebel (VP Investor Relations), Daniel J Paracka (VP Finance and Chief Financial Officer), Gerald B Rorer (VP Planning and Development)

PRINCIPAL ACTIVITIES: Holding company with interests in pharmaceutical products and surgical equipment
Principal Subsidiaries: William H Rorer Inc; Surgical Products; Rorer International Corp
Principal Bank: Philadelphia National Bank
Financial Information:

	Dec 31 1986
	$'000
Sales revenues	843,925
Net income	48,233
Earnings per share	$1.01
Shareholders equity	575,756

No of Employees: 8,000

ROSE'S STORES INC

P H Rose Building, 218 South Garnett Street, Henderson, NC 27536
Tel: (919) 492 8111

Chairman: Lucius H Harvin III (and Chief Executive Officer)
President: Jack E Bush (and Chief Operating Officer)
Senior Executive Officers: John W Little (Senior VP Merchandising), J Avery Roberts Jr (Senior VP Human Resources), R Edward Anderson (Senior VP Information Systems and Controller), David C Rose (Senior VP, Treasurer and Chief Financial Officer), George M Harvin (VP Corporate Development and Real Estate), Patricia D Hoffmeister (VP and General Manager), John H McElroy (VP Marketing), Joseph D Osowski (VP and General Manager), Thomas B Rose III (VP Distribution and Merchandising), Mike Sames (VP Information Services), George B Rush (Secretary and Assistant Treasurer), Nelson J Tucker (VP Operations), William Warren (VP Operations)

PRINCIPAL ACTIVITIES: Retail variety stores chain
Principal Bank: Wachovia Bank and Trust Co
Financial Information:

	$'000
Sales revenues	1,200,000

No of Employees: 12,700

ROSPATCH CORPORATION

3101 Walkent Drive NW, Walker, MI 49504
Tel: (616) 784-1000
Telex: WUT 226434 rospatch gdr

Chairman: Jones Y Pharr Jr
President: Joseph A Parini (and Chief Executive Officer)
Senior Executive Officers: Robert A Borlet (Group VP), David E Hoger (Group VP), Cecil M Jackson (Group VP), William E Malpass Jr (VP Finance and Treasurer)

PRINCIPAL ACTIVITIES: Manufacture of machinery for the production of cloth labels; processing of textiles; manufacture of printing machines, manufacture of furniture kits
Principal Bank: National Bank of Detroit
Financial Information:

	Dec 31 1985
	$'000
Sales revenues	97,110

No of Employees: 1,000

ROSS STORES INC

8333 Central Avenue, PO Box 728, Newark, CA 94560
Tel: (415) 790 4400

Chairman: Stuart G Moldaw
President: Donald E Rowlett (and Chief Executive Officer)
Senior Executive Officers: Greggory L Baldwin (Executive VP), Norman A Ferber (Executive VP), Herbert F Golden (Senior VP and Secretary), Richard Oppenheimer (Senior VP and Chief Financial Officer), Michael J Finn (VP), David Goldman (VP), Peter Hart (VP), David H Meckler (VP), David Morrison (VP), Michael E Signorelli (VP), J Bernard Tillotson (VP), Richard A Watson (VP), Earl T Benson (Treasurer, Assistant Secretary and Controller)

PRINCIPAL ACTIVITIES: Retail trade in clothing, footwear and miscellaneous household goods
Principal Bank: Bank of America
Financial Information:

	$'000
Sales revenues	350,000

No of Employees: 2,000

ROUNDY'S INC

11300 W Burleigh St, Wauwatosa, WI 53222
Tel: (414) 453-8200

President: John Dixon
Senior Executive Officers: John W Andorfer (Senior VP), Joseph Kosco (Senior VP), David H Maas (Senior VP, Secretary and Treasurer), A Patin (VP Retail Programs)

PRINCIPAL ACTIVITIES: Wholesale distribution of a wide range of food products including meat, dairy goods, frozen foods, groceries and fresh fruit and vegetables; also distribution of office equipment and supplies
Principal Bank: Marine National Exchange Bank of Milwaukee
Financial Information:

	Dec 31 1986
	$'000
Sales revenues	1,807,852
Shareholders equity	40,487

No of Employees: 4,700

ROUSE CO

10275 Little Patuxent Pkwy, Columbia, MD 21044
Tel: (301) 992-6000

Chairman: Mathias J DeVito (and President and Chief Executive Officer)
President: Michael D Spear
Senior Executive Officers: R Harwood Beville (Executive VP), Bruce D Alexander (Senior VP Commercial Development), Peyton S Cochran Jr (Senior VP New Business), Anthony W Deering (Senior VP and Chief Financial Officer), Richard G McCauley (Senior VP, Secretary and General Counsel), Douglas A McGregor (Senior VP), Larry M Wolf (Senior VP Retail Leasing)

PRINCIPAL ACTIVITIES: Building; operation of shopping center
Principal Bank: Chemical Bank
Financial Information:

	Dec 31 1985 $'000
Sales revenues	331,000

No of Employees: 3,400

ROWAN COMPANIES, INC

5051 Westheimer Rd, Houston, TX 77056
Tel: (713) 621-7800
Cable: ROWCO
Telex: 275542 ROWCO
Telefax: (713) 621-5264

Chairman: C R Palmer (and President and Chief Executive Officer)
Senior Executive Officers: C W Yeargain (Executive VP), D C Anderson (Senior VP, Secretary and Treasurer), R G Croyle (VP), Paul L Kelly (VP), D L Baumeister (VP), R A Watson (VP), R E McWilliams (VP), R A Keller (VP)

PRINCIPAL ACTIVITIES: Drilling for oil and gas; air transportation services
Principal Subsidiaries: ERA Helicopters Inc; Rowandrill Inc; Rowan International Inc; British American Offshore Ltd
Principal Bank: Citibank N.A.
Financial Information:

	Dec 31 1986 $'000
Sales revenues	167,163
Income before taxes	89,711
Net income (loss)	(42,147)
Dividends(1)	1,865
(Loss) per share(2)	($.81)
Common stock(3)	55,948
Retained income	360,203
Shareholders equity	578,925

(1) on pfa stock
(2) on common stock
(3) number of shares in thousands

No of Employees: 2,000

ROWE FURNITURE CORPORATION

239 Rowan Street, Salem, VA 24153
Tel: (703) 389-8671

Chairman: G M Birnbach (and President and Chief Executive Officer)
Senior Executive Officers: G O Woodlief (Senior VP), Keith J Rowe (VP), Harvey I Ptashek (Senior VP), A H Dunkin (Secretary-Treasurer)

PRINCIPAL ACTIVITIES: Manufacture of furniture
Financial Information:

	Nov 30 1986 $'000
Sales revenues	81,701
Income before taxes	3,635
Net income	2,171
Dividends	617
Dividends per	$0.26
Earnings per share	$0.95
Common stock	2,564
Retained income	20,773
Shareholders equity	20,521

No of Employees: 1,650

ROWE INTERNATIONAL, INC

75 Troy Hills Road, Whippany, NJ 07981
Tel: (201) 887-0400
Telex: RCA 219052 rowe ur

Presidents: M Krakauer; J Gordon (Distributor Operations)
Senior Executive Officers: R Freeman (Executive VP and Chief Operating Officer), E Wiler (VP Marketing), J Nitzberg (VP Finance), R Hendricks (VP and General Manager Grand Rapids)

PRINCIPAL ACTIVITIES: Manufacture of a range of leisure and entertainment equipment including vending machines and jukeboxes
Parent Company: Central Jersey Industries Inc
Financial Information:

	$'000
Sales revenues	147,000

No of Employees: 1,400

ROYAL CROWN BOTTLING COMPANY OF CHICAGO

2801 W 47th Street, Chicago, IL 60632
Tel: (312) 376-7000

President: Henry S Schimberg
Senior Executive Officers: Charles E Salatt (VP and General Manager)

PRINCIPAL ACTIVITIES: Bottling of soft drinks
Parent Company: Royal Crown Companies Inc, Atlanta, GA
Financial Information:

	$'000
Sales revenues	75,000

ROYAL CROWN COMPANIES, INC

41 Perimeter Center East NE, Atlanta, GA 30346
Tel: (404) 394-6120

Chairman: William T Young (and Chairman of Executive Committee)
President: Donald A McMahon
Senior Executive Officers: Richard St John (VP Administration), Arnold Belasco (VP Corporate Communications), Ronald L White (VP Finance), Fred M Adamany (VP and President Royal Crown Cola Co Soft Drink Division), W N Murrah Jr (VP Legal and Secretary), George Gray (VP and Controller)

PRINCIPAL ACTIVITIES: Manufacture of a range of products including fruit juice, soft drinks, fast food and household furnishings including furniture and lamps
Parent Company: Chesapeake Financial Corp
Principal Bank: First National City Bank
Financial Information:

	$'000
Sales revenues	490,000

No of Employees: 4,800

ROYAL INTERNATIONAL OPTICAL CORPORATION

2760 Irving Boulevard, Dallas, TX 75207
Tel: (214) 638-1397

Chairman: Gene T Schanbaum (and President and Chief Executive Officer); Vice Chairman: Benton W Markey
Senior Executive Officers: Clinton M DeWolfe (Executive VP), D F Coates (VP), Donald Gross (VP), Dwain M Robertson (VP), William J Storm (Chief Financial Officer)

PRINCIPAL ACTIVITIES: Retail of eyeglasses and contact lenses
Principal Subsidiaries: Styl-Rite Optical Manufacturing Co
Principal Bankers: Bank of Dallas
Financial Information:

	$'000
Sales revenues	70,000

No of Employees: 2,800

ROYALE AIRLINES INC

Shreveport Regional Airport, Shreveport, LA 71109
Tel: (318) 635 8168

Chairman: Douglas Y Smith Jr (and Chief Executive Officer)
President: John A Fasolino (and Chief Operating Officer)
Senior Executive Officers: Don Bethel (VP), A D Brannan Jr (VP), H Quan Elliott (VP Finance), Herman Williamson Jr (VP)

PRINCIPAL ACTIVITIES: Airline operating scheduled services
Principal Bank: Commercial National Bank
Financial Information:

	$'000
Sales revenues	33,500

No of Employees: 280

ROYDON WEAR, INC

1409 E Oak Street, McRae, GA 31055
Tel: (912) 868-6444

President: R T Lewis
Senior Executive Officers: D M Billing (VP Production), J Shenloogian (VP Marketing), B G Yingling (VP Finance), Alan L Vestal (Treasurer and Controller)

PRINCIPAL ACTIVITIES: Manufacture of clothing
Parent Company: Coordinated Apparel Inc
Principal Bank: Manufacturers Hanover Trust
Financial Information:

	$'000
Sales revenues	50,000

No of Employees: 1,200

RPC ENERGY SERVICES INC

2170 Piedmont Road North East, Atlanta, GA 30324
Tel: (404) 888 2000

Chairman: R Randall Rollins (and Chief Executive Officer, President and Chief Operating Officer)
Senior Executive Officers: Bobby Joe Cudd (Executive VP), Charles R Patterson Jr (Executive VP), Harrison Jones II (VP, Secretary, Treasurer and Chief Financial Officer)

PRINCIPAL ACTIVITIES: Leasing and rental of industrial equipment
Financial Information:

	$'000
Sales revenues	94,700

No of Employees: 1,350

RPM INC (OHIO)

2628 Pearl Road, Medina, OH 44256
Tel: (216) 225-3192
Telex: WUT 985418 r p m mina

Chairman: Thomas C Sullivan (and Chief Executive Officer)
President: James A Karman
Senior Executive Officers: John H Morris Jr (Executive VP), Julius K Nemeth (VP and Secretary), Clarence A Weltman (VP), Richard E Klar (VP and Treasurer)

PRINCIPAL ACTIVITIES: Manufacture of specialized chemical coatings
Principal Bank: National City Bank of Cleveland
Financial Information:

	$'000
Sales revenues	240,000

No of Employees: 1,600

RSI CORPORATION

One Shelter Centre, PO Box 6721, Suite 950, Greenville, SC 29606
Tel: (803) 271-7171

Chairman: Buck Mickel
President: C C Guy (and Treasurer)
Senior Executive Officers: C T Wyche (VP and Secretary)

PRINCIPAL ACTIVITIES: Wholesale trade in garden equipment, furniture and office equipment, machinery and power tools
Principal Bank: Citizens and Southern National Bank of South Carolina
Financial Information:

	$'000
Sales revenues	68,000

No of Employees: 388

RSR CORPORATION

1111 W Mockingbird Lane, Dallas, TX 75247
Tel: (214) 631-6070
Telex: WUT 732 402 rsr corp dal

President: Howard M Meyers
Senior Executive Officers: Albert P Lospinoso (Executive VP), John DePaul (VP Technical Service and Engineering), Jack L Pinkston (VP Operations), James Thrashey (VP Commercial Operations)

PRINCIPAL ACTIVITIES: Lead refining; lead alloys
Parent Company: RSR Holding Corp
Principal Bank: Chemical Bank
Financial Information:

	$'000
Sales revenues	131,000

No of Employees: 800

RTE CORPORATION

175 N Patrick Boulevard, Brookfield, WI 53005
Tel: (414) 792-9300
Telex: 260329

Chairman: L D Barre (and Chief Executive Officer)
President: Michael Allik (and Chief Operating Officer)
Senior Executive Officers: R C Lappin (Group VP Electronics), M W Gregg (VP Finance and Chief Financial Officer)

PRINCIPAL ACTIVITIES: Manufacture of electrical equipment for power distribution including transformers and transformer components, electronic power supplies and power conditioning equipment and capacitors
Trade Names: Aerovox, Deltec, Power Mate
Principal Subsidiaries: Aerovox Canada Ltd; RTE Far East; RTE International; Power/Mate Co; RTE Deltec; Aerovox Inc
Principal Bank: Continental First National Bank of Chicago

Financial Information:

	Dec 29 1985	Dec 28 1986
	$'000	$'000
Sales revenues	322,680	330,098
Income before taxes	27,225	19,017
Net income	15,225	11,417
Dividends	4,326	4,555
Dividends per share	$0.57	$0.60
Earnings per share	$2.01	$1.50
Common stock-par	7,653	7,707
Additional capital*	23,054	19,997
Retained income	73,218	80,080
Shareholders equity	103,235	95,910

*paid in

Number of shareholders: 4,200
No of Employees: 2,900

RUBATEX CORPORATION

Railroad Avenue, Bedford, VA 24523
Tel: (703) 586-2611
Telex: WUT 509 666 rubtx ud

Chairman: Burton I Koffman
President: Ronald L Adams
Senior Executive Officers: Leo P Serowik (VP), Kermit P Croft (VP Manufacturing), Cecil R Thaxton (VP Marketing), John T Evans Jr (Treasurer)

PRINCIPAL ACTIVITIES: Manufacture of rubber and vinyl products
Parent Company: Great American Industries Inc, San Diego, CA
Principal Bank: Sovran Bank
Financial Information:

	$'000
Sales revenues	50,000

No of Employees: 900

RUBBERMAID INC

1147 Akron Road, Wooster, OH 44691
Tel: (216) 264-6464
Telex: 986-491 sprubmd ur

Chairman: Stanley C Gault (and Chief Executive Officer)
President: Robert E Fowler Jr (and Chief Operating Officer)
Senior Executive Officers: Joseph G Meehan (Senior VP and Chief Financial Officer), James A Morgan (Senior VP and Secretary), Thomas W Ward (Senior VP Human Resources), Richard D Gates (VP and Treasurer), Carl R Bowers (VP and Controller)

PRINCIPAL ACTIVITIES: Manufacture of rubber and plastic products for domestic, commercial, institutional and industrial applications
Principal Subsidiaries: Rubbermaid Specialty Products Inc; Rubbermaid Canada Inc; Rubbermaid Commercial Products Inc; Dupol-Rubbermaid GmbH (Germany); Little Tikes, Inc; Gott Corporation
Principal Bank: National City Bank
Financial Information:

	Dec 31 1985	Dec 31 1986
	$'000	$'000
Sales revenues	671,362	795,184
Net income	57,130	70,050
Earnings per share	$1.58	$0.96
Shareholders equity	300,732	359,430

No of Employees: 5,429

RUDDICK CORPORATION

2000 First Union Plaza, Charlotte, NC 28282
Tel: (704) 372-5404

Chairman: R S Dickson
President: Alan T Dickson
Senior Executive Officers: Richard N Brigden (VP Finance), John L Chanon (Treasurer), Donald B Williford (Secretary)

PRINCIPAL ACTIVITIES: Holding company with interests in the retail trade, finance, the printing of business forms, yarns and threads
Principal Subsidiaries: American and Efird Mills Inc; Harris-Teeter Super Markets Inc; Jordan Business Forms Inc; Ruddick Investment Co
Principal Bank: North Carolina National Bank
Financial Information:

	$'000
Sales revenues	882,000

No of Employees: 3,000 full-time

RUSCO INDUSTRIES, INC

Millen Industrial Park, Magnolia Street, Millen, GA 30442
Tel: (912) 982-4334

President: Jasper S Licari (and Chief Executive Officer)
Senior Executive Officers: Douglas K McBean (Executive VP and Treasurer), A G Paganelli (Senior VP), Robert N Weingarten (Senior VP and Secretary)

PRINCIPAL ACTIVITIES: Manufacture of doors and windows
Financial Information:

	$'000
Sales revenues	70,000

No of Employees: 1,400

RUSS BERRIE & CO, INC

See BERRIE, RUSS, & CO, INC

RUSS TOGS, INC

1411 Broadway, New York, NY 10018
Tel: (212) 354-0700
Telex: WUI 620900 russ

President: Eli L Rousso
Senior Executive Officers: Irving L Rousso (Executive VP Sales and Merchandising), Herman Saporta (Executive VP Production), Michael McCabe (VP Data Processing), Mortimer F Zimmerman (VP and Treasurer), Louis Shantzer (Controller and Secretary), Richard J Lewis (Assistant Controller)

PRINCIPAL ACTIVITIES: Russ Togs, Inc is engaged in the manufacture and sale of apparel, including popularly priced sportswear and dresses for ladies, misses, children, pre-teens and juniors, as well as shirts and sweaters for men and boys. The Company's products are styled and manufactured with emphasis on color, fabric and design. They are sold by leading department stores, chain stores and specialty shops throughout the United States, with most items retailing between $20 and $80
Trade Names: Principal brand names include "Russ", "Russ Petites", "Ms Russ", "Russ Girl", "Russie", "Russ Teen", "New Attitude", "Crazy Horse", "Crazy Horse Girl", "Crazy Horse Teen", "Vicky Vaughn", "Toni Todd", "Lady Laura", "Kelli Kaye", "Sutton", "Bud Berma", "Brut", "Ashley Reid", and "Shore Things"
Principal Subsidiaries: Gerard Mills Inc; R T Realty Corp; Sutton Shirt Corp; Bud Berma Inc; Bud Berma International Ltd; Whitby Trading Ltd; Red Horse Inc
Principal Bank: Manufacturers Hanover Bank

Financial Information:

	Feb 1 1986	Jan 31 1987
	$'000	$'000
Sales revenues	276,815	274,992
Income before taxes	25,087	26,588
Net income	10,986	13,819
Common dividends	3,903	3,834
Preferred dividends	387	318
Dividends per common share	$0.76	$0.76
Earnings per share*	$2.07	$2.68
Common stock	5,027	5,024
Retained income	89,806	99,473
Shareholders equity	93,535	101,690
*shares outstanding in thousands		

No of Employees: 3,600

RUSSELL CORPORATION

PO Box 272, Alexander City, AL 35010
Tel: (205) 329-4000
Telex: 283306 RUSSUR

Chairman: E C Gwaltney (and Chief Executive Officer)
President: Dwight L Carlisle (and Chief Operating Officer)
Senior Executive Officers: Corporate Officers: Administrative:- Eugene C Gwaltney (Chairman and Chief Executive Officer), Dwight L Carlisle Jr (President and Chief Operating Officer), H Scott Howell (Executive VP, Apparel Group), James D Nabors (VP, Finance), Fletcher D Adamson (VP, Research), William P Dickson Jr (VP-Personnel and Industrial Relations), Larry E Workman (Controller), Steve R Forehand (Assistant Secretary). Marketing Divisions:- John C Adams (President Knit Apparel Division), Frank K Hall Jr (President Athletic Division), Donald F Logan (VP-Sales and Marketing Fabrics Division), Marvin Seals (VP-Apparel Marketing), Ward Wilson (VP-Apparel Merchandising), J T Taunton (VP-Operations-Fabrics Division). Manufacturing:- J Franklin Foy (VP Dyeing and Finishing), Gerald D McGill (VP Greige Fabric), Henry C Willis (VP Apparel), James D Peoples (VP-Services). Operating Vice Presidents: Marketing: Corporate:- J Lamar Latimer, Nancy Goldsmith. Knit Apparel Division:- Clarence L Abernathy (Marketing), Edward T Boylan (Sales), Ted Wilson (Merchandising). Athletic Division:- Mike Dodge (National Sales Manager), Charles R Gardner (Merchandising-Pro and College Department). Fabrics Division:- Joseph A Benedetto (Merchandising-Yarn Dyed Fabrics), Robert T Nadherny (Merchandising-Converted Fabrics). Manufacturing:- John I Argo (Knitting), David Major (Spinning and Weaving), H M Simpson (Cotton Buyer), Robert S White (Athletic Division), W J Spires (Materials Management)

PRINCIPAL ACTIVITIES: Russell Corporation is a vertically integrated designer, manufacturer and marketer of leisure apparel, athletic uniforms and a comprehensive line of lightweight woven fabrics. The manufacturing operations include the entire process of converting raw fibers into finished apparel in the Company's production facilities. The Company's products are sold through three marketing divisions-Athletic, Knit Apparel, and Fabrics
Trade Names: "Russel Athletic", "Jerzees"
Financial Information:

	Jan 4 1986	Jan 3 1987
	$'000	$'000
Sales revenues	385,433	437,520
Income before taxes	51,951	80,302
Net income	29,612	43,282
Dividends	5,929	6,334
Dividends per share	$0.15	$0.16
Earnings per share	$0.74	$1.08
Common stock	201	401
Retained earnings	194,490	231,438
Shareholders equity	219,733	248,347

No of Employees: 10,040

RUSTY PELICAN RESTAURANTS INC

2862 McGaw Avenue, Irvine, CA 92714
Tel: (714) 660 9011

Chairman: Louis A Siracusa (and Chief Executive Officer, Chief Financial Officer and Secretary)
President: T R Howatt
Senior Executive Officers: Gregory G Dollarhyde (VP Finance and Chief Financial Officer)

PRINCIPAL ACTIVITIES: Restaurants chain specializing in fresh seafood entrees
Principal Bank: Union Bank
Financial Information:

	$'000
Sales revenues	53,700

No of Employees: 2,325

RYAN HOMES, INC

100 Ryan Court, Pittsburgh, PA 15205
Tel: (412) 276-8000

Chairman: Malcolm M Prine (and Chief Executive Officer)
President: Steven J Smith (and Chief Operating Officer)
Senior Executive Officers: Arthur L Titus (Executive VP Operations), James D Bagley (Senior VP Operations), Joseph P Berghold (Senior VP Finance and Chief Financial Officer), James Brothers (Senior VP Operations), Michael J Cannizzo (Senior VP Operations), James J Miller (Senior VP Operations), Donald Solden (Senior VP Operations), Charles W Prine Jr (Senior VP Staff Service), C Lewis Wise (Senior VP Manufacturing), Donald E Gebhardt (VP Product Development), James C McDonough Jr (VP Customer Finance and President Ryan Financial Services Inc)

PRINCIPAL ACTIVITIES: House building; modular homes
Principal Subsidiaries: Lancaster Homes Inc; RHFC Servicing Corp; Ryan Financial Services Inc of Delaware; Cannon Properties Inc; Ryan Homes of Florida Inc; The Dillion Co; Ryan Financing Services Inc; Ryan Mortgage Acceptance Corp; Ryan Securities Inc
Principal Bank: Pittsburgh National Bank
Financial Information:

	$'000
Sales revenues	566,000

No of Employees: 1,900

RYAN'S FAMILY STEAK HOUSES, INC

405 Lancaster Avenue, Greer, SC 29651
Tel: (803) 879-1000
Telefax: (803) 877-0974

Chairman: Alvin A McCall Jr
President: T Mark McCall
Senior Executive Officers: Charles D Way (Executive VP), Charles F McWhorter (VP Operations)

PRINCIPAL ACTIVITIES: Restaurants
Principal Bank: Wachovia Bank and Trust Company N.A.
Financial Information:

	Dec 31 1985	Dec 31 1986
	$'000	$'000
Sales revenues	54,684	104,989
Income before taxes	9,463	20,502
Net income	5,425	10,811
Earnings per share	$0.35	$0.64
Common stock	15,702	16,895
Shareholders equity	38,287	67,907

No of Employees: 6,000

RYDER SYSTEM, INC

3600 NW 82nd Avenue, Miami, FL 33166
Tel: (305) 593-3726
Telex: WUT 519413 ryder sys mia

Chairman: M A Burns (and President and Chief Executive Officer)

Senior Executive Officers: Edwin A Huston (Senior Executive VP Transportation-Finance and Chief Financial Officer), David R Parker (Senior Executive VP and Chief Operating Officer-Business Services Group), Ronald H Dunbar (Executive VP-Human Resources and Administration), James M Herron (Executive VP and General Counsel), Daniel K O'Connell (Executive VP-Corporate Affairs)

PRINCIPAL ACTIVITIES: Ryder System, Inc is the parent of a group of companies which provide high-quality highway transportation, aviation and insurance management services

Principal Bank: The First National Bank of Boston

Financial Information:

	Dec 31 1985	Dec 31 1986
	$'000	$'000
Operating revenues	2,905,287	3,768,328
Income before taxes	202,122	277,471
Net income	125,316	160,935
Dividends per share	$0.40	$0.44
Earnings per share	$1.73	$2.09
Shareholders equity	973,335	1,239,231

No of Employees: 38,000

RYKOFF-SEXTON, INC

761 Terminal St, PO Box 21917, Los Angeles, CA 90021-0917
Tel: (213) 622-4131
Cable: RYKOFOOD
Telex: 67-4233

President: Roger W Coleman (and Chief Executive Officer)

Senior Executive Officers: Chris G Adams (President-S E Rykoff & Co Division), Harold Feather (President-John Sexton & Co Subsidiary), Victor Chavez (VP-Accounting), Tom Brant (VP), Herbert L Jaffe (VP and Treasurer), Neil Sell (Secretary)

PRINCIPAL ACTIVITIES: Distribution services to schools, colleges, health care operations, industrial catering facilities, hotels, restaurants, airlines and recreational facilities; products include food, foodservice equipment, paper and janitorial supplies; manufacture of cleaning products, specialty foods and plastic and paper products

Financial Information:

	May 2 1987
	$'000
Sales revenues	1,081,648
Income before taxes	16,507
Net income	8,001
Dividends	4,166
Dividends per share	$0.60
Earnings per share	$1.12
Common stock*	6,945
Retained income	62,815
Shareholders equity	94,463

*number of shares in thousands

No of Employees: 4,600

RYLAND GROUP, INC

10221 Wincopin Circle, Columbia, MD 21044
Tel: (301) 730-7222

Chairman: Charles E Peck (and President and Chief Executive Officer)

Senior Executive Officers: James F McEneaney (Executive VP), Robert J Gaw (Executive VP)

PRINCIPAL ACTIVITIES: Building contractors, mortgage financing

Principal Subsidiaries: Ryland Mortgage Company (wholly owned)

Principal Bank: Maryland National Bank

Financial Information:

	Dec 31 1985	Dec 31 1986
	$'000	$'000
Sales revenues	496,960	666,205
Income before taxes	24,177	34,159
Net income	15,982	26,051
Dividends	3,974	4,819
Dividends per share	$0.32	$0.38
Earnings per share	$1.27	$2.02
Common stock(1)	12,372(2)	12,547
Retained earnings	69,236	84,210
Shareholders equity	80,918	104,109

(1) $1 per share
(2) adjusted to reflect June 30 1986 two-for-one stock split

No of Employees: 1,781

RYMER COMPANY

1701 Golf Road, Rolling Meadows, IL 60008
Tel: (312) 952-2920

Chairman: Robert Rittmaster (and Chief Executive Officer)
President: Michael J Burns (and Chief Operating Officer)
Senior Executive Officers: Matthew Young (VP Finance), J B Katch (Secretary and Treasurer)

PRINCIPAL ACTIVITIES: Distribution of food to restaurants
Principal Subsidiaries: Rymer Corp
Principal Bank: Continental Illinois National Bank
Financial Information:

	$'000
Sales revenues	87,660

No of Employees: 450

S A SCHONBRUNN & CO, INC

See SCHONBRUNN, S A, & CO, INC

S B THOMAS INC

See THOMAS, S B, INC

S E NICHOLS INC

See NICHOLS, S E, INC

S S PIERCE CO INC

See PIERCE, S S, CO INC

S&K FAMOUS BRANDS INC

11100 West Broad Street, PO Box 31800, Richmond, VA 23294
Tel: (804) 346 2500

Chairman: Stuart C Siegel (and Chief Executive Officer)
President: Donald W Colbert (and Chief Operating Officer)
Senior Executive Officers: Robert E Knowles (Senior VP Finance and Chief Financial Officer), Daniel F Randolph (Senior VP and General Manager Merchandising), J Michael Desmond (VP Real Estate), Weldon J Wirick (VP Operations)

PRINCIPAL ACTIVITIES: Retail of clothing for men and boys
Principal Bank: Sovran Bank
Financial Information:

	$'000
Sales revenues	37,000

No of Employees: 600

SABINE CORPORATION

LTV Center, Suite 100, Lock Box 109, 2001 Ross Avenue, Dallas, TX 75201
Tel: (214) 979 6900

Chairman: Andrew J Shoup Jr (and Chief Executive Officer); Vice Chairman: Robert T Priddy
President: Harold D Carter (and Chief Operating Officer)
Senior Executive Officers: Peter R Vig (Senior VP and Chief Financial Officer), Jack L Blachly (VP and Legal Counsel),

Claude L Obar (VP and Divisional Manager), Joseph L Pritchett III (VP and Divisional Manager), Hervey A Priddy (Secretary and Assistant Treasurer)

PRINCIPAL ACTIVITIES: Production of oil, natural gas, uranium and coal

Principal Bank: InterFirst Bank Dallas

Financial Information:

	$'000
Sales revenues	99,330

No of Employees: 165

SABRELINER CORPORATION

6161 Aviation Drive, St Louis, MO 63134

Tel: (314) 731-2260

Telex: WUT 447227 sabre corp stl

Chairman: F H Lamoreux (and President and Chief Executive Officer)

Senior Executive Officers: Walter C Herter (Executive VP and Chief Operating Officer), Susan Seabury Aselage (VP and Secretary), Mark T Bond (VP Operations Perryville), Karl R Childs (VP Marketing), John P Dixon (VP Program Development), C R Espy (VP Sales Programs), Bob D Hanks (VP Engineering), Paul C Hans (VP Strategic Development), Jerry L Leath (VP Administration), Kevin Marsh (VP Material), Allen R McMahon (VP Fleet Support)

PRINCIPAL ACTIVITIES: Production of aerospace equipment and components; aircraft engine maintenance

Principal Bank: Manufacturers Hanover Trust Company

Financial Information:

	$'000
Sales revenues	51,000

No of Employees: 400

SAFECARD SERVICES INC

2995 North Dixie Highway, Ford Lauderdale, FL 33334

Tel: (305) 565 2131

Chairman: Steven J Halmos (and Chief Executive Officer

Senior Executive Officers: John Bochak (Executive VP Communications), John B McKinney (Executive VP Marketing), Joanne J Seehousen (Executive VP Marketing), W M Stalcup (Senior VP Operations), Harold T Stiles (Controller)

PRINCIPAL ACTIVITIES: Mail order services

Financial Information:

	$'000
Sales revenues	79,000

No of Employees: 400

SAFECO CORPORATION

SAFECO Plaza, Seattle, WA 98185

Tel: (206) 545-5000

Telex: WUT 821995

Chairman: R M Trafton

President: C B Maines (and Chief Executive Officer and Chief Operating Officer)

Senior Executive Officers: James Cannon (Executive VP), Roger H Eigsti (Executive VP), S F Bruhn (VP and General Counsel), B A Dickey (VP, Secretary and Controller), Richard Hubbard (VP and Treasurer), Karl Papenfus (VP Personnel)

PRINCIPAL ACTIVITIES: The company has interests in insurance, real estate and general financial services

Principal Bank: Seattle First National Bank

Financial Information:

	Dec 31 1985 $'000	Dec 31 1986 $'000
Revenues	2,164,890	2,518,977
Net income	170,390	228,687
Earnings per share	$4.74	$6.79
Shareholders equity	1,105,684	1,229,690

No of Employees: 9,000

SAFEGUARD BUSINESS SYSTEMS, INC

400 Maryland Drive, Fort Washington, PA 19034

Tel: (215) 641-5000

Telex: WUT 902759 s-b-s ftwn

Chairman: Vincent G Bell Jr (and President)

Senior Executive Officers: Marvin M Weinstein (VP), Donald S Alvin (VP), Robert J Bonfiglio (VP), Diane M Freaney (VP and Treasurer), Barry J Hartzell (VP), Robert J Hill (VP), Steven A Rosen (VP and Secretary)

PRINCIPAL ACTIVITIES: Manufacture of data processing equipment; office equipment; printing of commercial stationery

Principal Bank: Philadelphia National Bank

Financial Information:

	$'000
Sales revenues	223,600

No of Employees: 2,100

SAFEGUARD HEALTH ENTERPRISES INC

505 North Euclid Street, Suite 200, Anaheim, CA 92803

Tel: (714) 778 1284

Chairman: Alvin M Baileys (and Chief Executive Officer); Vice Chairman: Steven J Baileys (and President and Chief Operating Officer)

Senior Executive Officers: Ronald I Brendzel (Senior VP, Secretary and General Counsel), Larry Kay (Senior VP), Emelia Marko (Senior VP), Peter D Connolly (VP and Director, Marketing), Stefan J Dietrich (VP and Chief Financial Officer), Nathan C Kleinberg (VP and Director National Sales), Donald W Mead (VP Management Information Systems), Robert K Mehlman (VP), Norman J Pickell (VP), Susan Weiss (VP)

PRINCIPAL ACTIVITIES: Capitated dental insurance plans

Principal Subsidiaries: Safeguard Health Plans Inc (CA); Safeguard Health Plans Inc (WA); Safeguard Health Plans Inc (AZ); Community Dental Centers Inc

Principal Bank: Bank of America

Financial Information:

	$'000
Revenues	49,880

No of Employees: 335

SAFEGUARD SCIENTIFICS INC

630 Park Avenue, King of Prussia, PA 19406

Tel: (215) 265-4000

Telex: TWX 510 660 3388 safeguard kopr

Chairman: Warren V Musser (and Chief Executive Officer)

President: Adolf A Paier

Senior Executive Officers: Charles A Root (Executive VP), Gerald M Wilk (VP Finance), Raymond H Kraftson (VP and Secretary), Joseph F Waterman (VP), Ira M Lubert (VP), Gary J Anderson (VP)

PRINCIPAL ACTIVITIES: Production and sale of telecommunications systems, ergonomically designed workstations, specialized drive systems and microcomputer software systems, specialty metal finishing, ownership and operation of commercial real estate

Principal Subsidiaries: Safeguard PowerTech Systems; Center Core Inc; Penn El Service Company; Coherent Communications Systems Corp; Pioneer/Norelkote Metal

Finishing; Unison Technologies Inc; Safeguard Real Estate Division
Principal Bank: Fidelity Bank, N.A.
Financial Information:

	Dec 31 1985	Dec 31 1986
	$'000	$'000
Sales revenues	58,829	67,515
Income before taxes(1)	5,288	8,817
Net income(2)	3,323	7,109
Earnings per share	$0.75	$1.55(3)(4)
Common stock(5)	4,450	4,598
Retained income	10,007	17,116
Shareholders equity	25,599	32,429

(1) before extraordinary credit
(2) after extraordinary credit in 1986 of $1,378
(3) includes extraordinary credit of $1,378 or $.30 per share from the termination of the defined benefit pension plan
(4) assuming full dilution in 1986, net earnings per share is $1.48. Fully diluted earnings per share was not materially different from primary earnings per share in prior years
(5) average shares outstanding in thousands

No of Employees: 1,000

SAFETRAN SYSTEMS CORPORATION

7721 National Turnpike, Louisville, KY 40214
Tel: (502) 361-1691
Telex: TWX 8105353325 safetrain lvl

President: Paul L Wheeler
Senior Executive Officers: Joseph D Aldern (VP Cucamonga Division), Mike Keef (VP and General Manager), Robert Kennedy (VP and General Manager), Philip E Pierce (VP Sales), Donald F Remaley (VP Corporate Development)

PRINCIPAL ACTIVITIES: Manufacture of control systems including signals for railroads, traffic controls, mine safety controls
Parent Company: CCI Corp
Principal Bank: Citizens Fidelity Bank & Trust Company
Financial Information:

	$'000
Sales revenues	60,000

No of Employees: 1,100

SAFETY-KLEEN CORP.

777 Big Timber Road, Elgin, IL 60123
Tel: (312) 697-8460
Telex: 910-251-4479 ELG SK
Facsimile: (312) 697-4295

Chairman: Russell A Gwillim
President: Donald W Brinckman
Senior Executive Officers: David A Dattilo (VP, Corp Branch Sales and Service), Burton E Ericson (VP, General Counsel), Kenneth R Gordon (VP, Technical Services), Joseph F Hamlet (VP, International), William P Kasko (VP, Operations), Wallace K Louder (VP, Information Systems), Robert W Willmschen Jr (VP, Finance/Administration and Secretary), Robert J Burian (VP, Personnel), Michael H Carney (VP, Marketing), Scott E Fore (VP, Environment, Health and Safety), Joseph F Knott (VP, Strategic Planning)

PRINCIPAL ACTIVITIES: Safety-Kleen's principal business is providing parts cleaner services directly to customers in vehicular, industrial and related markets. Safety-Kleen's parts cleaner services make the degreasing of small, metal parts both efficient and safe. The Company supplies parts cleaning equipment, allied products and quantities of solvent to customers at regularly scheduled intervals. Spent solvent is later collected at customer locations and transported to company owned centers for recycling. Safety-Kleen continues to develop four new areas of business: bulk sales and recycling of industrial solvents; automotive paint refinishing; restaurant services and the recycling of dry cleaner filters and residues
Trade Names: Safety-Kleen
Principal Subsidiaries: Safety-Kleen (Canada); Safety-Kleen-UK
Principal Bank: Northern Trust Company
Financial Information:

	Dec 31 1985	Dec 31 1986
	$'000	$'000
Sales revenues	221,080	255,356
Income before taxes	41,271	50,347
Net income	27,185	28,254
Dividends	5,937	6,898
Dividends per share*	$0.19	$0.21
Earnings per share*	$0.84	$0.86
Common stock	21,441	32,434
Retained income	102,231	133,587
Shareholders equity	113,643	137,445

*all per share numbers have been restated to reflect 3-for-2 stock split of December 9 1985 and March 5 1987

No of Employees: 3,300

SAFEWAY STORES, INCORPORATED

Fourth and Jackson Street, Oakland, CA 94660
Tel: (415) 891-3000
Telex: 337-662 SFWYADMIN OAK

Chairman: Peter A Magowan (and Chief Executive Officer)
President: James A Rowland (and Chief Operating Officer)
Senior Executive Officers: Harry D Sunderland (Executive VP Chief Financial Officer), John Bell (Group VP), E Richard Jones (Group VP), William D Lowe (Group VP), Donald J Smith (Group VP), Robert H Kinnie (VP, Chairman, President and Chief Executive Oficer-Canada Safeway Limited), William M Albers (Senior VP, Distribution), Robert E Bradford (Senior VP, Public Affairs), F J Dale (Senior VP, Controller), Roderick W Davis (Senior VP, Management Information Systems), Philip G Horton (Senior VP, Real Estate and Engineering), John L Morris (Senior VP, Corporate Economist), Ronald F Zachary (Senior VP, Human Resources), Bernat Rosner (Senior VP Law, Secretary and General Counsel), Patrick S Totman (Senior VP, Finance)

PRINCIPAL ACTIVITIES: Grocery store retailing
Trade Names: Bel-air, Brocade, Busy Baker, Captain's Choice, Casa del Pueblo, Country Pure, Cragmont, Crown Colony, Edward's, Empress, Jell-Well, Lucerne, Manor House, Mrs Wright's, NuMade, Party Pride, Safeway, Sea Trader, SuPurb, Townhouse, Truly Fine, White Magic
Principal Subsidiaries: Canada Safeway Ltd; Johs Esmarch's EFTF A/S (Denmark)
Principal Bank: First National Bank of Boston
Financial Information:

	Sep 6 1986(1)	Jan 3 1987(2)
	(36 wks)	(17 wks)
	$'000	$'000
Sales revenues	13,699,356	6,612,124
Income (loss) before taxes	178,792	(84,429)
Net income (loss)	110,136	(124,396)
Dividends per share	$1.325	-
Earnings (loss) per share	$1.80	($1.93)
Shareholders equity	1,688,923	2,902

(1)Predecessor
(2)Successor

Principal Shareholders: Kohlberg Kravis Roberts & Co (an investment banking firm. Safeway was taken private on November 24 1986)
No of Employees: 150,000

SAGA CORPORATION

One Saga Lane, Menlo Park, CA 94025
Tel: (415) 854-5150

Chairman: Charles A Lynch (and Chief Executive Officer)
Senior Executive Officers: James W Morrell (Vice Chairman, Administration Group), Jeffrey O Henley (President Fast Service Restaurant Group), Laurence B Mindel (President Restaurant Group), Robert C Van Horn (President Contract Foodservices Group), Ernest W Collins (VP, General Counsel and Secretary), Leonard J LeBlanc (VP Finance and Treasurer), Earl C Royse (VP Human Resources)

PRINCIPAL ACTIVITIES: Saga Corporation owns and operates four restaurant businesses, Stuart Anderson's Black Angus/Cattle Company, The Velvet Turtle, Hotel Foodservices and Spectrum Foods; owns and franchises three fast service restaurant chains, Grandy's, Straw Hat Pizza and Spoons; and provides contract foodservice management to corporations, colleges and hospitals throughout the United States and Canada
Parent Company: Marriott Corporation
Principal Subsidiaries: Groups and Divisions: Black Angus Division; Grandy's Restaurant Division; Straw Hat Pizza Division; Spectrum Foods Division; Specialty Foodservices Group; The Velvet Turtle Restaurant Division; Hotel Foodservices Division; Spoons Grill & Bar Division; Contract Foodservices Group; Corporate Foodservices Division; Education Foodservices Division; Health Care Division; Canadian Division; Saga Canadian Management Services Ltd; The Company also has regional and district offices located throughout the United States and Canada
Principal Bank: Bank of America
Financial Information:

	$'000
Sales revenues	1,250,000

No of Employees: 58,000

SAGE-ALLEN & COMPANY INC

900 Main Street, Hartford, CT 06103
Tel: (203) 278 2570

Chairman: Lafayette Keeney (and Chief Executive Officer and Treasurer)
President: Charles Allen Haine (and Chief Operating Officer)
Senior Executive Officers: David R Bonney (Senior VP and Chief Financial Officer), Ronald Catania (VP and Director Corporate Planning), Michael T Dvorin (VP General Merchandise), Craig A Fleming (VP Merchandising), Rebecca Gilbert (VP Personnel Affairs), Norman G Novak (VP Management Information Systems), Harvey Syde (VP Operations), Frank L Toro (VP Operations), Allen Lynn Westphal (Secretary)

PRINCIPAL ACTIVITIES: Department stores trading
Principal Bank: Connecticut National Bank
Financial Information:

	$'000
Sales revenues	71,000

No of Employees: 1,000

SAHARA RESORTS

2535 Las Vegas Boulevard South, Las Vegas, NV 89109
Tel: (702) 737 2111

Chairman: Paul W Lowden (and President and Chief Executive Officer)
Senior Executive Officers: R J Radcliffe (Executive VP, Secretary and Treasurer), W J Raggio (VP)

PRINCIPAL ACTIVITIES: Management and operation of casinos, hotels and catering facilities
Principal Subsidiaries: Casino Properties Inc; Ever-Ski Properties Inc; Hacienda Hawaiian Properties; Resorts Marketing International; Sahara Las Vegas Corporation; Tempo Advertising Inc
Principal Bank: Valley Bank of Nevada
Financial Information:

	$'000
Sales revenues	96,000

No of Employees: 2,000

SALANT CORPORATION

290 Avenue of the Americas, New York, NY 10104
Tel: (212) 603-1600

Chairman: John S Rodgers
President: Ray W Williams (and Chief Executive Officer)
Senior Executive Officers: Martin F Tynan (VP Finance)

PRINCIPAL ACTIVITIES: Manufacture of clothing
Principal Subsidiaries: Salant Canada Ltd; Campbells Inc; Obion Company; Texas Apparel Company; Thompson Co; United Pioneer Co; Monarch Clothing Co
Principal Bank: Manufacturers Hanover Trust Co
Financial Information:

	$'000
Sales revenues	144,500

No of Employees: 2,700

SALEM CARPET MILLS, INC

Suite 1100 NCNB Plaza, NC 27101
Tel: (919) 727-1200

Chairman: W D Foster (and Chief Executive Officer)
President: Douglas A Cummins (and Chief Operating Officer)
Senior Executive Officers: Thomas F Lanier (Senior VP, Chief Financial Officer, Treasurer and Secretary), Jack Haselwander (Senior VP), J Terris Hagan (Senior VP), E A Myers Jr (Senior VP), Jon C Logue (Senior VP Marketing)

PRINCIPAL ACTIVITIES: Manufacture of carpets
Trade Names: "Salem", "Majestic", "Winston", "Ashley" - Carpet Divisions
Principal Bank: Dominion
Financial Information:

	Dec 31 1985	Dec 31 1986
	$'000	$'000
Sales revenues	276,381	325,396
Income before taxes	10,041	14,080
Net income	5,915	7,468
Earnings per share	$0.75	$0.94
Common stock	7,923	11,245*
Retained income	28,650	36,118
Shareholders equity	39,702	47,368

*includes $3,240,000 capital in excess of par value

Principal Shareholders: A G Foster; W N Hailey; A O Foster; W D Foster
No of Employees: 2,550

SALEM CORPORATION

PO Box 2222, Pittsburgh, PA 15230
Tel: (412) 923-2200

Chairman: Victor Posner (and Chief Executive Officer); Vice Chairman: Walter Sieckman
President: J A Scharbrough
Senior Executive Officers: Donald L Hoylman (Group VP), A A Fornataro (VP), L A Weaver (VP), George A Socher (Treasurer)

PRINCIPAL ACTIVITIES: Manufacture of hoists and cranes; mining machinery; mechanical handling plant; processing equipment; coal mining

Principal Subsidiaries: Salem Furnace Co; Herr Voss Corp; Industrial Resources Inc; Salem Industries Can Ltd; Salem Engineering Co Ltd; West Virginia Electric Corp; Salem Herr-Voss Co Ltd (UK); A L Lee Corp; Industrial Contracting of Fairmont Inc; McHal Corp; Mountainee and Resources Inc; Salem International Services Inc
Principal Bank: Pittsburgh National Bank
Financial Information:

	$'000
Sales revenues	75,800

No of Employees: 600

SALOMON INC

1221 Avenue of the Americas, New York, NY 10020
Tel: (212) 764-3700

Chairman: John H Gutfreund (and President and Chief Executive Officer); Vice Chairmen: Henry Kaufman, Thomas D O'Malley
Senior Executive Officers: Gedale B Horowitz (Executive VP), Richard J Schmeelk (Executive VP), William J Vouté (Executive VP), Thomas W Strauss (Executive VP), Walter E Baker (Senior VP and Controller), Richard A DiDonna (VP and Associate General Counsel), Gerald P Nagy (VP Taxes), Frederic G Schwarz (VP and Treasurer)

PRINCIPAL ACTIVITIES: Holding company with interests in a wide range of financial services and commodity trading operations
Principal Subsidiaries: Phibro Energy Inc; Philipp Brothers Inc; Salomon Brothers Inc
Principal Bank: The Chase Manhattan Bank NA
Financial Information:

	Dec 31 1986
	$'000
Revenues	6,790,000
Net income	516,000
Earnings per share	$3.45
Shareholders equity	3,454,000

No of Employees: 7,800

SAMSON PAPER BAG CO, INC

Arnold Drive, Huntington, NY 11743
Tel: (516) 271-8100
Telex: ITT 4758213 samson

Senior Executive Officers: Willis Fenwick (Senior VP Operations), Stan Kaufman (Senior VP Sales), Dante Pacifico (VP Administration), Norman Kaye (VP Sales)

PRINCIPAL ACTIVITIES: Manufacture of paper products including bags and sacks
Parent Company: Stone Container Corporation, Chicago, IL
Principal Bank: Citibank
Financial Information:

	$'000
Sales revenues	50,000

No of Employees: 180

SAN DIEGO GAS & ELECTRIC CO

PO Box 1831, San Diego, CA 92112
Tel: (619) 696-2000

Chairman: Thomas A Page (and President and Chief Executive Officer)
Senior Executive Officers: Jack E Thomas (Executive VP and Chief Operating Officer), Gary D Cotton (Senior VP Electricity Operations), Alton T Davis (Senior VP Gas Operations), Richard Korpan (Senior VP), Stephen L Baum (VP and General Counsel), Donald E Felsinger (VP Operational Services), Ronald K Fuller (VP Government and Regulatory Services), John E Hamrick (VP Customer Services), R Lee Haney (VP and Treasurer), Chris Harlow (VP), James C Holcombe (VP Fuel and Power Contracts), Richard L Manning (VP Public Relations), Ronald W Watkins (VP Administration Services), George A F Weida (VP Human Resources)

PRINCIPAL ACTIVITIES: Distribution of electricity
Principal Bankers: Bank of America
Financial Information:

	$'000
Sales revenues	1,600,000

No of Employees: 4,900

SANDERS ASSOCIATES, INC

Daniel Webster Highway S, Nashua, NH 03061
Tel: (603) 885-4321
Telex: TWX 710 2281894

Chairman: Jack L Bowers (and Chief Executive Officer)
President: Albert B Wight (and Chief Operating Officer)
Senior Executive Officers: Jay M Farrar (President Components Products Group), William B Conlin (President CalComp Group), Edward A Miller (Executive VP), Joseph A Scopelliti (Senior VP Finance and Chief Financial Officer), James P Woolnough (Senior VP, President Federal Systems Group), Charles A Glenday (VP Public Affairs)

PRINCIPAL ACTIVITIES: Production of advanced electronic equipment and systems for the defense industry
Principal Subsidiaries: CalComp BV (Netherlands); CalComp Europe Ltd (UK); CalComp GmbH (Germany); Calcomp Ltd (UK); CalComp Pacific Inc; Calcomp SA (France); CalComp SpA (Italy); CalComp of Canada Ltd; High Point Realty Corp; Hi-Tension Realty Corp; Sanders Developent Corp; SA Sales Corp; Analytyx Electronic Systems Inc; Nippon CalComp KK (Japan); Sanders Securities Corp; Image Resource Corp; Forjohn Ltd (Barbados); CalComp Foreign Sales Corp (Barbados); California Computer Products Inc
Financial Information:

	$'000
Sales revenues	885,790

No of Employees: 11,410

SANDERSON FARMS, INC

225 N Thirteenth Avenue, Laurel, MS 39440
Tel: (601) 649-4030

Chairman: Joe F Sanderson (and Chief Executive Officer and Treasurer)
President: Odell Johnson
Senior Executive Officers: Joe Sanderson Jr (VP), Wyatt Davis (Chief Financial Officer and Secretary)

PRINCIPAL ACTIVITIES: Poultry and meat processing
Trade Names: Miss Goldy
Principal Subsidiaries: Sanderson Farms Inc (Production Division), Sanderson Farms Inc (Processing Division); National Prepared Foods Inc
Principal Bank: Deposit Guaranty National Bank
Financial Information:

	Oct 31 1986	Oct 31 1987
	$'000	$'000
Sales revenues	150,973	149,995
Net income	15,582	10,956
Dividends per share(1)	$0.20	$0.20
Earnings per share	$1.85	$1.26
Common stock	8,435	9,075

(1) annual
(2) weighted average shares outstanding

No of Employees: 1,850

SANDOZ, INC

Rte 10, East Hanover, NJ 07936
Tel: (201) 386-7500
Telex: RCA 219346 a sand ur

Chairman: Marc Moret; Vice Chairman: Max E Link

Senior Executive Officers: Hansruedi Pulver (Executive VP and Chief Financial Officer), Herbert J Brennan (VP Legal Affairs), Craig D Burrell (VP External Affairs), Max E Link (President Pharmaceutical Division and Chief Executive Officer)

PRINCIPAL ACTIVITIES: Production of pharmaceuticals; general chemicals; chemicals for agricultural use; paints and dyestuffs
Parent Company: Sandoz Ltd, Basle, Switzerland
Principal Bank: Citibank
Financial Information:

	$'000
Sales revenues	340,000

No of Employees: 3,000

SANDVIK, INC

1702 Nevins Road, Fair Lawn, NJ 07410
Tel: (201) 797-6200
Telex: WUT 95099 sandvik

President: Bert A Fernaeus
Senior Executive Officers: Paul Hodgen (Treasurer and Assistant Secretary), Robert G Reveri (Purchasing Agent)

PRINCIPAL ACTIVITIES: Manufacture of machine tools and hand tools, steel tubes, wires and electrodes, conveying systems
Parent Company: Sandvik AB, Sweden
Principal Bank: Morgan Guaranty Trust Co of New York
Financial Information:

	$'000
Sales revenues	150,000

No of Employees: 1,300

SANMARK-STARDUST INC

145 Madison Avenue, New York, NY 10016
Tel: (212) 684 3400

Chairman: Abraham David (and Chief Executive Officer)
President: Mark M David (and Chief Operating Officer)
Senior Executive Officers: Marvin Rosen (Executive VP), Saul Pomerantz (VP and Secretary), Helen Samuels (Treasurer)

PRINCIPAL ACTIVITIES: Manufacture and wholesale of loungewear, daywear, nightwear and lingerie for ladies
Principal Bank: Republic National Bank of New York
Financial Information:

	$'000
Sales revenues	52,000

No of Employees: 1,500

SANTA ANITA OPERATING COMPANY

285 West Huntington Drive, Arcadia, CA 91006
Tel: (818) 574 7223

President: Robert P Strub (and Chief Executive Officer)
Senior Executive Officers: Glennon E King (VP Finance, Controller and Assistant Secretary), Alexander W Ingle (Secretary and Treasurer)

PRINCIPAL ACTIVITIES: Construction of race tracks; real estate development
Principal Subsidiaries: Los Angeles Turf Club Inc; Santa Anita Developers Corporation; Santa Anita Development Corporation
Principal Bank: Security Pacific National Bank
Financial Information:

	$'000
Sales revenues	88,000

No of Employees: 2,240

SANTA FE SOUTHERN PACIFIC CORPORATION

224 S Michigan Ave, Chicago, IL 60604
Tel: (312) 427-4900

Chairman: John J Schmidt (and Chief Executive Officer); Vice Chairmen: Alan C Furth; John W Swartz
President: Robert D Krebs (and Chief Operating Officer)
Senior Executive Officers: Orval M Adam (VP, Treasurer and Chief Financial Officer), C Ore Davis (VP Human Resources), William R Denton (VP and Chief Administration Officer), Glenn W Dodd (VP and Controller), Jerome F Donohue (VP Law), F N Grossman (VP Corporate Communications), Thomas I McKnew Jr (VP), Fred C Schulte (VP)

PRINCIPAL ACTIVITIES: Diversified corporation with interests in railroad operations, trucking, oil and gas pipelines, oil, gas and mineral exploration, leasing and the manufacture and sale of building materials
Financial Information:

	Dec 31 1985	Dec 31 1986
	$'000	$'000
Sales revenues	6,438,000	5,801,600
Net income (loss)	469,600	(137,900)
Earnings (loss) per share	$2.67	($0.84)
Shareholders equity	5,764,200	5,040,300

No of Employees: 53,400

SANYO MANUFACTURING CORPORATION

3333 Warwick Road, Forrest City, AR 72335
Tel: (501) 633-5030
Telex: WUT 536221 sanyo facy

President: M Iwasa
Senior Executive Officers: D Carter (VP Color Television Manufacturing), Charles L Green (VP Microwave Manufacturing), Tanemichi Sohma (VP Administration)

PRINCIPAL ACTIVITIES: Production of televisions
Parent Company: Sanyo Electric Co Ltd
Principal Bank: Sumitomo Bank
Financial Information:

	$'000
Sales revenues	416,000

No of Employees: 2,400

SARA LEE CORPORATION

3 First National Plaza, Chicago, IL 60602
Tel: (312) 726-2600
Telex: 4330147
Telefax: (312) 558-8567

Chairman: John H Bryan Jr (and Chief Executive Officer); Vice Chairman: Robert E Elberson
President: John B McKinnon
Senior Executive Officers: Michael E Murphy (Executive VP and Chief Financial and Administrative Officer), George W Bryan (Senior VP), Joseph F Neely (Senior VP Human Resources), Paul Fulton (Executive VP), C Steven McMillan (Senior VP-Strategy Development), Gordon H Newman (Senior VP, Secretary and General Counsel), Richard G Rademacher (Senior VP), Andrea Stack (VP), Cornelis Boonsta (Senior VP), Brian Healey (Senior VP), Keith L Alm (VP), Gary F Bernegger (VP), Philip R Courier (VP), William Hardison Jr (VP), Floyd Hoffman (VP, Associate General Counsel), Mary Ellen Johnson (VP and Treasurer), Daniel R Kulik (VP and Controller), Robert L Lauer (VP Corporate Affairs), Mark McCarville (VP Corporate Development), Thomas D MacLeod (VP), Leslie W Riley Jr (VP), M Weldon Schenck (VP), Vincent H Swoyer (VP Corporate Systems), Phillip A Temple (VP Human Resources), Lee Kramer (VP)

PRINCIPAL ACTIVITIES: Sara Lee Corporation is an international company primarily engaged in manufacturing and marketing consumer products, principally packaged goods; manufacturing and distributing food and non-food items for the foodservice industry; and manufacturing and marketing consumer products that are sold directly to the consumer. The company has many well-known brands that compete in markets around the world

Trade Names: Consumer Brands:- Ambi, Ambipur, Erdal, Miss Den, Odorex, Prodent, Radox, Roger Para, White King (personal care and household products), Isotoner (gloves, slippers and knitted accessories), Aspro, Rennie (home medicines), Bali, A-OK, Flexnit, Dici, Something Else, WonderBra (women's intimate apparel), Bryan*, Emmber's Lean'n Tender, Galileo*, Gallo Salame, Gianola, Hillshire Farm*, Jimmy Dean*, Kahn's*, King Cotton, MarTenn*, Prairie Belt, R B Rice*, Rudy's Farm*, Smoky Hollow (fresh smoked, processed and canned meat products), Chef Pierre*, Lloyd J Harriss (frozen pies and other bakery goods), Coach (leather handbags, belts and other accessories), Douwe Egberts*, Amphora, Chat Noir, Drum, Jacqmotte, La Maison du Café, Marcilla, Merrild, Moccona, Pickwick, Soley (coffee, tea and tobacco products), Fuller (brushes, cleaning accessories, personal care products and home maintenance aids), Hanes, Fitting Pretty, Hanes Too!, Just My Size, L'eggs, Sheer Elegance, Sheer Energy, Slenderalls, Today's Girl, Underalls (women's hoisery), Hanes (men's and boys' underwear; printable T-shirts), Jonker Fris* (processed fruits, vegetables and mushrooms), Kiwi, Tana, Tuxan (shoe care products), PayDay, ButterNut, Chocolaty Payday, MilkShake, Zero (candy bars), Sara Lee* (frozen baked goods), *Also distributed to foodservice market. Foodservice and Commercial Suppliers:-Booth Fisheries (fresh, frozen and processed fish and seafood distribution), Hi-Brand Foods, Peck Meat Packing, Standard Meat (fresh and processed meat products), Lyon's Restaurants (family-style restaurants), Moccomat (foodservice coffee and beverage systems), PYA/Monarch (foodservice distribution; institutional foods), Superior Coffee and Foods (foodservice coffee and tea)

Financial Information:

	Jun 28 1986	Jun 27 1987
	$'000	$'000
Net sales	7,938,000	9,155,000
Income before taxes	356,000	448,000
Net income	223,000	267,600
Dividends	83,379	102,148
Dividends per share*	$0.78	$0.95
Earnings per share*	$2.02	$2.35
Common stock	79,730	159,461
Retained earnings	1,320,475	1,408,504
Shareholders equity	1,155,000	1,416,000

*restated for the 2 for 1 stock split effective Dec 1 1986

No of Employees: 92,400

SARGENT INDUSTRIES, INC

1901 Building, Century City, Los Angeles, CA 90067
Tel: (213) 277-9111

Chairman: Dan W Burns (and Chief Executive Officer)
President: John M Jarboe
Senior Executive Officers: Bene J Cerrito (VP and Secretary), Ralph J Eschborn (VP Energy Control Group)

PRINCIPAL ACTIVITIES: Manufacture of energy control products; aerospace equipment and components; pumps and valves
Parent Company: Dover Corporation
Principal Bank: Bankers Trust Company
Financial Information:

	$'000
Sales revenues	100,700

No of Employees: 1,120

SARGENT-WELCH SCIENTIFIC COMPANY

7300 North Linder Avenue, PO Box 1026, Skokie, IL 60077-4326
Tel: (312) 677-0600
Telex: 72-4442 SARWELSCI SKO

Chairman: Thomas M Mints Jr (and President)
Senior Executive Officers: D Jeffrey Baddeley (VP, Secretary and General Counsel), Robert L Bieser (VP, Science Education Sales), Edward F Ewen (VP, Engineering), Ronald M Rodeo (VP, Manufacturing), Clark L Schmitz (VP, Operations), Gerald J Sweas (VP, Finance and Controller)

PRINCIPAL ACTIVITIES: Sargent-Welch Scientific Company is a supplier of materiel for scientific research, educational and applied science. The Company develops, manufactures, markets and distributes a broad, diverse line of analytical instruments, scientific apparatus, laboratory equipment, supplies, chemicals and furniture to industrial, educational and governmental markets
Trade Names: Bio-Perm, ChemAnal, CryoSource, Densichron, Densichrometer, Densi-Scan, DirecTorr, DuoCone, Duo Seal, Ed-Set, Lammert, Mangephot, Mathset, Polarograph, Rol-a-Lab, Rol-Labette, Sargent, SarVac, ScienCenter, ScienSet, Thermonitor, TurboTorr, Welch, Sargent-Welch (all Registered Trade Names)
Principal Subsidiaries: Sargent-Welch Scientific of Canada Ltd; SWS Inc; SWS International Ltd; Sargent-Welch Pte Ltd
Principal Bank: The First National Bank of Chicago; The Northern Trust Company
Financial Information:

	$'000
Sales revenues	82,000

No of Employees: 805

SAUDER WOODWORKING CO

502 Middle Street, Archbold, OH 43502
Tel: (419) 445-6010

Chairman: Erie J Sauder
President: Maynard Sauder (and Treasurer)
Senior Executive Officers: Lynn Aschliman (Purchasing Agent), Elvin D Yoder (Secretary), Gene Metz (Sales Manager)

PRINCIPAL ACTIVITIES: Manufacture of household furniture; plastic products
Principal Bank: First National Bank of Toledo
Financial Information:

	$'000
Sales revenues	90,000

No of Employees: 750

SAUNDERS SYSTEM INC

201 Office Park Drive, Birmingham, AL 35223
Tel: (205) 879 2131

Co-Chairmen: Harris Saunders Jr (and Chief Executive Officer), John R Saunders
President: A Gordon Shelfer Jr (and Chief Executive Officer)
Senior Executive Officers: Harris Saunders Sr (Chairman of Executive Committee), Joseph H Flemming Jr (Executive VP Finance and Administration), Ronald T Sorrow (Executive VP Marketing), Thomas P Dunn (VP Human Resources), Larry J Halbert (VP Corporate Services), Milton G Hauser (VP Employee Relations), V Aubrey Mince Jr (VP and Legal Counsel), William C Sims (VP Development), John H Traendly (VP Management Information Systems), Terry G Sledge (Treasurer)

PRINCIPAL ACTIVITIES: Haulage and freight carrying services; truck rental and leasing; contract carriers and all services related to truck transportation
Parent Company: Ryder System Inc
Principal Subsidiaries: Saunders Carriers; Tandem Advertising Inc; Transportation Industrial Consultants; Truck Central Inc
Principal Bank: SouthTrust Bank
Financial Information:

	$'000
Sales revenues	271,170

No of Employees: 2,270

SAVANNAH ELECTRIC AND POWER COMPANY

600 Bay Street East, PO Box 968, Savannah, GA 31402
Tel: (912) 238-2254
Telefax: (912) 238-2219

President: Arthur M Gignilliat Jr (and Chief Executive Officer)
Senior Executive Officers: E Olin Veale (Senior VP and Chief Financial Officer), Y Allen Beall (VP, Corporate Services), W Miles Greer (VP, Area Development and Governmental Affairs), Harold W Kraft (VP Power Supply and System Operation), James L Rayburn (VP Planning and Marketing), John W Spivey (VP Engineering and Power Delivery), Kirby R Willis (Treasurer and Secretary), Grace E Arnold (Assistant Secretary), Michael L Krick (Controller and Assistant Treasurer)

PRINCIPAL ACTIVITIES: Electric utility
Principal Bank: Citizens & Southern National Bank
Financial Information:

	Dec 31 1985	Dec 31 1986
	$'000	$'000
Sales revenues	158,727	175,585
Income before taxes	31,398	42,256
Net income	16,747	21,853
Dividends(1)	9,854	10,753
Dividends per share(2)	$0.80	$0.80
Earnings per share	$1.45	$1.91
Common stock	56,487	58,136
Retained income	53,898	64,997
Shareholders equity	110,385	123,133

(1) all stocks
(2) common only

No of Employees: 636

SAVANNAH FOODS & INDUSTRIES, INC

PO Box 339, Savannah, GA 31402
Tel: (912) 234-1261
Telex: TWX 910 3332648 savannahfoods

President: Wm W Sprague Jr
Senior Executive Officers: Walter C Scott (Executive VP and Secretary), George Fawcett (VP Operations), Benjamin A Oxnard Jr (VP Raw Sugar), James M Taylor (VP Corporate Development), F S Exley (VP Distribution), Ernest Flegenheimer (VP), William E Stainhauer (VP Finance), J C Williams Jr (VP Corporate Affairs)

PRINCIPAL ACTIVITIES: Sugar refining; manufacture of pet foods; warehousing; trucking
Principal Subsidiaries: Food Carrier Inc; Everglades Sugar Refinery Inc
Principal Bank: The Citizens and Southern National Bank
Financial Information:

	Dec 31 1985	Dec 31 1986
	$'000	$'000
Sales revenues	629,354	634,682
Net income	17,273	10,399
Earnings per share	$2.61	$1.56
Shareholders equity	106,270	112,078

No of Employees: 1,000

SAVIN CORPORATION

9 W Broad Street, Box 10270, Stamford, CT 06904
Tel: (203) 967-5000
Telex: ITT 495 1558 savn ui

Chairman: Serge Gouin; Vice Chairman: David G Sadler (and Chief Executive Officer)
President: Mel Mahler (and Chief Operating Officer)
Senior Executive Officers: Joan Cleveland (VP, Secretary and General Counsel), Gene Gage (VP and Controller), Woodrow Giezentanner (VP Field Operations Dealer Division), Daniel Harbison (VP Branch Development), Norman L Harritt (VP Finance and Chief Financial Officer), John Leary (VP Retail Operations), Robert Raffa (VP Major Account Marketing), Max E Schultes (VP Copier Products Development), Richard B Wilder (VP Human Resources)

PRINCIPAL ACTIVITIES: Manufacture of office copying equipment
Parent Company: Canada Development Corp
Principal Subsidiaries: Diversifed Equipment Leasing Corp; Magnetic Laboratories Inc; Savin Canada Inc; Savin GmbH (Germany); Savin World Trade Corp; Senox Limited
Financial Information:

	$'000
Sales revenues	431,710

No of Employees: 4,200

SAVOY INDUSTRIES, INC

150 E 58th St, New York, NY 10155
Tel: (212) 980-9670

Chairman: Benson A Selzer (and Executive VP)
President: Irwin L Feinberg (and Chief Executive Officer)
Senior Executive Officers: John A Selzer (Executive VP, Secretary, Treasurer and Chief Financial Officer)

PRINCIPAL ACTIVITIES: Manufacture of men's clothing, games and toys
Principal Bank: Chemical Bank
Financial Information:

	$'000
Sales revenues	40,700

No of Employees: 2,700

SAXON INDUSTRIES, INC

100 Fifth Avenue, New York, NY 10011
Tel: (212) 206-1000

President: William J Scharffenberger (and Chief Executive Officer)
Senior Executive Officers: Kenneth E Templin (Senior VP), Jay J Jacobson (VP Law), Louis L Broudy (VP Law), J H Wise (VP Human Resources), Carole G Donlin (VP Corporate Communications), Alan R Siegel (VP Finance and Chief Financial Officer)

PRINCIPAL ACTIVITIES: Manufacture of paper and paper products including industrial and fine papers, stationery and disposables for food packaging
Principal Bank: Chemical Bank
Financial Information:

	$'000
Sales revenues	710,000

No of Employees: 4,500

SBARRO INC

763 Larkfield Road, Commack, NY 11725
Tel: (516) 864 02 00

Chairman: Mario Sbarro (and President)
Senior Executive Officers: Anthony Sbarro (Executive VP and Treasurer), Joseph Sbarro (Executive VP and Secretary), Carmela Sbarro (VP), Jerold S Epstein (Controller)

PRINCIPAL ACTIVITIES: Restaurant franchise operation
Principal Bank: Marine Midland Bank
Financial Information:

	$'000
Sales revenues	35,000

No of Employees: 3,000

SCANA CORPORATION

1426 Main St, PO Box 764, Columbia, SC 29218
Tel: (803) 748-3000

Chairman: John A Warren (and Chief Executive Officer)
President: Lawrence M Gressette

Senior Executive Officers: T C Nichols Jr (Executive VP), E H Crews Jr (VP Operations), Max Earwood (VP Administration), C B Novinger (VP Administration), R W Stedman (VP and Controller), W B Timmermann (VP Finance and Treasurer), B C Bissell (Secretary)

PRINCIPAL ACTIVITIES: Distribution of electricity and natural gas
Principal Bankers: Citibank
Financial Information:

	$'000
Sales revenues	1,100,000

No of Employees: 4,400

SCHAAKE PACKING CO
PO Box 128, Ellensburg, WA 98926
Tel: (509) 925-5346

President: Donald E Schaake
Senior Executive Officers: Fred A Lienhard (VP Sales), Paul E Schaake (VP Manufacturing), Robert D Jackson (Secretary and Treasurer)

PRINCIPAL ACTIVITIES: Packaging of meat and meat products and cattle feeding
Principal Subsidiaries: Schaake International Corp
Principal Bank: Rainier National Bank
Financial Information:

	$'000
Sales revenues	155,000

No of Employees: 50

SCHAPER MANUFACTURING CO
9909 S Shore Drive, Minneapolis, MN 55441
Tel: (612) 540-0511
Telex: WUI 6879057 schaper

President: W L Garrity
Senior Executive Officers: Peter Wimsatt (Executive VP), Bob Beck (VP Research and Development), Robert Clifford (VP Materials), W J Daly (VP and Controller), Tony Martinson (VP Sales), Dennis Sharkey (VP Engineering), Dave Springer (VP Finance), Barry Tunick (VP Marketing)

PRINCIPAL ACTIVITIES: Manufacture of toys; plastics and plastic products
Parent Company: Kusan Inc
Principal Bank: Camden Northwestern State Bank
Financial Information:

	$'000
Sales revenues	95,000

No of Employees: 450

SCHEIB, EARL, INC
8737 Wilshire Boulevard, Beverly Hills, CA 90211
Tel: (213) 652 4880

Chairman: Earl A Scheib (and President)
Senior Executive Officers: Richard J Gariglio (VP Operations), Sam V La Monto (VP Operations), Donald R Scheib (VP Operations), John K Minnihan (VP Finance and Chief Financial Officer), Irwin R Buchalter (Secretary)

PRINCIPAL ACTIVITIES: Operation of auto paint centers
Principal Bank: Union Bank
Financial Information:

	$'000
Sales revenues	60,000

No of Employees: 1,800

SCHENLEY INDUSTRIES, INC
888 7th Avenue, New York, NY 10106
Tel: (212) 621-8000
Telex: WUT 12025 schenley nyk

Chairman: Howard S Feldman (and President and Chief Executive Officer); Vice Chairman: Marcia Riklis
Senior Executive Officers: David A Chernow (Senior Executive VP), Paul L Farber (Senior Executive VP), Adolph Slone (Executive VP), Alexander Berk (VP), Ephraim Spirn (VP and Treasurer), Arthur Waltzman (VP)

PRINCIPAL ACTIVITIES: Suppliers of wines and spirits
Parent Company: Rapid American Corp
Principal Bank: Manufacturers Hanover Trust Co
Financial Information:

	$'000
Sales revenues	693,000

No of Employees: 4,000

SCHERER, R P, CORPORATION
2075 W Big Beaver Road, Troy, MI 48084
Tel: (313) 649-0900
Telex: WUT 235745 rpscfin trly

Chairman: Wilber H Mack
President: Peter R Fink (and Chief Executive Officer)
Senior Executive Officers: Ernst A Scyoepe (Executive VP, Treasurer and Chief Operating Officer), David G Collins (VP Finance), J D Davies (VP Commercial Development), Erhard J Fuehrer (VP Marketing), Alberto S Inza (VP Operations)

PRINCIPAL ACTIVITIES: Manufacture of hardshell and soft elastic gelatin capsules for the packaging of drugs and cosmetics
Principal Bank: Manufacturers National Bank of Detroit
Financial Information:

	$'000
Sales revenues	167,400

No of Employees: 2,400

SCHERING-PLOUGH CORPORATION
One Giralda Farms, Madison, NJ 07940-1000
Tel: (201) 822-7000
Telex: 21-9165

Chairman: Robert P Luciano (and President and Chief Executive Officer)
Senior Executive Officers: Hugh A D'Andrade (Executive VP, Administration), R Lee Jenkins (Executive VP, Consumer Operations), Richard J Kogan (Executive VP, Pharmaceutical Operations), Stephen F Byrd (Senior VP, Human Resources), Harold R Hiser Jr (Senior VP, Finance), William E Keppler (Senior VP, Technical Operations and Management Systems), Allan S Kushen (Senior VP, Public Affairs), J Martin Comey (VP and Treasurer), Ralph W Golby (VP and General Counsel), Daniel A Nichols (VP, Taxes), Robert G Weiss (VP and Controller), John T Fogarty (Staff VP and Secretary), Jay T Ludwig (Staff VP and Assistant Treasurer), William J O'Hara (Staff VP and Assistant Treasurer), Benjamin Croce (Assistant Controller), Jane S Nixon (Assistant Secretary)

PRINCIPAL ACTIVITIES: Schering-Plough is a worldwide company primarily engaged in the discovery, development, manufacturing and marketing of pharmaceutical and consumer products. Pharmaceutical products include prescription drugs, over-the-counter medicines, vision care products and animal health products promoted to the medical and allied professions. The consumer products group consists of proprietary medicines, toiletries, cosmetics and foot care products marketed directly to the public
Trade Names: Pharmaceutical Products:- Principal prescription and over-the-counter products are GARAMYCIN, NETROMYCIN and sisomicin, antibiotics; AFRIN, CELESTAMINE, CHLOR-TRIMETON, CORICIDIN, DRIXORAL, OPTIMINE, POLARAMINE, PROVENTIL, TRINALIN, VANCENASE and VANCERIL, allergy, asthma/cold; DIPROLENE, DIPROSONE, DIPROSPAN, FULVICIN, GYNE-LOTRIMIN, LOTRIMIN, LOTRISONE, QUADRIDERM, TINACTIN and VALISONE, dermatologicals; ETRAFON and

TRILAFON, psychopharmaceuticals; NORMODYNE, an antihypertensive; EULEXIN, anti-cancer; and INTRON A, anti-viral/anti-cancer. Major vision care prodcuts are Wesley-Jessen DURASOFT, hard and soft contact lenses and lens accessories. Animal health biological and pharmaceutical products include antibiotics, steroids, antifungals and vaccines. Major animal health products are GENTOCIN and GARASOL, antibiotics; and BANAMINE, an analgesic. Consumer Products:- Principal consumer products are CORRECTOL and FEEN-A-MINT laxatives; ASPERGUM and ST JOSEPH aspirin and aspirin-free products for children and adults, analgesics; DI-GEL, an antacid; MAXSANA, a medicated powder, DURATION, a nasal decongestant; AFTATE, an antifungal; COPPERTONE, QT, and TROPICAL BLEND, suntan products; SOLARCAINE, a sunburn remedy; SHADE, sunscreens; MAYBELLINE, CHICOGO and RIMMEL, cosmetics; DR SCHOLL'S, foot pads, cushions, arch supports, sprays, powders, creams and sandals; MUSKOL, insect repellent; and PAAS Easter egg coloring and activity kits and Halloween make-up kits

Principal Subsidiaries: Argentina: Compañia Dr Scholl (SACI); Essex (Argentina) SAIC; UNIFA SAQI. Australia: Essex Laboratories Pty Ltd; Plough (Australia) Pty Ltd; Scholl (Australia) Ltd. Austria: AESCA Chemisch-Pharmazeutische Fabrik GmbH; Scholl-Oestereich Gesellschaft mbH. Belgium: Essex Laboratories NV; NV Essex (Belgium) SA; Scholl Belgique SA. Brazil: Dr Scholl SA (Comercio e Industria) Ltd; Industria Química e Farmacéutica Schering SA; Plough Produtos Farmacéuticos e Cosméticos; Schering Produtos Veterinarios Ltd. Canada: Plough Canada Inc; Schering Canada Inc; Scholl (Canada) Inc. Chile: Plough-Chile Ltda; Schering Cia Ltda. Colombia: Laboratorios Undra SA. Denmark: Essex Pharma A/S; Scholl Manufacturing Co A/S. Ecuador: Productos Farmacéuticos Ecuatorianos SA (PROFESA). Finland: Essex Laakkeet Oy; Wesley-Jessen of Scandinavia Oy. France: Rigaux Galena; Scholl France SA; UNICET. Greece: Essex Hellas SA; Scholl Hellas Ltd. Guatemala: Plough Export Inc. Hong Kong: Essex Asia Ltd; Plough Consumer Prods. (Asia) Ltd. India: Fulford (India) Limited. Indonesia: PT Essex Indonesia. Eire: Scholl (Ireland) Ltd. Italy: Essex (Italia) SpA; Plough Italia SpA. Japan: Central-Plough Ltd; Coppertone (Japan) Ltd; Essex Nippon Kabushiki Kaisha. Kenya: Sentipharm AG. Luxembourg: Essex Luxembourg SA. Malaysia: Warrick (Malaysia) Sdn Bhd. Mexico: Cia Dr Scholl SA de CV; Plough de México SA de CV,; Scheramex SA de CV. Nederlands: Essex (Nederland) BV; Warrick (Nederland) BV. New Zealand: Essex Laboratories (NZ) Ltd; Scholl (NZ) Ltd. Norway: Scholl (Norge) A/S; Sentipharm AG. Panama: Schering Corporation Centroamérica SA; Schering Overseas Limited. Peru: Schering Corp del Peru SA. Philippines: Plough Consumer Products (Phillippines) Inc; Schering Corporation (Philippines) Inc. Portugal: Essex Farmacéutica Portoguesa Ltda; Plough Portguesa Química Farmacéutica Ltda; SOPROL-Sociedad Pro-Farmacia Ltda. South Africa: (Pty) Ltd; Scholl-Plough South Africa (Pty) Ltd. South Korea: YuHan SP Corporation. Spain: Compañia Scholl SA; Desarrollos Farmacéuticos y Cosméticos SA; Essex (España) SA. Sweden: Essex Lakemedel AB; Pro Medica AB; Scholl (Sverige) AB. Switzerland: Essex Chemie AG; Plough-Scholl Trading Ltd; Wm Scholl AG. Taiwan: Essex Taiwan Limited Co. Thailand: Essex Thailand Ltd. UK: Kirby-Warrick Pharmaceuticals Ltd; Plough (UK) Ltd; Rimmel International Ltd; Scholl (UK) Ltd. USA: American Scientific Laboratories; Artra Cosmetics Inc; Continental Animal Health Products; Coppertone Corporation; Maybelline Company; Plough Broadcasting Company Inc; Plough Inc; Sardo Inc; Schering Corporation; Schering del Caribe Inc (Puerto Rico); Schering Veterinary Products; Scholl Inc; Wesley-Jessen Inc. Uruguay: Essex Uruguay SA. Venezuela: PROFAR; Scholl Venezolana CA. West Germany: Chicogo Cosmetic GmbH; Essex Pharma GmbH; Scholl-Werke GmbH.

Principal Bank: Morgan Guaranty; Citibank; Chase Manhattan

Financial Information:

	Dec 31 1986 $'000
Sales revenues	2,398,700
Net income	265,800
Earnings per share	$4.34
Shareholders equity	1,458,800

No of Employees: 24,000

SCHIAVONE-BONOMO CORPORATION

Foot of Jersey Avenue, Jersey City, NJ 07302
Tel: (201) 333-4300
Telex: RCA 219245 sbc ur

President: Gerard V Bonomo
Senior Executive Officers: Joseph Laraja (Executive VP Advertising Operations), Peter Avagliano (VP)

PRINCIPAL ACTIVITIES: Processing of, and wholesale trade in scrap metals
Principal Bank: Irving Trust Company
Financial Information:

	$'000
Sales revenues	70,000

No of Employees: 140

SCHLAGE LOCK CO

2401 Bayshore Blvd, San Francisco, CA 94134
Tel: (415) 467-1100
Telex: WUT 340409 schlage sfo

President: David W Lasier
Senior Executive Officers: Thomas R Lasier (VP LCN Division), Jerold H Tuft (VP Schlage Division), William L Parker (VP Von Duprin Inc), Stuart B Knott (VP Schlage Electronics), Robert N Rasmussen (VP and Treasurer)

PRINCIPAL ACTIVITIES: Manufacture of locks
Parent Company: Ingersoll-Rand Co, Woodcliff Lake, NJ
Financial Information:

	$'000
Sales revenues	290,000

No of Employees: 3,300

SCHLUDERBERG-KURDLE CO, INC

3800 E Baltimore Street, Baltimore, MD 21203
Tel: (301) 276-2000

Chairman: Joseph Luter III
President: Paul E Shank
Senior Executive Officers: Robert W Bossell (VP Marketing), Arron D Trub (Secretary and Treasurer), C Larry Pope Controller)

PRINCIPAL ACTIVITIES: Meat and meat processing; dairy products
Principal Bank: First Pennsylvania Bank
Financial Information:

	$'000
Sales revenues	50,000

No of Employees: 500

SCHLUMBERGER LTD

277 Park Avenue, New York, NY 10017
Tel: (212) 350-9400
Telex: ITT 4995828 sch ui

Chairman: Dugald E Baird (and President and Chief Executive Officer)
Senior Executive Officers: R Genin (Chairman Executive Committee), A Lendenauer (Executive VP Finance), Donald W Brooks (Executive VP), M Gouilloud (Executive VP Technical), J G Lee (Executive VP), R Mitieus (Executive VP), T C Roberts (Executive VP), Roy Shourd (Executive VP), J Babaud

(VP), V E Grijalva (VP Personnel), A D Klein (VP), W T Long (VP), A Misk (VP)

PRINCIPAL ACTIVITIES: Services to the oil and gas industries; electronic testing and measuring systems and components
Principal Bank: Morgan Guaranty Trust Co of New York
Financial Information:

	$'000
Sales revenues	4,600,000

No of Employees: 75,000

SCHMIDT, C, & SONS, INC

127 Edward Street, Philadelphia, PA 19123
Tel: (215) 928-4000
Telex: TWX 710 6700167 schmidts pha

Chairman: William H Pflaumer
President: William T Elliott
Senior Executive Officers: William A Hipp (VP Production), John P Jones (VP Marketing), Frederick H von Czoernig (VP Administration and Treasurer), Robert L Welty (VP and Secretary)

PRINCIPAL ACTIVITIES: Brewing; a subsidiary operates as a wholesale distributor of beer and other beverages
Trade Names: Schmidt's, Rheingold, Knickerbocker, Prior, Wunder Brau, Duke and others
Principal Subsidiaries: Midway Beverage Corporation
Principal Bank: Maryland National Bank
Financial Information:

	$'000
Sales revenues-over	125,000

Principal Shareholders: William H Pflaumer (100%)-privately held
No of Employees: 1,000

SCHOLASTIC INC

730 Broadway, New York, NY 10003
Tel: (212) 505-3000
Telex: TWX 7105812057 scholintl nyk

Chairman: Richard Robinson (and President and Chief Executive Officer); Vice Chairmen: G H McCracken, Joseph W Oliver
Senior Executive Officers: Richard M Spaulding (Executive VP), Richard A Krinsley (Executive VP), Frederic Bischoff (Executive VP Finance and Administration and Chief Financial Officer), David J Walsh (Senior VP International), James Carsley (Senior VP/Professional Relations)

PRINCIPAL ACTIVITIES: Educational publishers; publication of periodicals, software and books
Parent Company: SI Holdings Inc
Principal Subsidiaries: Ashton-Scholastic Pty Ltd (Australia); Scholastic TAB Publications Ltd (Canada); Ashton Scholastic Ltd (New Zealand); Scholastic Publications Ltd (UK)

Principal Shareholders: Privately held company as of July 16 1987
No of Employees: 1,200

SCHONBRUNN, S A, & CO, INC

Grand & Ruby, Palisades Park, NJ 07650
Tel: (201) 943-0600
Telex: WUT 517149 schonbrunn

Chairman: William Ziegler III
President: George M Brunner
Senior Executive Officers: Donald E McNicol (Secretary)

PRINCIPAL ACTIVITIES: Processing of coffee
Principal Bank: Citibank
Financial Information:

	$'000
Sales revenues	100,000

No of Employees: 2,200

SCHRADER (ABE) CORPORATION

530 Seventh Avenue, New York, NY 10018
Tel: (212) 840-7733
Telex: ITT 422122 shrader

Chairman: Abraham Schrader
President: M J Schrader
Senior Executive Officers: Tom Verola (VP)

PRINCIPAL ACTIVITIES: Production of clothing
Financial Information:

	$'000
Sales revenues	60,000

No of Employees: 420

SCHRADER AUTOMOTIVE PRODUCTS DIVISION

566 Mainstream Drive, Box 675, Nashville, TN 37202
Tel: (615) 256 3400

President: J K Nameth
Senior Executive Officers: D R Coker (Director Marketing), G W Edwards (Manager Manufacturing), P B Fox (Comptroller)

PRINCIPAL ACTIVITIES: Production of automotive components and equipment
Parent Company: Arvin Industries Inc
Principal Bank: Third National Bank in Nashville
Financial Information:

	$'000
Sales revenues	90,000

No of Employees: 2,300

SCHRODER, J HENRY, BANK & TRUST CO

One State Street, New York, NY 10015
Tel: (212) 269-6500
Telex: 232376

Chairman of the Board: Alva O Way; Chairman: Peter Rona (and Chief Operating Officer); Vice Chairmen: Takeo Kani, George W Mallinckrodt
Senior Executive Officers: Colin A Browning (Executive VP), Edward G Hamway Jr (Executive VP), Michael O Magdol (Executive VP), Harry J Arnold Jr (Senior VP), Edgar B Howard III (Senior VP), Ernst Luthi (Senior VP), Peter D Maffhy (Senior VP), Charles F Robbins (Senior VP), Frederick D Seeley (Senior VP), Paul Sicari (Senior VP), George R Sievers (Senior VP), Robert M Tomlin (Senior VP), Paul A Wan (Senior VP)

PRINCIPAL ACTIVITIES: Banking
Parent Company: Schroders PLC, London, UK through Schroders Inc; Industrial Bank of Japan Ltd

No of Employees: 700

SCHULMAN, A, INC

3550 W Market Street, Akron, OH 44313
Tel: (216) 666-3751
Telex: 6874422 SCHU AK

Chairman: William C Zekan (and President)
Senior Executive Officers: Robert A Stefanko (VP), Brian R Colbow (Treasurer), Larry A Kushkin (VP), Richard J Enders (VP), Alfred D Veale (VP), James H Berick (Secretary)

PRINCIPAL ACTIVITIES: Manufacturer and merchant of various plastic resins and compounds
Trade Names: Polyfort, Polyblak, Polytrope, Polyvin, Polyflam, Formion, (all Registered Trade Names)
Principal Subsidiaries: A Schulman GmbH; NV A Schulman Plastics SA; A Schulman Canada Ltd; A Schulman SA; A Schulman Inc Ltd; A Schulman AG
Principal Bank: Society National Bank

Financial Information:

	$'000
Sales revenues	318,900

No of Employees: 980

SCHULT HOMES CORPORATION

PO Box 151, Middlebury, IN 46540
Tel: (219) 825-5881

Chairman: Walter O Wells
Senior Executive Officers: John P Guequierre (Senior VP Administration, Chief Financial and Real Estate Officer), Francis M Kennard (Senior VP Marketing), Alan J Behling (VP Eastern Region), Ervin L Bontrager (VP National Sales), Harold M Copsey (VP Manufacturing), James M Gurch (VP Western Region)

PRINCIPAL ACTIVITIES: Manufacture of mobile homes
Principal Bank: St Joseph Valley Bank
Financial Information:

	$'000
Sales revenues	103,000

No of Employees: 900

SCHURZ COMMUNICATIONS, INC

225 W Colfax Avenue, South Bend, IN 46626
Tel: (219) 287-1001

President: Franklin D Schurz Jr (and Treasurer)
Senior Executive Officers: James M Schurz (VP), Scott C Schurz (VP), Mary Schurz (VP and Secretary)

PRINCIPAL ACTIVITIES: The company has interests in the publishing of newspapers; television and radio broadcasting and cable operations
Principal Subsidiaries: Advocate Messenger; Associated Desert Newspapers, Inc; The Herald-Mail Co; The Herald-Times, Inc; South Bend Tribune Corp; Cable TV of Coral Springs, Inc; Antietam Cable TV, Inc; WDBJ-TV, Inc; WSBT, Inc; WAGT-TV, Inc; KY3, Inc
Financial Information:

	$'000
Sales revenues	60,000

No of Employees: 1,100

SCHWARTZ BROTHERS INC

4901 Forbes Boulevard, Lanham, MD 20706
Tel: (301) 459 8000

Chairman: Stuart Schwartz (and Executive VP and Treasurer)
President: James Schwartz
Senior Executive Officers: Melvin C Davis (VP Finance and Advertising and Secretary), Jerome Jacobs (VP Sales)

PRINCIPAL ACTIVITIES: Cassettes, records and videos; computer services
Principal Bank: Maryland National Bank
Financial Information:

	$'000
Sales revenues	40,000

No of Employees: 180

SCHWEIGER INDUSTRIES, INC

116 W Washington Street, Jefferson, WI 53549
Tel: (414) 674-2440
Telex: WUT 265434 schweigerjfer

Chairman: J F Schweiger
Senior Executive Officers: Gerald Hirschhaut (VP Sales), Tom Lucas (VP Manufacturing), Walter Winding (VP Administration), Gary Mayhew (Treasurer), S L Schweiger (Secretary)

PRINCIPAL ACTIVITIES: Production of household furniture
Principal Bank: Marine National Bank
Financial Information:

	$'000
Sales revenues	60,000

No of Employees: 1,500

SCHWINN BICYCLE CO

1856 N Kostner Avenue, Chicago, IL 60639
Tel: (312) 292-2900
Telex: TWX 9102210091 schwinn cgo

Chairman: Frank V Schwinn (and Chief Executive Officer)
President: Edward R Schwinn Jr (and Chief Operating Officer)
Senior Executive Officers: William Austin (Group VP Marketing), John W Barker (VP Finance), Frank Brilando (VP Quality Assurance), Leland V Meader (VP Human Resources)

PRINCIPAL ACTIVITIES: Manufacture of bicycles and components; fitness equipment
Financial Information:

	$'000
Sales revenues	100,000

No of Employees: 450

SCI SYSTEMS, INC

5000 Technology Drive, Huntsville, AL 35805
Tel: (205) 882-4800
Telex: WUT 782421 sci htv

Chairman: Olin B King
President: A E Sapp Jr
Senior Executive Officers: J Sandoval (VP), J Thomas (VP), Bill Hebding (Treasurer), Harvey Harkness (Secretary)

PRINCIPAL ACTIVITIES: Manufacture of electronic equipment for the aerospace industry; electronic control systems for industry
Principal Bank: First Alabama
Financial Information:

	Jun 30 1986 $'000
Sales revenues	470,224
Net income	13,792
Earnings per share	$1.00
Shareholders equity	114,469

No of Employees: 3,000

SCIENCE MANAGEMENT CORPORATION

PO Box 0600, Basking Ridge, NJ 07920
Tel: (201) 647 7000

Chairman: James A Skidmore (and President and Chief Executive Officer)
Senior Executive Officers: Douglas A Davidson (Executive VP), Karl W Dieckmann (Executive VP), Edward J Hughes (Senior VP and Chief Financial Officer), Louis P Healey (VP, Controller and Assistant Secretary), Marion G Hilferty (VP and Secretary)

PRINCIPAL ACTIVITIES: Public relations and management consultancy services in engineering, high technology and computer industries
Principal Subsidiaries: Handy Associates International; Handy Associates Inc; SMC O'Donnell & Associates Inc; SMC Hendrick Inc; SMC Information Systems; SMC International GmbH; SMC Management Technology Inc; SMC Martin Inc; SMC McEver Inc; SMC Personal Support; SMC Wofac Inc; SMC Publications Marketing Group Inc; SMC Real Time Systems Inc
Principal Bank: National State Bank

Financial Information:

	1986 $'000
Sales revenues	69,149
Income before taxes	1,858
Net income	988
Dividends per share	$0.10
Earnings per share	$0.38
Common stock	319
Retained income	5,708
Shareholders equity	17,341

No of Employees: 850

SCIENTIFIC AMERICAN INC

415 Madison Avenue, New York, NY 10017
Tel: (212) 754-0550
Cable: SCIAMER NY
Telex: RCA 236115
Answerback: scan ur

Chairman: Gerard Piel
President: Dieter Von Holtzbrinck
Senior Executive Officers: Vincent Barger (VP and Treasurer), Harry Myers (Senior VP and Publisher), Claus Finchow (Executive VP), Linda Chaput (President-WH Freeman), Jonathen Piel (VP-Editor)

PRINCIPAL ACTIVITIES: Publishing of periodicals and academic books
Trade Names: Scientific American, W H Freeman, Scientific American Medicine
Parent Company: Georg Von Holtzbrinck GmbH
Principal Subsidiaries: W H Freeman & Company; Seam GmbH
Principal Banks: The Bank of New York; The Morgan Bank
Financial Information:

	Jun 30 1987 $'000
Sales revenues	56,000

No of Employees: 250

SCIENTIFIC LEASING INC

292 Colt Highway, Farmington, CT 06032
Tel: (203) 677 8700

Chairman: Robert A Bernhard (and Chief Executive Officer)
President: W Barry Tanner (and Chief Operating Officer)
Senior Executive Officers: Vincent T Jazwinski (Senior VP and Divisional Manager), Bryan K Hausman (VP Administration and Treasurer), Pierre D Lorio (VP National Accounts), Robert P Medwin (VP Finance), David J Spiegel (VP, Secretary and General Counsel), Mitchell D Weiss (VP National Sales)

PRINCIPAL ACTIVITIES: Leasing services for high-tec capital equipment
Principal Bank: Connecticut Bank and Trust Co NA
Financial Information:

	$'000
Sales revenues	37,750

No of Employees: 100

SCIENTIFIC MICRO SYSTEMS INC

339 North Bernado Avenue, Mountain View, CA 94043
Tel: (415) 964 5700

President: Charles A Mathews (and Chief Executive Officer)
Senior Executive Officers: D L Auclair (VP, OMTI Division), R A Forsyth (VP Operations), John Henry (VP Advance Development), Michael A Liccardo (VP and Divisional Manager), H Reusser (VP Sales)

PRINCIPAL ACTIVITIES: Manufacture of microcomputer equipment
Principal Subsidiaries: OMT Inc
Financial Information:

	$'000
Sales revenues	39,500

No of Employees: 310

SCIENTIFIC-ATLANTA, INC

One Technology Pkwy, Box 105600, Atlanta, GA 30348
Tel: (404) 441-4000
Telex: 4611081 SCIATLA-DORA
Telefax: (404) 441-4617

Chairman: Sidney Topol; Chief Executive Officer: William E Johnson
President: John H Levergood (and Chief Operating Officer)
Senior Executive Officers: Raymond M Hartnett (Senior VP Finance), Jules E Kadish (VP), H A Ecker (VP), William S Brown (VP), Sezer M Soylemez (VP Information Management), David A Eggers (VP and General Counsel), Julian W Eidson (VP and Controller), James A Hart (VP), Leo Ramsauer (VP)

PRINCIPAL ACTIVITIES: Worldwide manufacturer of communications products, defense systems and test instruments for industrial, telecommunications and government applications
Principal Subsidiaries: Scientific-Atlanta (UK) Ltd; Scientific-Atlanta (France) SA; Scientific-Atlanta GmbH (Germany); Scientific-Atlanta SpA (Italy); Scientific-Atlanta Pty, Ltd (Australia); Digital Video Systems (Canada)
Principal Bank: The C & S National Bank
Financial Information:

	Jun 30 1986 $'000	Jun 30 1987 $'000
Sales revenues	469,124	495,346
Income (loss) before taxes	(15,614)	48,250
Net income (loss)	(9,212)	24,260
Dividends	2,792	2,811
Dividends per share	$0.12	$0.12
Earnings(loss) per share	($0.39)	$1.04
Common stock	23,222	23,449
Retained income	62,774	82,835
Shareholders equity	179,863	201,603

No of Employees: 3,500

SCM CORPORATION

299 Park Avenue, New York, NY 10171
Tel: (212) 752-2700
Telex: RCA 224082 scm ur

Chairman: Paul H Elicker (and President)
Senior Executive Officers: George E Hall (Senior VP) Administration), Gerard F Stoddard (VP Corporate Communications)

PRINCIPAL ACTIVITIES: Manufacture of pulp and paper, typewriters, chemicals, resins and coatings, telecommunications equipment, groceries
Principal Bank: Manufacturers Hanover Trust Co
Financial Information:

	$'000
Sales revenues	2,175,000

No of Employees: 20,000

SCM GLIDCO ORGANICS

PO Box 389, Jacksonville, FL 32201
Tel: (904) 768-5800
Telex: 441763 SCM GLIDCO JAX

President: George W Robbins
Senior Executive Officers: Ralph E Close (VP Aromas and Flavors)

PRINCIPAL ACTIVITIES: Manufacture of special-purpose chemicals; plastics
Trade Names: GLIDCO

Parent Company: Hanson Trust PLC, UK
Financial Information:

	$'000
Sales revenues	120,000

No of Employees: 20

SCOA INDUSTRIES

15 Dan Rd, Canton, MA 02021
Tel: (617) 821-1000

Chairman: Herbert H Goldberger; Vice Chairman: George R Friese
President: Stephen A Goldberger (and Chief Operating Officer)
Senior Executive Officers: Raymond Brinkman (VP), John C Brouillard (VP Finance), Stephen A Feldman (VP and Controller), William K Friend (VP and Secretary), Eugene O'Donnell (VP), John G Reen (VP and Controller), Andrew J Samuto (VP Human Resources), Larry Voelker (VP Finance and Treasurer)

PRINCIPAL ACTIVITIES: Retailing; department stores and footwear stores
Parent Company: THL Holdings Inc
Principal Bank: Bankers Trust Company
Financial Information:

	$'000
Sales Revenues	1,480,000

No of Employees: 20,000

SCOT FORGE CO

PO Box 8, Spring Grove, IL 60081
Tel: (312) 587-1000
Telex: 754283 SCOT UD

Chairman: Peter I Georgeson
President: James F McKinley
Senior Executive Officers: Tom Cooper (VP Treasurer)

PRINCIPAL ACTIVITIES: Forged steel products; heat treatment of metals
Principal Bank: La Salle National Bank
Financial Information:

	$'000
Sales revenues	50,000

No of Employees: 185

SCOTT & FETZER COMPANY

28800 Clemens Road, Westlake, OH 44145
Tel: (216) 892-3000
Telex: TWX 810 4218128 scottfetz wlke

Chairman: Ralph Schey (and President and Chief Executive Officer)
President: Kenneth J Semelsberger (and Chief Operating Officer)
Senior Executive Officers: J F Bradley (VP), John Bebbington (VP), Walter A Rajki (Senior VP), Kearney K Kier (VP), K D Hughes (VP), William W Stephans (VP and Treasurer), R C Weber (VP and Secretary)

PRINCIPAL ACTIVITIES: Manufacture of domestic vacuum cleaners; educational and information systems; automobile components
Parent Company: Berkshire Hathaway Inc
Principal Subsidiaries: SFZ International Inc; World Book Inc; Scott & Fetzer Canada Ltd; Scott & Fetzer International Co; Melben Products Company Inc; World Book Finance Inc; Scott Fetzer Financial Service Company; The Kirby Sales Co Inc; SFZ Transportation Inc; United Consumer Financial Services Co; United Acceptance Ltd; Scott & Fetzer Financial Services of Canada Inc
Principal Bank: National Citibank
Financial Information:

	$'000
Sales revenues	695,000

No of Employees: 17,000

SCOTT, O M, & SONS COMPANY

14111 Scottslawn Road, Marysville, OH 43041
Tel: (513) 644-0011
Telex: WUT 245300 scotts mrvl

President: Tadd C Seitz (and Chief Executive Officer)
Senior Executive Officers: John E Cleveland (VP), Bernard R Ford (VP), E Peter Griffin (VP), Richard B Stahl (VP), Robert A Stern (VP), Paul D Yeager (VP)

PRINCIPAL ACTIVITIES: Manufacture of agricultural and horticultural supplies and equipment including fertilizers, seeds and farming machinery
Parent Company: ITT Corporation, New York, NY
Financial Information:

	$'000
Sales revenues	120,000

No of Employees: 900

SCOTT PAPER COMPANY

Scott Plaza, Philadelphia, PA 19113
Tel: (215) 522-5000
Telex: TWX 9103800420 scottpaper

Chairman: Philip E Lippincott (and Chief Executive Officer)
Senior Executive Officers: J R Leaman Jr (Executive VP), Robert E McAvoy (Executive VP), William H Nelson III (Executive VP), J L Shane (Executive VP), William S Wesson (Executive VP), Ashok N Bakhru (Senior VP and Chief Financial Officer), Norman M Heisman (Senior VP and General Counsel)

PRINCIPAL ACTIVITIES: Manufacture of pulp, paper and paper products including consumer and commercial non-wovens, specialty and publishing papers; interests in lumber and logs
Principal Subsidiaries: (100% owned unless stated): Scott Paper International Inc; Scott Timber Co; Hoffmaster Co, Inc; Escuhbia Oil Co; Skylark Inc; Sani-Fresh International Inc; Three Rivers Timber Co; Brunswick Pulp & Paper Co (50%); Brunswick Pulp Land Co (50%); Mountain Tree Farm Co (50%); Riscott Insurance Ltd; Owikeno Lake Timber Company; Cape Chignecto Lands Ltd; Scott Maritimes Ltd; Scott Finance Liberia Ltd; Canso Chemicals Ltd (33.3%); Celulosa Jujuy SA (33.3%) (Argentina); Bowater Scott Corp of Autralia Ltd (50%); Scott Continental (Belgium); COPA-Companhia de Papeis (49%) (Brazil); Scott Paper Ltd (50%) (Canada); Scott Paper Co de Costa Rica SA (50%); Bouton Brochard Scott SA (France); Scott Paper GmbH Nonwovens (Germany); Scott SpA (Italy); Sanyo Scott Co Ltd (50%) (Japan); Ssangyong Paper Co Ltd (34%) (Korea); Scott Paper (Malaysia) Sdn Bhd (50%); Compania Industrial de San Cristobel SA (48.8%) (Mexico); Scott Paper (Singapore) Pte Ltd (50%); Gureola-Scott SA (93%) (Spain); Productos Sanitarios e Higienicos Sancel SA (93%) (Spain); Taiwan Scott Paper Corp (66.7%) (Taiwan); Thai-Scott Paper Co Ltd (50%) (Thailand); Bowater Scott Corp Ltd (50%) (UK); Scott Graphics International (Belgium); Fiscott VI Ltd (Virgin Islands); Excell Paper Sales Co
Financial Information:

	Dec 31 1985	Dec 31 1986
	$'000	$'000
Sales revenues	3,049,000	3,437,000
Net income	201,100	186,500
Earnings per share	$4.52	$4.96
Retained income	1,282,400	1,359,300

No of Employees: 22,200 (Group); 16,500 (Affiliated Cos)

SCOTTY'S INC
5300 Recker Highway, Winter Haven, FL 33880
Tel: (813) 299 1111

Chairman: James W Sweet (and Chief Executive Officer); Vice Chairman: Ray H Cooney (and Chief Operating Officer)
President: Dennis W Stults
Senior Executive Officers: Harold W Taylor (Senior VP, Chief Financial Officer and Secretary), David J Bryant (VP and General Manager Sales Promotion), Robert G Cawein (VP and Director Transportation), James A Church (VP Management Information Systems), Richard D Clark (VP Real Estate), Thomas B Cook (VP and Regional General Manager), David Fender (VP), Kevin E Fitzgerald (VP and Director Purchasing), James E Howe (VP Employee Relations), Dan W Maffett (VP and General Manager Sales), Richard W Martineau (VP, Treasurer, Chief Accounting Officer and Controller), William J Sauder (VP Manufacturing), Orbin Sexon (VP), Hugh Tuttle (VP and Regional General Manager)

PRINCIPAL ACTIVITIES: Retail supply of lumber and building materials, home hardware and hand tools
Principal Bank: First National Bank of Florida
Financial Information:

	$'000
Sales revenues	453,400

No of Employees: 5,355

SCOVILL INC
1600 Summer St., Stamford, CT 06904
Tel: (203) 352 8500

Chairman: Richard E Bennett (and President and Chief Executive Officer)
Senior Executive Officers: Frederick F Schauder (Executive VP Finance, Treasurer, Controller and Chief Financial Officer), Sang C Lee (Senior VP Business Development and Operations), Dennis C J Grabham (VP and General Manager, International Yale Security Group), Stewart S Hudnut (VP, General Counsel and Secretary), J W Moore (VP Employee Relations), John J Flaherty (President Hamilton Beach Division), Roger W Hall (President Apparel Fastener Division), Patrick J McCord (President Yale Security Inc), James A Rankin (President NuTone Inc)

PRINCIPAL ACTIVITIES: Manufacture of household hardware products, plumbing hardware and bathroom accessories, domestic electrical appliances, fasteners for clothing, security equipment and automotive components
Parent Company: First City Industries Inc
Principal Subsidiaries: (100% owned unless stated): Scovill Mexicana SA de CV (57%) (Mexico); Cierres Ideal de Mexico SA (57%) (Mexico); Scovill UK Ltd; Schrader Bellows Ltd; Schrader Automotive Ltd; Yale Security Products Ltd; Whitecroft-Scovill Ltd; Zincast Ltd (UK); Schrader-Scovill Co Proprietary Ltd (Australia); Scovill Australia Pty Ltd; Scovill Industries Ltd (Canada); Schrader Bellows SpA (Italy); Yale Security Products SpA (Italy); Schrader SA (France); Schrader Bellows Ltd (Japan); Valvulas Schrader do Brasil SA (99.6%) (Brazil); AB FAS Lasfabrik (Sweden); NuTone International Corporation; NuTone Intercontinental Corp; Scovill Industries of Puerto Rico Inc
Principal Bank: Morgan Guaranty Trust Co of New York
Financial Information:

	$'000
Sales revenues	561,650

No of Employees: 10,000

SCRIPPS, E W, COMPANY INC
1100 Central Trust Tower, Cincinnati, OH 45202
Tel: (513) 977 3000

President: Charles E Scripps
Senior Executive Officers: Daniel A Castillini (VP Finance), E John Wolfzoin (Treasurer)

PRINCIPAL ACTIVITIES: Radio and television broadcasting; publication of newspapers
Principal Subsidiaries: Allied Newspapers Inc; Berkley Small Inc; Cordovan Corporation; Courier Company; Dataway Inc; Denver Publishing Company; Evansville Press Company; George R Hall Inc; Hall Systems Inc; Herald Post Publishing Company Inc; Memphis Publishing Company; New Mexico State Tribune Company; Newspaper Enterprise Association; Pittsburgh Press Company; Scripps-Howard Broadcasting Company; Scripps-Howard Supply Company; Stuart News Company Inc; Southern California Publishing Company; Standard Publishing Company Inc; Sun Tattler Company Inc; United Features Syndicate Inc; TV Data Inc; TV Watch Inc

No of Employees: 8,500

SCRIPPS HOWARD BROADCASTING CO
1100 Central Trust Tower, Cincinnati, OH 45202
Tel: (513) 977-3000

Chairman: Jack R Howard
President: Donald L Perris (and Chief Executive Officer)
Senior Executive Officers: Daniel J Castellini (Senior VP Finance and Administration), William R Burleigh (Senior VP)

PRINCIPAL ACTIVITIES: Broadcasting services including radio, television and cable
Parent Company: E W Scripps Co
Financial Information:

	$'000
Sales Revenues	211,000

No of Employees: 950

SCRIVNER, INC
1101 SE 59th St, Oklahoma City, OK 73129
Tel: (405) 6670-4571

Chairman: Jerry D Metcalf (and Chief Executive Officer)
President: D Clark Ogle (and Chief Operating Officer)
Senior Executive Officers: James Demmle (Senior VP), Burt P Flickinger Jr (Senior VP), William T Bishop (Senior VP), Larry W Kordisch (VP Finance and Treasurer)

PRINCIPAL ACTIVITIES: Wholesale and retail trade in food
Parent Company: Haniel Corp
Financial Information:

	$'000
Sales Revenues	2,170,000

No of Employees: 5,000

SCT YARNS
18th & Watkins Streets, Chattanooga, TN 37401
Tel: (615) 622-3131
Telex: TWX 810 5735 225 sct cta

Chairman: J W Thatcher
President: J Don Trotter
Senior Executive Officers: J E Moore (VP), D H Gunther (VP), David D Groves (Secretary and Treasurer)

PRINCIPAL ACTIVITIES: Industrial thread and yarn manufacturing
Principal Bank: First Tennesse Bank

Principal Shareholders: J E Moore; J D Trotter; D H Gunther
No of Employees: 2,000

SEA GALLEY STORES INC
6920-220th South West Mountlake Terrace, WA 98043
Tel: (206) 775 0411

Chairman: Steven B Dowen (and President and Chief Executive Officer)
Senior Executive Officers: Brian R Cook (Senior VP Corporate Development), Lawrence A Crowe (VP and Treasurer), Keith C Huetson (VP and Chief Accounting Officer), Ronald R Jackman (VP, Chief Financial Officer and Secretary), David A

Mahnke (VP and Director Operations), Suzanne M Scharz (VP Human Resources and Personnel), Kendall A Wilson (VP Marketing)

PRINCIPAL ACTIVITIES: Restaurants

Principal Bank: First Interstate Bank of Washington

Financial Information:

	$'000
Sales revenues	61,400

No of Employees: 2,300

SEABOARD CORPORATION

200 Boylston Street, Newton, MA 02167

Tel: (617) 332-8492

President: H H Bresky (and Chief Executive Officer)

Senior Executive Officers: Richard G Myers (Executive VP and Treasurer), Otto Bresky Jr (Senior VP), Jack Miller (VP), Donald Robohm (VP)

PRINCIPAL ACTIVITIES: Milling and wholesale distribution of flour, animal feedstuffs; grain storage

Parent Company: Seaboard Flour Corporation, Newton, MA

Principal Subsidiaries: Holsun Bakers of Puerto Rico; Seaboard Bakeries Inc; Seaboard Marine Ltd; Life Flour Mill Ltd; Delta Packaging Co Ltd; Seaboard Sales Corp; Western Coat Pad Co; Cape Fear Railways Inc; Seaboard Farms of Athens Inc; Seaboard Farms of Canton Inc; Seaboard Farms of Chattanooga Inc; Seaboard Overseas Ltd; Desarrollo Industrial Bioacutico SA; Miller Grain Co; Seaboard Trading Corp; Seaboard Export Corp; Penny Curtiss Baking Co Inc

Financial Information:

	$'000
Sales revenues	353,220

No of Employees: 2,500

SEACO INC

1155 Avenue of the Americas, New York, NY 10036

Tel: (212) 302 5055

President: James B Sherwood

Senior Executive Officers: Daniel J Sullivan (Senior VP Finance and Treasurer), Erik P Woit (Senior VP), David G Benson (VP Tourist Trains and Ferries), Edwin S Hetherington (Legal Counsel and Secretary), Kenneth N Hume (VP Ships), Nicholas J Novasic (VP Funding)

PRINCIPAL ACTIVITIES: Management of hotels and tourist facilities including travel agency and luxury train services; property development

Principal Bank: First National Bank of Boston

Financial Information:

	$'000
Sales revenues	51,860

No of Employees: 860

SEAFIRST MORTGAGE CORPORATION

Columbia Seafirst Center, Seattle, WA 98104

Tel: (206) 442-3550

Chairman: William R Jennings

President: William D Pettit Jr

Senior Executive Officers: Georgene Lee (Executive VP), James L Kirschbaum (Executive VP), Reah De Priest (Senior VP), Jerry Melton (Senior VP), Diane Ingram (Senior VP)

PRINCIPAL ACTIVITIES: Property finance-mortgage banking

Parent Company: Seattle-First National Bank, Seattle, WA

Principal Subsidiaries: Seafirst Capital Corporation

Principal Bank: Seattle-First National Bank

Financial Information:

	Dec 31 1985 $'000
Revenues	45,162
Income before taxes	9,167
Net income	4,950
Retained income	34,391
Shareholders equity	38,042
Total assets	548,290

Principal Shareholders: Seafirst Bank

No of Employees: 478

SEAGATE TECHNOLOGY

920 Disc Drive, Scotts Valley, CA 95066

Tel: (408) 438-6550

Telex: WUT 592527 seagate tech

President: David T Michell (and Chief Operations Officer)

Senior Executive Officers: Alan F Shugart (Chief Executive Officer), Douglas K Mahon (Senior VP and Chief Technical Officer), Donald L Waite (Senior VP and Chief Financial Officer), Sing C Tien (Senior VP Far East Operations), James H Bensen (VP Facilities), Joe Chen (VP Engineering Far East Operations), Sanjoy Ghose (VP), James O Jacques (VP Engineering), Thomas Maher (VP Manufacturing), Robert Martell (VP Sales), Anthony L Perlick (VP Engineering), Robert A Sandie (VP Corporate Materials), Fred Schudel (VP Marketing), Ronald D Verdoorn (VP Far East Operations)

PRINCIPAL ACTIVITIES: Manufacture of Winchester disc drives for computers

Principal Bank: Bank of America NT & SA

Financial Information:

	$'000
Sales revenues	460,000

No of Employees: 3,000

SEAGRAM, JOSEPH E, & SONS, INC

375 Park Avenue, New York, NY 10152

Tel: (212) 572-7000

Chairman: David G Sacks (and Chief Operating Officer)

Senior Executive Officers: Richard Karl Goeltz (Executive VP and Chief Financial Officer), Charles M Andolsek (VP), Arthur S Margolin (VP and Assistant to Chairman), Daniel R Paladino (VP, Secretary and General Counsel), Hannah S Sistare (VP Public Policy), Thomas Trainer (VP Management Information Systems)

PRINCIPAL ACTIVITIES: Production of wines and spirits

Parent Company: The Seagram Company Ltd, Canada

Principal Bank: Manufacturers Hanover Trust Co

Financial Information:

	Jan 31 1986 $'000
Revenues excl.tax	1,809,608
Net income	246,958
Shareholders equity	3,377,952

No of Employees: 10,900

SEAGULL ENERGY CORPORATION

1001 Fannin-Suite 1700, Houston, TX 77002

Tel: (713) 951-4700

Chairman: Barry J Galt (and President and Chief Executive Officer)

Senior Executive Officers: Dale Teel (President ENSTAR Natural Gas Company), John N Goodpasture (VP Marketing and Supply), Harold A Kergosien (VP Engineering and Operations), Joe T Rye (VP, Finance and Administration), G Thomas Wilkinson (VP, Exploration and Production), James M Booth (Treasurer), B Eugene Brown Jr (Controller) Sylvia Sanchez (Secretary)

PRINCIPAL ACTIVITIES: Distribution of natural gas and by-products; oil and gas exploration and production
Principal Bank: First Republic Bank, Houston, N.A.
Financial Information:

	Dec 31 1985	Dec 31 1986
	$'000	$'000
Sales revenues	98,222	176,971
Income (loss) before taxes	9,117	(1,436)
Net income (loss)	7,347	(2,189)
Earnings (loss) per share	$1.16	($0.34)
Common stock	639	642
Retained income	48,334	46,145
Shareholders equity	79,092	101,012

No of Employees: 350

SEA-LAND CORPORATION

10 Parsonage Rd, Edison, NJ 08837
Tel: (201) 632-2000
Telex: WUT 844432 sealand mepl

Chairman: Joseph F Abely (and Chief Executive Officer)
Senior Executive Officers: Jackson A Baker (Executive VP Operations), Jack A Drobnick (Senior VP Transport Systems), Robert J Fahey (Senior VP Planning and Development), Peter M Klein (Senior VP, General Counsel and Secretary), David J Tolan (Senior VP Labor Relations), George I Clover (VP Administration), Phillip C England (VP Tax), Peter J Finnerty (VP Public Affairs), Frank R Power (VP Corporate Planning), Richard H Sanger Jr (VP and Treasurer)

PRINCIPAL ACTIVITIES: Shipping transportation services
Principal Bank: BankAmerica International
Financial Information:

	$'000
Sales revenues	1,634,183

No of Employees: 9,000

SEALASKA CORPORATION

1 Sealaska Plaza, Juneau, AK 99801
Tel: (907) 586-1512
Telefax: (907) 463-4849

Chairman: Marlene A Johnson; Vice Chairman: Raymond Q Demmert; Chief Executive Officer: Byron I Mallott
President: William M Howe (and Chief Operating Officer)
Senior Executive Officers: William F Strafford (VP Finance and Treasurer), Robert W Loescher (Senior VP, Resource Management), Chris E McNeil (Senior VP and General Counsel), Robert Martin Jr (VP Administration), Richard P Harris (VP, Resource Planning and Administration), Maxine H Richert (Corporate Secretary)

PRINCIPAL ACTIVITIES: Holding company with interests in forestry, building materials including concrete products and ready-mixed concrete, fishing and fish processing
Principal Subsidiaries: Ocean Beauty Seafoods Inc; Alaska Aggregate Corporation; Sealaska Timber Corporation
Principal Bank: Bank of Tokyo
Financial Information:

	Mar 31 1986	Mar 31 1987
	$'000	$'000
Sales revenues	237,171	234,881
Income before taxes	256	23,960
Net income	256	23,960
Dividends	-	6,000
Dividends per share	-	$4.00
Earnings per share	$0.16	$15.18
Common stock	93,162	93,162
Retained income (deficit)	(20,760)	44
Shareholders equity	72,402	93,206

No of Employees: 1,250

SEALED AIR CORPORATION

Park 80 Plaza E, Saddle Brook, NJ 07662
Tel: (201) 791-7600
Telex: RCA 219719 sasb ur

President: T J Dunphy
Senior Executive Officers: Alfred W Fielding (Executive VP), Merle C Brown (Senior VP), Larry C Chandler (Senior VP), Elmer N Funkhouser III (Senior VP), George S Shegog Jr (Senior VP Finance), Donald R McGregor (VP Development), James F Lyons (VP), Jerry L Barnes (VP)

PRINCIPAL ACTIVITIES: Manufacture of plastic packaging and protective products
Principal Subsidiaries: Sealed Air of Canada Ltd; Seal Air BV; Sealed Air GmbH (Germany); Sibco SA; Sealed Air (Singapore) Pte Ltd; Sealed Air Ltd; Instapak (Italia) Srl; Plastic Iberica SA; Instapak Ltd (Japan) Instapak Ltd (Taiwan); Instapak (Far East) Ltd (Hong Kong); Seomyung Enterprises Co Ltd; Aire Sellado SA; Protective Packaging Pty Ltd; Cellu-Products Co; Static Inc
Principal Bank: United Jersey Bank
Financial Information:

	$'000
Sales revenues	183,220

No of Employees: 1,500

SEALED POWER CORPORATION

100 Terrace Plaza, Muskegon, MI 49443
Tel: (616) 724-5011
Telex: WUT 228464 seal pwr msk

Chairman: Robert D Tuttle (and Chief Executive Officer)
President: Dale A Johnson
Senior Executive Officers: Curtis T Atkinson (Group VP Power Products), Peter M Turner) Group VP General Products), Robert A Bishop (Group VP Kent-Moore), R B Werner (VP and Chief Financial Officer), Donald H Johnson (VP and Treasurer), A D Joseph (VP Research and Development), John M Day (VP Corporate Planning), James M Sheridan (VP and Secretary), Robert Hoffmeister (VP Technology)

PRINCIPAL ACTIVITIES: Sealed Power Corporation is a major manufacturer and worldwide distributor of a broad range of high quality, precision engineered parts and components for both the original equipment and replacement transportation industries, with a leadership position in the special service tool and equipment sector, and a growing presence in a number of industrial product markets. engineering
Principal Subsidiaries: Sealed Power Corp of Canada Ltd (40%); Sealed Power de Mexico SA (40%); Cia Americana-Mexicana SA (40%); Kent Moore Corp; Owatonna Tool Co; Truth Inc; Tri-Mark Corp; Twin Tool Inc; Kent-Moore Europe; Kent-Moore UK; Kent-Moore Germany; Kent-Moore Spain; Kent-Moore Australia; Kent-Moore Japan (50%); Kent-Moore Brazil (49%)
Principal Bank: Savings Bank of New York
Financial Information:

	Dec 31 1985	Dec 31 1986
	$'000	$'000
Sales revenues	624,546	665,807
Income before taxes	50,250	50,100
Net income	29,900	28,500
Dividends	12,246	12,884
Dividends per share	$1.00	$1.05
Earnings per share*	$2.44	$2.32
Common stock	122,515	122,783
Retained income	141,403	157,015
Shareholders equity	255,542	272,893

*primary

No of Employees: 7,025

SEAMEN'S CORPORATION

2777 Stemmons Frwy, Dallas, TX 75207
Tel: (214) 689-4280

Chairman: R T Enloe III; Vice Chairman: E V Conway
President: R K Utley III (and Chief Executive Officer)
Senior Executive Officers: M K Shaughnessy (Treasurer), Joan E Bennie (Secretary)

PRINCIPAL ACTIVITIES: Savings bank
Principal Subsidiaries: Seamen's Bank for Savings FSB
Financial Information:

	Dec 31 1986
	$'000
Net income	26,757
Earnings per share	$1.89
Shareholders equity	85,785
Deposits	2,418,300
Total assets	3,315,777

No of Employees: 458

SEARS, ROEBUCK & CO
Sears Tower, Chicago, IL 60684
Tel: (312) 875-2500
Telex: WUT 25211 seroco cgo

Chairman: Edward A Brennan (and Chief Executive Officer)
President: Richard M Jones (and Chief Financial Officer)
Senior Executive Officers: Henry D Sunderland (Senior VP, Corporate Administration), Randolf H Aires (VP, Governmental Affairs), Robert F Gurnee (VP and Corporate Treasurer), Charles W Harper (VP and Secretary), Philip M Knox Jr (VP and Corporate General Counsel), David P Norum (VP, Corporate Taxes), Charles J Ruder (VP, Corporate Public Affairs), William E Sanders (VP Corporate Personnel and Employee Relations), Allan B Stewart (VP, Corporate Planning), John S Vivian (VP and Corporate Comptroller)

PRINCIPAL ACTIVITIES: Retailers; investments, insurance, real estate and world trade
Principal Subsidiaries: Allstate; Coldwell Banker; Dean Witter
Financial Information:

	Dec 31 1985	Dec 31 1986
	$'000	$'000
Sales revenues	40,715,300	44,281,500
Net income	1,303,300	1,351,300
Earnings per share	$3.53	$3.62
Shareholders equity	11,793,600	13,046,600

No of Employees: 466,000

SEARS ROEBUCK ACCEPTANCE CORPORATION
One Customs House Square, Wilmington, DE 19899
Tel: (302) 656-9971

Chairman: Robert F Gurnee
President: Albert W James Jr
Senior Executive Officers: L T Pease Jr (Senior VP Finance), W T Cashman II (Senior VP Marketing), P M Schofield (VP and Treasurer), George F Slook (VP and Comptroller), Robert T Coyle (VP Data Processing)

PRINCIPAL ACTIVITIES: Financial services including short term business credit
Parent Company: Sears Roebuck & Co, Chicago, IL
Financial Information:

	$'000
Revenues	96,000

No of Employees: 40

SEASON-ALL INDUSTRIES, INC
Wayne Avenue, Indiana, PA 15701
Tel: (412) 349-4600
Telex: TWX 510 468 4909

President: F R Gorell
Senior Executive Officers: Roger W Barwick (VP Finance, Secretary and Treasurer), Wayne C Gorell (VP)

PRINCIPAL ACTIVITIES: Manufacture of doors and windows

Principal Bank: Mellon Bank NA
Financial Information:

	$'000
Sales revenues	65,000

No of Employees: 700

SEATTLE-FIRST NATIONAL BANK
PO Box 3977, Seattle, WA 98124
Tel: (206) 585-3131
Telex: 320249

Chairman: Richard P Cooley; Vice Chairman Administration Group: Alwyn Nelson
Senior Executive Officers: William D Pettit Jr (Executive VP and Manager Real Estate and Financial Group), Luke Helms (Executive VP and Manager World Banking Group), Roy Henderson (Executive VP and Manager Northwest Banking), Louis Mertes (Executive VP and Manager Operations Group), Richard Puz (Executive VP and Chief Credit Officer), James R Anderson (Senior VP National Division), Dorothy Bjorklund (Senior VP and Manager Management Services), Robert Burson (Senior VP and Manager Dealer Banking Division), Reah Defriest (Senior VP and Manager Real Estate Services), Brian J Ducey (Senior VP Credit Administration/World Banking), David Friedenberg (Senior VP and Manager Northwest National Accounts), Richard Fulp (Senior VP and Manager Trust Division), Josef E Gray (Senior VP and Manager Personal Banking Division), John C Herber (Senior VP and Manager Corporate Banking Division), James Per Lee (Senior VP and Manager Loan Services), F Bentley Lovejoy (Senior VP and Manager Business Banking Division), Jerry Melton (Senior VP and Manager Special Credit), Clark Mock (Senior VP, Chairman Senior Credit Committee), James R Monger (Senior VP and Manager Energy), Robert Rudder (Senior VP and Manager EDP Operations), Elaine Scherba (Senior VP and Manager Financial Planning and Reporting), John F Sheeran (Senior VP and Manager EDP Systems), Earl N Shulman (Senior VP and Manager Personnel), Dean J Torkelson (Senior VP and Manager Capital Markets), Len R Williamson (Senior VP Credit Administration), Randy C James (Senior VP Corporate Affairs)

PRINCIPAL ACTIVITIES: Banking services
Parent Company: Seafirst Corporation
Principal Subsidiaries: Seafirst Mortgage Co; Seattle First International Bank; Seattle-First International Corp

No of Employees: 8,600

SEAWAY FOOD TOWN INC
1020 Ford Street, Maumee, OH 43537
Tel: (419) 893 9401

President: Wallace D Iott
Senior Executive Officers: David J Walrod (Senior VP Operations), Waldo E Yeager (Senior VP Finance), Marvin S Damrauer (VP Produce Operations), John Gensler (VP Purchasing), Richard Iott (VP Marketing), William V Puckett (VP Wholesale and Transport), Donald E Spalding (VP Meat Operations), John Wines (VP Employee Relations)

PRINCIPAL ACTIVITIES: Supermarkets
Principal Subsidiaries: Grubers Food Town Inc; Northern Distributing Company; Tracy & Avery Food Town Inc; VF Inc
Principal Bank: First National Bank
Financial Information:

	$'000
Sales revenues	431,000

No of Employees: 3,345

SECOND NATIONAL FEDERAL SAVINGS BANK
PO Box 2558, Rt 50 & Phillip Morris Dr, Salisbury, MD 21801
Tel: (301) 749-8415
Telefax: (301) 548-2566

Chairman: Eugene F Ford Sr

President: Henry A Berliner Jr (and Chief Executive Officer)

Senior Executive Officers: William F Brooks Jr (Executive VP and Chief Operating Officer), Marion J Minker Jr (Executive VP Mortgage), Dennis F Davies (Senior VP Administration), Richard L Brake (Senior VP Accounting and Controller), Eric W Edstrom (Senior VP Branches), William T Hill (Senior VP Banking), William T Russell III (Senior VP and Treasurer), Gage Thomas (VP Residental Lending), Edward W Hynes (VP Administrative Services), Tracy T Morris (VP Human Resources), Bruce D Kimball (VP Management Information), Walton W Sanderson (Subsidiary Officer), Patricia A Gleason (Secretary), Ronald G Rayne (Legal Counsel)

PRINCIPAL ACTIVITIES: Provision of mortgage and loan facilities; savings and investment products

Principal Subsidiaries: Second National Service Corporation; Second National Insurance Corporation

Principal Bank: Signet Bank/Maryland

Financial Information:

	Sep 30 1987
	$'000
Revenues	59,552
Income before taxes	10,857
Net income	6,921
Dividends	1,497
Dividends per share	$0.21
Earnings per share	$0.97
Common stock	7,131
Retained income	17,775
Shareholders equity	35,232
Deposits	80,611
Total assets	829,270

No of Employees: 330

SECURITY BANCORP INC MICHIGAN

Security Circle, 16333 Trenton Road, Southgate, MI 48195

Tel: (313) 281 5000

Chairman: Douglas A Hayes (and Subsidiary Officer)

President: Lowell L Peacock (and Chief Executive Officer and Subsidiary Officer)

Senior Executive Officers: Philip D Caruso (Executive VP), Thomas R Stewart (Executive VP and Secretary), Robert A Welch (Senior VP and Treasurer), Carlton C Caza (VP Audit), Donald E Cooper (VP Marketing), Francis L Giuliani (VP Investment), James B Herzog (VP Affiliated Banks), Jerry D Ohlrich (VP Corporate Planning), Allen L Strang (VP and Legal Counsel)

PRINCIPAL ACTIVITIES: Holding company with interests in banking

Principal Subsidiaries: Securedata Corporation; Security Bank; Security Bank and Trust Company; Security Bank Oakland County; Security Realcorp Inc; United Bankers Life Insurance Company

Principal Bank: Security Bank and Trust Company

Financial Information:

	Dec 31 1985
	$'000
Revenues	177,880
Net income	12,910

No of Employees: 2,020

SECURITY CAPITAL CORPORATION

1290 Avenue of the Americas, New York, NY 10104

Tel: (212) 408-2900

Chairman: Melville Chapin; Vice Chairman: John M O'Mara

President: Thomas J Gochberg

Senior Executive Officers: William T Bozarth (Senior VP), Joseph P King (Senior VP Finance), Gary Wolf (1st VP), Gary J Yannazzo (1st VP)

PRINCIPAL ACTIVITIES: Holding company with interests in property and finance, banking and mortgage banking

Principal Subsidiaries: Benjamin Franklin Savings Association; Foster Mortgage Corporation; Security Capital Real Estate Corporation

Principal Bank: Chemical Bank

Financial Information:

	Sep 30 1985	Sep 30 1986
	$'000	$'000
Revenues	268,328	277,616
Net income (loss)	10,936	(8,935)
Earnings (loss) per share	$1.72	($1.52)
Shareholders equity	73,055	59,226

No of Employees: 1,300

SECURITY PACIFIC CORPORATION

333 S Hope Street, Los Angeles, CA 90071

Tel: (213) 613-6211

Chairman: Richard J Flamson 3rd

President: George F Moody

Senior Executive Officers: William F Ford (Vice Chairman), Roy D Hartmann (Vice Chairman), Robert H Smith (Vice Chairman)

PRINCIPAL ACTIVITIES: Holding Company which owns Security Pacific National Bank, the second largest bank in California and seventh largest in the US and The Arizona Bank, the third largest bank in Arizona. SPC has diversified into non-banking financial services, which account for a growing part of profits. The Corporation is organized into three major groups: The California Banking System, Security Pacific Merchant Bank and the specialized Financial Services System. The Company has over 1,100 offices worldwide

Principal Subsidiaries: Security Pacific National Bank; Arizona Bancwest Corp; The Bank of Canton Ltd (Hong Kong); Century Credit Corp; Clifford Drake & Co Inc; Hoare Govett Ltd (UK); Hoenig & Co Inc; Japan Security Pacific Finance Co Ltd (Japan); KMS Corporate Brokers Inc; Pacific Century Group; Security Pacific Euro Finances Ltd; Security Pacific Australia Ltd (Australia); Security Pacific Bank Asia Ltd (Singapore); Security Pacific Bank Canada Ltd (Canada); Security Pacific Bank SA (Switzerland); Security Pacific Brokers Inc; Security Pacific Business Credit Inc; Security Pacific Capital Markets Group Inc; Security Pacific Clearing & Services Corp; Security Pacific Credit (Hong Kong) Ltd (Hong Kong); Security Pacific Credit Corp; Security Pacific Finance Corp; Security Pacific Finance (Germany); Security Pacific Housing Services Inc; Security Pacific International Bank; Security Pacific International Leasing (Europe) Ltd (UK); Security Pacific Investment Managers Inc; Security Pacific Investments Arizona Inc; Security Pacific Leasing Corp; Security Pacific Leasing SA (Spain); Security Pacific Ltd (UK); Security Pacific Mortgage Banking Group; Security Pacific State Bank; Security Pacific Trade Finance; Security Pacific Trading Corp; Security Pacific Trust Ltd (UK); Security Pacific Venture Capital Group; SPB & Trust Co (Bahamas) Ltd (Bahamas); SPC Insurance Services Inc; SPC Securities Services Corp

Principal Bank: Security Pacific National Bank

Financial Information:

	Dec 31 1985	Dec 31 1986
	$'000	$'000
Income before taxes	577,600	587,500
Net income	322,800	385,900
Dividends(1)	98,000	121,000
Dividends per share	$1.31	$1.445
Earnings per share	$4.35	$4.86
Common stock(2)	76,789	77,437
Shareholders equity	2,439,000	2,875,000
Deposits	32,873,000	38,408,000
Total assets	53,503,000	62,606,000

(1) common and preferred
(2) shares outstanding in thousands

No of Employees: 35,000

SECURITY PACIFIC FINANCE SYSTEM INC

10089 Willow Creek Road, San Diego, CA 92131
Tel: (619) 578-6150
Telex: WUT 695 446 s p f c sdg

Chairman: William F Ford
President: James A Konvath (and Chief Executive Officer)
Senior Executive Officers: Timothy P Devlin (Executive VP), Richard P McManus (Executive VP Legal), K C Mead (Executive VP), Harold Owens (Executive VP), Charles G Dahl (Senior VP Finance), Carl F Detweiler (Senior VP and Controller), Thomas A Hobbs (Senior VP Human Resources), Dennis G O'Brien (Senior VP), Ray Osgood (Senior VP), R V Pinneker (Senior VP Marketing and Support Services), Gordon Thomasch (Senior VP Industry Relations)

PRINCIPAL ACTIVITIES: Financial services and insurance
Parent Company: Security Pacific Corporation, Los Angeles, CA

No of Employees: 1,520

SECURITY PACIFIC NATIONAL BANK

333 S Hope Street, Los Angeles, CA 90071
Tel: (213) 345-6211
Telex: WUT 674343 secbank Isa

Chairman: Richard J Flamson III; Vice Chairmen: David R Lovejoy, George H Benter
President: Robert H Smith (and Chief Executive Officer)
Senior Executive Officers: Nick Baker (Executive VP), Robert C Corteway (Executive VP), Russell A Freeman (Executive VP), L Peter Lowe (Executive VP and Chief Financial Officer)

PRINCIPAL ACTIVITIES: Banking services
Parent Company: Security Pacific Corporation, Los Angeles, CA
Principal Bank: Security Pacific National Bank
Financial Information: Sec Pac Nat'l Bank only

	Dec 31 1985	Dec 31 1986
	$'000	$'000
Shareholders equity	1,874,000	2,052,000
Deposits	32,884,000	34,574,000
Total assets	44,812,000	47,502,000

SEDCO, INC

1901 N Akard Street, Dallas, TX 75201
Tel: (214) 720-8700
Telex: ITT 4630026 seda ui

Chairman: W P Clements Jr
President: B G Clements (and Chief Executive Officer)
Senior Executive Officers: Stephen C Mahood (Executive VP), Spencer L Taylor (Executive VP), John Milem (VP Finance), Irving E Davis (VP Taxation)

PRINCIPAL ACTIVITIES: Exploration for oil; services to the offshore drilling industry
Principal Bank: Interfirst Bank Dallas
Financial Information:

	$'000
Sales revenues	517,000

No of Employees: 8,000

SEEQ TECHNOLOGY INC

1849 Fortune Drive, San Jose, CA 95131
Tel: (408) 262 5041

Chairman: E Floyd Kvamme
President: J Daniel McCranie (and VP Sales and Marketing)
Senior Executive Officers: Patrick B Brennan (VP and Chief Financial Officer), Gerald A Robinson (VP Operations), Phillip J Salsbury (VP, Chief Technical Officer and Secretary)

PRINCIPAL ACTIVITIES: Production of semiconductors and electronic components
Financial Information:

	$'000
Sales revenues	40,000

No of Employees: 470

SEE'S CANDY SHOPS, INC

210 El Camino Real, South San Francisco, CA 94080
Tel: (415) 583-7307

Chairman: Warren E Buffett
President: Charles N Huggins
Senior Executive Officers: Richard V Doren (VP and General Manager), Herman J Grothmann (Secretary, Treasurer and Chief Financial Officer)

PRINCIPAL ACTIVITIES: Manufacture and sale of confectionery
Parent Company: Ultimate Holding Company - Berkshire Hathaway Inc, New Bedford, MA
Principal Bank: Bank of America
Financial Information:

	$'000
Sales revenues	100,000

No of Employees: 1,200

SEI CORPORATION

680 East Swedesford Road, Wayne, PA 19087
Tel: (215) 687 1700

Chairman: Alfred P West Jr (and President and Chief Executive Officer)
Senior Executive Officers: William R Bullion (Executive VP), James E Minnick (Executive VP), Robert A Nesher (VP Administration Division), D Bruce Peterson (VP Information Services), Donald H Putnam (VP Research and Evaluation Division), David B Robb (VP Financial Products Division), Carmen V Romeo (VP and Chief Financial Officer), Antonia W Weisgrau (VP Human Resources), William M Doran (Secretary)

PRINCIPAL ACTIVITIES: Computer services including software supply, automated accounting services and other financial services
Principal Bank: Provident National Bank
Financial Information:

	$'000
Sales revenues	105,620

No of Employees: 1,145

SEIBELS BRUCE GROUP, INC

1501 Lady Street, Columbia, SC 29201
Tel: (803) 748-2000

Chairman: Sterling E Beale (and Treasurer and Chief Executive Officer)
President: Jack S Hupp (and Chief Operating Officer)
Senior Executive Officers: W Thomas Reichard III (Executive VP), Lucy L McDow (Secretary)

PRINCIPAL ACTIVITIES: Holding company with interests in insurance and computer software for insurance applications
Principal Bank: South Carolina National Bank
Financial Information:

	$'000
Revenues	249,000

No of Employees: 1,500

SEILER CORPORATION
153 Second Avenue, Waltham, MA 02254
Tel: (617) 890-6200

Chairman: Patrice Douce
President: James R Cochrane
Senior Executive Officers: Philip A Gorman (Executive VP and Treasurer), William Zammer (Senior VP Healthcare Division), Ned D Gardner (Senior VP Food Services Division), Robert D Hirtle (Senior VP Dining Services Division), Donald E Storer (Senior VP Marketing), Peter F Franzosa (VP Finance and Treasurer), Richard Spratley (VP Consumer Products Division), David Hayes (VP Legal and Industrial Relations)

PRINCIPAL ACTIVITIES: Contract food and general services management: manufacture of bakery products; design food service facilities; distribution of food service equipment and supplies
Parent Company: International Catering Corporation
Principal Bank: State Street Bank and Trust Company
Financial Information:

	$'000
Sales revenues	150,000

No of Employees: 2,750

SEIS PROS INC
16850 Park Row, Houston, TX 77084
Tel: (713) 492 0028

Chairman: W Peyton Weems (and VP)
President: Hugh R Ervin
Senior Executive Officers: Willis T Brown (VP), George E Pawley (VP), William A Stroud (VP), David L Treiger (VP, Secretary and Treasurer), Wayne L Underwood (VP)

PRINCIPAL ACTIVITIES: Exploration services for oil and gas
Principal Bank: First City National Bank of Houston
Financial Information:

	$'000
Sales revenues	53,420

No of Employees: 605

SEISCOM DELTA INC
PO Box 4610, Houston, TX 77210
Tel: (713) 556-1400
Telex: 3787780 SD INC A

Chairman: Marc K Rieke (and Chief Financial Officer and Controller)
President: Michael J Castelberg (and Chief Executive Officer)
Senior Executive Officers: Palmer L Greene (Senior VP-International Data Acquisition), W F Albers (VP-Non Exclusive Propriety Surveys, NEPS), Wayne A Heitshusen (Senior VP), Richard M Love (VP and General Counsel), Roderick M Macdonald (VP Brazilian Operations), Harry Morley (VP and Regional Manager E.A.M.E. Data Acquisition), Kenneth A Stewart (VP and General Manager-Seiscom Delta United (Canada) Ltd), D Wayne Turner (VP-Data Processing), Hugh Fraser (Manager Gulf Coast)

PRINCIPAL ACTIVITIES: Geophysical services to the oil and gas exploration industry. Seismic data acquisition, seismic data processing, conducting and licensing of speculative data surveys, development of seismic software technology; international drilling services
Trade Names: MEGASEIS(R) Seismic data processing computer systems, SEISCHROME(R) Laser digital plotter for seismic displays
Principal Subsidiaries: Seiscom Delta United (Canada) Ltd (Canada); Instrumentos Technicos E Pesquiras Ltda (Brazil); Seiscom Delta United (Int'l) Corp (UK); Seiscom Delta United (Int'l) Inc (UK); Seiscom Delta United (Int'l) Corp (Sudan); United Geophysical (Nigeria) Ltd (Nigeria); Seiscom Delta United (Int'l) Corp (Singapore); Seiscom Delta United (Australia) Pty Ltd (Australia); Seiscom Delta United (P.N.G.) Pty Ltd (Papua New Guinea)
Principal Bank: First City National Bank of Houston
Financial Information:

	$'000
Sales revenues	85,500

No of Employees: 2,000

SELIGMAN & LATZ, INC
1133 Avenue of the Americas, New York, NY 10036
Tel: (212) 382-7400

Chairman: John S Kubie (and Chief Executive Officer)
President: Arthur D Fabricant (and Chief Operating Officer)
Senior Executive Officers: Irving M Hird (Senior Executive VP and Treasurer)

PRINCIPAL ACTIVITIES: Beauty salons; cosmetics and beauty care products; retail and wholesale trade in jewelry
Principal Bank: Chase Manhattan Bank
Financial Information:

	$'000
Sales revenues	342,100

No of Employees: 10,000

SEMICON INC
15 New England Executive Park, Burlington, MA 01803
Tel: (617) 229 6290

President: Rolland V Robinson
Senior Executive Officers: Robert E House (Executive VP), Richard C Allard (VP Finance and Treasurer)

PRINCIPAL ACTIVITIES: Production of electronic components
Principal Subsidiaries: Microfab Inc; S-T Semicon Inc; Semicon Components Inc
Principal Bank: Fleet National Bank
Financial Information:

	$'000
Sales revenues	37,555

No of Employees: 800

SENECA FOODS CORPORATION
74 Seneca Street, Dundee, NY 14837
Tel: (607) 243-7171
Telex: TWX 510582 4577 sn fd cp dund

Chairman: A S Wolcott (and Chief Executive Officer)
President: J G Kayser
Senior Executive Officers: F W Leick (Executive VP), D P Naeye (Executive VP), D L Sprissler (VP, Secretary and Treasurer)

PRINCIPAL ACTIVITIES: Canning of fruit and vegetables
Parent Company: S S Pierce Co Inc, Dundee, NY
Principal Bank: Liberty National Bank & Trust
Financial Information:

	$'000
Sales revenues	225,000

No of Employees: 1,500

SENSORMATIC ELECTRONICS CORPORATION
500 W 12th Avenue, Deerfield Beach, FL 33442
Tel: (305) 427-9700
Telex: 264076

Chairman: Ronald G Assaf
President: Allen J Dusault (and Chief Executive Officer)
Senior Executive Officers: J Lineburger (Chairman, Executive Committee), M E Pardue (VP Finance), D C Gillette (VP Sales and Marketing), O S Giles (VP Engineering), G Witter (VP European Operations)

PRINCIPAL ACTIVITIES: Manufacture of electronic surveillance equipment and detection systems
Principal Subsidiaries: Senelco Ltd
Principal Bank: Wachovia Bank and Trust
Financial Information:

	May 31 1987
	$'000
Sales revenues	98,263
Income before taxes	21,254
Net income	13,754
Dividends	1,411
Dividends per share	$0.05
Earnings per share	$0.48
Common stock	283
Capital*	122,057
Retained income	86,271
Shareholders equity	203,282

*in excess of par value

No of Employees: 1,200

SEQUA CORPORATION (FORMERLY SUN CHEMICAL CORPORATION)

200 Park Avenue, New York, NY 10166
Tel: (212) 986-5500
Telex: WUT 147236

Chairman: Norman E Alexander (and Chief Executive Officer)
President: Robert E Davis (and Chief Operating Officer)
Senior Executive Officers: Stuart Z Krinsly (Senior Executive VP), Gerald S Gutterman (Executive VP Finance and Administration and Chief Financial Officer)

PRINCIPAL ACTIVITIES: Supplier of advanced metalurgical products and processers for jet engine components; operation of inland waterway barges and intracoastal tankers; manufacture of components for the automotive, aerospace, defense and two piece can industries
Principal Subsidiaries: (100% owned unless stated): Sequa plc (formerly Ault and Wiborg Group Ltd) (83%); Chromalloy American Corp; Casco Products Corp; Chromalloy Gas Turbine Corp
Financial Information:

	Dec 31 1986
	$'000
Sales revenues*	1,226,000
Income before taxes*	112,611
Net income*	60,297
Dividends	3,742
Earnings per share	$5.20
Shareholders equity	631,952

*sales and income data all pro forma to include Chromalloy Americas Corporation which was acquired in December 1986

No of Employees: 15,000

SERVAMATIC SYSTEMS INC

1641 Challenge Drive, Concord, CA 94520
Tel: (415) 680 8853

Chairman: Harvey R Anderson (and President and Chief Executive Officer)
Senior Executive Officers: Richard C Brown (Chief Operating Officer), Calvin R Edmonds (Executive VP and Secretary), Eric B Levine (Senior VP), Gary D Anderson (VP), Robert B Anderson (VP)

PRINCIPAL ACTIVITIES: Sale and installation of solar heating units for commercial and residential applications
Principal Subsidiaries: Energy Clinic Corporation
Principal Bank: Bank of America NT & SA
Financial Information:

	$'000
Sales revenues	73,160

No of Employees: 2,700

SERVBEST FOODS INC

1256 Old Skokie Road, Highland Park, IL 60035
Tel: (312) 831-4700
Telex: TWX 910 688 4168 servbest hipk

Chairman: William E Kentor (and President)
Senior Executive Officers: Roger Maina (VP)

PRINCIPAL ACTIVITIES: Processing of meat
Trade Names: Servbest, Meat Eater, Prime
Principal Subsidiaries: Haitian American Meat Co SA; Prime Packing Co Inc
Principal Bank: Continental Illinois National Bank and Trust Company

No of Employees: 600

SERVICE CORP INTERNATIONAL

1929 Allen Parkway, Houston, TX 77019
Tel: (713) 522 5141

Chairman: Robert L Waltrip (and President and Chief Executive Officer)
Senior Executive Officers: Donald R Campbell (Executive VP Operations), Victor M Evans (Senior VP Division), Jon David Gooch (Senior VP and Legal Counsel), William E Mercer (Executive VP Finance), Paul Page (Senior VP Investments), Don Gould (Senior VP Division), Greg Jewell (Senior VP Division), Blair Waltrip (Senior VP Division), Joe E Turner Jr (Senior VP Administration), G Kyle Guinn (Senior VP Corporate Development), Ben B Dees (Senior VP Finance and Treasurer), E Keith Payne (Secretary)

PRINCIPAL ACTIVITIES: Provision of funeral and related services
Principal Bank: Texas Commerce Bank
Financial Information:

	Apr 30 1987
	$'000
Sales Revenues	386,632
Income before taxes	86,004
Net income	51,604
Dividends per share	$0.29
Earnings per share	$1.21
Common stock	45,411
Retained income	204,433
Shareholders equity	478,581

No of Employees: 9,500

SERVICE MERCHANDISE CO, INC

2968 Foster Creighton Drive, Nashville, TN 37204
Tel: (615) 251-6666
Telex: WUT 509404 metro ud

Chairman: Raymond Zimmerman (and President and Chief Executive Officer)
Senior Executive Officers: Howard I Levy (Executive VP), S P Braud (VP Finance, Treasurer and Chief Financial Officer), Ron Sydes (VP Human Resources), Glen Bodzy (VP, Secretary and General Counsel)

PRINCIPAL ACTIVITIES: Retailers of a wide range of consumer products including giftware, household goods, toys, silver, jewelry, sports equipment, photographic equipment, home improvement goods, computerware
Principal Bank: First American Bank

Financial Information:

	Dec 28 1985	Jan 31 1987
	$'000	$'000
Sales revenues	2,244,806	2,527,300
Income (loss) before taxes(1)	37,295	(29,133)
Net income (loss)(1)	24,269	(17,098)
Net (loss)(2)	(13,536)	(29,800)
Dividends	2,663	2,665
Dividends per share	$0.08	$0.08
Earnings per share primary	$0.32	$1.41
Common stock	16,884	16,884
Retained income	238,110	188,547
Shareholders equity	328,150	278,566

(1) continuing operations

(2) discontinued operations

No of Employees: 24,000

SERVICEMASTER INDUSTRIES INC

2300 Warrenville Road, Downers Grove, IL 60515

Tel: (312) 964-1300

Telex: WUT 270069 servmaster dove

Chairman: Kenneth T Wessner (and Chairman of Executive Committee); Vice Chairman: Kenneth N Hansen

President: C William Pollard (and Chief Executive Officer)

Senior Executive Officers: Richard A Armstrong (Executive VP), Robert D Erickson (Executive VP), Edward F Morgan Jr (Executive VP), C W Stair (Executive VP), Alex Bale Jr (Corporate VP), K W Creasman (Group President Central), Ronald D Kuykendall (Group President East), John G Pollock (Group President West), Robert S Estabrooks (VP and Chief Accounting Officer), Vincent N Damle (VP Manufacturing)

PRINCIPAL ACTIVITIES: Operation of management services in the fields of health care and industrial plants; commercial cleaning services; food services for institutions

Principal Bank: Harris Trust and Savings Bank

Financial Information:

	Dec 31 1985	Dec 31 1986
	$'000	$'000
Sales revenues	1,002,213	1,122,503
Net income	32,705	32,775
Earnings per share	$1.00	$1.00
Shareholders equity	-	32,106

No of Employees: 12,291

SERVICO, INC

1601 Belvedere Rd, Suite 501 South, West Palm Beach, Florida, FL 33406

Tel: (305) 689-9700

Chairman: Arthur I Meyer (and Chief Executive Officer)

President: William A Meyer (and Chief Operating Officer)

Senior Executive Officers: Vartan Tchekmeian (Executive VP), Howard Feiertag (Senior VP Sales and Marketing), Donald Pavony (Secretary), Ivan Roth (Treasurer)

PRINCIPAL ACTIVITIES: Servico, Inc together with its subsidiaries, is engaged in the ownership, operation or management of hotels. At June 25, 1987, the Company owned, operated or managed 59 hotels, located in 19 states, the District of Columbia and Canada, containing a total of 13,016 guest rooms

Financial Information:

	Jun 26 1986	Jun 25 1987
	$'000	$'000
Sales revenues	168,928	180,801
Income before taxes	7,740	2,714
Net income	5,104	1,418
Earnings per share	$1.35	$0.37
Common stock	486	486
Retained income	15,641	17,059
Shareholders equity	36,445	37,875

Principal Shareholders: Southmark Corporation

No of Employees: 8,000

SERVISCO

470 Mundet Place, Hillside, NJ 07205

Tel: (201) 964-7500

Chairman: Philip A Lane

President: Bruce L Cohen (and Chief Executive Officer)

Senior Executive Officers: Alfred Berry (VP), Murray Bloomenfeld (VP), Carl G Cohen (VP and Secretary), Eric S Cohen (VP), Frank Felchlin (VP)

PRINCIPAL ACTIVITIES: Manufacture, rental and laundering of overalls and uniforms; operation of security and maintenance services

Principal Subsidiaries: Angus International Corp; Angus-America Corp; Atlas Guard Service Inc; Penn Protective Services Inc; Columbus Services Inc

Principal Bank: First Pennsylvania Bank

Financial Information:

	$'000
Sales revenues	98,500

No of Employees: 5,500

SESSIONS CO INC

PO Box 1336, Enterprise, AL 36331

Tel: (205) 347-9551

Telex: TWX 810 7443090 sessions entr

President: H M Sessions Sr

Senior Executive Officers: James F Curran (VP Sales and Production), Larry Milliner (VP Operations), H B Thompson (VP), H M Sessions Jr (Secretary and Treasurer)

PRINCIPAL ACTIVITIES: Manufacture of peanut products including peanut butter, peanut oil and shelled peanuts

Financial Information:

	$'000
Sales revenues	60,000

No of Employees: 120

SETON CO

949 Broadway, Newark, NJ 07104

Tel: (201) 485-4800

Telex: TWX 710 9954613 seton co nwk

Chairman: Philip D Kaltenbacher (and Chief Executive Officer)

President: Paul A Fertell (and Chief Operating Officer)

Senior Executive Officers: Leo Sender (Senior VP and Secretary), Robert K Rothman (VP)

PRINCIPAL ACTIVITIES: Leather tanning and finishing

Principal Subsidiaries: Wilmington Chemical Corp; Norwood Industries Inc; Seton Leather Co; Sepa Inc; A Mindel & Son Inc

Principal Bank: Citibank

Financial Information:

	$'000
Sales revenues	102,000

No of Employees: 850

SEVEN-UP COMPANY

121 S Meramec, St Louis, MO 63105
Tel: (314) 889-7777
Telex: TWX 9107610513 seven up day

President: Edward W Frantel (and Chief Executive Officer)
Senior Executive Officers: Charles W Schmid (Executive VP Soft Drink Group), Gerard J Martin (Executive VP Food Group)

PRINCIPAL ACTIVITIES: Production and distribution of soft drinks, flavorings, syrups, extracts, frozen vegetables and fruit, chemicals
Parent Company: Philip Morris Inc, New York, NY
Financial Information:

	$'000
Sales revenues	658,000

No of Employees: 4,000

SFE TECHNOLOGIES

1501 First Street, Box 351, San Fernando, CA 91340-2793
Tel: (818) 361-1176
Telex: 4720536 SFEUI

Chairman: Donald Rubendall
President: Alan D Rubendall
Senior Executive Officers: Jerome J Jahn (VP, Finance, Administration and Secretary and Legal Counsel), Robert O Roberg (VP, Operations), Michael A Rosenberg (VP, Technology), Joseph L Lucia (VP, Marketing and Sales), Robert W Bronson (VP, Quality Assurance), Robert Rubendall (VP), H Kermit Hawkins (VP). Division and Subsidiary Officers: Robert Kassell (President, San Fernando Electric Division), Robert Rabuck (President, West-Cap Arizona), Joe B Weddington Jr (President, Orchard Electronics, Inc), James Walsh (President, Polytronics Inc), Joseph M Scheer (Acting President, Electro Dynamics Division), Wolfgang O Furkert (President, SFE Technologies GMBH)

PRINCIPAL ACTIVITIES: Manufacture of electronic components, including multilayer ceramic capacitors, wound-film capacitors, magnetic components, electromagnetic interference filters, quartz crystal frequency control devices and circuit assemblies utilizing surface mount technology and thick-film hybrid techniques
Principal Bank: City National Bank
Financial Information:

	Oct 31 1985 $'000	Oct 31 1986 $'000
Sales revenues	57,024	42,672
Loss before taxes*	(10,628)	(19,707)
Net (loss)	(4,989)	(15,889)
Earnings (loss) per share	($0.80)	($2.53)
Common stock	6,265	6,604
Retained (deficit)	(3,007)	(18,897)
Shareholders equity	41,677	26,709

*and extraordinary credit

No of Employees: 2,900

SFN COMPANIES, INC

1900 E Lake Avenue, Glenview, IL 60025
Tel: (312) 657-3900

Chairman: John R Purcell (and President)
Senior Executive Officers: Richard T Morgan (Senior VP and President Scott, Foresman and Co), Richard B Sernett (Senior VP, General Counsel and Assistant Secretary), David H Soskin (Senior VP), Richard F Blake (VP, Secretary and Associate General Counsel), Robert F Fuson (VP Finance and Controller), Nelson B Heller, Thomas G Kennedy (VP Taxes), C LeMoyne Smith (VP, President South Western Publishing Co), Carl G Strub (VP Human Resources), Sherman C Wildman (VP)

PRINCIPAL ACTIVITIES: Publishing, including educational and professional books and journals; broadcasting and information services
Principal Subsidiaries: Scott Foresman & Co; South-Western Publishing Co; Silver Burdett Co; New York Law Publishing Co; Biomedical Information Corp; Broadcast Advertisers Reports Inc; Mindscape Inc; Data Acquisition Services Inc; SFN Communications Inc; Western Broadcasting Co
Principal Bank: First National Bank of Chicago
Financial Information:

	$'000
Sales revenues	382,000

No of Employees: 4,000

SHAKLEE CORPORATION

444 Market Street, San Francisco, CA 94111
Tel: (415) 954-3000
Telex: TWX 910-372-6016 SHAKLE SFO

Chairman: John C Lorini
President: David M Chamberlain (and Chief Executive Officer)
Senior Executive Officers: Richard B Stein (Senior VP and Chief Financial Officer), Hugh A Eyerly (VP and Corporate Controller), Allen Simon (Senior VP Operations)

PRINCIPAL ACTIVITIES: Manufacture of personal care products and cosmetics, nutritional products including vitamins and household goods
Principal Subsidiaries: Shaklee Canada Inc; Shaklee (Japan) KK; Shaklee Australia Pty Ltd; Shaklee Deutschland GmbH; Shaklee (UK) Ltd
Principal Bank: Crocker National Bank
Financial Information:

	$'000
Sales revenues	406,000

No of Employees: 1,500

SHAMROCK FOODS COMPANY

2228 N Black Canyon Hwy, Phoenix, AZ 85009
Tel: (602) 272-6721

President: Norman P McClelland
Senior Executive Officers: David B Hall (Senior VP), John W Harty (VP), Derrell Fairfield (Senior VP), Donald Van Wormer (VP), Charles D Roberts (VP), W Kent McClelland (VP), Frances H McClelland (Treasurer and Secretary)

PRINCIPAL ACTIVITIES: Process and distribute dairy products; distribute complete line of food and related items; have meat processing plant
Principal Subsidiaries: United Food Service, Inc
Principal Bank: Arizona Bank
Financial Information:

	$'000
Sales revenues	250,000

No of Employees: 1,000

SHARED MEDICAL SYSTEMS CORPORATION

51 Valley Stream Parkway, Malvern, PA 19355
Tel: (215) 296-6300

Chairman: R James MacAleer (and Chief Executive Officer)
Senior Executive Officers: James C Kelly (VP Secretary and Treasurer), T W Kyle (VP Finance)

PRINCIPAL ACTIVITIES: Computer services
Principal Bank: Provident National Bank
Financial Information:

	$'000
Sales revenues	372,000

No of Employees: 3,400

SHARON STEEL CORPORATION

PO Box 270, Farrell, PA 16121
Tel: (412) 981-1375
Telex: WUT 902 971 sharon stl shar

Chairman: Victor Posner (and President and Chief Executive Officer); Vice Chairman: Steven Posner (and Chairman of Executive Committee)
Senior Executive Officers: Walter Sieckman (Group Executive VP), Henry G Evans (Executive VP and Chief Operating Officer), Jack Coppersmith (Senior VP and Chief Financial Officer), Raymond J Dettore (Senior VP), Bernard I Posner (Senior VP), Robert R Albert Jr (VP Sales), Ted W Bowden (VP Planning), Melvin R Colvin (VP), Thomas W Evans (VP Materials Control), Mitchell V Gregory (VP), Robert C Griffin (VP, Treasurer and Assistant Secretary), William N Merchant (VP Finance), Maynard L Moore Jr (VP and General Counsel), Renée Mottram (VP Administration and Assistant Secretary), Martin J Posner (VP and General Manager Sharonsteel Products), Tracy Posner (VP), Philip A Smalley Jr (VP Personnel and Organisation)

PRINCIPAL ACTIVITIES: Steel industry
Parent Company: NVF Company, Yorklyn, DE
Principal Subsidiaries: Carpentertown Coal & Coke Co; Macomber Inc; Sharon Building and Land Corp; Sharonsteel Products Co; Union Steel Corp; Summit Systems Inc; Alaska Gold Co; Arava Exploration Co,; Kennet Co Ltd (Bermuda); Mueller Brass Co; Itawamba Industrial Gas Co Inc; Mueller Industrial Realty Co; Streamline Copper & Brass Ltd (Canada); United States Fuel Co; King Coal Co; Ussram Exploration Co; USS Lead Refinery Inc; United States Smelting, Refining & Mining Co; Utah Railway Co; Washington Mining Co; White Knob Mining Co
Financial Information:

	$'000
Sales revenues	800,000

No of Employees: 6,400

SHATTERPROOF GLASS CORPORATION

4815 Cabot Avenue, Detroit, MI 48210
Tel: (313) 582-6200
Telex: WUT 235 266 shatproof det

Chairman: W B Chase (and President and Chief Executive Officer); Vice Chairmen: C C Suchy, J S Svendor
Senior Executive Officers: H E McKelvey (VP Research and Development), T H Campbell (VP Sales), Philip G Myers (VP Corporate Development), Stanley E Nirider (VP), R C Urquhart (VP Purchasing), M G Robinson (VP Coatings Technology), M A Woodward (VP Labor Relations), L C Puchalski (Treasurer)

PRINCIPAL ACTIVITIES: Manufacture of glass including flat glass, safety glass, insulating, automobile and architectural glass
Principal Bank: Comerica Bank Detroit
Financial Information:

	$'000
Sales revenues	54,304

No of Employees: 740

SHAW INDUSTRIES, INC

616 E Walnut Avenue, Dalton, GA 30720
Tel: (404) 278-3812

President: Robert E Shaw (and Chief Executive Officer)
Senior Executive Officers: W N Little (Senior VP Manufacturing), William C Lusk Jr (Senior VP and Treasurer)

PRINCIPAL ACTIVITIES: Manufacture of carpets
Financial Information:

	Jun 30 1986 $'000
Sales revenues	550,024
Net income	24,095
Earnings per share	$1.41
Shareholders equity	141,218

No of Employees: 4,300

SHAWMUT CORPORATION

One Federal Street, Boston, MA 02211
Tel: (617) 292-2000

Chairman: John P LaWare (and Chief Executive Officer); Vice Chairmen: William F Craig, Neal F Finnegan
President: John P Hamill
Senior Executive Officers: John J Green (Executive VP and Chief Loan Officer), Timothy J Hansberry (Executive VP Community Banking), Carter H Harrison (Executive VP Financial Management), Paul A Miller (Executive VP and Treasurer), William C Schrader (Executive VP Information Systems and Bank Operations), Horace C Sylvester Jr (Executive VP Investments), Warren S Berg (Senior VP Corporate Relations), Charles M Bush (Senior VP Human Resources), David W Dailey (Senior VP and Controller), P Clarke Dwyer (Senior VP Loan Review), Charles H Eppinger (Senior VP Information Systems), John G Fallon (Senior VP Corporate Planning), John Gould (Senior VP Government and Investor Relations), C Keefe Hurley Jr (Senior VP and General Counsel), John H Kalchbrenner (Senior VP and Chief Economist), William L G Lester (Senior VP Corporate Finance), Ann M Moe (Senior VP Marketing), Thomas V Moriarty (Senior VP Consumer Products Wholesale), Paul J MacKinnon (VP and General Auditor), James E Nix (VP and Deputy Controller)

PRINCIPAL ACTIVITIES: Banking
Principal Subsidiaries: Shawmut Bank of Boston
Financial Information:

	Dec 31 1985 $'000	Dec 31 1986 $'000
Net income	57,290	78,642
Earnings per share	$5.17	$5.07
Shareholders equity	446,914	633,691
Deposits	5,527,350	7,751,252
Total assets	7,822,570	10,697,446

No of Employees: 6,730

SHEAFFER EATON INC

75 S Church Street, Pittsfield, MA 01201
Tel: (413) 499-2210
Telex: TWX 710 352 6931 sheaffer pfl

President: J E Biofore
Senior Executive Officers: C D Roberson (VP Administration), R T Asselta (VP Domestic Sales), B T Bessey (VP Operations Duo-Tang), D W Fore (VP Operations Shaeffer), E E Byrnes (VP Operations Eaton), K A McLusky (VP International Operations)

PRINCIPAL ACTIVITIES: Manufacture of a wide range of stationery products, pens, ballpoints, pencils, appointment books and desk sets
Trade Names: Sheaffer, Eaton, At-A-Glance, Duo-Tang
Principal Subsidiaries: Shaeffer Pen (Australia, Canada, England, France, Netherlands, Belgium, West Germany, Italy)
Principal Bank: National Westminster USA
Financial Information:

	$'000
Sales revenues	150,000

No of Employees: 2,000

SHEARSON LEHMAN BROTHERS INC.

2 World Financial Center, American Express Tower, New York, NY 10285
Tel: (212) 298-2000

Chairman: Peter A Cohen (and Chief Executive Officer): Vice Chairmen: Herbert S Freiman (Chairman of the Capital Markets Group), Richard J Fuld (Chairman, Shearson Lehman Commercial Paper Inc), David S Hershberg (Legal, Human Resources, Corporate and Government Affairs), Sherman R Lewis Jr (Co-Chairman of the Investment Banking Group), Joel Margolies (Director of the Domestic Branch System),

George W Phillips (Asset Management and Real Estate), George C Sheinberg (Firmwide Commitment Committees), Hardwick Simmons (Chairman of the Private Client Group), Peter J Solomon (Co-Chairman of the Investment Banking Group)
President: Jeffrey B Lane (and Chief Operating Officer)
Senior Executive Officers: Albert C Bellas (Senior Executive VP), Peter J Da Puzzo (Senior Executive VP), Richard H Darsky (Senior Executive VP), Peter M Dawkins (Senior Executive VP), Francois de St Phalle (Senior Executive VP), Francis L Fraenkel (Senior Executive VP), Edwin I Gill (Senior Executive VP), Henry D Gottmann (Senior Executive VP), Leonard V Haynes (Senior Executive VP), Jack H Lehman III (Senior Executive VP), John S Levy (Senior Executive VP), Louis B Lloyd (Senior Executive VP), John J McDougall (Senior Executive VP), Richard F Morrison (Senior Executive VP), George A Murray (Senior Executive VP), Kenneth R Natori (Senior Executive VP), T Christopher Pettit (Senior Executive VP), Joseph J Plumeri II (Senior Executive VP), Victor M Samra Jr (Senior Executive VP), M David Standridge (Senior Executive VP), Philip M Waterman Jr (Senior Executive VP)

PRINCIPAL ACTIVITIES: Shearson Lehman Brothers Inc provides a comprehensive range of investment products and services to individuals, institutions, corporations and governments throughout the world. These include stocks, bonds, options, futures, commercial paper, certificates of deposit, insurance and tax-advantaged investments as well as investment banking, pension and investment management, real estate and mortgage banking services. Approximately 5,500 financial consultants serve investors from a network of 354 offices in 44 states and 15 countries
Principal Subsidiaries: Foster & Marshall Inc; The Robinson-Humphrey Company, Inc; Shearson Lehman Mortgage Corporation; The Balcor Company; The Boston Company, Inc; Bernstein-Macaulay, Inc; Shearson Asset Management Inc; Lehman Management Co, Inc; *American Express Asset Management Limited; Shearson Management Inc; Lehman Commercial Paper Incorporated; The Ayco Corporation; Shearson Lehman Brothers Limited. *A wholly owned subsidiary of American Express Company
Financial Information:

	Dec 31 1986 (12 mths) $'000	Jun 30 1987 (6 mths) $'000
Revenues	4,600,000	2,575,000
Income before taxes	488,000	223,300
Net income	316,000	137,500
Dividends per share	-	$0.1875
Earnings per share	-	$1.60
Common stock(1)	-	85,900
Retained earnings	910,000	945,000
Shareholders equity	1,358,000	2,022,000
Total Capital(2)	2,800,000	3,300,000

(1) average shares and common equivalent shares outstanding in thousands
(2) including subordinated debt

Principal Shareholders: American Express Company (60%); Nippon Life Insurance Company (13%)
No of Employees: 28,000

SHELBY WILLIAMS INDUSTRIES, INC

1348 Merchandise Mart, Chicago, IL 60654
Tel: (312) 527-3593
Telex: WUT 253 228 shelby wm cgo

Chairman: Manfred Steinfeld; Vice Chairman: Leslie D Guyette
President: Robert P Coulter
Senior Executive Officers: Paul N Steinfeld (Executive VP), Peter W Barile (Senior VP), Dennis Gurley (VP Manufacturing), Kurt Keller (VP Sales), Sam Ferrell (Comptroller)

PRINCIPAL ACTIVITIES: Manufacture of office furniture
Principal Bank: Continental Illinois National Bank and Trust Co
Financial Information:

	$'000
Sales revenues	118,000

No of Employees: 1,650

SHELDAHL INC

Northfield, MN 55057
Tel: (612) 332 5371

President: James S Womack (and Chief Executive Officer)
Senior Executive Officers: B M Brumbaugh (VP), James H Kessler Jr (VP Finance), Patrick A O'Malley (VP), Richard J Slater (VP Business Development), Gerald E Magnuson (Secretary)

PRINCIPAL ACTIVITIES: Manufacture of components and parts for the electronics industry
Principal Bank: Norwest Bank
Financial Information:

	$'000
Sales revenues	59,390

No of Employees: 1,000

SHELL OIL COMPANY

One Shell Plaza, Houston, TX 77001
Tel: (713) 241-6161
Telex: WUT 76 2248 shell plz hou

Chairman: L C Van Wachem
President: John F Bookout (and Chief Executive Officer)
Senior Executive Officers: C L Blackburn (Executive VP Exploration and Production), Frank H Richardson (Executive VP Products), Jack E Little (Senior VP Administration), Donald G Russell (VP Production), Jack C Threet (VP Exploration), R G Dilliard, Jr (VP Manufacturing and Technical), Davis B Richardson (VP Refining and Marketing), S G Stiles (VP Products), James R Street (VP Chemical Products), Paul F Deisler Jr (VP Health, Safety and Environment), L L Drury (VP Purchasing and Administrative Services), J C Jacobsen (VP Finance), Jess Johnson Jr (VP Government Relations), D R Milton (VP Tax), Merrill K Seggerman (VP Public Affairs), V G Whittington (VP Employee Relations), C W Wilson (VP Corporate Planning), W T Wise (General Counsel), D E Cannon (Treasurer), N E Gautier (Controller), Thomas E Baker (Corporate Secretary)

PRINCIPAL ACTIVITIES: Shell Oil is one of America's leading oil, gas and petrochemical companies
Parent Company: Royal Dutch Petroleum Company (60%); The "Shell" Transport and Trading Company plc (40%)
Financial Information:

	Dec 31 1985 $'000	Dec 31 1986 $'000
Sales revenues	20,477,000	16,833,000
Net income	1,650,000	883,000
Shareholders equity	14,129,000	14,312,000

Principal Shareholders: SPNV Holdings, Inc
No of Employees: 35,170

SHELLER-GLOBE CORPORATION

1505 Jefferson Avenue, Toledo, OH 43697
Tel: (419) 255-8840
Telex: WUT 286428 shelglobdp tol

Chairman: Chester Devenow (and Chief Executive Officer); Vice Chairman: John R Eastman (and Chief Administration Officer)
President: James A Graham (and Chief Operating Officer)
Senior Executive Officers: George A Berry (Executive VP Industrial Sector), Alfred H Grava (Executive VP Auto and Light Truck Sector), William H Patterson (Executive VP), Sidney D Jeffe (Senior VP Operating Staff), Irvin M Zimet (VP and President Officer Products Group), Stanley Berlinghoff (VP Technical Services), John L Bradley (VP Human

Resources and Administration Services), Kenneth L Cation (VP, President Electrical Group), John S Harman (VP International), Ralph J Hill (VP and Controller), John F McCuen (VP and General Counsel)

PRINCIPAL ACTIVITIES: Manufacture of components and accessories for the automotive industry; manufacture of office products; manufacture of scientific measuring instruments
Principal Subsidiaries: Concorco Lda; Sheller-Globe International Corp; Sheller-Clifford Ltd; Leece-Neville de Mexico SA de CV; Sheller-Globe of Canada Ltd; Sheller-Globe Export Sales Corp; Victoreen Inc; Northern Fibre Products Co; Sheller-Globe Engineered Polymers Co; Nuclear Associate Division; Amoco Engineered Plastics Co; Establissement Mesnel (60%); Crawford Industries
Principal Bank: National Bank of Detroit
Financial Information:

	Sep 30 1985	Sep 30 1986
	$'000	$'000
Sales revenues	917,700	940,000

No of Employees: 12,300

SHELTER RESOURCES CORPORATION

24200 Chagrin Blvd, Beachwood, OH 44122
Tel: (216) 831-0076

Chairman: James P Maloney Jr (and Chief Executive and Chief Financial Officer)
Senior Executive Officers: Thomas F McWilliams (VP), Kenneth J Lorek (Treasurer), Edward I Gold (Secretary)

PRINCIPAL ACTIVITIES: Holding company with interests in the production of mobile homes
Principal Bank: Chase Commercial Corporation
Financial Information:

	$'000
Sales revenues	109,000

No of Employees: 1,230

SHEPARD NILES CRANE & HOIST CORPORATION

Schuyler Avenue, Montour Falls, NY 14865
Tel: (607) 535-7111
Telex: WUT 932 473 shepniles mtur

Chairman: Marshall L Berkman; Vice Chairman: Robert A Pall
President: Jim R Foster
Senior Executive Officers: Edward Cullen (VP Manufacturing), F W Dunning (VP Cleveland Tramrail Products), Keith C Hatsell (VP Shepard Niles Products), David C Lee (VP Finance)

PRINCIPAL ACTIVITIES: Manufacture of cranes and hoists
Parent Company: Ampco-Pittsburgh Corp
Principal Bank: Mellon Bank
Financial Information:

	$'000
Sales revenues	50,000

No of Employees: 500

SHEREX CHEMICAL CO, INC

5777 Frantz Road, Dublin, OH 43017
Tel: (614) 764-6500
Telex: ITT 4332067 sherex dboh

Chairman: Klaus-Peter Kantzer
President: C A Aldag (and Chief Executive Officer)
Senior Executive Officers: J R Stockton (VP Administration), C L Immel (VP Sales and Marketing), J F McGann (VP Business Development), W R Starkey (VP Operations), J W Sigan (VP Technology), G T Wyatt (Treasurer and VP Finance)

PRINCIPAL ACTIVITIES: Manufacture of chemicals
Parent Company: Schering AG, Berlin, West Germany
Principal Bank: Huntington Bank
Financial Information:

	$'000
Sales revenues	145,000

No of Employees: 620

SHERWIN-WILLIAMS CO

101 Prospect Avenue NW, Cleveland, OH 44115
Tel: (216) 566-2000
Telex: WUT 85 85 97 sherwil clv ud

Chairman: John G Breen (and Chief Executive Officer)
President: Thomas A Commes (and Chief Operating Officer)
Senior Executive Officers: Dr F Thomas Krotine (Senior VP-Corporate Research and Development), Thomas R Miklich (Senior VP, Finance and Chief Financial Officer), William B Eldredge (President, International Group), Robert B Venick (President-Paint Stores Group), John L Ault (VP-Corporate Controller), Conway G Ivy (VP, Corporate Planning and Development), Thomas Kroeger (VP-Human Resources), Larry J Pitorak (VP, Secretary-Treasurer and General Counsel), Francis C Piccirillo (Assistant Secretary and Corporate Director of Taxes), Len A Ward (VP-Administration)

PRINCIPAL ACTIVITIES: Sherwin-Williams completed 121 years of doing business in 1987. The company's core business is the manufacture, distribution and sale of coatings and related products. We sell Sherwin-Williams labeled architectural coatings, industrial finishes, and associated supplies through 1,829 company-operated paint and wallcovering stores in 48 states. We also manufacture and sell coatings such as Dutch Boy, Martin-Senour, Kem-Tone, plus private label brands to independent dealers, mass merchandisers, and home improvement centers. We produce coatings for original equipment manufacturers in a number of industries and special purpose coatings for the automotive aftermarket, industrial maintenance, and traffic paint markets
Principal Subsidiaries: Brazil:- Sherwin-Williams do Brasil Industria e Comercio Ltda. Canada:- Sherwin-Williams Canada Inc; Sherwin-Williams Automotive Finishes, Inc. Mexico:- Compania Sherwin-Williams, SA de CV. West Indies:- Sherwin Williams, Cayman Islands Ltd (Grand Cayman); The Sherwin-Williams Co Resources Limited (Jamaica); Sherwin-Williams (Caribbean) NV (Curaçao); Sherwin-Williams (West Indies) Ltd (Jamaica); Sherwin-Williams (Barbados) Ltd (Barbados); Sherwin-Williams Foreign Sales Corporation Limited (Virgin Islands). USA:- Sherwin-Williams Development Corporation; SWDC (Ohio) Inc; SWDC (Virginia) Inc; Contract Transportation Systems Co; CTS Brokerage Inc; Dupli-Color Products Company; Lyons Transportation Lines Inc; P-Y Transport Inc; Certified Distribution Services Inc; Ress Realty Co. Joint Ventures: Canada:- BAPCO; 128639 Canada, Inc. Ecuador:- Sherwin-Williams del Ecuador Fábrica Nacional de Pinturas, SA. Ireland:- F.S.W. Coatings Limited; F.S.W. Paints Ltd. Japan:- Nippon Sherwin-Williams Chemicals Co Ltd. Panama:- Sherwin-Williams de Panama SA. Saudi Arabia:-Sherwin Williams Saudi Arabia Ltd. UK:- F.S.W. Ltd
Principal Bank: AmeriTrust Company
Financial Information:

	Dec 31 1986	Dec 31 1987
	$'000	$'000
Sales revenues	1,552,931	1,792,736
Income before taxes	174,074	161,726
Net income	86,357	96,577
Dividends	(22,594)	(24,810)
Dividends per share	$0.50	$0.56
Earnings per share net	$2.31	$2.15
Common stock	47,131	47,603
Retained income	407,873	479,440
Shareholders equity	491,569	549,685

No of Employees: 15,901

SHERWOOD MEDICAL COMPANY

1831 Olive Street, St Louis, MO 63103
Tel: (314) 621-7788
Telex: TRT 193105 argyle stl

Chairman: J W Culligan
President: H E Wickstra
Senior Executive Officers: J T Broers (Senior VP), D A Low (Senior VP), D M Oliver (Senior VP), C D Canevari (VP)

PRINCIPAL ACTIVITIES: Manufacture of medical and surgical equipment and supplies
Parent Company: American Home Products Corporation, New York, NY
Financial Information:

	$'000
Sales revenues	330,000

No of Employees: 5,000

SHOE TOWN INC

994 Riverview Drive, Totowa, NJ 07512
Tel: (201) 785 1900

Chairman: George M Kaye (and Chief Executive Officer)
President: Charles C Cannon (and Chief Operating Officer)
Senior Executive Officers: Lionel M Levey (Chairman of Executive Committee), Irving Beckman (Senior VP), Howard Cohen (VP), Neal R Goldner (VP and Chief Financial Officer), Donald Lebowitz (VP), Robert Shubilla (VP), Mark Witkowsky (VP)

PRINCIPAL ACTIVITIES: Retail of a wide range of footwear
Principal Subsidiaries: Felsway Corporation; Footwear Unlimited Inc
Principal Bank: Citibank
Financial Information:

	$'000
Sales revenues	143,150

No of Employees: 2,150

SHONEY'S, INC

1727 Elm Hill Pike, Nashville, TN 37210
Tel: (615) 361-5201

Chairman: R L Danne; Vice Chairman: J Mitchell Boyd (and Chief Executive Officer)
President: Gary P Spoleta (and Chief Operating Officer)
Senior Executive Officers: James Arnett (Group VP), Frank Brown (Group VP), Veral Starnes (Group VP), Frank Dauscha (VP), Dick Early (VP), Leon Elrod (VP), T H Henry Jr (VP Finance), Louis Leppink (VP Purchasing), Bill Long (VP), Chuck Porter (VP), Steve Sanders (VP), Micky Skelton (VP Personnel), Steve Tidwell (VP Real Estate)

PRINCIPAL ACTIVITIES: Operation of restaurants
Principal Bank: First American National Bank of Nashville
Financial Information:

	$'000
Sales revenues	623,000

No of Employees: 20,000

SHONEY'S SOUTH, INC

2158 Union Ave, Memphis, TN 38104
Tel: (901) 725-6400

Chairman: James H Prentiss (and President and Chief Executive Officer)
Senior Executive Officers: Larry R Walker (Senior VP), Gary W Borth (VP Operations Captain D's), Jack D Gay (VP Personnel), John F Given (VP Operations), Ted F Goldthorpe Jr (VP Marketing)

PRINCIPAL ACTIVITIES: Restaurant operations; insurance broking
Principal Bank: NCNB National Bank of North Carolina
Financial Information:

	$'000
Sales revenues	179,000

No of Employees: 10,000

SHOPSMITH, INC

6640 Poe Avenue, Dayton, OH 45414
Tel: (513) 898-6070

Chairman: J R Folkerth (and Chief Executive Officer); Vice Chairman: H E Folkerth Sr
President: Joseph D Giacomo Jr (and Chief Operating Officer)
Senior Executive Officers: W C Becker (VP Finance), R A Bartlett (Division VP Engineering), M E Harris (Division VP Sales), B L Hile (Division VP Marketing), W A Hussong (Division VP Shopsmith Manufacturing), C I Jaynes (Division VP Missouri Manufacturing), J M Lerer (Division VP Personnel), W U Michel (Division VP Operations)

PRINCIPAL ACTIVITIES: Manufacture of electrically powered tools for carpentry
Principal Bank: Bank One Dayton
Financial Information:

	$'000
Sales revenues	71,000

No of Employees: 500

SHOPWELL INC

400 Walnut Avenue, Bronx, NY 10454
Tel: (212) 579 3400

Chairman: Jay M Rosengarten (and Chief Executive and Administration; Vice Chairman: Herbert B Daitch; Chairman of Office of Chief Executive: Martin Rosengarten
President: Glenn Rosengarten (and Chief Operating Officer)
Senior Executive Officers: Alan H Olstein (Senior VP Division), Laurence R S Buxbaum (VP Real Estate), Paul Farrow (VP Consumer Relations), Abraham Laxer (vP Advertising), Roy Marcus (VP and Chief Financial Officer), Louis Ruggiero (VP Merchandise), David Smithies (VP Human Resources), Stuart Spivak (VP and Controller)

PRINCIPAL ACTIVITIES: Retail food outlets and supermarkets
Principal Subsidiaries: Crystal Products Inc; Delaware County Dairies Inc; Manny's Meat & Vegetable Store; Shopmore Inc; Shopwell VT Inc
Principal Bank: Chase Manhattan
Financial Information:

	$'000
Sales revenues	463,535

No of Employees: 5,030

SHOWBOAT INC

2800 East Fremont Street, Las Vegas, NV 89104
Tel: (702) 385 9123

Chairman: Joseph H Kelley (and President and Chief Executive Officer); Vice Chairman: J K Houssels Jr (and Senior VP)
Senior Executive Officers: Frank A Modica (Chief Operating Officer and Executive Vice President), Fred Morledge (Senior VP), G Clifford Taylor (VP Finance and Treasurer), Randy Miller (Purchasing Agent), H Gregory Nasky (Secretary)

PRINCIPAL ACTIVITIES: Casinos, hotels and restaurants; leisure and entertainment facilities
Principal Subsidiaries: Showboat Operating Company; Showboat Sports Inc
Principal Bank: Valley Bank
Financial Information:

	$'000
Sales revenues	47,500

No of Employees: 1,200

SIEMENS CAPITAL CORPORATION

767 Fifth Avenue, 4th Floor, New York, NY 10022
Telex: WUT 125199 sie corp nyk

Chairman: Karlheinz Kaske; Vice Chairman: Heribald Naerger
President: Hans W Decker
Senior Executive Officers: Thomas E Bolas (VP Corporate Management Audit), Walter G Gans (VP Law), Joachim Hesse (VP and Treasurer), Thomas J Keller (VP Corporate Relations), Peter Kroener (VP and Controller), Leonard Levin (VP Taxes), Jürgen Mittag (VP and Assistant Controller)

PRINCIPAL ACTIVITIES: Holding company; financing operations through its subsidiaries the company has interests in the manufacture and marketing of teleprinter and telephone switching systems; the manufacture of power semiconductors and optoelectronic components, marketing of semiconductors, passive components, and electron tubes; the manufacture and marketing of medical equipment; the manufacture and marketing of electric motors, generators, switchgear and power switching installations, power electronics, regulator and control systems. Siemens Capital Corporation holds an interest in 2 other consolidated Siemens companies and in 2 financial corporations in the USA
Parent Company: Siemens AG, Munich, Germany
Principal Subsidiaries: Siemens Communications Systems Inc; Siemens Components Inc; Siemens Medical Systems Inc; Siemens-Allis Inc. (These four companies hold an interest in 28 other consolidated Siemens companies in the USA, Great Britain, the Netherlands, Austria, Canada, Barbados, and Malaysia)
Principal Bank: Citibank
Financial Information:

	$'000
Sales revenues	1,860,000

No of Employees: 100

SIEMENS ENERGY & AUTOMATION, INC

223 Perimeter Center Pkwy, Atlanta, GA 30346
Tel: (404) 393-8200
Telex: TWX 810 7573 663

President: H S Burker Jr (and Chief Executive Officer)
Senior Executive Officers: J K Radomski (Senior VP, Chief Financial Officer), R E Bailey (VP Marketing), W E Beringer (VP and Secretary), J J Hettich (VP Engineering and Technology Services), H K Stadlbauer (VP Power Engineering Marketing Division), C R Smelas (VP Controller), G L Bourassa (VP Human Resources)

PRINCIPAL ACTIVITIES: Manufacture of a wide range of electrical/electronic equipment and systems for electric utilities, commercial and residential construction and general industry
Trade Names: I-T-E electrical products
Parent Company: Siemens AG, Germany
Financial Information:

	$'000
Sales revenues	700,000

No of Employees: 8,000

SIERRA PACIFIC INDUSTRIES

PO Drawer Y, Arcata, CA 95521
Tel: (707) 443-3111

President: A A Emmerson
Senior Executive Officers: Ron Hoppe (Sales Manager), Francis B Mathews (General Counsel), Donald E Riewerts (Secretary), Richard L Smith (Treasurer)

PRINCIPAL ACTIVITIES: Production and processing of timber
Principal Bank: Bank of America
Financial Information:

	$'000
Sales revenues	225,000

No of Employees: 1,500

SIERRA PACIFIC RESOURCES

3301 South Virginia Street, PO Box 30150, Reno, NV 89520
Tel: (702) 789 4030

Chairman: Joe L Gremban (and President and Chief Executive Officer)
Senior Executive Officers: Richard E Hughs (VP Corporate Affairs), J Sargini (VP), Richard H Schmidt (Treasurer and Assistant Secretary)

PRINCIPAL ACTIVITIES: Supply of electricity
Financial Information:

	$'000
Sales revenues	373,000

No of Employees: 15

SIERRA RESEARCH DIVISION
LTV Missiles and Electronics Group

247 Cayuga Road, Buffalo, NY 14225-0222
Tel: (716) 631-6200
Telex: 685-4308

President: Thomas W Cobb
Senior Executive Officers: Goerge H Davidson (VP, General Manager, Advanced Technology Products Business Elements), John T Buck (VP, General Manager, Command Control and Navigation Business Element), Herman P Knocklein (VP, General Manager, Electronic Warfare Business Element), John Bathrick (VP, Engineering), William J Sullivan (VP, Finance)

PRINCIPAL ACTIVITIES: Manufacture of electronic and avionic equipment for aircraft, electronic warfare equipment, data links, flight inspection systems, and electronic integration
Parent Company: The LTV Corporation, Dallas, Texas
Principal Bank: Chemical Bank
Financial Information:

	$'000
Sales revenues	108,000

No of Employees: 1,108

SIERRA SPRING WATER COMPANY

1801 R Street, Sacramento, CA 95814
Tel: (916) 446 5341

Chairman: Ritz Naygrow
President: Tom Naygrow
Senior Executive Officers: Steven J Orlando (VP Finance and Treasurer), Louis W Panos (VP Production), Todd M Vansenten (VP and Legal Counsel), June Naygrow (Secretary)

PRINCIPAL ACTIVITIES: Production of bottled water and coffee
Financial Information:

	$'000
Sales revenues	34,570

No of Employees: 350

SIERRACIN CORPORATION

12780 San Fernando Road, Sylmar, CA 91342
Tel: (818) 362-6802
Telex: 677122
Fax: (818) 362-0603

Chairman: Christopher Tribull (and President and Chief Executive Officer and Chief Operating Officer)
Senior Executive Officers: Eldon Swanson (President Transflex, Formerly Thermal Systems Division), Errol Roy (President Harrison Division), James Romine (President Magnedyne Division), Terence Jacobsen (President Intrex Division),

Richard Monteferrante (President TransTech Division), Gary Roberts Sr (Senior VP Finance and Secretary)

PRINCIPAL ACTIVITIES: Sierracin Corporation manufactures high technology products for the aerospace, electronics and industrial markets

Principal Subsidiaries: Sierracin Research Corp

Principal Bank: California Federal Savings & Loan

Financial Information:

	Dec 31 1985	Dec 31 1986
	$'000	$'000
Revenues	61,445	72,670
Income (loss) before taxes	(2,280)	3,624
Net income (loss)	(2,718)	642
Dividends	676	-
Dividends per share	$0.20	-
Earnings (loss) per share	($0.80)	$0.19
Common stock	3,659	3,660
Retained income	13,711	14,270
Shareholders equity	14,645	15,366

No of Employees: 900

SIFCO INDUSTRIES, INC

970 E 64th Street, Cleveland, OH 44103

Tel: (216) 881-8600

Telex: WUT 980664 sifco clv

Chairman: Charles H Smith Jr

President: Kevin O'Donnell (and Chief Executive Officer)

Senior Executive Officers: Jeffrey P Gotschall (Executive VP and Chief Operating Officer), Edwin J Schmidt (VP), Richard A Demetter (VP Finance and Chief Financial Officer), Hudson D Smith (Treasurer), Mara L Babin (Secretary and General Counsel)

PRINCIPAL ACTIVITIES: SIFCO Industries Inc headquartered in Cleveland, Ohio is a global manufacturer, manager and marketer that focuses on metalworking and related industrial technologies. SIFCO links domestic with affiliated and independent foreign manufacturing facilities. In concert with its related trading company, SIFCO uses its management and marketing expertise to provide worldwide sourcing and selling capabilities. SIFCO's business segments are: Specialty Products and Services: Manufacture of original and replacement large-diameter bearings for specialized industrial markets; remanufacture and other services for the bearing aftermarket; equipment, solutions and contract services in selective electroplating for aerospace, shipbuilding and most other industrial markets; contract precision machining for aerospace, turbine power generation equipment and medical prostheses; remanufacture and modification of jet engine and land-based combustion turbine components; distribution of replacement components for trucks, off-highway and other heavy equipment; services in international technology transfer, trade and business development. Forgings: Specialized and commercial forgings for applications in virtually all major industrial markets. These are produced in carbon, alloy and stainless steels; titanium; high temperature and numerous exotic alloys. Processing is by hammers, upsetters, presses or cold/warm extrusion as required by application. SIFCO SA: A multifaceted industrial manufacturer operating six facilities in Brazil. The largest forging operation of a publicly held firm in the Southern Hemisphere provides the base for product diversification. Operations include finished components and sub-assemblies for automotive and truck manufacturers; induction heating and melting equipment for the forging and foundry industries; speed reducers, gears and castings for industry; pumping equipment for oilfields; and remanufacture, upgrading and repowering of tracked vehicles for military applications

Principal Subsidiaries: SIFCO Custom Machining Co; SIFCO Bearings Inc; SIFCO Replacement Components Co; SIFCO Turbine Components Ltd

Principal Bank: National City Bank

Financial Information:

	Sep 30 1985	Sep 30 1986
	$'000	$'000
Sales revenues	59,225	61,323
Income (loss) before taxes	(1,903)	2,289
Net income (loss)	(855)	1,784*
Dividends	214	215
Dividends per share	$0.10	$0.10
Earnings (loss) per share net	($0.40)	$0.83*
Common stock	2,150	2,152
Retained income	18,108	20,483
Shareholders equity	25,512	27,898
*before accounting method change		

No of Employees: 580

SIGMA-ALDRICH CORPORATION

3050 Spruce Street, St Louis, MO 63103

Tel: (314) 771-5765

Chairman: Alfred Bader

President: Carl T Cori (and Chief Executive Officer)

Senior Executive Officers: David R Harvey (Executive VP and Chief Operating Officer), Peter A Gleich (VP, Secretary and Treasurer)

PRINCIPAL ACTIVITIES: Holding company with interests in the manufacture of chemicals including biochemicals and diagnostics, inorganic and specialty chemicals; aluminum components

Principal Subsidiaries: Sigma Chamical Co; Aldrich Chemical Co Inc; B-Line Systems Inc; Alrich-Boranes Inc

Principal Bank: Boatmen's National Bank of St Louis

Financial Information:

	$'000
Sales revenues	253,000

No of Employees: 2,400

SIGNAL APPAREL COMPANY, INC

200A Manufacturers Rd, PO Box 4296, Chattanooga, TN 37405

Tel: (615) 756-8146

Chairman: George B Clairmont

President: J Franklin Joiner (and Chief Executive Officer)

Senior Executive Officers: James Brown (VP-Manufacturing), David Bryant (VP-Sales and Marketing), Jeremy Dick (VP-Administration), Leslie W Levy (VP and President of Heritage Sportswear Division), Dennis Roberts (VP-Human Resources), Paul Bradshaw (Secretary), Ted Grubbs (Treasurer)

PRINCIPAL ACTIVITIES: Manufacture of men's and children's clothing; sports clothes and women's knit apparel

Trade Names: Signal, Heritage USA, Joan Vass USA, Laura Pearson USA

Principal Bank: Continental Illinois National Bank & Trust Co

Financial Information:

	Dec 31 1985	Dec 31 1986
	$'000	$'000
Sales revenues	79,229	94,488
Income (loss) before taxes	(726)	8,145
Net income (loss)	(398)	4,238
Dividends	271	286
Dividends per share	$0.20	$0.20
Earnings (loss) per share	($0.31)	$1.35
Common stock	4,595	5,125
Retained income	17,147	20,438
Shareholders equity	27,845	31,018

No of Employees: 2,250

SIGNAL KNITTING MILLS, INC

Manufacturers Road, Box 4296, Chattanooga, TN 37405

Tel: (615) 266-2175

Chairman: Robert Colbert

President: R M Yount

Senior Executive Officers: Thomas N Parker (Executive VP), Peter Platt (VP Sales), Vijay Ralhan (VP Production), George Monson (Treasurer)

PRINCIPAL ACTIVITIES: Manufacture of knitted sports clothing and underwear
Parent Company: Wayne-Gossard Corp, Chattanooga, TN
Principal Bank: First Tennessee
Financial Information:

	$'000
Sales revenues	60,000

No of Employees: 1,900

SIGNET BANKING CO
PO Box 25970, Richmond, VA 23260
Tel: (804) 747-2000

Chairman: Frederick Deane Jr (and Chief Executive Officer); Vice Chairmen: William H Cowie Jr, Malcolm S McRonald
President: Robert M Freeman (and Chief Operating Officer)
Senior Executive Officers: Wallace B Millner III (Executive VP and Chief Financial Officer), David S Norris (Executive VP and Controller)

PRINCIPAL ACTIVITIES: Banking and financial services
Principal Subsidiaries: Signet Bank, Virginia; Signet Bank, Maryland; Signet Bank NA
Financial Information:

	Dec 31 1985	Dec 31 1986
	$'000	$'000
Net income	71,070	86,277
Dividends per share	-	$1.21
Earnings per share	$3.05	$3.53
Shareholders equity	417,750	527,415
Deposits	5,353,680	5,776,723
Total assets	7,744,630	8,286,431

No of Employees: 5,880

SIKES CORPORATION
One Sikes Blvd, Lakeland, FL 33801
Tel: (813) 687-7171
Telex: TWX 810 8670 465 sikes ikl

Chairman: Leon R Sikes Jr
President: Kelly Norton (and Chief Executive Officer)
Senior Executive Officers: Warren E Clegg (Executive VP Corporate Services), Rudolph H Thornberry (Senior VP Marketing), William R Boakes (VP), Phillip G Dunne (VP Finance), Sam LaNeave (VP Sales)

PRINCIPAL ACTIVITIES: Manufacture of ceramic tiles
Principal Bank: Sun Bank
Financial Information:

	$'000
Sales revenues	87,660

No of Employees: 1,100

SILER CITY MILLS, INC
118 W 2nd Street, Siler City, NC 27344
Tel: (919) 742-2166

Chairman: William M Wren (and President)
Senior Executive Officers: Roy McCollum (VP Purchasing), William McKeown (VP Administration and Secretary)

PRINCIPAL ACTIVITIES: Flour milling and production of animal feed
Parent Company: Wren Industries Inc, Siler City, NC
Principal Bank: First Union National Bank
Financial Information:

	$'000
Sales revenues	50,000

No of Employees: 320

SILICON GENERAL INC
11651 Monarch Street, Garden Grove, CA 92641
Tel: (714) 892 5531

Chairman: Q T Wiles (and Chief Executive Officer); Associate Chairman: Michael O Preletz
Presidents: William D Rasdel (and Chief Executive Officer); Robert Deinhammer (and Chief Operating Officer)
Senior Executive Officers: Ralph Brandi (Executive VP), Warren L Perry (Executive VP), Paul N Risinger (Executive VP), John L Kehoe (VP and Chief Financial Officer), Irwin Reuling (Secretary and Treasurer)

PRINCIPAL ACTIVITIES: Manufacture of electronic components including semiconductors and converters
Principal Bank: Bank of America NT & SA
Financial Information:

	$'000
Sales revenues	46,200

No of Employees: 400

SILICON SYSTEMS, INC
14351 Myford Road, Tustin, CA 92680
Tel: (714) 731-7110
Telex: TWX 910 595 2604 ss im kt

Chairman: Carmelo J Santoro (and President and Chief Executive Officer)
President: Stephen E Cooper (and Chief Operating Officer)
Senior Executive Officers: Richard Goerner (Senior VP), William Healey (Senior VP), Martin H Jurick (Senior VP), Gary Kelson (Senior VP), Nick E Yocca (Corporate Secretary)

PRINCIPAL ACTIVITIES: Manufacture of integrated circuits for computers and telecommunications equipment
Principal Bank: Wells Fargo Bank
Financial Information:

	$'000
Sales revenues	54,600

No of Employees: 330

SILICON VALLEY GROUP
541 East Trimble Road, San Jose, CA 95131
Tel: (408) 945 9300

Chairman: Gerald M Starek (and Chief Executive Officer)
President: Papken S Der Torossian (and Chief Operating Officer)
Senior Executive Officers: Kenneth D Giles (VP Marketing), Patrick C O'Connor (VP Corporate Development), Arthur G Silver (VP Manufacturing), Johann Tam (VP Engineering)

PRINCIPAL ACTIVITIES: Manufacture of specialty electronic equipment including semiconductor wafer processing equipment
Principal Bank: Bank of America NT & SA
Financial Information:

	$'000
Sales revenues	40,000

No of Employees: 300

SILICONIX INC
2201 Laurelwood Road, Santa Clara, CA 95054
Tel: (408) 988-8000
Telex: TWX 910 3380 227 siliconix snta
Telefax: (408) 727-5414

Chairman: Richard E Lee (and President and Chief Executive Officer)
Senior Executive Officers: Douglas R Sullivan (Executive VP and Chief Operating Officer), Peter W Weber (VP), Richard J Kulle (VP), Donald G Keefe (VP), John W Niem (VP), Walter Senges (VP)

PRINCIPAL ACTIVITIES: Manufacture of components equipment including transistors and integrated circuits

Principal Bank: First Interstate Bank
Financial Information:

	Dec 31 1986
	$'000
Sales revenues	111,185
Income before taxes	11,819
Net income	7,364
Earnings per share	$0.55
Common stock	12,780
Retained income	43,184
Shareholders equity	65,721

Principal Shareholders: Westinghouse Corp; Dr R E Lee
No of Employees: 2,730

SILTEC CORPORATION

190 Independence Drive, Menlo Park, CA 94025-1197
Tel: (415) 328-7600
Telex: 348336 SILEQ MNPK
Fax: (415) 853-5080

Chairman: Shigeru Masuda
President: Stanley T Myers (and Chief Executive Officer)
Senior Executive Officers: Yasuo Sawada (Executive VP), Kanegi Nagai (Executive VP/GP Manager for Cybeg Systems, a business unit of Siltec), Bradford M Wait (Senior VP, Administration and Chief Financial Officer)

PRINCIPAL ACTIVITIES: Manufacture of silicon wafers and processing equipment for the electronics industry
Parent Company: Mitsubishi Metal Corp, Tokyo, Japan
Principal Subsidiaries: Siltec Silicon (wafers mfg); Cybeg Systems (equipment)

No of Employees: 500

SILVERCREST INDUSTRIES, INC

299 N Smith Ave, Corona, CA 91720
Tel: (714) 734 6610

Chairman: Howard Sherman
President: Richard Simonian (and Chief Executive Officer)
Senior Executive Officers: Gary King (Senior VP and Chief Financial Officer), Ralph J Calzaretta Sr (VP and Treasurer), Victor Ewy (Regional VP South), Robert Servatius (Regional VP North)

PRINCIPAL ACTIVITIES: Manufacture of sectional homes, mobile homes and park development and operation
Principal Subsidiaries: Lynn Forest Products Inc; Lake Mountain Estates Inc; Santiago Corporation; Coastland Construction; Santiago Consulting
Principal Bank: Security Pacific National Bank
Financial Information:

	$'000
Sales revenues	56,451

No of Employees: 700

SIM KAR LIGHTING FIXTURE COMPANY INC

601 East Cayuga Street, Philadelphia, PA 19120
Tel: (215) 831 7700

Chairman: Charles A Trowbridge (and Secretary)
President: Barney Bernstein
Senior Executive Officers: Bernard Aronson (Executive VP), Scott Butville (VP), John Donahue (VP), Joseph Nasal (VP), Fred Shander (VP and Treasurer), Antonio Almazan (Controller), Nat Meerbaum (Purchasing Agent)

PRINCIPAL ACTIVITIES: Manufacture of a wide range of light fittings and equipment
Principal Bank: Continental Bank
Financial Information:

	$'000
Sales revenues	48,815

No of Employees: 575

SIMKINS INDUSTRIES INC

259 East Street, New Haven, CT 06511
Tel: (203) 787-7171

Chairman: Leon J Simkins (and President)
Senior Executive Officers: James N Galvin (Chief Financial Officer), S F Gadon (Secretary), Barbera P Camera (Assistant Secretary and Treasurer), Milton Anderson (Controller)

PRINCIPAL ACTIVITIES: Manufacture of packaging products and paper
Principal Subsidiaries: First Quip Leasing Co; Beveridge Paper Co Inc; Westfield Financial Corp; Westfield River Paper Co; Lowe Paper Co
Principal Bank: Mellon
Financial Information:

	Sep 30 1986	Sep 30 1987
	$'000	$'000
Sales revenues	145,957	182,361
Income before taxes	13,133	13,404
Net income	8,956	9,824
Common stock	1,882	1,882
Retained income	81,636	91,460
Shareholders equity*	67,156	73,701

*includes treasury stock

No of Employees: 1,550

SIMMONDS PRECISION PRODUCTS, INC

150 White Plains Road, Tarrytown, NY 10591
Tel: (914) 631-7500
Telex: WUT 925051 simmonds prec

President: Robert I August (and Chief Executive Officer)
Senior Executive Officers: Russell R Coyner (Group VP), Timothy S Kavanaugh (Secretary and General Counsel), Thomas S Seary (Controller)

PRINCIPAL ACTIVITIES: Manufacture of fuel gages, oil gages, temperature gages and ignition equipment for aircraft
Parent Company: Hercules Inc, Wilmington, DE
Principal Bank: The First National Bank of Boston
Financial Information:

	$'000
Sales revenues	153,000

No of Employees: 3,000

SIMMONS AIRLINES INC

900 N Franklin St, Chicago, IL 60610
Tel: (312) 280 8222

Chairman: Joel Murray (and Chief Executive Officer)
President: Marvin W Murray (and Chief Operating Officer)
Senior Executive Officers: Peter A Piper (Executive VP), James M Davis (Senior VP Service), James Forgan Ott (Senior VP and Chief Financial Officer), George R Hagens (VP Airline Reliability), Timothy J Harristhal (VP Operations), Gary S Holter (VP and Controller), Robert D Morrison (VP Real Estate and Facilities)

PRINCIPAL ACTIVITIES: Operation of air transport services
Financial Information:

	$'000
Sales revenues	72,000

No of Employees: 1,060

SIMMONS FIRST NATIONAL CORPORATION

501 Main Street, Pine Bluff, AR 71601
Tel: (501) 541 1350

President: Howell N Davis (and Chief Executive Officer)
Senior Executive Officers: W E Ayres (Senior Executive VP), John L Rush (Senior VP and Secretary)

PRINCIPAL ACTIVITIES: Holding company with interests in banking
Principal Subsidiaries: Simmons First National Bank

No of Employees: 400

SIMON & SCHUSTER INC
1230 Avenue of the Americas, New York, NY 10020
Tel: (12)435-6400
Telex: WUT 127806 sims schustr nyk

Chairman: Richard E Snyder (and President)
Senior Executive Officers: Enzo Vialardi (Executive VP), P J Russo (Senior VP Finance and Administration), Eric Rayman (VP), Harold Gordon (VP), Richard A Koplitz (VP Purchasing), Michael Korda (VP), Rudolph Sanson Jr (VP and Secretary)

PRINCIPAL ACTIVITIES: Simon & Schuster is one of the world's foremost book publishers. The company holds leadership positions in virtually every major segment of the book publishing industry and is building a growing position in information services
Parent Company: Gulf & Western Industries Inc, New York, NY
Principal Bank: Bankers Trust Company
Financial Information:

	$'000
Sales revenues	300,000

No of Employees: 2,000

SIMPLEX WIRE & CABLE CO
PO Box 479, Portsmouth, NH 03801
Tel: (603) 436-6100
Telex: TWX 510 297 4419 simplex porh

Chairman: John F Fort
President: John C McIntyre
Senior Executive Officers: Maurice L Fenderson (VP Engineering), Bernard C Duboise (VP Marketing and Sales)

PRINCIPAL ACTIVITIES: Manufacture of cables and wires for telecommunications and power transmission
Parent Company: Tyco Laboratories Inc, Exeter, NH
Financial Information:

	$'000
Sales revenues	50,000

No of Employees: 450

SIMPSON INDUSTRIES, INC
32100 Telegraph Road, Birmingham, MI 48010
Tel: (313) 540-6200
Telex: TWX 810 232 4810 smps ud

Chairman: Robert W Navarre (and President)
Senior Executive Officers: R H Behling (Executive VP Manufacturing Operations), C K Winter (VP Human Resources), K E Berman (VP Finance and Treasurer), D R Marsh (VP Sales and Marketing)

PRINCIPAL ACTIVITIES: Manufacture of machined parts, and automotive components
Principal Bank: Manufacturers National Bank of Detroit
Financial Information:

	Jun 30 1986 (12 mths) $'000	Dec 31 1986 (6 mths) $'000
Sales revenues	147,323	68,125
Income before taxes	12,437	1,787
Net income	9,238	192
Dividends	3,405	1,770
Dividends per share	$0.54	$0.28
Earnings per share	$1.47	$0.03
Common stock	6,318	6,321
Retained income	43,174	41,596
Shareholders equity	49,576	48,536

No of Employees: 1,342

SIMPSON INVESTMENT COMPANY
900 4th Avenue, Seattle, WA 98164
Tel: (206) 292-5000
Telex: WUT 329560 simpson hq sea

Chairman: Wm G Reed Jr; Vice Chairman: Gilbert L Oswald
President: Furman C Moseley
Senior Executive Officers: J Thurston Roach (VP and Chief Financial Officer), R James Day (VP and Treasurer), Joseph L Leitzinger (VP Public Affairs), Robert J Day (VP Planning and Control), Cindy P Sonstelie (VP Human Resources), Joseph R Breed (VP and General Counsel)

PRINCIPAL ACTIVITIES: Production of timber, lumber, plywood, doors, pulp and paper and extruded plastic pipe
Principal Subsidiaries: Simpson Paper Co; Simpson Timber Co; Pacific Western Extruded Plastics Co
Principal Bank: Seattle-First National Bank

No of Employees: 6,200

SIMPSON TIMBER COMPANY
900 Fourth Avenue, Seattle, WA 98164
Tel: (206) 292-5000
Telex: 261379

Chairman: William G Reed Jr
Directors: T R Ingham Jr
Senior Executives: J R Breed (VP and General Counsel), Robert J Day (VP and Treasurer), R R Grant (VP and Controller), J Thurston Roach (VP, Secretary and Chief Financial Officer), H P Sandstrom (VP and General Manager, Redwood), J L Walker (VP Land and Timber)

PRINCIPAL ACTIVITIES: Manufacture of plywood and hardwood veneer, building paper; sawmills and logging camps
Parent Company: Simpson Investment Co
Subsidiary Companies: Simpson Paper Co
Principal Bankers: Mellon Bank
Financial Information:

	$'000
Sales turnover	670,000

No of Employees: 2,600

SINGER COMPANY (THE)
110 Summit Avenue, PO Box 426, Montvale, NJ 07645
Tel: (201) 573-8016
Telex: WUI 681 9114 singer wh std

Chairman: Joseph B Flavin (and President and Chief Executive Officer)
Senior Executive Officers: F G Bitter (Senior VP and Chief Financial Officer), Terry W Heil (Executive VP Defense Electronics Group), T S Hoffman Jr (Senior VP, Human Resources), W D Turner (Group VP, Training Systems Group), P A Watson (Senior VP, General Counsel), T L Elliott Jr (VP, Corporate Relations)

PRINCIPAL ACTIVITIES: Manufacturer of electronic equipment for aerospace and defense
Financial Information:

	Dec 31 1986 $'000
Sales revenues	1,725,200
Income before taxes	65,300
Net income	82,600
Dividends	13,000
Dividends per share	$0.40
Earnings per share	$2.63
Common stock	209,600
Retained income	269,500
Shareholders equity	607,000

No of Employees: 28,000

SIPI METALS CORPORATION

1720 N Elston Avenue, Chicago, IL 60622
Tel: (312) 276-0070
Telex: TWX 910 221 6057 sipi metco cgo

Chairman: Philip Pinsof
President: Leslie S Pinsof
Senior Executive Officers: Robert S Glidden (VP Operations), Dennis Arakelian (VP Engineering), Marion A Cameron (Treasurer and VP Finance)

PRINCIPAL ACTIVITIES: Manufacture of metal products including those made from aluminum, lead, zinc, tin, copper and brass; precious metal refining
Principal Bank: American National Bank
Financial Information:

	$'000
Sales revenues	50,000

No of Employees: 125

SIPPICAN INC

7 Barnabas Road, Marion, MA 02738
Tel: (617) 748 1160

Chairman: Thayer Francis Jr
President: Richard I Arthur (and Chief Executive Officer)
Senior Executive Officers: Richard W Bixby (VP Engineering), David P Gagnon (VP Production), Stephen S Galliker (VP Finance and Treasurer), Henry C Hall (VP and Controller), Frank E Maddocks (VP Quality Control), John Kelso (VP Manufacturing), William E Walsh Jr (VP Marketing Software)

PRINCIPAL ACTIVITIES: Scientific and research equipment
Principal Bank: First National Bank of Boston
Financial Information:

	$'000
Sales revenues	32,065

No of Employees: 400

SIRCO INTERNATIONAL CORPORATION

700 South Fulton Avenue, Mount Vernon, NY 10550
Tel: (914) 664 4400

Chairman: Burt J Siris
President: Joseph Ganz
Senior Executive Officers: John Goldsmith (Executive VP), Sidney Jerris (VP Finance), Leonard Yolowitz (Secretary and Treasurer)

PRINCIPAL ACTIVITIES: Supply of leather goods, luggage, handbags and accessories
Principal Subsidiaries: Utility Company Inc
Principal Bank: Irving Trust Company
Financial Information:

	$'000
Sales revenues	41,000

No of Employees: 240

SIZZLER RESTAURANTS INTERNATIONAL INC

5400 Alla Road, Los Angeles, CA 90066
Tel: (213) 827 2300

Chairman: Joseph A Collins
President: Thomas L Gregory (and Chief Executive Officer)
Senior Executive Officers: Michael W Arthur (Executive VP Administration and Development), Michael M Minchin Jr (Executive VP), Michael R MacAtee (Senior VP Merchandise), W A Fitzgerald (VP), Ileen Garcia (VP, Treasurer and Chief Financial Officer), R E Harrod (VP), R G Knapp (VP), J S McGinnis (VP)

PRINCIPAL ACTIVITIES: Restaurants
Financial Information:

	$'000
Sales revenues	241,000

No of Employees: 5,100

SJW CORPORATION

374 West Santa Clara Street, San Jose, CA 95113
Tel: (408) 279 7819

President: J W Weinhardt (and Chief Executive Officer)
Senior Executive Officers: F R Meyer (VP, Chief Financial Officer and Treasurer), P J Schreiber (VP Operations)

PRINCIPAL ACTIVITIES: Water supply
Principal Bank: Bank of America NT & SA
Financial Information:

	$'000
Sales revenues	61,000

SKF INDUSTRIES, INC

1100 First Avenue, King of Prussia, PA 19406
Tel: (215) 265-1900
Telex: WUI 6851030 sffex

Chairman: Carl W Desch
President: James Skinner
Senior Executive Officers: Charles F Wuestner (VP and Group Executive), Thomas H Karlsson (VP and Group Executive), Adam H Herzig (VP and Group Executive), Tibor E Tallian (VP Technology), William H Vonier (VP Marketing), Daniel F Collins (VP and Corporate Controller)

PRINCIPAL ACTIVITIES: Manufacture of ball and roller bearings and automotive components
Parent Company: AB SKF, Göteborg, Sweden
Financial Information:

	$'000
Sales revenues	400,000

No of Employees: 5,000

SKI LIMITED

Killington Rd, Killington, UT 05751
Tel: (802) 422-3333

Chairman: Joseph D Sargent (and Treasurer)
President: Preston L Smith (and Chief Executive Officer)
Senior Executive Officers: Foster T Chandler Jr (VP Marketing), Christopher S Diamond (VP), Henry B Lunde (VP), Walter N Morrison (VP), Martel D Wilson Jr (VP and Controller)

PRINCIPAL ACTIVITIES: Holding company with interests in the leisure and entertainment industries
Principal Subsidiaries: Killington Ltd; Mount Snow Ltd
Principal Bank: First National Bank of Boston
Financial Information:

	$'000
Sales revenues	48,420

No of Employees: 1,260

SKIL CORPORATION

4801 W Peterson Avenue, Chicago, IL 60646
Tel: (312) 286-7330
Telex: TRT 190103 skil ut

President: George M Sherman
Senior Executive Officers: Carl Amrein (VP Engineering), L S Bailey (VP Sales and Service), Peter Bredehoeft (VP Materials Distribution), Gene Goode (VP National Accounts), James Healy (VP Finance), Cliff McRae (VP Management Information Services), James New (VP International), George D Slocum (VP Manufacturing), Ronald J Staub (VP Public Relations), Jack Watson (VP Marketing, Planning and Services)

PRINCIPAL ACTIVITIES: Manufacture of a wide range of power hand tools
Parent Company: Emerson Electric Company, St Louis, MO

Principal Bank: Continental Illinois National Bank and Trust Company
Financial Information:

	$'000
Sales revenues	164,000

No of Employees: 4,000

SKIPPER'S INC
14450 Northeast 29th Place, Bellevue, WA 98007
Tel: (206) 454 3456

Chairman: M Eugene Stone (and Chief Executive Officer)
President: Chris L LeSourd (and Chief Operating Officer)
Senior Executive Officers: Douglas C Bamford (VP), David Miller (VP Control), Carol L Nolan (VP and Controller), Mark Pass (VP Real Estate and Development), Jay W Switzer (VP, Secretary and Treasurer), John Torza (VP Purchasing)

PRINCIPAL ACTIVITIES: Seafood restaurant chain
Principal Subsidiaries: Skipper's Seafood'n Chowder House Inc; Seattle Restaurant Equipment Co Inc; Joe's Restaurants Ltd
Principal Bank: First Interstate Bank of Washington
Financial Information:

	$'000
Sales revenues	72,300

No of Employees: 2,520

SKYLINE CORPORATION
2520 By Pass Road, Elkhart, IN 46514
Tel: (219) 294-6521

Chairman: A J Declo (and Chief Executive Officer)
President: Ronald F Kloska
Senior Executive Officers: Donald A Barrow (VP), Terrence M Decio (VP Marketing), Pat J Divietro (VP), Joseph B Fanchi (VP Finance), Eugene A Gassere (VP), J P Kerich (VP Sales), Frederick C Mischke (VP and Treasurer), William H Murschel (VP)

PRINCIPAL ACTIVITIES: Manufacture of sectional homes and recreational vehicles
Principal Subsidiaries: Skyline Homes Inc; Homette Corp; Layton Homes Inc
Principal Bank: American National Bank & Trust Co Chicago
Financial Information:

	$'000
Sales revenues	316,200

No of Employees: 2,700

SL INDUSTRIES, INC
Three Greentree Centre, Marlton, NJ 08053
Tel: (609) 596-7800

Chairman: Byrne Litschgi
President: John C Instone (and Chief Executive Officer)
Senior Executive Officers: Robert T Cross (VP Finance and Secretary), Gordon C Mason (VP Corporate Development), Charles A Shipley (VP Finance), Raymond R Wright (VP Operations)

PRINCIPAL ACTIVITIES: Manufacture of plastic products; electroplating of metals; manufacture of magnetic components and printed circuits
Principal Subsidiaries: S G L Homalite; S G L Auburn Spark Plug Company; S G L Piping Systems
Principal Bank: Heritage Bank
Financial Information:

	$'000
Sales revenues	67,850

No of Employees: 900

SLATTERY GROUP INC
1044 Northern Boulevard, PO Box C, Roslyn, NY 11576
Tel: (516) 484 5858

Chairman: Milton Cooper
President: Bernard Richards (and Chief Executive Officer)
Senior Executive Officers: Joseph Catapano (VP and Treasurer), John D Saunders (VP Construction), Robert E Hartmann (Secretary)

PRINCIPAL ACTIVITIES: Civil engineering including construction of roads and bridges
Principal Subsidiaries: Slattery Equities Inc; Grow Tunneling Corporation; H Sand & Company; Underpinning Foundation Contractors
Principal Bank: Citibank
Financial Information:

	$'000
Sales revenues	134,000

No of Employees: 220

SLAUGHTER BROTHERS, INC
11050 Plano Road, Dallas, TX 75238
Tel: (214) 341-9000

President: Timothy J Thompson
Senior Executive Officers: Ronald Kephart (VP Finance, Secretary and Treasurer), George W Steele (VP)

PRINCIPAL ACTIVITIES: Timber production; building products
Parent Company: STK Enterprises Inc
Principal Bank: Republic Bank
Financial Information:

	$'000
Sales revenues	60,000

No of Employees: 170

SLEEPECK PRINTING CO
815 25th Avenue, Bellwood, IL 60104
Tel: (312) 544-8900

Chairman: William H Sleepeck Jr
President: Stanley Strotman
Senior Executive Officers: Robert R Kenyon (Executive VP), George Sinka (VP Manufacturing), Michael W Sleepeck (VP Sales)

PRINCIPAL ACTIVITIES: Printing services
Principal Bank: Continental Illinois National Bank and Trust Company
Financial Information:

	$'000
Sales revenues	50,000

No of Employees: 400

SLOANE, R & G, MANUFACTURING
7660 N Clybourn, Sun Valley, CA 91352
Tel: (213) 767-4726

President: N M Dye
Senior Executive Officers: Michael J Denehy (VP Plumbing and International Division), J Michael Hogan (VP Manufacturing), J Patrick Hopkins (VP Marketing), Henry J Medina (VP Finance and Controller), L L Murphy (VP Sales)

PRINCIPAL ACTIVITIES: Manufacture of plumbing supplies including plastic pipe, fittings and valves
Parent Company: Susquehanna Corporation, Englewood, CO
Principal Bank: Bank of America
Financial Information:

	$'000
Sales revenues	75,000

No of Employees: 900

SMD INDUSTRIES INC
190 North Main Street, Natick, MA 01760
Tel: (617) 237 6477

Chairman: David Knopping
President: Aaron H Knopping (and Executive VP)

Senior Executive Officers: Richard J Knopping (Executive VP and Treasurer), Paul R Yecies (VP Administration and Finance), Lawrence M Levinson (Clerk)

PRINCIPAL ACTIVITIES: Manufacture of picture frames, jewelry boxes, stationery and school supplies
Principal Bank: Bank of New England
Financial Information:

	$'000
Sales revenues	32,140

No of Employees: 600

SMIDTH, F L, & CO

300 Knickerbocker Road, Cresskill, NJ 07626
Tel: (201) 871-3300
Telex: WUT 135452 fl smidth cres

Chairman: Erik B Rasmussen
President: Julian B Lewis
Senior Executive Officers: Joseph S Katzel (VP and Treasurer), George F Grana (Secretary)

PRINCIPAL ACTIVITIES: Distribution of machinery and equipment for the cement and metallurgical industries
Parent Company: F L Smidth & Co A/S, Copenhagen, Denmark
Principal Bank: Bankers Trust Company
Financial Information:

	$'000
Sales revenues	64,000

No of Employees: 200

SMITH & WESSON

2100 Roosevelt Avenue, Springfield, MA 01102
Tel: (413) 781-8300
Telex: WUI 6817064 SMIWS UW

President: L J Deters (and Chief Executive Officer)
Senior Executive Officers: Robert I Hass (Senior VP Marketing), Robert A Metzger (Senior VP Manufacturing), G W Bachmann (VP Administration and Assistant to President), John M Prosser (VP Finance), Delbert E Shorb (VP Sales Sporting Goods), David G Simons (VP Sales Public and Industrial Safety Products)

PRINCIPAL ACTIVITIES: Manufacture of firearms
Parent Company: Lear Siegler Inc
Principal Bank: Bank of New England-West
Financial Information:

	$'000
Sales revenues	100,000

No of Employees: 2,000

SMITH, A O, CORPORATION

11270 West Park Place, Milwaukee, WI 53224-3690
Tel: (414) 359-4000
Telex: TWX 9102623388 aos milw

Chairman: Thomas I Dolan (and Chief Executive Officer)
President: Robert O'Toole (and Chief Operating Officer)
Senior Executive Officers: G R Bomberger (Executive VP and Chief Financial Officer), Donald L Dunaway (Executive VP), Rod A LeMense (Executive VP), John R Donnelly (VP and Chairman Electrical Products Company), Bill W Wilcock (VP and Chairman Automotive), Dr Charles J Bishop (VP-Corporate Technology), Edward J O'Connor (VP-Human Resources and Public Affairs), Tom W Ryan (VP and Treasurer), David A Fewkes (VP, Secretary and General Counsel), Earl R Milner (VP-Controller), Richard A Wendorf (VP and President Smith Fiberglass Products, Inc), Paul W Smaglick (VP and Executive VP Automotive Products Company)

PRINCIPAL ACTIVITIES: Water heating equipment, electric motors, agricultural feed storage and handling systems, auto and truck structural components, fiberglass reinforced plastic piping systems, agricultural financing and glass-based protective industrial coatings
Principal Subsidiaries: A O Smith Harvestore Products Inc; A O Smith Electric Motors (Ireland) Ltd (Eire); A O Smith Export Corporation Ltd; AgriStor Credit Corporation; AgriStor Credit Corporation Canada Ltd (Canada); AgriStor Leasing; AgriStor Financial Corporation; AgriStor Automation Leasing; Smith Fiberglass Products Inc; Metalsa SA (Mexico); Sterling Electric Inc; Productos de Aqua SA de CV (Mexico); Productos Aplicados SA de CV; Claymore Insurance Company Ltd (Bermuda); A O Smith Enterprises Ltd (Canada); Fabricantes de Motores Electricos de Mexico SA de CV (Mexico)
Financial Information:

	Dec 31 1985	Dec 31 1986
	$'000	$'000
Sales revenues*(1)	880,902	910,897
Earnings(1)	26,807	26,118
Earnings(2)	14,368	2,869
Net earnings	41,175	28,987
Earnings per share primary(1)	$3.41	$2.72
Earnings per share net	$5.35	$3.07
Earnings per share net(3)	$4.94	$2.81
Common stock(4)	7,421	8,241

(1) continuing operations
(2) discontinued operations
(3) fully diluted
(4) average number of shares outstanding in thousands

No of Employees: 9,900

SMITH INTERNATIONAL, INC

4343 Von Karman Avenue, Newport Beach, CA 92660
Tel: (714) 752-9000
Telex: WUT 655402 smithintl npbh

Chairman: Jerry W Neely (and Chief Executive Officer)
Senior Executive Officers: Dale E Boyer (Group VP Operations), Loren K Carroll (VP and Chief Financial Officer), Robert M Gubrud (VP and Treasurer), J H Hauke (VP Human Resources)

PRINCIPAL ACTIVITIES: Manufacture of tools and equipment for the exploration of oil and gas; mining equipment
Principal Subsidiaries: (100% owned unless stated): Barrenas de Mexico SA (Mexico); Smith International France (France); SIDEM SA (49%) (Mexico); Smith International Australia Pty Ltd (Australia); Smith International Canada Ltd (Canada); Smith International Deutschland GmbH (Germany); Smith International (North Sea) Ltd (UK); Smith International Italia (SpA (Italy); Smith International do Brasil Equipamentos e Servicos Ltda (Brazil); SI Nederland BV (Netherlands); Sii Mining Equipment Companies (Africa) (Pty) Ltd (South Africa); Smith International Gulf Services Ltd (49%) (UAE); Smith International de Venezuela CA (Venezuela); Willis Oil Tool Ireland Ltd (Eire); Smith Brocas CA (60%) (Venezuela); Omega Insurance Ltd (Bermuda); Smith International (Singapore) Pte Ltd (Singapore)
Principal Bank: Security Pacific National Bank
Financial Information:

	$'000
Sales revenues	697,300

No of Employees: 7,230

SMITH KLINE & FRENCH LABORATORIES

1500 Spring Garden Street, Box 7929, Philadelphia, PA 19101
Tel: (215) 751-4000
Cable: SMITHKLINE PHILADELPHIA PA
Telex: 83-4487

Presidents: J H Cavanaugh, Ph.D. (US), John Chappell (International)

Senior Executive Officers: Robert Bastan (VP Manufacturing Operations, US), William K Robinson (VP Planning and Finance), Walter J Graham (VP Sales), Roger Ross (VP Marketing), T M Collins (VP Corporate Affairs)

PRINCIPAL ACTIVITIES: Manufacture of pharmaceuticals
Trade Names: TAGMET, DYAZIDE, RIDAURA
Parent Company: SmithKline Beckman Corporation
Financial Information:

	$'000
Sales revenues	2,154,700

No of Employees: 12,074

SMITH TOOL DIVISION

PO Box C-19511, Irvine, CA 92713
Tel: (714) 660-6000
Telex: WUT 182715 smithtool irin

President: Doug Rock
Senior Executive Officers: Ken Grumbles (Senior VP Sales), M R Banks (VP Domestic Sales), Larry Bishop (VP International Operations), Art Hess (VP Finance), Jim Schmook (VP Quality), Hobie Smith (VP and Assistant to President), Joe Vincent (VP Technical Development), Karl Wicker (VP International Sales), Roy Yeager (VP Engineering)

PRINCIPAL ACTIVITIES: Manufacture of tools for the oil industry
Parent Company: Smith International Inc, Newport Beach, CA
Financial Information:

	$'000
Sales revenues	285,000

No of Employees: 3,000

SMITH VALVE CORPORATION

125 Fisher Street, Westboro, MA 01581
Tel: (617) 366-9171
Telex: RCA 200402 snul ur

Chairman: Anthony D Smith (and President)
Senior Executive Officers: Thomas A DiMarco (Senior VP), Donald W Bean (VP), Earle C Booth (VP), Richard W Gibney (VP), Howard Y Yang (VP)

PRINCIPAL ACTIVITIES: Manufacture of valves
Principal Bank: State Street Bank and Trust Company
Financial Information:

	$'000
Sales revenues	50,000

No of Employees: 500

SMITHFIELD FOODS, INC

1777 N Kent Street, Arlington, VA 22209
Tel: (703) 276-7200

Chairman: Joseph W Luter III (and Chief Executive Officer)
President: Alan T Anderson (and Chief Operating Officer)
Senior Executive Officers: Robert W Manly (Executive VP), Henry L Morris (VP Engineering), J S Sawyer (VP), John P Schroeder (VP Livestock Procurement), Aaron D Trub (VP, Secretary and Treasurer)

PRINCIPAL ACTIVITIES: Meat production and packing
Principal Bank: Sovran Bank
Financial Information:

	Apr 30 1986
	$'000
Sales revenues	864,324
Net income	4,660
Earnings per share	$1.95
Shareholders equity	24,298

No of Employees: 4,800

SMITHKLINE BECKMAN CORPORATION

One Franklin Plaza, Philadelphia, PA 19101
Tel: (215) 751-4000
Cable: SMITHKLINE PHILADELPHIAPA
Telex: 834487 sk corp pha

Chairman: Henry Wendt (and Chief Executive Officer)
President: George Ebright (and Chief Operating Officer)
Senior Executive Officers: Kenneth N Kermes (Executive VP, Corporate Finance), Norman H Blanchard (President, Animal Health), Robert J Byrnes (VP and General Manager Chemical Division), James H Cavanaugh (President, US Pharmaceutical Products), Thomas M Collins (VP Corporate Affairs), John F Chappell (President, International Pharmaceutical Products), Gavis S Herbert (President, Eye and Skin Care Products)

PRINCIPAL ACTIVITIES: Research, development, manufacture and marketing of a broad range of prescription and proprietary products for humans and animals, and diagnostic and analytical products and services to facilitate detection and treatment of disease and the advancement of biomedical research
Trade Names: "Tagarnet", "Dyazide"
Principal Subsidiaries: Smith Kline & French Laboratories (pharmaceuticals); SmithKline Consumer Products (non prescription products); SmithKline Animal Health Products (Norden Laboratories) (large and small animal pharmaceuticals and biologicals); Beckman Instruments; Allergan Inc (eye care products); Allergan Humphrey (eye instruments); SmithKline Bio-Science Laboratories (clinical laboratories)
Principal Bank: Girard Bank
Financial Information:

	Dec 31 1985	Dec 31 1986
	$'000	$'000
Sales revenues	3,256,600	3,745,400
Income before taxes	756,700	722,300
Net income	514,400	521,100
Dividends per share	$2.85	$3.00
Earnings per share	$6.56	6.78
Shareholders equity	2,268,100	1,296,000

Principal Shareholders: Publicly held
No of Employees: 32,824

SMITH'S TRANSFER CORPORATION

PO Box 1000, Staunton, VA 24401
Tel: (703) 248 6231

President: Joseph F Gilbert (and Chief Operating Officer)
Senior Executive Officers: R L Franco (Chief Executive Officer), Clark E Brown (VP), Roger T Burbage (VP, Treasurer and Chief Financial Officer), Lemuel W Houston Jr (VP), Gary F Paler (VP), D W Reich (VP Marketing), William B Wall (VP), Max M McFarlin (Secretary)

PRINCIPAL ACTIVITIES: Long-haul common carrier services
Parent Company: ARA Services Inc
Principal Bank: Bank of New York
Financial Information:

	$'000
Sales revenues	331,300

No of Employees: 6,000

SMO, INC

US Rte 301, Box E, La Plata, MD 20646
Tel: (301) 934-8101

President: J B Wills
Senior Executive Officers: Charles F Boyers (Senior VP Administration and Secretary), J B Wills Jr (VP)

PRINCIPAL ACTIVITIES: Distribution of petroleum
Principal Bank: Mercantile Safe Deposit and Trust Company

Financial Information:

	$'000
Sales revenues	80,000

No of Employees: 400

SMOKY HOLLOW FOODS, INC

32nd & Woodrow, Little Rock, AR 72203
Tel: (501) 664-5110

Senior Executive Officers: Larry Rice (Executive VP and General Manager), John Woolbright (Chief Financial Officer), William Cook (Chief Engineer)

PRINCIPAL ACTIVITIES: Meat processing; production of ham, sausages, bacon and specialties
Parent Company: Sara Lee Corporation through Bryan Foods Inc
Principal Bank: First Commercial Bank
Financial Information:

	$'000
Sales revenues	83,000

No of Employees: 370

SMUCKER, J M, CO

Strawberry Lane, Orrville, OH 44667
Tel: (216) 682-0015
Telex: WUT 241612 jmsmucker ohio

Chairman: Paul H Smucker (and Chief Executive Officer)
President: Timothy P Smucker (and Chief Operating Officer)
Senior Executive Officers: R K Smucker (Executive VP and Treasurer), Wm P Boyle Jr (Senior VP Marketing), Edwin Dountz (VP Sales), Fred A Duncan (VP Technical Services), Charles Laine (VP Grocery Market), J D Millken (VP Logistics), R R Morrison (VP Production), Vernon D Netzly (VP Processing)

PRINCIPAL ACTIVITIES: Manufacture of jellies, preserves, jams, frozen fruit and vegetables, fruit toppings for ice cream and syrups, relishes, sauces, peanut butter and fruit juices
Principal Subsidiaries: H B DeViney; A F Murch Company
Principal Bank: National City Bank Cleveland
Financial Information:

	$'000
Sales revenues	230,470

No of Employees: 1,200

SNAP-ON TOOLS CORPORATION

2801 80th Street, Kenosha, WI 53140
Tel: (414) 656-5200
Telex: ITT 4311080 snap on kne

Chairman: William B Rayburn (and Chief Executive Officer)
President: Marion F Gregory (and Chief Operating Officer)
Senior Executive Officers: Michael G Hassett (Senior VP Manufacturing and Engineering), Earl B Reed (Senior VP Marketing), Harry W Fry (Senior VP Administration), Lowell L Larson (Senior VP Finance), Michael F Montemurro (Treasurer), Clarence J Niemi (Director Public Relations), James Andersen (Director Purchasing), William Tower (Advertising Manager)

PRINCIPAL ACTIVITIES: Manufacture of mechanic hand tools and related service items
Trade Names: Snap-on, Blue Point, Torqometer, Flank Drive, Par X
Principal Subsidiaries: Snap-on Tools of Canada Ltd; Snap-on Tools Ltd; Snap-on Tools International Ltd; Snap-on AG; Henamientas Snap-on de Mexico SA; Snap-on Tools de Mexico SA de CV; Snap-on Tools GmbH; Snap-on Tools (Europe) Ltd
Principal Bank: Harris Bank

Financial Information:

	Dec 31 1985	Jan 31 1987
	$'000	$'000
Sales revenues	591,278	670,086
Income before taxes	111,832	126,496
Net income	59,732	65,496
Dividends	23,700	25,110
Dividends per share	$1.16	$0.61(1)
Earnings per share	$2.92	$1.59(1)
Common stock(2)	20,437	41,168
Retained income	310,490	348,405
Shareholders equity	337,328	382,952

(1) two for one stock split in 1986
(2) average shares outstanding in thousands

No of Employees: 6,500

SNAPPER POWER EQUIPMENT

PO Box 777, McDonough, GA 30253
Tel: (404) 957-9141
Telex: WUT 542182 snapper mdgh

Chairman: A A Malizia (and Chief Executive Officer)
President: R E Robinson
Senior Executive Officers: C H Boylston (Executive VP), Don B Weakley (Senior VP Corporate Development), W R Garner (VP Operations), N L Seibert (VP Marketing)

PRINCIPAL ACTIVITIES: Manufacture of garden equipment
Parent Company: Fuqua Industries Inc, Atlanta, GA
Principal Bank: The Citizens and Southern National Bank
Financial Information:

	$'000
Sales revenues	250,000

No of Employees: 1,300

SOCIETY CORPORATION

800 Superior Avenue, Cleveland, OH 44114
Tel: (216) 622-9000
Telex: International 98 5517 Society B CLV

Chairman: Gordon E Heffern; Vice Chairman: Roger Noall (and Chief Administrative Officer)
President: Robert W Gillespie (and Chief Executive Officer)
Senior Executive Officers: Henry L Meyer III (Executive VP, Retail Banking Sector), David L Stith (Executive VP, Credit Policy and Loan Administration Group), James W Wert (Executive VP, Corporate Finance Sector), Robert M Patrick (Senior VP, Chief Financial Officer and Treasurer), Anthony Heyworth (Senior VP, Trust and Investment Services Sector), D Allan McDaniel (Senior VP Corporate Planning and Development), Robert G Nemer (Senior VP, Human Resources Group), F Scott O'Donnell (Senior VP, Corporate Loan Quality), W Robert Perkins (Senior VP, Balance Sheet Management), Frank G Ponchak (Senior VP, Management Information Systems and Service Group), Michael N Trigg (Senior VP, Sales Management and Development), Lawrence J Carlini (General Counsel and Secretary), Thomas M Neel (Controller) and Edward J Seink (General Auditor)

PRINCIPAL ACTIVITIES: Commerical banking and associated financial services to consumers, businesses and corporations; domestic and international credit; cash management; trust services; mortgage banking; leasing; credit life reinsurance; data processing and discount brokerage services
Trade Names: Green Machine (Automated teller machine network)
Principal Subsidiaries: Society National Bank, Cleveland Ohio; Society Bank, N.A., Dayton, Ohio; Society Bank of Eastern Ohio N.A., Canton, Ohio; Society Bank, Columbus, Ohio; BancSystems Association Inc; Green Machine Network Corp; Investor Services Corp; SocietyLease Inc; Society Life Insurance Co; Society Management Company; Midwest Power Company; Society Capital Corporation

Principal Bank: Society National Bank, Cleveland, Ohio
Financial Information:

	Dec 31 1985	Dec 31 1986
	$'000	$'000
Income before taxes	74,312	101,867
Net income	60,307	84,122
Common dividends	18,235	21,473
Preferred dividends	1,344	3,460
Dividends per common share	$0.92(1)	$0.96(1)
Earnings per share	$3.01(1)	$3.43(1)
Common stock(2)	11,221	22,442(1)
Retained income	246,411	305,600
Shareholders equity	532,422	568,917
Deposits	7,094,718	7,327,461
Total assets	8,749,066	9,060,948

(1) adjusted for a two-for-one stock split, effected by means of a 100% stock dividend, paid February 24 1987
(2) $1 par value

No of Employees: 6,151

SOCIETY FOR SAVINGS

31 Pratt St, Hartford, CT 06101
Tel: (203) 727-5000

President: Elliott C Miller (and Chief Executive Officer)
Senior Executive Officers: Albert E Fiacre (Executive VP Finance), Todd B Ikard (Executive VP Retail Banking), William T Kosturko (Executive VP and Counsel), William W Wilcox (Executive VP), Paul M Aldrich (Senior VP Administration and Secretary), Karen Antion (Senior VP Community Banking), Richard P Clinton (Senior VP Real Estate Investment), Edward Cohen (Senior VP Finance), David M G Hammaker (Senior VP Operations), Charles L Hanscomb (Senior VP Trust Department), Henrietta J Michaels (Senior VP and Controller), Peter K Mulligan (Senior VP Marketing), Raymond V Rosa (Senior VP and Auditor), Stephen E Smith (Senior VP Investment), James H Vanderhoff (Senior VP Data Processing), Jon R Vining (Senior VP Personnel Resource)

PRINCIPAL ACTIVITIES: Banking and financial services
Financial Information:

	Dec 31 1985	Dec 31 1986
	$'000	$'000
Net income	14,290	23,036
Earnings per share	$1.51	$2.15
Shareholders equity	155,760	178,738
Deposits	-	2,228,376
Total assets	2,506,750	2,948,366

No of Employees: 1,200

SOCIETY NATIONAL BANK

127 Public Square, Cleveland, OH 44114
Tel: (216) 622-9000
Telex: 98 5517

Chairman: Gordon E Heffern
President: Robert W Gillespie
Senior Executive Officers: Richard C Garretson (Executive VP Credit Policy), Bruce C Murray (Executive VP Consumer/Business Banking), Robert G Nemer (Executive VP Human Resources), Robert M Patrick (Executive VP and Chief Financial Officer), Frank G Ponchak (Executive VP Management Information Systems), John P Reinartz (Executive VP Trusts), James W Wert (Executive VP Corporate Banking Money Market), James J Andrews (Senior VP Information Services), Patrick V Auletta (Senior VP Corporate Banking Northern Ohio), Janet Bullard (Senior VP Human Resources), Neil J Byrne (Senior VP Law and Secretary), Donald Cruse Jr (Senior VP Trust Investment), Michael T Doland (Senior VP Consumer Lending), James A Fishell (Senior VP Corporate Banking Southern Ohio), R B Heisler Jr (Senior VP and District President Akron), Kevin J McGinty (Senior VP Bond and Money Market Services), Richard J Rapacz (Senior VP National/Multinational Banking), Elroy W Schaedel (Senior VP Specialty Lending/Cash Management Services), Albert O Schupp (Senior VP International Banking), Arthur W Wootton (Senior VP Mortgage Loans)

PRINCIPAL ACTIVITIES: Banking services
Parent Company: Society Corporation, Cleveland, OH

No of Employees: 1,630

SOFTECH INC

460 Totten Pond Road, Waltham, MA 02254
Tel: (617) 890 6900

Chairman: Douglas T Ross
President: Justus F Lowe Jr (and Chief Executive Officer)
Senior Executive Officers: Jorge E Rodriguez (Senior VP), Philip B Baker (Group Vice President), Charles B Clark (VP Program Development), F William Helming III (VP Division), John K Maloy (Group Vice President), William J Mrachek (VP Personnel), William F Vail (VP Finance and Administration)

PRINCIPAL ACTIVITIES: Computer software and related services
Principal Bank: Shawmut Bank of Boston NA
Financial Information:

	$'000
Sales revenues	36,435

No of Employees: 545

SOFTSEL COMPUTER PRODUCTS

546 N Oak St, Inglewood, CA 90302
Tel: (213) 412 1700
Telex: WUT 516233 softsel uu

PRINCIPAL ACTIVITIES: Distribution of software for personal computers

SOFTWARE AG SYSTEMS INC

11800 Sunrise Valley Drive, Reston, VA 22091
Tel: (703) 860 5050

Chairman: John Norris Maguire
President: Stuart J Miller (and Chief Executive Officer)
Senior Executive Officers: E Linwood Pearce (Executive VP Sales and Marketing), Edward J Forman (Senior VP Technology), Michael E Jakes (Senior VP International), Carlton B Crenshaw (VP, Chief Financial Officer and Treasurer), Gilbert Markbein (VP and Controller)

PRINCIPAL ACTIVITIES: Holding company with interests in data processing, software and computer services
Principal Subsidiaries: Software AG North America Inc
Principal Bank: Bank of Virginia
Financial Information:

	$'000
Sales revenues	52,265

No of Employees: 315

SOFTWARE PUBLISHING CORPORATION

1901 Landings Drive, Mountain View, CA 94043
Tel: (415) 962-8910

President: Fred M Gibbons (and Chief Executive Officer)
Senior Executive Officers: Janelle Bedke (VP and General Manager), Kathleen Bailey (VP and Chief Financial Officer), John D Page (VP)

PRINCIPAL ACTIVITIES: Production of software for personal computers
Financial Information:

	$'000
Sales revenues	37,200

No of Employees: 130

SOLO CUP COMPANY

1505 E Main Street, Urbana, IL 61801
Tel: (217) 384-1800

Chairman: Leo J Hulseman
President: Robert L Hulseman
Senior Executive Officers: John F Hulseman (VP Manufacturing Paper and Secretary), Ray F Hulseman (VP), E L Carter (VP Industrial Relations)

PRINCIPAL ACTIVITIES: Manufacture of disposable cups and plates
Parent Company: SCC Holding Company, Urbana, IL
Principal Bank: First National Bank of Chicago
Financial Information:

	$'000
Sales revenues	228,000

No of Employees: 2,400

SOLTEX POLYMER CORPORATION

3333 Richmond Avenue, Houston, TX 77027
Tel: (713) 522-1781
Telex: TWX 908815788 soltex hou

Chairman: Jacques E Solvay; Vice Chairman: Claude Y Loutrel
President: M W Sadler (and Chief Executive Officer)
Senior Executive Officers: Yves Secousse (Executive VP and General Manager Plastics), Michel M Osterrieth (Group VP), E J Buckingham (VP, General Counsel and Secretary), René H Degreve (VP Finance), Maurice P Fitzgerald (VP Marketing), Frank T McKevitt (VP Human Resources)

PRINCIPAL ACTIVITIES: Manufacture of plastics
Parent Company: Solvay & Cie SA, Brussels, Belgium through Solvay America Inc
Principal Bank: First City National Bank of Houston
Financial Information:

	$'000
Sales revenues	380,000

No of Employees: 700

SONAT INC

PO Box 2563, Birmingham, AL 35202-2563
Tel: (205) 325-3586

Chairman: Ronald L Kuehn Jr (and President and Chief Executive Officer); Vice Chairman: J Robert Doody (and Chief Financial Officer)
Senior Executive Officers: William C O'Malley (Executive VP), William E Matthews IV (Senior VP), William A Smith (Senior VP and General Counsel), W F Ammentorp (VP), Thomas W Barker Jr (VP-Finance), Duane J Kerper (VP-Management Information Systems), Beverley T Krannich (VP-Human Resources and Secretary), Dan C Langford (VP-Tax), James E Moylan Jr (VP-Comptroller), Ralph F Spinnler (VP), James C Yardley (VP-Corporate Development), John M Musgrave (Treasurer)

PRINCIPAL ACTIVITIES: Sonat Inc, headquartered in Birmingham, Alabama, is a worldwide energy company involved in natural gas, oil, services, and oil and gas exploration and gas pipelines. Sonat and its subsidiaries own more than 13,300 miles of natural gas pipelines in eight states from Texas to South Carolina, including a jointly owned pipeline system that serves the fast-growing Florida market. Its oil services segment serves the energy industry around the world by operating an international fleet of marine drilling rigs and providing measurement-while-drilling services for exploration and development drilling. Sonat's exploration and production subsidiary explores for and produces oil and natural gas in the Gulf of Mexico and onshore in the United States
Principal Subsidiaries: Natural Gas:- Southern Natural Gas Co.Oil Services:-Sonat Offshore Drilling Inc; Teleco Oilfield Services Inc. Exploration and Production:- Sonat Exploration Co

Financial Information:

	Dec 31 1985 $'000	Dec 31 1986 $'000
Revenues	2,407,751	1,792,632
(Loss) before taxes	(115,259)	(515,393)
Net income (loss)	3,044	(304,300)
Dividends	77,885	80,948
Dividends per share	$1.925	$2.00
Earnings (loss) per share	$0.08	($7.52)
Common stock	40,949	40,949
Retained income	1,290,743	905,495
Shareholders equity	1,360,744	975,546

No of Employees: 4,10C

SONESTA INTERNATIONAL HOTELS CORPORATION

200 Clarendon Street, Boston, MA 02116
Tel: (617) 421 5400

Chairman: Roger P Sonnabend (and Chief Executive Officer)
President: Paul Sonnabend (and Vice Chairman)
Senior Executive Officers: Stephen Sonnabend (Senior VP), John J Duane (VP and Treasurer), Hans J Keller (VP International), Brian T Owen (VP, Controller and Secretary), Charles Popper (VP), Theodore Rosen (VP Design Development), Jules Sieburgh (VP Information Systems), Stephanie Sonnabend (VP Marketing)

PRINCIPAL ACTIVITIES: Management of hotels and motels
Principal Subsidiaries: Amsterdam Sonesta Corporation; Brewster Wholesale Corporation; Charterhouse of MA; Florida Sonesta Corporation; Hotel Corporation of ME; Royal Sonesta Inc; Sonesta Charitable Foundation
Principal Bank: Bank of New England
Financial Information:

	$'000
Sales revenues	80,000

No of Employees: 2,000

SONOCO PRODUCTS CO

N 2nd Street, Hartsville, SC 29550
Tel: (803) 383-7000
Cable: As telex
Telex: 4944994 Sonoco

Chairman: C W Coker (President and Chief Executive Officer)
Corporate Officers: P C Coggeshall (Senior Executive VP), D R Russell (Senior VP Corporate Development), Thomas C Coxe III (Executive VP), J G Caudle (VP International Division), P C Coggeshall Jr (Group VP), C R Koerwer Jr (VP Finance and Treasurer), H E DeLoach Jr (VP Administration and General Counsel), R C King Jr (Group VP), F B Williams (Group VP), J G McGee Jr (Group VP), J L Coker (Secretary)

PRINCIPAL ACTIVITIES: Manufacture of a wide range of paper and plastic products and metal containers
Principal Subsidiaries: Continental Fibre Drum, Inc; Paper Stock Dealers, Inc; Sonoco Ltd; Sonoco UK Ltd; Sonoco de'Mexico, SA
Principal Bank: North Carolina National Bank
Financial Information:

	Dec 31 1985 $'000	Dec 31 1986 $'000
Sales revenues	869,598	963,796
Income before taxes	88,784	97,166
Net income	49,409	54,676
Dividends	15,746	17,963
Dividends per share	$0.36	$0.41
Earnings per share	$1.13	$1.25
Common stock	7,175	7,175
Retained income	272,631	309,344
Shareholders equity	295,743	332,890

Principal Shareholders: Officers and Directors of the Company (8.51%)
No of Employees: 11,735

SONOMA VINEYARDS
11455 Old Redwood Hwy, Healdsburg, CA 95448
Tel: (707) 433-6511
Telex: TWX 5107468280 sonovnyds wdso

Chairman: Herman I Merinoff (and President and Chief Executive Officer)
Senior Executive Officers: Rodney D Strong (Chairman Wine Division and Winemaster)

PRINCIPAL ACTIVITIES: Wine production; manufacture of tools; operation of advertising services
Principal Bank: Wells Fargo Bank
Financial Information:

	$'000
Sales revenues	63,000

No of Employees: 300

SOO LINE CORPORATION
Soo Line Building, PO Box 530, Minneapolis, MN 55440
Tel: (612) 347-8000

Chairman: Dennis Cavanaugh (and Chief Executive Officer)
Senior Executive Officers: Robert C Gilmore (Vice Chairman), James A Lee (Senior VP Finance and Chief Financial Officer), Wayne C Serkland (Senior VP and Chief Legal Officer), James F Johnson (Senior VP Corporate), J Michael Fox (VP Information Systems), Earl J Currie (Executive VP Operations-Railroad), Robert S Ingram (Executive VP Distribution Services-Railroad)

PRINCIPAL ACTIVITIES: Holding company engaged in transportation
Principal Subsidiaries: Soo Line Railroad Company
Principal Bank: First National, Minneapolis
Financial Information:

	Dec 31 1985	Dec 31 1986
	$'000	$'000
Sales revenues	617,570	631,823
(Loss) before taxes	(23,591)	(84,515)
Net (loss)	(8,691)	(43,315)
Dividends	9,675	2,847
Dividends per share	$1.20	$0.30
(Loss) per share	($1.14)	($4.56)
Common stock	156,887	156,887
Retained income	150,991	104,829
Shareholders equity	307,878	261,716

Number of Shareholders: 3,540
No of Employees: 6,000

SOONER FEDERAL SAVINGS & LOAN ASSOCIATION
5100 East Skelly Drive, Box 1004, Tulsa, OK 74101-1004
Tel: (918) 665-6600

Chairman: W R Hagstrom (and Chief Executive Officer)
President: Rod L Reppe (and Chief Operating Officer)
Senior Executive Officers: Robin K Buerge (Executive VP), Mark R Graham (Executive VP), W Wayne Learned (Executive VP), Steven Berry (Senior VP), Kenyon J Blunt (Senior VP), (Senior VP), Jack Koepernik (Senior VP), Robert Payne (Senior VP), John Bryant (VP), Mark Adkisson (VP) Deborah L Andress (VP), Ed Carpenter (VP), Norma Cooper (VP), Ted Dubie (VP), Steven M Gobel (VP), Kathy Knight (VP), Darlene Martin (VP), Larry Morris (VP), Dwayne Moses (VP), Susan Neville (VP), Jack Staubus (VP), Dan Swaim (VP), Jeffrey L Thomas (VP)

PRINCIPAL ACTIVITIES: Financial services including savings and loans
Principal Subsidiaries and Affiliates: Texas Western Service Corporation; Texas Western Federal Savings and Loan; First Home Service Corporation; First Home Mortgage Corporation; First Home Development Corporation; Western Home Service Corporation; The Britton Insurance Agency Inc; Tandem Financial Corporation; Tandem Securities Corporation
Principal Bank: First of Tulsa
Financial Information:

	Jun 30 1986	Jun 30 1987
	$'000	S'000
Income (loss) before taxes	2,198	(17,157)
Net income (loss)	1,113	(14,906)
Dividends per share	$0.45	-
Earnings (loss) per share	$0.54	($7.29)
Shareholders equity	77,926	63,020
Deposits	1,270,705	1,221,770
Total assets	1,567,609	1,527,401

No of Employees: 400

SORG INCORPORATED
111 Eighth Avenue, New York, NY 10011
Tel: (212) 741-6600
Telex: WUT 530429 sorg

Chairman: Gilbert B Sorg
President: Roy A Cardia (and Chief Executive Officer)
Senior Executive Officers: Donn Q Powers (Secretary and Treasurer), Edmond P Sorg (Controller)

PRINCIPAL ACTIVITIES: Printing services
Principal Subsidiaries: Sorg Printing Company of California; Sorg Printing Company of Illinois; Sorg Printing Co of Minnesota; Sorg Printing Co of New York; Sorg Printing Co of Southern California; Appeal Printing Co Inc; Litigation Resources Inc; Harborview Communications Corp; Sorg Printing Company of Washington, D.C.
Principal Bank: Irving Trust Company
Financial Information:

	May 31 1985	May 31 1986
	$'000	$,000
Sales revenues	54,129	70,747
Income before taxes	450	4,657
Net income	377	2,316
Dividends	-	161
Dividends per share	-	$0.10
Earnings per share	$0.23	$1.30
Retained income	9,129	12,980
Shareholders equity	11,397	22,680

No of Employees: 500

SORG PAPER CO
901 Manchester Avenue, Middleton, OH 45042
Tel: (513) 422-3661
Telex: TWX 810 451 2942 sorg pap mdwn

President: William R Picard
Senior Executive Officers: H A Baumann Jr (VP Marketing), William D Smith (VP Finance and Treasurer), D A Driscoll (VP Personnel and Public Relations), T L Schuler (VP Materials), Frank Cessna (VP)

PRINCIPAL ACTIVITIES: Manufacture of paper
Parent Company: Mosinee Paper Corporation
Principal Bank: Bank One
Financial Information:

	$'000
Sales revenues	95,000

No of Employees: 600

SOUND WAREHOUSE INC
10911 Petal Street, Dallas, TX 75238
Tel: (214) 343 4700

Chairman: Kay Y Moran
President: Terry N Worrell (and Chief Executive Officer)
Senior Executive Officers: Sharon C Worrell (Executive VP and Assistant Secretary), Joe N Malone (VP), Walter E White (VP), Truong V Khuong (Secretary and Treasurer)

PRINCIPAL ACTIVITIES: Restaurants and catering outlets
Financial Information:

	$'000
Sales revenues	109,570

No of Employees: 1,620

SOUNDESIGN CORPORATION

34 Exchange Place, Jersey City, NJ 07302
Tel: (201) 434-1050
Telex: TWX 710 7305342 soundson j cty

Chairman: Saul E Ashkenazi
President: Ely E Ashkenazi
Senior Executive Officers: Morris Franco (Senior VP), Harry Franco (Senior VP), Chabetaye Chraime (Senior VP Procurement and Treasurer), Samuel Laniado (Senior VP Production), Robert Winer (Senior VP), Albert A Ades (VP Sales), Thomas R Greene (VP), Albert Hanowy (VP Domestic Purchasing), Bernard Weinstein (VP and Comptroller)

PRINCIPAL ACTIVITIES: Manufacture of consumer products including radios and hi-fi equipment
Principal Bank: Manufacturers Hanover Trust Company
Financial Information:

	$'000
Sales revenues	178,000

No of Employees: 800

SOUTH BAY GROWERS, INC

PO Box A, South Bay, FL 33493
Tel: (305) 996-2085

Chairman: C S H Mott
President: John B Boy
Senior Executive Officers: Frank D Teets (VP and General Manager), C D Lewis (Secretary and Treasurer), William G Norman (Sales Manager)

PRINCIPAL ACTIVITIES: Production of vegetables; fresh and frozen produce; plastic packaging products
Parent Company: United States Sugar Corporation, Clewiston, FL
Principal Bank: Citizens and Southern National Bank
Financial Information:

	$'000
Sales revenues	50,000

No of Employees: 2,000

SOUTH BOSTON SAVINGS BANK

460 West Broadway, South Boston, MA 02127
Tel: (617) 268 2500

Chairman: Alfred W Archibald
President: Richard R Laine (and Chief Executive Officer and Legal Counsel)
Senior Executives Officers: Paul A Archibald (Executive VP), J R Catalano (VP), Anita L Daniels (VP), R C Feeney (VP), Robert E Lee (VP), W D Powers (VP), R Ranieri (VP), David L Smart (VP and Treasurer)

PRINCIPAL ACTIVITIES: Financial services including savings and loans

No of Employees: 155

SOUTH CAROLINA NATIONAL CORPORATION

1426 Main St, Columbia, SC 29226
Tel: (803) 765-3000

Chairman: James G Lindley (and Chief Executive Officer); Vice Chairmen: Arthur M Bjontegard Jr
President: Robert S McCoy Jr
Senior Executive Officers: William W Murphy (Executive VP), Charles H Davis III (Senior VP), Gary M Duncan (Senior VP and Treasurer), T Stephen Lynch (Senior VP and General Counsel), James B Murphy Jr (Senior VP and Secretary), Sandra M Mathews (VP and General Auditor)

PRINCIPAL ACTIVITIES: Banking and financial services
Principal Bank: South Carolina National Bank
Financial Information:

	Dec 31 1985	Dec 31 1986
	$'000	$'000
Net income	31,730	48,925
Earnings per share	$2.97	$2.05
Shareholders equity	273,130	303,635
Deposits	3,050,063	3,294,601
Total assets	4,212,060	4,737,125

No of Employees: 4,131

SOUTH JERSEY INDUSTRIES INC

1 South Jersey Plaza, Route 54, Folsom, NJ 08037
Tel: (609) 561 9000

Chairman: W A Gemmel
President: William F Ryan (and Chief Executive Officer)
Senior Executive Officers: Harvey B Haslett Jr (VP), Gerald S Levitt (VP), Richard T Sigmund (VP), Richard B Tonielli (Treasurer), George L Baulig (Secretary and Assistant Treasurer)

PRINCIPAL ACTIVITIES: Holding company with interests in natural gas and fuel oil
Principal Subsidiaries: Delaware Valley Industrial Gases; Energy and Minerals Inc; Morie Company Inc; South Jersey Exploration Company; South Jersey Fuel Inc; South Jersey Gas Company
Financial Information:

	$'000
Sales revenues	258,225

No of Employees: 875

SOUTHDOWN, INC

1200 Smith Street, Houston, TX 77002
Tel: (713) 658-8921
Telex: WUT 791116 Southdown hou

Chairman: Donald E Peiser
President: Clarence C Comer (and Chief Operating Officer)
Senior Executive Officers: Kenneth D Cohn (Treasurer), James L Persky (Controller), Wendell E Phillips II

PRINCIPAL ACTIVITIES: Exploration and production of oil and natural gas; production of cement
Principal Subsidiaries: Southwestern Cement Enterprises Inc; Southwestern Portland Cement Company; Azusa Land Reclamation Company Inc; Pelto Oil Company; Southwestern Cement International Finance NV (Netherlands Antilles)
Principal Bank: Continental Illinois National Bank
Financial Information:

	$'000
Sales revenues	324,810

No of Employees: 2,500

SOUTHEAST BANK, NA

200 S Biscayne Blvd, Miami, FL 33131
Tel: (305) 375-7500
Telex: WUI 681 1519 semia uw

Chairman: Charles J Zwick (and Chief Executive Officer); Vice Chairmen: Alexander M Wolfe Jr, William H Dougherty Jr
President: John E Porta (and Chief Operating Officer)
Senior Executive Officers: R C Palmer (Executive VP), Karl M Shelton (Executive VP Asset and Liability), G D Mathias (Executive VP Operations Group), Oakley W Cheney (Senior VP International Banking), Lester Freeman (Senior VP Marketing)

PRINCIPAL ACTIVITIES: Banking services

Parent Company: Southeast Banking Corporation, Miami, FL
Principal Bank: Manufacturers Hanover Trust Co

No of Employees: 6,800

SOUTHEAST BANKING CORPORATION

One Southeast Financial Ctr, Miami, FL 33131
Tel: (305) 375-7500
Telex: WUI 6811519 semia uw

Chairman: Charles J Zwick (and Chief Executive Officer); Chairman of Executive Committee: Harry H Bassett; Vice Chairmen: William H Dougherty Jr, Alexander McW Wolfe Jr
President: John E Porta (and Chief Operating Officer)
Senior Executive Officers: G Dodson Mathias (Executive VP), William D Plechaty (Executive VP), Kristen M Hudak (Senior VP and Chief Financial Officer), Melvin M Kann (General Auditor), Samuel A Milne (Senior VP and Chief Accounting Officer), Thomas R Woolsey (Senior VP, Senior Counsel and Corporate Secretary)

PRINCIPAL ACTIVITIES: Holding company with banking and general financial interests
Principal Subsidiaries: Southeast Bank NA; Southeast Bank of Chipley; Southeast Bank of Madison County NA; Southeast Bank of Perry NA; Southeast Bank of Tallahassee; Southeast Mortgage Company; Southeast Properties Inc
Principal Bank: Southeast Bank NA
Financial Information:

	Dec 31 1985	Dec 31 1986
	$'000	$'000
Income before taxes	75,073	96,397
Net income	64,913	86,522
Dividends	19,913	21,919
Dividends per share	$0.80	$0.82
Earnings per share	$2.27	$3.00
Common stock	125,388	136,737
Retained income	248,831	307,417
Shareholders equity	551,381	666,284
Deposits	8,337,897	9,555,874
Total assets	11,052,012	12,468,984

No of Employees: 7,364

SOUTHEAST MEDIA INC

333 E Grace Street, Richmond, VA 23219
Tel: (804) 649-6000

Chairman: D T Bryan
President: Alan S Donnahoe
Senior Executive Officers: J C Barden (Treasurer), Andrew J Brent (Secretary)

PRINCIPAL ACTIVITIES: Publication of newspapers, printing and broadcasting
Parent Company: Media General Inc, Richmond, VA
Financial Information:

	$'000
Sales revenues	190,000

No of Employees: 3,000

SOUTHEASTERN MICHIGAN GAS ENTERPRISES INC

405 Water Street, Port Huron, MI 48060
Tel: (313) 987 7900

Chairman: William A Runyan
President: Robert J Thomson (and Chief Executive Officer)
Senior Executive Officers: James R Shaw Jr (Executive VP), Robert F Caldwell (Secretary and Treasurer)

PRINCIPAL ACTIVITIES: Holding company with interests in the supply of natural gas
Principal Subsidiaries: Southeastern Exploration Company; Southeastern MI Engineering Specialists; Southeastern MI Gas Company
Principal Bank: Michigan Bank
Financial Information:

	$'000
Sales revenues	105,100

No of Employees: 315

SOUTHEASTERN PUBLIC SERVICE CO

6917 Collins Avenue, Miami Beach, FL 33141
Tel: (305) 866-7771

Chairman: Victor Posner (and President and Chief Executive Officer); Vice Chairmen: Steven Posner (and Chairman of Executive Committee); Russell A Boyle
Senior Executive Officers: Frank E Autrey (Executive VP and Chief Operating Officer), Donald J Glazer (Executive VP), Melvin R Colvin (Senior VP), Jack Coppersmith (Senior VP and Chief Financial Officer), Raymond J Dettore (Senior VP Insurance), Renee Moltram (Senior VP Administration), Bernard I Posner (Senior VP), Walter Sieckman (Senior VP), Philip A Smalley Jr (Senior VP Human Resources), Gilbert L Bieger Jr (VP Operations), Harry T Clew (VP), Mitchell V Gregory (VP), Robert C Griffin (VP, Treasurer and Assistant Secretary), Leonard Leifert (VP), Jack Lubin (VP Purchasing), John C Luby (VP), Tracy Posner (VP)

PRINCIPAL ACTIVITIES: Operation of public services including cold storage facilities; gas supply and petroleum supply; civil engineering
Parent Company: DWG Corporation, Miami, FL (63%)
Financial Information:

	$'000
Sales revenues	496,840

No of Employees: 9,000

SOUTHEASTERN SAVINGS & LOAN COMPANY

112 South Tryon Street, 1st SE Center, Charlotte, NC 28284-1002
Tel: (704) 376 7283

Chairman: Wallace N Hyde
President: George S Currin (and Chief Executive Officer)
Senior Executive Officers: C L Pressley (Treasurer)

PRINCIPAL ACTIVITIES: Financial services including mortgage and loan facilities

No of Employees: 200

SOUTHERN CALIFORNIA EDISON CO

2244 Walnut Grove Avenue, Rosemead, CA 91770
Tel: (818) 302-1212
Telex: WUT 677268 edison co rsmd

Chairman: Howard P Allen (and Chief Executive Officer)
President: H Frederick Christie
Senior Executive Officers: John E Bryson (Executive VP and Chief Financial Officer), David J Fogarty (Executive VP), Michael R Peevey (Executive VP), Philip L Martin (Senior VP), L T Papay (Senior VP), Richard K Bushey (VP and Controller)

PRINCIPAL ACTIVITIES: Electricity supply
Principal Bank: Bank of America
Financial Information:

	Dec 31 1985	Dec 31 1986
	$'000	$'000
Sales revenues	5,168,850	5,311,733
Net income	774,110	768,617
Earnings per share	$3.26	3.38
Shareholders equity	4,575,400	5,159,929

No of Employees: 17,182

SOUTHERN CALIFORNIA WATER COMPANY

3625 West Sixth Street, Los Angeles, CA 90020
Tel: (213) 251 3600

Chairman: W W Franklin

President: W V Caveney (and Chief Executive Officer)
Senior Executive Officers: R L Anthony (Senior VP), R F Grusza (VP), Alexander Shipman (VP, Secretary and Treasurer), Keith Copp (Controller, Assistant Secretary and Assistant Treasurer)

PRINCIPAL ACTIVITIES: Water supply; purchase and distribution of electricity
Principal Bank: First Interstate Bank of California
Financial Information:

	$'000
Sales revenues	71,000

No of Employees: 375

SOUTHERN CO

PO Box 720071, Atlanta, GA 30346
Tel: (404) 393-0650

President: Edward L Addison
Senior Executive Officers: Alan R Barton (VP), A W Dahlberg (VP), Joseph M Farley (VP), Douglas L McCrary (VP), Robert W Scherer (VP), W L Westbrook (VP Finance)

PRINCIPAL ACTIVITIES: Holding company with interests in electricity supply
Principal Bank: First National Bank
Financial Information:

	Dec 31 1985 $'000	Dec 31 1986 $'000
Sales revenues	6,813,927	6,846,591
Net income	829,590	882,860
Earnings per share	$3.20	$3.17
Shareholders equity	5,332,400	6,009,574

No of Employees: 31,700

SOUTHERN CONTAINER CORPORATION

140 W Industry Ct, Deer Park, NY 11729
Tel: (212) 386-2224

President: Steven Grossman
Senior Executive Officers: Bernard Stebel (General Counsel)

PRINCIPAL ACTIVITIES: Manufacture of containers
Principal Bank: Chemical Bank
Financial Information:

	$'000
Sales revenues	75,000

No of Employees: 520

SOUTHERN FRUIT DISTRIBUTORS, INC

1 W Pineloch Avenue, Orlando, FL 32806
Tel: (305) 859-3550
Telex: TWX 810 8500216 soufruit orl

President: Austin A Caruso (and General Manager)
Senior Executive Officers: Joseph M Caruso (VP), John J Walsh (VP Engineering and Production), Philip P Caruso (Secretary and Treasurer)

PRINCIPAL ACTIVITIES: Canning and freezing of fruit and fruit products
Financial Information:

	$'000
Sales revenues	65,000

No of Employees: 300

SOUTHERN HOSPITALITY CORPORATION

PO Box 48, Nashville, TN 37202
Tel: (615) 327 3311

Chairman: R Wayne Oldham (and Chief Executive Officer)
President: Henry R Hillenmeyer
Senior Executive Officers: David McDaniel (Senior VP, Secretary and Treasurer)

PRINCIPAL ACTIVITIES: Chain of restaurants
Principal Bank: Commerce Union Bank
Financial Information:

	$'000
Sales revenues	50,300

No of Employees: 1,700

SOUTHERN INDIANA GAS AND ELECTRIC COMPANY

20 Northwest Fourth Street, Evansville, IN 47741
Tel: (812) 424-6411
Telex: 464-4554

Chairman: Norman P Wagner (and President and Chief Executive Officer)
Senior Executive Officers: Ronald G Reherman (Executive VP and General Manager of Operations), James S Luker (VP and Director of Corporate Services), J A VanMeter (VP and Director of Electric Operations), A E Goebel (VP, Secretary and Treasurer)

PRINCIPAL ACTIVITIES: Generation, transmission and distribution of electricity and purchase, distribution and sale of natural gas
Financial Information:

	Dec 31 1986 $'000	Dec 31 1987 $'000
Sales revenues	268,646	276,886
Income before taxes	61,722	70,880
Net income	31,822	33,321
Dividends	18,519	19,681
Dividends per share	$1.96	$2.12
Earnings per share	$3.18	$3.42
Common stock	102,734	102,734
Retained income	112,922	125,032
Shareholders equity	212,946	213,945

Principal Shareholders: Princeton Mining; Rose Hulman Institute; Black Hawk Coal Corp; Hulman & Company
No of Employees: 908

SOUTHERN MINNESOTA BEET SUGAR COOPERATIVE

PO Box 500, Renville, MN 56284
Tel: (612) 329-8305
Telex: TWX 910 5651140 smn sugar rnvl

Chairman: Arlo Gordon; Vice Chairman: George Kleven
President: Irvin Zitterkopf
Senior Executive Officers: Curtis Watson (Treasurer), Alan Roebke (Secretary)

PRINCIPAL ACTIVITIES: Production of sugar from sugar beet
Principal Subsidiaries: North Central Sugar Marketing Coop; Midwest Agri-Commodities Co
Principal Bank: Bank for Cooperatives
Financial Information:

	Aug 31 1985 $'000	Aug 31 1986 $'000
Sales revenues	56,200	83,000
Income before taxes	9,600	55
Common stock	5,693	6,149
Retained income	1,400	2,890
Shareholders equity	14,600	15,257

Number of shareholders: 300
No of Employees: 170

SOUTHERN NATIONAL CORPORATION

500 North Chestnut Street, Lumberton, NC 28358
Tel: (919) 671 2000

Chairman: Hector MacLean (and President and Chief Executive Officer)
Senior Executive Officers: Bonner Hudson (Executive VP and Controller), Charles Chatham (Senior VP and Secretary)

PRINCIPAL ACTIVITIES: Banking services

Principal Subsidiaries: Southern International Corporation; Southern National Bank of NC; Southern National Financial Corporation; Southern National Leasing Corporation; Southern National Mortgage Company
Principal Bank: Southern National Bank
Financial Information:

	$'000
Revenues	154,000

No of Employees: 1,300

SOUTHERN NEW ENGLAND TELEPHONE CO

227 Church St, New Haven, CT 06506
Tel: (203) 771-5200

Chairman: Walter H Monteith Jr (and President and Chief Executive Officer)
Senior Executive Officers: Richard M Donofrio (Senior VP Communications), Daniel J Miglio (Senior VP Finance), Robert F Neal (Senior VP Operations), James B Curtin (VP and General Counsel), Jean M Handley (VP Corporate Relations), Charles B Harrison (VP Technical), Ross L Miller (VP Information Systems), O Haydn Owens Jr (VP Directory and Support Services), Terry O Oulundsen (VP Regulatory Matters), Arthur E Parsons (VP)

PRINCIPAL ACTIVITIES: Telecommunications services
Parent Company: Southern New England Telecommunications Corp
Financial Information:

	$'000
Sales revenues	1,400,000

No of Employees: 13,800

SOUTHERN STATES COOPERATIVE, INC

6606 West Broad Street, Richmond, VA 23230
Tel: (804) 281-1000
Telex: 710-9560165

Chairman: Richard F Price; Vice Chairman: Dr Marvin R McClung
President: Gene A James (and Chief Executive Officer)
Senior Executive Officers: G R Anderson (Group VP, Corporate Services), W M Smith (Group VP Retail and Marketing Services), M T Ragsdale (Group VP, Manufacturing and Distribution Service), J A Hawkins (VP and Treasurer), Dr J D Coffey (VP Economics and Planning), C A Miller (VP Information Systems), R W Taylor (VP and Controller), N Hopper Ancarrow Jr (VP and Secretary)

PRINCIPAL ACTIVITIES: Agricultural supplies
Financial Information:

	Jun 30 1987 $'000
Sales revenues	645,694
Income before taxes	13,044
Net income	7,523
Shareholders equity	128,974

No of Employees: 3,400

SOUTHERN STEEL CO

PO Box 2021, San Antonio, TX 78297
Tel: (512) 533-1231

Chairman: Robert G Tointon
President: Michael M Holland
Senior Executive Officers: James H Caudill (VP), Eugene Daugherty (VP Engineering), Charles E Holycross (VP Manufacturing), Herb Wolverton (Comptroller)

PRINCIPAL ACTIVITIES: Manufacture of fabricated metal products including prison security equipment
Parent Company: Phelps Inc
Principal Bank: National Bank of Commerce
Financial Information:

	$'000
Sales revenues	250,000

No of Employees: 200

SOUTHERN UNION CO

First International Building, Dallas, TX 75270
Tel: (214) 748-8511

Chairman: Frank W Denis (and President and Chief Executive Officer)
Senior Executive Officers: James Purser (Chief Operating Officer), J O Carnes (Senior VP), D J Crowley (Senior VP), M R Baxter (VP Finance), Ronald J Endres (VP, Treasurer and Controller), Thomas E Morton Jr (VP, Secretary and General Counsel), Stanley D Smith (VP and Controller)

PRINCIPAL ACTIVITIES: Distribution of natural gas; petroleum refining; exploration and production of oil and gas
Pricipal Subsidiaries: Famariss Oil & Refining Co; Southern Union Refining Co
Principal Bank: Interfirst Bank
Financial Information:

	$'000
Sales revenues	305,200

No of Employees: 2,200

SOUTHERN UNION REFINING CO

1001 N Turner, Hobbs, NM 88240
Tel: (505) 393-6116
Telex: WUT 169015 surf hob

President: Randolph Scott
Senior Executive Officers: Bill Champlin (Senior VP Marketing), William L McDonnell (VP Operations), Ronald Grassarth (VP Marketing), Russel Buss (VP), Warren Franklin (VP Raw Material)

PRINCIPAL ACTIVITIES: Oil refining; production of asphalt; gas oils; petroleum by-products
Parent Company: Southern Union Co, Dallas, TX
Principal Bank: InterFirst Bank Dallas
Financial Information:

	$'000
Sales revenues	500,000

No of Employees: 210

SOUTHERN WOOD PIEDMONT CO

PO Box 5447, Spartanburg, SC 29304
Tel: (803) 576-7660
Telex: WUT 809467 sou wd spa

Chairman: R M Gross (and President and Chief Executive Officer)
Senior Executive Officers: T H Brannon (Executive VP and Chief Operating Officer), D F Lundy (VP), S A Everitt (Treasurer)

PRINCIPAL ACTIVITIES: Production of building materials
Parent Company: ITT Rayonier Inc
Principal Bank: North Carolina National Bank
Financial Information:

	$'000
Sales revenues	50,000

No of Employees: 600

SOUTHLAND CORPORATION (THE)

PO Box 719, Dallas, TX 75221
Tel: (214) 828-7011

Chairman: John P Thompson
President: Jere W Thompson (and Chief Executive Officer)
Senior Executive Officers: Clark J Matthews II (Senior Executive VP and Chief Executive Officer), Joe C Thompson Jr (Senior Executive VP, Retail), Walter Grayson III (Executive VP, Administration and Services), James W Parker (VP,

Manufacturing and Distribution), S R Dole (Senior VP Stores), Sam J Susser (Senior VP, Petroleum Products)

PRINCIPAL ACTIVITIES: Nation's largest convenience retailer, with 7,500 7-Eleven stores and numerous supporting operations. Nation's largest independent refiner/retailer of gasoline, with over 2 billion gallons of gasoline sold at retail through 7-Eleven and over another 2 billion gallons sold at wholesale to Citgo-branded stations owned by others. Nation's third largest processor/distributor of dairy products. Operate the nation's tenth largest refinery

Trade Names: 7-Eleven, Citgo, Southland Distribution Centers, Southland Food Centers, Quik Mart, Chief Auto Parts, Gristede's, Charles & Co, Reddy Ice, Adohr Farms, Bancroft, Cabell's, Embassy, Harbisons, Knowlton's, Merritt Foods, Oak Farms, Velda Farms

Principal Subsidiaries: Citgo Petroleum Corporation; CityPlace Development Corporation and numerous other operating subsidiaries

Principal Bank: Goldman Sachs & Co (Investment Banking); Citicorp (USA), Inc (Commercial Banking); Interfirst Bank Dallas, NA (Commercial Banking)

Financial Information:

	Dec 31 1986
	$'000
Total revenues	11,081,835
Net income	200,445
Earnings per share primary	$3.96
Shareholders equity	1,667,831

No of Employees: 41,000

SOUTHLAND FINANCIAL CORPORATION

5215 N O'Connor Blvd, Irving, TX 75039
Tel: (214) 556-0500

President: John W Carpenter III (and Chief Operating Officer)

Senior Executive Officers: David H Brune (Senior Executive VP Administration), Frank T Hundley (Senior Executive VP Finance), Richard W Douglas (Executive VP), J Michael Lewis (Executive VP and Treasurer), J Frank Miller III (Executive VP), James A Stockard (Executive VP and Secretary), B C Klinke (Senior VP), James E Olson (Senior VP Personnel), Frank B Schubert (Senior VP and Controller), W Brett Brown (VP), Jeffrey R Burgher (VP), Samuel L Fairchild (VP), Steven Hickock (VP), Judith A Hoffman (VP), Donald L Johnson (VP), W C Scarborough (VP), Richard W Wilhelm (VP)

PRINCIPAL ACTIVITIES: Holding company with interests in property development and management; insurance; finance; cattle ranching

Principal Bank: Republic National Bank

Financial Information:

	Dec 31 1986
	$'000
Sales revenues	58,803
Net (loss)	(16,330)
(Loss) per share	($0.97)
Shareholders equity	183,173

No of Employees: 800

SOUTHLAND OIL CO

5170 Galaxie Drive, Jackson, MS 39206
Tel: (601) 981-4151
Telex: TWX 810 966 2715 southland jks

Chairman: Charles W Else

President: Roger G McGrath

Senior Executive Officers: Daisy S Blackwell (Secretary), James D Bennett (Treasurer), Clyde Walters (Sales Manager), Tom Allmon (Personnel Director), Neal Riley (Data Processing Manager), James R Satcher (Product Manager)

PRINCIPAL ACTIVITIES: Oil refining; oil by-products

Parent Company: VGS Corporation

Principal Bank: First National Bank

Financial Information:

	$'000
Sales revenues	137,000

No of Employees: 140

SOUTHMARK CORPORATION

1601 LBJ Freeway, Dallas, TX 75234
Tel: (214) 241-8787
Telex: 62229200 SOUTHMARK DAL

Chairman: Gene E Phillips (and President and Chief Executive Officer)

Senior Executive Officers: D Vinson Marley (Executive VP), Thomas C Walker (Executive VP), Donald W Hair (Chief Financial Officer)

PRINCIPAL ACTIVITIES: Real estate-based financial services company

Principal Subsidiaries: (100% owned): Southmark/Envicon Capital Corp; Southmark Capital Corporation; Southmark Consolidated Resources Corp of America; Southmark Management/Retail Division, Office/Industrial Division, Residential Division; San Jacinto Savings Association; Southmark Financial Services Inc; Southmark Life Group Inc; Southmark Pacific Corp; National America Corporation; Parker & Parsley Petroleum Corporation; Southmark Retirement Corporation; Southmark/Autumn West Corporation; National Heritage; Integon Corporation; American Realty Trust; J M Peters Company Inc; National Realty LP; Realty World Inc

Financial Information:

	Jun 30 1985	Jun 30 1986
	$'000	$'000
Sales revenues	572,744	534,411
Net income	86,409	94,289
Earnings per share	$1.74	$1.54
Shareholders equity	528,135	753,121

Number of shareholders: 13,049
No of Employees: 25,000

SOUTHTRUST CORPORATION

112 N 20th St, PO Box 2554, Birmingham, AL 35290
Tel: (205) 254-5000
Telex: 810733656

Chairman: Wallace D Malone (and Chief Executive Officer)

President: Roy W Gilbert Jr

Senior Executive Officers: Frederick W Murray Jr (Executive VP), Aubrey D Barnard (Secretary, Treasurer and Controller), James W Rainer Jr (Executive VP)

PRINCIPAL ACTIVITIES: Bank holding company

Principal Bank: SouthTrust Bank of Alabama, National Association

Financial Information:

	Dec 31 1985	Dec 31 1986
	$'000	$'000
Income before taxes	49,882	55,371
Net income	44,249	53,737
Dividends	13,344	16,062
Dividends per share	$0.60	$0.68
Earnings per share	$1.98	$2.26
Common stock	57,760	61,686
Retained income	186,180	223,855
Shareholders equity	276,163	350,684
Deposits	3,293,218	3,973,842
Total assets	4,271,234	5,101,073

No of Employees: 3,400

SOUTHWEST AIRLINES CO

PO Box 37611, Love Field, 8008 Aviaition Place, Dallas, TX 75235
Tel: (214) 353-6100
Telex: 910-861-4300 SW AIRLINE DAL

Chairman: Herbert D Kelleher (and President and Chief Executive Officer)

Senior Executive Officers: Robert W Lawless (Executive VP and Chief Operating Officer), James G Amos (VP-Flight Operations), Gary A Barron (Executive VP-Corporate Services), J L Herring (VP, Energy and Provisioning), Camille T Keith (VP, Special Marketing), Marcy E Lawless (VP-Personnel), William Q Miller (VP-Inflight Service), Paul J Quinn (VP-Schedule Planning), Donald G Valentine (VP-Marketing), John A Vidal (VP-Maintenance), C James Brunjes (VP-Systems), James F Parker (VP-General Counsel), Ron Ricks (VP-Governmental Affairs), James C Wimberly (VP-Ground Operations), Colleen C Barrett (VP-Administration and Corporate Secretary), Gary C Kelly (Controller), John D Owen (Treasurer)

PRINCIPAL ACTIVITIES: Southwest Airlines provides single-class, high frequency air service to ten cities in Texas and to New Orleans, Oklahoma City, Tulsa, Albuquerque, Phoenix, Las Vegas, San Diego, Kansas City, Los Angeles, San Francisco, Detroit, Nashville, Birmingham, Chicago and Little Rock. The Company principally concentrates on short-haul markets and stresses high levels of aircraft utilization and employee productivity. In the Company's opinion its service is characterized by low fares, convenient schedules and reliability. The principal hub airports in Southwest's system are Dallas Love Field and Houston Hobby Airport, satellite airports located substantially closer to downtown business centers than the major airports serving these cities. Phoenix was added to the system in 1982 and is rapidly becoming a third hub airport. Southwest's two-tier fare structure is designed to provide "Executive Class" travelers with low cost air transportation and "Pleasure Class" travelers with an economically competitive alternative to various forms of ground transportation. Southwest does not carry the United States mail, interline passengers or engage in carrying large air freight shipments

Principal Bank: M Bank Dallas NA

Financial Information: Consolidated

	Dec 31 1985	Dec 31 1986
	$'000	$'000
Sales revenues	679,672	768,790
Income before taxes	60,784	65,446
Net income	47,278	50,035
Dividends	4,016	4,193
Dividends per share	$0.13	$0.13
Earnings per share(1)	$1.54	$1.55
Earnings per share(2)	$1.51	$1.55
Common stock(3)	32,254	32,254
Retained earnings	258,584	304,426
Total shareholders equity	466,004	511,850

(1) primary
(2) fully diluted
(3) par value $1

No of Employees: 5,819

SOUTHWEST BANCORP

1737 West Vista Way, PO Box 1748, Vista, CA 92083

Tel: (619) 726 5870

Chairman: R R Robinson

President: Sidney Fox (and Chief Executive Officer)

Senior Executive Officers: Frank Mercardante (Executive VP), Michael R Ernst (Senior VP and Chief Financial Officer), Paul M Weil (Secretary)

PRINCIPAL ACTIVITIES: Holding company with interests in banking

Principal Subsidiaries: Southwest Bank; SW Mortgage Inc; Southwest Mortgage Inc; Southwest Thrift & Loan

Principal Bank: Federal Reserve Bank of San Francisco

No of Employees: 680

SOUTHWEST FOREST INDUSTRIES

6225 N 24th Street, Phoenix, AZ 85016

Tel: (602) 956-6000

Telex: 165-713; 165-911 SOWEST FOR PHX; SWF PAPER PHX

President: W A Franke (and Chief Executive Officer)

Senior Executive Officers: J O Underwood (Executive VP, Paper Products Group), D A Graves (Executive VP, Building Products Group), R A Miller (Executive VP, Allied Operations), R P Elder (Executive VP, Chief Financial Officer), W J Rainey (VP, General Counsel and Corporate Secretary), D G Dahlmeier (VP, Purchasing and Transportation), E J Wren (VP, Public Affairs), J P Lall (Treasurer), K M Olsen (Controller)

PRINCIPAL ACTIVITIES: Manufacture and distribution of paper, packaging and building products

Principal Bank: Morgan Guaranty Trust Co of New York

Financial Information:

	Dec 31 1986
	$'000
Sales revenues	660,342
Net (loss)	(1,700)
(Loss) per common share	($0.62)
Common shareholders equity	215,254

No of Employees: 5,000

SOUTHWEST GAS CORPORATION

5241 Spring Mountain Road, PO Box 15015, Las Vegas, NV 89114

Tel: (702) 876 7011

Co-Chairmen: Edward M Berol, William M Laub Sr (and President and Chief Executive Officer)

Senior Executive Officers: Charles H McCrea (Executive VP and Legal Counsel), Judith A Ford (Senior VP), Michael O Maffie (Senior VP Finance and Secretary), John L Mayo (Senior VP Operations), Robert L Muirhead (Senior VP Engineering), Marvin R Shaw (Senior VP Government Relations), W B Down (VP Apache Division), A J Dubuc Jr (VP Materials), Frederick D Joels (VP Engineering), R Hammett (VP Sierra Division), Dennis M Hetherington (VP Communications), William M Morrison (VP Management Information Services), Donald H Sherlock (VP Real Estate), Tom Olson (VP Human Resources), Don Sherlock (VP Prop), L K Stewart (VP Papago Division), Preston W Thompson (VP and Controller)

PRINCIPAL ACTIVITIES: Natural gas supply

Principal Subsidiaries: Design Center Southwest; Don A Harris & Associates; Utility Mortgage Financial Corporation

Principal Bank: Bank of America

Financial Information:

	$'000
Sales revenues	451,020

No of Employees: 2,145

SOUTHWEST MARINE, INC

PO Box 13308, San Diego, CA 92113

Tel: (619) 238-1000

Telex: TWX 910 3351167 swm sdg

President: Arthur Engel

Senior Executive Officers: Herbert G Engel (Executive VP), Lloyd Schwartz (Secretary), William Johnston (VP), David Engel (VP), Alex Vinck (VP), Mark Leinenweber (Treasurer), Jim Nakamura (Chief Financial Officer)

PRINCIPAL ACTIVITIES: Marine engineering services

Trade Names: SWM

Principal Bank: Wells Fargo Bank

Financial Information:

	Feb 28 1986	Feb 28 1987
	$'000	$'000
Sales revenues	118,000	126,000
Income (loss) before taxes	2,945	(1,400)
Net income (loss)	1,301	(500)
Dividends	100	50
Dividends per share	$0.025	$0.063
Earnings (loss) per share	$0.325	($0.63)
Retained income	17,000	16,400
Shareholders equity	17,128	16,600

No of Employees: 1,700

SOUTHWEST MOBILE SYSTEMS CORPORATION

200 Sidney Street, St Louis, MO 63104
Tel: (314) 771-3950
Telex: 434347 SMS STL

Chairman: J Adorjan
President: E J McGuire
Senior Executive Officers: D R Keller (VP Business Development), Ross Leach (VP Finance), John Martin (VP Manufacturing)

PRINCIPAL ACTIVITIES: Design and production of vehicular and bridging systems for defense customers
Parent Company: Emerson Electric Co
Principal Bank: Centerre Bank
Financial information:

	$'000
Sales revenues	50,000

No of Employees: 500

SOUTHWEST NATIONAL CORPORATION

111 South Main Street, Greensburg, PA 15601
Tel: (412) 834 2310

President: Joseph L Blair (and Chief Executive Officer)
Senior Executive Officers: Robert B Troy (Executive VP and Treasurer), Donald A Lawry (Controller), Edwin F George (Secretary)

PRINCIPAL ACTIVITIES: Holding company with interests in banking
Principal Subsidiaries: Southwest National Bank of PA
Principal Bank: Southwest National Bank of PA

No of Employees: 300

SOUTHWESTERN BELL CORPORATION

One Bell Center, St Louis, MO 63101
Tel: (314) 247-9800

Chairman: Zane E Barnes (and Chief Executive Officer); Vice Chairmen: G D Blatherwick (Human Resources and Corporate Communications), R G Pope (Corporate Development); E E Whitacre Jr (Chief Financial Officer)
President: J B Ellis (Group)
Senior Executive Officers: J F Haake (Senior VP Administration), E Myafield (Senior VP and General Counsel), D G Boerger (VP Government and Industry Affairs), R A Dickemper (VP Strategic Planning), M Kaufman (VP Finance and Treasurer), D C Lottmann (VP Corporate Communications), G E Miller Jr (VP Human Resources)

PRINCIPAL ACTIVITIES: Telephone services
Principal Bank: Centerre Bank
Financial Information:

	Dec 31 1985	Dec 31 1986
	$'000	$'000
Sales revenues	7,925,000	7,902,400
Net income	996,200	1,022,700
Earnings per share	$10.00	$10.26
Shareholders equity	7,397,000	7,818,000

No of Employees: 67,500

SOUTHWESTERN ELECTRIC SERVICE COMPANY

1310 Mercantile Bank Building, Dallas, TX 75201
Tel: (214) 741 3125

Chairman: Charles D Goforth (and President)
Senior Executive Officers: John A Barton (VP), David C Fairbanks (VP), Glen H Hibbs (Secretary)

PRINCIPAL ACTIVITIES: Generation and distribution of electricity
Principal Bank: M Bank Dallas
Financial Information:

	$'000
Sales revenues	57,650

No of Employees: 160

SOUTHWESTERN ENERGY COMPANY

75 North East Street, 1 McIlroy Plaza, Suite 302, Fayetteville, AR 72701
Tel: (501) 521 1141

Chairman: Charles E Scharlau (and President and Chief Executive Officer)
Senior Executive Officers: William V Martin (VP, Treasurer and Secretary)

PRINCIPAL ACTIVITIES: Holding company with interests in exploration, production and sale of oil and natural gas
Principal Subsidiaries: AW Realty Company; Arkansas Western Gas Company Inc; Seeco Inc; Southwestern Energy Production Company
Principal Bank: McIlroy Bank and Trust
Financial Information:

	$'000
Sales revenues	99,230

No of Employees: 430

SOUTHWESTERN LIFE INSURANCE CO

Lincoln Plaza, 500 N Akard, Dallas, TX 75201
Tel: (214) 954-7111

President: Kenneth D Allen (and Chief Executive Officer)
Senior Executive Officers: Robert J Bruce (Executive VP Administration), James H Cobb (Executive VP Marketing), Robert L Pashby (Executive VP Eastern Home Office), George A Robinson (Executive VP Western Home Office), Joseph F Zullo (Executive VP Southwestern Home Office), Joseph J Baker (Senior VP and Chief Financial Officer), Donald E Caum (Senior VP Corporate Marketing), J Thomas Deitschel (Senior VP and Counsel), Steve Randall Johnson (Senior VP Marketing and Field Operations), Peter T Lellair (Senior VP and Chief Actuary), W H Mathis (Senior VP Human Resources), Henry H Powers (Senior VP Underwriting), George E Priest (Senior VP Management Information Services), F C Sullivan Jr (Senior VP Pensions), C Douglas Ward (Senior VP Finance)

PRINCIPAL ACTIVITIES: Life insurance, pensions and annuities
Parent Company: Tenneco Inc, Houston, TX
Principal Bank: Interfirst Bank Dallas
Financial Information:

	Dec 31 1985	Dec 31 1986
	$'000	$'000
Premium income	1,349,260	1,218,986
Investment income	172,340	181,840

No of Employees: 5,300

SOUTHWESTERN PIPE, INC

PO Box 2002, Houston, TX 77252
Tel: (713) 863-4300
Telex: WUT 590 254 spax inc

Chairman: J C Moore
President: P C Lewis

Senior Executive Officers: H R Alford (VP), W B Stuessy (Secretary/Treasurer and Controller)

PRINCIPAL ACTIVITIES: Production of steel tubes and pipes; distribution of explosives
Parent Company: Spax Incorporated, Houston, TX
Principal Bank: Texas Commerce Bank
Financial Information:

	$'000
Sales revenues	50,000

Principal Shareholders: Spax Incorporated
No of Employees: 250

SOUTHWESTERN PORTLAND CEMENT CO

3055 Wilshire Blvd, Los Angeles, CA 90010
Tel: (213) 487-4930

Chairman: W J Conway (and Chief Executive Officer)
President: J H Davies (and Chief Operating Officer)
Senior Executive Officers: D W Heineck (Executive VP), W H Strautman (Senior VP), E B Thorn (VP Operations), F R McGoey (VP and Secretary), J M Anderson (VP Administration), D G Dagnan (VP Engineering), C D Leibsle (VP Southwest Division), W I Gharst (VP Eastern Division), R M Ratekin (VP California Division), T F Swafford (VP Southwest Division), David O Tower (VP Mountain Division), Dennis M Thies (Treasurer)

PRINCIPAL ACTIVITIES: Production of cement
Parent Company: Southdown Inc, Houston, TX
Financial Information:

	$'000
Sales revenues	240,000

No of Employees: 1,250

SOUTHWESTERN PUBLIC SERVICE CO

PO Box 1261, Amarillo, TX 79170
Tel: (806) 378-2121

Chairman: Bert P Ballengee (and Chief Executive Officer)
President: W R Esler (and Chief Operating Officer)
Senior Executive Officers: J Bryan Austin (Senior VP Administration), W T Seitz (Senior VP Engineering and Operations), Coyt Webb (Senior VP and Controller), Doyle R Bunch II (VP Finance and Secretary), Gary L Gibson (VP Marketing), Bill D Helton (VP Corporate Services), Sam R Hunter (VP Rates and Economic Research), Carl E Jeans (VP Management Systems), Kenneth L Ladd Jr (VP Fuel Acquisition and Administration), J B Matthews (VP Generation Plant Design and Construction)

PRINCIPAL ACTIVITIES: Distribution of electricity
Principal Bankers: MBank Dallas
Financial Information:

	$'000
Sales revenues	808,000

No of Employees: 2,400

SOUTHWIRE CO

Fertilla Street, Carrollton, GA 30119
Tel: (404) 832-4242
Telex: WUT 542 799 southwire crll

President: Roy Richards (and Chief Executive Officer)
Senior Executive Officers: Gordon E Johnson III (Executive VP Wire and Cable Group), John C Chandler (Executive VP Primary Aluminum), D B Cofer (Senior VP Research and Development), James H Griffin (Senior VP Marketing), J F Holladay (Senior VP Corporate Engineering), John C Huffard (Senior VP Finance), Roger J Schoerner (Senior VP Corporate Development), H D Threadgill (VP International Operations)

PRINCIPAL ACTIVITIES: Manufacture of aluminum and copper wires and cables
Principal Bank: Continental Illinois National Bank of Chicago
Financial Information:

	$'000
Sales revenues	500,000

No of Employees: 3,195

SOVEREIGN CORPORATION

30 West Sola Street, Santa Barbara, CA 93101
Tel: (805) 963 7871

Chairman: Victor T Terry (and Chief Executive Officer)
President: Tim Terry (and Chief Operating Officer and Subsidiary Officer)
Senior Executive Officers: John F Ritchie (Executive VP and Chief Marketing Officer), Robert J Alcocer (Senior VP Underwriting), Craig L Rice (Senior VP, Treasurer and Chief Financial Officer), Burton Bernstein (VP), Jerry L Ewing (VP), Richard Williams (VP), Dennis W Woodall (VP and Controller), Gavin Miller (Secretary)

PRINCIPAL ACTIVITIES: Life insurance services
Principal Subsidiaries: Sovereign Life Insurance Company of California
Principal Bank: Security Pacific National Bank
Financial Information:

	Dec 31 1985 $'000
Revenues	48,765
Net income	4,250

No of Employees: 175

SOVRAN FINANCIAL CORPORATION

One Commercial Place, Norfolk, VA 23510
Tel: (804) 441-4000

Chairman: C A Cutchins III (and Chief Executive Officer); Vice Chairmen: John B Bernhardt; Randolph W McElroy
President: C Coleman McGehee (and Chief Operating Officer)
Senior Executive Officers: Albert B Gornto Jr (Senior Executive VP), L Ralph Hicks (Senior Executive VP), Doyle E Hull (Senior Executive VP and Chief Financial Officer), John B Werner (Senior Executive VP), Page D Cranford (Corporate General Counsel), George R Walls (Corporate Secretary), James E Jarvis (Corporate General Auditor), Donald R Fisher Jr (Treasurer and Chief Accounting Officer)

PRINCIPAL ACTIVITIES: Banking services
Principal Subsidiaries: Sovran Bank, N.A.; Sovran Bank/Maryland; Sovran Bank/DC National
Financial Information:

	Dec 31 1985 $'000	Dec 31 1986 $'000
Income before taxes	148,814	169,283
Net income	124,176	147,956
Dividends(1)	42,084	53,409
Dividends per share(2)	$1.20	$1.32
Earnings per share	$2.94	$3.48
Common stock	210,484	210,960
Retained income	561,711	626,258
Total shareholders equity	763,125	864,335
Deposits	9,716,331	11,610,599
Total assets	13,041,363	14,952,156

(1) Common and Preferred
(2) Declared-Common

No of Employees: 10,961

SPANG & CO

Brugh Avenue, Butler, PA 16001
Tel: (412) 287-8781

Chairman: Frank E Rath; Vice Chairman: Robert A Rath
President: Frank E Rath Jr
Senior Executive Officers: Robert W Olmsted (Executive VP), William T Marsh (VP and Secretary), Charles R Dorsch (VP and Treasurer), Loretta A Rath (VP Personnel)

PRINCIPAL ACTIVITIES: Manufacture of electronic components, specialty metals, power control equipment and toys
Trade Names: Magneties, Today's Kids
Principal Subsidiaries: Tok Inc
Principal Bank: The Union National Bank of Pittsburgh
Financial Information:

	$'000
Sales revenues	60,000

No of Employees: 1,000

SPARKMAN ENERGY CORPORATION

710 N Mesquite, Corpus Christi, TX 78401
Tel: (512) 883 6978

Chairman: Wallace C Sparkman (and President)
Senior Executive Officers: R Michael Hill (Senior VP and Chief Financial Officer), Earl D Coleman (VP), Max Emmert III (VP), David L Harvey (VP and Chief Financial Officer), Stevens G Herbst (VP), S Kennard Smith (Treasurer and Controller), Renee Wardrip (Secretary)

PRINCIPAL ACTIVITIES: Distribution of natural gas
Principal Subsidiaries: Di-Com Services Inc; Esperanza Transmission Company Inc; Key Yale E Inc; VPI/Di-Com Services Inc
Principal Bank: Bank of the Southwest
Financial Information:

	$'000
Sales revenues	139,200

No of Employees: 490

SPARTAN MILLS

Blackstock Road, Spartanburg, SC 29303
Tel: (803) 574-0211
Telex: TWX 810 2812178 spartanml spa

Chairman: Walter S Montgomery
President: Walter S Montgomery Jr (and Chief Executive Officer and Treasurer)
Senior Executive Officers: Mitchell Allen Jr (Group VP), E E Kirkland (Group VP), John M Nicholson (VP Manufacturing), Harold Thompson (VP Industrial Relations), Leslie Odom (VP Purchasing), Joe Herlong (VP Fiber Purchasing), Richard Baldwin (VP Administration), Lester Eledge (VP Engineering)

PRINCIPAL ACTIVITIES: Textile spinning, weaving and finishing
Principal Bank: Chemical Bank
Financial Information:

	$'000
Sales revenues	250,000

No of Employees: 3,250

SPARTECH CORPORATION

7777 Bonhomme, Suite 1001, Clayton, MO 63105
Tel: (314) 721 4242

Chairman: Lawrence M Powers (and Chief Executive Officer)
Senior Executive Officers: Bradley B Buechler (Executive VP and Chief Operating Officer), John D Minard (VP and Controller), William H Hiatt (General Manager), Donald H Hudson (General Manager), James O Huffman (General Manager), John G James (General Manager)

PRINCIPAL ACTIVITIES: Supply of a wide range of plastic products
Principal Subsidiaries: Alchem Plastics; Southwest Converting Inc; Spartech-Adams Inc
Principal Bank: Congress Financial Corporation
Financial Information:

	$'000
Sales revenues	75,000

No of Employees: 450

SPARTON CORPORATION

2400 E Ganson Street, Jackson, MI 49202
Tel: (517) 787-8600
Telex: TWX 810 2531925 sparton jkn

Chairman: John J Smith (and Chief Executive Officer)
President: David W Hockenbrocht
Senior Executive Officers: Blair H Thompson (VP and Treasurer), Lawson K Smith (VP and Secretary), Richard Mico (VP Sparton Technology Inc), William Becktell (VP Sparton Manufacturing Co), Richard H Nichols (VP Sparton Electronics Division), Tom Paul (VP Michigan Oil Company), R C French (VP Lake Odessa Machine Products Inc), L R Staszak (President Sparton of Canada Ltd), Stanley V Kostecki (VP Kent Products), Fred D Keister (Director Public Relations)

PRINCIPAL ACTIVITIES: Manufacture of electronic systems for the defense industry; automotive components; oil and gas exploration and production
Principal Subsidiaries: Michigan Oil Company; Sparton of Canada Ltd; Sparton Technology Inc; Sparton Manufacturing Co; Lake Odessa Machine Products Inc; Kent Products, Inc; Sparton Electronics Florida Inc; Sparton Indiana Inc
Principal Bank: Detroit Bank & Trust Company
Financial Information:

	$'000
Sales revenues	137,750

No of Employees: 3,000

SPECIALTY BRANDS INC

222 Sutter Street, Box 7004, San Francisco, CA 94120
Tel: (415) 981-7600
Telex: TWX 910 372 6115 specbrands sfo

Chairman: I P Rosow (and President)
Senior Executive Officers: Robert D Cameron (VP Sales), W Stephen Holmes III (VP Finance and Administration), Ronald L Colvin (VP Manufacturing)

PRINCIPAL ACTIVITIES: Manufacture of spices, salad dressings and olives
Trade Names: Spice Islands, Marie's Refrigerated Dressings, Early California Olives
Parent Company: United Biscuits (Holdings) PLC, UK
Principal Subsidiaries: Early California Foods, Inc
Principal Bank: Wells Fargo Bank
Financial Information:

	$'000
Sales revenues	83,642

Principal Shareholders: United Biscuits (100%)
No of Employees: 560

SPECIALTY PACKAGING PRODUCTS, INC

PO Box 1106, Richmond, VA 23208
Tel: (804) 344-0300
Telex: TWX 910-997-0617

Chairman: Phillips E Patton (and President)
Senior Executive Officers: E Paul Winslow (VP-Sales), James R Kopnisky (VP-Manufacturing and Technical), John E Willis (VP-Finance, Secretary and Treasurer)

PRINCIPAL ACTIVITIES: Manufacture of finger activated pumps, closures, metal tubes and cans for the cosmetic, toiletries, and household consumer goods industries
Parent Company: Specialty Acquisition Corp
Principal Subsidiaries: SPP Inc (Canada)
Principal Bank: United Virginia Bank
Financial Information:

	$'000
Sales revenues	70,000

No of Employees: 900

SPECTRADYNE INC

1501 North Plano Road, Richardson, TX 75081
Tel: (214) 234 2721

President: Howard T Buchanan
Senior Executive Officers: Sidney L Boyer (VP Operations), Robert S Briggs (VP Technology), James D Everett (VP Manufacturing), Daniel T Owen (VP Marketing), Donald P Snodgrass (VP Networking), R F Troy (VP Finance and Treasurer)

PRINCIPAL ACTIVITIES: Manufacture and installation of televisions for hotels for closed circuit pay TV movies
Principal Bank: BancTexas Dallas NA
Financial Information:

	$'000
Sales revenues	60,000

No of Employees: 370

SPECTRA-PHYSICS, INC

3333 N First Street, San Jose, CA 95134
Tel: (408) 946-6080
Telex: WUT 357460 spectrphys snj

Chairman: Herbert M Dwight Jr (and President and Chief Executive and Operating Officer)
Senior Executive Officers: Michael R Gaulke (Senior VP and Chief Financial Officer), Jan Blakslee (VP Human Resources), Kenneth A Ruddock (VP), Klaus F Derge (VP International), Michael Hodges (VP Auto Lab Division), John J Poggi Jr (VP and Secretary), William L Overell (VP and Controller), Ted L Teach (VP), Alfred P Hildebrand (VP Laser Products Division)

PRINCIPAL ACTIVITIES: Production of lasers
Principal Subsidiaries: Spectra-Physics International; Laserplane Corp; Spectra-Physics SARL (France); Spectra-Physics Ltd (UK); Spectra-Physics BV (Netherlands); Spectra-Physics International Finance NV (Netherlands Antilles); Laser Analytics Inc; Quanta-Ray Inc; Spectra-Physics Pty Ltd (Australia); Spectra-Physics KK (Japan); Spectra-Physics AG (Switzerland); Spectra-Physics Canada Inc (Canada); Spectra-Physics GmbH (Germany); Mathematical Sciences Northwest Inc
Principal Bank: Bank of America
Financial Information:

	$'000
Sales revenues	191,360

No of Employees: 2,500

SPECTRO INDUSTRIES, INC

Jenkintown Plaza, Jenkintown, PA 19046
Tel: (215) 885-3678

Chairman: Joseph L Garde (and President)
Senior Executive Officers: Philip Levin (VP and Secretary), James Eisenstock (VP Sales), Herbert G Altman (VP Finance), Joseph O'Brien (VP Manufacturing), Robert Peirce (VP Data Services), Herbert Garde (VP Operations), Joseph A Goldblum (VP and Corporate Counsel)

PRINCIPAL ACTIVITIES: The company has interests in the supply of pharmaceuticals; medical and surgical equipment; hospital furniture and health care equipment
Parent Company: McKesson Corporation
Principal Subsidiaries: Custom Kit Pack Co; District Hospital Supply Co Inc; District Wholesale Drug Corp; Goodman Manufacturing Co; Loewy Drug Co Inc; Massachusetts Wholesale Drug Co; Medical Equipment Unlimited Inc; Penn-Chem Corp; Sci-o-Tech/Goodman; Spectro Medical Inc; Toub Distributors Inc; West Wholesale Drug Co
Principal Bank: First Pennsylvania Bank
Financial Information:

	$'000
Sales revenues	400,000

No of Employees: 1,500

SPECTRUM GROUP INC

8641 Baypine Road, Jacksonville, FL 32216
Tel: (904) 636 7500

Chairman: Edward M Corey Sr; Vice Chairman: Carl A Steighner (and President and Treasurer)
Senior Executive Officers: Kenneth M Kirschner (VP and Secretary), William R Mabry III (Chief Accounting Officer and Controller)

PRINCIPAL ACTIVITIES: Supply of specialty chemicals including household pest control products
Principal Bank: Southeast Bank
Financial Information:

	$'000
Sales revenues	54,380

No of Employees: 130

SPENCER BEEF DIVISION

PO Box 116, Minneapolis, MN 55440
Tel: (612) 481-2900
Telex: WUT 297070 spncrbeef ardh

Senior Executive Officers: Ron Diven (Senior VP), Al Wood (VP Operations), James Whatron (VP Procurement)

PRINCIPAL ACTIVITIES: Beef processing
Parent Company: Land O'Lakes Inc
Financial Information:

	$'000
Sales revenues	624,000

No of Employees: 1,250

SPENCER COMPANIES INC

450 Summer Street, Boston, MA 02210
Tel: (617) 542 8120

Chairman: C Charles Marran; Vice Chairman: Herbert Rosen
President: Paul F O'Connor (and Chief Executive Officer)
Senior Executive Officers: Donald C Burgess (VP Merchandise), Irwin J Lakin (VP Store Operations), Frank L Marran (VP Manufacturing), James Morin (VP), W A Oliver (VP and Treasurer), Lewis H Weinstein (Clerk)

PRINCIPAL ACTIVITIES: Retail outlets for the sale of women's footwear and clothing
Principal Subsidiaries: Fashion Gallery Inc; Happy Legs Inc
Principal Bank: Chase Manhattan Bank
Financial Information:

	$'000
Sales revenues	114,920

No of Employees: 3,000

SPENDTHRIFT FARM INC

PO Box 996, Iron Works Pike, Lexington, KY 40588
Tel: (606) 299 5271

Chairman: Leslie Combs II (and Chief Executive Officer); Vice Chairman: Keith P Nally
Senior Executive Officers: Peter J Belanto (VP), Scott Peterson (Secretary and Treasurer), David Wilhite (Controller and Assistant Secretary)

PRINCIPAL ACTIVITIES: Breeding and care of horses
Financial Information:

	$'000
Sales revenues	34,400

No of Employees: 250

SPORTSCOACH CORPORATION OF AMERICA

1520 Mishawaka Street, Elkhart, IN 46515
Tel: (219) 522-6224

Chairman: T H Corson
President: D Olson

Senior Executive Officers: R A Gottschalk (Executive VP), P G Lux (Executive VP), J Skinner (Executive VP), J Todd (VP Sales and Marketing)

PRINCIPAL ACTIVITIES: Manufacture of motor homes

Parent Company: Coachmen Industries Inc, Middlebury, IN

Financial Information:

	$'000
Sales revenues	80,000

No of Employees: 600

SPRING AIR CO

20 N Wacker Drive, Chicago, IL 60606

Tel: (312) 782-2971

Chairman: James Brite; Vice Chairman: E M Salomon Jr

President: Donald P Pellegrini (and Chief Executive Officer)

Senior Executive Officers: Donald Balsguich (VP Marketing), LeRoy Simon (VP Manufacturing)

PRINCIPAL ACTIVITIES: Manufacture of mattresses and springs

Principal Bank: First National Bank of Chicago

Financial Information:

	$'000
Sales revenues	120,000

SPRINGFIELD INSTITUTION FOR SAVINGS

1441 Main Street, Springfield, MA 01103

Tel: (413) 781-8000

Chairman: William A James

President: Philip E Lamb

Senior Executive Officers: Lawrence D Beane (Chief Operating Officer), Roland G Desrochers (VP and Controller), Michael O Miller (VP and Treasurer), Harold A Smith (VP Mortgage), Robert D Piper (VP Commercial Loans)

PRINCIPAL ACTIVITIES: Banking and financial services

No of Employees: 500

SPRINGS INDUSTRIES, INC

205 N White Street, Fort Mill, SC 29715

Tel: (803) 547-3650

Telex: WUT 573458 SPNG MIL LCER B

Chairman: Walter Y Elisha (and Chief Executive Officer)

President: W Paul Tippett

Senior Executive Officers: Julius Lasnick (Executive VP), John V Cauthen (Executive VP), A W Peacock (Executive VP-Finance), H B Millican (Senior VP-Diversified Products), Robert L Thompson Jr (VP-Public Affairs), Ralph T Brannan (VP-Systems), Robert M Bruton (VP-Data Processing), J E Hendrix (VP-Research and Development), F E Williams (VP-Engineering), James F Zahrn (Treasurer), C M Harrell (VP-Financial Planning), John A Palmer (Controller), J S White (Senior VP-Human Resources/Corporate Secretary), Bruce Roberts (Senior VP), R S Hudspeth (VP-Purchasing), J D Hopkins (VP-Business Development)

PRINCIPAL ACTIVITIES: General textile manufacture

Trade Names: Springmaid, Wamsutta, Skinner, Ultrasuede, Performance, Pacific, Graber, FashionPleat, Custom Designs, Pacific Silvercloth

Principal Subsidiaries: Graber Industries Inc; Clark-Schwebel Fiber Glass Corporation

Financial Information:

	Jan 4 1986	Jan 3 1987
	$'000	$'000
Sales revenues	1,013,000	1,504,984
Net income	13,271	32,575
Dividends	13,400	13,400
Dividends per share*	$0.76	$0.76
Earnings per share*	$0.75	$1.83
Retained income	431,504	450,622
Shareholders equity	442,223	464,622

*restated to reflect the two-for-one stock split effective April 30 1987

No of Employees: 23,500

SPS TECHNOLOGIES INC

Corporate Offices, Newtown, PA 18940

Tel: (215) 860-3000

Telex: WUI 685 1214 corpsps nwtn

Chairman: John R Selby Jr (and Chief Executive Officer)

President: Harry J Wilkinson (and Chief Operating Officer)

Senior Executive Officers: Thomas R O'Neill (Group VP Fastener), Rockwell M Groves (VP Industrial Relations), Edward H Kottcamp Jr (Group VP, Manufacturing, Engineering and Special Materials), Joseph P Rhein (VP Finance), Harry W Antes (VP Research and Development), Arthur B Belden III (VP and Controller), Charles E Myslinski (Treasurer), Aaron Nerenberg (Corporate Counsel and Secretary)

PRINCIPAL ACTIVITIES: Manufacture of high-technology aerospace and industrial fasteners; materials handling equipment; computer controlled tightening equipment; and special materials

Principal Subsidiaries: Cannon-Muskegon Corporation; T J Brooks Ltd; The Arnold Engineering Co; Standco Canada Ltd; SPS Technologies Ltd; SPS International Ltd; Unbrako Mexicana SA de CV; Unbrako Steel Company Ltd; Unbrako Schrauben GmbH; Unbrako SRL; SPS-Unbrako SA; SPS/Unbrako KK; Alexander Socket Screws Ltd; Unbrako Pty Ltd; SPS Inc; Unbrako ApS; Precision Fasteners Ltd (36.75%); Metalac SA Industria e Comercio (46.1%)

Principal Bank: Philadelphia National Bank

Financial Information:

	Dec 31 1985	Dec 31 1986
	$'000	$'000
Sales revenues	289,900	341,400
Income before taxes	14,350	20,885
Net income	11,112	14,335
Dividends	3,916	4,367
Dividends per share	$0.82	$0.90
Earnings per share	$2.33	$2.96
Retained income	94,033	104,001
Shareholders equity	121,142	137,200

No of Employees: 6,277

SQUARE D CO

1415 S Roselle, Palatine, IL 60067

Tel: (312) 397-2600

Telex: WUT 281004 sqd corp palt

Chairman: Dalton L Knauss (and Chief Executive Officer)

President: Robert E King (Group)

Senior Executive Officers: Thomas L Bindley (VP Finance and Chief Financial Officer), Thomas H Brown (VP, Smyrna TN), John N Daniel (VP Asheville), Charles W Denny III (VP), Richard A Hegeman (VP Marketing), E A Kemper (VP), W W Kurczewski (VP, Secretary and General Counsel), A G Mueller (VP), G E Myers (VP), R M O'Neal (VP Sales), Charles E Quentel (VP Engineering), R A Sackett (VP), J M Vetta (VP Personnel), J Vikmanis (VP), Thomas W Wilbor (VP), Simon Yin (VP Research and Development)

PRINCIPAL ACTIVITIES: Manufacture of electrical machinery and components; power equipment; switchgear apparatus; heating and ventilation equipment; electronic components; measuring devices
Principal Bank: First National Bank of Chicago
Financial Information:

	Dec 31 1985	Dec 31 1986
	$'000	$'000
Sales revenues	1,402,200	1,403,472
Net income	87,190	98,928
Dividends per share	$3.02	$3.42
Shareholders equity	606,140	670,789

No of Employees: 22,100

SQUARE INDUSTRIES INC

921 Bergen Avenue, Jersey City, NJ 07306
Tel: (201) 798 0090

Chairman: Lowell Harwood (and Chief Executive Officer)
President: Sanford Harwood (and Chief Operating Officer)
Senior Executive Officers: Brett Harwood (Executive VP Real Estate), Steven Chiappa (VP Metro NY), John Hogan (VP), Dan Jeremitsky (VP Design), Jack Perry (VP Eastern Region), Aaron D Levey (Secretary and Treasurer)

PRINCIPAL ACTIVITIES: Operation of gas stations, parking lots and garages; property development
Principal Bank: National Westminster Bank USA
Financial Information:

	$'000
Sales revenues	37,150

No of Employees: 835

SQUIBB CORPORATION

PO Box 4000, Princeton, NJ 08540
Tel: (609) 921-4000
Telex: ITT 4754082 squibb prin

Chairman: Richard M Furlaud (and Chief Executive Officer)
Senior Executive Officers: Charles A Sanders (Executive VP), Jan Leschly (Executive VP), George B Mackaness (Group VP), Daniel A Cuoco (Senior VP), Robert E Humes (Senior VP), Anthony W Ruggiero (Senior VP), Joseph T Stewart Jr (Senior VP), Andrew Briskar (VP), Edward C Coleman (VP), Allan E Garb (VP), Jan M Z Kaczmarek (VP), Richard S Kahn (VP), James R Knill (VP), Robert D Popper (VP), Richard L Thompson (VP), G Walton Cottrell (Treasurer), Philip S Seydel (Controller)

PRINCIPAL ACTIVITIES: Manufacture of a wide range of pharmaceutical products
Principal Subsidiaries: E R Squibb & Sons Inc
Financial Information:

	Dec 31 1985*	Dec 31 1986
	$'000	$'000
Sales revenues	1,403,800	1,784,600
Income before taxes	323,447	377,700
Net income	226,599	396,300
Dividends	92,026	103,387
Dividends per share	$1.72	$1.94
Earnings per share	$4.03	$4.90
Common stock	54,093	53,824
Retained income	1,310,790	1,349,049
Shareholders equity	1,465,758	1,358,096

*Restated to reflect discontinued businesses

No of Employees: 16,915

SQUIBB, E R, & SONS, INC

PO Box 4000, Princeton, NJ 08540
Tel: (609) 921-4000

Chairman: Richard M Furlaud (and Chief Executive Officer)
President: Dennis C Fill (and Chief Operating Officer)
Senior Executive Officers: Charles A Sanders (Executive VP), Daniel A Cuoco (Senior VP and General Counsel), Robert E Humes (Senior VP), Leo S Martinuzzi Jr (VP), Anthony W Ruggiero (Senior VP and Chief Financial Officer), Joseph T Stewart Jr (Senior VP), Jan Leschly (Group VP), George B Mackaness (Group VP), Ernest Mario (Group VP), Robert H Miller (Group VP), Andrew Briskar (VP), Edward C Coleman (VP), William R Cox (VP), Robert T DeGavre (VP and Treasurer), Allan E Garb (VP), Richard S Kahn (VP Taxes), Ian M Z Kaczmarek (VP), James R Knill (VP), William R Luney (VP and Secretary), Robert T Popper (VP), Philip S Seydel (VP), Richard L Thompson (VP)

PRINCIPAL ACTIVITIES: Manufacture of pharmaceutical preparations; surgical instruments
Parent Company: Squibb Corporation, Princeton, NJ
Principal Bank: Morgan Guaranty Trust Co of NY
Financial Information:

	$'000
Sales revenues	980,000

No of Employees: 23,650

SQUIRT & COMPANY

777 Brooks Avenue, Holland, MI 49423
Tel: (616) 396-1281

Chairman: James F Brooks
President: James W F Brooks (and Chief Executive Officer)
Senior Executive Officers: George P Julius Jr (Executive VP), Michael R Mucciolo (Senior VP and Chief Financial Officer), Dennis H Eade (VP Human Resources), Charles B Thies (VP Franchise Administration)

PRINCIPAL ACTIVITIES: Production of non-alcoholic beverages; fruit drinks; flavorings
Principal Bank: First Michigan Bank Corporation
Financial Information:

	$'000
Sales revenues	65,000

No of Employees: 225

ST JOE GOLD CORPORATION

7733 Forsyth Boulevard, Clayton, MO 63105
Tel: (314) 726 9500

Chairman: Peter J Neff (and Chief Executive Officer)
President: Alvan H Sage (and Chief Operating Officer)
Senior Executive Officers: Dwight A Miller (VP, Legal Counsel and Secretary), Robert A Sherman (VP, Chief Financial Officer and Treasurer), Thomas N Walthier (VP), Kenneth R Werneburg (VP), Guy A McCormick (Controller)

PRINCIPAL ACTIVITIES: Mining and gold refining
Financial Information:

	$'000
Sales revenues	97,800

No of Employees: 1,520

ST JOE PAPER CO

803 Edward Ball Building, Jacksonville, FL 32202
Tel: (904) 356-8311

Chairman: J C Belin (and Chief Executive Officer)
President: W L Thornton (and Chief Operating Officer)
Senior Executive Officers: W W Carlson (VP), Stanley D Fraser (VP), W F Hudson (VP), E T Ford (VP), Robert E Nedley (VP)

PRINCIPAL ACTIVITIES: Manufacture of pulp and paper products; manufacture of packaging materials
Principal Bank: Florida National Bank
Financial Information:

	$'000
Sales revenues	500,000

No of Employees: 3,400

ST JOSEPH BANCORPORATION INC

River Bend Plaza at Jefferson Blvd, South Bend, IN 46601
Tel: (219) 237 5200

Chairman: Richard A Rosenthal (and Chief Executive Officer)
President: Arthur H McElwee Jr (and Chief Administration Officer)
Senior Executive Officers: Michael J Hammes (Executive VP), Edward A Mangone (Executive VP and Chief Operating)

PRINCIPAL ACTIVITIES: Holding company with interests in banking
Principal Bank: St Joseph Bank and Trust

No of Employees: 325

ST JOSEPH LIGHT AND POWER COMPANY

520 Francis Street, St Joseph, MO 64502
Tel: (816) 233 8888
Telex: (816) 233-7915

President: Terry F Steinbecker
Senior Executive Officers: Robert L Slater (VP Administration), Ralph B Mayer (VP Operations), Gary L Myers (Secretary), Larry J Stoll (VP Finance, Treasurer and Assistant Secretary)

PRINCIPAL ACTIVITIES: Supply of electricity, natural gas and steam
Principal Bank: Citibank NA
Financial Information:

	Dec 31 1985	Dec 31 1986
	$'000	$'000
Operating revenues	77,281	78,138
Operating income	14,461	15,497
Net income	9,798	11,024
Dividends	5,229	5,660
Dividends per share	$1.72	$1.835
Earnings per share	3.03	$3.50
Common stock	33,776	33,828
Retained income	29,007	34,136

No of Employees: 400

ST PAUL COMPANIES, INC

385 Washington Street, St Paul, MN 55102
Tel: (612) 221-7911

Chairman: Robert J Haugh (and President and Chief Executive Officer)
Senior Executive Officers: Douglas W Leatherdale (Executive VP), Thomas W McKeown (Executive VP), James J Mock (Executive VP), Tom H Swain (Executive VP), Richard W Tongen (Executive VP), Roger R Conant (Senior VP Investment), J Gerald Levey (Senior VP Accounting and Controller), L O Shervheim (Senior VP Law and Corporate Secretary), W T Gryska (VP Corporate Taxes), W J Hay (VP, General Counsel and Assistant Corporate Secretary), E G Pendergast (VP Fixed Income Investment), R W Worthing (VP Equity Investment)

PRINCIPAL ACTIVITIES: Financial services and insurance
Financial Information:

	Dec 31 1985	Dec 31 1986
	$'000	$'000
Revenues	2,671,630	3,181,587
Net income	94,168	217,114
Earnings per share	$4.70	$4.75
Shareholders equity	1,012,245	1,440,565

No of Employees: 10,200

STADLER PACKING CO

1333 Indiana Avenue, Columbus, IN 47201
Tel: (812) 379-9553

Chairman: Fritz Stadler
President: John Stadler
Senior Executive Officers: Fred Stadler (VP), Ernest L Stadler (Secretary), Thomas C Butler (Comptroller)

PRINCIPAL ACTIVITIES: Meat and meat processing
Principal Bank: The First National Bank of Columbus
Financial Information:

	$'000
Sales revenues	125,000

No of Employees: 300

STAFF BUILDERS INC

122 East 42nd Street, New York, NY 10168
Tel: (212) 867 2345

President: George Rubin (and Treasurer)
Senior Executive Officers: Walter E Ritter (VP Operations), Jesse Ulezalka (Secretary and Controller)

PRINCIPAL ACTIVITIES: Supply of temporary personnel for the health care and advertising industries
Principal Subsidiaries: Professional Detail Service; Rapid Computing Corporation; Staff Builders Temporary Personnel
Principal Bank: Chemical Bank
Financial Information:

	$'000
Sales revenues	83,875

No of Employees: 350

STALEY, A E, MFG CO

2200 Eldorado Street, Decatur, IL 62525
Tel: (217) 423-4411
Telex: WUI 6871552 staly uw

Chairman: Donald E Nordlund (and Chief Executive Officer)
President: Robert M Powers (and Chief Operating Officer)
Senior Executive Officers: William F Evans (VP Commodity Operations), Richard R Hahn (VP Research and Development), Edward J Koval (VP International), Wayne S Martin (VP Sweeteners), Reeder C Miller (VP Transport), Kent N Mittelberg (VP), George M Prust (VP Industrial Relations), Robert L Schwanke (VP Finance), Robert K Scott (VP and General Counsel), Henry M Staley (VP Business and Economic Analysis), Warren T Trask (VP Technical Operations)

PRINCIPAL ACTIVITIES: Corn milling products; soybean products; livestock feeds; food products for institutional catering
Parent Company: Staley Continental, Inc, Rolling Meadows, IL
Financial Information:

	$'000
Sales revenues	1,200,000

No of Employees: 4,390

STALEY CONTINENTAL, INC

One Continental Towers, 1701 Golf Rd, Rolling Meadows, IL 60008
Tel: (312) 981-1696

Chairman: Donald E Nordlund (and Chief Executive Officer); Vice Chairman: Alvin W Cohn, Robert H Cohn
Senior Executive Officers: Robert B Hoffman (Executive VP and Chief Financial Officer), Robert M Powers (Executive VP), G David Satterfield (VP Corporate Relations and Administrative Services), Leland B Miller (VP and Treasurer), Robert C Morgan II (VP Tax), Robert K Scott (VP, Secretary and General Counsel), E Raymond Stanhope (VP Human Resources and Government Relations), Michael Urbut (VP and Controller), Edward J Koval (VP International), Robert W Pirscin (VP Human Resources)

PRINCIPAL ACTIVITIES: Holding company whose subsidiaries are engaged in corn refining, food service distribution, and food manufacturing
Principal Bank: Continental Illinois National Bank and Trust Company of Chicago

Financial Information:

	Sep 30 1985	Sep 30 1986
	$'000	$'000
Sales revenues	2,707,862	2,988,396
Income before taxes	20,358	60,618
Net income	6,655	26,186
Dividends	23,816	23,908
Dividends per share	$0.80	$0.80
Earnings per share	$0.19	$0.88
Common stock	286	291,000
Retained income	373,620	375,898
Shareholders equity	658,181	674,621

No of Employees: 9,411

STAMBAUGH-THOMPSON CO

3745 Henricks Road, Youngstown, OH 44501

Tel: (216) 792-9071

Chairman: James B Thompson

President: Philip F Thompson (and Chief Executive Officer)

Senior Executive Officers: Fred Tod (VP), Daniel R Pringle (Treasurer), J Thompson (Secretary)

PRINCIPAL ACTIVITIES: Horticultural equipment and supplies; building materials and fittings; paints and varnishes

Principal Bank: Union National Bank

Financial Information:

	$'000
Sales revenues	54,000

No of Employees: 800

STANADYNE, INC

100 Deerfield Road, Windsor, CT 06095

Tel: (203) 525-0821

Telex: WUI 6813112 stanadyne wsor

Chairman: George J Michel Jr (and Chief Financial Officer)

President: Gerald R Bouwkamp (and Chief Executive Officer)

Senior Executive Officers: C E Brady (Executive VP Automotive Products), Robert E Stuart (Executive VP Moen and Western Steel), Mark I Jurras (VP Employee Relations), Edwin L Russell (VP Corporate Development), Michael J DiFranco (Treasurer), Bruce A Carbonari (Controller), Hargreaves V Tattersall, III (Secretary and General Counsel), Elizabeth W Davenport (Assistant Secretary)

PRINCIPAL ACTIVITIES: Stanadyne Inc is involved primarily in the design, manufacturing and marketing of complex precision metal products and components for industrial and consumer markets both foreign and domestic. The Company pioneered the development of two important products, diesel fuel injection systems for the farm, light construction, automobile and light-truck markets and the single-handle faucet for the plumbing industry. In addition, the Company is the country's third largest producer of cold drawn steel bars, and is one of the largest independent producers of hydraulic valve lifters and lash adjusters in the world

Principal Subsidiaries: Stanadyne International Inc; Stanadyne BV (Netherlands); Stanadyne do Brazil; Stanadyne Incorporated (Canada); Casa Buades SA (Spain); Stanadyne Ltd (Japan); Stanadyne of Pennsylvania Inc; Stanadyne Foreign Sales Corp

Financial Information:

	Dec 31 1986
	$'000
Sales revenues	492,763
Income before taxes	42,032
Net income	21,131
Dividends	10,662
Dividends per share	$1.11
Earnings per share	$2.20
Common stock	27,084
Retained income	195,972
Shareholders equity	216,642

No of Employees: 4,950

STANDARD BRANDS PAINT COMPANY

4300 W 190th Street, Torrance, CA 90509

Tel: (213) 214-2411

Telex: WUT 696158 std br pt tor

Chairman: Stuart D Buchalter (and Chief Executive Officer)

President: Marvin S Wager (and Chief Operating Officer)

Senior Executive Officers: Eric Beck (Executive VP), Alfred Applerose (VP, Real Estate), Sheldon S Abrams (Corporate Controller and Chief Accounting Officer), Victor Loewenstein (VP, Administration), Paul M Ozawa (VP Finance, Chief Financial Officer and Treasurer), Wallace Steadman (VP, Human Resources), Dorothy Cvetas (Corporate Secretary)

PRINCIPAL ACTIVITIES: Retail of paints and other home decorating products and paint manufacturing

Trade Names: DECADE, BENCHMARK, TOTAL CONCEPT, HIDE-ALL, KWAL, THE ART STORE, STYLEFAIRE, ZYNOLYTE, KLENK's, THE MASTER DECORATOR, THE MASTER PROTECTOR, THE WOOD PROTECTOR, CREATIVE, GALLERIE, SHIVA

Principal Subsidiaries: Standard Brands Paint Co Inc; Standard Brands Realty Co Inc; Enterprise Wallcoverings Inc; Zynolyte Products Co; KWAL Paints, Inc; Howells, Inc; Major Paint Co

Principal Bank: Bank of America, Long Beach, CA

Financial Information:

	Jan 26 1986
	$'000
Sales revenues	337,968
Income before taxes	27,105
Net income	15,808
Dividends	6,234
Dividends per share	$0.555
Earnings per share	$1.40
Common stock-equity	11,307
Retained income	150,329
Shareholders equity	169,185

Principal Shareholders: M.D. Sass Associates, Inc; Thompson, Siegel & Walmsley, Inc

No of Employees: 3,647

STANDARD COMMERCIAL CORPORATION

PO Box 450, Wilson, NC 27894-0450

Tel: (919) 291-5507

Telex: 802840 stancomm wisn

Chairman: Ery W Keyaha

President: Marvin W Coghill

Senior Executive Officers: J A Murray (Executive VP Finance), Eugene S DesPortes (Senior VP Sales), A W Peters (VP), Graham D Evans (VP), Harvey B Ruffin (VP), Duncan B Meech (VP), Alexander C Spies (VP), Y K Hsu (VP)

PRINCIPAL ACTIVITIES: Tobacco and wool processing and wholesaling

Principal Subsidiaries: (100% owned unless stated): Tobacco:- Jas I Miller Tobacco Company Inc; Standard Commercial Tobacco Company of Canada Limited (Canada); Werkhof GmbH (West Germany); Leafco Trading GmbH (West Germany); Standard Commercial Tobacco Company (UK) Limited (UK); Stancom Tobacco Company (Malawi) Limited

(Malawi); Trans-Continental Leaf Tobacco Corporation (Liechtenstein); Kortec Limited (Korea); Transhellenic Tobacco SA (51%) (Greece); Spierer Freres & Cie SA (51%) (Switzerland-Branches in Greece and Turkey); Exelka SA (51%) (Greece); Spierer Tutun Ihracat Sanayi Ticaret SA (Turkey). Wool:- Alphonse Six SA (France); Anselme Dewavrin Père et Fils Sa (ADPF) (France); Jacomb Hoare & Company Limited (UK); Lohmann & Company GmbH (West Germany); Lohmann & Company (Proprietary) Limited (South Africa); Peignage de la Tossée (France); Societe d'Investissements et de Commerce Dewavrin et Cie SA (SICOD) (France); Standard Wool (Australia) (Pty) Limited (Australia); Standard Wool (UK) Limited (UK). Other Subsidiaries:- Caro-Green Nursery Inc; Stancom Building Supplies Inc; Kraemer Mercantile Corporation; Standard Computer Systems Inc. Associated Companies: Tobacco:- Atitransco SpA (50%) (Italy); Fumex Exportadora de Tabacos SA (50%) (Brazil); Siam Tobacco Export Corporation Limited (49%) (Thailand); Trans-Continental Leaf Tobacco Company (Central Africa) (Private) Limited (49%) (Zimbabwe); Tobacco Packers (Private) Limited (44.1%) (Zimbabwe); Stancom Tobacco Packers (Malawi) Limited (34.84%) (Malawi); Tobacco Processors (Malawi) Limited (30%) (Malawi); Campbell Tobacco Rehandling Company (Malawi) Limited (25%) (Malawi); Cordillerana Tabacalera Paraguaya SA (Paraguay); Dibcom Tobacco Processors Limited (Canada)

Principal Bank: Bank of America

Financial Information:

	Mar 31 1986	Mar 31 1987
	$'000	$'000
Sales revenues	520,674	618,434
Income before taxes	14,586	20,557
Net income	11,930	13,315
Dividends	1,572	2,189
Dividends per share	$0.36	$0.42
Earnings per share	$2.73	$2.65
Common stock*	4,367	5,028
Retained income	91,429	102,555
Shareholders equity	87,945	128,353

*average shares outstanding in thousands

Principal Shareholders: E W Kehaya; M W Coghill

No of Employees: 1,385

STANDARD HAVENS, INC

PO Box 9430, 8800 East 63rd Street, Kansas City, MO 64133

Tel: (816) 737-0400

Telex: (US) 42-6165; (International) Via WU Domestic 42-6165 STD HAVENS KSC

Chairman: Fred R Havens

President: Lamson Rheinfrank Jr

Senior Executive Officers: William B Berk, Robert W Ittmann, Glenn A Smith Jr

PRINCIPAL ACTIVITIES: Manufacture of air pollution control and asphalt roadbuilding equipment

Trade Names: AC Tensioning Tool System, Alpha/Mark I Baghouse, Alpha/Mark II Baghouse, Alpha/Mark III Baghouse, Alpha/Module Plenum, APPCO Logo, Aqua Black Coal Water Slurry, Bag Sentry Monitoring Device, Beta/Mark I Baghouse, Beta/Mark II Baghouse, Beta/Mex Fabric, BHA Logo, Coneflight, Dacron, Delta/Mark I Baghouse, Disposable Filter Cartridge "Patented 1980, Canada", Dralon T, EEMCO Logo, Engineering Efficient Dryer Flights System, Glasgow Batcher System, Gortex, Low Rider Portable Drum-Mixer Plant, Magnum Hot-Mix Plant, Maxi-Spacer Support Cage, Maxi-Steel Wear Guard, Newplant I Retrofit System, Nomex, Orlon, Poly-Armor Fabric Filter, PrecipTech Logo, Protecta-Guard Metal Shield, Pulse-Pak Conversion, Standard Havens' Logo, S H-Filter Logo, S H-Intecon Logo, S H-Maintenance Logo, S H-Parts Logo, SHS Logo, Steel Timber Supports, Super Plant System, Super-Stor Bin, Teflon, Teflon TFE, Tensionor Suspension System, Thru-Put Processing, Vent-Vac Powerhead Vacuum System, Vistolite Leak Detection System

Principal Subsidiaries: Standard Havens Ltd (UK); Standard Havens (Canada) Ltd (Canada); Baghouse Accessories Co; Standard Havens Filtra GmbH (Germany); Ermont SA (France); SH Properties Inc; SH Research Corp; SH Research Associates

Principal Bank: Commerce Bank of Kansas City

Financial Information:

	$'000
Sales revenues	67,910

No of Employees: 700

STANDARD KNITTING MILLS, INC

Washington & Mitchell, Knoxville, TN 37901

Tel: (615) 546-3211

Telex: TWX 810 5830056 standard kxv

Chairman: James E Gettys

President: E R Chestnut

Senior Executive Officers: J G Maloy (Senior VP), Mansfield S Templeton (VP Sales), H L Johnson (VP Finance), F B Beal (VP Manufacturing), James R Dance (VP Sales)

PRINCIPAL ACTIVITIES: Manufacture of clothing

Parent Company: Stanwood Corporation

Principal Bank: First Tennessee Bank

Financial Information:

	$'000
Sales revenues	60,000

No of Employees: 2,500

STANDARD MEAT CO

3709 E First Street, Fort Worth, TX 76111

Tel: (817) 831-0981

Telex: TWX 910 3505233 standard meat

Chairman: E M Rosenthal

President: William Rosenthal

Senior Executive Officers: Conway Phillips (Executive VP Finance), Tom DeBroeck (VP Marketing)

PRINCIPAL ACTIVITIES: Meat and meat products; ready prepared food products

Parent Company: Sara Lee Foods Corporation, Chicago, IL

Financial Information:

	$'000
Sales revenues	100,000

No of Employees: 1,000

STANDARD MICROSYSTEMS CORPORATION

35 Marcus Blvd, Hauppauge, NY 11788

Tel: (516) 273-3100

Telex: RCA 221646 smc ur

Chairman: Paul Richman (and President)

Senior Executive Officers: Gerald E Gollub (Executive VP), Arthur Sidorsky (Executive VP), Walter J Kmeta (Senior (VP), Victor F Trizzino (Senior VP Finance), H P Zimbelmann (VP), Jay D Popper (VP), Jean-Pierre Chalmin (VP), John Tweedy (VP), Harry Horn (VP)

PRINCIPAL ACTIVITIES: Manufacture of integrated circuits

Principal Bank: Chemical Bank

Financial Information:

	$'000
Sales revenues	44,500

No of Employees: 670

STANDARD MOTOR PRODUCTS, INC

37-18 Northern Blvd, Long Island City, NY 11101

Tel: (718) 392-0200

Telex: ITT 422401 smp ui

Co-Chairmen: Bernard Fife (and Co-Chief Executive Officer), Nathaniel L Sills (and Co-Chief Executive Officer)
President: Lawrence I Sills (and Chief Operating Officer)
Senior Executive Officers: Steven Brown (VP), Richard Cannon (VP), Marvin S Chanko (VP, Secretary and Treasurer), Stanley Davidow (VP), Arthur Davis (VP), Joseph Forlenza (VP), Boris Jody (VP), Nitin Parikh (VP), Kenneth Rogers (VP), Jerry Sorrow (VP)

PRINCIPAL ACTIVITIES: Production of electrical equipment for the automotive industry
Principal Subsidiaries: Blue Streak-Hygrade Motor Products Ltd; Stanric Inc; Stantronics Incs; Champ Service Items
Principal Bank: Bankers Trust Company
Financial Information:

	$'000
Sales revenues	242,800

No of Employees: 2,200

STANDARD PRODUCTS COMPANY

2130 W 110th Street, Cleveland, OH 44102
Tel: (216) 281-8300
Telex: TWX 810 4218400 std prods cv

Chairman: James S Reid Jr (and President)
Senior Executive Officers: Charles Brooks (Senior VP), Robert C Jacob (VP Industrial Relations), Thomas E Judy (VP Manufacturing), R D Kitis (VP), J H Nussbaum (VP Product Development), Joseph A Robinson (VP Finance), Robert B Stevens (VP Sales), T Zampets (VP)

PRINCIPAL ACTIVITIES: Tread rubber for truck-hire retreading; rubber and plastic components for the automobile and truck industry; warehousing services
Principal Subsidiaries: Standard Products (Canada) Ltd; Westbourne Service Center Inc; Oliver Rubber Co; Silent Channel Products Ltd (UK)
Principal Bank: National City Bank, Cleveland
Financial Information:

	Jun 30 1986	Jun 30 1987
	$'000	$'000
Sales revenues	433,159	464,905
Income before taxes	48,818	59,845
Net income	27,184	31,525
Dividends	5,583	6,576
Dividends per share	$0.60	$0.72
Earnings per share	$2.92	$3.46
Common stock	9,313	8,914
Retained income	110,167	119,633
Shareholders equity	117,383	127,359

No of Employees: 5,800

STANDARD PUBLISHING CO

8121 Hamilton Avenue, Cincinnati, OH 45231
Tel: (513) 931-4050

President: Frederic D Mosher
Senior Executive Officers: Gene Wigginton (VP), John D Sharpe (VP Commercial Sales), James R Grogg (VP Religious Sales and Marketing), Robert J Hyde (VP Manufacturing), Robert J Dittrich (Executive VP), Daniel D Miles (VP Berean Bookservices)

PRINCIPAL ACTIVITIES: Publication of religious periodicals, Sunday School literature and supplies; operates a chain of 17 bookstores which distribute religious literature and supplies from Standard and other publishers to churches and school systems
Trade Names: Registered trademarks: Standard, Berean
Parent Company: Standex International Corp, Salem, NH
Financial Information:

	$'000
Sales revenues	75,000

No of Employees: 500

STANDARD REGISTER COMPANY

600 Albany Street, Dayton, OH 45401-1167
Tel: (513) 443-1000
Telex: TWX 810 459 1694 stanregico 1 dy

Chairman: Paul H Granzow
President: John K Darragh (and Chief Executive Officer)
Senior Executive Officers: William P Sherman (VP), J T Kerlin (Senior VP Manufacturing), F V Parenti (VP Engineering), Robert H Reeves (VP Purchasing), P S Redding (Senior VP Administration), C J O'Hara (VP and General Manager Communicolor Division), Norman C Young (VP Industrial Relations), Craig R Brown (VP Finance and Treasurer), G B Chadwick (VP Marketing)

PRINCIPAL ACTIVITIES: Printing of business forms; production of forms handling equipment; data systems
Principal Subsidiaries: The Rein Co
Principal Bank: Bank One
Financial Information:

	Dec 31 1985	Dec 31 1986
	$'000	$'000
Sales revenues	441,048	561,858
Net income	31,795	32,666
Dividends	7,864	9,833
Dividends per share	$0.60	$0.72
Earnings per share	$2.41	$2.42
Shareholders equity	170,196	243,054

No of Employees: 6,674

STANDARD SHARES INC

230 Park Avenue, New York, NY 10169
Tel: (212) 697 4767

Chairman: Neison Harris
President: Irving B Harris
Senior Executive Officers: Sidney Barrows (VP and Treasurer), Arnold Berke (VP and Secretary), Edward Schwartz (VP Finance)

PRINCIPAL ACTIVITIES: Manufacture of plumbing, heating and air conditioning products; security equipment
Principal Subsidiaries: Central Del & Messen Inc; Central Deliveries SV MA; Pittway Corporation; Alarm Device Manufacturing Company; Sontrix BRK Electronics; Penton/Industrial Publishing Company; Penton Learning Systems Inc; Reinhold Publishing Company; Pittway Disc; Pittway Real Estate Inc; Saddlebrook Resorts Inc; Seaquist Valve Company; Valmold; Standard Operations Inc; Brand Insulations Inc; Brand Industrial Services; Bisco Products Inc; DE Biscraft Inc; Brand Asbestos Control Inc; Brand Mid-Atlantic Inc; Brand Examination Services Inc; Brand Structures Inc; Brand/Sabine Industries Inc; S & K Equipment Installations; Thermo Tech
Financial Information:

	$'000
Sales revenues	571,870

No of Employees: 7,955

STANDARD-PACIFIC CORPORATION

1565 W Mac Arthur Blvd, Costa Mesa, CA 92626
Tel: (714) 546-1161

Chairman: Arthur Svendsen (and Chief Exeucitve Officer)
President: Ronald R Foell
Senior Executive Officers: Robert J St Lawrence (VP Finance, Secretary and Treasurer), Steve Scarborough (VP Orange County Division)

PRINCIPAL ACTIVITIES: Building of single family homes; acoustical office partitions; fiberglass and metal panels for the aerospace indsutry
Principal Bank: Crocker National Bank

Financial Information:

	$'000
Sales revenues	263,330

No of Employees: 300

STANDEX INTERNATIONAL CORPORATION

6 Manor Parkway, Salem, NH 03079
Tel: (603) 893-9701
Telex: 24 7821

Chairman: Daniel E Hogan
President: Thomas L King (and Chief Executive Officer)
Senior Executive Officers: Sol Sackel (Senior VP), Samuel S Dennis III (VP), Thomas H DeWitt (Executive VP Administration, Secretary and General Counsel), Sam Grillo (Executive VP, Operations), John M Wall (VP, Industrial Relations), John J Bentley (Corporate Controller), Lindsay Sedwick (Treasurer), Robert R Kettinger (Assistant Corporate Controller), Norman B Asher (Assistant Secretary), Charles F Hartsock (Assistant Secretary), Deborah A Rosen (Assistant Secretary), Tom L Peterson (Corporate Counsel and Assistant Secretary)

PRINCIPAL ACTIVITIES: Standex is a diversified manufacturing and marketing company with operations in five products groups or segments - Graphics, Consumer, Institutional, Electronics and Industrial. The major products are - Graphics:- educational and religious publishing, binding systems, commercial printing and office supplies. Consumer Products:- mail order and furniture. Institutional Products:- food service equipment and hospital equipment. Electronics:- switches and relays, inductors and electronic assemblies, capacitors, micro coils and electrical connectors. Industrial Products:- texturizing systems and metal products
Trade Names: Frank Lewis(R), Yield House(R), Standard(R), Wire-O(R), Mult-O(R), Doubleday, Standex, Roehlen(R), Mold-Tech(R), Perkins(R), Procon(R), Spincraft(R), Snappy(R), Harding, Greer, Master-Bilt(R), Barbecue King(R), Mason(R), Coors, Red Goat(R), General Slicing(R), EPCO, Jarvis & Jarvis, Zenith(R)
Principal Subsidiaries: Crest Fruit Company; Keller-Dorian Graveurs SA (France); S I de Mexico SA de CV (Mexico); Standex International FSC Inc (Virgin Islands); Standex International GmbH (Germany); Yield House Inc; Standex Holdings Ltd (UK); Standex International Ltd (UK); Roehlen Industries Pty Ltd (Australia); James Burn Ltd (UK); Standex Electronics (UK) Ltd (UK)
Principal Bank: The First National Bank of Boston
Financial Information:

	Jun 30 1986 $'000	Jun 30 1987 $'000
Sales revenues	376,322	409,173
Income before taxes	28,210	29,666
Net income	15,593	17,355
Dividends	6,752	6,375
Dividends per share	$0.52	$0.52
Earnings per share	$1.20	$1.41
Common stock	20,988	20,988
Retained income	146,283	157,264
Shareholders equity	146,784	159,664

No of Employees: 5,300

STANFORD TELECOMMUNICATIONS, INC

2421 Mission College Boulevard, Santa Clara, CA 95054
Tel: (408) 748-1010
Telex: TWX 910-339-9531

Chairman: Dr James J Spilker Jr (and President)
Senior Executive Officers: Walter Melton (Senior VP), Leonard Schuchman (Senior VP), Wayne Zachow (Senior VP), Robert Fair (VP), Charles Gandy (VP), Howard Gannes (VP), Gerald Laufman (VP), Dr John Ohlson (VP), Robert Warmke (VP), Gary Wolf (VP, Chief Financial Officer, Secretary)

PRINCIPAL ACTIVITIES: Stanford Telecommunications, Inc designs, manufactures and operates defense electronic systems for aerospace. These systems consist of earth terminals and airborne electronics which provide a variety of services including satellite communications, navigation and tracking, telemetry and control. In addition, the Company performs important engineering functions in design of the next-generation air traffic control systems and major new NASA and DoD space programs. Stanford Telecommunications is a technology leader in advanced digital signal processing and satellite communications and other system control software. These technologies include: Advanced high-speed digital signal processing. Proprietary semiconductor integrated circuits operating at speeds up to several hundred million computations per second. Information processing software-all of the Company's systems contain microprocessors or mainframe computers. Microwave electronics extending to the Extremely High Frequency (EHF) bands. Artificial Intelligence-Expert Systems for use in sophisticated control systems
Trade Names: Stanford Telecommunications, Inc
Principal Bank: Bank of America, Palo Alto, CA
Financial Information:

	Mar 31 1986 $'000	Mar 31 1987 $'000
Sales revenues	45,535	55,368
Income before taxes	4,930	5,220
Net income	2,682	2,742
Earnings per share	$0.60	$0.60
Common stock	12,242	13,142
Retained income	7,866	10,608
Shareholders equity	20,108	23,750

No of Employees: 643

STANGE CO

342 N Western Avenue, Chicago, IL 60612
Tel: (312) 733-6945
Telex: TWX 9102215389 stange cg

Chairman: T R Miles
President: Bailey Thomas
Senior Executive Officers: Francis W Skeans (VP Operations), Florian F Palac (Treasure)

PRINCIPAL ACTIVITIES: Production of specialty chemicals for the food industry
Parent Company: McCormick & Co Inc, Hunt Valley, MD
Principal Bank: The First National Bank of Chicago
Financial Information:

	$'000
Sales revenues	57,000

No of Employees: 500

STANHOME INC

333 Western Avenue, Westfield, MA 01085
Tel: (413) 562-3631
Telex: 955406

Chairman: H L Tower (and President and Chief Executive Officer)
Senior Executive Officers: Allan G Keirstead (Financial VP and Controller), Robert C Alsop (VP, General Counsel, Secretary and Clerk), J Robert Burns (VP, President, Stanley Home Products Division), Alejandro Diaz (VP, President, Stanhome Intnernational Division), Eugene Freedman (VP, President and Chief Executive Officer, Enesco Imports Corp), Bruno F Gedmin (VP, President, National Contracts Division), Ronald R Jalbert (VP, Human Resources and Public Affairs), Gary LaFountain (VP, President, Industrial Division), Thomas M Glynn (VP, President, Operations Division), Latimer B Eddy (VP Strategic Planning and Treasurer), Bruce H Wyatt (Assistant General Counsel, Assistant Clerk and Assistant Secretary), Richard L Thompson (Assistant Clerk and Assistant Secretary)

PRINCIPAL ACTIVITIES: Stanhome Inc is worldwide marketer of quality products with businesses in direct selling, design giftware and specialty industrial markets. These business are supported by a well-developed, international service network. The company and its multinational Direct Sales subsidiaries provide health, home and personal care products and career opportunities worldwide. The Enesco subsidiary distributes high quality, affordable family giftware and collectibles to domestic and international markets. The Industrial Division furnishes custom cleaning systems and products to specialty industrial markets

Trade Names: Principal Trade Marks: LI'L LUV BUNTING; BABY'S BREATH; RAG TAG TEDDIES; M'LADY'S TREASURES; ROSIE & ME; FAITH, HOPE & CHARITY; LUCY & ME; GARFIELD(R); PRECIOUS MOMENTS; MUPPET BABIES; MISS PIGGY; POPPYSEED COLLECTION; STRAWBERRY SHORTCAKE(R); DEAR GOD KIDS; COUNTRY COUSINS(R); COUNTRY CALICO MICE(R), GROWING UP(R); TREASURED MEMORIES(R); STANHOMME(R); TRY-IT(R); AQUILAUN(R); GRADU-WEIGHT(R); SEMIPLICE(R); SELECTIVES

Principal Subsidiaries: Division Offices: Stanhome International Division; Stanley Home Products Division; Operations Division; Stanhome Industrial Division. Subsidiaries: Enesco Imports Corp; Stanley Home Productos Para O Lar Ltda (Brazil); Stanhome SA (France); Enesco International (HK) Ltd (Hong Kong); Stanhome SpA (Italy); Stanhome de Mexico SA de CV (Mexico); Stanhome Inter-American Corporation (Puerto Rico); Stanhome SA (Spain); Cosmhogar SA (Spain); Stanhome Panamericana CA (Venezuela); Stanhome CA (Venezuela); Enesco Australia Pty Ltd (Australia); Enesco Import GmbH (West Germany)

Financial Information:

	Dec 31 1985	Dec 31 1986
	$'000	$'000
Sales revenues net	327,888	380,501
Income before taxes	34,743	50,548
Net income	18,059	25,648
Dividends	6,345	8,367
Dividends per share	$0.60	$0.80
Earnings per share*	$1.71	$2.35
Common stock	25,491	51,746
Retained earnings	135,232	152,514
Shareholders equity	109,742	100,764

*fully diluted

No of Employees: 6,000

STANLEY WORKS (THE)

1000 Stanley Drive, New Britain, CT 06050
Tel: (203) 827-3882
Telex: 99289 STANWORKS-NBT

Chairman: Donald W Davis
President: Richard H Ayers (and Chief Executive Officer)
Senior Executive Officers: R Alan Hunter (Chief Financial Officer and VP Finance), Matthew Bristow (VP and Controller), Thomas K Clarke (VP Corporate Development), Ronald F Gilrain (VP Public Affairs), David M Hadlow (Group VP), Robert E Johnson (VP and Treasurer), Thomas N Jones (VP Industrial Relations), Paul A Marier (VP Organization Development), Lloyd Wallis Jr (VP; President of Stanley Magic-Door Division), Stephen S Weddle (VP and General Counsel), Robert G Widham (Group VP)

PRINCIPAL ACTIVITIES: The Stanley Works is a worldwide marketer and manufacturer of quality consumer, builders and industrial products, including tools for professionals and Do-It-Yourselfers. Stanley also makes hardware and complementary products for the home, the factory and the building industry. Industry segments are: Consumer Products - A growing line of products for the Do-It-Yourself market, including hand tools, staplers, fasteners, consumer hardware, weatherproofing products, plumbing supplies and U-Install garage door openers and residential entry doors. Taylor Rental is the franchisor and operator of the nation's largest system of general equipment rental centers for Do-It-Yourselfers and commercial customers. Builders Products - Products for the professional construction industry, including architectural and residential hardware, stapling and fastening tools, fasteners, pedestrian power-operated doors, insulated steel entry doors, garage doors and openers, automatic parking gates. Industrial Products - Products sold to industrial customers, including professional and industrial hand tools, air tools, hydraulic tools, hardware, fastening tools and fasteners for industry, industrial storage and retrieval systems. This segment includes the products and services that Mac Tools provides to professional mechanics

Trade Names: Registered Trade marks:- Stanley, Magic-Door, U-Install, Mac Tools, Proto, Challenger, Helps You Do Things Right, Handyman, Surform, Yankee, Powerlock, 100 Plus, Steelmaster, Workmaster, Leverlock, Vidmar, Bostitch, Taylor Rental Center

Principal Subsidiaries: Mac Tools Inc; Stanley Proto Industrial Tools, Inc; Stanley-Bostitch; Acme General Corp; National Hand Tool Corp; Taylor Rental Corp; Stanley Canada Inc; Ferramentas Stanley SA; Herramientas Stanley SA de CV; Stanley Works de Mexico; Stanley Works (Italia) SRL; The Stanley Works Ltd; Stanley-Mabo SA; The Stanley Works (Australia) Pty Ltd; Herramientas Stanley SA; Stanley-Bostitch, Inc; National Hand Tool Corporation

Principal Bank: Morgan Guaranty; Citibank; Connecticut Bank & Trust Company

Financial Information:

	Jan 3 1986	Jan 2 1987
	$'000	$'000
Sales revenues	1,371,270	1,763,147
Income before taxes*	131,191	165,247
Net income	78,714	86,639
Dividends	30,723	35,563
Dividends per share	$0.726	$0.82
Earnings per share	$1.86	$2.00
Common stock	106,845	109,095
Retained income	521,874	575,361
Shareholders equity	555,462	625,558

*from continuing operations

No of Employees: 19,100

STANLINE INC

12851 Alondra Boulevard, Norwalk, CA 90650
Tel: (213) 921 0966

President: Stanley G Frahm (and Chief Executive Officer)
Senior Executive Officers: Frank D Hobbs (Senior VP), Kenneth N Christopher (VP), Roger G Lighthart (VP), Roger S Johnson (Secretary and Chief Financial Officer)

PRINCIPAL ACTIVITIES: Building materials including timber products

Financial Information:

	$'000
Sales revenues	49,360

No of Employees: 120

STANWOOD CORPORATION

PO Box 11813, Charlotte, NC 28220
Tel: (704) 527-5270

Chairman: Thomas N Roboz (and President and Chief Executive Officer)
Senior Executive Officers: Douglas F Bassitt (VP and Treasurer), Roy R Bowman (VP Operations), J B Haymes Jr (VP), Dee M Wyatt (Secretary)

PRINCIPAL ACTIVITIES: Manufacture of clothing for men, women and boys

Principal Subsidiaries: Carwood Manufacturing Co; International Apparel Co; Standard Knitting Mills Inc; Checkout Corp; Pony Sports Apparel Inc; Quail Hollow Inc

Financial Information:

	$'000
Sales revenues	117,300

No of Employees: 4,000

STANWYCK, E, COIL CO, INC

75 Carson Avenue, Newburgh, NY 12550
Tel: (914) 561-3030

Chairman: Edmund Stanwyck (and President)
Senior Executive Officers: Nicholas Stanwyck (VP Sales and Purchasing Agent), Arthur Wood (Production Manager)

PRINCIPAL ACTIVITIES: Manufacture of metal components for electric and electronic equipment
Principal Bank: Highland National Bank
Financial Information:

	$'000
Sales revenues	500,000

No of Employees: 90

STAR MFG CO OF OKLAHOMA

PO Box 94910, Oklahoma City, OK 73143
Tel: (405) 636-2010
Telex: 747120

Chairman: John F Fennessey
President: Edward G Edgren
Senior Executive Officers: Wayne E Curran (Senior VP), Arthur L Powell (VP Finance), J R Taylor (VP Operations), Robert F Barth (VP Sales), R T Helvenston (VP Marketing)

PRINCIPAL ACTIVITIES: Manufacture and sale of metal buildings
Trade Names: Star Manufacturing Co
Parent Company: Star Acquisition Company, Oklahoma City, OK
Principal Subsidiaries: Star Building Systems
Principal Bank: AmeriTrust, Cleveland, OH
Financial Information:

	$'000
Sales revenues	60,000

No of Employees: 700

STA-RITE INDUSTRIES, INC

777 E Wisconsin Avenue, Milwaukee, WI 53202
Tel: (414) 276-68885

Chairman: Stuart W Tisdale (and Chief Executive Officer)
President: Joseph P Wenzler (and Chief Operating Officer)
Senior Executive Officers: J L Marringa (VP), Stanley E Farnham (VP)

PRINCIPAL ACTIVITIES: Manufacture of pumps and valves; manufacture of water treatment products and components for heating equipment
Trade Names: STA-RITE, WEBSTER, SWIMQUIP, ONGA
Parent Company: WICOR Inc, Milwaukee, WI
Principal Subsidiaries: Webster Electric Company, Inc; WICOR Canada Inc (Canada); Onga Pty (Australia); Sta-Rite Foreign Sales Corporation; Sta-Rite Europa GmbH (West Germany)
Principal Bank: Harris Bank and Trust
Financial Information:

	Dec 31 1985	Dec 31 1986
	$'000	$'000
Sales revenues	193,241	207,256
Income before taxes	19,277	14,560

No of Employees: 2,300

STARRETT HOUSING CORPORATION

909 Third Avenue, New York, NY 10022
Tel: (212) 751 3100

Chairman: Henry Benach (and Chief Executive Officer)
President: Richard Bassuk
Senior Executive Officers: Robert C Rosenberg (Senior VP), Lewis A Weinfeld (Senior VP, Treasurer and Secretary), Joseph Zelazny (Senior VP), Murray Smith (VP)

PRINCIPAL ACTIVITIES: Real estate development; building and construction
Principal Subsidiaries: HRH Construction Corporation; Levitt Corporation; Levitt Homes Inc
Principal Bank: Chase Manhattan Bank
Financial Information:

	$'000
Sales revenues	98,260

No of Employees: 1,650

STARRETT, L S, CO

121 Crescent Street, Athol, MA 01331
Tel: (617) 249-3551

President: Douglas R Starrett
Senior Executive Officers: D A Starrett (VP), Charles H Morrow (VP Sales), George B Webber (VP), R Wellington Jr (Treasurer)

PRINCIPAL ACTIVITIES: Manufacture of measuring and cutting tools and measuring instruments
Principal Subsidiaries: Industria e Comercio L S Starrett SA (Brazil); L S Starrett Co Ltd (UK); L S Starrett Co of Canada Ltd
Principal Bank: First National Bank of Boston
Financial Information:

	$'000
Sales revenues	118,390

No of Employees: 2,252

STATE FARM LIFE INSURANCE CO

One State Farm Plaza, Bloomington, IL 61701
Tel: (309) 766-2311

Chairman: Marvin D Bower
President: Edward B Rust
Senior Executive Officers: Darrell W Beernink (VP and Actuary), William O Burns (VP and Treasurer), C R Charlson Jr (VP and Secretary), Robert N Fischer (VP Claims), John S Hindahl (VP Underwriting), James A Malay (VP Operations), Norman K Martin (VP), Walter G Nelson (VP and Counsel), Don D Reed (VP Agency), Dallas Reynolds (VP Personnel), James W Spellman (VP), Clifford Steinkraus (VP Municipal Securities), A L Van Ness (VP Medical), Frank Warber (VP Research)

PRINCIPAL ACTIVITIES: Insurance
Parent Company: State Farm Mutual Automobile Insurance Company
Financial Information:

	Dec 31 1985	Dec 31 1986
	$'000	$'000
Premium income	1,156,080	1,224,966
Investment income	576,470	657,872

No of Employees: 18,140

STATE INDUSTRIES, INC

Ashland City, TN 37015
Tel: (615) 792-4371
Telex: WUT 508539 stateindeng ud

Chairman: John R Lindahl
President: Herbert W Lindahl
Senior Executive Officers: Phil Loughrey (VP Marketing), Joseph V Lanier (VP Finance), Ernest Wenczl (VP Engineering), Jim Raymer (VP Purchasing), John Lindahl Jr (VP Sales), Hilda Wilsdorf (VP Customer Services)

PRINCIPAL ACTIVITIES: Manufacture of water heating equipment; trucking services
Principal Bank: Third National Bank

Financial Information:

	$'000
Sales revenues	200,000

No of Employees: 2,000

STATE MUTUAL LIFE ASSURANCE COMPANY OF AMERICA

440 Lincoln Street, Worcester, MA 01605
Tel: (617) 852-1000
Telex: WUT 920425 sma co wor a

President: Frederick Fedeli (and Chief Executive Officer)
Senior Executive Officers: Donald R Nelson (Executive VP Administration), John M Quinlan (Executive VP Individual Insurance), Benjamin R Schenck (Executive VP and Controller), Edmund T Bennett (Senior VP and Chief Investment Officer), John F Kelly (Senior VP and General Counsel), Arthur H Alie (VP Group Pension Administration), Bruce B Crawford (VP Group Marketing)

PRINCIPAL ACTIVITIES: Mutual life insurance company
Principal Bank: Manufacturers Hanover Trust Co
Financial Information:

	Dec 31 1985 $'000	Dec 31 1986 $'000
Premium income	1,100,340	1,142,833
Investment income	261,390	314,773

No of Employees: 4,500

STATE STREET BOSTON CORPORATION

225 Franklin St, Boston, MA 02101
Tel: (617) 786-3000

Chairman: William S Edgerly (and President)
President: Peter E Madden
Senior Executive Officers: David A Spina (Executive VP, Treasurer and Chief Financial Officer), Ronald A Golz (Executive VP), Norton Q Sloan (Executive VP), Bradford S Tripp (Senior VP), William S Tripp (Senior VP), William E Gundy (Executive VP), Howard H Fairweather (Executive VP)

PRINCIPAL ACTIVITIES: Banking and financial services
Principal Bank: State Street Bank and Trust Company
Financial Information:

	Dec 31 1986 $'000	Dec 31 1987 $'000
Income before taxes	110,089	132,992
Net income	71,395	83,133
Dividends	12,506	4,383
Dividends per share	$0.36	$0.12
Earnings per share(1)	$1.97	$2.23
Earnings per share(2)	$1.84	$2.12
Common stock	35,078	36,526
Retained income	318,615	386,274
Shareholders equity	392,364	471,364
Deposits	5,269,596	4,537,942
Total assets	7,189,818	6,955,225

(1) primary
(2) fully diluted

No of Employees: 6,943

STATER BROTHERS INC

21700 Barton Road, Colton, CA 92324
Tel: (714) 783 5000

Chairman: B R Garrett
President: Jack H Brown (and Chief Executive Officer)
Senior Executive Officers: Joseph E Davis (VP), H Harrison Lightfoot (VP), L D McKenzie (VP and Chief Financial Officer), Richard C Moseley (VP), M A Resnik (VP and Secretary), Ronald P Woodstra (VP)

PRINCIPAL ACTIVITIES: Retail food stores

Financial Information:

	$'000
Sales revenues	714,000

No of Employees: 4,700

STATESMAN GROUP INC

1400 Des Moines Building, Des Moines, IA 50309
Tel: (515) 284 7500

Chairman: D J Noble (and President and Chief Executive Officer)
Senior Executive Officers: O O Allen (VP), J M Matovina (VP and Treasurer), W R O'Donnell (VP), T A Reimer (Secretary)

PRINCIPAL ACTIVITIES: Holding company with interests in a wide range of insurance and financial services
Principal Subsidiaries: American Life and Casualty Insurance Company; State Automobile Insurance Association; Statesman Financial Service; R G Dickinson & Company; Statesman Insurance Company; Statesman Life Insurance Company; Techno Company; Vulcan Life Insurance Company
Principal Bank: American Fletcher National Bank
Financial Information:

	$'000
Revenues	252,670

No of Employees: 800

STATEWIDE BANCORP

40 Main Street, Toms River, NJ 08753
Tel: (201) 244 1011

Chairman: Richard D Sutton
President: Joseph W Robertson (and Chief Executive Officer)
Senior Executive Officers: William T Hiering (VP), Leonard G Lomell (VP), Richard Sambol (VP), Frank J Ewart (Secretary and Treasurer), Roger N Lane Jr (Assistant Secretary)

PRINCIPAL ACTIVITIES: Banking

No of Employees: 945

STAUFFER CHEMICAL COMPANY

Westport, CT 06881
Tel: (203) 222-3000
Telex: WUT 643 445 stauffer intl

Chairman: H B Morely (and Chief Executive Officer); Vice Chairman: Milton Stern
Senior Executive Officers: Robert E Crow (President, Basic Chemicals Division), Conrad S Kent (President, Specialty and Food Products Division), Joseph P Monteleone (President, International Division), Roy Sambrook (President, Chemical Products Group), Milan J Turk (President, Agricultural Products), Rocco Balestriere (VP and Controller)

PRINCIPAL ACTIVITIES: Manufacture of chemicals and plastics; manufacture of food additives, agricultural chemicals and pharmaceutical intermediates
Parent Company: Chesebrough Pond's Inc
Principal Bank: Bank of New York
Financial Information:

	$'000
Sales revenues	1,500,000

No of Employees: 11,650

STAUFFER COMMUNICATIONS, INC

616 Jefferson Street, Topeka, KS 66607
Tel: (913) 295-1111

Chairman: Stanley H Stauffer
President: John H Stauffer
Senior Executive Officers: William D Duckworth (VP/Treasurer), Gerald N Holley (VP Broadcasting), Kenneth C Bronson (VP Affiliated Dailies), E V Anderson (VP National Media)

PRINCIPAL ACTIVITIES: Publication of morning and evening newspapers and television and radio broadcasting

Principal Subsidiaries: Brainerd Dispatch Newspaper Company (Brainerd, MN); Capper's Insurance Service Inc (Topeka, KS); Communications & Signaling Inc (Topeka, KS); Grit Publishing Company (Williamsport, PA); Grit Printing Company (Williamsport, PA); Yankton Printing Company (Yankton, SD)
Principal Bank: The Merchants National Bank of Topeka
Financial Information:

	Dec 31 1985	Dec 31 1986
	$'000	$'000
Sales revenues	113,000	118,000
Income before taxes	12,000	33,000
Net income	6,000	20,000
Dividends	2,000	2,100
Dividends per share	$2.00	$2.10
Earnings per share	$6.70	$20.37
Common stock*	1,833	1,833
Retained income	41,665	59,939
Shareholders equity	43,499	61,773

*and Paid-in Capital

Principal Shareholders: Approx 427 shareholders
No of Employees: 2,250

STAYTON CANNING CO COOPERATIVE

930 W Washington Street, Stayton, OR 97383
Tel: (503) 769-2101

Chairman: Donald Nielson
President: Arthur Christianson (and General Manager)
Senior Executive Officers: Robert Winn (VP), David M Karr (Treasurer and Controller)

PRINCIPAL ACTIVITIES: Canning and freezing of fruit and vegetables
Principal Bank: United States National Bank of Oregon
Financial Information:

	$'000
Sales revenues	135,000

No of Employees: 600-4,000 (seasonal variations)

STC-DOCUMATION INC

150 Wickham Road, Melbourne, FL 32901
Tel: (305) 725-5520

President: R T H Higgins

PRINCIPAL ACTIVITIES: Manufacture of computer peripherals
Parent Company: Storage Technology Corporation, Louisville, CO
Financial Information:

	$'000
Sales revenues	90,000

No of Employees: 600

STEARNS & FOSTER BEDDING CO

1300 E 9th St, Cleveland, OH 44114
Tel: (216) 522 1310
Telex: TWX 810 4612618 s&f at lold

Chairman: Ernest M Wuliger
President: Ronald E Trzcinski (and Chief Executive Officer)
Senior Executive Officers: Perry E Doermann (Secretary), Thomas L Smudz (Treasurer)

PRINCIPAL ACTIVITIES: Manufacture of components for the manufacture of beds
Parent Company: Ohio Mattress Co
Financial Information:

	$'000
Sales revenues	100,000

No of Employees: 1,500

STEEGO CORPORATION

319 Clematis Street, Suite 900, West Palm Beach, FL 33402
Tel: (305) 655-9700
Faxsimile: (305) 659-0790

Chairman: J Russell Duncan (and President)
Senior Executive Officers: John H Schuler (Executive VP), William W Curtas (VP, Treasurer, Secretary and Controller), Robert A Lawton (Senior VP, Steego Corporation; President, Steego Parts Corporation), Arthur E Smith (VP, Steego Corporation), Gregory L Stone (Senior VP, Steego Corporation; President, McKerlie-Millen Inc)

PRINCIPAL ACTIVITIES: Distribution of automotive replacement parts and the manufacture and distribution of agri-equipment replacement parts; distribution of industrial tools and supplies; distribution of metal working machinery; manufacture and sale of transportation equipment; manufacture and sale of office products; engineering services; real estate activities; and financial services
Principal Subsidiaries: Steego Parts Corporation; McKerlie-Millen Inc; Elbe-Cesco Inc; Herschel Corporation; Homestead Corporation; King & Gavaris Consulting Engineers Inc; Nabors Trailers Inc; Steego Technical Corporation; Unisig Corporation; Steel & English Industrial Supplies Inc; Bayou Acceptance Corporation
Principal Bank: National Westminster Bank USA
Financial Information:

	Apr 30 1986	Apr 30 1987
	$'000	$'000
Sales revenues	207,592	215,560
Income before taxes	2,122	108
Net (loss)	(896)	(1,318)
Cash dividends	565	-
Stock dividends	3%	3%
Dividends per common share	$0.06	-
(Loss) per common share	($0.10)	($0.14)
Common stock	10,022	10,352
Retained income	12,977	10,420
Shareholders equity	44,274	43,708

No of Employees: 2,300

STEEL HEDDLE MANUFACTURING CO

1801 Rutherford Road, Box 1867, Greenville, SC 29602
Tel: (803) 244-4110
Telex: 570416

Chairman: James B Bowen
President: Albert J Kieny
Senior Executive Officers: Richard P Coen (Senior VP Administration), Frank J Scirica (VP Administration), Hugh I Cash (VP Sales), Gerhardt A Dobslaw (VP Engineering), Joseph K Leaphart (VP Industrial Relations and Secretary), Benjamin G Team (VP Reed Division), Edward A Rostick (VP Industrial Products Group), George R Smith (Treasurer)

PRINCIPAL ACTIVITIES: Manufacture of textile machinery and equipment; cast steel products; metal fabrication and electroplating
Principal Bank: South Carolina National Bank
Financial Information:

	$'000
Sales revenues	50,000

No of Employees: 1,000

STEEL TECHNOLOGIES INC

11605 Shelbyville Road, Louisville, KY 40243
Tel: (502) 245 2110

Chairman: Merwin J Ray (and Chief Executive Officer)
President: Daryl A Elser (and Chief Operating Officer)
Senior Executive Officers: Timothy M Graven (Executive VP, Chief Financial Officer, Secretary and Treasurer), Howard F Bates Jr (VP-Technical Services), Bradford T Ray (VP-Manufacturing), Michael J Carroll (VP-Sales)

PRINCIPAL ACTIVITIES: Production of hot and cold rolled steel and strip
Principal Subsidiaries: Mi-Tech Steel Inc
Principal Bank: Citizens Fidelity Bank

Financial Information:

	Sep 30 1986	Sep 30 1987
	$'000	$'000
Sales revenues	62,732	86,001
Income before taxes	7,682	9,105
Net income	3,927	4,880
Dividends	62,449	93,672
Dividends per share	$0.013	$0.020
Earnings per share	$0.84	$1.04
Common stock	3,122	3,122
Retained income	12,020	16,806
Shareholders equity	20,051	24,837

No of Employees: 200

STEELCASE INC

901 44th Street, Grand Rapids, MI 49508
Tel: (616) 247-2710
Telex: 226484 Steelcase GDR

Chairman: Robert C Pew; Vice Chairmen: David D Hunting Sr, Peter M Wege
President: Frank H Merlotti (and Chief Operating Officer)
Senior Executive Officers: David D Hunting Jr (Executive VP Subsidiaries), Alwyn Rougier-Chapman (Senior VP Finance), Jack Stegmier (Senior VP Operations), Paul Witting (Senior VP Marketing), Clifford O Boyce (VP Community Relations), Duane Bucklin (VP Administration Services), Howard Cooper (VP Marketing and Product Development), F James Delaney (VP and General Manager Western Division), David Donnelly (VP and General Sales Manager), Gerard Hekker (VP Manufacturing), William R Heyne (VP and Director Dealer Relations), Robert E Hubling (VP and Treasurer), Roger L Martin (VP Marketing, Administration and Distribution), James C Soule (VP Human Resources), James E Stievater (VP and Controller)

PRINCIPAL ACTIVITIES: Manufacture of furniture and office equipment
Principal Bank: Old Kent Bank and Trust Company
Financial Information:

	$'000
Sales revenues	1,300,000

No of Employees: 12,500

STEIGER TRACTOR INC

406 Main, Fargo, ND 58126
Tel: (701) 293-4400
Telex: WUT 292221 steiger qc fgo

Chairman: Eugene Dahl
President: Irvin E Aal (and Chief Executive Officer)
Senior Executive Officers: Dallas Lien (VP Engineering), Timothy P Lundberg (VP Finance, Secretary and Treasurer), Thomas St John (VP Marketing)

PRINCIPAL ACTIVITIES: Manufacture of tractors and agricultural equipment
Principal Bank: Northwestern National Bank
Financial Information:

	$'000
Sales revenues	80,300

No of Employees: 400

STEPAN COMPANY

Northfield, IL 60093
Tel: (312) 446-7500
Telex: 910-992-1437 STEPAN NFLD

Chairman: F Quinn Stepan (and President and Chief Executive Officer)
Senior Executive Officers: William W Meier (Senior VP-Finance and Administration), Edwin R Vath (Senior VP-Industrial Chemicals), James A Hartlage (VP-Technology), Edward A Knaggs (VP-Petroleum Products), Charles P Riley Jr (VP-Manufacturing and Engineering), Jeffrey W Bartlett (General Counsel and Corporate Secretary), Walter J Klein (Corporate Controller), Norma J Hedin (Assistant Corporate Secretary). Departmental Vice Presidents: Industrial Chemicals:- Gilbert B Eshoo (VP-Sales), Charles W Given (VP-Marketing), Norman R Smith (VP-Product Development), Edward D Tobey (VP-Naional Accounts). Manufacturing and Engineering:- M Mirghanbari (VP-Millsdale Operations), Henry Mork (VP-Plant Operations)

PRINCIPAL ACTIVITIES: Stepan Company, headquartered in Northfield, Illinois is a leading producer of basic and intermediate chemicals used in household, industrial, personal care, agricultural and energy-related products
Principal Subsidiaries: Stepan Europe SA (France)
Principal Bank: First National Bank of Chicago
Financial Information:

	$'000
Sales revenues	236,000

No of Employees: 890

STERCHI BROTHERS STORES INC

114-18 S Gay Street, Knoxville, TN 37901
Tel: (615) 523 4163

Chairman: C A Terrell
President: R H Beam (and Chief Executive Officer)
Senior Executive Officers: J P Childress (Senior VP, Secretary and Chief Financial Officer), S B Cash (VP), R H Dempster Jr (VP, Treasurer and Assistant Secretary)

PRINCIPAL ACTIVITIES: Furniture retail stores
Financial Information:

	$'000
Sales revenues	48,230

No of Employees: 765

STEREO VILLAGE INC

1833 Lawrenceville Highway, Decatur, GA 30033
Tel: (404) 325 0049

President: Larry Sarner
Senior Executive Officers: B J Dubler (Chief Executive Officer)

PRINCIPAL ACTIVITIES: Retail trade in television, radio and stereo equipment
Financial Information:

	$'000
Sales revenues	40,500

No of Employees: 230

STERLING BANCORP NEW YORK

540 Madison Avenue, New York, NY 10022
Tel: (212) 826 8000

Chairman: Theodore H Silbert (and Chief Executive Officer)
President: Ezra J Denerstein (and Chief Operating Officer)
Senior Executive Officers: Louis J Cappelli (Executive VP), Arthur F Silbert (Executive VP), Gerard P Griffin Jr (Senior VP and Legal Counsel), Fred J Howard (Senior VP), Sydney Meckler (VP and Assistant Secretary), Alexander O Saulon (VP Accounting), Joseph M Freeman (Treasurer and Chief Financial Officer), Jerrold Gilbert (Assistant Legal Counsel and Secretary)

PRINCIPAL ACTIVITIES: Holding company with interests in banking and financial services including loans and factoring
Principal Subsidiaries: Standard Financial Corporation; Security Industrial Loan Association; Standard Factors Corporation; Universal Finance Corporation; Sterling Banking Corporation; Sterling National Bank and Trust Company
Principal Bank: Sterling National Bank

No of Employees: 325

STERLING DRUG INC
90 Park Avenue, New York, NY 10016
Tel: (212) 907-2000
Telex: ITT 422850 chemgrp

Chairman: J M Pietruski Jr (and Chief Executive Officer)
President: J G Andress (and Chief Operating Officer)
Senior Executive Officers: James H Luther (Senior VP), Gary D Penisten (Senior VP Finance and Chief Financial Officer), Monroe E Trout (Senior VP Medical and Scientific Affairs), Arthur D Juceam (Group VP), John J McCarthy (Group VP), Herbert A McKenzie (Group VP), Bernard C Ouellette (Group VP), David W Wylie (Group VP), George S Benjamin (VP Financial Control), Earle K Borman (VP), Lawrence W Chaprin (VP Research), Willys D DeVoll (VP Employee Relations), Michael R Gallagher (VP), George S Goldstein (VP Medical Affairs), John R Gwilt (VP Commercial Development), Robert J Hennessey (VP Corporate Planning), J Gene Hinson (VP), A Douglas Lockwood (VP Tax Audits), Robin D Mills (VP), Frank J Petrocelli Jr (VP Real Estate and Treasurer), Andrew P Power (VP), Joseph Scarlata (VP), Pedro E Schwed (VP Manufacturing and Engineering)

PRINCIPAL ACTIVITIES: Manufacture of medicines, pharmaceutical products, household products and chemicals
Principal Bank: Chase Manhattan Bank
Financial Information:

	Dec 31 1985	Dec 31 1986
	$'000	$'000
Sales revenues	1,848,320	1,990,434
Net income	109,710	171,507
Earnings per share	$1.83	$2.91
Shareholders equity	936,450	973,548

No of Employees: 27,300

STERLING ELECTRONICS CORPORATION
4201 Southwest Freeway, Houston, TX 77027
Tel: (713) 623-6600
Telex: WUT 775299 steleco hou a

Chairman: Michael S Spolane (and Chief Executive Officer)
President: Leopold S Baer (and Chief Operating Officer)
Senior Executive Officers: Leon Webb Jr (VP and Chief Financial Officer), Byron Turner (VP and Area Manager), Tom McGinty (VP Materials Management), Jim McConkey (VP and Area Manager), Ronny Spolane (VP Marketing), David Spolane (VP Semi Marketing), Dave Goforth (VP Connector Marketing), Eugene Lax (VP Data Processing)

PRINCIPAL ACTIVITIES: Manufacture and distribution of electronic components including aircraft instruments and security equipment
Principal Subsidiaries: Airmark Plastics Corp; Kann Ellert Electronics Inc (89.6%); Meridian Electronics Inc (96.1%); Phaostron Instrument and Electronics Co Inc (91.7%); Sterling Computer Systems Inc (89.9%); Sterling Electronics and Instruments Co Inc
Principal Bank: Texas Commerce Bank
Financial Information:

	Mar 28 1987
	$'000
Sales revenues	51,480
Income before taxes	83
Net income	55
Earnings per share	$0.01
Common stock	3,707
Retained income	178
Shareholders equity	7,104

Principal Shareholders: M S Spolane; Woodland Investments
No of Employees: 441

STERLING SOFTWARE INC
8080 North Central Expressway, Suite 1140, Dallas, TX 75206
Tel: (214) 891 8600

Chairman: Sam Wyly; Vice Chairman: Charles J Wyly Jr
President: Sterling L Williams (and Chief Executive Officer)
Senior Executive Officers: Werner L Frank (Executive VP and Group President), A E Holland Jr (Executive VP and Treasurer), Edward J Lott (Executive VP and Group President), Phillip A Moore (Senior VP Business Development), Bill Newcomer (Senior VP Systems Software), W Mack Goforth (VP Finance)

PRINCIPAL ACTIVITIES: Data processing services and software
Principal Bank: Texas American Bank
Financial Information:

	$'000
Sales revenues	60,550

No of Employees: 2,940

STERNER LIGHTING SYSTEMS INC
Winsted, MN 55395
Tel: (612) 473 1251

Chairman: George F Nye
President: Frank M Feeney (and Chief Executive Officer)
Senior Executive Officers: Dale F Churchill (VP and Treasurer), Dale P Kunz (VP and Controller), Robert E Meyer (VP), Richard D Genty (Secretary)

PRINCIPAL ACTIVITIES: Industrial and commercial lighting equipment and related apparatus
Principal Subsidiaries: Electro-Static Finishing Inc; Sterner Power and Electrical Control Systems; Sternlite Transportation Company
Principal Bank: Irving Trust Company
Financial Information:

	$'000
Sales revenues	34,865

No of Employees: 410

STEVENS, J P, & CO, INC
1185 Avenue of the Americas, New York, NY 10036
Tel: (212) 930-2000
Telex: WUI 666878 jps

Chairman: Whitney Stevens (and Chief Executive Officer); Vice Chairman: David M Tracy
President: Ward Burns
Senior Executive Officers: Marvin B Crow (Executive Vice President and Managing Director Stevens Fabrics), Paul W Nipper Jr (Senior VP), Robert O Burger (VP), Thomas C Durst (VP), John W Wagner (VP and Treasurer), John J Zerrenner (VP and Controller)

PRINCIPAL ACTIVITIES: Manufacture of textiles
Trade Names: Utica, Tastemaker, Ralph Lauren, Gloria Vanderbilt, Laura Ashley, Gulistan
Principal Subsidiaries: Stevens Graphics Inc; Foote & Davies Inc; Ralph Lauren Home Furnishings Inc; Gloria Vanderbilt Creations Inc; Stevens Aviation Inc
Principal Banks: Bankers Trust Co; Chemical Bank
Financial Information:

	Oct 31 1985	Oct 31 1986
	$'000	$'000
Sales revenues	1,698,300	1,671,871
Net income (loss)	(15,500)	53,687
Earnings (loss) per share	($0.89)	$3.01
Shareholders equity	501,800	502,685

No of Employees: 27,200

STEWART & STEVENSON SERVICES, INC
2707 N Loop W, Box 1637, Houston, TX 77251
Tel: (713) 868-7700
Telex: TRT 166258 stewsteve jpi

Chairman: Jim Stewart II
President: Thomas H Langham III

Senior Executive Officers: Geneva Dye (VP and Secretary), Carsey Manning (VP), Robert Hargrave (VP and Treasurer), LaRoy Hammer (VP), Bob H Oneal (VP), T Michael Andrews (VP), Donald E Stevenson (VP), Richard R Stewart (VP), Keith T Stevenson (VP

PRINCIPAL ACTIVITIES: Manufacture of industrial engines and generator sets
Principal Bank: Texas Commerce Bank
Financial Information:

	Jan 31 1987 $'000
Sales revenues	248,993
Income before taxes	1,532
Common stock	21,521
Retained income	48,787
Shareholders equity	70,308

No of Employees: 2,000

STEWART INFORMATION SERVICES CORPORATION

2200 West Loop South, Houston, TX 77027
Tel: (713) 871 1100

Chairman: Carloss Morris (and Corporate Executive Officer)
President: Stewart Morris (and Corporate Executive Officer)
Senior Executive Officers: Malcolm Morris (VP Operations), Stewart Morris Jr (VP Operations), Max Crisp (VP Finance, Secretary and Treasurer)

PRINCIPAL ACTIVITIES: Title insurance
Principal Subsidiaries: Stewart Title Guaranty Company; Florida Land Title Company Inc; Security Abstract and Insurance Company; Security Abstract Wld County; Stewart Escrow and Title Services; Stewart Title; Data Concepts Inc; Citizens Title and Trust
Principal Bank: Texas Commerce Bank
Financial Information:

	$'000
Premium income	139,800

No of Employees: 2,260

STEWART SANDWICHES INC

5732 Curlew Drive, Norfolk, VA 23502
Tel: (804) 466 9200

Chairman: Theodore J Broecker (and President and Chief Executive Officer)
Senior Executive Officers: Donald Beard (VP and Chief Operating Officer), Philip R Sawyer Jr (Treasurer and Assistant Secretary), Robert Friend Boyd (Secretary)

PRINCIPAL ACTIVITIES: Sandwiches, coffee and beverages
Principal Bank: United Virginia Bank
Financial Information:

	$'000
Sales revenues	42,455

No of Employees: 650

STEWART-WARNER CORPORATION

1826 Diversey Pkwy, Chicago, IL 00614
Tel: (312) 883-6000
Telex: WUT 256268 stewart'c cgo

Chairman: Bennett Archambault (and President)
Senior Executive Officers: Donald A Potter (VP and Division General Manager), Harold B McMahon (VP and Division General Manager), T J McCook (VP and Division General Manager), Robert H Reid (VP and Division General Manager), J C Morrison (VP Treasurer and Controller), Wesley W Kiley (VP), Robin M Demouth (VP, Secretary and General Counsel)

PRINCIPAL ACTIVITIES: Electronic and electromechanical systems and products:- Electromechanical, electric and electronic instruments and auxiliary devices; military electronics equipment for shipborne, airborne and ground applications; electronic information display systems; photoelectric and numerical machine tool controls; and electromechanical devices, wiring and switching systems, and primary and secondary lighting for powered vehicles. Fabricated metal products and hardware:- Casters and related devices to provide mobility for industrial materials handling equipment, business machines, hospital and food service equipment, and in almost any application where ease of mobility is required. Casters, chair controls, hardware and decorative trim for office and home furniture. Vehicular service equipment and materials:- A broad range of lubricating and other service equipment for all types of automotive maintenance establishments and service station facilities, including wheel balancers and aligners, automotive test equipment and analyzers, spray and wash systems, lifts, fittings, and chemical additives. Pumps, controls, guns, couplings and hose, utilized in systems designed for the transfer and application of a wide variety of fluid materials in extensive industrial equipment installations. Specialty products and others:- Heat transfer products for aerospace applications, in heating or cooling liquid or gas streams on aircraft and space vehicles; for applications on mobile equipment, for use in controlling the temperatures of liquid or gaseous products in the power systems of heavy duty trucks, military and off-the-road vehicles, and in stationary engines; and for industrial applications (suspended in 1984), in the fields of hydrocarbon processing, oxygen and nitrogen production, ethylene purification, and natural gas liquefaction and separation. Combustion heating products, for personnel heating in many types of mobile equipment, both commercial and military, and for pre-heating heavy duty engines. Air- and hydraulically-powered tools for use by construction contractors, and in virtually every type of manufacturing and maintenance activity
Trade Names: Stewart-Warner instruments, Alemite, Bassick, South Wind, Stewart-Warner electronics, Hobbs, Bassick-Sack, Thor-
Principal Subsidiaries: Stewart-Warner Corp of Canada Ltd; Stewart-Warner Foreign Sales Corp (Virgin Islands); Stewart-Warner Display Systems Inc; Stewart-Warner Alemite GmbH (Germany); Thor Power Tool Co; Stewart-Warner Ltd (UK); Thor Power Tool GmbH (Germany); Thor-Fiap SpA (Italy); Herramientas Thor de Mexico SA de CV (Mexico); Ickneild Engineering Holding Ltd; Icknield Instruments Ltd (UK); Icknield Telecommunications Ltd (UK)
Principal Banks: Continental Bank (Chicago, IL); Harris Trust & Savings (Chicago, IL); Chase Manhattan (New York, NY)
Financial Information:

	$'000
Sales revenues	290,000

No of Employees: 5,100

STIFEL FINANCIAL CORPORATION

500 North Broadway, Saint Louis, MO 63102
Tel: (314) 342 2000

Chairman: George H Walker III (and President and Chief Executive Officer); Vice Chairman: William F White
Senior Executive Officers: J J Goebel (Secretary), James W Shafter (Treasurer and Chief Financial Officer)

PRINCIPAL ACTIVITIES: Financial services including dealing in securities and brokerage

No of Employees: 760

STIMSON LUMBER CO

Box 68, Forest Grove, OR 97116
Tel: (503) 357-2131

President: Darrell Schroeder
Senior Executive Officers: T Lilley (VP), Leo Graham (VP Petrochemical), Ronald Mundt (Secretary), John Dimeling (Sales Manager)

PRINCIPAL ACTIVITIES: Timber supplies and petrochemicals

Principal Bank: First Interstate Bank
Financial Information:

	$'000
Sales revenues	100,000

No of Employees: 270

STINNES CORPORATION

750 Third Avenue, New York, NY 10017
Tel: (212) 986-1515
Telex: RCA 234123 stin ur

Chairman: Guenther Winkelmann
President: Horst H Siedentopf
Senior Executive Officers: Dietrich Heitmueller (VP), Jochen Schwicking (VP), Heinrich Lange (VP and Treasurer)

PRINCIPAL ACTIVITIES: Trade in a wide range of products including metals, minerals, chemicals and energy prodcuts; manufacture of engineering equipment
Parent Company: Stinnes AG, Mülheim/Ruhr, Germany
Financial Information:

	$'000
Sales revenues	1,000,000

No of Employees: 1,000

STOCK EQUIPMENT CO

16490 Chillicothe Road, Chagrin Falls, OH 44022
Tel: (216) 543-6000
Telex: WUT 980 611 stockeqpt chag

President: Joseph K Tannehill (and Chief Executive Officer)
Senior Executive Officers: Arthur L Bennett (VP International Sales), Peter B Cadou (VP Engineering), Ronald A McIntyre (VP Finance), Paul C Williams (VP Nuclear and Energy Systems Sales)

PRINCIPAL ACTIVITIES: Manufacture of electricity generating equipment
Parent Company: General Signal Corp
Financial Information:

	$'000
Sales revenues	50,000

No of Employees: 530

STOKELY USA INC

626 East Wisconsin Avenue, Oconomowoc, WI 53066
Tel: (414) 567 1731

Chairman: Joseph B Weix (and Chief Executive Officer)
President: Thomas W Mount (and Chief Operating Officer)
Senior Executive Officers: Vernon L Wiersma (Executive VP), Eddie W Foster (VP Marketing), J Kohlhoff (VP Quality Management), Robert Lenz (VP Technical Services), R McMillen (VP Manufacturing), Patrick Muller (VP Distribution), Arthur Sandsmark (VP Sales), Steven Theobald (VP Investor Relations), R J Whelan (VP Industrial Relations)

PRINCIPAL ACTIVITIES: Production of canned vegetables and fruit
Principal Bank: First Bank NA
Financial Information:

	$'000
Sales revenues	140,000

No of Employees: 480

STOLPER INDUSTRIES, INC

W 156 N, 9073 Stolper Drive, Menomonee Falls, WI 53051
Tel: (414) 251-5000
Telex: WUT 26654 stolper mefs

Chairman: L A Gerlach
Senior Executive Officers: C L Harbeck (Executive VP and Secretary), John Love (VP Finance), W L Ludtke (President Stolper Division), P C Erdmann (President Fabralloy Division)

PRINCIPAL ACTIVITIES: Manufacture of steel and aluminum products including vehicle cabs and containers
Financial Information:

	$'000
Sales revenues	50,000

No of Employees: 800

STONE & WEBSTER INC

One Penn Plaza, 250 West 34th Street, New York, NY 10119
Tel: (212) 290-7500

Chairman: Raymond C Foster
President: William F Allen Jr (and Chief Executive Officer)
Senior Executive Officers: William M Egan (Executive VP), R V Whisnand (Executive VP), John A Carter Jr (VP)

PRINCIPAL ACTIVITIES: Provision of management, engineering, pharmaceutical and general industrial consultancy services
Principal Subsidiaries: Commercial Cold Storage Inc; Sabal Corp; Stone & Webster Engineering Corp; Stone & Webster Management Consultants Inc; Stone & Webster Oil Co Inc
Principal Bank: Chase Manhattan Bank
Financial Information:

	$'000
Sales revenues	270,000

No of Employees: 15,000

STONE CONTAINER CORPORATION

360 N Michigan Avenue, Chicago, IL 60601
Tel: (312) 346-6600
Telex: TWX 910 2212673 sccc bm cgo

Chairman: Roger W Stone (and Chief Executive Officer)
President: James E Frew (and Chief Operating Officer)
Senior Executive Officers: Arnold F Brookstone (Senior VP and Chief Financial/Planning Officer), George B Hills Jr (Senior VP and General Manager Paperboard Division), Morty Rosenkranz (Senior VP and General Manager Corrugated Container Division), James Doughan (Senior VP and General Manager Bag and Kraft Paper Marketing Division), Alan Stone (Senior VP Administration and General Manager Energy Division), Thomas P Cutilletta (VP and Controller), Gerald M Freeman (VP, General Manager Forest Products Division), Richard J Raskin (VP Planning and Legal Services), Covington Shackleford (VP Industrial Relations), Ira N Stone (VP, Secretary, Public Affairs), Michael B Wheeler (VP and Treasurer)

PRINCIPAL ACTIVITIES: Manufacture of packaging products
Principal Bank: First National Bank of Chicago
Financial Information:

	Dec 31 1985	Dec 31 1986
	$'000	$'000
Sales revenues	1,299,150	2,032,325
Net income	3,780	35,415
Dividends per share	$0.24	$1.95
Shareholders equity	294,730	481,804

No of Employees: 9,380

STOP & SHOP COMPANIES, INC (THE)

PO Box 369, Boston, MA 02101
Tel: (617) 770-8000
Telefax: (617) 770-8303

Chairman: Avram J Goldberg (and Chief Executive Officer)
President: Carol R Goldberg (and Chief Operating Officer)
Senior Executive Officers: Donald J Comeau (Senior VP), Harold Frank (Senior VP, Chairman and Chief Executive Officer of the Bradlees Discount Department Store Company), Jack Kushinsky (Senior VP), Samuel W W Mandell (Senior VP, General Counsel, Clerk and Secretary), Joseph D McGlinchey (Senior VP, Treasurer and Chief Financial Officer), Lewis G Schaeneman Jr (Senior VP, President and Chief Executive Officer, Stop & Shop Supermarket Company), Rufus E Lester Jr (Group VP for Public Policy and Technical Affairs), Harold

E Fine (VP, Construction and Engineering), Aileen Gorman (VP, Public Affairs), Robert Manson (VP, Information Systems), James V Morgan (VP, Labor Relations), Charles A Richards III (VP, Corporate Properties), Arthur S Robbins (VP, Financial Services and Assistant Treasurer), Glenn E Davis (Corporate Controller), Paul H Freischlag Jr (VP & Assistant Treasurer)

PRINCIPAL ACTIVITIES: Diversified retailer operating department stores, drug stores, supermarkets and tobacco shops. Also operates manufacturing facilities including a bakery, carbonated beverage plant, commissary, dairy, seafood processing plant, household chemical plant, photo finishing plant and recycling center

Principal Operating Companies or Divisions: Bradlees Department Store Company; Stop & Shop Supermarket Company

Principal Bank: The First National Bank of Boston

Financial Information:

	Feb 1 1986	Jan 31 1987
	$'000	$'000
Sales revenues	3,429,508	3,872,419
Income before taxes(1)	56,776	88,125
Net income	30,300	38,400
Dividends	14,817	15,247
Dividends per share	$1.08	$1.10
Earnings per share(2)	$2.20	$2.77
Earnings per share(3)	$2.20	$2.77
Common stock(4)	13,810	13,898
Retained income	263,716	286,869
Shareholders equity	405,670	431,028

(1) continuing operations
(2) primary
(3) fully diluted
(4) stores outstanding

No of Employees: 44,000

STORAGE TECHNOLOGY CORPORATION

StorageTek

2270 South 88th Street, Louisville, CO 80028-4310
Tel: (303) 673-5151
Telex: WUT 530226 storagetechcor

Chairman: R Poppa (and Chief Executive Officer)
President: S Jerritts (and Chief Operating Officer)
Senior Executive Officers: H Ravine (Chief Administrative Officer/General Counsel), W Mansfield (Finance/Chief Financial Officer), R Costain (Strategic Planning), R Benson (VP Corporate Quality), T Gooch (VP Corporate Manufacturing), A Higgins (VP General Manager/Printer Operations), F Gunn (VP Corporate OEM Operations), S Sleek (Corporate VP Systems Development), R Douglas (Corporate VP Marketing and Services), W Young (Corporate VP Human Resources), W Malmquist (Director Internal Audit), W Miller (Director Consulting Services), H Pforzheimer (Director Corporate Communications), K Smith (Director Corporate Services), G Tymn (Corporate VP/Corporate Controller), C Vertuca (Corporate VP/Corporate Treasurer), S Smith (Director International Finance), D Lacey (Director Tax), L Leir (VP Corporate Field Engineering), W Treadwell (VP Corporate Americas/Pacific), D Thompson (VP Europe/Africa), J Jeter (VP Corporate US Sales), C Raine (VP Corporate Worldwide Marketing)

PRINCIPAL ACTIVITIES: Storage Technology Corporation designs, develops, manufactures, markets and services information storage and retrieval subsystems for high-performance computers. StorageTek's principal products are high-performance tape and disk subsystems and impact and non-impact printer subsystems

Principal Subsidiaries: (100% owned unless stated): Storage Technology E.D.V. Service GmbH (Germany); Nippon STC Kabushiki Kaisha (Japan); Storage Technology Middle East Inc (Saudi Arabia); Media Technology Division; Dispositivos Magneticos SA (19%) (Mexico)

Principal Bank: Citibank

Financial Information:

	Dec 27 1985	Dec 26 1986
	$'000	$'000
Sales revenues	673,419	696,009
Income (loss) before taxes	(38,591)	34,592
Net income (loss)	(57,437)	36,180
Earnings (loss) per share net	($1.66)	$1.03
Common stock*	34,689	34,760
Retained (deficit)	(318,413)	(282,233)
Shareholders (deficit)	(54,421)	(18,060)

*shares outstanding in thousands

No of Employees: 8,540

STORER COMMUNICATIONS, INC

12000 Biscayne Blvd, Miami, FL 33181
Tel: (305) 899-1000

Chairman: Terry Lee (and President and Chief Executive Officer)
Senior Executive Officers: Kenneth Bagwell (Executive VP), Joseph C Dimino (President TV Stations Division), Daniel Berkery (VP, TV Operations), A A Church (VP, General Counsel and Secretary), Kenneth L Danielson (VP and Assistant Treasurer), William J Flynn (VP, TV Operations), Bill Fox (VP, TV Operations),James A Long (VP Personnel), Kenneth R Mosher (VP, Treasurer and Chief Financial Officer), Andrew P Potos (VP, TV Operations), H W Ray (VP, TV Operations), Paul Raymon (VP, TV Operations), Loraine H Strait (VP Law), C David Whitaker (VP, TV Operations), Warren C Zwicky (VP and Washington Counsel)

PRINCIPAL ACTIVITIES: Television communications services; cable television

Parent Company: SCI Holdings Inc

Principal Bank: Continental Illinois National Bank & Trust Co

Financial Information:

	$'000
Sales revenues	592,420

No of Employees: 4,800

STOUFFER CORPORATION

29800 Bainbridge Road, Solon, OH 44139
Tel: (216) 248-3600

Chairman: James M Biggar (and President)
Senior Executive Officers: William N Hulett (Executive VP Hotels), Anthony J Martino (Executive VP Finance and Treasurer), John Quagiata (Executive VP Prepared Foods and Stouffer Restaurants), Thomas G Stauffer (Executive VP Hotel Development), Ronald Baker (VP Management Information Systems), James H Ball (VP, Secretary and General Counsel), Martin H Elrad (VP Vending Services), Donald C Flagg (VP Personnel), Edwin T Frantz (VP Long Range Planning), Robert L McGuigan (VP Marketing and Sales Frozen Prepared Foods), David Mikolajczyk (VP Purchasing, Corporate Hotels and Restaurants), Fred Tippett (VP and General Manager Borel Restaurants)

PRINCIPAL ACTIVITIES: Management of hotels and restaurants; preparation of frozen foods; operation of vending services

Parent Company: Nestle Enterprises Inc-Ultimate Holding Company-Nestlé SA, Vevey, Switzerland

Financial Information:

	$'000
Sales revenues	400,000

No of Employees: 13,000

STRATUS COMPUTER INC

55 Fairbanks Boulevard, Marlborough, MA 01752
Tel: (617) 460 2000

President: William E Foster (and Chief Executive Officer)

Senior Executive Officers: John H Curtis (Executive VP and Chief Operating Officer), James E D Austin (Senior VP Manufacturing), Robert A Freiburghouse (Senior VP Engineering), J P Morgridge (Senior VP), Nicholas J Bologna (VP), Gary E Harolan (VP Finance and Administration, Chief Financial Officer and Treasurer), G C Hendrie (VP), R James Schroeder (VP)

PRINCIPAL ACTIVITIES: Manufacture of data processing equipment

Financial Information:

	$'000
Sales revenues	125,000

No of Employees: 780

STRAWBRIDGE & CLOTHIER

801 Market Street, Philadelphia, PA 19107

Tel: (215) 629 6779

Chairman: Francis R Strawbridge III

President: Peter S Strawbridge

Senior Executive Officers: G Stockton Strawbridge (Chairman of Executive Committee), James M Gassaway II (Executive VP Planning, Development and Research), Richard H Hall (Executive VP), Warren W White (Executive VP), Louis F Busico (VP General Merchandise Clover Stores), George L Compton (VP General Merchandise), Finley H Haiman (VP General Merchandise), Robert A Hoffner (VP Clover Stores), Alice T Kanigowski (VP General Merchandise Clover Stores), John J Leahy (VP), Robert G Muskas (VP Stores), Thomas S Rittenhouse (VP and Controller), William A Rittmayer (VP, Control and Operations Clover Stores), G Leonard Shea (VP Personnel Clover Stores), David W Strawbridge (VP Personnel), Steven L Strawbridge (VP, Treasurer and Secretary), William A Timmons (VP Publicity), Natalie B Weintraub (VP General Merchandise),

PRINCIPAL ACTIVITIES: Department stores trading

Principal Bank: Philadelphia National Bank

Financial Information:

	$'000
Sales revenues	686,900

No of Employees: 12,000

STRIDE RITE CORPORATION

5 Cambridge Center, Cambridge, MA 02142

Tel: (617) 491-8800

Telex: TWX 710 3207695 striderite cam

Chairman: Arnold S Hiatt (and Chief Executive Officer)

President: Michael Rayden

Senior Executive Officers: Irwin Miller (Executive VP), John Phelan (Executive VP and Treasurer), John Gravina (VP Purchasing), Marcia C Morris (VP, General Counsel)

PRINCIPAL ACTIVITIES: The Stride Rite Corporation is the leading marketer of high quality children's footwear in the United States. The Company is also a major marketer of athletic and casual footwear for children and adults and of adult work boots and outdoor recreational shoes. The Company manufactures products in its own facilities in the United States and Puerto Rico and imports products from abroad

Trade Names: Stride Rite, Keds, Sperry Top-Sider, Herman Suvivor

Principal Subsidiaries: Joseph M Herman Shoe Co Inc; Stride Rite Retail Corp; Stride Rite Footwear Inc; The Keds Corporation; Sperry Top-Sider Inc; Stride Rite International Ltd

Principal Bank: First National Bank of Boston

Financial Information:

	Nov 29 1985 $'000	Nov 28 1986 $'000
Sales revenues	277,310	283,457
Income before taxes*	17,552	27,630
Net income	11,178	17,014
Dividends	6,005	6,024
Dividends per share	$0.80	$0.80
Earnings per share net	$1.49	$2.25
Common stock	7,603	7,603
Retained income	74,276	85,266
Shareholders equity	111,526	122,729

*and extraordinary gain

No of Employees: 5,500

STROH BREWERY COMPANY

100 River Place, Detroit, MI 48207

Tel: (313) 446-2000

Telex: TWX 810 2211 212 strohpur det

Chairman: Peter W Stroh; Vice Chairman: Harold A Ruemenapp

President: Roger Fridholm

Senior Executive Officers: Arthur J Tonna (Executive VP Operations), Ralph A Caponigro (Senior VP Finance and Treasurer), Richard J Lodato (Senior VP Administration), John H Bissell (Senior VP Special Products), Kenneth A Tippery (Group VP Sales Operations and Market Development), William V Weatherston (VP Corporate Affairs)

PRINCIPAL ACTIVITIES: Brewing of beer; manufacture of ice cream

Principal Bank: Morgan Guaranty Trust Company of New York

Financial Information:

	$'000
Sales revenues	1,650,000

No of Employees: 5,500

STRUTHERS WELLS CORPORATION

PO Box 8, Warren, PA 16365

Tel: (814) 726-1000

Telex: WUT 914455 str wells wren

Chairman: Jerry Finkelstein

President: John C Wallace (and Chief Executive Officer)

Senior Executive Officers: Forest C Monkman (Executive VP), John M Carey (VP and Treasurer), Dale F Eyster (VP), Burton M Abrams (Secretary

PRINCIPAL ACTIVITIES: Heat exchangers, waste heat boilers, steam generators, process equipment

Principal Subsidiaries: Struthers Scientific and International Corp (80.1%)

Principal Bank: Chemical Bank

Financial Information:

	Nov 30 1985 $'000	Nov 30 1986 $'000
Sales revenues	49,420	13,134
Income (loss) before taxes	292	(2,480)
Net income (loss)	296	(17,107)
Earnings (loss) per share	$0.07	($5.72)
Common stock	3,085	3,085
Shareholders equity (deficit)	3,848	(12,189)

No of Employees: 285

STRYKER CORPORATION

420 Alcott, Kalamazoo, MI 49001

Tel: (616) 381-3811

Telex: WUT 224464 stryker kmz

Chairman: John W Brown (and President and Chief Executive Officer)

Senior Executive Officers: P H Chang (Executive VP/Surgical Division), R A Elenbaas (President/Surgical Division), W T Laube (President, Stryker Pacific), R D Monk (Treasurer), E G Phillips (President/Physical Therapy Incorporated), J W

Richmond (Senior VP/Global Marketing and Development), D J Simpson (VP Chief Financial Officer and Secretary), H H Woodworth (VP/Regulatory Affairs), T R Winkel (VP/Administration)

PRINCIPAL ACTIVITIES: Manufacture of medical equipment and surgical instruments
Principal Subsidiaries: Osteonics Corp; Physical Therapy Incorporated; Stryker Europe BV; Stryker Pacific Limited; StrykerVision Corporation
Principal Bank: Manufacturers Hanover Trust Company
Financial Information:

	Dec 31 1985(1)	Dec 31 1986(1)
	$'000	$'000
Sales revenues	108,377	129,183
Income before taxes	15,337	18,715
Net income	8,567	10,213
Earnings per share	$0.56	$0.66
Common stock(2)	15,382	15,470
Retained income	44,503	54,703
Shareholders equity	73,448	89,323

(1) restated for acquisition of Adel Medical Limited
(2) average shares outstanding in thousands

No of Employees: 1,008

STUART HALL COMPANY INC

2121 Central, Kansas City, MO 64108
Tel: (816) 221 8480

Chairman: Charles G Hanson (and Chief Executive Officer)
President: James E Freeman Jr (and Chief Operating Officer)
Senior Executive Officers: Patrick H Clifford (Executive VP), Robert G Bowen (VP), R Douglas Pomeroy (VP), Daniel S Rebeck (VP and Treasurer), James R Schmidt (VP and Secretary)

PRINCIPAL ACTIVITIES: Manufacture of a wide range of writing paper and related products
Principal Bank: Mellon Financial Services Corporation
Financial Information:

	$'000
Sales revenues	43,180

No of Employees: 250

STUARTS DEPARTMENT STORES INC

101 Hampton Ave, Needham Heights, MA 02194
Tel: (617) 444 9000

Chairman: Marc C Ostrow
Senior Executive Officers: Anthony J Cincotta (VP Merchandising), Gerald Davis (VP Real Estate and Construction), Joseph B Garb (VP Finance, Chief Financial Officer and Secretary), James H Lee (VP Administration and Treasurer)

PRINCIPAL ACTIVITIES: Holding company with interests in retail stores
Principal Subsidiaries: Newlee Corporation; Lee Shops Inc
Principal Bank: State Street Bank & Trust Co
Financial Information:

	$'000
Sales revenues	96,000

No of Employees: 700

STUDENT LOAN MARKETING ASSOCIATION

1050 Thomas Jefferson Street NW, Washington, DC 20007
Tel: (202) 333-8000

Chairman: Edward A McCabe
President: Edward A Fox (and Chief Executive Officer)
Senior Executive Officers: Ronald F Hunt (Executive VP), Oliver R Sockwell (Executive VP), Lawrence A Hough (Executive VP), Albert L Lord (Executive VP and Chief Financial Officer), Dennis A Kernahan (Senior VP), Michael A Wyatt (Senior VP), Gerald Cohen (Senior VP), Lydia M Gladney (Senior VP), Suzanne J Peck (Senior VP), Mitchell A Johnson (Senior VP)

PRINCIPAL ACTIVITIES: Financial services
Principal Bank: Irving Trust Company
Financial Information:

	Dec 31 1985	Dec 31 1986
	$'000	$'000
Revenues	1,283,130	1,376,785
Income before taxes	201,797	222,258
Net income	123,329	144,559
Common dividends	7,424	10,679
Preferred dividends	16,938	12,639
Dividends per common share	$0.18	$0.27
Earnings per share	$2.45	$3.08
Common stock(1)	10,150	7,250
Common stock(2)	10,473	13,390
Common stock(3)	-	161,172
Retained income	299,754	420,995
Shareholders equity	675,625	654,805

(1) voting-par
(2) non voting-par
(3) treasury-cost

No of Employees: 820

STUPP BROS BRIDGE & IRON CO

PO Box 6600, Lemay Sta, St Louis, MO 63125
Tel: (314) 638-5000
Telex: TWX 910 350 6493 stupp bros

President: John P Stupp (and Chief Executive Officer)
Senior Executive Officers: Robert P Stupp (Executive VP Sales), Erwin P Stupp Jr (Executive VP Operations), Thomas L Turner (Treasurer), John P Stupp Jr (Secretary)

PRINCIPAL ACTIVITIES: Fabrication of structural steel
Principal Subsidiaries: Stupp Corporation
Principal Bank: Centerre Bank
Financial Information:

	$'000
Sales revenues	50,000

No of Employees: 400

STUPP CORPORATION

PO Box 3558, Baton Rouge, LA 70821
Tel: (504) 775-8800
Telex: WUT 586422 stupp corp btr

Chairman: John P Stupp
President: Ralph V Schmidt
Senior Executive Officers: William H Bassett (Executive VP), Erwin P Stupp Jr (Senior VP), Robert P Stupp (Senior VP), N J LeBlanc (VP Plant), Howard E Midkiff (VP Sales), Howard LaBauve Jr (Treasurer and Comptroller)

PRINCIPAL ACTIVITIES: Manufacture of steel pipe for the energy industries
Parent Company: Stupp Bros Bridge & Iron Co, St Louis, MO
Principal Bank: Centerre Bank
Financial Information:

	$'000
Sales revenues	100,000

No of Employees: 350

STURM-RUGER & COMPANY, INC

Lacey Place, Southport, CT 06490
Tel: (203) 259-7843
Telex: TWX 710 459 3029 ruger ex sprt

President: William B Ruger (and Treasurer)
Senior Executive Officers: John M Kingsley Jr (Executive VP), William B Ruger Jr (Senior VP), Stanley B Terhune (VP), James T Ruger (VP), Gloria M Biagioni (Secretary), Robert J Cataldo (Assistant Controller)

PRINCIPAL ACTIVITIES: Sturm, Ruger & Company Inc is engaged principally in the design, manufacture, and sale of pistols, revolvers, rifles and shotguns for a variety of sporting purposes. The Company also produces and markets various models of police revolvers, automatic pistols, rifles, and selective firearms for law enforcement agencies and military establishments

Trade Names: Ruger M-77(R), Ruger 77/22(R), Ruger 10/22(R), Ruger XGI(R), Ruger Mini-14(R), Ruger P-85 (TM)

Financial Information:

	Dec 31 1985	Dec 31 1986
	$'000	$'000
Sales revenues	93,953	87,041
Income before taxes	19,103	12,442
Net income	9,555	6,026
Dividends	10,734	6,633
Dividends per share	$3.25	$2.00
Earnings per share	$2.89	$1.80
Common stock	3,303	3,321
Retained income	70,194	69,587
Shareholders equity	73,497	73,603

No of Employees: 1,147

STV ENGINEERS INC

11 Robinson Street, Pottstown, PA 19464
Tel: (215) 326 4600

Chairman: Richard L Holland (and Chief Executive Officer)
President: Alan F Richter (and Chief Operating Officer)
Senior Executive Officers: Charles E Defendorf (Executive VP), Edward E Gilvey (Executive VP Marketing and Director Business Development), Michael Haratunian (Executive VP Engineering), Frank E Lyon Jr (Executive VP), Maurice L Meier (Executive VP), W C Rex (VP), W A Sanders II (VP), Clyde F Umstead (Secretary and Treasurer)

PRINCIPAL ACTIVITIES: Consultancy services for the architectural, engineering and planning industries

Principal Subsidiaries: Lyon Associates Inc; Saunders & Thomas Inc

Principal Bank: First PA Bank

Financial Information:

	$'000
Sales revenues	64,220

No of Employees: 1,190

SUAVE SHOE CORPORATION

14100 NW 60 Avenue, Miami Lakes, FL 33014
Tel: (305) 822-7880
Telex: 441821 SUAVE UI

Chairman: David Egozi (and President and Chief Executive Officer)
Senior Executive Officers: Solomon Garazi (Senior VP, Shoe Import Division), Eugene D Ramos (Senior VP and General Manager, Shoe Manufacturing Divison), Pedro Mirones (Secretary, Assistant General Manager, and Treasurer Shoe Manufacturing Division), Luis Egozi (VP-Marketing, Shoe Manufacturing Division), Carlos Alvarado (VP-Management Information Systems, Shoe Manufacturing Division), Saul Ginzburg (VP-Merchandising and Sales Shoe Import Division), Luis Arrizurieta (VP Finance and Administration, Shoe Import Division), Francisco Llaca (VP-Marketing, Shoe Import Division), Sergio Echeverria (VP-Finance and Controller, Shoe Manufacturing Division), Jose Marroquin (Assistant Secretary)

PRINCIPAL ACTIVITIES: Manufacturer of unbranded and private label athletic and leisure shoes; importer of fashion, work and leisure footwear

Principal Subsidiaries: Oriental Trading Corporation

Principal Bank: SouthEast Bank NA

Financial Information:

	Sep 30 1986	Sep 30 1987
	$'000	$'000
Sales revenues	75,351	71,436
Income before taxes	4,863	3,734
Net income	2,623	1,989
Earnings per share	$0.99	$0.71
Common stock	36	28
Retained income	26,113	23,079
Shareholders equity	26,240	29,105

No of Employees: 800

SUBARU®

SUBARU OF AMERICA, INC

Subaru Plaza, PO Box 6000, Cherry Hill, NJ 08034
Tel: (609) 488-8500
Telex: WUT 834582 mabosan pesn a

Chairman: Harvey H Lamm (and Chief Executive Officer)
President: Thomas R Gibson (and Chief Operating Officer)
Senior Executive Officers: Marvin S Riesenbach (Executive VP and Chief Financial Officer), Katsuya Utada (VP-Corporate Liaison), Herman Berg (Group VP-Information and Administrative Services), J Paul Bubernak (Group VP-Parts and Service), Charles D Mahin (Group VP-Sales and Marketing), George T Muller (Group VP-Finance), Robert J Whitehead (Group VP-Product Engineering), Gilbert N Zitin (Group VP-Dealer Financial Services)

PRINCIPAL ACTIVITIES: Subaru of America, organized in 1968, distributes Subaru four-wheel drive and front-wheel drive passenger cars and replacement parts and accessories through fifteen distributors who sell those Subaru products to a nationwide dealer network

Trade Names: SBRU

Principal Subsidiaries: Subaru Atlantic, Inc; Southeast Subaru, Inc; Southwest Subaru, Inc; Subaru of Northern California, Inc; Subaru of Southern California, Inc; Subaru Mid-America; Subaru North West; Subaru Inter-Mountain; Subaru Great Lakes Inc

Principal Bank: Irving Trust Company

Financial Information:

	Oct 31 1986	Oct 31 1987
	$'000	$'000
Sales revenues	1,939,286	1,785,038
Income (loss) before taxes	159,342	(56,946)
Net income (loss)	93,960	(29,972)
Earnings (loss) per share	$1.92	($0.62)

Principal Shareholders: Fuji Heavy Industries, Ltd
No of Employees: 889

SUBURBAN PROPANE GAS CORPORATION

334 Madison Avenue, Morristown, NJ 07960
Tel: (201) 540-0300

Chairman: Mark J Anton (and President)
Senior Executive Officers: Salvadore G Pastore (Executive VP), Donald R Long (Senior VP Operations), William J Owen Jr (Senior VP Finance and Administration), Jack S Boyd (VP Area 6), Francis L Brophy (VP), William H Butcher (VP Supply and Wholesale Market), Neil M Carey (VP Marketing and Materials Supply Services), Dexter A Elsmore (VP Area 2), John R Kukucka (VP Safety, Engineering and Regulatory Services), Daryl F McClendon (VP Area 4), Albert M Miller (VP Area 5), Carl C Richardson (VP Area 1), John W Sweeney (VP Area 3), Thomas B Wheeler (VP Area 7)

PRINCIPAL ACTIVITIES: Refining and marketing of petroleum and propane gas; exploration and production of oil and

natural gas; gasoline stations; manufacture of air conditioning and heating products
Parent Company: National Distillers and Chemical Corp, New York, NY
Principal Bank: Manufacturers Hanover Trust Company
Financial Information:

	$'000
Sales revenues	575,000

No of Employees: 4,300

SUDBURY, INC
3733 Park East Drive, Suite 100, Cleveland, OH 44122
Tel: (216) 464-7026

Chairman: Tinkham Veale II
President: Charles W Walton (and Chief Executive Officer)
Senior Executive Officers: Jon E Denney (Executive VP/Chief Financial Officer), Floyd L Bishop (Executive VP/Chief Operating Officer)

PRINCIPAL ACTIVITIES: Diversified manufacturer of industrial products: automotive components; steel tubing; lubricants and greases; solid waste disposal and material handling equipment; machining
Trade Names: Accurate, Galbreath, Bobko, IMT, Lubriko
Principal Subsidiaries: Operating Units: Accurate Industries; Accurate Industries of Louisiana; Alpha Tube; American Metal Products; Bobko Industries; Cast-Matic; E-W Mold & Tool; R J Frisby Mfg; Galbreath; General Products; General Products-Angola; Graphite Products; Bert R Huncilman & Son; Industrial Powder Coatings; Iowa Mold Tooling; IMT Cranes Canada; Maro; Metalcote Grease & Oil; Midwest Rubber; James Miller Machine; Steel Products; Platt Manufacturing; RD&D; Reef-Baker; Schrader Machine & Tool; Shane Steel Processing; South Coast Terminals; Trans Plastics; United Industries; Wagner Castings
Principal Bank: Bank One, Columbus, Ohio
Financial Information:

	May 31 1986	May 30 1987
	$'000	$'000
Sales revenues	205,878	343,910
Income before taxes	12,054	21,650
Net income	10,028	11,258
Earnings per share net	$1.03	$0.79
Common stock	86	114
Retained income (deficit)	(5,508)	5,373
Shareholders equity	37,111	60,005

No of Employees: 5,000

SUGAR CANE GROWERS COOPERATIVE OF FLORIDA
PO Box 666, Belle Glade, FL 33430
Tel: (305) 996-5556
Telex: TWX 510 9517392 scgcoop bdge

President: George H Wedgworth
Senior Executive Officers: Enrique R Arais (Executive VP), Robert D Apelgren (VP), Harry Atwood (VP Marketing), Billy Rogers (VP), Walter J Krauz (Secretary and Treasurer)

PRINCIPAL ACTIVITIES: Sugar and molasses
Principal Bank: Bank of Belle Glade
Financial Information:

	$'000
Sales revenues	65,000

No of Employees: 500-2,500 (seasonal variations)

SUGARDALE FOODS INC
1600 Harmont Avenue, Canton, OH 44705
Tel: (216) 832-7491
Telex: TWX 910 3508614 sugardale food

Chairman: Neil Genshaft
President: Harry Valentino
Senior Executive Officers: Sam Applebaum (VP Sales), Richard Ashcroft (Controller)

PRINCIPAL ACTIVITIES: Meat packing
Parent Company: Superiors Brand Meats Inc, Massillon, OH
Principal Bank: Central National Bank of Cleveland
Financial Information:

	$'000
Sales revenues	215,000

No of Employees: 900

SULLAIR CORPORATION
3700 E Michigan Blvd, Michigan City, IN 46360
Tel: (219) 879-5451
Telex: WUT 258318 sullair mci a

President: Robert T Bloomberg (and Chief Executive Officer)
Senior Executive Officers: Jackson Sloan (Executive VP Sales and Marketing), Raymond P Klingler (VP Engineering), Lester W Lincke (VP and Controller)

PRINCIPAL ACTIVITIES: Manufcture of compressors, pumps and generating sets; manufacture of drills
Parent Company: Sundstrand Corporation
Principal Bank: Citibank
Financial Information:

	$'000
Sales revenues	120,000

No of Employees: 1,000

SUMITOMO BANK OF CALIFORNIA
320 California St, San Francisco, CA 94104
Tel: (415) 445-8000

Chairman: Chusuke Takahashi
President: Teruhisa Shimizu (and Chief Executive Officer)
Senior Executive Officers: Joichi Saito (Executive VP), Jack S Kusaba (Senior VP and Secretary), M Miyakoda (Senior VP and Manager Personnel), Shigeo Nagata (Senior VP and Manager Branch Business Department), Yashuhiko Okiyama (Senior VP and Manager Operations Administration and Computer Centre), Frank K Omatsu (Senior VP and Assistant to President), Katsuumi Shiba (Senior VP and Assistant to President), T Arishima (VP and Manager Loan Administration), Yasuaki Ikeda (VP and Manager Northern California Credit Administration), Robert C Johnsen (VP and Chief Auditor), Y Kitagawa (VP and Manager Marketing), Robert R McElroy (VP and Assistant to President), Kenichiro Miura (VP and Manager Southern California Credit Administration), T Sugie (VP, Treasurer, Cashier and Manager Administration and Properties)

PRINCIPAL ACTIVITIES: Banking
Financial Information:

	Dec 31 1985
	$'000
Revenues	297,000
Net income	12,900
Total assets	2,900,000

No of Employees: 1,700

SUMMCORP
1 Summit Square, PO Box 2345, Fort Wayne, IN 46801
Tel: (219) 427 8333

Chairman: Richard T Doermer (and Chief Executive Officer); Vice Chairman: Hiram Nally
President: Donnelly P McDonald Jr
Senior Executive Officers: Darrell L Blanton (Executive VP), Paul E Underwood (Executive VP), John D Auld (Senior VP Lending), Marvin V Basse (Senior VP, Secretary and Treasurer), Thomas G Blume (Senior VP Deposit Administration and Investment), Gordon O Johnson (Senior VP Operations), Donald E Simmons (Senior VP Financial

Planning and Asset Liability Management), William R White (Senior VP)

PRINCIPAL ACTIVITIES: Holding company with interests in banking

Principal Subsidiaries: Summit Bank

No of Employees: 610

SUMMIT BANCORPORATION

367 Springfield Avenue, Summit, NJ 07901
Tel: (201) 522 8400

Chairman: Thomas D Sayles Jr (Chief Executive Officer and Subsidiary Officer)
President: Robert G Cox (and Subsidiary Officer)
Senior Executive Officers: Douglas E Johnson (Vice Chairman, Subsidiary Officer), John R Feeney (Executive VP, Chief Financial Officer, Subsidiary Officer), Dennis McChesney (Executive VP, Senior Lending Officer, Subsidiary Officer)

PRINCIPAL ACTIVITIES: Holding company with interests in a wide range of banking services
Principal Subsidiaries: Chatham Trust Company; Maplewood Bank and Trust Company; Ocean National Bank; Summit Trust Company; Town & Country Bank; Bay State Bank; Trust Company of Princeton; National Machine Tool Finance Corp; Beechwood Securities Corp
Principal Bank: Manufacturers Hanover Trust Company
Financial Information:

	Dec 31 1985	Dec 31 1986
	$'000	$'000
Income before taxes	24,609	35,159
Net income	20,425	26,044
Dividends	8,310	9,754
Dividends per share(1)	$0.59	$0.63
Dividends per share(2)	$2.20	$1.28(5)
Dividends per share(3)	$2.13	$1.59
Earnings per share(4)	$1.51	$1.79
Common stock	17,133	20,256
Retained income	69,855	86,145
Shareholders equity	135,625	186,434
Deposits	1,698,645	2,081,827
Total assets	1,954,806	2,427,801

(1) common
(2) conv. pref.
(3) ARP
(4) fully diluted
(5) redeemed July 15 1986

No of Employees: 1,313

SUMMIT HEALTH LIMITED

1800 Avenue of the Stars, Los Angeles, CA 90067
Tel: (213) 201 4000

Chairman: Don Freeberg; Vice Chairman: John E Anderson
President: William L Pierpoint (and Chief Executive Officer)
Senior Executive Officers: Dorothy Crawford (VP and Secretary), Thomas Konig (VP Skilled Nursing Facilities), Clark D McQuay (VP), David E Morgan (VP Acute Hospitals), James Rush (VP and Treasurer)

PRINCIPAL ACTIVITIES: Operation of hospitals, nursing facilities, retirement hotels, a hemodialysis center, urgent care centers, a home health center and substance abuse centers; management of medical office buildings for hospital medical staff
Principal Bank: Crocker National Bank
Financial Information:

	$'000
Sales revenues	364,080

No of Employees: 6,000

SUN BANK OF TAMPA BAY

315 E Madison Street, Tampa, FL 33601
Tel: (813) 224-2121
Telex: 52626

Chairman: Thomas E Mundy (and Chief Executive Officer)
President: Wesley W Martin Jr (and Chief Administration Officer)
Senior Executive Officers: Wallace F Hood (Senior Executive VP Investment), Otis H Long (Senior Executive VP Investment), David J Dillon (Executive VP Finance and Administration), John M Tapley (Executive VP Fiduciary Services), Terry L Kors (Executive VP Retail), Rafael Martinez-Ybor (Executive VP International Division), Diane B Coates (Senior VP Marketing), Charles S Conklin (Senior VP, President Hillsborough County), James Rasmussen (Senior VP, President Pinellas County), Bonnie W Simon (Senior VP Human Resources)

PRINCIPAL ACTIVITIES: Banking services
Parent Company: Sun Banks Inc

No of Employees: 850

SUN BANKS INC

Sun Bank N A Bldg, Orlando, FL 32802
Tel: (305) 237-4585

Chairman: Philip F Searle; Vice Chairman: Donald T Senterfitt (and Senior Executive Officer)
President: Joel R Wells Jr (and Chief Executive Officer)
Senior Executive Officers: Buell G Duncan Jr (Senior Executive VP Banking), Daniel S Goodrum (Senior Executive VP), George A Snelling (Senior Executive VP and Treasurer), Robert H Bowen (Executive VP Personnel), Wendell H Colson (Executive VP Community Banking), Thomas C Duer (Executive VP Corporate Administration), Charles E LeGette (Executive VP Community Banking), Robert E Raymond (Executive VP Real Estate), Carl E Stallard (Executive VP Fiduciary Services), Hans W Tews (Executive VP Corporate/International Banking)

PRINCIPAL ACTIVITIES: Financial services
Principal Bank: Sun Bank

No of Employees: 250

SUN CITY INDUSTRIES, INC

1200 NW 78th Avenue, Miami, FL 33126
Tel: (305) 593-2355
Telex: WUT 853301 sun city

Chairman: Morton S Neiman (and Chief Executive Officer)
President: Marvin S Rosenberg (and Chief Operating Officer and Secretary)
Senior Executive Officers: Malvin Avchen (VP and Treasurer), Gustave Minkin (VP), Donald Neiman (VP), Harvey Neiman (VP), Vance Weibley (VP), Saul Zalka (VP)

PRINCIPAL ACTIVITIES: Holding company with interests in poultry farming and egg production and the wholesaling of dairy products and poultry
Principal Subsidiaries: Sun City of Georgia Inc; Sun City of Florida Inc; Oak Crest Enterprises Inc; Certified Poultry and Egg Co Inc; Carlisle Poultry and Egg Association Inc; Nearby Producers Egg & Poultry Marketing Corp; Owlkill Farm Inc; Southeast Marketing Association Inc; Nearby Eggs Inc
Principal Bank: Commercial Bank and Trust Company
Financial Information:

	$'000
Sales revenues	53,700

No of Employees: 500

SUN COMPANY, INC

100 Matsonford Road, Radnor, PA 19087
Tel: (215) 293-6000

Chairman: Robert McClements Jr (and Chief Executive Officer)
President: Robert P Hauptfuhrer (and Chief Operating Officer)

Senior Executive Officers: John P Neafsey (Executive VP and Chief Financial Officer), Bill N Rutherford (Senior VP Human Resources and Administration), Harlan T Snider (Senior VP Planning and Public Affairs), Donald P Walsh (Senior VP and General Counsel), Robert H Campbell (Group VP Refining and Marketing), James E McCormick (Group VP Exploration and Production), Richard W Ince (Group VP Coal)

PRINCIPAL ACTIVITIES: Exploration and production of crude oil and natural gas

Principal Subsidiaries: Sun Exploration and Production Co; Sun Refining and Marketing Co; Elk River Resources Inc; Suncor Inc (75%) (Canada)

Principal Bank: Philadelphia National Bank

Financial Information:

	Dec 31 1985	Dec 31 1986
	$'000	$'000
Sales revenues	14,435,000	10,047,000
Income before taxes	816,000	592,000
Net income	527,000	385,000
Dividends	257,000	324,000
Dividends per share	$2.30	$3.00
Earnings per share	$4.72	$3.54
Common stock	1,595,000	1,602,000
Retained income	4,584,000	4,643,000
Shareholders equity	5,289,000	5,287,000

No of Employees: 23,645

SUN DIAMOND GROWERS OF CALIFORNIA

1050 S Diamond Street, Stockton, CA 95201

Tel: (209) 467-6000

Telex: WUT 359470 diasun d sto

Chairman: William C Hosie; Vice Chairmen: Earl L Giacolini, Pete J Penner

President: David R Newstadt

Senior Executive Officers: L D Busboom (Senior VP and Chief Financial Officer), Donald J Soetaert (Senior VP Sales and Marketing), Thomas A Fossey (Controller), Gary H Mershburn (Secretary)

PRINCIPAL ACTIVITIES: Processing of fruit and nuts

Principal Bank: Chemical Bank

Financial Information:

	$'000
Sales revenues	517,000

No of Employees: 500

SUN ELECTRIC CORPORATION

One Sun Pkwy, Crystal Lake, IL 60014

Tel: (815) 459-7700

Telex: WUT 722486 sundelec cry s

Chairman: D B Davis (and President and Chief Executive Officer)

Senior Executive Officers: Craig A Loomis (Senior VP and Chief Financial Officer), Tony Zack (VP Sales and Marketing), H A Stark (VP Legal and Human Resources and Secretary), Adilson DeLuna (VP, President Sun, Electric Europe)

PRINCIPAL ACTIVITIES: Manufacture of electronic test equipment for the automotive industry

Principal Subsidiaries: Sun Electric UK Ltd; Sun Electric Deutschland GmbH; Sun Electric Systems BV; Sun Electric Belgium NV; Sun Electric Europe BV; Sun Electric Austria; Sun Electric do Brasil

Principal Bank: Harris Trust and Savings Bank

Financial Information:

	Oct 31 1985	Oct 31 1986
	$'000	$'000
Sales revenues	164,296	176,998
Income (loss) before taxes	(291)	3,660
Net income (loss)	(615)	1,932
Earnings (loss) per share	($0.09)	$0.28
Common stock	6,556	7,030
Retained income	19,790	21,722
Shareholders equity	64,475	71,430

No of Employees: 2,500

SUN MAID GROWERS OF CALIFORNIA

13525 S Bethel Avenue, Kingsburg, CA 93631

Tel: (209) 896-80000

Telex: WUT 355359 sunmaid kngb

Chairman: George Kaufman; Vice Chairman: Peter J Penner

President: F R Light (and Chief Executive Officer)

Senior Executive Officers: William K Dabney (Executive VP Finance and Administration), Donald J Soetaert (Senior VP Sales, Marketing and Distribution), Ben H Body (VP Sales US and Canada), Glenn E Olmstead (VP Sales International), Larry R Whorton (VP Operations), Fred D Allen Jr (VP and Controller), James R Santo (VP Industrial Sales and Marketing, US and Canada), Richard Douglas (VP Public Affairs), Lee W Halverstadt (VP and Secretary), Barry F Kriebel (VP and General Counsel)

PRINCIPAL ACTIVITIES: Production of dried fruit and snack mixes

Principal Bank: Wells Fargo Bank

Financial Information:

	$'000
Sales revenues	200,000

No of Employees: 750

SUN MICROSYSTEMS INC

2550 Garcia Avenue, Mountain View, CA 94043

Tel: (415) 960 1300

Chairman: Scott G McNealy (and President, Chief Executive Officer and Secretary)

Senior Executive Officers: Robert G Smith (VP, Chief Financial Officer and Assistant Secretary)

PRINCIPAL ACTIVITIES: Manufacture of computers; programming and software services

Financial Information:

	$'000
Sales revenues	115,250

No of Employees: 1,225

SUN REFINING AND MARKETING COMPANY

1801 Market Street, Philadelphia, PA 19103

Tel: (215) 977-3000

Cable: SUNCO

Telex: RCA 244941 SUNCO UR

Chairman: Robert McClements

President: R H Campbell

Senior Executive Officers: J D Helms (VP), K D Hill (VP), G D Kirk (VP), D I Hughes (Treasurer and Controller), D C Rippy (VP), D E Knoll (VP), R O Lewers (VP), J V D Fear (VP), H Z Shelton (VP), N Neuhausel (VP), H S Roe Jr, J I Plyler (VP)

PRINCIPAL ACTIVITIES: Refining and marketing of petroleum and related products

Trade Names: SUNOCO

Parent Company: Sun Company Inc

Principal Subsidiaries: Puerto Rico Sun Oil Co; Mid State Oil Co

Principal Bank: Philadelphia National Bank

Financial Information:

	Dec 31 1986
	$'000
Sales revenues	4,444,000
Shareholders equity	823,000

No of Employees: 5,000

SUN STUDS, INC

PO Box 1127, Roseburg, OR 97470
Tel: (503) 673-0141

President: Fred Sohn
Senior Executive Officers: Carl Allison (Sales Manager), Larry Berry (Chief Engineer), George Funk (Treasurer)

PRINCIPAL ACTIVITIES: Lumber, logging
Principal Bank: Timber Community Bank
Financial Information:

	$'000
Sales revenues	50,000

No of Employees: 400

SUNBEAM APPLIANCE COMPANY

2001 S York Road, Oak Brook, IL 60521
Tel: (312) 850-5000
Telex: WUT 253249 sunworld oakr a

President: James Connors
Senior Executive Officers: Steve Duffy (VP Human Resources), Jerry Gronwick (VP Research and Development), Donald E C Hak (VP Finance), Paul A Saxton (VP Sales and Marketing), Douglas O Smith (VP Operations)

PRINCIPAL ACTIVITIES: Manufacture of domestic electrical appliances
Parent Company: Allegheny International Inc, Pittsburgh, PA
Principal Bank: Mellon Bank
Financial Information:

	$'000
Sales revenues	200,000

No of Employees: 1,500

SUNDSTRAND CORPORATION

4751 Harrison Avenue, Box 7003, Rockford, IL 61125
Tel: (815) 226-6000
Telex: WUT 257440 sunavia rkd b

Chairman: Evans W Erikson (and Chief Executive Officer); Vice Chairman: Don R O'Hare
President: Harry C Stone Cipher (and Chief Operating Officer)
Senior Executive Officers: Bernard W Kittle (Group VP), William R Kopp (Group VP), Philip W Polgreen (VP Public Relations), Kenelm A Groff (VP Administration), Ted L Ross (VP Finance and Secretary), Richard M Schilling (VP and General Counsel), David MacMorris (Executive VP), A Adrian Kemper (Controller)

PRINCIPAL ACTIVITIES: Manufacture of fluid handling and power transmission equipment; manufacture of pumps and compressors; manufacture of gears and couplings; high technology products for the aircraft industry
Trade Names: Sundyne, Sunflo, Highmix, Omnibox
Principal Subsidiaries: Falk Corporation; Global Systems; Signatron Inc; Standard of America Financial Corporation; Sullair Corporation; Sundstrand Domestic and International Sales Corporation; Sundstrand Heat Transfer Disc; Sundstrand International Corporation; Sundstrand Service Corporation; Sundstrand Tubular Products; Sundstrand Electronics Inc
Principal Bank: Bankers Trust Company
Financial Information:

	Dec 31 1985	Dec 31 1986
	$'000	$'000
Sales revenues	1,284,100	1,433,900
Income before taxes	119,700	66,400
Net income	74,400	45,400
Dividends	33,300	33,700
Dividends per share	$1.80	$1.80
Earnings per share	$4.02	$2.42
Shareholders equity	589,129	604,669

No of Employees: 16,000

SUNDSTRAND DATA CONTROL, INC

15001 NE 36 St, PO Box 97001, Redmond, WA 98073-9701
Tel: (206) 885-3711
Telex: TWX 910 449 2860 sdc redmond

Senior Executive Officers: William R Kopp (Group VP), Robert H Ilgenfritz (VP and General Manager Avionic Systems Division), Robert J Wyma (VP and General Manager Instrument Systems Division), Basil J Cascio (VP Administration), John B Landstrom (VP and General Manager Technology Development Division)

PRINCIPAL ACTIVITIES: Manufacture of electronic equipment for the aerospace industry
Parent Company: Sundstrand Corporation, Rockford, IL
Financial Information:

	$'000
Sales revenues	100,000

No of Employees: 2,000

SUNKIST GROWERS, INC

PO Box 7888, Van Nuys, CA 91409
Tel: (213) 986-4800
Telex: TRT 188266 sunkist lsa

Chairman: J V Newman; Vice Chairmen: D E Armstrong, R E Bondine, H S Chase
President: R L Hanlin
Senior Executive Officers: C W Anderson (VP), D V Cunningham (Senior VP Law), H J Carnine Jr (VP), H B Flach (VP), M V Johnson Jr (VP), F R McGill (VP), D P Bernstein (VP Sales Advertising, International Operations), W K Quarles Jr (VP)

PRINCIPAL ACTIVITIES: Production of processing of fruit; fresh canned and frozen citrus fruits
Principal Bank: First Interstate Bank
Financial Information:

	$'000
Sales revenues	822,000

No of Employees: 1,330

SUNLAND REFINING CORPORATION

PO Box 1345, Bakersfield, CA 93302
Tel: (805) 589-9615

Chairman: Bernard B Roth (and Chief Executive Officer)
President: Dale A Snyder
Senior Executive Officers: Robert S Roth (VP), Robert Bimat (VP Finance and Treasurer)

PRINCIPAL ACTIVITIES: Oil refining
Parent Company: World Oil Company
Principal Bank: Wells Fargo Bank
Financial Information:

	$'000
Sales revenues	60,000

No of Employees: 80

SUNRISE MEDICAL INC

970 West 190th Street, Suite 280, Torrance, CA 90502
Tel: (213) 516-8568
Facsimile No: (213) 516-8106

Chairman: Richard H Chandler (and President)
Senior Executive Officers: Thomas H O'Donnell (Executive VP-Operations), Warren E Pinckert II (VP Finance, Chief Financial Officer and Secretary), Terry D Mulkey (VP-Sales-Homecare/Rehabilitation Products), Ted N Tarbet (Controller)

PRINCIPAL ACTIVITIES: Sunrise Medical Inc, designs, manufactures and markets a broad line of innovative medical products used in the preventive, recovery and rehabilitation phases of patient care. The company markets its products to home health care dealers, nursing homes, hospitals, doctor's offices and physical therapy clinics using specialized company salesforces organized by market segment. Products are manufactured in the United States, Canada and United Kingdom and are distributed in 32 other countries
Trade Names: Sciitas, *Eggcrate, *BioGard, Mighty Ramp, Easy-Care, Tru-Trac, *Registered Trade Names
Principal Subsidiaries: Operating Divisions:- A-BEC Mobility Inc; BEC Mobility Inc; Bio Clinic Corporation; Motion Designs Inc; Guardian Products Inc; Joerns Healthcare Inc; Sunrise Medical Canada Inc; Trans-Aid Corporation; Tru-Truc Therapy Products Inc; Akron Therapy Products Ltd; Performance USA
Principal Bank: Wells Fargo Bank
Financial Information:

	Jun 27 1986	Jun 26 1987
	$'000	$'000
Sales revenues	97,863	140,756
Income before taxes	5,288	1,708
Net income	1,874	850
Earnings per share	$0.20	$0.48
Common stock	4,011	4,423
Retained income	4,781	5,631
Shareholders equity	27,064	32,369

No of Employees: 1,000

SUNSHINE BISCUITS, INC

100 Woodbridge Center Drive, Woodbridge, NJ 07095
Tel: (202) 855-4000

President: Howard E Fraga (and Chief Executive Officer)
Senior Executive Officers: Arthur G Murray (Senior VP Operations), Charles J Griffin (VP Operations), John F Klarich (VP Sales), Reno Morandi (VP Materials Management), Richard D Schwartz (VP, Controller and Assistant Treasurer), Joseph P Simrany (VP Marketing)

PRINCIPAL ACTIVITIES: Manufacture of cookies and snack products
Trade Names: Krispy, Cheez-It, Hi Ho, Chip A Roos, Hydrox, Vanilla Wafers, Bell Brand Natural Style potato chips, Vienna Fingers
Parent Company: American Brands Inc, New York, NY
Financial Information:

	1986
	$'000
Sales revenues	510,639

No of Employees: 4,700

SUNSHINE MINING COMPANY

500 Plaza of the Americas-South, Dallas, TX 75201
Tel: (214) 979 0405

Chairman: G Michael Boswell (and President and Chief Executive Officer)
Senior Executive Officers: E Viet Howard (Executive VP and Chief Operating Officer), Paul L Hunter (Senior VP, President Precious Metals Group), David H Jardine (Senior VP and Chief Financial Officer), John S Simko (Senior VP and Legal Counsel)

PRINCIPAL ACTIVITIES: Mining of gold, antimony, copper and silver
Principal Subsidiaries: First Matagorda Corporation; Sunshine Bullion Company; Sunshine Energy Corporation; Texas Energies Inc; Republic Natural Gas Company; Wheatstate Oil Field Services; Woods Petroleum Corporation
Principal Bank: MBank
Financial Information:

	$'000
Sales revenues	169,465

No of Employees: 880

SUNSHINE-JR STORES INC

Seventeenth Street and June Avenue, Panama City, FL 32405
Tel: (904) 769 1661

Chairman: Leona J Lewis; Vice Chairman: Lana Jane Lewis-Brent (and President)
Senior Executive Officers: James C Burkhalter (VP Gasoline Marketing), John M Eaves (VP, Treasurer and Chief Financial Officer), Ralph W Lake (VP Merchandise/Store Operations), Harold Mills (VP)

PRINCIPAL ACTIVITIES: Retail food outlets
Financial Information:

	$'000
Sales revenues	183,100

No of Employees: 2,000

SUNSTAR FOODS, INC

7575 Golden Valley Road, Minneapolis, MN 55427
Tel: (612) 546-2506

Chairman: George B Keister (and President and Chief Executive Officer)
Senior Executive Officers: David L Schinke (VP Finance and Treasurer), Lee Campisi (VP), Gary Arndt (VP), Larry Perkins (VP), Tom Swanson (VP)

PRINCIPAL ACTIVITIES: Manufacture of a wide range of food products including meat, fruit juices, spreads, dressings, frozen and snack foods
Principal Bank: Northwestern National Bank of Minneapolis
Financial Information:

	$'000
Sales revenues	77,560

No of Employees: 400

SUNSTREAM AIRCRAFT, INC

Dupage Airport, West Chicago, IL 60185
Tel: (312) 584-8250
Telex: 722494; 270127 SUNSTREAM WCGO

Chairman: Norman E Lively
President: James H Higby

PRINCIPAL ACTIVITIES: Supply of aircraft, avionics, components and engines
Principal Bank: Northern Trust
Financial Information:

	Dec 31 1986
	$'000
Sales revenues	890,000

No of Employees: 56

SUNSWEET GROWERS INC

1050 S Diamond Street, Stockton, CA 95205
Tel: (209) 467-6000

Chairman: Charles T Yerxa; Vice Chairman: Earl Giacolini
President: F R Light
Senior Executive Officers: W K Dabney (Executive VP and Treasurer), D Soetart (Senior VP, Distribution, Marketing and Sales), B Body (VP Consumer Pkg Product, US and Canada), R Douglas (VP Public Affairs), H Jackson (VP Prune Operations), J Kramer (VP New Product Development), B F Kriebel (VP, Secretary and General Counsel), G Olmstead (VP International Sales and Raisin Marketing), X Regli (VP International Sales and Prune and Walnut Marketing)

PRINCIPAL ACTIVITIES: Production of dried fruit
Principal Bank: Chemical Bank
Financial Information:

	$'000
Sales revenues	116,000

No of Employees: 800

SUNTRUST BANKS, INC

25 Park Place NE, Atlanta, GA 30303
Tel: (404) 588-7455
Telex: WUT 542210

Chairman: Robert Strickland; Vice Chairmen: Donald T Senterfitt; James B Williams
President: Joel R Wells Jr
Senior Executive Officers: Jesse S Hall (Executive VP), George A Snelling (Executive VP), John W Spiegel (Executive VP)

PRINCIPAL ACTIVITIES: Bank holding company
Principal Subsidiaries: Sun Banks, Inc; Trust Company of Georgia; Third National Corporation
Principal Bank: Trust Company Bank
Financial Information:

	Dec 31 1985	Dec 31 1986
	$'000	$'000
Income before taxes	249,643	260,122
Net income	216,411	245,188
Common dividends	55,535	60,613
Dividends per common share	$0.56	$0.61
Earnings per common share	$1.65	$1.86
Common stock	131,220	129,172
Retained income	736,663	874,002
Shareholders equity	1,386,962	1,507,858
Deposits	18,967,845	21,284,007
Total assets	24,448,790	26,165,455

No of Employees: 19,711 (full-time equivalents)

SUNWEST FINANCIAL SERVICES INC

303 Roma Avenue NW, PO Box 25500, Albuquerque, NM 87125-0500
Tel: (505) 765-2403

Chairman: Daniel A Sisk
President: George S Jenks (and Chief Executive Officer)
Senior Executive Officers: Thomas C Roope (Executive VP and Chief Financial Officer), Ike Kalangis (Senior Executive VP), David A Mitchell (Chief Operating Officer), Chester W Wright (Treasurer), Olivia Kesler (Secretary)

PRINCIPAL ACTIVITIES: Banking services
Trade Names: SFSI
Financial Information:

	Dec 31 1986	Dec 31 1987
	$'000	$'000
Income before taxes	42,570	36,362
Net income	32,263	28,300
Dividends	10,646	10,646
Dividends per share	$1.10	$1.00
Earnings per share	$3.30	$2.91
Common stock	114,482	128,980
Retained income	74,015	53,148
Shareholders equity	188,497	182,128
Deposits	2,246,353	2,237,041
Total assets	2,621,964	2,588,639

No of Employees: 1,373

SUNWORLD INTERNATIONAL AIRWAYS INC

2333 Renaissance Drive, Las Vegas, NV 89119
Tel: (702) 798 0088

Chairman: G M Sage; Vice Chairman: H L Lucas
President: T J Volz (and Chief Executive Officer)
Senior Executive Officers: Robert J Sherer (Executive VP, Chief Financial Officer and Treasurer), Gene R Empey (VP), Jorge L Mayor (VP), George A McConnaughey (VP), Richard R Myler (VP), John L Puskarich (VP and Assistant Secretary), J R Sinis Jr (VP, Secretary and General Counsel), Robert A Warren (VP), Judith Ann Massa (Controller)

PRINCIPAL ACTIVITIES: Air transportation services
Financial Information:

	$'000
Sales revenues	41,300

No of Employees: 400

SUPER FOOD SERVICES, INC

3185 Elbee Road, Dayton, OH 45439
Tel: (513) 294-1731
Telex: TWX 810 459 1633 superfd day

Chairman: Jack Twyman (and President and Chief Executive Officer); Vice Chairman: John Demos (and Secretary and General Counsel)
President: Sam Robinson (and Chief Operating Officer)
Senior Executive Officers: I J Potter (Executive VP Operations), Al Burshtan (Executive VP and Secretary), John Batista (Senior VP), Larry G Dear (Senior VP), Robert F Koogler (Senior VP Finance and Treasurer), Richard Metzgar (Senior VP), Doug Koenig (VP)

PRINCIPAL ACTIVITIES: Wholesale trade in food products; management consultants
Principal Subsidiaries: Parkview Markets Inc; General Merchandise Services Inc
Principal Bank: Third National Bank of Dayton
Financial Information:

	Aug 31 1986
	$'000
Sales revenues	1,422,309
Net income	10,588
Earnings per share	$1.48
Shareholders equity	69,625

No of Employees: 1,860

SUPER RITE FOODS INC

3900 Industrial Road, Harrisburg, PA 17110
Tel: (717) 232 6821

Chairman: Alex Grass (and Chief Executive Officer)
President: Peter Vanderveen (and Chief Operating Officer)
Senior Executive Officers: David Gundling (Senior VP), Robert Anderson (VP), William K Schantzenbach (VP and Chief Financial Officer), Ben DeFrancesco (VP), Roger Grass (Treasurer), John Harrison (Controller)

PRINCIPAL ACTIVITIES: Retail and wholesale trade in food and tobacco
Financial Information:

	$'000
Sales revenues	602,460

No of Employees: 2,700

SUPER SKY INTERNATIONAL INC

10301 North Enterprise Drive, Mequon, WI 53092
Tel: (414) 242 2000

Chairman: Larry L Huffman (and Chief Executive Officer)
President: Robert L Pagel
Senior Executive Officers: James E Roesing (Executive VP), Douglas Carlson (VP Finance, Secretary and Treasurer)

PRINCIPAL ACTIVITIES: Holding company with interests in the manufacture of aluminum and glass skylights
Principal Subsidiaries: Super Sky Products Inc
Principal Bank: First WI National Bank
Financial Information:

	$'000
Sales revenues	36,250

No of Employees: 200

SUPER VALU STORES, INC

11840 Valley View Road, Eden Prairie, MN 55344
Tel: (612) 828-4000
Telex: WUT 290522 supervalu enpe

Chairman: Michael W Wright (and President and Chief Executive Officer); Chariman of Executive Committee: Jack J Crocker
Senior Executive Officers: John B Ferris (Senior VP), John E Morrissey (Senior VP Distribution), Charles D Dugan Jr (VP and Secretary), Gene D Hoffman (VP Marketing and President Wholesale Food Companies), Thomas L Dekko (VP Sales), Robert O Erickson (VP Development), Sumner H Goldman (VP Merchandising), John J Prior (VP), Lloyd K Stenbeck (VP Store Planning and Engineering), Ronald C Tortelli (VP Human Resources), William J Tyrell (VP, President Shopko Stores Inc), David A Cairns (Treasurer)

PRINCIPAL ACTIVITIES: Wholesale trade in food products
Principal Subsidiaries: The Lewis Grocer Co; Sunflower Stores Inc; J M Jones Co; ShopKo Stores Inc; Hornbacker Foods Inc; Risk Planners Inc; SVS Trucking Inc; Western Grocers Inc
Principal Bank: The First National Bank of Minneapolis
Financial Information:

	$'000
Sales revenues	9,100,000

No of Employees: 26,580

SUPERIOR CARE INC

200 Park Ave, New York, NY 10166-0005

Chairman: Michael J Sinclair
President: Anthony H Reeves (and Chief Executive Officer)
Senior Executive Officers: David M Barnes (VP, Chief Financial Officer and Secretary)

PRINCIPAL ACTIVITIES: Provision of home health care services
Principal Bank: Manufacturers Hanover Trust Company
Financial Information:

	$'000
Sales revenues	23,000

No of Employees: 100

SUPERIOR COFFEE CO

990 Supreme Drive, Bensenville, IL 60106
Tel: (312) 489-1000

President: James D Cockman
Senior Executive Officers: Tony Valvo (Executive VP Finance), Sheldon Pines (Treasurer), James F Polark (Controller)

PRINCIPAL ACTIVITIES: Manufacture of coffee
Parent Company: Sara Lee Corporation, Chicago, IL
Principal Bank: Continental Illinois National Bank and Trust Company
Financial Information:

	$'000
Sales revenues	136,000

No of Employees: 630

SUPERIOR ELECTRIC CO (THE)

383 Middle Street, Bristol, CT 06010
Tel: (203) 582-9561
Telex: 681-3196 SUPE
Fax: 584-1483

President: Maurice P Andrien Jr
Senior Executive Officers: Anthony E Balestro (VP-Manufacturing), John Crozier (General Counsel and Secretary), Gilbert Dinkins (VP-Engineering), Frank S Doyle (VP-Finance), Martin Kaplan (VP-Research and Development), Harold Lorenson (VP-Sales), Arthur C Savage (VP-Marketing)

PRINCIPAL ACTIVITIES: Electrical and electronic products:- motion control, voltage conditioning
Trade Names: SLO-SYN(R) (synchronous/stepping motors), SLO-SYN(R) (stepping control devices), MODULYNY(R) (motion controls), MITAS(TM) (motion controls), POWERSTAT(R) (variable transformers), STABILINE(R) (voltage control equipment), STABILINE(R) (UPS/conditioners), STABILINE(R) (AC voltage monitors), LUXTROL(R) (light controls)
Principal Subsidiaries: The American Superior Electric Company Ltd (Canada); Superior Electric Nederland BV (Netherlands)
Principal Bank: Connecticut Bank & Trust Company
Financial Information:

	$'000
Sales revenues	49,550

No of Employees: 900

SUPERIOR INDUSTRIES INTERNATIONAL, INC

7800 Woodley Avenue, Van Nuys, CA 91406
Tel: (818) 781-4973
Telex: 65-1454

Chairman: Louis L Borick (and President)
Senior Executive Officers: Raymond C Brown (Senior VP), R Jeffrey Ornstein (VP Finance and Treasurer), Ronald R Feiner (VP, Operations and Corporate Secretary), Morris Herstein (VP, Services), Charles B May (VP, Manufacturing), Delbert J Schmitz (VP, Sales Accessories), Joseph T D'Amico (VP, Material), James M Ferguson (VP, OEM Programs), Lewis H Oster (VP, Iowa Plant)

PRINCIPAL ACTIVITIES: The Company designs, manufactures and markets automotive products for Original Equipment Manufacturers (OEM) and the automotive aftermarket. During the past five years the Company has become a leading supplier of high quality stylized cast aluminum road wheels to Ford, General Motors and Chrysler. The Company designs and manufactures various products for the automotive and recreational vehicle aftermarkets, including custom road wheels, steering wheel covers, steering wheels, seat belts, suspension products and miscellaneous accessories
Trade Names: Superior Industries, SPORT GRIP(R), EZ SLIDER (TM), ELECTRA GUARD(R)
Principal Subsidiaries: Superior Performance-Canada; Superior Puerto Rico; Ideal Manufacturing
Principal Bank: Bankers Trust
Financial Information:

	Dec 31 1985	Dec 31 1986
	$'000	$'000
Sales revenues	130,836	148,550
Income before taxes	10,952	14,425
Net income	3,703	5,920
Dividends	1,193	1,350
Dividends per share	$0.23	$0.24
Earnings per share	$1.32	$1.43
Common stock	5,373	5,937
Retained income	20,022	19,215
Shareholders equity	39,988	47,223

Principal Shareholders: Mr L Borick; Mrs J Borick
No of Employees: 2,000

SUPERIOR OIL CO

PO Box 1521, Houston, TX 77001
Tel: (713) 751-4111
Telex: WUT 775 369 supco hou a

Chairman: Fred C Ackman (and President and Chief Executive Officer)
Senior Executive Officers: R A Barker (VP), David G Beerbower (VP), T E Burke (VP), Jack C Castleberry (VP Finance and Chief Financial Officer), Joseph O Carter (VP), Eugene C Hixson Jr (VP), William J Johnson (VP), Fines F Martin (VP), R B Rice (VP), Louis O Satterfield Jr (VP, Secretary and Assistant General Counsel), Robert I Schramm (VP)

PRINCIPAL ACTIVITIES: Production of oil and gas

Parent Company: Mobil Corporation
Principal Bank: First City National Bank
Financial Information:

	$'000
Sales revenues	1,800,000

No of Employees: 5,700

SUPERIOR SURGICAL MFG CO, INC

Seminole Blvd at 100th Terrace, Seminole, FL 33542
Tel: (813) 397-9611

Chairman: Gerald M Benstock (and President and Chief Executive Officer)
Senior Executive Officers: Saul Schechter (Executive VP), Alan D Schwartz (Executive VP), John W Johansen (Senior VP, Chief Financial Officer and Treasurer), Michael Benstock (Senior VP), Nathan L Belkin Ph D (VP), Spencer Cohen (VP), Anne Fasani (VP), Robert M Green (VP), Errol Pegler (VP), Irving Weissman (VP), Earl Marvin (Secretary). Corporate Managers: Leonard J Berman (Corporate Manager Healthcare Marketing), Mark Birenbaum (Corporate Manager Marketing Operations), Mark Decker (Corporate Manager Engineering), Thomas R Duntze (Corporate Manager Management Information Systems), Sherwin J Klein (Corporate Manager Martin's Divisions), John H Lord (Corporate Manager Manufacturing), Marvin Schane (Corporate Manager Textile Services), Richard Snyder (Corporate Manager Purchasing)

PRINCIPAL ACTIVITIES: Superior Surgical Mfg Co, Inc and its subsidiaries manufacture and sell a wide range of uniforms, career apparel and accessories. Products include hospital and health service uniforms, apparel and accessories; laundry bags; commercial, industrial, leisure services and government employee uniforms, apparel and accessories; career wardrobes and on-the-job uniforms and apparel
Principal Subsidiaries: Evansville Garment Corp; Providence Garment Corp
Financial Information:

	Dec 31 1985	Dec 31 1986
	$'000	$'000
Sales revenues	98,540	96,200
Income before taxes	7,267	6,855
Net income	4,027	3,645
Dividends	875	974
Dividends per share	$0.36	$0.40
Earnings per share	$1.66	$1.50
Common stock	2,431	2,440
Retained income	28,616	31,289
Shareholders equity	33,732	36,506

No of Employees: 2,100

SUPERIOR'S BRAND MEATS INC

Southway Street SE, Massillon, OH 44646
Tel: (216) 832-7491
Telex: WUT 883802 superior oh

President: Neil Genshaft (and Treasurer)
Senior Executive Officers: Joe Sekring (Executive VP), Harry Valentino (Executive VP Administration), Donald Heidmeyer (VP and General Manager)

PRINCIPAL ACTIVITIES: Packaging of meat products
Principal Bank: Central National Bank of Cleveland
Financial Information:

	$'000
Sales revenues	500,000

No of Employees: 2,400

SUPERMARKETS GENERAL CORPORATION

301 Blair Road, Woodbridge, NJ 07095
Tel: (201) 499-3000
Telex: WUT 138796 sgc pthmk wobe

Chairman: Alex Aidekman
President: Leonard Lieberman (and Chief Executive Officer)
Senior Executive Officers: James D Dougherty (Executive VP and Secretary), Murray Levine (Senior VP and Controller), Arnold J Pearl (VP), Jeffrey Girard (VP and Treasurer), Jerome F Katcher (VP)

PRINCIPAL ACTIVITIES: Operation of retail stores including supermarkets, drug stores, department stores and home centers
Principal Bank: Bank of New York
Financial Information:

	Dec 31 1985	Dec 31 1986
	$'000	$'000
Sales revenues	5,122,633	5,560,130
Net income	63,710	60,865
Earnings per share	$1.78	$1.60
Shareholders equity	346,980	465,791

No of Employees: 53,000

SUPERSCOPE INC

20525 Nordhoff Street, Chatsworth, CA 91311
Tel: (213) 998 9333
Telex: WUT 182853

Chairman: Joseph S Tushinsky (and President and Chief Executive Officer)
Senior Executive Officers: Fred C Tushinsky (Executive VP), Anthony M Blazina (VP), Ronald C Costa (VP), Robert M Fried (VP), William Morris (VP Finance and Administration and Chief Financial Officer)

PRINCIPAL ACTIVITIES: Supply of televisions and other home entertainment equipment; electrical equipment
Financial Information:

	$'000
Sales revenues	33,875

No of Employees: 310

SUPREME EQUIPMENT AND SYSTEMS CORPORATION

170 53rd Street, Brooklyn, NY 11232
Tel: (718) 439 3800

Chairman: Sam Nissenson (and Executive VP)
President: Martin Frederick (and Chief Executive Officer)
Senior Executive Officers: Allen S Fox (Executive VP Finance and Administration), Robert Stahl (Executive VP and Secretary), Robert DiSalvio (VP Human Resources), Hira Kochar (VP Manufacturing), Jack Nooney (VP Management Information Systems and Purchasing), Howard Wilkinson (VP Special Projects), Louis Zito (VP Engineering)

PRINCIPAL ACTIVITIES: Manufacture of filing systems and equipment for manual and electronic storage and retrieval
Principal Bank: Bank Leumi Trust Company of New York
Financial Information:

	$'000
Sales revenues	39,130

No of Employees: 515

SURFACE COMBUSTION DIVISION

PO Box 907, Toledo, OH 43691
Tel: (419) 537-6176
Telex: TWX 810 442 1651 surfce mr tol

Senior Executive Officers: Joe Andrews (VP and General Manager), T C McClain (Controller), T P Plunkett (Sales Manager), W Dempster (Director International Sales)

PRINCIPAL ACTIVITIES: Manufacture of process systems, incinerators and disposal systems for environmental protection
Parent Company: Midland-Ross Corporation

Financial Information:

	$'000
Sales revenues	60,000

No of Employees: 350

SUSQUEHANNA BANCSHARES INC

9 East Main Street, Lititz, PA 17543
Tel: (717) 626 4721

President: Robert S Bolinger (and Chief Executive Officer)
Senior Executive Officers: Franklin M Blubaugh (VP), Richard M Cloney (VP and Secretary), J Stanley Mull Jr (VP and Treasurer)

PRINCIPAL ACTIVITIES: Holding company with interests in banking
Principal Subsidiaries: Citizens National Bank and Trust Company; Farmers Agcredit Corporation; Farmers First Bank; Susque-Bancshares Life Insurance Company
Principal Bank: Farmers First Bank

No of Employees: 630

SUSQUEHANNA BROADCASTING CO

140 East Market Street, York, PA 17401
Tel: (717) 848-5500
Telex: WUT 8555 551 susquehanna ud

President: Louis J Appell Jr
Senior Executive Officers: Arthur W Carlson (VP Radio), William S Ripley (VP Marketing), William H Simpson (VP Manufacturing), John L Finlayson (VP Administration), Peter P Brubaker (VP Finance)

PRINCIPAL ACTIVITIES: Broadcasting; manufacture of giftware and domestic ceramic goods
Principal Bank: The York Bank and Trust Company
Financial Information:

	$'000
Sales revenues	110,000

No of Employees: 2,000

SUSQUEHANNA CORPORATION

PO Box 5170, Denver, CO 80217
Tel: (303) 779-0777
Telex: 5106004513 SQN CORP ENGLE

Chairman: Fred L Pundsack (and President and Chief Executive Officer)
Senior Executive Officers: R L Rasmussen (VP Finance, Treasurer and Secretary)

PRINCIPAL ACTIVITIES: Manufacture of plastic pipe
Principal Subsidiaries: R & G Sloane Manufacturing Co Inc; Accesorios Plasticos Centro Americanos SA (30%) (Costa Rica); Piezas Plasticas C por A (45%) (Dominican Republic)
Principal Bank: United Bank of Denver
Financial Information:

	Dec 31 1985 $'000	Dec 31 1986 $'000
Sales revenues	72,845	74,064
Net income (loss)	3,810	(8,786)
Earnings (loss) per share	$0.40	($0.92)
Shareholders equity	54,642	45,888

No of Employees: 708

SWANK, INC

6 Hazel Street, Attleboro, MA 02703
Tel: (617) 222-3400
Telex: WUT 927600 swanktwo abor

President: Marshall Tulin
Senior Executive Officers: John Tulin (Executive VP), Dennis Beardall (Senior VP-President, Prince Gardner Division), Richard S Blum (Senior VP-President Crestline Division), Andrew C Corsini (Senior VP-Treasurer and Secretary), Melvin Goldfeder (Senior VP-National Sales Manager Swank Division), Irving I Greene (Senior VP-General Merchandise Manager Swank Division), Raymond J Hill (Senior VP-Manufacturing Swank Division), Fred Stern (Senior VP-Customer Service Swank Division), James A Tulin (Senior VP-Men's Leather, Accessories, Fragrance Merchandise Manager), Henry R Delaive (VP-Systems and Information Services Swank Division), Paul Duckett (VP-Distribution Swank Division), Lawrence F Fleming (VP-Executive VP-Crestline Division), Arthur T Gately Jr (VP-Administration), John E Hirsch (VP-Belt Merchandise Manager Crestline Division), Lewis Valenti (VP-General Manager Women's Jewelry Division), Donald I Zeman (VP-Regional Sales Swank Division), Arthur N Ehlert (Assistant Secretary-VP, Prince Gardner Division)

PRINCIPAL ACTIVITIES: Swank, Inc is a leading manufacturer and distributor of men's and women's jewelry, personal leather goods, belts, fragrances, gifts and personal accessory items. The Company is dedicated to maintaining style and quality leadership in the broad diveristy of products it markets. Products are sold across more than 48,000 department and specialty store counters in the United States, as well as in 50 foreign countries. In order to appeal to a large economic cross-section of the buying public, most of Swank's collections are offered in a wide variety of styles and range of prices. The Company takes great pride in the strength of its consumer franchise and the brand name recognition of its products
Principal Bank: Chase Manhattan Bank
Financial Information:

	Dec 31 1985 $'000	Dec 31 1986 $'000
Sales revenues	140,074	137,926
Income before taxes	3,080	2,116
Net income	1,845	1,096
Dividends	2,376	414
Dividends per share	$0.69	$0.12
Earnings per share net	$0.54	$0.32
Common stock	3,473	3,476
Retained income	48,534	49,184
Shareholders equity	59,800	61,812

No of Employees: 2,700

SWEDLOW INC

12122 Western Avenue, Garden Grove, CA 92641
Tel: (714) 893 7531

Chairman: David A Swedlow (and Chief Executive Officer)
President: Charles J Deischter (and Chief Operating Officer and Chief Financial Officer)
Senior Executive Officers: Paul H Bottoms (Senior VP and Assistant Secretary), Jack Gold (Senior VP and Secretary), William F Fischer (VP)

PRINCIPAL ACTIVITIES: Manufacture of a wide range of plastic products including ballistic and abrasion resistant products and aircraft transparencies
Parent Company: PPG Industries Inc
Financial Information:

	$'000
Sales revenues	46,300

No of Employees: 750

SWIFT INDEPENDENT CORPORATION

115 W Jackson Blvd, Chicago, IL 60604
Tel: (312) 431-3500
Telex: RCA 210307 sipc ur

Chairman: John A Copeland (and Chief Executive Officer)
President: J D Gray (and Chief Operating Officer)
Senior Executive Officers: Richard W Jaracz (Senior VP Pork, Purchasing and Transport), Richard C Knight (Senior VP Beef and Lamb), William J Zautcke (Senior VP Sales), Charles Bedrosian (VP and Controller), Karl M Becker (VP and

Secretary), Richard A Hayden (VP Direct Sales), Harry A Niese (VP Employee Relations), William G Ross (VP Beef Marketing and Assistant General Manager), Ronald R Scoville (VP Operations and Engineering), Kenneth E Shockley (VP Hog Procurement and Pork Marketing)

PRINCIPAL ACTIVITIES: Holding company with interests in meat production and sales; prepared meat products for the foodservice industry
Principal Subsidiaries: Swift Independent Packing Co; Institutional Meat Purveyors Ltd; Swift International Sales Corp
Principal Bank: Mellon Bank
Financial Information:

	Oct 31 1986
	$'000
Sales revenues	2,763,235
Net profit	4,434
Shareholders equity	17,036

No of Employees: 6,830

SWIFTSHIPS INC
1105 Levee Road, Box 1908, Morgan City, LA 70380
Tel: (504) 384-1700
Telex: TWX 810 950 5700

Chairman: Keith A Cunningham
President: Jerry L Hoffpauir
Senior Executive Officers: Barnard Heaps (Senior VP), Sidney Mizell (VP Marketing), Patrick N Calelly (Treasurer)

PRINCIPAL ACTIVITIES: Shipbuilding and ship repair and maintenance
Parent Company: UNC Rescources Inc, Falls Church, VA
Principal Bank: Allied Bank
Financial Information:

	$'000
Sales revenues	60,000

No of Employees: 450

SWINGLINE INC
32-00 Skillman Avenue, Long Island City, NY 11101
Tel: (718) 729-9600
Telex: ITT 421 906 swin ui

Chairman: John P Clark
President: Kenneth X Miles (and Chief Executive Officer)
Senior Executive Officers: David B Miller (VP Sales and Marketing), Robert Pungello (VP, Controller and Assistant Secretary), John P Vota (VP Operations), Dudley L Bauerlein Jr (Treasurer), Theresa B Fealey (Secretary)

PRINCIPAL ACTIVITIES: Manufacture of staples and staplers, manufacture of manual and electric staple guns, glue guns, nail drivers and riveters sold in hardware and home product centers
Parent Company: American Brands Inc, New York, NY
Financial Information:

	1986
	$'000
Sales revenues	71,052

No of Employees: 1,100

SYBRON CORPORATION
Park 80, W Plaza I, Saddle Brook, NJ 07662
Tel: (201) 845-4990

Chairman: Howard H Leach
President: Kenneth F Yontz (and Chief Executive Officer)
Senior Executive Officers: James C McCulloch (VP Finance and Treasurer), Uldis Kordons (VP, Secretary and General Counsel)

PRINCIPAL ACTIVITIES: Manufacture of medical supplies and chemicals; treatment of water and waste
Principal Bank: Manufacturers Hanover Trust
Financial Information:

	$'000
Sales revenues	500,000

No of Employees: 13,400

SYMBOLICS INC
11 Cambridge Center, Cambridge, MA 02142
Tel: (617) 577 7500

Chairman: Russell Noftsker (and President)
Senior Executive Officers: Ronald L Derry (VP Manufacturing), B M Gras (VP), J T Holloway (VP), John L Kulp Jr (VP Research and Development), Robert B Lamkin (VP Sales), Minoru Tonai (VP Operations), Thomas F Farb (Treasurer, Director Corporate Development)

PRINCIPAL ACTIVITIES: Computer software
Financial Information:

	$'000
Sales revenues	69,000

No of Employees: 450

SYMONS CORPORATION
200 E Touhy Avenue, Des Plaines, IL 60018
Tel: (312) 298-3200
Telex: TWX 910 2330 163 symonscorp dsp

Chairman: M Nash (and Chief Executive Officer)
Senior Executive Officers: E O Gibson Jr (Executive VP and General Manager), S N Shukas (Secretary), B C Johnson (Controller), G Salisbury (Secretary and Treasurer), C A Springman (Advertising Manager)

PRINCIPAL ACTIVITIES: Manufacture of conveyors and concrete prodcuts
Parent Company: Gulf and Western Industries Inc, New York, NY
Principal Bank: Bank of America
Financial Information:

	$'000
Sales revenues	70,000

No of Employees: 1,200

SYMS CORPORATION
300 Chubb Avenue, Lyndhurst, NJ 07071
Tel: (201) 935 7500

Chairman: Sy Syms Merns (and Chief Executive Officer)
President: Marcy Syms Merns (and Chief Operating Officer)
Senior Executive Officers: Richard B Diamond (VP Finance and Treasurer), Robert Merns (VP and Secretary)

PRINCIPAL ACTIVITIES: Retail of men's and boys' clothes
Principal Bank: Chemical Bank
Financial Information:

	$'000
Sales revenues	215,170

No of Employees: 1,215

SYM-TEK SYSTEMS INC
3912 Calle Fortunada, San Diego, CA 92123
Tel: (619) 569 6800

President: Ray Twigg (and Chief Executive Officer)
Senior Executive Officers: R Bruce O'Connor (Executive VP), Ronald G Sidorchuk (VP Finance and Chief Financial Officer), Ralph Liberatore (Treasurer)

PRINCIPAL ACTIVITIES: Manufacture of handling equipment to position integrated circuits for testing
Principal Subsidiaries: General Thermionics Corporation
Principal Bank: Wells Fargo Bank; Bank of America NT & SA

Financial Information:

	$'000
Sales revenues	35,745

No of Employees: 385

SYNCOR INTERNATIONAL INC
12847 Arroyo Street, Sylmar, CA 91342
Tel: (818) 365 8151
Telex: WUT 182627

Chairman: Monty Fu (and VP)
President: Mark T Hebner (and Chief Executive Officer)
Senior Executive Officers: Charles F Panneciere (Executive VP), D M J Compton (VP), Robert F Irwin (VP), Richard E Keesee (VP), William A Kemmel Jr (VP), Jean E Ravold (VP), Peter R Chiarella (Chief Financial Officer), Robert A Krulisky (Treasurer), Michael E Mikity (Chief Financial Officer and Controller)

PRINCIPAL ACTIVITIES: Manufacture of pharmaceuticals
Financial Information:

	$'000
Sales revenues	38,000

No of Employees: 680

SYNERGEX CORPORATION
4974 E Clinton Way, Fresno, CA 93727
Tel: (209) 252-4000

Chairman: Philmore G Divine
President: Dwight A Steffensen (and Chief Executive Officer)
Senior Executive Officers: Robert A Allen (VP), Melburn G Whitmire (VP), Richard G Bacigalupi (Treasurer and Chief Financial Officer), Dyanna M Winn (Secretary)

PRINCIPAL ACTIVITIES: Wholesale trade in drugs, medical and surgical supplies
Parent Company: Bergen Brunswig Corporation
Principal Bank: Wells Fargo Bank
Financial Information:

	$'000
Sales revenues	253,600

No of Employees: 450

SYNTEX CORPORATION
3401 Hillview Avenue, Palo Alto, CA 94304
Tel: (415) 855-5050
Telex: ITT 4997273 syntec pla

Chairman: Albert Bowers (and President and Chief Executive Officer); Vice Chairmen: John H Fried (President Syntex Research); Hans A Wolf (and Chief Administration Officer)
Senior Executive Officers: Paul Freiman (Executive VP), Richard P Powers (Senior VP and Chief Financial Officer), Neil W Flanzraich (Senior VP), Thomas L Gutshall (Senior VP), Alan Jarrett (Senior VP), Anthony A Bourdakis (VP), Burleigh Cook (VP), Stephen W Corless (VP), Kathleen N Gary (VP), William M Gomez (VP), George Holder (VP), Roy Kuramoto (VP), John Munson (VP), Burton L Rogers (VP and Secretary), James E Williams (VP and Treasurer)

PRINCIPAL ACTIVITIES: Manufacture of pharmaceutical products, animal health products, dental equipment, hair care products and soft contact lenses
Principal Bank: The Chase Manhattan Bank
Financial Information:

	$'000
Sales revenues	980,000

No of Employees: 10,500

SYNTREX INC
246 Industrial Way West, Eatontown, NJ 07724
Tel: (201) 542-1500
Telex: 710-722-6604 SYNTREX ENTN

Chairman: Daniel Sinnott (and Chief Executive Officer)
President: James Bruno (and Chief Operating Officer)
Senior Executive Officers: Richard E Jones (Senior VP Development and Manufacturing), Jan C Koontz (Senior VP Marketing and Sales), Robert F Ahearn (VP Manufacturing), William J Alznauer (VP Finance and Administration), James R Folts (VP Corporate Development), Barry C Ross (VP International Sales), Edward H Smith (VP Customer Service), Louis G Turkaly (VP Marketing)

PRINCIPAL ACTIVITIES: Syntrex designs, manufactures, markets and supports office automation products and systems for text editing, electronic filing with automatic retrieval, personal computing and data communications
Trade Names: LEO, VIRGO, SynPro, Always-Up(R), GEMINI, Syntrex's Advanced Legal Software, Genie(R)
Principal Bank: Central Jersey Bank & Trust Co
Financial Information:

	$'000
Sales revenues	55,700

No of Employees: 700

SYRACUSE SUPPLY COMPANY
5921 Court Street Road, Syracuse, NY 13221
Tel: (315) 463-9511
Telex: WUT 937402 syrsupply syr

Chairman: Harold B Scott
President: Stephen J Suhowatsky (and Chief Executive Officer)
Senior Executive Officers: W E Forsthoff (VP), John C Hession (VP), Howard R Phipps (VP and Chief Financial Officer), James M Snyder (Corporate Controller)

PRINCIPAL ACTIVITIES: Wholesale trade in construction machinery and machine tools, handling systems, lift trucks for industry and highways, maintenance services. Provides financing for the lease, purchase or remarketing of new or used equipment. Provides durable medical equipment and respiratory support systems to home health care market
Principal Bank: Chemical Bank
Financial Information:

	Dec 31 1986 $'000
Sales revenues	110,727
Income before taxes	2,144
Net income	1,517
Dividends	303
Dividends per share	$0.28
Earnings per share	$1.40
Common stock	6,863
Retained income	18,715
Shareholders equity	19,598

No of Employees: 570

SYSCO CORPORATION
1390 Enclave Parkway, Houston, TX 77077-2027
Tel: (713) 584-1390
Telex: 910-881-3680 SYSCO CORP HOU
Fax: (713) 584-1188

Chairman: John F Woodhouse
President: Bill M Lindig (and Chief Operating Officer)
Senior Executive Officers: E J Lowrey (Executive VP Finance and Administration), James A Schlindwein (Executive VP-Procurement), Carl J Lange (Senior VP and Controller), Gregory K Marshall (Senior VP)

PRINCIPAL ACTIVITIES: Institutional marketer and distributor of food service products to supermarkets and retail stores; distributor of frozen food products
Principal Bank: First City National Bank of Houston

Financial Information:

	Jun 27 1986 $'000	Jun 28 1987 $'000
Sales revenues	3,655,912	3,172,269
Income before taxes	122,328	107,670
Net income	61,825	58,328
Earnings per share	$1.40	$1.34
Shareholders equity	456,000	397,800

No of Employees: 12,000

SYSCON CORPORATION

2000 Thomas Jefferson Street NW, Washington, DC 20007
Tel: (202) 342 4000

Chairman: Jose J Yglesias (and Chief Executive Officer)
President: Edwin E Tritch (and Chief Operating Officer)
Senior Executive Officers: Michael Burke (VP Projects), William Campbell (VP Administration), George E Christopher (VP and Contract Control Officer), Maurice Cove (Group VP), Nils Ericson (Group VP), John Gingrich (VP Projects), Donald D Horton (VP Eastern Group), Dan Howard (VP), Robert S Kidwell (VP), Robert Owens (VP Research and Development), James Perriello (VP Operations), Christine Reynolds (VP), David Rubin (VP), Alexander Sikorsky (VP Planning), Dennis Vaughan (VP), Harry P Ridenour Jr (Chief Financial Officer and Treasurer)

PRINCIPAL ACTIVITIES: Manufacture of computer systems and related software services
Financial Information:

	$'000
Sales revenues	117,290

SYSTEM INDUSTRIES, INC

560 Cottonwood St, Box 789, Milpitas, CA 95035
Tel: (408) 942-1212
Telex: TWX 910 350 6827 sys ind

Chairman: Eugene R White
President: James K Dutton (and Chief Executive Officer)
Senior Executive Officers: Paul Emery (Executive VP Finance, Chief Financial Officer and Secretary), Jay Greenberg (Senior VP Corporate Planning), Richard LaBarbara (Senior VP), Christopher J Ibbott (Senior VP), D Kent Winton (Senior VP Marketing), Rufus Crow (VP Manufacturing), Steven J Hammerslag (VP Sales)

PRINCIPAL ACTIVITIES: Manufacture of computer peripherals
Principal Bank: Bank of America
Financial Information:

	$'000
Sales revenues	98,650

No of Employees: 760

SYSTEM INTEGRATORS, INC

4111 N Freeway Blvd, Box 13626, Sacramento, CA 95853
Tel: (916) 929-9481
Telex: WUT 172829 sii sac

Chairman: James P Lennane (and President and Chief Executive Officer)
President: Alden L Edwards (and Chief Operating Officer)
Senior Executive Officers: William Aaronson (VP), John L Hatchett (VP Manufacturing), John-Paul Menard (VP), John Tedesco (VP International)

PRINCIPAL ACTIVITIES: Manufacture of data processing equipment
Principal Bank: Bank of America
Financial Information:

	$'000
Sales revenues	60,750

No of Employees: 420

SYSTEMATICS INC

4001 Rodney Parham Road, Little Rock, AR 72212
Tel: (501) 223 5100

Chairman: Walter V Smiley (and Chief Executive Officer)
President: Raymond R Maturi (and Chief Operating Officer)
Senior Executive Officers: Collins A Andrews (Executive VP), Drew P Kelso (Executive VP), David K Gray (Senior VP), Donald B Hatfield (Senior VP), James R Herbig (Senior VP), Joseph M McDaniel (Senior VP), Tom Medley (Senior VP Consulting), Louise M Miller (Senior VP), Michael E Montgomery (Senior VP), James H Wilkins Jr (Senior VP Finance, Law and Secretary)

PRINCIPAL ACTIVITIES: Computer services including programs and data processing
Principal Subsidiaries: New York Systematics Inc; St Joseph Systematics Inc; Systematics of Arkansas
Principal Bank: Northern Bank
Financial Information:

	$'000
Sales revenues	122,600

No of Employees: 2,000

SYSTEMS & COMPUTER TECHNOLOGY CORPORATION

Great Valley Corporate Center, 4 Country View Road, Malvern, PA 19355
Tel: (215) 647 5930
Telex: 800-423-5013

Chairman: Michael J Emmi (and President and Chief Executive Officer)
Senior Executive Officers: Michael Searcy (Senior VP Information Resource Management), Rodney L Everhart (VP Finance and Administration), Michael Chamberlain (VP Software and Technology Services), Richard Blumenthal (VP and General Counsel)

PRINCIPAL ACTIVITIES: Provision of computer and related software services including services to local education systems
Trade Names: SYMMETRY, BANNER, LINK*STATION
Principal Bank: Hamilton Bank, Lancaster, PA
Financial Information:

	Sep 30 1986 $'000	Sep 30 1987 $'000
Sales revenues	41,523	42,037
(Loss) before taxes	(23,377)(1)	(1,460)
Net income (loss)	(14,810)	100
Earnings (loss) per share	($1.08)	$0.01
Common stock(2)	13,696	13,841
Retained income	6,535	6,635
Shareholders equity	40,650	41,002

(1) includes Class Action and Related Settlements Totalling
(2) number of shares outstanding in thousands

Number of Shareholders: 919
No of Employees: 750

SYSTEMS ASSOCIATES INC

412 East Boulevard, Box 26305, Charlotte, NC 28203
Tel: (704) 333 1276

Chairman: John Weil (and President and Chief Executive Officer)
President: Larry R Ferguson (and Chief Operating Officer)
Senior Executive Officers: Berryman L Bourne (Executive VP and Treasurer), Darryl G Bowles (Executive VP), Anthony J Barretta (VP), Walter E Batchelor (VP), Allan W Lackey (VP), Keith H Mallinson (VP and General Manager), Michael G Mayberry (VP and General Manager), Curtis W McCain (VP), Richard Michelotti (VP)

PRINCIPAL ACTIVITIES: Design and marketing of computer systems for hospitals
Principal Bank: Wachovia Bank & Trust Co
Financial Information:

	$'000
Sales revenues	32,890

No of Employees: 360

SYSTEMS ENGINEERING & MANUFACTURING CORPORATION

44 Campanelli Parkway, Stoughton, MA 02702
Tel: (617) 344 1700
Telex: 924328

Chairman: Steven Baker (and President and Chief Executive Officer)
Senior Executive Officers: John J Skorupski (VP, Finance and Administration and Assistant Treasurer), R Stephen Manty (Corporate Controller), Walter D Wekstein (Secretary)

PRINCIPAL ACTIVITIES: Manufacture of waste treatment equipment and machinery for automated plating
Principal Bank: Bank of New England NA
Financial Information:

	Sep 30 1986	Sep 30 1987
	$'000	$'000
Sales revenues	20,631	24,876
Income (loss) before taxes	(1,263)	743
Net income (loss)	(661)	571
Earnings (loss) per share	($0.40)	$0.35
Common stock	20	20
Retained income	8,629	9,201
Shareholders equity	6,380	7,123

No of Employees: 245

SYSTEMS RESEARCH LABORATORIES, INC

2800 Indian Ripple Road, Dayton, OH 45440
Tel: (513) 426-6000
Telex: TWX 810 450 2621

Chairman: Fritz J Russ (and President)
Senior Executive Officers: Kenneth E Jarrett (Senior VP Finance and Administration), Kenneth J Langhout (VP Research and Development), William K Bishoff (VP Legal and Contracts), James E Clifford (VP Defense Electronic Systems), Richard A Johnson (VP Technology), L Stanley Bell (VP Visual and Training Services)

PRINCIPAL ACTIVITIES: Research into electronic systems
Principal Subsidiaries: Synergy, Inc; MBS Associates, Inc
Principal Bank: Miamibank
Financial Information:

	$'000
Sales revenues	51,000

No of Employees: 1,200

T BAR INC

141 Danbury Road, PO Box T, Wilton, CT 06897
Tel: (203) 834 8227

Chairman: A Henry Morgan (and Chief Executive Officer and Treasurer)
President: James B Lambert (and Chief Operating Officer)
Senior Executive Officers: Gerrit J Rohner (Senior VP Operations), Zygmund Reich (Senior VP Engineering), John P Ponziani (Senior VP Finance), Thomas J Infantino (VP Sales), Walter R Jonsson (VP Switching Products Sales), L J Seiden (VP Research and Engineering), Michael J Ushka (VP Marketing Operations)

PRINCIPAL ACTIVITIES: Manufacture of resource management products for computers
Principal Bank: National Bank
Financial Information:

	$'000
Sales revenues	40,415

No of Employees: 550

T M DUCHE NUT COMPANY, INC

See DUCHE, T M, NUT COMPANY, INC

T ROWE PRICE ASSOCIATES INC

See PRICE, T ROWE, ASSOCIATES INC

TAB PRODUCTS CO

1400 Page Mill Road, Palo Alto, CA 94304
Tel: (415) 852-2400
Telex: TWX 910 373 1285 tab prod pla

Chairman: Harry W Le Claire (and Chief Executive Officer)
President: Dennis R Searles (and Chief Operating Officer)
Senior Executive Officers: Frank F DeSafey (VP), K Lein (VP International), David A Price (VP), John Petry (VP), Brandt Brooksky (VP), Mike S Kelton (VP)

PRINCIPAL ACTIVITIES: Manufactures and markets filing systems for the general office
Principal Subsidiaries: Tab Sales Corp International (Virgin Islands); Tab Products of Canada Ltd (Canada); Tab Products (Europa) BV (Netherlands)
Principal Bank: Wells Fargo Bank
Financial Information:

	May 31 1986	May 31 1987
	$'000	$'000
Sales revenues	121,429	123,681
Income before taxes	11,275	13,470
Net income	5,685	6,790
Dividends	994	1,329
Dividends per share	$0.15	$0.20
Earnings per share	$0.85	$1.00
Common stock	5,832	67
Retained income	41,605	47,146
Shareholders equity	47,273	53,180

No of Employees: 950

TACO VILLA INC

1801 Royal Lane, Suite 902, Dallas, TX 75229
Tel: (214) 556 0955

Chairman: J Peter Grace; Vice Chairman: Anwar Soliman
President: B D Cox (and Chief Executive Officer)
Senior Executive Officers: Mark D Scherer (VP, Controller and Chief Financial Officer)

PRINCIPAL ACTIVITIES: Restaurants
Financial Information:

	$'000
Sales revenues	26,000

No of Employees: 4,000

TAFT BROADCASTING CO

1718 Young St, Cincinnati, OH 45210
Tel: (513) 721-1414

Chairman: Charles S Mechem Jr (and Chief Executive Officer)
President: Dudley S Taft (and Chief Operating Officer)
Senior Executive Officers: George E Castrucci (Executive VP Finance), Jack Sander (Executive VP Television), Carl J Wagner (Executive VP Radio and Cable), William T Baumann (Senior VP Planning and Corporate Development), John D Chapman (Senior VP Corporate Affairs), Gregory C Thomas (Senior VP Finance, Chief Financial Officer and Controller), S Donald Urban (Senior VP Administration and Personnel)

PRINCIPAL ACTIVITIES: Television and radio broadcasting services; production of motion pictures; interests in amusement parks
Principal Bank: The Fifth Third Bank

Financial Information:

	$'000
Sales revenues	500,000

No of Employees: 1,600

TALLEY INDUSTRIES, INC

2702 N 44th Street, Phoenix, AZ 85008
Tel: (602) 957-7711
Telex: WUT 668473 tal ind phx

Chairman: William H Mallender (and Chief Executive Officer)
President: Jack C Crim (and Chief Operating Officer)
Senior Executive Officers: Richard H Allen (VP Operations), Donald L Corey (VP Corporate Development), Thomas A Dickey (VP Operations), Edward T Ryan Jr (VP)

PRINCIPAL ACTIVITIES: Manufacture of watches and clocks, clothing, aerospace and industrial products; high technology products for the defense industry
Trade Names: Big Ben, Westclox, Seth Thomas (all registered Trade Marks)
Principal Bank: First Interstate Bank of Arizona
Financial Information:

	$'000
Sales revenues	316,050

No of Employees: 4,400

TAMBRANDS INC

One Marcus Avenue, Lake Success, NY 11042
Tel: (516) 358-8300

Chairman: Edwin H Shutt Jr (and President and Chief Executive Officer)
Senior Executive Officers: John F Bard (Executive VP), Dustin L Allred (Group VP), Peter J Perkinson (VP and Chief Financial Officer), M Richard Wadley (VP Advertising), Harry W Rowe (VP Sales)

PRINCIPAL ACTIVITIES: Manufacturer and marketer of feminine hygiene products, home diagnostics, cosmetics and other personal care products
Trade Names: TAMPAX, Maxithins, First Response, Physicians Formula
Principal Subsidiaries: Tambrands Canada Inc; Tambrands Ltd (UK); Tambrands AG (Switzerland); Tambrands Ireland Ltd; Tambrands France SA; Hygeia Sciences Inc; Physicians Formula Cosmetics Inc; Industria Corporativa Sanitaria SA de CV; Pro Higiene Tambrands Sa; Shenyang Tambrands Company Limited (People's Republic of China)
Principal Bank: Irving Trust Company
Financial Information:

	Dec 31 1986	Dec 31 1987
	$'000	$'000
Sales revenues	486,564	538,861
Net income	69,130	76,601
Dividends	38,279	40,693
Dividends per share	$1.725	$1.83
Earnings per share	$3.12	$3.45
Shareholders equity	260,303	313,914

No of Employees: 4,700

TAMKO ASPHALT PRODUCTS INC

601 N High Street, PO Box 1404, Joplin, MO 64802
Tel: (417) 624-6644
Telex: TWX 910 774 4521

Chairman: Ethelmae C Humphreys (and Secretary)
President: J P Humphreys
Senior Executive Officers: Leland W Browne Jr (Executive VP), Leo J Faneuf (VP manufacturing), James McCauley (VP Sales)

PRINCIPAL ACTIVITIES: Manufacture of asphalt materials and dry felt for roofing
Principal Bank: Mercantile Bancorporation Inc
Financial Information:

	$'000
Sales revenues	50,000

No of Employees: 800

TAMPA SHIPYARDS INC

1130 McCloskey Blvd, Tampa, FL 33605
Tel: (813) 247-1183
Telex: WUT 52637 tampa ship tpa

Chairman: Sam Davis
President: Ralph Anselmi
Senior Executive Officers: H A Fernstrom (Executive VP), Donald Coss (VP Operations), Edward Goerke (VP Personnel), Emory Washington (VP Facilities)

PRINCIPAL ACTIVITIES: Ship maintenance and repair; conversion of ships
Parent Company: American Ship Building Company, Tampa, FL
Principal Bank: The First National Bank of Florida
Financial Information:

	$'000
Sales revenues	100,000

No of Employees: 1,200

TANDEM COMPUTERS INC

19333 Vallco Pkwy, Cupertino, CA 95014
Tel: (408) 725-6000
Telex: WUT 516 745 tamdem

Chairman: T S Perkins
President: J G Treybig (and Chief Executive Officer)
Senior Executive Officers: R C Marshall (Senior VP and Chief Operating Officer), M K Bateman (VP), T A Bechler (VP), J W Chapman (VP), Thomas L Chun (VP and Secretary), G C Eckert (VP), J Jensen (VP), Thomas J Klitgaard (VP and Secretary), L A Laurich (VP), D L McEvoy (VP), Lawrence W McGraw (VP), M C Moore (VP), G L Peterson (VP), David J Rynne (VP and Chief Financial Officer), Stephen C Schmidt (VP), Alois J Strnad (VP Management Information Services), Jeanne D Wohlers (VP and Controller), Barry Young (VP)

PRINCIPAL ACTIVITIES: Manufacture of computers
Principal Bank: Bank of America
Financial Information:

	Sep 30 1985	Sep 30 1986
	$'000	$'000
Sales revenues	624,140	767,793
Net income	34,374	63,766
Earnings per share	$0.82	$1.44
Shareholders equity	420,408	534,680

No of Employees: 5,494

TANDON CORPORATION

20320 Prairie Street, Chatsworth, CA 91311
Tel: (213) 993-6644
Telex: WUT 820819 tandon ud

Chairman: Sirjang L Tandon (and President)
President: Dan H Wilkie (and Chief Operating Officer)
Senior Executive Officers: Stephen Huenemeier (VP Operations), Ranjit Sitlani (VP Planning), Jack Reynolds (VP Management Systems), Steven R Elsner (VP), Hari Apte (VP Singapore Operations), Michel Fromont (VP Marketing), Dennis J Trafecanty (VP and Treasurer)

PRINCIPAL ACTIVITIES: Manufacture of Winchester disk drives and floppy disks
Financial Information:

	$'000
Sales revenues	268,800

No of Employees: 3,500

TANDY BRANDS, INC

550 Bailey Avenue, Suite 400, Fort Worth, TX 76107
Tel: (817) 334-8200

Chairman: Carson R Thompson (and President and Chief Executive Officer)
Senior Executive Officers: Harold DeHart (VP and Treasurer), Britt Jenkins (Executive VP), Timm Mikulenka (VP), Michael J Veitenheimer (Secretary)

PRINCIPAL ACTIVITIES: Manufacture of leather products; retail trade and mail order service in furniture and home improvement products
Principal Subsidiaries: The Bombay Furniture Co of Canada
Principal Bank: InterFirst Bank, Fort Worth
Financial Information:

	$'000
Sales revenues	52,647

No of Employees: 900

TANDY CORPORATION

1800 One Tandy Center, Fort Worth, TX 76102
Tel: (817) 390-3700
Cable: AMATAYAMA
Telex: RCA 203934 TANDY FTW

Chairman: John V Roach (and President and Chief Executive Officer)
Senior Executive Officers: Paul L Hill (Senior VP and Treasurer), Herschel C Winn (Senior VP and Secretary), John H McDaniel (Senior VP and Controller)

PRINCIPAL ACTIVITIES: Retail trade in consumer electronic equipment
Trade Names: Radio Shack, Tandy, Tandy Electronics, McDuff
Principal Bank: Chemical Bank; Bank of Boston
Financial Information:

	Jun 30 1986 $'000	Jun 30 1987 $'000
Sales revenues	3,035,969	3,452,178
Income before taxes	387,014	458,791
Net income	197,659	242,329
Dividends	-	33,693
Dividends per share	-	$0.375*
Earnings per share	$2.22	$2.70
Common stock	95,645	95,645
Retained income	1,301,016	1,344,394
Shareholders equity	1,306,458	1,380,039

*a quarterly dividend of $0.125 was instituted during the second quarter of fiscal 1987

Principal Shareholders: None over 5%
No of Employees: 39,000

TANDYCRAFTS, INC

2727 W Seventh Street, Fort Worth, TX 76101
Tel: (817) 870-0361

Chairman: William H Michero
President: Kenneth L Gregson (and Chief Executive Officer)
Senior Executive Officers: C G Crow (VP and Treasurer), Michael J Walsh (Secretary)

PRINCIPAL ACTIVITIES: Manufacture of leather products and wooden picture frames; retail trade in furnishing products
Principal Subsidiaries: Tandy Leather Co; Magee Co Inc; Casual Concepts Inc
Principal Bank: InterFirst Bank
Financial Information:

	$'000
Sales revenues	72,700

No of Employees: 1,500

TANNER COMPANIES

PO Box 20128, Phoenix, AZ 85036
Tel: (602) 262-1211
Telex: TWX 910 350 2228 tanner cos

Chairman: Maurice R Tanner (and Chief Executive Officer)
President: Robert G Wallace
Senior Executive Officers: D H Tanner (Executive VP and President Central Arizona Region), Richard F Martin (Executive VP Administration), S L Tanner (Senior VP Finance, Secretary and Chief Financial Officer), T E Blizzard (VP, President and General Manager TPAC Prestressed Group), Anthony M Burd (VP), Nancy J Cork (VP), John L Fowler (VP, Senior VP and General Manager United Metro Materials Division), William G Heeter (VP, Senior VP United Metro Materials Division), Bradley E Larson (VP, General Manager Western Arizona Region), Grant P Lungren (VP, Senior VP and General Manager Construction Division), Billy J Murray (VP, President and General Manager Southern Arizona Region), Harold D Salem (VP Safety, Insurance and Union Relations), Royce L Smith (VP, Senior VP Estimating Construction Division), John H Tanner (VP, President Tanner Southwest Inc), Robert G Trehearne (VP, VP Administration Central Arizona Region)

PRINCIPAL ACTIVITIES: Manufacture of materials for building and construction including concrete and concrete products, ready mixed concrete and aggregates
Principal Bank: Valley National Bank of Arizona
Financial Information:

	$'000
Sales revenues	150,000

No of Employees: 2,000

TANNER, O C, CO

1930 S State Street, Salt Lake City, UT 84115
Tel: (801) 486-2430

Chairman: Obert C Tanner; Chief Executive Officer: O D Ostler
Presidents: Lenard T Hilton (Manufacturing), William J Paul (Sales)
Senior Executive Officers: W L Benson (Executive VP)

PRINCIPAL ACTIVITIES: Manufacture of jewelry, service awards and emblems
Principal Bank: First Security Bank of Utah
Financial Information:

	$'000
Sales revenues	80,000

No of Employees: 1,200

TASTY BAKING CO

2801 Hunting Park Avenue, Philadelphia, PA 19129
Tel: (215) 221-8500

Chairman: Philip J Baur Jr
President: Nelson G Harris (and Chief Executive Officer)
Senior Executive Officers: Joseph H Phillips III (VP), John M Pettine (VP Finance and Treasurer)

PRINCIPAL ACTIVITIES: Holding company with interests in the manufacture of bakery products; interests in graphic arts materials
Principal Subsidiaries: Tastykake Inc; Phillips & Jacobs Inc; Buckeye Biscuit Co
Principal Bank: Central Penn National Bank
Financial Information:

	$'000
Sales revenues	239,260

No of Employees: 2,000

TATE & LYLE INC

One Federal Street, Yonkers, NY 10702
Tel: (914) 963-2400

Chairman: Neil M Shaw

President: John C Mitchell
Senior Executive Officers: Samuel I Edelman (Executive VP and Treasurer)

PRINCIPAL ACTIVITIES: Sugar refining
Parent Company: Tate & Lyle PLC, London, UK
Principal Bank: Bank of New York
Financial Information:

	$'000
Sales revenues	360,000

No of Employees: 600

TATUNG COMPANY OF AMERICA, INC

2850 El Presidio Street, Long Beach, CA 90810
Tel: (213) 979-7055
Telex: ITT 4720341 ustatung

Chairman: L C Chen
President: Chieh Sun
Senior Executive Officers: George A Chen (Senior VP Marketing), C C Liu (VP Manufacturing and Production), Steve Wang (VP)

PRINCIPAL ACTIVITIES: Domestic electrical appliances and consumer electronics
Principal Bank: Bank of America

No of Employees: 165

TAUBER OIL CO

55 Waugh Drive, PO Box 4645, Houston, TX 77210
Tel: (713) 869-8700
Telex: TWX 910 881 1645 tauboil hou

Chairman: Orner J Tauber
President: O J Tauber Jr
Senior Executive Officers: William W Kyle (VP Petrochemicals), Richard E Tauber (VP Refined Products), H L Mayes (VP Crude Oil and Refined Products), James E Marquardt (VP Marketing), James N Click (VP Petrochemicals), W L Sallee (VP LPG Products), Theresa P Witt (VP Administration and Public Relations)

PRINCIPAL ACTIVITIES: Wholesale trade in petroleum products, petrochemicals and crude oil
Principal Bank: First City National Bank
Financial Information:

	$'000
Sales revenues	500,000

No of Employees: 35

TAYLOR MACHINE WORKS, INC

Hwy 15 N, Louisville, MS 39339
Tel: (601) 773-3421
Telex: 504159

President: William A Taylor Jr
Senior Executive Officers: James M Ward (VP Finance, Secretary and Treasurer), W A Taylor III (VP and General Manager)

PRINCIPAL ACTIVITIES: Manufacture of mechanical handling equipment
Principal Bank: National Bank of Commerce
Financial Information:

	$'000
Sales revenues	50,000

No of Employees: 500

TAYLOR WINE CO

County Rte 88, Hammondsport, NY 14840
Tel: (607) 569-2111
Telex: WUT 646838 taylor hadt

President: Michael J Doyle
Senior Executive Officers: Andrew C Rice (VP Production), Ralph I Brown (VP Finance and Treasurer), David C Katz (VP)

PRINCIPAL ACTIVITIES: Production of wines
Parent Company: Joseph E Seagram & Sons Inc
Principal Bank: Lincoln First Bank
Financial Information:

	$'000
Sales revenues	80,000

No of Employees: 500

TBC CORPORATION

4770 Hickory Hill Road, Memphis, TN 38115
Tel: (901) 363 8030

Chairman: Irving E Krantzman
President: Marvin E Bruce (and Chief Executive Officer)
Senior Executive Officers: Ronald E McCollough (Senior VP Operations), Bob M Hubbard (Senior VP Purchasing and Engineering), Charles B Quinn Jr (VP and Treasurer), Stanley A Freedman (Secretary), J H deJongh (VP), Kenneth P Dick (VP Sales), G M Tucker (VP)

PRINCIPAL ACTIVITIES: Supply of tires and inner tubes
Financial Information:

	$'000
Sales revenues	389,000

No of Employees: 220

TCA CABLE TV INC

3015 Southeast Loop 323, Tyler, TX 75701
Tel: (214) 595 3701

Chairman: Robert M Rogers (and President and Chief Executive Officer); Vice Chairman: R Don Cowan
Senior Executive Officers: Fred R Nichols (Executive VP, Chief Operating Officer and Secretary), Alton C Rye (Chief Financial Officer and Treasurer)

PRINCIPAL ACTIVITIES: Cable television services
Principal Subsidiaries: Teleservice Corp of America
Principal Bank: First National Bank
Financial Information:

	$'000
Sales revenues	43,620

No of Employees: 440

TCBY ENTERPRISES INC

11300 Rodney Parham, Little Rock, AR 72212
Tel: (501) 225-0349

Chairman: Frank D Hickingbotham (and President)
Senior Executive Officers: Herren C Hickingbotham (Executive VP), Gale Law (VP and Chief Financial Officer), Walter B Winters (VP), Donald W Terry (VP), Harold Walden (VP)

PRINCIPAL ACTIVITIES: Retail of frozen yogurt desserts through over 700 stores
Financial Information:

	$'000
Sales revenues	40,000

TCF BANKING & SAVINGS FA

801 Marquette Ave, Minneapolis, MN 55402
Tel: (612) 370-7000

Chairman: William A Cooper (and Chief Executive Officer)
Senior Executive Officers: Edward M Burger (Executive VP, Treasurer and Chief Financial Officer), Neil I Whitehouse (Executive VP and Secretary), Robert E Evans (Executive VP), Thomas A Cusick (Executive VP), William E Dove (Executive VP), Joseph P Clifford (Executive VP Lending)

PRINCIPAL ACTIVITIES: Savings and loans
Principal Bank: Federal Home Loan Bank of Des Moines

Financial Information:

	Dec 31 1986 $'000
Net income	21,401
Earnings per share	$3.00
Shareholders equity	211,792
Deposits	3,405,961
Total assets	6,517,650

No of Employees: 1,800

TEACHERS INSURANCE & ANNUITY ASSOCIATION-COLLEGE RETIREMENT EQUITIES FUND

730 Third Avenue, New York, NY 10017
Tel: (212) 490-9000
Telex: 961636 CREF invest NYK

Chairman: James G MacDonald (and Chief Executive Officer)
President: Walter G Ehlers
Senior Executive Officers: Russell E Bone (Executive VP), Francis P Gunning (Executive VP), J Daniel Lee Jr (Executive VP), James S Martin (Executive VP), John J McCormack Jr (Executive VP), John A Putney Jr (Executive VP), Donald S Willard (Executive VP)

PRINCIPAL ACTIVITIES: Pensions and insurance (Life, Group Disability and Group Major Medical)
Trade Names: TIAA-CREF
Parent Company: Carnegie Foundation for the Advancement of Teaching (1918)
Principal Banks: Bankers Trust Company; Chase Manhattan; Morgan Guaranty; Citibank
Financial Information:

	Dec 31 1985 $'000	Dec 31 1986 $'000
Premium income*	3,500,000	2,654,607
Investment income	3,100,000	2,778,127

*TIAA-CREF is a non-profit pension and insurance organization serving higher education. Principal policyholders are employees of US colleges, universities, independent schools and related non-profit educational organizations

No of Employees: 2,500

TECHAMERICA GROUP INC

Elkan Estates Industrial Park, Elwood, KS 66024
Tel: (913) 365-9076

Chairman: C W Remington
President: David Hein
Senior Executive Officers: J K Hornbuckle (VP Finance, Secretary and Treasurer), S J Gore (Controller)

PRINCIPAL ACTIVITIES: Manufacture of a range of pharmaceutical products
Principal Subsidiaries: Biologics Corp; Dellen Laboratories Inc; Medico Industries Inc
Principal Bank: First National Bank
Financial Information:

	$'000
Sales revenues	37,000

No of Employees: 200

TECHNIC, INC

1 Spectacle Street, Cranston, RI 02910
Tel: (401) 781-6100
Telex: WUT 927514 technic crnt

Chairman: A Meigel Weisberg
President: H K Shoushanian
Senior Executive Officers: Geo de Q David (VP Sales), L Hurbour (VP West), A M Weisberg (Treasurer)

PRINCIPAL ACTIVITIES: Manufacture of products for the electroplating industry including precious metal compounds
Trade Names: Orosene, Pallaspeed, Trushade, Technispeed-R, Oroflow, Rhodium S-Less
Principal Bank: Fleet National Bank
Financial Information:

	$'000
Sales revenues	80,000+

Principal Shareholders: A Meigel Weisberg; A M Weisberg; Geo de Q David; Geo Haverhill; Lloyd Bass
No of Employees: 100

TECHNICAL EQUITIES CORPORATION

1922 The Alameda, San Jose, CA 95126
Tel: (408) 246-7502

Chairman: Thomas G Wiley (and President and Chief Executive Officer)
President: Paul C Knauff
Senior Executive Officers: Herbert L Barovsky (Senior VP and Chief Financial Officer), Joel S Baylson (VP), H Conrad Blackerby (VP Operations), Joseph C Brooks (VP), Craig A Foster (VP, Treasurer and Chief Financial Officer), Albert J Green (VP), John A Lindberg (VP), Linda A Penny (VP and Associate Secretary), Ray M Wahba (VP), Paul A Wehner (VP and Controller)

PRINCIPAL ACTIVITIES: Management and financial services; real estate; manufacturing interests include rubber and plastic products; metal fabricating and the heat treatment of metals
Principal Subsidiaries: (100% owned unless stated): Badger Paper Co Inc (72.5%); Noel J Brown Manufacturing Co Inc (55%); Coast Fabrication Inc; Downey Heat Treating Company; GTS Engineering Inc; The Hybrid House Inc; Holtz Rubber Company Inc; Idaho Norland Corporation; Junction Devices Inc; Lark Engineering Company Inc; Little Giant Industries Inc; National Heat Treating Co Inc; Spectrum Molding and Engineering; Tamik Manufacturing Inc; Technical Equities Financial Services Inc; Technical Equities Intermountain Inc; Technical Heat Treating Inc (52.4%); Technical Real Estate Investments Inc; West American Rubber Co Inc (55%); Yale Engineering Company (84%); Technical Equities Financial Group Inc; Technical Athletic Programs
Principal Bank: Security Pacific National Bank
Financial Information:

	$'000
Sales revenues	159,700

No of Employees: 1,700

TECHNICAL TAPE, INC

LeFevre Lane, New Rochelle, NY 10801
Tel: (914) 235-1000
Telex: 131506 TUCK IND NRCH

Chairman: Peter Harvey
President: Austin A Iodice (and Chief Executive Officer)
Senior Executive Officers: Michael C McMahon (VP and Chief Financial Officer), James J Daniels (Secretary)

PRINCIPAL ACTIVITIES: Technical Tape, Inc is engaged through its tape manufacturing subsidiaries in one line of business; the production, sale, marketing and distribution of a broad line of pressure sensitive tapes for business, industrial and household use
Principal Subsidiaries: Tuck Industries Inc; Dominion Tape of Canada Ltd; Tuck Tape Ltd (UK); Tuck Tape of Europe Inc (Switzerland)
Principal Bank: National Westminster Bank, USA

Financial Information:

	Dec 31 1985	Dec 31 1986
	$'000	$'000
Sales revenues	66,559	68,179
Income before taxes	3,895	3,858
Net income	2,300	2,017
Earnings per share	$0.49	$0.43
Common stock*	4,618	46,195
Retained income	12,565	14,582
Shareholders equity	22,022	24,103

*outstanding

Principal Shareholders: Peter Harvey
No of Employees: 900

TECHNICOM INTERNATIONAL, INC

5 Research Drive, Shelton, CT 06484
Tel: (201) 926-2000

President: Thomas L Kelly Jr
Senior Executive Officers: William A Merritt Jr (Executive VP), Robert J Luth (Treasurer), Paul B Gaynor (Secretary)

PRINCIPAL ACTIVITIES: Telephones and telecommunications equipment
Parent Company: TIE Communications Inc, Shelton, CT
Principal Bank: Chemical Bank
Financial Information:

	$'000
Sales revenues	138,000

No of Employees: 30

TECHNITROL, INC

8200 Flourtown Avenue, Suite 10, Wyndmoor, PA 19118
Tel: (215) 233-9500
Telex: 8 34245 Technitrol PHA

Chairman: Roy E Hock (and President)
Senior Executive Officers: James J Rafferty Jr, Thomas J Flakoll, Robert J Citrino (Treasurer), J Barton Harrison (Secretary)

PRINCIPAL ACTIVITIES: Manufacturer of: electronic components, transformers, currency counting and handling products, force measuring instruments, scales, springs, electrical contacts, contact assemblies; also perform electronic engineering
Trade Names: Technicount, Automated Cash Drawer, Chatillon
Principal Subsidiaries: John Chatillon & Sons Inc; Advanced Metallurgy Inc; Technitrol International Inc; Technitrol Foreign Sales Corporation
Principal Bank: First Pennsylvania Bank
Financial Information:

	Dec 31 1985	Dec 31 1986
	$'000	$'000
Sales revenues	39,009	37,385
Income before taxes	6,435	6,257
Net income	3,314	3,321
Dividends	646	810
Dividends per share	$0.32	$0.405
Earnings per share	$1.64	$1.65
Common stock	2,003	2,014
Retained income	22,070	22,581
Shareholders equity	19,894	21,285

No of Employees: 563

TECHNOLOGY INC

1115 Talbott Tower, Dayton, OH 45402
Tel: (513) 224-9066

Chairman: Maurice F Krug (and President)
Senior Executive Officers: Ronald T Deger (Executive VP), Betty A Krug (VP Administration), Richard J Swanson (VP and Treasurer), James J Mulligan (Secretary)

PRINCIPAL ACTIVITIES: Research and production of electronic equipment for defense and general industrial use; solid waste handling equipment; fabricated metal products; biotechnology
Principal Bank: Bank One
Financial Information:

	$'000
Sales revenues	67,700

No of Employees: 760

TECH-SYM CORPORATION

10500 Westoffice Drive, Houston, TX 77042
Tel: (713) 785-7790

Chairman: Wendell W Gamel (and President)
Senior Executive Officers: Robert E Moore (VP and Secretary), Coy J Scribner (VP), Ray F Thompson (Treasurer)

PRINCIPAL ACTIVITIES: Production of electronic industrial equipment; property development; timber distribution
Principal Subsidiaries: All Woods/Schroeder Inc; Enterprise Electronics Corp; Metric Systems Corp; Trak Microwave Corp and subsidiaries; Tecom Industries Inc
Principal Bank: Allied Bank of Texas
Financial Information:

	$'000
Sales revenues	91,440

No of Employees: 1,330

TECO ENERGY INC

702 N Franklin St, PO Box 111, Tampa, FL 33601
Tel: (813) 228-4111

Chairman: Hugh L Culbreath (and President)
Senior Executive Officers: David N Campbell (VP), A D Oak (VP Finance and Chief Financial Officer), G Pierce Wood (VP), James K Taggart (VP)

PRINCIPAL ACTIVITIES: Electricity supply
Principal Bankers: NCNB National Bank of Florida
Financial Information:

	$'000
Sales revenues	902,000

No of Employees: 4,000

TECUMSEH PRODUCTS CO

100 E Patterson Street, Tecumseh, MI 49286
Tel: (517) 423-8411
Telex: WUT 223445 tec prod tecu

Chairman: Kenneth G Herrick
President: Todd W Herrick (and Chief Executive Officer)
Senior Executive Officers: H L Hans (Executive VP), R T Heglin (VP), C E Schmid (VP), W O Hermanson (VP), J S Sullivan (VP), L D Thompson (VP), F D Randall (VP), E B Rapin (VP Industrial Relations), J H Foss (VP and Treasurer)

PRINCIPAL ACTIVITIES: Manufacture of refrigeration equipment and components; internal combustion engines
Principal Bank: Manufacturers National Bank
Financial Information:

	Dec 31 1985	Dec 31 1986
	$'000	$'000
Sales revenues	829,033	821,122
Net income	60,054	50,715
Earnings per share	$10.98	$9.27
Shareholders equity	481,493	517,943

No of Employees: 8,000

TEEPAK, INC

1211 W 22nd St, Oak Brook, IL 60521
Tel: (312) 986-6200

President: W J Canavan

Senior Executive Officers: J E Hermesdorf (VP Danville Manufacturing Operation), P B Carter (VP Finance and Secretary)

PRINCIPAL ACTIVITIES: Manufacture of edible cellulose and plastic products for use in the food industry, including sausage casings
Parent Company: Hillside Capital Inc
Principal Bank: Chemical Bank
Financial Information:

	$'000
Sales revenues	194,000

No of Employees: 1,900

TEKTRONIX, INC

4900 SW Griffith Drive, Beaverton, OR 97077
Tel: (503) 627-7111

Chairman: John D Gray; Vice Chairman: Howard Vollum
President: Earl Wantland (and Chief Executive Officer)
Senior Executive Officers: Willem B Velsink (Executive VP), Larry N Choruby (Senior VP Finance), John L Landis (Senior VP), Kevin T Considine (VP), Francis Doyle (VP), David p Friedley (VP), Charles H Frost (VP), Frederick L Hanson (VP), George Kersels (VP), Stanley F Kouba (VP), R Allan Leedy Jr (VP, Secretary and General Counsel), Tom Long (VP), Jon S Reed (VP), Philip J Robinson (VP)

PRINCIPAL ACTIVITIES: Manufacture of control and measurement systems and instruments for industrial, scientific and educational applications; computer peripherals
Principal Subsidiaries: Citra Inc; Grass Valley Group Inc; Grass Valley International Inc; Tektronix Export Corp; VR Information Systems
Principal Bank: Morgan Guaranty Trust Co
Financial Information:

	May 31 1986 $'000
Sales revenues	1,352,212
Net income	39,327
Earnings per share	$1.97
Shareholders equity	837,059

No of Employees: 20,525

TELCO SYSTEMS, INC

333 Twin Dolphin Drive, Redwood City, CA 94065
Tel: (415) 593 9300

Chairman: R L Bowman (and Chief Executive Officer)
President: Jack Shirman (and Chief Operating Officer)
Senior Executive Officers: K L Robertson (VP and Chief Financial Officer), E N Lenowitz (VP and Assistant Secretary)

PRINCIPAL ACTIVITIES: The company has interests in the production of fiber optics and electronic components for use in the telecommunications industry
Principal Bank: Bank of America
Financial Information:

	$'000
Sales revenues	93,050

No of Employees: 900

TELECO OILFIELD SERVICES, INC

105 Pondview Drive, Meriden, CT 06450
Tel: (203) 237-9655

President: R F Spinnler
Senior Executive Officers: T J Collins (Senior VP Operations), J Bogert (VP, Treasurer and Controller), R A Britts (VP Western Region Operations), D Rader (VP Research and Development and Engineering), L G Schoonover (VP Corporate Development), W A Smith (VP Operations Eastern Region), F A Stone (VP and Chief Engineer), H F Wintsch (VP Personnel)

PRINCIPAL ACTIVITIES: Oil and gas industry equipment
Parent Company: Sonat Inc, Birmingham, AL
Principal Bank: Colonial Bank
Financial Information:

	$'000
Sales revenues	52,000

No of Employees: 1,000

TELECOM CORPORATION

1341 West Mockingbird Lane, Suite 1250E, Dallas, TX 75247
Tel: (214) 638-0638

Chairman: Thomas M Gaubert (and President)
Senior Executive Officers: W Grogan Lord (Senior Chairman of the Board), Lawrence W Schumann (Executive VP, Chief Operating Officer and Secretary), Larry T Marek (Senior VP, Treasurer and Assistant Secretary), Eric A Young (Controller)

PRINCIPAL ACTIVITIES: TeleCom Corporation is a holding company engaged primarily in manufacturing and wholesale distribution. Comfort Supply, Inc is a wholesale distributor with a full line of air conditioning and heating equipment as well as installation accessories and backup parts necessary to support the needs of the installing contractor. Comfort distributes the equipment of Rheem and Sanyo Electric, Inc and operates 13 branches in Texas and Louisiana. Allen-Lewis Manufacturing Company imports a broad line of souvenir and novelty items from the Far East which are sold nationally to theme parks, national and state parks and souvenir shops. Meyer Machine Company and its wholly-owned subsidiary, Precision Metal Fabricators, Inc designs and manufactures a broad line of mechanical and air conveying machinery and systems for food, chemical, beverage and similar industries. Meyer's principal products lines include Simplex Conveying Elevators and Vibratory Conveyors. PMF's principal product lines include Air Mass Conveyors, Vertical Air Single Filers and Air Elevators and Lowerators
Trade Names: Simplex Conveying Elevators, ConveyAir, Meyer Plier
Principal Subsidiaries: Allen-Lewis Manufacturing Company; Comfort Supply Inc; Meyer Machine Company; Precision Metal Fabricators Inc
Principal Bank: MBank, Dallas
Financial Information:

	Dec 31 1985 $'000	Dec 31 1986 $'000
Sales revenues	36,794	29,887
Income (loss) before taxes	104	(2,259)
Net income (loss)	2,990	(6,117)
Earnings (loss) per share	$0.81	($1.65)
Common stock	3,707	3,707
Retained income (deficit)	2,990	(3,127)
Shareholders equity	13,981	7,733

No of Employees: 260

TELECOM PLUS INTERNATIONAL INC

8000 North Federal Highway, Boca Raton, FL 33431
Tel: (305) 997 9999

Chairman: Stephen R Cohen (and Chief Executive Officer)
President: Thomas J Burger (and Chief Operating Officer)
Senior Executive Officers: Robert A Kennedy (Executive VP), Ira M Lieberman (Executive VP and Secretary), Malcolm Cheek (VP Corporate Development), Jospeh P Gowan (Chief Financial Officer)

PRINCIPAL ACTIVITIES: Supply of electronic products for the telecommunications industry
Principal Subsidiaries: Tel Plus Communications Inc; Triboro Communications Inc
Principal Bank: European American Bank
Financial Information:

	$'000
Sales revenues	240,930

No of Employees: 2,800

TELE-COMMUNICATIONS, INC

Call Box 22595, Wellshire Station, Denver, CO 80222
Tel: (303) 771-8200

Chairman: Bob Magness
President: John C Malone
Senior Executive Officers: Donne F Fisher (Senior VP and Treasurer)

PRINCIPAL ACTIVITIES: Cable television and motion picture theatres services
Trade Names: TCI
Principal Subsidiaries: United Artists Communications Inc; TCI West Inc; TCI Central Inc; TCI North Central Inc; TCI East Inc; TCI Southeast Inc; TCI Northeast Inc
Principal Banks: The Bank of New York; Toronto-Dominion Bank; Mellon Bank
Financial Information:

	Dec 31 1985	Dec 31 1986
	$'000	$'000
Sales revenues	577,251	645,724
Income (loss) before taxes	(1,322)	118,904
Net income	10,119	72,296
Earnings per share	$0.11	$0.72
Common stock(1)	47,667	97,750(2)
Retained income	62,083	134,379
Shareholders equity(3)	373,807	716,012

(1) $1 par value
(2) 2-for-1 stock split during 1986
(3) including common stock, paid-in capital and retained income

Principal Shareholders: Bob Magness; Various institutional investors; The Kearns-Tribune Corporation
No of Employees: 14,800

TELECREDIT INC

1901 Avenue of the Stars, Los Angeles, CA 90067
Tel: (213) 277 4061

Chairman: Lee A Ault III (and Chief Executive Officer and President)
Senior Executive Officers: Daniel Norwich (Senior VP), Barbara Kheel (VP and Legal Counsel), Charles R McDermott (VP and General Manager Service), Dewaine A Olson (VP and Controller), Donald D Inberg (VP Finance and Chief Financial Officer), Bertram K Massing (Secretary)

PRINCIPAL ACTIVITIES: Operation of credit card services; financial data processing and protection against counterfeting services
Principal Subsidiaries: Light Signatures Inc; Telecredit Collection Service; Telecredit Corp GA; Telecredit Service Center Inc; Telecredit Service Corp
Principal Bank: Bank of America
Financial Information:

	$'000
Sales revenues	121,000

No of Employees: 1,000

TELEDYNE, INC

1901 Avenue of the Stars, Los Angeles, CA 90067-6046
Tel: (213) 277-3311
Cable: TELEDYNE
Telex: 67-4181 TDYAINC LSA; Easylink: 62859812

Chairman: Henry E Singleton
President: George A Roberts (and Chief Executive Officer)
Senior Executive Officers: Leo W Killen (VP), Jerrold V Jerome (VP), G W Rutherford (VP), Charles E Rinsch (VP and Treasurer), Allen H Orbuch (VP), Hudson B Drake (VP), William P Rutledge (VP)

PRINCIPAL ACTIVITIES: Teledyne, Inc is a high technology multiproduct corporation consisting of some 130 individual companies. Teledyne's activities include advanced microelectronic hybrid devices, electromechanical and solid state relays, analog and digital components and systems, high speed general purpose airborne computers, large-scale instrumentation systems, radar, microwave, guidance and navigation equipment, electronic monitoring instruments, electronic warfare systems integration and management and a complete line of military identification (IFF) equipment. Design and manufacture of military fighting vehicles, both wheeled and tracked. The production of specialty metals and alloys. Manufacture of a variety of industrial machines. Also a complete line of internal combustion piston engines and heavy-duty turbocharged diesel engines for military tanks and heavy construction machinery with outputs up to 1500 horsepower. Aerial surveying and mapping. Teledyne also produces a variety of seismic instruments. Production of a variety of electrical equipment including generators and transformers. Among Teledyne's products used more directly by the general public are the well-known Teledyne Water Pik Oral Hygiene Appliances, Shower Massage, Pulsating Showerheads, Instapure, Acoustic Research AR high fidelity speaker systems, electronic components and systems, battery operated hand lanterns, swimming pool and spa heaters, commercial water heaters and residential heating boilers, drafting room instruments, furniture and supplies, diazowhiteprint machines, and a broad line of instruments, equipment and consumable products for professional dental use. Teledyne is also active in casualty and life insurance, and finance
Principal Subsidiaries: Teledyne Acoustic Research; Teledyne Adams; Teledyne Aero-Cal; Teledyne Aerospace Systems; Teledyne Allvac; Teledyne Amco; Teledyne Analytical Instruments; Teledyne Ansonia; Teledyne Avionics; Teledyne AWD; Teledyne Battery Products; Teledyne Big Beam; Teledyne Brown Engineering; Teledyne CAE; Teledyne Camera Systems; Teledyne Canada; Teledyne Cast Products; Teledyne Casting Service; Teledyne Columbia-Summerill; Teledyne Continental Motors-Aircraft Products; Teledyne Continental Motors-General Products; Teledyne Continental Motors-Industrial Products; Teledyne Controls; Teledyne Crittenden; Teledyne Crystalonics; Teledyne Densco; Teledyne Economic Development; Teledyne Efficient Industries; Teledyne Electro-Mechanisms; Teledyne Electronics; Teledyne Energy Systems; Teledyne Engineering Services; Teledyne Exploration; Teledyne Farris Engineering; Teledyne Firth Sterling; Teledyne Geotech; Teledyne Getz; Teledyne Gurley; Teledyne Hanau; Teledyne Hastings-Raydist; Teledyne Howell Penncraft; Teledyne Hydra-Power; Teledyne Hyson; Teledyne Inet; Teledyne Irby Steel; Teledyne Isotopes; Teledyne Kinetics; Teledyne Laars; Teledyne Landis Machine; Teledyne Lewisburg; Teledyne Linair Engineering; Teledyne McCormick Selph; Teledyne McKay; Teledyne MEC; Teledyne Mecca; Teledyne Meria; Teledyne Metal Finishers; Teledyne Metal Forming; Teledyne Microelectronics; Teledyne Microwave; Teledyne Monarch Rubber; Teledyne Movible Offshore; Teledyne National Tracing Paper; Teledyne Neosho; Teledyne Ohio Steel; Teledyne Osco Steel; Teledyne Oster; Teledyne Owen; Teledyne Peer; Teledyne Penn-Union; Teledyne Philbrick; Teledyne Picco; Teledyne Pines; Teledyne Pipe; Teledyne Pittsburgh Tool Steel; Teledyne Portland Forge; Teledyne Post; Teledyne Powder Alloys; Teledyne Precision-Cincinnati; Teledyne Readco; Teledyne Relays; Teledyne Republic; Teledyne Rodney Metals; Teledyne Rotolite; Teledyne Ryan Aeronautical; Teledyne Ryan Electronics; Teledyne Semiconductor; Teledyne Sprague Engineering; Teledyne Still-Man; Teledyne Systems; Teledyne Taber; Teledyne TAC; Teledyne Thermatics; Teledyne Tungsten; Teledyne Vasco; Teledyne Wah Chang Albany; Teledyne Wah Chang Huntsville; Teledyne Water Pik; Teledyne Wirz; Teledyne Wisconsin Motor. Insurance & Finance Companies: Financial Indemnity; Fireside Thrift; General Life Insurance; Pyramid Life Insurance; Trinity Universal Insurance; United Insurance Home Service; United Group Insurance; Coastal Plain Life

Principal Bank: Bank of America
Financial Information:

	Dec 31 1985	Dec 31 1986
	$'000	$'000
Sales revenues	3,256,200	3,241,400
Income before taxes	315,400	230,300
Net income	546,400	238,300
Earnings per share	$46.66	$20.35
Shareholders equity	1,577,400	1,636,600

No of Employees: 47,200

TELEDYNE MONARCH RUBBER
Ten Lincoln Park, Hartville, OH 44632
Tel: (216) 877-1211

President: R M Barrett
Senior Executive Officers: G C Caplea (VP Sales), J M Nelson (VP Human Resources), M F Vincent (VP Finance), T E Wills (VP Materials)

PRINCIPAL ACTIVITIES: Manufacture of rubber and rubber products
Parent Company: Teledyne Industries Inc-Ultimate Holding Company-Teledyne Inc
Financial Information:

	$'000
Sales revenues	115,000

No of Employees: 1,200

TELEFLEX INC
155 S Limerick Road, Limerick, PA 19468
Tel: (215) 948-5100
Telex: WUT 846335 teleser limk

Chairman: Lennox K Black (and Chief Executive Officer)
President: David S Boyer (and Chief Operating Officer)
Senior Executive Officers: John H Remer (Senior VP Administration), John J Sickler (Senior VP and Chief Financial Officer), Ira Albom (President Defense Aerospace Group), Roy C Carriker (President Sermetel Inc), John F Schoenfelder (VP, Secretary and Treasurer), August E Tschanz (VP), Harold L Zuber Jr (VP and Controller)

PRINCIPAL ACTIVITIES: Production of electrical and electronic equipment for aerospace, medical and general industrial applications; plastic and metal components
Principal Subsidiaries: Teleflex International Sales Corp; Teleflex (Canada) Ltd; Sermatech International Inc; Sermatech (UK) Ltd; Sermatech Canada Inc; Sermatech (Germany) GmbH; Hoover Electric Co; Hutson Aerospace Inc; Albert H Suprenant Inc; TFX Engineering Ltd; Merriman-Yacht Specialties Inc; Tele-Aim Inc; Capro Inc; Teleflex Fluid Systems Inc; TFX International Corp; TFX Medical Inc; Aries Medical Inc; Tact Inc; Airfoil Inc; Gator-Gard Inc; Sermetal Technical Services (STS) GmbH; TFX Foreign Sales Corp
Principal Bank: First Pennsylvania Bank
Financial Information:

	$'000
Sales revenues	175,000

No of Employees: 2,200

TELEPHONE & DATA SYSTEMS INC
79 West Monroe Street, Chicago, IL 60603
Tel: (312) 630 1900

Chairman: LeRoy T Carlson (and Chief Executive Officer)
President: LeRoy T Carlson Jr
Senior Executive Officers: D R Brown (VP and Regional Manager Wisconsin), R J Collins (VP and Regional Manager Northeast), George L Dienes (VP Corporate Development), C T Herbert (VP Human Resources), A R Hocker (VP Revenue Requirements), Rudolph E Hornacek (VP Engineering), Lester O Johnson (VP), Robert M Laurion (VP Special Projects), Vincent J Reed (VP Plant), Louis D Reilly (VP Customer Services), Albert E Serewicz (VP), Murray L Swanson (VP Finance)

PRINCIPAL ACTIVITIES: Operation of telephone systems and services
Principal Bank: LaSalle National Bank
Financial Information:

	$'000
Sales revenues	119,100

No of Employees: 1,700

TELEPICTURES CORPORATION
1 Dag Hammarskgold Plaza, New York, NY 10017-2201
Tel: (212) 838 1122

Chairman: Michael Jay Solomon (and Chief Executive Officer); Vice Chairman: David E Salzman
President: Michael N Garin (and Chief Operating Officer)
Senior Executive Officers: Richard T Robertson (Executive VP), J H Goldfarb (Senior VP), James McGillan (Senior VP), Stephen Ross (Senior VP and General Counsel), Arthur Loomis (VP)

PRINCIPAL ACTIVITIES: Production of motion pictures; publication of magazines
Principal Bank: Chemical Bank
Financial Information:

	$'000
Sales revenues	106,760

No of Employees: 340

TELERATE, INC
One World Trade Center, New York, NY 10048
Tel: (212) 938-5200
Telex: TWX 710 5812249 telerate nyk

President: Neil S Hirsch (and Chief Executive Officer)
Senior Executive Officers: John P Terranova (Executive VP), William P Miller (Senior VP), Richard J Cowles (Executive VP Telerate Systems Inc), John D Jessop (Managing Director Interfinet (UK) Ltd, Senior VP Telerate Systems Inc), Scott Rumbold (Senior VP, Telerate Systems Inc), Alan L Zimmermann (Treasurer and Chief Financial Officer), Steven N Rapport (Secretary)

PRINCIPAL ACTIVITIES: Telerate, Inc occupies a growing and highly profitable niche in the worldwide financial markets through the Telerate Financial Information Network. The computerized network provides over 20,000 video pages of prices, rates, market data and news covering major financial markets, including US Treasury and Agency securities, US and world money markets, foreign exchange and Eurodeposits, US mortgage-backed securities and financial futures. Professional traders and investors in the US the UK and more than 40 other countries use the network to receive up-to-the-second information which is not available on any central exchange or ticker. More than 1,000 banks, brokers, dealers and other financial institutions around the world feed their quotations into the system, gaining immediate exposure on over 30,000 video display screens worldwide. Telerate's concentration on its basic business-selling information-has resulted in the steady expansion of innovative services, an increasing subscriber and contributor base and strong earnings growth
Principal Bank: Manufacturers Hanover Trust Co
Financial Information:

	$'000
Sales revenues	210,000

No of Employees: 200

TELESCIENCES, INC
124 Gaither Drive, Mount Laurel, NJ 08054
Tel: (609) 866-1000
Telex: ITT 4761210 ittsimrltn

Chairman: Fred Cohen (and President and Chief Executive Officer)
President: Leopold P Oberst (and Chief Operating Officer)
Senior Executive Officers: Seymour I Hernes (Executive VP, Secretary and Treasurer), G Daly (Senior VP Operations), Alfred E Franks (VP), Alexander S Micko (VP and Controller), Robert P White (VP Engineering, Warminster)

PRINCIPAL ACTIVITIES: Production of telecommunications apparatus including telephones and PABX systems
Principal Subsidiaries: Telesciences Capital Corp; Telesciences UK Ltd; Telesciences International Inc; Telesciences Management Services Inc (83%); URIX Corp
Principal Bank: Mellon Bank (EAST)
Financial Information:

	$'000
Sales revenues	45,300

No of Employees: 500

TELESPHERE INTERNATIONAL, INC

2 Mid-America Plaza, Oak Brook, IL 60181-4451
Tel: (312) 655-2169
Telex: WUT 728354 tsph corp oakr

Chairman: D R Casey
President: Arthur McCauley
Senior Executive Officers: Toomas Mitt (VP Research and Development), E J Ptacek (VP Marketing), Tom Clark (VP and Treasurer), Michael Stewart (VP National Sales), Louis Merdoza (VP Engineering)

PRINCIPAL ACTIVITIES: Telecommunications services and equipment
Principal Bank: Oak Brook Bank
Financial Information:

	$'000
Sales revenues	80,700

No of Employees: 260

TELETYPE CORPORATION

5555 West Touhy Avenue, Skokie, IL 60076
Tel: (312) 982-2000

President: John J Pappas
Senior Executive Officers: Joseph E Sciulli (Executive VP), D M Printz (VP Sales and Marketing), Joseph P Baldwin (Secretary)

PRINCIPAL ACTIVITIES: Manufacture and sale of telecommunications equipment
Parent Company: American Telephone & Telegraph Co, New York, NY
Principal Subsidiaries: Teletype International Sales Corporation
Principal Bank: Northern Trust Company
Financial Information:

	$'000
Sales revenues	416,000

No of Employees: 4,700

TELEVIDEO SYSTEMS, INC

1170 Morse Avenue, Sunnyvale, CA 94088
Tel: (408) 971-0255
Telex: ITT 4745021 tsi sj

Chairman: K P Hwang (and President and Chief Executive Officer)
Senior Executive Officers: William Leung (Executive VP), Elson Park (Executive VP), Howard Oringer (Executive VP and Chief Operating Officer), A D Platt (Senior VP), M G Snyder (Senior VP), Kent Anderson (VP)

PRINCIPAL ACTIVITIES: Manufacture of microcomputers and video display terminals
Principal Bank: Bank of the West
Financial Information:

	$'000
Sales revenues	109,000

No of Employees: 800

TELEX COMPUTER PRODUCTS, INC

6422 E 41st Street, Tulsa, OK 74135
Tel: (918) 627-1111

Chairman: George L Bragg (and President and Chief Executive Officer)
Senior Executive Officers: H L Eberly (Executive VP), Roy L King (Executive VP), R B Davie (Senior VP), Ronald J Wilson (Senior VP), E G Frank (VP and Treasurer), Alfred T Mockett (Senior VP)

PRINCIPAL ACTIVITIES: Manufacture of data processing equipment and peripherals
Trade Names: Telex
Parent Company: Telex Corporation, Tulsa, OK
Principal Bank: Continental Illinois
Financial Information:

	$'000
Sales revenues	520,330

Principal Shareholders: Telex Corporation
No of Employees: 6,500

TELEX CORPORATION (THE)

6422 E 41st Street, Tulsa, OK 74101
Tel: (918) 627-2333
Telex: 492-489

Chairman: Stephen J Jatras
President: George L Bragg
Senior Executive Officers: Ansel Kleiman (Group VP and Chairman of the Board of Telex Communications Inc), J B Bailey (VP, General Counsel and Secretary), E G Frank (VP-Finance and Treasurer)

PRINCIPAL ACTIVITIES: The Company is engaged in two business segments and is organized with a subsidiary for each segment. One subsidiary, Telex Computer Products Inc, designs, manufactures, markets and services a diverse group of computer terminal and peripheral equipment. The other subsidiary, Telex Communications Inc, designs, manufactures and sells a wide range of specialized audio, audio visual and communication-related products
Trade Names: Telex Terminals, Telex Tape Drives, Hy-Gain, Telex, Telex/Magnecord
Principal Subsidiaries: Telex Computer Products Inc; Telex Communications Inc
Principal Bank: Continental Illinois National Bank
Financial Information:

	Mar 31 1986 $'000	Mar 31 1987 $'000
Sales revenues	709,220	840,683
Income before taxes	125,676	150,317
Net income	67,493	77,856
Earnings per share	$4.60	$5.28
Common stock	14,567	14,645
Retained income	217,562	291,799
Shareholders equity	270,282	351,381

No of Employees: 8,000

TELLABS, INC

4951 Indiana Avenue, Lisle, IL 60532
Tel: (312) 969-8800
Telex: 910-695-3530

President: Michael J Birck
Senior Executive Officers: Charles C Cooney (VP, Sales), Peter S Fuss (VP, Engineering), Brian J Jackman (VP, Marketing), James L Melsa (VP, Research), David C Sneider (Secretary and Treasurer)

PRINCIPAL ACTIVITIES: Tellabs Inc, designs, assembles and markets a wide range of telephone-related signaling and transmission products, echo control modules and systems, voice and data multiplexers, teleconferencing and emergency alerting systems and other products used by providers of telecommunication services in public and private voice and data communication networks. These products are marketed (under the Tellabs' name and under private labels) through its own field sales force and selected distributors to independent telephone operating companies, Bell Operating Companies ("BOCs"), non-telephone operating company providers of long distance telephone service ("Other Common Carriers" or "OCCs"), Original Equipment Manufacturers ("OEMs") and business end-users

Trade Names: TELLABS, Xplexer, T-Plexer, T-Coder, T-Carrier Cross-Connect System

Principal Subsidiaries: Tellabs Communications Canada Ltd (Canada); Tellabs (Texas) Inc; Tellabs Export Inc; Tellabs Caribe Inc (Puerto Rico); Best-Tronics Mfg Inc; Tellabs (VI) Inc

Principal Bank: American National Bank and Trust Company of Chicago

Financial Information:

	$'000
Sales revenues	100,000

No of Employees: 1,217

TELOS CORPORATION

3420 Ocean Park Boulevard, Santa Monica, CA 90405
Tel: (213) 450 2424
Telex: (000) 452-9051
Telefax: (213) 450-1705

Chairman: Lin Conger
President: Howard H Metcalfe (and Chief Executive Officer)
Senior Executive Officers: Phil Schaefer (Executive VP), Richard A Brewer (Senior VP), Richard Hansen (Senior VP Finance, Chief Financial Officer, Treasurer and Secretary), Paul E Ostrom (Senior VP), Kenneth A Holcomb jr (VP of Administration), Raymond L Thompson (VP), Steven S Robinson (Controller)

PRINCIPAL ACTIVITIES: Founded in 1969, Telos Corporation today has evolved into a diversified national computer software and hardware services company with more than 1,400 employees in 31 states. Telos provides computer software design, development and maintenance; consulting services; and computer hardware and peripheral equipment maintenance. About 90% of the Company's revenues are derived from US government contracts and subcontracts, primarily with the US Army, the National Aeronautics and Space Administration (NASA) and industrial Aerospace and defense firms. About 80% of revenues are earned on a cost-reimbursement or time-and-materials basis

Trade Names: Telos Field Engineering, Telos Federal Systems, Telos Consulting Services, Telos Aerospace Systems, Telos Systems Development

Principal Subsidiaries: DMA, Inc

Principal Bank: First Interstate Bank of California

Financial Information:

	Mar 31 1986	Mar 31 1987
	$'000	$'000
Sales revenues	69,222	78,787
Income before taxes	3,033	5,122
Net income	1,077	2,586
Earnings per share	$0.36	$0.73
Common stock	6,641	6,683
Retained income	3,862	6,448
Shareholders equity	10,503	13,131

Principal Shareholders: Lin Conger
No of Employees: 1,600

TELSMITH DIVISION

PO Box 723, Milwaukee, WI 53201
Tel: (414) 962-5710

Senior Executive Officers: R G Stafford (VP Operations and Engineering)

PRINCIPAL ACTIVITIES: Manufacture of mining and quarrying equipment

Parent Company: Barber-Greene Company, Aurora, IL
Principal Bank: Marshall & Ilsley Bank
Financial Information:

	$'000
Sales revenues	25,000

No of Employees: 200

TELXON CORPORATION

3330 West Market Street, Akron, OH 44313
Tel: (216) 867 3700

Chairman: Robert F Meyerson
President: Raymond D Meyo (and Chief Executive Officer and Chief Operating Officer)
Senior Executive Officers: John W Shumar (Executive VP), William E Beller (VP Systems), Ronald D Bufton (VP Operations), Donna H DeLamatter (VP and Secretary), Steven A Galvanoni (VP National Sales), Robert G Hess (VP Software Applications), George D Kostell (VP Engineering), Raj Kumar (VP Research and Development), Eugene A Novak (VP Finance and Treasurer), Gary J Sniadak (VP Field Services)

PRINCIPAL ACTIVITIES: Manufacture of a range of microcomputer equipment

Principal Bank: BancOhio National Bank
Financial Information:

	$'000
Sales revenues	64,020

No of Employees: 650

TEMPEL STEEL CO

5990 W Touhy Avenue, Niles, IL 60648
Tel: (312) 282-9400
Telex: 255246 TEMPEL NILE

President: Tempel Smith Jr
Senior Executive Officers: Stephen A Foerster (VP, of Corporate Planning), Ron Bailitz (VP Finance), Bob Breither (Transformer Sales Manager), Dick Mandahl (Motor Sales Manager)

PRINCIPAL ACTIVITIES: Manufacturer of magnetic steel; laminations for electric motors; transformers, alternators, ballasts

Trade Names: TEMPCOR, TEMPEL
Principal Subsidiaries: Portage Tool Company
Principal Bank: Continental Illinois National Bank

No of Employees: 1,100

TEMPLE-EASTEX INC

PO Box Drawer N, Diboll, TX 75941
Tel: (409) 829-5511
Telex: WUT 511078 temple eastex

Chairman: Joe C Denman Jr (and President and Chief Executive Officer)
Senior Executive Officers: David Ashcraft (Group VP), Harold Maxwell (Group VP), Glenn Chancellor (Group VP), W W McDonald (VP), M R Warner (VP), Robert G Luttrell (VP Administration and Treasurer), George S Vorpahl (VP Law)

PRINCIPAL ACTIVITIES: Timber and timber processing; production of pulp and paper

Parent Company: Temple-Inland Inc, Diboll, TX
Principal Bank: Republic Bank Dallas

Financial Information:

	$'000
Sales revenues	560,000

No of Employees: 5,200

TEMPLE-INLAND INC

303 S Temple Drive, Diboll, TX 75941

Tel: (409) 829-2211

Chairman: Arthur Temple

Directors: Clifford J Grum (and Chief Executive Officer)

Senior Executives: Clinton G Ames Jr (Executive VP), Joe C Denman Jr (Executive VP), Wayne W McDonald (Executive VP and Chief Financial Officer)

PRINCIPAL ACTIVITIES: Holding company with interests in paperboard manufacture and the production of packaging materials

Principal Bankers: Republic Bank Dallas

Financial Information:

	Dec 31 1985	Dec 31 1986
	$'000	$'000
Sales revenues	1,243,125	1,328,800
Net income	85,090	80,800
Earnings per share	$3.50	$2.64
Shareholders funds	863,705	928,900

No of Employees: 9,800

TEMPLETON, KENLY & CO

7No15 York Road, Bensenville, IL 60106

Tel: 312 865-1500

Telex: WUI 6871027 tmplen

Chairman: John B Rhinelander

President: Gordon H Fromm

Senior Executive Officers: Dennis Keller (Chairman of Executive Committee), Harry M Sloate (Senior VP), Jeffrey K Clemmens (President and General Manager Miller Fluid Power Division), Ralph Mueller (President and General Manager Simplex Division)

PRINCIPAL ACTIVITIES: Manufacture of lifts and conveyors; mechanical handling equipment; industrial machinery

Principal Bank: Northern Trust Co

Financial Information:

	$'000
Sales revenues	55,000

No of Employees: 570

TENNANT COMPANY

701 N Lilac Drive, Minneapolis, MN 55440

Tel: (612) 540-1200

Telex: TWX 910 3508793 tennantco

President: Roger L Hale (and Chief Executive Officer)

Senior Executive Officers: Lyle D Delwiche (Senior VP), Douglas R Hoelscher (VP Manufacturing), Richard A Snyder (VP, Treasurer and Chief Finance Officer), Robert D Langford (VP, Secretary and General Counsel)

PRINCIPAL ACTIVITIES: Manufacture of floor cleaning machinery and maintenance materials; general commercial and industrial surface cleaning equipment; floor coatings

Principal Subsidiaries: Tennant Trend Inc; Contract Applications Inc; Tennant NV; Tennant Maintenance Systems

Principal Bank: First National Bank of Minneapolis

Financial Information:

	Dec 31 1985	Dec 31 1986
	$'000	$'000
Sales revenues	136,512	151,497
Income before taxes	15,149	16,808
Net income	8,722	8,816
Dividends	4,899	4,937
Dividends per share	$0.92	$0.93
Earnings per share	$1.63	$1.65
Common stock	1,998	1,992
Retained income	57,790	61,401
Shareholders equity	59,912	65,356

No of Employees: 1,728

TENNECO AUTOMOTIVE

108 Wilmot Road, Deerfield, IL 60015

Tel: (414) 632-8871

President: James K Ashford (Chief Executive Officer)

Senior Executive Officers: James R Breen (Executive VP International), Ronald G Foster (Senior VP, General Manager Monroe), John P Reilly (Senior VP, General Manager Walker), A Davidson (VP), Paul R Frank (VP Sales and Marketing Monroe), J Kendrick (VP), Richard W Krant (VP Marketing), Ron J Martoia (VP Original Equipment Sales), J Mills (VP), Doug N Pearson (VP Development and Planning), William J Rankin (VP Manufacturing Monroe), Fred Shaddick (VP Sales Monroe), Keith M Thompson (VP Sales and Marketing, Walker), Richard L Touve (VP Finance)

PRINCIPAL ACTIVITIES: Manufacture of automotive components including shock absorbers and exhaust systems

Parent Company: Tenneco Inc, Houston, TX

Financial Information:

	$'000
Sales revenues	900,000

No of Employees: 12,000

TENNECO CORPORATION

PO Box 2482, Houston, TX 77001

Tel: (713) 757-2131

Telex: WUT 762283 tenneco hou

Chairman: J L Ketelsen (and President)

Senior Executive Officers: Robert T Blakeley (VP), J L Daily Jr (VP), Peter Menikoff (VP), M W Meyer (VP), Kenneth W Reese (VP)

PRINCIPAL ACTIVITIES: The company has interests in gas and oil exploration and production; petrochemicals and related products; real estate management

Parent Company: Tenneco Inc, Houston, TX

Principal Bank: Morgan Guaranty Trust Co

Financial Information:

	$'000
Sales revenues	9,600,000

No of Employees: 111,000

TENNECO INC

Tenneco Building, Houston, TX 77002

Tel: (713) 757-2131

Telex: WUT 762283 tenneco hou

Chairman: James L Ketelsen (and Chief Executive Officer)

President: John P Diesel

Senior Executive Officers: Joe B Foster (Executive VP), Allen T McInnes (Executive VP), Kenneth W Reese (Executive VP), Gordon B Bonfield Jr (Senior VP and Group Executive), C W Rackley (Senior VP and Group Executive), Robert T Blakely (Senior VP and Chief Financial Officer), Raymond H Marks (Senior VP), Kenneth L Otto (Senior VP), Jack H Ray (Senior VP), Walter W Sapp (Senior VP and Secretary)

PRINCIPAL ACTIVITIES: Oil and gas exploration and production; refining and distribution; chemicals; construction

of agricultural and building machinery; interests in packaging materials including paperboard, shipbuilding, real estate and insurance
Principal Subsidiaries: Tenneco Corporation; Tenneco Oil Exploration and Production; Tennessee Gas Transmission Co; JI Case Co; Tenngasco Corp; Albright & Wilson Ltd (UK); Newport News Shipbuilding and Dry Dock Co; Packaging Corpn of America; Tenneco West Inc; Philadelphia Life Insurance Co; Southwestern Life Insurance Co; Southwestern General Life Insurance Co; Tenneco Oil Processing & Marketing; Tenneco Automotive; Tenneco Europe; Tenneco Minerals; Tenneco Synfuels; Tenneco International Holdings Ltd
Principal Bank: Republic Bank
Financial Information:

	Dec 31 1986 $'000
Sales revenues	14,558,000
Net (loss)	(39,000)
(Loss) per share	($0.72)
Shareholders equity	4,412,000

No of Employees: 98,000

TENNECO OIL COMPANY

PO Box 2511, Houston, TX 77001
Tel: (713) 757 2131
Telex: WUT 762283 tenneco hou

Chairman: C W Rackley
President: Philip Oxley
Senior Executive Officers: Ralph S Cunningham (Executive VP), C W Nance (Executive VP), S D Cheseboro (Senior VP), H H Daniel (Senior VP), A R Dudley (Senior VP), D B Johnson (Senior VP), Ralph J Maynard (Senior VP, General Counsel and Assistant Secretary), L L Parish (Senior VP and Assistant Secretary), Charles M Rampacek (Senior VP), D S Taylor (Senior VP), Glen E Taylor (Senior VP and Associate General Counsel)

PRINCIPAL ACTIVITIES: Production of oil and gas; related chemicals
Parent Company: Tenneco Inc through Tenneco Corp
Principal Bank: Continental Illinois National Bank & Trust Co of Chicago
Financial Information:

	$'000
Sales revenues	3,700,000

No of Employees: 10,000

TENNESSEE VIRGINIA ENERGY CORPORATION

108 West Tenth Avenue, Johnson City, TN 37601
Tel: (615) 926 7171

Chairman: Paul C Walser
President: A E Johnson (and Chief Executive Officer)
Senior Executive Officers: C W Guy (VP, Secretary and Treasurer)

PRINCIPAL ACTIVITIES: Distribution of natural gas
Principal Bank: Hamilton Bank of Upper East Tennessee
Financial Information:

	$'000
Sales revenues	47,480

No of Employees: 160

TENSION ENVELOPE CORPORATION

19th & Campbell Streets, Kansas City, MO 64108
Tel: (816) 471-3800
Telex: WUT 857981 tension kcmo

Chairman: E B Berkley (and President)
Senior Executive Officers: Walter L Hiersteiner (Executive VP), Kenneth H Krueger (VP Sales), Larry R Denton (VP Finance), Richard Kranz (VP Manufacturing)

PRINCIPAL ACTIVITIES: Production of envelopes
Principal Bank: Commerce Bank of Kansas City
Financial Information:

	$'000
Sales revenues	125,000

No of Employees: 1,600

TERADYNE INC

321 Harrison Avenue, Boston, MA 02118
Tel: (617) 472-2700
Telex: TWX 710 3211552 teradynes bsn

Chairman: Alexander d'Arbeloff (and President)
Senior Executive Officers: R Ashdown (VP), G Chamillard (VP), George d'Arbeloff (VP), Loren Eaton (VP), Windsor Hunter (VP), Lennart Johnson (VP), Joseph B Lassiter III (VP), Thomas Newman (VP), D O'Connell (VP), James Prestridge (VP), Owen Robbins (VP), Edward Rogas (VP), Frederick Van Veen (VP Corporate Relations), S Osattin (Treasurer)

PRINCIPAL ACTIVITIES: Manufacture of electronic measuring and testing equipment and electrical components
Principal Bank: First National Bank of Boston
Financial Information:

	$'000
Sales revenues	306,000
*number of shares outstanding in thousands	

No of Employees: 4,300

TERMINAL DATA CORPORATION

21221 Oxnard Street, Woodland Hills, CA 91367
Tel: (818) 887 4900

Chairman: Michael Rothbart (and President)
President: James R Schwartz (and Chief Operating Officer)
Senior Executive Officers: Herman W Pass (Senior VP Special Projects), Sharon Franzen (VP and Secretary), Samuel Greene (VP Marketing and Sales), Stephen Shelton (VP Finance)

PRINCIPAL ACTIVITIES: Manufacture of high speed computer controlled micrographic and video based information systems; microfilm duplicating equipment
Principal Subsidiaries: Terminal Data International Sales Corp; TDC Properties Corp; Terminal Data Service Corp
Principal Bank: Bank of America NT & SA
Financial Information:

	$'000
Sales revenues	34,850

No of Employees: 460

TERRA CHEMICALS INTERNATIONAL, INC

600 Fourth Street, Sioux City, IA 51101
Tel: (712) 277-1340
Telex: TWX 910 9681700 terrachm a sou

Chairman: Reuben F Richard
President: William T Dible
Senior Executive Officers: P D Foster (VP Retail Sales), Raymond W Nason (VP Finance), Charles G Nevaril (VP Supply), James F Wokosin (VP Information Systems), Gene A Hallauer (VP Human Resources)

PRINCIPAL ACTIVITIES: Production of chemicals and feedstuffs for the agricultural industry
Parent Company: Inspiration Resources Corporation, New York, NY
Principal Bank: Citibank
Financial Information:

	$'000
Sales revenues	300,000

No of Employees: 1,000

TERSON CO, INC

310 S Michigan Avenue, Chicago, IL 60604
Tel: (312) 461-9111

Chairman: Joe A Masterson (and Chief Executive Officer)
President: Richard A Peterson (and Chief Operating Officer)
Senior Executive Officers: Martin Zoberman (VP Finance, Secretary and Treasurer)

PRINCIPAL ACTIVITIES: Manufacture of confectionery products; meat processing; milling; snacks
Parent Company: Terson Holdings Ltd
Principal Bank: CitiCorp
Financial Information:

	$'000
Sales revenues	150,000

No of Employees: 1,100

TESORO PETROLEUM CORPORATION

8700 Tesoro Drive, San Antonio, TX 78286
Tel: (512) 828-8484
Telex: WUT 767317 tesoro snt

Chairman: Robert V West Jr (and Chief Executive Officer); Vice Chairman: Z D Bonner
President: Dennis F Juren
Senior Executive Officers: J P Schmalz (Executive VP), Jack Charles (Group VP Oilfield Services), James F Smith (Group VP Refining and Crude Oil), Milton E Young (Group VP), John T Tagliarino (Senior VP Refining), Donald N Bonacci (Senior VP Administration), James W Queen (Senior VP and Controller), M R Stewart (Senior VP), Perry W Woofter (Senior VP), William M Sims (VP Financial Relations)

PRINCIPAL ACTIVITIES: Exploration and production of oil and gas; refining and related services
Principal Subsidiaries: Tesoro Alaska Petroleum Co; Tesoro Bolivia Petroleum Co; Tesoro Crude Oil Co; Tesoro Drilling Co; Tesoro Gasoline Marketing Co; Tesoro Indonesia Petroleum Co; Land & Marine Rental Co; Tesoro Alaska Pipeline Co; Tesoro Petroleum Distributing Co; Tesoro Pipeline Co; Tesoro Refining, Marketing & Supply Co; Tesoro United Kingdom Co; Tesoro Natural Gas Co
Principal Bank: Manufacturers Hanover Trust Co
Financial Information:

	Sep 30 1985 $'000	Sep 30 1986 $'000
Sales revenues	2,293,051	1,472,789
Net (loss)	(87,028)	(124,842)
(Loss) per share	($7.01)	($9.76)
Shareholders equity	337,349	197,543

No of Employees: 2,300

TEXACO INC

2000 Westchester Avenue, White Plains, NY 10650
Tel: (914) 253-4000
Telex: ITT 427763 texaco

President: James W Kinnear (and Chief Executive Officer)
Chairman: Alfred C DeCrone Jr
Senior Executive Officers: William S Barrack Jr (Senior VP), James L Dunlop (Senior VP), Robert R McCall (Senior VP), Willis B Reals (Senior VP), Roland M Routhier (Senior VP), William K Tell Jr (Senior VP), Elton G Yates (Senior VP), Richard G Brinkman (Senior VP and Chief Financial Officer), Paul B Hicks Jr (Senior VP), William C Weitzel Jr (Senior VP and General Counsel), David C Crickelair (Treasurer), Carl B Davidson (VP and Secretary), Albert J Bradford (Comptroller)

PRINCIPAL ACTIVITIES: Exploration and production of oil and gas; refining and distribution of oil and gas products
Principal Subsidiaries: Texaco USA:- Getty Oil Company; Riverway Gas Pipeline Company; Texaco Pipeline Inc; Texaco Producing Inc; Texaco Refining and Marketing Inc; Texaco Trading and Transportation Inc. Texaco Europe:-Deutsche Texaco AG (Germany); Norsk Texaco Oil A/S (Norway); SA Texaco Belgium NV (Belgium); SA Texaco Petroleum NV (Belgium); Texaco A/S (Denmark); Texaco Britain Limited (UK); Texaco Denmark Inc (Denmark); Texaco Investments (Netherlands), Inc (Netherlands); Texaco (Ireland) Limited (Eire); Texaco Limited (UK); Texaco North Sea UK Company (UK); Texaco Oil Aktiebolag (Sweden); Texaco Petroleum Maatschappij (Nederland) BV (Netherlands). Texaco Latin America/West Africa:- Refineria Panama SA (Panama); Refineria Texaco de Honduras, SA (Honduras); Texaco Brasil SA-Produtos de Petroleo (Brazil); Texaco Caribbean Inc; Texaco Nigeria Limited (Nigeria); Texaco Panama Inc (Panama); Texaco Petroleum Company; Texaco Trinidad, Inc; Texas Petroleum Company. Texaco Chemical:- Texaco Butadiene Company; Texaco Chemical Company. Texaco Canada: Texaco Canada Inc; Texaco Canada Resources Ltd; Texco Canada Resources. Other significant subsidiaries not handled by the above divisions:- Getty Marine Corporation (Liberia); Texaco International Trader Inc; Texaco Overseas Holdings Inc; Texaco Overseas Petroleum Company; Texaco Overseas Tankship Ltd (UK)
Financial Information:

	Dec 31 1985 $'000	Dec 31 1986 $'000
Sales revenues	46,297,000	31,613,000
Income before taxes	3,989,000	1,820,000
Net income	1,233,000	725,000
Dividends	730,000	722,000
Dividends per share	$3.00	$3.00
Earnings per share	$5.11	$3.01
Common stock(1)	238,121	240,523
Common stock(2)	238,921	242,274
Retained income	12,879,000	12,882,000
Shareholders equity	13,628,000	13,739,000

(1) average shares outstanding in thousands
(2) shares outstanding year end in thousands

No of Employees: 51,978

TEXAS AIR CORPORATION

4044 Capital Bank Plaza, Houston, TX 77002
Tel: (713) 658-9588

President: Francisco A Lorenzo (and Chief Executive Officer); Vice Chairman: Frank Borman
Senior Executive Officers: Charles T Goolsbee (Senior VP and General Counsel), Robert D Snedeker (Senior VP and Treasurer), Cynthia R Creager (VP), Larry S Dickenson (VP), J John Keenan (VP), Clark H Onstad (VP)

PRINCIPAL ACTIVITIES: Air transportation services
Principal Bank: Chase Manhattan Bank
Financial Information:

	Dec 31 1985 $'000	Dec 31 1986 $'000
Sales revenues	1,944,190	4,406,897
Net income	90,980	72,703
Earnings per share	$5.03	$1.75
Shareholders equity	-	803,869

No of Employees: 68,000

TEXAS AMERICAN BANCSHARES INC

PO Box 2050, Fort Worth, TX 76113
Tel: (817) 338-8671
Telex: TAB758275FTW

Chairman: Joseph M Grant
President: L O Brightbill III
Senior Executive Officers: Gary W Cage (Executive VP and Chief Financial Officer), Gene Gray (Executive VP, Credit), Robert L Herchert (Executive VP, Human Resources), Bill Lucas (Executive VP), A James Grant (Executive VP, Regional Manager Dallas), Joseph E Burns (Senior VP, Economist), Sam Fuller (Senior VP and Auditor), Jack L Gregory (Senior

VP and Controller), Bruce Petty (Senior VP Trust), Bob G Scott (Senior VP and Treasurer), Ann Quinn (Senior VP, Marketing), Gene E Miller Jr (Senior VP), Thomas C Sassman (Senior VP)

PRINCIPAL ACTIVITIES: Texas American Bancshares Inc ("TAB"), a multi-bank holding company with headquarters in Fort Worth, Texas, owns thirty-one banks located in the Fort Worth/Dallas Metroplex (14), Houston (5), Austin (2), Longview, Amarillo, Breckenbridge, Denison, Fredeicksburg, Levelland, McKinney, Midland, Temple and Wichita Falls. The Company's member banks are in the general commercial banking business. Other wholly-owned subsidiaries provide credit life insurance, investment advisory services and data processing and bank operations services

Principal Subsidiaries: Texas American Bank/Fort Worth, NA; Texas American Bank/Dallas; Texas American Bank/Galleria, NA; Texas American Bank/Amarillo, NA; Texas American Bank/West Side; Texas American Bank/Austin; Texas American Bank/Riverside; Texas American Bank/Levelland; Texas American Bank/Midland; Texas American Bank/McKinney, NA; Texas American Bank/Duncanville, NA; Texas American Bank/Denison, NA; Texas American Bank/Fredericksburg, NA; Texas American Bank/Breckenridge, NA; Texas American Bank/LBJ; Texas American Bank/Southwest; Texas American Bank/Prestonwood, NA; Texas American Bank/Westlake, NA; Texas American Bank/Fondren; Texas American Bank/Longview, NA; Texas American Bank/Spring Branch; Texas American Bank/Temple, NA; Texas American Bank/Forum; Texas American Bank/Wichita Falls; Texas American Bank/Farmers Branch; Texas American Bank/Greater Southwest; Texas American Bank/Town North, NA; Texas American Bank/Gulfway, NA; Texas American Bank/Richardson, NA; Texas American Bank/Plano, NA; Texas American Services Inc; Texas American Investment Management Inc; Texas American Life Insurance Company; American AgCredit Corporation

Principal Bank: Texas American Bank/Fort Worth, NA

Financial Information:

	Dec 31 1986 (12 mths) $'000	Jun 30 1987 (6 mths) $'000
Income(1)	607,939	270,564
(Loss) before taxes	(117,643)	(6,129)
Net (loss)	(115,159)	(6,129)
Dividends	9,095	-
Dividends per share	$0.83	-
(Loss) per share	($10.51)	($0.56)
Common stock(2)	10,962	11,036
Retained earnings	100,407	94,278
Total shareholders equity	257,183	253,121
Deposits	5,152,193	4,790,393
Total assets	5,985,740	5,264,841

(1) Interest and other income
(2) thousands

No of Employees: 2,990

TEXAS AMERICAN BANK/FORT WORTH, NA

500 Throckmorton, Box 2050, Fort Worth, TX 76113
Tel: (817) 338-8011
Telex: WU 758275

Chairman: Joseph M Grant (and Chief Executive Officer)
President: Gene Gray
Senior Executive Officers: Martin Bowen (Executive VP Retail Banking), Wayne C Jordan (Executive VP Special Industries), John J Koslow (Executive VP Commercial Division), Royce L Lee (Executive VP Real Estate), B W Lucas (Executive VP Investment Division), Bruce Petty (Executive VP), Ann Quinn (Executive VP Marketing Group)

PRINCIPAL ACTIVITIES: Banking and related services
Parent Company: Texas American Bancshares Inc, Fort Worth, TX

No of Employees: 1,000

TEXAS AMERICAN ENERGY CORPORATION

300 West Wall Avenue, Suite 400, Midland, TX 79701
Tel: (915) 683 4811

Acting Chairman: David B Blanchard (and President)
Senior Executive Officers: John W Galuchio Jr (VP)

PRINCIPAL ACTIVITIES: Distribution of natural gas
Principal Subsidiaries: Texas American Oil Corp; Texas American Petrochemicals; Western Kentucky Gas Resources Co
Principal Bank: InterFirst Bank
Financial Information:

	$'000
Sales revenues	185,700

No of Employees: 600

TEXAS AUSTIN INDUSTRIES, INC

PO Box 1827, Austin, TX 78767
Tel: (512) 476-6407

Chairman: Wm C Milstead
President: Kenneth P Johnson
Senior Executive Officers: John Davol (Executive VP and Treasurer), T N Morris Jr (VP and General Manager CALCO), Ron Lindsay (VP and General Manager Milstead), C R Messer (VP and General Manager Security)

PRINCIPAL ACTIVITIES: Timber products and building materials; distribution of heating, ventilation and industrial equipment
Parent Company: Calcasieu Lumber Co, Austin, TX
Principal Bank: First City National Bank
Financial Information:

	$'000
Sales revenues	60,000

No of Employees: 400

TEXAS BITULITHIC CO

PO Box 10365, Dallas, TX 75207
Tel: (214) 741-3531

President: J Melhorn (Divisional)
Senior Executive Officers: B Kemp (Divisional VP), B C Ragsdale (Divisional VP), K C Rochelle (Divisional VP), E W Webb (Divisional VP)

PRINCIPAL ACTIVITIES: Production of bituminous construction materials; civil engineering
Principal Bank: InterFirst Bank Dallas
Financial Information:

	$'000
Sales revenues	50,000

No of Employees: 600

TEXAS BOOT DIVISION

Western Avenue, Hartsville, TN 37074
Tel: (615) 374-2211

Chairman: Harry Vise (and President and Chief Executive Officer)
Senior Executive Officers: B Reed (Executive VP Manufacturing), D Strayfinger (Executive VP Branded Sales), L Hubbard (Senior VP Styles and Research), Donald Taylor (VP and Chief Financial Officer), Hugh Hankins (VP Volume Sales)

PRINCIPAL ACTIVITIES: Manufacture of cowboy boots
Parent Company: United States Shoe Corporation, Cincinnati, OH
Principal Bank: Commerce Union Bank

Financial Information:

	$'000
Sales revenues	50,000

No of Employees: 1,200

TEXAS CITY REFINING, INC

Box 1271, Texas City, TX 77592-1271
Tel: (713) 945-4451
Telex: TWX 910 8804109; TLX 765454 (TEXCITYTK TECY)

Chairman: W A Hiller; Vice Chairman: G A James
President: A T Rowe (and Chief Executive Officer)
Senior Executive Officers: J L Stratman (Senior VP), R G Sherman (VP Administrative Services), R L Williams (VP Finance), R L Youngblood (VP Refining)

PRINCIPAL ACTIVITIES: Oil refining and petroleum product marketing
Trade Names: TCR
Parent Company: Agway Inc through Agway Petroleum Corp
Principal Subsidiaries: TCR, Inc
Principal Bank: Chase Manhattan Bank, New York
Financial Information:

	Mar 31 1986	Mar 31 1987
	$'000	$'000
Sales revenues	885,000	750,000

No of Employees: 480

TEXAS COMMERCE BANCSHARES, INC

712 Main, Houston, TX 77252
Tel: (713) 236-4865
Telex: WUT 77548 texcombk hou a

Chairman: Ben F Love (and Chief Executive Officer); Vice Chairmen: James B Goodson, Marc J Shapiro, R Bruce LaBoon
Senior Executive Officers: John L Adams (Executive VP), Donald L Hawk (Executive VP), Robert C Hunter (Executive VP), W Merriman Morton (Executive VP), David P Shearer (Executive VP), Kenneth H Thorn (Executive VP), Kenneth L Tilton (Executive VP), John P Townley (Executive VP), Marshall C Tyndall Jr (Executive VP), H Michael Tyson (Executive VP)

PRINCIPAL ACTIVITIES: Banking and financial services
Parent Company: Chemical New York Corporation (from May 1 1987)
Principal Bank: Texas Commerce Bank, Houston
Financial Information:

	Dec 31 1985	Dec 31 1986
	$'000	$'000
Net income	53,000	20,000
Earnings per share	$1.62	$0.61
Deposits	14,612,000	14,139,000
Total assets	20,076,000	19,192,000

No of Employees: 8,270

TEXAS COMMERCE BANK, NA

712 Main Street, Houston, TX 77002
Tel: (713) 236-4865
Telex: 775418

Chairman: Charles C Beall Jr; Vice Chairmen: Lloyd L Bolton, Marc J Shapiro, John P Townley
President: John L Adams
Senior Executive Officers: Ben H Cohen (Executive VP Investment), William H Davis Jr (Executive VP and Executive Trust Officer), Stephen H Field (Executive VP Real Estate), W Carl Galloway (Executive VP Metro), Everett C Gambrell (Executive VP Customer Services), Donald L Hawk (Executive VP Administration), Richard G Hickson (Executive VP US Group), W Ben Kuenemann (Executive VP Data Services), Joe C McKinney (Executive VP Regional Group), Richard L Melten (Executive VP Trust and Corporate Services), Keith D Oldfield (Executive VP International), Geoffrey P Raymond (Executive VP, Chief Investment and Trust Officer), Larry L Shryock (Executive VP Metro), William A Swank (Executive VP and Trust Officer), Kenneth L Tilton (Executive VP Financial Accounting and Controller), Gary G Wright (Executive VP Energy)

PRINCIPAL ACTIVITIES: Banking and related services
Parent Company: Texas Commerce Bancshares Inc

No of Employees: 2,560

TEXAS EASTERN CORPORATION

PO Box 2521, Houston, TX 77252
Tel: (713) 759-3131
Cable: TETCO HOU
Telex: ITT 4620157 texern

Chairman: I D Bufkin
President: D R Hendrix (and Chief Executive Officer)
Senior Executive Officers: J M Conaway (Senior VP and Chief Financial Officer), B C Andrews (VP and General Counsel), H H King (Vice Chairman), P A McKim (Senior VP), H C Homeyer (Senior VP), W H McCollough (Senior VP), E E Hickam (Senior VP), J D Cody (Executive VP), P M Anderson (Senior VP), G L Mazanec (Senior VP)

PRINCIPAL ACTIVITIES: Principal activities include: natural gas and petroleum products; international oil and gas exploration and production; refining and marketing of petroleum products at wholesale; development of a mixed-use real estate project in downtown Houston; marketing of LP-Gas (Through its Petrolane Incorporated subsidiary, Texas Eastern is general partner for Petroland Partners, LP, one of the nation's largest marketers of LP-Gas)
Trade Names: Texas Eastern Gas Pipeline Co; Texas Eastern Products Pipeline Co
Principal Subsidiaries: Texas Eastern Transmission Co; Texas Eastern Gas Pipeline Co; Algonquin Gas Transmission Co; Texas Eastern Products Pipeline Co; Texas Eastern North Sea Inc; Texas Eastern Norwegian Inc; Petrolane Incorporated; La Gloria Oil and Gas Co; Houston Center Corp
Principal Bank: Manufacturers Hanover Trust Co
Financial Information:

	Dec 31 1985(1)	Dec 31 1986
	$'000	$'000
Sales revenues	5,249,742	4,074,106
Income before taxes	284,400	154,410
Net income	2,826	1,267
Dividends(2)	20,754	15,438
Dividends per share(3)	$2.20	$1.60
Earnings per share	$0.05	$0.02
Common stock	186,437	186,828
Retained income	892,125	808,101
Shareholders equity	1,320,995	1,241,988

(1) Results have been restated to reflect the change during second quarter 1986 in the method of accounting for oil and gas operations from the full cost to the successful efforts method
(2) Preferred
(3) Common stock

Principal Shareholders: (49.5%) institutional holdings
No of Employees: 8,800

TEXAS FARM PRODUCTS CO

915 S Fredonia Street, Nacogdoches, TX 75961
Tel: (713) 564-3711

President: Tom Wright
Senior Executive Officers: Cecil R Bomar (Executive VP and Controller), DeVant Beard (VP Production), Ray D Rinker Jr (VP Farm Supplies), John J Rudisill Jr (VP Sales), M S Wright III (VP Pet Food Division)

PRINCIPAL ACTIVITIES: Production of livestock and animal feeds; supply of fertilizers
Principal Subsidiaries: C J Martin & Son Inc
Principal Bank: Fredonia State Bank
Financial Information:

	$'000
Sales revenues	53,000

No of Employees: 450

TEXAS GAS RESOURCES CORPORATION

3800 Frederica Street, Owensboro, KY 42301
Tel: (502) 926-8686

Chairman: Hays T Watkins
President: R L Hintz (and Chief Executive Officer)
Senior Executive Officers: G T Smith (Senior VP), Jerry L Keller (VP), James Ermer (VP and Treasurer)

PRINCIPAL ACTIVITIES: The company has interests in the distribution of gas; river and canal transportation; production and exploration of gas and oil
Parent Company: CSX Corporation, Richmond, VA
Financial Information:

	$'000
Sales revenues	1,910,000

No of Employees: 2,000

TEXAS INDUSTRIES, INC

8100 Carpenter Freeway, Dallas, TX 75247
Tel: (14)37-3100

Chairman: Ralph B Rogers
President: Robert D Rogers (and Chief Executive Officer)
Senior Executive Officers: Fergus J Walker Jr (Executive VP and Chief Operating Officer), Robert H Foley (Senior VP Planning), J N Ball III (VP, LA Region), Brooke E Brewer (VP Human Resources), Kenneth R Darden (VP and Treasurer), Philip H Harris (VP Cement Planning), Robert E May (VP Concrete Division), Robert C Moore (VP, Secretary and General Counsel)

PRINCIPAL ACTIVITIES: Supply of quarry products, bricks, cement and ready mixed concrete; real estate management
Principal Bank: InterFirst Bank Dallas
Financial Information:

	May 31 1986 $'000
Sales revenues	648,230
Net income	22,114
Earnings per share	$2.44
Shareholders equity	194,083

No of Employees: 3,000

TEXAS INSTRUMENTS INCORPORATED

PO Box 655474, Dallas, TX 75265
Tel: (214) 995-2011
Telex: 73324 TEXINS DAL; TWX 910-867-4702

Chairman: Mark Shepherd Jr
President: Jerry R Junkins (and Chief Executive Officer)
Senior Executive Officers: William I George (Executive VP), William B Mitchell (Executive VP), William N Sick Jr (Executive VP), William P Weber (Executive VP), William A Aylesworth (VP, Treasurer and Chief Financial Officer)

PRINCIPAL ACTIVITIES: Worldwide development, manufacture and sale of semiconductors, defense electronics systems, computer systems, industrial control systems, electrical controls, metallurgical materials, geophysical exploration services, and consumer electronics products

Financial Information:

	Dec 31 1985 $'000	Dec 31 1986 $'000
Sales revenues	4,924,500	4,974,000
Income (loss) before taxes(1)	(115,000)	98,700
Net income (loss)	(118,700)	29,100
Dividends per share(2)	$2.00	$2.00
Earnings (loss) per share	($4.76)	$0.71
Retained income	1,072,500	1,039,300
Shareholders equity	1,427,700	1,727,100

(1) and extraordinary item
(2) common stock

No of Employees: 77,270

TEXAS INTERNATIONAL COMPANY

6525 North Meridan, Oklahoma City, OK 73116
Tel: (405) 728 5100

Chairman: J A Kishpaugh (and President and Chief Executive Officer)
Senior Executive Officers: Konstantinos Bakalis (Senior VP), Charles M Reimer (Senior VP), Russell L Burget (VP Investor Relations), Robert S Flaniken (VP, Secretary and General Counsel), Joseph J Romano (VP, Treasurer, Controller and Chief Financial Officer)

PRINCIPAL ACTIVITIES: Production of natural gas and crude oil
Principal Subsidiaries: Phoenix Resources Co; Texas International Petroleum
Principal Bank: Chemical Bank
Financial Information:

	$'000
Sales revenues	106,850

No of Employees: 200

TEXAS OIL & GAS CORPORATION

First City Center, 1700 Pacific Avenue, Dallas, TX 75201
Tel: (214) 954 2000

Chairman: William L Hutchison
President: Forrest E Hoglund (and Chief Executive Officer)
Senior Executive Officers: A D Carter Jr (Executive VP), T E Lohman (Executive VP), Charles L Canfield (Senior VP), John R Morgan (Senior VP), Richard F Doyle (Senior VP Finance and Administration), Larry H Carpenter (VP), David M Kihneman (VP), Martin B McNamara (VP, Legal Counsel and Secretary), R G Schweers (VP and Controller), Theodore R Warren (VP), Bob F Young (VP and Legal Counsel), Hamilton P Schrauff (VP Finance and Treasurer)

PRINCIPAL ACTIVITIES: Transmission of natural gas
Parent Company: USX Corporation
Principal Subsidiaries: Acadian Gas Pipeline Corp; Bayou Interstate Pipeline Corp; Calcasieu Gas Gathering Corp; California Natural Gas Pipeline; Delhi Gas Pipeline Corp; FWA Drilling Co Inc; FWA Equipment & Mud Co Inc; Nueces Co; Ozark Finance Corp; Ozark Gas Pipeline Corp; Pelican Interstate Gas Corp; Pelican Transmission Corp; Red River Gas Pipeline Corp; Spindletop Gas Distribution Corp; Tonkawa Gas Processing Co; TXO Gas Marketing Corp; TXO Gas Ventures Corp; TXO Minerals Inc; TXO Oil Co Inc; TXO Producing Properties Corp; TXO Production Corp; TXO Acadian Gas Pipeline Corp; TXO Bayou Interstate Pipeline Corp; TXO Calcasieu Gas Gathering Corp; TXO Louisiana Industrial Gas Supply Corp; TXO Pelican Interstate Gas Corp; TXO Pelican Transmission Corp; TXO Pontchartrain Natural Gas Corp; TXO Spindletop Gas Distribution Corp; Western Transmission Corp
Principal Bank: InterFirst Bank
Financial Information:

	$'000
Sales revenues	2,900,000

No of Employees: 3,600

TEXAS REFINERY CORPORATION

One Refinery Pl, Fort Worth, TX 76101
Tel: (817) 332-1161
Telex: WUT 821583 trc flw ud

Chairman: A M Pate Jr (and Chief Executive Officer); Vice Chairman: S L Pate
President: Jerry W Hopkins
Senior Executive Officers: Mrs Vivian Sharp (VP and Treasurer), Jimmy E Peel (VP Advertising and Public Relations)

PRINCIPAL ACTIVITIES: Production of industrial cleaners; coatings and paint; adhesives and sealants; lubricants
Principal Subsidiaries: Texas Refinery Corp of Canada; Texas Refinery Corp of Mexico; Texas Refinery Corp International; Panther Chemical Co
Principal Bank: First Republic Bank Fort Worth
Financial Information:

	$'000
Sales revenues	45,000

No of Employees: 600

TEXAS UTILITIES COMPANY

2001 Bryan Tower, Dallas, TX 75201
Tel: (214) 653-4600
Telex: WUT 730854 tx utility dal

Chairman: Jerry S Farrington (and Chief Executive Officer); Vice Chairman: Burl B Hulsey Jr
Senior Executive Officers: Earl Nye (Executive VP and Chief Financial Officer)

PRINCIPAL ACTIVITIES: Supply of electricity; coal mining interests
Principal Subsidiaries: Texas Utilities Electric Company; Dallas Power & Light Co; Texas Electric Service Co; Texas Power & Light Co; Texas Utilities Fuel Co; Texas Utilities Generating Co; Texas Utilities Services Inc; Chaco Energy Co; Basic Resources Inc; Texas Utilities Mining Co
Principal Bank: Morgan Guaranty Trust Co
Financial Information:

	Dec 31 1985	Dec 31 1986
	$'000	$'000
Sales revenues	4,170,160	3,932,045
Net income	587,760	626,851
Earnings per share	$4.35	$4.45
Shareholders equity	-	4,460,821

No of Employees: 17,000

TEXFI INDUSTRIES, INC

400 English Road, Rocky Mount, NC 27801
Tel: (919) 443 5001

Chairman: L T Sovey Jr (and Chief Executive Officer)
President: F B Lineweaver
Senior Executive Officers: Carroll Gibson (VP Manufacturing), Michael A Miller (VP Finance)

PRINCIPAL ACTIVITIES: Textile manufacture including knits and wovens
Principal Bank: First Union National Bank
Financial Information:

	$'000
Sales revenues	109,000

No of Employees: 900

TEXIZE DIVISION

PO Box 368, Greenville, SC 29602
Tel: (803) 271-9100
Telex: WUT 570499 texize grv

President: J F Mayer
Senior Executive Officers: W D West (Senior VP), A G Hansen (VP Finance), S J Price (VP Scientific and Technical Affairs), C K Sycks (VP Operations), B D Barfield (VP Sales), G E Mercer (VP Marketing), R J Egan (VP and Counsel), J W Spongberg (VP Commercial and International)

PRINCIPAL ACTIVITIES: Production of soaps, detergents and other household products
Parent Company: Dow Chemical Company
Principal Bank: First National Bank
Financial Information:

	$'000
Sales revenues	250,000

No of Employees: 1,000

TEXSCAN CORPORATION

7320 E Butherus Drive, Ste 200, Scottsdale, AZ 85261
Tel: (602) 998-1788

Chairman: James R Bonfiglio (and Chief Executive Officer and President)
Senior Executive Officers: Rene L Flores (VP Finance/Chief Financial Officer, Secretary), Dr William Firestone (VP and General Manager Texscan Communications Products Division), William P Dawson (VP and General Manager Texscan Instruments), David Keller (VP and General Manager Texscan MSI), John Smith (VP and General Manager Texscan European Operations), Bert L Hencheid (VP Engineering R & D), Norman R Barnard (VP Operations Communications Products Division), Raymond Pastie (VP Sales and Marketing Communications Products Division)

PRINCIPAL ACTIVITIES: Electronic testing and measuring apparatus; computing equipment; communications equipment; CATV transmission and distribution equipment; Lans equipment
Trade Names: Texscan, Theta-Com, Pathmaker
Principal Subsidiaries and Divisions: Texscan Instruments Ltd (UK); Texscan GmbH (Germany); Texscan Instruments; Société Texscan SA; Texscan MSI/Compuvid; Texscan de Mexico; Texscan Communications Products Division; Texscan Instruments Division
Principal Bank: United Bank of Arizona
Financial Information:

	Apr 30 1986	Apr 30 1987
	$'000	$'000
Sales revenues	47,078	35,992
Income (loss) before taxes	(51,863)	5,641
Net income (loss)	(51,850)	5,440
Earnings (loss) per share	($7.77)	$0.82
Common stock	35,884	35,884
Retained (deficit)	(85,770)	(80,330)
Shareholders (deficit)	(49,809)	(44,369)

No of Employees: 1,200

TEXTILE BANKING CO

51 Madison Ave, New York, NY 10010
Tel: (212) 481-3000

President: David Goldberg
Senior Executive Officers: Joseph J Rizzo (Executive VP), F V Celentano (VP), Al Jeter (VP), L G Hupfer (VP), P J Kelly (VP), W J Sweeney (VP), W C Eaker (VP and Secretary), M G Stipicevic (Treasurer)

PRINCIPAL ACTIVITIES: Credit and financial services
Parent Company: Control Data Corporation thru Commercial Credit Company

No of Employees: 260

TEXTILE RUBBER & CHEMICAL CO

Tiarco Dr SW, Dalton, GA 30720
Tel: (404) 277-1300
Telex: WUT 543458 tex rub dto

President: F H Howalt Jr
Senior Executive Officers: Neil E Tillotson (Treasurer), Grafton J Corbett III (Secretary)

PRINCIPAL ACTIVITIES: Fabrication of plastic and rubber products for carpet manufacture
Financial Information:

	$'000
Sales revenues	50,000

No of Employees: 400

TEXTRON INC

40 Westminster Street, Providence, RI 02903
Tel: (401) 421-2800
Cable: TEXTRON PVD
Telex: RCA 200160 TEXTRON UR
Telecopy: (401) 421-2878

Chairman: Beverly F Dolan (and President and Chief Executive Officer)
Senior Executive Officers: William J Ledbetter (Senior Executive VP Administration and Planning), William A Anders (Senior Executive VP-Operations), Donald K Farrar (Senior Executive VP-Operations), Dennis G Little (Executive VP and Chief Financial Officer), Thomas D Soutter (Executive VP and General Counsel)

PRINCIPAL ACTIVITIES: The Corporation's interests include aerospace technology, commercial products and financial services
Principal Subsidiaries: Avco Corporation
Financial Information:

	Dec 31 1985	Dec 31 1986
	$'000	$'000
Total revenues*	5,721,200	6,950,900
Income before taxes	300,000	444,800
Net income	251,800	239,200
Dividends	63,700	71,200
Dividends per share	$1.80	$1.80
Earnings per share	$6.75	$5.79
Common stock	10,100	10,200
Retained income	1,337,600	1,502,800
Shareholders equity	1,633,300	1,847,200

*including unconsolidated finance and insurance subsidiaries

No of Employees: 72,000

TEX-TUBE DIVISION

1503 N Post Oak Road, Houston, TX 77055
Tel: (713) 686-4351

President: David W Biggers (and Sales Manager)
Senior Executive Officers: Arthur T Jones (Divisional Manager), Carl G Farnsworth (Plant Manager), James E Wylie (Manager Industrial Relations), Corrinne Brandt (Purchasing Agent), Robert S Sudman (Data Processing Manager), Clifford H Price (Chief Engineer), J Writer (Controller)

PRINCIPAL ACTIVITIES: Production of steel and plastic pipes
Parent Company: Cyclops Corporation, Pittsburgh, PA
Principal Bank: Chase Manhattan Bank
Financial Information:

	$'000
Sales revenues	75,000

No of Employees: 200

TGI FRIDAY'S INC

14665 Midway Road, Addison, TX 75244
Tel: (214) 450 5400

Chairman: Curtis L Carlson
President: Daniel R Scoggin (and Chief Executive Officer)
Senior Executive Officers: Stephen G Milks (Executive VP), Edward G Engaron (Executive Group VP), James R Holland Jr (Executive Group VP), Frank H Steed (Executive Group VP), Kenneth A Hill (Senior VP and Chief Accounting Officer), Malcolm McRae (VP Operations), Roger L Zingle (VP Operations)

PRINCIPAL ACTIVITIES: Franchising and licensing of theme restaurants
Parent Company: Carlson Companies Inc
Principal Bank: First City Bank of Dallas
Financial Information:

	$'000
Sales revenues	314,400

No of Employees: 13,160

THACKERAY CORPORATION

One Penn Plaza, New York, NY 10119-0001
Tel: (212) 967-8600

Chairman: Lester Pollack (and Chief Executive Officer)
President: Stanley B Frieze (and Chief Operating Officer)
Senior Executive Officers: Russell E Mooney Jr (Executive VP and Treasurer), Kevin M Coffey (VP Finance and Chief Financial Officer)

PRINCIPAL ACTIVITIES: The company has interests in the manufacture of Christmas decorations and ribbon for giftware and florists; the production of cables and wires; construction equipment and tools
Principal Bank: Manufacturers Hanover Trust
Financial Information:

	$'000
Sales revenues	74,000

No of Employees: 400

THE NEW ENGLAND MUTUAL LIFE INSURANCE CO

See NEW ENGLAND MUTUAL LIFE INSURANCE CO, THE,

THERMO ELECTRON CORPORATION

101 First Avenue, Waltham, MA 02154
Tel: (617) 890-8700
Telex: WUT 923411 teco esd wha

Chairman: George N Hatsopoulos (and President and Chief Executive Officer)
Senior Executive Officers: Peter G Pantazelos (Executive VP Finance), Robert C Howard (Executive VP), John N Hatsopoulos (Senior VP Corporate Strategy), Walter J Bornhorst (Senior VP), Arvin Smith (Senior VP), John P Appleton (VP Technical), Jerry Davis (VP), Paris L Nicolaides (VP, Group Executive), Firooz Rufeh (VP)

PRINCIPAL ACTIVITIES: Industrial process equipment; papermaking machinery; pollution monitoring equipment; metal treatment
Principal Bank: The First National Bank of Boston
Financial Information:

	$'000
Sales revenues	322,000

No of Employees: 2,700

THETFORD CORPORATION

7101 Jackson Road, PO Box 1285, Ann Arbor, MI 48106
Tel: (313) 769 6000

Chairman: Charles L Sargent (and Chief Executive Officer)
President: John R Arlen (and Chief Operating Officer)
Senior Executive Officers: Edwin T Charles (VP Operations), Victor Silles (Treasurer), Morris Milmet (Secretary and Legal Counsel)

PRINCIPAL ACTIVITIES: Manufacture of a range of plastic products including sanitation systems
Principal Bank: First of America Bank
Financial Information:

	$'000
Sales revenues	33,300

No of Employees: 290

THIES COMPANIES, INC
S Main Street, Great Bend, KS 67530
Tel: (316)-792-1311

Chairman: Hubert P Thies
President: John M Thies
Senior Executive Officers: James J Graham (Secretary and Treasurer), Phil Roth (VP and Controller)

PRINCIPAL ACTIVITIES: Meat processing
Principal Bank: American State Bank & Trust Co
Financial Information:

	$'000
Sales revenues	50,000

No of Employees: 150

THIRD NATIONAL BANK & TRUST CO
34 N Main Street, Dayton, OH 45402
Tel: (513) 226-6000
Telex: ITT 4333042 third bank dtn

Chairman: Perry B Wydman (and Chief Executive Officer)
President: Douglas L Hawthorne (and Chief Operating Officer)
Senior Executive Officers: Joseph F Connelly (Executive VP), Michael N Trigg (Senior VP), John P Dale Jr (Senior VP), Peter O Knapp (Senior VP), Bruce A Jaquish (VP International), Sebastian J Meluzzo (VP Corporate Relations)

PRINCIPAL ACTIVITIES: Banking and financial services
Parent Company: Society Corporation, Cleveland, OH

No of Employees: 650

THIRD NATIONAL CORPORATION
Third National Bank Building, Nashville, TN 37244
Tel: (615) 748-4992

Chairman: Charles J Kane
President: Charles J Cook Jr

PRINCIPAL ACTIVITIES: Banking
Principal Subsidiaries: Third National Bank in Nashville; American National Bank and Trust Company of Chattanooga; Third National Bank in Knoxville; Hamilton Bank of Upper East Tennessee; Third National Bank in Anderson County; Merchants Bank; The First National Bank of Lawrenceburg; The Union Bank; Third National in Sevier County; Citizens Bank; Bank of Obion County; Third National Mortgage Company; Third Lease Corporation; Third National Life Insurance Company
Principal Bank: Third National Bank in Nashville

No of Employees: 3,480

THOMAS & BETTS CORPORATION
920 Rte 202, Raritan, NJ 08869
Tel: (201) 685-1600
Telex: WUT 511161 tnbr ud

Chairman: J David Parkinson
President: T Kevin Dunnigan (and Chief Executive Officer)
Senior Executive Officers: Robert V Berry (Senior VP), David M Hunihan (Group VP International), N G Shultis (Group VP Electrical), Ronald P Babcock (VP Finance), James D Hay (VP), E D Thomas (VP Corporate Development), John F Walsh (VP Human Resources)

PRINCIPAL ACTIVITIES: Manufacture of electrical and electronic components
Principal Subsidiaries: Thomas & Betts Ltd (Canada); Thomas & Betts International Inc; T & B/Ansley Corp; Thomas & Betts Caribe Inc; Doylestown Manufacturing Corp; Thomas & Betts (Pa) Inc; Excel Products Co Inc; Quelcor Inc
Principal Bank: Morgan Guaranty Trust Co
Financial Information:

	$'000
Sales revenues	386,000

No of Employees: 3,000

THOMAS INDUSTRIES INC
4360 Brownsboro Road, Suite 300, PO Box 35120, Louisville, KY 40232
Tel: (502) 893-4600
Telex: WUT 881221 thom inds lsvl

Chairman: Walter S Davis
President: Thomas R Fuller (and Chief Executive Officer)
Senior Executive Officers: Jackson W Smart Jr (Chairman Executive Committee), Gerald W P'Pool (Executive VP, Manager, Lighting Group), C Barr Schuler (VP Chief Financial Officer), Lars O Frey (VP International), Allan E Eggers (VP Public Relations), Gilbert R Grady Jr (VP Industrial Relations), Timothy C Brown (VP, Manager, Specialty Products), Michael T Fuller (VP, Marketing Services), John S Kahler (VP, Manufacturing Services), Phillip J Stuecker (Secretary and Treasurer), David J Stumler (Controller, Assistant Secretary)

PRINCIPAL ACTIVITIES: Manufacture of lighting equipment; compressors and paint application apparatus; domestic hardware and household fittings
Principal Subsidiaries: C & M Products Co Ltd (Canada); Pouliot Designs Corp; Thomas Industries of Tennesse Inc; Oliver-Macleod Ltd; Builders Brass Works; Capri Lighting Inc; Gardco Manufacturing Inc
Principal Bank: Wachovia Bank & Trust Co
Financial Information:

	Dec 31 1985 $'000	Dec 31 1986 $'000
Sales revenues	294,711	296,195
Income before taxes	27,480	24,216
Net income	16,233	12,756
Dividends	5,794	6,130
Dividends per share*	$0.59	$0.62
Earnings per share*	$1.65	$1.29
Shareholders equity	109,962	117,411
*adjusted for 10% stock dividend paid January 1 1987		

No of Employees: 3,080

THOMAS J LIPTON, INC
See LIPTON, THOMAS J, , INC

THOMAS NELSON INC
See NELSON, THOMAS, INC

THOMAS, S B, INC
930 N Riverview Drive, Totowa, NJ 07512
Tel: (201) 256-8200
Telex: TWX 710 9885720 tffi 2 towa

President: R Miller
Senior Executive Officers: Robert Anderson (VP Sales), N Henderson (VP Marketing), J Keith (VP Finance), Arthur Weren (VP Operations)

PRINCIPAL ACTIVITIES: Bakery products including bread
Parent Company: CPC International Inc
Financial Information:

	$'000
Sales revenues	100,000

No of Employees: 1,000

THOMASTON MILLS, INC
PO Box 311, Thomaston, GA 30286
Tel: (404) 647-7131
Telex: 804511 THST Mill TMST

President: Neil H Hightower (and Chief Executive Officer)
Senior Executive Officers: H Stewart Davis (Executive VP), George H Hightower Jr (Executive VP), O R Lewis (Senior VP-Director of Sales), S Richard Sargent (VP-Industrial Relations), John R Carson (VP-Household Sales), W Harrison Hightower III (VP-Administration), Harry W Ormand Jr (VP-

Finishing), John M Ormand (VP-Manufacturing), Robert E L Greene (VP-Engineering), Garner M Ellerbee (Secretary), Rosser R Raines (Treasurer)

PRINCIPAL ACTIVITIES: Thomaston Mills, Inc, manufactures textile products for the apparel, home furnishings and industrial markets. Apparel fabrics, including indigo denims and piece dyed fabrics, both rigid and stretch, are sold to apparel cutters in a wide range of finishes and blends. Thomaston markets a line of fashion blended sheets and pillowcases sold under the New Era label. Other home furnishing fabrics are sold to manufacturers of tablecloths, beddings and other domestic items. Industrial fabrics are manufactured for use in sporting goods, luggage, conveyor belts, fire hose, wall covering and flocking. Specialty items are fabricated for industrial and recreational markets. Yarns are made for knitting, industrial weaving and sewing operations, such as bag closure. Commission dyeing and finishing services are offered to outside converters

Trade Names: New Era

Financial Information:

	Jun 29 1985	Jun 28 1986
	$'000	$'000
Sales revenues	132,495	139,063
(Loss) before taxes	(1,565)	(1,047)
Net (loss)	(162)	(1,047)
Dividends	821	821
Dividends per share	$1.00	$1.00
(Loss) per share	($0.20)	($1.27)
Common stock	9,368	9,368
Retained income	40,136	38,268
Shareholders equity	48,389	46,521

No of Employees: 2,509

THOMPSON HAYWARD CHEMICAL CO

5200 Speaker Road, Kansas City, KS 66106
Tel: (913) 321-3131
Telex: WUT 426211 th chemco ksck

Chairman: Murray P Wilson
President: Ralph Ripley
Senior Executive Officers: James Nye (Secretary), R S Voda (Treasurer)

PRINCIPAL ACTIVITIES: Manufacture of agricultural and specialty chemicals
Parent Company: Harrisons & Crossfield plc, London, UK
Principal Bank: First National Bank
Financial Information:

	$'000
Sales revenues	250,000

No of Employees: 700

THOMPSON MEDICAL CO INC

919 Third Avenue, New York, NY 10022
Tel: (212) 688 4420

Chairman: S Daniel Abraham; Vice Chairman: Edward L Steinberg
President: Moses Ratowsky
Senior Executive Officers: Jack Cox (Executive VP), Louis J Guerci (VP Finance and Treasurer), Eric Sorensen (VP Manufacturing), Paul Craniotes (VP Development), Ronald Stern (VP Corporate Development and Production)

PRINCIPAL ACTIVITIES: Supply of pharmaceutical products
Principal Bank: Bankers Trust Co
Financial Information:

	$'000
Sales revenues	136,800

No of Employees: 125

THOMSON CO

1290 Avenue of the Americas, New York, NY 10019
Tel: (212) 397-3000

President: J Neff
Senior Executive Officers: E Lightman (Executive VP), Herbert A Cohen (VP Sales), Robert C Fazekas (VP Sales), Donald G Newsome (VP Operations)

PRINCIPAL ACTIVITIES: Manufacture of clothing
Parent Company: Salant Corporation, New York, NY
Principal Bank: Manufacturers Hanover Trust
Financial Information:

	$'000
Sales revenues	90,000

No of Employees: 2,600

THOR INDUSTRIES INC

419 West Pike Street, Jackson Center, OH 45334
Tel: (513) 596 6849

Chairman: Peter B Orthwein (and Treasurer)
President: F B Wade Thompson (and Chief Executive Officer)
Senior Executive Officers: Gerard N Letourneau (Executive VP), Kirby Gemberling (VP), Walter L Bennett (VP Finance and Secretary)

PRINCIPAL ACTIVITIES: Manufacture of a range of travel trailers, motor homes and camping equipment
Financial Information:

	$'000
Sales revenues	97,750

No of Employees: 790

THORN APPLE VALLEY, INC

18700 W Ten Mile, Southfield, MI 48075
Tel: (313) 552-0700

Chairman: Henry S Dorfman (and Chief Executive Officer); Vice Chairman: Allen Chariupski
President: Joel Dorfman (and Chief Operating Officer)
Senior Executive Officers: Donald Braam (Senior VP), John W Stein (Senior VP Sales and Marketing), Isaac Gold (VP Sales), Julius Schaumberg (VP Transport), Louis Glazier (VP Finance), Lawrence Charlupski (VP Sales)

PRINCIPAL ACTIVITIES: Slaughtering and processing of meat; specialty products; by-products; trucking services
Financial Information:

	May 31 1986
	$'000
Sales revenues	611,010
Net (loss)	(5,493)
(Loss) per share	($1.53)
Shareholders equity	28,095

No of Employees: 2,700

THORPE & RICKS, INC

Barnum Road, Rocky Mount, NC 27801
Tel: (919) 977-3151

Chairman: J L Parker
President: Alexander P Thorpe III
Senior Executive Officers: George W Thorpe (Executive VP), Robert L Minor (Senior VP), Robert Zalrneck (Senior VP), Henry Gregory (VP)

PRINCIPAL ACTIVITIES: Processing of tobacco
Financial Information:

	$'000
Sales revenues	100,000

No of Employees: 410

THOUSAND TRAILS, INC

15325 SE 30th Pl, Bellevue, WA 98007
Tel: (206) 644 1100

Chairman: James Jensen (and Chief Executive Officer)
President: Howard P Behar (and Chief Operating Officer)

Senior Executive Officers: R Craig Kirsch (Senior VP and Treasurer), Robert M Mayes (Senior VP), Jerol E Andres (VP), Ronald L Bidleman (VP), Julie A Brooks (VP and General Counsel), Duke Campbell (VP), James E Claus (VP Finance, Controller and Chief Financial Officer), Kathleen M Hornsby (VP and Secretary), Donald D Kent (VP), Alan B Schriber (VP)

PRINCIPAL ACTIVITIES: Operation of campgrounds in Texas, Nevada, Washington, Oregon, California, British Columbia, Virginia, Ohio, Arizona and Illinois
Principal Bank: First National Bank of Boston
Financial Information:

	$'000
Sales revenues	127,600

No of Employees: 1,800

THRALL CAR MANUFACTURING CO
26th & State, Box 218, Chicago Heights, IL 60411
Tel: (312) 757-5900

Chairman: Richard L Duchossois (and President)
Senior Executive Officers: Chester H Wright (Executive VP), J P Lynch (VP Sales), Robert J Ladecky (VP Finance)

PRINCIPAL ACTIVITIES: Supply of railroad cars and equipment; leasing
Principal Bank: Continental Illinois National Bank & Trust Co of Chicago
Financial Information:

	$'000
Sales revenues	150,000

No of Employees: 1,000

THREE D DEPARTMENTS INC
801 Silver Lane, East Hartford, CT 06118
Tel: (203) 569 6720

Chairman: Bernard Abrams (and Chief Executive Officer)
President: Donald L Abrams
Senior Executive Officers: John B Abrams (Senior VP and Assistant Treasurer), Ira Durlester (VP Operations), Robert C Lee (VP Operations), Ronald Dow (Controller), Robert Shutsky (VP Finance and Administration and Treasurer), David Kotkin (Secretary), Abe Markowicz (VP Merchandising)

PRINCIPAL ACTIVITIES: Wholesale and retail trade in drapery and upholstery fabrics
Principal Bank: Connecticut National Bank
Financial Information:

	$'000
Sales revenues	59,600

No of Employees: 600

THRIFTY CORPORATION
3424 Wilshire Blvd, Los Angeles, CA 90010
Tel: (213) 251 6000

Chairman: Leonard H Straus (and Chief Executive Officer)
President: Richard G Eils (and Chief Operating Officer)
Senior Executive Officers: Ellis H Axelrod (Senior VP Store Operations), Christian Bement (Senior VP Industrial Relations), Kenneth M Crosby (Senior VP Buying and Merchandising), James T Haight (Senior VP, Secretary and Chief Corporate Counsel), Robert W Henry Jr (Senior VP Real Estate and Construction), John Onestinghel (Senior VP Manufacturing and Distribution), Richard Ramsey (Senior VP Finance and Treasurer)

PRINCIPAL ACTIVITIES: Drugstores, discount stores, stores for sporting goods, restaurants
Principal Bank: Bank of America
Financial Information:

	$'000
Sales revenues	1,404,850

No of Employees: 14,000

THYSSEN-BORNEMISZA, INC
1211 Avenue of the Americas, New York, NY 10036
Tel: (212) 556-8500
Telex: TWX 710 5812429 tbi inhd nyk

President: Marshall F Smith (and Chief Executive Officer)
Senior Executive Officers: H R Looney (Executive VP), John D Rome (Executive VP), George E Furguson (Executive VP), Kim D Taggart (Executive VP), James E Dawson (Executive VP), William A Blue (Senior VP and Controller)

PRINCIPAL ACTIVITIES: Manufacture of containers and packaging products; motor vehicle components; electrical equipment components
Financial Information:

	$'000
Sales revenues	1,000,000

No of Employees: 13,000

TI-CARO INC
PO Box 699, Gastonia, NC 28053
Tel: (704) 867-7271

Chairman: James C Fry (and President and Chief Executive Officer)
Senior Executive Officers: James H Patterson (VP Finance), A G Myers III (VP Manufacturing), V E Stanley Jr (VP Manufacturing), John Land (VP Corporate Planning), J R Rawlings (Assistant VP Cotton), Lee O Waters (Assistant VP Employee Relations), Ray Jimison (Assistant VP Public Relations)

PRINCIPAL ACTIVITIES: Manufacture of yarns and threads from natural and synthetic fibers; knitted textiles
Principal Bank: Branch Banking & Trust Co

No of Employees: 5,000

TICOR
6300 Wilshire Blvd, Los Angeles, CA 90048
Tel: (213) 852-6300
Telex: WUT 559331 ticor mortgage

Chairman: Harold S Geneen
President: Winston V Morrow
Senior Executive Officers: Leonard T Wood (Executive VP and Chief Financial Officer), Erich E Everbach (Senior VP Secretary and General Counsel), Ellis Peter Miller (VP Government Affairs), Kurt G Pahl (VP and Treasurer), John W Uhlman (VP and Controller)

PRINCIPAL ACTIVITIES: General insurance services
Parent Company: New TC Holding Corporation
Financial Information:

	$'000
Premium income	619,000

No of Employees: 7,000

TIDEWATER INC
1440 Canal Street, New Orleans, LA 70112
Tel: (504) 568-1010
Telex: 584216 TIDEWATER NLN (Domestic); 460050 TIDE UI (International)

Chairman: John P Laborde
President: Damon B Bankston
Senior Executive Officers: Richard M Currence (Senior VP), Ken C Tamblyn (Senior VP), William R Croyle (Senior VP), H E Northcott (Senior VP), William M Wiseman (VP), Richard B Weir (VP), Victor I Koock (VP), Bill J Ramey (VP), (VP), Paul J Angelle (VP), William C Hightower (VP)

PRINCIPAL ACTIVITIES: Tidewater Inc, owns and operates one of the world's largest fleets of vessels supporting the offshore oil and gas industry and is active in oil and gas exploration and production and in the natural gas and air compression business. The company also has modest interests in real estate and insurance

Principal Subsidiaries: Tidewater Marine Service, Inc; Tidewater Compression Service, Inc; Tidwater Realty Inc; Pental Insurance

Principal Banks: Whitney National Bank of New Orleans-Registrar; Hibernia National Bank

Financial Information:

	Mar 31 1986 $'000	Mar 31 1987 $'000
Sales revenues	244,743	173,051
(Loss) before taxes	(49,589)	(52,839)
Net (loss)	(18,645)	(56,678)
(Loss) per common share	($1.25)	($2.62)
Common stock*	19,480	22,198
Retained earnings	188,175	130,485
Shareholders equity	272,366	206,150

*thousands

No of Employees: 2,300

TIDWELL INDUSTRIES, INC

PO Box 679, Haleyville, AL 35565
Tel: 205 486-9221
Telex: TWX 810 7300020 tidwell halv

Chairman: Don N Tidwell (and Chief Executive Officer)
President: Troy B Oliver (and Chief Operating Officer)
Senior Executive Officers: Edna M Frederick (VP Administration), D L Creen (VP Sales)

PRINCIPAL ACTIVITIES: Production of modular buildings and mobile homes

Principal Subsidiaries: Tidwell Motor Carriers Inc; Tidwell Insurance Brokers Inc; Tidwell Housing Systems International Inc; Lumber Components Inc; Pine Designs of Alabama Inc; Tidwell Housing SA (Pty) Ltd; Tidwell Properties SA (Pty) Ltd; Precision Bilt Homes Inc; Tidwell Building Systems; Tidwell Mortgage Corp; Berry Furniture Inc; Winston Homes Inc

Principal Bank: Morgan Guaranty Trust Co of New York

Financial Information:

	$'000
Sales revenues	169,730

No of Employees: 2,300

TIE COMMUNICATIONS, INC

8 Progress Drive, Shelton, CT 06484
Tel: (203) 926-2000
Telex: 179051

Chairman: T L Kelly Jr (and President)
Senior Executive Officers: W A Merritt Jr (Executive VP), G H Engels (Senior VP), Dr P Courtin (VP), P B Gaynor (VP), Eric V Carter (VP), J Lederhaas (VP), R Luth (Treasurer), Polly Parke (VP), David Ruberg (VP)

PRINCIPAL ACTIVITIES: Designer, manufacturer and distributor of advanced, digital key telephone, hybrids and switching systems

Principal Subsidiaries: International Components Corporation; TIE Industries Inc; TIE International Inc; TIE/Communications (UK) Ltd; TIE/Italia Spa; TIE/Telecommunications Canada Inc; Technicom International Inc; Technicom Systems Inc; Turret Equipment Corp; Chatlos Systems Inc

Principal Bank: Morgan Guarantee Bank, NY

Financial Information:

	Dec 31 1985 $'000	Dec 31 1986 $'000
Sales revenues	321,263	298,154
(Loss) before taxes	(102,322)	(55,470)
Net (loss)	(77,889)	(56,590)
(Loss) per share	($2.17)	($1.57)
Shareholders equity	211,452	156,346

No of Employees: 1,500

TIGER INTERNATIONAL, INC

1888 Century Park East, Los Angeles, CA 90067
Tel: (213) 552-6300
Telex: (213) 557-2860 tiger intl lsa

Chairman: Stephen M Wolf (and President and Chief Executive Officer)
Senior Executive Officers: Larry G Morris (Senior VP Finance and Administration), Robert J Harter Jr (Senior VP Law), Rolf Bodenburg (VP Taxes), Joseph K McDonnell (VP, Controller and Treasurer)

PRINCIPAL ACTIVITIES: The company has interests in airfreight and road transportation services

Principal Subsidiaries: The Flying Tiger Line Inc; Warren Transport, Inc

Principal Bank: Union Bank (Tiger Int'l)

Financial Information:

	Dec 31 1985 $'000	Dec 31 1986 $'000
Sales revenues	1,147,000	1,110,948
Net (loss)	(72,687)	(45,063)
(Loss) per share	($2.69)	($1.45)
Shareholders (deficit)	(4,462)	(43,160)

Principal Shareholders: Reliance Financial Services Corp (4,019,900 shares); Neuberger & Berman (1,854,881 shares)

No of Employees: 6,300

TII INDUSTRIES INC

1375 Akron Street, Copiague, NY 11726
Tel: (516) 789 5000

Chairman: Alfred J Roach (and Chief Executive Officer)
President: Timothy J Roach (and Vice Chairman and Joint Chief Executive Officer)
Senior Executive Officers: Steve L Takacs (Executive VP and Chief Operating Officer), Jack Cawley (VP Engineering), John T Hyland Jr (VP Finance), Dorothy Roach (Secretary and Treasurer), James R Grover Jr (Legal Counsel), C Bruce Barksdale (VP Division)

PRINCIPAL ACTIVITIES: Manufacture of electronic equipment for the telecommunications industry

Principal Subsidiaries: TII Computer Systems Inc

Principal Bank: Chase Manhattan Bank

Financial Information:

	$'000
Sales revenues	31,350

No of Employees: 500

TILCON INC

Blackrock Avenue, New Britain, CT 06050
Tel: (203) 223-3651

Chairman: Hugh W Laughland
President: Angelo Tomasso Jr (and Chief Executive Officer)
Senior Executive Officers: Charles McDonald (VP and Chief Financial Officer), William J Tomasso (VP)

PRINCIPAL ACTIVITIES: Supply of construction materials; civil engineering

Parent Company: BTR plc, London, UK

Principal Bank: European American Bank

Financial Information:

	$'000
Sales revenues	200,000

No of Employees: 1,500

TILLAMOOK COUNTY CREAMERY ASSOCIATION

PO Box 313, Tillamook, OR 97141
Tel: (503) 842-4481

Chairman: Edward Myers (and President)
Senior Executive Officers: Rudolph Fenk (VP), Robert C Berkey (Treasurer)

PRINCIPAL ACTIVITIES: Supply of milk and dairy products
Principal Bank: United States National Bank of Oregon
Financial Information:

	$'000
Sales revenues	66,000

No of Employees: 240

TILLIE LEWIS FOODS
PO Drawer J, Fresno & Navy Drive, Stockton, CA 95201
Tel: (209) 946-4011

Senior Executive Officers: T Wise (Senior VP Production), Albert S Heiser (VP Private Label), Tom Hickey (VP Pacific Sales), Stephen P Kilroy (VP Industrial Relations), Donald A Krenz (VP Legal), Don Enberg (VP Purchasing)

PRINCIPAL ACTIVITIES: Supply of canned vegetables and specialty foods
Principal Bank: Bank of America
Financial Information:

	$'000
Sales revenues	100,000

No of Employees: 1,200

TILLOTSON CORPORATION
59 Water Street, Everett, MA 02149
Tel: (617) 387-9400

President: Neil E Tillotson (and Treasurer)
Senior Executive Officers: Grafton J Corbett (Assistant Treasurer)

PRINCIPAL ACTIVITIES: Production of special purpose gloves for industrial, medical and surgical use; heavy duty gloves; novelty rubber goods; boatbuilding
Principal Bank: Bay Bank of Norfolk County Trust
Financial Information:

	$'000
Sales revenues	90,000

No of Employees: 2,200

TIMBERLAND COMPANY
Main Street, Newmarket, NH 03857
Tel: (603) 659-3111
Telex: TWX 710 3660001 timberland ud

President: Herman Swartz
Senior Executive Officers: Stanley Kravetz (Executive VP and Secretary), Douglas Eldridge (VP Finance and Administration)

PRINCIPAL ACTIVITIES: Manufacture of specialty footwear including hand made shoes, work shoes and outdoor boots
Principal Bank: The First National Bank of Boston
Financial Information:

	$'000
Sales revenues	70,000

No of Employees: 1,400

TIMBERLAND INDUSTRIES INC
3805 108th Avenue NE, Box 3546, Bellevue, WA 98009
Tel: (206) 828-3565

Chairman: J Allen MacDonald (and Chief Executive Officer)
President: R G Hess Jr (and Chief Operating Officer)

PRINCIPAL ACTIVITIES: Production of wooden cabinets, doors, windows and other building products; wholesale trade in lighting equipment and hardware
Principal Bank: Seattle First National Bank
Financial Information:

	$'000
Sales revenues	51,700

No of Employees: 500

TIME INC
Time & Life Building, New York, NY 10020
Tel: (212) 586-1212
Telex: TRT 177976 time inc ut

Chairman: J Richard Munro (and Chief Executive Officer)
President: N J Nicholas Jr (and Chief Operating Officer)
Senior Executive Officers: Ralph P Davidson (Chairman of Executive Committee), Gerald M Levin (Executive VP), Kelso F Sutton (Executive VP), Reginald K Brack Jr (Group VP), William M Guttman (VP, Secretary and Legal Counsel), R Bruce Hiland (VP and Chief Administration Officer), Donald M Wilson (Corporate VP Public Affairs)

PRINCIPAL ACTIVITIES: Publishing of newspapers, magazines and books; information services; cable and pay television interests
Principal Bank: Morgan Guaranty Trust Co
Financial Information:

	Dec 31 1985	Dec 31 1986
	$'000	$'000
Sales revenues	3,403,554	3,762,087
Net income	199,820	376,388
Earnings per share	$3.15	$5.95
Shareholders equity	1,210,510	1,301,657

No of Employees: 19,000

TIMEPLEX, INC
400 Chestnut Ridge Road, Woodcliff Lake, NJ 07675
Tel: (201) 930-4672
Telex: TWX 910 3506475 clock

Chairman: Edward Botwinick (and President); Vice Chairman: Bernard Furman (and Secretary, General Counsel and Chief Administration Officer)
Senior Executive Officers: Victoria A Brown (Senior VP), Bryan Gray (VP), Alan Guibord (VP), Rick MacPherson (VP), Wayne McPhearson (VP), Steve Ottersten (VP Human Resources), Harry Thomas (VP), Joseph Wechter (VP Operations)

PRINCIPAL ACTIVITIES: Manufacture of data transmission equipment
Principal Subsidiaries: Timeplex Canada (Canada); Timeplex Ltd (UK); Controleware GmbH (Germany)
Principal Bank: United Jersey Bank
Financial Information:

	$'000
Sales revenues	96,040

No of Employees: 1,250

TIMES FIBER COMMUNICATIONS, INC
1000 Research Pky, Meriden, CT 06450
Tel: (203) 634-2000

Chairman: Colin J O'Brien (and President and Chief Executive Officer)
Senior Executive Officers: Kenneth L Coleman (Senior VP), William F Tuxbury (Senior VP), David S Lenzer (VP Human Resources), Kirk Evans (VP and Treasurer), Robert T Brown (VP), Andrew C Marx (VP), Lemuel A Tarshis (VP and General Manager Communication Systems Division)

PRINCIPAL ACTIVITIES: Manufacture of fiber optic cables; communications equipment components
Parent Company: Insilco Corporation, Meriden, CT
Principal Bank: The Chase Manhattan Bank
Financial Information:

	$'000
Sales revenues	124,410

No of Employees: 800

TIMES MIRROR COMPANY (THE)
Time Mirror Square, Los Angeles, CA 90053
Tel: (213) 237-3700
Telex: TWX 910 3210050 tnmn la

Chairmen: Robert F Erbury (Chairman of the Board and Chief Executive Officer); Otis Chandler (Chairman of the Executive Committee)
President: David A Laventhol
Senior Executive Officers: Phillip L Williams (Vice Chairman of the Board), W Thomas Johnson Jr (Vice Chairman of the Board), Dow W Carpenter Jr (Senior VP), Charles R Redmond (Executive VP), Patrick H Butler (VP), Peter C Goldmark (Group VP), Edward E Johnson (VP, Planning and Development), Donald S Kellermann (VP, Public Affairs), Donald S Maxwell (VP), John J McCrory (VP), Jack L Plank (VP, Taxes), Jerome S Rubin (Group VP), Herbert K Schnall (Group VP), Charles I Schneider (Group VP), James R Simpson (VP, Human Resources), Stender E Sweeney (VP), Larry W Wangberg (VP), James W Wallace (Associate General Counsel and Secretary), Joyce M Fields (Treasurer), Duane L Storhaug (Controller)

PRINCIPAL ACTIVITIES: Newspaper publishing; book, magazine and other publishing; broadcast television; and cable television. Other operations include commercial printing and timberland management
Principal Subsidiaries: Los Angeles Times; Times Mirror Cable Television; The Baltimore Sun Newspapers and others
Financial Information:

	Dec 31 1985	Dec 31 1986
	$'000	$'000
Sales revenues	803,609	806,764
Income before taxes	125,152	174,537
Net income	58,207	99,324
Dividends	91,806	96,705
Dividends per share	$1.36	$1.50
Earnings per share	$0.90	$1.53
Common stock(1)	64,433	64,450
Retained income	893,752	1,204,271
Shareholders equity(2)	1,116,115	1,434,823

(1) number of shares in thousands
(2) includes retained earnings

No of Employees: 28,382

TIMES MIRROR MAGAZINES

380 Madison Avenue, New York, NY 10017
Tel: (212) 687-3000

Chairman: Herbert K Schnall
President: John A Scott
Senior Executive Officers: John Condon (Executive VP), Michael J Haugh (Treasurer)

PRINCIPAL ACTIVITIES: Publishing of magazines and books; book club services
Parent Company: The Times Mirror Company, Los Angeles, CA
Principal Bank: Bankers Trust Co
Financial Information:

	$'000
Sales revenues	100,000

No of Employees: 400

TIMES PUBLISHING CO

490 First Avenue S, St Petersburg, FL 33701
Tel: (813) 893-8111
Telex: WUT 523413 times new stb

Chairman: Eugene C Patterson
President: Andrew E Barnes (and Editor)
Senior Executive Officers: John H O'Hearn (Executive VP), Clifton D Camp Jr (Senior VP and Secretary), Norman P Dusseault (VP and Assistant General Manager)

PRINCIPAL ACTIVITIES: Publishing of newspapers
Principal Bank: Florida National Bank
Financial Information:

	$'000
Sales revenues	100,000

No of Employees: 1,200

TIMEX GROUP LTD

Waterbury, CT 06720
Tel: (203) 573-5000
Telex: ITT 4994309 timexnj

Chairman: T F Olsen
President: James W Binns
Senior Executive Officers: R DeAngelis (VP Finance), R Werner (Treasurer)

PRINCIPAL ACTIVITIES: Manufacture of clocks, watches and timing devices
Financial Information:

	$'000
Sales revenues	600,000

No of Employees: 20,000

TIMKEN COMPANY

1835 Dueber Avenue SW, Canton, OH 44706
Tel: (216) 438-3000
Telex: TWX 910 3502 425 timken

Chairman: W R Timken Jr (and Chairman of the Executive and Finance Committees)
President: J F Toot Jr
Senior Executive Officers: P J Ashton (Executive VP Bearings), C H West (Executive VP Steel), R W Lang (VP Personnel), A B Glossbrenner (VP Steel Operations), J H Fellows (VP Marketing), D L Hart (VP Bearings, North and South America), R L Leibensperger (VP Technical), J K Ramsey (VP Finance and Law, Secretary, Treasurer and Real Estate Officer), John J Schubach (VP Strategic Management)

PRINCIPAL ACTIVITIES: Manufacture of bearings and specialty steels; mining machinery components
Principal Bank: AmeriTrust
Financial Information:

	Dec 31 1985	Dec 31 1986
	$'000	$'000
Sales revenues	1,090,674	1,058,055
Net income (loss)	(3,903)	2,736
Earnings per share	-	$0.22
Shareholders equity	789,280	806,622

No of Employees: 17,560

TIPPERARY CORPORATION

511 W Ohio, Midland, TX 79701
Tel: (915) 684-7151

Chairman: Deane H Stolz (and Chief Executive Officer)
President: James D Ross (aned Chief Operating Officer)
Senior Executive Officers: Harlow W Gary R Chancellor (Group VP Gas Processing)

PRINCIPAL ACTIVITIES: Oil and gas exploration and production
Principal Bank: RepublicBank
Financial Information:

	$'000
Sales revenues	38,600

No of Employees: 100

TITAN CORPORATION

16000 Ventura Blvd, Encino, CA 91436
Tel: (818) 995 1755

Chairman: J Sidney Webb
President: Gene W Ray (and Chief Executive Officer and Secretary)
Senior Executive Officers: Edward F Kavanaugh (Senior VP Finance and Chief Financial Officer), Rolf B Erickson (Senior

VP Corporate Development), Albert E Knauf Jr (VP), John R McDougall (VP), James G Turner (VP), D Marshall Nelson (VP, Secretary and General Counsel)

PRINCIPAL ACTIVITIES: Manufacture of electronic products including semiconductors; magnetic cores; permanent and ferrite magnets; memory systems for computers
Principal Bank: Bank of America
Financial Information:

	$'000
Sales revenues	97,860

No of Employees: 3,000

TITANIUM METALS CORPORATION OF AMERICA

PO Box 2824, Pittsburgh, PA 15230
Tel: (412) 262-4200

President: Joseph W Byrne
Senior Executive Officers: J B Bruhn (VP Sales and Marketing), Dennis P Kelly (VP Finance)

PRINCIPAL ACTIVITIES: Titanium products
Parent Company: Allegheny International Inc
Principal Bank: Mellon Bank
Financial Information:

	$'000
Sales revenues	200,000

No of Employees: 1,500

TMBR DRILLING INC

500 Empire Plaza Building, PO Box 2608, Midland, TX 79701
Tel: (915) 682 9715

Chairman: Joe G Roper
President: Donald L Evans
Senior Executive Officers: James M Alsup (Secretary), J R Geltemeyer (Treasurer)

PRINCIPAL ACTIVITIES: Drilling of oil and gas wells
Financial Information:

	$'000
Sales revenues	46,770

No of Employees: 570

TNP ENTERPRISES INC

4100 International Plaza, PO Box 2943, Fort Worth, TX 76113
Tel: (817) 731 0099

Chairman: R D Woofter (and President and Chief Executive Officer)
Senior Executive Officers: D R Barnard (VP and Treasurer), J M Tarpley (VP), F G Von Huben (Secretary)

PRINCIPAL ACTIVITIES: Supply of electricity
Principal Bank: InterFirst Bank Fort Worth
Financial Information:

	$'000
Sales revenues	429,850

No of Employees: 1,050

TODD SHIPYARDS CORPORATION

1 Evertrust Plaza, Jersey City, NJ 07302
Tel: (201) 434-0200
Cable: ROBIN NEWJERSEY
Telex: TWX 710 5816139 TODD NJ

Chairman: Hans K Schaefer (and Chief Executive Officer)
President: John T Kilbride Jr (and Chief Operating Officer)
Senior Executive Officers: John B Burguieres (VP Marketing), Clifford E Jones (VP Resources)

PRINCIPAL ACTIVITIES: Todd Shipyards Corporation, the largest independent shipbuilding company in the United States, is engaged in the construction and overhaul/repair of naval and other government ships, as well as commercial ships, both domestic and foreign. Todd operates full-service shipyards in Seattle, San Francisco and Los Angeles that serve naval ships assigned to the Pacific fleet and commercial vessels engaged in coastal and Pacific Basin trade. On the Gulf Coast, its Galveston Division also serves naval ships and, with the New Orleans Division, provides complete services to vessels engaged in Caribbean Basin trade, intercoastal transport, offshore oil support and inland waterway commerce
Principal Subsidiaries: Todd Pacific Shipyards Corporation; The Aro Corporation
Principal Bank: Marine Midland Bank
Financial Information:

	$'000
Sales revenues	413,674

No of Employees: 5,000

TOKHEIM CORPORATION

1602 Wabash Avenue, PO Box 360, Fort Wayne, IN 46801
Tel: (219) 423-2552
Telecopier: 219-482-2677
Telex: 023-2439 Tokheim FWA

President: John E Overmeyer
Senior Executive Officers: Peter L Vlaskamp (VP Petroleum Equipment Division), Randolph J Straka (VP, Treasurer and Secretary), Huffman R Heisey (VP and General Manager, Process Controls Division), Robert P Seay (VP, Advanced Products and Electronics Division), Norman D Hottman (VP, International Division)

PRINCIPAL ACTIVITIES: Manufacturer of systems for the movement and measurement of liquids, including service station equipment with electronics, meters, hand, transfer and automotive electric fuel pumps
Principal Subsidiaries: Tokheim International Sales Inc; Tokheim Investment Corp; Central Die Casting & Mfg Co; National Controls Corp; Tokheim of Canada Ltd; Tokheim Electronic Systems ApS (Denmark); Tokheim BV (Netherlands); Tokheim GmbH (Germany); Tokheim Ltd (UK); Tokheim South Africa (Pty) Ltd (South Africa); Tokheim Service (Pty) Ltd (South Africa); Tokheim Sales BV (Netherlands)
Principal Bank: Summit Bank
Financial Information:

	Nov 30 1985	Nov 30 1986
	$'000	$'000
Sales revenues	147,380	157,232
Income before taxes	18,119	8,463
Net income	7,097	2,799
Dividends	3,174	3,176
Dividends per share	$0.48	$0.48
Earnings per share	$1.67	$0.85
Common stock	7,858	8,066
Retained income	69,993	72,481
Shareholders equity	74,088	73,904

No of Employees: 1,875

TOLEDO TRUSTCORP INC

Three SeaGate, Toledo, OH 43603
Tel: (419) 259-8598

President: George W Haigh (and Chief Executive Officer)
Senior Executive Officers: Edwin M Bergsmark (Executive VP and General Counsel), Richard E Caufman (Chief Financial Officer)

PRINCIPAL ACTIVITIES: Banking services
Principal Subsidiaries: The Toledo Trust Company

No of Employees: 1,700

TOLL BROTHERS INC

101 Witmer Rd, Horsham, PA 19044
Tel: (215) 441-4400

Chairman: Robert I Toll (and Chief Executive Officer)

President: B E Toll (and Secretary)
Senior Executive Officers: J H Rassman (Senior VP, Chief Financial Officer and Treasurer), Zvi Barzilay (Senior VP), G E Casey (Senior VP)

PRINCIPAL ACTIVITIES: Design and construction of family homes
Financial Information:

	$'000
Sales revenues	126,000

No of Employees: 230

TOMY CORPORATION

PO Box 6252, Carson, CA 90749
Tel: (213) 549-2721
Telex: WUT 653493 tomy toy crsn

President: David Iida
Senior Executive Officers: John van der Hulst (Senior VP and Controller), Frank Ward (Senior VP Marketing and Sales), William Yarbrough (VP Operations), Larry Anderson (VP Sales), Charles Cleveland (VP), William Uglow (VP Marketing)

PRINCIPAL ACTIVITIES: Manufacture of toys and games
Parent Company: Tomy Kogyo Co Inc
Principal Bank: Mitsubishi Bank
Financial Information:

	$'000
Sales revenues	150,000

No of Employees: 400

TONKA CORPORATION

4144 Shoreline Blvd, Spring Park, MN 55384
Tel: (612) 475-9500
Telex: WUI 6879061 tonka sppk

President: Stephen G Shank (and Chief Executive Officer)
Senior Executive Officers: David J Anderson (VP Human Resources), Patrick S Feely (Senior VP Commercial Operations), Robert H Kelsey (VP Research and Development), Raymond E McDonald (VP Marketing), Donald Holton (VP Operations), James D Miller (Chief Financial Officer), Gerald V Cleary (VP Sales)

PRINCIPAL ACTIVITIES: Manufacture of toys
Principal Subsidiaries: Tonka Corp (Canada) Ltd; Tonka Corp Pty Ltd (Australia); Tonka DISC Corp (50%); Tonka Manufacturing Inc; Tonka Mexico SA de CV; Tonka New Zealand Ltd; Tonka Transportation Inc
Principal Bank: First National Bank Minneapolis
Financial Information:

	$'000
Sales revenues	244,400

No of Employees: 1,900

TONY LAMA CO INC

See LAMA, TONY, CO INC

TOOTSIE ROLL INDUSTRIES, INC

7401 South Cicero Avenue, Chicago, IL 60629
Tel: (312) 838-3400
Telex: 910-221-4070 TWX

Chairman: Melvin J Gordon
President: Ellen R Gordon
Senior Executive Officers: F T Kushnir (VP, Finance), John W Newlin Jr (VP, Manufacturing), Thomas E Corr (VP, Marketing and Sales), G Howard Ember (Treasurer), William Touretz (Secretary), Daniel P Drechney (Controller)

PRINCIPAL ACTIVITIES: Tootsie Roll Industries Inc has engaged in the manufacture and sale of candy since 1896
Trade Names: TOOTSIE, TOOTSIE ROLL, TOOTSIE POP, TOOTSIE POP DROPS, TOOTSIE ROLL FLAVOR ROLLS, TOOTSIE GUMDROPS, MASON DOTS, MASON CROWS, BONOMO'S, TURKISH TAFFY, CELLA'S CHOCOLATE COVERED CHERRIES (all Registered Trademarks)
Principal Subsidiaries: Arrendadora Gorvac SA de CV; Henry Eisen Advertising Agency Inc; Tootsie Roll of Canada Ltd; Tootsie Roll Express Inc; Tootsie Roll Industries of New York Inc; Tootsie Roll Marketing Ltd; Tootsie Rolls-Latin America Inc; The Sweets Company Inc; The Sweets Mix Company Inc; TRI International Co; Tutsi SA de CV; Cella's Confections Inc
Principal Banks: American National Bank & Trust Company of Chicago; Manufacturers Hanover Trust Company
Financial Information:

	Dec 31 1985	Dec 31 1986
	$'000	$'000
Sales revenues	106,729	111,403
Income before taxes	22,660	25,701
Net income	10,917	12,802
Cash dividends	1,324	1,620
Stock dividends	2,902	5,124
Dividends per share	$0.31	$0.38
Earnings per share	$2.54	$2.99
Common stock	2,777	4,289
Retained income	37,094	41,635
Shareholders equity	53,501	64,583

No of Employees: 1,300

TOP BRASS ENTERPRISES INC

2174 Hewlett Avenue, Merrick, NY 11566
Tel: (516) 379 9800

Chairman: Phillip J Zeller Jr (and Secretary and Treasurer)
President: Jerome Greenberg (and Chief Executive Officer)

PRINCIPAL ACTIVITIES: Retail trade in televisions, electronic equipment and domestic appliances
Financial Information:

	$'000
Sales revenues	48,050

No of Employees: 470

TOPP ELECTRONICS INC

465 NW 77th Avenue, Miami, FL 33166
Tel: (305) 592-5023
Telex: WUT 519531 topp intl mia

President: Allen Rubin
Senior Executive Officers: Carlos Villalobos (Executive VP)

PRINCIPAL ACTIVITIES: Consumer electrical and electronic products
Principal Bank: South East Bank
Financial Information:

	$'000
Sales revenues	50,000

No of Employees: 260

TOPPS CHEWING GUM, INC

254 36th Street, Brooklyn, NY 11232
Tel: (718) 768-8900
Telex: RCA 232034 topps ur

Chairman: Arthur T Shorin (and Chief Executive Officer)
President: Joel J Shorin (and Chief Operating Officer)
Senior Executive Officers: Louis Walker (VP Finance and Chief Financial Officer), Seymour P Berger (VP Sports), Edward R Dulworth (VP Manufacturing), James McBrearty (VP Sales), John F Sullivan (VP Marketing and Sales)

PRINCIPAL ACTIVITIES: Manufacture of chewing gum and confectionery
Parent Company: Topps Holding Co Inc
Principal Bank: Manufacturers Hanover Trust Co
Financial Information:

	$'000
Sales revenues	73,000

No of Employees: 1,000

TOPS MARKETS INC

60 Dingens Street, Buffalo, NY 14206
Tel: (716) 823 3712

Chairman: Armand J Castellani
President: Savino Nanula (and Chief Executive Officer)
Senior Executive Officers: Paul D Bauer (Senior VP and Chief Financial Officer), Lawrence P Castellani (Senior VP), John S Dimiceli (Senior VP), Thomas J Shanahan (Senior VP and Secretary)

PRINCIPAL ACTIVITIES: Supermarkets
Financial Information:

	$'000
Sales revenues	742,920

No of Employees: 8,000

TORCHMARK CORPORATION

2001 Third Avenue South, Birmingham, AL 35233
Tel: (205) 325-4200

Chairman: Ronald K Richey (and Chief Executive Officer)
President: Jon W Rotenstreich
Senior Executive Officers: William T Graves (Executive VP), Herbert P Evert (Executive VP), John W Lovin Jr (Senior VP), William H Ray Jr (Senior VP), Michael L Avery (VP), Michael K Fagin (VP), Paul E Rutledge III (VP), Samuel E Upchurch Jr (VP and Legal Counsel), Terry G White (VP and Controller)

PRINCIPAL ACTIVITIES: Provision of general insurance and financial services
Principal Subsidiaries: American Life and Accident Insurance Co; CMI Corpn; Evaluation Associates Inc; Globe Life and Accident Insurance Co; J Gordon Gaines Inc; Liberty National Fire Insurance Co; Liberty National Reinsurance Co Ltd; Liberty Real Estate Corp; Torch Energy Corp; Torchmark Financial Services Inc; Torchmark Leasing Programs Inc; United American Leasing Programs Inc; United American Insurance Co; United Investors Life Insurance Co; Waddell & Reed Asset Management Co; Waddell & Reed Inc; Torchmark Reinsurance Co Ltd
Principal Bank: First National Bank of Chicago
Financial Information:

	$'000
Revenues	1,600,000

No of Employees: 6,300

TORO COMPANY

8111 Lyndale Avenue S, Minneapolis, MN 55420
Tel: (612) 888-8801
Telex: WUI 669706 torob

Chairman: Stephen F Keating (and Chairman of Executive Committee)
President: Kendrick B Melrose (and Chief Executive Officer)
Senior Executive Officers: Kenneth D Larson (Executive VP), Robert J Moeller (Executive VP), Terry M Anstett (VP Manufacturing), Robert B Carlson (VP and General Manager Fitness Equipment), Richard J Hargarten (VP Physical Distribution), Ram N Kumar (VP International Equipment), Vernon A Johnson (VP, General Counsel and Secretary), J David McIntosh (VP and General Manager Home Improvement), David H Morris (VP and General Manager Irrigation), Ralph D Murray (VP and General Manager Consolidated Products), Robert A Peterson (VP Finance), John G Szafranski (VP and General Manager Commercial Products), James R Watson (VP Customer Relations)

PRINCIPAL ACTIVITIES: Garden and lawn care equipment; agricultural and horticultural irrigation equipment and sprinklers
Principal Subsidiaries: Toro Sales Co; Toro International Sales Co; Toro Western Corp; Toro Irrigation Inc; Toro Irrigation Ltd (UK); Toro Australia Pty Ltd (Australia); Toro Credit Co; Irrigation Engineering Inc
Principal Bank: First National Bank of Minneapolis
Financial Information:

	$'000
Sales revenues	336,810

No of Employees: 1,900

TORRINGTON CO

59 Field Street, Torrington, CT 06790
Tel: (203) 482-9511
Telex: WUT 882377 tormorr ud

President: T E Bennett
Senior Executive Officers: N L Cook (VP and General Manager Heavy Bearings), A M Nixon (VP and General Manager Needle Bearings), H Degioanni (VP and General Manager Torrington International), M J Hartnett (VP Technical), G R Kelleher (VP and Controller), S T Martin (VP and General Manager Engineered Bearings Division), A A Padovano (VP North American Sales), J J Palker (VP Human Resources), W P Rausch (VP Business Systems), R B Wassung (VP), J H Williams (VP)

PRINCIPAL ACTIVITIES: Precision engineering; production of ball bearings
Parent Company: Ingersoll-Rand Co, Woodcliff Lake, NJ
Financial Information:

	$'000
Sales revenues	100,000

No of Employees: 12,000

TOSCO CORPORATION

2401 Colorado Avenue, Box 2401, Santa Monica, CA 90406-2401
Tel: (213) 207-6000
Telex: WUT 691523 TOSCOPETRO LSA

Chairman: Clarence G Frame (and Chief Executive Officer)
President: John G Drosdick (and Chief Operating Officer)
Senior Executive Officers: Eric Schwartz (Executive VP, Finance and Administration, General Counsel, and Secretary), William A Floyd (Senior VP, Marketing), James M Cleary (VP, Refining), Thomas K Nance (Treasurer), Michael L Chase (Controller), Robert E Sears (Corporate Communications Director)

PRINCIPAL ACTIVITIES: Refining and distribution of oil products
Principal Bank: The First National Bank of Boston
Financial Information:

	Dec 31 1985 $'000	Dec 31 1986 $'000
Sales revenues	1,513,094	780,278
Net income	8,867	17,580
Earnings per share(1)	$0.29	$0.53
Common stock(2)	25,017	28,779
Total equity (deficit)	(234,926)	150,253

(1) fully diluted
(2) outstanding in thousands

Principal Shareholders: Colorado Place Limited; Solomon Asset Management, Inc; Continental Casualty Company; Loews Corporation; Delaware Management Co, Inc; The First National Bank of Boston; Security Pacific National Bank; Manufacturers Hanover Trust Company; TCW Asset Management Company
No of Employees: 898

TOSHIBA AMERICA, INC

375 Park Avenue, New York, NY 10152
Tel: (212) 308 2040

Chairman: Nobuo Ishizaka (and Chief Executive Officer)
Presidents: Kazuo Ishiguro, Takahisa Ohira, Ryoui Suzuki
Senior Executive Officers: Toshioki Masuda (Executive VP Manufacturing), J P Michie (Executive VP Consumer Products), Kiyoaki Shimagami (Senior VP Consumer Products), Kazuhiro Hirose (Senior VP and General Manager

Electronics Components Business Sector), Takashi Ishida (Senior VP Industrial Electronics), Masahiro Matsuo (Senior VP Electronics Components Business Sector), Motoya Oghino (Senior VP Consumer Products), Sadao Takeda (Senior VP Manufacturing Division)

PRINCIPAL ACTIVITIES: Production of domestic electrical and electronic equipment; medical equipment, telecommunications equipment and electronic components
Parent Company: Toshiba Corporation, Japan
Principal Bank: Bank of Tokyo Trust Co
Financial Information:

	$'000
Sales revenues	1,000,000

No of Employees: 2,000

TOTAL PETROLEUM (NORTH AMERICA) LTD

999-18th St, PO Box 500, Denver, CO 80201
Tel: (303) 291-2000
Telex: 450198

Chairman: Philippe Dunoyer (and President and Chief Executive Officer)
Senior Executive Officers: Raymond C F Leeks (VP Finance, Treasurer and Controller)

PRINCIPAL ACTIVITIES: Oil refining and gasoline distribution
Trade Names: TOTAL, BEST, APCO, VICKERS gasoline
Parent Company: TOTAL Compagnie Française des Pétroles, Paris, France (49%)
Principal Bank: National Bank of Detroit
Financial Information:

	Dec 31 1985 $'000	Dec 31 1986 $'000
Sales revenues	2,372,100	1,597,400
Net income	88,100	38,000
Dividends	9,661	11,300
Shareholders equity	343,700	278,900

Principal Shareholders: TOTAL Compagnie Française de Petroles
No of Employees: 4,500

TOTAL SYSTEM SERVICES

PO Box 120, Columbus, GA 31902
Tel: (404) 571-2347

Chairman: James H Blanchard
President: Richard W Ussery (and Chief Executive Officer)
Senior Executive Officers: Philip W Tomlinson (Executive VP), Bill Blizard (Senior VP), Bill Pruett (Senior VP)

PRINCIPAL ACTIVITIES: Credit card services
Financial Information:

	$'000
Revenues	36,000

No of Employees: 300

TOWLE MANUFACTURING CO

144 Addison Street, Boston, MA 02128
Tel: (617) 569-7600

Chairman: William W Treat; Vice Chairman: Paul R Duncan
President: Paul J Dunphy (and Chief Executive and Chief Financial Officer)
Senior Executive Officers: William L Butts (Executive VP and Chief Operating Officer), Walter J Robbie (Senior VP), Barry Florence (VP)

PRINCIPAL ACTIVITIES: Manufacture of giftware including sterling silver and silver plated holloware and flatware, watches, crystal and glass products, class emblems and jewelry
Principal Subsidiaries: Leonard Silver Manufacturing Co Inc; Poole Silver Co; PMC (Sheffield) Ltd; Raimond Silver Mfg Co Inc; Rosemar Silver Co Inc; Shelton Ware Inc; Towle/Sigma Giftware Corp; Towle Silversmiths; Carvel Hall Cutlery; Oxford Hall Cutlery; Gailstyn-Sutton; Javit Crystal; Tiffin Crystal; Gold Lance; Irvinware; National Silver Industries Inc; F B Rogers Co; Galway Crystal Ltd; Seiden Brass; Old Harbor Co; Westfield Designs Ltd
Principal Bank: First National Bank of Boston
Financial Information:

	$'000
Sales revenues	264,613

No of Employees: 2,000

TOWN & COUNTRY JEWELRY MANUFACTURING CORPORATION

25 Union Street, Chelsea, MA 02150
Tel: (617) 884-8500

President: C William Carey (and Treasurer)
Senior Executive Officers: Francis X Correra (VP and Controller)

PRINCIPAL ACTIVITIES: Manufacture of jewelry
Financial Information:

	$'000
Sales revenues	60,820

No of Employees: 650

TOYS R US, INC

395 W Passaic Street, Rochelle Park, NJ 07662
Tel: (201) 845-5033
Telex: 7109905165

Chairman: Charles Lazarus (and Chief Executive Officer)
President: Norman Ricken (and Chief Operating Officer)
Senior Executive Officers: Michael Goldstein (Executive VP-Finance and Administration), Michael P Miller (Senior VP-Real Estate), Stephen W Austin (VP-Real Estate), Dennis Healey (VP-Management Information Systems), Louis Lipschitz (VP-Treasurer), Donald L Margolis (VP-Controller), Michael L Tumolo (VP-Real Estate Counsel), Lester Yassky (Secretary-Attorney-at-law-Partner-Shea & Gould)

PRINCIPAL ACTIVITIES: Retail selling of toys, games, sporting goods, bicycles, children's clothing, electronic and video games, home computers, records, books and juvenile furniture
Principal Subsidiaries: Interstate Department Stores Inc; TRU Inc; TRU (HK) Ltd; Toys R US (UK) Ltd; Toys R US (Canada) Ltd
Principal Bank: Bankers Trust Company; Morgan Guaranty Trust Co
Financial Information:

	Feb 2 1986 $'000	Feb 1 1987 $'000
Sales revenues	1,976,134	2,444,903
Income before taxes	219,774	284,217
Net income	119,774	152,217
Earnings per share	$0.93	$1.17
Common stock	8,405	12,711
Retained income	502,595	650,499
Shareholders equity	717,394	901,041

No of Employees: 28,000 (over 50,000 during Christmas)

TRACOR, INC

6500 Tracor Lane, Austin, TX 78725
Tel: (512) 926-2800
Telex: 77 6410 Tracor AUS

Chairman: Frank W McBee Jr (and Chief Executive Officer)
President: Mellon C Baird
Senior Executive Officers: J D Baird, (VP, Financial Services), W J Buffo (Group VP, Tracor Instruments), W A Clements (Group VP, Tracor Components), J O Colley (VP, Taxes), A T Dearing (Corporate Secretary), W C Moyer Ph D (Group VP, Tracor Applied Sciences), J A Newby (VP, Public Relations), R E Painton (VP and General Counsel), D A Ross (Group VP, Iracor Aerospace), F S Schulte (VP and Controller), M Shaw

(VP, Industrial Relations), J A Smith (VP, Treasurer and Chief Financial Officer), S C Warrick Jr (Group VP, Flight Systems)

PRINCIPAL ACTIVITIES: The Company is a a leader in the development and production of electronic countermeasures systems and other advanced defense electronics; a significant engineering and support contractor in sonar, communications, and aviation, and a major manufacturer of scientific instruments and electrical and electromechanical components
Trade Names: autofuse, Tracor, Littelfuse, Westronics
Principal Subsidiaries: Tracor Applied Sciences Group:- Tracor Applied Sciences Inc; Tracor Hydronautics Inc; Tracor Hydro-Services Inc; Tracor Jitco Inc; Tracor Marcon Inc; Tracor Marine Inc. Tracor Aerospace Group:-Tracor Aerospace Inc. Tracor Flight Systems Group:- Tracor Flight Systems Inc; Tracor Aviation Inc; Tracor Flight Services Inc. Tracor Instruments Group:- Tracor Atlas Inc; Tracor Europa BV; Tracor Instruments Austin Inc; Tracor Northern Inc; Tracor Westronics; Tracor Xray Inc. Tracor Components Group:- Littelfuse Tracor Inc. Other:- Electro Source Inc
Principal Bank: Bank of America
Financial Information:

	Dec 31 1985	Dec 31 1986
	$'000	$'000
Sales revenues	546,534	632,119
Income before taxes	31,209	28,411
Net income	13,371	18,837
Dividends per share	$0.32	$0.36
Earnings per share(1)	$0.97	$0.97
Common stock(2)	19,425	19,558
Retained income	122,822	137,337
Shareholders equity	196,301	212,957

(1) assuming full dilution
(2) outstanding-historical in thousands

Principal Shareholders: estimated 18,000
No of Employees: 10,500

TRAILWAYS CORPORATION

1500 Jackson St, Dallas, TX 78521
Tel: (214) 655-7711

Chairman: James Kerrigan
President: Harry Lasko
Senior Executive Officers: B A Robinson (Executive VP)

PRINCIPAL ACTIVITIES: Production of motor vehicles; interests in passenger bus transportation
Principal Subsidiaries: Trailways Inc; Trailways of New England Inc; Trailways Manufacturing Group
Financial Information:

	$'000
Sales revenues	380,000

No of Employees: 750

TRAK AUTO CORPORATION

3300 75th Avenue, Landover, MD 20785
Tel: (301) 731 1200

Chairman: Herbert H Haft
President: Robert M Haft
Senior Executive Officers: James Gauntlett (VP), Gloria G Haft (VP), Ben S Kovalsky (VP), Charles D Shipe (VP and Secretary)

PRINCIPAL ACTIVITIES: Retail trade in motor accessories and household products
Principal Bank: Riggs National Bank of Washington DC
Financial Information:

	$'000
Sales revenues	97,830

No of Employees: 770

TRANE CO

3600 Pammel Creek Road, La Crosse, WI 54601
Tel: (608) 787-2000
Telex: WUI 661450 tranela lcr

Chairman: William G Roth (and Chief Executive Officer)
President: Richard J Campbell (and Chief Operating Officer)
Senior Executive Officers: George H Kerckhove (Executive VP), James C Workman (Executive VP), John H Shuey (VP Finance)

PRINCIPAL ACTIVITIES: Production of ventilation and air-conditioning equipment
Parent Company: American Standard Inc, New York, NY
Financial Information:

	$'000
Sales revenues	866,000

No of Employees: 10,700

TRANS WORLD AIRLINES, INC
TWA

605 3rd Avenue, New York, NY 10158
Tel: (212) 557-3000

Chairman: L E Smart; Vice Chairman: D Joseph Corr (and Chief Executive Officer)
Senior Executive Officers: C J Bradshaw (Senior VP), Mark A Buckstein (Senior VP and General Counsel), S G Long (Senior VP), M S Mulvany (Senior VP and Controller), C R Strand (Senior VP), J E Frankum (Senior VP), J F Ash (VP), C L Glass (VP and Controller), J C Hilly (VP), U V Hoffmann (VP and General Counsel), B J Kennedy (VP), J M Kennedy (VP), R J Kenny (VP), W T Lagow (VP), R A Peiser (VP and Treasurer), W D Slattery (VP)

PRINCIPAL ACTIVITIES: Operation of airline passenger services; freight and mail services
Financial Information:

	Dec 31 1985	Dec 31 1986
	$'000	$'000
Sales revenues	3,725,420	3,145,429
Net (loss)	(193,090)	(106,328)
(Loss) per share	($6.10)	($3.87)
Shareholders equity	-	241,362

No of Employees: 27,500

TRANSAMERICA CORPORATION

600 Montgomery Street, San Francisco, CA 94111
Tel: (415) 983-4000

Chairman: James R Harvey (and Chief Executive Officer)
President: Frank C Herringer
Senior Executive Officers: Arthur E Van Leuven (Executive VP), Maryellen B Cattani (Senior VP, General Counsel and Corporate Secretary), Blair C Pascoe (Senior VP), Kent L Colwell (VP-Real Estate Services), James P Conn (VP-Investment Services), Gary L Depolo (Senior VP), Lawrence W Briscoe (VP-Corporate Development), Herbert L Cunningham (VP-Administration), Ronald C Gilbert (VP and Treasurer), James F Kiraly (VP-Financial Planning and Analysis), James B Lockhart (VP-Public Affairs), Richard J Olsen (VP-Corporate Relations), Burton E Broome (VP and Controller), Peter J Dawson (VP-Information Systems), H Reed Gregg (VP-Auditing), Robert R Lindberg (VP-Financial Relations), William H McClave Jr (VP-Corporate Communications), James C Peirano (VP-Taxes)

PRINCIPAL ACTIVITIES: Transamerica Corporation is a diversified company engaged through subsidiaries in insurance, finance, manufacturing and transportation. Transamerica's insurance services include life insurance, insurance brokerage and property and casualty insurance. Finance services include consumer lending and title operations. Transportation services include equipment leasing, air travel and car and truck rental

Principal Subsidiaries: Transamerica Operating Companies: Transamerica Life Companies; Transamerica Insurance Group; Transamerica Title Insurance Company; Transamerica Real Estate Tax Service; Transamerica Financial Corporation; Transamerica Interway Inc. Other Operations: Transamerica Investment Services Inc; Transamerica Realty Services Inc; Transamerica Information Services Corporation
Financial Information:

	Dec 31 1985 $'000	Dec 31 1986 $'000
Revenues	5,590,441	6,075,547
Premium income(1)	2,769,341	3,012,906
Premium income(2)	949,199	1,079,535
Investment income	690,142	853,770
Net income	145,843	267,541
Common dividends	109,122	125,063
Dividends per share	$1.66	$1.72
Net income per share	$2.15	$3.57
Common stock	65,938	72,684
Retained income	1,567,361	1,501,460
Shareholders equity	2,145,374	2,304,362
Total assets	13,750,504	16,181,783

(1) Life Insurance
(2) Property/Casualty

No of Employees: 15,200

TRANSAMERICA FINANCIAL CORPORATION

1150 S Olive Street, Los Angeles, CA 90015
Tel: (213) 742-4321
Telex: TWX 910 3213091 transfinan lsa

Chairman: A E Van Leuven (and Chief Executive Officer)
President: Richard A Greenwalt
Senior Executive Officers: E Senott (Executive VP), Juho Arends (Senior VP), R A Golan (VP and Controller), David H Hawkins (VP and Treasurer), S R White (VP), C R Warfel (VP)

PRINCIPAL ACTIVITIES: Provision of financial services including loans; insurance and real estate interests
Parent Company: Transamerica Corporation
Financial Information:

	$'000
Revenues	2,000,000

No of Employees: 5,300

TRANSAMERICA LIFE INSURANCE & ANNUITY CO

1150 Olive St, Los Angeles, CA 90015
Tel: (213) 742-3111

Chairman: David R Carpenter
President: Gilbert F Cronin (and Chief Executive Officer)
Senior Executive Officers: Richard J Eskoff (Senior VP), Robert W McCarty (Senior VP), John Cook (VP), Donald Peter Radisich (VP), Penny Baron Ribnik (VP), Folke Norman Nordin (Treasurer)

PRINCIPAL ACTIVITIES: Life insurance and pension schemes
Parent Company: Transamerica Corporation, San Francisco, CA
Financial Information:

	Dec 31 1985 $'000	Dec 31 1986 $'000
Premium income	2,595,830	2,931,496
Investment income	314,050	412,221

No of Employees: 1,290

TRANSAMERICA OCCIDENTAL LIFE INSURANCE COMPANY

1150 South Olive Street, Los Angeles, CA 90015
Tel: (213) 742-2111
Telex: 342-2111

Chairman: David R Carpenter (and President and Chief Executive Officer)
Senior Executive Officers: James B Roszak (President-Canadian Division), Simon C Baitler (Executive VP), Gilbert F Cronin, (Executive VP), Ronald W Moreland (Executive VP), William A Simpson (Executive VP-Individual Insurance), David J Beed (Senior VP), Raymond A Bierschbach (Senior VP), A Lad Burgin (Senior VP), James W Dederer (Senior VP and General Counsel), David E Gooding (Senior VP-Corporate Marketing and Planning), George H G Hall (Senior VP and Chief Financial Officer), Sherman Kerner (Senior VP), William F Krumm (Senior VP), Robert W McCarty (Senior VP and Actuary), Fred C Morrow (Senior VP), Gerald E Pelzl (Senior VP-Information Systems), James P Conn (Chief Investment Officer), Gary U Rolle (Chief Investment Officer)

PRINCIPAL ACTIVITIES: Life and accident and health insurance - group and ordinary
Parent Company: Transamerica Corporation
Principal Subsidiaries: Transamerica Life Insurance Company of Canada; Transamerica Occidental Life Insurance Company of Illinois. Affiliates: Arbor Life Insurance Company; Transamerica Assurance Company; Transamerica Life INsurance and Annuity Company
Principal Bank: Bank of America NT & SA
Financial Information:

	Dec 31 1986 $'000
Premium income	1,453,705
Investment income	298,289

No of Employees: 4,991

TRANSCO ENERGY CO

2800 Post Oak Blvd, Houston, TX 77056
Tel: (713) 439-2000
Telex: WUT 775267 transco hou

Chairman: George S Slocum (and Chief Executive Officer)
Senior Executive Officers: Jim P Wise (Executive VP and Chief Financial Officer), Robert M Chiste (Senior VP Corporate Planning and Development), Larry J Dagley (Senior VP and Controller), Thomas W Spencer (Senior VP and Chief Administration Officer), David E Varner (Senior VP, General Counsel and Secretary), Susan K Chism (VP Information Systems), John V Clarke (VP Finance), William H Cook (VP and Associate General Counsel), Reynaldo Garcia (VP Tax and Risk Management), R V Loftin Jr (VP and Associate General Counsel), Lee E McDuff (VP Corporate Services), William A Paling (VP Information Systems and Chief Information Officer), Curtis E Whalen (VP Government Affairs), Larry T Wolfe (VP Personnel)

PRINCIPAL ACTIVITIES: Holding company with interests in oil and gas exploration and production; natural gas supply; coal products
Principal Bank: Citibank
Financial Information:

	Dec 31 1985 $'000	Dec 31 1986 $'000
Sales revenues	3,732,514	3,690,767
Net income (loss)	25,660	(4,307)
Earnings (loss) per share	$0.91	($0.92)
Shareholders equity	-	774,651

No of Employees: 4,800

TRANSCON INC

625 The City Drive South, Orange, CA 92668
Tel: (714) 385-1591

Chairman: Burke G Piper
President: Joe E Hall (and Chief Executive Officer)
Senior Executive Officers: James R Chisolm (Senior VP Finance and Chief Financial Officer), Joseph F DeBella (Senior VP Sales and Marketing), Joseph B Gentry (Senior VP Operations), Benjamin C Throop (Senior VP Administration), Larry R Corn (VP Central Division), Philip R Dobb (VP Eastern Division), James E Fox (VP and Treasurer), Max R Gramly

(VP Maintenance), John W Hollingsworth (VP and Controller), Robert L Reed (VP Western Division), James E Fox (VP and Treasurer)

PRINCIPAL ACTIVITIES: Holding company with interests in coast to coast common carrier motor freight line
Principal Subsidiaries: Transcon Lines; Keystone Lines
Principal Bank: Wells Fargo National Bank
Financial Information:

	$'000
Sales revenues	324,000

No of Employees: 4,120

TRANSITRON ELECTRONIC CORPORATION
100 Unicorn Park Drive, Woburn, MA 01801
Tel: (617) 933-9640

Chairman: David Bakalar
President: Howard A Hull (and Chief Executive Officer)
Senior Executive Officers: H K Fish (Secretary)

PRINCIPAL ACTIVITIES: Manufacture of cables and wires; electronic components
Principal Bank: Citicorp
Financial Information:

	$'000
Sales revenues	105,000

No of Employees: 1,000

TRANSOHIO SAVINGS BANK, FSB
One Penton Plaza, Cleveland, OH 44114
Tel: (216) 579-7700

Chairman: Myron Filarski (and President and Chief Executive Officer)
Senior Executive Officers: Philip M Essig (Executive VP Retail Banking), Mark D Grossi (Executive VP and Chief Financial Officer), C William Landefeld (Senior VP Branch Administration), John Moore (Senior VP Savings), Gregory L Teare (Senior VP Mortgage Banking), Robert D Swope (Senior VP Lending), David M Sweeney (Secretary)

PRINCIPAL ACTIVITIES: The company has interests in savings and loan operations and public relations services
Parent Company: TransCapital Financial Corporation
Principal Bank: National City Bank

No of Employees: 1,900

TRANSPORTATION SYSTEMS & INDUSTRIAL GROUP
2550 Golf Road, Arlington Heights, IL 60008
Tel: (312) 640-7000

President: John C Felten
Senior Executive Officers: Paul R Leak (VP Administration), Donald G Heffner (VP Personnel), Thomas L Schoenbeck (Treasurer)

PRINCIPAL ACTIVITIES: Manufacture of railcars and equipment; truck trailers; general engineering; cast steel products; leasing
Parent Company: Evans Products Company, Miami, FL
Principal Bank: Continental Illinois National Bank
Financial Information:

	$'000
Sales revenues	300,000

No of Employees: 4,000

TRANSTECHNOLOGY CORPORATION
15233 Ventura Blvd, Sherman Oaks, CA 91403
Tel: (213) 990-5920

Chairman: Arch C Scurlock
President: Dan McBride (and Chief Executive Officer and Treasurer)
Senior Executive Officers: Paul Grosher (Senior VP and Treasurer), Burl Alison (VP and Secretary), William F Bakker (VP), Joseph R Cabaret (VP), Thomas E Hanrahan (VP Gessner Co), Ralph E Hutchins (VP Lloyd Manufacturing Co), Jeffrey A Norton (VP), John B Reilly (VP Belfort Instrument Co)

PRINCIPAL ACTIVITIES: Production of explosives and ammunition; electronic control systems; scientific instruments; textile machinery
Principal Subsidiaries: Belfort Instrument Co; Lloyd Manufacturing Co Inc; Mass Tech Corp; Gessner Curtis & Marble Corp; SSP Industries (94%)
Principal Bank: Bank of America
Financial Information:

	$'000
Sales revenues	113,000

No of Employees: 1,400

TRANSWAY INTERNATIONAL CORPORATION
81 Main Street, White Plains, NY 10601
Tel: (914) 682-7100

Chairman: John W Wolcott (and President and Chief Executive Officer)
Senior Executive Officers: Lawrence Berman (Senior VP Administration), David C Bevan Jr (Senior VP Finance), John O Foran (VP and Secretary), Charles A Huebner (VP Planning), James D McCormick (VP), P J West (VP Operations), J R Wilkinson (VP and Controller)

PRINCIPAL ACTIVITIES: Freight transportation; shipping services; storage and warehousing; manufacture of truck trailers
Principal Subsidiaries: Lasham Cartage Co; Robertson Drayage Co Inc; Transport Distribution Services Inc; Wescartage Co Inc; Westland Freight Lines Inc; Wescar Freight System Inc; Universal Transcontinental Corp; Coordinated Caribbean Transport Inc; Great Dane Trailers Inc; Transway Finance Co; Tropigas International Corp
Financial Information:

	$'000
Sales revenues	866,717

No of Employees: 5,750

TRANSWORLD CORPORATION
605 Third Avenue, New York, NY 10158
Tel: (212) 557-5500

Chairman: L E Smart (and President and Chief Executive Officer); Vice Chairman: Frank L Salizzoni
Senior Executive Officers: Nicholas C Moren (VP and Treasurer), John J O'Keeffe Jr (VP and General Counsel), James R Painter (VP and Controller)

PRINCIPAL ACTIVITIES: Retailing interests; air transportation services foodservice operations for hotels; property management services
Financial Information:

	$'000
Sales revenues	2,151,556

No of Employees: 85,000

TRANZONIC COMPANIES (THE)
30195 Chagrin Blvd, Pepper Pike, OH 44124
Tel: (216) 831-5757

Chairman: Robert S Reitman (and President and Chief Executive Officer)
Senior Executive Officers: Morton L Reitman (Executive VP), David J Golden (Senior VP), Larry L Wymor (Senior VP)

PRINCIPAL ACTIVITIES: Manufacture of disposable diapers, feminine napkins and other sanitary disposable products; toiletries
Principal Bank: AmeriTrust Co

Financial Information:

	Feb 28 1986	Feb 28 1987
	$'000	$'000
Sales revenues	54,028	58,591
Income before taxes	3,101	4,169
Net income	2,012	2,379
Dividends	526	524
Dividends per share	$0.43	$0.44
Earnings per share	$1.64	$2.00
Common stock	686	686
Retained income	19,383	21,239
Shareholders equity	24,440	34,811

No of Employees: 750

TRAVELERS CORPORATION (THE)

One Tower Square, Hartford, CT 06183
Tel: (203) 277-0111

Chairman: Edward H Budd (and President and Chief Executive Officer)
Senior Executive Officers: Thomas H McAboy (Executive VP), Richard W McLaughlin (Executive VP), Richard J Shima (Executive VP), Thomas O Thorsen (Executive VP and Chief Financial Officer), Frank E Walton (Executive VP), F Peter Libassi (Senior VP Corporate Communications)

PRINCIPAL ACTIVITIES: The Travelers Corporation is one of the world's largest multi-line insurance and financial services institutions. Through its four customer-oriented groups, The Travelers and its subsidiaries and affiliates offer a wide range of products and services, including property and casualty insurance, life, accident, and health insurance, annuities, pension and investment management services, private placement loans, financial planning, mutual funds, trust services, cash management, home and commercial mortgages, real estate development, individual retirement accounts, Keogh plans, and stock-brokerage clearing and execution
Financial Information:

	Dec 31 1985	Dec 31 1986
	$'000	$'000
Premium income	10,922,700	12,229,000
Investment income	3,671,700	3,817,600
Income before taxes	359,800	443,600
Net income	373,100	545,800
Dividends	189,400	212,300
Dividends per share	$2.04	$2.16
Earnings per share	$4.00	$4.45
Common stock	114,600	124,800
Retained earnings	3,521,600	3,845,100
Shareholders equity	3,952,200	4,705,800

No of Employees: 29,000

TRAVELERS INSURANCE CO

One Tower Square, Hartford, CT 06183
Tel: (203) 277-0111

Chairman: Edward H Budd (and President and Chief Executive Officer)
Senior Executives: Morrison H Beach (Chairman of Executive Committee), Alva O Way (Chairman Finance Committee), John W Heilshorn (Executive VP), Thomas H McAboy (Executive VP), Richard W McLaughlin (Executive VP), Richard J Shima (Executive VP), Thomas O Thorsen (Executive VP and Chief Financial Officer), Frank E Walton (Executive VP)

PRINCIPAL ACTIVITIES: Insurance services
Parent Company: Travelers Corporation, Hartford, CT
Principal Bankers: Connecticut National Bank

Financial Information:

	Dec 31 1985	Dec 31 1986
	$'000	$'000
Premium income	4,270,704	4,023,926
Investment income	2,311,460	2,371,822

No of Employees: 45,940

TRE CORPORATION

3030 S Red Hill Ave, Santa Ana, CA 92705-5866
Tel: (714) 250 8717

Chairman: Leopold S Wyler (and Chief Executive Officer)
President: George A Sawyer (and Chief Operating Officer)
Senior Executive Officers: W C Bertrand (VP Finance and Treasurer), Aaron L Kolom (VP), Steven A Wyler (VP)

PRINCIPAL ACTIVITIES: Production of aerospace, aircraft, shipbuilding and semiconductor equipment and components; household hardware and plumbing products
Principal Subsidiaries: Weslock Co; Modern Faucet Manufacturing Co; Electromask Inc; MDS Data Systems Inc (90%); TRE Financial Corp; TRE Semiconductor Equipment Corp; Fiber Technology Corp
Financial Information:

	$'000
Sales revenues	151,550

No of Employees: 2,000

TREASURE CHEST ADVERTISING CO, INC

511 W Citrus Edge, Glendora, CA 91740
Tel: (213) 914-3981
Telex: TWX 910 5841350 corporate glda

Chairman: Robert E Milhous
President: Sanford G Scheller
Senior Executive Officers: John F Whitney (Senior VP Finance and Administration, Secretary and Treasurer), Richard Olerich (Senior VP Sales and Marketing), Donald E Roland (Senior VP Operations)

PRINCIPAL ACTIVITIES: Commercial printing
Principal Bank: BT Commercial Corp
Financial Information:

	$'000
Sales revenues	520,000

No of Employees: 4,000

TREASURE ISLE, INC

PO Box 1126, Tampa, FL 33601
Tel: (813) 659-1104

President: Marshall E Levinson
Senior Executive Officers: Donald R Levinson (VP and Secretary), G C Hartley (VP), Rick B Levinson (VP), Robert D Hastings (VP Food Services), Ira F Smith (VP Special Commodities)

PRINCIPAL ACTIVITIES: Seafood processing including fresh and frozen shrimp
Principal Bank: Southeast Bank
Financial Information:

	$'000
Sales revenues	100,000

No of Employees: 600

TREE TOP INC

2nd & Railroad Avenue, Selah, WA 98942
Tel: (509) 697-7251
Telex: TWX 910 3509 636 treetop

Chairman: Chuck Peters; Vice Chairman: Pete Van Well
President: Dennis J Colleran
Senior Executive Officers: Ken Davidson (VP Sales), Ron Flagg (VP Labor Relations), LeRoy Fletcher (VP Operations), George Chapman (Secretary and Treasurer)

PRINCIPAL ACTIVITIES: Fruit processing; dried fruit and fruit juice
Principal Bank: Spokane Bank for Cooperatives
Financial Information:

	$'000
Sales revenues	190,000

No of Employees: 500

TREMCO INC

10701 Shaker Blvd, Cleveland, OH 44104
Tel: (216) 296-5000
Telex: WUT 241419 tremco clv

Chairman: Leigh Carter
President: Gordon D Harnett (and Chief Executive Officer)
Senior Executive Officers: Paul Broer (VP and Divisional Manager Incon Division), George W Snider (VP International Operations), David Warren (President Tremco Canada), Greg Smith (Secretary and Treasurer)

PRINCIPAL ACTIVITIES: Manufacture of adhesives and coatings; technical services
Parent Company: B F Goodrich Company, Akron, OH
Principal Bank: National City Bank of Cleveland
Financial Information:

	$'000
Sales revenues	190,000

No of Employees: 1,800

TRI VALLEY GROWERS INC

1255 Battery, San Francisco, CA 94111
Tel: (415) 445-1600

President: Travis Mullinex
Senior Executive Officers: Al Spina (Executive VP), Dan Schulak (VP Finance), Richard Garabedian (Senior VP Marketing)

PRINCIPAL ACTIVITIES: Production, processing and canning of fruit and vegetables
Principal Bank: Security Pacific National Bank
Financial Information:

	$'000
Sales revenues	630,000

No of Employees: 1,000 (7,000 in the season)

TRIAD SYSTEMS CORPORATION

1252 Orleans Drive, Sunnyvale, CA 94086
Tel: (408) 734-9720
Telex: 910 3399593

Chairman: William W Stevens
President: James R Porter (and Chief Executive Officer)
Senior Executive Officers: Ronald W Edinger (Group VP), Robert L West (Group VP), Jerome Carlson (VP and Chief Financial Officer), Shane Gorman (VP and General Manager Auto Division), Bruce J Hansen (VP Engineering), Steven J LaCommare (VP Manufacturing), Ralph C Montelius (VP Customer Services), David O Morgan (VP Technical), David M Stout (VP), Anthony J Zuanich (VP)

PRINCIPAL ACTIVITIES: Manufacture of electronic computing equipment for use in the hardware, tire and automotive components industry
Principal Bank: Bank of America
Financial Information:

	$'000
Sales revenues	107,000

No of Employees: 1,500

TRIANGLE CORPORATION (THE)

72 Cummings Point Rd, PO Box 1881, Stamford, CT 06904
Tel: (203) 327-9050
Telex: WUT 643421 triangle std

Chairman: H Arthur Bellows Jr (and President and Chief Executive Officer)
Senior Executive Officers: R William Metzger (VP and President, The Triangle Tool Group Inc), Don R Gifford (VP Finance and Treasurer), Earl F Cornwell (VP and President, Miller Special Tools Division), Alan J Ritter (Controller), Charles L McLafferty (Assistant Treasurer), E Susan Goldberg (Secretary)

PRINCIPAL ACTIVITIES: The Triangle Corporation, is engaged through its subsidiaries in the manufacture and sale of mechanics' hand tools, special tools, farrier (horseshoer) tools and horsehoes and related products
Trade Names: UTICA, UTICA-SWISS, BONNEY, DIAMOND
Principal Subsidiaries: Utica Tool Co Inc; Diamond Tool and Horseshoe Co; The Triangle Tool Group Inc
Principal Bank: Norwest Bank of Minneapolis, N.A.
Financial Information:

	Dec 31 1985	Dec 31 1986
	$'000	$'000
Sales revenues	55,297	56,530
Income before taxes	1,180	2,216
Net income	1,760	1,352
Earnings per share net	$0.78	$0.59
Common stock	719	1,088
Retained income	4,345	5,697
Shareholders equity	12,019	13,449

No of Employees: 1,200

TRIANGLE INDUSTRIES, INC

900 Third Avenue, New York, NY 10022-4702
Tel: (212) 230-3000
Telex: 510 60 7622

Chairman: Nelson Peltz (and Chief Executive Officer); Vice Chairman: Frank W Considine
President: Peter W May (and Chief Operating Officer)
Senior Executive Officers: Bruce K Cowles (Executive VP), Anthony W Graziano Jr (Senior VP-Legal Affairs), Jeffrey C Hennig (Senior VP-Mergers and Acquisitions), Joseph A Levato (Senior VP and Chief Financial Officer), Charles W McGovern (Senior VP and Treasurer), John G Polk (Senior VP), William R Pollert (Senior VP-Operations Services), Robert P Freeman (VP-Corporate Services), Curtis S Gimson (VP and Associate General Counsel), James F Hart (VP and Corporate Controller), Richard A Hintz (VP-Taxes), Jerry Hostetter (VP-Corporate Communications), Richard M Inserra (VP-Risk Management), Henry J Leingang (VP-Information Services), Russell B Mallett Jr (VP-Operations Controller), Robert H Metchick (VP-Human Resources), Fred H Schaefer (VP-Financial Reporting), Manuel Schultz (VP and General Counsel and Secretary)

PRINCIPAL ACTIVITIES: Triangle Industries Inc is primarily engaged in the manufacture and sale of packaging products under the name American National Can. American National Can is a combination of the operations of National Can Corporation which Triangle acquired effective April 16, 1985, and of the packaging business of American Can Company, which Triangle acquired effective October 31, 1986. Triangle intends in the forseeable future to merge its National Can and American Can Packaging subsidiaries, and the resulting subsidiary will be named American National Can Company. Triangle also manufactures and distributes fabricated metal products consisting of copper electrical wire and cable, steel electrical conduit and related products through Triangle PWC, Inc, a wholly-owned subsidiary. Triangle has a controlling interest in Avery, Inc and CJI Industries, Inc. Avery, through Uniroyal Chemical Company, Inc, an indirect wholly owned subsidiary, is primarily engaged in the development, manufacture and marketing of specialty chemicals and elastomers for use worldwide. CJI manufacturers and distributes coin and currency handling products and coin and currency operated products

Trade Names: American Can Packaging, American National Can, GAMMA, Glaminate, National Can, OMNI, Salad Bar Fresh, Triangle, Triangle PWC. Avery and Uniroyal Chemical are trademarks of Avery, Inc or its subsidiaries. CJI and Rowe/Brandt Group are trademarks of CJI Industries Inc or its subsidiaries
Principal Subsidiaries: American National Can; National Can Corp; Triangle PWC Inc; Avery Inc; CJI Industries Inc; Uniroyal Chemical Company Inc
Principal Bank: Manufacturers Hanover Trust Co
Financial Information:

	Dec 31 1985	Dec 31 1986
	$'000	$'000
Sales revenues net	1,645,721	2,667,912
Income before taxes(1)	71,682	102,769
Net income	36,823	12,928
Common dividends	781	1,220
Dividends per share	$0.10	$0.115
Earnings per share net(2)	$3.35	$0.45
Earnings per share net(3)	$3.24	$0.63
Common stock	4,014	23,240
Retained income	67,545	72,825
Shareholders equity	101,568	455,005

(1) and extraordinary charge
(2) primary
(3) fully diluted

No of Employees: 23,000

TRIANGLE PACIFIC CORPORATION

16803 Dallas Pkwy, Box 660100, Dallas, TX 75266
Tel: (214) 931-3000

Chairman: Abraham Meltzer
President: Floyd Sherman
Senior Executive Officers: Joseph Nussbaum (Senior Executive VP), M J McHugh (Senior Executive VP Finance), John G Conklin (VP), Robert J Symon (VP and Controller), Charles A Engle (VP), James T Fidler (VP), Darryl T Marchand (VP Legal)

PRINCIPAL ACTIVITIES: Manufacture of wooden bathroom and kitchen cabinets and hardwood flooring
Principal Bank: Republic National Bank
Financial Information:

	$'000
Sales revenues	270,615

No of Employees: 3,370

TRIANGLE PUBLICATIONS, INC

100 Matsonford Road, Radnor, PA 19088
Tel: (215) 293-8500

Chairman: W H Annenberg
President: William J Henrich Jr (and General Counsel)
Senior Executive Officers: Harry C Coles Jr (VP and Secretary), Albert V Grifone (VP and Treasurer)

PRINCIPAL ACTIVITIES: Printing and publication of magazines, periodicals and newspapers
Principal Bank: Fidelity Bank Philadelphia
Financial Information:

	$'000
Sales revenues	280,000

No of Employees: 2,000

TRIANGLE PWC, INC

Triangle & Jersey Avenues, New Brunswick, NJ 08903
Tel: (201) 745-5500

President: Bruce K Cowles
Senior Executive Officers: Peter W May (VP), Raymond S Pearman (VP and General Sales Manager), Richard Bishof (VP Sales), Joseph J Bendavid (VP Purchasing), Nelson Peltz (VP), Gerald Morrow (VP Finance and Controller), George Viegel (VP Marketing), Arthur Pollock (VP Materials)

PRINCIPAL ACTIVITIES: Production of cables and wires; electroplating
Parent Company: Triangle Industries Inc, New Brunswick, NJ
Principal Bank: Manufacturers Hanover Trust Company
Financial Information:

	$'000
Sales revenues	180,000

No of Employees: 1,500

TRIBUNE COMPANY

202 S Parker Street, Tampa, FL 33606
Tel: (813) 272-2711

Chairman: David T Bryan
President: Richard F Pittman (and Treasurer and Publisher)
Senior Executive Officers: James F Urbanski (VP), W S Trandle (VP)

PRINCIPAL ACTIVITIES: Publishing and printing of newspapers
Parent Company: Media General Inc, Richmond, VA
Principal Bank: NCNB Bank of Tampa
Financial Information:

	$'000
Sales revenues	113,000

No of Employees: 1,200

TRIBUNE COMPANY

435 N Michigan Avenue, Chicago, IL 60611
Tel: (312) 222-9100
Telex: TWX 910 3501945 tribune co cgo

President: S R Cook (and Chief Executive Officer)
Senior Executive Officers: J W Madigan (Executive VP), S C Smith (VP and Controller), S J Gradowski Jr (VP and Secretary), L Gunnels (VP Legal), J E Hayes (VP Corporate Relations), P E Heraty (VP Employee Relations), J N Longson (VP Technical Development)

PRINCIPAL ACTIVITIES: Publishing of newspapers and periodicals; radio and television broadcasting; forest products and manufacture of newsprint
Principal Subsidiaries: Chicago Tribune Co; Penny Saver Publications Inc; New York News Inc; News & Sun-Sentinel Co; Sentinel Communications Co; Suncoast Publications; Tribune Newspapers West Inc; Tribune Media Services Inc; Ontario Paper Co Ltd; QNS Paper Company Ltd (60%); Manicouagan Power Co; Tribune Broadcasting Company; WPIX Inc; WGN Continental Broadcasting Co; WGN of Colorado Inc; Connecticut Broadcasting Co Inc; WGN of California Inc; Tribune Entertainment Co; WGNO Inc; WGNX Inc; Tribune Cable Communications Inc (90%); Chicago National League Ball Club Inc (40%); Scierie des Outardes Enr and Tribune Co Overseas Finance NV; Tribune Marketing Company
Principal Bank: First National Bank of Chicago
Financial Information:

	Dec 31 1986
	$'000
Sales revenues	2,029,813
Net income	292,870
Earnings per share	$7.26
Shareholders equity	1,101,274

No of Employees: 18,400

TRIBUNE/SWAB-FOX COMPANIES INC

2407 East Skelly Drive, Tulsa, OK 74104
Tel: (918) 747 2600

Chairman: Jenkin Lloyd Jones
President: G Douglas Fox (and Chief Executive Officer)
Senior Executive Officers: Howard G Barnett Jr (Executive VP), Clifford R Muselman (VP Gas Division), J Gary Mourton (VP Finance, Treasurer and Chief Financial Officer)

PRINCIPAL ACTIVITIES: Newspaper publishing; oil and gas exploration; gas supply; real estate
Principal Subsidiaries: Swab Corp
Principal Bank: Bank of Oklahoma
Financial Information:

	$'000
Sales revenues	50,000

No of Employees: 90

TRICO INDUSTRIES, INC

15707 South Main Street, Gardena, CA 90248
Tel: (213) 516-5000
Telex: WUT 673496 tricomon gdna

Chairman: William T Box
President: William D Wagner
Senior Executive Officers: Walter Losk (Chairman Executive Committee), Dwight L Chapman (VP), Louis Johnston (VP), Robert Litschi (VP and Chief Financial Officer), Charles C Moody (VP), Lance Poulsen (VP)

PRINCIPAL ACTIVITIES: Manufacture of oil and gas production equipment
Principal Bank: California Canadian Bank
Financial Information:

	$'000
Sales revenues	114,000

No of Employees: 900

TRICO PRODUCTS CORPORATION

817 Washington Street, Buffalo, NY 14203
Tel: (716) 852-5700
Telex: WUT 916479
Answerback: trico buf

Chairman: R John Oshei (and Chief Executive Officer)
President: Richard L Wolf (and Chief Operating Officer)
Senior Executive Officers: Leslie W Baker (VP-Manufacturing), Frank F Breese (VP-Human Resources), J Walter Frey (VP-Finance and Administration and Secretary), J P Crisfield (Treasurer), David M Wood (VP-Engineering), J Robert Wasko (Controller)

PRINCIPAL ACTIVITIES: Manufacture of Safe Driving Products including windshield wiper systems (electrical and air pressure); windshield wiper arms, blades, refills, linkage mechanisms; windshield washers; headlight actuators and controls; rear wiper systems; reserve vacuum tanks; windshield washer solvent; die cast, screw machine and plastic fittings; air pressure motors and controls; rubber and plastic small tubing; sintered metal parts
Affiliated Companies: Trico Technologies Corporation; Trico Componentes, SA de CV (Mexico); Trico-Folberth Limited (UK); Trico Pty Limited (Australia)
Financial Information:

	Dec 31 1985 $'000	Dec 31 1986 $'000
Sales revenues	145,910	157,576
Net income (loss)	(5,950)	17,575
Dividends	1,847	1,847
Dividends per share	$1.00	$1.00
Earnings (loss) per share	($3.22)	$9.51
Common stock	20,925	20,925
Retained earnings	73,983	89,711
Shareholders equity	80,366	95,545

No of Employees: 3,700

TRINITY INDUSTRIES, INC

2525 Stemmons Freeway, Box 10587, Dallas, TX 75207
Tel: (214) 631-4420
Telex: WUT 856678 trindal

President: W Ray Wallace (and Chief Executive Officer)
Senior Executive Officers: Ralph A Banks Jr (Senior VP), E B Breeding (Senior VP and Treasurer), K W Lewis (Senior VP), Lee D McElroy (Senior VP)

PRINCIPAL ACTIVITIES: Manufacture of railroad vehicles and equipment; metal fabrication; marine engineering
Principal Subsidiaries: Hackney Inc; Gambles Inc; Equitable Shipyards Inc; Mosher Steel Co; Texas Metal Fabricating Co; Trinity Industries Transportation Inc; Trinity Railcar Leasing Corp; Trinity Industries Leasing Co; Gretna Machine and Iron Works Inc; Halter Marine Inc; General Steel Co; AESCO Steel Inc; Industrial Steel Products Inc; Pullman Standard Inc; Tank Lining Corp
Principal Bank: Republic Bank Dallas
Financial Information:

	$'000
Sales revenues	491,000

No of Employees: 5,400

TRINOVA CORPORATION (FORMERLY LIBBEY-OWENS-FORD CO)

1705 Indian Wood, Circle, Maumee, OH 43537
Tel: (419) 891-2200

Chairman: Don T McKone
President: Darryl F Allen (Chief Executive Officer and Chief Operating Officer)
Senior Executive Officers: Carl E LaRue (VP, General Counsel and Secretary), D R Bastian (VP), B Susan Bishop (VP Management Resources, Planning and Development), William R Ammann (VP Administration), Charles A Lupien (VP Management Information Services), G William Moody (VP, President Aeroquip Corporation), Stephen W Nagy (VP Finance), Philip G Simonds (VP Taxation), Richard C De Cook (VP and Treasurer), T N Duncan (VP, President Vickers Inc), Howard M Sellan (VP, President Sterling Engineered Products)

PRINCIPAL ACTIVITIES: Manufacture of molded and laminated plastic products; fluid power systems; hydraulic systems
Principal Subsidiaries: LOF Glass; LOF Plastics Inc; Aeroquip Corporation; Libbey-Owens-Ford Export Co; Photon Power Inc; Vickers Inc; Aeroquip GmbH (West Germany); Aeroquip (Canada) Inc (Canada); Aeroquip Vickers do Brazil SA (Brazil); Aeroquip Italia SpA (Italy); Aeroquip SA (France); Aeroquip Iberica SA (Spain)
Financial Information:

	Dec 31 1985 $'000	Dec 31 1986 $'000
Sales revenues	1,921,981	1,447,292
Net income	74,634	122,564
Earnings per share	$5.71	$6.96
Shareholders equity	-	549,732

No of Employees: 26,070

TRI-STAR PICTURES INC

711 Fifth Avenue, New York, NY 10022
Tel: (212) 758 3900

Chairman: Victor A Kaufman (and Chief Executive Officer)
Presidents: David A Matalon; Jeffrey Sagansky (Production)
Senior Executive Officers: Arnold W Messer (Senior Executive VP), Leslie H Jacobson (Executive VP, Legal Counsel and Secretary), M Jay Walkingshaw (Executive VP and Chief Financial Officer), Jerome Esbin (Executive VP National Sales), Stephen F Randall (Executive VP Marketing)

PRINCIPAL ACTIVITIES: Production of motion pictures
Financial Information:

	$'000
Sales revenues	254,000

No of Employees: 200

TRI-STATE MOTOR TRANSIT CO OF DELAWARE

East Seventh Street Road, Business 1-44, PO Box 113, Joplin, MO 64802

Tel: (417) 624 3131

Chairman: H Lang Rogers; Vice Chairman: Harold F Nickels (and President and Chief Executive Officer)

Senior Executive Officers: George F Boyd Jr (Executive VP), Charles O Gillogly (Executive VP), George W Carter (Senior VP Operations), Donald E Bassett (Treasurer), C Gerald Hendren (VP Finance and Assistant Secretary), Albert Thomson (Secretary and Legal Counsel)

PRINCIPAL ACTIVITIES: Road haulage

Principal Subsidiaries: Aero Body & Truck Equipment; Contract Operator Accounting Services; HGO Rigging & Storage Co; LKO Leasing Co Inc; Loadus Truck Leasing Inc; Tri-State Motor Transit Co

Principal Bank: First National Bank & Trust Co

Financial Information:

	$'000
Sales revenues	123,260

No of Employees: 1,120

TRITON ENERGY CORPORATION

1400 One Energy Square, Dallas, TX 75206

Tel: (214) 691-5200

Telex: 730454

Telecopy: (214) 987-0571

Chairman: William I Lee (and Chief Executive Officer)

President: Thomas A Goff (and Chief Operating Officer)

Senior Executive Officers: David E Gore (Executive VP), Herbert L Brewer (Senior VP, Exploration), W H Maloch Jr (Senior VP and President, Triton Oil & Gas Corp), John P Tatum (Senior VP, Operations), J J Ciavarra Jr (VP, Special Projects), Charles B Crowell (VP and General Counsel), Michael P McInerney (VP, Corporate Development and Investor Relations), Robert W Puetz (VP, Finance and Treasurer), Gordon M Smart (VP, Exploration), J W Janecek (Controller), J Sanderson (Corporate Secretary), Gregory A Austin (Assistant Treasurer), Frank M Cheatham Jr (Assistant Controller)

PRINCIPAL ACTIVITIES: Triton Energy Corporation is an international petroleum and mineral exploration and development company, with interests in producing oil and gas reserves in the United States, Canada, Australia, The Netherlands, France and the Republic of Côte d'Ivoire in western Africa. The Company's current exploration activities are conducted in these areas as well as the United Kingdom, Colombia, New Zealand, Tunisia, Thailand and Nepal. While new reserves are acquired principally by exploration, producing properties are acquired from time to time for cash or the Company's securities. The Company operates principally in the oil and gas industry. The Company also operates in the coal mining industry through an Australian affiliate

Principal Subsidiary and Affiliated Companies: Allied Queensland Coalfields Ltd (Australia); Crusader Limited (Australia); New Zealand Petroleum Company Limited (New Zealand); Pacific Basin Company; Tricorp Oil & Gas NV (Netherlands Antilles); Triton Colombia Inc (Colombia); Triton Côte D'Ivoire; Triton Europe plc (UK); Triton France SA (France); Triton Nepal Inc; Triton Oil Company of Thailand (Thailand); Triton Oil & Gas Corp; Triton Petroleum Limited (Canada); Triton Tunisia Inc; Whalen Corporation

Financial Information:

	May 31 1985	May 31 1986
	$'000	$'000
Sales revenues	51,025	86,187
Income (loss) before taxes	18,029	(27,315)
Net income (loss)	9,847	(42,387)
Dividends per share	$0.94	$0.99
Earnings (loss) per share	$1.05	($5.91)
Common stock	7,379	8,971
Retained income	21,148	-
Shareholders equity	96,867	104,293

TRITON GROUP LTD

1900 Avenue of the Stars, Suite 2700, Los Angeles, CA 90067

Tel: (213) 553 3900

Chairman: J B Fuqua

President: Ralph O Briscoe (and Chief Executive Officer)

Senior Executive Officers: George A Daniels (Senior VP Finance), John L Olson (VP and Controller), Albert M Bensusen (Treasurer), Anita J Cutchall (Assistant Secretary)

PRINCIPAL ACTIVITIES: Holding company with interests in steel, building products, commercial printing services, sewing patterns, photo processing and film services to the motion picture and TV industries

Principal Subsidiaries: Republic Corp; Dauman Displays Inc; Delmar Printing & Photographic Inc; National Airmotive Corp; Trans Air Supply Co; Simplicity Pattern Co Inc; Maxxam Properties Inc; Twin Fair Properties Inc; Simplicity Patterns International Ltd

Principal Bank: Manufacturers Hanover Trust Co

Financial Information:

	$'000
Sales revenues	304,400

No of Employees: 4,400

TROSTEL, ALBERT, & SONS CO

10201 W Lincoln Avenue, Milwaukee, WI 53227

Tel: (414) 273-3421

President: Everett G Smith

Senior Executive Officers: Frank D Fermano (President Albert Trostel Packing Division), Anders Segerdahl (VP and President Eagle Ottawa Leather Division), Charles D Krull (Treasurer)

PRINCIPAL ACTIVITIES: Leather tanning and finishing; rubber processing; manufacture of sealing and packaging equipment

Principal Bank: Continental Illinois National Bank and Trust Co

Financial Information:

	$'000
Sales revenues	70,000

No of Employees: 700

TRUE TEMPER CORPORATION

465 Railroad Avenue, Box 3500, Shiremanstown, PA 17011

Tel: (717) 737-1500

Telex: RCA 247662 aihg ur

President: D G Meckley

Senior Executive Officers: George Algire (VP and General Sales Manager), Raymond J Busam (VP), Russell H Mavis (VP), Timothy L Guzzle (VP), Lawrence Weber (VP)

PRINCIPAL ACTIVITIES: Production of hand and garden tools; sports and athletic equipment; cutlery; railroad track

Parent Company: Allegheny International Inc, Pittsburgh, PA

Principal Bank: Mellon Bank

Financial Information:

	$'000
Sales revenues	170,000

No of Employees: 3,000

TRUMBULL CORPORATION

PO Box 98100, Pittsburgh, PA 15227
Tel: (412) 462-9300

President: Perry J Dick
Senior Executive Officers: Robert Hecht (VP), Arthur B Hopperstead (VP Engineering), Louise H Dick (Secretary and Treasurer)

PRINCIPAL ACTIVITIES: Civil engineering and construction; manufacture of paving materials
Principal Bank: Pittsburgh National Bank
Financial Information:

	$'000
Sales revenues	50,000

No of Employees: 600

TRUS JOIST CORPORATION

9777 W Chinden Blvd, Box 60, Boise, ID 83707
Tel: (208) 375-4450

Chairman: Harold E Thomas (and Chief Executive Officer)
President: Walter C Minnick (and Chief Operating Officer)
Senior Executive Officers: Thomas H Denig (VP Eastern Operations), David L DeWitte (VP Divisional Operations), Robert J Dingman (VP Western Operations), Richard C Hansen (VP Mid America Operations), Larry R Henderson (VP Technical and Development), Arthur L Troutner (VP Research), Walter J Wadman (VP Finance and Treasurer)

PRINCIPAL ACTIVITIES: Production of joists and other structural building products
Principal Bank: First Interstate Bank
Financial Information:

	$'000
Sales revenues	133,670

No of Employees: 1,300

TRUST COMPANY OF GEORGIA

PO Box 4418, Atlanta, GA 30302
Tel: (404) 588-7711
Telex: 54 2210 (International); 4611057 (Domestic)
Fax: (404) 588-8129

Chairman: Robert Strickland (and Chief Executive Officer); Vice Chairman: Edward P Gould
President: James B Williams
Senior Executive Officers: Claude H Booker Jr (Executive VP)

PRINCIPAL ACTIVITIES: Holding company whose subsidiaries are engaged in banking
Principal Subsidiaries: Trust Company Bank (Atlanta, GA); Trust Company Bank (Savannah, GA); Trust Company Bank of Carroll County (Bowden, GA); Trust Company Bank of Clayton County (Jonesboro, GA); Trust Company Bank of Coffee County (Douglas, GA); Trust Company Bank of Douglas County (Douglasville, GA); Trust Company Bank of Henry County (Mcdonough, GA); Trust Company Bank of Rockdale (Conyers, GA); Trust Company Bank of South Georgia (Albany, GA); Trust Company Bank (Augusta, GA); Trust Company Bank of Northeast GA (Rome, GA); Trust Company Bank of Southeast GA (Brunswick, GA); Trust Company Bank of Northwest GA (Athens, GA); Trust Company Mortgage (Atlanta, GA)
Financial Information:

	Dec 31 1986 $'000
Net income	111,238
Deposits	6,128,800
Total assets	8,775,800

No of Employees: 2,560

TRUSTCO BANK CORP NY

320 State Street, Schenectady, NY 12305
Tel: (518) 377 3311

President: Robert A McCormick (and Chief Executive Officer)
Senior Executive Officers: William H Milton III (Executive VP and Secretary), Donald L Gaudette (Senior VP Operations), Ralph A Pidgeon (Senior VP Administration), Paul A Schwartz (Senior VP Division), Peter A Zakriski (Treasurer)

PRINCIPAL ACTIVITIES: Banking

No of Employees: 310

TRW INC

1900 Richmond Road, Cleveland, OH 44124
Tel: (216) 291-7000
Telex: TWX 810 4218350 trw cleve

Chairman: Ruben F Mettler (and Chief Executive Officer)
President: Joseph T Gorman (and Chief Operating Officer)

PRINCIPAL ACTIVITIES: Manufacture of high technology electronic equipment and components for the space and defense industries; telecommunications and data information systems; automotive components and systems
Financial Information:

	Dec 31 1985 $'000	Dec 31 1986 $'000
Sales revenues	5,917,200	6,035,900
Income before taxes	235,200	369,900
Net income (loss)	(7,100)	217,700
Dividends paid per share(1)	$1.50	$1.525
Net income (loss) per share(1)	($0.14)	$3.55
Common stock(1)(2)	58,100	58,900
Retained income	930,100	1,054,800
Shareholders equity	1,014,900	1,197,900

(1) shares and per share amounts reflect the split of the common stock effective May 8 1987
(2) shares outstanding in thousands

No of Employees: 75,000

TSO FINANCIAL CORPORATION

3515 Silverside Road, Wilmington, DE 19810
Tel: (302) 478 4846

Chairman: Denis Alter
President: James Diamond
Senior Executive Officers: Michael J Sexton (VP, Legal Counsel and Secretary)

PRINCIPAL ACTIVITIES: Financial services including loans
Principal Subsidiaries: Colonial National Bank; Colonial National Leasing Inc; Teachers Service Consumer Discount Co
Principal Bank: Fidelity Bank

No of Employees: 200

TUCK INDUSTRIES, INC

1 Lefevre Lane, New Rochelle, NY 10801
Tel: (914) 235-1000

President: Austin A Iodice (and Chief Executive Officer)
Senior Executive Officers: Michael C McMahon (VP Finance), Jack Lulla (Senior VP Research and Development), John G Iodice (VP Consumer Products Division), David D Krassner (VP Marketing), Mark Harrison (VP Planning), Attilio Cozzi (VP International Division), John A Praitano (VP Engineering), John F Mell (VP Manufacturing), John G Iodice (VP Consumer Products), John A Praitano (VP Engineering), James J Daniels (VP Customer Relations), Ted P Milewski (Treasurer), Joseph A LaFalce (Controller)

PRINCIPAL ACTIVITIES: Manufacture of sensitive tapes
Trade Names: TUCK TAPE
Parent Company: Technical Tape Inc, New Rochelle, NY
Principal Bank: National Westminster Bank, USA

Financial Information:

	$'000
Sales revenues	60,000

No of Employees: 800

TUCSON ELECTRIC POWER CO

22 W Sixth St, PO Box 711, Tucson, AZ 85702
Tel: (602) 622-6661

Chairman: J Luther Davis
President: Einar Greve (and Chief Executive Officer)
Senior Executive Officers: Steven M Banzhaf (Senior VP, Secretary and General Counsel), Herbert A Heim (Senior VP and Chief Operating Officer), Kenneth L Saul (Senior VP and Chief Financial Officer), Robert K Alexander (VP), Joe G Coykendall (VP and Treasurer), Thomas A Delawder (VP Power Supply and Systems Control), Sam G Minter (VP Operations), Joseph B Wilcox (VP)

PRINCIPAL ACTIVITIES: Electricity supply
Principal Bankers: Irving Trust Company
Financial Information:

	$'000
Sales revenues	425,000

No of Employees: 1,000

TULTEX CORPORATION

PO Box 5191, Martinsville, VA 24115
Tel: (703) 632-2961

Chairman: William F Franck (and Chief Executive Officer)
President: H R Hunnicutt Jr (and Chief Operating Officer)
Senior Executive Officers: W C Cole III (VP Personnel), John M Franck (VP), John S Hairfield (VP Marketing), C W Lawhon (VP Administration), Clarence F Williams (VP Yarn), B A Ratliff (VP Operations), D P Shook (Controller), W B Harris (Treasurer), M B Lopez (Secretary)

PRINCIPAL ACTIVITIES: Manufacture of fleeced knit apparel, a producer of jersey and interlock apparel and spun yarns
Principal Subsidiaries: Tulstar Factors Inc
Principal Bank: Sovran Bank, NA
Financial Information:

	$'000
Sales revenues	259,579

No of Employees: 7,820

TURNER BROADCASTING SYSTEM INC

One CNN Center, Box 105366, Atlanta, GA 3035
Tel: (404) 827-1700

Chairman: R E Turner (and President)
Senior Executive Officers: Robert Wussler (Executive VP), Paul D Beckham (VP and Controller), William C Bevins Jr (VP Finance, Secretary and Treasurer), Gerald C Hogan (VP Sales), William M Shaw (VP Personnel)

PRINCIPAL ACTIVITIES: Television broadcasting
Principal Bankers: Manufacturers Hanover Trust
Financial Information:

	$'000
Sales revenues	557,000

No of Employees: 2,000

TURNER CORPORATION

633 Third Avenue, New York, NY 10017
Tel: (212) 878-0300

Chairman: H D Conant (and Chief Executive Officer)
Senior Executive Officers: K H Wanderer (Senior VP), A H Wahlberg (VP, Controller and Chief Financial Officer)

PRINCIPAL ACTIVITIES: On June 1st 1984 Turner Corporation was formed as a holding company for the Turner Construction Company which is engaged in property development, civil engineering and construction

Financial Information:

	Dec 31 1985	Dec 31 1986
	$'000	$'000
Sales revenues	2,149,230	2,497,235
Net income	11,070	10,147
Earnings per share	$2.64	$2.41
Shareholders equity	-	71,488

No of Employees: 3,103

TUTHILL CORPORATION

908 North Elm Street, Hinsdale, IL 60521
Tel: (312) 655-2266

President: J G Tuthill
Senior Executive Officers: Glen R Ostdiek (Secretary and Treasurer), J G Tuthill Jr (President Fill-Rite Division), F S Galssini (President Superior Linkage Division), H H Flock (President Tuthill Pump Division), Dickey Londahl (President Tuthill Co of Cal Subsidiary), B W Manning (President Hansen Coupling Division), R A Rybak (President Hansen Plastics Division), Keith Clarno (President Cablecraft Subsidiary)

PRINCIPAL ACTIVITIES: Manufacture of pumps linkages, quick corrective couplings and control cables
Principal Bank: Harris Trust and Savings Bank
Financial Information:

	$'000
Sales revenues	75,000

No of Employees: 900

TW SERVICES INC

605 Third Avenue, New York, NY 10158
Tel: (212) 972-4700

Chairman: F L Salizzoni
Directors: J R Richardson
Senior Executives: J J O'Keefe Jr (Senior VP), J R Painter (Senior VP)

PRINCIPAL ACTIVITIES: Food services; restaurants; retirement care
Trade Names: Canteen, Spartan Food Systems, Denny's, El Pollo Loco, Quincy's, Hardee's (Franchises)
Subsidiary Companies: Denny's Inc; American Medical Services Inc
Principal Bankers: Bankers Trust Co
Financial Information:

	Dec 31 1986
	S'000
Sales revenues	1,918,051
Income before taxes	42,296
Net income	15,683
Earnings per share	$0.27
Common stock	485
Retained earnings	165,491
Shareholders equity	412,137

No of Employees: 59,000

TWENTIETH CENTURY FOX-FILM CORPORATION

940 Santa Monica Boulevard, Beverly Hills, CA 90210
Tel: (312) 372 1584
Telex: WUT 674875 tcfhqco lsa

Chairman: Barry Diller (and Chief Executive Officer); Vice Chairman: Norman Levy
Senior Executive Officers: Gerald K Bergman (Executive VP), Burton I Monasch (Executive VP), J M Hattendorf (VP), Martin B Shindler (Controller), Jerry Greenberg (Director Public Relations)

PRINCIPAL ACTIVITIES: Production of movies, video films and television programs; operators of ski resorts
Principal Subsidiaries: (100% owned unless stated): Amcoho Co (50%); Aspen Skiing Co (50%); National Wiz Co (60%); Studio

Properties Co (50%); Pebble Beach Co (50%); CinemaScope Products Inc; Twentieth Century-Fox Theatre Productions Inc; Twentieth Century-Fox Video Inc (50%); Twentieth Century-Fox Film (East) Ltd (Singapore); Twentieth Century-Fox Film (SA) (Pty) Ltd (South Africa); Hispano Fox Film SAE (Spain); Aktiebolaget Fox Film (Sweden); Twentieth & Century-Fox Film Corp Sd 'EP la S (Switzerland); Twentieth Century-Fox Film del Uruguay Ltd (Uruguay); Twentieth Century-Fox Trinidad Ltd (Trinidad); Zambia Film Services Ltd (Zambia)
Financial Information:

	$'000
Sales revenues	847,000

No of Employees: 3,300

TWIN CITY BARGE INC

222 W Grand Avenue, South St Paul, MN 55075
Tel: (612) 450-4700

President: James W Sullivan (and Chief Executive Officer)
Senior Executive Officers: David A Heider (Executive VP, Chief Operating Officer and Chief Financial Officer), Robert E Maher (Secretary and Chief Administrative Officer)

PRINCIPAL ACTIVITIES: River and ocean barge transportation and towing services
Principal Subsidiaries: Knappton Corporation
Principal Bank: United States National Bank of Oregon
Financial Information:

	Dec 31 1985	Dec 31 1986
	$'000	$'000
Sales revenues	53,534	52,090
Income (loss) before taxes	(11,257)	18,732
Net income (loss)	(11,257)	18,732
Income (loss) per share	($2.65)	$5.45
Common stock	4,325	4,325
Capital in excess par value	32,572	32,572
Accumulated (deficit)	(73,613)	(54,881)
Less treasury stock	(102)	(102)
Shareholders (deficit)	(36,818)	(18,086)

No of Employees: 301

TWIN CITY FOODS, INC

10120 269th Place NW, Stanwood, WA 98292
Tel: (206) 629-2111
Telex: TWX 910449 2908 twinctyfd stnd

Chairman: Arne T Lervick; Vice Chairman: Magnar O Lervick
President: Roger O Lervick
Senior Executive Officers: Richard C Cleary (VP Operations), Ray McClure (VP Sales), Ronald H Keolker (VP Finance, Secretary, Treasurer and Controller)

PRINCIPAL ACTIVITIES: Production of frozen vegetables
Principal Bank: Rainier National Bank
Financial Information:

	$'000
Sales revenues	100,000

No of Employees: 1,000

TWIN DISC INC

1328 Racine Street, Racine, WI 53403
Tel: (14)34-1981
Telex: TWX 910 2712384 twindiscrac

Chairman: John H Batten;
President: Michael E Batten (and Chief Executive Officer)
Senior Executive Officers: Leroy J Burlingame (Executive VP), Michael J Hablewitz (VP Manufacturing), Charles R Gibson (VP Industrial Relations), James O Parrish (VP Finance and Chief Financial Officer), Wendell E Richmond (VP Engineering), Lance J Melik (VP Marketing)

PRINCIPAL ACTIVITIES: Manufacture of gears and clutches for industrial and automotive use
Principal Subsidiaries: Twin Disc International; Twin Disc (Pacific) Pty Ltd (Australia); Twin Disc (South Africa) Pty (South Africa); Twin Disc (Far East) Ltd (Singapore)
Principal Bank: Northern Trust Company
Financial Information:

	Jun 30 1986	Jun 30 1987
	$'000	$'000
Sales revenues	121,221	129,709
Income (loss) before taxes	(6,225)	4,879
Net income (loss)	(3,738)	2,284
Dividends	2,881	2,228
Dividends per share	$0.90	0.70
Earnings (loss) per share	($1.17)	$0.72
Retained income	68,118	71,737

No of Employees: 1,434

TYCO LABORATORIES, INC

One Tyco Park, Exeter, NH 03833
Tel: (603) 778-7331
Telex: WUT 943524 tycolabs eter

Chairman: John F Fort (and President and Chief Executive Officer)
Senior Executive Officers: William A Hartley (VP-Tax Counsel), Richard D Power (VP-Chief Financial Officer), Irving Gutin (VP)

PRINCIPAL ACTIVITIES: Fire protection/flow control products, electronic components and packaging materials
Principal Subsidiaries: Armin Corp; Armin Plastics California Inc; Armin Plastics New Jersey Inc; Armin Plastics Oklahoma Inc; Armin Plastics South Carolina Inc; Armin Poly-Version Inc; Roto-Lith Ltd; Thermodynamics Corp; Armin Plastics Corp; Ludlow Corp; Twitchell Corp; Grinnell Corporation; Grinnell Fire Protection Systems Co Ltd (Canada); Incendio (Mexico); James H Merritt & Co; Pyrotector Inc; Simplex Wire & Cable Co; Tyco International Finance NV (Netherlands Antilles); Tyco Engineered Products Inc; Hersey Products Inc
Financial Information:

	May 31 1987
	$'000
Sales revenues	1,061,788
Income (1) before taxes	76,763
Income(1)	44,097
Dividends	7,300
Dividends per share	$0.40
Earnings per share(2)	$2.54
Common stock	9,118
Retained income	215,223
Shareholders equity	235,399

(1) from continuing operations
(2) primary

No of Employees: 11,000

TYLAN CORPORATION

23301 South Wilmington Avenue, Carson, CA 90745
Tel: (213) 518 3610

Chairman: Charles F Drexel (and President)
President: Kenneth Cleveland (and Chief Executive Officer)
Senior Executive Officers: William E Standring Jr (Executive VP and Secretary), Klaus K Schuegraf (VP and Chief Technical Officer), John L Olson (VP Finance)

PRINCIPAL ACTIVITIES: Manufacture of equipment for processing silicon wafers used in the semiconductor industry
Principal Bank: Bank of America NT & SA
Financial Information:

	$'000
Sales revenues	33,190

No of Employees: 300

TYLER CORPORATION

3200 San Jacinto Tower, Dallas, TX 75201
Tel: (214) 754-7800

Chairman: Joseph F McKinney (and Chief Executive Officer)
President: Frederick R Meyer (and Chief Operating Officer)
Senior Executive Officers: Richard W Margerison (VP), James E Russell (VP Finance), William E Scott (VP and Controller), David L Smart (VP and Treasurer)

PRINCIPAL ACTIVITIES: The company has interests in the production of building and construction materials and fittings; explosives; trucking services
Principal Subsidiaries: Atlas Powder Co; Hall-Mark Electronics; Reliance Universal Inc; Tyler Aviation Inc; Tyler Pipe Industries Inc
Principal Bank: InterFirst Bank Dallas
Financial Information:

	Dec 31 1985	Dec 31 1986
	$'000	$'000
Sales revenues	912,415	961,411
Net income	15,363	11,945
Earnings per share	$0.82	$0.66
Shareholders equity	200,135	181,989

No of Employees: 6,700

TYLER PIPE INDUSTRIES, INC

PO Box 2027, Tyler, TX 75710
Tel: (214) 882-5511
Telex: WUT 880175 tyler pipe

President: John A Warner (and Chief Executive Officer)
Senior Executive Officers: Glen C Uzzel (Executive VP), D K McKie (VP Industrial Relations), James B Horan (VP Marketing), J P Johnson (VP Cast Iron), Gene Mason (VP and Controller), Dan Gerhardstein (VP), Dale Meador (VP Utility Sales), M E Davis (VP Purchasing), James Milstead (VP Engineering)

PRINCIPAL ACTIVITIES: Production of plastic and cast-iron pipes and tubes
Parent Company: Tyler Corporation, Dallas, TX
Financial Information:

	$'000
Sales revenues	200,000

No of Employees: 2,700

TYLER REFRIGERATION CORPORATION

1329 Lake Street, Niles, MI 49120
Tel: (616) 683-2000
Telex: WUT 234240 tyler nles

President: James E Mack
Senior Executive Officers: Richard Dittoe (VP Marketing), John Geer (VP and Assistant Secretary), Joseph Humphrey (VP Engineering), Ed Ryan (VP Human Resources), Fayez Ibrahim (VP Research and Development), D G O'Donnell (VP), Roland Hedstrom (VP International Operations), John Shuey (VP Finance)

PRINCIPAL ACTIVITIES: Manufacture of frozen food display cabinets for supermarkets; cold rooms and freezers; catering equipment and air conditioning components
Parent Company: American Standard Inc, New York, NY
Principal Bank: Irving Trust Co
Financial Information:

	$'000
Sales revenues	110,000

No of Employees: 500

TYLER, W S, , INC

8200 Tyler Blvd, Mentor, OH 44060
Tel: (216) 255-9131
Telex: WUT 985416 wstylerco ment

President: Charles R Cox (and General Manager)
Senior Executive Officers: W F Roche (VP), Mitchell Kiamie (VP), L J Ruppe (VP Finance, Secretary, Treasurer and Controller), Raymond Dubois (VP Marketing)

PRINCIPAL ACTIVITIES: Manufacture of wire products including woven wire and screening sections; industrial equipment and machinery
Parent Company: Combustion Engineering Inc, Stamford, CT
Financial Information:

	$'000
Sales revenues	50,000

No of Employees: 600

TYSON FOODS, INC

2210 W Oaklawn Drive, Springdale, AR 72764
Tel: (501) 756-4000
Telex: TWX 910 7206421 tysonsale spge

Chairman: Don Tyson (and Chief Executive Officer); Vice Chairman: Joe F Starr
President: Leland E Tollett (and Chief Operating Officer)
Senior Executive Officers: Gerald Johnston (Executive VP and Chief Financial Officer), Wayne Britt (VP, Secretary and Treasurer), Howard Baird (VP Industrial Relations)

PRINCIPAL ACTIVITIES: Poultry processing and distribution; frozen poultry products
Principal Bank: The First National Bank of Chicago
Financial Information:

	Sep 30 1986
	$'000
Sales revenues	1,503,719
Net income	50,289
Earnings per share	$1.18
Shareholders equity	203,631

No of Employees: 11,000

UARCO INC

West County Line Road, Barrington, IL 60010
Tel: (312) 381-7000
Telex: TWX 910 651 1901 uarco bgtn

Chairman: H L Koelling
President: B H Moses
Senior Executive Officers: D W McGrath (Senior VP Marketing), L C Dille (VP Education and Development), R W Hinding (VP Manufacturing), R Lane (VP Sales), J K Marshall (VP and Controller), D R Mofett (VP), L S Richards (VP Marketing Programs), E F Werhand (VP Engineering)

PRINCIPAL ACTIVITIES: Manufacture of forms for business use
Parent Company: Pace Industries Inc
Principal Bank: Harris Trust and Savings Bank
Financial Information:

	$'000
Sales revenues	400,000

No of Employees: 4,000

U-BRAND CORPORATION

820 Clark Street, Ashland, OH 44805
Tel: (419) 289-1100
Telex: WUT 987428 u brand alnd

Senior Executive Officers: J Paul Herrmann (Executive VP), Michael McKibben (VP Industrial Relations), David Mickley (VP Marketing), Robert Schultz (VP Puerto Rican Operations), Doug Dever (Controller)

PRINCIPAL ACTIVITIES: Manufacture of malleable iron castings and steel and plastic fittings
Parent Company: Worthington Industries Inc, Columbus, OH
Principal Bank: Bank One of Ashland
Financial Information:

	$'000
Sales revenues	52,000

No of Employees: 950

UCCEL CORPORATION
UCCEL Tower, PO Box 660054, 6303 Forest Park Road, Dallas, TX 75235
Tel: (214) 353 7100

Chairman: Gregory J Liemandt (and Chief Executive Officer)
Senior Executive Officers: B Tom Carter Jr (Executive VP and Secretary), Peter E Dios (Senior VP), Paul E Newton (Senior VP and General Manager), Ron W Brittian (VP), Peter J Burris (VP), Michael G Locks (VP), W Daniel Johnson (VP), B Wade Monroe (VP), Donald L Steele (VP and General Manager), Selby F Little III (Treasurer)

PRINCIPAL ACTIVITIES: Computer services and software
Principal Subsidiaries: Digital Systems of Florida Inc
Principal Bank: First National Bank
Financial Information:

	$'000
Sales revenues	204,715

No of Employees: 1,500

UDISCO
2700 S 900 W, Salt Lake City, UT 84119
Tel: (801) 972-1330
Telex: WUT 453067 udisco slc

President: William Condon

PRINCIPAL ACTIVITIES: Manufacture of sports equipment and sportswear
Parent Company: Malone & Hyde Inc
Principal Bank: First Security Bank of Utah
Financial Information:

	$'000
Sales revenues	90,000

No of Employees: 1,000

UGI CORPORATION
460 North Gulph Road, Box 858, Valley Forge, PA 19482
Tel: (215) 337 1000

Chairman: Thomas V Lefevre
President: James A Sutton (and Chief Executive Officer)
Senior Executive Officers: R L Bunn (Senior VP Energy), C L Ladner (Senior VP Finance), G W Westerman (Senior VP Administration), A C Bullman (VP Human Resources), R L Casselberry (VP Resources), M J Cuzzolina (VP Accounting), W M Graff (VP), L R Greenberg (VP and Legal Counsel), P A Heckel (VP Corporate Development), R J Jablonski (VP Information Systems), R C Mauch (VP), F F Wilcox (VP Division), W W Warfel (Auditor)

PRINCIPAL ACTIVITIES: Gas supply
Principal Subsidiaries: Amerigas Inc; UGI Development Company; Universal Well Service Inc
Principal Bank: Mellon Bank
Financial Information:

	$'000
Sales revenues	605,515

No of Employees: 3,450

UI GROUP INC
PO Box 2308, Tri Cities, WA 99302
Tel: (509) 735-6461

Chairman: Royden G Derrick
President: R Q Gardner (and Chief Executive Officer)
Senior Executive Officers: Martin Wistisen (Senior VP Northwest Operations), Bruce Kenner (Senior VP Manufacturing), Charles R Whipple (VP Administration), Earl Banner (VP Employee Relations)

PRINCIPAL ACTIVITIES: Freezing of vegetable products; trade in agricultural produce
Financial Information:

	$'000
Sales revenues	76,500

No of Employees: 1,500

UIS, INC
600 Fifth Avenue, New York, NY 10020
Tel: (212) 581-7660

Chairman: Harry Lebensfeld
President: Andrew G Pietrini
Senior Executive Officers: Melvin L Spencer (Senior Executive VP), Richard Pasculano (Executive VP), Joseph Arrigo (VP, Treasurer and Secretary)

PRINCIPAL ACTIVITIES: Manufacture of replacement parts for the automotive industry; iron and steel castings and forgings; metal fabrication; institutional furniture; motion picture projectors and sound equipment; wholesale trade in hardware, plumbing and heating supplies and electrical appliances; interests in the manufacture of confectionery
Principal Bank: The First National Bank of Boston
Financial Information:

	$'000
Sales revenues	400,000

No of Employees: 5,700

ULBRICH STAINLESS STEELS & SPECIAL METALS, INC
PO Box 294, North Haven, CT 06473
Tel: (203) 239-4481
Telex: TWX 710 465 2039 ulbrich steel

Chairman: Fred C Ulbrich Jr
President: Richard J Ulbrich
Senior Executive Officers: Chris Ulbrich (Executive VP), Walter Kaczor (VP Sales), Bernard Campbell (VP Operations), Dana Stanziale (VP Finance and Chief Financial Officer), Anthony Medeiros (VP Corporate Development and Human Resources)

PRINCIPAL ACTIVITIES: Manufacture of stainless steel and special metal products
Financial Information:

	$'000
Sales revenues	50,000

No of Employees: 300

ULTIMATE CORPORATION (THE)
717 Ridgedale Avenue, East Hanover, NJ 07936
Tel: (201) 887-9222

Chairman: Theodore M Sabarese (and President)
Senior Executive Officers: John W Keough (Executive VP), Ernest J Sabato (Executive VP), Michael J O'Donnell (Executive VP and Chief Financial Officer), Roger T Hanley (VP, Administration and Manufacturing), Frank J Kacerek (VP, Technical Services), Ronald A Croen (VP, Secretary and General Counsel)

PRINCIPAL ACTIVITIES: The Ultimate Corp designs, develops, assembles and markets computer systems for data base management. These systems integrate Ultimate's co-processor technology and proprietary operating system software with hardware supplied by major manufacturers and are sold to organizations of all sizes for a range of business applications. Ultimate systems are distinguished by an enhanced proprietary version of the sophisticated PICK operating system which permits their use without trained data processing personnel. The Company distributes its products through independent and company-owned dealers, here and abroad
Trade Names: ULTIMATE
Principal Subsidiaries: Ultimate Midlantic Inc; Ultimate Southern Florida Inc; Ultimate Southern California Inc; Ultimate Data

Systems Inc; Ultimate France SARL (France); Ultimate UK Ltd (UK); Ultimate Computer Ltd (Australia)
Principal Bank: Midlantic National Bank
Financial Information:

	$'000
Sales revenues	140,000

No of Employees: 400

ULTRA BANCORPORATION

1125 Route 22 West, Bridgewater, NJ 08807
Tel: (201) 685 8486

Chairman: Paul Mallon (and President and Chief Executive Officer); Vice Chairman: James T Gibbons
Senior Executive Officers: Gerald A Johnson (Senior VP, Chief Financial Officer and Secretary), Robert N Nelson (VP), Howard M Pettebone (VP)

PRINCIPAL ACTIVITIES: Holding company with interests in banking
Principal Subsidiaries: First National Bank of Central Jersey; Peoples National Bank of Central Jersey
Principal Bank: First National Bank of Central Jersey

No of Employees: 710

ULTRASYSTEMS INCORPORATED

16845 Von Karman Avenue, Irvine, CA 92714
Tel: (714) 863-7000
Telex: 69-2356 ULTRA SYS IRIN

Chairman: Phillip J Stevens (and President)
Senior Executive Officers: John H Dean, Ying-Tzyong Du, Russell L Greengard

PRINCIPAL ACTIVITIES: Ultrasystems Incorporated and its subsidiaries provide a wide range of high-technology engineering services to government and industry in the areas of energy and defense. The Company's innovative energy projects include alternative energy facilities and the design and construction of power, chemical, petrochemical and food-processing plants. Ultrasystems also is involved with numerous defense and space systems projects, including command, control communication and intelligence (C3I) activities and missile, satellite and ground combat systems
Trade Names: Ultrapower, UltraSweet
Principal Subsidiaries: Ultrasystems Defense and Space Systems Inc; Ultrasystems Engineers and Constructors Inc; Ultrapower Inc; Ofcco Construction Co Inc; Ultrasystems Western Constructors Inc; Ultrasystems Technology Inc; Ultrafuels Inc
Principal Bank: Bank of America; National Trust and Savings Association
Financial Information:

	$'000
Sales revenues	152,700

No of Employees: 1,200

UNA CORPORATION

Federal Reserve Plaza, 600 Atlantic Avenue, Boston, MA 02210
Tel: (617) 973 9600

Chairman: Richard J Potischman (and Chief Executive Officer)
President: Seymour N Schwartz (and Treasurer and Chief Operating Officer)
Senior Executive Officers: Edward Motyl (VP), Stephen E Kaufman (Secretary)

PRINCIPAL ACTIVITIES: Production of steel
Principal Subsidiaries: UN Alloy Steel Sales Inc
Principal Bank: Bank of New England
Financial Information:

	$'000
Sales revenues	31,000

No of Employees: 110

UNC INC

175 Admiral Cochrane Drive, Annapolis, MD 21401-7394
Tel: (301) 266-7333

Chairman: Walter B Holmes Jr
President: Dan A Colussy (and Chief Executive Officer)
Senior Executive Officers: Robert J Waugh (Executive VP and Chief Operating Officer), G Vern Diedrick (Senior VP and Chief Financial Officer), John A Hollansworth (Senior VP and Chief Administrative Officer), Bernard M Kostelnik (Senior VP, General Counsel and Secretary), Frederick G Becker (VP), Donald Carruth (VP Planning and Development), Paul X McLain (VP Financial Control), Ronald L Messenheimer (VP), William Yeo (VP Human Resources)

PRINCIPAL ACTIVITIES: The company has interests in a wide range of nuclear activities, the manufacture and servicing of aircraft engines and components space technology and high technology telecommunications
Principal Subsidiaries: Airwork Corp; Pacific Air Motive Corp; TRT Communications Inc; UNC Nuclear Industries; UNC Naval Products (Division)
Principal Bank: Mellon Bank
Financial Information:

	$'000
Sales revenues	352,900

No of Employees: 4,350

UNC NAVAL PRODUCTS

67 Sandy Desert Road, Uncasville, CT 06382
Tel: (203) 848-1511
Telex: TWX 710 432 1243 unc mtve

President: Glenn O Amy
Senior Executive Officers: George Waugh (Executive VP), R B Andress (VP Engineering), Richard W Barrett (VP Business Planning and Marketing)

PRINCIPAL ACTIVITIES: Manufacture of nuclear equipment for the navy; manufacture of equipment and components for the aerospace industry
Parent Company: UNC Inc
Financial Information:

	$'000
Sales revenues	130,000

No of Employees: 1,200

UNGERMANN-BASS, INC

2560 Mission College Blvd, Santa Clara, CA 95050
Tel: (408) 496-0111
Telex: TWX 910 338 2096 u b inc snta

President: R K Ungermann (and Chief Executive Officer)
Senior Executive Officers: Robert K Dahl (VP and Chief Financial Officer), C C Bass (VP), J F Jordan (VP), K W Sickler (VP Manufacturing), J M Davidson (VP Research), L P Quilici (VP Administration and Information Service), T W Hubbs (Secretary)

PRINCIPAL ACTIVITIES: Manufacture of data communications equipment
Principal Bank: Bank of America
Financial Information:

	$'000
Sales revenues	72,170

No of Employees: 490

UNIBANCORP INC

Sears Tower, Chicago, IL 60606
Tel: (312) 876 4200

Chairman: Donald D Thornburg (and President)
Senior Executive Officers: Michael E Godwin (VP Finance and Treasurer)

PRINCIPAL ACTIVITIES: Holding company with interests in banking
Principal Subsidiaries: Unibanctrust Company; Unibancleasing Company
Principal Bank: UnibancTrust Company

No of Employees: 420

UNIBANCTRUST

Sears Tower, Chicago, IL 60606
Tel: (312) 876-4200
Telex: WUI 687 1300 unibt uw

Chairman: Donald D Thornburg (and Chief Executive Officer)
President: Ben T Reidy
Senior Executive Officers: Andrew B Bernhardt (Executive VP), Richard M Pollack (Executive VP), George W Vander Vennet (Executive VP and Secretary), Edward Berkheimer (Senior VP), Peter B Stickler (VP and Cashier)

PRINCIPAL ACTIVITIES: Banking services
Parent Company: Unibancorp Inc

No of Employees: 350

UNICORP AMERICAN CORPORATION

1133 Avenue of the Americas, Suite 2516, New York, NY 10036
Tel: (212) 398 6300

Chairman: George S Mann
President: Wayne J Stemmer
Senior Executive Officers: Michael R Kordyback (Senior VP Finance and Treasurer), James W Leech (Senior VP), Thomas P Lydon Jr (Senior VP), Ralph V Marra (Senior VP and Controller), John R Korylak (VP), Laurie J Becker (Secretary)

PRINCIPAL ACTIVITIES: Property and real estate
Parent Company: Unicorp Canada Corporation, Canada
Principal Bank: Morgan Guaranty Trust Company of New York
Financial Information:

	$'000
Sales revenues	83,810

No of Employees: 21

UNIDYNAMICS DEFENSE SYSTEMS

472 Paul Ave, St Louis, MO 63135
Tel: (314) 522-6700

Chairman: Robert S Evans
Presidents: Edwin F Phelps (Crane/UniDynamics), Melvin Appelman (Defense Systems)
Senior Executive Officers: John B McLemore (VP Finance)

PRINCIPAL ACTIVITIES: Manufacture of launching equipment; components fcr the nuclear and space industries; aerospace systems and ordnance devices
Parent Company: Crane Co
Principal Bank: Morgan Guaranty Trust Company
Financial Information:

	$'000
Sales revenues	100,000

No of Employees: 1,100

UNIFI INC

PO Box 19109, Greensboro, NC 27419
Tel: (919) 294-4410
Telex: TWX 510 922 7496 unifi ab gbo

Chairman: G A Mebane
Presidents: William T Kretzer; J Richard Hardin (Unifi Consulting Division)
Senior Executive Officers: Jerry W Eller (Executive VP Manufacturing), Robert A Ward (Executive VP Finance), G Alfred Webster (Executive VP Sales)

PRINCIPAL ACTIVITIES: Manufacture of man-made fibers
Principal Bank: North Carolina National Bank
Financial Information:

	$'000
Sales revenues	216,000

No of Employees: 900

UNIFIRST CORPORATION

15 Olympia Avenue, Woburn, MA 01888
Tel: (617) 933 5800

Chairman: Aldo Croatti; Vice Chairman: Ronald D Croatti (and Chief Executive Officer)
President: Anthony F Difillipo
Senior Executive Officers: John B Bartlett (VP), Robert L Croatti (VP), Ronald D Croatti (VP), Cynthia C Brown (Treasurer)

PRINCIPAL ACTIVITIES: Industrial dry-cleaning and laundry services
Principal Bank: Bank of New England
Financial Information:

	$'000
Sales revenues	104,800

No of Employees: 1,800

UNIFORCE TEMPORARY PERSONNEL INC

1335 Jericho Turnpike, New Hyde Park, NY 11040
Tel: (516) 437 3300

Chairman: John Fanning (and President)
Senior Executive Officers: Rosemary Maniscalco (Executive VP), Gordon Robinett (VP, Secretary and Treasurer)

PRINCIPAL ACTIVITIES: Temporary personnel services
Principal Bank: Chase Manhattan Bank
Financial Information:

	$'000
Sales revenues	52,270

No of Employees: 70

UNIGATE INC

6250 LBJ Freeway, Dallas, TX 75240
Tel: (214) 385-3302

President: Daniel Hodson
Senior Executive Officers: Clare Whitley (VP Finance), Jack Davis (Secretary)

PRINCIPAL ACTIVITIES: Holding company with interests in dairy products and fast food restaurants
Parent Company: Unigate PLC (UK) through Unigate International Ltd (UK)
Principal Bank: European American Bank and Trust Company
Financial Information:

	$'000
Sales revenues	250,000

No of Employees: 3,000

UNIMATION INC

Shelter Rock Lane, Danbury, CT 06810
Tel: (203) 744-1800
Telex: WUT 551445 unimation

Chairman: Chester A Sadlow
President: Paul H Ockerman
Senior Executive Officers: Hal H Bloch (VP Marketing and Sales), Michael P Comiskey (VP Operations), Maurice J Dunne (VP Product Planning), Gil R Legnard (VP Procurement), I W Pence (VP Engineering)

PRINCIPAL ACTIVITIES: Manufacture of industrial robots
Parent Company: Westinghouse Electric Corporation, Pittsburgh, PA
Principal Bank: Union Trust Company

Financial Information:

	$'000
Sales revenues	49,000

No of Employees: 730

UNIMAX CORPORATION

54 East 64th Street, New York, NY 10021
Tel: (212) 755-8800

Chairman: Arthur L Carter (Executive Committee)
President: Tom Scheinman (and Chief Executive Officer)
Senior Executive Officers: Richard S Wiesenthal (Executive VP), Jules Martinez (Senior VP), Peter Giosa (VP), John D Sicher Jr (VP)

PRINCIPAL ACTIVITIES: Manufacture of electrical and electronic equipment including electronic components, current carrying wiring devices, control equipment; printing services
Parent Company: Shepaug Corporation
Principal Subsidiaries: Unimax Switch Corp; Ward Leonard Electric Co; The Type Group Inc; Lee Spring Co Inc; Master-Eagle Photoengraving Corp; Craftsman Color Lithographers Inc
Principal Bank: Chemical Bank
Financial Information:

	$'000
Sales revenues	65,280

No of Employees: 1,200

UNION BANCORP INC

200 Ottawa Avenue NW, Grand Rapids, MI 49503
Tel: (616) 451 7393

Chairman: James W Carpenter (and Chief Executive Officer and Subsidiary Officer)
President: Craig W Schopf
Senior Executive Officers: Craig A Woodman (Senior VP, Chief Financial Officer and Treasurer)

PRINCIPAL ACTIVITIES: Holding company with interests in banking
Principal Subsidiaries: Bankers Leasing Services Inc; First National Bank & Trust Company; Peoples Bank & Trust Company; Union Bank & Trust Company

No of Employees: 715

UNION BANK

445 South Figueroa Street, Los Angeles, CA 90071
Tel: (213) 236-5000
Telex: 4999030

Chairman: John F Harrigan
President: John M Heidt
Senior Executive Officers: Donne P Moen (Senior Executive VP, Commercial Banking Division), Steven D Broidy (Executive VP Support Division), Mark E Buchman (Executive VP Institutional Markets Division), Jack A Frazee (Executive VP Finance Division), Neil E Kennedy (Executive VP Strategic Planning), Michael G Palin (Group Executive VP Asia-Pacific Regional Coordination), Ray M Williams (Executive VP Marketing Resources Division), Charles D Kenny (General Counsel and Secretary)

PRINCIPAL ACTIVITIES: Regarded as the premier business bank in California, Union Bank has been serving middle market businesses for more than 70 years. It offers specific expertise in foreign trade with the Pacific Rim, asset based financing, treasury operations and cash management. Union Bank has long been a leader in providing interim construction financing and also specializes in serving the needs of the telecommunications and energy-related industries. Union Bank is based in Los Angeles and is the 31st largest bank in the nation with offices throughout California. It is a member of the Standard Chartered Group, an international banking network with more than 2,000 offices in over 60 countries
Principal Subsidiaries: Institutional Credit Services Corporation; Market Investment Services Corporation; Stanchart Business Credit; Stanchart Equities Inc; Stanchart Export Trading Company; Stanchart Real Estate Investment Advisors Inc; Standard Chartered Bank International; Union Venture Corporation; Unionbank Leasing Corporation

No of Employees: 4,900

UNION BOILER CO

PO Box 425, Nitro, WV 25143
Tel: (304) 755-8171

Chairman: R S McDavid (and President)
Senior Executive Officers: Roger W Magaw (Executive VP and Treasurer), Oney McDavid (Executive VP Equipment), Robert L Mahaffey (Senior VP Branch), Tommy A Withrow (VP Projects), Joseph V Larkin (VP Construction), Philip Morrison (VP Quality Control), Arnold E Burdette (VP Purchasing), Billy D Price (VP)

PRINCIPAL ACTIVITIES: Electrical and mechanical engineering contractors; structural steel fabrication and erection
Parent Company: Concorp, Inc
Principal Subsidiaries: Graver Tank; Crown Union
Principal Bank: Continental Illinois National Bank and Trust Co
Financial Information:

	$'000
Sales revenues	97,000

Principal Shareholders: McDavid Family

UNION CAMP CORPORATION

1600 Valley Road, Wayne, NJ 07470
Tel: (201) 628-2000
Telex: TWX 710 988 5843 unioncamp wyne

Chairman: R E Cartledge (and President and Chief Executive Officer); Chairman of Executive Committee: Alexander Calder Jr
Senior Executive Officers: J M Piette (Senior Executive VP), J D Munford (Executive VP), J M Reed (Executive VP), William H Trice (Executive VP), Jerry H Ballengee (Senior VP), Russell W Boekenheide (Senior VP), William B Howes (Senior VP), Robert L Webb (Senior VP), James O Crisp (VP), Harold R Hoss (VP and Treasurer), J G McGowin II (VP), R E Moore (VP and Comptroller), Dirk R Soutendijk (VP, Secretary and General Counsel), D E Stahl (VP), William B Stewart (VP), W A Williams (VP), W S D Woods Jr (VP)

PRINCIPAL ACTIVITIES: Manufacture of pulp and paper, packaging products and machinery, timber, building materials, petrochemicals, specialty chemicals and land development
Principal Bank: Morgan Guaranty Trust Co of New York
Financial Information:

	Dec 31 1985	Dec 31 1986
	$'000	$'000
Sales revenues	1,865,870	2,045,215
Net income	95,092	129,934
Earnings per share	$1.73	$2.65
Shareholders equity	1,315,090	1,370,569

No of Employees: 17,700

UNION CARBIDE CORPORATION

39 Old Ridgebury Road, Danbury, CT 06817-0001
Tel: (203) 794-2000
Telex: ITT 420542 ucc ui

Chairman: Warren M Anderson
President: R D Kennedy (and Chief Executive Officer)
Senior Executive Officer: J C Stephenson (Executive VP and Chief Financial and Administrative Officer)

PRINCIPAL ACTIVITIES: Manufacture of chemicals, gases and carbon products

Financial Information:

	Dec 31 1985	Dec 31 1986
	$'000	$'000
Sales revenues	9,003,000	7,828,000
Net income (loss)	(581,000)	496,000
Earnings (loss) per share	($2.86)	$4.78
Shareholders equity	4,019,000	1,005,000

No of Employees: 91,459

UNION CHEMICALS DIVISION

PO Box 60455, Los Angeles, CA 90060
Tel: (213) 977-7600
Telex: WUT 698 288 union chem lsa

President: T C Henderson
Senior Executive Officers: T D Renfer (VP Finance), D E Barth (VP Carbon Marketing), C F Merrill (VP Chemical Marketing Domestic), E E Johnson (VP Chemical Manufacturing), P C Schmid (VP International Marketing)

PRINCIPAL ACTIVITIES: Manufacture of a wide range of chemicals
Parent Company: Union Oil Co of California-Ultimate Holding Company-UNOCAL Corp
Financial Information:

	$'000
Sales revenues	1,000,000

No of Employees: 2,500

UNION CORPORATION

50 Washington St, South Norwalk, CT 06854
Tel: (203) 866-1099

Chairman: Melvin L Cooper; Vice Chairman: John S Moeller
President: Robert H Sabel
Senior Executive Officers: Deke C Abbott Jr (Executive VP and Chief Operating Officer), Michael Strauss (Executive VP), Charles E Atwood (VP and Chief Financial Officer), Richard W Pickert (VP), Anthony P Spagnol (VP), Raymond M Beacha (VP Operations), Peter F Early (VP), James A Ceresa (VP)

PRINCIPAL ACTIVITIES: Manufacture of a wide range of products including electrical and electronic equipment, metal products, recycled metals, castings, springs and pollution control equipment
Principal Bank: Pittsburgh National Bank
Financial Information:

	$'000
Sales revenues	114,000

No of Employees: 3,100

UNION ELECTRIC CO

PO Box 149, St Louis, MO 63166
Tel: (314) 621-3222

President: William E Cornelius (and Chief Executive Officer)
Senior Executive Officers: Earl K Dille (Executive VP), Stewart W Smith Jr (Executive VP), J J Beisman (VP Customer Service), D E Brandt (VP and Controller), C A Bremer (VP Supply Services), D C Harrison (VP Regional West), G J Haven (VP Engineering and Construction), W E Jaudes (VP and General Counsel), F R Lengefeld (VP), H W Loeh (VP Human Resources), H G Meyer (VP Computer Services), C W Mueller (VP Finance), R O Piening (VP Rates), W A Sanford (VP Industrial Relations), D F Schnell (VP Nuclear), C J Schukai (VP Transmission and Distribution), E J Telthorst (VP Power Operations), H E Wuertenbaecher (VP Public Relations), J C Thompson (Secretary), L E Esswein (Treasurer)

PRINCIPAL ACTIVITIES: Electricity, gas and water supply
Principal Bank: Chemical Bank

Financial Information:

	Dec 31 1985	Dec 31 1986
	$'000	$'000
Sales revenues	1,591,763	1,807,182
Income before taxes	569,879	617,804
Net income	337,225	343,893
Dividends	178,717	189,950
Dividends per share	$1.78	$1.86
Earnings per share	$2.86	$2.89
Common stock*	100,403	102,124
Retained earnings	661,359	766,154
Common shareholders equity	1,887,750	1,992,545

*average shares outstanding in thousands

No of Employees: 7,400

UNION EQUITY CO-OPERATIVE EXCHANGE

10th & Willow Street, Enid, OK 73701
Tel: (405) 233-5100
Telex: WUT 747 169 equity enid

President: Erwin Duerksen
Senior Executive Officers: William R Allen Jr (Executive VP and General Manager), Darwin Francis (VP), Edwin Wallace (VP Administrative Services), Irvine Clubine (VP Business Development), Leonard Edwards (VP Grain Marketing), Ed O'Rourke (VP Export Marketing)

PRINCIPAL ACTIVITIES: Marketing of grain
Principal Bank: Wichita Bank for Cooperatives
Financial Information:

	$'000
Sales revenues	400,000

No of Employees: 300

UNION FEDERAL SAVINGS AND LOAN ASSOCIATION

523 West Sixth Street, Los Angeles, CA 90014
Tel: (213) 688 8400

Chairman: William S Martin Jr (and Chief Executive Officer)
President: Roger L Kringen (and Chief Operating Officer)
Senior Executive Officers: Richard S Lewis (Executive VP), J K MacCabe (Senior VP), W M McNeil (Senior VP), Melvin E Smith (Senior VP), R L Spinoglio (Senior VP)

PRINCIPAL ACTIVITIES: Savings and loans
Principal Subsidiaries: Uni-Cal Financial Corporation; Uni-Cal Insurance Inc; Uni-Cal Mortgage Corporation
Principal Bank: Union Bank

No of Employees: 400

UNION MUTUAL LIFE INSURANCE CO

2211 Congress Street, Portland, ME 04122
Tel: (207) 780-2211
Telex: WUT 944 421 umlifeins por

President: Colin C Hampton
Senior Executive Officers: Richard B Dalbeck (1st Senior VP Corporate), Francis R Noonan (Senior VP and Chief Financial Officer), William F Brennan (Senior VP Corporate Strategic Planning and Development), Stephen B Center (Senior VP Employee Benefits Division), Terry P Cohen (Senior VP Human Resources), Francis J Guthrie Jr (Senior VP Individual Life Division), David E Hughes (Senior VP and General Counsel), John C Roberts (Senior VP Individual Disability Division), David M Tourangeau (Senior VP Investment)

PRINCIPAL ACTIVITIES: Insurance

No of Employees: 3,450

UNION NATIONAL CORPORATION

670 Washington Rd, Mt Lebanon, PA 15228
Tel: (412) 644-8782

Chairman: Robert F Patton
President: George F Kesel (and Chief Executive Officer)
Senior Executive Officers: John R Echement (Executive VP and Treasurer), William E Walker (Executive VP), Fred H Gardner (Senior VP and Chief Financial Officer), Robert H Stevenson (Senior VP, Secretary and General Counsel)

PRINCIPAL ACTIVITIES: Banking services
Financial Information:

	Dec 31 1985
	$'000
Revenues	252,000
Net income	20,700
Total assets	2,500,000

No of Employees: 1,900

UNION OIL CO OF CALIFORNIA

1201 W 5th St, Los Angeles, CA 90017
Tel: (213) 977-7600
Telex: WUT 677593 unionoil lsa a

Chairman: Fred L Hartley (and President and Chief Executive Officer)
Senior Executive Officers: Claude S Brinegar (Senior VP Administration), Ray A Burke (Senior VP Energy Resources), William S McConnor (Senior VP), T C Henderson (Senior VP and President Union Chemical Division), Richard J Stegemeier (Senior VP Corporate Development), Philip Blamey (VP Finance)

PRINCIPAL ACTIVITIES: Manufacture of a wide range of oil related products including heating fuels, chemicals, lubricants and gasoline
Parent Company: UNOCAL Corporation

No of Employees: 20,000

UNION PACIFIC CORPORATION

345 Park Avenue, New York, NY 10154
Tel: (212) 418-7800
Telex: TWX 710 581 5440 up corp nyk

Chairman: William S Cook (and President and Chief Executive Officer and Chairman of Executive Committee); Vice Chairmen: J C Kenefick, W T Smith
Senior Executive Officers: C L Eaton (Senior VP Planning and External Affairs), W J McDonald (Senior VP Law), C B Schaefer (Senior VP Planning and Corporate Development), W F Surette (Senior VP Finance), T W Boswell (VP Strategic Planning), J P Halan (VP Employee Relations), E R Hill (VP Financial Administration), E P Kopp (VP Washington Affairs), L W Matthews III (VP and Treasurer), J R Mendenhall (VP Taxes), J W Otto (VP and Controller)

PRINCIPAL ACTIVITIES: Operation of railroad system; exploration and production of oil and gas; mining
Principal Subsidiaries: Union Pacific System; Champlin Petroleum Co; Rocky Mountain Energy Co; Upland Industries Co
Financial Information:

	Dec 31 1985	Dec 31 1986
	$'000	$'000
Sales revenues	7,797,890	6,688,000
Net income (loss)	501,207	(460,000)
Earnings (loss) per share	$4.18	($4.56)
Shareholders equity	4,356,150	3,408,000

No of Employees: 33,000

UNION PLANTERS CORPORATION

67 Madison Avenue, Memphis, TN 38147
Tel: (901) 523-6000

Chairman: Richard A Trippeer
President: Benjamin W Rawlins (and Chief Executive Officer)
Senior Executive Officers: James A Gurley (VP), M Kirk Walters (VP and Treasurer), David L Wark (VP and Chief Financial Officer)

PRINCIPAL ACTIVITIES: Banking services
Principal Subsidiaries: Union Planters National Bank of Memphis
Financial Information:

	$'000
Revenues	248,715

No of Employees: 1,770

UNION SPECIAL CORPORATION

400 N Franklin Street, Chicago, IL 60610
Tel: (312) 266-4000
Telex: ITT 4330213 union ui

Chairman: J G Beadle (and Chief Executive Officer)
President: Carlo A Kaiser
Senior Executive Officers: Donald R Meyer (Executive VP Marketing), Edward J O'Connell (VP Finance and Treasurer), John O Kleinschmidt (VP Research and Development), John W Aldridge (VP Manufacturing), J R Heggestad (VP Manufacturing and Materials)

PRINCIPAL ACTIVITIES: Manufacture of industrial sewing machines
Principal Bank: Harris Trust & Savings Bank
Financial Information:

	$'000
Sales revenues	97,100

No of Employees: 1,800

UNION TEXAS PETROLEUM HOLDINGS INC

1330 Post Oak Blvd, Houston, TX 77252
Tel: (713) 623-6544

Chairman: A C Johnson (and Chief Executive Officer)
Senior Executive Officers: A C Berman (Senior VP), W M Krips (Senior VP), J O Langley (Senior VP), A E Van Dyke (Senior VP), N W Wilson III (VP, Secretary and General Counsel), W L Brabham (VP), S M Lobliner (VP), A W Peabody (VP), D J Redlinger (VP), R L Ryan (VP)

PRINCIPAL ACTIVITIES: Oil and gas exploration and production; distribution of natural gas
Financial Information:

	Dec 31 1986
	$'000
Sales revenues	1,255,698
Net (loss)	(57,488)
(Loss) per share	($1.02)
Shareholders (deficit)	(382,094)

No of Employees: 3,000

UNION WARREN SAVINGS BANK

133 Federal Street, Boston, MA 02110
Tel: (617) 482 4590

Chairman: Francis P Brennan (and Chief Executive Officer); Vice Chairman: Herbert V Gearty (and Treasurer)
President: Luis C Roever
Senior Executive Officers: Francis J Shea Jr (Executive VP), R W Clifford (Senior VP), Paul E Dion (Senior VP and Controller), Gerard F Linskey (Senior VP), C W Swinton (Senior VP)

PRINCIPAL ACTIVITIES: Banking
Principal Subsidiaries: Colonial Car Lease Company Inc

No of Employees: 245

UNISTRUT INTERNATIONAL

35005 Michigan Avenue W, Wayne, MI 48184
Tel: (313) 721-4040
Telex: 235457

President: Constantine J Malfese
Senior Executive Officers: W B Attfield (VP and General Counsel), Edward C Cady (VP Finance), Ruthanne Kelly (VP Human Resources), Richard L Snyder (VP Sales)

PRINCIPAL ACTIVITIES: Manufacture of metal frames and tubes
Principal Bank: City National Bank of Detroit
Financial Information:

	$'000
Sales revenues	100,000

No of Employees: 1,000

UNISYS CORPORATION

One Unisys Place, PO Box 418, Detroit, MI 48232
Tel: (313) 972-7000 (World Headquarters, Detroit, MI); (215) 542-3501 (Corporate Offices, Blue Bell, PA)
Cable: BURAD, Detroit, Mich.; PO Box 500, Blue Bell, Pennsylvania
Telex: TRT 164125 BURR M UT; WU 224015 Burroughs E UD (Detroit); 846465 Univac BLUL (Blue Bell)
Facsimile: (313) 972-0311 DEX 3500 (Detroit); (215) 542-6850 (Blue Bell)

Chairman: W Michael Blumenthal (and Chief Executive Officer); Vice Chairman: Joseph J Kroger
President: Paul G Stern
Senior Executive Officers: James A Unruh (Executive VP), Vincent M Donovan (VP and President, Customer Services), John F Horton (VP and President, Federal Information Systems Div), O G Greene (VP, President, Financial Systems Div), John J Holton (SVP, President, Americas Div), Edward P Gilbert (Senior VP, Chief Financial Officer), Hollis L Caswell (Senior VP President, Office of Corp Product Operation), Philip S Dauber (Senior VP, President, Office of Corp Product Operation), Richard H Bierly (Senior VP, Human Resources), Robert F Holmes (Senior VP, Worldwide Marketing), Frederick F Jenny (Senior VP, President, Defense Systems), Curtis A Hessler (Senior VP Corp Development and General Counsel), Dewaine L Osman (VP, President, Communications and Airlines Systems Div), Leroy W Beers (VP, Engineering and Manufacturing Staff), Martin A Belsky (Executive VP Financial Systems Div), George R Gazerwitz (VP, Customer Services Engineering-United States), Jeanette P Lerman (VP Corporate Communications), Leon J Level (VP and Treasurer), Fred R Meier (VP, Corp Program Management), Robert D Merrell (VP), Kenneth L Miller (VP and Secretary), W Lee Shevel (VP, Systems and Technology), Jack F McHale (VP, Public and Investor Relations), Jack F Thompson (VP, Plans and Initiatives), Richard B Williams (VP, Market Strategy and Development), Alexander C Wilson (VP, Procurement), Jan Lindelow (Senior VP, Worldwide Marketing), Reto Braun (VP, President, Pacific Asia Div), G Graham Murphy (VP, Europe/Africa Div), A G Jones (VP Information Systems), D G Ludvigson (VP, Real Estate and Construction), Gary D Alexander (VP, President, Industrial and Commercial Systems Div), J M Tucci (President, Public Sector Systems Div), D L Osman (President, Communications and Airlines Systems Div), V Puritano (VP, Government Affairs), H N Ghosh (VP, Corp Quality Management)

PRINCIPAL ACTIVITIES: Unisys (the new company created by the merger of Burroughs Corporation and Sperry Corporaton, formally completed on September 16, 1986) provides advanced computer-based information systems, networks, and related products, services, and support to select commercial and defense markets. The company offers a wide range of processing systems, from proprietary and IBM-compatible PCs and small business systems, to systems that are among the most powerful in the world, plus a full line of peripheral attachments, including terminals, printers, and storage devices. It also offers system software (database management and development and productivity tools) and application software products that address particular customers operations, along with related support and professional services, and communications products that tie together its systems, as well as the systems of other vendors. Unisys is line-of-business oriented. Its marketing efforts are supported by Product Operations, which covers all Unisys engineering and manufacturing worldwide and has nearly 25,000 employees, and by Customer Service, with over 10,000 employees worldwide. Unisys commits about 10 percent of its nondefense revenues to research and development.
Principal Subsidiaries: Memorex Corporation; System Development Corporation; Graftek Inc
Principal Bank: Harris Trust Company of New York
Financial Information:

	Dec 31 1985	Dec 31 1986
	$'000	$'000
Revenues	5,037,700	7,432,400
Income (loss) before taxes	359,500	(91,800)
Net income (loss)	248,200	(43,400)
Dividends*	118,200	119,300
Dividends per share*	$2.60	$2.60
Earnings (loss) per share	$5.46	($1.63)
Common stock	228,000	231,000
Retained income	1,872,400	1,678,600
Shareholders equity	2,492,400	3,828,300

*common stock

No of Employees: 90,000 worldwide

UNIT DRILLING AND EXPLORATION COMPANY

1000 Galleria Tower 1, 7130 South Lewis, Tulsa, OK 74136
Tel: (918) 493 7700

Chairman: King P Kirchner (and Chief Executive Officer)
President: John G Nikkel (and Chief Operating Officer)
Senior Executive Officers: Philip M Keeley (Senior VP), O Earle Lamborn (Senior VP), Bill W Cobb (VP), J Richard Zieren (Secretary and Legal Counsel)

PRINCIPAL ACTIVITIES: Oil and gas exploration
Principal Bank: Bank of Oklahoma
Financial Information:

	$'000
Sales revenues	47,000

No of Employees: 550

UNITED AIRCRAFT PRODUCTS INC

PO Box 90007, Dayton, OH 45490
Tel: (513) 898 1811

Chairman: Maury L Spanier (and Chief Executive Officer)
President: Nick G Harris (and Chief Operating Officer)
Senior Executive Officers: Milton S Cohn (Chairman of Executive Committee), Henry Cozzolino (VP Marketing), Charles A Gockel Jr (VP and Treasurer), Robert R Pfouts (VP Engineering), Carl E Simmons (VP and Division President), John F Unger (VP Manufacturing), Carolyn J Allen (Secretary)

PRINCIPAL ACTIVITIES: Manufacture of aircraft components
Parent Company: Parker Hannifin Corporation
Financial Information:

	$'000
Sales revenues	36,100

No of Employees: 530

UNITED AIRLINES, INC

1200 Algonquin Rd, Elk Grove Township, IL 60666
Tel: (312) 952-4000
Telex: RCA 275362 UAL UR; WU 287419 UNITEDEXO ELGR

Chairman: James J Hartigan
President: Frank A Olson (and Chief Executive Officer)
Senior Executive Officers: John R Zeeman (Executive VP Marketing and Planning), Edward H Hoenicke (Senior VP, General Counsel and Secretary)

PRINCIPAL ACTIVITIES: Air transportation services, hotels and insurance

Financial Information:

	Dec 31 1985	Dec 31 1986
	$'000	$'000
Sales revenues	5,291,609	7,105,141
(Loss) before taxes	(198,738)	(170,719)
Net (loss)	(88)	(81)
Dividends per share	$1.00	$1.00
Earnings (loss) per share	($2.09)	$0.25
Common stock	35,262	50,172
Shareholders equity	1,789,470	2,292,610

No of Employees: 60,000

UNITED ARTISTS COMMUNICATIONS, INC

172 Golden Gate Ave, San Francisco, CA 94102
Tel: (415) 928-3200

Chairman: D Stewart Blair (and Chief Executive Officer)
President: Robert A Naify
Senior Executive Officers: Salah M Hassanein (Executive VP), A C Childhouse (Senior VP), John H Rowley (Senior VP), Marvin Luboff (VP, Secretary and General Counsel), Richard R Naify (VP), Irving Palace (VP), Allen Pinsker (VP), John A Treadwell (VP), Gladstone T Whitman (VP Finance)

PRINCIPAL ACTIVITIES: Operation of motion picture theaters; cable television services; building of non-residential property
Principal Bank: Chemical Bank
Financial Information:

	$'000
Sales revenues	529,000

No of Employees: 7,500

UNITED BANCORP OF ARIZONA

3300 North Central Avenue, Phoenix, AZ 85012
Tel: (602) 248 2200

Chairman: James P Simmons (and President and Chief Executive Officer)
Senior Executive Officers: Jack D Davis (VP), H S Pickrell (VP)

PRINCIPAL ACTIVITIES: Holding company with interests in a wide range of banking and financial services
Parent Company: Standard Chartered PLC, UK
Principal Subsidiaries: H S Pickrell Company; United Bank of Arizona; United Bancorp Realty Company; United Security Corporation
Principal Bank: United Bank of Arizona

No of Employees: 1,000

UNITED BANCORPORATION ALASKA INC

440 East 36th Avenue, Anchorage, AK 99503
Tel: (907) 276 1911

Chairman: William L Hensley; Vice Chairman: Eugene B Erskine (and Chief Executive Officer)
President: Earl M Miller
Senior Executive Officers: James M Hackett (Executive VP and Secretary), Richard D Barnhart (Senior VP Data Processing), Youngju K Murphy (Senior VP Planning), Valorie F Walker (Senior VP Finance)

PRINCIPAL ACTIVITIES: Holding company with interests in the provision of banking services
Principal Subsidiaries: United Bank Alaska
Principal Bank: United Bank Alaska

No of Employees: 300

UNITED BANK OF DENVER NA

1700 Broadway, Denver, CO 80274
Tel: (303) 861-8811

Chairman: Richard A Kirk (and Chief Executive Officer)

President: Charles R Hazelrigg

Senior Executive Officers: Donald W Robotham (Senior Executive VP), Carroll D Speckman (Senior Executive VP), Thomas C Stokes (Senior Executive VP), Jed J Burnham (Executive VP), Robert H Dressel (Executive VP), Michael J Fowles (Executive VP), Thomas W Swanson (Executive VP), Roger E Johnson (Senior VP and Comptroller)

PRINCIPAL ACTIVITIES: All banking services including deposits and loans, personal trust, international banking, municipal bond and other services

Parent Company: United Banks of Colorado

No of Employees: 1,450

UNITED BANKERS INC

510 N Valley Mills Drive, Suite 600, Waco, TX 76710

Tel: (817) 776 7600

Chairman: Robert A Mann; Vice Chairman: Walter J Rusek

President: Matt Landry Jr

Senior Executive Officers: Patrick L Rominger (Executive VP), Ben Y Kerr (Senior VP, Secretary and Treasurer)

PRINCIPAL ACTIVITIES: Holding company with interests in banking

Principal Subsidiaries: Farmers State Bank; First Bank & Trust; First National Bank; First State Bank; Sabine Bank; Southwest Bank; Travis Bank & Trust; United Data Services Inc; United Bank

Principal Bank: Westview National Bank

No of Employees: 580

UNITED BANKS OF COLORADO, INC

1700 Lincoln, Suite 3200, Denver, CO 80274

Tel: (303) 861-4700

Fax: 303-863-4605

Chairman: N Berne Hart

Senior Executive Officers: Richard A Kirk, Charles R Hazelrigg, Dennis Erickson, Tucker Hart Adams, R Bradford Laughlin, Robert L Schaep, Thomas W Swanson, Alvin W Naggerty, Charles H Powers, Candice W Rogers, William J Rundarff, Roger E Johnson, Robert G Boucher, Donald W Rowbotham, susan K Koonsman

PRINCIPAL ACTIVITIES: United Banks is the largest bank holding company in Colorado and one of the largest in the Rocky Mountain region. It owns the controlling interest in 41 Colorado banks (the subsidiary banks) as well as other subsidiaries engaged in data processing, equity investment, finance, insurance and mortgage banking. All the Company's banks provide a full range of deposit and loan services, while United Bank of Denver also provides personal trust, international banking, municipal bond and other services

Principal Subsidiaries: Banks: United Bank of:- Academy Place; Arapahoe; Arvada; Aurora; Aurora-City Center; Aurora-South; Bear Valley; Boulder; Brighton; Broomfield; Buckingham Square; Cherry Creek; Colorado Springs; Colorado Springs-East; Delta; Denver; Durango; Fort Collins; Fort Collins-South; Garden of the Gods; Grand Junction; Grand Junction-Downtown; Greeley; Highlands Ranch; Ignacio; Lakewood; LaSalle; Littleton; Longmont; Monaco; Montrose; Northglenn; Pueblo; Skyline; Southglenn; Southwest Plaza; Steamboat Springs; Sterling; Sunset Park; University Hills; Westminster. Bank Related Subsidiaires:- Fidelity National Life Insurance Company and Lincoln Agency, Inc; United Banks Service Company; United Financial Centers, Inc; United Mortgage Company

Principal Bank: United Bank of Denver

Financial Information:

	Dec 31 1985 $'000	Dec 31 1986 $'000
Income before taxes	38,211	5,181
Net income	41,781	22,177
Preferred dividends	2,921	2,201
Common dividends	13,400	13,354
Dividends per common share	$1.08	$1.08
Earnings per common share	$2.83	$1.36
Common stock	38,036	38,211
Retained income	178,243	184,860
Shareholders equity	397,826	409,950
Deposits	4,756,332	4,743,720
Total assets	6,018,306	6,038,826

No of Employees: 4,141

UNITED BRANDS COMPANY

One East Fourth St, Cincinnati, OH 45202
Tel: (513) 579-2115

Chairman: Carl H Lindner (and Chief Executive Officer and Chairman of the Executive Committee)
President: Ronald F Walker (and Chief Operating Officer)
Senior Executive Officers: Keith E Lindner (Senior Executive VP), Dennis M Doyle (VP, General Counsel and Secretary), James E Evans (VP), Thomas E Mischell (VP), Fred J Runk (VP, Chief Financial Officer and Treasurer), William A Tsacalis (Controller), Robert E Crowe (Assistant VP), John J Gerah (Assistant Secretary), David Groelinger (Assistant Treasurer), James J McLaughlin (Assistant Controller)

PRINCIPAL ACTIVITIES: United Brands is one of the world's leading producers, processors and distributors of quality food products. The products are marketed worldwide under the Chiquita, John Morrell and other brand names. Chiquita Brands products include bananas and other fresh fruit (pineapples, melons and grapefruit), frozen deserts and beverages sold under the Chiquita name, as well as margarine, shortening, salad dressings and dehydrated soups sold under various regional brand names. John Morrell products include fresh, frozen and processed meat (pork, beef and lamb), including sausage, frankfurters, bacon, canned hams and luncheon meats sold under the John Morrell, Rath Black Hawk and various regional brand names
Trade Names: Chiquita, Chiquita Pops, Brander, California Natural, Clover, Cremelado, Don Paco, Numar, Petite 150, Chico, John Morrell, *Nathan's Famous, Tobin's First Prize, Hunter, Tom Sawyer, Krey, Krey Gourmet, Peyton, Buckboard, Rath Black Hawk, Patridge, Rodeo, Scott Petersen, Bob Ostrow, E-Z Cut, Table Trim, Golden Smoked, *by license agreement
Principal Subsidiaries: United Fruit Company: John Morrell & Co; Numar Processed Foods Group; Polymer United
Financial Information:

	Dec 31 1985 (9 mths) $'000	Dec 31 1986 (12 mths) $'000
Sales revenues	2,288,182	3,306,733
Income before taxes(1)	48,147	102,924
Net income	22,647	53,824
Dividends per share	$0.05	$0.05
Earnings per share net(2)	$1.37	$3.38
Earnings per share net(3)	$1.37	$3.26
Shareholders equity	387,825	406,811

(1) and extraordinary item
(2) primary
(3) fully diluted

No of Employees: 39,000

UNITED CABLE TELEVISION CORPORATION

4700 South Syracuse Parkway, Suite 1100, Denver, CO 80237
Tel: (303) 779 5999

Chairman: Gene W Schneider (and Chief Executive Officer)
President: Fred A Vierra (and Chief Operating Officer)
Senior Executive Officers: William J Elsner (Senior VP and Chief Financial Officer), Richard C Schneider (Senior VP), Edward J Callahan (VP Research and Development), Gary S Howard (Treasurer), Nimrod J Kovacs (VP Marketing Software Systems), Donald J Masters (VP and Geneal Counsel), James W Neese (VP Engineering), Virgil Reed (VP Western Region), Mark Savage (VP), Daniel W Shields (VP), Barry L Wilson (VP Operations), Kenneth P Warner (Controller)

PRINCIPAL ACTIVITIES: Cable television services
Principal Subsidiaries: Comtronics Cable TV Inc; Tulsa Cable Television Inc; United Cable TV Eastern Share Inc; United Cable TV IL Valley; United Cable TV of CT; United Cable TV Illinois
Principal Bank: First National Bank; Mellon Bank
Financial Information:

	$'000
Sales revenues	196,000

No of Employees: 1,200

UNITED CAROLINA BANCSHARES CORPORATION

306 South Madison Street, Whiteville, NC 28472
Tel: (919) 642 5131

Chairman: E Rhone Sasser (and President and Chief Executive Officer)
Senior Executive Officers: Lawrence R Bowers (Chairman of Executive Committee), J W Adams (VP), Ronald C Monger (VP and Chief Financial Officer), Robert D Williams (VP Investment), William R Lathan (Secretary and Legal Counsel)

PRINCIPAL ACTIVITIES: Holding company with interests in a range of banking services
Principal Subsidiaries: First Credit Corporation; First Credit Corporation GA Inc; UCB Data Services Corporation; United Carolina Bank
Principal Bank: United Carolina Bank

No of Employees: 1,665

UNITED CATALYSTS INC

1227 Twelfth Street, Louisville, KY 40210
Tel: (502) 637-9751
Telex: WUT 204239 catalyst b lvl

Chairman: Joseph L Parker
President: C B Knight
Senior Executive Officers: William J Monin (Executive VP), Earl Englert (VP International Sales), John F Lombard (VP Marketing), J H Wright (VP Operations), E O Northcutt Jr (VP International), Paul B Boyd (VP Sales), William V Miller (VP Sales), Larry D Mulcahy (VP Finance and Secretary), Karl J Russ (VP Technical)

PRINCIPAL ACTIVITIES: Manufacture of catalysts
Parent Company: Sud-Chemie Inc
Principal Bank: First National Bank of Louisville
Financial Information:

	$'000
Sales revenues	75,000

No of Employees: 650

UNITED CITIES GAS COMPANY

5300 Maryland Way, Brentwood, TN 37027
Tel: (615) 373 0104

Chairman: Dwight C Baum
President: Gene C Koonce (and Chief Executive Officer)
Senior Executive Officers: L E Jirikovec (Senior VP Operations), Glenn G Rogers (Senior VP Supply), Thomas R Blose Jr (VP and Chief Engineer), James B Ford (Senior VP and Controller), Donald L Howard (VP and General Manager), Glenn R King (VP Administration), Victor G Pappas (VP

Marketing), Shirley M Hawkins (Assistant VP Human Resources)

PRINCIPAL ACTIVITIES: Natural gas supply
Principal Subsidiaries: UCG Energy Corporation
Principal Bank: Harris Bank
Financial Information:

	$'000
Sales revenues	132,150

No of Employees: 665

UNITED COATINGS, INC

3050 N Rockwell, Chicago, IL 60618
Tel: (312) 583-3700
Telex: TWX 910 221 1179

President: Jules F Knapp
Senior Executive Officers: Jim Perry (Senior VP), Tony Janus (VP Finance), F Schaffer (VP Sales)

PRINCIPAL ACTIVITIES: Manufacture of industrial coatings
Principal Bank: Exchange National Bank
Financial Information:

	$'000
Sales revenues	70,000

No of Employees: 400

UNITED COMPANIES FINANCIAL CORPORATION

4041 Essen Lane, PO Box 1591, Baton Rouge, LA 70821
Tel: (504) 924 6007

Chairman: Lloyd F Collete (and Chief Executive Officer); Vice Chairman: Harris J Chustz
President: J Terrell Brown
Senior Executive Officers: Daniel J Burns (Executive VP), Joseph P Griffon (VP), James B Harris (VP), Michael H Sause (VP Marketing), Dale E Redman (Treasurer)

PRINCIPAL ACTIVITIES: Holding company with interests in insurance including health and life
Principal Subsidiaries: Southern Mortgage Company Inc; United Communications Corporation LA; United Companies Life Insurance Company; United Companies Mortgage Alabama; United Companies Mortgage Florida; United Companies Mortgage Georgia; United Companies Mortgage Mississipi; United Companies Mortgage South Carolina; United Companies Mortgage Tennessee; United Companies Mortgage Virginia; United General Title Insurance Company; United Plan Insurance Agency; United Printing Company Inc; United Real Estate Development Company
Principal Bank: Manufacturers Hanover Trust Company
Financial Information:

	$'000
Revenues	138,135

No of Employees: 750

UNITED COUNTIES BANCORPORATION

4 Commerce Drive, Cranford, NJ 07016
Tel: (201) 931 6600

Chairman: Raymond W Bauer
President: Eugene H Bauer (and Chief Executive Officer)
Senior Executive Officers: Richard O Nowicki (VP, Treasurer and Subsidiary Officer), Richard O Woodfield (VP, Treasurer and Subsidiary Officer), Mary E Tierney (Secretary and Subsidiary Officer)

PRINCIPAL ACTIVITIES: Financial holding company

UNITED ENERGY RESOURCES, INC

PO Box 1478, Houston, TX 77001
Tel: (713) 229-4123

Chairman: J Hugh Roff (and President and Chief Executive Officer); Vice Chairmen: John S Davis; Stephen A Wakefield (and General Counsel)
Senior Executive Officers: James C Cooper (Executive VP and Chief Financial Officer), Gene P Morrell (Senior VP Energy Products and Services), D Lamar Smith (Senior VP Government Affairs and Public Relations), Paul M Adams (VP Administration), Fred T Baker Jr (VP), Paul F Ferguson (VP and Treasuere), Larry J Gunn (VP and Associate General Counsel), Stan M Haley (VP Human Resources), Sherwood O Jones (VP and Secretary), Harry H Jordan (VP Management Systems and Risk Management), E G Parks (VP and Controller), Steven B Toon (VP Finance), James A Tramuto (VP Public Affairs)

PRINCIPAL ACTIVITIES: Oil and gas exploration and production; gas supply
Parent Company: Midcon Corp
Principal Bank: Texas Commerce Bank
Financial Information:

	$'000
Sales revenues	4,000,000

No of Employees: 3,650

UNITED ENGINEERS & CONSTRUCTORS INTERNATIONAL INC

30 South 17th Street, PO Box 8223, Philadelphia, PA 19101
Tel: (215) 422-3000
Cable: UNTDGRS
Telex: 83-4203; TWX: 710-670-1267; ITT: 476-1045
Telecopier: (215) 422-4648

President: Gunnar E Sarsten
Senior Executive Officers: B Anz (President, Yeargin Inc), Isak Arditi (VP, Industrial Div), Henry P Burress (VP, Administration), Stanley L Clewett (President, UE&C-Catalytic Inc), Alan M Ebner (VP, General Engineering Div), Dennis Ferrigno (VP, General Technology), Harry G Kreider (VP, Stearns-Roger Div), Charles Q Miller (VP, Power Div), Mohan Pai (VP, Project Controls and Services), Pat R Pennell (VP, Western Construction), Werner J Poelck (VP, Maintenance), John W Renouf (Director, Industrial Relations), Robert A Simmers (VP, Stearns Catalytic Div), D Watson (President, Stearns Catalytic International), Conrad E Wysocki (VP, Petroleum and Mining), Thomas H Zarges (VP Business Development)

PRINCIPAL ACTIVITIES: An international engineering, construction and maintenance firm with 100 years of experience serving industry and government with technological expertise in energy, power generation and fuels, mining, petroleum and petrochemicals, pharmaceuticals, biotechnology, chemicals, electronics, aerospace and space launch facilities, metals facilities, research facilities, light industry, and environmental systems. Innovators in cost-effective engineering, design and modular construction, and pioneers in contract maintenance for utilities and industry
Parent Company: Raytheon Company, Lexington, MA
Principal Subsidiaries: United Engineers & Construction Inc, UE&C-Catalytic Inc; Yeargin Inc; Stearns Catalytic International Ltd

UNITED FEDERAL BANK FSB

156 Hanover Street, Manchester, NH 03101
Tel: (603) 625 2600

Chairman: William F Stone
President: John J McCarthy (and Chief Executive Officer)
Senior Executive Officers: Ralph P Tetreault (VP and Secretary)

PRINCIPAL ACTIVITIES: Banking

No of Employees: 200

UNITED FINANCIAL GROUP, INC
1033 Harwin, Houston, TX 77036
Tel: (713) 981-2300

Chairman: C E Bentley (and Chief Executive Officer)
President: Charles E Hurwitz (and Chief Executive Officer)
Senior Executive Officers: Robert M Dawson (VP), David E Barrett (VP and Treasurer), James L Pledger (Secretary and General Counsel)

PRINCIPAL ACTIVITIES: Financial services including savings and loans
Financial Information:

	Dec 31 1985	Dec 31 1986
	$'000	$'000
Net (loss)	(3,150)	(36,250)
(Loss) per share	($0.50)	($4.55)
Shareholders equity	114,224	77,013
Deposits	-	3,101,427
Total assets	4,989,030	6,464,869

No of Employees: 712

UNITED FIRE AND CASUALTY COMPANY
118 Second Avenue SE, Cedar Rapids, IA 52407
Tel: (319) 399 5700

Chairman: Scott McIntyre Jr (and President)
Senior Executive Officers: Harold A Hagen (Executive VP Marketing), Wallace H Horner (Senior VP), Kent G Baker (VP and Chief Financial Officer), Richard J Ehlinger (VP), Roy L Ewen (VP Insurance), Richard L Halsor (VP), Theodore H Hiller Jr (VP), Maynard L Hansen (Secretary), Gerald D Seidl (Legal Counsel), Glen H Smith Jr (Secretary), Galen E Underwood (Treasurer)

PRINCIPAL ACTIVITIES: Fire and casualty insurance
Principal Subsidiaries: Lafayette Insurance Inc; United Life Insurance Company
Principal Bank: Merchants National Bank
Financial Information:

	$'000
Revenues	99,145

No of Employees: 400

UNITED FIRST FEDERAL SAVINGS & LOAN ASSOCIATION
1390 Main Street, Sarasota, FL 33577
Tel: (813) 366-33577

Chairman: G K Page (and Chief Executive Officer)
President: D I Good (and Chief Operating Officer)
Senior Executive Officers: D D King (Executive VP), W M Blake (Senior VP Tampa Region), W F Hermanson (Senior VP Systems Management), Kemper M Hetzler (Senior VP Corporate Banking), J A Hobbs (Senior VP Deposit Account Administration), C E Long III (Senior VP Retail Banking), Rita E Moran (Senior VP Human Resources), W D Mossbarger (Senior VP Finance and Treasurer), W M Ross (Senior VP Residential Mortgage Lending)

PRINCIPAL ACTIVITIES: Financial services including savings and loans

No of Employees: 500

UNITED FOAM CORPORATION
615 S Flower, Los Angeles, CA 90017-2812

Chairman: Leonard Graff
Senior Executive Officers: Charles W Morgan (Senior VP), Philip C Ashov (VP Administration and Treasurer), H J Lee (VP Marketing)

PRINCIPAL ACTIVITIES: Manufacture of foam for the furniture and packaging industries
Principal Bank: Security Pacific National Bank
Financial Information:

	$'000
Sales revenues	50,000

No of Employees: 700

UNITED FOODS, INC
100 Dawson Avenue, Bells, TN 38006
Tel: (901) 663-2335
Telex: TWX 810 566 20604 united foods

Chairman: J I Tankersley (and President and Chief Executive Officer)
Senior Executive Officers: Norman A Rodriguez (Executive VP), D B Tankersley (Senior VP and Secretary), Carl W Gruenewald II (Senior VP and Treasurer), B M Ennis (Senior VP), W Donald Dresser (VP and General Counsel), Mason Leonard (VP)

PRINCIPAL ACTIVITIES: Freezing of fruit and vegetables and prepared food products
Principal Subsidiaries: United Foods International Corp
Principal Bank: Citicorp Industrial Credit Inc
Financial Information:

	$'000
Sales revenues	163,000

No of Employees: 1,600

UNITED GAS PIPE LINE CO
600 Travis, Houston, TX 77002
Tel: (713) 229-4123
Telex: WUT 774391 uer ugpl hou

Chairman: J H Roff Jr (and Chief Executive Officer)
President: John F Brown (and Chief Operating Officer)
Senior Executive Officers: Pat W Burnett (Executive VP Operations and Engineering), James E Haynes (Executive VP Marketing, Rates, Transportation and Exchange), R J Simmons Jr (Executive Senior VP Gas Supply, Personnel, Administration and Pipeline Ventures), J R Angell (Senior VP Government Affairs), T L Aubin Jr (Senior VP Gas Supply and Administration), J R Templeton (Senior VP Gas Imports and Joint Ventures), M Phyllis Bourque (VP Gas Supply), Ralph M Hall (VP Engineering), D A James (VP Rates and Regulatory Affairs), Francis S Kalman (VP and Controller), B G Lambert (VP Operations), G A Sanders (VP North Region Operations), Alvin White (VP Personnel), Gary N Willis (VP Sales), C H Young Jr (VP South Region Operations), C Kenneth Zinnecker (VP Transport and Exchange)

PRINCIPAL ACTIVITIES: Natural gas supply and distribution of fuels
Parent Company: United Energy Resources Inc, Houston, TX
Principal Bank: Texas Commerce Bank
Financial Information:

	$'000
Sales revenues	2,320,000

No of Employees: 2,300

UNITED HEALTHCARE CORPORATION
300 Opus Center, 9900 Bren Road East, Minnetonka, MN 55443
Tel: (612) 936 1380

Chairman: Richard T Burke (and President and Chief Executive Officer)
Senior Executive Officers: J G Degen Jr (Executive VP and Chief Executive Officer), R J Holloway (Secretary)

PRINCIPAL ACTIVITIES: Holding company with interests in healthcare organisations
Financial Information:

	$'000
Revenues	101,225

No of Employees: 1,700

UNITED ILLUMINATING CO

80 Temple St, New Haven, CT 06506
Tel: (203) 787-7200

Chairman: John D Fassett
President: George W Edwards Jr (and Chief Executive Officer)
Senior Executive Officers: Robert L Fiscus (Executive VP and Chief Financial Officer), Richard J Grossi (Executive VP and Chief Operating Officer), Rollie Comstock (Senior VP Corporate Affairs), Charles W Cook Jr (Senior VP Corporate Planning and Development), James F Crowe (Senior VP Marketing), David W Hoskinson (Senior VP Operations), Leon A Morgan (Senior VP Finance and Accounting), Albert Harary (VP Management Services), Albert N Henricksen (VP Engineering), Marcus R McCraven (VP Environmental Engineering), Harold J Moore Jr (VP Human Resources), E Jon Majkowski (VP Public Affairs)

PRINCIPAL ACTIVITIES: Electricity supply
Principal Bankers: Citibank
Financial Information:

	$'000
Sales revenues	470,000

No of Employees: 1,500

UNITED INDUSTRIAL CORPORATION

18 E 48th Street, New York, NY 10017
Tel: (212) 752-8787

Chairman: Bernard Fein (and President)
Senior Executive Officers: Irwin W Barr (VP and President, AAI Corp), Russell A Wills (President, Detroit Stoker Co), Howard M Bloch (Treasurer), Michael J Klitus Jr (Assistant Treasurer), Michael P Coppins (Assistant Secretary)

PRINCIPAL ACTIVITIES: United Industrial Corporation makes electronics, aerospace systems and weaponry for America and its allies. The company also produces energy systems and specialized plastic products
Principal Subsidiaries: Detroit Stoker Co; AAI Corp; Neo Products Co
Principal Bank: Morgan Guaranty Trust Co
Financial Information:

	Dec 31 1985	Dec 31 1986
	$'000	$'000
Sales revenues	269,378	272,508
Income (loss) before taxes	29,017	(17,582)
Net income (loss)	29,054	(9,154)
Dividends	6,157	7,776
Dividends per share	$0.49	$0.58
Earnings (loss) per share	$1.43	($0.69)
Common stock	13,117	14,348
Retained income (deficit)	19,898	(6,645)
Shareholders equity	109,954	93,267

No of Employees: 3,740

UNITED INNS, INC

5100 Poplar Avenue, Memphis, TN 38137
Tel: (901) 767-2880
Telex: WUI 6828042 uninn

Chairman: William B Cockroft; Vice Chairman: J T Kizer (and Treasurer)
President: Don W Cockroft
Senior Executive Officers: J H Lammons (Executive VP), John M Dollar (VP Construction), Ben M Gaines (VP Furniture Division), J D Miller (VP Finance), George W Akers (VP Carwash), David L Potts (VP Hotel Operations)

PRINCIPAL ACTIVITIES: Hotel management; retail trade in gasoline; operation of car wash services; furniture manufacture
Principal Bank: First Tennessee Bank
Financial Information:

	$'000
Sales revenues	173,873

No of Employees: 5,000

UNITED JERSEY BANKS

301 Carnegie Center, PO Box 2066, Princeton, NJ 08540
Tel: (609) 987-3200

Chairman: T Joseph Semrod (Chairman of the Board and President)
Senior Executive Officers: John R Haggerty (Executive VP/Finance), Stephen H Paneyko (Executive VP/Commercial Banking), Alan N Posencheg (Executive VP/Corporate Operations), Robert A Bonelli (Senior VP/Corporate Planning), William E Cosgrove Jr (Senior VP/Item Processing), Alfred M D'Augusta (Senior VP/Human Resources), William J Healy (Senior VP and Comptroller), John F Hoff III (Senior VP/Government Banking), James J Holzinger (Senior VP/Commercial Banking), Hubert C Mott (Senior VP/Loan Policy and Administration), Richard F Ober Jr (Senior VP, Corporate Counsel and Secretary), Dennis Porterfield (Senior VP/Bank Investments), Lenore Smith (Senior VP/Marketing), Edmund C Weiss Jr (Senior VP and Auditor)

PRINCIPAL ACTIVITIES: United Jersey Banks is a $8.0 billion holding company with six member banks and six non-bank subsidiaries that provide a wide range of financial services to consumers, businesses, government entities and financial institutions
Principal Subsidiaries: United Jersey Bank; United Jersey Bank/Northwest; United Jersey Bank/Mid State; United Jersey Bank/Southwest; United Jersey Bank/Cumberland National; United Jersey Bank, NA
Principal Bank: United Jersey Bank, Hackensack, NJ
Financial Information:

	Dec 31 1986
	$'000
Net income	71,505
Earnings per share	$2.17
Shareholders equity	510,205
Deposits	6,672,853
Total assets	8,023,961

No of Employees: 5,346

UNITED MEDICAL CORPORATION

56 Haddon Avenue, Haddonfield, NJ 08033
Tel: (609) 354 2200

Chairman: John Aglialoro (and Chief Executive Officer)
President: Joan P Carter (and Secretary and Chief Operating Officer)
Senior Executive Officers: Theodore P Heininger (VP and Chief Financial Officer)

PRINCIPAL ACTIVITIES: Wholesale trade in surgical and medical products; hospital cardiac treatment centers; medical software
Principal Subsidiaries: Brotherston Hospital Supply Corporation; Research Data Corporation; Trotter Treadmills Inc; UM Graphics Corporation
Principal Bank: Midlantic National Bank
Financial Information:

	$'000
Sales revenues	46,645

No of Employees: 310

UNITED MERCHANTS & MANUFACTURERS, INC

1407 Broadway, New York, NY 10018
Tel: (212) 930-3900

Chairman: Martin J Schwab (and Chief Executive Officer)
President: Uzi Ruskin (and Chief Operating Officer)

Senior Executive Officers: Tomas Furth (Executive VP), Sidney O Margolis (Executive VP), Robert D Mathews (Executive VP), Judith A Nadzick (Executive VP, Comptroller and Chief Financial Officer), Lawrence B Danza (Senior VP), James R Henderson (Senior VP), William E Iannone (Senior VP), H C Nixon (Senior VP), Thomas F G Abraham (VP), Edmund M Bamberger (VP), William H Carroll (VP), Arthur C Charwat (VP), William J Courtad (VP), Bernard G Mayers (VP), Cleland T Reed (VP), Robert M Smith (VP), James Spallina (VP), Herbert J Tamres (VP)

PRINCIPAL ACTIVITIES: Manufacture of textiles
Principal Bank: Manufacturers Hanover Trust Company
Financial Information:

	Jun 30 1986
	$'000
Sales revenues	802,105
Net (loss)	(35,340)
(Loss) per share	($3.88)
Shareholders equity	115,290

No of Employees: 9,000

UNITED MISSOURI BANCSHARES INC

PO Box 1771, Kansas City, MO 64141
Tel: (816) 556-5600

Chairman: R C Kemper (and Chief Executive Officer); Vice Chairmen: Peter J Genovese
President: Malcolm P Aslin (and Chief Operating Officer)
Senior Executive Officers: Douglas F Page (Executive VP), James E Street (Executive VP), William M Teiwes (Executive VP, Treasurer and Chief Financial Officer), Stephen W Gwartney (Senior VP), Marshall D Hendrickson (Senior VP Administration), Gary L Lasche (Senior VP and Assistant Treasurer), Marian S George (VP), Margie Hurley (VP Marketing), Chuck Lewis (VP Compliance), Charlotte Shelton (VP Training)

PRINCIPAL ACTIVITIES: Banking services
Principal Bankers: United Missouri Bank of Kansas City

No of Employees: 2,000

UNITED NEW MEXICO FINANCIAL CORPORATION

PO Box 1081, 200 Lomas NW, Albuquerque, NM 87103
Tel: (505) 765 5086

Chairman: Robert O Anderson
President: Gerald J Ford (and Chief Executive Officer)
Senior Executive Officers: Larry D Willard (Executive VP and Chief Operating Officer), Clifton E Fodge (Senior VP and Executive Officer), Clifford Aldrich (VP Data Processing), James H Donaldson (VP Item Processing), Carl G Guist (VP Finance, Secretary and Treasurer), Marvin Kallsen (VP and Auditor), Thomas Rogers (VP Review)

PRINCIPAL ACTIVITIES: Holding company with interests in banking
Principal Subsidiaries: United New Mexico Bank; United New Mexico Bank at Mimbres Valley; United New Mexico Bank at Vaughn; United New Mexico Trust Company
Principal Bank: United New Mexico Bank
Financial Information:

Net income	3,105

No of Employees: 720

UNITED OF OMAHA LIFE INSURANCE CO

Mutual of Omaha Plaza, Omaha, NE 68175
Tel: (402) 342-7600
Telex: WUT 484564 mut un oma a

Chairman: V J Skutt (and Chief Executive Officer); First Chairman: Thomas J Skutt (and Chief Executive Officer); Vice Chairman: Hugh V Plunkett Jr
President: Conrad S Young (and Chief Operating Officer)
Senior Executive Officers: M T Crummer (Senior Executive VP and Chief Investment Officer), William J Hetzler (Senior Executive VP Operations), John D Minton (Senior Executive VP), John W Weekly (Senior Executive VP Computer Data Services and Group Insurance), G Ronald Ames (Executive VP Computer Data Services), Milton W Beal (Executive VP Marketing Administration), Boyd A Carnaby (Executive VP Mortgage Loans and Real Estate), Robert J Collins (Executive VP International Development), John R Dixon (Executive VP Personnel), John F Gaule Jr (Executive VP General Agency Sales), Robert G Gundry (Executive VP Marketing Support), Lawrence F Harr (Executive VP and General Counsel), Lon G Heinitz (Executive VP Divisional Office Sales), Burton D Jay (Executive VP and Chief Actuary), Ernest B Johnson (Executive VP), D E Laughlin (Executive VP Life Marketing), John L Maginn (Executive VP Investment and Treasurer), Donald R McCormick (Executive VP Life Underwriting Division), John F Nauss (Executive VP Specialty Group Markets), Richard J Sampson (Executive VP Group Insurance), Donna L Schissler (Executive VP Policyowner Services), John A Sturgeon (Executive VP and General Comptroller), Emil L Sulentic (Executive VP Administration), Leslie I Telford (Executive VP Military Sales), William L Wiseman (Executive VP Advertising and Community and Public Affairs)

PRINCIPAL ACTIVITIES: Insurance

Parent Company: Mutual of Omaha Insurance Co

Principal Bank: The Omaha National Bank

Financial Information:

	$'000
Premium income	496,000

No of Employees: 3,000

UNITED OKLAHOMA BANKSHARES INC

1217 South Agnew, Oklahoma City, OK 73108
Tel: (405) 239 5800

Chairman: Morrison G Tucker (and President and Chief Executive Officer)

Senior Executive Officers: Neil S West (Executive VP), A Thomas Loy (Senior VP and Chief Financial Officer), June O'Steen (Senior VP), Robert F Dilg Jr (VP, Treasurer and Controller), Martha J Williams (Secretary)

PRINCIPAL ACTIVITIES: Holding company with interests in banking

Principal Subsidiaries: United Oklahoma Bank; United Bankcard Association Inc; United Bankers Mortgage Corporation; United Bank Advisory Services; United Check Processing Center; United Data Services Inc

Principal Bank: United Oklahoma Bank

No of Employees: 370

UNITED PARCEL SERVICE OF AMERICA, INC

51 Weaver Street, Greenwich, CT 06830

Tel: (203) 622-6000

Telex: 965 857

Chairman: John W Rogers (and Chief Executive Officer)

Senior Executive Officers: John W Alden (Senior VP), Larry P Breakiron (Senior VP), Vernard F Cormie (Senior VP), Donald W Layden (Senior VP), Kent C Nelson (Executive VP and Chief Financial Officer), Robert Smith (Senior VP), J R Peterson (Senior VP and Secretary), Bruce M Barone (Treasurer)

PRINCIPAL ACTIVITIES: Holding company with interests in trucking and parcel delivery by ground and air, full service truck leasing and trucking

Financial Information:

	Dec 31 1985	Dec 31 1986
	$'000	$'000
Sales revenues	7,686,719	8,619,703
Net income	567,627	668,966
Earnings per share	$3.36	$3.96
Shareholders equity	2,026,417	2,469,798

No of Employees: 168,200

UNITED PRESIDENTIAL CORPORATION

217 Southway Boulevard East, Kokomo, IN 46902
Tel: (317) 453 0602

President: D L Wilhelm
Senior Executive Officers: Arthur H Stonebraker (Executive VP), Peter F Huse (VP and Legal Counsel), Louis C Schmidt (VP and Treasurer), James R Martin (Secretary)

PRINCIPAL ACTIVITIES: Holding company with interests in life insurance
Principal Subsidiaries: Diversified National Corporation; United Presidential Life Insurance Company
Principal Bank: Union Bank and Trust Company

No of Employees: 130

UNITED REFINING CO OF PENNSYLVANIA

15 Bradley Street, Warren, PA 16365
Tel: (814) 723-1500
Telex: TWX 510 695 4781

Chairman: David B Chalmers (and President)
Senior Executive Officers: Peter R Hunter (Executive VP), James E Sadler (Executive VP), James G Gray (Senior VP Marketing), Young J Boozer III (VP), Robert L Daye (VP), Myron Turfit (VP Administration and Accounting)

PRINCIPAL ACTIVITIES: Oil refining
Parent Company: United Refining Co
Principal Bank: Chase Manhattan Bank
Financial Information:

	$'000
Sales revenues	611,000

No of Employees: 2,000

UNITED SAVER'S BANCORP INC

85 Main Street, Littleton, NH 03561
Tel: (603) 444 5321

Chairman: Raymond E Closson
President: Daniel G Edgar (and Chief Executive Officer)
Senior Executive Officers: Robert L Reynells Jr (Executive VP and Chief Financial Officer), John J McCarthy (Executive VP and Treasurer), Shirley K Wentzell (Secretary)

PRINCIPAL ACTIVITIES: Banking activities

No of Employees: 200

UNITED SAVINGS BANK

8219 Leesburg Pike, Vienna, VA 22180
Tel: (703) 749 8500

Chairman: Robert J Lewis
President: Howard D Orebaugh (and Chief Executive Officer)
Senior Executive Officers: Cynthia L Fisher (Executive VP), Christopher W Burch (Senior VP and Treasurer), Susan M Browning (VP), Francine D Maestri (VP), F Buddy McCombs (VP), John C Savanosh (VP), Richard A Duffy (Controller), Harold R Evans (Secretary)

PRINCIPAL ACTIVITIES: Banking services

Financial Information:

	Dec 31 1985
	$'000
Revenues	38,470
Net income	1,530

No of Employees: 205

UNITED STATES BRASS CORPORATION

901 Tenth Street, Plano, TX 75074
Tel: (214) 423-3576

President: Delwin D Renfroe (and General Manager)
Senior Executive Officers: Roy E Baxter (VP Purchasing), Rich Gleitsmann (VP Operations), Jack Miller (VP Marketing), Wesley Thompson (VP Finance)

PRINCIPAL ACTIVITIES: Manufacture of brass fittings for the plumbing industry
Parent Company: Household International Inc, Prospect Hts, IL
Principal Bank: Republic National Bank
Financial Information:

	$'000
Sales revenues	85,000

No of Employees: 1,200

UNITED STATES HEALTH CARE SYSTEMS INC

980 Jolly Rd, PO Box 1109, Blue Bell, PA 19422
Tel: (215) 628-4800

President: Leonard Abramson
Senior Executive Officers: W B Skillman (Executive VP), J R Weiner (Executive VP), Frederick C Berger (Senior VP), Jayne E Ashenfelter (VP), E J Doerr Jr (VP), Eugene J Fluehr (VP Operations), A M Friedman (VP), W L Horrocks (VP), Lawrence T Longacre (VP Finance), Milton W Williams (Secretary)

PRINCIPAL ACTIVITIES: Hospital management
Financial Information:

	$'000
Sales revenues	363,000

No of Employees: 800

UNITED STATES LEASING INTERNATIONAL, INC

733 Battery Street, San Francisco, CA 94111
Tel: (415) 627-9000
Telex: 278602

Chairman: Brooks Walker Jr
President: D E Mundell (and Chief Executive Officer)
Senior Executive Officers: Michael J O'Shea (Executive VP), C S La Follette (Executive VP), David B Hudnut (Senior VP, Corporate Development), Peter Mezey (Senior VP and General Counsel), C P Apple (VP and Controller), Gary P Stern (Senior VP), Daniel N Swisher (Senior VP, International Operations), M J O'Shea (President, U.S. Leasing Corporation), H J L Bosman (President, U.S. Fleet Leasing), R E Laing (President, U.S. instrument Rentals), John F Longinotti (President U.S. Portfolio Leasing), David A Summers (President U.S. Rail Services), Dennis Demontigny (President, Crest Medical Inc), Douglas E Scudamore (President, Orient-U.S. Leasing), Roy H Findlay (Managing Director, Instrument Rentals U.K.), Glyn A Jenkins (Managing Director U.S. Leasing Ltd)

PRINCIPAL ACTIVITIES: Sales-aid equipment leasing programs; commercial auto fleet leasing and management services; business and computer equipment rentals; electronic test equipment rentals; rail car leasing and management; home health-care equipment rentals; leased equipment income fund management; large lease arrangement and portfolio management
Trade Names: U.S. Leasing

Principal Subsidiaries: United States Leasing Corporation; United States Fleet Leasing, Inc; United States Instruments Rentals, Inc; Instrument Rentals (UK); United States Portfolio Leasing, Inc; United States Rail Services, Inc; United States Lease Financing, Inc; Crest Medical, Inc; Orient-U.S. Leasing Corporation; United States Airlease Inc
Principal Banks: Various (about three dozen in total)
Financial Information:

	Dec 31 1985 $'000	Dec 31 1986 $'000
Sales revenues	380,582	434,060
Income before taxes	56,915	49,012
Net income	29,303	29,303
Dividends	5,787	5,999
Dividends per share	$0.80	$0.82
Income per share	$3.25	$3.96
Common stock	8,015	7,391
Retained income	185,583	208,887
Shareholders equity	250,670	276,917

No of Employees: 1,700

UNITED STATES PIPE & FOUNDRY CO

3300 First Avenue N, Birmingham, AL 35202
Tel: (205) 254-7000
Telex: TWX 810 733 3684 us pipe bhm

Chairman: J B Cordell
President: Stanley Gurak
Senior Executive Officers: Kenneth E Hyatt (VP), Russell E Lloyd (VP), K J Matlock (VP), E J Mize Jr (VP and Controller), Peter Petro (VP), H C Winsor (VP)

PRINCIPAL ACTIVITIES: Manufacture of cast iron pipe and metal fasteners
Parent Company: Jim Walter Corporation
Financial Information:

	$'000
Sales revenues	370,000

No of Employees: 5,000

UNITED STATES PLAYING CARD CORPORATION

360 Madison Avenue, New York, NY 10017
Tel: (212) 907-0100

Chairman: Howard R Curd
President: Leslie J Racey (and Chief Executive Officer)
Senior Executive Officers: Raymond F Ostrander (Executive VP, Chief Operating Officer and Secretary), William C Biehl (VP and Treasurer), Stewart E Moore (VP Sales), Louis B Eichhold (VP Industrial Relations), Dan F Edelschick (VP Marketing), G D Murphy (VP Business Development)

PRINCIPAL ACTIVITIES: Manufacture of playing cards; lithographic printing services
Principal Subsidiaries: United States Playing Card Co
Financial Information:

	$'000
Sales revenues	46,000

No of Employees: 720

UNITED STATES SHOE CORPORATION

One Eastwood Drive, Cincinnati, OH 45227
Tel: (513) 527-7000
Telex: ITT 4333064 usshoe cin

Chairman: Philip G Barach (and President and Chief Executive Officer)
Senior Executive Officers: Henry A Billeter (VP-Marketing and Corporate Development), James J Crowe (VP-Secretary and General Counsel), Edwin C Gerth (VP-Corporate Controller), Seymour Glabman (Group VP-Women's Footwear), Edward J Klee (VP-Finance), Joseph C Lamb (VP-Treasurer), Louis Neusner (VP-Merchandising Operations), Howard Platt (Executive VP-President Footwear Wholesaling and Retailing), Harry S Robinson (Group VP-Chairman Red Cross Shoe Division), Martin Sherman (Senior VP-Chief Executive Officer Retail Development and Services Division), Robert Stix (Senior VP-Manufacturing and Operations), James L Vadis (Senior VP-President, Specialty Retailing)

PRINCIPAL ACTIVITIES: The United States Shoe Corporation is a consumer goods company with operations in specialty retailing and in footwear manufacturing and distribution
Trade Names: Red Cross, Amalfi, Pappagallo, Selby, Joyce, Freeman, French Shriner, Texas Brand Boots, Casual Corner, J Riggings
Principal Subsidiaries: The shops for Pappagallo Inc; Community Urban Redevelopment of Duck Creek Inc; The Winterbrook Corp; Delaware Financing Corp
Principal Banks: Bankers Trust, NY; Wells Fargo, San Francisco
Financial Information:

	Dec 31 1986 $'000
Sales revenues	2,003,246
Net income	25,472
Earnings per share	$0.57
Shareholders equity	488,818

No of Employees: 35,000

UNITED STATES SUGAR CORPORATION

PO Box 1207, Clewiston, FL 33440
Tel: (813) 983-8121

Chairman: C S H Mott
President: John B Boy
Senior Executive Officers: H T Vaughn Jr (Executive VP), J N Fairbanks (Senior VP Corporate Development), A R Mayo (Senior VP Sugar Houses), H J Andreis (VP Research), Robert H Buker Jr (VP Legal Affairs), R C Lee (VP Community Affairs and Personnel), Robert A Miller (VP Engineering), Mike Milicevic (VP Cattle), Frank L Polhill (VP Agriculture), Joseph P Sexton Jr (VP Agriculture Equipment Shops), Frank D Teets (VP Vegetable Operations), James E Terrill (VP Administration)

PRINCIPAL ACTIVITIES: Sugar refining; molasses; vegetables; beef cattle
Principal Bank: Chemical Bank
Financial Information:

	$'000
Sales revenues	274,813

No of Employees: 2,500

UNITED STATES SURGICAL CORPORATION

150 Glover Avenue, Norwalk, CT 06856
Tel: (203) 866-5050
Telex: RCA 221904 ussc ur

Chairman: Zanvyl Krieger
President: Leon C Hirsch (and Chief Executive Officer)
Senior Executive Officers: Turi Josefsen (Executive VP Marketing), Bruce S Lustman (Executive VP Finance), Herbert W Korthoff (Executive VP Operations), David Fisher (Senior VP Law), David T Green (Senior VP Research), Marianne Scipione (VP Corporate Communications)

PRINCIPAL ACTIVITIES: Design, manufacture and market surgical stapling instruments
Trade Names: Registered trademark: AUTO SUTURE
Principal Subsidiaries: Auto Suture Benelux BV; Auto Suture Canada Ltd; Auto Suture (Deutschland) GmbH; Merlin Medical SA; Auto Suture UK Limited; Auto Suture (Australia) Pty Ltd; Automated Instruments
Principal Bank: Connecticut Bank and Trust
Financial Information:

	$'000
Sales revenues	206,000

Principal Shareholders: Leon C Hirsch (8.66%); Zanvyl Kreiger (8.46%)
No of Employees: 2,083

UNITED STATES TOBACCO CO

100 W Putnam Avenue, Greenwich, CT 06830
Tel: (203) 661-1100
Telex: WUT 996624 us tobacco grc

Chairman: Louis F Bantle (and Chief Executive Officer); Vice Chairmen: Thomas B O'Grady; Ralph L Rossi
President: Nicholas A Buoniconti (and Chief Operating Officer)
Senior Executive Officers: Jack Africk (Executive VP), Manuel Leitao (Executive VP and President Tobacco Division), Stanley W Beetham (Senior VP Marketing), James W Chapin (Senior VP and General Counsel), Timothy M Cornell (Senior VP), Vincent A Gierer Jr (Senior VP, Controller and Principal Financial Officer), Per Erik Lindqvist (Senior VP), Henry A Schones Jr (Senior VP), Yannis S Stephano (Senior VP), Donald J Turck (Senior VP), Walter A Wuchiski (Senior VP), Walter B Garrison (VP), I Robert Levine (VP), Richard A Manning (VP), Jonathan P Nelson (VP and Secretary), Joseph R Taddeo (VP)

PRINCIPAL ACTIVITIES: Tobacco processing and manufacture of cigars, smokeless tobaccos and chewing tobaccos; smokers requisites; pens and pencils
Principal Bank: First National Bank of Boston
Financial Information:

	Dec 31 1986
	$'000
Sales revenues	511,573
Net income	103,938
Earnings per share	$1.86
Shareholders equity	371,559

No of Employees: 3,673

UNITED STATIONERS INC

2200 East Golf Road, Des Plaines, IL 60016
Tel: (312) 699 5000

Chairman: Howard M Wolf (and Chief Executive Officer)
President: Joel D Spungin (and Chief Operating Officer)
Senior Executive Officers: Marshall A Gardner (Senior VP and Chief Financial Officer), Arnold W Johnsen (Senior VP Marketing and Sales), Harold B Sheahan (Senior VP Management Information Systems), Ronald W Weissman (Senior VP Distribution), Robert W Welnhofer (Senior VP Corporate Development), David A Carter (VP Marketing and Sales), Jerold A Hecktman (VP Advertising and Secretary), Allen B Kravis (VP, Treasurer and Assistant Secretary), Ted S Rzeszuto (Controller)

PRINCIPAL ACTIVITIES: Stationery and office supplies
Principal Subsidiaries: Johnson and Staley Inc; Microunited Inc; United Stationers Supply Company
Principal Bank: Northern Trust Company
Financial Information:

	$'000
Sales revenues	546,320

UNITED TECHNOLOGIES CORPORATION

United Technologies Bldg, Hartford, CT 06101
Tel: (203) 728-7000
Telex: WUT 99212 utc hfd a

Chairman: Robert F Daniell (and Chief Executive Officer)
Senior Executive Officers: John A Rolls (Executive VP-Finance), Arthur E Wegner (Senior VP-Power), Edward W Large (Executive VP-Corporate Development), Edward M Irving (Senior VP-Industrial), Sidney F McKenna (Senior VP-Employee and External Relations), William F Paul (Senior VP-Defense and Space), Stephen C Groth (Director-Investor Relations)

PRINCIPAL ACTIVITIES: Manufacture of a wide range of high technology equipment. Sales and balanced among the aerospace, defense, building and automotive businesses
Principal Divisional and Subsidiaries: Pratt & Whitney Aircraft; Hamilton Standard; Norden Systems; Sikorsky Aircraft; Carrier; Otis; United Technologies Automotive; Essex
Financial Information:

	Dec 31 1985	Dec 31 1986
	$'000	$'000
Sales revenues	15,748,674	15,669,000
Income before taxes	1,083,000	124,000(1)
Net income	312,724	73,000
Dividends per share	$1.40	$1.40
Earnings per share	$2.12	$0.27
Common stock(2)	138,997,346	133,694,697
Retained income	2,604,707	2,281,000
Shareholders equity	4,373,344	3,803,000

(1) net of $593m restructuring provision recorded in 4th quarter 1986
(2) Aug-fully diluted

No of Employees: 193,500

UNITED TELECOMMUNICATIONS, INC

PO Box 11315, Kansas City, MO 64112
Tel: (913) 676-3000
Telex: 42-244 UNITEL A WESN

Chairman: Paul H Henson
President: William T Esrey
Senior Executive Officers: Charles W Battey (Vice Chairman, Chief Financial Officer), John F Dodd (Executive VP, General Counsel), John C Hancock (Executive VP), Donald A Jensen (VP and Secretary), William J Gunter (VP and Treasurer), Thomas A Benedett (VP), Hayward D Fisk (VP), Donald G Forsythe (VP), Sushil G Munshi (VP), Ralph T Whiteside (VP), Curtis G Fields (Executive VP), Ronald T LeMay (Executive VP), Richard H Brown (Senior VP), J Richard Devlin (VP), Joe B Gibson (VP), Daniel J Evanoff (VP), John A Mihalovich (VP), David J Nicol (VP), Thomas A Norman (VP), William E Roche (VP), M Jeannine Strandford (VP and Controller), Alan J Sykes (VP)

PRINCIPAL ACTIVITIES: United Telecom is a diversified telecommunications company. It provides local and long distance telephone services and related communications services. The United Telephone System serves more than 3,000 communities in 19 states, with principal operations in Florida, North Carolina and Ohio. In partnership with GTE, United offers long distance voice, data and video communications services through US Sprint, which is constructing a nationwide fiber optic communications network. North Supply Company, a distributor of telecommunications equipment and supplies, is the largest company in United Telecom's complementary business group
Principal Subsidiaries: Carolina Telephone and Telegraph Company; United Telephone Company of Florida; United Telephone Company of Indiana; United Telephone Company of the Northwest; United Telephone Company of Ohio; United Telephone Company of Texas; United Telephone System-Midwest Group; United Telephone System-Eastern Group; United Telephone System-Southeast Group; United Data Services; United TeleSentinel; United TeleSpectrum; Vista-United Telecommunications; Directories America; Template Graphics Software; Information Systems of America; Megatek; North Supply; NorthCom

Financial Information:

	Dec 31 1986
	$'000
Sales revenues	3,058,783
Income before taxes	235,035
Net income	180,561
Dividends	190,346
Dividends per share	$1.92
Earnings per share	$1.81
Common stock	246,340
Retained income	662,033
Shareholders equity	1,783,952

No of Employees: 23,245

UNITED TELEVISION INC

8501 Wilshire Boulevard, Suite 340, Beverly Hills, CA 90211
Tel: (213) 854 0426

Chairman: Herbert J Siegel (and Chief Executive Officer); Vice Chairman: Lawrence R Barnett
President: Evan C Thompson (and Chief Operating Officer)
Senior Executive Officers: Garth S Lindsey (Executive VP, Chief Financial Officer and Secretary), Gerard R Braet (VP), Edward V Cheviot (VP), Robert P Donohue (VP), Robert J Queen (VP), Stuart Z Swartz (VP), David J Woodcock (VP), Thomas L Muir (Treasurer and Controller)

PRINCIPAL ACTIVITIES: Broadcasting of television programs
Parent Company: Chris-Craft Industries Inc
Principal Bank: First National Bank of Minneapolis
Financial Information:

	$'000
Sales revenues	77,140

No of Employees: 500

UNITED VAN LINES, INC

1 United Drive, Fenton, MO 63026
Tel: (314) 326-3100
Telex: RCA 297 302 uvl intdv fent

Chairman: Maurice Greenblatt (and Chief Executive Officer); Vice Chairman: Gerald P Stadler
President: Robert J Baer (and Chief Operating Officer)
Senior Executive Officers: David R Hollis (Senior VP Operations), James R Kendrick (Senior VP and Chief Financial Officer), Alan C Richter (Senior VP Administration), James L Wilson (Senior VP Marketing), Charles R Childers (Senior VP and Chief Information Officer), Morton I Golder (Senior VP and General Counsel)

PRINCIPAL ACTIVITIES: Operation of domestic and international transportation services
Principal Subsidiaries: United Leasing, Inc; Matlock Trailer Corp; Transprotection Service Company; Vanliner Limited
Principal Bank: Mercantile Commerce Trust Co
Financial Information:

	Dec 31 1985	Dec 31 1986
	$'000	$'000
Sales revenues	562,101	589,871
Net income	3,164	3,464
Shareholders equity	28,911	32,091

No of Employees: 982

UNITED WATER RESOURCES INC

200 Old Hook Road, Harrington Park, NJ 07640
Tel: (201) 784 9434

Chairman: Robert H Mulreany
President: Robert A Gerber (and Chief Executive Officer)
Senior Executive Officers: Donald L Correll (VP, Treasurer and Chief Financial Officer), O F Laurino (VP Legal Affairs and Real Estate), Donald L Schlenger (VP Corporate Development), Douglas W Hawes (Secretary)

PRINCIPAL ACTIVITIES: Water supply
Principal Subsidiaries: Hackensack Water Company Inc; Spring Valley Water Company Inc
Principal Bank: United Jersey Bank
Financial Information:

	$'000
Sales revenues	95,490

No of Employees: 575

UNITEK CORPORATION

2724 South Peck Road, Monrovia, CA 91016
Tel: (818) 445-7960
Telex: TWX 910 585 3236 unitek corp

President: Randall J Wall
Senior Executive Officers: Richard C Jackson (VP Finance), V N Anderson (VP Marketing), Nat A Cantampner (VP Operations), Steven L Getrain (VP Finance), Joseph L Laub (VP and General Manager Equipment Division), Dennis J Smith (VP Personnel)

PRINCIPAL ACTIVITIES: Manufacture of dental equipment and supplies; equipment for dental laboratories
Parent Company: Bristol-Myers Co, New York, NY
Principal Bank: Security Pacific National Bank
Financial Information:

	$'000
Sales revenues	110,000

No of Employees: 1,400

UNITOG CO

101 W 11th Street, Kansas City, MO 64105
Tel: (816) 474-7000
Telex: WUT 42583 unitog co ksc

Chairman: Robert F Hagans
President: Arthur D Brookfield II
Senior Executive Officers: Ernest A Rylander (Senior VP Rental Systems), John W Hall (Senior VP Human Resources), Thomas F Pearson (Senior VP Finance), Bruce A Ames (VP Manufacturing), Bob O Brown (VP International Audit), Jack L Leisure (VP Rental Operations), Keith Schreiman (VP Field Sales), O Wayne Snyder (VP Management Information Systems)

PRINCIPAL ACTIVITIES: Manufacture of clothing including uniforms and men's workwear; rental services
Principal Bank: Merchants Bank
Financial Information:

	$'000
Sales revenues	77,000

No of Employees: 2,300

UNITRODE CORPORATION

5 Forbes Road, Lexington, MA 02173
Tel: (617) 861-6540
Telex: TWX 910 333 1528 unitrode ariz

Chairman: George M Berman; Vice Chairman: William B Mitchell
President: Howard Wasserman
Senior Executive Officers: Gerald C Bellis (Executive VP), Walter B Gates (Senior VP Finance and Treasurer), Arthur Bruno (VP), William Campbell (VP and Controller), Norman DeVolder (VP), Robert F Feier (VP), Michael T O'Connor (VP), Edward Simon (VP Technical)

PRINCIPAL ACTIVITIES: Manufacture of electrical and electronic components
Principal Subsidiaries: Powercube Corp; Unitrode Semiconductor Products Corp; Unitrode Mexicana SA de CV; Unitrode International Sales Corp; Unitrode Investment Corp; Unitrode Electronics GmbH; United Integrated Circuits Corp; Unitrode UK Ltd; Unitrode SRL; Unitrode BV; Unitrode Europe BV; Unitrode Cheland Ltd; Power General Corp; US Micioted Component Corp
Principal Bank: The First National Bank of Boston

Financial Information:

	$'000
Sales revenues	167,970

No of Employees: 3,000

UNIVAR CORPORATION
1600 Norton Building, Seattle, WA 98104
Tel: (206) 447-5911
Telex: WUT 320 174 univar sea

Chairman: James H Wiborg; Chairman of Executive Committee: Lowry Wyatt; Vice Chairman: M M Harris
President: James W Bernard (and Chief Operating Officer)
Senior Executive Officers: N S Rogers (Senior VP Finance), Clarence W Bengston (VP and Treasurer), Albert C McNeight (VP), Robert A Steinseifer (VP), Guenter Zimmer (VP)

PRINCIPAL ACTIVITIES: Through its subsidiaries and divisions the company distributes industrial and agricultural chemicals; graphic arts and laboratory products, furnishing fabrics
Principal Subsidiaries: Van Waters & Rogers Division; Van Waters & Rogers Ltd (Canada); VWR Scientific Division; VWR & R Home Furnishing Division
Principal Bank: Seattle-First National Bank
Financial Information:

	$'000
Sales revenues	538,000

No of Employees: 1,480

UNIVERSAL CIGAR CORPORATION
654 Madison Avenue, New York, NY 10021
Tel: (212) 753-5700
Telex: ITT 423331 ucc ui

Senior Executive Officers: Edward Gropper (Chief Executive Officer), Henry M Hafer (Executive VP), Edward W Schwartz (VP), Juan Cueva (VP), Louis Torano (VP)

PRINCIPAL ACTIVITIES: Manufacture of cigars
Principal Bank: Marine Midland Bank New York
Financial Information:

	$'000
Sales revenues	54,000

No of Employees: 750

UNIVERSAL COMMUNICATION SYSTEMS INC
1401 Municipal Road NW, Roanoke, VA 24012
Tel: (703) 362 3701

President: Frederick K Shaftman (and Chief Executive Officer and Legal Counsel)
Senior Executive Officers: W Thomas Craig (VP Sales), Dallas G Jarrell (VP Finance and Treasurer), Fred T Adams (VP Operations), Clyde H Snavely Jr (Controller)

PRINCIPAL ACTIVITIES: Sale and installation of privately owned telephone equipment
Parent Company: American Motor Inns Inc
Principal Bank: First National Bank of Boston
Financial Information:

	$'000
Sales revenues	66,400
Net income	6,330

No of Employees: 650

UNIVERSAL COOPERATIVES, INC
7801 Metro Parkway, Minneapolis, MN 55420
Tel: (612) 854-0800

President: Donald R Armstrong
Senior Executive Officers: L Bryan Morrison (VP Human Resources), Patrick M Finley (VP Finance), Albert J Oukrop (VP Procurement), Richard Hutchings (VP Ag Chemical and Manufacturing)

PRINCIPAL ACTIVITIES: Manufacture of agricultural equipment and supplies; wholesale trade in agricultural supplies and household appliances
Principal Bank: First National Bank of Minneapolis
Financial Information:

	$'000
Sales revenues	320,000

No of Employees: 500

UNIVERSAL FLAVORS, INC
5600 W Raymond Street, Indianapolis, IN 46241
Tel: (317) 243-3521

Chairman: Lewis A Enkema (and Secretary)
President: Lawrence J Noling
Senior Executive Officers: Dennis M Maude (Treasurer)

PRINCIPAL ACTIVITIES: Manufacture of food flavorings
Principal Bank: Merchants National Bank and Trust
Financial Information:

	$'000
Sales revenues	100,000

No of Employees: 650

UNIVERSAL FOODS CORPORATION
433 E Michigan Street, Milwaukee, WI 53202
Tel: (414) 271-6755
Telex: GRT 3797206 ufwpmil

Chairman: John L Murray (and Chief Executive Officer)
President: Guy A Osborn
Senior Executive Officers: Darrell E Wilde (Senior VP), David B Essner (VP Finance and Treasurer), Herbert Feuerstein (VP and General Manager Commodity Foods), Richard W Gochnauer (VP and General Manager Cheese), James F Palo (VP and General Manager Dehydrated), Frank J Listi (VP and General Manager-Flavors), Thomas J Dignan (VP and General Manager-Bakery Products), Kenneth R Scheffel (VP and General Manager-Industrial Fermentation Products), Richard F Hobbs (Corporate Controller), Robert S Wright (VP and General Manager-Frozen Foods), Don L Allan (VP and General Manager, Gourmet Products), F Preston Mottram (Senior VP and General Manager-Fermentation), James E Noonan (VP and General Manager-Color), Terrence M O'Reilly (VP, Secretary and General Counsel)

PRINCIPAL ACTIVITIES: Manufacture of a wide range of food products including cheeses, bakery products, food colors/flavors, frozen potatoes and dehydrated seasonings
Principal Subsidiaries: Red Star de Puerto Rico SA; Universal Food Products International Co Ltd; Universal Foods Export Corp; Universal Group Limited
Principal Bank: First Wisconsin National Bank of Milwaukee
Financial Information:

	Sep 30 1986 $'000
Sales revenues	602,679
Income before taxes	29,129
Net income	15,438
Dividends per share	$0.76
Earnings per share	$1.42
Common stock*	10,875
Retained income	103,265
Shareholders equity	165,163

*number of shares in thousands

Principal Shareholders: Bartar Ltd; Pioneer Management
No of Employees: 4,700

UNIVERSAL HEALTH SERVICES INC
Universal Corporation Center, 367 S Gulph Rd, King of Prussia, PA 19406
Tel: (215) 768 3300

Chairman: Alan B Miller (and President and Chief Executive Officer)

Senior Executive Officers: Sidney Miller (Executive VP), Robert W Fleming Jr (VP Corporate Development), Joseph P Gaynor III (VP and Treasurer), Richard C White (VP Operations), Steven L Volla (Senior VP Operations), Robert M Dubbs (Secretary and Legal Counsel)

PRINCIPAL ACTIVITIES: Management of hospitals
Financial Information:

	$'000
Sales revenues	650,000

No of Employees: 10,000

UNIVERSAL INSTRUMENTS CORPORATION

Kirkwood Industrial Park, Binghamton, NY 13902
Tel: (607) 772-7522
Telex: WUI 685 4515 univ inst

President: John E Pomeroy (and Chief Executive Officer)
Senior Executive Officers: John F Peebles (Executive VP), D Whitney Ackerman (VP Technical), Thomas E Bell (VP Finance), Ronald Budacz (VP Mechanized Electronic Assembly), Gerhard D Meese (VP Systems Division), James P Roth (VP Marketing), John E Wedge (VP Human Resources)

PRINCIPAL ACTIVITIES: Manufacture of special machinery; automation systems for electronics assembly, electronic components
Parent Company: Dover Corporation, New York, NY
Principal Bank: First City National Bank of Binghampton
Financial Information:

	$'000
Sales revenues	210,000

No of Employees: 1,600

UNIVERSAL LEAF TOBACCO CO, INC

Hamilton Street at Broad, Richmond, VA 23230
Tel: (804) 359-9311
Telex: WUT 828 377 ultoco a rch

Chairman: Gordon L Crenshaw (and Chief Executive Officer); Vice Chairmen: Wallace L Chandler; Thomas R Towers
President: Henry H Harrell
Senior Executive Officers: M N Howe Jr (Senior VP), A B King (Senior VP), W C Lacy (Senior VP Purchasing), O K Dozier (Treasurer)

PRINCIPAL ACTIVITIES: Tobacco processing and tobacco trading
Principal Subsidiaries: Lawyers Title Insurance Co; Continental Land Title Co
Financial Information:

	$'000
Sales revenues	1,100,000

No of Employees: 14,000

UNIVERSAL MANUFACTURING CORPORATION

200 Robin Road, Paramus, NJ 07652
Tel: (201) 967-7600
Telex: TWX 710 988 5934

President: Otto A Payonzeck
Senior Executive Officers: Thomas Ettz (VP MIS), S Steinberger (VP Manufacturing), Michael Stein (VP Ballast Engineering), A Pucillo (VP Sales), S J Cohen (VP Manufacturing and Operations), Chestina Hughes (VP Finance)

PRINCIPAL ACTIVITIES: Manufacture of electrical machinery including transformers
Parent Company: Northwest Industries Inc, Chicago, IL
Principal Bank: Valley National Bank
Financial Information:

	$'000
Sales revenues	200,000

No of Employees: 3,700

UNIVERSAL RESOURCES CORPORATION

5400 Valley View Trail, PO Box 802426, Dallas, TX 75380
Tel: (214) 661 3876

Chairman: Robert G Brown (and Chairman Executive Committee)
President: Charles B Ponder (and Chief Executive Officer)
Senior Executive Officers: Joe Coffman (Senior VP, Secretary and Chief Financial Officer), James R Cobb (VP), James R Nichols (VP), Melvin L Owen (Treasurer)

PRINCIPAL ACTIVITIES: Oil and gas exploration and production; supply of related services and equipment
Principal Subsidiaries: Loyal Construction Inc; Loyal Mud and Chemical Company Inc; Loyal Supply Company
Principal Bank: Interfirst Bank
Financial Information:

	$'000
Sales revenues	43,540

No of Employees: 140

UNIVERSAL-RUNDLE CORPORATION

PO Box 29, New Castle, PA 16103
Tel: (412) 658-6631
Telex: WUI 6711166 urun uw

Chairman: Ralph R Papitto (and Chief Executive Officer)
President: D C Cooke (and Chief Operating Officer)
Senior Executive Officers: R H Carlson (Senior VP Finance, Secretary and Treasurer), J A Woulf (Senior VP Sales and Marketing), W L Morris (VP Industrial Relations)

PRINCIPAL ACTIVITIES: Manufacture of plumbing supplies and bathroom equipment including vitreous china and fiber glass fixtures; plastic molded products and packaging
Parent Company: Nortek Inc
Financial Information:

	$'000
Sales revenues	126,000

No of Employees: 2,000

UNIVERSITY FEDERAL SAVINGS BANK

6400 Roosevelt Way Northeast, Seattle, WA 98115
Tel: (206) 256-1000

Chairman: Donald A Lockwood
President: Brian P Dempsey (and Chief Executive Officer)
Senior Executive Officers: Donald E Wahlquist (Executive VP), Larry L Bain (Senior VP and Treasurer), Ann M Durrigan (VP), Arden R Johnson (VP), Richard W Pickering (VP)

PRINCIPAL ACTIVITIES: Banking
Principal Subsidiaries: Unisav Service Corporation Inc; University Financial Services Inc; University Insurance Services Inc; University Investment Advisory Services; University Mortgage Services; Express Escrow Service Inc
Principal Bank: Peoples National Bank

No of Employees: 315

UNOCAL CORPORATION

UnoCal Center, Los Angeles, CA 90017
Tel: (213) 977-7600

Chairman: Fred L Hartley (and Chief Executive Officer)
President: Richard J Stegemeier (and Chief Operating Officer)
Senior Executive Officers: Claude S Brinegar (Executive VP and Chief Financial Officer), R A Burke (Senior VP Energy Resources), Joseph Byrne (VP Corporate Human Resources), C P Reeg (VP, President Unocal Science and Technical Division), Neal E Schmale (VP Budgets, Planning and Economics), Sam A Snyder (VP and General Counsel)

PRINCIPAL ACTIVITIES: Holding company with interests in the exploration and production of oil, natural gas and minerals; manufacture and sale of petroleum products, fertilizers, chemicals and metals

Financial Information:

	Dec 31 1985	Dec 31 1986
	$'000	$'000
Sales revenues	10,738,000	7,482,000
Net income	325,000	176,000
Earnings per share	$2.36	$1.51
Shareholders equity	1,630,000	1,681,000

No of Employees: 20,214

UNR INDUSTRIES, INC

332 S Michigan Avenue, Chicago, IL 60604
Tel: (312) 341-1234
Telex: WUT 466507 unr cgo ci

Chairman: Edwin E Hokin
President: Robert J Penn (and Chief Executive Officer)
Senior Executive Officers: Louis B Guthmann Jr (VP Purchasing), William Leavitt (VP), Ronald P Zenner (VP Finance), David F Starling (Treasurer and Controller)

PRINCIPAL ACTIVITIES: Manufacture of a wide range of welded steel products including shop fittings, lighting and communication towers, railroad equipment and household goods
Principal Bank: Exchange National Bank of Chicago
Financial Information:

	$'000
Sales revenues	305,500

No of Employees: 3,000

UPJOHN CO

7000 Portage Road, Kalamazoo, MI 49001
Tel: (616) 323-4000
Telex: WUT 224401 upjohn

Chairman: Theodore Cooper, MD (and Chief Executive Officer)
President: Lawrence C Hoff (and Chief Operating Officer)
Senior Executive Officers: W U Parfet (VP and Treasurer), Gerard Thomas (Senior VP and Secretary), D A Phillipson (Senior VP Agriculture), J C Stucki (VP Pharmaceutical Research), Charles T Mangee (VP Public Relations), D D Witcher (Senior VP Worldwide Pharmaceuticals), M Novitch (Senior VP Scientific Affairs)

PRINCIPAL ACTIVITIES: Manufacture of pharmaceutical products, ethical drugs, agricultural chemicals and fine chemicals
Trade Names: MOTRIN, CLEOCIN, XANAX, HALCION, MICRONASE
Financial Information:

	Dec 31 1985	Dec 31 1986
	$'000	$'000
Sales revenues	2,017,200	2,291,400
Income before taxes	295,664	358,000
Net income	203,193	252,600
Dividends	82,840	92,600
Dividends per share	$1.34	$0.50
Earnings per share	$3.29	$1.35
Common stock	-	187,300
Retained income	1,259,254	1,388,400
Shareholders equity	1,129,085	1,470,200

No of Employees: 20,600

UPPER PENINSULA POWER COMPANY

616 Shelden Avenue, Houghton, MI 49931
Tel: (906) 482 0220

Chairman: Elio Argentati (and President)
Senior Executive Officers: William L Veeser (Senior VP Public and Corporate Relations), Rodney H Carlson (VP), Clarence R Fisher (VP), George Gildersleeve (VP), Burton C Arola (Treasurer), Dennis G Barrette (Secretary)

PRINCIPAL ACTIVITIES: Distribution of electricity
Principal Bank: Chase Manhattan Bank NA
Financial Information:

	$'000
Sales revenues	56,700

No of Employees: 600

UP-RIGHT INC

1013 Pardee Street, Berkeley, CA 94710
Tel: (415) 843 0770

President: Theodore S Ockels (and Chief Executive Officer)
Senior Executive Officers: George N Rufenacht (Executive VP and Chief Operating Officer), Hugo C Kapelke (VP and General Manager), E Donald Reichert (VP Administration and Safety Affairs), James O Hartman (Legal Counsel and Secretary), Tom M Thompson (Controller and Assistant Treasurer)

PRINCIPAL ACTIVITIES: Manufacture of portable work platforms and grape harvesters
Principal Bank: Bank of California
Financial Information:

	$'000
Sales revenues	49,000

No of Employees: 750

UPSTATE MILK COOPERATIVES, INC

7115 W Main Street, Leroy, NY 14482
Tel: (716) 768-2247

President: William Zuber
Senior Executive Officers: Donald M Bay (Executive VP and General Manager), Frank Wiley (VP), Herbert Nobles (Treasurer)

PRINCIPAL ACTIVITIES: Manufacture and distribution of dairy produce
Financial Information:

	$'000
Sales revenues	175,000

No of Employees: 500

URS CORPORATION

2000 Alameda de las Pugas, San Mateo, CA 94403
Tel: (415) 574 5000

Chairman: Arthur H Stromberg (and President and Chief Executive Officer)
Senior Executive Officers: Franklin J Agardy (Executive VP and Chief Operating Officer), Richard H Towle (Senior VP, Chief Financial Officer and Chief Administrative Officer), Thomas E Leep (VP), Michael J McDevitt (VP Communications), Arthur O Whipple (VP, Treasurer and Chief Accounting Officer), Shirlee Allen (Secretary and Assistant VP)

PRINCIPAL ACTIVITIES: Architectural and engineering services
Principal Subsidiaries: Advanced Production Service Inc; Caillou Rental Service Inc; URS Company Inc; URS John A Blume Assoc Engineers; URS Company; URS Company Inc; URS Rental Services Company; Wood Evelyn Reading Dynamics Inc
Principal Bank: First Interstate Bank
Financial Information:

	$'000
Sales revenues	96,705

No of Employees: 1,800

US BANCORP

111 SW 5th Avenue, Portland, OR 97204
Tel: (503) 225-6111

Chairman: Roger L Breezley (and Chief Executive Officer)
Presidents: Edmund P Jensen (US Bancorp); Robert R Mitchell (US Bank)

Senior Executive Officers: Gerry B Cameron (Executive VP), Donald W Magnusen (Executive VP), Paul M Devore, Anthony P Yasiello, William R Ulrich, Kevin R Kelly (Executive VP)

PRINCIPAL ACTIVITIES: Banking
Principal Subsidiaries: US National Bank of Oregon
Principal Bank: United States National Bank of Oregon
Financial Information:

	Dec 31 1985	Dec 31 1986
	$'000	$'000
Net income	66,240	77,200
Dividends	-	22,100
Dividends per share	-	$0.74
Earnings per share	$2.22	$2.56
Shareholders equity	574,155	633,200
Deposits	5,166,800	5,762,500
Total assets	8,349,720	9,491,400

No of Employees: 5,468

US CAPITAL CORPORATION SOUTH CAROLINA

1400 Main Street, Columbia, SC 29201
Tel: (803) 779 2170

Chairman: Donald R Tomlin Jr (and President and Chief Executive Officer); Vice Chairman: Billy J Bobo (and Secretary)
President: P L Tomlin
Senior Executive Officers: Donald A Points (Senior VP), Daniel L Kingsbury (VP)

PRINCIPAL ACTIVITIES: Civil engineering and construction
Principal Subsidiaries: Capital Resort Inc; US Capital Mortgage Corporation
Principal Bank: Philadelphia National Bank
Financial Information:

	$'000
Sales revenues	114,015

No of Employees: 250

US HEALTH INC

300 East Joppa Road, Towson, MD 21204
Tel: (301) 296 8800

Chairman: Frank Bond (and President and Chief Executive Officer)
Senior Executive Officers: William J Fleischer (Senior VP and Chief Financial Officer), Barry Mandel (Senior VP Operations), Allen D Greif (VP and Legal Counsel), Austin E Hubbard (VP Administration), Blaine G Leidy (VP Construction), John M Stern Jr (Treasurer and Controller)

PRINCIPAL ACTIVITIES: Fitness and health facilities
Principal Bank: First National Bank of Maryland
Financial Information:

	$'000
Sales revenues	69,600

No of Employees: 1,160

US HOME CORPORATION

1800 West Loop S, Houston, TX 77027
Tel: (713) 877-2311
Telex: WUT 791 451 us home hou

Chairman: Robert J Strudler (and Chief Executive Officer); Chairman of Executive Committee: Kenneth J Hanau Jr
President: Isaac Heimbender (and Chief Operating Officer)
Senior Executive Officers: Tim W Humphrey (VP Audit), Larry D Kelley (VP Land Development), Chester P Sadawski (VP and Controller), William Weidmann (VP Operations)

PRINCIPAL ACTIVITIES: House building and manufacture of sectional buildings
Principal Bank: Bankers Trust Company

Financial Information:

	Dec 31 1985	Dec 31 1986
	$'000	$'000
Sales revenues	922,080	890,472
Net (loss)	(8,980)	(80,071)
(Loss) per share	($0.26)	($2.05)
Shareholders equity	281,480	220,917

No of Employees: 1,702

US INTEC INC

1212 Brai Drive, Port Arthur, TX 77643
Tel: (409) 724 7024

President: Danny J Adair (and Chief Executive Officer)
Senior Executive Officers: John J Chamberlin (VP), John E Davis (VP and Secretary), Bailey C King (VP), Ken D Latiolais (VP), S Craig Noble (VP)

PRINCIPAL ACTIVITIES: Production of asphalt
Financial Information:

	$'000
Sales revenues	36,000

No of Employees: 150

US MUTUAL FINANCIAL CORPORATION

200 Renaissance Center, Suite 3060, Detroit, MI 48243
Tel: (313) 259 3300

Vice Chairman: P Philip Mathews (and Senior VP and Chief Operating Officer)
President: Stephen P Banicki (and Chief Operating Officer)
Senior Executive Officers: Joseph E Krul (Executive VP and Chief Financial Officer), James B Quinlan (Executive VP), P Philip Matthews (Senior VP and Chief Operating Officer), Edward Mannino (VP and Controller)

PRINCIPAL ACTIVITIES: Mortgages and loans
Principal Bank: National Bank of Detroit
Financial Information:

	$'000
Revenues	44,610

No of Employees: 235

US REDUCTION CO

9200 Calumet Avenue, Munster, IN 46321
Tel: (312) 785-5000
Telex: RCA 210237 usred ur

President: R S Neufeld
Senior Executive Officers: B E Ronco (VP Finance, Secretary and Treasurer)

PRINCIPAL ACTIVITIES: Manufacture of non-ferrous metals including aluminum alloys and zinc; international metals trading
Parent Company: American Can Co, Greenwich, CT
Principal Bank: Continental Illinois National Bank and Trust Co
Financial Information:

	$'000
Sales revenues	140,000

No of Employees: 1,400

US SHELTER CORPORATION

1 Shelter Place, PO Box 1089, Greenville, SC 29602
Tel: (803) 239 1000

Chairman: N Barton Tuck Jr (and Chief Executive Officer); Vice Chairman: Buck Mickel
President: Carol D Vinson (and Chief Operating Officer)
Senior Executive Officers: Gary R Hediger (Executive VP), William N Page (Executive VP), Robert O Taylor (Executive VP), Donald R Waldrop (Executive VP), James A Aston (VP Finance and Treasurer), Douglas G Brown (VP and Legal Counsel)

PRINCIPAL ACTIVITIES: Property and real estate

Principal Subsidiaries: Amreal Corporation; Smithy Company; Malibu Savings and Loan Association; Sullivan Company Inc
Principal Bank: Citizens and Southern National Bank
Financial Information:

	$'000
Sales revenues	140,000

No of Employees: 1,500

US TRUCK LINES INC OF DELAWARE

500 National City Bank Building, Cleveland, OH 44114
Tel: (216) 241 5326

Chairman: W G Bernet Jr
President: J J Bernet
Senior Executive Officers: M L Hobzek (VP), W J Strazinsky (VP Operations), W R Fifner (Secretary and Legal Counsel), N B Romito (Treasurer)

PRINCIPAL ACTIVITIES: Holding company with interests in motor carrier transportation
Principal Subsidiaries: Be-Mac Transport Company Inc; Brown Express Inc; Central Truck Lines Inc; Cleveland Columbus Cincinnati Hwy; Consolidated Cartage and Storage; Delta Drayage Company; Detroit Delivery Inc; Kanawha Cartage Company Inc; Michigan Delivery Inc; Motor Express Inc NJ; Motor Express Inc of IN; National Tank Truck Delivery Inc; Ohio Delivery Inc; Parts Transport Inc; Republic Supply Corporation; Superior Transfer Company
Principal Bank: National City Bank
Financial Information:

	$'000
Sales revenues	123,085

No of Employees: 1,500

US TRUST CO OF NEW YORK

45 Wall St, New York, NY 1005
Tel: (212) 806-4500

Chairman: P Daniel P Davison (and President and Chief Executive Officer); Vice Chairman: Edwin A Heard (and Treasurer)
President: H Marshall Schwarz
Senior Executive Officers: Frederick B Taylor (Chairman Investment Policy, Personal and Institutional Equity Management), James E Bacon (Executive VP Corporate Trust and Computer Services Group), Jeffrey S Maurer (Executive VP Asset Management Group), Donald M Roberts (Executive VP Bank Group), Frederick S Wonham (Executive VP Planning and Administration Group)

PRINCIPAL ACTIVITIES: Banking services

No of Employees: 1,800

US WEST, INC

7800 E Orchard Rd, Englewood, CO 80111
Tel: (303) 793-6500

President: Jack A MacAllister (and Chief Executive Officer)
Senior Executive Officers: Lawrence W Demuth Jr (Executive VP), H P Doerr (Executive VP, General Counsel and Secretary), J M Travers (VP and Controller)

PRINCIPAL ACTIVITIES: Telephone services
Financial Information:

	Dec 31 1985	Dec 31 1986
	$'000	$'000
Sales revenues	7,812,600	8,308,400
Net income	925,600	924,300
Earnings per share	$9.68	$4.86
Shareholders equity	6,943,500	7,278,500

No of Employees: 69,400

USAIR GROUP, INC

1911 Jefferson Davis Highway, Arlington, VA 22202
Tel: (703) 892-7000

Chairman: Edwin I Colodny (and President)
Senior Executive Officers: Officers of USAir Group Inc:- Edwin I Colodny (Chairman ofthe Board and President), P Jackson Bell (VP-Finance), W Dale Hay (VP-Corporate Affairs and Assistant Secretary), G Jack King (VP-Public Affairs), Lawrence L Stentzel (VP, General Counsel and Secretary), John W Funkhouser (Controller), Juliette C Heintze (Treasurer). USAir, Inc Executive Committee:- Edwin I Colodny (Chairman of the Board and President), Randall Malin (Executive VP-Marketing), Seth E Schofield (Executive VP-Operations), Lawrence L Stentzel (Executive VP and General Counsel), P Jackson Bell (VP and Senior VP-Finance), John R Long III (Senior VP-Administration), Garner W Miller (Senior VP-Maintenance and Engineering)

PRINCIPAL ACTIVITIES: USAir Inc. - Scheduled airline service
Principal Subsidiaries: USAir, Inc; Pennsylvania Commuter Airlines, Inc; Clark Leasing Corp; USAir Finance, NV
Principal Bank: The Chase Manhattan Bank NA
Financial Information:

	Dec 31 1986
	$'000
Sales revenues	1,835,199
Net income	98,352
Earnings per share	$3.34
Shareholders equity	1,057,953

No of Employees: 14,976

USF&G CORPORATION

100 Light Street, Baltimore, MD 21202
Tel: (301) 547-3000
Telex: (301) 625-5618

Chairman: Jack Moseley (and President)
Senior Executive Officers: Paul J Scheel (Executive VP), James M Raley Jr (VP-Finance and Treasurer), William F Spliedt (Secretary), Samuel H McCoy III (General Counsel). Principal Subsidiary: United States Fidelity & Guaranty Company:- Jack Moseley (Chairman of the Board), Paul J Scheel (President), E Donald Bangs (Executive VP), Karl H Doerre (Executive VP), David H Meehan (Executive VP), Robert R Treweek (Executive VP)

PRINCIPAL ACTIVITIES: Property/casualty insurance; life insurance; financial services
Trade Names: USF&G Insurance
Principal Subsidiaries: United States Fidelity & Guaranty Company; Fidelity Insurance Company of Canada; F&G Re, Inc; Fidelity and Guaranty Life Insurance Company; USF&G Financial Services Corporation; E W Axe & Company, Inc; USF&G Realty Inc; Megatron, Inc
Financial Information:

	Dec 31 1986
	$'000
Revenues	4,336,783
Net income	296,330
Earnings per share	$4.43
Shareholders equity	1,576,161
Total assets	8,935,993

No of Employees: 9,000

USG CORPORATION

101 S Wacker Drive, Chicago, IL 60606-4385
Tel: (312) 321-4000
Telex: 253035 USGYPSUM C60

Chairman: Robert J Day (and Chief Executive Officer)
President: Ralph C Joynes (and Chief Operating Officer)
Senior Executive Officers: Eugene Miller (Executive VP), William J White (Executive VP), Eugene Connolly (Executive VP), Robert D Carnahan (Senior VP Science and Technology), Stanton T Hadley (Senior VP, Staff Services)

PRINCIPAL ACTIVITIES: Produces and markets products for the building products and industrial processes markets

Trade Names: Sheetrock(R) Brand Gypsum Panels, Acoustone(R) and Auratone(R) Ceiling Panels, Kinkead(R) tub and shower enclosures, Castlegate(R) thermal doors, Thermafiber(R) mineral fiber insulation, Ultrawall(R) partition systems
Principal Subsidiaries: United States Gypsum Company; Masonite Corporation; USG Interiors Inc; USG Industries Inc; Canadian Gypsum Company Ltd
Financial Information:

	Dec 31 1985 $'000	Dec 31 1986 $'000
Sales revenues	2,333,387	2,723,664
Income before taxes	426,690	497,759
Net income	223,797	225,508
Dividends	56,198	67,201
Dividends per share	$0.84	$1.04
Earnings per share	$3.36	$3.54
Common stock	129,624	209,738
Retained income	889,295	398,011
Shareholders equity	984,331	584,615

Number of shareholders: 17,000
No of Employees: 22,000

USI CHEMICALS, DIVISION OF NATIONAL DISTILLERS & CHEMICAL CORP

11500 Northlake Drive, Cincinnati, OH 45249
Tel: (513) 530-6500
Telex: TRT 155116

Chairman: John Hoyt Stookey (Chairman NDCC)
President: James F Schorr
Senior Executive Officers: A P Flaim (Group VP, Polyolefins), James R Crozier (Group VP, Chemicals and Specialty Products), D Spiess (Group VP, Sales and Marketing Services), P B Nolan (Group VP, Manufacturing Services), R Yocum (Group VP, R&D), D Snyder (Controller)

PRINCIPAL ACTIVITIES: USI is one of the world's largest merchant suppliers of pure and denatured ethyl alcohol, is the third largest domestic manufacturer of high density polyethylene and largest US producer of polyethylene in general. USI's vinyl acetate monomer plant is the world's largest and the company produces its own acetic acid as feedstock for USI VAM as well as for sale to others. USI's lines of polyethylene resins, polypropylene and ethylene-vinyl acetate copolymers are some of the industry's broadest. Resins are available for a wide variety of applications: blow molding, injection molding, sheet and profile extrusion, adhesives and coatings, film extrusion, extrusion coating, rotational molding, powder coating, and wire and cable. USI also produces a wide variety of colorants and additives which are useable with most plastics. USI operates the first US grass roots plant for ethylene vinyl alcohol, barrier resin production in a joint venture with Kuraray, Inc of Japan. USI also produces ethylene glycol and ethylene oxide, industrial coolants and cleaners and ethyl ether
Trade Names: Registered Trademarks: Punctilious, Petrothene, Ultrathene, Microthene, Spectrathene, Vynathene, Plexar, EVAL, Norkool, Nortuff
Parent Company: National Distillers & Chemical Corp, New York, NY
Principal Bank: The Chase Manhattan Bank
Financial Information:

	$'000
Sales revenues	729,600

No of Employees: 4,100

USLIFE CORPORATION

125 Maiden Lane, New York, NY 10038
Tel: (212) 709-6000

Chairman: Gordon E Crosby Jr (Chairman of the Board, President and Chief Executive Officer)
Senior Executive Officers: Greer F Henderson (Vice Chairman-Chief Financial Officer), Wesley E Forte (Executive VP-General Counsel), John D Gavrity (Executive VP-Chief Actuary), Edward H Goodstone (Executive VP-Marketing Support), David E Ayres (Senior VP-Field Marketing), A Scott Bushey (Senior VP-Corporate Planning), H Scott Condit (Senior VP-Field Marketing), William B Ipema (Senior VP-Field Marketing), Frederick S Gallo (Senior VP-Audit and Control), John G Kelly (Senior VP-Corporate Affairs and Corporate Secretary), James B Lynch Jr (Senior VP-Controller), George W McQueen (Senior VP-Financial Operations), Christopher S Ruisi (Senior VP-Human Resources), Melvin D Schursky (Senior VP-Field Marketing), Jerry J Wakefield (Senior VP Marketing Support), Robert H Wall (Senior VP-Actuary)

PRINCIPAL ACTIVITIES: Life insurance
Principal Subsidiaries: Ordinary Life Insurance:- The United States Life Insurance Company In the City of New York; All American Life Insurance Company; USLIFE Life Insurance Company; The Old Line Life Insurance Company of America. Credit Life Insurance:- USLIFE Credit Life Insurance Company; Security of America Life Insurance Company; Sooner Life Insurance Company. Service Subsidiaries:- USLIFE Advisers, Inc; USLIFE Agency Services Inc; USLIFE Equity Sales Corporation; USLIFE Insurance Services Corporation; USLIFE Real Estate Services Corporation; USLIFE Systems Corporation
Principal Bank: Stock Transfer Agent and Stock Registrar: Manufacturers Hanover Trust Company
Financial Information:

	Dec 31 1985 $'000	Dec 31 1986 $'000
Premium income	777,143	902,064
Investment income	230,046	255,741
Income before taxes	107,637	107,686
Net income	76,224	92,332
Dividends	20,806	22,061
Dividends per share	$1.06	$1.14
Net income per share	$3.66	$4.63
Common stock	24,805	24,934
Retained income	852,330	921,572
Shareholders equity	832,772	906,025

No of Employees: 1,910

USPCI INC

US Pollution Control Inc

2000 Classen Center Buildings, Suite 400 South Oklahoma City, OK 73106
Tel: (405) 528 8371

Chairman: W M Beard; Vice Chairman: Herb Mee Jr
President: Gerald J Gagner (and Chief Executive Officer)
Senior Executive Officers: L F Centofanti (Senior VP), Larry M Shelton (VP Finance, Chief Financial Officer, Secretary and Treasurer), Forrest Moseley (Controller)

PRINCIPAL ACTIVITIES: Pollution control services including disposal of hazardous waste
Financial Information:

	$'000
Sales revenues	33,245

No of Employees: 160

UST CORPORATION

40 Court Street, Boston, MA 02108
Tel: (617) 726 7000

Chairman: Paul M Siskind (and Legal Counsel)
President: James V Sidell (and Chief Executive Officer)
Senior Executive Officers: Quinlan J Sullivan Jr (Executive VP), William C Brooks (Senior VP, Treasurer and Chief Financial Officer), Eric R Fischer (Senior VP and General Counsel), Stephen R Lewinstein (Senior VP), Alan R Morse Jr (Senior VP), Frank A Morse (Senior VP), Arthur F Snyder (Senior VP),

John A Dobra (VP), Robert Kaiser (VP), Louisa Kasdon-Ellis (VP Marketing), Paul V Montesino (VP Financial Services), Charles M Goldman (Clerk)

PRINCIPAL ACTIVITIES: Banking
Financial Information:

	$'000
Revenues	122,700

No of Employees: 800

USX CORPORATION (FORMERLY US STEEL CORPORATION)

600 Grant Street, Pittsburgh, PA 15230
Tel: (412) 433-1121
Telex: WUT 866425 us steel pgh

Chairman: David M Roderick (Chief Executive Officer); Vice Chairman: W Bruce Thomas (Administrative and Chief Financial Officer)
Senior Executive Officers: Thomas C Graham (Executive Director, President USS Corp), Forest E Hoglund (Executive Director, President Texas Oil & Gas Corp), J Bruce Johnston (Executive VP Employee Relations), William F Swales (Executive Director, President Marathon Oil Co), David H Hopton (Group VP Manufactured Products and Engineering Services), Guiseppe Colombari (Senior VP Related Resources), Charles A Corry (Senior VP and Comptroller), William E Llewellen (Senior VP Finance), Reuben L Perin Jr (Senior VP Sheet and Tin Products), Thomas J Usher (Senior VP Heavy Products), Francis P Adams (VP Accounting), Drummond C Bell (VP Realty), Donald K Frick (VP Taxes), Charles C Gedeon (VP Raw Materials), Harold C Haase (VP Purchasing and Traffic), Robert M Hernandez (VP and Treasurer), Keith K Kappmeyer (VP Reserach and Technology), Earl W Mallick (VP Public Affairs), Philip X Masciantonio (VP Environmental Affairs), Anthony F Mastro (VP Accounting and Finance, US Diversified Group), Peter B Mulloney (VP and Assistant to Chairman), James D Short (VP Benefits Administration), Thomas W Sterling III (VP Employee Relations), Louis A Valli (VP Personnel), Charles D Williams (VP Investor Relations)

PRINCIPAL ACTIVITIES: Production of steel and iron ore; exploration, production and distribution of oil and gas; mining of minerals; general engineering and provision of related services
Principal Subsidiaries: Bessemer and Lake Erie Railroad Co; Birmingham Southern Railroad Co; Carnegie Natural Gas Co; Duluth Missabe and Iron Range Railway Co; Elgin Joliet and Eastern Railway Co; Marathon Oil Company; Marathon Petroleum Company; Texas Oil and Gas Corp; Union Railroad Co; Warrior and Gulf Navigation Co
Financial Information:

	Dec 31 1985 $'000	Dec 31 1986 $'000
Sales revenues	18,429,000	14,000,000
Net income (loss)	409,000	(1,883,000)
Earnings (loss) per share	$2.56	($7.46)
Shareholders equity	6,305,000	5,634,000

No of Employees: 79,650

UTAH POWER & LIGHT CO

1407 W N Temple St, PO Box 899, Salt Lake City, UT 84110
Tel: (801) 535-2000

Chairman: E Allan Hunter
President: Frank N Davis (and Chief Executive Officer)
Senior Executive Officers: Sidney G Baucom (Executive VP and General Counsel), Arvin A Gibson (Executive VP), Curtis L Hoskins (Executive VP), Dean L Bryner (Senior VP), Verl R Topham (Senior VP and Chief Financial Officer), Robert Gordon (VP and Secretary), Harry A Haycock (VP Operations)

PRINCIPAL ACTIVITIES: Electricity supply
Financial Information:

	$'000
Sales revenues	985,000

No of Employees: 4,900

UTILICORP UNITED INC

922 Walnut, Kansas City, MO 64199
Tel: (816) 472 7329

Chairman: Avis G Tucker; Vice Chairman: William I Owen (and Chief Operating Officer)
President: Richard C Green Jr (and Chief Executive Officer)
Senior Executive Officers: John R Baker (Senior VP), James E Franklin (VP), Dale J Wolf (VP Finance), Roger K Sallee (Secretary)

PRINCIPAL ACTIVITIES: Electricity and natural gas supply
Principal Bank: Commerce Bank of Kansas City NA
Financial Information:

	$'000
Sales revenues	243,150

No of Employees: 1,000

VALERO ENERGY CORPORATION

530 McCullough, San Antonio, TX 78292
Tel: (512) 246-2000
Telex: TWX 910 3501545 valero eng cor

Chairman: William E Greehey (and Chief Executive Officer)
President: Palmer Moe (and Chief Operating Officer)
Senior Executive Officers: Richard A Upton (Senior VP Exploration and Production), John H Hoelscher (Senior VP Finance), Stan L McLelland (Senior VP Legal), Martin Zanotti (Senior VP Refining and Marketing), Wayne H King (Senior VP Natural Gas Liquids), Diana J Shiller (VP Administration), Gregory Wright (Director Investor Relations)

PRINCIPAL ACTIVITIES: Distribution of natural gas; exploration and production of oil and gas
Principal Subsidiaries: Valero Transmission Co; Valero Interstate Transmission Co; Valero Hydrocarbons Co; Valero Marketing Co; Valero Gathering Co; Val Gas Co; Rio Grande Valley Gas Co; Valero Consumer Service Co; Esco Supply Co; Valero Storage Cos; Valero Realty Cos; Valero Management Co; Valero Coal Cos; Valero Producing Co; Valero Natural Gas Co; Reata Industrial Gas Co; Valero Industrial Gas Co; Valero Land Co; Valero Communications Co; Valero Refining & Marketing
Principal Bank: Continental Illinois National Bank
Financial Information:

	Dec 31 1985 $'000	Dec 31 1986 $'000
Sales revenues	2,661,622	1,880,083
Net income (loss)	34,718	(99,888)
Earnings (loss) per share	$1.06	($4.36)
Shareholders equity	482,942	377,425

No of Employees: 2,230

VALLEY BANK OF NEVADA

PO Box 15427, Las Vegas, NV 89114
Tel: (702) 386-1000
Telex: TWX 910 3976972 val bk nv lv

Chairman: Richard A Etter (and Chief Executive Officer); Chairman of Executive Committee: E P Thomas; Vice Chairman: Jerome D Mack
President: Peter M Thomas
Senior Executive Officers: Richard H Taggart (Senior Executive VP), Bill K Hull (Executive VP Reno), Kenneth Miller (Executive VP, Cashier and Chief Financial Officer), Dennis Carroll (Senior VP and Controller), Clifford L Chaddick (Senior VP Marketing and Sales), Thomas E Hodson (Senior VP Banking), Jon A Joseph (Senior VP and General Counsel), Robert J Kolesar (Senior VP and Trust Officer), Sidney F Perzy (Senior VP Resource Management)

PRINCIPAL ACTIVITIES: Banking services
Parent Company: Valley Capital Corp

No of Employees: 850

VALLEY FEDERAL SAVINGS & LOAN ASSOCIATION

6842 Van Nuys Blvd, Van Nuys, CA 91405
Tel: (818) 904-3000

Chairman: Joseph R Biafora
President: Donald C Headlund (and Chief Executive Officer)
Senior Executive Officers: Michael Laurin (Senior Executive VP and Chief Operations Officer), Jack R Allewaert (Executive VP, Chief Financial Officer and Treasurer), Dan E Nelms (Executive VP and Chief Landing Officer), Paul F Chesley (Senior VP and Savings Administrator), Joseph S Huber (Senior VP and Branch Administrator), John R Marquis (Senior VP and Marketing Administrator), Linda M Martin (Senior VP and Information Systems Administrator)

PRINCIPAL ACTIVITIES: Financial services including savings and loans
Principal Subsidiaries: All Valley Financial Corp; All Valley Mortgage; All Valley Acceptance Corp; ALCAL Financial Corp (58%)
Principal Bank: Bank of America
Financial Information:

	Dec 31 1985	Dec 31 1986
	$'000	$'000
Revenues	316,220	313,831
Income before taxes	18,721	31,406
Net income	10,409	17,033
Earnings per share	$1.61	$2.75
Common stock	2,603	2,876
Retained income	31,669	41,335
Shareholders equity	77,546	94,169
Deposits	1,959,453	2,067,106
Total assets	2,478,485	2,661,651

No of Employees: 1,000

VALLEY INDUSTRIES, INC

900 Walnut Street, St Louis, MO 63102
Tel: (314) 231-2160

Chairman: Lester A Crancer Jr (and Chief Executive Officer)
President: Patrick J Gilligan (and Chief Financial Officer)
Senior Executive Officers: Thomas R Carrico (VP Administration and Secretary), Harold R Mabrey (VP), Bradley T Melchior (VP)

PRINCIPAL ACTIVITIES: Manufacture of steel pipe and pipe fittings; oil drilling equipment
Principal Subsidiaries: Valley Steel Products Company
Principal Bank: First National Bank of Chicago
Financial Information:

	Nov 30 1985	Nov 30 1986
	$'000	$'000
Sales revenues	96,352	75,581
Net income (loss)	340	(13,222)
Retained income	13,357	135

No of Employees: 550

VALLEY NATIONAL BANK OF ARIZONA

PO Box 71, Phoenix, AZ 85001
Tel: (602) 261-2900
Telex: 667 371

Chairman: Howard C McCrady (and Chief Executive Officer)
President: Leonard W Huck (and Chief Administration Officer)
Senior Executive Officers: Nathan C Collins (Executive VP Commercial Banking Group), Timothy Creedon (Executive VP Personal Banking Group), B Paul Jones (Executive VP Funds Management and Economic Planning Group), Ronald C McLaughlin (Executive VP Finance and Corporate Planning), James H Alltop (Senior VP Human Resources), Harley H Barnes (Senior VP Commercial Banking Group), Arthur K Carlson (Senior VP Trust Division), Michael W Hard (Senior VP Southern Division), Roy J Johnson (Senior VP Western Division), Donald W Kirkman (Senior VP Audit Division), Darrel McIntyre (Senior VP Commercial Banking Loan Administration), Mike Michalis (Senior VP and Controller), Harold Mosanko (Senior VP Central Division), George L Mullinax (Senior VP Consumer Lending Division), Richard A Picard (Senior VP Systems and Data Processing Administration), Norwood W Pope (Senior VP Marketing Division), Donald E Ruff (Senior VP Eastern Division), V Lamoine Saunders (Senior VP Bank Operations/Transaction Services), Gene Wright (Senior VP and Cashier)

PRINCIPAL ACTIVITIES: Banking services
Parent Company: Valley National Corporation

No of Employees: 6,940

VALLEY NATIONAL CORPORATION

PO Box 71, Phoenix, AZ 85001
Tel: (602) 261-2900

Chairman: Howard C McCrady (and Chief Executive Officer)
President: Leonard W Huck (and Chief Administration Officer)
Senior Executive Officers: Nathan Collins (Executive VP), Timothy Creedon (Executive VP), B P Jones (Executive VP), Ronald C McLaughlin (Executive VP)

PRINCIPAL ACTIVITIES: Financial services including trust services and commercial banking
Principal Subsidiaries: Valley National Bank of Arizona; Valley Utah Bancorporation
Principal Bank: Valley National Bank of Arizona
Financial Information:

	Dec 31 1985	Dec 31 1986
	$'000	$'000
Income before taxes	109,200	81,923
Net income	77,000	83,222
Dividends	20,591	22,610
Dividends per share	$1.23	$1.35
Earnings per share	$4.60	$4.97
Retained income	-	450,718
Shareholders equity	531,700	592,518
Deposits	8,136,000	9,186,694
Total assets	9,931,000	10,715,497

No of Employees: 7,914

VALLEY STEEL PRODUCTS CO

900 Walnut Street, St Louis, MO 63102
Tel: (314) 231-2160

President: Bradley T Melchior
Senior Executive Officers: Patrick J Gilligan (VP), Ray Guthrie (VP Operations), James C Barnes (Senior VP Sales and Marketing), Thomas R Carrico (VP), Harold Mabrey (VP)

PRINCIPAL ACTIVITIES: Manufacture of steel products including pipes, tubes, sheets and plates; manufacture of pumps and drilling equipment
Parent Company: Valley Industries Inc, St Louis, MO
Principal Bank: First National Bank of Chicago
Financial Information:

	$'000
Sales revenues	216,000

No of Employees: 1,700

VALLEYLAB, INC

5920 Longbow Drive, Boulder, CO 80301
Tel: (303) 530-2300
Telex: TWX 910 9402514 valleylab bdr

Chairman: Robert K Anderson
President: William D Reichenberg (and Chief Executive Officer)
Senior Executive Officers: Bruce A Murray (VP), R Toler (VP), William Goslau (VP)

PRINCIPAL ACTIVITIES: Manufacture and sale of medical supplies and surgical instruments
Parent Company: Pfizer Inc, New York, NY
Principal Bank: First National Bank in Boulder
Financial Information:

	1986 $'000
Sales revenues	76,760

No of Employees: 1,000

VALMAC INDUSTRIES, INC
855 Ridge Lake Blvd, Memphis, TN 38119
Tel: (901) 685-8251

Chairman: Shelby D Massey (and President and Chief Executive Officer)
Senior Executive Officers: Richard C Bevier (Executive VP, Secretary and Treasurer)

PRINCIPAL ACTIVITIES: Poultry processing; cotton trading and processing
Parent Company: Tyson Foods Inc
Principal Bank: Morgan Guaranty Trust Co
Financial Information:

	$'000
Sales revenues	360,000

No of Employees: 5,000

VALMONT INDUSTRIES, INC
Valley, NE 68064
Tel: (402) 359-2201
Telex: WUT 484459 vmtully

Presidents: William Welsh II (and Chief Operating Officer); William Welsh (Industrial Products Group); Melvin Bannister (AgriProducts Group)
Senior Executive Officers: Paul Lienemann (Senior VP), Gary Crouch (VP and Controller), Thomas P Egan Jr (VP, Secretary and Corporate Counsel), Richard Galberaith (VP), Gerald C Gray (VP), William C Eaton (VP), J Lee Salmans (VP), Tom L Whalen (VP)

PRINCIPAL ACTIVITIES: Manufacture of steel tubes, poles and structures for irrigation equipment, lighting and electricity transmission
Principal Bank: Continental Illinois National Bank and Trust Co
Financial Information:

	$'000
Sales revenues	313,400

No of Employees: 1,800

VALSPAR CORPORATION
1101 Third Street S, Minneapolis, MN 55415
Tel: (612) 332-7371

Chairman: C A Wurtele (and Chief Executive Officer)
President: Robert E Pajor (and Chief Operating Officer)
Senior Executive Officers: J D Bennett (VP), Paul Fritzke (VP), Sam Guerrera (VP), O W Huggard (VP), D C Olfe (VP), Richard D Radford (VP), J F Whealy (VP), J L Seiberlich (VP), V J Greci (VP), D Ochs (VP), Paul C Reyelts (VP Finance), J Stevenson (VP)

PRINCIPAL ACTIVITIES: Manufacture of paint
Principal Subsidiaries: Valspar Corp Ltd; McWhorter Inc; Color Corp of Europe BV
Principal Bank: Norwest Bank of Minneapolis
Financial Information:

	$'000
Sales revenues	347,160

No of Employees: 2,350

VALUE LINE INC
711 Third Avenue, New York, NY 10017
Tel: (212) 687-3965

Chairman: Arnold Bernhard (and Chief Executive Officer); Vice Chairman: Jean B Buttner (and President and Chief Operating Officer)
Senior Executive Officers: M K Tavel (Executive VP), Samuel Eisenstadt (Senior VP), Edward Havasy (VP), Louis Kirschbaum (VP Securities Analysis), Thomas J Sextion (VP)

PRINCIPAL ACTIVITIES: Financial advice and publication of financial literature; data processing services; advertising agency services
Parent Company: Arnold Bernhard & Co Inc, New York, NY
Principal Bank: Bankers Trust Company
Financial Information:

	$'000
Sales revenues	53,000

No of Employees: 435

VAN DORN CO
2700 E 79th Street, Cleveland, OH 44104
Tel: (216) 361-5234
Telex: TWX 810 4218668 van dorn

Chairman: Lawrence C Jones (and President)
Senior Executive Officers: Campbell W Elliott (VP Public Affairs), Robert N Jones (VP), George J Milton (VP Finance), James W Milton (VP), George M Smart (VP), Samuel H Smith Jr (VP)

PRINCIPAL ACTIVITIES: Manufacture of machinery for the plastics industry; manufacture of containers
Principal Bank: Huntington Bank
Financial Information:

	$'000
Sales revenues	314,330

No of Employees: 2,200

VAN HUFFEL TUBE CORPORATION
PO Box 1540, Dietz Road, Warren, OH 44482
Tel: (216) 372-1711
Telex: 810 436 2671

Chairman: R Q Anderson
President: J McAllister (and Chief Executive Officer)
Senior Executive Officers: James Cochran (Executive VP), James A Reed (Senior VP), John W Ferry (VP Engineering), James Poss (VP Power Strut Division), George McZie (VP Manufacturing)

PRINCIPAL ACTIVITIES: Manufacture of steel tubes
Principal Bank: Chemical Bank
Financial Information:

	$'000
Sales revenues	100,000

No of Employees: 1,000

VARCO INTERNATIONAL, INC
800 E Eckhoff Street, Orange, CA 92668
Tel: (714) 978-1900
Telex: WUT 678336 varco orge

Chairman: Walter B Reinhold (and Chief Executive Officer)
President: George I Boyadjieff (and Chief Operating Officer)
Senior Executive Officers: Donald L Stichler (Corporate Controller), Jim Kremidas (Director Engineering)

PRINCIPAL ACTIVITIES: Manufacture of tools and equipment for the oil industry
Principal Subsidiaries: Best Industries Inc; Varco Oil Tools; Varco Electronics Inc; Varcomarine Tools Inc
Principal Bank: Crocker National Bank
Financial Information:

	$'000
Sales revenues	60,620

No of Employees: 700

VARCO-PRUDEN
6000 Poplar, Memphis, TN 38119-3954
Tel: (901) 767-5910
Telex: WUT 53802 varcoprdn mfs

President: John E Johnston
Senior Executive Officers: Jim Drake (VP Marketing), George McSparren (VP Manufacturing), Charles Rauscher (VP Human Resources), John Sullivan (VP Finance), Samuel L Love (VP Technical Services)

PRINCIPAL ACTIVITIES: Manufacture of metal buildings
Parent Company: AMCA International Corporation
Principal Bank: Wachovia National Bank and Trust Co
Financial Information:

	$'000
Sales revenues	100,000

No of Employees: 1,000

VARIABLE ANNUITY LIFE INSURANCE CO
2727 Allen Pkwy, Houston, TX 77019
Tel: (713) 526-5251

Senior Chairman: Harold S Hook; Chairman: Michael J Poulos
President: Joe D Heusi (and Chief Executive Officer)
Senior Executive Officers: Wayne D Baker (Senior VP Operations), Sam E Magee (Senior VP), Joe C Osborne (Senior VP Marketing), Nicholas R Rasmussen (Senior VP Investment), Mark W Shartle (Senior VP and Treasurer), Frank J Aten (VP Portfolio), Gregory J Carney (VP and Chief Actuary), J David Crank (VP Group Planning Services), Walter B Colvin (VP Investment), Diane G D'Agostino (VP External Affairs and Assistant to President), Kenneth C Emery (VP Systems Development), Duane C Hendricks (VP), Campbell D McHugh (VP, General Counsel and Secretary), D Ann Mobley (VP Research), Edwin W Pfaff (VP Investment), Herschell C Pittenger (VP Investment), Leonard M Richards (VP and Senior Portfolio Manager), Jules E Schneider (VP and Portfolio Manager), Julia S Tucker (VP Investment)

PRINCIPAL ACTIVITIES: Insurance
Parent Company: American General Corporation, Houston, TX
Principal Bank: Texas Commerce Bank
Financial Information:

	Dec 31 1985	Dec 31 1986
	$'000	$'000
Premium income	695,250	1,004,512
Investment income	477,390	562,186

No of Employees: 1,220

VARIAN ASSOCIATES, INC
611 Hansen Way, Palo Alto, CA 94303-0883
Tel: (415) 493-4000
Telex: 348476
Telefax: (415) 493-0307

Chairman: Thomas D Sege (and President)
Senior Executive Officers: Robert A Lemos (VP Finance), Larry L Hansen (Executive VP Corporate Technology and Planning), Norman H Pond (Executive VP), Vincent J Battaglia (VP Corporate; President Electron Device Group), Alan J Bennett (VP, Research), Stanley Z Cole (VP and Director of Patents and Licensing), John J Cooper (VP, General Counsel and Secretary), William E Finney (VP, Corporate; and President, Medical and Industrial Products Group), Tony Jurvetson (President, Semiconductor Equipment Group), Allen J Lauer (VP, Corporate; and President, Instrument Group), James A Taylor (Treasurer), Wayne P Somrak (Controller), David F Minnery (VP, Corporate; and President International Group), Ernest M Felago (VP, Human Resources), Gary E Simpson (VP, Corporate Communications)

PRINCIPAL ACTIVITIES: Varian Associates, Inc, is an international electronics company that designs, manufactures and markets high-technology systems and components. These products include microwave, power and special-purpose electron tubes, solid state components and equipment for defense and communications; analytical instruments for science and industry; wafer-fabrication equipment for the semiconductor industry; radiation equipment for cancer therapy; vacuum equipment and leak detectors for industrial and scientific processes
Trade Names: Varian, Clinac, Eimac, Extrion, Gartek, StarCell, Techtron, TEM
Principal Subsidiaries: Electron Device Group: Divisions:- Microwave Equipment Division; Microwave Tube Division; EIMAC San Carlos; EIMAC Salt Lake; Image Tube Division; Solid State Microwave Division; Beverly Microwave Division; Canada Microwave Division (Canada); Varian Taiwan Ltd. Affiliate: Thorn EMI-Varian Ltd (UK); Varian TVT (UK); Continental Electronics (Texas). Instrument Group: Divisions:- Palo Alto Instrument Division; Walnut Creek Instrument Division (Eire); Varian Techtron, Pty Ltd (Australia); Analytichem Inc. Affiliate: Siemens Joint Venture. Medical and Industrial Products Group: Divisions:- Radiation Division (USA and UK). Vacuum Products Division (USA and Italy). Associated Operations: Memory Disk Project; Varian TEM (UK); Semiconductor Equipment Group: Specialty Metals Division; Divisions:- Extrion Division; Thin Film Technology Division; Fremont Division. Affiliate: TEL-Varian Ltd (Japan)
Financial Information:

	Sep 30 1986	Oct 31 1987
	$'000	$'000
Sales revenues	891,139	982,776
Income (loss) before taxes	(40,173)	31,895
Net income (loss)	(14,863)	21,365
Dividends	5,552	5,700
Dividends per share	$0.26	$0.26
Earnings (loss) per share	($0.70)	$0.98
Common stock	21,448	21,834
Retained income	232,006	247,700
Shareholders equity	410,930	438,100

No of Employees: 12,000

VARIAN/BEVERLY MICROWAVE DIVISION
Salem Road, Beverly, MA 01915
Tel: (617) 922-6000
Telex: WUT 940795 varian bvly

Senior Executive Officers: H C Warner (General Manager), Chester G Lob (Technical Director), Gerald Karlsruher (Marketing Manager), Ronald Lawler (Materials Manager), Frank Herlihy (Controller)

PRINCIPAL ACTIVITIES: Manufacture of magnetrons, crossed-field amplifiers, ring-loop traveling-wave tubes, receiver protectors, solid-state components, modulators, radar subsystems
Parent Company: Varian Associates
Financial Information:

	$'000
Sales revenues	49,000

No of Employees: 750

VARITYPER
11 Mt Pleasant Avenue, East Hanover, NJ 07936
Tel: (201) 887-8000
Telex: TWX 910 3802816 varittyper

President: J A Verderber
Senior Executive Officers: K Brunell (VP Marketing), M Daly (VP Sales), R Smith (VP Customer Services), R Zeisler (VP Finance), T Markley (VP Engineering), D Hubbard (VP Manufacturing), C Burlingame (VP Human Resources), T Wellman (VP Product Management)

PRINCIPAL ACTIVITIES: The Varityper Division markets computer-based composing and phototypesetting systems for the commercial and in-plant markets. The Division's line of products includes direct-entry phototypesetter models covering a spectrum of capabilities, off-line text entry and editing terminals including value-added personal computers, new on-line shared resource text processing systems, machine options and accessories such as image previewers, telecommunications interfaces, photographic processors, photographic papers and chemicals, other consumable supplies and type

Parent Company: AM International Inc

Financial Information:

	$'000
Sales revenues	100,000

No of Employees: 1,600

VARLEN CORPORATION

200 Park Plaza, Naperville, IL 60566
Tel: (312) 420-0400
Telex: WUT 283407 varln roms

Chairman: John A Moran
President: Richard Wellek (and Chief Executive Officer)
Senior Executive Officers: Thomas E Berger (Executive VP), Richard E Sullivan (VP and Treasurer), Melvin A Adelman (VP), David J Breault (VP)

PRINCIPAL ACTIVITIES: Manufacture of metal products for the automotive, agricultural and railroad industries
Principal Bank: Mellon Bank
Financial Information:

	$'000
Sales revenues	119,000

No of Employees: 1,400

VARO INC

2203 W Walnut Street, Box 461426, Garland, TX 75046
Tel: (214) 272-1571
Telex: TWX 910 8605093 varoinc garl

Chairman: Samuel Yanagisawa
President: James F Gero (and Chief Executive Officer)
Senior Executive Officers: Stanley J Sadlowski (Senior VP), David L Dollob (VP and Chief Operating Officer), Leo J Eveleth Jr (VP and Chief Personnel Officer), William R Mason (VP Corporate Planning and Development), Clifford L Steward (VP, Secretary, Treasurer and Chief Financial Officer)

PRINCIPAL ACTIVITIES: Manufacture of electronic equipment for navigation and weapon guidance
Principal Subsidiaries: Varo-Semiconductor Inc; Applied Optics Center Corp
Principal Bank: Republic Bank Dallas
Financial Information:

	$'000
Sales revenues	94,500

No of Employees: 1,630

VAUGHAN & SONS, INC

Petroleum Commerce Bldg, San Antonio, TX 78294
Tel: (512) 222-1311

Chairman: Curtis Vaughan Jr (and President and Chief Executive Officer)
President: Norman Harwell (and Chief Operating Officer)
Senior Executive Officers: Melvin Follis (VP Lumber Purchasing), Denis C Parker (VP and Comptroller), Thomas R Rice (VP Operations), Steve Sims (VP Houston Operations), Tracy F Smith (VP Finance), William E Thomas (VP), Curtis Vaughan III (VP and Secretary), George C Vaughan (VP Marketing), Robert L Vaughan (VP Planning), Richard W Wood (VP Dallas Operations)

PRINCIPAL ACTIVITIES: Production of timber; manufacture of building supplies
Principal Bank: Frost National Bank
Financial Information:

	$'000
Sales revenues	90,000

No of Employees: 600

VAUGHAN PRODUCTS, INC

5300 Katrine Avenue, Downers Grove, IL 60515
Tel: (312) 969-6300

Chairman: John C Vaughan
President: John F Moates
Senior Executive Officers: Michael Novovesky (VP), Charles Walkiewicz (VP), Michael Sullivan (Treasurer), James O'Connell (Secretary)

PRINCIPAL ACTIVITIES: Wholesale distributor and manufacturer of professionally used horticultural products and home garden supply items
Principal Bank: Continental Illinois National Bank and Trust Co
Financial Information:

	Sep 30 1985	Sep 30 1986
	$'000	$'000
Sales revenues	73,000	82,000
Income before taxes	1,312	2,730
Net income	757	1,380
Common stock	21	21*
Retained income	1,212	2,592
Shareholders equity	3,282	4,697

*and Paid in Capital 2,084

No of Employees: 500

VAW OF AMERICA, INC

Ellenville, NY 12428
Tel: (914) 647-7510
Telex: WUT 926479 vawamrica elve

Chairman: Rudolf J Escherich
President: Manfred F Schroeder
Senior Executive Officers: Leon A Smith (VP Operations Ellenville), Albert F Styring (VP Operations St Augustine), James F Wilcox (VP Finance and Secretary)

PRINCIPAL ACTIVITIES: Manufacture of aluminum products including tube and pipe
Parent Company: Vereinigte Aluminum-Werke AG, Bonn, Germany
Financial Information:

	$'000
Sales revenues	95,000

No of Employees: 600

VECTOR CABLE CO

555 Industrial Road, Sugar Land, TX 77478
Tel: (713) 491-9196
Telex: TWX 910 880 4891 vector sugl

Senior Executive Officers: Robert Olson (VP Research and Development), John H Winkler (General Manager), James D English (Controller), Alan Faraizl (Marketing Director)

PRINCIPAL ACTIVITIES: Manufacture of cables and wires
Parent Company: Schlumberger Ltd, New York, NY
Principal Bank: Bank of the Southwest
Financial Information:

	$'000
Sales revenues	28,000

No of Employees: 240

VEECO INSTRUMENTS INC

515 Broad Hollow Road, Melville, NY 11747
Tel: (516) 694-4200

Chairman: Albert Nerken
President: Allen E Busching (and Chief Executive Officer)

Senior Executive Officers: Edward H Braun (Executive VP-Instrument Group, Automation and Semiconductor Equipment Group and Chief Operating Officer), Joshua A Hauser (Executive VP-Lambda Group), Steven M Goldschein (VP Administration, Treasurer and Chief Financial Officer), Thomas E Heftler (Secretary), Rikihiro Madarame (VP-Lambda Far East Operations), B Alan Ross (VP-Automation and Semiconductor Equipment Group), Michael J Speiller (Controller)

PRINCIPAL ACTIVITIES: Manufacture of power supplies, vacuum instrumentation and semiconductor processing equipment and specialty power semiconductors
Principal Subsidiaries: Veeco Integrated Automation Inc (90%); Lambda Electronics (1979) Ltd (Israel), Veeco SA (France); Lambda Electronique SA (France); Veeco GmbH (Germany); Lambda Netzgerate GmbH (Germany); Veeco Instruments Ltd (UK); Lambda Electronics (UK); Lambda Electronica de Mexico SA (Mexico); Veeco Lambda Inc (Canada); IsLAMBDA Electronics Ltd (Israel); NEMIC-Lambda (Singapore) Pte Ltd (Singapore); Lambda Semiconductor SA (Mexico); NEMIC-LAMBDA KK (72%) (Japan); Lambda Novatronics Inc; Lambda Magnapower Inc; Sloan Technology Corp; UPA Technology Inc
Principal Bank: Chemical Bank
Financial Information:

	Sep 30 1985	Sep 30 1986
	$'000	$'000
Sales revenues	161,900	167,769
Income before taxes	19,003	613
Net income	9,836	380
Dividends	3,654	3,932
Dividends per share	$0.35	$0.37
Earnings per share	$0.94	$0.04
Common stock	10,467	10,487
Retained income	73,336	75,059
Shareholders equity	89,389	92,821

Principal Shareholders: A Nerken (14.1%)
No of Employees: 2,500

VEEDER INDUSTRIES, INC

345 Park Avenue, New York, NY 10154
Tel: (203) 278-5960

Chairman: Howard A Newman (and Chief Executive Officer)
President: William C Scott (and Chief Operating Officer)
Senior Executive Officers: Michael Greenberg (VP), Roger F Haskell (Treasurer)

PRINCIPAL ACTIVITIES: Manufacture of plastic products; screws; calculating and computing equipment
Parent Company: Western Pacific Industries Inc, New York, NY
Financial Information:

	$'000
Sales revenues	168,000

No of Employees: 2,750

VELAN VALVE CORPORATION

Avenue C, Griswold Industrial Park, Williston, VT 05495
Tel: (802) 863-2562
Telex: WUT 954613 velvalve wivt

President: A K Velan
Senior Executive Officers: I C Velan (Executive VP), P O Velan (VP Manufacturing), T C Velan (VP Export Sales), R Maasik (VP Sales)

PRINCIPAL ACTIVITIES: Manufacture of valves
Principal Bank: First National Bank
Financial Information:

	$'000
Sales revenues	120,000

No of Employees: 920

VENDO CO

7209 N Ingram Avenue, Fresno, CA 93650
Tel: (209) 439-1770
Telex: WUT 355427 vendo bcs fso

Chairman: Spencer L Childers
President: Joe R Town (and Chief Executive Officer)
Senior Executive Officers: Robert F Williams (Senior VP Vending Sales and Marketing), David L McDonald (Senior VP Operations and Metal Products), Donald H Bradford (VP/Controller)

PRINCIPAL ACTIVITIES: Manufacture of vending machines
Principal Subsidiaries: (100% owned unless stated): Vendo International Service Corp; Ven Par Vending Equipment Sales Ltd; Vendo (Japan) Ltd (87%); Vendo (France) SARL (France); Vendo GmbH (Germany); Vendo (Hong Kong) Ltd (Hong Kong); Vendo Iberia SA (Spain); Vendo International SA (Belgium); Vendo (Italy) SpA (Italy)
Principal Bank: Bank of America
Financial Information:

	$'000
Sales revenues	88,582

No of Employees: 1,170

VENTRON DIVISION

150 Andover Street, Danvers, MA 01923
Tel: (617) 774-3100
Telex: TWX 710 3476480 ventron dans

Chairman: Charles S Locke (and Chief Executive Officer)
President: Tyrone G Goodart
Senior Executive Officers: Steve A Bayless (VP and General Manager Carstab Products), Herve M Bellego (VP and General Manager Ventron Products), Larence J Guilbault (VP Research and Development Ventron Products), Lynwood J Krischke (VP Manufacturing Ventron Products), Thomas G Kugele (VP Research and Development Carstab Products), Joseph A Mazzei (VP Manufacturing Carstab Products), William D Van Lokeren (VP Finance)

PRINCIPAL ACTIVITIES: Manufacture of specialty chemicals and metal powders
Parent Company: Morton Thiokol Inc, Chicago, IL
Principal Bank: First National Bank of Chicago
Financial Information:

	$'000
Sales revenues	150,000

No of Employees: 700

VERBATIM CORPORATION

323 Soquel Way, PO Box 3477, Sunnyvale, CA 94088-3477
Tel: (408) 245-4400
Telex: 340-692

Chairman: J R Anderson
President: Richard T Bourns (and Chief Executive Officer)
Senior Executive Officers: James C Olsen (Senior VP Human Resources)

PRINCIPAL ACTIVITIES: Manufacture of floppy disks, mini cassettes and data cassettes
Trade Names: DataLife
Parent Company: Eastman-Kodak Company
Principal Subsidiaries: Verbatim SA (Switzerland); ITC International (Disc); Varbatim Ltd SA (Eire); Verbatim Ltd (UK); Verbatim GmbH (Germany); Verbatim Australia Pty Ltd (Australia); Varbatim do Amazonas Industrial Ltd (49%) (Brazil); Varbatim de Mexico SA de cv (49%) (Mexico); Kasei Verbatim Corp (50%) (Japan); Verbatim do Commercial Ltda (51%) (Brazil); Data Encore Inc; Verbatim France SARL (France); Verbatim Italia SpA (Italy)
Principal Bank: Bank of America

Financial Information:

	$'000
Sales revenues	150,000

No of Employees: 1,500

VERMONT AMERICAN CORPORATION

100 E Liberty Street, Louisville, KY 40202
Tel: (502) 587-6851
Telex: TWX 810 535 3340 v a corp ud

Chairman: Lee B Thomas Jr; Chairman of Executive Committee: Lee B Thomas Sr
President: Robert I Baker (and Chief Executive Officer)
Senior Executive Officers: Wilfred M McCord (VP Engineering), Timothy T Shea (VP Finance and Treasurer), George Chapman (VP Manufacturing), Glenn E Thomas (VP and General Manager Corporate Engineering)

PRINCIPAL ACTIVITIES: Manufacture of a wide range of tools including cutting tools, power tool accessories, hand tools and lawn and garden products
Principal Subsidiaries: Larsan Manufacturing Co; VAC Data Management Inc; DML Inc; Vermont American Corp-Fountain Inn; Atkinson Manufacturing Co; Gilmour Manufacturing Co; Seymour Smith & Son Inc; Westa Werkzeugbau; Vermont American Australia Ltd; Vermont American Canada Inc
Principal Bank: Citizens Fidelity Bank and Trust Co
Financial Information:

	Dec 31 1985	Dec 31 1986
	$'000	$'000
Sales revenues	230,118	255,427
Income before taxes	5,932	25,548
Net income	4,662	13,548
Dividends per share	$0.36	$0.37
Earnings per share	$0.54	$1.61
Common stock	8,576	8,184
Retained income	16,551	10,982
Shareholders equity	110,300	113,365

Principal Shareholders: Lee B Thomas Jr; Ellen Thomas Dunbar
No of Employees: 3,520

VERNITRON CORPORATION

2001 Marcus Avenue, Lake Success, NY 11042
Tel: (516) 775-8200
Telex: TWX 510 223 0409 vernitron laks

Chairman: Herman S Nathanson (and President and Chief Executive Officer); Vice Chairman: Bernard Levine
Senior Executive Officers: Daniel A Nathanson (Executive VP Corporate Planning), Michael J Goldman (VP, Treasurer and Chief Financial Officer), Benjamin Kittner (VP), Benjamin K Sachs (VP and Secretary)

PRINCIPAL ACTIVITIES: Manufacture of electronic equipment, ignition devices, communication equipment and medical equipment
Principal Subsidiaries: AEI Magnetics Division; Vernitron Ltd; AST/Servo Systems Inc; VRN International; BEAU Products Division; Brevel Motors Inc; Lafayette Precision Products Inc; LIFEMED Division; Magnetic Technology Division; PED-O-JET Intl Inc; Vernitech Division; Vernitron Control Components Division; Vernitron Medical Products Division; Vernitron Piezaelectric Division; Lorch Electronics Corp; Brevel Motors of Canada Ltd
Principal Bank: Bankers Trust Company
Financial Information:

	$'000
Sales revenues	136,000

No of Employees: 2,800

VERNON CO

604 W Fourth Street N, Newton, IA 50208
Tel: (515) 792-2880
Telex: WUT 882579 vernon nwt ud

President: William F Vernon
Senior Executive Officers: Joseph D Geneser (Executive VP), Joseph L Pugel (VP Manufacturing), George Riley (VP Sales), Dan Stevenson (VP Finance)

PRINCIPAL ACTIVITIES: Manufacture of advertising specialties including business gifts and calendars
Principal Bank: Jasper County Savings
Financial Information:

	$'000
Sales revenues	50,000

No of Employees: 1,000

VERSATEC

2710 Walsh Avenue, Santa Clara, CA 95051
Tel: (408) 988-2800
Telex: TWX 910 3380243 versatec snta

President: Renn Zaphiropoulos
Senior Executive Officers: Bill Lloyd (VP Research and Development), Tony Taroni (VP Manufacturing)

PRINCIPAL ACTIVITIES: Manufacture of electrographic printing equipment
Parent Company: Xerox Corp, Stamford, CT
Financial Information:

	$'000
Sales revenues	100,000

No of Employees: 1,250

VERSON ALLSTEEL PRESS CO

1355 E 93rd Street, Chicago, IL 60619
Tel: (312) 933-8200
Telex: WUT 253444 verson cgo

Chairman: Melvin D Verson
President: C J Kelleher
Senior Executive Officers: L Novak (Executive VP and General Manager Verson-Chicago), D D Smith (Executive VP and General Manager Marketing), Vincent Pisciotta (Corporate VP Systems and Planning), J Demetral (VP Manufacturing), R W Hoefler (VP Sales Administration), W C Johnson (VP Systems Sales), K Otsuka (VP Research and Development and Engineering)

PRINCIPAL ACTIVITIES: Manufacture of presses for a wide range of industrial applications
Parent Company: Allied Products Corp
Principal Bank: Continental Illinois National Bank
Financial Information:

	$'000
Sales revenues	120,000

No of Employees: 1,500

VERTAC CHEMICAL CORPORATION

5100 Poplar Avenue, Memphis, TN 38137
Tel: (901) 767-6851
Telex: WUT 53927 vertacorp mfs

Chairman: C P Bomar Jr
President: J R Tomblin (and Chief Executive Officer)
Senior Executive Officers: R A Guidi (VP Operations), J L Hanna (VP Finance, Secretary and Treasurer), G T Manley (VP Marketing)

PRINCIPAL ACTIVITIES: Manufacture of chemicals and fertilizers
Principal Bank: First Tennessee Bank
Financial Information:

	$'000
Sales revenues	60,000

No of Employees: 60

VERTIPILE, INC
Scott Drive, Leominster, MA 01453
Tel: (617) 534-6191
Telex: WUT 508717 vertipile leom

Chairman: Alan E Symonds (and President and Chief Executive Officer)
Senior Executive Officers: Arthur W Hall (Senior VP, Treasurer, Secretary and Chief Financial Officer), H D Harmoning (VP Manufacturing), Hemendra Shah (VP), Carl F Steinfield (VP Flock Sales)

PRINCIPAL ACTIVITIES: Manufacture of flock for the textile industry
Principal Subsidiaries: Claremont Flock Corp; Quaker Fabric Corp
Principal Bank: First National Bank of Boston
Financial Information:

	$'000
Sales revenues	118,300

No of Employees: 1,600

VESPER CORPORATION
301 City Line Avenue, Bala-Cynwyd, PA 19004
Tel: (215) 667-8440

Chairman: James Benenson Jr (and President)
Senior Executive Officers: John V Curci (VP and Treasurer), Gerald J Carroll (VP and Secretary)

PRINCIPAL ACTIVITIES: Manufacture of metal storage equipment and gears
Principal Bank: Bankers Trust Company
Financial Information:

	$'000
Sales revenues	75,000

No of Employees: 800

VESTRON INC
1011 High Ridge Road, Stamford, CT 06905
Tel: (203) 968 0000

Chairman: Austin O Furst Jr (and Chief Executive Officer)
President: Jon R Peisinger (and Chief Operating Officer)
Senior Executive Officers: Stephen L Einhorn (Executive VP, Chief Financial Officer and Secretary)

PRINCIPAL ACTIVITIES: Pre-recorded video cassette publishing
Principal Bank: Connecticut National Bank
Financial Information:

	$'000
Sales revenues	182,630

No of Employees: 170

VF CORPORATION
1047 N Park Road, Wyomissing, PA 19610
Tel: (215) 378-1151
Telex: WUT 836427 vf wyms

Chairman: Lawrence R Pugh (and Chief Executive Officer)
President: Robert E Gregory Jr (and Principal Operating Officer)
Senior Executive Officers: Harold E Addis (VP), Prakash C Bhatt (VP), Wayne L Bildahl (VP), Norman L Cochran (VP), Ardys A Kussman (VP), Harold D McKemy (VP Treasury and Financial Services), Janet J Peters (VP), Frederick J Rowan II (VP), Christopher L Schaller (VP), Lori M Tarnoski (VP and Secretary), Jerome M Wiggins (VP and Chief Financial Officer), Kenneth E Beyers (Controller), Louis J Fecile (Assistant VP), Frank C Pickard III (Treasurer), Gary E Dunham (Assistant Controller), Robert K Shearer (Assistant Controller)

PRINCIPAL ACTIVITIES: VF Corporation is the world's largest publicly-owned apparel company, is a leader in the jeanswear, sportswear, intimate apparel and occupational apparel markets. Its principal brands are Lee, Wrangler, Rustler, Girbaud, Bassett-Walker, Jantzen, JanSport, Vanity Fair, Lollipop by Modern Globe, Big Ben by Wrangler
Principal Subsidiaries/Divisions: The Lee Apparel Company, Inc; Vanity Fair Mills, Inc; Basset-Walker, Inc; Modern Globe, Inc; VF International Division, Inc; Girbaud; JanSport; Jantzen; Red Kap; Wrangler
Financial Information:

	Jan 4 1986 $'000	Jan 31 1987 $'000
Sales revenues	1,481,182	1,544,574
Income before taxes	272,117	249,443
Net income	139,417	129,350
Dividends	36,026	42,124
Dividends per share	$1.16	$0.66*
Earnings per share	$4.50	$2.05*
Common stock	31,097	63,068*
Retained income	499,407	555,446
Shareholders equity	554,223	824,141

*2 for 1 stock split April 1986

No of Employees: 50,000

VIACOM INTERNATIONAL INC
1211 Avenue of the Americas, New York, NY 10036
Tel: (212) 575-5175

Chairman: Ralph M Baruch
President: Terence A Elkes (and Chief Executive Officer)
Senior Executive Officers: Kenneth F Gorman (Executive VP), John W Goddard (Senior VP), Ronald Lightstone (Senior VP), Gordon E Belt (VP, Treasurer and Chief Financial Officer), George C Castell (VP Corporate Development), Kenneth Meyer (VP Human Resources), George S Smith Jr (VP and Controller), Mark M Weinstein (VP, General Counsel and Assistant Secretary)

PRINCIPAL ACTIVITIES: Production of motion pictures and broadcasting
Principal Bankers: Mellon Bank
Financial Information:

	$'000
Sales revenues	444,000

No of Employees: 4,200

VICKERS, INC
1401 Croosk Road, Troy, MI 48084
Tel: (313) 280-3000
Telex: TWX 910 3509107 vickers try mi

President: T N Duncan
Senior Executive Officers: Jim McKee (Executive VP Operations), L J Lyng (VP and General Manager North America Commercial), T Van Meter (VP), A G Goudreau (VP Manufacturing), C Kolioudiz (VP Corporate Communications), O Langosch (VP Engineering and Licensing), C Naudi (VP and Controller)

PRINCIPAL ACTIVITIES: Manufacture of hydraulic machinery
Parent Company: Trinova Corporation
Financial Information:

	$'000
Sales revenues	200,000

No of Employees: 6,700

VICORP RESTAURANTS, INC
400 W 48th Ave, Denver, CO 80216
Tel: (303) 296-2121

Chairman: Gordon H Miles
President: Charles R Frederickson
Senior Executive Officers: Peter F Doane (Executive VP, Chief Financial Officer, Secretary and Treasurer), Thomas W Doan (Executive VP Dinnerhouse Operations), Emerson B Kendall (Executive VP Bakery Operations), Joseph H Mohr (Executive VP and Chief Administration Officer), Ronald Sacks (Executive VP Family Restaurant Operations), Kenneth H Card (VP Real

Estate), Stanley Erickson Jr (VP and Counsel), Dennis L Kuper (VP and Controller), James T Orr (VP Franchise Operations and Field Services), Peter E Palumbo (VP Management Information Services), James E Shamis (VP Administration Services), James T Strohan (VP Strategic Planning)

PRINCIPAL ACTIVITIES: Restaurant interests
Principal Bank: United Bank of Denver
Financial Information:

	$'000
Sales revenues	383,830

No of Employees: 25,000

VICTOR F WEAVER INC

See WEAVER, VICTOR F, INC

VIE DE FRANCE CORPORATION

8201 Greensboro Drive, McLean, VA 22102-3805

Chairman: Jean-Louis Vilgrain (and Chief Executive Officer); Vice Chairman: Claude Bauduin (and Secretary and Treasurer)
President: L J Faul (and Chief Operating Officer)
Senior Executive Officers: Anita M Difanis (VP), R S Merritt (VP), W N Peachey (VP)

PRINCIPAL ACTIVITIES: Manufacture and sale of bakery products; restaurants
Financial Information:

	$'000
Sales revenues	63,120

No of Employees: 1,300

VIENNA SAUSAGE MFG CO

2501 N Damen Avenue, Chicago, IL 60647
Tel: (312) 278-7800
Telex: WUT 206295 vienna cgo
Fax: (312) 278-4759

Chairman: James Eisenberg (and Chief Executive Officer and Treasurer)
President: James W Bodman (and Chief Operating Officer and Secretary)
Senior Executive Officers: Stanley Kouba (Senior VP Marketing), Dennis Wilson (Senior VP), Tom Pierce (Senior VP), George Sklenicka (Senior VP), James McGuire (VP Sales), Hy Ramis (Senior VP Production)

PRINCIPAL ACTIVITIES: Meat processing; production of pastrami, corned beef and frankfurters, desserts, soups and pickles
Parent Company: Vienna Sausage Mfg Co/Vienna Beef Company
Principal Subsidiaries: Pie Piper; Bistro Soup; Mr Kitzel's Pickles
Principal Bank: American National Bank
Financial Information:

	$'000
Sales revenues	80,000

No of Employees: 660

VIKING CORPORATION

210 N Industrial Park Road, Hastings, MI 49058
Tel: (616) 945-9501
Telex: WUT 226400 viking hasg

President: Richard T Groos
Senior Executive Officers: Jack A Wood (VP), Clifford W Dolan (VP Marketing), George Hamaty (VP Purchasing and Personnel), Robert E Hollister (VP Manufacturing), James G Retzloff (VP Design and Development), John A Panfil (VP Finance and Administration, Secretary and Treasurer)

PRINCIPAL ACTIVITIES: Manufacture of fire extinguishing systems and automotive seals, industrial equipment; metal fabrication
Principal Bank: Old Kent Bank and Trust Company
Financial Information:

	$'000
Sales revenues	65,000

No of Employees: 1,120

VIRCO MFG CORPORATION

15134 S Vermont Avenue, Los Angeles, CA 90247
Tel: (213) 532-3570

Chairman: Julian K Virtue; Vice Chairman: Donald C Heyl
President: Robert A Virtue (and Chief Executive Officer)
Senior Executive Officers: James R Braam (VP Finance, Secretary and Treasurer), George S Ackerman (VP Educational Sales), Donald S Friesz (VP Sales Marketing), Robert C Gann (VP), Arthur J Millane (VP Manufacturing)

PRINCIPAL ACTIVITIES: Manufacture of furniture
Principal Subsidiaries: Delkay Plastics Corp; Pride-Trimble Corp; Virtue of California Inc; Virsan SA de CV
Principal Bank: Security Pacific National Bank
Financial Information:

	$'000
Sales revenues	168,750

No of Employees: 3,000

VIRGINIA IRON, COAL & COKE CO

PO Box 1871, Roanoke, VA 24008
Tel: (703) 342-1801
Telex: TWX 710 8700415 anr c.s.roa

President: James L Van Lanen
Senior Executive Officers: Robert H Warnick (Executive VP), William S Hudgins (VP, General Counsel, Assistant Secretary)

PRINCIPAL ACTIVITIES: Coal production
Parent Company: The Coastal Corporation through American Natural Resources Company through ANR Coal Co Inc
Financial Information:

	$'000
Sales revenues	80,000

No of Employees: 359

VLSI TECHNOLOGY INC

1101 McKay Drive, San Jose, CA 95131
Tel: (408) 942-1810
Telex: WUT 176151 vti snk

Chairman: A J Stein (and Chief Executive Officer)
President: H A Jarrat (and Chief Operating Officer)
Senior Executive Officers: K A Goldman (VP Finance and Chief Financial Officer), D G Fairbairn (VP), R C Kasper (VP), David Ledvina (VP)

PRINCIPAL ACTIVITIES: Manufacture of integrated circuits
Principal Bank: Bank of Boston
Financial Information:

	$'000
Sales revenues	78,670

No of Employees: 830

VODAVI TECHNOLOGY CORPORATION

8300 East Raintree Drive, Scottsdale, AZ 85260
Tel: (602) 998 2200

Chairman: Steven A Sherman (and Chief Executive Officer)
President: Gerhart F Klaiber
Senior Executive Officers: Kent R Burgess (Executive VP), John M Barr (VP Operations), Emmett E Mitchell (VP Finance, Secretary and Treasurer), Glenn R Fitchet (VP Marketing), Edward P Termini (VP Engineering)

PRINCIPAL ACTIVITIES: Telephone equipment

Principal Bank: First Interstate Bank of Arizona
Financial Information:

	$'000
Sales revenues	63,450

No of Employees: 70

VOEST ALPINE INTERNATIONAL CORPORATION

60 E 42nd Street, New York, NY 10165
Tel: (212) 661-1060
Telex: RCA 233228 voest ur

President: Hans H Schumacher
Senior Executive Officers: Joseph J Sieghart (Executive VP and Secretary), I Nemling (VP Forgings and Castings), R Doerre (VP Oil Pipes, Hot and Cold Rolled Steel, Plate), H Muller (VP Continuous Casting Machinery), Joseph J Gobris (Treasurer)

PRINCIPAL ACTIVITIES: Manufacture of a range of steel products and mining equipment
Parent Company: Voest-Alpine AG, Linz, Austria
Principal Subsidiaries: Virginia Crews Coal Company; Voest Alpine Trading USA Corp
Principal Bank: Chase Manhattan Bank
Financial Information:

	1987* $'000
Sales revenues	262,000
Income before taxes	7,500
Shareholders equity	28,000

*Voest Alpine International unconsolidated-1987 estimated

No of Employees: 150

VOLKSWAGEN OF AMERICA INC

888 W Big Beaver, Troy, MI 48077
Tel: (313) 362-6000
Telex: WUT 230628 vw-moa try

Chairman: Carl H Hahn
President: Noel Phillips (and Chief Executive Officer)
Senior Executive Officers: Iain M Anderson (Executive VP Finance and Administration and Treasurer), Bodo Dencker (VP Manufacturing Operations), Ulrich Fahrun (VP Parts Division), Peter Fischer (VP Audi of America, Inc), James R Fuller (VP Volkswagen United States, Inc)

PRINCIPAL ACTIVITIES: Manufacture of motor vehicles; import of motor vehicles and spare parts
Parent Company: Volkswagen AG, Wolfsburg, Germany
Financial Information:

	$'000
Sales revenues	3,800,000

No of Employees: 6,600

VOLT INFORMATION SCIENCES, INC

101 Park Avenue, New York, NY 10178
Tel: (212) 309-0200

Chairman: William Shaw (and President)
Senior Executive Officers: Jerome Shaw (Executive VP and Secretary), Irwin B Robins (VP and General Counsel), Julius J Lucks (VP, Treasurer and Controller), Michael E Grejtak (VP), Henry L Bechard (VP), Nicholas DiPadova (VP), John A Hunter (VP)

PRINCIPAL ACTIVITIES: Computer systems and services; electronic publication and typesetting systems; directory and publication services; human resources including technical services, temporary services and sales and sales support services; telecommunications services
Principal Subsidiaries: Volt Technical Services; Volt Delta Resources; Volt Alphanumeric Publications Systems; Volt Directory Data; Telecommunications Voltelcon; Volt Energy Systems; Volt Temporary Services; Autologic Inc; Autologic SA (Switzerland); Volt-Autologic Pty Ltd (Australia); Volt-Autologic SA (France); Autologic GmbH (Germany); Volt-Autologic Ltd (UK); Volt-Autologic Ltd (Israel); Volt-Autologic SpA (Italy); Volt-Autologic SA (Spain); Volt-Autologic AB (Sweden); Volt-Autologic SA Ltd (Uruguay)
Principal Bank: Manufacturers Hanover Trust Co
Financial Information:

	$'000
Revenues	410,000

No of Employees: 13,400

VOPLEX CORPORATION

1100 Pittsford-Victor Road, Pittsford, NY 14534
Tel: (716) 248-5350

Chairman: Raymond A Lander Jr (and Chief Executive Officer)
President: Joseph C Tolley (and Chief Operating Officer)
Senior Executive Officers: Donald C Greenhouse (Financial VP and Treasurer), Donald B Smart (Sales VP), John D Harman (Secretary)

PRINCIPAL ACTIVITIES: Manufacture of plastic products for the automotive industry and other industrial applications
Principal Subsidiaries/Divisions: Lapeer Fabricators Division; Vassar Fiber Coating and Metallizing Division; Allerton Chemical Division
Financial Information:

	$'000
Sales revenues	79,533

Principal Shareholders: Raymond A Lander Jr
No of Employees: 1,372

VORNADO INC

174 Passaic Street, Garfield, NJ 07026
Tel: (201) 773-4000

Chairman: Frederick Zissu
Senior Executive Officers: Steven Roth (Chairman of Executive Committee), Lawrence Schaen (Executive VP), Joseph Macnow (VP and Chief Financial Officer), Richard Rowan (VP Real Estate)

PRINCIPAL ACTIVITIES: Manufacture and wholesale of apparel for the family; leasing of property
Principal Bankers: National Westminster Bank
Financial Information:

	$'000
Sales revenues	68,000

No of Employees: 100

VSI CORPORATION

600 N Rosemead Blvd, Pasadena, CA 91107
Tel: (213) 681-4415

President: Frank Marra
Senior Executive Officers: R H Kauffman (Executive VP), G R Bartolme (Senior VP), R L Woodworth (VP Industrial and Building Products Division), Jerry R Lirette (VP Tooling for Plastics), Thomas F Spoehr (Aerospace Division), Raymond S O'Connor (VP), E A Bettin (VP and Corporate Controller), John J Theiss (VP Access Control Division), H D Weeks (VP Fluid Energy Division)

PRINCIPAL ACTIVITIES: Manufacture of equipment for the plastics industry, fasteners for the aerospace industry and hardware
Parent Company: Fairchild Industries Inc, Germantown, MD
Principal Bank: Security Pacific National Bank
Financial Information:

	$'000
Sales revenues	390,000

No of Employees: 5,000

VULCAN CHEMICALS
PO Box 7689, Birmingham, AL 35253
Tel: (205) 877-3484

President: M J Ferris
Senior Executive Officers: J A Heilala (VP Manufacturing), G L Fish (VP Research and Engineering), B L Crone (VP Marketing), R D Shilling (VP Commercial Development)

PRINCIPAL ACTIVITIES: The Chemicals Division is the world's second largest producer of the chlorinated solvents it manufactures, and is a major producer of chlorine and liquid caustic soda, two of the most important industrial chemicals. It also produces a number of other basic industrial chemicals. The division's chemicals are used in a variety of products and systems that are essential to the standard of living of advanced industrial societies. The division and its predecessor companies have been serving the chloralkali and chlorosolvent markets for some 35 years
Trade Names: GLAZD(R) PENTA, SOLVENT III(R), TEXSAN(R)
Parent Company: Vulcan Materials Company, Birmingham, AL
Financial Information:

	$'000
Sales revenues	250,000

No of Employees: 1,200

VULCAN HART CORPORATION
PO Box 696, Louisville, KY 40201
Tel: (502) 778-2791
Telex: WUT 204181 vulihart lul

President: Gordon F Oates
Senior Executive Officers: W J Vandrick (VP Sales), M T Dore (VP and Treasurer)

PRINCIPAL ACTIVITIES: Manufacture of appliances and equipment for the food industry
Principal Bank: The Equitable Trust Company
Financial Information:

	$'000
Sales revenues	70,000

Principal Shareholders: Dart & Kraft Inc
No of Employees: 900

VULCAN INC
PO Box 70, Latrobe, PA 15650
Tel: (412) 537-3356

Chairman: Gerald N Potts (and President and Chief Executive Officer)
Senior Executive Officers: Chris F Moersch Jr (VP), Edward G Nemanic (Secretary and Treasurer)

PRINCIPAL ACTIVITIES: Manufacture of molds and accessories for the cast iron industry; manufacture of cast iron products, tools and lifting equipment
Parent Company: Ampco-Pittsburgh Corp, Pittsburgh, PA
Principal Bank: Mellon Bank
Financial Information:

	$'000
Sales revenues	85,000

No of Employees: 1,500

VULCAN MATERIALS CO
PO Box 7497, Birmingham, AL 35253
Tel: (205) 877-3000
Telex: 59709 VULCANMATL-BHM

Chairman: W Houston Blount
President: Herbert A Sklenar (and Chief Executive Officer)
Senior Executive Officers: Lee K Bailey (Executive VP-Construction Materials), William J Grayson Jr (Executive VP-Corporate Development), Peter J Clemens III (Senior VP-Finance), R Morrieson Lord (Senior VP-Human Resources), James O Screven (Senior VP and General Counsel), W Joe Shaw (Senior VP), John D Dwyer (VP, Technical and Marketing Services, Construction Materials), Willis W Lake (VP, Industrial Relations), Robert W Lee (VP, Compensation and Risk Management), William F Denson III (Secretary and General Attorney), C Kent Garner (Treasurer), William L Glusac (Controller)

PRINCIPAL ACTIVITIES: Vulcan is a multi-industry company with strong positions in three basic businesses. It is the nation's foremost producer of construction aggregates; a leading chemicals manufacturer, producing a diversified line of chlorinated solvents and other industrial chemicals; and a principal producer of secondary aluminum, detinned steel scrap and tin chemicals. Additionaly, Vulcan conducts domestic oil and gas exploration and production operations through its wholly owned subsidiary, Southport Exploration, Inc
Principal Subsidiaries: Southport Exploration, Inc
Principal Bank: AmSouth Bank NA
Financial Information:

	$'000
Sales revenues	958,000

No of Employees: 5,900

W A KRUEGER CO
See KRUEGER, W A, CO

W BELL & CO INC
See BELL, W, & CO INC

W F HALL PRINTING CO
See HALL, W F, PRINTING CO

W H BRADY CO
See BRADY, W H, CO

W M BARR CO INC
See BARR, W M, CO INC

W R BERKLEY CORPORATION
See BERKLEY, W R, CORPORATION

W R GRACE & CO
See GRACE, W R, & CO

W S BADCOCK CORPORATION
See BADCOCK, W S, CORPORATION

W S TYLER, INC
See TYLER, W S, , INC

W W GRAINGER INC
See GRAINGER, W W, INC

W W WILLIAMS COMPANY
See WILLIAMS, W W, COMPANY

WABASH ALLOYS INC
US 24 West, Wabash, IN 46993
Tel: (219) 563-7461

President: J R Hahn
Senior Executive Officers: George Veverka (VP Sales), Ralph Bruner (VP Technical Sales), Howard Sinclair (VP Finance), John Minniear (Comptroller)

PRINCIPAL ACTIVITIES: Secondary smelting and refining of aluminum
Parent Company: Ogden Corp, New York, NY
Principal Bank: Chase Manhattan Bank
Financial Information:

	$'000
Sales revenues	150,000

No of Employees: 425

WABASH RELAY & ELECTRONICS DIVISION

810 N Cass Street, Wabash, IN 46992
Tel: (219) 563-3111

Senior Executive Officers: J A Cook (Group VP)

PRINCIPAL ACTIVITIES: Manufacture of electrical and electronic components
Parent Company: Kearney-National Inc
Principal Bank: Continental Illinois National Bank and Trust Company of Chicago
Financial Information:

	$'000
Sales revenues	110,000

No of Employees: 1,850

WACKENHUT CORPORATION

1500 San Remo Ave, Coral Gables, FL 33146
Tel: (305) 666-5656

Chairman: George R Wackenhut (and Chief Executive Officer)
President: Richard R Wackenhut (and Chief Operating Officer)
Senior Executive Officers: Frederick T Thornburg (Executive VP), Alan Bernstein (Senior VP Domestic Operations, Calvin G Harris (Senior VP and Treasurer), J C Bachmann (VP Business Development Administration), Jess J Boytell (VP Southern Region), A Robert Frye (VP Proposal Development), James E Hastings (VP and General Counsel), William E Jackson (VP Western Region), Kenneth C Ketterer (VP Human Resources), Murray Levine (VP South Florida Region), Norbert J Novotny (VP National and International Accounts), James P Rowan (VP Administration), Michael J Simpson (VP Management Information Servics and Cost Control), George A Zeiss (VP Client Relations)

PRINCIPAL ACTIVITIES: Security services
Principal Bank: Southeast Bank
Financial Information:

	$'000
Sales revenues	300,900

No of Employees: 24,000

WADSWORTH, INC

10 Davis Drive, Belmont, CA 94002
Tel: (415) 595-2350
Telex: WUT 348383 wadsworth blmt

President: Jack N Thornton (and Chief Executive Officer)
Senior Executive Officers: Richard L Greenberg (Executive VP and Chief Operating Officer), Wayne A Barcomb (VP and Group Executive), William C Smith (VP Finance and Chief Financial Officer), Robert W Sass (VP Administration)

PRINCIPAL ACTIVITIES: Academic publishing; reference books
Parent Company: International Thomson Organisation Ltd
Principal Bank: Bank of America
Financial Information:

	$'000
Sales revenues	76,000

No of Employees: 700

WAGNER CASTINGS CO

1275 E Sangamon Street, Decatur, IL 62525
Tel: (217) 428-7791

Chairman: Ross D Lake (and President); Vice Chairman: John A Wagner Jr
Senior Executive Officers: Philip R Wiant (VP Marketing), John R Koucky (VP Engineering), Donald C Lawson (VP Manufacturing), Wm A Huber (VP and Treasurer)

PRINCIPAL ACTIVITIES: Production of metal castings
Principal Bank: Harris Trust & Savings Bank
Financial Information:

	$'000
Sales revenues	50,000

No of Employees: 1,250

WAGNER SPRAY TECH CORPORATION

1770 Fernbrook Lane, Minneapolis, MN 55441
Tel: (612) 559-7000
Telex: 29-0186
Facsimile: (612) 553-7288

President: Max Ruff
Senior Executive Officers: Peter E Bader (Exexutive VP), John E Somers (VP Finance, Secretary, Treasurer), Ken R Ester (VP Manufacturing), Richard C Swenson (VP Human Resources and Customer Relations)

PRINCIPAL ACTIVITIES: Manufacture of airless paint sprayers for consumer, commercial and industrial use, as well as power tools, hand tools and accessories connected with the painting industry
Trade Names: Wagner Power Painters and Power Painter Systems, Wagner Power Roller, Wagner Power Stripper, Wagner Power Scraper, Wagner Mask-it tape applicator, Wagner Glass Mask, Wagner Added Touches (touch-up and repair kits), Wagner Pro Series (Power Roller, Paint Sprayers), Wagner Gold Power, Wagner Line Crew
Parent Company: Wagner International AG, Switzerland
Principal Banks: Union Bank of Switzerland; Deutsche Bank AG; Swiss Bank Corporation
Financial Information:

	$'000
Sales revenues	130,000

No of Employees: 700

WAIALUA SUGAR CO, INC

Waialua, Oahi, HI 96791
Tel: (808) 637-4520

Chairman: Michael M Rotolo
President: John Hewetson
Senior Executive Officers: Geo B Fraser (VP Production), Jaime Rovelo (VP and Treasurer), Patrick J Doherty (VP)

PRINCIPAL ACTIVITIES: Sugar refining
Parent Company: Castle & Cook Inc
Principal Bank: Bank of Hawaii
Financial Information:

	$'000
Sales revenues	50,000

No of Employees: 600

WAINOCO OIL CORPORATION

1200 Smith Street, Suite 1500, Houston, TX 77002
Tel: (713) 658 9900

President: John B Ashmun
Senior Executive Officers: James R Gibbs (Executive VP), George E Aldrich (VP and Controller), Denis F Bacon (VP Operations), Edward D Cole (VP Production), Darcy D Schindewolf (VP, Secretary and Treasurer)

PRINCIPAL ACTIVITIES: Exploration and production of oil and gas
Principal Subsidiaries: Wainoco Australia Ltd; Wainoco Indonesia Inc; Wainoco International Inc; Wainoco Oil and Gas Co; Wainoco Resources Inc
Principal Bank: First City National Bank
Financial Information:

	$'000
Sales revenues	43,000

No of Employees: 135

WALBAR, INC
Peabody Industrial Center, PO Box 3369, Peabody, MA 01960
Tel: (617) 532-2700
Telex: TWX 710 3470287 walbar peab

Chairman: David I Margolis
President: Francis Novak (and Chief Executive Officer)
Senior Executive Officers: Andrew J Cox (VP Human Resources), Salvatore J Cozzolino (VP and Treasurer), Anthony J DiBuono (VP and Secretary), Jack M Fischer (VP and Chief Financial Officer), Joseph D Lisa (VP and Controller)

PRINCIPAL ACTIVITIES: Production of aircraft engine components
Parent Company: Colt Industries Inc
Principal Subsidiaries: Walbar Metals Inc; Ellis Tool and Die Co Inc; Walbar of Arizona Inc; Walbar of Canada Inc; Turbo Tool Division
Principal Bank: First National Bank of Boston
Financial Information:

	$'000
Sales revenues	80,000

No of Employees: 1,250

WALBRO CORPORATION
6242 Garfield Street, Cass City, MI 48726
Tel: (517) 872-2131
Telex: TWX 810 2655199 walbro cacy

Chairman: W E Walpole
President: Lambert E Althaver (and Chief Executive Officer)
Senior Executive Officers: R H Walpole (Executive VP), Louis Horner (VP Carburetor Group), Clarke Searl (VP Auto Products), J L Ware (Custom Manufacturing)

PRINCIPAL ACTIVITIES: Manufacture of carburetors and other automotive components; pumps; metal castings
Principal Bank: Citizens Bank
Financial Information:

	$'000
Sales revenues	73,000

No of Employees: 1,320

WALCO NATIONAL CORPORATION
743 Fifth Avenue, New York, NY 10022
Tel: (212) 688-4685

Chairman: Thomas G Wyman (and Chairman Executive Committee)
President: Frederic Ouweleen
Senior Executive Officers: James Lynam (VP Finance), Timothy E Wyman (VP Corporate Planning)

PRINCIPAL ACTIVITIES: Manufacture of industrial engines; plastic products; lifts and conveyors; industrial equipment for the timber and machine tool industries; fabricated steel products
Principal Subsidiaries: Federal Forge Inc; Carthage Machine Co Inc; General Industries Co; Husky Hydraulics Inc; Transue & Williams; Walco National Realty Co
Principal Bank: Mellon Bank
Financial Information:

	$'000
Sales revenues	165,945

No of Employees: 2,360

WALDBAUM, INC
Hemlock & Boulevard, Central Islip, NY 11722
Tel: (516) 248-5600

President: Ira Waldbaum
Senior Executive Officers: Aaron Malinsky (Executive VP), Ernest Brown (VP Sales), Erwin Hartman (VP Appetizing and Delicatessen), Jack Kaufman (VP Finance), Melvin Levy (VP Industrial Relations), Martin Krichmar (VP Produce), Stanley Lang (VP Store Operations), Dominic Piccininni (VP Safety and Claims), Sidney Zuckerman (VP Advertising), Robert Perfido (VP Warehousing), Louis Sollicito (VP Meat), Martin Waldbaum (VP Non Foods), Arthur Waldbaum (VP Frozen Foods)

PRINCIPAL ACTIVITIES: Operation of supermarket chain
Principal Bank: Chemical Bank
Financial Information:

	Dec 31 1985	Dec 31 1986
	$'000	$'000
Sales revenues	1,764,040	1,800,000
Net income	17,110	12,500
Earnings per share	$3.08	$2.10
Shareholders equity	145,584	155,000

No of Employees: 11,000

WALGREEN CO
200 Wilmot Road, Deerfield, IL 60015
Tel: (312) 940-2500
Telex: TWX 910 6922151 walgreens dfld

Chairman: Charles R Walgreen III (and Chief Executive Officer)
President: F F Canning (and Chief Operating Officer)
Senior Executive Officers: Charles D Hunter (Executive VP), John R Brown (Senior VP Distribution and Manufacturing), L Daniel Jorndt (Senior VP and Treasurer), Glenn S Kraiss (Senior VP Drug Store Operations), Vernon A Brunner (Senior VP Marketing), L A Crotty (VP Administration), J A Rubino (VP Human Resources), John B Seastone (VP Food Services), William Shiel (VP Facilities Development), Wm O Shank (VP Legal)

PRINCIPAL ACTIVITIES: Operation of drug stores
Principal Bank: First National Bank of Chicago
Financial Information:

	Aug 31 1986
	$'000
Sales revenues	3,660,553
Net income	103,137
Earnings per share	$1.67
Shareholders equity	553,611

No of Employees: 40,000

WALKER, B B, COMPANY
East Dixie Drive, PO Drawer 1167, Asheboro, NC 27203
Tel: (919) 625 1380

Chairman: M R Williams
President: Kent T Anderson (and Chief Operating Officer)
Senior Executive Officers: Robert L Donnell Jr (Executive VP), C L Richardson (Executive VP), Lawrence M Shaw (Executive VP), Thomas W White (Executive VP), James H Finison Jr (VP, Controller and Chief Accounting Officer), James P McDermott (VP, Legal Counsel and Secretary), Edna Mae Phillips (VP Credit), Dorothy L Walker (Treasurer)

PRINCIPAL ACTIVITIES: Manufacture of footwear
Principal Bank: First National Bank of Randolph County
Financial Information:

	$'000
Sales revenues	42,400

No of Employees: 800

WALKER TELECOMMUNICATIONS CORPORATION
200 Oser Avenue, Hauppauge, NY 11788
Tel: (516) 435 1100

Chairman: Burt Walker
President: Howard Laffler
Senior Executive Officers: M D Brozinsky (VP and Chief Operating Officer), Irwin R Eyerman (VP Finance and Treasurer), David Linker (VP), Barry J Pinkowitz (Secretary)

PRINCIPAL ACTIVITIES: Engineering and consultancy services to the data processing industry
Financial Information:

	$'000
Sales revenues	33,000

No of Employees: 85

WALL TO WALL SOUND & VIDEO INC
200 South Route 130, Cinnaminson, NJ 08077
Tel: (609) 786 8300

Chairman: Jerome Shulman (and President and Chief Executive Officer)
Senior Executive Officers: Bruce Bell (Senior VP), Stephen Bell (Senior VP), Gary Shulman (VP Music), Scott Shulman (VP Audio), L Swede (Secretary and Treasurer)

PRINCIPAL ACTIVITIES: Retail trade in TV and audio equipment
Principal Bank: Midlantic National Bank
Financial Information:

	$'000
Sales revenues	100,500

No of Employees: 1,400

WALLACE COMPUTER SERVICES INC
4600 Roosevelt Road, Hillside, IL 60162
Tel: (312) 626-2000
Telex: TWX 910 2344464 wallacecs hsid

Chairman: Theodore Dimitriou (and President and Chief Executive Officer)
Senior Executive Officers: John Hill (Senior VP), Gerald L Governile (Senior VP, Treasurer and Secretary), Anthony Grassi (VP Human Resources), James Parilli (VP)

PRINCIPAL ACTIVITIES: Data processing services and software; printing of business forms and continuous stationery, catalogs and price lists
Principal Subsidiaries: Visible Computer Supply Corporation
Principal Bank: First National Bank of Chicago
Financial Information:

	$'000
Sales revenues	305,000

No of Employees: 2,000

WAL-MART STORES, INC
702 S W Eighth Street, Bentonville, AR 72712
Tel: (501) 273-4000

Chairman: Sam M Walton (and Chief Executive Officer); Vice Chairmen: Jack Shewmaker (and Chief Financial Officer), S R Walton (and Secretary)
President: David D Glass (and Chief Operating Officer)
Senior Executive Officers: Paul R Carter (Executive VP Specialty Divisions), Donald G Soderquist (Executive VP Administration), A L Johnson (Executive VP Merchandise), Thomas Jefferson (Executive VP Store Operations), Bill Fields (Senior VP Distribution and Transport), Joseph P Hatfield (Senior VP General Merchandise, Home Seasonal), Harold E Johnson (Senior VP Div 1-B), Ronald L Loveless (Senior VP Sam's Wholesale Club Division), A L Miles (Senior VP Div 1-A), Dean L Sanders (Senior VP General Merchandise Hardlines), Thomas P Seay (Senior VP Real Estate and Construction), J L Walton (Senior VP), Colon Washburn (Senior VP Merchandise, Apparel)

PRINCIPAL ACTIVITIES: Operation of department stores
Financial Information:

	Dec 31 1985	Dec 31 1986
	$'000	$'000
Sales revenues	8,580,910	11,909,076
Net income	327,470	450,086
Earnings per share	$1.16	$1.59
Shareholders equity	1,277,660	1,690,493

No of Employees: 141,000

WALNUT GROVE PRODUCTS
Second & Linn, Atlantic, IA 50022
Tel: (712) 243-1030

Senior Executive Officers: R L Crom (General Manager), Ray Underwood (Director Marketing), Wayne Schope (Director Product Control), Bernard Elming (Director Business Administration and Control)

PRINCIPAL ACTIVITIES: Production of livestock and animal feeds
Parent Company: W R Grace & Co, New York, NY
Financial Information:

	$'000
Sales revenues	80,000

No of Employees: 750

WALT DISNEY PRODUCTIONS
See DISNEY, WALT, PRODUCTIONS

WALTER CARPETS
14528 E Bonelli Street, City of Industry, CA 91749
Tel: (213) 968-1464
Telex: WUT 670429 walter c coid

Senior Executive Officers: William Kaiser (VP Marketing), Jack Lickhalter (General Sales Manager), Richard Giguere (Operations Manager), Walt James (Credit Manager)

PRINCIPAL ACTIVITIES: Manufacture of carpets
Parent Company: West Point-Pepperell Inc
Principal Bank: Trust Company Bank
Financial Information:

	$'000
Sales revenues	100,000

No of Employees: 150

WALTER, JIM, CORPORATION
1500 North Dale Mabry, Tampa, FL 33607
Tel: (813) 871-4811
Telex: 52859 J W WALTER TPA

Chairman: James W Walter
President: Joe B Cordell (and Chief Executive Officer)
Senior Executive Officers: James O Alston (Vice Chairman), James W Kynes (Executive VP and Secretary), Kenneth J Matlock (Senior VP/Chief Financial Officer)

PRINCIPAL ACTIVITIES: Homebuilding and related financing; building materials production and development of natural resources, including coal, oil, gas, marble, granite, limestone and gypsum. Production of coke and industrial chemicals, distribution of quality printing papers, retail and wholesale jewelry sales, and insurance services
Principal Subsidiaries: Jim Walter Homes; The Celotex Corporation; United States Pipe and Foundry Company; The Georgia Marble Company; Jim Walter Resources Inc
Principal Bank: Citibank; Chase Manhattan; Manufacturers Hanover Trust
Financial Information:

	Aug 31 1985	Aug 31 1986
	$'000	$'000
Sales revenues	2,292,275	2,320,466
Net income	111,670	138,552
Earnings per share	$5.11	$4.64
Shareholders equity	906,321	1,132,869

No of Employees: 17,700

WALTER, JIM, RESOURCES, INC
3300 First Avenue N, Birmingham, AL 35202
Tel: (205) 254-7481

President: J B Cordell
Senior Executive Officers: W Carr (Senior Executive VP)

PRINCIPAL ACTIVITIES: Production of coal and related by-products
Parent Company: Jim Walter Corporation
Financial Information:

	$'000
Sales revenues	242,000

WALTER W MOYER COMPANY, INC
See MOYER, WALTER W, COMPANY, INC

WANG LABORATORIES INC
One Industrial Avenue, Lowell, MA 01851
Tel: (617) 459-5000
Telex: TWX 710 3436769 wanglll lowe

Chairman: An Wang (and President and Chief Executive Officer); Vice Chairman: Harry H Chou (and Treasurer and Chief Financial Officer)
Senior Executive Officers: Frederick A Wang (Executive VP and Treasurer), Eugene M Bullis (Senior VP), Dodge Chu (Senior VP Americas and Asia Pacific Operations), Raymond Cullen (Senior VP Customer Services Operation), Edward Devin (Senior VP Human Resources), Ian Diery (Senior VP European Operations), Robert L Doretti (Senior VP, US Operations), Edward Grayson (Senior VP and Secretary), Paul Guzzi (Senior VP Administration Services), Johannes Spanjaard (Senior VP and Controller, International), Horace Tsiang (Senior VP)

PRINCIPAL ACTIVITIES: Manufacture of electronic data processing equipment and peripherals
Principal Bank: The First National Bank of Boston
Financial Information:

	Jun 30 1986 $'000
Sales revenues	2,642,500
Net income	50,900
Earnings per share	$0.35
Shareholders equity	1,447,600

No of Employees: 31,060

WARNACO INC
350 Lafayette Street, Bridgeport, CT 06601
Tel: (203) 579-8272
Telex: WUT 852248 complete

Chairman: Andrew G Galef
President: Linda Wachner
Senior Executive Officers: Robert D Walter (Executive VP), Carol Leslie (VP Corporate Communications), Paul R Olson (VP and Chief Financial Officer), Gerard F Sullivan (VP Human Resources)

PRINCIPAL ACTIVITIES: Manufacture of underwear, shirts, sports clothes, knitted clothing and ties
Principal Subsidiaries: C F Hathaway Co; Warnaco Trucking Corp; White Stag Manufacturing Co; Warnaco Int'l Inc; Warnaco Men's Sportswear Inc; Warnaco Outlet Stores Inc; Warmana Ltd; Olga Co; Hirsh Weis Inc; Warnaco of Canada Ltd
Principal Bank: The First National Bank of Boston
Financial Information:

	Dec 31 1985 $'000	Dec 31 1986 $'000
Sales revenues	591,285	630,000

No of Employees: 10,500

WARNACO KNITWEAR DIVISION
5416 6th Avenue, Altoona, PA 16603
Tel: (814) 696-2011

President: Arthur H Warshaw
Senior Executive Officers: Larry S Bloom (President Thane Division), Daniel Kriegel (President Puritan Sportswear Division), Herbert S McMullen (President Spalding Division), John R Welch (Executive VP Operations), Robert J Pulkka (Executive VP Finance)

PRINCIPAL ACTIVITIES: Manufacture of knitted clothing including sweaters and sportswear
Parent Company: Warnaco Inc
Financial Information:

	$'000
Sales revenues	100,000

No of Employees: 1,500

WARNER BROS, INC
4000 Warner Blvd, Burbank, CA 91505
Tel: (213) 954-6000
Telex: ITT 4720389 warners bubk

Chairman: Bob Daly; Vice Chiarman: Frank Wells
President: Terry Semel (and Chief Operating Officer)
Senior Executive Officers: Bob Shapiro (Executive VP World Products), Myron Karlin (Executive VP Foreign Sales), Sandy Risenbeck (Executive VP), Mark Rosenberg (Senior VP), Stanley Belkin (VP and Assistant General Counsel), Mark Cantin (VP Production), L Fisher (VP Purchasing), Fred Gallo (VP Studio), Arthur Kananack (VP), Edward Morey (VP), Ralph Peterson (VP and Treasurer), Barry Reardon (VP), Edward Romano (VP), Diane Sokolow (VP, EC Production)

PRINCIPAL ACTIVITIES: Production and distribution of motion pictures and television programs; records and cassettes; music publishing
Parent Company: Warner Communications Inc, New York, NY
Financial Information:

	$'000
Sales revenues	410,000

No of Employees: 3,000

WARNER COMMUNICATIONS INC
75 Rockefeller Plaza, New York, NY 10019
Tel: (212) 484-8000
Telex: ITT 424602 wrco ui

Chairman: Steven J Ross (and Chief Executive Officer); Vice Chairman: Ted Ashley
Senior Executive Officers: Bert W Wasserman (Office of the President), Deane F Johnson (Office of the President), Martin D Payson (Executive VP), Edwin W Hamowy (Senior VP), Albert Sarnoff (Senior VP and Treasurer), Jason S Berman (VP Public Affairs), David Haas (VP and Controller), Geoffrey W Holmes (VP)

PRINCIPAL ACTIVITIES: Production of motion pictures, television programs, music, book and magazine publishing, entertainment services
Principal Subsidiaries: (100% owned unless stated): Warner Bros; Warner Bros Television; Warner Home Video; Licensing Co of America; Warner Bros Records; Atlantic Records; Elektra/Asylum/Nonesuch Records; WEA Corpn; WEA International; WEA Manufacturing; Warner Special Products; Warner Bros Music; Warner Books; DC Comics; Mad Magazine; Warner Publisher Services; Warner Audio Publishing; Warner Amex Cable Communications (50%); MTV Networks Inc (33%); Showtime/The Movie Channel Inc (40.5%); BHC Inc (42.5%)
Principal Bank: Manufacturers Hanover Trust Co
Financial Information:

	Dec 31 1985 $'000	Dec 31 1986 $'000
Sales revenues	2,234,890	2,848,324
Net income	195,305	185,795
Earnings per share	$1.43	$0.17
Shareholders equity	-	1,172,520

No of Employees: 11,660

WARNER ELECTRIC BRAKE & CLUTCH CO
449 Gardner Street, South Beloit, IL 61080
Tel: (815) 389-3771
Telex: TWX 910 3505873 warnerelectric

Chairman: William Keefer (and Chief Executive Officer)
President: Frank E Bauchiero (and Chief Operating Officer)
Senior Executive Officers: Jack Simpson (Executive VP Finance, Secretary and Chief Financial Officer), Wayne Filichowski (VP and General Manager Beloit Division), Rene Frachon (VP International Operations), H E Klinkenberg (VP and General Manager Beaver Precision), Rodney MacFarlane (VP and General Manager MCSD Division)

PRINCIPAL ACTIVITIES: Manufacture of industrial control equipment; motor vehicle components; industrial fasteners
Parent Company: Dana Corporation
Principal Bank: Harris Trust and Savings Bank
Financial Information:

	$'000
Sales revenues	165,000

No of Employees: 1,800

WARNER-LAMBERT COMPANY
201 Tabor Road, Morris Plains, NY 07950
Tel: (201) 540-2000
Telex: WUT 136376 warnlam mops

Chairman: Joseph D Williams (and Chief Executive Officer), Vice Chairman: George Hromadko (and Chief Financial Officer)
President: Melvin R Goodes (and Chief Operating Officer)
Senior Executive Officers: Donald E O'Neill (Executive VP), Robert J Dircks (Senior VP and Chief Financial Officer), James E Wavle Jr (Senior VP, President Parke Davis Group), John C Carroll (VP, President American Chicle Group), Gustavo J Figueirido (VP, President Canada, Latin-America Group), Raymond M Fino (VP Human Resources), William F Gilroy (VP and Controller), Jay M Gwynne (VP Consumer Health Products Group), Elias K Hebeka (VP Technical Operations), Gregory L Johnson (VP and General Counsel), Raymond P LeFebvre (VP, President Europe, Middle East, Africa Group), Edward Marlowe (VP, President ConsProd, Research and Development Division), Jerry A Weisbach (VP, President Pharmaceutical Research Division), Fred G Weiss (VP Corporate Planning and Development), Stephen A Wilgar (VP, President Asia, Australia Group), Ronald E Zier (VP Public Affairs)

PRINCIPAL ACTIVITIES: Production of pharmaceutical products and medical supplies; health care products; toiletries
Principal Bank: Irving Trust Co
Financial Information:

	Dec 31 1985	Dec 31 1986
	$'000	$'000
Sales revenues	3,200,070	3,102,918
Net income (loss)	(315,596)	309,484
Earnings per share	-	$4.18
Shareholders equity	891,192	907,322

No of Employees: 45,000

WARREN COMMUNICATIONS
Newtown Road, Littleton, MA 01460
Tel: (617) 486-9551
Telex: TWX 710 3470650 warren lttn

President: J J Beville
Senior Executive Officers: E Rhyne (VP Engineering), A C Restaino (Controller and Financial Officer), Vic Fasino (General Manager), James Hunt (Manufacturing Director), Ken Cameron (Director Employee Relations), W J Vandertulip (Director Marketing)

PRINCIPAL ACTIVITIES: Manufacture of telecommunications equipment and components
Parent Company: General Signal Corporation
Principal Bank: Marine Midland Bank
Financial Information:

	$'000
Sales revenues	1,000,000

No of Employees: 25,000

WARREN GORHAM & LAMONT, INC
210 South Street, Boston, MA 02111
Tel: (800) 225-2363

Chairman: Rae Smith
President: Joseph M Palazzolo (and Chief Executive Officer)
Senior Executive Officers: Robert Becker (VP Finance), John Petrino (VP Operations)

PRINCIPAL ACTIVITIES: Publishing of reference books
Parent Company: Thompson Organization
Principal Bank: First National Bank of Boston
Financial Information:

	$'000
Sales revenues	60,000

No of Employees: 290

WASHINGTON ENERGY COMPANY
815 Mercer Street, Seattle, WA 98109
Tel: (206) 622 6767

Chairman: James A Thorpe (and Chief Executive Officer)
President: Robert R Golliver (and Chief Operating Officer)
Senior Executive Officers: Charles H Petek (Senior VP Finance), Robert J Tomlinson (Senior VP and Secretary), H B Simpson (VP and Treasurer)

PRINCIPAL ACTIVITIES: Holding company with interests in natural gas distribution
Principal Subsidiaries: Thermal Energy Inc; Washington Natural Gas Co
Principal Bank: Seattle First National Bank
Financial Information:

	$'000
Sales revenues	411,410

No of Employees: 1,000

WASHINGTON FEDERAL SAVINGS AND LOAN ASSOCIATION
425 Pike Street, Seattle, WA 98101
Tel: (206) 624 7930

Chairman: Elliot K Knutson (and President and Chief Executive Officer)
Senior Executive Officers: W Alden Harris (Executive VP), Guy C Pinkerton (Executive VP and Treasurer), Charles R Richmond (Executive VP and Secretary), Jerry L Molitor (Senior VP), Douglas A Rowell (Senior VP and Divisional Manager), William A Cassels (VP Data Processing), William P Clements (VP Loan Services), Robert E Hawkins (VP Marketing, Communications and Investor Relations), Charles W Hoag (VP Operations)

PRINCIPAL ACTIVITIES: Financial services including savings and loans
Principal Subsidiaries: First Appraisal; First Insurance Agency Inc; Washington Services Inc
Principal Bank: Seattle First National Bank

No of Employees: 200

WASHINGTON GAS LIGHT COMPANY
1100 H Street NW, Washington, DC 20080
Tel: (703) 750 4440

Chairman: Donald J Heim (and President and Chief Executive Officer)
Senior Executive Officers: Jeremiah K Hughitt (Executive VP and VP Planning), Patrick J Maher (Executive VP and Chief Financial Officer), J L Blincoe (VP Consumer Services and Public Affairs), Lewis Carroll (VP and General Counsel),

James W Freeman (VP Research and Marketing), Reginald G Fuller (VP Corporate Planning), Frank J Hollewa (VP), Roy J Kahn (VP Human Resources), Edmund W Smallwood (VP Rates and Regulatory Affairs), Andrew Tarapchak (VP Distribution), Kenneth H Tracy (VP Community Affairs), Herbert L Munday (Treasurer), Douglas V Pope (Secretary)

PRINCIPAL ACTIVITIES: Distribution of natural gas
Principal Subsidiaries: Brandywood Estates Inc; Washington Gas Approved Services; Crab Run Gas Co; Davenport Insulation Inc; Cellin Manufacturing Inc; Universal Insulation Inc; Frederick Gas Company; Hampshire Gas Co; Rock Creek Properties Inc; Shenandoah Gas Co
Principal Bank: Riggs National Bank
Financial Information:

	$'000
Sales revenues	720,000

No of Employees: 3,285

WASHINGTON HOMES INC

Chandler Center, PO Box 1006, Waldorf, MD 20601
Tel: (301) 843 8900

Chairman: William J Harnett (and Chief Executive Officer)
President: Lawrence M Breneman (and Chief Operating Officer)
Senior Executive Officers: John F Motzer (Executive VP), Sherrie L Kubala (Secretary)

PRINCIPAL ACTIVITIES: House construction
Principal Bank: Suburban Bank
Financial Information:

	$'000
Sales revenues	61,500

No of Employees: 170

WASHINGTON MUTUAL SAVINGS BANK

1101 2nd Ave, Seattle, WA 98101
Tel: (206) 464-4400

Chairman: Louis H Pepper (and President and Chief Executive Officer)
Senior Executive Officers: Kerry K Killinger (Senior Executive VP), William A Longbrake (Senior Executive VP)

PRINCIPAL ACTIVITIES: Banking
Financial Information:

	Dec 31 1985	Dec 31 1986
	$'000	$'000
Revenues	442,590	526,402
Income before taxes	28,162	108,522
Net income	18,555	70,654
Dividends	664	2,671
Dividends per share	$0.07	$0.27
Earnings per share	$1.93	$7.11
Common stock	80,391	80,135
Retained income	134,263	202,174
Shareholders equity	214,654	282,309
Deposits	3,251,111	3,293,169
Total assets	4,238,080	5,392,597

WASHINGTON NATIONAL CORPORATION

1630 Chicago Avenue, Evanston, IL 60201
Tel: (312) 570-3200

Chairman: Stanley P Hutchinson (and President and Chief Executive Officer); Vice Chairman: G P Kendall Jr
President: T R Strubbe
Senior Executive Officers: George A Condos (Executive VP and Chief Financial Officer), Thomas Pontarelli (Senior VP, Secretary and General Counsel), John M Watts (Senior VP Marketing), Brett H Bowen (VP Auditing), Herman G Schiller (VP and Controller)

PRINCIPAL ACTIVITIES: Insurance services including life and health insurance

Principal Bankers: Continental Illinois National Bank & Trust Co of Chicago
Financial Information:

	$'000
Revenues	762,000

No of Employees: 5,600

WASHINGTON POST COMPANY (THE)

1150 15th Street NW, Washington, DC 20071
Tel: (202) 223-6000
Telex: WUT 89545 washpost wsh a

Chairman: Katharine Graham (and Chief Executive Officer)
President: Richard D Simmons (and Chief Operating Officer)
Senior Executive Officers: Joel Chaseman (VP, President, Post-Newsweek Stations), Alan Spoon (VP-Finance), Christopher M Little (VP, President, Newsweek), Alan R Finberg (VP, General Counsel and Secretary), Ross F Hamachek (VP-Planning and Development), Beverly R Keil (VP-Human Resources), Gordon C King Jr (VP), Guyon Knight (VP-Corporate Communications), Edward N Van Gombos (VP-Information Systems), Howard E Wall (VP, President, Post-Newsweek Cable), Martin Cohen (VP)

PRINCIPAL ACTIVITIES: Publishing of newspapers and magazines; television broadcasting and cable activities
Principal Subsidiaries: Newsweek Inc; Newsweek Services Inc; The Daily Herald Co; Newsprint Inc; Post-Newsweek Stations Inc; Post-Newsweek Stations Connecticut Inc; Post-Newsweek Stations Florida Inc; Post-Newsweek Stations Michigan Inc; Post-Newsweek Cable; Robinson Terminal Warehouse Corp; Legi-Slate Inc; Stanley H Kaplan Educational Centers. Affiliates: Los Angeles Times-Washington Post News Service, Inc (50%); Bowater Mersey Paper Company Limited (49%); Bear Island Paper Company (33.33%); Bear Island Timberland Company (33.33%); International Herald Tribune, SA (33.33%); Cowles Media Company (20%)
Financial Information:

	Dec 31 1985	Dec 31 1986
	$'000	$'000
Operating revenues	1,078,650	1,215,064
Income before taxes	221,434	204,623
Net income	114,261	100,173
Dividends	12,881	14,365
Dividends per share	$0.96	$1.12
Earnings per share	$8.66	$7.80
Common stock class A	2,199	2,109
Common stock class B	17,801	17,891
Retained income	549,909	635,717
Shareholders equity	885,079	1,145,227

No of Employees: 6,300

WASHINGTON SCIENTIFIC INDUSTRIES

2605 W Wayzata Blvd, Long Lake, MN 55356
Tel: (612) 473 1271

Chairman: Stewart Pfannstiehl
President: Clifford W Dinsmore (and Chief Executive Officer)
Senior Executive Officers: Terry J Blount (VP Human Resources), B E Kinney (VP and Treasurer), W J Lucke (VP), Gerald E Magnuson (Secretary)

PRINCIPAL ACTIVITIES: Precision engineering; machined metal components for the aerospace and computer industries; transmission products, gear boxes and hydraulic motors for agricultural and industrial use
Principal Subsidiaries: K Y Rogers Inc
Principal Bank: Northwestern National Bank
Financial Information:

	$'000
Sales revenues	34,930

No of Employees: 500

WASHINGTON WATER POWER CO

E 1411 Mission Avenue, Spokane, WA 99202
Tel: (509) 489-0500

Chairman: Paul A Redmond (and President and Chief Executive Officer)
Senior Executive Officers: James R Harvey (Executive VP), Donald L Olson (Senior VP Resources), W L Bryan (VP Power Supply), D A Damiano (VP Engineering), J E Eliassen (VP Finance and Chief Financial Officer), G G Ely (VP Marketing), Robert D Fukai (VP Operations), E J Leary (VP and Secretary), R T McLendon (VP Gas Supply), J R Piedmont (VP Public Relations and Public Affairs), O I Quarta (VP Administration)

PRINCIPAL ACTIVITIES: Electricity supply
Principal Bankers: Seattle First National Bank
Financial Information:

	$'000
Sales revenues	390,000

No of Employees: 1,400

WASTE MANAGEMENT, INC

3003 Butterfield Road, Oak Brook, IL 60521
Tel: (312) 654-8800
Telex: RCA 210099 wmob ur

Chairman: Dean L Buntrock (and Chief Executive Officer); Vice Chairman: Jerry Dempsey
President: Phillip B Rooney (and Chief Operating Officer)
Senior Executive Officers: Donald F Flynn (Senior VP and Chief Financial Officer), Harold Gershowitz (Senior VP), J Steven Bergerson (VP and General Counsel), David C Coleman (VP Labor Relations), James G DeBoer (VP), Jerome D Girsch (VP), Peter H Huizenga (VP and Secretary), William P Hulligan (VP), Francis B Moore (VP Government Affairs), R A Paul (VP Administration), Peter Vardy (VP Environmental Management), Fred J Weinert (VP)

PRINCIPAL ACTIVITIES: Collection and processing of waste products, refuse and radioactive waste
Principal Bank: Harris Trust & Savings Bank
Financial Information:

	Dec 31 1985	Dec 31 1986
	$'000	$'000
Sales revenues	1,625,428	2,017,775
Net income	171,550	370,930
Earnings per share	$1.72	$1.46
Shareholders equity	1,137,200	1,580,264

No of Employees: 18,800

WATERS ASSOCIATES, INC

34 Maple Street, Milford, MA 01757
Tel: (617) 478-2000
Telex: WUT 948413 waters milf a

Chairman: Dee d'Arbeloff
President: Gary Frashier (and Chief Executive Officer)
Senior Executive Officers: Tom Feller (Senior VP Operations), William Shippey (Senior VP), Steve Peltzman (VP Marketing), John Nelson (VP Research and Development), Carl Rausch (VP Process Division), Brian McGuinn (VP International), Ernie Godshalk (VP Finance), Ted Hickey VP Human Resources), George Grippo (VP Chemical Products Division), E J Jones (VP International), Robert Limpert (VP World Wide Services)

PRINCIPAL ACTIVITIES: Manufacture of liquid chromatography equipment, laboratory equipment and chemicals
Parent Company: Millipore Corporation
Principal Bank: State Street Bank and Trust Company
Financial Information:

	$'000
Sales revenues	100,000

No of Employees: 1,500

WATKINS-JOHNSON CO

3333 Hillview Avenue, Palo Alto, CA 94304
Tel: (415) 493-4141
Telex: WUT 348415 wi pla

Chairman: Dr Dean A Watkins
President: Dr H Richard Johnson (and Chief Executive Officer)
Senior Executive Officers: Dr William E Kunz (VP Systems Group), Dr W Keith Kennedy, Jr (VP), Bernard Rosen (VP), Keith D Gilbert (VP, Devices Group), Robert C Lowe (VP), Ronald D Lessack (VP), Barry R Hoglund (VP), Paul Y Lin (VP), Bruce G Bleecker (VP), Kenneth W Bach (VP), Peter S Pao (VP), C Louise Beer (Secretary), H Edward Beckmeyer (Treasurer), Carl L Avelar (Controller)

PRINCIPAL ACTIVITIES: Watkins-Johnson Company is a technologically oriented company engaged primarily in the design, development, manufacture, sale and service of advanced electronic systems, electron devices and related equipment for military, industrial and space applications. The Company's products perform reconnaissance, surveillance, communications, telemetry, semiconductor production, frequency measurement and testing functions. They are used in strategic and tactical military systems, aboard guided missiles and spacecraft and in a wide range of government and commercial operations requiring automatic test, heat processing and frequency measurement equipment
Principal Subsidiaries: Watkins-Johnson International; Watkins-Johnson Italiana SpA; Watkins-Johnson Limited; Watkins-Johnson Associates; Watkins-Johnson FSC. Groups: Systems Group; Devices Group
Principal Bank: Bank of America
Financial Information:

	Dec 31 1985	Dec 31 1986
	$'000	$'000
Sales revenues	232,587	255,382
Income before taxes	30,567	29,981
Net income	18,437	17,241
Dividends	3,406	3,500
Dividends per share	$0.36	$0.40
Earnings per share	$1.94	$1.97
Common stock	7,935	7,263
Retained income	97,933	95,294
Shareholders equity	105,868	102,557

No of Employees: 3,150

WATTS REGULATOR CO

10 Embankment Street, Lawrence, MA 01842
Tel: (617) 688-1811
Telex: WUT 855820 wattsreg ud

Chairman: Timothy P Horne (and President and Treasurer)
Senior Executive Officers: Charles W Gregg (Executive VP), Robert J Tesar (Senior VP Marketing), Frederic B Horne (VP and General Manager), Kenneth J McAvoy (VP Finance)

PRINCIPAL ACTIVITIES: Production of valves, meters and control devices
Principal Bank: Bank of New England
Financial Information:

	$'000
Sales revenues	102,000

No of Employees: 1,000

WAUSAU PAPER MILLS CO

One Clark's Island, Wausau, WI 54417
Tel: (715) 845-5266

President: Richard L Radt (and Chief Executive Officer)
Senior Executive Officers: Daniel R Olvey (VP, Secretary and Treasurer), John W Peterman (VP Marketing), Thomas B Pitcher (VP and General Manager Brokaw Division), Larry A Baker (VP Administration), William L Goggins (VP Operations)

PRINCIPAL ACTIVITIES: Production of pulp and paper
Principal Bank: Harris Trust and Savings Bank

Financial Information:

	$'000
Sales revenues	205,500

No of Employees: 1,400

WAVERLY PRESS, INC

428 E Preston Street, Baltimore, MD 21202
Tel: (301) 528-4000
Telex: GRT 3746419 wilco bal

President: William M Passano Jr (and Chief Executive Officer)
Senior Executive Officers: G James Gallagher (VP Publishing), Samuel G Macfarlane (VP Finance), E M Passano Jr (VP and Secretary), Constance B Kiley (VP Printing), Robert W Grose (Executive VP and Chief Operating Officer)

PRINCIPAL ACTIVITIES: Publishing text books and journals; printing journals
Trade Names: Williams & Wilkins
Principal Bank: The First National Bank of Maryland
Financial Information:

	Dec 31 1985	Dec 31 1986
	$'000	$'000
Sales revenues	65,219	68,830
Income before taxes	3,910	5,645
Net income	2,592	3,501
Dividends	1,065	1,092
Dividends per share*	$0.29	$0.30
Earnings per share*	$0.71	$0.96
Common stock	4,876	7,304
Retained income	19,610	22,246
Shareholders equity	27,030	29,550

*adjusted for 3 for 2 stock split in September 1986

Principal Shareholders: William M and Edward M Passano; Trustees of Life Estate under will of E B Passano
No of Employees: 1,000

WAVETEK CORPORATION

9191 Towne Centre Drive, San Diego, CA 92122
Tel: (619) 450-9971

Chairman: John M Thornton; Vice Chairman: David M Goodman
President: John W Battin
Senior Executive Officers: Henry Reinecke Jr (Senior VP), Louis W Abbott (VP and Chief Operating Officer), Robert J Croshaw (VP International Sales), Lawrence C Dolan (VP)

PRINCIPAL ACTIVITIES: Manufacture of electronic industrial measuring and testing instruments and equipment
Principal Bank: Lloyds Bank California
Financial Information:

	$'000
Sales revenues	75,410

No of Employees: 1,050

WAXMAN INDUSTRIES INC

24460 Aurora Road, Bedford Heights, OH 44146
Tel: (216) 439 1830

Chairman: Melvin Waxman (and Chief Executive Officer)
President: Armond Waxman (and Chief Operating Officer and Treasurer)
Senior Executive Officers: Jerome C Jacques (VP Finance and Chief Financial Officer), John Peters (VP Operations), Florian Schmidhammer (VP and General Manager), Tom Walsh (VP and General Manager), Lawrence S Waxman (VP Sales), George N Aronoff (Secretary)

PRINCIPAL ACTIVITIES: Wholesale trade and mail order services in plumbing and heating supplies
Principal Subsidiaries: Barnett Brass and Copper Inc
Principal Bank: National City Bank

Financial Information:

	$'000
Sales revenues	97,800

No of Employees: 530

WD-40 COMPANY

1061 Cudahy Place, PO Box 80607, San Diego, CA 92138-9021
Tel: (619) 275-1400
Telex: 312466

President: John S Barry (and Treasurer)
Senior Executive Officers: Gerald C Schleif (Senior VP Marketing), Harlan F Harmsen (Secretary)

PRINCIPAL ACTIVITIES: Production of a petrochemical based lubricant product which is also a moisture displacer and rust preventative
Trade Names: WD-40
Principal Subsidiaries: WD-40 Products (Canada) Ltd; WD-40 Company Ltd (UK)
Principal Bank: Wells Fargo Bank
Financial Information:

	Aug 31 1985	Aug 31 1986
	$'000	$'000
Sales revenues	57,289	69,384
Income before taxes	19,338	22,653
Net income	9,354	11,570
Dividends	6,749	7,804
Dividends per share	$0.90	$1.04
Earnings per share	$1.25	$1.54
Common stock	1,714	1,750
Retained income	27,103	30,869
Shareholders equity	28,582	32,471

No of Employees: 56

WEAN UNITED INC

948 Fort Duquesne Blvd, Pittsburgh, PA 15222
Tel: (412) 456-5300
Telex: TRT 199122 wean united pgh

Chairman: R J Wean Jr (and Chief Executive Officer)
President: R J Wean III
Senior Executive Officers: Walter R Tarbert Jr (Executive VP), A P Cipriano (Senior VP), Walter W Stasik (Senior VP and Chief Financial Officer), Richard J Connors (VP Finance), John Upton Jr (VP)

PRINCIPAL ACTIVITIES: Manufacture of machinery for processing steel; manufacture of machinery for the timber, rubber and plastic industries
Principal Subsidiaries: Stedman Machine Co Inc; Berkeley-Davis Inc; Wean United Canada Ltd; Wean United of Australia (Pty) Ltd; Wean United (Africa) (Pty) Ltd; Wean Technology Corp; Wean United International Automated Production Systems Corp; Schaming Industries Inc
Principal Bank: Manufacturers Hanover Trust Co
Financial Information:

	$'000
Sales revenues	171,520

No of Employees: 1,500

WEATHERFORD INTERNATIONAL, INC

1360 Post Oak Blvd, Box 27608, Houston, TX 77227
Tel: (713) 439-9400
Telex: RCA 203337 a wii ur

Chairman: Robert K Moses Sr
President: Eugene L Butler (and Chief Executive Officer)
Senior Executive Officers: Kurt K Bushati (Executive VP and Chief Operating Officer), Fritz H Langer (Senior VP New Product Development), Robert E Haine (VP Corporate Relations), H Suzanne Thomas (Corporate Counsel and Secretary), George G Petty (VP, Finance, Controller and Treasurer)

PRINCIPAL ACTIVITIES: Manufacture of tools for the oil industry; operation of services for the oil industry
Principal Subsidiaries: Weatherford US Inc; Weatherford Oil Tool GmbH; Weatherford (UK) Ltd; Weatherford Oil Tool GesmbH; Weatherford Oil Tool Nederland BV; Weatherford Italiana SpA; Weatherford Norge Inc; Weatherford Oil Tool Middle East Limited; Weatherford (Saudi Arabia) Ltd; Weatherford Oil Tool (Pte) Ltd; Weatherford/Stabylia SA; Weatherford/Fabrumex SA de CV
Principal Bank: First City National Bank of Houston
Financial Information:

	$'000
Sales revenues	165,065

No of Employees: 2,100

WEAVER, VICTOR F, INC

403 S Custer Avenue, New Holland, PA 17557
Tel: (717) 354-4211
Telex: TWX 510 6720610 v weaver nh

Chairman: Victor F Weaver
President: Dale M Weaver
Senior Executive Officers: Benjamin L Burkholder (VP Production), Melvin S Mitchell (VP Marketing), R J Lafferty (VP Finance), Allon Lefever (VP Operations), Paul M Martin (VP Human Resources)

PRINCIPAL ACTIVITIES: Manufacture of convenience food products; processing of poultry
Principal Bank: Central Penn National Bank
Financial Information:

	$'000
Sales revenues	155,000

No of Employees: 2,200

WEBB CO (THE)

1999 Shepard Road, St Paul, MN 55116
Tel: (612) 690-7200

President: Robert J Sallman (and Chief Executive Officer)
Senior Executive Officers: Bert O Lund (Group VP), Richard A Reese (VP), John A Carlson (VP, Secretary/Treasurer), Borghild M Ruesink (Assistant Secretary)

PRINCIPAL ACTIVITIES: Printing and publishing. In printing the company concentrates on four markets: catalogs, magazines, circulars/inserts, and directories. The company specializes in long-run four-color printing, and has developed technological leadership in the high-growth markets of mail-order catalogs and magazines. In publishing the company-owned magazines serve millions of readers monthly in the areas of agriculture, recreation, and home improvement, and are among the leaders in their markets. The company is also recognized as one of the nation's largest custom publishers of magazines for sponsoring corporations and associations
Trade Names: The Farmer, Farm Industry News, BEEF, Dairy, National Hog Farmer, Seedsmen's Digest, Irrigation Age, MotorCycle, The Family Handyman
Principal Subsidiaries: Major Operating Groups:- Midwest Printing Company; Volkmuth Printers Inc; Publishing Group. The Company also has Advertising Sales Offices in Atlanta, Chicago, Los Angeles, New York and St Paul and Printing Sales Offices in Chicago, Minneapolis, New York, St Cloud (MI) and St Paul
Principal Bank: First Bank, St Paul
Financial Information:

	$'000
Sales revenues	177,340

No of Employees: 1,500

WEBB, DEL E, CORPORATION

3800 N Central Ave, Phoenix, AZ 85012
Tel: (602) 264-8011

Chairman: Robert K Swanson (and Chief Executive Officer)
President: Philip J Dion (and Chief Operating Officer)
Senior Executive Officers: William W Acton (VP Public Affairs), John A Bogert (VP Corp Internal Auditing), Ernest E East (VP, Secretary and General Counsel), Carl F Freeman (VP and Director of Security), Erik L Johnson (VP and Director of Risk Management), Anne L Mariucci (VP Planning and Development), Donald V Mickus (VP and Treasurer), Alan P O'Connor (VP Human Resources), David E Rau (VP Taxes), Robert L Rush (VP of Management Services), John A Spencer (VP and Controller)

PRINCIPAL ACTIVITIES: Management and development of retirement communities; real estate and leisure operations
Subsidiary Companies: Del E. Webb Communities, Inc; Del E. Webb Commercial Properties Corp; Del E. Webb Construction Services Co; Del Webb Hotels; Del Webb Recreational Properties, Inc
Principal Banks: Morgan Guaranty Trust Co; Valley National Bank
Financial Information:

	Dec 31 1985	Dec 31 1986
	$'000	$'000
Sales revenues	270,768	282,202
Income before taxes	39,300	20,700
Net income	16,200	19,600
Dividends	1,561	1,584
Dividends per share	$0.20	$0.20
Earnings per share	$1.98	$2.37
Common stock	7,849	7,953
Retained income	123,586	141,046
Shareholders equity	131,909	151,145
*shares outstanding in thousands		

No of Employees: 7,500

WEBB, JERVIS B, COMPANY

World Headquarters, Webb Drive, Farmington Hills, MI 48018
Tel: (313) 553-1000
Cable: JERWEB FMHL
Telex: RCA 211892 jwebb ur

Chairman: Jervis C Webb (and President)
Senior Executive Officers: George H Webb (Executive VP, Secretary and General Manager), David C Clark (VP Purchasing and Tresurer), E Owen Newell (VP Finance), Norris M Colley (VP Field Operations), David W Clark (VP Engineering), Robert L Richardson (VP Marketing), Steve Kurtis (VP International), Keith R Scrutton (VP Personnel), Jervis H Webb (VP Manufacturing), George Ramsden (VP Sales)

PRINCIPAL ACTIVITIES: Manufacture of material handling equipment, automation products and control systems
Principal Bank: National Bank of Detroit
Financial Information:

	$'000
Sales revenues	350,000

No of Employees: 3,000

WEBER MARKING SYSTEMS, INC

711 W Algonquin Road, Arlington Heights, IL 60005
Tel: (312) 364-8500
Cable: WAMCO
Telex: TWX 910-222-1602 weber mkg sy
Telefax: (312) 364-8575

Chairman: Joseph A Weber
President: Joseph A Weber Jr
Senior Executive Officers: James B Crassweller (VP Sales), James E Thomas (VP Manufacturing), William J Darras (VP International Sales), Nate Drucker (VP Controller)

PRINCIPAL ACTIVITIES: Manufacture of labelling machines and printing inks and equipment
Principal Bank: Mount Prospect State Bank, Mt Prospect, IL

Financial Information:

	$'000
Sales revenues	55,000

No of Employees: 750

WEBSTER INDUSTRIES, INC

58 Pulaski Street, Peabody, MA 01960
Tel: (617) 532-2000

President: David L Phillips
Senior Executive Officers: Brian O'Donnohue (Executive VP)

PRINCIPAL ACTIVITIES: Manufacture of plastic products for packaging and plastic consumer products
Parent Company: Chelsea Indsutries Inc, Boston, MA
Financial Information:

	$'000
Sales revenues	70,000

No of Employees: 500

WEDTECH CORPORATION

595 Gerard Avenue, Bronx, NY 10451
Tel: (212) 993-0500
Telex: WUT 147281 wedtech nyk

Chairman: Fred Neuberger (and Chief Executive Officer); Vice Chairman: Mario E Moreno (President Coting Division)
President: Anthony Guariglia (and Chief Operating Officer)
Senior Executive Officers: Lawrence Shorten (Executive VP Financial Operations), Alfred Rivera (VP and Treasurer)

PRINCIPAL ACTIVITIES: Manufacture of machined parts for military vehicles
Principal Subsidiaries: (100% owned unless stated): Vanora Ltd (70%); Fleetwood Metals Corp
Financial Information:

	$'000
Sales revenues	117,500

No of Employees: 750

WEHR CORPORATION

10201 W Lincoln Avenue, Milwaukee, WI 53227
Tel: (414) 327-53227

Chairman: R L Manegold
President: Brian L Nahey (and Chief Executive Officer)
Senior Executive Officers: Bruce A Beda (VP, Secretary, Treasurer and Chief Financial Officer)

PRINCIPAL ACTIVITIES: Manufacture of castings, ventilation equipment and pollution control equipment
Principal Bank: First Wisconsin National Bank of Milwaukee
Financial Information:

	$'000
Sales revenues	100,000

No of Employees: 1,600

WEIGHT WATCHERS INTERNATIONAL INC

500 N Broadway, Jericho, NY 11753-2196
Tel: (516) 939-0400

Chairman: Albert Lippert
President: Charles M Berger (and Chief Executive Officer)
Senior Executive Officers: Andrew Barrett (Executive VP North American and Pacific Operations), Richard A Samber (VP Finance and Administration), Warren Adamsbaum (VP North American Classroom Operations), D T Fisher (VP Franchise and Licensing), Louis J Pacini (Executive VP Business Development), Lelio G Parducci (VP Marketing and Operations)

PRINCIPAL ACTIVITIES: Operation of classes for weight watchers; frozen and other foods; leisure camps
Parent Company: H J Heinz Co, Pittsburgh, PA
Principal Bank: Citibank
Financial Information:

	$'000
Sales revenues	78,000

No of Employees: 7,700

WEIL-MCLAIN

Blaine Street, Michigan City, IN 46360
Tel: (219) 879-6561

President: Ben A Radi
Senior Executive Officers: M Jadvani (VP Manufacturing), Robert B Duggan (VP Research), L V Herker (VP Marketing/Sales), William A Jackson (Controller)

PRINCIPAL ACTIVITIES: Manufacture of cast iron and sheet metal
Parent Company: The Marley Co
Financial Information:

	$'000
Sales revenues	70,000

No of Employees: 700

WEIMAN CO INC

4801 West Peterson Avenue, Chicago, IL 60646
Tel: (312) 286 1121

Chairman: Richard D Goddard (and President and Chief Executive Officer)
Senior Executive Officers: Ronald Meyers (Executive VP), Paul F Bohlmann (Secretary and Treasurer)

PRINCIPAL ACTIVITIES: Manufacture and trade in home furnishing products; photographic processing
Principal Subsidiaries: Company Products Inc
Principal Bank: American National Bank & Trust Company of Chicago
Financial Information:

	$'000
Sales revenues	37,600

No of Employees: 475

WEINGARTEN REALTY INC

2600 Citadel Plaza Drive, PO Box 94133, Houston, TX 77292
Tel: (713) 868 6361

President: Stanford Alexander (and Chief Executive Officer)
Senior Executive Officers: Joseph W Robertson Jr (Senior VP and Chief Financial Officer), C T Friday (VP), M Candace Dufour (Secretary and Treasurer), Steven C Roosth (Secretary)

PRINCIPAL ACTIVITIES: Real estate management
Principal Bank: Texas Commerce Bank
Financial Information:

	$'000
Sales revenues	52,900

No of Employees: 20

WEIRTON STEEL CORPORATION

400 Three Springs Drive, Weirton, WV 26062-4989
Tel: (304) 797-2000
Telex: 7109368300 WSX WEIR

Chairman: Herbert Elish (and President and Chief Executive Officer)
Senior Executive Officers: R A Prosswimmer (VP Chief Financial Officer and Treasurer), J J Gilmore (Acting VP-Operations), J B Bruhn (VP-Tin Mill Products Sales), D M Gould (VP-Sales, Sheet Products), R S Miltenberger (VP-Quality Control), R B Morgan Jr (VP-Technical Development), D A Pengidore (VP-Engineering), W T Saunders (VP-Product Development and Research), W C Brenneisen (Director-Industrial Relations), C R Cronin (Director-Public Relations), G T Kilavos (Director-Production Planning), F T Malloy (Director-Corporate Long Range Planning), A J Santilli (Director-Management Services),

H R Wood (Director-Environmental Control and Governmental Relations), T V Evans (VP-Purchasing and Traffic), W R Kiefer (Corporate Attorney)

PRINCIPAL ACTIVITIES: Steel industry-flat rolled products
Trade Names: Registered Trademarks: WEIRKOTE PLUS, WEIRITE, WEIRLITE, WEIRCHROME, WEIRKOTE, WEIRZIN, WSQ
Principal Banks: Pittsburgh National; Ameritrust; CoAmerica; Mellon; Continental Illinois; Chase Manhattan; Irving Trust Co; Citizens & Southern National Bank
Financial Information:

	Dec 31 1985 $'000	Dec 31 1986 $'000
Sales revenues	1,156,000	1,173,812
Income before taxes	61,035	45,085
Net income	61,035	45,085
Common stock	301,240	303,139
Retained income	2,458	58
Shareholders equity	101,312	131,369

Principal Shareholders: Employee Owned (100%)
No of Employees: 8,400

WEIS MARKETS INC
1000 S Second St, Sunbury, PA 17801
Tel: (717) 286-4571

President: Sigfried Weis
Senior Executive Officers: Michael C Rheam (VP and Secretary), Robert F Weis (VP and Treasurer), Richard D Madison (VP Merchandising)

PRINCIPAL ACTIVITIES: Supermarkets
Principal Bankers: First National Trust Bank
Financial Information:

	$'000
Sales revenues	1,017,000

No of Employees: 10,000

WEISFIELD'S INC
800 South Michigan Street, Seattle, WA 98108
Tel: (206) 767 5011

President: Herman Blumenthal
Senior Executive Officers: Sam Arnsteim (VP Operations), Jerry Denning (VP Operations), E Robert Nelsen (VP, Secretary and Legal Counsel), Leslie Rosenberg (VP Merchandising), G A Prosio (Treasurer and Chief Financial Officer)

PRINCIPAL ACTIVITIES: Retail trade in jewelry
Principal Bank: Rainier National Bank
Financial Information:

	$'000
Sales revenues	48,750

No of Employees: 585

WELBILT CORPORATION
3333 New Hyde Park Road, PO Box 3618, New Hyde Park, NY 11042
Tel: (516) 365-5040
Telex: 277051 WELB UR

President: Richard L Hirsch
Senior Executive Officers: David A Hirsch (Treasurer), Lawrence R Gross (Executive VP), Robert M Leach (Senior VP), Donald Shack (Secretary), Peter Fuerst (VP), Gerald Sauk (VP), Bruce Wright (VP), Clem Luebke (VP)

PRINCIPAL ACTIVITIES: Manufacture of food service eqiupment; manufacture and distribution of consumer appliances
Trade Names: GARLAND(R), FRYMASTER(R), ICE-O-MATIC(R)
Principal Subsidiaries: Garland Commercial Ranges Ltd (Canada); Garland Catering Equipment Ltd (UK); Garland Commercial Industries Inc; The Frymaster Corporation; Mile High Equipment Company; Belshaw Bros, Inc; Welbilt Commercial Industries, Inc; Welbilt Catering BV (Netherlands); Consolidated Industries Corp; Appliance Industries, Inc; WEL Trading Corp, Ltd (Switzerland)
Principal Bank: First Pennsylvania Bank
Financial Information:

	Dec 27 1986 $'000
Revenues	201,051
Income before taxes	19,280
Net income	10,462
Earnings per share	$2.03
Common stock*	5,317
Retained income	42,799
Shareholders equity	66,697

*number of shares in thousands

No of Employees: 1,500

WELCH FOODS INC
100 Main Street, Concord, MA 01742
Tel: (617) 371-1000
Telex: TWX 710 3470063 welchmass wcrd

Chairman: J R Orton
President: Everett N Baldwin
Senior Executive Officers: T J Wolfe (Executive VP), P Rembert (Senior VP Operations), Carl Barba Jr (VP Finance), Dan P Dillon (VP Marketing), C R Fulton (VP, General Counsel and Secretary), Tom Gettig (VP Personnel), H K Kelley (VP Sales), A W Luddington (VP International), A B Wright (VP Corporate Planning)

PRINCIPAL ACTIVITIES: Manufacture of fruit products including juices and frozen concentrates
Parent Company: National Grape Co-operative Association, Westfield, NY
Principal Bank: Springfield Bank for Cooperatives
Financial Information:

	$'000
Sales revenues	240,000

No of Employees: 1,230

WELDED TUBE COMPANY OF AMERICA
36th Floor, 1818 Market Street, Philadelphia, PA 19103
Tel: (215) 557 9777

Chairman: Louis Bailis (and Chief Executive Officer)
President: William O Nostrand (and Chief Operating Officer)
Senior Executive Officers: Samuel H Landy (Executive VP and Treasurer), David Alligood (VP Engineering and Planning), H Melvyn Bailis (VP Purchasing), Raymond G Didinger (VP Facilities), Arthur A Stark (VP Sales), Jean S Wexler (Secretary)

PRINCIPAL ACTIVITIES: Manufacture of steel tubes and pipes
Principal Bank: Philadelphia National Bank
Financial Information:

	$'000
Sales revenues	46,390

No of Employees: 200

WELDOTRON CORPORATION
1532 South Washington Avenue, Piscataway, NJ 08854
Tel: (201) 752 6700

Chairman: Martin Siegel (and President)
Senior Executive Officers: Albert W Sanders (VP and Controller), Seymour G Siegel (VP, Secretary and Treasurer), Seymour Zelnick (VP Engineering), Isidore Siegel (Assistant Secretary and Legal Counsel)

PRINCIPAL ACTIVITIES: Industrial equipment, food packaging equipment, automation controls, safety controls, computer equipment

Financial Information:

	$'000
Sales revenues	33,570

No of Employees: 1,750

WELLCO CARPET CORPORATION
PO Box 281, Calhoun, GA 30701
Tel: (404) 629-7301
Telex: TWX 810 7663974 wellco carpet

Chairman: John B Campbell
President: B R Weddle
Senior Executive Officers: Al Cox (VP Marketing), Wallace C Hawkins (VP Manufacturing), Robert S Evans (VP Product Development), Howard E Baggett (VP Operations Planning), Norman Markle (VP Sales), Emil Helbing (Treasurer)

PRINCIPAL ACTIVITIES: Manufacture of carpets and rugs
Parent Company: Mannington Mills Inc, Salem, NJ
Financial Information:

	$'000
Sales revenues	55,000

No of Employees: 370

WELLCRAFT MARINE CORPORATION
8151 Bradenton Road, Sarasota, FL 33580
Tel: (813) 355-9711
Telex: WUT 803790 wellcraft sara

President: J R Long
Senior Executive Officers: Donald M Spencer (Senior VP Administration), C B Andrews (Senior VP Operations), William W Erickson (Senior VP Marketing), Gus Anastasi (VP Performance Boats), William C Mudgett (VP Sales), Paul W Perry (VP Sales Californian), Robert P Trolian (VP Production Runabouts and Fishing Boats), Howard L Bleser (Treasurer)

PRINCIPAL ACTIVITIES: Boat building
Parent Company: Genmar Industries Inc
Principal Bank: Norwest Bank
Financial Information:

	$'000
Sales revenues	86,000

No of Employees: 1,500

WELLINGTON INDUSTRIES INC
PO Box 244, Madison, GA 30650
Tel: (404) 342-1916

President: Richard Wellington
Senior Executive Officers: Andy Postnicks (Chief Financial Officer), John Massengale (Secretary)

PRINCIPAL ACTIVITIES: Manufacture of garden furniture and patio products; equipment for water skiing and other water sports; manufacture of twine and textiles; printing and binding
Principal Bank: Connecticut Bank and Trust Co
Financial Information:

	$'000
Sales revenues	69,000

No of Employees: 1,700

WELLMAN, INC
67 Walnut Avenue, Clark, NJ 07066
Tel: (201) 388 0120

President: Thomas M Duff
Senior Executive Officers: Clifford J Christenson (Chief Financial Officer), David Duffie (Secretary and General Counsel)

PRINCIPAL ACTIVITIES: Manufacture of synthetic fibers, furnishing fabrics and plastics

Financial Information:

	$'000
Sales revenues	100,000

No of Employees: 100

WELLS FARGO & CO
420 Montgomery, San Francisco, CA 94104
Tel: (415) 396-0123
Telex: TRT 184904 wells ut

Chairman: Carl E Reichardt (and Chief Executive Officer)
President: Paul Hazen (and Chief Operating Officer)
Senior Executive Officers: Thomas A Bigelow (Executive VP), Richard J Borda (Executive VP), George F Casey Jr (Executive VP), R T Decker (Executive VP), Gordon S Grout (Executive VP), John F Grundhofer (Executive VP), E Alan Holroyde (Executive VP), Robert L Joss (Executive VP), Frank N Newman (Executive VP Finance), Richard Oppenheimer (Executive VP), Jesun Paik (Executive VP), David M Petrone (Executive VP), William F Zuendt (Executive VP), Alan C Gordon (Senior VP), Guy Jounsaville Jr (Senior VP), Clyde W Ostler (Senior VP), Alan J Pabst (Senior VP)

PRINCIPAL ACTIVITIES: The company has interests in banking and general credit and financial services
Principal Subsidiaries: Wells Fargo Bank International; Wells Fargo Corporate Service Inc; Wells Fargo International Ltd; Wells Fargo Leasing Corpn; Wells Fargo Realty Advisors; Wells Fargo Securities Clearance Corp; Well Fargo Insurance Services; Central Western Insurance Co; Wells Fargo Business Credit; Wells Fargo Ag Credit; Wells Fargo Capital Markets Inc; Wells Fargo Equity Corp; Wells Fargo Investment Advisors; Wells Fargo Credit Corp; Wells Fargo Realty Finance
Financial Information:

	Dec 31 1985 $'000	Dec 31 1986 $'000
Net income	190,034	276,202
Earnings per share	$4.15	$5.03
Shareholders equity	-	2,347,377
Deposits	19,501,300	27,024,943
Total assets	29,429,394	44,577,100

No of Employees: 21,500

WELLS LAMONT CORPORATION
6640 W Touhy Avenue, Chicago, IL 60648
Tel: (312) 763-1100
Telex: RCA 210032 wlcorp ur

President: R A Pritzker
Senior Executive Officers: R C Gluth (VP), R W Webb (Secretary)

PRINCIPAL ACTIVITIES: Manufacture of gloves
Parent Company: Marmon Group Inc
Financial Information:

	$'000
Sales revenues	128,000

No of Employees: 2,300

WEMBLEY INDUSTRIES, INC
966 S White Street, New Orleans, LA 70125
Tel: (504) 822-3700
Telex: TWX 810 9515389 wembley nln

Chairman: Sidney C Pulitzer (and Chief Operating Officer)
President: Arthur C Pulitzer
Senior Executive Officers: Sam C Pulitzer (Chief Executive Officer), A M Wolff (VP and Treasurer)

PRINCIPAL ACTIVITIES: Manufacture of men's clothing
Principal Bank: Whitney National Bank

Financial Information:

	$'000
Sales revenues	50,000

No of Employees: 750

WENDY'S INTERNATIONAL, INC

4288 W Dublin-Granville Rd, PO Box 256, Dublin, OH 43017
Tel: (614) 764-3100
Telefax: (614) 764-3459

Senior Chairman and Founder: R David Thomas; Chairman: Robert L Barney (and Chief Executive Officer)
President: James W Near (and Chief Operating Officer)
Senior Executive Officers: Executive Vice Presidents: John K Casey, Thomas C Copeland III, Joseph E Madigan (Chief Financial Officer), Richard C Postle (President, Company Operations), William M Welter. Senior Vice Presidents: George Condos (Company Operations), Gilles M Gallant (Chicago Operations), Lee H Hess, Ronald E Musick (Corporate Development), Edwin L Ourant (Special Projects). Vice Presidents: Robert E Bauer (Product Research and Development), John F Brownley (Treasurer), Earl Burden (Staff Services), Donald F Calhoon (Field Marketing), Dennis Campbell (Special Projects), Charles D Finlay (Equipment Engineering), H James Graham (National Development), W Glenn Gulledge (Operations, Special Projects), Stephen D Harness (Planning, Engineering), Richard L Hill (Purchasing and Distribution), John M Houck (Construction), Stanley S Jeska (Site Acquisition), Rosalyn S Jinkens (Transportation), R Michael Kennedy Jr (General Counsel and Secretary), Lawrence A Laudick (General Controller and Assistant Secretary), Bruce M Ley (Corporate Marketing), Dennis L Lynch (Corporate Communications), Thomas M Nash (Site Acquisition), M H Notowidigdo (Information Systems), Michael M Sapienza (Marketing Analysis and New Products), Henry J Sherowski (Engineering and Development), Kenneth W Tipton (Training), Ronald E Wallace (Site Acquisition), Stevan J Wilt (Chicago Operations), Frank B Young Jr (Franchise Business Development), Richard W Zborowski (Human Resources). Division Vice Presidents Company Operations: Ronald E Dury, Steven M Meyer, Dale A Naftzger, Fred C Poesel, Gary A Rozanczyk, John T Schuessler. Regional Vice Presidents Franchise Operations: Edward L Austin, Stephen D Farrar, Robert A Melberth, Robert P Pratt. International Operations: John L Rome (President), Fred D Younker (Vice President). Additional: Mark R Liebel (President, Wendy's Restaurants of Canada Inc), Donald E Tincher (General Manager and Vice President The New Bakery Co of Ohio Inc), Thomas W Carton Jr (Assistant Secretary)

PRINCIPAL ACTIVITIES: Fast service restaurants
Financial Information:

	Dec 31 1985	Dec 31 1986
	$'000	$'000
Sales revenues	1,125,617	1,139,852
Income before taxes	133,411	11,328
Net income (loss)	76,191	(4,926)
Dividends	15,969	19,920
Dividends per share	$0.17	$0.21
Earnings (loss) per share	$0.82	($0.05)
Common stock	9,530	9,622
Retained income	325,081	300,235
Shareholders equity	443,529	424,699

No of Employees: 50,000

WESCO FINANCIAL CORPORATION

315 East Colarado Boulevard, Pasadena, CA 91109
Tel: (818) 449 2345

Chairman: Charles Munger
Senior Executive Officers: John R Armetta (VP), H R Dettman (VP), P E Lynn (VP), Robert E Sahm (VP), Dolores Henderson (Secretary), Jeanne Leach (Treasurer)

PRINCIPAL ACTIVITIES: Financial services including savings and loans
Parent Company: Berkshire Hathaway Inc
Principal Bank: Bank of America

No of Employees: 70

WEST BEND CO

400 Washington Street, West Bend, WI 53095
Tel: (414) 334-2311
Telex: ITT 4311104 wbcoui

President: A J English
Senior Executive Officers: D F Parlow (Senior VP Finance), R C Indermuehle (Senior VP Manufacturing Operations), L E Grescoviak (VP Human Resources), T W Kieckhafer (VP Sales), F W Ladwig (VP Manufacturing), G H Miller (VP Marketing)

PRINCIPAL ACTIVITIES: Manufacture of domestic electrical goods and other household products
Parent Company: Dart Industries Inc
Principal Bank: First Wisconsin National Bank
Financial Information:

	$'000
Sales revenues	170,000

No of Employees: 1,700

WEST CO, INC (THE)

West Bridge Street, Phoenixville, PA 19460
Tel: (215) 935-4500
Telex: 84 6410

Chairman: William S West
President: Rene L Guerster (and Chief Executive Officer)
Senior Executive Officers: George R Bennyhoff (Senior VP, Human Resources and Public Affairs), Jack C Girton (Group President), Robert J Jonik (Controller), Carl J Melone Jr (Treasurer), John C Mueller (Senior VP-Finance and Secretary), D Bruce Pattison (Group Executive VP), Robert C Simpson (Group President, International), Victor E Ziegler (Group Executive VP)

PRINCIPAL ACTIVITIES: The West Company, Incorporated is the world's largest manufacturer of specialized packaging components for the pharmaceutical and medical device industries with over 85% of its revenue generated by the health care markets. Its products include stoppers, closures, containers, medical device components and assemblies made from rubber, metal, plastic, glass and combinations thereof, plus related packaging machinery
Principal Bank: Morgan Guaranty Trust Co
Financial Information:

	Dec 31 1985	Dec 31 1986
	$'000	$'000
Sales revenues	190,093	235,635
Income before taxes	23,437	29,405
Net income	14,964	17,020
Dividends	3,566	3,923
Dividends per share	$0.45	$0.49
Earnings per share	$1.90	$2.11
Common stock*	7,877	8,063
Retained income	113,386	126,483
Shareholders equity	119,506	138,905

*average shares outstanding in thousands

No of Employees: 2,480

WEST POINT-PEPPERELL, INC

PO Box 71, West Point, GA 31833
Tel: (404) 645-4000
Telex: WUT 540446 wppeppcoa wtpt

Chairman: Joseph L Lanier Jr (and Chief Executive Officer)
President: Donald J Keller (and Chief Operating Officer)

Senior Executive Officers: Charles Crowder (VP Manufacturing), Vance L Cathey (VP Personnel), Clayton Sauers (VP Finance), Robert L Brightman (VP Synthetic Fiber Purchasing), R L Allen (VP Cotton Purchasing), R H Monk Jr (VP), Marshall N Morton (VP, Treasurer and Controller)

PRINCIPAL ACTIVITIES: Manufacture of cotton and synthetic fabrics and industrial clothing
Principal Subsidiaries: West-Point-Pepperell Export Inc; Chattahoochee Valley Railway Co; Bond-Cote Inc; Cluett Peabody & Co Inc
Financial Information:

	Aug 31 1986
	$'000
Sales revenues	1,813,354
Net income	54,465
Earnings per share	$4.09
Shareholders equity	674,977

No of Employees: 21,000

WESTAMERICA BANCORPORATION
PO Box 567, San Rafael, CA 94915
Tel: (415) 457-8790

Chairman: Rex T Silvernale
President: Richard N Hall (and Chief Executive Officer)
Senior Executive Officers: Dennis Hansen (VP and Controller), E Joseph Bowler (VP and Treasurer), M Kitty Jones (VP and Secretary)

PRINCIPAL ACTIVITIES: Banking services
Principal Bank: Westamerica Bank

No of Employees: 960

WESTBRIDGE CAPITAL CORPORATION
777 Main Street, Suite 900, Fort Worth, TX 76102
Tel: (817) 878 3300

Chairman: Martin E Kantor (and President and Chief Executive Officer); Vice Chairman: Raymond S Troubh
Senior Executive Officers: Scott R Munse (VP and Actuary), William R Riddell (VP, Legal Counsel and Secretary), James W Thigpen (VP), Wayne E Williams (VP and Treasurer)

PRINCIPAL ACTIVITIES: Insurance
Principal Subsidiaries: National Foundation Life Insurance
Principal Bank: Texas American Bank

No of Employees: 220

WESTCHESTER FINANCIAL SERVICES CORPORATION
North Avenue and Huguenot Street, New Rochelle, NY 10802
Tel: (914) 636 6400

Chairman: Kenneth R Biederman (and Chief Executive Officer)
President: Raymond W Kerr (and Secretary)
Senior Executive Officers: Carl Cirino (VP and Chief Financial Officer), Sabatino DiGiambattista Jr (VP) Thomas K Hernly (VP Financial Public Relations), Kenneth J Kaul (VP Corporate Planning), Rainer J Olbrich (VP)

PRINCIPAL ACTIVITIES: Financial services including savings and loans
Parent Company: Marine Midland Banks Inc

No of Employees: 315

WESTCORP
1111 East Katella Avenue, Orange, CA 92667
Tel: (714) 532 7200

Chairman: Ernest S Rady (and Chief Executive Officer)
President: Robert W Jenkins

Senior Executive Officers: Robert S Waligore (Senior VP and Chief Financial Officer), Regan A Kelly (VP, Secretary and Legal Counsel),

PRINCIPAL ACTIVITIES: Bank holding company

No of Employees: 360

WESTERN & SOUTHERN LIFE INSURANCE CO
400 Broadway, Cincinnati, OH 45202
Tel: (513) 629-1800

Chairman: Charles M Barrett (and Chief Executive Officer; Chairman of Executive Committee: Charles M Williams
President: William J Williams (and Chief Operating Officer)
Senior Executive Officers: James N Clark (Executive VP, Secretary and Assistant to President), Milton W Gwinner (Senior VP Medical), Carroll R Hutchinson (Senior VP and Chief Actuary), J J Miller (Senior VP and Chief Marketing Officer), E W Bates (Executive VP), Raymond M Blankenship (Executive VP Data Processing), James R Barton (VP Mortgage Loans), James R Cullinan (VP and Auditor), Donald H Deidesheimer (VP), Thomas X Dillon (VP), John W Donovan (VP), Ralph E Ellis (VP and Counsel), Gavin D Gray (VP Real Estate), E Channing Headley (VP Personnel), Dale P Hennie (VP), Jay E Johnson (VP and Comptroller), Turner E Kirby (VP), William F Ledwin (VP and Chief Investment Officer), John F Letscher (VP), J Gibbs MacVeigh (VP and Treasurer), William F Meyer (VP and Senior Counsel), Kenneth A Palmer (VP), Richard L Siegel (VP), Wendall Sullivan (VP and Chief Counsel), Rex Tate (VP), Paul D Yeary (VP and Actuary)

PRINCIPAL ACTIVITIES: Life insurance
Financial Information:

	Dec 31 1985	Dec 31 1986
	$'000	$'000
Premium income	422,672	423,088
Investment income	218,336	206,436

No of Employees: 6,195

WESTERN AIR LINES, INC
6060 Avion Drive, Los Angeles, CA 90045
Tel: (213) 216-3000

Chairman: Gerald Grinstein (and Chief Executive Officer)
President: Donald J Lloyd-Jones (and Chief Operating Officer)
Senior Executive Officers: Thomas J Roeck Jr (Senior VP and Chief Financial Officer), Harold L Achtziger (VP Airport Services), Adam M Aron (VP Marketing Programs), Richard J Carter (VP Sales), Gregory P Chambers (VP and Controller), William C Farrell (VP Corporate and Financial Planning), Thomas J Greene (VP, General Counsel and Secretary), Larry M Hecker (VP Flight Operations), Joseph C Hilly (VP Employee Relations), Ronald D Marasco (VP Maintenance and Engineering), Robert L Moore (VP Market Planning), William Semos (VP Corporate Communications), Douglas B Swets (VP and Treasurer), Glen L Stewart (VP Operations Administration), Jorge Valencia (VP and General Manager Mexico)

PRINCIPAL ACTIVITIES: Operation of air transportation services
Principal Bank: Citibank
Financial Information:

	$'000
Sales revenues	1,306,550

No of Employees: 10,250

WESTERN CAPITAL INVESTMENT CORP
1675 Broadway, Suite 1700, Denver, CO 80202
Tel: (303) 623-5577

Chairman: Junius F Baxter (and Chief Executive Officer)
President: R D Barnard (and Vice Chairman)

Senior Executive Officers: M W Buckels (Executive VP), R L Schwarz (Executive VP and Treasurer), R L Green (Senior VP), R V Stailey (Secretary)

PRINCIPAL ACTIVITIES: Banking services
Financial Information:

	Dec 31 1985	Dec 31 1986
	$'000	$'000
Net income (loss)	17,700	(7,170)
Earnings (loss) per share	$2.07	($0.77)
Shareholders equity	-	286,900
Deposits	-	2,354,490
Total assets	3,030,000	3,563,600

No of Employees: 1,956

WESTERN CO OF NORTH AMERICA
6000 Western Pl, Fort Worth, TX 76107
Tel: (817) 731-5100
Telex: WUT 559119 western co ftw

Chairman: H E Chiles
President: Sheldon R Erikson (and Chief Executive Officer)
Senior Executive Officers: Sam R Morrow (VP and Chief Financial Officer), Graham L Adelman (VP, General Counsel and Secretary), Steven P Beatty (Controller)

PRINCIPAL ACTIVITIES: Onshore oilfield services and offshore contract drilling
Principal Subsidiaries: Western Oceanic Inc; Western Towers Inc; Western Oceanic Services Inc; Western Services International Inc; Western Petroleum Services International Co; Western Petroleum Services Inc; Western Oceanic International Inc; Western Oceanic (Cameroon) Ltd; Altomar Perfuracoes-Maritimas Limitada (99%); Saturn Energy Co; Colony Drilling Co; Western Oceanic (UK) Ltd; Western Oceanic (Overseas) Ltd; Western Oilfield Supply & Rental Inc
Principal Bank: Manufacturers Hanover, New York
Financial Information:

	Dec 31 1985	Dec 31 1986
	$'000	$'000
Sales revenues	500,186	197,025
(Loss) before taxes	(84,929)	(366,249)
Net (loss)	(67,269)	(340,516)
Preferred dividends	7,250	7,250
(Loss) per share	($1.66)	($7.46)
Retained earnings (deficit)	124,354	(219,823)
Shareholders equity (deficit)	315,686	(32,280)

Principal Shareholders: H E Chiles; Jerry E Chiles; Carol Chiles Ballard
No of Employees: 2,100

WESTERN CONSUMER INDUSTRIES INC
7768 E Jackson Street, Paramount, CA 90723
Tel: (213) 636-1191

Chairman: William Schaffer; Vice Chairman: Jack Herron
President: Frank K Doyle (and Chief Executive Officer)
Senior Executive Officers: Bill Boersong (VP Sales), Ed Reyes (VP and Division Manager Paramount)

PRINCIPAL ACTIVITIES: Production of animal feeds
Principal Bank: Bank of America
Financial Information:

	$'000
Sales revenues	60,000

No of Employees: 100

WESTERN DIGITAL CORPORATION
2445 McCabe Way, Irvine, CA 92714
Tel: (714) 863-0102
Telex: TRT 188742 westdigco irin

Chairman: Roger W Johnson (and President and Chief Executive Officer); Vice Chairman: Joseph Baia (and Assistant to Chief Executive Officer)
Senior Executive Officers: Terry N Holdt (Executive VP), Chester A Brown (VP Strategic Business Development), H D Gray (VP Administration), James L Hodges (VP Quality), Alan J Mattal (VP Marketing and Major Accounts), A J Moyer (VP Finance and Chief Financial Officer), John J Petersen (VP Engineering), Joseph F Pleso (VP Sales US), Charles A Von Urff (VP Sales International)

PRINCIPAL ACTIVITIES: Manufacture of semiconductors for use in data processing and telecommunications equipment
Principal Subsidiaries: Western Digital (Malaysia) SDN BHD; Western Digital Development Corp; Western Digital Assembly Corp; Western Digital Ireland Ltd; Western Digital UK Ltd; Western Digital Japan Inc; Western Digital Deutschland GmbH
Principal Bank: First Interstate Bank of California
Financial Information:

	$'000
Sales revenues	279,000

No of Employees: 1,000

WESTERN ENGINE CO
500 Lombard, Addison, IL 60101
Tel: (312) 620-2000
Telex: WUT 728468 western adis

President: John R Lundahl
Senior Executive Officers: Robert Bowles (Executive VP), E O'Brien (VP Finance and Treasurer), L J Smith (VP and General Manager)

PRINCIPAL ACTIVITIES: Manufacture of generators
Principal Bank: First National Bank
Financial Information:

	$'000
Sales revenues	40,000

No of Employees: 200

WESTERN HEALTH PLANS INC
3702 Ruffin Road, San Diego, CA 92123
Tel: (619) 571 3102

Chairman: Allan H Goodman; Vice Chairman: Robert Penner
President: Douglas Werner
Senior Executive Officers: Ray Mendoza (Executive VP, Secretary, Treasurer and Chief Operating Officer), John H Gindorff (VP), Georgia E Needham (VP), Susan L Jones (VP and Chief Financial Officer), Barry L Showe (VP)

PRINCIPAL ACTIVITIES: Health and medical services
Financial Information:

	$'000
Sales revenues	70,300

No of Employees: 200

WESTERN INDUSTRIES, INC
1211 N 62nd Street, Milwaukee, WI 53213
Tel: (414) 771-7700

President: Jack F Kellner
Senior Executive Officers: Richard Lynch (VP)

PRINCIPAL ACTIVITIES: Manufacture of metal stampings and forgings
Principal Bank: M & I Marshall & Ilsey Bank
Financial Information:

	$'000
Sales revenues	90,000

No of Employees: 1,200

WESTERN MICROTECHNOLOGY INC
10040 Bubb Road, Cupertino, CA 95014
Tel: (408) 725 1660

Chairman: Marshall G Cox (and Chief Executive Officer)
President: Bernard T Marren

Senior Executive Officers: John H Hughes III (VP and General Manager), Paul A Araquistane (Chief Financial Officer), Paul I Myers Jr (Secretary)

PRINCIPAL ACTIVITIES: High-tec electronic components and computer systems
Principal Bank: Bank of the West
Financial Information:

	$'000
Sales revenues	46,230

No of Employees: 160

WESTERN PACIFIC INDUSTRIES, INC
345 Park Ave, New York, NY 10154
Tel: (212) 751-6464

Chairman: Howard A Newman (and Chief Executive Officer)
President: William C Scott
Senior Executive Officers: Roger F Haskell (VP, Treasurer and Secretary)

PRINCIPAL ACTIVITIES: Holding company with interests in the manufacture of plastic products, industrial fasteners and computer products
Principal Bank: Manufacturers Hanover Trust Co
Financial Information:

	$'000
Sales revenues	167,800

No of Employees: 2,750

WESTERN PLASTICS CORPORATION
1019 Pacific Ave, Tacoma, WA 98402
Tel: (206) 572-5111

Chairman: Robert Freeman (and President)
Senior Executive Officers: Ken Holt (VP Engineering and Production), Kenneth Johnson (VP Finance and Treasurer)

PRINCIPAL ACTIVITIES: Manufacture of a range of plastic products including pipe, containers and insulating material
Parent Company: Hepworth Ceramic Holdings PLC, Sheffield, UK
Principal Bank: Puget Sound National Bank
Financial Information:

	$'000
Sales revenues	30,000

No of Employees: 350

WESTERN PUBLISHING CO
1220 Mound Avenue, Racine, WI 53404
Tel: (414) 633-2431
Telex: RCA 297860 west ur

Chairman: Richard A Bernstein (and Chief Executive Officer, Western Publishing Group, Inc)
President: Joseph A Marino (and Chief Executive Officer)
Senior Executive Officers: William Nahikian (Group VP Consumer Products Marketing), Bruce A Bernberg (Senior VP Finance), George P Oess (VP Consumer Products), Ralph L Donnelly (VP Diversified Products), Doris Dunewald (Publisher-Golden Books)

PRINCIPAL ACTIVITIES: Publishing, children's activities, videos and games, printing
Trade Names: Golden Books, Golden Press, Whitman
Parent Company: Western Publishing Group Inc
Principal Subsidiaries: Les Editions Deux Coqs d'Or; Whitman-Golden, Canada; Datapage
Principal Bank: Chemical Bank
Financial Information:

	$'000
Sales revenues	300,000

No of Employees: 2,600

WESTERN SAVINGS & LOAN ASSOCIATION
6001 N 24th Street, Phoenix, AZ 85016
Tel: (602) 468-5900
Telex: WUT 595154 western svgs

Chairman: John D Driggs
President: Gary Driggs
Senior Executive Officers: Clark P Cederlof (Executive VP), Gerald D Miller (Executive VP), Fred Stutenroth (Senior VP and Treasurer), Don C Driggs (Senior VP and Secretary)

PRINCIPAL ACTIVITIES: Savings and loans; real estate interests
Principal Bank: The Arizona Bank
Financial Information:

	Dec 31 1985 $'000	Dec 31 1986 $'000
Income before taxes	54,387	46,671
Net income	36,667	30,171
Dividends per share	$0.17	$0.21
Earnings per share	$2.32	$1.80
Common stock	12,096	12,087
Shareholders equity	113,075	127,984
Deposits	3,279,691	3,813,475
Total assets	4,807,367	5,547,105

No of Employees: 1,978

WESTERN STEER-MOM'N'POP'S INC
PO Box 399, Claremont, NC 28610
Tel: (704) 459 7626

Chairman: Marshall E Digh (and President and Treasurer)
Senior Executive Officers: Charles F Connor Jr (Executive VP and Secretary), Richard S Howard (VP Franchising), J Frank Buff (VP Operations), Jack B Busic (VP Purchasing Manager), Ronnie L Digh (VP Bakery), Jack L Harmon (VP Administration), Fred H Keller (VP Smokehouse), Thomas W Turner (VP Marketing), James W Berry (Controller)

PRINCIPAL ACTIVITIES: Restaurants and catering
Principal Subsidiaries: Mom'N'Pop's Smoke House Inc
Principal Bank: First Union National Bank
Financial Information:

	$'000
Sales revenues	45,450

No of Employees: 1,000

WESTERN TELE-COMMUNICATIONS INC
4643 South Ulster St, Suite 400, Denver, CO 80237
Tel: (303) 796 9100
Telex: 454426
Telefax: (303) 721-5566

Chairman: Bob Magness
President: Carter F Page
Senior Executive Officers: Larry Romrell (Executive VP and Secretary), Russell F Johnson (VP, Engineering), C C Thomas (VP, Operations), James L Downing (Controller and Principal Accounting Officer), Ben Summers (VP, Network Development), Robert L Ottmann (VP, Marketing)

PRINCIPAL ACTIVITIES: Western Tele-Communications, Inc (WTCI) is a diversified communications company based in Englewood, Colorado. WTCI provides a vital link in today's communications network. Looked to as a leader in providing quality service and the latest technologies, WTCI serves a wide variety of communications needs. An understanding of WTCI is best achieved by categorizing its services as follows: 1) WTCI owns and operates microwave relay systems throughout the western half of the United States which allow customers leasing those facilities to transmit voice and data messages from the point of origin to the point of reception. 2) Another area of WTCI involvement in the communications industry is the acquisition and operation of cable television systems throughout the United States. In 1986 WTCI acquired Televents Group, Inc. 3) A variety of WTCI activities can best be placed in a category described as "other services". These services include: Leasing transportable earth stations for receiving and transmitting broadcast signals via satellite in "remote" areas; constructing permanent earth station facilities for domestic communications satellite systems; receiving television broadcast signals and relaying those signals to the headends of cable companies; providing communications engineering and turn-key microwave system construction and maintenance services to private companies and federal agencies. As broadcast, cable, satellite and data transmission services increasingly utilize shares technologies, WTCI is ideally positioned as an important link in meeting the communications needs of the future.

Principal Subsidiaries: Televents Group, Inc
Principal Bank: First National Bank of Chicago
Financial Information:

	Dec 31 1985	Dec 31 1986
	$'000	$'000
Sales revenues	32,026	47,842
Income before taxes	14,171	25,168
Net income	12,135	13,607
Earnings per share	$1.42	$1.56
Class A common stock	67	70
Class B common stock	18	17
Retained income	17,171	30,778
Shareholders equity	31,090	45,275

No of Employees: 280

WESTERN UNION CORPORATION

1 Lake St, Upper Saddle River, NJ 07458
Tel: (201) 825-5000

Chairman: Robert S Leventhal (and President and Chief Executive Officer)
Senior Executive Officers: John E Fox (VP), John W Pope Jr (VP), Stephan E Smiszko (VP and Treasurer)

PRINCIPAL ACTIVITIES: Telecommunications services
Principal Bank: Chase Manhattan Bank
Financial Information:

	$'000
Sales revenues	1,082,500

No of Employees: 13,800

WESTERN WASTE INDUSTRIES

19803 S Main Street, Carson, CA 90745
Tel: (213) 321 2533

Chairman: Kosti Shirvanian (and President)
Senior Executive Officers: Anatol Gendal (VP Operations), John Gerardi (VP), R A Haft Jr (VP and Legal Counsel), Allen Hicks (VP), L F McQuaide (VP Finance), Bernard Nash (VP), George Osepian (VP Corporate Development), Clarence Pine (VP), Jacob Shirvanian (VP Public Relations), Ralph Tufenkian (VP Special Projects), Charles Wilson (VP Operations), Morris Wolfe (VP Operations), Savey Tufenkian (Secretary and Treasurer)

PRINCIPAL ACTIVITIES: Industrial waste disposal services
Principal Subsidiaries: Western Waste Industries TX Inc
Principal Bank: Bank of America
Financial Information:

	$'000
Sales revenues	69,100

No of Employees: 600

WESTINGHOUSE CREDIT CORPORATION

One Oxford Centre, Pittsburgh, PA 15219
Tel: (412) 393-3000
Telecopier: (412) 393-3388 (Law Dept)

President: J R McClester
Senior Executive Officers: R T Barbour (Senior VP Commercial Services Group), W A Powe (Senior VP Capital Financing Group), R L Bencke (VP Finance), R C Jacobs (VP Corporate Marketing and Development)

PRINCIPAL ACTIVITIES: Domestic business financing, including leasing
Parent Company: Westinghouse Financial Services, Inc, a wholly owned subsidiary of Westinghouse Electric Corporation
Principal Banks: Chase Manhattan Bank; Citibank; First Interstate Bank of California; First Republic Bank; Mellon Bank NA; Morgan Guaranty Trust Company of New York; Security Pacific National Bank
Financial Information:

	Dec 31 1986(1)	Jun 30 1987(2)
	(12 mths)	(6 mths)
	$'000	$'000
Revenues	689,436	326,720
Income before taxes	117,147	87,073
Net income	106,244	58,079
Common stock(3)	8,000	8,000
Retained income	552,075	610,154
Shareholders equity	647,575	705,654

(1) audited
(2) unaudited
(3) par value $100,100,000 shares authorized, 80,000 shares issued and outstanding

Principal Shareholders: Wholly owned by Westinghouse Financial Services Inc
No of Employees: 750

WESTINGHOUSE ELECTRIC CORPORATION

Gateway Center Westinghouse Bldg, Pittsburgh, PA 15222
Tel: (412) 642-3800
Telex: WUT 866194 westinghse pgh

Chairmen: D D Danforth (and Chief Executive Officer), D L Ritchie (and Chief Executive Officer Broadcasting)
President: N M Nelson
Senior Executive Officers: W C Carlsen (President Latin-America), J L Davis (President Longines-Wittnauer Watch Co), H J Frazier (President Community Development), J C Marous (President Industries and International Group), J R McClester (President Westinghouse Credit Corporation), T J Murrin (President Energy and Advanced Technology Group), N M Nelson (President Learning Corporation), G E Nietfeld (President Westinghouse Electric Supply Co), C F Obermesser (President Asia-Pacific), J C Sheehan (President Thermo King Corporation), F H Tyaack (President Westinghouse Canada Inc), J B Yasinski (President, Europe, Africa and Middle East), E V Clarke Jr (Senior Executive VP Corporate Resources), Leo W Yochum (Senior Executive VP Finance), W A Coates (Executive VP International), T Stern (Executive VP Nuclear Energy Systems), R V Gavert Jr (Executive VP Marketing), H B Smith (Executive VP Defense), Douglas D Stark (Executive VP Commercial), E J Cattabiania (Executive VP Power Generation), Paul E Lego (Executive VP)

PRINCIPAL ACTIVITIES: Production of machinery for the generation and transmission of electricity; electrical equipment and appliances; telecommunications; weapons and armaments systems; aerospace components
Principal Bank: Philadelphia National Bank
Financial Information:

	Dec 31 1985	Dec 31 1986
	$'000	$'000
Sales revenues	10,700,200	10,731,000
Net income	605,300	670,800
Earnings per share	$3.52	$4.42
Shareholders equity	3,234,700	3,009,600

No of Employees: 12,570

WESTMORELAND COAL CO

2500 Fidelity Building, Philadelphia, PA 19109

Tel: (215) 545-2500

Chairman: E B Leisenring Jr (and Chief Executive Officer)

President: Pemberton Hutchinson (and Chief Operating Officer)

Senior Executive Officers: Martin J McDonnell (Senior VP Finance and Administration), Charles E Brinley II (Senior VP Planning and Development), Alvey B Rushton (Senior VP Operations), Hershiel H Hayden (VP Virginia Operations), Larry B Correll (VP Human Resources), R Page Henley (VP Planning and Development), Clarence Justice (VP West Virginia Operations)

PRINCIPAL ACTIVITIES: Coal mining

Financial Information:

	$'000
Sales revenues	544,550

No of Employees: 2,410

WESTVACO CORPORATION

299 Park Avenue, New York, NY 10171

Tel: (212) 688-5000

Telex: WUT 353946 westvaco

Chairman: David L Luke III (and Chief Executive Officer)

President: John A Luke

Senior Executive Officers: George E Cruser (Senior VP Finance), Victor S Luke (Senior VP and Division Manager Bleached Board Division), Frederick C Haas (Senor VP), Harold A Sutphen Jr (Senior VP and Division Manager Fine Papers), Robert A Powers (Senior VP), John C Callihan (VP Public Relations), Thomas R Long (Senior VP/General Counsel), John A Luke Jr (VP/Treasurer), James E Stovekin (VP/Comptroller), John W Glomb (VP, Corporate Research), Charles Hill (VP, Manager U.S. Envelope Division)

PRINCIPAL ACTIVITIES: Manufacture of paper and board

Principal Bank: Irving Trust Co

Financial Information:

	Oct 31 1985	Oct 31 1986
	$'000	$'000
Sales revenues	1,721,783	1,811,937
Net income	104,625	108,096
Earnings per share	$2.74	$2.50
Shareholders equity	1,012,860	1,082,791

No of Employees: 15,080

WESTVACO-US ENVELOPE DIVISION

20001 Roosevelt Avenue, Springfield, MA 01104

Tel: (413) 736-7211

Senior Executive Officers: Charles E Hill (Division Manager), Edward Parker (Administration Manager), William Murphy (Manufacturing Manager), Donald F Reed (Marketing Manager)

PRINCIPAL ACTIVITIES: Manufacture of envelopes and disposable cups

Parent Company: Westvaco Corporation, New York, NY

Financial Information:

	$'000
Sales revenues	150,000

No of Employees: 2,000

WESTWORLD COMMUNITY HEALTHCARE INC

23832 Rockfield Road, Lake Forest, CA 92630

Tel: (714) 768 2981

Chairman: Michael D Dunn (and Chief Executive Officer)

President: Peter C Donald

Senior Executive Officers: Walter J Kaczor Jr (Senior VP and Chief Financial Officer), Richard Barnett (VP), J A Calderone (VP), M B Files (VP), Ronald Kuperstein (VP), Richard Mulry (VP), Jeffrey R Smith (Senior VP Development), J S Wilson (VP)

PRINCIPAL ACTIVITIES: Hospitals, healthcare facilities; operates air ambulance services

Financial Information:

	$'000
Sales revenues	133,000

No of Employees: 1,300

WETTERAU INC

8920 Pershall Road, Hazelwood, MO 63042

Tel: (314) 524-5000

Chairman: Ted C Wetterau (and Chief Executive Officer)

President: Robert K Crutsinger (and Chief Operating Officer)

Senior Executive Officers: John D Ryan (Executive VP), Robert J Livingston (Senior VP), Robert E Mohrmann (Executive VP Finance), George H Thomazin (Executive VP), George Chirtea (Senior VP), Donald D Bennett (First VP), Kurt D Blumenthal (First VP Finance), Leroy Holdman (First VP), Andrew Levy (First VP Human Resources), Matthew M McCarthy (First VP, Secretary and General Counsel), William R Miller (First VP Personnel), William E Patton (First VP Property and Facilities), Robert L Pomeroy (First VP), W Robert Tannehill (First VP), Michael L Waitukaitus (First VP), Roger D Beard (VP Data Processing), Charles A Gauen (VP Risk Management), Lawrence C Hild (VP and Assistant Secretary), Ronald S Humiston (VP Public Relations), Joseph W Lintzenich (VP Air Transport), James V Mroczkowski (VP and Controller), Richard H Schaefer (VP), H Wallace Truelock (VP), William B Winkeler (VP Corporate Taxes)

PRINCIPAL ACTIVITIES: Diversified company with interests in food retailing, wholesaling, warehousing and distribution; frozen dough; insurance and financial interests

Principal Bank: Centerre Bank St Louis

Financial Information:

	Mar 31 1986
	$'000
Sales revenues	3,482,315
Net income	31,825
Earnings per share	$2.90
Shareholders equity	243,127

No of Employees: 10,200

WEYENBERG SHOE MFG CO

234 E Reservoir Avenue, Milwaukee, WI 53201

Tel: (414) 374-8900

Telex: TWX 910 2621101 weyenberg mil

Chairman: Thomas W Florsheim (and Chief Executive Officer)

President: Robert Feitler

Senior Executive Officers: James Gorman (VP), Peter S Grossman (VP), Thomas McArdle (VP), David Couper (VP), Roland Keuler (Treasurer)

PRINCIPAL ACTIVITIES: Manufacture of men's footwear; retail footwear

Trade Names: Weyenberg, Nunn Bush, Stacy Adams, Brass Boot

Principal Subsidiaries: Nunn Bush Shoe Company (Delaware); Adler Shoe Shops Inc (New York); Stedfast Limited (Ireland)

Principal Bank: Marine Bank, Milwaukee, WI

Financial Information:

	Dec 31 1985 $'000	Dec 31 1986 $'000
Sales revenues	111,512	106,703
Income before taxes	9,009	7,803
Net income	4,779	4,310
Dividends	770	803
Dividends per share	$1.34	$1.42
Earnings per share	$8.01	$7.32
Common stock	1,335	1,335
Retained income	47,565	51,072
Shareholders equity	32,483	32,559

Principal Shareholders: Thomas W Florsheim; Robert Feitler
No of Employees: 1,300

WEYERHAEUSER CO

Tacoma, WA 98477
Tel: (206) 924-2345
Telex: TRT 140142 185116 weyhq ut

President: George H Weyerhaeuser (and Chief Executive Officer)
Senior Executive Officers: Charles W Bingham (Executive VP), John W Creighton Jr (Executive VP), Robert L Schuyler (Executive VP and Chief Financial Offier), Fred R Fosmire (Senior VP)

PRINCIPAL ACTIVITIES: Production and processing of timber; manufacture of paper and board products
Principal Subsidiaries: Weyerhaeuser Real Estate Co
Financial Information:

	Dec 28 1986 $'000
Sales revenues	5,652,029
Income before taxes	420,585
Net income	276,685
Dividends*	197,654
Dividends per share	$1.30
Earnings per share	$1.91
Common stock	248,667
Retained income	2,562,484
Shareholders equity	3,253,165

*on preferred, preference and common shares

No of Employees: 37,497

WHEATLAND TUBE CO

900 Haddon Avenue, Colingswood, NJ 08110
Tel: (609) 854-5400
Telex: WUT 834372 wheatland clgd

Chairman: James O'Donnell (and President)
Senior Executive Officers: C R Wahl (Senior VP, Secretary and Treasurer), James Feeney (Senior VP Operations), Peter S Dooner Jr (VP Electrical Sales), Edwin Hopkinson (VP Pipe Sales)

PRINCIPAL ACTIVITIES: Manufacture of steel tubes and pipes
Parent Company: John Maneely Co
Principal Bank: Philadelphia National Bank
Financial Information:

	Feb 28 1988 $'000
Sales revenues	200,000

No of Employees: 600

WHEATLEY PUMP & VALVE CO

3303 Charles Page Blvd, Tulsa, OK 74127
Tel: (918) 587-6731

President: Gene Kaefer (and General Manager)
Senior Executive Officers: Steven Thompson (VP and General Manager, David Moore (Controller), Malcolm Cloyd (General Manager Pumps)

PRINCIPAL ACTIVITIES: Manufacture of pumps and valves
Parent Company: Moorco International Inc
Financial Information:

	$'000
Sales revenues	60,000

No of Employees: 580

WHEATON INDUSTRIES

Wheaton Avenue, Millville, NJ 08332
Tel: (609) 825-1400
Telex: WUT 551523 wheatonindust

President: Frank H Wheaton Jr (and Chief Executive Officer)
Senior Executive Officers: Fred Allen (VP Corporate Research and Development), J E Goff (VP Legal and Secretary), Jack Sheridan (VP Plastics), George J Straubmuller III (VP Tubing), James E Gutknecht (Controller), Daniel M Replogle Jr (Treasurer)

PRINCIPAL ACTIVITIES: Manufacture of a range of glass products; manufacture of plastic bottles
Financial Information:

	$'000
Sales revenues	325,000

No of Employees: 6,000

WHEEL HORSE PRODUCTS, INC

515 W Ireland Road, South Bend, IN 46614
Tel: (219) 291-3112
Telex: WUT 258462 wheelhorse sbn

Chairman: John S Munn (and President); Vice Chairman: Robert F Hawkins (and Treasurer)
Senior Executive Officers: A W Coye Jr (VP), S B Esbenshade (VP), D J Masini (VP), J P Nelson (VP), S P Wolfe (VP), R G Wasielewski (Controller)

PRINCIPAL ACTIVITIES: Manufacture of garden machinery
Principal Bank: First Source Bank
Financial Information:

	$'000
Sales revenues	50,000

No of Employees: 350

WHEELING-PITTSBURGH STEEL CORPORATION

PO Box 118, Pittsburgh, PA 15230
Tel: (412) 288-3600
Telex: TWX 710 6644820 wheel pitt hdq

Chairman: Allen E Paulson; Vice Chairman: George A Ferris (and Chief Executive Officer)
President: John D Fry (and Chief Operating Oficer)
Senior Executive Officers: Richard A Barcelona (VP Purchasing, Traffic and Raw Materials), Fred G Chbosky (VP Purchasing), Robert F Good (VP Commercial), Francis P Masco (VP, Secretary and General Counsel), William J Miller (VP Human Resources), John W Testa (VP and Treasurer)

PRINCIPAL ACTIVITIES: Manufacture of steel
Principal Subsidiaries: Consumers Mining Co; Three Rivers Coal CO; W-P Coal CO; Mingo Oxygen Co; Monessen Southwestern Ry Co; Gateway Coal Co (75%); Wheeling Gateway Coal Co; Pittsburgh-Canfield Corp; Ft Duquesne Coal Co; Wheeling Pittsburgh Trading Co; Wheeling-Itasca Co; Harmar Coal Co (75%), Wheeling-Minmentals International Inc
Principal Bank: Manufacturers Hanover Trust Co

Financial Information:

	Dec 31 1985	Dec 31 1986
	$'000	$'000
Sales revenues	681,057	934,450
Net (loss)	(303,072)	(250,923)
(Loss) per share	($60.87)	($50.75)
Shareholders equity (deficit)	33,977	(216,946)

No of Employees: 8,000

WHIRLPOOL CORPORATION

Administrative Center, Benton Harbor, MI 49022
Tel: (616) 926-5000
Telex: TWX 910 3508848 whirlpool mich

Chairman: David R Whitwam (and President and Chief Executive Officer); Vice Chairman: George E Wardberg (and Chief Operating Officer)
Senior Executive Officers: Samuel M Bateman (Executive VP), Robert J Flautt (Senior VP and Treasurer), Stephen E Upton (Senior VP), Lloyd A Wampach (Senior VP), Robert E Bartley (VP), H W Bowman (VP), August Brogno (VP), Robert J Collins-Wright (VP), E R Dunn (VP), Robert I Frey (VP), Glenn E Holubar (VP), Charles Z Jespersen (VP), Lawrence J Kremer (VP), William D Marohn (VP), Glenn S Olinger (VP)

PRINCIPAL ACTIVITIES: Manufacture of domestic electrical appliances; heating and ventilation equipment
Principal Subsidiaries: Heil-Quaker Corp; Inglis Ltd (Canada); Whirlpool Acceptance Corp; Whirlpool Trading Co
Principal Bank: Chase Manhattan Bank
Financial Information:

	Dec 31 1985	Dec 31 1986
	$'000	$'000
Sales revenues	3,474,456	4,008,702
Net income	182,319	199,649
Earnings per share	$4.98	$2.70
Shareholders equity	1,206,602	1,349,791

No of Employees: 25,524

WHITE CASTLE SYSTEM INC

555 W Goodale Street, Columbus, OH 43215
Tel: (614) 228-5781

Chairman: E W Ingram Jr
President: Edgar W (Bill) Ingram III (and Chief Executive Officer)
Senior Executive Officers: Robert D Hays (Senior VP, Secretary and General Counsel), William D Johnston (VP Engineering and Construction), Robert D Giroux (VP, Purchasing), Richard E Allen (Assistant Purchasing Agent), James W Bricker (Treasurer and Tax Manager), Jack L Trador (Assistant Secretary and Director of Administrative Services), Michael R Smith (Assistant Director of Administrative Services), G Roger Post (Assistant Secretary and Corporate Counsel), Nicholas W Zuk (Associate Counsel), Barry L Elder (Controller), Frederick P Schindler (Director of Advertising), Robert B Goldberg (Assistant Director of Advertising), John E Huffner (Director of Construction), Craig R Martin (Assistant Director of Construction), Mark I Gelderloos (Director of Engineering), David B Rister (Director of Location Research), John J Ransom (Director of Management Information Services), Sandra E Montgomery (Assistant Director of Management Information Services), Russell J Crouthers (Director of Meat Purchasing and Quality Assurance), Fred G Gunderson (Director of Personnel), Jerry R Richardson (Assistant Director of Personnel), Gail D Turley (Director of Public Relations), James F Sipp (Director of Real Estate), Salvatore J Grani (Assistant Director of Real Estate), John R Edison (Director of Risk Management and Benefits), Richard D Randall (Assistant Director of Risk Management and Benefits), Russell J Meyer (Auditor)

PRINCIPAL ACTIVITIES: Operation of restaurants; fabrication of sheet metal; PSB Company does plastic injection molding and electrostatic painting in addition to metal fabrication
Trade Names: PSB PrizeLAWN (lawn fertilizer spreaders)
Principal Subsidiaries: Division: PSB Company
Principal Bank: Bank One
Financial Information:

	$'000
Sales revenues	244,198

No of Employees: 9,000

WHITE CONSOLIDATED INDUSTRIES, INC

11770 Berea Road, Cleveland, OH 44111
Tel: (216) 252-3700
Telex: 980629

Chairman: Roy H Holdt (and Chief Executive Officer)
President: Ward Smith (and Chief Operating Officer)
Senior Executive Officers: Karl E Ware (Vice Chairman and Chief Administrative Officer), Vincent A Chiarucci (President-Domestic Consumer Products Group), Joseph L McGowan (President-International Products Group), John B Schulze (President-Industrial Products Group), Alfred G Mugford (Senior Executive VP), William F Burrows (VP-Machinery and Equipment Engineering), James L Calhoun (VP-Environmental and Energy Affairs), Leonard C Dook (VP-Procurement and Material Planning), Charles J Conlin Jr (VP-Industrial Relations), Daniel R Elliott Jr (VP-Law and Secretary), Ronald G Fountain (VP-Finance and Treasurer), John A Gehling (VP-Consumer Products), Robert Gross (VP and Inventory Controller), Frederick H Hallett (VP-Industry and Government Relations), W Derald Hunt (VP and Controller), Richard E Isaacson (VP-Consumer Products), Richard L Puterbaugh (VP-Consumer Products Engineering), Richard D Rinehart (VP and Operating Controller), Harold E Schafer (VP-Consumer Products Domestic Marketing), Bernard Zweifach (VP and General Credit Manager)

PRINCIPAL ACTIVITIES: WCI operates in two principal segments: products for the home and industrial machinery and equipment. The products for the home segment consists principally of the manufacture and selling of major home appliances. The industrial machinery and equipment segment manufactures principally machine tools, highway construction equipment, valves, controls and instrumentation, commercial air conditioning, heating and refrigeration products
Trade Names: Frigidaire, Gibson, Kelvinator, White-Westinghouse, Bullard, White-Sundstrand, Blaw-Knox, Jerguson, Copes-Vulcan, Kelvinator Commercial Products
Principal Subsidiaries: Products for the Home:- Americold Compressor Company; Webster City Products Company (Jefferson, IA); Webster City Products Company (Webster City, IA); Belding Products Company; GR Manufacturing Company; Kelvinator International Company; General Appliance Authorized Parts; Gibson Appliance Company; Gibson International Company; Greenville Products Company; Franklin Manufacturing Company; Edison (NJ) Products Company; White Sewing Machine Company; Standard Sewing Equipment Company; Columbus Products Company; Frigidaire Company; Frigidaire Parts & Service Company; Frigidaire International Company; Mansfield Products Company; White-Westinghouse Consumer Service Company; Newark Parts Depot; Philco International Corporation; Kelvinator Appliance Company; White-Westinghouse Consumer Service Company; White-Westinghouse International Company; Productos de Control Corox Inc (Puerto Rico); Kelvinator Sales of Puerto Rico Inc (Puerto Rico); White-Westinghouse Puerto Rico Corporation (Puerto Rico); Athens Products Company; Athens Stove Works; Franklin Canada Manufacturing Division (Canada); WCI Manufacturing Ltd (Canada); WCI Canada Ltd (Canada); Resco Division (Canada); White Sewing Machine Company (A Division of WCI Canada Ltd) (Canada); Hupp Canada Division (Canada); WCI Manufacturing Ltd (Canada); White Westinghouse GmbH (Germany). Industrial Machinery and Equipment:- WCI Machine Tools & Systems (Fairfield, CT); Aurora Steel Products; Richards-Wilcox Manufacturing Company; WCI Machine Tools & Systems (Belvidere, IL);

Blaw-Knox Construction Equipment Company; WCI Machine Tools & Systems (Rockford, IL); WCI Machine Tools & Systems (Dexter, ME); Jerguson Gage & Valve Company; Copes-Vulcan (Charlotte NC); WCI Machine Tools & Systems (Charlotte, NC); Hupp Company; WCI Machine Tools & Systems (Cincinatti, OH) Copes Vukan (Lake City, PA); KCP Company; WCI Machine Tool Group Ltd (UK); Blaw-Knox Construction Equipment Co Ltd (UK); Copes-Vulcan Ltd (UK); White-Sundstrand Machine Tool-Europe SARL (France)

Principal Bank: AmeriTrust Company

Financial Information:

	$'000
Sales revenues	1,900,000

No of Employees: 16,118

WHITE FARM EQUIPMENT CO

2625 Butterfield Road, Oak Brook, IL 60521
Tel: (312) 887-0110
Telex: WUT 25209 whitefarm oakr

Chairman: S J Georgoulis (and President and Chief Executive Officer)
Senior Executive Officers: R E Prunty (VP Manufacturing and Engineering), J H Slife (VP Finance), D L Hays (VP Marketing and Sales)

PRINCIPAL ACTIVITIES: Manufacture of agricultural machinery
Parent Company: Ultimate Holding Company-TIC United Corporation
Financial Information:

	$'000
Sales revenues	150,000

No of Employees: 1,200

WHITE LILY FOODS COMPANY

218 Depot Avenue NE, Knoxville, TN 37901
Tel: (615) 546-5511

Chairman: John T Stout
President: T A Pedas
Senior Executive Officers: J D Kuhn (VP Operations), Lloyd L Montgomery (VP Marketing), Charles J Smiddy (VP Sales), James W Stamper (VP Distribution and Supply), John F Keasling (Secretary and Treasurer)

PRINCIPAL ACTIVITIES: Flour milling
Parent Company: Federal Company through Dixie Portland Flour Mills Inc
Principal Bank: Park National Bank
Financial Information:

	$'000
Sales revenues	50,000

No of Employees: 170

WHITEHALL CORPORATION

2659 Nova Drive, PO Box 29709, Dallas, TX 75229
Tel: (214) 247-8747
Telex: 6829-187 WHT DAL

Chairman: Lee D Webster (and President)
Senior Executive Officers: Carl R Anderson (VP and Treasurer)

PRINCIPAL ACTIVITIES: Seismic and geophysical exploration; manufacture of electronic components; aircraft rebuilding services; anti-submarine warfare systems
Principal Subsidiaries: Seismic Engineering Co; Hydroscience, Inc; Aero Corp; Rogers Explorations Inc; Seismic Explorations International SA; Crystek Crystals Division; Avionics Division; Electroscience Division; Whitehall Export, Inc; Seismic Export Corp
Principal Bank: First Republic Bank Dallas
Financial Information:

	Dec 31 1985	Dec 31 1986
	$'000	$'000
Sales revenues	55,721	36,931
Income before taxes	16,623	2,763
Net income	9,313	2,198
Earnings per share	$2.52	$0.60
Common stock	3,703	3,670
Retained income	56,390	58,588
Shareholders equity	55,557	57,343

No of Employees: 1,369

WHITLOCK CORPORATION

2 Gannett Drive, White Plains, NY 10604
Tel: (914) 694-4650

Chairman: William J Fox (and Chief Executive Officer)
President: Norman Helft (and Chief Operating Officer)
Senior Executive Officers: W J Fox Jr (VP), L Schilz (VP), W Edvenson (VP), Edward Stevens (Treasurer)

PRINCIPAL ACTIVITIES: Manufacture of motor vehicle components
Parent Company: LCP Holdings PLC, UK
Principal Bank: Bank of America
Financial Information:

	$'000
Sales revenues	80,000

No of Employees: 750

WHITNEY HOLDING CORPORATION

228 St Charles Avenue, New Orleans, LA 70103
Tel: (504) 586-7272

Chairman: Patrick A Delaney (and Chief Executive Officer); Vice Chairman: Morgan Whitney
President: R King Milling
Senior Executive Officers: George J Mayer (Senior VP), Harry C Stahel (Senior VP), David F Andignac (VP), Dorothy R Archer (VP), Charles N Monsted III (VP), M Cleland Powell III (VP), Michael J Rapier (VP)

PRINCIPAL ACTIVITIES: Banking services

No of Employees: 900

WHITNEY-FIDALGO SEAFOODS, INC

2360 W Commodore Way, Seattle, WA 98133
Tel: (206) 285-0300

Chairman: Larry Kaner (and Executive VP)
President: G L Salkield
Senior Executive Officers: Elmer Burgess (VP), John Lyon (VP), Ivar Reitan (VP), Paul Palmer (VP), Lloyd Whaley (VP), Wilfred L DeRosier (VP), Wayne Axelson (VP), Arvid Tellevik (Treasurer)

PRINCIPAL ACTIVITIES: Seafoods; fresh, frozen and canned products
Principal Bank: National Bank of Alaska
Financial Information:

	$'000
Sales revenues	50,000

No of Employees: 4,000

WHITTAKER CORPORATION

10880 Wilshire Blvd, Los Angeles, CA 90024
Tel: (213) 475-9411
Telex: 674891

Chairman: Joseph F Alibrandi (and Chief Executive Officer)
President: Gregory T Parkos (and Chief Operating Officer)
Senior Executive Officers: Alan D Jacobson (Senior VP, Administration)

PRINCIPAL ACTIVITIES: Specialty chemical products and technology

Trade Names: Whittaker
Principal Bank: Manufacturers Hanover Trust Company
Financial Information:

	Oct 31 1985	Oct 31 1986
	$'000	$'000
Sales revenues	308,563	399,144
Income (loss) before taxes	(16,228)	8,252
Net income (loss)	19,867	(4,946)
Common dividends	8,267	7,175
Dividends per share	$0.60	$0.60
Earnings (loss) per share	$1.40	($0.44)
Common stock	20,708	15,253
Retained income	235,652	107,665
Shareholders equity	390,162	204,668

No of Employees: 4,000

WHITTET-HIGGINS CO

33 Higginson Avenue, Central Falls, RI 02863
Tel: (401) 728-0700

President: David A Brown (and Chief Executive Officer)

PRINCIPAL ACTIVITIES: Retaining devices including threaded adjustable components for bearing and numerous other power transmission assemblies
Trade Names: Bearhug, Bearlok, Shoenut
Principal Bank: Rhode Island Hospital Trust National Bank

No of Employees: 55

WHOLESALE CLUB INC

7260 Shadeland Station, Indianapolis, IN 46256
Tel: (317) 842 0351

Chairman: John F Geisse (and Chief Executive Officer)
President: Arthur L Coller (and Chief Operating Officer)
Senior Executive Officers: Charles H Huber (Executive VP and Manager Finance), John L Hall (Senior VP, Secretary and Treasurer), C Dennison Brooke (VP), Kenneth E Crawford (VP), Thomas J Geisse (VP), Frank E Hysell (VP and Controller)

PRINCIPAL ACTIVITIES: Wholesale warehouse
Financial Information:

	$'000
Sales revenues	46,145

No of Employees: 360

WICK BUILDING SYSTEMS, INC

403 Walter Road, Box 490, WI 53560-0490
Tel: (608) 795-4281

Chairman: John F Wick (and Chief Executive Officer)
President: Jeffrey Wick (and Chief Operating Officer)
Senior Executive Officers: Helen Wick (VP), Roger E Oimoen (VP), Warren Davis (Senior VP), Darrell Kolstad (VP Administrative Service)

PRINCIPAL ACTIVITIES: Production of prefabricated buildings and mobile homes
Principal Bank: First Wisconsin National Bank
Financial Information:

	$'000
Sales revenues	50-100,000

No of Employees: 700

WICKES COMPANIES, INC

3340 Ocean Park Blvd, Santa Monica, CA 90405
Tel: (213) 452-0161
Telex: TWX 910 3436258 wickes cos

Chairman: Sanford C Sigoloff (and President and Chief Executive Officer)
Corporate Officers: Lawrence P Friedman (Senior VP-Human Resources), Syemour Strasberg (Senior VP-Strategic Planning), James M Van Tatenhove (Senior VP-Administration), Wilhelm A Mallory (Senior Executive VP and Chief Financial Officer), Alvin G Segel (Senior VP, General Counsel and Secretary), Ronald D Strongwater (Senior VP-Real Estate), Michael S Sitrick (Senior VP-Communications), Ervin J Bolks (VP and Treasurer), James N Castleberry (VP-Controls Evaluation and Compliance), Robert S Fenton (VP-Tax), M Douglas Fisher (VP-Risk Management), Michael Jamieson (VP and Controller), Bill J Mann (VP-Wickes Data Services Division), Raymond J Byrne (VP)

PRINCIPAL ACTIVITIES: Principal Businesses:- Building materials and home furnishings, apparel and hosiery, and manufacturing and automotive parts distribution
Financial Information:

	$'000
Sales revenues	4,800,000

No of Employees: 50,000

WICOR, INC

777 E Wisconsin Avenue, Milwaukee, WI 53202
Tel: (414) 291-7000

President: Stuart W Tisdale (and Chief Executive Officer)
Senior Executive Officers: B William Kostecke (VP Treasurer and Secretary), John W Brady (VP)

PRINCIPAL ACTIVITIES: The company has interests in oil and gas exploration and production; fuel distribution; manufacture of fluid control apparatus and pumps
Principal Subsidiaries: Wisconsin Gas Company; STA-RITE Industries Inc; WEXCO of Delaware, Inc
Principal Bank: Citibank
Financial Information:

	Dec 31 1985	Dec 31 1986
	$'000	$'000
Sales revenues	831,772	740,054
Income before taxes	49,236	37,744
Net income	26,251	21,103
Dividends	15,845	17,264
Dividends per share	$2.36	$2.56
Earnings per share	$4.14	$3.18
Common stock*	5,890	6,012
Retained income	67,848	71,687
Shareholders equity	169,431	198,652

*number of shares in thousands

No of Employees: 3,381

WIEGAND, EDWIN L,

641 Alpha Drive, Pittsburgh, PA 15238-2819
Tel: (412) 323-3800
Telex: WUT 866124 wiegand pgh cc

President: William H Davis
Senior Executive Officers: Stephen Campanella (Executive VP), E Blystone (Executive VP Operations), L Hill (VP Personnel), Thomas L Watson (VP Finance), Ross Werner (VP International)

PRINCIPAL ACTIVITIES: Production of electrical heating systems
Parent Company: Emerson Electric Co, St Louis, MO
Financial Information:

	$'000
Sales revenues	100,000

No of Employees: 2,000

WIENER ENTERPRISES INC

5725 Powell Street, PO Box 23607, Harahan, LA 70183
Tel: (504) 733 7055

Chairman: Sander N Wiener (and President and Chief Executive Officer)
Senior Executive Officers: Norris J Gremillion (Executive VP and Chief Operating Officer), Michael J Doherty (Senior VP,

Secretary and Treasurer), Jules Watsky (Senior VP), Randy Ferguson (VP Apparel), Frank C Shows (VP)

PRINCIPAL ACTIVITIES: Retail trade in clothing and footwear
Principal Subsidiaries: Apparel Specialty Inc; Danny's Men and Boys Wear Inc; Shoe Lodge Inc; Shoe Town Inc
Principal Bank: Texas Commerce Bank
Financial Information:

	$'000
Sales revenues	58,000

No of Employees: 870

WILEY, JOHN, & SONS, INC
605 Third Avenue, New York, NY 10158
Tel: (212) 850-6000
Telex: WUT 127063 jonwile nyk

Chairman: W B Wiley
President: Andrew H Neilly Jr (and Chief Executive Officer)
Senior Executive Officers: Anthony W Molnar Jr (Senior VP and Chief Financial Officer), William Smith (VP and Treasurer), R C Douglas (Senior VP), Warren Sullivan (VP), Andrew E Ford (VP), J A Higham (Senior VP), Deborah E Wiley (VP)

PRINCIPAL ACTIVITIES: Publishers of academic and professional books and periodicals; training
Principal Subsidiaries: Wilson Learning Corporation
Principal Bank: Morgan Guaranty Trust Company
Financial Information:

	$'000
Sales revenues	213,300

No of Employees: 1,900

WILFRED AMERICAN EDUCATIONAL CORPORATION
1657 Boradway, New York, NY 10019
Tel: (212) 582 6690

Chairman: Philip E Jakeway Jr (and President)
Senior Executive Officers: Anthony B Colletti (Executive VP and Secretary)

PRINCIPAL ACTIVITIES: Training schools for careers
Financial Information:

	$'000
Sales revenues	75,365

No of Employees: 1,545

WILLAMETTE INDUSTRIES, INC
1300 SW Fifth Avenue, Portland, OR 97201
Tel: (503) 227-5581
Telex: TWX 910 4648033 westkrvt ptd

Chairman: William Swindells Jr (and President and Chief Executive Officer)
Senior Executive Officers: C W Knodell (Executive VP and Secretary), Felix M Hammack (Executive VP), William P Kinnune (Executive VP), William M Shields (Executive VP), David W Morthland (VP Personnel and Industrial Relations), J A Parsons (VP and Controller)

PRINCIPAL ACTIVITIES: Wood and wood products; paper and paper products
Principal Bank: Chase Manhattan Bank
Financial Information:

	Dec 31 1985	Dec 31 1986
	$'000	$'000
Sales revenues	1,152,067	1,200,155
Net income	60,244	74,665
Earnings per share	$3.95	$2.94
Shareholders equity	473,050	521,795

No of Employees: 8,110

WILLCOX & GIBBS INC
1440 Broadway, New York, NY 10018
Tel: (212) 869-1800

Chairman: Sidney B Becker
President: John K Ziegler (and Chief Executive Officer)
Senior Executive Officers: Richard J Mackey (Executive VP and Treasurer), Wayne Campbell (VP), Jeffrey B Koch (VP), Richard Warsoff (VP)

PRINCIPAL ACTIVITIES: Supply of sewing machines and equipment; manufacture of die cut paperboard and sample cards
Principal Subsidiaries: Willcox & Gibbs Ltd (UK); W & G Export Corp; F W Peighton & Co Ltd; MEC Sewing Machines Ltd; Robin Service Corp; Willcox & Gibbs Delaware Inc; Willcox & Gibbs Engineering Ltd; Steinthal Sample Co Inc; Unique Sewing Machine Parts & SUpply Corp; W & G Jolier Inc; W & G Development AG; Willcox & Gibbs-Kennedy of Delaware Inc; Willcox & Gibbs (France), SA; Kennedy Sewing Machine Co; Regal Manufacturing Co
Financial Information:

	$'000
Sales revenues	224,750

No of Employees: 1,650

WILLIAM CARTER COMPANY
See CARTER, WILLIAM, COMPANY

WILLIAM L BONNELL CO
See BONNELL, WILLIAM L, CO

WILLIAMHOUSE-REGENCY INC
28 West 23rd Street, New York, NY 10010
Tel: (212) 691-2000

Chairman: Saul Olzman
President: Martin R Lewis (and Chief Executive Officer)
Senior Executive Officers: Edward F Downs (VP Finance), John E Slough (VP and Secretary), C W Holloman (VP and Group Chairman Converting), Edward L Norton (VP and Group Vice-Chairman Converting), Arthur R Fugazzi (VP Manufacturing), David L Gersman (VP Marketing), Antony Urgola (VP Group Chairman Personalizing), Diane C Brandt (VP), James C Mendicino (VP Business Product Development), David L Mittelman (VP)

PRINCIPAL ACTIVITIES: Printers of commercial and social stationery; greetings cards
Principal Bank: Continental Illinois National Bank of Chicago
Financial Information:

	$'000
Sales revenues	240,000

No of Employees: 3,800

WILLIAMS, A L, CORPORATION (THE)
3120 Breckinridge Boulevard, Duluth, GA 30199
Tel: (404) 381-1674

Chairman: Arthur L Williams Jr (and Chief Executive Officer)
President: Robert J Miller
Senior Executive Officers: William C Keane (Executive VP), Robert L Whitney (Executive VP and Actuary), Robert T Buisson (VP Sales), Barbara T King (VP Public Relations), Barry W Turk (VP Finance, Treasurer and Controller)

PRINCIPAL ACTIVITIES: Insurance
Principal Bank: National Bank of Georgia
Financial Information:

	$'000
Revenues	202,000

WILLIAMS COMPANIES
One Williams Center, Tulsa, OK 74172
Tel: (918) 588-2000

Chairman: Joseph H Williams (and Chief Executive Officer)
President: Vernon T Jones
Senior Executive Officers: Keith E Bailey (Executive VP Finance and Administration), John C Bumgarner Jr (Senior VP), Robert G Harbison (Senior VP), M Fred Droege (VP), John C Fischer (VP), John T Miller (VP), Barry N Roth (VP Government Affairs)

PRINCIPAL ACTIVITIES: The company has interests in the distribution of natural gas and petroleum products and telecommunications
Principal Bank: Citibank
Financial Information:

	$'000
Sales revenues	1,900,000

No of Employees: 7,000

WILLIAMS ELECTRONICS, INC

3401 N California Avenue, Chicago, IL 60618
Tel: (312) 267-2240
Telex: WUT 270273 wilelacct cgo

Chairman: Louis J Nicastro (and President, Chief Executive and Operating Officer)
Senior Executive Officers: Norman Menell (Executive VP and Chief Operating Officer), Thomas Cutti (VP Finance, Chief Financial and Accounting Officer), John Masterson (VP Manufacturing), Kenneth Fedesna (VP Engineering), Joseph Dillon (VP Sales), Neil Nicastro (VP and Treasurer), Barbara M Norman (VP, Secretary and General Counsel), Richard J Wilkus (VP)

PRINCIPAL ACTIVITIES: Manufacture of slot machines
Principal Subsidiaries: Williams Electronics Games Inc; Williams Video Games Inc; Williams Innovative Technologies Inc; Williams Int'l Sales Corp; Williams Hotel Corp; Posadas de Puerto Rico; Williams Hospitality Mgmt; Williams Entertainment Corp
Principal Bank: Continental Illinois National Bank & Trust Co of Chicago
Financial Information:

	$'000
Sales revenues	65,000

No of Employees: 500

WILLIAMS GOLD REFINING CO

2978 Main Street, Buffalo, NY 14214
Tel: (716) 837-1000
Telex: WUT 91224 willgold buf

President: John A Williams
Senior Executive Officers: Reginald V Williams Jr (Executive VP Dental Sales), Malcolm A Williams (Executive VP), David G Hecht (VP Administration), George Keller (VP Industrial Sales), Kevin M Dillon (VP Dental Sales), Joseph P Quinn (VP Manufacturing), Robert A Ganley (Treasurer)

PRINCIPAL ACTIVITIES: Gold alloys for dentistry; processing of scrap precious metals; metals for precious metal electroplating
Principal Bank: Marine Midland Bank
Financial Information:

	$'000
Sales revenues	100,000

No of Employees: 330

WILLIAMS INDUSTRIES INC

2849 Meadow View Road, Falls Church, VA 22042
Tel: (703) 560 1505

President: Frank E Williams
Senior Executive Officers: William R Weadon (VP), F Everett Williams (VP), Arthur V Conover (Secretary and Treasurer)

PRINCIPAL ACTIVITIES: Steel erection, fabrication and related services
Principal Subsidiaries: Bridge and Paving Services Inc; SIP Inc; Commercial Manufacturing and Repair Company Inc; Allied Engineered Products Inc; Cranes Unlimited Inc; Delaware Valley Erectors Inc; Dominion Caisson Corporation; Williams Enterprises Inc; Arthur Phillips & Company Inc; Williams Mescellaneous Erection Company Inc; Williams Steel Erection Company Inc
Principal Bank: Sovran Bank
Financial Information:

	$'000
Sales revenues	45,000

No of Employees: 1,000

WILLIAMS, W W, COMPANY

835 West Goodale Boulevard, Columbus, OH 43212
Tel: (614) 228 5000

Chairman: David F Williams (and Chief Executive Officer)
President: Edward J Mullaney (and Chief Operating Officer)
Senior Executive Officers: Richard M Gilbert (VP Finance), Douglas E Nunnery (VP and General Manager TN & MS Construction Equipment Division), Jean A Patrick (VP Marketing), Gordon W Rosencrans Jr (VP and General Manager FL Construction Equipment Division), Thomas A Ables (Controller), Stephen E Auch (Secretary), Donald F Campbell (Treasurer)

PRINCIPAL ACTIVITIES: Mining and construction equipment
Principal Subsidiaries: Atlantic Power Systems Inc; Great Lakes Energy Systems Inc; W W Williams Co Florida; W W Williams Co Pennsylvania
Principal Bank: BancOhio National Bank
Financial Information:

	$'000
Sales revenues	110,755

No of Employees: 730

WILLIAMSON-DICKIE MFG CO

509 W Vickery Blvd, Fort Worth, TX 76104
Tel: (817) 336-7201

Chairman: C D Williamson (and Chief Executive Officer)
President: J D Williamson
Senior Executive Officers: William G Bush (VP Finance), Charles M Crane (VP Sales), Stephen Lefler (VP Merchandise)

PRINCIPAL ACTIVITIES: Manufacture of clothing for men and boys
Principal Bank: First National Bank of Fort Worth
Financial Information:

	$'000
Sales revenues	200,000

No of Employees: 3,000

WILLIAMS-SONOMA INC

5750 Hollis Street, Emeryville, CA 94608
Tel: (415) 652 1555

Chairman: Charles E Williams
President: W Howard Lester (and Chief Executive Officer)
Senior Executive Officers: C Thomas Egan (VP and General Manager), James D Abrams (Chief Financial Officer and Secretary), Patrick J Conolly (VP Sales), Robert K Early (VP Distribution), Donna Moore (VP)

PRINCIPAL ACTIVITIES: Retail trade in cookware and related items; mail order services
Principal Bank: Wells Fargo Bank
Financial Information:

	$'000
Sales revenues	68,000

No of Employees: 840

WILMINGTON SAVINGS FUND SOCIETY

838 Market Street, Wilmington, DE 19899
Tel: (302) 571-7000

President: J W St Clair Jr (and Chief Executive Officer)
Senior Executive Officers: Arthur C Annone (Executive VP Commercial Lending), Ronald C Smith (Executive VP and Secretary), John M Mason (Executive VP and Chief Financial Officer), David J Feeser (Executive VP Operations and Data Processing), Thomas K Kerstetter (Executive VP Marketing), Ralph L Baldwin (Senior VP Consumer Loans), Gordon M Dyott (Senior VP Marketing), Ronald E Anderson (VP Operations), David L Burton (VP Personnel), Richard E Coning (VP Commercial Oans), Donald Hale Hadley II (VP Branch Administration), Richard Hirtzell (VP Residential Mortgages), Samuel Lam (VP Commercial Mortgages), Constance McCarthy (VP Commercial Loans), Scott L Morrison (VP Consumer Banking), John J Parker III (VP Community Banking), Jack L Ratcliffe (VP Commercial Loans), Robert Shadduck (VP Commercial Credit and Loan Review), Barbara L Testa (VP and Controller)

PRINCIPAL ACTIVITIES: Mutual Savings Bank
Principal Bank: Fidelity Bank

No of Employees: 430

WILMINGTON TRUST CO

Rodney Square N, Wilmington, DE 19890
Tel: (302) 651-1000

Chairman: Bernard J Taylor II (and Chief Executive Officer)
President: A Samuel Gray (and Chief Operating Officer)
Senior Executive Officers: Henry F Acquaotta (Senior VP), Ted T Cecala (Senior VP), Donald A Corkran (Senior VP), George D Craig (Senior VP), Robert V A Harra Jr (Senior VP), Nathan Hayward III (Senior VP), Joseph M Moran (Senior VP, Secretary and Real Estate Officer), Leonard W Quill (Senior VP)

PRINCIPAL ACTIVITIES: Banking services

No of Employees: 1,500

WILSEY FOODS, INC

14840 Don Julian Road, City of Industry, CA 91746
Tel: (213) 264-2160
Telex: WUT 670351 wilsey corp ci

Chairman: Henry Poelt III
President: Jack J Davis
Senior Executive Officers: Art Cayley (Senior VP), Warren Mitchell (Senior VP), Greg McIntosh (Senior VP), Ray Bennett (VP)

PRINCIPAL ACTIVITIES: Production of vegetable oils
Principal Bank: Bank of America
Financial Information:

	$'000
Sales revenues	200,000

No of Employees: 600

WILSON BROTHERS

43 West 42nd Street, New York, NY 10036
Tel: (212) 302 8460

Chairman: Victor Posner (and President and Chief Executive Officer); Vice Chairman: Steven N Posner (and Chairman Executive Committee)
Senior Executive Officers: Donald J Glazer (Executive VP), V J Kaplan (Executive VP and Chief Operating Officer), Melvin R Colvin (Senior VP), Jack Coppersmith (Senior VP and Chief Financial Officer), Raymond J Dettore (Senior VP), Renee Mottram-Doss (Senior VP Administration), Bernard I Posner (Senior VP), Walter Sieckman (Senior VP), Philip A Smalley Jr (Senior VP Human Resources), Edward A Christensen (VP and Secretary), Harry T Clew (VP), David T Glasser (VP Finance and Administration), Mitchell V Gregory (VP and Controller), Leonard Leifert (VP), Jack Lubin (VP), Tracy Posner (VP)

PRINCIPAL ACTIVITIES: Manufacture of shirts; production of glass; manufacture of ceramic tiles
Principal Subsidiaries: The Enro Shirt Co Inc; Levin & Hecht Inc; Houze Grass Corp; Enno-at-East Inc; Foxcroft Shirt Ltd
Principal Bank: Manufacturers Hanover Trust
Financial Information:

	$'000
Sales revenues	64,780

No of Employees: 870

WILSON FOODS CORPORATION

4545 N Lincoln Blvd, Oklahoma City, OK 73105
Tel: (405) 525-4545

Chairman: Kenneth J Griggy (Chief Exeutive Officer)
President: Richard T Berg (Chief Operating Officer)
Senior Executive Officers: John T Hanes (Executive VP Sales and Marketing), Vincent P Cotter (Executive VP and Chief Financial Officer), John M Groom (Senior VP-Plant Management), David R Almond (VP and General Counsel), William L Brady (VP and Controller), James D Desherow (Senior VP-Food Service Sales), James D Hartson (VP-Retail Sales)

PRINCIPAL ACTIVITIES: Wilson Foods produces a variety of fresh, frozen and processed meat products and cuts including canned and boneless hams; boneless, vacuum-packed, fresh pork cuts; sausages; cold cuts and deli products; sliced bacon; canned luncheon meats; fried pork rinds; bacon crumbles; and meat by-products such as hydrogenated shortening and cooking and salad oils. Sales are made to retail grocery organizations, foodservice operators, other food processors and regional distributors throughout the country
Principal Subsidiaries: Anderson Meat & Provisions, Inc; Brennan Packing Co Inc; Fischer Packing Company; Toppers Meat Company; Wilson Certified Express, Inc; Wilson & Co, Inc; Wilson Foods Ltd (New Zealand)
Financial Information:

	Aug 3 1985 $'000	Aug 2 1986 $'000
Sales revenues	1,533,155	1,454,210
(Loss) before taxes*	(16,978)	(25,028)
Net (loss)	(16,185)	(23,514)
(Loss) per share	($2.71)	($3.80)
Common stock	3,000	94,128
Retained (deficit)	(33,868)	(57,382)
Shareholders equity	50,100	36,746

*and extraordinary gains

No of Employees: 4,950

WILSON INDUSTRIES, INC

1301 Conti Street, Houston, TX 77251
Tel: (713) 237-3700
Cable: TWX 910 8817156
Answerback: wilsco hou

Chairman: Wallace S Wilson
President: Preston Moore Jr
Senior Executive Officers: G W Gist Jr

PRINCIPAL ACTIVITIES: Oil and gas services and equipment; livestock feeding equipment
Financial Information:

	$'000
Sales revenues	500,000

No of Employees: 1,000

WILSON JONES CO

6150 Touhy Avenue, Chicago, IL 60648
Tel: (312) 774-7700
Telex: WUT 724467 wlsnjones nile

President: Winthrop W Hamilton (and Chief Executive Officer)
Senior Executive Officers: Vernon S Schroeder (Executive VP and Chief Operating Officer), Gene Angel (VP Sales), Jerry Peters (VP Marketing)

PRINCIPAL ACTIVITIES: Manufacture of a broad line of office products, including columnar pads, loose-leaf binders, accounting forms, computer printout binders, supplies and furniture and through its Acme Visible Division, Record Systems. Also sale of paper shredders
Parent Company: American Brands Inc, New York, NY
Principal Bank: First National Bank of Chicago
Financial Information:

	1986
	$'000
Sales revenues	169,142

No of Employees: 1,700

WILTON ENTERPRISES, INC

2240 W 75th Street, Woodridge, IL 60517
Tel: (312) 963-7100
Telex: WUT 857497 wilton ent ud

Chairman: William G Henderson; Vice Chairman: Vincent A Naccarato (and Chief Executive Officer)
Senior Executive Officers: Walter Kelly (VP Finance), Harry Levy (VP Sales), W Howard McClennan (VP, Secretary and Chief Financial Officer), Marvin Oakes (VP Marketing), Joseph M Snayd (VP Operations)

PRINCIPAL ACTIVITIES: Sale of home baking equipment
Principal Bank: The Northern Trust Company
Financial Information:

	$'000
Sales revenues	48,000

No of Employees: 320

WINDMERE CORPORATION

4920 NW 165th Street, Hialeah, FL 33014
Tel: (305) 621 2611

Chairman: Belvin Friedson (and Chief Executive Officer)
President: David M Friedson (and Chief Operating Officer)
Senior Executive Officers: Lucille K Friedson (Senior VP), Barbara F Hornsby (Senior VP Professional Group), Arnold Thaler (Senior VP Product Development and Imports), Burton A Honig (VP Finance), David A Ruben (VP Consumer Group), Neil E Wallach (VP Marketing and Advertising), Joseph Reid (Treasurer and Controller) Secretary), Jerald I Rosen (Secretary)

PRINCIPAL ACTIVITIES: Import, manufacture and sale of electrical appliances for hair care and personal and hair care products
Principal Bank: Continental Illinois National Bank & Trust Co of Chicago
Financial Information:

	$'000
Sales revenues	91,000

No of Employees: 400

WINFIELD MFG CO INC

350 5th Avenue, Empire State Bldg-Suite 6608, New York, NY 10118
Tel: (212) 695-2860
Telex: 710581 2572 winfield nyk

Chairman: Milton Weinsten
President: Jeffrey J Weinsten
Senior Executive Officers: Lee Weinsten (Secretary), Bill Martin (VP), S J Elias (Chief Financial Officer)

PRINCIPAL ACTIVITIES: Manufacturer of apparel equipage and chemical protective clothing for Defense Department (USA) and other allies. Tents, field packs, field coats, combat trousers and combat coats, chemical protective suits and outfits
Trade Names: Winfield International Ltd
Principal Subsidiaries: MJM Management Corp in New York, NY with plants in Belmont (MS); Cherokee (AL); Burnsville (MS)
Principal Bank: National Westminster; Manufacturers Hanover; First Citizens Bank
Financial Information:

	Jun 30 1987
	$'000
Sales revenues	42,187
Net income	1,036
Retained income	9,593
Shareholders equity	10,207

No of Employees: 450 (plus contractors)

WINN ENTERPRISES

5500 East Santa Ana Canyon Rd, Anaheim, CA 92807
Tel: (714) 637-2720

Chairmen: Daniel C Montano
President: John P Brinco (and Chief Executive Officer)

PRINCIPAL ACTIVITIES: The company has interests in financial and investment services; dairy food products, food flavorings and the operation of convenience food stores
Principal Subsidiaries: Knudsen Foods Inc; Mountain West Savings and Loan Association
Principal Bank: Wells Fargo
Financial Information:

	$,000
Sales revenues	546,000

No of Employees: 2,500

WINN-DIXIE STORES, INC

5050 Edgewood Court, Jacksonville, FL 32203
Tel: (904) 783-5000
Telex: WUT 56266 winn dixie mgy

Chairman: Robert D Davis (and Chief Financial Office)
President: A Dano Davis (and Chief Executive Officer)
Senior Executive Officers: Frank L James (Executive VP), S W Evans (Senior VP), R J Holmes (Senior VP), James Kufeldt (Senior VP), C H McKellar (Senior VP), T Wayne Davis Jr (VP), Richard P McCook (VP Finance)

PRINCIPAL ACTIVITIES: Operation of a chain of grocery stores
Principal Bank: Atlantic National Bank
Financial Information:

	Jun 30 1985	Jun 30 1986
	$'000	$'000
Sales revenues	7,774,480	8,225,244
Net income	107,900	116,391
Earnings per share	$2.64	$2.84
Shareholders equity	646,777	704,558

No of Employees: 76,900

WINNEBAGO INDUSTRIES, INC

PO Box 152, Forest City, IA 50436
Tel: (515) 582-3535
Telex: TWX 910 5236810 winnebago forr

Chairman: John K Hanson; Deputy Chairman: John V Hanson
President: Gerald W Gilbert (and Chief Executive Officer)
Senior Executive Officers: Gerald E Boman (Senior VP), Raymond M Beebe (VP, Secretary and General Counsel), Richard Berreth (VP Operations), Barbara H Bulman (VP Administration), Clyde L Church (VP Product Planning and Engineering), H W Dahl (VP Finance), Fred G Emmert (VP Marketing)

PRINCIPAL ACTIVITIES: Manufacture of motor homes
Principal Subsidiaries: Winnebago Acceptance Corp; Winnebago Realty Corp; Winnebago International Corp
Principal Bank: Northwestern National Bank of Minneapolis

Financial Information:

	$'000
Sales revenues	424,170

No of Employees: 2,600

WINNERS CORPORATION

PO Box 184, Two Maryland Farms, Suite 100, Brentwood, TN 37027
Tel: (615) 377 4400

Chairman: Jack C Massey
President: Lonnie J Stout (and Chief Executive Officer)
Senior Executive Officers: Charles W Porter-Shirley (Executive VP and Chief Operating Officer), Gary T Custer (VP), William E Hall Jr (VP), Gregory R Lewis (VP, Chief Financial Officer and Secretary), Richard D May (VP), John A Weber (VP), Stephen R Meek (VP and Controller)

PRINCIPAL ACTIVITIES: Restaurants and catering
Principal Subsidiaries: Union Leasing Corporation; Volunteer Capital East Inc; Volunteer Capital West Inc
Principal Bank: Nashville City Bank
Financial Information:

	$'000
Sales revenues	112,160

No of Employees: 5,600

WINTER, JACK, INC

8100 North Teutonia Avenue, Milwaukee, WI 53209
Tel: (414) 357 4840

Chairman: Jack A Winter (and Chief Executive Officer)
President: Jack R Winter (and Treasurer)
Senior Executive Officers: Michael Winter (VP), Ken J Pleimann (VP Finance and Secretary)

PRINCIPAL ACTIVITIES: Manufacture of sports clothing for women
Principal Subsidiaries: Jack Winter Apparel Inc
Principal Bank: First Wisconsin National Bank
Financial Information:

	$'000
Sales revenues	40,500

No of Employees: 610

WIRE ROPE CORPORATION OF AMERICA, INC

609 N 2nd Street, St Joseph, MO 64501
Tel: (816) 233-0287
Telex: WUT 426157 wire rope stj

President: J P Barclay Jr (and Chief Executive Officer)
Senior Executive Officers: Charles W Salanski (Executive VP), R L Kessler (VP Manufacturing), Stephen D Wurtzler (VP Finance, Secretary and Treasurer)

PRINCIPAL ACTIVITIES: Manufacture of wire rope and related products
Principal Bank: State Bank of Albany
Financial Information:

	$'000
Sales revenues	75,000

No of Employees: 700

WISCONSIN CENTRIFUGAL INC

905 E St Paul Avenue, Waukesha, WI 53186
Tel: (414) 544-7777
Telex: 26 9553

President: Robert Piper
Senior Executive Officers: John M Nevins (Senior VP), Herbert E Pritzlaff (VP Engineering), Robert Smickley (VP Operations)

PRINCIPAL ACTIVITIES: Centrifugally cast parts and automotive and industrial components
Parent Company: Southern Centrifugal Inc
Principal Bank: Barnett Bank of Florida
Financial Information:

	$'000
Sales revenues	42,000

No of Employees: 500

WISCONSIN DAIRIES COOPERATIVE

Route 3, Baraboo, WI 53913
Tel: (608) 356-8316

Chairman: Herbert Selbrede
President: Don Storhoff
Senior Executive Officers: Richard Krueger (1st VP), Duane Solum (2nd VP), Werner Bailweg (Treasurer), Eldon Netz (Secretary)

PRINCIPAL ACTIVITIES: Dairy products cooperative
Financial Information:

	Mar 31 1986 $'000
Sales revenues	459,242
Shareholders equity	48,605

No of Employees: 650

WISCONSIN ELECTRIC POWER CO

231 W Michigan St, PO Box 2046, Milwaukee, WI 53201
Tel: (414) 277-2345

Chairman: Charles S McNeer (and Chief Executive Officer); Vice Chairman: Sol Burstein
President: Russell W Britt (and Chief Operating Officer)
Senior Executive Officers: Thomas Cassidy (Executive VP), Richard A Abdoo (Senior VP), George W Bomier (VP), John W Boston (Senior VP), Carlyle W Fay (VP Nuclear Power), Robert H Gorske (VP and General Counsel), Russell A Niles (VP Operations), H R Platz (VP Engineering and Construction), Jerry G Remmel (VP and Treasurer), Richard E Skogg (VP Operations), John E Speaker (VP Communications), Kenneth E Walters (VP Operations)

PRINCIPAL ACTIVITIES: Distribution of electricity and natural gas
Principal Bankers: First WI National Bank
Financial Information:

	$'000
Sales revenues	1,441,000

No of Employees: 6,200

WISCONSIN POWER & LIGHT CO

PO Box 192, Madison, WI 53701-0192
Tel: (608) 252-3311

Chairman: James R Underkofler (and President and Chief Executive Officer)
Senior Executive Officers: Erroll B Davis Jr (Executive VP), Eugene O Gehl (Executive VP and General Counsel), William L Keepers (Executive VP), Robert A Carlsen (VP Customer Services and Corporate Communications), David E Ellestad (VP Electrical Engineering and Processing), Edward M Gleason (VP Finance, Treasurer and Secretary), William D Harvey (VP and Associate General Counsel), James E Johnson (VP Natural Gas), Edward F Killeen (VP Administration), William C Register (VP Power Production and Systems Planning)

PRINCIPAL ACTIVITIES: Natural gas and electricity supply
Principal Bankers: First WI National Bank of Milwaukee
Financial Information:

	$'000
Sales revenues	569,000

No of Employees: 2,500

WISCONSIN PUBLIC SERVICE CORPORATION

PO Box 19001, Green Bay, WI 54307-9001
Tel: (414) 433-1598

Chairman: Paul D Ziemer
President: Linus M Stoll (and Chief Executive Officer)
Senior Executive Officers: Daniel A Bollom (Senior VP Operations), James H Liethen (Senior VP Finance), John V Henderson (Senior VP Corporate Services), Eugene R Mathews (Senior VP-Power Supply and Engineering)

PRINCIPAL ACTIVITIES: Electricity supply; distribution of natural gas
Principal Subsidiaries: Dolores Bench General Partner Inc; WPS Development Inc; Wisconsin Public Service Resources Inc; WPS Communications Inc
Financial Information:

	Dec 31 1986
	$'000
Sales revenues	592,270
Income before taxes	87,202
Net income	51,541
Common dividends	34,257
Preferred dividends	4,392
Dividends per share	$1.46
Earnings per share	$2.02
Common stock	92,802
Retained income	203,258
Shareholders equity	346,445

No of Employees: 2,497

WISCONSIN SOUTHERN GAS COMPANY INC

120 East Sheridan Springs Road, Lake Geneva, WI 53147
Tel: (414) 248 8861

Chairman: Thomas C Jacobs
President: Willard L Decker (and Chief Executive Officer)
Senior Executive Officers: Edward A Labelle (VP Operations), Charles D Larson (VP Utilization), Richard E Johnson (Treasurer), Glen H Bell (Secretary)

PRINCIPAL ACTIVITIES: Distribution of natural gas
Principal Bank: Harris Trust & Savings Bank
Financial Information:

	$'000
Sales revenues	43,518

No of Employees: 130

WISCONSIN TISSUE MILLS

Menasha, WI 54952
Tel: (414) 725-7031
Telex: WUT 262744 wistissue mnsh

President: George P Mueller
Senior Executive Officers: Charles S Cianciola (Executive VP), Wm L New (Executive VP), Jack E Carstens (VP Sales and Marketing), Bill Raaths (VP Finance and Planning), Daniel Waselchek (VP Engineering)

PRINCIPAL ACTIVITIES: Manufacture of paper napkins, facial tissues and toilet tissue
Parent Company: Chesapeake Corporation
Principal Bank: Bank of Menasha
Financial Information:

	$'000
Sales revenues	100,000

No of Employees: 1,000

WISE/OLD LONDON FOODS

228 Raseley Street, Berwick, PA 18603
Tel: (717) 759-4000

President: George Waydo
Senior Executive Officers: George Cooper (General Manager), Bob Paquette (General Manager Southwest Zone), Ed Chapman (Director Management Information Systems)

PRINCIPAL ACTIVITIES: Manufacture of potato snack products
Parent Company: Borden Inc
Principal Bank: Chase Manhattan Bank
Financial Information:

	$'000
Sales revenues	180,000

No of Employees: 1,200

WISER OIL COMPANY (THE)

210 Charles Street, Sistersville, WV 26175
Tel: (304) 652 3861

President: John C Wright (and Chief Executive Officer)
Senior Executive Officers: Milton G Bailes (VP and Secretary), Charles P LaRue (VP Production), Paul H C Eddy (Treasurer)

PRINCIPAL ACTIVITIES: Production of oil and natural gas
Financial Information:

	$'000
Sales revenues	46,513

No of Employees: 230

WITCO CORPORATION

520 Madison Avenue, New York, NY 10022
Tel: (212) 605-3800
Telex: ITT 422186 witco

Chairman: William Wishnick (and Chief Executive Officer)
President: Thomas J Bickett (and Chief Operating Officer)
Senior Executive Officers: J L Kennedy (Senior Executive VP), Dennis Andreuzzi (Executive VP Commercial Services), William E Setzler (Executive VP Chemical Group), William J Toller (Executive VP Finance and Administration), Alan M Abrams (VP and General Counsel), Peter J Biancotti (VP and Controller), Howard S Bryant (VP Engineering), Eric Davies (VP Management Information Services), Paul M Feeney (VP and Treasurer), Gerald Katz (VP Corporate Development), Arthur R Kuhn (VP Industrial Relations), Joseph Russo (VP and Secretary), Carl R Soderlind (VP Corporate Communications), Tom M Uhoda (VP Purchasing, Distribution and Traffic)

PRINCIPAL ACTIVITIES: Manufacture of specialty chemicals; petrochemicals; fertilizers
Principal Subsidiaries: Witco Chemical Canada Ltd; Savon-Majestic Ltee; Witco Chemical Ltd; Baxenden Chemical Co Ltd (53.5%); Witco Chemical SA; Witco Chemical Ltd (60%); Argus Quimica Mexicana SA de CV; Witco Chemical BV; Jonk BV; Southwest Petro-Chem Inc; Surpass Chemicals Ltd; Witco Chemical Italiana SRL; Witco Chemical Espanola SA; Witco Chemical Australia Pty Ltd
Financial Information:

	Dec 31 1985	Dec 31 1986
	$'000	$'000
Sales revenues	1,448,929	1,355,018
Net income	56,774	65,215
Earnings per share	$3.85	$2.93
Shareholders equity	415,410	465,465

No of Employees: 8,060

W-K-M DIVISION

PO Box 4334, Houston, TX 77210
Tel: (713) 780-8888

Senior Executive Officers: C L Harper (General Manager), Glen A Tableman (Assistant General Manager), H E Conway (Controller), C J Lockstedt (Director Operations), G L Robertson (Director Human Resources)

PRINCIPAL ACTIVITIES: Manufacture of equipment for production of gas and oil; manufacture of valves
Parent Company: Joy Manufacturing Co

Principal Bank: Houston National Bank

Financial Information:

	$'000
Sales revenues	170,000

No of Employees: 1,650

WM B REILY & CO

See REILY, WM B, & CO

WM E WRIGHT CO

See WRIGHT, WM E, CO

WM WRIGLEY JR CO

See WRIGLEY, WM, JR CO

WOLOHAN LUMBER COMPANY

1740 Midland Road, PO Box 3235, Saginaw, MI 48605

Tel: (517) 793 4532

Chairman: David F Wallace

President: James L Wolohan (and Chief Executive Officer)

Senior Executive Officers: Robert F Anderson (Executive VP, Secretary and Chief Financial Officer), David G Honaman (VP Administration), Gary D Sellers (VP Operations), Edward J Dean (Corporate Controller), James R Krapohl (Treasurer and Assistant Secretary), Timothy J Stein (VP Merchandising), Thomas R Wolohan (VP Corporate Development). District Operations Managers: Larry R Croucher, Harold L Erskine, Thomas E Farrell, Leonard J Gutierrez, Mark H Hershberger, James G White

PRINCIPAL ACTIVITIES: Wolohan Lumber Co is a full-line retailer of lumber and building materials and related products used primarily for new home construction and home-improvement and maintenance projects serving both consumer/do-it-yourself (DIY) and professional contractor customers

Financial Information:

	Dec 31 1985	Dec 31 1986
	$'000	$'000
Sales revenues	150,732	194,351
Income before taxes	6,421	9,927
Net income	3,492	5,278
Dividends	936	996
Dividends per share	$0.16	$0.17
Earnings per share	$0.60	$0.90
Common stock	5,883	5,893
Retained income	24,823	29,105
Shareholders equity	31,296	35,637

No of Employees: 630

WOLVERINE TECHNOLOGIES INC

Four Parklane Blvd, Dearborn, MI 48126

Tel: (313) 337-7100

Chairman: Gregory C Smith (and Chief Executive Officer)

President: James K Cassedy (and Chief Operating Officer)

Senior Executive Officers: Thomas A Jeffers (VP, Treasurer and Chief Financial Officer), C W Peek (VP Manufacturing)

PRINCIPAL ACTIVITIES: Residential exterior building materials

Trade Names: Ashland Davis Company

Principal Bank: Manufacturers National Bank of Detroit

Financial Information:

	Dec 31 1985	Dec 31 1986
	$'000	$'000
Sales revenues	84,782	99,760
Income before taxes	5,124	7,265
Net income	2,864	4,245
Dividends	435	504
Dividends per share	$0.13*	$0.15*
Earnings per share	$0.89*	$1.26*
Common stock	2,074	3,441
Retained income	12,922	16,663
Shareholders equity	19,574	26,911

*adjusted for 50% stock distribution of June 1986

No of Employees: 625

WOLVERINE WORLD WIDE INC

9341 Courtland Drive, Rockford, MI 49351

Tel: (616) 874-8448

Telex: TWX 810 2736160 www rkfd

Chairman: Thomas D Gleason (and President and Chief Executive Officer); Vice Chairman: Frank J Flood

Senior Executive Officers: Charles F Morgo (Senior Executive VP), Timothy J O'Donovan (Executive VP), Prasad Reddy (Group VP), John P Stevenson (Group VP), George A Andrews (VP Finance), John D Bunbury (VP), Robert S Burch (VP), Peter Panter (VP), Nunzio J Vaccaro (VP), Robert S Wolff (VP)

PRINCIPAL ACTIVITIES: Tanning of leather; production of footwear and leather goods

Principal Subsidiaries: WWW Retail Inc; Hush Puppies AG (Switzerland); Wolverine International Inc; Institutional Shoe Corp; Wolverine World Wide BV; Aguadilla Shoe Corp (Puerto Rico); Town and Country Shoes Inc; Lustig's Shoes Inc; Viner Bros Inc; VBI Inc; Brooks Shoe Inc

Principal Bank: Harris Trust & Savings Bank

Financial Information:

	$'000
Sales revenues	389,460

No of Employees: 8,000

WOODHEAD INDUSTRIES INC

3411 Woodhead Drive, Northbrook, IL 60062

Tel: (312) 272 7990

President: Robert S Lamantia (and Chief Executive Officer)

Senior Executive Officers: Gene G Armiger (Group VP), Donald A Kauth (Group VP), Lloyd J Kurkowski (VP Finance), James E Robinson (Treasurer and Controller), Helen Pachniak (Secretary), Alan Reed (VP Corporate Development)

PRINCIPAL ACTIVITIES: Power transmission products and telecommunications equipment

Principal Subsidiaries: Aero-Motive Manufacturing Company; Armiger and Associates Inc; Central Rubber Company; Woodhead El Paso Inc; Woodhead International Sales

Principal Bank: Harris Trust and Savings Bank

Financial Information:

	$'000
Sales revenues	59,720

No of Employees: 860

WOODS DIVISION OF HESSTON CORP

Rte 2, Oregon, IL 61061

Tel: (815) 732-2141

Telex: WUT 257411 woods div oreg

Senior Executive Officers: Fred Scharer (General Manager), Harry D Kasper (Marketing Manager), Carol Long (Controller), David Rosenow (Manufacturing Manager), Mike Dawson (Engineering Manager)

PRINCIPAL ACTIVITIES: Manufacture and distribution of agricultural and horticultural machinery
Parent Company: Hesston Corporation
Financial Information:

	$'000
Sales revenues	60,000

No of Employees: 580

WOODSTREAM CORPORATION

69 North Locust Street, Lititz, PA 17543
Tel: (717) 626 2125

Chairman: Richard G Woolworth (and Chief Executive Officer)
President: Frederick O Schweizer (and Chief Operating Officer)
Senior Executive Officers: J Hibbard Robertson (Senior VP), Joseph H Bumstead (VP), Bruce A Hepburn (VP, Treasurer and Secretary), J H Kadel (VP and Controller)

PRINCIPAL ACTIVITIES: Fishing equipment; pet supplies
Financial Information:

	$'000
Sales revenues	43,590

No of Employees: 650

WOODWARD GOVERNOR COMPANY

5001 North 2nd Street, Rockford, IL 61125-7001
Tel: (815) 877-7441

Chairman: Calvin C Covert (and Chief Executive Officer)
President: Mark E Leum (and Chief Operating Officer)
Senior Executive Officers: Vern H Cassens (VP), Peter A Gomm (VP), Gavin M Van De Mark (VP), Plato J Leeson (VP), C Phillip Turner (Secretary and Treasurer), Arnold B Swenson (Assistant Secretary)

PRINCIPAL ACTIVITIES: The Woodward Governor Company is engaged in the design, manufacture and sale of prime mover controls and accessories. The company is the world's oldest and largest manufacturer, exclusively of prime mover controls. Prime movers are machines which convert either heat or hydraulic energy into mechanical or electrical energy. The company provides controls for prime movers of all sizes including diesel engines, hydraulic turbines, steam engines, aircraft propellers, industrial gas turbines and aircraft gas turbines. Woodward products are used to control the rotational speed as well as other functions of these machines. The company distributes its products by direct sale to original equipment manufacturers, service providers and equipment users worldwide. Woodward products are designed and manufactured to precisely govern prime movers operating under the most demanding specifications and conditions.
Principal Subsidiaries: Woodward Governor Nederland BV (Netherlands); Woodward Governor (UK) Ltd (UK); Woodward Governor GmbH (Switzerland and Netherlands); Woodward Governor (Japan) Ltd (Japan); Woodward Governor (Reguladores) Limitada (Brazil); Woodward Governor (Quebec) Limited (Canada)
Financial Information:

	Sep 30 1986 $'000
Sales revenues	244,656
Earnings before taxes	32,162
Net earnings	17,657
Dividends	5,617
Dividends per share	$4.10
Earnings per share	$12.89
Common stock	1,372
Retained earnings	143,338
Shareholders equity	138,318

No of Employees: 2,947 (worker members)

WOOLFOLK CHEMICAL WORKS, INC

124 East Main Street, Fort Valley, PO Box 938, GA 31030
Tel: (912) 825-5511

President: Virgil H Young Jr
Senior Executive Officers: John C Alden (VP Research and Development), Ralph W Fuller Jr (VP Finance)

PRINCIPAL ACTIVITIES: Production of agrichemicals
Principal Bank: Bank of the South
Financial Information:

	$'000
Sales revenues	50,000

No of Employees: 235

WOOLRICH WOOLEN MILLS, INC

Woolrich, PA 17779
Tel: (717) 769-6464
Telex: TWX 510 6558737 woolrich wool

Chairman: Roswell Brayton Sr (and Chief Executive Officer)
President: S Wade Judy (and Chief Operating Officer)
Senior Executive Officers: K Alan Himes (Senior VP Marketing and Sales), Rodney Bailey (VP Human Resources), Robert Lamphere (VP Western Division), James Lawrence (VP Piece Goods Sales), Richard Holcombe (VP Sales Services and Distribution), Edward Howell (VP National Apparel Sales), Chester Pribble (VP Apparel)

PRINCIPAL ACTIVITIES: Manufacture of woolen fabrics, apparel, blankets and upholstery fabric; a subsidiary is engaged in water supply
Principal Subsidiaries: Chatham Water Co
Principal Bank: Mellon Bank
Financial Information:

	$'000
Sales revenues	142,000

No of Employees: 2,000

WOOLWORTH, F W, CO

Woolworth Building, 233 Broadway, New York, NY 10279
Tel: (212) 553-2000

Chairman: Harold E Sells (and Chief Executive Officer)
President: Frederick E Hennig (and Chief Operating Officer)
Senior Executive Officers: Arnold S Anderson (Executive VP Administration and General Counsel), William K Lavin (Executive VP Finance and Chief Financial Officer), Ted M Annenberg (VP Deputy General Counsel), John H Cannon (VP Treasurer), Joseph F Carroll (VP Public Affairs), William F Forcht (VP Human Resources), Roy L Garofalo (VP Investor Relations), C Jackson Gray (VP Corporate Planning and Development), Aubrey C Lewis (VP Corporate Liaison), Henry C Miner III (VP Taxation), Thomas E Page (VP and Controller), Charles T Young (VP Management Information Systems), William B Thomson (Secretary), Glen R Goff (General Auditor), Jacqueline D Delafuente (Assistant VP Law Department) James J O'Neill (Assistant VP Taxation), Laura T Kirsner (Assistant Controller), Michael T Steven (Assistant Controller), Gary M Bahler (Assistant Secretary), Christopher J Hoey (Assistant Secretary), S William Manteria (Assistant Secretary), James J Pirretti (Assistant Secretary), George K Schubert (Assistant Secretary), Frances E Trachter (Assistant Secretary), Alfonso Tino (Assistant Treasurer)

PRINCIPAL ACTIVITIES: The Company and its subsidiaries are engaged in the retail sale of general merchandise, apparel and footwear in USA, Canada, Australia and Germany
Principal Subsidiaries: Consolidated Operations:- US Woolworth Division; F W Woolworth Co Ltd (Canada); F W Woodworth Co GmbH (Germany); Kinney Shoe Corporation; The Richman Brothers Company; Holtzman's Little Folk Shop Inc; The Rx Place Division; Woolworth Overseas Corp. Unconsolidated Operation:-Woolworth Mexicana, SA de CV (Mexico)

Financial Information:

	Jan 31 1986	Jan 31 1987
	$'000	$'000
Sales revenues	5,958,000	6,501,000
Income before taxes	314,000	374,000
Net income	177,000	214,000
Dividends(1)	64,000	73,000
Dividends per share(1)	$1.00	$1.12
Earnings per share(1)	$2.75	$3.25
Common stock(2)	128,000	236,000
Retained income(2)	1,181,000	1,239,000
Shareholders equity	1,223,000	1,484,000

(1) Common stock
(2) End of year

No of Employees: 120,500

WORK WEAR CORPORATION INC

1768 East 25th Street, Cleveland, OH 44114
Tel: (216) 771-4040
Telex: 212 542 WORKW UR

President: Earle G Poole
Senior Executive Officers: Alan R Nutson (Executive VP Sales and Marketing-US Apparel Division), Robert J Sislian (Executive VP and President-Healthcare Products Division), D Richard Williams (VP, Treasurer and Chief Financial Officer), Curtis Hoogland (Executive VP-Manufacturing), E Stanley Hale (VP, European Operations), Byron N Cohen (VP General Counsel and Secretary), Carl H Hulsman (Controller)

PRINCIPAL ACTIVITIES: Work Wear Corporation Inc is a leading manufacturer of occupational and specialized apparel for business and industry, as well as disposable products for the health care, food service and transportation industries. The Company also operates the major industrial garment rental services facilities in Canada
Trade Names: Action-Line, Mars, Mars White Knight, Precept, Sir Shirtmakers, White Knight Textiles, Wiz-Wipes, Wearwell Overall, The World of Work Wear, Brew Apparel
Principal Subsidiaries: Business Segments: US Apparel; US Health Care & Disposables; Canadian Apparel & Dental Operations and European Apparel
Principal Banks: National Bank of Detroit; Society National Bank of Cleveland; Huntington National Banks
Financial Information:

	Dec 31 1986
	$'000
Revenues	124,850
Income before taxes*	4,367
Net income	798
Common stock	12,500
Retained income	798
Shareholders equity	13,841

*and extraordinary item

No of Employees: 6,469

WORLD AIRWAYS, INC

Oakland International Airport, PO Box 2330, Oakland, CA 94614
Tel: (415) 577-2000
Cable: WORLDAIR, OAKLAND
Telex: 335479, WORLDAIROAK

President: T Coleman Andrews III (and Chief Executive Officer)
Senior Executive Officers: Arthur H Hutton (Vice Chairman), John D Phillips (Senior VP Finance), Daulton J Lewis (VP-Legal Affairs and Secretary), Terry D Hall (VP-Administration and Labor Relations), Franco Mancassola (VP-Marketing), Merrill F Reese (VP/General Manager-Cargo), Edward P Rich (VP and Chief Financial Officer), Warren K Vest (VP/Director of Operations), Norm Dargie (VP/General Manager of Airline Maintenance Center)

PRINCIPAL ACTIVITIES: Air transportation services; scheduled and charter passenger flights; cargo services; aircraft leasing and maintenance services
Principal Bank: Bank of America
Financial Information:

	$'000
Sales revenues	360,240

No of Employees: 2,428

WORLD BOOK INC

510 Merchandise Mart Plaza, Chicago, IL 60654
Tel: (312) 245-3456
Telex: TRT 190169 wb ci cgo

Chairman: Stephan H Fuller (and Chief Executive Officer)
President: Michael J Goodkin
Senior Executive Officers: John E Frere (Senior VP and Chief Financial Officer), Harold M Ross (VP and Secretary)

PRINCIPAL ACTIVITIES: Publishing of reference books
Parent Company: Scott Fetzer, Cleveland, OH
Principal Bank: LaSalle National Bank
Financial Information:

	$'000
Sales revenues	260,000

No of Employees: 8,200

WORLD CARPETS INC

World Plaza, Dalton, GA 30720
Tel: (404) 278-8000
Telex: TWX 8107594401 world dto

Chairman: Shaheen Shaheen; Vice Chairman: Piera Shaheen
President: Joe B Maffett
Senior Executive Officers: David Shaheen (Executive VP), John A Shaheen (Executive VP), W B Coffey (Comptroller)

PRINCIPAL ACTIVITIES: Manufacture of carpets and rugs
Principal Bank: Hardwick Bank & Trust Company
Financial Information:

	$'000
Sales revenues	250,000

No of Employees: 2,000

WORLD COLOR PRESS, INC

401 Industrial Drive, Box 1248, Effingham, IL 62401
Tel: (217) 342-8241
Telex: TWX 910 6633911 wldclrps effi

Chairman: Clyde Oberlin (and Chief Executive Officer)
President: Robert A Huey (and Chief Operating Officer)
Senior Executive Officers: Robert K Bockhorn (Senior VP Manufacturing), James A Dawson (Senior VP Sales), Fred D Jacobus (Senior VP Personnel), Eugene L Ferretti (Senior VP and Chief Finance Officer), F D Carpenter (Senior VP Marketing), Robert W Young (Senior VP Corporate Services), Bruce A Baker (VP Western Sales), Patrick W Bryan (VP Eastern Sales), J Richard Cassady (VP Management Information Systems), Joe M Collier (VP Midwestern Sales), Richard P Hartman (VP, Regional Manager Spartan Printing Co), Kenneth J Maleske (VP Sales Administration), John F O'Connor (VP, Regional Manager Salem Gravure), Robert H Pillers (VP, Regional Manager Crossroads Press), Leon L Woodland (VP Computer Applications Engineering Group)

PRINCIPAL ACTIVITIES: Printing of periodicals and directories
Parent Company: Pace Industries
Principal Bank: Continental Bank
Financial Information:

	$'000
Sales revenues	160,000

WORLD'S FINEST CHOCOLATE, INC

4801 South Lawndale Avenue, Chicago, IL 60632
Tel: (312) 847-4600
Telex: WUT 25276 worfincho cgo

Chairman: Edmond Opler (and Chief Executive Officer)
President: Edmond Opler Jr (and Treasurer)

Senior Executive Officers: Thomas F Morris (Comptroller), Francis J Nudd (VP Sales)

PRINCIPAL ACTIVITIES: Confectionery and chocolate products
Principal Bank: The First National Bank of Chicago

No of Employees: 600

WORLDWIDE ENERGY CORPORATION

4849 Greenville Ave, Dallas, TX 75206-4123

President: Robert B Tenison (and Chief Executive Officer)
Senior Executive Officers: Ronald J Cargo (Senior VP), A H Hurley Jr (VP Operations), Walter V Pelepchan (VP Administration), Mark A Hellerstein (VP Finance and Treasurer), John E Vermillion (Secretary and Legal Counsel), Roger L Nelson (VP Real Estate)

PRINCIPAL ACTIVITIES: Production of oil and gas; minerals mining
Principal Subsidiaries: Semco Gas Inc; Weco Energy Inc; Worldwide Energy (UK) Limited
Principal Bank: United Bank
Financial Information:

	$'000
Sales revenues	68,890

No of Employees: 210

WORTHEN BANKING CORPORATION

200 West Capitol Avenue, Little Rock, AR 72201
Tel: (501) 378 1433

Chairman: William L Cravens (and Chief Executive Officer)
President: Curtis F Bradbury Jr (and Chief Operating Officer)
Senior Executive Officers: Mochtar Riady (Chairman of Executive Committee), Donald B Hayes (Executive VP), Robert L Trammel (Executive VP and Chief Financial Officer), Fred C Burns (VP and Secretary), Woodlief A Thomas (VP, Treasurer and Controller), E Steve Watson (VP and General Counsel)

PRINCIPAL ACTIVITIES: Banking
Principal Subsidiaries: First AR Leasing Corporation; First National Bank; First SBIC of Arkansas; First State Bank; First State Bank and Trust Company; Metro Properties Inc; National Bank of Commerce; National Credit Corporation; Peoples Bank and Trust Company; Worthen Bank and Trust Company; Continental Finance Corporation; First Bank Finance Services; Worthen First Mortgage Company Inc

No of Employees: 1,600

WORTHINGTON DIAGNOSTIC SYSTEMS INC

Halls Mills Road, Freehold, NJ 07728
Tel: (201) 462-3838
Telex: TWX 710 7223847 worth diag

President: Patrick Leonard
Senior Executive Officers: William Baker (VP Operations), James Montenegro (VP Finance), Samuel Tata (VP Sales), Thomas Foley (VP Research and Development)

PRINCIPAL ACTIVITIES: Biotechnology; diagnostics and reagents
Parent Company: Flow General Inc, McLean, VA
Principal Bank: The National State Bank
Financial Information:

	$'000
Sales revenues	50,000

No of Employees: 550

WORTHINGTON INDUSTRIES, INC

1205 Dearborn Drive, Columbus, OH 43085
Tel: (614) 438-3210

Chairman: John H McConnell (and Chief Executive Officer)
President: Donal Malenick
Senior Executive Officers: Robert J Borel (VP Engineering), Robert J Klein (Executive VP), Joseph Stegmayer (VP and Treasurer)

PRINCIPAL ACTIVITIES: Processing of flat rolled steel; cast steel products; low pressure cylinders and molded plastic products
Principal Bank: Bank One of Columbus
Financial Information:

	May 31 1986 $'000	May 31 1987 $'000
Sales revenues	754,317	818,847
Income before taxes	80,394	78,124
Net income	41,987	42,145
Dividends	12,335	14,515
Dividends per share	$0.298	$0.350
Earnings per share	$1.01	$1.02
Common stock	62,717	63,619
Retained income	170,889	197,307
Shareholders equity	233,606	260,926

No of Employees: 5,800

WRATHER CORPORATION

270 North Cannon Drive, Beverly Hills, CA 90210
Tel: (213) 278 8521

Chairman: Bonita Granville Wrather
President: Christopher Wrather (and Chief Executive Officer)
Senior Executive Officers: Roy M Rawls (Executve VP Finance and Chief Financial Officer), Eugene L Saenger (Executive VP Development), Wendy L Shurtleff (VP and Controller), Gerald L Weisberger (VP and Secretary)

PRINCIPAL ACTIVITIES: Restaurants, hotels and amusement facilities
Principal Subsidiaries: Wrather Hotels Inc; WCO Hotel Supply Corporation; Wrather Leisure Inc; Wrather Port Properties Limited
Principal Bank: Security Pacific National Bank
Financial Information:

	$'000
Sales revenues	113,800

No of Employees: 2,200

WRIGHT LINE INC

160 Gold Star Blvd, Worcester, MA 01606
Tel: (617) 852-4300
Telex: RCA 200401 wline ur

President: Philip M Croel
Senior Executive Officers: J Goes (VP International), Naresh Kapahi (VP Administration and Finance), Alex Pais (VP Sales), D Peters (VP Manufacturing)

PRINCIPAL ACTIVITIES: Wright Line's business is to design, manufacture and market products for the accessing, organizing, filing and protection of diversified information media. The products, designed and manufactured for use in automated office applications, help people become more productive by enabling them to access the right information at the right time. Wright Line's major product families, including media devices, cabinets and work surfaces, assist in effective management of information media at every level in the automated office
Trade Names: Docu-Mate (R), Tape-Seal (R)
Parent Company: Barry Wright Corporation, Newton Lower Falls, MA
Principal Bank: State Street Bank & Trust Co
Financial Information:

	$'000
Sales revenues	104,000

No of Employees: 1,000

WRIGHT, WM E, CO

South Street, West Warren, MA 01092
Tel: (413) 436-7732
Telex: TWX 910 3500421 wrightw warren

Chairman: Daniel C Ferguson
President: John J Lynch
Senior Executive Officers: Gordon B Ruesch (Secretary), Edward M Milko (Controller), William Smith (Purchasing Manager), Anthony Sinkewich (Public Relations), Verna Hogencamp (Traffic Manager)

PRINCIPAL ACTIVITIES: Production of trimmings and accessories for sewing and home furnishing
Financial Information:

	$'000
Sales revenues	52,000

No of Employees: 1,150

WRIGLEY, WM, JR CO

410 N Michigan Avenue, Chicago, IL 60611
Tel: (312) 644-2121
Telex: TWX 910 2212583 Wrigleyspear cg

President: William Wrigley (and Chief Executive Officer)
Senior Executive Officers: R D Ewers (Executive VP), Douglas S Barrie (Group VP International), Graham T Morgan (VP International), Ronald O Cox (Group VP Marketing), J E Dy-Liacco (VP International), E E Fisher (VP Research and Development), Ake Frisk (VP international), Martin J Geraghty (VP Manufacturing), Alfons Jakob (VP International), Edmund R Meyer (VP Finance), Paul W Rogers (Senior VP), E W Swanson Jr (VP Personnel), Norman E Zibell (VP Purchasing), Anthony Cipollina (VP Sales), Hollis W Moyse (Treasurer), Wm M Piet (Corporate Secretary)

PRINCIPAL ACTIVITIES: Manufacture of chewing gum
Financial Information:

	Dec 31 1985	Dec 31 1986
	$'000	$'000
Sales revenues	620,267	698,982
Income before taxes	80,461	103,658
Net income	43,498	53,818
Dividends	21,825	27,905
Dividends per share	$1.03	$1.28
Earnings per share	$2.06	$2.55
Common stock	19,200	19,200
Retained income	303,766	329,679
Shareholders equity	258,809	292,962

No of Employees: 5,500

WRITER CORPORATION

27 Inverness Drive East, Englewood, CO 80112
Tel: (303) 790 2870

Chairman: George S Writer Jr (and Chief Executive Officer)
President: William E Nollsch (and Treasurer)
Senior Executive Officers: Charles R Polk (Executive VP), Marty Josephs (Senior VP), Don F Rampy (Senior VP), Robert H Klatsky (VP Finance), Steven G Delva (Senior VP Planning), Jeffrey D Engebretson (Controller), Ronald S Loser (Secretary), Gary L Carlson (VP Sales and Marketing), Edgar W Nichols (VP Technical Services), Robert R Reid (VP Construction), Sidney J Montague (VP Development), Larry E Reichert (VP Development)

PRINCIPAL ACTIVITIES: Building and construction
Principal Subsidiaries: Writer Square Inc
Principal Bank: First Interstate Bank
Financial Information:

	$'000
Sales revenues	61,711

No of Employees: 170

WURLITZER CO

403 E Gurler Road, DeKalb, IL 60115
Tel: (815) 756-2771
Telex: WUT 854316 wurlitzer co

Chairman: A D Arsem
President: George B Howell (and Chief Executive Officer)
Senior Executive Officers: Wallace R Borgeson (Senior VP Finance), William J Young (Senior VP), Robert W Donaldson (VP), James M Graham (VP National Sales), Fred P Youssi (VP Manufacturing)

PRINCIPAL ACTIVITIES: Production of musical instruments including electronic organs; vending machines
Principal Subsidiaries: Wurlitzer Distribution Corporation; Wurlitzer International Ltd; Deutsche Wurlitzer GmbH (Germany); Wurlitzer Australia Pty Ltd (Australia); Wurlitzer Canada Ltd (Canada)
Principal Bank: Chase Manhattan Bank
Financial Information:

	$'000
Sales revenues	49,000

No of Employees: 1,200

WYLE LABORATORIES

128 Maryland Street, El Segundo, CA 90245
Tel: (213) 678-4251
Telex: TWX 910 3486699 wyle labs els

Chairman: Stanley A Wainer (and Chief Executive Officer)
President: Charles M Clough (and Cheif Operating Officer)
Senior Executive Officers: John R Herring (Executive VP), Theodore M Freedman (Executive VP Finance and Chief Financial Officer), R Van Ness Holland Jr (VP and Controller), Ralph L Ozorkiewicz (VP), Joseph E Sullivan (VP)

PRINCIPAL ACTIVITIES: Trade in data processing equipment and electronic components; services to the aerospace, energy and defense industries
Principal Subsidiaries: Elmar Electronics Inc; Redwing of California Inc; Wyle Distribution Group-Santa Clara Inc
Principal Bank: Security Pacific National Bank
Financial Information:

	Jan 31 1987
	$'000
Sales revenues	307,000
Income before taxes	6,999
Net income	4,307
Dividends	2,641
Dividends per share	$0.28*
Earnings per share	$0.44*
Shareholders equity	80,612

*restated for 5 for 4 stock split distributed October 1987

No of Employees: 2,000

WYMAN-GORDON CO

105 Madison Street, Worcester, MA 01601
Tel: (617) 756-5111

Chairman: Joseph R Carter
President: John R Bullock (and Chief Executive Officer)
Senior Executive Officers: Henry Dormitzer (Executive VP and Chief Operating Officer), Edward W Bettke (VP Finance), James E Coyne (VP and Technical Director), Paul Hausmann (VP and General Manager Midwest Division), William C Kunkler (VP Corporate Development), John E Odell (VP Sales and Marketing), Paul J Wisniewski (VP and General Manager Eastern Division)

PRINCIPAL ACTIVITIES: Manufacture of metal forgings in ferrous and non ferrous metals; metal forgings
Principal Bank: Old Stone Corporation

Financial Information:

	$'000
Sales revenues	384,000

No of Employees: 3,400

WYNN'S INTERNATIONAL, INC

2600 E Nutwood Avenue, Fullerton, CA 92631
Tel: (714) 992-2000
Telex: 181591 WYN

Chairman: Wesley E Bellwood
President: John F Lillicrop (and Chief Executive Officer)
Senior Executive Officers: Roberto J Martinez (VP and Controller), John W Huber (VP Corporate Development), Gregg M Gibbons (VP General Counsel and Secretary)

PRINCIPAL ACTIVITIES: The company has interests in the production of motor vehicle components; petrochemical products; hardware products for the building industry; O-rings and other seals and molded rubber products for the automotive, industrial and various industries
Trade Names: Air conditioning units for the automotive aftermarket are marketed by the Company under the trademark "Frostemp". O-rings and other molded rubber products are marketed under the trademarks "Precision" and "Hercules". Petrochemical specialties are marketed under various trademarks, including "Wynn's", "Friction Proofing", "X-Tend", "Spit-Fire" and "Classic".
Principal Subsidiaries: Wynn Oil Company; Wynn's Climate Systems, Inc; Precision Products Corporation; Robert Skeels & Company
Principal Bank: First Interstate Bank
Financial Information:

	Dec 31 1985	Dec 31 1986
	$'000	$'000
Sales revenues	207,104*	306,129
Income (loss) before taxes	(715)*	11,862
Net income (loss)	(1,957)	6,455
Dividends	2,230	2,233
Dividends per share	$0.60	$0.60
Earnings (loss) per share	($0.53)	$1.70
Common stock	3,800	3,806
Retained income	63,294	67,516
Shareholders equity	71,848	77,382
*restated for discontinued operations		

Principal Shareholders: Carl E Wynn (18.4%)
No of Employees: 2,372

WYO-BEN, INC

1242 N 28th Street, Box 1979, Billings, MT 59103
Tel: (406) 252-6351
Telex: WUT 319430 wyoben bil

Chairman: Alfred K Brown (and President)
Senior Executive Officers: David L Auer (Executive VP), Rockwood Brown (Senior VP, Secretary and General Counsel), David S Brown (VP Industrial Division), Harry R Funk (VP Operations)

PRINCIPAL ACTIVITIES: Mineral mining; supply of specialty chemicals for drilling activities
Principal Bank: First Bank Billings
Financial Information:

	$'000
Sales revenues	50,000

No of Employees: 100

WYSE TECHNOLOGY

3571 North First Street, San Jose, CA 95134
Tel: (408) 946 3075

Chairman: B K Tse
President: Phillip E White (and Chief Executive Officer)
Senior Executive Officers: Douglas G G Levick III (VP Finance and Chief Financial Officer), Craig W Johnson (Secretary)

PRINCIPAL ACTIVITIES: Data processing equipment
Financial Information:

	$'000
Sales revenues	165,000

No of Employees: 600

XEBEC

3579 Hwy 50, Carson City, NV 89701
Tel: (702) 883-4000

Chairman: J S Toreson (and President and Chief Executive Officer)
Senior Executive Officers: Marcia A Glow (Executive VP), John M Nosek (VP), M K Rainey (VP), Donald Redmond (VP), Christian C Hoebich (Chief Financial Officer)

PRINCIPAL ACTIVITIES: Production of disk drive controllers and disk storage subsystems
Principal Subsidiaries: Information Memories Corp; Disk Drive Systems Inc
Financial Information:

	$'000
Sales revenues	149,250

No of Employees: 960

XEROX CORPORATION

PO Box 1600, Stamford, CT 06904
Tel: (203) 968-3000
Telex: 221981 Xerox UR

Chairman: David T Kearns (and Chief Executive Officer)
President: Paul A Allaire
Senior Executive Officers: William F Glavin (Vice Chairman), Melvin Howard (Vice Chairman), Robert V Adams (Executive VP), Wayland R Hicks (Executive VP), Frank J Pipp (Group VP), A Barry Rand (Group VP), Robert F Reiser (Group VP), Dwight F Ryan (Group VP), William J Spencer (VP), Robert S Banks (VP and General Counsel), William T Blair (VP), Ronald B Campbell Jr (VP), Eunice M Filter (VP and Secretary), L Lyndon Haddon (VP), Robert J Kammerer (VP), Norbett H Kaupp (VP), Roger E Levien (VP), John J McGinty (VP), Ronald L Mercer (VP), David R Myerscough (VP), Douglas M Reid (Senior VP), Stuart B Ross (VP and Controller), M Norton Rosner (VP), Joseph C Sanchez (VP), James E Shapiro (VP), Renn Zaphiropoulos (VP), Donald R Altieri (Assistant Controller), Alan Z Senter (Treasurer), Eliott D James (VP), Charles E Otto (VP), Norman E Rickard (VP), John C Shoemaker (VP), Michael Smith (VP), Eric L Steenburgh (VP)

PRINCIPAL ACTIVITIES: Xerox is a multinational company in the business products and systems and financial services markets worldwide. Our business products and systems activities encompass the developing, manufacturing, marketing and servicing of a complete range of document processing products and systems designed to make offices more productive. Xerox copiers, duplicators, electronic printers, electronic typewriters, workstations, networks and other related products, software and supplies are marketed in over 130 countries by our direct sales force and a growing network of dealers and distributors. Our financial services businesses provide financial products and services primarily on a wholesale basis. Our largest financial services companies are Crum and Forster, Inc, a property and casualty insurer; Van Kampen Merritt Inc, a specialized investment banking firm; and Xerox Credit Corporation, a commercial and industrial financing unit whose primary business is financing purchases of Xerox equipment by our customers. We also participate in specialty markets such as bond and life insurance and real estate through joint ventures and other partnerships. The objective of each of the

Company's businesses is to maximize growth and the return to Xerox shareholders

Trade Names: Xerox, Memorywriter (Electronic Typewriter), 10 series (Copiers)

Principal Subsidiaries: Rank Xerox; Fuji Xerox; Crum and Forster Inc; Van Kampen Merritt Inc; Xerox Canada Inc; Kurzweil Computer Products Inc; Xerox Realty Corp; Versatec Inc; Furman Selz Holding Corp; Xerox Financial Services Inc; Xerox Credit Corp

Principal Bank: Citibank

Financial Information:

	Dec 31 1985	Dec 31 1986
	$'000	$'000
Total revenues	11,761,000	13,046,000
Income(1)	381,000	488,000
Net income	475,000	465,000
Dividends per share	$3.00	$3.00
Net income per share	$4.44	$4.28
Common stock(2)	96,159	97,260
Shareholders equity	4,386,000	4,687,000

(1) continuing operations
(2) average shares outstanding in thousands

No of Employees: 100,367

XICOR INC

1511 Buckeye Drive, Milpitas, CA 95035
Tel: (408) 432-8888
Telex: 910-379-0033
Telefax: (408) 432-0640

Chairman: Raphael Klein (and President and Chief Financial Officer)

Senior Executive Officers: Arieh Schifrin (Executive VP, Sales, Marketing and Operations), John Caywood (VP, Technology, Reliability and Quality Assurance), Kalus G Hendig (VP and Controller), Manuel Mere (VP, Manufacturing), William H Owen III (VP, Research and Development), Wallace E Tchon (VP, Strategic Planning), Paul L Myers Jr (Secretary)

PRINCIPAL ACTIVITIES: Electronic components including semiconductors

Trade Names: Xicor (R)

Financial Information:

	Dec 31 1986	Dec 31 1987
	$'000	$'000
Sales revenues	44,279	64,688
Income (loss) before taxes	(3,812)	7,737
Net income (loss)	(3,812)	7,564
Earnings (loss) per share	($0.32)	$0.52
Common stock*	11,927	14,631
Retained (deficit)	(40,740)	(44,552)
Shareholders equity	61,862	27,296

*number of shares in thousands

No of Employees: 670

XIDEX CORPORATION

305 Soquel Way, Sunnyvale, CA 94086
Tel: (408) 739-4170

Chairman: Lester L Colbert Jr (and President)

Senior Executive Officers: Gary B Filler (Executive VP, Treasurer and Secretary), Bert L Zaccaria (Executive VP), Stanley Gula (VP Solvent Coating), William L Harry (VP Rigid Disk Division), Douglas M McBurnie (VP Magnetics Operations), Glenham C Mezher (VP International Operations), Philip J Micciche (VP Magnetics Marketing), John P O'Neil (VP Industrial Relations), Richard F Polhemus (VP Domestic Marketing)

PRINCIPAL ACTIVITIES: Manufacture of data storage products including floppy disks

Principal Bank: Bank of California

Financial Information:

	Jun 30 1986
	$'000
Sales revenues	432,300
Net income	32,248
Earnings per share	$0.75
Shareholders equity	484,963

No of Employees: 4,000

XL/DATACOMP INC

907 North Elm Street, Hinsdale, IL 60521
Tel: (312) 323 1200

President: Thomas M Owens

Senior Executive Officers: Robert J Passaneau (Executive VP), Robert L Biddle (VP), William A Conwell (VP), Michael J Laforte (VP), James J McCarthy (VP), William P Quinn (VP and Assistant Secretary), Thomas A Skalitzky (Treasurer and Secretary), Frederick A Spreadbury (Controller)

PRINCIPAL ACTIVITIES: Office equipment

Financial Information:

	$'000
Sales revenues	63,160

No of Employees: 200

XOMOX CORPORATION

4444 Cooper Road, Cincinnati, OH 45242
Tel: (513) 745-6000
Telex: TWX 910 3501225 xomox

President: Thomas Burns

Senior Executive Officers: John Colvin (VP and Chief Financial Officer)

PRINCIPAL ACTIVITIES: Production of valves and control equipment

Parent Company: Emerson Electric Co, St Louis, MO

Principal Bank: Central Trust Company

Financial Information:

	$'000
Sales revenues	100,000

No of Employees: 1,300

XTEK, INC

11451 Reading Road, Cincinnati, OH 45241
Tel: (513) 733-2800
Telex: 241916 Xtek Inc Sare

Chairman: James D Kiggen (and President and Chief Executive Officer)

Senior Executive Officers: Arthur Pehrson (VP Sales), Robert C Wood (VP Finance)

PRINCIPAL ACTIVITIES: Manufacture of machinery parts; gear drives; steel pipes

Principal Subsidiaries: Xtek Canada; Xtek Goldman

Principal Bank: The Fifth Third Bank

Financial Information:

	$'000
Sales revenues	50,000

Principal Shareholders: ESOP

No of Employees: 400

XTRA CORPORATION

2625 Concord Pike, Wilmington, DE 19803
Tel: (302) 478 0705

Chairman: Charles F Kaye (and President and Chief Executive Officer)

Senior Executive Officers: Selwyn A Kudisch (VP and Secretary), Michael J Soja (VP Finance and Administration), Francis C Ventre (Treasurer and Secretary)

PRINCIPAL ACTIVITIES: Leasing of road haulage vehicles and equipment

Principal Subsidiaries: AJF Industries Inc; AJF Warehouse Distributors; MMX Corporation; Dunham Manufacturing Company; Mercury Motor Express Inc; XTR Inc; X-L-Co Inc; Xtra Inc
Principal Bank: State Street Bank and Trust
Financial Information:

	$'000
Sales revenues	199,540

No of Employees: 1,500

YANKEE COMPANIES INC

49 Margin Street, Cohasset, MA 02025
Tel: (617) 383 1500

Chairman: Graham E Jones
President: Paul J Montle (and Chief Executive Officer)
Senior Executive Officers: Lance W Schneier (Executive VP), Michael R Kutch (Senior VP, Treasurer and Chief Financial Officer), Richard N Morash (Senior VP), Carolyn Thayer Ross (Senior VP, Secretary and General Counsel)

PRINCIPAL ACTIVITIES: Natural gas supply; oil and gas exploration and production; oilfield services
Principal Bank: First National Bank of Boston
Financial Information:

	$'000
Sales revenues	213,000

No of Employees: 200

YARWAY CORPORATION

Blue Bell, PA 19422
Tel: (215) 825-2100
Telex: WUI 6851071 yarwy

Chairman: O R Yarnall Jr
President: Theodore B Palmer III (and Chief Executive Officer)
Senior Executive Officers: J F Barclay Jr (VP and General Manager North America Operations), David W Dupert (VP Finance, Secretary and Treasurer), Rudolph V Dutzman (VP Human Development), Heinz K Hetz (VP Product Planning and Development), Richard J Mattie (VP International Operations)

PRINCIPAL ACTIVITIES: Valves and expansion joints; pollution control equipment; industrial recording pens
Parent Company: Keystone International Inc
Financial Information:

	$'000
Sales revenues	80,000

No of Employees: 850

YATES INDUSTRIES, INC

US Highway 130, Bordentown, NJ 08505
Tel: (609) 298-4800
Telex: WUT 642896 corp btwn

President: Derek Roberts (and Treasurer)
Senior Executive Officers: Michael Hacart (VP), Peter A Inverso (VP and Secretary)

PRINCIPAL ACTIVITIES: Manufacture of metal foil and leaf
Parent Company: Square D Co
Principal Bank: New Jersey National Bank
Financial Information:

	$'000
Sales revenues	116,000

No of Employees: 1,000

YELLOW FREIGHT SYSTEM, INC OF DELAWARE

10990 Roe Avenue, Box 7270, Overland Park, KS 66207
Tel: (913) 383-3000
Telex: WUT 426351 yellow ft swms

Chairman: George E Powell Jr
President: Raymond A Stewart Jr
Senior Executive Officers: Robert W Burdick (Senior VP Marketing), Forrest H Burm (Senior VP), Paul M Eaton (Senior VP), David E Loeffler (Senior VP Finance), Stephen P Murphy (Senior VP and Secretary), George E Powell III (Senior VP Operations), Glenn M Brown (VP Traffic), Robert K Callaghan (VP Information Services), William H Curry (VP Labor Relations), Robert W Dro (VP Maintenance), Douglas A Fisher (VP), Newton A Graves (VP Sales), Mike Haughton (VP Human Resources), Austin E Hocklander (BP Insurance and Claims), William F Martin (VP Legal), Richard H Palmer (VP Sales), Gail A Parris (VP and Controller), Donald T Robertson (VP and Controller), Donald T Robertson (VP Corporate Sales), Edward C Schneider (VP International), Phillip A Spangler (VP and Treasurer), Kenneth A Thompson (VP Safety)

PRINCIPAL ACTIVITIES: Freight forwarding; trucking
Principal Bank: First National Bank of Kansas City
Financial Information:

	Dec 31 1985	Dec 31 1986
	$'000	$'000
Sales revenues	1,530,310	1,731,731
Net income	55,536	69,719
Earnings per share	$1.95	$2.44
Shareholders equity	-	376,370

No of Employees: 23,500

YORK BANK & TRUST CO

Market & Beaver Streets, Box 869, York, PA 17401
Tel: (717) 843-8651
Telex: TWX 510 6574 228 yby yorkbank

President: John C Schmidt (and Chief Executive Officer)
Senior Executive Officers: Rodney E Rohrbaugh (Senior Executive VP), Richard H Brown (Executive VP), Noah B Hershey (Senior VP and Treasurer), Paul R Summers (Senior VP), William E Groft (Senior VP Operations), Donald C McVay (Senior VP Commercial Lending)

PRINCIPAL ACTIVITIES: Banking and financial services
Parent Company: Continental Bancorp Inc

No of Employees: 480

YORK INTERNATIONAL CORPORATION

631 S Richland Ave, York, PA 17403
Tel: (717) 771-7400

President: R J M Fisher (also Chief Executive Officer)
Senior Executive Officers: R J Doyle (Executive VP), R G Meisenhelder (VP Human Resources), R C Barnett (VP), D L McEwan (VP), J R Walsh (VP), K D Schulz (VP), W M Valiant (Treasurer), S N Rosenfeld (Secretary and General Counsel)

PRINCIPAL ACTIVITIES: Manufacture of heating, industrial refrigeration and air conditioning equipment
Parent Company: Borg-Warner Corporation
Financial Information:

	Dec 31 1986
	$'000
Sales revenues	689,979
Net income	8,217
Earnings per share	$0.88
Shareholders equity	179,752

No of Employees: 4,100

YOUNG RADIATOR COMPANY

2825 Four Mile Road, Racine, WI 53404
Tel: (414) 639-1010
Telex: TWX 910 2712397 young racine

Chairman: Fred M Young Jr (and President)
Senior Executive Officers: Harry T Gant (Secretary and Treasurer), D O Klompmaker (Sales Manager Auto Division),

R J Dezek (Sales Manager Industrial Division), Alan Pretzel (Marketing Manager), William V Astrup (VP Engineering)

PRINCIPAL ACTIVITIES: Manufacture of components for heating and ventilation equipment; motor vehicle components

Principal Bank: The First National Bank of Chicago

No of Employees: 600

ZALE CORPORATION

PO Box 152777, Irving, TX 75015-2777

Tel: (214) 257-4980

Chairman: Donald Zale (and Chief Executive Officer); Vice Chairmen: Richard F Mitchell (and Chief Administrative Officer), Marvin Zale

President: Bruce A Lipshy (and Chief Operating Officer); Executive Vice President: H R Lively Jr

Senior Executive Officers: Senior Vice Presidents: Paul M Cholak, Jerold Grubstein, William R Gutow, Michael B Hacker, E Dean Liles Jr, Gene Morphis, William H Pavony, Dolph B H Simon. Vice Presidents: Jean S Barrow, Don L Bolen, Mary A Garza, Jerry B Gray, Walter H Harvey (Treasurer), Edward Jaben, Harry Johnson, Gary I Kastel, John I Mitchell, Dennis P Mullin, Barry Pasarew, Lynn Reynolds, Michael Romaine PhD, Leonard H Schwartz, Craig B Sorrels, Merrill J Wertheimer (Controller). Other Corporate Officers: C Scott Litten (Assistant Controller), B F Godfrey Jr (Assistant Secretary), Richard A Wiggins (Assistant Treasurer)

PRINCIPAL ACTIVITIES: The world's largest retailer of fine jewelry and one of this nation's dominant specialty retail organizations. There are two major jewelry divisions; the Zale Division serves middle America in 749 stores, while the Fine Jewelers Guild Division is comprised of 321 carriage trade jewelry stores operating under 38 trade names. Other divisions include leased jewelry departments, promotional jewelry stores, catalog showrooms, newsstand shops at airport and hotel locations, international jewelry operations and various financial services. In total there are more than 1,500 outlets worldwide. Retail activities span 49 states, Guam, Puerto Rico, the United Kingdom, West Germany, Switzerland and Japan. Additionally Zale's jewelry operations are vertically integrated in that the Company purchases diamonds and other precious gems and metals and operates its own jewelry manufacturing facilities

Principal Subsidiaries: Retail Divisions:- Zale Jewelers; Fine Jewelers Guild; Diamond Park Fine Jewelers; Mission Jewelers; Catalog Showrooms; Aeroplex; Willoughby & Taylor; Zale Jewellers, Ltd (UK); Christ Jewellers Europe

Principal Bank: Republic Bank Dallas

Financial Information:

	$'000
Net sales	1,054,330

No of Employees: 12,633

ZAPATA CORPORATION

Zapata Tower, PO Box 4240, Houston, TX 77210

Tel: (713) 226-6000

Chairman: Ronald C Lassiter (and Chief Executive Officer)

Senior Executive Officers: Thomas H Bowersox (Senior VP, Assistant Secretary, General Counsel and Chief Administration Officer), Peter C Forbes (Senior VP and Chief Financial Officer), Davis Allen (VP Co-ordination and Planning), Robert A Jones (VP Human Resources), Marvin J Migura (VP Finance and Accounting), William P Sanford Jr (VP), George A O'Brien Jr (VP), George K Sherwood (VP Taxes), Kent R Stephenson (VP and Secretary)

PRINCIPAL ACTIVITIES: Interests in offshore oil and gas drilling; marine services; fishing and fish processing

Principal Bank: First City National Bank of Houston

Financial Information:

	$'000
Sales revenues	288,674

No of Employees: 3,800

ZAYRE CORPORATION

Framingham, MA 01701

Tel: (617) 620-5000

Chairman: Sumner L Feldberg

President: Maurice Segall (and Chief Executive Officer)

Senior Executive Officers: Stanley H Feldberg (Chairman Executive Committee), Arthur F Loewy (Executive VP Finance), Malcolm L Sherman (Executive VP), Herbert Zarkin (Executive VP Marketing and Real Estate), Michael Bilotti (Senior VP Systems and Technical Services), John Nagy (Senior VP Construction), Donald G Campbell (VP and Controller), George Freeman (VP Financial Planning), Gerald P Donini (Senior VP), Jay H Meltzer (VP), Irving Ritz (VP Labor Relations), Robert Shedd (VP)

PRINCIPAL ACTIVITIES: Operation of department stores

Principal Bank: Bank of New England

Financial Information:

	Dec 31 1985	Dec 31 1986
	$'000	$'000
Sales revenues	4,036,018	5,350,630
Net income	94,647	88,974
Earnings per share	$1.61	$1.49
Shareholders equity	-	652,314

No of Employees: 63,500

ZEHNTEL INC

2625 Shadelands Drive, Walnut Creek, CA 94598

Tel: (415) 932-6900

Chairman: T C Taylor

President: Ronald N Borelli (and Chief Operating Officer)

Senior Executive Officers: James R Donley (VP Personnel), Robert C Hood (VP and Chief Financial Officer), Craig T Pynn (VP)

PRINCIPAL ACTIVITIES: Electrical measuring equipment

Financial Information:

	$'000
Sales revenues	66,400

No of Employees: 820

ZEMEX CORPORATION

280 Park Avenue, New York, NY 10017-1216

Tel: (212) 557-2020

Telex: 383873 ZMX NYK

Chairman: Peter Lawson-Johnston

President: Harry A Durney

Senior Executive Officers: Donald G Shanks (VP Secretary and Treasurer), Laurence G Luedy (Controller and Assistant Secretary), Paul G Milcetic (Assistant Treasurer), E Clark Jenkins (Chairman, The Feldspar Corporation) Richard L Barber (President, The Feldspar Corporation), Michael G Holloway (VP-Marketing), G Russell Lewis (President, Pyron Corporation), James H Smyth (VP-Production)

PRINCIPAL ACTIVITIES: The principal products of Zemex are industrial minerals, iron powders and tin ore which serve major markets that include home building and construction, packaging and containers, automobiles and other vehicles, household fixtures and appliances

Principal Subsidiaries: The Feldspar Corporation; Pyron Corporation; Perangsang Pasifik Sdn Berhad

Principal Bank: The Bank of New York, New York, NY

Financial Information:

	Dec 31 1985	Dec 31 1986
	$'000	$'000
Sales Revenues	36,017	35,130
Income before taxes	1,536	739
Net income	1,340	1,883
Dividends	435	504
Dividends per share	$0.10	$0.10
Earnings per share	$1.23	$1.57
Common stock*	1,777	1,777
Retained income	15,896	17,275
Shareholders equity	18,861	26,050

*number of shares in thousands

No of Employees: 550

ZENITH ELECTRONICS CORPORATION

1000 Milwaukee Avenue, Glenview, IL 60025
Tel: (312) 391-7000

Chairman: Jerry K Pearlman (and President)
Senior Executive Officers: Corporate Officers: John Borst Jr (VP-General Counsel), David W Denton (VP-Human Resources and Public Affairs), Howard H Graham (VP-Finance), David S Levin (Treasurer), Dennis J Waldeck (Secretary). Consumer Products Group: Robert B Hansen (President, Consumer Products Group), Gerald M McCarthy (President, Zenith Sales Company), Bruce A Huber (VP-Marketing, Consumer Products), H Vincent Kamler (VP-Manufacturing, Consumer Products), Peter C Skerlos (VP-Engineering, Consumer Products), James A Stark (VP-Purchasing, Consumer Products), James L Faust (President, Zenith Cable Products). Computer Group: Carl A Michelotti (President, Computer Group), John P Frank (President, Zenith Data Systems). Components Group: Otto M Genutis (President, Components Group), Michael S Tamkin (VP-Video Display Operations). CRT Group: Melvin L Moore (President, CRT Group), Leonard Dietch (VP-CRT Research and Development)

PRINCIPAL ACTIVITIES: Zenith Electronics Corporation introduced more new products in 1986 than in any year in the company's history, establishing a foundation for continued growth and a return to profitability. This strategy was strongly evident in Zenith's color television business, where unique new digital and stereo TV products are shaping the industry's state of the art for home entertainment. Future Zenith developments in consumer electronics (including color television, video cassette recorder and cable technology) will continue to expand television's role as the primary source of home entertainment and information into the 21st Century. Zenith's fastest-growing business area, computer systems and components, applies the company's traditional strengths-innovative research and engineering, efficient high-volume production and broad marketing expertise-to personal computers and to electronic components for other manufacturers. Today, all of these skills, products and technologies are evolving and interacting to make the company even more competitive. In 1987, Zenith will continue to strengthen its position as an industry leader, a leader committed to value, performance and quality
Financial Information:

	Dec 31 1985	Dec 31 1986
	$'000	$'000
Sales revenues	1,623,700	1,892,100
(Loss) before taxes	(20,900)	(20,200)
Net (loss)	(7,700)	(10,000)
(Loss) per share	($0.33)	($0.43)
Common stock	23,100	23,300
Retained income	348,600	338,600
Shareholders equity	437,200	431,600

No of Employees: 37,000

ZENITH LABORATORIES INC

50 Williams Drive, Ramsey, NJ 07446
Tel: (201) 327 3100

President: James O Leonard (and Chief Executive Officer)
Senior Executive Officers: Kevin G Conway (Senior VP Legal, Finance and Administration and Chief Financial Officer), Philip Blick (Senior VP Sales), Victor Bakian (VP Facilities Planning and Corporate Services), Frederick Shainfeld (VP New Product and Business Development), Robert Rees (VP Medicine), Edward W Thwaite (VP Marketing), David R Willcox (VP Human Resources), Ruth Wallestad (Treasurer and Assistant VP)

PRINCIPAL ACTIVITIES: Pharmaceuticals
Principal Bank: Marine Midland Bank
Financial Information:

	$'000
Sales revenues	80,545

No of Employees: 470

ZENITH NATIONAL INSURANCE CORPORATION

15760 Ventura Boulevard, Encino, CA 91436
Tel: (818) 990 9300

Chairman: Stanley R Zax (and President)
Senior Executive Officers: Arlington C Ansbro (Senior VP), Alex S Chernow (Senior VP and Secretary), William L Gentz (Senior VP), James R Ross (Senior VP and Actuary), Goran Ryden (Senior VP and Treasurer), William J Saake (Senior VP)

PRINCIPAL ACTIVITIES: Insurance
Principal Subsidiaries: Zenith Insurance Company
Principal Bank: City National Bank
Financial Information:

	$'000
Revenues	410,000

No of Employees: 350

ZEP MANUFACTURING CO

1310 Seaboard Industrial Blvd NW, Atlanta, GA 30318
Tel: (404) 352-1680
Telex: TWX 810 7513209 zep mfg co ntl

President: Harry Maziar
Senior Executive Officers: John Harper (VP Operations), Harold B Friedman (VP), Manny Fineman (VP Research and Development), Garland Monroe (VP Finance), Bob Blitz (VP Sales), Allen Soden (VP Marketing)

PRINCIPAL ACTIVITIES: Production of specialty cleaning chemicals
Parent Company: National Service Industries Inc, Atlanta, GA
Principal Bank: First National Bank of Atlanta
Financial Information:

	$'000
Sales revenues	140,000

No of Employees: 1,800

ZERO CORPORATION

444 So. Flower Street, Suite 2100, Los Angeles, CA 90071-2922
Tel: (213) 629-7000
Telex: EASYLINK 358020 ZERO CORP

Chairman: John B Gilbert
President: Wilford D Godbold Jr
Senior Executive Officers: James F Hermanson (VP), Ronald L Hess (VP), Mark Tranckino (Controller), George A Daniels (VP and Chief Financial Officer), James E Osterman (VP), Howard W Hill (Vice Chairman)

PRINCIPAL ACTIVITIES: Zero has established itself as the leading producer of specialized enclosures, cooling equipment and accessories for the electronics industry. Zero also markets a high-value line of luggage and camera cases under the Zero Halliburton name. The enclosures include instrument housings, carrying cases for portable equipment, cabinets for electronics equipment and consoles for controls. To support the needs of customer systems, Zero also offers a wide range of complementary products, including blowers, cooling systems, PCB card files, chassis slides, and other accessories. These products are manufactured in two European and fifteen US Locations, thus allowing Zero to fulfill its customers' needs for availability and service

Trade Names: Halliburton, Centurion

Principal Subsidiaries: Divisions and Subsidiaries:- McLean Engineering; McLean Midwest; Samuel Groves & Co Ltd (UK); Scanbe; Zero-East; Zero-Halliburton; Zero-West

Principal Bank: Security Pacific Bank

Financial Information:

	Mar 31 1986	Mar 31 1987
	$'000	$'000
Sales revenues	123,253	125,699
Income before taxes	27,380	22,474
Net income	12,777	11,602
Dividends	3,311	3,801
Dividends per share	$0.272	$0.306
Earnings per share	$1.03	$0.93
Common stock	12,333	12,474
Retained income	52,640	60,303
Shareholders equity	73,935	83,123

No of Employees: 1,700

ZEUS COMPONENTS INC

100, Midland Avenue, Port Chester, NY 10573
Tel: (914) 937-7400
Telex: Domestic 646610; International 681 8102 (MCI); International 178977 (TRT)
Telefax: (914) 937-2553

Chairman: Robert E Schrader (and President)

Senior Executive Officers: John M Burrows (VP of Finance), Joseph P Camarda (VP of Product Management), Wayne A Schrader (Senior VP of Sales and Marketing), Kenneth A Seybold (VP-Marketing), Eugene Sheinman (VP of International Sales), Martin S Fawer (Treasurer), Thomas J Ross (Controller), Deborah J Schrader (Secretary)

PRINCIPAL ACTIVITIES: Distribution of electronic components (semiconductors and passive components), to the military/aerospace industry

Principal Subsidiaries: Barclay's Bank & Trust P.L.C.

Financial Information:

	Sep 30 1986	Sep 30 1987
	$'000	$'000
Sales revenues	90,400	89,110
Income (loss) before taxes	746	(1,720)
Net income (loss)	507	(903)
Earnings (loss) per share	$0.19	($0.36)
Common stock	13,106	13,112
Retained income	4,263	3,301
Shareholders equity	17,369	16,413

Principal Shareholders: At Sep 30 1987: Robert Schrader 947,211 shares; Total 2,678,968 shares

No of Employees: 308

ZIDELL EXPLORATIONS, INC

3121 S W Moody Avenue, Portland, OR 97201
Tel: (503) 228-8691
Telex: WUT 360503 zidell ptl

President: Emery N Zidell (and Chief Executive Officer)

Senior Executive Officers: Jay N Zidell (VP), David W Scott (VP Value Division), Larry Richards (Treasurer)

PRINCIPAL ACTIVITIES: Shipbuilding and maintenance; industrial equipment

Principal Bank: US National Bank of Oregon

Financial Information:

	$'000
Sales revenues	30,000

No of Employees: 250

ZIMMER CORPORATION

5801 Congress Avenue, Box 3058, Boca Raton, FL 33431
Tel: (305) 997-0700

Chairman: Paul H Zimmer (and President)

Senior Executive Officers: Richard S Thompson (Senior VP and Treasurer), Richard E Roughton (VP, President of Manufactured Housing Operations), Myron K Fulle (VP and Controller), Terry P McMahan (VP (Legal) and Secretary)

PRINCIPAL ACTIVITIES: Zimmer Corporation produces and sells manufactured housing, luxury automobiles, van conversions, motor coaches and sport-fishing yachts. Zimmer distributes its quality products nationally through l200 independent dealers

Manufacturing Divisions and Subsidiaries: Zimmer Homes of Indiana; Crestridge Homes; Zimmer Homes of Kansas; Zimmer Homes of Pennsylvania; Zimmer Homes of Ohio; Zimmer Homes of Idaho; Zimmer Homes of North Carolina; Zimmer Homes of Florida; Zimmer Motor Vans; Zimmer Motor Cars Corporation; Black Fin Yacht Corporation; Zimmer Motor Coach Corp; Zimmer Product Development Center

Principal Bank: Southeast Bank, N.A.

Financial Information:

	Dec 31 1985	Dec 31 1986
	$'000	$'000
Sales revenues	145,194	134,638
(Loss) before taxes	(9,476)	(7,934)
Net (loss)	(5,688)	(7,934)
Dividends	232	-
Dividends per share	$0.05	-
(Loss) per share	($1.22)	($1.70)
Common stock	4,654	4,662
Retained income	11,569	3,635
Shareholders equity	46,456	9,256

Principal Shareholders: P H Zimmer

No of Employees: 600

ZIMMER INC

727 N Detroit Street, Box 708, Warsaw, IN 46580
Tel: (219) 267-6131
Telex: WUT 852194 zimmer inc

President: Thomas H Hughes

Senior Executive Officers: R L Davis (Executive VP), R L Fuson (Senior VP Medical and Scientific), J D Shinneman (VP Finance), N Keeney (VP Finance), D Berry (VP Corporate Planning), L Dagnall (VP Manufacturing), M Fisher (VP Employee Relations), J Halcomb (VP), T M Wendt (VP)

PRINCIPAL ACTIVITIES: Manufacture of orthopedic and surgical supplies and health care products

Parent Company: Bristol-Myers Co

Financial Information:

	$'000
Sales revenues	100,000

No of Employees: 1,000

ZIMPRO INC

Rothschild, WI 54474
Tel: (715) 359-7211
Telex: WUT 290495 zimpro rhco

President: Gerald H Teletzke

Senior Executive Officers: Charles N Watts (VP Sales), Louis A Pradt (VP Project Operations), J R Nicholson (VP Government Affairs), George Nugent (VP Marketing)

PRINCIPAL ACTIVITIES: Production of refuse cleaning systems; pollution control equipment
Parent Company: Sterling Drug Inc, New York, NY
Financial Information:

	$'000
Sales revenues	50,000

No of Employees: 300

ZIONS UTAH BANCORPORATION

1190 Kennecott Building, Salt Lake City, CT 84133
Tel: (801) 524-4787

Chairman: Roy W Simmons (and Chief Executive Officer)
President: Harris H Simmons

PRINCIPAL ACTIVITIES: Banking services
Principal Subsidiaries: Zions First National Bank

No of Employees: 1,700

ZOECON CORPORATION

975 California Avenue, Palo Alto, CA 94304
Tel: (415) 857-1130
Telex: WUT 345550 zoecon pla

Chairman: Carl Djerassi
President: Alexander D Cross
Senior Executive Officers: R S Brakke (VP Consumer and Animal Health), John D Diekman (Crop Protection Division and Manufacturing), Geoffrey Powell (VP Finance), Daniel Lazare (VP International Division), Terry Burkoth (VP Product Development), James Young (VP Research)

PRINCIPAL ACTIVITIES: Research services and production of pesticides
Parent Company: Sandoz United States Inc
Principal Bank: Wells Fargo Bank
Financial Information:

	$'000
Sales revenues	105,000

Principal Shareholders: Sandoz AG, Switzerland
No of Employees: 1,000

ZONDERVAN CORPORATION

1415 Lake Drive SE, Grand Rapids, MI 49506
Tel: (616) 698-6000
Telex: WUT 226300 zondervan ud
Fax: (616) 698-3 235

Chairman: Gordon Buter
President: James G Buick (and Chief Executive and Operating Officer)
Senior Executive Officers: Bruce E Ryskamp (Group President Bible Group), George Buck (Music and Consumer Group Executive), Hugh F Madden (Treasurer), Brent D Clark (Corporate Secretary and Counsel), Daniel T Caldon (VP and Chief Financial Officer)

PRINCIPAL ACTIVITIES: The Zondervan Corporation is a leading Christian communications company which publishes, distributes, and retails Bibles, books, and printed and recorded music. Zondervan sells its products principally through distributors who supply some 10,000 Christian bookstores and religious supply outlets. Zondervan also markets through its own 82 store chain of family bookstores strategically located in shopping malls nationwide. Publishing divisions are located in Michigan, Tennessee, and the United Kingdom
Principal Subsidiaries: The Benson Company; Tapley-Rutter Company Inc
Principal Bank: Old Kent Bank & Trust Co
Financial Information:

	Dec 31 1985	Dec 31 1986
	$'000	$'000
Sales revenues	98,620	103,492
Income before taxes	291	418
Net income (loss)	(96)	24
Dividends	342	-
Dividends per share	$0.8	-
Earnings (loss) per share	($0.02)	$0.01
Common stock	4,083	4,135
Retained income	11,620	13,793
Shareholders equity	31,298	28,512

No of Employees: 1,089

ZURN INDUSTRIES, INC

One Zurn Pl, Erie, PA 16505
Tel: (814) 452-2111

Chairman: George H Schofield (and President and Chief Executive Officer)
Senior Executive Officers: Charles L Hedrick (Senior Executive VP), Donald F Fessler (Executive VP), Richard J Nanula (Executive VP), Edward J Donn (Senior VP), William A Freeman (Senior VP Finance and Administration), David H Lund (Senior VP, Secretary and General Counsel), James A Zurn (Senior VP), James A Baldauf (VP and Controller), Lawrence J MacBean (VP Corporate Planning and Development and President International Division), W Weber (VP Human Resources)

PRINCIPAL ACTIVITIES: The company has interests in the manufacture of pollution control equipment; mining machinery; compressors and leisure and entertainment goods
Principal Subsidiaries: Lamar Corp; Robert Irsay Co; Advanco Constructors Inc; Nat'l Energy Production Corp; Bumstead-Woolford Co; Lynx Golf Co; Linear-Flo Systems Co; NEPCP Constructors Inc; Permtek Ltd; Permutit Co Inc; Permutit Co of Canada Inc; Gary Concrete Products Inc; Atlantic Gulf Co; Firetrol Protection Systems Inc; Nuevo Camino Construction Co
Principal Bank: Morgan Guaranty Trust
Financial Information:

	$'000
Sales revenues	345,000

No of Employees: 3,670

ZWICKER KNITTING MILLS

410 N Richmond Street, Appleton, WI 54913
Tel: (414) 731-7000
Telex: TWX 910272 1133 zwicker aple

President: Thomas Zwicker (and Chief Executive Officer)
Senior Executive Officers: Clifford Schupbach (VP Marketing), James Ertl (VP Research and Design), Sheldon Sontag (VP National Sales), Earl Bilsky (VP and General Manager Apparel), Larry Maples (Treasurer and Chief Financial Officer)

PRINCIPAL ACTIVITIES: Manufacture of knitted goods
Principal Bank: Firstar Bank of Appleton
Financial Information:

	$'000
Sales revenues	60,000

No of Employees: 1,200

Alphabetical Index

Index by State

Alabama

Alaska

Arizona

Arkansas

California

Colorado

Connecticut

Delaware

District of Columbia

Florida

Indiana

Iowa

Kansas

Kentucky

Louisiana

Maine

Maryland

Massachusetts

Michigan

Minnesota

Mississippi

Missouri

Montana

Nebraska

Nevada

New Hampshire

New Mexico

New York

North Carolina

North Dakota

Ohio

Oklahoma

Oregon

Pennsylvania

Rhode Island

South Carolina

South Dakota

Tennessee

Texas

Utah

Vermont

Virginia

Washington

West Virginia

Wisconsin

Wyoming

Index to Business Activities

Abrasives

Advertising and public relations

Aerospace equipment and components

Agricultural and horticultural equipment and services

Agriculture and horticulture

Air transportation and airport services

Aluminum

Architecture and town planning

Baking and flour milling

Banks, finance and investment

Betting and gambling

Biotechnology

Brewing, wines and spirits

Broadcasting, films, theater

Building materials, fittings and modular homes

Cables and wires

Carpets

Cement and bricks

Cereal products

Chemical plant

Civil engineering and construction

Civil engineering consultants

Cleaning and waste disposal services

Clothing

Coal mining

Coal products

Coffee

Commodity trading

Computer software and services

Confectionery

Construction equipment and plant hire

Copper and copper alloys

Dairy products

Data processing equipment

Defense and armaments

Defense electronics

Domestic ceramics

Domestic electrical appliances

Education and training services

Educational equipment

Electrical and electronic equipment

Electrical engineering

Electrical engineering consultants

Electrical machinery and components

Electricity supply

Elevators, lifting equipment and conveyors

Explosives

Fertilizers and agricultural chemicals

Fish and fish processing

Fishing

Food and beverage plant

Food and drink retailing

Footwear

Forestry

Freight forwarding

Frozen and ready prepared food products

Fruit products

Fuel distribution

Funeral homes, cemeteries and related services

Furniture and components

Furs

General chemicals

General mechanical engineering

General trading

Generators

Glass

Hand tools

Health care

Heating, ventilation and refrigeration

Home hardware

Hotels, restaurants and catering

Industrial ceramics

Industrial engines

Industrial equipment

Industrial gases

Infant and dietetic foods

Insulation products

Insurance

Iron and steel

Irrigation equipment

Jewelry

Knitted goods

Laundries and dry cleaning

Leasing and rental services

Leather goods

Livestock and animal feeds

Machine tools

Mail order services

Management services and consultants

Man-made fibers

Manpower services

Meat and meat processing

Mechanical engineering consultants

Mechanical engineering plant

Mechanical handling equipment

Medical and surgical equipment

Medical instruments

Medical supplies

Metal castings

Metal fabrication

Metal treatment and related services

Mining and quarrying

Mining equipment

Mobile homes, trailers and campers

Motor vehicle components

Motor vehicles

Motorcycles and bicycles

Natural gas supply

Non-alcoholic beverages

Non-ferrous metals

Non-food retailing

Nuclear engineering

Office equipment

Oil and gas exploration and production

Oil and gas services and equipment

Oil refining

Oils and fats

Optical equipment

Other textiles

Packaging

Paints, inks and dyestuffs

Paper and board

Paper and packaging machinery

Petrochemicals

Pharmaceuticals

Photographic and copying equipment and services

Plastics and plastic products

Pollution control equipment

Postal services

Power equipment

Precious metals

Printing and binding

Printing machinery and equipment

Process engineering

Property, real estate

Public services

Publishing and information services

Pumps, valves and compressors

Railroad and bus services

Railroad vehicles and equipment

Ready mixed concrete

Recreational goods and giftware

Recreational services

Road haulage

Rubber and rubber goods

Safety equipment

Scientific instruments

Security equipment

Security services

Ship and boat building and marine engineering

Shipping and port services

Snack products

Soaps, detergents and other cleaning products

Soups, sauces and other relishes

Specialty chemicals

Spinning and weaving

Storage and warehousing

Sugar

Tea

Telecommunications

Telecommunications services

Textile finishing

Textile machinery

Timber industries

Tobacco

Toiletries and cosmetics

Toys and games

Travel and tourism

Vegetable products

Watches and clocks

Water supply and treatment services

Welding equipment and services

Wholesalers

Woolen goods

Writing equipment

MIX
Papier aus verantwortungsvollen Quellen
Paper from responsible sources
FSC® C105338

If you have any concerns about our products,
you can contact us on
ProductSafety@springernature.com

In case Publisher is established outside the EU,
the EU authorized representative is:
Springer Nature Customer Service Center GmbH
Europaplatz 3, 69115 Heidelberg, Germany

Printed by Libri Plureos GmbH
in Hamburg, Germany